The
Merriam-Webster
Thesaurus

The Merriam-Webster Thesaurus

Merriam-Webster, Incorporated
Springfield, Massachusetts

A GENUINE MERRIAM-WEBSTER

The name *Webster* alone is no guarantee of excellence. It is used by a number of publishers and may serve mainly to mislead an unwary buyer.

Merriam-Webster™ is the name you should look for when you consider the purchase of dictionaries or other fine reference books. It carries the reputation of a company that has been publishing since 1831 and is your assurance of quality and authority.

ISBN: 978-0-87779-850-7

A powerful agent is the right word: it lights the reader's way and makes it plain; a close approximation to it will answer, and much traveling is done in a well-enough fashion by its help, but we do not welcome it and applaud it and rejoice in it as we do when the right one blazes out on us. Whenever we come upon one of those intensely right words in a book or a newspaper the resulting effect is physical as well as spiritual, and electrically prompt: it tingles exquisitely around through the walls of the mouth and tastes as tart and crisp and good as the autumn-butter that creams the sumac-berry.

—Mark Twain

PREFACE

This thesaurus is specially designed for those who want to enlarge their vocabularies and learn more about the rich variety of the English language. We hope and expect that users will readily turn to a dictionary whenever they need a better understanding of the meaning of any word used in the thesaurus.

In creating this thesaurus, the editors have drawn on years of experience with a thesaurus format that is at once easy to use, broad in its scope, and especially helpful to the user in the selection of the right word. We also believe that this thesaurus will prove to be highly useful as a vocabulary builder. We have parted ways with the more traditional approach of presenting long, undifferentiated lists of words that are tied to some topic or intellectual concept. Instead, we present a strictly alphabetical ordering of entries. These entries consist of lists of words that are centered on a specific—and specified—meaning. Main entries consist of lists of synonyms and related words, as well as antonyms and near antonyms whenever applicable. Phrases and idioms that function as synonyms are occasionally offered as well.

The purpose of the differentiated lists is to accommodate the various purposes for which a thesaurus is used. People use a thesaurus generally because they are dissatisfied with the word they already have in mind. They want a different word. The question is: how different?

If users of this thesaurus are trying to avoid a boring repetition of the same word, or are seeking to vary and enrich their vocabulary, then they will wish to select from the list of synonyms a word that shares the same basic meaning as the one they already have but differs from it in suggestion and tone. If they are seeking a word that is different from but still related to what they already have, then they will want to scan the lists of related words for a rewarding journey through the variety of possibilities that English offers.

If users are seeking a word that is to some degree opposite in meaning to what they have, then they will want to consult the lists of antonyms or near antonyms. By specifying the meaning under consideration, and by making distinctions between words that are truly synonymous and those that are only somewhat synonymous, we hope that we have given users the guidance they desire. We believe that this system minimizes the need to guess and to grope.

What makes this thesaurus unique is the content of the separate entries for each and every word appearing in the lists of synonyms. Since a user's search for the right word may start anywhere, the thesaurus is arranged so that any member of a synonym group can serve as the starting point. An entry for a listed synonym consists of a restatement of the meaning common to all the members of the group. A user who happens to use a particular synonym as a starting point should follow the cross-reference to the main entry for the complete listing of synonyms, related words, and any antonyms or near antonyms.

The thesaurus format is intended to encourage and facilitate users in finding the right word, which results in writing of greater precision and clarity. The word *thesaurus* literally means "treasury" in Latin, and we hope that the treasure trove of words contained in these pages will enhance the user's interest in and appreciation of the English language. We urge all users to read carefully the following sections entitled Introduction and Using Your Thesaurus in order to make the most of what the book has to offer. The Introduction contains an informative discussion of what distinguishes a synonym from a related word, an antonym from a near antonym. The section Using Your Thesaurus explains in detail the organization of the thesaurus and discusses the differences between the two basic types of entries. Study of this section is especially important.

The editor has been ably assisted in its composition by the editors Rose Martino Bigelow, Daniel B. Brandon, Adam Groff, Kory L. Stamper, and Deanna Stathis. The entire project was supervised by Madeline L. Novak, and Robert D. Copeland served as editor in charge of production. Stephen J. Perrault devised ways to facilitate the creation of the manuscript electronically. The difficult task of cross-referencing the text was accomplished by Christopher Chapin Connor and Allison S. Crawford. Credit for proofreading the text goes to Ilya A. Davidovich, Donna L. Rickerby, Maria Sansalone, Adrienne M. Scholz, Peter A. Sokolowski, Emily A. Vezina, and Judy Yeh. Michael D. Roundy acted as a consultant on miscellaneous scientific questions. Finally, John M. Morse, Merriam-Webster's President and Publisher, must be acknowledged and thanked for his unfailing support for this thesaurus.

Michael G. Belanger,
Editor

INTRODUCTION

Synonyms

The English language contains a wealth of words, and perhaps no other language has as many synonyms as English. Synonyms give color, precision, and variety to a person's writing, breaking up the dullness that can come from too many overused words.

So, just what are synonyms? Put simply, synonyms are words that mean the same thing. Words that are only somewhat similar in meaning—but do not mean the same thing—are not true synonyms. They are merely related words, and they belong in a different category. In this thesaurus a word is classified as a synonym if and only if it shares with another word at least one basic meaning.

Here's an example of how we arrived at a basic meaning shared by one group of words. The word *freight* can be defined as "goods or cargo carried by ship, train, truck, or airplane." We can break up the definition like this:

Since a person using *freight* as the starting point in his or her search for the right word is probably dissatisfied with that term, the word that he or she is seeking will most likely come under a broader or more basic meaning. We can phrase that more basic meaning as: "a mass or quantity of something taken up and carried, conveyed, or transported." The list of synonyms for *freight—burden, cargo, draft, haul, lading, load, loading, payload, weight*—can all be said to share this basic meaning.

If a word is more limited in scope than the basic meaning given at a main entry, then it cannot be regarded as a synonym. Hence, *truckload*, which refers specifically to the load carried by a truck, cannot be a synonym of *freight* and the other members of *freight's* synonym group. Likewise, the words *mass* and *quantity* cannot themselves be regarded as synonyms because the notion of being carried, conveyed, or transported is not an essential part of their meaning.

Related Words

Oftentimes thesaurus users are not looking for something that means exactly the same as the word they already have. To help in this situation, this thesaurus includes lists of related words, which are words whose meanings are close enough to the synonymy group to be of interest to the user. These related words do not qualify as synonyms because they have meanings that differ from the basic meaning shared by the synonymy group in some significant way.

For example, the word *funny* has the meaning of "causing or intended to cause laughter." A person who is making "funny faces" is causing, or at least trying to cause, others to laugh. *Witty*, which is certainly closely related to *funny*, has a slightly different meaning: "given to or marked by mature intelligent humor." A witty person is someone who has a habit of making clever remarks that display a grown-up sense of humor. Thus, *funny* and *witty* are related, but the words are not synonymous. Because of the close relationship between two words like *funny* and *witty*, all of the words listed as synonyms at *witty* are given as related words at *funny*.

The lists of related words at a main entry in the thesaurus may be likened to the hyperlinks that connect one Web site to another on the Internet. Following the links between Web sites often takes one to new and unexpected places. Thesaurus users are encouraged to go from one related entry to another in their search for just the right word.

Some words are not true synonyms of anything, but because they are so fundamentally useful, they have been included in this thesaurus among the lists of related words and in places where they are likely to be most helpful. For example, the word *ballast*, which refers to any type of "heavy material used to make a ship steady," is too narrow in meaning to have any synonyms of its own. It is related to the more general term *load*, however, and so, fittingly, it is included as a related word at the entry for *load*.

Antonyms

An antonym is a word whose meaning is directly opposite to another word's meaning. In this thesaurus, an antonym is a word that has a meaning that completely cancels out another word's meaning. *Short* and *tall* are complete opposites. Something cannot be both short and tall at the same time, and both words suggest about the same degree of difference from the norm or average in height. *Good* and *evil* are another pair of exact opposites. Logically, something cannot be both *good* and *evil* in the same way and at the same time.

Words that are only opposite in some aspect of their meaning cannot be said to be true antonyms. For example, *sad*, which means "causing unhappiness," is not a true antonym of *funny*, which means "causing or intended to cause laughter." The opposite of unhappiness is happiness, and so the opposite of sad is happy. There are things, like a frowning clown, that can be both funny and sad, so these words can't be antonyms. Pairs of words like *sad* and *funny* are better regarded as near antonyms.

Near Antonyms

Near antonyms are words that do not qualify as antonyms under the strict definition used for this thesaurus but that clearly have meanings in marked contrast with the members of a synonym group. For example, *afraid* is not so exactly opposite to *courageous* as *cowardly* is, but *afraid* and *courageous* certainly have markedly contrasting meanings and so are considered near antonyms. And just as a user may not be seeking a word that is exactly synonymous with another, he or she may likewise not be seeking a word that is exactly opposite. The user may simply want a word that lies somewhere on the opposite side of the range of meaning.

Phrases

This thesaurus also includes phrases that, taken as a whole, are synonymous with individual words. Within this category are some words that are commonly used in combination with one another but are not necessarily included as entry words in most dictionaries. Some of these fixed phrases represent virtually the only way in which the word is used in contemporary English. For example, *in jeopardy* appears as a synonymous phrase at *liable* because a person exposed to something dangerous or undesirable is a person in jeopardy. The word *jeopardy* is generally only used in the phrase *in jeopardy*.

Idioms constitute the other major class of word combinations that are entered under the heading of Phrases. Idioms are phrases that have a special meaning that is different from the literal meaning that a person would get if adding together the individual meanings of the components of the phrase. For example, the phrase *make good* is virtually meaningless if one attempts to piece together the literal meanings of *make* and *good*. As a fixed phrase, however, *make good* means "to reach a desired level of accomplishment" and is a synonym of *succeed*.

What this thesaurus does not enter are phrases that are simple restatements of the basic meaning shared by the members of the synonym group. The verb *remark*, for example, might be defined as "to express as an opinion." Such rewordings of a basic definition have no place in a thesaurus because they contribute nothing useful to the user's vocabulary.

Choosing the Right Word—Using Your Dictionary

Even after you have mastered all of these categories, deciding which word in a thesaurus entry is best for your purposes is not always easy. The basic meaning shared by the members of a synonym group cannot tell you everything you need to know in order to choose the word that best suits your needs.

Something that is "very pleasing to look at" can be described as *attractive, beauteous, beautiful, bonny, comely, cute, fair, gorgeous, handsome, knockout, lovely, pretty, ravishing, sightly, stunning,* or *taking,* but which word is best for describing a sunset? A city? Should you use *knockout* to describe a cathedral or *ravishing* for a sports car?

If after reviewing the synonyms, you decide that you still have not found the right word, then you have the list of related words to consider:

related words alluring, appealing, charming, delightful, eye-catching, glamorous (*also* glamourous), prepossessing; elegant, exquisite, glorious, resplendent, splendid, statuesque, sublime, superb; flawless, perfect, radiant; dainty, delicate; personable, presentable

Now you have 38 words that mean the same thing or nearly the same thing as *beautiful*. Here's where you need a good dictionary. You can consult the dictionary to get a precise definition of any word in the lists, and perhaps an example of its use. You should always use this thesaurus along with a good dictionary.

EXPLANATORY NOTES

Every user of this thesaurus should read this section of the book carefully in order to use it effectively.

A thesaurus consists mostly of lists of words, and it is often difficult to know which word is best for a particular purpose. Because the English language has so many different ways of combining words with different shades of meaning, you should always use this thesaurus along with a reliable dictionary.

ENTRY ORDER

The first word of a thesaurus entry is called a **headword**. Headwords are printed in boldface type and are in alphabetical order. Alphabetization is by first letter, then second letter, and so on, regardless of any spaces or hyphens that may appear in them:

make *vb*
make–believe *adj*
make out *vb*

make over *vb*
Maker *n*
makeshift *adj*

When a headword contains a numeral, the numeral is alphabetized as though it were a spelled-out word:

anywise *adv*
A1 *adj*
apace *adv*

Homographs are words that are spelled the same, but each is a different part of speech or has a different etymology (word origin). Homographs that are different parts of speech are separate headwords:

hail *n* 1 a heavy fall of objects
hail *vb* 1 to declare enthusiastic approval of

Homographs that have a different etymology, even when they are the same part of speech, are entered as separate headwords.

Those that are the same part of speech are grouped together and numbered in sequence:

¹**list** *n* a record of a series of items (as names or titles) usually arranged according to some system
²**list** *n* the act of positioning or an instance of being positioned at an angle
³**list** *n* a long narrow piece of material
¹**list** *vb* 1 to make a list of
²**list** *vb* to set or cause to be at an angle

Verbs that are used in combination with a preposition or an adverb are entered with the verb in boldface type followed by the preposition or adverb in parentheses in lightface type. Such combinations immediately follow the base verb in alphabetical order:

go *vb*
go (for) *vb*
go (on) *vb*
go (to) *vb*

When main entries are compound words, a closed form is entered before a hyphenated form and a hyphenated form is entered before a form that contains spaces:

nosedive *n*
nose–dive *vb*

open–air *adj*
open air *n*

PLURAL NOUNS

Some nouns are always pluralized when they are used a certain way. When there are no thesaurus entries which include the singular form of a such a noun, the plural form is given as the headword:

leavings *n pl* a remaining group or portion — see REMAINDER 1

When a noun is usually, but not always, used in plural form in a certain sense, the singular form is the headword, and the plural follows the label *usually*:

habiliment *n usually* **habiliments** *pl* covering for the human body — see CLOTHING

Such nouns are followed by *s* in parentheses in the synonym list:

clothing *n* covering for the human body

synonyms apparel, attire, clothes, dress, duds, habiliment(s), rags, raiment, togs, wear

When a noun is used in the singular form in one sense and in the plural form in another, the singular form is given as the headword. The plural form is indicated at the individual sense or senses:

provision *n* **1** something upon which the carrying out of an agreement or offer depends — see CONDITION 2 **2 provisions** *pl* substances intended to be eaten — see FOOD

VARIANTS

An alternate spelling or form of a headword is called a **variant**. Variants are shown in boldface after the headword and are preceded by *or* or *also*. The label *or* means that the variant is as common or nearly as common as the headword. The headword is usually the form that comes first alphabetically:

egotistic *or* **egotistical** *adj*
lighted *or* **lit** *adj*
OK *or* **okay** *vb*

However, if one of the spellings or forms is used slightly more frequently, the more common one is entered first even though it may not fall first alphabetically:

gizmo *or* **gismo** *n*

A variant that is preceded by the label *also* is not as common as the headword:

among *also* **amongst** *prep*
facade *also* **façade** *n*
naught *also* **nought** *n*

When two variants are separated from the headword by *also* but from each other by *or*, it means that they are both less common than the headword:

bogey *also* **bogy** *or* **bogie** *n*

Variants are also given in the word lists:

zero *n* the numerical symbol 0 or the absence of number or quantity represented by it ⟨anything multiplied by *zero* comes out to zero⟩
synonyms aught, cipher, goose egg, naught (*or* nought), nil, nothing, oh, zilch, zip

PARTS OF SPEECH

Every headword is followed by a part-of-speech label. The abbreviations for the parts of speech are *adj* (adjective), *adv* (adverb), *conj* (conjunction), *interj* (interjection), *n* (noun), *prep* (preposition), *pron* (pronoun), and *vb* (verb).

KINDS OF ENTRIES

There are two kinds of entries: main entries and secondary entries. Every headword with its part-of-speech label is followed by either one or more main entries, one or more secondary entries, or a combination of the two. If there is more than one entry, each one begins on a new line introduced by a boldface sense number. Main entries come first. A **main entry** consists of the meaning shared by the members of the synonym group, a verbal illustration, and lists of synonyms as well as any related words, phrases, near antonyms, and antonyms:

> **eagerness** *n* urgent desire or interest
>   *synonyms* appetite, ardor, avidity, desirousness, enthusiasm, excitement, hunger, impatience, keenness, thirst
>   *related words* alacrity, quickness; ambition, gusto, zest
>   *near antonyms* unconcern; aloofness, detachment; impassivity, languor
>   *antonyms* apathy, indifference

A **secondary entry** has the same shared meaning that is shown at the main entry. The secondary entry does not contain lists of synonyms, antonyms, related words, phrases, or near antonyms. Instead, at the end of the entry, there is a direction to "see" the appropriate main entry at another headword. Secondary entries follow any main entries at a headword:

> **gain** *vb* 1 to increase in
>   *synonyms* build (up), gather, grow (in), pick up . . .
>   **2** to receive as return for effort — see EARN 1
>   **3** to become healthy and strong again after illness or weakness — see CONVALESCE

> **fade** *vb* 1 to cease to be visible — see DISAPPEAR
>   **2** to make white or whiter by removing color — see WHITEN

CROSS-REFERENCES

The direction at the end of every secondary entry to see another entry is called a **cross-reference**. The cross-reference tells you where the main entry for a word's synonym group is located. No matter which member of a synonym group you used to begin your search, you can always find your way to the entry that has the lists of all the synonyms and any related words, phrases, near antonyms, or antonyms. If there is more than one sense at the headword referred to in the cross-reference, the cross-reference will also include a sense number. If the headword has more than one numbered homograph, the cross-reference will send you to the right homograph number as well:

pain *vb* to feel or cause physical pain — see HURT 1

ranking *n* 1 a scheme of rank or order — see ³SCALE 1

If a headword appears as more than one part of speech, the cross-reference is sending you to the same part of speech as the word you looked up. The cross-reference in the **ranking** example above tells you that the main

entry where you will find *ranking* as a member of the synonym group with the shared meaning "a scheme of rank or order" is at sense 1 of the noun entry ³**scale**:

³**scale** *n* 1 a scheme of rank or order ⟨how would you rate your experience on a *scale* of one to ten?⟩
synonyms graduation, ladder, ordering, ranking

SPECIAL USAGE LABELS

You will find special usage labels in italics after a headword whenever they apply. The labels are *chiefly British, British, chiefly Scottish, Scottish, Australian, chiefly dialect, chiefly Southern & Midland*, and *slang*.

These labels are placed directly after the part-of-speech label when the word has only one sense or when the label applies to all the senses:

afore *prep, chiefly dialect* 1
bairn *n, chiefly Scottish*
bobby *n, British*
dis *vb, slang* 1

The label comes after the sense number when the word has more

than one sense and the label applies only to that sense:

jack *n* 1 *slang* something (as pieces of stamped metal or printed paper) customarily and legally used as a medium of exchange, a measure of value, or a means of payment — see MONEY

Special usage labels also appear in the word lists:

before *prep* 1 earlier than ⟨since I'm a faster runner, I got there *before* him⟩
synonyms afore [*chiefly dialect*], ahead of, ere, of, previous to, prior to, to

SHARED MEANING

The shared meaning follows the sense number when there is more than one sense and the part-of-speech label when there is only one sense. It is a meaning shared equally by the headword and the other members of the synonym group. This shared meaning is the "thing" that is referred to when we say that two or more words "mean the same thing" and thus are synonyms.

Sometimes there are words in parentheses within a shared meaning:

district *n* an area (as of a city) set apart for some purpose or having some special feature ⟨Independence Hall in Philadelphia's historic *district*⟩
synonyms neighborhood, quarter, section
related words belt, zone; department, . . .

In the shared meaning at **district**, the words in parentheses indicate that *district, neighborhood, quarter*, and *section* are synonyms when they refer to an area of a city or something like that, and that the words in the related words list also refer specifically to this type of area.

For information regarding the use and purpose of parentheses around certain words in entries for verbs, read below.

SOME NOTES ABOUT VERBS

A boldface verb headword followed by a lightface word in parentheses tells you to use the parenthetical word with the verb:

comply (with) *vb* 1 to act according to the commands of
hold off (on) *vb* to assign to a later time
knock (about) *vb* to move about from place to place aimlessly

If there are two words inside the parentheses and they are separated by *or*, then either word can be used with the verb:

fit (in *or* into) *vb* to put among or between others

These verbs appear in the synonym lists followed by their customary adverb or preposition in parentheses. These entries are treated this way in the thesaurus because such verb combinations are not the usual form of dictionary entries, but it is only when the verb is used with the adverb or preposition that it matches the shared meaning of its synonym group.

When the meaning of a verb requires a direct object, all of the words in the synonym list take a direct object. If a verb does not take an object, none of the synonyms will take an object.

VERBAL ILLUSTRATIONS

Every main entry in this thesaurus shows an example of typical use. The **verbal illustration**, as it is called, follows the shared meaning, is enclosed in angle brackets, and italicizes the synonym:

fight *vb* 1 to oppose (someone) in physical conflict ⟨a proud people who have fiercely *fought* all invaders of their homeland⟩
rich *adj* 1 having goods, property, or money in abundance ⟨Tanya's dad works as a chauffeur for the *richest* man in town, a big oil baron⟩

Words in parentheses after a boldface headword are italicized in the verbal illustration:

stick (to *or* with) *vb* to give steadfast support to ⟨thanks for *sticking with* me when all my other so-called friends have turned their backs⟩

Some verbal illustrations in the thesaurus are complete sentences and others are only sentence fragments. Though it may look a little odd, for the sake of consistency, all verbal illustrations in this thesaurus begin with a lowercase letter unless the initial word is normally capitalized. Question marks and exclamation points are used when appropriate at the end of a verbal illustration, but otherwise no ending punctuation is used.

A WORD ABOUT SYNONYMS

If a word is used as the defining term in a shared meaning, it will not be listed as one of the synonyms. Since words can only be defined in terms of other words, the result of this restriction is that some terms that might be rightly regarded as synonyms do not appear in the synonym lists. Here is an example:

> **go** *vb* . . . **2** to leave a place often for another
> **synonyms** begone, clear out, depart, exit, get, get off, move, pull (out), quit, sally (forth), shove (off), take off, walk out

Leave, used as the defining term, could be considered another synonym, but it is not entered as such in this thesaurus because it has been used as a defining term.

RELATED WORDS

You will see that in most cases there are more related words than synonyms. That is because there is much more flexibility in choosing words for these lists. They do not have to match the shared meaning: they only need to relate to some aspect of it. Related words are often divided into subgroups separated by a semicolon. Words within each subgroup are generally closer in meaning to each other than to the members of the following subgroups. The subgroups tend to be presented in order of most relevant to least relevant.

> **object** *n* **1** something material that can be perceived by the senses
> **synonyms** thing
> **related words** article, item, piece; being, entity, substance; commodity, good, ware; accessory, accompaniment; bauble, curio, knickknack, spangle, token, trinket

PHRASES

Listed in alphabetical order after the heading **phrases** at some of the main entries are expressions that are synonymous with the headword and the other members of the synonym group. Although they have essentially the same meaning as the synonyms, these phrases tend to be used only in certain ways, and you should be careful about substituting one of them for a word in the synonym list. Since phrases are not entered as headwords in the thesaurus, they do not come with verbal illustrations. It's a good idea to look them up in a dictionary before considering them.

NEAR ANTONYMS

Just as related words are not exact synonyms, near antonyms are not exact antonyms. Not every synonym group has near antonyms. As is the case with related words, when there are near antonyms, they are often divided into subgroups separated by a semicolon, with the members of each subgroup listed alphabetically.

have *vb* **1** to keep, control, or experience as one's own
synonyms command, enjoy, hold, occupy, own, possess, retain
related words keep, reserve, withhold; bear, carry; boast, show off, sport

near antonyms abandon, cede, disclaim, disown, hand over, relinquish, renounce, surrender, yield; discard, dump; decline, reject, repudiate, spurn; need, require
antonyms lack, want

ANTONYMS

The words in the antonym lists are the exact opposites of the headword and the words in the synonym lists. Not every synonym group has antonyms, and antonym lists tend to be shorter than near antonym lists. Antonyms are listed alphabetically, just as synonyms are. They appear as boldface headwords at their own alphabetical places in the thesaurus only if they are part of a synonym group elsewhere.

Ordinarily, all the words in an antonym list are synonyms of each other. Sometimes, however, a semicolon in an antonym list divides words which, while they are exact opposites of the words in the synonym group, are not synonyms of each other.

Here is an example:

present *adj* **1** existing or in progress right now
synonyms current, extant, ongoing, present-day
antonyms ago, past; future

The opposite of "existing or in progress right now" is "*not* existing or in progress right now." All three of the words in the antonyms list fit that meaning. *Ago* and *past*, separated by a comma, are synonyms of each other; they both can mean "earlier than the present time." But *ago* and *past* are not synonyms of *future*, which means, of course, "occurring at a later time."

A NOTE ABOUT THE LISTS: WORD DUPLICATION

No word appears in more than one list at any single main entry. Some words have slight variations in meaning. If they are used one way, they are synonymous with a headword; if they are used another way, they are merely closely related. To avoid confusion, such words have been entered in a main entry's synonym list only. For example, *nice* is in the synonym list at *pleasant* where the shared meaning is "giving pleasure or contentment to the mind or senses." *Nice* is also in the synonym list at *amiable*, where the shared meaning is "having an easygoing and pleasing manner especially in social situations." If you go back to *pleasant*, you will find *amiable* among the related words. So it would stand to reason that *nice*, having the same meaning as *amiable*, would also be entered in the related word list at *pleasant*. Since it's already in the synonym list, however, it was left out of the related words.

Some words can have two meanings that are opposite of each other—or nearly so. *Nervy* can mean both "fearless" and "fearful, timid." Thus, at the thesaurus entry for bold, where the shared meaning is "inclined or willing to take risks," *nervy* might qualify as both a synonym and an antonym (or near antonym). And, indeed, *nervy* appears as a synonym, along with *adventuresome,* *adventurous, audacious, daring, dashing, emboldened, enterprising, gutsy, hardy, nerved, venturesome,* and *venturous.* Although the near antonym list contains *fearful* and *timid* as expected, *nervy* is left off the list. Again, this is to avoid confusion.

GUIDE WORDS

The two boldface words separated by a dot at the top of each page are **guide words,** and they show the alphabetical range of entries on the page. You can use them to find a word more quickly.

The first guide word is the headword of the first entry beginning on that page, and the second guide is the headword of the last entry on the page.

The
Merriam-Webster
Thesaurus

A

aback *adv* without warning — see UN-AWARES

abaft *adv* near, toward, or in the stern of a ship or the tail of an aircraft — see AFT

abaft *prep* at, to, or toward the rear of — see BEHIND 1

abandon *n* carefree freedom from constraint ⟨added spices to the stew with complete *abandon*⟩

syn abandonment, ease, lightheartedness, naturalness, spontaneity, unrestraint

rel ardor, enthusiasm, exuberance, fervor, spirit, warmth, zeal; carelessness, heedlessness, impulsiveness, indiscretion, insouciance, recklessness, thoughtlessness; excess, excessiveness, immoderacy, incontinence, indulgence, intemperance, licentiousness, permissiveness, wantonness, wildness

near ant embarrassment, reserve, reticence, self-consciousness, uneasiness; inhibition, repression, self-restraint, suppression; carefulness, discreetness, discretion, heedfulness; discipline, self-control, self-discipline, willpower

ant constraint, restraint

abandon *vb* to cause to remain behind — see LEAVE 1

abandoned *adj* left unoccupied or unused ⟨Marlene avoided walking past the *abandoned* house, with its broken windows and sagging porch⟩

syn derelict, deserted, disused, forgotten, forsaken, rejected, vacated

rel ignored, neglected, unattended, untended; castaway, cast-off, discarded, jettisoned, junked; desolate, godforsaken, miserable, shabby, wretched; empty, idle, vacant

near ant reclaimed, recovered, redeemed, rescued, retrieved, salvaged, saved; reconditioned, rehabilitated, restored; repeopled

abandonment *n* **1** carefree freedom from constraint — see ABANDON

2 the act of abandoning — see DERELICTION 1

abase *vb* **1** to lower in character or dignity — see DEBASE 1

2 to reduce to a lower standing in one's own eyes or in others' eyes — see HUMBLE

abash *vb* to throw into a state of self-conscious distress — see EMBARRASS 1

abashment *n* the emotional state of being made self-consciously uncomfortable — see EMBARRASSMENT 1

abate *vb* **1** to grow less in scope or intensity especially gradually — see DECREASE 2

2 to make smaller in amount, volume, or extent — see DECREASE 1

abatement *n* **1** something that is or may be subtracted — see DEDUCTION 1

2 the amount by which something is lessened — see DECREASE

abbey *n* a residence for men under religious vows — see MONASTERY

abbreviate *vb* to make less in extent or duration — see SHORTEN

abbreviation *n* a shortened version of a written work — see ABRIDGMENT

abdicate *vb* to give up (as a position of authority) formally ⟨the revolutionary government forced Nicholas II to *abdicate* the Russian throne⟩

syn abnegate, cede, relinquish, renounce, resign, step down (from), surrender

rel abjure, deny, disavow, disclaim, disown, waive; forsake, give up, hand over, yield; abandon, desert, quit, vacate

near ant appropriate, arrogate, assume, claim, confiscate; seize, take over, usurp, wrest; defend, guard, protect, safeguard, secure

abdomen *n* the part of the body between the chest and the pelvis — see STOMACH

abduct *vb* to carry a person away by unlawful force or against his or her will — see KIDNAP

aberrant *adj* **1** being out of the ordinary — see EXCEPTIONAL

2 departing from some accepted standard of what is normal — see DEVIANT

aberration *n* a serious mental disorder that prevents one from living a safe and normal life — see INSANITY 1

abet *vb* **1** to cause or encourage the development of — see INCITE 1

2 to provide (someone) with what is useful or necessary to achieve an end — see HELP 1

abettor *also* **abetter** *n* **1** one associated with another in wrongdoing — see ACCOMPLICE

2 someone associated with another to give assistance or moral support — see ALLY

abeyance *n* a state of temporary inactivity ⟨our weekend plans were held in *abeyance* until we could get a weather forecast⟩

syn doldrums, dormancy, latency, quiescence, suspense, suspension

rel inaction, inertia, inertness, motionlessness; impasse, standstill; coma, hibernation, hypnosis, repose, rest, sleep, slumber, torpor; recession, remission; idleness

near ant recommencement, renewal, resumption, resuscitation

ant continuance, continuation

abhor *vb* to dislike strongly — see HATE

abhorrence *n* something or someone that is hated — see HATE 2

2 a very strong dislike — see HATE 1

abhorrent *adj* causing intense displeasure, disgust, or resentment — see OFFENSIVE 1

abide *vb* **1** to continue to be in a place for a significant amount of time — see STAY 1

2 to have a home — see LIVE 1

3 to put up with (something painful or difficult) — see BEAR 2

4 to remain indefinitely in existence or in the same state — see CONTINUE 1

ability *n* the physical or mental power to do something ⟨as a result of the accident he lost the *ability* to walk⟩

syn capability, capacity, competence, competency, faculty

rel aptitude, aptness, endowment, facility, gift, knack, talent; adroitness, deftness, dexterity, prowess, skill; gray matter, instinct, intelligence, reason, understanding; potency, staying power, stuff; adequacy, effectiveness, effectualness, fitness, form, influence, resourcefulness, usefulness; means, resources, wherewithal

near ant helplessness, impotence, paralysis, powerlessness, weakness; defectiveness, deficiency, inadequacy, ineffectiveness, ineffectualness, uselessness; debilitation, disablement, impairment, incapacitation

ant disability, inability, incapability, incapacity, incompetence, incompetency, ineptitude, ineptness

abjure *vb* to solemnly or formally reject or go back on (as something formerly adhered to) ⟨*abjured* some long-held beliefs when she converted to another religion⟩

syn recant, renounce, retract, take back, unsay, withdraw

rel contradict, deny, disavow, disclaim, disown, gainsay, negate, negative, repudiate; abandon, abnegate, forsake, give up, relinquish, spurn, surrender; controvert, disagree (with), disprove, dispute, rebut, refute; back down, back off, backtrack; disallow, recall, renege, revoke

near ant acknowledge, admit, affirm, assert, avow, claim, contend, declare, maintain, proclaim, profess, state; back, confirm, defend, endorse (*also* indorse), espouse, maintain, support, uphold; accept, adopt, embrace

ant adhere (to)

ablaze *adj* **1** being on fire ⟨the entire block was *ablaze* by the time fire fighters arrived⟩

syn afire, aflame, blazing, burning, combusting, fiery, flaming, ignited, inflamed, kindled, lighted (*or* lit)

rel aglow, alight, flaring, flickering, glowing, live, smoldering; broiling, hot, piping hot, red-hot, roasting, scalding, scorching, searing, sizzling; burnt, charred, incinerated, scorched, seared, singed

near ant choked, damped, dead, doused, extinguished, quenched, smothered, snuffed (out), stamped (out), suffocated

2 filled with much light — see BRIGHT 2

able *adj* having the required skills for an acceptable level of performance — see COMPETENT

able–bodied *adj* enjoying health and vigor — see HEALTHY 1

ably *adv* in a skillful or expert manner — see WELL 3

abnegate *vb* to give up (as a position of authority) formally — see ABDICATE

abnegation *n* the act or practice of giving up or rejecting something once enjoyed or desired — see RENUNCIATION

abnormal *adj* **1** being out of the ordinary — see EXCEPTIONAL

2 departing from some accepted standard of what is normal — see DEVIANT

abnormality *n* a person, thing, or event that is not normal — see FREAK 1

abode *n* the place where one lives — see HOME 1

abolish *vb* to put an end to by formal action ⟨the U.S. *abolished* slavery by constitutional amendment on December 6, 1865⟩

syn abrogate, annul, cancel, dissolve, invalidate, negate, nullify, quash, repeal, rescind, void

rel countermand, override, overrule, overturn, veto; retract, reverse, revoke, suspend, withdraw; ban, enjoin, forbid, outlaw, prohibit; disallow, dismiss, reject; eliminate, eradicate, erase, liquidate, remove, throw out, write off

phrases do away with

near ant establish, found, institute; formalize, legalize, legitimate, legitimize, validate; pass, ratify; allow, approve, authorize, clear, endorse (*also* indorse), permit, sanction, warrant; command, decree, mandate, prescribe, order

abominable *adj* causing intense displeasure, disgust, or resentment — see OFFENSIVE 1

abominate *vb* to dislike strongly — see HATE

abomination *n* something or someone that is hated — see HATE 2

2 a very strong dislike — see HATE 1

aboriginal *adj* belonging to a particular place by birth or origin — see NATIVE 1

abort *vb* to put an end to (something planned or previously agreed to) — see CANCEL 1

abortion *n* the act of putting an end to something planned or previously agreed to — see CANCELLATION

abortive *adj* producing no results — see FUTILE

abounding *adj* possessing or covered with great numbers or amounts of something specified — see RIFE

about *adv* **1** on all sides or in every direction — see AROUND 1

2 toward the opposite direction — see AROUND 2

3 very close to but not completely — see ALMOST

about *prep* **1** having to do with ⟨a story *about* a young man who goes off to war⟩

---

syn synonym(s)   *rel* related words
ant antonym(s)   *near ant* near antonym(s)

syn apropos of, concerning, of, on, regarding, respecting, toward (*or* towards)

rel as to, over

phrases as regards

2 close to — see AROUND 1

3 in random positions within the boundaries of — see AROUND 2

above *prep* higher than ⟨one minute our kite was *above* the telephone wires; the next minute it was tangled in them⟩

syn over

rel atop

near ant underneath

ant below, beneath, under

above *adv* to or in a higher place ⟨we eventually got used to the planes constantly flying *above*⟩

syn aloft, over, overhead, skyward

near ant underneath

ant below, beneath, under

abrade *vb* **1** to damage or diminish by continued friction ⟨ropes *abraded* by the rocks were a huge danger to the climbers⟩

syn chafe, erode, fray, fret, gall, rub, wear

rel file, gnaw, grate, graze, grind, nibble, rasp, sandblast, sandpaper, scour, scrape, scuff, shave; erase, reduce, rub out, wear out, wipe (away); bite, break down, break up, chew, corrode, decompose, disintegrate, dissolve, eat; hone, sharpen, whet

2 to make sore by continued rubbing — see CHAFE 1

3 to damage by rubbing against a sharp or rough surface — see SCRAPE 2

abreast *adj* having information especially as a result of study or experience — see FAMILIAR 2

abridge *vb* to make less in extent or duration — see SHORTEN

abridgment *or* **abridgement** *n* a shortened version of a written work ⟨this Italian-English pocket dictionary is an *abridgment* of the hardback edition⟩

syn abbreviation, condensation, digest

rel abstract, brief, outline, overview, précis, recap, recapitulation, résumé (*or* resume *also* resumé), review, sketch, sum, summarization, summary, summation, survey, syllabus, synopsis, wrap-up

near ant amplification, elaboration, enlargement, expansion

abrogate *vb* to put an end to by formal action — see ABOLISH

abrupt *adj* **1** being or characterized by direct, brief, and potentially rude speech or manner — see BLUNT 1

2 having an incline approaching the perpendicular — see STEEP 1

abruptly *adv* with great suddenness — see SHORT

abscond *vb* to get free from a dangerous or confining situation — see ESCAPE 1

absence *n* **1** a state of being without something necessary, desirable, or useful — see NEED 1

2 the fact or state of being absent — see LACK 1

absent *adj* **1** not at a certain place ⟨three students were *absent* because of the flu⟩

syn away, missing, out

rel AWOL, truant; departed, gone, retired; abroad, vacationing

near ant accompanying, attending, participating

ant here, present

2 not present or in evidence ⟨the usual stir of activity was *absent* in the city due to the report of an escaped lion from the zoo⟩

syn lacking, missing, nonexistent, wanting

rel dead, departed, extinct, lost, perished, vanished; defunct, done, expired, finished, lapsed, obsolete, over, passé; inadequate, insufficient, rare, scarce, sparse, uncommon

near ant active, alive, animate, living, thriving; current, going, prevailing, uncanceled; common, prevalent; apparent, conspicuous, evident, obvious, plain

ant existent, present

3 lost in thought and unaware of one's surroundings or actions — see ABSENT-MINDED 1

absentminded *adj* **1** lost in thought and unaware of one's surroundings or actions ⟨the grieving woman was so *absentminded* that she left her key in the lock after opening the door⟩

syn absent, abstracted, preoccupied

rel absorbed, daydreaming, distracted, dreaming, dreamy, engrossed, faraway, intent, pensive, rapt; heedless, inattentive, insensible, oblivious, unaware, unconscious, unheeding, unknowing, unmindful, unobservant, unobserving, unperceiving, unperceptive, unseeing, unthinking, unwary, unwitting, vacant; befogged, befuddled, bemused, bewildered, confused, dazed, flighty, foggy, forgetful, forgetting, hazy, muddled, scatterbrained, unfocused

near ant alive, attentive, aware, conscious, heedful, mindful, observant, observing, open-eyed, sharp, vigilant, wary, watchful, wide-awake; clearheaded, unconfused

ant alert

2 inclined to forget what one has learned or to do what one should — see FORGETFUL

absolute *adj* **1** exercising power or authority without interference by others ⟨the *absolute* monarchy of Russia ended when Czar Nicholas II promised to share power with a legislative body⟩

syn autocratic, despotic, dictatorial, tyrannical (*also* tyrannic), tyrannous

rel authoritarian, totalitarian; arbitrary, high-handed, magisterial; domineering, imperious, masterful; all-powerful, almighty, omnipotent; autonomous, self-governing, sovereign; unconditional, unlimited

near ant circumscribed, restrained, restricted; constitutional, lawful

ant limited

2 having no exceptions or restrictions ⟨ironing is an *absolute* bore⟩ ⟨I want the *absolute* truth⟩

syn all-out, arrant, categorical (*also* categoric), complete, consummate, dead, downright, flat, out-and-out, outright, perfect, profound, pure, regular, sheer, simple, stark, thorough, thoroughgoing, total, unadulterated, unalloyed, unconditional, unequivocal, unmitigated, unqualified, utter

rel authentic, classic, genuine, real, veritable; constant, endless, eternal, perpetual, undying, unremitting; extreme, rank, unrestricted; confirmed, habitual, hopeless, inveterate; deadly, extraordinary, frightful, horrible, huge, main, superlative, supreme, surpassing, terrible, terrific

near ant doubtful, dubious, equivocal, qualified, questionable, restricted, uncertain

3 being entirely without fault or flaw — see PERFECT 1

4 free from added matter — see PURE 1

5 serving to put an end to all debate or questioning — see CONCLUSIVE 1

absolution *n* release from the guilt or penalty of an offense — see PARDON

absolve *vb* to free from a charge of wrongdoing — see EXCULPATE

absorb *vb* **1** to take in (something liquid) through small openings ⟨most of the spilled water was *absorbed* by the tablecloth⟩

syn drink, imbibe, soak (up), sponge, suck (up)

rel gulp, guzzle, quaff, sip, slurp, swallow, swig, swill

2 to hold the attention of — see ENGAGE 1

absorbed *adj* having the mind fixed on something — see ATTENTIVE

absorbing *adj* holding the attention or provoking interest — see INTERESTING

absorption *n* a focusing of the mind on something — see ATTENTION 1

abstain (from) *vb* to resist the temptation of — see FORBEAR

abstract *adj* **1** dealing with or expressing a quality or idea ⟨the book deals with *abstract* matters such as honesty and integrity on the job as well as practical subjects such as asking for a raise⟩

syn conceptual, theoretical (*also* theoretic)

rel conjectural, hypothetical, speculative; intellectual, mental, spiritual; ethereal, immaterial, incorporeal, insubstantial, metaphysical, nonmaterial, nonphysical, unsubstantial; impalpable, imperceptible, insensible, intangible, invisible; impractical, romantic, transcendent, transcendental, unreal, utopian, visionary

near ant material, physical; appreciable, detectable, discernable, noticeable, observable, palpable, perceptible, sensible,

substantial, tangible, visible; defined, definite, distinct; actual, factual, real

ant concrete

2 using elements of form (as color, line, or texture) with little or no attempt at creating a realistic picture ⟨Cubism is a style of *abstract* art in which natural forms are broken up into geometric shapes⟩

syn nonrealistic

rel impressionist, impressionistic; symbolist, symbolistic

near ant lifelike, natural

ant realistic, representational

abstract *n* a short statement of the main points — see SUMMARY

abstract *vb* to make into a short statement of the main points (as of a report) — see SUMMARIZE

abstracted *adj* lost in thought and unaware of one's surroundings or actions — see ABSENTMINDED 1

abstruse *adj* difficult for one of ordinary knowledge or intelligence to understand — see PROFOUND 1

absurd *adj* **1** conceived or made without regard for reason or reality — see FANTASTIC 1

2 showing or marked by a lack of good sense or judgment — see FOOLISH 1

3 so foolish or pointless as to be worthy of scornful laughter — see RIDICULOUS 1

absurdity *n* **1** a foolish act or idea — see FOLLY 1

2 lack of good sense or judgment — see FOOLISHNESS 1

abundance *n* **1** a considerable amount — see LOT 2

2 an amount or supply more than sufficient to meet one's needs — see PLENTY 1

abundant *adj* being more than enough without being excessive — see PLENTIFUL

abuse *n* **1** harsh insulting language ⟨spectators hurled *abuse* at the visiting team⟩

syn fulmination, invective, vitriol, vituperation

rel blasphemy, curse, execration, imprecation, malediction, profanity; epithet, insult, put-down, slur; expletive, swearword; aspersion, bad-mouthing, belittlement, disparagement, revilement, vilification; castigation, chastisement, criticism, excoriation, opprobrium, rebuke, reprimand, reproof; broadside, diatribe, harangue, polemic, tirade

near ant acclaim, applause, commendation, praise; compliments, congratulations, endearments, felicitations; adulation, blarney, flattery, overpraise, soft soap

2 incorrect or improper use — see MISUSE

abuse *vb* **1** to inflict physical or emotional harm upon ⟨if you *abuse* your pet, he will always have an ugly disposition⟩

syn ill-treat, ill-use, maltreat, manhandle, mishandle, mistreat, misuse

---

syn synonym(s)   *rel* related words
ant antonym(s)   *near ant* near antonym(s)

rel molest, outrage, violate; harass, harm, hurt, injure, oppress, persecute, torment, torture, victimize, wrong

near ant care (for), cherish, foster, nurture; baby, cater (to), coddle, favor, gratify, humor, indulge, mollycoddle, pamper, spoil

2 to criticize harshly and usually publicly — see ATTACK 2

3 to put to a bad or improper use — see MISAPPLY

4 to take unfair advantage of — see EXPLOIT 1

abut *vb* to be adjacent to — see ADJOIN 1

abutting *adj* having a border in common — see ADJACENT

abysmal *adj* extending far downward or inward — see DEEP 1

abyss *n* an immeasurable depth or space ⟨looking down at the dark ocean from the ship's rail, Malcolm felt as though he was staring into an *abyss*⟩

syn chasm, gulf

rel cleft, crevasse, crevice, fissure; cavern, hole, hollow, pit; breadth, expanse, extent, reach, spread, stretch; emptiness, nothingness, vacuity, vacuum, void

academic *adj* of or relating to schooling or learning especially at an advanced level ⟨"If you spent more time in *academic* pursuits and less time in social ones, you could easily make good grades," the dean told Valerie⟩

syn educational, scholarly, scholastic

rel bookish, pedantic, professorial; curricular; educative, instructive; collegiate, graduate, postgraduate

near ant extracurricular; noncollegiate

ant nonacademic, unacademic

academy *n* a place or establishment for teaching and learning — see SCHOOL

accelerate *vb* to cause to move or proceed fast or faster — see HURRY 1

accent *n* a special notice or importance given to something — see EMPHASIS 1

accent *vb* to indicate the importance of by giving prominent display — see EMPHASIZE

accentuate *vb* to indicate the importance of by giving prominent display — see EMPHASIZE

accentuation *n* a special notice or importance given to something — see EMPHASIS 1

accept *vb* **1** to agree to receive whether willingly or reluctantly — see TAKE 2

2 to have a favorable opinion of — see APPROVE 1

3 to regard as right or true — see BELIEVE 1

4 to take to or upon oneself — see ASSUME 1

acceptability *n* the quality or state of meeting one's needs adequately — see SUFFICIENCY

acceptable *adj* of a level of quality that meets one's needs or standards — see ADEQUATE

acceptably *adv* in a satisfactory way — see WELL 1

accepting *adj* showing or expressing acceptance or approval — see POSITIVE

access *n* the means or right of entering or participating in — see ENTRANCE 1

access *vb* to go or come in or into — see ENTER 1

accessible *adj* **1** possible to get — see AVAILABLE 1

2 situated within easy reach — see CONVENIENT

accessory *adj* available to supply something extra when needed — see AUXILIARY

accessory *n* **1** something that is not necessary in itself but adds to the convenience or performance of the main piece of equipment ⟨bought a new car with lots of high-tech *accessories*⟩

syn accoutrement (*or* accouterment), adjunct, appendage, attachment

rel accompaniment, additive, complement, supplement; auxiliary, subsidiary; amenity, extra, filler, frill, incidental, luxury, nonessential, nonnecessity; equipment, furnishings, paraphernalia, trappings; adornment, decoration, embellishment, enhancement, garnish, ornament, trim

near ant essential, necessity, requirement, requisite

2 one associated with another in wrongdoing — see ACCOMPLICE

accident *n* **1** a chance and usually sudden event bringing loss or injury ⟨was involved in an *accident* on her way home from work⟩

syn casualty, mischance, mishap

rel calamity, cataclysm, catastrophe, cropper, deathblow, disaster, tragedy; bummer, knock, misadventure, misfortune; collision, crack-up, crash, smashup, wreck

near ant boon, break, fluke, godsend, miracle, strike, windfall; fortune, luck, serendipity

2 the uncertain course of events — see CHANCE 1

accidental *adj* happening by chance ⟨finding the gold was all the more remarkable because its discovery was entirely *accidental*⟩

syn casual, chance, fluky, fortuitous, inadvertent, incidental, unintended, unintentional, unplanned, unpremeditated, unwitting

rel coincidental; freak, odd; aimless, arbitrary, desultory, haphazard, random; uncertain, unexpected, unforeseeable, unforeseen; coerced, forced, involuntary; unconscious, unexpected, unprompted

near ant certain, destined, expected, fixed, foreordained, foreseeable, foreseen, inevitable, predestined, predetermined, predictable, preordained, prescribed, sure; conscious, freewill, knowing, unforced, voluntary, volunteer, willful (*or* wilful)

ant deliberate, intended, intentional, planned, premeditated

acclaim *n* public acknowledgment or admiration for an achievement — see GLORY 1

acclaim *vb* to declare enthusiastic approval of ⟨she was *acclaimed* by the critics for her realistic acting⟩

syn applaud, cheer, crack up, hail, laud, praise, salute, tout

rel ballyhoo; approve, commend, endorse (*also* indorse), favor, recommend, support; celebrate, emblazon, eulogize, extol (*also* extoll), glorify, sing; adulate, flatter, overpraise; deify, idolize

near ant belittle, disparage, put down; blame, censure, reprehend, reprobate; admonish, chide, criticize, rebuke, reprimand, reproach, reprove; castigate, excoriate, lambaste

ant knock, pan, slam

acclamation *n* enthusiastic and usually public expression of approval — see APPLAUSE

acclimate *vb* to change (something) so as to make it suitable for a new use or situation — see ADAPT

acclimatize *vb* to change (something) so as to make it suitable for a new use or situation — see ADAPT

accolade *n* 1 a formal expression of praise — see ENCOMIUM

2 public acknowledgment or admiration for an achievement — see GLORY 1

accommodate *vb* 1 to make or have room for ⟨the back seat *accommodates* three people comfortably⟩

syn fit, hold, take

rel carry, contain, seat; enclose (*also* inclose), encompass; harbor, house

2 to bring to a state free of conflicts, inconsistencies, or differences — see HARMONIZE 2

3 to change (something) so as to make it suitable for a new use or situation — see ADAPT

4 to do a service or favor for — see OBLIGE 1

5 to provide with living quarters or shelter — see HOUSE 1

accommodation *n* the act or practice of each side giving up something in order to reach an agreement — see CONCESSION 1

accompaniment *n* something that is found along with something else ⟨the sound of crickets was the perfect *accompaniment* to our summer evenings on the porch⟩

syn companion, concomitant

rel accessory, adjunct, appendage; complement, supplement; counterpart, fellow, mate; consequence, corollary, follow-up; fixings, trimmings

accompany *vb* to go along with in order to provide assistance, protection, or companionship ⟨children must be *accompanied* by a parent at all times⟩

syn attend, chaperone (*or* chaperon), convoy, escort, squire

rel associate, consort, pal (around), team (up); defend, guard, protect; bring, conduct, guide, lead, pilot, see, steer, usher; follow, shadow, tag, tag along, tail; hang (around), hover (over)

near ant abandon, desert, ditch, dump, forsake

accompanying *adj* present at the same time and place — see COINCIDENT

accomplice *n* one associated with another in wrongdoing ⟨the thief and his *accomplices* were eventually caught and brought to justice⟩

syn abettor (*also* abetter), accessory, cohort, confederate

rel collaborator, collaborationist, informant, informer; companion, comrade, crony, henchman, partner; conspirator, plotter, traitor; gangster, mobster, racketeer

accomplish *vb* to carry through (as a process) to completion — see PERFORM 1

accomplished *adj* having or showing exceptional knowledge, experience, or skill in a field of endeavor — see PROFICIENT

accomplishment *n* 1 a successful result brought about by hard work ⟨Jared's biggest *accomplishment* this week was finishing his art project⟩

syn achievement, attainment, coup, success, triumph

rel blockbuster, hit, jackpot, megahit, smash, winner; conquest, gain, victory, win; acquirement, skill; deed, feat, performance; completion, consummation, culmination, execution, fruition, fulfillment, implementation, realization

phrases a feather in one's cap

near ant botch, mess, muddle, shambles; bummer, bust, catastrophe, debacle (*also* débâcle), dud, failure, fiasco, fizzle, flop, washout; disappointment, letdown, loss, setback

2 the doing of an action — see COMMISSION 2

3 the state of being actual or complete — see FRUITION

accord *n* 1 a formal agreement between two or more nations or peoples — see TREATY

2 a state of consistency — see CONFORMITY 1

3 an arrangement about action to be taken — see AGREEMENT 2

4 the act or fact of being of one opinion about something — see AGREEMENT 1

5 the act or power of making one's own choices or decisions — see FREE WILL

accord *vb* 1 to be in agreement on every point — see CHECK 1

2 to give the ownership or benefit of (something) formally or publicly — see CONFER 1

accordance *n* a state of consistency — see CONFORMITY 1

accordingly *adv* for this or that reason — see THEREFORE

account *n* 1 a relating of events usually in the order in which they happened ⟨news-

---

syn synonym(s)   *rel* related words
ant antonym(s)   *near ant* near antonym(s)

paper reporters must strive to provide an accurate *account* of what happened⟩

syn chronicle, history, narrative, record, report, story

rel version; deposition, documentation, testament, testimonial, testimony, witness; annals, diary, journal, log, logbook, memoir; anecdote, tale, yarn; epic, saga; recital, recitation

2 a record of goods sold or services performed together with the costs due — see ¹BILL 1

3 a sum of money set aside for a particular purpose — see FUND 1

4 the capacity for being useful for some purpose — see USE 2

5 the relative usefulness or importance of something as judged by specific qualities — see WORTH 1

account *vb* to think of in a particular way — see CONSIDER 1

account (for) *vb* to give the reason for or cause of — see EXPLAIN 2

accountable *adj* being the one who must meet an obligation or suffer the consequences for failing to do so — see RESPONSIBLE 1

accoutre *or* **accouter** *vb* to provide (someone) with what is needed for a task or activity — see FURNISH 1

accoutrement *or* **accouterment** *n* **1** something that is not necessary in itself but adds to the convenience or performance of the main piece of equipment — see ACCESSORY 1

2 accoutrements *or* accouterments *pl* items needed for the performance of a task or activity — see EQUIPMENT

accredit *vb* **1** to explain (something) as being the result of something else — see CREDIT 1

2 to give official or legal power to — see AUTHORIZE 1

accreditation *n* the granting of power to perform various acts or duties — see COMMISSION 1

accretion *n* something added (as by growth) — see INCREASE 1

accrual *n* something added (as by growth) — see INCREASE 1

accumulate *vb* **1** to become greater in extent, volume, amount, or number — see INCREASE 2

2 to bring together in one body or place — see GATHER 1

3 to gradually form into a layer, pile, or mass — see COLLECT 2

accumulating *n* the act or process of becoming greater in number — see MULTIPLICATION

accumulation *n* **1** a mass or quantity that has piled up or that has been gathered ⟨a vast *accumulation* of evidence about the dangers of smoking⟩

syn assemblage, collection, gathering

rel agglomerate, assortment, conglomerate, conglomeration, hodgepodge, hotchpotch, jumble, medley, mélange, mishmash, mix, mixture, motley, potpourri; agglomeration, clutter, hash, heap, litter,

mass, pile; aggregate, aggregation, sum, totality; cache, fund, hoard, inventory, nest egg, reserve, stock, stockpile, store, supply

2 the act or process of becoming greater in number — see MULTIPLICATION

accuracy *n* the quality or state of being very accurate — see PRECISION

accurate *adj* **1** being in agreement with the truth or a fact or a standard — see CORRECT 1

2 following an original exactly — see FAITHFUL 2

3 meeting the highest standard of accuracy — see PRECISE 1

accuse *vb* to make a claim of wrongdoing against ⟨she was *accused* of cheating on the test⟩

syn charge, impeach, incriminate, indict

rel blame, castigate, censure, condemn, criticize, damn, denounce, fault, impugn, reproach, reprobate; chide, rebuke, reprove, tax; arraign, book, cite, summon; prosecute, sue, try; frame, implicate, inform (against), report; recriminate, retaliate

near ant advocate, champion, defend; excuse, forgive, justify, pardon, remit, shrive

ant absolve, acquit, clear, exculpate, exonerate, vindicate

accustomed *adj* being in the habit or custom ⟨Josh felt uncomfortably full, as he was not *accustomed* to eating so much⟩

syn given, habituated, used, wont

rel apt, inclined, liable, prone; hardened, inured; experienced, practiced (*or* practised), seasoned, veteran; addicted, hooked

near ant averse, disinclined, opposed; inexperienced, new, unseasoned

ant unaccustomed, unused

ace *adj* having or showing exceptional knowledge, experience, or skill in a field of endeavor — see PROFICIENT 1

ace *n* **1** a person with a high level of knowledge or skill in a field — see EXPERT

2 a very small amount — see PARTICLE 1

3 a very small distance or degree — see HAIR 1

ache *n* a sharp unpleasant sensation usually felt in some specific part of the body — see PAIN 1

ache *vb* to feel or cause physical pain — see HURT 1

ache (for) *vb* to have an earnest wish to own or enjoy — see DESIRE

achievable *adj* capable of being done or carried out — see POSSIBLE 1

achieve *vb* **1** to obtain (as a goal) through effort ⟨finally *achieved* stardom⟩

syn attain, hit, make, score, win

rel acquire, capture, carry, draw, garner, get, land, make, obtain, procure, realize, secure; amount (to), approach, equal, match, measure up (to), meet, rival, tie, touch; beat, excel, outdo, surpass, top

near ant fall short (of); fail (at); lose

2 to carry through (as a process) to completion — see PERFORM 1

achievement *n* **1** a successful result brought about by hard work — see ACCOMPLISHMENT 1

2 the doing of an action — see COMMISSION 2

3 the state of being actual or complete — see FRUITION

aching *adj* causing or feeling bodily pain — see PAINFUL 1

acid *adj* causing or characterized by the one of the four basic taste sensations that is produced chiefly by acids — see SOUR 1

acidic *adj* causing or characterized by the one of the four basic taste sensations that is produced chiefly by acids — see SOUR 1

acidity *n* **1** a harsh or sharp quality — see EDGE 1

2 biting sharpness of feeling or expression — see ACRIMONY 1

acidness *n* biting sharpness of feeling or expression — see ACRIMONY 1

acknowledge *vb* to accept the truth or existence of (something) usually reluctantly — see ADMIT 1

acknowledgment *also* **acknowledgement** *n* **1** a formal recognition of an achievement or praiseworthy deed — see COMMENDATION 1

2 an open declaration of something (as a fault or the commission of an offense) about oneself — see CONFESSION

acme *n* the highest part or point — see HEIGHT 1

acoustic *or* **acoustical** *adj* of, relating to, or experienced through the sense of hearing — see AUDITORY

acquaint *vb* **1** to impart knowledge of a new thing or situation to ⟨Mr. King spent the first week of class *acquainting* everyone with the new computers⟩
syn familiarize, initiate, introduce, orient, orientate
rel apprise, brief, clue (in), fill in, inform; educate, enlighten, ground, instruct, school, train; expose, present, subject; advise, tell, tip off, warn, wise up

2 to give information to — see ENLIGHTEN 1

3 to make (one person) known (to another) socially — see INTRODUCE 1

acquaintance *n* knowledge gained by personal experience ⟨Tiffany's *acquaintance* with cows is limited to a visit to a petting zoo when she was three⟩
syn cognizance, familiarity
rel association, experience, exposure, intimacy, involvement; initiation, introduction; awareness, comprehension, conception, inkling, notion, understanding; education, enlightenment, grounding, information, instruction, learning, schooling, training
near callowness, greenness, ignorance, inexperience
ant unfamiliarity

acquainted *adj* having information especially as a result of study or experience — see FAMILIAR 2

acquiescent *adj* receiving or enduring without offering resistance — see PASSIVE

acquirable *adj* possible to get — see AVAILABLE 1

acquire *vb* **1** to come to have gradually — see DEVELOP 2

2 to receive as return for effort — see EARN 1

acquisitive *adj* having or marked by an eager and often selfish desire especially for material possessions — see GREEDY 1

acquisitiveness *n* an intense selfish desire for wealth or possessions — see GREED

acquit *vb* **1** to free from a charge of wrongdoing — see EXCULPATE

2 to manage the actions of (oneself) in a particular way — see BEHAVE

acrid *adj* **1** having or showing deep-seated resentment — see BITTER 1

2 marked by the use of wit that is intended to cause hurt feelings — see SARCASTIC

acridness *n* **1** a harsh or sharp quality — see EDGE 1

2 biting sharpness of feeling or expression — see ACRIMONY 1

acrimonious *adj* having or showing deep-seated resentment — see BITTER 1

acrimoniousness *n* a harsh or sharp quality — see EDGE 1

acrimony *n* **1** biting sharpness of feeling or expression ⟨she responded with such *acrimony* that he never brought the subject up again⟩
syn acidity, acidness, acridness, asperity, bitterness, cattiness, tartness, virulence, vitriol
rel gruffness, harshness, hostility, relentlessness, severity, sternness, vehemence; coldness, crossness, discourteousness, iciness, impoliteness, incivility, nastiness, rudeness, sourness, surliness, ungraciousness; anger, animosity, bile, jaundice, malevolence, malice, rancor, scorn, spite, spleen, venom; jealousy, pique, resentment
near civility, cordiality, courtesy, diplomacy, geniality, graciousness, politeness, tactfulness; compassion, softness, sweetness, sympathy, tenderness, warmth; oiliness, smoothness, suaveness, unctuousness, urbanity

2 a harsh or sharp quality — see EDGE 1

across *adv* from one side to the other of an intervening space — see OVER 1

across *prep* to the opposite side of ⟨we swam *across* the lake and visited the other summer camp⟩
syn athwart, over, through
rel around, round; beyond, past

act *n* **1** a display of emotion or behavior that is insincere or intended to deceive — see MASQUERADE

2 a rule of conduct or action laid down by a governing authority and especially a legislator — see LAW 1

---

3 something done by someone — see ACTION 1

act *vb* **1** to present a portrayal or performance of ⟨a very talented student *acted* the part of Tiny Tim in our production of *A Christmas Carol*⟩

syn impersonate, perform, play, portray

rel depict, dramatize, enact, pantomime, render, represent, role-play, take on; overact, underplay; ape, clown, ham, imitate, masquerade, mime, mimic, pose (as); star (in)

2 to produce a desired effect ⟨the painkiller *acted* quickly⟩

syn operate, perform, take, work

rel behave, react, respond; affect, influence, sway; pan out, redound, result

phrases take effect

near ant backfire; fizzle

3 to give the impression of being — see SEEM

4 to have a certain purpose — see FUNCTION

act (toward) *vb* to behave toward in a stated way — see TREAT 1

action *n* **1** something done by someone ⟨judge people by their *actions*, not by their words⟩

syn act, deed, doing, exploit, feat, thing

rel accomplishment, achievement, attainment; adventure, experience; enterprise, initiative, undertaking; handiwork, performance, work; stunt, trick; activity, dealing; maneuver, measure, move, operation, procedure, proceeding, step, tactic

2 a court case for enforcing a right or claim — see LAWSUIT

3 active fighting during the course of a war — see COMBAT 1

4 actions *pl* the way or manner in which one conducts oneself — see BEHAVIOR

activate *vb* to cause to function ⟨the thermostat is set to *activate* the heating system only when the temperature drops below 65 degrees⟩

syn actuate, crank (up), drive, move, propel, run, set off, spark, start, touch off, trigger, turn on

rel charge, electrify, energize, fire, fuel, generate, power, push; discharge, launch, release, switch, trip; reactivate, recharge; arouse, excite, stimulate, vitalize; incite, instigate, provoke, quicken, stir up; accelerate, catalyze, speed up, step up

near ant arrest, brake, chock, cut off, draw up, halt, jam, stall, stick, stop; decelerate, repress, slow, stunt, suppress

ant cut, deactivate, kill, shut off, turn off

active *adj* **1** being in effective operation ⟨the abandoned factory had not been *active* for years⟩

syn alive, functional, functioning, going, living, on, operating, operational, operative, running, working

rel effective, effectual; employable, operable, usable, viable, workable; performing, producing, productive, serving, useful, yielding; astir, bustling, busy, dynamic, flourishing, humming, roaring, thriving

phrases in commission

near ant deactivated, decommissioned; ineffective, ineffectual, useless; inoperable, unusable, unworkable; arrested, asleep, dormant, fallow, idle, inert, latent, lifeless, nonproductive, quiescent, sleepy, stagnating, unproductive, vegetating

ant broken, dead, inactive, inoperative, nonfunctional, nonfunctioning, nonoperating

2 having much high-spirited energy and movement — see LIVELY 1

3 involved in often constant activity — see BUSY 1

activity *n* energetic movement of the body for the sake of physical fitness — see EXERCISE 1

actor *n* one who acts professionally (as in a play, movie, or television show) ⟨my sister went to drama school to become an *actor*⟩

syn impersonator, mummer, player, trouper

rel barnstormer, entertainer, performer; actress, starlet; lead, leading lady, leading man, star; monologuist (*or* monologist); prima donna, scene-stealer, understudy; comedian, tragedian; ape, aper, ham, imitator, impressionist, masquerader, mime, mimic, pantomime, pantomimist, poser; buffoon, clown, harlequin, stooge, zany

actual *adj* existing in fact and not merely as a possibility ⟨the *actual* outcome of the election was quite different from what everybody expected⟩

syn concrete, existent, factual, real, true, very

rel attested, authenticated, confirmed, demonstrated, established, proven, substantiated, validated, verified; incontestable, incontrovertible, indisputable, indubitable, inescapable, irrefutable, undeniable, unquestionable; believable, convincing, literal, realistic, unmistakable, verifiable; authentic, bona fide, genuine, real-life; absolute, certain, final, hard, palpable, positive, substantial, tangible; authoritative, certifiable, certified

near ant alleged, assumed, reputed, supposed; conceived, envisaged, imagined, pictured, visualized; chimerical, fabled, fanciful, fictional, fictitious, legendary, illusory; fabricated, fake, imaginary, invented, made-up, make-believe, pretend, romantic; abstract, unreal

ant conjectural, hypothetical, ideal, nonexistent, possible, potential, theoretical (*also* theoretic)

actuality *n* **1** the fact of being or of being real — see EXISTENCE

2 the quality of being actual — see FACT 1

3 the state of being actual or complete — see FRUITION

actually *adv* **1** to tell the truth ⟨*actually*, I'd rather spend the evening at home⟩

syn forsooth, frankly, honestly, really, truly, truthfully, verily *rel* absolutely, certainly, indisputably, indubitably, positively, realistically, undoubtedly, unquestionably, veritably

phrases in point of fact, in reality, in truth

2 in actual fact — see VERY 2

actuate *vb* **1** to cause to function — see ACTIVATE

2 to set or keep in motion — see MOVE 2

act up *vb* **1** to behave badly — see MISBEHAVE

2 to engage in attention-getting playful or boisterous behavior — see CUT UP

acute *adj* **1** able to sense slight impressions or differences ⟨dogs, with their *acute* sense of smell, are used for finding toxic substances undetectable by humans⟩

syn delicate, keen, perceptive, sensitive, sharp

rel accurate, clear, discerning, fine, good, piercing, precise, quick, receptive, sensible, subtle; hypersensitive, oversensitive, supersensitive

near ant bad, deadened, dimmed, dull, dulled, fading; dead, imperceptive, insensible, insensitive, numb; imprecise, inaccurate

2 needing immediate attention ⟨famine caused by an *acute* shortage of grain⟩

syn critical, crying, dire, imperative, imperious, instant, pressing, urgent

rel compelling, demanding, extreme, immediate, insistent, intense, overriding; crucial, desperate, grave, life-and-death, serious, severe, vital; dangerous, explosive, hazardous, perilous, precarious, unstable

near ant incidental, low-pressure, minor, negligible, trivial, unimportant; nonthreatening, safe, stable

ant noncritical, nonurgent

3 causing intense mental or physical distress — see SHARP 2

4 having a high musical pitch or range — see SHRILL

acuteness *n* a harsh or sharp quality — see EDGE 1

ad *n* a published statement informing the public of a matter of general interest — see ANNOUNCEMENT

adage *n* an often stated observation regarding something from common experience — see SAYING

adamant *adj* sticking to an opinion, purpose, or course of action in spite of reason, arguments, or persuasion — see OBSTINATE

adamantine *adj* sticking to an opinion, purpose, or course of action in spite of reason, arguments, or persuasion — see OBSTINATE

adapt *vb* to change (something) so as to make it suitable for a new use or situation ⟨it always takes freshmen a little while to *adapt* themselves to high school⟩

syn acclimate, acclimatize, accommodate, adjust, condition, conform, fit, shape

rel readapt, readjust; customize, tailor; attune, harmonize, reconcile, suit, tune; establish, root, settle; acquaint, familiarize, orient, orientate; equip, prepare, prime, rehearse; harden, inure, season, toughen; alter, convert, make over, modify, redo, refashion, refit, remake, remodel, revamp, revise, rework, transform

adaptable *adj* **1** able to do many different kinds of things — see VERSATILE

2 capable of being readily changed — see FLEXIBLE 1

add *vb* **1** to join (something) to a mass, quantity, or number so as to bring about an overall increase ⟨the band recently *added* a saxophonist and a keyboard player to its ranks⟩ ⟨*add* another cup of flour to the mixture⟩

syn adjoin, annex, append, tack (on)

rel affix, attach, fasten, fix, graft, hitch, tie; infuse, inject, insert, introduce

near ant detach, disconnect, disjoin, separate, unfasten; amputate, cut, excise, lop off, sever

ant deduct, remove, subtract, take

2 to combine (numbers) into a single sum ⟨when she *added* all the phone charges she discovered an error in her bill⟩

syn foot (up), sum, total

rel calculate, cast, cipher, compute, figure, reckon, tally; count, enumerate, number

add (to) *vb* to make greater in size, amount, or number — see INCREASE 1

added *adj* resulting in an increase in amount or number — see ADDITIONAL

addendum *n* something added (as by growth) — see INCREASE 1

addict *n* **1** a person who regularly uses drugs especially illegally — see DOPER

2 a person with a strong and habitual liking for something — see FAN

addition *n* **1** a smaller structure added to a main building — see ANNEX

2 something added (as by growth) — see INCREASE 1

3 the act or process of becoming greater in number — see MULTIPLICATION

additional *adj* resulting in an increase in amount or number ⟨there turned out to be *additional* reasons for her absence besides those she had given⟩

syn added, another, else, farther, further, more, other

rel accessory, collateral, extraneous, side, supplemental, supplementary; fresh, new; extra, plus, spare, surplus

near ant fewer, less

additionally *adv* in addition to what has been said — see MORE 1

additive *adj* produced by a series of additions of identical or similar things — see CUMULATIVE

addle *vb* to throw into a state of mental uncertainty — see CONFUSE 1

addled *adj* having undergone organic breakdown — see ROTTEN 1

---

syn synonym(s)   *rel* related words
ant antonym(s)   *near ant* near antonym(s)

address *n* a usually formal discourse delivered to an audience — see SPEECH 1

address *vb* to occupy (oneself) diligently or with close attention — see APPLY 2

adduce *vb* to give as an example — see QUOTE 1

add up (to) *vb* **1** to be the same in meaning or effect — see AMOUNT (TO) 2

2 to have a total of — see AMOUNT (TO) 1

adept *adj* having or showing exceptional knowledge, experience, or skill in a field of endeavor — see PROFICIENT

adept *n* a person with a high level of knowledge or skill in a field — see EXPERT

adeptly *adv* in a skillful or expert manner — see WELL 3

adeptness *n* subtle or imaginative ability in inventing, devising, or executing something — see SKILL 1

adequacy *n* the quality or state of meeting one's needs adequately — see SUFFICIENCY

adequate *adj* of a level of quality that meets one's needs or standards ⟨this old computer is probably *adequate* if you just want to type a book report⟩
syn acceptable, all right, decent, fine, OK (*or* okay), passable, respectable, satisfactory, tolerable
rel agreeable, bearable, endurable, sufferable; average, fair, mediocre, middling, minimal, unexceptional; appropriate, correct, due, fitting, good, meet, proper, right, seemly, suitable, useful, worthy; gratifying, satisfying
near ant disreputable, improper, indecent, objectionable, unfit, unsuitable, unworthy; bad, defective, faulty, imperfect, incomplete, lamentable, pitiful; dissatisfying, unsatisfying; insufficient, meager, mean, miserly, niggardly, poor, scanty, shabby, short, skimpy, spare, stingy; insufferable, intolerable, unbearable, unendurable; exceptional, exquisite, extreme, first-class, matchless, maximized, maximum, optimal, optimum, peerless, preeminent, superior, supreme, unmatched, unparalleled, unsurpassed
ant deficient, inadequate, lacking, unacceptable, unsatisfactory, wanting

adequately *adv* **1** in a satisfactory way — see WELL 1

2 in or to a degree or quantity that meets one's requirements or satisfaction — see ENOUGH 1

adhere *vb* to hold to something firmly as if by adhesion — see STICK 1

adhere (to) *vb* to give steadfast support to ⟨our coach *adheres to* the belief that we can win this game if we just have a positive attitude⟩
syn cling (to), hew (to), keep (to), stick (to *or* with)
rel cleave (to), hang on (to); back, confirm, defend, endorse (*also* indorse), espouse, support, uphold; accept, adopt, cherish, cultivate, embrace, follow, foster, heed
phrases abide by, live up to, stand by

near ant abandon, desert, forsake, give up, relinquish, spurn, surrender; abjure, disavow, disclaim, disown, recall, recant, reconsider, renege, renounce, retract, revoke, take back, unsay, withdraw
ant defect (from)

adherence *n* a physical sticking to as if by glue — see ADHESION

adherent *n* one who follows the opinions or teachings of another — see FOLLOWER

adhesion *n* a physical sticking to as if by glue ⟨mom prefers photo albums that keep the pictures in place by *adhesion* to the pages⟩
syn adherence, bonding
rel agglutination, clumping, cohesion; adhesiveness, attachment, cohesiveness, tenacity; cementing, glueing

adhesive *adj* being of such a thick consistency as to readily cling to objects upon contact — see STICKY 1

adhesive *n* a substance used to stick things together — see GLUE

adieu *n* an expression of good wishes at parting — see GOOD-BYE

adipose *adj* containing animal fat especially in unusual amounts — see FATTY

adiposity *n* the condition of having an excess of body fat — see CORPULENCE

adjacent *adj* having a border in common ⟨Crystal's house is *adjacent* to a wooded park⟩
syn abutting, adjoining, bordering, contiguous, flanking, fringing, joining, juxtaposed, skirting, touching, verging
rel close, closest, immediate, near, nearest, nearby, neighboring, next, next-door, nigh; attached, communicating, connecting, interconnecting, linked; bounding, embracing, encircling, enclosing, fencing, rimming, surrounding; marginal, peripheral, tangent, tangential
near ant apart, detached, free-standing, removed, separate, unattached, unconnected, unlinked; away, distant, far, far-off, farthest, remote; discontinuous, noncontinuous
ant nonadjacent

adjoin *vb* **1** to be adjacent to ⟨Colleen, whose bedroom *adjoins* her little brother's room, sometimes hears him talking in his sleep⟩
syn abut, border (on), flank, fringe, join, skirt, touch, verge (on)
rel attach (to), communicate (with), connect (with), link (with); bound, embrace, encircle, enclose (*also* inclose), fence, line, rim, surround; contact, converge, meet, neighbor

2 to join (something) to a mass, quantity, or number so as to bring about an overall increase — see ADD 1

adjoining *adj* having a border in common — see ADJACENT

adjourn *vb* to bring to a formal close for a period of time ⟨the meeting was *adjourned* by the chairperson until further notice⟩
syn recess, suspend

rel break off, discontinue, intermit, interrupt; defer, hold off, postpone, put off, reserve, shelve, table; abort, call off, cancel, dissolve, terminate; break up, close, conclude, wind up, wrap up

near ant inaugurate, launch, open; carry on, continue, draw out, extend, proceed, prolong; renew, reopen, resume; convene, convoke

adjudge *vb* to give an opinion about (something at issue or in dispute) — see JUDGE 1

adjudicate *vb* to give an opinion about (something at issue or in dispute) — see JUDGE 1

adjunct *n* something that is not necessary in itself but adds to the convenience or performance of the main piece of equipment — see ACCESSORY 1

adjure *vb* to issue orders to (someone) by right of authority — see COMMAND 1

adjust *vb* to change (something) so as to make it suitable for a new use or situation — see ADAPT

adjustable *adj* capable of being readily changed — see FLEXIBLE 1

adjutant *n* a person who helps a more skilled person — see HELPER

ad-lib *adj* made or done without previous thought or preparation — see EXTEMPORANEOUS

ad-lib *vb* to perform, make, or do without preparation — see IMPROVISE

administer *vb* 1 to give out (something) in appropriate amounts or to appropriate individuals ⟨the principal *administers* discipline fairly when students break the rules⟩

syn allocate, apportion, deal (out), dispense, distribute, dole (out), mete (out), parcel (out), portion, prorate

rel allot, allow, appropriate, assign, dish (out), divide, measure (out), ration, redistribute, split; bestow, disburse, furnish, issue, provide, share, supply; circulate, disperse, disseminate, scatter, spread; chip in, contribute, donate, pledge

near ant begrudge, deny, deprive (of), pinch, refuse, skimp, stint, withhold

2 to carry out effectively — see ENFORCE

3 to look after and make decisions about — see CONDUCT 1

administration *n* 1 lawful control over the affairs of a political unit (as a nation) — see RULE 2

2 the act or activity of looking after and making decisions about something — see CONDUCT 1

administrative *adj* suited for or relating to the directing of things — see EXECUTIVE

administrator *n* a person who manages or directs — see EXECUTIVE

admirable *adj* deserving of high regard or great approval ⟨it's *admirable* the way Kory helps her grandmother with chores and errands every Saturday⟩

syn commendable, creditable, laudable, meritorious, praiseworthy

rel awesome, distinctive, distinguished, excellent, honorable, noteworthy, noticeable, outstanding, reputable, worthy; invaluable, precious, priceless, valuable; delightful, enjoyable, pleasing, satisfying

near ant contemptible, deplorable, infamous, notorious, sorry, unlikable, unworthy, worthless; disgraceful, dishonorable, disreputable, low, mean, scandalous, seamy, shady, shameful, shocking, sordid, unsavory

ant censurable, discreditable, reprehensible

admiration *n* 1 a feeling of great approval and liking ⟨my *admiration* for Yoko increased when I discovered she had learned English only since coming to the U.S.⟩

syn appreciation, esteem, estimation, favor, regard, respect

rel acclamation, adoration, approbation, deference, homage, honor, praise, reverence, veneration, worship; delight, enjoyment, fancy; amazement, awe, wonder, wonderment

near ant condemnation, disapproval, disdain, opprobrium, scorn; disappointment, discontent, disenchantment, disgruntlement, disillusionment, displeasure, indignation, unhappiness; aversion, contempt, disgust, dislike, disregard, distaste

ant disfavor

2 the rapt attention and deep emotion caused by the sight of something extraordinary — see WONDER 2

admire *vb* to think very highly or favorably of ⟨I *admire* the way you handled such a touchy situation⟩

syn appreciate, esteem, regard, respect

rel acclaim, accredit, applaud, approve, commend, compliment, credit, praise; delight (in), drink (in), enjoy, relish, revel (in), savor; dig, fancy, favor, groove (on), like, love; adore, deify, idolize, revere, reverence, venerate, worship; cherish, prize, treasure, value

phrases set store by (*or* on)

near ant condemn, decry, deplore, disapprove, discount, discountenance, disdain, disfavor, dislike, dismiss, disregard, frown (on), scorn

admiring *adj* expressing approval — see FAVORABLE 1

admissible *adj* that may be permitted — see PERMISSIBLE

admission *n* 1 an open declaration of something (as a fault or the commission of an offense) about oneself — see CONFESSION

2 the means or right of entering or participating in — see ENTRANCE 1

admit *vb* to accept the truth or existence of (something) usually reluctantly ⟨Eliza readily *admitted* she hadn't read the assignment⟩ ⟨you can't bring yourself to *admit* your mistakes⟩

---

syn synonym(s)	*rel* related words	
ant antonym(s)	*near ant* near antonym(s)	

syn acknowledge, agree, allow, concede, confess, grant, own (up)

rel disburden, unburden, unload; affirm, avow, confirm, profess; accept, recognize, yield; announce, break, broadcast, communicate, declare, disclose, divulge, impart, publish, reveal, spill, tell, unveil; betray, blab, expose, give away, inform, leak, rat, squeal, talk, tattle, tip off, warn, wise up; breathe, whisper

near ant disallow, disavow, disclaim, disown; contradict, dispute, gainsay, negate, negative; rebut, refute, reject, repudiate; conceal, cover (up), hide, obscure, veil

ant deny

admittance *n* the means or right of entering or participating in — see ENTRANCE 1

admixture *n* a distinct entity formed by the combining of two or more different things — see BLEND

admonish *vb* to criticize (someone) usually gently so as to correct a fault — see REBUKE 1

admonishing *adj* serving as or offering a warning — see CAUTIONARY

admonition *n* the act or an instance of telling beforehand of danger or risk — see WARNING 1

admonitory *adj* serving as or offering a warning — see CAUTIONARY

adolescent *adj* **1** being in the early stage of life, growth, or development — see YOUNG

2 having or showing the annoying qualities (as silliness) associated with children — see CHILDISH

3 lacking in adult experience or maturity — see CALLOW

adopt *vb* to take for one's own use (something originated by another) ⟨the family *adopted* the American tradition of having turkey for Thanksgiving after they moved to the U.S.⟩

syn borrow, embrace, take up

rel domesticate, naturalize; appropriate, arrogate, take over, usurp; absorb, assimilate, incorporate; cherish, prize, treasure; cultivate, follow, heed, honor; use, utilize; bring up, foster, nurture, raise, rear; affect, assume, copy, imitate, pretend, put on, simulate

near ant abandon, forsake, give up, relinquish, surrender; abjure, abnegate, disown; reject, renounce, repudiate, spurn; discard, jettison, junk, throw away, throw out

adorable *adj* having qualities that tend to make one loved — see LOVABLE

adore *vb* **1** to feel passion, devotion, or tenderness for — see LOVE 2

2 to love or admire too much — see IDOLIZE

3 to offer honor or respect to (someone) as a divine power — see WORSHIP 1

4 to take pleasure in — see ENJOY 1

adoring *adj* **1** feeling or showing love — see LOVING

2 reflecting great admiration or devotion — see WORSHIPFUL

adorn *vb* to make more attractive by adding something that is beautiful or becoming — see DECORATE

adorning *adj* serving to add beauty — see DECORATIVE

adornment *n* something that decorates or beautifies — see DECORATION 1

adroit *adj* accomplished with trained ability — see SKILLFUL

adroitness *n* **1** mental skill or quickness — see DEXTERITY 1

2 subtle or imaginative ability in inventing, devising, or executing something — see SKILL 1

adulate *vb* **1** to love or admire too much — see IDOLIZE

2 to praise too much — see FLATTER 1

adulation *n* **1** excessive admiration of or devotion to a person — see WORSHIP

2 excessive praise — see FLATTERY

adulatory *adj* **1** overly or insincerely flattering — see FULSOME

2 reflecting great admiration or devotion — see WORSHIPFUL

adult *adj* fully grown or developed — see MATURE 1

adult *n* a fully grown person ⟨at the beach, the *adults* sat under broad umbrellas while the children splashed in the water⟩

syn grown-up

rel ancient, elder, graybeard, oldster, old-timer, senior, senior citizen

near ant kid, moppet, tad, toddler, tot, tyke; baby, infant; adolescent, juvenile, minor, youngster, youth; preteen, teenager, youngster, teenybopper

ant child

adulterant *n* something that is or that makes impure — see IMPURITY

adulterate *vb* to alter (something) for the worse with the addition of foreign or lower-grade substances ⟨the company was fined for *adulterating* its "all beef" frankfurters with cereal⟩

syn dilute, thin, water (down), weaken

rel befoul, contaminate, corrupt, defile, dirty, foul, infect, poison, pollute, soil, spoil, sully, taint; cheapen, debase, degrade; manipulate, misrepresent, tamper (with); counterfeit, fake, falsify, fudge; doctor, spike

near ant fertilize, lard; augment, supplement; clarify, clean, cleanse, distill, filter, flush, leach, pasteurize, purge, purify, refine; better, enhance, improve

ant enrich, fortify, richen, strengthen

adulterated *adj* containing foreign or lower-grade substances — see IMPURE

adulthood *n* the state of being fully grown or developed — see MATURITY

advance *n* **1** forward movement in time or place ⟨during her long convalescence, Penny was barely aware of the *advance* of the seasons⟩

syn advancement, furtherance, going, headway, march, onrush, passage, process, procession, progress, progression

rel current, drift, flow, flux, stream, way; advent, approach, arrival, coming, nearing; bound, jump, leap, step, stride; impetus, momentum

near ant backwash, ebb, reflux; retraction, retreat, return, reversal, reverse; about-face, turnabout, turnaround

ant recession, regression, retrogression

2 an instance of notable progress in the development of knowledge, technology, or skill ⟨with her new violin teacher, Nadia has made noticeable *advances* in her technique in just a few weeks⟩

syn advancement, breakthrough, enhancement, improvement, refinement

rel amelioration, boost, heightening, increase, melioration, strengthening, upgrade, uplift, upswing, uptrend, upturn; betterment, evolution, maturation, perfection, ripening; civilization, edification, education, enlightenment; renaissance, renascence, revival; discovery, find, windfall; innovation, invention

near ant breakdown, collapse, crash; hindrance, impediment, stumbling block; decline, decrease, deterioration, diminishment, failing, flagging, languishment, lapse, lessening, reduction, sinking, slowing, weakening, worsening; detriment, disablement, drawback, glitch, impairment, shortcoming

ant setback

advance *vb* 1 to give to another for temporary use with the understanding that it or a like thing will be returned — see LEND

2 to help the growth or development of — see FOSTER 1

3 to move forward along a course — see GO 1

4 to move higher in rank or position — see PROMOTE 1

5 to set before the mind for consideration — see PROPOSE 1

6 to move closer to — see COME 1

advanced *adj* 1 being far along in development ⟨an *advanced* civilization, among the first anywhere to use the plow, developed on the banks of the Nile River thousands of years ago⟩

syn developed, evolved, high, higher, improved, progressive, refined

rel full-blown, full-fledged, full-grown, full-scale; aged, grown, mature, matured, perfected, ripe, ripened; civilized, educated, enhanced, enlightened; contemporary, latest, modern, newest, newfangled, new-fashioned, novel, recent, up-to-date; early, precocious

near ant green, immature, underdeveloped, undersized, underweight, unripe, unripened; uncivilized, uneducated; early, primeval, primordial; antediluvian, antiquated, Neanderthal, oldfangled, old-fashioned

ant backward, low, lower, nonprogressive, primitive, retarded, rudimentary, undeveloped

---

2 being at a higher level than average — see HIGH 2

advancement *n* 1 a raising or a state of being raised to a higher rank or position ⟨Paul's rapid *advancement* in the company came as no surprise to those who knew he was the president's nephew⟩

syn ascent, elevation, preferment, promotion, rise, upgrade

rel aggrandizement, ennoblement, exaltation, glorification

near ant deposition, dethronement, dismissal, expulsion, impeachment, ouster, overthrow, removal, suspension, unmaking, unseating; downfall, fall

ant abasement, demotion, downgrade, reduction

2 an instance of notable progress in the development of knowledge, technology, or skill — see ADVANCE 2

3 forward movement in time or place — see ADVANCE 3

advantage *n* 1 the more favorable condition or position in a competition ⟨your experience volunteering at the hospital will put you at an *advantage* when you're applying for a job there⟩

syn better, drop, edge, jump, upper hand, vantage

rel allowance, head start, lead, margin, odds, start; ascendancy, command, dominance, mastery, predominance, superiority, supremacy, transcendence; favoritism, nepotism, precedence, preference, privilege, seniority; break, foothold, opportunity

near ant detriment, drawback, penalty, stranglehold; disparity, imbalance, inequality, unevenness; disability, impairment, shortcoming

ant disadvantage, handicap, liability

2 a thing that helps — see HELP 2

advantageous *adj* conferring benefits; promoting or contributing to personal or social well-being — see BENEFICIAL

advent *n* the act of coming upon a scene — see ARRIVAL

adventitious *adj* not being a vital part of or belonging to something — see EXTRINSIC

adventure *n* an exciting or noteworthy event that one experiences firsthand ⟨our quiet hike turned into quite an *adventure* when we encountered a bear and her cub⟩

syn experience, happening, time

rel escapade, lark; act, action, deed, doing, exploit; episode, occasion; baptism, ordeal, test, trial, tribulation; enterprise, risk, venture; expedition, exploration, feat, mission, performance, quest, stunt

near ant bore, bummer, bust, drag

adventure *vb* to place in danger — see ENDANGER

adventuresome *adj* inclined or willing to take risks — see BOLD 1

adventurous *adj* inclined or willing to take risks — see BOLD 1

adversary n **1** one that is hostile toward another — see ENEMY

2 one that takes a position opposite another in a competition or conflict — see OPPONENT 1

adverse adj **1** opposed to one's interests ⟨all the *adverse* publicity really caused the movie star's popularity to suffer⟩

syn counter, disadvantageous, hostile, inimical, negative, prejudicial, unfavorable, unfriendly, unsympathetic

rel bad, baleful, baneful, evil; damaging, deleterious, destructive, detrimental, fatal, harmful, hurtful, injurious, lethal, murderous, poisonous, ruinous, threatening, troublesome, unhealthy, wounding; dangerous, hazardous, imperiling, jeopardizing, parlous, perilous, risky, unsafe; defamatory, detractive, offensive, scathing, slanderous; antagonistic, antipathetic, inhospitable, intolerant, uncongenial, uncooperative; competing, conflicting, counteracting, countering, opposing, resistant, resisting

near ant beneficial, good, helpful, propitious, useful; harmless, innocent, innocuous, inoffensive, nondestructive, nonfatal, nonlethal, nonthreatening; unresisting, unresistant; tolerant, understanding; agreeable, affable, amiable, amicable, benign, benignant, congenial, cordial, complying, friendly, hospitable

ant advantageous, favorable, friendly, positive, supportive, sympathetic, well-disposed

2 causing or capable of causing harm — see HARMFUL

adversity n **1** bad luck or an example of this — see MISFORTUNE

2 something that is a cause for suffering or special effort especially in the attainment of a goal — see DIFFICULTY 1

advert (to) vb to make reference to or speak about briefly but specifically — see MENTION 1

advertise vb to make known openly or publicly — see ANNOUNCE

advertisement n a published statement informing the public of a matter of general interest — see ANNOUNCEMENT

advice n an opinion suggesting a wise or proper course of action ⟨Stephanie got some good *advice* from the vet about dealing with her dog's habit of chasing cars⟩

syn counsel, guidance

rel recommendation, suggestion; hint, pointer, tip; data, feedback, information; answer, solution; advisement, consideration, thought; admonishment, admonition, caution, cautioning, expostulation, remonstration, urging, warning; judgment (*or* judgement), observation, verdict; assistance, briefing, coaching, direction, instruction, mentoring, priming, prompting, teaching, tutoring; interference, kibitzing, meddling; moralizing, pontificating, preaching; exhortation, lecture, lesson, sermon, speech

advisable adj suitable for bringing about a desired result under the circumstances — see EXPEDIENT

advise vb **1** to give advice to ⟨a popular guidance counselor who has been *advising* students about their college plans for two decades⟩

syn counsel

rel admonish, caution, warn; brief, clue (in), fill in, inform, wise (up); coach, direct, lead, guide, instruct, mentor, teach, tutor; acquaint, apprise, familiarize; convince, encourage, induce, persuade, talk (into); beg, exhort, implore, prevail (upon), urge; propose, recommend, suggest

2 to put forward as one's choice for a wise or proper course of action ⟨she *advised* calling ahead for a reservation at the new restaurant⟩

syn counsel, recommend, suggest

rel advocate, back, favor, support; exhort, urge; advance, propose, submit

3 to exchange viewpoints or seek advice for the purpose of finding a solution to a problem — see CONFER 2

4 to give information to — see ENLIGHTEN 1

advised adj decided on as a result of careful thought — see DELIBERATE 1

adviser or **advisor** n a person who gives advice especially professionally — see CONSULTANT

advocate n **1** a person who actively supports or favors a cause — see EXPONENT

2 a person whose profession is to conduct lawsuits for clients or to advise about legal rights and obligations — see LAWYER

advocate vb to promote the interests or cause of — see SUPPORT 1

aegis n means or method of defending — see DEFENSE 1

aeon or **eon** n a long or seemingly long period of time — see AGE 2

aerodrome n, *British* a place from which aircraft operate that usually has paved runways and a terminal — see AIRPORT

affability n the state or quality of having a pleasant or agreeable manner in socializing with others — see AMIABILITY 1

affable adj **1** having a relaxed, casual manner — see EASYGOING 1

2 having an easygoing and pleasing manner especially in social situations — see AMIABLE

3 showing a natural kindness and courtesy especially in social situations — see GRACIOUS 1

affair n **1** a brief romantic relationship ⟨an *affair* between two teenagers spending the summer at the same beach resort⟩

syn love affair, romance

rel amour, intrigue; attachment, infatuation; entanglement, fling, flirtation; liaison, passion

2 a social gathering — see PARTY 1

3 something produced by physical or intellectual effort — see PRODUCT 1

4 something that happens — see EVENT 1

5 something to be dealt with — see MATTER 2

¹**affect** *vb* **1** to act upon (a person or a person's feelings) so as to cause a response ⟨Gary claims that scary movies don't *affect* him in the least⟩

syn impact, impress, influence, move, strike, sway, tell (on), touch

rel bias, color; inspire, stir; carry, engage, interest, involve, penetrate, pierce; afflict, agitate, bother, discomfort, discompose, disquiet, distress, disturb, fluster, harass, harry, perturb, pester, plague, smite, strain, stress, trouble, try, upset, worry, wring; allure, attract, bewitch, captivate, charm, dazzle, enchant

phrases get to

near ant bore, jade, pall, tire, weary

2 to be the business or affair of — see CONCERN 2

²**affect** *vb* to present a false appearance of — see FEIGN

affectation *n* the quality or state of appearing or trying to appear more important or more valuable than is the case — see PRETENSE 1

affected *adj* **1** lacking in natural or spontaneous quality — see ARTIFICIAL 1

2 self-consciously trying to present an appearance of grandeur or importance — see PRETENTIOUS 1

affectedness *n* the quality or state of appearing or trying to appear more important or more valuable than is the case — see PRETENSE 1

affecting *adj* having the power to affect the feelings or sympathies — see MOVING

¹**affection** *n* a feeling of strong or constant regard for or dedication to someone — see LOVE 1

²**affection** *n* an abnormal state that disrupts a plant's or animal's normal bodily functioning — see DISEASE

affectionate *adj* feeling or showing love — see LOVING

affianced *adj* pledged in marriage — see ENGAGED

affiliate *n* a local unit of an organization — see CHAPTER

affiliated *adj* having a close connection like that between family members — see RELATED

affiliation *n* the state of having shared interests or efforts (as in social or business matters) — see ASSOCIATION 1

affirm *vb* **1** to state as a fact usually forcefully — see CLAIM 1

2 to state clearly and strongly — see ASSERT 1

affirmation *n* a solemn and often public declaration of the truth or existence of something — see PROTESTATION

affirmative *adj* showing or expressing acceptance or approval — see POSITIVE

affix *vb* to cause (something) to hold to another — see FASTEN 1

---

syn synonym(s)   *rel* related words
ant antonym(s)   *near ant* near antonym(s)

afflict *vb* to cause persistent suffering to ⟨the South was *afflicted* by a severe drought⟩ ⟨he's been *afflicted* by nightmares ever since the accident⟩

syn agonize, bedevil, curse, harrow, martyr, persecute, plague, rack, torment, torture

rel assail, attack, beset, set upon; badger, dog, hound, ride; agitate, annoy, bother, distress, disturb, harass, harry, irk, molest, pester; discomfort, discompose, disquiet, fluster, perturb, strain, stress, trouble, try, upset, vex, worry; crush, oppress, overpower, overwhelm, smite, strike, tyrannize; pain, prick, stab, sting, wring

near ant abet, aid, assist, help; deliver, release, relieve, reprieve; comfort, console, solace, soothe, succor

afflicting *adj* hard to accept or bear especially emotionally — see BITTER 2

affliction *n* **1** a state of great suffering of body or mind — see DISTRESS 1

2 deep sadness especially for the loss of someone or something loved — see SORROW

affluent *adj* having goods, property, or money in abundance — see RICH 1

affray *n* a rough and often noisy fight usually involving several people — see BRAWL 1

affright *vb* to strike with fear — see FRIGHTEN

affrighted *adj* filled with fear or dread — see AFRAID 1

affront *n* an act or expression showing scorn and usually intended to hurt another's feelings — see INSULT

affront *vb* to cause hurt feelings or deep resentment in — see INSULT

aficionado *n* a person with a strong and habitual liking for something — see FAN

afield *adv* off the desired or intended path or course — see WRONG 1

afire *adj* being on fire — see ABLAZE 1

aflame *adj* being on fire — see ABLAZE 1

aflutter *adj* feeling or showing uncomfortable feelings of uncertainty — see NERVOUS 1

afoot *adj* being in progress or development — see ONGOING 1

afore *adv, chiefly dialect* so as to precede something in order of time — see AHEAD 1

afore *prep, chiefly dialect* **1** earlier than — see BEFORE 1

2 preceding in space — see BEFORE 2

afraid *adj* **1** filled with fear or dread ⟨Melissa is *afraid* of flying, so she takes a train from Boston to visit her brother in Chicago⟩

syn affrighted, aghast, alarmed, fearful, frightened, horrified, scared, spooked, terrified, terrorized

rel fainthearted, fearsome, shrinking, shy, timid, timorous, tremulous; agitated, anxious, apprehensive, disconcerted, disquieted, disturbed, jittery, jumpy, nervous, panicky, perturbed, skittish, uneasy, upset, worried; appalled, dismayed, shocked, startled; cowed, daunted, intimidated, unnerved; coward, cowardly, craven, gutless, lily-livered, pusillanimous; careful, cautious, heedful, prudent, unadventurous, wary

near ant adventuresome, adventurous, audacious, bold, daredevil, daring, dashing, gutsy, plucky, spirited, spunky, venturesome, venturous; brave, courageous, gallant, hardy, heroic, intrepid, lionhearted, manful, stalwart, stout, stouthearted, valiant, valorous; assured, collected, composed, confident, cool, sanguine, sure, unperturbed; dauntless, resolute, undaunted

ant fearless, unafraid

2 having doubts about the wisdom of doing something — see HESITANT

afresh *adv* yet another time — see AGAIN 1

aft *adv* near, toward, or in the stern of a ship or the tail of an aircraft ⟨after transferring the controls to the copilot, the captain went *aft* to see what the disturbance was⟩

syn abaft, astern

rel after, back, backward, behind, posteriorly, rearward (*also* rearwards), rearwardly

near ant anteriorly; ahead, before

ant fore, forward

after *adj* being, occurring, or carried out at a time after something else — see SUBSEQUENT

after *adv* following in time or place ⟨upon seeing *The Nutcracker* for the first time, and for a long time *after*, Irma wanted to play the part of the Mouse King⟩

syn afterward (*or* afterwards), later, subsequently, thereafter

rel next; by and by, hereafter, presently, since, soon, then, thereupon

near ant antecedently, formerly; heretofore, theretofore

ant afore [*chiefly dialect*], before, beforehand, earlier, previously

after *prep* subsequent to in time or order ⟨the high school band came right *after* the mayor in the parade⟩

syn behind, following

rel next; since

near ant of, to, toward (*or* towards)

ant afore [*chiefly dialect*], ahead of, before, ere, previous to, prior to

aftereffect *n* a condition or occurrence traceable to a cause — see EFFECT 1

afterlife *n* unending existence after death — see ETERNITY 2

aftermath *n* a condition or occurrence traceable to a cause — see EFFECT 1

afterward *or* **afterwards** *adv* following in time or place — see AFTER

again *adv* **1** yet another time ⟨now I have to mop the floor *again* because you didn't wipe your feet⟩

syn afresh, anew, over

rel always, constantly, continuously, endlessly, ever, evermore, perpetually; frequently, often; recurrently, repeatedly; freshly, newly

near ant ne'er, never

ant nevermore

2 in addition to what has been said — see MORE 1

3 just the opposite being true — see CONTRARIWISE

against *prep* in or into contact with ⟨he leaned *against* the fence and it collapsed⟩ ⟨unwittingly rubbed his leg *against* some poison ivy⟩

syn on, upon

rel alongside, next, next to

agape *adj* having or showing signs of eagerly awaiting something — see EXPECTANT 1

age *n* **1** an extent of time associated with a particular person or thing ⟨the Bronze *Age* marks the beginning of the use of metal by ancient peoples⟩

syn day, epoch, era, period, time

rel cycle, generation, year; span, spell, stretch, while

2 a long or seemingly long period of time ⟨it took *ages* for the clerk to ring up three items⟩

syn aeon (*or* eon), cycle, eternity

rel infinity; lifetime

near ant flash, instant, jiffy, minute, moment, second, trice, twinkle, twinkling, wink; microsecond, nanosecond

age *vb* to become mature — see MATURE

aged *adj* **1** being of advanced years and especially past middle age — see ELDERLY

2 dating or surviving from the distant past — see ANCIENT 1

agency *n* something used to achieve an end — see AGENT 1

agenda *n* a listing of things to be presented or considered (as at a concert or play) — see PROGRAM 1

agent *n* **1** something used to achieve an end ⟨the whitening *agent* in the detergent is chlorine bleach⟩ ⟨the Church has been the traditional *agent* for social justice in impoverished countries⟩

syn agency, instrument, instrumentality, machinery, means, medium, organ, vehicle

rel determinant, expedient, factor, influence, ingredient, mechanism, tool; activator, catalyst, driver, energizer, executor, generator, instigator, launcher, mover, power, stimulus, trigger

2 a person who acts or does business for another ⟨the sports *agent* negotiated a record-breaking contract for the baseball player⟩

syn attorney, commissary, delegate, deputy, envoy, factor, procurator, proxy, representative

rel ambassador, emissary, foreign minister, legate, minister; alternate, backup, pinch hitter, relief, replacement, stand-in, sub, substitute, surrogate, understudy; informer, operative, spy; broker, distributor, manager; arbiter, arbitrator, go-between, intercessor, intermediary, interposer, liaison, mediator, middleman; mouthpiece, spokesperson

age-old *adj* dating or surviving from the distant past — see ANCIENT 1

agglomerate *vb* to form into a round compact mass — see WAD

aggrandize *vb* **1** to enhance the status of — see EXALT

2 to make greater in size, amount, or number — see INCREASE 1

aggravate *vb* to disturb the peace of mind of (someone) especially by repeated disagreeable acts — see IRRITATE 1

aggravating *adj* **1** causing annoyance — see ANNOYING

aggravation *n* **1** something that is a source of irritation — see ANNOYANCE 3

2 the act of making unwelcome intrusions upon another — see ANNOYANCE 1

3 the feeling of impatience or anger caused by another's repeated disagreeable acts — see ANNOYANCE 2

aggregate *n* a complete amount of something — see WHOLE

aggression *n* **1** an inclination to fight or quarrel — see BELLIGERENCE

2 the act or action of setting upon with force or violence — see ATTACK 1

aggressive *adj* **1** having or showing a bold forcefulness in the pursuit of a goal ⟨if you don't take a more *aggressive* approach to this yard pretty soon, the weeds are going to take over completely⟩

syn ambitious, assertive, enterprising, fierce, go-getting, high-pressure, in-your-face, militant, self-assertive

rel dynamic, energetic, gung ho, hustling, scrappy, strenuous, vigorous; emphatic, obtrusive; adventuresome, adventurous, venturesome, venturous; audacious, bold, brash, brassy, cheeky, cocksure, cocky, confident, determined, forward, impudent, insolent, overconfident, presumptuous, unapologetic, unsubdued, unyielding; dominating, domineering, imperious, lordly, magisterial, overbearing

near ant easygoing, laid-back, relaxed; acquiescent, compliant, deferential, resigned, submissive, yielding; cowering, cringing, groveling (*or* grovelling), shrinking; bashful, diffident, meek, mousy (*or* mousey), overmodest, passive, quiet, reserved, retiring, shy, subdued, timid, unobtrusive

ant low-pressure, unaggressive, unambitious, unassertive, unenterprising

2 feeling or displaying eagerness to fight — see BELLIGERENT

3 marked by or uttered with forcefulness — see EMPHATIC 1

aggressiveness *n* **1** readiness to engage in daring or difficult activity — see ENTERPRISE 2

2 the quality or state of being forceful (as in expression) — see VEHEMENCE 1

3 an inclination to fight or quarrel — see BELLIGERENCE

aggressor *n* one that starts armed conflict against another especially without reasonable cause ⟨the countries formed an alliance to deter potential *aggressors*⟩

syn invader, raider

rel initiator, instigator; ambuscader, assailant, attacker, pillager, plunderer; hawk, militarist, warmonger; belligerent, combatant

near ant defender; dove, pacifist, peacemaker; nonbelligerent

aggrieved *adj* having a feeling that one has been wronged or thwarted in one's ambitions — see DISCONTENTED

aghast *adj* filled with fear or dread — see AFRAID 1

agile *adj* moving easily — see GRACEFUL 1

agility *n* ease and grace in physical activity — see DEXTERITY 2

aging *adj* being of advanced years and especially past middle age — see ELDERLY

agitate *vb* **1** to cause (as a liquid) to move about in a circle especially repeatedly — see STIR 1

2 to trouble the mind of; to make uneasy — see DISTURB 1

3 to make a series of small irregular or violent movements — see SHAKE 1

agitated *adj* **1** being in a state of increased activity or agitation — see FEVERISH 1

2 feeling overwhelming fear or worry — see FRANTIC 1

agitating *adj* marked by or causing agitation or uncomfortable feelings — see NERVOUS 2

agitation *n* **1** a state of wildly excited activity or emotion — see FRENZY

2 an uneasy state of mind usually over the possibility of an anticipated misfortune or trouble — see ANXIETY 1

agitator *n* a person who stirs up public feelings especially of discontent ⟨a political *agitator* who led an unsuccessful revolt against the government⟩

syn demagogue (*also* demagog), exciter, firebrand, fomenter, incendiary, inciter, instigator, rabble-rouser

rel demonstrator, marcher, objector, picketer, protester (*or* protestor); advocate, champion, exponent, persuader, promoter, proponent, reformer, supporter; alarmist, extremist, insurgent, insurrectionist, radical, rebel, revolter, revolutionary, revolutionist, subversive, troublemaker

aglow *adj* having or being an outward sign of good feelings (as of love, confidence, or happiness) — see RADIANT 1

agog *adj* **1** having or showing signs of eagerly awaiting something — see EXPECTANT 1

2 showing urgent desire or interest — see EAGER

agonize *vb* **1** to cause persistent suffering to — see AFFLICT

2 to feel deep sadness or mental pain — see GRIEVE

agonizing *adj* **1** hard to accept or bear especially emotionally — see BITTER 2

2 intensely or unbearably painful — see EXCRUCIATING 1

3 causing intense mental or physical distress — see SHARP 2

---

syn synonym(s)   *rel* related words
ant antonym(s)   *near ant* near antonym(s)

agonizingly *adv* with feelings of bitterness or grief — see HARD 2

agony *n* **1** a situation or state that causes great suffering and unhappiness — see HELL 2

2 a state of great suffering of body or mind — see DISTRESS 1

3 a sudden intense expression of strong feeling — see OUTBURST 1

agrarian *adj* engaged in or concerned with agriculture — see AGRICULTURAL

agree *vb* **1** to have or come to the same opinion or point of view ⟨since we couldn't *agree*, we tossed a coin to decide the matter⟩
syn coincide, concur
rel accede (to), accept, acquiesce, assent (to), comply (with), consent (to), go (by), subscribe; affiliate, ally, associate, unite; collaborate, cooperate, get along
phrases see eye to eye
near ant clash, collide, conflict; bicker, counter, dispute, dissent, diverge, fall out, object, oppose, protest, quarrel, resist, rival; dissociate, separate, split
ant differ, disagree

2 to accept the truth or existence of (something) usually reluctantly — see ADMIT

3 to be in agreement on every point — see CHECK 1

4 to form a pleasing relationship — see HARMONIZE 1

agreeable *adj* **1** being to one's liking — see SATISFACTORY 1

2 giving pleasure or contentment to the mind or senses — see PLEASANT

3 having an easygoing and pleasing manner especially in social situations — see AMIABLE

4 having or marked by agreement in feeling or action — see HARMONIOUS 3

agreeableness *n* the state or quality of having a pleasant or agreeable manner in socializing with others — see AMIABILITY 1

agreeably *adv* in a pleasing way — see WELL 5

agreement *n* **1** the act or fact of being of one opinion about something ⟨I only had the energy to nod in *agreement* when Cheryl said we'd never worked so hard in all our lives⟩
syn accord, concurrence, consensus, unanimity, unison
rel accession, assent, consent; acceptance, acquiescence, compliance, concession, conformity; approbation, approval, favor; alliance, collaboration, collusion, complicity, conspiracy; concord, consonance, harmony, oneness, solidarity, understanding, union; empathy, rapport, sympathy
near ant conflict, discord, dissension; opposition, resistance; disapprobation, disapproval, disfavor
ant disagreement, dissent

2 an arrangement about action to be taken ⟨we finally reached an *agreement* regarding a fair division of the housework⟩
syn accord, bargain, compact, contract, convention, covenant, deal, pact, settlement, understanding
rel charter, treaty; pledge, promise; alliance, association, league, partnership; acceptance, assent, assent, concurrence, consent, OK (*or* okay)

3 a state of consistency — see CONFORMITY 1

agricultural *adj* engaged in or concerned with agriculture ⟨he grew up in an *agricultural* community⟩
syn agrarian, farming
rel pastoral, rural
near ant metropolitan, urban; industrial, industrialized
ant nonagricultural

agriculture *n* the science or occupation of cultivating the soil, producing crops, and raising livestock ⟨the forest was cut down, and the land given over to *agriculture*⟩
syn farming, husbandry
rel agronomy; animal husbandry

agriculturist *or* **agriculturalist** *n* a person who cultivates the land and grows crops on it — see FARMER

agronomist *n* a person who cultivates the land and grows crops on it — see FARMER

aground *adj* resting on the shore or bottom of a body of water ⟨the villagers came to stare at the foreign ship that was *aground* on their beach and at the strangely dressed sailors on board⟩
syn beached, grounded, stranded
rel landed; alongshore
near ant offshore
ant afloat

ah *interj* how surprising, doubtful, or unbelievable — see NO

aha *interj* how surprising, doubtful, or unbelievable — see NO

ahead *adv* **1** so as to precede something in order of time ⟨we were cautioned not to fill out any of the test answers *ahead* of time⟩ ⟨call *ahead* for reservations⟩
syn afore [*chiefly dialect*], antecedently, anteriorly, before, beforehand, previously
rel formerly
phrases in advance
near ant behind, by and by, next, presently, subsequently
ant after, afterward (*or* afterwards), later

2 toward a point ahead in space or time — see ONWARD 1

3 toward or at a point lying in advance in space or time — see ALONG

ahead of *prep* **1** earlier than — see BEFORE 1

2 preceding in space — see BEFORE 2

aid *n* **1** a person who helps a more skilled person — see HELPER

2 a thing that helps — see HELP 2

3 an act or instance of helping — see HELP 1

aid *vb* to provide (someone) with what is useful or necessary to achieve an end — see HELP 1

aide *n* a person who helps a more skilled person — see HELPER

ailing *adj* **1** chronically or repeatedly suffering from poor health — see SICKLY 1

2 temporarily suffering from a disorder of the body — see SICK 1

ailment *n* an abnormal state that disrupts a plant's or animal's normal bodily functioning — see DISEASE

aim *n* something that one hopes or intends to accomplish — see GOAL

aim *vb* **1** to point or turn (something) toward a target or goal ⟨the anti-drug campaign was *aimed* primarily at preteens⟩
syn bend, cast, direct, head, level, set, train
rel bear, face; concentrate, focus; incline, orient, steer
near ant avert, curve, deflect, detour, divert, rechannel, shunt, sidetrack

2 to have in mind as a purpose or goal — see INTEND

aimless *adj* lacking a definite plan, purpose, or pattern — see RANDOM

aimlessly *adv* without definite aim, direction, rule, or method — see HIT OR MISS

air *n* **1** a rhythmic series of musical tones arranged to give a pleasing effect — see MELODY

2 a slight or gentle movement of air — see BREEZE 1

3 a special quality or impression associated with something — see AURA

4 airs *pl* a display of emotion or behavior that is insincere or intended to deceive — see MASQUERADE

air *vb* to make known (as an idea, emotion, or opinion) — see EXPRESS 1

airdrome *n* a place from which aircraft operate that usually has paved runways and a terminal — see AIRPORT

airfield *n* a place from which aircraft operate that usually has paved runways and a terminal — see AIRPORT

airman *n* one who flies or is qualified to fly an aircraft or spacecraft — see PILOT

airport *n* a place from which aircraft operate that usually has paved runways and a terminal ⟨the *airport* nearest us has plane service on only one major airline⟩
syn aerodrome [*British*], airdrome, airfield
rel air base, heliport; airstrip, landing field, landing strip, runway; launchpad, pad

airy *adj* **1** resembling air in lightness ⟨Aunt Helen's lemon pies are famous for their *airy* meringues⟩
syn ethereal, fluffy, gossamer, gossamery, light
rel dainty, delicate, downy, feathery, flimsy, insubstantial, tender, wispy; buoyant, lighter-than-air, lightweight, rarefied, unsubstantial, weightless

---

near ant firm, solid, substantial; bulky, burdensome, cumbersome, hefty, hulking, lumpish, ponderous, unwieldy, weighty
ant heavy, leaden

2 having little weight — see ¹LIGHT 1

3 located at a greater height than average or usual — see HIGH 3

akin *adj* **1** having a close connection like that between family members — see RELATED

2 having qualities in common — see ALIKE

alacritous *adj* having or showing the ability to respond without delay or hesitation — see QUICK 1

alacrity *n* cheerful readiness to do something ⟨having just acquired his driver's license that morning, Sam agreed with *alacrity* to drive his cousin to the airport⟩
syn amenability, gameness, goodwill, willingness
rel celebrity, quickness, rapidity, speed, speediness, swiftness; dispatch, promptitude, promptness; ardor, avidity, eagerness, enthusiasm, exuberance, fervor, gusto, keenness, relish, zeal, zest; agreeableness, geniality, good-naturedness, heartiness, warmth; open-mindedness, receptivity, responsiveness
near ant leisureliness, pokiness, slowness, sluggishness; apathy, disinterestedness, halfheartedness, indifference, lukewarmness, perfunctoriness; delay, dilatoriness, doubt, equivocation, hesitance, hesitancy, hesitation, reluctance, reservation, uncertainty, vacillation; disinclination, indisposition, recalcitrance, resistance, unwillingness; antipathy, averseness, aversion

à la mode *also* **a la mode** *adj* being in the latest or current fashion — see STYLISH

alarm *n* **1** suspicion or fear of future harm or misfortune — see APPREHENSION 1

2 the act or an instance of telling beforehand of danger or risk — see WARNING 1

3 the emotion experienced in the presence or threat of danger — see FEAR

alarm *vb* to strike with fear — see FRIGHTEN

alarmed *adj* filled with fear or dread — see AFRAID 1

alarming *adj* causing fear — see FEARFUL 1

albeit *conj* in spite of the fact that — see ALTHOUGH

album *n* a collection of writings — see ANTHOLOGY

alcohol *n* a fermented or distilled beverage that can make a person drunk ⟨once he joined the swim team, Sergei never again touched *alcohol*⟩
syn booze, drink, grog, intoxicant, liquor, moonshine, spirits
rel ale, beer, mead, sake (*or* saki), table wine, wine; brandy, gin, mescal, rum, tequila, vodka, whiskey (*or* whisky)

alcove *n* a hollowed-out space in a wall — see NICHE 1

---

alert *adj* **1** paying close attention usually for the purpose of anticipating approaching danger or opportunity ⟨Susan needed to stay *alert* throughout the train ride so as not to miss her stop⟩
syn attentive, awake, open-eyed, vigilant, watchful, wide-awake
rel alive, aware, conscious, sensitive; heedful, mindful, observant, observing, sharp, sharp-eyed; sleepless, wakeful; careful, cautious, chary, wary; prepared, ready
phrases on guard, on the alert
near ant absent, absentminded, absorbed, abstracted, daydreaming, dazed, distracted, dreaming, dreamy, engrossed, faraway, insensible, oblivious, preoccupied; asleep, sleeping, unaware, unconscious, unknowing, unperceiving, unseeing, unwitting; careless, heedless, inattentive, unheeding, unmindful, unobservant, unobserving, unthinking, unwary; unprepared, unready
2 having or showing a close attentiveness to avoiding danger or trouble — see CAREFUL 1
3 having or showing quickness of mind — see INTELLIGENT 1
4 having or showing the ability to respond without delay or hesitation — see QUICK 1
alert *n* the act or an instance of telling beforehand of danger or risk — see WARNING 1
alert *vb* to give notice to beforehand especially of danger or risk — see WARN
alertness *n* **1** a close attentiveness to avoiding danger — see CAUTION 1
2 the act or state of being constantly attentive and responsive to signs of opportunity, activity, or danger — see VIGILANCE
alias *n* **1** a descriptive or familiar name given instead of or in addition to the one belonging to an individual — see NICKNAME
2 a fictitious or assumed name — see PSEUDONYM
alibi *n* an explanation that frees one from fault or blame — see EXCUSE
alien *adj* **1** being, relating to, or characteristic of a country other than one's own — see FOREIGN 1
2 not being a vital part of or belonging to something — see EXTRINSIC
alienate *vb* **1** to cause to change from friendly or loving to unfriendly or uncaring — see ESTRANGE
2 to give over the legal possession or ownership of — see TRANSFER 1
alienation *n* the loss of friendship or affection — see ESTRANGEMENT
alight *adj* filled with much light — see BRIGHT 2
alight *vb* to come to rest after descending from the air ⟨a flock of eight swans circled above, then *alighted* on the pond⟩
syn land, light, perch, roost, settle, touch down
rel belly-land, crash-land

near ant arise, ascend, climb, rise; float, fly, glide, plane, soar, wing; hang, hover
ant take off
alike *adj* having qualities in common ⟨all the houses in the neighborhood are *alike* in that they all have a one-car garage and a fenced-in backyard⟩
syn akin, analogous, comparable, correspondent, corresponding, like, matching, parallel, resembling, similar, such, suchlike
rel commensurate, proportionate; tantamount, virtual; allied, kindred, related; approaching, approximating, close, coextensive, coincident, conformable, conforming, consistent, consonant, equal, equivalent, identical, indistinguishable, interchangeable, same, selfsame, synonymous, twin; homogeneous, unchanging, uniform, unvaried, unvarying
phrases on the order of
near ant disparate, distinct, distinguishable; variable, varied, varying; imprecise, inaccurate, inexact; unallied, unconnected, unrelated
ant different, dissimilar, diverse, unlike
alike *adv* in like manner — see ALSO 1
alikeness *n* the quality or state of having many qualities in common — see SIMILARITY 1
alive *adj* **1** having or showing life ⟨after crashing into the plate glass window the little bird was not only still *alive*, it seemed merely dazed⟩
syn animate, breathing, live, living
rel active, animated, dynamic, lively, thriving, vibrant, vital, vivacious; current, existent, existing, extant, going, prevailing, surviving
near ant dying, fading, moribund; stillborn; absent, extinct, fallen, finished, gone, lapsed, lost, nonexistent, perished, terminated, vanished, wiped out; barren, desert
ant breathless, dead, deceased, defunct, departed, expired, inanimate, lifeless, nonliving
2 marked by much life, movement, or activity ⟨the mall was *alive* with holiday shoppers⟩
syn animated, astir, bustling, busy, buzzing, flourishing, humming, lively, thriving, vibrant
rel abounding, crowded, overflowing, populous, swarming, teeming, thronging
ant asleep, dead, inactive, lifeless, sleepy
3 being in effective operation — see ACTIVE 1
4 having being at the present time — see EXTANT 1
5 having specified facts or feelings actively impressed on the mind — see CONSCIOUS
all *adj* not divided or scattered among several areas of interest or concern — see WHOLE 1
all *adv* **1** to a full extent or degree — see FULLY 1
2 for each one — see APIECE
all *pron* every person — see EVERYBODY

Allah *n* the being worshipped as the creator and ruler of the universe — see DEITY 2

all–around *also* **all–round** *adj* **1** not limited or specialized in application or purpose — see GENERAL 4

2 relating to the main elements and not to specific details — see GENERAL 2

3 able to do many different kinds of things — see VERSATILE

allay *vb* **1** to free from distress or disturbance — see CALM 1

2 to make more bearable or less severe — see HELP 2

allege *vb* to state as a fact usually forcefully — see CLAIM 1

allegiance *n* adherence to something to which one is bound by a pledge or duty — see FIDELITY

allegory *n* a story intended to teach a basic truth or moral about life ⟨Dr. Seuss's story "The Sneetches" is an *allegory* about tolerance for people's differences⟩

syn fable, parable

rel morality play; legend, myth, narrative, tale

allergic *adj* having a natural dislike for something — see ANTIPATHETIC

allergy *n* a strong feeling of not liking or approving — see DISLIKE 1

alleviate *vb* to make more bearable or less severe — see HELP 2

alleviation *n* reduction of or freedom from pain — see EASE 1

alliance *n* **1** a formal agreement between two or more nations or peoples — see TREATY

2 an association of persons, parties, or states for mutual assistance and protection — see CONFEDERACY

3 the state of having shared interests or efforts (as in social or business matters) — see ASSOCIATION 1

allied *adj* having a close connection like that between family members — see RELATED

all–important *adj* impossible to do without — see ESSENTIAL 1

allocate *vb* **1** to give as a share or portion — see ALLOT

2 to give out (something) in appropriate amounts or to appropriate individuals — see ADMINISTER 1

3 to keep or intend for a special purpose — see DEVOTE 1

allocation *n* **1** a sum of money allotted for a specific use by official or formal action — see APPROPRIATION

2 the act or process of giving out something to each member of a group — see DISTRIBUTION 1

allot *vb* to give as a share or portion ⟨each speaker was *allotted* five minutes to present his or her opinion in the debate⟩

syn allocate, allow, apportion, assign, ration

rel deal, dispense, distribute, divide, dole (out), measure, mete (out), parcel (out), portion, prorate, reserve; accord, award, grant; chip in, contribute, donate

near ant begrudge, deny, deprive (of); keep, retain, stint, withhold; appropriate, arrogate, confiscate

allotment *n* **1** a sum of money allotted for a specific use by official or formal action — see APPROPRIATION

2 something belonging to, due to, or contributed by an individual member of a group — see SHARE 1

all–out *adj* **1** having no exceptions or restrictions — see ABSOLUTE 2

2 trying all possibilities — see EXHAUSTIVE

all out *adv* with all power or resources being used — see FULL BLAST

all over *adv* in every place or in all places — see EVERYWHERE

allow *vb* **1** to give permission for or to approve of ⟨flash photography is not *allowed* inside the church⟩

syn have, permit, suffer

rel authorize, commission, license (*also* licence); accede (to), acquiesce, agree (to), assent (to), consent (to), OK (*or* okay), warrant; accord, concede, grant, sanction, vouchsafe; admit, brook, condone, countenance, endure, support, tolerate

near ant hinder, impede, obstruct; censure, disallow, disapprove, deny, interdict, refuse, reject, revoke, suppress, withhold; deplore, discountenance, dislike, disfavor, frown (at *or* on); check, curb, repress, restrain

ant ban, enjoin, forbid, prohibit, proscribe, veto

2 to give permission to ⟨Cindy's parents sometimes *allow* her to take the bus by herself downtown⟩

syn let, permit, suffer

rel authorize, commission, empower, license (*also* licence); approve, endorse (*also* indorse), sanction; free, liberate, release; cater (to), give in (to), humor, indulge

near ant deter, discourage; bar, block, constrain, curb, frustrate, hold back, impede, inhibit, obstruct, prevent

ant enjoin, forbid, prohibit

3 to accept the truth or existence of (something) usually reluctantly — see ADMIT

4 to give as a share or portion — see ALLOT

5 to make able or possible — see ENABLE 1

allowable *adj* that may be permitted — see PERMISSIBLE

allowance *n* **1** something belonging to, due to, or contributed by an individual member of a group — see SHARE 1

2 the approval by someone in authority for the doing of something — see PERMISSION

alloyed *adj* containing foreign or lower-grade substances — see IMPURE

---

syn synonym(s)   *rel* related words
ant antonym(s)   *near ant* near antonym(s)

all–powerful *adj* having unlimited power or authority — see OMNIPOTENT

all–purpose *adj* not limited or specialized in application or purpose — see GENERAL 4

all right *adj* **1** being to one's liking — see SATISFACTORY 1

2 not exposed to the threat of loss or injury — see SAFE 1

3 of a level of quality that meets one's needs or standards — see ADEQUATE

all right *adv* **1** in a satisfactory way — see WELL 1

2 used to express agreement — see YES

allude *vb* to convey an idea indirectly — see HINT

allure *n* the power of irresistible attraction — see CHARM 2

allure *vb* **1** to attract or delight as if by magic — see CHARM 1

2 to lead away from a usual or proper course by offering some pleasure or advantage — see LURE

allurement *n* **1** something that persuades one to perform an action for pleasure or gain — see LURE 1

2 the act or pressure of giving in to a desire especially when ill-advised — see TEMPTATION 1

alluring *adj* having an often mysterious or magical power to attract — see FASCINATING 1

ally *n* someone associated with another to give assistance or moral support ⟨in trying to convince his parents to send him to soccer camp, Toby had a real *ally* in his coach⟩

syn abettor (*also* abetter), backer, confederate, supporter, sympathizer

rel well-wisher; accessory, accomplice, collaborationist, collaborator; adjunct, assistant, coadjutor, helper; associate, cohort, colleague, fellow, partner; buddy, chum, companion, comrade, confidant, crony, familiar, friend, intimate, mate, pal

near ant belittler, detractor; adversary, enemy, foe, opponent

ally *vb* to form or enter into an association that furthers the interests of its members ⟨the area's small grape growers have *allied* and formed a cooperative that will help them get the best prices⟩

syn associate, band, club, confederate, conjoin, cooperate, federate, league, unite

rel collaborate, gang (up), team (up); incorporate, organize, unionize; affiliate; amalgamate, combine, conglomerate, consolidate, converge, group, join, merge; knot, link, tie, wed

near ant detach, disengage, dissolve, disunite, divorce, part, segregate, separate, sever, split, sunder; alienate, estrange, fall out

ant break up, disband

almighty *adj* having unlimited power or authority — see OMNIPOTENT

Almighty *n* the being worshipped as the creator and ruler of the universe — see DEITY 2

almost *adv* very close to but not completely ⟨we were *almost* finished with dinner when Uncle Richard showed up⟩ ⟨there were *almost* enough seats for everybody on the bus⟩

syn about, more or less, most, much, near, nearly, next to, nigh, practically, some, virtually, well-nigh

rel appreciably, by and large, chiefly, largely, mainly, mostly; partially, partly, somewhat

phrases as good as

near ant absolutely, altogether, completely, entirely, fully, plumb [*chiefly dialect*], quite, thoroughly; totally, utterly, wholly; barely, hardly, scarcely

alms *n* a gift of money or its equivalent to a charity, humanitarian cause, or public institution — see CONTRIBUTION

almsgiving *n* the giving of necessities and especially money to the needy — see CHARITY 1

aloft *adv* to or in a higher place — see ABOVE

alone *adj* **1** not being in the company of others ⟨no one realized Jeff was *alone* in his room so they all left for the movies without him⟩

syn lone, lonely, lonesome, solitary, solo, unaccompanied

rel unattended, unchaperoned; forlorn, friendless; cloistered, insulated, isolated, remote, retired, secluded, withdrawn; quarantined, segregated, separated, sequestered; separate, unattached, unconnected, unlinked; detached, disconnected, disjointed, dissociated, disunited, divided, fractionated; abandoned, adrift, deserted, desolate, forgotten, forsaken, lorn, neglected

near ant attended, chaperoned, escorted; adjacent, adjoining, communicating, contiguous, neighboring, next-door; attached, connected, coupled, linked

ant accompanied

2 being the one or ones of a class with no other members — see ONLY 2

alone *adv* **1** without aid or support ⟨Rebecca managed to find her way home *alone*⟩

syn independently, single-handedly, singly, solely, unaided, unassisted

rel individually, separately

phrases by oneself

near ant collectively, conjointly, cooperatively, jointly, mutually, together; en masse

2 for nothing other than — see SOLELY 1

along *adv* toward or at a point lying in advance in space or time ⟨traffic was inching *along* at a snail's pace⟩ ⟨work on the project is moving right *along*⟩

syn ahead, forth, forward, on, onward (*also* onwards)

rel before

near ant back, backward (*or* backwards), behind, rearward (*or* rearwards)

aloof *adj* having or showing a lack of friendliness or interest in others — see COOL 1

aloud *adv* with one's normal voice speaking the words ⟨Mr. Gripp likes to call on the sleepiest-looking students to read *aloud* from the textbook⟩

syn audibly, out, out loud

rel clearly, discernibly, distinctly, distinguishably, perceptibly, plainly; blatantly, boisterously, clamorously, loudly, lustily, mightily, noisily, resoundingly, stridently, thunderously, uproariously, vociferously

near ant faintly, feebly, low, noiselessly, quietly, softly

ant inaudibly, silently, soundlessly

alp *n* an elevation of land higher than a hill — see MOUNTAIN 1

alpha *n* the point at which something begins — see BEGINNING

alright *adj* 1 being to one's liking — see SATISFACTORY 1

2 not exposed to the threat of loss or injury — see SAFE 1

alright *adv* used to express agreement — see YES

also *adv* 1 in like manner ⟨we stayed at an historic London hotel, the same establishment that had *also* welcomed our grandparents many years ago⟩

syn alike, correspondingly, likewise, similarly, so

rel equally, equivalently, identically

near ant contrarily, conversely, inversely, oppositely, vice versa; diversely, unequally, variously

ant differently, dissimilarly, otherwise

2 in addition to what has been said — see MORE 1

alter *vb* 1 to make different in some way — see CHANGE 1

2 to remove the sex organs of — see NEUTER

alterable *adj* capable of being readily changed — see FLEXIBLE 1

alteration *n* the act, process, or result of making different — see CHANGE

altercation *n* an often noisy or angry expression of differing opinions — see ARGUMENT 1

alternative *n* the power, right, or opportunity to choose — see CHOICE 1

although *also* **altho** *conj* in spite of the fact that ⟨*although* I've been to his house several times, I still can't remember how to get there⟩

syn albeit, howbeit, though, when, while, whilst [*chiefly British*]

rel but, whereas

altitude *n* 1 the distance of something or someone from bottom to top — see HEIGHT 3

2 the most extreme or advanced point — see HEIGHT 2

3 *usually* **altitudes** *pl* an area of high ground — see HEIGHT 4

altogether *adv* 1 for the most part — see CHIEFLY

2 to a full extent or degree — see FULLY 1

altruistic *adj* having or showing a concern for the welfare of others — see CHARITABLE 1

always *adv* 1 on every relevant occasion ⟨Aunt Trina *always* insists we stay for dinner⟩

syn consistently, constantly, continually, ever, forever, incessantly, invariably, perpetually, unfailingly

rel commonly, frequently, oft, often, oftentimes (*or* ofttimes), recurrently, repeatedly; continuously, steadily, uninterruptedly; dependably, normally, ordinarily, regularly, routinely, typically, usually; inevitably; eternally, everlastingly

near ant intermittently, occasionally, periodically, sometimes, sporadically; infrequently, rarely, seldom, unusually

ant ne'er, never

2 for all time — see EVER 1

amalgam *n* a distinct entity formed by the combining of two or more different things — see BLEND

amalgamate *vb* 1 to mix thoroughly so that the things mixed cannot be recognized — see BLEND 1

2 to turn into a single mass that is more or less the same throughout — see BLEND 1

amalgamated *adj* made from the joining of two or more parts or elements — see COMPOSITE

amalgamation *n* a distinct entity formed by the combining of two or more different things — see BLEND

amass *vb* to bring together in one body or place — see GATHER 1

amateur *adj* lacking or showing a lack of expert skill — see AMATEURISH

amateur *n* a person who regularly or occasionally engages in an activity without being or becoming an expert at it ⟨a homemade doghouse that looked like it was built by an *amateur* who hadn't mastered basic carpentry⟩

syn dabbler, dilettante, potterer, putterer

rel apprentice, trainee; beginner, freshman, greenhorn, learner, neophyte, newcomer, novice, rookie, tenderfoot, tyro; hobbyist, tinkerer, trifler; layman, nonprofessional

near ant authority, pro, professional; maestro, virtuoso, whiz, wizard; artisan, artist, craftsman, workman; initiate, journeyman; specialist, technician; old hand, old-timer, vet, veteran

ant ace, adept, crackerjack, expert, master, past master

amateurish *adj* lacking or showing a lack of expert skill ⟨that's an *amateurish* wallpapering job—the pattern doesn't match at the seams⟩

syn amateur, dilettante, inexperienced, inexpert, nonprofessional, unprofessional, unskilled, unskillful

rel primitive, self-taught, uninitiated, unprepared, unqualified, unschooled, untaught, untrained, untutored; clumsy, crude, defective, faulty, flawed, unfin-

---

ished, unpolished; beginning, green, new, raw, unpracticed, unseasoned, untested, untried); incapable, incompetent, unable, unfit, ungifted, untalented

near ant able, accomplished, capable, competent, dexterous (*also* dextrous), gifted, proficient, skilled, skillful, talented; experienced, practiced (*or* practised), seasoned, veteran; educated, fitted, initiated, knowledgeable, prepared, qualified, schooled, taught, trained, tutored, versed; all-around (*also* all-round), versatile, well-rounded; finished, polished

ant ace, adept, consummate, crackerjack, expert, master, masterful, masterly, professional, virtuoso

amatory *adj* of, relating to, or expressing sexual attraction — see EROTIC

amaze *vb* to make a strong impression on (someone) with something unexpected — see SURPRISE 1

amazed *adj* 1 affected with sudden and great wonder or surprise — see THUNDERSTRUCK

2 filled with amazement or wonder — see OPENMOUTHED

amazement *n* 1 the rapt attention and deep emotion caused by the sight of something extraordinary — see WONDER 2

2 the state of being strongly impressed by something unexpected or unusual — see SURPRISE 2

amazing *adj* 1 causing a strong emotional reaction because unexpected — see SURPRISING 1

2 causing wonder or astonishment — see MARVELOUS 1

ambassador *n* a person sent on a mission to represent another ⟨a beloved entertainer who has often been sent abroad by the president as his country's goodwill *ambassador*⟩

syn delegate, emissary, envoy, minister, legate, representative

rel agent, attaché, consul, deputy, diplomat, foreign minister, nuncio, procurator, proxy; apostle, evangelist, missionary; deputation, detachment, legation; courier, messenger; mouthpiece, spokesperson

ambiguity *n* the quality or state of having a veiled or uncertain meaning — see OBSCURITY 1

ambiguous *adj* having an often intentionally veiled or uncertain meaning — see OBSCURE 1

ambiguousness *n* the quality or state of having a veiled or uncertain meaning — see OBSCURITY 1

ambition *n* 1 eager desire for personal advancement ⟨"Talent without *ambition* will not make you a star," McKenzie's dance instructor liked to remind her⟩

syn aspiration, go-getting

rel determination, diligence, drive, energy, enterprise, go, hustle, industry, initiative, motivation, push; opportunism; aggression, assertiveness, daring, spirit; ardor, avidity, eagerness, keenness, passion; avarice, greed

near ant apathy, indifference, unconcern; idleness, indolence, inertia, laziness, lethargy, shiftlessness, sloth

2 readiness to engage in daring or difficult activity — see ENTERPRISE 2

3 something that one hopes or intends to accomplish — see GOAL

ambitious *adj* 1 having a strong desire for personal advancement ⟨an *ambitious* child actor and his even more ambitious mother, who will do anything to get him in commercials⟩

syn aspiring, go-getting, self-seeking

rel determined, diligent, driving, dynamic, enterprising, gung ho, hustling, industrious, motivated, scrappy, venturesome, venturous; animated, lively, spirited; ardent, avid, eager, energetic, impassioned, keen, raring, vigorous; aggressive, assertive, opportunistic, pushy, self-assertive

near ant apathetic, disinterested, indifferent, uneager, unenthusiastic, unexcited, uninterested; casual, easygoing, lackadaisical; halfhearted, lukewarm, tepid; lazy, lethargic, listless, shiftless, sluggish, spiritless; unaggressive, unassertive

2 having or showing a bold forcefulness in the pursuit of a goal — see AGGRESSIVE 1

ambrosial *adj* 1 having a pleasant smell — see FRAGRANT

2 very pleasing to the sense of taste — see DELICIOUS 1

ambuscade *n* a scheme in which hidden persons wait to attack by surprise — see AMBUSH 1

ambush *n* 1 a scheme in which hidden persons wait to attack by surprise ⟨revolutionaries laid an *ambush* for the king along the route his carriage would travel⟩

syn ambuscade, surprise, trap

rel assault, attack, charge, sally; capture, entrapment, snare; hunting, stalking

2 a device or scheme for capturing another by surprise — see TRAP 1

ambush *vb* to lie in wait for and attack by surprise ⟨the king's enemies planned to *ambush* the royal coach on the way to Paris and capture the king⟩

syn surprise, waylay

rel assail, assault, attack, storm, strike; jump, pounce (on); tackle; charge, sally; capture, ensnare, entrap, net, snare, trap; hunt, prey (on *or* upon), stalk

phrases lay for

ameliorate *vb* to make better — see IMPROVE

amenability *n* 1 a desire or disposition to please — see COMPLAISANCE

2 cheerful readiness to do something — see ALACRITY

amenable *adj* 1 having a desire or inclination (as for a specified course of action) — see WILLING 1

2 readily giving in to the command or authority of another — see OBEDIENT

amend *vb* **1** to make better — see IMPROVE

2 to remove errors, defects, deficiencies, or deviations from — see CORRECT 1

amendment *n* a change designed to correct or improve a written work — see CORRECTION 1

amenity *n* **1** an act or utterance that is a customary show of good manners — see CIVILITY 1

2 something adding to pleasure or comfort but not absolutely necessary — see LUXURY 1

3 something that adds to one's ease — see COMFORT 2

4 the state or quality of having a pleasant or agreeable manner in socializing with others — see AMIABILITY 1

American Indian *n* a member of any of the native peoples of the western hemisphere usually not including the Eskimos ⟨Jeremy's great-grandfather was an *American Indian*, a member of the Shoshones⟩

syn Amerindian (*also* Amerind), Indian, Native American

rel mestizo

Amerindian *also* **Amerind** *n* a member of any of the native peoples of the western hemisphere usually not including the Eskimos — see AMERICAN INDIAN

amiability *n* **1** the state or quality of having a pleasant or agreeable manner in socializing with others ⟨the waitress's *amiability* is what makes eating at the diner so much fun⟩

syn affability, agreeableness, amenity, amiableness, geniality, good-naturedness, good-temperedness, graciousness, niceness, pleasantness, sweetness

rel amenability, complaisance; amicability, amity, cordiality, friendliness; benignity, gentleness, kindness; cheeriness, cheeriness, sunniness; civility, comity, considerateness, consideration, courteousness, courtesy, politeness, thoughtfulness; attractiveness, delightfulness, enjoyableness

near ant boorishness, discourtesy, impoliteness, incivility, rudeness, ungraciousness; biliousness, cantankerousness, churlishness, crankiness, fussiness, grouchiness, grumpiness, irascibility, irritability, peevishness, petulance, testiness; contentiousness, contrariness, orneriness, querulousness; hostility, unfriendliness

ant disagreeableness, unpleasantness

2 a desire or disposition to please — see COMPLAISANCE

amiable *adj* having an easygoing and pleasing manner especially in social situations ⟨the owner of the inn is an *amiable*, talkative widow who treats guests like family⟩

syn affable, agreeable, genial, good-natured, good-tempered, gracious, nice, sweet, well-disposed

rel amicable, cordial, friendly, neighborly; benign, gentle, kind; cheerful, cheery, sunny; companionable, sociable; civil, considerate, courteous, polite, thoughtful; accommodating, amenable, obliging; attractive, delightful, enjoyable

near ant boorish, discourteous, ill-mannered, impolite, inconsiderate, rude, surly, uncivil, unmannerly; bearish, bilious, cantankerous, choleric, churlish, crabby, cranky, dyspeptic, fussy, grouchy, grumpy, ill-humored, irascible, irritable, peevish, petulant, quick-tempered, snappish, testy, touchy; argumentative, contentious, contrary, ornery, querulous; unappealing, unattractive

ant disagreeable, ill-natured, ill-tempered, ungracious, unpleasant

amiableness *n* the state or quality of having a pleasant or agreeable manner in socializing with others — see AMIABILITY 1

amicable *adj* **1** having or marked by agreement in feeling or action — see HARMONIOUS 3

2 having or showing kindly feeling and sincere interest — see FRIENDLY 1

amid *or* **amidst** *prep* in or into the middle of — see AMONG

amiss *adv* **1** in a mistaken or inappropriate way — see WRONGLY

2 off the desired or intended path or course — see WRONG 1

amity *n* kindly concern, interest, or support — see GOODWILL 1

ammunition *n* means or method of defending — see DEFENSE 1

amnesty *n* release from the guilt or penalty of an offense — see PARDON

amok *or* **amuck** *adv* in a confused and reckless manner — see HELTER-SKELTER 1

among *also* **amongst** *prep* in or into the middle of ⟨a gull landed *among* the burgers-and-fries eaters at the outdoor snack bar, clearly looking for handouts⟩

syn amid (*or* amidst), mid, midst, through

rel between, betwixt

phrases in the thick of

near ant from, out of

amorous *adj* of, relating to, or expressing sexual attraction — see EROTIC

amorphous *adj* having no definite or recognizable form — see FORMLESS

amount *n* a given or particular mass or aggregate of matter ⟨is this small *amount* of food supposed to feed the whole hockey team?⟩

syn measure, quantity, volume

rel body, portion; many, number

amount (to) *vb* **1** to have a total of ⟨the expenses of the trip *amounted to* nearly double what we'd budgeted for⟩

syn add up (to), come (to), number, sum (to *or* into), total

rel average, equal, measure, reach; aggregate, comprise

2 to be the same in meaning or effect ⟨it makes no difference whether you're going to the game or to the movies, for it

---

syn synonym(s)   *rel* related words
ant antonym(s)   *near ant* near antonym(s)

amounts to your unavailability for babysitting⟩

syn add up (to), come (to), correspond (to), equal

rel approach, match, measure (up), meet, rival, touch; connote, denote, express, import, mean, signify, smack (of), spell, suggest

ample *adj* 1 being more than enough without being excessive — see PLENTIFUL

2 more than adequate or average in capacity — see SPACIOUS

amplify *vb* 1 to express more fully and in greater detail — see EXPAND 1

2 to make greater in size, amount, or number — see INCREASE 1

3 to make markedly greater in measure or degree — see INTENSIFY

amplitude *n* an area over which activity, capacity, or influence extends — see RANGE 2

amulet *n* something worn or kept to bring good luck or keep away evil — see CHARM 1

amuse *vb* to cause (someone) to pass the time agreeably occupied ⟨Christie *amused* her four-year-old sister at the family reunion by showing her off to all the relatives⟩

syn disport, divert, entertain, regale

rel absorb, busy, distract, engage, engross, immerse, interest, involve, occupy; beguile, bewitch, captivate, charm, delight, enchant, enthrall (*or* enthral), fascinate; grip, hypnotize, intrigue, mesmerize; coddle, gratify, humor, indulge, mollycoddle, pamper, please, pleasure, spoil; appease, comfort, conciliate, console, content, mollify, oblige, pacify, placate, propitiate, soothe

near ant bore, jade; drain, enervate, exhaust, fatigue, tire, wear, wear out, weary; aggravate, annoy, bother, bug, chafe, disturb, exasperate, fret, gall, grate, harass, harry, irk, nettle, peeve, perturb, pester, pique, upset, vex

amusement *n* the act or activity of providing pleasure or amusement especially for the public — see ENTERTAINMENT 1

amusing *adj* providing amusement or enjoyment — see FUN

analgesic *n* something (as a drug) that relieves pain — see PAINKILLER

analogous *adj* having qualities in common — see ALIKE

analysis *n* 1 the separation and identification of the parts of a whole ⟨investigators took the mysterious powder to the lab for *analysis*⟩

syn anatomizing, assay, breakdown, dissection

rel assessment, evaluation, examination, inspection, investigation, scrutiny; arrangement, assortment, cataloging (*or* cataloguing), categorization, classification, codification, indexing; enumeration, inventory, itemization, tabulation; division, reduction, segmentation, separation, subdivision

near ant agglomeration, aggregation, amalgamation, assimilation, coalescence, conglomeration, consolidation, integration, synthesis, unification

2 a series of explanations or observations on something (as an event) — see COMMENTARY

analytic *or* **analytical** *adj* according to the rules of logic — see LOGICAL 1

analyze *vb* to identify and examine the basic elements or parts of (something) especially for discovering interrelationships ⟨*analyze* the park's ecosystem before deciding whether hunting should be allowed⟩

syn anatomize, assay, break down, dissect

rel assess, evaluate, examine, inspect, investigate, scrutinize; arrange, assort, catalog (*or* catalogue), categorize, classify, codify, diagram, index, order, schematize, sort, tabulate; divide, reduce, segment, separate, subdivide

near ant agglomerate, aggregate, amalgamate, assimilate, coalesce, conglomerate, consolidate, integrate, synthesize, unify

anarchic *adj* not restrained by or under the control of legal authority — see LAWLESS

anarchy *n* a state in which there is widespread wrongdoing and disregard for rules and authority ⟨the *anarchy* that the country experienced after the dictator drained the treasury and fled the country⟩

syn lawlessness, misrule

rel commotion, tumult, uproar; chaos, confusion, disarray, disorder, disorderliness, disorganization; disruption, disturbance, havoc, riot, strife, turbulence, turmoil, unrest, upheaval; mutiny, rebellion, revolution, uprising; criminality, outlawry

near ant law, lawfulness, legality, legitimacy, rule; calmness, harmony, order, orderliness, peace, peacefulness, quiet, tranquillity (*or* tranquility)

anathema *n* 1 a prayer that harm will come to someone — see CURSE 1

2 something or someone that is hated — see HATE 2

anatomize *vb* to identify and examine the basic elements or parts of (something) especially for discovering interrelationships — see ANALYZE

anatomizing *n* the separation and identification of the parts of a whole — see ANALYSIS 1

ancestor *n* 1 a person who is several generations earlier in an individual's line of descent ⟨Bridie's Irish *ancestors* immigrated to the United States in the 19th century during the Great Potato Famine⟩

syn father, forebear (*also* forbear), forefather, grandfather

rel grandmother, matriarch, patriarch; ancestry, antecedents

near ant children, issue, offspring, posterity, progeny, seed; heir, inheritor, son, successor

ant descendant (*or* descendent)

2 something belonging to an earlier time from which something else was later developed ⟨pinball machines—the *ancestors* of today's video games—go back to the 19th century⟩

syn antecedent, foregoer, forerunner, precursor, predecessor

rel archetype, model, original, prototype; father, mother

near ant by-product, derivative, offshoot, outgrowth, spin-off; daughter, son

ant descendant (*or* descendent)

ancestry *n* the line of ancestors from whom a person is descended ⟨a Cambodian immigrant who can trace her Khmer *ancestry* as far back as the 16th century⟩

syn birth, blood, bloodline, breeding, descent, extraction, family tree, genealogy, line, lineage, origin, parentage, pedigree, stock, strain

rel heredity, succession; family, house; kin, kindred, relations, relatives; race

near ant offspring; child, heir, inheritor, son, successor

ant issue, posterity, progeny, seed

anchor *n* one who reads and introduces news reports on a news program — see ANCHORPERSON

anchor *vb* **1** to put securely in place or in a desired position — see FASTEN 1

2 to stop at or near a place along the shore — see LAND 1

anchorage *n* a part of a body of water protected and deep enough to be a place of safety for ships — see HARBOR 1

anchorite *n* a person who lives away from others — see RECLUSE

anchorperson *n* one who reads and introduces news reports on a news program ⟨the new *anchorperson* did an admirable job of dealing with the late-breaking news story⟩

syn anchor

rel anchorman, anchorwoman; broadcaster, newscaster, telecaster; correspondent, interviewer, reporter; journalist, newsman

ancient *adj* dating or surviving from the distant past ⟨Rome's *ancient* ruins are carefully preserved in the midst of the bustle of the modern city⟩

syn aged, age-old, antediluvian, antique, dateless, hoar, hoary, old, venerable

rel aging, mature; antiquated, obsolete, outmoded, out-of-date, passé; old-fashioned, old-time, old-world; durable, enduring, lasting, long-lived, permanent; ageless, hallowed, time-honored, timeless, time-tested, traditional, tried, tried-and-true; classic, classical; prehistoric, primeval, primordial

near ant fresh, new, youthful; contemporary, current, latest, mod, novel, present-day, ultramodern; untested, untried; brand-new, unused, unworn

ant modern, new, recent

2 being of advanced years and especially past middle age — see ELDERLY

3 relating to or occurring near the beginning of a process, series, or time period — see EARLY 1

ancient *n* a person of advanced years — see SENIOR CITIZEN

anecdote *n* a brief account of something interesting that happened especially to one personally — see STORY 2

anesthetic *n* something (as a drug) that relieves pain — see PAINKILLER

anew *adv* yet another time — see AGAIN 1

angel *n* **1** an innocent or gentle person — see LAMB

2 one that announces or indicates the later arrival of another — see FORERUNNER 1

anger *n* an intense emotional state of displeasure with someone or something ⟨Dave stifled his *anger* when the kids on the bus made fun of him⟩

syn angriness, furor, fury, indignation, irateness, ire, outrage, rage, spleen, wrath, wrathfulness

rel aggravation, annoyance, exasperation, irritation, vexation; animosity, antagonism, antipathy, bile, bitterness, contempt, enmity, grudge, hostility, rancor; envy, jaundice, jealousy, pique, resentment; malevolence, malice, spite, venom, virulence, vitriol; belligerence, contentiousness, contrariness, disputatiousness, orneriness, pugnacity, querulousness; blowup, flare-up, outburst; dander, dudgeon, huff, pet, rise, ruffle, temper; delirium, heat, passion, warmth

near ant calmness, forbearance, patience

ant delight, pleasure

anger *vb* to make angry ⟨it's virtually impossible to *anger* Mrs. Peterson—she's the most easygoing person I've ever known⟩

syn antagonize, enrage, incense, inflame, infuriate, madden, outrage, rankle, rile, roil

rel affront, aggravate, annoy, cross, exasperate, get, irritate, nettle, offend, peeve, pique, provoke, put out, ruffle, vex; embitter, envenom

phrases get one's goat, rub the wrong way

near ant allay, assuage, relieve; comfort, console, soothe; appease, conciliate, mollify, pacify, placate; calm, lull, quiet, settle; beguile, bewitch, captivate, charm, disarm, enchant

ant delight, gratify, please

angered *adj* feeling or showing anger — see ANGRY

angle *n* **1** a certain way in which something appears or may be regarded — see ASPECT 1

2 a way of looking at or thinking about something — see POINT OF VIEW

3 something that curves or is curved — see BEND 1

angle *vb* to set or cause to be at an angle — see LEAN 1

---

syn synonym(s)   **rel** related words

ant antonym(s)   **near ant** near antonym(s)

angling *n* the act of positioning or an instance of being positioned at an angle — see TILT

angriness *n* an intense emotional state of displeasure with someone or something — see ANGER

angry *adj* feeling or showing anger ⟨my sister gets really *angry* and practically throws a tantrum if her soccer team loses⟩

syn angered, apoplectic, enraged, foaming, fuming, furious, incensed, indignant, inflamed, infuriated, irate, ireful, mad, outraged, rabid, riled, roiled, shirty [*chiefly British*], sore, steaming, wrathful, wroth

rel ranting, raving, stormy; bristling, burning, cross, huffy, livid, seething, smoldering, worked up, wrought (up); acrid, acrimonious, antagonistic, antipathetic, bitter, embittered, inimical, malevolent, piqued, rancorous, resentful, spiteful, vindictive, virulent; antisocial, cold, cool, disagreeable, disapproving, distant, frigid, icy, ill-tempered, sulky, unfriendly, unpleasant; aggravated, annoyed, bearish, bilious, cantankerous, choleric, churlish, crabby, cranky, dyspeptic, exasperated, fretful, fussy, grouchy, grumpy, ill-humored, irascible, irritable, peevish, perturbed, petulant, put out, quick-tempered, snappish, testy, touchy; argumentative, belligerent, contentious, contrary, disputatious, ornery, pugnacious, quarrelsome, querulous

near ant accepting, accommodating, obliging; agreeable, amenable, complaisant; amicable, cordial, friendly; content, happy, satisfied; empathetic, sympathetic, tolerant, understanding; calm, pacific, peaceable, placid, serene, tranquil; affable, amiable, easygoing, genial, good-natured, good-tempered, kind, pleasant, sweet

ant delighted, pleased

anguish *n* **1** a state of great suffering of body or mind — see DISTRESS 1

2 deep sadness especially for the loss of someone or something loved — see SORROW

anguished *adj* expressing or suggesting mourning — see MOURNFUL 1

animal *adj* of or relating to the human body — see PHYSICAL 1

animal *n* one of the lower animals as distinguished from human beings ⟨we saw a lot of *animals* at the wildlife refuge—cranes, alligators, deer, a fox, even an armadillo⟩

syn beast, brute, creature, critter

rel varmint, vermin; biped, quadruped; carnivore, herbivore, insectivore; invertebrate, vertebrate

animate *adj* **1** having much high-spirited energy and movement — see LIVELY 1

2 having or showing life — see ALIVE 1

animate *vb* to give life, vigor, or spirit to ⟨Mr. Clark *animates* history for his sixth graders by frequently showing up for class dressed like some famous historical figure⟩

syn brace, energize, enliven, fire, invigorate, jazz (up), liven (up), pep (up), quicken, stimulate, vitalize, vivify

rel arouse, awake, awaken, raise, rouse, stir, wake (up); activate, actuate, drive, impel, motivate, move, propel; charge, electrify, galvanize; excite, ferment, foment, incite, inflame, instigate, kindle, provoke, set off, spark, trigger, turn on, whip (up); abet, boost, buoy, cheer, embolden, fortify, hearten, inspire, lift, rally, steel, strengthen; reactivate, reanimate, reawake, reawaken, recharge, recreate, reenergize, refresh, regenerate, rejuvenate, rekindle, renew, resurrect, resuscitate, revitalize, revive

near ant burn out, debilitate, do in, drain, enervate, enfeeble, exhaust, fag, fatigue, sap, tucker (out), undermine, weaken, wear, wear out; check, curb, inhibit, jade, quell, quench, repress, restrain, slow, still, stunt, suppress; daunt, demoralize, discourage, dishearten, dispirit

ant damp, dampen, deaden, dull

animated *adj* **1** having much high-spirited energy and movement — see LIVELY 1

2 marked by much life, movement, or activity — see ALIVE 2

animatedly *adv* in a quick and spirited manner — see GAILY 2

animately *adv* in a quick and spirited manner — see GAILY 2

animation *n* the quality or state of having abundant or intense activity — see VITALITY 1

animosity *n* a deep-seated ill will — see ENMITY

annalist *n* a student or writer of history — see HISTORIAN

annals *n pl* an account of important events in the order in which they happened — see HISTORY 1

annex *n* a smaller structure added to a main building ⟨a new *annex* that will serve as the permanent home for the school library⟩

syn addition, extension, penthouse

rel arm, ell, wing

annex *vb* to join (something) to a mass, quantity, or number so as to bring about an overall increase — see ADD 1

annihilate *vb* **1** to destroy all traces of ⟨the family's attempts to *annihilate* the roach population in their apartment had met with little success⟩

syn blot out, efface, eradicate, expunge, exterminate, extirpate, liquidate, obliterate, root (out), rub out, snuff (out), stamp (out), wipe out

rel decimate, demolish, destroy, devastate; dismantle, flatten, mow (down), raze, tear down; ruin, total, waste, wreck; blast, blow up, dash, dynamite, smash; atomize, consume, devour, dissolve, fragment, powder, pulverize, shatter, splinter; doom, finish, kill, terminate, zap; cancel, cut, discard, ditch, eject, excise, expel, jettison, oust, throw out *near ant* conserve, preserve, protect, save; build, construct, create, fabricate, fashion, forge, form, frame, make, manufacture, shape; fix, mend, patch, rebuild, recondition, reconstruct, renew, renovate, repair, restore, revamp

2 to bring to a complete end the physical soundness, existence, or usefulness of — see DESTROY 1

annihilation *n* the state or fact of being rendered nonexistent, physically unsound, or useless — see DESTRUCTION

announce *vb* to make known openly or publicly ⟨Jeannie *announced* to everyone within hearing distance that she didn't care if she failed the test⟩

syn advertise, blaze, broadcast, declare, enunciate, placard, post, proclaim, promulgate, publicize, publish, sound

rel advise, apprise, inform, notify; communicate, impart, intimate; disclose, divulge, report, reveal; disseminate, spread

near ant conceal, hush (up), silence, suppress, withhold; recall, recant, retract, revoke

announcement *n* a published statement informing the public of a matter of general interest ⟨an *announcement* was in today's paper regarding the merger of the two banks⟩

syn ad, advertisement, bulletin, notice, notification, posting, release

rel broadside, circular, flier (*or* flyer), handbill, handout; bill, billboard, placard, poster, sign; broadcast, newscast, telecast; advertising, commercial, message, spot, word; communication, dispatch, report; ballyhoo, boost, buildup, campaign, plug, promotion, propaganda, publicity

annoy *vb* to disturb the peace of mind of (someone) especially by repeated disagreeable acts — see IRRITATE 1

annoyance *n* **1** the act of making unwelcome intrusions upon another ⟨they have an unlisted number in the hopes that it will reduce the constant *annoyance* by telephone salespeople⟩

syn aggravation, bedevilment, bothering, bugging, disturbance, harassment, harrying, pestering, teasing, vexation

rel molestation, offense (*or* offence), persecution, provocation, torment, torture

2 the feeling of impatience or anger caused by another's repeated disagreeable acts ⟨Carlene made known her *annoyance* at having to pick up her sister's dirty clothes⟩

syn aggravation, bother, exasperation, frustration, irritation, vexation

rel agitation, anger, angriness, discomfort, displeasure, distress, disturbance, indignation, irateness, ire, outrage, perturbation, resentment; dander, dudgeon, huff, peeve, pet, pique, umbrage, upset

near ant delight, pleasure

3 something that is a source of irritation ⟨flashing ads, visual clutter, and other *annoyances* that are the price for free information on the Internet⟩

syn aggravation, bother, exasperation, frustration, hassle, headache, inconvenience, irritant, nuisance, peeve, pest, problem, thorn

rel affront, insult, offense; upset, worry; affliction, cross, curse, menace, plague; plight, predicament, trial, tribulation; annoyer, disturber, offender

near ant delight, joy, pleasure

4 one who is obnoxiously annoying — see NUISANCE 1

annoyer *n* one who is obnoxiously annoying — see NUISANCE 1

annoying *adj* causing annoyance ⟨Sheldon has the *annoying* habit of eating all the pickles and leaving a jar full of pickle juice in the refrigerator⟩

syn aggravating, bothersome, disturbing, exasperating, frustrating, galling, irksome, irritating, maddening, nettling, peeving, pesty, rankling, riling, vexatious, vexing

rel burdensome, discomforting, displeasing, disquieting, distressing, importunate, inconveniencing; angering, enraging, infuriating; mischievous, offensive, pesky, troublesome, upsetting; stressful, tiresome, troubling, trying, worrisome

near ant delightful, pleasing

annuity *n* a sum of money allotted for a specific use by official or formal action — see APPROPRIATION

annul *vb* **1** to balance with an equal force so as to make ineffective — see OFFSET

2 to put an end to by formal action — see ABOLISH

anoint *vb* to rub an oily or sticky substance over — see SMEAR 1

anomalous *adj* departing from some accepted standard of what is normal — see DEVIANT

anomaly *n* a person, thing, or event that is not normal — see FREAK 1

anon *adv* at or within a short time — see SHORTLY 2

anonymity *n* the quality or state of being mostly or completely unknown — see OBSCURITY 2

anonymous *adj* **1** known but not named — see CERTAIN 1

2 not named or identified by a name — see NAMELESS 1

3 not widely known — see OBSCURE 2

another *adj* resulting in an increase in amount or number — see ADDITIONAL

answer *n* **1** something spoken or written in reaction especially to a question ⟨the standard *answer* of "Nothing" when asked, "What did you do in school today?"⟩

syn comeback, rejoinder, reply, response, retort, return

rel banter, persiflage, repartee; acknowledgment (*also* acknowledgement), comment, communication, correspondence, feedback, observation, reaction, remark;

---

defense, explanation, justification, rebuttal, refutation

near ant challenge, cross-examination, grilling, interrogation, quiz; poll, questionnaire, survey

ant inquiry, query, question

2 something attained by mental effort and especially by computation ⟨the *answers* to the odd-numbered problems are at the back of the book⟩

syn result, solution

rel conclusion, determination, explanation, finding; clue, key

answer *vb* **1** to speak or write in reaction to a question or to another reaction ⟨Ryan didn't *answer* right away when Mrs. Jacobs asked him where he'd been for the last three hours⟩

syn rejoin, reply, respond, retort, return

rel acknowledge, comment, communicate, correspond, react, remark; explain, rebut, refute

near ant challenge, cross-examine, examine, grill, interrogate, pump, quiz; poll, query, survey

ant inquire, question

2 to be in agreement on every point — see CHECK 1

3 to do what is required by the terms of — see FULFILL 1

4 to find an answer for through reasoning — see SOLVE

answerable *adj* **1** being the one who must meet an obligation or suffer the consequences for failing to do so — see RESPONSIBLE 1

2 capable of having the reason for or cause of determined — see SOLVABLE

antagonism *n* a deep-seated ill will — see ENMITY

antagonist *n* **1** one that is hostile toward another — see ENEMY

2 one that takes a position opposite another in a competition or conflict — see OPPONENT 1

antagonistic *adj* marked by opposition or ill will — see HOSTILE 1

antagonize *vb* **1** to implant bitter feelings in — see EMBITTER

2 to make angry — see ANGER

antecedent *adj* going before another in time or order — see PREVIOUS

antecedent *n* **1** someone or something responsible for a result — see CAUSE 1

2 something belonging to an earlier time from which something else was later developed — see ANCESTOR 2

antecedently *adv* so as to precede something in order of time — see AHEAD 1

antedate *vb* to go or come before in time — see PRECEDE

antediluvian *adj* dating or surviving from the distant past — see ANCIENT 1

antediluvian *n* a person with old-fashioned ideas — see FOGY

anterior *adj* going before another in time or order — see PREVIOUS

anteriorly *adv* so as to precede something in order of time — see AHEAD 1

anthem *n* a religious song — see HYMN

anthology *n* a collection of writings ⟨an *anthology* of American short stories⟩

syn album, compilation, miscellany

rel archives; digest

antic *adj* **1** causing or intended to cause laughter — see FUNNY 1

2 given to good-natured joking or teasing — see PLAYFUL

antic *n* a playful or mischievous act intended as a joke — see PRANK

anticipate *vb* **1** to believe in the future occurrence of (something) — see EXPECT 1

2 to realize or know about beforehand — see FORESEE

anticipated *adj* being in accordance with the prescribed, normal, or logical course of events — see DUE 2

anticipatory *adj* having or showing signs of eagerly awaiting something — see EXPECTANT 1

antipathetic *adj* having a natural dislike for something ⟨a series of adventure books that turned boys who had been *antipathetic* to reading into avid readers⟩

syn allergic, averse

rel disinclined, loath (*or* loth), reluctant, unwilling; adverse, antagonistic, hostile, intolerant, negative, opposed, opposing, resistant, resisting, uncongenial, unfriendly, unsympathetic; disgusted, nauseated, repelled, repulsed, revolted, shocked, squeamish, turned off

near ant friendly, sympathetic, tolerant, understanding; admiring, appreciative, charmed, delighted, fond, pleased, tickled

antipathy *n* **1** a deep-seated ill will — see ENMITY

2 something or someone that is hated — see HATE 2

antipodal *adj* being as different as possible — see OPPOSITE

antipode *n* something that is as different as possible from something else — see OPPOSITE

antipodean *adj* being as different as possible — see OPPOSITE

antiquated *adj* having passed its time of use or usefulness — see OBSOLETE

antique *adj* **1** dating or surviving from the distant past — see ANCIENT 1

2 pleasantly reminiscent of an earlier time — see OLD-FASHIONED 1

antique *n* something belonging to or surviving from an earlier period ⟨Shamika's house is filled with *antiques*, including a collection of 19th-century African masks⟩

syn relic

rel artifact, fossil; antiquities, ruins; remains, remnant, trace, vestige

antisocial *adj* having or showing a lack of friendliness or interest in others — see COOL 1

antithesis *n* something that is as different as possible from something else — see OPPOSITE

antithetical *adj* being as different as possible — see OPPOSITE

anxiety *n* **1** an uneasy state of mind usually over the possibility of an anticipated misfortune or trouble ⟨Dorothy's *anxiety* about her brother's operation kept her awake all night⟩

syn agitation, anxiousness, apprehension, apprehensiveness, care, concern, disquiet, nervousness, perturbation, solicitude, uneasiness, worry

rel strain, stress, tension; alarm, anguish, consternation, desperation, desperateness, discomfort, discomposure, dismay, distraction, distress, disturbance, edginess, jitters, jumpiness; fear, fearfulness, torment, upset, vexation; doubt, dread, foreboding, incertitude, misgiving, presentiment, suspense, uncertainty

near ant calm, calmness, content, contentment, ease, peace, placidity, quiet, quietude, serenity, tranquillity (*or* tranquility); comfort, consolation, relief, solace

2 the emotion experienced in the presence or threat of danger — see FEAR

anxious *adj* **1** feeling or showing uncomfortable feelings of uncertainty — see NERVOUS 1

2 marked by or causing agitation or uncomfortable feelings — see NERVOUS 2

3 showing urgent desire or interest — see EAGER

anxiousness *n* an uneasy state of mind usually over the possibility of an anticipated misfortune or trouble — see ANXIETY 1

any *adj* being one of a group — see EACH

anyhow *adv* **1** in spite of everything — see REGARDLESS

2 without definite aim, direction, rule, or method — see HIT OR MISS

anymore *adv* at the present time — see NOW 1

anyway *adv* **1** in spite of everything — see REGARDLESS

2 without definite aim, direction, rule, or method — see HIT OR MISS

anywise *adv* **1** in any way or respect — see AT ALL

2 without definite aim, direction, rule, or method — see HIT OR MISS

A1 *adj* of the very best kind — see EXCELLENT

apace *adv* with great speed — see FAST 1

apart *adv* into parts or to pieces ⟨the fancy new adjustable rake came *apart* the first time Chad tried to use it⟩

syn asunder, piecemeal

ant together

apartment *n* **1** a room or set of rooms in a private house or a block used as a separate dwelling place ⟨a spacious six-room *apartment* that occupies the entire upper floor of a two-family house⟩

syn flat, lodgings, suite, tenement

rel condominium, duplex, penthouse, salon, studio, triplex; apartment house, tenement house, walk-up

2 an area within a building that has been set apart from surrounding space by a wall — see ROOM 2

apathetic *adj* **1** having or showing a lack of interest or concern — see INDIFFERENT 1

2 not feeling or showing emotion — see IMPASSIVE 1

apathy *n* **1** a lack of emotion or emotional expressiveness ⟨the *apathy* of the people of that war-torn country comes from their having seen too many horrors⟩

syn impassivity, insensibility, numbness, phlegm

rel callousness, coldness, coolness, hardheartedness, hardness, heartlessness, insensitivity, obduracy; blankness, deadness, emptiness, vacancy; aloofness, detachment, indifference, unconcern; stiffness, woodenness

near ant compassion, empathy, pity, sympathy; responsiveness, sensitivity; solicitude, tenderness, understanding, warmth; histrionics, hysteria, hysterics, melodrama

ant emotion, feeling, sensibility

2 lack of interest or concern — see INDIFFERENCE

ape *vb* to use (someone or something) as the model for one's speech, mannerisms, or behavior — see IMITATE 1

aper *n* a person who adopts the appearance or behavior of another especially in an obvious way — see COPYCAT

aperture *n* a place in a surface allowing passage into or through a thing — see HOLE 1

apex *n* **1** the highest part or point — see HEIGHT 1

2 the last and usually sharp or tapering part of something long and narrow — see POINT 2

aphorism *n* **1** an idea or statement about all of the members of a group or all the instances of a situation — see GENERALIZATION

2 an often stated observation regarding something from common experience — see SAYING

aphoristic *adj* marked by the use of few words to convey much information or meaning — see CONCISE

apiece *adv* for each one ⟨when you figure that it comes to six dollars *apiece*, it's too much to pay for used CDs⟩

syn all, each, per capita

rel apart, independently, individually, respectively, separately, singly

near ant altogether, collectively, together

apish *adj* using or marked by the use of something else as a basis or model — see IMITATIVE

aplomb *n* **1** evenness of emotions or temper — see EQUANIMITY

2 great faith in oneself or one's abilities — see CONFIDENCE 1

apologetic *adj* feeling sorrow for a wrong that one has done — see CONTRITE 1

apoplectic *adj* feeling or showing anger — see ANGRY

---

syn synonym(s)   *rel* related words
ant antonym(s)   *near ant* near antonym(s)

apostate *n* one who betrays a trust or an allegiance — see TRAITOR

apostle *n* a person who actively supports or favors a cause — see EXPONENT

apothecary *n* a person who prepares drugs according to a doctor's prescription — see DRUGGIST

appall *vb* to cause an often unpleasant surprise for — see SHOCK 1

appalling *adj* 1 causing intense displeasure, disgust, or resentment — see OFFENSIVE 1

2 extremely disturbing or repellent — see HORRIBLE 1

appanage *n* 1 something granted as a special favor — see PRIVILEGE

2 something to which one has a just claim — see RIGHT 1

apparatus *n* items needed for the performance of a task or activity — see EQUIPMENT

apparel *n* covering for the human body — see CLOTHING

apparel *vb* to outfit with clothes and especially fine or special clothes — see CLOTHE 1

apparent *adj* 1 appearing to be true on the basis of evidence that may or may not be confirmed ⟨at the start of the investigation, the *apparent* cause of the plane crash was mechanical failure⟩

syn assumed, evident, ostensible, presumed, reputed, seeming, supposed

rel external, outward, visible; conceivable, plausible; likely, probable; clear, distinct, manifest, obvious, plain; deceptive, delusive, delusory, illusive, illusory, imaginary; misleading, specious; fake, faked, feigned, phony (*also* phoney), pretended, pseudo, put-on; alleged, professed, purported, so-called

near ant authenticated, confirmed, corroborated, established, real, substantiated, valid, validated, verified

2 capable of being seen — see VISIBLE

3 not subject to misinterpretation or more than one interpretation — see CLEAR 2

apparently *adv* to all outward appearances ⟨*apparently*, Phil didn't know the cake was for the raffle, since he helped himself to a piece⟩

syn evidently, ostensibly, presumably, seemingly, supposedly

rel externally, outwardly, visibly; believably, credibly; maybe, mayhap, perchance, perhaps, possibly, professedly; allegedly, reputedly; clearly, distinctly, obviously, plainly; assuredly, positively, surely

near ant implausibly, impossibly, improbably, incredibly

apparition *n* the soul of a dead person thought of especially as appearing to living people — see GHOST

appeal *n* 1 an earnest request — see PLEA 1

2 the power of irresistible attraction — see CHARM 2

appeal (to) *vb* to make a request to (someone) in an earnest or urgent manner — see BEG

appealing *adj* having an often mysterious or magical power to attract — see FASCINATING 1

appear *vb* 1 to come into view ⟨a police car *appeared* just as Michael ran a red light⟩

syn come out, materialize, show up, turn up

rel reappear, resurface; bulk, loom; arrive, come; dawn, debut; arise, break, break out, emanate, erupt, issue, rise, spring (up); surface; happen, occur

near ant depart, leave, retire, withdraw

ant clear, disappear, dissolve, evanesce, evaporate, fade, go (away), melt (away), vanish

2 to give the impression of being — see SEEM

appearance *n* 1 the outward form of someone or something especially as indicative of a quality ⟨the dignified *appearance* of this church leader⟩ ⟨the country club's manicured lawns and well-groomed *appearance* in general⟩

syn aspect, look, mien, presence

rel air, attitude, bearing, behavior, comportment, demeanor, deportment, manner, poise, pose; carriage, posture, stance; color, complexion; countenance, face, features, physiognomy, visage

2 outward and often deceptive indication ⟨can't you at least give the *appearance* of listening to what I say?⟩

syn face, guise, name, semblance, show

rel affectation, display, fiction, imposture, make-believe, pose, pretense (*or* pretence), simulation; cloak, disguise, exterior, facade (*also* façade), front, mask, masquerade, shell, surface

3 the act of coming upon a scene — see ARRIVAL

appease *vb* to lessen the anger or agitation of — see PACIFY

appeasing *adj* tending to lessen or avoid conflict or hostility — see PACIFIC 1

appellation *n* a word or combination of words by which a person or thing is regularly known — see NAME 1

append *vb* to join (something) to a mass, quantity, or number so as to bring about an overall increase — see ADD 1

appendage *n* something that is not necessary in itself but adds to the convenience or performance of the main piece of equipment — see ACCESSORY 1

appertain *vb* 1 to be the property of a person or group of persons — see BELONG 2

2 to have a relation or connection — see APPLY 1

appetite *n* 1 a need or desire for food — see HUNGER 1

2 a strong wish for something — see DESIRE

3 positive regard for something — see LIKING

4 urgent desire or interest — see EAGERNESS

appetizing *adj* very pleasing to the sense of taste — see DELICIOUS 1

applaud *vb* to declare enthusiastic approval of — see ACCLAIM

applauding *adj* expressing approval — see FAVORABLE 1

applause *n* enthusiastic and usually public expression of approval ⟨a design for a memorial for the victims of the attack that has received nothing but *applause* from officials, commentators, and the general public⟩
syn acclamation, cheering, cheers, ovation, plaudit(s), rave(s)
rel clapping; bravo, hallelujah, hosanna; acclaim, accolade, citation, commendation, compliment, encomium, eulogy, homage, paean, panegyric, salutation, tribute
near ant boo, hiss, hoot, jeer, raspberry, smirk, sneer, snicker, snigger, snort, whistle; gibe (*or* jibe), put-down, taunt
ant booing, hissing

appliance *n* an interesting and often novel device with a practical use — see GADGET

applicability *n* the fact or state of being pertinent — see PERTINENCE

applicable *adj* 1 capable of being put to use or account — see PRACTICAL 1
2 having to do with the matter at hand — see PERTINENT
3 meeting the requirements of a purpose or situation — see FIT 1

applicant *n* one who seeks an office, honor, position, or award — see CANDIDATE

application *n* the act or practice of employing something for a particular purpose — see USE 1

apply *vb* 1 to have a relation or connection ⟨does your rule about calling home *apply* to me as well?⟩
syn appertain, bear, pertain, refer, relate
rel affect, concern, interest, involve, touch; associate, connect, couple, interrelate, link, tie in; deal (with), treat
phrases have to do with
2 to occupy (oneself) diligently or with close attention ⟨Sam *applied* himself to writing thank-you letters to everyone who'd helped sponsor him for the jamboree⟩
syn address, bend, buckle, devote, give
rel readdress, reapply; knuckle down, set (to), settle (down); busy, commit, concern, engage, involve; exert, exhaust, put out, spend, strain, stress, tax, trouble, wear out; carry on, pitch in, plunge (in); grind, hump, hustle, peg (away), plod, plow, plug (away), work
near ant dally, dawdle, dillydally, fiddle, fool (around), idle, mess (around), monkey (around), play, potter, putter, trifle
3 to put a layer of on a surface — see SPREAD 2

4 to put into action or service — see USE 1
5 to bring to bear especially forcefully or effectively — see EXERT
6 to carry out effectively — see ENFORCE

appoint *vb* 1 to decide upon (the time or date for an event) usually from a position of authority ⟨at the *appointed* hour we were in our places⟩
syn designate, fix, name, set
rel adopt, assign, choose, determine, establish, opt (for), pick, pin down, prefer, select, settle, single (out); specify; arrange, coordinate, orchestrate; advertise, announce, declare, publish
2 to pick (someone) by one's authority for a specific position or duty ⟨Igor was *appointed* hall monitor for May⟩
syn assign, attach, commission, constitute, designate, detail, name
rel authorize, delegate, depute, deputize; inaugurate, induct, install, instate, ordain, invest; crown, enthrone, throne; choose, elect, handpick, nominate, select, single (out), vote (in)
near ant depose, dethrone, displace, eject, oust, overthrow, remove, throw out, uncrown, unmake
ant discharge, dismiss, expel, fire

appointment *n* 1 the state or fact of being chosen for a position or duty ⟨the *appointment* of the mayor's husband to the Board of Health came as a surprise⟩
syn assignment, commission, designation
rel billet, job, office, place, position, situation, spot, station; authorization, delegation, deputation, placement, ranking; induction, installation, installment (*or* instalment), instating, investiture, investment, ordination; choosing, election, nomination, picking, selection, singling out
near ant deposition, dethronement, ejection, ouster, overthrow, rejection, removal
ant discharge, dismissal, expulsion, firing
2 an agreement to be present at a specified time and place — see ENGAGEMENT 2
3 an assignment at which one regularly works for pay — see JOB 1
4 appointments *pl* the movable articles in a room — see FURNITURE

apportion *vb* 1 to give as a share or portion — see ALLOT
2 to give out (something) in appropriate amounts or to appropriate individuals — see ADMINISTER 2

apportionment *n* the act or process of giving out something to each member of a group — see DISTRIBUTION 1

apposite *adj* having to do with the matter at hand — see PERTINENT

appraisal *n* 1 an opinion on the nature, character, or quality of something — see ESTIMATION 1
2 the act of placing a value on the nature, character, or quality of something — see ESTIMATE 1

---

syn synonym(s)   *rel* related words
ant antonym(s)   *near ant* near antonym(s)

appraise vb to make an approximate or tentative judgment regarding — see ESTIMATE 1

appraisement n **1** an opinion on the nature, character, or quality of something — see ESTIMATION 1
2 the act of placing a value on the nature, character, or quality of something — see ESTIMATE 1

appreciable adj able to be perceived by a sense or by the mind — see PERCEPTIBLE

appreciate vb **1** to become greater in extent, volume, amount, or number — see INCREASE 2
2 to hold dear — see LOVE 1
3 to recognize the meaning of — see COMPREHEND 1
4 to think very highly or favorably of — see ADMIRE

appreciation n **1** a feeling of great approval and liking — see ADMIRATION 1
2 acknowledgment of having received something good from another — see THANKS
3 the knowledge gained from the process of coming to know or understand something — see COMPREHENSION

appreciative adj **1** expressing approval — see FAVORABLE 1
2 feeling or expressing gratitude — see GRATEFUL 1

appreciativeness n acknowledgment of having received something good from another — see THANKS

apprehend vb **1** to recognize the meaning of — see COMPREHEND 1
2 to take or keep under one's control by authority of law — see ARREST 1

apprehended adj taken and held prisoner — see CAPTIVE

apprehension n **1** suspicion or fear of future harm or misfortune ⟨Erica entered the dark cave with a great deal of *apprehension*⟩
syn alarm, apprehensiveness, dread, foreboding, misgiving
rel agitation, anxiousness, concern, disquiet, distress, disturbance, fearfulness, perturbation, solicitude, uneasiness; scruple, worry; doubt, incertitude, suspense, uncertainty, wariness; defeatism, pessimism; foreknowledge, premonition, presage, presentiment
near ant anticipation, excitement, hope, hopefulness; confidence, optimism, sanguinity
2 the act of taking or holding under one's control by authority of law — see ARREST
3 the emotion experienced in the presence or threat of danger — see FEAR
4 an uneasy state of mind usually over the possibility of an anticipated misfortune or trouble — see ANXIETY 1
5 the knowledge gained from the process of coming to know or understand something — see COMPREHENSION

apprehensiveness n **1** an uneasy state of mind usually over the possibility of an anticipated misfortune or trouble — see ANXIETY 1
2 suspicion or fear of future harm or misfortune — see APPREHENSION 1

apprentice n a person who helps a more skilled person — see HELPER

apprise vb to give information to — see ENLIGHTEN 1

approach n **1** an established course for traveling from one place to another — see PASSAGE 1
2 the means or procedure for doing something — see METHOD

approach vb **1** to come near or nearer ⟨The parade's *approaching* ! I can hear the band playing!⟩
syn close, draw on, near
rel arrive, attain, come, gain, hit, land, make, reach, show up, turn up; adjoin, border, touch, verge
near ant clear out, depart, exit, go, leave, light out, pull (out), quit, remove, run away, shove (off), take off, walk out
ant back (up or away), recede, retire, retreat, withdraw
2 to move closer to — see COME 1
3 to come near or nearer to in character or quality — see APPROXIMATE

approaching adj being soon to appear or take place — see FORTHCOMING

approbation n an acceptance of something as satisfactory — see APPROVAL 1

appropriate adj meeting the requirements of a purpose or situation — see FIT 1

appropriate vb **1** to take or make use of without authority or right ⟨archaeologists once *appropriated* artifacts excavated at ancient African sites for their museums in Europe⟩
syn arrogate, commandeer, preempt, usurp
rel annex, claim, confiscate, expropriate, preoccupy, sequester; grab, grasp, seize, snatch, steal, take over, wrench, wrest; encroach, infringe, invade, trespass
2 to take (something) without right and with an intent to keep — see STEAL 1

appropriately adv in a manner suitable for the occasion or purpose — see PROPERLY

appropriateness n the quality or state of being especially suitable or fitting ⟨Mrs. Bryce-Jones remarked on the *appropriateness* of window boxes on the cottage, noting they gave it a quaint, cheerful look⟩
syn aptness, felicitousness, fitness, fittingness, rightness, seemliness, suitability, suitableness
rel agreeableness, compatibility, congruity, harmoniousness; applicability, bearing, connection, materiality, pertinence, relevance; acceptability, adequacy, adequateness, satisfactoriness, serviceableness, usefulness
near ant inapplicability, irrelevance; meaninglessness, pointlessness; incompatibility, incongruity
ant inappropriateness, inaptness, infelicity, unfitness

appropriation *n* a sum of money allotted for a specific use by official or formal action ⟨the National Park Service received an increased *appropriation* for wildlife management⟩

syn allocation, allotment, annuity, grant, subsidy

rel advance, allowance, benefit, endowment, fund, stipend, trust

approval *n* an acceptance of something as satisfactory ⟨Does this dress I bought for the wedding meet with your *approval* ?⟩

syn approbation, blessing, favor, imprimatur, OK (*or* okay)

rel backing, endorsement, sanction, support; benediction, goodwill; agreement, assent, concurrence, consent; countenance, liking, satisfaction

near ant refusal, rejection, repudiation; dislike, dissatisfaction; censure, condemnation, criticism, denunciation, deprecation, depreciation, disparagement, opprobrium, reprehension, reproach, reprobation

ant disapprobation, disapproval, disfavor

approve *vb* to give official acceptance of something as satisfactory ⟨as soon as the pond project was *approved*, the bulldozers were at the site⟩

syn authorize, clear, OK (*or* okay), ratify, sanction, warrant

rel accept, acknowledge, affirm, confirm; accredit, certify, endorse (*also* indorse), validate; initial, sign; allow, license (*or* licence), permit; reapprove

near ant ban, enjoin, forbid, interdict, prohibit; disregard, ignore, neglect, overlook; rebuff, rebut, refuse, spurn

ant decline, deny, disallow, disapprove, negative, reject, turn down

approve (of) *vb* to have a favorable opinion of ⟨Mrs. Pinkerton doesn't *approve of* people who stand in the "12 items or less" lane with 13 items⟩

syn accept, care (for), countenance, favor, OK (*or* okay), subscribe (to)

rel acclaim, applaud, laud, praise, salute; back (up), stand by, support, sustain, uphold; bear, endure, tolerate; assent (to), concur (with), consent (to); commend, recommend; enjoy, like

phrases go for, hold with

near ant censure, condemn, criticize, damn, denounce, deprecate, depreciate, disparage, reprehend, reprobate; detest, dislike, hate, loathe; object (to), oppose

ant disapprove (of), discountenance, disfavor, frown (on *or* upon)

approving *adj* **1** expressing approval — see FAVORABLE 1

2 showing or expressing acceptance or approval — see POSITIVE

approximate *adj* being such only when compared to something else — see COMPARATIVE

approximate *vb* to come near or nearer to in character or quality ⟨Rob's violin performance last night didn't even *approximate* what he's really capable of when he's not feeling sick⟩

syn approach, compare (with), measure up (to), stack up (against *or* with)

rel add up (to), amount (to), come (to); duplicate, equal, match; mirror, parallel, reflect; border (on), touch (on), verge (on)

apropos *adj* having to do with the matter at hand — see PERTINENT

apropos of *prep* having to do with — see ABOUT 1

apt *adj* **1** having a tendency to be or act in a certain way — see PRONE 1

2 meeting the requirements of a purpose or situation — see FIT 1

aptitude *n* a special and usually inborn ability — see TALENT

aptness *n* **1** an established pattern of behavior — see TENDENCY 1

2 the quality or state of being especially suitable or fitting — see APPROPRIATENESS

aquatic *adj* living, lying, or occurring below the surface of the water — see UNDERWATER

aqueduct *n* an open man-made passageway for water — see CHANNEL 1

arbiter *n* one who works with opposing sides in order to bring about an agreement — see MEDIATOR

arbitrary *adj* **1** having or showing a tendency to force one's will on others without any regard to fairness or necessity ⟨an *arbitrary* piano teacher who makes all her students do the same exercises over and over again⟩

syn dictatorial, high-handed, imperious, peremptory, willful (*or* wilful)

rel arrogant, commanding, demanding, dominant, domineering, haughty, imperative, lordly, masterful, overbearing, presumptuous; authoritarian, autocratic, despotic, totalitarian, tyrannical (*also* tyrannic), tyrannous; capricious, changeable, erratic, mercurial, whimsical; biased, inequitable, partisan, prejudiced, unequal, unfair, unjust, unreasonable; unconscionable, unethical, unprincipled, unscrupulous

near ant balanced, disinterested, dispassionate, equal, equitable, evenhanded, fair, impartial, just, nonpartisan, objective; rational, reasonable, understanding; unbiased, unprejudiced; ethical, honorable, irreproachable, law-abiding, moral, principled, unimpeachable

2 lacking a definite plan, purpose, or pattern — see RANDOM

arbitrate *vb* to give an opinion about (something at issue or in dispute) — see JUDGE 1

arbitrator *n* one who works with opposing sides in order to bring about an agreement — see MEDIATOR

arc *n* something that curves or is curved — see BEND 1

---

syn synonym(s)   *rel* related words
ant antonym(s)   *near ant* near antonym(s)

arc *vb* to turn away from a straight line or course — see CURVE 1

arch *adj* **1** coming before all others in importance — see FOREMOST 1

2 displaying or marked by rude boldness — see NERVY 1

arch *n* something that curves or is curved — see BEND 1

arch *vb* **1** to cause to turn away from a straight line — see BEND 1

2 to turn away from a straight line or course — see CURVE 1

archaic *adj* having passed its time of use or usefulness — see OBSOLETE

archetypal *adj* **1** constituting, serving as, or worthy of being a pattern to be imitated — see MODEL

2 having or showing the qualities associated with the members of a particular group or kind — see TYPICAL 1

archetype *n* something from which copies are made — see ORIGINAL

archive *n* a place where books, periodicals, and records are kept for use but not for sale — see LIBRARY

arctic *adj* having a low or subnormal temperature — see COLD 1

ardent *adj* **1** having or expressing great depth of feeling — see FERVENT

2 showing urgent desire or interest — see EAGER

ardor *n* **1** depth of feeling ⟨candidates for citizenship reciting the oath of allegiance to the United States with all the *ardor* that they could muster⟩

syn emotion, fervency, fervidness, fervor, heat, intensity, passion, vehemence, warmth

rel histrionics, mawkishness, melodrama, sappiness, sentimentality; eagerness, earnestness, enthusiasm, excitement, gusto, zest; fanaticism, fever, fire, hot-bloodedness, infatuation, mania, obsession, zeal; compassion, responsiveness, sympathy, tenderness

near ant aloofness, calmness, coldness, collectedness, composure, coolness, detachedness, dryness, phlegm, reserve, reservedness, reticence, taciturnity; apathy, indifference, unconcern; stiffness, woodenness

ant impassivity

2 urgent desire or interest — see EAGERNESS

arduous *adj* **1** requiring considerable physical or mental effort — see HARD 2

2 requiring much time, effort, or careful attention — see DEMANDING 1

arduously *adv* with great effort or determination — see HARD 1

area *n* **1** a part or portion having no fixed boundaries — see REGION 1

2 a region of activity, knowledge, or influence — see FIELD 2

arena *n* **1** a large room or building for enclosed public gatherings — see HALL 3

2 a region of activity, knowledge, or influence — see FIELD 2

argot *n* the special terms or expressions of a particular group or field — see TERMINOLOGY

argue *vb* **1** to state (something) as a reason in support of or against something under consideration ⟨Luis *argued* that a bake sale would make a lot less money than a car wash⟩

syn assert, contend, maintain, plead, reason

rel claim, insist; affirm, aver, avouch, avow; advance, offer, propose, submit; advise, counsel, recommend, suggest, urge; convince, persuade; advocate, champion, espouse, support; explain, justify, rationalize; consider, debate, discuss; counter, disprove, rebut, refute

2 to express different opinions about something often angrily ⟨Francesca didn't *argue* with her little brother the whole time they were at Walt Disney World⟩

syn bicker, brawl, dispute, fall out, fight, hassle, quarrel, row, scrap, spat, squabble, wrangle

rel challenge, dare, defy; clash, contend, contest; cavil, fuss, nitpick, quibble; consider, debate, discuss; kick, object, protest

phrases bandy words, fall foul

near ant coexist, get along; accept, agree, assent, concur, consent

3 to cause (someone) to agree with a belief or course of action by using arguments or earnest requests — see PERSUADE

4 to talk about (an issue) usually from various points of view and for the purpose of arriving at a decision or opinion — see DISCUSS

arguer *n* a person who takes part in a dispute — see DISPUTANT

argument *n* **1** an often noisy or angry expression of differing opinions ⟨the couple's *arguments* were often loud enough to be heard all over the neighborhood⟩

syn altercation, bicker, brawl, cross fire, disagreement, dispute, falling-out, fight, hassle, misunderstanding, quarrel, row, scrap, spat, squabble, tiff, wrangle

rel clash, run-in, skirmish, tussle; feud, vendetta; attack, contention, dissension; controversy, debate; fuss, objection, protest, protestation; affray, feud, fisticuffs, fracas, fray, free-for-all, melee

2 a statement given to explain a belief or act — see REASON 1

3 an exchange of views for the purpose of exploring a subject or deciding an issue — see DISCUSSION 1

4 an idea or opinion that is put forth in a discussion or debate — see CONTENTION

argumentative *adj* **1** given to arguing ⟨Ryan's *argumentative* nature is such that he's always insisting he didn't make the fouls that the referee calls⟩

syn contentious, disputatious, quarrelsome, scrappy

rel bellicose, belligerent, combative, pugnacious, truculent; balky, contrary, ornery, perverse, restive, wayward; disobedient, froward, insubordinate, intractable, recalcitrant, refractory; hardheaded, headstrong, mulish, obdurate, obstinate, pigheaded, resistant, self-willed, stubborn, unbending, uncompromising, uncooperative, unreasonable, unyielding, willful (or wilful)

near ant acquiescent, agreeable, amenable, complaisant, compliant, complying, conciliatory, cooperative, obliging; docile, obedient, submissive, tractable

2 feeling or displaying eagerness to fight — see BELLIGERENT

arid *adj* marked by little or no precipitation or humidity — see DRY 1

arise *vb* 1 to leave one's bed ⟨the travelers *arose* before dawn and were on their way as the sun came up⟩

syn get up, rise, uprise

rel arouse, awake, awaken, bestir, stir, wake

near ant doze, drop (off), nap, nod, sleep, slumber; bunk, perch, roost, settle; couch, lie (down), recline

ant bed (down), retire, turn in

2 to come to one's attention especially gradually or unexpectedly ⟨note in your report any problems that *arise* while you are conducting the experiment⟩

syn crop (up), emerge, materialize, spring (up), surface

rel appear, come out, show up, turn up; chance, come, come about, fall out, go (on), go off, hap, happen, occur, pass, transpire; interfere, interpose, intervene, intrude

3 to come into existence — see BEGIN 2

4 to move or extend upward — see ASCEND

aristocracy *n* the highest class in a society ⟨at one time in China only the *aristocracy* could own land⟩

syn gentry, upper class, upper crust

rel elect, elite, establishment, gentlefolk, jet set, nobility, quality, royalty, society

near ant commoners, (the) crowd, (the) masses, peasantry, peonage, (the) people, plebeians, (the) populace, (the) public, rank and file; bourgeoisie, middle class, working class; dregs, (the) herd, (the) mob, rabble, riffraff, scum, trash

ant proletarians, proletariat

aristocrat *n* a man of high birth or social position — see GENTLEMAN 1

aristocratic *adj* of high birth, rank, or station — see NOBLE 1

arithmetic *n* the act or process of performing mathematical operations to find a value — see CALCULATION

¹**arm** *n* a portable weapon from which a shot is discharged by gunpowder — see GUN 1

²**arm** *n* 1 an area of land that juts out into a body of water — see ²CAPE

2 the right or means to command or control others — see POWER 1

armada *n* a group of vehicles traveling together or under one management — see FLEET

armed forces *n pl* the combined army, air force, and navy of a nation ⟨our nation's *armed forces* are stationed throughout the world⟩

syn military, service, troops

rel GI's (or GIs), men-at-arms, rank and file, servicemen, servicewomen, soldiers, soldiery; militia, reserves; armor, defense

near ant civilians, noncombatants

armistice *n* a temporary stopping of fighting — see TRUCE

armor *n* 1 means or method of defending — see DEFENSE 1

2 something that encloses another thing especially to protect it — see ¹CASE

armory *n* a place where military arms are stored ⟨the soldier was sent to the *armory* to get a replacement weapon for the one that had been stolen⟩

syn arsenal, depot, dump, magazine

rel fort, fortress, stronghold; repository, storehouse, warehouse

army *n* 1 a large body of men and women organized for land warfare ⟨In 218 B.C., Hannibal marched into Italy with an *army* of 26,000, and even a few elephants, after crossing the Alps⟩

syn battalion, host, legion

rel infantry, ranks, regulars, soldiers, troops, troopers

2 a great number of persons or things gathered together — see CROWD 1

aroma *n* a sweet or pleasant smell — see FRAGRANCE

aromatic *adj* having a pleasant smell — see FRAGRANT

around *adv* 1 on all sides or in every direction ⟨he looked *around*⟩ ⟨butterflies were flying all *around*⟩

syn about, round

rel all over, everyplace, everywhere; abroad, afloat, hereabouts (or hereabout)

2 toward the opposite direction ⟨she turned *around* and saw him⟩

syn about, back, round

rel backward (or backwards), behind, down, downward, rearward (or rearwards); across, athwart, counter, counterclockwise

3 at, within, or to a short distance or time — see NEAR 1

4 from beginning to end — see THROUGH 1

around *prep* 1 close to ⟨I wouldn't stand *around* those rocks—there could be snakes under them⟩

syn about, by, near, next to

rel alongside, beside; across, along, at; circa

2 in random positions within the boundaries of ⟨huge, strangely shaped rocks were scattered *around* the canyon floor⟩

syn about, over, round, through, throughout

rel on

arouse *vb* 1 to cause to stop sleeping — see WAKE 1

2 to cease to be asleep — see WAKE 2

3 to rouse to strong feeling or action — see PROVOKE 1

---

syn synonym(s) *rel* related words
ant antonym(s) *near ant* near antonym(s)

arrange *vb* **1** to come to an agreement or decision concerning the details of ⟨*arrange* a time for the meeting⟩ ⟨*arrange* money matters for your trip⟩

syn decide, fix, set, settle

rel agree, contract, pledge, promise; draft, frame, hammer (out), intrigue, lay out, maneuver, map (out), plan, program, schematize, scheme, shape, square away, work out; affirm, approve, authorize, clear, confirm, OK (*or* okay), sanction, warrant; close, complete, conclude, end, finalize, finish, round (off *or* out), wind up, wrap up; bargain, chaffer, deal, dicker, haggle, horse-trade, negotiate

phrases dispose of

2 to put into a particular arrangement — see ORDER 1

3 to bring about through discussion and compromise — see NEGOTIATE 1

4 to work out the details of (something) in advance — see PLAN 1

arrangement *n* **1** a method worked out in advance for achieving some objective — see PLAN 1

2 the way in which something is sized, arranged, or organized — see FORMAT 1

3 the way in which the elements of something (as a work of art) are arranged — see COMPOSITION 3

4 the way objects in space or events in time are arranged or follow one another — see ORDER 1

arrant *adj* having no exceptions or restrictions — see ABSOLUTE 2

array *n* **1** a number of things considered as a unit — see GROUP 1

2 a usually small number of persons considered as a unit — see GROUP 2

3 dressy clothing — see FINERY

4 the way objects in space or events in time are arranged or follow one another — see ORDER 1

array *vb* **1** to make more attractive by adding something that is beautiful or becoming — see DECORATE

2 to outfit with clothes and especially fine or special clothes — see CLOTHE 1

3 to put into a particular arrangement — see ORDER 1

arrest *n* the act of taking or holding under one's control by authority of law ⟨there have been only two *arrests* for driving while intoxicated in the county in the last six months⟩

syn apprehension, pinch

rel bust [*slang*]; raid; capture, entrapment, seizure; captivity, confinement, detention, enchainment, immurement, imprisonment, incarceration, restraint

near ant emancipation, liberation, release

ant discharge

arrest *vb* **1** to take or keep under one's control by authority of law ⟨the inept robber was promptly *arrested* by the off-duty policeman he had tried to hold up⟩

syn apprehend, bust [*slang*], nab, pick up, pinch, restrain, seize

rel bag, capture, catch, collar, get, grab, grapple, hook, land, nail, snare, snatch, trap; confine, detain, hold, immure, imprison, incarcerate, intern, jail, lock (up); bind, enchain, fetter, handcuff, manacle, shackle, trammel

near ant emancipate, free, liberate, loose, loosen, release, spring; unbind, unchain

ant discharge

2 to bring (something) to a standstill — see ¹HALT 1

3 to hold the attention of as if by a spell — see ENTHRALL 1

arrested *adj* taken and held prisoner — see CAPTIVE

arresting *adj* **1** holding the attention or provoking interest — see INTERESTING

2 likely to attract attention — see NOTICEABLE

arrival *n* the act of coming upon a scene ⟨spring's late *arrival* meant we were still skiing in mid-April⟩ ⟨the groom blamed his belated *arrival* for the wedding on a huge traffic snarl⟩

syn advent, appearance

rel approach, entrance, ingress; beginning, birth, commencement, dawn, dawning, debut, genesis, inception, morning, onset, start

near ant dissipation, dissolution, evaporation, fading, melting, passing, vanishing; clearing out, egress, exit, exiting, leaving, retirement, withdrawal

ant departing, departure, disappearance, going

arrive *vb* to get to a destination — see COME 2

arrogance *n* an exaggerated sense of one's importance that shows itself in the making of excessive or unjustified claims ⟨in his *arrogance* the president of the club made all the arrangements for the annual banquet without consulting the members⟩

syn haughtiness, imperiousness, loftiness, lordliness, masterfulness, peremptoriness, pompousness, presumptuousness, pretense (*or* pretence), pretension, pretentiousness, self-importance, superciliousness, superiority

rel authoritativeness, bossiness, dominance, high-handedness; condescension, disdain, scorn; snobbery, snobbishness, snobbism, snootiness; cheek, cheekiness, impertinence, impudence, sauciness; boastfulness, bombast, braggadocio, swagger, vaingloriousness, vainglory; cockiness, complacence, conceit, egoism, egotism, pride, pridefulness, self-centeredness, self-conceit, self-satisfaction, smugness, vanity

near ant bashfulness, demureness, retiringness, shyness; diffidence, self-doubt, timidity; meekness, passiveness, passivity, submissiveness; quietness, reserve, reservedness

ant humility, modesty

arrogant *adj* having a feeling of superiority that shows itself in an overbearing attitude ⟨the *arrogant* young lawyer elbowed his way to the head of the line of customers, declaring that he was too busy to wait like everybody else⟩

syn cavalier, haughty, highfalutin, high-handed, high-hat, imperious, important, lofty, lordly, masterful, overweening, peremptory, pompous, presumptuous, pretentious, supercilious, superior, uppish, uppity

rel authoritarian, bossy, dominant, dominating, domineering, magisterial, pontificating; condescending, disdainful, patronizing; impertinent, impudent, saucy; snobbish, snobby, snooty; boastful, bombastic, braggart, bragging, cocky, swaggering, vain, vainglorious; complacent, conceited, egocentric, egoistic, egotistic (*or* egotistical), prideful, proud, self-centered, self-conceited, self-satisfied, smug, stuck-up

near ant bashful, cowering, cringing, demure, diffident, mousy (*or* mousey), overmodest, self-doubting, shrinking, shy, subdued, timid; acquiescent, compliant, deferential, meek, passive, submissive, unaggressive, unassertive, unassuming, unobtrusive, yielding; quiet, reserved, retiring

ant humble, modest

arrogate *vb* to take or make use of without authority or right — see APPROPRIATE 1

arsenal *n* a place where military arms are stored — see ARMORY

arsonist *n* a person who deliberately and unlawfully sets fire to a building or other property ⟨they finally caught the *arsonist*, but only after he'd set fire to four barns⟩

syn firebug, incendiary

rel igniter (*or* ignitor)

art *n* subtle or imaginative ability in inventing, devising, or executing something — see SKILL 1

artery *n* a passage cleared for public vehicular travel — see WAY 1

artful *adj* **1** clever at attaining one's ends by indirect and often deceptive means ⟨the lawyer, by her *artful* questioning, got the witness to admit he had been lying⟩

syn beguiling, cagey (*also* cagy), crafty, cunning, devious, foxy, guileful, slick, sly, subtle, wily

rel astute, cute, facile, glib, sharp, shrewd; crooked, deceitful, deceptive, dishonest, insidious, insinuating, Machiavellian, shady, shifty, slippery, sneaky, treacherous, tricky, underhand, underhanded, unscrupulous; backhanded, double-dealing, hypocritical, insincere, mealymouthed, smooth-tongued, two-faced; circuitous, circular, roundabout; clandestine, concealed, covert, furtive, hugger-mugger, secret, stealthy, surreptitious, undercover; calculating, designing, scheming, plotting

near ant obvious, patent, plain, public, unconcealed; aboveboard, candid, direct, forthright, frank, honest, natural, outspoken, plainspoken, real, sim-

ple, sincere, straightforward, unaffected, unpretending

ant artless, guileless, ingenuous

2 showing a use of the imagination and creativity especially in inventing — see CLEVER 1

3 accomplished with trained ability — see SKILLFUL

artfulness *n* **1** skill in achieving one's ends through indirect, subtle, or underhanded means — see CUNNING 1

2 subtle or imaginative ability in inventing, devising, or executing something — see SKILL 1

article *n* a short piece of writing typically expressing a point of view — see ESSAY 1

articulate *adj* able to express oneself clearly and well ⟨the television crew covering the science fair were looking for photogenic and *articulate* students to explain their projects on the air⟩

syn eloquent, fluent, well-spoken

rel facile, glib, smooth-tongued, voluble; expressive, outspoken, verbal, vocal; blabby, chatty, garrulous, loquacious, talkative, verbose; unfaltering, unhesitating

near ant faltering, halting, hesitant, maundering, mumbling, muttering, sputtering, stammering, stumbling, stuttering; mute, speechless, tongue-tied, voiceless

ant inarticulate

articulate *vb* **1** to utter clearly and distinctly ⟨uses a very measured tone and *articulates* every syllable when issuing scoldings⟩

syn enunciate

rel express, pronounce, say, verbalize, vocalize, voice; speak out, speak up

near ant falter, grunt, halt, hesitate, maunder, sputter, stammer, stumble, stutter; mouth, mumble, murmur, mutter, whisper

2 to convey in appropriate or telling terms — see PHRASE

3 to express (a thought or emotion) in words — see SAY 1

articulateness *n* the art or power of speaking or writing in a forceful and convincing way — see ELOQUENCE

articulation *n* **1** an act, process, or means of putting something into words — see EXPRESSION 1

2 the clear and accurate pronunciation of words especially in public speaking — see DICTION 1

artifice *n* **1** a clever often underhanded means to achieve an end — see TRICK 1

2 skill in achieving one's ends through indirect, subtle, or underhanded means — see CUNNING 1

3 subtle or imaginative ability in inventing, devising, or executing something — see SKILL 1

4 the inclination or practice of misleading others through lies or trickery — see DECEIT

5 the use of clever underhanded actions to achieve an end — see TRICKERY

---

syn synonym(s)   **rel** related words
ant antonym(s)   **near ant** near antonym(s)

artificer *n* a person whose occupation requires skill with the hands — see ARTISAN

artificial *adj* 1 lacking in natural or spontaneous quality ⟨the beauty-pageant contestants' *artificial* smiles looked like they were glued on their faces⟩

syn affected, assumed, bogus, contrived, factitious, fake, false, feigned, forced, mechanical, mock, phony (*also* phoney), pretended, pseudo, put-on, sham, simulated, spurious, strained, unnatural

rel automatic, canned, concocted, fabricated, labored, manufactured, unauthentic, unreal, unrealistic; empty, facile, hollow, hypocritical, insincere, left-handed; exaggerated, histrionic, melodramatic, overacted, overdone, theatrical; cute, cutesy, goody-goody, mincing, overrefined, simpering; conventional, formal, impersonal, inflexible, rigid, stiff, stylized, wooden; artful, calculated, conscious, cultivated, deliberate, premeditated, studied

near ant authentic, bona fide, real, realistic, true; honest, ingenuous, sincere, unpretending; easy, effortless, smooth; extemporaneous, impromptu, impulsive, instinctive, unconscious, unprompted, unrehearsed

ant artless, genuine, natural, spontaneous, unaffected, unfeigned, unforced

2 not being or expressing what one appears to be or express — see INSINCERE

3 being such in appearance only and made with or manufactured from usually cheaper materials — see IMITATION

artillery *n* large firearms (as cannon or rockets) ⟨during the *artillery* attack families hid in their cellars⟩

syn guns, ordnance

rel ammunition, armament, arms, munitions, weaponry, weapons

artisan *n* a person whose occupation requires skill with the hands ⟨we visited a re-created 19th-century New England village that features an array of *artisans* —a cooper, a carpenter, a blacksmith, a potter, a glassblower⟩

syn artificer, craftsman, handicrafter, tradesman

rel artist, maker; journeyman, master; mechanic, smith, technician, wright; handyman

artist *n* a person with a high level of knowledge or skill in a field — see EXPERT

artistic *adj* of or relating to the fine arts — see CULTURAL

artistry *n* subtle or imaginative ability in inventing, devising, or executing something — see SKILL 1

artless *adj* 1 free from any intent to deceive or impress others — see GUILELESS

2 hastily or roughly constructed — see RUDE 1

artlessly *adv* without any attempt to impress by deception or exaggeration — see NATURALLY 3

artlessness *n* the quality or state of being simple and sincere — see NAÏVETÉ 1

as *conj* for the reason that — see SINCE

ascend *vb* to move or extend upward ⟨the path *ascended* so steeply at one point that we had to scramble up on our hands and knees⟩

syn arise, climb, lift, mount, rise, soar, up, uprise, upsweep, upturn

rel boost, elevate, raise, uplift, upraise; take off, zoom; crest, scale, surmount, top

near ant dive, nose-dive, plummet, plunge, sink, slide

ant decline, descend, dip, drop, fall (off)

ascendancy *n* controlling power or influence over others — see SUPREMACY 1

ascension *n* the act or an instance of rising or climbing up — see ASCENT 1

ascent *n* 1 the act or an instance of rising or climbing up ⟨our plane broke through some heavy low clouds during its *ascent* and leveled off once we were above them⟩

syn ascension, climb, rise, rising, soar

rel boost, hike, increase, raise; elevation, levitation, lift-off, raising, takeoff; heave, upheaval, uplifting, upraising, upsurge, upsweep, upswing, uptrend, upturn, upwelling

near ant dive, nosedive, plop, plummeting, plunge, sinking; decline, decrease

ant descent, dip, drop, fall

2 an upward slope ⟨we'd reached the final *ascent* of the trail to the summit⟩

syn rise, upgrade

rel grade, incline; climb, hump, mound, ridge, swell

near ant basin, depression, hollow

ant declension, decline, declivity, descent, downgrade

3 a raising or a state of being raised to a higher rank or position — see ADVANCEMENT 1

ascertain *vb* 1 to come to an awareness — see DISCOVER 1

2 to come upon after searching, study, or effort — see FIND 1

ascribe *vb* to explain (something) as being the result of something else — see CREDIT 1

aseptic *adj* free from filth, infection, or dangers to health — see SANITARY

ashamed *adj* suffering from or expressive of a feeling of responsibility for wrongdoing — see GUILTY 2

ashen *adj* lacking a healthy skin color — see PALE 2

ashes *n pl* the portion or bits of something left over or behind after it has been destroyed — see REMAINS 1

ashy *adj* lacking a healthy skin color — see PALE 2

aside from *prep* not including — see EXCEPT

as if *conj* the way it would be or one would do if ⟨she looked *as if* she wanted to ask one more question before we left⟩

syn as though, like

asinine *adj* showing or marked by a lack of good sense or judgment — see FOOLISH 1

asininity *n* **1** a foolish act or idea — see FOLLY 1

2 lack of good sense or judgment — see FOOLISHNESS 1

ask *vb* **1** to put a question or questions to ⟨my grandfather *asked* me all about my trip⟩

syn inquire (of), interrogate, query, question, quiz

rel cross-examine, examine, grill, pump; poll, survey

near ant rejoin, retort; comment, observe, remark

ant answer, reply, respond

2 to make a request of ⟨*ask* the sales clerk for assistance⟩

syn request, solicit

rel appeal (to), beg, beseech, entreat, implore, importune, invoke, petition, pray, supplicate; demand, enjoin, exact, press, require

phrases call on (*or* upon)

3 to set or receive as a price — see CHARGE 1

ask (for) *vb* **1** to make a request for ⟨don't be afraid to *ask for* help if you need it⟩

syn call (for), plead (for), quest, request, seek, solicit, sue (for)

rel apply (for), beg (for), clamor (for), urge; demand, enjoin, exact, insist (on), require, requisition

2 to act so as to make (something) more likely — see COURT 1

3 to give a request or demand for — see ORDER 2

askance *adv* with distrust ⟨we looked *askance* at the dealer's assertion that the car had never been in an accident⟩

syn distrustfully, doubtfully, doubtingly, dubiously, mistrustfully, skeptically, suspiciously

rel hesitantly, hesitatingly, incredulously, questioningly, quizzically, unbelievingly; charily, guardedly, warily; captiously, critically, cynically, deprecatingly, disapprovingly, disparagingly, negatively, reproachfully, unfavorably; anxiously, apprehensively, uncomfortably, uneasily

phrases with a grain of salt

near ant approvingly, favorably, positively; confidently, sanguinely; credulously, uncritically

ant trustfully, trustingly

askew *adj* inclined or twisted to one side — see AWRY

aslant *adj* inclined or twisted to one side — see AWRY

asleep *adj* **1** being in a state of suspended consciousness ⟨Paul was *asleep* when the earthquake struck⟩

syn dormant, dozing, napping, resting, sleeping, slumbering

rel drowsy, nodding, sleepy, slumberous (*or* slumbrous), somnolent; dreaming, reposing; hypnotized, mesmerized, semiconscious

near ant aware, conscious; sleepless; aroused, astir, up

ant awake, wakeful, wide-awake

2 lacking in sensation or feeling — see NUMB

aspect *n* **1** a certain way in which something appears or may be regarded ⟨depending on what *aspect* of college life you consider most important, there are several colleges which might be good for you⟩

syn angle, facet, hand, phase, side

rel air, appearance, character, color, complexion, condition, face, look, semblance, shape, state, visage; period, stage, step; point of view, position, posture, stance, standpoint, view, viewpoint; interpretation, reading, rendering, translation, version; article, case, component, count, detail, element, factor, instance, item, matter, part, particular, point, regard, respect

2 the outward form of someone or something especially as indicative of a quality — see APPEARANCE 1

asperity *n* **1** a harsh or sharp quality — see EDGE 1

2 biting sharpness of feeling or expression — see ACRIMONY 1

3 something that is a cause for suffering or special effort especially in the attainment of a goal — see DIFFICULTY 1

asperse *vb* to make untrue and harmful statements about — see SLANDER

aspersing *n* the making of false statements that damage another's reputation — see SLANDER

aspirant *n* one who seeks an office, honor, position, or award — see CANDIDATE

aspiration *n* **1** eager desire for personal advancement — see AMBITION 1

2 something that one hopes or intends to accomplish — see GOAL

aspire *vb* to have in mind as a purpose or goal — see INTEND

aspiring *adj* having a strong desire for personal advancement — see AMBITIOUS 1

ass *n* a sturdy and patient domestic mammal that is used especially to carry things — see DONKEY 1

assail *vb* **1** to criticize harshly and usually publicly — see ATTACK 2

2 to take sudden, violent action against — see ATTACK 1

assassin *n* a person who kills another person ⟨shot down by an unknown *assassin*⟩

syn killer, murderer

rel butcher, executioner, slaughterer, slayer

assault *n* the act or action of setting upon with force or violence — see ATTACK 1

assault *vb* to take sudden, violent action against — see ATTACK 1

assay *n* the separation and identification of the parts of a whole — see ANALYSIS 1

assay *vb* **1** to identify and examine the basic elements or parts of (something) es-

---

syn synonym(s)   *rel* related words
ant antonym(s)   *near ant* near antonym(s)

pecially for discovering interrelationships — see ANALYZE

2 to make an effort to do — see ATTEMPT

assemblage *n* **1** a body of people come together in one place — see GATHERING 1

2 a mass or quantity that has piled up or that has been gathered — see ACCUMULATION 1

3 a number of things considered as a unit — see GROUP 1

4 an organized group of objects acquired and maintained for study, exhibition, or personal pleasure — see COLLECTION 1

assemble *vb* **1** to come together into one body or place ⟨the graduates were told to *assemble* in the cafeteria an hour before the ceremony⟩

syn cluster, collect, concentrate, conglomerate, congregate, convene, converge, forgather (*or* foregather), gather, meet, rendezvous

rel affiliate, ally, associate, band (together), club, collaborate, confederate, conjoin, consolidate, consort, cooperate, couple, federate, gang (up), join, merge, unite

near ant depart, leave, take off; disjoin, dissociate, disunite

ant break up, disband, disperse, split up

2 to form by putting together parts or materials — see BUILD

3 to bring together in assembly by or as if by command — see CONVOKE

4 to bring together in one body or place — see GATHER 1

assembly *n* **1** a body of people come together in one place — see GATHERING 1

2 a body of persons gathered for religious worship — see CONGREGATION 1

3 a coming together of a number of persons for a specified purpose — see MEETING 1

assert *vb* **1** to state clearly and strongly ⟨Mrs. Cartwright is never afraid to *assert* her allegiance to flag and country⟩

syn affirm, aver, avouch, avow, declare, lay down, profess

rel advance, advertise, boost, plug, promote, publicize; announce, blaze, call, proclaim, pronounce, say; accent, accentuate, emphasize, stress, underline, underscore; advocate, champion, defend, espouse, support, uphold; assure, convince, persuade; explain, justify, rationalize

near ant minimize, understate; disregard, ignore, neglect, overlook

2 to state (something) as a reason in support of or against something under consideration — see ARGUE 1

3 to state as a fact usually forcefully — see CLAIM 1

assertion *n* **1** a solemn and often public declaration of the truth or existence of something — see PROTESTATION

2 an idea or opinion that is put forth in a discussion or debate — see CONTENTION

assertive *adj* **1** having or showing a bold forcefulness in the pursuit of a goal — see AGGRESSIVE 1

2 marked by or uttered with forcefulness — see EMPHATIC 1

assertiveness *n* the quality or state of being forceful (as in expression) — see VEHEMENCE 1

assess *vb* **1** to establish or apply as a charge or penalty — see IMPOSE

2 to make an approximate or tentative judgment regarding — see ESTIMATE 1

assessment *n* **1** a charge usually of money collected by the government from people or businesses for public use — see TAX

2 an opinion on the nature, character, or quality of something — see ESTIMATION 1

3 the act of placing a value on the nature, character, or quality of something — see ESTIMATE 1

assets *n pl* the total of one's money and property — see WEALTH 1

assiduity *n* attentive and persistent effort — see DILIGENCE

assiduous *adj* involved in often constant activity — see BUSY 1

assiduously *adv* with great effort or determination — see HARD 1

assiduousness *n* attentive and persistent effort — see DILIGENCE

assign *vb* **1** to give a task, duty, or responsibility to — see ENTRUST 1

2 to give as a share or portion — see ALLOT

3 to give over the legal possession or ownership of — see TRANSFER 1

4 to pick (someone) by one's authority for a specific position or duty — see APPOINT 2

assignment *n* **1** a piece of work that needs to be done regularly — see CHORE 1

2 a specific task with which a person or group is charged — see MISSION

3 something assigned to be read or studied — see LESSON

4 the state or fact of being chosen for a position or duty — see APPOINTMENT 1

assimilate *vb* to make a part of a body or system — see EMBODY 1

assist *n* an act or instance of helping — see HELP 1

assist *vb* to provide (someone) with what is useful or necessary to achieve an end — see HELP 1

assistance *n* an act or instance of helping — see HELP 1

assistant *n* a person who helps a more skilled person — see HELPER

associate *n* **1** a person frequently seen in the company of another ⟨after he took up skateboarding, Michael gained a whole new set of *associates*⟩

syn cohort, companion, comrade, crony, fellow, hobnobber, mate

rel colleague, coworker, equal, peer, workmate; accomplice, affiliate, ally, collaborator, confederate, partner; buddy, chum, confidant, familiar, friend, hearty, intimate, pal; compatriot, countryman; classmate, housemate, messmate, playmate, roommate, schoolmate, shipmate, teammate; attendant, escort; hanger-on, leech, parasite

2 a fellow worker — see COLLEAGUE

associate *vb* **1** to come or be together as friends ⟨a boy who would *associate* only with other hard-core basketball fans⟩

syn chum, consort, fraternize, hang around, hobnob, pal (around)

rel affiliate, ally, attach, band, bond, club, collaborate, collude, confederate, conjoin, connect, cooperate, couple, gang, get along, group, hook, interrelate, join, knot, league, link, mingle, mix, rally, relate, side, socialize, team, tie, wed

phrases rub elbows (with), rub shoulders (with), take up with

near ant avoid, cold-shoulder, shun, snub; alienate, estrange; break up, disband, disperse, split up; disjoin, dissociate, disunite, divorce, sever, split, sunder

2 to think of (something) in combination ⟨Kelly *associates* getting shots with ice cream cones, her treat every time she goes to the doctor⟩

syn connect, correlate, identify, link, relate

rel compare, equate, liken; group, join, lump (together); tie (together)

near ant contrast, differentiate, discriminate, distinguish, separate, set off

3 to come together to form a single unit — see UNITE 1

4 to form or enter into an association that furthers the interests of its members — see ALLY

5 to take part in social activities — see SOCIALIZE

association *n* **1** the state of having shared interests or efforts (as in social or business matters) ⟨Rita was honored for her long *association* with the Montgomery Benevolent Society⟩

syn affiliation, alliance, collaboration, confederation, connection, cooperation, hookup, liaison, linkup, partnership, relation, relationship, tie-up, union

rel business, dealings, interaction; exchange, interconnection, interrelation, mutuality, reciprocity, symbiosis; incorporation, integration, merger, unification; affinity, attachment, closeness, intimacy, rapport, sympathy; kinship, oneness, solidarity, togetherness, unity; companionship, company, fellowship

near ant breakup, dissolution, disunion; division, parting, separation, severance, split; alienation, divorce, estrangement

ant dissociation

2 a group of persons formally joined together for some common interest ⟨all *associations* meeting on school property must be registered with and approved by the principal's office⟩

syn brotherhood, club, college, congress, council, fellowship, fraternity, guild (*also* gild), institute, institution, junto, league, order, organization, society, sodality

rel collective, commune, community, co-operative; alliance, bloc, coalition, partnership; body, group; circle, clan, clique, coterie, lot, set; crew, outfit, party, squad, team; branch, chapter, local; faithful, fold, membership; sisterhood, sorority; cabal, confederacy, conspiracy; band, gang, ring; cartel, combine, syndicate

3 the fact or state of having something in common — see CONNECTION 1

assort *vb* to arrange or assign according to type — see CLASSIFY 1

assorted *adj* consisting of many things of different sorts — see MISCELLANEOUS

assortment *n* **1** an unorganized collection or mixture of various things — see MISCELLANY 1

2 the quality or state of being composed of many different elements or types — see VARIETY 1

assuage *vb* **1** to make more bearable or less severe — see HELP 2

2 to put a complete end to (a physical need or desire) — see SATISFY 1

assume *vb* **1** to take to or upon oneself ⟨Josh promised to *assume* responsibility for any damage to the flower beds caused by the volleyball game in the backyard⟩

syn accept, bear, shoulder, take over, undertake

rel adopt, embrace; back, endorse (*also* indorse), espouse, stand by, support, uphold; accede, acquiesce, agree, assent, consent

near ant abjure, recant, renounce, retract, take back; decline, refuse, reject, spurn, turn down; abstain, forbear, refrain; avoid, bypass, detour

ant disavow, disclaim, disown, repudiate

2 to take as true or as a fact without actual proof ⟨everyone *assumed*, wrongly, that someone else was bringing dessert⟩

syn postulate, premise, presume, presuppose, suppose

rel accept, believe, credit, swallow; conclude, deduce, gather, judge, infer, take; conjecture, figure, guess, reckon [*chiefly dialect*], surmise, suspect, think; conceive, dream, fancy, imagine, perceive, preconceive; hypothesize, speculate, theorize; affirm, allege, assert, aver, avouch, avow, claim, contend, declare, insist, maintain, profess

phrases take for granted

near ant challenge, disbelieve, discount, discredit, dispute, distrust, doubt, mistrust, question, suspect, wonder (about); deny, disavow, disclaim, disown, reject, repudiate; confute, disprove, rebut, refute

3 to form an opinion from little or no evidence — see GUESS 1

4 to present a false appearance of — see FEIGN

assumed *adj* **1** appearing to be true on the basis of evidence that may or may not be confirmed — see APPARENT 1

2 lacking in natural or spontaneous quality — see ARTIFICIAL 1

---

assumption *n* something taken as being true or factual and used as a starting point for a course of action or reasoning ⟨the widespread *assumption* that violent entertainment leads to violent behavior in children⟩ ⟨your argument is faulty because it's based on erroneous *assumptions*⟩

syn postulate, premise, presumption, presupposition, supposition

rel hypothesis, proposition, theory, thesis; axiom, truism, verity; belief, canon, doctrine, dogma, gospel, law; precept, principle, rule, standard, tenet; basis, foundation, ground; conclusion, deduction, inference; affirmation, assertion, avouchment, declaration

assurance *n* 1 a state of mind in which one is free from doubt — see CONFIDENCE 2

2 great faith in oneself or one's abilities — see CONFIDENCE 1

assure *vb* 1 to ease the grief or distress of — see COMFORT 1

2 to make sure, certain, or safe — see ENSURE

assured *adj* 1 having or showing a mind free from doubt — see CERTAIN 2

2 having or showing great faith in oneself or one's abilities — see CONFIDENT 1

assuredly *adv* without any question — see INDEED 1

assuredness *n* a state of mind in which one is free from doubt — see CONFIDENCE 2

astern *adv* near, toward, or in the stern of a ship or the tail of an aircraft — see AFT

as though *conj* the way it would be or one would do if — see AS IF

astir *adj* marked by much life, movement, or activity — see ALIVE 2

astonish *vb* to make a strong impression on (someone) with something unexpected — see SURPRISE 1

astonished *adj* 1 affected with sudden and great wonder or surprise — see THUNDERSTRUCK

2 filled with amazement or wonder — see OPENMOUTHED

astonishing *adj* 1 causing a strong emotional reaction because unexpected — see SURPRISING 1

2 causing wonder or astonishment — see MARVELOUS 1

astonishment *n* 1 the rapt attention and deep emotion caused by the sight of something extraordinary — see WONDER 2

2 the state of being strongly impressed by something unexpected or unusual — see SURPRISE 2

astound *vb* to make a strong impression on (someone) with something unexpected — see SURPRISE 1

astounded *adj* 1 affected with sudden and great wonder or surprise — see THUNDERSTRUCK

2 filled with amazement or wonder — see OPENMOUTHED

astounding *adj* 1 causing a strong emotional reaction because unexpected — see SURPRISING 1

2 causing wonder or astonishment — see MARVELOUS 1

astral *adj* of or relating to the stars — see STELLAR 1

astray *adv* off the desired or intended path or course — see WRONG 1

astronomical *also* **astronomic** *adj* unusually large — see HUGE

astronomically *adv* to a large extent or degree — see GREATLY 2

astute *adj* having or showing a practical cleverness or judgment — see SHREWD

asunder *adv* into parts or to pieces — see APART

as well as *prep* in addition to — see BESIDES 1

asylum *n* 1 a place where insane people are cared for — see MADHOUSE 1

2 something (as a building) that offers cover from the weather or protection from danger — see SHELTER

at all *adv* in any way or respect ⟨Ted wasn't *at all* pleased with the way his mother's birthday cake came out⟩

syn anywise, ever, half

rel somehow, someway; remotely

phrases by any means

athirst *adj* showing urgent desire or interest — see EAGER

athwart *adv* in a line or direction running from corner to corner — see CROSSWISE

athwart *prep* to the opposite side of — see ACROSS

atmosphere *n* 1 a special quality or impression associated with something — see AURA

2 the circumstances, conditions, or objects by which one is surrounded — see ENVIRONMENT

atom *n* a very small piece — see BIT 1

atomic *adj* very small in size — see TINY

atomize *vb* to reduce to fine particles — see POWDER

atone (for) *vb* to make up for (an offense) — see EXPIATE

atrocious *adj* 1 extremely disturbing or repellent — see HORRIBLE 1

2 extremely unsatisfactory — see WRETCHED 1

atrociousness *n* 1 the quality of inspiring intense dread or dismay — see HORROR 1

2 the state or quality of being utterly evil — see ENORMITY 1

atrocity *n* 1 the quality of inspiring intense dread or dismay — see HORROR 1

2 the state or quality of being utterly evil — see ENORMITY 1

attach *vb* 1 to cause (something) to hold to another — see FASTEN 1

2 to pick (someone) by one's authority for a specific position or duty — see APPOINT 2

attached *adj* having a liking or affection — see FOND 1

attachment *n* 1 a feeling of strong or constant regard for and dedication to someone — see LOVE 1

2 something that is not necessary in itself but adds to the convenience or performance of the main piece of equipment — see ACCESSORY 1

attack *n* **1** the act or action of setting upon with force or violence ⟨The USS Constitution was nicknamed "Old Ironsides" after its oaken hull successfully withstood a British *attack*⟩

syn aggression, assault, blitzkrieg, charge, descent, offense (*or* offence), offensive, onset, onslaught, raid, rush, strike

rel ambuscade, ambush; counterattack, counteroffensive, sally, sortie; foray, incursion, invasion; pillage, ravage, sack; air raid, blitz, bombardment; siege, storm

near ant defense, defensive, guard, shield; opposition, resistance; protection, security, shelter

2 a sudden experiencing of a physical or mental disorder ⟨malaria is characterized by periodic *attacks* of chills and fever⟩

syn bout, case, fit, seizure, siege, spell

rel recurrence, relapse; brainstorm, convulsion, pang, paroxysm, spasm, throe; breakdown, collapse, prostration

near ant arrest, relief, remission

attack *vb* **1** to take sudden, violent action against ⟨my dog unexpectedly *attacked* the mailman, sinking his teeth into the startled man's leg⟩

syn assail, assault, beset, charge, descend (on *or* upon), jump (on), pounce (on *or* upon), raid, rush, storm, strike

rel gang (up on), mob, swarm; mug, rob; ambuscade, ambush, surprise, waylay; blitz, bomb, bombard; beleaguer, besiege; harry, loot, pillage, plunder, ravage, sack; foray, invade, overrun

phrases fly at, give it to, go at, set upon

near ant cover, defend, guard, protect, secure, shield

2 to criticize harshly and usually publicly ⟨the mayor and all his aides were *attacked* mercilessly in the press when the scandal erupted⟩

syn abuse, assail, belabor, blast, castigate, excoriate, jump (on), lambaste (*or* lambast), scathe, slam, vituperate

rel berate, harangue, harass, harry, revile, scold; blaspheme, curse, execrate, imprecate, profane; affront, insult, slur; asperse, bad-mouth, belittle, disparage, put down; libel, slander, traduce; chastise, chide, criticize, rebuke, reprimand, reproof; fulminate, lash (out)

near ant acclaim, commend, compliment, laud, praise

3 to start work on energetically ⟨Courtney *attacked* the huge mess in her room with determination and enthusiasm⟩

syn tackle, wade (into)

rel address, approach, face; buckle (to), concentrate (on), focus (on), knuckle down (to), zero in (on); fall (to), pitch in,

plunge (in), settle (down); pursue, take up, undertake

phrases go at, have at, sail into

near ant avoid, evade, shun; dally, dawdle, dillydally, fiddle, fool, idle, lag, mess, monkey, play, poke, potter, putter, trifle

attain *vb* **1** to obtain (as a goal) through effort — see ACHIEVE 1

2 to receive as return for effort — see EARN 1

attainable *adj* **1** capable of being done or carried out — see POSSIBLE 1

2 possible to get — see AVAILABLE 1

attainment *n* **1** a successful result brought about by hard work — see ACCOMPLISHMENT 1

2 the state of being actual or complete — see FRUITION

attempt *n* an effort to do or accomplish something ⟨it took several *attempts* before we made good ice cream with an old-fashioned hand-cranked ice cream freezer⟩

syn crack, endeavor, essay, fling, go, pass, shot, stab, trial, try, whack

rel bid, striving, struggle, throes, undertaking; trial and error

attempt *vb* to make an effort to do ⟨after *attempting*— and failing—to start the lawn mower on my own, I finally succeeded with Dad's help⟩ ⟨don't even *attempt* walking on your broken foot⟩

syn assay, endeavor, essay, seek, strive, try

rel fight, strain, struggle, toil, trouble, work; aim, aspire, hope; assume, take up, undertake

phrases have a go at

near ant drop, give up, quit

attend *vb* **1** to go along with in order to provide assistance, protection, or companionship — see ACCOMPANY

2 to pay attention especially through the act of hearing — see LISTEN

3 to take charge of especially on behalf of another — see ²TEND 1

attendant *adj* **1** coming as a result — see RESULTANT

2 present at the same time and place — see COINCIDENT

attendant *n* one that accompanies another for protection, guidance, or as a courtesy — see ESCORT

attending *adj* **1** being within the confines of a specified place — see PRESENT 2

2 present at the same time and place — see COINCIDENT

attention *n* **1** a focusing of the mind on something ⟨I need your full *attention* right now⟩

syn absorption, concentration, engrossment, enthrallment, immersion

rel fixation, obsession, preoccupation; alertness, application, awareness, consciousness, consideration, heedfulness, intentness, raptness

near ant absence, absentmindedness, abstractedness, abstraction, detachment, distraction, obliviousness, remoteness, unawareness, unconsciousness, with-

---

drawal; disinterest, indifference, mindlessness, unconcern; befuddlement, bemusement, bewilderment, confusion

ant inattention

2 a state of being aware ⟨several mothers brought to the committee's *attention* the deplorable condition of the playground⟩

syn awareness, cognizance, ear, eye, heed, notice, observance, observation

rel advisement, care, concern, consideration, regard, watch; apprehension, discernment, grasp, mind, perception, recognition, thought, understanding

near ant disregard, neglect, obliviousness, unawareness

attentive *adj* **1** having the mind fixed on something ⟨Susan became particularly *attentive* when the sportscaster turned to field hockey, her favorite sport⟩

syn absorbed, engrossed, enthralled, focused (*also* focussed), immersed, intent, observant, rapt

rel interested, intrigued, involved; hypnotized, mesmerized; alert, alive, conscious, open-eyed, watchful, wide-awake

near ant daydreaming, dreamy, faraway, foggy, hazy, oblivious, preoccupied, remote; apathetic, disinterested, uninterested

ant absent, absentminded, abstracted, distracted, inattentive, unabsorbed, unfocused (*also* unfocussed), unobservant

2 given to or made with heedful anticipation of the needs and happiness of others — see THOUGHTFUL 1

3 paying close attention usually for the purpose of anticipating approaching danger or opportunity — see ALERT 1

attentiveness *n* the act or state of being constantly attentive and responsive to signs of opportunity, activity, or danger — see VIGILANCE

attest *vb* **1** to declare (something) to be true or genuine — see CERTIFY 1

2 to make a solemn declaration under oath for the purpose of establishing a fact — see TESTIFY

attestation *n* something presented in support of the truth or accuracy of a claim — see PROOF

attire *n* covering for the human body — see CLOTHING

attire *vb* to outfit with clothes and especially fine or special clothes — see CLOTHE 1

attorney *n* **1** a person who acts or does business for another — see AGENT 2

2 a person whose profession is to conduct lawsuits for clients or to advise about legal rights and obligations — see LAWYER

attraction *n* something that attracts interest — see MAGNET

attractive *adj* **1** having an often mysterious or magical power to attract — see FASCINATING 1

2 very pleasing to look at — see BEAUTIFUL

attractiveness *n* **1** the power of irresistible attraction — see CHARM 2

2 the qualities in a person or thing that as a whole give pleasure to the senses — see BEAUTY 1

attribute *n* something that sets apart an individual from others of the same kind — see CHARACTERISTIC

attribute *vb* to explain (something) as being the result of something else — see CREDIT 1

attrition *n* a gradual weakening, loss, or destruction — see CORROSION

atypical *adj* **1** being out of the ordinary — see EXCEPTIONAL

2 departing from some accepted standard of what is normal — see DEVIANT

audacious *adj* inclined or willing to take risks — see BOLD 1

audacity *n* shameless boldness — see EFFRONTERY

audibly *adv* with one's normal voice speaking the words — see ALOUD

audit *n* a close look at or over someone or something in order to judge condition — see INSPECTION

audit *vb* to look over closely (as for judging quality or condition) — see INSPECT

auditorium *n* a large room or building for enclosed public gatherings — see HALL 3

auditory *adj* of, relating to, or experienced through the sense of hearing ⟨I have a bad *auditory* memory—unless I see a word in writing, and not just hear it, I forget it easily⟩

syn acoustic (*or* acoustical), aural, auricular

rel audible, clear, discernible, distinct, distinguishable, heard, perceptible

near ant faint, feeble, imperceptible, inaudible, indistinguishable, indistinct; low, noiseless, quiet, silent, soft, soundless

aught *n* the numerical symbol 0 or the absence of number or quantity represented by it — see ZERO 1

augment *vb* to make greater in size, amount, or number — see INCREASE 1

augmentation *n* something added (as by growth) — see INCREASE 1

augur *n* one who predicts future events or developments — see PROPHET

augur *vb* **1** to show signs of a favorable or successful outcome — see BODE

2 to tell of or describe beforehand — see FORETELL

auguring *n* a declaration that something will happen in the future — see PREDICTION

augury *n* something believed to be a sign or warning of a future event — see OMEN

august *adj* **1** having or showing a serious and reserved manner — see DIGNIFIED

2 large and impressive in size, grandeur, extent, or conception — see GRAND 1

augustness *n* **1** a dignified bearing or appearance befitting royalty — see MAJESTY 1

2 impressiveness of beauty on a large scale — see MAGNIFICENCE

auld lang syne *n* the events or experience of former times — see PAST

aura *n* a special quality or impression associated with something ⟨the monastery perched high on a mountaintop had an *aura* of unreality and mystery about it⟩
syn air, atmosphere, climate, flavor, mood, note, temper
rel feel, feeling, sensation, sense, spirit; attribute, character, characteristic, image, mark, notion, peculiarity, picture, property, trait; color, illusion, overtone, semblance, suggestion, tone

aural *adj* of, relating to, or experienced through the sense of hearing — see AUDITORY

au revoir *n* an expression of good wishes at parting — see GOOD-BYE

auricular *adj* of, relating to, or experienced through the sense of hearing — see AUDITORY

aurora *n* the first appearance of light in the morning or the time of its appearance — see DAWN 1

auspice *n* something believed to be a sign or warning of a future event — see OMEN

auspicious *adj* 1 having qualities which inspire hope — see HOPEFUL 1
2 pointing toward a happy outcome — see FAVORABLE 2

austere *adj* 1 given to exacting standards of discipline and self-restraint — see SEVERE 1
2 harsh and threatening in manner or appearance — see GRIM 1

authentic *adj* 1 being exactly as appears or as claimed ⟨found an *authentic* Native American arrowhead⟩
syn bona fide, genuine, real, right, true
rel actual, historical, original; lawful, legal, legitimate; identifiable, recognizable, verifiable; proven, substantiated, validated, verified; incontestable, incontrovertible, indisputable, indubitable, irrefutable, undeniable, undoubted, unmistakable, unquestionable; veritable, very; accurate, correct, proper; pure, unadulterated, unalloyed
near ant artificial, factitious, imitation, man-made, simulated, synthetic, unnatural; concocted, fabricated, manufactured; deceptive, delusive, delusory, misleading; unauthenticated, unverified
ant bogus, counterfeit, fake, false, mock, phony (*also* phoney), pseudo, sham, spurious, unauthentic, unreal
2 following an original exactly — see FAITHFUL 2

authentically *adv* in actual fact — see VERY 2

authenticate *vb* to declare (something) to be true or genuine — see CERTIFY 1

author *n* 1 a person who creates a written work ⟨a brilliant novel by a first-time *author*⟩
syn penman, writer
rel coauthor, ghostwriter, hack, scribbler; autobiographer, biographer; novelist; essayist, pamphleteer; dramatist, play-

wright, scenarist, screenwriter, scriptwriter; bard, poet, rhymer (*or* rimer); columnist, journalist, newspaperman, reporter, sportswriter
2 a person who establishes a whole new field of endeavor — see FATHER 2

author *vb* to compose and set down on paper the words of — see WRITE 1

authoritarian *adj* 1 fond of ordering people around — see BOSSY
2 given to exacting standards of discipline and self-restraint — see SEVERE 1

authoritative *adj* 1 being the most accurate and apparently thorough — see DEFINITIVE 1
2 having power over the minds or behavior of others — see INFLUENTIAL 1

authority *n* 1 a person with a high level of knowledge or skill in a field — see EXPERT
2 lawful control over the affairs of a political unit (as a nation) — see RULE 2
3 the power to direct the thinking or behavior of others usually indirectly — see INFLUENCE 1
4 the right or means to command or control others — see POWER 1

authorization *n* 1 the approval by someone in authority for the doing of something — see PERMISSION
2 the granting of power to perform various acts or duties — see COMMISSION 1
3 the right to act or move freely — see FREEDOM 2

authorize *vb* 1 to give official or legal power to ⟨only the school nurse is *authorized* to give any necessary shots⟩
syn accredit, certify, commission, empower, enable, invest, license (*or* licence), qualify
rel approve, clear, endorse (*also* indorse), OK (*or* okay), sanction; affirm, confirm, validate; inaugurate, induct, initiate, install, instate, swear in; allow, let, permit; enfranchise, entitle, privilege
near ant ban, bar, block, constrain, deny, disallow, disbar, discourage, disenfranchise, disfranchise, disqualify, exclude, hinder, hold back, impede, inhibit, obstruct, prevent, shut out, stop; enjoin, forbid, interdict, outlaw, prohibit, proscribe, veto
2 to give a right to — see ENTITLE 1
3 to give official acceptance of something as satisfactory — see APPROVE

authorized *adj* ordered or allowed by those in authority — see OFFICIAL

auto *n* a self-propelled passenger vehicle on wheels — see CAR

autocracy *n* a system of government in which the ruler has unlimited power — see DESPOTISM

autocrat *n* 1 a person who uses power or authority in a cruel, unjust, or harmful way — see DESPOT
2 one who rules over a people with a sole, supreme, and usually hereditary authority — see MONARCH

---

syn synonym(s)   *rel* related words
ant antonym(s)   *near ant* near antonym(s)

autocratic *adj* **1** exercising power or authority without interference by others — see ABSOLUTE 1

2 fond of ordering people around — see BOSSY

autograph *vb* to write one's name on (as a document) — see SIGN

automated *adj* designed to replace or decrease human labor and especially physical labor — see LABORSAVING

automatic *adj* **1** done instantly and without conscious thought or decision ⟨Carl's *automatic* use of the brakes prevented a serious accident⟩

syn instinctive, instinctual, involuntary, mechanical, spontaneous

rel conditioned, natural, reactive, reflex, simple, subliminal, unconscious, unforced; blind, inadvertent, unintended, unintentional, unwilling, unwitting; abrupt, quick, ready, sudden; ad-lib, extemporaneous, extempore, impromptu, improvised, offhand, offhanded, snap, spur-of-the-moment, unconsidered, unplanned, unpremeditated, unprepared, unprompted, unreasoned, unrehearsed, unstudied; casual, chance, chancy, haphazard, hasty, hit-or-miss, impetuous, impulsive, perfunctory, random, rash

near ant calculated, conscious, cultivated, deliberate, designed, intended, intentional, predetermined, prepared, projected, refined, rehearsed, volitional, voluntary, willed, willful (*or* wilful); advised, aforethought, careful, considered, foresighted, forethoughtful, measured, meticulous, reasoned, studied, thoughtful

2 designed to replace or decrease human labor and especially physical labor — see LABORSAVING

automobile *n* a self-propelled passenger vehicle on wheels — see CAR

automobile *vb* to travel by a motorized vehicle — see DRIVE 2

automobilist *n* a person who travels by automobile — see MOTORIST

autonomous *adj* not being under the rule or control of another — see FREE 1

autonomy *n* the state of being free from the control or power of another — see FREEDOM 1

autopsy *n* examination of a dead body especially to find out the cause of death ⟨the *autopsy* revealed an advanced stage of cancer⟩

syn postmortem, postmortem examination

rel dissection

near ant biopsy, vivisection

auxiliary *adj* available to supply something extra when needed ⟨the auditorium has an *auxiliary* cooling system used only on particularly sweltering days⟩

syn accessory, peripheral, supplemental, supplementary

rel backup, makeshift, substitute; added, additional, another, further; complementary, contributory; assistant, assisting, helping, supportive, tributary; secondary, subordinate, subservient, subsidiary; dis-

pensable, excess, nonessential, superfluous, surplus, unessential

near ant basic, fundamental, primary, prime; all-important, essential, imperative, indispensable, integral, necessary, needed, needful, required, requisite, vital

ant chief, main, principal

avail *n* the capacity for being useful for some purpose — see USE 2

avail *vb* to provide with something useful or desirable — see BENEFIT

available *adj* **1** possible to get ⟨the nursery's orchids are *available* by mail order only⟩ ⟨fare information is readily *available* by using the toll-free number⟩

syn accessible, acquirable, attainable, obtainable, procurable

rel purchasable, rentable; furnished, provided, supplied; common, omnipresent, prevalent, ubiquitous, universal, widespread; free, free-for-all, open, public, unrestricted

phrases on hand

near ant limited, off-limits, restricted; deficient, lacking, missing, rare, scarce, uncommon

ant inaccessible, unattainable, unavailable, unobtainable

2 capable of or suitable for being used for a particular purpose — see USABLE 1

avarice *n* an intense selfish desire for wealth or possessions — see GREED

avaricious *adj* having or marked by an eager and often selfish desire especially for material possessions — see GREEDY 1

avariciousness *n* an intense selfish desire for wealth or possessions — see GREED

avenge *vb* to punish in kind the wrongdoer responsible for ⟨a play about a prince who struggles to *avenge* his father's death⟩

syn requite, retaliate, revenge

rel castigate, fix, get, penalize, punish, scourge; chasten, chastise, correct, discipline; redress, right; compensate, pay (back), recompense, repay

phrases get even (for)

near ant absolve, condone, excuse, forgive, pardon, remit

avenger *n* one who inflicts punishment in return for an injury or offense — see NEMESIS 1

avenue *n* **1** a passage cleared for public vehicular travel — see WAY 1

2 an established course for traveling from one place to another — see PASSAGE 1

aver *vb* **1** to state as a fact usually forcefully — see CLAIM 1

2 to state clearly and strongly — see ASSERT 1

average *adj* **1** being about midway between extremes of amount or size — see MIDDLE 2

2 being of the type that is encountered in the normal course of events — see ORDINARY 1

3 having or showing the qualities associated with the members of a particular group or kind — see TYPICAL 1

average *n* what is typical of a group, class, or series ⟨my cat's a cut above the *average* when it comes to being a finicky eater⟩

syn norm, normal, par, standard

rel golden mean, mean, median, middle; commonplace, ordinary, rule, run, status quo, usual; exemplar, representative

near ant abnormality, anomaly, deviation, exception, rarity

averse *adj* having a natural dislike for something — see ANTIPATHETIC

averseness *n* a strong feeling of not liking or approving — see DISLIKE 1

aversion *n* 1 a dislike so strong as to cause stomach upset or queasiness — see DISGUST

2 a strong feeling of not liking or approving — see DISLIKE 1

3 something or someone that is hated — see HATE 2

avert *vb* to keep from happening by taking action in advance — see PREVENT

averting *n* the act or practice of keeping something from happening — see PREVENTION

aviator *n* one who flies or is qualified to fly an aircraft or spacecraft — see PILOT

avid *adj* 1 having or marked by an eager and often selfish desire especially for material possessions — see GREEDY 1

2 showing urgent desire or interest — see EAGER

avidity *n* 1 an intense selfish desire for wealth or possessions — see GREED

2 urgent desire or interest — see EAGERNESS

avoid *vb* to get or keep away from (as a responsibility) through cleverness or trickery — see ESCAPE 2

avoidance *n* the act or a means of getting or keeping away from something undesirable — see ESCAPE 2

avoirdupois *n* the state or quality of being heavy — see WEIGHTINESS 1

avouch *vb* 1 to declare (something) to be true or genuine — see CERTIFY 1

2 to state as a fact usually forcefully — see CLAIM 1

3 to state clearly and strongly — see ASSERT 1

avouchment *n* a solemn and often public declaration of the truth or existence of something — see PROTESTATION

avow *vb* 1 to state as a fact usually forcefully — see CLAIM 1

2 to state clearly and strongly — see ASSERT 1

avowal *n* 1 a solemn and often public declaration of the truth or existence of something — see PROTESTATION

2 an open declaration of something (as a fault or the commission of an offense) about oneself — see CONFESSION

await *vb* 1 to believe in the future occurrence of (something) — see EXPECT

2 to remain in place in readiness or expectation of something — see WAIT

awaited *adj* being in accordance with the prescribed, normal, or logical course of events — see DUE 2

awake *adj* 1 not sleeping or able to sleep — see WAKEFUL

2 paying close attention usually for the purpose of anticipating approaching danger or opportunity — see ALERT 1

awake *vb* 1 to cause to stop sleeping — see WAKE 1

2 to cease to be asleep — see WAKE 2

awaken *vb* 1 to cause to stop sleeping — see WAKE 1

2 to cease to be asleep — see WAKE 2

award *n* something given in recognition of achievement ⟨Faye received the highest *award* in the 16 and under category for her poem⟩

syn decoration, distinction, honor, plume, premium, prize

rel badge, crown, cup, laurel, medal, order, ribbon, trophy; accolade, applause, bravo, encomium, eulogy, hallelujah, homage, paean, panegyric, plaudit, tribute; citation, commendation, compliment

award *vb* 1 to give something as a token of gratitude or admiration for a service or achievement — see REWARD

2 to give the ownership or benefit of (something) formally or publicly — see CONFER 1

aware *adj* having specified facts or feelings actively impressed on the mind — see CONSCIOUS

awareness *n* a state of being aware — see ATTENTION 2

awash *adj* containing, covered with, or thoroughly penetrated by water — see WET

away *adj* 1 not close in time or space — see DISTANT 1

2 not at a certain place — see ABSENT 1

away *adv* from this or that place ⟨don't walk *away* while I'm still talking to you⟩

syn hence, off

rel apart, aside, elsewhere; abroad, afar, afield, astray

awe *n* the rapt attention and deep emotion caused by the sight of something extraordinary — see WONDER 2

awed *adj* filled with amazement and wonder — see OPENMOUTHED

awesome *adj* causing wonder or astonishment — see MARVELOUS 1

awestruck *adj* 1 affected with sudden and great wonder or surprise — see THUNDERSTRUCK

2 filled with amazement and wonder — see OPENMOUTHED

awful *adj* 1 causing intense displeasure, disgust, or resentment — see OFFENSIVE 1

2 causing wonder or astonishment — see MARVELOUS 1

3 extremely disturbing or repellent — see HORRIBLE 1

4 extremely unsatisfactory — see WRETCHED 1

---

syn synonym(s)   *rel* related words

ant antonym(s)   *near ant* near antonym(s)

awful *adv* to a great degree — see VERY 1

awfully *adv* to a great degree — see VERY 1

awfulness *n* the quality of inspiring intense dread or dismay — see HORROR 1

awkward *adj* 1 lacking social grace and assurance ⟨preteens feeling *awkward* at their first formal dance⟩

syn clumsy, gauche, graceless, inelegant, roughhewn, stiff, stilted, uncomfortable, uneasy, ungraceful, wooden

rel gawky, lubberly, ungainly; boorish, clownish, uncouth; abashed, discomfited, discomforted, discomposed, disconcerted, discountenanced, embarrassed; agitated, bothered, chagrined, dismayed, disquieted, distressed, disturbed, fazed, flustered, jittery, jumpy, mortified, nervous, nonplussed (*also* nonplused), perturbed, rattled, unhinged, unsettled, upset; diffident, insecure, meek, modest, self-doubting, timid, unassertive, unassuming, unpretentious

near ant assured, calm, collected, composed, confident, cool, placid, poised, serene, secure, self-assured, self-confident, self-possessed, tranquil, undisturbed, unperturbed

ant graceful, suave, urbane

2 showing or marked by a lack of skill and tact (as in dealing with a situation) ⟨her *awkward* handling of the seating arrangements at the wedding reception resulted in many hurt feelings⟩

syn botched, bungling, clumsy, fumbled, inept, inexpert, maladroit

rel amateur, amateurish, crude, green, incompetent, ineffectual, inefficient, inexperienced, unpolished, unprofessional, unskilled, unskillful; careless, sloppy, tacky, tactless, undiplomatic; ill-advised, ineffective, ineffectual, misdirected, misguided

near ant able, accomplished, adept, capable, clever, competent, consummate, crackerjack, expert, masterful, masterly, polished, professional, proficient, skilled,

skillful, talented; diplomatic, easy, effortless, gracious, smooth, tactful

ant adroit, deft, dexterous (*also* dextrous), facile

3 causing embarrassment ⟨the *awkward* situation of having to listen in as your teacher talks about you to your parents⟩

syn discomfiting, disconcerting, disturbing, embarrassing, flustering, uncomfortable

rel confusing, difficult, disagreeable, impossible, inconvenient, intolerable, troublesome, unpleasant, unwieldy; debasing, degrading, demeaning, humbling, humiliating, mortifying

near ant agreeable, comfortable, convenient, pleasing

4 causing difficulty, discomfort, or annoyance — see INCONVENIENT 1

5 difficult to use or operate especially because of size, weight, or design — see CUMBERSOME

6 lacking in physical ease and grace in movement or in the use of the hands — see CLUMSY 1

awning *n* a raised covering over something for decoration or protection — see CANOPY

awry *adj* inclined or twisted to one side ⟨the shutters that still remained on the run-down old house were all *awry*⟩

syn askew, aslant, cockeyed, crooked, listing, lopsided, oblique, skewed, slanted, slanting, slantwise, tilted, tipping, uneven

rel asymmetrical (*or* asymmetric), unbalanced, unsymmetrical; contorted, disordered, distorted, irregular

near ant ordered, orderly, regular, uniform; balanced, symmetrical (*or* symmetric)

ant even, level, straight

awry *adv* off the desired or intended path or course — see WRONG 1

¹aye *also* **ay** *adv* for all time — see EVER 1

²aye *also* **ay** *adv* used to express agreement — see YES

B

babble *n* unintelligible or meaningless talk — see GIBBERISH

babble *vb* 1 to speak rapidly, inarticulately, and usually unintelligibly ⟨in such a rush to tell us the news that she just *babbled*⟩

syn chatter, drivel, gabble, gibber, jabber, prattle, sputter

rel gab, jaw, patter, prate, rattle, run on; maunder, mouth, mumble, murmur, mutter; stammer, stutter; chat, converse, palaver, rap, visit; discourse; screech, shout, shriek

near ant articulate, enunciate, pronounce

2 to engage in casual or rambling conversation — see CHAT

babbler *n* a person who talks constantly — see CHATTERBOX

babe *n* a recently born person — see BABY

babel *n* a place of uproar or confusion — see MADHOUSE 2

babushka *n* a scarf worn on the head — see BANDANNA

baby *n* a recently born person ⟨the *baby* is just learning to sit up, so be careful⟩

syn babe, child, infant, newborn

rel cherub; foundling, nursling, suckling; papoose; kid, moppet, toddler, tot, tyke;

boy, nipper, tad; juvenile, minor, youngster, youth; brat, imp, squirt, urchin, whippersnapper; girl, hoyden, tomboy

phrases babe in arms

near ant adult, grown-up; elder, graybeard, oldster, old-timer, senior citizen

baby *vb* to treat with great or excessive care ⟨he babied his car, faithfully washing it every week⟩

syn coddle, dandle, mollycoddle, nurse, pamper, spoil

rel cater (to), humor, indulge; gratify, mother, oblige, please, satisfy

near ant control, discipline, restrain; oppress; neglect, overlook, slight

ant abuse, ill-treat, ill-use, maltreat, mishandle, mistreat, misuse

babyish *adj* having or showing the annoying qualities (as silliness) associated with children — see CHILDISH

babysitter *n* a girl or woman employed to care for a young child or children — see NURSE

back *adj* being at or in the part of something opposite the front part ⟨she carried all the presents in the *back* door, as the children were playing in the front yard⟩

syn hind, hindmost, posterior, rear, rearward

ant anterior, fore, forward, front

back *adv* toward the opposite direction — see AROUND 2

back up *vb* 1 to promote the interests or cause of — see SUPPORT 1

2 to provide (someone) with what is useful or necessary to achieve an end — see HELP 1

back away *vb* to move back or away (as from something difficult, dangerous, or disagreeable) — see RETREAT 1

backbone *n* 1 a column of bones supporting the trunk of a vertebrate animal — see SPINE

2 the strength of mind that enables a person to endure pain or hardship — see FORTITUDE

back down *vb* to break a promise or agreement — see RENEGE

backdrop *n* the physical conditions or features that form the setting against which something is viewed — see BACKGROUND 1

backer *n* 1 a person who actively supports or favors a cause — see EXPONENT

2 a person who takes the responsibility for some other person or thing — see SPONSOR

3 someone associated with another to give assistance or moral support — see ALLY

background *n* 1 the physical conditions or features that form the setting against which something is viewed ⟨they got married on a mountain top with the sunset as *background*⟩

syn backdrop, ground

rel scene, scenery, set, stage; environment, milieu, setting, surroundings

near ant foreground; center, focal point, focus, heart

2 the place and time in which the action for a portion of a dramatic work (as a movie) is set — see SCENE 1

backhanded *adj* not being or expressing what one appears to be or express — see INSINCERE

backing *n* an act or instance of helping — see HELP 1

back of *prep* at, to, or toward the rear of — see BEHIND 1

back off *vb* to break a promise or agreement — see RENEGE

backpack *n* a soft-sided case designed for carrying belongings especially on the back — see PACK 1

backside *n* the part of the body upon which someone sits —'see BUTTOCKS

backslider *n* a person who has sunk below the normal moral standard — see DEGENERATE

backstage *adj or adv* off or away from the part of the stage visible to the audience — see OFFSTAGE

back talk *n* disrespectful or argumentative talk given in response to a command or request ⟨his mother sent him to his room because of his constant *back talk*⟩

syn cheek, impertinence, impudence, insolence, sass, sauce

rel comeback, rejoinder, retort, riposte, wisecrack; discourtesy, disrespect, impoliteness, rudeness, tactlessness; audaciousness, audacity, boldness, brazenness; coarseness, crassness, crudity, vulgarity; abruptness, bluffness, bluntness, brusqueness, crossness, curtness, gruffness, surliness

near ant civility, cordiality, courtesy, diplomacy, politeness, tactfulness; consideration, gallantry, gentility, graciousness, smoothness, suaveness; deference, respect; affability

backup *adj* taking the place of one that came before — see NEW 1

backup *n* a person or thing that takes the place of another — see SUBSTITUTE

backward *adj* directed, turned, or done toward the back ⟨a *backward* turn on ice skates is hard to learn, because you can't see where you're going⟩

syn rearward, retrograde

rel reversed; hind, posterior, rear

near ant forward

backwater *n* a rural region that forms the edge of the settled or developed part of a country — see FRONTIER 2

backwoods *n* a rural region that forms the edge of the settled or developed part of a country — see FRONTIER 2

bad *adj* 1 falling short of a standard ⟨a *bad* first attempt at making meat loaf resulted in a soggy inedible mess⟩

syn deficient, inferior, lousy, off, poor, punk, rotten, substandard, unacceptable, ungodly, unsatisfactory, wanting, wretched, wrong

---

syn synonym(s)   *rel* related words
ant antonym(s)   *near ant* near antonym(s)

rel defective, faulty, flawed; execrable, lesser, low-grade, mediocre, reprehensible, second-rate, unspeakable; bum, useless, valueless, worthless; inadequate, insufficient, lacking; astray; scurrilous, villainous

phrases below (or under) par

near ant choice, excellent, exceptional, first-class, first-rate, premium, prime, superior; adequate, sufficient

ant acceptable, satisfactory

2 not conforming to a high moral standard; morally unacceptable ⟨stealing is just plain *bad*⟩

syn black, evil, immoral, iniquitous, nefarious, rotten, sinful, unethical, unrighteous, unsavory, vicious, vile, villainous, wicked, wrong

rel base, contemptible, despicable, dirty, disreputable, evil-minded, ignoble, ill, infernal, low, mean; atrocious, cruel, nasty; blamable, blameworthy, censurable, reprehensible; corrupt, debased, debauched, degenerate, depraved, dissolute, libertine, loose, perverted, reprobate; banned, barred, condemned, discouraged, forbidden, interdicted, outlawed, prohibited, proscribed, unauthorized, unclean; disallowed; execrable, lousy, miserable, wretched; erring, fallen, unprincipled, unscrupulous; improper, incorrect, indecent, indecorous, unbecoming

near ant high-minded, honest, honorable, law-abiding, legitimate, principled, reputable, right-minded, scrupulous, straight, upright; allowed, authorized, legal, licensed, permissible, permitted; approved, endorsed, sanctioned; abetted, encouraged, promoted, supported; clean, correct, decent, decorous, exemplary, proper, seemly; blameless, commendable, creditable, guiltless; chaste, immaculate, innocent, irreproachable, lily-white, perfect, pure, spotless

ant good, ethical, moral, right, righteous, virtuous

3 causing or capable of causing harm — see HARMFUL

4 engaging in or marked by childish misbehavior — see NAUGHTY

5 feeling unhappiness — see SAD 1

6 having a fault — see FAULTY

7 having undergone organic breakdown — see ROTTEN 1

8 not giving pleasure to the mind or senses — see UNPLEASANT

9 of low quality — see CHEAP 2

10 temporarily suffering from a disorder of the body — see SICK 1

bad *n* that which is morally unacceptable — see EVIL

badly *adv* in an unsatisfactory way ⟨I'm afraid you performed quite *badly* in our last rehearsal⟩

syn inadequately, poorly, unacceptably, unsatisfactorily

rel rottenly; intolerably, unbearably; inappropriately, incorrectly, indecently, rakishly, unsuitably; naughtily

near ant appropriately, congruously, correctly, decently, decorously, felicitously, fittingly, genteelly, rightly, seemly, suitably

ant acceptably, adequately, all right, fine, good, palatably, passably, so-so, tolerably

bad–mouth *vb* to express scornfully one's low opinion of — see DECRY 1

badness *n* the state or quality of being utterly evil — see ENORMITY 1

baffle *vb* **1** to prevent from achieving a goal — see FRUSTRATE

2 to throw into a state of mental uncertainty — see CONFUSE 1

bafflement *n* a state of mental uncertainty — see CONFUSION 1

bag *n* **1** a container made of a flexible material (as paper or plastic) ⟨she carries her towel and other supplies to the beach in a bright, colorful *bag* slung over her arm⟩

syn poke [*chiefly Southern & Midland*], pouch, sack

rel carryall, portmanteau, traveling bag; bundle, pack, package, packet, parcel; backpack, duffel bag, haversack, knapsack, rucksack; handbag, pocketbook, purse, tote bag

2 a container for carrying money and small personal items — see PURSE

bag *vb* **1** to extend outward beyond a usual point — see BULGE

2 to take physical control or possession of (something) suddenly or forcibly — see CATCH 1

bail out *vb* to remove from danger or harm — see SAVE 2

bairn *n*, *chiefly Scottish* a young person who is between infancy and adulthood — see CHILD 1

bait *n* **1** something used to attract animals to a hook or into a trap ⟨cheese is the traditional *bait* for trapping mice⟩

syn decoy, lure

rel ambush, trap; hook, snare, troll; appeal, attraction, call, draw, incentive, pull; enticement, seduction, temptation

near ant repellent

2 something that persuades one to perform an action for pleasure or gain — see LURE 1

bait *vb* to attack repeatedly with mean putdowns or insults — see TEASE 2

baiter *n* **1** a person who causes repeated emotional pain, distress, or annoyance to another — see TORMENTOR

2 one that tries to get a person to give in to a desire — see TEMPTER

balance *n* **1** a condition in which opposing forces are equal to one another ⟨in order to determine the weight of that beaker, you need to get the two pans of the scale in perfect *balance*⟩

syn equilibrium, equipoise, poise

rel counterbalance, counterpoise; firmness, fixedness, security, stability, steadiness

near ant changeability, fluctuation, inconstancy, insecurity, instability, mutability, precariousness, shakiness, unsteadiness, volatility

ant imbalance

2 a balanced, pleasing, or suitable arrangement of parts — see HARMONY 1

3 a device for measuring weight — see ¹SCALE

4 a force or influence that makes an opposing force ineffective or less effective — see COUNTERBALANCE

5 a remaining group or portion — see REMAINDER 1

balance *vb* to make equal in amount, degree, or status — see EQUALIZE

balanced *adj* **1** having full use of one's mind and control over one's actions — see SANE

2 having the parts agreeably related — see HARMONIOUS 2

bald *adj* **1** lacking a usual or natural covering — see NAKED 2

2 free from all additions or embellishment — see PLAIN 1

baleful *adj* **1** being or showing a sign of evil or calamity to come — see OMINOUS

2 causing or capable of causing harm — see HARMFUL

3 likely to cause or capable of causing death — see DEADLY

balk *vb* to prevent from achieving a goal — see FRUSTRATE

balky *adj* given to resisting authority or another's control — see DISOBEDIENT

¹ball *n* **1** a more or less round body or mass ⟨the little rubber *ball* used in racquetball⟩ ⟨a *ball* of string⟩

syn globe, orb, sphere

rel egg, oval; circle, ring, round; chunk, clump, gob, hunk, lump, nugget, wad

near ant block, cube, rectangle, square

2 a usually round or cone-shaped little piece of lead to be fired from a firearm — see BULLET

²ball *n* a social gathering for dancing — see DANCE

ball *vb* to form into a round compact mass — see WAD

ballad *n* a short musical composition for the human voice often with instrumental accompaniment — see SONG 1

balloon *vb* **1** to become greater in extent, volume, amount, or number — see INCREASE 2

2 to extend outward beyond a usual point — see BULGE

ballot *n* a piece of paper indicating a person's preferences in an election ⟨we collected all of the *ballots* from the students voting for class president⟩

syn vote

rel aye (*also* ay), nay, no, yea; blackball; referendum; ticket

ballyhoo *n* newsworthy information released to the media that is designed to gain public attention or support for a person, business, or cause — see PUBLICITY

ballyhoo *vb* **1** to praise or publicize lavishly and often excessively — see TOUT 1

2 to provide publicity for — see PUBLICIZE 1

balminess *n* lack of good sense or judgment — see FOOLISHNESS 1

balmy *adj* **1** having or showing a very abnormal or sick state of mind — see INSANE 1

2 marked by temperatures that are neither too high nor too low — see CLEMENT

3 not harsh or stern especially in manner, nature, or effect — see GENTLE 1

4 showing or marked by a lack of good sense or judgment — see FOOLISH 1

balustrade *n* a protective barrier consisting of a horizontal bar and its supports — see RAILING

ban *n* an order that something not be done or used — see PROHIBITION 2

ban *vb* **1** to order not to do or use or to be done or used — see FORBID

2 to prevent the participation or inclusion of — see EXCLUDE

banal *adj* **1** lacking in qualities that make for spirit and character — see WISHY-WASHY 1

2 used or heard so often as to be dull — see STALE

banality *n* an idea or expression that has been used by many people — see COMMONPLACE

bananas *adj* having or showing a very abnormal or sick state of mind — see INSANE 1

¹band *n* **1** a circular strip — see RING 2

2 something that physically prevents free movement — see BOND 1

3 a line or long narrow section differing in color from the background — see STRIPE

²band *n* **1** a usually large group of musicians playing together ⟨that traveling *band* needs to find a new singer⟩

syn orchestra, philharmonic, symphony, symphony orchestra

rel brass band; brasses, strings, woodwinds; combo, ensemble, group; company, troupe; duo, octet, quartet (*also* quartette), quintet, septet (*also* septette), sextet, trio

2 a group of people working together on a task — see GANG 1

band *vb* **1** to encircle or bind with or as if with a belt — see GIRD 1

2 to form or enter into an association that furthers the interests of its members — see ALLY

3 to gather into a tight mass by means of a line or cord — see TIE 1

4 to make stripes on — see STRIPE

bandage *vb* to cover with a bandage ⟨her mother always *bandages* her scraped knees very carefully⟩

syn bind, dress

rel care (for), doctor, medicate, minister (to), nurse, treat; mend, heal

bandanna *or* **bandana** *n* a scarf worn on the head ⟨she uses her colorful print *bandanna* to keep the hair out of her eyes⟩

---

syn synonym(s)   **rel** related words
ant antonym(s)   **near ant** near antonym(s)

syn babushka, handkerchief, kerchief, mantilla

rel shawl

bandwagon *n* a series of activities undertaken to achieve a goal — see CAMPAIGN

bandy *vb* to talk about (an issue) usually from various points of view and for the purpose of arriving at a decision or opinion — see DISCUSS

bane *n* a substance that by chemical action can kill or injure a living thing — see POISON

baneful *adj* causing or capable of causing harm — see HARMFUL

bang *n* **1** a hard strike with a part of the body or an instrument — see ¹BLOW

2 a loud explosive sound — see CLAP 1

3 a pleasurably intense stimulation of the feelings — see THRILL

bang *vb* **1** to come into usually forceful contact with something — see HIT 2

2 to deliver a blow to (someone or something) usually in a strong vigorous manner — see HIT 1

3 to shove into a closed position with force and noise — see SLAM 1

bangle *n* an ornament worn on a chain around the neck or wrist — see PENDANT

bang–up *adj* of the very best kind — see EXCELLENT

banish *vb* **1** to force to leave a country ⟨in the old days, criminals were sometimes *banished*⟩

syn deport, displace, exile, expatriate, transport

rel dismiss, eject, eliminate, evict, exclude, expel, oust, throw out; excommunicate, ostracize, reject, repudiate, spurn; dispossess

near ant naturalize, repatriate; accept, admit, receive, take in; entertain, harbor, house, shelter

2 to drive or force out — see EJECT 1

banishment *n* the forced removal from a homeland — see EXILE 1

banister *n* a protective barrier consisting of a horizontal bar and its supports — see RAILING

¹bank *n* **1** a number of things considered as a unit — see GROUP 1

2 a series of people or things arranged side by side — see ROW 1

²bank *n* a pile or ridge of granular matter (as sand or snow) ⟨he likes to play on the *bank* of dirt the construction workers left⟩

syn bar, drift, mound

rel snowbank, snowdrift; embankment, sandbar; heap, hill, mass, mountain, stack

bank *vb* **1** to form into a pile or ridge of earth — see MOUND 1

2 to put into an account — see DEPOSIT 1

bank note *n* a piece of printed paper used as money — see ¹BILL 2

bankroll *n* available money — see FUND 2

bankrupt *vb* to cause to lose one's fortune and become unable to pay one's debts — see RUIN 1

banned *adj* that may not be permitted — see IMPERMISSIBLE

banner *adj* of the very best kind — see EXCELLENT

banner *n* a piece of cloth with a special design that is used as an emblem or for signaling — see FLAG 1

banning *n* the act of ordering that something not be done or used — see PROHIBITION 1

banquet *n* a large fancy meal often accompanied by ceremony or entertainment — see FEAST

banquet *vb* to entertain with a fancy meal — see FEAST

bantam *adj* of a size that is less than average — see SMALL 1

banter *n* good-natured teasing or exchanging of clever remarks ⟨those particular students are known for their brilliant and witty *banter* at lunchtime⟩

syn chaff, give-and-take, jesting, joshing, persiflage, raillery, repartee

rel barb, crack, dig, gag, jest, joke, quip, sally, wisecrack, witticism; facetiousness, humorousness; fooling, kidding, mocking, razzing, ribbing, ridiculing; humor, wit, wordplay; chatter, chitchat, gossip, small talk

banter *vb* to make jokes — see JOKE

bantering *adj* marked by or expressive of mild or good-natured teasing — see QUIZZICAL

baptism *n* the process or an instance of being formally placed in an office or organization — see INSTALLATION 1

baptize *vb* **1** to give a name to — see NAME 1

2 to put into an office or welcome into an organization with special ceremonies — see INSTALL 1

bar *n* **1** a straight piece (as of wood or metal) that is longer than it is wide ⟨all of the prison's windows are partially covered with steel *bars*⟩

syn billet, rod

rel beam, board; band, strip; ingot, slab, stick

2 a line or long narrow section differing in color from the background — see STRIPE

3 a pile or ridge of granular matter (as sand or snow) — see ²BANK

4 a place of business where alcoholic beverages are sold to be consumed on the premises — see BARROOM

5 an assembly of persons for the administration of justice — see COURT 3

6 something that makes movement or progress more difficult — see ENCUMBRANCE

bar *prep* not including — see EXCEPT

bar *vb* **1** to make stripes on — see STRIPE

2 to order not to do or use or to be done or used — see FORBID

3 to prevent the participation or inclusion of — see EXCLUDE

barb *n* an act or expression showing scorn and usually intended to hurt another's feelings — see INSULT

barbarian *n* an uncivilized person — see HEATHEN 2

barbaric *adj* having or showing the desire to inflict severe pain and suffering on others — see CRUEL 1

barbarity *n* the willful infliction of pain and suffering on others — see CRUELTY

barbarous *adj* 1 having or showing the desire to inflict severe pain and suffering on others — see CRUEL 1

2 not civilized — see SAVAGE 1

bard *n* a person who writes poetry — see POET

bare *adj* 1 being this and no more — see MERE

2 free from all additions or embellishment — see PLAIN 1

3 lacking a usual or natural covering — see NAKED 2

4 lacking or shed of clothing — see NAKED 1

5 lacking contents that could or should be present — see EMPTY 1

bare *vb* to make known (as information previously kept secret) — see REVEAL 1

barely *adv* by a very small margin — see JUST 2

bareness *n* the quality or state of being empty — see VACANCY 2

bargain *n* 1 something bought or offered for sale at a desirable price ⟨those shoes were a *bargain* because the store was going out of business⟩
syn buy, steal
rel markdown; bonus, freebie, gift, giveaway, premium, present; sale; boon, windfall
near ant overcharge, rip-off; markup; extravagance, luxury

2 an arrangement about action to be taken — see AGREEMENT 2

bargain *vb* to talk over or dispute the terms of a purchase ⟨they *bargained* with the car salesman for half an hour before settling on a price⟩
syn chaffer, deal, dicker, haggle, horse-trade, negotiate, palter
rel argue, bicker, clash, quibble, squabble, wrangle; comparison shop, shop (around); barter, exchange, trade; hawk, peddle; buy, purchase

barge *vb* to move heavily or clumsily — see LUMBER 1

bark *n* a boat equipped with one or more sails — see SAILBOAT

¹**bark** *vb* to remove the natural covering of — see PEEL

²**bark** *vb* to speak sharply or irritably — see SNAP 1

baron *n* a person of rank, power, or influence in a particular field — see MAGNATE

baronial *adj* large and impressive in size, grandeur, extent, or conception — see GRAND 1

barrage *n* a rapid or overwhelming outpouring of many things at once ⟨the teacher's rapid-fire *barrage* of homework assignments went by too fast for me to write them all down⟩

syn bombardment, cannonade, fusillade, hail, salvo, shower, storm, volley
rel broadside, burst, deluge, flood, flood tide, flush, gush, inundation, outburst, outflow, outpouring, overflow, spate, surge, torrent; current, river, stream, tide; excess, glut, overabundance, overage, overkill, overmuch, oversupply, superabundance, superfluity, surfeit, surplus
near ant dribble, drip, trickle

barred *adj* 1 having stripes — see STRIPED

2 that may not be permitted — see IMPERMISSIBLE

barrel *n* 1 a considerable amount — see LOT 2

2 a metal container in the shape of a cylinder — see CAN

3 an enclosed wooden vessel for holding beverages — see CASK

barrel *vb* to proceed or move quickly — see HURRY 2

barren *adj* 1 producing inferior or only a small amount of vegetation ⟨if tobacco fields aren't allowed to lie idle once every few years, they will become *barren*⟩
syn impoverished, infertile, poor, stark, unproductive, weak
rel bleak, dead, desolate, inhospitable, lifeless; bankrupted, consumed, debilitated, depleted, diminished, drained, dried up, enfeebled, exhausted, expended, lessened, reduced, spent, used up; arid, desert, dry
near ant arable, tillable; green, verdant
ant fertile, fruitful, lush, luxuriant, productive, rich

2 not able to produce fruit or offspring — see STERILE 1

barren *n* land that is uninhabited or not fit for crops — see WASTELAND

barricade *n* a physical object that blocks the way — see BARRIER

barrier *n* a physical object that blocks the way ⟨there was a big *barrier* plastered with signs saying "Keep Out" around the trash compactor⟩
syn barricade, fence, hedge, wall
rel bar, encumbrance, handicap, hindrance, hurdle, impediment, obstacle, obstruction, roadblock, stop; fetter, hobble, manacle, shackle; constraint, curb, restraint, snag
near ant door, doorway, entrance, entry, entryway, gate, portal

barring *n* the act of ordering that something not be done or used — see PROHIBITION 1

barring *prep* not including — see EXCEPT

barroom *n* a place of business where alcoholic beverages are sold to be consumed on the premises ⟨her mother didn't like her even to walk past the *barroom* because she was worried that there might be drunk people inside⟩
syn bar, café (*also* cafe), groggery, grogshop, pub, public house [*chiefly British*], saloon, tavern
rel cabaret, dive, joint, nightclub, roadhouse, speakeasy; package store

---

syn synonym(s)   *rel* related words
ant antonym(s)   *near ant* near antonym(s)

barter *n* a giving or taking of one thing of value in return for another — see EX-CHANGE 1

base *adj* not following or in accordance with standards of honor and decency — see IGNOBLE 2

base *n* 1 an immaterial thing upon which something else rests ⟨the firm belief that complete trust between husband and wife is the *base* of any successful marriage⟩
syn basis, bedrock, cornerstone, footing, foundation, ground, groundwork, keystone, underpinning
rel buttress, framework, prop, substructure, support; assumption, justification, premise, presumption, presupposition, theory, thesis, warrant; center, core, eye, focus, heart, hub, nucleus, seat; essence, quintessence, soul
2 a place from which an advance (as for military operations) is made ⟨the Army's *base* of attack was kept top secret until the battle began⟩
syn bridgehead, foothold
rel beachhead, center, front, headquarters; bastion, fastness, fórtress, stronghold
3 a thing or place that is of greatest importance to an activity or interest — see CENTER 1
4 the lowest part, place, or point — see BOTTOM 3
5 the place from which a commander runs operations — see COMMAND 3

base *vb* to find a basis ⟨she *based* her argument against the death penalty on careful research⟩
syn ground, predicate, rest
rel establish, found; assume, postulate, premise, presume, presuppose, suppose

baseborn *adj* 1 belonging to the class of people of low social or economic rank — see IGNOBLE 1
2 born to a father and mother who are not married — see ILLEGITIMATE 1

basement *n* a room or set of rooms below the surface of the ground — see CELLAR

bash *vb* 1 to come into usually forceful contact with something — see HIT 2
2 to deliver a blow to (someone or something) usually in a strong vigorous manner — see HIT 1
3 to strike repeatedly — see BEAT 1

bashful *adj* not comfortable around people — see SHY 1

basic *adj* of or relating to the simplest facts or theories of a subject — see ELEMENTARY

basically *adv* for the most part — see CHIEFLY

basics *n pl* general or basic truths on which other truths or theories can be based — see PRINCIPLES 1

basis *n* an immaterial thing upon which something else rests — see BASE 1

bask *vb* to refrain from labor or exertion — see REST 1

bass *adj* having a low musical pitch or range — see DEEP 2

bastard *adj* born to a father and mother who are not married — see ILLEGITIMATE 1

bastion *n* a structure or place from which one can resist attack — see FORT

bat *n* 1 a hard strike with a part of the body or an instrument — see ¹BLOW
2 a heavy rigid stick used as a weapon or for punishment — see CLUB 1

bat *vb* 1 to deliver a blow to (someone or something) usually in a strong vigorous manner — see HIT 1
2 to strike repeatedly — see BEAT 1

batch *n* 1 a number of things considered as a unit — see GROUP 1
2 a usually small number of persons considered as a unit — see GROUP 2

bath *n* a room furnished with a fixture for flushing body waste — see TOILET

bathe *vb* to make wet — see WET

bathed *adj* containing, covered with, or thoroughly penetrated by water — see WET

bathroom *n* a room furnished with a fixture for flushing body waste — see TOILET

battalion *n* a large body of men and women organized for land warfare — see ARMY 1

batter *vb* to strike repeatedly — see BEAT 1

battery *n* 1 a number of things considered as a unit — see GROUP 1
2 a usually small number of persons considered as a unit — see GROUP 2

battle *n* 1 a forceful effort to reach a goal or objective — see STRUGGLE 1
2 a physical dispute between opposing individuals or groups — see FIGHT 1
3 active fighting during the course of a war — see COMBAT 1
4 an earnest effort for superiority or victory over another — see CONTEST 1

battle *vb* 1 to engage in a contest — see COMPETE
2 to enter into contest or conflict with — see ENGAGE 2
3 to oppose (someone) in physical conflict — see FIGHT 1
4 to strive to reduce or eliminate — see FIGHT 2

batty *adj* having or showing a very abnormal or sick state of mind — see INSANE 1

bauble *n* a small object displayed for its attractiveness or interest — see KNICK-KNACK

bawdiness *n* the quality or state of being obscene — see OBSCENITY 1

bawdy *adj* 1 depicting or referring to sexual matters in a way that is unacceptable in polite society — see OBSCENE 1
2 hinting at or intended to call to mind matters regarded as indecent — see SUGGESTIVE 1

bawl *vb* 1 to shed tears often while making meaningless sounds as a sign of pain or distress — see CRY 1
2 to speak so as to be heard at a distance — see CALL 1

bay *n* **1** a part of a body of water that extends beyond the general shoreline — see GULF 1

2 one of the parts into which an enclosed space is divided — see COMPARTMENT

bay *vb* to make a long loud mournful sound — see HOWL 1

bazaar *n* an establishment where goods are sold to consumers — see SHOP 1

be *vb* **1** to have life ⟨stories that begin with the familiar line "once upon a time there *was* a beautiful maiden"⟩

syn breathe, exist, live, subsist

rel abide, continue, endure, last, lead, persist, survive; move; flourish, prosper, thrive

near ant disappear, evaporate, vanish; cease, end, stop

ant depart, die, expire, pass away, perish, succumb

2 to occupy a place or location — see STAND 1

3 to take or have a certain position within a group arranged in vertical classes — see RANK 1

4 to take place — see HAPPEN

be (to) *vb* to behave toward in a stated way — see TREAT 1

beach *n* the usually sandy or gravelly land bordering a body of water ⟨she loves walking along the *beach*, looking for shells that the waves cast up⟩

syn shore, strand

rel seaboard, seacoast, seashore, seaside; coast, coastline, shoreline; waterfront; bank, riverbank, riverside; esplanade; littoral

beached *adj* resting on the shore or bottom of a body of water — see AGROUND

beacon *n* something that provides illumination — see LIGHT 2

beak *n* the jaws of a bird together with their hornlike covering ⟨the bird cracked the walnut shell with its *beak* and ate its nut⟩

syn bill, nib

rel mouth; muzzle; mandible, maw, maxilla

beam *n* a narrow sharply defined line of light radiating from an object — see SHAFT 1

beam *vb* **1** to emit rays of light — see SHINE 1

2 to express an emotion (as amusement) by curving the lips upward — see SMILE 1

beaming *adj* **1** giving off or reflecting much light — see BRIGHT 1

2 having or being an outward sign of good feelings (as of love, confidence, or happiness) — see RADIANT 1

bear *n* an irritable and complaining person — see GROUCH

bear *vb* **1** to bring forth from the womb ⟨luckily, she turned out to be able to *bear* children after all⟩

syn drop, have, produce

rel deliver; create; breed, multiply, propagate, reproduce, spawn; beget, father, generate, get, mother, sire

phrases to give birth to

near ant abort, lose, miscarry

2 to put up with (something painful or difficult) ⟨I can't *bear* having to eat my vegetables in order to have ice cream⟩

syn abide, brook, countenance, endure, meet, stand, stick out, stomach, support, sustain, take, tolerate

rel accept, allow, permit, suffer, swallow; acquiesce, agree (with *or* to), assent (to), capitulate, consent (to), respect, submit (to), yield (to)

near ant decline, dismiss, refuse, reject, repudiate, spurn, turn down; combat, contest, fight, oppose, resist; avoid, bypass, circumvent, dodge, elude, escape, evade, miss; abstain, forbear, refrain

3 to have a relation or connection — see APPLY 1

4 to go on a specified course or in a certain direction — see HEAD 1

5 to hold up or serve as a foundation for — see SUPPORT 3

6 to keep in one's mind or heart — see HARBOR 1

7 to manage the actions of (oneself) in a particular way — see BEHAVE

8 to support and take from one place to another — see CARRY 1

9 to take to or upon oneself — see ASSUME 1

10 to wear or have on one's person — see CARRY 2

bearable *adj* capable of being endured ⟨the pain from a sprained ankle is annoying but *bearable*⟩

syn endurable, sufferable, supportable, sustainable, tolerable

rel livable (*also* liveable); acceptable, allowable, reasonable

near ant agonizing, appalling, awful, bad, cruel, dire, dreadful, excruciating, ghastly, harrowing, harsh, horrible, nasty, painful, rotten, terrible, tormenting, torturous, unfortunate, vicious, vile, wretched; unacceptable; acute, extreme, intense, piercing

ant insufferable, insupportable, intolerable, unbearable, unendurable, unsupportable

beard *vb* to oppose (something hostile or dangerous) with firmness or courage — see FACE 2

bear down on *vb* to push steadily against with some force — see PRESS 1

bearing *n* **1** the fact or state of being pertinent — see PERTINENCE

2 the fact or state of having something in common — see CONNECTION 1

3 the way or manner in which one conducts oneself — see BEHAVIOR

bearish *adj* having or showing a habitually bad temper — see ILL-TEMPERED

bear out *vb* to give evidence or testimony to the truth or factualness of — see CONFIRM

---

syn synonym(s)   *rel* related words
ant antonym(s)   *near ant* near antonym(s)

beast *n* **1** a mean, evil, or unprincipled person — see VILLAIN

2 a person whose behavior is offensive to others — see JERK 1

3 one of the lower animals as distinguished from human beings — see ANIMAL

beastly *adv* to a great degree — see VERY 1

beat *adj* depleted in strength, energy, or freshness — see WEARY 1

beat *n* **1** a hard strike with a part of the body or an instrument — see ¹BLOW

2 a rhythmic expanding and contracting — see PULSATION

3 the recurrent pattern formed by a series of sounds having a regular rise and fall in intensity — see RHYTHM

beat *vb* **1** to strike repeatedly ⟨they attacked and *beat* him, but fortunately he'll be fine⟩

syn bash, bat, batter, belt, bludgeon, buffet, bung (up), club, drub, flog, hammer, hide, lace, lambaste (*or* lambast), lick, maul, pelt, pommel, pound, pummel, thrash, thump, wallop, whale, whip

rel assail, attack, box, bust, cane, chop, clobber, clout, crack, cudgel, cuff, hit, horsewhip, knock, lam, lash, lay on, paste, punch, slap, smack, smash, sock, spank, swat, swipe, thwack, whack; gore, lacerate, wound; maim, mangle, mutilate

2 to achieve a victory over ⟨she always *beats* everyone at checkers, but she's not as good at chess⟩

syn best, clobber, conquer, crush, defeat, drub, lick, master, overbear, overcome, overmatch, prevail (over), rout, skunk, subdue, surmount, thrash, trim, triumph (over), trounce, wallop, whip, win (against), worst

rel nose out; excel, flourish, score, succeed; overpower, overthrow, subjugate, vanquish; exceed, outdo, surpass

phrases get around, get the better of

near ant fail

ant lose (to)

3 to be greater, better, or stronger than — see SURPASS 1

4 to expand and contract in a rhythmic manner — see PULSATE

5 to move or cause to move with a striking motion — see FLAP

6 to prevent from achieving a goal — see FRUSTRATE

7 to shape with a hammer — see HAMMER 1

8 to shine with a bright harsh light — see GLARE 1

9 to strike or cause to strike lightly and usually rhythmically — see ¹TAP

beater *n* one that defeats an enemy or opponent — see VICTOR 1

beating *n* failure to win a contest — see DEFEAT 1

beau *n* a male romantic companion — see BOYFRIEND

beau ideal *n* **1** someone of such unequaled perfection as to deserve imitation — see IDEAL 1

2 the most perfect type or example — see QUINTESSENCE 1

beauteous *adj* very pleasing to look at — see BEAUTIFUL

beauteousness *n* the qualities in a person or thing that as a whole give pleasure to the senses — see BEAUTY 1

beautiful *adj* very pleasing to look at ⟨a strikingly *beautiful* child who is being eagerly pursued by all the modeling agencies⟩

syn attractive, beauteous, bonny [*chiefly British*], comely, cute, fair, gorgeous, handsome, knockout, lovely, pretty, ravishing, sightly, stunning, taking

rel alluring, appealing, charming, delightful, eye-catching, glamorous (*also* glamourous), prepossessing; elegant, exquisite, glorious, resplendent, splendid, statuesque, sublime, superb; flawless, perfect, radiant; dainty, delicate; personable, presentable

near ant abhorrent, abominable, bad, disagreeable, disgusting, dreadful, foul, frightful, ghastly, hideous, horrible, loathsome, nasty, nauseating, objectionable, offensive, repellent, repugnant, repulsive, revolting, shocking, sickening, terrible; unappealing, unappetizing, unpleasant, unpleasing, unprepossessing

ant homely, ill-favored, plain, ugly, unattractive, unbeautiful, unhandsome, unlovely, unpretty, unsightly

beautify *vb* to make more attractive by adding something that is beautiful or becoming — see DECORATE

beautifying *adj* serving to add beauty — see DECORATIVE

beauty *n* **1** the qualities in a person or thing that as a whole give pleasure to the senses ⟨her *beauty* was enough to take your breath away⟩

syn attractiveness, beauteousness, comeliness, cuteness, fairness, gorgeousness, handsomeness, looks, loveliness, prettiness

rel allure, appeal, attraction, glamour (*also* glamor); charm, elegance, exquisiteness, flawlessness, gloriousness, perfection, radiance, resplendence; desirability, desirableness

near ant dreadfulness, foulness, ghastliness, grotesqueness, hideousness, loathsomeness, nastiness, offensiveness, repellency, repulsiveness, unattractiveness; blemish, flaw, imperfection

ant homeliness, plainness, ugliness, unsightliness

2 a lovely woman ⟨she was quite a *beauty* in her younger days⟩

syn eyeful, goddess, knockout, stunner

rel belle, charmer, honey

near ant hag, horror, witch

3 something very good of its kind — see JIM-DANDY

because *conj* for the reason that — see SINCE

because of *prep* as the result of ⟨I was late for school *because of* the snowstorm, which made driving very hazardous⟩

syn due to, owing to, through, with

beckon *vb* to direct or notify by a movement or gesture — see MOTION

becloud *vb* **1** to make (something) unclear to the understanding — see CONFUSE 2
2 to make dark, dim, or indistinct — see CLOUD 1

beclouded *adj* **1** covered over by clouds — see OVERCAST
2 filled with or dimmed by fine particles (as of dust or water) in suspension — see HAZY 1

become *vb* to eventually have as a state or quality ⟨many people *became* sick with the flu⟩ ⟨with autumn the days *become* crisper and breezier⟩
syn come, get, go, grow, run, turn, wax
rel alter, change, metamorphose, modify, mutate, transfigure, transform, transmute
near ant abide, be, continue, linger, remain, stay

becoming *adj* meeting the requirements of a purpose or situation — see FIT 1

bed *n* **1** a place set aside for sleeping ⟨the sofa in the living room will be your *bed* for the night⟩
syn bunk, pad, sack
rel bedstead, mattress, pallet; cot, couch, daybed, feather bed, four-poster, hammock, sofa, sofa bed, studio couch, trundle bed, water bed; bassinet, cradle, crib
2 the surface upon which a body of water lies — see BOTTOM 2

bed *vb* to go to one's bed in order to sleep ⟨the campers all *bedded* down for the night around 9 pm⟩
syn retire, turn in
rel bunk, perch, roost, settle; doze, drop (off), nap, nod, sleep, slumber, snooze; couch, lie (down), recline
near ant arouse, awake, awaken, rouse, wake, waken; bestir, stir, wake; reawake, reawaken; shift, stir
ant arise, get up, rise, uprise

bedaub *vb* to rub an oily or sticky substance over — see SMEAR 1

bedazzle *vb* to overpower with light — see DAZZLE

bedazzling *adj* giving off or reflecting much light — see BRIGHT 1

bedeck *vb* to make more attractive by adding something that is beautiful or becoming — see DECORATE

bedevil *vb* to cause persistent suffering to — see AFFLICT

bedevilment *n* the act of making unwelcome intrusions upon another — see ANNOYANCE 1

bedim *vb* to make dark, dim, or indistinct — see CLOUD 1

bedizen *vb* to make more attractive by adding something that is beautiful or becoming — see DECORATE

bedizened *adj* elaborately and often excessively decorated — see ORNATE

bedlam *n* a place of uproar or confusion — see MADHOUSE 2

bedrock *n* an immaterial thing upon which something else rests — see BASE 1

bedspread *n* a decorative cloth used as a top covering for a bed — see COUNTERPANE

beef *n* an expression of dissatisfaction, pain, or resentment — see COMPLAINT 1

beef *vb* to express dissatisfaction, pain, or resentment usually tiresomely — see COMPLAIN

beef (up) *vb* **1** to increase the ability of (as a muscle) to exert physical force — see STRENGTHEN 1
2 to make markedly greater in measure or degree — see INTENSIFY

beefy *adj* strongly and heavily built — see ¹HUSKY

beetle *vb* to extend outward beyond a usual point — see BULGE

befall *vb* to take place — see HAPPEN

befit *vb* to be fitting or proper — see DO 1

befitting *adj* meeting the requirements of a purpose or situation — see FIT 1

befog *vb* **1** to make (something) unclear to the understanding — see CONFUSE 2
2 to make dark, dim, or indistinct — see CLOUD 1
3 to throw into a state of mental uncertainty — see CONFUSE 1

befogged *adj* filled with or dimmed by fine particles (as of dust or water) in suspension — see HAZY 1

before *adv* so as to precede something in order of time — see AHEAD 1

before *prep* **1** earlier than ⟨since I'm a faster runner, I got there *before* him⟩
syn afore [*chiefly dialect*], ahead of, ere, of, previous to, prior to, to
rel till, until, up to
phrases in advance of
near ant next, next to, since
ant after, following
2 preceding in space ⟨the children always insisted on running *before* their parents⟩
syn afore [*chiefly dialect*], ahead of
rel against
phrases in advance of, in front of
ant after, following

beforehand *adv* **1** before the usual or expected time — see EARLY
2 so as to precede something in order of time — see AHEAD 1

befoul *vb* **1** to make dirty — see DIRTY
2 to make unfit for use by the addition of something harmful or undesirable — see CONTAMINATE

befuddle *vb* to throw into a state of mental uncertainty — see CONFUSE 1

befuddled *adj* suffering from mental confusion — see DIZZY 2

befuddlement *n* a state of mental uncertainty — see CONFUSION 1

beg *vb* to make a request to (someone) in an earnest or urgent manner ⟨she *begged* her mother to let her go on the Girl Scout camporee⟩
syn appeal (to), beseech, conjure, entreat, implore, importune, petition, plead (to), pray, solicit, supplicate

---

rel mooch, sponge; ask, desire, invoke, request, sue; claim, coerce, command, compel, demand, force, insist, require

phrases call on (*or* call upon)

near ant hint, imply, intimate, suggest; appease, conciliate, gratify, mollify, oblige, pacify, placate, please, satisfy; comfort, console, content, quiet

beget *vb* to become the father of — see FATHER

begetter *n* a person who establishes a whole new field of endeavor — see FATHER 2

beggar *n* a person who lives by public begging 〈the poor *beggars* that are such a common sight in underdeveloped countries〉

syn mendicant, panhandler

rel bum, drifter, hobo, tramp, vagabond, vagrant; pauper; hanger-on, leech, moocher, parasite, sponge, sponger; dependent; deadbeat, derelict, idler, ne'er-do-well

beggared *adj* lacking money or material possessions — see POOR 1

beggary *n* the state of lacking sufficient money or material possessions — see POVERTY 1

begin *vb* 1 to take the first step in (a process or course of action) 〈she *began* walking to school〉

syn commence, embark (on *or* upon), enter (into *or* upon), get off, kick off, launch, open, start, strike (into)

rel create, generate, inaugurate, initiate, innovate, invent, originate; adopt, embrace, take on, take up; establish, father, found, institute, organize, pioneer, set up, spawn

phrases get to, set about

near ant cease, desist, discontinue, halt, lay off, quit, stop; close, complete; abandon, forsake, leave; abolish, demolish, destroy, exterminate, extinguish, phase out

ant conclude, end, finish, terminate

2 to come into existence 〈the storm *began* late in the day and lasted all night〉

syn arise, commence, dawn, form, materialize, originate, set in, spring, start

rel be, breathe, exist, live, subsist; appear, arrive, emerge; continue, endure, last, persist, survive

near ant conclude, desist, discontinue, finish, halt, quit, terminate; disappear, dissolve, evaporate, vanish; depart, die, expire, pass away, perish

ant cease, end, stop

beginner *n* a person who is just starting out in a field of activity 〈although he is only a *beginner* at swimming, he is making excellent progress〉

syn colt, fledgling, freshman, greenhorn, neophyte, newcomer, novice, recruit, rookie, tenderfoot, tyro

rel apprentice, cub; boot, novitiate; amateur, dilettante; learner, student, trainee; candidate, entrant, probationer

near ant expert, master, pro, professional

ant old hand, old-timer, vet, veteran

beginning *n* the point at which something begins 〈the actual *beginning* of the universe is still under debate, with some scientists believing in the big bang theory〉

syn alpha, birth, commencement, dawn, genesis, inception, incipiency, launch, morning, onset, outset, start, threshold

rel creation, inauguration, initiation, institution, origination; cradle, fountainhead, origin, root, source, spring, well, wellspring; dawning, opening; appearance, arrival, emergence; infancy

near ant cessation, closing, closure, completion, finale, finish, period, stop, termination, windup

ant close, conclusion, end, ending

begone *vb* to leave a place often for another — see GO 2

begrime *vb* to make dirty — see DIRTY

beguile *vb* 1 to attract or delight as if by magic — see CHARM 1

2 to cause to believe what is untrue — see DECEIVE

3 to lead away from a usual or proper course by offering some pleasure or advantage — see LURE

beguiling *adj* 1 clever at attaining one's ends by indirect and often deceptive means — see ARTFUL 1

2 tending or having power to deceive — see DECEPTIVE 1

behave *vb* to manage the actions of (oneself) in a particular way 〈if she *behaves* herself properly and sits quietly during church, she will get ice cream afterward〉

syn acquit, bear, comport, conduct, demean, deport, quit

rel check, collect, compose, constrain, contain, control, curb, handle, inhibit, quiet, repress, restrain; moderate, modulate, temper; act, impersonate, play

near ant act up, carry on, cut up, misbehave, misconduct

behavior *n* the way or manner in which one conducts oneself 〈he promised to be on his best *behavior* for the party〉

syn actions, bearing, comportment, conduct, demeanor, deportment

rel etiquette, form, manners, mores, proprieties; amenity, civility, courtesy, decorum, politeness; air, attitude, carriage, poise, pose, posture, presence; aspect, look, mien; formality, protocol, rules; custom, habit, pattern, practice (*also* practise), trick, wont; convention, fashion, form, mode, style; affectation, attribute, characteristic, mark, trait; distinctiveness, oddity, peculiarity, singularity, strangeness, uniqueness, weirdness

behead *vb* to cut off the head of — see DECAPITATE

behemoth *n* something that is unusually large and powerful — see GIANT

behest *n* a statement of what to do that must be obeyed by those concerned — see COMMAND 1

behind *adj* not arriving, occurring, or settled at the due, usual, or proper time — see LATE 1

behind *prep* **1** at, to, or toward the rear of ⟨she preferred to be *behind* the lead hikers, who were always too much in a rush to enjoy the scenery⟩
syn abaft, back of
near ant ahead of
ant before, in front of
2 subsequent to in time or order — see AFTER

behindhand *adj* not arriving, occurring, or settled at the due, usual, or proper time — see LATE 1

behold *vb* to make note of (something) through the use of one's eyes — see SEE 1

being *n* **1** a member of the human race — see HUMAN
2 one that has a real and independent existence — see ENTITY

belabor *vb* to criticize harshly and usually publicly — see ATTACK 2

belated *adj* not arriving, occurring, or settled at the due, usual, or proper time — see LATE 1

belatedness *n* the quality or state of being late — see LATENESS

belch *vb* to throw out or off (something from within) often violently — see ERUPT 1

beldam *or* **beldame** *n* a mean or ugly old woman — see CRONE

beleaguer *vb* to surround (as a fortified place) with armed forces for the purpose of capturing or preventing commerce and communication — see BESIEGE

belie *vb* **1** to give a false idea of ⟨his bright smile *belied* his actual mood, which was really one of great sadness⟩
syn misrepresent
rel contradict; camouflage, cloak, conceal, counterfeit, disguise, hide, mask, obscure; color, deceive, distort, falsify, garble, mislead, twist; dissemble, feign, pretend
near ant bare, demonstrate, disclose, discover, exhibit, expose, evince, reveal; flaunt, parade, show off
ant betray, represent
2 to prove to be false — see DISPROVE

belief *n* **1** mental conviction of the truth of some statement or the reality of some being or phenomenon ⟨a *belief* in unicorns led him to look for them every time he walked through the woods⟩
syn credence, credit, faith
rel axiom, law, precept, principle, tenet; assurance, certainty, certitude, conviction, positiveness, sureness; confidence, dependance, reliance, trust; hope; doctrine, dogma, philosophy; dogmatism, fanaticism, insistence
near ant distrust, mistrust, skepticism, suspicion, uncertainty
ant disbelief, discredit, doubt, unbelief
2 an idea that is believed to be true or valid without positive knowledge — see OPINION 1

believable *adj* worthy of being accepted as true or reasonable ⟨she had a *believable* story for why her homework was late, so she didn't receive any punishment⟩
syn credible, likely, plausible, probable
rel acceptable, conceivable, imaginable, possible, practical, reasonable; dependable, reliable, trustworthy
near ant absurd, doubtful, dubious, fantastic, flimsy, outlandish, preposterous, questionable, ridiculous; impossible, inconceivable, unimaginable, unthinkable; skeptical, suspect, suspicious, uncertain, unsure; hopeless, unworkable, useless
ant far-fetched, implausible, improbable, incredible, unbelievable, unlikely

believe *vb* **1** to regard as right or true ⟨the teacher *believed* the student's explanation that the assignment was late because she was sick, even though she didn't bring in a note from the doctor⟩
syn accept, credit, swallow, trust
rel account, accredit, understand; assume, presume, suppose; conclude, deduce, infer
phrases set store by (*or* on)
near ant distrust, doubt, mistrust, question, suspect; challenge, dispute
ant disbelieve, discredit, reject
2 to have as an opinion ⟨he *believed* that his favorite tennis player was the best in the world⟩
syn consider, deem, feel, figure, guess, hold, imagine, reckon [*chiefly dialect*], suppose, think
rel esteem, regard, view; accept, conceive, perceive; depend, rely, trust; assume, presume, presuppose; conclude, deduce, infer
near ant distrust, doubt, mistrust, question, suspect; disbelieve, discredit, reject

belittle *vb* to express scornfully one's low opinion of — see DECRY 1

belittlement *n* the act of making a person or a thing seem little or unimportant — see DEPRECIATION

belittling *adj* intended to make a person or thing seem of little importance or value — see DEROGATORY

bellicose *adj* feeling or displaying eagerness to fight — see BELLIGERENT

bellicosity *n* an inclination to fight or quarrel — see BELLIGERENCE

belligerence *n* an inclination to fight or quarrel ⟨among the Native American tribes of the Colonial period, the Iroquois were known for their *belligerence*⟩
syn aggression, aggressiveness, bellicosity, combativeness, contentiousness, disputatiousness, fight, militancy, pugnacity, scrappiness, truculence
rel antagonism, fierceness, hostility, unfriendliness; acidity, biliousness, crabbiness, crankiness, crossness, disagreeableness, fretfulness, grouchiness, grumpiness, huffiness, irascibility, irritability, irritableness, orneriness, peevishness, pettishness, petulance, querulousness, rudeness, surliness, testiness, waspishness

---

syn synonym(s)   *rel* related words
ant antonym(s)   *near ant* near antonym(s)

phrases chip on one's shoulder

near ant affability, amiability, amicability, benevolence, complaisance, cordiality, friendliness, geniality, graciousness, pleasantness, sociability; gentleness, kindliness, mildness

ant pacifism

belligerent *adj* feeling or displaying eagerness to fight ⟨the coach became quite *belligerent* and spit on an umpire after being thrown out of the game⟩

syn aggressive, argumentative, bellicose, combative, contentious, discordant, disputatious, gladiatorial, militant, pugnacious, quarrelsome, scrappy, truculent, warlike

rel antagonistic, fierce, hostile, hot-tempered; acidic, bearish, bilious, choleric, crabby, cranky, cross, disagreeable, dyspeptic, fretful, grouchy, grumpy, huffy, ill-humored, ill-natured, ill-tempered, irascible, irritable, ornery, peevish, pettish, petulant, querulous, rude, snappish, snappy, surly, testy, touchy, ugly, waspish; battling, fighting, warring

phrases on the warpath

near ant affable, amiable, amicable, benevolent, complaisant, conciliatory, cordial, easygoing, friendly, genial, good-natured, good-tempered, gracious, ingratiating, obliging, pleasant, sociable; calm, quiet, relaxed, serene, tranquil; benign, gentle, kindly, mild

ant nonbelligerent, pacific, peaceable, peaceful

bellow *vb* to make a long loud deep noise or cry — see ROAR

belly *n* the part of the body between the chest and the pelvis — see STOMACH

belly *vb* to extend outward beyond a usual point — see BULGE

bellyache *n* abdominal pain especially when focused in the digestive organs — see STOMACHACHE

bellyache *vb* to express dissatisfaction, pain, or resentment usually tiresomely — see COMPLAIN

belong *vb* 1 to have or be in a usual or proper place ⟨your shoes *belong* in the closet, not out on the floor where people will trip on them⟩

syn go

rel place, stay; fit (in)

2 to be the property of a person or group of persons ⟨those textbooks *belong* to the school system, and you have to give them back at the end of the year⟩

syn appertain, pertain

rel have, hold, own, possess

belongings *n pl* transportable items that one owns — see POSSESSION 2

beloved *adj* granted special treatment or attention — see DARLING 1

beloved *n* a person with whom one is in love — see SWEETHEART

below *adv* in or to a lower place ⟨he climbed *below* to fix the engine⟩

syn beneath, under, underneath

rel beside, near, nearby

near ant aloft, overhead

ant up

2 toward or in a lower position — see DOWN

below *prep* in a lower position than ⟨she sat *below* everyone else, on the floor⟩

syn beneath, under

rel underneath

ant above, over

¹**belt** *n* a hard strike with a part of the body or an instrument — see ¹BLOW

²**belt** *n* a strip of flexible material (as leather) worn around the waist ⟨he loves his fancily decorated *belt*, but only gets to wear it on special occasions⟩

syn cincture, cummerbund, girdle, sash

rel band, waistband; circle, loop, ribbon, ring; baldric, bandolier (*or* bandoleer)

2 a broad geographical area — see REGION 2

belt *vb* 1 to deliver a blow to (someone or something) usually in a strong vigorous manner — see HIT 1

2 to encircle or bind with or as if with a belt — see GIRD 1

3 to strike repeatedly — see BEAT 1

bemoan *vb* 1 to feel or express sorrow for — see LAMENT 1

2 to feel sorry or dissatisfied about — see REGRET

bemoaning *adj* expressing or suggesting mourning — see MOURNFUL 1

bemuse *vb* to throw into a state of mental uncertainty — see CONFUSE 1

bench *n* a public official having authority to decide questions of law — see JUDGE 1

benchmark *n* something set up as an example against which others of the same type are compared — see STANDARD 1

bend *n* 1 something that curves or is curved ⟨it's hard to see around that *bend* in the road, so be careful⟩

syn angle, arc, arch, bow, crook, curvature, curve, turn, wind

rel kink, warp; circle, ring, ringlet, round; coil, curl, curlicue (*also* curlycue), flexure, fold, loop, spiral, swirl, twist; decline, inclination, incline, slope; corner, turnoff

ant straight line

2 the act of positioning or an instance of being positioned at an angle — see TILT

bend *vb* 1 to cause to turn away from a straight line ⟨she *bent* the knife when she got it stuck in the drawer⟩

syn arch, bow, crook, curve, hook, swerve

rel arc, bow, round; deflect, divert; entwine, kink, swirl, turn, twine, twist, veer, warp; coil, curl, loop, spiral; dent, dimple; meander, weave, wind; decline, incline, slope

ant straighten, unbend, uncurl

2 to occupy (oneself) diligently or with close attention — see APPLY 2

3 to point or turn (something) toward a target or goal — see AIM 1

4 to turn away from a straight line or course — see CURVE 1

bending *adj* marked by a long series of irregular curves — see CROOKED 1

beneath *adv* in or to a lower place — see BELOW 1

beneath *prep* in a lower position than — see BELOW

benediction *n* a prayer calling for divine care, protection, or favor — see BLESSING 1

benefaction *n* a gift of money or its equivalent to a charity, humanitarian cause, or public institution — see CONTRIBUTION

benefactor *n* one that helps another with gifts or money ⟨an anonymous *benefactor* gave our school a dozen new computers⟩
syn donator, donor, patron
rel almsgiver, philanthropist; contributor, giver; subscriber, supporter, helper

beneficence *n* a gift of money or its equivalent to a charity, humanitarian cause, or public institution — see CONTRIBUTION

beneficent *adj* **1** having or marked by sympathy and consideration for others — see HUMANE 1
2 having or showing a concern for the welfare of others — see CHARITABLE 1

beneficial *adj* conferring benefits; promoting or contributing to personal or social well-being ⟨tutoring can often be as *beneficial* and rewarding for the tutor as for the student receiving the help⟩
syn advantageous, favorable, helpful, profitable, salutary
rel gratifying, rewarding, satisfying; promising, propitious; advisable, desirable, healthful, healthy, salubrious, wholesome
near ant bad, damaging, deleterious, harmful, injurious, unfavorable, unhelpful
ant disadvantageous, unfavorable, unhelpful

benefit *n* **1** a thing that helps — see HELP 1
2 something that provides happiness or does good for a person or thing — see BLESSING 2

benefit *vb* to provide with something useful or desirable ⟨his summer job *benefited* him in two ways: by giving him spending money and by offering some work experience⟩
syn avail, profit, serve
rel succeed, work (for); aid, assist, help, improve; content, delight, gladden, gratify, please, satisfy; bless
near ant hinder, impede; damage, harm, hurt, impair, injure; afflict, distress, upset

benevolence *n* kindly concern, interest, or support — see GOODWILL 1

benevolent *adj* **1** having or marked by sympathy and consideration for others — see HUMANE 1
2 having or showing a concern for the welfare of others — see CHARITABLE 1

benighted *adj* lacking in education or the knowledge gained from books — see IGNORANT 1

benign *adj* not harsh or stern especially in manner, nature, or effect — see GENTLE 1

benignant *adj* having or marked by sympathy and consideration for others — see HUMANE 1

benison *n* a prayer calling for divine care, protection, or favor — see BLESSING 1

bent *n* a habitual attraction to some activity or thing — see INCLINATION 1

bent (on *or* upon) *adj* fully committed to achieving a goal — see DETERMINED

benumb *vb* to reduce or weaken in strength or feeling — see DULL 1

benumbed *adj* lacking in sensation or feeling — see NUMB

bequeath *vb* to give by means of a will — see LEAVE 2

bequest *n* something that is or may be inherited — see INHERITANCE

berate *vb* to criticize (someone) severely or angrily especially for personal failings — see SCOLD

bereaved *adj* suffering the death of a loved one ⟨the *bereaved* parents cried often in the first year⟩
syn bereft
rel orphaned, widowed; distressed, grieving, melancholy, miserable, mournful, mourning, sad, sorrowing, suffering, unhappy, upset; bemoaning, crying, lamenting, wailing, weeping

bereft *adj* **1** suffering the death of a loved one — see BEREAVED
2 utterly lacking in something needed, wanted, or expected — see DEVOID 1

berserk *adv* in a confused and reckless manner — see HELTER-SKELTER 1

berth *n* an assignment at which one regularly works for pay — see JOB 1

beseech *vb* to make a request to (someone) in an earnest or urgent manner — see BEG

beseeching *adj* asking humbly — see SUPPLIANT

beset *vb* to take sudden, violent action against — see ATTACK 1

beside *prep* **1** in addition to — see BESIDES 1
2 not including — see EXCEPT

besides *adv* in addition to what has been said — see MORE 1

besides *prep* **1** in addition to ⟨*besides* me, there are five people working on this project⟩
syn as well as, beside, over and above
rel plus; including
phrases along with, together with
near ant except (*also* excepting); less, minus
2 not including — see EXCEPT

besiege *vb* to surround (as a fortified place) with armed forces for the purpose of capturing or preventing commerce and communication ⟨the army *besieged* the fort for six months before it finally surrendered⟩
syn beleaguer, blockade, invest
rel barricade, block, cut off, dam, encircle; assail, assault, attack, beset; confine, insulate, isolate, quarantine
phrases lay siege to

---

syn synonym(s)   *rel* related words
ant antonym(s)   *near ant* near antonym(s)

near ant emancipate, free, liberate, release, rescue

besmear *vb* to rub an oily or sticky substance over — see SMEAR 1

besmirch *vb* to make dirty — see DIRTY

besmirched *adj* not clean — see DIRTY 1

bespatter *vb* to wet or soil by striking with something liquid or mushy — see SPLASH 2

bespeak *vb* 1 to arrange to have something (as a hotel room) held for one's future use — see RESERVE 1

2 to make known (something abstract) through outward signs — see SHOW 2

best *n* 1 dressy clothing — see FINERY

2 individuals carefully selected as being the best of a class — see ELITE

best *vb* to achieve a victory over — see BEAT 2

bestow *vb* to make a present of — see GIVE 1

bestowal *n* something given to someone without expectation of a return — see GIFT 1

bestrew *vb* to cover by or as if by scattering something over or on — see SCATTER 2

bet *n* the money or thing risked on the outcome of an uncertain event ⟨she offered the *bet* of a free lunch if her team won the World Series⟩
syn stake, wager
rel collateral; jackpot, kitty, pot

bet *vb* to risk (something) on the outcome of an uncertain event ⟨he *bet* a month's allowance on the World Series⟩
syn gamble, go, lay, stake, wager
rel bid, offer; adventure, chance, hazard, speculate, venture; endanger, imperil, jeopardize

bête noire *n* 1 something or someone that causes fear or dread especially without reason — see BOGEY 1

2 something or someone that is hated — see HATE 2

betide *vb* to take place — see HAPPEN

betray *vb* 1 to be unfaithful or disloyal to ⟨childhood friends of movie stars often *betray* them by telling their secrets to the supermarket tabloids⟩
syn cross, double-cross, sell (out)
rel give away; inform (on), rat (on), snitch (on), split (on) [*British*], tell (on)
phrases go back on
near ant defend, guard, protect, safeguard, save, shield

2 to make known (something abstract) through outward signs — see SHOW 2

betrayal *n* the act or fact of violating the trust or confidence of another ⟨the terrible *betrayal* of having her best friend reveal her confidences to others⟩
syn disloyalty, double cross, faithlessness, falseness, falsity, infidelity, perfidy, sellout, treachery, treason, unfaithfulness
rel abandonment, desertion; deceit, deception, double-dealing, duplicity, guile; fraud, informing, lying, snitching, talebearing, trickery

near ant dependability, reliability, trustworthiness; allegiance, devotion, faithfulness, fealty, fidelity, loyalty, staunchness, steadfastness; defense, protection, safeguard, shield

betrayer *n* 1 a person who provides secret information about another's wrongdoing — see INFORMER

2 one who betrays a trust or an allegiance — see TRAITOR

betrothal *n* the act or state of being engaged to be married — see ENGAGEMENT 1

betrothed *adj* pledged in marriage — see ENGAGED

betrothed *n* the person to whom one is engaged to be married ⟨he gazed lovingly at his *betrothed* throughout dinner⟩
syn fiancé, fiancée, intended
rel admirer, beau, beloved, boyfriend, darling, dear, favorite, fellow, flame, girlfriend, honey, love, lover, steady, swain, sweet, sweetheart, valentine; bride, groom

better *adv* to a greater or higher extent — see MORE 2

better *n* 1 one who is above another in rank, station, or office — see SUPERIOR

2 the more favorable condition or position in a competition — see ADVANTAGE 1

better *vb* 1 to be greater, better, or stronger than — see SURPASS 1

2 to make better — see IMPROVE

bettor *or* **better** *n* one that bets (as on the outcome of a contest or sports event) ⟨*bettors* on the horse race have to place their bets at least 20 minutes before the start of the race⟩
syn gambler, wagerer
rel dicer; speculator

beverage *n* a liquid suitable for drinking — see DRINK 1

bewail *vb* to feel or express sorrow for — see LAMENT 1

bewailing *adj* expressing or suggesting mourning — see MOURNFUL 1

beware (of) *vb* to be cautious of or on guard against ⟨*beware* of that parrot because it bites⟩
syn guard (against), mind, watch out (for)
rel attend, heed, mark, note, notice; behold, discern, observe, perceive, see, watch
phrases be on the lookout for, look out for
near ant discount, disregard, ignore, miss, overlook

bewilder *vb* to throw into a state of mental uncertainty — see CONFUSE 1

bewildered *adj* suffering from mental confusion — see DIZZY 2

bewilderment *n* a state of mental uncertainty — see CONFUSION 1

bewitch *vb* 1 to cast a spell on ⟨a wicked fairy *bewitched* Sleeping Beauty so that she would sleep for a hundred years⟩
syn charm, enchant, hex, spell

rel curse, jinx, possess; attract, beguile, captivate, fascinate, mesmerize, spellbind; entice, lure, seduce, tempt

near ant bless

2 to attract or delight as if by magic — see CHARM 1

bewitched *adj* being or appearing to be under a magic spell — see ENCHANTED

bewitching *adj* having an often mysterious or magical power to attract — see FASCINATING 1

bewitchment *n* **1** a spoken word or set of words believed to have magic power — see SPELL 1

2 the power to control natural forces through supernatural means — see MAGIC 1

beyond *adv* at or to a greater distance or more advanced point — see FARTHER

beyond *prep* **1** on or to the farther side of ⟨the arrow flew *beyond* the fence and in the woods⟩

syn over, past

rel outside

near ant inside

2 out of the reach or sphere of ⟨although the school can keep you from screaming during school hours, making someone be quiet after school is *beyond* their authority⟩

syn outside, outside of, without

rel except (*also* excepting)

near ant inside

ant within

bias *n* an attitude that always favors one way of feeling or acting especially without considering any other possibilities ⟨he had a powerful *bias* towards doing all math problems by the same method, regardless of the problem⟩

syn favor, one-sidedness, partiality, partisanship, prejudice

rel favoritism, nepotism; bent, inclination, leaning, penchant, predilection, predisposition, proclivity, propensity, tendency; preconception, prejudgment

near ant calm, detachment, dispassion, indifference; aversion, dislike, distaste

ant impartiality, neutrality, objectivity, open-mindedness

bias *vb* to cause to have often negative opinions formed without sufficient knowledge — see PREJUDICE

biased *adj* inclined to favor one side over another — see PARTIAL 1

Bible *n* a book made up of the writings accepted by Christians as coming from God ⟨she received a lovely *Bible* as a First Communion gift⟩

syn Book, Good Book, Holy Writ, Scripture

bicker *n* an often noisy or angry expression of differing opinions — see ARGUMENT 1

bicker *vb* to express different opinions about something often angrily — see ARGUE 2

---

syn synonym(s)   *rel* related words

ant antonym(s)   *near ant* near antonym(s)

bid *vb* to issue orders to (someone) by right of authority — see COMMAND 1

bide *vb* to remain in place in readiness or expectation of something — see WAIT

big *adj* **1** having great meaning or lasting effect — see IMPORTANT 1

2 of a size greater than average of its kind — see LARGE

bight *n* a part of a body of water that extends beyond the general shoreline — see GULF 1

bigness *n* the quality or state of being large in size — see LARGENESS

bigoted *adj* unwilling to grant other people social rights or to accept other viewpoints — see INTOLERANT 2

bilious *adj* having or showing a habitually bad temper — see ILL-TEMPERED

biliousness *n* readiness to show annoyance or impatience — see PETULANCE

¹**bill** *n* **1** a record of goods sold or services performed together with the costs due ⟨luckily, the amount due on our electric *bill* wasn't too high this month, because we finally convinced everyone to stop wasting electricity⟩

syn account, check, invoice, statement, tab

rel receipt, reckoning; document, record; charge, cost, expense, fee, price, rate, toll; score, tally

2 a piece of printed paper used as money ⟨the United States twenty-dollar *bill* has a picture of Andrew Jackson on the front⟩

syn bank note, greenback, note

rel paper money, scrip; buck, dollar; cash, chips, currency, dough, legal tender, lucre, money, pelf; check, draft, money order

3 a sheet bearing an announcement for posting in a public place — see POSTER

4 the amount owed at a bar or restaurant or the slip of paper stating the amount — see CHECK 1

²**bill** *n* **1** the jaws of a bird together with their hornlike covering — see BEAK

2 the projecting front part of a hat or cap — see VISOR

¹**billet** *n* a straight piece (as of wood or metal) that is longer than it is wide — see BAR 1

²**billet** *n* an assignment at which one regularly works for pay — see JOB 1

billet *vb* to provide with living quarters or shelter — see HOUSE 1

bill of fare *n* a list of foods served at or available for a meal — see MENU 1

billow *n* a moving ridge on the surface of water — see WAVE

billow *vb* to extend outward beyond a usual point — see BULGE

billy *n* a heavy rigid stick used as a weapon or for punishment — see CLUB 1

binary *adj* consisting of two members or parts that are usually joined — see DOUBLE 1

bind *vb* **1** to confine or restrain with or as if with chains ⟨prisons tend to *bind* convicted criminals for transport⟩ ⟨Angie feels *bound* to her boyfriend by love and loyalty⟩

syn chain, enchain, fetter, handcuff, manacle, shackle, trammel

rel lash, pinion, secure, tie, truss; attach, fasten, join, link; confine, constrain, curb, hamper, hinder, limit, restrict; entangle, tangle

near ant emancipate, free, liberate, loose, release, rescue; undo, unfasten, untangle, untie; detach, disengage

ant unbind, unfetter

2 to cover with a bandage — see BANDAGE

3 to gather into a tight mass by means of a line or cord — see TIE 1

binge *n* a time or instance of carefree fun — see FLING 1

biography *n* a history of a person's life ⟨an unauthorized *biography* of the actor made him very unhappy⟩

syn life, memoir

rel autobiography; chronicle, history, past, story; obituary; character sketch

bipartite *adj* consisting of two members or parts that are usually joined — see DOUBLE 1

birch *vb* to strike repeatedly with something long and thin or flexible — see WHIP 1

bird *n* a member of the human race — see HUMAN

birdman *n* one who flies or is qualified to fly an aircraft or spacecraft — see PILOT

bird's–eye *adj* relating to the main elements and not to specific details — see GENERAL 2

birth *n* **1** the act or instance of being born ⟨biology class will be showing a movie of the *birth* of kittens⟩

syn nativity

rel creation, genesis, origination, rise; bearing, childbearing, labor, parturition; begetting, breeding, fathering, generation, mothering, reproduction, siring, spawning; fatherhood, maternity, motherhood, parenthood, paternity

near ant abortion, miscarriage

2 the line of ancestors from whom a person is descended — see ANCESTRY

3 the point at which something begins — see BEGINNING

birthright *n* **1** something that is or may be inherited — see INHERITANCE

2 something to which one has a just claim — see RIGHT 1

bisect *vb* to divide by passing through or across — see INTERSECT

bit *n* **1** a very small piece ⟨she left only a *bit* of the broccoli on her plate, so she was allowed to have dessert⟩

syn atom, crumb, fleck, flyspeck, grain, granule, molecule, morsel, mote, nubbin, particle, patch, scrap, scruple, snippet, speck, tittle

rel ace, dab, glimmer, hint, hoot, iota, jot, lick, little, mite, modicum, ounce, peanuts, pinch, ray, shade, shred, smidgen (*also* smidgeon *or* smidgin), spot, strain, streak, suspicion, taste, touch, trace,

whisper, whit; dash, driblet, drop; fragment, part, portion, section; bite, mouthful, nibble; handful, scattering, smattering, sprinkling; dose, shot; damn, darn; chip, flake, shard, shiver, sliver, splinter; clipping, paring, shaving; smithereens

near ant chunk, gob, lump, hunk, slab; abundance, barrel, bucket, bushel, deal, heaps, loads, mass, mountain, much, peck, pile, plenty, pot, profusion, quantity, raft, scads, stack, volume, wad, wealth

2 a broken or irregular part of something that often remains incomplete — see FRAGMENT

3 a very small amount — see PARTICLE 1

4 an indefinite but usually short period of time — see WHILE 1

bite *n* **1** a harsh or sharp quality — see EDGE 1

2 a small piece or quantity of food — see MORSEL 1

3 an uncomfortable degree of coolness — see CHILL

bite (at) *vb* to consume or wear away gradually — see EAT 2

bite (on) *vb* to crush or grind with the teeth ⟨she likes to *bite on* her pencils when she thinks hard⟩

syn champ, chew, chomp (on), crunch (on), gnaw (on), masticate, nibble

rel lap, lick, munch; consume, ingest, eat, swallow; bolt, devour, gobble (up *or* down), gorge, gulp, scarf, scoff, snack, wolf; peck (at), pick (at)

biting *adj* **1** causing intense discomfort to one's skin — see CUTTING 1

2 causing intense mental or physical distress — see SHARP 2

3 marked by the use of wit that is intended to cause hurt feelings — see SARCASTIC

bitter *adj* **1** having or showing deep-seated resentment ⟨a *bitter* attitude about always having to work on Saturday⟩ ⟨she's still *bitter* about the way her boyfriend broke up with her⟩

syn acrid, acrimonious, embittered, hard, rancorous, resentful, sore

rel disaffected, discontented, disgruntled, malcontent; contemptuous, cynical, disdainful, scornful; angry, cruel, harsh, irritated, mad, rough, savage, vicious; acid, caustic, cutting, mordant, sarcastic, trenchant

near ant caring, forgiving, gentle, kind, loving, sweet, sympathetic, tender, warm, warmhearted

2 hard to accept or bear especially emotionally ⟨discovering that he had been cut from the team was a *bitter* disappointment⟩

syn afflicting, agonizing, cruel, excruciating, galling, grievous, harrowing, harsh, heartrending, hurtful, painful, tormenting, tortuous

rel insufferable, insupportable, intolerable, unacceptable, unbearable, unendurable, unsupportable; appalling, awful, bad, dire, dreadful, ghastly, horrible, miserable, nasty, rotten, terrible, vile,

wretched; acute, extreme, intense, piercing
near ant bearable, endurable, supportable, sustainable, tolerable; livable (*also* liveable), sufferable, survivable; acceptable, allowable, reasonable
ant gratifying, pleasing, sweet
3 causing intense discomfort to one's skin — see CUTTING 1
4 difficult to endure — see HARSH 1
5 having a low or subnormal temperature — see COLD 1
6 uncomfortably cool — see CHILLY 1
bitterly *adv* with feelings of bitterness or grief — see HARD 2
bitterness *n* **1** a deep-seated ill will — see ENMITY
2 a harsh or sharp quality — see EDGE 1
3 an uncomfortable degree of coolness — see CHILL
4 biting sharpness of feeling or expression — see ACRIMONY 1
bitty *adj* very small in size — see TINY
bivouac *n* a place where a group of people live for a short time in tents or cabins — see CAMP 1
bivouac *vb* to live in a camp or the outdoors — see CAMP
bizarre *adj* **1** conceived or made without regard for reason or reality — see FANTASTIC 1
2 different from the ordinary in a way that causes curiosity or suspicion — see ODD 2
blab *vb* **1** to engage in casual or rambling conversation — see CHAT
2 to relate sometimes questionable or secret information of a personal nature — see GOSSIP
blabber *n* **1** a person who talks constantly — see CHATTERBOX
2 unintelligible or meaningless talk — see GIBBERISH
black *adj* **1** having the color of soot or coal ⟨a little *black* dress blends into the night very well⟩
syn ebony, pitch-black, pitch-dark, pitchy, raven, sable
rel dark, dusky, inky; blackish, brunet (*or* brunette)
near ant bright, brilliant, light, pale
ant white
2 causing or marked by an atmosphere lacking in cheer — see GLOOMY 1
3 not conforming to a high moral standard; morally unacceptable — see BAD 2
black art *n* the power to control natural forces through supernatural means — see MAGIC 1
blackball *vb* to reject by or as if by a vote — see NEGATIVE 1
blacken *vb* **1** to make dirty — see DIRTY
2 to make untrue and harmful statements about — see SLANDER
3 to make dark, dim, or indistinct — see CLOUD 1
blackened *adj* not clean — see DIRTY 1

blackening *n* the making of false statements that damage another's reputation — see SLANDER
black magic *n* the power to control natural forces through supernatural means — see MAGIC 1
blackmailer *n* a person who gets money from another by using force or threats — see RACKETEER
blackness *n* a time or place of little or no light — see DARK 1
blackout *n* a temporary or permanent state of unconsciousness — see FAINT
black out *vb* to lose consciousness — see FAINT
blade *n* **1** a hand weapon with a length of metal sharpened on one or both sides and usually tapered to a sharp point — see SWORD
2 an instrument with a sharp edge for cutting — see KNIFE
blamable *adj* **1** deserving reproach or blame — see BLAMEWORTHY
2 responsible for a wrong — see GUILTY 1
blame *n* **1** responsibility for wrongdoing or failure ⟨willingly accepted the *blame* for not seeing that the kitchen was properly cleaned⟩
syn culpability, fault, guilt, rap
rel regret, remorse, self-reproach, shame; accountability, liability, complicity; blameworthiness, reprehensibleness, sinfulness; censure, condemnation, denunciation
near ant acclaim, plaudits, praise; achievement, success
ant blamelessness, faultlessness, guiltlessness, innocence
2 the state of being held as the cause of something that needs to be set right — see RESPONSIBILITY 1
blame *vb* to express one's unfavorable opinion of the worth or quality of — see CRITICIZE
blameless *adj* free from guilt or blame — see INNOCENT 1
blamelessness *n* the quality or state of being free from guilt or blame — see INNOCENCE 1
blameworthy *adj* deserving reproach or blame ⟨copying another student's work was certainly a *blameworthy* act⟩
syn blamable, censurable, culpable, reprehensible, reproachable
rel bad, guilty, sinful, wicked; foolish, irresponsible, reckless; chargeable, impeachable, indictable, punishable; criminal, illegal, illicit, unlawful; illegitimate, improper, wrongful
phrases at fault
near ant flawless, perfect, pure; guiltless, innocent
ant blameless, faultless, impeccable, irreproachable
blanch *vb* to make white or whiter by removing color — see WHITEN
blanched *adj* lacking a healthy skin color — see PALE 2
bland *adj* not harsh or stern especially in manner, nature, or effect — see GENTLE 1

---

blandish *vb* to get (someone) to do something by gentle urging, special attention, or flattery — see COAX

blank *adj* **1** not expressing any emotion ⟨the teacher knew no one was paying attention when she looked out and saw all those *blank* faces⟩

syn deadpan, expressionless, impassive, inexpressive, stolid, vacant

rel dull, empty, vacuous, vapid; enigmatic (*also* enigmatical), impenetrable, inscrutable, mysterious; dead, inactive, quiescent, sleepy, sluggish; indolent, languorous, lazy, lethargic, listless; motionless, static, still, wooden; reserved, restrained, reticent, taciturn; aloof, apathetic, detached, indifferent, phlegmatic; cold, cool

near ant active, alive, animated, bright, busy, dynamic, effervescent, energetic, expansive, exuberant, lively, vigorous, vital, vivacious; eloquent, revealing, revelatory, significant, vivid; emotional, melodramatic, theatrical, unreserved, unrestrained

ant demonstrative, expressive

2 lacking contents that could or should be present — see EMPTY 1

blank *n* **1** a piece of paper with information written or to be written on it — see FORM 2

2 empty space — see VACANCY 1

blanket *adj* belonging or relating to the whole — see GENERAL 1

blanket *vb* **1** to form a layer over — see COVER 2

2 to keep secret or shut off from view — see ¹HIDE 2

blankness *n* empty space — see VACANCY 1

blaring *adj* marked by a high volume of sound — see LOUD 1

blarney *n* excessive praise — see FLATTERY

blarney *vb* **1** to get (someone) to do something by gentle urging, special attention, or flattery — see COAX

2 to praise too much — see FLATTER 1

blaspheme *vb* to use offensive or indecent language — see SWEAR 1

blasphemous *adj* not showing proper reverence for the holy or sacred — see IRREVERENT

blasphemy *n* an act of great disrespect shown to God or to sacred ideas, people, or things ⟨in the 17th century the Quakers were persecuted for beliefs and practices that older churches regarded as *blasphemies*⟩

syn defilement, desecration, impiety, irreverence, sacrilege

rel cursing, profanity, swearing; affront, insult; violation; contamination, corruption, debasement, pollution; sin, trespass

near ant consecration, purification, sanctification; reverence, veneration

ant adoration, glorification, worship

blast *n* **1** a loud explosive sound — see CLAP 1

2 a sudden brief rush of wind — see GUST 1

3 the act or an instance of exploding — see EXPLOSION 1

blast *vb* **1** to cause to break open or into pieces by or as if by an explosive ⟨the highway engineers will have to *blast* that hill in order to put a road through it⟩

syn blow up, burst, demolish, explode, pop, shatter, smash

rel dynamite; annihilate, decimate, destroy; ruin, wreck; detonate, discharge; fragment, splinter

near ant collapse, implode

2 to cause (a projectile) to be driven forward with force — see SHOOT 1

3 to cause a weapon to release a missile with great force — see SHOOT 2

4 to criticize harshly and usually publicly — see ATTACK 2

blasting *adj* marked by a high volume of sound — see LOUD 1

blasting *n* a directed propelling of a missile from a firearm or artillery piece — see SHOT

blatant *adj* **1** engaging in or marked by loud and insistent cries especially of protest — see VOCIFEROUS

2 very noticeable especially for being incorrect or bad — see EGREGIOUS

blaze *n* the steady giving off of the form of radiation that makes vision possible — see LIGHT 1

blaze *vb* **1** to be on fire especially brightly — see BURN 1

2 to make known openly or publicly — see ANNOUNCE

3 to shine with a bright harsh light — see GLARE 1

blazing *adj* **1** being on fire — see ABLAZE 1

2 having or expressing great depth of feeling — see FERVENT

bleach *vb* to make white or whiter by removing color — see WHITEN

bleak *adj* **1** causing or marked by an atmosphere lacking in cheer — see GLOOMY 1

2 marked by wet and windy conditions — see FOUL 1

3 uncomfortably cool — see CHILLY 1

bleakness *n* an uncomfortable degree of coolness — see CHILL

bleary *adj* not seen or understood clearly — see FAINT 1

bleed *vb* **1** to feel deep sadness or mental pain — see GRIEVE

2 to flow forth slowly through small openings — see EXUDE

3 to remove (liquid) gradually or completely — see DRAIN 1

4 to rob by the use of trickery or threats — see FLEECE

bleed (for) *vb* to have sympathy for — see PITY

blemish *n* something that spoils the appearance or completeness of a thing ⟨a slight *blemish* on the mirror was the only break in the gleaming surface⟩

syn defect, deformity, disfigurement, fault, flaw, imperfection, mark, pock-mark, scar

rel abnormality, distortion, irregularity, malformation; bug, glitch, kink; blot, blotch, spot, stain; failing, vice, weakness

near ant adornment, decoration, embellishment, enhancement, ornament

blemish *vb* **1** to affect slightly with something morally bad or undesirable — see TAINT 1

2 to reduce the soundness, effectiveness, or perfection of — see DAMAGE 1

¹blench *vb* to draw back in fear, pain, or disgust — see FLINCH

²blench *vb* to make white or whiter by removing color — see WHITEN

blend *n* a distinct entity formed by the combining of two or more different things ⟨that fabric is a cotton and polyester *blend*, so it shouldn't shrink as much as pure cotton⟩

syn admixture, amalgam, amalgamation, combination, composite, compound, fusion, intermixture, mix, mixture

rel coalescence, concoction, incorporation, intermingling, mingling; assortment, hash, hodgepodge, hotchpotch, jumble, medley, mélange, mishmash, motley, patchwork, potpourri, variety; accumulation, aggregation, conglomeration

near ant component, constituent, element, ingredient

blend *vb* **1** to turn into a single mass that is more or less the same throughout ⟨she *blended* the ingredients for the brownies very thoroughly to eliminate lumps in the batter⟩

syn amalgamate, combine, commingle, fuse, incorporate, integrate, intermingle, intermix, merge, mingle, mix

rel fold, mix, stir, toss; coalesce, combine, compound, conjoin, join, link, unite

near ant cleave, disjoin, disunite, divide, divorce, part, rupture, sever, sunder; disperse, dissolve, scatter; detach, disengage, split

ant break down, break up, separate

2 to form a pleasing relationship — see HARMONIZE 1

bless *vb* **1** to make holy through prayers or ritual ⟨the priest *blessed* the water, thus allowing it to be used as holy water for various rites⟩

syn consecrate, hallow, sanctify

rel cleanse, purify; commit, dedicate, devote; reconsecrate

near ant defile, desecrate, profane; dirty, foul, pollute, soil, taint; curse, damn, execrate; cast out, condemn, damn, punish

2 to proclaim the glory of — see PRAISE 1

blessed *adj* **1** of, relating to, or being God — see HOLY 3

2 set apart or worthy of veneration by association with God — see HOLY 2

blessedness *n* **1** a feeling or state of well-being and contentment — see HAPPINESS 1

2 the quality or state of being spiritually pure or virtuous — see HOLINESS

blessing *n* **1** a prayer calling for divine care, protection, or favor ⟨that rabbi also always ends the service with a short *blessing*⟩

syn benediction, benison

rel Godspeed; appeal, entreaty, grace, invocation, orison, petition, plea, prayer, supplication; sanctification

ant anathema, curse, execration, imprecation, malediction

2 something that provides happiness or does good for a person or thing ⟨finding money on the sidewalk just when he needed to buy new sneakers was an unexpected *blessing*⟩

syn benefit, boon, felicity, godsend, good, manna, windfall

rel bonus, extra, lagniappe; advantage, aid, assistance, gift, help, relief, support; comfort, consolation, solace; delight, joy, pleasure

near ant hex, hoodoo, jinx; bother, irritant, nuisance, pest

ant affliction, bane, curse, evil, plague, scourge

3 an acceptance of something as satisfactory — see APPROVAL 1

4 the act of making something holy through religious ritual — see CONSECRATION

blind *adj* lacking the power of sight ⟨our old *blind* cat kept walking into walls and furniture⟩

syn eyeless, sightless, stone blind

rel unobservant, unobserving; blinded, purblind

near ant observant, observing

ant sighted

blind *vb* to overpower with light — see DAZZLE

blink *vb* **1** to shine with light at regular intervals ⟨she loves to sit in the dark and watch the lights on the Christmas tree *blink* in ever-changing patterns⟩

syn flash, twinkle, wink

rel flicker, glance, glimmer, glint, glisten, glister, glitter, scintillate, shimmer, sparkle; beam, gleam, irradiate, radiate

2 to rapidly open and close one's eyes — see WINK 1

bliss *n* a feeling or state of well-being and contentment — see HAPPINESS 1

blissful *adj* experiencing pleasure, satisfaction, or delight — see GLAD 1

blissfulness *n* a feeling or state of well-being and contentment — see HAPPINESS 1

blithe *adj* **1** having or showing a good mood or disposition — see CHEERFUL 1

2 indicative of or marked by high spirits or good humor — see MERRY

blithesome *adj* **1** having or showing a good mood or disposition — see CHEERFUL 1

---

syn synonym(s)   *rel* related words
ant antonym(s)   *near ant* near antonym(s)

2 indicative of or marked by high spirits or good humor — see MERRY

blitz *vb* to use bombs or artillery against — see BOMBARD

blitzkrieg *n* the act or action of setting upon with force or violence — see ATTACK 1

blob *n* **1** a small uneven mass — see LUMP 1

2 the quantity of fluid that falls naturally in one rounded mass — see DROP 1

bloc *n* **1** a group of people acting together within a larger group — see FACTION

2 an association of persons, parties, or states for mutual assistance and protection — see CONFEDERACY

block *n* **1** a number of things considered as a unit — see GROUP 1

2 something that makes movement or progress more difficult — see ENCUMBRANCE

block *vb* **1** to close up so that no empty spaces remain — see FILL 2

2 to prevent passage through — see CLOG 1

blockade *n* the cutting off of an area by military means to stop the flow of people or supplies ⟨it was the *blockade* of all the enemy's major ports that finally won the war⟩
syn investment, siege
rel encompassment, encirclement; confinement, insulation, isolation, quarantine, seclusion, segregation, sequestration; incarceration, internment
near ant emancipation, freedom, liberation, release, rescue

blockade *vb* to surround (as a fortified place) with armed forces for the purpose of capturing or preventing commerce and communication — see BESIEGE

blockbuster *n* **1** a person or thing that is successful — see HIT 1

2 something that is unusually large and powerful — see GIANT

blockhead *n* a stupid person — see IDIOT

bloke *n*, *chiefly British* an adult male human being — see MAN 1

blond *or* **blonde** *adj* of a pale yellow or yellowish brown color ⟨the little boy's *blond* hair darkened to brown as he grew older⟩
syn fair, flaxen, golden, sandy, straw, tawny
rel gold, light, white
near ant brunet (*or* brunette), dark, swarthy; black, ebony, raven
ant dark

blood *n* **1** a group of persons who come from the same ancestor — see FAMILY 1

2 the line of ancestors from whom a person is descended — see ANCESTRY

bloodline *n* the line of ancestors from whom a person is descended — see ANCESTRY

bloodstained *adj* containing, smeared, or stained with blood — see BLOODY 1

bloodthirsty *adj* eager for or marked by the shedding of blood, extreme violence,

or killing ⟨the Goths were a wild and *bloodthirsty* people⟩
syn bloody, homicidal, murdering, murderous, sanguinary, sanguine
rel barbaric, barbarous, cruel, heartless, inhumane, sadistic, savage, vicious, wanton; antagonistic, fierce, gladiatorial, hostile; aggressive, assertive, bellicose, belligerent, combative, contentious, discordant, pugnacious, quarrelsome, scrappy, truculent, violent; merciless, pitiless, ruthless; fell, ferocious, grim; despiteful, hateful, malevolent, malicious, malign, malignant, mean, nasty, spiteful; destructive, devastating, ruinous
near ant appeasing, conciliatory, disarming, dovish, mollifying, pacific, pacifying, peaceable, peaceful, peacemaking, placating, propitiatory; unaggressive, unassertive; benign, benignant, compassionate, good-hearted, humane, kind, kindhearted, sympathetic, tenderhearted; tender, warm, warmhearted; clement, lenient, merciful; affable, amiable, amicable, benevolent, gentle, kindly; submissive, surrendering, yielding

bloody *adj* **1** containing, smeared, or stained with blood ⟨after the fight, her shirt was all *bloody*⟩
syn bloodstained, gory
rel carmine, crimson, red, ruby, sanguine; bloodthirsty, sanguinary

2 eager for or marked by the shedding of blood, extreme violence, or killing — see BLOODTHIRSTY

bloom *n* **1** a state or time of great activity, thriving, or achievement ⟨a handsome young man in the full *bloom* of youth⟩
syn blossom, flower, flush, heyday, prime
rel acme, apex, climax, meridian, peak, pinnacle, summit, zenith; glory, grandeur, splendor; haleness, heartiness; energy, force, potency, power, vigor
near ant decline; bottom, nadir; feebleness, fragility, frailty, weakness; illness, infirmity, sickness; shriveling, wilting, withering

2 a rosy appearance of the cheeks ⟨after a snowball fight, she came inside with a *bloom*⟩
syn blush, flush
rel brightness, brilliance, glow; pinkness, rosiness

3 the usually showy plant part that produces seeds — see FLOWER 1

bloom *vb* **1** to produce flowers ⟨forsythias only *bloom* at the beginning of spring⟩
syn blossom, blow, burgeon, flower, unfold
rel leaf, leave; bud; open
near ant dry (up), fade, shrivel, wilt, wither; die, drop, expire, perish

2 to develop a rosy facial color (as from excitement or embarrassment) — see BLUSH

blooming *adj* having a healthy reddish skin tone — see RUDDY

blossom *n* **1** a state or time of great activity, thriving, or achievement — see BLOOM 1

2 the usually showy plant part that produces seeds — see FLOWER 1

blossom *vb* to produce flowers — see BLOOM

blot *n* a mark of guilt or disgrace — see STAIN 1

blotch *n* a small area that is different (as in color) from the main part — see SPOT 1

blotch *vb* **1** to mark with blotches especially of different colors or shades — see MOTTLE 1

2 to mark with small spots especially unevenly — see SPOT

blotched *adj* having blotches of two or more colors — see PIED

blot out *vb* **1** to destroy all traces of — see ANNIHILATE 1

2 to keep secret or shut off from view — see ¹HIDE 2

¹**blow** *n* a hard strike with a part of the body or an instrument ⟨he was dizzy for the rest of the day after the *blow* to his head⟩
syn bang, bat, beat, belt, bop, box, buffet, bust, chop, clap, clip, clout, crack, cuff, hit, hook, knock, lick, pound, punch, rap, slam, slap, slug, smack, smash, sock, spank, stroke, swat, swipe, thud, thump, thwack, wallop, whack
rel flick, jab, poke, roundhouse, stab; beating, battering, bludgeoning, clobbering, drubbing, hammering, lambasting, licking, pasting, pounding, pummeling, thrashing; flogging, walloping, whipping

²**blow** *n* a sudden brief rush of wind — see GUST 1

¹**blow** *vb* **1** to breathe hard, quickly, or with difficulty — see GASP

2 to use up carelessly — see WASTE 1

²**blow** *vb* to produce flowers — see BLOOM

blow (out) *vb* to let or force out of the lungs — see EXHALE 1

blowout *n* a social gathering — see PARTY 1

blowup *n* an outburst or display of excited anger — see TANTRUM

blow up *vb* **1** to become very angry ⟨she *blew up* at everybody after a very long and very bad day⟩
syn flare (up), flip
rel fulminate, rant, vituperate; bristle, burn, foam, fume, rage, seethe; burst, explode; enrage, incense, inflame, infuriate, madden; aggravate, anger, annoy, bother, bug, displease, distress, exasperate, gall, get, irk, irritate, nettle, peeve, pique, provoke, put out, rile, vex; agitate, disturb, perturb, upset
phrases fly into a rage, fly off the handle, forget oneself, lose one's temper
near ant appease, conciliate, mollify, pacify, placate; comfort, console, quiet, soothe
ant calm (down)

2 to break open or into pieces usually because of internal pressure — see EXPLODE 1

3 to cause to break open or into pieces by or as if by an explosive — see BLAST 1

blowy *adj* marked by strong wind or more wind than usual — see WINDY 1

blubber *vb* to shed tears often while making meaningless sounds as a sign of pain or distress — see CRY 1

bludgeon *n* a heavy rigid stick used as a weapon or for punishment — see CLUB 1

bludgeon *vb* **1** to deliver a blow to (someone or something) usually in a strong vigorous manner — see HIT 1

2 to strike repeatedly — see BEAT 1

blue *adj* feeling unhappiness — see SAD 1

blue *n* **1** the expanse of air surrounding the earth — see SKY

2 the whole body of salt water that covers nearly three-fourths of the earth — see OCEAN

blueprint *n* a method worked out in advance for achieving some objective — see PLAN 1

blueprint *vb* to work out the details of (something) in advance — see PLAN 1

blues *n pl* a state or spell of low spirits — see SADNESS

bluff *adj* being or characterized by direct, brief, and potentially rude speech or manner — see BLUNT 1

bluff *n* a steep wall of rock, earth, or ice — see CLIFF

bluff *vb* to cause to believe what is untrue — see DECEIVE

blunder *n* an unintentional departure from truth or accuracy — see ERROR 1

blunt *adj* **1** being or characterized by direct, brief, and potentially rude speech or manner ⟨he values honesty and is quite *blunt* about telling people their flaws⟩
syn abrupt, bluff, brusque, crusty, curt, downright, snippy
rel gruff, rough, short; hearty, honest, sincere; candid, direct, forthright, foursquare, frank, free-spoken, open, outspoken, plain, plainspoken, straightforward; discourteous, disrespectful, impertinent, impolite, inconsiderate, rude, tactless, undiplomatic; closemouthed, laconic, reserved, reticent, terse, tight-lipped; artless, earnest, sincere; coarse, crass, crude, low, uncouth, vulgar
near ant civil, considerate, courteous, diplomatic, gracious, polite, politic, smooth, suave, tactful; loquacious, talkative, voluble; long-winded, prolix, verbose; courtly, cultivated, gallant, genteel, polished, refined
ant circuitous, mealymouthed

2 lacking sharpness of edge or point — see DULL 1

blunt *vb* to reduce or weaken in strength or feeling — see DULL 1

blunted *adj* lacking sharpness of edge or point — see DULL 1

blur *vb* **1** to make (something) unclear to the understanding — see CONFUSE 2

2 to make dark, dim, or indistinct — see CLOUD 1

blurt (out) *vb* to utter with a sudden burst of strong feeling — see EXCLAIM

---

syn synonym(s) **rel** related words
ant antonym(s) **near ant** near antonym(s)

blush *n* a rosy appearance of the cheeks — see BLOOM 2

blush *vb* to develop a rosy facial color (as from excitement or embarrassment) ⟨she *blushed* when she realized she had walked into the boys' bathroom by mistake⟩

syn bloom, color, crimson, flush, glow, redden

rel rouge; abash, chagrin, discomfit, disconcert, embarrass, faze, humiliate, mortify

bluster *n* 1 boastful speech or writing — see BOMBAST 1

2 loud, confused, and usually unharmonious sound — see NOISE 1

bluster *vb* to talk loudly and wildly — see RANT

blustery *adj* marked by strong wind or more wind than usual — see WINDY 1

board *n* a leg-mounted piece of furniture with a broad flat top designed for the serving of food — see TABLE 1

board *vb* 1 to provide food or meals for — see FEED 1

2 to provide with living quarters or shelter — see HOUSE 1

boarder *n* one who rents a room or apartment in another's house — see TENANT

boast *n* an asset that brings praise or renown — see GLORY 2

boast *vb* to praise or express pride in one's own possessions, qualities, or accomplishments often to excess ⟨he *boasted* that he was the best hockey goalie in the whole school⟩

syn brag, crow, swagger

rel puff (up); pride; gush; exult, glory, rejoice; brandish, display, exhibit, expose, flaunt, parade, show off; magnify, maximize

near ant bad-mouth, belittle, decry, deprecate, depreciate, diminish, discount, disparage, minimize; bemoan, lament, mourn, regret

boat *n* 1 a small buoyant structure for travel on water ⟨paddling the little *boat* across the lake is great exercise, but tiring⟩

syn bottom, craft, vessel, watercraft

rel canoe, catamaran, catboat, cockleshell, coracle, dinghy, dory, dugout, flatboat, float, gig, gondola, houseboat, ironclad, kayak, launch, life boat, longboat, motorboat, outrigger, pirogue, pontoon, punt, raft, rowboat, sail, sampan, scow, scull, shallop, shell, sloop, tender, umiak; bark, brig, brigantine, caravel, clipper, galleon, galley, junk, ketch, pinnace, sailboat, schooner, ship, square-rigger, windjammer, xebec, yacht; corvette, cutter, destroyer, fireship, flagship, gunboat, landing craft, privateer, torpedo boat, warship; argosy, barge, coaster, collier, containership, ferryboat, icebreaker, lighter, lightship, liner, merchantman, merchant ship, packet, revenuer, riverboat, showboat, steamboat, steamer, supertanker, taxi, towboat, trader, tugboat; sealer, shrimper, trawler, whaler; derelict,

hulk, tub; air-cushion vehicle, hovercraft; hydrofoil, hydroplane

2 a large craft for travel by water — see SHIP

boat *vb* to travel on water in a vessel — see SAIL 1

¹**bob** *vb* to make (as hair) shorter with or as if with the use of shears — see CLIP

²**bob** *vb* to make short up-and-down movements — see NOD

bobble *vb* 1 to make or do (something) in a clumsy or unskillful way — see BOTCH

2 to make short up-and-down movements — see NOD

bobby *n, British* a member of a force charged with law enforcement at the local level — see OFFICER 1

bobby-soxer *n* a young usually unmarried woman — see GIRL 1

bode *vb* to show signs of a favorable or successful outcome ⟨her natural gift for reading *boded* well for her future in school⟩

syn augur, forebode (*also* forbode), promise

rel forecast, foretell, predict, presage, prognosticate, prophesy; anticipate, divine, foreknow, foresee; foreshadow, portend, prefigure; allude, connote, hint, imply, insinuate, intimate, suggest

phrases bid fair, give promise of

bodiless *adj* not composed of matter — see IMMATERIAL 1

bodily *adj* of or relating to the human body — see PHYSICAL 1

boding *n* something believed to be a sign or warning of a future event — see OMEN

body *n* 1 the main or greater part of something as distinguished from its appendages ⟨the *body* of the novel was quite good, even if the beginning was a bit slow⟩

syn bulk, core, generality, main, mass, staple, weight

rel majority; aggregate, amount, entirety, sum, sum total, total, totality, whole; bottom, essence, essentiality, marrow, nature, quintessence, soul, stuff, substance; center, heart, hub, middle, nucleus, seat; affair, argument, burden, crux, focus, gist, kernel, nub, pitch, point, purport; matter, motif, subject, text, theme, topic

near ant accessory, adjunct, appendage, extension, offshoot; component, constituent, element, ingredient; division, part, piece, section, segment; angle, aspect, facet, feature, quality, side

2 a distinct and separate portion of matter ⟨the Atlantic is a gigantic *body* of water⟩

syn mass

rel aggregate, amount, bulk, quantity, volume; item, object, thing; material, stuff, substance; entirety, totality, whole

3 a group of people acting together within a larger group — see FACTION

4 a group of people sharing a common interest and relating together socially — see GANG 2

5 a member of the human race — see HUMAN

6 a usually small number of persons considered as a unit — see GROUP 2

bog *n* spongy land saturated or partially covered with water — see SWAMP

bog (down) *vb* to place in conflict or difficulties — see EMBROIL

bogey *also* **bogy** *or* **bogie** *n* **1** something or someone that causes fear or dread especially without reason ⟨math and math tests have long been *bogeys* for many students⟩

syn bête noire, bugaboo, bugbear, hobgoblin, ogre

rel apparition, ghost, phantasm, phantom, poltergeist, shade, specter (*or* spectre), spirit, spook, wraith; banshee, bogeyman, demon, devil, fiend, imp, incubus; fright, horror, monster, monstrosity, terror; bane, curse, plague, scourge, torment; abomination, anathema

2 the soul of a dead person thought of especially as appearing to living people — see GHOST

bogus *adj* **1** being such in appearance only and made with or manufactured from usually cheaper materials — see IMITATION

2 being such in appearance only and made or manufactured with the intention of committing fraud — see COUNTERFEIT

3 lacking in natural or spontaneous quality — see ARTIFICIAL 1

bohemian *n* a person who does not conform to generally accepted standards or customs — see NONCONFORMIST 1

boil *vb* **1** to be excited or emotionally stirred up with anger ⟨she was *boiling* at the thought of her so-called best friend trying to steal her boyfriend⟩

syn burn, fume, rage, seethe, steam

rel fulminate, rant, rave; smolder; bristle, flare (up); chafe, fret, stew; agitate, convulse, shake; disturb, perturb, upset

2 to cook in a liquid heated to the point that it gives off steam ⟨*boil* the potatoes very well before you try to mash them⟩

syn coddle, parboil, poach, simmer, stew

rel scald; braise, fricassee, pressure-cook, steam; reboil

3 to be in a state of violent rolling motion — see SEETHE 1

boisterous *adj* being rough or noisy in a high-spirited way ⟨the fans at the baseball game became particularly *boisterous* after the home run⟩

syn knockabout, rambunctious, raucous, rowdy

rel rampageous, riotous, stormy, tempestuous, turbulent, violent; disorderly, raffish, ruffianly; headstrong, intractable, obstreperous, recalcitrant, uncontrollable, uncontrolled, undisciplined, ungovernable, uninhibited, unmanageable, unruly, wild, willful (*or* wilful); bubbly, buoyant,

effervescent, exuberant, high-spirited, impassioned, lively, passionate, sprightly, vivacious; clamorous, loudmouthed, noisy, strident, vociferous; howling, screaming, yelling

near ant sedate, sober, solemn, somber (*or* sombre), staid; decorous, dignified, proper, seemly; calm, hushed, noiseless, peaceful, placid, quiet, restrained, serene, silent, soundless, tranquil; collected, composed, constrained, controlled, imperturbable, inhibited, repressed, self-controlled, unflappable, unruffled; moderate, reasonable, subdued, temperate; impassive, phlegmatic, stoic (*or* stoical), stolid; depressed; aloof, detached, indifferent

ant orderly

bold *adj* **1** inclined or willing to take risks ⟨our youngest brother was the *boldest* one in the family, instantly taking to everything from skiing to skateboarding⟩

syn adventuresome, adventurous, audacious, daring, dashing, emboldened, enterprising, gutsy, hardy, nerved, nervy, venturesome, venturous

rel brash, daredevil, foolhardy, heedless, hotheaded, impetuous, imprudent, impulsive, incautious, madcap, overbold, overconfident, rash, reckless, spirited, thoughtless, wild; brave, courageous, dauntless, fearless, gallant, greathearted, heroic, intrepid, lionhearted, stalwart, stout, stouthearted, unafraid, undaunted, valiant, valorous; gritty, plucky, spirited, spunky; hasty, headlong, precipitate; absurd, asinine, balmy, brainless, crazy, foolish, half-witted, harebrained, insane, lunatic, mad, nutty, scatterbrained, silly, wacky, witless; unnecessary; dumb, idiotic, moronic, stupid; irrational, unreasonable

near ant chickenhearted, coward, cowardly, craven, lily-livered, pusillanimous, shy, timid, timorous; careful, cautious, heedful, prudent, wary; overcareful, overcautious; affrighted, afraid, alarmed, fainthearted, fearful, frightened, horrified, scared, shocked, spooked, startled, terrified, terrorized; unnerved; calm, cool, levelheaded, rational, reasonable, sage, sane, sensible, sound, wise; appalled, concerned, dismayed, upset, worried

ant unadventurous, unenterprising

2 displaying or marked by rude boldness — see NERVY 1

3 likely to attract attention — see NOTICEABLE

4 showing a lack of proper social reserve or modesty — see PRESUMPTUOUS 1

5 having an incline approaching the perpendicular — see STEEP 1

bold–faced *adj* displaying or marked by rude boldness — see NERVY 1

bolster *vb* to hold up or serve as a foundation for — see SUPPORT 3

bolt *n* something that makes a strong impression because it is so unexpected — see SURPRISE 1

---

syn synonym(s) *rel* related words
ant antonym(s) *near ant* near antonym(s)

bolt *vb* **1** to move suddenly and sharply (as in surprise) — see START 1

2 to proceed or move quickly — see HURRY 2

3 to hasten away from something dangerous or frightening — see RUN 2

4 to utter with a sudden burst of strong feeling — see EXCLAIM

bomb *vb* to use bombs or artillery against — see BOMBARD

bombard *vb* to use bombs or artillery against ⟨the Allies *bombarded* Germany for a great many months during World War II⟩

syn blitz, bomb, shell

rel rake, strafe; assail, assault, attack, devastate, hit, pound, ravage, strike

bombardment *n* a rapid or overwhelming outpouring of many things at once — see BARRAGE

bombast *n* **1** boastful speech or writing ⟨filling a speech with *bombast* about one's unique qualifications for student council is usually a bad idea⟩

syn bluster, brag, braggadocio, gas, grandiloquence, hot air, rant

rel rhapsody, rhetoric; babble, blab, chatter, drivel, gabble, gibber, jabber, prattle; jawing, patter, prating, yammering; egotism, self-conceit, self-importance

2 language that is impressive-sounding but not meaningful or sincere — see RHETORIC 1

bombastic *adj* marked by the use of impressive-sounding but mostly meaningless words and phrases — see RHETORICAL

bombshell *n* something that makes a strong impression because it is so unexpected — see SURPRISE 1

bona fide *adj* being exactly as appears or as claimed — see AUTHENTIC 1

bond *n* **1** something that physically prevents free movement ⟨before they could release the captive, they had to undo a number of *bonds*⟩

syn band, bracelet, chain, fetter, handcuff(s), irons, ligature, manacle, shackle

rel confinement, constraint, curb, hamper, hindrance, restraint, restriction; entanglement, net, trammel, trap; collar, straitjacket (*also* straightjacket); hobble, tie

2 a uniting or binding force or influence ⟨the *bond* of love between them was so strong that even death could not break it⟩

syn cement, knot, ligature, link, tie

rel attachment, connection, entanglement, fastening, joint, linkage; affection, fondness, sympathy; fetter, handcuff, manacle, shackle, trammel; constraint, curb, hampering, limit, limitation, restraint, restriction

near ant detaching, disengaging, parting, separation; unbinding, unfastening, unfettering, untying; emancipation, freedom, liberation, release

3 a formal agreement to fulfill an obligation — see GUARANTEE 1

bondage *n* the state of being a slave — see SLAVERY 1

bonding *n* a physical sticking to as if by glue — see ADHESION

bondman *n* a person who is considered the property of another person — see SLAVE 1

bondsman *n* a person who is considered the property of another person — see SLAVE 1

bone *n, usually* **bones** *pl* a small cube marked on each side with one to six spots and usually played in pairs in various games — see DIE

bone (up) *vb* to use the mind to acquire knowledge — see STUDY 1

bonny *adj, chiefly British* very pleasing to look at — see BEAUTIFUL

bonus *n* something given in addition to what is ordinarily expected or owed ⟨this job offers a nice Christmas *bonus* in addition to the salary⟩

syn dividend, extra, gratuity, gravy, lagniappe, perquisite, tip

rel fillip; bestowal, presentation; benefaction, benevolence, bounty, charity, generosity, largess (*or* largesse), philanthropy; contribution, donation, gift, offering, present; grant, subsidy; boon, manna, windfall; favor, freebie (*or* freebee), giveaway, premium; award, prize, reward; fringe benefit

bon voyage *n* an expression of good wishes at parting — see GOOD-BYE

boo *n* a vocal sound made to express scorn or disapproval — see CATCALL

booby *n* a person who lacks good sense or judgment — see FOOL 1

boobytrap *vb* to place hidden explosive devices in or under — see MINE

booby trap *n* **1** a usually concealed explosive device designed to go off when disturbed ⟨luckily, the bomb squad didn't find any *booby traps*⟩

syn mine

rel bomb, explosive; pitfall, snare, trap; ambush

2 a danger or difficulty that is hidden or not easily recognized — see PITFALL 1

book *n* **1** a set of printed sheets of paper bound together between covers and forming a work of fiction or nonfiction ⟨I bought another new *book* yesterday, and I can't wait to read it⟩

syn tome, volume

rel hardback, paperback, pocket book; folio, quarto; guidebook, handbook, manual; catalog (*or* catalogue), dictionary, encyclopedia; booklet, brochure, circular, flier (*or* flyer), folder, leaflet, magazine, pamphlet, program; textbook, tract, treatise; novel, novelette, pulp

2 *cap* a book made up of the writings accepted by Christians as coming from God — see BIBLE

book *vb* to arrange to have something (as a hotel room) held for one's future use — see RESERVE 1

bookish *adj* suggestive of the vocabulary used in books ⟨*fealty* is a *bookish* synonym for *loyalty*⟩
   syn erudite, learned, literary
   rel academic, pedantic, scholastic; highbrow, intellectual; educated, schooled; formal
   near ant chatty, conversational; familiar, informal; slangy
   ant colloquial, nonliterary

booklet *n* a short printed publication with no cover or with a paper cover — see PAMPHLET

bookworm *n* a person slavishly devoted to intellectual or academic pursuits — see NERD

boom *n* a loud explosive sound — see CLAP 1

boom *vb* to make a long loud deep noise or cry — see ROAR

booming *adj* **1** marked by a high volume of sound — see LOUD 1
   2 marked by vigorous growth and wellbeing especially economically — see PROSPEROUS 1

boon *adj* likely to seek or enjoy the company of others — see CONVIVIAL

boon *n* **1** a thing that helps — see HELP 2
   2 an act of kind assistance — see FAVOR 1
   3 something granted as a special favor — see PRIVILEGE
   4 something that provides happiness or does good for a person or thing — see BLESSING 2

boor *n* a person whose behavior is offensive to others — SEE JERK 1

boorish *adj* having or showing crudely insensitive or impolite manners — see CLOWNISH

boost *n* **1** an act or instance of helping — see HELP 1
   2 something added (as by growth) — see INCREASE 1
   3 something that arouses action or activity — see IMPULSE

boost *vb* **1** to lift with effort — see HEAVE 1
   2 to make greater in size, amount, or number — see INCREASE 1
   3 to make markedly greater in measure or degree — see INTENSIFY
   4 to move from a lower to a higher place or position — see RAISE 1
   5 to provide publicity for — see PUBLICIZE 1

booster *n* a person who actively supports or favors a cause — see EXPONENT

boot (out) *vb* to drive or force out — see EJECT 1

bootleg *n* illegally produced liquor — see MOONSHINE 1

bootless *adj* producing no results — see FUTILE

booty *n* valuables stolen or taken by force — see LOOT

booze *n* a fermented or distilled beverage that can make a person drunk — see ALCOHOL

bop *n* a hard strike with a part of the body or an instrument — see ¹BLOW

bop *vb* to deliver a blow to (someone or something) usually in a strong vigorous manner — see HIT 1

border *n* **1** the line or relatively narrow space that marks the outer limit of something ⟨a rug with a fancily embroidered *border*⟩
   syn bound, boundary, brim, circumference, compass, confines, edge, end, fringe, margin, perimeter, periphery, rim, skirt, verge
   rel crest, hem, lip; ceiling, maximum; demarcation, extent, limitation, measure, restriction, termination; borderland, frontier, march, pale
   near ant center; inner, inside, interior
   2 a region along the dividing line between two countries — see FRONTIER 1

border *vb* to serve as a border for ⟨that velvet *bordered* the sleeves on this shirt, until it fell off⟩
   syn bound, fringe, margin, rim, skirt
   rel edge, hem, trim; circumscribe, define, delineate, demarcate, frame, outline; circle, compass, encircle, girdle, girth, loop, ring, round, surround; check, confine, control, curb, limit, restrain, restrict

border (on) *vb* **1** to come very close to being ⟨that comment *borders on* insubordination, and you should be more careful in the future⟩
   syn verge (on)
   rel approach, near; appear, look, resemble, seem, suggest
   2 to be adjacent to — see ADJOIN 1

bordering *adj* having a border in common — see ADJACENT

borderland *n* a region along the dividing line between two countries — see FRONTIER 1

bore *n* someone or something boring — see DRAG 1

¹bore *vb* to make a hole or series of holes in — see PERFORATE

²bore *vb* to make weary and restless by being dull or monotonous ⟨the teacher's lifeless and unimaginative teaching style *bored* the students to death⟩
   syn jade, tire, weary
   rel pall; drain, enervate, exhaust, fatigue, wear, wear out; debilitate, disable, enfeeble; deject, demoralize, discourage, dishearten, dispirit
   phrases put to sleep
   near ant animate, energize, enliven, excite, galvanize, invigorate, stimulate, vitalize; amuse, entertain; allure, attract, beguile, bewitch, captivate, charm, enchant, enthrall (*or* enthral), fascinate, hypnotize, mesmerize; monopolize, preoccupy; busy, immerse, involve, occupy; rally, rouse, stir
   ant absorb, engage, engross, grip, interest, intrigue

---

syn synonym(s)   **rel** related words
ant antonym(s)   **near ant** near antonym(s)

bored *adj* having one's patience, interest, or pleasure exhausted — see WEARY 2

boredom *n* the state of being bored ⟨she spends that whole class in a state of complete *boredom*, waiting for lunch⟩

syn doldrums, ennui, listlessness, restlessness, tedium, tiredness, weariness

rel cheerlessness, dispiritedness, joylessness, melancholy; languor, lassitude, lethargy, lifelessness, torpor; dullness (*also* dulness), monotonousness, monotony, sameness; apathy, indifference, unconcern

near ant beguilement, bewitchment, captivation, enchantment, fascination; absorption, engagement, engrossment, immersion, involvement; animation, enlivenment, excitement, invigoration, stimulation; amusement, entertainment

boring *adj* causing weariness, restlessness, or lack of interest ⟨I wish this book weren't so *boring*; I keep falling asleep whenever I try to read it⟩

syn drab, dreary, dry, dull, flat, heavy, humdrum, jading, leaden, monotonous, pedestrian, ponderous, stodgy, stuffy, stupid, tame, tedious, tiresome, tiring, unanimated, uninteresting, wearisome, weary, wearying

rel undramatic, unentertaining, uneventful, unexciting, uninspiring, unnewsworthy, unrewarding, unsatisfying, unsensational, unspectacular; annoying, bothersome, irksome, irritating; drudging, palling, draining, enervating, exhausting, fatiguing, wearing; debilitating, enfeebling; demoralizing, discouraging, disheartening, dispiriting; common, commonplace, ordinary, stale, unexceptional; lumbering, plodding, slow

near ant amazing, astonishing, astounding, awesome, eye-opening, fabulous, marvelous (*or* marvellous), sensational, spectacular, surprising, wonderful, wondrous; animating, energizing, enlivening, exciting, galvanizing, invigorating, stimulating; amusing, diverting, entertaining; alluring, attracting, attractive, beguiling, bewitching, captivating, charming, enchanting, enthralling, entrancing, fascinating; mesmerizing

ant absorbing, engaging, engrossing, gripping, interesting, intriguing, involving

born *adj* 1 being such from birth or by nature — see NATURAL 1

2 belonging to a particular place by birth or origin — see NATIVE 1

borrow *vb* to take for one's own use (something originated by another) — see ADOPT

bosom *adj* closely acquainted — see FAMILIAR 1

boss *adj, slang* of the very best kind — see EXCELLENT

boss *n* the person (as an employer or supervisor) who tells people and especially workers what to do ⟨every morning the *boss* hands out a list of top-priority tasks⟩

syn captain, chief, foreman, head, headman, helmsman, kingpin, leader, master, taskmaster

rel administrator, commander, director, executive, general, manager, overseer, principal, standard-bearer, straw boss, superintendent, superior, supervisor; dominator, lord, overlord, potentate, ruler; figurehead; slave driver; baron, czar (*also* tsar *or* tzar), king, magnate, mogul, president, prince

near ant dependent, inferior, secondary, subject, subordinate, underling

boss *vb* 1 to be in charge of ⟨she *bossed* that project for years, until she was promoted again⟩

syn captain, head, oversee, superintend, supervise

rel command, control, direct, guide, manage, order, run, shepherd, show, steer; quarterback; administer; monitor; govern, reign, rule

2 to exercise authority or power over — see GOVERN 1

3 to serve as leader of — see LEAD 2

boss (**around**) *vb* to issue orders to (someone) by right of authority — see COMMAND 1

bossy *adj* fond of ordering people around ⟨I don't want to work with him because he's so *bossy* and always runs roughshod over me⟩

syn authoritarian, autocratic, despotic, dictatorial, domineering, imperious, masterful, overbearing, peremptory, tyrannical (*also* tyrannic), tyrannous

rel arrogant, disdainful, haughty, lofty, lordly, proud, supercilious, superior; commanding, dictating; arbitrary, highhanded, imperial; authoritative, directorial, magisterial; aggressive, assertive, self-assertive; conceited, narcissistic, pompous, vain; all-powerful, almighty, omnipotent; firm, stern

near ant humble, meek, modest, unassuming; amenable, docile, obedient, tractable; indecisive, irresolute; acquiescent, compliant, passive, resigned, submissive, yielding

botch *vb* to make or do (something) in a clumsy or unskillful way ⟨the first time we tried to make a cake, we *botched* the job completely⟩

syn bobble, bungle, butcher, flub, foozle, foul up, fumble, louse up, mangle, mess (up), muff, murder

rel blunder, goof (up), gum (up); blemish, blight, damage, flaw, harm, hurt, impair, injure, mar, mutilate, ruin, spoil, vitiate; destroy, wreck; mishandle, mismanage

near ant ameliorate, better, enhance, help, improve, meliorate, rectify, refine, reform, remedy

botched *adj* showing or marked by a lack of skill and tact (as in dealing with a situation) — see AWKWARD 2

bother *n* 1 a state of noisy, confused activity — see COMMOTION

2 one who is obnoxiously annoying — see NUISANCE 1

3 something that is a source of irritation
— see ANNOYANCE 3

4 the feeling of impatience or anger
caused by another's repeated disagreeable acts — see ANNOYANCE 2

bother *vb* **1** to thrust oneself upon (another) without invitation ⟨I am never going
to get this work done if people don't stop
wandering into the room and *bothering*
me⟩

syn bug, chivy, disturb, intrude (upon),
pester

rel inconvenience, trouble; aggravate,
anger, annoy, bedevil, devil, exasperate,
fret, gall, get, gnaw, hassle, irritate, nettle,
peeve, pique, put out, rile, torment, vex,
worry; beleaguer, beset, besiege; distress,
plague; afflict, harass, torment; grate, inflame, provoke; enrage, incense, inflame,
infuriate, madden; agitate, perturb

near ant ignore, leave; appease, conciliate, mollify, oblige, placate; delight, gladden, gratify, please, satisfy; comfort, console, content

2 to disturb the peace of mind of (someone) especially by repeated disagreeable
acts — see IRRITATE 1

3 to experience concern or anxiety — see
WORRY 1

4 to trouble the mind of; to make uneasy
— see DISTURB 1

bothering *n* the act of making unwelcome
intrusions upon another — see ANNOY-
ANCE 1

bothersome *adj* causing annoyance —
see ANNOYING

bottom *n* **1** the side or part facing downward from something ⟨that side of the
shelf is supposed to be the *bottom*, so turn
it over before you assemble the book-
case⟩

syn underbelly, underbody, underside,
undersurface

rel belly, sole; base, floor, foot, ground,
seat, underpinning

near ant acme, apex, crest, crown,
height, peak, pinnacle, roof, summit;
cusp, head, point, tip

ant face, top

2 the surface upon which a body of water
lies ⟨my missing fishing pole is probably
lying on the *bottom* of the lake⟩

syn bed, floor

rel riverbed; base, basement, foundation,
ground

near ant surface

3 the lowest part, place, or point ⟨sliding
all the way to the *bottom* of the snow-cov-
ered slope⟩

syn base, foot, rock bottom

rel basis, bed, bedrock, foundation,
ground, groundwork, keystone, seat, underpinning

near ant acme, apex, climax, crest, face,
height, peak, pinnacle, summit, tip-top,
zenith

ant head, top

4 the part of the body upon which someone sits — see BUTTOCKS

5 a small buoyant structure for travel on
water — see BOAT 1

bottomless *adj* extending far downward
or inward — see DEEP 1

bough *n* a major outgrowth from the main
stem of a woody plant — see BRANCH 1

boulevard *n* a passage cleared for public
vehicular travel — see WAY 1

bounce *n* active strength of body or mind
— see VIGOR 1

bounce *vb* **1** to drive or force out — see
EJECT 1

2 to strike and fly off at an angle — see
GLANCE 1

bouncing *adj* **1** enjoying health and vigor
— see HEALTHY 1

2 having much high-spirited energy and
movement — see LIVELY 1

bound *adj* fully committed to achieving a
goal — see DETERMINED 1

¹**bound** *n* **1** a real or imaginary point beyond which a person or thing cannot go
— see LIMIT

2 the line or relatively narrow space that
marks the outer limit of something — see
BORDER 1

²**bound** *n* an act of leaping into the air —
see JUMP 1

¹**bound** *vb* **1** to mark the limits of — see
LIMIT 2

2 to serve as a border for — see BORDER

²**bound** *vb* **1** to move with a light bouncing
step — see SKIP 1

2 to propel oneself upward or forward
into the air — see JUMP 1

boundary *n* **1** a real or imaginary point
beyond which a person or thing cannot
go — see LIMIT

2 the line or relatively narrow space that
marks the outer limit of something — see
BORDER 1

bounded *adj* having distinct or certain
limits — see LIMITED 1

boundless *adj* being or seeming to be
without limits — see INFINITE

bounteous *adj* giving or sharing in abundance and without hesitation — see GEN-
EROUS 1

bountiful *adj* **1** being more than enough
without being excessive — see PLENTI-
FUL

2 giving or sharing in abundance and
without hesitation — see GENEROUS 1

bountifully *adv* in a generous manner —
see WELL 2

bountifulness *n* the quality or state of
being generous — see LIBERALITY

bounty *n* **1** something offered or given in
return for a service performed — see RE-
WARD

2 the quality or state of being generous —
see LIBERALITY

bouquet *n* **1** a bunch of flowers ⟨I bought
my mother a nice *bouquet* for her birth-
day⟩

syn nosegay, posy

rel boutonniere, corsage; arrangement;
garland, lei

---

syn synonym(s)   *rel* related words
ant antonym(s)   *near ant* near antonym(s)

2 a sweet or pleasant smell — see FRA-GRANCE

bout *n* **1** a competitive encounter between individuals or groups carried on for amusement, exercise, or in pursuit of a prize — see GAME 1

2 a sudden experiencing of a physical or mental disorder — see ATTACK 2

bow *n* something that curves or is curved — see BEND 1

¹bow *vb* **1** to cease resistance (as to another's arguments, demands, or control) — see YIELD 3

2 to give up and cease resistance (as to a liking, temptation, or habit) — see YIELD 1

²bow *vb* to turn away from a straight line or course — see CURVE 1

bowed *adj* bending downward or forward — see NODDING

bowing *adj* bending downward or forward — see NODDING

bowl *n* a large usually roofless building for sporting events with tiers of seats for spectators — see STADIUM

bowl *vb* **1** to move or proceed smoothly and readily — see FLOW 2

2 to proceed or move quickly — see HURRY 2

bowl (down *or* over) *vb* to strike (someone) so forcefully as to cause a fall — see FELL 1

bowl (over) *vb* **1** to cause an often unpleasant surprise for — see SHOCK 1

2 to make a strong impression on (someone) with something unexpected — see SURPRISE 1

bowled over *adj* affected with sudden and great wonder or surprise — see THUN-DERSTRUCK

¹box *n* a covered rectangular container for storing or transporting things — see CHEST

²box *n* a hard strike with a part of the body or an instrument — see ¹BLOW

boxer *n* one that engages in the sport of fighting with the fists ⟨that *boxer* is quite famous for being the youngest heavyweight champion ever⟩

syn fighter, prizefighter, pugilist

rel bantamweight, featherweight, flyweight, heavyweight, light heavyweight, lightweight, middleweight, welterweight

boy *n* a male person who has not yet reached adulthood ⟨a giggling little *boy* ran by⟩

syn lad, laddie, nipper, shaver, sonny, stripling, tad, youth

rel adolescent, juvenile, kid, minor, moppet, teenager, youngster; brat, gamin, hobbledehoy, imp, squirt, urchin, whippersnapper; schoolboy

boyfriend *n* a male romantic companion ⟨her *boyfriend* always brings her flowers for Valentine's Day⟩

syn beau, fellow, man, swain

rel admirer, crush, steady; gallant, suitor, wooer; beloved, darling, dear, favorite, flame, honey, love, lover, sweet, sweet-heart, valentine; date, escort; groom, husband; fiancé, intended

brace *n* **1** something that holds up or serves as a foundation for something else — see SUPPORT 1

2 two things of the same or similar kind that match or are considered together — see PAIR

brace *vb* **1** to give life, vigor, or spirit to — see ANIMATE

2 to hold up or serve as a foundation for — see SUPPORT 3

3 to prepare (oneself) mentally or emotionally — see FORTIFY 1

bracelet *n* something that physically prevents free movement — see BOND 1

bracing *adj* having a renewing effect on the state of the body or mind — see TONIC

bracket *n* one of the units into which a whole is divided on the basis of a common characteristic — see CLASS 2

bracket *vb* to describe as similar — see COMPARE 1

brag *n* boastful speech or writing — see BOMBAST 1

brag *vb* to praise or express pride in one's own possessions, qualities, or accomplishments often to excess — see BOAST

braggadocio *n* boastful speech or writing — see BOMBAST 1

braid *n* a length of something formed of three or more strands woven together ⟨until she was fifteen, she had a *braid* that reached to her knees⟩

syn lace, lacing, plait

rel rickrack (*or* ricrac), stripe; pigtail

braid *vb* to form into a braid ⟨they taught each other how to *braid* yarn into bracelets⟩

syn plait, pleat

rel interlace, interweave, weave

brain *n* **1** a very smart person — see GE-NIUS 1

2 *often* **brains** *pl* the ability to learn and understand or to deal with problems — see INTELLIGENCE 1

brainless *adj* **1** not having or showing an ability to absorb ideas readily — see STU-PID 1

2 showing or marked by a lack of good sense or judgment — see FOOLISH 1

brainlessness *n* **1** lack of good sense or judgment — see FOOLISHNESS 1

2 the quality or state of lacking intelligence or quickness of mind — see STU-PIDITY 1

brainstorm *vb* to engage in an exchange of information or ideas — see COMMUNI-CATE 2

brainy *adj* having or showing quickness of mind — see INTELLIGENT 1

brake *n* a thick patch of shrubbery, small trees, or underbrush — see THICKET

brake *vb* to cause to move or proceed at a less rapid pace — see SLOW 1

braking *n* a usually gradual decrease in the pace or level of activity of something — see SLOWDOWN

brambly *adj* likely to cause a scratch — see SCRATCHY 1

branch *n* 1 a major outgrowth from the main stem of a woody plant ⟨I loved climbing among the *branches* of that old tree⟩

syn bough, limb

rel offshoot, outgrowth, shoot; spray, sprig, twig

2 a local unit of an organization — see CHAPTER

branch *vb* to extend outwards from or as if from a central point — see RADIATE 1

branch (out) *vb* to go or move in different directions from a central point — see SEPARATE 2

brand *n* 1 a device (as a word) identifying the maker of a piece of merchandise and legally reserved for the exclusive use of that person or company — see TRADEMARK 1

2 a mark of guilt or disgrace — see STAIN 1

brand—new *adj* 1 being in an original and unused or unspoiled state — see FRESH 1

2 recently made and never used before — see NEW 3

brash *adj* 1 displaying or marked by rude boldness — see NERVY 1

2 foolishly adventurous or bold — see FOOLHARDY 1

brashness *n* shameless boldness — see EFFRONTERY

brass *n* shameless boldness — see EFFRONTERY

brassiness *n* shameless boldness — see EFFRONTERY

brassy *adj* displaying or marked by rude boldness — see NERVY 1

brave *adj* feeling or displaying no fear by temperament ⟨the *brave* little boy sat still for the flu shot⟩

syn courageous, dauntless, doughty, fearless, gallant, greathearted, heroic, intrepid, lionhearted, manful, stalwart, stout, stouthearted, undaunted, valiant, valorous

rel determined, firm, game, plucky, resolute, undeterred, undismayed, unflinching, unswerving; mettlesome, spirited, spunky; adventuresome, adventurous, audacious, bold, daring, dashing, gutsy, hardy, venturesome, venturous; crazy, foolish, half-witted, insane, lunatic, mad, nutty; brash, brazen, daredevil, foolhardy, heedless, hotheaded, impetuous, imprudent, impulsive, incautious, madcap, overbold, overconfident, rash, reckless, thoughtless, wild; hasty, headlong, precipitate; comforted, emboldened, encouraged, heartened, reassured, unafraid

near ant mousy (*or* mousey), scary, shy, skittish, timid, timorous; anxious, apprehensive, nervous; careful, cautious, heedful, prudent, unadventurous; afraid, agitated, disconcerted, disquieted, disturbed, frightened, horrified, panicked, perturbed, scared, shocked, spooked, startled, terrified, terrorized, unnerved, upset; appalled, concerned, dismayed, worried

ant chicken, chickenhearted, coward, cowardly, craven, fainthearted, fearful, lily-livered, pusillanimous, timorous

brave *vb* to oppose (something hostile or dangerous) with firmness or courage — see FACE 2

bravery *n* 1 dressy clothing — see FINERY

2 strength of mind to carry on in spite of danger — see COURAGE

brawl *n* 1 a rough and often noisy fight usually involving several people ⟨they were thrown out of the party after starting a *brawl*⟩

syn affray, fracas, fray, free-for-all, melee, row, ruckus, ruction

rel battle, clash, combat, conflict, contest, fight, fisticuffs, scrap, scrimmage, scuffle, struggle, tussle; horseplay, roughhousing; altercation, argument, dispute, quarrel, spat, squabble, tiff, wrangle

2 an often noisy or angry expression of differing opinions — see ARGUMENT 1

brawl *vb* to express different opinions about something often angrily — see ARGUE 2

brawn *n* muscular strength — see MUSCLE 1

brawny *adj* 1 having muscles capable of exerting great physical force — see STRONG 1

2 marked by a well-developed musculature — see MUSCULAR 1

3 strongly and heavily built — see ¹HUSKY

brazen *adj* displaying or marked by rude boldness — see NERVY 1

brazen *vb* to oppose (something hostile or dangerous) with firmness or courage — see FACE 2

brazenness *n* shameless boldness — see EFFRONTERY

breach *n* 1 a failure to uphold the requirements of law, duty, or obligation ⟨the president's deliberate misstatements were widely seen as a *breach* of the public trust⟩

syn infraction, infringement, transgression, trespass, violation

rel offense, sin, wrong; disregard, forgetting, ignoring, nonobservance, overlooking; delinquency, dereliction, neglect; intrusion, invasion

near ant respecting, upholding

ant nonviolation, observance

2 a breaking of a moral or legal code — see OFFENSE 1

3 an open space in a barrier (as a wall or hedge) — see GAP 1

breach *vb* to fail to keep — see VIOLATE 1

bread *n* 1 *slang* something (as pieces of stamped metal or printed paper) customarily and legally used as a medium of exchange, a measure of value, or a means of payment — see MONEY

2 substances intended to be eaten — see FOOD

---

syn synonym(s)   *rel* related words
ant antonym(s)   *near ant* near antonym(s)

breadbasket *n, slang* the part of the body between the chest and the pelvis — see STOMACH

breadth *n* 1 a wide space or area — see EXPANSE

2 an area over which activity, capacity, or influence extends — see RANGE 2

break *n* 1 a momentary halt in an activity — see PAUSE

2 a period during which the usual routine of school or work is suspended — see VACATION

3 an open space in a barrier (as a wall or hedge) — see GAP 1

break *vb* 1 to cause to separate into pieces usually suddenly or forcibly ⟨I hated admitting to Mom that I had *broken* her favorite glass vase⟩

syn bust, fracture, fragment

rel blast, blow up, burst, detonate, explode; pop, shatter, shiver, smash; sliver, splinter, split; collapse, implode; demolish, destroy, ruin, wreck

near ant fix, heal, mend, patch, rebuild, reconstruct, repair

2 to bring (as an action or operation) to an immediate end — see STOP 1

3 to bring to a lower grade or rank — see DEMOTE

4 to change (as a secret message) from code into ordinary language — see DECODE

5 to come to a temporary halt in one's activity — see PAUSE

6 to cut into and turn over the sod of (a piece of land) using a bladed implement — see PLOW 1

7 to fail to keep — see VIOLATE 1

8 to find an answer for through reasoning — see SOLVE

9 to reduce the soundness, effectiveness, or perfection of — see DAMAGE 1

10 to stop functioning — see FAIL 1

11 to hasten away from something dangerous or frightening — see RUN 2

breakable *adj* easily broken — see FRAGILE 1

breakdown *n* 1 the process by which dead organic matter separates into simpler substances — see CORRUPTION 1

2 the separation and identification of the parts of a whole — see ANALYSIS 1

break down *vb* 1 to arrange or assign according to type — see CLASSIFY 1

2 to go through decomposition — see DECAY 1

3 to identify and examine the basic elements or parts of (something) especially for discovering interrelationships — see ANALYZE

4 to stop functioning — see FAIL 1

5 to yield to mental or emotional stress — see CRACK 2

break in *vb* 1 to enter a house or building by force usually with illegal intent ⟨the burglars *broke in* by smashing a window⟩

syn burglarize

rel invade, trespass; hold up, loot, plunder, rip off, rob, stick up; ransack, rifle;

despoil, devastate, maraud, pillage, ravage, sack

2 to cause a disruption in a conversation or discussion — see INTERRUPT

breakneck *adj* moving, proceeding, or acting with great speed — see FAST 1

break off *vb* 1 to bring (as an action or operation) to an immediate end — see STOP 1

2 to come to an end — see CEASE 1

break out *vb* to develop suddenly and violently — see ERUPT 2

breakthrough *n* an instance of notable progress in the development of knowledge, technology, or skill — see ADVANCE 2

breakup *n* the act or process of a whole separating into two or more parts or pieces — see SEPARATION 1

break up *vb* 1 to cease to exist or cause to cease to exist as a group or organization — see DISBAND 1

2 to come to an end — see CEASE 1

3 to set or force apart — see SEPARATE 1

breast *n* the seat of one's deepest thoughts and emotions — see CORE 1

breast *vb* to oppose (something hostile or dangerous) with firmness or courage — see FACE 2

breath *n* 1 a momentary halt in an activity — see PAUSE

2 a slight or gentle movement of air — see BREEZE 1

breathe *vb* 1 to inhale and exhale air ⟨sometimes it gets so hot in here that it's hard to even *breathe*⟩

syn respire

rel expire, inspire; gasp, huff, pant, puff, wheeze; sniff, snore, snort, snuffle; yawn

near ant asphyxiate, choke, gag, smother, suffocate; garrotte (*or* garrote), stifle, strangle, throttle

2 to have life — see BE 1

breathe (out) *vb* to let or force out of the lungs — see EXHALE 1

breather *n* a momentary halt in an activity — see PAUSE

breathing *adj* having or showing life — see ALIVE 1

breathless *adj* 1 lacking fresh air — see STUFFY 1

2 moving, proceeding, or acting with great speed — see FAST 1

3 no longer living — see DEAD 1

breathtaking *adj* causing great emotional or mental stimulation — see EXCITING 1

breech *n* 1 the part of the body upon which someone sits — see BUTTOCKS

2 **breeches** *pl* an outer garment covering each leg separately from waist to ankle — see PANTS

breed *n* a number of persons or things that are grouped together because they have something in common — see SORT 1

breed *vb* 1 to bring forth offspring — see PROCREATE

2 to bring to maturity through care and education — see BRING UP 1

breeding *n* the line of ancestors from whom a person is descended — see ANCESTRY

breeze *n* 1 a slight or gentle movement of air ⟨a warm spring *breeze* ruffled our hair⟩

syn air, breath, puff, waft, zephyr

rel draft, whiff; land breeze, sea breeze; blast, blow, flurry, gale, northeaster, norther, northwester, southeaster, southwester, westerly, wind; squall, tempest, tornado, windstorm; airflow

near ant calm

2 something that is easy to do — see CINCH

breeze *vb* 1 to move or proceed smoothly and readily — see FLOW 2

2 to proceed or move quickly — see HURRY 2

breezy *adj* 1 having a relaxed, casual manner — see EASYGOING 1

2 marked by strong wind or more wind than usual — see WINDY 1

brevity *n* 1 the condition of being short ⟨the best quality a graduation speech can have is *brevity*⟩

syn briefness, conciseness, shortness

rel abbreviation, abridgment (*or* abridgement), compression, condensation, contraction, curtailment; decreasing, diminishing, lessening, reducing, shortening, shrinking; abruptness, brusqueness, curtness; pithiness, succinctness, terseness; littleness, minuteness, smallness, tininess

near ant extensiveness; elongating, elongation, extending, extension, prolongation, prolonging, protraction, stretching; expansion, growth, spread; diffuseness, prolixity, talkativeness, verboseness, volubility, wordiness; bigness, bulkiness, greatness, heftiness, largeness

ant lengthiness

2 the quality or state of being marked by or using only few words to convey much meaning — see SUCCINCTNESS

brew *vb* to be about to happen — see LOOM

bribable *adj* open to improper influence and especially bribery — see VENAL

bribe *n* something given or promised in order to improperly influence a person's conduct or decision ⟨that judge refused a huge *bribe* to dismiss the charges against the wealthy defendant⟩

syn fix, sop

rel incentive, incitement, motivation, spur, stimulation, stimulus; boost, goad, inducement; allurement, bait, enticement, lure, temptation; flattery, persuasion; decoy, snare, trap

bribe *vb* to influence someone with a bribe ⟨meat inspectors were *bribed*, and the contaminated beef was sold to the public⟩

syn have, square

rel fix, tamper (with); corrupt, debase, defile, dishonor, taint; allure, bait, entice, lure, tempt; motivate, provoke, spur, stimulate; goad, induce; flatter, persuade; snare, trap

bridal *n* a ceremony in which two people are united in matrimony — see WEDDING

bridgehead *n* a place from which an advance (as for military operations) is made — see BASE 2

bridle *vb* to keep from exceeding a desirable degree or level (as of expression) — see CONTROL 1

brief *adj* 1 marked by the use of few words to convey much information or meaning — see CONCISE

2 not lasting for a considerable time — see SHORT 2

brief *vb* to give information to — see ENLIGHTEN 1

briefly *adv* in a few words — see SHORTLY 1

briefness *n* 1 the condition of being short — see BREVITY 1

2 the quality or state of being marked by or using only few words to convey much meaning — see SUCCINCTNESS

brig *n* a place of confinement for persons held in lawful custody — see JAIL

bright *adj* 1 giving off or reflecting much light ⟨in the desert the sun was so *bright* that it hurt my eyes⟩ ⟨the moon is *bright* tonight⟩

syn beaming, bedazzling, brilliant, dazzling, effulgent, glowing, incandescent, lambent, lucent, lucid, luminous, lustrous, radiant, refulgent, shining, shiny

rel blazing, burning, combusting, fiery, flaming; agleam, aglitter, blinding, flaring, flashing, flickering, glaring, gleaming, glimmering, glinting, glistening, glittering, scintillating, shimmering, sparkling, twinkling; burnished, polished; sunny

near ant blackened, dark, darkened, darkish, darkling, darksome, dimmed, dusky, gloomy, murky, obscure, obscured, pitch-black, pitch-dark, somber (*or* sombre), sunless; cloudy, shadowy, shady; gray (*also* grey), leaden, pale

ant dim, dull, lackluster

2 filled with much light ⟨the display windows of department stores are especially *bright* at Christmastime⟩

syn ablaze, alight, brightened, illuminated, illumined, light, lighted (*or* lit)

rel floodlit (*or* floodlighted), highlighted, spotlighted (*or* spotlit); kindled, ignited

near ant gloomy, somber, sunless; cloudy, murky, obscured, shadowy; gray (*also* grey), leaden, pale

ant blackened, dark, darkened, darkish, darkling, dimmed, dusky, pitch-black, pitch-dark

3 having or showing a good mood or disposition — see CHEERFUL 1

4 having or showing quickness of mind — see INTELLIGENT 1

5 having qualities which inspire hope — see HOPEFUL 1

6 pointing toward a happy outcome — see FAVORABLE 2

---

syn synonym(s) *rel* related words

ant antonym(s) *near ant* near antonym(s)

7 serving to lift one's spirits — see CHEERFUL 2

brighten *vb* to become glad or hopeful — see CHEER (UP) 1

brightened *adj* filled with much light — see BRIGHT 1

brightness *n* the quality or state of having or giving off light — see BRILLIANCE 1

brilliance *n* 1 the quality or state of having or giving off light ⟨the *brilliance* of the flash from the camera was so intense that I was blinded for a moment afterwards⟩
syn brightness, brilliancy, dazzle, effulgence, illumination, lightness, lucidity, luminosity, radiance, refulgence, splendor
rel blaze, flare, flicker, light; fluorescence, incandescence, luminescence; burnish, gloss, luster, polish, sheen, shine; fire, flame, glare, glow; flash, gleam, glimmer, glint, glisten, glitter, scintillation, shimmer, sparkle, twinkle
near ant dimness, dullness (*also* dulness), gloominess, somberness; cloudiness, haziness, murkiness, obscurity; colorlessness, grayness, paleness
ant blackness, dark, darkness, duskiness
2 impressiveness of beauty on a large scale — see MAGNIFICENCE

brilliancy *n* the quality or state of having or giving off light — see BRILLIANCE 1

brilliant *adj* 1 giving off or reflecting much light — see BRIGHT 1
2 having or showing quickness of mind — see INTELLIGENT 1

brilliant *n* a usually valuable stone cut and polished for ornament — see GEM 1

brim *n* 1 the line or relatively narrow space that marks the outer limit of something — see BORDER 1
2 the projecting front part of a hat or cap — see VISOR

brimful *adj* containing or seeming to contain the greatest quantity or number possible — see FULL 1

brimming *adj* containing or seeming to contain the greatest quantity or number possible — see FULL 1

brine *n* the whole body of salt water that covers nearly three-fourths of the earth — see OCEAN

bring *vb* to have a price of — see COST

bring about *vb* to be the cause of (a situation, action, or state of mind) — see EFFECT

bring up *vb* 1 to bring to maturity through care and education ⟨it takes an immense commitment and a lot of love to *bring up* a child properly⟩
syn breed, foster, raise, rear
rel father, mother; attend, care (for), cultivate, mind, minister (to), nurse, nurture, watch; discipline, educate, instruct, mentor, school, teach, train, tutor; edify, enlighten, indoctrinate; feed, nourish, provide (for), supply; advance, forward, further, promote; prepare; direct, guide, lead, shepherd, show
near ant abuse, ill-treat, ill-use, maltreat, mishandle, mistreat; ignore, neglect; harm, hurt, injure

2 to present or bring forward for discussion — see INTRODUCE 2

brininess *n* the quality or state of being salty — see SALTINESS

briny *adj* of, relating to, or containing salt — see SALTY 1

brisk *adj* 1 having much high-spirited energy and movement — see LIVELY 1
2 moving, proceeding, or acting with great speed — see FAST 1

briskly *adv* with great speed — see FAST 1

briskness *n* the quality or state of having abundant or intense activity — see VITALITY 1

bristle *vb* to express one's anger usually violently — see RAGE 1

bristly *adj* covered with or as if with hair — see HAIRY 1

brittle *adj* having a texture that readily breaks into little pieces under pressure — see CRISP 1

broach *vb* 1 to penetrate the surface (as of water) from below ⟨the immense whales *broaching* was a magnificent sight⟩
syn surface
rel break, emerge, rise
near ant dive, drop, founder, plunge, sink, submerge, submerse
2 to present or bring forward for discussion — see INTRODUCE 2

broad *adj* 1 having a greater than usual measure across — see WIDE 1
2 having considerable extent — see EXTENSIVE
3 not subject to misinterpretation or more than one interpretation — see CLEAR 2
4 relating to the main elements and not to specific details — see GENERAL 2

broadcast *vb* 1 to cause to be known over a considerable area or by many people — see SPREAD 1
2 to make known openly or publicly — see ANNOUNCE

broadly *adv* to a large extent or degree — see GREATLY 2

broad-minded *adj* 1 not bound by traditional ways or beliefs — see LIBERAL 1
2 willing to consider new or different ideas — see OPEN-MINDED 1

broadside *adv* with one side faced forward — see SIDEWAYS

brochure *n* a short printed publication with no cover or with a paper cover — see PAMPHLET

broiling *adj* having a notably high temperature — see HOT 1

broke *adj* lacking money or material possessions — see POOR 1

broken *adj* 1 having an uneven edge or outline — see RAGGED 1
2 not having a level or smooth surface — see UNEVEN 1

brokenhearted *adj* feeling unhappiness — see SAD 1

brood *vb* to cover and warm eggs to hatch them — see SET 1

brook *n* a natural body of running water smaller than a river — see CREEK 1

brook *vb* to put up with (something painful or difficult) — see BEAR 2

brooklet *n* a natural body of running water smaller than a river — see CREEK 1

brotherhood *n* **1** a group of persons formally joined together for some common interest — see ASSOCIATION 2

2 the body of people in a profession or field of activity — see CORPS

brotherly *adj* of, relating to, or befitting brothers — see FRATERNAL

browbeat *vb* to make timid or fearful by or as if by threats — see INTIMIDATE

brownie *n* an imaginary being usually having a small human form and magical powers — see FAIRY

browse *vb* **1** to feed on grass or herbs — see GRAZE

2 to take a quick or hasty look — see ¹GLANCE 2

bruise *n* a bodily injury in which small blood vessels are broken but the overlying skin is not — see CONTUSION

bruit (about) *vb* to make (as a piece of information) the subject of common talk without any authority or confirmation of accuracy — see RUMOR

brush *n* a brief clash between enemies or rivals — see ENCOUNTER

brush *vb* to pass lightly across or touch gently especially in passing ⟨spiderwebs *brushed* her cheek as she walked through the basement⟩

syn graze, kiss, nudge, shave, skim

rel bump, contact, scrape, strike, sweep, swipe, touch; bounce, carom, glance, rebound, ricochet, sideswipe, skip; caress, cuddle, fondle, pet, stroke

near ant clash, collide, hit, knock, punch, slap, smack, smash, thwack, whack

brush (aside *or* off) *vb* to overlook or dismiss as of little importance — see EXCUSE 1

brush–off *n* treatment that is deliberately unfriendly — see COLD SHOULDER

brushwood *n* a thick patch of shrubbery, small trees, or underbrush — see THICKET

brusque *adj* being or characterized by direct, brief, and potentially rude speech or manner — see BLUNT 1

brutal *adj* **1** difficult to endure — see HARSH 1

2 having or showing the desire to inflict severe pain and suffering on others — see CRUEL 1

brutality *n* the willful infliction of pain and suffering on others — see CRUELTY

brute *n* **1** one of the lower animals as distinguished from human beings — see ANIMAL

2 a mean, evil, or unprincipled person — see VILLAIN

bubble *vb* to flow in a broken irregular stream — see GURGLE

bubbly *adj* joyously unrestrained — see EXUBERANT

buccaneer *n* someone who engages in robbery of ships at sea — see PIRATE

buck *n* **1** a man extremely interested in his clothing and personal appearance — see DANDY

2 an adult male human being — see MAN 1

buck *vb* **1** to move or cause to move with a sharp quick motion — see JERK 1

2 to refuse to give in to — see RESIST

buckaroo *n* a hired hand who tends cattle or horses at a ranch or on the range — see COWBOY

bucket *n* **1** a considerable amount — see LOT 2

2 a round container that is open at the top and outfitted with a handle — see PAIL

buckle *vb* to occupy (oneself) diligently or with close attention — see APPLY 2

bucolic *adj* of, relating to, associated with, or typical of open areas with few buildings or people — see RURAL

buddy *n* a person who has a strong liking for and trust in another — see FRIEND 1

budge *vb* **1** to cease resistance (as to another's arguments, demands, or control) — see YIELD 3

2 to change one's position — see MOVE 3

3 to change the place or position of — see MOVE 1

budget *n* **1** a sum of money set aside for a particular purpose — see FUND 1

2 the number of individuals or amount of something available at any given time — see SUPPLY

buff *n* a person with a strong and habitual liking for something — see FAN

buff *vb* **1** to make smooth by friction — see GRIND 1

2 to make smooth or glossy usually by repeatedly applying surface pressure — see POLISH

buffed *adj* having a shiny surface or finish — see GLOSSY

buffer *n* something that serves as a protective barrier — see CUSHION

buffer *vb* to lessen the shock of — see CUSHION

¹**buffet** *n* a hard strike with a part of the body or an instrument — see ¹BLOW

²**buffet** *n* a storage case typically having doors and shelves — see CABINET

buffet *vb* to strike repeatedly — see BEAT 1

buffoon *n* a comically dressed performer (as at a circus) who entertains with playful tricks and ridiculous behavior — see CLOWN 1

bug *n* **1** a person with a strong and habitual liking for something — see FAN

2 an abnormal state that disrupts a plant's or animal's normal bodily functioning — see DISEASE

bug *vb* **1** to attack repeatedly with mean put-downs or insults — see TEASE 2

2 to disturb the peace of mind of (someone) especially by repeated disagreeable acts — see IRRITATE 1

3 to thrust oneself upon (another) without invitation — see BOTHER 1

---

syn synonym(s)   *rel* related words
ant antonym(s)   *near ant* near antonym(s)

bugaboo *n* something or someone that causes fear or dread especially without reason — see BOGEY 1

bugbear *n* something or someone that causes fear or dread especially without reason — see BOGEY 1

bugging *n* the act of making unwelcome intrusions upon another — see ANNOYANCE

build *n* the type of body that a person has — see PHYSIQUE

build *vb* to form by putting together parts or materials ⟨he spent hours *building* a model airplane from a kit⟩

syn assemble, construct, erect, fabricate, make, make up, piece, put up, raise, rear, set up

rel fashion, forge, frame, manufacture, mold, produce, shape; prefabricate; begin, coin, create, generate, inaugurate; initiate, innovate, invent, originate; constitute, establish, father, found, institute, organize; conceive, concoct, contrive, cook up, design, devise, imagine, think (up); rebuild; rig up

phrases put together

near ant dismember; demolish, destroy, devastate, flatten, pulverize, raze, ruin, shatter, smash, wreck; blow up, explode
ant disassemble, dismantle, take down

build (up) *vb* **1** to become greater in extent, volume, amount, or number — see INCREASE 2

2 to increase in — see GAIN 1

3 to produce or bring about especially by long or repeated effort — see HAMMER (OUT)

building *n* something built as a dwelling, shelter, or place for human activity ⟨English class will be in that big stone *building* over there⟩

syn edifice, structure

rel construction, erection; bungalow, cabin, chalet, cottage, house, lodge, summerhouse; hovel, hut, shack, shanty, shed; castle, château, estate, hall, manor, mansion, palace, villa; skyscraper, tower

bulge *n* a part that sticks out from the general mass of something ⟨several *bulges* in the old vinyl flooring in the dingy bathroom⟩

syn jut, overhang, projection, protrusion, protuberance

rel dome; blob, bump, knob, lump, nub, swelling; block, piece, portion, section; enlargement, escalation, expansion, increase

near ant cavity, crater, hole; basin, dip, valley

ant concavity, dent, depression, hollow, indentation, pit

bulge *vb* to extend outward beyond a usual point ⟨the sides of the returning camper's suitcase *bulged* with a month's worth of dirty laundry⟩

syn bag, balloon, beetle, belly, billow, jut, overhang, poke, project, protrude, stand out, start, stick out

rel dome; blow up, inflate; distend, expand, swell; mushroom, snowball; elongate, extend, lengthen, stretch

near ant compress, condense, constrict, contract, shrink

bulk *n* the main or greater part of something as distinguished from its appendages — see BODY 1

bulkiness *n* the quality or state of being large in size — see LARGENESS

bulky *adj* of a size greater than average of its kind — see LARGE

bull *n, slang* a member of a force charged with law enforcement at the local level — see OFFICER 1

bulldoze *vb* to force one's way — see PRESS 4

bullet *n* a usually round or cone-shaped little piece of lead made to be fired from a firearm ⟨it is possible to make your own *bullets*, but it takes a lot of patience and some extra money⟩

syn ball, pellet

rel ammunition, cannonball, cap, cartridge, charge, gunshot, lead, load, missile, pop, projectile, round, shell, shot, slug; twenty-two

near ant blank

bulletin *n* a published statement informing the public of a matter of general interest — see ANNOUNCEMENT

bully *n* **1** a person who teases, threatens, or hurts smaller or weaker persons ⟨the *bully* spent most of the afternoon in detention for pushing people down on the playground⟩

syn intimidator

rel antagonist, enemy; harrier, nuisance, persecutor, pest, tease, teaser; heckler; goon, hood, hoodlum, punk, rough, roughneck, rowdy, ruffian, thug, tough; cutthroat, felon, gangster, gunman, mobster, racketeer

2 a violent, brutal person who is often a member of an organized gang — see HOODLUM

bully *vb* to make timid or fearful by or as if by threats — see INTIMIDATE

bulwark *n* something that holds up or serves as a foundation for something else — see SUPPORT 1

bum *adj* of low quality — see CHEAP 2

bum *n* a homeless wanderer who may beg or steal for a living — see TRAMP

bummer *n* **1** something (as a situation or event) that is depressing — see DOWNER

2 something that disappoints — see DISAPPOINTMENT 2

3 something that has failed — see FAILURE 3

bump *n* **1** a small rounded mass of swollen tissue ⟨that's a nasty *bump* on your arm where you hit the table⟩

syn knot, lump, node, nodule, swelling

rel growth, tumor, wart; hump, hunch; bruise, contusion; blob, chunk, clod, clump, gob, gobbet, hunk, knob, nub, nubble, nugget, wad

2 a forceful coming together of two things — see IMPACT 1

bump *vb* to come into usually forceful contact with something — see HIT 2

bumper *adj* unusually large — see HUGE

bumper *n* something that serves as a protective barrier — see CUSHION

bumpkin *n* an awkward or simple person especially from a small town or the country — see HICK

bumpy *adj* **1** marked by a series of sharp quick motions — see JERKY 1

2 not having a level or smooth surface — see UNEVEN 1

bunch *n* **1** a group of people sharing a common interest and relating together socially — see GANG 2

2 a number of things considered as a unit — see GROUP 1

3 a usually small number of persons considered as a unit — see GROUP 2

bunch *vb* to gather into a closely packed group — see PRESS 3

bundle *n* a wrapped or sealed case containing an item or set of items — see PACKAGE 1

bung *vb* to close up so that no empty spaces remain — see FILL 2

bungle *vb* to make or do (something) in a clumsy or unskillful way — see BOTCH

bungling *adj* showing or marked by a lack of skill and tact (as in dealing with a situation) — see AWKWARD 2

¹bunk *n* a place set aside for sleeping — see BED 1

²bunk *n* **1** language, behavior, or ideas that are absurd and contrary to good sense — see NONSENSE 1

2 unintelligible or meaningless talk — see GIBBERISH

bunk *vb* to provide with living quarters or shelter — see HOUSE 1

buoy (up) *vb* to fill with courage or strength of purpose — see ENCOURAGE 1

buoyant *adj* **1** having or showing a good mood or disposition — see CHEERFUL 1

2 joyously unrestrained — see EXUBERANT

burden *n* **1** a mass or quantity of something taken up and carried, conveyed, or transported — see LOAD 1

2 a part of a song or hymn that is repeated every so often — see CHORUS 2

3 something one must do because of prior agreement — see OBLIGATION

burden *vb* **1** to place a weight or burden on — see LOAD 1

2 to make sad — see DEPRESS 1

burdensome *adj* **1** difficult to endure — see HARSH 1

2 requiring much time, effort, or careful attention — see DEMANDING 1

bureau *n* a large unit of a governmental, business, or educational organization — see DIVISION 2

bureaucrat *n* a worker in a government agency ⟨the *bureaucrats* at the town hall seem to think that we need a building permit to build a tree house⟩

syn functionary, public servant

rel clerk, officeholder, official; employee, underling, worker

burg *n* a thickly settled, highly populated area — see CITY

burgeon *vb* **1** to become greater in extent, volume, amount, or number — see INCREASE 2

2 to grow vigorously — see THRIVE 1

3 to produce flowers — see BLOOM

burgher *n* a person who lives in a town on a permanent basis ⟨many of the college students are regarded by the local *burghers* as obnoxious louts⟩

syn citizen, townie, villager

rel denizen, dweller, habitant, homeowner, inhabitant, national, native, occupant, resident, resider; town, townsfolk, townspeople; suburbanite, urbanite

near ant foreigner, guest, tourist, transient, visitor

burglarize *vb* **1** to enter a house or building by force usually with illegal intent — see BREAK IN 1

2 to remove valuables from (a place) unlawfully — see ROB

burial *n* the act or ceremony of putting a dead body in its final resting place ⟨the children wanted to give the dead bird a proper *burial* in the backyard⟩

syn burying, entombing, entombment, interment, interring, sepulture

rel embalmment, funeral

near ant cremation

ant disinterment, exhumation, unearthing

burlesque *n* a work that imitates and exaggerates another work for comic effect — see PARODY 1

burlesque *vb* to copy or exaggerate (someone or something) in order to make fun of — see MIMIC 1

burly *adj* strongly and heavily built — see ¹HUSKY

burn *vb* **1** to be on fire especially brightly ⟨all evening long we just sat there, contentedly watching the Yule log *burn*⟩

syn blaze, combust, flame, glow

rel fire, ignite, kindle; flare (up), light (up); flicker, gutter, waver; bake, broil, char, cook, melt, roast, scorch, swelter; smolder, spark, sputter; beam, brighten, radiate; beat (down), flash, glare, gleam, glimmer, glint, glisten, glitter, scintillate, shimmer, shine, sparkle, twinkle

2 to set (something) on fire ⟨it is not a good idea to try to *burn* old papers in the sink⟩

syn fire, ignite, inflame, kindle, light

rel char, scorch; bake, cremate, incinerate, kiln; brighten, illumine, illuminate, irradiate, lighten, radiate; scald, scathe, sear; rekindle, relight

near ant choke, smother, suffocate; stamp (out); blacken, darken, dim, dull, obscure

ant douse, extinguish, put out, quench, snuff (out)

3 to be excited or emotionally stirred up with anger — see BOIL 1

---

4 to shine with a bright harsh light — see GLARE 1

burnable *adj* capable of catching or being set on fire — see COMBUSTIBLE

burned–out *or* **burnt–out** *adj* depleted in strength, energy, or freshness — see WEARY 1

burning *adj* **1** being on fire — see ABLAZE 1

2 having a notably high temperature — see HOT 1

3 having or expressing great depth of feeling — see FERVENT

burnish *vb* to make smooth or glossy usually by repeatedly applying surface pressure — see POLISH

burnished *adj* having a shiny surface or finish — see GLOSSY

burnout *n* a complete depletion of energy or strength — see FATIGUE

burn out *vb* to use up all the physical energy of — see EXHAUST 1

burro *n* a sturdy and patient domestic mammal that is used especially to carry things — see DONKEY 1

burrow *n* the shelter or resting place of a wild animal — see DEN 1

burst *n* **1** a sudden and usually temporary growth of activity — see OUTBREAK

2 a sudden intense expression of strong feeling — see OUTBURST 1

burst *vb* **1** to break open or into pieces usually because of internal pressure — see EXPLODE 1

2 to cause to break open or into pieces by or as if by an explosive — see BLAST 1

burst (forth) *vb* to develop suddenly and violently — see ERUPT 1

bursting *adj* containing or seeming to contain the greatest quantity or number possible — see FULL 1

bursting *n* the act or an instance of exploding — see EXPLOSION 1

bury *vb* **1** to place (a dead body) in the earth, a tomb, or the sea ⟨he died on Tuesday and was *buried* on Friday⟩

syn entomb, inter

rel enshrine; conceal, cover, ensconce, hide; obscure, shade, shield; cloak, curtain, enshroud, shroud

near ant burn, cremate; bare, disclose, discover, display, exhibit, expose, reveal, show

ant disinter, exhume, unearth

2 to put into a hiding place — see ¹HIDE 1

burying *n* the act or ceremony of putting a dead body in its final resting place — see BURIAL

bush *n* a rural region that forms the edge of the settled or developed part of a country — see FRONTIER 2

bushed *adj* depleted in strength, energy, or freshness — see WEARY 1

bushel *n* a considerable amount — see LOT 2

business *n* **1** a commercial or industrial activity or organization — see ENTERPRISE 1

2 something to be dealt with — see MATTER 2

3 the buying and selling of goods especially on a large scale and between different places — see COMMERCE

bust *n* **1** a hard strike with a part of the body or an instrument — see ¹BLOW

2 something that has failed — see FAILURE 3

bust *vb* **1** to bring to a lower grade or rank — see DEMOTE

2 to cause to lose one's fortune and become unable to pay one's debts — see RUIN 1

3 to cause to separate into pieces usually suddenly or forcibly — see BREAK 1

4 to deliver a blow to (someone or something) usually in a strong vigorous manner — see HIT 1

5 *slang* to take or keep under one's control by authority of law — see ARREST 1

bustle *n* a state of noisy, confused activity — see COMMOTION

bustling *adj* marked by much life, movement, or activity — see ALIVE 2

busy *adj* **1** involved in often constant activity ⟨the deadline is in two days, so everyone at work has been extremely *busy*⟩

syn active, assiduous, diligent, employed, engaged, industrious, laborious, occupied, sedulous, working

rel absorbed, concentrating, engrossed, focused (*also* focussed), immersed, intent, preoccupied; alive, functional, functioning, going, living, operating, operational, operative, running; energetic, vigorous; indefatigable, tireless, untiring

near ant asleep, dormant, latent, quiescent, sleepy; inert, passive; dead, dull, slow; inoperative, nonoperating

ant idle, inactive, unemployed, unengaged, unoccupied

2 marked by much life, movement, or activity — see ALIVE 2

busy *vb* to hold the attention of — see ENGAGE 1

busybody *n* a person who meddles in the affairs of others ⟨that *busybody* across the street is always telling me how to tend to my own garden⟩

syn interferer, interloper, intruder, kibitzer, meddler

rel peeper, peeping Tom, snoop, snooper, spy; blabber, discloser, gossip, gossiper, prattler, revealer, teller; betrayer, talebearer, tattletale; snake, sneak; informer, snitcher, squealer, stool pigeon

but *adv* nothing more than — see JUST 3

but *conj* **1** if it were not for the fact that — see EXCEPT

2 in spite of that — see HOWEVER

but *prep* not including — see EXCEPT

butcher *vb* **1** to kill on a large scale — see MASSACRE

2 to make or do (something) in a clumsy or unskillful way — see BOTCH

butchery *n* the killing of a large number of people — see MASSACRE

¹butt *n* the part of the body upon which someone sits — see BUTTOCKS

²**butt** *n* **1** a person or thing that is made fun of — see LAUGHINGSTOCK

2 a person or thing that is the object of abuse, criticism, or ridicule — see TARGET 1

butt in *vb* to interest oneself in what is not one's concern — see INTERFERE

buttocks *n pl* the part of the body upon which someone sits ⟨she slipped in the mud puddle and hit the ground square on her *buttocks*⟩

syn backside, bottom, breech, butt, fanny, hams, haunches, posterior, rear, rump, seat

buttress *n* **1** something or someone to which one looks for support — see DEPENDENCE 2

2 something that holds up or serves as a foundation for something else — see SUPPORT 1

buttress *vb* to hold up or serve as a foundation for — see SUPPORT 3

buy *n* something bought or offered for sale at a desirable price — see BARGAIN 1

buy *vb* to get possession of (something) by giving money in exchange for ⟨I really want to *buy* that new book, but I don't have enough money right now⟩

syn pick up, purchase, take

rel acquire, get, obtain, procure, secure; finance, pay (for), spring (for); barter (for), deal (for), exchange (for), trade (for); bargain (with), chaffer (with), dicker (over), horse-trade (with), negotiate (about), palter (with); bid, offer; rebuy, repurchase

buzz *n* **1** a communication by telephone — see CALL 3

2 a monotonous sound like that of an insect in motion — see HUM

buzz *vb* to fly, turn, or move rapidly with a fluttering or vibratory sound — see WHIRR

buzzing *adj* marked by much life, movement, or activity — see ALIVE 2

by *adv* at, within, or to a short distance or time — see NEAR 1

by *prep* **1** along the way of ⟨went *by* the woods to get to the summer cottage⟩

syn through, via

rel across, along, alongside, beyond, near, nearby, over; below, beneath, under, underneath; outside, past

phrases by way of

2 using the means or agency of ⟨try to convince them *by* reason alone, if possible⟩

syn per, through, with

phrases by means of, by (*or* in) virtue of, through the medium of

3 close to — see AROUND 1

by-and-by *n* time that is to come — see FUTURE 1

by and large *adv* for the most part — see CHIEFLY

bygone *adj* no longer existing — see EXTINCT

bylaw *n* a statement spelling out the proper procedure or conduct for an activity — see RULE 1

bypass *vb* to avoid by going around — see DETOUR 1

by-product *n* something that naturally develops or is developed from something else — see DERIVATIVE

byword *n* an often stated observation regarding something from common experience — see SAYING

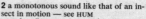

cab *n* an automobile that carries passengers for a fare usually determined by the distance traveled — see TAXI

cabal *n* a group involved in secret or criminal activities — see RING 1

cabaret *n* a bar or restaurant offering special nighttime entertainment (as music, dancing, or comedy acts) — see NIGHTCLUB

cabin *n* **1** a small, simply constructed, and often temporary dwelling — see SHACK

2 an often small house for recreational or seasonal use — see COTTAGE

3 one of the parts into which an enclosed space is divided — see COMPARTMENT

cabinet *n* a storage case typically having doors and shelves ⟨the most precious knickknacks were kept in a *cabinet* with glass doors⟩

syn buffet, closet, cupboard, hutch, locker, sideboard

rel bookcase, secretary; shelving; console

cabinetwork *n* the movable articles in a room — see FURNITURE

cable *n* a length of braided, flexible material that is used for tying or connecting things — see CORD

cache *n* **1** a collection of things kept available for future use or need — see STORE 1

2 a supply stored up and often hidden away — see HOARD 1

cache *vb* **1** to put (something of future use or value) in a safe or secret place — see HOARD

2 to put into a hiding place — see ¹HIDE 1

---

syn synonym(s)   *rel* related words
ant antonym(s)   *near ant* near antonym(s)

caching *n* the placing of something out of sight — see CONCEALMENT 1

cackle *n* an explosive sound that is a sign of amusement — see LAUGH 1

cackle *vb* to engage in casual or rambling conversation — see CHAT

cackler *n* a person who talks constantly — see CHATTERBOX

cacophony *n* loud, confused, and usually unharmonious sound — see NOISE 1

cad *n* a person whose behavior is offensive to others — see JERK 1

cadaver *n* a dead body — see CORPSE

cadaverous *adj* 1 lacking a healthy skin color — see PALE 2

2 suffering extreme weight loss as a result of hunger or disease — see EMACIATED

caddy *n* a covered rectangular container for storing or transporting things — see CHEST

cadence *n* the recurrent pattern formed by a series of sounds having a regular rise and fall in intensity — see RHYTHM

cadenced *adj* marked by or occurring with a noticeable regularity in the rise and fall of sound — see RHYTHMIC

café *also* **cafe** *n* 1 a bar or restaurant offering special nighttime entertainment (as music, dancing, or comedy acts) — see NIGHTCLUB

2 a place of business where alcoholic beverages are sold to be consumed on the premises — see BARROOM

3 a public establishment where meals are served to paying customers for consumption on the premises — see RESTAURANT

cage *n* an enclosure with an open framework for keeping animals ⟨the dogs and cats at the animal shelter looked so sad in their *cages*⟩

syn coop, corral, pen, pound
rel fence; cote, dovecote, fold; aquarium, terrarium

cage *vb* to close or shut in by or as if by barriers — see ENCLOSE 1

cagey *also* **cagy** *adj* clever at attaining one's ends by indirect and often deceptive means — see ARTFUL 1

caginess *n* skill in achieving one's ends through indirect, subtle, or underhanded means — see CUNNING 1

cajole *vb* to get (someone) to do something by gentle urging, special attention, or flattery — see COAX

cake *n* a small usually rounded mass of minced food that has been fried ⟨the rich, tender *cakes* of crabmeat had been lightly fried⟩

syn croquette, cutlet, fritter, patty (*also* pattie)
rel finger, stick

cake *vb* to cover with a hardened layer — see ENCRUST

calamitous *adj* 1 bringing about ruin or misfortune — see FATAL 1

2 causing or tending to cause destruction — see DESTRUCTIVE 1

calamity *n* a sudden violent event that brings about great loss or destruction — see DISASTER

calculate *vb* 1 to determine (a value) by doing the necessary mathematical operations ⟨the family has been *calculating* what a week at the beach resort would end up costing⟩

syn compute, figure, reckon, work out
rel conjecture, estimate, guess, judge, suppose; add up, sum, tally, total; add, cipher, divide, multiply, subtract; calibrate, gauge (*also* gage), measure, scale; ascertain, discover, dope (out), figure out, find out; recompute, refigure

2 to decide the size, amount, number, or distance of (something) without actual measurement — see ESTIMATE 2

3 to work out the details of (something) in advance — see PLAN 1

calculated *adj* decided on as a result of careful thought — see DELIBERATE 1

calculation *n* the act or process of performing mathematical operations to find a value ⟨by my *calculation*, it should take me a month to save up for the sneakers⟩

syn arithmetic, ciphering, computation, figures, figuring, reckoning
rel mathematics; addition, division, multiplication, subtraction; appraisal, assessment, estimation, evaluation, judgment (*or* judgement)

calendar *n* a listing of things to be presented or considered (as at a concert or play) — see PROGRAM 1

caliber *or* **calibre** *n* degree of excellence — see QUALITY 1

call *n* 1 a natural vocal sound made by an animal ⟨a ranger who could immediately identify the *call* of every creature in the forest⟩

syn cry, note
rel bark, bay, bellow, bleat, bray, caterwaul, caw, cheep, chirp, grunt, hoot, howl, low, meow, moo, neigh, peep, roar, screech, squawk, squeak, squeal, twitter, whinny, yap, yelp, yip, yowl

2 a coming to see another briefly for social or business reasons ⟨we paid a *call* on the new neighbors the day after they moved in⟩

syn visit, visitation
rel meeting, rendezvous, tryst; stopover

3 a communication by telephone ⟨give me a *call* as soon as you arrive, so I'll know you got there safely⟩

syn buzz, ring
rel callback; toll call; message

4 an act or instance of asking for information — see QUESTION 2

5 an entitlement to something — see CLAIM 1

call *vb* 1 to speak so as to be heard at a distance ⟨we could hear someone *calling* for help from the other side of the wall⟩

syn bawl, cry, holler, shout, vociferate, yell
rel bellow, roar; whoop; scream, screech, shriek, shrill, squeak, squeal; caterwaul, howl, wail, yawp (*or* yaup), yowl
near ant breathe, mumble, murmur, mutter, whisper

2 to make a telephone call to 〈use this cell phone to *call* me if there's an emergency〉
syn dial, phone, ring (up) [*chiefly British*], telephone
rel beep, buzz

3 to make a brief visit 〈the hospital posts the hours during which friends and relatives may *call*〉
syn drop (by *or* in), pop (in), stop (by *or* in), visit
rel barge (in); look up, see; frequent, hang around (in), hang out (at), haunt, resort (to)

4 to put an end to (something planned or previously agreed to) — see CANCEL 1

5 to think of in a particular way — see CONSIDER 1

6 to utter one's distinctive animal sound — see CRY 1

7 to bring together in assembly by or as if by command — see CONVOKE

8 to decide the size, amount, number, or distance of (something) without actual measurement — see ESTIMATE 2

9 to demand or request the presence or service of — see SUMMON 1

10 to give a name to — see NAME 1

call (for) *vb* **1** to ask for (something) earnestly or with authority — see DEMAND 1
2 to make a request for — see ASK (FOR) 1

call (on *or* upon) *vb* to make a social call upon — see VISIT 1

caller *n* a person who visits another — see GUEST 1

calligraphy *n* writing done by hand — see HANDWRITING 2

calling *n* **1** the act of putting an end to something planned or previously agreed to — see CANCELLATION
2 the activity by which one regularly makes a living — see OCCUPATION

calling off *n* the act of putting an end to something planned or previously agreed to — see CANCELLATION

call off *vb* **1** to put an end to (something planned or previously agreed to) — see CANCEL 1

callous *adj* having or showing a lack of sympathy or tender feelings — see HARD 1

callow *adj* lacking in adult experience or maturity 〈a story about a *callow* youth who learns the value of hard work and self-reliance〉
syn adolescent, green, immature, inexperienced, juvenile, puerile, raw, unfledged, unripe, unripened
rel babyish, childish, infantile; boyish, girlish, maidenly, virginal, youthful; ingenuous, innocent, naive (*or* naïve); unpracticed, unseasoned, untrained, untried
near ant advanced, precocious; knowing, sophisticated, worldly-wise
ant adult, experienced, grown-up, mature, ripe

calm *adj* **1** free from storms or physical disturbance 〈after a stormy night of high winds and driving rains, the day dawned on a *calm* sea〉
syn halcyon, hushed, peaceful, placid, quiet, serene, still, stilly, tranquil, untroubled
rel calming, pacific, restful, soothing; inactive, inert, quiescent, reposing, resting; smooth, unruffled; clear, cloudless, fair, rainless, sunny, sunshiny
near ant bleak, cloudy, dirty, foul, nasty, overcast, rainy, raw, rough, squally
ant agitated, angry, stormy, turbulent

2 free from emotional or mental agitation 〈bystanders tried to help the injured person remain *calm* while they waited for the ambulance to arrive〉
syn collected, composed, cool, coolheaded, placid, self-possessed, serene, tranquil, undisturbed, unperturbed, unshaken, untroubled, unworried
rel imperturbable, nerveless, unflappable, unshakable; disciplined, self-contained, self-controlled; affable, breezy, devil-may-care, easygoing, happy-go-lucky, laid-back, low-pressure; carefree, nonchalant, unconcerned; assured, confident, self-assured; aloof, detached, dispassionate, indifferent; impassive, phlegmatic, stolid
near ant anxious, bothered, distressed, worried; jittery, jumpy, nervous, skittish, tense; high-strung, uptight
ant agitated, discomposed, disturbed, flustered, perturbed, upset

3 free from disturbing noise or uproar — see QUIET 1

calm *n* a state of freedom from storm or disturbance 〈vacationing city dwellers who are tired of the hustle and bustle enjoy the *calm* of the secluded mountain village〉
syn calmness, hush, peace, peacefulness, placidity, quiet, quietness, quietude, repose, restfulness, sereneness, serenity, still, stillness, tranquillity (*or* tranquility)
rel lull, pause, respite; silence; comity, concord, harmony
near ant clamor, din, noise, racket
ant bustle, commotion, hubbub, hurly-burly, pandemonium, tumult, turmoil, uproar

calm *vb* **1** to free from distress or disturbance 〈the president's reassuring words did much to *calm* the public during the national emergency〉
syn allay, compose, quiet, settle, soothe, still, tranquilize (*also* tranquillize)
rel alleviate, assuage, ease, mitigate, relieve; appease, conciliate, mollify, pacify, placate; lull, relax, stupefy
near ant aggravate, heighten, intensify; arouse, excite, foment, incite, rouse, stir (up)
ant agitate, discompose, disquiet, disturb, perturb, upset

2 to gain emotional or mental control of — see COLLECT 1

calm (down) *vb* to become still and orderly — see QUIET 1

---

syn synonym(s)   *rel* related words
ant antonym(s)   *near ant* near antonym(s)

calming *adj* tending to calm the emotions and relieve stress — see SOOTHING 1

calmness *n* 1 a state of freedom from storm or disturbance — see CALM

2 evenness of emotions or temper — see EQUANIMITY

camaraderie *n* the feeling of closeness and friendship that exists between companions — see COMPANIONSHIP

camouflage *n* clothing put on to hide one's true identity or imitate someone or something else — see DISGUISE

camouflage *vb* to change the dress or looks of so as to conceal true identity — see DISGUISE

camp *n* 1 a place where a group of people live for a short time in tents or cabins ⟨the war forced people to flee their homes and to live in crowded *camps* along the border⟩
syn bivouac, campground, campsite, encampment
rel barracks; colony, plantation, settlement; shantytown; concentration camp, prison camp

2 a small, simply constructed, and often temporary dwelling — see SHACK

3 an often small house for recreational or seasonal use — see COTTAGE

camp *vb* to live in a camp or the outdoors ⟨rather than stay in motels, my family usually *camps* when we're on vacation⟩
syn bivouac, encamp
rel tent; backpack
phrases rough it

campaign *n* a series of activities undertaken to achieve a goal ⟨an all-out *campaign* to bring a minor league baseball team to the city⟩
syn bandwagon, cause, crusade, drive, movement
rel attack, march, offensive

campaigner *n* one who seeks an office, honor, position, or award — see CANDIDATE

camper *n* a motor vehicle that is specially equipped for living while traveling ⟨the family loaded up the *camper* and headed off for the tour of several national parks⟩
syn caravan, mobile home, motor home, trailer
rel van

campground *n* a place where a group of people live for a short time in tents or cabins — see CAMP 1

campsite *n* a place where a group of people live for a short time in tents or cabins — see CAMP 1

can *vb* 1 to bring (as an action or operation) to an immediate end — see STOP 1
2 to let go from office, service, or employment — see DISMISS 1

can *n* a metal container in the shape of a cylinder ⟨the shelter stores huge *cans* of water for an emergency⟩
syn barrel, drum
rel tube; tin

canal *n* an open man-made passageway for water — see CHANNEL 1

cancel *vb* 1 to put an end to (something planned or previously agreed to) ⟨please call to *cancel* your appointment with the dentist if you can't make it⟩
syn abort, call, call off, drop, recall, repeal, rescind, revoke
rel abrogate, annul, invalidate, nullify, void, write off; recant, retract, take back, withdraw; countermand, reverse; end, halt, stop, terminate; give up, relinquish, surrender
near ant engage, pledge, promise; begin, commence, initiate, start; take on, take up, undertake
ant continue, keep

2 to put an end to by formal action — see ABOLISH

3 to show (something written) to be no longer valid by drawing a cross over or a line through it — see X (OUT)

cancel (out) *vb* to balance with an equal force so as to make ineffective — see OFFSET

canceler *or* **canceller** *n* a force or influence that makes an opposing force ineffective or less effective — see COUNTERBALANCE

cancellation *n* the act of putting an end to something planned or previously agreed to ⟨the misbehavior of a few bad apples at the end of the football game resulted in the *cancellation* of the victory party⟩
syn abortion, calling, calling off, dropping, recall, repeal, rescission, revocation
rel annulment, invalidation, neutralization, nullification; abolishment, abolition, ending, halting, stopping, termination; giving up, relinquishment, surrender
near ant beginning, commencement, initiation; engagement, undertaking
ant continuation

candid *adj* free in expressing one's true feelings and opinions — see FRANK

candidate *n* one who seeks an office, honor, position, or award ⟨each *candidate* for student council was allowed to speak at the school assembly⟩
syn applicant, aspirant, campaigner, contender, hopeful, prospect, seeker
rel competitor, contestant, entrant; also-ran, dark horse, favorite, finisher, has-been, runner-up; nominee; claimant, pretender
near ant incumbent, officeholder; dropout

candor *n* the free expression of one's true feelings and opinions ⟨an interview in which the members of the rock band speak with *candor* about their recent squabbling⟩
syn directness, forthrightness, frankness, openheartedness, openness, plainness, straightforwardness
rel earnestness, sincerity, sobriety; artlessness, genuineness, naïveté (*also* naivete), simplicity, unsophistication; bluffness, bluntness, brusqueness; freedom, license (*or* licence), unrestraint

near ant inhibition, reserve, restraint; diplomacy, tact

ant dissembling, pretense (*or* pretence)

cane *n* a heavy rigid stick used as a weapon or for punishment — see CLUB 1

canine *n* a domestic mammal that is related to the wolves and foxes — see DOG

canniness *n* skill in achieving one's ends through indirect, subtle, or underhanded means — see CUNNING 1

cannonade *n* a rapid or overwhelming outpouring of many things at once — see BARRAGE

canny *adj* having or showing a practical cleverness or judgment — see SHREWD

canon *n* **1** a statement or body of statements concerning faith or morals proclaimed by a church — see DOCTRINE 1

2 a record of a series of items (as names or titles) usually arranged according to some system — see ¹LIST

canonize *vb* **1** to declare to be a saint and worthy of public respect — see SAINT

2 to love or admire too much — see IDOLIZE

canopy *n* a raised covering over something for decoration or protection ⟨trees line both sides of the garden path, with their foliage forming a leafy *canopy* for walkers⟩

syn awning, ceiling, roof, tent

rel screen, shade, shelter, shield, sunshade; canvas, fly

¹**cant** *n* the degree to which something rises up from a position level with the horizon — see SLANT

²**cant** *n* **1** the pretending of having virtues, principles, or beliefs that one in fact does not have — see HYPOCRISY

2 the special terms or expressions of a particular group or field — see TERMINOLOGY

cant *vb* to set or cause to be at an angle — see LEAN 1

cantankerous *adj* having or showing a habitually bad temper — see ILL-TEMPERED

canted *adj* running in a slanting direction — see DIAGONAL

canticle *n* a religious song — see HYMN

canvas *n* a picture created with usually oil paint — see PAINTING

canvass *vb* to go around and approach (people) with a request for opinions or information ⟨we *canvassed* people all over town, asking if they would be interested in participating in a recycling program⟩

syn poll, solicit, survey

rel interrogate, interview, question; feel (out), sound (out)

near ant report

canyon *also* **cañon** *n* a narrow opening between hillsides or mountains that can be used for passage ⟨as the scouts made their way through the *canyon*, they marveled at the sheer walls of rock on both sides⟩

syn defile, flume, gap, gorge, gulch, gulf, notch, pass, ravine

rel abyss, chasm, cirque, cleft, crevasse, crevice, fissure; dale, glen, hollow, vale, valley; basin, floodplain, plain; arroyo, coulee, gully, gutter, wash [*Western*]

cap *n* **1** a covering for the head usually having a shaped crown — see HAT

2 a piece placed over an open container to hold in, protect, or conceal its contents — see COVER 1

capability *n* **1** a skill, an ability, or knowledge that makes a person able to do a particular job — see QUALIFICATION 1

2 the physical or mental power to do something — see ABILITY

capable *adj* having the required skills for an acceptable level of performance — see COMPETENT

capably *adv* in a skillful or expert manner — see WELL 3

capacious *adj* more than adequate or average in capacity — see SPACIOUS

capacity *n* **1** the largest number or amount that something can hold ⟨the seating *capacity* of the school auditorium is 800 people⟩

syn complement, content

rel area, room, space, volume; fill, load, measure

2 an assignment at which one regularly works for pay — see JOB 1

3 the action for which a person or thing is specially fitted or used or for which a thing exists — see ROLE

4 the physical or mental power to do something — see ABILITY

caparison *n* **1** dressy clothing — see FINERY

2 something that decorates or beautifies — see DECORATION 1

caparison *vb* to outfit with clothes and especially fine or special clothes — see CLOTHE 1

¹**cape** *n* a sleeveless garment worn so as to hang over the shoulders, arms, and back ⟨the mysterious figure wrapped his *cape* tightly around his shoulders⟩

syn cloak, mantle, roquelaure

rel frock, gown, robe; shawl, stole, wrap; poncho, serape (*or* sarape)

²**cape** *n* an area of land that juts out into a body of water ⟨residents fled the *cape* as the hurricane roared up the coast⟩

syn arm, headland, peninsula, point, promontory, spit

rel breakwater, jetty

caper *n* a playful or mischievous act intended as a joke — see PRANK

caper *vb* to play and run about happily — see FROLIC 1

capital *adj* of the very best kind — see EXCELLENT

capital *n* **1** a thing or place that is of greatest importance to an activity or interest — see CENTER 1

2 the total of one's money and property — see WEALTH

capitalize *vb* to provide money for — see FINANCE 1

---

syn synonym(s)   *rel* related words
ant antonym(s)   *near ant* near antonym(s)

capitalize (on) *vb* to take unfair advantage of — see EXPLOIT 1

capitol *n* the building in which a state legislature meets ⟨the legislators were called to the *capitol* for an emergency session⟩
syn state house
rel meetinghouse; chamber, hall

capitulate *vb* **1** to cease resistance (as to another's arguments, demands, or control) — see YIELD 3
2 to yield to the control or power of enemy forces — see FALL 2

capitulating *n* the usually forced yielding of one's person or possessions to the control of another — see SURRENDER

capitulation *n* the usually forced yielding of one's person or possessions to the control of another — see SURRENDER

caprice *n* a sudden impulsive and apparently unmotivated idea or action — see WHIM

capricious *adj* **1** likely to change frequently, suddenly, or unexpectedly — see FICKLE 1
2 prone to sudden illogical changes of mind, ideas, or actions — see WHIMSICAL

capriciousness *n* an inclination to sudden illogical changes of mind, ideas, or actions — see WHIMSICALITY

capsize *vb* to turn on its side or upside down ⟨a huge wave out of nowhere caused our little sailboat to *capsize*⟩
syn overturn, upset
rel invert, topple; keel over; heel, list, tilt; founder, sink, swamp
phrases turn turtle
ant right

capsule *n* **1** a small mass containing medicine to be taken orally — see PILL
2 something that encloses another thing especially to protect it — see ¹CASE 1

captain *n* **1** a person in overall command of a ship ⟨the *captain* is responsible for everything that happens to his ship in the course of a voyage⟩
syn commander, skipper
rel master; commanding officer; admiral, commodore, vice admiral
2 one in official command especially of a military force or base — see COMMANDER 1
3 the person (as an employer or supervisor) who tells people what to do — see BOSS

captain *vb* **1** to be in charge of — see BOSS 1
2 to exercise authority or power over — see GOVERN 1
3 to serve as leader of — see LEAD 2

caption *n* **1** an explanation or description accompanying a pictorial illustration ⟨for the school yearbook, funny *captions* were written for snapshots showing a typical day at school⟩
syn legend
rel key; subtitle, translation; motto, tag line
2 a word or series of words often in larger letters placed at the beginning of a passage or at the top of a page in order to introduce or categorize — see HEADING

captious *adj* given to making or expressing unfavorable judgments about things — see CRITICAL 1

captivate *vb* to attract or delight as if by magic — see CHARM 1

captivating *adj* having an often mysterious or magical power to attract — see FASCINATING 1

captivation *n* the power of irresistible attraction — see CHARM 2

captive *adj* taken and held prisoner ⟨the *captive* soldiers were treated humanely by the guards⟩
syn apprehended, arrested, captured, caught, imprisoned, incarcerated, interned, jailed
rel bound, enslaved, indentured; subdued, subjugated
near ant emancipated, enfranchised, freed, liberated, released
ant free

captive *n* one that has been taken and held in confinement ⟨the *captives* in the concentration camp had devised a daring plan of escape⟩
syn capture, internee, prisoner
rel convict, jailbird; parolee
near ant custodian, guard, guardian, jailer (*or* jailor), keeper, warden
ant captor

captivity *n* the act of confining or the state of being confined — see INTERNMENT

capture *n* one that has been taken and held in confinement — see CAPTIVE

capture *vb* **1** to receive as return for effort — see EARN 1
2 to take physical control or possession of (something) suddenly or forcibly — see CATCH 1

captured *adj* taken and held prisoner — see CAPTIVE

car *n* a self-propelled passenger vehicle on wheels ⟨every teenager's dream of getting a driver's license and a first *car*⟩
syn auto, automobile, machine, motor, motorcar, motor vehicle
rel bus, coach, minibus; beach buggy, brougham, compact, convertible, coupe, dune buggy, fastback, gas-guzzler, hardtop, hatchback, hot rod, jeep, limousine, roadster, sedan, sports car, station wagon, stock car, subcompact, van; flivver, jalopy

caravan *n* **1** a group of vehicles traveling together or under one management — see FLEET
2 a motor vehicle that is specially equipped for living while traveling — see CAMPER

caravansary *or* **caravanserai** *n* a place that provides rooms and usually a public dining room for overnight guests — see HOTEL

carbon copy *n* **1** something or someone that strongly resembles another — see IMAGE 1
2 something that is made to look exactly like something else — see COPY

carcass *n* a dead body — see CORPSE

card *n* a person (as a writer) noted for or specializing in humor — see HUMORIST

cardinal *adj* coming before all others in importance — see FOREMOST 1

care *n* 1 strict attentiveness to what one is doing ⟨that's an extremely valuable violin, so handle it with *care*⟩

syn carefulness, conscientiousness, heed, heedfulness, pains, scrupulousness

rel exactness, meticulousness, particularity, punctiliousness; dutifulness, responsibility; bother, effort, trouble; alertness, vigilance, watchfulness

ant carelessness, heedlessness

2 a close attentiveness to avoiding danger — see CAUTION 1

3 an uneasy state of mind usually over the possibility of an anticipated misfortune or trouble — see ANXIETY 1

4 responsibility for the safety and well-being of someone or something — see CUSTODY

5 the duty or function of watching or guarding for the sake of proper direction or control — see SUPERVISION 1

care *vb* to have an interest or concern for ⟨a teacher who *cares* what happens to her students long after they leave her classroom⟩

syn mind, watch

rel attend, heed, regard; note, notice, observe; empathize (with), feel (for), sympathize (with)

phrases look out for

near ant disregard, ignore, overlook

care (for) *vb* 1 to take charge of especially on behalf of another — see ²TEND 1

2 to attend to the needs and comforts of — see NURSE 1

3 to have a favorable opinion of — see APPROVE (OF)

4 to wish to have — see LIKE 1

careen *vb* 1 to make a series of unsteady side-to-side motions — see ROCK 1

2 to move forward while swaying from side to side — see STAGGER 1

career *vb* to proceed or move quickly — see HURRY 2

carefree *adj* having or showing a lack of concern or seriousness ⟨passengers on a luxury cruise ship enjoying a *carefree* vacation⟩ ⟨*carefree* college students on spring break⟩

syn breezy, cavalier, devil-may-care, easygoing, gay, happy-go-lucky, insouciant, lighthearted, unconcerned

rel breezy, nonchalant; casual, informal, laid-back, low-pressure, relaxed; heedless, irresponsible, lackadaisical, negligent, reckless

near ant earnest, grave, serious, somber (*or* sombre); careful, cautious, heedful, wary; concerned, upset, worried; long-suffering, overburdened, sorrowful

ant careworn

careful *adj* 1 having or showing a close attentiveness to avoiding danger or trouble ⟨*careful* drivers slow down on slick or icy roadways⟩

syn alert, cautious, circumspect, considerate, gingerly, guarded, heedful, safe, wary

rel attentive, chary, observant, vigilant, watchful; foresighted, forethoughtful, provident; cagey (*also* cagy), noncommittal; calculating, scheming, shrewd; considerate, thoughtful; deliberate, slow

near ant bold, impetuous, rash, reckless; inattentive, unobservant; inconsiderate, thoughtless; lax, neglectful, negligent; imprudent, indiscreet, injudicious

ant careless, heedless, incautious, unguarded, unsafe, unwary

2 taking great care and effort — see PAINSTAKING

carefulness *n* 1 a close attentiveness to avoiding danger — see CAUTION 1

2 strict attentiveness to what one is doing — see CARE 1

careless *adj* 1 not paying or showing close attention especially for the purpose of avoiding trouble ⟨a *careless* reporter who often doesn't get his facts straight⟩ ⟨a *careless* mistake that caused the plane to crash⟩

syn heedless, incautious, mindless, unguarded, unsafe, unwary

rel bold, impetuous, rash, reckless; inattentive, unobservant; blithe, inconsiderate, thoughtless; absentminded, forgetful, unmindful; lax, neglectful, negligent, remiss; imprudent, indiscreet, injudicious; inadvertent, unintentional, unplanned

near ant attentive, chary, observant, vigilant, watchful; foresighted, forethoughtful, provident; calculating, scheming, shrewd; considerate, thoughtful

ant alert, cautious, circumspect, gingerly, guarded, heedful, safe, wary

2 failing to give proper care and attention — see NEGLIGENT

3 having or showing a lack of concern or seriousness — see CAREFREE

carelessness *n* failure to take the care that a cautious person usually takes — see NEGLIGENCE 1

caress *vb* to touch or handle in a tender or loving manner — see FONDLE

caretaker *n* a person who takes care of a property sometimes for an absent owner — see CUSTODIAN 1

cargo *n* a mass or quantity of something taken up and carried, conveyed, or transported — see LOAD 1

caricature *n* 1 a poor, insincere, or insulting imitation of something — see MOCKERY 1

2 a work that imitates and exaggerates another work for comic effect — see PARODY 1

3 the representation of something in terms that go beyond the facts — see EXAGGERATION

caricature *vb* to copy or exaggerate (someone or something) in order to make fun of — see MIMIC 1

carnage *n* the killing of a large number of people — see MASSACRE

carnal *adj* 1 having to do with life on earth especially as opposed to that in heaven — see EARTHLY

2 of or relating to the human body — see PHYSICAL 1

3 pleasing to the physical senses — see SENSUAL

carnival *n* a time or program of special events and entertainment in honor of something — see FESTIVAL

carol *n* a religious song — see HYMN

carol *vb* to produce musical sounds with the voice — see SING 1

caroler *or* **caroller** *n* one who sings — see SINGER

carom *vb* to strike and fly off at an angle — see GLANCE 1

carousal *n* a bout of drinking — see CAROUSE

carouse *n* a bout of drinking ⟨the Old West custom of heading to the saloon at night for a *carouse* and some poker playing⟩

syn carousal, drunk, wassail

rel binge, jag, spree; blowout, orgy

carp *vb* 1 to express dissatisfaction, pain, or resentment usually tiresomely — see COMPLAIN

2 to make often peevish criticisms or objections about matters that are minor, unimportant, or irrelevant — see QUIBBLE

carper *n* a person given to harsh judgments and to finding faults — see CRITIC 1

carpet *vb* to form a layer over — see COVER 2

carping *adj* given to making or expressing unfavorable judgments about things — see CRITICAL 1

carriage *n* 1 a horse-drawn wheeled vehicle for carrying passengers ⟨a museum with a large collection of beautiful, old *carriages*⟩

syn equipage, rig

rel brougham, buckboard, cab, chaise, coach, hackney, hansom, surrey

2 a general way of holding the body — see POSTURE 1

carry *vb* 1 to support and take from one place to another ⟨each camper must be able to *carry* his or her own backpack⟩

syn bear, cart, convey, ferry, haul, lug, pack, tote, transport

rel deliver, hand over, transfer; forward, send, ship, transmit; bring, fetch, take; move, remove, shift

2 to wear or have on one's person ⟨I always *carry* a camera with me so as to never miss a great shot⟩

syn bear, pack

rel flaunt, show off, sport; display, exhibit, parade, show

3 to bring before the public in performance or exhibition — see PRESENT 1

4 to have as part of a whole — see INCLUDE

5 to hold up or serve as a foundation for — see SUPPORT 3

6 to receive as return for effort — see EARN 1

carryall *n* a bag carried by hand and designed to hold a traveler's clothing and personal articles — see TRAVELING BAG

carry away *vb* 1 to fill with overwhelming emotion (as wonder or delight) — see ENTRANCE

2 to subject to incapacitating emotional or mental stress — see OVERWHELM 1

carry on *vb* 1 to behave badly — see MISBEHAVE

2 to continue despite difficulties, opposition, or discouragement — see PERSEVERE

3 to look after and make decisions about — see CONDUCT 1

carry out *vb* to carry through (as a process) to completion — see PERFORM 1

cart *n* a wheeled usually horse-drawn vehicle used for hauling ⟨an old *cart* piled up with hay⟩

syn wagon, wain

rel barrow, pushcart, wheelbarrow; oxcart

cart *vb* to support and take from one place to another — see CARRY 1

cartel *n* a number of businesses or enterprises united for commercial advantage ⟨a *cartel* of oil-producing nations that controls production and influences prices⟩

syn combination, combine, syndicate, trust

rel chain, conglomerate, multinational; association, organization, pool

cartoon *n* 1 a picture using lines to represent the chief features of an object or scene — see DRAWING

2 a series of drawings that tell a story or part of a story — see COMIC STRIP

carve *vb* to create a three-dimensional representation of (something) using solid material — see SCULPT

carve (out) *vb* to produce or bring about especially by long or repeated effort — see HAMMER (OUT)

cascade *n* a fall of water usually from a great height — see WATERFALL

¹case *n* 1 something that encloses another thing especially to protect it ⟨those binoculars come with their own *case*⟩

syn armor, capsule, casing, cocoon, cover, covering, housing, husk, jacket, pod, sheath, shell

rel bark, crust; mail, plate, plating, shield; hide, skin; envelope, wrapper; backing, coating, facing

2 a covered rectangular container for storing or transporting things — see CHEST

²case *n* 1 an individual awaiting or under medical care and treatment — see PATIENT

2 one of a group or collection that shows what the whole is like — see EXAMPLE

3 something that actually exists — see FACT 1

4 a statement given to explain a belief or act — see REASON 1

5 a sudden experiencing of a physical or mental disorder — see ATTACK 2

6 something that might happen — see EVENT 2

7 something that requires thought and skill for resolution — see PROBLEM 1

cash n something (as pieces of stamped metal or printed paper) customarily and legally used as a medium of exchange, a measure of value, or a means of payment — see MONEY

cashier vb to let go from office, service, or employment — see DISMISS 1

cash in (on) vb to take unfair advantage of — see EXPLOIT 1

casing n something that encloses another thing especially to protect it — see ¹CASE 1

cask n an enclosed wooden vessel for holding beverages ⟨casks of wine that had been in the castle for many years⟩
syn barrel, firkin, hogshead, keg, pipe, puncheon
rel tub, vat; can, drum

casket n **1** a box for holding a dead body — see COFFIN

2 a covered rectangular container for storing or transporting things — see CHEST

cast n **1** a declaration that something will happen in the future — see PREDICTION

2 a property that becomes apparent when light falls on an object and by which things that are identical in form can be distinguished — see COLOR 1

3 an instance of looking especially briefly — see LOOK 2

4 facial appearance regarded as an indication of mood or feeling — see LOOK 1

5 the outward appearance of something as distinguished from its substance — see FORM 1

cast vb **1** to get rid of as useless or unwanted — see DISCARD

2 to point or turn (something) toward a target or goal — see AIM 1

3 to put (something) into proper and usually carefully worked out written form — see COMPOSE 1

4 to send through the air especially with a quick forward motion of the arm — see THROW

cast (off) vb to throw or give off — see EMIT 1

cast (out) vb to drive or force out — see EJECT 1

cast about (for) vb to go in search of — see SEEK 1

cast around (for) vb to go in search of — see SEEK 1

castaway n one who is cast out or rejected by society — see OUTCAST

caste n one of the segments of society into which people are grouped — see CLASS 1

castigate vb **1** to criticize (someone) severely or angrily especially for personal failings — see SCOLD

2 to criticize harshly and usually publicly — see ATTACK 2

3 to inflict a penalty on for a fault or crime — see PUNISH

castigating adj inflicting, involving, or serving as punishment — see PUNITIVE

castigation n suffering, loss, or hardship imposed in response to a crime or offense — see PUNISHMENT

castigator n **1** a person given to harsh judgments and to finding faults — see CRITIC 1

2 one who inflicts punishment in return for an injury or offense — see NEMESIS 1

castle n a large impressive residence — see MANSION

castoff n one who is cast out or rejected by society — see OUTCAST

casual adj **1** not designed for special occasions ⟨a restaurant where people in *casual* clothes are always welcome⟩
syn everyday, informal, workaday
rel sporty; shabby, sloppy, slovenly, unkempt
near ant best, Sunday; chic, elegant, fashionable, smart, stylish; neat, tidy, trim; semiformal
ant dressy, formal

2 happening by chance — see ACCIDENTAL

3 having or showing a lack of interest or concern — see INDIFFERENT 1

4 lacking in steadiness or regularity of occurrence — see FITFUL

casualness n lack of interest or concern — see INDIFFERENCE

casualty n **1** a person or thing harmed, lost, or destroyed ⟨the real *casualties* in the war against drugs are millions of innocent children⟩
syn fatality, loss, victim
rel failure, loser
near ant gainer, victor, winner

2 a chance and usually sudden event bringing loss or injury — see ACCIDENT 1

cat n **1** a small domestic animal known for catching mice ⟨the family's *cat* did a good job of keeping the house and yard free of all rodents⟩
syn feline, house cat, kitty, puss, pussy
rel mouser; kit, kitten; tabby, tomcat

2 *slang* an adult male human being — see MAN 1

cataclysm n **1** a great flow of water or of something that overwhelms — see FLOOD

2 a sudden violent event that brings about great loss or destruction — see DISASTER

3 a violent disturbance (as of the political or social order) — see CONVULSION

cataclysmal or **cataclysmic** adj **1** bringing about ruin or misfortune — see FATAL 1

2 causing or tending to cause destruction — see DESTRUCTIVE 1

3 marked by sudden or violent disturbance — see CONVULSIVE

catacomb n, usually **catacombs** pl an underground burial chamber — see CRYPT

---

syn synonym(s)   *rel* related words
ant antonym(s)   *near ant* near antonym(s)

catalog or **catalogue** n a record of a series of items (as names or titles) usually arranged according to some system — see ¹LIST

catalog or **catalogue** vb to put (someone or something) on a list — see ¹LIST 2

catamount n a large tawny cat of the wild — see COUGAR

catapult vb to send through the air especially with a quick forward motion of the arm — see THROW

cataract n 1 a fall of water usually from a great height — see WATERFALL

2 a great flow of water or of something that overwhelms — see FLOOD

catastrophe n 1 a sudden violent event that brings about great loss or destruction — see DISASTER

2 something that has failed — see FAILURE 3

catastrophic adj bringing about ruin or misfortune — see FATAL 1

catcall n a vocal sound made to express scorn or disapproval ⟨the band's sloppy playing produced only *catcalls* from the crowd⟩

syn boo, hiss, hoot, jeer, raspberry, snort

rel smirk, sneer, snicker, snigger; gibe (or jibe), put-down, taunt; whistle

near ant applause, clapping

ant cheer

catch n 1 a danger or difficulty that is hidden or not easily recognized — see PITFALL 1

2 someone or something unusually desirable — see PRIZE 1

3 the total amount collected or obtained especially at one time — see HAUL 1

catch vb 1 to take physical control or possession of (something) suddenly or forcibly ⟨we tried to *catch* the kitten before she could sneak out the door⟩

syn bag, capture, collar, corral, get, grab, grapple, hook, land, nab, nail, seize, snap (up), snare, snatch, trap

rel lasso, rope; apprehend, arrest, detain; clasp, clutch, grasp, grip, hold, secure; rend, wrest; ensnare, entangle, entrap; abduct, kidnap, spirit (away or off)

phrases lay hold of

near ant discharge, free, liberate, release; drop, loosen

ant miss

2 to become affected with (a disease or disorder) — see CONTRACT 1

3 to bring (something) to a standstill — see ¹HALT 1

4 to put securely in place or in a desired position — see FASTEN 2

5 to recognize the meaning of — see COMPREHEND 1

catching adj 1 capable of being passed by physical contact from one person to another — see CONTAGIOUS 1

2 exciting a similar feeling or reaction in others — see CONTAGIOUS 2

catch on vb to come to an awareness — see DISCOVER 1

catch on (to) vb to recognize the meaning of — see COMPREHEND 1

catch up (with) vb to move fast enough to get even with — see OVERTAKE

catchy adj 1 likely to attract attention — see NOTICEABLE

2 requiring exceptional skill or caution in performance or handling — see TRICKY

categorical also **categoric** adj having no exceptions or restrictions — see ABSOLUTE 2

categorize vb to arrange or assign according to type — see CLASSIFY 1

category n one of the units into which a whole is divided on the basis of a common characteristic — see CLASS 2

cater vb to provide food or meals for — see FEED 1

cater (to) vb to give in to (a desire) — see INDULGE

catnap n a short sleep — see ¹NAP

catnap vb 1 be in a state of sleep — see SLEEP 1

2 to sleep lightly or briefly — see NAP 1

catnapping n a natural periodic loss of consciousness during which the body restores itself — see SLEEP 1

cattily adv in a mean or spiteful manner — see NASTILY

cattiness n 1 biting sharpness of feeling or expression — see ACRIMONY 1

2 the desire to cause pain for the satisfaction of doing harm — see MALICE

catty adj having or showing a desire to cause someone pain or suffering for the sheer enjoyment of it — see HATEFUL

caught adj taken and held prisoner — see CAPTIVE

cause n 1 someone or something responsible for a result ⟨the much-debated *causes* of the American Civil War⟩

syn antecedent, occasion, reason

rel consideration, determinant, factor; impetus, incentive, inspiration, instigation, stimulus; mother, origin, root, source, spring

near ant ramification; denouement, repercussion; conclusion, end; by-product, side effect

ant aftereffect, aftermath, consequence, corollary, development, effect, fate, fruit, issue, outcome, outgrowth, product, result, resultant, sequel, sequence, upshot

2 a series of activities undertaken to achieve a goal — see CAMPAIGN

cause vb to be the cause of (a situation, action, or state of mind) — see EFFECT

caustic adj marked by the use of wit that is intended to cause hurt feelings — see SARCASTIC

caution n 1 a close attentiveness to avoiding danger ⟨the extreme *caution* with which the zookeeper handled the snake⟩

syn alertness, care, carefulness, cautiousness, circumspection, heedfulness, wariness

rel attentiveness, chariness, vigilance, watchfulness; foresight, foresightedness, providence; calculation, canniness, deliberateness, deliberation, shrewdness

near ant abruptness, hastiness, impetuousness, precipitousness, rashness, suddenness; inconsideration, thoughtlessness
ant brashness, carelessness, heedlessness, incautiousness, recklessness, unwariness
2 something extraordinary or surprising — see WONDER 1
3 something that tells of approaching danger or risk — see WARNING 1
4 the act or an instance of telling beforehand of danger or risk — see WARNING 1

caution *vb* to give notice to beforehand especially of danger or risk — see WARN

cautionary *adj* serving as or offering a warning ⟨the story of King Midas is a *cautionary* tale about the perils of wishing for something—you just might get it⟩
syn admonishing, admonitory, cautioning, warning
rel didactic, moralistic, moralizing; advisory, counseling (*or* counselling); punishing, punitive

cautioning *adj* serving as or offering a warning — see CAUTIONARY

cautious *adj* having or showing a close attentiveness to avoiding danger or trouble — see CAREFUL 1

cautiousness *n* a close attentiveness to avoiding danger — see CAUTION 1

cavalcade *n* **1** a group of vehicles traveling together or under one management — see FLEET
2 a staged presentation often with music that consists of a procession of narrated or enacted scenes — see PAGEANT

cavalier *adj* **1** having a feeling of superiority that shows itself in an overbearing attitude — see ARROGANT
2 having or showing a lack of concern or seriousness — see CAREFREE

cavalier *n* an honorable and courteous man ⟨a novel about the dashing *cavaliers* and gracious ladies of the South before the Civil War⟩
syn gentleman
rel knight, prince; blade, buck, dandy, fop, gallant; charmer, smoothy (*or* smoothie); aristocrat, patrician

cave *n* a naturally formed underground chamber with an opening to the surface ⟨Kentucky's Mammoth *Cave* is actually a series of large chambers on five levels⟩
syn cavern, grot, grotto
rel abyss, chasm, gulf, hollow; subway, tunnel; excavation, mine, pit, shaft, well; bunker, dugout, foxhole; burrow, covert, den, hole, lair, lodge, shelter

cave (in) *vb* to fall down or in as a result of physical pressure — see COLLAPSE 1

cavern *n* a naturally formed underground chamber with an opening to the surface — see CAVE

cavil *vb* to make often peevish criticisms or objections about matters that are minor, unimportant, or irrelevant — see QUIBBLE

caviler *or* **caviller** *n* a person given to harsh judgments and to finding faults — see CRITIC 1

caviling *or* **cavilling** *adj* given to making or expressing unfavorable judgments about things — see CRITICAL 1

cavity *n* a sunken area forming a separate space — see HOLE 2

cavort *vb* to play and run about happily — see FROLIC 1

cease *vb* **1** to come to an end ⟨the rain finally *ceased*, and we were able to continue the baseball game⟩
syn break off, break up, close, conclude, die, discontinue, elapse, end, expire, finish, halt, lapse, leave off, let up, pass, quit, stop, terminate, wind up
rel desist (from), lay off (of), refrain (from); knock off; break down, conk (out), cut out, stall; pause, stay, suspend
near ant draw out, extend, prolong, protract
ant continue, hang on, persist
2 to bring (as an action or operation) to an immediate end — see STOP 1

cease-fire *n* a temporary stopping of fighting — see TRUCE

ceaseless *adj* **1** going on and on without any interruptions — see CONTINUOUS
2 lasting forever — see EVERLASTING

cede *vb* **1** to give (something) over to the control or possession of another usually under duress — see SURRENDER 1
2 to give over the legal possession or ownership of — see TRANSFER 1
3 to give up (as a position of authority) formally — see ABDICATE

ceiling *n* **1** a real or imaginary point beyond which a person or thing cannot go — see LIMIT
2 a raised covering over something for decoration or protection — see CANOPY

celebrant *n* one who engages in merrymaking especially in honor of a special occasion ⟨all of the *celebrants* at the birthday party received a favor to take home⟩
syn celebrator, merrymaker, reveler (*or* reveller), roisterer
rel carouser, wassailer; cutup, skylarker
ant killjoy, party pooper

celebrate *vb* to act properly in relation to — see KEEP 1

celebrated *adj* widely known — see FAMOUS

celebration *n* a time or program of special events and entertainment in honor of something — see FESTIVAL

celebrator *n* one who engages in merrymaking especially in honor of a special occasion — see CELEBRANT

celebrity *n* **1** a person who is widely known and usually much talked about ⟨*celebrities* from sports and entertainment attended the opening ceremonies of the Olympic Games⟩
syn figure, light, luminary, notable, personage, personality, somebody, standout, star, superstar, VIP

---

syn synonym(s)   ***rel*** related words
ant antonym(s)   ***near ant*** near antonym(s)

rel favorite, hero, idol; demigod, dignitary, eminence, immortal, pillar, worthy; baron, big shot, bigwig, magnate, mogul, nabob

near ant lightweight, mediocrity; hasbeen

ant nobody

2 the fact or state of being known to the public — see FAME

celerity *n* a high rate of movement or performance — see SPEED

celestial *adj* of, relating to, or suggesting heaven ⟨movie scenes depicting life after death are usually accompanied by *celestial* music⟩

syn Elysian, empyreal, empyrean, heavenly, supernal

rel ethereal, supernatural, transcendent, transcendental, unearthly, unworldly; angelic, beatific, blissful; Olympian, utopian; cosmic, stellar

near ant earthly, mundane, terrestrial, worldly

ant hellish, infernal

cell *n* **1** an area within a building that has been set apart from surrounding space by a wall — see ROOM 2

2 one of the parts into which an enclosed space is divided — see COMPARTMENT

cellar *n* a room or set of rooms below the surface of the ground ⟨an amazing variety of interesting things were found in the *cellar* of the old house⟩

syn basement

rel bunker, crawlway, foundation, hold

cement *n* **1** a substance used to stick things together — see GLUE

2 a uniting or binding force or influence — see BOND 2

cemetery *n* a piece of land used for burying the dead ⟨many of the soldiers who died in the battle are buried in a *cemetery* nearby⟩

syn graveyard, potter's field

rel catacombs, churchyard; crypt, grave, mausoleum, sepulcher (*or* sepulchre), sepulture, tomb, vault

censor *vb* to remove objectionable parts from ⟨the producers were told that they would have to *censor* their movie if they wanted a PG rating⟩

syn clean (up), expurgate

rel cleanse, purge, purify; abbreviate, edit, shorten; cut (out), delete, excise, expunge; repress, silence, suppress; censure, condemn, denounce; examine, review, screen, scrutinize

near ant approve, authorize, sanction

censurable *adj* **1** deserving reproach or blame — see BLAMEWORTHY

2 provoking or likely to provoke protest — see OBJECTIONABLE

censure *n* an often public or formal expression of disapproval ⟨a rare *censure* of a senator by the full United States Senate for misconduct⟩

syn condemnation, denunciation, rebuke, reprimand, reproach, reproof, stricture

rel admonishment, admonition, castigation, chastisement, punishment; belittlement, criticism, deprecation, depreciation, disparagement

near ant acclamation, honor, tribute; encomium, eulogy, panegyric, plaudit(s), praise; approval, blessing, sanction

ant citation, commendation, endorsement

censure *vb* **1** to express public or formal disapproval of ⟨a vote to *censure* the President for conduct that was unbecoming to his office⟩

syn condemn, denounce, rebuke, reprimand, reproach, reprove

rel admonish, castigate, chastise, punish; belittle, criticize, deprecate, depreciate, disparage

near ant acclaim, applaud, honor; eulogize, laud, praise; approve, bless, sanction

ant cite, commend, endorse (*also* indorse)

2 to declare to be morally wrong or evil — see CONDEMN 1

3 to express one's unfavorable opinion of the worth or quality of — see CRITICIZE

censurer *n* a person given to harsh judgments and to finding faults — see CRITIC 1

center *n* **1** a thing or place that is of greatest importance to an activity or interest ⟨a stretch of coastline that has long been the area's *center* of tourism⟩

syn base, capital, core, cynosure, eye, focus, heart, hub, mecca, nucleus, seat

rel focus, headquarters; kernel, nub, pith; deep, thick; essence, quintessence, soul; attraction, lodestone, magnet

2 an area or point that is an equal distance from all points along an edge or outer surface ⟨the *center* of the earth⟩

syn core, middle, midpoint, midst

rel inside, interior

ant perimeter, periphery

center *vb* to bring (something) to a central point or under a single control — see CENTRALIZE

central *adj* coming before all others in importance — see FOREMOST 1

centralize *vb* to bring (something) to a central point or under a single control ⟨the company decided to *centralize* all of its operations at its Ohio plant⟩

syn center, compact, concentrate, consolidate, unify, unite

rel coordinate, harmonize, integrate, orchestrate; blend, coalesce, combine, fuse, incorporate, merge; conjoin, join, link; assemble, collect, gather; reunify, reunite

near ant segregate, separate

ant decentralize, spread (out)

cerebral *adj* **1** much given to learning and thinking — see INTELLECTUAL 1

2 of or relating to the mind — see MENTAL 1

cerebrum *n* the part of a person that feels, thinks, perceives, wills, and especially reasons — see MIND 1

ceremonial *adj* following or agreeing with established form, custom, or rules — see FORMAL 1

ceremonial *n* an oft-repeated action or series of actions performed in accordance with tradition or a set of rules — see RITE

ceremonious *adj* 1 marked by or showing careful attention to set forms and details ⟨a century ago everyday life was much more *ceremonious* than in our anything-goes era⟩

syn correct, decorous, formal, proper, starchy

rel sober, solemn, stately; chivalrous, courtly, gallant; genteel, polished, refined; civil, courteous, polite, red-carpet

near ant improper, indecorous, unmannerly; discourteous, impolite, rude

ant casual, easygoing, informal, laid-back

2 following or agreeing with established form, custom, or rules — see FORMAL 1

ceremony *n* an oft-repeated action or series of actions performed in accordance with tradition or a set of rules — see RITE

certain *adj* 1 known but not named ⟨a *certain* person told me that today is your birthday⟩

syn anonymous, one, some, unidentified, unnamed, unspecified

rel particular, specific

near ant known, named, specified

2 having or showing a mind free from doubt ⟨I'm *certain* that they'll arrive on time⟩

syn assured, clear, cocksure, confident, doubtless, positive, sanguine, sure

rel self-assured, self-conceited, self-confident; decisive, resolute, unfaltering, unhesitating, unwavering

near ant hesitant, indecisive; wavering; diffident, unassuming

ant doubtful, dubious, uncertain, unsure

3 having been established and usually not subject to change — see FIXED 1

4 impossible to avoid or evade — see INEVITABLE

5 not likely to fail — see INFALLIBLE 2

certainly *adv* without any question — see INDEED 1

certainty *n* a state of mind in which one is free from doubt — see CONFIDENCE 2

certificate *n* a written or printed paper giving information about or proof of something ⟨a *certificate* will be awarded to each person who completes the course in lifesaving⟩

syn document, instrument

rel credentials; diploma, parchment; warrant, writ; warranty; coupon, voucher

certify *vb* 1 to declare (something) to be true or genuine ⟨experts *certified* the letter as indeed having been written by Abraham Lincoln⟩

syn attest, authenticate, avouch, testify (to), vouch (for), witness

rel guarantee, warrant; affirm, assert, aver, avow, profess

2 to give official or legal power to — see AUTHORIZE 1

certitude *n* a state of mind in which one is free from doubt — see CONFIDENCE 2

cessation *n* the stopping of a process or activity — see END 1

chafe *vb* 1 to make sore by continued rubbing ⟨ill-fitting boots that had badly *chafed* my heels⟩

syn abrade, gall, irritate

rel graze, scrape, scratch; burn, inflame; flay, peel, skin

2 to damage or diminish by continued friction — see ABRADE 1

3 to disturb the peace of mind of (someone) especially by repeated disagreeable acts — see IRRITATE 1

chaff *n* 1 discarded or useless material — see GARBAGE

2 good-natured teasing or exchanging of clever remarks — see BANTER

chaff *vb* to make fun of in a good-natured way — see TEASE 1

chaffer *vb* to talk over or dispute the terms of a purchase — see BARGAIN

chaffing *adj* marked by or expressive of mild or good-natured teasing — see QUIZZICAL

chaffy *adj* having no usefulness — see WORTHLESS

chain *n* 1 a series of things linked together ⟨the *chain* of events that led the American colonies to seek independence from Great Britain⟩

syn concatenation, progression, sequence, string, train

rel chain reaction; belt, circle, cycle; continuum, gamut, scale, spectrum; flow, river, stream; file, line, queue, row, succession

2 something that makes movement or progress more difficult — see ENCUMBRANCE

3 something that physically prevents free movement — see BOND 1

chain *vb* 1 to confine or restrain with or as if with chains — see BIND 1

2 to put or bring together so as to form a new and longer whole — see CONNECT 1

chair *n* 1 a person in charge of a meeting ⟨all questions and comments should be directed to the *chair*⟩

syn chairman, chairperson, moderator, president, speaker

rel chairwoman

2 the place of leadership or command — see HEAD 2

chairman *n* a person in charge of a meeting — see CHAIR 1

chairperson *n* a person in charge of a meeting — see CHAIR 1

chalet *n* an often small house for recreational or seasonal use — see COTTAGE

challenge *n* a feeling or declaration of disapproval or dissent — see OBJECTION

challenge *vb* 1 to demand proof of the truth or rightness of ⟨don't hesitate to *challenge* any statement that generalizes about people⟩

syn contest, dispute, query, question

rel doubt, mistrust; kick (about), object (to), protest; combat, fight, oppose, resist *near ant* back, defend, support; advocate, champion, promote; abide, endure, stomach, tolerate

ant accept, believe, embrace, swallow

2 to invite (someone) to take part in a contest or to perform a feat ⟨I *challenge* you to swim to the other side of the pond⟩

syn dare, defy, stump

rel beard, brave, brazen, breast, confront, face, outbrave

challenged *adj* deprived of the power to perform one or more natural bodily activities — see DISABLED

challenger *n* one who strives for the same thing as another — see COMPETITOR

challenging *adj* requiring much time, effort, or careful attention — see DEMANDING 1

chamber *n* **1** an area within a building that has been set apart from surrounding space by a wall — see ROOM 2

2 one of the parts into which an enclosed space is divided — see COMPARTMENT

chamber *vb* to provide with living quarters or shelter — see HOUSE 1

champ *n* the person who comes in first in a competition — see CHAMPION 1

champ *vb* to crush or grind with the teeth — see BITE (ON)

champion *n* **1** the person who comes in first in a competition ⟨the *champion* of the national spelling bee⟩

syn champ, victor, winner

rel finalist, semifinalist; medalist, prizewinner; star, superstar

near ant loser

2 a person who actively supports or favors a cause — see EXPONENT

champion *vb* to promote the interests or cause of — see SUPPORT 1

championship *n* the position occupied by the one who comes in first in a competition — see CROWN 2

chance *adj* happening by chance — see ACCIDENTAL

chance *n* **1** the uncertain course of events ⟨rather than leave everything to *chance*, let's plan how we're going to spend our time in New York City⟩

syn accident, circumstance, hap, hazard, luck

rel fortuitousness, randomness, uncertainty; fluke; destiny, doom, fate, fortune, lot; danger, peril, risk

near ant intent, intention, purpose; design, outline, plan, scheme

2 a favorable combination of circumstances, time, and place — see OPPORTUNITY

3 a measure of how often an event will occur instead of another — see PROBABILITY 2

4 a risky undertaking — see GAMBLE

chance *vb* **1** to take a chance on — see RISK 1

2 to take place — see HAPPEN

chance (upon) *vb* **1** to come upon face-to-face or as if face-to-face — see MEET

2 to come upon unexpectedly or by chance — see HAPPEN (ON OR UPON)

change *n* the act, process, or result of making different ⟨the positive *change* in our students' attitude toward people who are somehow different was a long and gradual process⟩

syn alteration, difference, modification, redoing, refashioning, remaking, remodeling, revamping, revise, revision, reworking, variation

rel amendment, correction, rectification; conversion, deformation, distortion, metamorphosis, mutation, transfiguration, transformation; fluctuation, oscillation, shift; displacement, replacement, substitution; adjustment, modulation, regulation

ant fixation, stabilization

change *vb* **1** to make different in some way ⟨Mother has *changed* the look of our living room more times than we care to remember⟩

syn alter, make over, modify, recast, redo, refashion, remake, remodel, revamp, revise, rework, vary

rel deform, metamorphose, mutate; revolutionize, transfigure, transform, transmute; commute, convert, exchange

ant fix, freeze, set, stabilize

2 to pass from one form, state, or level to another ⟨the weather in New England is constantly *changing*⟩

syn fluctuate, mutate, shift, vary

rel metamorphose, transmute; better, improve; deteriorate, worsen; seesaw, teeter, vacillate, waver

ant stabilize

3 to give up (something) and take something else in return ⟨would you mind *changing* your seat so my friends can sit together?⟩

syn commute, exchange, shift, substitute, swap, switch, trade

rel interchange; displace, replace, supersede; cede, surrender, yield

changeable *adj* **1** capable of being readily changed — see FLEXIBLE 1

2 likely to change frequently, suddenly, or unexpectedly — see FICKLE 1

changeful *adj* likely to change frequently, suddenly, or unexpectedly — see FICKLE 1

changeless *adj* not undergoing a change in condition — see CONSTANT 1

changelessness *n* the state of continuing without change — see CONSTANCY 1

changeover *n* a change in form, appearance, or use — see CONVERSION

changing *adj* not staying constant — see UNEVEN 2

channel *n* **1** an open man-made passageway for water ⟨water was drained from the swamp through a specially constructed *channel*⟩

syn aqueduct, canal, conduit, flume, raceway, watercourse, waterway

rel millrace, millstream; river, rivulet, stream

2 a narrow body of water between two land masses ⟨the world record for swimming the *channel* between France and Great Britain⟩

syn narrows, sound, strait

rel arm, bay, gulf, inlet; roads, roadstead; reach, stretch

3 a direct way of passing along information or supplies — see PIPELINE

4 a long hollow cylinder for carrying a substance (as a liquid or gas) — see PIPE 1

channel *vb* to cause to move to a central point or along a restricted pathway ⟨an athletic youth who *channeled* all of his energy into sports⟩

syn channelize, conduct, direct, funnel, pipe, siphon

rel carry, convey, transmit; concentrate, consolidate, focus

channelize *vb* to cause to move to a central point or along a restricted pathway — see CHANNEL

chant *vb* **1** to utter in musical or drawn out tones ⟨the frustrated crowd at the rock concert started to *chant*, "We want the show to start!"⟩

syn intone, sing

rel bellow, belt, roar; chime, chorus

2 to produce musical sounds with the voice — see SING 1

chaos *n* a state in which everything is out of order ⟨your room is in such *chaos* that it looks as though a tornado had struck⟩

syn confusion, disarrangement, disarray, disorder, disorganization, havoc, hell, jumble, mess, muddle, shambles

rel anarchy, lawlessness, misrule; knot, snarl, tangle; labyrinth, maze, web; maelstrom, storm; clutter, litter, mishmash, shuffle; hodgepodge, medley, miscellany, motley

near ant method, pattern, plan, system

ant order, orderliness

chaotic *adj* lacking in order, neatness, and often cleanliness — see MESSY

chap *n, chiefly British* an adult male human being — see MAN 1

chaparral *n* a thick patch of shrubbery, small trees, or underbrush — see THICKET

chaperone *or* **chaperon** *vb* to go along with in order to provide assistance, protection, or companionship — see ACCOMPANY

chapter *n* a local unit of an organization ⟨our *chapter* of the 4-H Club came in first in the competition⟩

syn affiliate, branch, local

rel arm, division, wing; offshoot; lodge, post

char *vb* to burn on the surface — see SCORCH

character *n* **1** a written or printed mark that is meant to convey information to the reader ⟨the pictorial *characters* of the ancient Egyptians were long a mystery⟩

syn sign, symbol

rel cipher, letter, numeral; hieroglyph, pictogram, pictograph; rune

2 a person of odd or whimsical habits — see ECCENTRIC

3 conduct that conforms to an accepted standard of right and wrong — see MORALITY 1

4 overall quality as seen or judged by people in general — see REPUTATION

5 something that sets apart an individual from others of the same kind — see CHARACTERISTIC

6 the set of qualities that make a person different from other people — see INDIVIDUALITY

7 the set of qualities that makes a person, a group of people, or a thing different from others — see NATURE 1

characteristic *adj* **1** serving to identify as belonging to an individual or group ⟨the *characteristic* taste of licorice⟩

syn classic, distinct, distinctive, distinguishing, identifying, individual, peculiar, proper, symptomatic, typical

rel idiosyncratic; identifiable, pronounced, unmistakable; general, generic; common, normal, regular, usual; particular, special, specific; archetypal, model, paradigmatic

ant atypical, nontypical

2 having or showing the qualities associated with the members of a particular group or kind — see TYPICAL 1

characteristic *n* something that sets apart an individual from others of the same kind ⟨the ability to fashion tools and other *characteristics* that distinguish human beings from other animals⟩

syn attribute, character, feature, mark, peculiarity, point, property, quality, trait

rel badge, indication, sign; emblem, symbol, token; excellence, merit, virtue; individuality, singularity, uniqueness

characterize *vb* **1** to point out the chief quality or qualities of an individual or group ⟨how would you *characterize* the mission of this environmental organization?⟩

syn define, depict, describe, portray, represent

rel categorize, classify, pigeonhole, type; identify, indicate, name, specify; distinguish, individualize, mark, particularize, stamp

2 to be an important feature of ⟨an unsightly rash *characterizes* chicken pox⟩

syn distinguish, mark

rel differentiate; customize, individualize, particularize

characterless *adj* lacking strength of will or character — see WEAK 2

charade *n* a display of emotion or behavior that is insincere or intended to deceive — see MASQUERADE

charge *n* **1** a formal claim of criminal wrongdoing against a person ⟨*charges* of burglary and armed robbery that have yet to be proved⟩

syn complaint, count, indictment, rap

rel accusation, allegation; arraignment, impeachment; implication, innuendo, insinuation; censure, condemnation, denunciation; incrimination

2 a specific task with which a person or group is charged — see MISSION

3 a statement of what to do that must be obeyed by those concerned — see COMMAND 1

4 something one must do because of prior agreement — see OBLIGATION

5 the act or action of setting upon with force or violence — see ATTACK 1

6 the amount of money that is demanded as payment for something — see PRICE 1

7 the duty or function of watching or guarding for the sake of proper direction or control — see SUPERVISION 1

charge *vb* **1** to set or receive as a price ⟨any shop would *charge* $100 to repair that thing⟩

syn ask, command, demand

rel overcharge, undercharge; bring, fetch, sell (for); discount, mark down, mark up; assess, price, value

2 to establish or apply as a charge or penalty — see IMPOSE

3 to give a task, duty, or responsibility to — see ENTRUST 1

4 to issue orders to (someone) by right of authority — see COMMAND 1

5 to make a claim of wrongdoing against — see ACCUSE

6 to put into (something) as much as can be held or contained — see FILL 1

7 to take sudden, violent action against — see ATTACK 1

charged *adj* having or expressing great depth of feeling — see FERVENT

charisma *n* the power of irresistible attraction — see CHARM 2

charitable *adj* **1** having or showing a concern for the welfare of others ⟨a *charitable* couple who have donated a sizable chunk of their fortune to the local university⟩

syn altruistic, beneficent, benevolent, humanitarian, philanthropic

rel selfless, self-sacrificing; bounteous, bountiful, free, freehanded, generous, greathearted, handsome, liberal, magnanimous, munificent, openhanded, openhearted, unselfish, unsparing; compassionate, humane, kind

near ant self-indulgent, self-seeking; cheap, closefisted, miserly, niggardly, parsimonious, stingy, tight, tightfisted; hardhearted, pitiless, unfeeling

ant self-centered, selfish

2 giving or sharing in abundance and without hesitation — see GENEROUS 1

charity *n* **1** the giving of necessities and especially money to the needy ⟨after amassing a fortune in the computer industry, they devoted themselves to *charity*⟩

syn almsgiving, philanthropy

rel altruism, humanitarianism; beneficence, benevolence, goodwill; alms, benefaction, contribution, donation; dole, relief, welfare; endowment, fund, grant, subsidy

2 a gift of money or its equivalent to a charity, humanitarian cause, or public institution — see CONTRIBUTION

3 kind, gentle, or compassionate treatment especially towards someone who is undeserving of it — see MERCY 1

4 the capacity for feeling for another's unhappiness or misfortune — see HEART 1

charlatan *n* one who makes false claims of identity or expertise — see IMPOSTOR

charley horse *n* a painful sudden tightening of a muscle — see CRAMP

charm *n* **1** something worn or kept to bring good luck or keep away evil ⟨an old cap that I use as a *charm* for whenever I play softball⟩

syn amulet, fetish (*also* fetich), mascot, mojo, phylactery, talisman

rel emblem, symbol, token, totem

near ant curse, hex, spell

ant hoodoo, jinx

2 the power of irresistible attraction ⟨a young singer with the kind of *charm* that turns a performer into a star⟩

syn allure, appeal, attractiveness, captivation, charisma, enchantment, fascination, glamour (*also* glamor), magic, magnetism, seductiveness, witchery

rel allurement, attraction, call, lure, seduction; agreeableness, delightfulness, desirableness, niceness, pleasantness, sweetness

near ant disagreeableness, distastefulness, obnoxiousness, offensiveness, unpleasantness

ant repulsion, repulsiveness

3 a spoken word or set of words believed to have magic power — see SPELL 1

4 an ornament worn on a chain around the neck or wrist — see PENDANT

charm *vb* **1** to attract or delight as if by magic ⟨a quaint seaside village that *charms* all who visit it⟩

syn allure, beguile, bewitch, captivate, enchant, fascinate, magnetize, wile

rel disarm, draw, entice, lure, pull, seduce, tempt; delight, gratify, please; arrest, enrapture, enthrall (*or* enthral), entrance; appeal (to), interest, intrigue; beckon, court, invite, solicit, woo

near ant disgust, offend, repel, revolt; annoy, displease, irk; bore, tire, weary

2 to cast a spell on — see BEWITCH 1

charmed *adj* being or appearing to be under a magic spell — see ENCHANTED

charmer *n* a person skilled in using supernatural forces — see MAGICIAN 1

charming *adj* having an often mysterious or magical power to attract — see FASCINATING 1

chart *n* an illustration of certain features of a geographical area — see MAP

chart *vb* to work out the details of (something) in advance — see PLAN 1

charter *vb* to take or get the temporary use of (something) for a set sum — see HIRE 1

charwoman *n* a female domestic servant — see MAID 1

chase n 1 an animal that is hunted or killed — see PREY

2 the act of going after or in the tracks of another — see PURSUIT

chase vb 1 to drive or force out — see EJECT 1

2 to go after or on the track of — see FOLLOW 1

3 to seek out (game) for food or sport — see HUNT 1

chasing n the act of going after or in the tracks of another — see PURSUIT

chasm n an immeasurable depth or space — see ABYSS

chaste adj free from any trace of the coarse or indecent ⟨as one would expect, the minister's small talk is always *chaste*, even though he likes a joke as much as the next person⟩

syn clean, decent, immaculate, modest, pure

rel spotless, stainless, unblemished, undefiled, unsoiled, unspotted, unstained, unsullied, untainted, untarnished; decorous, proper, seemly; cultivated, refined, tasteful; harmless, innocent, innocuous, inoffensive

near ant blemished, defiled, soiled, spotted, stained, sullied, tainted, tarnished; improper, indecorous, ribald, unseemly; crude, tacky, tasteless, unrefined

ant coarse, dirty, filthy, immodest, impure, indecent, obscene, smutty, unchaste, unclean, vulgar

chastely adv with purity of thought and deed — see PURELY

chasten vb to inflict a penalty on for a fault or crime — see PUNISH

chasteness n the quality or state of being morally pure — see CHASTITY

chastening adj inflicting, involving, or serving as punishment — see PUNITIVE

chastise vb to inflict a penalty on for a fault or crime — see PUNISH

chastisement n suffering, loss, or hardship imposed in response to a crime or offense — see PUNISHMENT

chastiser n one who inflicts punishment in return for an injury or offense — see NEMESIS 1

chastising adj inflicting, involving, or serving as punishment — see PUNITIVE

chastity n the quality or state of being morally pure ⟨a saint who is often held up as a model of *chastity*⟩

syn chasteness, modesty, purity

rel goodness, righteousness, virtuousness, morality, probity, rectitude; decency, decorum, propriety, seemliness

near ant badness, evil, sinfulness, unrighteousness, wickedness; impropriety, indecency

ant immodesty, impurity, unchastity

chat n friendly, informal conversation or an instance of this ⟨short *chats* between parents and teachers during the school's open house⟩

syn chatter, chitchat, gabfest, gossip, palaver, rap, small talk, table talk, talk, tête-à-tête

rel colloquy, conference, discourse, parley, powwow, symposium; debate, dialogue (or dialog), exchange, give-and-take

chat vb to engage in casual or rambling conversation ⟨the coffeehouse is a great place to meet friends and *chat* for hours⟩

syn babble, blab, cackle, chatter, converse, gab, gabble, gas, jabber, jaw, palaver, patter, prate, prattle, rap, rattle, run on, talk, twitter, visit

rel gossip, tattle; descant, discuss, expatiate

phrases shoot the breeze

chat (with) vb to communicate with by means of spoken words — see TALK 1

château n a large impressive residence — see MANSION

chattel n 1 a person who is considered the property of another person — see SLAVE 1

2 **chattels** pl transportable items that one owns — see POSSESSION 2

chatter n friendly, informal conversation or an instance of this — see CHAT

chatter vb 1 to engage in casual or rambling conversation — see CHAT

2 to speak rapidly, inarticulately, and usually unintelligibly — see BABBLE 1

chatterbox n a person who talks constantly ⟨my seat companion was a *chatterbox* who never once shut up during the whole trip⟩

syn babbler, blabber, cackler, chatterer, conversationalist, gabbler, jabberer, magpie, prattler, talker

rel blabbermouth, gossip, gossiper, talebearer, tattler, tattletale; converser

chatterer n a person who talks constantly — see CHATTERBOX

chatty adj 1 having the style and content of everyday conversation ⟨a time when campers were expected to write a *chatty* letter to their folks every week⟩

syn colloquial, conversational, gossipy, newsy

rel casual, familiar, informal, intimate; digressive, discursive, rambling; communicative, expansive, garrulous, talkative

near ant ceremonious, dignified, elevated, formal, solemn, stately

ant bookish, literary

2 fond of talking or conversation — see TALKATIVE

chauvinism n excessive favoritism towards one's own country ⟨their *chauvinism* blinded them to their country's faults⟩

syn jingoism, nationalism

rel loyalty, patriotism; xenophobia

near ant internationalism

chauvinist n one who shows excessive favoritism towards his or her country — see NATIONALIST

cheap adj 1 costing little ⟨e-mail is so popular because it's a *cheap* way to send messages⟩

syn cut-rate, inexpensive, low, reasonable

rel moderate, popular; discounted, lowered, reduced; wholesale

near ant precious, priceless, valuable; increased, inflated

ant costly, dear, expensive, high, premium

2 of low quality ⟨a *cheap* sweater that started to unravel almost as soon as I bought it⟩

syn bad, bum, cheesy, coarse, common, cut-rate, execrable, inferior, junky, lousy, low-grade, mediocre, miserable, poor, rotten, rubbishy, second-rate, shoddy, sleazy, terrible, trashy, trumpery, wretched

rel useless, valueless, worthless; flashy, garish, gaudy, meretricious, showy, tawdry; seedy, shabby, tacky; counterfeit, fake, phony (*also* phoney), sham

near ant elegant, handsome, tasteful; handcrafted, polished, refined

ant excellent, fine, first-class, first-rate, good, high-grade, superior, top-notch

3 giving or sharing as little as possible — see STINGY 1

cheapen *vb* to lower the price or value of — see DEPRECIATE 1

cheapness *n* the quality of being overly sparing with money — see PARSIMONY

cheapskate *n* a mean grasping person who is usually stingy with money — see MISER

cheat *n* a dishonest person who uses clever means to cheat others out of something of value — see TRICKSTER 1

cheat *vb* **1** to use dishonest methods to achieve a goal ⟨students who *cheat* on tests end up never knowing anything⟩

syn fudge

rel distort, falsify, misrepresent, twist; doctor, fake, tamper (with); color, elaborate, embellish, embroider, exaggerate, magnify, pad, stretch; dodge, evade, hedge

2 to fall short in satisfying the expectation or hope of — see DISAPPOINT

3 to rob by the use of trickery or threats — see FLEECE

cheater *n* a dishonest person who uses clever means to cheat others out of something of value — see TRICKSTER 1

check *n* **1** the amount owed at a bar or restaurant or the slip of paper stating the amount ⟨diners at the fancy restaurant often look shocked when they receive the *check*⟩

syn bill, tab

rel invoice; receipt; account, record, statement; charge, fee; score, tally

2 a close look at or over someone or something in order to judge condition — see INSPECTION

3 a record of goods sold or services performed together with the costs due — see ¹BILL 1

4 a small sheet of plastic, paper, or paperboard showing that the bearer has a claim to something (as admittance) — see TICKET 1

5 something that limits one's freedom of action or choice — see RESTRICTION 1

check *vb* **1** to be in agreement on every point ⟨their story of what happened *checks* with the report of the eyewitness⟩

syn accord, agree, answer, cohere, coincide, comport, conform, correspond, dovetail, fit, go, harmonize, jibe, square, tally

rel equal, match, parallel

near ant contradict, dispute, gainsay; negate, nullify; clash, conflict, jar

ant differ (from), disagree (with)

2 to bring (something) to a standstill — see ¹HALT 1

3 to keep from exceeding a desirable degree or level (as of expression) — see CONTROL 1

check (out) *vb* to look over closely (as for judging quality or condition) — see INSPECT

checklist *n* a record of a series of items (as names or titles) usually arranged according to some system — see ¹LIST

checkmate *vb* to prevent from achieving a goal — see FRUSTRATE

checkup *n* a close look at or over someone or something in order to judge condition — see INSPECTION

cheek *n* **1** disrespectful or argumentative talk given in response to a command or request — see BACK TALK

2 shameless boldness — see EFFRONTERY

cheekiness *n* shameless boldness — see EFFRONTERY

cheeky *adj* displaying or marked by rude boldness — see NERVY 1

cheep *vb* to make a short sharp sound like a small bird — see CHIRP

cheer *n* **1** a mood characterized by high spirits and amusement and often accompanied by laughter — see MIRTH

2 a feeling of ease from grief or trouble — see COMFORT 1

3 a state of mind dominated by a particular emotion — see MOOD 1

4 cheers *pl* enthusiastic and usually public expression of approval — see APPLAUSE

cheer *vb* **1** to declare enthusiastic approval of — see ACCLAIM

2 to ease the grief or distress of — see COMFORT 1

cheer (up) *vb* **1** to become glad or hopeful ⟨*cheer up* —things are bound to get better⟩

syn brighten, perk (up)

rel rejoice; liven (up), revive; beam, glow, radiate, sparkle; encourage, gladden, hearten

near ant despair, despond; brood, fret, mope

ant darken, sadden

2 to fill with courage or strength of purpose — see ENCOURAGE 1

cheerful *adj* **1** having or showing a good mood or disposition ⟨a *cheerful* person who is always fun to work with and a pleasure to be around⟩

syn blithe, blithesome, bright, buoyant, cheery, chipper, gay, gladsome, lightsome, sunny, upbeat

rel hopeful, optimistic, sanguine; jaunty, lively, perky, sprightly, vivacious; carefree, careless, cavalier, devil-may-care, easygoing, happy-go-lucky, insouciant, lighthearted, unconcerned; boon, jolly, jovial, merry, mirthful; glad, happy, pleased

near ant dull, lethargic, listless, sluggish, torpid; blue, dejected, depressed, heavyhearted, melancholy, sorrowful; discontented, disgruntled, unhappy

ant dour, gloomy, glum, morose, saturnine, sulky, sullen

2 serving to lift one's spirits ⟨a hospital with sunny, *cheerful* rooms that are designed to make a patient's stay as pleasant as possible⟩

syn bright, cheering, cheery, gay, glad

rel gladdening, heartening, heartwarming; gleaming, radiant, sparkling

near ant discouraging, disheartening; colorless, drab, dull, lackluster, lusterless

ant bleak, cheerless, dark, depressing, dismal, dreary, gloomy, gray (*also* grey)

cheerfully *adv* in a cheerful or happy manner — see GAILY 1

cheerfulness *n* a mood characterized by high spirits and amusement and often accompanied by laughter — see MIRTH

cheeriness *n* a mood characterized by high spirits and amusement and often accompanied by laughter — see MIRTH

cheering *adj* making one feel good inside — see HEARTWARMING

2 serving to lift one's spirits — see CHEERFUL 2

cheering *n* enthusiastic and usually public expression of approval — see APPLAUSE

cheerless *adj* causing or marked by an atmosphere lacking in cheer — see GLOOMY 1

cheery *adj* **1** having or showing a good mood or disposition — see CHEERFUL 1

2 serving to lift one's spirits — see CHEERFUL 2

cheesy *adj* **1** marked by an obvious lack of style or good taste — see TACKY 1

2 of low quality — see CHEAP 2

chef *n* a person who prepares food by some manner of heating — see COOK

cherish *vb* **1** to feel passion, devotion, or tenderness for — see LOVE 2

2 to hold dear — see LOVE 1

3 to keep in one's mind or heart — see HARBOR 1

cherished *adj* granted special treatment or attention — see DARLING 1

chest *n* a covered rectangular container for storing or transporting things ⟨a *chest* containing almost every tool that the home do-it-yourselfer is likely to need⟩

syn box, caddy, case, casket, locker, trunk

rel crate; footlocker; coffer, safe, safe-deposit box, strongbox; coffin; compartment, vault

chesterfield *n* a long upholstered piece of furniture designed for several sitters — see COUCH

chew *vb* to crush or grind with the teeth — see BITE (ON)

chew out *vb* to criticize (someone) severely or angrily especially for personal failings — see SCOLD

chew over *vb* **1** to give serious and careful thought to — see PONDER

2 to talk about (an issue) usually from various points of view and for the purpose of arriving at a decision or opinion — see DISCUSS

chewy *adj* not easily chewed — see TOUGH 1

chic *adj* being in the latest or current fashion — see STYLISH

chicanery *n* the use of clever underhanded actions to achieve an end — see TRICKERY

chick *n, slang* a young usually unmarried woman — see GIRL 1

chicken *adj* having or showing a shameful lack of courage — see COWARDLY

chicken *n* a person who shows a shameful lack of courage in the face of danger — see COWARD

chickenhearted *adj* having or showing a shameful lack of courage — see COWARDLY

chide *vb* to criticize (someone) usually gently so as to correct a fault — see REBUKE 1

chief *adj* **1** coming before all others in importance — see FOREMOST 1

2 highest in rank or authority — see HEAD

chief *n* the person (as an employer or supervisor) who tells people and especially workers what to do — see BOSS

chiefly *adv* for the most part ⟨our video collection consists *chiefly* of comedies, but we have a few horror movies⟩

syn altogether, basically, by and large, generally, largely, mainly, mostly, overall, predominantly, primarily, principally, substantially

rel nearly, practically, virtually; approximately, broadly, roughly; commonly, frequently, normally, ordinarily, usually; incompletely, partially, partly

phrases in general, on the whole

near ant completely, entirely, fully, totally, wholly; barely, hardly, marginally, minimally, scarcely

child *n* **1** a young person who is between infancy and adulthood ⟨an imaginative animated film that appeals to adults as well as *children*⟩

syn bairn [*chiefly Scottish*], cub, juvenile, kid, youngster, youth

rel adolescent, minor; schoolboy, schoolchild, schoolgirl; moppet, nestling, toddler, tot, tyke; brat, imp, squirt, urchin, whippersnapper; cherub; preteen, subteen, teenager, teenybopper; lad, nipper,

---

syn synonym(s)   **rel** related words
ant antonym(s)   **near ant** near antonym(s)

shaver, stripling, tad; bobby-soxer, hoyden, tomboy

near ant golden-ager, oldster, senior citizen

ant adult, grown-up

2 a recently born person — see BABY

childbearing *n* the act or process of giving birth to children — see CHILDBIRTH

childbirth *n* the act or process of giving birth to children ⟨women who choose to undergo *childbirth* without the use of anesthetics and other drugs⟩

syn childbearing, delivery, labor, parturition

rel pains; pregnancy; abortion, miscarriage; cesarean section (*also* cesarian section)

childhood *n* the state or time of being a child ⟨enjoy your *childhood* —it won't last forever⟩

syn youth

rel boyhood, girlhood; adolescence, minority; immaturity, juvenility; babyhood, infancy

near ant majority

ant adulthood

childish *adj* having or showing the annoying qualities (as silliness) associated with children ⟨you almost spoiled the ceremony for everyone with your *childish* giggling⟩

syn adolescent, babyish, immature, infantile, juvenile, kiddish, puerile

rel boyish, girlish; childlike, innocent, naive (*or* naïve), simple, unsophisticated

near ant experienced, sophisticated, worldly-wise

ant adult, grown-up, mature

child's play *n* **1** something of little importance — see TRIFLE

2 something that is easy to do — see CINCH

chill *adj* **1** lacking in friendliness or warmth of feeling — see COLD 2

2 uncomfortably cool — see CHILLY 1

chill *n* an uncomfortable degree of coolness ⟨there's a *chill* in the air, so you'd better wear a sweater⟩

syn bite, bitterness, bleakness, chilliness, nip, rawness, sharpness

rel briskness, crispness; coldness, frigidity, frigidness, frostiness, iciness; cold, freeze, snap

near ant balminess, warmth

chill *vb* to cause to lose heat — see COOL 1

chilliness *n* an uncomfortable degree of coolness — see CHILL

chilling *adj* uncomfortably cool — see CHILLY 1

chilly *adj* **1** uncomfortably cool ⟨those *chilly* nights when a warm fire can be especially comforting⟩

syn bitter, bleak, chill, chilling, nippy, raw, sharp

rel brisk, crisp; arctic, cold, freezing, frigid, frosty, icy

near ant balmy, warm

2 lacking in friendliness or warmth of feeling — see COLD 2

chime *vb* to make the clear sound heard when metal vibrates — see RING 1

chime *n*, usually **chimes** *pl* a series of short high ringing sounds — see TINKLE

chime in *vb* to cause a disruption in a conversation or discussion — see INTERRUPT

chimera *n* a conception or image created by the imagination and having no objective reality — see FANTASY 1

chimerical *adj* not real and existing only in the imagination — see IMAGINARY

chine *n* a column of bones supporting the trunk of a vertebrate animal — see SPINE

chink *n* an irregular usually narrow break in a surface created by pressure — see CRACK 1

chink *vb* to make a repeated sharp light ringing sound — see JINGLE

chip *n* **1** a small flat piece separated from a whole ⟨wood *chips* were spread over the ground between the plants⟩

syn flake, sliver, splint, splinter

rel bit, disk (*or* disc), fragment, particle, scrap, shard; shiver, smithereens; shred, tatter; clipping, paring, shaving, snippet; leaf, sheet, slice; chunk, hunk, lump, slab

2 a V-shaped cut usually on an edge or a surface — see NOTCH 1

3 chips *pl* something (as pieces of stamped metal or printed paper) customarily and legally used as a medium of exchange, a measure of value, or a means of payment — see MONEY

chip in *vb* to make a donation as part of a group effort — see CONTRIBUTE 1

chipper *adj* **1** enjoying health and vigor — see HEALTHY 1

2 having or showing a good mood or disposition — see CHEERFUL 1

chirp *vb* to make a short sharp sound like a small bird ⟨the sparrows were *chirping* up a storm in the backyard⟩

syn cheep, chirrup, peep, pipe, tweet, twitter

rel cackle, chatter, jabber; sing, trill, warble

chirr *n* a monotonous sound like that of an insect in motion — see HUM

chirrup *vb* to make a short sharp sound like a small bird — see CHIRP

chisel *vb* to rob by the use of trickery or threats — see FLEECE

chitchat *n* friendly, informal conversation or an instance of this — see CHAT

chivalrous *adj* having, characterized by, or arising from a dignified and generous nature — see NOBLE 2

chivy *vb* to thrust oneself upon (another) without invitation — see BOTHER 1

chock–full *or* **chockful** *adj* containing or seeming to contain the greatest quantity or number possible — see FULL 1

choice *adj* having qualities that appeal to a refined taste ⟨*choice* chocolates for which chocolate lovers are willing to pay extra⟩

syn dainty, delicate, elegant, exquisite, rare, select

rel elite, exclusive; excellent, outstanding, premium, prime, superior

near ant coarse, gross, vulgar; commercial, mass-produced, popular; common, ordinary; average, mediocre, run-of-the-mill, second-rate

choice *n* **1** the power, right, or opportunity to choose ⟨you have no *choice* : you have to go to school⟩

syn alternative, discretion, option, pick, preference, way

rel say, voice, vote; inclination, liking, partiality, penchant, predilection, proclivity, propensity, tendency; discernment, judgment (*or* judgement), perspicacity

near ant coercion, duress, force; duty, obligation

2 a person or thing that is chosen ⟨my *choice* for best song of all time⟩

syn pick, selection

rel favorite, like, liking, preference; elective, option; appointment, designation, nomination; appointee, candidate, nominee

3 individuals carefully selected as being the best of a class — see ELITE

4 the act or power of making one's own choices or decisions — see FREE WILL

5 the act or process of selecting — see SELECTION 1

choir *n* an organized group of singers — see CHORUS 1

choke *vb* **1** to keep (someone) from breathing by exerting pressure on the windpipe ⟨let go of my throat—you're *choking* me!⟩

syn garrote (*or* garotte), strangle, throttle

rel asphyxiate, smother, suffocate

near ant restore, resuscitate, revive

2 to experience complete or partial blockage of the windpipe ⟨the recommended procedure for helping someone who is *choking*⟩

syn gag

rel heave, retch, throw up, vomit; asphyxiate, smother, suffocate

near ant breathe, respire

3 to be or cause to be killed by lack of breathable air — see SMOTHER 1

4 to prevent passage through — see CLOG 1

choke (back) *vb* to refrain from openly showing or uttering — see SUPPRESS 2

choker *n* an ornamental chain or string (as of beads) worn around the neck — see NECKLACE

choleric *adj* easily irritated or annoyed — see IRRITABLE

chomp (on) *vb* to crush or grind with the teeth — see BITE (ON)

choose *vb* **1** to decide to accept (someone or something) from a group of possibilities ⟨*choose* a computer that best suits your needs⟩

syn cull, elect, handpick, name, opt (for), pick, prefer, select, single (out), take

rel appoint, designate, nominate, tab; accept, adopt, embrace, espouse

near ant discard, jettison, throw away, throw out

ant decline, refuse, reject, turn down

2 to see fit ⟨you can wear whatever you *choose* to the party⟩

syn like, want, will, wish

rel crave, desire, fancy, hanker (for), hunger (for), long (for), yearn (for); decide, determine, resolve

3 to come to a judgment after discussion or consideration — see DECIDE 1

chooser *n* someone with the right or responsibility for making a selection — see SELECTOR

choosing *n* the act or process of selecting — see SELECTION 1

choosy *or* **choosey** *adj* **1** hard to please — see FINICKY

2 tending to select carefully — see SELECTIVE

chop *n* a hard strike with a part of the body or an instrument — see ¹BLOW

chop *vb* to cut into small pieces ⟨*chop* the onions before adding them to the pot⟩

syn dice, hash, mince

rel chip, grind, mash, puree, slice

chop (down) *vb* to bring down by cutting — see FELL 2

choppy *adj* lacking in steadiness or regularity of occurrence — see FITFUL

chorale *n* **1** a religious song — see HYMN

2 an organized group of singers — see CHORUS 1

chore *n* **1** a piece of work that needs to be done regularly ⟨everyone in this household is expected to do weekly *chores*⟩

syn assignment, duty, job, stint, task

rel endeavor, enterprise, project, undertaking; care, charge, commission, responsibility; function, mission, office; errand; circuit, round, route

2 a dull, unpleasant, or difficult piece of work ⟨cleaning everything out of the attic was a real *chore*⟩

syn headache, labor

rel drudgery, grind; effort, strain, sweat; burden, load, weight; bother, nuisance, trouble

near ant breeze, child's play, cinch, duck soup, snap

chortle *n* an explosive sound that is a sign of amusement — see LAUGH 1

chorus *n* **1** an organized group of singers ⟨the annual Christmas program presented by the school's *chorus*⟩

syn choir, chorale, glee club

rel ensemble; minstrelsy

2 a part of a song or hymn that is repeated every so often ⟨the whole congregation will join in for the *chorus*⟩

syn burden, refrain

rel repeat

chosen *adj* singled out from a number or group as more to one's liking — see SELECT 1

chow *n* **1** food eaten or prepared for eating at one time — see MEAL

2 substances intended to be eaten — see FOOD

---

christen vb to give a name to — see NAME 1

Christian name n a name that is placed before one's family name — see FORENAME

Christmastime n the season celebrating Christmas — see YULETIDE

chronic adj being such by habit and not likely to change — see HABITUAL 1

chronicle n 1 a relating of events usually in the order in which they happened — see ACCOUNT 1

2 an account of important events in the order in which they happened — see HISTORY 1

chronicler n a student or writer of history — see HISTORIAN

chronometer n a device to measure time — see TIMEPIECE

chubbiness n the condition of having an excess of body fat — see CORPULENCE

chubby adj having an excess of body fat — see FAT 1

chuck vb to send through the air especially with a quick forward motion of the arm — see THROW

chuckle n an explosive sound that is a sign of amusement — see LAUGH 1

chum n a person who has a strong liking for and trust in another — see FRIEND 1

chum vb to come or be together as friends — see ASSOCIATE 1

chumminess n the state of being in a very personal or private relationship — see FAMILIARITY 1

chummy adj closely acquainted — see FAMILIAR 1

chump n one who is easily deceived or cheated — see DUPE

chunk n a small uneven mass — see LUMP 1

chunky adj 1 having small pieces or lumps spread throughout ⟨*chunky* peanut butter adds an interesting layer of texture when paired with jelly⟩

syn clumpy, curdy, lumpy, nubbly, nubby

rel ropy, thick, viscous; clabbered [*dialect*], clotted, coagulated, congealed, curdled, gelled, thickened

ant smooth

2 being compact and broad in build and often short in stature — see STOCKY

3 having or being of relatively great depth or extent from one surface to its opposite — see THICK 1

church n 1 a building for public worship and especially Christian worship ⟨a city that is noted for its many historic *churches*⟩

syn kirk [*chiefly Scottish*], tabernacle, temple

rel abbey, bethel, cathedral, chapel, oratory, sanctuary, shrine; meetinghouse; mosque, pagoda, synagogue (or synagog)

2 a body of persons gathered for religious worship — see CONGREGATION 1

churchly adj of or relating to a church — see ECCLESIASTICAL

churl n a person whose behavior is offensive to others — see JERK 1

churlish adj having or showing crudely insensitive or impolite manners — see CLOWNISH

churn vb 1 to be in a state of violent rolling motion — see SEETHE 1

2 to cause (as a liquid) to move about in a circle especially repeatedly — see STIR 1

chutzpah also **chutzpa** or **hutzpah** or **hutzpa** n shameless boldness — see EFFRONTERY

cinch n something that is easy to do ⟨the clear instructions made setting up the audiovisual system a *cinch*⟩

syn breeze, child's play, duck soup, picnic, pushover, snap

rel nothing; sitting duck

phrases piece of cake

near ant bother, nuisance, trouble

ant chore, headache, labor

cinch vb to make sure, certain, or safe — see ENSURE

cincture n a strip of flexible material (as leather) worn around the waist — see ²BELT

cinema n 1 the art or business of making a movie — see MOVIE 2

2 a building or part of a building where movies are shown — see THEATER 1

cipher n the numerical symbol 0 or the absence of number or quantity represented by it — see ZERO 1

ciphering n the act or process of performing mathematical operations to find a value — see CALCULATION

circle n 1 something with a perfectly round circumference ⟨a *circle* of columns surrounds the memorial to the fallen heroes⟩

syn ring, round

rel circlet; ellipse, loop, oval; ball, globe, orb, sphere

2 a circular strip — see RING 2

3 a group of people sharing a common interest and relating together socially — see GANG 2

4 a series of events or actions that repeat themselves regularly and in the same order — see CYCLE 1

circle vb 1 to form a circle around — see SURROUND

2 to pass completely around — see ENCIRCLE 1

circuitous adj 1 not straightforward or direct — see INDIRECT

2 using or containing more words than necessary to express an idea — see WORDY

circular adj not straightforward or direct — see INDIRECT

circular n a short printed publication with no cover or with a paper cover — see PAMPHLET

circulate vb 1 to cause to be known over a considerable area or by many people — see SPREAD 1

2 to make (as a piece of information) the subject of common talk without any au-

thority or confirmation of accuracy —
see RUMOR

circumference *n* **1** the distance around a
round body ⟨the *circumference* of the
earth at the equator⟩
syn girth
rel waistline; equator; diameter, perimeter
2 the line or relatively narrow space that
marks the outer limit of something — see
BORDER 1

circumlocution *n* the use of too many
words to express an idea — see VERBIAGE

circumlocutory *adj* using or containing
more words than necessary to express an
idea — see WORDY

circumnavigate *vb* to pass completely
around — see ENCIRCLE 1

circumscribe *vb* **1** to set bounds or an
upper limit for — see LIMIT 1
2 to mark the limits of — see LIMIT 2

circumscribed *adj* having distinct or certain limits — see LIMITED 1

circumspect *adj* having or showing a
close attentiveness to avoiding danger or
trouble — see CAREFUL 1

circumspection *n* a close attentiveness to
avoiding danger — see CAUTION 1

circumstance *n* **1** a state or end that
seemingly has been decided beforehand
— see FATE 1
2 something that happens — see EVENT 1
3 the uncertain course of events — see
CHANCE 1

circumstantial *adj* including many small
descriptive features — see DETAILED 1

circumvent *vb* **1** to avoid having to comply with (something) especially through
cleverness ⟨students who try to *circumvent* the school's dress code⟩
syn dodge, sidestep, skirt
rel avoid, duck, elude, escape, eschew,
evade, shake, shun; disobey, disregard,
flout, ignore
phrases get around
near ant accede (to), acquiesce (to), assent (to)
ant comply (with), follow, keep, obey, observe
2 to avoid by going around — see DETOUR 1

circus *n* **1** a large usually roofless building
for sporting events with tiers of seats for
spectators — see STADIUM
2 a place of uproar or confusion — see
MADHOUSE 2

citadel *n* a structure or place from which
one can resist attack — see FORT

citation *n* **1** a formal expression of praise
— see ENCOMIUM
2 a formal recognition of an achievement
or praiseworthy deed — see COMMENDATION 1
3 a passage referred to, repeated, or offered as an example — see QUOTATION

cite *vb* **1** to give as an example — see
QUOTE 1

2 to make reference to or speak about
briefly but specifically — see MENTION 1

citify *vb* to accustom to the ways of the
city ⟨we've become so *citified* that many
people have no idea where their food
comes from⟩
syn urbanize
rel civilize, cultivate

citizen *n* **1** a person who owes allegiance
to a government and is protected by it
⟨conscientious *citizens* who regard voting
as a duty as well as a right⟩
syn national, subject
rel compatriot, countryman; inhabitant,
native, nonimmigrant, resident
near ant foreigner, stranger; immigrant,
nonnative
ant alien, noncitizen
2 a person who lives in a town on a permanent basis — see BURGHER

city *n* a thickly settled, highly populated
area ⟨commuters who drive every day between their homes in the suburbs and
their jobs in the *city*⟩
syn burg, megalopolis, metropolis, municipality, town
rel borough; conurbation; urban sprawl;
suburbia

civil *adj* **1** of or relating to a nation — see
NATIONAL
2 showing consideration, courtesy, and
good manners — see POLITE 1

civility *n* **1** an act or utterance that is a
customary show of good manners ⟨after
the usual *civilities*, the parents and the
principal had a serious talk about the
boy⟩
syn amenity, courtesy, formality, gesture
rel ceremony, observance, rite, ritual; etiquette, manners, proprieties; greetings,
regards, respects; favor, grace, kindness
2 speech or behavior that is a sign of good
breeding — see POLITENESS

civilization *n* **1** the way people live at a
particular time and place ⟨a study unit on
the advanced *civilization* created by the
Mayas over a thousand years ago⟩
syn culture, life, lifestyle, society
rel customs, manners, mores, values;
folklore, heritage, tradition
2 a high level of taste and enlightenment
as a result of extensive intellectual training and exposure to the arts — see CULTURE 1

civilized *adj* having or showing a taste for
the fine arts and gracious living — see
CULTIVATED

clack *vb* to make a series of short sharp
noises — see RATTLE 1

claim *n* **1** an entitlement to something ⟨I'm
announcing my *claim* to that last slice of
pizza⟩
syn call, pretense (*or* pretence), pretension, right
rel birthright, prerogative; favor, privilege; refusal
2 a legal right to participation in the advantages, profits, and responsibility of
something — see INTEREST 1

---

syn synonym(s)   **rel** related words
ant antonym(s)   **near ant** near antonym(s)

3 a solemn and often public declaration of the truth or existence of something — see PROTESTATION

4 something that someone insists upon having — see DEMAND 1

claim *vb* **1** to state as a fact usually forcefully ⟨people who *claim* that they have been kidnapped by aliens from other worlds⟩

syn affirm, allege, assert, aver, avouch, avow, contend, declare, insist, maintain, profess, protest, warrant

rel announce, broadcast, proclaim; argue, rationalize, reason; confirm, justify, vindicate; defend, support, uphold

near ant disavow, disclaim, disown; challenge, dispute, question; confute, disprove, rebut, refute; contradict

ant deny, gainsay

2 to ask for (something) earnestly or with authority — see DEMAND 1

clairvoyance *n* the power of seeing or knowing about things that are not present to the senses ⟨people who claim to have *clairvoyance* are sometimes asked to help locate missing persons⟩

syn extrasensory perception, sixth sense

rel foreknowledge, foresight, prescience; telepathy

clamber *vb* to move (as up or over something) often with the help of the hands in holding or pulling — see CLIMB 1

clamor *n* **1** a violent shouting ⟨a *clamor* arose from the crowd as the prisoner was brought forward⟩

syn howl, hubbub, hue and cry, hullabaloo, noise, outcry, roar, tumult, uproar

rel clangor, din, jangle, racket

near ant mumble, mumbling, murmur, murmuring, rumble, rumbling

2 loud, confused, and usually unharmonious sound — see NOISE 1

clamor (for) *vb* to ask for (something) earnestly or with authority — see DEMAND 1

clamorous *adj* **1** engaging in or marked by loud and insistent cries especially of protest — see VOCIFEROUS

2 full of or characterized by the presence of noise — see NOISY 2

3 marked by a high volume of sound — see LOUD 1

clamp *vb* to put securely in place or in a desired position — see FASTEN 2

clamp down (on) *vb* to put a stop to (something) by the use of force — see QUELL 1

clam up *vb* to stop talking — see SHUT UP

clan *n* **1** a group of people sharing a common interest and relating together socially — see GANG 2

2 a group of persons who come from the same ancestor — see FAMILY 1

clandestine *adj* undertaken or done so as to escape being observed or known by others — see SECRET 1

clang *n* the loud sound made when metal strikes metal ⟨the horseshoe hit the stake with a satisfying *clang*⟩

syn clangor, clank, clash

rel chime, dingdong, peel, ring; clink, jangle, jingle, tinkle; clap, clop, crack, crash

clangor *n* **1** loud, confused, and usually unharmonious sound — see NOISE 1

2 the loud sound made when metal strikes metal — see CLANG

clangorous *adj* **1** full of or characterized by the presence of noise — see NOISY 2

2 making loud, confused, and usually unharmonious sounds — see NOISY 1

3 marked by a high volume of sound — see LOUD 1

clank *n* the loud sound made when metal strikes metal — see CLANG

clannish *adj* bound together by feelings of very close association — see CLOSE-KNIT

clap *n* **1** a loud explosive sound ⟨a *clap* of thunder that woke the whole house up⟩

syn bang, blast, boom, crack, crash, pop, report, slam, smash, snap, thwack, whack

rel clang, clangor, clank, clash; knock, rap, tap; clamor, howl, hubbub, hue and cry, hullabaloo, outcry, roar, tumult, uproar

2 a hard strike with a part of the body or an instrument — see ¹BLOW

clap *vb* to deliver a blow to (someone or something) usually in a strong vigorous manner — see HIT 1

claptrap *n* **1** language, behavior, or ideas that are absurd and contrary to good sense — see NONSENSE 1

2 unintelligible or meaningless talk — see GIBBERISH

clarification *n* a statement that makes something clear — see EXPLANATION 1

clarify *vb* **1** to remove usually visible impurities from ⟨*clarify* the melted butter by skimming off the milky bits⟩

syn clear, distill, filter, purify

rel process, refine; clean, cleanse, purge; extract, leach; screen, sieve, sift

near ant cloud, dull, muddy; contaminate, dirty, soil

2 to make plain or understandable — see EXPLAIN 1

clarity *n* **1** the state or quality of being easily seen through ⟨mountain streams with water of incredible *clarity*⟩

syn clearness, limpidity, limpidness, transparency

rel lucidity, lucidness, translucency; brightness, brilliance, effulgence, luminosity, luminousness; definition, resolution, sharpness

near ant fogginess, haziness, murkiness

ant cloudiness, opacity, opaqueness

2 clearness of expression — see SIMPLICITY 2

clash *n* **1** a physical dispute between opposing individuals or groups — see FIGHT 1

2 the loud sound made when metal strikes metal — see CLANG

clash *vb* to be out of harmony or agreement usually noticeably ⟨the colors of your shirt and pants *clash*⟩ ⟨Mom's idea of proper dress often *clashes* with mine⟩

syn collide, conflict, jar

rel mismatch; battle, combat, fight, war (against); chafe, gall, grate, jangle; differ, disagree

near ant agree, coincide, correspond

ant blend, harmonize, match

clash (with) *vb* to oppose (someone) in physical conflict — see FIGHT 1

clashing *adj* not being in agreement or harmony — see INCONSISTENT

clasp *n* the act or manner of holding — see HOLD 1

clasp *vb* 1 to put one's arms around and press tightly — see EMBRACE 1

2 to reach for and take hold of by embracing with the fingers or arms — see TAKE 1

class *n* 1 one of the segments of society into which people are grouped ⟨a politician who appeals to people of every *class*⟩

syn caste, estate, folk, order, stratum

rel bracket, echelon, grade, layer, level, tier; place, position, rank, standing, status; grouping, hierarchy, stratification; clan, family, people, race, tribe

2 one of the units into which a whole is divided on the basis of a common characteristic ⟨a new *class* of wireless devices that could be used for Internet access as well as personal communication⟩

syn bracket, category, division, family, grade, group, kind, order, rank(s), set, species, type

rel description, feather, ilk, nature, sort; branch, section, subdivision, subgroup, variety; breed, race; classification, heading, label, rubric, title

3 a number of persons or things that are grouped together because they have something in common — see SORT 1

4 a series of lectures on a subject — see COURSE 2

5 degree of excellence — see QUALITY 1

6 dignified or restrained beauty of form, appearance, or style — see ELEGANCE

7 high position within society — see RANK 2

class *vb* to arrange or assign according to type — see CLASSIFY 1

classic *adj* 1 constituting, serving as, or worthy of being a pattern to be imitated — see MODEL

2 of the very best kind — see EXCELLENT

3 serving to identify as belonging to an individual or group — see CHARACTERISTIC 1

classic *n* 1 someone of such unequaled perfection as to deserve imitation — see IDEAL 1

2 something (as a work of art) that is a great achievement and often its creator's greatest achievement — see MASTERPIECE

3 the most perfect type or example — see QUINTESSENCE 1

classical *adj* based on customs usually handed down from a previous generation — see TRADITIONAL 1

classify *vb* 1 to arrange or assign according to type ⟨*classify* the baseball cards in your collection on the basis of rarity⟩

syn assort, break down, categorize, class, grade, group, peg, place, range, rank, separate, sort

rel arrange, order, organize, systematize; alphabetize, catalog (*or* catalogue), codify, file, index, list; pigeonhole, shelve; distinguish, identify, recognize; cull, screen, sift, winnow

near ant confuse, disarrange, jumble, lump, mix (up), scramble

2 to put into a particular arrangement — see ORDER 1

clatter *n* a state of noisy, confused activity — see COMMOTION

clatter *vb* to make a series of short sharp noises — see RATTLE 1

clattering *adj* full of or characterized by the presence of noise — see NOISY 2

clattery *adj* full of or characterized by the presence of noise — see NOISY 2

clean *adj* 1 free from dirt or stain ⟨although the soccer team always starts out with *clean* uniforms, they don't stay that way for long⟩

syn immaculate, spick-and-span (*or* spic-and-span), spotless, stainless, unsoiled, unsullied

rel pure, taintless, undefiled, unpolluted, untainted, wholesome; cleanly, hygienic, sanitary; bleached, cleansed, purified, whitened; milky, snowy, white; flawless, unblemished; bright, shiny, sparkling

near ant dingy, greasy, grimy, mucky, muddy; defiled, polluted, tainted; blackened, discolored

ant besmirched, dirty, filthy, foul, grubby, soiled, spotted, stained, sullied, unclean

2 following or according to the rules — see FAIR 3

3 free from any trace of the coarse or indecent — see CHASTE

4 trying all possibilities — see EXHAUSTIVE

clean *adv* to a full extent or degree — see FULLY 1

clean *vb* 1 to make clean ⟨we *cleaned* the clothes before donating them to charity⟩

syn cleanse

rel decontaminate, purge, purify; disinfect, sanitize; brush, dry-clean, dust, launder, mop, rinse, scour, scrub, sweep, wash, wipe; brighten, deodorize, freshen, spruce (up), sweeten; pick up, straighten (up), tidy

near ant begrime, muddy; defile, pollute, taint; blacken, discolor

ant besmirch, dirty, foul, soil, spot, stain, sully

2 to take the internal organs out of — see GUT

clean (out) *vb* to make complete use of — see DEPLETE

clean (up) *vb* to remove objectionable parts from — see CENSOR

---

syn synonym(s)　　**rel** related words
ant antonym(s)　　**near ant** near antonym(s)

cleaner *n* a substance used for cleaning ⟨a kitchen shelf loaded with household *cleaners*⟩

syn cleanser, detergent, soap

rel disinfectant, purifier, solvent

cleanse *vb* 1 to free from moral guilt or blemish especially ceremonially — see PURIFY 1

2 to make clean — see CLEAN 1

cleanser *n* a substance used for cleaning — see CLEANER

cleansing *n* the act or fact of freeing from sin or moral guilt — see PURIFICATION

clear *adj* 1 easily seen through ⟨the *clear* glass walls of the aquarium's giant ocean tank⟩

syn limpid, liquid, lucent, pellucid, transparent

rel colorless, uncolored; lucid, translucent; crystal, crystalline, glassy, sparkling; bright, brilliant, effulgent, luminous

near ant foggy, hazy, misty, murky, smoky (*also* smokey)

ant cloudy, nontransparent, opaque

2 not subject to misinterpretation or more than one interpretation ⟨the meaning of her broad smile was *clear* to the whole class⟩

syn apparent, broad, clear-cut, decided, distinct, evident, lucid, manifest, obvious, open-and-shut, palpable, patent, perspicuous, plain, transparent, unambiguous, unequivocal, unmistakable

rel comprehendible, comprehensible, decipherable, fathomable, graspable, intelligible, knowable, understandable; self-evident, self-explanatory; simple, uncomplicated; overt, undisguised; appreciable, perceptible, recognizable, sensible, tangible; discernible, noticeable, observable, visible

near ant incomprehensible, unfathomable, unintelligible, unknowable; imperceptible, inappreciable, insensible; delicate, subtle

ant dark, enigmatic, indistinct, mysterious, obscure, unclear; ambiguous, equivocal

3 having or showing a mind free from doubt — see CERTAIN 2

4 not stormy or cloudy — see FAIR 1

5 serving to put an end to all debate or questioning — see CONCLUSIVE 1

6 allowing passage without obstruction — see OPEN 1

7 free from guilt or blame — see INNOCENT 2

clear *vb* 1 to rid the surface of (as an area) from things in the way ⟨the early settlers worked hard to *clear* the land for crops⟩

syn free, open, unblock

rel ease, facilitate, loosen (up), smooth, unclog, unstop

near ant clog, dam, obstruct, plug, stop

ant block

2 to set (a person or thing) free of something that encumbers — see RID

3 to give what is owed for — see PAY 1

4 to remove the contents of — see EMPTY

5 to remove usually visible impurities from — see CLARIFY 1

6 to set free from entanglement or difficulty — see EXTRICATE

7 to arrange clear passage of (something) by removing obstructions — see OPEN 2

8 to free from a charge of wrongdoing — see EXCULPATE

9 to give official acceptance of something as satisfactory — see APPROVE

10 to take away from a place or position — see REMOVE 2

clear (up) *vb* to make plain or understandable — see EXPLAIN 1

clearance *n* the approval by someone in authority for the doing of something — see PERMISSION

clear-cut *adj* 1 not subject to misinterpretation or more than one interpretation — see CLEAR 2

2 so clearly expressed as to leave no doubt about the meaning — see EXPLICIT

cleared *adj* allowing passage without obstruction — see OPEN 1

clearheaded *adj* 1 having full use of one's mind and control over one's actions — see SANE

2 not having one's mind affected by alcohol — see SOBER 1

clearing *n* a small area of usually open land — see FIELD 1

clearness *n* the state or quality of being easily seen through — see CLARITY 1

clear out *vb* 1 to cause (members of a group) to move widely apart — see SCATTER 1

2 to get free from a dangerous or confining situation — see ESCAPE 1

3 to leave a place often for another — see GO 2

clear-sighted *adj* 1 having or showing a practical cleverness or judgment — see SHREWD

2 having unusually keen vision — see SHARP-EYED

cleave *vb* to hold to something firmly as if by adhesion — see STICK 1

cleft *n* an irregular usually narrow break in a surface created by pressure — see CRACK 1

clemency *n* kind, gentle, or compassionate treatment especially towards someone who is undeserving of it — see MERCY 1

clement *adj* marked by temperatures that are neither too high nor too low ⟨Hawaii is known for its delightfully *clement* climate⟩

syn balmy, equable, gentle, mild, moderate, temperate

rel clear, cloudless, fair, rainless, sunny, sunshiny; calm, halcyon, peaceful, placid, tranquil; delightful, fine, pleasant

near ant blustering, blustery, breezy, gusty; foggy, hazy, misty; bleak, cloudy, dirty, foul, nasty, overcast, rainy, raw, rough, squally, stormy, sunless

ant harsh, inclement, intemperate, severe

clench *vb* to have or keep in one's hands — see HOLD 1

clergyman *n* a person specially trained and authorized to conduct religious services in a Christian church ⟨a special memorial service that attracted *clergymen* from all over the city⟩

  syn cleric, deacon, divine, dominie, ecclesiastic, father, minister, padre, parson, preacher, priest, reverend

  rel evangelist, missionary; deaconess, priestess; dean, pastor, rector, vicar; chaplain, confessor; canon, curate; friar, mendicant, monastic, monk, religious

  ant layman

cleric *n* a person specially trained and authorized to conduct religious services in a Christian church — see CLERGYMAN

clerical *adj* of, relating to, or characteristic of the clergy ⟨*clerical* duties such as providing spiritual counseling and leading classes in Bible study⟩

  syn ministerial, pastoral, priestly, sacerdotal

  rel evangelical, missionary; apostolic, canonical, episcopal, papal, patriarchal, pontifical; churchly, ecclesiastical (*or* ecclesiastic); divine, holy, religious, sacramental; rabbinic (*or* rabbinical)

  ant lay, nonclerical

clerk *n* **1** a person whose job is to keep records ⟨you'll need to get a copy of your birth certificate from the office of the town *clerk*⟩

  syn register, registrar, scribe

  rel archivist, bookkeeper, recorder; annalist, chronicler

  2 a person employed to sell goods or services especially in a store — see SALESPERSON

clever *adj* **1** showing a use of the imagination and creativity especially in inventing ⟨an inventor who was constantly coming up with *clever* devices for doing everyday chores⟩

  syn artful, creative, imaginative, ingenious

  rel innovative, novel, original; convenient, handy, practical, useful; complex, sophisticated; adroit, deft, dexterous (*also* dextrous); brainy, intelligent, sharp, smart

  near ant dull, pedestrian, stodgy

  ant uncreative, unimaginative

  2 having or showing quickness of mind — see INTELLIGENT 1

  3 skillful with the hands — see DEXTEROUS 1

  4 given to or marked by mature intelligent humor — see WITTY

cleverness *n* **1** mental skill or quickness — see DEXTERITY 1

  2 subtle or imaginative ability in inventing, devising, or executing something — see SKILL 1

cliché *n* an idea or expression that has been used by many people — see COMMONPLACE

click *vb* **1** to form a close personal relationship — see COMMUNE

  2 to turn out as planned or desired — see SUCCEED 1

client *n* a person who buys a product or uses a service from a business — see CUSTOMER 1

cliff *n* a steep wall of rock, earth, or ice ⟨the *cliff* rises 200 feet from the island's south shore⟩

  syn bluff, crag, escarpment, palisade, precipice, scarp

  rel tor; bulwark, embankment

climate *n* **1** a special quality or impression associated with something — see AURA

  2 the circumstances, conditions, or objects by which one is surrounded — see ENVIRONMENT

climax *n* **1** a point in a chain of events at which an important change (as in one's fortunes) occurs — see TURNING POINT

  2 the highest part or point — see HEIGHT 1

climax *vb* to bring to a triumphant conclusion — see CROWN

climb *n* the act or an instance of rising or climbing up — see CROWN

climb *vb* **1** to move (as up or over something) often with the help of the hands in holding or pulling ⟨visitors should use caution when *climbing* over the wet rocks along the shore⟩

  syn clamber, scramble

  rel shin, shinny; inch; mount, scale, surmount; claw, struggle

  2 to move or extend upward — see ASCEND

clinch *vb* to make final, definite, or beyond dispute ⟨the rain *clinched* the matter: we would have the party indoors⟩

  syn decide, settle

  rel demonstrate, determine, establish, prove, show; clarify, clear (up), illuminate; conclude, end, finish

  near ant confuse, muddle, muddy

clincher *n* something (as a fact or argument) that is decisive or overwhelming ⟨the fact that the resort had tennis courts was the *clincher* in our deciding to stay there⟩

  syn crusher, topper

  rel deathblow, knockout; coup

cling *vb* to hold to something firmly as if by adhesion — see STICK 1

cling (to) *vb* **1** to give steadfast support to — see ADHERE

  2 to have or keep in one's hands — see HOLD 1

clink *vb* to make a repeated sharp light ringing sound — see JINGLE

clip *n* a hard strike with a part of the body or an instrument — see ¹BLOW

clip *vb* to make (as hair) shorter with or as if with the use of shears ⟨toddlers are often fearful the first time they get their hair *clipped*⟩

  syn bob, crop, curtail, cut, cut back, dock, lop (off), nip, pare, prune, shave, shear, snip, trim

---

syn synonym(s)   **rel** related words
ant antonym(s)   **near ant** near antonym(s)

rel manicure, mow; abbreviate, abridge, shorten

near ant elongate, extend, lengthen

clique *n* a group of people sharing a common interest and relating together socially — see GANG 2

cloak *n* **1** something that covers or conceals like a piece of cloth ⟨the *cloak* of mystery that surrounds the royal family⟩

syn curtain, hood, mantle, mask, shroud, veil

rel cover, screen, shield; facade (*also* façade), face, veneer

2 a sleeveless garment worn so as to hang over the shoulders, arms, and back — see ¹CAPE

cloak *vb* **1** to change the dress or looks of so as to conceal true identity — see DISGUISE

2 to keep secret or shut off from view — see ¹HIDE 2

clobber *vb* **1** to deliver a blow to (someone or something) usually in a strong vigorous manner — see HIT 1

2 to defeat by a large margin — see WHIP 2

3 to achieve a victory over — see BEAT 2

clock *n* a device to measure time — see TIMEPIECE

clod *n* **1** a big clumsy often slow-witted person — see OAF

2 a small uneven mass — see LUMP 1

cloddish *adj* having or showing crudely insensitive or impolite manners — see CLOWNISH

clodhopper *n* an awkward or simple person especially from a small town or the country — see HICK

clog *n* something that makes movement or progress more difficult — see ENCUMBRANCE

clog *vb* **1** to prevent passage through ⟨the discovery that a ton of hair was *clogging* the drain in the tub⟩

syn block, choke, close (off), congest, dam, jam, obstruct, plug (up), stop (up), stuff

rel bung, fill, pack; flood, glut, inundate, overwhelm, swamp

near ant excavate, hollow (out), scoop (out); empty, lighten

ant clear, free, open (up), unclog

2 to create difficulty for the work or activity of — see HAMPER

cloister *n* a residence for men under religious vows — see MONASTERY

cloistered *adj* hidden from view — see SECLUDED

close *adj* **1** having little space between items or parts ⟨the soldiers marched in *close* formation against the enemy⟩

syn compact, crowded, dense, jam-packed, packed, serried, thick, tight

rel airtight, snug; compacted, compressed, condensed; firm, hard, solid; impenetrable, impermeable, impervious

near ant commodious, roomy, spacious

ant loose, uncrowded

2 not being distant in time, space, or significance ⟨my birthday is *close* to Christ-

mas⟩ ⟨a shopping mall that is very *close* to the highway⟩ ⟨these words are *close* synonyms⟩

syn immediate, near, nearby, neighboring, next-door, nigh

rel abutting, adjacent, adjoining, bordering, contiguous; approaching, coming, forthcoming, oncoming, upcoming; accessible, convenient, handy

phrases at hand

near ant divorced, removed, separated

ant away, distant, far, faraway, far-off, remote

3 showing little difference in the standing of the competitors ⟨the election results were so *close* that the votes had to be recounted⟩

syn narrow, nip and tuck, tight

rel crowded

4 closely acquainted — see FAMILIAR 1

5 given to keeping one's activities hidden from public observation or knowledge — see SECRETIVE

6 giving or sharing as little as possible — see STINGY 1

7 lacking fresh air — see STUFFY 1

8 meeting the highest standard of accuracy — see PRECISE 1

close *adv* at, within, or to a short distance or time — see NEAR 1

¹**close** *n* an open space wholly or partly enclosed (as by buildings or walls) — see COURT 2

²**close** *n* **1** the stopping of a process or activity — see END 1

2 the last part of a process or action — see FINALE

close *vb* **1** to position (something) so as to prevent passage through an opening ⟨be sure to *close* the gate when you leave⟩

syn shut

rel bar, batten (down), bolt, chain, fasten, latch, lock; plug, seal, stopper; secure; bang, clap, slam

near ant unbar, unbolt, unchain, unfasten, unlatch, unlock, unseal

ant open

2 to stop the operations of ⟨the merchant will *close* the store if business doesn't improve⟩

syn shut

rel phase out, turn off; extinguish, quell, suppress; gag, muzzle, silence; fail, fold

near ant build, expand

ant open, start

3 to bring (an event) to a natural or appropriate stopping point ⟨we'll *close* the assembly with the singing of our national anthem⟩

syn conclude, end, finish, round (off *or* out), terminate, wind up, wrap up

rel climax, crown; complete, consummate, perfect; halt, stop, suspend

ant begin, commence, inaugurate, open, start

4 to come to an end — see CEASE 1

5 to come near or nearer — see APPROACH 1

close (off) *vb* to prevent passage through — see CLOG 1

closefisted *adj* giving or sharing as little as possible — see STINGY 1

close–knit *adj* bound together by feelings of very close association ⟨a *close-knit* family that constantly keeps in touch⟩
syn clannish
rel bosom, chummy, close, familiar, friendly, intimate, thick; exclusive, snobbish, snobby; forbidding, inhospitable, unfriendly

closely *adv* to a close degree — see NEAR 2

closemouthed *adj* 1 given to keeping one's activities hidden from public observation or knowledge — see SECRETIVE
2 tending not to speak frequently (as by habit or inclination) — see SILENT 2

closeness *n* 1 the practice or habit of keeping secrets or keeping one's affairs secret — see SECRECY
2 the quality of being overly sparing with money — see PARSIMONY
3 the quality or state of being very accurate — see PRECISION
4 the state of being in a very personal or private relationship — see FAMILIARITY 1
5 the state or condition of being near — see PROXIMITY

closer *adj* being the less far of two — see NEAR 1

closet *n* 1 a storage case typically having doors and shelves — see CABINET
2 an area within a building that has been set apart from surrounding space by a wall — see ROOM 2

closet *vb* to close or shut in by or as if by barriers — see ENCLOSE 1

closing *adj* following all others of the same kind in order or time — see LAST

closing *n* the last part of a process or action — see FINALE

closure *n* the stopping of a process or activity — see END 1

clot *vb* to turn from a liquid into a substance resembling jelly — see COAGULATE

cloth *n* a woven or knitted material (as of cotton or nylon) ⟨cotton canvas was the *cloth* traditionally used for a ship's sails⟩
syn fabric, textile
rel fiber, thread, yarn

clothe *vb* 1 to outfit with clothes and especially fine or special clothes ⟨they liked to *clothe* the twins in identical outfits just to confuse people⟩
syn apparel, array, attire, caparison, costume, deck, dress, garb, garment, gown, invest, rig (out), robe, suit
rel cloak, mantle; drape, swaddle, swathe; accoutre (*or* accouter), equip, furnish, outfit
near ant divest, uncover, undrape, unveil
ant disrobe, strip, unclothe, undress
2 to convey in appropriate or telling terms — see PHRASE

clothes *n pl* covering for the human body — see CLOTHING

clothing *n* covering for the human body ⟨a store that sells both men's and women's *clothing*⟩
syn apparel, attire, clothes, dress, duds, habiliment(s), rags, raiment, togs, wear
rel garment, vestment; array, bravery, finery; tatters; costume, garb, getup, guise, outfit, rig, wardrobe; haberdashery

cloud *vb* 1 to make dark, dim, or indistinct ⟨unfortunately, smog *clouds* the view of the city from the hilltop⟩
syn becloud, bedim, befog, blacken, blur, darken, dim, fog, haze, mist, obscure, overcast, overcloud, overshadow, shadow, shroud
rel blot out, conceal, hide, screen, shade; camouflage, cloak, cover, curtain, disguise, mask, veil; distort, falsify, garble, misrepresent
near ant expose, reveal, uncover, unveil; clarify, clear, purify; highlight, spotlight
ant brighten, illuminate, illumine, light (up), lighten
2 to make (something) unclear to the understanding — see CONFUSE 2

cloudburst *n* a steady falling of water from the sky in significant quantity — see RAIN 1

clouded *adj* 1 covered over by clouds — see OVERCAST
2 filled with or dimmed by fine particles (as of dust or water) in suspension — see HAZY 1

cloudless *adj* not stormy or cloudy — see FAIR 1

cloudy *adj* 1 having visible particles in liquid suspension ⟨the water coming out of the faucet was unusually *cloudy*⟩
syn muddy, roiled, turbid
rel dingy, filmy, hazy, unfiltered; inky, murky; nontransparent, opaque
near ant clarified, filtered, purified
ant clear
2 covered over by clouds — see OVERCAST
3 filled with or dimmed by fine particles (as of dust or water) in suspension — see HAZY 1

clout *n* 1 a hard strike with a part of the body or an instrument — see ¹BLOW
2 the power to direct the thinking or behavior of others usually indirectly — see INFLUENCE 1

clout *vb* to deliver a blow to (someone or something) usually in a strong vigorous manner — see HIT 1

clown *n* 1 a comically dressed performer (as at a circus) who entertains with playful tricks and ridiculous behavior ⟨a *clown* wearing big floppy shoes and a red wig⟩
syn buffoon, harlequin, zany
rel cutup, madcap; fool, jester, motley; mime, mummer; comedian, comedienne, comic, joker, jokester, wag
2 a person whose behavior is offensive to others — see JERK 1

clown (around) *vb* to engage in attention-getting playful or boisterous behavior — see CUT UP

clowning *n* wildly playful or mischievous behavior — see HORSEPLAY

clownish *adj* having or showing crudely insensitive or impolite manners ⟨the *clownish* antics of some of the teenagers at the wedding reception⟩

syn boorish, churlish, cloddish, loutish, uncouth

rel coarse, ill-bred, uncultivated, unpolished, unrefined; tasteless, vulgar; beastly, bestial; doltish, oafish, stupid; discourteous, impolite, rude, uncivil

ant cultivated, polished, refined, well-bred; courtly, genteel, gentlemanly, lady-like; civil, courteous, polite

club *n* 1 a heavy rigid stick used as a weapon or for punishment ⟨hit the prisoner with a *club* if he tries anything funny⟩

syn bat, billy, bludgeon, cane, cudgel, nightstick, rod, shillelagh, staff, truncheon

rel blackjack, mace; birch, switch; hammer, mallet, maul; walking stick

2 the meeting place of an organization ⟨the Scouts gather at their *club* every Monday evening⟩

syn clubhouse, lodge

rel den, hangout, haunt, hideaway, hideout, lair; camp, headquarters; meeting-house

3 a group of persons formally joined together for some common interest — see ASSOCIATION 2

club *vb* 1 to form or enter into an association that furthers the interests of its members — see ALLY

2 to strike repeatedly — see BEAT 1

clubhouse *n* the meeting place of an organization — see CLUB 2

clue *n* a slight or indirect pointing to something (as a solution or explanation) — see HINT 1

clue *vb* to give information to — see ENLIGHTEN 1

clump *n* 1 a number of things considered as a unit — see GROUP 1

2 a small uneven mass — see LUMP 1

clump *vb* to move heavily or clumsily — see LUMBER 1

clumpy *adj* having small pieces or lumps spread throughout — see CHUNKY 1

clumsy *adj* 1 lacking in physical ease and grace in movement or in the use of the hands ⟨diamond cutting is no job for a *clumsy* person⟩

syn awkward, gawky, graceless, heavy-handed, lubberly, lumbering, lumpish, ungainly, unhandy

rel butterfingered, uncoordinated; oafish; bungling, gauche, inept, inexpert, maladroit, unskilled, unskillful; cumbersome, unwieldy

near ant expert, masterly, skilled, skillful; lissome (*also* lissom), lithe, nimble; light, light-footed, surefooted

ant deft, dexterous (*also* dextrous), graceful, handy

2 lacking social grace and assurance — see AWKWARD 1

3 showing or marked by a lack of skill and tact (as in dealing with a situation) — see AWKWARD 2

4 difficult to use or operate especially because of size, weight, or design — see CUMBERSOME

5 hastily or roughly constructed — see RUDE 1

cluster *n* 1 a number of things considered as a unit — see GROUP 1

2 a usually small number of persons considered as a unit — see GROUP 2

cluster *vb* 1 to come together into one body or place — see ASSEMBLE 1

2 to gather into a closely packed group — see PRESS 3

clutch *n* 1 a time or state of affairs requiring prompt or decisive action — see EMERGENCY

2 the right or means to command or control others — see POWER 1

clutch *vb* to have or keep in one's hands — see HOLD 1

clutter *n* an unorganized collection or mixture of various things — see MISCELLANY 1

cluttered *adj* lacking in order, neatness, and often cleanliness — see MESSY

coach *n* a person who trains performers or athletes ⟨a *coach* who is highly respected by all of the baseball players⟩

syn trainer

rel instructor, teacher; driller, drillmaster; adviser (*or* advisor), counselor (*or* counsellor), mentor

coach *vb* to give advice and instruction to (someone) regarding the course or process to be followed — see GUIDE 1

coadjutor *n* a person who helps a more skilled person — see HELPER

coagulate *vb* to turn from a liquid into a substance resembling jelly ⟨the blood *coagulated*, and a scab formed on the wound⟩

syn clot, congeal, gel, jell, jelly, set

rel concrete, firm (up), freeze, harden, solidify, stiffen; condense, thicken; curdle, lump (up)

near ant deliquesce, flux, fuse, liquefy, melt, thaw

coalesce *vb* to come together to form a single unit — see UNITE 1

coalition *n* 1 a group of people acting together within a larger group — see FACTION

2 an association of persons, parties, or states for mutual assistance and protection — see CONFEDERACY

coarse *adj* 1 made up of large particles ⟨*coarse* rock salt was sprinkled on the icy walkway⟩

syn grainy, granular, granulated

rel rough; unfiltered, unrefined; gravelly, gritty, sandy; pebbly, rocky, stony (*also* stoney); lumpy, mealy

near ant smooth; filtered, pulverized, refined

ant dusty, fine, floury, powdery

2 lacking in refinement or good taste ⟨the hockey player's *coarse* manners turned his date off completely⟩

syn common, crass, crude, gross, ill-bred, low, lowbred, lowbrow, raffish, rough, roughhewn, rude, tasteless, uncouth, uncultivated, uncultured, unpolished, unrefined, vulgar

rel boorish, churlish, cloddish, clownish, loutish, ungentlemanly; clumsy, lubberly, lumpish, oafish; inconsiderate, insensitive, thoughtless; countrified (*also* countryfied), provincial, rustic; graceless, inelegant, tacky

near ant aristocratic, courtly, patrician; elegant, graceful, gracious; considerate, sensitive, thoughtful; citified, sophisticated, urbane

ant cultivated, cultured, genteel, polished, refined, smooth, tasteful, well-bred

3 depicting or referring to sexual matters in a way that is unacceptable in polite society — see OBSCENE 1

4 harsh and dry in sound — see HOARSE

5 not having a level or smooth surface — see UNEVEN 1

6 of low quality — see CHEAP 2

coarseness *n* 1 the quality or state of being obscene — see OBSCENITY 1

2 the quality or state of lacking refinement or good taste — see VULGARITY 1

coast *vb* to move or proceed smoothly and readily — see FLOW 2

coat *n* the hairy covering of a mammal especially when fine, soft, and thick — see FUR 1

coat *vb* to form a layer over — see COVER 2

coax *vb* to get (someone) to do something by gentle urging, special attention, or flattery ⟨trying to *coax* Dad into taking us on a ski trip, we mentioned what a great skier he is⟩

syn blandish, blarney, cajole, soft-soap, wheedle

rel adulate, flatter, overpraise; compliment, praise; beguile, charm, woo; beg, importune, urge; bug, nag, pester

near ant browbeat, bulldoze, bully, cow, intimidate; coerce, compel, constrain, force, oblige

cobble (together) *vb* to make or assemble roughly or hastily ⟨the stranded hikers *cobbled* together a rickety shelter for the night⟩

syn patch (together), throw up

rel dash (off)

phrases knock together

near ant craft, handcraft; fashion, forge, hammer (out), pound (out)

¹**cock** *n* a fixture for controlling the flow of a liquid — see FAUCET

²**cock** *n* a quantity of things thrown or stacked on one another — see ¹PILE 1

³**cock** *n* the act of positioning or an instance of being positioned at an angle — see TILT

cock *vb* to set or cause to be at an angle — see LEAN 1

cockcrow *n* the first appearance of light in the morning or the time of its appearance — see DAWN 1

cockeyed *adj* 1 inclined or twisted to one side — see AWRY

2 showing or marked by a lack of good sense or judgment — see FOOLISH 1

cocksure *adj* having or showing a mind free from doubt — see CERTAIN 2

cocky *adj* displaying or marked by rude boldness — see NERVY 1

cocoon *n* something that encloses another thing especially to protect it — see ¹CASE 1

coddle *vb* 1 to cook in a liquid heated to the point that it gives off steam — see BOIL 2

2 to treat with great or excessive care — see BABY

code *n* a collection or system of rules of conduct ⟨Hammurabi was an ancient king of Babylon with a famous *code* of laws⟩

syn decalogue, law

rel constitution

codger *n* a person of odd or whimsical habits — see ECCENTRIC

codify *vb* to put into a particular arrangement — see ORDER 1

coequal *adj* resembling another in every respect — see SAME 1

coerce *vb* to cause (a person) to give in to pressure — see FORCE

coerced *adj* not made or done willingly or by choice — see INVOLUNTARY 1

coercion *n* the use of power to impose one's will on another — see FORCE 2

coeval *adj* existing or occurring at the same period of time — see CONTEMPORARY 1

coeval *n* a person who lives at the same time or is about the same age as another — see CONTEMPORARY

coexist *vb* to occur or exist at the same time — see COINCIDE 1

coexistence *n* the occurrence or existence of several things at once — see CONCURRENCE 1

coexistent *adj* 1 existing or occurring at the same period of time — see CONTEMPORARY 1

2 present at the same time and place — see COINCIDENT

coexisting *adj* 1 existing or occurring at the same period of time — see CONTEMPORARY 1

2 present at the same time and place — see COINCIDENT

coextensive *adj* existing or occurring at the same period of time — see CONTEMPORARY 1

coffer *n* a specially reinforced container to keep valuables safe — see SAFE

coffin *n* a box for holding a dead body ⟨*coffins* are said to be the preferred sleeping places of vampires⟩

syn casket

---

syn synonym(s)   **rel** related words
ant antonym(s)   **near ant** near antonym(s)

rel sarcophagus, vault; urn; sepulcher (*or* sepulchre), sepulture

cogency *n* 1 the capacity to persuade 〈the *cogency* of Thomas Paine's case for American independence〉

syn effectiveness, force, forcefulness, persuasiveness

rel impact, punch, strength; soundness, validity; pertinence, relevance

near ant invalidity, unsoundness; weakness

ant ineffectiveness

2 the quality of an utterance that provokes interest and produces an effect — see ¹PUNCH 1

cogent *adj* having the power to persuade 〈the results of the DNA fingerprinting were the most *cogent* evidence for acquittal〉

syn compelling, conclusive, convincing, decisive, effective, forceful, persuasive, strong, telling

rel sound, valid, well-founded; important, significant, weighty; material, pertinent, relevant

near ant groundless, invalid, unfounded, unsound; inconsequential, insignificant, unimportant; immaterial, irrelevant

ant inconclusive, indecisive, ineffective, unconvincing

cogitate *vb* to give serious and careful thought to — see PONDER

cognizance *n* 1 a state of being aware — see ATTENTION 2

2 knowledge gained by personal experience — see ACQUAINTANCE

cognizant *adj* having specified facts or feelings actively impressed on the mind — see CONSCIOUS

cognomen *n* 1 a descriptive or familiar name given instead of or in addition to the one belonging to an individual — see NICKNAME

2 a word or combination of words by which a person or thing is regularly known — see NAME 1

cohere *vb* to be in agreement on every point — see CHECK 1

coherence *n* a balanced, pleasing, or suitable arrangement of parts — see HARMONY 1

coherent *adj* according to the rules of logic — see LOGICAL 1

cohort *n* 1 a person frequently seen in the company of another — see ASSOCIATE 1

2 one associated with another in wrongdoing — see ACCOMPLICE

coil *vb* to follow a circular or spiral course — see WIND

coiling *adj* turning around an axis like the thread of a screw — see SPIRAL

coinage *n* something (as a device) created for the first time through the use of the imagination — see INVENTION 1

coincide *vb* 1 to occur or exist at the same time 〈the heaviest snowfall of the season *coincided* with the start of our week-long ski vacation〉

syn coexist, concur

rel chance, happen, transpire

near ant antedate, precede, predate; follow, succeed

2 to be in agreement on every point — see CHECK 1

3 to have or come to the same opinion or point of view — see AGREE 1

coincidence *n* the occurrence or existence of several things at once — see CONCURRENCE 1

coincident *adj* present at the same time and place 〈the hard economic times and the *coincident* increase in crime were a double strain on the city's social services〉

syn accompanying, attendant, attending, coexistent, coexisting, coincidental, concomitant, concurrent

rel contemporaneous, contemporary, simultaneous, synchronous; associated, collateral, connected, linked, related; consequent, resultant, resulting; ensuing, following, subsequent; accidental, casual, chance, fluky, fortuitous, freak, incident, incidental

near ant unassociated, unconnected, unrelated

coincidental *adj* present at the same time and place — see COINCIDENT

coincidentally *adv* at one and the same time — see TOGETHER 1

coincidently *adv* at one and the same time — see TOGETHER 1

coitus *n* sexual union involving penetration of the vagina by the penis — see SEXUAL INTERCOURSE

cold *adj* 1 having a low or subnormal temperature 〈the *cold* climate of the Yukon〉 〈an unusually *cold* spring that was followed by a sweltering summer〉

syn arctic, bitter, cool, coolish, freezing, frigid, frosty, glacial, ice-cold, icy, nipping, nippy, numbing, polar, shivery, snappy, wintry

rel subfreezing, subzero; cutting, keen, penetrating, piercing, sharp; bracing, brisk, crisp, invigorating, rigorous; chilled, cooled, frosted, frozen, iced, refrigerated, unheated

near ant lukewarm, tepid; heated, warmed

ant broiling, burning, fiery, hot, piping hot, red-hot, roasting, scalding, scorching, searing, sultry, summery, sweltering, torrid, tropical, warm, warming

2 lacking in friendliness or warmth of feeling 〈the prisoners got only a *cold* stare when they tried to befriend the guard〉

syn chill, chilly, cold-blooded, cool, frigid, frosty, glacial, icy, unfriendly, unsympathetic, wintry

rel hardhearted, heartless, pitiless, uncaring, unfeeling; reserved, soulless, undemonstrative, unemotional, unresponsive; apathetic, indifferent, unenthusiastic, uninterested; aloof, detached, impersonal

near ant compassionate, kind, kindhearted; demonstrative, emotional, expressive; eager, enthusiastic, passionate *ant* cordial, friendly, genial, hearty, sympathetic, warm, warm-blooded, warm-hearted

3 having or showing a lack of friendliness or interest in others — see COOL 1

4 having lost consciousness — see UNCONSCIOUS 1

cold *n* a weather condition marked by low temperatures ⟨the *cold* will stay with us for another day, then temperatures should rise⟩

syn freeze, snap

rel frost; glaciation; ice age; bite, chill, nip, wintriness

near ant heat wave; dog days

cold-blooded *adj* **1** having or showing a lack of sympathy or tender feelings — see HARD 1

2 lacking in friendliness or warmth of feeling — see COLD 2

3 not feeling or showing emotion — see IMPASSIVE 1

cold-shoulder *vb* to deliberately ignore or treat rudely — see SNUB 1

cold shoulder *n* treatment that is deliberately unfriendly ⟨at the party the two former friends gave each other the *cold shoulder*⟩

syn brush-off, rebuff, repulse, snub

rel dismissal, rejection; banishment, ostracism

near ant welcome

coliseum *n* a large usually roofless building for sporting events with tiers of seats for spectators — see STADIUM

collaborate *vb* to participate or assist in a joint effort to accomplish an end — see COOPERATE 1

collaboration *n* **1** the state of having shared interests or efforts (as in social or business matters) — see ASSOCIATION 1

2 the work and activity of a number of persons who individually contribute toward the efficiency of the whole — see TEAMWORK

collapse *n* **1** a complete depletion of energy or strength — see FATIGUE

2 a falling short of one's goals — see FAILURE 2

collapse *vb* **1** to fall down or in as a result of physical pressure ⟨the motel balcony *collapsed* under the weight of so many people⟩

syn cave (in), crumple, give, go, yield

rel deflate, flatten, melt; break, break down, conk (out), crash, die, fail, give out, stall; burst, shatter, smash; crack, pop, snag

phrases give way

near ant inflate, rise, swell

2 to be unsuccessful — see FAIL 2

collar *vb* to take physical control or possession of (something) suddenly or forcibly — see CATCH 1

colleague *n* a fellow worker ⟨on her first day at work her *colleagues* went out of their way to make her feel welcome⟩

syn associate, coworker

rel equal, fellow, peer; accomplice, ally, cohort, collaborator, confederate, partner; buddy, chum, companion, comrade, crony, pal; compatriot, countryman

collect *vb* **1** to gain emotional or mental control of ⟨applicants should *collect* their thoughts while waiting to be interviewed⟩

syn calm, compose, contain, control, recollect, settle

rel allay, lull, quiet, soothe, still, tranquilize (*also* tranquillize)

phrases pull oneself together

2 to gradually form into a layer, pile, or mass ⟨dust has been *collecting* under my bed for years⟩

syn accumulate, conglomerate, gather, heap, pile (up)

rel bank, drift, ridge

near ant disperse, dissipate, scatter

3 to bring together from several sources into a single volume or list — see COMPILE

4 to bring together in one body or place — see GATHER 1

5 to come together into one body or place — see ASSEMBLE 1

collected *adj* free from emotional or mental agitation — see CALM 2

collection *n* **1** an organized group of objects acquired and maintained for study, exhibition, or personal pleasure ⟨his stamp *collection* has become quite valuable⟩

syn assemblage, library

rel cache, hoard, repertory, reserve, stock, stockpile, store, supply; accumulation, gathering, heap, pile; clutter, jumble, litter

2 a mass or quantity that has piled up or that has been gathered — see ACCUMULATION 1

3 a number of things considered as a unit — see GROUP 1

collective *adj* used or done by a number of people as a group ⟨the cleanup of the neighborhood park was a *collective* effort for which many people should be thanked⟩

syn combined, common, communal, concerted, conjoint, joint, mutual, public, shared, united

rel cooperative, reciprocal, symbiotic; mass, popular; general, generic, universal

near ant personal, private; independent, separate; particular, special, specialized

ant individual, single, sole

college *n* a group of persons formally joined together for some common interest — see ASSOCIATION 2

collide *vb* **1** to be out of harmony or agreement usually noticeably — see CLASH

2 to come into usually forceful contact with something — see HIT 2

collision *n* **1** a forceful coming together of two things — see IMPACT 1

2 the violent coming together of two bodies into destructive contact — see CRASH 1

---

syn synonym(s)   *rel* related words
ant antonym(s)   *near ant* near antonym(s)

colloquial *adj* **1** used in or suitable for speech and not formal writing 〈the new kid's rudeness soon began—to use a *colloquial* expression—to rub me the wrong way〉

syn conversational, informal, nonliterary, unliterary, vernacular, vulgar

rel dialectal, dialectical, nonstandard, substandard, uneducated; slang, slangy

near ant educated, standard; correct, genteel, grammatical, proper

ant bookish, formal, learned, literary

2 having the style and content of everyday conversation — see CHATTY 1

colloquy *n* **1** a meeting featuring a group discussion — see FORUM

2 an exchange of views for the purpose of exploring a subject or deciding an issue — see DISCUSSION 1

3 talking or a talk between two or more people — see CONVERSATION

collusion *n* a secret agreement or cooperation between two parties for an illegal or dishonest purpose 〈there was *collusion* between the two companies to fix prices〉

syn complicity, connivance, conspiracy

rel chicanery, foul play, skulduggery (*or* skullduggery); double-dealing, duplicity; cover-up, frame-up; intrigue, plot, scheme

colonist *n* a person who settles in a new region — see FRONTIERSMAN

colonizer *n* a person who settles in a new region — see FRONTIERSMAN

colony *n* **1** a settlement in a new country or region 〈the early history of New York City when it was a Dutch *colony*〉

syn plantation

rel outpost; dependency, mandate, possession, protectorate, territory

2 a group of people with a common interest living in one place — see COMMUNITY 2

color *n* **1** a property that becomes apparent when light falls on an object and by which things that are identical in form can be distinguished 〈a shirt that is available in every *color* of the rainbow〉

syn cast, hue, shade, tinge, tint, tone

rel complementary color, primary color, secondary color; brightness, saturation, value; coloration, coloring

2 a substance used to color other materials — see PIGMENT

3 the hue or appearance of the skin and especially of the face — see COMPLEXION 1

4 colors *pl* a piece of cloth with a special design that is used as an emblem or for signaling — see FLAG 1

color *vb* **1** to give color or a different color to 〈she's *colored* her hair for so long and so often that no one knows what her natural color is〉

syn dye, paint, stain, tinge, tint

rel brighten, lighten; darken, tone (down); daub

near ant blanch, bleach, whiten

ant decolorize

2 to add to the interest of by including made-up details — see EMBROIDER

3 to change so much as to create a wrong impression or alter the meaning of — see GARBLE

4 to develop a rosy facial color (as from excitement or embarrassment) — see BLUSH

colorful *adj* marked by a variety of usually vivid colors 〈the *colorful* robes and blankets of the Native Americans of the Southwest〉

syn motley, multicolored, polychromatic, polychrome, varicolored, variegated

rel brave, bright, brilliant, gay; flashy, garish, gaudy, loud, showy, splashy; deep, rich, unbleached; checkered, dotted, plaid, striped; colored, pigmented; dappled, shaded; marbled, mottled, piebald, pied, pinto; flecked, spotted, streaked; specked, speckled; banded, barred, brindled (*or* brindle)

near ant achromatic; bleached, decolorized, faded, washed out; dull, faint, gray (*also* grey), neutral, pale, pallid

ant colorless; monochromatic, solid

coloring *n* **1** a substance used to color other materials — see PIGMENT

2 the hue or appearance of the skin and especially of the face — see COMPLEXION 1

3 the representation of something in terms that go beyond the facts — see EXAGGERATION

colorless *adj* lacking an addition of color 〈since we can't decide what color to paint the doghouse, our latest home project remains *colorless* for the time being〉

syn uncolored, undyed, unpainted, unstained, white

rel clear, limpid, liquid, lucent, pellucid, transparent; bleached, faded, washed; dull, faint, gray (*also* grey), neutral, pale, pallid

near ant colorful, multicolored, polychromatic, polychrome, varicolored, variegated

ant colored, dyed, painted, stained, tinged

colossal *adj* unusually large — see HUGE

colossally *adv* to a large extent or degree — see GREATLY 2

colosseum *n* a large usually roofless building for sporting events with tiers of seats for spectators — see STADIUM

colossus *n* something that is unusually large and powerful — see GIANT

colt *n* a person who is just starting out in a field of activity — see BEGINNER

coltish *adj* given to good-natured joking or teasing — see PLAYFUL

column *n* **1** a series of persons or things arranged one behind another — see LINE 1

2 an upright shaft that supports an overhead structure — see PILLAR 1

coma *n* a temporary or permanent state of unconsciousness — see FAINT

comb *vb* to look through (as a place) carefully or thoroughly in an effort to find or discover something — see SEARCH 1

combat *n* **1** active fighting during the course of a war ⟨a soldier who served through the war without actually seeing *combat*⟩
syn action, battle
rel attack, fire; hostilities, operations, warfare; duty, service
2 a physical dispute between opposing individuals or groups — see FIGHT 1
3 an earnest effort for superiority or victory over another — see CONTEST 1

combat *vb* **1** to oppose (someone) in physical conflict — see FIGHT 1
2 to strive to reduce or eliminate — see FIGHT 2

combative *adj* feeling or displaying eagerness to fight — see BELLIGERENT

combativeness *n* an inclination to fight or quarrel — see BELLIGERENCE

combination *n* **1** a distinct entity formed by the combining of two or more different things — see BLEND
2 the act or an instance of joining two or more things into one — see UNION 1
3 a number of businesses or enterprises united for commercial advantage — see CARTEL
4 an association of persons, parties, or states for mutual assistance and protection — see CONFEDERACY

combine *n* **1** a number of businesses or enterprises united for commercial advantage — see CARTEL
2 an association of persons, parties, or states for mutual assistance and protection — see CONFEDERACY

combine *vb* **1** to come together to form a single unit — see UNITE 1
2 to turn into a single mass that is more or less the same throughout — see BLEND 1

combined *adj* used or done by a number of people as a group — see COLLECTIVE

combining *n* the act or an instance of joining two or more things into one — see UNION 1

combust *vb* to be on fire especially brightly — see BURN 1

combustible *adj* capable of catching or being set on fire ⟨don't store oily rags and other *combustible* materials in a hot attic⟩
syn burnable, flammable, ignitable, inflammable
rel explosive, incendiary
near ant nonexplosive
ant fireproof, incombustible, noncombustible, nonflammable, noninflammable

combusting *adj* being on fire — see ABLAZE 1

come *vb* **1** to move closer to ⟨*come* here and sit by the fire⟩
syn advance, approach, near
rel drop (in), enter, pop (in)
near ant depart, exit, leave
ant go, retreat, withdraw

2 to get to a destination ⟨when do you think they'll *come* ?⟩
syn arrive, land, show up, turn up
rel hit, make, reach; pull (in), touch down; debark, disembark; barge (in), breeze (in), burst (in *or* into), waltz (in)
ant go
3 to eventually have as a state or quality — see BECOME
4 to take place — see HAPPEN

come (to) *vb* **1** to have a total of — see AMOUNT (TO) 1
2 to be the same in meaning or effect — see AMOUNT (TO) 2

come about *vb* to take place — see HAPPEN

come around *vb* to gain consciousness again — see COME TO

comeback *n* **1** a quick witty response — see RETORT 1
2 something spoken or written in reaction especially to a question — see ANSWER 1
3 the process or period of gradually regaining one's health and strength — see CONVALESCENCE

comedian *n* a person (as a writer) noted for or specializing in humor — see HUMORIST

comedown *n* a loss of status ⟨after a rapid rise to stardom, the rock band's *comedown* was just as quick⟩
syn decline, descent, down, downfall, fall
rel breakdown, collapse, crash, meltdown, ruin, undoing; defeat, disappointment, reversal, setback; bottom, nadir
near ant advance, headway, progress; flower, heyday, prime
ant aggrandizement, ascent, exaltation, rise, up

come down (with) *vb* to become affected with (a disease or disorder) — see CONTRACT 1

comedy *n* humorous entertainment ⟨presented a night of *comedy* as part of the week-long celebrations⟩
syn farce, humor, slapstick
rel burlesque, parody, satire; banter, persiflage, wit; foolery, fun, horseplay, monkeyshines, shenanigans

comeliness *n* the qualities in a person or thing that as a whole give pleasure to the senses — see BEAUTY 1

comely *adj* very pleasing to look at — see BEAUTIFUL

come out *vb* **1** to come to be ⟨in the end everything *came out* OK⟩
syn pan out, prove, turn out
rel develop, emerge, evolve, play out, unfold, work out
2 to come into view — see APPEAR 1
3 to become known — see GET OUT 1

come round *vb* to gain consciousness again — see COME TO

come to *vb* to gain consciousness again ⟨after being in a coma for months, the patient suddenly *came to*⟩
syn come around, come round, revive
rel pull through, rally, recover; awake, awaken, wake up
near ant black out, faint, pass out

---

syn synonym(s) *rel* related words
ant antonym(s) *near ant* near antonym(s)

comfort n 1 a feeling of ease from grief or trouble ⟨the mourners found *comfort* in their pastor's words⟩
syn cheer, consolation, relief, solace
rel encouragement, inspiration, uplift; assurance, reassurance; alleviation, assuagement, mitigation; contentment, gladness, happiness; commiseration, empathy, sympathy
near ant anguish, distress, heartache, heartbreak, torment, torture
2 something that adds to one's ease ⟨a family campground with all the *comforts* of home⟩
syn amenity, convenience, luxury
rel extra; benefit, help, service; delight, indulgence, joy, pleasure
ant burden, millstone, weight
3 reduction of or freedom from pain — see EASE 1
4 something adding to pleasure or comfort but not absolutely necessary — see LUXURY 1

comfort vb 1 to ease the grief or distress of ⟨the minister did his best to *comfort* the victims of the terrible tornado⟩
syn assure, cheer, console, reassure, solace, soothe
rel commiserate, condole, empathize, sympathize; boost, buoy (up), elevate, lift, uplift; allay, alleviate, assuage, relieve; calm, quiet, relax, tranquilize (*also* tranquillize)
near ant demoralize, discourage, dishearten; fret, upset, worry; aggravate, intensify, worsen; annoy, irk, irritate; harass, pester
ant distress, torment, torture, trouble
2 to fill with courage or strength of purpose — see ENCOURAGE 1

comfortable adj 1 providing physical comfort ⟨a large, overstuffed chair that is very *comfortable*⟩
syn cozy, cushy, easy, snug, soft
rel relaxing, reposeful, restful; genial, hospitable, inviting, pleasant; commodious, roomy, spacious; homelike, homely, homey
near ant hard, harsh, severe; inhospitable, uninviting, unpleasant
ant uncomfortable
2 enjoying physical comfort ⟨make yourself *comfortable* in the living room while I fix us some snacks⟩
syn cozy, relaxed, snug
rel content, contented, pleased, satisfied; peaceful, resting; easygoing, laid-back; undisturbed, unperturbed, untroubled
phrases at ease, at home
near ant discontented, displeased, dissatisfied; agitated, disturbed, perturbed, troubled
ant uncomfortable
3 being more than enough without being excessive — see PLENTIFUL

comforting adj 1 making one feel good inside — see HEARTWARMING
2 tending to calm the emotions and relieve stress — see SOOTHING 1

comforting n the giving of hope and strength in times of grief, distress, or suffering — see CONSOLATION 1

comfortless adj 1 causing discomfort — see UNCOMFORTABLE 1
2 causing or marked by an atmosphere lacking in cheer — see GLOOMY 1

comic adj 1 causing or intended to cause laughter — see FUNNY 1

comic n 1 a person (as a writer) noted for or specializing in humor — see HUMORIST
2 a series of drawings that tell a story or part of a story — see COMIC STRIP

comical adj 1 causing or intended to cause laughter — see FUNNY 1
2 so foolish or pointless as to be worthy of scornful laughter — see RIDICULOUS 1

comic strip n a series of drawings that tell a story or part of a story ⟨a *comic strip* that is beloved by both children and adults⟩
syn cartoon, comic, funny
rel comic book, funny paper(s); animated cartoon, animation; caricature

coming adj 1 being soon to appear or take place — see FORTHCOMING
2 being the one that comes immediately after another — see NEXT
3 of a time after the present — see FUTURE

comity n peaceful coexistence — see HARMONY 2

command n 1 a statement of what to do that must be obeyed by those concerned ⟨the captain's *commands* were followed without question⟩
syn behest, charge, commandment, decree, dictate, direction, directive, edict, instruction, order, word
rel demand, requirement; injunction, mandate; law, precept, rule; ordinance, regulation, statute
near ant appeal, entreaty, petition, plea, urging; proposal, recommendation, suggestion
2 a highly developed skill in or knowledge of something ⟨a *command* of French that is the result of a year spent in France as an exchange student⟩
syn mastership, mastery, proficiency
rel virtuosity; fluency, literacy; experience, expertise, know-how, practice (*also* practise); skill(s); acquaintance, familiarity, intimacy
near ant incompetence, incompetency; ignorance, illiteracy, unfamiliarity
3 the place from which a commander runs operations ⟨the general set up his *command* in the old port city⟩
syn base, headquarters
rel home, seat
4 a place from which authority is exercised — see SEAT 1
5 the right or means to command or control others — see POWER 1

command vb 1 to issue orders to (someone) by right of authority ⟨the general *commanded* the troops to advance⟩

syn adjure, bid, boss (around), charge, direct, enjoin, instruct, order, tell

rel ask, petition, request; beg, beseech, entreat; advise, counsel, warn; appoint, assign, authorize, commission; oversee, superintend, supervise; conduct, control, lead, manage; coerce, compel, constrain, force, oblige, require

near ant comply (with), follow, keep, observe

ant mind, obey

2 to give an order ⟨the governor has *commanded* that all state flags be flown at half-mast⟩

syn decree, dictate, direct, ordain, order

rel ask, petition, request; demand, require

phrases call for

3 to ask for (something) earnestly or with authority — see DEMAND 1

4 to exercise authority or power over — see GOVERN 1

5 to keep, control, or experience as one's own — see HAVE 1

6 to look down on — see OVERLOOK 1

7 to serve as leader of — see LEAD 2

8 to set or receive as a price — see CHARGE 1

commandant *n* one in official command especially of a military force or base — see COMMANDER 1

commandeer *vb* **1** to take control of (a vehicle) by force ⟨an airliner *commandeered* by terrorists⟩

syn hijack (*also* highjack)

rel appropriate, confiscate, expropriate, seize

2 to take or make use of without authority or right — see APPROPRIATE 1

commander *n* **1** one in official command especially of a military force or base ⟨a surrender of the fort by the *commander* without a single shot having been fired⟩

syn captain, commandant, commanding officer

rel commissioned officer

phrases commander in chief

2 a person in overall command of a ship — see CAPTAIN 1

commanding *adj* highest in rank or authority — see HEAD

commanding officer *n* one in official command especially of a military force or base — see COMMANDER 1

commandment *n* a statement of what to do that must be obeyed by those concerned — see COMMAND 1

commemorate *vb* **1** to be a memorial of ⟨a stone obelisk *commemorates* the Battle of Bunker Hill⟩

syn memorialize

rel celebrate, keep, observe, remember; enshrine, exalt, glorify, honor; bless, consecrate, sanctify, solemnize

near ant disgrace, dishonor

2 to act properly in relation to — see KEEP 1

commemorating *adj* serving to preserve the memory of a person, thing, or an event — see COMMEMORATIVE

commemorative *adj* serving to preserve the memory of a person, thing, or an event ⟨*commemorative* stamps for the stars of American popular music⟩

syn commemorating, memorial, memorializing

rel dedicatory, testimonial; enshrining, glorifying, honorary

commemorative *n* something that serves to keep alive the memory of a person or event — see MEMORIAL

commence *vb* **1** to take the first step in (a process or course of action) — see BEGIN 1

2 to come into existence — see BEGIN 2

commencement *n* the point at which something begins — see BEGINNING

commend *vb* to put (something) into the possession or safekeeping of another — see GIVE 2

commendable *adj* deserving of high regard or great approval — see ADMIRABLE

commendation *n* **1** a formal recognition of an achievement or praiseworthy deed ⟨a firefighter who has been awarded several *commendations* for bravery⟩

syn acknowledgment (*also* acknowledgement), citation

rel decoration, medal, ribbon; accolade, award, prize, tribute; dedication

2 a formal expression of praise — see ENCOMIUM

commendatory *adj* expressing approval — see FAVORABLE 1

commensurate *adj* corresponding in size, amount, extent, or degree — see PROPORTIONAL

comment *n* **1** a briefly expressed opinion — see REMARK

2 **comments** *pl* a series of explanations or observations on something (as an event) — see COMMENTARY

comment *vb* to make a statement of one's opinion — see REMARK 1

commentary *n* a series of explanations or obser-vations on something (as an event) ⟨the TV anchors provided a running *commentary* on the parade⟩

syn analysis, comment, exposition

rel annotation, explication; note, observation, remark; report, review, write-up

commerce *n* the buying and selling of goods especially on a large scale and between different places ⟨a government agency in charge of regulating interstate *commerce*⟩

syn business, marketplace, trade, traffic

rel free trade; dealings, horse-trading; merchandising, retailing, wholesaling; bartering

commercial *adj* fit or likely to be sold especially on a large scale ⟨the *commercial* fare produced by the Hollywood movie studios⟩

syn marketable, salable (*or* saleable)

rel mass-produced, wholesale

---

syn synonym(s)   *rel* related words
ant antonym(s)   *near ant* near antonym(s)

ant noncommercial, nonsalable, uncommercial, unmarketable, unsalable

commingle *vb* to turn into a single mass that is more or less the same throughout — see BLEND 1

commiserate (with) *vb* to have sympathy for — see PITY

commiseration *n* **1** sorrow or the capacity to feel sorrow for another's suffering or misfortune — see SYMPATHY 1

2 the capacity for feeling for another's unhappiness or misfortune — see HEART 1

commissary *n* a person who acts or does business for another — see AGENT 2

commission *n* **1** the granting of power to perform various acts or duties ⟨President Jefferson's *commission* to Lewis and Clark to explore the Louisiana Territory⟩

syn accreditation, authorization, delegation, license (*or* licence), mandate

rel commendation, consignment, entrustment; facilitation, fostering, promotion; commanding, directing, ordering

2 the doing of an action ⟨a single burglar was responsible for the *commission* of all the break-ins⟩

syn accomplishment, achievement, discharge, enactment, execution, fulfillment, implementation, performance, perpetration

rel dispatch, expedition; administration, direction, handling, management; application, operation, practice (*also* practise)

ant nonfulfillment, nonperformance

3 a select group of persons assigned to consider or take action on some matter — see COMMITTEE

4 the state or fact of being chosen for a position or duty — see APPOINTMENT 1

commission *vb* **1** to appoint as one's representative — see DELEGATE 1

2 to give official or legal power to — see AUTHORIZE 1

3 to give a task, duty, or responsibility to — see ENTRUST 1

4 to pick (someone) by one's authority for a specific position or duty — see APPOINT 2

commit *vb* **1** to carry through (as a process) to completion — see PERFORM 1

2 to obligate by prior agreement — see PLEDGE 1

3 to put (something) into the possession or safekeeping of another — see GIVE 2

4 to put in or as if in prison — see IMPRISON

commitment *n* something one must do because of prior agreement — see OBLIGATION

committee *n* a select group of persons assigned to consider or take action on some matter ⟨a *committee* in charge of planning the organization's annual Christmas party⟩

syn commission, panel

rel subcommittee; delegation, mission; assembly, body, congress, convocation, council, synod

commodious *adj* more than adequate or average in capacity — see SPACIOUS

commodities *n pl* products that are bought and sold in business — see MERCHANDISE

common *adj* **1** often observed or encountered ⟨horse ranches are a *common* sight in that part of the state⟩

syn commonplace, everyday, familiar, frequent, garden, household, ordinary, routine, ubiquitous, usual

rel normal, regular, standard; general, universal; ceaseless, constant, continual, continuous, incessant, unceasing; popular, prevailing, prevalent, rampant; perennial, recurrent, repeated

near ant aberrant, abnormal, irregular, unnatural; intermittent, occasional, sporadic

ant extraordinary, infrequent, rare, uncommon, unfamiliar, unusual

2 being of the type that is encountered in the normal course of events — see ORDINARY 1

3 belonging or relating to the whole — see GENERAL 1

4 belonging to the class of people of low social or economic rank — see IGNOBLE 1

5 held by or applicable to a majority of the people — see GENERAL 3

6 used or done by a number of people as a group — see COLLECTIVE

7 of average to below average quality — see MEDIOCRE 1

8 of low quality — see CHEAP 2

9 lacking in refinement or good taste — see COARSE 2

commoners *n pl* the body of the community as contrasted with the elite — see MASS 1

commonly *adv* according to the usual course of things — see NATURALLY 2

commonness *n* **1** the fact or state of happening often — see FREQUENCY

2 the quality or state of lacking refinement or good taste — see VULGARITY 1

commonplace *adj* **1** being of the type that is encountered in the normal course of events — see ORDINARY 1

2 often observed or encountered — see COMMON 1

3 used or heard so often as to be dull — see STALE

commonplace *n* an idea or expression that has been used by many people ⟨the familiar summertime *commonplace* that "it's not the heat, it's the humidity"⟩

syn banality, cliché, platitude, shibboleth, truism

rel inanity; generality, generalization, simplification; adage, proverb, saw, saying; old wives' tale, stereotype

near ant profundity

commonsense *adj* based on sound reasoning or information — see GOOD 1

common sense *n* the ability to make intelligent decisions especially in everyday matters ⟨*common sense* should tell you not to meet face-to-face with someone who is just an online acquaintance⟩

syn discreetness, discretion, horse sense, levelheadedness, prudence, sense, sensibleness, wisdom, wit

rel street smarts; farsightedness, foresight, foresightedness, judgment (*or* judgement); brains, gray matter, intelligence; logicalness, practicality, rationality; discernment, discrimination, insight, sagacity, sapience; acumen, astuteness, keenness, penetration, perspicacity, shrewdness; care, caution, circumspection, precaution, premeditation

near ant shortsightedness; brainlessness, foolishness, idiocy, senselessness, stupidity; carelessness, heedlessness

ant imprudence, indiscretion

commonwealth *n* a body of people composed of one or more nationalities usually with its own territory and government — see NATION

commotion *n* a state of noisy, confused activity ⟨the *commotion* created when the nation's top rock band arrived in town⟩

syn bother, bustle, clatter, disturbance, furor, furore, fuss, hubbub, hullabaloo, hurly-burly, pandemonium, pother, row, ruckus, ruction, rumpus, shindy, squall, stew, stir, storm, to-do, tumult, turmoil, uproar, welter, whirl

rel cacophony, clamor, din, howl, hue and cry, outcry, noise, racket, roar; disorder, unrest, upheaval; eruption, flare-up, flurry, outbreak, outburst; brawl, fracas, fray, hassle, melee, scuffle; dither, fever, fret, lather, tizzy

near ant calm, hush, peace, quiet, quietude, rest, stillness, tranquillity (*or* tranquility); order, orderliness

communal *adj* used or done by a number of people as a group — see COLLECTIVE

commune *vb* to form a close personal relationship ⟨after a week in the wilderness, the scouts were really starting to *commune* with nature⟩

syn click, relate

rel bond; befriend

communicable *adj* capable of being passed by physical contact from one person to another — see CONTAGIOUS 1

communicate *vb* 1 to cause (something) to pass from one to another ⟨the infected cook unknowingly *communicated* the disease to hundreds of people⟩

syn convey, impart, spread, transfer, transfuse, transmit

rel deliver, hand over, surrender, turn over; broadcast, diffuse, disseminate, propagate; contaminate, infect, poison

near ant catch, come down (with), contract

2 to engage in an exchange of information or ideas ⟨for decades the two medical centers have been *communicating* about cancer research⟩

syn brainstorm, intercommunicate

rel correspond; converse, talk; bond, commune, relate; accost, approach, contact

communicate (with) *vb* to transmit information or requests to — see CONTACT

communication *n* a piece of conveyed information ⟨the latest *communication* from the crew of the space station⟩

syn dispatch, message

rel bulletin, communiqué, report; memo, memorandum, notice; epistle, letter, missive, note; electronic mail, e-mail; intelligence, news, tidings, word; command, directive, instruction, order

communion *n* a friendly relationship marked by ready communication and mutual understanding — see RAPPORT

community *n* 1 the people living in a particular area ⟨the whole *community* rallied to the aid of the family who had lost its home⟩

syn neighborhood

rel city, commune, town, village; denizens, dwellers, inhabitants, residents; citizenry, culture, people, populace, public, society

2 a group of people with a common interest living in one place ⟨a picturesque seacoast village that is known for its sizable *community* of artists⟩

syn colony

rel circle, clique, coterie, set, society; band, company, troop; clan, family

3 a group of people sharing a common interest and relating together socially — see GANG 1

4 the body of people in a profession or field of activity — see CORPS

5 the quality or state of having many qualities in common — see SIMILARITY 1

commutation *n* a giving or taking of one thing of value in return for another — see EXCHANGE 1

commute *vb* to give up (something) and take something else in return — see CHANGE 3

compact *adj* 1 having a consistency that does not easily yield to pressure — see FIRM 2

2 having little space between items or parts — see CLOSE 1

3 marked by the use of few words to convey much information or meaning — see CONCISE

compact *n* 1 a formal agreement between two or more nations or peoples — see TREATY

2 an arrangement about action to be taken — see AGREEMENT 2

compact *vb* 1 to bring (something) to a central point or under a single control — see CENTRALIZE

2 to reduce in size or volume by or as if by pressing parts or members together — see COMPRESS 1

compacting *n* the act or process of reducing the size or volume of something by or as if by pressing — see COMPRESSION

compactly *adv* in a few words — see SHORTLY 1

---

syn synonym(s)   *rel* related words
ant antonym(s)   *near ant* near antonym(s)

compactness *n* the quality or state of being marked by or using only few words to convey much meaning — see SUCCINCTNESS

companion *n* 1 a person frequently seen in the company of another — see ASSOCIATE 1

2 one that accompanies another for protection, guidance, or as a courtesy — see ESCORT

3 either of a pair matched in one or more qualities — see MATE 1

4 something that is found along with something else — see ACCOMPANIMENT

companionable *adj* 1 having or showing kindly feeling and sincere interest — see FRIENDLY 1

2 likely to seek or enjoy the company of others — see CONVIVIAL

companionship *n* the feeling of closeness and friendship that exists between companions ⟨the widow's pet cats provided her with her only *companionship*⟩

syn camaraderie, company, comradeship, fellowship, society

rel amity, benevolence, cordiality, friendliness, friendship, goodwill, kindliness, civility, comity, concord, harmony, rapport; charity, generosity; affinity, compassion, empathy, sympathy; chumminess, familiarity, inseparability, intimacy, nearness; affection, devotion, fondness, love

near ant forlornness, loneliness, lonesomeness

company *n* 1 an organized group of stage performers ⟨a city that is fortunate enough to have two thriving opera *companies*⟩

syn troop, troupe

rel stock company; cast, dramatis personae, ensemble

2 a group of people working together on a task — see GANG 1

3 a commercial or industrial activity or organization — see ENTERPRISE 1

4 the feeling of closeness and friendship that exists between companions — see COMPANIONSHIP

comparable *adj* having qualities in common — see ALIKE

comparative *adj* being such only when compared to something else ⟨if you consider the multimillionaire's yearly income, we're living in *comparative* poverty⟩

syn approximate, near, relative

rel alike, comparable, similar; equal, equivalent

near ant genuine, real, true

ant absolute, complete, downright, out-and-out, outright, perfect, pure, unqualified

compare *vb* 1 to describe as similar ⟨reviews that *compared* the adventure movie to a thrilling ride on a roller coaster⟩

syn bracket, equate, liken

rel associate, connect, couple, link; allude, refer, relate; equal, match, parallel

ant contrast

2 to regard or represent as equal or comparable — see EQUATE 1

compare (with) *vb* to come near or nearer to in character or quality — see APPROXIMATE

compartment *n* one of the parts into which an enclosed space is divided ⟨a backpack with many handy *compartments* for storing your camping gear⟩

syn bay, cabin, cell, chamber, cubicle

rel cubbyhole, pigeonhole, snuggery [*chiefly British*]; alcove, niche, nook, recess; cabinet, drawer; cavity, hole, hollow; booth, crib, stall; crypt, vault

compass *n* 1 an area over which activity, capacity, or influence extends — see RANGE 2

2 the line or relatively narrow space that marks the outer limit of something — see BORDER 1

compass *vb* 1 to carry through (as a process) to completion — see PERFORM 1

2 to pass completely around — see ENCIRCLE 1

compassion *n* 1 sorrow or the capacity to feel sorrow for another's suffering or misfortune — see SYMPATHY 1

2 the capacity for feeling for another's unhappiness or misfortune — see HEART 1

compassionate *adj* 1 having or marked by sympathy and consideration for others — see HUMANE 1

2 having or showing the capacity for sharing the feelings of another — see SYMPATHETIC 1

compatibility *n* peaceful coexistence — see HARMONY 2

compatible *adj* 1 having or marked by agreement in feeling or action — see HARMONIOUS 3

2 not having or showing any apparent conflict — see CONSISTENT

compatriot *n* a person living in or originally from the same country as another ⟨an appeal to all of his *compatriots* to come to their country's aid in its hour of need⟩

syn countryman

rel nationalist, patriot; citizen, national, subject; aborigine, native; homeboy, resident

near ant alien, foreigner, immigrant, outsider

compel *vb* to cause (a person) to give in to pressure — see FORCE

compelling *adj* having the power to persuade — see COGENT

compendious *adj* 1 covering everything or all important points — see ENCYCLOPEDIC

2 marked by the use of few words to convey much information or meaning — see CONCISE

compensate *vb* 1 to provide (someone) with a just payment for loss or injury ⟨you'll have to *compensate* the neighbors for cutting down their tree⟩

syn indemnify, recompense, recoup, remunerate, requite

rel refund, reimburse, repay; redress, remedy, repair; discharge, pay, quit

2 to give (someone) the sum of money owed for goods or services received — see PAY 1

compensate (for) *vb* to balance with an equal force so as to make ineffective — see OFFSET

compensation *n* **1** payment to another for a loss or injury ⟨a warehouse worker who received a large *compensation* for his crippling injury while on the job⟩

syn damages, indemnification, indemnity, quittance, recompense, recoupment, redress, remuneration, reparation, requital, restitution, satisfaction

rel amends, atonement, expiation; refund, reimbursement, repayment; adjustment, settlement; punishment, reprisal, retaliation

2 something (as money) that is given or received in return for goods or services — see PAYMENT 2

3 the act of offering money in exchange for goods or services — see PAYMENT 1

compete *vb* to engage in a contest ⟨prizefighters *competing* for the world heavyweight championship⟩

syn battle, contend, fight, race, vie

rel challenge, engage, play; jockey, maneuver; go out, try out; train, work

competence *n* the physical or mental power to do something — see ABILITY

competency *n* the physical or mental power to do something — see ABILITY

competent *adj* having the required skills for an acceptable level of performance ⟨any *competent* mechanic should be able to fix that⟩

syn able, capable, fit, good, qualified, suitable

rel accomplished, ace, adept, experienced, expert, master, masterful, masterly, practiced (*or* practised), proficient, seasoned, skilled, skillful, veteran; prepared, schooled, trained

near ant inexperienced, inexpert, unseasoned, unskilled, unskillful; unprepared, unschooled, untrained; beginning, green, new, raw, untested, untried

ant incompetent, inept, poor, unfit, unqualified

competently *adv* in a skillful or expert manner — see WELL 3

competition *n* **1** a competitive encounter between individuals or groups carried on for amusement, exercise, or in pursuit of a prize — see GAME 1

2 one who strives for the same thing as another — see COMPETITOR

competitor *n* one who strives for the same thing as another ⟨the *competitors* for the science award come from the best high schools in the country⟩

syn challenger, competition, contender, contestant, rival

rel finalist, semifinalist; entrant; player; adversary, antagonist, opponent

compilation *n* a collection of writings — see ANTHOLOGY

compile *vb* to bring together from several sources into a single volume or list ⟨*compiled* the best short stories ever written into one fat book⟩

syn collect

rel edit, redraft, revamp, revise, rework; accumulate, amass, assemble, gather, group

complacence *n* an often unjustified feeling of being pleased with oneself or with one's situation or achievements ⟨the *complacence* of some of the rich kids at the exclusive private school⟩

syn complacency, conceit, conceitedness, ego, egotism, pompousness, pride, pridefulness, self-admiration, self-conceit, self-esteem, self-importance, self-satisfaction, smugness, vaingloriousness, vainglory, vainness, vanity

rel assurance, confidence, self-assurance, self-confidence; self-righteousness; arrogance, disdainfulness, haughtiness, imperiousness, lordliness, self-assertion, snobbishness, superciliousness, superiority; overconfidence, presumption; pretense (*or* pretence), pretension, pretentiousness; egoism, self-centeredness, selfishness; self-respect

near ant diffidence, self-doubt; altruism, unselfishness; bashfulness, demureness, shyness, timidity, timidness; passiveness, passivity

ant humbleness, humility, modesty

complacency *n* an often unjustified feeling of being pleased with oneself or with one's situation or achievements — see COMPLACENCE

complacent *adj* having too high an opinion of oneself — see CONCEITED

complain *vb* to express dissatisfaction, pain, or resentment usually tiresomely ⟨the time-honored tradition of students *complaining* about the food in the cafeteria⟩

syn beef, bellyache, carp, crab, croak, fuss, gripe, grouse, growl, grumble, kick, moan, murmur, mutter, repine, squawk, wail, whine, yammer

rel object (to), protest, quarrel (with); cavil, quibble; fret, stew, worry; blubber, cry, sob; bemoan, bewail, deplore, lament

near ant accept, bear, countenance, endure, tolerate; applaud, cheer, commend

ant rejoice

complainant *n* the person in a legal proceeding who makes a charge of wrongdoing against another ⟨the *complainant* charged that the defendant had broken the ironclad contract that both had signed⟩

syn plaintiff, suer

rel accuser; litigant, party, suitor; appellant, petitioner, pleader

near ant accused

ant defendant

---

syn synonym(s)	*rel* related words
ant antonym(s)	*near ant* near antonym(s)

complainer *n* **1** a person who makes frequent complaints usually about little things — see CRYBABY

2 an irritable and complaining person — see GROUCH

complaint *n* **1** an expression of dissatisfaction, pain, or resentment ⟨a warning that if there were any more *complaints*, we were turning around and not going to the beach after all⟩

syn beef, fuss, grievance, gripe, grumble, murmur, plaint, squawk

rel challenge, demur, expostulation, kick, objection, protest, quibble, remonstrance

near ant commendation, compliment, plaudit; acclaim, applause, praise; approval, endorsement, sanction

2 a feeling or declaration of disapproval or dissent — see OBJECTION

3 a formal claim of criminal wrongdoing against a person — see CHARGE 1

4 an abnormal state that disrupts a plant's or animal's normal bodily functioning — see DISEASE

complaisance *n* a desire or disposition to please ⟨the *complaisance* of his girlfriend is such that she goes along with everything he says⟩

syn amenability, amiability, good-naturedness

rel affability, amicability, congeniality, cordiality, friendliness, geniality, sociability; agreeableness, graciousness, pleasantness; kindheartedness, kindliness, warmheartedness; compliance, docility, passivity, submissiveness

near ant disagreeableness, sullenness, surliness, ungraciousness; disobedience, intractability, recalcitrance

complement *n* **1** something that serves to complete or make up for a deficiency in something else ⟨with his practicality and her refreshing enthusiasm, they are perfect *complements* to each other⟩

syn supplement

rel addendum, addition, appendix; adjunct, annex, appendage, extension; accessory, appliance, attachment; additive, filler

2 the largest number or amount that something can hold — see CAPACITY 1

complement *vb* to serve as a completing element to ⟨this cap *complements* your Boy Scout uniform⟩

syn complete, round (off *or* out)

rel finish (off), flesh (out); adorn, beautify, decorate, embellish; better, enhance, improve; constitute, form, make up

complementary *adj* related to each other in such a way that one completes the other ⟨the *complementary* contributions of the cooking and cleanup committees were essential to the success of the church barbecue⟩

syn reciprocal, supplementary

rel cooperative, mutual, symbiotic; collective, combined, common, communal, conjoint, joint, shared, united

ant noncomplementary, nonreciprocal

complete *adj* **1** not lacking any part or member that properly belongs to it ⟨a *complete* deck of cards⟩

syn comprehensive, entire, full, grand, intact, integral, perfect, plenary, total, whole

rel unabridged, uncut, undiminished; all-out, exhaustive, extensive; full-blown, full-fledged, full-scale

near ant abbreviated, abridged, cut, diminished, reduced

ant imperfect, incomplete, partial

2 brought or having come to an end ⟨your education is never *complete* — there's always something more to learn⟩

syn completed, concluded, done, down, ended, finished, over, terminated, through, up

rel accomplished, achieved, attained, compassed, realized; dead, defunct, extinct, obsolete; expired

ant continuing, incomplete, ongoing, uncompleted, unfinished

3 covering everything or all important points — see ENCYCLOPEDIC

4 having no exceptions or restrictions — see ABSOLUTE 2

5 trying all possibilities — see EXHAUSTIVE

complete *vb* **1** to bring (something) to a state where nothing remains to be done — see FINISH 1

2 to serve as a completing element to — see COMPLEMENT

completed *adj* brought or having come to an end — see COMPLETE 2

completely *adv* **1** to a full extent or degree — see FULLY 1

2 with attention to all aspects or details — see THOROUGHLY 1

complex *adj* **1** having many parts or aspects that are usually interrelated ⟨this camera is a *complex* instrument that requires careful handling⟩ ⟨*complex* issues regarding free speech and school discipline⟩

syn complicated, convoluted, elaborate, intricate, involved, knotty, labyrinthine, sophisticated

rel composite, compound, heterogeneous, mixed, multifarious, varied; challenging, difficult, tough; impenetrable, incomprehensible, inexplicable, unfathomable, unintelligible

near ant oversimplified, simplified; homogeneous, uniform, unvaried

ant plain, simple, uncomplicated

2 made or done with great care or with much detail — see ELABORATE 1

complex *n* **1** a structure that is designed and built for a particular purpose — see FACILITY

2 something made up of many interdependent or related parts — see SYSTEM 1

complexion *n* **1** the hue or appearance of the skin and especially of the face ⟨a sunscreen for people with very light *complexions*⟩

syn color, coloring

rel shade, tint, tone; features, lineaments, looks; countenance, face, visage

2 the set of qualities that makes a person, a group of people, or a thing different from others — see NATURE 1

complexity *n* **1** the state or quality of having many interrelated parts or aspects ⟨the *complexity* of the company's computer system is such that a full-time repairman is needed⟩

syn complicatedness, elaborateness, intricacy, involution, sophistication

rel diversity, heterogeneousness; impenetrability, incomprehensibility, inexplicability

near ant simplification; homogeneity, uniformity

ant plainness, simpleness, simplicity

2 something that makes a situation more complicated or difficult — see COMPLICATION 1

compliance *n* **1** a readiness or willingness to yield to the wishes of others ⟨a strong-willed pop star who is not known for her *compliance*⟩

syn compliancy, deference, docility, obedience, submissiveness

rel amenability, amiability, complaisance, good-naturedness; servility, slavishness, subservience, subserviency; conformity; cooperativeness, receptiveness, receptivity; humoring, indulgence; acceptance, acquiescence, assent, consent; capitulation, submission, surrender; affability, amicability, congeniality, cordiality, friendliness, geniality, sociability

near ant animosity, antipathy, enmity, hostility, ill will

ant defiance, disobedience, intractability, recalcitrance

2 a bending to the authority or control of another — see OBEDIENCE 1

compliancy *n* a readiness or willingness to yield to the wishes of others — see COMPLIANCE 1

compliant *adj* readily giving in to the command or authority of another — see OBEDIENT

complicate *vb* to make complex or difficult ⟨the need to go to both a soccer game and band practice really *complicates* tonight's schedule⟩

syn perplex, sophisticate

rel develop, elaborate, expand; intensify, magnify; confound, confuse, mess (up), mix (up), muddle; entangle, snarl, tangle

near ant abbreviate, cut, shorten; ease, facilitate; disentangle, straighten (out), untangle; oversimplify

ant simplify, streamline

complicated *adj* **1** having many parts or aspects that are usually interrelated — see COMPLEX 1

2 made or done with great care or with much detail — see ELABORATE 1

complicatedness *n* the state or quality of having many interrelated parts or aspects — see COMPLEXITY 1

complication *n* **1** something that makes a situation more complicated or difficult ⟨the food allergies of the guests were just another *complication* for the couple trying to plan their wedding reception⟩

syn complexity, difficulty, intricacy

rel aftereffect, ramification, side effect; subtlety, technicality; annoyance, bother, headache, inconvenience, matter, trouble

phrases fly in the ointment

2 an abnormal state that disrupts a plant's or animal's normal bodily functioning — see DISEASE

complicity *n* a secret agreement or cooperation between two parties for an illegal or dishonest purpose — see COLLUSION

compliment *vb* to express to (someone) admiration for his or her success or good fortune — see CONGRATULATE

complimentary *adj* **1** expressing approval — see FAVORABLE 1

2 not costing or charging anything — see FREE 4

compliments *n pl* best wishes ⟨please extend our *compliments* to the chef for a great meal⟩

syn congratulations, felicitations, greetings, regards, respects

rel approval, blessing, endorsement; acknowledgment (*also* acknowledgement), citation, commendation; adulation, flattery, praise

near ant dig, gibe (*or* jibe), insult, putdown, taunt

comply (with) *vb* **1** to act according to the commands of — see OBEY

2 to do what is required by the terms of — see FULFILL 1

component *n* one of the parts that make up a whole — see ELEMENT 1

comport *vb* **1** to be in agreement on every point — see CHECK 1

2 to manage the actions of (oneself) in a particular way — see BEHAVE

comportment *n* the way or manner in which one conducts oneself — see BEHAVIOR

compose *vb* **1** to put (something) into proper and usually carefully worked out written form ⟨the whole class *composed* a request to the governor asking that the endangered species be adopted as the official state animal⟩

syn cast, craft, draft, draw (up), formulate, frame, prepare

rel fabricate, fashion, form, mold, sculpture, shape; couch, express, phrase, state, verbalize, word; author, pen, write; conceive, concoct, devise; build, construct, make; assemble, compound, piece (together)

phrases put together

2 to be all the substance of — see CONSTITUTE 1

3 to free from distress or disturbance — see CALM 1

---

syn synonym(s)   *rel* related words
ant antonym(s)   *near ant* near antonym(s)

4 to gain emotional or mental control of — see COLLECT 1

composed *adj* free from emotional or mental agitation — see CALM 2

composer *n* a person who writes musical compositions ⟨a versatile *composer* whose works include operas, symphonies, concertos, and sonatas⟩
syn musician, songwriter
rel arranger, scorer; librettist

composite *adj* made from the joining of two or more parts or elements ⟨the movie's special effects included the use of many *composite* photographs⟩
syn amalgamated, compound
rel blended, combined, commingled, mingled, mixed; fused, integrated; interlaced, intermixed, intertwined, interwoven
near ant uncombined, unmixed
ant simple

composite *n* a distinct entity formed by the combining of two or more different things — see BLEND

composition *n* **1** a literary, musical, or artistic production ⟨the *compositions* of Michelangelo include the dome of St. Peter's, the ceiling of the Sistine Chapel, and his monumental statue of David⟩
syn opus, piece, work
rel classic, magnum opus, masterpiece, pièce de résistance, showpiece; model, outline, sketch; étude
2 a short piece of writing done as a school exercise ⟨a teacher who is fond of having her class write *compositions*⟩
syn paper, theme
rel article, essay, story
3 the way in which the elements of something (as a work of art) are arranged ⟨student photographers learn the importance of *composition* in creating striking images⟩
syn arrangement, configuration, design, form, format, layout, makeup, pattern
rel motif, theme
4 a short piece of writing typically expressing a point of view — see ESSAY 1

composure *n* evenness of emotions or temper — see EQUANIMITY

compound *adj* made from the joining of two or more parts or elements — see COMPOSITE

compound *n* a distinct entity formed by the combining of two or more different things — see BLEND

compound *vb* **1** to make greater in size, amount, or number — see INCREASE 1
2 to put or bring together so as to form a new and longer whole — see CONNECT 1

comprehend *vb* **1** to recognize the meaning of ⟨the age at which children can *comprehend* the difference between right and wrong⟩
syn appreciate, apprehend, catch, catch on (to), dig [*slang*], get, grasp, make, make out, perceive, see, seize, tumble (to), understand
rel absorb, assimilate, digest, take in; know, realize, sense; fathom, penetrate

near ant misapprehend, misconstrue, misinterpret, misunderstand
ant miss
2 to have a practical understanding of — see KNOW 1
3 to have as part of a whole — see INCLUDE

comprehension *n* the knowledge gained from the process of coming to know or understand something ⟨the president's *comprehension* of the current situation in the Middle East⟩
syn appreciation, apprehension, grasp, grip, perception, understanding
rel absorption, assimilation, uptake; conception, visualization; awareness, consciousness, realization
near ant misapprehension, misinterpretation, misunderstanding

comprehensive *adj* **1** covering everything or all important points — see ENCYCLOPEDIC
2 not lacking any part or member that properly belongs to it — see COMPLETE 1
3 trying all possibilities — see EXHAUSTIVE

comprehensively *adv* with attention to all aspects or details — see THOROUGHLY 1

compress *vb* **1** to reduce in size or volume by or as if by pressing parts or members together ⟨a science textbook that *compresses* a lot of information about human reproduction into a few short chapters⟩
syn compact, condense, constrict, contract, squeeze
rel cram, crowd, jam, jam-pack, pack; abbreviate, abridge, curtail, shorten; downsize, shrink; concentrate, consolidate; simplify, streamline; decrease, diminish, lessen
near ant disperse, dissipate, scatter; distend, inflate, swell
ant expand, open, outspread, outstretch
2 to become smaller in size or volume through the drawing together of particles of matter — see CONTRACT 2

compression *n* the act or process of reducing the size or volume of something by or as if by pressing ⟨the *compression* of a long, complicated story into a two-hour movie is never easy⟩
syn compacting, condensation, constriction, contraction, squeezing
rel abbreviation, abridgment (*or* abridgement), curtailment, shortening; concentration, consolidation; simplification, streamlining; decreasing, diminishment, lessening
near ant dispersion, dissipation, scattering; distension (*or* distention), inflation, swelling
ant expansion

comprise *vb* **1** to be made up of ⟨the mall *comprises* three department stores and eighty smaller shops selling specialized goods⟩
syn consist (of), contain
rel embrace, encompass, entail, include, involve, take in; assimilate, embody, incorporate

2 to be all the substance of — see CONSTITUTE 1

compromise *n* the act or practice of each side giving up something in order to reach an agreement — see CONCESSION 1

compromise *vb* to place in danger — see ENDANGER

compulsion *n* the use of power to impose one's will on another — see FORCE 2

compulsive *adj* caused by or suggestive of an irresistible urge ⟨his *compulsive* clowning around can sometimes be annoying⟩

syn impulsive, obsessive

rel uncontrollable, irrepressible; automatic, instinctive, involuntary, reflex, spontaneous; conditioned, mechanical; unconscious, unthinking, unwitting

near ant unforced, voluntary, willful (*or* wilful); controllable, manageable, resistible

compulsory *adj* forcing one's compliance or participation by or as if by law — see MANDATORY

compunction *n* an uneasy feeling about the rightness of what one is doing or going to do — see QUALM

computation *n* the act or process of performing mathematical operations to find a value — see CALCULATION

compute *vb* to determine (a value) by doing the necessary mathematical operations — see CALCULATE 1

comrade *n* **1** a person frequently seen in the company of another — see ASSOCIATE 1

2 a person who has a strong liking for and trust in another — see FRIEND 1

comradely *adj* having or showing kindly feeling and sincere interest — see FRIENDLY 1

comradeship *n* the feeling of closeness and friendship that exists between companions — see COMPANIONSHIP

con *vb* to commit to memory — see MEMORIZE

concatenate *vb* to put together into a series by means of or as if by means of a thread — see THREAD 2

concatenation *n* a series of things linked together — see CHAIN 1

concave *adj* curved inward — see HOLLOW

concavity *n* a sunken area forming a separate space — see HOLE 2

conceal *vb* **1** to put into a hiding place — see ¹HIDE 1

2 to keep secret or shut off from view — see ¹HIDE 2

concealment *n* **1** the placing of something out of sight ⟨your choice of the oven for the *concealment* of the money was unwise⟩

syn caching, hiding, secretion, stashing

rel burial, burying, entombment, interment, interring

near ant disinterment, unearthing

---

ant display, exhibition, exposure, parading, showing

2 a place where a person goes to hide — see HIDEOUT

concede *vb* **1** to accept the truth or existence of (something) usually reluctantly — see ADMIT

2 to cease resistance (as to another's arguments, demands, or control) — see YIELD 3

conceit *n* **1** an elaborate or fanciful way of expressing something ⟨the *conceit* that the crowd at the outdoor rock concert was a vast sea of people waving to the beat of the music⟩

syn metaphor

rel analogy, circumlocution, euphemism, simile

phrases figure of speech

2 a conception or image created by the imagination and having no objective reality — see FANTASY 1

3 an often unjustified feeling of being pleased with oneself or with one's situation or achievements — see COMPLACENCE

conceited *adj* having too high an opinion of oneself ⟨a *conceited* basketball player who was always too busy even to sign autographs⟩

syn complacent, egoistic, egotistic (*or* egotistical), important, overweening, pompous, prideful, proud, self-conceited, self-important, self-satisfied, smug, stuck-up, vain, vainglorious

rel boastful, braggart, bragging; arrogant, cavalier, disdainful, haughty, lordly, self-assertive, snobbish, supercilious, superior, uppity; domineering, high-handed, imperious; highfalutin, pretentious; overconfident, presumptuous; confident, self-assured, self-confident; self-centered, selfish

near ant diffident, self-doubting; meek, unassertive; down-to-earth, unassuming, unpretentious; bashful, retiring, shy

ant humble, modest

conceitedness *n* an often unjustified feeling of being pleased with oneself or with one's situation or achievements — see COMPLACENCE

conceivably *adv* it is possible — see PERHAPS

conceive *vb* to form a mental picture of — see IMAGINE 1

concentrate *vb* **1** to increase the amount of (a substance in a mixture) by removing other substances ⟨prolonged boiling is required to *concentrate* the sap when making maple syrup⟩

syn condense

rel distill (*or* distil), purify, refine; compact, harden, solidify; deepen, enhance, heighten, intensify; evaporate, extract, remove

near ant weaken

ant dilute, water (down)

2 to fix (as one's attention) steadily toward a central objective ⟨a president who

---

syn synonym(s)   *rel* related words
ant antonym(s)   *near ant* near antonym(s)

will try to *concentrate* public attention on
the problems of inner cities⟩
syn fasten, focus, rivet, train
rel aim, direct, level, point, zero (in on);
attend, heed, mind
3 to bring (something) to a central point
or under a single control — see CEN-
TRALIZE
4 to bring together in one body or place
— see GATHER 1
5 to come together into one body or place
— see ASSEMBLE 1
concentrated *adj* 1 having an abundance
of some characteristic quality (as flavor)
— see FULL-BODIED
2 not divided or scattered among several
areas of interest or concern — see
WHOLE 1
concentration *n* a focusing of the mind
on something — see ATTENTION 1
concept *n* something imagined or pictured in the mind — see IDEA
conception *n* something imagined or pictured in the mind — see IDEA
conceptual *adj* dealing with or expressing
a quality or idea — see ABSTRACT 1
concern *n* 1 a commercial or industrial
activity or organization — see ENTER-
PRISE 1
2 an uneasy state of mind usually over the
possibility of an anticipated misfortune
or trouble — see ANXIETY 1
concern *vb* 1 to have (something) as a subject matter ⟨the book *concerns* the challenges faced by children growing up in
single-parent households⟩
syn cover, deal (with), pertain (to), treat
(of)
rel appertain (to), bear (on *or* upon), refer
(to), relate (to); allude (to), glance
(upon), mention, touch (upon); offer,
present; contain, embrace, encompass,
entail, include, incorporate
phrases have to do with
near ant exclude, omit; disregard, ignore,
neglect, overlook, pass over, slight
2 to be the business or affair of ⟨the problems of air and water pollution that *concern* all of us⟩
syn affect, involve, touch
rel apply (to), relate (to); embroil, ensnare, entangle, implicate
3 to trouble the mind of; to make uneasy
— see DISTURB 1
concerning *prep* having to do with — see
ABOUT 1
concert *n* an entertainment featuring singing or the playing of musical instruments
⟨during the summer various groups give
concerts on the town green⟩
syn musicale
rel performance, presentation; recital;
hootenanny, jam session, sing, songfest;
festival
concert *vb* 1 to bring about through discussion and compromise — see NEGOTI-
ATE 1
2 to participate or assist in a joint effort to
accomplish an end — see COOPERATE 1

concerted *adj* used or done by a number
of people as a group — see COLLECTIVE
concession *n* 1 the act or practice of each
side giving up something in order to
reach an agreement ⟨when trying to get a
raise in your allowance, it's good to know
the art of *concession*⟩
syn accommodation, compromise, give-
and-take, negotiation
rel arrangement, bargain, deal, understanding; agreement, settlement
2 an open declaration of something (as a
fault or the commission of an offense)
about oneself — see CONFESSION 1
3 something granted as a special favor —
see PRIVILEGE
conciliate *vb* 1 to bring to a state free of
conflicts, inconsistencies, or differences
— see HARMONIZE 2
2 to lessen the anger or agitation of — see
PACIFY
conciliating *adj* tending to lessen or avoid
conflict or hostility — see PACIFIC 1
conciliator *n* one who works with opposing sides in order to bring about an agreement — see MEDIATOR
conciliatory *adj* tending to lessen or avoid
conflict or hostility — see PACIFIC 1
concise *adj* marked by the use of few
words to convey much information or
meaning ⟨a *concise* article on violence in
the media that manages to say more than
most books on the subject⟩
syn aphoristic, brief, compact, compendious, crisp, epigrammatic, laconic, pithy,
succinct, summary, terse
rel abrupt, blunt, brusque, curt, short,
snippy; abbreviated, abridged, condensed, shortened; meaty, substantial;
meaningful, significant
near ant redundant, repetitious, tautological; enlarged, expanded, supplemented;
embellished, embroidered, exaggerated
ant diffuse, long-winded, prolix, rambling, verbose, wordy
concisely *adv* in a few words — see
SHORTLY 1
conciseness *n* 1 the condition of being
short — see BREVITY 1
2 the quality or state of being marked by
or using only few words to convey much
meaning — see SUCCINCTNESS
conclude *vb* 1 to bring (an event) to a natural or appropriate stopping point — see
CLOSE 3
2 to come to an end — see CEASE 1
3 to bring about through discussion and
compromise — see NEGOTIATE 1
4 to come to a judgment after discussion
or consideration — see DECIDE 1
5 to form an opinion through reasoning
and information — see INFER 1
concluded *adj* brought or having come to
an end — see COMPLETE 2
concluding *adj* following all others of the
same kind in order or time — see LAST
conclusion *n* 1 an opinion arrived at
through a process of reasoning ⟨the detective's *conclusion* that the murderer
had to be left-handed⟩

syn deduction, determination, inference
rel decision, judgment (*or* judgement),
ruling, verdict; conjecture, guess, surmise; assumption, presumption, supposition

2 a position arrived at after consideration
— see DECISION 1

3 a condition or occurrence traceable to a
cause — see EFFECT 1

4 the last part of a process or action — see
FINALE

5 the stopping of a process or activity —
see END 1

conclusive *adj* **1** serving to put an end to
all debate or questioning ⟨the archeolog-
ical discovery was *conclusive* proof that
the Vikings had indeed settled in North
America around 1000 A.D.⟩
syn absolute, clear, decisive, definitive
rel incontestable, incontrovertible, indisputable, indubitable, irrefutable, undeniable, unquestionable; unchallenged, uncontested, undisputed; unambiguous,
unequivocal; certain, definite, positive,
sure
near ant debatable, disputable, questionable, refutable; ambiguous, equivocal
ant inconclusive, indecisive, unclear

2 having the power to persuade — see
COGENT

concoct *vb* to create or think of by clever
use of the imagination — see INVENT

concoction *n* something (as a device) created for the first time through the use of
the imagination — see INVENTION 1

concomitant *n* something that is found
along with something else — see ACCOM-
PANIMENT

concomitant *adj* present at the same time
and place — see COINCIDENT

concord *n* peaceful coexistence — see
HARMONY 2

concourse *n* a typically long narrow way
connecting parts of a building — see
HALL 2

concrete *adj* **1** existing in fact and not
merely as a possibility — see ACTUAL

2 relating to or composed of matter —
see MATERIAL 1

concrete *vb* to become physically firm or
solid — see HARDEN 1

concur *vb* **1** to have or come to the same
opinion or point of view — see AGREE 1

2 to occur or exist at the same time — see
COINCIDE 1

concurrence *n* **1** the occurrence or existence of several things at once ⟨the *concurrence* of my birthday and the concert
by my favorite rock band made my preference for a birthday present pretty obvi-
ous⟩
syn coexistence, coincidence
rel development, happening, occurrence

2 the act or fact of being of one opinion
about something — see AGREEMENT 1

3 the approval by someone in authority
for the doing of something — see PER-
MISSION

concurrent *adj* **1** existing or occurring at
the same period of time — see CONTEM-
PORARY 1

2 present at the same time and place —
see COINCIDENT

concurrently *adv* at one and the same
time — see TOGETHER 1

concussion *n* a forceful coming together
of two things — see IMPACT 1

condemn *vb* **1** to declare to be morally
wrong or evil ⟨it is a sign of human
progress that slavery, which was once
common, is now universally *condemned*⟩
syn censure, damn, decry, denounce, execrate, reprehend, reprobate
rel attack, blast, criticize, knock, pan,
slam; belittle, deprecate, disparage;
doom, sentence; convict; blacklist, excommunicate, ostracize; rebuke, reprimand, reproach; admonish, chide, reprove; berate, lambaste (*or* lambast),
scold, upbraid; curse, imprecate; abhor,
abominate, detest, hate, loathe, revile
near ant approve, endorse (*also* indorse),
sanction; eulogize, exalt, extol (*also* extoll), glorify, laud, praise; acclaim, applaud, commend, hail; consecrate, hallow, sanctify; honor, revere, venerate
ant bless

2 to express one's unfavorable opinion of
the worth or quality of — see CRITICIZE

3 to express public or formal disapproval
of — see CENSURE 1

4 to find or pronounce guilty — see CON-
VICT

5 to impose a judicial punishment on —
see SENTENCE

condemnation *n* an often public or formal expression of disapproval — see
CENSURE

condensation *n* **1** a shortened version of a
written work — see ABRIDGMENT

2 the act or process of reducing the size
or volume of something by or as if by
pressing — see COMPRESSION

condense *vb* **1** to become smaller in size
or volume through the drawing together
of particles of matter — see CONTRACT 2

2 to reduce in size or volume by or as if
by pressing parts or members together —
see COMPRESS 1

3 to increase the amount of (a substance
in a mixture) by removing other substances — see CONCENTRATE 1

condensed *adj* not lasting for a considerable time — see SHORT 2

condescend *vb* **1** to descend to a level
that is beneath one's dignity ⟨I will not
condescend to answer the sore loser's
charge that I cheated in order to win the
race⟩
syn deign, stoop
rel debase, degrade, demean, humble, humiliate, lower
near ant rise

2 to assume or treat with an air of superiority ⟨wealthy people who tend to be

condescending toward their poor relations⟩

syn lord (it over), patronize

rel cold-shoulder, cut, high-hat, snub

condiment *n* something used to enhance the flavor of cooked or prepared food ⟨the cafeteria's self-serve table has a full array of *condiments*⟩

syn seasoning

rel herb, savory, spice; relish, sauce; flavoring

condition *n* 1 a state of being or fitness ⟨a car that was ten years old but in still good *condition*⟩

syn estate, fettle, form, kilter, order, repair, shape, trim

rel practice (*also* practise); pass, phase, stage

near ant disorder, disrepair

2 something upon which the carrying out of an agreement or offer depends ⟨you'll get a raise in your allowance with the *condition* that you'll do a better job of keeping your room clean⟩

syn provision, proviso, qualification, reservation, stipulation

rel strings, terms; prerequisite, requirement, requisite; limitation, modification, restriction; exception, exemption; essential, must, necessity

3 an abnormal state that disrupts a plant's or animal's normal bodily functioning — see DISEASE

4 something necessary, indispensable, or unavoidable — see ESSENTIAL 1

5 something that limits one's freedom of action or choice — see RESTRICTION 1

condition *vb* 1 to bring to a proper or desired state of fitness ⟨the length of time that it takes for runners to *condition* their bodies for a marathon⟩

syn season, train

rel fit, prepare, ready; acclimate, acclimatize, break in, orient, orientate; accustom, familiarize, habituate; harden, inure

2 to change (something) so as to make it suitable for a new use or situation — see ADAPT

conditional *adj* determined by something else — see DEPENDENT 2

conditioning *n* energetic movement of the body for the sake of physical fitness — see EXERCISE 1

condole (with) *vb* to have sympathy for — see PITY

condone *vb* to overlook or dismiss as of little importance — see EXCUSE 1

conduct *n* 1 the act or activity of looking after and making decisions about something ⟨the president was happy to leave the *conduct* of foreign affairs to his secretary of state⟩

syn administration, control, direction, governance, government, guidance, handling, management, operation, oversight, regulation, running, superintendence, supervision

rel care, custody, guardianship, protection, tutelage; engineering, machination, manipulation

2 the way or manner in which one conducts oneself — see BEHAVIOR

conduct *vb* 1 to look after and make decisions about ⟨the company's president continues to *conduct* the everyday affairs of the software firm he founded many years ago⟩

syn administer, carry on, control, direct, govern, guide, handle, manage, operate, oversee, regulate, run, superintend, supervise

rel care (for), keep, mind, tend, watch; lead, pilot, steer; guard, protect, safeguard

2 to cause to move to a central point or along a restricted pathway — see CHANNEL

3 to manage the actions of (oneself) in a particular way — see BEHAVE

4 to point out the way for (someone) especially from a position in front — see LEAD 1

conduit *n* 1 a long hollow cylinder for carrying a substance (as a liquid or gas) — see PIPE 1

2 an open man-made passageway for water — see CHANNEL 1

confection *n* a food having a high sugar content — see SWEET 1

confederacy *n* an association of persons, parties, or states for mutual assistance and protection ⟨a *confederacy* of several small nations who had promised to come to one another's aid if any were attacked⟩

syn alliance, bloc, coalition, combination, combine, confederation, federation, league, union

rel cabal, conspiracy, junto; cartel, syndicate, trust; faction, side, wing; association, group, organization; affiliation, cooperative, partnership

confederate *n* 1 one associated with another in wrongdoing — see ACCOMPLICE

2 someone associated with another to give assistance or moral support — see ALLY

confederate *vb* to form or enter into an association that furthers the interests of its members — see ALLY

confederation *n* 1 an association of persons, parties, or states for mutual assistance and protection — see CONFEDERACY

2 the state of having shared interests or efforts (as in social or business matters) — see ASSOCIATION 1

confer *vb* 1 to give the ownership or benefit of (something) formally or publicly ⟨the British monarch continues to *confer* knighthood on those who are outstanding in their fields⟩

syn accord, award, grant

rel bestow, contribute, donate, give, present; furnish, provide, supply; extend, offer, proffer; allocate, appropriate, assign

near ant rescind, revoke

2 to exchange viewpoints or seek advice for the purpose of finding a solution to a problem ⟨my parents are going to *confer*

with a financial advisor about saving for my college education⟩

syn advise, consult, counsel, parley, pow-wow, treat

rel debate, deliberate, discuss, hash (over); coach, guide, tutor; recommend, suggest; direct, refer (to)

conference *n* **1** a body of people come together in one place — see GATHERING 1

2 a coming together of a number of persons for a specified purpose — see MEETING 1

3 a meeting featuring a group discussion — see FORUM

4 an exchange of views for the purpose of exploring a subject or deciding an issue — see DISCUSSION 1

confess *vb* to accept the truth or existence of (something) usually reluctantly — see ADMIT

confession *n* an open declaration of something (as a fault or the commission of an offense) about oneself ⟨a *confession* that he had been lying all along⟩

syn acknowledgment (*also* acknowledgement), admission, avowal, concession

rel allowance; betrayal, disclosure, divulgence, revelation; announcement, declaration, proclamation; contrition, regret, remorse, repentance

confidant *n* a person who has a strong liking for and trust in another — see FRIEND 1

confidence *n* **1** great faith in oneself or one's abilities ⟨a lifelong *confidence* that enabled her to achieve great things despite powerful obstacles⟩

syn aplomb, assurance, self-assurance, self-confidence, self-esteem

rel cockiness, complacence, complacency, conceit, conceitedness, ego, egotism, overconfidence, pompousness, pride, self-admiration, self-conceit, self-importance, self-satisfaction, smugness, vainglory, vanity; calmness, composure, coolness, equanimity; self-possession

near ant apprehension, doubt, misgiving

ant diffidence, self-doubt

2 a state of mind in which one is free from doubt ⟨the *confidence* with which the game show contestant answered every question⟩

syn assurance, assuredness, certainty, certitude, conviction, positiveness, sureness

rel authoritarianism, dogmatism; decisiveness, firmness, resolution

near ant hesitancy, hesitation, indecisiveness, irresolution

ant doubt, incertitude, nonconfidence, uncertainty

3 firm belief in the integrity, ability, effectiveness, or genuineness of someone or something — see TRUST 1

4 information shared only with another or with a select few — see SECRET 1

confidence game *n* a scheme in which the victim is cheated out of his money after first gaining his trust ⟨the old *confidence game* in which the victims are told that they must pay a fee in order to collect their prize money⟩

syn hustle, racket, swindle

rel double cross, fix; gyp, rip-off; squeeze, ruse, subterfuge, trick

confidence man *n* a dishonest person who uses clever means to cheat others out of something of value — see TRICKSTER 1

confident *adj* **1** having or showing great faith in oneself or one's abilities ⟨you'll need to be *confident* —even in the face of rejection—if you want to pursue a career in show business⟩

syn assured, secure, self-assured, self-confident

rel hopeful, optimistic, rosy, sanguine, upbeat; complacent, conceited, egoistic, egotistic (*or* egotistical), important, overweening, pompous, prideful, proud, self-conceited, self-important, self-satisfied, smug, stuck-up, vain, vainglorious; calm, collected, composed, cool, placid, self-possessed, serene, tranquil, undisturbed, unperturbed

near ant meek, timid, unassertive; modest, unassuming, unpretentious; jittery, jumpy, nervous

ant diffident, insecure, self-doubting

2 having or showing a mind free from doubt — see CERTAIN 2

confidential *adj* not known or meant to be known by the general populace — see PRIVATE 1

confiding *adj* having or showing trust in another — see TRUSTING 1

configuration *n* **1** the arrangement of parts that gives something its basic form — see FRAME 1

2 the way in which something is sized, arranged, or organized — see FORMAT 1

3 the way in which the elements of something (as a work of art) are arranged — see COMPOSITION 3

4 the outward appearance of something as distinguished from its substance — see FORM 1

confine *vb* **1** to set bounds or an upper limit for — see LIMIT 1

2 to put in or as if in prison — see IMPRISON

confinement *n* **1** the act of confining or the state of being confined — see INTERNMENT

2 the act or practice of keeping something (as an activity) within certain boundaries — see RESTRICTION 2

confines *n pl* **1** a real or imaginary point beyond which a person or thing cannot go — see LIMIT

2 the line or relatively narrow space that marks the outer limit of something — see BORDER 1

confirm *vb* to give evidence or testimony to the truth or factualness of ⟨several

---

syn synonym(s)   **rel** related words
ant antonym(s)   **near ant** near antonym(s)

eyewitnesses who can *confirm* the youngster's account of what happened⟩

syn bear out, corroborate, substantiate, support, validate, verify, vindicate

rel attest, authenticate, avouch, certify, testify (to), vouch (for); witness; guarantee, warrant; affirm, assert, aver, avow, profess

near ant contradict, gainsay; deny, disavow, disclaim

ant disprove, rebut, refute

confirmable *adj* capable of being proven as true or real — see VERIFIABLE

confirmation *n* something presented in support of the truth or accuracy of a claim — see PROOF

confirmatory *adj* serving to give support to the truth or factualness of something — see CORROBORATIVE

confirmed *adj* 1 being such by habit and not likely to change — see HABITUAL 1

2 firmly established over time — see INVETERATE 1

confirming *adj* serving to give support to the truth or factualness of something — see CORROBORATIVE

confiscate *vb* to take ownership or control of (something) by right of one's authority ⟨anything that might be used as a weapon will be *confiscated* by the security guards⟩

syn expropriate, sequester

rel appropriate, arrogate, preempt, usurp; commandeer, seize, take over

near ant release, relinquish, surrender, yield

conflagration *n* a destructive burning — see FIRE

conflict *n* 1 a lack of agreement or harmony — see DISCORD

2 a physical dispute between opposing individuals or groups — see FIGHT 1

3 a state of armed violent struggle between states, nations, or groups — see WAR 1

4 an earnest effort for superiority or victory over another — see CONTEST 1

conflict *vb* to be out of harmony or agreement usually noticeably — see CLASH

conflicting *adj* not being in agreement or harmony — see INCONSISTENT

confluence *n* the coming together of two or more things to the same point — see CONVERGENCE

conform *vb* 1 to be in agreement on every point — see CHECK 1

2 to form a pleasing relationship — see HARMONIZE 1

3 to bring to a state free of conflicts, inconsistencies, or differences — see HARMONIZE 2

4 to change (something) so as to make it suitable for a new use or situation — see ADAPT

conform (to) *vb* to act according to the commands of — see OBEY

conformable *adj* readily giving in to the command or authority of another — see OBEDIENT

conformable (to) *adj* not having or showing any apparent conflict — see CONSISTENT

conformation *n* 1 the outward appearance of something as distinguished from its substance — see FORM 1

2 the way in which something is sized, arranged, or organized — see FORMAT 1

conformity *n* 1 a state of consistency ⟨the simple lifestyle of the Amish is in *conformity* with their ascetic religious beliefs⟩

syn accord, accordance, agreement, congruity, consonance, harmony, tune

rel assimilation, integration; oneness, solidarity, togetherness; affinity, empathy, sympathy

near ant discrepancy, disparity, dissimilarity

ant conflict, disagreement

2 a bending to the authority or control of another — see OBEDIENCE 1

confound *vb* 1 to throw into a state of mental uncertainty — see CONFUSE 1

2 to throw into a state of self-conscious distress — see EMBARRASS 1

confront *vb* to oppose (something hostile or dangerous) with firmness or courage — see FACE 2

confrontation *n* an earnest effort for superiority or victory over another — see CONTEST 1

confuse *vb* 1 to throw into a state of mental uncertainty ⟨the similar-sounding words "censure" and "censor" often *confuse* people⟩

syn addle, baffle, befog, befuddle, bemuse, bewilder, confound, disorient, muddle, muddy, mystify, perplex, puzzle

rel stick, stump; abash, discomfit, disconcert, discountenance, embarrass, faze, fluster, mortify, nonplus, rattle; agitate, bother, chagrin, discomfort, discompose, dismay, disquiet, distress, disturb, perturb, stun, unhinge, unsettle, upset; deceive, misguide, mislead

near ant assure, reassure, satisfy; enlighten, inform

2 to make (something) unclear to the understanding ⟨stop *confusing* the issue with irrelevant facts⟩

syn becloud, befog, blur, cloud, fog, muddy

rel complicate, perplex, sophisticate; entangle, snarl, tangle; disorder, jumble, mess (up), mix (up)

near ant simplify, streamline; disentangle, straighten (out), untangle

ant clarify

3 to throw into a state of self-conscious distress — see EMBARRASS 1

4 to undo the proper order or arrangement of — see DISORDER

confused *adj* 1 lacking in order, neatness, and often cleanliness — see MESSY

2 suffering from mental confusion — see DIZZY 2

confusion *n* 1 a state of mental uncertainty ⟨the farmer's driving directions to the fairground just left us in total *confusion*⟩

syn bafflement, befuddlement, bewilderment, distraction, muddle, mystification, perplexity, puzzlement, whirl

rel abashment, discomfiture, embarrassment, fluster, mortification; agitation, chagrin, discomfort, dismay, disquiet, distress, disturbance, perturbation, upset

near ant assurance, certainty, certitude, confidence, conviction, positiveness, sureness

2 a state in which everything is out of order — see CHAOS

3 the emotional state of being made self-consciously uncomfortable — see EMBARRASSMENT 1

confute *vb* to prove to be false — see DISPROVE

congeal *vb* **1** to become physically firm or solid — see HARDEN 1

2 to turn from a liquid into a substance resembling jelly — see COAGULATE

congenial *adj* **1** giving pleasure or contentment to the mind or senses — see PLEASANT

2 having or marked by agreement in feeling or action — see HARMONIOUS 3

congenital *adj* being such from birth or by nature — see NATURAL 1

congest *vb* to prevent passage through — see CLOG 1

conglomerate *n* a group of businesses or enterprises under one control ⟨the huge media *conglomerate* owns TV and radio stations, a cable company, and a movie studio⟩

syn empire

rel multinational; cartel, combination, syndicate, trust; chain; association, corporation, organization; pool

conglomerate *vb* **1** to come together into one body or place — see ASSEMBLE 1

2 to gradually form into a layer, pile, or mass — see COLLECT 2

congratulate *vb* to express to (someone) admiration for his or her success or good fortune ⟨let me be the first to *congratulate* you on winning the award⟩

syn compliment, felicitate

rel applaud, cheer, commend, hail; extol (*also* extoll), glorify, laud, praise

near ant bad-mouth, belittle, decry, disparage, put down; jeer, mock, ridicule, taunt, tease

congratulations *n pl* best wishes — see COMPLIMENTS

congregate *vb* to come together into one body or place — see ASSEMBLE 1

congregation *n* **1** a body of persons gathered for religious worship ⟨the whole *congregation* began to sing with great fervor⟩

syn assembly, church

rel laity, parish; communion, denomination, fold, sect

2 a body of people come together in one place — see GATHERING 1

congress *n* **1** the highest lawmaking body of a political unit ⟨the national emergency required a special session of *congress*⟩

syn parliament

rel assembly, chamber, council, diet, house, legislature

2 a coming together of a number of persons for a specified purpose — see MEETING 1

3 a group of persons formally joined together for some common interest — see ASSOCIATION 2

congruity *n* a state of consistency — see CONFORMITY 1

congruous *adj* **1** having the parts agreeably related — see HARMONIOUS 2

2 not having or showing any apparent conflict — see CONSISTENT

congruously *adv* in a manner suitable for the occasion or purpose — see PROPERLY

conjectural *adj* existing only as an assumption or speculation — see THEORETICAL 1

conjecture *n* an opinion or judgment based on little or no evidence ⟨the many *conjectures* about the true identity of Jack the Ripper⟩

syn guess, supposition, surmise

rel hypothesis, theory, thesis; guesswork, speculation; hunch, intuition; belief, faith

conjecture *vb* **1** to decide the size, amount, number, or distance of (something) without actual measurement — see ESTIMATE 2

2 to form an opinion from little or no evidence — see GUESS 1

conjoin *vb* **1** to come together to form a single unit — see UNITE 1

2 to form or enter into an association that furthers the interests of its members — see ALLY

conjoint *adj* used or done by a number of people as a group — see COLLECTIVE

conjointly *adv* in or by combined action or effort — see TOGETHER 2

conjugal *adj* of or relating to marriage — see MARITAL

conjugate *vb* **1** to come together to form a single unit — see UNITE 1

2 to put or bring together so as to form a new and longer whole — see CONNECT 1

conjunction *n* the coming together of two or more things to the same point — see CONVERGENCE

conjuration *n* a spoken word or set of words believed to have magic power — see SPELL 1

conjure *vb* to make a request to (someone) in an earnest or urgent manner — see BEG

conjure (up) *vb* to call into being through the use of one's inner resources or powers — see SUMMON 2

conjurer *or* **conjuror** *n* **1** a person skilled in using supernatural forces — see MAGICIAN 1

2 one who practices tricks and illusions for entertainment — see MAGICIAN 2

---

syn synonym(s)   *rel* related words
ant antonym(s)   *near ant* near antonym(s)

conjuring n 1 the power to control natural forces through supernatural means — see MAGIC 1

2 the art or skill of performing tricks or illusions for entertainment — see MAGIC 2

conk (out) vb to stop functioning — see FAIL 1

connect vb 1 to put or bring together so as to form a new and longer whole ⟨*connect* all the sets of lights and attach them to the branches of the Christmas tree⟩

syn chain, compound, conjugate, couple, hitch, hook, join, link, yoke

rel dovetail; concatenate, string; cement, coalesce, combine, fuse, unite

ant disconnect, disjoin, separate, unchain, uncouple, unhitch, unlink, unyoke

2 to come together to form a single unit — see UNITE 1

3 to think of (something) in combination — see ASSOCIATE 2

connecting n the act or an instance of joining two or more things into one — see UNION 1

connection n 1 the fact or state of having something in common ⟨the endless debate about the *connection* between crime and poverty⟩

syn association, bearing, kinship, liaison, linkage, relation, relationship

rel correlation, interrelation; materiality, pertinence, relevance; bond, link, tie; affiliation, alliance, union; likeness, resemblance, similarity

2 a place where two or more things are united — see JOINT 1

3 an acquaintance who has influence especially in the business or political world — see CONTACT

4 the act or an instance of joining two or more things into one — see UNION 1

5 the fact or state of being pertinent — see PERTINENCE

6 the state of having shared interests or efforts (as in social or business matters) — see ASSOCIATION 2

connivance n a secret agreement or cooperation between two parties for an illegal or dishonest purpose — see COLLUSION

connive vb to secretly sympathize with or pretend ignorance of something improper or unlawful ⟨the principal *connived* at all the school absences that were recorded on the day of the city's celebration of its Super Bowl victory⟩

syn wink

rel condone, disregard, excuse, ignore, overlook, tolerate

near ant disapprove (of), frown (on *or* upon); deny, disallow, refuse

connoisseur n a person having a knowledgeable and fine appreciation of the arts ⟨a forthcoming exhibit at the art museum that is eagerly awaited by *connoisseurs* of ancient Greek pottery⟩

syn dilettante

rel adept, authority, expert, master; critic, reviewer; amateur, dabbler; collector

near ant materialist, philistine

connubial adj of or relating to marriage — see MARITAL

conquer vb 1 to bring under one's control by force of arms ⟨before his final defeat, Napoleon had managed to *conquer* much of Europe⟩

syn dominate, overpower, subdue, subject, subjugate, vanquish

rel beat, crush, defeat, drub, lick, mow (down), rout, smash, thrash, trounce; enslave; break, put down, quell, suppress

near ant emancipate, free, liberate, manumit, release

2 to achieve a victory over — see BEAT 2

3 to achieve victory (as in a contest) — see WIN 1

conqueror n one that defeats an enemy or opponent — see VICTOR 1

conquest n the act or process of bringing someone or something under one's control ⟨the *conquest* of much of North and South America by the Spanish during the 16th century⟩

syn dominating, domination, overpowering, subduing, subjecting, subjection, subjugating, subjugation, vanquishing

rel triumph, victory, winning; beating, defeat, drubbing, licking, trouncing; enslavement

near ant emancipation, freeing, liberation, manumission, release

conscientious adj 1 guided by or in accordance with one's sense of right and wrong ⟨operated on the belief that most people are *conscientious*, the unattended farm stand has a price list and a money drawer for customers to leave payment for their purchases⟩

syn ethical, honest, honorable, just, moral, principled, scrupulous

rel good, righteous, upright, virtuous; dutiful, observant, respectful; overconscientious; reliable, trustworthy, trusty

near ant unreliable, untrustworthy

ant cutthroat, dishonest, dishonorable, immoral, unethical, unjust, unprincipled, unscrupulous

2 taking great care and effort — see PAINSTAKING

conscientiousness n strict attentiveness to what one is doing — see CARE 1

conscious adj having specified facts or feelings actively impressed on the mind ⟨*conscious* of the fact that my hands were sweating the whole time that I was making my presentation⟩

syn alive, aware, cognizant, mindful, sensible, sentient

rel attentive, heedful, observant, regardful, vigilant, watchful

near ant inattentive, unheeding, unobservant, unobserving

ant insensible, unaware, unconscious, unmindful

consciously adv with full awareness of what one is doing — see INTENTIONALLY

conscript n a person forced or required to enroll in military service ⟨as the war continued, the body of enlisted soldiers was

supplemented by an increasing number of *conscripts*⟩
syn draftee, inductee
rel recruit, rookie

conscript *vb* to pick especially for required military service — see DRAFT 1

consecrate *vb* 1 to keep or intend for a special purpose — see DEVOTE 1
2 to make holy through prayers or ritual — see BLESS 1

consecrated *adj* set apart or worthy of veneration by association with God — see HOLY 2

consecration *n* the act of making something holy through religious ritual ⟨the *consecration* of the Host during Communion⟩
syn blessing, hallowing, sanctification
rel dedication
near ant defilement, desecration, profanation

consecutive *adj* following one after another without others coming in between ⟨the team's winning streak has lasted for seven *consecutive* games⟩
syn sequential, succeeding, successional, successive
rel serial; constant, continuous, uninterrupted; ensuing, following, later, next, subsequent

consensus *n* the act or fact of being of one opinion about something — see AGREEMENT 1

consent *n* the approval by someone in authority for the doing of something — see PERMISSION

consequence *n* 1 a condition or occurrence traceable to a cause — see EFFECT 1
2 the quality or state of being important — see IMPORTANCE

consequent *adj* coming as a result — see RESULTANT

consequential *adj* 1 coming as a result — see RESULTANT
2 having great meaning or lasting effect — see IMPORTANT 1

consequently *adv* for this or that reason — see THEREFORE

conservation *n* 1 the careful maintaining and protection of something valuable especially in its natural or original state ⟨everyone has a duty to aid in the *conservation* of our nation's wilderness areas⟩
syn preservation
rel care, maintenance, upkeep; salvation, saving; guardianship, protection, safeguarding, safekeeping; economy, husbandry, management
near ant neglect, squandering, waste; destruction, ruin; damage, injury
2 the act or activity of keeping something in an existing and usually satisfactory condition — see MAINTENANCE

conservative *adj* 1 tending to favor established ideas, conditions, or institutions ⟨*conservative* baseball fans consider the

new ballpark too modern-looking and plain ugly⟩
syn old-fashioned, orthodox, reactionary, traditional, unprogressive
rel conventional; faithful, loyal, steadfast, true-blue
near ant extremist, radical, revolutionary; nonconformist
ant liberal, nonorthodox, nontraditional, progressive, unorthodox
2 not excessively showy — see QUIET 2

conservative *n* a person whose political beliefs are centered on tradition and keeping things the way they are ⟨proposed legislation that was opposed by *conservatives* throughout the state⟩
syn reactionary, rightist
rel conformist
near ant extremist, radical, revolutionary, revolutionist
ant leftist, liberal, progressive

conservatory *n* a glass-enclosed building for growing plants ⟨the college's *conservatory* is entirely devoted to cultivating and displaying orchids⟩
syn greenhouse, hothouse
rel cold frame; nursery

conserve *vb* to keep in good condition — see MAINTAIN 1

conserving *n* the act or activity of keeping something in an existing and usually satisfactory condition — see MAINTENANCE

consider *vb* 1 to think of in a particular way ⟨I *consider* him a very good friend⟩
syn account, call, count, esteem, hold, rate, reckon, regard, take (for)
rel believe, feel, sense, think; conceive, fancy, imagine
phrases look on (*or* upon)
2 to give serious and careful thought to — see PONDER
3 to have as an opinion — see BELIEVE 2

considerable *adj* 1 sufficiently large in size, amount, or number to merit attention ⟨the *considerable* number of auto accidents that resulted from the surprise snowstorm⟩
syn good, goodly, good-sized, healthy, largish, respectable, significant, sizable (*or* sizeable), substantial, tidy
rel big, colossal, enormous, gigantic, great, huge, immense, mammoth
near ant piddling, puny, trivial, unimportant; marginal, meager, slight; little, small, tiny
ant inconsiderable, insignificant, insubstantial
2 of a size greater than average of its kind — see LARGE

considerably *adv* to a large extent or degree — see GREATLY 2

considerate *adj* 1 given to or made with heedful anticipation of the needs and happiness of others — see THOUGHTFUL 1
2 having or showing a close attentiveness to avoiding danger or trouble — see CAREFUL 1

considerately *adv* with good reason or courtesy — see WELL 4

---

syn synonym(s)   **rel** related words
ant antonym(s)   **near ant** near antonym(s)

consideration n 1 a careful weighing of the reasons for or against something ⟨after much *consideration* we decided to make an offer on the house⟩

syn debate, deliberation, thought

rel cogitation, contemplation, meditation, pondering, rumination; introspection, reflection; agonizing, hesitation, indecision

2 something (as money) that is given or received in return for goods or services — see PAYMENT 2

considered adj decided on as a result of careful thought — see DELIBERATE 1

consign vb 1 to cause to go or be taken from one place to another — see SEND

2 to put (something) into the possession or safekeeping of another — see GIVE 2

consist (of) vb to be made up of — see COMPRISE 1

consistency n the degree to which a fluid can resist flowing ⟨beat the egg whites until they take on the *consistency* of whipped cream⟩

syn density, thickness, viscosity

rel compactness, firmness, solidity; ropiness, stickiness

consistent adj not having or showing any apparent conflict ⟨the clothes you wear to class must be *consistent* with the school's dress code⟩

syn compatible, conformable (to), congruous, consonant, correspondent (with or to), harmonious, nonconflicting

rel appropriate, fitting, meet, suitable

phrases of a piece

ant conflicting, incompatible, incongruous, inconsistent, inharmonious, unharmonious

consistently adv on every relevant occasion — see ALWAYS 1

consolation n 1 the giving of hope and strength in times of grief, distress, or suffering ⟨the *consolation* of the grieving family by their pastor⟩

syn comforting, consoling, solace, solacing

rel commiseration, condolence, sympathy; counseling (or counselling)

2 a feeling of ease from grief or trouble — see COMFORT 1

console vb to ease the grief or distress of — see COMFORT 1

consolidate vb 1 to bring (something) to a central point or under a single control — see CENTRALIZE 1

2 to make markedly greater in measure or degree — see INTENSIFY

consolidation n the act or an instance of joining two or more things into one — see UNION 1

consoling n the giving of hope and strength in times of grief, distress, or suffering — see CONSOLATION 1

consonance n 1 a balanced, pleasing, or suitable arrangement of parts — see HARMONY 1

2 a state of consistency — see CONFORMITY 1

consonant adj 1 having the parts agreeably related — see HARMONIOUS 2

2 not having or showing any apparent conflict — see CONSISTENT

consort n the person to whom another is married — see SPOUSE

consort vb to come or be together as friends — see ASSOCIATE 1

conspicuous adj 1 likely to attract attention — see NOTICEABLE

2 very noticeable especially for being incorrect or bad — see EGREGIOUS

conspiracy n 1 a group involved in secret or criminal activities — see RING 1

2 a secret agreement or cooperation between two parties for an illegal or dishonest purpose — see COLLUSION

3 a secret plan for accomplishing evil or unlawful ends — see PLOT 1

conspire vb to engage in a secret plan to accomplish evil or unlawful ends — see PLOT

constable n a member of a force charged with law enforcement at the local level — see OFFICER 1

constabulary n a body of officers of the law — see POLICE 2

constancy n 1 the state of continuing without change ⟨the mistaken notion that there is *constancy* in language—words do indeed change their meanings over time⟩

syn changelessness, fixedness, immutability, invariability, stability, steadiness, unchangeableness

rel consistency, regularity, sameness, uniformity; durability, lastingness, permanence

near ant inconsistency, irregularity, unevenness; evanescence, impermanence

ant changeability, changeableness, instability, mutability, unsteadiness, variability

2 adherence to something to which one is bound by a pledge or duty — see FIDELITY

constant adj 1 not undergoing a change in condition ⟨change is the only *constant* thing in the world of fashion⟩

syn changeless, stable, stationary, steady, unchanging, unvarying

rel fast, fixed, hard-and-fast, immutable, inflexible, invariable, unalterable, unchangeable; established, set, settled; durable, enduring, lasting, permanent

near ant alterable, changeable, flexible, mutable, variable; ephemeral, evanescent, fleeting, momentary, transient, transitory

ant changeful, changing, fluctuating, inconstant, unstable, unsteady, varying

2 appearing or occurring repeatedly from time to time — see REGULAR 1

3 firm in one's allegiance to someone or something — see FAITHFUL 1

constantly adv 1 many times — see OFTEN

2 on every relevant occasion — see ALWAYS 1

consternation n the emotion experienced in the presence or threat of danger — see FEAR

constituent n one of the parts that make up a whole — see ELEMENT 1

constitute vb 1 to be all the substance of ⟨nine players *constitute* a baseball team⟩
syn compose, comprise, form, make up
rel embody, incorporate, integrate; complement, complete, supplement; fill out, flesh (out)
2 to be responsible for the creation and early production or use of — see FOUND
3 to pick (someone) by one's authority for a specific position or duty — see APPOINT 2

constitution n 1 the set of qualities that makes a person, a group of people, or a thing different from others — see NATURE 1
2 the type of body that a person has — see PHYSIQUE

constitutional n a relaxed journey on foot for exercise or pleasure — see WALK

constitutionally adv by natural character or ability — see NATURALLY 1

constrain vb 1 to cause (a person) to give in to pressure — see FORCE
2 to keep from exceeding a desirable degree or level (as of expression) — see CONTROL 1

constraint n 1 the checking of one's true feelings and impulses when dealing with others ⟨in civilized society people do not just say or do whatever they feel like—they exercise some *constraint*⟩
syn inhibition, repression, reserve, restraint, self-control, self-restraint, suppression
rel control, discipline, self-denial, self-discipline; composure, self-possession; aloofness, detachment, distance; bashfulness, modesty, shyness; reticence, silence, taciturnity
near ant self-indulgence; bluntness, candor, frankness
2 something that limits one's freedom of action or choice — see RESTRICTION 1
3 the use of power to impose one's will on another — see FORCE 2

constrict vb 1 to become smaller in size or volume through the drawing together of particles of matter — see CONTRACT 2
2 to reduce in size or volume by or as if by pressing parts or members together — see COMPRESS 1

constriction n the act or process of reducing the size or volume of something by or as if by pressing — see COMPRESSION

construct vb to form by putting together parts or materials — see BUILD

construction n 1 something put together by arranging or connecting an array of parts ⟨the swing set turned out to be a more complicated *construction* than the "some assembly required" warning suggested⟩
syn erection, structure
rel arrangement, assembly; frame, framework, skeleton
2 a statement that makes something clear — see EXPLANATION 1

constructive adj having a role in deciding something's final form — see FORMATIVE

construe vb to make plain or understandable — see EXPLAIN 1

consult vb to exchange viewpoints or seek advice for the purpose of finding a solution to a problem — see CONFER 2

consultant n a person who gives advice especially professionally ⟨a *consultant* in public relations to a number of large corporations⟩
syn adviser (*or* advisor), counselor (*or* counsellor)
rel authority, expert, professional; confidant

consume vb 1 to destroy all trace of ⟨massive fires had *consumed* hundreds of square miles of forest⟩
syn devour, eat (up)
rel gut; deplete, exhaust, use up; raze, ruin, waste; annihilate, extinguish
2 to make complete use of — see DEPLETE
3 to take in as food — see EAT 1

consummate adj 1 having or showing exceptional knowledge, experience, or skill in a field of endeavor — see PROFICIENT
2 having no exceptions or restrictions — see ABSOLUTE 2
3 of the greatest or highest degree or quantity — see ULTIMATE 1

consummate vb to bring (something) to a state where nothing remains to be done — see FINISH 1

consummation n 1 the last part of a process or action — see FINALE
2 the state of being actual or complete — see FRUITION

contact n an acquaintance who has influence especially in the business or political world ⟨an intern who got her summer job in the governor's office through *contacts*⟩
syn connection
rel big shot, bigwig, somebody, VIP; go-between, intermediary, mediator

contact vb to transmit information or requests to ⟨you can *contact* me at this number⟩
syn communicate (with), reach
rel apprise, fill in, inform, notify; buzz, call, phone, ring [*chiefly British*], telephone
phrases get (*or* keep) in touch with

contagious adj 1 capable of being passed by physical contact from one person to another ⟨chicken pox, measles, German measles, and other *contagious* diseases⟩
syn catching, communicable, transmittable
rel infectious, infective
near ant noninfectious
ant noncommunicable
2 exciting a similar feeling or reaction in others ⟨the enthusiasm of the new club members was *contagious*⟩
syn catching, infectious, spreading
rel palpable, perceptible, tangible; irresistible, overpowering, overwhelming; fetching, inviting, winning

---

syn synonym(s)   *rel* related words
ant antonym(s)   *near ant* near antonym(s)

contain vb 1 to have within ⟨the top drawer of the cabinet *contains* my stamp collection⟩
syn hold
rel accommodate, fit; encase, enclose (*also* inclose), encompass; harbor, house, lodge, shelter
2 to have as part of a whole — see INCLUDE
3 to be made up of — see COMPRISE 1
4 to gain emotional or mental control of — see COLLECT 1
5 to keep from exceeding a desirable degree or level (as of expression) — see CONTROL 1

container n something into which a liquid or smaller objects can be put for storage or transportation ⟨save the plastic *containers* from the deli for other uses⟩
syn holder, receptacle, vessel
rel cartridge; bin, box, carton, case, crate; bag, pocket, sack; cooler, warmer

contaminant n something that is or that makes impure — see IMPURITY

contaminate vb to make unfit for use by the addition of something harmful or undesirable ⟨a supply of drinking water that was *contaminated* by a toxic waste dump⟩
syn befoul, defile, foul, poison, pollute, taint
rel infect; besmirch, dirty, soil, sully; corrupt, rot, spoil; adulterate, doctor; dilute, water (down)
near ant clean, cleanse, purge; filter; disinfect, sanitize
ant decontaminate, purify

contaminated adj containing foreign or lower-grade substances — see IMPURE

contemplate vb 1 to give serious and careful thought to — see PONDER
2 to have in mind as a purpose or goal — see INTEND

contemplation n long or deep thinking about spiritual matters ⟨the decision to enter a monastery and to spend one's life in prayer and *contemplation*⟩
syn meditation
rel introspection, reflection, retrospection; cogitation, deliberation, musing, pondering, rumination

contemplative adj given to or marked by long, quiet thinking ⟨a *contemplative* person who likes to go on solitary walks⟩ ⟨the *contemplative* life of the monks at the abbey⟩
syn meditative, melancholy, pensive, reflective, ruminant, thoughtful
rel introspective, retrospective; earnest, serious, sober, somber (*or* sombre); analytic (*or* analytical), logical, rational; deliberate, purposeful
near ant flighty, flippant, frivolous; brainless, mindless, silly, thoughtless, unthinking
ant unreflective

contemporaneous adj existing or occurring at the same period of time — see CONTEMPORARY 1

contemporaneously adv at one and the same time — see TOGETHER 1

contemporary adj 1 existing or occurring at the same period of time ⟨the absurd notion that early cave dwellers were *contemporary* with the dinosaurs⟩
syn coeval, coexistent, coexisting, coextensive, concurrent, contemporaneous, simultaneous, synchronous
rel accompanying, attendant, attending, coincident, concomitant
ant noncontemporary
2 being or involving the latest methods, concepts, information, or styles — see MODERN

contemporary n a person who lives at the same time or is about the same age as another ⟨Abraham Lincoln and Charles Darwin were exact *contemporaries*, actually being born on the same day in 1809⟩
syn coeval
rel accompaniment, companion, concomitant; equal, peer

contempt n open dislike for someone or something considered unworthy of one's concern or respect ⟨my undying *contempt* for people who abuse animals⟩
syn despite, despitefulness, disdain, scorn
rel abhorrence, abomination, execration, hate, hatred, loathing; cattiness, hatefulness, invidiousness, malevolence, malice, maliciousness, malignancy, malignity, meanness, spite, spitefulness; aversion, disgust, distaste, horror, odium, repugnance, repulsion, revulsion; animosity, antagonism, antipathy, bitterness, enmity, grudge, hostility, jealousy, pique, resentment; bile, jaundice, rancor, spleen, venom, virulence, vitriol
near ant acceptance, tolerance; adoration, veneration, worship; affection, fondness, liking
ant admiration, esteem, regard, respect

contemptible adj 1 arousing or deserving of one's loathing and disgust ⟨the *contemptible* thieves who stole the Christmas gifts intended for needy children⟩
syn despicable, lousy, nasty, pitiable, pitiful, scabby, scummy, scurvy, sorry, wretched
rel abhorrent, abominable, detestable, execrable, hateful, loathsome, odious; disgusting, repugnant, repulsive; disgraceful, dishonorable, shameful; base, ignoble, low, mean; shabby, sordid, squalid, vile; cowardly, craven, dastardly
near ant high-minded, honorable, noble, principled; commendable, creditable, laudable, praiseworthy
ant admirable
2 deserving pitying scorn (as for inadequacy) — see PITIFUL 1
3 not following or in accordance with standards of honor and decency — see IGNOBLE 2

contemptuous adj 1 feeling or showing open dislike for someone or something regarded as undeserving of respect or concern ⟨loutish tourists who are *con-*

temptuous of the ways and traditions of their host countries⟩

syn disdainful, scornful

rel discourteous, disrespectful, impudent, insolent; arrogant, cavalier, high-handed; haughty, lofty, lordly, prideful, sniffish, snobbish, supercilious; pompous, self-important, superior

near ant deferential, respectful; accepting, tolerant; courteous, polite

ant admiring, appreciative

2 intended to make a person or thing seem of little importance or value — see DEROGATORY

contend *vb* **1** to engage in a contest — see COMPETE

2 to state (something) as a reason in support of or against something under consideration — see ARGUE 1

3 to state as a fact usually forcefully — see CLAIM 1

contend (with) *vb* **1** to deal with (something) usually skillfully or efficiently — see HANDLE 1

2 to strive to reduce or eliminate — see FIGHT 2

contender *n* **1** one who seeks an office, honor, position, or award — see CANDIDATE

2 one who strives for the same thing as another — see COMPETITOR

content *adj* feeling that one's needs or desires have been met ⟨are you *content* with your present allowance?⟩

syn contented, gratified, happy, pleased, satisfied

rel delighted, glad, joyful, joyous, jubilant; ecstatic, elated, enraptured, euphoric, overjoyed, rapturous, thrilled; appeased, mollified, pacified, placated

near ant disaffected, disgruntled; discouraged, disheartened, dispirited

ant discontent, discontented, displeased, dissatisfied, malcontent, unhappy

¹content *n* **1** a major object of interest or concern (as in a discussion or artistic composition) — see MATTER 1

2 the amount of something (as subject matter) included — see COVERAGE

3 the largest number or amount that something can hold — see CAPACITY 1

²content *n* the feeling experienced when one's wishes are met — see PLEASURE 1

content *vb* to give satisfaction to — see PLEASE

contented *adj* feeling that one's needs or desires have been met — see CONTENT

contentedness *n* the feeling experienced when one's wishes are met — see PLEASURE 1

contention *n* an idea or opinion that is put forth in a discussion or debate ⟨my *contention* is that today's lower batting averages are the result of better pitching⟩

syn argument, assertion, thesis

rel hypothesis, theory; proposal, proposition; assumption, presupposition, supposition; position, stand

contentious *adj* **1** feeling or displaying eagerness to fight — see BELLIGERENT

2 given to arguing — see ARGUMENTATIVE 1

contentiousness *n* an inclination to fight or quarrel — see BELLIGERENCE

contentment *n* the feeling experienced when one's wishes are met — see PLEASURE 1

contest *n* **1** an earnest effort for superiority or victory over another ⟨the eternal *contest* between the forces of good and the forces of evil⟩

syn battle, combat, conflict, confrontation, duel, face-off, rivalry, struggle, tug-of-war, warfare

rel showdown; contention, discord, friction, strife; controversy, debate, disagreement

near ant concord, harmony, peace

2 a competitive encounter between individuals or groups carried on for amusement, exercise, or in pursuit of a prize — see GAME 1

3 a physical dispute between opposing individuals or groups — see FIGHT 1

contest *vb* to demand proof of the truth or rightness of — see CHALLENGE 1

contestant *n* one who strives for the same thing as another — see COMPETITOR

contiguity *n* the state or condition of being near — see PROXIMITY

contiguous *adj* having a border in common — see ADJACENT

continent *n* one of the great divisions of land on the globe or the main part of such a division — see MAINLAND

contingency *n* something that might happen — see EVENT 2

contingent *n* a body of persons chosen as representatives of a larger group ⟨our Scout troop sent a large *contingent* to the jamboree⟩

syn delegation

rel embassy, legation, mission; crew, detachment, gang, outfit, squad

contingent (on *or* **upon)** *adj* determined by something else — see DEPENDENT 2

continual *adj* **1** going on and on without any interruptions — see CONTINUOUS

2 occurring or appearing at intervals — see INTERMITTENT 1

continually *adv* **1** many times — see OFTEN

2 on every relevant occasion — see ALWAYS 1

continuance *n* **1** continuing existence — see PERSISTENCE 1

2 uninterrupted or lasting existence — see CONTINUATION

continuation *n* uninterrupted or lasting existence ⟨the *continuation* of high unemployment has cost the government much support⟩

syn continuance, duration, endurance, persistence, subsistence

---

rel elongation, extension, lengthening, prolongation

near ant abridgment (*or* abridgement), curtailment, shortening

ant ending, termination

continue *vb* **1** to remain indefinitely in existence or in the same state ⟨the heavy snow *continued* throughout the night⟩

syn abide, endure, hold (up), hold on, keep up, last, persist, run on

rel linger, remain, stay, stick around, tarry

near ant abate, die (down), ebb, let up, moderate, subside, wane

ant cease, desist, discontinue, quit, stop

2 to begin again or return to after an interruption — see RESUME

continuous *adj* going on and on without any interruptions ⟨a city that has been under *continuous* bombardment for three days⟩

syn ceaseless, continual, incessant, unbroken, unceasing, uninterrupted, unremitting

rel endless, eternal, everlasting, interminable, perpetual, unending; changeless, constant, stable, steady, unchanging, unvarying

near ant intermittent, periodic, recurrent, recurring

ant noncontinuous

contort *vb* to twist (something) out of a natural or normal shape or condition ⟨the acrobat is able to *contort* his body so that it almost looks like a pretzel⟩

syn deform, distort, screw, squinch, warp

rel deface, disfigure; wrench, wrest, wring; coil, curl, twine, wind, wreathe

contortion *n* the twisting of something out of its natural or normal shape or condition ⟨the comedian is renowned for his seemingly endless variety of facial *contortions*⟩

syn deformation, distortion, screwing, squinching, warping

rel defacement, disfigurement

contour *n* a line that traces the outer limits of an object or surface — see OUTLINE 1

contract *n* **1** a formal agreement to fulfill an obligation — see GUARANTEE 1

2 an arrangement about action to be taken — see AGREEMENT 2

contract *vb* **1** to become affected with (a disease or disorder) ⟨before vaccines were invented, people lived in fear of *contracting* polio⟩

syn catch, come down (with), get, sicken (with), take

rel break out (with); die (from), succumb (to); fail, sink, weaken

near ant recover (from), shake (off)

2 to become smaller in size or volume through the drawing together of particles of matter ⟨metal *contracts* at low temperatures⟩

syn compress, condense, constrict, shrink

rel collapse, deflate; dry (up), shrivel, wither; decrease, diminish, dwindle, lessen; recede, retreat, withdraw

near ant accumulate, grow, increase; balloon, inflate, puff (up)

ant expand, swell

3 to reduce in size or volume by or as if by pressing parts or members together — see COMPRESS 1

contraction *n* the act or process of reducing the size or volume of something by or as if by pressing — see COMPRESSION

contradict *vb* **1** to make an assertion that is contrary to one made by (another) ⟨no matter what I say, you always have to *contradict* me⟩

syn disagree (with), gainsay

rel challenge, contest, dispute, question; confute, rebut, refute; cross, fight, oppose, resist

near ant concur (with); confirm, corroborate, substantiate, verify

ant agree (with)

2 to declare not to be true — see DENY 1

contradiction *n* **1** someone or something with qualities or features that seem to conflict with one another ⟨a loving father as well as a ruthless killer, the gangster is a living *contradiction*⟩

syn incongruity, paradox

rel conundrum, enigma, mystery, puzzle, riddle

2 a refusal to confirm the truth of a statement — see DENIAL 2

contradictory *adj* being as different as possible — see OPPOSITE

contraption *n* an interesting and often novel device with a practical use — see GADGET

contrariness *n* refusal to obey — see DISOBEDIENCE

contrariwise *adv* just the opposite being true ⟨the rock singer is hardly a carouser; *contrariwise*, he totally abstains from alcohol⟩

syn again, conversely

phrases on the contrary

near ant even, indeed, nay, truly, verily, yea

contrary *adj* **1** being as different as possible — see OPPOSITE

2 engaging in or marked by childish misbehavior — see NAUGHTY

3 given to resisting authority or another's control — see DISOBEDIENT

contrary *n* something that is as different as possible from something else — see OPPOSITE

contrast *n* the quality or state of being different — see DIFFERENCE 1

contribute *vb* **1** to make a donation as part of a group effort ⟨would you like to *contribute* to the Thanksgiving fund for needy families?⟩

syn chip in, kick in, pitch in

rel bestow, donate, give, present

2 to make a present of — see GIVE 1

contribution *n* a gift of money or its equivalent to a charity, humanitarian cause, or public institution ⟨*contributions* for the victims of the earthquake began pouring in⟩

syn alms, benefaction, beneficence, charity, donation, philanthropy

rel offering, tithe; bequest, endowment, legacy; aid, assistance, relief, welfare; grant, subsidy

contrite *adj* **1** feeling sorrow for a wrong that one has done ⟨being *contrite* is not enough to spare you an arrest if you're caught shoplifting⟩

syn apologetic, penitent, regretful, remorseful, repentant, rueful, sorry

rel sad, grieving, mournful, sorrowful, woeful

near ant merciless, pitiless, ruthless

ant impenitent, remorseless, unapologetic, unrepentant

2 suffering from or expressive of a feeling of responsibility for wrongdoing — see GUILTY 2

contriteness *n* a feeling of responsibility for wrongdoing — see GUILT 1

contrition *n* a feeling of responsibility for wrongdoing — see GUILT 1

contrivance *n* **1** an interesting and often novel device with a practical use — see GADGET

2 something (as a device) created for the first time through the use of the imagination — see INVENTION 1

contrive *vb* **1** to create or think of by clever use of the imagination — see INVENT

2 to engage in a secret plan to accomplish evil or unlawful ends — see PLOT

3 to plan out usually with subtle skill or care — see ENGINEER

contrived *adj* lacking in natural or spontaneous quality — see ARTIFICIAL 1

contriver *n* one who creates or introduces something new — see INVENTOR

control *n* **1** a mechanism for adjusting the operation of a device, machine, or system ⟨the *controls* for the player are well marked⟩

syn regulator

rel button, dial, key, knob, lever, push button, switch

2 the ability to direct the course of something ⟨after the tail fell off, the plane went out of the pilot's *control*⟩ ⟨firefighters keeping *control* of the blaze⟩

syn grasp, hand(s)

rel clutch, grip, hold, mastery; command, dominion, helm; authority, jurisdiction, might, power

3 the act or activity of looking after and making decisions about something — see CONDUCT 1

4 the fact or state of having (something) at one's disposal — see POSSESSION 1

5 the right or means to command or control others — see POWER 1

control *vb* **1** to keep from exceeding a desirable degree or level (as of expression) ⟨you must learn to *control* your temper⟩

syn bridle, check, constrain, contain, curb, govern, hold in, inhibit, regulate, rein (in), restrain, tame

rel bottle (up), repress, suppress; arrest, interrupt, stop; block, hinder, impede, obstruct; gag, muzzle, silence

near ant liberate, loose, loosen, unleash; air, express, take out, vent

2 to gain emotional or mental control of — see COLLECT 1

3 to exercise authority or power over — see GOVERN 1

4 to look after and make decisions about — see CONDUCT 1

controversy *n* variance of opinion on a matter — see DISAGREEMENT 1

contusion *n* a bodily injury in which small blood vessels are broken but the overlying skin is not ⟨*contusions* occurred as a result of a car accident⟩

syn bruise

rel black eye; discoloration

conundrum *n* something hard to understand or explain — see MYSTERY

convalesce *vb* to become healthy and strong again after illness or weakness ⟨the long months that the soldier spent in the hospital slowly *convalescing*⟩

syn gain, heal, mend, rally, recover, recuperate, snap back

rel come around, come round, come to, improve, pick up, revive; cheer (up), perk (up); pull through, survive; recruit

near ant ail, collapse, come down, sicken; decline, degenerate, deteriorate, fade, fail, languish, sink, waste (away), weaken, wilt, wither, worsen; relapse

convalescence *n* the process or period of gradually regaining one's health and strength ⟨her release from the hospital was followed by a long *convalescence* at home⟩

syn comeback, healing, mending, rally, recovery, recuperation, rehabilitation, snapback

rel resuscitation, revival; survival

near ant decline, deterioration, failing, languishing, sinking, wasting (away), weakening

convene *vb* **1** to bring together in assembly by or as if by command — see CONVOKE

2 to come together into one body or place — see ASSEMBLE 1

convenience *n* something that adds to one's ease — see COMFORT 2

convenient *adj* situated within easy reach ⟨the shopping mall is *convenient* to all of the area's major highways⟩

syn accessible, handy, reachable

rel close, near, nigh; abutting, adjacent, adjoining

near ant distant, far, remote

ant inaccessible, inconvenient, unhandy, unreachable

convention *n* **1** a coming together of a number of persons for a specified purpose — see MEETING 1

2 a formal agreement between two or more nations or peoples — see TREATY

---

syn synonym(s)   **rel** related words
ant antonym(s)   **near ant** near antonym(s)

3 an arrangement about action to be taken — see AGREEMENT 2

4 an inherited or established way of thinking, feeling, or doing — see TRADITION 1

conventional *adj* **1** accepted, used, or practiced by most people — see CURRENT 1

2 based on customs usually handed down from a previous generation — see TRADITIONAL 1

3 following or agreeing with established form, custom, or rules — see FORMAL 1

converge *vb* to come together into one body or place — see ASSEMBLE 1

convergence *n* the coming together of two or more things to the same point ⟨the *convergence* of the city's major arteries on a single rotary⟩

syn confluence, conjunction, meeting

rel joining, juncture, merging, union

ant divergence

conversant *adj* having information especially as a result of study or experience — see FAMILIAR 2

conversation *n* talking or a talk between two or more people ⟨Thomas Jefferson was celebrated for his brilliant, wide-ranging *conversations* with a host of friends and acquaintances⟩

syn colloquy, dialogue (*also* dialog), discourse, discussion, exchange

rel banter, cross fire, give-and-take, repartee; conference, parley, powwow; babble, chat, chatter, chitchat, gabfest, gossip, palaver, prate, prattle, rap, small talk, table talk; roundtable, symposium; debate, deliberation

conversational *adj* **1** fond of talking or conversation — see TALKATIVE

2 having the style and content of everyday conversation — see CHATTY 1

3 used in or suitable for speech and not formal writing — see COLLOQUIAL 1

conversationalist *n* a person who talks constantly — see CHATTERBOX

converse *vb* to engage in casual or rambling conversation — see CHAT

converse (with) *vb* to communicate with by means of spoken words — see TALK (TO)

conversely *adv* just the opposite being true — see CONTRARIWISE

conversion *n* a change in form, appearance, or use ⟨the *conversion* of the spare bedroom into a home office was easily accomplished⟩

syn changeover, metamorphosis, transfiguration, transformation

rel shift, transition; adjustment, alteration, modification; redoing, refashioning, remaking, remodeling, revamping, revision, reworking, variation; deformation, disfigurement, distortion, mutation, transmutation; displacement, replacement, substitution, supplantation

convert *n* **1** a person who has recently been persuaded to join a religious sect ⟨the *converts* were the most vocal and fervent worshippers in the church⟩

syn proselyte

rel newcomer, novice, recruit

2 one who follows the opinions or teachings of another — see FOLLOWER

convert *vb* **1** to persuade to change to one's religious faith ⟨young missionaries who go door-to-door trying to *convert* people⟩

syn proselytize

rel brainwash, influence, sway; propagate

near ant dissuade

2 to change in form, appearance, or use ⟨the old factory was *converted* into an apartment building⟩

syn make over, metamorphose, transfigure, transform

rel adjust, alter, modify; redo, refashion, remake, remodel, revamp, revise, rework, vary; deform, disfigure, distort, mutate, transmute; displace, replace, substitute, supplant

convey *vb* **1** to cause (something) to pass from one to another — see COMMUNICATE 1

2 to support and take from one place to another — see CARRY 1

conveyance *n* something used to carry goods or passengers ⟨the covered wagon was the major *conveyance* that transported settlers and their belongings across the frontier⟩

syn transport, transportation, vehicle

rel carrier, hauler, mover; transit

convict *n* a person convicted as a criminal and serving a prison sentence ⟨a warning that the three escaped *convicts* were armed and dangerous⟩

syn jailbird

rel captive, capture, inmate, internee, prisoner

convict *vb* to find or pronounce guilty ⟨an accused person is presumed innocent until *convicted* in a court of law⟩

syn condemn

rel censure, denounce, rebuke, reprimand, reproach, reprove; admonish, castigate, chastise; penalize, punish, sentence

near ant cite, commend, endorse (*also* indorse); approve, bless, sanction

ant absolve, acquit, clear, exonerate, vindicate

conviction *n* **1** a state of mind in which one is free from doubt — see CONFIDENCE 2

2 an idea that is believed to be true or valid without positive knowledge — see OPINION 1

convince *vb* to cause (someone) to agree with a belief or course of action by using arguments or earnest requests — see PERSUADE

convincing *adj* having the power to persuade — see COGENT

convincing *n* the act of reasoning or pleading with someone to accept a belief or course of action — see PERSUASION 1

convivial *adj* likely to seek or enjoy the company of others ⟨the hiking club attracts a wide range of *convivial* people who share a love of the outdoors〉

syn boon, companionable, extroverted (*also* extraverted), gregarious, outgoing, sociable, social

rel cordial, friendly, hospitable; affable, genial, gracious; animated, lively, sprightly, vivacious; communicative, expansive, garrulous, talkative

near ant misanthropic; aloof, reserved, standoffish; reticent, silent, taciturn

ant antisocial, introverted, reclusive, unsociable

conviviality *n* **1** joyful or festive activity — see MERRYMAKING

2 the quality or state of being social — see SOCIABILITY

convocation *n* **1** a body of people come together in one place — see GATHERING 1

2 a coming together of a number of persons for a specified purpose — see MEETING 1

convoke *vb* to bring together in assembly by or as if by command 〈*convoked* the leading experts on juvenile delinquency to study the situation〉

syn assemble, call, convene, muster, summon

rel amass, collect, gather, group, round up

near ant break up, dissolve

convoluted *adj* having many parts or aspects that are usually interrelated — see COMPLEX 1

convoy *vb* to go along with in order to provide assistance, protection, or companionship — see ACCOMPANY

convulse *vb* to make a series of small irregular or violent movements — see SHAKE 1

convulsion *n* a violent disturbance (as of the political or social order) 〈the Russian Revolution was one of the major *convulsions* of the 20th century〉

syn cataclysm, paroxysm, storm, tempest, tumult, upheaval, uproar

rel overthrow, overturn, revolution, subversion, upset; fit, seizure, spasm; eruption, flare-up, outbreak, outburst; commotion, furor, fuss, hubbub, hullabaloo, row, ruckus, stew, turmoil; quaking, rocking, shaking, trembling

convulsive *adj* marked by sudden or violent disturbance 〈the assassination of Martin Luther King was one of the most *convulsive* events of the 1960s〉

syn cataclysmal (*or* cataclysmic), stormy, tempestuous, tumultuous

rel fitful, spasmodic, sporadic

near ant calm, peaceful, serene, tranquil

cook *n* a person who prepares food by some manner of heating 〈the hearty meals prepared by the *cook* at summer camp〉

syn chef, cooker

rel baker

cook (up) *vb* to create or think of by clever use of the imagination — see INVENT

cooker *n* **1** an appliance that prepares food for consumption by heating it 〈a portable gas-fired *cooker* that's perfect for camping trips〉

syn cookstove, range

rel broiler, fryer (*also* frier), microwave oven, oven, roaster, rotisserie, stove, toaster, toaster oven

2 a person who prepares food by some manner of heating — see COOK

cookery *n* the art or style of preparing food (as in a specified region) 〈tacos represented my introduction to Mexican *cookery*〉

syn cooking, cuisine

cooking *n* the art or style of preparing food (as in a specified region) — see COOKERY

cookstove *n* an appliance that prepares food for consumption by heating it — see COOKER 1

cool *adj* **1** having or showing a lack of friendliness or interest in others 〈the locals were *cool* towards outsiders〉 〈the schoolmaster's *cool* manner did not encourage chitchat〉

syn aloof, antisocial, cold, detached, distant, frosty, remote, standoffish, unsociable

rel introverted, reclusive, reserved, withdrawn; misanthropic; apathetic, indifferent, unconcerned; disinterested, incurious, uninterested; reticent, silent, taciturn; diffident, shy, timid

near ant companionable, convivial, extroverted (*also* extraverted), gregarious, outgoing; communicative, expansive, garrulous, talkative

ant cordial, friendly, sociable, warm

2 free from emotional or mental agitation — see CALM 2

3 having a low or subnormal temperature — see COLD 1

4 lacking in friendliness or warmth of feeling — see COLD 2

cool *vb* **1** to cause to lose heat 〈*cool* your drinks in the icy mountain stream〉

syn chill, refrigerate

rel air-condition; freeze, ice, quick-freeze, supercool; air-cool, ventilate

near ant bake, boil, broil, steam

ant heat, warm

2 to become still and orderly — see QUIET 1

coolheaded *adj* free from emotional or mental agitation — see CALM 2

coolheadedness *n* evenness of emotions or temper — see EQUANIMITY

coolish *adj* having a low or subnormal temperature — see COLD 1

coolness *n* evenness of emotions or temper — see EQUANIMITY

coop *n* an enclosure with an open framework for keeping animals — see CAGE

coop (up) *vb* to close or shut in by or as if by barriers — see ENCLOSE 1

cooperate *vb* **1** to participate or assist in a joint effort to accomplish an end 〈conser-

---

syn synonym(s) **rel** related words
ant antonym(s) **near ant** near antonym(s)

vation groups *cooperated* with state authorities to find a humane way to manage the area's overpopulation of deer⟩
syn collaborate, concert, join, team (up)
rel connive, conspire; affiliate, ally, associate, band, combine, confederate, league, unite
phrases play ball

2 to form or enter into an association that furthers the interests of its members — see ALLY

cooperation *n* 1 the state of having shared interests or efforts (as in social or business matters) — see ASSOCIATION 1

2 the work and activity of a number of persons who individually contribute toward the efficiency of the whole — see TEAMWORK

coordinate *n* one that is equal to another in status, achievement, or value — see EQUAL

coordinate *vb* 1 to bring to a state free of conflicts, inconsistencies, or differences — see HARMONIZE 2

2 to form a pleasing relationship — see HARMONIZE 1

coordination *n* the work and activity of a number of persons who individually contribute toward the efficiency of the whole — see TEAMWORK

cop *n* a member of a force charged with law enforcement at the local level — see OFFICER 1

copacetic *also* **copasetic** *or* **copesetic** *adj* being to one's liking — see SATISFACTORY 1

cope *vb* to meet one's day-to-day needs — see GET ALONG 1

cope (with) *vb* to deal with (something) usually skillfully or efficiently — see HANDLE 1

copious *adj* pouring forth in great amounts — see PROFUSE

cop-out *n* the act or a means of getting or keeping away from something undesirable — see ESCAPE 2

cop out *vb* to break a promise or agreement — see RENEGE

coppice *n* a thick patch of shrubbery, small trees, or underbrush — see THICKET

copse *n* a thick patch of shrubbery, small trees, or underbrush — see THICKET

copulate *vb* to engage in sexual intercourse ⟨the time of year when deer in the wild are likely to *copulate*⟩
syn mate, sleep
rel fornicate

copulating *n* sexual union involving penetration of the vagina by the penis — see SEXUAL INTERCOURSE

copulation *n* sexual union involving penetration of the vagina by the penis — see SEXUAL INTERCOURSE

copy *n* something that is made to look exactly like something else ⟨a *copy* of the famous painting "Washington Crossing the Delaware"⟩

syn carbon copy, duplicate, duplication, facsimile, imitation, reduplication, replica, replication, reproduction
rel counterfeit, fake, forgery, phony (*also* phoney), sham; dummy, mock-up, simulation; reconstruction, re-creation; image, likeness, semblance, shadow; impression, imprint, print
ant original

copy *vb* 1 to make an exact likeness of ⟨for the movie, set designers *copied* the Oval Office in the White House down to the smallest detail⟩
syn duplicate, imitate, reduplicate, replicate, reproduce
rel counterfeit, fake, forge; simulate; reconstruct, re-create
near ant create, imagine, initiate, invent
ant originate

2 to use (someone or something) as the model for one's speech, mannerisms, or behavior — see IMITATE 1

copycat *n* a person who adopts the appearance or behavior of another especially in an obvious way ⟨every rock singer who makes it big soon has a whole cluster of *copycats*⟩
syn aper, copyist, imitator
rel parrot

copyist *n* a person who adopts the appearance or behavior of another especially in an obvious way — see COPYCAT

coquettish *adj* affecting shyness or modesty in order to attract masculine interest — see COY 1

cord *n* a length of braided, flexible material that is used for tying or connecting things ⟨a vacuum cleaner with an extra long *cord*⟩
syn cable, lace, lacing, line, rope, string, wire
rel guy, lanyard, stay

cordial *adj* 1 having or showing kindly feeling and sincere interest — see FRIENDLY 1

2 showing a natural kindness and courtesy especially in social situations — see GRACIOUS 1

cordiality *n* kindly concern, interest, or support — see GOODWILL 1

core *n* 1 the seat of one's deepest thoughts and emotions ⟨in my very *core* I knew that an injustice was being committed⟩
syn breast, heart, quick, soul
rel conscience, mind
phrases bottom of one's heart

2 a thing or place that is of greatest importance to an activity or interest — see CENTER 1

3 the central part or aspect of something under consideration — see CRUX

4 the main or greater part of something as distinguished from its appendages — see BODY 1

5 an area or point that is an equal distance from all points along an edge or outer surface — see CENTER 2

corker *n* something very good of its kind — see JIM-DANDY

corkscrew *adj* turning around an axis like the thread of a screw — see SPIRAL

corn *n* something (as a work of literature or music) that is too sentimental ⟨a story about a lost puppy that was pure *corn*⟩
syn mush, schmaltz (*also* schmalz)
rel claptrap, drivel, rubbish, slush

corner *n* **1** a difficult, puzzling, or embarrassing situation from which there is no easy escape — see PREDICAMENT
2 a place where roads meet — see CROSSROAD 1

cornerstone *n* an immaterial thing upon which something else rests — see BASE 1

cornet *n* something shaped like a hollow cone and used as a container ⟨*cornets* of pastry dough that were baked and later filled with cream⟩
syn cornucopia, horn
rel funnel, tube

cornucopia *n* something shaped like a hollow cone and used as a container — see CORNET

corny *adj* appealing to the emotions in an obvious and tiresome way ⟨*corny* violin music during the movie's love scenes⟩
syn maudlin, mawkish, mushy, saccharine, sappy, schmaltzy, sentimental, sloppy, sugarcoated, sugary
rel dreamy, moonstruck, nostalgic; flat, insipid, tasteless, vapid, watery
near ant unadulterated, unvarnished; cynical, hard-boiled, hardheaded
ant unsentimental

corollary *n* a condition or occurrence traceable to a cause — see EFFECT 1

coronet *n* a decorative band or wreath worn about the head as a symbol of victory or honor — see CROWN 1

corporal *adj* of or relating to the human body — see PHYSICAL 1

corporeal *adj* of or relating to the human body — see PHYSICAL 1

corps *n* the body of people in a profession or field of activity ⟨a reporter who is widely respected throughout the press *corps*⟩
syn brotherhood, community, fellowship, fraternity
rel calling, profession; association, club, federation, guild (*also* gild), organization, society, sodality

corpse *n* a dead body ⟨the discovery of a *corpse* required a call to the police⟩
syn cadaver, carcass, remains
rel deceased, decedent

corpulence *n* the condition of having an excess of body fat ⟨the doctor warned that *corpulence* is unhealthy and not just unattractive⟩
syn adiposity, chubbiness, fatness, fleshiness, grossness, obesity, plumpness, portliness, pudginess, rotundity
rel bulkiness, heaviness; huskiness, stoutness; brawniness, burliness
near ant fitness, trimness; scrawniness, skinniness

ant leanness, slenderness, slimness, thinness

corpulent *adj* having an excess of body fat — see FAT 1

corral *n* an enclosure with an open framework for keeping animals — see CAGE

corral *vb* **1** to close or shut in by or as if by barriers — see ENCLOSE 1
2 to take physical control or possession of (something) suddenly or forcibly — see CATCH

correct *adj* **1** being in agreement with the truth or a fact or a standard ⟨a real brainteaser with only one *correct* solution to it⟩
syn accurate, exact, precise, proper, right, so, true
rel legitimate, logical, valid; errorless, faultless, flawless, impeccable, letter-perfect, perfect; rigorous, strict, stringent
near ant defective, faulty, flawed, imperfect
ant false, improper, inaccurate, incorrect, inexact, untrue, wrong
2 following the established traditions of refined society and good taste — see PROPER 1
3 marked by or showing careful attention to set forms and details — see CEREMONIOUS 1

correct *vb* **1** to remove errors, defects, deficiencies, or deviations from ⟨students who never take the time to *correct* their own compositions before handing them in⟩
syn amend, debug, emend, rectify, reform, remedy
rel redraft, redraw, restyle, revise, rework, rewrite; redress, right; ameliorate, better, improve; perfect, polish, touch up; fix, mend, repair; adjust, modulate, regulate; alter, change, modify
near ant damage, harm, hurt, impair, injure, mar, spoil; aggravate, worsen
2 to balance with an equal force so as to make ineffective — see OFFSET
3 to inflict a penalty on for a fault or crime — see PUNISH

correctable *adj* capable of being corrected — see REMEDIABLE

correcting *adj* inflicting, involving, or serving as punishment — see PUNITIVE

correction *n* **1** a change designed to correct or improve a written work ⟨here's your theme back with the *corrections* marked in blue⟩
syn amendment, emendation
rel cut, deletion; addition, amplification, supplement; alteration, modification, revision; improvement, renovation; clarification, explanation, explication
2 suffering, loss, or hardship imposed in response to a crime or offense — see PUNISHMENT

correctional *adj* inflicting, involving, or serving as punishment — see PUNITIVE

corrective *adj* **1** serving to raise or adjust something to some standard or proper condition ⟨eyeglasses are called *corrective*

---

syn synonym(s)   *rel* related words
ant antonym(s)   *near ant* near antonym(s)

lenses by the department of motor vehicles⟩

syn rectifying, remedial, remedying, reformative, reformatory

rel curative, medicinal, therapeutic; reparative, restorative; beneficial, helpful, salutary, wholesome

2 inflicting, involving, or serving as punishment — see PUNITIVE

corrective n something that corrects or counteracts something undesirable — see CURE 1

correctly adv in a manner suitable for the occasion or purpose — see PROPERLY

correlate vb to think of (something) in combination — see ASSOCIATE 2

correspond vb **1** to engage in an exchange of written messages ⟨old friends who had been *corresponding* for years⟩

syn write

rel communicate, intercommunicate; airmail, e-mail, telegraph; mail, post; answer, reply

2 to be in agreement on every point — see CHECK 1

correspond (to) vb **1** to be the exact counterpart of — see MATCH 1

2 to be the same in meaning or effect — see AMOUNT (TO) 2

correspondence n **1** a point which two or more things share in common — see SIMILARITY 2

2 the quality or state of having many qualities in common — see SIMILARITY 1

correspondent n a person employed by a newspaper, magazine, or radio or television station to gather, write, or report news — see REPORTER

correspondent adj having qualities in common — see ALIKE

correspondent (with or to) adj not having or showing any apparent conflict — see CONSISTENT

corresponding adj having qualities in common — see ALIKE

correspondingly adv in like manner — see ALSO 1

corridor n a typically long narrow way connecting parts of a building — see HALL 1

corroborate vb to give evidence or testimony to the truth or factualness of — see CONFIRM

corroborating adj serving to give support to the truth or factualness of something — see CORROBORATIVE

corroboration n something presented in support of the truth or accuracy of a claim — see PROOF

corroborative adj serving to give support to the truth or factualness of something ⟨the results of the DNA fingerprinting was all the *corroborative* evidence the jury needed to convict⟩

syn confirmatory, confirming, corroborating, corroboratory, substantiating, supporting, supportive, verifying, vindicating

rel auxiliary, supplementary; beneficial, helpful

near ant contradictory, contrary, counter, opposing

ant confuting, disproving, refuting

corroboratory adj serving to give support to the truth or factualness of something — see CORROBORATIVE

corrode vb to consume or wear away gradually — see EAT 2

corrosion n a gradual weakening, loss, or destruction ⟨the *corrosion* of family values that is often brought on by great wealth⟩

syn attrition, erosion

rel breakdown, decay, decomposition, disintegration, dissolution

near ant gain, increase

ant buildup

corrupt adj having or showing lowered moral character or standards ⟨*corrupt* businessmen who are out to fleece the public⟩ ⟨*corrupt* business practices that should be investigated⟩

syn debased, debauched, decadent, degenerate, degraded, demoralized, depraved, dissipated, dissolute, perverse, perverted, reprobate, warped

rel crooked, cutthroat, dishonest, unethical, unprincipled, unscrupulous; contaminated, spoiled, tainted; bad, evil, immoral, iniquitous, nefarious, sinful, vicious, wicked

near ant incorruptible, uncorruptible; ethical, honest, principled; good, moral, righteous, virtuous

ant uncorrupted

corrupt vb **1** to go through decomposition — see DECAY 1

2 to lower in character or dignity — see DEBASE 1

corrupted adj having undergone organic breakdown — see ROTTEN 1

corruptible adj open to improper influence and especially bribery — see VENAL

corruption n **1** the process by which dead organic matter separates into simpler substances ⟨the ancient Egyptians used special preservatives to spare their dead from complete *corruption*⟩

syn breakdown, decay, decomposition, putrefaction, rot, spoilage

rel crumbling, disintegration, dissolution; curdling, fermentation, moldering, souring

near ant growth, maturation, ripening

2 a sinking to a state of low moral standards and behavior ⟨the *corruption* of the upper classes eventually led to the fall of the Roman empire⟩

syn corruptness, debasement, debauchery, decadence, degeneracy, degeneration, degradation, demoralization, depravity, dissipatedness, dissipation, dissoluteness, perversion

rel evil, immorality, nefariousness, sinfulness, wickedness

near ant goodness, morality, righteousness, virtue

3 immoral conduct or practices harmful or offensive to society — see VICE 1

corruptness *n* a sinking to a state of low moral standards and behavior — see CORRUPTION 2

corsair *n* someone who engages in robbery of ships at sea — see PIRATE

cortege *also* **cortège** *n* 1 a body of employees or servants who accompany and wait on a person ⟨the movie star's *cortege* included her hair stylist, makeup artist, personal assistant, and press agent⟩
syn following, retinue, suite, train
rel crew, personnel, staff; assistant, attendant, helper, retainer
2 a body of individuals moving along in an orderly and often ceremonial way ⟨the funeral *cortege* of mourners stretched for three city blocks⟩
syn parade, procession
rel column, line, string, train

cosmetics *n pl* preparations intended to beautify the face or hair — see MAKEUP 1

cosmic *adj* unusually large — see HUGE

cosmopolitan *adj* having a wide and refined knowledge of the world especially from personal experience — see WORLDLY-WISE

cosmopolitan *n* a person with the outlook, experience, and manners thought to be typical of big city dwellers ⟨as someone who had lived in Paris for a year as an exchange student, she seemed very much the *cosmopolitan* to her old classmates⟩
syn metropolitan, sophisticate
rel urbanite; worldling
ant bumpkin, hick, provincial, rustic, yokel

cosmos *n* the whole body of things observed or assumed — see UNIVERSE

cost *n* 1 a payment made in the course of achieving a result — see EXPENSE
2 the amount of money that is demanded as payment for something — see PRICE 1
3 the loss or penalty involved in achieving a goal — see PRICE 2

cost *vb* to have a price of ⟨the raffle tickets *cost* a dollar each⟩
syn bring, fetch, go (for), sell (for)
rel amount (to), come (to), total; command, exact; ask, demand

costly *adj* commanding a large price ⟨running is one sport that does not require a lot of *costly* equipment⟩
syn dear, expensive, high, precious, premium, valuable
rel exorbitant, extravagant, overpriced, prohibitive, steep, stiff, unreasonable; invaluable, priceless
near ant moderate, reasonable; valueless, worthless; discounted
ant cheap, inexpensive

costume *n* 1 clothing chosen as appropriate for a specific situation — see OUTFIT 1
2 clothing put on to hide one's true identity or imitate someone or something else — see DISGUISE

costume *vb* to outfit with clothes and especially fine or special clothes — see CLOTHE 1

coterie *n* a group of people sharing a common interest and relating together socially — see GANG 2

cotillion *n* a social gathering for dancing — see DANCE

cottage *n* an often small house for recreational or seasonal use ⟨for a month every summer we rent a *cottage* on the ocean⟩
syn cabin, camp, chalet, lodge
rel bungalow, cot; hut, shack, shanty

cottony *adj* smooth or delicate in appearance or feel — see SOFT 2

couch *n* a long upholstered piece of furniture designed for several sitters ⟨find yourself a place on the *couch* and make yourself at home⟩
syn chesterfield, davenport, divan, lounge, settee, sofa
rel love seat; day bed, sofa bed; bench

couch *vb* to convey in appropriate or telling terms — see PHRASE

cougar *n* a large tawny cat of the wild ⟨in many areas suburban developments have encroached upon the habitat of the *cougar*⟩
syn catamount, mountain lion, panther, puma

council *n* 1 a coming together of a number of persons for a specified purpose — see MEETING 1
2 a group of persons formally joined together for some common interest — see ASSOCIATION 2
3 a meeting featuring a group discussion — see FORUM

counsel *n* 1 a person whose profession is to conduct lawsuits for clients or to advise about legal rights and obligations — see LAWYER
2 an opinion suggesting a wise or proper course of action — see ADVICE

counsel *vb* 1 to exchange viewpoints or seek advice for the purpose of finding a solution to a problem — see CONFER 2
2 to give advice and instruction to (someone) regarding the course or process to be followed — see GUIDE 1
3 to give advice to — see ADVISE 1
4 to put forward as one's choice for a wise or proper course of action — see ADVISE 2

counselor *or* **counsellor** *n* 1 a person who gives advice especially professionally — see CONSULTANT
2 a person whose profession is to conduct lawsuits for clients or to advise about legal rights and obligations — see LAWYER

count *n* 1 a total number obtained or recorded by noting each thing as it was being added ⟨my *count* for the number of bird species and subspecies that visited the sanctuary that weekend was 43⟩
syn tally
rel score; amount, gross, sum, total, whole
2 a formal claim of criminal wrongdoing against a person — see CHARGE 1

count *vb* 1 to find the sum of (a collection of things) by noting each one as it is being added ⟨*count* the baseball gloves in the storage locker to see if there are enough to go around⟩
syn enumerate, number, tell
rel add (up), tally, total; calculate, compute, reckon, table, tabulate; check, mark, tick (off)
2 to be of importance — see MATTER
3 to place reliance or trust — see DEPEND 2
4 to think of in a particular way — see CONSIDER 1

countenance *n* 1 facial appearance regarded as an indication of mood or feeling — see LOOK 1
2 the front part of the head — see FACE 1

countenance *vb* 1 to have a favorable opinion of — see APPROVE (OF)
2 to put up with (something painful or difficult) — see BEAR 2

counter *adj* opposed to one's interests — see ADVERSE 1

counter *vb* to strive to reduce or eliminate — see FIGHT 2

counteract *vb* to balance with an equal force so as to make ineffective — see OFFSET

counteraction *n* a force or influence that makes an opposing force ineffective or less effective — see COUNTERBALANCE

counterattack *n* an attack made to counter an enemy's attack ⟨suddenly the tide of battle turned, and the rebels, who had been falling back, made a furious *counterattack*⟩
syn counteroffensive
rel sally, sortie; blitzkrieg, charge; assault, attack, offensive, onslaught

counterbalance *n* a force or influence that makes an opposing force ineffective or less effective ⟨charitable giving is usually a good *counterbalance* to the self-indulgent commercialism of the Christmas season⟩
syn balance, canceler (*or* canceller), counteraction, counterpoise, counterweight, equipoise, neutralizer, offset
rel trade-off

counterbalance *vb* to balance with an equal force so as to make ineffective — see OFFSET

counterfeit *adj* being such in appearance only and made or manufactured with the intention of committing fraud ⟨*counterfeit* money that had been passed all over town⟩
syn bogus, fake, false, forged, inauthentic, phony (*also* phoney), sham, spurious, unauthentic
rel artificial, factitious, imitation, manmade, mimic, mock, simulated, substitute, synthetic; dummy, nonfunctioning, ornamental; cultured, fabricated, manufactured; deceptive, delusive, misleading
near ant natural; actual, true, valid
ant authentic, bona fide, genuine, real

counterfeit *n* an imitation that is passed off as genuine — see FAKE 1

counterfeit *vb* 1 to imitate or copy especially in order to deceive — see FAKE 1
2 to present a false appearance of — see FEIGN

counteroffensive *n* an attack made to counter an enemy's attack — see COUNTERATTACK

counterpane *n* a decorative cloth used as a top covering for a bed ⟨a beautiful *counterpane* that was a family heirloom⟩
syn bedspread, coverlet, spread
rel comforter, puff, quilt; bedclothes, bedding

counterpart *n* 1 one that is equal to another in status, achievement, or value — see EQUAL
2 something or someone that strongly resembles another — see IMAGE 1

counterpoise *n* a force or influence that makes an opposing force ineffective or less effective — see COUNTERBALANCE

counterpoise *vb* to balance with an equal force so as to make ineffective — see OFFSET

countersign *n* a word or phrase that must be spoken by a person in order to pass a guard — see PASSWORD

counterweight *n* a force or influence that makes an opposing force ineffective or less effective — see COUNTERBALANCE

countless *adj* too many to be counted ⟨I've told you *countless* times not to do that⟩
syn innumerable, numberless, uncountable, uncounted, unnumbered, untold
rel endless, infinite, unlimited, vast; many, multitudinous, numerous
near ant finite, limited
ant countable

count out *vb* to prevent the participation or inclusion of — see EXCLUDE

country *adj* of, relating to, associated with, or typical of open areas with few buildings or people — see RURAL

country *n* 1 the land of one's birth, residence, or citizenship ⟨a great love for my *country*⟩
syn fatherland, home, homeland, motherland, sod
rel old country; community, neighborhood
2 the open rural area outside of big towns and cities ⟨out in the *country*, where the air is fresh and the rivers are clean⟩
syn countryside, sticks
rel exurbia; backwater, backwoods, bush, frontier, hinterland, up-country; wild, wilderness
near ant conurbation, megalopolis, urban sprawl
3 a body of people composed of one or more nationalities usually with its own territory and government — see NATION

countryman *n* 1 a person living in or originally from the same country as another — see COMPATRIOT
2 an awkward or simple person especially from a small town or the country — see HICK

countryseat *n* a large impressive residence — see MANSION

countryside *n* the open rural area outside of big towns and cities — see COUNTRY 2

coup *n* a successful result brought about by hard work — see ACCOMPLISHMENT

couple *n* two things of the same or similar kind that match or are considered together — see PAIR

couple *vb* **1** to come together to form a single unit — see UNITE 1

2 to put or bring together so as to form a new and longer whole — see CONNECT 1

coupling *n* **1** a place where two or more things are united — see JOINT 1

2 the act or an instance of joining two or more things into one — see UNION 1

coupon *n* a small sheet of plastic, paper, or paperboard showing that the bearer has a claim to something (as admittance) — see TICKET 1

courage *n* strength of mind to carry on in spite of danger ⟨the moral *courage* to speak out against injustice when no one else will⟩

   syn bravery, courageousness, daring, dauntlessness, doughtiness, fearlessness, gallantry, greatheartedness, guts, hardihood, heart, heroism, intrepidity, intrepidness, nerve, stoutness, valor

   rel backbone, fiber, fortitude, grit, gumption, mettle, pluck, spunk; determination, perseverance, resolution; endurance, stamina, tenacity; audacity, boldness, brazenness, cheek, effrontery, gall, temerity

   near ant faintheartedness, fearfulness, timidity, timorousness; feebleness, softness, weakness; impotence, ineffectualness; hesitation, indecision, indecisiveness, irresolution

   ant cowardice, cowardliness, cravenness, dastardliness, spinelessness, yellowness

courageous *adj* feeling or displaying no fear by temperament — see BRAVE

courageousness *n* strength of mind to carry on in spite of danger — see COURAGE

courier *n* one that carries a message or does an errand — see MESSENGER

course *n* **1** a way of acting or proceeding ⟨the president's usual *course* has been to obtain advice from several people and then make up his own mind⟩

   syn line, policy, procedure, program

   rel blueprint, design, plan, scheme, strategy; intent, intention, purpose; approach, direction, path, pathway, tack

2 a series of lectures on a subject ⟨a *course* on American history from the colonial period to the present⟩

   syn class

   rel elective, refresher, seminar; core, curriculum

3 a usually fixed or ordered series of actions or events leading to a result — see PROCESS 1

4 the direction along which something or someone moves — see PATH 1

course *vb* to proceed or move quickly — see HURRY 2

court *n* **1** the residence of a ruler ⟨Hampton *Court* was the residence of King Henry VIII⟩

   syn palace

   rel castle, château, estate, mansion, villa

2 an open space wholly or partly enclosed (as by buildings or walls) ⟨the art museum boasts a glass-sided *court* that is filled with an array of greenery and sculpture⟩

   syn close, courtyard, enclosure (*also* inclosure), patio, quadrangle, yard

   rel place, plaza, square; deck, terrace

3 an assembly of persons for the administration of justice ⟨this *court* is now called to order⟩

   syn bar, tribunal

   rel judiciary; court-martial; inquisition, kangaroo court

4 a public official having authority to decide questions of law — see JUDGE 1

court *vb* **1** to act so as to make (something) more likely ⟨you're *courting* disaster if you keep playing with matches⟩

   syn ask (for), invite, woo

   rel angle (for), fish (for); hunt, search, seek

   phrases look for

2 to go out on dates that may eventually lead to marriage ⟨they *courted* for a year before getting married⟩

   syn date

   rel romance, spark, woo; escort, see, take out

   phrases go steady, make love

courteous *adj* showing consideration, courtesy, and good manners — see POLITE 1

courteously *adv* with good reason or courtesy — see WELL 4

courteousness *n* speech or behavior that is a sign of good breeding — see POLITENESS

courtesy *n* **1** an act of kind assistance — see FAVOR 1

2 an act or utterance that is a customary show of good manners — see CIVILITY 1

3 speech or behavior that is a sign of good breeding — see POLITENESS

courting *n* the series of social engagements shared by a couple looking to get married — see COURTSHIP

courtship *n* the series of social engagements shared by a couple looking to get married ⟨a long-married couple who look back on their whirlwind *courtship* with fondness and laughter⟩

   syn courting, dating

   rel affair, love affair, romance; betrothal, engagement

courtyard *n* an open space wholly or partly enclosed (as by buildings or walls) — see COURT 2

cove *n* a part of a body of water that extends beyond the general shoreline — see GULF 1

---

syn synonym(s)	**rel** related words	
ant antonym(s)	**near ant** near antonym(s)	

covenant n 1 a formal agreement between two or more nations or peoples — see TREATY

2 a formal agreement to fulfill an obligation — see GUARANTEE 1

3 an arrangement about action to be taken — see AGREEMENT 2

covenant vb to make a solemn declaration of intent — see PROMISE 1

cover n 1 a piece placed over an open container to hold in, protect, or conceal its contents ⟨where's the *cover* for the cookie jar?⟩

syn cap, lid, top

rel dome, hood, roof; capsule, case, casing, covering, housing, jacket, sheath, shell

2 means or method of defending — see DEFENSE 1

3 something that encloses another thing especially to protect it — see ¹CASE 1

cover vb 1 to serve as a replacement usually for a time only ⟨a friend *covered* for me as a hospital volunteer while my family went on vacation⟩

syn fill in, pinch-hit, stand in, sub, substitute, take over

rel understudy; relieve, spell; double (as)

2 to form a layer over ⟨by morning a foot of snow *covered* the ground⟩

syn blanket, carpet, coat, overlay, overlie, overspread, sheet

rel enclose (*also* inclose), enshroud, envelop, enwrap, mantle, shawl, shroud, swathe, wrap; cloak, clothe, curtain, veil; circle, encircle, encompass

3 to place a protective layer over ⟨*cover* your skin with sunblock so you won't get sunburned⟩

syn screen, shield

rel cloak, clothe, veil; disguise, mask, obscure

near ant bare, expose, uncover

4 to have (something) as a subject matter — see CONCERN 1

5 to keep secret or shut off from view — see ¹HIDE 2

6 to make one's way through, across, or over — see TRAVERSE

7 to pay continued close attention to (something) for a particular purpose — see MONITOR

8 to drive danger or attack away from — see DEFEND 1

cover (up) vb to keep from being publicly known — see SUPPRESS 1

coverage n the amount of something (as subject matter) included ⟨the biographical dictionary's *coverage* is limited to people no longer living⟩

syn content

rel compass, gamut, range, scope, sweep; membership, participation

covering n something that encloses another thing especially to protect it — see ¹CASE 1

coverlet n a decorative cloth used as a top covering for a bed — see COUNTERPANE

covert adj 1 hidden from view — see SECLUDED

2 undertaken or done so as to escape being observed or known by others — see SECRET 1

covert n 1 a place where a person goes to hide — see HIDEOUT

2 a thick patch of shrubbery, small trees, or underbrush — see THICKET

covet vb to have an earnest wish to own or enjoy — see DESIRE

coveting adj having or marked by an eager and often selfish desire especially for material possessions — see GREEDY 1

covetous adj 1 having or marked by an eager and often selfish desire especially for material possessions — see GREEDY 1

2 having or showing mean resentment of another's possessions or advantages — see ENVIOUS

covetousness n 1 a painful awareness of another's possessions or advantages and a desire to have them too — see ENVY

2 an intense selfish desire for wealth or possessions — see GREED

cow vb to make timid or fearful by or as if by threats — see INTIMIDATE

coward n a person who shows a shameful lack of courage in the face of danger ⟨the soldiers who ran as soon as the first shots were fired were branded as *cowards*⟩

syn chicken, craven, dastard, poltroon, recreant, sissy

rel defeatist, quitter; pushover, weakling, wimp; snake, sneak

near ant daredevil

ant hero, stalwart, valiant

cowardice n a shameful lack of courage in the face of danger ⟨the *cowardice* shown by political leaders who were willing to give the Nazis whatever they wanted⟩

syn cowardliness, cravenness, dastardliness, spinelessness, yellowness

rel diffidence, faintheartedness, fearfulness, timidity, timorousness; carefulness, cautiousness, wariness; bashfulness, shyness; feebleness, softness, weakness

near ant audacity, boldness, brazenness; backbone, fiber, fortitude, grit, gumption, mettle, pluck, spunk; determination, perseverance, resolution; endurance, stamina, tenacity

ant bravery, courage, courageousness, daring, dauntlessness, doughtiness, fearlessness, gallantry, greatheartedness, guts, hardihood, heart, heroism, intrepidity, intrepidness, nerve, stoutness, valor

cowardliness n a shameful lack of courage in the face of danger — see COWARDICE

cowardly adj having or showing a shameful lack of courage ⟨a *cowardly* bully who picks on much smaller kids⟩ ⟨vile charges that were made in a *cowardly*, unsigned letter⟩

syn chicken, chickenhearted, craven, dastardly, lily-livered, pusillanimous, recreant, spineless, unheroic, yellow

rel diffident, fainthearted, fearful, timid, timorous; afraid, frightened, scared; careful, cautious, wary; bashful, coy, shy; feeble, soft, weak

near ant audacious, bold, brazen, cheeky, nervy; plucky, spirited, spunky; determined, resolute

ant brave, courageous, daring, dauntless, doughty, fearless, gallant, greathearted, gutsy, hardy, heroic, intrepid, lionhearted, stalwart, stout, stouthearted, valiant, valorous

cowboy *n* a hired hand who tends cattle or horses at a ranch or on the range ⟨*cowboys* were rounding up the cattle for branding⟩

syn buckaroo, cowhand, cowman, cowpoke, cowpuncher

rel cowgirl; gaucho, vaquero; horseman, horsewoman, wrangler; cattleman, rancher; herdsman

cower *vb* to draw back or crouch down in fearful submission ⟨the abused dog always *cowered* in the presence of its master⟩

syn cringe, grovel, quail

rel flinch, recoil, shrink, squinch; blanch, blench, whiten; fawn, kowtow, toady

cowhand *n* a hired hand who tends cattle or horses at a ranch or on the range — see COWBOY

cowhide *vb* to strike repeatedly with something long and thin or flexible — see WHIP 1

cowman *n* a hired hand who tends cattle or horses at a ranch or on the range — see COWBOY

coworker *n* a fellow worker — see COLLEAGUE

cowpoke *n* a hired hand who tends cattle or horses at a ranch or on the range — see COWBOY

cowpuncher *n* a hired hand who tends cattle or horses at a ranch or on the range — see COWBOY

coy *adj* 1 affecting shyness or modesty in order to attract masculine interest ⟨not wanting him to know that she was interested in him, she acted very *coy* at the dance⟩

syn coquettish, demure, kittenish

rel flirtatious, goody-goody, overmodest, priggish, prim, prudish

2 not comfortable around people — see SHY 2

cozen *vb* 1 to cause to believe what is untrue — see DECEIVE

2 to rob by the use of trickery or threats — see FLEECE

cozener *n* a dishonest person who uses clever means to cheat others out of something of value — see TRICKSTER 1

cozy *adj* 1 enjoying physical comfort — see COMFORTABLE 2

2 providing physical comfort — see COMFORTABLE 1

crab *n* an irritable and complaining person — see GROUCH

crab *vb* to express dissatisfaction, pain, or resentment usually tiresomely — see COMPLAIN

---

syn synonym(s)   **rel** related words
ant antonym(s)   **near ant** near antonym(s)

crabby *adj* 1 easily irritated or annoyed — see IRRITABLE

2 given to complaining a lot — see FUSSY 1

crack *adj* having or showing exceptional knowledge, experience, or skill in a field of endeavor — see PROFICIENT

crack *n* 1 an irregular usually narrow break in a surface created by pressure ⟨a pebble struck the car's windshield and left a *crack* in it⟩

syn chink, cleft, cranny, crevice, fissure, rift, split

rel craze, hairline; fracture, rupture; breach, gap, opening; cut, gash, incision, slit

2 a hard strike with a part of the body or an instrument — see ¹BLOW

3 a loud explosive sound — see CLAP 1

4 an effort to do or accomplish something — see ATTEMPT

5 something said or done to cause laughter — see JOKE 1

crack *vb* 1 to break suddenly with an explosive sound ⟨the tree branch unexpectedly *cracked* under our weight⟩

syn pop, snap

rel crackle, hiss, sizzle, sputter; burst, explode, shatter; clack, click, clatter

2 to yield to mental or emotional stress ⟨after hours of tough questioning the suspect finally *cracked* and blurted out a confession⟩

syn break (down), flip, freak (out)

phrases go to pieces

3 to change (as a secret message) from code into ordinary language — see DECODE

4 to deliver a blow to (someone or something) usually in a strong vigorous manner — see HIT 1

5 to find an answer for through reasoning — see SOLVE

crackbrain *n* 1 a person judged to be legally or medically insane — see LUNATIC 1

2 a person of odd or whimsical habits — see ECCENTRIC

crackbrained *adj* having or showing a very abnormal or sick state of mind — see INSANE 1

crack down (on) *vb* to put a stop to (something) by the use of force — see QUELL 1

cracked *adj* having or showing a very abnormal or sick state of mind — see INSANE 1

crackerjack *adj* 1 having or showing exceptional knowledge, experience, or skill in a field of endeavor — see PROFICIENT

2 of the very best kind — see EXCELLENT

crackerjack *n* 1 a person with a high level of knowledge or skill in a field — see EXPERT

2 something very good of its kind — see JIM-DANDY

crackpot *n* a person of odd or whimsical habits — see ECCENTRIC

crack–up *n* the violent coming together of two bodies into destructive contact — see CRASH 1

crack up vb 1 to declare enthusiastic approval of — see ACCLAIM

2 to praise or publicize lavishly and often excessively — see TOUT 1

craft n 1 an occupation requiring skillful use of the hands ⟨the *craft* of cabinet-making was much admired in colonial times⟩

syn handcraft, handicraft, trade

rel art, skill; calling, occupation, profession, vocation

2 a small buoyant structure for travel on water — see BOAT 1

3 the inclination or practice of misleading others through lies or trickery — see DECEIT

4 skill in achieving one's ends through indirect, subtle, or underhanded means — see CUNNING 1

5 subtle or imaginative ability in inventing, devising, or executing something — see SKILL 1

craft vb to put (something) into proper and usually carefully worked out written form — see COMPOSE 1

craftiness n 1 skill in achieving one's ends through indirect, subtle, or underhanded means — see CUNNING 1

2 the inclination or practice of misleading others through lies or trickery — see DECEIT

craftsman n a person whose occupation requires skill with the hands — see ARTISAN

crafty adj clever at attaining one's ends by indirect and often deceptive means — see ARTFUL 1

crag n a steep wall of rock, earth, or ice — see CLIFF

craggy adj having an uneven edge or outline — see RAGGED 1

cram vb 1 to fit (something) into a tight space — see CROWD 1

2 to put into (something) as much as can be held or contained — see FILL 1

crammed adj containing or seeming to contain the greatest quantity or number possible — see FULL 1

cramp n a painful sudden tightening of a muscle ⟨I was suddenly awakened by a *cramp* in my leg⟩

syn charley horse, crick, spasm

rel contraction, jerk, stitch, twinge, twitch

cramp vb to create difficulty for the work or activity of — see HAMPER

crane vb to move from a lower to a higher place or position — see RAISE 1

cranium n the case of bone that encloses the brain and supports the jaws of vertebrates — see SKULL

crank n 1 a person of odd or whimsical habits — see ECCENTRIC

2 an irritable and complaining person — see GROUCH

crank (up) vb to cause to function — see ACTIVATE

crankiness n readiness to show annoyance or impatience — see PETULANCE

cranky adj 1 difficult to use or operate especially because of size, weight, or design — see CUMBERSOME

2 easily irritated or annoyed — see IRRITABLE

3 given to complaining a lot — see FUSSY 1

cranny n an irregular usually narrow break in a surface created by pressure — see CRACK 1

crash n 1 the violent coming together of two bodies into destructive contact ⟨the fiery *crash* of two jumbo jet airplanes in midair⟩

syn collision, crack-up, smash, smashup, wreck

rel accident; demolishment, destruction, ruin

2 a falling short of one's goals — see FAILURE 2

3 a loud explosive sound — see CLAP 1

4 a forceful coming together of two things — see IMPACT 1

crash vb 1 to cause to break with violence and much noise — see SMASH 1

2 to come into usually forceful contact with something — see HIT 2

3 to stop functioning — see FAIL 1

crass adj lacking in refinement or good taste — see COARSE 2

crassness n the quality or state of lacking refinement or good taste — see VULGARITY 1

crave vb to have an earnest wish to own or enjoy — see DESIRE

craven adj having or showing a shameful lack of courage — see COWARDLY

craven n a person who shows a shameful lack of courage in the face of danger — see COWARD

cravenness n a shameful lack of courage in the face of danger — see COWARDICE

craving n a strong wish for something — see DESIRE

crawl vb 1 to move slowly with the body close to the ground ⟨the time we had to *crawl* through a narrow passageway from one cave to another⟩

syn creep, grovel, slither, snake, worm, wriggle

rel crouch, squat; slide; edge, inch, nose; skulk, sneak, steal, tiptoe

2 to move slowly ⟨the weekend traffic on the road to the beach just *crawled*⟩

syn creep, drag, inch, plod, poke

rel lumber, shamble, shuffle, tramp, trudge

near ant float, glide, sail; hurry, tear

ant fly, race, speed, whiz (or whizz), zip

3 to move or act slowly — see DELAY 1

crawler n someone who moves slowly or more slowly than others — see SLOWPOKE

crawling adj moving or proceeding at less than the normal, desirable, or required speed — see SLOW 1

craze n a practice or interest that is very popular for a short time — see FAD

craze vb to cause to go insane or as if insane ⟨soldiers who had been *crazed* by months of combat and chaos in the countryside⟩

syn derange, madden, unbalance, unhinge, unstring

rel agitate, bother, confuse, discompose, disquiet, distract, disturb, perturb, unsettle, upset; annoy, irritate, vex

near ant calm, quiet, relax, settle, soothe, tranquilize (*or* tranquillize)

crazed *adj* having or showing a very abnormal or sick state of mind — see INSANE 1

craziness *n* lack of good sense or judgment — see FOOLISHNESS 1

crazy *adj* 1 conceived or made without regard for reason or reality — see FANTASTIC 1

2 having or showing a very abnormal or sick state of mind — see INSANE 1

3 showing or marked by a lack of good sense or judgment — see FOOLISH 1

4 showing urgent desire or interest — see EAGER

crazy (*about or* over) *adj* filled with an intense or excessive love for — see ENAMORED (OF)

creak *n* a harsh grating sound — see RASP

creak *vb* to make a short shrill noise — see SQUEAK

cream *n* individuals carefully selected as being the best of a class — see ELITE

crease *n* a small fold in a soft and otherwise smooth surface — see WRINKLE 1

crease *vb* to develop creases or folds — see WRINKLE 1

create *vb* to be the cause of (a situation, action, or state of mind) — see EFFECT

creation *n* 1 something (as a device) created for the first time through the use of the imagination — see INVENTION 1

2 the whole body of things observed or assumed — see UNIVERSE

creative *adj* 1 having the skill and imagination to create new things ⟨Thomas Edison's status as perhaps America's greatest *creative* genius⟩

syn imaginative, ingenious, innovative, inventive, original

rel gifted, inspired, talented; resourceful; fecund, fertile, fruitful, productive, prolific

near ant imitative, uninspired; infertile, unproductive

ant uncreative, unimaginative, unoriginal

2 showing a use of the imagination and creativity especially in inventing — see CLEVER 1

creativeness *n* the skill and imagination to create new things — see CREATIVITY 1

creativity *n* 1 the skill and imagination to create new things ⟨the arts and crafts fair showed the remarkable *creativity* of local artists and artisans⟩

syn creativeness, imaginativeness, ingeniousness, ingenuity, invention, inventiveness, originality

rel resourcefulness; fecundity, fertility, fruitfulness, productiveness, productivity; freshness, newness, novelty; genius, inspiration, talent

near ant dryness, dullness (*also* dulness)

2 the ability to form mental images of things that either are not physically present or have never been conceived or created by others — see IMAGINATION

creator *n* 1 a person who establishes a whole new field of endeavor — see FATHER 2

2 *cap* the being worshipped as the creator and ruler of the universe — see DEITY 2

creature *n* 1 a member of the human race — see HUMAN

2 one of the lower animals as distinguished from human beings — see ANIMAL

credence *n* 1 firm belief in the integrity, ability, effectiveness, or genuineness of someone or something — see TRUST 1

2 mental conviction of the truth of some statement or the reality of some being or phenomenon — see BELIEF 1

credentials *n pl* a skill, an ability, or knowledge that makes a person able to do a particular job — see QUALIFICATION 1

credible *adj* worthy of being accepted as true or reasonable — see BELIEVABLE

credit *n* 1 the right to take possession of goods before paying for them ⟨because of their reputation for not paying their bills, no store will extend the family *credit*⟩

syn trust

rel installment plan, layaway

2 an asset that brings praise or renown — see GLORY 2

3 mental conviction of the truth of some statement or the reality of some being or phenomenon — see BELIEF 1

4 public acknowledgment or admiration for an achievement — see GLORY 1

credit *vb* 1 to explain (something) as being the result of something else ⟨has to *credit* his success in picking winning lottery numbers to pure luck⟩

syn accredit, ascribe, attribute, impute

rel blame, pin (on); associate, connect, link

2 to regard as right or true — see BELIEVE 1

creditable *adj* deserving of high regard or great approval — see ADMIRABLE

credo *n* 1 a body of beliefs and practices regarding the supernatural and the worship of one or more deities — see RELIGION 1

2 the basic beliefs or guiding principles of a person or group — see CREED 1

credulity *n* readiness to believe the claims of others without sufficient evidence ⟨the quack pushing the phony medicine was taking advantage of the *credulity* of people hoping for miracle cures⟩

syn credulousness, gullibility, naïveté (*also* naivete)

rel artlessness, simplicity, unsophistication; trust, unwariness

---

syn synonym(s)   **rel** related words
ant antonym(s)   **near ant** near antonym(s)

near ant sophistication, worldliness; distrust, mistrust, suspicion, wariness; doubt, uncertainty
ant incredulity, skepticism

credulousness *n* readiness to believe the claims of others without sufficient evidence — see CREDULITY

creed *n* 1 the basic beliefs or guiding principles of a person or group ⟨central to the *creed* of this organization of medical volunteers is the belief that health care is a basic human right⟩
syn credo, doctrine, gospel, ideology, philosophy
rel manifesto
2 a body of beliefs and practices regarding the supernatural and the worship of one or more deities — see RELIGION 1

creek *n* 1 a natural body of running water smaller than a river ⟨the shallow *creek* that runs in back of our house⟩
syn brook, brooklet, rill, rivulet, run [*chiefly Midland*], streamlet
rel freshet, runoff; river, stream, watercourse, waterway; canal, millrace, millstream, race
2 *chiefly British* a part of a body of water that extends beyond the general shoreline — see GULF 1

creep *n* a person whose behavior is offensive to others — see JERK 1

creep *vb* 1 to advance gradually beyond the usual or desirable limits — see ENCROACH
2 to move or act slowly — see DELAY 1
3 to move slowly with the body close to the ground — see CRAWL 1
4 to move slowly — see CRAWL 2

creeper *n* someone who moves slowly or more slowly than others — see SLOWPOKE

creeping *adj* moving or proceeding at less than the normal, desirable, or required speed — see SLOW 1

creepy *adj* fearfully and mysteriously strange or fantastic — see EERIE

crest *n* the line formed when two sloping surfaces come together along their topmost edge — see RIDGE

crestfallen *adj* feeling unhappiness — see SAD 1

cretin *n* 1 a person whose behavior is offensive to others — see JERK 1
2 a stupid person — see IDIOT

crevice *n* an irregular usually narrow break in a surface created by pressure — see CRACK 1

crew *n* a group of people working together on a task — see GANG 1

crick *n* a painful sudden tightening of a muscle — see CRAMP

crime *n* 1 activities that are in violation of the laws of the state ⟨a promise by the president to step up the war against *crime*⟩
syn criminality, lawbreaking, lawlessness
rel malfeasance, misconduct; wrongdoing; evil, immorality, sin, wickedness; corruption, depravity; malefaction, misdeed,

misdoing, offense (*or* offence), transgression, trespass
2 a regrettable or blameworthy act ⟨it's a *crime* to waste food, so give the rest of the pizza to me⟩
syn disgrace, pity, shame, sin
rel outrage, scandal
3 a breaking of a moral or legal code — see OFFENSE 1
4 a cause of shame — see DISGRACE 2

criminal *adj* contrary to or forbidden by law — see ILLEGAL 1

criminal *n* a person who has committed a crime ⟨car thieves, pickpockets, burglars, and other *criminals*⟩
syn crook, culprit; felon, lawbreaker, malefactor, offender
rel desperado, outlaw; convict, jailbird; perpetrator; evildoer, sinner, transgressor, trespasser, wrongdoer; gangster, gunman, hoodlum, mobster, racketeer, thug; backslider, relapser, repeater

criminality *n* activities that are in violation of the laws of the state — see CRIME 1

crimp *n* 1 a small fold in a soft and otherwise smooth surface — see WRINKLE 1
2 something that makes movement or progress more difficult — see ENCUMBRANCE

crimson *vb* to develop a rosy facial color (as from excitement or embarrassment) — see BLUSH

cringe *vb* to draw back or crouch down in fearful submission — see COWER

crinkle *n* a small fold in a soft and otherwise smooth surface — see WRINKLE 1

crinkle *vb* 1 to create (as by crushing) an irregular mass of creases in — see CRUMPLE 1
2 to develop creases or folds — see WRINKLE 1

cripple *vb* 1 to cause severe or permanent injury to — see MAIM
2 to reduce the soundness, effectiveness, or perfection of — see DAMAGE 1
3 to render powerless, ineffective, or unable to move — see PARALYZE

crisis *n* a time or state of affairs requiring prompt or decisive action — see EMERGENCY

crisp *adj* 1 having a texture that readily breaks into little pieces under pressure ⟨the bag of *crisp* cookies had a lot of crumbs on the bottom⟩
syn brittle, crispy, crumbly, flaky, friable, short
rel crunchy; breakable, delicate, fragile
near ant elastic, flexible, pliable, pliant, resilient; strong, sturdy, tough
2 being clean and in good order — see NEAT 1
3 marked by the use of few words to convey much information or meaning — see CONCISE

crisply *adv* in a few words — see SHORTLY 1

crispness *n* the quality or state of being marked by or using only few words to convey much meaning — see SUCCINCTNESS

crispy *adj* having a texture that readily breaks into little pieces under pressure — see CRISP 1

crisscross *vb* to make one's way through, across, or over — see TRAVERSE

criterion *n* something set up as an example against which others of the same type are compared — see STANDARD 1

critic *n* **1** a person given to harsh judgments and to finding faults 〈the president's hard-core *critics* are going to criticize him no matter what he does〉
syn carper, castigator, caviler (*or* caviller), censurer, faultfinder, nitpicker, railer, scold
rel belittler, derider, detractor; pettifogger, quibbler; complainer, crybaby, fusser, whiner
2 a person who makes or expresses a judgment on the quality of offerings in some field of endeavor 〈the restaurant *critic* said that the fries at that fast-food outlet were the worst that she had ever eaten〉
syn reviewer
rel analyst, columnist, commentator; appraiser, evaluator, judge

critical *adj* **1** given to making or expressing unfavorable judgments about things 〈adults tend to be *critical* of teenagers' taste in music and movies〉
syn captious, carping, caviling (*or* cavilling), faultfinding, hypercritical, overcritical
rel discerning, discriminating, judicious; demanding, exacting, fastidious, finicky, fussy, particular
near ant undiscerning
ant uncritical
2 needing immediate attention — see ACUTE 2
3 of the greatest possible importance — see CRUCIAL

criticism *n* an essay evaluating or analyzing something 〈every *criticism* of the movie has noted that there are major holes in its plot〉
syn notice, review
rel rave; appraisal, assessment, evaluation; analysis, examination, study

criticize *vb* to express one's unfavorable opinion of the worth or quality of 〈students who feel the need to *criticize* every single idea by the principal for improving the school〉
syn blame, censure, condemn, denounce, dis [*slang*], fault, knock, pan, reprehend
rel assail, attack, blast, slam, slash; beef, bellyache, carp, complain, crab, croak, fuss, gripe, grouse, growl, grumble, kick, moan, murmur, mutter, repine, squawk, wail, whine, yammer; admonish, chide, rebuke, reprimand, reproach, reprove; berate, castigate, crucify, excoriate, flay, lambaste (*or* lambast), lash, pillory, scold, upbraid; bad-mouth, belittle, disparage, put down

phrases find fault (with), take to task
near ant approve, endorse (*also* indorse), recommend, sanction
ant extol (*also* extoll), laud, praise

critter *n* one of the lower animals as distinguished from human beings — see ANIMAL

croak *vb* **1** to express dissatisfaction, pain, or resentment usually tiresomely — see COMPLAIN
2 *slang* to stop living — see DIE 1
3 *slang* to deprive of life — see KILL 1

croaker *n* an irritable and complaining person — see GROUCH

croaking *adj* harsh and dry in sound — see HOARSE

crockery *n* articles made of baked clay 〈a display of beautifully hand-painted *crockery* on the kitchen countertop〉
syn earthenware, pottery, stoneware
rel ceramics; china, porcelain

crone *n* a mean or ugly old woman 〈a run-down house that was inhabited by a cantankerous *crone* who kept to herself〉
syn beldam (*or* beldame), hag, witch
rel grandam (*or* grandame); harpy, shrew, virago

crony *n* **1** a person frequently seen in the company of another — see ASSOCIATE 1
2 a person who has a strong liking for and trust in another — see FRIEND 1

crook *n* **1** a person who has committed a crime — see CRIMINAL
2 something that curves or is curved — see BEND 1

crook *vb* **1** to cause to turn away from a straight line — see BEND 1
2 to turn away from a straight line or course — see CURVE 1

crooked *adj* **1** marked by a long series of irregular curves 〈a long, *crooked* line of people had formed in front of the ticket booth〉
syn bending, curled, curling, curved, curving, devious, serpentine, sinuous, tortuous, twisted, twisting, winding
rel zigzag, zigzagging; circling, coiled, coiling, corkscrew, looping, spiral, spiraling (*or* spiralling), swirling; circuitous, indirect, roundabout; meandering, rambling, wandering
near ant direct, linear
ant straight, straightaway
2 given to or marked by cheating and deception — see DISHONEST 2
3 inclined or twisted to one side — see AWRY
4 marked by, based on, or done by the use of dishonest methods to acquire something of value — see FRAUDULENT 1

crookedness *n* the inclination or practice of misleading others through lies or trickery — see DECEIT

crop *n* **1** the quantity of an animal or vegetable product gathered at the end of a season 〈the wheat *crop* is going to be exceptionally large this year〉
syn harvest
rel return, yield

---

syn synonym(s)	**rel** related words
ant antonym(s)	**near ant** near antonym(s)

2 a usually small number of persons considered as a unit — see GROUP 2

crop *vb* **1** to look after or assist the growth of by labor and care — see GROW 1

2 to make (as hair) shorter with or as if with the use of shears — see CLIP

crop (**up**) *vb* to come to one's attention especially gradually or unexpectedly — see ARISE 2

cropper *n* a falling short of one's goals — see FAILURE 1

croquette *n* a small usually rounded mass of minced food that has been fried — see CAKE

cross *adj* easily irritated or annoyed — see IRRITABLE

cross *n* **1** a test of faith, patience, or strength — see TRIAL 1

2 an offspring of parents with different genes especially when of different races, breeds, species, or genera — see HYBRID

cross *vb* **1** to be unfaithful or disloyal to — see BETRAY 1

2 to divide by passing through or across — see INTERSECT

3 to make one's way through, across, or over — see TRAVERSE

cross (**out**) *vb* to show (something written) to be no longer valid by drawing a cross over or a line through it — see X (OUT)

crossbred *adj* being offspring produced by parents of different races, breeds, species, or genera — see MIXED 1

crossbreed *n* an offspring of parents with different genes especially when of different races, breeds, species, or genera — see HYBRID

cross fire *n* an often noisy or angry expression of differing opinions — see ARGUMENT 1

crossing *n* **1** a journey over water in a vessel — see SAIL

2 a place where roads meet — see CROSSROAD 1

crossness *n* readiness to show annoyance or impatience — see PETULANCE

crossroad *n* **1** *usually* **crossroads** *pl* a place where roads meet ⟨the fast-food chain has a restaurant at practically every *crossroads*⟩
syn corner, crossing, intersection
rel overpass, underpass

2 *usually* **crossroads** *pl* a time or state of affairs requiring prompt or decisive action — see EMERGENCY

cross section *n* a number of things selected from a group to stand for the whole — see SAMPLE 1

crossways *adv* in a line or direction running from corner to corner — see CROSSWISE

crosswise *adv* in a line or direction running from corner to corner ⟨first cut the sandwiches *crosswise* and then trim the crusts⟩
syn athwart, crossways, obliquely, transversely

crotchet *n* an odd or peculiar habit — see IDIOSYNCRASY

crotchetiness *n* readiness to show annoyance or impatience — see PETULANCE

crotchety *adj* easily irritated or annoyed — see IRRITABLE

crouch *vb* to lie low with the limbs close to the body ⟨the cat *crouched* in the bushes, waiting for the right moment to pounce on the chipmunk⟩
syn huddle, hunch, scrunch, squat, squinch
rel curl up

crow *vb* **1** to feel or express joy or triumph — see EXULT

2 to praise or express pride in one's own possessions, qualities, or accomplishments often to excess — see BOAST

crowd *n* **1** a great number of persons or things gathered together ⟨a huge *crowd* of fans was on hand to greet the returning Super Bowl champions⟩
syn army, crush, drove, flock, horde, host, legion, mob, multitude, press, swarm, throng
rel masses, rabble, riffraff; gaggle, herd; heap, mountain, pile

2 a group of people sharing a common interest and relating together socially — see GANG 2

crowd *vb* **1** to fit (something) into a tight space ⟨*crowded* all the boats into the harbor before the storm struck⟩
syn cram, jam, ram, sandwich, squeeze, stuff, wedge
rel fill, heap, jam-pack, load, pack

2 to move upon or fill (something) in great numbers ⟨cars *crowded* the roads over the long holiday weekend⟩
syn flock, mob, swarm, throng
rel beset, infest, invade, overrun; clog, dam, obstruct, plug (up)

3 to gather into a closely packed group — see PRESS 3

crowded *adj* **1** containing or seeming to contain the greatest quantity or number possible — see FULL 1

2 having little space between items or parts — see CLOSE 1

crown *n* **1** a decorative band or wreath worn about the head as a symbol of victory or honor ⟨the *crown* of laurel leaves that is traditionally placed on the winner of the marathon⟩
syn coronet, diadem
rel tiara; garland, laurel

2 the position occupied by the one who comes in first in a competition ⟨his lifelong dream of someday winning the heavyweight boxing *crown*⟩
syn championship, title

3 the highest part or point — see HEIGHT 1

crown *vb* to bring to a triumphant conclusion ⟨the Olympic Games were *crowned* by spectacular closing ceremonies⟩
syn climax, culminate
rel complete, conclude, finish, round (off *or* out), terminate, wrap up

crucial *adj* of the greatest possible importance ⟨water is *crucial* to our survival⟩
syn critical, key, pivotal, vital

rel decisive, life-and-death; basic, elementary, fundamental; essential, indispensable, necessary, requisite; pressing, urgent

near ant inconsequential, insignificant, trivial, unimportant

crucible *n* a test of faith, patience, or strength — see TRIAL 1

crude *adj* **1** being such as found in nature and not altered by processing or refining ⟨a spill of *crude* oil along a coastline is the worst kind of environmental disaster⟩

syn native, natural, raw, undressed, unprocessed, unrefined, untreated

rel undeveloped; roughhewn, unfinished, unpolished; unbaked, uncooked; impure, unfiltered, unpurified

phrases in the rough

near ant filtered, pure, purified

ant dressed, processed, refined, treated

2 belonging to or characteristic of an early level of skill or development — see PRIMITIVE 1

3 depicting or referring to sexual matters in a way that is unacceptable in polite society — see OBSCENE 1

4 lacking in refinement or good taste — see COARSE 2

5 hastily or roughly constructed — see RUDE 1

crudeness *n* **1** the quality or state of being obscene — see OBSCENITY 1

2 the quality or state of lacking refinement or good taste — see VULGARITY 1

cruel *adj* **1** having or showing the desire to inflict severe pain and suffering on others ⟨a *cruel* dictator who tortured anyone who dared to speak out against him⟩ ⟨*cruel* and unusual punishments are forbidden by the U.S. Constitution⟩

syn barbaric, barbarous, brutal, heartless, inhumane, sadistic, savage, vicious, wanton

rel cutthroat, merciless, pitiless, ruthless; fell, ferocious, grim; bloodthirsty, murderous, sanguinary, sanguine; catty, despiteful, hateful, malevolent, malicious, malign, malignant, mean, nasty, spiteful

near ant tender, warm, warmhearted; charitable, clement, lenient, merciful, pitying; pacific, peaceable, peaceful

ant benign, benignant, compassionate, good-hearted, humane, kind, kindhearted, sympathetic, tenderhearted

2 difficult to endure — see HARSH 1

3 hard to accept or bear especially emotionally — see BITTER 2

4 having or showing a desire to cause someone pain or suffering for the sheer enjoyment of it — see HATEFUL

cruelness *n* the willful infliction of pain and suffering on others — see CRUELTY

cruelty *n* the willful infliction of pain and suffering on others ⟨centuries after he ravaged Europe, Attila the Hun remains notorious for his *cruelty*⟩

syn barbarity, brutality, cruelness, heartlessness, inhumanity, sadism, savageness, savagery, viciousness, wantonness

rel mercilessness, ruthlessness; ferocity, fierceness; bloodthirstiness, sanguinity; cattiness, despitefulness, hatefulness, malevolence, maliciousness, malignity, meanness, nastiness, spitefulness

near ant tenderness, warmheartedness, warmth; clemency, leniency, mercifulness, mercy, pity

ant benignity, compassion, good-heartedness, humanity, kindheartedness, kindness, sympathy

cruise *n* a journey over water in a vessel — see SAIL

cruise *vb* to travel on water in a vessel — see SAIL 1

crumb *n* **1** a very small amount — see PARTICLE 1

2 a very small piece — see BIT 1

crumble *vb* to become worse or of less value — see DETERIORATE

crumbly *adj* having a texture that readily breaks into little pieces under pressure — see CRISP 1

crumple *vb* **1** to create (as by crushing) an irregular mass of creases in ⟨*crumpled* the piece of paper and angrily threw it in the wastebasket⟩

syn crinkle, rumple, scrunch, wrinkle

rel corrugate, crease, crimp, fold, furrow, pleat; ripple, ruffle; disarrange, jumble, mess (up), muss (up)

ant iron out, smooth

2 to fall down or in as a result of physical pressure — see COLLAPSE 1

crunch *n* a time or state of affairs requiring prompt or decisive action — see EMERGENCY

crunch *vb* to press or strike against or together so as to make a scraping sound — see GRIND 1

crunch (on) *vb* to crush or grind with the teeth — see BITE (ON)

crusade *n* a series of activities undertaken to achieve a goal — see CAMPAIGN

crusader *n* one who is intensely or excessively devoted to a cause — see ZEALOT

crush *n* **1** a strong but often short-lived liking for another person ⟨the *crush* that she had on a boy whom she had met over the summer⟩

syn infatuation, passion

rel fixation, obsession; affection, devotion, fondness, love; craze, fad, rage, vogue

2 a great number of persons or things gathered together — see CROWD 1

crush *vb* **1** to cause to become a pulpy mass ⟨dark-colored grapes that will be *crushed* to make red wine⟩

syn mash, pulp, squash

rel press, squeeze; beat, pound, powder, pulverize

2 to achieve a victory over — see BEAT 2

3 to put a stop to (something) by the use of force — see QUELL 1

4 to reduce to fine particles — see POWDER

---

syn synonym(s)	**rel** related words
ant antonym(s)	**near ant** near antonym(s)

5 to subject to incapacitating emotional or mental stress — see OVERWHELM 1

6 to apply external pressure on so as to force out the juice or contents of — see PRESS 2

crusher *n* something (as a fact or argument) that is decisive or overwhelming — see CLINCHER

crusty *adj* being or characterized by direct, brief, and potentially rude speech or manner — see BLUNT 1

crux *n* the central part or aspect of something under consideration ⟨the *crux* of the problem is that the school's current budget is totally inadequate⟩

syn core, gist, heart, nub, pith, pivot

rel course, direction, drift, tenor; body, essence, substance

cry *n* **1** a loud vocal expression of strong emotion — see SHOUT

2 a natural vocal sound made by an animal — see CALL 1

3 an attention-getting word or phrase used to publicize something (as a campaign or product) — see SLOGAN

4 an earnest request — see PLEA 1

cry *vb* **1** to shed tears often while making meaningless sounds as a sign of pain or distress ⟨some kids started to *cry* even before the doctor had given them their shot⟩

syn bawl, blubber, sob, weep

rel grieve, keen, lament, mourn; howl, scream, squall, wail, yowl; pule, whimper, whine; sniffle, snivel; groan, moan, sigh

2 to utter one's distinctive animal sound ⟨we knew that we were getting very close to the ocean when we could hear sea gulls *crying*⟩

syn call, sing

3 to speak so as to be heard at a distance — see CALL 1

cry (out) *vb* to utter with a sudden burst of strong feeling — see EXCLAIM

crybaby *n* a person who makes frequent complaints usually about little things ⟨car trips that were often spoiled by a couple of *crybabies* in the back seat⟩

syn complainer, fusser, griper, growler, grumbler, whiner

rel malcontent; carper, critic, faultfinder, nitpicker, squawker; bawler, wailer, weeper

cry down *vb* to express scornfully one's low opinion of — see DECRY 1

crying *adj* needing immediate attention — see ACUTE 2

crypt *n* an underground burial chamber ⟨the old church's *crypt* is the final resting place for the president and his beloved wife⟩

syn catacomb(s), vault

rel mausoleum, sepulcher (*or* sepulchre), tomb

cryptic *adj* **1** being beyond one's powers to know, understand, or explain — see MYSTERIOUS 1

2 having an often intentionally veiled or uncertain meaning — see OBSCURE 1

crystallize *vb* to take on a definite form — see FORM 1

cub *n* a young person who is between infancy and adulthood — see CHILD 1

cubicle *n* one of the parts into which an enclosed space is divided — see COMPARTMENT

cuckoo *adj* **1** having or showing a very abnormal or sick state of mind — see INSANE 1

2 showing or marked by a lack of good sense or judgment — see FOOLISH 1

cuddle *vb* **1** to lie close — see NUZZLE

2 to sit or recline comfortably or cozily — see SNUGGLE 1

cudgel *n* a heavy rigid stick used as a weapon or for punishment — see CLUB 1

cue *n* **1** a series of persons or things arranged one behind another — see LINE 1

2 a slight or indirect pointing to something (as a solution or explanation) — see HINT 1

cuff *n* a hard strike with a part of the body or an instrument — see ¹BLOW

cuisine *n* the art or style of preparing food (as in a specified region) — see COOKERY

cull *n* something separated from a group or lot for not being as good as the others ⟨the unbruised apples will be packed in bags, and the *culls* will be used for cider⟩

syn discard, reject, rejection

rel second, throwaway

cull *vb* to decide to accept (someone or something) from a group of possibilities — see CHOOSE 1

culminate *vb* to bring to a triumphant conclusion — see CROWN

culmination *n* the highest part or point — see HEIGHT 1

culpability *n* responsibility for wrongdoing or failure — see BLAME 1

culpable *adj* **1** deserving reproach or blame — see BLAMEWORTHY

2 responsible for a wrong — see GUILTY 1

culprit *n* a person who has committed a crime — see CRIMINAL

cult *n* **1** a group of people showing intense devotion to a cause, person, or work (as a film) ⟨long after it had gone off the air, the TV series continued to have a huge *cult*⟩

syn following

rel discipleship

2 a body of beliefs and practices regarding the supernatural and the worship of one or more deities — see RELIGION 1

cultivate *vb* **1** to come to have gradually — see DEVELOP 2

2 to promote the growth or development of — see FOSTER 1

3 to look after or assist the growth of by labor and care — see GROW 1

4 to work by plowing, sowing, and raising crops on — see FARM

cultivated *adj* having or showing a taste for the fine arts and gracious living ⟨the museum's annual gala for charity usually attracts a *cultivated* crowd⟩

syn civilized, cultured, genteel, polished, refined

rel cerebral, highbrow, intellectual; educated, erudite, knowledgeable, learned, literate, scholarly, well-read; civil, courteous, mannerly, polite, well-bred; cosmopolitan, sophisticated, urbane

near ant ignorant, illiterate, uneducated, unlettered; lowbrow, unintelligent; coarse, ill-bred, ill-mannered; provincial, rustic, unsophisticated; boorish, churlish, cloddish, clownish, crude, uncouth, vulgar

ant philistine, uncivilized, uncultured, unpolished, unrefined

cultivation n a high level of taste and enlightenment as a result of extensive intellectual training and exposure to the arts — see CULTURE 1

cultivator n a person who cultivates the land and grows crops on it — see FARMER

cultural adj of or relating to the fine arts ⟨with its many museums, theaters, and opera and ballet companies, the city is a *cultural* paradise⟩
syn artistic
rel aesthetic, tasteful

culture n 1 a high level of taste and enlightenment as a result of extensive intellectual training and exposure to the arts ⟨because of its wide reputation as a place of *culture*, Boston became known as "the Athens of America"⟩
syn civilization, cultivation, polish, refinement
rel education, erudition, learning, literacy, scholarship; sophistication, urbanity; breeding, gentility, manners; class, elegance, grace, taste; civility, courtesy, politeness
near ant ignorance, illiteracy, parochialism, provincialism, unsophistication; boorishness, churlishness, clownishness, coarseness, crudeness, vulgarity
ant philistinism

2 the way people live at a particular time and place — see CIVILIZATION 1

culture vb to look after or assist the growth of by labor and care — see GROW 1

cultured adj having or showing a taste for the fine arts and gracious living — see CULTIVATED

cumbersome adj difficult to use or operate especially because of size, weight, or design ⟨a long-handled wrench that is too *cumbersome* for tight spots, like under the sink⟩
syn awkward, clumsy, cranky, cumbrous, ungainly, unhandy, unwieldy
rel uncontrollable, unmanageable; bulky, heavy, massive; impracticable, impractical
near ant functional, practicable, practical, serviceable, useful
ant handy

cumbrous adj difficult to use or operate especially because of size, weight, or design — see CUMBERSOME

---

syn synonym(s)   **rel** related words
ant antonym(s)   **near ant** near antonym(s)

---

cummerbund n a strip of flexible material (as leather) worn around the waist — see ²BELT

cumulative adj produced by a series of additions of identical or similar things ⟨a *cumulative* weight gain of 20 pounds over the course of a year⟩
syn additive, incremental
rel gradual, step-by-step

cunning adj 1 clever at attaining one's ends by indirect and often deceptive means — see ARTFUL 1

2 skillful with the hands — see DEXTEROUS 1

cunning n 1 skill in achieving one's ends through indirect, subtle, or underhanded means ⟨the *cunning* with which Tom Sawyer was able to get others to whitewash the fence for him⟩
syn artfulness, artifice, caginess, canniness, craft, craftiness, deviousness, foxiness, guile, slickness, slyness, sneakiness, subtleness, subtlety, wiliness
rel calculation, care, design; savvy, sharpness, shrewdness; cleverness, ingeniousness, ingenuity, inventiveness; ease, facility, finesse; deceitfulness, duplicity, shiftiness

2 subtle or imaginative ability in inventing, devising, or executing something — see SKILL 1

3 the inclination or practice of misleading others through lies or trickery — see DECEIT

cup n a round vessel equipped with a handle and designed for drinking ⟨a large *cup* that can hold almost a pint of hot chocolate⟩
syn mug
rel stein, tankard; demitasse, noggin; teacup

cupboard n a storage case typically having doors and shelves — see CABINET

cupidity n an intense selfish desire for wealth or possessions — see GREED

cur n a person whose behavior is offensive to others — see JERK 1

curb n something that limits one's freedom of action or choice — see RESTRICTION 1

curb vb to keep from exceeding a desirable degree or level (as of expression) — see CONTROL 1

curdy adj having small pieces or lumps spread throughout — see CHUNKY 1

cure n 1 something that corrects or counteracts something undesirable ⟨a fun hobby is always a good *cure* for boredom⟩
syn corrective, remedy
rel cure-all, elixir, panacea; answer, solution; aid, help, relief, succor; balm, palliative

2 a substance or preparation used to treat disease — see MEDICINE

cure vb 1 to bring about recovery from ⟨do you have anything that will *cure* my headache?⟩
syn heal, remedy

rel allay, alleviate, assuage, relieve; palliate, salve, soothe; ease, lighten, moderate, temper; doctor, treat

near ant aggravate, worsen

2 to restore to a healthy condition — see HEAL 1

cure–all *n* something that cures all ills or problems ⟨raising a young person's self-esteem is not the *cure-all* that some people think⟩

syn elixir, panacea

rel corrective, cure, remedy

curio *n* **1** a small object displayed for its attractiveness or interest — see KNICK-KNACK

2 something strange or unusual that is an object of interest — see CURIOSITY 2

curiosity *n* **1** an eager desire to find out about things that are often none of one's business ⟨the neighbors' *curiosity* about what we paid for our new car was really offensive⟩

syn curiousness, inquisitiveness, nosiness

rel attentiveness, concern, interest, regard; inquiry, interrogation, questioning; intrusiveness, obtrusiveness, officiousness; eavesdropping, rubbernecking

near ant apathy, disinterestedness, disregard, indifference, unconcern

2 something strange or unusual that is an object of interest ⟨the museum's *curiosities* include items constructed entirely out of toothpicks⟩

syn curio, exotic, oddity, rarity

rel marvel, prodigy, wonder; abnormality, anomaly, freak, monster, monstrosity; malformation, mutant, mutation

3 a small object displayed for its attractiveness or interest — see KNICKKNACK

curious *adj* **1** interested in what is not one's own business ⟨*curious* neighbors peered out of their windows as the new people moved in⟩

syn inquisitive, nosy (*or* nosey), prying, snoopy

rel interfering, intrusive, meddlesome, meddling, obtrusive, officious; inquisitional, inquisitorial; concerned, interested

near ant apathetic, disinterested, indifferent, unconcerned, uninterested

ant incurious, uncurious

2 different from the ordinary in a way that causes curiosity or suspicion — see ODD 2

3 noticeably different from what is generally found or experienced — see UNUSUAL 1

curiousness *n* an eager desire to find out about things that are often none of one's business — see CURIOSITY 1

curl *n* a length of hair that forms a loop or series of loops ⟨a young girl with beautiful golden *curls*⟩

syn ringlet

rel kink, wave; lock, tress

curl *vb* to follow a circular or spiral course — see WIND

curled *adj* **1** forming or styled into loops — see CURLY

2 marked by a long series of irregular curves — see CROOKED 1

curling *adj* marked by a long series of irregular curves — see CROOKED 1

curl up *vb* to sit or recline comfortably or cozily — see SNUGGLE 1

curly *adj* forming or styled into loops ⟨the boy's naturally *curly* hair⟩

syn curled

rel frizzy, kinky, waved, wavy

near ant lank, limp

ant straight

curmudgeon *n* an irritable and complaining person — see GROUCH

currency *n* something (as pieces of stamped metal or printed paper) customarily and legally used as a medium of exchange, a measure of value, or a means of payment — see MONEY

current *adj* **1** accepted, used, or practiced by most people ⟨the *current* theories on parenting favor allowing children lots of self-expression⟩

syn conventional, customary, going, popular, prevailing, prevalent, standard, stock, usual

rel average, common, everyday, normal, ordinary; regular, routine; ubiquitous, universal, widespread; accustomed, wonted; fashionable, in, modish, stylish

near ant abnormal, exceptional, extraordinary, uncommon

ant nonstandard, unconventional, unpopular, unusual

2 being or involving the latest methods, concepts, information, or styles — see MODERN

3 existing or in progress right now — see PRESENT 1

current *n* **1** a prevailing or general movement or inclination — see TREND 1

2 noticeable movement of air in a particular direction — see ¹WIND 1

currently *adv* at the present time — see NOW 1

curse *n* **1** a prayer that harm will come to someone ⟨the victim's *curse* that the man who robbed her never receive any pleasure from her money⟩

syn anathema, execration, imprecation, malediction

rel censure, condemnation, damnation, denunciation; hex, spell

near ant citation, commendation, endorsement

ant benediction, benison, blessing

2 a disrespectful or indecent word or expression — see SWEARWORD

curse *vb* **1** to ask a divine power to send harm or evil upon ⟨I *curse* the guy who had the idea of having annoying salespeople call up innocent people to sell them things they don't want⟩

syn imprecate

rel condemn, damn, denounce, execrate, reprobate; hex, jinx; fulminate (against), rail (against), revile

near ant applaud, commend, congratulate

ant bless

2 to cause persistent suffering to — see AFFLICT

3 to use offensive or indecent language — see SWEAR 1

cursorily *adv* with excessive or careless speed — see HASTILY 1

cursory *adj* acting or done with excessive or careless speed — see HASTY 1

curt *adj* being or characterized by direct, brief, and potentially rude speech or manner — see BLUNT 1

curtail *vb* **1** to make (as hair) shorter with or as if with the use of shears — see CLIP

2 to make less in extent or duration — see SHORTEN

curtain *n* **1** something that covers or conceals like a piece of cloth — see CLOAK 1

2 curtains *pl* pieces of cloth hung to darken, decorate, or divide a room — see DRAPERY

curtain *vb* to keep secret or shut off from view — see ¹HIDE 1

curvature *n* something that curves or is curved — see BEND 1

curve *n* something that curves or is curved — see BEND 1

curve *vb* **1** to turn away from a straight line or course ⟨after following a straight path most of the way down the mountain, the ski trail abruptly *curves* to the right⟩

syn arc, arch, bend, bow, crook, hook, round, sweep, swerve, wheel

rel circle, coil, curl, loop, spiral; turn, twist, wind; deviate, veer

ant straighten

2 to cause to turn away from a straight line — see BEND 1

curved *adj* marked by a long series of irregular curves — see CROOKED 1

curving *adj* marked by a long series of irregular curves — see CROOKED 1

cushion *n* something that serves as a protective barrier ⟨used a blanket as a *cushion* between the two tables in the moving van⟩

syn buffer, bumper, fender, pad

rel baffle, muffler; padding; safeguard, shield; barricade, cordon

cushion *vb* to lessen the shock of ⟨a substantial nest egg helped to *cushion* the sudden loss of her job⟩

syn buffer, gentle, soften

rel baffle, dampen, deaden, dull; moderate, modulate, temper; allay, alleviate, assuage, ease; lighten, mitigate, relieve

near ant heighten, intensify, sharpen

cushy *adj* providing physical comfort — see COMFORTABLE 1

cusp *n* the last and usually sharp or tapering part of something long and narrow — see POINT 2

cuss *n* a disrespectful or indecent word or expression — see SWEARWORD

cuss *vb* to use offensive or indecent language — see SWEAR 1

custodian *n* **1** a person who takes care of a property sometimes for an absent owner ⟨the *custodian* made his usual rounds of the building to make sure that everything was OK⟩

syn caretaker, guardian, janitor, keeper, warden, watchman

rel curator; sexton; steward

2 a person or group that watches over someone or something — see GUARD 1

3 someone that protects — see PROTECTOR

custody *n* responsibility for the safety and well-being of someone or something ⟨the divorcing parents will share *custody* of the children⟩

syn care, guardianship, keeping, safekeeping, trust, ward

rel control, governorship, management, superintendence, supervision

custom *adj* made or fitted to the needs or preferences of a specific customer — see CUSTOM-MADE

custom *n* **1** a usual manner of behaving or doing — see HABIT

2 an inherited or established way of thinking, feeling, or doing — see TRADITION 1

customary *adj* **1** accepted, used, or practiced by most people — see CURRENT 1

2 based on customs usually handed down from a previous generation — see TRADITIONAL 1

customer *n* **1** a person who buys a product or uses a service from a business ⟨the store greatly values its regular *customers*⟩

syn client, guest, patron

rel consumer, end user, user; buyer, purchaser; browser, prospect, shopper, window-shopper

near ant merchant, seller, vendor (*also* vender)

2 a member of the human race — see HUMAN

customized *adj* made or fitted to the needs or preferences of a specific customer — see CUSTOM-MADE

custom–made *adj* made or fitted to the needs or preferences of a specific customer ⟨an odd-sized window that will require the purchase of *custom-made* curtains⟩

syn custom, customized, tailored, tailor-made

rel particular, special, specialized; handcrafted, handmade

ant mass-produced, ready-made

cut *n* **1** a piece that has been separated from the whole by cutting ⟨choose *cuts* of meat that have very little visible fat⟩

syn cutting, slice

rel chop, cutlet; chunk, hunk, lump; clipping, paring, shaving, snippet; sliver, splinter

2 an individual part of a process, series, or ranking — see DEGREE 1

3 something belonging to, due to, or contributed by an individual member of a group — see SHARE 1

cut *vb* **1** to penetrate with a sharp edge (as a knife) ⟨I *cut* my hand on a piece of broken glass⟩

---

syn synonym(s) *rel* related words
ant antonym(s) *near ant* near antonym(s)

syn gash, incise, rip, slash, slice, slit

rel saw, scissor; cleave, rive, split; pierce, stab; bruise, hack, lacerate, mangle; rend, tear; butcher, carve, dissect; chop, dice, mince; amputate, cut off, sever

2 to fail to attend ⟨a warning that she had been *cutting* too many classes without valid excuses⟩

syn miss, skip

rel ignore, neglect, pass over

phrases absent oneself, play hooky

ant attend, show up (for)

3 to deliberately ignore or treat rudely — see SNUB 1

4 to make (as hair) shorter with or as if with the use of shears — see CLIP

5 to shorten the standing leafy plant cover of — see MOW 1

cut (across) *vb* to make one's way through, across, or over — see TRAVERSE

cut (down) *vb* to bring down by cutting — see FELL 2

cut (out) *vb* to bring (as an action or operation) to an immediate end — see STOP 1

cut back *vb* **1** to make (as hair) shorter with or as if with the use of shears — see CLIP

2 to make less in extent or duration — see SHORTEN

cute *adj* very pleasing to look at — see BEAUTIFUL

cuteness *n* the qualities in a person or thing that as a whole give pleasure to the senses — see BEAUTY 1

cut in *vb* to cause a disruption in a conversation or discussion — see INTERRUPT

cutlet *n* a small usually rounded mass of minced food that has been fried — see CAKE

cut off *vb* to set or keep apart from others — see ISOLATE

cut out *vb* to stop functioning — see FAIL 1

cut-rate *adj* **1** costing little — see CHEAP 1

2 of low quality — see CHEAP 2

cutter *n* an instrument with a sharp edge for cutting — see KNIFE

cutthroat *adj* not guided by or showing a concern for what is right — see UNPRINCIPLED

cutting *adj* **1** causing intense discomfort to one's skin ⟨a frigid day with a *cutting* wind that made it seem even colder⟩

syn biting, bitter, keen, penetrating, piercing, raw, sharp, smarting, stinging

rel brisk, invigorating, nippy, snappy; needlelike, prickly, tingling; caustic, corrosive

near ant balmy, gentle, mild, soothing

2 having an edge thin enough to cut or pierce something — see SHARP 1

3 marked by the use of wit that is intended to cause hurt feelings — see SARCASTIC

cutting *n* a piece that has been separated from the whole by cutting — see CUT 1

cut up *vb* to engage in attention-getting playful or boisterous behavior ⟨high-spirited cousins who *cut up* at every family gathering⟩

syn act up, clown (around), fool (around), horse (around), monkey (around), show off, skylark

rel carry on, misbehave; roughhouse; caper, cavort, disport, frisk, frolic, gambol, lark, rollick, romp; carouse, revel, wassail

cycle *n* **1** a series of events or actions that repeat themselves regularly and in the same order ⟨the *cycle* of birth, growth, decline, and death that is experienced by all life forms⟩

syn circle, round

rel pattern, syndrome; course, development, progression, run; circuit, loop, ring; rotation, revolution, turn; chain, sequence, series, string, succession, train

2 a long or seemingly long period of time — see AGE 2

cynic *n* a person who distrusts other people and believes that everything is done for selfish reasons ⟨a *cynic* who believes that nobody does a good deed without expecting something in return⟩

syn misanthrope, pessimist

rel misogynist; doubter, skeptic; belittler, derider, detractor, scoffer; malcontent; defeatist, quitter

near ant optimist; idealist; sentimentalist

cynical *adj* having or showing a deep distrust of human beings and their motives ⟨so *cynical* that he can't understand why anyone would volunteer to help out at a homeless shelter⟩

syn misanthropic, pessimistic

rel distrustful, mistrustful, skeptical, suspicious; derisive, mocking, sardonic, scornful; defeatist, fatalistic, negative; ironic (*or* ironical), sarcastic; jaded, sophisticated, worldly-wise; hard-bitten, hard-boiled, unsentimental

near ant trustful, trusting, unsuspicious; cheerful, optimistic, rose-colored; ingenuous, innocent, naive (*or* naïve), unsophisticated; idealistic, impractical, romantic; maudlin, mushy, saccharine, sappy, sentimental

cynosure *n* a thing or place that is of greatest importance to an activity or interest — see CENTER 1

czar *also* **tsar** *or* **tzar** *n* a person of rank, power, or influence in a particular field — see MAGNATE

¹dab *n* a quick thrust — see ¹POKE

²dab *n* a very small amount — see PARTICLE 1

dabbler *n* a person who regularly or occasionally engages in an activity without being or becoming an expert at it — see AMATEUR

dad *n* a male human parent — see FATHER 1

daddy *n* a male human parent — see FATHER 1

daffy *adj* **1** having or showing a very abnormal or sick state of mind — see INSANE 1

2 showing or marked by a lack of good sense or judgment — see FOOLISH 1

daft *adj* **1** having or showing a very abnormal or sick state of mind — see INSANE 1

2 showing or marked by a lack of good sense or judgment — see FOOLISH 1

daftness *n* lack of good sense or judgment — see FOOLISHNESS 1

daily *adj* occurring, done, produced, or appearing every day ⟨they made their *daily* stop at the coffee shop after work to relax before dinner⟩
syn day-to-day, diurnal
rel alternate, cyclical, intermittent, periodic, recurrent, recurring, regular; continuous, frequent, incessant
near ant nightly, nocturnal; monthly, weekly, yearly; erratic, infrequent, irregular; occasional, spasmodic, sporadic; interrupted

daintiness *n* the state or quality of having a delicate structure — see DELICACY 2

dainty *adj* **1** hard to please — see FINICKY

2 having qualities that appeal to a refined taste — see CHOICE

3 satisfying or pleasing because of fineness or mildness — see DELICATE 1

dainty *n* something that is pleasing to eat because it is rare or a luxury — see DELICACY 1

dais *n* a level usually raised surface — see PLATFORM

dale *n* an area of lowland between hills or mountains — see VALLEY

dalliance *n* activity engaged in to amuse oneself — see PLAY 1

dallier *n* someone who moves slowly or more slowly than others — see SLOWPOKE

dally *vb* **1** to engage in activity for amusement — see PLAY 1

2 to move or act slowly — see DELAY 1

3 to show a liking for someone of the opposite sex just for fun — see FLIRT

4 to spend time doing nothing — see IDLE

dallying *adj* moving or proceeding at less than the normal, desirable, or required speed — see SLOW 1

dam *n* a bank of earth constructed to control water ⟨the river backed up behind the *dam* until it formed a new lake⟩
syn dike, embankment, levee
rel breakwater, jetty, seawall; breastwork, bulwark, earthwork, rampart; canal, channel, ditch, gutter, trough; lock; barricade, barrier, block; floodgate, sluice

dam *vb* **1** to prevent passage through — see CLOG 1

2 to close up so that no empty spaces remain — see FILL 2

damage *n* **1** something that causes loss or pain — see INJURY 1

2 **damages** *pl* a sum of money to be paid as a punishment — see FINE

3 **damages** *pl* payment to another for a loss or injury — see COMPENSATION 1

damage *vb* **1** to reduce the soundness, effectiveness, or perfection of ⟨the explosion in the sewers *damaged* the entire city's water supply⟩
syn blemish, break, cripple, deface, disfigure, flaw, harm, hurt, impair, injure, mar, spoil, vitiate
rel enfeeble, undermine, weaken; erode, scour, wash out, wear (away); blight, tarnish; dent, dint; botch, gum (up); lacerate, wound; maim, mangle, mutilate, torment, torture; annihilate, crush, dash, decimate, demolish, destroy, devastate, pulverize, raze, ruin, scourge, shatter, smash, tear down, waste, wipe out, wreck
near ant cure, heal, help, rectify, remedy; edit, remodel, revise; ameliorate, better, enhance, improve, meliorate
ant fix, mend, patch, rebuild, recondition, reconstruct, renovate, repair, revamp

2 to cause bodily damage to — see INJURE 1

damaging *adj* causing or capable of causing harm — see HARMFUL

dame *n* **1** a dignified usually elderly woman of some rank or authority — see MATRIARCH

2 a woman of high birth or social position — see GENTLEWOMAN

damn *vb* **1** to declare to be morally wrong or evil — see CONDEMN 1

2 to impose a judicial punishment on — see SENTENCE

damp *adj* slightly or moderately wet — see MOIST

damp *vb* to reduce or weaken in strength or feeling — see DULL 1

---

syn synonym(s)   *rel* related words
ant antonym(s)   *near ant* near antonym(s)

dampen *vb* 1 to make or become slightly or moderately wet — see MOISTEN

2 to reduce or weaken in strength or feeling — see DULL 1

damper *n* a device on a musical instrument that deadens or softens its tone — see MUTE

dampness *n* the amount of water suspended in the air in tiny droplets — see MOISTURE

damsel *n* a young usually unmarried woman — see GIRL 1

dance *n* a social gathering for dancing ⟨who are you taking to the *dance* Saturday night?⟩

syn ball, cotillion, formal, hop, prom

rel blowout, celebration, event, festival, festivity, fete (*or* fête), gala, masquerade, mixer, party, reception, shindig, soiree (*or* soirée)

dance *vb* 1 to perform a series of usually rhythmic bodily movements to music ⟨she liked to *dance* to her favorite rock bands⟩

syn foot (it), hoof (it), step

rel prance, strut, trip; gavotte, jig, jitterbug, jive, mambo, polka, tango, tap-dance, waltz; tread

2 to make an irregular series of quick, sudden movements — see FLIT

dandle *vb* to treat with great or excessive care — see BABY

dandy *adj* of the very best kind — see EXCELLENT

dandy *n* 1 a man extremely interested in his clothing and personal appearance ⟨that *dandy* was willing to spend all day and hundreds of dollars just to get the perfect pair of shoes⟩

syn buck, dude, fop, gallant

rel coxcomb, popinjay; blade, cavalier; swell; clotheshorse

near ant slattern, slob, sloven, slut

2 something very good of its kind — see JIM-DANDY

danger *n* 1 the state of not being protected from injury, harm, or evil ⟨he knew he was in *danger* when he received the threatening phone calls at home⟩

syn distress, endangerment, imperilment, jeopardy, peril, risk, trouble

rel exposure, liability, vulnerability; precariousness, threat

near ant preservation, salvation; defense, protection; exemption, immunity, impunity

ant safeness, safety, security

2 something that may cause injury or harm ⟨she was willing to face the *dangers* of the construction site in order to get her Frisbee back⟩

syn hazard, menace, peril, pitfall, risk, threat, trouble

rel snare, trap

near ant guard, protection, safeguard, shield, ward

dangerous *adj* involving potential loss or injury ⟨the soldiers were commanded to go on a *dangerous* mission behind enemy lines⟩

syn grave, grievous, hazardous, jeopardizing, menacing, parlous, perilous, risky, serious, threatening, unhealthy, unsafe, venturesome

rel insecure, precarious, treacherous, uncertain; chance, haphazard, random; distressing, sickening, unpleasant; ugly, wicked; adverse, bad, baleful, baneful, deleterious, detrimental, evil, harmful, hurtful, ill, inimical, injurious, malignant, nasty, noxious, pernicious, pestilent; deadly, deathly, destructive, dire, fatal, fateful, fell, killer, lethal, mortal, murderous

near ant advantageous, beneficial, good

ant harmless, innocent, innocuous, safe

dangle *vb* to place on an elevated point without support from below — see HANG 1

dangling *adj* extending freely from a support from above — see DEPENDENT 1

dank *adj* slightly or moderately wet — see MOIST

dapper *adj* being strikingly neat and trim in style or appearance — see SMART 1

dapple *n* a small area that is different (as in color) from the main part — see SPOT 1

dapple *vb* to mark with small spots especially unevenly — see SPOT

dappled *also* **dapple** *adj* 1 marked with spots — see SPOTTED 1

2 having blotches of two or more colors — see PIED

dare *vb* 1 to invite (someone) to take part in a contest or to perform a feat — see CHALLENGE 2

2 to oppose (something hostile or dangerous) with firmness or courage — see FACE 2

daredevil *adj* 1 foolishly adventurous or bold — see FOOLHARDY 1

2 having or showing a lack of concern for the consequences of one's actions — see RECKLESS 1

daring *adj* inclined or willing to take risks — see BOLD 1

daring *n* strength of mind to carry on in spite of danger — see COURAGE

dark *adj* 1 being without light or without much light ⟨a *dark* alley that most people wisely avoided⟩

syn darkened, darkish, darkling, darksome, dim, dimmed, dusky, gloomy, murky, obscure, obscured, pitch-black, pitch-dark, somber (*or* sombre)

rel moonless, sunless; cloudy, dull, dulled, lackluster; shadowy, shady; gray (*also* grey), leaden, pale

near ant beaming, effulgent, glowing, lambent, radiant, shining; glossy, lustrous, shiny

ant bright, brightened, brilliant, illuminated, illumined, light, lighted (*or* lit), lucent, lucid, luminous

2 causing or marked by an atmosphere lacking in cheer — see GLOOMY 1

3 given to keeping one's activities hidden from public observation or knowledge — see SECRETIVE

4 having an often intentionally veiled or uncertain meaning — see OBSCURE 1

5 lacking in education or the knowledge gained from books — see IGNORANT 1

dark *n* 1 a time or place of little or no light ⟨I have a bad habit of running into tables in the *dark*⟩
syn blackness, darkness, dusk, gloaming, gloom, murk, night, semidarkness, shade, shadows, twilight, umbra
rel blackout, brownout; shadiness; dullness (*also* dulness), somberness; cloudiness, fogginess, haziness, mistiness, murkiness; dimness, faintness, gloominess, grayness, paleness
near ant moonlight, starlight, sunlight; effulgence, radiance, shine, sunshine; incandescence, luminescence, luminosity
ant blaze, brightness, brilliance, day, daylight, glare, glow, light, lightness

2 the time from sunset to sunrise when there is no visible sunlight — see NIGHT 1

darken *vb* 1 to take on a gloomy or forbidding look ⟨his face slowly *darkened* as we told him the sad news⟩
syn gloom, glower, lower (*also* lour)
rel frown, scowl; glare, stare; brood, mope, pout, sulk; anger, fume, rage, steam; intimidate, menace, threaten
ant brighten, cheer (up), lighten, perk (up)

2 to make dark, dim, or indistinct — see CLOUD 1

darkened *adj* being without light or without much light — see DARK 1

darkening *adj* causing or marked by an atmosphere lacking in cheer — see GLOOMY 1

darkish *adj* being without light or without much light — see DARK 1

darkling *adj* 1 being beyond one's powers to know, understand, or explain — see MYSTERIOUS 1

2 being without light or without much light — see DARK 1

3 having an often intentionally veiled or uncertain meaning — see OBSCURE 1

darkness *n* 1 a time or place of little or no light — see DARK 1

2 the quality or state of having a veiled or uncertain meaning — see OBSCURITY 1

3 the time from sunset to sunrise when there is no visible sunlight — see NIGHT 1

darksome *adj* being without light or without much light — see DARK 1

darling *adj* 1 granted special treatment or attention ⟨they poured gifts and affection on their *darling* child⟩
syn beloved, cherished, dear, favored, favorite, loved, pet, precious, special, sweet
rel admired, adored, appreciated, esteemed, relished, revered; prized, treasured; preferred
near ant despised, detested, disdained, disfavored, disliked, execrated, hated, loathed; abandoned, forgotten, ignored

2 having qualities that tend to make one loved — see LOVABLE

3 giving pleasure or contentment to the mind or senses — see PLEASANT

darling *n* 1 a person or thing that is preferred over others — see FAVORITE

2 a person with whom one is in love — see SWEETHEART

darn *vb* to close up with a series of interlacing stitches — see SEW

dart *n* an act or expression showing scorn and usually intended to hurt another's feelings — see INSULT

dart *vb* to make an irregular series of quick, sudden movements — see FLIT

dash *n* active strength of body or mind — see VIGOR 1

dash *vb* 1 to go at a pace faster than a walk — see RUN 1

2 to proceed or move quickly — see HURRY 2

3 to send through the air especially with a quick forward motion of the arm — see THROW

4 to wet or soil by striking with something liquid or mushy — see SPLASH 2

dashing *adj* inclined or willing to take risks — see BOLD 1

dashingly *adv* 1 in a bright and showy way — see GAILY 3

2 in a strikingly neat and trim manner — see SMARTLY

dastard *n* a person who shows a shameful lack of courage in the face of danger — see COWARD

dastardliness *n* a shameful lack of courage in the face of danger — see COWARDICE

dastardly *adj* having or showing a shameful lack of courage — see COWARDLY

date *n* 1 an agreement to be present at a specified time and place — see ENGAGEMENT 2

2 the period during which something exists, lasts, or is in progress — see DURATION 1

date *vb* 1 to go on a social engagement with ⟨I don't want to *date* him—I'd rather just be friends⟩
syn take out
rel accompany, escort, see; court, woo

2 to go on dates that may eventually lead to marriage — see COURT 2

dated *adj* having passed its time of use or usefulness — see OBSOLETE

dateless *adj* 1 dating or surviving from the distant past — see ANCIENT 1

2 lasting forever — see EVERLASTING

dating *n* the series of social engagements shared by a couple looking to get married — see COURTSHIP

datum *n* a single piece of information — see FACT 3

daub *vb* to rub an oily or sticky substance over — see SMEAR 1

daunt *vb* to lessen the courage or confidence of — see DISCOURAGE 1

dauntless *adj* feeling or displaying no fear by temperament — see BRAVE

---

dauntlessness *n* strength of mind to carry on in spite of danger — see COURAGE

davenport *n* a long upholstered piece of furniture designed for several sitters — see COUCH

dawdle *vb* 1 to move or act slowly — see DELAY 1

2 to spend time doing nothing — see IDLE

dawdler *n* someone who moves slowly or more slowly than others — see SLOWPOKE

dawdling *adj* moving or proceeding at less than the normal, desirable, or required speed — see SLOW 1

dawn *n* 1 the first appearance of light in the morning or the time of its appearance ⟨we stayed up talking until *dawn*⟩
syn aurora, cockcrow, dawning, daybreak, daylight, morn, morning, sunrise, sunup
rel day, daytime, light; twilight; forenoon
near ant dark, darkness, night, nighttime; afternoon, dusk, evening, gloaming
ant nightfall, sundown, sunset

2 the point at which something begins — see BEGINNING

dawn *vb* to come into existence — see BEGIN 2

dawn (on) *vb* to come into the mind of — see OCCUR (TO)

dawning *n* the first appearance of light in the morning or the time of its appearance — see DAWN 1

day *n* 1 the hours of light between one night and the next ⟨during the *day*, we like to go play ball in the park⟩
syn daylight, daytime
rel light, sunlight, sunshine; dawn, dawning, daybreak, morn, morning, sunrise, sunset; dusk, evening, gloaming, nightfall, sundown, twilight
near ant dark, darkness
ant night, nighttime

2 an extent of time associated with a particular person or thing — see AGE 1

daybreak *n* the first appearance of light in the morning or the time of its appearance — see DAWN 1

daydream *n* a conception or image created by the imagination and having no objective reality — see FANTASY 1

daydreaming *n* the state of being lost in thought — see REVERIE

daylight *n* 1 the first appearance of light in the morning or the time of its appearance — see DAWN 1

2 the hours of light between one night and the next — see DAY 1

daytime *n* the hours of light between one night and the next — see DAY 1

day-to-day *adj* occurring, done, produced, or appearing every day — see DAILY

daze *n* a state of mental confusion — see HAZE 2

daze *vb* 1 to make senseless or dizzy by a blow — see STUN 1

2 to overpower with light — see DAZZLE

dazed *adj* suffering from mental confusion — see DIZZY 2

dazzle *n* the quality or state of having or giving off light — see BRILLIANCE 1

dazzle *vb* to overpower with light ⟨skiers were *dazzled* by the glare off of the slopes of freshly packed snow⟩
syn bedazzle, blind, daze
rel confuse, overpower, overwhelm, stun

dazzling *adj* giving off or reflecting much light — see BRIGHT 1

deacon *n* a person specially trained and authorized to conduct religious services in a Christian church — see CLERGYMAN

dead *adj* 1 no longer living ⟨I inherited this heirloom from my *dead* great-grandfather⟩
syn breathless, deceased, defunct, departed, fallen, gone, late, lifeless
rel extinct; dying, fading, moribund; stillborn; finished, lapsed, terminated; barren, desert; inanimate, insensate, nonliving, unanimated
phrases bitten the dust, passed away, passed on
near ant animate, animated; dynamic, lively, thriving, vibrant, vital, vivacious; active, functioning, operative, running
ant alive, breathing, going, living

2 depleted in strength, energy, or freshness — see WEARY 1

3 having no exceptions or restrictions — see ABSOLUTE 2

4 lacking in sensation or feeling — see NUMB

5 no longer existing — see EXTINCT

6 not being in a state of use, activity, or employment — see INACTIVE 2

7 of, relating to, or suggestive of death — see DEATHLY 1

dead *adv* 1 in a direct line or course — see DIRECTLY 1

2 to a full extent or degree — see FULLY 1

deaden *vb* to reduce or weaken in strength or feeling — see DULL 1

dead heat *n* a situation in which neither participant in a contest, competition, or struggle comes out ahead of the other — see TIE 1

deadlock *n* a point in a struggle where neither side is capable of winning or willing to give in — see IMPASSE

deadly *adj* likely to cause or capable of causing death ⟨the doctors were alarmed about the outbreak of the *deadly* new virus⟩
syn baleful, deathly, fatal, fell, killer, lethal, mortal, murderous, pestilent, vital
rel baneful, destructive, harmful, noxious, pernicious; poisonous, toxic, virulent; dangerous, grave, grievous, hazardous, jeopardizing, menacing, parlous, perilous, risky, serious, threatening, ugly, unhealthy, unsound; capital; bloody, internecine, sanguinary, sanguine
near ant beneficial, restorative; nonpoisonous, nontoxic, safe
ant healthful, healthy, nonfatal, nonlethal, wholesome

deadly *adv* to a great degree — see VERY 1

deadness *n* the state of being dead — see DEATH 2

deadpan *adj* not expressing any emotion — see BLANK 1

deadwood *n* discarded or useless material — see GARBAGE

deafening *adj* marked by a high volume of sound — see LOUD 1

¹deal *n* a considerable amount — see LOT 2

²deal *n* **1** an arrangement about action to be taken — see AGREEMENT 1

2 the transfer of ownership of something from one person to another for a price — see SALE

deal *vb* **1** to carry on the business of buying and selling goods or other property — see TRADE 1

2 to talk over or dispute the terms of a purchase — see BARGAIN

deal (in) *vb* to offer for sale to the public — see MARKET

deal (out) *vb* to give out (something) in appropriate amounts or to appropriate individuals — see ADMINISTER 1

deal (with) *vb* **1** to behave toward in a stated way — see TREAT 1

2 to have (something) as a subject matter — see CONCERN 1

dealer *n* **1** a buyer and seller of goods for profit — see MERCHANT

2 the person in a business deal who hands over an item in exchange for money — see VENDOR

dealings *n pl* doings between individuals or groups — see RELATION 1

dean *n* the senior member of a group ⟨the *dean* of the Aspen ski instructors oversaw the training of the rescue team⟩

syn elder, elder statesman, senior

rel better, superior

near ant inferior, subordinate, underling; beginner, freshman, newcomer, rookie

ant baby

dear *adj* **1** commanding a large price — see COSTLY

2 granted special treatment or attention — see DARLING 1

3 having qualities that tend to make one loved — see LOVABLE

dear *n* a person with whom one is in love — see SWEETHEART

dearth *n* **1** a falling short of an essential or desirable amount or number — see DEFICIENCY

2 the fact or state of being absent — see LACK 1

death *n* **1** the permanent stopping of all the vital bodily activities ⟨we were all saddened by the *death* of our teacher⟩

syn decease, demise, doom, end, passing, quietus

rel casualty, fatality; martyrdom, self-destruction, suicide; annihilation, destruction, ending, expiration, extermination, ruin

near ant existence, life; creation

---

ant birth

2 the state of being dead ⟨*death* is one of the few constants in the universe⟩

syn deadness, lifelessness, sleep

ant existence, life

3 the act of ceasing to exist ⟨the *death* of the Soviet economic system in the wake of the breakup of the USSR⟩

syn demise, expiration, termination

rel dispersion, dissolution; shutdown; decease, doom, end, ending, passing, quietus; suicide; annihilation, destruction, ruin

near ant existence

ant beginning, creation, start

deathless *adj* lasting forever — see EVERLASTING

deathlike *adj* of, relating to, or suggestive of death — see DEATHLY 1

deathly *adj* **1** of, relating to, or suggestive of death ⟨his *deathly* pallor suggested that any attempt to find a pulse would be futile⟩

syn dead, deathlike, mortal

rel ghostly, phantom, spectral; inactive, inert, inoperative, lifeless, quiescent, still; macabre; baleful, fatal, fateful, fell, killer, lethal, murderous, pestilent

near ant active, alive, living; animated, energetic, lively, vigorous, vivacious; hale, healthy, hearty, robust, sound

2 likely to cause or capable of causing death — see DEADLY

debacle *also* **débâcle** *n* **1** a sudden violent event that brings about great loss or destruction — see DISASTER

2 something that has failed — see FAILURE 3

debar *vb* to prevent the participation or inclusion of — see EXCLUDE

debark *vb* to go ashore from a ship — see DISEMBARK

debase *vb* to lower in character or dignity ⟨we *debased* ourselves when we cheated on the test⟩

syn abase, corrupt, debauch, degrade, demean, deprave, pervert, poison, profane, prostitute, subvert, warp

rel contaminate, pollute, taint; descend; disgrace, humble, humiliate; blemish, damage, deface, destroy, flaw, harm, hurt, impair, mar, ruin, spoil, stain, tarnish, vitiate, wreck; depreciate, downgrade

near ant dignify, exalt, honor; amend, improve; cleanse, purify, restore; respect

ant elevate, ennoble, uplift

2 to reduce to a lower standing in one's own eyes or in others' eyes — see HUMBLE

debased *adj* having or showing lowered moral character or standards — see CORRUPT

debasement *n* a sinking to a state of low moral standards and behavior — see CORRUPTION 2

debatable *adj* **1** open to question or dispute ⟨it's always *debatable* which college football team is really number one, since there's more than one ranking system⟩

syn disputable, doubtable, doubtful, moot, questionable

rel refutable; controversial, debated, disputed; dubious, inconclusive, indecisive, problematic (*also* problematical), uncertain; academic, hypothetical, speculative, theoretical (*also* theoretic); ambiguous, equivocal

near ant irrefutable; certain, definite, positive, sure; unambiguous, unequivocal; absolute, clear, conclusive, decisive; uncontested, undisputed

ant incontestable, incontrovertible, indisputable, indubitable, undeniable, unquestionable

2 giving good reason for being doubted, questioned, or challenged — see DOUBTFUL 2

debate *n* **1** a careful weighing of the reasons for or against something — see CONSIDERATION 1

2 variance of opinion on a matter — see DISAGREEMENT 1

debate *vb* **1** to give serious and careful thought to — see PONDER

2 to talk about (an issue) usually from various points of view and for the purpose of arriving at a decision or opinion — see DISCUSS

debater *n* a person who takes part in a dispute — see DISPUTANT

debauch *vb* to lower in character or dignity — see DEBASE 1

debauched *adj* having or showing lowered moral character or standards — see CORRUPT

debaucher *n* a person who has sunk below the normal moral standard — see DEGENERATE

debauchery *n* **1** immoral conduct or practices harmful or offensive to society — see VICE 1

2 a sinking to a state of low moral standards and behavior — see CORRUPTION 2

debilitate *vb* to diminish the physical strength of — see WEAKEN 1

debilitated *adj* lacking bodily strength — see WEAK 1

debilitation *n* **1** a gradual sinking and wasting away of mind or body — see DECLINE 1

2 the quality or state of lacking physical strength or vigor — see WEAKNESS 1

debility *n* the quality or state of lacking physical strength or vigor — see WEAKNESS 1

debonair *adj* having or showing very polished and worldly manners — see SUAVE

debris *n* the portion or bits of something left over or behind after it has been destroyed — see REMAINS 1

debt *n* a breaking of a moral or legal code — see OFFENSE 1

debug *vb* to remove errors, defects, deficiencies, or deviations from — see CORRECT 1

debunk *vb* to reveal the true nature of — see EXPOSE 1

decadence *n* **1** a change to a lower state or level — see DECLINE 2

2 a sinking to a state of low moral standards and behavior — see CORRUPTION 2

decadent *adj* **1** having lost forcefulness, courage, or spirit — see EFFETE 1

2 having or showing lowered moral character or standards — see CORRUPT

decadent *n* a person who has sunk below the normal moral standard — see DEGENERATE

decalogue *n* a collection or system of rules of conduct — see CODE

decamping *n* the act of leaving a place — see DEPARTURE

decampment *n* the act of leaving a place — see DEPARTURE

decapitate *vb* to cut off the head of ⟨he started *decapitating* wildflowers with his walking stick as they strolled through the park⟩

syn behead, guillotine

rel prune, shorten, trim; scalp

decay *n* **1** a gradual sinking and wasting away of mind or body — see DECLINE 1

2 the process by which dead organic matter separates into simpler substances — see CORRUPTION 1

decay *vb* **1** to go through decomposition ⟨the logs *decayed* on the rain forest floor⟩ ⟨the atom of plutonium *decayed* in the test chamber⟩

syn break down, corrupt, decompose, disintegrate, molder, putrefy, rot, spoil

rel sour, turn; contaminate, defile, pollute, taint; curdle, ferment; crumble, degenerate, deteriorate

phrases go to seed, run to seed

near ant develop, grow, mature, ripen; refresh, renew, restore; cleanse, purify; assemble, compose, integrate

2 to become worse or of less value — see DETERIORATE

3 to lose bodily strength or vigor — see WEAKEN 2

decayed *adj* **1** having lost forcefulness, courage, or spirit — see EFFETE 1

2 having undergone organic breakdown — see ROTTEN 1

decaying *n* a gradual sinking and wasting away of mind or body — see DECLINE 1

decease *n* the permanent stopping of all the vital bodily activities — see DEATH 1

decease *vb* to stop living — see DIE 1

deceased *adj* no longer living — see DEAD 1

deceit *n* the inclination or practice of misleading others through lies or trickery ⟨the evil queen in the story was full of *deceit*⟩

syn artifice, craft, craftiness, crookedness, cunning, deceitfulness, dishonesty, dissembling, dissimulation, double-dealing, duplicity, fakery, foxiness, guile, wiliness

rel equivocation, prevarication; chicanery, skulduggery (*or* skullduggery), subterfuge, trickery; hypocrisy, insincerity; deviousness, shrewdness; treacherousness, underhandedness, unscrupulousness; covertness, furtiveness, secrecy, shadiness, sneakiness, stealthiness; oiliness, shiftiness, slickness, slipperiness, slyness, smoothness

near ant candidness, candor, directness, frankness, ingenuousness, openness, plainness; honesty; probity; reliability, trustworthiness

ant artlessness, forthrightness, good faith, guilelessness, sincerity

deceitful *adj* **1** marked by, based on, or done by the use of dishonest methods to acquire something of value — see FRAUDULENT 1

2 tending or having power to deceive — see DECEPTIVE 1

deceitfulness *n* **1** the inclination or practice of misleading others through lies or trickery — see DECEIT

2 the tendency to tell lies — see DISHONESTY 1

deceive *vb* to cause to believe what is untrue ⟨he went to great lengths to *deceive* his younger brother about the nature of his new job at the mall⟩

syn beguile, bluff, cozen, delude, dupe, fool, gull, have, hoax, hoodwink, humbug, misguide, misinform, mislead, snow, string along, take in, trick

rel cheat, chisel, defraud, fleece, gyp, hustle, rook, swindle

near ant debunk, expose, reveal, show up, uncloak, uncover, unmask; disclose, divulge, tell, unveil; disabuse, disenchant, disillusion; edify, enlighten

ant undeceive

deceiving *adj* tending or having power to deceive — see DECEPTIVE 1

decelerate *vb* to cause to move or proceed at a less rapid pace — see SLOW 1

deceleration *n* a usually gradual decrease in the pace or level of activity of something — see SLOWDOWN

decency *n* **1** socially acceptable behavior ⟨the standards of basic *decency* demanded that they help the old lady with her groceries⟩

syn decorum, form, propriety

rel civility, courtesy, politeness; dignity, grace, refinement; discretion, prudence; correctness, decorousness, fitness, rightness, seemliness; attention, attentiveness, care, carefulness; goodness, high-mindedness, honesty, morality, probity, rectitude, righteousness, straightness, uprightness, virtue, virtuousness

near ant coarseness, crudeness, gracelessness; discourtesy, impoliteness, incivility; imprudence, indiscretion; badness, evil, immorality, wickedness

ant impropriety, indecency, indecorum

2 conduct that conforms to an accepted standard of right and wrong — see MORALITY 1

decent *adj* **1** conforming to a high standard of morality or virtue — see GOOD 2

2 following the accepted rules of moral conduct — see HONORABLE 1

3 following the established traditions of refined society and good taste — see PROPER 1

4 free from any trace of the coarse or indecent — see CHASTE

5 of a level of quality that meets one's needs or standards — see ADEQUATE

deceptive *adj* **1** tending or having power to deceive ⟨in his *deceptive* answer about the vehicle's history, the salesman said that the used car had never been hit by another car⟩

syn beguiling, deceitful, deceiving, deluding, delusive, delusory, fallacious, false, misleading, specious

rel devious, guileful, shady, shifty, sly, sneaking, sneaky, trick, tricky, underhand, underhanded; inaccurate, incorrect, wrong; bewildering, confounding, distracting, perplexing, puzzling; crooked, dishonest, double-dealing, faithless, fast, fraudulent, knavish, lying, mendacious, untrustworthy, untruthful; insidious, perfidious, treacherous; artificial, backhanded, feigned, hypocritical, insincere, left-handed, two-faced

near ant candid, frank, open, plain; clarifying, elucidative, explanatory, illuminating; revealing, revelatory; honest, trustworthy, truthful

ant aboveboard, forthright, straightforward

2 given to or marked by cheating and deception — see DISHONEST 2

decide *vb* **1** to come to a judgment after discussion or consideration ⟨they *decided* to go out for pizza after the movie was over⟩

syn choose, conclude, determine, figure, opt, resolve

rel decree, rule; cull, elect, handpick, pick, prefer, select, single (out), take

phrases make up one's mind

near ant abstain, decline, refuse, reject, turn down; delay, hesitate, stall, temporize; shilly-shally, vacillate, waver

2 to give an opinion about (something at issue or in dispute) — see JUDGE 1

3 to come to an agreement or decision concerning the details of — see ARRANGE 1

4 to make final, definite, or beyond dispute — see CLINCH

decided *adj* not subject to misinterpretation or more than one interpretation — see CLEAR 2

decidedness *n* firm or unwavering adherence to one's purpose — see DETERMINATION 1

decimate *vb* to bring to a complete end the physical soundness, existence, or usefulness of — see DESTROY 1

decimation *n* the state or fact of being rendered nonexistent, physically unsound, or useless — see DESTRUCTION

decipher *vb* to change (as a secret message) from code into ordinary language — see DECODE

decision *n* **1** a position arrived at after consideration ⟨after much deliberation,

---

syn synonym(s)   *rel* related words
ant antonym(s)   *near ant* near antonym(s)

we made a *decision* about what to have on our pizza⟩

syn conclusion, deliverance, determination, diagnosis, judgment (*or* judgement), opinion, resolution, verdict

rel decree, mandate, order; say-so; doom, finding, ruling, sentence; choice, option, selection

near ant deadlock, draw, stalemate, stand-off, tie

2 firm or unwavering adherence to one's purpose — see DETERMINATION 1

decisive *adj* **1** fully committed to achieving a goal — see DETERMINED 1

2 having the power to persuade — see COGENT

3 serving to put an end to all debate or questioning — see CONCLUSIVE 1

decisiveness *n* firm or unwavering adherence to one's purpose — see DETERMINATION 1

deck *vb* **1** to make more attractive by adding something that is beautiful or becoming — see DECORATE

2 to outfit with clothes and especially fine or special clothes — see CLOTHE 1

declaim *vb* **1** to give a formal often extended talk on a subject — see TALK 1

2 to talk as if giving an important and formal speech — see ORATE 1

declamation *n* a usually formal discourse delivered to an audience — see SPEECH 1

declaration *n* a solemn and often public declaration of the truth or existence of something — see PROTESTATION

declare *vb* **1** to make known openly or publicly — see ANNOUNCE

2 to state as a fact usually forcefully — see CLAIM 1

3 to state clearly and strongly — see ASSERT 1

declension *n* **1** a gradual sinking and wasting away of mind or body — see DECLINE 1

2 a change to a lower state or level — see DECLINE 2

decline *n* **1** a gradual sinking and wasting away of mind or body ⟨her sad *decline* from a robust athlete to an old woman with arthritis⟩

syn debilitation, decay, decaying, declension, degeneration, descent, deterioration, ebbing, enfeeblement, weakening

rel atrophy; exhaustion; drooping, flagging, limping; relapse, setback

near ant invigoration, strengthening; progress

ant improvement, recovery, revitalization

2 a change to a lower state or level ⟨the *decline* of the Roman Empire⟩

syn decadence, declension, degeneracy, degeneration, degradation, descent, deterioration, downfall, downgrade, fall

rel decay, rotting, spoiling; breakup, crumbling, decomposition, disintegration, dissolution; abasement, debasement; depreciation, lessening; decimation, demolishment, demolition, desolation, destruction, havoc, ruin, ruination; abatement, decrease, decrement, de-escalation,

deflation, diminishment, diminution, dip, drop, fall, loss, lowering, reduction, sag, shrinkage

near ant advancement, development, evolution, growth; blossoming, flourishing, flowering; renewal, restoration, revitalization; heightening; accretion, accrual, addendum, addition, augmentation, boost, enhancement, gain, increase, increment, raise, supplement

ant ascent, rise, upswing

3 a loss of status — see COMEDOWN

4 the amount by which something is lessened — see DECREASE

decline *vb* **1** to show unwillingness to accept, do, engage in, or agree to ⟨he *declined* the invitation to the party⟩ ⟨she *declined* to participate in the soccer game⟩

syn disapprove, negative, refuse, reject, repudiate, spurn, turn down

rel overrule, veto; forbid, prohibit, proscribe; dismiss; abstain, forbear, refrain; deny, dispute, gainsay; balk, stick; abjure, renounce; avoid, bypass, detour

near ant condone, countenance, swallow, tolerate; adopt, embrace, receive, take; accede, acquiesce, agree, assent, consent; choose, select; espouse, support

ant accept, agree (to), approve

2 to be unwilling to grant — see DENY 1

3 to go to a lower level — see DROP 2

4 to become worse or of less value — see DETERIORATE

5 to grow less in scope or intensity especially gradually — see DECREASE 2

6 to lead or extend downward — see DESCEND 1

declined *adj* bending downward or forward — see NODDING

declining *adj* bending downward or forward — see NODDING

decode *vb* to change (as a secret message) from code into ordinary language ⟨the agents worked into the night to *decode* the transmission from the enemy spy⟩

syn break, crack, decipher

rel render, translate; dope (out), figure out, puzzle (out), solve, unravel, work, work out

ant cipher, code, encode

decolorize *vb* to make white or whiter by removing color — see WHITEN

decompose *vb* to go through decomposition — see DECAY 1

decomposed *adj* having undergone organic breakdown — see ROTTEN 1

decomposition *n* the process by which dead organic matter separates into simpler substances — see CORRUPTION 1

decorate *vb* to make more attractive by adding something that is beautiful or becoming ⟨they *decorated* the hallway with paintings and tapestries⟩

syn adorn, array, beautify, bedeck, bedizen, deck, do, dress, embellish, enrich, garnish, grace, ornament, trim

rel doll up, dress up, trick (out); brighten, freshen, smarten, spruce (up); boss, chase, emboss; embroider, figure, flounce, fringe, garland, hang, lace, wreathe; gild, paint; redecorate, redo

near ant simplify, streamline; bare, denude, dismantle, display, divest, expose, reveal, strip, uncover

ant blemish, deface, disfigure, mar, scar, spoil

decoration *n* **1** something that decorates or beautifies ⟨they put lots of *decorations* on and around the Christmas tree⟩

syn adornment, caparison, embellishment, frill, garnish, ornament, trim

rel finery, frippery; flounce, flourish, furbelow, ruffle; enhancement, enrichment, improvement; embossment, embroidery, fancywork; gilt, glitter; design, figure, pattern; furnishings, regalia, trappings

near ant blemish, defacement, disfigurement, scar; blot, spot, stain

2 something given in recognition of achievement — see AWARD

decorative *adj* serving to add beauty ⟨they planted *decorative* flowers all along the path to the cottage⟩

syn adorning, beautifying, embellishing, ornamental

rel alluring, appealing, attractive, charming, delightful, glamorous (*also* glamourous), pleasing, prepossessing; beauteous, beautiful, bonny, comely, fair, gorgeous, handsome, lovely, pretty, stunning; detailed, elaborate, fancy, ornate

ant functional, utilitarian

decorous *adj* **1** following the established traditions of refined society and good taste — see PROPER 1

2 marked by or showing careful attention to set forms and details — see CEREMONIOUS 1

decorum *n* socially acceptable behavior — see DECENCY 1

decoy *n* something used to attract animals to a hook or into a trap — see BAIT 1

decoy *vb* to lead away from a usual or proper course by offering some pleasure or advantage — see LURE

decrease *n* the amount by which something is lessened ⟨the average *decrease* in the price of milk was five cents per gallon⟩

syn abatement, decline, decrement, diminishment, diminution, drop, fall, loss, reduction, shrinkage

rel deduction, dent, depression; slip, slump; curtailment, cut, cutback

near ant accretion, accrual, accumulation, addition, supplement; continuation, extension; upswing, uptrend, upturn

ant boost, enlargement, gain, increase, increment, raise, rise

decrease *vb* **1** to make smaller in amount, volume, or extent ⟨they *decreased* the amount of water flowing through the pipes in order to prevent an overflow⟩

syn abate, de-escalate, diminish, downsize, dwindle, lessen, lower, reduce

rel compress, condense, constrict, contract; abbreviate, abridge, clip, crop, curtail, cut, cut back, cut down, dock, pare, prune, retrench, shorten, slash, trim, truncate, whittle; deflate, shrink; moderate, modify, modulate, qualify

near ant blow up, dilate, distend, inflate, swell; elongate, extend, lengthen, prolong, protract; add (to), complement, supplement; enhance, heighten, intensify

ant aggrandize, amplify, augment, boost, enlarge, escalate, expand, increase, raise

2 to grow less in scope or intensity especially gradually ⟨the force of the wind slowly *decreased* until the flowers were standing upright again⟩

syn abate, decline, de-escalate, die (down), diminish, dwindle, ebb, fall, lessen, let up, lower, moderate, recede, relent, remit, shrink, subside, taper, taper off, wane

rel compress, condense, constrict, contract; evaporate, fade (away), give out, melt (away), peter (out), vanish; slacken, slow (down); alleviate, ease, relax; flag, sink, weaken; cave (in), collapse, deflate, give out

near ant appear, emerge, show up; blow up, distend, elongate, lengthen

ant accumulate, balloon, build, burgeon, enlarge, escalate, expand, grow, increase, intensify, mount, mushroom, pick up, rise, snowball, soar, swell, wax

decree *n* **1** a statement of what to do that must be obeyed by those concerned — see COMMAND 1

2 an order publicly issued by an authority — see EDICT 1

decree *vb* to give an order — see COMMAND 2

decrement *n* the amount by which something is lessened — see DECREASE

decry *vb* **1** to express scornfully one's low opinion of ⟨scientists were quick to *decry* the claims of the psychic⟩

syn bad-mouth, belittle, cry down, deprecate, depreciate, diminish, discount, disparage, minimize, put down, write off

rel abuse, scold; disapprove (of), dislike; censure, condemn, criticize, denounce, reprehend, reprobate; asperse, defame, malign, slander, traduce, vilify; discredit, disgrace

near ant approve, countenance, endorse (*also* indorse), favor, recommend, sanction; commend, compliment, eulogize

ant acclaim, applaud, exalt, extol (*also* extoll), glorify, laud, magnify, praise

2 to declare to be morally wrong or evil — see CONDEMN 1

decrying *adj* intended to make a person or thing seem of little importance or value — see DEROGATORY

dedicate *vb* to keep or intend for a special purpose — see DEVOTE 1

dedication *n* adherence to something to which one is bound by a pledge or duty — see FIDELITY

deduce *vb* to form an opinion through reasoning and information — see INFER 1

deducible *adj* being or provable by reasoning in which the conclusion follows necessarily from given information — see DEDUCTIVE

deduct *vb* to take away (an amount or number) from a total — see SUBTRACT

deduction *n* 1 something that is or may be subtracted ⟨contestants get a *deduction* from their scores for every incorrect guess⟩

syn abatement, discount, reduction

rel kickback, rebate; dent, depreciation; decline, decrement, diminishment, diminution, drop, fall, loss; forfeit, forfeiture, penalty

near ant accretion, accrual, augmentation, boost, gain, increase, increment, raise, rise; appreciation

ant accession, addition

2 the act or an instance of taking away from a total — see SUBTRACTION

3 an opinion arrived at through a process of reasoning — see CONCLUSION 1

deductive *adj* being or provable by reasoning in which the conclusion follows necessarily from given information ⟨using *deductive* reasoning we must conclude that since everyone eventually dies, sooner or later it's going to be our turn⟩

syn deducible, derivable, inferable, reasoned

rel conjectural, hypothetical, purported, supposed, suppositional; academic, speculative, theoretical (*also* theoretic); logical, rational ·

near ant inducible, inductive; absolute, categorical (*also* categoric), definite, explicit, express; instinctive, intuitive; illogical, irrational

deed *n* 1 an act of notable skill, strength, or cleverness — see FEAT 1

2 something done by someone — see ACTION 1

deed *vb* to give over the legal possession or ownership of — see TRANSFER 1

deem *vb* to have as an opinion — see BELIEVE 1

deep *adj* 1 extending far downward or inward ⟨they dropped their bucket down a *deep* well⟩ ⟨the knife made a *deep* cut into the wood⟩

syn abysmal, bottomless

rel abyssal, unfathomable; boundless, endless, immeasurable, inestimable, infinite, limitless, measureless, unlimited, vast

near ant depthless, two-dimensional; even, flat, flush, horizontal, level, plane, smooth; confined, finite, limited, measured, restricted

ant shallow, shoal, skin-deep, superficial, surface

2 having a low musical pitch or range ⟨the tour guide had a very *deep* voice⟩

syn bass, low, throaty

rel gruff, hoarse, husky, rough

near ant squeaking, squeaky, squealing, thin; earsplitting, penetrating, piercing, strident; peeping, tinny

ant acute, high, high-pitched, piping, sharp, shrill, treble

3 being beyond one's powers to know, understand, or explain — see MYSTERIOUS 1

4 difficult for one of ordinary knowledge or intelligence to understand — see PROFOUND 1

5 having an often intentionally veiled or uncertain meaning — see OBSCURE 1

6 extreme in degree, power, or effect — see INTENSE

deep *n* 1 the most intense or characteristic phase of something — see THICK

2 the whole body of salt water that covers nearly three-fourths of the earth — see OCEAN

deepen *vb* to make markedly greater in measure or degree — see INTENSIFY

deep–rooted *adj* firmly established over time — see INVETERATE 1

deep–seated *adj* firmly established over time — see INVETERATE 1

de–escalate *vb* 1 to make smaller in amount, volume, or extent — see DECREASE 1

2 to grow less in scope or intensity especially gradually — see DECREASE 2

deface *vb* 1 to deliberately cause the damage or destruction of another's property — see VANDALIZE 1

2 to reduce the soundness, effectiveness, or perfection of — see DAMAGE 1

defacement *n* deliberate damaging or destroying of another's property — see VANDALISM

defacer *n* a person who damages or destroys property on purpose — see VANDAL

defamation *n* the making of false statements that damage another's reputation — see SLANDER

defamatory *adj* causing or intended to cause unjust injury to a person's good name — see LIBELOUS

defame *vb* to make untrue and harmful statements about — see SLANDER

defaming *n* the making of false statements that damage another's reputation — see SLANDER

default *n* the nonperformance of an assigned or expected action — see FAILURE 1

defeat *n* 1 failure to win a contest ⟨sore losers griping about their *defeat* in the basketball game earlier that week⟩

syn beating, drubbing, licking, loss, overthrow, rout, shellacking, trimming, trouncing, whipping

rel collapse, debacle (*also* débâcle), failure, fizzle, flop, nonsuccess, setback, upset, washout; lurch, shutout

near ant accomplishment, achievement; landslide, sweep

ant success, triumph, victory, win

2 a falling short of one's goals — see FAILURE 2

defeat *vb* to achieve a victory over — see BEAT 2

defeatist *adj* emphasizing or expecting the worst — see PESSIMISTIC 1

defeatist *n* one who emphasizes bad aspects or conditions and expects the worst — see PESSIMIST 1

defect *n* something that spoils the appearance or completeness of a thing — see BLEMISH

defect (from) *vb* to leave (a cause or party) often in order to take up another ⟨many soldiers *defected from* the rebel army as soon as they realized the uprising was hopeless⟩

syn desert, rat (on)

rel abandon, abdicate, abjure, cut off, disown, forsake, quit, reject, renounce, repudiate, spurn; renege; depart, go, leave, withdraw

phrases go back on, walk out on

near ant adhere (to), cling (to), stick (to *or* with); cherish, cultivate, foster

defective *adj* having a fault — see FAULTY

defector *n* a person who abandons a cause or organization usually without right — see RENEGADE

defend *vb* **1** to drive danger or attack away from ⟨a solemn oath to *defend* the country at any cost⟩

syn cover, guard, protect, safeguard, screen, secure, shield, ward

rel avert, prevent; fend (off), oppose, resist, withstand; battle, contend, fight, war; conserve, keep, preserve, save; buffer, palisade, picket, wall

phrases look out for, stand up for

near ant bombard, storm; beset, besiege, overrun; capitulate, cave, submit, yield

ant assail, assault, attack

2 to continue to declare to be true or proper despite opposition or objections — see MAINTAIN 2

defendable *adj* capable of being defended with good reasoning against verbal attack — see TENABLE 2

defender *n* someone that protects — see PROTECTOR

defense *n* **1** means or method of defending ⟨thorns are a rose's *defense* against grazing animals⟩

syn aegis, ammunition, armor, cover, guard, protection, safeguard, screen, security, shield, wall, ward

rel arm, armament, munitions, weapon, weaponry; fastness, fort, fortress, palisade, stronghold

near ant aggression, assault, attack, offense (*or* offence), offensive

2 an explanation that frees one from fault or blame — see EXCUSE

defenseless *adj* lacking protection from danger or resistance against attack — see HELPLESS 1

defenselessness *n* the quality or state of having little resistance to some outside agent — see SUSCEPTIBILITY

defensible *adj* capable of being defended with good reasoning against verbal attack — see TENABLE 1

defensive *adj* intended to resist or prevent attack or aggression ⟨a *defensive* alliance against the aggressors⟩

syn protective, self-protective

rel deterrent, preventive; safe, secure

near ant aggressive, bellicose, belligerent, combative, contentious, militant, pugnacious, quarrelsome, scrappy, truculent, warlike

ant offensive

defensive *n* a position or readiness to oppose actual or expected attack ⟨their harsh words put him on the *defensive*⟩

syn guard

rel alert, watch

ant offensive

defer *vb* to assign to a later time — see POSTPONE

deference *n* a readiness or willingness to yield to the wishes of others — see COMPLIANCE 1

deferential *adj* marked by or showing proper regard for another's higher status — see RESPECTFUL

deferentially *adv* in manner showing no signs of pride or self-assertion — see LOWLY

defiance *n* **1** refusal to obey — see DISOBEDIENCE

2 the inclination to resist — see RESISTANCE 1

defiant *adj* given to resisting authority or another's control — see DISOBEDIENT

deficiency *n* a falling short of an essential or desirable amount or number ⟨there was a *deficiency* of fresh food in the house⟩

syn dearth, deficit, failure, famine, inadequacy, insufficiency, lack, paucity, poverty, scantiness, scarceness, scarcity, shortage, want

rel absence, omission; meagerness, poorness, skimpiness; necessity, need, privation

near ant bountifulness, copiousness; excess, overabundance, oversupply, surfeit, surplus

ant abundance, adequacy, amplitude, plenitude, plenty, sufficiency

deficient *adj* **1** lacking some necessary part — see INCOMPLETE

2 falling short of a standard — see BAD 1

3 not coming up to a usual standard or meeting a particular need — see SHORT 3

deficit *n* a falling short of an essential or desirable amount or number — see DEFICIENCY

defile *n* a narrow opening between hillsides or mountains that can be used for passage — see CANYON

defile *vb* **1** to make unfit for use by the addition of something harmful or undesirable — see CONTAMINATE

2 to treat (a sacred place or object) shamefully or with great disrespect — see DESECRATE

---

syn synonym(s)   *rel* related words
ant antonym(s)   *near ant* near antonym(s)

defilement *n* **1** an act of great disrespect shown to God or to sacred ideas, people, or things — see BLASPHEMY

2 something that is or that makes impure — see IMPURITY

define *vb* **1** to draw or make apparent the outline of — see OUTLINE 1

2 to mark the limits of — see LIMIT 2

3 to point out the chief quality or qualities of an individual or group — see CHARACTERIZE 1

4 to give the rules about (something) clearly and exactly — see PRESCRIBE

defined *adj* having distinct or certain limits — see LIMITED 1

definite *adj* **1** having distinct or certain limits — see LIMITED 1

2 so clearly expressed as to leave no doubt about the meaning — see EXPLICIT

definitely *adv* without any question — see INDEED 1

definitive *adj* **1** being the most accurate and apparently thorough ⟨the *definitive* work on the attack on Pearl Harbor⟩

syn authoritative

rel conclusive, decisive; official; accurate, correct; complete, thorough

2 serving to put an end to all debate or questioning — see CONCLUSIVE 1

3 so clearly expressed as to leave no doubt about the meaning — see EXPLICIT

deflect *vb* to change the course or direction of (something) — see TURN 2

deform *vb* to twist (something) out of a natural or normal shape or condition — see CONTORT

deformation *n* the twisting of something out of its natural or normal shape or condition — see CONTORTION

deformed *adj* badly or imperfectly formed — see MALFORMED

deformity *n* something that spoils the appearance or completeness of a thing — see BLEMISH

defraud *vb* to rob by the use of trickery or threats — see FLEECE

defrauder *n* a dishonest person who uses clever means to cheat others out of something of value — see TRICKSTER 1

defrauding *adj* marked by, based on, or done by the use of dishonest methods to acquire something of value — see FRAUDULENT 1

defrosted *adj* freed from a frozen state by exposure to warmth — see THAWED

deft *adj* skillful with the hands — see DEXTEROUS

deftness *n* **1** ease and grace in physical activity — see DEXTERITY 1

2 subtle or imaginative ability in inventing, devising, or executing something — see SKILL 1

defunct *adj* **1** no longer existing — see EXTINCT

2 no longer living — see DEAD 1

defy *vb* **1** to go against the commands, prohibitions, or rules of — see DISOBEY

2 to invite (someone) to take part in a contest or to perform a feat — see CHALLENGE 2

3 to oppose (something hostile or dangerous) with firmness or courage — see FACE 2

4 to refuse to give in to — see RESIST

degeneracy *n* **1** a change to a lower state or level — see DECLINE 2

2 a sinking to a state of low moral standards and behavior — see CORRUPTION 2

degenerate *adj* **1** having lost forcefulness, courage, or spirit — see EFFETE 1

2 having or showing lowered moral character or standards — see CORRUPT

degenerate *n* a person who has sunk below the normal moral standard ⟨the *degenerate* would stop at nothing to get satisfaction⟩

syn backslider, debaucher, decadent, libertine, pervert, profligate

rel delinquent, derelict, incorrigible; blackguard, cad, heel, knave, rascal, miscreant, reprobate, rogue, scoundrel, villain; playboy, satyr

near ant saint

degenerate *vb* to become worse or of less value — see DETERIORATE

degeneration *n* **1** a change to a lower state or level — see DECLINE 2

2 a gradual sinking and wasting away of mind or body — see DECLINE 1

3 a sinking to a state of low moral standards and behavior — see CORRUPTION 2

degradation *n* **1** a change to a lower state or level — see DECLINE 2

2 a sinking to a state of low moral standards and behavior — see CORRUPTION 2

degrade *vb* **1** to bring to a lower grade or rank — see DEMOTE

2 to lower in character or dignity — see DEBASE 1

3 to reduce to a lower standing in one's own eyes or in others' eyes — see HUMBLE

degraded *adj* having or showing lowered moral character or standards — see CORRUPT

degrading *adj* intended to make a person or thing seem of little importance or value — see DEROGATORY

degree *n* **1** an individual part of a process, series, or ranking ⟨they completed the project by *degrees*⟩

syn cut, grade, inch, notch, peg, phase, point, stage, step

rel amount, measure, plane; decrement, increment

2 the placement of someone or something in relation to others in a vertical arrangement — see RANK 1

dehydrate *vb* to make dry — see DRY 1

deification *n* excessive admiration of or devotion to a person — see WORSHIP

deify *vb* **1** to love or admire too much — see IDOLIZE

2 to offer honor or respect to (someone) as a divine power — see WORSHIP 1

deifying *adj* reflecting great admiration or devotion — see WORSHIPFUL

deign *vb* to descend to a level that is beneath one's dignity — see CONDESCEND 1

deity *n* 1 a being having superhuman powers and control over a particular part of life or the world ⟨to the ancient Greeks, Zeus was the *deity* who ruled over the sky and weather, and Poseidon was god of the sea⟩
syn divinity, god
rel angel, demigod, demon (*or* daemon), devil, spirit, supernatural
2 *cap* the being worshipped as the creator and ruler of the universe ⟨we prayed to the *Deity* for salvation⟩
syn Allah, Almighty, Creator, Divinity, Father, God, Godhead, Jehovah, Lord, Maker, Providence, Supreme Being
3 the quality or state of being divine — see DIVINITY

dejected *adj* feeling unhappiness — see SAD 1

dejection *n* a state or spell of low spirits — see SADNESS

delay *n* an instance or period of being prevented from going about one's business ⟨there was a *delay* for our boarding while the airplane unloaded incoming passengers⟩
syn detainment, holdup, wait
rel deferment, postponement; reprieve, respite; hesitation, lag, pause, setback, slowdown
near ant haste, rush; dispatch, promptness

delay *vb* 1 to move or act slowly ⟨she told them to stop *delaying* and get to bed⟩
syn crawl, creep, dally, dawdle, dillydally, drag, lag, linger, loiter, poke, tarry
rel hang around, hang out, idle, loaf, loll, lounge; amble, ease, inch, lumber, plod, saunter, shuffle, stagger, stroll; decelerate, slow (down *or* up); filibuster, procrastinate, stall, temporize
phrases mark time
near ant bowl, breeze, dart, hump, hurtle, hustle, scramble, stampede; gallop, jog, run, sprint, trot; accelerate, quicken, speed up; catch up, fast-forward, outpace, outrun, outstrip, overtake
ant barrel, bolt, career, course, dash, fly, hasten, hotfoot (it), hurry, race, rip, rocket, run, rush, scoot, scud, scurry, speed, tear, whirl, whisk, whiz (*or* whizz), zip
2 to assign to a later time — see POSTPONE
3 to create difficulty for the work or activity of — see HAMPER

delectable *adj* 1 giving pleasure or contentment to the mind or senses — see PLEASANT
2 very pleasing to the sense of taste — see DELICIOUS 1

delectably *adv* in a pleasing way — see WELL 5

delectation *n* 1 a source of great satisfaction — see DELIGHT 1
2 the feeling experienced when one's wishes are met — see PLEASURE 1

delegate *n* 1 a person sent on a mission to represent another — see AMBASSADOR
2 a person who acts or does business for another — see AGENT 2

delegate *vb* 1 to appoint as one's representative ⟨he *delegated* his son to go pick up the tickets for him⟩
syn commission, depute, deputize
rel assign, charge; appoint, designate, name, nominate
near ant abrogate; abdicate
2 to put (something) into the possession or safekeeping of another — see GIVE 2

delegation *n* 1 a body of persons chosen as representatives of a larger group — see CONTINGENT
2 the granting of power to perform various acts or duties — see COMMISSION 1

delete *vb* to show (something written) to be no longer valid by drawing a cross over or a line through it — see X (OUT)

deleterious *adj* causing or capable of causing harm — see HARMFUL

deletion *n* something left out — see OMISSION

deliberate *adj* 1 decided on as a result of careful thought ⟨the judge made a *deliberate* decision to impose the maximum sentence⟩
syn advised, calculated, considered, measured, reasoned, studied, thoughtful, weighed
rel aforethought, premeditated; educated, informed; intentional, purposeful; designed, intended, planned, projected; careful, meticulous; foresighted, forethoughtful, provident, prudent
near ant ill-advised; chance, haphazard, hit-or-miss, random; aimless, desultory, purposeless; hasty, hurried, rushed; abrupt, impetuous, sudden; automatic, extemporaneous, impromptu, instinctive, spontaneous
ant casual
2 made, given, or done with full awareness of what one is doing — see INTENTIONAL

deliberate *vb* to give serious and careful thought to — see PONDER

deliberately *adv* with full awareness of what one is doing — see INTENTIONALLY

deliberation *n* 1 a careful weighing of the reasons for or against something — see CONSIDERATION 1
2 an exchange of views for the purpose of exploring a subject or deciding an issue — see DISCUSSION 1

delicacy *n* 1 something that is pleasing to eat because it is rare or a luxury ⟨they were given a plate of *delicacies* while they waited for the queen⟩
syn dainty, goody, tidbit (*also* titbit), treat
rel morsel; candy, dessert, junket, sweet, sweetmeat
2 the state or quality of having a delicate structure ⟨they marvelled at the *delicacy* of a snowflake⟩
syn daintiness, delicateness, exquisiteness, fineness, fragility
rel flimsiness, insubstantiality, wispiness

---

syn synonym(s)   *rel* related words
ant antonym(s)   *near ant* near antonym(s)

near ant firmness, solidity; strength

ant coarseness, crudeness, crudity, roughness, rudeness

3 the tendency to be or state of being squeamish ⟨the urgent need for blood prompted many people to overcome their habitual *delicacy* and become first-time donors⟩

syn qualmishness, queasiness, squeamishness

rel daintiness, fastidiousness, finickiness, fussiness

near ant boldness

ant indelicacy

4 the quality or state of being very accurate — see PRECISION

5 the quality or state of lacking physical strength or vigor — see WEAKNESS 1

delicate *adj* 1 satisfying or pleasing because of fineness or mildness ⟨a heavy sauce would spoil the *delicate* flavor of this fish⟩

syn dainty, exquisite, refined, subtle

rel choice, elegant, extraordinary, incomparable, peerless, preeminent, prime, rare, select, superior, superlative, supreme, transcendent, unsurpassed; picked, selected; fine, fragile, frail

near ant coarse, crude, rough; common, ordinary; average, fair, indifferent, mediocre, medium, middling, run-of-the-mill, second-rate

ant robust, strong, sturdy

2 able to sense slight impressions or differences — see ACUTE 1

3 accomplished with trained ability — see SKILLFUL

4 easily broken — see FRAGILE 1

5 easily injured without careful handling — see TENDER 1

6 hard to please — see FINICKY

7 having qualities that appeal to a refined taste — see CHOICE

8 lacking bodily strength — see WEAK 1

9 made or done with extreme care and accuracy — see FINE 2

10 meeting the highest standard of accuracy — see PRECISE 1

11 not harsh or stern especially in manner, nature, or effect — see GENTLE 1

12 requiring exceptional skill or caution in performance or handling — see TRICKY

delicateness *n* 1 the quality or state of lacking physical strength or vigor — see WEAKNESS 1

2 the state or quality of having a delicate structure — see DELICACY 2

delicious *adj* 1 very pleasing to the sense of taste ⟨the family sat down to a *delicious* Thanksgiving dinner⟩

syn ambrosial, appetizing, delectable, flavorful, luscious, palatable, savory, scrumptious, tasty, toothsome, yummy

rel digestible, eatable, edible; delightful, heavenly, pleasing; agreeable, gratifying, pleasant; satisfying; choice, dainty, delicate, exquisite, rare

near ant banal, boring, commonplace, tedious; noisome, smelly, stinky; noxious,

unwholesome; miserable, wretched; abhorrent, abominable, awful, detestable, disagreeable, disgusting, distasteful, foul, horrid, nauseating, offensive, repellent, repugnant, repulsive, sickening, unpleasant

ant flat, flavorless, insipid, stale, tasteless, unappetizing, unpalatable

2 giving pleasure or contentment to the mind or senses — see PLEASANT

deliciously *adv* in a pleasing way — see WELL 5

deliciousness *n* the quality of being delicious ⟨the fancy feast was *deliciousness* itself⟩

syn lusciousness, savor, savoriness, tastiness

delight *n* 1 a source of great satisfaction ⟨the school play was a *delight* for the parents⟩

syn delectation, gas [*slang*], joy, kick, manna, pleasure, treat

rel amusement, diversion, entertainment, fun, recreation; comfort, relief, solace; gratification, indulgence; ambrosia

2 someone or something that provides amusement or enjoyment — see FUN

3 the feeling experienced when one's wishes are met — see PLEASURE 1

delight *vb* 1 to feel or express joy or triumph — see EXULT

2 to give satisfaction to — see PLEASE

delight (in) *vb* to take pleasure in — see ENJOY 1

delighted *adj* experiencing pleasure, satisfaction, or delight — see GLAD 1

delightful *adj* 1 giving pleasure or contentment to the mind or senses — see PLEASANT

2 providing amusement or enjoyment — see FUN

delightfully *adv* in a pleasing way — see WELL 5

delimit *vb* to mark the limits of — see LIMIT 2

delineate *vb* 1 to draw or make apparent the outline of — see OUTLINE 1

2 to give a representation or account of in words — see DESCRIBE 1

delineated *adj* producing a mental picture through clear and impressive description — see GRAPHIC 1

delineation *n* 1 a picture using lines to represent the chief features of an object or scene — see DRAWING

2 a vivid representation in words of someone or something — see DESCRIPTION 1

delinquency *n* 1 the nonperformance of an assigned or expected action — see FAILURE 1

2 the quality or state of being late — see LATENESS

delinquent *adj* not arriving, occurring, or settled at the due, usual, or proper time — see LATE 1

deliquesce *vb* to go from a solid to a liquid state — see LIQUEFY

delirious *adj* 1 feeling overwhelming fear or worry — see FRANTIC 1

2 marked by great and often stressful excitement or activity — see FURIOUS 1

delirium *n* a state of wildly excited activity or emotion — see FRENZY

deliver *vb* 1 to free from the penalties or consequences of sin — see SAVE 1

2 to remove from danger or harm — see SAVE 2

3 to give (something) over to the control or possession of another usually under duress — see SURRENDER 1

4 to put (something) into the possession of someone for use or consumption — see FURNISH 2

5 to put (something) into the possession or safekeeping of another — see GIVE 2

6 to turn out as planned or desired — see SUCCEED 1

deliverance *n* 1 the saving from danger or evil — see SALVATION

2 a position arrived at after consideration — see DECISION 1

deliverer *n* 1 a person who delivers goods to customers usually over a regular local route — see DELIVERYMAN

2 one that saves from danger or destruction — see SAVIOR

delivery *n* 1 a freeing from an obligation or responsibility — see RELEASE 1

2 the act or process of giving birth to children — see CHILDBIRTH

deliveryman *n* a person who delivers goods to customers usually over a regular local route ⟨the *deliveryman* dropped off a package for us while we were at the store⟩

syn deliverer

rel beárer, carrier, courier, go-between, liaison, messenger

delude *vb* to cause to believe what is untrue — see DECEIVE

deluding *adj* tending or having power to deceive — see DECEPTIVE 1

deluge *n* 1 a great flow of water or of something that overwhelms — see FLOOD

2 a steady falling of water from the sky in significant quantity — see RAIN 1

deluge *vb* to cover or become filled with a flood — see FLOOD

delusion *n* a conception or image created by the imagination and having no objective reality — see FANTASY 1

delusive *adj* tending or having power to deceive — see DECEPTIVE 1

delusory *adj* tending or having power to deceive — see DECEPTIVE 1

deluxe *adj* showing obvious signs of wealth and comfort — see LUXURIOUS

delve (into) *vb* to search through or into — see EXPLORE 1

delving *n* a systematic search for the truth or facts about something — see INQUIRY 1

demagogue *also* **demagog** *n* a person who stirs up public feelings especially of discontent — see AGITATOR

demand *n* 1 something that someone insists upon having ⟨the terrorists presented their list of *demands*⟩

syn claim, dun, requisition, ultimatum

rel desire, request, want, wish; drive, need, requirement, stipulation; basic, essential, must; imposition; condition, provision

2 something necessary, indispensable, or unavoidable — see ESSENTIAL 1

demand *vb* 1 to ask for (something) earnestly or with authority ⟨the losing party *demanded* a recount of the votes cast in the election⟩

syn call (for), claim, clamor (for), command, enjoin, exact, insist (on), press (for), quest, stipulate (for)

rel ask, plead (for), request, want; cry (for), necessitate, need, require, take, warrant; requisition; impose; badger, dun, hound

near ant give up, relinquish, surrender, yield

2 to have as a requirement — see NEED 1

3 to set or receive as a price — see CHARGE 1

demanding *adj* 1 requiring much time, effort, or careful attention ⟨the *demanding* assignment kept them working all night⟩

syn arduous, burdensome, challenging, exacting, grueling (*or* gruelling), laborious, onerous, taxing, toilsome

rel difficult, formidable, hard, herculean, rough, rugged, stiff, strenuous, tough; oppressive, trying; rigid, rigorous, severe, stern, strict, stringent

near ant easy, effortless, facile, simple, smooth

ant light, undemanding

2 hard to please — see FINICKY

3 requiring considerable physical or mental effort — see HARD 2

demarcate *vb* to mark the limits of — see LIMIT 2

demarcation *n* the state of being kept distinct — see SEPARATION 2

¹**demean** *vb* 1 to lower in character or dignity — see DEBASE 1

2 to reduce to a lower standing in one's own eyes or in others' eyes — see HUMBLE

²**demean** *vb* to manage the actions of (oneself) in a particular way — see BEHAVE

demeaning *adj* intended to make a person or thing seem of little importance or value — see DEROGATORY

demeanor *n* the way or manner in which one conducts oneself — see BEHAVIOR

demented *adj* having or showing a very abnormal or sick state of mind — see INSANE 1

dementia *n* a serious mental disorder that prevents one from living a safe and normal life — see INSANITY 1

demerit *n* a defect in character — see FAULT 1

demesne *n* 1 a part or portion having no fixed boundaries — see REGION 1

2 a region of activity, knowledge, or influence — see FIELD 2

---

syn synonym(s)   *rel* related words
ant antonym(s)   *near ant* near antonym(s)

3 the area around and belonging to a building — see GROUND 1

demilitarization *n* the reduction or elimination of a country's armed forces or weapons — see DISARMAMENT

demilitarize *vb* to reduce the size and strength of the armed forces of — see DISARM 1

demise *n* **1** the permanent stopping of all the vital bodily activities — see DEATH 1

2 the act of ceasing to exist — see DEATH 3

democracy *n* government in which the supreme power is held by the people and used by them directly or indirectly through representation ⟨under our *democracy* the people have some control over their lives by being able to decide who their political leaders will be⟩

syn republic, self-government, self-rule

rel home rule, self-determination; autonomy, sovereignty

near ant despotism, dictatorship, monarchy, totalitarianism, tyranny

democratic *adj* of, relating to, or favoring political democracy ⟨the *democratic* system ensured that every citizen's voice was heard⟩

syn popular, republican, self-governing, self-ruling

rel representative; libertarian

near ant autocratic, despotic, dictatorial, monarchal (*or* monarchial), monarchical (*also* monarchic), tyrannical (*also* tyrannic)

ant undemocratic

demolish *vb* **1** to destroy (as a building) completely by knocking down or breaking to pieces ⟨they *demolished* the old warehouse to make room for the new shopping mall⟩

syn raze, tear down

rel blow up, dynamite; abolish, annihilate, crack up, crush, dash, decimate, destroy, devastate, devour, dissolve, do in, eradicate, extirpate, finish, flatten, obliterate, overturn, pulverize, ravage, ruin, scourge, smash, total, unmake, waste, wipe out, wreck

near ant build, construct, erect, put up, raise; rebuild, renew, renovate, restore; create, fabricate, fashion, forge, form, make, manufacture, shape

2 to bring to a complete end the physical soundness, existence, or usefulness of — see DESTROY 1

3 to cause to break open or into pieces by or as if by an explosive — see BLAST 1

demolishment *n* the state or fact of being rendered nonexistent, physically unsound, or useless — see DESTRUCTION

demolition *n* the state or fact of being rendered nonexistent, physically unsound, or useless — see DESTRUCTION

demon *or* **daemon** *n* an evil spirit ⟨only in rare cases is the ancient rite of exorcism performed to cast out a troublesome *demon*⟩

syn devil, fiend, ghoul, imp, incubus

rel apparition, bogey (*also* bogy *or* bogie), familiar, ghost, phantasm, phantom, poltergeist, shade, shadow, specter (*or* spectre), spirit, spook, vision, wraith; brownie, dwarf, elf, faerie (*also* faery), fairy, fay, gnome, goblin, gremlin, hobgoblin, leprechaun, pixie (*also* pixy), puck, sprite, troll; monster, ogre

near ant angel

demoniac *also* **demoniacal** *adj* of, relating to, or worthy of an evil spirit — see FIENDISH

demonic *adj* of, relating to, or worthy of an evil spirit — see FIENDISH

demonstrable *adj* capable of being proven as true or real — see VERIFIABLE

demonstrate *vb* **1** to gain full recognition or acceptance of — see ESTABLISH 1

2 to show the existence or truth of by evidence — see PROVE 1

3 to make known (something abstract) through outward signs — see SHOW 2

4 to make plain or understandable — see EXPLAIN 1

5 to show or make clear by using examples — see ILLUSTRATE 1

demonstration *n* **1** a mass meeting for the purpose of displaying or arousing support for a cause or person — see RALLY 2

2 an outward and often exaggerated indication of something abstract (as a feeling) for effect — see SHOW 1

demonstrative *adj* showing feeling freely ⟨my grandmother was always very *demonstrative* when we visited, showering us with hugs and kisses⟩

syn effusive, emotional, uninhibited, unreserved, unrestrained

rel dramatic, histrionic, melodramatic, theatrical; gushing, maudlin, mawkish, mushy, schmaltzy, sentimental; communicative, expansive; extroverted (*also* extraverted), outgoing; affectionate, feeling, intense, loving, passionate, sensitive, soulful, warm; blunt, candid, frank, outspoken, plain

near ant constrained; quiet, reticent, silent, taciturn; bashful, modest, retiring, shy; introverted, self-directed; aloof, detached, dispassionate, impassive, indifferent, phlegmatic, stolid, unconcerned, unfeeling; chilly, cold, frigid, glacial, hard-boiled, hardhearted, icy, unfriendly

ant inhibited, reserved, restrained, undemonstrative, unemotional

demoralization *n* **1** a sinking to a state of low moral standards and behavior — see CORRUPTION 2

2 the state of being discouraged — see DISCOURAGEMENT

demoralize *vb* **1** to deprive of courage or confidence — see UNNERVE 1

2 to lessen the courage or confidence of — see DISCOURAGE 1

demoralized *adj* having or showing lowered moral character or standards — see CORRUPT

demote *vb* to bring to a lower grade or rank ⟨the court-martial's decision was to

demote the officer responsible for the failed mission⟩
syn break, bust, degrade, downgrade, reduce
rel can, dismiss, fire, lay off, sack; abase, debase, demean, humble, humiliate, lower
near ant hire
ant advance, elevate, promote, raise

demount *vb* to take apart — see DISASSEMBLE

demur *n* a feeling or declaration of disapproval or dissent — see OBJECTION

demur *vb* to present an opposing opinion or argument — see OBJECT

demure *adj* 1 affecting shyness or modesty in order to attract masculine interest — see COY 1

2 not comfortable around people — see SHY 2

3 not having or showing any feelings of superiority, self-assertiveness, or showiness — see HUMBLE 1

demureness *n* the absence of any feelings of being better than others — see HUMILITY

den *n* 1 the shelter or resting place of a wild animal ⟨the foxes hid in their *den* until the bear left the area⟩
syn burrow, hole, lair, lodge
rel nest

2 a place where a person goes to hide — see HIDEOUT

denial *n* 1 an unwillingness to grant something asked for ⟨our principal's *denial* of our request to come to school on Halloween dressed in costumes⟩
syn disallowance, nay, no, refusal, rejection
rel decline, rebuff, repudiation; negative
near ant acceptance, accession, consent, leave, permission, sufferance
ant allowance, grant

2 a refusal to confirm the truth of a statement ⟨the senator issued a flat *denial* of the accusation against her⟩
syn contradiction, disallowance, disavowal, disclaimer, negation, rejection, repudiation
rel disproof, rebuttal, refutation; negative
near ant confession; affirmation, assertion, declaration
ant acknowledgment (*also* acknowledgement), admission, avowal, confirmation

denizen *n* one who lives permanently in a place — see INHABITANT

denominate *vb* to give a name to — see NAME 1

denomination *n* a word or combination of words by which a person or thing is regularly known — see NAME 1

denotation *n* 1 a word or combination of words by which a person or thing is regularly known — see NAME 1

2 the idea that is conveyed or intended to be conveyed to the mind by language, symbol, or action — see MEANING 1

denotative *adj* indicating something — see INDICATIVE

denote *vb* to communicate or convey (as an idea) to the mind — see MEAN 1

denoting *adj* indicating something — see INDICATIVE

denounce *vb* 1 to declare to be morally wrong or evil — see CONDEMN 1

2 to express one's unfavorable opinion of the worth or quality of — see CRITICIZE

3 to express public or formal disapproval of — see CENSURE 1

dense *adj* 1 having little space between items or parts — see CLOSE 1

2 not having or showing an ability to absorb ideas readily — see STUPID 1

denseness *n* the quality or state of lacking intelligence or quickness of mind — see STUPIDITY 1

density *n* 1 the degree to which a fluid can resist flowing — see CONSISTENCY

2 the quality or state of lacking intelligence or quickness of mind — see STUPIDITY 1

dent *n* a sunken area forming a separate space — see HOLE 2

dented *adj* curved inward — see HOLLOW

denuded *adj* lacking a usual or natural covering — see NAKED 2

denunciation *n* an often public or formal expression of disapproval — see CENSURE

deny *vb* 1 to declare not to be true ⟨the congressman *denied* all charges of wrongdoing⟩
syn contradict, disallow, disavow, disclaim, gainsay, negate, negative, reject, repudiate
rel disown, renounce; challenge, confute, disprove, rebut, refute; disagree (with), dispute
near ant accept, adopt, embrace, espouse; affirm, announce, assert, aver, claim, declare, maintain, profess, submit; authenticate, corroborate, substantiate, validate, verify
ant acknowledge, admit, allow, avow, concede, confirm, own

2 to be unwilling to grant ⟨he *denied* access to the top secret files to the nosy reporters⟩
syn decline, disallow, refuse, reject, withhold
rel rebuff, repel, spurn; check, constrain, hold, keep, restrain, restrict
near ant afford, furnish, give, provide, supply
ant allow, concede, grant, let, permit

depart *vb* 1 to leave a place often for another — see GO 2

2 to stop living — see DIE 1

departed *adj* 1 no longer existing — see EXTINCT

2 no longer living — see DEAD 1

departing *n* the act of leaving a place — see DEPARTURE

department *n* 1 a large unit of a governmental, business, or educational organization — see DIVISION 2

---

syn synonym(s)   **rel** related words
ant antonym(s)   **near ant** near antonym(s)

2 a region of activity, knowledge, or influence — see FIELD 2

departure *n* the act of leaving a place ⟨his sudden *departure* left them wondering if they'd upset him⟩

syn decamping, decampment, departing, exit, exiting, farewell, going, leave-taking, lighting out, parting, quitting, walking out

rel flight, retirement, retreat, running away, withdrawal; emigration, evacuation, exodus; egress; abandonment, forsaking, relinquishment

near ant advent, coming; entrance, ingress

ant arrival

depend *vb* **1** to be determined by, based on, or subject (to) ⟨whether or not we play baseball will *depend* on how much rain we get⟩

syn hang, hinge

rel base, establish, found, rest, stay; ground

2 to place reliance or trust ⟨I know I can always *depend* on you for help when I really need it⟩

syn count, lean, reckon, rely

rel commit, confide, entrust, trust

phrases bank on, figure on

near ant distrust, mistrust

dependability *n* worthiness as the recipient of another's trust or confidence — see RELIABILITY

dependable *adj* worthy of one's trust ⟨Boy Scouts are supposed to be always *dependable*⟩

syn good, reliable, responsible, safe, solid, steady, sure, tried, tried-and-true, true, trustworthy, trusty

rel constant, devoted, faithful, fast, loyal, staunch (*or* stanch), steadfast; honest, sincere, single-minded; infallible, unerring; firm, sound, strong; effective, telling; attested, authenticated, confirmed, proven, valid, validated, verified; blameless, irreproachable, unimpeachable, unquestionable

near ant disloyal, faithless, false, unfaithful; deceitful, dishonest; doubtful, dubious, questionable, suspect, uncertain, unsound; hazardous, risky; unauthenticated, unconfirmed, untried, unverified

ant irresponsible, undependable, unreliable, untrustworthy

dependence *n* **1** the quality or state of needing something or someone ⟨a baby's total *dependence* upon his or her parents for every one of life's needs⟩

syn dependency, reliance

rel reciprocity, relativity; confidence, faith, stock, trust

near ant autonomy, sovereignty

ant independence, self-reliance

2 something or someone to which one looks for support ⟨ultimately rice became the chief *dependence* in that state⟩

syn buttress, mainstay, pillar, reliance, standby, support

rel backbone, spine; crutch, prop, stay

dependency *n* the quality or state of needing something or someone — see DEPENDENCE 1

dependent *adj* **1** extending freely from a support from above ⟨the *dependent* willow branches swayed in the gentle breeze⟩

syn dangling, hanging, pendent (*or* pendant), pendulous

2 determined by something else ⟨our going to the movies tonight is *dependent* on whether or not we have any money left after we eat out⟩

syn conditional, contingent (on *or* upon), subject (to), tentative

rel liable, open, susceptible; limited, modified, qualified, restricted; doubtful, iffy, problematic (*also* problematical), questionable, uncertain

near ant absolute, categorical (*also* categoric); ultimate; basal, basic, fundamental, primary

ant independent, unconditional

depict *vb* **1** to give a representation or account of in words — see DESCRIBE 1

2 to point out the chief quality or qualities of an individual or group — see CHARACTERIZE 1

3 to present a picture of — see PICTURE 1

depiction *n* a vivid representation in words of someone or something — see DESCRIPTION 1

deplete *vb* to make complete use of ⟨miners *depleted* the vein of copper ore after months of working⟩

syn clean (out), consume, drain, exhaust, expend, spend, use up

rel decrease, diminish, lessen, reduce; eat, use; bankrupt, impoverish; cripple, debilitate, disable, enfeeble, sap, undermine, weaken; dry up, empty; dissipate, squander, waste

near ant augment, enlarge, increase; bolster, fortify, reinforce, strengthen; rebuild, repair, restore, revive

ant renew, replace

deplorable *adj* of a kind to cause great distress — see REGRETTABLE

deplore *vb* **1** to feel or express sorrow for — see LAMENT 1

2 to feel sorry or dissatisfied about — see REGRET

deploring *adj* expressing or suggesting mourning — see MOURNFUL 1

deport *vb* **1** to force to leave a country — see BANISH 1

2 to manage the actions of (oneself) in a particular way — see BEHAVE

deportation *n* the forced removal from a homeland — see EXILE 1

deportee *n* a person forced to emigrate for political reasons — see ÉMIGRÉ 1

deportment *n* the way or manner in which one conducts oneself — see BEHAVIOR

depose *vb* **1** to remove from a position of prominence or power (as a throne) ⟨they *deposed* the dictator after he had bankrupted the country⟩

syn dethrone, oust, uncrown, unmake, unseat, unthrone

rel discharge, dismiss; overthrow, usurp, subvert, topple; eject, throw out

near ant inaugurate, induct, install, instate, invest; appoint, designate, elect

ant crown, enthrone, throne

2 to make a solemn declaration under oath for the purpose of establishing a fact — see TESTIFY

deposit *n* **1** matter that settles to the bottom of a body of liquid ⟨a *deposit* of silt on the river bed⟩

syn deposition, dregs, grounds, precipitate, sediment

rel lees; ooze, sludge; dross, slag, waste

2 a collection of things kept available for future use or need — see STORE 1

3 a sum of money set aside for a particular purpose — see FUND 1

deposit *vb* **1** to put in an account ⟨we *deposited* the check in a bank account⟩

syn bank

rel cache, hoard, lay away, reserve, salt away, save, squirrel (away), stash, store, stow; invest

near ant remove, take out; disburse, expend, lay out, spend

ant withdraw

2 to arrange something in a certain spot or position — see PLACE 1

deposition *n* matter that settles to the bottom of a body of liquid — see DEPOSIT 1

depository *n* a building for storing goods — see STOREHOUSE

depot *n* **1** a building for storing goods — see STOREHOUSE

2 a place where military arms are stored — see ARMORY

deprave *vb* to lower in character or dignity — see DEBASE 1

depraved *adj* having or showing lowered moral character or standards — see CORRUPT

depravedness *n* the state or quality of being utterly evil — see ENORMITY 1

depravity *n* **1** a sinking to a state of low moral standards and behavior — see CORRUPTION 2

2 immoral conduct or practices harmful or offensive to society — see VICE 1

3 the state or quality of being utterly evil — see ENORMITY 1

deprecate *vb* **1** to express scornfully one's low opinion of — see DECRY 1

2 to hold an unfavorable opinion of — see DISAPPROVE

deprecation *n* **1** refusal to accept as right or desirable — see DISAPPROVAL

2 the act of making a person or a thing seem little or unimportant — see DEPRECIATION

depreciate *vb* **1** to lower the price or value of ⟨a faded finish will really *depreciate* your car when you decide to trade it in⟩

syn cheapen, depress, mark down, write off

rel underrate, undervalue; abate, abridge, compress, contract, de-escalate, deflate, diminish, dwindle, lessen, lower, moderate, reduce, shrink

near ant bloat, blow up, inflate; add, aggrandize, amplify, augment, balloon, boost, dilate, enlarge, escalate, expand, extend, heighten, increase, maximize, raise, swell

ant appreciate, mark up

2 to express scornfully one's low opinion of — see DECRY 1

depreciation *n* the act of making a person or a thing seem little or unimportant ⟨the boys' *depreciation* of the girls' basketball victories only showed how jealous they were⟩

syn belittlement, deprecation, detraction, diminishment, disparagement, put-down

rel aspersion, backbiting, defamation, libel, slander, vilification; derision, mockery, ridicule; abuse, invective, vituperation; censure, condemnation, denunciation

near ant acclaim, praise; approbation, approval, commendation

ant aggrandizement, ennoblement, exaltation, glorification, magnification

depreciative *adj* intended to make a person or thing seem of little importance or value — see DEROGATORY

depreciatory *adj* intended to make a person or thing seem of little importance or value — see DEROGATORY

depress *vb* **1** to make sad ⟨the thought of failing the test *depressed* me⟩

syn burden, oppress, sadden

rel ail, distress, trouble; afflict, torment, torture; discourage, dishearten, dispirit; bother, disquiet, disturb, perturb, upset

near ant animate, enliven, invigorate; comfort, console, solace; excite, inspire, stimulate; elate, exhilarate; encourage, hearten; delight, gratify, please

ant brighten, buoy, cheer, gladden

2 to cause to fall intentionally or unintentionally — see DROP 1

3 to lower the price or value of — see DEPRECIATE 1

4 to push steadily against with some force — see PRESS 1

depressed *adj* **1** curved inward — see HOLLOW

2 feeling unhappiness — see SAD 1

depressing *adj* **1** causing or marked by an atmosphere lacking in cheer — see GLOOMY 1

2 causing unhappiness — see SAD 2

depression *n* **1** a period of decreased economic activity ⟨during the 1930s the U.S. suffered a great *depression*⟩

syn recession, slump

rel crash, panic; stagnation

near ant development, growth; advancement, progress

ant boom

2 a state or spell of low spirits — see SADNESS

3 a sunken area forming a separate space — see HOLE 2

deprivation *n* the state of being robbed of something normally enjoyed — see PRIVATION

deprived *adj* kept from having the necessities of life or a healthful environment ⟨*deprived* children growing up in the slums⟩
syn disadvantaged, underprivileged
rel impoverished, needy, poor; hapless, ill-fated, ill-starred, unfortunate, unlucky
near ant fortunate, lucky; affluent, rich, wealthy; coddled, indulged, pampered, spoiled
ant privileged

depth *n* **1** distance measured from the top to the bottom of something ⟨be sure to check the *depth* of the water before diving off the dock⟩
syn drop
rel lowness; draft, sounding
near ant shallowness; altitude, elevation, height
2 the quality of being great in extent (as of insight) ⟨the *depth* of the poet's understanding of human nature has given his works a timeless appeal⟩
syn profoundness, profundity
rel discernment, sense, wisdom; brain, intellect, intelligence; acuteness, keenness, penetration, sharpness
near ant shallowness, superficiality; smattering
3 the most intense or characteristic phase of something — see THICK

depthless *adj* lacking significant physical depth — see SHALLOW 1

depute *vb* to appoint as one's representative — see DELEGATE 1

deputize *vb* to appoint as one's representative — see DELEGATE 1

deputy *n* **1** a person who acts or does business for another — see AGENT 2
2 a person who helps a more skilled person — see HELPER

derange *vb* **1** to cause to go insane or as if insane — see CRAZE
2 to undo the proper order or arrangement of — see DISORDER

deranged *adj* having or showing a very abnormal or sick state of mind — see INSANE 1

derangement *n* **1** a serious mental disorder that prevents one from living a safe and normal life — see INSANITY 1
2 an act or instance of the order of things being disturbed — see UPSET

derelict *adj* **1** failing to give proper care and attention — see NEGLIGENT
2 left unoccupied or unused — see ABANDONED

dereliction *n* **1** the act of abandoning ⟨the family's shameful *dereliction* of their pets at the end of the summer season⟩
syn abandonment, desertion, forsaking
rel defection; discard, dumping, jettison
near ant retention
ant reclamation
2 failure to take the care that a cautious person usually takes — see NEGLIGENCE 1

3 the nonperformance of an assigned or expected action — see FAILURE 1

deride *vb* to make (someone or something) the object of unkind laughter — see RIDICULE

derision *n* the making of unkind jokes as a way of showing one's scorn for someone or something — see RIDICULE

derisive *adj* so foolish or pointless as to be worthy of scornful laughter — see RIDICULOUS 1

derisory *adj* so foolish or pointless as to be worthy of scornful laughter — see RIDICULOUS 1

derivable *adj* being or provable by reasoning in which the conclusion follows necessarily from given information — see DEDUCTIVE

derivative *adj* taken or created from something original or basic — see SECONDARY 1

derivative *n* something that naturally develops or is developed from something else ⟨the whole field of industrial robots is a *derivative* of technology developed for the space program⟩
syn by-product, offshoot, outgrowth, spin-off
rel descendant (*or* descendent); aftermath, consequence, result; aftereffect, side effect; copy, duplicate, facsimile, replica, reproduction
near ant archetype, original, prototype; antecedent, cause, determinant
ant origin, root, source

derogatory *adj* intended to make a person or thing seem of little importance or value ⟨fans made a steady stream of *derogatory* remarks about the players on the visiting team⟩
syn belittling, contemptuous, decrying, degrading, demeaning, depreciative, depreciatory, disdainful, disparaging, scornful, slighting, uncomplimentary
rel aspersing, defamatory, detractive, insulting, libelous, maligning, slandering, slanderous, vilifying; abusive, opprobrious, scurrilous; despiteful, malevolent, malicious, spiteful
near ant admiring, adulatory, laudatory; appreciative, respectful
ant commendatory, complimentary

descant *vb* **1** to give a formal often extended talk on a subject — see TALK 1
2 to produce musical sounds with the voice — see SING 1

descend *vb* **1** to lead or extend downward ⟨the pathway *descends* to the river bank⟩
syn decline, dip, drop, fall, plunge
rel cant, incline, lean, list, recline, slant, slope, tilt, tip
near ant even, flatten, level, straighten
ant ascend, climb, rise
2 to become worse or of less value — see DETERIORATE
3 to go to a lower level — see DROP 2

descend (on *or* upon) *vb* to take sudden, violent action against — see ATTACK 1

descendant *or* **descendent** *adj* bending downward or forward — see NODDING

descending *adj* bending downward or forward — see NODDING

descent *n* **1** the act or process of going to a lower level or altitude ⟨the airplane began its gradual *descent* to the landing field⟩
syn dip, dive, down, drop, fall, nosedive, plunge
rel comedown, downfall, downgrade; sinking
near ant advance, headway, progress, progression; betterment, improvement
ant ascent, climb, rise, upswing, upturn
2 a gradual sinking and wasting away of mind or body — see DECLINE 1
3 a change to a lower state or level — see DECLINE 2
4 a loss of status — see COMEDOWN
5 a sudden attack and entrance into hostile territory — see RAID 1
6 the act or action of setting upon with force or violence — see ATTACK 1
7 the line of ancestors from whom a person is descended — see ANCESTRY

describe *vb* **1** to give a representation or account of in words ⟨he tried to *describe* the dream he had last night as accurately as he could⟩
syn delineate, depict, draw, image, paint, picture, portray, sketch
rel characterize, qualify, represent; demonstrate, illustrate; narrate, recite, recount, relate; display, exhibit, show; hint, suggest; draft, outline
near ant color, distort, falsify, garble, misrepresent, pervert, twist, warp
2 to give an oral or written account of in some detail — see TELL 1
3 to point out the chief quality or qualities of an individual or group — see CHARACTERIZE 1

description *n* **1** a vivid representation in words of someone or something ⟨we recognized his cousin from his *description*⟩
syn delineation, depiction, picture, portrait, portrayal, sketch
rel account, chronicle, narrative, report, story, tale; demonstration, exemplification, illustration
2 a number of persons or things that are grouped together because they have something in common — see SORT 1

descry *vb* **1** to come upon after searching, study, or effort — see FIND 1
2 to make note of (something) through the use of one's eyes — see SEE 1

desecrate *vb* to treat (a sacred place or object) shamefully or with great disrespect ⟨vandals *desecrated* the cemetery last night with graffiti⟩
syn defile, profane, violate
rel blaspheme, curse, swear; befoul, contaminate, foul, pollute; affront, insult, offend; crush, decimate, demolish, destroy, devastate, ravage, raze, ruin, waste, wreck; despoil, loot, pillage, plunder, raid, ransack, rob, sack, spoil, strip

near ant bless, consecrate, dedicate, hallow, sanctify; honor, respect; cleanse, purify

desecration *n* an act of great disrespect shown to God or to sacred ideas, people, or things — see BLASPHEMY

¹desert *n* land that is uninhabited or not fit for crops — see WASTELAND

²desert *n* suffering, loss, or hardship imposed in response to a crime or offense — see PUNISHMENT

desert *vb* **1** to leave (a cause or party) often in order to take up another — see DEFECT
2 to cause to remain behind — see LEAVE 1

deserted *adj* left unoccupied or unused — see ABANDONED

deserter *n* a person who abandons a cause or organization usually without right — see RENEGADE

desertion *n* the act of abandoning — see DERELICTION 1

deserve *vb* to be or make worthy of (as a reward or punishment) — see EARN 2

deserved *adj* being what is called for by accepted standards of right and wrong — see JUST 1

deserving *adj* having sufficient worth or merit to receive one's honor, esteem, or reward — see WORTHY

desex *vb* to remove the sex organs of — see NEUTER

design *n* **1** a method worked out in advance for achieving some objective — see PLAN 1
2 a secret plan for accomplishing evil or unlawful ends — see PLOT 1
3 something that one hopes or intends to accomplish — see GOAL
4 a unit of decoration that is repeated all over something (as a fabric) — see PATTERN 1
5 the way in which the elements of something (as a work of art) are arranged — see COMPOSITION 3

design *vb* **1** to have in mind as a purpose or goal — see INTEND
2 to work out the details of (something) in advance — see PLAN 1

designate *vb* **1** to decide upon (the time or date for an event) usually from a position of authority — see APPOINT 1
2 to pick (someone) by one's authority for a specific position or duty — see APPOINT 2
3 to give a name to — see NAME 1

designation *n* **1** a word or combination of words by which a person or thing is regularly known — see NAME 1
2 the state or fact of being chosen for a position or duty — see APPOINTMENT 1

designedly *adv* with full awareness of what one is doing — see INTENTIONALLY

designer *n* one who creates or introduces something new — see INVENTOR

desirable *adj* suitable for bringing about a desired result under the circumstances — see EXPEDIENT

---

syn synonym(s)   *rel* related words
ant antonym(s)   *near ant* near antonym(s)

desire *n* a strong wish for something ⟨a *desire* for adventure and excitement prompted him to travel to Africa⟩
syn appetite, craving, drive, hankering, hunger, itch, longing, lust, passion, pining, thirst, urge, yearning, yen
rel compulsion, impulse, urge, will, zeal; liking, love, taste; eagerness, impatience; wish, want; necessity, need, requirement; avarice, cupidity, greed, rapacity
near ant abhorrence, aversion, disfavor, disgust, dislike, distaste, hatred, repugnance, repulsion; apathy, indifference, unconcern

desire *vb* to have an earnest wish to own or enjoy ⟨he greatly *desired* a new mountain bike for his next birthday⟩
syn ache (for), covet, crave, die (for), hanker (for *or* after), hunger (for), itch (for), long (for), lust (for *or* after), pant (after), pine (for), repine (for), sigh (for), thirst (for), want, wish (for), yearn (for)
rel delight (in), enjoy, fancy, like, relish
near ant abhor, abominate, detest, hate, loathe; decline, refuse, reject, spurn

desirous *adj* showing urgent desire or interest — see EAGER

desirousness *n* urgent desire or interest — see EAGERNESS

desist (from) *vb* to bring (as an action or operation) to an immediate end — see STOP 1

desk *n* a large unit of a governmental, business, or educational organization — see DIVISION 2

desolate *adj* **1** causing or marked by an atmosphere lacking in cheer — see GLOOMY 1
2 sad from lack of companionship or separation from others — see LONESOME 1

desolate *vb* to bring to a complete end the physical soundness, existence, or usefulness of — see DESTROY 1

desolation *n* **1** a state or spell of low spirits — see SADNESS
2 land that is uninhabited or not fit for crops — see WASTELAND
3 the state of being unattended to or not cared for — see NEGLECT 1
4 the state or fact of being rendered nonexistent, physically unsound, or useless — see DESTRUCTION

despair *n* **1** utter loss of hope ⟨the endless drought drove the farmers to *despair*⟩
syn desperation, despondency, forlornness, hopelessness
rel blues, depression, dejection, desolation, doldrums, dolor, downheartedness, dumps, gloom, melancholy, mopes, oppression, sadness, sorrow, unhappiness; cynicism, pessimism; acceptance, resignation
near ant cheer, cheerfulness, sunniness; optimism
ant hope, hopefulness
2 the state of being discouraged — see DISCOURAGEMENT

despair *vb* to lose all hope or confidence ⟨we *despaired* when we saw how little time we had left to complete our project⟩

syn despond
rel give up, surrender, yield; darken, sadden; grieve, mourn, sorrow; discourage, dishearten, dispirit
near ant assure, encourage, hearten, reassure; hope
ant brighten, cheer (up), perk (up)

despairing *adj* emphasizing or expecting the worst — see PESSIMISTIC 1

desperation *n* utter loss of hope — see DESPAIR 1

despicable *adj* **1** arousing or deserving of one's loathing and disgust — see CONTEMPTIBLE 1
2 not following or in accordance with standards of honor and decency — see IGNOBLE 2
3 deserving pitying scorn (as for inadequacy) — see PITIFUL 1

despise *vb* **1** to dislike strongly — see HATE
2 to ignore in a disrespectful manner — see SCORN 2

despite *n* **1** open dislike for someone or something considered unworthy of one's concern or respect — see CONTEMPT
2 the desire to cause pain for the satisfaction of doing harm — see MALICE

despite *prep* without being prevented by ⟨we went to the party *despite* the bad weather outside⟩
syn notwithstanding, with
phrases in despite of, in spite of

despiteful *adj* having or showing a desire to cause someone pain or suffering for the sheer enjoyment of it — see HATEFUL

despitefully *adv* in a mean or spiteful manner — see NASTILY

despitefulness *n* open dislike for someone or something considered unworthy of one's concern or respect — see CONTEMPT

despoil *vb* to search through with the intent of committing robbery — see RANSACK 1

despond *vb* to lose all hope or confidence — see DESPAIR

despondency *n* **1** a state or spell of low spirits — see SADNESS
2 the state of being discouraged — see DISCOURAGEMENT
3 utter loss of hope — see DESPAIR 1

despondent *adj* feeling unhappiness — see SAD 1

despot *n* a person who uses power or authority in a cruel, unjust, or harmful way ⟨the *despot* threw anyone who dared to criticize his rule into jail⟩
syn autocrat, dictator, oppressor, potentate, tyrant
rel dominator, master, overlord, ruler; king, lord, monarch, prince, queen, sovereign; baron, czar (*also* tsar *or* tzar), magnate, mogul, tycoon; authoritarian, disciplinarian, discipliner, martinet

despotic *adj* **1** exercising power or authority without interference by others — see ABSOLUTE 1
2 fond of ordering people around — see BOSSY

despotism *n* a system of government in which the ruler has unlimited power ⟨by the end of the 20th century many countries around the world had rejected *despotism* in favor of democracy⟩

syn autocracy, dictatorship, totalitarianism, tyranny

rel monarchy; authoritarianism, fascism; domination, oppression

near ant democracy; freedom; anarchy

destine *vb* to determine the fate of in advance ⟨his extreme height seemed to *destine* him for a career in basketball⟩

syn doom, fate, foredoom, foreordain, ordain, predestine, predetermine

rel forecast, foretell, predict, prognosticate, prophesy; preconceive, prejudge; condemn, sentence

destiny *n* a state or end that seemingly has been decided beforehand — see FATE 1

destitute *adj* 1 lacking money or material possessions — see POOR 1
2 utterly lacking in something needed, wanted, or expected — see DEVOID 1

destitution *n* the state of lacking sufficient money or material possessions — see POVERTY 1

destroy *vb* 1 to bring to a complete end the physical soundness, existence, or usefulness of ⟨they practically *destroyed* the safe in order to get at the money inside⟩ ⟨their poor scores on the final exam *destroyed* any chance they might have had to pass the course⟩

syn annihilate, decimate, demolish, desolate, devastate, do in, extinguish, pulverize, raze, ruin, shatter, smash, tear down, waste, wreck

rel gut; beat, best, clobber, conquer, crush, defeat, lick, master, overbear, overcome, prevail (over), scotch, subdue, surmount, thrash, triumph (over), win (against); blow up, break, damage, deface, disintegrate, dynamite, mangle, mar, mutilate, spoil, vitiate; erode, scour, wash out, wear (away); dismantle, undo, unmake; blot out, eradicate, exterminate, extirpate, obliterate, remove, rub out, stamp (out), wipe out; despoil, loot, pillage, plunder, ravage, sack, vandalize; assassinate, butcher, cut down, dispatch, execute, kill, massacre, murder, slaughter, slay, zap

near ant create, invent; fabricate, fashion, forge, form, make, manufacture, shape; bring about, establish, found, institute, organize; conserve, preserve, protect, save; rebuild, reconstruct, remodel, renovate, restore

ant build, construct, erect, put up, raise
2 to bring destruction to (something) through violent action — see RAVAGE
3 to deprive of life — see KILL 1

destruction *n* the state or fact of being rendered nonexistent, physically unsound, or useless ⟨the violent storm re-

---

sulted in the *destruction* of their tree house⟩

syn annihilation, decimation, demolishment, demolition, desolation, devastation, extermination, extinction, havoc, loss, obliteration, ruin, ruination, wastage, wreckage

rel depredation, despoilment, despoliation; breakup, disintegration, dissolution; assassination, execution, killing, massacre, slaughter

near ant conservation, preservation, protection; reconstruction, re-creation, remodeling, renovation, restoration

ant building, construction, erection, raising

destructive *adj* 1 causing or tending to cause destruction ⟨the *destructive* storm blew down trees all over town, and blew the roof off our neighbor's house⟩

syn calamitous, cataclysmal (*or* cataclysmic), devastating, disastrous, ruinous

rel deadly, fatal, lethal, mortal, vital; deleterious, detrimental, harmful, pernicious

near ant preservative, protective; creative, formative; harmless, innocuous, inoffensive, nondestructive; ameliorative, helpful, useful

ant constructive
2 bringing about ruin or misfortune — see FATAL 1

desultorily *adv* without definite aim, direction, rule, or method — see HIT OR MISS

desultory *adj* 1 lacking a definite plan, purpose, or pattern — see RANDOM
2 passing from one topic to another — see DISCURSIVE

detached *adj* 1 having or showing a lack of friendliness or interest in others — see COOL 1
2 not physically attached to another unit — see SEPARATE 2

detachment *n* 1 lack of favoritism toward one side or another ⟨the judge showed great *detachment* when deciding the controversial case⟩

syn disinterestedness, impartiality, neutrality, objectivity

rel equitableness, fairness; apathy, indifference, unconcern; broad-mindedness, open-mindedness, tolerance

near ant chauvinism, nepotism; subjectivity; bent, inclination, leaning, penchant, predilection, predisposition, proclivity, propensity, tendency; preconception, prejudgment

ant bias, favor, favoritism, one-sidedness, partiality, partisanship, prejudice
2 a small military unit with a special task or function ⟨the general sent a *detachment* ahead to scout the enemy's position⟩

syn detail

rel commando, firing squad, paratroops, patrol, picket; battalion, command, company, corps, division, platoon, regiment, squad, troop, wing

detail *n* 1 a separate part in a list, account, or series — see ITEM 1

---

2 a single piece of information — see
FACT 3

3 a small military unit with a special task
or function — see DETACHMENT 2

detail *vb* 1 to assign to a place or position
— see ²POST

2 to pick (someone) by one's authority
for a specific position or duty — see AP-
POINT 2

3 to specify one after another — see
ENUMERATE 1

detailed *adj* 1 including many small descriptive features ⟨a *detailed* report on all
the activities that their Scout troop had
been involved in over the past year⟩
syn circumstantial, elaborate, full,
minute, particularized, thorough
rel enumerated, inventoried, itemized,
listed; delineated, specific, specified;
abundant, copious; comprehensive, exhausting, exhaustive, thoroughgoing; accurate, exact, precise; complete, entire,
replete; distinct, explicit, precise, sharp;
inclusive, mapped (out); descriptive,
graphic (*also* graphical), picturesque,
vivid
near ant concise, pithy, short, succinct;
abbreviated, abridged, curtailed, cut,
pruned, shortened, trimmed; indeterminate, nebulous, nondescript, sketchy,
vague; bird's-eye, broad, general, nonspecific, overall, unspecified
ant compendious, summary

2 made or done with great care or with
much detail — see ELABORATE 1

detailedly *adv* with attention to all aspects
or details — see THOROUGHLY 1

detainment *n* an instance or period of
being prevented from going about one's
business — see DELAY

detect *vb* to come upon after searching,
study, or effort — see FIND 1

detectable *adj* able to be perceived by a
sense or by the mind — see PERCEPTIBLE

detection *n* the act or process of sighting
or learning the existence of something for
the first time — see DISCOVERY 1

detective *n* a person whose business is
solving crimes and catching criminals or
gathering information that is not easy to
get ⟨the *detective* tracked the criminals to
an abandoned warehouse on the south
side of town⟩
syn investigator, operative, plainclothesman, shadow, sleuth, tail
rel Federal, G-man, narc (*or* nark) [*slang*]

detector *n* a device that detects some
physical quantity and responds usually
with a transmitted signal — see SENSOR

deter *vb* to steer (a person) from an activity or course of action — see DISCOUR-
AGE 2

detergent *n* a substance used for cleaning
— see CLEANER

deteriorate *vb* to become worse or of less
value ⟨the garden slowly *deteriorated*
after months of neglect⟩
syn crumble, decay, decline, degenerate,
descend, ebb, rot, sink, worsen

rel recede, wane; decompose, degrade,
disintegrate; sour, spoil; lessen, lower, reduce; debilitate, undermine, weaken
phrases go to pot
near ant better, upgrade; enhance, enrich,
fortify, heighten, intensify, strengthen;
advance, develop, progress
ant ameliorate, improve, meliorate

deterioration *n* 1 a gradual sinking and
wasting away of mind or body — see DE-
CLINE 1

2 a change to a lower state or level — see
DECLINE 2

determinate *adj* 1 having been established
and usually not subject to change — see
FIXED 1

2 having distinct or certain limits — see
LIMITED 1

determination *n* 1 firm or unwavering adherence to one's purpose ⟨the *determination* with which the pioneers settled the
land despite many hardships and set-
backs⟩
syn decidedness, decision, decisiveness,
firmness, granite, purposefulness, resoluteness, resolution, resolve
rel doggedness, obstinacy, perseverance,
persistence, stubbornness, tenaciousness,
tenacity; backbone, fortitude, grit, pluck
near ant uncertainty
ant hesitation, indecision, irresolution,
vacillation

2 a position arrived at after consideration
— see DECISION 1

3 an opinion arrived at through a process
of reasoning — see CONCLUSION 1

determine *vb* 1 to give an opinion about
(something at issue or in dispute) — see
JUDGE 1

2 to come to a judgment after discussion
or consideration — see DECIDE 1

3 to come upon after searching, study, or
effort — see FIND 1

determined *adj* 1 fully committed to
achieving a goal ⟨his *determined* opponent would not be bluffed or shaken⟩
syn bent (on *or* upon), bound, decisive,
firm, intent, purposeful, resolute, resolved, set
rel certain, cocksure, positive, sure; earnest, serious; steady, unfaltering, unhesitating, unswerving, unwavering
near ant doubtful, dubious, uncertain,
unsure
ant faltering, hesitant, indecisive, irresolute, undetermined, unresolved, vacillating, wavering

2 showing no signs of slackening or yielding in one's purpose — see UNYIELDING 1

determinedly *adv* with great effort or determination — see HARD 1

deterrent *n* something that makes movement or progress more difficult — see
ENCUMBRANCE

detest *vb* to dislike strongly — see HATE

detestable *adj* not following or in accordance with standards of honor and decency — see IGNOBLE 2

dethrone *vb* to remove from a position of prominence or power (as a throne) — see DEPOSE 1

detonate *vb* to break open or into pieces usually because of internal pressure — see EXPLODE 1

detonation *n* the act or an instance of exploding — see EXPLOSION 1

detour *vb* 1 to avoid by going around ⟨we had to *detour* the construction zone in order to get to the stadium⟩
    syn bypass, circumvent, skirt
    rel circumnavigate; avoid, dodge, duck, elude, escape, eschew, evade, shake, shun
    near ant confront, face, meet; accept, court, embrace, pursue, seek, welcome
2 to change one's course or direction — see TURN 3

detraction *n* the act of making a person or a thing seem little or unimportant — see DEPRECIATION

detriment *n* something that causes loss or pain — see INJURY 1

detrimental *adj* causing or capable of causing harm — see HARMFUL

devastate *vb* 1 to bring destruction to (something) through violent action — see RAVAGE
2 to bring to a complete end the physical soundness, existence, or usefulness of — see DESTROY 1
3 to subject to incapacitating emotional or mental stress — see OVERWHELM 1

devastating *adj* causing or tending to cause destruction — see DESTRUCTIVE 1

devastation *n* the state or fact of being rendered nonexistent, physically unsound, or useless — see DESTRUCTION

develop *vb* 1 to gradually become clearer or more detailed ⟨as the story of the bombing *developed*, the scope of the tragedy became more apparent⟩
    syn evolve, unfold
    rel advance, proceed, progress; mature, ripen; materialize
2 to come to have gradually ⟨they *developed* a taste for green olives⟩
    syn acquire, cultivate, form
    rel gain, get, obtain; achieve, attain, reach; foster, nourish, nurture, promote
    ant lose
3 to become mature — see MATURE
4 to express more fully and in greater detail — see EXPAND 1

developed *adj* being far along in development — see ADVANCED 1

developer *n* one who creates or introduces something new — see INVENTOR

development *n* 1 the act or process of going from the simple or basic to the complex or advanced ⟨the *development* of an idea into a marketable product⟩
    syn elaboration, evolution, expansion, growth, progress, progression
    rel advancement, betterment, improvement, perfection, refinement; maturation

near ant decadence, decay, decaying, declension, decline, degeneration, descent, deterioration, downgrade, ebbing, weakening
    ant regression, retrogression
2 a condition or occurrence traceable to a cause — see EFFECT 1
3 the process of becoming mature — see MATURATION

deviant *adj* departing from some accepted standard of what is normal ⟨some studies show that many violent criminals begin exhibiting *deviant* behavior in early childhood⟩
    syn aberrant, abnormal, anomalous, atypical, irregular, unnatural
    rel extraordinary, preternatural; rare, uncommon, uncustomary, unusual, unwonted; odd, peculiar, strange, weird
    near ant common, familiar, ordinary; customary, usual, wonted
    ant natural, normal, regular, standard, typical

deviant *n* a person who does not conform to generally accepted standards or customs — see NONCONFORMIST

deviate *vb* to change one's course or direction — see TURN 3

device *n* 1 a clever often underhanded means to achieve an end — see TRICK 1
2 an article intended for use in work — see IMPLEMENT
3 **devices** *pl* a habitual attraction to some activity or thing — see INCLINATION 1

devil *n* 1 *cap* the supreme personification of evil often represented as the ruler of Hell ⟨the *Devil* is traditionally seen as a being who relentlessly tempts people to commit evil⟩
    syn Lucifer, Satan
    rel deuce, dickens
    phrases Prince of Darkness
2 an evil spirit — see DEMON
3 a member of the human race — see HUMAN
4 an appealingly mischievous person — see SCAMP 1
5 a mean, evil, or unprincipled person — see VILLAIN

devilfish *n* any of several extremely large rays ⟨they saw a *devilfish* when they went scuba diving in the Caribbean, but it swam away quickly⟩
    syn devil ray, manta, manta ray, sea devil
    rel ray, skate

devilish *adj* 1 going beyond a normal or acceptable limit in degree or amount — see EXCESSIVE
2 of, relating to, or worthy of an evil spirit — see FIENDISH
3 tending to or exhibiting reckless playfulness — see MISCHIEVOUS 1

devilishly *adv* beyond a normal or acceptable limit — see TOO 1

devilishness *n* playful, reckless behavior that is not intended to cause serious harm — see MISCHIEF 1

devil—may—care *adj* 1 having a relaxed, casual manner — see EASYGOING 1

---

syn synonym(s)   **rel** related words
ant antonym(s)   **near ant** near antonym(s)

2 having or showing a lack of concern or seriousness — see CAREFREE

3 having or showing a lack of concern for the consequences of one's actions — see RECKLESS 1

devilment *n* playful, reckless behavior that is not intended to cause serious harm — see MISCHIEF 1

devil ray *n* any of several extremely large rays — see DEVILFISH

devilry *or* **deviltry** *n* playful, reckless behavior that is not intended to cause serious harm — see MISCHIEF 1

devious *adj* **1** clever at attaining one's ends by indirect and often deceptive means — see ARTFUL 1

2 marked by a long series of irregular curves — see CROOKED 1

deviousness *n* skill in achieving one's ends through indirect, subtle, or underhanded means — see CUNNING 1

devise *vb* to create or think of by clever use of the imagination — see INVENT

deviser *n* one who creates or introduces something new — see INVENTOR

devoid *adj* utterly lacking in something needed, wanted, or expected ⟨the so-called comedy is totally *devoid* of intelligence, originality, and even laughs⟩
syn bereft, destitute, void
rel bare, barren, blank, empty, lacking, stark, vacant, wanting; deficient, fragmental, fragmentary, incomplete, partial; absent, missing
near ant filled, full; furnished, provided, supplied
ant replete

2 lacking contents that could or should be present — see EMPTY 1

devote *vb* **1** to keep or intend for a special purpose ⟨he *devoted* several hours every weekend to playing with his dog⟩
syn allocate, consecrate, dedicate, earmark, reserve, save
rel hallow, sanctify; commit, confide, consign, entrust
phrases set apart, set aside

2 to occupy (oneself) diligently or with close attention — see APPLY

devoted *adj* **1** feeling or showing love — see LOVING

2 firm in one's allegiance to someone or something — see FAITHFUL 1

devotedness *n* **1** a feeling of strong or constant regard for and dedication to someone — see LOVE 1

2 adherence to something to which one is bound by a pledge or duty — see FIDELITY

devotee *n* a person with a strong and habitual liking for something — see FAN

devotion *n* **1** a feeling of strong or constant regard for and dedication to someone — see LOVE 1

2 adherence to something to which one is bound by a pledge or duty — see FIDELITY

3 belief and trust in and loyalty to God — see FAITH 1

devotional *adj* of, relating to, or used in the practice or worship services of a religion — see RELIGIOUS 1

devour *vb* to destroy all trace of — see CONSUME 1

devout *adj* showing a devotion to God and to a life of virtue — see HOLY 1

devoutness *n* the quality or state of being spiritually pure or virtuous — see HOLINESS

dexterity *n* **1** mental skill or quickness ⟨the ambassador showed great *dexterity* in his handling of the touchy situation⟩
syn adroitness, cleverness, finesse, sleight
rel ability, prowess, talent; competence, efficiency, expertise, know-how, proficiency; ingeniousness, ingenuity, resourcefulness
near ant inadequacy, ineptitude, ineptness; slowness, stupidity

2 ease and grace in physical activity ⟨the juggler needed lots of *dexterity* in order to keep all five balls in the air at the same time⟩
syn agility, deftness, nimbleness, sleight, spryness
rel coordination
ant awkwardness, clumsiness, gawkiness

dexterous *also* **dextrous** *adj* **1** skillful with the hands ⟨the *dexterous* watchmaker was able to repair the tiny gears and parts in the antique watch⟩
syn clever, cunning, deft, handy
rel agile, flexible, graceful, limber, lissome (*also* lissom), lithe, nimble, spry; coordinated; adept, competent, expert, masterful, masterly, proficient, skilled, skillful; double-jointed, loose-jointed
near ant awkward, bungling, clumsy, fumbling, gawky; uncoordinated; incompetent, inept, maladroit
ant butterfingered, heavy-handed, unhandy

2 accomplished with trained ability — see SKILLFUL

diabolical *or* **diabolic** *adj* of, relating to, or worthy of an evil spirit — see FIENDISH

diadem *n* a decorative band or wreath worn about the head as a symbol of victory or honor — see CROWN 1

diagnosis *n* a position arrived at after consideration — see DECISION 1

diagonal *adj* running in a slanting direction ⟨the *diagonal* design ran up the wall all the way from the lower left to the upper right-hand corner⟩
syn canted, inclined, leaning, listing, oblique, pitched, slanted, slantwise, sloped, sloping, tilted, tilting
near ant horizontal, vertical; parallel, perpendicular

diagonal *n* the degree to which something rises up from a position level with the horizon — see SLANT

diagram *n* something that visually explains or decorates a text — see ILLUSTRATION 1

dial *vb* to make a telephone call to — see CALL 2

dialect *n* the special terms or expressions of a particular group or field — see TERMINOLOGY

dialogue *also* **dialog** *n* talking or a talk between two or more people — see CONVERSATION

diametric *or* **diametrical** *adj* being as different as possible — see OPPOSITE

diatribe *n* a long angry speech or scolding — see TIRADE

dice *n* a small cube marked on each side with one to six spots and usually played in pairs in various games — see DIE

dice *vb* to cut into small pieces — see CHOP

dicker *vb* to talk over or dispute the terms of a purchase — see BARGAIN

dictate *n* a statement of what to do that must be obeyed by those concerned — see COMMAND 1

dictate *vb* to give an order — see COMMAND 1

dictator *n* a person who uses power or authority in a cruel, unjust, or harmful way — see DESPOT

dictatorial *adj* 1 exercising power or authority without interference by others — see ABSOLUTE 1

2 fond of ordering people around — see BOSSY

3 having or showing a tendency to force one's will on others without any regard to fairness or necessity — see ARBITRARY 1

dictatorship *n* a system of government in which the ruler has unlimited power — see DESPOTISM

diction *n* 1 the clear and accurate pronunciation of words especially in public speaking ⟨the actors had very good *diction*, clearly speaking every single word of the Shakespearean play that they were performing⟩
syn articulation, enunciation
rel elocution; speech, wording

2 the way in which something is put into words — see WORDING

dictionary *n* a reference book giving information about the meanings, pronunciations, uses, and origins of words listed in alphabetical order ⟨try to develop the habit of going to the *dictionary* whenever you encounter an unfamiliar word⟩
syn lexicon, wordbook
rel glossary, thesaurus, vocabulary

die *n* a small cube marked on each side with one to six spots and usually played in pairs in various games ⟨he rolled the *die*, hoping for a six⟩
syn bone(s), dice

die *vb* 1 to stop living ⟨the king *died* of old age after ruling for many years⟩
syn croak [*slang*], decease, depart, expire, pass (on), pass away, perish, succumb
rel disappear, fade
phrases bite the dust
near ant be, exist, subsist; flourish, prosper, thrive

ant breathe, live

2 to come to an end — see CEASE 1

3 to stop functioning — see FAIL 1

die (down) *vb* to grow less in scope or intensity especially gradually — see DECREASE 2

die (for) *vb* to have an earnest wish to own or enjoy — see DESIRE

differ *vb* 1 to be unlike; to not be the same ⟨my brother and I *differ* in looks⟩
syn disagree, vary
rel clash, conflict, jar; distinguish, divide, separate
near ant blend, harmonize
ant accord, agree, conform, correspond

2 to have a different opinion — see DISAGREE 1

difference *n* 1 the quality or state of being different ⟨there's a great *difference* between claiming to care about the environment and living like you really do⟩
syn contrast, disagreement, discrepancy, disparateness, disparity, dissimilarity, distinction, distinctiveness, distinctness, diverseness, diversity, unlikeness
rel deviance, divergence; change, modification, variation; conflict, discord, discordance, dissension, dissent, dissidence, disunity, friction, strife; variability, variance; incompatibility, incongruity, incongruousness; disproportion
near ant identicalness, identity; analogy, similitude; accordance, agreement, conformity, congruity, correspondence; equality, equivalence, equivalency; parallelism
ant alikeness, community, likeness, resemblance, sameness, similarity

2 variance of opinion on a matter — see DISAGREEMENT 1

3 the act, process, or result of making different — see CHANGE

different *adj* 1 being not of the same kind ⟨apples are *different* from oranges⟩
syn disparate, dissimilar, distinct, distinctive, distinguishable, diverse, other, unalike, unlike
rel divers, miscellaneous, several, sundry, variant, varied, various; individual, particular, peculiar, single; unequal; disproportionate
near ant identical, selfsame; equal, equivalent, tantamount; akin, analogous, comparable, related; homogeneous, uniform
ant alike, indistinguishable, like, parallel, same, similar

2 not the same or shared — see SEPARATE 1

differential *adj* favoring, applying, or being unequal treatment of different classes of people — see DISCRIMINATORY

differentiate *vb* to understand or point out the difference — see DISTINGUISH 1

differently *adv* in a different way — see OTHERWISE

difficult *adj* 1 requiring considerable physical or mental effort — see HARD 2

2 requiring exceptional skill or caution in performance or handling — see TRICKY

---

syn synonym(s)   *rel* related words
ant antonym(s)   *near ant* near antonym(s)

difficulty n 1 something that is a cause for suffering or special effort especially in the attainment of a goal ⟨the many *difficulties* that he encountered on the road from poor orphan to head of a major corporation⟩

syn adversity, asperity, hardness, hardship, rigor

rel discomfort, inconvenience, nuisance; affliction, trial, tribulation; knock, misfortune, mishap, tragedy; bar, catch, check, clog, crimp, embarrassment, handicap, hindrance, hitch, hurdle, impediment, interference, let, manacle, obstacle, obstruction, rub, shackle, snag, stop, trammel; block, chain, deterrent, encumbrance, fetter, inhibition; hump

near ant advantage, break, opportunity

2 something that makes a situation more complicated or difficult — see COMPLICATION 1

diffident adj not comfortable around people — see SHY 2

diffuse adj using or containing more words than necessary to express an idea — see WORDY

diffuseness n the use of too many words to express an idea — see VERBIAGE

dig n 1 a quick thrust — see ¹POKE

2 an act or expression showing scorn and usually intended to hurt another's feelings — see INSULT

dig vb 1 to hollow out or form (something) by removing earth ⟨a backhoe *dug* a hole in the backyard to make a swimming pool⟩

syn excavate, shovel

rel dredge; burrow, claw, grub; dig in; scoop, spade; delve; mine, quarry

near ant fill (in); smooth (out *or* over)

2 to take pleasure in — see ENJOY 1

3 slang to recognize the meaning of — see COMPREHEND 1

dig (into) vb to search through or into — see EXPLORE 1

dig (through) vb to look through (as a place) carefully or thoroughly in an effort to find or discover something — see SEARCH 1

dig (up) vb to come upon after searching, study, or effort — see FIND 1

digest n 1 a short statement of the main points — see SUMMARY

2 a shortened version of a written work — see ABRIDGMENT

digest vb to make into a short statement of the main points (as of a report) — see SUMMARIZE

diggings n pl the place where one lives — see HOME 1

digit n a character used to represent a mathematical value — see NUMBER

dignified adj having or showing a serious and reserved manner ⟨the chief justice of the U.S. Supreme Court is always very *dignified* when swearing in the new president⟩ ⟨*dignified* funeral services for the fallen firemen⟩

syn august, imposing, solemn, staid, stately

rel decorous, formal, proper, seemly; grim, sober, somber (*or* sombre); aristocratic, lordly, majestic, noble

near ant coarse, crass, crude, improper, indecent, uncouth, unseemly, vulgar

ant flighty, frivolous, giddy, goofy, silly, undignified

dignify vb to enhance the status of — see EXALT

dignity n high position within society — see RANK 2

digression n a departure from the subject under consideration — see TANGENT

digressive adj passing from one topic to another — see DISCURSIVE

dike n 1 a bank of earth constructed to control water — see DAM

2 a long narrow channel dug in the earth — see DITCH

dilapidated adj showing signs of advanced wear and tear and neglect — see SHABBY 1

dilapidation n the state of being unattended to or not cared for — see NEGLECT 1

dilatory adj moving or proceeding at less than the normal, desirable, or required speed — see SLOW 1

dilemma n a situation in which one has to choose between two or more equally unsatisfactory choices ⟨they were faced with a *dilemma* : either they could spend the night out in the cold or they could walk back into their house and face their father⟩

syn quandary

rel deadlock, halt, impasse, quagmire, stalemate, standoff; knot, problem; difficulty, fix, hole, jam, pickle, pinch, plight, predicament, spot

near ant breeze, cinch, duck soup, snap

dilettante adj lacking or showing a lack of expert skill — see AMATEURISH

dilettante n 1 a person having a knowledgeable and fine appreciation of the arts — see CONNOISSEUR

2 a person who regularly or occasionally engages in an activity without being or becoming an expert at it — see AMATEUR

diligence n attentive and persistent effort ⟨through the *diligence* and ingenuity of a single detective, the gang's ringleader was finally caught⟩

syn assiduity, assiduousness, industriousness, industry

rel application, concentration; doggedness, perseverance, persistence, tenacity, tirelessness

near ant carelessness; idleness, indolence, laziness

diligent adj involved in often constant activity — see BUSY 1

diligently adv with great effort or determination — see HARD 1

dillydally vb 1 to move or act slowly — see DELAY 1

2 to spend time doing nothing — see IDLE

dillydallying *adj* moving or proceeding at less than the normal, desirable, or required speed — see SLOW 1

dilute *adj* **1** not containing very much of some important element — see WEAK 3

2 containing foreign or lower-grade substances — see IMPURE

dilute *vb* to alter (something) for the worse with the addition of foreign or lower-grade substances — see ADULTERATE

diluted *adj* **1** not containing very much of some important element — see WEAK 3

2 containing foreign or lower-grade substances — see IMPURE

dim *adj* **1** being without light or without much light — see DARK 1

2 lacking a surface luster or gloss — see MATTE

3 not seen or understood clearly — see FAINT 1

dim *vb* to make dark, dim, or indistinct — see CLOUD 1

dimension *n* **1** the total amount of measurable space or surface occupied by something — see SIZE 1

2 dimensions *pl* an area over which activity, capacity, or influence extends — see RANGE 2

diminish *vb* **1** to express scornfully one's low opinion of — see DECRY 1

2 to make smaller in amount, volume, or extent — see DECREASE 1

3 to grow less in scope or intensity especially gradually — see DECREASE 2

diminishment *n* **1** the act of making a person or a thing seem little or unimportant — see DEPRECIATION

2 the amount by which something is lessened — see DECREASE

diminution *n* the amount by which something is lessened — see DECREASE

diminutive *adj* of a size that is less than average — see SMALL 1

diminutive *n* a living thing much smaller than others of its kind — see DWARF 1

diminutiveness *n* the quality or state of being little in size — see SMALLNESS

dimmed *adj* being without light or without much light — see DARK 1

din *n* loud, confused, and usually unharmonious sound — see NOISE 1

din *vb* to say or state again — see REPEAT 1

dine *vb* **1** to take a meal ⟨they *dined* elegantly at the city's finest restaurant before taking in an opera downtown⟩

syn eat, fare, feed

rel banquet, feast, fete (*or* fête); board, mess; breakfast, lunch, sup; picnic

2 to entertain with a fancy meal — see FEAST

diner *n* a public establishment where meals are served to paying customers for consumption on the premises — see RESTAURANT

dinghy *n* a boat equipped with one or more sails — see SAILBOAT

dinginess *n* the state or quality of being dirty — see DIRTINESS 1

dingy *adj* not clean — see DIRTY 1

dinky *adj* of a size that is less than average — see SMALL 1

dinner *n* a large fancy meal often accompanied by ceremony or entertainment — see FEAST

dinnerware *n* dishes used for eating or serving food or drink — see TABLEWARE 2

dinning *adj* making loud, confused, and usually unharmonious sounds — see NOISY 1

dint *n* a sunken area forming a separate space — see HOLE 2

dip *n* the act or process of going to a lower level or altitude — see DESCENT 1

dip *vb* **1** to sink or push (something) briefly into or as if into a liquid ⟨he went to *dip* a paper towel in water and clean off the window⟩ ⟨she *dipped* a hand into her pocket and pulled out a piece of candy⟩

syn douse, duck, dunk, immerse, souse, submerge, submerse

rel drench, flood, soak, wet; plunge, thrust

2 to lift out with something that holds liquid ⟨they *dipped* water from the bucket to pour into the kettle⟩

syn lade, ladle, scoop, spoon

rel bail; deplete, drain, eliminate, exhaust; bleed, draw (off); dish; draw, siphon

near ant pour; fill

3 to go to a lower level — see DROP 2

4 to lead or extend downward — see DESCEND 1

5 to take a quick or hasty look — see GLANCE 1

diplomacy *n* the ability to deal with others in touchy situations without offending them — see TACT

diplomatic *adj* having or showing tact — see TACTFUL

dipper *n* a utensil with a bowl and a handle that is used especially in cooking and serving food — see SPOON

dire *adj* **1** being or showing a sign of evil or calamity to come — see OMINOUS

2 causing fear — see FEARFUL

3 needing immediate attention — see ACUTE 2

direct *adj* **1** done or working without something else coming in between ⟨a zoologist whose works are based entirely on her *direct* observation of animals in the wild⟩ ⟨the virus was the *direct* cause of the disease⟩

syn firsthand, immediate, primary

rel clinical

ant indirect, secondhand

2 free in expressing one's true feelings and opinions — see FRANK

3 going straight to the point clearly and firmly — see STRAIGHTFORWARD 1

direct *adv* in a direct line or course — see DIRECTLY 1

---

syn synonym(s)   **rel** related words
ant antonym(s)   **near ant** near antonym(s)

direct *vb* **1** to cause to move to a central point or along a restricted pathway — see CHANNEL

2 to issue orders to (someone) by right of authority — see COMMAND 1

3 to give an order — see COMMAND 2

4 to look after and make decisions about — see CONDUCT 1

5 to point or turn (something) toward a target or goal — see AIM 1

6 to point out the way for (someone) especially from a position in front — see LEAD 1

direction *n* **1** a statement of what to do that must be obeyed by those concerned — see COMMAND 1

2 the act or activity of looking after and making decisions about something — see CONDUCT 1

directive *n* **1** a statement of what to do that must be obeyed by those concerned — see COMMAND 1

2 an order publicly issued by an authority — see EDICT 1

3 a written communication giving information or directions — see MEMORANDUM 1

directly *adv* **1** in a direct line or course ⟨we went *directly* to the school without stopping⟩

syn dead, direct, due, plumb, plump, right, straight

phrases as the crow flies

near ant circuitously, deviously

ant indirectly

2 in an honest and direct manner — see STRAIGHTFORWARD

3 in the same words — see VERBATIM

4 without delay — see IMMEDIATELY

directness *n* the free expression of one's true feelings and opinions — see CANDOR

director *n* a person who manages or directs — see EXECUTIVE

directorial *adj* suited for or relating to the directing of things — see EXECUTIVE

direful *adj* causing fear — see FEARFUL 1

dirge *n* a composition expressing one's grief over a loss — see LAMENT 2

dirt *n* **1** the loose spongue material in which plants naturally grow ⟨dig into the *dirt* to a depth of about three inches⟩

syn earth, ground, soil

rel clay, duff, dust, gravel, humus, loam, loess, marl, mud, sand, silt, subsoil, topsoil

2 the solid part of our planet's surface as distinguished from the sea and air — see EARTH 2

3 foul matter that mars the purity or cleanliness of something — see FILTH 1

4 the quality or state of being obscene — see OBSCENITY 1

dirtiness *n* **1** the state or quality of being dirty ⟨when the maid arrived, she exclaimed over the *dirtiness* of the china⟩

syn dinginess, dustiness, filthiness, foulness, griminess, grubbiness, nastiness, squalidness, uncleanliness, uncleanness

rel impurity; messiness, sloppiness, untidiness; shabbiness; squalor; smuttiness, sootiness

near ant purity

ant cleanliness, immaculateness, spotlessness

2 the quality or state of being obscene — see OBSCENITY 1

dirty *adj* **1** not clean ⟨after playing in the mud all day, his clothes were very *dirty*⟩

syn besmirched, blackened, dingy, dusty, filthy, foul, grimy, grubby, mucky, muddy, nasty, smutty, soiled, sordid, stained, sullied, unclean, uncleanly

rel contaminated, defiled, impure, polluted, tainted; uncleaned, unsanitary, unsterile, unsterilized, unwashed; discolored; bedraggled, draggled, chaotic, cluttered, confused, disarranged, disarrayed, disheveled (or dishevelled), disordered, jumbled, littered, messed, messy, muddled, mussed, mussy, rumpled, scruffy, sloppy, slovenly, unkempt, untidy; shabby, sleazy, squalid; smutty, sooty

near ant clear, limpid, pure; cleaned, cleansed, combed, groomed, neat, ordered, orderly, tidy; bleached, purified, whitened; bright, flawless, perfect, shiny, sparkling, unspotted, untouched; taintless, unblemished, undefiled, unpolluted, untainted; wholesome

ant clean, cleanly, immaculate, spick-and-span (or spic-and-span), spotless, stainless, unsoiled, unstained, unsullied

2 depicting or referring to sexual matters in a way that is unacceptable in polite society — see OBSCENE 1

3 marked by wet and windy conditions — see FOUL 1

4 not being in accordance with the rules or standards of what is fair in sport — see FOUL 2

5 not following or in accordance with standards of honor and decency — see IGNOBLE 2

dirty *vb* to make dirty ⟨she *dirtied* her new shoes when she splashed in the puddle⟩

syn befoul, begrime, besmirch, blacken, foul, grime, mire, muddy, smirch, smudge, soil, stain, sully

rel contaminate, defile, pollute, taint; discolor; confuse, disarrange, disarray, dishevel, disorder, jumble, mess, muddle

near ant decontaminate, purge, purify; disinfect, sanitize; brush, dry-clean, dust, launder, mop, rinse, scour, scrub, sweep, wash, wipe; brighten, deodorize, freshen, renew, spruce (up); straighten (up), tidy (up)

ant clean, cleanse

dis *vb, slang* **1** to cause hurt feelings or deep resentment in — see INSULT

2 to express one's unfavorable opinion of the worth or quality of — see CRITICIZE

disable *vb* **1** to cause severe or permanent injury to — see MAIM

2 to render powerless, ineffective, or unable to move — see PARALYZE

disabled *adj* deprived of the power to perform one or more natural bodily activities ⟨the *disabled* man was unable to climb the stairs without help⟩
syn challenged, incapacitated
rel blind, deaf, mute; halt, lame, paralyzed, quadriplegic; immobile, immobilized; ailing, diseased, ill, sick, unfit, unhealthy, unsound, unwell
near ant bouncing, chipper, fit, hale, healthy, hearty, robust, sound, well, whole, wholesome
ant able-bodied, nondisabled

disabuse *vb* to free from mistaken beliefs or foolish hopes — see DISILLUSION

disadvantage *n* a feature of someone or something that creates difficulty for achieving success ⟨their lack of height was a *disadvantage* on the basketball court⟩
syn drawback, handicap, liability, minus, penalty, strike
rel stranglehold; detriment, disability, impairment; failing, shortcoming; bar, catch, check, clog, crimp, embarrassment, hindrance, hitch, hurdle, impediment, interference, let, manacle, obstacle, obstruction, rub, shackle, stop, trammel
near ant vantage; head start, jump, lead, margin, start; ascendancy, better, command, control, drop, mastery, predominance, superiority, supremacy, transcendence, upper hand; prerogative, privilege; break, opportunity; aid, assistance, help
ant advantage, asset, edge, plus

disadvantaged *adj* kept from having the necessities of life or a healthful environment — see DEPRIVED

disadvantageous *adj* opposed to one's interests — see ADVERSE 1

disaffect *vb* 1 to cause to change from friendly or loving to unfriendly or uncaring — see ESTRANGE
2 to make discontented — see DISCONTENT

disaffection *n* the loss of friendship or affection — see ESTRANGEMENT

disagree *vb* 1 to have a different opinion ⟨she thought we were still headed north on the trail, but I *disagreed*⟩
syn differ, dissent
rel clash, collide, conflict, contrast; counter, debate, object, oppose, protest, resist; contest, dispute; argue, bicker, fall out, quarrel
near ant accede, accept, acquiesce, comply, consent, subscribe; affiliate, ally, associate, collaborate, collude, compromise, cooperate, get along, side
ant agree, assent, concur
2 to be unlike; to not be the same — see DIFFER 1

disagree (with) *vb* to make an assertion that is contrary to one made by (another) — see CONTRADICT 1

disagreeable *adj* 1 having or showing a habitually bad temper — see ILL-TEMPERED
2 not giving pleasure to the mind or senses — see UNPLEASANT

disagreeing *adj* not being in agreement or harmony — see INCONSISTENT

disagreement *n* 1 variance of opinion on a matter ⟨there was some *disagreement* about what the color of the missing sweater actually was⟩
syn controversy, debate, difference, disputation, dispute, dissension
rel clash, collision, conflict, contention, discord, strife; discussion; altercation, argument, bicker, falling-out, fight, quarrel
near ant acceptance, compliance; concord, peace
ant accord, agreement, consensus, harmony, unanimity
2 an often noisy or angry expression of differing opinions — see ARGUMENT 1
3 the quality or state of being different — see DIFFERENCE 1

disallow *vb* 1 to declare not to be true — see DENY 1
2 to be unwilling to grant — see DENY 2

disallowance *n* 1 an unwillingness to grant something asked for — see DENIAL 1
2 a refusal to confirm the truth of a statement — see DENIAL 2

disappear *vb* to cease to be visible ⟨the stranger *disappeared* into the mists, never to be seen again⟩
syn dissolve, evanesce, evaporate, fade, flee, go (away), melt, vanish
rel clear, dissipate
near ant arrive, break out, come out, emerge, issue, loom, show up
ant appear, materialize

disappoint *vb* to fall short in satisfying the expectation or hope of ⟨they were *disappointed* by the outcome of the big game⟩
syn cheat, dissatisfy, fail, let down
rel discontent, disgruntle, displease; disenchant, disillusion
near ant gladden
ant satisfy

disappointment *n* 1 the emotion felt when one's expectations are not met ⟨we felt *disappointment* after failing a test that we thought would be easy⟩
syn dismay, dissatisfaction, frustration, letdown
rel disenchantment, disillusionment; blues, dejection, depression, desolateness, desolation, despondency, disconsolateness, distress, doldrums, dolefulness, dolor, downheartedness, dreariness, dumps, gloom, gloominess, joylessness, melancholy, mopes, oppression, sadness, sorrow, unhappiness; alarm, concern, consternation; chagrin, discomfiture
near ant bliss, felicity, gladness, happiness, joy
ant contentment, gratification, satisfaction
2 something that disappoints ⟨after all the publicity and high expectations, the se-

---

quel to the movie blockbuster was a *disappointment*⟩

syn bummer, letdown

rel anticlimax, failure, fiasco, fizzle; lemon, loser

near ant success, winner; relief

disapprobation *n* refusal to accept as right or desirable — see DISAPPROVAL

disapproval *n* refusal to accept as right or desirable ⟨thus far, every one of her boyfriends has met with her parents' *disapproval*⟩

syn deprecation, disapprobation, disfavor, dislike, displeasure

rel blame, censure, criticism, condemnation, denunciation, dressing down, opprobrium, reproach, reprobation; antagonism, antipathy, hostility; belittlement, disparagement, opposition

near ant acclaim, commendation, praise; endorsement, sanction; empathy, sympathy

ant approbation, approval, favor

disapprove *vb* to show unwillingness to accept, do, engage in, or agree to — see DECLINE 1

disapprove (of) *vb* to hold an unfavorable opinion of ⟨my sister *disapproves* of smoking and refuses to date anyone who thinks it's cool⟩

syn deprecate, discountenance, disfavor, dislike, frown (on), reprove

rel blame, censure, condemn, criticize, denounce, reprehend, reprobate; chide, rebuke, reproach, scold

near ant endorse (*also* indorse), sanction, support; adore, delight (in), dig, enjoy, fancy, groove (on), love, relish, revel (in)

ant approve, favor, like

disarm *vb* 1 to reduce the size and strength of the armed forces of ⟨the defeated nation was *disarmed* so that it would never again be a threat to international order⟩

syn demilitarize

rel demobilize

near ant equip, mobilize

ant arm, militarize

2 to lessen the anger or agitation of — see PACIFY

disarmament *n* the reduction or elimination of a country's armed forces or weapons ⟨the ambassador spoke at length about the possible unilateral *disarmament* of his country⟩

syn demilitarization

rel demobilization

near ant mobilization

ant militarization

disarming *adj* 1 having qualities that tend to make one loved — see LOVABLE

2 likely to win one's affection — see INGRATIATING

3 tending to lessen or avoid conflict or hostility — see PACIFIC 1

disarrange *vb* to undo the proper order or arrangement of — see DISORDER

disarranged *adj* lacking in order, neatness, and often cleanliness — see MESSY

disarrangement *n* a state in which everything is out of order — see CHAOS

disarray *n* a state in which everything is out of order — see CHAOS

disarray *vb* to undo the proper order or arrangement of — see DISORDER

disarrayed *adj* lacking in order, neatness, and often cleanliness — see MESSY

disassemble *vb* to take apart ⟨they had to *disassemble* the television set in order to replace the wiring⟩

syn demount, dismantle, dismember, knock down, strike, take down

rel detach, disengage; disconnect, disjoin, disunite, divide, separate

near ant build, erect; combine, unite

ant assemble, construct, put together

disaster *n* a sudden violent event that brings about great loss or destruction ⟨hurricanes are natural *disasters*⟩

syn calamity, cataclysm, catastrophe, debacle (*also* débâcle), tragedy

rel collapse, crash, meltdown; convulsion, paroxysm, upheaval; accident, casualty, fatality; misadventure, mischance, misfortune, mishap, woe; bummer, downer

near ant godsend, manna, windfall

disastrous *adj* 1 bringing about ruin or misfortune — see FATAL 1

2 causing or tending to cause destruction — see DESTRUCTIVE 1

disavow *vb* 1 to declare not to be true — see DENY 1

2 to refuse to acknowledge as one's own or as one's responsibility — see DISCLAIM 1

disavowal *n* a refusal to confirm the truth of a statement — see DENIAL 2

disband *vb* 1 to cease to exist or cause to cease to exist as a group or organization ⟨they *disbanded* the committee after the report had been submitted⟩ ⟨the rock group *disbanded* upon finishing the tour⟩

syn break up, disperse, dissolve

near ant incorporate; consolidate

ant band, join, unite

2 to cause (members of a group) to move widely apart — see SCATTER 1

disbandment *n* an act or process in which something scatters or is scattered — see SCATTERING 1

disbelief *n* refusal to accept as true ⟨their story explaining their absence was met with frank *disbelief*⟩

syn incredulity, unbelief

rel distrust, doubt, mistrust, skepticism, suspicion, uncertainty; denial, rejection, repudiation

near ant acceptance, faith; trust

ant belief, credence, credit

disbelieve *vb* to think not to be true or real ⟨many *disbelieved* the medium's claims that she could communicate with the spirits of the dead⟩

syn discredit, negate

rel deny, reject, repudiate; distrust, doubt, mistrust, suspect; debunk, disprove; deride, pooh-pooh, scoff (at)

near ant trust

ant accept, believe, credit, swallow

disbeliever *n* a person who is always ready to doubt or question the truth or existence of something — see SKEPTIC

disbelieving *adj* inclined to doubt or question claims — see SKEPTICAL 1

disburden *vb* 1 to empty or rid of cargo — see UNLOAD 1

2 to set (a person or thing) free of something that encumbers — see RID

disburse *vb* to hand over or use up in payment — see SPEND 1

disbursement *n* 1 a payment made in the course of achieving a result — see EXPENSE

2 the act of offering money in exchange for goods or services — see PAYMENT 1

discard *n* something separated from a group or lot for not being as good as the others — see CULL

discard *vb* to get rid of as useless or unwanted ⟨*discard* an old, torn sweater⟩
syn cast, ditch, dump, fling (off *or* away), jettison, junk, lose, reject, scrap, shed, shuck (off), slough (*also* sluff), throw away, throw out, unload
rel abandon, desert, forsake; dismiss; abolish, annihilate, eliminate, eradicate, expunge, exterminate, extinguish, extirpate, liquidate, remove, root (out), stamp (out), wipe out
phrases dispose of, set aside
near ant adopt, embrace, take on; employ, use, utilize; hold, hold back, keep, retain

discarding *n* the getting rid of whatever is unwanted or useless — see DISPOSAL 1

discern *vb* 1 to make note of (something) through the use of one's eyes — see SEE 1

2 to understand or point out the difference — see DISTINGUISH 1

discernible *adj* able to be perceived by a sense or by the mind — see PERCEPTIBLE

discerning *adj* having or showing deep understanding and intelligent application of knowledge — see WISE 1

discernment *n* the ability to understand inner qualities or relationships — see WISDOM 1

discharge *n* 1 a directed propelling of a missile from a firearm or artillery piece — see SHOT

2 a freeing from an obligation or responsibility — see RELEASE 1

3 the termination of the employment of an employee or a work force often temporarily — see LAYOFF

4 the doing of an action — see COMMISSION 2

discharge *vb* 1 to cause (a projectile) to be driven forward with force — see SHOOT 1

2 to empty or rid of cargo — see UNLOAD 1

3 to give what is owed for — see PAY 2

4 to set free (as from slavery or confinement) — see FREE 1

5 to throw or give off — see EMIT 1

6 to cause a weapon to release a missile with great force — see SHOOT 2

disciple *n* one who follows the opinions or teachings of another — see FOLLOWER

disciplinary *adj* inflicting, involving, or serving as punishment — see PUNITIVE

discipline *n* 1 a region of activity, knowledge, or influence — see FIELD 2

2 suffering, loss, or hardship imposed in response to a crime or offense — see PUNISHMENT

discipline *vb* to inflict a penalty on for a fault or crime — see PUNISH

disciplining *adj* inflicting, involving, or serving as punishment — see PUNITIVE

disclaim *vb* 1 to refuse to acknowledge as one's own or as one's responsibility ⟨the prisoner *disclaimed* any part in the prank⟩
syn disavow, disown, repudiate
rel contradict, deny, disallow, gainsay, negate, negative, refuse, reject; challenge, confute, criticize, disprove, rebut, refute; dispute, question
near ant accept, adopt, embrace, espouse; admit, concede, confess, grant; announce, assert, aver, declare, maintain, profess, submit; authenticate, confirm, corroborate, substantiate, validate, verify
ant acknowledge, avow, claim, own, recognize

2 to declare not to be true — see DENY 1

disclaimer *n* a refusal to confirm the truth of a statement — see DENIAL 2

disclose *vb* to make known (as information previously kept secret) — see REVEAL 1

disclosure *n* the act or an instance of making known something previously unknown or concealed — see REVELATION

disco *n* a bar or restaurant offering special nighttime entertainment (as music, dancing, or comedy acts) — see NIGHTCLUB

discomfit *vb* to throw into a state of self-conscious distress — see EMBARRASS 1

discomfiting *adj* causing embarrassment — see AWKWARD 3

discomfiture *n* the emotional state of being made self-consciously uncomfortable — see EMBARRASSMENT 1

discomfort *vb* to trouble the mind of; to make uneasy — see DISTURB 1

discomforting *adj* 1 causing discomfort — see UNCOMFORTABLE 1

2 causing worry or anxiety — see TROUBLESOME

discommode *vb* to cause discomfort to or trouble for — see INCONVENIENCE

discommoding *adj* causing difficulty, discomfort, or annoyance — see INCONVENIENT 1

discompose *vb* 1 to trouble the mind of; to make uneasy — see DISTURB 1

2 to undo the proper order or arrangement of — see DISORDER

discomposing *adj* causing worry or anxiety — see TROUBLESOME

disconcert *vb* to throw into a state of self-conscious distress — see EMBARRASS 1

---

syn synonym(s)   *rel* related words
ant antonym(s)   *near ant* near antonym(s)

disconcerting *adj* causing embarrassment — see AWKWARD 3

disconnect *vb* to set or force apart — see SEPARATE 1

disconnected *adj* 1 not clearly or logically connected — see INCOHERENT 1

2 not physically attached to another unit — see SEPARATE 2

disconsolate *adj* feeling unhappiness — see SAD 1

disconsolateness *n* a state or spell of low spirits — see SADNESS

discontent *adj* having a feeling that one has been wronged or thwarted in one's ambitions — see DISCONTENTED

discontent *n* the condition of being dissatisfied with one's life or situation ⟨the rebels tried to stir up *discontent* among the citizens⟩

syn discontentedness, discontentment, disgruntlement, displeasure, dissatisfaction

rel bitterness, resentment; disquiet, perturbation, uneasiness; blues, dejection, depression, desolateness, desolation, despondency, disconsolateness, doldrums, dolefulness, dolor, downheartedness, dreariness, dumps; misery, sadness, sorrow, unhappiness, wretchedness

near ant bliss, felicity, gladness, happiness, joy, lightheartedness; elatedness, exultation, jubilation, triumph

ant contentedness, contentment, pleasure, satisfaction

discontent *vb* to make discontented ⟨the ongoing lack of decent food *discontented* and demoralized the soldiers in the rebel army⟩

syn disaffect, disgruntle, displease, dissatisfy

rel alienate, estrange; agitate, discompose, disquiet, disturb, perturb, upset; annoy, irk, irritate, nettle, peeve; depress, sadden

near ant delight, gladden, tickle; calm, soothe, tranquilize (*also* tranquillize)

ant content, gratify, please, satisfy

discontented *adj* having a feeling that one has been wronged or thwarted in one's ambitions ⟨he was *discontented* with his small role in the school play⟩

syn aggrieved, discontent, disgruntled, displeased, dissatisfied, malcontent

rel disappointed, frustrated, unfulfilled; disquieted, disturbed, perturbed, upset; dejected, depressed, despairing, despondent, disconsolate, doleful, down, downcast, downhearted, forlorn, hangdog, inconsolable, joyless, low-spirited, miserable, mournful, sad, sorrowful, unhappy

near ant blissful, delighted, glad, happy, joyful, joyous; elated, exultant, jubilant, triumphant

ant content, contented, gratified, pleased, satisfied

discontentedness *n* the condition of being dissatisfied with one's life or situation — see DISCONTENT

discontentment *n* the condition of being dissatisfied with one's life or situation — see DISCONTENT

discontinuance *n* the stopping of a process or activity — see END 1

discontinue *vb* 1 to bring (as an action or operation) to an immediate end — see STOP 1

2 to stop doing (something) permanently — see QUIT 2

3 to come to an end — see CEASE 1

discontinuity *n* 1 an open space in a barrier (as a wall or hedge) — see GAP 1

2 a break in continuity — see GAP 2

discontinuous *adj* lacking in steadiness or regularity of occurrence — see FITFUL

discord *n* a lack of agreement or harmony ⟨the *discord* between the two scout leaders threatened to tear our troop apart⟩

syn conflict, discordance, dissension, dissent, dissidence, disunity, friction, schism, strife, variance, war, warfare

rel clash, collision, competition, contention; altercation, argument, bicker, brawl, debate, disagreement, dispute, falling-out, fight, hassle, jar, quarrel, row, run-in, scrap, spat, squabble, tiff, wrangle; incompatibility, incongruity, inconsistency, inconsonance; animosity, antagonism, antipathy, enmity, hostility, ill will, rancor

near ant concurrence, cooperation

ant accord, agreement, concord, concordance, harmony, peace

discordance *n* 1 a lack of agreement or harmony — see DISCORD

2 loud, confused, and usually unharmonious sound — see NOISE 1

discordant *adj* 1 marked by or producing a harsh combination of sounds — see DISSONANT

2 making loud, confused, and usually unharmonious sounds — see NOISY 1

3 feeling or displaying eagerness to fight — see BELLIGERENT

4 not being in agreement or harmony — see INCONSISTENT

discotheque *n* a bar or restaurant offering special nighttime entertainment (as music, dancing, or comedy acts) — see NIGHTCLUB

discount *n* something that is or may be subtracted — see DEDUCTION 1

discount *vb* to express scornfully one's low opinion of — see DECRY 1

discountenance *vb* 1 to hold an unfavorable opinion of — see DISAPPROVE

2 to throw into a state of self-conscious distress — see EMBARRASS 1

discourage *vb* 1 to lessen the courage or confidence of ⟨I didn't let losing *discourage* me from trying again⟩

syn daunt, demoralize, dishearten, dismay, dispirit, unman, unnerve

rel browbeat, bully, cow, intimidate; depress, sadden, weigh; afflict, try; damp, dampen, deaden; distress, trouble; bother, irk, vex, worry; debilitate, enfeeble, undermine, weaken; frighten, horrify, scare *near ant* buoy (up), cheer, gladden; animate, enliven, invigorate; fortify, reinforce, strengthen; assure, reassure; boost, energize, excite, galvanize, inspire, lift, provoke, quicken, rally, stimulate, stir

ant embolden, encourage, hearten, nerve, steel

2 to steer (a person) from an activity or course of action ⟨the higher fines may help *discourage* drivers from speeding on the highway⟩

syn deter, dissuade, inhibit

rel divert

near ant egg (on), exhort, goad, prod, urge; impel, induce, prompt

ant encourage, persuade

discouragement *n* the state of being discouraged ⟨we tried to avoid *discouragement* after failing the test twice⟩

syn demoralization, despair, despondency, disheartenment, dismay, dispiritedness

rel blues, dejection, depression, dumps, gloom, melancholy, mopes; defeatism, pessimism, resignation

near ant optimism, sanguinity

ant encouragement

discourse *n* **1** an exchange of views for the purpose of exploring a subject or deciding an issue — see DISCUSSION 1

2 talking or a talk between two or more people — see CONVERSATION

discourse *vb* **1** to give a formal often extended talk on a subject — see TALK 1

2 to talk as if giving an important and formal speech — see ORATE 1

discourteous *adj* showing a lack of manners or consideration for others — see IMPOLITE

discourteousness *n* rude behavior — see DISCOURTESY

discourtesy *n* rude behavior ⟨the courtiers shuddered at the *discourtesy* shown to the king⟩

syn discourteousness, disrespect, impertinence, impoliteness, impudence, incivility, inconsideration, insolence, rudeness, ungraciousness

rel audacity, boldness, brashness, brassiness, sauciness, shamelessness; boorishness, churlishness, clownishness, crudeness, loutishness, vulgarity; abruptness, bluntness, brusqueness, crustiness, curtness, gruffness, sharpness; crabbedness, crossness, disagreeableness, grumpiness, sullenness, surliness; impropriety, inappropriateness, incorrectness, indecency, unfitness, unsuitability; arrogance, conceit, conceitedness, presumption, pretense (*or* pretence), pretension, pretentiousness

near ant humility, meekness, modesty; deference, dutifulness, respectfulness, submissiveness; acceptability, appropriateness, correctness, decency, decorousness, fitness, goodness, propriety, respectability, respectableness, rightness,

seemliness, suitability, suitableness; affability, cordiality, friendliness, geniality, hospitality; felicitousness, grace, gracefulness

ant civility, considerateness, consideration, courtesy, genteelness, gentility, graciousness, politeness, thoughtfulness

discover *vb* **1** to come to an awareness ⟨I was startled to *discover* that my keys were missing⟩

syn ascertain, catch on, find out, hear, learn, realize, see

rel hit (on *or* upon), tumble (to); descry, detect, encounter, espy, spot; dope (out), figure out, puzzle (out); discern, note, observe, perceive; divine

near ant miss, overlook; disregard, ignore; forget, unlearn; blanket, blot out, cloak, conceal, cover, curtain, enshroud, hide, mask, occult, screen, shroud, veil

2 to come upon after searching, study, or effort — see FIND 1

3 to make known (as information previously kept secret) — see REVEAL 1

discovery *n* **1** the act or process of sighting or learning the existence of something for the first time ⟨the *discovery* of a new species of starfish⟩

syn detection, finding, spotting, unearthing

rel disclosure, exposure, revelation, uncovering, unveiling; creation, invention; exploration; rediscovery

near ant concealment, hiding

2 something discovered ⟨his many zoological *discoveries* included several species of birds⟩

syn find

rel pay dirt, strike, treasure trove; breakthrough

discredit *n* the state of having lost the esteem of others — see DISGRACE 1

discredit *vb* **1** to reduce to a lower standing in one's own eyes or in others' eyes — see HUMBLE

2 to think not to be true or real — see DISBELIEVE

discreditable *adj* not respectable — see DISREPUTABLE

discreet *adj* having or showing good judgment and restraint especially in conduct or speech ⟨he was very *discreet*, only saying what was necessary⟩

syn judicious, prudent

rel cautious, chary, circumspect; foresighted, forethoughtful; discerning, discrim-inating, sage, sane, sapient, sensible, wise; canny, provident; astute, perspicacious, sagacious, shrewd

near ant careless, heedless; improvident, shortsighted; foolish, unwise

ant imprudent, indiscreet, injudicious

discreetness *n* the ability to make intelligent decisions especially in everyday matters — see COMMON SENSE

discrepancy *n* the quality or state of being different — see DIFFERENCE 1

discrepant *adj* not being in agreement or harmony — see INCONSISTENT

---

syn synonym(s)   *rel* related words
ant antonym(s)   *near ant* near antonym(s)

discrete *adj* not physically attached to another unit — see SEPARATE 2

discreteness *n* the state of being kept distinct — see SEPARATION 2

discretion *n* **1** the ability to make intelligent decisions especially in everyday matters — see COMMON SENSE
2 the power, right, or opportunity to choose — see CHOICE 1

discretionary *adj* subject to one's freedom of choice — see OPTIONAL

discriminate *vb* to understand or point out the difference — see DISTINGUISH 1

discriminating *adj* favoring, applying, or being unequal treatment of different classes of people — see DISCRIMINATORY

discrimination *n* the state of being kept distinct — see SEPARATION 2

discriminational *adj* favoring, applying, or being unequal treatment of different classes of people — see DISCRIMINATORY

discriminative *adj* favoring, applying, or being unequal treatment of different classes of people — see DISCRIMINATORY

discriminatory *adj* favoring, applying, or being unequal treatment of different classes of people ⟨a company that was fined for its *discriminatory* practices in the hiring of women⟩
syn differential, discriminating, discriminational, discriminative
rel biased, inequitable, partial, partisan, prejudiced, prejudicial, unequal, unfair, unjust
near ant equal, equitable, fair, just; impartial, neutral, objective, unbiased, uncolored, unprejudiced
ant nondiscriminatory

discursive *adj* passing from one topic to another ⟨the speaker's *discursive* style made it difficult to understand his point⟩
syn desultory, digressive, leaping, maundering, rambling
rel circuitous, deviating, devious, roundabout
near ant focused (*also* focussed)

discuss *vb* to talk about (an issue) usually from various points of view and for the purpose of arriving at a decision or opinion ⟨we *discussed* the new proposal for the school stadium⟩
syn argue, bandy, chew over, debate, dispute, hash (over), moot, talk over
rel descant (on), lecture (on *or* about), speak (about), talk (about); broach, introduce; forge, hammer (out), thrash (out); consider, deliberate, weigh; reason (with)

discussion *n* **1** an exchange of views for the purpose of exploring a subject or deciding an issue ⟨the *discussion* about the club budget went on for hours⟩
syn argument, colloquy, conference, deliberation, discourse, give-and-take, parley, talk
rel debate, dialogue (*also* dialog); forum, meeting, powwow, roundtable, seminar, symposium; chat, conversation, rap
2 talking or a talk between two or more people — see CONVERSATION

disdain *n* open dislike for someone or something considered unworthy of one's concern or respect — see CONTEMPT

disdain *vb* to show contempt for — see SCORN 1

disdainful *adj* **1** feeling or showing open dislike for someone or something regarded as undeserving of respect or concern — see CONTEMPTUOUS 1
2 having or displaying feelings of scorn for what is regarded as beneath oneself — see PROUD 1
3 intended to make a person or thing seem of little importance or value — see DEROGATORY

disease *n* an abnormal state that disrupts a plant's or animal's normal bodily functioning ⟨they caught a rare *disease* while they were traveling in Africa and were sick for weeks⟩
syn affection, ailment, bug, complaint, complication, condition, disorder, fever, ill, illness, infirmity, malady, sickness, trouble
rel contagion, contagious disease; infection, infectious disease; deficiency disease; attack, bout, fit, spell; debility, decrepitude, feebleness, frailness, lameness, weakness; malaise, matter; pest, pestilence, plague
near ant fitness, healthiness, heartiness, robustness, soundness, wholeness, wholesomeness
ant health, wellness

disembark *vb* to go ashore from a ship ⟨the cruise passengers *disembarked* as soon as they got to the terminal in Miami⟩
syn debark, land
rel beach; anchor, dock, put in
near ant board, get (on); weigh (anchor)
ant embark

disembowel *vb* to take the internal organs out of — see GUT

disenchant *vb* to free from mistaken beliefs or foolish hopes — see DISILLUSION

disencumber *vb* **1** to empty or rid of cargo — see UNLOAD 1
2 to set (a person or thing) free of something that encumbers — see RID

disencumbered *adj* no longer burdened with something unpleasant or painful — see FREE 2

disengage *vb* to set free from entanglement or difficulty — see EXTRICATE

disentangle *vb* **1** to separate the various strands of — see UNRAVEL 1
2 to set free from entanglement or difficulty — see EXTRICATE

disfavor *n* **1** a strong feeling of not liking or approving — see DISLIKE 1
2 refusal to accept as right or desirable — see DISAPPROVAL

disfavor *vb* **1** to feel dislike for — see DISLIKE 1
2 to hold an unfavorable opinion of — see DISAPPROVE

disfigure *vb* to reduce the soundness, effectiveness, or perfection of — see DAMAGE 1

disfigurement *n* something that spoils the appearance or completeness of a thing — see BLEMISH

disgorge *vb* to throw out or off (something from within) often violently — see ERUPT 1

disgrace *n* 1 the state of having lost the esteem of others ⟨the players who threw the game were in *disgrace* with their schoolmates⟩

syn discredit, dishonor, disrepute, ignominy, infamy, odium, opprobrium, reproach, shame

rel contempt, disdain, scorn; deprecation, disapprobation, disapproval, disfavor; abasement, debasement, debasing, degradation, humbling, humiliation; blot, brand, slur, smirch, spot, stain, stigma

near ant admiration, regard; awe, fear, reverence; fame, glory, renown, repute

ant esteem, honor, respect

2 a cause of shame ⟨the exposure of his criminal activities was a huge *disgrace* for the councilman⟩

syn crime, dishonor, reflection, reproach, scandal

rel brand, smirch, spot, stain, stigma

ant credit, honor

3 a regrettable or blameworthy act — see CRIME 2

disgrace *vb* to reduce to a lower standing in one's own eyes or in others' eyes — see HUMBLE

disgraceful *adj* not respectable — see DISREPUTABLE

disgruntle *vb* 1 to cause to change from friendly or loving to unfriendly or uncaring — see ESTRANGE

2 to make discontented — see DISCONTENT

disgruntled *adj* having a feeling that one has been wronged or thwarted in one's ambitions — see DISCONTENTED

disgruntlement *n* 1 the condition of being dissatisfied with one's life or situation — see DISCONTENT

2 the loss of friendship or affection — see ESTRANGEMENT

disguise *n* clothing put on to hide one's true identity or imitate someone or something else ⟨Mardi Gras revelers dressed in a colorful array of outlandish *disguises*⟩

syn camouflage, costume, guise

rel domino, mask, veil, vizard; dress, get-up, outfit, rig; coloring, cosmetic, make-up, paint

disguise *vb* to change the dress or looks of so as to conceal true identity ⟨the spies *disguised* themselves as harmless tourists⟩

syn camouflage, cloak, dress up, mask

rel blanket, blot out, conceal, cover, curtain, enshroud, hide, obscure, occult, screen, shroud, veil; affect, assume, counterfeit, dissemble, dissimulate, feign, pose, pretend, sham, simulate

near ant display, exhibit, expose, flaunt, parade, show, uncover, unmask; betray, disclose, discover, reveal

disgust *n* a dislike so strong as to cause stomach upset or queasiness ⟨we turned from the grisly scene with *disgust*⟩

syn aversion, distaste, loathing, nausea, repugnance, repulsion, revulsion

rel abhorrence, abomination, execration, hate, hatred; disapproval, disfavor, disinclination, dislike, disliking, displeasure

near ant appetite, bent, fondness, like, liking, partiality, penchant, predilection, preference, propensity, taste

disgust *vb* to cause to feel disgust ⟨the usual school lunch *disgusted* us, so we started bringing our lunches from home⟩

syn nauseate, repel, repulse, revolt, sicken, turn off

rel displease, distress; appall, horrify; affront, insult, offend, outrage, shock

near ant attract, charm, entice, tempt; delight, gratify, please, rejoice, tickle

disgusted *adj* filled with disgust — see SICK 2

dish *n* a usually circular utensil for holding something (as food) ⟨we threw all of the ingredients for the salsa into a *dish* and mixed them together⟩

syn vessel

rel bowl, casserole, charger, cup, plate, platter, salver, saucer, tray

dishearten *vb* to lessen the courage or confidence of — see DISCOURAGE 1

disheartenment *n* the state of being discouraged — see DISCOURAGEMENT

dishevel *vb* to undo the proper order or arrangement of — see DISORDER

disheveled *or* **dishevelled** *adj* lacking in order, neatness, and often cleanliness — see MESSY

dishonest *adj* 1 telling or containing lies ⟨*dishonest* kids who lie about their ages in order to get into R-rated movies⟩ ⟨*dishonest* statements about the fight in the locker room⟩

syn lying, mendacious, untruthful

rel erroneous, fallacious, false, misleading; double-dealing, hypocritical, two-faced

near ant candid, open, straightforward; earnest, sincere, true

ant honest, truthful, veracious

2 given to or marked by cheating and deception ⟨*dishonest* car dealers who roll back mileage gauges⟩ ⟨*dishonest* business deals that landed him in jail⟩

syn crooked, deceptive, fast, fraudulent, shady, sharp, shifty, underhand, underhanded

rel unconscionable, unethical, unprincipled, unscrupulous; deceitful, deceiving, deluding, delusive, delusory; artful, cunning; devious, furtive, sneaking, sneaky, tricky; insidious, perfidious, treacherous

near ant conscientious, honorable, just, scrupulous, upright; forthright, straightforward

ant aboveboard, honest, straight

syn synonym(s)   *rel* related words
ant antonym(s)   *near ant* near antonym(s)

3 marked by, based on, or done by the use of dishonest methods to acquire something of value — see FRAUDULENT 1

dishonesty *n* **1** the tendency to tell lies ⟨if you gain a reputation for *dishonesty*, no one will believe you even when you're telling the truth⟩

syn deceitfulness, mendacity, untruthfulness

rel artifice, craft, craftiness, crookedness, cunning, deceit, dissembling, dissimulation, double-dealing, duplicity, fakery, foxiness, guile, wiliness; falseness; hypocrisy

near ant honor, incorruptibility; candidness, candor, frankness, good faith, sincerity, straightforwardness; dependability, reliability, reliableness, trustworthiness; accuracy, objectivity; authenticity, correctness, genuineness; credibility

ant honesty, integrity, probity, truthfulness, veracity, verity

2 the inclination or practice of misleading others through lies or trickery — see DECEIT

dishonor *n* **1** the state of having lost the esteem of others — see DISGRACE 1

2 a cause of shame — see DISGRACE 2

dishonor *vb* to reduce to a lower standing in one's own eyes or in others' eyes — see HUMBLE

dishonorable *adj* **1** not following or in accordance with standards of honor and decency — see IGNOBLE 2

2 not respectable — see DISREPUTABLE

disillusion *vb* to free from mistaken beliefs or foolish hopes ⟨we were *disillusioned* when we saw how the movie star acted in real life⟩

syn disabuse, disenchant, undeceive

rel debunk, expose, show up, unclook, uncover, unmask; disclose, divulge, tell, unveil

near ant beguile, bluff, cozen, delude, dupe, fool, gull, hoax, hoodwink, kid, misguide, misinform, mislead, misrepresent, snow, take in, trick

disinclination *n* **1** a lack of willingness or desire to do or accept something — see RELUCTANCE

2 a strong feeling of not liking or approving — see DISLIKE 1

disinclined *adj* having doubts about the wisdom of doing something — see HESITANT

disintegrate *vb* to go through decomposition — see DECAY 1

disinter *vb* to remove from place of burial — see EXHUME

disinterested *adj* **1** having or showing a lack of interest or concern — see INDIFFERENT 1

2 marked by justice, honesty, and freedom from bias — see FAIR 2

disinterestedness *n* **1** lack of favoritism toward one side or another — see DETACHMENT 1

2 lack of interest or concern — see INDIFFERENCE

disjoin *vb* to set or force apart — see SEPARATE 1

disjoint *vb* to set or force apart — see SEPARATE 1

disjointed *adj* not clearly or logically connected — see INCOHERENT 1

dislike *n* **1** a strong feeling of not liking or approving ⟨we have a strong *dislike* for olives and wouldn't eat them even if we were paid⟩

syn allergy, averseness, aversion, disfavor, disinclination, disliking

rel disgust, distaste, loathing, nausea, repugnance, repulsion, revulsion; abomination, antipathy, detestation, hate, hatred; deprecation, disapproval, displeasure, dissatisfaction; jaun-dice

near ant affection, attachment, love; bent, leaning, penchant, predilection, propensity, tendency

ant appetite, fondness, like, liking, partiality, preference, taste

2 refusal to accept as right or desirable — see DISAPPROVAL

dislike *vb* **1** to feel dislike for ⟨the two dogs *disliked* each other the first time they met, and never did become friends⟩

syn disfavor

rel abhor, abominate, detest, hate, loathe; condemn, despise, scorn; disapprove (of), frown (on *or* upon), object (to)

near ant admire, appreciate, cherish, revere, venerate, worship; prize, treasure, value; drink (in), savor; dote (on), idolize; favor, prefer

ant adore, cotton (to), delight (in), dig, enjoy, fancy, groove (on), like, love, relish, revel (in)

2 to hold an unfavorable opinion of — see DISAPPROVE

disliking *n* a strong feeling of not liking or approving — see DISLIKE 1

dislocate *vb* **1** to change the place or position of — see MOVE 1

2 to undo the proper order or arrangement of — see DISORDER

dislocation *n* an act or instance of the order of things being disturbed — see UPSET

disloyal *adj* not true in one's allegiance to someone or something — see FAITHLESS

disloyalty *n* **1** lack of faithfulness especially to one's husband or wife — see INFIDELITY 1

2 the act or fact of violating the trust or confidence of another — see BETRAYAL

dismal *adj* **1** causing or marked by an atmosphere lacking in cheer — see GLOOMY 1

2 causing unhappiness — see SAD 2

dismantle *vb* to take apart — see DISASSEMBLE

dismay *n* **1** the emotion felt when one's expectations are not met — see DISAPPOINTMENT 1

2 the state of being discouraged — see DISCOURAGEMENT

dismay *vb* to lessen the courage or confidence of — see DISCOURAGE 1

dismember vb to take apart — see DISASSEMBLE

dismiss vb 1 to let go from office, service, or employment ⟨the secretary was *dismissed* after it was discovered that she was stealing office supplies⟩

syn can, cashier, fire, muster out, remove, retire, sack

rel downsize, furlough, lay off; boot (out), bounce

near ant contract, subcontract

ant employ, hire

2 to drive or force out — see EJECT 1

dismissal n the termination of the employment of an employee or a work force often temporarily — see LAYOFF

disobedience n refusal to obey ⟨they gave up on training the dog to fetch because of his constant *disobedience*⟩

syn contrariness, defiance, frowardness, insubordination, intractability, rebelliousness, recalcitrance, refractoriness, unruliness, willfulness

rel disrespect, impudence, insolence, rudeness; doggedness, hardheadedness, mulishness, obstinacy, pertinaciousness, pertinacity, perversity, stubbornness; mischievousness, naughtiness

near ant agreeability, amiability; slavishness, submissiveness, subservience

ant amenability, compliance, docility, obedience

disobedient adj given to resisting authority or another's control ⟨the *disobedient* child refused to eat his vegetables⟩

syn balky, contrary, defiant, froward, insubordinate, intractable, rebellious, recalcitrant, refractory, restive, ungovernable, unruly, untoward, wayward, willful (*or* wilful)

rel insurgent, mutinous; dogged, hardheaded, headstrong, mulish, obdurate, obstinate, peevish, pertinacious, pigheaded, self-willed, stubborn, unyielding; obstreperous, uncontrollable, unmanageable, wild; perverse, resistant, wrongheaded; bad, disorderly, errant, misbehaving, mischievous, monkeying, monkeyish, naughty; undisciplined; dissident, nonconformist; disrespectful, ill-mannered, ill-natured, impolite, impudent, insolent, ornery, rude, uncouth

near ant acquiescent, agreeable, amiable, deferential, obliging; submissive, yielding; behaved, disciplined, well-bred; courteous, polite, respectful; servile, slavish, subservient; decorous, orderly, proper; controllable, governable, manageable

ant amenable, compliant, docile, obedient, tractable

disobey vb to go against the commands, prohibitions, or rules of ⟨students who *disobey* their teachers and use cell phones in class⟩ ⟨drivers who consistently *disobey* traffic laws⟩

syn defy, rebel (against)

rel mutiny (against), revolt (against); disregard, ignore, tune out; dismiss, flout, pooh-pooh, reject, scoff (at), scorn, shrug off; break, transgress, violate; combat, contest, dispute, fight, oppose, resist, withstand

near ant defer (to), serve, submit (to); surrender (to), yield (to); keep, observe; accede (to), acquiesce (to), agree (to), assent (to), comply (with), conform (to), oblige; attend, hear, heed, listen (to), mark, note, notice, regard, watch

ant follow, mind, obey

disoblige vb to cause discomfort to or trouble for — see INCONVENIENCE

disobliging adj causing difficulty, discomfort, or annoyance — see INCONVENIENT 1

disorder n 1 a state in which everything is out of order — see CHAOS

2 an abnormal state that disrupts a plant's or animal's normal bodily functioning — see DISEASE

disorder vb to undo the proper order or arrangement of ⟨be careful not to *disorder* the carefully arranged contents of the dresser⟩

syn confuse, derange, disarrange, disarray, discompose, dishevel, dislocate, disorganize, disrupt, disturb, hash, jumble, mess (up), mix (up), muddle, muss, rumple, scramble, shuffle, tousle, tumble, upset

rel embroil, entangle, snarl, tangle; agitate, stir (up), unsettle

near ant align, line, line up; systematize; adjust, fix

ant arrange, array, draw up, marshal, order, organize, range, regulate, straighten (up), tidy

disordered adj lacking in order, neatness, and often cleanliness — see MESSY

disorderly adj 1 not restrained by or under the control of legal authority — see LAWLESS

2 lacking in order, neatness, and often cleanliness — see MESSY

disorganization n a state in which everything is out of order — see CHAOS

disorganize vb to undo the proper order or arrangement of — see DISORDER

disorient vb to throw into a state of mental uncertainty — see CONFUSE 1

disown vb to refuse to acknowledge as one's own or as one's responsibility — see DISCLAIM 1

disparage vb to express scornfully one's low opinion of — see DECRY 1

disparagement n the act of making a person or a thing seem little or unimportant — see DEPRECIATION

disparaging adj intended to make a person or thing seem of little importance or value — see DEROGATORY

disparate adj being not of the same kind — see DIFFERENT 1

disparateness n the quality or state of being different — see DIFFERENCE 1

disparity n the quality or state of being different — see DIFFERENCE 1

dispassionate *adj* marked by justice, honesty, and freedom from bias — see FAIR 2

dispatch *n* 1 a message on paper from one person or group to another — see LETTER

2 a piece of conveyed information — see COMMUNICATION

dispatch *vb* 1 to cause to go or be taken from one place to another — see SEND

2 to deprive of life — see KILL 1

3 to put to death deliberately — see MURDER 1

dispel *vb* 1 to cause (members of a group) to move widely apart — see SCATTER 1

dispensable *adj* not needed by the circumstances or to accomplish an end — see UNNECESSARY

dispensation *n* the act or process of giving out something to each member of a group — see DISTRIBUTION 1

dispense *vb* to give out (something) in appropriate amounts or to appropriate individuals — see ADMINISTER 1

dispersal *n* an act or process in which something scatters or is scattered — see SCATTERING 1

disperse *vb* 1 to cause (members of a group) to move widely apart — see SCATTER 1

2 to cease to exist or cause to cease to exist as a group or organization — see DISBAND 1

dispersion *n* an act or process in which something scatters or is scattered — see SCATTERING 1

dispirit *vb* to lessen the courage or confidence of — see DISCOURAGE 1

dispiritedness *n* 1 a state or spell of low spirits — see SADNESS

2 the state of being discouraged — see DISCOURAGEMENT

displace *vb* 1 to change the place or position of — see MOVE 1

2 to force to leave a country — see BANISH 1

3 to take the place of — see REPLACE 1

displacement *n* the forced removal from a homeland — see EXILE 1

display *n* 1 a public showing of objects of interest — see EXHIBITION 1

2 an outward and often exaggerated indication of something abstract (as a feeling) for effect — see SHOW 1

display *vb* 1 to present so as to invite notice or attention — see SHOW 1

2 to make known (something abstract) through outward signs — see SHOW 2

displease *vb* to make discontented — see DISCONTENT

displeased *adj* having a feeling that one has been wronged or thwarted in one's ambitions — see DISCONTENTED

displeasing *adj* not giving pleasure to the mind or senses — see UNPLEASANT

displeasure *n* 1 refusal to accept as right or desirable — see DISAPPROVAL

2 the condition of being dissatisfied with one's life or situation — see DISCONTENT

disport *vb* 1 to cause (someone) to pass the time agreeably occupied — see AMUSE

2 to engage in activity for amusement — see PLAY 1

3 to play and run about happily — see FROLIC 1

4 to present so as to invite notice or attention — see SHOW 1

disposal *n* 1 the getting rid of whatever is unwanted or useless ⟨trash *disposal* is on Wednesday in our neighborhood⟩

syn discarding, disposition, dumping, jettison, junking, removal, riddance, scrapping, throwing away

rel clearance, clearing; decimation, demolishment, demolition, destruction

near ant accumulation, acquirement, acquisition, collection, deposit

2 the way objects in space or events in time are arranged or follow one another — see ORDER 1

dispose *vb* 1 to arrange something in a certain spot or position — see PLACE 1

2 to put into a particular arrangement — see ORDER 1

disposed *adj* having a desire or inclination (as for a specified course of action) — see WILLING 1

disposition *n* 1 one's characteristic attitude or mood ⟨he had a cheerful *disposition* and was very rarely depressed⟩

syn grain, nature, temper, temperament

rel cheer, frame, humor, mode, mood; attitude, outlook, perspective, point of view, standpoint, viewpoint; emotion, feeling, heart, passion, sentiment; strain; belief, conviction, mind, opinion, persuasion; expression, tone, vein; character, individuality, personality; responsiveness, sensibility, sensitiveness, sensitivity

2 a habitual attraction to some activity or thing — see INCLINATION 1

3 the getting rid of whatever is unwanted or useless — see DISPOSAL 1

4 the way objects in space or events in time are arranged or follow one another — see ORDER 1

disprove *vb* to prove to be false ⟨Magellan's circumnavigation of the globe *disproved* any lingering notions that the earth is flat⟩

syn belie, confute, rebut, refute

rel overthrow, overturn

phrases give the lie to

near ant evidence, show; demonstrate, display, illustrate, manifest; argue, reason

ant confirm, prove, verify

disputable *adj* 1 giving good reason for being doubted, questioned, or challenged — see DOUBTFUL

2 open to question or dispute — see DEBATABLE 2

disputant *n* a person who takes part in a dispute ⟨there were only three *disputants* in the argument, but they made enough noise for a dozen⟩

syn arguer, debater, disputer, quarreler (*or* quarreller), squabbler, wrangler *rel* advocate, defendant, plaintiff, pleader; nitpicker, pettifogger, quibbler

disputation *n* variance of opinion on a matter — see DISAGREEMENT 1

disputatious *adj* 1 feeling or displaying eagerness to fight — see BELLIGERENT
2 given to arguing — see ARGUMENTATIVE 1

disputatiousness *n* an inclination to fight or quarrel — see BELLIGERENCE

dispute *n* 1 variance of opinion on a matter — see DISAGREEMENT 1
2 an often noisy or angry expression of differing opinions — see ARGUMENT 1

dispute *vb* 1 to demand proof of the truth or rightness of — see CHALLENGE 1
2 to express different opinions about something often angrily — see ARGUE 2
3 to talk about (an issue) usually from various points of view and for the purpose of arriving at a decision or opinion — see DISCUSS

disputer *n* a person who takes part in a dispute — see DISPUTANT

disquiet *n* 1 a disturbed or uneasy state — see UNREST
2 an uneasy state of mind usually over the possibility of an anticipated misfortune or trouble — see ANXIETY 1

disquiet *vb* to trouble the mind of; to make uneasy — see DISTURB 1

disquieting *adj* 1 causing worry or anxiety — see TROUBLESOME
2 marked by or causing agitation or uncomfortable feelings — see NERVOUS 2

disregard *n* lack of interest or concern — see INDIFFERENCE

disregard *vb* 1 to ignore in a disrespectful manner — see SCORN 2
2 to fail to give proper attention to — see NEGLECT 1
3 to overlook or dismiss as of little importance — see EXCUSE 1

disrepair *n* the state of being unattended to or not cared for — see NEGLECT 1

disreputable *adj* not respectable ⟨a *disreputable* Internet retailer that had a record of hundreds of complaints for shoddy merchandise and slow refunds⟩
syn discreditable, disgraceful, dishonorable, ignominious, infamous, notorious, shameful
rel bad, immoral, seamy, shady, sordid, unethical, unsavory, wicked; base, contemptible, despicable, detestable, dirty, low, mean, vile, wretched
near ant ethical, good, moral
ant honorable, reputable, respectable

disrepute *n* the state of having lost the esteem of others — see DISGRACE 1

disrespect *n* rude behavior — see DISCOURTESY

disrobe *vb* to remove clothing from — see UNDRESS

disrobed *adj* lacking or shed of clothing — see NAKED 1

disrupt *vb* to undo the proper order or arrangement of — see DISORDER

disruption *n* an act or instance of the order of things being disturbed — see UPSET

dissatisfaction *n* 1 the condition of being dissatisfied with one's life or situation — see DISCONTENT
2 the emotion felt when one's expectations are not met — see DISAPPOINTMENT 1

dissatisfied *adj* having a feeling that one has been wronged or thwarted in one's ambitions — see DISCONTENTED

dissatisfy *vb* 1 to fall short in satisfying the expectation or hope of — see DISAPPOINT
2 to make discontented — see DISCONTENT

dissect *vb* to identify and examine the basic elements or parts of (something) especially for discovering interrelationships — see ANALYZE

dissection *n* the separation and identification of the parts of a whole — see ANALYSIS 1

dissemble *vb* to take on a false or deceptive appearance — see PRETEND 1

dissembling *n* 1 the inclination or practice of misleading others through lies or trickery — see DECEIT
2 the pretending of having virtues, principles, or beliefs that one in fact does not have — see HYPOCRISY

disseminate *vb* to cause to be known over a considerable area or by many people — see SPREAD 1

dissension *n* 1 a lack of agreement or harmony — see DISCORD
2 variance of opinion on a matter — see DISAGREEMENT 1

dissent *n* 1 a lack of agreement or harmony — see DISCORD
2 departure from a generally accepted theory, opinion, or practice — see HERESY

dissent *vb* to have a different opinion — see DISAGREE 1

dissenter *n* a person who believes or teaches something opposed to accepted beliefs — see HERETIC

dissentient *adj* deviating from commonly accepted beliefs or practices — see HERETICAL

dissenting *adj* deviating from commonly accepted beliefs or practices — see HERETICAL

disservice *n* unfair or inadequate treatment of someone or something or an instance of this ⟨you do a great *disservice* to the professionals at the day-care center when you refer to them as "babysitters"⟩
syn injury, injustice, raw deal, wrong
rel insult, offense, outrage; complaint, grievance
near ant cricket
ant justice

dissever *vb* to set or force apart — see SEPARATE 1

---

dissidence n 1 a lack of agreement or harmony — see DISCORD

2 departure from a generally accepted theory, opinion, or practice — see HERESY

dissident adj deviating from commonly accepted beliefs or practices — see HERETICAL

dissident n a person who believes or teaches something opposed to accepted beliefs — see HERETIC

dissimilar adj being not of the same kind — see DIFFERENT 1

dissimilarity n the quality or state of being different — see DIFFERENCE 1

dissimulation n 1 the inclination or practice of misleading others through lies or trickery — see DECEIT

2 the pretending of having virtues, principles, or beliefs that one in fact does not have — see HYPOCRISY

dissipate vb 1 to cause (members of a group) to move widely apart — see SCATTER 1

2 to use up carelessly — see WASTE 1

dissipated adj having or showing lowered moral character or standards — see CORRUPT

dissipatedness n a sinking to a state of low moral standards and behavior — see CORRUPTION 2

dissipation n 1 a sinking to a state of low moral standards and behavior — see CORRUPTION 2

2 an act or process in which something scatters or is scattered — see SCATTERING 1

dissociate vb to set or force apart — see SEPARATE 1

dissolute adj having or showing lowered moral character or standards — see CORRUPT

dissoluteness n a sinking to a state of low moral standards and behavior — see CORRUPTION 2

dissolution n the act or process of a whole separating into two or more parts or pieces — see SEPARATION 1

dissolve vb 1 to cease to be visible — see DISAPPEAR

2 to cease to exist or cause to cease to exist as a group or organization — see DISBAND 1

3 to put an end to by formal action — see ABOLISH

dissonant adj marked by or producing a harsh combination of sounds ⟨a *dissonant* chorus of noises arose from the busy construction site⟩

syn discordant, inharmonious, unmelodious, unmusical

rel blaring, clanging, clashing, clattering, grating, harsh, jangling, jarring, metallic, raspy, raucous, scratching, screeching, shrill, squeaky, strident; disagreeable, unpleasant, unpleasing; atonal, off-key

near ant dulcet, euphonious, mellifluous, mellow, melodic, sweet, tuneful; resonant, sonorous; quavering, trilling, warbling; agreeable, appealing, pleasant; ca-

denced, lilting, lyric, lyrical, rhythmic (*or* rhythmical); chordal, harmonic, homophonic, orchestral, polyphonic, symphonic, tonal

ant harmonious, harmonizing, melodious, musical

dissuade vb to steer (a person) from an activity or course of action — see DISCOURAGE 2

distance n the space or amount of space between two points, lines, surfaces, or objects ⟨the *distance* between the earth and the sun is about 93 million miles⟩

syn lead, length, remove, spacing, spread, stretch, way

rel altitude, area, breadth, depth, height, rise, space, volume, width; extension, extent; cast, range, reach, scope, shot, sweep, throw; drop, fall, flight, haul; berth, clearance

phrases a far cry

distant adj 1 not close in time or space ⟨the *distant* towers were barely visible in the fog⟩

syn away, far, faraway, far-off, remote, removed

rel apart, isolated, obscure, outlying, out-of-the-way, retired, secluded, secret, sequestered

near ant adjacent, adjoining, contiguous

ant close, near, nearby, nigh

2 having or showing a lack of friendliness or interest in others — see COOL 1

distaste n a dislike so strong as to cause stomach upset or queasiness — see DISGUST

distasteful adj 1 disagreeable or disgusting to the sense of taste ⟨cod-liver oil is so *distasteful* that it's worse than anything it cures⟩

syn unappetizing, unpalatable, unsavory

rel abominable, awful, bad, filthy, foul, horrible, loathsome, nasty, nauseating, noisome, obnoxious, offensive, repellent, repugnant, repulsive, revolting, shocking, sickening; bland, flat, flavorless, insipid, savorless, tasteless

near ant appealing, attractive, flavorful, piquant, rich

ant appetizing, delectable, delicious, palatable, savory, tasty

2 not giving pleasure to the mind or senses — see UNPLEASANT

3 causing intense displeasure, disgust, or resentment — see OFFENSIVE 1

distill vb to remove usually visible impurities from — see CLARIFY 1

distinct adj 1 being not of the same kind — see DIFFERENT 1

2 not subject to misinterpretation or more than one interpretation — see CLEAR 2

3 of a particular or exact sort — see EXPRESS 1

4 serving to identify as belonging to an individual or group — see CHARACTERISTIC 1

distinction n 1 exceptionally high quality — see EXCELLENCE 1

2 a quality that gives something special worth — see EXCELLENCE 2

3 public acknowledgment or admiration for an achievement — see GLORY 1

4 the fact or state of being above others in rank or importance — see EMINENCE 1

5 something given in recognition of achievement — see AWARD

6 the quality or state of being different — see DIFFERENCE 1

7 the state of being kept distinct — see SEPARATION 2

distinctive *adj* **1** being not of the same kind — see DIFFERENT 1

2 serving to identify as belonging to an individual or group — see CHARACTERISTIC 1

distinctiveness *n* the quality or state of being different — see DIFFERENCE 1

distinctness *n* the quality or state of being different — see DIFFERENCE 1

distinguish *vb* **1** to understand or point out the difference ⟨even at such a young age, he could *distinguish* between right and wrong⟩

syn differentiate, discern, discriminate, separate

rel comprehend, grasp, know, understand; divide, part, sever; demarcate, mark (off), set off

near ant confound, lump (together), mingle

ant confuse, mistake, mix (up)

2 to be an important feature of — see CHARACTERIZE 2

3 to find out or establish the identity of — see IDENTIFY 1

4 to make note of (something) through the use of one's eyes — see SEE 1

distinguishable *adj* **1** able to be perceived by a sense or by the mind — see PERCEPTIBLE

2 being not of the same kind — see DIFFERENT 1

distinguished *adj* standing above others in rank, importance, or achievement — see EMINENT

distinguishing *adj* serving to identify as belonging to an individual or group — see CHARACTERISTIC 1

distort *vb* **1** to change so much as to create a wrong impression or alter the meaning of — see GARBLE

2 to twist (something) out of a natural or normal shape or condition — see CONTORT

distorted *adj* badly or imperfectly formed — see MALFORMED

distortion *n* the twisting of something out of its natural or normal shape or condition — see CONTORTION

distract *vb* **1** to draw the attention or mind to something else ⟨we were *distracted* from our homework by the noise outside⟩

syn divert

rel amuse, entertain; stray, wander

near ant focus

2 to trouble the mind of; to make uneasy — see DISTURB 1

distraction *n* **1** a state of mental uncertainty — see CONFUSION 1

2 a state of wildly excited activity or emotion — see FRENZY

3 the act or activity of providing pleasure or amusement especially for the public — see ENTERTAINMENT 1

distraught *adj* feeling overwhelming fear or worry — see FRANTIC 1

distress *n* **1** a state of great suffering of body or mind ⟨the upcoming final exam is causing us considerable *distress*⟩ ⟨the survivors were in extreme *distress* after having been stranded on the island for a week with no food⟩

syn affliction, agony, anguish, misery, pain, strait(s), torment, torture, tribulation, woe

rel discomfort; cross, crucible, trial; heartbreak, joylessness, sadness, sorrow, unhappiness; emergency, pinch; asperity, difficulty, hardship, rigor; ache, hurt, pang, smarting, soreness, stitch, throe, twinge; danger, jeopardy, trouble

near ant comfort, consolation, solace; alleviation, assuagement, ease, relief; peace, security

2 the state of not being protected from injury, harm, or evil — see DANGER 1

distress *vb* to trouble the mind of; to make uneasy — see DISTURB 1

distressful *adj* **1** marked by or causing agitation or uncomfortable feelings — see NERVOUS 2

2 of a kind to cause great distress — see REGRETTABLE

distressing *adj* **1** causing worry or anxiety — see TROUBLESOME

2 of a kind to cause great distress — see REGRETTABLE

3 marked by or causing agitation or uncomfortable feelings — see NERVOUS 2

distribute *vb* to give out (something) in appropriate amounts or to appropriate individuals — see ADMINISTER 1

distribution *n* **1** the act or process of giving out something to each member of a group ⟨we oversaw the *distribution* of medicine to the natives⟩

syn allocation, apportionment, dispensation, division, issuance

rel disbursement; reapportionment, redistribution

2 the way objects in space or events in time are arranged or follow one another — see ORDER 1

district *n* an area (as of a city) set apart for some purpose or having some special feature ⟨Independence Hall in Philadelphia's historic *district*⟩

syn neighborhood, quarter, section

rel belt, zone; department, division, part; precinct, ward; area, locality, place, region; barrio, enclave, ghetto

distrust *n* a feeling or attitude that one does not know the truth, truthfulness, or

---

syn synonym(s)   *rel* related words
ant antonym(s)   *near ant* near antonym(s)

trustworthiness of someone or something — see DOUBT

distrust *vb* to have no trust or confidence in ⟨we *distrusted* the stranger when he offered us free candy⟩
syn doubt, mistrust, question, suspect
rel disbelieve, discount, discredit, negate
phrases look askance at
near ant bank (on *or* upon), count (on *or* upon), depend (on *or* upon), rely (on *or* upon)
ant trust

distrustful *adj* **1** inclined to doubt or question claims — see SKEPTICAL 1
2 not feeling sure about the truth, wisdom, or trustworthiness of someone or something — see DOUBTFUL 1

distrustfully *adv* with distrust — see ASKANCE

distrustfulness *n* a feeling or attitude that one does not know the truth, truthfulness, or trustworthiness of someone or something — see DOUBT

disturb *vb* **1** to trouble the mind of; to make uneasy ⟨all that talk of war *disturbed* us⟩
syn agitate, bother, concern, discomfort, discompose, disquiet, distract, distress, exercise, freak (out), perturb, undo, unhinge, unsettle, upset, worry
rel aggravate, anger, annoy, bug, chafe, chivy, exasperate, fret, gall, get, grate, harass, harry, irk, irritate, nettle, peeve, pester, pique, put out, rile, vex; bedevil, haunt, plague; abash, confound, confuse, discomfit, disconcert, discountenance, embarrass, faze, fluster, mortify, nonplus, rattle; daunt, demoralize, discourage, dishearten, dismay, dispirit
near ant allay, alleviate, assuage; appease, conciliate, mollify, pacify, placate, propitiate
ant calm, compose, quiet, settle, soothe, tranquilize (*also* tranquillize)
2 to change the place or position of — see MOVE 1
3 to undo the proper order or arrangement of — see DISORDER
4 to thrust oneself upon (another) without invitation — see BOTHER 1
5 to cause discomfort to or trouble for — see INCONVENIENCE

disturbance *n* **1** a state of noisy, confused activity — see COMMOTION
2 an act or instance of the order of things being disturbed — see UPSET
3 the act of making unwelcome intrusions upon another — see ANNOYANCE 1

disturbing *adj* **1** causing annoyance — see ANNOYING
2 causing embarrassment — see AWKWARD 3
3 causing worry or anxiety — see TROUBLESOME
4 marked by or causing agitation or uncomfortable feelings — see NERVOUS 2

disunion *n* the act or process of a whole separating into two or more parts or pieces — see SEPARATION 1

disunite *vb* to set or force apart — see SEPARATE 1

disunited *adj* disagreeing with each other — see DIVIDED

disunity *n* a lack of agreement or harmony — see DISCORD

disuse *n* lack of use ⟨the old farmhouse showed signs of *disuse*⟩
syn idleness, inactivity
rel abandonment, desertion, neglect; dormancy, latency, quiescence
ant use

disused *adj* left unoccupied or unused — see ABANDONED

ditch *n* a long narrow channel dug in the earth ⟨after skidding on the ice, our car went right into the *ditch*⟩
syn dike, gutter, trench, trough
rel culvert, drain, draw, gully, ravine; drill, furrow

ditch *vb* to get rid of as useless or unwanted — see DISCARD

dither *n* **1** a state of nervous or irritated concern — see FRET
2 a sense of panic or extreme nervousness — see JITTERS

dithery *adj* feeling or showing uncomfortable feelings of uncertainty — see NERVOUS 1

ditty *n* a short musical composition for the human voice often with instrumental accompaniment — see SONG 1

diurnal *adj* occurring, done, produced, or appearing every day — see DAILY

divan *n* a long upholstered piece of furniture designed for several sitters — see COUCH

dive *n* **1** an act or instance of diving ⟨the penguin took a *dive* off of the ice sheet⟩
syn pitch, plunge
rel dip, immersion, submersion; fall, slip, spill, stumble, tumble; descent, drop; belly flop, header, jackknife
near ant jump, leap
2 the act or process of going to a lower level or altitude — see DESCENT 1

dive *vb* to cast oneself head first into deep water ⟨we watched her *dive* in after the drowning man⟩
syn pitch, plunge, sound
rel dip, immerse, submerge; belly flop
near ant surface

diverge *vb* **1** to extend outwards from or as if from a central point — see RADIATE 1
2 to go or move in different directions from a central point — see SEPARATE 2

divergence *n* a movement in different directions away from a common point ⟨a growing *divergence* of opinion about that U.S. president's place in history⟩
syn separation
rel difference, disagreement, discrepancy, disparateness, disparity, dissidence, dissimilarity, distinction, distinctiveness, distinctness, diversity, unlikeness
near ant accord, agreement; likeness, similarity
ant convergence

divers *adj* being of many and various kinds — see MANIFOLD

diverse *adj* being not of the same kind — see DIFFERENT 1

diverseness *n* **1** the quality or state of being composed of many different elements or types — see VARIETY 1
2 the quality or state of being different — see DIFFERENCE 1

diversion *n* **1** someone or something that provides amusement or enjoyment — see FUN 1
2 the act or activity of providing pleasure or amusement especially for the public — see ENTERTAINMENT 1

diversity *n* **1** the quality or state of being composed of many different elements or types — see VARIETY 1
2 the quality or state of being different — see DIFFERENCE 1

divert *vb* **1** to cause (someone) to pass the time agreeably occupied — see AMUSE
2 to change the course or direction of (something) — see TURN 2
3 to draw the attention or mind to something else — see DISTRACT 1

diverting *adj* providing amusement or enjoyment — see FUN

divide *vb* **1** to set or force apart — see SEPARATE 1
2 to go or move in different directions from a central point — see SEPARATE 2

divided *adj* disagreeing with each other ⟨the club members were *divided* on the need for more fundraising⟩
syn disunited, split
phrases at loggerheads, at odds
ant undivided, united

dividend *n* something given in addition to what is ordinarily expected or owed — see BONUS

divider *n* something that divides, separates, or marks off — see DIVISION 1

divine *adj* **1** of the very best kind — see EXCELLENT
2 of, relating to, or being God — see HOLY 3

divine *n* a person specially trained and authorized to conduct religious services in a Christian church — see CLERGYMAN

divine *vb* to realize or know about beforehand — see FORESEE

diviner *n* one who predicts future events or developments — see PROPHET

divinity *n* **1** the quality or state of being divine ⟨Henry David Thoreau felt the presence of *divinity* in every part of nature⟩
syn deity, godhead, godhood
2 a being having superhuman powers and control over a particular part of life or the world — see DEITY 1
3 *cap* the being worshipped as the creator and ruler of the universe — see DEITY 2

divisible *adj* capable of being split into two or more parts or pieces — see SEPARABLE

division *n* **1** something that divides, separates, or marks off ⟨we poked our heads

over the *division* between the yards to see what the fuss was about⟩
syn divider, partition
rel barrier, fence, wall; border, boundary, limit
2 a large unit of a governmental, business, or educational organization ⟨the complaints *division* handled all of the calls from the angry townsfolk⟩
syn bureau, department, desk, office
3 one of the units into which a whole is divided on the basis of a common characteristic — see CLASS 2
4 the act or process of a whole separating into two or more parts or pieces — see SEPARATION 1
5 the act or process of giving out something to each member of a group — see DISTRIBUTION 1

divorce *vb* to set or force apart — see SEPARATE 1

divulge *vb* to make known (as information previously kept secret) — see REVEAL 1

divulgence *n* the act or an instance of making known something previously unknown or concealed — see REVELATION

dizzy *adj* **1** having a feeling of being whirled about and in danger of falling down ⟨I felt very *dizzy* after I got off of the roller coaster⟩
syn giddy, light-headed, reeling, whirling
rel faint, weak; addled, befuddled, confused, dazed
near ant clearheaded; stable, steady
2 suffering from mental confusion ⟨he felt *dizzy* from trying to remember all of the dates and names that were sure to be asked on the test⟩
syn befuddled, bewildered, confused, dazed, stunned, stupefied
rel senseless, unconscious
phrases at sea
near ant alert, conscious
ant clearheaded, unconfused
3 moving, proceeding, or acting with great speed — see FAST 1

do *vb* **1** to be fitting or proper ⟨Oh, that outfit just won't *do* for the opera⟩
syn befit, fit, go, serve, suit
rel satisfy, suffice; function, work
2 to be enough — see SERVE 2
3 to carry through (as a process) to completion — see PERFORM 1
4 to make more attractive by adding something that is beautiful or becoming — see DECORATE
5 to meet one's day-to-day needs — see GET ALONG 1

doable *adj* capable of being done or carried out — see POSSIBLE 1

docile *adj* readily giving in to the command or authority of another — see OBEDIENT

docility *n* a readiness or willingness to yield to the wishes of others — see COMPLIANCE 1

dock *n* a structure used by boats and ships for taking on or landing cargo and passengers ⟨the boat remained tied up at the *dock* for a week, waiting for the weather to clear⟩

syn float, jetty, landing, levee, pier, quay, wharf

rel berth, mooring, slip; dockyard, marina, shipyard

¹**dock** *vb* to make (as hair) shorter with or as if with the use of shears — see CLIP

²**dock** *vb* to stop at or near a place along the shore — see LAND 1

docket *n* a listing of things to be presented or considered (as at a concert or play) — see PROGRAM 1

dockworker *n* one who loads and unloads ships at a port ⟨the *dockworkers* spent all afternoon taking crates off of the ship⟩

syn longshoreman, stevedore

doctor *n* a person specially trained in healing human medical disorders ⟨we called a *doctor* as soon as we realized the baby was sick⟩

syn medic, physician

rel dermatologist, general practitioner, gynecologist, internist, neurologist, obstetrician, ophthalmologist, orthopedist, pediatrician, specialist, surgeon; intern, resident; nurse, paramedic

doctor *vb* 1 to give medical treatment to ⟨a pledge to *doctor* the burn victims until they were whole again⟩

syn treat

rel cure, heal, mend, rehabilitate, remedy; attend, care (for), dose, drug, minister (to), nurse

2 to put into good shape or working order again — see MEND 1

doctrine *n* 1 a statement or body of statements concerning faith or morals proclaimed by a church ⟨the Catholic Church's *doctrine* on the Eucharist⟩

syn canon, dogma

rel belief, conviction, tenet; credo, creed, ideology, philosophy, theology; axiom, precept, principle

2 the basic beliefs or guiding principles of a person or group — see CREED 1

document *n* 1 a piece of paper with information written or to be written on it — see FORM 2

2 a written or printed paper giving information about or proof of something — see CERTIFICATE

document *vb* to show the existence or truth of by evidence — see PROVE 1

documentary *adj* restricted to or based on fact — see FACTUAL 1

documentation *n* something presented in support of the truth or accuracy of a claim — see PROOF

dodder *vb* to move forward while swaying from side to side — see STAGGER 1

dodge *n* a clever often underhanded means to achieve an end — see TRICK 1

dodge *vb* 1 to move suddenly aside or to and fro ⟨*dodging* through the crowd on his way to the exit⟩

syn duck, sidestep, zigzag

rel avoid, elude, escape, evade, parry, shirk, skirt; deflect, turn; slide, slip

2 to avoid having to comply with (something) especially through cleverness — see CIRCUMVENT 1

3 to get or keep away from (as a responsibility) through cleverness or trickery — see ESCAPE 2

dodger *n* a dishonest person who uses clever means to cheat others out of something of value — see TRICKSTER 1

dodging *n* the act or a means of getting or keeping away from something undesirable — see ESCAPE 2

dodo *n* 1 a person with old-fashioned ideas — see FOGY

2 a stupid person — see IDIOT

doff *vb* to rid oneself of (a garment) — see REMOVE 1

dog *n* a domestic mammal that is related to the wolves and foxes ⟨we got a *dog* from the pound to keep as a pet⟩

syn canine, doggy (*or* doggie), hound, pooch

rel cur, mongrel, mutt; bitch; lapdog, pup, puppy, whelp; bird dog, hunter, police dog, sheepdog, sled dog, watchdog, wolf dog, wolfhound

dog *vb* to go after or on the track of — see FOLLOW 2

dog-eared *adj* showing signs of advanced wear and tear and neglect — see SHABBY 1

dogged *adj* 1 continuing despite difficulties, opposition, or discouragement — see PERSISTENT

2 sticking to an opinion, purpose, or course of action in spite of reason, arguments, or persuasion — see OBSTINATE

3 showing no signs of slackening or yielding in one's purpose — see UNYIELDING 1

doggedness *n* a steadfast adherence to an opinion, purpose, or course of action — see OBSTINACY

dogging *n* the act of going after or in the tracks of another — see PURSUIT

doggy *or* **doggie** *n* a domestic mammal that is related to the wolves and foxes — see DOG

dogma *n* a statement or body of statements concerning faith or morals proclaimed by a church — see DOCTRINE 1

do in *vb* 1 to bring to a complete end the physical soundness, existence, or usefulness of — see DESTROY 1

2 to deprive of life — see KILL 1

3 to put to death deliberately — see MURDER 1

4 to use up all the physical energy of — see EXHAUST 1

doing *n* something done by someone — see ACTION 1

doldrums *n pl* 1 a state of temporary inactivity or abeyance — see ABEYANCE

2 a state or spell of low spirits — see SADNESS

3 the state of being bored — see BOREDOM

dole (out) *vb* to give out (something) in appropriate amounts or to appropriate individuals — see ADMINISTER 1

doleful adj 1 expressing or suggesting mourning — see MOURNFUL 1
2 feeling unhappiness — see SAD 1

dolefulness n deep sadness especially for the loss of someone or something loved — see SORROW

doll n 1 a small figure often of a human being used especially as a child's plaything ⟨there was a row of *dolls* along the shelf in the bedroom⟩
syn dolly, puppet
rel rag doll; figure, figurine; plaything, toy
2 a young usually unmarried woman — see GIRL 1

doll up vb to put on one's best or formal clothes — see DRESS UP

dolly n a small figure often of a human being used especially as a child's plaything — see DOLL 1

dolor n deep sadness especially for the loss of someone or something loved — see SORROW

dolorous adj expressing or suggesting mourning — see MOURNFUL 1

dolt n a stupid person — see IDIOT

doltish adj not having or showing an ability to absorb ideas readily — see STUPID 1

doltishness n the quality or state of lacking intelligence or quickness of mind — see STUPIDITY 1

domain n a region of activity, knowledge, or influence — see FIELD 2

domestic adj 1 of or relating to a household or family ⟨the surest way to maintain *domestic* peace and harmony is to have everyone pitch in on chores⟩
syn familial, household
rel homelike, homely, homey; residential
2 changed from the wild state so as to become useful and obedient to humans — see TAME 1

domestic n 1 a female domestic servant — see MAID 1
2 a person hired to perform household or personal services — see SERVANT

domesticated adj changed from the wild state so as to become useful and obedient to humans — see TAME 1

domicile n the place where one lives — see HOME 1

domicile vb to provide with living quarters or shelter — see HOUSE 1

dominance n 1 controlling power or influence over others — see SUPREMACY 1
2 the fact or state of being above others in rank or importance — see EMINENCE 1

dominant adj coming before all others in importance — see FOREMOST 1

dominate vb 1 to bring under one's control by force of arms — see CONQUER 1
2 to look down on — see OVERLOOK 1
3 to serve as leader of — see LEAD 2

dominating n the act or process of bringing someone or something under one's control — see CONQUEST

domination n the act or process of bringing someone or something under one's control — see CONQUEST

domineering adj fond of ordering people around — see BOSSY

dominie n a person specially trained and authorized to conduct religious services in a Christian church — see CLERGYMAN

dominion n 1 controlling power or influence over others — see SUPREMACY 1
2 the right or means to command or control others — see POWER 1

don vb to place on one's person — see PUT ON 1

donate vb to make a present of — see GIVE 1

donation n 1 a gift of money or its equivalent to a charity, humanitarian cause, or public institution — see CONTRIBUTION
2 something given to someone without expectation of a return — see GIFT 1

donator n one that helps another with gifts or money — see BENEFACTOR

done adj brought or having come to an end — see COMPLETE 2

done in adj depleted in strength, energy, or freshness — see WEARY 1

donkey n 1 a sturdy and patient domestic mammal that is used especially to carry things ⟨we put our bags on the *donkey* and headed down the canyon⟩
syn ass, burro, jackass
rel jack, jenny; hinny, mule; pack animal
2 a stupid person — see IDIOT

donor n one that helps another with gifts or money — see BENEFACTOR

doom n 1 a decision made by a court or tribunal regarding a case it has heard — see SENTENCE
2 a state or end that seemingly has been decided beforehand — see FATE 1
3 the permanent stopping of all the vital bodily activities — see DEATH 1

doom vb 1 to determine the fate of in advance — see DESTINE
2 to impose a judicial punishment on — see SENTENCE

door n 1 a barrier by which an entry is closed and opened ⟨we locked the *door* to the room so that no one could get in⟩
syn gate, hatch, portal
rel Dutch door, French door, lattice, portcullis, postern, trapdoor, wicket
2 the opening through which one can enter or leave a structure ⟨a steady stream of visitors through the front *door*⟩
syn doorway, entrance, gate, gateway, way
rel hatch, hatchway

doorkeeper n a person who tends a door ⟨the *doorkeeper* held the door open for us so we didn't have to put down our packages⟩
syn doorman, gatekeeper, janitor, porter [*chiefly British*]

doorman n a person who tends a door — see DOORKEEPER

doorway n 1 the means or right of entering or participating in — see ENTRANCE 1

---

syn synonym(s)   *rel* related words
ant antonym(s)   *near ant* near antonym(s)

2 the opening through which one can enter or leave a structure — see DOOR 2

dope *n* **1** information not generally available to the public ⟨he gave us the *dope* on the deal taking place that night at the warehouse⟩
syn lowdown, scoop, tip
rel dirt, gossip, rumor, story; hint, pointer; information, intelligence, news, tidings, word
2 a stupid person — see IDIOT

dope (out) *vb* to find an answer for through reasoning — see SOLVE

doper *n* a person who regularly uses drugs especially illegally ⟨the *doper* had to go straight, since he couldn't keep a steady job while using drugs⟩
syn addict, fiend, junkie (*also* junky), substance abuser, user
rel pothead

dopey *adj* not having or showing an ability to absorb ideas readily — see STUPID 1

dopiness *n* the quality or state of lacking intelligence or quickness of mind — see STUPIDITY 1

dork *n, slang* a stupid person — see IDIOT

dorky *adj, slang* not having or showing an ability to absorb ideas readily — see STUPID 1

dormancy *n* **1** a state of temporary inactivity — see ABEYANCE
2 lack of action or activity — see INACTION

dormant *adj* **1** being in a state of suspended consciousness — see ASLEEP 1
2 not being in a state of use, activity, or employment — see INACTIVE 2

dot *n* a small area that is different (as in color) from the main part — see SPOT 1

dot *vb* **1** to cover by or as if by scattering something over or on — see SCATTER 2
2 to mark with small spots especially unevenly — see SPOT

dote (on) *vb* to love or admire too much — see IDOLIZE

dotted *adj* marked with spots — see SPOTTED 1

dotty *adj* showing or marked by a lack of good sense or judgment — see FOOLISH 1

double *adj* **1** consisting of two members or parts that are usually joined ⟨an egg with a *double* yolk⟩
syn binary, bipartite, dual, duplex, twin
rel mated, paired
ant single
2 being twice as great or as many ⟨after it was ranked the best in the country, the college had *double* the usual number of applicants⟩
syn twofold

double *adv* to two times the amount or degree — see DOUBLY

double *n* something or someone that strongly resembles another — see IMAGE 1

double *vb* **1** to make twice as great or as many ⟨we *doubled* our efforts to find a solution to the problem⟩
syn duplicate, redouble

rel compound, multiply; accumulate, balloon, build (up), burgeon, enlarge, escalate, expand, increase, mount, mushroom, proliferate, rise, snowball, swell, wax
2 to lay one part over or against another part of — see FOLD 1

double–cross *vb* to be unfaithful or disloyal to — see BETRAY 1

double cross *n* the act or fact of violating the trust or confidence of another — see BETRAYAL

double–crosser *n* one who betrays a trust or an allegiance — see TRAITOR

double–dealing *adj* **1** marked by, based on, or done by the use of dishonest methods to acquire something of value — see FRAUDULENT 1
2 not being or expressing what one appears to be or express — see INSINCERE

double–dealing *n* the inclination or practice of misleading others through lies or trickery — see DECEIT

doubly *adv* to two times the amount or degree ⟨we were *doubly* certain of her guilt after we read the article in the newspaper⟩
syn double, twice, twofold

doubt *n* a feeling or attitude that one does not know the truth, truthfulness, or trustworthiness of someone or something ⟨from the beginning I had my *doubts* about the new kid in school⟩
syn distrust, distrustfulness, incertitude, misgiving, mistrust, mistrustfulness, skepticism, suspicion, uncertainty
rel disbelief, incredulity, unbelief; anxiety, concern; compunction, qualm, scruple
near ant credence, faith
ant assurance, belief, certainty, certitude, confidence, conviction, sureness, surety, trust

doubt *vb* to have no trust or confidence in — see DISTRUST

doubtable *adj* **1** giving good reason for being doubted, questioned, or challenged — see DOUBTFUL 2
2 open to question or dispute — see DEBATABLE 1

doubter *n* a person who is always ready to doubt or question the truth or existence of something — see SKEPTIC

doubtful *adj* **1** not feeling sure about the truth, wisdom, or trustworthiness of someone or something ⟨he was *doubtful* about the decision to complete the project despite its mounting problems⟩
syn distrustful, dubious, mistrustful, skeptical, suspicious, uncertain, unconvinced, undecided, unsettled, unsure
rel diffident, insecure; hesitant, indecisive, irresolute, vacillating, wavering
phrases on the fence
near ant assured, confident, sanguine, self-assured; decisive, determined, resolute
ant certain, convinced, positive, sure
2 giving good reason for being doubted, questioned, or challenged ⟨the election

results were highly *doubtful*, so an investigation was begun⟩

syn debatable, disputable, doubtable, dubious, equivocal, fishy, problematic (*also* problematical), questionable, shady, shaky, suspect, suspicious

rel moot; ambiguous, open, unclear; uncertain, undecided, undetermined; far-fetched, flimsy, improbable, unlikely

near ant decisive, definitive; clear, obvious, open-and-shut, positive

ant certain, incontestable, indisputable, indubitable, sure, undeniable, undoubted, unquestionable

3 not likely to be true or to occur — see IMPROBABLE

4 open to question or dispute — see DEBATABLE 1

doubtfully *adv* with distrust — see ASKANCE

doubting *adj* inclined to doubt or question claims — see SKEPTICAL 1

doubtingly *adv* with distrust — see ASKANCE

doubtless *adj* having or showing a mind free from doubt — see CERTAIN 2

doubtless *adv* **1** without any question — see INDEED 1

2 without much doubt — see PROBABLY

dough *n* something (as pieces of stamped metal or printed paper) customarily and legally used as a medium of exchange, a measure of value, or a means of payment — see MONEY

doughtiness *n* strength of mind to carry on in spite of danger — see COURAGE

doughty *adj* feeling or displaying no fear by temperament or appearance — see BRAVE

dour *adj* harsh and threatening in manner or appearance — see GRIM 1

douse *vb* **1** to cause to cease burning — see EXTINGUISH 1

2 to make wet — see WET

3 to sink or push (something) briefly into or as if into a liquid — see DIP 1

doused *adj* containing, covered with, or thoroughly penetrated by water — see WET

dove *n* **1** a person who opposes war or warlike policies ⟨the *doves* were in favor of using the money to improve the school system instead of the army⟩

syn pacifist

rel peacemaker

near ant militarist; chauvinist, nationalist

ant hawk, jingo, warmonger

2 an innocent or gentle person — see LAMB

dovetail *vb* to be in agreement on every point — see CHECK 1

dowager *n* a dignified usually elderly woman of some rank or authority — see MATRIARCH

dowdily *adv* in a careless or unfashionable manner — see SLOPPILY

dowdy *adj* **1** lacking neatness in dress or person — see SLOPPY 1

---

syn synonym(s)   **rel** related words
ant antonym(s)   **near ant** near antonym(s)

---

2 marked by an obvious lack of style or good taste — see TACKY 1

down *adj* **1** brought or having come to an end — see COMPLETE 2

2 directed down — see DOWNCAST 1

3 feeling unhappiness — see SAD 1

4 temporarily suffering from a disorder of the body — see SICK 1

down *adv* toward or in a lower position ⟨the stairs went *down* to the basement⟩

syn below, downward, over

rel facedown; low; downgrade, downhill, downstairs

near ant aloft

ant up, upward (*or* upwards), upwardly

¹down *n* a soft airy substance or covering — see FUZZ

²down *n* **1** the act or process of going to a lower level or altitude — see DESCENT 1

2 a loss of status — see COMEDOWN

down *vb* **1** to strike (someone) so forcefully as to cause a fall — see FELL 1

2 to take into the stomach through the mouth and throat — see SWALLOW 1

downcast *adj* **1** directed down ⟨her *downcast* gaze made us realize that she was shy⟩

syn down, downward, lowered

near ant elevated, lifted, raised, uplifted, upward

2 feeling unhappiness — see SAD 1

downer *n* something (as a situation or event) that is depressing ⟨that math exam was a real *downer*⟩

syn bummer

rel bore, drag; accident, fatality, mishap, woe; calamity, catastrophe, debacle (*also* débâcle), misfortune, tragedy

near ant pick-me-up

downfall *n* **1** a change to a lower state or level — see DECLINE 2

2 a loss of status — see COMEDOWN

downgrade *n* a change to a lower state or level — see DECLINE 2

downgrade *vb* to bring to a lower grade or rank — see DEMOTE

downhearted *adj* feeling unhappiness — see SAD 1

downheartedness *n* a state or spell of low spirits — see SADNESS

downpour *n* a steady falling of water from the sky in significant quantity — see RAIN 1

downright *adj* **1** being or characterized by direct, brief, and potentially rude speech or manner — see BLUNT 1

2 having no exceptions or restrictions — see ABSOLUTE 2

downs *n pl* a broad area of level or rolling treeless country — see PLAIN

downsize *vb* to make smaller in amount, volume, or extent — see DECREASE 1

down-to-earth *adj* willing to see things as they really are and deal with them sensibly — see REALISTIC 1

downward *adv* toward or in a lower position — see DOWN

downward *adj* directed down — see DOWNCAST 1

downwind *adj* being in the direction that the wind is blowing ⟨we were *downwind* of the deer, so it couldn't smell us⟩
syn leeward
ant upwind, windward

downy *adj* smooth or delicate in appearance or feel — see SOFT 2

doze *n* a short sleep — see ¹NAP

doze *vb* **1** to be in a state of sleep — see SLEEP 1
2 to sleep lightly or briefly — see NAP 1

dozer *n* one who sleeps — see SLEEPER

dozing *adj* being in a state of suspended consciousness — see ASLEEP 1

dozing *n* a natural periodic loss of consciousness during which the body restores itself — see SLEEP 1

drab *adj* causing weariness, restlessness, or lack of interest — see BORING

draft *n* **1** a mass or quantity of something taken up and carried, conveyed, or transported — see LOAD 1
2 the portion of a serving of a beverage that is swallowed at one time — see DRINK 2
3 noticeable movement of air in a particular direction — see ¹WIND 1

draft *vb* **1** to pick especially for required military service ⟨my grandfather was *drafted* to fight in the war, even though he didn't want to go⟩
syn conscript
rel impress, press; enlist, enroll (*also* enrol); sign up, volunteer
near ant discharge
2 to put (something) into proper and usually carefully worked out written form — see COMPOSE 1

draftee *n* a person forced or required to enroll in military service — see CONSCRIPT

drag *n* **1** someone or something boring ⟨that lecture was such a *drag* that half of the audience fell asleep⟩
syn bore
rel bummer, downer; pill
near ant gas [*slang*]
2 a passage cleared for public vehicular travel — see WAY 1
3 something that makes movement or progress more difficult — see ENCUMBRANCE
4 the portion of a serving of a beverage that is swallowed at one time — see DRINK 2

drag *vb* **1** to cause to follow by applying steady force on — see PULL 1
2 to move or act slowly — see DELAY 1
3 to move slowly — see CRAWL 2

dragger *n* someone who moves slowly or more slowly than others — see SLOWPOKE

dragging *adj* moving or proceeding at less than the normal, desirable, or required speed — see SLOW 1

drain *vb* **1** to remove (liquid) gradually or completely ⟨we *drained* the water from the tank before cleaning it⟩
syn bleed, draw (off), pump, siphon, tap

rel milk; suck; clear, empty, evacuate, exhaust, vacate, void
ant fill
2 to make complete use of — see DEPLETE 1
3 to use up all the physical energy of — see EXHAUST 1

drained *adj* depleted in strength, energy, or freshness — see WEARY 1

drainpipe *n* a pipe or channel for carrying off water from a roof — see GUTTER 1

drama *n* **1** the public performance of plays ⟨he has been interested in *drama* from the first time he ever saw a play⟩
syn dramatics, stage, theater (*or* theatre), theatricals
rel boards; acting, footlights; entertainment, show business
2 a written work in which the story is told through speech and action that is intended to be acted out on stage — see PLAY 2

dramatic *adj* **1** having the general quality or effect of a stage performance ⟨the basketball player's *dramatic* announcement of his sudden retirement held everybody spellbound⟩
syn histrionic, melodramatic, theatrical
rel affected, emotional, sensational
near ant matter-of-fact, monotonous
ant undramatic, untheatrical
2 given to or marked by attention-getting behavior suggestive of stage acting — see THEATRICAL 1
3 likely to attract attention — see NOTICEABLE

dramatics *n pl* the public performance of plays — see DRAMA 1

dramatization *n* a written work in which the story is told through speech and action that is intended to be acted out on stage — see PLAY 2

drapery *n* pieces of cloth hung to darken, decorate, or divide a room ⟨the *drapery* for the picture window matched the color of the furniture in the center of the room⟩
syn curtains, drapes
rel hanging(s), tapestry, window shade

drapes *n pl* pieces of cloth hung to darken, decorate, or divide a room — see DRAPERY

draw *n* **1** a situation in which neither participant in a contest, competition, or struggle comes out ahead of the other — see TIE 1
2 something that attracts interest — see MAGNET
3 the act or an instance of applying force on something so that it moves in the direction of the force — see PULL 1

draw *vb* **1** to cause to follow by applying steady force on — see PULL 1
2 to give a representation or account of in words — see DESCRIBE 1
3 to receive as return for effort — see EARN 1
4 to take away from a place or position — see REMOVE 2
5 to take the internal organs out of — see GUT

draw (off) *vb* to remove (liquid) gradually or completely — see DRAIN 1

draw (up) *vb* to put (something) into proper and usually carefully worked out written form — see COMPOSE 1

drawback *n* a feature of someone or something that creates difficulty for achieving success — see DISADVANTAGE

drawing *n* a picture using lines to represent the chief features of an object or scene ⟨he made a *drawing* of the tree in his sketchpad while he was waiting for the bus⟩

syn cartoon, delineation, sketch

rel outline, silhouette; caricature, doodle, illustration; depiction, image, likeness, portrait, representation; engraving, etching; blueprint

drawing out *n* the act of making longer — see EXTENSION 1

drawn *adj* stretched with little or no give — see TAUT

draw on *vb* to come near or nearer — see APPROACH 1

draw out *vb* to make longer — see EXTEND 1

draw up *vb* 1 to bring (something) to a standstill — see ¹HALT 1

2 to put into a particular arrangement — see ORDER 1

dread *n* 1 suspicion or fear of future harm or misfortune — see APPREHENSION 1

2 the emotion experienced in the presence or threat of danger — see FEAR

dreadful *adj* 1 causing fear — see FEARFUL 1

2 causing intense displeasure, disgust, or resentment — see OFFENSIVE 1

3 extremely disturbing or repellent — see HORRIBLE 1

dreadfulness *n* the quality of inspiring intense dread or dismay — see HORROR 1

dream *n* 1 a series of often striking pictures created by the imagination during sleep ⟨I had a *dream* last night about flying without any support⟩

syn nightmare, vision

rel daydream, pipe dream, reverie (*also* revery); chimera, delusion, fancy, fantasy (*also* phantasy), figment, hallucination, illusion, mirage, phantasm

2 a conception or image created by the imagination and having no objective reality — see FANTASY 1

3 something that one hopes or intends to accomplish — see GOAL

dream *vb* to form a mental picture of — see IMAGINE 1

dreamer *n* one whose conduct is guided more by the image of perfection than by the real world — see IDEALIST

dreamily *adv* in a pleasing way — see WELL 5

dreamy *adj* giving pleasure or contentment to the mind or senses — see PLEASANT

2 tending to calm the emotions and relieve stress — see SOOTHING 1

drear *adj* 1 causing or marked by an atmosphere lacking in cheer — see GLOOMY 1

2 causing unhappiness — see SAD 2

dreariness *n* a state or spell of low spirits — see SADNESS

dreary *adj* 1 causing or marked by an atmosphere lacking in cheer — see GLOOMY 1

2 causing unhappiness — see SAD 2

3 causing weariness, restlessness, or lack of interest — see BORING

dredge *vb* to look through (as a place) carefully or thoroughly in an effort to find or discover something — see SEARCH 1

dregs *n pl* matter that settles to the bottom of a body of liquid — see DEPOSIT 1

drench *vb* 1 to make wet — see WET

2 to wet thoroughly with liquid — see SOAK 1

drenched *adj* containing, covered with, or thoroughly penetrated by water — see WET

dress *adj* relating to or suitable for wearing to an event requiring elegant dress and manners ⟨the naval commander wore his *dress* uniform to the ball⟩

syn dressy, formal

rel costume; chic, dapper, fashionable, modish, natty, sharp, smart, stylish; custom-made, fitted, tailored; state

near ant street; dowdy, unfashionable, unstylish

ant casual, informal, sporty

dress *n* 1 a garment with a joined blouse and skirt for a woman or girl ⟨what a lovely *dress* you're wearing today!⟩

syn frock, gown

rel chemise, granny, housedress, jumper, Mother Hubbard, muumuu (*or* mumu), overdress

2 clothing chosen as appropriate for a specific situation — see OUTFIT 1

3 covering for the human body — see CLOTHING

dress *vb* 1 to cover with a bandage — see BANDAGE

2 to make more attractive by adding something that is beautiful or becoming — see DECORATE

3 to make smooth or glossy usually by repeatedly applying surface pressure — see POLISH

4 to outfit with clothes and especially fine or special clothes — see CLOTHE 1

5 to put on one's best or formal clothes — see DRESS UP

dress down *vb* to criticize (someone) severely or angrily especially for personal failings — see SCOLD

dressing *n* a medicated covering used to heal an injury ⟨nurses put a *dressing* over his cuts so they wouldn't get infected⟩

syn plaster, poultice

rel balm, cream, liniment, lotion, ointment, salve, unguent

---

syn synonym(s)   *rel* related words
ant antonym(s)   *near ant* near antonym(s)

2 a savory fluid-food used as a topping or accompaniment to a main dish — see SAUCE 1

dress up vb 1 to put on one's best or formal clothes ⟨we always like to *dress up* when going to parties⟩

syn doll up, dress

rel apparel, array, attire, bedeck, bedizen, caparison, clothe, costume, deck, garb, garment, invest, rig (out), robe

2 to change the dress or looks of so as to conceal true identity — see DISGUISE

dressy adj relating to or suitable for wearing to an event requiring elegant dress and manners — see DRESS

dribble vb 1 to fall or let fall in or as if in drops — see DRIP

2 to flow in a broken irregular stream — see GURGLE

3 to let saliva or some other substance flow from the mouth — see DROOL

driblet n 1 a very small amount — see PARTICLE 1

2 the quantity of fluid that falls naturally in one rounded mass — see DROP 1

drift n 1 a pile or ridge of granular matter (as sand or snow) — see ²BANK

2 a prevailing or general movement or inclination — see TREND 1

3 the idea that is conveyed or intended to be conveyed to the mind by language, symbol, or action — see MEANING 1

drift vb 1 to move or proceed smoothly and readily — see FLOW 2

2 to rest or move along the surface of a liquid or in the air — see FLOAT

drifter n a person who roams about without a fixed route or destination — see NOMAD

drill n something done over and over in order to develop skill — see EXERCISE 2

¹drill vb 1 to make a hole or series of holes in — see PERFORATE

2 to strike with a missile from a gun — see SHOOT 3

²drill vb to put or set into the ground to grow — see PLANT

drink n 1 a liquid suitable for drinking ⟨we went inside to have a *drink* after mowing the lawn⟩

syn beverage, libation, quencher

rel potion; pop, soda, soda pop, soft drink; alcohol, brew, intoxicant, liquor, spirits

2 the portion of a serving of a beverage that is swallowed at one time ⟨the thirsty scout took a long *drink* from his canteen⟩

syn draft, drag, gulp, nip, quaff, shot, sip, slug, snort, sup, swallow, swig, swill

3 a fermented or distilled beverage that can make a person drunk — see ALCOHOL

drink vb 1 to swallow in liquid form ⟨the doctor wants her to *drink* lots of water before the examination⟩

syn gulp, guzzle, imbibe, quaff, sip, slurp, sup, swig, swill, toss (down or off)

rel lap, lick; consume, down, mouth (down); tipple; toast, wine

2 to take in (something liquid) through small openings — see ABSORB 1

drinkable adj suitable for drinking — see POTABLE

drip n the quantity of fluid that falls naturally in one rounded mass — see DROP 1

drip vb to fall or let fall in or as if in drops ⟨water from the leaky roof was *dripping* all over the floor⟩ ⟨the cracked bottle *dripped* wine⟩

syn dribble, trickle

rel bleed, exude, ooze, seep, weep; discharge

dripping adj containing, covered with, or thoroughly penetrated by water — see WET

drive n 1 a passage cleared for public vehicular travel — see WAY 1

2 a series of activities undertaken to achieve a goal — see CAMPAIGN

3 a strong wish for something — see DESIRE

4 active strength of body or mind — see VIGOR 1

5 readiness to engage in daring or difficult activity — see ENTERPRISE 2

drive vb 1 to urge, push, or force onward ⟨cowboys *drove* the herd of cattle from San Antonio to San Francisco⟩

syn herd, punch, run

rel shepherd; wrangle; egg, exhort, goad, prick, prod, spur, urge

2 to travel by a motorized vehicle ⟨I'm going to *drive* across the country—want to come?⟩

syn automobile, motor

rel roll, wheel; chauffeur, taxi; ride; drag, race

3 to apply force to (someone or something) so that it moves in front of one — see PUSH 1

4 to cause (a person) to give in to pressure — see FORCE

5 to cause to function — see ACTIVATE

6 to set or keep in motion — see MOVE 2

drivel n 1 language, behavior, or ideas that are absurd and contrary to good sense — see NONSENSE 1

2 unintelligible or meaningless talk — see GIBBERISH

drivel vb 1 to let saliva or some other substance flow from the mouth — see DROOL

2 to speak rapidly, inarticulately, and usually unintelligibly — see BABBLE 1

driver n a person who travels by automobile — see MOTORIST

drizzle n a light or fine rain ⟨the intermittent *drizzle* was just heavy enough to spoil all of our outdoor activities⟩

syn mist, sprinkle

rel precipitation, rainfall, shower

near ant cloudburst, deluge, downpour, storm; rainstorm, thunderstorm; monsoon

droll adj causing or intended to cause laughter — see FUNNY 1

drollness n the amusing quality or element in something — see HUMOR 1

¹drone n a lazy person — see LAZYBONES

²**drone** *n* a monotonous sound like that of an insect in motion — see HUM

drone *vb* to fly, turn, or move rapidly with a fluttering or vibratory sound — see WHIRR

drool *vb* to let saliva or some other substance flow from the mouth ⟨the dog *drooled* when we put the steak down on the floor⟩
syn dribble, drivel, salivate, slaver, slobber
rel water; expectorate, spit; foam, froth; sputter

droop *n* the extent to which something hangs or dips below a straight line — see SAG

droop *vb* **1** to be limp from lack of water or vigor ⟨the flowers *drooped* on their stalks in the blazing sun⟩
syn flag, hang, loll, sag, wilt
rel slouch, slump; collapse, drop, fall, sink, subside
near ant distend, stiffen; rise, straighten
2 to lose bodily strength or vigor — see WEAKEN 2

drooping *adj* bending downward or forward — see NODDING

droopy *adj* **1** bending downward or forward — see NODDING
2 not stiff in structure — see LIMP 1
3 feeling unhappiness — see SAD 1

drop *n* **1** the quantity of fluid that naturally in one rounded mass ⟨a *drop* of water fell from the leaky faucet every few seconds⟩
syn blob, driblet, drip, droplet, glob, globule
rel dewdrop, raindrop, tear; spatter; dribble, trickle
2 distance measured from the top to the bottom of something — see DEPTH 1
3 the act or process of going to a lower level or altitude — see DESCENT 1
4 the amount by which something is lessened — see DECREASE
5 the more favorable condition or position in a competition — see ADVANTAGE 1

drop *vb* **1** to cause to fall intentionally or unintentionally ⟨I *dropped* the fly ball⟩ ⟨*drop* the anchor⟩
syn depress, lower
rel flatten, floor, level; bobble, bungle, foozle, fumble; immerse, sink, submerge
ant lift, pick up, raise
2 to go to a lower level ⟨although they start out high, prices for home electronics eventually *drop*⟩
syn decline, descend, dip, fall, lower, nose-dive, plummet, plunge, sink, tumble
rel decrease, diminish, lessen; recede, retreat
ant arise, lift, rise, soar
3 to bring (as an action or operation) to an immediate end — see STOP 1
4 to stop doing (something) permanently — see QUIT 1

5 to lead or extend downward — see DESCEND 1
6 to put an end to (something planned or previously agreed to) — see CANCEL 1
7 to bring forth from the womb — see BEAR 1
8 to strike (someone) so forcefully as to cause a fall — see FELL 1

drop (*by* or *in*) *vb* to make a brief visit — see CALL 3

droplet *n* the quantity of fluid that falls naturally in one rounded mass — see DROP 1

dropping *n* **1** **droppings** *pl* solid matter discharged from an animal's alimentary canal ⟨the only bad part about owning a rabbit was cleaning the *droppings* out of the cage every night⟩
syn dung, excrement, excreta, feces, slops, waste
rel stool; dunghill, guano, manure, muck; spoor; sewage
2 the act of putting an end to something planned or previously agreed to — see CANCELLATION

dross *n* discarded or useless material — see GARBAGE

droughty *adj* marked by little or no precipitation or humidity — see DRY 1

drove *n* **1** a great number of persons or things gathered together — see CROWD 1
2 a group of domestic animals assembled or herded together — see HERD

drown *vb* **1** to cover or become filled with a flood — see FLOOD
2 to wet thoroughly with liquid — see SOAK 1

drowse *n* a short sleep — see ¹NAP

drowse *vb* to sleep lightly or briefly — see NAP 1

drowsiness *n* the quality or state of desiring or needing sleep — see SLEEPINESS

drowsy *adj* **1** desiring or needing sleep — see SLEEPY 1
2 tending to cause sleep — see HYPNOTIC

drub *vb* **1** to strike repeatedly — see BEAT 1
2 to achieve a victory over — see BEAT 2
3 to defeat by a large margin — see WHIP 2

drubbing *n* failure to win a contest — see DEFEAT 1

drudge *n* a person who does very hard or dull work — see SLAVE 2

drudge *vb* to devote serious and sustained effort — see LABOR

drudger *n* a person who does very hard or dull work — see SLAVE 2

drudgery *n* very hard or unpleasant work — see TOIL

drug *n* a substance or preparation used to treat disease — see MEDICINE

druggist *n* a person who prepares drugs according to a doctor's prescription ⟨she got her prescription for antibiotics filled by the *druggist*⟩
syn apothecary, pharmacist
rel pharmacologist

drugstore *n* a retail store where medicines and miscellaneous articles are sold

---

syn synonym(s) *rel* related words
ant antonym(s) *near ant* near antonym(s)

⟨we picked up her medicine and some toothpaste at the *drugstore*⟩

syn pharmacy

rel dispensary

drum *n* a metal container in the shape of a cylinder — see CAN

drum *vb* to strike or cause to strike lightly and usually rhythmically — see ¹TAP

drum (out) *vb* to drive or force out — see EJECT 1

drunk *adj* being under the influence of alcohol ⟨several wedding guests who got a little *drunk*⟩

syn drunken, high, inebriate, inebriated, intoxicated, loaded [*slang*], soused, tipsy

rel maudlin; befuddled, stupefied; debauched, dissipated, dissolute

near ant abstemious, abstinent, temperate; clearheaded, cool, level, steady

ant sober

drunk *n* **1** a person who makes a habit of getting drunk ⟨you can't trust anything that old *drunk* says⟩

syn drunkard, inebriate, soak, sot, souse, tippler

rel alcoholic, substance abuser; drinker

near ant abstainer

2 a bout of drinking — see CAROUSE

drunkard *n* a person who makes a habit of getting drunk — see DRUNK 1

drunken *adj* being under the influence of alcohol — see DRUNK

dry *adj* **1** marked by little or no precipitation or humidity ⟨the *dry* climate of the American Southwest⟩

syn arid, droughty, sere, thirsty, waterless

rel baked, dehydrated, parched, sunbaked; rainless

near ant drenched, dripping, saturated, soaked, soaking, sodden, sopping, soppy, soused

ant damp, dank, humid, moist, wet

2 causing weariness, restlessness, or lack of interest — see BORING

dry *vb* **1** to make dry ⟨they *dried* the grapes to make raisins⟩

syn dehydrate, parch, sear

rel dehumidify; evaporate; shrivel, wither

near ant deluge, douse, drench, saturate, soak, sop, souse; damp, dampen, moisten; rehydrate

ant hydrate, wet

2 to lose liveliness, force, or freshness — see WITHER

dryad *n* a mythical goddess represented as a young girl and said to live outdoors — see NYMPH 1

dry run *n* a private performance or session in preparation for a public appearance — see REHEARSAL

dual *adj* consisting of two members or parts that are usually joined — see DOUBLE 1

dub *vb* to give a name to — see NAME 1

dubious *adj* **1** giving good reason for being doubted, questioned, or challenged — see DOUBTFUL 2

2 having doubts about the wisdom of doing something — see HESITANT

3 not likely to be true or to occur — see IMPROBABLE

4 not feeling sure about the truth, wisdom, or trustworthiness of someone or something — see DOUBTFUL 1

dubiously *adv* with distrust — see ASKANCE

duck *vb* **1** to get or keep away from (as a responsibility) through cleverness or deception — see ESCAPE 1

2 to move suddenly aside or to and fro — see DODGE 1

3 to sink or push (something) briefly into or as if into a liquid — see DIP 1

ducking *n* the act or a means of getting or keep-ing away from something undesirable — see ESCAPE 2

duck soup *n* something that is easy to do — see CINCH

duct *n* a long hollow cylinder for carrying a substance (as a liquid or gas) — see PIPE 1

dud *n* **1** something that has failed — see FAILURE 3

2 duds *pl* covering for the human body — see CLOTHING

dude *n* **1** a man extremely interested in his clothing and personal appearance — see DANDY 1

2 an adult male human being — see MAN 1

dudgeon *n* the feeling of being offended or resentful after a slight or indignity — see PIQUE

due *adj* **1** having reached the date at which payment is required ⟨the loan is *due* next April⟩

syn mature

rel delinquent, outstanding, overdue, owed, owing, receivable, unpaid, unsettled; payable

2 being in accordance with the prescribed, normal, or logical course of events ⟨their train is *due* to arrive in half an hour⟩

syn anticipated, awaited, expected, scheduled, slated

near ant belated, delinquent, dilatory, latish, overdue, tardy

3 being what is called for by accepted standards of right and wrong — see JUST 1

due *adv* in a direct line or course — see DIRECTLY 1

due (to) *adj* coming as a result — see RESULTANT

duel *n* an earnest effort for superiority or victory over another — see CONTEST 1

due to *prep* as the result of — see BECAUSE OF

dull *adj* **1** lacking sharpness of edge or point ⟨the *dull* knife just bounced off the skin of the tomato without cutting it⟩

syn blunt, blunted, dulled, obtuse

rel rounded

near ant cutting, edged, edgy, ground, honed, stropped; jagged, needlelike, prickly, spiked, spiky, spiny

ant keen, pointed, sharp, sharpened, whetted

2 causing weariness, restlessness, or lack of interest — see BORING

3 covered over by clouds — see OVERCAST

4 lacking a surface luster or gloss — see MATTE

5 lacking intensity of color — see PALE 1

6 not having or showing an ability to absorb ideas readily — see STUPID 1

7 not loud in pitch or volume — see SOFT 1

8 slow to move or act — see INACTIVE 1

dull *vb* **1** to reduce or weaken in strength or feeling ⟨the aspirin *dulled* his headache and he was soon feeling better⟩
syn benumb, blunt, damp, dampen, deaden, numb
rel muffle, mute, tone (down); decrease, diminish, lessen, let up (on), reduce, subdue; debilitate, enfeeble, weaken; dwindle, recede, subside, taper (off), wane; alleviate, ease, lighten; abate, moderate
near ant amplify, beef (up), boost, consolidate, deepen, enhance, heighten, intensify, magnify, redouble, step up, strengthen; animate, arouse, stimulate
ant sharpen, whet

2 to make white or lighter by removing color — see WHITEN

dulled *adj* **1** lacking a surface luster or gloss — see MATTE

2 lacking intensity of color — see PALE 1

3 lacking sharpness of edge or point — see DULL 1

dullness *also* **dulness** *n* the quality or state of lacking intelligence or quickness of mind — see STUPIDITY 1

dumb *adj* **1** deliberately refraining from speech — see SILENT 1

2 not having or showing an ability to absorb ideas readily — see STUPID 1

dumbbell *n* a stupid person — see IDIOT

dumbfound *also* **dumfound** *vb* to make a strong impression on (someone) with something unexpected — see SURPRISE 1

dumbfounded *or* **dumfounded** *adj* **1** affected with sudden and great wonder or surprise — see THUNDERSTRUCK

2 filled with amazement or wonder — see OPENMOUTHED

dumbfounding *or* **dumfounding** *adj* causing a strong emotional reaction because unexpected — see SURPRISING 1

dumbness *n* **1** incapacity for or restraint from speaking — see SILENCE 1

2 the quality or state of lacking intelligence or quickness of mind — see STUPIDITY 1

dummy *n* **1** a stupid person — see IDIOT

2 a three-dimensional representation of the human body used especially for displaying clothes — see MANNEQUIN 1

dump *n* **1** a place where discarded materials (as trash) are dumped ⟨all of the used packaging eventually ends up in a *dump*⟩
syn landfill, sanitary landfill

rel pigpen, pigsty

2 a place where military arms are stored — see ARMORY

dump *vb* to get rid of as useless or unwanted — see DISCARD

dumping *n* the getting rid of whatever is unwanted or useless — see DISPOSAL 1

dumps *n pl* a state or spell of low spirits — see SADNESS

dumpy *adj* being compact and broad in build and often short in stature — see STOCKY

dun *n* something that someone insists upon having — see DEMAND 1

dunce *n* a stupid person — see IDIOT

dung *n* solid matter discharged from an animal's alimentary canal — see DROPPING 1

dunk *vb* to sink or push (something) briefly into or as if into a liquid — see DIP 1

duo *n* two things of the same or similar kind that match or are considered together — see PAIR

dupe *n* one who is easily deceived or cheated ⟨the swindler was able to escape with all of the *dupe's* money⟩
syn chump, gull, pigeon, sap, sucker, tool
rel victim; schlemiel; butt, derision, laughingstock, mark, mock, mockery; booby, dodo, fool, goose, half-wit, jackass, lunatic, monkey, nincompoop, ninny, nitwit, simpleton, turkey; pushover; loser
near ant confidence man, shark, sharper, swindler, trickster

dupe *vb* to cause to believe what is untrue — see DECEIVE

duplex *adj* consisting of two members or parts that are usually joined — see DOUBLE 1

duplicate *adj* resembling another in every respect — see SAME 1

duplicate *n* **1** something or someone that strongly resembles another — see IMAGE 1

2 something that is made to look exactly like something else — see COPY 1

duplicate *vb* **1** to make an exact likeness of — see COPY 1

2 to make or do again — see REPEAT 4

3 to make twice as great or as many — see DOUBLE 2

duplication *n* **1** something or someone that strongly resembles another — see IMAGE 1

2 something that is made to look exactly like something else — see COPY·

3 the act of saying or doing over again — see REPEAT

duplicity *n* the inclination or practice of misleading others through lies or trickery — see DECEIT

durability *n* continuing existence — see PERSISTENCE 1

duration *n* **1** the period during which something exists, lasts, or is in progress ⟨for the whole *duration* of the speech the bored audience fidgeted⟩
syn date, life, life span, lifetime, run, standing, time

---

syn synonym(s)   *rel* related words
ant antonym(s)   *near ant* near antonym(s)

rel spell, stretch; span, tenure, term; hitch, tour, turn

2 uninterrupted or lasting existence — see CONTINUATION

duress *n* the use of power to impose one's will on another — see FORCE 2

during *prep* in the course of ⟨we wrote notes *during* the boring lecture⟩
syn over, through, throughout

dusk *n* 1 the time from when the sun begins to set to the onset of total darkness ⟨we stopped playing at *dusk*, since it was getting too dark to see the ball⟩
syn evening, eventide, gloaming, nightfall, sundown, sunset, twilight
rel dark, darkness, night, nighttime
near ant day, daytime, light
ant aurora, cockcrow, dawn, dawning, daybreak, daylight, morn, morning, sunrise, sunup

2 a time or place of little or no light — see DARK 1

dusky *adj* being without light or without much light — see DARK 1

dust *n* 1 discarded or useless material — see GARBAGE

2 the solid part of our planet's surface as distinguished from the sea and air — see EARTH 2

dustiness *n* the state or quality of being dirty — see DIRTINESS 1

dusty *adj* 1 consisting of very small particles — see FINE 1

2 not clean — see DIRTY 1

dutiful *adj* marked by or showing proper regard for another's higher status — see RESPECTFUL

duty *n* 1 a charge usually of money collected by the government from people or businesses for public use — see TAX

2 a piece of work that needs to be done regularly — see CHORE 1

3 something one must do because of prior agreement — see OBLIGATION

dwarf *adj* of a size that is less than average — see SMALL 1

dwarf *n* 1 a living thing much smaller than others of its kind ⟨Shetland ponies are the *dwarfs* of the horse world⟩
syn diminutive, midget, mite, peewee, pygmy, runt, scrub, shrimp
rel mini, miniature
near ant whale
ant behemoth, colossus, giant, jumbo, leviathan, mammoth, monster, titan

2 an imaginary being usually having a small human form and magical powers — see FAIRY

dwarf *vb* to hold back the normal growth of — see STUNT

dwarfish *adj* of a size that is less than average — see SMALL 1

dwell *vb* 1 to continue to be in a place for a significant amount of time — see STAY 1

2 to have a home — see LIVE 1

dweller *n* one who lives permanently in a place — see INHABITANT

dwelling *n* the place where one lives — see HOME 1

dwindle *vb* 1 to make smaller in amount, volume, or extent — see DECREASE 1

2 to grow less in scope or intensity especially gradually — see DECREASE 2

dye *n* a substance used to color other materials — see PIGMENT

dye *vb* to give color or a different color to — see COLOR 1

dyestuff *n* a substance used to color other materials — see PIGMENT

dying *adj* nearly dead — see MORIBUND

dynamic *adj* 1 having active strength of body or mind — see VIGOROUS 1

2 marked by or uttered with forcefulness — see EMPHATIC 1

dyspeptic *adj* having or showing a habitually bad temper — see ILL-TEMPERED

each *adj* being one of a group ⟨*each* park visitor receives a free souvenir⟩
syn any, every
rel all; several, various; particular; respective, specific
phrases each and every

each *adv* for each one — see APIECE

eager *adj* showing urgent desire or interest ⟨Tom was *eager* to try out his new pair of skis⟩
syn agog, anxious, ardent, athirst, avid, crazy, desirous, enthusiastic, excited, gung ho, hot, hungry, impatient, keen, nuts, raring, solicitous, thirsty, voracious
rel engaged, interested; hung up, obsessed; ambitious, covetous, craving, hankering, longing, pining; restive, restless;

disposed, inclined, ready, unreluctant, willing
phrases champing at the bit
near ant incurious, unconcerned, uninterested; aloof, detached, disinterested; impassive, stolid; halfhearted, lackadaisical, languid, languorous, spiritless; averse, disinclined, hesitant, loath (*or* loth), reluctant, unwilling
ant apathetic, indifferent, uneager

eagerness *n* urgent desire or interest ⟨students with an *eagerness* to learn⟩
syn appetite, ardor, avidity, desirousness, enthusiasm, excitement, hunger, impatience, keenness, thirst
rel alacrity, quickness; ambition, gusto, zest

near ant unconcern; aloofness, detachment; impassivity, languor

ant apathy, indifference

ear *n* a state of being aware — see ATTENTION 2

earliest *adj* coming before all others in time or order — see FIRST 1

early *adj* 1 relating to or occurring near the beginning of a process, series, or time period ⟨*early* birds of the Jurassic period⟩

syn ancient, primal, primeval, primitive, primordial

rel aged, antediluvian, antiquated, antique, hoary

near ant advanced, complex

ant late

2 occurring before the usual or expected time ⟨we had an *early* dinner so as not to miss the concert⟩

syn inopportune, precocious, premature, unseasonable, untimely

rel unanticipated, unexpected; abrupt, sudden

near ant slow, tardy; anticipated, expected

ant late

early *adv* before the usual or expected time ⟨that year spring arrived *early*⟩

syn beforehand, inopportunely, precociously, prematurely, unseasonably

rel immediately, promptly, punctually; betimes, seasonably

near ant belatedly, tardily

ant late

earmark *vb* to keep or intend for a special purpose — see DEVOTE 1

earn *vb* 1 to receive as return for effort ⟨for years I've *earned* pocket money by mowing lawns⟩

syn acquire, attain, capture, carry, draw, gain, garner, get, land, make, obtain, procure, realize, secure, win

rel clear, net; accomplish, achieve, notch (up), score; accumulate, draw, rack up; catch, pick up; occupy, take over; reacquire, recapture, regain, remake

phrases come by

near ant give up, hand over, part (with), relinquish, surrender, yield

ant forfeit, lose

2 to be or make worthy of (as a reward or punishment) ⟨you've *earned* the afternoon off after all that hard work⟩

syn deserve, merit, rate

rel entitle, qualify

earnest *adj* not joking or playful in mood or manner — see SERIOUS 1

earnestness *n* a mental state free of jesting or trifling ⟨practiced the art of acting with great *earnestness*⟩

syn gravity, intentness, seriousness, soberness, sobriety, solemnity

rel deliberation, determination, firmness, purposefulness, resolve; absorption, attentiveness, concentration, engrossment

near ant lightness, shallowness, superficiality; dalliance, dilettantism

ant frivolity, levity, lightheartedness

earnings *n pl* 1 an increase usually measured in money that comes from labor, business, or property — see INCOME

2 the amount of money left when expenses are subtracted from the total amount received — see PROFIT 1

earshot *n* range of hearing ⟨babysitters should remain within *earshot* of young children⟩

syn hearing, sound

rel volume; distance, sight

earsplitting *adj* marked by a high volume of sound — see LOUD 1

earth *n* 1 the celestial body on which we live ⟨environmentalists who are committed to preserving the *earth*⟩

syn globe, planet, world

rel cosmos, creation, universe; orb, sphere; macrocosm, microcosm

2 the solid part of our planet's surface as distinguished from the sea and air ⟨after nearly drowning, I was glad to feel the *earth* under my feet⟩

syn dirt, dust, ground, land, soil

rel continent, landmass; island, isthmus, mainland, peninsula

3 the loose surface material in which plants naturally grow — see DIRT 1

earthenware *n* articles made of baked clay — see CROCKERY

earthlike *adj* consisting or suggestive of earth — see EARTHY 1

earthly *adj* having to do with life on earth especially as opposed to that in heaven ⟨a sermon against our obsession with *earthly* pursuits⟩

syn carnal, fleshly, material, mundane, temporal, terrestrial, worldly

rel bodily, corporal, corporeal, physical; daily, diurnal; unspiritual

near ant celestial, empyreal, empyrean; divine, spiritual, utopian; extraterrestrial

ant heavenly, nontemporal

earthquake *n* a shaking of the earth ⟨the San Andreas Fault is notorious for its *earthquakes*⟩

syn quake, tremor

rel shock; cataclysm, convulsion, upheaval

earthy *adj* 1 consisting or suggestive of earth ⟨the unmistakably *earthy* aroma of a greenhouse⟩

syn earthlike, loamy

rel clayey, dusty, muddy, sandy

2 willing to see things as they really are and deal with them sensibly — see REALISTIC 1

ease *n* 1 reduction of or freedom from pain ⟨the sunburn medication brought me instant *ease*⟩

syn alleviation, comfort, relief

rel appeasement, assuagement, decrease, diminishment, moderation, mollification; calming, salving, soothing

near ant discomfort, unrest; agony, anguish, pain

2 carefree freedom from constraint — see ABANDON

3 freedom from activity or labor — see ¹REST 1

---

syn synonym(s)	**rel** related words
ant antonym(s)	**near ant** near antonym(s)

ease *vb* 1 to free from obstruction or difficulty <measures intended to *ease* the flow of traffic during rush hour>

syn facilitate, loosen (up), smooth, unclog

rel accelerate, expedite, hasten, speed; advance, further, promote; aid, assist, help, improve

phrases pave the way (for)

near ant hinder, impede; retard

ant complicate

2 to make less taut — see SLACKEN

3 to make more bearable or less severe — see HELP 2

easily *adv* without difficulty <a skater who *easily* executes even the most difficult jumps>

syn effortlessly, facilely, fluently, freely, handily, lightly, painlessly, readily, smoothly

rel ably, adeptly, adroitly, competently, dexterously, efficiently, expertly, proficiently, skillfully; instinctively, intuitively, naturally, spontaneously

near ant awkwardly, clumsily, gracelessly, ineptly, maladroitly; painfully, painstakingly

ant arduously, laboriously

easy *adj* 1 involving minimal difficulty or effort <a minor problem with an *easy* solution>

syn effortless, facile, fluent, fluid, light, painless, ready, simple, smooth, snap, soft

rel apparent, clear, distinct, evident, manifest, obvious, plain; clear-cut, straightforward, uncomplicated

near ant painful, troublesome; abstruse, complex, complicated, intricate, knotty

ant arduous, difficult, hard, labored

2 readily taken advantage of <senior citizens who are *easy* prey for scam artists>

syn exploitable, gullible, naive (*or* naïve), susceptible, trusting

rel credulous, trustful, uncritical, unsuspecting, unsuspicious; artless, simple, unsophisticated

near ant critical, cynical, mistrustful, skeptical, suspicious; sophisticated

3 providing physical comfort — see COMFORTABLE 1

easygoing *adj* 1 having a relaxed, casual manner <counselors at the summer camp are pretty *easygoing*>

syn affable, breezy, devil-may-care, happy-go-lucky, laid-back, low-pressure

rel carefree, lackadaisical, nonchalant, unaffected, unconcerned; familiar, homey, informal; lax, lenient, permissive, soft

near ant ceremonious, decorous, formal, rigid, strict

ant uptight

2 not bound by rigid standards <boys are pretty *easygoing* about housekeeping>

syn flexible, lax, loose, relaxed, slack, unrestrained, unrestricted

rel careless, heedless, negligent, slipshod, sloppy, slovenly, unfussy

near ant constrained, restrained, restricted, rigid, strict, tight; exact, fussy, meticulous, scrupulous

ant rigorous

3 having or showing a lack of concern or seriousness — see CAREFREE

eat *vb* 1 to take in as food <having gone all day without food, we greedily *ate* the hamburgers>

syn consume, ingest

rel digest, down, mouth (down), swallow; bolt, devour, gobble (up *or* down), gorge, gulp, wolf; chew, gnaw (at *or* on), lap, lick, nibble (on); relish, savor, taste; banquet, dine, feast, gormandize, pig out; dispatch, polish off; breakfast, lunch, sup; munch, snack

2 to consume or wear away gradually <the pot's protective coating was *eaten* away by the acid>

syn bite (at), corrode, erode, fret

rel break down, break up, decompose, disintegrate, dissolve; destroy, ruin, wreck

3 to take a meal — see DINE 1

eat (up) *vb* to destroy all trace of — see CONSUME 1

eatable *adj* suitable for use as food — see EDIBLE

eatables *n pl* substances intended to be eaten — see FOOD

eavesdrop (on) *vb* to listen to (another in private conversation) <a nosy traveler who likes to *eavesdrop on* his fellow airline passengers>

syn listen in (on), overhear

rel bug, tap, wiretap; monitor, snoop, spy; hear, hearken

eaves trough *n* a pipe or channel for carrying off water from a roof — see GUTTER 1

ebb *vb* 1 to become worse or of less value — see DETERIORATE

2 to grow less in scope or intensity especially gradually — see DECREASE 2

ebbing *n* a gradual sinking and wasting away of mind or body — see DECLINE 1

ebony *adj* having the color of soot or coal — see BLACK 1

eccentric *n* a person of odd or whimsical habits <an *eccentric* who designed his house to look like a Scottish castle>

syn character, codger, crackbrain, crackpot, crank, kook, nut, oddball, screwball, weirdo

rel bohemian, maverick, nonconformist, coot, rarity; freak

near ant conformer, conformist, follower, sheep

eccentricity *n* an odd or peculiar habit — see IDIOSYNCRASY

ecclesiastic *n* a person specially trained and authorized to conduct religious services in a Christian church — see CLERGYMAN

ecclesiastical *or* **ecclesiastic** *adj* of or relating to a church <*ecclesiastical* laws that have been in existence for centuries>

syn churchly

rel divine, holy, religious, sacramental; apostolic, canonical, clerical, episcopal, evangelical, ministerial, papal, pastoral,

patriarchal, pontifical, priestly, rabbinical, sacerdotal

near ant lay, profane, secular, temporal

echo *vb* **1** to continue or be repeated in a series of reflected sound waves — see REVERBERATE

2 to say after another — see REPEAT 3

eclipse *vb* to be greater, better, or stronger than — see SURPASS 1

economical *adj* careful in the management of money or resources — see FRUGAL

economize *vb* to avoid unnecessary waste or expense ⟨in tough times people learn how to *economize*⟩

syn save, scrimp, skimp

rel conserve, husband, manage; scrape; cut back, cut down, retrench

near ant dissipate, fritter (away), squander, throw away

ant waste

economizing *adj* careful in the management of money or resources — see FRUGAL

economy *n* careful management of material resources ⟨people on fixed incomes are used to practicing *economy*⟩

syn frugality, husbandry, providence, scrimping, skimping, thrift

rel conservation, saving; miserliness, stinginess; discretion, prudence

near ant extravagance, improvidence, lavishness, prodigality, squandering

ant wastefulness

ecstasy *n* a state of overwhelming usually pleasurable emotion ⟨actors are typically in *ecstasy* upon winning an Oscar⟩

syn elation, euphoria, exhilaration, heaven, intoxication, paradise, rapture, rhapsody, transport

rel exaltation; bliss, blissfulness, delight, enchantment, gladness, happiness, joy, joyfulness, pleasure; reverie, trance; inspiration; fervor, frenzy, madness, passion

near ant blues, dejection, despondency, doldrums, downheartedness, dumps, melancholy, mopes

ant depression

ecstatic *adj* experiencing or marked by overwhelming usually pleasurable emotion ⟨a football player who was *ecstatic* upon receiving a full athletic scholarship to the college of his choice⟩

syn elated, enraptured, entranced, euphoric, exhilarated, intoxicated, rapturous, rhapsodic (*also* rhapsodical)

rel exultant, jubilant, triumphant; enthusiastic, excited, gung ho, thrilled; blissful, delighted, glad, gratified, happy, joyful, joyous, pleased, satisfied, tickled

near ant blue, dejected, despondent, disconsolate, disheartened, downhearted, melancholy

ant depressed

Eden *n* a place or state of great happiness — see PARADISE 1

edge *n* **1** a harsh or sharp quality ⟨the teacher's voice had a sarcastic *edge* as she welcomed the tardy student to class⟩

syn acidity, acridness, acrimoniousness, acrimony, acuteness, asperity, bite, bitterness, harshness, keenness, poignancy, pungency, roughness, sharpness, tartness

rel ginger, punch, spice, tang; severity, shrillness, virulence; pointedness, thorniness

2 the line or relatively narrow space that marks the outer limit of something — see BORDER 1

3 the more favorable condition or position in a competition — see ADVANTAGE 1

edge *vb* to make sharp or sharper — see SHARPEN

edged *adj* having an edge thin enough to cut or pierce something — see SHARP 1

edgewise *adv* with one side faced forward — see SIDEWAYS

edginess *n* a state of nervousness marked by sudden jerky movements — see JUMPINESS

edgy *adj* **1** feeling or showing uncomfortable feelings of uncertainty — see NERVOUS 1

2 having an edge thin enough to cut or pierce something — see SHARP 1

edible *adj* suitable for use as food ⟨*edible* plant products⟩

syn eatable, esculent

rel absorbable, chewable, digestible; nourishing, nutritious, nutritive; appetizing, delicious, flavorful, palatable, savory, succulent, tasty, toothsome

near ant indigestible, nondigestible

ant inedible

edibles *n pl* substances intended to be eaten — see FOOD

edict *n* **1** an order publicly issued by an authority ⟨the school board's *edict* put a new student dress code into effect⟩

syn decree, directive, fiat, ruling

rel call, decision, judgment (*or* judgement); announcement, declaration, dictum, manifesto, proclamation, pronouncement; canon, encyclical

2 a statement of what to do that must be obeyed by those concerned — see COMMAND 1

edifice *n* **1** a large, magnificent, or massive building ⟨the U.S. Capitol is one of our nation's most impressive *edifices*⟩

syn hall, palace, tower

rel construction, erection, structure; castle, château, estate, manor, mansion, villa; mausoleum, memorial, monument

2 something built as a dwelling, shelter, or place for human activity — see BUILDING

edify *vb* to provide (someone) with moral or spiritual understanding — see ENLIGHTEN 2

edit *vb* to prepare for publication by correcting, rewriting, or updating ⟨the publisher *edited* a new version of its best-selling school dictionary⟩

syn redraft, revamp, revise, rework

---

syn synonym(s)   *rel* related words
ant antonym(s)   *near ant* near antonym(s)

rel amend, correct, emend, rectify; collect, compile; issue, print, publish

educate *vb* **1** to cause to acquire knowledge or skill in some field — see TEACH 2 **2** to provide (someone) with moral or spiritual understanding — see ENLIGHTEN 2

educated *adj* having or displaying advanced knowledge or education ⟨*educated* people are often more aware and tolerant of cultural and ethnic diversity⟩

syn erudite, knowledgeable, learned, literate, scholarly, well-read

rel civilized, cultivated, cultured; cerebral, highbrow, intellectual; polished, refined, well-bred; academic, bookish, didactic, pedantic, professorial; instructed, schooled, skilled, trained; homeschooled, self-educated, self-taught; briefed, enlightened, informed, versed

near ant uncivilized, uncultivated, uncultured; lowbrow, unintelligent; ill-bred, unpolished, unrefined; uninformed

ant ignorant, illiterate, uneducated

education *n* **1** the act or process of imparting knowledge or skills to another ⟨a teacher who devoted herself to the *education* of children with special needs⟩

syn instruction, schooling, teaching, training, tutelage, tutoring

rel coaching, conditioning, cultivation, preparation, readying; development, direction, guidance, nurturance, nurturing; edification, enlightenment, improvement **2** the understanding and information gained from being educated ⟨a person whose extensive *education* was obvious to all who met him⟩

syn erudition, knowledge, learnedness, learning, scholarship, science

rel culture, edification, enlightenment; literacy, reading; bookishness, pedantry

near ant ignorance, illiteracy

educational *adj* **1** providing useful information or knowledge — see INFORMATIVE **2** of or relating to schooling or learning especially at an advanced level — see ACADEMIC

educative *adj* providing useful information or knowledge — see INFORMATIVE

educator *n* a person whose occupation is to give formal instruction in a school — see TEACHER

educe *vb* to draw out (something hidden, latent, or reserved) ⟨the gift of a puppy finally *educed* a response from the shy boy⟩

syn elicit, evoke, raise

rel drag, dredge (up), extort, pull, wangle, wrest, wring; gain, get, obtain, procure, secure; expose, reveal, uncover

near ant miss, overlook, pass over

eerie *adj* fearfully and mysteriously strange or fantastic ⟨*eerie* noises would occasionally come from locked rooms in the castle⟩

syn creepy, haunting, spooky, uncanny, unearthly, weird

rel ghostly, spectral; odd, strange, uncommon, unusual; preternatural, supernatural; enigmatic (*also* enigmatical), inscrutable, mysterious, puzzling; dreadful, fearsome, horrible, horrifying, terrible, terrifying

near ant common, commonplace, everyday, normal, ordinary, usual

efface *vb* to destroy all traces of — see ANNIHILATE 1

effect *n* **1** a condition or occurrence traceable to a cause ⟨better health is always one of the *effects* of improved hygiene⟩

syn aftereffect, aftermath, conclusion, consequence, corollary, development, fate, fruit, issue, outcome, outgrowth, product, result, resultant, sequel, sequence, upshot

rel ramification; denouement, repercussion; conclusion, end; by-product, side effect

phrases matter of course

near ant consideration, determinant, factor; base, basis, foundation, ground, groundwork

ant antecedent, cause, occasion, reason **2** the power to bring about a result on another ⟨religion has a profound *effect* on our lives⟩

syn impact, influence, mark, repercussion, sway

rel authority, clout, prestige, weight; command, domination, dominion; consequence, importance, significance

3 effects *pl* transportable items that one owns — see POSSESSION 2

effect *vb* to be the cause of (a situation, action, or state of mind) ⟨classroom discussions designed to *effect* a change in racial attitudes⟩

syn bring about, cause, create, effectuate, engender, generate, induce, make, produce, prompt, result (in), spawn, work, yield

rel decide, determine; begin, establish, father, found, inaugurate, initiate, institute, introduce, set, set up; advance, encourage, forward, foster, promote; enact, render, turn out

phrases bring forth, give rise to

near ant impede, limit, restrict; dampen, repress, smother, stifle, suppress; arrest, check, curb, restrain, retard; can, kill, snuff (out), still; abolish, demolish, destroy, extinguish, liquidate, quash, quell, quench

effective *adj* **1** producing or capable of producing a desired result ⟨an *effective* treatment of the once-dreaded disease⟩

syn effectual, efficacious, efficient, fruitful, potent, productive

rel adequate, capable, competent; adept, expert, masterly, proficient, skilled, skillful; cogent, convincing, killer, sound, striking, telling, valid; active, dynamic, operative, useful, working; feasible, practical, realizable, workable

near ant incapable, incompetent, inexpert, unqualified; abortive, bootless, fu-

tile, vain; empty, hollow, idle, pointless; inoperative, useless, worthless
ant fruitless, ineffective, ineffectual, inefficient, unproductive
2 having the power to persuade — see COGENT

effectiveness *n* **1** the capacity to persuade — see COGENCY
2 the power to produce a desired result — see EFFICACY
3 the quality of an utterance that provokes interest and produces an effect — see ¹PUNCH 1

effectual *adj* producing or capable of producing a desired result — see EFFECTIVE 1

effectualness *n* the power to produce a desired result — see EFFICACY

effectuate *vb* to be the cause of (a situation, action, or state of mind) — see EFFECT

effeminate *adj* having or displaying qualities more suitable for women than for men ⟨a comedian deliberately affecting *effeminate* mannerisms⟩
syn feminine, girlish, sissy, unmanly, womanish, womanlike, womanly
rel old-maidish, overnice, spinsterish; dandyish, foppish, sappy
ant manlike, manly, mannish, masculine

effervescent *adj* joyously unrestrained — see EXUBERANT

effete *adj* **1** having lost forcefulness, courage, or spirit ⟨the soft, *effete* society that marked the final years of the Roman empire⟩
syn decadent, decayed, degenerate, overripe, washed-up
rel decaying, declining, dying, failing, waning; soft, weak; dissolute, immoral
2 depleted in strength, energy, or freshness — see WEARY 1
3 lacking bodily strength — see WEAK 1
4 lacking strength of will or character — see WEAK 2

efficacious *adj* producing or capable of producing a desired result — see EFFECTIVE 1

efficaciousness *n* the power to produce a desired result — see EFFICACY

efficacy *n* the power to produce a desired result ⟨questioned the *efficacy* of the alarms in actually preventing auto theft⟩
syn effectiveness, effectualness, efficaciousness, efficiency, productiveness
rel ability, capability, capacity; potency, strength
near ant inability, inadequacy, incompetence
ant ineffectiveness, ineffectualness, inefficiency

efficiency *n* the power to produce a desired result — see EFFICACY

efficient *adj* producing or capable of producing a desired result — see EFFECTIVE 1

effort *n* the active use of energy in producing a result ⟨the finished parade float was well worth the *effort*⟩
syn elbow grease, exertion, expenditure, labor, pains, sweat, trouble, while, work
rel drudgery, grind, toil, travail; dint, energy; force, might, muscle, power, puissance; attempt, endeavor, essay
near ant adroitness, ease, facility, fluency, smoothness; idleness, inaction, inactivity, indolence, inertia, languor, laziness

effortless *adj* involving minimal difficulty or effort — see EASY 1

effortlessly *adv* without difficulty — see EASILY

effrontery *n* shameless boldness ⟨the little squirt had the *effrontery* to deny eating any cookies, even with the crumbs still on his lips⟩
syn audacity, brashness, brass, brassiness, brazenness, cheek, cheekiness, chutzpah (*also* chutzpa *or* hutzpah *or* hutzpa), gall, nerve, nerviness, pertness, presumption, presumptuousness, sauce, sauciness, temerity
rel arrogance, assurance, cockiness, confidence, overconfidence, sanguinity, self-assurance, self-confidence; impertinence, impudence, insolence, rudeness
near ant bashfulness, diffidence, hesitancy, modesty, shyness, timidity

effulgence *n* the quality or state of having or giving off light — see BRILLIANCE 1

effulgent *adj* giving off or reflecting much light — see BRIGHT 1

effusive *adj* showing feeling freely — see DEMONSTRATIVE

egg (on) *vb* to try to persuade (someone) through earnest appeals to follow a course of action — see URGE

ego *n* **1** a reasonable or justifiable sense of one's worth or importance — see PRIDE 1
2 an often unjustified feeling of being pleased with oneself or with one's situation or achievements — see COMPLACENCE

egocentric *adj* overly concerned with one's own desires, needs, or interests ⟨the cult attracts *egocentric* people who are preoccupied with reaching their potential as individuals⟩
syn egoistic, egotistic (*or* egotistical), self-centered, selfish, self-seeking
rel complacent, conceited, self-conceited, self-directed, self-important, self-indulgent, self-satisfied, smug, vain
near ant altruistic, generous, greathearted, magnanimous, self-sacrificing
ant selfless

egoism *n* excessive interest in oneself ⟨because of her *egoism*, she never gave a thought to asking how the others felt⟩
syn egotism, self-centeredness, self-interest, selfishness, self-regard
rel conceit, self-admiration, self-conceit, self-esteem, self-importance, self-indulgence, self-respect, self-satisfaction, self-sufficiency

---

near ant altruism, generosity, magnanimity, self-sacrifice

ant selflessness

egoistic *adj* 1 having too high an opinion of oneself — see CONCEITED

2 overly concerned with one's own desires, needs, or interests — see EGOCENTRIC

egotism *n* 1 an often unjustified feeling of being pleased with oneself or with one's situation or achievements — see COMPLACENCE

2 excessive interest in oneself — see EGOISM

egotistic *or* **egotistical** *adj* 1 having too high an opinion of oneself — see CONCEITED

2 overly concerned with one's own desires, needs, or interests — see EGOCENTRIC

egregious *adj* very noticeable especially for being incorrect or bad ⟨the student's theme was marred by a number of *egregious* errors in spelling⟩

syn blatant, conspicuous, flagrant, glaring, gross, obvious, patent, pronounced, rank, striking

rel clear, distinct, evident, notable, outstanding, plain, salient; absolute, arrant, downright, out-and-out, outright, sheer, stark, utter; abominable, atrocious, awful, deplorable, execrable, heinous, monstrous, outrageous, preposterous, shameful, shocking

near ant imperceptible, inconspicuous, insignificant, slight, trifling, trivial; concealed, hidden, invisible

egress *n* a place or means of going out — see EXIT 1

ejaculate *vb* to utter with a sudden burst of strong feeling — see EXCLAIM

eject *vb* 1 to drive or force out ⟨we quickly *ejected* the unwanted guest from our party⟩

syn banish, boot (out), bounce, cast (out), chase, dismiss, drum (out), expel, extrude, oust, rout, run off, throw out

rel deport, displace, dispossess, evict, exile, expatriate, ostracize, shut out; discharge, fire, sack

phrases send packing

near ant accept, admit, receive, take in; welcome; entertain, harbor, house, lodge, shelter

2 to throw out or off (something from within) often violently — see ERUPT 1

eke out *vb* to get with great difficulty ⟨*eked out* a living from the family's small farm⟩

syn scrape, scrounge, squeeze, wrest, wring

rel acquire, earn, gain, obtain, procure, secure

elaborate *adj* 1 made or done with great care or with much detail ⟨*elaborate* festivities for the 200th anniversary of the town's founding⟩

syn complex, complicated, detailed, fancy, intricate, involved, sophisticated

rel elegant, grand, ornate, magnificent, splendid; extravagant, flamboyant, frilly, grandiose, ostentatious, overwrought; labyrinthine

near ant modest, plain, uncomplicated, unsophisticated

ant simple

2 including many small descriptive features — see DETAILED 1

3 having many parts or aspects that are usually interrelated — see COMPLEX 1

elaborate (on) *vb* 1 to add to the interest of by including made-up details — see EMBROIDER

2 to express more fully and in greater detail — see EXPAND 1

elaborateness *n* the state or quality of having many interrelated parts or aspects — see COMPLEXITY 1

elaboration *n* 1 the act or process of going from the simple or basic to the complex or advanced — see DEVELOPMENT 1

2 the representation of something in terms that go beyond the facts — see EXAGGERATION

elapse *vb* to come to an end — see CEASE 1

elastic *adj* 1 able to revert to original size and shape after being stretched, squeezed, or twisted ⟨*elastic* rubber bands⟩

syn flexible, resilient, rubberlike, rubbery, springy, stretch, stretchable, supple

rel adaptable, ductile, malleable, moldable, plastic, pliable, pliant; limber, lissome (*also* lissom), lithe

near ant firm, hard, solid; brittle, crisp, friable

ant inelastic, inflexible, nonelastic, rigid, stiff

2 capable of being readily changed — see FLEXIBLE 1

elate *vb* to fill with great joy ⟨the winning of the state basketball championship *elated* the whole student body⟩

syn elevate, enrapture, exhilarate, overjoy, transport

rel excite, inspire, stimulate, uplift; delight, gladden, gratify, please

near ant demoralize, discourage, dishearten, dispirit; distress, oppress, sadden

ant depress

elated *adj* experiencing or marked by overwhelming usually pleasurable emotion — see ECSTATIC

elation *n* a state of overwhelming usually pleasurable emotion — see ECSTASY

elbow *vb* to force one's way — see PRESS 4

elbow grease *n* the active use of energy in producing a result — see EFFORT

elbowroom *n* an extent or area available for or used up by some activity or thing — see ROOM 1

elder *n* 1 a person of advanced years — see SENIOR CITIZEN

2 one who is above another in rank, station, or office — see SUPERIOR

3 one who is older than another — see SENIOR 1

4 the senior member of a group — see DEAN

elderly *adj* being of advanced years and especially past middle age ⟨*elderly* people who stay active are usually the healthiest and the happiest⟩

syn aged, aging, ancient, geriatric, long-lived, old, older, senior

rel adult, grown-up, mature, middle-aged; pensioned, retired, superannuated; matriarchal, patriarchal, venerable; doddering, senile, tottery

near ant youngish; adolescent, immature, juvenile, puerile

ant young, youthful

elder statesman *n* the senior member of a group — see DEAN

elect *adj* singled out from a number or group as more to one's liking — see SELECT 1

elect *n* individuals carefully selected as being the best of a class — see ELITE

elect *vb* to decide to accept (someone or something) from a group of possibilities — see CHOOSE 1

election *n* the act or process of selecting — see SELECTION 1

elective *adj* subject to one's freedom of choice — see OPTIONAL

electric *adj* causing great emotional or mental stimulation — see EXCITING 1

electrify *vb* to cause a pleasurable stimulation of the feelings — see THRILL

electrifying *adj* causing great emotional or mental stimulation — see EXCITING 1

elegance *n* dignified or restrained beauty of form, appearance, or style ⟨the *elegance* of the hotel's French furnishings⟩

syn class, elegancy, grace, gracefulness, handsomeness, majesty, refinement, stateliness

rel grandeur, lavishness, luxuriousness, magnificence, ornateness, richness, splendor; artfulness, chic, polish, sophistication, taste, tastefulness; choiceness, classicism, dignity, exquisiteness, restraint, simplicity; affectedness, grandiosity, pretentiousness

near ant coarseness, crudeness, flashiness, garishness, gaudiness, gracelessness, grotesqueness, tastelessness, tawdriness

elegancy *n* dignified or restrained beauty of form, appearance, or style — see ELEGANCE

elegant *adj* 1 having or showing elegance ⟨the most *elegant* First Lady in the nation's history⟩ ⟨the bride's *elegant* gown received nothing but praise⟩

syn graceful, handsome, majestic, refined, stately, tasteful

rel grand, lavish, luxurious, magnificent, ornate, rich, splendid; artful, genteel, polished, sophisticated; classic, exquisite, restrained, simple; chic, fashionable, posh, smart, stylish; affected, grandiose, pretentious

near ant coarse, crude, flashy, garish, gaudy, grotesque, tacky, tawdry

ant graceless, inelegant, tasteless, unhandsome

2 having qualities that appeal to a refined taste — see CHOICE

elegiac *adj* causing or marked by an atmosphere lacking in cheer — see GLOOMY 1

elegy *n* a composition expressing one's grief over a loss — see LAMENT 2

element *n* 1 one of the parts that make up a whole ⟨a free press is an essential *element* of a democracy⟩

syn component, constituent, factor, ingredient, member

rel detail, item, particular, point; aspect, characteristic, facet, feature, trait; division, fragment, particle, piece, portion, section, sector, segment

near ant aggregate, composite, compound, sum, total, totality

ant whole

2 **elements** *pl* general or basic truths on which other truths or theories can be based — see PRINCIPLES 1

elemental *adj* of or relating to the simplest facts or theories of a subject — see ELEMENTARY

elementary *adj* of or relating to the simplest facts or theories of a subject ⟨students who do not have even an *elementary* knowledge of geography⟩

syn basic, elemental, essential, fundamental, rudimentary, underlying

rel primal, primary, prime; primitive; beginning, introductory, preliminary

near ant complex, sophisticated; detailed, extensive, intricate

ant advanced

elephantine *adj* unusually large — see HUGE

elevate *vb* 1 to fill with great joy — see ELATE

2 to move from a lower to a higher place or position — see RAISE 1

3 to move higher in rank or position — see PROMOTE 1

elevated *adj* 1 being positioned above a surface ⟨an *elevated* monorail that transports visitors all over the theme park⟩

syn lifted, raised, uplifted, upraised

rel aerial, suspended; erect, upright

near ant low-lying

ant sunken

2 very dignified in form, tone, or style ⟨the *elevated* language of Lincoln's Gettysburg Address⟩

syn eloquent, formal, high-flown, lofty, majestic, stately, towering

rel bombastic, declamatory, florid, flowery, grandiloquent, highfalutin, pompous, stilted

near ant casual, colloquial, conversational, informal, slangy; coarse, crude, indecent, vulgar

ant low, undignified

3 being at a higher level than average — see HIGH 2

4 having, characterized by, or arising from a dignified and generous nature — see NOBLE 2

5 located at a greater height than average or usual — see HIGH 3

elevation *n* **1** a raising or a state of being raised to a higher rank or position — see ADVANCEMENT 1

2 an area of high ground — see HEIGHT 4

3 the distance of something or someone from bottom to top — see HEIGHT 3

4 the most extreme or advanced point — see HEIGHT 2

elf *n* an imaginary being usually having a small human form and magical powers — see FAIRY

elfin *adj* having an often mysterious or magical power to attract — see FASCINATING 1

elfish *adj* given to good-natured joking or teasing — see PLAYFUL

elicit *vb* to draw out (something hidden, latent, or reserved) — see EDUCE

eliminate *vb* to prevent the participation or inclusion of — see EXCLUDE

elite *n* individuals carefully selected as being the best of a class ⟨the winners of this science award represent the *elite* of our high schools⟩
syn best, choice, cream, elect, fat, flower, pick, prime, upper crust
rel aristocracy, (the) establishment, gentry, nobility, society, (the) top, upper class
phrases cream of the crop
near ant commoners, masses, rank and file

elixir *n* something that cures all ills or problems — see CURE-ALL

elliptic *or* **elliptical** *adj* having the shape of an egg — see OVAL

elocution *n* the art of speaking in public eloquently and effectively — see ORATORY 1

elongate *vb* to make longer — see EXTEND 1

elongated *adj* of great extent from end to end — see LONG 1

elongation *n* the act of making longer — see EXTENSION 1

eloquence *n* the art or power of speaking or writing in a forceful and convincing way ⟨the *eloquence* of Martin Luther King's "I Have a Dream" speech⟩
syn articulateness, poetry, rhetoric
rel expression, expressiveness; declamation, elocution, oratory; forcefulness, meaningfulness, persuasiveness; ardor, fervor, passion, power

eloquent *adj* **1** able to express oneself clearly and well — see ARTICULATE

2 clearly conveying a special meaning (as one's mood) — see EXPRESSIVE

3 very dignified in form, tone, or style — see ELEVATED 2

else *adj* resulting in an increase in amount or number — see ADDITIONAL

else *adv* in a different way — see OTHERWISE

elucidate *vb* to make plain or understandable — see EXPLAIN 1

elucidation *n* a statement that makes something clear — see EXPLANATION 1

elucidative *adj* serving to explain — see EXPLANATORY

elude *vb* to get or keep away from (as a responsibility) through cleverness or trickery — see ESCAPE 2

eluding *n* the act or a means of getting or keeping away from something undesirable — see ESCAPE 2

elusive *adj* hard to find, capture, or isolate ⟨the giant squid is one of the ocean's most *elusive* inhabitants⟩
syn evasive, fugitive, slippery
rel cagey (*also* cagy), shifty; ephemeral, evanescent, fleeting, momentary, passing, short-lived, transitory; unavailable, unobtainable
near ant accessible, approachable, attainable, available, obtainable

elvish *adj* tending to or exhibiting reckless playfulness — see MISCHIEVOUS 1

Elysian *adj* of, relating to, or suggesting heaven — see CELESTIAL

Elysium *n* **1** a dwelling place of perfect bliss for the soul after death — see HEAVEN 1

2 a place or state of great happiness — see PARADISE 1

emaciated *adj* suffering extreme weight loss as a result of hunger or disease ⟨the *emaciated* bodies of the survivors of the concentration camps⟩
syn cadaverous, gaunt, haggard, skeletal, wasted
rel bony, rawboned, scrawny, skinny, thin; starved, underfed, undernourished; shriveled, withered, wizened
near ant beefy, brawny, burly, fit, hale, healthy, hearty, husky; chubby, corpulent, fat, fleshy, heavyset, plump, portly, stocky, thickset

emancipate *vb* to set free (as from slavery or confinement) — see FREE 1

emancipation *n* the act of setting free from slavery — see LIBERATION

emasculate *vb* to deprive of courage or confidence — see UNNERVE 1

embankment *n* a bank of earth constructed to control water — see DAM

embargo *n* an order that something not be done or used — see PROHIBITION 2

embark (on *or* upon) *vb* to take the first step in (a process or course of action) — see BEGIN 1

embarrass *vb* **1** to throw into a state of self-conscious distress ⟨the young soldier was *embarrassed* by the public praise for his heroism⟩
syn abash, confound, confuse, discomfit, disconcert, discountenance, faze, fluster, mortify, nonplus, rattle
rel agitate, bother, chagrin, discomfort, discompose, dismay, disquiet, distress, disturb, perturb, unhinge, unsettle, upset; debase, degrade, demean, humble, humiliate
near ant calm, comfort, console, relieve, soothe; buoy, cheer, embolden, encourage, hearten; assure, reassure

2 to create difficulty for the work or activity of — see HAMPER

embarrassing *adj* causing embarrassment — see AWKWARD 3

embarrassment *n* **1** the emotional state of being made self-consciously uncomfortable ⟨experienced the great *embarrassment* of tripping while on stage⟩

syn abashment, confusion, discomfiture, fluster, mortification

rel agitation, bother, chagrin, discomfort, discomposure, dismay, disquiet, distress, disturbance, perturbation, uneasiness, upset; debasement, degradation, humiliation

near ant aplomb, assurance, composure, confidence, coolness, equanimity, poise, self-assurance, self-confidence, self-possession

2 something that makes movement or progress more difficult — see ENCUMBRANCE

embed *also* **imbed** *vb* to set solidly in or as if in surrounding matter — see ENTRENCH

embellish *vb* **1** to add to the interest of by including made-up details — see EMBROIDER

2 to make more attractive by adding something that is beautiful or becoming — see DECORATE

embellishing *adj* serving to add beauty — see DECORATIVE

embellishment *n* **1** something that decorates or beautifies — see DECORATION 1

2 the representation of something in terms that go beyond the facts — see EXAGGERATION

embitter *vb* to implant bitter feelings in ⟨the family refused to allow their collision with a drunk driver *embitter* them⟩

syn antagonize, envenom

rel aggravate, anger, enrage, incense, infuriate, madden; alienate, disaffect, disgruntle, estrange; sour

near ant endear, ingratiate; appease, assuage, mollify, pacify, placate, propitiate; sweeten

embittered *adj* having or showing deep-seated resentment — see BITTER 1

emblem *n* a device, design, or figure used as an identifying mark (as a quality) ⟨the oil company uses a scallop shell as its *emblem*⟩

syn hallmark, logo, symbol, trademark

rel icon, pictograph; badge, coat of arms, crest, insignia; monogram, stamp, token

emblematic *also* **emblematical** *adj* having the function or meaning of a symbol — see SYMBOLIC

embodiment *n* a visible representation of something abstract (as a quality) ⟨Mother Theresa was often regarded as the *embodiment* of selfless devotion to others⟩

syn epitome, incarnation, manifestation, personification

rel exemplification, incorporation, substantiation; essence, quintessence; arche-

type, exemplar, model, paradigm, pattern; acme, apex, culmination, peak, pinnacle, summit, zenith

embody *vb* **1** to make a part of a body or system ⟨concepts of moral behavior that we should *embody* into our daily life⟩

syn assimilate, incorporate, integrate

rel amalgamate, blend, combine, commingle, fuse, intermingle, merge, mingle

2 to represent in visible form ⟨George Washington *embodied* so many of the virtues that Americans hold dear⟩

syn epitomize, incarnate, manifest, materialize, personalize, personify, substantiate

rel actualize, realize; symbolize; exemplify, illustrate

embolden *vb* to fill with courage or strength of purpose — see ENCOURAGE 1

emboldened *adj* inclined or willing to take risks — see BOLD 1

embosom *vb* to surround or cover closely — see ENFOLD 1

embower *vb* to surround or cover closely — see ENFOLD 1

embrace *vb* **1** to put one's arms around and press tightly ⟨upon being finally reunited, the overjoyed father *embraced* his son⟩

syn clasp, enfold, grasp, hug

rel cling, cradle, grab, grip, hold; embosom, encircle, entwine, envelop; fold, lock, twine, wrap; cuddle, fondle, nestle, nuzzle, pat, pet, snuggle, stroke

2 to surround or cover closely — see ENFOLD 1

3 to take for one's own use (something originated by another) — see ADOPT

4 receive or accept gladly or readily — see WELCOME

5 to have as part of a whole — see INCLUDE

embroider *vb* to add to the interest of by including made-up details ⟨Dad likes to *embroider* his fishing stories⟩

syn color, elaborate (on), embellish, exaggerate, magnify, pad, stretch

rel amplify, enhance, enlarge (upon), expand, flesh (out); fudge, hedge; overdo, overdraw, overemphasize, overplay, overstate; caricature; satirize

near ant belittle, minimize, play (down), understate

embroidering *n* the representation of something in terms that go beyond the facts — see EXAGGERATION

embroidery *n* decorative stitching done on cloth with the use of a needle — see NEEDLEWORK

embroil *vb* to place in conflict or difficulties ⟨the town has been *embroiled* in controversy over the building of the huge shopping mall⟩

syn bog (down), mire

rel enmesh, ensnare, entangle, entrap, snare, tangle, trap

near ant emancipate, free, liberate, release

---

syn synonym(s)   **rel** related words
ant antonym(s)   **near ant** near antonym(s)

emend *vb* to remove errors, defects, deficiencies, or deviations from — see CORRECT 1

emendation *n* a change designed to correct or improve a written work — see CORRECTION 1

emerge *vb* to come to one's attention especially gradually or unexpectedly — see ARISE 2

emergency *n* a time or state of affairs requiring prompt or decisive action ⟨an alert, quick-thinking girl who is good to have around in an *emergency*⟩
syn clutch, crisis, crossroad(s), crunch, exigency, head, juncture, zero hour
rel contingency, possibility; climax, landmark, milestone, turning point; condition, pass, situation, strait; deadlock, impasse, stalemate; corner, fix, hole, hot water, jam, pinch, predicament, scrape, spot

emigrant *n* one that leaves one place to settle in another ⟨a city teeming with *emigrants* from many lands⟩
syn émigré (*also* emigré), immigrant, migrant, settler
rel defector, deportee, evacuee, exile, expatriate, refugee; alien, foreigner, noncitizen, nonnative; colonist, newcomer, squatter
near ant aborigine, native; citizen, inhabitant, national, resident
ant nonimmigrant

émigré *also* **emigré** *n* 1 a person forced to emigrate for political reasons ⟨the revolution resulted in a flood of *émigrés* into neighboring countries⟩
syn deportee, evacuee, exile, expatriate, refugee
rel alien, fugitive; castoff, outcast, pariah; loyalist, patriot
2 one that leaves one place to settle in another — see EMIGRANT

eminence *n* 1 the fact or state of being above others in rank or importance ⟨the *eminence* of the Nobel Prize in the field of awards and prizes⟩
syn distinction, dominance, noteworthiness, preeminence, superiority
rel celebrity, fame, famousness, glory, honor, renown, reputation, repute; authority, greatness, influence, power, weight
near ant insignificance, unimportance; inferiority, mediocrity; obscurity
2 an area of high ground — see HEIGHT 4

eminent *adj* standing above others in rank, importance, or achievement ⟨many *eminent* surgeons are on the hospital's staff⟩
syn distinguished, illustrious, noble, notable, noteworthy, outstanding, preeminent, prestigious, signal, star, superior
rel celebrated, famed, famous, glorious, honored, renowned, reputable; infamous, notorious; dominant, paramount, predominant
near ant insignificant, minor, unimportant; average, inferior, mediocre; obscure, uncelebrated, unsung

emissary *n* a person sent on a mission to represent another — see AMBASSADOR

emit *vb* 1 to throw or give off ⟨the cabin's chimney *emitted* smoke⟩
syn cast (off), discharge, exhale, expel, issue, release, shoot, vent
rel eliminate, evacuate, excrete, exude, ooze, secrete; gush, pour, spew
near ant absorb, inhale
2 to send forth using the vocal chords — see UTTER 1

emolument *n* the money paid regularly to a person for labor or services — see WAGE

emotion *n* 1 a subjective response to a person, thing, or situation — see FEELING 1
2 depth of feeling — see ARDOR 1

emotional *adj* 1 having or expressing great depth of feeling — see FERVENT
2 having the power to affect the feelings or sympathies — see MOVING
3 showing feeling freely — see DEMONSTRATIVE

emphasis *n* 1 a special notice or importance given to something ⟨a prep school with a long-established *emphasis* on sports⟩
syn accent, accentuation, stress, weight
rel attention, concentration, consideration, heed, note, regard; value, worth; consequence, import, moment, significance; precedence, primacy, priority
near ant apathy, disregard, indifference
2 the quality or state of being forceful (as in expression) — see VEHEMENCE 1

emphasize *vb* to indicate the importance of by giving prominent display ⟨supermarket tabloids that *emphasize* sensational news stories⟩
syn accent, accentuate, feature, highlight, play (up), point (up), stress, underline, underscore
rel focus, identify, pinpoint, spotlight; advertise, boost, plug, promote, publicize
near ant tone (down), understate; belittle, discount, disparage, minimize
ant play (down)

emphatic *adj* 1 marked by or uttered with forcefulness ⟨the governor issued an *emphatic* denial of all charges⟩
syn aggressive, assertive, dynamic, energetic, forceful, resounding, strenuous, vehement, vigorous
rel decided, insistent, marked, pointed; arresting, compelling, conspicuous, noticeable, striking; absolute, categorical (*also* categoric); clear, plain, unambiguous, unequivocal
near ant guarded, mild, weak, wishy-washy; ambiguous, equivocal; understated
ant unemphatic
2 likely to attract attention — see NOTICEABLE

empire *n* a group of businesses or enterprises under one control — see CONGLOMERATE

empirical *adj* based on observation or experience ⟨guidelines for raising children that are based on *empirical* evidence⟩

syn experimental, objective, observational

rel actual, factual, genuine, hard, real; accepted, established, tried, tried-and-true; indisputable, undeniable; demonstrable, provable, verifiable

near ant conjectural, hypothetical, speculative; unproven, unsubstantiated, unverified

ant nonempirical, theoretical (*also* theoretic)

employ *n* the state of being provided with a paying job — see HIRE 1

employ *vb* **1** to provide with a paying job ⟨a new factory that will *employ* 500 people⟩

syn engage, hire, retain, take on

rel recruit, sign on; keep

near ant furlough, lay off

ant can, discharge, dismiss, fire, sack

2 to put into action or service — see USE 1

employable *adj* capable of or suitable for being used for a particular purpose — see USABLE 1

employed *adj* involved in often constant activity — see BUSY 1

employee *n* one who works for another for wages or a salary ⟨an employer who was loved and admired by generations of *employees*⟩

syn hand, hireling, jobholder, worker

rel assistant, cog, flunky (*also* flunkey), subordinate, underling, yes-man; drudge, grub, laborer, navvy [*chiefly British*], toiler, workingman, workman; associate, colleague, coworker

near ant boss, superior, supervisor

ant employer

employment *n* **1** the act or practice of employing something for a particular purpose — see USE 1

2 the activity by which one regularly makes a living — see OCCUPATION

3 the state of being provided with a paying job — see HIRE 1

emporium *n* an establishment where goods are sold to consumers — see SHOP 1

empower *vb* to give official or legal power to — see AUTHORIZE 1

emptiness *n* **1** a need or desire for food — see HUNGER 1

2 empty space — see VACANCY 1

3 the quality or state of being empty — see VACANCY 2

empty *adj* **1** lacking contents that could or should be present ⟨the refrigerator is *empty*, so we'll have to eat out⟩

syn bare, blank, devoid, stark, vacant, void

rel barren, hollow; available, clear, free, open; unfilled, unfurnished; unattended, uninhabited, unoccupied; abandoned, deserted, emptied, forsaken, vacated; depleted, drained, dry, exhausted

---

near ant complete; replete; furnished, provided, supplied; filled, occupied; flush, overflowing, packed, teeming

ant full

2 feeling a desire or need for food — see HUNGRY 1

3 having no meaning — see MEANINGLESS

4 having no usefulness — see WORTHLESS

5 producing no results — see FUTILE

empty *vb* to remove the contents of ⟨*empty* the room before starting to paint the ceiling⟩

syn clear, evacuate, vacate, void

rel deplete, drain, eliminate, exhaust; bleed, draw (off); clean, flush, purge, scour, sweep

ant fill, load

empyreal *adj* of, relating to, or suggesting heaven — see CELESTIAL

empyrean *adj* of, relating to, or suggesting heaven — see CELESTIAL

emulate *vb* to use (someone or something) as the model for one's speech, mannerisms, or behavior — see IMITATE 1

emulative *adj* using or marked by the use of something else as a basis or model — see IMITATIVE

enable *vb* **1** to make able or possible ⟨my new glasses *enable* me to read⟩

syn allow, let, permit

rel fit, prepare, qualify, ready; approve, endorse (*also* indorse), sanction; condition, equip

near ant inhibit, preclude; disallow, enjoin, forbid, prohibit

ant prevent

2 to give official or legal power to — see AUTHORIZE 1

enact *vb* to put into effect through legislative or authoritative action ⟨Congress *enacts* all laws relating to foreign trade and immigration⟩

syn lay down, legislate, make, pass

rel bring about, effect; allow, authorize, permit, sanction; decree, dictate, proclaim; administer, execute; approve, confirm, ratify

near ant abolish, abrogate, annul, cancel, invalidate, nullify; overturn, reverse

ant repeal, rescind, revoke

enactment *n* **1** a rule of conduct or action laid down by a governing authority and especially a legislator — see LAW 1

2 the doing of an action — see COMMISSION 2

enamored (of) *adj* filled with an intense or excessive love for ⟨many teenage girls became *enamored of* the movie idol for his boyish good looks⟩

syn crazy (about *or* over), enraptured (by), infatuated (with), mad (about), nuts (about)

rel hung up, obsessed; foolish, silly, wild; bewitched, captivated, charmed, enchanted, entranced, fascinated

phrases sweet on

near ant cool, detached, unimpressed; disenchanted, disillusioned

---

syn synonym(s)	*rel* related words	
ant antonym(s)	*near ant* near antonym(s)	

encamp vb **1** to live in a camp or the outdoors — see CAMP

2 to provide with living quarters or shelter — see HOUSE 1

encampment n a place where a group of people live for a short time in tents or cabins — see CAMP

encapsulate vb to make into a short statement of the main points (as of a report) — see SUMMARIZE

encapsulation n a short statement of the main points — see SUMMARY

encase vb to close or shut in by or as if by barriers — see ENCLOSE 1

enchain vb to confine or restrain with or as if with chains — see BIND 1

enchant vb **1** to attract or delight as if by magic — see CHARM 1

2 to cast a spell on — see BEWITCH 1

3 to hold the attention of as if by a spell — see ENTHRALL 1

enchanted adj being or appearing to be under a magic spell ⟨an *enchanted* isle of the South Pacific⟩

  syn bewitched, charmed, entranced, magic, magical, spellbound

  rel dreamy, fairy, fairylike; fantastic, miraculous, utopian, wondrous; hypnotized, mesmerized; captivated, fascinated

enchanter n a person skilled in using supernatural forces — see MAGICIAN 1

enchanting adj having an often mysterious or magical power to attract — see FASCINATING 1

enchantment n **1** a spoken word or set of words believed to have magic power — see SPELL 1

2 the power of irresistible attraction — see CHARM 1

3 the power to control natural forces through supernatural means — see MAGIC 1

enchantress n **1** a woman believed to have often harmful supernatural powers — see WITCH 1

2 a woman whom men find irresistibly attractive — see SIREN

encircle vb **1** to pass completely around ⟨communication satellites *encircling* the earth⟩

  syn circle, circumnavigate, compass, girdle, girth, loop, orbit, ring, round

  rel cross, perambulate, traverse

2 to form a circle around — see SURROUND

enclose also **inclose** vb **1** to close or shut in by or as if by barriers ⟨dogs who spend the day *enclosed* in small cages⟩

  syn cage, closet, coop (up), corral, encase, envelop, fence (in), hedge, hem, house, immure, pen, wall (in)

  rel bound, circumscribe, confine, contain, limit, restrict; encircle, encompass, ring, surround

2 to form a circle around — see SURROUND

3 to surround or cover closely — see ENFOLD 1

enclosure also **inclosure** n an open space wholly or partly enclosed (as by buildings or walls) — see COURT 2

encomium n a formal expression of praise ⟨the *encomiums* bestowed on a teacher at her retirement ceremonies⟩

  syn accolade, citation, commendation, eulogy, homage, paean, panegyric, salutation, tribute

  rel award, decoration, honor, prize; acclaim, acclamation, approval, compliment, recommendation; applause, plaudits; bravo, hallelujah

  near ant censure, condemnation, denunciation, indictment, rebuke, reprimand, reproof; admonition, correction, lecture, sermon

encompass vb **1** to form a circle around — see SURROUND

2 to have as part of a whole — see INCLUDE

3 to surround or cover closely — see ENFOLD 1

encounter n a brief clash between enemies or rivals ⟨survived an *encounter* with the school bully at the local park⟩

  syn brush, hassle, run-in, scrape, skirmish

  rel argument, fight, quarrel, row, spat, squabble, tiff; battle, brawl, fray, wrangle

encounter vb **1** to come upon face-to-face or as if face-to-face — see MEET 1

2 to come upon unexpectedly or by chance — see HAPPEN (ON OR UPON)

3 to enter into contest or conflict with — see ENGAGE 2

encourage vb **1** to fill with courage or strength of purpose ⟨a pep talk that *encouraged* the team to get out there and win⟩

  syn buoy (up), cheer (up), comfort, embolden, hearten, inspire, steel

  rel animate, enliven, invigorate; fortify, reinforce, strengthen; assure, reassure; boost, energize, excite, galvanize, provoke, quicken, rally, stimulate, stir

  near ant demoralize, depress, sadden; debilitate, enfeeble, undermine, weaken

  ant daunt, discourage, dishearten, dispirit

2 to help the growth or development of — see FOSTER 1

3 to rouse to strong feeling or action — see PROVOKE 1

4 to try to persuade (someone) through earnest appeals to follow a course of action — see URGE

encouragement n something that arouses action or activity — see IMPULSE

encouraging adj **1** having qualities which inspire hope — see HOPEFUL 1

2 making one feel good inside — see HEARTWARMING

3 pointing toward a happy outcome — see FAVORABLE 2

encroach vb to advance gradually beyond the usual or desirable limits ⟨each year the sea continues to *encroach* upon the island's beaches⟩

  syn creep, inch, worm

rel snake, sneak; entrench (*also* intrench), impinge, infringe, intrude, invade; overpass, overreach, overrun, overshoot, overstep

encrust *also* **incrust** *vb* to cover with a hardened layer ⟨refrigerator shelves that were *encrusted* with the residue of many spills⟩

syn cake, rime

rel besmear, coat, smear, spread; cover, daub; coagulate, congeal, harden

encumber *vb* **1** to create difficulty for the work or activity of — see HAMPER

2 to place a weight or burden on — see LOAD 1

encumbrance *n* something that makes movement or progress more difficult ⟨without the *encumbrance* of a heavy backpack, I could sprint along the trail⟩

syn bar, block, chain, clog, crimp, deterrent, drag, embarrassment, fetter, handicap, hindrance, hurdle, impediment, inhibition, interference, let, manacle, obstacle, obstruction, shackles, stop, stumbling block, trammel

rel catch, hitch, rub, snag; hobble; arrest, check, constraint, curb, rein, restraint, stop; delay, holdup; burden, load; danger, hazard, peril; adversity, difficulty, disadvantage, hardship

near ant catalyst, goad, impetus, incentive, spur, stimulant, stimulus; advantage, edge; break

ant aid, assistance, benefit, help

encyclopedic *also* **encyclopaedic** *adj* covering everything or all important points ⟨a tour guide with an *encyclopedic* knowledge of New York City and its people⟩

syn compendious, complete, comprehensive, full, global, inclusive, in-depth, omnibus, panoramic, universal

rel broad, catholic, extensive, far-reaching, general, overall, sweeping, vast, wide; blanket, indiscriminate, unrestricted

near ant circumscribed, limited, narrow, restricted, specialized; exact, precise; individual, singular, specific

end *n* **1** the stopping of a process or activity ⟨the *end* of hostilities brought general rejoicing⟩

syn cessation, close, closure, conclusion, discontinuance, ending, expiration, finish, halt, lapse, shutdown, shutoff, stop, stoppage, surcease, termination

rel abeyance, interruption, moratorium, suspension

near ant extension, persistence, prolongation

ant continuation

2 a real or imaginary point beyond which a person or thing cannot go — see LIMIT

3 an unused or unwanted piece or item typically of small size or value — see ¹SCRAP 1

4 something that one hopes or intends to accomplish — see GOAL

5 the last and usually sharp or tapering part of something long and narrow — see POINT 2

6 the last part of a process or action — see FINALE

7 the line or relatively narrow space that marks the outer limit of something — see BORDER 1

8 the permanent stopping of all the vital bodily activities — see DEATH 1

end *vb* **1** to bring (an event) to a natural or appropriate stopping point — see CLOSE 3

2 to bring (as an action or operation) to an immediate end — see STOP 1

3 to come to an end — see CEASE 1

endanger *vb* to place in danger ⟨a reckless use of fireworks that *endangered* the lives of many people⟩

syn adventure, compromise, gamble (with), hazard, imperil, jeopardize, menace, risk, venture

rel intimidate, threaten; expose; subject; chance, wager

near ant guard, protect, shelter, shield; preserve, resume, save

endangered *adj* being in a situation where one is likely to meet with harm — see LIABLE 1

endangerment *n* the state of not being protected from injury, harm, or evil — see DANGER 1

endearing *adj* **1** having qualities that tend to make one loved — see LOVABLE

2 likely to win one's affection — see INGRATIATING

endeavor *n* an effort to do or accomplish something — see ATTEMPT

endeavor *vb* **1** to devote serious and sustained effort — see LABOR

2 to make an effort to do — see ATTEMPT

ended *adj* brought or having come to an end — see COMPLETE 2

endemic *adj* belonging to a particular place by birth or origin — see NATIVE 1

ending *n* **1** the last part of a process or action — see FINALE

2 the stopping of a process or activity — see END 1

endless *adj* **1** being or seeming to be without limits — see INFINITE

2 lasting forever — see EVERLASTING

endorse *also* **indorse** *vb* to promote the interests or cause of — see SUPPORT 1

endow *vb* **1** to furnish with something freely or naturally ⟨a young performer *endowed* with a great singing voice⟩

syn endue, invest

rel equip, provide, supply; bestow, confer; accord, award, grant; empower, enable, enhance, enrich, heighten; bless, favor, grace; bequeath, will

near ant dispossess, divest, strip; deplete, drain, exhaust; skimp, stint

2 to furnish (as an institution) with a regular source of income ⟨a wealthy businessman who *endowed* several museums⟩

syn finance, fund, subsidize

---

syn synonym(s)   *rel* related words
ant antonym(s)   *near ant* near antonym(s)

rel establish, found, organize; bequeath, contribute, donate, subscribe, support; award, grant; back, promote, sponsor
near ant draw, receive; subsist

3 to provide money for — see FINANCE 1

endowment *n* a special and usually inborn ability — see TALENT

endue *vb* to furnish with something freely or naturally — see ENDOW 1

endurable *adj* capable of being endured — see BEARABLE

endurance *n* **1** continuing existence — see PERSISTENCE 1

2 uninterrupted or lasting existence — see CONTINUATION

endure *vb* **1** to come to a knowledge of (something) by living through it — see EXPERIENCE

2 to put up with (something painful or difficult) — see BEAR 2

3 to remain indefinitely in existence or in the same state — see CONTINUE 1

enemy *n* one that is hostile toward another ⟨a beloved minister with no known *enemies*⟩
syn adversary, antagonist, foe, opponent
rel archenemy; (the) opposition; nemesis; bane, bête noire; assailant, attacker, combatant, invader; competitor, emulator, rival
near ant ally, collaborator, colleague, confederate, friendly, partner; adherent, disciple, follower; backer, benefactor, supporter
ant friend

energetic *adj* **1** having active strength of body or mind — see VIGOROUS 1

2 having much high-spirited energy and movement — see LIVELY 1

3 marked by or uttered with forcefulness — see EMPHATIC 1

energetically *adv* in a vigorous and forceful manner — see HARD 3

energize *vb* to give life, vigor, or spirit to — see ANIMATE

energized *adj* made or become fresh in spirits or vigor — see NEW 4

energy *n* **1** active strength of body or mind — see VIGOR 1

2 something with a usable capacity for doing work — see FUEL

3 the ability to exert effort for the accomplishment of a task — see POWER 2

enervate *vb* to diminish the physical strength of — see WEAKEN 1

enervated *adj* **1** lacking bodily energy or motivation — see LISTLESS

2 lacking bodily strength — see WEAK 1

enfeeble *vb* to diminish the physical strength of — see WEAKEN 1

enfeebled *adj* lacking bodily strength — see WEAK 1

enfeeblement *n* **1** a gradual sinking and wasting away of mind or body — see DECLINE 1

2 the quality or state of lacking physical strength or vigor — see WEAKNESS 1

enfold *vb* **1** to surround or cover closely ⟨darkness began to *enfold* the lonely house on the hill⟩

syn embosom, embower, embrace, enclose (*also* inclose), encompass, enshroud, envelop, enwrap, invest, lap, mantle, shroud, swathe, veil, wrap
rel curtain, drape; encase; swaddle; blanket, overlay, overspread; camouflage, cloak, disguise, mask; circle, encircle, encompass
near ant bare, denude, expose, strip

2 to put one's arms around and press tightly — see EMBRACE 1

enforce *vb* to carry out effectively ⟨the duty of the police is to *enforce* the law⟩
syn administer, apply, execute, implement
rel effect, effectuate; discharge, fulfill (*or* fulfil), render; cite, invoke; enact, legislate; honor, observe; prosecute; promulgate
near ant disregard, ignore, neglect

enfranchise *vb* to set free (as from slavery or confinement) — see FREE 1

enfranchisement *n* **1** the act of setting free from slavery — see LIBERATION

2 the right to formally express one's position or will in an election — see VOTE 1

engage *vb* **1** to hold the attention of ⟨the challenging jigsaw puzzle *engaged* us all evening⟩
syn absorb, busy, engross, enthrall (*or* enthral), fascinate, grip, immerse, interest, intrigue, involve, occupy
rel allure, attract, bewitch, captivate, charm, enchant; hypnotize, mesmerize; monopolize, preoccupy
near ant bore, jade, pall, tire, weary

2 to enter into contest or conflict with ⟨the daring young captain was eager to *engage* the enemy⟩
syn battle, encounter, face, meet, take on
rel emulate, rival; contend, fight, oppose
near ant elude, escape, evade; retreat

3 to obligate by prior agreement — see PLEDGE 1

4 to provide with a paying job — see EMPLOY 1

5 to take or get the temporary use of (something) for a set sum — see HIRE 1

engaged *adj* **1** involved in often constant activity — see BUSY 1

2 pledged in marriage ⟨the *engaged* couple make a charming pair⟩
syn affianced, betrothed
rel committed
ant unengaged

engagement *n* **1** the act or state of being engaged to be married ⟨the fun couple recently announced their *engagement*⟩
syn betrothal, espousal, troth
ant disengagement

2 an agreement to be present at a specified time and place ⟨a lifelong practice of marking all of my *engagements* on a weekly calendar⟩
syn appointment, date, rendezvous, tryst
rel arrangement; invitation; interview; get-together, meeting; call, visit; schedule

3 the state of being provided with a paying job — see HIRE 1

engaging *adj* **1** having an often mysterious or magical power to attract — see FASCINATING 1

2 holding the attention or provoking interest — see INTERESTING

engender *vb* to be the cause of (a situation, action, or state of mind) — see EFFECT

engine *n* a device that changes energy into mechanical motion ⟨a car with a 200-horsepower *engine*⟩
syn machine, motor
rel converter, transformer; appliance, mechanism; equipment; mill

engineer *vb* to plan out usually with subtle skill or care ⟨the mayor *engineered* an agreement to have a major league team play in our city⟩
syn contrive, finagle, finesse, frame, machinate, maneuver, manipulate, mastermind, negotiate, wangle
rel intrigue, plot, scheme; connive; concoct, cook (up), hatch; captain, command, conduct, direct, handle, manage, quarterback, run; gerrymander
near ant blow, bobble, botch, bungle, butcher, flub, fumble, gum (up), louse up, mangle, mess (up), mishandle, muff

engrave *vb* **1** to cut (as letters or designs) on a hard surface ⟨*engraved* the birth and death dates on the tombstone⟩
syn etch, grave, incise, inscribe
rel carve, chisel, sculpt, sculpture; chase; score

2 to produce a vivid impression of ⟨a scar that forever *engraved* the killer's face in the witness's mind⟩
syn etch, impress, imprint, ingrain
rel imbue, implant, inculcate, infuse, instill

engross *vb* to hold the attention of — see ENGAGE 1

engrossed *adj* having the mind fixed on something — see ATTENTIVE

engrossing *adj* holding the attention or provoking interest — see INTERESTING

engrossment *n* a focusing of the mind on something — see ATTENTION 1

engulf *vb* to cover or become filled with a flood — see FLOOD

enhance *vb* **1** to make better — see IMPROVE

2 to make markedly greater in measure or degree — see INTENSIFY

enhancement *n* an instance of notable progress in the development of knowledge, technology, or skill — see ADVANCE 2

enigma *n* something hard to understand or explain — see MYSTERY

enigmatic *also* **enigmatical** *adj* **1** being beyond one's powers to know, understand, or explain — see MYSTERIOUS 1

2 having an often intentionally veiled or uncertain meaning — see OBSCURE 1

enjoin *vb* **1** to ask for (something) earnestly or with authority — see DEMAND 1

2 to issue orders to (someone) by right of authority — see COMMAND 1

3 to order not to do or use or to be done or used — see FORBID

enjoining *n* the act of ordering that something not be done or used — see PROHIBITION 1

enjoy *vb* **1** to take pleasure in ⟨TV and videos are OK, but we still *enjoy* seeing movies on the big screen⟩
syn adore, delight (in), dig, fancy, groove (on), like, love, relish, revel (in)
rel admire, appreciate, cherish, revere, venerate, worship; prize, treasure, value; devour, drink (in), savor; dote (on), idolize; cotton (to), favor, prefer
phrases be partial to, get a kick (*or* charge) out of, go for, have a soft spot for, take to
near ant abhor, abominate, detest, dislike, hate, loathe; condemn, despise, scorn

2 to keep, control, or experience as one's own — see HAVE 1

enjoyable *adj* **1** giving pleasure or contentment to the mind or senses — see PLEASANT

2 providing amusement or enjoyment — see FUN

enjoyment *n* the feeling experienced when one's wishes are met — see PLEASURE 1

enlarge *vb* **1** to become greater in extent, volume, amount, or number — see INCREASE 2

2 to make greater in size, amount, or number — see INCREASE 1

enlarge (on) *vb* to express more fully and in greater detail — see EXPAND 1

enlighten *vb* **1** to give information to ⟨the lecturer at the planetarium *enlightened* us about the latest astronomical discoveries⟩
syn acquaint, advise, apprise, brief, clue, familiarize, fill in, inform, instruct, tell, wise (up)
rel clarify, clear (up), construe, elucidate, explain, explicate, expound, illuminate, illustrate, interpret, spell out; announce, disclose, report; disabuse, disenchant, disillusion
near ant misinform, mislead

2 to provide (someone) with moral or spiritual understanding ⟨many people around the world have been *enlightened* by the teachings of Gautama Buddha⟩
syn edify, educate, nurture
rel elevate, ennoble, lift, uplift; better, improve, transform; exalt, glorify, transfigure
near ant confuse, perplex, puzzle; becloud, cloud, darken, obscure

enlist (in) *vb* to become a member of — see ENTER 2

enliven *vb* to give life, vigor, or spirit to — see ANIMATE

enmesh *vb* to catch or hold as if in a net — see ENTANGLE 2

enmity *n* a deep-seated ill will ⟨*enmity* had existed between the two families for generations⟩

---

syn synonym(s)   *rel* related words
ant antonym(s)   *near ant* near antonym(s)

syn animosity, antagonism, antipathy, bitterness, gall, grudge, hostility, jaundice, rancor

rel hate, hatred, loathing; vindictiveness, virulence, vitriol; alienation, disaffection, estrangement; abhorrence, aversion, repugnance, repulsion; disgust, horror; conflict, coolness, friction, strain, tension; discord, unfriendliness; malice, malignancy, malignity, spite, spitefulness, venom

near ant amiability, amicability, civility, cordiality, friendliness, hospitality, neighborliness; comity, empathy, friendship, goodwill, sympathy, understanding

ant amity

ennoble *vb* to enhance the status of — see EXALT

ennui *n* the state of being bored — see BOREDOM

enormity *n* **1** the state or quality of being utterly evil ⟨the *enormity* of the crimes committed by the Nazis⟩

syn atrociousness, atrocity, badness, depravedness, depravity, evilness, heinousness, monstrousness, nefariousness, sinfulness, vileness, wickedness

rel accursedness, baseness, devilishness, execrableness, fiendishness, hellishness; corruption, decadence, degeneracy; immorality; infamy, notoriety

near ant morality; chasteness, innocence, purity

ant goodness, righteousness, virtuousness

2 the quality or state of being very large — see IMMENSITY

enormous *adj* unusually large — see HUGE

enormously *adv* to a large extent or degree — see GREATLY 2

enormousness *n* the quality or state of being very large — see IMMENSITY

enough *adv* **1** in or to a degree or quantity that meets one's requirements or satisfaction ⟨the elevator is big *enough* to hold everyone⟩

syn adequately, satisfactorily, sufficiently

rel acceptably, decently, fairly, moderately, passably, tolerably; abundantly, amply; commensurately, proportionately

ant inadequately, insufficiently, unsatisfactorily

2 to some degree or extent — see FAIRLY

enrage *vb* to make angry — see ANGER

enraged *adj* feeling or showing anger — see ANGRY

enrapture *vb* **1** to fill with great joy — see ELATE

2 to fill with overwhelming emotion (as wonder or delight) — see ENTRANCE

enraptured *adj* experiencing or marked by overwhelming usually pleasurable emotion — see ECSTATIC

enraptured (by) *adj* filled with an intense or excessive love for — see ENAMORED (OF)

enrich *vb* **1** to make better — see IMPROVE

2 to make more attractive by adding something that is beautiful or becoming — see DECORATE

enroll *also* **enrol** *vb* **1** to enter in a list or roll ⟨the school *enrolls* about 800 students⟩

syn inscribe, list, matriculate, register

rel catalog (*or* catalogue), itemize, tabulate, tally; file, index; book, log, post; program, schedule; check in

near ant cancel, delete, exclude, expel, expunge, reject; omit, overlook

2 to put (someone or something) on a list — see ¹LIST 2

enroll (in) *vb* to become a member of — see ENTER 2

enrollment *n* the number of individuals registered — see REGISTRATION

ensconce *vb* **1** to establish or place comfortably or snugly ⟨the kids had contentedly *ensconced* themselves on the couch before the TV⟩

syn install, lodge, perch, roost, settle

rel curl up; park, plant; anchor, bivouac, camp; burrow; locate, situate

2 to put into a hiding place — see ¹HIDE 1

enshrine *vb* to enhance the status of — see EXALT

enshroud *vb* **1** to keep secret or shut off from view — see ¹HIDE 2

2 to surround or cover closely — see ENFOLD 1

ensign *n* a piece of cloth with a special design that is used as an emblem or for signaling — see FLAG 1

enslavement *n* the state of being a slave — see SLAVERY 1

ensnare *vb* to catch or hold as if in a net — see ENTANGLE 2

ensuing *adj* **1** being the one that comes immediately after another — see NEXT

2 being, occurring, or carried out at a time after something else — see SUBSEQUENT

ensure *vb* to make sure, certain, or safe ⟨regulations that *ensure* the wholesomeness of our food⟩

syn assure, cinch, guarantee, guaranty, insure, secure

rel attest, certify, vouch, warrant, witness; pledge, promise, swear

near ant enfeeble, undermine, weaken

entail *vb* to have as part of a whole — see INCLUDE

entangle *vb* **1** to twist together into a usually confused mass ⟨in the process of taking down the Christmas tree, we managed to *entangle* the string of lights into a hopeless mess of wires⟩

syn interlace, intertwine, interweave, knot, snarl, tangle

rel weave, wind, wreathe; braid, plait

ant disentangle

2 to catch or hold as if in a net ⟨the young runaway gradually became *entangled* in a web of lies⟩

syn enmesh, ensnare, entrap, mesh, snare, tangle, trap

rel bag, capture, collar; embroil, implicate, involve, mire

near ant extricate, untangle; detach, disengage; clear, free, liberate

ant disentangle

entanglement *n* something that catches and holds — see WEB 1

enter *vb* **1** to go or come in or into ⟨the hikers *entered* the cave with considerable caution⟩

syn access, penetrate, pierce

rel barge (in), breeze (in), burst (in *or* into), waltz (in); drop (in), pop (in)

phrases set foot in, step in

ant depart, exit, leave

2 to become a member of ⟨patriotic young men and women *entering* the armed services⟩

syn enlist (in), enroll (in), join, sign on (for), sign up (for)

rel reenlist, reenroll, reenter

3 to put (someone or something) on a list — see ¹LIST 2

enter (into *or* upon) *vb* to take the first step in (a process or course of action) — see BEGIN 1

enterprise *n* **1** a commercial or industrial activity or organization ⟨the booming economy witnessed the launch of many small *enterprises*⟩

syn business, company, concern, establishment, firm, house, outfit

rel conglomerate, corporation, multinational; association, cartel, chain, combine, syndicate, trust; agency, dealer, outlet

2 readiness to engage in daring or difficult activity ⟨the *enterprise* shown by the early developers and promoters of personal computers⟩

syn aggressiveness, ambition, drive, go, hustle, initiative

rel gumption, pluck, snap, spirit, spunk, starch; assertiveness, self-reliance; energy, hardihood, pep, vigor, vitality

near ant inactivity, inertia, passivity; diffidence, faintheartedness, timidity; hesitation, reluctance; indolence, laziness, lethargy

3 a risky undertaking — see GAMBLE

enterprising *adj* **1** having or showing a bold forcefulness in the pursuit of a goal — see AGGRESSIVE 1

2 inclined or willing to take risks — see BOLD 1

entertain *vb* **1** to cause (someone) to pass the time agreeably occupied — see AMUSE

2 to give serious and careful thought to — see PONDER

3 to keep in one's mind or heart — see HARBOR 1

entertaining *adj* providing amusement or enjoyment — see FUN

entertainment *n* **1** the act or activity of providing pleasure or amusement especially for the public ⟨a variety show was staged as *entertainment* for the scouts at the jamboree⟩

syn amusement, distraction, diversion, recreation

---

syn synonym(s)   *rel* related words
ant antonym(s)   *near ant* near antonym(s)

rel show business; delectation, delight, enjoyment, joy, mirth; gratification, relaxation, relief, satisfaction; exhibition, performance, presentation, production, show, spectacle; escapism

2 someone or something that provides amusement or enjoyment — see FUN 1

enthrall *or* **enthral** *vb* **1** to hold the attention of as if by a spell ⟨*enthralled* by the flickering fire in the hearth, we lost all track of time⟩

syn arrest, enchant, fascinate, grip, hypnotize, mesmerize, spellbind

rel enrapture, entrance, thrill; beguile, bewitch, charm; absorb, engage, engross, involve

phrases cast a spell on

2 to fill with overwhelming emotion (as wonder or delight) — see ENTRANCE

3 to hold the attention of — see ENGAGE 1

enthralled *adj* having the mind fixed on something — see ATTENTIVE

enthralling *adj* holding the attention or provoking interest — see INTERESTING

enthrallment *n* a focusing of the mind on something — see ATTENTION 1

enthuse *vb* to make an exaggerated display of affection or enthusiasm — see GUSH 2

enthusiasm *n* **1** a practice or interest that is very popular for a short time — see FAD

2 urgent desire or interest — see EAGERNESS

enthusiast *n* a person with a strong and habitual liking for something — see FAN

enthusiastic *adj* showing urgent desire or interest — see EAGER

enthusiastically *adv* in an enthusiastic manner — see SKY-HIGH

entice *vb* to lead away from a usual or proper course by offering some pleasure or advantage — see LURE

enticement *n* **1** something that persuades one to perform an action for pleasure or gain — see LURE 1

2 the act or pressure of giving in to a desire especially when ill-advised — see TEMPTATION 1

entire *adj* **1** not divided or scattered among several areas of interest or concern — see WHOLE 1

2 not lacking any part or member that properly belongs to it — see COMPLETE 1

entirely *adv* to a full extent or degree — see FULLY 1

entitle *vb* **1** to give a right to ⟨the card *entitles* my grandmother to the discount for senior citizens⟩

syn authorize, qualify

rel empower, enable, license (*also* licence); approve, endorse (*also* indorse); allow, let, permit; certify, ratify, sanction, validate

ant disqualify

2 to give a name to — see NAME 1

entity *n* one that has a real and independent existence ⟨the question of whether

extrasensory perception will ever be a scientifically recognized *entity*⟩
syn being, individual, object, something, substance, thing
rel body; material, matter, stuff

entomb *vb* to place (a dead body) in the earth, a tomb, or the sea — see BURY 1

entombing *n* the act or ceremony of putting a dead body in its final resting place — see BURIAL

entombment *n* the act or ceremony of putting a dead body in its final resting place — see BURIAL

entrails *n pl* the internal organs of the body — see GUT 1

entrance *n* 1 the means or right of entering or participating in ⟨*entrance* to the club is by invitation only⟩
syn access, admission, admittance, doorway, entrée (*or* entree), entry, gateway
rel approval, certification, qualification
2 the opening through which one can enter or leave a structure — see DOOR 2

entrance *vb* to fill with overwhelming emotion (as wonder or delight) ⟨a production of *The Nutcracker* ballet that will *entrance* audiences⟩
syn carry away, enrapture, enthrall (*or* enthral), overjoy, ravish, transport
rel delight, gladden, gratify, please, satisfy; bewitch, captivate, charm, enchant, fascinate; elate, excite, exhilarate, stir

entranced *adj* 1 being or appearing to be under a magic spell — see ENCHANTED
2 experiencing or marked by overwhelming usually pleasurable emotion — see ECSTATIC

entrancing *adj* having an often mysterious or magical power to attract — see FASCINATING 1

entrap *vb* to catch or hold as if in a net — see ENTANGLE 2

entreat *vb* to make a request to (someone) in an earnest or urgent manner — see BEG

entreating *adj* asking humbly — see SUPPLIANT

entreaty *n* an earnest request — see PLEA 1

entrée *or* **entree** *n* the means or right of entering or participating in — see ENTRANCE 1

entrench *also* **intrench** *vb* to set solidly in or as if in surrounding matter ⟨a father who *entrenched* in our minds the belief that hard work pays off⟩
syn embed (*also* imbed), fix, implant, ingrain, lodge, root
rel imbue, infuse, instill; establish, place, put, settle, stick
near ant eliminate, eradicate; eject, expel; detach, disconnect, disengage, remove
ant dislodge, root (out), uproot

entrenched *also* **intrenched** *adj* firmly established over time — see INVETERATE 1

entrust *vb* 1 to give a task, duty, or responsibility to ⟨we *entrusted* our financial adviser with the investment of all of our savings⟩
syn assign, charge, commission, trust

rel confer, impose; commit, consign, delegate, relegate; allocate, allot; authorize, empower, invest
2 to put (something) into the possession or safekeeping of another — see GIVE 2

entry *n* 1 the entrance room of a building — see HALL 1
2 the means or right of entering or participating in — see ENTRANCE 1

entryway *n* the entrance room of a building — see HALL 1

entwine *vb* to follow a circular or spiral course — see WIND

enumerate *vb* 1 to specify one after another ⟨I proceeded to *enumerate* the reasons why my allowance needed raising⟩
syn detail, itemize, list, numerate, rehearse, tick (off)
rel outline; tabulate, tally; catalog (*or* catalogue), inventory; chart, diagram, graph; calculate, compute, estimate, figure, reckon; cite, mention, name
2 to find the sum of (a collection of things) by noting each one as it is being added — see COUNT 1
3 to make a list of — see ¹LIST 1

enunciate *vb* 1 to utter clearly and distinctly — see ARTICULATE 1
2 to make known openly or publicly — see ANNOUNCE

enunciation *n* the clear and accurate pronunciation of words especially in public speaking — see DICTION 1

envelop *vb* 1 to close or shut in by or as if by barriers — see ENCLOSE 1
2 to surround or cover closely — see ENFOLD 1

envenom *vb* to implant bitter feelings in — see EMBITTER

envenomed *adj* containing or contaminated with a substance capable of injuring or killing a living thing — see POISONOUS

envious *adj* having or showing mean resentment of another's possessions or advantages ⟨a family that is *envious* of their neighbors' big house⟩
syn covetous, invidious, jaundiced, jealous, resentful
rel begrudging, grudging; avaricious, grasping, greedy; distrustful, suspicious; malicious, petty, spiteful
phrases green with envy
near ant generous, kind, kindhearted; altruistic, benevolent, charitable; well-meaning

enviousness *n* a painful awareness of another's possessions or advantages and a desire to have them too — see ENVY

environment *n* the circumstances, conditions, or objects by which one is surrounded ⟨the joys of growing up in the *environment* that a small town offers⟩
syn atmosphere, climate, environs, medium, milieu, setting, surroundings
rel backdrop, background, context; element; situation, status; habitat

environs *n pl* 1 the area around a city ⟨the city and its *environs* total about a million in population⟩

syn exurbia, outskirts, purlieu, suburbia

rel backwater, backwoods, hinterland

2 the circumstances, conditions, or objects by which one is surrounded — see ENVIRONMENT

envisage *vb* to form a mental picture of — see IMAGINE 1

envoy *n* **1** a person sent on a mission to represent another — see AMBASSADOR

2 a person who acts or does business for another — see AGENT 2

envy *n* a painful awareness of another's possessions or advantages and a desire to have them too ⟨her *envy* of her neighbor's fancy clothes wrecked their friendship⟩

syn covetousness, enviousness, invidiousness, jealousy, resentment

rel animosity, enmity, hatred, ill will; malice, maliciousness, spitefulness

near ant benevolence, goodwill, kindness, sympathy

enwrap *vb* to surround or cover closely — see ENFOLD 1

ephemeral *adj* lasting only for a short time — see MOMENTARY

epicure *n* a person with refined tastes in food and wine ⟨Thomas Jefferson was one of America's first great *epicures*⟩

syn gourmand, gourmet

rel connoisseur, dilettante; savorer

near ant glutton, gorger, hog, trencherman

epigram *n* an often stated observation regarding something from common experience — see SAYING

epigrammatic *adj* marked by the use of few words to convey much information or meaning — see CONCISE

episode *n* something that happens — see EVENT 1

episodic *adj* appearing in parts or numbers that follow regularly — see SERIAL

epistle *n* a message on paper from one person or group to another — see LETTER

epithet *n* **1** a descriptive or familiar name given instead of or in addition to the one belonging to an individual — see NICKNAME

2 an act or expression showing scorn and usually intended to hurt another's feelings — see INSULT

epitome *n* **1** a short statement of the main points — see SUMMARY

2 a visible representation of something abstract (as a quality) — see EMBODIMENT

3 the most perfect type or example — see QUINTESSENCE 1

epitomize *vb* **1** to make into a short statement of the main points (as of a report) — see SUMMARIZE

2 to represent in visible form — see EMBODY 2

epoch *n* an extent of time associated with a particular person or thing — see AGE 1

---

equable *adj* marked by temperatures that are neither too high nor too low — see CLEMENT

equal *vb* **1** to produce something equal to (as in quality or value) ⟨no one has *equaled* Shakespeare's plays⟩

syn match, meet, tie

rel beat, excel, outdo, surpass, top; amount (to), approach, touch; measure (up), rival

2 to be the same in meaning or effect — see AMOUNT (TO) 2

3 to be the exact counterpart of — see MATCH 1

equal *adj* **1** marked by justice, honesty, and freedom from bias — see FAIR 2

2 resembling another in every respect — see SAME 1

equal *n* one that is equal to another in status, achievement, or value ⟨a basketball player who truly has no *equal* in his sport⟩

syn coordinate, counterpart, equivalent, fellow, like, match, parallel, peer, rival

rel analogue (*or* analog); double, mate, twin; associate, colleague, companion, partner; competitor

equality *n* the state or fact of being exactly the same in number, amount, status, or quality — see EQUIVALENCE 1

equalize *vb* to make equal in amount, degree, or status ⟨a plan to *equalize* educational opportunities for all the state's children, rich and poor alike⟩

syn balance, equate, even, level

rel accommodate, adjust, compensate, fit; homogenize, normalize, regularize, standardize; democratize

equanimity *n* evenness of emotions or temper ⟨an Olympic diver who always displays remarkable *equanimity* on the platform⟩

syn aplomb, calmness, composure, coolheadedness, coolness, imperturbability, placidity, self-possession, serenity, tranquillity (*or* tranquility)

rel assurance, confidence, poise, self-assurance, self-confidence; apathy, detachment, indifference, phlegm

near ant alarm, anxiety, apprehension, disquiet; excitability, nervousness; disturbance

ant agitation, discomposure, perturbation

equate *vb* **1** to regard or represent as equal or comparable ⟨a value system that *equates* money with success⟩

syn compare, liken

rel associate, connect, join, link, match; group, lump (together)

near ant differentiate, discriminate, distinguish

2 to describe as similar — see COMPARE 1

3 to make equal in amount, degree, or status — see EQUALIZE

equatorial *adj* being near the equator — see LOW 1

equilibrium *n* a condition in which opposing forces are equal to one another — see BALANCE 1

---

syn synonym(s)   *rel* related words
ant antonym(s)   *near ant* near antonym(s)

equine *n* a large hoofed domestic animal that is used for carrying or drawing loads and for riding — see HORSE

equip *vb* 1 to make competent (as by training, skill, or ability) for a particular office or function — see QUALIFY 2

2 to provide (someone) with what is needed for a task or activity — see FURNISH 1

equipage *n* a horse-drawn wheeled vehicle for carrying passengers — see CARRIAGE 1

equipment *n* items needed for the performance of a task or activity ⟨the *equipment* for the polar expedition included ships, instruments, sleds, dogs, and provisions⟩

syn accoutrements (*or* accouterments), apparatus, gear, material(s), matériel (*or* materiel), outfit, paraphernalia, tackle

rel accessories, attachments, fittings; baggage, belongings, impedimenta; appliances, facilities, instruments, machinery, tools; apparel, attire, habiliments, raiment, trappings; battery

equipoise *n* 1 a condition in which opposing forces are equal to one another — see BALANCE 1

2 a force or influence that makes an opposing force ineffective or less effective — see COUNTERBALANCE

equitable *adj* marked by justice, honesty, and freedom from bias — see FAIR 2

equity *n* the act or practice of giving to others what is their due — see JUSTICE 1

equivalence *n* the state or fact of being exactly the same in number, amount, status, or quality ⟨moviegoers who mistakenly believe that there is an *equivalence* between the personality of an actor and that of his character⟩

syn equality, equivalency, par, parity, sameness

rel compatibility, correlation, correspondence; likeness, similarity; exchangeability, interchangeability

near ant difference, discrepancy, disparity, divergence; incompatibility; dissimilarity, unlikeness

ant inequality

equivalency *n* the state or fact of being exactly the same in number, amount, status, or quality — see EQUIVALENCE

equivalent *n* one that is equal to another in status, achievement, or value — see EQUAL

equivocal *adj* 1 giving good reason for being doubted, questioned, or challenged — see DOUBTFUL 2

2 having an often intentionally veiled or uncertain meaning — see OBSCURE 1

equivocalness *n* the quality or state of having a veiled or uncertain meaning — see OBSCURITY 1

equivocate *vb* to avoid giving a definite answer or position ⟨the candidate *equivocated* as long as he could on controversial issues⟩

syn fudge, hedge, pussyfoot

rel dodge, duck, evade, sidestep, skirt; bypass, circumvent; cavil, quibble

phrases beat around (*or* about) the bush, dance around, hem and haw

equivocation *n* the quality or state of having a veiled or uncertain meaning — see OBSCURITY 1

era *n* an extent of time associated with a particular person or thing — see AGE 1

eradicate *vb* to destroy all traces of — see ANNIHILATE 1

ere *prep* earlier than — see BEFORE 1

erect *adj* rising straight up ⟨a lone tree remained *erect* after the terrible tornado had passed⟩

syn perpendicular, plumb, raised, standing, upright, upstanding, vertical

rel elevated, lifted, upended, upraised; freestanding

near ant prostrate, supine; hanging, sagging, slanted, slanting

ant flat, recumbent

erect *vb* 1 to fix in an upright position ⟨the tribes of the Pacific Northwest *erected* totem poles in front of their dwellings⟩

syn pitch, put up, raise, rear, set up, upend, upraise

rel brace, buttress, prop (up), shore (up), support; elevate, hoist, lift

near ant demolish, flatten, knock down, level, raze, tear down

2 to form by putting together parts or materials — see BUILD

erection *n* something put together by arranging or connecting an array of parts — see CONSTRUCTION 1

ergo *adv* for this or that reason — see THEREFORE

erode *vb* 1 to consume or wear away gradually — see EAT 2

2 to damage or diminish by continued friction — see ABRADE 1

erosion *n* a gradual weakening, loss, or destruction — see CORROSION

erotic *adj* of, relating to, or expressing sexual attraction ⟨the *erotic* aspects of the story of Beauty and the Beast⟩

syn amatory, amorous, sexy

rel carnal, sensual, sensuous; bawdy, lascivious, lewd, lustful, obscene, prurient, spicy

err *vb* to commit an offense — see OFFEND 1

errant *adj* 1 engaging in or marked by childish misbehavior — see NAUGHTY

2 traveling from place to place — see ITINERANT

erratic *adj* 1 lacking a definite plan, purpose, or pattern — see RANDOM

2 lacking in steadiness or regularity of occurrence — see FITFUL

3 not staying constant — see UNEVEN 2

erratically *adv* without definite aim, direction, rule, or method — see HIT OR MISS

erroneous *adj* not being in agreement with what is true — see FALSE 1

erroneously *adv* in a mistaken or inappropriate way — see WRONGLY

erroneousness *n* the quality or state of being false — see FALLACY 2

error *n* **1** an unintentional departure from truth or accuracy ⟨a report on the earthquake contained several unfortunate *errors*⟩
　syn blunder, fault, flub, fumble, goof, inaccuracy, lapse, miscue, misstep, mistake, oversight, slip, slipup, stumble
　rel boner, howler; foul-up, muff; misapprehension, miscalculation, misconception, misjudgment, misstatement, misunderstanding
　near ant accuracy, correctness, precision
2 a breaking of a moral or legal code — see OFFENSE 1
3 a false idea or belief — see FALLACY 1
erstwhile *adj* having been such at some previous time — see FORMER
erudite *adj* **1** having or displaying advanced knowledge or education — see EDUCATED
2 suggestive of the vocabulary used in books — see BOOKISH
erudition *n* the understanding and information gained from being educated — see EDUCATION 2
erupt *vb* **1** to throw out or off (something from within) often violently ⟨the volcano *erupted* clouds of poisonous gas and tons of hot ash⟩
　syn belch, disgorge, eject, expel, jet, spew, spout, spurt
　rel gush, pour, stream, surge; emanate, issue, spring; discharge, emit, fire; cast, fling, heave, hurl, launch, pitch, toss
　near ant bottle (up), contain, restrain, shut (in *or* up)
2 to develop suddenly and violently ⟨a fire *erupted*, and flames soon engulfed the room⟩
　syn break out, burst (forth), explode, flame, flare (up)
　rel burgeon, mushroom, snowball; blow up, detonate, touch off
eruption *n* **1** a sudden intense expression of strong feeling — see OUTBURST 1
2 the act or an instance of exploding — see EXPLOSION 1
escalate *vb* **1** to become greater in extent, volume, amount, or number — see INCREASE 2
2 to make greater in size, amount, or number — see INCREASE 1
escalated *adj* being at a higher level than average — see HIGH 2
escapade *n* a playful or mischievous act intended as a joke — see PRANK
escape *n* **1** the act or an instance of getting free from danger or confinement ⟨a daring prison *escape*⟩
　syn flight, getaway, lam, slip
　rel deliverance, liberation, redemption, release, rescue, salvation
　near ant imprisonment, incarceration; custody, detention, hold, holding, retention; danger, hazard, jeopardy, peril, risk
2 the act or a means of getting or keeping away from something undesirable ⟨the

reading of science fiction novels as an *escape* from boring reality⟩
　syn avoidance, cop-out, dodging, ducking, eluding, eschewing, evasion, out, shaking, shunning
　rel bypassing, circumvention; averting, deflection, prevention
　near ant abidance, endurance, submission, toleration
escape *vb* **1** to get free from a dangerous or confining situation ⟨everyone managed to *escape* from the burning building in time⟩
　syn abscond, clear out, flee, fly, get away, get out, lam, run away, run off
　rel avoid, elude, evade, lose, shun; decamp, depart, exit, leave; disentangle, extricate; emancipate, free, liberate, redeem, release
　phrases fly the coop, free oneself
　near ant abide, linger, remain, stay, tarry; come back, return
2 to get or keep away from (as a responsibility) through cleverness or trickery ⟨a judge who is very determined not to let criminals *escape* punishment⟩
　syn avoid, dodge, duck, elude, eschew, evade, shake, shirk, shun
　rel miss; avert, deflect, divert, obviate, parry, prevent, ward (off); debar, exclude, preclude; bypass, circumvent, skirt; foil, frustrate, outwit, thwart
　phrases get around, have nothing to do with, shy away from, steer clear of
　near ant accept, court, embrace, pursue, seek, welcome; catch, contract, incur
escarpment *n* a steep wall of rock, earth, or ice — see CLIFF
eschew *vb* to get or keep away from (as a responsibility) through cleverness or trickery — see ESCAPE 2
eschewing *n* the act or a means of getting or keeping away from something undesirable — see ESCAPE 2
escort *n* one that accompanies another for protection, guidance, or as a courtesy ⟨the mayor served as the First Lady's *escort* for her tour of the city⟩
　syn attendant, companion, guard, guide
　rel chaperone (*or* chaperon), squire; shadow, sidekick; conductor, leader, pilot
escort *vb* to go along with in order to provide assistance, protection, or companionship — see ACCOMPANY
esculent *adj* suitable for use as food — see EDIBLE
esoteric *adj* difficult for one of ordinary knowledge or intelligence to understand — see PROFOUND 1
especial *adj* of a particular or exact sort — see EXPRESS 1
especially *adv* to a great degree — see VERY 1
espionage *n* the secret gathering of information on others ⟨the acts of *espionage* on behalf of the Confederacy carried on by Belle Boyd and Rose Greenhow⟩
　syn spying
　rel dope, goods, lowdown; counterintelligence, intelligence; observation, recon-

---

syn synonym(s)　　*rel* related words
ant antonym(s)　　*near ant* near antonym(s)

naissance, surveillance; bugging, eavesdropping, wiretapping

espousal *n* **1** a ceremony in which two people are united in matrimony — see WEDDING

2 the act or state of being engaged to be married — see ENGAGEMENT 1

espouse *vb* **1** to give in marriage — see MARRY 2

2 to take as a spouse — see MARRY 3

esprit *n* active strength of body or mind — see VIGOR 1

espy *vb* to make note of (something) through the use of one's eyes — see SEE 1

essay *n* **1** a short piece of writing typically expressing a point of view ⟨school *essays* on what it means to be a patriot⟩

syn article, composition, paper, theme

rel column, commentary, editorial, feature, report, review, write-up; dissertation, thesis; tract, treatise; discourse, discussion, exposition, study

2 an effort to do or accomplish something — see ATTEMPT

essay *vb* to make an effort to do — see ATTEMPT

essence *n* the quality or qualities that make a thing what it is ⟨the belief that power ultimately rests with the people is the very *essence* of democracy⟩

syn essentiality, nature, quintessence, soul, stuff, substance

rel heart, spirit; center, core, keynote, marrow, pith, seat; embodiment, epitome, incarnation, manifestation, personification; aspect, attribute, feature, property; gist, kernel, nub

essential *adj* **1** impossible to do without ⟨a well-stocked public library is *essential* for the well-being of a community⟩

syn all-important, imperative, indispensable, integral, necessary, needed, needful, required, requisite, vital

rel prerequisite; compulsory, mandatory, obligatory; important, momentous, significant; basic, central, fundamental, key, organic; insistent, persistent, pressing, urgent

near ant undesired, unwanted; inconsequential, insignificant, unimportant; excess, extra, superfluous, surplus

ant dispensable, needless, nonessential, unnecessary, unneeded

2 of or relating to the simplest facts or theories of a subject — see ELEMENTARY

3 being a part of the innermost nature of a person or thing — see INHERENT

essential *n* **1** something necessary, indispensable, or unavoidable ⟨the *essentials* for success include a willingness to work and the right attitude⟩

syn condition, demand, must, necessity, need, requirement, requisite

rel precondition, prerequisite; advantage, edge, plus

near ant extra, extravagance, frill, luxury, superfluity

ant nonessential, nonnecessity

2 essentials *pl* general or basic truths on which other truths or theories can be based — see PRINCIPLES 1

essentiality *n* the quality or qualities that make a thing what it is — see ESSENCE

establish *vb* **1** to gain full recognition or acceptance of ⟨the teenagers accused of shoplifting were able to *establish* their innocence⟩

syn demonstrate, prove, show, substantiate

rel attest, authenticate, bear out, document, evidence, support, sustain, uphold; confirm, corroborate, justify, validate, verify

phrases prove beyond a reasonable doubt

near ant confute, discredit, invalidate, rebut, refute

ant disprove

2 to show the existence or truth of by evidence — see PROVE 1

3 to be responsible for the creation and early operation or use of — see FOUND

establisher *n* a person who establishes a whole new field of endeavor — see FATHER 2

establishment *n* **1** a building, room, or suite of rooms occupied by a service business — see PLACE 2

2 a commercial or industrial activity or organization — see ENTERPRISE 1

3 a public organization with a particular purpose or function — see INSTITUTION 1

4 a structure that is designed and built for a particular purpose — see FACILITY

estate *n* **1** a large impressive residence — see MANSION

2 a state of being or fitness — see CONDITION 1

3 one of the segments of society into which people are grouped — see CLASS 1

esteem *n* a feeling of great approval and liking — see ADMIRATION 1

esteem *vb* **1** to think of in a particular way — see CONSIDER 1

2 to think very highly or favorably of — see ADMIRE

esteemed *adj* having a good reputation especially in a field of knowledge — see RESPECTABLE 1

estimate *n* **1** the act of placing a value on the nature, character, or quality of something ⟨what we owe our war veterans is beyond *estimate*⟩

syn appraisal, appraisement, assessment, estimation, evaluation, reckoning, valuation

rel calculation, computation, measurement

2 an opinion on the nature, character, or quality of something — see ESTIMATION 1

estimate *vb* **1** to make an approximate or tentative judgment regarding ⟨experts *estimated* the value of the painting at a million dollars⟩

syn appraise, assess, evaluate, rate, set, value

rel adjudge, deem, judge; ascertain, determine, discover, learn; price, prize; decide, settle; analyze, assay, survey, test; reappraise, reassess, reevaluate, revalue

2 to decide the size, amount, number, or distance of (something) without actual measurement ⟨we *estimated* the snowfall to be about a foot⟩

syn calculate, call, conjecture, figure, gauge (*also* gage), guess, judge, make, place, put, reckon, suppose

near ant calibrate, measure, scale; compute

estimation *n* **1** an opinion on the nature, character, or quality of something ⟨the teacher's *estimation* of her student's scientific aptitude proved to be well-founded when he won a national science award⟩

syn appraisal, appraisement, assessment, estimate, evaluation, judgment (*or* judgement)

rel impression, notion, perception; confidence, faith, stock, trust

2 the act of placing a value on the nature, character, or quality of something — see ESTIMATE 1

3 a feeling of great approval and liking — see ADMIRATION 1

estrange *vb* to cause to change from friendly or loving to unfriendly or uncaring ⟨Carrie's tendency to tattle *estranged* her classmates⟩

syn alienate, disaffect, disgruntle, sour

rel antagonize, embitter, envenom; aggravate, anger, enrage, incense, infuriate, madden; disunite, divide, separate, sever, sunder; disappoint, disenchant, disillusion

near ant endear, ingratiate; appease, conciliate, mollify, pacify, propitiate

ant reconcile

estrangement *n* the loss of friendship or affection ⟨a silly quarrel that resulted in a complete and lasting *estrangement* between the onetime friends⟩

syn alienation, disaffection, disgruntlement, souring

rel antagonism, embitterment, envenoming; aggravation, incensing, infuriation; disunion, division, divorce, schism, separation; disenchantment, disillusionment

near ant endearment, ingratiation; appeasement, conciliation, mollification, pacification, propitiation

ant reconciliation

estuary *n* a part of a body of water that extends beyond the general shoreline — see GULF 1

etch *vb* **1** to cut (as letters or designs) on a hard surface — see ENGRAVE 1

2 to produce a vivid impression of — see ENGRAVE 2

eternal *adj* lasting forever — see EVERLASTING

eternally *adv* for all time — see EVER 1

eternity *n* **1** endless time ⟨the question whether the universe will end someday or continue to exist in *eternity*⟩

syn infinity, perpetuity

rel boundlessness, endlessness, interminableness, permanence, timelessness

2 unending existence after death ⟨a firm belief in the *eternity* of the soul⟩

syn afterlife, hereafter, immortality

rel otherworld

phrases life after death

3 a long or seemingly long period of time — see AGE 2

ethereal *adj* resembling air in lightness — see AIRY 1

ethical *adj* **1** conforming to a high standard of morality or virtue — see GOOD 2

2 following the accepted rules of moral conduct — see HONORABLE 1

3 guided by or in accordance with one's sense of right and wrong — see CONSCIENTIOUS 1

ethics *n pl* the code of good conduct for an individual or group ⟨the *ethics* of scouting require scouts to be loyal, clean, and reverent⟩

syn morality, morals, principles, standards

rel customs, etiquette, manners, mores; beliefs, dogma, faith, tenets

ethnic *adj* of, relating to, or reflecting the traits exhibited by a group of people with a common ancestry and culture — see RACIAL

etiquette *n* personal conduct or behavior as evaluated by an accepted standard of appropriateness for a social or professional setting — see MANNER 1

eulogy *n* a formal expression of praise — see ENCOMIUM

euphonious *adj* **1** having a pleasantly flowing quality suggestive of music — see LYRIC 1

2 having a pleasing mixture of notes — see HARMONIOUS 1

euphoria *n* a state of overwhelming usually pleasurable emotion — see ECSTASY

euphoric *adj* experiencing or marked by overwhelming usually pleasurable emotion — see ECSTATIC

evacuate *vb* to remove the contents of — see EMPTY

evacuee *n* a person forced to emigrate for political reasons — see ÉMIGRÉ 1

evade *vb* to get or keep away from (as a responsibility) through cleverness or trickery — see ESCAPE 2

evaluate *vb* to make an approximate or tentative judgment regarding — see ESTIMATE 1

evaluation *n* **1** an opinion on the nature, character, or quality of something — see ESTIMATION 1

2 the act of placing a value on the nature, character, or quality of something — see ESTIMATE 1

evanesce *vb* to cease to be visible — see DISAPPEAR

evanescent *adj* lasting only for a short time — see MOMENTARY

evaporate *vb* to cease to be visible — see DISAPPEAR

---

syn synonym(s)   *rel* related words
ant antonym(s)   *near ant* near antonym(s)

evasion n the act or a means of getting or keep-ing away from something undesir-able — see ESCAPE 2

evasive adj hard to find, capture, or iso-late — see ELUSIVE

even adj 1 being neither more nor less than a certain amount, number, or extent ⟨the distance to town is an *even* mile⟩
syn exact, flat, precise, round
near ant approximate, comparative, rela-tive
2 having a surface without bends, breaks, or irregularities — see LEVEL
3 resembling another in every respect — see SAME 1

even adv not merely this but also ⟨the blue whale is a huge, *even* awesome animal by any measure⟩
syn indeed, nay, truly, verily, yea
rel assuredly, certainly, decidedly, defi-nitely, positively, really, surely, undeni-ably, unquestionably
phrases in fact, in reality, in truth

even vb 1 to make free from breaks, curves, or bumps ⟨*even* the filling before adding the top layer of the cake⟩
syn flatten, level, plane, smooth
rel clip, crop, pare, prune, shave, trim; lay, spread; card, comb, rake
near ant coarsen, rumple, wrinkle
ant rough, roughen
2 to make equal in amount, degree, or status — see EQUALIZE

evening n the time from when the sun be-gins to set to the onset of total darkness — see DUSK 1

event n 1 something that happens ⟨dinner-time was devoted to talking over the day's *events*, not to watching television⟩
syn affair, circumstance, episode, hap, happening, incident, occasion, occur-rence, thing
rel coincidence, fluke, freak; landmark, milestone, page, phenomenon, turning point; adventure, experience; accident, crisis, emergency, juncture; achievement, deed, exploit, feat; news, tidings
2 something that might happen ⟨in the *event* of rain, graduation ceremonies will be held indoors⟩
syn case, contingency, eventuality, possi-bility
rel probability; chance, risk
3 a competitive encounter between indi-viduals or groups carried on for amuse-ment, exercise, or in pursuit of a prize — see GAME 1
4 a social gathering — see PARTY 1

eventful adj having great meaning or last-ing effect — see IMPORTANT 1

eventide n the time from when the sun be-gins to set to the onset of total darkness — see DUSK 1

eventuality n 1 something that can devel-op or become actual — see POTENTIAL
2 something that might happen — see EVENT 2

eventually adv at a later time — see YET 1

ever adv 1 for all time ⟨the name of Bene-dict Arnold will *ever* be linked with trea-son⟩
syn always, aye (*also* ay), eternally, ever-lastingly, evermore, forever, forevermore, permanently, perpetually
rel enduringly, long, perennially
phrases forever and a day, forever and ever, for good, to (*or* until) the end of time
ant never, nevermore
2 in any way or respect — see AT ALL
3 on every relevant occasion — see AL-WAYS 1

everlasting adj lasting forever ⟨valentines typically express the giver's *everlasting* love and devotion⟩
syn ceaseless, dateless, deathless, endless, eternal, immortal, permanent, perpetual, undying, unending
rel durable, enduring, lasting, persistent; imperishable, indestructible; timeless; abiding, steadfast, steady, unfailing, un-faltering
near ant ephemeral, evanescent, fleeting, momentary, passing, short-lived, transi-tory
ant impermanent, mortal, temporary

everlastingly adv for all time — see EVER 1

evermore adv for all time — see EVER 1

every adj being one of a group — see EACH

everybody pron every person ⟨*everybody* must do what his or her conscience dic-tates⟩
syn all, everyone
phrases each and everyone, one and all
ant nobody

everyday adj 1 being of the type that is en-countered in the normal course of events — see ORDINARY 1
2 having to do with the practical details of regular life — see MUNDANE 1
3 not designed for special occasions — see CASUAL 1
4 often observed or encountered — see COMMON 1

everyone pron every person — see EVERYBODY

everyplace adv in every place or in all places — see EVERYWHERE

everywhere adv in every place or in all places ⟨freedom and happiness are the goals of people *everywhere*⟩
syn all over, everyplace, throughout
phrases all over the place (*or* map), far and near, far and wide, high and low, in every corner (*or* quarter)
ant nowhere

evidence n something presented in sup-port of the truth or accuracy of a claim — see PROOF

evident adj 1 appearing to be true on the basis of evidence that may or may not be confirmed — see APPARENT 1
2 not subject to misinterpretation or more than one interpretation — see CLEAR 2

evidently *adv* to all outward appearances — see APPARENTLY

evil *adj* **1** causing or capable of causing harm — see HARMFUL

2 not conforming to a high moral standard; morally unacceptable — see BAD 2

evil *n* that which is morally unacceptable ⟨our free will allows us to choose between good and *evil*⟩

syn bad, evildoing, ill, immorality, iniquity, sin, villainy, wrong

rel atrociousness, badness, evilness, heinousness, nefariousness, sinfulness, vileness, wickedness; devilry (*or* deviltry), fiendishness; cancer, decay, rot, squalor; corruption, debauchery, degeneracy, depravity, indecency, perversion; abomination, anathema, taboo (*also* tabu)

near ant integrity, probity, rectitude, uprightness; goodness, righteousness, virtuousness

ant good, morality, right, virtue

evildoer *n* **1** a person who commits moral wrongs ⟨if good people stand by and do nothing, *evildoers* will triumph⟩

syn malefactor, sinner, wrongdoer

rel criminal, crook, felon, lawbreaker, miscreant, reprobate, transgressor, villain

near ant angel, saint

2 a mean, evil, or unprincipled person — see VILLAIN

evildoing *n* that which is morally unacceptable — see EVIL

evilness *n* the state or quality of being utterly evil — see ENORMITY 1

evince *vb* to make known (something abstract) through outward signs — see SHOW 2

eviscerate *vb* to take the internal organs out of — see GUT

evocative *adj* provoking a memory or mental association — see SUGGESTIVE 2

evoke *vb* to draw out (something hidden, latent, or reserved) — see EDUCE

evolution *n* the act or process of going from the simple or basic to the complex or advanced — see DEVELOPMENT 1

evolve *vb* to gradually become clearer or more detailed — see DEVELOP 1

evolved *adj* being far along in development — see ADVANCED 1

exact *adj* **1** being in agreement with the truth or a fact or a standard — see CORRECT 1

2 being neither more nor less than a certain amount, number, or extent — see EVEN 1

3 following an original exactly — see FAITHFUL 2

4 made or done with extreme care and accuracy — see FINE 2

5 meeting the highest standard of accuracy — see PRECISE 1

exact *vb* **1** to ask for (something) earnestly or with authority — see DEMAND 1

2 to establish or apply as a charge or penalty — see IMPOSE

3 to get (as money) by the use of force or threats — see EXTORT

exacting *adj* **1** hard to please — see FINICKY

2 not allowing for any exceptions or loosening of standards — see RIGID 1

3 requiring considerable physical or mental effort — see HARD 2

4 requiring much time, effort, or careful attention — see DEMANDING 1

exactitude *n* the quality or state of being very accurate — see PRECISION

exactly *adv* **1** as stated or indicated without the slightest difference ⟨we will meet at *exactly* six o'clock⟩

syn just, precisely, right, sharp, smack-dab, squarely

2 in a like manner — see JUST 1

3 in the same words — see VERBATIM

4 without any relaxation of standards or precision — see STRICTLY

exactness *n* the quality or state of being very accurate — see PRECISION

exaggerate *vb* **1** to add to the interest of by including made-up details — see EMBROIDER

2 to describe or express in too strong terms — see OVERSTATE

exaggeration *n* the representation of something in terms that go beyond the facts ⟨their *exaggeration* was such that a rainstorm became a hurricane⟩

syn caricature, coloring, elaboration, embellishment, embroidering, hyperbole, magnification, overstatement, padding, stretching

rel amplification, enhancement; fabrication, misrepresentation; fudging, hedging

near ant belittlement, disparagement, minimizing

ant understatement

exalt *vb* to enhance the status of ⟨popular support and media hype have *exalted* Super Bowl Sunday to the level of a national holiday⟩

syn aggrandize, dignify, ennoble, enshrine, glorify, magnify

rel boost, elevate, lift, promote, raise, upgrade, uplift; heighten, intensify; idealize, romanticize, sanitize, sugarcoat; canonize, deify; acclaim, extol, extoll (*also* extoll), honor, laud, praise

near ant belittle, decry, depreciate, detract, disparage, minimize

ant abase, degrade, demean, humble, humiliate

exam *n* a set of questions or problems designed to assess knowledge, skills, or intelligence — see EXAMINATION 1

examination *n* **1** a set of questions or problems designed to assess knowledge, skills, or intelligence ⟨applicants to the prep school are required to take an *examination*⟩

syn exam, quiz, test

rel catechism; audition; final; checkup, inspection, review; inquiry, interrogation, investigation, probe, research

2 a systematic search for the truth or facts about something — see INQUIRY 1

---

syn synonym(s)   *rel* related words
ant antonym(s)   *near ant* near antonym(s)

3 a close look at or over someone or something in order to judge condition — see INSPECTION

examine vb **1** to put a series of questions to ⟨the defense attorney was eager to *examine* her star witness⟩

syn grill, interrogate, pump, query, question, quiz

rel debrief; cross-examine; catechize; annoy, harass, hound, pester

phrases give the third degree to

2 to look over closely (as for judging quality or condition) — see INSPECT

example n one of a group or collection that shows what the whole is like ⟨a war bonnet that is a fine *example* of Native American handicraft⟩

syn case, exemplar, illustration, instance, representative, sample, specimen

rel cross section; evidence, indication, manifestation, sign

phrases case in point

exasperate vb to disturb the peace of mind of (someone) especially by repeated disagreeable acts — see IRRITATE 1

exasperating adj causing annoyance — see ANNOYING

exasperation n **1** something that is a source of irritation — see ANNOYANCE 3

2 the feeling of impatience or anger caused by another's repeated disagreeable acts — see ANNOYANCE 2

excavate vb to hollow out or form (something) by removing earth — see DIG 1

exceed vb to go beyond the limit of ⟨by resorting to corporal punishment, the teacher had *exceeded* his authority⟩

syn overreach, overrun, overshoot, overstep, surpass

rel encroach, entrench (*also* intrench), infringe, invade, trespass; overdo, overuse, overwork

exceedingly *also* **exceeding** adv to a great degree — see VERY 1

excel vb to be greater, better, or stronger than — see SURPASS 1

excellence n **1** exceptionally high quality ⟨the annual awards honor *excellence* in children's literature⟩

syn distinction, excellency, greatness, preeminence, superbness, superiority, supremacy

rel faultlessness, flawlessness, impeccability, perfection; goodness, value, worth; consequence, importance, notability

near ant averageness, badness, inferiority, mediocrity, ordinariness, worthlessness

2 a quality that gives something special worth ⟨the particular *excellence* of down in clothing and sleeping bags is its lightness⟩

syn distinction, excellency, merit, value, virtue

rel advantage, edge, superiority

near ant blemish, defect, failing, fault, flaw

ant deficiency

excellency n **1** a quality that gives something special worth — see EXCELLENCE 2

2 exceptionally high quality — see EXCELLENCE 1

excellent adj of the very best kind ⟨fast-food fans rate this chain's fries as *excellent*⟩

syn A1, bang-up, banner, boss [*slang*], capital, classic, crackerjack, dandy, divine, fabulous, fine, first-class, first-rate, grand, great, groovy, heavenly, jim-dandy, keen, marvelous (*or* marvellous), mean, neat, nifty, noble, par excellence, prime, sensational, splendid, stellar, sterling, superb, superior, superlative, supernal, swell, terrific, tip-top, top, top-notch, unsurpassed, wonderful

rel acceptable, adequate, all right, decent, good, OK, passable, satisfactory, tolerable; better, exceptional, fancy, high-grade, premium, special

phrases out of sight

near ant bad, inferior, low-grade, substandard, unsatisfactory; mediocre, second-class, second-rate; atrocious, execrable, vile, wretched

ant poor

except *also* **excepting** conj if it were not for the fact that ⟨I'd go, *except* it's too far⟩

syn but, only, saving, yet

except *also* **excepting** prep not including ⟨the store is open daily *except* Sundays⟩

syn aside from, bar, barring, beside, besides, but, except for, excluding, outside, outside of, save, saving

except vb to prevent the participation or inclusion of — see EXCLUDE

except for prep not including — see EXCEPT

exceptionable adj provoking or likely to provoke protest — see OBJECTIONABLE

exceptional adj being out of the ordinary ⟨an *exceptional* amount of snow fell in March⟩

syn aberrant, abnormal, atypical, extraordinary, freak, odd, peculiar, phenomenal, rare, singular, uncommon, uncustomary, unique, unusual, unwonted

rel conspicuous, notable, noticeable, outstanding, prominent, remarkable, salient, striking; bizarre, deviant, eccentric, outlandish, quaint, strange, weird; incomprehensible, inconceivable, incredible, unimaginable, unthinkable

near ant everyday, familiar, frequent

ant common, customary, normal, ordinary, typical, unexceptional, usual

excerpt n a part taken from a longer work ⟨we'll read an *excerpt* from the novel⟩

syn extract, passage

rel snippet; citation, quotation; context; selection

excess adj being over what is needed — see SPARE 1

excess n the state or an instance of going beyond what is usual, proper, or needed ⟨a new television season with an *excess* of wisecracking teenagers⟩

syn fat, overabundance, overage, overflow, overkill, overmuch, oversupply, superabundance, superfluity, surfeit, surplus

rel abundance, bounty, plentitude, plenty, profusion, sufficiency; overproduction, overstock

near ant dearth, lack, scarcity

ant deficiency, deficit, insufficiency

excessive *adj* going beyond a normal or acceptable limit in degree or amount ⟨nerdy hackers who spend an *excessive* amount of time sitting in front of their computers⟩

syn devilish, exorbitant, extravagant, extreme, immoderate, inordinate, lavish, overmuch, overweening, steep, stiff, towering, unconscionable, undue

rel boundless, endless, immeasurable, infinite, limitless; intolerable, unbearable, unjustifiable, unwarranted; improper, inappropriate, thick, unseemly

near ant deficient, inadequate, insufficient; minimal, minimum

ant moderate, modest, reasonable, temperate

excessively *adv* beyond a normal or acceptable limit — see TOO 1

exchange *n* 1 a giving or taking of one thing of value in return for another ⟨*exchanges* of commemorative pins are common among Olympic athletes⟩

syn barter, commutation, swap, trade, truck

rel replacement, substitution; reciprocation, recompense, requital; bargain, deal, horse trade, negotiation, transaction; bargaining, dealing, dickering, haggling, horse trading; logrolling

2 talking or a talk between two or more people — see CONVERSATION

exchange *vb* to give up (something) and take something else in return — see CHANGE 3

excitable *adj* easily excited by nature ⟨an *excitable* child who needed a stable home life⟩

syn flighty, fluttery, high-strung, jittery, jumpy, nervous, skittish, spooky

rel hot-blooded, mercurial, temperamental, unstable, volatile, volcanic; anxious, edgy, jumpy, nervy, tense, uptight; emotional, hypersensitive, intense, sensitive, soulful; dramatic, histrionic, melodramatic; irascible, irritable, prickly, testy, touchy

near ant calm, collected, cool, serene, tranquil; easy, easygoing, laid-back, relaxed

ant unflappable

excite *vb* 1 to cause a pleasurable stimulation of the feelings — see THRILL

2 to rouse to strong feeling or action — see PROVOKE 1

excited *adj* 1 being in a state of increased activity or agitation — see FEVERISH 1

2 showing urgent desire or interest — see EAGER

excitement *n* 1 something that arouses a strong response from another — see PROVOCATION 1

2 urgent desire or interest — see EAGERNESS

exciter *n* a person who stirs up public feelings especially of discontent — see AGITATOR

exciting *adj* 1 causing great emotional or mental stimulation ⟨an *exciting*, come-from-behind victory for the underdogs in the last game of the World Series⟩

syn breathtaking, electric, electrifying, exhilarating, galvanizing, inspiring, riproaring, rousing, stimulating, stirring, thrilling

rel arresting, interesting, intriguing, provocative, tantalizing; absorbing, engrossing, gripping, riveting; moving, poignant, touching; enchanting, enthralling, fascinating, spellbinding

near ant boring, tedious, tiresome; dreary, dull, humdrum, monotonous, uninteresting

ant unexciting

2 serving or likely to arouse a strong reaction — see PROVOCATIVE

exclaim *vb* to utter with a sudden burst of strong feeling ⟨the whole team *exclaimed* with one voice, "We won!"⟩

syn blurt (out), bolt, cry (out), ejaculate

rel blunder, leak; bellow, bleat, crow, holler, hoot, howl, roar, shout, whoop, yowl; interject

exclude *vb* to prevent the participation or inclusion of ⟨troublemakers were *excluded* from the club⟩

syn ban, bar, count out, debar, eliminate, except, rule out

rel blackball, blacklist, ostracize; banish, deport, exile, expel, oust, throw out; block, hinder, impede, obstruct; cease, discontinue, halt, suspend; deter, stave off, ward (off)

near ant accept, entertain, receive, welcome

ant admit, include

excluding *prep* not including — see EXCEPT

exclusive *adj* 1 belonging only to the one person, unit, or group named — see SOLE 1

2 not divided or scattered among several areas of interest or concern — see WHOLE 1

exclusively *adv* for nothing other than — see SOLELY 1

excoriate *vb* to criticize harshly and usually publicly — see ATTACK 2

excrement *n* solid matter discharged from an animal's alimentary canal — see DROPPING 1

excrescence *n* an abnormal mass of tissue — see GROWTH 1

excreta *n pl* solid matter discharged from an animal's alimentary canal — see DROPPING 1

excruciating *adj* 1 intensely or unbearably painful ⟨those who publicly disagreed with the government were subjected to *excruciating* torture⟩

syn agonizing, harrowing, racking, tormenting, torturing, torturous

rel acute, exquisite, extreme, fierce, intense, vehement, violent; piercing, sharp, shooting, stabbing, stinging, tearing, tingling

2 causing intense mental or physical distress — see SHARP 2

3 difficult to endure — see HARSH 1

4 hard to accept or bear especially emotionally — see BITTER 2

exculpate *vb* to free from a charge of wrongdoing ⟨I will present evidence that will *exculpate* my client⟩

syn absolve, acquit, clear, exonerate, vindicate

rel atone (for); expiate; discharge, liberate, redeem, release, unburden; condone, excuse, forgive, pardon, remit; avenge, redress, revenge

near ant accuse, arraign, charge, impeach, indict; convict

ant incriminate

excursion *n* **1** a short trip for pleasure ⟨our weekend *excursions* have been to all parts of our home state⟩

syn jaunt, junket, outing, sally

rel journey, travel(s); circuit, tour; expedition, odyssey, safari; detour; hike, peregrination, trek, walk; pilgrimage

2 a departure from the subject under consideration — see TANGENT

excursionist *n* a person who travels for pleasure — see TOURIST

excusable *adj* worthy of forgiveness — see VENIAL

excuse *n* an explanation that frees one from fault or blame ⟨a whole evening of must-see TV is no *excuse* for not having your homework done⟩

syn alibi, defense, justification, plea, reason

rel guise, pretense (*or* pretence), pretext, rationale, rationalization; cop-out, out; acknowledgment (*also* acknowledgement), apology, atonement, confession

excuse *vb* **1** to overlook or dismiss as of little importance ⟨the student's theme is so good that I'm willing to *excuse* the spelling errors⟩

syn brush (aside *or* off), condone, disregard, forgive, gloss (over), gloze (over), ignore, pardon, pass over, remit, shrug off, wink (at)

rel explain, justify, rationalize, whitewash; absolve, acquit, clear, exculpate, exonerate, vindicate

phrases forgive and forget

near ant heed, mark, mind, note, object (to)

2 to be an acceptable reason for — see JUSTIFY 1

3 to make (something) seem less bad by offering excuses — see PALLIATE 1

execrable *adj* **1** extremely unsatisfactory — see WRETCHED 1

2 of low quality — see CHEAP 2

execrate *vb* **1** to declare to be morally wrong or evil — see CONDEMN 1

2 to dislike strongly — see HATE

execration *n* **1** a prayer that harm will come to someone — see CURSE 1

2 a very strong dislike — see HATE 1

execute *vb* **1** to carry out effectively — see ENFORCE

2 to carry through (as a process) to completion — see PERFORM 1

3 to put to death deliberately — see MURDER 1

execution *n* the doing of an action — see COMMISSION 2

executive *adj* suited for or relating to the directing of things ⟨the *executive* skills needed to manage a large business office⟩

syn administrative, directorial, managerial, supervisory

rel bureaucratic, governmental, ministerial, official, parliamentary; regulatory; authoritarian, despotic, dictatorial

executive *n* a person who manages or directs ⟨a program that teaches company *executives* how to better manage their staffs⟩

syn administrator, director, manager, superintendent, supervisor

rel officer, official; commissioner, minister; boss, chief, head, leader, president

exemplar *n* **1** one of a group or collection that shows what the whole is like — see EXAMPLE

2 someone of such unequaled perfection as to deserve imitation — see IDEAL 1

3 the most perfect type or example — see QUINTESSENCE 1

exemplary *adj* constituting, serving as, or worthy of being a pattern to be imitated — see MODEL

exemplify *vb* to show or make clear by using examples — see ILLUSTRATE 1

exemption *n* freedom from punishment, harm, or loss — see IMPUNITY

exercise *n* **1** energetic movement of the body for the sake of physical fitness ⟨the doctor ordered plenty of fresh air and *exercise*⟩

syn activity, conditioning, exertion

rel training, warm-up, workout; toning, trimming; aerobics, bodybuilding, calisthenics, isometrics, weight lifting; physical therapy

2 something done over and over in order to develop skill ⟨a young piano student dutifully going through the standard finger *exercises*⟩

syn drill, practice (*also* practise), routine, training, workout

rel assignment, homework, lesson

3 the act or practice of employing something for a particular purpose — see USE 1

exercise *vb* **1** to bring to bear especially forcefully or effectively — see EXERT

2 to do over and over so as to become skilled — see PRACTICE

3 to put into action or service — see USE 1

4 to trouble the mind of; to make uneasy — see DISTURB 1

exert *vb* to bring to bear especially forcefully or effectively ⟨*parental involvement has been shown to* exert *the most influence over a child's success in school*⟩
syn apply, exercise, ply, put out, wield
rel employ, use, utilize

exertion *n* **1** energetic movement of the body for the sake of physical fitness — see EXERCISE 1
2 the active use of energy in producing a result — see EFFORT

exfoliate *vb* to cast (a natural bodily covering or appendage) aside — see SHED 1

exhale *vb* **1** to let or force out of the lungs ⟨*before answering, the suspect* exhaled *a cloud of cigarette smoke*⟩
syn blow (out), breathe (out), expire
rel expectorate
ant inhale, inspire
2 to throw or give off — see EMIT 1

exhaust *vb* **1** to use up all the physical energy of ⟨*the long day at the county fair had* exhausted *everyone*⟩
syn burn out, do in, drain, fag, fatigue, tire, tucker (out), wash out, wear, wear out, weary
rel debilitate, enervate, enfeeble, sap, waste, weaken
phrases wear to a frazzle
near ant activate, energize, invigorate, strengthen, vitalize; relax, rest, unwind
2 to make complete use of — see DEPLETE

exhausted *adj* depleted in strength, energy, or freshness — see WEARY 1

exhaustion *n* a complete depletion of energy or strength — see FATIGUE

exhaustive *adj* trying all possibilities ⟨*after an* exhaustive *search of our house, we still hadn't found the cat*⟩
syn all-out, clean, comprehensive, full-scale, out-and-out, thorough, thoroughgoing, total
rel broad, extensive, far-reaching, in-depth, wide; general, global, inclusive
near ant aimless, desultory, haphazard, hit-or-miss, random; cursory, shallow, slipshod, superficial; limited, narrow, restricted

exhaustively *adv* with attention to all aspects or details — see THOROUGHLY 1

exhibit *n* a public showing of objects of interest — see EXHIBITION 1

exhibit *vb* to present so as to invite notice or attention — see SHOW 1

exhibition *n* **1** a public showing of objects of interest ⟨*an* exhibition *of valuable and fascinating artifacts from a recovered pirate ship*⟩
syn display, exhibit, exposition, fair, show
rel demonstration, performance, presentation, production; extravaganza, pageant, spectacle; auction, offering, sale

2 an outward and often exaggerated indication of something abstract (as a feeling) for effect — see SHOW 1

exhilarate *vb* **1** to cause a pleasurable stimulation of the feelings — see THRILL
2 to fill with great joy — see ELATE

exhilarated *adj* experiencing or marked by overwhelming usually pleasurable emotion — see ECSTATIC

exhilarating *adj* causing great emotional or mental stimulation — see EXCITING 1

exhilaration *n* **1** a pleasurably intense stimulation of the feelings — see THRILL
2 a state of overwhelming usually pleasurable emotion — see ECSTASY

exhort *vb* to try to persuade (someone) through earnest appeals to follow a course of action — see URGE

exhume *vb* to remove from place of burial ⟨*the remains of John Paul Jones were* exhumed *in Paris and transported with great ceremony to the U.S. Naval Academy*⟩
syn disinter, unearth
ant bury, entomb, inter

exigency *n* a time or state of affairs requiring prompt or decisive action — see EMERGENCY

exile *n* **1** the forced removal from a homeland ⟨*the* exile *of French settlers from Nova Scotia resulted in the birth of the Cajun community in the U.S.*⟩
syn banishment, deportation, displacement, expatriation, expulsion
rel ostracism; extradition; dispersion, scattering; emigration, migration; evacuation
near ant repatriation, return; immigration
2 a person forced to emigrate for political reasons — see ÉMIGRÉ 1

exile *vb* to force to leave a country — see BANISH 1

exist *vb* to have life — see BE 1

existence *n* the fact of being or of being real ⟨*the* existence *of UFOs is something that people continue to argue about*⟩
syn actuality, reality, subsistence
rel genuineness, realness; activity, animation, life; currency, presence, prevalence
near ant absence, dearth, lack, want
ant nonexistence

existent *adj* **1** existing in fact and not merely as a possibility — see ACTUAL
2 having being at the present time — see EXTANT 1

existing *adj* having being at the present time — see EXTANT 1

exit *n* **1** a place or means of going out ⟨*all of the building's* exits *were being watched by security guards*⟩
syn egress, issue, outlet
rel escape, release; opening, passage, vent
near ant access, entrée (*or* entree)
ant entrance, entry, entryway, ingress
2 the act of leaving a place — see DEPARTURE

exit *vb* to leave a place often for another — see GO 2

---

syn synonym(s)   *rel* related words
ant antonym(s)   *near ant* near antonym(s)

exiting *n* the act of leaving a place — see DEPARTURE

exodus *n* a flowing or going out — see OUTFLOW

exonerate *vb* to free from a charge of wrongdoing — see EXCULPATE

exorbitant *adj* going beyond a normal or acceptable limit in degree or amount — see EXCESSIVE

exorbitantly *adv* beyond a normal or acceptable limit — see TOO 1

exotic *adj* excitingly or mysteriously unusual ⟨the dream of someday traveling to *exotic* lands⟩

syn fantastic, glamorous (*also* glamourous), marvelous (*or* marvellous), outlandish, romantic, strange

rel colorful, picturesque, quaint; alien, foreign; distant, faraway, remote; alluring, captivating, enchanting, fascinating

exotic *n* something strange or unusual that is an object of interest — see CURIOSITY 2

expand *vb* 1 to express more fully and in greater detail ⟨an article on the First Ladies that the author later *expanded* into a book⟩

syn amplify, develop, elaborate (on), enlarge (on)

rel add (to), complement, supplement; discourse, expatiate, ramble, run on

near ant compress, contract; outline, summarize, sum up

ant abbreviate, abridge, condense, shorten

2 to make greater in size, amount, or number — see INCREASE 1

3 to arrange the parts of (something) over a wider area — see OPEN 3

4 to become greater in extent, volume, amount, or number — see INCREASE 2

expanse *n* a wide space or area ⟨the great explorers who crossed the vast *expanse* of the ocean in small ships⟩

syn breadth, extent, reach, spread, stretch

rel domain, field, sphere, territory; compass, range, scope, sweep; gamut, scale, spectrum; depth, emptiness, void; distance, extension, latitude, length, span; amplitude, immensity, magnitude

expansion *n* 1 something added (as by growth) — see INCREASE 1

2 the act or process of going from the simple or basic to the complex or advanced — see DEVELOPMENT 1

expansive *adj* having considerable extent — see EXTENSIVE

expatiate *vb* to give a formal often extended talk on a subject — see TALK 1

expatriate *n* a person forced to emigrate for political reasons — see ÉMIGRÉ 1

expatriate *vb* to force to leave a country — see BANISH 1

expatriation *n* the forced removal from a homeland — see EXILE 1

expect *vb* to believe in the future occurrence of (something) ⟨we *expect* their arrival late this afternoon⟩

syn anticipate, await, hope (for), watch (for)

rel bank on, count (on *or* upon), depend (on *or* upon), rely (on *or* upon); envisage, foresee; foretell, predict, prophesy; assume, presume, presuppose; contemplate, eye, view

phrases look for, look forward to

near ant doubt, question

expectant *adj* 1 having or showing signs of eagerly awaiting something ⟨*expectant* crowds gathered at the spot where the President was scheduled to make an appearance⟩

syn agape, agog, anticipatory

rel open-eyed, openmouthed; alert, vigilant, watchful; anxious, breathless, eager, enthusiastic, raring; impatient, restive, restless

near ant apathetic, indifferent, unconcerned, unimpressed, uninterested, unmoved

2 containing unborn young within the body — see PREGNANT 1

expected *adj* being in accordance with the prescribed, normal, or logical course of events — see DUE 2

expedient *adj* suitable for bringing about a desired result under the circumstances ⟨made the *expedient* decision to sell the land to whomever offered the most money⟩

syn advisable, desirable, judicious, politic, prudent, tactical, wise

rel advantageous, beneficial, profitable; useful, utilitarian; feasible, possible, practicable, practical; opportune, seasonable, timely; opportunistic, self-seeking

near ant impractical, unfeasible, unprofitable; inopportune, unseasonable, untimely

ant imprudent, inadvisable, inexpedient, injudicious, unwise

expedient *n* 1 a temporary replacement — see MAKESHIFT

2 an action planned or taken to achieve a desired result — see MEASURE 1

3 something that one uses to accomplish an end especially when the usual means is not available — see RESOURCE 1

expedition *n* a going from one place to another usually of some distance — see JOURNEY

expeditious *adj* having or showing the ability to respond without delay or hesitation — see QUICK 1

expel *vb* 1 to drive or force out — see EJECT 1

2 to throw or give off — see EMIT 1

3 to throw or cast off (something from within) often violently — see ERUPT 1

expend *vb* 1 to hand over or use up in payment — see SPEND 1

2 to make complete use of — see DEPLETE

expenditure *n* 1 a payment made in the course of achieving a result — see EXPENSE

2 the active use of energy in producing a result — see EFFORT

expense *n* a payment made in the course of achieving a result ⟨they spared no *expense* in building the house of their dreams⟩
syn cost, disbursement, expenditure, outgo, outlay
rel overhead; outflow; spending money; charge, price, rate, tab, tariff, toll

expensive *adj* commanding a large price — see COSTLY

expensively *adv* in a luxurious manner — see HIGH

experience *n* 1 knowledge gained by actually doing or living through something ⟨the hospital is looking for nurses with operating-room *experience*⟩
syn expertise, know-how, proficiency, savvy, skills
rel background; command, mastery; acquaintance, familiarity, intimacy
near ant ignorance, unawareness, unfamiliarity
ant inexperience
2 an exciting or noteworthy event that one experiences firsthand — see ADVENTURE

experience *vb* to come to a knowledge of (something) by living through it ⟨eventually we all have to *experience* the loss of a loved one⟩
syn endure, feel, have, know, see, suffer, sustain, taste, undergo
rel encounter, meet; accept, receive
phrases go through

experienced *adj* having or showing exceptional knowledge, experience, or skill in a field of endeavor — see PROFICIENT

experiment *n* a procedure or operation carried out to resolve an uncertainty ⟨Benjamin Franklin's famous *experiment* in which he flew a kite in a thunderstorm to see if lightning and electricity were identical⟩
syn experimentation, test, trial
rel trial and error; dry run, shakedown; exercise, practice (*also* practise), rehearsal, tryout, workout; crucible, ordeal; attempt, effort, try

experimental *adj* 1 made or done as an experiment ⟨an *experimental* procedure for patients suffering from leukemia⟩
syn pilot, trial
rel developmental, investigative, preparatory; preliminary, provisional, temporary, tentative; conjectural, hypothetical, speculative, theoretical (*also* theoretic); untested, untried; unproved, unproven
near ant accepted, established, standard; tested, tried; advanced, developed; proved, proven; conclusive, decisive, definitive, final, permanent
2 based on observation or experience — see EMPIRICAL

experimentation *n* a procedure or operation carried out to resolve an uncertainty — see EXPERIMENT

expert *adj* 1 accomplished with trained ability — see SKILLFUL
2 having or showing exceptional knowledge, experience, or skill in a field of endeavor — see PROFICIENT

expert *n* a person with a high level of knowledge or skill in a field ⟨*experts* at the crime lab were able to tell the sex, race, and approximate age of the murderer⟩
syn ace, adept, artist, authority, crackerjack, maestro, master, past master, scholar, shark, virtuoso, whiz, wizard
rel pro, professional; specialist; addict, aficionado, buff, devotee, enthusiast, fan; craftsman, journeyman; jack-of-all-trades
near ant apprentice, beginner, neophyte, novice; dabbler, dilettante; layman, nonprofessional
ant amateur

expertise *n* knowledge gained by actually doing or living through something — see EXPERIENCE 1

expertly *adv* in a skillful or expert manner — see WELL 3

expiate *vb* to make up for (an offense) ⟨Yom Kippur is the holy day on which Jews are expected to *expiate* sins committed during the past year⟩
syn atone (for)
rel compensate, recompense, reimburse, remunerate, repay; amend, correct, rectify, redress; propitiate
phrases make amends for, make good for

expiration *n* 1 the act of ceasing to exist — see DEATH 3
2 the stopping of a process or activity — see END 1

expire *vb* 1 to come to an end — see CEASE 1
2 to let or force out of the lungs — see EXHALE 1
3 to stop living — see DIE 1

expired *adj* no longer existing — see EXTINCT

explain *vb* 1 to make plain or understandable ⟨write an essay that *explains* the meaning of the poem⟩
syn clarify, clear (up), construe, demonstrate, elucidate, explicate, expound, illuminate, illustrate, interpret, spell out
rel decipher, decode; analyze, break down; disentangle, undo, unravel, unscramble, untangle; resolve, solve; define, specify
phrases get across
near ant befog, cloud; confound, confuse
ant obscure
2 to give the reason for or cause of ⟨can you *explain* your very odd behavior at the wedding reception?⟩
syn account (for), explain away, rationalize
rel condone, excuse, forgive, justify; absolve, acquit, exculpate, exonerate, vindicate

explainable *adj* capable of having the reason for or cause of determined — see SOLVABLE

---

syn synonym(s)   **rel** related words
ant antonym(s)   **near ant** near antonym(s)

explain away *vb* to give the reason for or cause of — see EXPLAIN 2

explanation *n* **1** a statement that makes something clear ⟨an *explanation* of photosynthesis that the whole class was able to understand⟩

syn clarification, construction, elucidation, explication, exposition, illumination, illustration, interpretation

rel paraphrase, restatement, translation; deciphering, decoding; disentanglement, unscrambling; analysis; definition, meaning; demonstration, enactment; justification, rationale, rationalization, reasoning

2 a statement given to explain a belief or act — see REASON 1

explanatory *adj* serving to explain ⟨the *explanatory* section has as its heading "Using Your Dictionary"⟩

syn elucidative, expository, illuminative, illustrative, interpretive

rel analytic (*also* analytical), demonstrative, discursive; exculpatory

expletive *n* a disrespectful or indecent word or expression — see SWEARWORD

explicable *adj* capable of having the reason for or cause of determined — see SOLVABLE

explicate *vb* to make plain or understandable — see EXPLAIN 1

explication *n* a statement that makes something clear — see EXPLANATION 1

explicit *adj* so clearly expressed as to leave no doubt about the meaning ⟨*explicit* instructions about what to do in an emergency⟩

syn clear-cut, definite, definitive, express, specific, unambiguous, unequivocal

rel avowed, declared, stated; categorical (*also* categoric), complete, comprehensive, exhaustive, full; certain, sure, unmistakable; clear, distinct, lucid; exact, precise; direct, literal, plain, simple, straightforward; comprehensible, intelligible, understandable

near ant cryptic, dark, enigmatic (*also* enigmatical), obscure, unclear; imprecise, inaccurate, incorrect, inexact; incomprehensible, unintelligible

ant implicit, implied, inferred; ambiguous, circuitous; equivocal, indefinite

explicitness *n* **1** careful thoroughness of detail — see PARTICULARITY 1

2 clearness of expression — see SIMPLICITY 2

explode *vb* **1** to break open or into pieces usually because of internal pressure ⟨the building was wrecked when a powerful bomb *exploded*⟩

syn blow up, burst, detonate, go off, pop

rel fragment, shatter, smash, splinter; discharge, fire, shoot; balloon, burgeon, mushroom

near ant collapse, fizzle

ant implode

2 to cause to break open or into pieces by or as if by an explosive — see BLAST 1

3 to develop suddenly and violently — see ERUPT 2

exploit *n* **1** an act of notable skill, strength, or cleverness — see FEAT 1

2 something done by someone — see ACTION 1

exploit *vb* **1** to take unfair advantage of ⟨a student who *exploits* his friend's good nature by always sponging off him⟩

syn abuse, capitalize (on), cash in (on), impose (on *or* upon), play (on *or* upon), use

rel manipulate, mistreat; bleed, cheat, fleece, overcharge, skin, soak, stick; commercialize

2 to control or take advantage of by artful, unfair, or insidious means — see MANIPULATE 1

3 to put into action or service — see USE 1

exploitable *adj* **1** capable of or suitable for being used for a particular purpose — see USABLE 1

2 readily taken advantage of — see EASY 2

exploration *n* a systematic search for the truth or facts about something — see INQUIRY 1

explore *vb* **1** to search through or into ⟨let's *explore* new ways of raising money for the school band⟩

syn delve (into), dig (into), inquire (into), investigate, look (into), probe, research

rel examine, inspect, sift, study, view; browse, peruse, scan, skim (through), thumb (through)

2 to go into or range over for purposes of discovery ⟨we must continue to *explore* the depths of the ocean⟩

syn hunt, probe, prospect, search

rel reconnoiter (*or* reconnoitre), scout; disclose, discover, reveal, unearth; fathom, plumb, sound

explosion *n* **1** the act or an instance of exploding ⟨the *explosion* of the first atomic bomb at Hiroshima⟩

syn blast, bursting, detonation, eruption

rel discharge, firing, shooting; blowout, flare-up; bang, boom, pop

ant implosion

2 a sudden intense expression of strong feeling — see OUTBURST 1

3 an outburst or display of excited anger — see TANTRUM

explosive *adj* **1** extreme in degree, power, or effect — see INTENSE

2 marked by bursts of destructive force or intense activity — see VIOLENT 1

exponent *n* a person who actively supports or favors a cause ⟨*exponents* of space exploration called for more missions to the outer reaches of the solar system⟩

syn advocate, apostle, backer, booster, champion, friend, promoter, proponent, supporter

rel loyalist, partisan, stalwart; adherent, cohort, disciple, follower; expounder, interpreter; cheerleader

near ant enemy, foe, rival; belittler, critic, faultfinder

ant adversary, antagonist, opponent

expose *vb* **1** to reveal the true nature of ⟨a well-researched article that *exposes* the UFO story as a hoax⟩

syn debunk, show up, uncloak, uncover, unmask

rel discredit, disprove; disclose, divulge, tell, unveil

near ant conceal, hide, secrete

ant camouflage, cloak, disguise, mask

2 to make known (as information previously kept secret) — see REVEAL 1

3 to make known (something abstract) through outward signs — see SHOW 2

4 to present so as to invite notice or attention — see SHOW 1

exposed *adj* **1** being in a situation where one is likely to meet with harm — see LIABLE 1

2 lacking a usual or natural covering — see NAKED 2

3 lacking protection from danger or resistance against attack — see HELPLESS 1

exposition *n* **1** a public showing of objects of interest — see EXHIBITION 1

2 a series of explanations or observations on something (as an event) — see COMMENTARY

3 a statement that makes something clear — see EXPLANATION 1

expository *adj* serving to explain — see EXPLANATORY

expostulate (with) *vb* to present an opposing opinion or argument — see OBJECT

expostulation *n* a feeling or declaration of disapproval or dissent — see OBJECTION

exposure *n* **1** the state of being left without shelter or protection against something harmful ⟨some people avoid situations in which there is a high level of *exposure* to germs⟩

syn liability, openness, vulnerability

rel susceptibility; defenselessness, helplessness, weakness; danger, jeopardy, peril, risk

near ant protection, safeguarding, sheltering, shielding

2 the act or an instance of making known something previously unknown or concealed — see REVELATION

expound *vb* to make plain or understandable — see EXPLAIN 1

express *adj* **1** of a particular or exact sort ⟨a trip to the supermarket with the *express* purpose of buying milk⟩

syn distinct, especial, precise, set, special, specific

rel lone, only, separate, single, sole, solitary; distinctive, exclusive, individual, peculiar, unique; limited, restricted; specified

near ant general, generic, nonexclusive, universal

ant nonspecific

2 so clearly expressed as to leave no doubt about the meaning — see EXPLICIT

---

syn synonym(s)   *rel* related words
ant antonym(s)   *near ant* near antonym(s)

express *vb* **1** to make known (as an idea, emotion, or opinion) ⟨in a true democracy, a person can freely *express* his or her views⟩

syn air, give, look, sound, state, vent, ventilate, voice

rel advertise, announce, declare, enunciate, proclaim, publish; describe, write, write up; sound off, speak out, speak up; chime in; communicate, convey, put across, put over; offer, submit

phrases put forth

near ant censor, restrain, restrict

ant stifle, suppress

2 to apply external pressure on so as to force out the juice or contents of — see PRESS 2

3 to communicate or convey (as an idea) to the mind — see MEAN 1

4 to convey in appropriate or telling terms — see PHRASE

expression *n* **1** an act, process, or means of putting something into words ⟨the poem is his *expression* of his grief upon the loss of his beloved dog⟩

syn articulation, formulation, statement, utterance, voice

rel outlet, vent; observation, reflection, remark, thought; speech, tongue

2 facial appearance regarded as an indication of mood or feeling — see LOOK 1

3 a pronounceable series of letters having a distinct meaning especially in a particular field — see WORD 1

4 a sequence of words having a specific meaning — see PHRASE

expressionless *adj* not expressing any emotion — see BLANK 1

expressive *adj* clearly conveying a special meaning (as one's mood) ⟨the teacher's *expressive* sigh showed that she had heard that excuse many times before⟩

syn eloquent, meaning, meaningful, pregnant, revealing, significant, suggestive

rel graphic (*also* graphical), pictorial, vivid; evocative, redolent, reminiscent; sententious, weighty; flavorful, rich

expressway *n* a passage cleared for public vehicular travel — see WAY 1

expropriate *vb* to take ownership or control of (something) by right of one's authority — see CONFISCATE

expulsion *n* the forced removal from a homeland — see EXILE 1

expunge *vb* to destroy all traces of — see ANNIHILATE 1

expurgate *vb* to remove objectionable parts from — see CENSOR

exquisite *adj* **1** extreme in degree, power, or effect — see INTENSE

2 having qualities that appeal to a refined taste — see CHOICE

3 satisfying or pleasing because of fineness or mildness — see DELICATE 1

exquisiteness *n* the state or quality of having a delicate structure — see DELICACY 2

extant *adj* **1** having being at the present time ⟨a celebrated author who is generally regarded as America's greatest novelist *extant*⟩

syn alive, existent, existing, living

rel active, busy, flourishing, functioning, operating, working

near ant defunct, destroyed, exterminated; departed, gone, lost; nonexistent; idle, inactive, inert

ant dead, extinct

2 existing or in progress right now — see PRESENT 1

extemporaneous *adj* made or done without previous thought or preparation ⟨caught by surprise, I had to make an *extemporaneous* speech at the awards banquet⟩

syn ad-lib, extempore, impromptu, improvised, offhand, offhanded, snap, spur-of-the-moment, unconsidered, unplanned, unpremeditated, unprepared, unrehearsed

rel automatic, impulsive, instinctive, involuntary, spontaneous; casual, informal, unauthorized

near ant deliberate, intended, intentional

ant considered, planned, premeditated, prepared, rehearsed

extempore *adj* made or done without previous thought or preparation — see EXTEMPORANEOUS

extemporize *vb* to perform, make, or do without preparation — see IMPROVISE

extend *vb* **1** to make longer ⟨our guests from out of town *extended* their visit by a week⟩

syn draw out, elongate, lengthen, prolong, protract, stretch

rel amplify, enlarge, expand, increase; attenuate, thin

near ant decrease, diminish, lessen, reduce; thicken

ant abbreviate, abridge, curtail, cut, cut back, shorten

2 to put before another for acceptance or consideration — see OFFER 1

3 to arrange the parts of (something) over a wider area — see OPEN 3

4 to be positioned along a certain course or in a certain direction — see RUN 3

5 to make greater in size, amount, or number — see INCREASE 1

extended *adj* **1** expressing one thing in terms normally used for another — see FIGURATIVE

2 having considerable extent — see EXTENSIVE

3 lasting for a considerable time — see LONG 2

4 of great extent from end to end — see LONG 1

extended family *n* those who live as a family in one house — see HOUSEHOLD

extension *n* **1** the act of making longer ⟨the board's *extension* of the school year drew howls of protest⟩

syn drawing out, elongation, lengthening, prolongation, prolonging, stretching

ant abbreviation, abridgment (*or* abridgement), curtailment, cutback, shortening

2 a smaller structure added to a main building — see ANNEX

extensive *adj* having considerable extent ⟨a rock hound whose *extensive* reading enables him to identify just about any rock or mineral⟩

syn broad, expansive, extended, far-flung, far-reaching, wide, widespread

rel comprehensive, general, global, inclusive; boundless, endless, limitless, unlimited; capacious, commodious, roomy, spacious

near ant circumscribed, limited, restricted

ant narrow

extensively *adv* to a large extent or degree — see GREATLY 2

extent *n* **1** a real or imaginary point beyond which a person or thing cannot go — see LIMIT

2 a wide space or area — see EXPANSE

3 an area over which activity, capacity, or influence extends — see RANGE 2

4 the total amount of measurable space or surface occupied by something — see ¹SIZE

extenuate *vb* to make (something) seem less bad by offering excuses — see PALLIATE 1

exterior *adj* situated on the outside or farther out — see OUTER

exterior *n* an outer part or layer ⟨the *exterior* of the tooth consists of very hard enamel⟩

syn face, outside, skin, surface, veneer

rel facade (*also* façade), front, top; cover, covering, facing; appearance, disguise, guise, mask, semblance, show

ant inside, interior

exterminate *vb* to destroy all traces of — see ANNIHILATE 1

extermination *n* the state or fact of being rendered nonexistent, physically unsound, or useless — see DESTRUCTION

external *adj* situated on the outside or farther out — see OUTER

extinct *adj* no longer existing ⟨a few overgrown ruins are all that remain of that once mighty but now *extinct* civilization⟩

syn bygone, dead, defunct, departed, expired, gone, vanished

rel nonexistent; dying, faded, moribund; collapsed, fallen, overthrown; antiquated, dated, obsolete, passé; finished, lapsed, terminated; lost, missing

near ant active, dynamic, thriving, vibrant

ant alive, existent, existing, extant, living

extinction *n* the state or fact of being rendered nonexistent, physically unsound, or useless — see DESTRUCTION

extinguish *vb* **1** to cause to cease burning ⟨the fire in the skillet was quickly *extinguished* by slamming the lid on⟩

syn douse, put out, quench, snuff (out)

rel choke, smother, suffocate; stamp (out)

ant fire, ignite, inflame, kindle

2 to bring to a complete end the physical soundness, existence, or usefulness of — see DESTROY 1

extirpate *vb* to destroy all traces of — see ANNIHILATE 1

extol *also* **extoll** *vb* to proclaim the glory of — see PRAISE 1

extort *vb* to get (as money) by the use of force or threats ⟨a school bully who was used to *extorting* lunch money from weaker kids⟩
syn exact, wrest, wring
rel bleed, fleece, gouge, milk, skin, squeeze; cheat, gyp, racketeer, swindle; coerce, compel, force

extortioner *n* a person who gets money from another by using force or threats — see RACKETEER

extortionist *n* a person who gets money from another by using force or threats — see RACKETEER

extra *adj* being over what is needed — see SPARE 1

extra *adv* to a great degree — see VERY 1

extra *n* 1 an interchangeable part or piece of equipment that is kept on hand for replacement of an original — see SPARE
2 something adding to pleasure or comfort but not absolutely necessary — see LUXURY 1
3 something given in addition to what is ordinarily expected or owed — see BONUS

extract *n* a part taken from a longer work — see EXCERPT

extract *vb* to draw out by force or with effort ⟨*extracted* a splinter from my hand⟩
syn prize, pry, pull, root (out), tear (out), uproot, wrest, yank
rel remove, take (out), withdraw
near ant implant, insert, install, instill; cram, jam, ram, stuff, wedge

extraction *n* the line of ancestors from whom a person is descended — see ANCESTRY

extraneous *adj* 1 not being a vital part of or belonging to something — see EXTRINSIC
2 not having anything to do with the matter at hand — see IRRELEVANT

extraneousness *n* the quality or state of not having anything to do with the matter at hand — see IRRELEVANCE

extraordinary *adj* 1 being out of the ordinary — see EXCEPTIONAL
2 noticeably different from what is generally found or experienced — see UNUSUAL 1

extrapolate *vb* to form an opinion through reasoning and information — see INFER 1

extrasensory perception *n* the power of seeing or knowing about things that are not present to the senses — see CLAIRVOYANCE

extravagance *n* 1 the quality or fact of being free or wasteful in the expenditure of money ⟨Hollywood stars are famous for the *extravagance* of their parties⟩
syn lavishness, prodigality, wastefulness

rel bountifulness, generosity, liberality; improvidence, squandering; indulgence, overindulgence, self-indulgence; excess, immoderacy, overkill
near ant austerity, moderation, restraint, temperance
ant economy, frugality
2 an instance of spending money or resources without care or restraint — see WASTE 1

extravagant *adj* 1 given to spending money freely or foolishly — see PRODIGAL
2 going beyond a normal or acceptable limit in degree or amount — see EXCESSIVE

extravagantly *adv* in a luxurious manner — see HIGH

extreme *adj* 1 most distant from a center ⟨spacecraft that is specially designed to explore the *extreme* edge of our solar system⟩
syn farthermost, farthest, furthermost, furthest, outermost, outmost, remotest, ultimate, utmost
near ant intermediate, medial, median, mid, middle, middlemost, midmost
ant inmost, innermost, nearest
2 being very far from the center of public opinion ⟨their *extreme* political views attracted only a small band of followers⟩
syn extremist, fanatic (*or* fanatical), rabid, radical, revolutionary, revolutionist, ultra
rel subversive, violent, wild; reactionary
near ant conservative, moderate, temperate; conventional, orthodox, traditional; liberal, progressive
ant middle-of-the-road
3 going beyond a normal or acceptable limit in degree or amount — see EXCESSIVE

extremely *adv* to a great degree — see VERY 1

extremist *adj* being very far from the center of public opinion — see EXTREME 2

extremist *n* a person who favors rapid and sweeping changes especially in laws and methods of government — see RADICAL

extricate *vb* to set free from entanglement or difficulty ⟨you've woven such a web of lies that it's hard to see how you can *extricate* yourself now⟩
syn clear, disengage, disentangle, free, liberate, release, untangle
rel deliver, redeem, rescue, save; disburden, disencumber, unburden; unravel, unsnarl, untie, untwine
near ant block, hamper, hinder, impede, obstruct; burden, encumber, load, weigh
ant embroil, entangle

extrinsic *adj* not being a vital part of or belonging to something ⟨the fact that the ring belonged to your grandmother is *extrinsic* to its value to a jeweler⟩
syn adventitious, alien, extraneous, foreign

---

rel exterior, external, outside; immaterial, inapplicable, insignificant, irrelevant; nonessential, unessential, unnecessary

near ant congenital, deep-seated, inborn, inbred; inside, interior, internal; basic, essential, necessary

ant inherent, innate, intrinsic

extroverted *also* **extraverted** *adj* likely to seek or enjoy the company of others — see CONVIVIAL

extrude *vb* to drive or force out — see EJECT 1

exuberance *n* the quality or state of having abundant or intense activity — see VITALITY 1

exuberant *adj* joyously unrestrained ⟨*exuberant* crowds rushed to greet the returning national champions in collegiate basketball⟩

syn bubbly, buoyant, effervescent, frolicsome, high-spirited, vivacious

rel extroverted (*also* extraverted), outgoing, uninhibited; carefree, insouciant, joyful, lighthearted, lively, sprightly; boisterous, raucous, rollicking, rowdy; giddy, light-headed, silly; ecstatic, euphoric, rapturous; audacious, bold, brash, brazen, impertinent, impudent, insolent, saucy

near ant constrained, inhibited, repressed, restrained, subdued; impassive, phlegmatic, stoic (*or* stoical), stolid; depressed, dour, glum, morose, surly

ant low-spirited, noneffervescent, sullen

exuberantly *adv* 1 in a quick and spirited manner — see GAILY 2

2 in an enthusiastic manner — see SKY-HIGH

exude *vb* to flow forth slowly through small openings ⟨a sticky resin *exudes* from the bark of the tree⟩

syn bleed, ooze, percolate, seep, strain, sweat, weep

rel dribble, drip, trickle; discharge, emit, give off, vent; emanate, flow, spring

near ant flood, gush, pour, stream, surge

exult *vb* to feel or express joy or triumph ⟨the winners of the Super Bowl spent the next week *exulting* in their victory⟩

syn crow, delight, glory, joy, rejoice, triumph

rel gloat; boast, brag; flaunt, parade, show off, strut, swagger

near ant bemoan, bewail, grieve, lament, weep

exultant *adj* having or expressing feelings of joy or triumph ⟨the *exultant* winner of the award for best country artist of the year⟩

syn exulting, glorying, jubilant, rejoicing, triumphant

rel ecstatic, elated, euphoric; arrogant, boastful, cocky; conquering, victorious, winning

near ant crestfallen, defeated, dejected, depressed, disconsolate, dispirited, downcast

exulting *adj* having or expressing feelings of joy or triumph — see EXULTANT

exurbia *n* the area around a city — see ENVIRONS 1

eye *n* 1 a circular strip — see RING 2

2 a state of being aware — see ATTENTION 2

3 a thing or place that is of greatest importance to an activity or interest — see CENTER 1

4 an idea that is believed to be true or valid without positive knowledge — see OPINION 1

5 an instance of looking especially briefly — see LOOK 2

6 the ability to see — see EYESIGHT

eye *vb* 1 to keep one's eyes on — see WATCH 1

2 to make note of (something) through the use of one's eyes — see SEE 1

eye–catching *adj* likely to attract attention — see NOTICEABLE

eyeful *n* a lovely woman — see BEAUTY 2

eyeglasses *n pl* a pair of lenses set in a frame that is held in place with ear supports and which are usually worn to correct vision — see GLASSES 1

eyeless *adj* lacking the power of sight — see BLIND

eye–opening *adj* 1 causing a strong emotional reaction because unexpected — see SURPRISING 1

2 causing wonder or astonishment — see MARVELOUS 1

eyesight *n* the ability to see ⟨the keen *eyesight* of a bird of prey⟩

syn eye, sight, vision

rel myopia, nearsightedness; farsightedness; astigmatism

eyesore *n* something unpleasant to look at ⟨the old abandoned house was a neighborhood *eyesore*⟩

syn fright, horror, mess, monstrosity, sight

rel blot, smear, smudge, spot, stain

eyespot *n* a small area that is different (as in color) from the main part — see SPOT 1

fable *n* **1** a story intended to teach a basic truth or moral about life — see ALLEGORY

2 a traditional but unfounded story that gives the reason for a current custom, belief, or fact of nature — see MYTH 1

3 something that is the product of the imagination — see FICTION

fabled *adj* based on, described in, or being a myth — see MYTHICAL 1

fabric *n* a woven or knitted material (as of cotton or nylon) — see CLOTH

fabricate *vb* **1** to bring into being by combining, shaping, or transforming materials — see MAKE 1

2 to create or think of by clever use of the imagination — see INVENT

3 to form by putting together parts or materials — see BUILD

4 to make a statement one knows to be untrue — see LIE 1

fabrication *n* **1** a statement known by its maker to be untrue and made in order to deceive — see LIE

2 something that is the product of the imagination — see FICTION

fabricator *n* a person who tells lies — see LIAR

fabulous *adj* **1** based on, described in, or being a myth — see MYTHICAL 1

2 causing wonder or astonishment — see MARVELOUS 1

3 not real and existing only in the imagination — see IMAGINARY

4 of the very best kind — see EXCELLENT

facade *also* **façade** *n* **1** a forward part or surface — see FRONT 1

2 a display of emotion or behavior that is insincere or intended to deceive — see MASQUERADE

face *n* **1** the front part of the head ⟨the criminal hid his *face* from the news cameras as he slumped into the patrol car⟩
syn countenance, kisser [*slang*], mug, puss [*slang*], visage
rel appearance, features, lineaments, looks; expression, physiognomy

2 a forward part or surface — see FRONT 1

3 a twisting of the facial features in disgust or disapproval — see GRIMACE

4 an outer part or layer — see EXTERIOR

5 facial appearance regarded as an indication of mood or feeling — see LOOK 1

6 outward and often deceptive indication — see APPEARANCE 2

face *vb* **1** to stand or sit with the face or front toward ⟨the house *faces* the sparkling blue waters of the Pacific Ocean⟩

syn front, look (toward), point (toward)
rel abut, adjoin, border, meet, neighbor, touch; command, dominate, overlook

2 to oppose (something hostile or dangerous) with firmness or courage ⟨movie superheroes who are ever ready to *face* danger without blinking an eye⟩
syn beard, brave, brazen, breast, confront, dare, defy, outbrave
rel encounter, meet; accost, approach; repel, resist, withstand; battle, combat, contend (with), fight, oppose, square (off)
phrases stand up to
near ant avoid, eschew, shun; elude, escape, evade
ant dodge, duck, shirk, sidestep

3 to cover with something that protects — see SHEATHE

4 to enter into contest or conflict with — see ENGAGE 2

face–off *n* an earnest effort for superiority or victory over another — see CONTEST 1

facet *n* a certain way in which something appears or may be regarded — see ASPECT 1

facetious *adj* **1** given to or marked by mature intelligent humor — see WITTY

2 making light of something usually regarded as serious or sacred — see FLIPPANT

facetiousness *n* a lack of seriousness often at an improper time — see FRIVOLITY 1

face–to–face *adv* in person and usually privately — see TÊTE-À-TÊTE

facile *adj* **1** having or showing a lack of depth of understanding or character — see SUPERFICIAL 2

2 involving minimal difficulty or effort — see EASY 1

facilely *adv* without difficulty — see EASILY

facilitate *vb* to free from obstruction or difficulty — see EASE 1

facility *n* a structure that is designed and built for a particular purpose ⟨the city is known for its outstanding medical *facilities*⟩
syn complex, establishment, installation
rel building, edifice; institute, institution; business, company, concern, outfit

facsimile *n* **1** something or someone that strongly resembles another — see IMAGE 1

2 something that is made to look exactly like something else — see COPY

fact *n* **1** the quality of being actual ⟨scientists deal in the realm of *fact*, not speculation⟩
syn actuality, factuality, materiality, reality
rel authenticity, genuineness, truth

---

syn synonym(s)   *rel* related words
ant antonym(s)   *near ant* near antonym(s)

near ant fancy, fantasy (*also* phantasy), fiction; fictitiousness

ant unreality

2 something that actually exists ⟨once considered a wild fantasy, the Internet is now a *fact* of everyday life⟩

syn case, materiality, reality

rel certainty, inevitability; circumstance, event, occurrence, phenomenon; element, item, particular, thing

near ant eventuality, possibility, potentiality, probability

ant fantasy (*also* phantasy), fiction, illusion

3 a single piece of information ⟨a book of little-known *facts* about famous people⟩

syn datum, detail, nicety, particular, particularity, point

rel article, item; element, ingredient, part; aspect, facet, factor; evidence, exhibit; database, information, knowledge

near ant error, fallacy, falsehood, misconception, myth

faction *n* a group of people acting together within a larger group ⟨several *factions* within the environmental movement have joined forces⟩

syn bloc, body, coalition, party, sect, set, side, wing

rel crew, gang, pack, team; denomination, persuasion, schism

factitious *adj* **1** being such in appearance only and made with or manufactured from usually cheaper materials — see IMITATION

2 lacking in natural or spontaneous quality — see ARTIFICIAL 1

factor *n* **1** a person who acts or does business for another — see AGENT 2

2 one of the parts that make up a whole — see ELEMENT 1

factory *n* a building or set of buildings for the manufacturing of goods ⟨the new *factory* will create hundreds of much-needed jobs⟩

syn manufactory, mill, plant, shop, works, workshop

rel sweatshop; workroom; yard

factual *adj* **1** restricted to or based on fact ⟨a *factual* biography of George Washington that scoffs at the story about the cherry tree⟩

syn documentary, hard, historical, literal, matter-of-fact, nonfictional, objective, true

rel actual, authentic, genuine, real; documented, established; reliable, verifiable; demonstrable, provable; incontestable, incontrovertible, indisputable, irrefutable, undeniable, unquestionable; plain, simple, unexaggerated; certain, undoubted

near ant hypothetical, speculative, theoretical (*also* theoretic); fabulous, fanciful, imaginary, legendary, mythical (*or* mythic); embroidered, exaggerated

ant fictional, fictionalized, fictitious, nondocumentary, nonhistorical

2 existing in fact and not merely as a possibility — see ACTUAL

factuality *n* **1** agreement with fact or reality — see TRUTH

2 the quality of being actual — see FACT 1

faculty *n* **1** a natural ability of the mind or body — see POWER 3

2 a special and usually inborn ability — see TALENT

3 the physical or mental power to do something — see ABILITY

fad *n* a practice or interest that is very popular for a short time ⟨the *fad* for that kind of music had long passed⟩

syn craze, enthusiasm, fashion, go, last word, mode, rage, sensation, style, trend, vogue

rel crush, infatuation; fervor, passion; furor, fuss, hullabaloo, to-do, uproar; bandwagon, crusade, cult, movement; novelty, wrinkle; caprice, fancy, whim

near ant classic, standard

fade *vb* **1** to cease to be visible — see DISAPPEAR

2 to make white or whiter by removing color — see WHITEN

faded *adj* lacking intensity of color — see PALE 1

faerie *also* **faery** *n* an imaginary being usually having a small human form and magical powers — see FAIRY

fag *n* a person who does very hard or dull work — see SLAVE 2

fag *vb* **1** to devote serious and sustained effort — see LABOR

2 to use up all the physical energy of — see EXHAUST 1

fag end *n* an unused or unwanted piece or item typically of small size or value — see ¹SCRAP 1

fail *vb* **1** to stop functioning ⟨my video camera *failed* just as I was about to shoot the big mo-ment⟩

syn break, break down, conk (out), crash, cut out, die, give out, stall

rel fizzle, sputter, wheeze; malfunction

ant start (up)

2 to be unsuccessful ⟨despite all the publicity, the movie *failed* miserably at the box office⟩

syn collapse, flop, flunk, fold, wash out

rel flounder, struggle; decline, slip, slump, wane

phrases fall flat

near ant flourish, prosper, thrive

ant succeed

3 to fall short in satisfying the expectation or hope of — see DISAPPOINT

4 to lose bodily strength or vigor — see WEAKEN 2

5 to miss the opportunity or obligation — see NEGLECT 3

failing *n* a defect in character — see FAULT 1

failure *n* **1** the nonperformance of an assigned or expected action ⟨your *failure* to check the batteries in the smoke detector could have tragic results⟩

syn default, delinquency, dereliction, neglect, negligence, oversight

rel carelessness, heedlessness, laxity

near ant compliance, discharge, fulfillment

2 a falling short of one's goals ⟨the *failure* of the school's fund-raising drive was a big disappointment to all⟩

syn collapse, crash, cropper, defeat, fizzle, nonsuccess

rel futility, uselessness; ineffectiveness, ineffectualness; deficiency, inadequacy, insufficiency; disappointment, letdown, setback

ant accomplishment, achievement, success

3 something that has failed ⟨the students' first attempt to build a homemade rocket was a disappointing *failure*⟩

syn bummer, bust, catastrophe, debacle (*also* débâcle), dud, fiasco, fizzle, flop, lemon, loser, turkey, washout

rel also-ran, disappointment, has-been; botch, hash, mess, muddle, shambles

near ant corker, crackerjack, dandy, jim-dandy, phenomenon

ant blockbuster, hit, smash, success, winner

4 a falling short of an essential or desirable amount or number — see DEFICIENCY

faint *adj* **1** not seen or understood clearly ⟨after wandering in the woods for hours, we had only a *faint* idea of where we were⟩

syn bleary, dim, foggy, fuzzy, hazy, indefinite, indistinct, indistinguishable, murky, nebulous, obscure, opaque, shadowy, unclear, undefined, undetermined, vague

rel dark, dusky, gloomy; impalpable, inappreciable, intangible, invisible; incomprehensible, inexplicable, mysterious, puzzling

near ant bright, distinct, evident, obvious; certain, firm, strong, sure

ant clear, definite

2 lacking bodily strength — see WEAK 1

faint *n* a temporary or permanent state of unconsciousness ⟨shocking news can cause a person to fall into a *faint*⟩

syn blackout, coma, insensibility, knockout, swoon

rel daze, stupor, trance; drowsiness, narcosis, sleep, somnolence

faint *vb* to lose consciousness ⟨the kind of person who *faints* at the sight of blood⟩

syn black out, pass out, swoon

rel break down, collapse

ant come around, come round, come to, revive

fainthearted *adj* easily frightened — see SHY 1

faintheartedness *n* lack of willingness to assert oneself and take risks — see TIMIDITY

faintness *n* the quality or state of lacking physical strength or vigor — see WEAKNESS 1

fair *adj* **1** not stormy or cloudy ⟨we prayed that there would be *fair* weather during our vacation at the beach⟩

syn clear, cloudless, sunny, sunshiny, unclouded

rel balmy, clement, gentle, mild, temperate; calm, halcyon, peaceful, placid, tranquil; fine, pleasant

near ant harsh, inclement, severe; blustering, blustery, breezy, gusty; foggy, hazy, misty

ant bleak, cloudy, dirty, foul, nasty, overcast, rainy, raw, rough, squally, stormy, sunless

2 marked by justice, honesty, and freedom from bias ⟨a commanding officer who enjoyed the respect of his soldiers because his decisions were always *fair*⟩

syn disinterested, dispassionate, equal, equitable, impartial, just, nonpartisan, objective, square, unbiased, unprejudiced

rel candid, frank, forthright, open, straightforward; balanced, rational, reasonable

near ant deceitful, deceptive, dishonest; arbitrary, unconscionable, unreasonable

ant biased, inequitable, partisan, prejudiced, unequal, unjust

3 following or according to the rules ⟨a hockey player who is respected for his *fair* play⟩

syn clean, legal, sportsmanlike, sportsmanly

rel just, law-abiding; ethical, moral, principled; honorable, irreproachable, unimpeachable

near ant immoral, unethical, unprincipled, unscrupulous

ant dirty, foul, nasty, unfair, unsportsmanlike

4 of light complexion ⟨*fair* people tend to sunburn easily⟩

syn light

rel ashen, pale, pallid, pasty, peaked, sallow, wan, white

ant black, brunet (*or* brunette), dark, swarthy

5 having qualities which inspire hope — see HOPEFUL 1

6 of a pale yellow or yellowish brown color — see BLOND

7 of average to below average quality — see MEDIOCRE 1

8 very pleasing to look at — see BEAUTIFUL

fair *n* a public showing of objects of interest — see EXHIBITION 1

fairly *adv* to some degree or extent ⟨for someone without professional training, she sings *fairly* well⟩

syn enough, kind of, like, moderately, more or less, pretty, quite, rather, relatively, something, somewhat, sort of

rel acceptably, decently, passably, tolerably

near ant awfully, exceedingly (*also* exceeding), exceptionally, extremely, greatly, surpassingly, very

---

syn synonym(s)   *rel* related words
ant antonym(s)   *near ant* near antonym(s)

fairness *n* the qualities in a person or thing that as a whole give pleasure to the senses — see BEAUTY 1

fairy *n* an imaginary being usually having a small human form and magical powers ⟨*fairies* are part of the folklore of many countries and cultures⟩

syn brownie, dwarf, elf, faerie (*also* faery), fay, gnome, goblin, gremlin, hobgoblin, leprechaun, pixie (*also* pixy), puck, sprite, troll

rel changeling; imp; banshee, ghoul, ogre

fairy tale *n* a statement known by its maker to be untrue and made in order to deceive — see LIE

faith *n* 1 belief and trust in and loyalty to God ⟨a people who are known for their strong and steadfast *faith*⟩

syn devotion, piety, religion

rel devoutness, piousness, religiousness; adoration, reverence, veneration, worship

near ant disbelief, doubt, unbelief

ant atheism, godlessness

2 a body of beliefs and practices regarding the supernatural and the worship of one or more deities — see RELIGION 1

3 adherence to something to which one is bound by a pledge or duty — see FIDELITY

4 firm belief in the integrity, ability, effectiveness, or genuineness of someone or something — see TRUST 1

5 mental conviction of the truth of some statement or the reality of some being or phenomenon — see BELIEF 1

faithful *adj* 1 firm in one's allegiance to someone or something ⟨fans of the Chicago Cubs are famously *faithful*⟩

syn constant, devoted, fast, good, loyal, pious, staunch (*or* stanch), steadfast, steady, true, true-blue

rel dependable, dutiful, reliable, tried, trustworthy; unfaltering, unhesitating, unwavering; determined, intent, resolute; confirmed, dyed-in-the-wool, inveterate, sworn; ardent, fervent, fervid, impassioned, passionate

near ant undependable, unreliable, untrustworthy; faltering, hesitant, vacillating, wavering; dubious, irresolute, uncertain; apathetic, dispassionate, uninterested

ant disloyal, faithless, false, fickle, inconstant, perfidious, recreant, traitorous, treacherous, unfaithful, untrue

2 following an original exactly ⟨a *faithful* filming of Robert Louis Stevenson's novel *Treasure Island*⟩

syn accurate, authentic, exact, precise, right, strict, true, veracious

rel lifelike, realistic; careful, conscientious, meticulous, punctilious, scrupulous; authoritative; bona fide, genuine, real

near ant careless, slack, slipshod, slovenly

ant false, imprecise, inaccurate, inauthentic, inexact, loose, unfaithful

faithfulness *n* adherence to something to which one is bound by a pledge or duty — see FIDELITY

faithless *adj* not true in one's allegiance to someone or something ⟨*faithless* friends who deserted him in his time of need⟩

syn disloyal, false, fickle, inconstant, perfidious, recreant, traitorous, treacherous, unfaithful, untrue

rel undependable, unreliable, untrustworthy; faltering, hesitant, vacillating, wavering; dubious, irresolute, uncertain; apathetic, dispassionate, uninterested

near ant dependable, reliable, tried, trustworthy; unfaltering, unhesitating, unwavering; determined, intent, resolute; confirmed, dyed-in-the-wool, inveterate, sworn; ardent, fervent, fervid, impassioned, passionate

ant constant, devoted, faithful, fast, loyal, staunch (*or* stanch), steadfast, steady, true

faithlessness *n* 1 lack of faithfulness especially to one's husband or wife — see INFIDELITY 1

2 the act or fact of violating the trust or confidence of another — see BETRAYAL

fake *adj* 1 being such in appearance only and made with or manufactured from usually cheaper materials — see IMITATION

2 being such in appearance only and made or manufactured with the intention of committing fraud — see COUNTERFEIT

3 lacking in natural or spontaneous quality — see ARTIFICIAL 1

fake *n* 1 an imitation that is passed off as genuine ⟨experts declared that one of the museum's prized paintings was actually a *fake*⟩

syn counterfeit, forgery, hoax, humbug, phony (*also* phoney), sham

rel copy, reproduction; dummy; fraud, imposture, swindle; simulation, synthetic

near ant original

2 one who makes false claims of identity or expertise — see IMPOSTOR

fake *vb* 1 to imitate or copy especially in order to deceive ⟨pranksters *faked* giant footprints and then claimed that they had seen Bigfoot⟩

syn counterfeit, forge

rel simulate; crib, plagiarize; adulterate, doctor, fudge, juggle, manipulate, tamper (with); concoct, cook (up), fabricate, invent

2 to present a false appearance of — see FEIGN

faker *n* one who makes false claims of identity or expertise — see IMPOSTOR

fakery *n* the inclination or practice of misleading others through lies or trickery — see DECEIT

fall *n* 1 the act of going down from an upright position suddenly and involuntarily ⟨a bad *fall* that resulted in several broken bones⟩

syn slip, spill, stumble, tumble

rel header, pratfall; trip; descent, dive, plunge, slide; free-fall

2 a change to a lower state or level — see
DECLINE 2

3 a loss of status — see COMEDOWN

4 the act or process of going to a lower
level or altitude — see DESCENT 1

5 the amount by which something is lessened — see DECREASE

6 *usually* **falls** *pl* a fall of water usually
from a great height — see WATERFALL

fall *vb* **1** to go down from an upright position suddenly and involuntarily ⟨better
sand that walkway before somebody *falls*
on the ice⟩

syn slip, stumble, topple, trip, tumble

rel collapse, crumple, drop, keel over,
slump (over); nose-dive, plunge, precipitate

ant get up, rise, stand (up), uprise

2 to yield to the control or power of
enemy forces ⟨the city *fell* after weeks of
merciless bombardment⟩

syn capitulate, give up, knuckle under,
submit, succumb, surrender

rel bow, buckle, cave (in), collapse; hand
over, relinquish, yield; lose; fail, fold

near ant fight, oppose, resist, withstand;
beat, overcome, win; prevail, triumph

ant stand

3 to go to a lower level — see DROP 2

4 to grow less in scope or intensity especially gradually — see DECREASE 2

5 to lead or extend downward — see DE-
SCEND 1

fallacious *adj* **1** not using or following
good reasoning — see ILLOGICAL

2 tending or having power to deceive —
see DECEPTIVE 1

fallaciousness *n* the quality or state of
being false — see FALLACY 2

fallacy *n* **1** a false idea or belief ⟨the once-
common *fallacy* that girls just weren't
any good at math⟩

syn error, falsehood, falsity, illusion, misconception, myth, old wives' tale, untruth

rel superstition; distortion, inaccuracy,
misinterpretation, misrepresentation, misstatement, misunderstanding; sophism,
sophistry; fib, lie, story, tale

ant truth, verity

2 the quality or state of being false ⟨the
fallacy of the notion of spontaneous generation was demonstrated by the Dutch
naturalist Leeuwenhoek⟩

syn erroneousness, fallaciousness, falseness, falsity, untruth

rel speciousness, spuriousness; deception,
deceptiveness, delusion

near ant accuracy, correctness, factualness, genuineness

ant truth

fall back *vb* to move back or away (as
from something difficult, dangerous, or
disagreeable) — see RETREAT 1

fallen *adj* no longer living — see DEAD 1

fall guy *n* a person or thing taking the
blame for others — see SCAPEGOAT

falling–out *n* an often noisy or angry expression of differing opinions — see AR-
GUMENT 1

fall out *vb* to express different opinion
about something often angrily — see
ARGUE 2

fallow *adj* not being in a state of use, activity, or employment — see INACTIVE 2

false *adj* **1** not being in agreement with
what is true ⟨early reports about the explosion contained much *false* informa-
tion⟩

syn erroneous, inaccurate, incorrect, inexact, invalid, off, unsound, untrue, untruthful, wrong

rel specious, spurious; deceptive, delusive, delusory, distorted, fallacious, misleading; amiss, askew, awry; deceitful,
dishonest, fraudulent, lying, mendacious,
untruthful; unconfirmed, unproven, untested; fabricated, invented, made-up,
trumped-up

near ant confirmed, demonstrated, established, proven, tested

ant accurate, correct, errorless, factual,
right, sound, true, valid

2 being such in appearance only and
made with or manufactured from usually
cheaper materials — see IMITATION

3 being such in appearance only and
made or manufactured with the intention
of committing fraud — see COUNTER-
FEIT

4 lacking in natural or spontaneous quality — see ARTIFICIAL 1

5 marked by, based on, or done by the
use of dishonest methods to acquire
something of value — see FRAUDULENT 1

6 not true in one's allegiance to someone
or something — see FAITHLESS

7 tending or having power to deceive —
see DECEPTIVE 1

falsehood *n* **1** a false idea or belief — see
FALLACY 1

2 a statement known by its maker to be
untrue and made in order to deceive —
see LIE

falseness *n* **1** lack of faithfulness especially to one's husband or wife — see INFI-
DELITY 1

2 the act or fact of violating the trust or
confidence of another — see BETRAYAL

3 the quality or state of being false — see
FALLACY 2

falsify *vb* to change so much as to create a
wrong impression or alter the meaning of
— see GARBLE

falsity *n* **1** a false idea or belief — see FAL-
LACY 1

2 a statement known by its maker to be
untrue and made in order to deceive —
see LIE

3 lack of faithfulness especially to one's
husband or wife — see INFIDELITY 1

4 the act or fact of violating the trust or
confidence of another — see BETRAYAL

5 the quality or state of being false — see
FALLACY 2

falter *vb* **1** to show uncertainty about the
right course of action — see HESITATE

2 to swing unsteadily back and forth or from side to side — see TEETER 1

faltering *n* the act or an instance of pausing because of uncertainty about the right course of action — see HESITATION

fame *n* the fact or state of being known to the public ⟨many go to Hollywood in search of *fame* and fortune⟩

syn celebrity, notoriety, renown

rel infamy; name, report, reputation, repute; cachet, position, prestige, rank, standing, stature; distinction, eminence, glory, greatness, honor, illustriousness, note, preeminence, prominence; acclaim, acknowledgment (*also* acknowledgement), praise, recognition; adoration, idolization

near ant disgrace, dishonor, disrepute, ignominy, odium, opprobrium, shame; unimportance

ant anonymity, obscurity

famed *adj* widely known — see FAMOUS

familial *adj* of or relating to a household or family — see DOMESTIC 1

familiar *adj* **1** closely acquainted ⟨the little inside jokes that people who have long been *familiar* like to share⟩

syn bosom, chummy, close, friendly, intimate, thick

rel affable, boon, companionable, convivial, cordial, genial, gracious, hearty, gregarious, sociable, social; comfortable, cozy, easy, snug; amicable, neighborly; confidential, secretive; affectionate, dear, devoted, fond, loving, warm

near ant aloof, cold, cool, reserved, standoffish, unfriendly, unsociable, withdrawn

ant distant

2 having information especially as a result of study or experience ⟨book editors who are *familiar* with what is being taught in the schools⟩

syn abreast, acquainted, conversant, informed, knowledgeable, up, up-to-date, versed

rel aware, cognizant, conscious, heedful, mindful

phrases in the know

near ant unaware, unconscious, unmindful; blind, oblivious, unknowing, unwitting

ant ignorant, unacquainted, unfamiliar, uninformed

3 often observed or encountered — see COMMON 1

4 showing a lack of proper social reserve or modesty — see PRESUMPTUOUS 1

familiar *n* a person who has a strong liking for and trust in another — see FRIEND 1

familiarity *n* **1** the state of being in a very personal or private relationship ⟨the elderly couple enjoys a *familiarity* that is the result of many years of happy marriage⟩

syn chumminess, closeness, inseparability, intimacy, nearness

rel immediacy; affinity, kinship; commitment, devotion; affection, fondness, love; constancy, faithfulness, fidelity; amity, fellowship, friendship, goodwill; affability, conviviality, cordiality, geniality

near ant aloofness, coldness, coolness, reserve

ant distance

2 a socially improper or unsuitable act or remark — see IMPROPRIETY 2

3 knowledge gained by personal experience — see ACQUAINTANCE

familiarize *vb* **1** to give information to — see ENLIGHTEN 1

2 to impart knowledge of a new thing or situation to — see ACQUAINT 1

family *n* **1** a group of persons who come from the same ancestor ⟨the Adams *family* made remarkable contributions to American life for more than two centuries⟩

syn blood, clan, folks, house, kin, kindred, kinfolk, kinsfolk, line, lineage, people, race, stock, tribe

rel nuclear family; extended family, kith; brood; descendant (*or* descendent), issue, offspring, progeny, scion, seed; clansman, kinsman, kinswoman, relative; dynasty

near ant ancestry, birth, descent, extraction, origin, pedigree

2 one of the units into which a whole is divided on the basis of a common characteristic — see CLASS 2

family tree *n* the line of ancestors from whom a person is descended — see ANCESTRY

famine *n* a falling short of an essential or desirable amount or number — see DEFICIENCY

famished *adj* feeling a desire or need for food — see HUNGRY 1

famishment *n* a need or desire for food — see HUNGER 1

famous *adj* widely known ⟨a book about some of the most *famous* people of the last century⟩

syn celebrated, famed, noted, notorious, prominent, renowned, star, well-known

rel fabled, fabulous, legendary; infamous; distinguished, eminent, exceptional, great, illustrious, leading, notable, outstanding, prestigious, remarkable; important, significant; favorite, popular, preferred; estimable, honorable, reputable, respectable; formidable, redoubtable

near ant insignificant, unimportant; inconspicuous; undistinguished, unexceptional; unpopular

ant anonymous, obscure, unknown

fan *n* a person with a strong and habitual liking for something ⟨life-long *fans* of country and western music⟩

syn addict, aficionado, buff, bug, devotee, enthusiast, fanatic, fancier, fiend, freak, lover, maniac, nut

rel groupie; admirer, collector, connoisseur, dilettante; authority, expert; cultist, disciple, follower, votary; backer, patron, promoter, supporter; partisan, zealot; booster, rooter, well-wisher; faddist

near ant belittler, carper, critic, detractor

fan (out) *vb* **1** to arrange the parts of (something) over a wider area — see OPEN 3

2 to extend outwards from or as if from a central point — see RADIATE 1

fanatic *n* **1** a person with a strong and habitual liking for something — see FAN

2 one who is intensely or excessively devoted to a cause — see ZEALOT

fanatic *or* **fanatical** *adj* being very far from the center of public opinion — see EXTREME 2

fancier *n* a person with a strong and habitual liking for something — see FAN

fanciful *adj* **1** conceived or made without regard for reason or reality — see FANTASTIC 1

2 not real and existing only in the imagination — see IMAGINARY

fancy *adj* made or done with great care or with much detail — see ELABORATE 1

fancy *n* **1** a conception or image created by the imagination and having no objective reality — see FANTASY 1

2 a sudden impulsive and apparently unmotivated idea or action — see WHIM

3 positive regard for something — see LIKING

4 the ability to form mental images of things that either are not physically present or have never been conceived or created by others — see IMAGINATION

fancy *vb* **1** to form a mental picture of — see IMAGINE 1

2 to take pleasure in — see ENJOY 1

fanny *n* the part of the body upon which someone sits — see BUTTOCKS

fantastic *adj* **1** conceived or made without regard for reason or reality ⟨a *fantastic* scheme for getting rich quick⟩

syn absurd, bizarre, crazy, fanciful, foolish, insane, nonsensical, preposterous, unreal, wild

rel inconceivable, incredible, unbelievable; extravagant, grotesque; eccentric, odd, peculiar, strange, weird; farcical, laughable, ludicrous, ridiculous

ant realistic, reasonable

2 excitingly or mysteriously unusual — see EXOTIC

3 not real and existing only in the imagination — see IMAGINARY

4 too extraordinary or improbable to believe — see INCREDIBLE

fantasy *also* **phantasy** *n* **1** a conception or image created by the imagination and having no objective reality ⟨a constant daydreamer who started to believe his own *fantasies*⟩

syn chimera, conceit, daydream, delusion, dream, fancy, figment, hallucination, illusion, phantasm, pipe dream, unreality, vision

rel mirage; brainchild, idea; concoction, fabrication, fiction, invention; envisaging, imaging, visualization

near ant actuality, fact, reality

2 the ability to form mental images of things that either are not physically present or have never been conceived or created by others — see IMAGINATION

3 something that is the product of the imagination — see FICTION

far *adj* **1** lasting for a considerable time — see LONG 2

2 not close in time or space — see DISTANT 1

far *adv* to a great degree — see VERY 1

faraway *adj* not close in time or space — see DISTANT 1

farce *n* **1** a poor, insincere, or insulting imitation of something — see MOCKERY 1

2 humorous entertainment — see COMEDY

farcical *adj* **1** causing or intended to cause laughter — see FUNNY 1

2 so foolish or pointless as to be worthy of scornful laughter — see RIDICULOUS 1

fare *n* substances intended to be eaten — see FOOD

fare *vb* **1** to meet one's day-to-day needs — see GET ALONG 1

2 to move forward along a course — see GO 1

3 to take a meal — see DINE 1

farewell *adj* given, taken, or performed at parting — see PARTING 1

farewell *n* **1** an expression of good wishes at parting — see GOOD-BYE

2 the act of leaving a place — see DEPARTURE

3 the act or process of two or more persons going off in different directions — see PARTING

far-fetched *adj* not likely to be true or to occur — see IMPROBABLE

far-flung *adj* having considerable extent — see EXTENSIVE

farm *n* a piece of land and its buildings used to grow crops or raise livestock ⟨a *farm* that has been in the same family for five generations⟩

syn farmstead, grange, ranch

rel cropland, farmland, farmyard; farmhouse, homestead, manor, plantation; croft [*chiefly British*], station; garden, orchard

farm *vb* to work by plowing, sowing, and raising crops on ⟨we're planning on *farming* 50 acres the first year⟩

syn cultivate, tend, till

rel crop, plant; harvest, reap; harrow, hoe

farmer *n* a person who cultivates the land and grows crops on it ⟨a young *farmer* whose family has been growing wheat for many generations⟩

syn agriculturist (*or* agriculturalist), agronomist, cultivator, grower, planter, tiller

rel farmhand, gleaner, harvester, reaper; crofter [*chiefly British*], cropper, sharecropper; homesteader, nester [*West*]; granger; rancher, ranchero, ranchman

farming *adj* engaged in or concerned with agriculture — see AGRICULTURAL

farming *n* the science or occupation of cultivating the soil, producing crops, and raising livestock — see AGRICULTURE

---

syn synonym(s)   *rel* related words
ant antonym(s)   *near ant* near antonym(s)

farmstead *n* a piece of land and its buildings used to grow crops or raise livestock — see FARM

far-off *adj* not close in time or space — see DISTANT 1

far-out *adj* different from the ordinary in a way that causes curiosity or suspicion — see ODD 2

far-reaching *adj* having considerable extent — see EXTENSIVE

farsighted *adj* having or showing awareness of and preparation for the future — see FORESIGHTED

farsightedness *n* concern or preparation for the future — see FORESIGHT 2

farther *adj* resulting in an increase in amount or number — see ADDITIONAL

farther *adv* at or to a greater distance or more advanced point ⟨they had traveled *farther* down the Colorado River than any previous explorers⟩
syn beyond, further, yon, yonder

farthermost *adj* most distant from a center — see EXTREME 1

farthest *adj* most distant from a center — see EXTREME 1

fascinate *vb* 1 to attract or delight as if by magic — see CHARM 1
2 to hold the attention of as if by a spell — see ENTHRALL 1
3 to hold the attention of — see ENGAGE 1

fascinating *adj* 1 having an often mysterious or magical power to attract ⟨the *fascinating* cities and peoples of central Asia have been intriguing travelers at least since the time of Marco Polo⟩
syn alluring, appealing, attractive, bewitching, captivating, charming, elfin, enchanting, engaging, entrancing, fetching, glamorous (*also* glamourous), luring, magnetic, seductive
rel enthralling, gripping, hypnotizing, mesmerizing, riveting, spellbinding; enticing, tantalizing, tempting; exciting, haunting, interesting, intriguing, titillating; beckoning, inviting, winning; darling, delightful, pleasing
near ant boring, irksome, tedious, tiresome; abhorrent, distasteful, invidious, loathsome, obnoxious, offensive
ant repellant, repelling, repugnant, repulsive, revolting
2 holding the attention or provoking interest — see INTERESTING

fascination *n* the power of irresistible attraction — see CHARM 2

fashion *n* 1 a practice or interest that is very popular for a short time — see FAD
2 a distinctive way of putting ideas into words — see STYLE 1
3 a usual manner of behaving or doing — see HABIT
4 the means or procedure for doing something — see METHOD

fashion *vb* to bring into being by combining, shaping, or transforming materials — see MAKE 1

fashionable *adj* 1 being in the latest or current fashion — see STYLISH

2 enjoying widespread favor or approval — see POPULAR 1

fashionableness *n* the state of enjoying widespread approval — see POPULARITY

fast *adj* 1 moving, proceeding, or acting with great speed ⟨the *fast* pace of construction resulted in our new house being done ahead of schedule⟩
syn breakneck, breathless, brisk, dizzy, fleet, fleet-footed, flying, hasty, lightning, nippy, quick, rapid, rapid-fire, rattling, snappy, speedy, swift, whirlwind
rel expeditious, prompt, ready; hurried, quickened; breathtaking; energetic, strenuous, strong, vigorous
near ant crawling, dawdling, laggard, lingering, plodding, poky (*or* pokey), slowish, sluggish, unhurried; deliberate, leisurely, measured; dilatory, late
ant slow
2 firm in one's allegiance to someone or something — see FAITHFUL 1
3 firmly positioned in place and difficult to dislodge — see TIGHT 2
4 given to or marked by cheating and deception — see DISHONEST 2
5 marked by the ability to withstand stress without structural damage or distortion — see STABLE 1

fast *adv* 1 with great speed ⟨run as *fast* as you can to get help⟩
syn apace, briskly, fleetly, full tilt, hastily, posthaste, presto, pronto, quick, quickly, rapidly, snappily, soon, speedily, swift, swiftly
rel immediately, promptly, readily; impetuously, impulsively, rashly, recklessly; abruptly, suddenly; energetically, vigorously
phrases at full tilt, by leaps and bounds, in short order
near ant laggardly, lingeringly, ploddingly, sluggishly; deliberately, leisurely
ant slow, slowly
2 to a full extent or degree — see FULLY 1

fasten *vb* 1 to cause (something) to hold to another ⟨use this paperclip to *fasten* your picture to the application form⟩
syn affix, attach, fix
rel adhere, bolt, clamp, clasp, clinch, clip, glue, hang, harness, lace, lash, latch, nail, paste, pin, rivet, screw, staple, stick, strap, tack, tie, yoke; connect, join, link, unite; reattach, refasten, refix
near ant part, separate, sever; loose, loosen
ant detach, undo, unfasten
2 to put securely in place or in a desired position ⟨don't forget to *fasten* all the lines on your tent⟩
syn anchor, catch, clamp, fix, hitch, moor, secure, set
rel embed (*also* imbed), entrench (*also* intrench), implant, ingrain, lodge, wedge
near ant extract, pry, yank
ant loose, loosen, unfasten, unloose, unloosen
3 to fix (as one's attention) steadily toward a central objective — see CONCENTRATE 2

fastidious *adj* hard to please — see
FINICKY

fastness *n* **1** a high rate of movement or
performance — see SPEED

2 a structure or place from which one can
resist attack — see FORT

3 adherence to something to which one is
bound by a pledge or duty — see FIDELI-
TY

fat *adj* **1** having an excess of body fat ⟨the
popular image of Santa Claus as a *fat* man
in a red suit⟩

syn chubby, corpulent, fleshy, full, gross,
obese, overweight, plump, portly, pudgy,
roly-poly, rotund, round, tubby

rel beefy, bulky, chunky, heavy, heavyset,
stocky, stout, thick, thickset, weighty;
brawny, burly, husky; dumpy, squat, stubby; paunchy, potbellied; flabby, soft;
buxom

near ant angular, bony, gaunt, lank,
lanky, rawboned, sinewy, skinny; cadaverous, haggard, skeletal, wasted; puny,
scraggy, scrawny, slight; reedy, twiggy,
willowy

ant lean, slender, slim, spare, thin

2 containing or seeming to contain the
greatest quantity or number possible —
see FULL 1

3 having a greater than usual measure
across — see WIDE 1

4 having or being of relatively great
depth or extent from one surface to its
opposite — see THICK 1

5 producing abundantly — see FERTILE

6 yielding a profit — see PROFITABLE 1

fat *n* **1** individuals carefully selected as
being the best of a class — see ELITE

2 the state or an instance of going beyond
what is usual, proper, or needed — see
EXCESS

fatal *adj* **1** bringing about ruin or misfortune ⟨I made the *fatal* mistake of sharing
my secret with the school's biggest blab-
bermouth⟩

syn calamitous, cataclysmal (*or* cataclysmic), catastrophic, destructive, disastrous, fateful, ruinous, unfortunate

rel hapless, ill-fated, ill-starred, luckless

near ant fluky, fortuitous, fortunate,
happy, lucky, providential; auspicious,
bright, encouraging, golden, heartening,
hopeful, promising, propitious

2 likely to cause or capable of causing
death — see DEADLY

fatality *n* a person or thing harmed, lost, or
destroyed — see CASUALTY 1

fate *n* **1** a state or end that seemingly has
been decided beforehand ⟨the belief that
it was this country's *fate* to extend from
sea to sea⟩

syn circumstance, destiny, doom, fortune, lot, portion

rel accident, chance, hazard, luck; pre-
destination; consequence, effect, issue,
outcome, result, upshot

2 a condition or occurrence traceable to
a cause — see EFFECT 1

fate *vb* to determine the fate of in advance
— see DESTINE

fateful *adj* bringing about ruin or misfortune — see FATAL 1

fathead *n* a stupid person — see IDIOT

father *n* **1** a male human parent ⟨the special relationship that exists between *fathers* and sons⟩

syn dad, daddy, old man, pa, papa, pop

rel patriarch

2 a person who establishes a whole new
field of endeavor ⟨Sir Isaac Newton is regarded by many as the *father* of modern
science⟩

syn author, begetter, creator, establisher,
founder, generator, inaugurator, initiator,
instituter (*or* institutor), originator

rel conceiver, contriver, designer, formulator, innovator, inventor, spawner;
builder, maker, producer; developer, pioneer, researcher; organizer, promoter; en-
courager, inspiration, inspirer

near ant disciple, follower, supporter

3 a person specially trained and authorized to conduct religious services in a
Christian church — see CLERGYMAN

4 a person who is several generations earlier in an individual's line of descent —
see ANCESTOR 1

5 *cap* the being worshipped as the creator
and ruler of the universe — see DEITY 2

father *vb* to become the father of ⟨Paul
Revere somehow found room in his small
house for the large family he had *fa-
thered*⟩

syn beget, get, sire

rel breed, multiply, procreate, propagate,
reproduce, spawn; bear, engender, generate, produce

fatherland *n* the land of one's birth, residence, or citizenship — see COUNTRY 1

fathom *vb* to measure the depth of (as a
body of water) typically with a weighted
line — see ²SOUND 1

fatigue *n* a complete depletion of energy
or strength ⟨the day-long battle against
the blaze left firefighters in a state of utter
fatigue⟩

syn burnout, collapse, exhaustion, lassitude, prostration, tiredness, weariness

rel debilitation, enervation, faintness, feebleness, weakness; languor, lethargy, listlessness; sluggishness, slumber, stupor,
torpor; apathy, inertia, passivity

near ant energy, go, liveliness, pep, vigor,
vitality; might, potency, strength

ant refreshment, rejuvenation, revitalization

fatigue *vb* to use up all the physical energy
of — see EXHAUST 1

fatigued *adj* depleted in strength, energy,
or freshness — see WEARY 1

fatness *n* the condition of having an excess of body fat — see CORPULENCE

fatty *adj* containing animal fat especially in
unusual amounts ⟨*fatty* ground beef that
was the cheapest available⟩

syn adipose

---

syn synonym(s) *rel* related words
ant antonym(s) *near ant* near antonym(s)

rel greasy, oily

near ant fibrous, gristly, stringy, tough; nonfat

ant lean

fatuity *n* 1 a foolish act or idea — see FOLLY 1

2 lack of good sense or judgment — see FOOLISHNESS 1

3 the quality or state of lacking intelligence or quickness of mind — see STUPIDITY 1

fatuous *adj* 1 not having or showing an ability to absorb ideas readily — see STUPID 1

2 showing or marked by a lack of good sense or judgment — see FOOLISH 1

faucet *n* a fixture for controlling the flow of a liquid ⟨don't forget to turn off the *faucet*⟩

syn cock, gate, spigot, stopcock, tap, valve

rel hydrant, spout

fault *n* 1 a defect in character ⟨the common *fault* of being quick to judge others⟩

syn demerit, failing, foible, frailty, shortcoming, vice, weakness

rel blot, spot, stain; blemish, deficiency, flaw; Achilles' heel; corruption, depravity, evil, immorality, sinfulness, wickedness

near ant excellence, perfection; goodness, integrity, morality, probity, rectitude, righteousness

ant merit, virtue

2 an unintentional departure from truth or accuracy — see ERROR 1

3 responsibility for wrongdoing or failure — see BLAME 1

4 something that spoils the appearance or completeness of a thing — see BLEMISH

5 the state of being held as the cause of something that needs to be set right — see RESPONSIBILITY 1

fault *vb* to express one's unfavorable opinion of the worth or quality of — see CRITICIZE

faultfinder *n* a person given to harsh judgments and to finding faults — see CRITIC 1

faultfinding *adj* given to making or expressing unfavorable judgments about things — see CRITICAL 1

faultily *adv* in a mistaken or inappropriate way — see WRONGLY

faultless *adj* 1 being entirely without fault or flaw — see PERFECT 1

2 free from guilt or blame — see INNOCENT 2

faultlessly *adv* without any flaws or errors — see PERFECTLY 1

faultlessness *n* the quality or state of being free from guilt or blame — see INNOCENCE 1

faulty *adj* having a fault ⟨the cause of the plane crash was traced to *faulty* wiring⟩

syn bad, defective, flawed, imperfect

rel fallible; blemished, broken, damaged, defaced, disfigured, impaired, injured, marred, spoiled; deficient, inadequate, incomplete, insufficient, wanting

near ant complete, entire, intact, whole; undamaged, unimpaired, unspoiled

ant faultless, flawless, impeccable, perfect

favor *n* 1 an act of kind assistance ⟨a good and generous friend who is always doing *favors* for others⟩

syn boon, courtesy, grace, indulgence, kindness, mercy, service, turn

rel dispensation, waiver; advantage, benefit, blessing, godsend, manna; liberty, license (*or* licence), privilege

near ant hindrance, impediment, obstacle

2 a feeling of great approval and liking — see ADMIRATION 1

3 an acceptance of something as satisfactory — see APPROVAL 1

4 an attitude that always favors one way of feeling or acting especially without considering any other possibilities — see BIAS

5 positive regard for something — see LIKING

6 the state of enjoying widespread approval — see POPULARITY

favor *vb* 1 to do a service or favor for — see OBLIGE 1

2 to have a favorable opinion of — see APPROVE (OF)

3 to show partiality toward — see PREFER 1

favorable *adj* 1 expressing approval ⟨*favorable* reviews for the movie were few⟩

syn admiring, applauding, appreciative, approving, commendatory, complimentary, friendly, good, positive

rel eulogistic, laudatory, praiseful; respectful, supportive; adulatory, worshipful

near ant captious, carping, caviling (*or* cavilling), censuring, hypercritical, overcritical

ant adverse, disapproving, negative, unappreciative, uncomplimentary, unfavorable, unfriendly

2 pointing toward a happy outcome ⟨*favorable* conditions for opening a new business⟩

syn auspicious, bright, encouraging, golden, heartening, hopeful, promising, propitious

rel fortunate, happy, lucky, providential; advantageous, beneficial, profitable

near ant unfortunate, unhappy, unlucky; calamitous, catastrophic, disastrous, fatal, ruinous

ant discouraging, disheartening, futureless, hopeless, inauspicious, unfavorable, unpromising

3 conferring benefits; promoting or contributing to personal or social well-being — see BENEFICIAL

4 showing or expressing acceptance or approval — see POSITIVE

favorably *adv* in a pleasing way — see WELL 5

favored *adj* 1 granted special treatment or attention — see DARLING 1

2 singled out from a number or group as more to one's liking — see SELECT 1

favorite *adj* granted special treatment or attention — see DARLING 1

favorite *n* a person or thing that is preferred over others ⟨the youngest child was always Mother's *favorite*⟩
syn darling, minion, pet, preference
rel beloved, dear; jewel, prize, treasure
near ant abomination, anathema, bête noire, bugbear

fawn *vb* to use flattery or the doing of favors in order to win approval especially from a superior ⟨a student who could not wait to *fawn* over the new teacher⟩
syn fuss, kowtow, toady
rel drool, gush, slaver, slobber; endear, ingratiate; court, woo; adulate, idolize, worship; blandish, cajole, coax, flatter, soft-soap; cower, cringe, grovel; abase, debase, demean; defer, submit, yield
phrases curry favor
near ant despise, disdain, scorn; gibe (*or* jibe), jeer, scoff; brave, challenge, defy

fawner *n* a person who flatters another in order to get ahead — see SYCOPHANT

fay *adj* given to good-natured joking or teasing — see PLAYFUL

fay *n* an imaginary being usually having a small human form and magical powers — see FAIRY

faze *vb* to throw into a state of self-conscious distress — see EMBARRASS 1

fealty *n* adherence to something to which one is bound by a pledge or duty — see FIDELITY

fear *n* the emotion experienced in the presence or threat of danger ⟨the sight of the headless horseman filled the schoolmaster with *fear*⟩
syn alarm, anxiety, apprehension, consternation, dread, fearfulness, fright, horror, panic, terror, trepidation
rel phobia; creeps, jitters, nervousness, willies; pang, qualm, twinge; agitation, discomposure, disquiet, perturbation; concern, dismay, worry; cowardice, faint-heartedness, timidity, timorousness
near ant aplomb, assurance, boldness, confidence, self-assurance, self-confidence; courage, dauntlessness, fearlessness, fortitude

fear *vb* to experience concern or anxiety — see WORRY 1

fearful *adj* **1** causing fear ⟨the *fearful* roar of a lion⟩
syn alarming, dire, direful, dreadful, fearsome, forbidding, formidable, frightening, frightful, hair-raising, horrendous, horrible, horrifying, intimidating, redoubtable, scary, shocking, terrible, terrifying
rel daunting, disconcerting, discouraging, dismaying, disquieting, distressing, disturbing, perturbing, startling, threatening, troubling, trying; creepy, eerie (*also* eery), weird; ghastly, gruesome, nightmarish

near ant comforting, consoling, inviting, reassuring, soothing; nonthreatening
2 easily frightened — see SHY 1
3 extreme in degree, power, or effect — see INTENSE
4 filled with fear or dread — see AFRAID 1

fearfulness *n* the emotion experienced in the presence or threat of danger — see FEAR

fearless *adj* feeling or displaying no fear by temperament — see BRAVE

fearlessness *n* strength of mind to carry on in spite of danger — see COURAGE

fearsome *adj* causing fear — see FEARFUL 1

feasible *adj* capable of being done or carried out — see POSSIBLE 1

feast *n* a large fancy meal often accompanied by ceremony or entertainment ⟨some 90 Native Americans showed up for the *feast* put on by the Pilgrims at Plymouth⟩
syn banquet, dinner, feed, spread
rel chow, repast; blowout, festival, fete (*or* fête), gala, party, shindig; festivity; barbecue, clambake, cookout, fry, luau, roast

feast *vb* to entertain with a fancy meal ⟨the returning war heroes were *feasted* all over the country⟩
syn banquet, dine, junket, regale
rel cater, feed; fete (*or* fête), honor

feat *n* **1** an act of notable skill, strength, or cleverness ⟨Washington's legendary *feat* of tossing a silver dollar across the Rappahannock River⟩
syn deed, exploit, stunt, trick
rel accomplishment, achievement, coup; adventure; performance
2 something done by someone — see ACTION 1

feather *n* **1** a number of persons or things that are grouped together because they have something in common — see SORT 1
2 dressy clothing — see FINERY

featherbrained *adj* lacking in seriousness or maturity — see GIDDY 1

feathery *adj* having little weight — see ¹LIGHT 1

feature *n* something that sets apart an individual from others of the same kind — see CHARACTERISTIC

feature *vb* to indicate the importance of by giving prominent display — see EMPHASIZE

feces *n pl* solid matter discharged from an animal's alimentary canal — see DROPPING 1

fecund *adj* producing abundantly — see FERTILE

fed up *adj* having one's patience, interest, or pleasure exhausted — see WEARY 2

federate *vb* to form or enter into an association that furthers the interests of its members — see ALLY

federation *n* an association of persons, parties, or states for mutual assistance and protection — see CONFEDERACY

fee *n* the amount of money that is demanded as payment for something — see PRICE 1

feeble *adj* lacking bodily strength — see WEAK 1

feebleness *n* the quality or state of lacking physical strength or vigor — see WEAKNESS 1

feed *n* 1 a large fancy meal often accompanied by ceremony or entertainment — see FEAST

2 food eaten or prepared for eating at one time — see MEAL

feed *vb* 1 to provide food or meals for ⟨a charity dedicated to *feeding* the hungry⟩
syn board, cater, provision
rel serve, wait; nourish, nurture; banquet, dine, feast, regale; mess

2 to put (something) into the possession of someone for use or consumption — see FURNISH

3 to take a meal — see DINE 1

feed (on) *vb* to seize and eat (something) as prey — see PREY

feel *n* an indefinite physical response to a stimulus — see SENSATION 1

feel *vb* 1 to have a vague awareness of ⟨I *feel* trouble brewing in the town⟩
syn perceive, scent, see, sense, smell, taste
rel behold, discern, observe, view; ascertain, discover, learn; anticipate, expect, foresee

2 to come into bodily contact with (something) so as to perceive a slight pressure on the skin — see TOUCH 1

3 to come to a knowledge of (something) by living through it — see EXPERIENCE

4 to have as an opinion — see BELIEVE 2

5 to search for something blindly or uncertainly — see GROPE

feel (for) *vb* to have sympathy for — see PITY

feeling *n* 1 a subjective response to a person, thing, or situation ⟨an overall *feeling* of happiness about their new home⟩
syn emotion, passion, sentiment
rel impression, perception, sense; attitude, outlook, perspective, viewpoint; belief, opinion, view; responsiveness, sensibility, sensitiveness, sensitivity

2 **feelings** *pl* general emotional condition ⟨a remark that thoughtlessly hurt her *feelings*⟩
syn heartstrings, passions, sensibilities
rel cheer, frame, humor, mode, mood, temper

3 an idea that is believed to be true or valid without positive knowledge — see OPINION 1

4 an indefinite physical response to a stimulus — see SENSATION 1

5 sorrow or the capacity to feel sorrow for another's suffering or misfortune — see SYMPATHY 1

6 the capacity for feeling for another's unhappiness or misfortune — see HEART 1

feign *vb* to present a false appearance of ⟨I would never *feign* illness just to get out of a test⟩
syn affect, assume, counterfeit, fake, pretend, profess, put on, sham, simulate

rel act, dissemble, impersonate, masquerade; forge, imitate; camouflage, conceal, disguise, mask; bluff, feint; malinger

feigned *adj* 1 lacking in natural or spontaneous quality — see ARTIFICIAL 1

2 not being or expressing what one appears to be or express — see INSINCERE

felicitate *vb* to express to (someone) admiration for his or her success or good fortune — see CONGRATULATE

felicitations *n pl* best wishes — see COMPLIMENTS

felicitous *adj* 1 giving pleasure or contentment to the mind or senses — see PLEASANT

2 meeting the requirements of a purpose or situation — see FIT 1

felicitously *adv* in a pleasing way — see WELL 5

felicitousness *n* the quality or state of being especially suitable or fitting — see APPROPRIATENESS

felicity *n* 1 a feeling or state of well-being and contentment — see HAPPINESS 1

2 something that provides happiness or does good for a person or thing — see BLESSING 2

feline *n* a small domestic animal known for catching mice — see CAT 1

fell *adj* 1 likely to cause or capable of causing death — see DEADLY

2 violently unfriendly or aggressive in disposition — see FIERCE 1

fell *vb* 1 to strike (someone) so forcefully as to cause a fall ⟨a boxer who was often *felled* in the first round⟩
syn bowl (down *or* over), down, drop, floor, knock (down *or* over), level
rel hit, jab, poke, punch, smite, sock, strike, whack

2 to bring down by cutting ⟨the settlers began the daunting task of *felling* the mighty trees that blanketed the island⟩
syn chop (down), cut (down), hew, mow
rel bulldoze, flatten, level, raze, tear down

3 to deprive of life — see KILL 1

fellow *n* 1 a male romantic companion — see BOYFRIEND

2 a person frequently seen in the company of another — see ASSOCIATE 1

3 an adult male human being — see MAN 1

4 either of a pair matched in one or more qualities — see MATE 1

5 one that is equal to another in status, achievement, or value — see EQUAL

fellowship *n* 1 a friendly relationship marked by ready communication and mutual understanding — see RAPPORT

2 a group of persons formally joined together for some common interest — see ASSOCIATION 2

3 kindly concern, interest, or support — see GOODWILL 1

4 the body of people in a profession or field of activity — see CORPS

5 the feeling of closeness and friendship that exists between companions — see COMPANIONSHIP

female *adj* of, relating to, or marked by qualities traditionally associated with women — see FEMININE 1

female *n* an adult female human being — see WOMAN

feminine *adj* **1** of, relating to, or marked by qualities traditionally associated with women ⟨the *feminine* furnishings suggested that the bedroom was intended for a girl⟩

syn female, womanish, womanlike, womanly

rel effeminate, girlish, sissy, unmanly; ladylike; distaff, petticoat

near ant boyish, hoydenish, tomboyish; gentlemanly

ant male, manlike, manly, mannish, masculine

2 having or displaying qualities more suitable for women than for men — see EFFEMINATE

fen *n* spongy land saturated or partially covered with water — see SWAMP

fence *n* a physical object that blocks the way — see BARRIER

fence (in) *vb* to close or shut in by or as if by barriers — see ENCLOSE 1

fend (off) *vb* to drive back — see REPEL 1

fender *n* something that serves as a protective barrier — see CUSHION

feral *adj* living outdoors without taming or domestication by humans — see WILD 1

ferment *n* a disturbed or uneasy state — see UNREST

ferment *vb* to cause or encourage the development of — see INCITE 1

ferocious *adj* **1** extreme in degree, power, or effect — see INTENSE

2 marked by bursts of destructive force or intense activity — see VIOLENT 1

3 violently unfriendly or aggressive in disposition — see FIERCE 1

ferry *vb* to support and take from one place to another — see CARRY 1

fertile *adj* producing abundantly ⟨the *fertile* mind of Leonardo da Vinci explored art, architecture, engineering, mathematics, and many other fields⟩

syn fat, fecund, fruitful, luxuriant, productive, prolific, rich

rel bearing, producing, yielding; abounding, abundant, bountiful; copious, plenteous, plentiful; blooming, bursting, flourishing, swarming, teeming, thriving; creative, inventive, original

near ant meager (*or* meagre), scant, scanty, skimpy, spare, sparse

ant barren, infertile, sterile, unfruitful, unproductive

fervency *n* depth of feeling — see ARDOR 1

fervent *adj* having or expressing great depth of feeling ⟨a *fervent* speech that called for tolerance and compassion for those who are different⟩

syn ardent, blazing, burning, charged, emotional, fervid, feverish, fiery, flaming, glowing, hot-blooded, impassioned, passionate, red-hot, vehement, warm, warm-blooded

rel gushing, maudlin, mawkish, mushy, sentimental; histrionic, melodramatic; enthusiastic, gung ho, zealous; enamored, infatuated, obsessed

phrases on fire

near ant detached, dry, impersonal, objective; reserved, undemonstrative

ant cold, cool, dispassionate, impassive, unemotional

fervid *adj* having or expressing great depth of feeling — see FERVENT

fervidness *n* depth of feeling — see ARDOR 1

fervor *n* depth of feeling — see ARDOR 1

festival *n* a time or program of special events and entertainment in honor of something ⟨tourists flock to the town for its annual strawberry *festival*⟩

syn carnival, celebration, festivity, fete (*or* fête), fiesta, gala, jubilee

rel jamboree, jollification, merrymaking, revel, revelry; exhibit, exhibition, exposition, fair, show; exercises, honors

festive *adj* indicative of or marked by high spirits or good humor — see MERRY

festivity *n* **1** a mood characterized by high spirits and amusement and often accompanied by laughter — see MIRTH

2 a time or program of special events and entertainment in honor of something — see FESTIVAL

3 joyful or festive activity — see MERRYMAKING

fetch *vb* to have a price of — see COST

fetching *adj* having an often mysterious or magical power to attract — see FASCINATING 1

fetch up *vb* to bring (something) to a standstill — see ¹HALT 1

fete *or* **fête** *vb* to show appreciation, respect, or affection for (someone) with a public celebration — see HONOR

fete *or* **fête** *n* **1** a social gathering — see PARTY 1

2 a time or program of special events and entertainment in honor of something — see FESTIVAL

fetid *adj* having an unpleasant smell — see MALODOROUS

fetish *also* **fetich** *n* **1** something about which one is constantly thinking or concerned — see FIXATION

2 something worn or kept to bring good luck or keep away evil — see CHARM 1

fetter *n* **1** something that limits one's freedom of action or choice — see RESTRICTION 1

2 something that makes movement or progress more difficult — see ENCUMBRANCE

3 something that physically prevents free movement — see BOND 1

fetter *vb* **1** to confine or restrain with or as if with chains — see BIND 1

2 to create difficulty for the work or activity of — see HAMPER

---

syn synonym(s)   **rel** related words
ant antonym(s)   **near ant** near antonym(s)

fettle *n* a state of being or fitness — see CONDITION 1

fever *n* an abnormal state that disrupts a plant's or animal's normal bodily functioning — see DISEASE

feverish *adj* **1** being in a state of increased activity or agitation ⟨scary stories that were the product of a *feverish* imagination⟩
syn agitated, excited, frenzied, heated, hectic, overactive, overwrought
rel ardent, burning, fervent, fiery, impassioned; high-strung, jittery, jumpy, nervous
phrases keyed up
near ant calm, composed, cool, serene, tranquil
2 having or expressing great depth of feeling — see FERVENT
3 marked by great and often stressful excitement or activity — see FURIOUS 1

few *n* a small number ⟨a *few* of the songs on the album are good, but most are forgettable⟩
syn handful, scattering, smattering, sprinkle, sprinkling
rel minority
near ant majority, most; abundance, excess, plenty, surplus
ant army, crowd, flock, horde, host, legion, many, mountain, multitude

fiancé *n* the person to whom one is engaged to be married — see BETROTHED

fiancée *n* the person to whom one is engaged to be married — see BETROTHED

fiasco *n* something that has failed — see FAILURE 3

fiat *n* an order publicly issued by an authority — see EDICT 1

fib *n* a statement known by its maker to be untrue and made in order to deceive — see LIE

fib *vb* to make a statement one knows to be untrue — see LIE 1

fibber *n* a person who tells lies — see LIAR

fiber *n* the strength of mind that enables a person to endure pain or hardship — see FORTITUDE

fibrous *adj* resembling or having the texture of a mass of strings — see STRINGY

fickle *adj* **1** liable to change frequently, suddenly, or unexpectedly ⟨a *fickle* friendship that was on and off over the years⟩
syn capricious, changeable, changeful, flickery, fluctuating, fluid, inconstant, mercurial, mutable, temperamental, uncertain, unpredictable, unsettled, unstable, unsteady, variable, volatile
rel aimless, erratic, haphazard, irregular, random; hesitating, shilly-shallying, vacillating, wavering; undependable, unreliable, untrustworthy; adaptable, mobile, protean, versatile
near ant equable, even, uniform; abiding, durable, lasting, permanent, persistent; dependable, reliable, trustworthy
ant certain, changeless, constant, immutable, invariable, settled, stable, steady, unchangeable

2 not true in one's allegiance to someone or something — see FAITHLESS

fiction *n* something that is the product of the imagination ⟨most stories about famous outlaws of the Old West are *fictions* that have little or nothing to do with fact⟩
syn fable, fabrication, fantasy (*also* phantasy), figment, invention
rel anecdote, narrative, novel, story, tale, yarn; falsehood, fib, lie, misrepresentation, untruth
near ant actuality, reality
ant fact

fictional *adj* not real and existing only in the imagination — see IMAGINARY

fictitious *adj* not real and existing only in the imagination — see IMAGINARY

fiddle *vb* to make jerky or restless movements — see FIDGET

fiddle (around) *vb* to spend time in aimless activity ⟨we spent the snow day just *fiddling around*⟩
syn fool (around), mess (around), monkey (around), play, potter (around), putter (around), trifle
rel dally, dawdle, dillydally, hang around, hang out, idle, loaf, loll, lounge; clown (around), horse (around); tinker
near ant buckle (down)

fiddle (with) *vb* to handle thoughtlessly, ignorantly, or mischievously — see TAMPER

fiddlesticks *n pl* language, behavior, or ideas that are absurd and contrary to good sense — see NONSENSE 1

fidelity *n* adherence to something to which one is bound by a pledge or duty ⟨they have never wavered in their *fidelity* to the cause of freedom⟩
syn allegiance, constancy, dedication, devotedness, devotion, faith, faithfulness, fastness, fealty, loyalty, steadfastness
rel affection, attachment, fondness; determination, firmness, resolution; dependability, reliability, trustworthiness
near ant alienation, disaffection, estrangement, separation
ant disloyalty, faithlessness, falseness, inconstancy, infidelity, perfidiousness, perfidy, treachery

fidget *vb* to make jerky or restless movements ⟨small children are likely to *fidget* in church⟩
syn fiddle, jerk, squirm, toss, twitch, wiggle, wriggle, writhe
rel flit, flutter, twitter; quake, quiver, shake, shiver, tremble; pace
near ant relax, rest, unwind

fidgets *n pl* a state of nervousness marked by sudden jerky movements — see JUMPINESS

fie *interj* how surprising, doubtful, or unbelievable — see NO

field *n* **1** a small area of usually open land ⟨a *field* that is the frequent site of neighborhood softball games⟩
syn clearing, ground, lot, parcel, plat, plot, tract

rel common(s); grass, green, greensward, lawn; glade, grassland, heath, lea, meadow, moor, pasture

2 a region of activity, knowledge, or influence ⟨the first woman to enter the *field* of medicine⟩

syn area, arena, demesne, department, discipline, domain, line, province, realm, specialty, sphere

rel study, subject; territory, turf; business, occupation, profession, pursuit, racket, vocation

3 a part or portion having no fixed boundaries — see REGION 1

fiend *n* **1** a mean, evil, or unprincipled person — see VILLAIN

2 a person who regularly uses drugs especially illegally — see DOPER

3 a person with a strong and habitual liking for something — see FAN

4 an evil spirit — see DEMON

fiendish *adj* of, relating to, or worthy of an evil spirit ⟨a *fiendish* delight in playing cruel tricks⟩

syn demoniac (*also* demoniacal), demonic, devilish, diabolical (*or* diabolic), satanic

rel hellish, infernal; baleful, evil, sinister; malevolent, malicious, malignant; heinous, monstrous; barbarous, cruel, ferocious, inhuman, savage, vicious

near ant celestial, heavenly; beneficent, benevolent, benign, benignant; godly, holy, saintly

ant angelic

fierce *adj* **1** violently unfriendly or aggressive in disposition ⟨the Vikings had a well-earned reputation for being *fierce* warriors⟩

syn fell, ferocious, grim, savage, vicious

rel bellicose, belligerent, pugnacious, warlike; contentious, quarrelsome, truculent; menacing, threatening; bestial, brute, inhuman, inhumane; barbaric, uncivilized, wild; heartless, implacable, merciless, pitiless, relentless, ruthless, unrelenting, wanton; bloodthirsty, bloody, murderous; rapacious, ravenous, voracious

near ant amicable, congenial, friendly; compliant, submissive, tame, unaggressive; compassionate, kind, merciful; pacific, peaceable, peaceful; amiable, complaisant, obliging; human, humane; civilized, cultured

ant gentle, mild

2 extreme in degree, power, or effect — see INTENSE

3 harsh and threatening in manner or appearance — see GRIM 1

4 having or showing a bold forcefulness in the pursuit of a goal — see AGGRESSIVE 1

5 marked by bursts of destructive force or intense activity — see VIOLENT 1

6 marked by great and often stressful excitement or activity — see FURIOUS 1

fierceness *n* the quality or state of being forceful (as in expression) — see VEHEMENCE 1

fiery *adj* **1** being on fire — see ABLAZE 1

2 having a notably high temperature — see HOT 1

3 having or expressing great depth of feeling — see FERVENT

4 marked by a lively display of strong feeling — see SPIRITED 1

fiesta *n* a time or program of special events and entertainment in honor of something — see FESTIVAL

fight *n* **1** a physical dispute between opposing individuals or groups ⟨a troubled youth who got into one *fight* after another⟩

syn battle, clash, combat, conflict, contest, fracas, fray, hassle, scrap, scrimmage, scuffle, skirmish, struggle, tussle

rel pitched battle; brawl, free-for-all, melee; fisticuffs; confrontation, duel, face-off; altercation, argument, disagreement, quarrel, row, wrangle

2 a forceful effort to reach a goal or objective — see STRUGGLE 1

3 an inclination to fight or quarrel — see BELLIGERENCE

4 an often noisy or angry expression of differing opinions — see ARGUMENT 1

fight *vb* **1** to oppose (someone) in physical conflict ⟨a proud people who have fiercely *fought* all invaders of their homeland⟩

syn battle, clash (with), combat, scrimmage (with), skirmish (with), war (against)

rel duel; bash, batter, beat, buffet, hit, punch, slug, strike; box, spar; brawl; grapple, scuffle, tussle, wrestle; bump, collide

phrases fall foul (of)

near ant give up, submit, surrender

2 to strive to reduce or eliminate ⟨a civil rights leader who dedicated his life to *fighting* prejudice⟩

syn battle, combat, contend (with), counter, oppose

rel baffle, foil, frustrate, resist, thwart, withstand; confront, defy, face, meet

near ant abide, bear, endure, suffer; advocate, back, support, uphold

ant advance, encourage, foster, further, promote

3 to engage in a contest — see COMPETE

4 to express different opinions about something often angrily — see ARGUE 2

5 to refuse to give in to — see RESIST

fighter *n* **1** a person engaged in military service — see SOLDIER

2 one that engages in the sport of fighting with the fists — see BOXER

figment *n* **1** a conception or image created by the imagination and having no objective reality — see FANTASY 1

2 something that is the product of the imagination — see FICTION

figurative *adj* expressing one thing in terms normally used for another ⟨the *figurative* meaning of "allergy" is "a feeling of dislike"⟩

---

syn synonym(s)   *rel* related words
ant antonym(s)   *near ant* near antonym(s)

syn extended, metaphorical

rel allegorical, emblematic (*also* emblematical), symbolic (*also* symbolical); euphemistic

near ant nonsymbolic

ant literal, nonfigurative

figure *n* **1** a character used to represent a mathematical value — see NUMBER

2 a line that traces the outer limits of an object or surface — see OUTLINE 1

3 a person who is widely known and usually much talked about — see CELEBRITY 1

4 a small statue — see FIGURINE

5 a three-dimensional representation of the human body used especially for displaying clothes — see MANNEQUIN 1

6 a unit of decoration that is repeated all over something (as a fabric) — see PATTERN 1

7 something that visually explains or decorates a text — see ILLUSTRATION 1

8 the amount of money that is demanded as payment for something — see PRICE 1

9 the outward appearance of something as distinguished from its substance — see FORM 1

10 the type of body that a person has — see PHYSIQUE

11 figures *pl* the act or process of performing mathematical operations to find a value — see CALCULATION

figure *vb* **1** to come to a judgment after discussion or consideration — see DECIDE 1

2 to decide the size, amount, number, or distance of (something) without actual measurement — see ESTIMATE 2

3 to determine (a value) by doing the necessary mathematical operations — see CALCULATE 1

4 to have as an opinion — see BELIEVE 2

figure out *vb* to find an answer for through reasoning — see SOLVE

figurine *n* a small statue ⟨his collection of *figurines* includes toy soldiers from every war that America has fought⟩

syn figure, statuette

rel doll, marionette, puppet; bust, figurehead; carving, model, sculpture; dummy, form, mannequin

ant colossus

figuring *n* the act or process of performing mathematical operations to find a value — see CALCULATION

filch *vb* to take (something) without right and with an intent to keep — see STEAL 1

file *n* a series of persons or things arranged one behind another — see LINE 1

¹file *vb* to make smooth by friction — see GRIND 1

²file *vb* to move along with a steady regular step especially in a group — see MARCH 1

fill *n* soft material that is used to fill the hollow parts of something — see FILLING

fill *vb* **1** to put into (something) as much as can be held or contained ⟨*fill* the basket with apples⟩

syn charge, cram, heap, jam, jam-pack, load, pack, stuff

rel flood, glut, swamp; crowd, crush, press, ram, shove, squash, squeeze; refill, reload, repack

near ant lighten

ant empty

2 to close up so that no empty spaces remain ⟨before starting to paint, *fill* all the cracks with putty⟩

syn block, bung, dam, pack, plug, stop, stuff

rel choke, clog, obstruct; caulk, chink

near ant excavate, hollow (out), scoop (out)

3 to do what is required by the terms of — see FULFILL 1

filled *adj* containing or seeming to contain the greatest quantity or number possible — see FULL 1

filler *n* soft material that is used to fill the hollow parts of something — see FILLING

fill in *vb* **1** to give information to — see ENLIGHTEN 1

2 to serve as a replacement usually for a time only — see COVER 1

filling *n* soft material that is used to fill the hollow parts of something ⟨the *filling* for the parka is goose down⟩

syn fill, filler, padding, stuffing

rel interlining, lining, wadding; cushion

film *n* **1** a story told by means of a series of continuously projected pictures and a sound track — see MOVIE 1

2 the art or business of making a movie — see MOVIE 2

filmy *adj* **1** being of a material lacking in sturdiness or substance — see FLIMSY 1

2 very thin and easy to see through — see SHEER 1

filter *vb* **1** to pass through a filter — see STRAIN 2

2 to remove usually visible impurities from — see CLARIFY 1

filth *n* **1** foul matter that mars the purity or cleanliness of something ⟨the *filth* in the restaurant's kitchen was unbelievable⟩

syn dirt, grime, muck, smut, soil

rel scum, sewage, slime, sludge, swill; garbage, refuse, trash; soot; dirtiness, filthiness, foulness, griminess, grubbiness, nastiness, squalidness, uncleanliness, uncleanness

near ant cleanliness, cleanness

2 the quality or state of being obscene — see OBSCENITY 1

filthiness *n* **1** the quality or state of being obscene — see OBSCENITY 1

2 the state or quality of being dirty — see DIRTINESS 1

filthy *adj* **1** depicting or referring to sexual matters in a way that is unacceptable in polite society — see OBSCENE 1

2 not clean — see DIRTY 1

finagle *vb* to plan out usually with subtle skill or care — see ENGINEER

final *adj* **1** following all others of the same kind in order or time — see LAST

2 having been established and usually not subject to change — see FIXED 1

finale *n* the last part of a process or action ⟨the *finale* to the festivities was a grand display of fireworks⟩
syn close, closing, conclusion, consummation, end, ending, finis, finish, windup
rel apex, climax, crescendo, culmination, peak, summit, zenith; aftermath, anticlimax, coda, epilogue, postscript; tag end, tail end
near ant introduction, overture, prelude, prologue
ant beginning, dawn, opening, start

finalize *vb* to bring (something) to a state where nothing remains to be done — see FINISH 1

finally *adv* at a later time — see YET 1

finance *vb* 1 to provide money for ⟨a local business kindly *financed* the high school band's trip to New York City⟩
syn capitalize, endow, fund, stake, subsidize, underwrite
rel grubstake; aid, back, patronize, sponsor, support
2 to furnish (as an institution) with a regular source of income — see ENDOW 2

finances *n pl* available money — see FUND 2

financial *adj* of or relating to money, banking, or investments ⟨the *financial* world was watching the stock market closely⟩
syn fiscal, monetary, pecuniary
rel capitalist (*or* capitalistic), commercial, economic

find *n* something discovered — see DISCOVERY 2

find *vb* 1 to come upon after searching, study, or effort ⟨we finally *found* the information after searching dozens of Internet sites⟩
syn ascertain, descry, detect, determine, dig (up), discover, find out, get, hit (on *or* upon), hunt (down *or* up), learn, locate, run down, scare up, scout (up), track (down)
rel espy, sight, spot; look for, search (for *or* out), seek
near ant lose, mislay, misplace
ant miss, overlook, pass over
2 to come upon unexpectedly or by chance — see HAPPEN (ON *OR* UPON)

finding *n* 1 a decision made by a court or tribunal regarding a case it has heard — see SENTENCE
2 the act or process of sighting or learning the existence of something for the first time — see DISCOVERY 2

find out *vb* 1 to come to an awareness — see DISCOVER 1
2 to come upon after searching, study, or effort — see FIND 1

fine *adj* 1 consisting of very small particles ⟨the *fine* sand found on the island's beaches⟩
syn dusty, floury, powdery
rel smooth; filtered, pulverized, refined

near ant rough; unfiltered, unrefined; gravelly, gritty, sandy; pebbly, rocky, stony (*also* stoney); lumpy, mealy
ant coarse, grainy, granular, granulated
2 made or done with extreme care and accuracy ⟨the *fine* distinction between bravery and recklessness⟩
syn delicate, exact, hairline, hairsplitting, minute, nice, refined, subtle
rel nitpicking, quibbling; petty, piddling, trifling, trivial; fastidious, finicky, fussy, particular
near ant apparent, clear, obvious; broad, indefinite; careless, slapdash, slipshod, sloppy
ant coarse, inexact, rough
3 being of less than usual width — see NARROW 1
4 being to one's liking — see SATISFACTORY 1
5 free from added matter — see PURE 1
6 meeting the highest standard of accuracy — see PRECISE 1
7 of a level of quality that meets one's needs or standards — see ADEQUATE
8 of a size that is less than average — see SMALL 1
9 of the very best kind — see EXCELLENT

fine *adv* in a satisfactory way — see WELL 1

fine *n* a sum of money to be paid as a punishment ⟨a $50 *fine* for speeding⟩
syn damages, forfeit, forfeiture, mulct, penalty
rel reparations; award, compensation; indemnity

fine *vb* to establish or apply as a charge or penalty — see IMPOSE

fineness *n* 1 the quality or state of being little in size — see SMALLNESS
2 the quality or state of being very accurate — see PRECISION
3 the state or quality of having a delicate structure — see DELICACY 2

finery *n* dressy clothing ⟨the guests arrived at the wedding in all their *finery*⟩
syn array, best, bravery, caparison, feather, frippery, full dress, gaiety (*also* gayety), regalia
rel apparel, attire, costume, duds, raiment
near ant rags, tatters

finesse *n* mental skill or quickness — see DEXTERITY 1

finesse *vb* to plan out usually with subtle skill or care — see ENGINEER

finicky *adj* hard to please ⟨cats have a reputation for being *finicky* eaters⟩
syn choosy (*or* choosey), dainty, delicate, demanding, exacting, fastidious, fussy, nice, old-maidish, particular, picky
rel discerning, discriminating, insightful, knowledgeable; carping, critical; careful, meticulous, punctilious, scrupulous; queasy (*also* queazy), squeamish; peevish, petulant, prickly, touchy
near ant affable, breezy, devil-may-care, happy-go-lucky, laid-back; flexible, lax, loose; lenient, permissive; uncritical
ant undemanding, unfussy

finis *n* the last part of a process or action — see FINALE

---

syn synonym(s) *rel* related words
ant antonym(s) *near ant* near antonym(s)

finish *n* **1** the last part of a process or action — see FINALE

2 the stopping of a process or activity — see END 1

finish *vb* **1** to bring (something) to a state where nothing remains to be done ⟨we should *finish* the painting of the house by tomorrow⟩

syn complete, consummate, finalize, perfect

rel follow through, see out, stick out; accomplish, achieve, effect; discharge, execute, fulfill (*or* fulfil), perform; machine, polish, refine, round (off *or* out), shine, touch up

near ant abandon, desert, drop, forsake, quit

2 to bring (an event) to a natural or appropriate stopping point — see CLOSE 3

3 to come to an end — see CEASE 1

finished *adj* brought or having come to an end — see COMPLETE 2

finite *adj* **1** having a limit ⟨our nation's natural resources are abundant, but they are also *finite*⟩

syn limited

rel confined, restricted; definable, defined, definite, determinate; decided, established, fixed, set; exact, precise, specific

near ant unconfined, unrestricted; indefinite, indeterminate, undefinable, undefined

ant boundless, infinite, unbounded, unlimited

2 having distinct or certain limits — see LIMITED 1

fire *n* a destructive burning ⟨a number of suspicious *fires* in the neighborhood recently⟩

syn conflagration, holocaust, inferno

rel blaze, flare-up; backfire, bonfire, forest fire, wildfire; arson

fire *vb* **1** to cause (a projectile) to be driven forward with force — see SHOOT 1

2 to cause a weapon to release a missile with great force — see SHOOT 2

3 to give life, vigor, or spirit to — see ANIMATE

4 to let go from office, service, or employment — see DISMISS 1

5 to send through the air especially with a quick forward motion of the arm — see THROW

6 to set (something) on fire — see BURN 2

fire (up) *vb* to rouse to strong feeling or action — see PROVOKE 1

firearm *n* a portable weapon from which a shot is discharged by gunpowder — see GUN 1

firebrand *n* a person who stirs up public feelings especially of discontent — see AGITATOR

firebug *n* a person who deliberately and unlawfully sets fire to a building or other property — see ARSONIST

fireproof *adj* incapable of being burned — see INCOMBUSTIBLE

fireside *n* the place where one lives — see HOME 1

fireworks *n pl* an outburst or display of excited anger — see TANTRUM

firing *n* a directed propelling of a missile by a firearm or artillery piece — see SHOT

firkin *n* an enclosed wooden vessel for holding beverages — see CASK

firm *adj* **1** not showing weakness or uncertainty ⟨a friendly fellow with a ready smile and a *firm* handshake⟩

syn forceful, hearty, iron, lusty, robust, solid, stout, strong, sturdy, vigorous

rel mighty, powerful, tough, unyielding; animated, energetic, lively, spirited; certain, confident, sanguine, sure

near ant feeble, fragile, frail; limp, listless, spiritless

ant uncertain, weak

2 having a consistency that does not easily yield to pressure ⟨cold butter that was too *firm* to spread⟩

syn compact, hard, rigid, solid, stiff, unyielding

rel case-hardened, compacted, compressed, hardened, indurated, stiffened, tempered; close, dense, heavy, thick, thickset; inelastic, inflexible, ramrod, unbending; compressed, condensed; sturdy, substantial; impenetrable, impermeable, nonporous

near ant loose, scattered, thin; bendable, elastic, flexible, malleable, pliable; flaccid, floppy, limp, slack; airy, light; permeable, porous

ant flabby, soft, spongy, squashy, squishy

3 firmly positioned in place and difficult to dislodge — see TIGHT 2

4 fully committed to achieving a goal — see DETERMINED 1

5 having been established and usually not subject to change — see FIXED 1

6 marked by the ability to withstand stress without structural damage or distortion — see STABLE 1

firm *n* a commercial or industrial activity or organization — see ENTERPRISE 1

firm (up) *vb* to become physically firm or solid — see HARDEN 1

firmament *n* the expanse of air surrounding the earth — see SKY

firmly *adv* in a vigorous and forceful manner — see HARD 3

firmness *n* **1** firm or unwavering adherence to one's purpose — see DETERMINATION 1

2 the ability to withstand force or stress without being distorted, dislodged, or damaged — see STABILITY 1

first *adj* **1** coming before all others in time or order ⟨the much-studied *first*—and last—voyage of the *Titanic*⟩

syn earliest, inaugural, initial, maiden, original, pioneer, premier

rel ancient, early, primal, primary, primeval, primitive, primordial; antecedent, preceding, previous

near ant advanced, late; ensuing, following, subsequent, succeeding

ant final, last, terminal, ultimate

2 coming before all others in importance — see FOREMOST 1

3 highest in rank or authority — see HEAD

first *adv* 1 as a substitute — see INSTEAD
2 by choice or preference — see RATHER 1

first–class *adj* of the very best kind — see EXCELLENT

firsthand *adj* done or working without something else coming in between — see DIRECT 1

firstly *adv* in the beginning — see ORIGINALLY

first–rate *adj* of the very best kind — see EXCELLENT

firth *n* a part of a body of water that extends beyond the general shoreline — see GULF 1

fiscal *adj* of or relating to money, banking, or investments — see FINANCIAL

fish *vb* to search for something blindly or uncertainly — see GROPE

fishy *adj* giving good reason for being doubted, questioned, or challenged — see DOUBTFUL 2

fissure *n* an irregular usually narrow break in a surface created by pressure — see CRACK 1

fit *adj* 1 meeting the requirements of a purpose or situation ⟨clothing that is *fit* for horseback riding⟩
syn applicable, appropriate, apt, becoming, befitting, felicitous, fitting, good, happy, meet, proper, right, suitable
rel just, justified, right; needed, required, requisite; able, capable, competent, qualified, trained; acceptable, adequate, decent, satisfactory, tolerable; correct, decorous, respectable, seemly
near ant incompetent, unqualified, untrained; inadequate, intolerable, unacceptable, unsatisfactory; incorrect, indecorous, unseemly
ant improper, inapplicable, inappropriate, inapt, infelicitous, unhappy, unsuitable, wrong
2 being in a state of fitness for some experience or action — see READY 1
3 capable of or suitable for being used for a particular purpose — see USABLE 1
4 enjoying health and vigor — see HEALTHY 1
5 having the required skills for an acceptable level of performance — see COMPETENT

fit *n* 1 a sudden experiencing of a physical or mental disorder — see ATTACK 2
2 a sudden intense expression of strong feeling — see OUTBURST 1
3 an outburst or display of excited anger — see TANTRUM

fit *vb* 1 to be fitting or proper — see DO 1
2 to be in agreement on every point — see CHECK 1
3 to change (something) so as to make it suitable for a new use or situation — see ADAPT

4 to make competent (as by training, skill, or ability) for a particular office or function — see QUALIFY 2
5 to make or have room for — see ACCOMMODATE 1
6 to make ready in advance — see PREPARE 1

fit (in *or* **into)** *vb* to put among or between others — see INSERT

fit (out) *vb* to provide (someone) with what is needed for a task or activity — see FURNISH 1

fitful *adj* lacking in steadiness or regularity of occurrence ⟨a night of *fitful* sleep did not leave me feeling well rested the next morning⟩
syn casual, choppy, discontinuous, erratic, intermittent, irregular, occasional, spasmodic, sporadic, spotty, unsteady
rel convulsive, sudden, violent; broken, disconnected, fragmentary, interrupted; desultory, haphazard, hit-or-miss, random; changing, fluctuating, unstable, varying, wavering; changeable, fickle, variable
near ant equable, even, stable, uniform; unchanging, unvarying, unwavering; methodical, orderly, systematic
ant constant, continuous, regular, steady

fitness *n* 1 the condition of being sound in body — see HEALTH
2 the quality or state of being especially suitable or fitting — see APPROPRIATENESS

fitting *adj* meeting the requirements of a purpose or situation — see FIT 1

fittingly *adv* in a manner suitable for the occasion or purpose — see PROPERLY

fittingness *n* the quality or state of being especially suitable or fitting — see APPROPRIATENESS

fix *n* 1 a difficult, puzzling, or embarrassing situation from which there is no easy escape — see PREDICAMENT
2 something given or promised in order to improperly influence a person's conduct or decision — see BRIBE

fix *vb* 1 to arrange something in a certain spot or position — see PLACE 1
2 to cause (something) to hold to another — see FASTEN 1
3 to come to an agreement or decision concerning the details of — see ARRANGE
4 to decide upon (the time or date for an event) usually from a position of authority — see APPOINT 1
5 to make ready in advance — see PREPARE 1
6 to put into good shape or working order again — see MEND 1
7 to put securely in place or in a desired position — see FASTEN 2
8 to set solidly in or as if in surrounding matter — see ENTRENCH

fixable *adj* capable of being corrected — see REMEDIABLE

fixation *n* something about which one is constantly thinking or concerned ⟨their

syn synonym(s)   *rel* related words
ant antonym(s)   *near ant* near antonym(s)

weight is an unfortunate *fixation* for many teenagers⟩

syn fetish (*also* fetich), idée fixe, mania, obsession, preoccupation, prepossession

rel complex, hang-up, problem; compulsion, craving, enthusiasm, fascination, infatuation, passion; idiosyncrasy, quirk; penchant, predilection, proclivity

near ant apathy, indifference, unconcern

fixed *adj* **1** having been established and usually not subject to change ⟨the baseball card dealer's prices were *fixed*, so bargaining was not an option⟩

syn certain, determinate, final, firm, flat, frozen, hard, hard-and-fast, set, settled, stable

rel nonadjustable, nonnegotiable, unchangeable; constant, steady, unchanging, uniform, unwavering; definite, exact, explicit, specific; stated, stipulated

near ant adjustable, changeable, negotiable; indefinite, unspecified

2 not capable of changing or being changed — see INFLEXIBLE 1

fixedness *n* the state of continuing without change — see CONSTANCY 1

fizz *n* a sound similar to the speech sound \s\ stretched out — see HISS 1

fizz *vb* to make a sound like that of stretching out the speech sound \s\ — see HISS

fizzle *n* **1** a falling short of one's goals — see FAILURE 2

2 something that has failed — see FAILURE 3

fjord *or* **fiord** *n* a part of a body of water that extends beyond the general shoreline — see GULF 1

flabbergast *vb* to make a strong impression on (someone) with something unexpected — see SURPRISE 1

flabbergasted *adj* **1** affected with sudden and great wonder or surprise — see THUNDERSTRUCK

2 filled with amazement or wonder — see OPENMOUTHED

flabbergasting *adj* causing a strong emotional reaction because unexpected — see SURPRISING 1

flabby *adj* giving easily to the touch — see SOFT 3

flaccid *adj* not stiff in structure — see LIMP 1

flag *n* **1** a piece of cloth with a special design that is used as an emblem or for signaling ⟨the *flags* of both countries were prominently displayed at the treaty signing⟩

syn banner, colors, ensign, guidon, jack, pennant, pennon, standard, streamer

rel bunting; black flag, Jolly Roger, union jack, white flag; semaphore, signaler; badge, coat of arms, crest, insignia

2 an object intended to give public notice or warning — see SIGNAL 1

¹flag *vb* **1** to be limp from lack of water or vigor — see DROOP

2 to lose bodily strength or vigor — see WEAKEN 2

²flag *vb* to direct or notify by a movement or gesture — see MOTION

flagellate *vb* to strike repeatedly with something long and thin or flexible — see WHIP 1

flagon *n* a handled container for holding and pouring liquids that usually has a lip or a spout — see PITCHER

flagrant *adj* very noticeable especially for being incorrect or bad — see EGREGIOUS

flail *vb* **1** to move or cause to move with a striking motion — see FLAP

2 to strike repeatedly with something long and thin or flexible — see WHIP 1

flair *n* a special and usually inborn ability — see TALENT

flake *n* a small flat piece separated from a whole — see CHIP 1

flaky *adj* having a texture that readily breaks into little pieces under pressure — see CRISP 1

flamboyance *n* excessive or unnecessary display — see OSTENTATION

flamboyant *adj* **1** likely to attract attention — see NOTICEABLE

2 excessively showy — see GAUDY

flamboyantly *adv* in a bright and showy way — see GAILY 3

flame *n* a person with whom one is in love — see SWEETHEART

flame *vb* **1** to be on fire especially brightly — see BURN 1

2 to develop suddenly and violently — see ERUPT 2

3 to shine with a bright harsh light — see GLARE 1

4 to shoot forth bursts of light — see FLASH 1

flaming *adj* **1** being on fire — see ABLAZE 1

2 having or expressing great depth of feeling — see FERVENT

flammable *adj* capable of catching or being set on fire — see COMBUSTIBLE

flank *n* a place, space, or direction away from or beyond a central point or line — see SIDE 1

flank *vb* to be adjacent to — see ADJOIN 1

flanking *adj* having a border in common — see ADJACENT

flap *vb* to move or cause to move with a striking motion ⟨the stirring sight of a huge flock of geese *flapping* their wings⟩

syn beat, flail, flop, flutter, whip

rel bang, batter, buffet, knock, pound, smack, spank, thump; flick, flicker, flit; oscillate, sway, swing; undulate, wave; palpitate, pulse, throb

flapjack *n* a flat cake made from thin batter and cooked on both sides (as on a griddle) — see PANCAKE

flare *n* **1** a sudden and usually temporary growth of activity — see OUTBREAK

2 a sudden intense expression of strong feeling — see OUTBURST 1

3 the steady giving off of the form of radiation that makes vision possible — see LIGHT 1

flare *vb* to shine with a bright harsh light — see GLARE 1

flare (out) *vb* to arrange the parts of (something) over a wider area — see OPEN 3

flare (up) *vb* 1 to become very angry — see BLOW UP

2 to develop suddenly and violently — see ERUPT 2

flare–up *n* 1 a sudden and usually temporary growth of activity — see OUTBREAK

2 a sudden intense expression of strong feeling — see OUTBURST 1

flash *adj* lasting only for a short time — see MOMENTARY

flash *n* 1 a sudden and usually temporary growth of activity — see OUTBREAK

2 a sudden intense expression of strong feeling — see OUTBURST 1

3 a very small space of time — see INSTANT

4 something extraordinary or surprising — see WONDER 1

flash *vb* 1 to shoot forth bursts of light ⟨the actress's diamond necklace *flashed* as she hurried on stage to accept the award⟩

syn flame, glance, gleam, glimmer, glint, glisten, glister, glitter, scintillate, shimmer, sparkle, twinkle, wink

rel beam, radiate, shine; bedazzle, blind, daze, dazzle; blaze, burn, flare, glare, glow

2 to present so as to invite notice or attention — see SHOW 1

3 to shine with light at regular intervals — see BLINK 1

flashily *adv* in a bright and showy way — see GAILY 3

flashiness *n* excessive or unnecessary display — see OSTENTATION

flashy *adj* 1 attractively eye-catching in style — see JAZZY 1

2 excessively showy — see GAUDY

flat *adj* 1 being neither more nor less than a certain amount, number, or extent — see EVEN 1

2 causing weariness, restlessness, or lack of interest — see BORING

3 having a surface without bends, breaks, or irregularities — see LEVEL

4 having been established and usually not subject to change — see FIXED 1

5 having no exceptions or restrictions — see ABSOLUTE 2

6 lacking a surface luster or gloss — see MATTE

7 lacking in qualities that make for spirit and character — see WISHY-WASHY 1

8 lacking in taste or flavor — see INSIPID 1

flat *adv* to a full extent or degree — see FULLY 1

flat *n, chiefly British* a room or set of rooms in a private house or a block used as a separate dwelling place — see APARTMENT 1

flatten *vb* to make free from breaks, curves, or bumps — see EVEN 1

flatter *vb* 1 to praise too much ⟨the billionaire had an army of assistants who *flattered* him at every opportunity⟩

syn adulate, blarney, overpraise, softsoap

rel blandish, cajole, coax, wheedle; fawn, kowtow, toady; idolize, worship; eulogize, extol (*also* extoll), laud, praise; applaud, commend, compliment; congratulate, felicitate; drool, gush, slaver, slobber; endear, ingratiate; court, woo

near ant bad-mouth, belittle, decry, depreciate, disparage, put down

2 to think highly of (oneself) — see PRIDE

flattery *n* excessive praise ⟨a talk show host who is known for charming her guests with *flattery*⟩

syn adulation, blarney, overpraise, soft soap

rel allurements, blandishments, endearments; compliments, congratulations, felicitations, greetings, regards, respects; adoration, idolatry, worship; cajolery, endearment, ingratiation; acclaim, applause, commendation, praise

near ant bad-mouthing, belittlement, depreciation, detraction, disparagement, put-down

flatware *n* eating and serving utensils — see TABLEWARE 1

flaunt *vb* to present so as to invite notice or attention — see SHOW 1

flaunting *n* an outward and often exaggerated indication of something abstract (as a feeling) for effect — see SHOW 1

flavor *n* 1 a special quality or impression associated with something — see AURA

2 something (as a spice or herb) that adds an agreeable or interesting taste to food — see SEASONING 1

3 the property of a substance that can be identified by the sense of taste — see TASTE 1

flavor *vb* to make more pleasant to the taste by adding something intensely flavored — see SEASON 1

flavorful *adj* very pleasing to the sense of taste — see DELICIOUS 1

flavoring *n* something (as a spice or herb) that adds an agreeable or interesting taste to food — see SEASONING 1

flavorless *adj* lacking in taste or flavor — see INSIPID 1

flaw *n* something that spoils the appearance or completeness of a thing — see BLEMISH

flaw *vb* to reduce the soundness, effectiveness, or perfection of — see DAMAGE 1

flawed *adj* having a fault — see FAULTY

flawless *adj* being entirely without fault or flaw — see PERFECT 1

flawlessly *adv* without any flaws or errors — see PERFECTLY 1

flaxen *adj* of a pale yellow or yellowish brown color — see BLOND

flay *vb* 1 to criticize (someone) severely or angrily especially for personal failings — see SCOLD

---

syn synonym(s)   *rel* related words
ant antonym(s)   *near ant* near antonym(s)

2 to remove the natural covering of — see PEEL

fleck *n* **1** a small area that is different (as in color) from the main part — see SPOT 1

2 a very small piece — see BIT 1

fleck *vb* to mark with small spots especially unevenly — see SPOT

flecked *adj* marked with spots — see SPOTTED 1

fledgling *n* a person who is just starting out in a field of activity — see BEGINNER

flee *vb* **1** to cease to be visible — see DISAPPEAR

2 to get free from a dangerous or confining situation — see ESCAPE 1

3 to hasten away from something dangerous or frightening — see RUN 2

fleece *n* the hairy covering of a mammal especially when fine, soft, and thick — see FUR 1

fleece *vb* to rob by the use of trickery or threats ⟨swindlers who use the telephone to *fleece* senior citizens out of their savings⟩

syn bleed, cheat, chisel, cozen, defraud, gyp, hustle, mulct, rook, shortchange, skin, squeeze, stick, sting, swindle, victimize

rel extort, wrench, wrest, wring; gouge, overcharge, soak; exploit, milk; deceive, dupe, fool, gull, trick; rope (in); betray, double-cross

fleecy *adj* covered with or as if with hair — see HAIRY 1

fleet *adj* moving, proceeding, or acting with great speed — see FAST 1

fleet *n* a group of vehicles traveling together or under one management ⟨a *fleet* of buses rolling down the highway⟩

syn armada, caravan, cavalcade, line, motorcade, train

rel convoy, flotilla, navy; column, cortege (*also* cortège), parade, procession

fleet–footed *adj* moving, proceeding, or acting with great speed — see FAST 1

fleeting *adj* lasting only for a short time — see MOMENTARY

fleetly *adv* with great speed — see FAST 1

fleetness *n* a high rate of movement or performance — see SPEED

flesh *n* animal and especially mammal tissue used as food — see MEAT 1

fleshiness *n* **1** the condition of having an excess of body fat — see CORPULENCE

2 the quality or state of being full of juice — see SUCCULENCE

fleshly *adj* **1** having to do with life on earth especially as opposed to that in heaven — see EARTHLY

2 of or relating to the human body — see PHYSICAL 1

3 pleasing to the physical senses — see SENSUAL

fleshy *adj* **1** full of juice — see JUICY

2 having an excess of body fat — see FAT 1

flexible *adj* **1** capable of being readily changed ⟨fortunately, Mom has a very *flexible* schedule for her office job⟩

syn adaptable, adjustable, alterable, changeable, elastic, fluid, malleable, modifiable, variable

rel changing, fluctuating, inconstant, unstable, unsteady, varying

near ant constant, stable, steady, unchanging, uniform, unvarying

ant established, fixed, immutable, inelastic, inflexible, invariable, nonmalleable, ramrod, set, unalterable, unchangeable

2 not bound by rigid standards — see EASYGOING 2

3 able to bend easily without breaking — see WILLOWY

4 able to revert to original size and shape after being stretched, squeezed, or twisted — see ELASTIC 1

flick *vb* to make an irregular series of quick, sudden movements — see FLIT

flicker *n* a sudden and usually temporary growth of activity — see OUTBREAK

flicker *vb* to make an irregular series of quick, sudden movements — see FLIT

flickery *adj* likely to change frequently, suddenly, or unexpectedly — see FICKLE 1

flier *or* **flyer** *n* **1** a risky undertaking — see GAMBLE

2 one who flies or is qualified to fly an aircraft or spacecraft — see PILOT

3 a short printed publication with no cover or with a paper cover — see PAMPHLET

¹flight *n* the act or an instance of getting free from danger or confinement — see ESCAPE 1

²flight *n* travel through the air by the use of wings ⟨for centuries people had been fascinated by the *flight* of birds⟩

syn flying

rel aviation; aeronautics; ballooning, gliding, skydiving, soaring

flightiness *n* **1** a lack of seriousness often at an improper time — see FRIVOLITY 1

2 a state of nervousness marked by sudden jerky movements — see JUMPINESS

flighty *adj* **1** easily excited by nature — see EXCITABLE

2 lacking in seriousness or maturity — see GIDDY 1

flimsy *adj* **1** being of a material lacking in sturdiness or substance ⟨a *flimsy* scarf that was more for decoration than for warmth⟩

syn filmy, gauzy, gossamer, gossamery, insubstantial, unsubstantial

rel dainty, delicate, fine; feeble, fragile, frail; sheer, transparent

near ant durable, lasting, tough; coarse, heavy, rough, rude

ant sturdy, substantial

2 not likely to be true or to occur — see IMPROBABLE

flinch *vb* to draw back in fear, pain, or disgust ⟨there are some patients who *flinch* at the mere sight of a needle⟩

syn blench, quail, recoil, shrink, wince

rel blanch, pale, whiten; quake, quiver, shake, shudder, tremble; crouch, squinch;

jerk, start, twitch; recede, retire, retreat, withdraw; falter, hesitate, reel, waver

near ant advance, approach, near; confront, challenge, defy, face

fling *n* **1** a time or instance of carefree fun ⟨most families spend Labor Day weekend having one last summer *fling*⟩

syn binge, frolic, gambol, lark, revel, rollick, romp, spree

rel caper, escapade, prank; antic, monkeyshine(s), shenanigans; field day; festivity, merriment, merrymaking; enjoyment, indulgence, pleasure, self-indulgence; amusement, diversion, entertainment, recreation

2 an effort to do or accomplish something — see ATTEMPT

fling *vb* to send through the air especially with a quick forward motion of the arm — see THROW

fling (off or away) *vb* to get rid of as useless or unwanted — see DISCARD

flinty *adj* **1** given to exacting standards of discipline and self-restraint — see SEVERE 1

2 harsh and threatening in manner or appearance — see GRIM 1

flip *adj* making light of something usually regarded as serious or sacred — see FLIPPANT

flip *vb* **1** to become very angry — see BLOW UP

2 to change the position of (an object) so that the opposite side or end is showing — see REVERSE 2

3 to yield to mental or emotional stress — see CRACK 1

flippancy *n* a lack of seriousness often at an improper time — see FRIVOLITY 1

flippant *adj* making light of something usually regarded as serious or sacred ⟨his *flippant* comment that the poor save on taxes offended many people⟩

syn facetious, flip, pert, smart, smart-alecky (*or* smart-aleck)

rel flighty, frivolous; cheeky, cocky, cute, fresh, impertinent, impish, impudent, mischievous, playful, roguish, sassy, saucy, waggish; disrespectful, rude; breezy, casual, glib, inappropriate, thoughtless

near ant grave, serious, sober, solemn, somber (*or* sombre)

ant earnest, sincere

flirt *vb* to show a liking for someone of the opposite sex just for fun ⟨the servers at that restaurant *flirt* with all the customers⟩

syn dally, frivol, trifle

rel josh, kid, put on, razz, rib, tease; fool, lead on, string along; play (with), toy (with)

flit *vb* to make an irregular series of quick, sudden movements ⟨bargain hunters at the flea market *flitted* from table to table like hummingbirds in a garden⟩

syn dance, dart, flick, flicker, flutter, zip

rel dash, fly, sail, shoot, speed, sprint, zoom; scamper, scud, scurry, scuttle, skip, skitter; meander, ramble, roam, wander

near ant float, hang, hover

float *n* a structure used by boats and ships for taking on or landing cargo and passengers — see DOCK

float *vb* to rest or move along the surface of a liquid or in the air ⟨a canoe *floating* down the river⟩ ⟨particles of dust *floating* in the air⟩

syn drift, glide, hang, hover, poise, ride, sail, waft

rel bob, dangle, suspend; buoy; balloon, raft

near ant dive, lunge, plunge; dip, immerse, submerge, submerse

ant settle, sink

flock *n* **1** a great number of persons or things gathered together — see CROWD 1

2 a group of domestic animals assembled or herded together — see HERD

flock *vb* to move upon or fill (something) in great numbers — see CROWD 2

flog *vb* **1** to strike repeatedly with something long and thin or flexible — see WHIP 1

2 to strike repeatedly — see BEAT 1

flogger *n* a long thin or flexible tool for striking — see WHIP

flood *n* a great flow of water or of something that overwhelms ⟨a *flood* nearly wiped out the town⟩ ⟨a *flood* of messages on my computer⟩

syn cataclysm, cataract, deluge, flood tide, inundation, overflow, spate, torrent

rel current, river, stream, tide; discharge, flush, gush, outflow, outpouring; flux, inflow, influx; engulfment, washout; avalanche; cascade, waterfall; excess, glut, overabundance, overage, overkill, overmuch, oversupply, superabundance, superfluity, surfeit, surplus

near ant dribble, drip, trickle

ant drought

flood *vb* to cover or become filled with a flood ⟨the lowlands were completely *flooded*⟩ ⟨angry calls *flooded* the radio station⟩

syn deluge, drown, engulf, inundate, overflow, overwhelm, submerge, submerse, swamp

rel overcome, overrun; flow, flush, gush, pour, sluice, spout, spurt, stream; douse, drench, soak, wet

near ant dehydrate, dry, parch

ant drain

flood tide *n* a great flow of water or of something that overwhelms — see FLOOD

floor *n* the surface upon which a body of water lies — see BOTTOM 2

floor *vb* **1** to cause an often unpleasant surprise for — see SHOCK 1

2 to make a strong impression on (someone) with something unexpected — see SURPRISE 1

3 to strike (someone) so forcefully as to cause a fall — see FELL 1

---

syn synonym(s)   **rel** related words
ant antonym(s)   **near ant** near antonym(s)

4 to subject to incapacitating emotional or mental stress — see OVERWHELM 1

flop *n* something that has failed — see FAILURE 3

flop *vb* **1** to throw or set down clumsily or casually ⟨they *flopped* themselves onto the couch to watch the game⟩ ⟨*flopped* the bag of groceries onto the counter⟩

syn plop, plump, plunk

rel fling, heave, sling, toss; ensconce, install, plant, settle

2 to be unsuccessful — see FAIL 2

3 to move or cause to move with a striking motion — see FLAP

floppy *adj* not stiff in structure — see LIMP 1

flora *n* green leaves or plants — see GREENERY 1

floral *adj* of or relating to flowers ⟨wallpaper with a *floral* pattern for the bedroom⟩

syn flowered, flowery

rel florid; abloom

florid *adj* **1** elaborately and often excessively decorated — see ORNATE

2 full of fine words and fancy expressions — see FLOWERY 1

3 having a healthy reddish skin tone — see RUDDY

floss *n* a soft airy substance or covering — see FUZZ

flounce *n* a strip of fabric gathered or pleated on one edge and used as trimming — see RUFFLE

flounder *vb* **1** to make progress in a clumsy, struggling manner ⟨unprepared choristers who *floundered* helplessly through the musical number⟩

syn limp, lumber, plod, stumble, trudge

rel shamble, shuffle; wallow, welter; falter, lurch, reel, stagger, sway, teeter, totter; blunder, fumble, muddle

near ant coast, fly, glide, sail, zip, zoom

2 to move heavily or clumsily — see LUMBER 1

flourish *vb* **1** to grow vigorously — see THRIVE 1

2 to reach a desired level of accomplishment — see SUCCEED 2

flourishing *adj* **1** having attained a desired end or state of good fortune — see SUCCESSFUL 1

2 marked by much life, movement, or activity — see ALIVE 1

3 marked by vigorous growth and well-being especially economically — see PROSPEROUS 1

floury *adj* consisting of very small particles — see FINE 1

flout *vb* to ignore in a disrespectful manner — see SCORN 2

flow *vb* **1** to move in a stream ⟨water was *flowing* over the dam at a tremendous rate⟩

syn pour, roll, run, stream

rel arise, emanate, issue, spring; course, race, rush; gush, spout, spurt; deluge, engulf, flood, inundate, overflow, swamp; cascade, dribble, drip, gutter, riffle, ripple, trickle; flush, wash out

near ant clot, coagulate, congeal, gel, harden, set

ant back up

2 to move or proceed smoothly and readily ⟨as everyone relaxed, the conversation really started to *flow*⟩

syn bowl, breeze, coast, drift, glide, roll, sail, skim, slide, slip, stream, sweep, whisk

rel fly, race, rush, speed

near ant limp, lumber, plod, stumble, trudge; shamble, shuffle; stamp, stomp, stump, tramp; labor, toil

ant flounder, struggle

flower *n* **1** the usually showy plant part that produces seeds ⟨*flowers* are always a thoughtful gift⟩

syn bloom, blossom

rel bud, floret; bouquet, nosegay, posy; arrangement, boutonniere, corsage, garland, lei, spray, wreath

2 a state or time of great activity, thriving, or achievement — see BLOOM 2

3 individuals carefully selected as being the best of a class — see ELITE

flower *vb* to produce flowers — see BLOOM

flowered *adj* of or relating to flowers — see FLORAL

flowery *adj* **1** full of fine words and fancy expressions ⟨the *flowery* verses that always appear on valentines⟩

syn florid, grandiloquent, highfalutin, high-flown, high-sounding

rel affected, grandiose, inflated, pompous, pretentious, stilted; excessive, flattering, fulsome; boastful, bombastic; elevated, eloquent, lofty

near ant prosaic, unpoetic; bald, direct, matter-of-fact, plain, plainspoken, simple, stark, straightforward, unadorned; natural, unaffected, unpretentious

2 of or relating to flowers — see FLORAL

flowing *adj* capable of moving like a liquid — see FLUID 1

flub *n* an unintentional departure from truth or accuracy — see ERROR 1

flub *vb* to make or do (something) in a clumsy or unskillful way — see BOTCH

fluctuate *vb* to pass from one form, state, or level to another — see CHANGE 2

fluctuating *adj* **1** likely to change frequently, suddenly, or unexpectedly — see FICKLE 1

2 not staying constant — see UNEVEN 2

fluent *adj* **1** able to express oneself clearly and well — see ARTICULATE

2 capable of moving like a liquid — see FLUID 1

3 involving minimal difficulty or effort — see EASY 1

fluently *adv* without difficulty — see EASILY

fluff *n* a soft airy substance or covering — see FUZZ

fluffy *adj* resembling air in lightness — see AIRY 1

fluid *adj* **1** capable of moving like a liquid ⟨warm the jam until it is *fluid*, then spread it over the cake⟩

syn flowing, fluent, liquid

rel diluted, thin, watery, weak

near ant clotted, coagulated, gelatinous, gelled, jelled, jellied, thick; gluey, glutinous, gooey, gummy, viscous

ant hard, solid

2 capable of being readily changed — see FLEXIBLE 1

3 involving minimal difficulty or effort — see EASY 1

4 likely to change frequently, suddenly, or unexpectedly — see FICKLE 1

fluky *adj* **1** coming or happening by good luck especially unexpectedly — see FORTUNATE 1

2 happening by chance — see ACCIDENTAL

flume *n* **1** a narrow opening between hillsides or mountains that can be used for passage — see CANYON

2 an open man-made passageway for water — see CHANNEL 1

flunk *vb* to be unsuccessful — see FAIL 2

flunky *also* **flunkey** *n* **1** a person hired to perform household or personal services — see SERVANT

2 a person who flatters another in order to get ahead — see SYCOPHANT

fluorescence *n* the steady giving off of the form of radiation that makes vision possible — see LIGHT 1

flurry *n* **1** a sudden and usually temporary growth of activity — see OUTBREAK

2 a sudden brief rush of wind — see GUST 1

flush *adj* **1** having a healthy reddish skin tone — see RUDDY

2 having a surface without bends, breaks, or irregularities — see LEVEL

3 having active strength of body or mind — see VIGOROUS 1

4 having goods, property, or money in abundance — see RICH 1

5 possessing or covered with great numbers or amounts of something specified — see RIFE

flush *n* **1** a rosy appearance of the cheeks — see BLOOM 2

2 a state or time of great activity, thriving, or achievement — see BLOOM 1

3 a sudden intense expression of strong feeling — see OUTBURST 1

flush *vb* **1** to pour liquid over or through in order to cleanse ⟨use this cleaner to *flush* the drain in the sink⟩

syn irrigate, rinse, sluice, wash

rel deluge, engulf, flood, inundate, swamp; flow, gush, rush, stream; douche, hose; drench, saturate, soak; douse, slosh, splash

2 to develop a rosy facial color (as from excitement or embarrassment) — see BLUSH

fluster *n* **1** a state of nervous or irritated concern — see FRET

2 the emotional state of being made self-consciously uncomfortable — see EMBARRASSMENT 1

fluster *vb* to throw into a state of self-conscious distress — see EMBARRASS 1

flustering *adj* causing embarrassment — see AWKWARD 3

flutter *n* a sudden and usually temporary growth of activity — see OUTBREAK

flutter *vb* **1** to make an irregular series of quick, sudden movements — see FLIT

2 to move or cause to move with a striking motion — see FLAP

fluttery *adj* easily excited by nature — see EXCITABLE

flux *n* a flowing or coming in — see INFLUX

flux *vb* to go from a solid to a liquid state — see LIQUEFY

fly *vb* **1** to move through the air with or as if with outstretched wings ⟨the Wright brothers realized mankind's age-old wish to *fly*⟩

syn glide, plane, soar, wing

rel drift, float, hang, hover, waft; coast, cruise, sail, sweep; dart, flit, flutter; catapult, jet, orbit, rocket

2 to get free from a confining or confining situation — see ESCAPE 1

3 to proceed or move quickly — see HURRY 2

4 to hasten away from something dangerous or frightening — see RUN 2

flying *adj* **1** acting or done with excessive or careless speed — see HASTY 1

2 moving, proceeding, or acting with great speed — see FAST 1

flying *n* travel through the air by the use of wings — see ¹FLIGHT

flyspeck *n* a very small piece — see BIT 1

foam *n* a light mass of fine bubbles formed in or on a liquid ⟨a steaming cup of hot cocoa with a sprinkling of marshmallows drifting through the *foam*⟩

syn froth, head, lather, spume, suds, surf

rel mousse; mist, spindrift; spray; scum

foaming *adj* feeling or showing anger — see ANGRY

foamy *adj* covered with, consisting of, or resembling foam ⟨*foamy* milky shakes⟩

syn frothy, lathery, sudsy

rel bubbly, effervescent, fizzy, sparkling; soapy

focus *n* a thing or place that is of greatest importance to an activity or interest — see CENTER 1

focus *vb* to fix (as one's attention) steadily toward a central objective — see CONCENTRATE 2

focused *also* **focussed** *adj* **1** having the mind fixed on something — see ATTENTIVE

2 not divided or scattered among several areas of interest or concern — see WHOLE 1

foe *n* one that is hostile toward another — see ENEMY

fog *n* **1** a state of mental confusion — see HAZE 2

---

syn synonym(s)   *rel* related words

ant antonym(s)   *near ant* near antonym(s)

2 an atmospheric condition in which suspended particles in the air rob it of its transparency — see HAZE 1

fog *vb* **1** to make (something) unclear to the understanding — see CONFUSE 2

2 to make dark, dim, or indistinct — see CLOUD 1

foggy *adj* **1** filled with or dimmed by fine particles (as of dust or water) in suspension — see HAZY 1

2 not seen or understood clearly — see FAINT 1

fogy *also* **fogey** *n* a person with old-fashioned ideas ⟨old *fogies* who said that rap music would never last⟩

syn antediluvian, dodo, fossil, fuddy-duddy, reactionary, stick-in-the-mud

rel conservative, rightist, tory; old hand, old-timer, veteran; old maid

near ant liberal, progressive, radical

ant modern

foible *n* a defect in character — see FAULT 1

foil *vb* to prevent from achieving a goal — see FRUSTRATE

foist *vb* to offer (something fake, useless, or inferior) as genuine, useful, or valuable ⟨shopkeepers who *foist* shoddy souvenirs on unsuspecting tourists⟩

syn palm off, pass off

rel force, impose, inflict; counterfeit, fake, forge; distort, falsify, misrepresent

fold *n* a group of people sharing a common interest and relating together socially — see GANG 2

fold *vb* **1** to lay one part over or against another part of ⟨*fold* the blanket so that it will fit inside the trunk⟩

syn double

rel overlap, overlay, overlie; collapse, telescope; close, shut

ant extend, open, spread, unfold

2 to be unsuccessful — see FAIL 2

folder *n* a short printed publication with no cover or with a paper cover — see PAMPHLET

foliage *n* green leaves or plants — see GREENERY 1

folk *n* **1** *folks pl* a group of persons who come from the same ancestor — see FAMILY 1

2 one of the segments of society into which people are grouped — see CLASS 1

3 *folks pl* human beings in general — see PEOPLE 1

folklore *n* the body of customs, beliefs, stories, and sayings associated with a people, thing, or place ⟨the Scottish Highlands are rich in *folklore*⟩

syn legend, lore, myth, mythology, tradition

rel information, knowledge, wisdom; anecdote, fable, folktale, old wives' tale, tale, yarn

follow *vb* **1** to come after in time ⟨a wrap-up always *follows* the Super Bowl broadcast⟩

syn postdate, succeed, supervene

rel displace, replace, supersede, supplant; ensue

ant antedate, precede, predate

2 to go after or on the track of ⟨let's *follow* the boys to their hiding place⟩

syn chase, dog, hound, pursue, shadow, tag, tail, trace, track, trail

rel accompany, chaperone (*or* chaperon), escort; hunt, search (for), seek; eye, observe, watch

near ant head

ant guide, lead, pilot

3 to act according to the commands of — see OBEY

4 to make one's way through, across, or over — see TRAVERSE

5 to take notice of and be guided by — see HEED 1

follower *n* one who follows the opinions or teachings of another ⟨the *followers* of Gandhi have spread his philosophy of nonviolence all over the world⟩

syn adherent, convert, disciple, partisan, pupil, votary

rel apostle; faithful, loyalist; advocate, backer, champion, supporter; scholar, student; ideologist, sectarian; admirer, cultist, devotee, enthusiast, fan, idolater (*or* idolator), worshipper (*or* worshiper), zealot; flunky (*also* flunkey), hanger-on, henchman, lackey, satellite, stooge, sycophant, toady, yes-man

near ant apostate, defector, renegade, traitor, turncoat

ant leader

following *prep* subsequent to in time or order — see AFTER

following *adj* being the one that comes immediately after another — see NEXT

following *n* **1** a body of employees or servants who accompany and wait on a person — see CORTEGE 1

2 a group of people showing intense devotion to a cause, person, or work (as a film) — see CULT 1

3 the act of going after or in the tracks of another — see PURSUIT

follow through *vb* to carry through (as a process) to completion — see PERFORM 1

folly *n* **1** a foolish act or idea ⟨the American purchase of Alaska was originally considered a grand *folly*⟩

syn absurdity, asininity, fatuity, foolery, idiocy, imbecility, inanity, insanity, lunacy, stupidity

rel absurdness, craziness, foolishness, madness, senselessness, witlessness; monkeyshine(s), shenanigans, tomfoolery; drivel, humbug, nonsense, twaddle; blunder, bungle, flub, goof, howler

near ant discretion, forethought, prudence, sagacity, wisdom; brainstorm, inspiration

2 lack of good sense or judgment — see FOOLISHNESS 1

3 language, behavior, or ideas that are absurd and contrary to good sense — see NONSENSE 1

foment *vb* to cause or encourage the development of — see INCITE 1

fomenter *n* a person who stirs up public feelings especially of discontent — see AGITATOR

fond *adj* **1** having a liking or affection ⟨even lots of city people are *fond* of country music⟩

syn attached, inclined, partial

rel crazy (about *or* over), enamored, enraptured, gone (on), infatuated, mad (about), nuts (about); desirous, eager, enthusiastic, excited, gung ho, keen

near ant apathetic, cool, indifferent, uninterested; contemptuous, disdainful, scornful; antagonistic, antipathetic, hostile; alienated, disaffected, disenchanted, estranged

ant allergic, averse, disinclined

2 feeling or showing love — see LOVING

fondle *vb* to touch or handle in a tender or loving manner ⟨a cat who enjoys being *fondled* by his loving owners⟩

syn caress, love, pat, pet, stroke

rel cuddle, nestle, nose, nuzzle, snuggle; cradle, embrace, enfold, hug; bounce, dandle; knead, massage; baby, coddle, indulge, mollycoddle, pamper, spoil

fondness *n* **1** a feeling of strong or constant regard for and dedication to someone — see LOVE 1

2 positive regard for something — see LIKING

food *n* substances intended to be eaten ⟨a simple, little restaurant with excellent *food*⟩

syn bread, chow, eatables, edibles, fare, foodstuffs, grub, meat, provender, provisions, table, viands, victuals, vittles

rel rations; aliment, nutriment; diet, nurture, sustenance; mess, pap; feed, fodder, forage, slop, swill; feast, meal, refreshments, repast, spread; board; dish, plate, serving

near ant poison

foodstuffs *n pl* substances intended to be eaten — see FOOD

fool *n* **1** a person who lacks good sense or judgment ⟨only a *fool* would attempt to climb that mountain unprepared⟩

syn booby, goose, half-wit, jackass, lunatic, nincompoop, ninny, nitwit, nut, simpleton, turkey, yo-yo

rel daredevil; madman, madwoman; blockhead, cretin, dodo, dolt, dope, dumbbell, dummy, dunce, idiot, imbecile, moron; featherbrain, scatterbrain; butt, dupe, laughingstock, mockery, monkey; chump, loser, schlemiel

near ant sage, thinker; brain, genius

2 a person formerly kept in a royal or noble household to amuse with jests and pranks ⟨a king's *fool* could get away with saying things that others in the palace couldn't⟩

syn jester, motley

rel buffoon, clown, comedian, comedienne, comic, cutup, harlequin, zany

fool *vb* **1** to cause to believe what is untrue — see DECEIVE

2 to make jokes — see JOKE

fool (around) *vb* **1** to engage in attention-getting playful or boisterous behavior — see CUT UP

2 to spend time in aimless activity — see FIDDLE (AROUND)

fool (with) *vb* to handle thoughtlessly, ignorantly, or mischievously — see TAMPER

foolery *n* **1** a foolish act or idea — see FOLLY 1

2 wildly playful or mischievous behavior — see HORSEPLAY

foolhardy *adj* **1** foolishly adventurous or bold ⟨hikers who were *foolhardy* enough to remain on the summit during a thunderstorm⟩

syn brash, daredevil, madcap, overbold, overconfident, reckless

rel adventuresome, adventurous, audacious, bold, daring, venturesome, venturous; brave, courageous, dauntless, fearless, intrepid, lionhearted, stouthearted, undaunted, valiant; hotheaded; impetuous, impulsive, rash; brainless, foolish, harebrained, scatterbrained; careless, heedless, thoughtless; hasty, headlong, precipitate

near ant unadventurous, unambitious; fainthearted, timid, timorous; calm, cool, levelheaded, sensible; alert, intelligent, quick-witted, sharp

ant careful, cautious, heedful, prudent

2 having or showing a lack of concern for the consequences of one's actions — see RECKLESS 1

fooling *adj* marked by or expressive of mild or good-natured teasing — see QUIZZICAL

foolish *adj* **1** showing or marked by a lack of good sense or judgment ⟨*foolish* people who thought that the world would end in the year 2000⟩ ⟨a *foolish* scheme that was supposed to make us all rich⟩

syn absurd, asinine, balmy, brainless, cockeyed, crazy, cuckoo, daffy, daft, dotty, fatuous, harebrained, half-witted, insane, jerky, kooky, loony (*also* looney), lunatic, mad, nonsensical, nutty, preposterous, sappy, screwball, senseless, silly, simpleminded, stupid, unwise, wacky, weak-minded, witless, zany

rel dumb, idiotic, imbecilic, moronic; fallacious, illogical, invalid, irrational, unreasonable; farcical, laughable, ludicrous, ridiculous

near ant brainy, bright, clever, intelligent, smart; logical, rational, reasonable, valid

ant judicious, prudent, sage, sane, sapient, sensible, sound, wise

2 conceived or made without regard for reason or reality — see FANTASTIC 1

foolishness *n* **1** lack of good sense or judgment ⟨the *foolishness* of going off to search for the fountain of youth⟩

syn absurdity, asininity, balminess, brainlessness, craziness, daftness, fatuity, folly, inanity, insanity, lunacy, madness, nonsensicalness, nuttiness, preposterousness, senselessness, silliness, simplicity, wackiness, witlessness, zaniness

rel idiocy, imbecility, stupidity; fallacy, irrationality, unreasonableness; laughableness, ludicrousness, ridiculousness

near ant logicalness, rationality, reasonableness, validity

ant prudence, sageness, sanity, sapience, sensibleness, soundness, wisdom

2 language, behavior, or ideas that are absurd and contrary to good sense — see NONSENSE 1

3 the quality or state of lacking intelligence or quickness of mind — see STUPIDITY 1

foot *n* the lowest part, place, or point — see BOTTOM 3

foot *vb* to give what is owed for — see PAY 2

foot (it) *vb* **1** to go on foot — see WALK

2 to perform a series of usually rhythmic bodily movements to music — see DANCE 1

foot (up) *vb* to combine (numbers) into a single sum — see ADD 2

foothold *n* a place from which an advance (as for military operations) is made — see BASE 2

footing *n* **1** an immaterial thing upon which something else rests — see BASE 1

2 position with regard to conditions and circumstances — see SITUATION 1

3 the placement of someone or something in relation to others in a vertical arrangement — see RANK 1

footloose *adj* **1** not bound, confined, or detained by force — see FREE 3

2 not held back by rules, duties, or worries — see FREEWHEELING

footpath *n* a rough course or way formed by or as if by repeated footsteps — see TRAIL 1

footprint *n* the mark or impression made by a foot ⟨mysterious *footprints* along the beach⟩

syn footstep, step

rel hoofprint; spoor, track; sign, trace, vestige

footstep *n* the mark or impression made by a foot — see FOOTPRINT

foozle *vb* to make or do (something) in a clumsy or unskillful way — see BOTCH

fop *n* a man extremely interested in his clothing and personal appearance — see DANDY 1

for *conj* for the reason that — see SINCE

forage *vb* to feed on grass or herbs — see ¹GRAZE

forage (for) *vb* to go in search of — see SEEK 1

foray *n* a sudden attack on and entrance into hostile territory — see RAID 1

foray (into) *vb* to enter for conquest or plunder — see INVADE

forbear *vb* to resist the temptation of ⟨she's old enough to make her own decisions, so we must *forbear* criticizing her taste in clothes⟩

syn abstain (from), forgo (*also* forego), keep (from), refrain (from)

rel avoid, eschew, shun; check, constrain, curb, inhibit; deny, refuse, withhold; buck, combat, fight

near ant capitulate, knuckle under, submit, surrender

ant give in (to), succumb (to), yield (to)

forbearance *n* the capacity to endure what is difficult or disagreeable without complaining — see PATIENCE

forbearing *adj* accepting pains or hardships calmly or without complaint — see PATIENT 1

forbid *vb* to order not to do or use or to be done or used ⟨smoking is *forbidden* throughout the building⟩ ⟨we *forbid* you to see him⟩

syn ban, bar, enjoin, interdict, outlaw, prohibit, proscribe

rel deter, discourage, dissuade; repress, suppress; halt, preclude, prevent, stop; embargo, exclude, rule out, shut out; debar, deprive, disallow, reject, veto; check, curb, inhibit, restrain; block, hinder, impede, obstruct

near ant approve, endorse (*also* indorse), sanction; authorize, license (*also* licence); abet, encourage, promote, support; bid, command, order; abide, bear, endure, tolerate

ant allow, let, permit, suffer

forbidden *adj* that may not be permitted — see IMPERMISSIBLE

forbidding *adj* **1** causing fear — see FEARFUL 1

2 harsh and threatening in manner or appearance — see GRIM 1

forbidding *n* the act of ordering that something not be done or used — see PROHIBITION 1

force *n* **1** a body of persons at work or available for work ⟨the nation's labor *force*⟩

syn help, manpower, personnel, pool, staff

rel labor, proletariat, rank and file; band, company, crew, gang, outfit, party, team; employee, helper, hireling, worker

2 the use of power to impose one's will on another ⟨a cruel tyrant who disbanded the parliament and ruled by *force*⟩

syn coercion, compulsion, constraint, duress, pressure

rel browbeating, bulldozing, bullying; fear, intimidation, menace, sword, terror, terrorism, threat, violence; might, muscle, strength; hardheadedness, self-will, willfulness; strain, stress

near ant agreement, approval, consent, permission; persuasion, reason

3 the ability to exert effort for the accomplishment of a task — see POWER 2

4 the capacity to persuade — see COGENCY 1

5 the quality of an utterance that provokes interest and produces an effect — see ¹PUNCH 1

6 the use of brute strength to cause harm to a person or property — see VIOLENCE

force *vb* to cause (a person) to give in to pressure ⟨*forced* the natives to sell their land⟩ ⟨hunger *forced* the refugees to steal⟩

syn coerce, compel, constrain, drive, make, muscle, obligate, oblige, press, pressure

rel browbeat, bulldoze, bully; high-pressure, intimidate, menace, terrorize, threaten

near ant allow, let, permit; convince, induce, persuade

forced *adj* 1 forcing one's compliance or participation by or as if by law — see MANDATORY

2 lacking in natural or spontaneous quality — see ARTIFICIAL 1

3 not made or done willingly or by choice — see INVOLUNTARY 1

forceful *adj* 1 having the power to persuade — see COGENT

2 marked by or uttered with forcefulness — see EMPHATIC 1

3 not showing weakness or uncertainty — see FIRM 1

4 having power over the minds or behavior of others — see INFLUENTIAL 1

forcefully *adv* in a vigorous and forceful manner — see HARD 3

forcefulness *n* 1 the capacity to persuade — see COGENCY 1

2 the quality of an utterance that provokes interest and produces an effect — see ¹PUNCH 1

3 the quality or state of being forceful (as in expression) — see VEHEMENCE 1

forcibly *adv* in a vigorous and forceful manner — see HARD 3

ford *n* a place where a body of water (as a sea or river) is shallow — see SHOAL

forearm *vb* to prepare (oneself) mentally or emotionally — see FORTIFY 1

forebear *also* **forebar** *n* a person who is several generations earlier in an individual's line of descent — see ANCESTOR 1

forebode *also* **forbode** *vb* to show signs of a favorable or successful outcome — see BODE

foreboding *adj* being or showing a sign of evil or calamity to come — see OMINOUS

foreboding *n* 1 a feeling that something bad will happen — see PREMONITION

2 something believed to be a sign or warning of a future event — see OMEN

3 suspicion or fear of future harm or misfortune — see APPREHENSION 1

forecast *n* a declaration that something will happen in the future — see PREDICTION

forecast *vb* to tell of or describe beforehand — see FORETELL

forecaster *n* one who predicts future events or developments — see PROPHET

forecasting *n* a declaration that something will happen in the future — see PREDICTION

foredoom *vb* to determine the fate of in advance — see DESTINE

forefather *n* a person who is several generations earlier in an individual's line of descent — see ANCESTOR 1

forefront *n* the leading or most important part of a movement ⟨a politician who was in the *forefront* of women's rights⟩

syn vanguard

rel spearhead

near ant rank and file

forego *vb* to go or come before in time — see PRECEDE

foregoer *n* 1 one that announces or indicates the later arrival of another — see FORERUNNER 1

2 something belonging to an earlier time from which something else was later developed — see ANCESTOR 2

foregoing *adj* going before another in time or order — see PREVIOUS

forehanded *adj* having or showing awareness of and preparation for the future — see FORESIGHTED

foreign *adj* 1 being, relating to, or characteristic of a country other than one's own ⟨more Americans should take an interest in *foreign* languages⟩

syn alien, nonnative

rel imported, introduced, naturalized, transplanted; international, multicultural, multinational; distant, far-off, overseas, remote; bizarre, exotic, outlandish, strange

near ant endemic, local; aboriginal, indigenous

ant domestic, native

2 not being a vital part of or belonging to something — see EXTRINSIC

foreigner *n* a person who is not native to or known to a community — see STRANGER

foreknow *vb* to realize or know about beforehand — see FORESEE

foreknowledge *n* the special ability to see or know about events before they actually occur — see FORESIGHT 1

foreman *n* the person (as an employer or supervisor) who tells people and especially workers what to do — see BOSS

foremost *adj* 1 coming before all others in importance ⟨Albert Einstein is regarded by many as the *foremost* figure of the 20th century⟩

syn arch, cardinal, central, chief, dominant, first, grand, greatest, highest, key, leading, main, paramount, predominant, preeminent, premier, primary, principal, sovereign, supreme

rel distinguished, eminent, notable, noteworthy, illustrious, outstanding, prestigious, stellar, superior; important, major, momentous, significant; incomparable, matchless, unequaled (*or* unequalled), unparalleled, unsurpassed

near ant inconsequential, insignificant, minor, trivial, unimportant; collateral, inferior, secondary, subordinate, subsidiary

ant last, least

---

syn synonym(s)   *rel* related words
ant antonym(s)   *near ant* near antonym(s)

2 highest in rank or authority — see HEAD

forename *n* a name that is placed before one's family name ⟨a long string of *forenames* was given to the latest addition to the royal family⟩
syn Christian name, given name
rel appellation, denomination, designation; epithet, handle, nickname, sobriquet (*also* soubriquet); alias, nom de plume, pen name, pseudonym

forenoon *n* the time from sunrise until noon — see MORNING 1

foreordain *vb* to determine the fate of in advance — see DESTINE

forepart *n* a forward part or surface — see FRONT 1

forerunner *n* **1** one that announces or indicates the later arrival of another ⟨the return of the swallows is traditionally regarded as a *forerunner* of spring⟩
syn angel, foregoer, harbinger, herald, precursor
rel foreboder, foreshadower, foretaste, forewarning; advertiser, announcer, crier, proclaimer; courier, messenger, runner; augury, omen, portent, presage; mark, sign, symptom; bellwether
2 something belonging to an earlier time from which something else was later developed — see ANCESTOR 2

foresee *vb* to realize or know about beforehand ⟨a freak accident that no one could possibly have *foreseen*⟩
syn anticipate, divine, foreknow
rel augur, forecast, foretell, presage, prognosticate, prophesy; envisage, foreshadow, prefigure, visualize; forewarn; preview; descry, discern, perceive; apprehend, dread, fear

foreseeing *adj* having or showing awareness of and preparation for the future — see FORESIGHTED

foreseer *n* one who predicts future events or developments — see PROPHET

foreshadow *vb* to give or show a slight indication of beforehand ⟨a series of small tremors that *foreshadowed* the massive earthquake the next day⟩
syn prefigure
rel anticipate, foreknow, foresee; forecast, foretell, predict, prognosticate, prophesy; forewarn; augur, bode, forebode (*also* forbode), portend, presage, promise; connote, hint, imply, insinuate, intimate, suggest

foreshadowing *n* something believed to be a sign or warning of a future event — see OMEN

foresight *n* **1** a special ability to see or know about events before they actually occur ⟨a mysterious woman who claims to have the gift of *foresight*⟩
syn foreknowledge, prescience
rel premonition, presentiment; clairvoyance, extrasensory perception, sixth sense; omniscience; divination
2 concern or preparation for the future ⟨had the *foresight* to realize the global importance of the Internet⟩
syn farsightedness, foresightedness, forethought, prescience, providence
rel precaution, premeditation; discretion, insight, prudence, sagacity, wisdom
near ant hindsight
ant improvidence, shortsightedness

foresighted *adj* having or showing awareness of and preparation for the future ⟨the *foresighted* conservationists who worked to create the national park system⟩
syn farsighted, forehanded, foreseeing, forethoughtful, prescient, provident
rel careful, cautious; insightful, perceptive, prudent, sage, wise
near ant careless, heedless, incautious
ant improvident, shortsighted

foresightedness *n* concern or preparation for the future — see FORESIGHT 2

forest *n* a dense growth of trees and shrubs covering a large area ⟨the endless *forest* that the first European settlers encountered⟩
syn timber, timberland, wood(s), woodland
rel coppice, copse, grove, scrubland, stand, thicket; greenwood, wildwood; woodlot

forestall *vb* to keep from happening by taking action in advance — see PREVENT

forestallment *n* the act or practice of keeping something from happening — see PREVENTION

foretell *vb* to tell of or describe beforehand ⟨a 16th century astrologer who, some claim, accurately *foretold* 20th century events⟩
syn augur, forecast, predict, presage, prognosticate, prophesy
rel forewarn; bode, forebode (*also* forbode), portend; anticipate, divine, foreknow, foresee; announce, declare, proclaim
near ant recount, relate, report

foreteller *n* one who predicts future events or developments — see PROPHET

foretelling *n* a declaration that something will happen in the future — see PREDICTION

forethought *n* concern or preparation for the future — see FORESIGHT 2

forethoughtful *adj* having or showing awareness of and preparation for the future — see FORESIGHTED

forever *adv* **1** for all time — see EVER 1
2 on every relevant occasion — see ALWAYS 1

forevermore *adv* for all time — see EVER 1

forewarn *vb* to give notice to beforehand especially of danger or risk — see WARN

forewarning *n* the act or an instance of telling beforehand of danger or risk — see WARNING 1

foreword *n* a short section (as of a book) that leads to or explains the main part — see INTRODUCTION

forfeit *n* a sum of money to be paid as a punishment — see FINE

forfeiture *n* a sum of money to be paid as a punishment — see FINE

forgather or **foregather** vb to come together into one body or place — see ASSEMBLE 1

¹**forge** vb 1 to imitate or copy especially in order to deceive — see FAKE 1

2 to produce or bring about especially by long or repeated effort — see HAMMER (OUT)

3 to shape with a hammer — see HAMMER 1

²**forge** vb to move forward along a course — see GO 1

forged adj being such in appearance only and made or manufactured with the intention of committing fraud — see COUNTERFEIT

forgery n an imitation that is passed off as genuine — see FAKE 1

forget vb 1 to be unable to recall or think of ⟨I *forget* exactly on which street the house is⟩
syn unlearn
rel lose, miss; blank; disregard, ignore, neglect, overlook
near ant reminisce; remind
ant mind [*chiefly dialect*], recall, recollect, remember

2 to fail to give proper attention to — see NEGLECT 1

3 to leave undone or unattended to especially through carelessness — see NEGLECT 2

4 to miss the opportunity or obligation — see NEGLECT 3

forgetful adj inclined to forget what one has learned or to do what one should ⟨we become more *forgetful* as we get older⟩
syn absentminded
rel absent, abstracted, lost, oblivious, preoccupied, unmindful; amnesiac, senile; lax, neglectful, negligent, remiss, slack; careless, heedless, inconsiderate, thoughtless
near ant alert, keen, sharp; careful, conscientious, heedful, thoughtful
ant retentive

forgetfulness n a state of being disregardful or unconscious of one's surroundings, concerns, or obligations — see OBLIVION

forgivable adj worthy of forgiveness — see VENIAL

forgive vb 1 to cease to have feelings of anger or bitterness toward ⟨it is not easy to *forgive* those who have hurt us⟩
syn pardon
rel absolve, acquit, clear, exculpate, exonerate, vindicate; remit, shrive; condone, disregard, excuse, ignore, pass over, shrug off
near ant smart; despise, detest, dislike, hate, loathe; avenge, redress, revenge
ant resent

2 to overlook or dismiss as of little importance — see EXCUSE 1

forgiveness n release from the guilt or penalty of an offense — see PARDON

---

syn synonym(s)   *rel* related words
ant antonym(s)   *near ant* near antonym(s)

forgo also **forego** vb to resist the temptation of — see FORBEAR

forgotten adj left unoccupied or unused — see ABANDONED

fork vb to go or move in different directions from a central point — see SEPARATE 2

forlorn adj 1 feeling unhappiness — see SAD 1

2 sad from lack of companionship or separation from others — see LONESOME 1

forlornness n 1 a state or spell of low spirits — see SADNESS

2 utter loss of hope — see DESPAIR 1

form n 1 the outward appearance of something as distinguished from its substance ⟨carved the block of wood into the *form* of a duck⟩
syn cast, configuration, conformation, figure, geometry, shape
rel contour, outline, profile, silhouette; framework, skeleton, situation; arrangement, layout, organization, pattern, plan, setup
near ant composition, material, matter, stuff, substance

2 a piece of paper with information written or to be written on it ⟨I filled out all the *forms* for applying to the school⟩
syn blank, document, paper
rel instrument, writ

3 personal conduct or behavior as evaluated by an accepted standard of appropriateness for a social or professional setting — see MANNER 1

4 a state of being or fitness — see CONDITION 1

5 a three-dimensional representation of the human body used especially for displaying clothes — see MANNEQUIN 1

6 an oft-repeated action or series of actions performed in accordance with tradition or a set of rules — see RITE

7 socially acceptable behavior — see DECENCY 1

8 the means or procedure for doing something — see METHOD

9 the type of body that a person has — see PHYSIQUE

10 the way in which the elements of something (as a work of art) are arranged — see COMPOSITION 3

form vb 1 to take on a definite form ⟨my ideas on the subject are just starting to *form*⟩
syn crystallize, jell, shape (up), solidify
rel coalesce, cohere, fuse; combine, connect, join, unite
near ant break down, decompose, disintegrate

2 to be all the substance of — see CONSTITUTE 1

3 to bring into being by combining, shaping, or transforming materials — see MAKE 1

4 to come into existence — see BEGIN 2

5 to come to have gradually — see DEVELOP 2

formal adj 1 following or agreeing with established form, custom, or rules ⟨a *formal* meeting of the school board⟩ ⟨a *formal* contract that was legally binding⟩

syn ceremonial, ceremonious, conventional, orthodox, regular, routine

rel authorized, certified, official; accepted, correct, decorous, proper; formalistic, ritual, ritualistic; methodical, orderly, systematic

near ant unauthorized, unofficial; improper, incorrect, indecorous

ant informal, irregular, unceremonious, unconventional, unorthodox

2 being something in name or form only — see NOMINAL 1

3 marked by or showing careful attention to set forms and details — see CEREMONIOUS 1

4 relating to or suitable for wearing to an event requiring elegant dress and manners — see DRESS

5 very dignified in form, tone, or style — see ELEVATED 2

formal *n* a social gathering for dancing — see DANCE

formality *n* **1** an act or utterance that is a customary show of good manners — see CIVILITY 1

2 an oft-repeated action or series of actions performed in accordance with tradition or a set of rules — see RITE

formalize *vb* to make agree with a single established standard or model — see STANDARDIZE

format *n* **1** the way in which something is sized, arranged, or organized ⟨the book's *format* is very user-friendly⟩

syn arrangement, configuration, conformation, formation, layout, setup

rel design, plan, scheme; composition, constitution, makeup; build, construction, structure

2 the way in which the elements of something (as a work of art) are arranged — see COMPOSITION 3

formation *n* the way in which something is sized, arranged, or organized — see FORMAT 1

formative *adj* having a role in deciding something's final form ⟨a teacher who was a *formative* influence on generations of students⟩

syn constructive, productive

rel causal, creative; consequential, influential

ant nonconstructive, nonproductive, unproductive

former *adj* having been such at some previous time ⟨the coach is a *former* professional baseball player⟩

syn erstwhile, late, old, onetime, past, sometime, whilom

rel bygone, dead, extinct

near ant contemporary, current, present; future, prospective

formidable *adj* **1** causing fear — see FEARFUL 1

2 requiring considerable physical or mental effort — see HARD 2

formless *adj* having no definite or recognizable form ⟨a *formless* mass of clay that

the potter transformed into an attractive bowl⟩

syn amorphous, shapeless, unformed, unshaped, unstructured

rel characterless, featureless, nondescript; chaotic, disorganized, incoherent, unordered, unorganized; fuzzy, hazy, indeterminate, indistinct, obscure, unclear, vague

near ant coherent, ordered, organized; clear, definite, distinct

ant formed, shaped, structured

formulaic *adj* using or marked by the use of something else as a basis or model — see IMITATIVE

formulate *vb* **1** to convey in appropriate or telling terms — see PHRASE

2 to put (something) into proper and usually carefully worked out written form — see COMPOSE 1

formulation *n* an act, process, or means of putting something into words — see EXPRESSION 1

formulator *n* one who creates or introduces something new — see INVENTOR

forsake *vb* to cause to remain behind — see LEAVE 1

forsaken *adj* left unoccupied or unused — see ABANDONED

forsaking *n* the act of abandoning — see DERELICTION 1

forsooth *adv* **1** to tell the truth — see ACTUALLY 1

2 without any question — see INDEED 1

fort *n* a structure or place from which one can resist attack ⟨a series of *forts* along the frontier⟩

syn bastion, citadel, fastness, fortification, fortress, hold, stronghold

rel breastwork, bulwark, parapet, rampart; bunker, dugout

forte *n* something for which a person shows a special talent ⟨doing funny impressions of people has always been my *forte*⟩

syn speciality, specialty

rel area, demesne, department, discipline, domain, field, line, province, realm, sphere; element; aptness, bent, faculty, flair, genius, gift, knack, talent

forth *adv* **1** toward a point ahead in space or time — see ONWARD 1

2 toward or at a point lying in advance in space or time — see ALONG

forthcoming *adj* being soon to appear or take place ⟨everyone's excited about the *forthcoming* school vacation⟩

syn approaching, coming, imminent, impending, nearing, oncoming, pending, upcoming

rel future; anticipated, awaited, expected, foreseen, predicted

near ant bygone, former, past

ant late, recent

forthright *adj* **1** free in expressing one's true feelings and opinions — see FRANK

2 going straight to the point clearly and firmly — see STRAIGHTFORWARD 1

forthrightly *adv* in an honest and direct manner — see STRAIGHTFORWARD

forthrightness *n* the free expression of one's true feelings and opinions — see CANDOR

forthwith *adv* without delay — see IMMEDIATELY

fortification *n* a structure or place from which one can resist attack — see FORT

fortify *vb* **1** to prepare (oneself) mentally or emotionally ⟨Kelly *fortified* herself for the basketball tournament with a series of confidence-boosting exercises⟩

syn brace, forearm, nerve, ready, steel, strengthen

rel harden, inure, season, toughen; bolster, boost, buoy (up), buttress, prop (up), reinforce, support, sustain; embolden, encourage, hearten; rally, rouse, stir

near ant demoralize, discourage, dishearten, unnerve; debilitate, enfeeble, undermine, weaken

2 to increase the ability of (as a muscle) to exert physical force — see STRENGTHEN 1

3 to make able to withstand physical hardship, strain, or exposure — see HARDEN 2

fortitude *n* the strength of mind that enables a person to endure pain or hardship ⟨it was only with the greatest *fortitude* that the Pilgrims were able to survive their first winter in Plymouth⟩

syn backbone, fiber, grit, guts, pluck, spunk

rel determination, purposefulness, resoluteness, resolution; bravery, courage, fearlessness, intrepidity; endurance, stamina, tolerance; heart, mettle, spirit; audacity, boldness, brass, cheek, chutzpah (*also* chutzpa *or* hutzpah *or* hutzpa), effrontery, hardihood, nerve, temerity

near ant indecisiveness, irresoluteness, irresolution, vacillation; cowardliness, cravenness, faintheartedness, timidity, timorousness

ant spinelessness

fortress *n* a structure or place from which one can resist attack — see FORT

fortuitous *adj* **1** coming or happening by good luck especially unexpectedly — see FORTUNATE 1

2 happening by chance — see ACCIDENTAL

fortunate *adj* **1** coming or happening by good luck especially unexpectedly ⟨a *fortunate* turn of events, the motel had one last vacancy⟩

syn fluky, fortuitous, happy, lucky, providential

rel convenient, opportune, seasonable, timely; unexpected, unforeseen, unlooked-for; accidental, chance, coincidental; auspicious, bright, fair, promising, propitious; benign, favorable, golden, good; advantageous, beneficial, profitable

near ant inconvenient, inopportune, unseasonable, untimely; anticipated, expected, foreseen; deliberate, intentional, planned; inauspicious, unpromising

ant luckless, unfortunate, unhappy, unlucky

2 having good luck — see LUCKY 1

fortunateness *n* success that is partly the result of chance — see LUCK 1

fortune *n* **1** what is going to happen to someone in the time ahead ⟨the telephone psychic proceeded to tell me my *fortune*—at great length⟩

syn future

rel circumstance, destiny, doom, lot, portion; futurities, outlook, prospect

near ant present

ant past

2 a very large amount of money ⟨the billionaire's huge mansion must have cost a *fortune*⟩

syn king's ransom, mint, wad

rel heap, pile, pot; bonanza, mine, treasure trove; assets, property, riches, wealth

ant mite, pittance

3 a state or end that seemingly has been decided beforehand — see FATE 1

4 success that is partly the result of chance — see LUCK 1

5 the total of one's money and property — see WEALTH 1

fortune-teller *n* one who predicts future events or developments — see PROPHET

forty winks *n pl* a short sleep — see ¹NAP

forum *n* a meeting featuring a group discussion ⟨a public *forum* called to find out how residents felt about a large high school being built in their neighborhood⟩

syn colloquy, conference, council, panel, parley, powwow, roundtable, seminar, symposium

rel caucus, town meeting; assembly, conclave, congregation, congress, convention, convocation, synod; debate, deliberation; brainstorming

forward *adv* **1** toward or at a point lying in advance in space or time — see ALONG

2 toward a point ahead in space or time — see ONWARD 1

forward *adj* showing a lack of proper social reserve or modesty — see PRESUMPTUOUS 1

forward *vb* to help the growth or development of — see FOSTER 1

fossil *n* a person with old-fashioned ideas — see FOGY

foster *vb* **1** to help the growth or development of ⟨the head librarian firmly declared that it is indeed the duty of local government to *foster* learning and a love of reading⟩

syn advance, cultivate, encourage, forward, further, nourish, nurture, promote

rel back, champion, support, uphold; endow, finance, fund, patronize, subsidize; abet, aid, assist; advertise, boost, plug, publicize, tout; agitate (for), campaign (for), work (for)

near ant forbid, prevent, prohibit; battle, combat, counter, fight, oppose; repress, stifle, suppress; arrest, check, halt, retard

ant discourage, frustrate, hinder, inhibit

---

syn synonym(s)   *rel* related words
ant antonym(s)   *near ant* near antonym(s)

2 to bring to maturity through care and education — see BRING UP 1

foul *adj* **1** marked by wet and windy conditions ⟨the *foul* weather brought out the windbreakers and rain slickers as everyone braced for a day of rough sailing⟩

syn bleak, dirty, inclement, nasty, raw, rough, squally, stormy, tempestuous, turbulent

rel blustering, blustery, breezy, gusty, windblown, windswept; cloudy, overcast, sunless; rainy, snowy; foggy, hazy, misty

near ant clear, cloudless, rainless, sunny; balmy, calm, halcyon, peaceful, placid

ant clement, fair

2 not being in accordance with the rules or standards of what is fair in sport ⟨an aggressive hockey player who is known for his *foul* play and readiness for a fight⟩

syn dirty, illegal, unfair, unsportsmanlike

rel dishonorable, shabby, shameful; ignoble, low, mean, ungentlemanly; immoral, unethical, unjust, unprincipled, unrighteous, unscrupulous

near ant just, law-abiding; ethical, moral, principled, righteous; honorable, irreproachable, unimpeachable

ant clean, fair, legal, sportsmanlike, sportsmanly

3 causing intense displeasure, disgust, or resentment — see OFFENSIVE 1

4 depicting or referring to sexual matters in a way that is unacceptable in polite society — see OBSCENE 1

5 having an unpleasant smell — see MALODOROUS

6 not clean — see DIRTY 1

foul *vb* **1** to make dirty — see DIRTY

2 to make unfit for use by the addition of something harmful or undesirable — see CONTAMINATE

foulness *n* **1** the quality or state of being obscene — see OBSCENITY 1

2 the state or quality of being dirty — see DIRTINESS 1

foul play *n* **1** the intentional and unlawful taking of another person's life — see HOMICIDE

2 the use of brute strength to cause harm to a person or property — see VIOLENCE

foul–up *n* an instance of confusion ⟨there was a *foul-up* with our mail order, and not one item arrived as ordered⟩

syn mix-up

rel bobble, botch, bungle, fumble; blunder, error, flub, goof, mistake, slipup; chaos, confusion, disarrangement, disarray, disorder, hash, jumble, mess, muddle, shambles

foul up *vb* to make or do (something) in a clumsy or unskillful way — see BOTCH

found *vb* to be responsible for the creation and early operation or use of ⟨John Harvard did not actually *found* the university that now bears his name⟩

syn constitute, establish, inaugurate, initiate, innovate, institute, introduce, launch, pioneer, set up, start

rel author, father, originate; create, invent, produce; construct, erect, put up;

develop, enlarge, expand; endow, finance, fund, subsidize; arrange, organize, systematize

near ant abolish, annihilate, annul, nullify; end, finish, stop, terminate

ant close (down), phase out, shut (up)

foundation *n* **1** a public organization with a particular purpose or function — see INSTITUTION 1

2 an immaterial thing upon which something else rests — see BASE 1

founder *n* a person who establishes a whole new field of endeavor — see FATHER 2

foursquare *adj* **1** free in expressing one's true feelings and opinions — see FRANK

2 going straight to the point clearly and firmly — see STRAIGHTFORWARD 1

foursquare *adv* in an honest and direct manner — see STRAIGHTFORWARD

fox *vb* to get the better of through cleverness — see OUTWIT

foxiness *n* **1** skill in achieving one's ends through indirect, subtle, or underhanded means — see CUNNING 1

2 the inclination or practice of misleading others through lies or trickery — see DECEIT

foxy *adj* clever at attaining one's ends by indirect and often deceptive means — see ARTFUL 1

foyer *n* **1** a centrally located room in a building that serves as a gathering or waiting area or as a passageway into the interior ⟨theatergoers crowded the *foyer* during the play's intermission⟩

syn hall, lobby

rel entry, entryway, hallway, vestibule; concourse, corridor, gallery, passageway; antechamber, anteroom, waiting room

2 the entrance room of a building — see HALL 1

fracas *n* **1** a physical dispute between opposing individuals or groups — see FIGHT 1

2 a rough and often noisy fight usually involving several people — see BRAWL 1

fractionation *n* the act or process of a whole separating into two or more parts or pieces — see SEPARATION 1

fracture *vb* to cause to separate into pieces usually suddenly or forcibly — see BREAK 1

fragile *adj* **1** easily broken ⟨attaching the beautiful but *fragile* ornaments to the Christmas tree is always a touchy operation⟩

syn breakable, delicate, frail

rel dainty, fine, gossamer; flimsy, slight, tenuous; brittle, crisp, crumbly, flaky, friable, short; feeble, infirm, weak; inelastic, inflexible, stiff

near ant firm, solid, substantial; elastic, flexible, resilient

ant nonbreakable, strong, sturdy, tough, unbreakable

2 easily injured without careful handling — see TENDER 1

fragility *n* the state or quality of having a delicate structure — see DELICACY 2

fragment *n* a broken or irregular part of something that often remains incomplete ⟨charred *fragments* of the exploded rocket were scattered over a huge area of ground⟩

syn bit, piece, scrap

rel shred, tatter; end, leftover, remainder, remnant; part, portion, section, segment

fragment *vb* to cause to separate into pieces usually suddenly or forcibly — see BREAK 1

fragmental *adj* lacking some necessary part — see INCOMPLETE

fragmentary *adj* lacking some necessary part — see INCOMPLETE

fragrance *n* a sweet or pleasant smell ⟨the *fragrance* of lilac trees in full bloom⟩

syn aroma, bouquet, incense, perfume, redolence, scent, spice

rel odor

ant reek, stench, stink

fragrant *adj* having a pleasant smell ⟨the balsam fir is a favorite as a Christmas tree because it is so *fragrant*⟩

syn ambrosial, aromatic, perfumed, redolent, savory, scented, sweet

rel flowery, fruity, pungent, spicy; odoriferous, odorous; clean, fresh, pure

near ant odorless, unscented; fusty, musty, stale; gamy (*or* gamey)

ant fetid, foul, malodorous, noisome, putrid, rancid, rank, reeking, reeky, smelly, stinking, stinky, strong

frail *adj* 1 easily broken — see FRAGILE 1

2 easily injured without careful handling — see TENDER 1

3 lacking bodily strength — see WEAK 1

4 lacking strength of will or character — see WEAK 2

frailness *n* 1 the quality or state of lacking physical strength or vigor — see WEAKNESS 1

2 the quality or state of lacking strength of will or character — see WEAKNESS 2

frailty *n* 1 a defect in character — see FAULT 1

2 the quality or state of lacking physical strength or vigor — see WEAKNESS 1

3 the quality or state of lacking strength of will or character — see WEAKNESS 2

frame *n* 1 the arrangement of parts that gives something its basic form ⟨now that the *frame* has been built, we have a better idea of the size of our new house⟩

syn configuration, framework, shell, skeleton, structure

rel lattice, network; contour, figure, outline, profile, shape, silhouette; frame

2 a state of mind dominated by a particular emotion — see MOOD 1

3 the type of body that a person has — see PHYSIQUE

frame *vb* 1 to bring into being by combining, shaping, or transforming materials — see MAKE 1

2 to plan out usually with subtle skill or care — see ENGINEER

3 to put (something) into proper and usually carefully worked out written form — see COMPOSE 1

4 to work out the details of (something) in advance — see PLAN 1

framework *n* the arrangement of parts that gives something its basic form — see FRAME 1

franchise *n* the right to formally express one's position or will in an election — see VOTE 1

frank *adj* free in expressing one's true feelings and opinions ⟨our ballet teacher is very *frank* about telling her students whether she thinks they have the talent for a career in dance⟩

syn candid, direct, forthright, foursquare, free-spoken, honest, open, openhearted, outspoken, plain, plainspoken, straight, straightforward, unguarded, unreserved

rel artless, earnest, sincere; outgoing, uninhibited, unrestrained; vocal, vociferous; abrupt, bluff, blunt, brusque, curt, gruff, sharp; impolite, inconsiderate, rude, tactless, undiplomatic, unsubtle

near ant inhibited, reserved, restrained; close-mouthed, reticent, tight-lipped; ambiguous, circuitous, equivocal, evasive; diplomatic, politic, tactful; civil, considerate, courteous, polite

ant dissembling

frankly *adv* to tell the truth — see ACTUALLY 1

frankness *n* the free expression of one's true feelings and opinions — see CANDOR

frantic *adj* 1 feeling overwhelming fear or worry ⟨the *frantic* parents were searching all over the fairgrounds for their lost child⟩

syn agitated, delirious, distraught, frenzied, hysterical

rel alarmed, anxious, disquieted, disturbed, troubled, upset, worried, wrought (up); berserk, crazed, demented, deranged, mad, maniacal (*also* maniac); raging, ranting, raving

near ant calm, peaceful, serene, tranquil; cool, coolheaded, undisturbed, unperturbed, untroubled

ant collected, composed, self-possessed

2 marked by great and often stressful excitement or activity — see FURIOUS 1

frantically *adv* in a confused and reckless manner — see HELTER-SKELTER 1

fraternal *adj* of, relating to, or befitting brothers ⟨there was a *fraternal* bond between the two boys all throughout their school years⟩

syn brotherly

rel familial, sisterly; chummy, friendly, neighborly

fraternity *n* 1 a group of persons formally joined together for some common interest — see ASSOCIATION 2

2 the body of people in a profession or field of activity — see CORPS

fraternize *vb* 1 to come or be together as friends — see ASSOCIATE 1

---

2 to take part in social activities — see
SOCIALIZE

fraud *n* one who makes false claims of
identity or expertise — see IMPOSTOR

fraudulent *adj* **1** marked by, based on, or
done by the use of dishonest methods to
acquire something of value ⟨hoping to
get millions from the insurance company,
the man made the *fraudulent* claim that
he had been seriously injured in the acci-
dent⟩

syn crooked, deceitful, defrauding, dishonest, double-dealing, false

rel deceptive, misleading, specious

near ant legitimate, true, valid

ant aboveboard, honest, truthful

2 given to or marked by cheating and deception — see DISHONEST 2

fraught *adj* possessing or covered with
great numbers or amounts of something
specified — see RIFE

fray *n* **1** a forceful effort to reach a goal or
objective — see STRUGGLE 1

2 a physical dispute between opposing individuals or groups — see FIGHT 1

3 a rough and often noisy fight usually involving several people — see BRAWL 1

fray *vb* to damage or diminish by continued friction — see ABRADE 1

frayed *adj* worn or torn into or as if into
rags — see RAGGED 2

freak *adj* being out of the ordinary — see
EXCEPTIONAL

freak *n* **1** a person, thing, or event that is
not normal ⟨that snowstorm in April was
a *freak*, since our weather is usually much
balmier by then⟩

syn abnormality, anomaly, monster, monstrosity

rel malformation, mutant, mutation;
character, crackbrain, crackpot, eccentric, kook, oddball, screwball, weirdo; deviant; maverick, nonconformist

near ant sample, specimen; standard

ant average, norm

2 a person with a strong and habitual liking for something — see FAN

3 a sudden impulsive and apparently unmotivated idea or action — see WHIM

freak (out) *vb* **1** to trouble the mind of; to
make uneasy — see DISTURB 1

2 to yield to mental or emotional stress —
see CRACK 2

freakish *adj* prone to sudden illogical
changes of mind, ideas, or actions — see
WHIMSICAL

freakishness *n* an inclination to sudden
illogical changes of mind, ideas, or actions — see WHIMSICALITY

freckle *vb* to mark with small spots especially unevenly — see SPOT

freckled *adj* marked with spots — see
SPOTTED 1

free *adj* **1** not being under the rule or control of another ⟨the 20th century saw
many African countries become *free* after
many years of European rule⟩

syn autonomous, independent, self-governing, separate, sovereign

rel freeborn; delivered, emancipated,
freed, liberated, manumitted, redeemed,
released; unconquered, ungoverned, un-
ruled, unsupervised; empowered, enfranchised; democratic, republican

near ant captive, conquered, enslaved,
subdued, subjugated; inferior, subordinate, subservient

ant dependent, subject, unfree

2 no longer burdened with something unpleasant or painful ⟨after our son arrived
home safely, we were grateful to be *free*
from worry⟩

syn disencumbered, quit, unburdened

rel delivered, freed, liberated, released;
unhampered, unimpeded

3 not bound, confined, or detained by
force ⟨all of the animals in the game preserve are *free* to roam all over its vast
area⟩

syn footloose, loose, unbound, unconfined, unrestrained

rel escaped; uncaged, unchained, unfet-
tered, unleashed; uncaught; unanchored,
unbolted, undone, unfastened, untied;
clear, disengaged, unengaged

phrases at large, at liberty

near ant caught; caged, chained, leashed;
anchored, bolted, fastened, shackled, tied

ant bound, confined, restrained, unfree

4 not costing or charging anything ⟨al-
though the museum normally charges admission, on Wednesdays it is *free* to all⟩

syn complimentary, gratis, gratuitous

rel nominal; discretionary, freewill, optional, voluntary; honorary, uncompen-
sated, unpaid

near ant paid

5 allowing passage without obstruction
— see OPEN 1

6 giving or sharing in abundance and
without hesitation — see GENEROUS 1

7 not being in a state of use, activity, or
employment — see INACTIVE 2

8 showing a lack of proper social reserve
or modesty — see PRESUMPTUOUS 1

free *vb* **1** to set free (as from slavery or
confinement) ⟨a global crusade to *free*
Nelson Mandela from a South African
prison had emerged⟩

syn discharge, emancipate, enfranchise,
liberate, loose, loosen, manumit, release,
spring, unbind, uncage, unchain, unfetter

rel bail (out), deliver, parole, ransom, redeem, rescue; disengage, disentangle, extricate

near ant manacle, shackle, trammel; immure, imprison, incarcerate, intern, jail;
conquer, enslave, subdue, subjugate

ant bind, confine, enchain, fetter, restrain

2 to arrange clear passage of (something)
by removing obstructions — see OPEN 2

3 to rid the surface of (as an area) from
things in the way — see CLEAR 1

4 to set (a person or thing) free of something that encumbers — see RID

5 to set free from entanglement or difficulty — see EXTRICATE

freebie *or* **freebee** *n* something given to someone without expectation of a return — see GIFT 1

freebooter *n* someone who engages in robbery of ships at sea — see PIRATE

freedom *n* 1 the state of being free from the control or power of another ⟨we owe our *freedom* to the untold numbers of soldiers who have fought in our nation's wars since its founding⟩

syn autonomy, independence, liberty, self-government, sovereignty

rel emancipation, enfranchisement, liberation, manumission, release

near ant captivity, enchainment, enslavement, imprisonment, incarceration, subjugation

ant dependence, subjection

2 the right to act or move freely ⟨as special guests of the owners, the youngsters had full *freedom* of the resort and its private beach⟩

syn authorization, free hand, latitude, license (*or* licence), run

rel authority, mandate, power; range, room, space

free-for-all *adj* freely available for use or participation by all — see OPEN 2

free-for-all *n* a rough and often noisy fight usually involving several people — see BRAWL 1

free hand *n* the right to act or move freely — see FREEDOM 2

freehanded *adj* giving or sharing in abundance and without hesitation — see GENEROUS 1

freeing *n* the act of setting free from slavery — see LIBERATION

freely *adv* 1 of one's own free will — see VOLUNTARILY

2 without difficulty — see EASILY

free-spoken *adj* free in expressing one's true feelings and opinions — see FRANK

freestanding *adj* not physically attached to another unit — see SEPARATE 1

freeway *n* a passage cleared for public vehicular travel — see WAY 1

freewheeling *adj* not held back by rules, duties, or worries ⟨James Bond has long been the model of the *freewheeling* hero who encounters danger and excitement in every corner of the globe⟩

syn footloose

rel easygoing, nonchalant, relaxed; unattached, uncommitted, unbridled, ungoverned, unrestrained; uninhibited, unsuppressed; self-assured, self-confident, self-reliant

near ant attached, committed

ant tied

freewill *adj* 1 made, given, or done with one's own free will — see INTENTIONAL 1

2 done, made, or given with one's own free will — see VOLUNTARY 1

free will *n* the act or power of making one's own choices or decisions ⟨all of the workers at the homeless shelter are unpaid and are there of their own *free will*⟩

syn accord, choice, option, self-determination, volition, will

rel election, preference; inclination, penchant, predilection, predisposition

near ant coercion, compulsion, constraint, duress, force

freeze *n* a weather condition marked by low temperatures — see COLD

freeze *vb* to become physically firm or solid — see HARDEN 1

freezing *adj* having a low or subnormal temperature — see COLD 1

freight *n* a mass or quantity of something taken up and carried, conveyed, or transported — see LOAD 1

frenetic *adj* marked by great and often stressful excitement or activity — see FURIOUS 1

frenzied *adj* 1 being in a state of increased activity or agitation — see FEVERISH 1

2 feeling overwhelming fear or worry — see FRANTIC 1

3 marked by great and often stressful excitement or activity — see FURIOUS 1

frenziedly *adv* in a confused and reckless manner — see HELTER-SKELTER 1

frenzy *n* a state of wildly excited activity or emotion ⟨in its *frenzy* to flee the danger the crowd became uncontrollable, and a number of people were trampled to death⟩

syn agitation, delirium, distraction, furor, furore, fury, hysteria, rage, rampage, uproar

rel chaos, confusion, disorder, turmoil; clamor, commotion, hubbub, hurly-burly, tumult

near ant calm, peacefulness, serenity, tranquillity (*or* tranquility)

frequency *n* the fact or state of happening often ⟨the *frequency* of twins in that family is remarkable⟩

syn commonness, prevalence

rel constancy, continualness, regularity; appearance, incidence, occurrence

ant infrequency, uncommonness, unusualness

frequent *adj* 1 appearing or occurring repeatedly from time to time — see REGULAR 1

2 often observed or encountered — see COMMON 1

frequent *vb* to go to or to spend time in often ⟨like their counterparts elsewhere, the town's teenagers like to *frequent* the local malls⟩

syn hang around (in), hang out (at), haunt, resort (to), visit

rel attend, take in; infest, invade, swarm, overrun; drop (in *or* by), pop (in *or* in), stop (in *or* by); sojourn (at), stay (at), stop (over), tarry (in)

near ant elude, escape, evade

ant avoid, shun

frequenter *n* a person who visits another — see GUEST 1

frequently *adv* many times — see OFTEN

---

syn synonym(s)   *rel* related words
ant antonym(s)   *near ant* near antonym(s)

fresh *adj* **1** being in an original and unused or unspoiled state ⟨the restaurant uses only really *fresh* ingredients in all of its dishes⟩

syn brand-new, pristine, virgin

rel unaltered, unblemished, unbruised, uncontaminated, undamaged, undefiled, unharmed, unhurt, unimpaired, uninjured, unpolluted, unsoiled, unspoiled, unsullied, untainted, untouched, unused, unworn

near ant blemished, bruised, damaged, defiled, harmed, hurt, impaired, injured, soiled, sullied, tainted; faded, shopworn, used, worn; contaminated, polluted, spoiled

ant stale

2 displaying or marked by rude boldness — see NERVY 1

3 not known or experienced before — see NEW 2

freshen *vb* to bring back to a former condition or vigor — see RENEW 1

freshened *adj* made or become fresh in spirits or vigor — see NEW 4

freshly *adv* not long ago — see NEWLY

freshman *n* a person who is just starting out in a field of activity — see BEGINNER

freshness *n* the quality or appeal of being new — see NOVELTY 1

fret *n* a state of nervous or irritated concern ⟨one of my customers always gets into a *fret* if I'm so much as 15 minutes late delivering his newspaper⟩

syn dither, fluster, fuss, huff, lather, pother, stew, tizzy, twitter

rel dudgeon, pique; alarm, panic; ado, agitation, delirium, distraction, furor, hysteria, uproar; nervous breakdown

fret *vb* **1** to consume or wear away gradually — see EAT 2

2 to damage or diminish by continued friction — see ABRADE 1

3 to experience concern or anxiety — see WORRY 1

friable *adj* having a texture that readily breaks into little pieces under pressure — see CRISP 1

friary *n* a residence for men under religious vows — see MONASTERY

friction *n* a lack of agreement or harmony — see DISCORD

frictionless *adj* having or marked by agreement in feeling or action — see HARMONIOUS 3

friend *n* **1** a person who has a strong liking for and trust in another ⟨really close *friends* who like to do everything together and are always sharing secrets⟩

syn buddy, chum, comrade, confidant, crony, familiar, intimate, pal

rel acquaintance; associate, cohort, colleague, companion, fellow, hearty, hobnobber, mate, partner, peer; brother, sister; accomplice, ally, collaborator, confederate; benefactor, supporter, sympathizer, well-wisher; friendly

near ant adversary, antagonist, opponent, rival; archenemy, nemesis

ant enemy, foe

2 a person who actively supports or favors a cause — see EXPONENT

friendliness *n* kindly concern, interest, or support — see GOODWILL 1

friendly *adj* **1** having or showing kindly feeling and sincere interest ⟨all of the kids at Stacy's new school seemed *friendly*⟩ ⟨as a *friendly* gesture, we presented our new neighbors with a plate of homemade cookies⟩

syn amicable, companionable, comradely, cordial, genial, hearty, neighborly, warm, warmhearted

rel affable, approachable, gracious; convivial, gregarious, hospitable, sociable, social; jolly, jovial, merry; extroverted (*also* extraverted), outgoing; brotherly, fraternal, sisterly; close, familiar, intimate; affectionate, devoted, loving

near ant cold, cool, frigid; bellicose, belligerent, contentious, quarrelsome

ant antagonistic, hostile, unfriendly

2 closely acquainted — see FAMILIAR 1

3 expressing approval — see FAVORABLE 1

friendship *n* kindly concern, interest, or support — see GOODWILL 1

fright *n* **1** something unpleasant to look at — see EYESORE

2 the emotion experienced in the presence or threat of danger — see FEAR

frighten *vb* to strike with fear ⟨around the campfire the campers tried to *frighten* one another with ghostly legends and grisly tales⟩

syn affright, alarm, horrify, panic, scare, shock, spook, startle, terrify, terrorize

rel appall, dismay; amaze, astound, awe; chill, daunt, demoralize, dispirit, unman, unnerve; discompose, disconcert, disquiet, disturb, perturb, upset

near ant cheer, comfort, console, solace, soothe; embolden, encourage, hearten

ant reassure

frightened *adj* filled with fear or dread — see AFRAID 1

frightening *adj* causing fear — see FEARFUL 1

frightful *adj* **1** causing fear — see FEARFUL 1

2 extremely disturbing or repellent — see HORRIBLE 1

frightfully *adv* to a great degree — see VERY 1

frightfulness *n* the quality of inspiring intense dread or dismay — see HORROR 1

frigid *adj* **1** having a low or subnormal temperature — see COLD 1

2 lacking in friendliness or warmth of feeling — see COLD 2

frill *n* **1** a strip of fabric gathered or pleated on one edge and used as trimming — see RUFFLE

2 something adding to pleasure or comfort but not absolutely necessary — see LUXURY 1

3 something that decorates or beautifies — see DECORATION 1

fringe *n* the line or relatively narrow space that marks the outer limit of something — see BORDER 1

fringe *vb* **1** to be adjacent to — see ADJOIN 1

2 to serve as a border for — see BORDER

fringing *adj* having a border in common — see ADJACENT

frippery *n* **1** dressy clothing — see FINERY

2 something of little importance — see TRIFLE

frisk *vb* to play and run about happily — see FROLIC 1

friskiness *n* a natural disposition for playful behavior — see PLAYFULNESS

frisky *adj* **1** given to good-natured joking or teasing — see PLAYFUL

2 having much high-spirited energy and movement — see LIVELY 1

fritter *n* a small usually rounded mass of minced food that has been fried — see CAKE

fritter (away) *vb* to use up carelessly — see WASTE 1

frivol *vb* to show a liking for someone of the opposite sex just for fun — see FLIRT

frivolity *n* a lack of seriousness often at an improper time ⟨the boys were scolded for joking during the funeral service, which was hardly the time for *frivolity*⟩
syn facetiousness, flightiness, flippancy, frivolousness, levity, light-headedness, lightness
rel cheerfulness, gaiety (*also* gayety), glee, high-spiritedness, lightheartedness, merriment, mirth
near ant gloom, melancholy, moroseness, sadness, sullenness
ant gravity, intentness, seriousness, soberness, sobriety

frivolous *adj* **1** lacking importance — see UNIMPORTANT

2 lacking in seriousness or maturity — see GIDDY 1

frivolousness *n* a lack of seriousness often at an improper time — see FRIVOLITY 1

frock *n* a garment with a joined blouse and skirt for a woman or girl — see DRESS 1

frolic *n* **1** a playful or mischievous act intended as a joke — see PRANK

2 a time or instance of carefree fun — see FLING 1

3 activity engaged in to amuse oneself — see PLAY 1

frolic *vb* **1** to play and run about happily ⟨scores of swimmers were *frolicking* in the ocean surf along the beach⟩
syn caper, cavort, disport, frisk, gambol, lark, rollick, romp, sport
rel bound, leap, skip, spring, tumble; curvet, dance, prance; carouse, revel, roister; carry on, fool (around), horse (around); clown, cut up; joyride, roughhouse, skylark
phrases kick up one's heels
near ant mope, stew, sulk

2 to engage in activity for amusement — see PLAY 1

frolicking *n* activity engaged in to amuse oneself — see PLAY 1

frolicsome *adj* **1** given to good-natured joking or teasing — see PLAYFUL

2 joyously unrestrained — see EXUBERANT

front *n* **1** a forward part or surface ⟨the *front* of the church features a magnificent stained-glass window⟩
syn exterior, facade (*also* façade), face, forepart, outside, skin, surface, veneer
near ant innards, inside, interior
ant back, rear, reverse

2 a display of emotion or behavior that is insincere or intended to deceive — see MASQUERADE

front *vb* to stand or sit with the face or front toward — see FACE 1

frontier *n* **1** a region along the dividing line between two countries ⟨the Apaches were once feared on both sides of the U.S.-Mexico *frontier*⟩
syn border, borderland, march
rel no-man's-land

2 a rural region that forms the edge of the settled or developed part of a country ⟨Alaska has been called America's last *frontier*⟩
syn backwater, backwoods, bush, hinterland, up-country
rel country, countryside, sticks

frontiersman *n* a person who settles in a new region ⟨the *frontiersmen* were willing to brave harsh living conditions in order to achieve a better life⟩
syn colonist, colonizer, homesteader, pioneer, settler
rel explorer, pathfinder, trailblazer

frost *n* a covering of tiny ice crystals on a cold surface ⟨the wintertime routine of scraping the *frost* off the car's windshield every morning⟩
syn hoar, hoarfrost, rime
rel frostwork

frosty *adj* **1** having a low or subnormal temperature — see COLD 1

2 having or showing a lack of friendliness or interest in others — see COOL 1

3 lacking in friendliness or warmth of feeling — see COLD 2

froth *n* a light mass of fine bubbles formed in or on a liquid — see FOAM

frothy *adj* covered with, consisting of, or resembling foam — see FOAMY

froward *adj* **1** engaging in or marked by childish misbehavior — see NAUGHTY

2 given to resisting authority or another's control — see DISOBEDIENT

3 given to resisting control or discipline by others — see UNCONTROLLABLE

frowardness *n* refusal to obey — see DISOBEDIENCE

frown *n* a twisting of the facial features in disgust or disapproval — see GRIMACE

frown *vb* to look with anger or disapproval ⟨the principal just stood there and *frowned* at the student who, once again, was in trouble⟩

---

syn synonym(s)   *rel* related words
ant antonym(s)   *near ant* near antonym(s)

syn glare, gloom, glower, lower (*also* lour), scowl

rel gape, gaze, ogle, stare; grimace, pout; growl, snarl, sneer

phrases look daggers

ant beam, smile

frown (on) *vb* to hold an unfavorable opinion of — see DISAPPROVE

frowsy *or* **frowzy** *adj* lacking neatness in dress or person — see SLOPPY 1

frozen *adj* 1 firmly positioned in place and difficult to dislodge — see TIGHT 2

2 having been established and usually not subject to change — see FIXED 1

frugal *adj* careful in the management of money or resources ⟨by being *frugal*, the family is able to stretch its monthly budget⟩

syn economical, economizing, provident, scrimping, sparing, thrifty

rel conserving, preserving, saving; forehanded, foresighted, prudent; pennywise; cheap, close, closefisted, miserly, niggardly, parsimonious, stingy, stinting, tight, tightfisted

near ant improvident, shortsighted; freehanded, generous, liberal, openhanded, unsparing; extravagant, indulgent, lavish

ant prodigal, wasteful

frugality *n* careful management of material resources — see ECONOMY

fruit *n* 1 a condition or occurrence traceable to a cause — see EFFECT 1

2 something produced by physical or intellectual effort — see PRODUCT 1

fruitful *adj* 1 producing abundantly — see FERTILE

2 producing or capable of producing a desired result — see EFFECTIVE 1

fruition *n* the state of being actual or complete ⟨when she landed the lead in a Broadway play, a lifelong dream was brought to *fruition*⟩

syn accomplishment, achievement, actuality, attainment, consummation, fulfillment, realization

ant naught (*also* nought), nonfulfillment

fruitless *adj* producing no results — see FUTILE

frustrate *vb* to prevent from achieving a goal ⟨a multitude of conflicting opinions *frustrated* me in my attempt to find a computer that best suits my needs⟩

syn baffle, balk, beat, checkmate, foil, thwart

rel bar, block, hinder, impede, obstruct; arrest, check, halt, stop; forestall, obviate, preclude; negate, neutralize, nullify; counteract, offset; conquer, defeat, overcome

near ant abet, aid, assist; ease, facilitate, smooth;

ant advance, cultivate, encourage, forward, foster, further, nurture, promote

frustrating *adj* causing annoyance — see ANNOYING

frustration *n* 1 something that is a source of irritation — see ANNOYANCE 3

2 the emotion felt when one's expectations are not met — see DISAPPOINTMENT 1

3 the feeling of impatience or anger caused by another's repeated disagreeable acts — see ANNOYANCE 2

fuddy–duddy *n* a person with old-fashioned ideas — see FOGY

fudge *n* 1 language, behavior, or ideas that are absurd and contrary to good sense — see NONSENSE 1

2 unintelligible or meaningless talk — see GIBBERISH

fudge *vb* 1 to avoid giving a definite answer or position — see EQUIVOCATE

2 to use dishonest methods to achieve a goal — see CHEAT 1

fuel *n* something with a usable capacity for doing work ⟨such fossil *fuels* as coal, petroleum, and natural gas⟩

syn energy, power

rel kindling, propellant

fugitive *adj* 1 hard to find, capture, or isolate — see ELUSIVE

2 lasting only for a short time — see MOMENTARY

fulfill *or* **fulfil** *vb* 1 to do what is required by the terms of ⟨the football player must remain with the team one more year to *fulfill* his contract⟩

syn answer, comply (with), fill, keep, meet, redeem, satisfy

rel complete, conclude, finalize, finish; accomplish, achieve, bring about, bring off, effect; discharge, execute, perform

phrases abide by, make good

near ant disregard, ignore, neglect, overlook, slight

ant breach, break, violate

2 to carry through (as a process) to completion — see PERFORM 1

fulfilling *adj* making one feel good inside — see HEARTWARMING

fulfillment *n* 1 the doing of an action — see COMMISSION 2

2 the state of being actual or complete — see FRUITION

full *adj* 1 containing or seeming to contain the greatest quantity or number possible ⟨at the start of the game everyone was *full* of energy and hope⟩ ⟨the boy's bedroom is *full* of sports trophies and medals⟩

syn brimful, brimming, bursting, chockfull (*or* chockful), crammed, crowded, fat, filled, jammed, jam-packed, loaded, packed, stuffed

rel overcrowded, overfilled, overflowing, overfull, overloaded, overstuffed; abounding, fraught, replete, rife, swarming, teeming

near ant deficient, incomplete, insufficient, short; depleted, drained, exhausted

ant bare, blank, devoid, empty, stark, vacant, void

2 of the highest degree ⟨even at the age of eighteen he hadn't reached his *full* height⟩ ⟨a boat going at *full* speed⟩

syn greatest, maximum, top, topmost, utmost

rel high

near ant low
ant least, lowest, minimal, minimum

3 having one's appetite completely satisfied ⟨even the heartiest eaters are sure to be *full* when they leave that restaurant⟩
syn sated, satiate, satiated, stuffed, surfeited
rel glutted, gorged, overfed, overfull, overstuffed
near ant underfed, undernourished
ant empty, hungry, starving

4 covering everything or all important points — see ENCYCLOPEDIC

5 having an abundance of some characteristic quality (as flavor) — see FULL-BODIED

6 having an excess of body fat — see FAT 1

7 including many small descriptive features — see DETAILED 1

8 not lacking any part or member that properly belongs to it — see COMPLETE 1

full *adv* **1** to a full extent or degree — see FULLY 1

2 to a great degree — see VERY 1

full *n* a complete amount of something — see WHOLE

full blast *adv* with all power or resources being used ⟨Mom and Dad arrived home to find the stereo going *full blast* and the kitchen a mess⟩
syn all out, full steam ahead, full tilt, tooth and nail
rel completely, fully, totally; extremely, utterly
phrases in full career, to the hilt

full–blooded *adj* of unmixed ancestry — see PUREBRED

full–blown *adj* fully grown or developed — see MATURE 1

full–bodied *adj* having an abundance of some characteristic quality (as flavor) ⟨after that huge Sunday brunch, Mom and Dad needed a *full-bodied* coffee⟩
syn concentrated, full, potent, rich, robust, strong
rel heavy; straight, undiluted, unmixed
near ant diluted, watered (down), watery
ant light, thin, thin, weak

full dress *n* dressy clothing — see FINERY

full–fledged *adj* fully grown or developed — see MATURE 1

full–grown *adj* fully grown or developed — see MATURE 1

full–scale *adj* trying all possibilities — see EXHAUSTIVE

full steam ahead *adv* with all power or resources being used — see FULL BLAST

full tilt *adv* **1** with all power or resources being used — see FULL BLAST

2 with great speed — see FAST 1

fully *adv* **1** to a full extent or degree ⟨only with daybreak did we *fully* realize the extent of the damage from the storm⟩
syn all, altogether, clean, completely, dead, entirely, fast, flat, full, perfectly,

plumb [*chiefly dialect*], quite, thoroughly, totally, utterly, well, wholly
rel absolutely, categorically, unqualifiedly; by and large, chiefly, generally, largely, mainly, more or less, mostly, predominately, primarily, principally
phrases at length, to pieces, to the hilt
near ant barely, hardly, just, scarcely
ant partially, partly

2 with attention to all aspects or details — see THOROUGHLY 1

fulminate *vb* to talk loudly and wildly — see RANT

fulmination *n* harsh insulting language — see ABUSE 1

fulsome *adj* overly or insincerely flattering ⟨the player's *fulsome* praise for the coach showed just how hard he was trying to be named captain of the team⟩
syn adulatory, gushing, unctuous
rel drooling, slavering, slobbering; cloying, sickening; demonstrative, effusive, mushy; hypocritical, insincere, sanctimonious; endearing, ingratiating; extravagant, lavish, unrestrained; abundant, copious, profuse
near ant earnest, genuine, heartfelt, sincere, unfeigned

fumble *n* an unintentional departure from truth or accuracy — see ERROR 1

fumble *vb* **1** to make or do (something) in a clumsy or unskillful way — see BOTCH

2 to search for something blindly or uncertainly — see GROPE

fumbled *adj* showing or marked by a lack of skill and tact (as in dealing with a situation) — see AWKWARD 2

fume *vb* **1** to be excited or emotionally stirred up with anger — see BOIL 1

2 to express one's anger usually violently — see RAGE 1

fuming *adj* feeling or showing anger — see ANGRY

fun *adj* providing amusement or enjoyment ⟨there were so many *fun* things to do at summer camp that I really hated to leave⟩
syn amusing, delightful, diverting, enjoyable, entertaining, pleasurable ·
rel agreeable, beguiling, pleasant; funny, hilarious, humorous; gay, happy, jolly, merry; exciting, stimulating, thrilling
near ant disagreeable, unpleasant
ant boring, dull

fun *n* **1** someone or something that provides amusement or enjoyment ⟨theme parks with their rides, shows, and games are great *fun* for the whole family⟩
syn delight, diversion, entertainment, pleasure, recreation
rel binge, fling, frolic, gambol, lark, revel, rollick, romp, spree; carousing, festivity, gaiety (*also* gayety), hilarity, merrymaking, revelry; picnic; laugh, riot, scream
ant bore, bummer, downer, drag

2 an attitude or manner not to be taken seriously ⟨when I said that playing the piano like that could get you arrested, I only said it in *fun*⟩
syn game, jest, play, sport

rel facetiousness, flippancy, levity
near ant earnestness, gravity, seriousness
ant earnest

3 activity engaged in to amuse oneself — see PLAY 1

fun *vb* to make jokes — see JOKE

function *n* **1** a social gathering — see PARTY 1

2 an assignment at which one regularly works for pay — see JOB 1

3 the action for which a person or thing is specially fitted or used or for which a thing exists — see ROLE

function *vb* to have a certain purpose ⟨the heart *functions* as a pump for the blood⟩
syn act, perform, serve, work
rel operate, run; control, direct, manage

functional *adj* **1** being in effective operation — see ACTIVE 1

2 capable of being put to use or account — see PRACTICAL 1

3 capable of or suitable for being used for a particular purpose — see USABLE 1

functionary *n* **1** a person who holds a public office — see OFFICIAL

2 a worker in a government agency — see BUREAUCRAT

functioning *adj* being in effective operation — see ACTIVE 1

fund *n* **1** a sum of money set aside for a particular purpose ⟨our club has a *fund* for parties—which we like to have as often as possible⟩
syn account, budget, deposit, kitty, nest egg, pool
rel chest, coffer(s); assets, savings, savings account; bankroll, cache, collection, hoard, reserve, treasure; petty cash, pin money, pocket money, spending money

2 funds *pl* available money ⟨my *funds* were a little low, so I asked my favorite lending institution—Dad—for a small advance on my allowance⟩
syn bankroll, finances, pocket, resources, wherewithal
rel cash, money; assets, capital, means, wealth; purse, treasury

3 the number of individuals or amount of something available at any given time — see SUPPLY

fund *vb* **1** to furnish (as an institution) with a regular source of income — see ENDOW 2

2 to provide money for — see FINANCE 1

fundamental *adj* of or relating to the simplest facts or theories of a subject — see ELEMENTARY

fundamentals *n pl* general or basic truths on which other truths or theories can be based — see PRINCIPLES 1

funeral *adj* expressing or suggesting mourning — see MOURNFUL 1

funeral director *n* a person who manages funerals and prepares the dead for burial or cremation ⟨the *funeral director* instructed the pallbearers on how to proceed⟩
syn mortician, undertaker
rel embalmer

funereal *adj* causing or marked by an atmosphere lacking in cheer — see GLOOMY 1

funnel *vb* to cause to move to a central point or along a restricted pathway — see CHANNEL

funniness *n* the amusing quality or element in something — see HUMOR 1

funning *adj* marked by or expressive of mild or good-natured teasing — see QUIZZICAL

funny *adj* **1** causing or intended to cause laughter ⟨a very *funny* movie that had audiences rolling in the aisles⟩
syn antic, comic, comical, droll, farcical, hilarious, humorous, hysterical, laughable, ludicrous, ridiculous, riotous, risible, screaming, side-splitting, uproarious
rel amusing, diverting, entertaining; clownish, slapstick, zany; facetious, flip, flippant, pert, smart, smart-alecky (*or* smart-aleck); jocular, playful, waggish; priceless, rich, whimsical, witty; gleeful, merry, mirthful
near ant grave, serious, sober, solemn, somber (*or* sombre); affecting, moving, poignant, touching, tragic; lachrymose, mournful, sad, tearful
ant humorless, lame, uncomic, unfunny

2 different from the ordinary in a way that causes curiosity or suspicion — see ODD 2

3 noticeably different from what is generally found or experienced — see UNUSUAL 1

funny *n* a series of drawings that tell a story or part of a story — see COMIC STRIP

fur *n* **1** the hairy covering of a mammal especially when fine, soft, and thick ⟨the chinchilla is known for its exceptionally soft *fur*⟩
syn coat, fleece, hair, pelage, pile, wool
rel hide, pelt, skin

2 a soft airy substance or covering — see FUZZ

3 the outer covering of an animal removed for its commercial value — see HIDE 1

furbelow *n* a strip of fabric gathered or pleated on one edge and used as trimming — see RUFFLE

furious *adj* **1** marked by great and often stressful excitement or activity ⟨everyone worked at a *furious* pace in order to get the float ready for the parade⟩
syn delirious, feverish, fierce, frantic, frenetic, frenzied, mad, rabid, violent, wild
rel concentrated, high-pressured, intense, vehement; excessive, extreme, inordinate; crazy, demented, insane, irrational
near ant calm, peaceful, quiet, subdued, tranquil; moderate, reasonable, temperate; casual, easygoing, low-pressure
ant relaxed

2 extreme in degree, power, or effect — see INTENSE

3 feeling or showing anger — see ANGRY

4 marked by bursts of destructive force or intense activity — see VIOLENT 1

furlough *n* the termination of the employment of an employee or a work force often temporarily — see LAYOFF

furnish *vb* **1** to provide (someone) with what is needed for a task or activity ⟨the students were *furnished* with brushes, crayons, pencils, and various other art supplies⟩

syn accoutre (*or* accouter), equip, fit (out), outfit, rig, supply

rel stock, store; bestow, donate, give, present; deal, dispense, distribute, dole (out); allocate, allot, assign

near ant deprive, dispossess, divest, strip

2 to put (something) into the possession of someone for use or consumption ⟨we'll gladly *furnish* the food for any out-of-town guests⟩

syn deliver, feed, give, hand, hand over, provide, supply

rel administer, dispense, distribute, dole (out), mete (out), parcel (out); cede, deed, transfer

near ant conserve, preserve, save

ant hold (back), keep (back), reserve, retain, withhold

furnishings *n pl* the movable articles in a room — see FURNITURE

furniture *n* the movable articles in a room ⟨we bought all new *furniture* for our new house⟩

syn appointments, cabinetwork, furnishings, movables (*or* moveables)

rel effects, goods, possessions

near ant fixtures

furor *n* **1** a state of noisy, confused activity — see COMMOTION

2 a state of wildly excited activity or emotion — see FRENZY

3 an intense emotional state of displeasure with someone or something — see ANGER

furore *n* **1** a state of noisy, confused activity — see COMMOTION

2 a state of wildly excited activity or emotion — see FRENZY

furrow *n* a small fold in a soft and otherwise smooth surface — see WRINKLE 1

furrow *vb* **1** to cut into and turn over the sod of (a piece of land) using a bladed implement — see PLOW 1

2 to develop creases or folds — see WRINKLE 1

furry *adj* **1** covered with or as if with hair — see HAIRY 1

2 made of or resembling hair — see HAIRY 2

further *adj* resulting in an increase in amount or number — see ADDITIONAL

further *adv* **1** at or to a greater distance or more advanced point — see FARTHER

2 in addition to what has been said — see MORE 1

further *vb* to help the growth or development of — see FOSTER 1

furtherance *n* forward movement in time or place — see ADVANCE 1

furthermore *adv* in addition to what has been said — see MORE 1

furthermost *adj* most distant from a center — see EXTREME 1

furthest *adj* most distant from a center — see EXTREME 1

furtive *adj* **1** given to acting in secret and to concealing one's intentions — see SNEAKY 1

2 undertaken or done so as to escape being observed or known by others — see SECRET 1

fury *n* **1** a bad-tempered scolding woman — see SHREW

2 a state of wildly excited activity or emotion — see FRENZY

3 an intense emotional state of displeasure with someone or something — see ANGER

fuse *vb* **1** to come together to form a single unit — see UNITE 1

2 to go from a solid to a liquid state — see LIQUEFY

3 to turn into a single mass that is more or less the same throughout — see BLEND 1

fusillade *n* a rapid or overwhelming outpouring of many things at once — see BARRAGE

fusion *n* a distinct entity formed by the combining of two or more different things — see BLEND

fuss *n* **1** a feeling or declaration of disapproval or dissent — see OBJECTION

2 a state of nervous or irritated concern — see FRET

3 a state of noisy, confused activity — see COMMOTION

4 an expression of dissatisfaction, pain, or resentment — see COMPLAINT 1

fuss *vb* **1** to express dissatisfaction, pain, or resentment usually tiresomely — see COMPLAIN

2 to make an exaggerated display of affection or enthusiasm — see GUSH 2

3 to make often peevish criticisms or objections about matters that are minor, unimportant, or irrelevant — see QUIBBLE

4 to use flattery or the doing of favors in order to win approval especially from a superior — see FAWN

fusser *n* **1** a person who makes frequent complaints usually about little things — see CRY-BABY

2 an irritable and complaining person — see GROUCH

fussy *adj* **1** given to complaining a lot ⟨the kids riding in the back were *fussy* passengers, always asking "Are we there yet?"⟩

syn crabby, cranky, grouchy, grumpy, querulous

rel fidgety, restive, restless, squirmy, uneasy; discontented, disgruntled, displeased, dissatisfied; fretful, nervous, worrisome; cantankerous, crotchety, irascible, irritable, ornery

near ant amiable, genial, good-humored, good-natured, good-tempered; accommodating, complaisant, obliging; easygoing, laid-back, relaxed

---

syn synonym(s)   *rel* related words
ant antonym(s)   *near ant* near antonym(s)

ant uncomplaining

2 hard to please — see FINICKY

3 taking great care and effort — see PAINSTAKING

fusty *adj* having an unpleasant smell — see MALODOROUS

futile *adj* producing no results ⟨the prison is so well guarded that all attempts to escape have proven *futile*⟩

syn abortive, bootless, empty, fruitless, ineffective, ineffectual, unavailing, unproductive, unprofitable, unsuccessful, useless, vain

rel hollow, idle, meaningless, pointless, worthless; hopeless, impossible; inadequate, insufficient

phrases in vain, of no avail

near ant meaningful, worthwhile; adequate, sufficient

ant effective, effectual, efficacious, efficient, fruitful, productive, profitable, successful

future *adj* of a time after the present ⟨we must preserve our national parks in all their glory so that *future* generations can experience the majesty of nature⟩

syn coming, unborn

rel approaching, forthcoming, imminent, impending, nearing, oncoming, pending, upcoming; later, posterior, subsequent; anticipated, awaited, expected, planned, predicted, projected; eventual, final, last, ultimate

near ant ancient, olden

ant bygone, past

future *n* **1** time that is to come ⟨in the *future*, there may be medical discoveries that are beyond our fondest dreams⟩

syn by-and-by, futurity, hereafter, offing

rel eventuality, finality; posterity

near ant yesterday, yesteryear; antiquity, old, yore

ant past

2 what is going to happen to someone in the time ahead — see FORTUNE 1

futurist *n* one who predicts future events or developments — see PROPHET

futurity *n* time that is to come — see FUTURE 1

fuzz *n* a soft airy substance or covering ⟨a comfortable old sweater with clumps of *fuzz* all over it⟩

syn down, floss, fluff, fur, lint, nap, pile

rel batting

fuzzy *adj* **1** made of or resembling hair — see HAIRY 2

2 not clearly expressed — see VAGUE 1

3 not seen or understood clearly — see FAINT 1

G

---

gab *vb* to engage in casual or rambling conversation — see CHAT

gabble *n* unintelligible or meaningless talk — see GIBBERISH

gabble *vb* **1** to engage in casual or rambling conversation — see CHAT

2 to speak rapidly, inarticulately, and usually unintelligibly — see BABBLE 1

gabbler *n* a person who talks constantly — see CHATTERBOX

gabby *adj* fond of talking or conversation — see TALKATIVE

gabfest *n* friendly, informal conversation or an instance of this — see CHAT

gad (about) *vb* to move about from place to place aimlessly — see WANDER

gadabout *n* a person who roams about without a fixed route or destination — see NOMAD

gadfly *n* one who is obnoxiously annoying — see NUISANCE 1

gadget *n* an interesting and often novel device with a practical use ⟨she tried out a new *gadget* for weeding the garden⟩

syn appliance, contraption, contrivance, gimmick, gizmo (*or* gismo), jigger

rel implement, instrument, tool, utensil; ingenuity, innovation, invention; accessory, adjunct; mechanism, trick

gaffe *n* a socially improper or unsuitable act or remark — see IMPROPRIETY 2

gag *n* something said or done to cause laughter — see JOKE 1

gag *vb* **1** to discharge the contents of the stomach through the mouth — see VOMIT

2 to experience complete or partial blockage of the windpipe — see CHOKE 2

gage *n* something given or held to assure that the giver will keep a promise — see PLEDGE 1

gaiety *also* **gayety** *n* **1** dressy clothing — see FINERY

2 joyful or festive activity — see MERRYMAKING

gaily *also* **gayly** *adv* **1** in a cheerful or happy manner ⟨we sat around the table, *gaily* teasing each other and laughing about the good old days⟩

syn cheerfully, happily, heartily, jocosely, jovially, merrily, mirthfully

rel blithely, blithesomely, breezily, brightly, buoyantly, cheerily, gladly, gladsomely, sanguinely, sunnily; good-humoredly, good-naturedly

near ant abjectly, dejectedly, despondently, disconsolately, dispiritedly, wretchedly; dolefully, dolorously, forlornly, mournfully, plaintively, sorrowfully; dourly, glumly, sternly, sulkily, sullenly; dismally, drearily, gloomily *ant* bleakly, cheerlessly, darkly, heavily, miserably, morosely, unhappily

2 in a quick and spirited manner ⟨children *gaily* running to the buses on the last day of school⟩

syn animatedly, animately, exuberantly, high-spiritedly, jauntily, pertly, sprightly, trippingly

rel friskily, playfully, skittishly, sportively; briskly, crisply, snappily, springily; breezily, cockishly; allegro

near ant idly, indolently, lazily, slothfully; heavily, inactively, listlessly

ant dully, inanimately, sluggishly, tardily

3 in a bright and showy way ⟨the Mexican dancers were *gaily* dressed in lavish, bright costumes⟩

syn dashingly, flamboyantly, flashily, jauntily, rakishly, swankily

rel garishly, gaudily, loud, loudly, ostentatiously; fancily, gallantly, ornately; nattily, neatly, smartly; conspicuously, luridly, spectacularly, strikingly; gorgeously, splendidly

near ant inconspicuously, unobtrusively, unpretentiously; chastely, demurely, homely, modestly; plainly, simply; colorlessly, dirtily, drably, dully; bleakly, severely, somberly

ant conservatively, plain, quietly

gain *n* **1** something added (as by growth) — see INCREASE 1

2 the amount of money left when expenses are subtracted from the total amount received — see PROFIT 1

3 *gains pl* an increase usually measured in money that comes from labor, business, or property — see INCOME

gain *vb* **1** to increase in ⟨as the car coasted downhill, it gradually *gained* speed and momentum⟩

syn build (up), gather, grow (in), pick up

rel accrue, accumulate, amass; excite, stimulate; enhance, enrich, maximize; boost, jack (up), mount, step up

near ant abate, diminish (in), dip, dwindle, fall (in), lessen, taper, taper off

ant decrease (in), lose

2 to receive as return for effort — see EARN 1

3 to become healthy and strong again after illness or weakness — see CONVALESCE

gainful *adj* yielding a profit — see PROFITABLE 1

gainsay *vb* **1** to declare not to be true — see DENY 1

2 to make an assertion that is contrary to one made by (another) — see CONTRADICT 1

gal *n* **1** a woman with whom one is in love — see GIRLFRIEND

2 a young usually unmarried woman — see GIRL 1

gala *n* a time or program of special events and entertainment in honor of something — see FESTIVAL

gale *n* a sudden intense expression of strong feeling — see OUTBURST 1

gall *n* **1** a deep-seated ill will — see ENMITY

2 shameless boldness — see EFFRONTERY

gall *vb* **1** to damage or diminish by continued friction — see ABRADE 1

2 to disturb the peace of mind of (someone) especially by repeated disagreeable acts — see IRRITATE 1

3 to make sore by continued rubbing — see CHAFE 1

gallant *adj* **1** feeling or displaying no fear by temperament — see BRAVE

2 having, characterized by, or arising from a dignified and generous nature — see NOBLE 2

3 large and impressive in size, grandeur, extent, or conception — see GRAND 1

gallant *n* **1** a man extremely interested in his clothing and personal appearance — see DANDY 1

2 a man who courts a woman usually with the goal of marrying her — see SUITOR 1

gallantly *adv* in a manner befitting a person of the highest character and ideals — see GREATLY 1

gallantry *n* strength of mind to carry on in spite of danger — see COURAGE

gallery *n* **1** a building or part of a building in which objects of interest are displayed — see MUSEUM

2 a typically long narrow way connecting parts of a building — see HALL 2

galling *adj* **1** causing annoyance — see ANNOYING

2 hard to accept or bear especially emotionally — see BITTER 2

gallivant *also* **galavant** *vb* to move about from place to place aimlessly — see WANDER

gallivanting *also* **galavanting** *adj* traveling from place to place — see ITINERANT

gallop *vb* to go at a pace faster than a walk — see RUN 1

galore *adj* pouring forth in great amounts — see PROFUSE

galvanize *vb* to cause a pleasurable stimulation of the feelings — see THRILL

galvanizing *adj* causing great emotional or mental stimulation — see EXCITING 1

gamble *n* a risky undertaking ⟨would never take a *gamble* on such a poorly researched business deal⟩

syn chance, enterprise, flier (*or* flyer), speculation, venture

rel bet, hazard, stake, wager; liberty; dark horse, long shot, play

gamble *vb* to risk (something) on the outcome of an uncertain event — see BET

gamble (on) *vb* to take a chance on — see RISK 1

gamble (with) *vb* to place in danger — see ENDANGER

gambler *n* one that bets (as on the outcome of a contest or sports event) — see BETTOR

gambol *n* a time or instance of carefree fun — see FLING 1

---

syn synonym(s)   *rel* related words
ant antonym(s)   *near ant* near antonym(s)

gambol *vb* to play and run about happily — see FROLIC 1

game *adj* having a desire or inclination (as for a specified course of action) — see WILLING 1

game *n* 1 a competitive encounter between individuals or groups carried on for amusement, exercise, or in pursuit of a prize ⟨decided he would indulge in a friendly basketball *game* with his friends before dinner⟩

syn bout, competition, contest, event, match, meet, sweepstakes, tournament, tourney

rel athletics, sport; battle, conflict, scrimmage, skirmish, struggle, tug-of-war, tussle; championship, final, nightcap, playoff, semifinal; derby, field day, open; marathon, race; heat, round, run, set; rally, volley; rubber, runoff, sudden death; dead heat, photo finish, seesaw; classic

2 a method worked out in advance for achieving some objective — see PLAN 1

3 an attitude or manner not to be taken seriously — see FUN 2

gameness *n* cheerful readiness to do something — see ALACRITY

gamut *n* the distance or extent between possible extremes — see RANGE 3

gander *n* an instance of looking especially briefly — see LOOK 2

gang *n* 1 a group of people working together on a task ⟨a *gang* of neighborhood residents spent the weekend cleaning up the park⟩

syn band, company, crew, outfit, party, squad, team

rel army, battalion, brigade, corps, troop; force, host, posse, stable, troupe; administration, department, help, personnel, staff

2 a group of people sharing a common interest and relating together socially ⟨the whole *gang* went out for pizza⟩ ⟨the school's computer hackers had their own little *gang*⟩

syn body, bunch, circle, clan, clique, community, coterie, crowd, fold, lot, ring, set

rel bevy, covey, flock, herd, horde, mob, swarm, throng; club, college, fellowship, guild (*also* gild), league, organization, society; cohort, pack; camp, faction, sect, side, tribe; mess, squad; brotherhood, fraternity, order, sisterhood, sodality, sorority; commune; alliance, bloc, coalition, confederation, congress, council, federation, union

near ant loner; individualist

3 a group involved in secret or criminal activities — see RING 1

gangling *adj* being tall, thin and usually loose-jointed — see LANKY

gangly *adj* being tall, thin and usually loose-jointed — see LANKY

gangster *n* a violent, brutal person who is often a member of an organized gang — see HOODLUM

gaol *n, chiefly British* a place of confinement for persons held in lawful custody — see JAIL

gap *n* 1 an open space in a barrier (as a wall or hedge) ⟨there were several visible *gaps* in the wall where the drywall had pulled away from the wall framing⟩

syn breach, break, discontinuity, gulf, hole, interval, opening, rent, rift, separation

rel chink, cleft, crack, cranny, crevice, fissure; notch, slit, slot, split; interspace, pore, space; abyss, aperture, cavity, chasm, gape, orifice; fracture, rupture, severance, sundering

2 a break in continuity ⟨there was a 15-minute *gap* between the two televised sporting events⟩

syn discontinuity, hiatus, interim, interlude, intermission, interruption, interval

rel caesura, pause, space; lapse, suspension; lull, recess, respite, rest

near ant continuum, run, stretch; procession, progression

ant continuation, continuity

3 a narrow opening between hillsides or mountains that can be used for passage — see CANYON

gape *vb* to look long and hard in wonder or surprise ⟨she *gaped* openmouthed at the young man in the mall with purple and green hair⟩

syn gawk, gaze, goggle, peer, rubberneck, stare

rel glare, gloat, glower; eye, observe, watch; leer, ogle

near ant glance, glimpse, peek, peep; browse, dip (into), scan; blink, wink

garb *n* clothing chosen as appropriate for a specific situation — see OUTFIT 1

garb *vb* to outfit with clothes and especially fine or special clothes — see CLOTHE 1

garbage *n* discarded or useless material ⟨the stray dogs were looking for leftover food in the family's *garbage*⟩

syn chaff, deadwood, dross, dust, junk, litter, refuse, riffraff, rubbish, scrap, trash, waste

rel offal, sewage, slop, swill, wash; debris, detritus, rubble, ruins; lumber, odds and ends; flotsam, jetsam; castoff, cull, discard, reject, throwaway; nothing, straw, two bits

near ant catch, treasure, treasure trove

ant find, prize

garble *vb* to change so much as to create a wrong impression or alter the meaning of ⟨the candidate complained that his views had been deliberately *garbled* by his opponent⟩

syn color, distort, falsify, misinterpret, misrepresent, misstate, pervert, twist, warp

rel belie, camouflage, disguise, mask, veil; complicate, confound, confuse, mix up; mystify, obscure, puzzle; equivocate, fib, lie, palter, prevaricate

near ant clarify, clear (up), explain, illuminate, illustrate, interpret, spell out; decipher

garden *adj* **1** being of the type that is encountered in the normal course of events — see ORDINARY 1

2 often observed or encountered — see COMMON 1

garish *adj* excessively showy — see GAUDY

garishness *n* excessive or unnecessary display — see OSTENTATION

garment *vb* to outfit with clothes and especially fine or special clothes — see CLOTHE 1

garner *vb* **1** to bring together in one body or place — see GATHER 1

2 to receive as return for effort — see EARN 1

garnish *n* something that decorates or beautifies — see DECORATION 1

garnish *vb* to make more attractive by adding something that is beautiful or becoming — see DECORATE

garrote *or* **garotte** *vb* to keep (someone) from breathing by exerting pressure on the windpipe — see CHOKE 1

garrulous *adj* fond of talking or conversation — see TALKATIVE

gas *n* **1** boastful speech or writing — see BOMBAST 1

2 language that is impressive-sounding but not meaningful or sincere — see RHETORIC 1

3 *slang* a source of great satisfaction — see DELIGHT 1

gas *vb* to engage in casual or rambling conversation — see CHAT

gaseous *adj* marked by the use of impressive-sounding but mostly meaningless words and phrases — see RHETORICAL

gash *n* a long deep cut ⟨got a *gash* in his knee that required four stitches⟩
syn incision, laceration, rent, rip, slash, slit, tear
rel abrasion, score, scrape, scratch; injury, wound

gash *vb* to penetrate with a sharp edge (as a knife) — see CUT 1

gasp *vb* to breathe hard, quickly, or with difficulty ⟨the runner was *gasping* by the end of the marathon⟩
syn blow, hyperventilate, pant, puff, wheeze
rel choke, gulp, huff; exhale, expire
phrases to be out of breath

gassy *adj* marked by the use of impressive-sounding but mostly meaningless words and phrases — see RHETORICAL

gate *n* **1** a barrier by which an entry is closed and opened — see DOOR 1

2 the opening through which one can enter or leave a structure — see DOOR 2

3 a fixture for controlling the flow of a liquid — see FAUCET

gatekeeper *n* a person who tends a door — see DOORKEEPER

gateway *n* **1** something that allows someone to achieve a desired goal — see PASSPORT

2 the means or right of entering or participating in — see ENTRANCE 1

3 the opening through which one can enter or leave a structure — see DOOR 2

gather *vb* **1** to bring together in one body or place ⟨he *gathered* the leftovers from the table and gave them to the dog⟩ ⟨let's *gather* the students and have them line up on the playground before going in from recess⟩
syn accumulate, amass, assemble, collect, concentrate, garner, group, lump, pick up, round up, scrape (together)
rel agglomerate, aggregate, ball, bunch, cluster, huddle; heap, pile, stack; muster, raise, rally; flock, herd, hive, pack, press, swarm, throng, troop; congregate, forgather (*or* foregather), meet, rendezvous; affiliate, ally, combine, connect, join, link, merge, unite; arrange, organize, systematize; regather, regroup
phrases get together
near ant break up, disband, disintegrate, dissolve, separate, sever, split (up); dismiss, send
ant dispel, disperse, dissipate, scatter

2 to catch or collect (a crop or natural resource) for human use — see HARVEST

3 to come together into one body or place — see ASSEMBLE 1

4 to form an opinion through reasoning and information — see INFER 1

5 to gradually form into a layer, pile, or mass — see COLLECT 2

6 to increase in — see GAIN 1

gather (up) *vb* to call into being through the use of one's inner resources or powers — see SUMMON 2

gathering *n* **1** a body of people come together in one place ⟨the President spoke before the *gathering* of student leaders⟩
syn assemblage, assembly, conference, congregation, convocation, meeting, muster
rel aggregation, collection, conglomeration; company, coterie, gang, pack; caucus, forum, market, panel, rally, symposium, synod; crowd, flock, horde, legion, multitude, press, swarm, throng; crush, mob, rabble

2 a coming together of a number of persons for a specified purpose — see MEETING 1

3 a mass or quantity that has piled up or that has been gathered — see ACCUMULATION 1

gauche *adj* lacking social grace and assurance — see AWKWARD 1

gaud *n* a small object displayed for its attractiveness or interest — see KNICKKNACK

gaudiness *n* excessive or unnecessary display — see OSTENTATION

gaudy *adj* excessively showy ⟨the bright purple sequined miniskirt she wore to the wedding was *gaudy*⟩
syn flamboyant, flashy, garish, glitzy, loud, ostentatious, splashy, swank (*or* swanky), tawdry

---

syn synonym(s)   *rel* related words
ant antonym(s)   *near ant* near antonym(s)

rel meretricious, pretentious; graceless, inelegant, tacky, tasteless, vulgar; bedizened, extravagant, fancy, florid, glittery, spectacular; lurid, ornate, overdone, overwrought

near ant appropriate, fitting, proper; inconspicuous, muted, restrained, subdued, toned (down), unobtrusive; elegant, graceful, tasteful; modest, plain, simple, unpretentious

ant conservative, quiet, understated

gauge *also* **gage** *vb* **1** to decide the size, amount, number, or distance of (something) without actual measurement — see ESTIMATE 2

2 to find out the size, extent, or amount of — see MEASURE

gaunt *adj* suffering extreme weight loss as a result of hunger or disease — see EMACIATED

gauntlet *also* **gantlet** *n* a test of faith, patience, or strength — see TRIAL

gauzy *adj* **1** being of a material lacking in sturdiness or substance — see FLIMSY 1

2 very thin and easy to see through — see SHEER 1

gawk *n* a big clumsy often slow-witted person — see OAF

gawk *vb* to look long and hard in wonder or surprise — see GAPE

gawky *adj* lacking in physical ease and grace in movement or in the use of the hands — see CLUMSY 1

gay *adj* **1** having much high-spirited energy and movement — see LIVELY 1

2 having or showing a lack of concern or seriousness — see CAREFREE

3 indicative of or marked by high spirits or good humor — see MERRY

4 having or showing a good mood or disposition — see CHEERFUL 1

5 serving to lift one's spirits — see CHEERFUL 2

gaze *vb* to look long and hard in wonder or surprise — see GAPE

gazette *n* a publication that appears at regular intervals — see JOURNAL

gear *n* items needed for the performance of a task or activity — see EQUIPMENT

gel *vb* to turn from a liquid into a substance resembling jelly — see COAGULATE

gelatinous *adj* being of such a thick consistency as to readily cling to objects upon contact — see STICKY 1

gem *n* **1** a usually valuable stone cut and polished for ornament ⟨a ring set with diamonds and other precious *gems*⟩

syn brilliant, gemstone, jewel

rel birthstone; baguette, cameo, scarab, solitaire, teardrop; paste, rhinestone, zircon

near ant rough

2 someone or something unusually desirable — see PRIZE 1

gemstone *n* a usually valuable stone cut and polished for ornament — see GEM 1

genealogy *n* the line of ancestors from whom a person is descended — see ANCESTRY

general *adj* **1** belonging or relating to the whole ⟨a *general* increase in postage rates⟩ ⟨there's been a *general* improvement in the economy⟩

syn blanket, common, generic, global, overall, universal

rel broad, collective, comprehensive, extensive, pervasive, sweeping, ubiquitous, wholesale, wide, widespread; complete, full, plenary; planetary, worldwide

near ant component, constituent; cross-sectional, divisional, fragmentary, partial; local, localized, regional, sectional

ant individual, particular

2 relating to the main elements and not to specific details ⟨gave the *general* impression of being kindhearted⟩ ⟨a *general* course of study in American history⟩

syn all-around (*also* all-round), bird's-eye, broad, nonspecific, overall

rel comprehensive, inclusive; absolute, boundless, expansive, extensive, infinite, panoramic, sweeping, vast, wide; indeterminate, nebulous, nondescript, vague; nonspecific, unlimited, unrestricted, unspecified

near ant limited, restricted, specified; distinct, explicit, precise, sharp; comprehensive, elaborate, full, mapped (out), thorough; enumerated, inventoried, itemized, listed; individual, singular; particular, peculiar

ant delineated, detailed, particularized, specific

3 held by or applicable to a majority of the people ⟨it was the *general* opinion that the politician was a liar⟩ ⟨the *general* mood of the nation was one of hope and optimism⟩

syn common, public, popular, prevailing, vulgar

rel unanimous, universal; pop; everyday, familiar, household, usual, well-known; contemporary, current, present; dominant, predominant, preponderant; characteristic, typical, pandemic, pervasive, prevalent, rife, widespread; communal, shared

near ant rare, strange, unknown, unusual; distinctive, especial, idiosyncratic, peculiar, special, unique; individual, separate, singular; nonpublic, personal, private

ant uncommon, unpopular

4 not limited or specialized in application or purpose ⟨a new kitchen tool of *general* usefulness⟩

syn all-around (*also* all-round), all-purpose, unlimited, unqualified, unrestricted, unspecialized

rel broad, wide; nonspecific, unspecified, vague

near ant bounded, circumscribed, confined, definite, demarcated, determinate, finite, qualified

ant limited, restricted, specialized, technical

generality *n* **1** an idea or statement about all of the members of a group or all the

instances of a situation — see GENERAL-
IZATION

2 the main or greater part of something
as distinguished from its appendages —
see BODY 1

generalization *n* an idea or statement
about all of the members of a group or all
the instances of a situation ⟨the *generalization* that children who like violent entertainment grow up to be violent crimi-
nals⟩

syn aphorism, generality, maxim, stereotype

rel concept, conception, notion; precept,
rule, rule of thumb; adage, proverb, saw,
saying; cliché, commonplace, platitude,
truism; hypothesis, proposition, theory

generally *adv* **1** according to the usual
course of things — see NATURALLY 2

2 for the most part — see CHIEFLY

generate *vb* to be the cause of (a situation,
action, or state of mind) — see EFFECT

generator *n* a person who establishes a
whole new field of endeavor — see FA-
THER 2

generic *adj* belonging or relating to the
whole — see GENERAL 1

generosity *n* the quality or state of being
generous — see LIBERALITY

generous *adj* **1** giving or sharing in abundance and without hesitation ⟨a civic
leader who is very *generous* with his
money and time⟩

syn bounteous, bountiful, charitable,
free, freehanded, liberal, munificent,
openhanded, unselfish, unsparing

rel extravagant, handsome, lavish, profuse, unstinting; altruistic, beneficent,
benevolent, hospitable, humanitarian,
philanthropic; compassionate, good-
hearted, greathearted, kindly, magnanimous, openhearted

near ant mean, petty, small; frugal, spare,
sparing, thrifty, chary, stinting; acquisitive, avaricious, avid, coveting, covetous,
desirous, grasping, hoggish, itchy, mercenary, rapacious; begrudging, envious,
grudging, resentful

ant cheap, close, closefisted, miserly, niggardly, parsimonious, penurious, selfish,
stingy, tight, tightfisted, uncharitable

2 being more than enough without being
excessive — see PLENTIFUL

generously *adv* in a generous manner —
see WELL 2

genesis *n* the point at which something
begins — see BEGINNING

genetic *also* **genetical** *adj* genetically
passed or capable of being passed from
parent to offspring — see HEREDITARY

genial *adj* **1** having an easygoing and pleasing manner especially in social situations
— see AMIABLE

2 having or showing kindly feeling and
sincere interest — see FRIENDLY 1

3 showing a natural kindness and courtesy especially in social situations — see
GRACIOUS 1

geniality *n* the state or quality of having a
pleasant or agreeable manner in socializing with others — see AMIABILITY 1

genius *n* **1** a very smart person ⟨the 16-
year-old college graduate was considered
to be a *genius*⟩

syn brain, intellect, thinker, whiz, wizard

rel egghead, highbrow, intellectual; master, virtuoso; ace, crackerjack, natural;
sage, savant

near ant ignoramus, illiterate, know-
nothing; ass, donkey, fool, jackass; beast,
boor, cad, churl, clown, creep, cretin,
cur, heel, jerk, louse, lout, skunk, snake,
stinker

ant blockhead, dodo, dolt, dope, dumbbell, dummy, dunce, fathead, goon, half-
wit, idiot, imbecile, knothead, moron,
nitwit, numskull (*or* numbskull), pinhead

2 a special and usually inborn ability —
see TALENT

3 a habitual attraction to some activity or
thing — see INCLINATION 1

4 the set of qualities that makes a person,
a group of people, or a thing different
from others — see NATURE 1

gent *n* an adult male human being — see
MAN 1

genteel *adj* **1** following the established traditions of refined society and good taste
— see PROPER 1

2 having or showing a taste for the fine
arts and gracious living — see CULTIVAT-
ED

3 of high birth, rank, or station — see
NOBLE 1

4 showing consideration, courtesy, and
good manners — see POLITE 1

gentile *n* a person who does not worship
the God of the Bible — see HEATHEN 1

gentility *n* speech or behavior that is a sign
of good breeding — see POLITENESS

gentle *adj* **1** not harsh or stern especially
in manner, nature, or effect ⟨use a *gentle*
detergent on that delicate silk blouse⟩
⟨the pastor had a *gentle* disposition that
calmed everyone he met⟩

syn balmy, benign, bland, delicate, light,
mellow, mild, soft, soothing, tender

rel sleek, slick, smooth; calm, pacific,
peaceful, placid, quiet, serene, tranquil;
clement, compassionate, easy, lenient,
merciful; buffering, cushioning, softening

near ant exquisite, fierce, intense, powerful, severe; forceful, forcible, savage, violent; roughened, rugged; strong; abrad-
ing, irritating, roughening; grim, gruff,
rude, stiff; heavy-handed, oppressive,
tyrannical (*also* tyrannic)

ant abrasive, caustic, coarse, hard, harsh,
rough, scathing, stern, ungentle

2 marked by temperatures that are neither too high nor too low — see
CLEMENT

3 of high birth, rank, or station — see
NOBLE 1

---

syn synonym(s)   *rel* related words
ant antonym(s)   *near ant* near antonym(s)

gentle *vb* to lessen the shock of — see CUSHION

gentleman *n* **1** a man of high birth or social position ⟨many of the signers of the Declaration of Independence were *gentlemen* who were risking everything⟩

syn aristocrat, grandee, noble, nobleman, patrician

rel squire; cavalier, knight; don, nawab, seigneur, seignior, sheikh (*or* sheik); baron, baronet, count, duke, earl, esquire, lord, marquess, marquis, prince, thane, viscount; czar (*also* tsar *or* tzar), magnate, mogul, nabob; socialite, swell

near ant boor, churl, cotter (*or* cottar), fellah, peasant, peon; commoner, plebeian; proletarian; toiler

2 an adult male human being — see MAN 1

3 an honorable and courteous man — see CAVALIER

gentlewoman *n* a woman of high birth or social position ⟨in the 19th century a number of American *gentlewomen* used their wealth and influence to further abolitionism, women's rights, and other worthy causes⟩

syn dame, lady, noblewoman

rel ladyship, madam; baroness, countess, duchess, marchioness; czarina (*also* tsarina *or* tzarina), empress, queen; dowager, matriarch, matron, mistress

gentry *n* the highest class in a society — see ARISTOCRACY

genuine *adj* **1** being exactly as appears or as claimed — see AUTHENTIC 1

2 free from any intent to deceive or impress others — see GUILELESS

genuinely *adv* in actual fact — see VERY 2

geometry *n* the outward appearance of something as distinguished from its substance — see FORM 1

geriatric *adj* being of advanced years and especially past middle age — see ELDERLY

germane *adj* having to do with the matter at hand — see PERTINENT

germfree *adj* free from filth, infection, or dangers to health — see SANITARY

gestation *n* the state of containing unborn young within the body — see PREGNANCY

gesticulation *n* a movement of the body or limbs that expresses or emphasizes an idea or feeling — see GESTURE 1

gesture *n* **1** a movement of the body or limbs that expresses or emphasizes an idea or feeling ⟨a teenager who often shrugs his shoulders in a *gesture* of indifference⟩

syn gesticulation, pantomime, sign, signal

rel beck, flourish, shrug, wave; body language, posture; indication, motion

2 an act or utterance that is a customary show of good manners — see CIVILITY 1

gesture *vb* to direct or notify by a movement or gesture — see MOTION

get *vb* **1** to acquire complete knowledge, understanding, or skill in — see LEARN 1

2 to become affected with (a disease or disorder) — see CONTRACT 1

3 to become the father of — see FATHER

4 to cause (someone) to agree with a belief or course of action by using arguments or earnest requests — see PERSUADE

5 to come upon after searching, study, or effort — see FIND 1

6 to disturb the peace of mind of (someone) especially by repeated disagreeable acts — see IRRITATE 1

7 to eventually have as a state or quality — see BECOME

8 to receive as return for effort — see EARN 1

9 to recognize the meaning of — see COMPREHEND 1

10 to take physical control or possession of (something) suddenly or forcibly — see CATCH 1

11 to leave a place often for another — see GO 2

get along *vb* **1** to meet one's day-to-day needs ⟨most college students can *get along* with just a few hours of sleep at night⟩

syn cope, do, fare, get by, get on, make out, manage, shift

rel carry on, contrive, fend, handle, scrape (by *or* through), survive; eke out, scrape (out), scrounge, squeeze, wrest, wring; afford, swing

phrases make shift

near ant collapse, fail, fall short, fizzle, flounder; decline, peter (out), slump, wane; give up

2 to move forward along a course — see GO 1

getaway *n* the act or an instance of getting free from danger or confinement — see ESCAPE 1

get by *vb* to meet one's day-to-day needs — see GET ALONG 1

get off *vb* **1** to leave a place often for another — see GO 2

2 to take the first step in (a process or course of action) — see BEGIN 1

get on *vb* to meet one's day-to-day needs — see GET ALONG 1

get out *vb* **1** to become known ⟨news of the rock star's secret wedding *got out* to the news media⟩

syn come out, leak (out), out, spread

rel break, develop, transpire, unfold; circulate, disclose, reveal, spill, tell

near ant hush (up), suppress; conceal, disguise, hide, mask; secrete

2 to get free from a dangerous or confining situation — see ESCAPE 1

3 to produce and release for distribution in printed form — see PUBLISH 1

get–together *n* **1** a coming together of a number of persons for a specified purpose — see MEETING 1

2 a social gathering — see PARTY 1

getup *n* clothing chosen as appropriate for a specific situation — see OUTFIT 1

get up *vb* to leave one's bed — see ARISE 1

gewgaw *n* a small object displayed for its attractiveness or interest — see KNICK-KNACK

ghastliness *n* the quality of inspiring intense dread or dismay — see HORROR 1

ghastly *adj* extremely disturbing or repellent — see HORRIBLE 1

ghost *n* the soul of a dead person thought of especially as appearing to living people ⟨looked for *ghosts* in the graveyard on Halloween⟩
syn apparition, bogey (*also* bogy *or* bogie), phantasm, phantom, poltergeist, shade, shadow, specter (*or* spectre), spirit, spook, vision, wraith
rel banshee, demon (*or* daemon), familiar (*or* familiar spirit), genie, imp, incubus, puck; vampire, zombie

ghoul *n* an evil spirit — see DEMON

giant *adj* unusually large — see HUGE

giant *n* something that is unusually large and powerful ⟨the Great Pyramids of Egypt are *giants*⟩
syn behemoth, blockbuster, colossus, jumbo, leviathan, mammoth, monster, titan, whale, whopper
rel amazon; bulk, hulk; heavyweight
near ant lightweight, weakling, wimp, wisp; nonentity, twerp, whippersnapper
ant dwarf, midget, mini, miniature, peewee, pygmy, runt, shrimp

gibber *vb* to speak rapidly, inarticulately, and usually unintelligibly — see BABBLE 1

gibberish *n* unintelligible or meaningless talk ⟨was so excited he could only talk *gibberish*⟩
syn babble, blabber, bunk, claptrap, drivel, fudge, gabble, gobbledygook (*also* gobbledegook), hogwash, jabber, jabberwocky, jazz, moonshine, mumbo jumbo, nonsense, piffle, prattle, rigmarole, rot
rel abracadabra; chatter, clatter, gab, gibber, prate, tattle, twaddle; double-talk, hocus-pocus, jive; gas, hot air, wind

gibe *or* **jibe** *vb* to make (someone or something) the object of unkind laughter — see RIDICULE

giddy *adj* 1 lacking in seriousness or maturity ⟨the *giddy* youngsters continued to laugh, joke, and make faces during the ceremonies⟩
syn featherbrained, flighty, frivolous, goofy, harebrained, light-headed, puerile, scatterbrained, silly
rel fatuous, foolish, inane, nonsensical, thoughtless, witless; crazy, daffy, daft, exuberant, flippant, fluttery, light, lighthearted, playful; sappy, shallow, superficial
near ant grave, melancholy, somber (*or* sombre), thoughtful; dignified, heavy, nononsense, sedate, severe, solemn, staid
ant earnest, serious, serious-minded, sober

2 having a feeling of being whirled about and in danger of falling down — see DIZZY 1

gift *n* 1 something given to someone without expectation of a return ⟨gave him a *gift* for his birthday⟩
syn bestowal, donation, freebie (*or* freebee), giveaway, lagniappe, largess (*or* largesse), present, presentation
rel alms, benefaction, beneficence, benevolence, charity, contribution, dole, generosity, offering, philanthropy; grant, subsidy; remembrance, tribute; bonus, boon, windfall; favor, valentine; gratuity, tip; award, prize, reward; bequest, legacy; sacrifice
near ant advance, loan; bribe, sop

2 a special and usually inborn ability — see TALENT

gigantic *adj* unusually large — see HUGE

giggle *n* an explosive sound that is a sign of amusement — see LAUGH 1

gimmick *n* 1 a clever often underhanded means to achieve an end — see TRICK 1

2 an interesting and often novel device with a practical use — see GADGET

ginger *n* active strength of body or mind — see VIGOR 1

gingerbread *adj* elaborately and often excessively decorated — see ORNATE

gingerly *adj* having or showing a close attentiveness to avoiding danger or trouble — see CAREFUL 1

gingery *adj* 1 having active strength of body or mind — see VIGOROUS 1

2 marked by a lively display of strong feeling — see SPIRITED 1

gird *vb* 1 to encircle or bind with or as if with a belt ⟨for the celebration of the heroes' return, well-wishers *girded* hundreds of trees with yellow ribbons⟩ ⟨she *girded* her waist with a delicate sash⟩
syn band, belt, girdle, girt, girth, wrap
rel tie up, truss; circle, loop, wind, wreathe; bandage, swathe; chain, cord, enchain, lash, rope, shackle, tape, wire
near ant loose, loosen, unbind, unlash, undo, unfasten, unlash, untie, unwind
ant unwrap

2 to gather into a tight mass by means of a line or cord — see TIE 1

girdle *n* a strip of flexible material (as leather) worn around the waist — see ²BELT

girdle *vb* 1 to encircle or bind with or as if with a belt — see GIRD 1

2 to pass completely around — see ENCIRCLE 1

girl *n* 1 a young usually unmarried woman ⟨a book that discusses the special challenges that *girls* face as they enter their teenage years⟩
syn bobby-soxer, chick [*slang*], damsel, doll, gal, lass, lassie, mademoiselle, maid, maiden, miss
rel gamine; hoyden, tomboy; hussy; ingenue; belle, deb, debutante, sylph; schoolgirl; teenybopper; senorita (*or* señorita)

2 a woman with whom one is in love — see GIRLFRIEND

girlfriend *n* a woman with whom one is in love ⟨he proposed to his *girlfriend* of seven years⟩

syn gal, girl, ladylove

rel mistress; beloved, darling, dear, favorite, flame, honey, love, lover, sweet, sweetheart, valentine

girlish *adj* having or displaying qualities more suitable for women than for men — see EFFEMINATE

girt *vb* to encircle or bind with or as if with a belt — see GIRD 1

girth *n* the distance around a round body — see CIRCUMFERENCE 1

girth *vb* 1 to encircle or bind with or as if with a belt — see GIRD 1

2 to pass completely around — see ENCIRCLE 1

gist *n* the central part or aspect of something under consideration — see CRUX

give *vb* 1 to make a present of ⟨tutors *gave* their time to help students after school⟩

syn bestow, contribute, donate, present

rel chip in, kick in, pitch in; award, confer, dole (out); afford, furnish, provide; lavish, regale; aid, assist, benefit, help; administer, dispense, impart, issue, render; extend, offer, pay, proffer, tender; sacrifice

near ant hold, keep, pocket, retain, withhold; preserve, save; advance, lend, loan; sell

2 to put (something) into the possession or safekeeping of another ⟨*gave* my camera to my father to hold while I went swimming⟩

syn commend, commit, consign, delegate, deliver, entrust, hand over, leave, pass, transfer, transmit, trust, turn over, vest

rel confer, grant; assign, deal (out), dispense, disperse, distribute, divide; release, relinquish, submit, surrender, turn in, yield; bequeath, hand down, will; advance, lend, loan; furnish, supply

near ant detain, hold back, reserve, withhold; own, possess; accept, receive, take in; occupy, take, take over

ant hold, keep, retain

3 to bring before the public in performance or exhibition — see PRESENT 1

4 to fall down or in as a result of physical pressure — see COLLAPSE 1

5 to hand over or use up in payment — see SPEND 1

6 to make known (as an idea, emotion, or opinion) — see EXPRESS 1

7 to occupy (oneself) diligently or with close attention — see APPLY 2

8 to produce as revenue — see YIELD 2

9 to put (something) into the possession of someone for use or consumption — see FURNISH 1

10 to put before another for acceptance or consideration — see OFFER 1

give–and–take *n* 1 an exchange of views for the purpose of exploring a subject or deciding an issue — see DISCUSSION 1

2 the act or practice of each side giving up something in order to reach an agreement — see CONCESSION 1

3 good-natured teasing or exchanging of clever remarks — see BANTER

giveaway *n* something given to someone without expectation of a return — see GIFT 1

give away *vb* to make known (something abstract) through outward signs — see SHOW 2

give in *vb* 1 to give up and cease resistance (as to a liking, temptation, or habit) — see YIELD 1

2 to cease resistance (as to another's arguments, demands, or control) — see YIELD 3

given *adj* 1 being in the habit or custom — see ACCUSTOMED

2 having a tendency to be or act in a certain way — see PRONE 1

given name *n* a name that is placed before one's family name — see FORENAME

give out *vb* to stop functioning — see FAIL 1

give up *vb* 1 to give (something) over to the control or possession of another usually under duress — see SURRENDER 1

2 to stop doing (something) permanently — see QUIT 2

3 to yield to the control or power of enemy forces — see FALL 2

giving *n* the act of offering money in exchange for goods or services — see PAYMENT 1

gizmo or **gismo** *n* an interesting and often novel device with a practical use — see GADGET

glacial *adj* 1 having a low or subnormal temperature — see COLD 1

2 lacking in friendliness or warmth of feeling — see COLD 2

glad *adj* 1 experiencing pleasure, satisfaction, or delight ⟨the husband was *glad* to see his wife again, after so long an absence⟩

syn blissful, delighted, gratified, happy, joyful, joyous, pleased, satisfied, tickled

rel beaming, blithe, blithesome, buoyant, cheerful, cheery, gay, gladsome, lighthearted, sunny, upbeat; gleeful, jocund, jolly, jovial, laughing, merry, mirthful, smiling; carried away, ecstatic, elated, enraptured, entranced, euphoric, exhilarated, intoxicated, rapturous, rhapsodic; exuberant, exultant, jubilant, rapt, rejoicing, thrilled; hopeful, optimistic, rosy, sanguine

near ant abject, aggrieved, anguished, blue, brokenhearted, dejected, depressed, despondent, disconsolate, disheartened, downcast, downhearted, forlorn, melancholy; doleful, dolorous, lachrymose, mournful, plaintive, sorrowful, sorry, woeful; black, dark, desolate, dispirited, gloomy, glum, gray (*also* grey), grieved, heartbroken, heartsick, miserable, woebegone, wretched

ant displeased, joyless, sad, unhappy, unsatisfied

2 having a desire or inclination (as for a specified course of action) — see WILLING 1

3 serving to lift one's spirits — see CHEERFUL 2

gladden *vb* to give satisfaction to — see PLEASE

gladdening *adj* making one feel good inside — see HEARTWARMING

gladiatorial *adj* feeling or displaying eagerness to fight — see BELLIGERENT

gladness *n* **1** a feeling or state of well-being and contentment — see HAPPINESS 1

2 the feeling experienced when one's wishes are met — see PLEASURE 1

gladsome *adj* having or showing a good mood or disposition — see CHEERFUL 1

glamorize *also* **glamourize** *vb* to represent or think of as better than reality — see IDEALIZE

glamorous *also* **glamourous** *adj* **1** excitingly or mysteriously unusual — see EXOTIC

2 having an often mysterious or magical power to attract — see FASCINATING 1

glamour *also* **glamor** *n* the power of irresistible attraction — see CHARM 2

glance *n* an instance of looking especially briefly — see LOOK 2

glance *vb* **1** to strike and fly off at an angle ⟨the basketball *glanced* off the rim⟩ ⟨her wild pitch *glanced* off my shoulder and landed in the dugout⟩
  syn bounce, carom, rebound, ricochet, skim, skip
  rel brush, graze, nudge, shave, sweep; bump, contact, hit, kiss, touch; sideswipe; reflect

2 to take a quick or hasty look ⟨just *glanced* at the instructions before assembling the bike⟩ ⟨*glanced* over his shoulder to see if she was still there⟩
  syn browse, dip, glimpse, peek, skim
  rel peep; blink, squint; look over, scan
  near ant examine, overlook, oversee, question, survey; study, view; peer, pry; gawk, goggle, rubberneck; leer, ogle
  ant gaze, stare

3 to shoot forth bursts of light — see FLASH 1

glare *n* the steady giving off of the form of radiation that makes vision possible — see LIGHT 1

glare *vb* **1** to shine with a bright harsh light ⟨the spotlight *glared* down on the suspect as the police questioned him relentlessly⟩
  syn beat, blaze, burn, flame, flare
  rel beam, glow, radiate; flash, glance, gleam, glimmer, glint, glisten, glister, glitter, scintillate, shimmer, sparkle, twinkle; bedazzle, blind, daze, dazzle

2 to look with anger or disapproval — see FROWN

glaring *adj* very noticeable especially for being incorrect or bad — see EGREGIOUS

glasses *n pl* a pair of lenses set in a frame that is held in place with ear supports and which are usually worn to correct vision ⟨I'm a little nearsighted, so I'm going to need *glasses*⟩
  syn eyeglasses, specs, spectacles
  rel bifocals; monocle, pince-nez; sunglasses; goggles; contact lens

gleam *n* the steady giving off of the form of radiation that makes vision possible — see LIGHT 1

gleam *vb* to shoot forth bursts of light — see FLASH 1

glee *n* a mood characterized by high spirits and amusement and often accompanied by laughter — see MIRTH

glee club *n* an organized group of singers — see CHORUS 1

gleeful *adj* indicative of or marked by high spirits or good humor — see MERRY

gleefulness *n* a mood characterized by high spirits and amusement and often accompanied by laughter — see MIRTH

glide *vb* **1** to move or proceed smoothly and readily — see FLOW 2

2 to move through the air with or as if with outstretched wings — see FLY 1

3 to rest or move along the surface of a liquid or in the air — see FLOAT

glimmer *n* a very small amount — see PARTICLE 1

glimmer *vb* to shoot forth bursts of light — see FLASH 1

glimpse *n* an instance of looking especially briefly — see LOOK 2

glimpse *vb* to take a quick or hasty look — see GLANCE 2

glint *vb* to shoot forth bursts of light — see FLASH 1

glisten *vb* to shoot forth bursts of light — see FLASH 1

glistening *adj* having a shiny surface or finish — see GLOSSY

glister *vb* to shoot forth bursts of light — see FLASH 1

glitter *vb* to shoot forth bursts of light — see FLASH 1

glitz *n* excessive or unnecessary display — see OSTENTATION

glitzy *adj* excessively showy — see GAUDY

gloaming *n* **1** a time or place of little or no light — see DARK 1

2 the time from when the sun begins to set to the onset of total darkness — see DUSK 1

glob *n* **1** a small uneven mass — see LUMP 1

2 the quantity of fluid that falls naturally in one rounded mass — see DROP 1

global *adj* **1** belonging or relating to the whole — see GENERAL 1

2 covering everything or all important points — see ENCYCLOPEDIC

3 having every part of the surface the same distance from the center — see ROUND 1

globe *n* **1** a more or less round body or mass — see ¹BALL 1

2 the celestial body on which we live — see EARTH 1

globule *n* the quantity of fluid that falls naturally in one rounded mass — see DROP 1

gloom *n* **1** a state or spell of low spirits — see SADNESS

2 a time or place of little or no light — see DARK 1

gloom *vb* **1** to look with anger or disapproval — see FROWN

2 to take on a gloomy or forbidding look — see DARKEN 1

gloominess *n* a state or spell of low spirits — see SADNESS

gloomy *adj* **1** causing or marked by an atmosphere lacking in cheer ⟨the cold rain made for a *gloomy* day⟩

syn black, bleak, cheerless, comfortless, dark, darkening, depressing, desolate, dismal, drear, dreary, elegaic, funereal, glum, gray (*also* grey), miserable, morbid, morose, murky, saturnine, sepulchral, somber (*or* sombre), sullen, wretched

rel dejected, depressed, despondent, disconsolate, droopy, inconsolable, low, melancholy, sad, unhappy, woebegone, woeful; discomfiting, discouraging, disheartening, dismaying, dispiriting, distressful, distressing, upsetting; desperate, hopeless, pessimistic; lamentable, lugubrious, mournful, sorrowful; cloudy, colorless, drab, dull; dour, grim, lowering (*also* louring), menacing, negative, oppressive, threatening

near ant blithe, blithesome, buoyant, gay, jocund, jolly, joyful, joyous, merry, mirthful; encouraging, hopeful, optimistic; lighthearted, lightsome

ant bright, cheerful, cheering, cheery, comforting, cordial, gay, festive, friendly, heartwarming, sunshiny

2 feeling unhappiness — see SAD 1

3 being without light or without much light — see DARK 1

glorify *vb* **1** to enhance the status of — see EXALT

2 to offer honor or respect to (someone) as a divine power — see WORSHIP 1

3 to praise or publicize lavishly and often excessively — see TOUT 1

4 to proclaim the glory of — see PRAISE 1

5 to represent or think of as better than reality — see IDEALIZE

glorious *adj* large and impressive in size, grandeur, extent, or conception — see GRAND 1

gloriously *adv* in a pleasing way — see WELL 5

gloriousness *n* impressiveness of beauty on a large scale — see MAGNIFICENCE

glory *n* **1** public acknowledgment or admiration for an achievement ⟨the drama teacher gave the stage crew all the *glory* for the successful production⟩

syn acclaim, accolade, credit, distinction, homage, honor, laurels

rel celebrity, fame, renown, repute; compliment, encomium, eulogy, panegyric, toast, tribute; acclamation, ovation, plaudit, praise, rave, rhapsody; citation, commendation, note, recommendation; elevation, exaltation, glorification

2 an asset that brings praise or renown ⟨the new computer lab was the *glory* of the middle school⟩

syn boast, credit, honor, jewel, pride, treasure

rel pièce de résistance, showpiece; attraction, feature, highlight; distinction, excellence, merit, value, virtue

phrases a feather in one's cap

near ant disgrace, dishonor; blemish, blot, defect, shame, slur, smirch, smudge, stain, stigma; eyesore, fright, horror, mess

3 impressiveness of beauty on a large scale — see MAGNIFICENCE

glory *vb* to feel or express joy or triumph — see EXULT

glorying *adj* having or expressing feelings of joy or triumph — see EXULTANT

gloss *n* brightness created by light reflected from a surface — see SHINE 1

gloss *vb* to make smooth or glossy usually by repeatedly applying surface pressure — see POLISH

gloss (over) *vb* **1** to make (something) seem less bad by offering excuses — see PALLIATE 1

2 to overlook or dismiss as of little importance — see EXCUSE 1

glossy *adj* having a shiny surface or finish ⟨the *glossy* finish on the gym floor⟩ ⟨a sports car with an interior upholstered with *glossy* leather⟩

syn buffed, burnished, glistening, lustrous, polished, rubbed, satin, satiny, sleek

rel silken, silky, slick, slippery; glassy, glazed, lacquered, shellacked, varnished; gleaming, glittering, reflective, shining

near ant lackluster

ant dim, dull, flat, lusterless, matte (*also* mat *or* matt)

glow *n* the steady giving off of the form of radiation that makes vision possible — see LIGHT 1

glow *vb* **1** to be on fire especially brightly — see BURN 1

2 to develop a rosy facial color (as from excitement or embarrassment) — see BLUSH

glower *vb* **1** to look with anger or disapproval — see FROWN

2 to take on a gloomy or forbidding look — see DARKEN 1

glowing *adj* **1** giving off or reflecting much light — see BRIGHT 1

2 having a healthy reddish skin tone — see RUDDY

3 having or being an outward sign of good feelings (as of love, confidence, or happiness) — see RADIANT 1

4 having or expressing great depth of feeling — see FERVENT

gloze (over) *vb* **1** to make (something) seem less bad by offering excuses — see PALLIATE 1

2 to overlook or dismiss as of little importance — see EXCUSE 1

glue *n* a substance used to stick things together ⟨used *glue* to stick the photo in the album⟩
syn adhesive, cement, size
rel epoxy, epoxy resin, library paste, mucilage, superglue; dope, goo, gum

gluey *adj* being of such a thick consistency as to readily cling to objects upon contact — see STICKY 1

glum *adj* 1 causing or marked by an atmosphere lacking in cheer — see GLOOMY 1
2 feeling unhappiness — see SAD 1
3 given to or displaying a resentful silence and often irritability — see SULKY

glut *vb* to fill with food to capacity — see GORGE 1

glutinous *adj* being of such a thick consistency as to readily cling to objects upon contact — see STICKY 1

glutton *n* one who eats greedily or too much ⟨he's such a *glutton* that he ate the whole cake⟩
syn gorger, gormandizer, gourmand, hog, overeater, stuffer, swiller
rel feaster, trencherman; muncher; guzzler
near ant dieter, nibbler, picker

gluttonous *adj* having a huge appetite — see VORACIOUS 1

gnash *vb* to press or strike against or together so as to make a scraping sound — see GRIND 2

gnaw (on) *vb* to crush or grind with the teeth — see BITE (ON)

gnawer *n* one who is obnoxiously annoying — see NUISANCE 1

gnome *n* an imaginary being usually having a small human form and magical powers — see FAIRY

go *adj* being in a state of fitness for some experience or action — see READY 1

go *n* 1 a practice or interest that is very popular for a short time — see FAD
2 active strength of body or mind — see VIGOR 1
3 an effort to do or accomplish something — see ATTEMPT
4 readiness to engage in daring or difficult activity — see ENTERPRISE 2

go *vb* 1 to move forward along a course ⟨everything is *going* according to our plans⟩
syn advance, fare, forge, get along, march, proceed, progress
rel accelerate, fast-forward, speed; approach, near; journey, pass, repair, run, travel, wend; actuate, drive, impel, propel, push; do, go off, take out
phrases gain ground
near ant arrest, balk, block, check, detain, halt, hinder, hold back, impede, nip, obstruct, slow (down *or* up), stem; repress, retard, stunt, suppress; delay, interrupt, stall; cramp, hamper, inhibit; cease, let up, pause; regress
ant remain, stand, stay, stop

2 to leave a place often for another ⟨will *go* on vacation at the end of the year⟩ ⟨decided it would be better to *go* before she got any angrier⟩
syn begone, clear out, depart, exit, get, get off, move, pull (out), quit, sally (forth), shove (off), take off, walk out
rel set out, start, strike out; abscond, decamp, escape, evacuate, flee, fly, get out, run away, scat, scram, skip; go out, light out, step out; abandon, desert, forsake, vacate; emigrate; remove, retire, retreat, withdraw
phrases beat it
near ant abide, dwell, lodge, remain, settle, stay, tarry; approach, close, near; hit, land, reach
ant arrive, come, show up, turn up
3 to be fitting or proper — see DO 1
4 to be in agreement on every point — see CHECK 1
5 to be positioned along a certain course or in a certain direction — see RUN 3
6 to eventually have as a state or quality — see BECOME
7 to fall down or in as a result of physical pressure — see COLLAPSE 1
8 to have or be in a usual or proper place — see BELONG 1
9 to lose bodily strength or vigor — see WEAKEN 2
10 to make one's way through, across, or over — see TRAVERSE
11 to occur within a continuous range of variation — see RUN 4
12 to risk (something) on the outcome of an uncertain event — see BET

go (for) *vb* to have a price of — see COST

go (on) *vb* to take place — see HAPPEN

go (to) *vb* to use or seek out as a source of aid, relief, or advantage — see RESORT (TO) 1

goad *n* something that arouses action or activity — see IMPULSE

goad *vb* 1 to try to persuade (someone) through earnest appeals to follow a course of action — see URGE
2 to urge or push forward with or as if with a pointed object — see PROD 1

goal *n* something that one hopes or intends to accomplish ⟨graduating from high school with honors is one of my main *goals*⟩
syn aim, ambition, aspiration, design, dream, end, intent, intention, mark, meaning, object, objective, plan, pretension, purpose, target, thing
rel plot, project, scheme; desire, hope, wish; destination, terminus
near ant means, method, way

goat *n* a person or thing taking the blame for others — see SCAPEGOAT

¹gob *n* 1 a small uneven mass — see LUMP 1
2 **gobs** *pl* a considerable amount — see LOT 2

²gob *n* one who operates or navigates a seagoing vessel — see SAILOR

gobbet *n* a small uneven mass — see LUMP 1

gobbledygook also **gobbledegook** n unintelligible or meaningless talk — see GIBBERISH

go-between n 1 one that carries a message or does an errand — see MESSENGER

2 one who works with opposing sides in order to bring about an agreement — see MEDIATOR

goblin n an imaginary being usually having a small human form and magical powers — see FAIRY

god n 1 a being having superhuman powers and control over a particular part of life or the world — see DEITY 1

2 cap the being worshipped as the creator and ruler of the universe — see DEITY 2

goddess n a lovely woman — see BEAUTY 2

godhead n 1 the quality or state of being divine — see DIVINITY

2 cap the being worshipped as the creator and ruler of the universe — see DEITY 2

godhood n the quality or state of being divine — see DIVINITY

godless adj lacking religious emotions, principles, or practices — see IRRELIGIOUS

godlike adj of, relating to, or being God — see HOLY 3

godliness n the quality or state of being spiritually pure or virtuous — see HOLINESS

godly adj showing a devotion to God and to a life of virtue — see HOLY 1

godsend n something that provides happiness or does good for a person or thing — see BLESSING 1

Godspeed n an expression of good wishes at parting — see GOOD-BYE

go-getter n an ambitious person who eagerly goes after what is desired ⟨a *go-getter* with his sights set on the presidency⟩
syn hummer, hustler, live wire, powerhouse, rustler, self-starter
rel dasher; doer, enterpriser; he-man
near ant dawdler, idler, loafer, lounger, putterer, trifler; goldbrick, malingerer, procrastinator, shirker, slacker; drone, lazybones, sluggard; dallier, laggard, lingerer, loiterer, slowpoke, stick-in-the-mud; ignorer, ne'er-do-well, neglecter; daydreamer, dreamer; dropout, quitter

go-getting adj 1 having a strong desire for personal advancement — see AMBITIOUS 1

2 having or showing a bold forcefulness in the pursuit of a goal — see AGGRESSIVE 1

go-getting n eager desire for personal advancement — see AMBITION 1

goggle vb to look long and hard in wonder or surprise — see GAPE

going adj 1 accepted, used, or practiced by most people — see CURRENT 1

2 being in effective operation — see ACTIVE 1

3 having attained a desired end or state of good fortune — see SUCCESSFUL 1

going n 1 forward movement in time or place — see ADVANCE 1

2 the act of leaving a place — see DEPARTURE

gold n something (as pieces of stamped metal or printed paper) customarily and legally used as a medium of exchange, a measure of value, or a means of payment — see MONEY

goldbrick n one who deliberately avoids work or duty — see SLACKER

golden adj 1 having qualities which inspire hope — see HOPEFUL 1

2 marked by conspicuously full and rich sounds or tones — see RESONANT

3 marked by vigorous growth and well-being especially economically — see PROSPEROUS 1

4 of a pale yellow or yellowish brown color — see BLOND

5 pointing toward a happy outcome — see FAVORABLE 2

golden-ager n a person of advanced years — see SENIOR CITIZEN

golden mean n a middle point between extremes — see MEAN 1

gone adj 1 no longer existing — see EXTINCT

2 no longer living — see DEAD 1

3 no longer possessed — see LOST

good adj 1 based on sound reasoning or information ⟨had enough information to make a *good* assessment of the situation⟩
syn commonsense, hard, informed, just, justified, levelheaded, logical, rational, reasonable, reasoned, sensible, sober, solid, valid, well-founded
rel actual, real, true; certain, sure; certified, validated, verified; confirmed, corroborated, substantiated; cogent, convincing, credible
near ant unsubstantiated, unsupported, unwarranted; flimsy, implausible, unconvincing, weak; fallacious, false, misled
ant groundless, illogical, invalid, irrational, nonrational, nonsensical, nonvalid, unfounded, ungrounded, uninformed, unjustified, unreasonable, unsound

2 conforming to a high standard of morality or virtue ⟨a *good* person who seldom did wrong⟩ ⟨*good* behavior will earn you the respect of others⟩
syn decent, ethical, honest, honorable, just, moral, right, righteous, right-minded, straight, upright, virtuous
rel correct, decorous, proper, seemly; high-minded, noble, principled; commendable, creditable, exemplary, legitimate; esteemed, law-abiding, reputable, respected, upstanding, worthy; blameless, clean, guiltless, immaculate, incorruptible, innocent, inoffensive, irreproachable, unobjectionable; lily-white, pure, scrupulous, spotless, uncorrupted, unerring; goody-goody, moralistic, sanctimonious, self-righteous
near ant improper, incorrect, indecorous, naughty, unbecoming, unseemly; corrupt, debased, debauched, degenerate,

depraved, dissolute, perverted, reprobate; unprincipled, unscrupulous; atrocious, infamous, villainous; base, low, mean, vicious, vile; blameworthy, objectionable, offensive; iniquitous, nefarious; errant, erring, fallen

ant bad, black, dishonest, dishonorable, evil, evil-minded, immoral, indecent, sinful, unethical, unrighteous, wicked, wrong

3 according to the rules of logic — see LOGICAL 1

4 being to one's liking — see SATISFACTORY 1

5 expressing approval — see FAVORABLE 1

6 firm in one's allegiance to someone or something — see FAITHFUL 1

7 giving pleasure or contentment to the mind or senses — see PLEASANT

8 having or showing exceptional knowledge, experience, or skill in a field of endeavor — see PROFICIENT

9 having sufficient worth or merit to receive one's honor, esteem, or reward — see WORTHY

10 having the required skills for an acceptable level of performance — see COMPETENT

11 meeting the requirements of a purpose or situation — see FIT 1

12 showing or expressing acceptance or approval — see POSITIVE

13 sufficiently large in size, amount, or number to merit attention — see CONSIDERABLE 1

14 worthy of one's trust — see DEPENDABLE

good *adv* in a satisfactory way — see WELL 1

good *n* **1** something that provides happiness or does good for a person or thing — see BLESSING 2

2 the state of doing well especially in relation to one's happiness or success — see WELFARE

3 goods *pl* products that are bought and sold in business — see MERCHANDISE

Good Book *n* a book made up of the writings accepted by Christians as coming from God — see BIBLE

good–bye *or* **good–by** *n* an expression of good wishes at parting ⟨said our *good-byes* and headed for home⟩

syn adieu, au revoir, bon voyage, farewell, Godspeed

rel leave-taking, send-off

near ant greeting(s), salutation, salute; welcome

ant hello

good–hearted *adj* having or marked by sympathy and consideration for others — see HUMANE 1

goodly *adj* **1** of a size greater than average of its kind — see LARGE

2 sufficiently large in size, amount, or number to merit attention — see CONSIDERABLE 1

good–natured *adj* having an easygoing and pleasing manner especially in social situations — see AMIABLE

good–naturedness *n* **1** a desire or disposition to please — see COMPLAISANCE

2 the state or quality of having a pleasant or agreeable manner in socializing with others — see AMIABILITY 1

goodness *n* conduct that conforms to an accepted standard of right and wrong — see MORALITY 1

good–sized *adj* **1** of a size greater than average of its kind — see LARGE

2 sufficiently large in size, amount, or number to merit attention — see CONSIDERABLE 1

good–tempered *adj* having an easygoing and pleasing manner especially in social situations — see AMIABLE

good–temperedness *n* the state or quality of having a pleasant or agreeable manner in socializing with others — see AMIABILITY 1

goodwill *n* **1** kindly concern, interest, or support ⟨the long tradition of *goodwill* that exists between the United States and Canada⟩

syn amity, benevolence, cordiality, fellowship, friendliness, friendship, kindliness

rel camaraderie, community, companionship, comradeship; civility, comity, concord, harmony, rapport; charity, generosity, neighborliness; affinity, communion, empathy, sympathy, tolerance; altruism, philanthropy, selflessness

near ant disfavor, intolerance; animosity, antagonism, antipathy, enmity, hate, hatred, hostility, incivility, malice, rancor

ant ill will, malevolence

2 cheerful readiness to do something — see ALACRITY

goody *n* something that is pleasing to eat because it is rare or a luxury — see DELICACY 1

gooey *adj* being of such a thick consistency as to readily cling to objects upon contact — see STICKY 1

goof *n* an unintentional departure from truth or accuracy — see ERROR 1

go off *vb* to break open or into pieces usually because of internal pressure — see EXPLODE 1

goofy *adj* lacking in seriousness or maturity — see GIDDY 1

goon *n* **1** a stupid person — see IDIOT

2 a violent, brutal person who is often a member of an organized gang — see HOODLUM

goose *n* a person who lacks good sense or judgment — see FOOL 1

goose egg *n* the numerical symbol 0 or the absence of number or quantity represented by it — see ZERO 1

go over *vb* to turn out as planned or desired — see SUCCEED 1

---

syn synonym(s)   *rel* related words
ant antonym(s)   *near ant* near antonym(s)

gore *vb* to penetrate or hold (something) with a pointed object — see IMPALE

gorge *n* a narrow opening between hillsides or mountains that can be used for passage — see CANYON

gorge *vb* **1** to fill with food to capacity ⟨they *gorged* themselves on the four pies Aunt Martha brought for Thanksgiving⟩
syn glut, sate, stuff, surfeit
rel gobble, gormandize, pig out; gulp, guzzle; cloy, fill; banquet, feast, regale
near ant diet, fast
2 to eat greedily or to excess ⟨the kids *gorged* on Halloween candy when they got home from trick-or-treating⟩
syn gormandize, overeat, pig out, swill
rel devour, glut, sate, stuff, surfeit, wolf; banquet, feast, regale; bolt, cram, gulp, guzzle
near ant nibble, peck, pick, taste

gorgeous *adj* very pleasing to look at — see BEAUTIFUL

gorgeousness *n* the qualities in a person or thing that as a whole give pleasure to the senses — see BEAUTY 1

gorger *n* one who eats greedily or too much — see GLUTTON

gormandize *vb* to eat greedily or to excess — see GORGE 2

gormandizer *n* one who eats greedily or too much — see GLUTTON

gory *adj* containing, smeared, or stained with blood — see BLOODY 1

gospel *n* the basic beliefs or guiding principles of a person or group — see CREED 1

gossamer *adj* **1** being of a material lacking in sturdiness or substance — see FLIMSY 1
2 resembling air in lightness — see AIRY 1
3 very thin and easy to see through — see SHEER 1

gossamery *adj* **1** being of a material lacking in sturdiness or substance — see FLIMSY 1
2 resembling air in lightness — see AIRY 1
3 very thin and easy to see through — see SHEER 1

gossip *n* friendly, informal conversation or an instance of this — see CHAT

gossip *vb* to relate sometimes questionable or secret information of a personal nature ⟨likes to *gossip* with others about our neighbors' arguments⟩
syn blab, talk, tattle
rel bandy (about), circulate, noise (about), rumor; disclose, divulge, reveal, tell; hint, imply, insinuate, intimate, let on, suggest; inform, report, snitch, squeal, tip (off); babble, spill; confide
phrases spill the beans
near ant clam up, shut up

gossipy *adj* having the style and content of everyday conversation — see CHATTY 1

gouge *vb* to charge (someone) too much for goods or services — see OVERCHARGE 1

gourmand *n* **1** a person with refined tastes in food and wine — see EPICURE

2 one who eats greedily or too much — see GLUTTON

gourmet *n* a person with refined tastes in food and wine — see EPICURE

govern *vb* **1** to exercise authority or power over ⟨the president is elected in order to *govern* the country⟩
syn boss, captain, command, control, preside (over), rule
rel conduct, direct, head, lead; administer, manage, oversee, regulate, superintend, supervise; dictate, dominate, domineer, lord (it over), master, oppress, reign (over), tyrannize; conquer, subdue, subjugate
2 to keep from exceeding a desirable degree or level (as of expression) — see CONTROL 1
3 to look after and make decisions about — see CONDUCT 1

governance *n* **1** lawful control over the affairs of a political unit (as a nation) — see RULE 2
2 the act or activity of looking after and making decisions about something — see CONDUCT 1

government *n* **1** lawful control over the affairs of a political unit (as a nation) — see RULE 2
2 the act or activity of looking after and making decisions about something — see CONDUCT 1

gown *n* a garment with a joined blouse and skirt for a woman or girl — see DRESS 1

gown *vb* to outfit with clothes and especially fine or special clothes — see CLOTHE 1

grab *n* an instance of theft — see THEFT 2

grab *vb* to take physical control or possession of (something) suddenly or forcibly — see CATCH 1

grace *n* **1** an act of kind assistance — see FAVOR 1
2 dignified or restrained beauty of form, appearance, or style — see ELEGANCE

grace *vb* to make more attractive by adding something that is beautiful or becoming — see DECORATE

graceful *adj* **1** moving easily ⟨the *graceful* ballerina effortlessly leapt across the dance floor⟩
syn agile, light, light-footed, lissome (*also* lissom), lithe, lithesome, nimble, spry
rel flexible, limber, loose-jointed, pliable, pliant, supple; adroit, deft, dexterous (*also* dextrous); fleet-footed, surefooted
near ant inflexible, rigid, stiff; bungling, inept, maladroit
ant awkward, clumsy, gawky, graceless, lumbering, ungainly, ungraceful
2 having or showing elegance — see ELEGANT 1

gracefulness *n* dignified or restrained beauty of form, appearance, or style — see ELEGANCE

graceless *adj* **1** lacking in physical ease and grace in movement or in the use of the hands — see CLUMSY 1

2 lacking social grace and assurance — see AWKWARD 1

3 not appropriate for a particular occasion or situation — see INAPPROPRIATE

gracious *adj* **1** showing a natural kindness and courtesy especially in social situations ⟨a *gracious* teacher who made the new student feel welcome⟩

syn affable, cordial, genial, hospitable, sociable

rel agreeable, amiable, benignant, congenial, convivial, friendly, kind, kindly, neighborly; accommodating, obliging; considerate, courteous, polite, thoughtful; sophisticated, urbane; approachable, attentive, outgoing

near ant boorish, churlish; abrupt, blunt, brusque, curt, gruff, sharp, snippy; antisocial, disagreeable, discourteous, illmannered, impolite, rude, sullen, surly, uncivil, unfriendly, unkind, unmannerly; crabbed, crabby, cross, crusty, grumpy

ant inhospitable, ungracious, unsociable

2 having an easygoing and pleasing manner especially in social situations — see AMIABLE

3 showing consideration, courtesy, and good manners — see POLITE 1

graciousness *n* **1** speech or behavior that is a sign of good breeding — see POLITENESS

2 the state or quality of having a pleasant or agreeable manner in socializing with others — see AMIABILITY 1

gradational *adj* proceeding or changing by steps or degrees — see GRADUAL

gradationally *adv* by small steps or amounts — see GRADUALLY

grade *n* **1** an individual part of a process, series, or ranking — see DEGREE 1

2 degree of excellence — see QUALITY 1

3 one of the units into which a whole is divided on the basis of a common characteristic — see CLASS 2

4 something set up as an example against which others of the same type are compared — see STANDARD 1

5 the degree to which something rises up from a position level with the horizon — see SLANT

grade *vb* **1** to arrange or assign according to type — see CLASSIFY 1

2 to take or have a certain position within a group arranged in vertical classes — see RANK 1

gradient *n* the degree to which something rises up from a position level with the horizon — see SLANT

gradual *adj* proceeding or changing by steps or degrees ⟨a *gradual* drop in gas prices will take place over the next several months⟩

syn gradational, incremental, phased, piecemeal, step-by-step

rel progressive, stepped, tapered; imperceptible, inching

near ant abrupt, acute, sharp; changeable, dynamic, volatile

ant sudden

gradually *adv* by small steps or amounts ⟨*gradually* worked his way down the class roster⟩ ⟨add the sugar to the beaten egg whites *gradually* to make the meringue⟩

syn gradationally, little by little, piece by piece, piecemeal

rel hierarchically, increasingly, progressively; fractionally, imperceptibly; slowly

near ant acutely, sharply, steeply, unprogressively; hastily, precipitously

ant abruptly, suddenly

graduation *n* a scheme of rank or order — see ³SCALE 1

grain *n* **1** a very small piece — see BIT 1

2 one's characteristic attitude or mood — see DISPOSITION 1

grainy *adj* made up of large particles — see COARSE 1

grand *adj* **1** large and impressive in size, grandeur, extent, or conception ⟨the *grand* ceremonies that typically mark the opening of the Olympic Games⟩

syn august, baronial, gallant, glorious, grandiose, heroic, imposing, magnificent, majestic, monumental, noble, proud, regal, royal, splendid, stately

rel colossal, monstrous, prodigious, stupendous, tremendous; kingly, lordly, princely, queenly; awesome, awful, cosmic, sublime, wondrous; formidable, impressive, prepossessing, redoubtable; marvelous (*or* marvellous), superb, terrific, wonderful; extravagant, lavish, luxurious, opulent, sumptuous; gorgeous, resplendent, splendiferous; extraordinary, killer, remarkable, sensational, striking; celestial, divine, heavenly

near ant lowly, modest, unprepossessing; average, common, mediocre, ordinary, run-of-the-mill, second-rate; abject, mean, meretricious, shabby, sordid; insignificant, measly, paltry, petty, puny, trifling, trivial

ant humble, unheroic, unimposing, unimpressive

2 coming before all others in importance — see FOREMOST 1

3 not lacking any part or member that properly belongs to it — see COMPLETE 1

4 of a size greater than average of its kind — see LARGE

5 of high birth, rank, or station — see NOBLE 1

6 of the very best kind — see EXCELLENT 1

7 unusually large — see HUGE

grandee *n* a man of high birth or social position — see GENTLEMAN 1

grandeur *n* impressiveness of beauty on a large scale — see MAGNIFICENCE

grandfather *n* a person who is several generations earlier in an individual's line of descent — see ANCESTOR 1

grandiloquence *n* **1** boastful speech or writing — see BOMBAST 1

2 language that is impressive-sounding but not meaningful or sincere — see RHETORIC 1

---

syn synonym(s) **rel** related words
ant antonym(s) **near ant** near antonym(s)

grandiloquent *adj* **1** full of fine words and fancy expressions — see FLOWERY 1

2 marked by the use of impressive-sounding but mostly meaningless words and phrases — see RHETORICAL

grandiose *adj* **1** large and impressive in size, grandeur, extent, or conception — see GRAND 1

2 self-consciously trying to present an appearance of grandeur or importance — see PRETENTIOUS 1

grandiosity *n* the quality or state of appearing or trying to appear more important or more valuable than is the case — see PRETENSE 1

grandly *adv* **1** in a luxurious manner — see HIGH

2 in a manner befitting a person of the highest character and ideals — see GREATLY 1

grandness *n* **1** impressiveness of beauty on a large scale — see MAGNIFICENCE

2 the quality or state of being large in size — see LARGENESS

grange *n* a piece of land and its buildings used to grow crops or raise livestock — see FARM

granite *n* firm or unwavering adherence to one's purpose — see DETERMINATION 1

grant *n* a sum of money allotted for a specific use by official or formal action — see APPROPRIATION

grant *vb* **1** to accept the truth or existence of (something) usually reluctantly — see ADMIT

2 to give the ownership or benefit of (something) formally or publicly — see CONFER 1

granting *n* the approval by someone in authority for the doing of something — see PERMISSION

granular *adj* made up of large particles — see COARSE 1

granulated *adj* made up of large particles — see COARSE 1

granule *n* a very small piece — see BIT 1

graphic *also* **graphical** *adj* **1** producing a mental picture through clear and impressive description ⟨the report offered many *graphic* details about the huge earthquake that rocked the area⟩

syn delineated, pictorial, picturesque, vivid

rel depicted, descriptive, expressive; concrete, explicit, specific; faithful, lifelike, natural, realistic; fresh, incisive, sharp

near ant indeterminate, nebulous, obscure, sketchy, unclear, vague; blurry, dark, dim, muddy, murky, shadowy

2 consisting of or relating to pictures — see PICTORIAL 1

graphic *n* something that visually explains or decorates a text — see ILLUSTRATION 1

grapple *n* the act or manner of holding — see HOLD 1

grapple *vb* **1** to seize and attempt to unbalance one another for the purpose of achieving physical mastery — see WRESTLE

2 to take physical control or possession of (something) suddenly or forcibly — see CATCH 1

grapple (with) *vb* to deal with (something) usually skillfully or efficiently — see HANDLE 1

grasp *n* **1** the ability to direct the course of something — see CONTROL 2

2 the act or manner of holding — see HOLD 1

3 the knowledge gained from the process of coming to know or understand something — see COMPREHENSION

grasp *vb* **1** to have a practical understanding of — see KNOW 1

2 to put one's arms around and press tightly — see EMBRACE 1

3 to reach for and take hold of by embracing with the fingers or arms — see TAKE 1

4 to recognize the meaning of — see COMPREHEND 1

grasping *adj* having or marked by an eager and often selfish desire especially for material possessions — see GREEDY 1

grassland *n* a broad area of level or rolling treeless country — see PLAIN

grate *vb* **1** to disturb the peace of mind of (someone) especially by repeated disagreeable acts — see IRRITATE 1

2 to pass roughly and noisily over or against a surface — see SCRAPE 1

3 to press or strike against or together so as to make a scraping sound — see GRIND 2

grateful *adj* **1** feeling or expressing gratitude ⟨was *grateful* for her neighbor's help after she broke her foot⟩

syn appreciative, obliged, thankful

rel beholden, indebted; gratified, pleased; thanking

ant thankless, unappreciative, ungrateful, unthankful

2 giving pleasure or contentment to the mind or senses — see PLEASANT

gratefulness *n* acknowledgment of having received something good from another — see THANKS

gratification *n* the feeling experienced when one's wishes are met — see PLEASURE 1

gratified *adj* **1** experiencing pleasure, satisfaction, or delight — see GLAD 1

2 feeling that one's needs or desires have been met — see CONTENT

gratify *vb* **1** to give in to (a desire) — see INDULGE

2 to give satisfaction to — see PLEASE

gratifying *adj* **1** giving pleasure or contentment to the mind or senses — see PLEASANT

2 making one feel good inside — see HEARTWARMING

grating *adj* **1** disagreeable to one's aesthetic or artistic sense — see HARSH 2

2 harsh and dry in sound — see HOARSE

gratis *adj* not costing or charging anything — see FREE 4

gratitude *n* acknowledgment of having received something good from another — see THANKS

gratuitous *adj* **1** not costing or charging anything — see FREE 4

2 not needed by the circumstances or to accomplish an end — see UNNECESSARY

gratuity *n* **1** a small sum of money given for a service over and above what is due — see ²TIP 1

2 something given in addition to what is ordinarily expected or owed — see BONUS

grave *adj* **1** having a matter of importance as its topic — see SERIOUS 2

2 involving potential loss or injury — see DANGEROUS

3 not joking or playful in mood or manner — see SERIOUS 1

grave *n* a final resting place for a dead person ⟨put flowers on his mother's *grave*⟩

syn sepulcher (*or* sepulchre), sepulture, tomb

rel catacomb, charnel, crypt, mausoleum, vault; cemetery, churchyard, graveyard, potter's field; barrow, mound, tumulus

grave *vb* to cut (as letters or designs) on a hard surface — see ENGRAVE 1

gravel *adj* harsh and dry in sound — see HOARSE

gravelly *adj* harsh and dry in sound — see HOARSE

gravestone *n* a shaped stone laid over or erected near a grave and usually bearing an inscription to identify and preserve the memory of the deceased — see TOMBSTONE

graveyard *n* a piece of land used for burying the dead — see CEMETERY

gravid *adj* containing unborn young within the body — see PREGNANT 1

gravity *n* a mental state free of jesting or trifling — see EARNESTNESS

gravy *n* **1** a savory fluid food used as a topping or accompaniment to a main dish — see SAUCE 1

2 something given in addition to what is ordinarily expected or owed — see BONUS

gray *also* **grey** *adj* **1** of the color gray ⟨the *gray* elephant and the gaudily dressed circus performer created a striking contrast⟩

syn grayish, leaden, pewter, silver, silvery, slate, slaty, steely

rel achromatic, neutral; dirty, dull, faded, washed-out; ashen, ashy, chalky, livid, mousy (*or* mousey), pale, white, whitish; chocolate, dun, sandy, sepia; brindled, grizzled, hoar, hoary

near ant ablaze, bright, deep, gay, rich; chromatic, colored

2 causing or marked by an atmosphere lacking in cheer — see GLOOMY 1

grayish *adj* of the color gray — see GRAY 1

gray matter *n* the ability to learn and understand or to deal with problems — see INTELLIGENCE 1

¹graze *vb* to feed on grass or herbs ⟨cows *grazing* in the meadow⟩

syn browse, forage, pasture

rel eat, feed, nibble

²graze *vb* **1** to damage by rubbing against a sharp or rough surface — see SCRAPE 2

2 to pass lightly across or touch gently especially in passing — see BRUSH

grease *vb* to coat (something) with a slippery substance in order to reduce friction — see LUBRICATE

greased *adj* having or being a surface so smooth as to make sliding or falling likely — see SLICK 1

greasy *adj* having or being a surface so smooth as to make sliding or falling likely — see SLICK 1

great *adj* **1** having or showing exceptional knowledge, experience, or skill in a field of endeavor — see PROFICIENT

2 having, characterized by, or arising from a dignified and generous nature — see NOBLE 2

3 lasting for a considerable time — see LONG 2

4 of a size greater than average of its kind — see LARGE

5 of the very best kind — see EXCELLENT

greatcoat *n* a warm outdoor coat — see OVERCOAT

greatest *adj* **1** coming before all others in importance — see FOREMOST

2 of the highest degree — see FULL 2

greathearted *adj* **1** feeling or displaying no fear by temperament — see BRAVE

2 having, characterized by, or arising from a dignified and generous nature — see NOBLE 2

greatheartedness *n* strength of mind to carry on in spite of danger — see COURAGE

greatly *adv* **1** in a manner befitting a person of the highest character and ideals ⟨as commander of the Union army's first black regiment, Robert Gould Shaw died as *greatly* as he had lived⟩

syn gallantly, grandly, heroically, highmindedly, honorably, magnanimously, nobly

rel loftily, venerably; magnificently, majestically

near ant abominably, contemptibly, despicably, detestably, hatefully; degenerately

ant basely, dishonorably, ignobly

2 to a large extent or degree ⟨Todd has *greatly* increased the scope of his theme on civic responsibility⟩

syn astronomically, broadly, colossally, considerably, enormously, extensively, hugely, largely, massively, monstrously, much, sizably, stupendously, tremendously, utterly, vastly

rel appreciably, noticeably, significantly; abundantly, amply, copiously, healthily, plentifully

---

syn synonym(s)   **rel** related words
ant antonym(s)   **near ant** near antonym(s)

***near* ant** modestly; fractionally; imperceptibly, infinitesimally, insignificantly, invisibly, microscopically, minutely, negligibly; barely, hardly, just, scarcely

ant little, slightly

3 to a great degree — see VERY 1

greatness *n* **1** exceptionally high quality — see EXCELLENCE 1

2 the quality or state of being large in size — see LARGENESS

greed *n* an intense selfish desire for wealth or possessions ⟨don't let *greed* for riches control you⟩

syn acquisitiveness, avarice, avariciousness, avidity, covetousness, cupidity, greediness, rapaciousness, rapacity

rel materialism, possessiveness; appetite, craving, hankering, hunger, itch, longing, lust, passion, ravenousness, thirst, voracity, yearning, yen

***near* ant** contentment, fulfillment, satisfaction; bounteousness, bounty, charity, generosity, generousness, liberality, openhandedness, openheartedness, unselfishness

greediness *n* an intense selfish desire for wealth or possessions — see GREED

greedy *adj* **1** having or marked by an eager and often selfish desire especially for material possessions ⟨a young rocker who was *greedy* for fame and riches⟩ ⟨the *greedy* exploitation of the land by developers⟩

syn acquisitive, avaricious, avid, coveting, covetous, grasping, mercenary, rapacious

rel materialistic, philistine; desirous, eager, itchy, miserly; hoggish, piggish, swinish; devouring, gluttonous, gobbling, insatiable, ravenous, unquenchable, voracious; discontent, discontented, malcontent, unquenched, unsatisfied; begrudging, grudging, resentful

***near* ant** bounteous, bountiful, charitable, freehanded, generous, greathearted, handsome, liberal, munificent, openhanded, openhearted, unselfish, unsparing; controlled, moderate, restrained, temperate; content, sated, satisfied

2 having a huge appetite — see VORACIOUS 1

green *adj* **1** covered with a thick, healthy natural growth — see LUSH 1

2 lacking in adult experience or maturity — see CALLOW

3 lacking in worldly wisdom or informed judgment — see NAIVE 1

4 lacking the warm skin color indicative of or associated with good health — see SICKLY 2

green *n* green leaves or plants — see GREENERY 1

greenback *n* a piece of printed paper used as money — see ¹BILL 2

greenery *n* green leaves or plants ⟨Scottish highlands covered with lush *greenery*⟩

syn flora, foliage, green, herbage, leafage, vegetation, verdure

rel grassland, prairie; underbrush, undergrowth

greenhorn *n* a person who is just starting out in a field of activity — see BEGINNER

greenhouse *n* a glass-enclosed building for growing plants — see CONSERVATORY

greenness *n* the quality or state of being simple and sincere — see NAÏVETÉ 1

greeting *n* **1** an expression of goodwill upon meeting — see HELLO

2 **greetings** *pl* best wishes — see COMPLIMENT

gregarious *adj* likely to seek or enjoy the company of others — see CONVIVIAL

gregariousness *n* the quality or state of being social — see SOCIABILITY

gremlin *n* an imaginary being usually having a small human form and magical powers — see FAIRY

griddle cake *n* a flat cake made from thin batter and cooked on both sides (as on a griddle) — see PANCAKE

grief *n* deep sadness especially for the loss of someone or something loved — see SORROW

grievance *n* **1** a lingering ill will towards a person for a real or imagined wrong — see GRUDGE 1

2 an expression of dissatisfaction, pain, or resentment — see COMPLAINT 1

grieve *vb* to feel deep sadness or mental pain ⟨*grieved* over the lost cat⟩

syn agonize, bleed, hurt, mourn, sorrow, suffer

rel ache, long (for), pine (away); rack, torment, torture; bemoan, bewail, deplore, lament, rue; bawl, cry, groan, howl, keen, moan, take on, wail, weep, yammer

***near* ant** beam, cheer, exult, joy, laugh, overjoy, ravish, rejoice; comfort, console

grieve (for) *vb* to feel or express sorrow for — see LAMENT 1

grieving *adj* expressing or suggesting mourning — see MOURNFUL 1

grievous *adj* **1** difficult to endure — see HARSH 1

2 hard to accept or bear especially emotionally — see BITTER 2

3 involving potential loss or injury — see DANGEROUS

4 of a kind to cause great distress — see REGRETTABLE

grievously *adv* with feelings of bitterness or grief — see HARD 2

grill *n* a public establishment where meals are served to paying customers for consumption on the premises — see RESTAURANT

grill *vb* to put a series of questions to — see EXAMINE 1

grim *adj* **1** harsh and threatening in manner or appearance ⟨a *grim* and desolate landscape⟩ ⟨a *grim* and short-tempered shopkeeper who didn't exactly invite friendly conversation⟩

syn austere, dour, fierce, flinty, forbidding, gruff, intimidating, lowering (*also* louring), rough, rugged, severe, stark, steely, stern, ungentle *rel* bleak, cold, hostile, unfriendly; adamant, determined, firm, resolute, steadfast, unflinching; fixed, hard, immovable, implacable, inflexible, obdurate, rigid, set, stiff, unbending, uncompromising, unyielding; immutable, unchangeable; black, cheerless, dark, gloomy, glum, joyless, moody, morose, sulky, sullen, surly; brooding, grave, melancholy, serious, sober, solemn, somber (*or* sombre), unsmiling, weighty

near ant bland, meek, mellow, soft; easy, quiet, tranquil; agreeable, bright, cheerful, inviting, pleasant, pleasing, sweet; glad, happy, lighthearted, merry, mirthful, sunny; featherbrained, flighty, frivolous, giddy, goofy, light-headed, playful

ant benign, benignant, gentle, mild, tender

2 difficult to endure — see HARSH 1

3 showing no signs of slackening or yielding in one's purpose — see UNYIELDING 1

4 violently unfriendly or aggressive in disposition — see FIERCE 1

grimace *n* a twisting of the facial features in disgust or disapproval ⟨made a *grimace* when he tasted the medicine⟩

syn face, frown, lower (*also* lour), mouth, pout, scowl

rel flinch, squinch, wince; growl, snarl; simper, smirk; scoff, sneer; glare, glower, look, stare

near ant grin, smile

grimace *vb* to distort one's face — see MUG 1

grime *n* foul matter that mars the purity or cleanliness of something — see FILTH 1

grime *vb* to make dirty — see DIRTY 1

griminess *n* the state or quality of being dirty — see DIRTINESS 1

grimy *adj* not clean — see DIRTY 1

grin *vb* to express an emotion (as amusement) by curving the lips upward — see SMILE 1

grind *n* **1** a harsh grating sound — see RASP

2 a person slavishly devoted to intellectual or academic pursuits — see NERD

3 very hard or unpleasant work — see TOIL

grind *vb* **1** to make smooth by friction ⟨after they are *ground* and polished, these stones can be used for jewelry⟩

syn buff, file, hone, rasp, rub, sand

rel plane, scrape; sandblast, scour; burnish, polish; sharpen, whet; regrind

near ant coarsen, roughen

2 to press or strike against or together so as to make a scraping sound ⟨everyone in the car winced when the driver *ground* the gears trying to shift into second⟩

syn crunch, gnash, grate, grit, scrape, scrunch

rel creak, groan, rasp, scratch; clash, jangle, jar

3 to make sharp or sharper — see SHARPEN

---

4 to make smooth or glossy usually by repeatedly applying surface pressure — see POLISH

5 to pass roughly and noisily over or against a surface — see SCRAPE 1

6 to reduce to fine particles — see POWDER

grind (out) *vb* to produce or bring about especially by long or repeated effort — see HAMMER (OUT)

grinder *n* a large sandwich on a long split roll — see SUBMARINE

grip *n* **1** a bag carried by hand and designed to hold a traveler's clothing and personal articles — see TRAVELING BAG

2 the act or manner of holding — see HOLD 1

3 the knowledge gained from the process of coming to know or understand something — see COMPREHENSION

4 the right or means to command or control others — see POWER 1

grip *vb* **1** to have or keep in one's hands — see HOLD 1

2 to hold the attention of as if by a spell — see ENTHRALL 1

3 to hold the attention of — see ENGAGE 1

4 to reach for and take hold of by embracing with the fingers or arms — see TAKE 1

gripe *n* an expression of dissatisfaction, pain, or resentment — see COMPLAINT 1

gripe *vb* to express dissatisfaction, pain, or resentment usually tiresomely — see COMPLAIN

griper *n* **1** a person who makes frequent complaints usually about little things — see CRYBABY

2 an irritable and complaining person — see GROUCH

gripping *adj* holding the attention or provoking interest — see INTERESTING

grisliness *n* the quality of inspiring intense dread or dismay — see HORROR 1

grisly *adj* extremely disturbing or repellent — see HORRIBLE 1

grit *n* the strength of mind that enables a person to endure pain or hardship — see FORTITUDE

grit *vb* to press or strike against or together so as to make a scraping sound — see GRIND 2

groan *n* **1** a crying out in grief — see LAMENT 1

2 a long low sound indicating pain or grief — see MOAN 1

groan *vb* to utter a moan — see MOAN 1

grog *n* a fermented or distilled beverage that can make a person drunk — see ALCOHOL

groggery *n* a place of business where alcoholic beverages are sold to be consumed on the premises — see BARROOM

grogshop *n* a place of business where alcoholic beverages are sold to be consumed on the premises — see BARROOM

groomed *adj* being clean and in good order — see NEAT 1

groove n an established and often automatic or monotonous series of actions followed when engaging in some activity — see ROUTINE 1

groove vb to mark with or as if with a line or groove — see SCORE 1

groove (on) vb to take pleasure in — see ENJOY 1

groovy adj of the very best kind — see EXCELLENT

grope vb to search for something blindly or uncertainly ⟨groped for her car keys⟩ ⟨groping for the right answer⟩
syn feel, fish, fumble
rel cast about, hunt, look, reach, seek (out); clutch, grab, scrabble, snatch

gross adj 1 depicting or referring to sexual matters in a way that is unacceptable in polite society — see OBSCENE 1

2 having an excess of body fat — see FAT 1

3 lacking in refinement or good taste — see COARSE 2

4 very noticeable especially for being incorrect or bad — see EGREGIOUS

grossness n 1 the condition of having an excess of body fat — see CORPULENCE

2 the quality or state of being obscene — see OBSCENITY 1

3 the quality or state of lacking refinement or good taste — see VULGARITY 1

grot n a naturally formed underground chamber with an opening to the surface — see CAVE

grotesque adj 1 disagreeable to one's aesthetic or artistic sense — see HARSH 2

2 unpleasant to look at — see UGLY 1

grotto n a naturally formed underground chamber with an opening to the surface — see CAVE

grouch n an irritable and complaining person ⟨an uncle who is a real grouch when he's sick⟩
syn bear, complainer, crab, crank, croaker, curmudgeon, fusser, griper, grouser, growler, grumbler, grump, murmurer, mutterer, whiner
rel fulminator, malcontent, sorehead; killjoy, party pooper, spoilsport; defeatist, pessimist; faultfinder, kicker, nagger, nitpicker, quibbler
near ant optimist; rejoicer

grouchiness n readiness to show annoyance or impatience — see PETULANCE

grouchy adj 1 easily irritated or annoyed — see IRRITABLE

2 given to complaining a lot — see FUSSY 1

ground adj having an edge thin enough to cut or pierce something — see SHARP 1

ground n 1 **grounds** pl the area around and belonging to a building ⟨an escorted tour of the White House and its surrounding grounds⟩
syn demesne, park, premises, yard
rel acres, estate, land, lot, parcel, plot, property, real estate, realty; campus; backyard, churchyard, dooryard, schoolyard

2 **grounds** pl matter that settles to the bottom of a body of liquid — see DEPOSIT 1

3 **grounds** pl something (as a belief) that serves as the basis for another thing — see REASON 2

4 a small area of usually open land — see FIELD 1

5 an immaterial thing upon which something else rests — see BASE 1

6 the loose surface material in which plants naturally grow — see DIRT 1

7 the physical conditions or features that form the setting against which something is viewed — see BACKGROUND 1

8 the solid part of our planet's surface as distinguished from the sea and air — see EARTH 2

ground vb to find a basis — see BASE

grounded adj resting on the shore or bottom of a body of water — see AGROUND

groundless adj having no basis in reason or fact ⟨please stop making groundless accusations against the teachers you dislike⟩ ⟨fears of extinction proved groundless⟩
syn invalid, nonvalid, unfounded, ungrounded, unreasonable, unsubstantiated, unsupported, unwarranted
rel illogical, irrational, nonlogical, unconscionable, unsound; fallacious, false, misled, wrong; gratuitous, uncalled-for, unnecessary; flimsy, implausible, misleading, specious, unconvincing, unsatisfying, untenable, weak; ill-advised, unreasoned; inconsistent; absurd, asinine, foolish, meaningless, nonsensical, preposterous, senseless, silly; insane, nutty, mad, wacky
near ant certified, validated, verified; confirmed, corroborated; informed, logical, rational; commonsense, sane, sensible, sober, wise; actual, genuine, real, true; certain, sure; clear, cogent, compelling, convincing, credible, persuasive, plausible, satisfying, solid
ant good, hard, just, justified, reasonable, reasoned, substantiated, valid, well-founded

ground plan n a method worked out in advance for achieving some objective — see PLAN 1

ground rule n a statement spelling out the proper procedure or conduct for an activity — see RULE 1

groundwork n an immaterial thing upon which something else rests — see BASE 1

group n 1 a number of things considered as a unit ⟨car buffs stood around admiring a group of classic cars in the parking lot⟩
syn array, assemblage, bank, batch, battery, block, bunch, clump, cluster, collection, grouping, huddle, knot, lot, package, parcel, passel, set, suite
rel accumulation, aggregate, aggregation, conglomeration; agglomeration, assortment, hodgepodge, jumble, miscellany, mixture, odds and ends, sundries, variety; series, suit
phrases the whole kit and caboodle

near ant entity, item, single, unit

2 a usually small number of persons considered as a unit ⟨the next *group* of guests were being seated for dinner⟩

syn array, batch, battery, body, bunch, cluster, crop, grouping, huddle, knot, lot, parcel, party, passel

rel assembly, congregation, gathering, organization; circle, clan, clique, coterie, fellowship, gang, ring, set; faction, guild (*also* gild), order, school, sect; brigade, crew, outfit, platoon, posse; alliance, bloc, coalition, confederacy, confederation, federation, league, union; bevy, covey

phrases the whole kit and caboodle

near ant individual, single

3 one of the units into which a whole is divided on the basis of a common characteristic — see CLASS 2

group *vb* **1** to arrange or assign according to type — see CLASSIFY 1

2 to bring together in one body or place — see GATHER 1

grouping *n* **1** a number of things considered as a unit — see GROUP 1

2 a usually small number of persons considered as a unit — see GROUP 2

grouse *vb* to express dissatisfaction, pain, or resentment usually tiresomely — see COMPLAIN

grouser *n* an irritable and complaining person — see GROUCH

grovel *vb* **1** to draw back or crouch down in fearful submission — see COWER

2 to move slowly with the body close to the ground — see CRAWL 1

grow *vb* **1** to look after or assist the growth of by labor and care ⟨a dedicated home gardener who *grows* tomatoes in her small garden every summer⟩

syn crop, cultivate, culture, promote, raise, rear, tend

rel breed, produce, propagate; plant, sow; gather, glean, harvest, reap; germinate, quicken, root, sprout

near ant kill; dig, extirpate, pick, pluck, pull (up), uproot; cut, hay, mow

2 to become mature — see MATURE

3 to eventually have as a state or quality — see BECOME

grow (in) *vb* to increase in — see GAIN 1

grower *n* a person who cultivates the land and grows crops on it — see FARMER

growl *vb* **1** to express dissatisfaction, pain, or resentment usually tiresomely — see COMPLAIN

2 to make a long loud deep noise or cry — see ROAR

3 to make a low heavy rolling sound — see RUMBLE

growler *n* **1** a person who makes frequent complaints usually about little things — see CRYBABY

2 an irritable and complaining person — see GROUCH

grown–up *n* a fully grown person — see ADULT

growth *n* **1** an abnormal mass of tissue ⟨found a *growth* on the dog's neck under her collar⟩

syn excrescence, lump, neoplasm, tumor

rel outgrowth; cancer, carcinoma, lymphoma, malignancy, melanoma; cyst, tubercle, wart

2 the act or process of going from the simple or basic to the complex or advanced — see DEVELOPMENT 1

3 the process of becoming mature — see MATURATION

grow up *vb* to become mature — see MATURE

grub *n* substances intended to be eaten — see FOOD

grub *vb* to devote serious and sustained effort — see LABOR

grubber *n* a person who does very hard or dull work — see SLAVE 2

grubbiness *n* the state or quality of being dirty — see DIRTINESS 1

grubby *adj* not clean — see DIRTY 1

grudge *n* **1** a lingering ill will towards a person for a real or imagined wrong ⟨he's had a *grudge* against her ever since she snubbed him at the dance⟩

syn grievance, resentment, score

rel condemnation; offense (*or* offence), umbrage; complaint; peeve, pique

2 a deep-seated ill will — see ENMITY

grueling *or* **gruelling** *adj* **1** requiring considerable physical or mental effort — see HARD 2

2 requiring much time, effort, or careful attention — see DEMANDING 1

gruesome *adj* extremely disturbing or repellent — see HORRIBLE 1

gruesomeness *n* the quality of inspiring intense dread or dismay — see HORROR 1

gruff *adj* **1** harsh and dry in sound — see HOARSE

2 harsh and threatening in manner or appearance — see GRIM 1

grumble *n* an expression of dissatisfaction, pain, or resentment — see COMPLAINT 1

grumble *vb* **1** to express dissatisfaction, pain, or resentment usually tiresomely — see COMPLAIN

2 to make a low heavy rolling sound — see RUMBLE

grumbler *n* **1** a person who makes frequent complaints usually about little things — see CRY-BABY

2 an irritable and complaining person — see GROUCH

grump *n* an irritable and complaining person — see GROUCH

grumpiness *n* readiness to show annoyance or impatience — see PETULANCE

grumpy *adj* **1** easily irritated or annoyed — see IRRITABLE

2 given to complaining a lot — see FUSSY 1

grungy *adj* **1** not clean — see DIRTY 1

2 showing signs of advanced wear and tear and neglect — see SHABBY 1

---

syn synonym(s)   *rel* related words
ant antonym(s)   *near ant* near antonym(s)

grunt *n* speech that is not clear enough to be understood — see MUMBLE

grunt *vb* to speak softly and unclearly — see MUMBLE

grunting *n* speech that is not clear enough to be understood — see MUMBLE

guarantee *n* 1 a formal agreement to fulfill an obligation ⟨the contractors gave us a written *guarantee* that the work on the house would be done by Christmas⟩
syn bond, contract, covenant, guaranty, surety, warranty
rel oath, pledge, vow, word; bargain, compact, pact, treaty; assurance, insurance; bail, deposit, pawn, security
2 something given or held to assure that the giver will keep a promise — see PLEDGE 1

guarantee *vb* 1 to assume responsibility for the satisfactory quality or performance of — see WARRANT 1
2 to make sure, certain, or safe — see ENSURE

guarantor *n* a person who takes the responsibility for some other person or thing — see SPONSOR

guaranty *n* 1 a formal agreement to fulfill an obligation — see GUARANTEE 1
2 something given or held to assure that the giver will keep a promise — see PLEDGE 1

guaranty *vb* to make sure, certain, or safe — see ENSURE

guard *n* 1 a person or group that watches over someone or something ⟨checked in with the security *guard* at the gate⟩
syn custodian, guardian, keeper, lookout, picket, sentinel, sentry, warden, warder, watch, watchman
rel observer, patrol, spotter, watchdog; bodyguard, convoy, defender, escort, honor guard
2 a position or readiness to oppose actual or expected attack — see DEFENSIVE
3 a protective device (as on a weapon) to prevent accidental operation — see SAFETY 2
4 means or method of defending — see DEFENSE 1
5 one that accompanies another for protection, guidance, or as a courtesy — see ESCORT
6 someone that protects — see PROTECTOR

guard *vb* to drive danger or attack away from — see DEFEND 1

guard (against) *vb* to be cautious of or on guard against — see BEWARE (OF)

guarded *adj* having or showing a close attentiveness to avoiding danger or trouble — see CAREFUL 1

guardian *n* 1 a person or group that watches over someone or something — see GUARD 1
2 a person who takes care of a property sometimes for an absent owner — see CUSTODIAN 1

guardianship *n* responsibility for the safety and well-being of someone or something — see CUSTODY

guardrail *n* a protective barrier consisting of a horizontal bar and its supports — see RAILING

guardroom *n* a place of confinement for persons held in lawful custody — see JAIL

guess *n* an opinion or judgment based on little or no evidence — see CONJECTURE

guess *vb* 1 to form an opinion from little or no evidence ⟨though she does not speak with an accent, I would still *guess* that she is a foreigner⟩
syn assume, conjecture, presume, speculate, suppose, surmise, suspect, suspicion [*chiefly dialect*]
rel conclude, deduce, gather, infer; hypothesize, theorize; believe, conceive, expect, imagine, reckon [*chiefly dialect*], take, think
near ant demonstrate, establish, prove; ascertain, determine, find out
2 to decide the size, amount, number, or distance of (something) without actual measurement — see ESTIMATE 2
3 to have as an opinion — see BELIEVE 2

guest *n* 1 a person who visits another ⟨invited the afternoon *guests* to stay for dinner⟩
syn caller, frequenter, visitant, visitor
rel company; crasher, hanger-on
near ant denizen, dweller, habitant, inhabitant, occupant, resident, resider
2 a person who buys a product or uses a service from a business — see CUSTOMER 1

guffaw *n* an explosive sound that is a sign of amusement — see LAUGH 1

guidance *n* 1 an opinion suggesting a wise or proper course of action — see ADVICE
2 the act or activity of looking after and making decisions about something — see CONDUCT 1
3 the duty or function of watching or guarding for the sake of proper direction or control — see SUPERVISION 1

guide *n* one that accompanies another for protection, guidance, or as a courtesy — see ESCORT

guide *vb* 1 to give advice and instruction to (someone) regarding the course or process to be followed ⟨the famous chef *guided* her through the creation of the wedding cake, showing her how to ice the layers, fashion the elaborate decorations, and assemble the whole shebang⟩
syn coach, counsel, lead, mentor, pilot, shepherd, show, tutor
rel direct, steer; accompany, escort, see; oversee, superintend, supervise; drill, train; brief, enlighten, inform; instruct, school, teach; inculcate, indoctrinate; cultivate, foster, nurture
2 to look after and make decisions about — see CONDUCT 1
3 to point out the way for (someone) especially from a position in front — see LEAD 1

guidon *n* a piece of cloth with a special design that is used as an emblem or for signaling — see FLAG 1

guild also **gild** n a group of persons formally joined together for some common interest — see ASSOCIATION 2

guile n 1 skill in achieving one's ends through indirect, subtle, or underhanded means — see CUNNING 1

2 the inclination or practice of misleading others through lies or trickery — see DECEIT

guileful adj clever at attaining one's ends by indirect and often deceptive means — see ARTFUL 2

guileless adj free from any intent to deceive or impress others ⟨she was an easygoing, *guileless* young woman who was comfortable just being herself⟩

syn artless, genuine, honest, ingenuous, innocent, naive (*or* naïve), natural, real, simple, sincere, true, unaffected, unpretending, unpretentious

rel childlike, impressionable, inexperienced, malleable, persuadable, simpleminded, unsophisticated, unworldly; unforced, unstudied; candid, frank, free, openhearted, plain, plainspoken, singleminded; trustful, trusting

phrases on the level

near ant sophisticated, worldly, worldlywise; crooked, deceitful, deceptive, devious, double-dealing, hypocritical, two-faced; arch, calculating, canny, crafty, cunning, designing, scheming, sharp, shifty, shrewd, slick, slippery, sly, tricky, underhanded, wily; flattering, mealymouthed, smooth, sycophantic, unctuous; feigned, forced, strained

ant affected, artful, artificial, assuming, dishonest, dissembling, dissimulating, fake, false, guileful, insincere, phony (*also* phoney), pretentious

guilelessly adv without any attempt to impress by deception or exaggeration — see NATURALLY 3

guilelessness n the quality or state of being simple and sincere — see NAÏVETÉ 1

guillotine vb to cut off the head of — see DECAPITATE

guilt n 1 a feeling of responsibility for wrongdoing ⟨he was wracked with *guilt* after he accidentally broke his sister's antique grandfather clock⟩

syn contriteness, contrition, penitence, regret, remorse, remorsefulness, repentance, rue, self-reproach, shame

rel compunction, misgiving, qualm, scruple; blame, fault, responsibility; chagrin, embarrassment; anguish, distress, grief, sadness, sorrow

ant impenitence, remorselessness

2 responsibility for wrongdoing or failure — see BLAME 1

guiltless adj free from guilt or blame — see INNOCENT 2

guiltlessness n the quality or state of being free from guilt or blame — see INNOCENCE 1

guilty adj 1 responsible for a wrong ⟨he was found *guilty* on all charges brought against him⟩

syn blamable, culpable

rel blameworthy, censurable, impeachable, indictable, punishable, reprehensible, reproachable; accused, arraigned, impeached, implicated, indicted; accountable, answerable; condemned, convicted

phrases at fault

near ant absolved, acquitted, exonerated, vindicated; faultless, impeccable, irreproachable, unimpeachable

ant blameless, guiltless, innocent

2 suffering from or expressive of a feeling of responsibility for wrongdoing ⟨she was burdened with a *guilty* conscience after stealing the newspaper from the newsstand⟩

syn ashamed, contrite, hangdog, penitent, remorseful, repentant, shamed, shamefaced

rel apologetic, sorry; regretful, rueful, penitential; blushing, chagrined, embarrassed, sheepish

near ant unapologetic; brazen, cheeky, impudent

ant impenitent, remorseless, shameless, unashamed, unrepentant

guise n 1 a display of emotion or behavior that is insincere or intended to deceive — see MASQUERADE

2 clothing chosen as appropriate for a specific situation — see OUTFIT 1

3 clothing put on to hide one's true identity or imitate someone or something else — see DISGUISE

4 outward and often deceptive indication — see APPEARANCE 2

gulch n a narrow opening between hillsides or mountains that can be used for passage — see CANYON

gulf n 1 a part of a body of water that extends beyond the general shoreline ⟨dipped our feet in the warm waters of the *gulf*⟩

syn bay, bight, cove, creek [*chiefly British*], estuary, firth, fjord (*or* fiord), inlet, loch [*Scottish*]

rel harbor, port, road(s), roadstead; narrow, sound, strait; bayou

2 an immeasurable depth or space — see ABYSS

3 a narrow opening between hillsides or mountains that can be used for passage — see CANYON

4 an open space in a barrier (as a wall or hedge) — see GAP 1

gull n one who is easily deceived or cheated — see DUPE

gull vb to cause to believe what is untrue — see DECEIVE

gullibility n readiness to believe the claims of others without sufficient evidence — see CREDULITY

gullible adj readily taken advantage of — see EASY 2

---

syn synonym(s)   **rel** related words
ant antonym(s)   **near ant** near antonym(s)

gulp *n* the portion of a serving of a beverage that is swallowed at one time — see DRINK 2

gulp *vb* to swallow in liquid form — see DRINK 1

gummy *adj* being of such a thick consistency as to readily cling to objects upon contact — see STICKY 1

gun *n* 1 a portable weapon from which a shot is discharged by gunpowder ⟨while her father preferred hunting with a crossbow, she preferred a *gun*⟩

   syn arm, firearm, piece, small arm

   rel forty-five (*or* .45), gat [*slang*], handgun, pistol, revolver, rod [*slang*], six-gun, six-shooter, zip gun; blunderbuss, flintlock, harquebus (*or* arquebus), matchlock, musket, muzzleloader, rifle, shotgun; automatic, machine gun, repeater, submachine gun, tommy gun; speargun

   2 guns *pl* large firearms (as cannon or rockets) — see ARTILLERY

gun *vb* to strike with a missile from a gun — see SHOOT 3

gung ho *adj* showing urgent desire or interest — see EAGER

gurgle *vb* to flow in a broken irregular stream ⟨the tiny stream *gurgled* down the rocky slope and joined the larger river at the bottom of the hill⟩

   syn bubble, dribble, lap, plash, ripple, splash, trickle, wash

   rel eddy, purl, swirl; swash, swish, whish; drip, drop; gush, jet, rush, spout, spurt, squirt

   near ant run

   ant pour, roll, stream

gush *n* 1 a flowing or going out — see OUTFLOW

   2 a sudden intense expression of strong feeling — see OUTBURST 1

gush *vb* 1 to flow out in great quantities or with force ⟨the dam cracked and water *gushed* from the break⟩

   syn jet, pour, rush, spew, spout, spurt, squirt

   rel cascade, issue, roll, run, stream; plash, slosh, splash; surge, swell; flush, sluice; deluge, engulf, flood, inundate, overflow, overwhelm, submerge, swamp

   near ant spatter, sprinkle; exude, leak, ooze, seep, weep

   ant dribble, drip, drop, trickle

   2 to make an exaggerated display of affection or enthusiasm ⟨he *gushed* about his favorite basketball player, calling him "the best there ever was"⟩

   syn enthuse, fuss, rave, rhapsodize, slobber

   rel dote (on), fawn; emote

gushing *adj* 1 overly or insincerely flattering — see FULSOME

   2 pouring forth in great amounts — see PROFUSE

gust *n* 1 a sudden brief rush of wind ⟨a *gust* tore her umbrella from her grip and blew it down the street⟩

   syn blast, blow, flurry, williwaw

   rel breeze, zephyr; air, breath, waft; puff, whiff; gale, hurricane, squall, tempest, tornado, windstorm; northeaster, norther, northerly, northwester, southeaster, southwester, westerly

   2 a sudden intense expression of strong feeling — see OUTBURST 1

gusty *adj* marked by strong wind or more wind than usual — see WINDY 1

gut *n* 1 **guts** *pl* the internal organs of the body ⟨dissected the frog and looked at its *guts*⟩

   syn entrails, innards, inside(s), viscera, vitals

   rel bowel(s), intestine(s); giblet(s), variety meat

   2 guts *pl* strength of mind to carry on in spite of danger — see COURAGE

   3 guts *pl* the strength of mind that enables a person to endure pain or hardship — see FORTITUDE

   4 the part of the body between the chest and the pelvis — see STOMACH

gut *vb* to take the internal organs out of ⟨you'll need to *gut* the fish and wash it out before you can cook it⟩

   syn clean, disembowel, draw, eviscerate

   rel bone, dress; cut, excise, extract, remove, withdraw; transplant

gutsy *adj* inclined or willing to take risks — see BOLD 1

gutter *n* 1 a pipe or channel for carrying off water from a roof ⟨one of his chores is to clean leaves and sticks out of the *gutters* before winter sets in⟩

   syn drainpipe, eaves trough, spout, trough, waterspout

   rel drain, flume, sluice; conduit, duct

   2 a long narrow channel dug in the earth — see DITCH

guy *n* 1 a member of the human race — see HUMAN

   2 an adult male human being — see MAN 1

guzzle *vb* to swallow in liquid form — see DRINK 1

gym *n* a building or room used for sports activities and exercising ⟨decided to get up early and go to the *gym* to lift weights⟩

   syn gymnasium, spa

   rel arena, bowl, coliseum, colosseum, stadium

gymnasium *n* a building or room used for sports activities and exercising — see GYM

gyp *vb* to rob by the use of trickery or threats — see FLEECE

gyrate *vb* to move in circles around an axis or center — see SPIN 1

gyration *n* a rapid turning about on an axis or central point — see SPIN 1

habiliment *n, usually* **habiliments** *pl* covering for the human body — see CLOTHING

habit *n* a usual manner of behaving or doing ⟨it was his *habit* to rise early⟩
syn custom, fashion, pattern, practice (*also* practise), trick, way, wont
rel addiction; disposition; bent, inclination, proclivity, tendency, turn; convention, form, mode, style; usage; manners, mores; groove, rote, routine, rut; affectation, airs, pose; attribute, characteristic, mark, trait; oddity, peculiarity, quirk, singularity, tic; strangeness, weirdness

habitable *adj* suitable for living in — see LIVABLE

habitant *n* one who lives permanently in a place — see INHABITANT

habitat *n* the place where a plant or animal is usually or naturally found — see HOME 2

habitation *n* the place where one lives — see HOME 1

habitual *adj* 1 being such by habit and not likely to change ⟨Sarah admits she's an *habitual* procrastinator, but she still manages to complete her assignments on time⟩
syn chronic, confirmed, inveterate
rel incorrigible, unregenerate; born, natural; persistent, regular, steady, unfailing; addicted; accustomed, habituated, used; deep-rooted, entrenched (*also* intrenched), inbred, inherent, innate
near ant unaccustomed, unused; occasional
2 appearing or occurring repeatedly from time to time — see REGULAR 1

habituated *adj* being in the habit or custom — see ACCUSTOMED

hacienda *n* a large impressive residence — see MANSION

¹hack *n* a V-shaped cut usually on an edge or a surface — see NOTCH 1

²hack *n* an automobile that carries passengers for a fare usually determined by the distance traveled — see TAXI

hackney *adj* used or heard so often as to be dull — see STALE

hackneyed *adj* used or heard so often as to be dull — see STALE

hag *n* 1 a mean or ugly old woman — see CRONE
2 a woman believed to have often harmful supernatural powers — see WITCH 1

haggard *adj* suffering extreme weight loss as a result of hunger or disease — see EMACIATED

haggle *vb* to talk over or dispute the terms of a purchase — see BARGAIN

hail *n* 1 a heavy fall of objects — see RAIN 2
2 a rapid or overwhelming outpouring of many things at once — see BARRAGE

hail *vb* 1 to declare enthusiastic approval of — see ACCLAIM
2 to demand or request the presence or service of — see SUMMON 1

hair *n* 1 a very small distance or degree ⟨a race that was won by a *hair*⟩
syn ace, hairbreadth (*or* hairsbreadth), inch
rel bit, crumb, jot, mite, particle, smidgen, trace, trifle
2 the hairy covering of a mammal especially when fine, soft, and thick — see FUR 1

hairbreadth *or* **hairsbreadth** *n* a very small distance or degree — see HAIR 1

hairline *adj* 1 being of less than usual width — see NARROW 1
2 made or done with extreme care and accuracy — see FINE 2
3 meeting the highest standard of accuracy — see PRECISE 1

hair-raising *adj* causing fear — see FEARFUL 1

hairsplitting *adj* made or done with extreme care and accuracy — see FINE 2

hairy *adj* 1 covered with or as if with hair ⟨a *hairy* spider⟩
syn bristly, fleecy, furry, hirsute, rough, shaggy, unshorn, woolly (*also* wooly)
rel bearded, mustachioed, whiskered; downy, fluffy, fuzzy, nappy
near ant beardless, shaved, shaven
ant bald, furless, hairless, shorn, smooth
2 made of or resembling hair ⟨enough *hairy* clumps around the house to make another cat⟩ ⟨a *hairy* mass of fiberglass insulation⟩
syn furry, fuzzy, rough, shaggy, woolly (*also* wooly)
rel downy, fluffy, nappy

halcyon *adj* free from storms or physical disturbance — see CALM 1

hale *adj* enjoying health and vigor — see HEALTHY 1

hale *vb* to cause to follow by applying steady force on — see PULL 1

half *adv* in any way or respect — see AT ALL

half *n* 1 one of two equal or nearly equal parts ⟨to be fair, we each get *half* the pie⟩
syn moiety
rel hemisphere, meridian, semicircle; component, division, fraction, part, piece, portion, section, segment
near ant aggregate, whole

---

syn synonym(s)   **rel** related words
ant antonym(s)   **near ant** near antonym(s)

2 either of a pair matched in one or more qualities — see MATE 1

halfhearted *adj* showing little or no interest or enthusiasm — see TEPID 1

halfway *adj* **1** lacking some necessary part — see INCOMPLETE

2 occupying a position equally distant from the ends or extremes — see MIDDLE 1

half-wit *n* **1** a person who lacks good sense or judgment — see FOOL 1

2 a stupid person — see IDIOT

half-witted *adj* **1** not having or showing an ability to absorb ideas readily — see STUPID 1

2 showing or marked by a lack of good sense or judgment — see FOOLISH 1

hall *n* **1** the entrance room of a building ⟨the guests hung their coats in the *hall*⟩

syn entry, entryway, foyer, lobby, vestibule

rel antechamber, anteroom, waiting room; doorway, entrance, threshold

2 a typically long narrow way connecting parts of a building ⟨the bedroom is at the end of the *hall*⟩

syn concourse, corridor, gallery, hallway, passage, passageway

rel arcade, breezeway, cloister

3 a large room or building for enclosed public gatherings ⟨the concert *hall* was full⟩

syn arena, auditorium, theater (*or* theatre)

rel amphitheater, hippodrome, house, playhouse; ballroom; lyceum; chamber, senate

4 a centrally located room in a building that serves as a gathering or waiting area or as a passageway into the interior — see FOYER 1

5 a large impressive residence — see MANSION

6 a large, magnificent, or massive building — see EDIFICE 1

hallmark *n* a device, design, or figure used as an identifying mark — see EMBLEM

hallow *vb* to make holy through prayers or ritual — see BLESS 1

hallowed *adj* **1** deserving honor and respect especially by reason of age — see VENERABLE 1

2 set apart or worthy of veneration by association with God — see HOLY 2

hallowing *n* the act of making something holy through religious ritual — see CONSECRATION

hallucination *n* a conception or image created by the imagination and having no objective reality — see FANTASY 1

hallway *n* a typically long narrow way connecting parts of a building — see HALL 2

halt *n* **1** a point in a struggle where neither side is capable of winning or willing to give in — see IMPASSE

2 the stopping of a process or activity — see END 1

¹halt *vb* **1** to bring (something) to a standstill ⟨traffic was *halted* by the parade⟩

syn arrest, catch, check, draw up, fetch up, hold up, stall, stay, still, stop

rel balk, block, blockade, dam, detain, hinder, hold, hold back, impede, obstruct, stem; conclude, end, terminate; call, discontinue, suspend; clamp down, rein (in), squash, squelch, stamp, stanch (*also* staunch), stunt, suppress, turn back

near ant carry on, continue, follow through, keep on, keep up, run on; advance, fare, move, proceed, progress, wend; actuate, budge, drive, impel, propel, push, stir

2 to bring (as an action or operation) to an immediate end — see STOP 1

3 to come to an end — see CEASE 1

²halt *vb* to walk while favoring one leg — see LIMP 1

hammer *vb* **1** to shape with a hammer ⟨medieval artisans *hammered* brass into bowls and trays which they embossed with elaborate designs⟩

syn beat, forge, pound

rel chase, fashion, form, knead, model, mold, work; coin, mint, stamp; carve, chisel, hew, sculpt, sculpture

2 to deliver a blow to (someone or something) usually in a strong vigorous manner — see HIT 1

3 to strike repeatedly — see BEAT 1

hammer (out) *vb* to produce or bring about especially by long or repeated effort ⟨the school committee *hammered out* a new sports-participation policy with input from students, parents, and administrators⟩

syn build (up), carve (out), forge, grind (out), work out

rel cobble (together *or* up), create, construct, fabricate, fashion, form, frame, manufacture, model, shape, tailor; conceive, concoct, contrive, cook (up), devise, hatch, invent, originate; bring forth, effect; accomplish, achieve, bring off

near ant demolish, destroy, dismantle, raze, tear down; ruin, undo, unmake, wreck

hamper *vb* to create difficulty for the work or activity of ⟨fallen branches *hampered* the hikers as they made their way along the narrow path⟩

syn clog, cramp, delay, embarrass, encumber, fetter, handicap, hinder, hobble, hold back, hold up, impede, inhibit, interfere (with), manacle, obstruct, shackle, tie up, trammel

rel arrest, brake, check, constrain, curb, rein, restrain, snag; bind, chain, handcuff, leash, muzzle, strap, tether, tie; barricade, block, blockade, dam, head (off), plug; balk, choke, hurt, repress, retard, stifle, straiten, strangle, stunt; baffle, foil, frustrate, interrupt, sabotage, thwart; bog (down), confine, hedge (in), hem (in), limit, tie (down)

phrases cramp one's style, give a hard time

near ant clear, make way, open, unclog, unplug, unstop; free, liberate, release, untie; loosen, smooth; further, promote *ant* aid, assist, facilitate, help

hams *n pl* the part of the body upon which someone sits — see BUTTOCKS

hamstring *vb* to render powerless, ineffective, or unable to move — see PARALYZE

hand *n* **1** a certain way in which something appears or may be regarded — see ASPECT 1

2 a place, space, or direction away from or beyond a central point or line — see SIDE 1

3 an arrow-shaped piece on a dial or scale for registering information — see POINTER 1

4 one who works for another for wages or a salary — see EMPLOYEE

5 the form or style of a particular person's writing — see HANDWRITING 1

6 *usually* **hands** *pl* the ability to direct the course of something — see CONTROL 2

7 hands *pl* the fact or state of having (something) at one's disposal — see POSSESSION 1

hand *vb* **1** to put (something) into the possession of someone for use or consumption — see FURNISH 2

2 to shift possession of (something) from one person to another — see PASS 1

handbag *n* **1** a bag carried by hand and designed to hold a traveler's clothing and personal articles — see TRAVELING BAG

2 a container for carrying money and small personal items — see PURSE

handbook *n* a book used for instruction in a subject — see TEXTBOOK

handcraft *n* an occupation requiring skillful use of the hands — see CRAFT 1

handcuff *vb* to confine or restrain with or as if with chains — see BIND 1

handcuff *n usually* **handcuffs** *pl* something that physically prevents free movement — see BOND 1

handful *n* a small number — see FEW

handicap *n* **1** a feature of someone or something that creates difficulty for achieving success — see DISADVANTAGE

2 something that makes movement or progress more difficult — see ENCUMBRANCE

handicap *vb* to create difficulty for the work or activity of — see HAMPER

handicraft *n* an occupation requiring skillful use of the hands — see CRAFT 1

handicrafter *n* a person whose occupation requires skill with the hands — see ARTISAN

handily *adv* without difficulty — see EASILY

handiwork *n* something produced by physical or intellectual effort — see PRODUCT 1

handkerchief *n* a scarf worn on the head — see BANDANNA

handle *n* a word or combination of words by which a person or thing is regularly known — see NAME 1

handle *vb* **1** to deal with (something) usually skillfully or efficiently ⟨as host of a live TV talk show, she must *handle* any situation that comes up⟩

syn contend (with), cope (with), grapple (with), manage, maneuver, manipulate, negotiate, swing, treat

rel bring off, carry out, pull, swing; command, direct, guide, steer; control, regulate, run

phrases have a grip on

near ant botch, bungle, goof (up), louse up, mess (up)

ant fumble, muddle (through)

2 to behave toward in a stated way — see TREAT 1

3 to control the mechanical operation of — see OPERATE 1

4 to look after and make decisions about — see CONDUCT 1

handling *n* the act or activity of looking after and making decisions about something — see CONDUCT 1

hand over *vb* **1** to give (something) over to the control or possession of another usually under duress — see SURRENDER 1

2 to put (something) into the possession of someone for use or consumption — see FURNISH 2

3 to put (something) into the possession or safekeeping of another — see GIVE 2

4 to shift possession of (something) from one person to another — see PASS 1

handpick *vb* to decide to accept (someone or something) from a group of possibilities — see CHOOSE 1

handsome *adj* **1** having or showing elegance — see ELEGANT 1

2 of a size greater than average of its kind — see LARGE

3 very pleasing to look at — see BEAUTIFUL

handsomely *adv* in a generous manner — see WELL 2

handsomeness *n* **1** dignified or restrained beauty of form, appearance, or style — see ELEGANCE

2 the qualities in a person or thing that as a whole give pleasure to the senses — see BEAUTY 1

hand-to-mouth *adj* less plentiful than what is normal, necessary, or desirable — see MEAGER

handwriting *n* **1** the form or style of a particular person's writing ⟨she immediately recognized the *handwriting* on the envelope as that of her old college roommate⟩

syn hand, penmanship, script

rel scratch, scrawl, scribble; backhand, print; autograph, signature

2 writing done by hand ⟨most students are taught the value of good *handwriting*⟩

syn calligraphy, longhand, manuscript, penmanship, script

rel lettering; shorthand

ant print, type

---

syn synonym(s)   *rel* related words
ant antonym(s)   *near ant* near antonym(s)

handy *adj* **1** situated within easy reach — see CONVENIENT

2 skillful with the hands — see DEXTEROUS 1

hang *vb* **1** to place on an elevated point without support from below ⟨*hang* your coats on the coat rack in the hall⟩

syn dangle, sling, suspend, swing

rel hook, pin, tack; drape, festoon, garland, string; extend (out), jut, project, stick out; overhang, protrude; cascade, depend, fall

2 to be determined by, based on, or subject (to) — see DEPEND 1

3 to be limp from lack of water or vigor — see DROOP 1

4 to rest or move along the surface of a liquid or in the air — see FLOAT

hang (over) *vb* to remain poised to inflict harm, danger, or distress on — see THREATEN

hang around *vb* **1** to come or be together as friends — see ASSOCIATE 1

2 to continue to be in a place for a significant amount of time — see STAY 1

3 to spend time doing nothing — see IDLE

hang around (in) *vb* to go to or spend time in often — see FREQUENT

hang back *vb* to show uncertainty about the right course of action — see HESITATE

hangdog *adj* suffering from or expressive of a feeling of responsibility for wrongdoing — see GUILTY 2

hanger-on *n* a person who is supported or seeks support from another without making an adequate return — see LEECH

hanging *adj* **1** bending downward or forward — see NODDING

2 extending freely from a support from above — see DEPENDENT 1

hang on (to) *vb* **1** to continue to have in one's possession or power — see KEEP 2

2 to have or keep in one's hands — see HOLD 1

hangout *n* a place for spending time or for socializing ⟨Jake's favorite *hangout* is the local community center⟩

syn haunt, rendezvous, resort

rel camp, canteen, club, clubhouse, den, harbor, haven, nest, refuge, retreat

hang out *vb* to spend time doing nothing — see IDLE

hang out (at) *vb* to go to or spend time in often — see FREQUENT

hanker (for *or* after) *vb* to have an earnest wish to own or enjoy — see DESIRE

hankering *n* a strong wish for something — see DESIRE

hanky-panky *n* the use of clever underhanded actions to achieve an end — see TRICKERY

hap *n* **1** something that happens — see EVENT 1

2 the uncertain course of events — see CHANCE 1

hap *vb* to take place — see HAPPEN

haphazard *adj* lacking a definite plan, purpose, or pattern — see RANDOM

haphazard *adv* without definite aim, direction, rule, or method — see HIT OR MISS

haphazardly *adv* without definite aim, direction, rule, or method — see HIT OR MISS

hapless *adj* having, prone to, or marked by bad luck — see UNLUCKY

happen *vb* to take place ⟨did anything exciting *happen* over the summer?⟩

syn be, befall, betide, chance, come, come about, go (on), hap, occur, pass, transpire

rel arise, crop (up), develop, materialize, spring (up); intervene; fall out, go off, proceed, turn out

phrases come to pass

happen (on *or* upon) *vb* to come upon unexpectedly or by chance ⟨*happened* on the filming of a movie⟩

syn chance (upon), encounter, find, hit (upon), meet, stumble (on *or* onto)

rel confront, face; discover, turn up

phrases bump into, come across, run across, run into

happen (upon) *vb* to come upon face-to-face or as if face-to-face — see MEET 1

happening *n* **1** an exciting or noteworthy event that one experiences firsthand — see ADVENTURE

2 something that happens — see EVENT 1

happily *adv* **1** in a cheerful or happy manner — see GAILY 1

2 in a manner suitable for the occasion or purpose — see PROPERLY

happiness *n* **1** a feeling or state of well-being and contentment ⟨Marta's *happiness* was complete when she got her very own horse⟩

syn blessedness, bliss, blissfulness, felicity, gladness, joy

rel elatedness, elation, exhilaration, exultation, intoxication; ecstasy, euphoria, heaven, rapture, rapturousness; delectation, delight, enjoyment, pleasure; cheer, cheerfulness, exuberance, gaiety (*also* gayety), gladsomeness, glee, gleefulness, jollity, joyfulness, joyousness, jubilation, lightheartedness; content, contentedness, gratification, satisfaction

near ant anguish, desolation, joylessness, sorrow, woe, woefulness; blues, dejection, depression, despondency, disheartenment, dispiritedness, doldrums, downheartedness, gloom, gloominess, melancholy, mournfulness

ant misery, sadness, unhappiness, wretchedness

2 the feeling experienced when one's wishes are met — see PLEASURE 1

happy *adj* **1** coming or happening by good luck especially unexpectedly — see FORTUNATE 1

2 experiencing pleasure, satisfaction, or delight — see GLAD 1

3 feeling that one's needs or desires have been met — see CONTENT

4 having good luck — see LUCKY 1

5 meeting the requirements of a purpose or situation — see FIT 1

happy–go–lucky *adj* **1** having a relaxed, casual manner — see EASYGOING 1

2 having or showing a lack of concern or seriousness — see CAREFREE

harangue *n* **1** a long angry speech or scolding — see TIRADE

2 a usually formal discourse delivered to an audience — see SPEECH 1

harangue *vb* **1** to give a formal often extended talk on a subject — see TALK 1

2 to talk as if using an important and formal speech — see ORATE 1

harassment *n* the act of making unwelcome intrusions upon another — see ANNOYANCE 1

harbinger *n* one that announces or indicates the later arrival of another — see FORERUNNER 1

harbor *n* **1** a part of a body of water protected and deep enough to be a place of safety for ships ⟨the tanker stayed in Boston *harbor* three days to undergo repairs⟩

syn anchorage, harborage, haven, port

rel seaport; arm, bay, bight, cove, creek [*chiefly British*], estuary, firth, fjord (*or* fiord), gulf, inlet, loch [*Scottish*], narrow, roads, roadstead; canal, channel, sound, strait

2 something (as a building) that offers cover from the weather or protection from danger — see SHELTER

harbor *vb* **1** to keep in one's mind or heart ⟨Grandpa *harbored* a grudge against his first boss for nearly 50 years⟩

syn bear, cherish, entertain, have, hold, nurse

rel cultivate, foster, nurture, sustain, support; carry, keep, maintain, preserve, remember, retain, treasure; cleave (to), cling (to), hang on (to), stick (to)

near ant disregard, drop, forget, ignore, neglect, overlook; abjure, decline, deny, disdain, refuse, reject, repudiate, scorn; abandon, desert, discard, forsake, give up, quit, renounce, throw out

2 to provide with living quarters or shelter — see HOUSE 1

3 to be or provide a shelter for — see SHELTER 1

harborage *n* **1** a part of a body of water protected and deep enough to be a place of safety for ships — see HARBOR 1

2 something (as a building) that offers cover from the weather or protection from danger — see SHELTER

hard *adj* **1** having or showing a lack of sympathy or tender feelings ⟨a *hard* man, who never had a kind word for anyone⟩

syn callous, cold-blooded, hard-boiled, hardhearted, heartless, inhuman, inhumane, insensate, insensitive, merciless, obdurate, pitiless, ruthless, soulless, stony (*also* stoney), uncharitable, unfeeling, unmerciful, unsparing, unsympathetic

rel inconsiderate, thoughtless, uncaring, unfriendly, unloving, unthinking; grim,

hard-bitten, harsh, heavy-handed, oppressive, rough, severe, stern, tough, ungentle; abusive, acrimonious, disagreeable, hateful, ill-natured, ill-tempered, malevolent, malicious, mean, rancorous, spiteful, surly, virulent; barbarous, bestial, brutal, brutish, cruel, evil-minded, savage, vicious

near ant benevolent, benignant, gentle, kind; clement, lenient, mild; cordial, friendly, good-natured, good-tempered, gracious; tolerant, understanding; affectionate, loving

ant charitable, compassionate, humane, merciful, sensitive, softhearted, sympathetic, tender, tenderhearted, warm, warmhearted

2 requiring considerable physical or mental effort ⟨clearing land is *hard* work⟩ ⟨a *hard* Spanish test⟩

syn arduous, demanding, difficult, exacting, formidable, grueling (*or* gruelling), herculean, killer, laborious, murderous, rough, severe, stiff, strenuous, tall, toilsome, tough

rel abstract, abstruse, complex, complicated, insoluble, intricate, involved, knotty, problematic (*also* problematical), recondite, serious, spiny, thorny, ticklish, tricky, stubborn; burdensome, exhausting, labored, onerous, oppressive, problem, sore, stressful, taxing, tight, trying, uphill; annoying, bothersome, distressing, irksome, troublesome, vexatious; grievous, grim, heavy, strict, stringent; brutal, cruel, inhuman, painful

near ant achievable, clear, doable, elementary, manageable, uncomplicated; comforting, gentle, painless, relaxed; smooth, soothing

ant easy, effortless, facile, simple, soft, undemanding

3 able to withstand hardship, strain, or exposure — see HARDY 1

4 based on sound reasoning or information — see GOOD 1

5 difficult to endure — see HARSH 1

6 extreme in degree, power, or effect — see INTENSE

7 given to exacting standards of discipline and self-restraint — see SEVERE 1

8 having a consistency that does not easily yield to pressure — see FIRM 2

9 having been established and usually not subject to change — see FIXED 1

10 having or showing deep-seated resentment — see BITTER 1

11 sticking to an opinion, purpose, or course of action in spite of reason, arguments, or persuasion — see OBSTINATE

12 restricted to or based on fact — see FACTUAL 1

hard *adv* **1** with great effort or determination ⟨we took a much-needed break after working *hard* all week⟩ ⟨a *hard*-won victory⟩

syn arduously, assiduously, determinedly, diligently, hardly, indefatigably, industriously, intensely, intensively, intently, laboriously, mightily, sedulously, slavishly, strenuously, tirelessly

rel actively, animatedly, briskly, busily, dynamically, energetically, feverishly, spiritedly, vehemently, vigorously, zealously; continuously, ploddingly, steadily, unabatedly, unrelentingly, unremittingly; ardently, attentively, conscientiously, earnestly, exhaustively, meticulously, painstakingly, seriously, thoroughly

near ant casually, desultorily, indolently, lackadaisically, languidly, lazily, listlessly, shiftlessly, sluggishly, spiritlessly, tiredly, wearily

2 with feelings of bitterness or grief ⟨took the news of their grandfather's death *hard*⟩

syn agonizingly, bitterly, grievously, hardly, mournfully, painfully, regretfully, resentfully, ruefully, sadly, sorely, sorrowfully, unhappily, woefully, wretchedly

rel abjectly, dejectedly, despondently, dispiritedly; blackly, darkly, distressfully, distressingly, forlornly, gloomily, miserably; acutely, harshly, keenly, poignantly, severely, sharply; cruelly, hurtfully, ill, rancorously

near ant cheerfully, cheerily, delightedly, gaily (*also* gayly), gleefully, good-naturedly, lightheartedly, merrily; blithely, calmly, casually, dispassionately, easily, indifferently, lightly, nonchalantly, unconcernedly; favorably, well

ant gladly, happily, joyfully, joyously

3 in a vigorous and forceful manner ⟨Terry hit the ball *hard* and it soared out of bounds⟩ ⟨the wind blew *hard* all day⟩

syn energetically, firmly, forcefully, forcibly, mightily, powerfully, stiffly, stoutly, strenuously, strongly, sturdily, vigorously

rel robustly, sharply, vehemently, violently; animatedly, briskly, crisply, dynamically, heartily, lustily, snappily, spiritedly, vivaciously; decidedly, determinedly, directly, emphatically, fast, fixedly, intensively, intently, resolutely, rigidly, smartly, solidly, soundly, squarely, steadfastly, steadily, surely; aggressively, assertively, manfully, potently

phrases with might and main

near ant delicately, faintly, fraily, shakily; indirectly, languidly, listlessly, spiritlessly; impotently, ineffectively, ineffectually, nervelessly, spinelessly, uncertainly

ant feebly, gently, softly, weakly

4 at, within, or to a short distance or time — see NEAR 1

5 in a manner so as to cause loss or suffering — see HARDLY 1

hard-and-fast *adj* **1** having been established and usually not subject to change — see FIXED 1

2 not capable of changing or being changed — see INFLEXIBLE 1

hard-bitten *adj* able to withstand hardship, strain, or exposure — see HARDY 1

hard-boiled *adj* having or showing a lack of sympathy or tender feelings — see HARD 1

hard-core *adj* firmly established over time — see INVETERATE 1

harden *vb* **1** to become physically firm or solid ⟨waited for the bubbly caramel-and-nut sauce to cool and *harden* into peanut brittle⟩

syn concrete, congeal, firm (up), freeze, set, solidify

rel cake, callus, encrust (*also* incrust); coagulate, clot, gel, jell, jelly, stiffen, thicken; calcify, crystallize, ossify, petrify; anneal, case harden, temper

near ant deliquesce, dissolve, flux, fuse, liquefy, melt, smelt, thaw

ant soften

2 to make able to withstand physical hardship, strain, or exposure ⟨pioneer women who had been *hardened* by years of living on the plains⟩

syn fortify, inure, season, steel, strengthen, toughen

rel acclimate, acclimatize, adapt, adjust; anneal, temper; invigorate, vitalize; immunize; bolster, boost, brace, buttress, forearm, prop (up), reinforce, support; break in, limber (up), train; accustom, condition, habituate, naturalize

near ant emasculate, enervate, enfeeble, exhaust, sap, weaken; cripple, debilitate, incapacitate; sensitize

ant soften

3 to increase the ability of (as a muscle) to exert physical force — see STRENGTHEN 1

hardened *adj* **1** able to withstand hardship, strain, or exposure — see HARDY 1

2 sticking to an opinion, purpose, or course of action in spite of reason, arguments, or persuasion — see OBSTINATE

hardheaded *adj* **1** having or showing a practical cleverness or judgment — see SHREWD

2 sticking to an opinion, purpose, or course of action in spite of reason, arguments, or persuasion — see OBSTINATE

3 willing to see things as they really are and deal with them sensibly — see REALISTIC 1

hardheadedness *n* a steadfast adherence to an opinion, purpose, or course of action — see OBSTINACY

hardhearted *adj* **1** having or showing a lack of sympathy or tender feelings — see HARD 1

2 sticking to an opinion, purpose, or course of action in spite of reason, arguments, or persuasion — see OBSTINATE

hardihood *n* **1** active strength of body or mind — see VIGOR 1

2 strength of mind to carry on in spite of danger — see COURAGE

hardly *adv* **1** in a manner so as to cause loss or suffering ⟨the new judge vowed to deal *hardly* with repeat offenders⟩

syn hard, harshly, ill, oppressively, roughly, severely, sternly, stiffly

rel callously, cold-bloodedly, hardheartedly, heartlessly, inhumanely, inhumanly, insensately, insensitively, mercilessly, obdurately, pitilessly, ruthlessly, tyrannically, uncharitably, unfeelingly, unmercifully, unsparingly; abusively, brutally, brutishly, savagely, viciously; aggressively, assertively, decidedly, determinedly, firmly, grimly, gruffly, resolutely, strongly, toughly

near ant benevolently, benignantly, considerately, cordially, graciously, kindly, lovingly, tenderly; charitably, compassionately, humanely, mercifully, softheartedly, sympathetically, tolerantly, understandingly

ant clemently, gently, leniently, lightly, mildly, softly

2 certainly not ⟨it's *hardly* surprising that our team won, considering how weak the opponents are⟩

syn no, none, no way, scarcely

rel near, never, nothing, nowhere, nowise

phrases by no means, nothing doing, on no account

near ant awful, awfully, enormously, exceedingly (*also* exceeding), extremely, greatly, highly, hugely, immensely, mighty, most, quite, terribly, very; assuredly, clearly, perfectly, plainly, positively, really, truly, unequivocally, unquestionably, utterly; doubtless, more or less, mostly, rather, slightly, somewhat

ant absolutely, certainly, completely, definitely, positively, surely

3 by a very small margin — see JUST 2

4 with feelings of bitterness or grief — see HARD 2

5 with great effort or determination — see HARD 1

hardness *n* **1** something that is a cause for suffering or special effort especially in the attainment of a goal — see DIFFICULTY 1

2 the quality or state of being demanding or unyielding (as in discipline or criticism) — see SEVERITY

hardship *n* something that is a cause for suffering or special effort especially in the attainment of a goal — see DIFFICULTY 1

hardy *adj* **1** able to withstand hardship, strain, or exposure ⟨*chrysanthemums* are *hardy* enough to survive a light frost⟩ ⟨the men and women who settled the West were a *hardy* lot⟩

syn hard, hard-bitten, hardened, inured, rugged, stout, strong, sturdy, tough, toughened, vigorous

rel flinty, leathery, resilient, stalwart; durable, enduring, everlasting, immortal, imperishable, lasting, permanent, stable, staunch (*or* stanch), staying, tenacious, unyielding; flourishing, prospering, thriving; able-bodied, brawny, muscular; fit, fortified, hale, healthy, husky, lusty, redblooded, robust, sound, strapping, virile; annealed, seasoned, tempered

near ant emasculated, enervated, enfeebled, exhausted, run-down, sapped, wasted, weakened, worn, worn out; crippled, debilitated, diseased, incapacitated, infirm, unsound; fragile, frail, puny; resist-

less, sensitive, susceptible, unresistant, vulnerable, yielding; mortal, perishable, temporary, transient

ant delicate, nonhardy, soft, tender, weak

2 inclined or willing to take risks — see BOLD 1

harebrained *adj* **1** lacking in seriousness or maturity — see GIDDY 1

2 showing or marked by a lack of good sense or judgment — see FOOLISH 1

hark *vb* to pay attention especially through the act of hearing — see LISTEN

hark back (to) *vb* to bring back to mind — see REMEMBER

harlequin *n* a comically dressed performer (as at a circus) who entertains with playful tricks and ridiculous behavior — see CLOWN 1

harlot *n* a woman who engages in sexual activities for money — see PROSTITUTE

harlotry *n* the practice of engaging in sexual activities for money — see PROSTITUTION

harm *n* something that causes loss or pain — see INJURY 1

harm *vb* **1** to cause bodily damage to — see INJURE 1

2 to reduce the soundness, effectiveness, or perfection of — see DAMAGE 1

harmful *adj* causing or capable of causing harm ⟨DDT has been proven extremely *harmful* to the environment⟩

syn adverse, bad, baleful, baneful, damaging, deleterious, detrimental, evil, hurtful, ill, injurious, mischievous, noxious, pernicious, prejudicial

rel hostile, inimical, unfriendly; contagious, deadly, infectious, pestilent, pestilential, poisonous, venomous; insidious, menacing, ominous, sinister, threatening; dangerous, hazardous, imperiling, jeopardizing, parlous, perilous, risky, unsafe, unsound; nasty, noisome, unhealthful, unhealthy, unwholesome; destructive, fatal, lethal, malignant, ruinous

near ant advantageous, beneficial, useful; favorable, good, propitious; curative, healthful, healthy, helpful, palliative, remedial, salubrious, salutary, wholesome; secure, sound; benign, benignant; noncorrosive, nondestructive, nonfatal, noninfectious, nonlethal, nonpoisonous, nonpolluting, nontoxic, nonvenomous

ant harmless, innocent, innocuous, inoffensive, safe

harmless *adj* not causing injury or hurt ⟨a perfectly *harmless* little spider⟩

syn innocent, innocuous, inoffensive, safe, white

rel healthful, healthy, salubrious, wholesome; benign, benignant; sound, trustworthy; gentle, gracious, mild; nonthreatening, painless, unobjectionable; noncorrosive, nondestructive, nonfatal, noninfectious, nonlethal, nonpoisonous, nonpolluting, nontoxic, nonvenomous

near ant poisonous, venomous; menacing, ominous, sinister, threatening; dangerous, hazardous, imperiling, jeopardizing, parlous, perilous, risky, unsafe,

---

syn synonym(s) **rel** related words
ant antonym(s) **near ant** near antonym(s)

unsound; nasty, noisome, unhealthful, unhealthy, unwholesome; offensive, painful, scathing, wounding; deadly, fatal, lethal, ruinous; contaminated, corrosive, malignant, noxious, pestilent, polluted, tainted

ant adverse, bad, baleful, baneful, damaging, deleterious, detrimental, evil, harmful, hurtful, ill, injurious, mischievous, noxious, pernicious, prejudicial

harmonious *adj* **1** having a pleasing mixture of notes 〈the naturally *harmonious* sounds of a forest glen in springtime〉

syn euphonious, harmonizing, melodious, musical, symphonic, tuneful

rel blending, chiming, flowing, mellifluous; dulcet, mellow, melodic, sweet; echoing, resonant, sonorous, quavering, trilling, warbling; agreeable, appealing, pleasant; cadenced, lilting, lyric, lyrical, rhythmic (*or* rhythmical); chordal, harmonic, homophonic, orchestral, polyphonic, tonal

near ant blaring, clanging, clashing, clattering, grating, harsh, jangling, jarring, metallic, raspy, raucous, scratching, screeching, shrill, squeaky, strident; disagreeable, unpleasant, unpleasing; atonal, off-key

ant discordant, dissonant, inharmonious, unharmonious, unmelodious, unmusical

2 having the parts agreeably related 〈a *harmonious* arrangement of archways and doorways in the palace courtyard〉

syn balanced, congruous, consonant

rel even, proportioned, regular, symmetrical (*or* symmetric); aesthetic (*or* esthetic), artistic, becoming, elegant, graceful, tasteful; agreeable, felicitous, pleasant, pleasing, satisfying; compatible, coordinated, correspondent, matched, matching

near ant asymmetrical, disordered, irregular, skewed, unequal, uneven, unsymmetrical; distasteful, graceless, inartistic, inelegant, tasteless, unaesthetic, unbecoming, ungraceful, unlovely; disagreeable, displeasing, dissatisfying, infelicitous, unfortunate, unpleasant, unsightly; clashing, conflicting, disunited, incompatible, uncoordinated

ant incongruous, inharmonious, unbalanced

3 having or marked by agreement in feeling or action 〈an unusually *harmonious* meeting among the leaders resulted in a quick peace agreement〉

syn agreeable, amicable, compatible, congenial, frictionless, kindred, unanimous, united

rel pacific, peaceable, peaceful; collaborating, cooperative, symbiotic; noncompetitive, nonconflicting, uncompetitive; sympathetic, tolerant, understanding; affable, amiable, cordial, friendly, genial, neighborly; collaborating

near ant antagonistic, antipathetic, clashing, conflicting, hostile, inimical, unfriendly; belligerent, contentious, quarrelsome; contradicting, contradictory, contrary, opposing, opposite; competing, competitive, rivaling (*or* rivalling)

ant disagreeable, disunited, incompatible, inharmonious, uncongenial

4 not having or showing any apparent conflict — see CONSISTENT

harmonize *vb* **1** to form a pleasing relationship 〈the color of the walls *harmonized* nicely with the blue tones in the carpet〉

syn agree, blend, conform, coordinate

rel balance, correlate, correspond, dovetail; match; meet, parallel; bond, coalesce, cohere, conjoin, fuse, merge, square, tally

near ant contradict, contrast, counter, differ, diverge, jar; cancel (out), counteract, negate, offset

ant clash, collide, conflict

2 to bring to a state free of conflicts, inconsistencies, or differences 〈an attempt to *harmonize* the New Testament version of events with the accounts of the ancient Romans〉

syn accommodate, conciliate, conform, coordinate, key, reconcile

rel adapt, attune, tune; blend, combine, connect, correlate, dovetail, fit, fuse, integrate, join, match, merge, orchestrate, pair, square, suit, synchronize, synthesize, unify, unite; align, arrange, array, balance, equalize, even, order, proportion, regularize, standardize

near ant confuse, disarray, disorder, disorganize, disrupt, disturb, skew, upset

ant alienate, disjoin

3 to be in agreement on every point — see CHECK 1

harmonizing *adj* having a pleasing mixture of notes — see HARMONIOUS 1

harmony *n* **1** a balanced, pleasing, or suitable arrangement of parts 〈her face had an angelic *harmony* that fascinated the leading painters of her day〉

syn balance, coherence, consonance, proportion, symmetry, symphony, unity

rel coordination, correlation, correspondence, equalization, equilibrium, evenness, order, orderliness, regularity, uniformity

near ant confusion, disorganization, dissonance, disturbance, tension; disconnectedness, disjointedness, incompatibility; irregularity, unevenness

ant asymmetry, discordance, disproportion, disunity, imbalance, incoherence

2 peaceful coexistence 〈Mary Beth was determined to live in *harmony* with her new stepsister〉

syn comity, compatibility, concord, peace

rel amity, congeniality, fellowship, fraternization, friendship; collaboration, reciprocity, symbiosis; consensus, unanimity, unity; affinity, connection, empathy, kinship, oneness, rapport, solidarity, sympathy, understanding; peacefulness, serenity, tranquillity (*or* tranquility)

near ant antagonism, antipathy, enmity, hatred, hostility, unfriendliness; alienation, breach, divorce, estrangement,

rupture, schism, severance; dissent, dissidence; disturbance, strife, turmoil
ant conflict, discord, dissension
3 a state of consistency — see CONFORMITY 1

harness *vb* to put into action or service — see USE 1

harpoon *vb* to penetrate or hold (something) with a pointed object — see IMPALE

harpy *n* a bad-tempered scolding woman — see SHREW

harrow *vb* to cause persistent suffering to — see AFFLICT

harrowing *adj* **1** hard to accept or bear especially emotionally — see BITTER 2
2 intensely or unbearably painful — see EXCRUCIATING 1

harrying *n* the act of making unwelcome intrusions upon another — see ANNOYANCE 1

harsh *adj* **1** difficult to endure ⟨*harsh* conditions in the refugee camp⟩
syn bitter, brutal, burdensome, cruel, excruciating, grievous, grim, hard, heavy, inhuman, murderous, onerous, oppressive, rough, rugged, severe, stiff, tough, trying
rel austere, bleak, comfortless, discomforting, forbidding, hostile, inhospitable, Spartan, uncomfortable; biting, inclement, intemperate; rigorous, strict, stringent; agonizing, heartbreaking, heartrending, painful, wretched; crushing, grinding, overwhelming, wearing; insufferable, insupportable, intolerable, unbearable, unendurable; harrowing, tortuous; bad, disagreeable, hostile, unfriendly, unpleasant
near ant comfortable, cozy, luxurious, snug; agreeable, friendly, genial, hospitable, pleasant; peaceful, relaxing, reposeful, restful; bearable, endurable, painless, tolerable; balmy, calm, clement, gentle, mild, moderate, temperate
ant easy, light, soft
2 disagreeable to one's aesthetic or artistic sense ⟨the *harsh* lighting in the cafeteria makes the food look slightly off-color⟩
syn grating, grotesque, jarring, unaesthetic
rel flashy, garish, gaudy, loud, tawdry; tacky, tasteless, vulgar; inartistic, unartistic; artless, clumsy, crude, graceless, inelegant, rude; uncouth, uncultured, unrefined; disgusting, gross, obscene, repugnant, repulsive, ugly; disagreeable, jolting, unpleasant, unpleasing; blaring, clashing, discordant, dissonant, inharmonious, off-key, jangling, raspy, raucous, unharmonious, unmelodious, unmusical; bizarre, kinky, odd, outlandish, shocking
near ant artful, artistic; attractive, beautiful, becoming, comely; agreeable, appealing, felicitous, good, harmonious, harmonizing, pleasing, seemly; calming,

comforting, soothing; softened, subdued; cultured, elegant, graceful, gracious, polished, refined, tasteful
ant aesthetic (*or* esthetic)
3 causing discomfort — see UNCOMFORTABLE 1
4 given to exacting standards of discipline and self-restraint — see SEVERE 1
5 hard to accept or bear especially emotionally — see BITTER 2

harshly *adv* in a manner so as to cause loss or suffering — see HARDLY 1

harshness *n* **1** a harsh or sharp quality — see EDGE 1
2 the quality or state of being demanding or unyielding (as in discipline or criticism) — see SEVERITY

harum–scarum *adv* in a confused and reckless manner — see HELTER-SKELTER 1

harvest *n* the quantity of an animal or vegetable product gathered at the end of a season — see CROP 1

harvest *vb* to catch or collect (a crop or natural resource) for human use ⟨*harvest* salmon from nearby rivers⟩ ⟨every year we *harvest* corn from our own garden⟩
syn gather, pick, reap
rel clam, fish, seal, shrimp, whale; accumulate, garner; glean; cut, hay, mow; bag, capture, hunt, net, snare, trap; crop, grow, raise
near ant plant, seed, sow

hash *n* an unorganized collection or mixture of various things — see MISCELLANY 1

hash *vb* **1** to cut into small pieces — see CHOP
2 to undo the proper order or arrangement of — see DISORDER

hash (over) *vb* to talk about (an issue) usually from various points of view and for the purpose of arriving at a decision or opinion — see DISCUSS

hassle *n* **1** a brief clash between enemies or rivals — see ENCOUNTER
2 a physical dispute between opposing individuals or groups — see FIGHT 1
3 an often noisy or angry expression of differing opinions — see ARGUMENT 1
4 something that is a source of irritation — see ANNOYANCE 3

hassle *vb* **1** to attack repeatedly with mean put-downs or insults — see TEASE 2
2 to express different opinions about something often angrily — see ARGUE 2

haste *n* **1** a high rate of movement or performance — see SPEED
2 excited and often showy or disorderly speed — see HURRY 1

hasten *vb* **1** to cause to move or proceed fast or faster — see HURRY 1
2 to proceed or move quickly — see HURRY 2

hastily *adv* **1** with excessive or careless speed ⟨the *hastily* put together report contained a lot of errors⟩
syn cursorily, headlong, hotfoot, hurriedly, pell-mell, precipitately, precipitously, rashly

---

syn synonym(s)   *rel* related words
ant antonym(s)   *near ant* near antonym(s)

rel headily, hotheadedly, impatiently, impetuously, impulsively, recklessly, thoughtlessly; automatically, glancingly, haphazardly; impromptu, spontaneously; abruptly, suddenly; offhand, offhandedly

phrases on the spur of the moment

near ant calculatingly, circumspectly, designedly; falteringly, hesitantly, hesitatingly, tentatively; leisurely, slowly

ant deliberately, studiedly

2 with great speed — see FAST 1

hastiness *n* excited and often showy or disorderly speed — see HURRY 1

hasty *adj* **1** acting or done with excessive or careless speed ⟨Anna later regretted her *hasty* decision to sell her car⟩

syn cursory, flying, headlong, hurried, pell-mell, precipitate, precipitous, rash, rushed

rel breakneck, breathtaking; headstrong, heady, hotheaded, impatient, impetuous, impulsive, madcap, reckless, unadvised; quick, rapid, speedy, swift; impromptu, makeshift, offhand, offhanded, slap-dash, snap, spontaneous, spur-of-the-moment; abrupt, sudden

near ant calculated, calculating, measured; circumspect, foresighted, forethoughtful; drawn-out, extended, longterm, prolonged; faltering, hesitant, hesitating, tentative; dallying, dawdling, laggard, leisurely, poky (*or* pokey), shilly-shallying, slow

ant deliberate, unhurried

2 moving, proceeding, or acting with great speed — see FAST 1

hat *n* a covering for the head usually having a shaped crown ⟨Paul brought back warm fur *hats* for everyone from Russia⟩

syn cap, headdress, headgear, headpiece, lid [*slang*]

rel beret, biretta, boater, bonnet, bowler, derby, fedora, fez, hard hat, helm, helmet, homburg, hood, leghorn, miter, nightcap, panama, pillbox, poke bonnet, shako, skullcap, sombrero, sou'wester, Stetson, stocking cap, stovepipe, sunbonnet, tam-o'-shanter, top hat, topper, toque, turban; war bonnet; coronet, crown, diadem, headband, tiara; babushka, coif, kerchief, mantilla, scarf, shawl, tallith, veil, wimple

hatch *n* a barrier by which an entry is closed and opened — see DOOR 1

hatch *vb* to cover and warm eggs to hatch them — see SET 1

hate *n* **1** a very strong dislike ⟨*hate* can sometimes be replaced with tolerance when people meet face to face⟩

syn abhorrence, abomination, execration, hatred, loathing

rel cattiness, despite, despitefulness, hatefulness, invidiousness, malevolence, malice, maliciousness, malignancy, malignity, meanness, spite, spitefulness; aversion, disgust, distaste, horror, odium, repugnance, repulsion, revulsion; animosity, antagonism, antipathy, bitterness, contempt, disdain, enmity, grudge, hostility, jealousy, pique, resentment, scorn; bile, jaundice, rancor, spleen, venom, virulence, vitriol

near ant appetite, inclination, liking; adoration, veneration, worship; acceptance, tolerance; passion, relish, taste

ant affection, devotion, fondness, love

2 something or someone that is hated ⟨the Alaska pipeline is a pet *hate* of environmentalists⟩

syn abhorrence, abomination, anathema, antipathy, aversion, bête noire

rel dread, hang-up, horror, phobia; bogey (*also* bogy *or* bogie), bugaboo, bugbear; adversary, enemy; annoyance, grievance, hassle, nuisance, peeve

near ant beloved, darling, dear, honey; delight, enjoyment, felicity, joy, pleasure; favorite, like, preference; treasure

ant love

hate *vb* to dislike strongly ⟨Pete *hated* the farm and dreamed of working in the city⟩

syn abhor, abominate, despise, detest, execrate, loathe

rel deplore, deprecate, disapprove (of), discountenance, disdain, disfavor, scorn

phrases have it in for

near ant fancy, favor, like, prefer; enjoy, relish; adore, esteem, idolize, revere, venerate, worship; cherish, prize, treasure

ant love

hateful *adj* having or showing a desire to cause someone pain or suffering for the sheer enjoyment of it ⟨a *hateful* bully who loved to pick on little kids⟩ ⟨Janet's *hateful* remarks drove Penny to tears⟩

syn catty, cruel, despiteful, malevolent, malicious, malign, malignant, mean, nasty, spiteful, virulent

rel devious, scoundrelly, scurvy, snakelike; acrimonious, bitter, envious, jaundiced, jealous, rancorous, resentful; contemptuous, deprecating, disdainful, obnoxious, opprobrious, scornful, snide, unkind, unkindly, unloving; baleful, baneful, evil; harsh, hostile, inimical; acrid, caustic, scathing, venomous

near ant compassionate, good, goodhearted, kind, kindhearted, kindly, sympathetic, warm, warmhearted; affable, agreeable, amiable, cordial, friendly, genial, gracious, nice, pleasant; affectionate, amorous, sweet, tender, tenderhearted; altruistic, high-minded, humanitarian, magnanimous, noble, philanthropic

ant benevolent, benign, benignant, loving, unmalicious

hatefully *adv* in a mean or spiteful manner — see NASTILY

hatefulness *n* the desire to cause pain for the satisfaction of doing harm — see MALICE

hatred *n* a very strong dislike — see HATE 1

haughtiness *n* an exaggerated sense of one's importance that shows itself in the making of excessive or unjustified claims — see ARROGANCE

haughty *adj* **1** having a feeling of superiority that shows itself in an overbearing attitude — see ARROGANT

2 having or displaying feelings of scorn for what is regarded as beneath oneself — see PROUD 1

haul *n* **1** the total amount collected or obtained especially at one time ⟨the trick-or-treaters showed off their *haul*⟩

syn catch, take, yield

rel bag; earnings, gain, gross, income, net, payoff, proceeds, profit, receipts, return, revenue, winnings; booty, loot, plunder, spoils, swag; appropriation, collection

near ant deduction, loss, subtraction

2 a mass or quantity of something taken up and carried, conveyed, or transported — see LOAD 1

3 the act or an instance of applying force on something so that it moves in the direction of the force — see PULL 1

haul *vb* **1** to cause to follow by applying steady force on — see PULL 1

2 to support and take from one place to another — see CARRY 1

haunches *n pl* the part of the body upon which someone sits — see BUTTOCKS

haunt *n* a place for spending time or for socializing — see HANGOUT

haunt *vb* to go to or spend time in often — see FREQUENT

haunting *adj* fearfully and mysteriously strange or fantastic — see EERIE

have *vb* **1** to keep, control, or experience as one's own ⟨Aunt Chloe *has* 31 pairs of red shoes⟩

syn command, enjoy, hold, occupy, own, possess, retain

rel keep, reserve, withhold; bear, carry; boast, show off, sport

near ant abandon, cede, disclaim, disown, hand over, relinquish, renounce, surrender, yield; discard, dump; decline, reject, repudiate, spurn; need, require

ant lack, want

2 to agree to receive whether willingly or reluctantly — see TAKE 2

3 to bring forth from the womb — see BEAR 1

4 to cause to believe what is untrue — see DECEIVE

5 to come to a knowledge of (something) by living through it — see EXPERIENCE

6 to give permission for or to approve of — see ALLOW 1

7 to influence someone with a bribe — see BRIBE

8 to keep in one's mind or heart — see HARBOR 1

have (to) *vb* to be under necessity or obligation to — see NEED 2

haven *n* **1** a part of a body of water protected and deep enough to be a place of safety for ships — see HARBOR 1

2 something (as a building) that offers cover from the weather or protection from danger — see SHELTER

havoc *n* **1** a state in which everything is out of order — see CHAOS

2 the state or fact of being rendered nonexistent, physically unsound, or useless — see DESTRUCTION

hawk *n* one who urges or attempts to cause a war — see WARMONGER

hawk *vb* to sell from place to place usually in small quantities — see PEDDLE

hawker *n* one who sells things outdoors — see PEDDLER

hazard *n* **1** something that may cause injury or harm — see DANGER 2

2 the uncertain course of events — see CHANCE 1

hazard *vb* **1** to place in danger — see ENDANGER

2 to take a chance on — see RISK 1

hazardous *adj* involving potential loss or injury — see DANGEROUS

haze *n* **1** an atmospheric condition in which suspended particles in the air rob it of its transparency ⟨Jim could barely make out the tall buildings through the *haze*⟩

syn fog, mist, murk, reek, smog, soup

rel cloud, fume, miasma, smoke, steam

2 a state of mental confusion ⟨people wandered around in a *haze* in the days following the earthquake⟩

syn daze, fog, muddle, spin

rel reverie, stupor, trance; befuddlement, bewilderment, perplexity, puzzlement; delirium, malaise, paralysis; cloudiness, fogginess

near ant alertness, levelheadedness

haze *vb* to make dark, dim, or indistinct — see CLOUD 1

hazed *adj* covered over by clouds — see OVERCAST

hazy *adj* **1** filled with or dimmed by fine particles (as of dust or water) in suspension ⟨*hazy* skies made it dangerous to fly⟩ ⟨the *hazy* sunshine so common in August⟩

syn beclouded, befogged, clouded, cloudy, foggy, misty, murky, smoggy, soupy

rel overcast, rainy, stormy, thick; dirty, miry, mucky, muddy, slimy, slushy, turbid; smoky (*also* smokey), sooty; filmy, milky, opaque

near ant bright, clean; fair, rainless, sunny, sunshiny; translucent, transparent

ant clear, cloudless, limpid, pellucid, unclouded

2 covered over by clouds — see OVERCAST

3 not seen or understood clearly — see FAINT 1

head *adj* highest in rank or authority ⟨Mr. Pendergast, *head* editor at the TV station for 17 years, has hired and fired innumerable staff members⟩

syn chief, commanding, first, foremost, high, lead, leading, managing, preeminent, premier, presiding, primary, prime, principal, supreme

rel high-level, senior; controlling, directing, officiating, overseeing, reigning, rul-

---

syn synonym(s)   *rel* related words
ant antonym(s)   *near ant* near antonym(s)

ing, supervisory; main, major, paramount, predominant; dominant, grand, superior, topmost, upmost, upper, uppermost

phrases in charge

near ant inferior, last, lesser, lower, lowly, second, secondary, subordinate; assistant, assisting, coadjutor, deputy, junior, under

head *n* **1** the upper or front part of the body that contains the brain, the major sense organs, and the mouth ⟨I hit my *head* as I went through the low doorway⟩

syn noddle, noggin, pate, poll

rel cranium, crown, scalp, skull

2 the place of leadership or command ⟨every year a different parent is placed at the *head* of the troop's cookie drive⟩

syn chair, headship, helm, rein

rel chieftaincy, commandership, directorship; forefront, lead, preferment; chairmanship, deanship, dictatorship, governorship, kingship, mastership, mastery, presidency, superintendency; dominance, dominion, jurisdiction, sovereignty, sway, upper hand; eminence, height, pedestal, pinnacle, seat, throne, top

near ant ranks

3 a light mass of fine bubbles formed in or on a liquid — see FOAM

4 a member of the human race — see HUMAN

5 a time or state of affairs requiring prompt or decisive action — see EMERGENCY

6 the beginning part of a stream — see HEADWATER

7 the highest part or point — see HEIGHT 1

8 the normal or healthy condition of the mental abilities — see MIND 2

9 the part of a person that feels, thinks, perceives, wills, and especially reasons — see MIND 1

10 the person (as an employer or supervisor) who tells people and especially workers what to do — see BOSS

head *vb* **1** to go on a specified course or in a certain direction ⟨the migrant workers were *heading* for California for the grape harvest⟩

syn bear, make

rel aim, bend, direct, point, turn; put, put out, set forth, set off, set out, strike, take off; face, orient, steer; about-face, back, come about, come round, cut, incline, put about, reverse, swerve, tack, veer, yaw, wheel

2 to be at the front of — see LEAD 3

3 to be in charge of — see BOSS 1

4 to be positioned along a certain course or in a certain direction — see RUN 3

5 to point or turn (something) toward a target or goal — see AIM

6 to serve as leader of — see LEAD 2

headache *n* **1** a dull, unpleasant, or difficult period of work — see CHORE 2

2 something that is a source of irritation — see ANNOYANCE 3

headdress *n* a covering for the head usually having a shaped crown — see HAT

headgear *n* a covering for the head usually having a shaped crown — see HAT

heading *n* a word or series of words often in larger letters placed at the beginning of a passage or at the top of a page in order to introduce or categorize ⟨Fran found the recipe for turkey gumbo under the *heading* "stews" rather than under "soups"⟩

syn caption, headline, rubric, title

rel guide word, legend; greeting, salutation; superscript, superscription; subhead, subheading, subtitle

headland *n* **1** an area of high ground jutting out into a body of water beyond the line of the coast ⟨the lighthouse, situated on a narrow, rocky *headland*, commands an expansive view of the coast⟩

syn point, promontory

rel cape, peninsula; breakwater, jetty, levee; spit

2 an area of land that juts out into a body of water — see [2]CAPE

headline *n* **1** a word or series of words often in larger letters placed at the beginning of a passage or at the top of a page in order to introduce or categorize — see HEADING

headlong *adj* acting or done with excessive or careless speed — see HASTY 1

headlong *adv* with excessive or careless speed — see HASTILY 1

headman *n* the person (as an employer or supervisor) who tells people and especially workers what to do — see BOSS

headpiece *n* a covering for the head usually having a shaped crown — see HAT

headquarters *n pl* **1** a place from which authority is exercised — see SEAT 1

2 the place from which a commander runs operations — see COMMAND 3

headship *n* **1** the duty or function of watching or guarding for the sake of proper direction or control — see SUPERVISION 1

2 the place of leadership or command — see HEAD 2

headstone *n* a shaped stone laid over or erected near a grave and usually bearing an inscription to identify and preserve the memory of the deceased — see TOMBSTONE

headstrong *adj* **1** given to resisting control or discipline by others — see UNCONTROLLABLE

2 sticking to an opinion, purpose, or course of action in spite of reason, arguments, or persuasion — see OBSTINATE

headwater *n usually* **headwaters** *pl* the beginning part of a stream ⟨the first exploration of the Missouri River from its mouth to its *headwaters* was made by Meriwether Lewis and William Clark in the early 1800s⟩

syn head, source

rel fountain, fountainhead, geyser, hot spring, spring, thermal spring, wellspring

headway *n* forward movement in time or place — see ADVANCE 1

heal *vb* **1** to restore to a healthy condition ⟨a low-fat vegetarian diet, moderate exercise, and stress management help *heal* a diseased heart⟩ ⟨*heal* the sick⟩

syn cure, mend, rehabilitate

rel attend (to), care (for), doctor, minister (to), nurse, treat; fortify, rejuvenate, renew, resuscitate, revive; alleviate, fix, relieve, remedy, repair

phrases take care of

near ant damage, disable, harm, hurt, impair, injure, lacerate, lame, maim, mangle, mutilate, wound; afflict, ail, debilitate, enervate, enfeeble, lay up, sap, sicken, waste, weaken

2 to become healthy and strong again after illness or weakness — see CONVALESCE

3 to bring about recovery from — see CURE 1

healing *n* the process or period of gradually regaining one's health and strength — see CONVALESCENCE

health *n* the condition of being sound in body ⟨Sam gradually regained his *health* after a long bout with cholera⟩

syn fitness, healthiness, heartiness, robustness, soundness, wellness, wholeness, wholesomeness

rel fettle, shape; cleanliness, hygiene; hardiness, lustiness, ruggedness, stamina, strength, toughness, vigor, vigorousness, vitality; bloom, flush, flushness; activeness, agility, liveliness, spryness; weal, welfare, well-being

near ant debility, decrepitude, feebleness, frailness, infirmity, lameness, weakness; ailment, condition, disease, disorder, malady, trouble

ant illness, sickness, unhealthiness, unsoundness

healthful *adj* good for the health ⟨one of the most *healthful* forms of exercise is a brisk walk⟩

syn healthy, restorative, salubrious, salutary, wholesome

rel alleviative, corrective, curative, remedial, tonic; advantageous, beneficial, useful; antiseptic, clean, hygienic, sanitary; nonfattening, nonpoisonous, nontoxic

near ant deleterious, injurious, pernicious; infectious, poisonous, toxic; insanitary, unhygienic, unsanitary

ant insalubrious, noxious, unhealthful, unhealthy, unwholesome

healthiness *n* the condition of being sound in body — see HEALTH

healthy *adj* **1** enjoying health and vigor ⟨always a hard worker, Grandma has remained *healthy* into her eighties⟩

syn able-bodied, bouncing, chipper, fit, hale, hearty, robust, sound, well, whole, wholesome

rel hardy, lusty, rugged, stalwart, strong, sturdy, tough; nondisabled, nonhandicapped, uncrippled; active, agile, lively, sprightly, spry, vigorous, vital; blooming,

clean-cut, flourishing, flush, thriving; all right, good, right

phrases in fine fettle

near ant decrepit, enfeebled, feeble, infirm, run-down, sickened, sickly, weak, weakened, weakly, worn-out; challenged, crippled, debilitated, disabled, incapacitated, lame; delicate, fragile, frail; undernourished; afflicted, troubled; bad, poorly

ant ailing, diseased, ill, sick, unfit, unhealthy, unsound, unwell

2 good for the health — see HEALTHFUL

3 sufficiently large in size, amount, or number to merit attention — see CONSIDERABLE 1

heap *n* **1** a considerable amount — see LOT 2

2 a quantity of things thrown or stacked on one another — see ¹PILE 1

heap *vb* **1** to give readily and in large quantities — see RAIN 2

2 to gradually form into a layer, pile, or mass — see COLLECT 2

3 to lay or throw on top of one another — see PILE

4 to put into (something) as much as can be held or contained — see FILL 1

hear *vb* **1** to come to an awareness — see DISCOVER 1

2 to pay attention especially through the act of hearing — see LISTEN

hearing *n* range of hearing — see EARSHOT

hearken *vb* to pay attention especially through the act of hearing — see LISTEN

heart *n* **1** the capacity for feeling for another's unhappiness or misfortune ⟨when her parents refused her request for a puppy, Jessica asked, "Have you no *heart?*"⟩

syn charity, commiseration, compassion, feeling, humanity, kindheartedness, kindliness, kindness, mercy, pity, softheartedness, sympathy

rel responsiveness, sensitivity; affection, love, regard; affinity, empathy, rapport; altruism, benevolence, benignity, generosity, goodwill, humanitarianism, philanthropy

near ant callousness, coldness, indifference, unconcern; cruelty, harshness; animosity, antipathy, dislike, hatred, hostility

ant hardheartedness, inhumanity, mercilessness

2 the body of knowledge that has been retained in one's mind or the use of it ⟨Dan can recite the entire Declaration of Independence by *heart*⟩

syn memory, rote

rel association, conning, memorization

3 a thing or place that is of greatest importance to an activity or interest — see CENTER 1

4 strength of mind to carry on in spite of danger — see COURAGE

5 the central part or aspect of something under consideration — see CRUX

6 the seat of one's deepest thoughts and emotions — see CORE 1

heartache *n* deep sadness especially for the loss of someone or something loved — see SORROW

heartbreak *n* deep sadness especially for the loss of someone or something loved — see SORROW

heartbreaking *adj* 1 causing unhappiness — see SAD 2

2 of a kind to cause great distress — see REGRETTABLE

3 deserving of one's pity — see PATHETIC 1

heartbroken *adj* 1 feeling unhappiness — see SAD 1

2 expressing or suggesting mourning — see MOURNFUL 1

hearten *vb* to fill with courage or strength of purpose — see ENCOURAGE 1

heartening *adj* 1 having qualities which inspire hope — see HOPEFUL 1

2 making one feel good inside — see HEARTWARMING

3 pointing toward a happy outcome — see FAVORABLE 2

hearth *n* the place where one lives — see HOME 1

hearthstone *n* the place where one lives — see HOME 1

heartily *adv* in a cheerful or happy manner — see GAILY 1

heartiness *n* the condition of being sound in body — see HEALTH

heartless *adj* 1 having or showing a lack of sympathy or tender feelings — see HARD 1

2 having or showing the desire to inflict severe pain and suffering on others — see CRUEL 1

heartlessness *n* the willful infliction of pain and suffering on others — see CRUELTY

heartrending *adj* 1 causing unhappiness — see SAD 2

2 hard to accept or bear especially emotionally — see BITTER 2

3 of a kind to cause great distress — see REGRETTABLE

4 deserving of one's pity — see PATHETIC 1

heartsick *adj* feeling unhappiness — see SAD 1

heartsickness *n* a state or spell of low spirits — see SADNESS

heartsore *adj* feeling unhappiness — see SAD 1

heartstrings *n pl* general emotional condition — see FEELING 2

heartwarming *adj* making one feel good inside ⟨Sarah appreciated the *heartwarming* welcome she received from her relatives in Israel⟩
syn cheering, comforting, encouraging, fulfilling, gladdening, gratifying, heartening, rewarding, satisfying
rel affecting, inspiring, moving, poignant, stirring, touching; edifying, elevating, uplifting; sympathetic, tender; kind, kindly, loving, warm; exciting, exhilarating, rousing, stimulating, thrilling; pleasing, welcoming

near ant cheerless, depressing, disappointing, discouraging, disgruntling, disheartening, displeasing, dissatisfying, saddening; cold, unfeeling, unfriendly, unkind, unloving, unpleasant
ant depressing, discouraging, disheartening, dispiriting

hearty *adj* 1 characterized by unqualified enthusiasm ⟨Frank expressed *hearty* approval of his aunt's suggestion to rendezvous in Tokyo⟩
syn wholehearted
rel single-minded; ardent, avid, eager, enthusiastic, excited, exuberant, gung ho, impassioned, keen, raring, vehement, warm, zealous; alacritous, immediate, prompt, ready, willing, unhesitating; animated, energetic, lively, spirited, vigorous; absolute, bona fide, genuine, unaffected, undisguised, unequivocal, unrestrained
near ant apathetic, disinterested, indifferent, uninterested; lackadaisical, listless, perfunctory, spiritless, uneager, unenthusiastic, unexcited; equivocal, hesitant, qualified, tentative, uncertain; delayed, dilatory, doubtful, hedging, hesitating; forced, reluctant, resistant, unwilling
ant grudging, halfhearted, lukewarm, tepid

2 enjoying health and vigor — see HEALTHY 1

3 having or showing kindly feeling and sincere interest — see FRIENDLY 1

4 not showing weakness or uncertainty — see FIRM 1

heat *n* depth of feeling — see ARDOR 1

heat *vb* to cause to have or give off heat to a moderate degree — see WARM 1

heated *adj* 1 being in a state of increased activity or agitation — see FEVERISH 1

2 having or giving off heat to a moderate degree — see WARM 1

heathen *adj* not civilized — see SAVAGE 1

heathen *n* 1 a person who does not worship the God of the Bible ⟨a missionary sent to distant lands to convert the *heathens*⟩
syn gentile, idolater (*or* idolator), pagan
rel atheist, infidel, nonbeliever, non-Christian, unbeliever; polytheist, theist
near ant Christian, Jew, Muslim

2 an uncivilized person ⟨European colonizers, who considered the New World peoples to be *heathens*, forced them to conform to European ways⟩
syn barbarian, savage
rel Neanderthal, primitive

heathenish *adj* not civilized — see SAVAGE 1

heave *vb* 1 to lift with effort ⟨I *heaved* my duffel bag into the bus's overhead compartment⟩
syn boost, heft, hoist, jack (up)
rel elevate, hike, raise, rear, up, uplift, upraise
near ant drop, lower; sink, submerge, submerse

2 to discharge the contents of the stomach through the mouth — see VOMIT

3 to move from a lower to a higher place or position — see RAISE 1

4 to send through the air especially with a quick forward motion of the arm — see THROW

heaven *n* **1** a dwelling place of perfect bliss for the soul after death ⟨prayed that the souls of the deceased would go to *heaven*⟩

syn Elysium, kingdom come, paradise

rel empyrean; glory; otherworld

phrases on high

near ant inferno; limbo, purgatory; hades, netherworld, underworld

ant hell, perdition

2 a place or state of great happiness — see PARADISE 1

3 a state of overwhelming usually pleasurable emotion — see ECSTASY

4 *usually* heavens *pl* the expanse of air surrounding the earth — see SKY

heavenly *adj* **1** of the very best kind — see EXCELLENT

2 of, relating to, or being God — see HOLY 3

3 of, relating to, or suggesting heaven — see CELESTIAL

4 giving pleasure or contentment to the mind or senses — see PLEASANT

heavily *adv* to a great degree — see VERY 1

heaviness *n* **1** the amount that something weighs — see WEIGHT 1

2 the state or quality of being heavy — see WEIGHTINESS 1

heavy *adj* **1** having great weight ⟨this trunk full of books is much too *heavy* for one person to lift⟩

syn hefty, massive, ponderous, weighty

rel burdensome, leaden, lumpish; bulky, elephantine, outsize; overweight, topheavy; solid, substantial

near ant airy, ethereal, feathery, gossamer, gossamery; flimsy, fluffy, insubstantial

ant light, lightweight, weightless

2 causing weariness, restlessness, or lack of interest — see BORING

3 containing much seasoning, fat, or sugar — see RICH 2

4 covered over by clouds — see OVERCAST

5 difficult to endure — see HARSH 1

6 extreme in degree, power, or effect — see INTENSE

7 having a matter of importance as its topic — see SERIOUS 2

heavy *n* a mean, evil, or unprincipled person — see VILLAIN

heavy–handed *adj* **1** given to exacting standards of discipline and self-restraint — see SEVERE 1

2 lacking in physical ease and grace in movement or in the use of the hands — see CLUMSY 1

---

syn synonym(s) *rel* related words
ant antonym(s) *near ant* near antonym(s)

---

heavyset *adj* being compact and broad in build and often short in stature — see STOCKY

heckle *vb* to attack repeatedly with mean put-downs or insults — see TEASE 2

heckler *n* a person who causes repeated emotional pain, distress, or annoyance to another — see TORMENTOR

hectic *adj* being in a state of increased activity or agitation — see FEVERISH 1

hectically *adv* in a confused and reckless manner — see HELTER-SKELTER 1

hector *vb* to make timid or fearful by or as if by threats — see INTIMIDATE

hedge *n* a physical object that blocks the way — see BARRIER

hedge *vb* **1** to avoid giving a definite answer or position — see EQUIVOCATE

2 to close or shut in by or as if by barriers — see ENCLOSE 1

heed *n* **1** a state of being aware — see ATTENTION 2

2 strict attentiveness to what one is doing — see CARE 1

heed *vb* **1** to take notice of and be guided by ⟨if Paul had *heeded* his brother's advice, he might not have gotten lost⟩

syn follow, listen (to), mind, note, observe, regard, watch

rel consider, contemplate, mull, ponder, weigh; comply (with), keep, obey, respect; hark (to), hear, hearken (to); mark, notice, sense

near ant brush (off), dismiss, pooh-pooh, scorn, shrug off; defy, flout; slight, snub

ant disregard, ignore, tune out

2 to pay attention especially through the act of hearing — see LISTEN

heedful *adj* having or showing a close attentiveness to avoiding danger or trouble — see CAREFUL 1

heedfulness *n* **1** a close attentiveness to avoiding danger — see CAUTION 1

2 strict attentiveness to what one is doing — see CARE 1

heedless *adj* not paying or showing close attention especially for the purpose of avoiding trouble — see CARELESS 1

heedlessness *n* failure to take the care that a cautious person usually takes — see NEGLIGENCE 1

heel *n* a person whose behavior is offensive to others — see JERK 1

heel *vb* to set or cause to be at an angle — see LEAN 1

heft *n* the amount that something weighs — see WEIGHT 1

heft *vb* **1** to lift with effort — see HEAVE 1

2 to move from a lower to a higher place or position — see RAISE 1

heftiness *n* **1** the quality or state of being large in size — see LARGENESS

2 the state or quality of being heavy — see WEIGHTINESS 1

hefty *adj* **1** having great weight — see HEAVY 1

2 of a size greater than average of its kind — see LARGE

height *n* **1** the highest part or point ⟨many regard the painting of the Sistine Chapel as the *height* of Michelangelo's career⟩
syn acme, apex, climax, crown, culmination, head, high-water mark, meridian, peak, pinnacle, summit, tip-top, top, zenith
rel bloom, flood tide, flower, glory, heyday; high; cap, ceiling, crest, roof; crescendo, extremity, maximum, tip, vertex
near ant abyss, base, foot; minimum
ant bottom, nadir

2 the most extreme or advanced point ⟨the student's defiant use of a cell phone during class was regarded by the teacher as the *height* of insolence⟩
syn depth, extremity, limit
rel consummation, epitome, quintessence, ultimate

3 the distance of something or someone from bottom to top ⟨the average *height* of the players on the volleyball team is well over six feet⟩
syn altitude, elevation, stature
rel rise; highness; loftiness, tallness

4 an area of high ground ⟨Gulliver, standing on a *height* near the shore, saw an island suspended above the sea⟩
syn altitude(s), elevation, eminence, highland, hill, mound, prominence, rise, upland
rel alp, mount, mountain, peak; butte, mesa, plateau, table, tableland; cliff, crag, precipice, tor; ridge, sierra; dome, sugarloaf; foothill, hillock, knob, knoll; down
near ant dale, dell, dingle, glen, hollow, vale, valley; basin, bottom, bottomland, fen, flat, floodplain, plain, tidewater
ant lowland

5 the most intense or characteristic phase of something — see THICK

heighten *vb* **1** to make markedly greater in measure or degree — see INTENSIFY
2 to move from a lower to a higher place or position — see RAISE 1

heightened *adj* being at a higher level than average — see HIGH 2

heinousness *n* the state or quality of being utterly evil — see ENORMITY 1

heir *n* a person who has the right to inherit property ⟨upon his death, Mr. Parkworth's property was divided evenly among his *heirs*, four sons and three daughters⟩
syn inheritor, legatee
rel claimant; heir apparent, successor; heiress; assignee, beneficiary, grantee; descendant (*or* descendent), scion (*also* cion)

helical *adj* turning around an axis like the thread of a screw — see SPIRAL

hell *n* **1** the place of punishment for the wicked after death ⟨condemned to *hell* for their sins⟩
syn perdition
rel inferno; purgatory; hades, netherworld, underworld
near ant empyrean; glory

ant Elysium, heaven, kingdom come, paradise

2 a situation or state that causes great suffering and unhappiness ⟨picking cotton under the hot summer sun was *hell*⟩
syn agony, horror, misery, murder, nightmare, torment, torture
rel cross, ordeal, trial, tribulation; gall, thorn; bummer, downer, drag
near ant delight, diversion, entertainment, fun, pleasure, recreation; lark, picnic, riot
ant heaven, paradise

3 a place of uproar or confusion — see MADHOUSE 2

4 a state in which everything is out of order — see CHAOS

hellion *n* an appealingly mischievous person — see SCAMP 1

hello *n* an expression of goodwill upon meeting ⟨we said our *hellos* and got right down to business⟩
syn greeting, salutation, salute, welcome
rel amenities, civilities, pleasantries; regards, respects, wishes
ant adieu, bon voyage, farewell, Godspeed, good-bye (*or* good-by)

helm *n* the place of leadership or command — see HEAD 2

helmsman *n* the person (as an employer or supervisor) who tells people and especially workers what to do — see BOSS

help *n* **1** an act or instance of helping ⟨Andrew didn't get any *help* with his homework⟩
syn aid, assist, assistance, backing, boost, lift, support
rel advancement, encouragement, facilitation, forwarding, furtherance, furthering, nurturance; benefaction, patronage, promotion, sponsorship; advice, care, counsel, guidance, mentoring; attendance, attention, service; beneficence, charity, favor, kindness, philanthropy; relief, succor
near ant constraint, frustration, inhibition, interference, obstruction, repression, restraint; deterrence, discouragement
ant hindrance

2 a thing that helps ⟨the computer is a great *help* for writing reports⟩
syn advantage, aid, benefit, boon
rel lift, pick-me-up; support, sustenance; blessing, godsend, windfall; recourse, resort, resource; asset
near ant constraint, inhibitor, liability, obstacle, obstruction, restraint, stranglehold
ant disadvantage, drawback, hindrance, impediment

3 a body of persons at work or available for work — see FORCE 1

help *vb* **1** to provide (someone) with what is useful or necessary to achieve an end ⟨Mary Beth flew to Chicago to *help* her dad when he moved into an apartment⟩
syn abet, aid, assist, back, prop (up), support

rel advance, facilitate, forward, foster, further; champion, endorse (*also* indorse), patronize, promote, sponsor; attend, care (for), comfort, minister (to), succor; bolster, boost, buttress, reinforce; advise, counsel, guide, mentor, nurture; bail out, deliver, rescue, save; embolden, encourage, hearten; benefit, favor, profit, serve

phrases to stand one in good stead

near ant balk, bar, block, constrain, hamper, hold back, impede, inhibit, obstruct, restrain, strangle; baffle, foil, frustrate, interfere, oppose, sabotage, thwart; desert, disappoint, fail, let down; discourage, dishearten; repress, retard, stifle, straiten, stunt; damage, harm, hurt, injure
ant hinder

2 to make more bearable or less severe ⟨the new ointment didn't *help* Josh's sunburn one bit⟩

syn allay, alleviate, assuage, ease, mitigate, mollify, palliate, relieve, soothe
rel abate, lighten, moderate, soften, temper; cure, heal, remedy; amend, correct, emend, fix, mend, rectify, reform, repair; ameliorate, better, enhance, enrich, improve, meliorate, perfect, refine
near ant harm, hurt, impair, injure; heighten, intensify, sharpen
ant aggravate

3 to keep from happening by taking action in advance — see PREVENT

helper *n* a person who helps a more skilled person ⟨over the summer Chris worked as a carpenter's *helper*⟩
syn adjutant, aid, aide, apprentice, assistant, coadjutor, deputy, helpmate, helpmeet, mate, sidekick
rel attendant, handmaiden (*also* handmaid), maid, maidservant, scullion, servant; auxiliary, subordinate, underling; employee, hand, help, hireling, laborer, worker

helpful *adj* conferring benefits; promoting or contributing to personal or social well-being — see BENEFICIAL

helpless *adj* **1** lacking protection from danger or resistance against attack ⟨after the storm we found a *helpless* baby bird that had fallen out of its nest⟩
syn defenseless, exposed, susceptible, undefended, unguarded, unprotected, unresistant, unshielded, vulnerable
rel indefensible, untenable; uncovered, unsafe, unsheltered; overcome, preyed (on *or* upon); disarmed, passive, resistless, unarmed; feeble, frail, weak; abandoned, marooned
phrases in the lurch
near ant defensible; covered, fortified, safe, secure, screened, sheltered; armed, armored; immune, impenetrable, impregnable, invincible, strong, unassailable, unbeatable, unconquerable
ant guarded, invulnerable, protected, resistant, shielded

2 unable to act or achieve one's purpose — see POWERLESS

helpmate *n* **1** a person who helps a more skilled person — see HELPER

2 the female partner in a marriage — see WIFE

helpmeet *n* **1** a person who helps a more skilled person — see HELPER

2 the female partner in a marriage — see WIFE

helter–skelter *adv* **1** in a confused and reckless manner ⟨the sheep ran *helter-skelter* inside their pen when the coyote appeared in their midst⟩
syn amok (*or* amuck), berserk, frantically, frenziedly, harum-scarum, hectically, madly, pell-mell, wild, wildly
rel agitatedly, confusedly, crazily, desperately, feverishly, skittishly, uncontrollably; heedlessly, hotheadedly, recklessly, wantonly; chaotically, riotously, tumultuously, turbulently; aimlessly, haphazardly, hit-or-miss
near ant calmly, collectedly, composedly, coolly, imperturbably, peacefully, placidly, serenely, unconcernedly; meekly, mildly, passively, tamely; methodically, orderly, systematically

2 without definite aim, direction, rule, or method — see HIT OR MISS

hem *vb* to close or shut in by or as if by barriers — see ENCLOSE 1

hence *adv* **1** for this or that reason — see THEREFORE

2 from this or that place — see AWAY

henceforth *adv* from this point on ⟨*henceforth*, there will be no more prolonged coffee breaks⟩
syn henceforward, hereafter

henceforward *adv* from this point on — see HENCEFORTH

henpeck *vb* to subject (someone) to constant scoldings and sharp reminders — see NAG

herald *n* one that announces or indicates the later arrival of another — see FORERUNNER 1

herbage *n* green leaves or plants — see GREENERY 1

herculean *adj* **1** requiring considerable physical or mental effort — see HARD 2

2 unusually large — see HUGE

herd *n* **1** a group of domestic animals assembled or herded together ⟨the great *herds* of cattle that cowboys once drove across the plains⟩
syn drove, flock
rel colony, covey, gaggle, pack, school, swarm

2 the body of the community as contrasted with the elite — see MASS 1

herd *vb* to urge, push, or force onward — see DRIVE 1

herder *n* a tender of livestock ⟨the nomadic reindeer *herders* of Siberia live in reindeer-skin tents⟩
syn herdsman
rel buckaroo, cowboy, cowgirl, cowhand, cowherd, cowman, cowpoke, cowpuncher, gaucho, ranchero, vaquero; shepherd,

sheepherder, shepherdess; goatherd; wrangler; drover

herdsman *n* a tender of livestock — see HERDER

hereafter *adv* from this point on — see HENCEFORTH

hereafter *n* **1** time that is to come — see FUTURE 1

2 unending existence after death — see ETERNITY 2

hereditary *adj* genetically passed or capable of being passed from parent to offspring ⟨eye and hair color are *hereditary*⟩
syn genetic (*also* genetical), heritable, inborn, inheritable, inherited
rel congenital, inbred, inherent, innate, native, natural
near ant acquired

heresy *n* departure from a generally accepted theory, opinion, or practice ⟨the *heresy* of asserting that Shakespeare was not a great writer⟩
syn dissent, dissidence, heterodoxy, nonconformity
rel error, fallacy, falsehood, misbelief, misconception, myth; apostasy, defection, schism, sectarianism, separatism; deviance, deviation, unconventionality; disagreement, discord, dissension
near ant agreement, conformation, conventionality
ant conformity, orthodoxy

heretic *n* a person who believes or teaches something opposed to accepted beliefs ⟨Galileo was condemned as a *heretic* for supporting Copernicus's thesis that the earth revolves around the sun and not vice versa⟩
syn dissenter, dissident, nonconformist
rel apostate, defector, renegade; schismatic, sectarian, separatist; disbeliever, infidel, unbeliever; bohemian, individualist
near ant believer
ant conformer, conformist

heretical *adj* deviating from commonly accepted beliefs or practices ⟨the belief that women should be allowed to have careers outside the home was once considered *heretical*⟩
syn dissentient, dissenting, dissident, heterodox nonconformist, nonorthodox, unconventional, unorthodox
rel nontraditional; apostate, defecting, renegade; schismatic, sectarian, separatist
ant conforming, conformist, conventional, orthodox

heretofore *adv* up to this or that time — see HITHERTO

heritable *adj* genetically passed or capable of being passed from parent to offspring — see HEREDITARY

heritage *n* something that is or may be inherited — see INHERITANCE

hermit *n* a person who lives away from others — see RECLUSE

hero *n* a large sandwich on a long split roll — see SUBMARINE

heroic *adj* **1** feeling or displaying no fear by temperament — see BRAVE

2 large and impressive in size, grandeur, extent, or conception — see GRAND 1

3 unusually large — see HUGE

heroically *adv* in a manner befitting a person of the highest character and ideals — see GREATLY 1

heroism *n* strength of mind to carry on in spite of danger — see COURAGE

hesitance *n* **1** a lack of willingness or desire to do or accept something — see RELUCTANCE

2 the act or an instance of pausing because of uncertainty about the right course of action — see HESITATION

hesitancy *n* **1** a lack of willingness or desire to do or accept something — see RELUCTANCE

2 the act or an instance of pausing because of uncertainty about the right course of action — see HESITATION

hesitant *adj* having doubts about the wisdom of doing something ⟨Ivan was *hesitant* about lending CDs to his friends after he'd lost several of them that way⟩
syn afraid, disinclined, dubious, indisposed, loath (*or* loth), reluctant
rel uneager, unenthusiastic; averse, unwilling; doubtful, faltering, irresolute, questioning, uncertain, undecided, unsure, vacillating, wobbly; fainthearted, shy, timid
near ant eager, enthusiastic, glad, happy, keen; ready, willing; certain, decided, resolute, sure, unquestioning
ant disposed, inclined

hesitate *vb* to show uncertainty about the right course of action ⟨Keri didn't *hesitate* before answering the question⟩
syn falter, hang back, shilly-shally, stagger, teeter, vacillate, waver, wobble
rel haw, hem; dally, dawdle, delay, linger, procrastinate, pause, wait; back down, chicken (out); consider, debate, deliberate, ponder, weigh; oscillate, equivocate, hedge, pussyfoot
near ant budge, stir; advance, continue
ant dive (in), plunge (in)

hesitation *n* the act or an instance of pausing because of uncertainty about the right course of action ⟨one moment's *hesitation* on my part, and the elusive butterfly was lost to me forever⟩
syn faltering, hesitance, hesitancy, indecision, irresolution, shilly-shallying, vacillation, wavering, wobbling
rel delay, hawing, procrastination, waiting; consideration, debate, deliberation, doubt, incertitude, indetermination, uncertainty; avoidance, equivocation; aversion, disinclination, indisposition, reluctance, unwillingness; faintheartedness, shyness, timidness
near ant certainty, certitude, confidence, decisiveness, determination, firmness, resoluteness, resolution, sureness; alacrity, eagerness, readiness

heterodox *adj* deviating from commonly accepted beliefs or practices — see HERETICAL

heterodoxy *n* departure from a generally accepted theory, opinion, or practice — see HERESY

heterogeneous *adj* consisting of many things of different sorts — see MISCELLANEOUS

het up *adj* feeling or showing uncomfortable feelings of uncertainty — see NERVOUS 1

hew *vb* **1** to bring down by cutting — see FELL 2

2 to hold to something firmly as if by adhesion — see STICK 1

hew (to) *vb* to give steadfast support to — see ADHERE

hex *n* **1** a woman believed to have often harmful supernatural powers — see WITCH 1

2 something that brings bad luck — see JINX

hex *vb* to cast a spell on — see BEWITCH 1

heyday *n* a state or time of great activity, thriving, or achievement — see BLOOM 1

hiatus *n* a break in continuity — see GAP 2

hick *n* an awkward or simple person especially from a small town or the country ⟨city dwellers who looked down on their cousins from northern Maine as *hicks*⟩
syn bumpkin, clodhopper, countryman, hillbilly, provincial, rustic, yokel
rel boor, clod, gawk, lout, oaf; greenhorn, tenderfoot; peasant, peon; mountaineer
near ant slicker, smoothy (*or* smoothie); suburbanite, urbanite
ant cosmopolitan, sophisticate

hide *n* **1** the outer covering of an animal removed for its commercial value ⟨seal *hides* are used by Eskimos to make footwear, boats, shelters, bags, and clothing⟩
syn fur, leather, pelt, skin
rel badger, beaver, chamois, chinchilla, ermine, fisher, fox, mink, muskrat, otter, Persian lamb, rabbit, raccoon (*also* racoon), sable, seal, silver fox; bearskin, buckskin, calfskin, coonskin, cowhide, deerskin, doeskin, goatskin, horsehide, kidskin, lambskin, pigskin, rawhide, sealskin, sharkskin, sheepskin, snakeskin; fleece, mouton; alligator; cordovan, morocco, patent leather, suede

2 the hairless natural covering of an animal prepared for use — see LEATHER 1

¹hide *vb* **1** to put into a hiding place ⟨the thief *hid* the stolen jewelry under the floorboards⟩
syn bury, cache, conceal, ensconce, secrete
rel hoard, squirrel (away), stash; entomb, inter
near ant bare, expose, reveal, show, uncover, unmask, unveil, unwrap; flaunt, parade, show off; disinter, unearth
ant display, exhibit

2 to keep secret or shut off from view ⟨he tried to *hide* his criminal past⟩ ⟨she *hid* the cat's litter box behind a screen⟩

syn synonym(s)   *rel* related words
ant antonym(s)   *near ant* near antonym(s)

syn blanket, blot out, cloak, conceal, cover, curtain, enshroud, mask, obscure, occult, screen, shroud, veil
rel camouflage, cover (up), disguise, smother; gild, gloss (over), varnish, whitewash; becloud, bedim, befog, cloud, darken, eclipse, overcast, overshadow, shade
near ant bring out, present; clarify, illuminate; advertise, air, broadcast, proclaim, publicize
ant bare, disclose, display, divulge, expose, reveal, show, unclock, uncover, unmask, unveil

3 to strike repeatedly with something long and thin or flexible — see WHIP 1

²hide *vb* to strike repeatedly — see BEAT 1

hideaway *n* a place where a person goes to hide — see HIDEOUT

hideous *adj* **1** causing intense displeasure, disgust, or resentment — see OFFENSIVE 1

2 extremely disturbing or repellent — see HORRIBLE 1

3 unpleasant to look at — see UGLY 1

hideousness *n* the quality of inspiring intense dread or dismay — see HORROR 1

hideout *n* a place where a person goes to hide ⟨they found the stolen jewels under the floorboards in the thief's *hideout*, a cabin deep in the woods⟩
syn concealment, covert, den, hideaway, lair, nest
rel blind, cover, nook, recess; hangout, harbor, haunt, haven, refuge, retreat, shelter

hiding *n* the placing of something out of sight — see CONCEALMENT 1

higgledy-piggledy *adj* lacking in order, neatness, and often cleanliness — see MESSY

high *adj* **1** extending to a great distance upward ⟨Mt. Everest is the *highest* mountain in the world⟩
syn lofty, tall, towering
rel dominant, dominating, eminent, prominent; elevated, lifted, raised, uplifted, upswept; high-rise, statuesque
near ant flat, stubby, stumpy
ant low, low-lying, short, squat

2 being at a higher level than average ⟨gasoline prices are *high* right now⟩ ⟨a *high* fever⟩ ⟨people with *high* incomes⟩
syn advanced, elevated, escalated, heightened, increased, jacked (up), raised, up
rel extreme, full, maximized, maximum, peaked, sky-high, utmost; inflated, over, overfilled, overflowing, overfull, overlarge, overloaded, oversize (*or* oversized)
near ant decreased, depressed, dropped, receded, under
ant down, low

3 located at a greater height than average or usual ⟨an eagle's nest *high* on the cliff⟩ ⟨an old house with *high* ceilings⟩
syn airy, elevated
rel aerial, ascendant, ascending, soaring; overhead, overlooking, raised, upheld, uplifted, upraised; topmost, upmost, upper, uppermost, upward

near ant depressed, descendant (*or* descendent), descending, down, dropped, fallen, grounded, lowered, sunken; lowermost, nethermost, undermost; abreast, even, level

ant low, low-lying

4 being far along in development — see ADVANCED 1

5 being under the influence of alcohol — see DRUNK

6 commanding a large price — see COSTLY

7 having, characterized by, or arising from a dignified and generous nature — see NOBLE 2

8 highest in rank or authority — see HEAD

high *n* the expanse of air surrounding the earth — see SKY

high *adv* in a luxurious manner ⟨after he won the lottery Philip lived *high* until all the money was gone⟩

syn expensively, extravagantly, grandly, lavishly, luxuriously, opulently, richly, sumptuously

rel imposingly, impressively, magnificently, splendidly; grandiosely, ostentatiously, pretentiously; affluently, comfortably, fine; immoderately, indulgently, intemperately, prodigally, wantonly, wastefully

near ant unassumingly, unpretentiously; cheaply, economically, frugally, inexpensively, meagerly, poorly, skimpily, sparely, sparingly, thriftily; conservatively, moderately, prudently, reasonably, restrainedly, sensibly, temperately

ant austerely, humbly, modestly, plainly, simply

highborn *adj* of high birth, rank, or station — see NOBLE 1

highbrow *adj* much given to learning and thinking — see INTELLECTUAL 1

higher *adj* being far along in development — see ADVANCED 1

highest *adj* **1** being at a point or level higher than all others — see TOP 1

2 coming before all others in importance — see FOREMOST 1

highfalutin *adj* **1** full of fine words and fancy expressions — see FLOWERY 1

2 having a feeling of superiority that shows itself in an overbearing attitude — see ARROGANT

3 having or displaying feelings of scorn for what is regarded as beneath oneself — see PROUD 1

4 self-consciously trying to present an appearance of grandeur or importance — see PRETENTIOUS 1

high–flown *adj* **1** full of fine words and fancy expressions — see FLOWERY 1

2 very dignified in form, tone, or style — see ELEVATED 2

high–handed *adj* **1** having a feeling of superiority that shows itself in an overbearing attitude — see ARROGANT

2 having or showing a tendency to force one's will on others without any regard to fairness or necessity — see ARBITRARY 1

high–hat *adj* having a feeling of superiority that shows itself in an overbearing attitude — see ARROGANT

high–hat *vb* to show contempt for — see SCORN 1

high jinks *n pl* wildly playful or mischievous behavior — see HORSEPLAY

highland *n* an area of high ground — see HEIGHT 4

highlight *vb* to indicate the importance of by giving prominent display — see EMPHASIZE

highly *adv* to a great degree — see VERY 1

high–minded *adj* having, characterized by, or arising from a dignified and generous nature — see NOBLE 2

high–mindedly *adv* in a manner befitting a person of the highest character and ideals — see GREATLY 1

high noon *n* the middle of the day — see NOON

high–pitched *adj* having a high musical pitch or range — see SHRILL

high–pressure *adj* having or showing a bold forcefulness in the pursuit of a goal — see AGGRESSIVE 1

highroad *n* a passage cleared for public vehicular travel — see WAY 1

high–sounding *adj* full of fine words and fancy expressions — see FLOWERY 1

high–spirited *adj* **1** joyously unrestrained — see EXUBERANT

2 marked by a lively display of strong feeling — see SPIRITED 1

high–spiritedly *adv* in a quick and spirited manner — see GAILY 2

high–strung *adj* easily excited by nature — see EXCITABLE

high–water mark *n* the highest part or point — see HEIGHT 1

highway *n* a passage cleared for public vehicular travel — see WAY 1

hijack *also* **highjack** *vb* to take control of (a vehicle) by force — see COMMANDEER 1

hike *vb* to move from a lower to a higher place or position — see RAISE 1

hilarious *adj* causing or intended to cause laughter — see FUNNY 1

hilariousness *n* the amusing quality or element in something — see HUMOR 1

hilarity *n* a mood characterized by high spirits and amusement and often accompanied by laughter — see MIRTH

hill *n* **1** a quantity of things thrown or stacked on one another — see ¹PILE 1

2 an area of high ground — see HEIGHT 4

hill *vb* to form into a pile or ridge of earth — see MOUND 1

hillbilly *n* an awkward or simple person especially from a small town or the country — see HICK

hind *adj* being at or in the part of something opposite the front part — see BACK

hinder *vb* to create difficulty for the work or activity of — see HAMPER

hindmost *adj* **1** being at or in the part of something opposite the front part — see BACK

2 following all others of the same kind in order or time — see LAST

hindrance *n* **1** something that makes movement or progress more difficult — see ENCUMBRANCE

2 something that stands in the way of one's progress or achievement — see OBSTACLE 1

hinge *vb* to be determined by, based on, or subject (to) — see DEPEND 1

hint *n* **1** a slight or indirect pointing to something (as a solution or explanation) ⟨can't you give me some *hint* as to where you're taking me?⟩

syn clue, cue, indication, inkling, intimation, lead, suggestion

rel breath, flicker, glimmer, glimpse, mention, scent, whiff, wind; hunch, idea, inspiration, notion; allusion, implication, inference, innuendo, insinuation; evidence, mark, overtone, pointer, sign, signal, telltale, token; assistance, nod, prompt, tip, tip-off, wink; feeling, foreboding, intuition, premonition, presentiment, suspicion; augury, foreshadower, foretaste, omen, portent, prefigurement, symptom

near ant answer, solution

2 a piece of advice or useful information especially from an expert — see ¹TIP 1

3 a very small amount — see PARTICLE 1

hint *vb* to convey an idea indirectly ⟨Cecilia kept *hinting* that she wanted an invitation to Patty's party⟩

syn allude, imply, indicate, infer, insinuate, intimate, suggest

rel advert, mention, point, refer, signal, signify; smack (of), smell (of)

near ant announce, declare, proclaim; elucidate, explain, spell out

hinterland *n* a rural region that forms the edge of the settled or developed part of a country — see FRONTIER 2

hip *adj* having inside information — see WISE 2

hire *n* **1** the state of being provided with a paying job ⟨college graduates seeking *hire* by big corporations⟩

syn employ, employment, engagement

rel appointment, assignment, conscription, enlistment, recruitment; incumbency, tenure; occupation, place, position, post, situation, work

near ant boot, discharge, dismissal, firing, removal, sack; demotion, suspension; furlough, layoff, leave, liberty, retirement

ant joblessness, unemployment

2 the money paid regularly to a person for labor or services — see WAGE

hire *vb* **1** to take or get the temporary use of (something) for a set sum ⟨the Young's *hired* a limousine for their daughter's wedding⟩

syn charter, engage, lease, rent

rel sublease, sublet; check out; arrange (for), bespeak, book, contract (for), order, reserve, sign up (for)

2 to provide with a paying job — see EMPLOY 1

hireling *n* one who works for another for wages or a salary — see EMPLOYEE

hirsute *adj* covered with or as if with hair — see HAIRY 1

hiss *n* **1** a sound similar to the speech sound \s\ stretched out ⟨the *hiss* of air escaping from a balloon⟩

syn fizz, sizzle, swish, whish, whiz (*or* whizz)

rel wheeze, whistle, whoosh, zip; sibilant

2 a vocal sound made to express scorn or disapproval — see CATCALL

hiss *vb* to make a sound like that of stretching out the speech sound \s\ ⟨the frightened kitten *hissed* at us when we tried to pick it up⟩

syn fizz, sizzle, swish, whish, whiz (*or* whizz)

rel wheeze, whistle, whoosh, zip; bubble, effervesce; buzz, drone, hum

historian *n* a student or writer of history ⟨*historians* are still trying to sort out fact from fiction in the story of Kateri Tekakwitha, the Lily of the Mohawks⟩

syn annalist, chronicler

rel autobiographer, biographer; archivist, chronologist, genealogist

historical *adj* restricted to or based on fact — see FACTUAL 1

history *n* **1** an account of important events in the order in which they happened ⟨a *history* of the American civil rights movement during the 1960s⟩

syn annals, chronicle, record

rel autobiography, diary, journal, memoir, reminiscence(s); biography, life; epic, legend, narrative, saga, story, tale; archives, documentation, log, register, report; chronology, genealogy

2 a relating of events usually in the order in which they happened — see ACCOUNT 1

3 the events or experience of former times — see PAST

histrionic *adj* **1** given to or marked by attention-getting behavior suggestive of stage acting — see THEATRICAL 1

2 having the general quality or effect of a stage performance — see DRAMATIC 1

hit *n* **1** a person or thing that is successful ⟨the new babysitter turned out to be a great *hit* with the kids⟩

syn blockbuster, megahit, smash, success, winner

rel corker, crackerjack, dandy, jim-dandy, pip, prizewinner; gem, jewel, treasure; marvel, phenomenon, sensation, wonder; coup, triumph, victory

near ant disappointment, fizzle, lemon, loser

ant bummer, bust, catastrophe, debacle (*also* débâcle), dud, failure, fiasco, flop, turkey, washout

2 a hard strike with a part of the body or an instrument — see ¹BLOW

hit *vb* **1** to deliver a blow to (someone or something) usually in a strong vigorous manner ⟨a good carpenter *hits* a nail just two or three times to drive it in⟩

---

syn synonym(s)   *rel* related words
ant antonym(s)   *near ant* near antonym(s)

syn bang, bash, bat, belt, bludgeon, bop, bust, clap, clobber, clout, crack, hammer, knock, paste, pound, punch, rap, slam, slap, slog, slug, smack, smite, sock, strike, swat, swipe, thump, thwack, wallop, whack, whale, zap

rel batter, beat, buffet, bung, chop, drub, lace, lambaste (*or* lambast), lick, mangle, maul, pelt, pepper, pummel, rough; bunt, flick, stroke, tap; bump, butt, jab, jostle, kick, knee, poke, prod, push, shove, stamp; bowl (over), knock (down); cane, club, cudgel, flail, flog, lash, slash, spear, stab, switch, thrash, whip; brain

2 to come into usually forceful contact with something ⟨when she fell on the ice, she *hit* hard and badly bruised her elbow⟩

syn bang, bash, bump, collide, crash, impact, impinge, knock, ram, slam, smash, strike, swipe, thud

rel bounce, carom, glance, rebound, ricochet, skim, skip; contact, land, touch; brush, graze, kiss, nudge, scrape, shave, sweep; bulldoze, jostle, muscle, press, push

near ant miss, skirt

3 to obtain (as a goal) through effort — see ACHIEVE 1

hit (on *or* upon) *vb* to come upon after searching, study, or effort — see FIND 1

hit (upon) *vb* to come upon unexpectedly or by chance — see HAPPEN (ON *or* UPON)

hitch *n* a fixed period of time during which a person holds a job or position — see TERM 1

hitch *vb* **1** to move or cause to move with a sharp quick motion — see JERK 1

2 to put or bring together so as to form a new and longer whole — see CONNECT 1

3 to put securely in place or in a desired position — see FASTEN 2

4 to travel by securing free rides — see HITCHHIKE

hitcher *n* one who hitchhikes — see HITCHHIKER

hitchhike *vb* to travel by securing free rides ⟨Andrew *hitchhiked* from Baltimore to attend his sister's wedding in New Jersey⟩

syn hitch, thumb

rel bum; stow away; hijack (*also* highjack)

hitchhiker *n* one who hitchhikes ⟨on the highway out of town we picked up a *hitchhiker* who was trying to get to his sister's wedding⟩

syn hitcher

rel stowaway; hijacker

hither *adj* being the less far of two — see NEAR 1

hitherto *adv* up to this or that time ⟨at the talent show Kyle revealed his *hitherto* unknown gift for doing impressions⟩

syn heretofore, theretofore, thus far, yet

rel before, formerly, previously

near ant afterward (*or* afterwards), later, subsequently; hereupon, thereupon

ant henceforth, henceforward, hereafter, thenceforth, thenceforward (*also* thenceforwards), thereafter

hit–or–miss *adj* lacking a definite plan, purpose, or pattern — see RANDOM

hit or miss *adv* without definite aim, direction, rule, or method ⟨Angelo was learning Spanish *hit or miss*, mostly just by hearing his friends speak it⟩

syn aimlessly, anyhow, anyway, anywise, desultorily, erratically, haphazard, haphazardly, helter-skelter, irregularly, randomly

rel capriciously, carelessly, casually, indiscriminately, informally, offhand, offhandedly, promiscuously, whimsically; accidentally, fortuitously, inadvertently, unconsciously, unintentionally, unwittingly; disconnectedly, disjointedly, fitfully, intermittently, spottily, unpredictably; higgledy-piggledy, topsy-turvy

phrases at random

near ant carefully, formally, meticulously, orderly, punctiliously; deliberately, intentionally, purposefully, purposely

ant methodically, systematically

hoagie *n* a large sandwich on a long split roll — see SUBMARINE

hoar *adj* dating or surviving from the distant past — see ANCIENT 1

hoar *n* a covering of tiny ice crystals on a cold surface — see FROST

hoard *n* **1** a supply stored up and often hidden away ⟨Dad was upset when Mom put his entire *hoard* of empty yogurt containers in the recycling bin⟩

syn cache, stash, stockpile, store

rel coffers, deposit, funds, nest egg, savings, sinking fund, treasure; inventory, reserve, reservoir, stock; provisions, resources; accumulation, collection; repertory

2 a collection of things kept available for future use or need — see STORE 1

hoard *vb* to put (something of future use or value) in a safe or secret place ⟨Dad's been *hoarding* empty yogurt containers all winter, with the intention of using them to start seedlings in the spring⟩

syn cache, lay away, lay up, put by, salt away, squirrel (away), stash, stockpile, store, stow

rel accumulate, acquire, amass, assemble, collect, concentrate, garner, gather, round up, scrape (together); heap, pile, stack; conserve, husband, preserve; bank, deposit, hold, keep, reserve, retain, save, stock, withhold; conceal, ensconce, secrete

phrases set aside

near ant discard, dump, throw away, throw out; consume, squander, use up, waste; hand over, relinquish, surrender; blow, dissipate, fritter (away), lavish, misspend, run through, spend; deplete, exhaust, expend; dispel, disperse, dissipate, scatter

hoarfrost *n* a covering of tiny ice crystals on a cold surface — see FROST

hoarse *adj* harsh and dry in sound ⟨the dying man spoke in a *hoarse* whisper⟩

syn coarse, croaking, grating, gravel, gravelly, gruff, husky, rasping, raspy, scratchy, throaty

rel guttural; abrasive, cacophonous, discordant, grinding, jarring, rough, scraping, scratching; cawing, raucous, squawking, strident; choked, cracked, strained, strangled

near ant gentle, gliding, golden, liquid, mellifluous, mellow, sweet, tender; satiny, silken, smooth, soft, velvety

hoary *adj* dating or surviving from the distant past — see ANCIENT 1

hoax *n* an imitation that is passed off as genuine — see FAKE 1

hoax *vb* to cause to believe what is untrue — see DECEIVE

hoaxer *n* **1** a dishonest person who uses clever means to cheat others out of something of value — see TRICKSTER 1

2 one who makes false claims of identity or expertise — see IMPOSTOR

hob *n* playful, reckless behavior that is not intended to cause serious harm — see MISCHIEF 1

hobble *vb* **1** to create difficulty for the work or activity of — see HAMPER

2 to walk while favoring one leg — see LIMP 1

hobgoblin *n* **1** an imaginary being usually having a small human form and magical powers — see FAIRY

2 something or someone that causes fear or dread especially without reason — see BOGEY 1

hobnob *vb* **1** to come or be together as friends — see ASSOCIATE 1

2 to take part in social activities — see SOCIALIZE

hobnobber *n* a person frequently seen in the company of another — see ASSOCIATE 1

hobo *n* a homeless wanderer who may beg or steal for a living — see TRAMP

hock *vb* to leave as a guarantee of repayment of a loan — see PAWN

hodgepodge *n* an unorganized collection or mixture of various things — see MISCELLANY 1

hog *n* one who eats greedily or too much — see GLUTTON

hoggish *adj* having a huge appetite — see VORACIOUS 1

hogshead *n* an enclosed wooden vessel for holding beverages — see CASK

hogwash *n* **1** language, behavior, or ideas that are absurd and contrary to good sense — see NONSENSE 1

2 unintelligible or meaningless talk — see GIBBERISH

hoist *vb* **1** to lift with effort — see HEAVE 1

2 to move from a lower to a higher place or position — see RAISE 1

hold *n* **1** the act or manner of holding ⟨make sure you have a firm *hold* on the chain saw before you turn it on⟩

syn clasp, grapple, grasp, grip

rel anchorage, leverage, purchase; grab, seizure; foothold, footing, toehold; embrace, hug

near ant release, relinquishment

2 a structure or place from which one can resist attack — see FORT

3 the right or means to command or control others — see POWER 1

hold *vb* **1** to have or keep in one's hands ⟨this casserole dish is too hot to *hold*, so grab a potholder⟩

syn clench, cling (to), clutch, grip, hang on (to), hold on (to)

rel bear, carry; catch, grapple, nab, seize, snatch, take; feel, finger, handle, paw; clasp, embrace, grasp, hug

near ant drop, give, hand, unclasp, unhand; release, relinquish

2 to continue to have in one's possession or power — see KEEP 2

3 to have as an opinion — see BELIEVE 2

4 to have within — see CONTAIN 1

5 to keep in one's mind or heart — see HARBOR 1

6 to keep, control, or experience as one's own — see HAVE 1

7 to make or have room for — see ACCOMMODATE 1

8 to reach for and take hold of by embracing with the fingers or arms — see TAKE 1

9 to think of in a particular way — see CONSIDER 1

hold (up) *vb* **1** to continue to operate or to meet one's needs — see HOLD OUT

2 to remain indefinitely in existence or in the same state — see CONTINUE 1

hold back *vb* to create difficulty for the work or activity of — see HAMPER

holder *n* **1** one who has a legal or rightful claim to ownership — see PROPRIETOR

2 something into which a liquid or smaller objects can be put for storage or transportation — see CONTAINER

hold in *vb* to keep from exceeding a desirable degree or level (as of expression) — see CONTROL 1

holding *n* **1** a decision made by a court or tribunal regarding a case it has heard — see SENTENCE

2 *usually* **holdings** *pl* transportable items that one owns — see POSSESSION 2

hold off (on) *vb* to assign to a later time — see POSTPONE

hold on *vb* **1** to remain indefinitely in existence or in the same state — see CONTINUE 1

2 to remain in place in readiness or expectation of something — see WAIT

hold on (to) *vb* to have or keep in one's hands — see HOLD 1

hold out *vb* to continue to operate or to meet one's needs ⟨we hoped our supply of firewood would *hold out* until power was restored⟩ ⟨luckily, the old outboard motor *held out* till we made it to shore⟩

---

syn synonym(s)   *rel* related words
ant antonym(s)   *near ant* near antonym(s)

syn hold (up), last, keep up, prevail, survive

rel bear up, carry on, cope, endure, go, hang in, persevere; continue, draw out, hang on, linger, persist, remain, stretch

near ant break down, collapse, conk (out), crash, die, expire, stall, stop; run down, wane

ant fail, fizzle, give out, go out, peter (out), run out

holdup *n* an instance or period of being prevented from going about one's business — see DELAY

hold up *vb* 1 to assign to a later time — see POSTPONE

2 to bring (something) to a standstill — see ¹HALT 1

3 to create difficulty for the work or activity of — see HAMPER

hole *n* 1 a place in a surface allowing passage into or through a thing ⟨Mark was beside himself after seeing that his little sister had punched *holes* in his homework⟩

syn aperture, opening, orifice, perforation

rel chink, cleft, crack, cranny, crevice, cut, breach, break, fissure, gash, notch, rent, rift, rupture, slash, slit, split; gap, slot, space; exit, mouth, outlet, pore, vent; entrance, inlet, intake; pinprick, punch, puncture; armhole, buttonhole, knothole, peephole, pinhole, wormhole

near ant fill, filler, filling, patch, plug, seal, stopper; barrier, blockage, obstacle, obstruction

2 a sunken area forming a separate space ⟨Ann dug a *hole* big enough to plant the tree⟩

syn cavity, concavity, dent, depression, dint, hollow, indentation, pit, recess

rel burrow, cave, cavern, ditch, excavation, furrow, groove, trench, trough; basin, bowl, valley; alcove, cleft, niche, nook, opening, recess, socket; alveolus, dimple, gouge, notch, impression, pocket; chuckhole, crater, posthole, pothole, sinkhole, wallow, waterhole, well; abyss, chasm, gulf, vacuity, vacuum, void

near ant hill, mound, projection, rise; bump, lump, pimple, swell, swelling, tumor

ant bulge, convexity, protrusion, protuberance

3 a difficult, puzzling, or embarrassing situation from which there is no easy escape — see PREDICAMENT

4 a dirty or messy place — see PIGPEN

5 an open space in a barrier (as a wall or hedge) — see GAP 1

6 the shelter or resting place of a wild animal — see DEN 1

hole *vb* to make a hole or series of holes in — see PERFORATE

holiday *n, chiefly British* a period during which the usual routine of school or work is suspended — see VACATION

holiday *vb* to take or spend a vacation — see VACATION

holiness *n* the quality or state of being spiritually pure or virtuous ⟨known throughout the world for his *holiness,* the prophet was visited daily by hundreds of pilgrims⟩

syn blessedness, devoutness, godliness, piety, piousness, sainthood, saintliness, saintship, sanctity

rel asceticism, devotion, morality, prayerfulness, religiousness, spirituality; righteousness, virtuousness

near ant blasphemousness, irreverence, sacrilegiousness; depravity, sinfulness, wickedness

ant godlessness, impiety, ungodliness, unholiness

holler *n* a loud vocal expression of strong emotion — see SHOUT

holler *vb* to speak so as to be heard at a distance — see CALL 1

hollow *adj* curved inward ⟨there's a *hollow* spot in the mattress where Jim sleeps⟩

syn concave, dented, depressed, indented, recessed, sunken

rel alveolar, cavernous, cuplike, cupped; dimpled, pockmarked; compressed, condensed, contracted, diminished, reduced

near ant ballooning, bloated, blown up, bulbous, distended, enlarged, expanded, extended, inflated, jutting, projecting, puffed (up), puffy, risen, swollen; domed, globular, rounded, spherical

ant bulging, convex, protruding, protuberant

hollow *n* 1 a sunken area forming a separate space — see HOLE 2

2 an area of lowland between hills or mountains — see VALLEY

holocaust *n* a destructive burning — see FIRE

holy *adj* 1 showing a devotion to God and to a life of virtue ⟨the *holy* monk spent many hours on his knees in prayer⟩

syn devout, godly, pious, religious, sainted, saintly

rel ascetic, prayerful, reverent, reverential, spiritual, worshipful; beatified, blessed, canonized, venerable; angelic (or angelical); cherubic; chaste, pure, righteous, virtuous

near ant blasphemous, desecrating, irreverent, profane, sacrilegious, unspiritual; backsliding, unfaithful; sinful, sinning, wicked

ant faithless, godless, impious, irreligious, ungodly, unholy

2 set apart or worthy of veneration by association with God ⟨the Torah contains the *holy* writings of Judaism⟩

syn blessed, consecrated, hallowed, sacred, sacrosanct, sanctified

rel adored, enshrined, glorified, revered, venerated, worshipped (*also* worshiped); ceremonial, liturgical, priestly, religious, ritual, spiritual; biblical, scriptural

near ant nonreligious, unspiritual; earthly, mundane, secular, temporal, worldly

ant unconsecrated, unhallowed, unsanctified

3 of, relating to, or being God ⟨the *Holy* Trinity⟩
syn blessed, divine, godlike, heavenly, sacred, supernatural
rel eternal, everlasting, immortal; almighty, omnipotent, omniscient, supreme
near ant human, mortal
4 not to be violated, criticized, or tampered with — see SACRED 1

Holy Writ *n* a book made up of the writings accepted by Christians as coming from God — see BIBLE

homage *n* **1** a formal expression of praise — see ENCOMIUM
2 public acknowledgment or admiration for an achievement — see GLORY 1

hombre *n* an adult male human being — see MAN 1

home *n* **1** the place where one lives ⟨as we entered his 34-room mansion, Ernest said, "Welcome to my humble *home* !"⟩
syn abode, diggings, domicile, dwelling, fireside, habitation, hearth, hearthstone, house, lodging, pad, place, quarters, residence, roof
rel accommodations, housing, nest, residency, shelter; bungalow, cabin, chalet, cottage; duplex, ranch, split level, town house, tract house, triplex; apartment, apartment house, condominium, flat, tenement, tenement house, walk-up; penthouse, salon, suite; barracks, boardinghouse, dorm, dormitory, lodgment (*or* lodgement), lodging house, room(s), rooming house; castle, château, country seat, estate, manor, manor house, mansion, palace, villa; farmhouse, grange, hacienda, homestead, ranch house; houseboat, mobile home, motor home, trailer; hermitage, manse, parsonage, vicarage; hovel, hut, shack
2 the place where a plant or animal is usually or naturally found ⟨the American south, the *home* of the armadillo⟩
syn habitat, niche, range, territory
rel element, environment, environs, haunt, locality, milieu, neighborhood, setting, surroundings
3 the land of one's birth, residence, or citizenship — see COUNTRY 1

homeboy *n* a violent, brutal person who is often a member of an organized gang — see HOODLUM

homeland *n* the land of one's birth, residence, or citizenship — see COUNTRY 1

homely *adj* unpleasant to look at — see UGLY 1

homesteader *n* a person who settles in a new region — see FRONTIERSMAN

homicidal *adj* eager for or marked by the shedding of blood, extreme violence, or killing — see BLOODTHIRSTY

homicide *n* the intentional and unlawful taking of another person's life ⟨the missing man was thought to be the victim of a *homicide*, but his body was never found⟩
syn foul play, murder, slaying

rel killing, manslaughter; bloodshed, butchery, carnage, decimation, destruction, massacre, slaughter; assassination, execution; euthanasia, mercy killing

homily *n* a public speech usually by a member of the clergy for the purpose of giving moral guidance or uplift — see SERMON

homogenize *vb* to make agree with a single established standard or model — see STANDARDIZE

Homo sapiens *n* the human race — see MANKIND

hone *vb* **1** to make sharp or sharper — see SHARPEN
2 to make smooth by friction — see GRIND 1

honed *adj* having an edge thin enough to cut or pierce something — see SHARP 1

honest *adj* **1** being in the habit of telling the truth — see TRUTHFUL
2 conforming to a high standard of morality or virtue — see GOOD 2
3 following the accepted rules of moral conduct — see HONORABLE 1
4 free from any intent to deceive or impress others — see GUILELESS
5 free in expressing one's true feelings and opinions — see FRANK
6 guided by or in accordance with one's sense of right and wrong — see CONSCIENTIOUS 1

honestly *adv* to tell the truth — see ACTUALLY 1

honesty *n* **1** devotion to telling the truth ⟨George Washington has gone down in history for his *honesty*⟩
syn integrity, probity, truthfulness, veracity, verity
rel honor, incorruptibility; candidness, candor, frankness, good faith, sincerity, straightforwardness; dependability, reliability, reliableness, trustworthiness; accuracy, objectivity; authenticity, correctness, genuineness; credibility
near ant deception, dissembling, dissimulation, duplicity, fakery, falseness, falsity, fraudulentness, hypocrisy, insincerity; beguilement, craftiness, cunning, furtiveness, guile, insidiousness, oiliness, slickness, slipperiness, slyness, smoothness, trickery, underhandedness, wiliness; equivocation, prevarication; exaggeration, inaccuracy
ant deceit, deceitfulness, dishonesty, lying, mendacity, untruthfulness
2 conduct that conforms to an accepted standard of right and wrong — see MORALITY 1
3 faithfulness to high moral standards — see HONOR 1

honey *n* a person with whom one is in love — see SWEETHEART

honor *n* **1** faithfulness to high moral standards ⟨the mayor, a man of *honor*, never broke a promise to the voters⟩
syn honesty, integrity, probity, rectitude, righteousness, uprightness
rel blamelessness, character, conscientiousness, decency, fairness, high-mind-

edness, incorruptibility, justice, morality, nobility, reputability, respectability, scrupulousness, virtue, virtuousness

near ant corruptibility, corruption, corruptness, debasement, decadence, degeneracy, depravity, disgracefulness, disreputableness, dissipation, dissoluteness, looseness, perversion, profligacy, shamelessness, venality; blameworthiness, criminality, crookedness, dishonesty, immorality, unrighteousness, unscrupulousness; knavery, rascality, roguishness; meanness, reprehensibleness, rottenness, sinfulness, vileness, villainy, wretchedness

ant baseness, lowness

2 an asset that brings praise or renown — see GLORY 2

3 public acknowledgment or admiration for an achievement — see GLORY 1

4 something given in recognition of achievement — see AWARD

5 something granted as a special favor — see PRIVILEGE

honor *vb* to show appreciation, respect, or affection for (someone) with a public celebration ⟨the newlyweds were *honored* with a dinner given by the bride's grandmother⟩

syn fete (*or* fête), recognize

rel acknowledge, cite, commend, compliment, credit, thank; extol (*also* extoll), glorify, laud, praise; acclaim, applaud, cheer, hail, salute; celebrate, commemorate, memorialize, observe; congratulate, felicitate

near ant bad-mouth, defame, libel, malign, slander; boo, hiss, hoot, jeer; censure, condemn, damn, denounce, reprobate; mock, put down, ridicule, slight

honorable *adj* **1** following the accepted rules of moral conduct ⟨the only *honorable* thing to do is to admit that you were wrong and apologize⟩

syn decent, ethical, honest, just, noble, principled, respectable, righteous, upright, upstanding

rel decorous, proper, seemly; blameless, guiltless, irreproachable, unassailable, unimpeachable; chivalrous, highminded, right-minded; conscientious, fair, good, incorruptible, moral, reputable, respected, scrupulous, uncorrupted, virtuous

near ant bad, blackguardly, corrupt, criminal, crooked, immoral, iniquitous, knavish, mean, rascally, reprehensible, roguish, rotten, scoundrelly, sinful; unfair, unscrupulous, vile, villainous, wicked, wretched; blamable, blameworthy, censurable; debased, debauched, decadent, degenerate, depraved, disgraceful, disreputable, dissipated, dissolute, libertine, loose, perverted, profligate, reprobate, shameful, unscrupulous, venal

ant base, dishonest, ignoble, low, unethical, unjust, unprincipled, unrighteous

2 conforming to a high standard of morality or virtue — see GOOD 2

3 guided by or in accordance with one's sense of right and wrong — see CONSCIENTIOUS 1

honorably *adv* in a manner befitting a person of the highest character and ideals — see GREATLY 1

¹**hood** *n* a violent, brutal person who is often a member of an organized gang — see HOODLUM

²**hood** *n* something that covers or conceals like a piece of cloth — see CLOAK 1

hoodlum *n* a violent, brutal person who is often a member of an organized gang ⟨a couple of *hoodlums* held up the convenience store⟩

syn bully, gangster, goon, homeboy, hood, mobster, mug, punk, roughneck, rowdy, ruffian, thug, tough, toughie

rel cutthroat, scoundrel, villain; assassin, bandit, bravo, brigand, criminal, crook, desperado, felon, gunman, highwayman, lawbreaker, mafioso, outlaw, perpetrator, pickpocket, racketeer, robber, swindler, thief

hoodoo *n* something that brings bad luck — see JINX

hoodwink *vb* to cause to believe what is untrue — see DECEIVE

hoof (it) *vb* **1** to go on foot — see WALK

2 to perform a series of usually rhythmic bodily movements to music — see DANCE 1

hook *n* a hard strike with a part of the body or an instrument — see ¹BLOW

hook *vb* **1** to cause to turn away from a straight line — see BEND 1

2 to put or bring together so as to form a new and larger whole — see CONNECT 1

3 to take (something) without right and with an intent to keep — see STEAL 1

4 to take physical control or possession of (something) suddenly or forcibly — see CATCH 1

5 to turn away from a straight line or course — see CURVE 1

hookup *n* the state of having shared interests or efforts (as in social or business matters) — see ASSOCIATION 1

hoop *n* a circular strip — see RING 2

hoosegow *n* a place of confinement for persons held in lawful custody — see JAIL

hoot *n* **1** a loud vocal expression of strong emotion — see SHOUT

2 a vocal sound made to express scorn or disapproval — see CATCALL

3 the smallest amount or part imaginable — see JOT

hop *n* **1** a social gathering for dancing — see DANCE

2 an act of leaping into the air — see JUMP 1

hop *vb* **1** to move with a light bouncing step — see SKIP 1

2 to propel oneself upward or forward into the air — see JUMP 1

hope (for) *vb* to believe in the future occurrence of (something) — see EXPECT

hopeful *adj* **1** having qualities which inspire hope ⟨economists are offering a *hopeful* forecast for a healthy economy in the coming year⟩

syn auspicious, bright, encouraging, fair, golden, heartening, likely, optimistic, promising, propitious, rose-colored, rosy, upbeat

rel cheering, comforting, reassuring; assured, confident, decisive, doubtless, positive, sure, unhesitating; bullish, favorable, good

near ant cheerless, comfortless; doubtful, dubious, uncertain; bearish, grim, negative, unfavorable

ant bleak, dark, desperate, discouraging, disheartening, dismal, dreary, gloomy, hopeless, inauspicious, pessimistic, unlikely, unpromising

2 pointing toward a happy outcome — see FAVORABLE 2

hopeful *n* one who seeks an office, honor, position, or award — see CANDIDATE

hopeless *adj* **1** not capable of being cured or reformed ⟨a *hopeless* optimist who looked for the good in everyone and everything⟩ ⟨a *hopeless* criminal who spent most of his life in jail⟩

syn incorrigible, incurable, irrecoverable, irredeemable, irremediable, irretrievable, unrecoverable, unredeemable

rel irreparable, irreversible; unpromising; impenitent, unreformed, unregenerate, unrepentant

near ant reversible; promising; penitent, repentant; repairable, reparable, salvageable

ant correctable, curable, reclaimable, recoverable, redeemable, reformable, remediable, retrievable

2 emphasizing or expecting the worst — see PESSIMISTIC 1

3 incapable of being solved or accomplished — see IMPOSSIBLE

hopelessness *n* utter loss of hope — see DESPAIR 1

horde *n* a great number of persons or things gathered together — see CROWD 1

horn *n* something shaped like a hollow cone and used as a container — see CORNET

horrendous *adj* **1** causing fear — see FEARFUL 1

2 causing intense displeasure, disgust, or resentment — see OFFENSIVE 1

3 extremely disturbing or repellent — see HORRIBLE 1

horrible *adj* **1** extremely disturbing or repellent ⟨a *horrible* car accident that left eyewitnesses in a state of shock⟩

syn appalling, atrocious, awful, dreadful, frightful, ghastly, grisly, gruesome, hideous, horrendous, horrid, horrifying, lurid, macabre, monstrous, nightmarish, shocking, terrible

rel bloodcurdling, dire, direful, fearful, fearsome, forbidding, formidable, frightening, hair-raising, terrifying; abhorrent, deplorable, disagreeable, disgusting, dis-

tasteful, loathsome, nauseating, obnoxious, offensive, repugnant, repulsive, revolting, sickening; abominable, evil, foul, heinous, noxious, odious, unspeakable, vile

near ant agreeable, appealing, attractive, enticing, inviting; cheering, comforting, soothing

2 causing fear — see FEARFUL 1

3 causing intense displeasure, disgust, or resentment — see OFFENSIVE 1

horrid *adj* **1** causing intense displeasure, disgust, or resentment — see OFFENSIVE 1

2 extremely disturbing or repellent — see HORRIBLE 1

horridness *n* the quality of inspiring intense dread or dismay — see HORROR 1

horrified *adj* filled with fear or dread — see AFRAID 1

horrify *vb* to strike with fear — see FRIGHTEN

horrifying *adj* **1** causing fear — see FEARFUL 1

2 extremely disturbing or repellent — see HORRIBLE 1

horror *n* **1** the quality of inspiring intense dread or dismay ⟨it's difficult to even begin to comprehend the *horror* of the Holocaust⟩

syn atrociousness, atrocity, awfulness, dreadfulness, frightfulness, ghastliness, grisliness, gruesomeness, hideousness, horridness, monstrosity, repulsiveness

rel badness, baseness, diabolicalness, evil, foulness, heinousness, immorality, iniquity, invidiousness, nefariousness, ungodliness, viciousness, vileness, wickedness; accursedness, cursedness, deplorableness, despicableness, detestableness, execrableness, hatefulness, loathsomeness, reprehensibleness; creepiness, eeriness, fearfulness, fearsomeness, ghostliness, scariness; agony, hellishness, misery, torture

near ant agreeableness, delightfulness, pleasantness; allurement, appeal, attraction, attractiveness, desirability, desirableness

2 a situation or state that causes great suffering and unhappiness — see HELL 2

3 something unpleasant to look at — see EYESORE

4 the emotion experienced in the presence or threat of danger — see FEAR

horse *n* a large hoofed domestic animal that is used for carrying or drawing loads and for riding ⟨the mounted police stable their *horses* in the city park⟩

syn equine, nag, steed

rel colt, filly, foal, gelding, mare, stallion; bronco, mustang, pony; charger, courser, cow pony, mount, palfrey, prancer, quarter horse, racehorse, saddle horse, trotter, war-horse, workhorse; bay, black, buckskin, chestnut, dun, palomino, pinto, roan, sorrel; cob, jade, plug

horse (around) *vb* to engage in attention-getting playful or boisterous behavior — see CUT UP

---

horseplay *n* wildly playful or mischievous behavior ⟨when he saw us spraying each other with the hose instead of washing the car, Dad yelled, "Cut out the *horseplay*!"⟩

syn clowning, foolery, high jinks, horsing (around), monkeying, monkeyshines, roughhouse, roughhousing, shenanigans, skylarking, tomfoolery

rel buffoonery, clownishness, foolishness, funning; jesting, joking, nonsense, waggery; boisterousness, rowdiness; devilry (*or* deviltry), impishness, mischief, mischievousness, prankishness, roguishness, trickery; cavorting, frivolity, frolicking, gamboling (*or* gambolling), merrymaking, playfulness, revelry, roistering, romping, sporting, sportiveness

horse sense *n* the ability to make intelligent decisions especially in everyday matters — see COMMON SENSE

horse–trade *vb* to talk over or dispute the terms of a purchase — see BARGAIN

horsewhip *vb* to strike repeatedly with something long and thin or flexible — see WHIP 1

horsing (around) *n* wildly playful or mischievous behavior — see HORSEPLAY

hose *n* a close-fitting covering for the foot and leg — see STOCKING

hospice *n* a place that provides rooms and usually a public dining room for overnight guests — see HOTEL

hospitable *adj* showing a natural kindness and courtesy especially in social situations — see GRACIOUS 1

host *n* 1 a great number of persons or things gathered together — see CROWD 1
2 a large body of men and women organized for land warfare — see ARMY 1

hostel *n* a place that provides rooms and usually a public dining room for overnight guests — see HOTEL

hostelry *n* a place that provides rooms and usually a public dining room for overnight guests — see HOTEL

hostile *adj* 1 marked by opposition or ill will ⟨our landlord has a *hostile* attitude toward foreigners and refuses to rent to them⟩

syn antagonistic, inhospitable, inimical, jaundiced, negative, unfriendly, unsympathetic

rel adverse, bellicose, belligerent, clashing, conflicting, contentious, contrary, opposed, pugnacious, quarrelsome, resisting; antisocial, cold, cool, disagreeable, disapproving, distant, frigid, icy, biased, prejudiced; discourteous, impolite, rude, surly, uncivil, unfavorable, unkind, unpleasant, unsociable; acrimonious, antipathetic, bitter, hateful, malevolent, opprobrious, rancorous, spiteful, unloving, vindictive, virulent

near ant affable, amiable, amicable, companionable, convivial, cordial, civil, genial, gracious, gregarious, neighborly, pleasant, sociable, social, warm; affectionate, devoted, kind, loving, nice, sweet; accepting, agreeable, approving,

benign, empathetic, favorable, understanding, warmhearted, welcoming

ant friendly, hospitable, sympathetic
2 opposed to one's interests — see ADVERSE 1

hostility *n* 1 a deep-seated ill will — see ENMITY
2 **hostilities** *pl* a state of armed violent struggle between states, nations, or groups — see WAR 1

hot *adj* 1 having a notably high temperature ⟨the casserole, just out of the oven, was too *hot* to eat⟩

syn broiling, burning, fiery, piping hot, red-hot, roasting, scalding, scorching, searing, sultry, superheated, sweltering, torrid

rel blazing, glowing, molten, sizzling; heated, overheated, reheated, warmed; snug, toasty, warm; feverish, flushed, inflamed; muggy, steamy, summery, tropical

near ant chilly, cool, frosty, nippy, snowy, subzero, wintry; cooled, refrigerated, unheated, unthawed; benumbed, numb, shivering; lukewarm, temperate, tepid

ant arctic, chill, chilled, cold, freezing, frigid, frozen, glacial, ice-cold, iced, icy
2 being or involving the latest methods, concepts, information, or styles — see MODERN
3 enjoying widespread favor or approval — see POPULAR 1
4 marked by bursts of destructive force or intense activity — see VIOLENT 1
5 showing urgent desire or interest — see EAGER

hot air *n* 1 boastful speech or writing — see BOMBAST 1
2 language that is impressive-sounding but not meaningful or sincere — see RHETORIC 1

hot–blooded *adj* having or expressing great depth of feeling — see FERVENT

hotcake *n* a flat cake made from thin batter and cooked on both sides (as on a griddle) — see PANCAKE

hotchpotch *n* an unorganized collection or mixture of various things — see MISCELLANY 1

hotel *n* a place that provides rooms and usually a public dining room for overnight guests ⟨for their 50th anniversary they stayed at one of the finest *hotels* in San Francisco⟩

syn caravansary (*or* caravanserai), hospice, hostel, hostelry, inn, lodge, public house, tavern

rel bed-and-breakfast; accommodations, lodgings, rest; motel, motor court, resort, spa, youth hostel; camp, campground; bunkhouse, dorm, dormitory; boardinghouse, lodging house, rooming house

hotfoot *adv* with excessive or careless speed — see HASTILY 1

hotfoot (it) *vb* to proceed or move quickly — see HURRY 2

hothouse *n* a glass-enclosed building for growing plants — see CONSERVATORY

hotness *n* the state of enjoying widespread approval — see POPULARITY

hot war *n* a state of armed violent struggle between states, nations, or groups — see WAR 1

hound *n* a domestic mammal that is related to the wolves and foxes — see DOG

hound *vb* **1** to go after or on the track of — see FOLLOW 2

2 to subject (someone) to constant scoldings and sharp reminders — see NAG

hounding *n* the act of going after or in the tracks of another — see PURSUIT

house *n* **1** a commercial or industrial activity or organization — see ENTERPRISE 1

2 a group of persons who come from the same ancestor — see FAMILY 1

3 the place where one lives — see HOME 1

4 those who live as a family in one house — see HOUSEHOLD

house *vb* **1** to provide with living quarters or shelter ⟨some of the freshmen were temporarily *housed* in the gym while the new dorm was being finished⟩

syn accommodate, billet, board, bunk, chamber, domicile, encamp, harbor, lodge, put up, quarter, roof, shelter, take in

rel ensconce, home, roost, secure, stable, tent

near ant eject, evict

2 to close or shut in by or as if by barriers — see ENCLOSE 1

house cat *n* a small domestic animal known for catching mice — see CAT 1

household *adj* **1** of or relating to a household or family — see DOMESTIC 1

2 often observed or encountered — see COMMON 1

household *n* those who live as a family in one house ⟨a *household* that consists of a single mom, her two kids, and her widowed mother⟩

syn extended family, house, ménage

rel folks, kin, kindred, kinfolk, kinsfolk, kith; brood; nuclear family; clan, community

housekeeper *n* a female domestic servant — see MAID 1

housemaid *n* a female domestic servant — see MAID 1

housing *n* something that encloses another thing especially to protect it — see ¹CASE 1

hovel *n* a small, simply constructed, and often temporary dwelling — see SHACK

hover *vb* to rest or move along the surface of a liquid or in the air — see FLOAT

hover (over) *vb* to remain poised to inflict harm, danger, or distress on — see THREATEN

howbeit *adv* in spite of that — see HOWEVER

howbeit *conj* in spite of the fact that — see ALTHOUGH

however *adv* in spite of that ⟨I'm all out of eggs; *however,* I can still make us a nice breakfast⟩

syn howbeit, nevertheless, nonetheless, notwithstanding, still, though, withal, yet

rel after all, anyhow, regardless

howl *n* **1** a crying out in grief — see LAMENT 1

2 a loud vocal expression of strong emotion — see SHOUT

3 a violent shouting — see CLAMOR 1

howl *vb* **1** to make a long loud mournful sound ⟨several coyotes began *howling* close by as the sun went down⟩ ⟨the wind *howled* on the open plain⟩

syn bay, keen, wail, yowl

rel bawl, caterwaul, squall, yawp (*or* yaup), yell, yelp

2 to cry out loudly and emotionally — see SCREAM

hoydenish *adj* having qualities or traits that are traditionally considered inappropriate for a girl or woman — see UNFEMININE

hub *n* a thing or place that is of greatest importance to an activity or interest — see CENTER 1

hubbub *n* **1** a state of noisy, confused activity — see COMMOTION

2 a violent shouting — see CLAMOR 1

huckster *n* one who sells things outdoors — see PEDDLER

huddle *n* **1** a coming together of a number of persons for a specified purpose — see MEETING 1

2 a number of things considered as a unit — see GROUP 1

3 a usually small number of persons considered as a unit — see GROUP 2

huddle *vb* **1** to gather into a closely packed group — see PRESS 3

2 to lie low with the limbs close to the body — see CROUCH

hue *n* a property that becomes apparent when light falls on an object and by which things that are identical in form can be distinguished — see COLOR 1

hue and cry *n* a violent shouting — see CLAMOR 1

huff *n* **1** a state of nervous or irritated concern — see FRET

2 an outburst or display of excited anger — see TANTRUM

3 the feeling of being offended or resentful after a slight or indignity — see PIQUE

huffiness *n* readiness to show annoyance or impatience — see PETULANCE

hug *vb* to put one's arms around and press tightly — see EMBRACE 1

huge *adj* unusually large ⟨the old stadium was replaced by a *huge* new one that seats 100,000 spectators⟩

syn astronomical (*also* astronomic), bumper, colossal, cosmic, elephantine, enormous, giant, gigantic, grand, herculean, heroic, immense, jumbo, king-size (*or* king-sized), mammoth, massive, monster, monstrous, monumental, mountainous, prodigious, super, titanic,

---

syn synonym(s)   *rel* related words
ant antonym(s)   *near ant* near antonym(s)

tremendous, vast, vasty, whacking, whopping

rel big, bulky, considerable, extensive, good, goodly, good-sized, great, gross, handsome, hefty, hulking, largish, major, sizable (*or* sizeable), substantial, voluminous; august, formidable, grandiose, imposing, lofty, majestic; cavernous, monolithic, overwhelming, staggering, stupendous, towering; boundless, cosmic, immeasurable, infinite

near ant little, petite, pint-size (*or* pintsized), puny, small, smallish, undersized *ant* bitty, diminutive, microscopic (*or* microscopical), midget, miniature, minute, pocket, pygmy, teeny, teeny-weeny, tiny, wee

hugely *adv* **1** to a great degree — see VERY 1

2 to a large extent or degree — see GREATLY 2

hugeness *n* the quality or state of being very large — see IMMENSITY

hugger-mugger *adj* **1** lacking in order, neatness, and often cleanliness — see MESSY

2 undertaken or done so as to escape being observed or known by others — see SECRET 1

hulk *n* a big clumsy often slow-witted person — see OAF

hulking *adj* **1** of a size greater than average of its kind — see LARGE

2 strongly and heavily built — see ¹HUSKY

hull *vb* to remove the natural covering of — see PEEL

hullabaloo *n* **1** a state of noisy, confused activity — see COMMOTION

2 a violent shouting — see CLAMOR 1

hum *n* a monotonous sound like that of an insect in motion ⟨we heard the *hum* of an outboard motor and a few minutes later the small craft came into sight⟩

syn buzz, chirr, drone, purr, thrum, whir (*also* whirr), whiz (*or* whizz), zoom

rel babble, coo, gurgle, hiss, moan, murmur, rustle, sigh, whisper; whish, zing, zip

near ant bawl, howl, roar, scream, screech, shriek

hum *vb* to fly, turn, or move rapidly with a fluttering or vibratory sound — see WHIRR

human *adj* relating to or characteristic of human beings ⟨it's *human* nature to care about what people think of us⟩

syn mortal, natural

rel anthropoid, hominid, humanlike, humanoid

near ant angelic (*or* angelical), divine, godlike, superhuman, supernatural; immortal, omnipotent, omniscient; animal, beastly, bestial, brute; inhuman, robotic *ant* nonhuman

human *n* a member of the human race ⟨*humans* are the only mammals not endowed with a natural defense against the elements, such as fur or a thick hide⟩

syn being, bird, body, creature, customer, devil, guy, head, individual, life, man,

mortal, party, person, scout, sort, soul, specimen, thing, wight

rel hominid, homo, humanoid; brother, fellow, fellowman, neighbor; celebrity, personage, personality, self, somebody

near ant animal, beast, brute

humane *adj* **1** having or marked by sympathy and consideration for others ⟨*humane* guards who treated the prisoners decently⟩ ⟨the Geneva conventions spelled out standards for *humane* treatment of prisoners of war⟩

syn beneficent, benevolent, benignant, compassionate, good-hearted, kind, kindhearted, kindly, softhearted, sympathetic, tender, tenderhearted, warmhearted

rel attentive, considerate, thoughtful; affable, benign, cordial, friendly, gentle, good, good-natured, good-tempered, gracious, mild, nice, pleasant; clement, forbearing, forgiving, lenient, merciful, soft; patient, pitying, tolerant, understanding; altruistic, brotherly, charitable, generous, greathearted, humanitarian, magnanimous, noble, openhearted, philanthropic, unselfish, unsparing

near ant merciless, pitiless, ruthless; inconsiderate, insensitive, thoughtless, uncaring, unthinking; grim, hard-boiled, harsh, heavy-handed, severe, stern, tough, unsentimental; hateful, malevolent, malicious, mean, spiteful, virulent

ant barbarous, bestial, brutal, brutish, callous, cold-blooded, cruel, hardhearted, heartless, inhuman, inhumane, insensate, savage, unfeeling, unkind, unkindly, unsympathetic

2 having or showing the capacity for sharing the feelings of another — see SYMPATHETIC 1

humanitarian *adj* having or showing a concern for the welfare of others — see CHARITABLE 1

humanity *n* **1** human beings in general — see PEOPLE 1

2 the capacity for feeling for another's unhappiness or misfortune — see HEART 1

3 the human race — see MANKIND

humankind *n* **1** human beings in general — see PEOPLE 1

2 the human race — see MANKIND

humble *adj* **1** not having or showing any feelings of superiority, self-assertiveness, or showiness ⟨a medical scientist who remained remarkably *humble* even after winning the Nobel Prize⟩ ⟨even though she'd been twice proven wrong, Janet's attitude was still far from *humble*⟩

syn demure, lowly, meek, modest, retiring, unassuming, unpretentious

rel acquiescent, compliant, deferential, resigned, submissive, unaggressive, unassertive, yielding; cowering, cringing, shrinking; ingenuous, naive (*or* naïve), plain, simple, unaffected; bashful, diffident, mousy (*or* mousey), overmodest, passive, quiet, reserved, shy, subdued, timid, unobtrusive

near ant aggressive, assertive, audacious, bold, brash, brassy, cheeky, forward;

cocksure, cocky, confident, overconfident, self-confident; egocentric, egoistic, self-centered, self-satisfied; boastful, bombastic, vain, vainglorious; condescending, disdainful, dominant, dominating, domineering, imperious, lofty, lordly, magisterial, masterful, overbearing, patronizing, pontificating; flamboyant, flaunting, highfalutin, parading, ostentatious, showy

ant arrogant, conceited, egotistic (*or* egotistical), haughty, high-hat, pompous, presumptuous, pretentious, prideful, proud, self-assertive, self-conceited, self-important, stuck-up, supercilious, superior

2 belonging to the class of people of low social or economic rank — see IGNOBLE 1

humble *vb* to reduce to a lower standing in one's own eyes or in others' eyes ⟨Philip was utterly *humbled* by a crushing defeat in the first round of the state chess tournament⟩

syn abase, debase, degrade, demean, discredit, disgrace, dishonor, humiliate, lower, shame, smirch, take down

rel abash, discomfit, discountenance, embarrass, fluster, mortify; belittle, castigate, criticize, decry, depreciate, detract, disparage, minimize, put down, ridicule; bad-mouth, defame, defile, libel, malign, slander; affront, insult; censure, condemn, damn, denounce, reprobate

near ant acclaim, applaud, boast, celebrate, cite, commend, compliment, congratulate, decorate, eulogize, extol (*also* extoll), fete (*or* fête), hail, honor, laud, praise, salute, tout; acknowledge, recognize; highlight, play up, spotlight; dignify, ennoble, enshrine, glorify, magnify; lift, promote, raise, upgrade, uplift

ant aggrandize, elevate, exalt

humbleness *n* the absence of any feelings of being better than others — see HUMILITY

humbly *adv* in manner showing no signs of pride or self-assertion — see LOWLY

humbug *n* **1** an imitation that is passed off as genuine — see FAKE 1

2 language, behavior, or ideas that are absurd and contrary to good sense — see NONSENSE 1

3 one who makes false claims of identity or expertise — see IMPOSTOR

humbug *vb* to cause to believe what is untrue — see DECEIVE

humbuggery *n* language, behavior, or ideas that are absurd and contrary to good sense — see NONSENSE 1

humdrum *adj* causing weariness, restlessness, or lack of interest — see BORING

humid *adj* containing or characterized by an uncomfortable amount of moisture ⟨the air was so *humid* that our beach towels hanging on the line never really got dry⟩

syn muggy, sticky, sultry

rel summery, sweltering, torrid; semitropical (*also* semitropic), subtropical (*also* subtropic), tropic, tropical; close, heavy, oppressive, smothering, stifling, stuffy, suffocating; clammy, damp, dank, moist; drenched, dripping, soaked, sodden, soggy, sopping, soppy, waterlogged, wet

near ant bracing, cool, crisp, fresh, invigorating, refreshing; arid, baked, burned, burnt, dehydrated, desert, droughty, dusty, parched, scorched, seared, semiarid, sere, thirsty

ant dry

humidity *n* the amount of water suspended in the air in tiny droplets — see MOISTURE

humiliate *vb* to reduce to a lower standing in one's own eyes or in others' eyes — see HUMBLE

humility *n* the absence of any feelings of being better than others ⟨displaying genuine *humility*, the peace activist accepted the Nobel Prize on behalf of all who worked to end the violence⟩

syn demureness, humbleness, lowliness, meekness, modesty, retiringness

rel acquiescence, compliance, deference, resignedness, submission, submissiveness; ingenuousness, naïveté (*also* naivete); directness, plainness, simpleness; bashfulness, diffidence, passiveness, passivity, quietness, reserve, reservedness, shyness, timidity, timidness

near ant aggressiveness, assertiveness; audaciousness, boldness, brashness, brassiness, cheek, cheekiness, cockiness, forwardness, overconfidence, presumptuousness, temerity; impudence, insolence, nerve; boastfulness, self-centeredness, self-satisfaction; vanity, vaingloriousness; condescension, disdain, imperiousness, lordliness, masterfulness; flamboyance, ostentation, ostentatiousness, showiness

ant arrogance, conceit, egoism, egotism, haughtiness, pompousness, pretense (*or* pretence), pretension, pretentiousness, pride, pridefulness, superciliousness, superiority

hummer *n* an ambitious person who eagerly goes after what is desired — see GO-GETTER

humming *adj* marked by much life, movement, or activity — see ALIVE 2

humor *n* **1** the amusing quality or element in something ⟨Sarah failed to see any *humor* in being chased by the dog, but Tom thought it was quite funny⟩

syn drollness, funniness, hilariousness, humorousness, richness

rel amusement, enjoyment, fun, pleasure; absurdity, irony, laughableness, ludicrousness, ridiculousness; burlesque, caricature, comedy, farce, jest, lampoon, parody, satire, slapstick

near ant agony, anguish, heartache, misery, sorrow, woe

ant pathos

2 humorous entertainment — see COMEDY

---

syn synonym(s)   **rel** related words
ant antonym(s)   **near ant** near antonym(s)

3 a state of mind dominated by a particular emotion — see MOOD 1

humor vb to give in to (a desire) — see INDULGE

humorist n a person (as a writer) noted for or specializing in humor ⟨Mark Twain is perhaps America's most beloved *humorist*⟩

syn card, comedian, comic, jester, joker, jokester, wag, wit

rel comedienne, entertainer; banterer; cut up, kidder, practical joker, prankster, teaser, wisecracker; buffoon, clown, fool, harlequin, zany; caricaturist, lampooner, parodist, satirist

humorless adj not joking or playful in mood or manner — see SERIOUS 1

humorous adj 1 causing or intended to cause laughter — see FUNNY 1

2 given to or marked by mature intelligent humor — see WITTY

humorousness n the amusing quality or element in something — see HUMOR 1

hump vb 1 to devote serious and sustained effort — see LABOR

2 to proceed or move quickly — see HURRY 2

hunch vb to lie low with the limbs close to the body — see CROUCH

hung *also* **hanged** adj bending downward or forward — see NODDING

hunger n 1 a need or desire for food ⟨no amount of *hunger* would induce me to eat octopus⟩

syn appetite, emptiness, famishment

rel rapaciousness, ravenousness, voracity; malnutrition, starvation, undernourishment; craving, sweet tooth; stomach; famine, fast, hunger strike; gluttony, gourmandism, greed, hoggishness

near ant fill, fullness, glut, repletion, satiation, satiety, satisfaction

2 a strong wish for something — see DESIRE

3 urgent desire or interest — see EAGERNESS

hunger (for) vb to have an earnest wish to own or enjoy — see DESIRE

hungry adj 1 feeling a desire or need for food ⟨John was still *hungry* after eating only a muffin for breakfast⟩

syn empty, famished, starved, starving

rel rapacious, ravenous, voracious, wolfish; malnourished, underfed, undernourished; gluttonous, gormandizing, greedy, hoggish, insatiable, piggish

near ant engorged, glutted, gorged, overfed, overfull, replete, sated, satiated, stuffed, surfeited

ant full, satisfied

2 showing urgent desire or interest — see EAGER

hung up adj 1 having extreme or relentless concern ⟨Stephanie's parents are already *hung up* about her getting into a good college, and she's only six years old⟩

syn obsessed

rel absorbed, anxious, concerned, distracted, engaged, engrossed, full, involved, occupied, prepossessed, preoccupied, worried; ardent, crazy, fervent, fervid, foolish, impassioned, nuts, passionate, silly

near ant apathetic, cool, detached, dispassionate, unconcerned, unenthusiastic, uninterested, uninvolved

2 feeling or showing uncomfortable feelings of uncertainty — see NERVOUS 1

hunk n a small uneven mass — see LUMP 1

hunt n an act or process of looking carefully or thoroughly for someone or something — see SEARCH

hunt vb 1 to seek out (game) for food or sport ⟨Indians of the plains *hunted* buffalo for food, clothing, and shelter⟩

syn chase, stalk

rel capture, drag, net, snare, trap; ferret, dog, hawk, hound; pursue, run down, track, trail; gun (for), harpoon, kill, shoot; poach

2 to go in search of — see SEEK 1

3 to go into or range over for purposes of discovery — see EXPLORE 2

hunt (down *or* up) vb to come upon after searching, study, or effort — see FIND 1

hunt (through) vb to look through (as a place) carefully or thoroughly in an effort to find or discover something — see SEARCH 1

hunter n a person who hunts game ⟨*hunters* must have a license to shoot deer⟩

syn huntsman

rel huntress, sportsman, sportswoman; archer, gunner; falconer, hawker; hunter-gatherer, trapper; poacher

huntsman n a person who hunts game — see HUNTER

hurdle n something that makes movement or progress more difficult — see ENCUMBRANCE

hurl vb to send through the air especially with a quick forward motion of the arm — see THROW

hurly–burly n a state of noisy, confused activity — see COMMOTION

hurried adj acting or done with excessive or careless speed — see HASTY 1

hurriedly adv with excessive or careless speed — see HASTILY 1

hurry n 1 excited and often showy or disorderly speed ⟨after all her *hurry* to get her history report done on time, Elizabeth learned that it wasn't due till the following week⟩

syn haste, hastiness, hustle, precipitation, precipitousness, rush

rel bustle, flurry, flutter, scurry, scuttle, stir, whirl; beeline, dash, scramble, stampede; hotheadedness, impetuosity, impetuousness, impulsiveness, rashness; fleetness, quickness, rapidity, rapidness, speed, speediness, swiftness; celerity, dispatch, expeditiousness, promptness

near ant dilatoriness, lateness, pokiness, procrastination, slowness; languor, leisureliness, lethargy, sluggishness, torpor; inaction, inactivity, inertia, inertness, quiescence

ant deliberateness, deliberation

2 a high rate of movement or performance — see SPEED

hurry *vb* 1 to cause to move or proceed fast or faster ⟨the new nursing staff was *hurried* through the orientation because they were so desperately needed on the ward⟩

syn accelerate, hasten, quicken, rush, speed (up), whisk

rel drive, goad, prod, propel, push, race, spur, stir, urge; advance, aid, dispatch, ease, encourage, expedite, facilitate, forward, further

near ant delay, hamper, hinder, restrain; brake, check, stay

ant decelerate, retard, slow (down)

2 to proceed or move quickly ⟨if we *hurry*, we'll make the four o'clock train⟩

syn barrel, bolt, bowl, breeze, career, course, dash, fly, hasten, hotfoot (it), hump, hurtle, hustle, pelt, race, rip, rocket, run, rush, rustle, scoot, scurry, scuttle, shoot, speed, step (along), tear, trot, whirl, whisk, zip, zoom

rel dart, flit, scamper, scud, scuffle; stampede, streak, whiz (*or* whizz); gallop, jog, sprint; accelerate, quicken; catch up, fast-forward, outpace, outrun, outstrip, overtake

phrases shake a leg

near ant dally, dawdle, drag, lag, linger, loiter, tarry; amble, lumber, plod, saunter, shuffle, stroll; decelerate, slow (down *or* up)

ant crawl, creep, poke

hurt *n* something that causes loss or pain — see INJURY 1

hurt *vb* 1 to feel or cause physical pain ⟨my head *hurts*⟩ ⟨a bad sprain that really *hurts*⟩ ⟨I *hurt* all over⟩

syn ache, pain, smart

rel bleed, bite, burn, chafe, cramp, fester, itch, nag, pinch, pound, rack, sting, swell, throb, tingle, twinge; agonize, suffer

2 to reduce the soundness, effectiveness, or perfection of — see DAMAGE 1

3 to cause bodily damage to — see INJURE 1

4 to feel deep sadness or mental pain — see GRIEVE

hurtful *adj* 1 causing or capable of causing harm — see HARMFUL

2 hard to accept or bear especially emotionally — see BITTER 2

hurting *adj* causing or feeling bodily pain — see PAINFUL 1

hurtle *vb* 1 to proceed or move quickly — see HURRY 2

2 to send through the air especially with a quick forward motion of the arm — see THROW

husband *n* the male partner in a marriage ⟨she and her *husband* just celebrated their 50th wedding anniversary⟩

syn man, old man

rel consort, mate, partner, spouse; bridegroom, groom; widower

husbandry *n* 1 careful management of material resources — see ECONOMY

2 the science or occupation of cultivating the soil, producing crops, and raising livestock — see AGRICULTURE

hush *n* 1 a state of freedom from storm or disturbance — see CALM

2 the near or complete absence of sound — see SILENCE 2

hush *vb* 1 to become still and orderly — see QUIET 1

2 to stop talking — see SHUT UP

3 to stop the noise or speech of — see SILENCE 1

hush (up) *vb* to keep from being publicly known — see SUPPRESS 1

hushed *adj* 1 free from disturbing noise or uproar — see QUIET 1

2 free from storms or physical disturbance — see CALM 1

3 mostly or entirely without sound — see SILENT 3

4 not known or meant to be known by the general populace — see PRIVATE 1

husk *n* something that encloses another thing especially to protect it — see ¹CASE 1

husk *vb* to remove the natural covering of — see PEEL

¹**husky** *adj* strongly and heavily built ⟨a *husky* weight lifter⟩

syn beefy, brawny, burly, hulking

rel able-bodied, athletic, heavy, hefty, herculean, mighty, muscle-bound, muscular, powerful, robust, rugged, stalwart, strapping, strong, sturdy; chunky, compact, heavyset, solid, squat, squatty, stocky, thickset; dumpy, lumpish, portly, pudgy, stout

near ant lean, light, lightweight, slender, slight, slim, svelte, sylphlike, thin, willowy; bony, gangling, gangly, gaunt, gawky, lanky, scrawny, skinny, spare, twiggy; sinewy, spidery, wiry; delicate, emaciated, fragile, frail, puny, weakly

²**husky** *adj* harsh and dry in sound — see HOARSE

hustle *n* 1 a scheme in which the victim is cheated out of his money after first gaining his trust — see CONFIDENCE GAME

2 excited and often showy or disorderly speed — see HURRY 1

3 readiness to engage in daring or difficult activity — see ENTERPRISE 2

hustle *vb* 1 to devote serious and sustained effort — see LABOR

2 to proceed or move quickly — see HURRY 2

3 to rob by the use of trickery or threats — see FLEECE

hustler *n* an ambitious person who eagerly goes after what is desired — see GO-GETTER

hut *n* a small, simply constructed, and often temporary dwelling — see SHACK

hutch *n* 1 a small, simply constructed, and often temporary dwelling — see SHACK

2 a storage case typically having doors and shelves — see CABINET

hybrid *adj* being offspring produced by parents of different races, breeds, species, or genera — see MIXED 1

hybrid *n* an offspring of parents with different genes, breeds, or species, or genera ⟨a tangelo is a *hybrid* of the tangerine and the grapefruit⟩

syn cross, crossbreed, mongrel

rel mulatto

near ant purebred, thoroughbred

hygienic *adj* free from filth, infection, or dangers to health — see SANITARY

hymn *n* a religious song ⟨our Sunday church services always open with a *hymn*⟩

syn anthem, canticle, carol, chorale, psalm, spiritual

rel dirge, lament, requiem, threnody; Gloria Patri, hallelujah, paean; mass, oratorio; processional, recessional

hymnal *n* a book of hymns ⟨*hymnals* are distributed among the congregation before the church service so everyone can join in the singing⟩

syn hymnbook, psalmody

rel breviary, missal, Psalter, songster

hymnbook *n* a book of hymns — see HYMNAL

hyperbole *n* the representation of something in terms that go beyond the facts — see EXAGGERATION

hypercritical *adj* given to making or expressing unfavorable judgments about things — see CRITICAL 1

hyperventilate *vb* to breathe hard, quickly, or with difficulty — see GASP

hypnosis *n* the art or act of inducing in a person a sleep-like state during which he or she readily follows suggestions ⟨with *hypnosis* there's some question as to just how involuntary the actions of the hypnotized person really are⟩

syn hypnotism, mesmerism

rel bewitchment, enchantment, spellbinding

hypnotic *adj* tending to cause sleep ⟨her eyes soon grew heavy from the *hypnotic* rhythm of the train's wheels⟩

syn drowsy, narcotic, opiate, slumberous (*or* slumbrous)

rel depressant, relaxant, sedative, tranquilizing (*also* tranquillizing); calming, lulling, quieting, relaxing, restful, settling, soothing; analgesic, anesthetic, anesthetizing, benumbing, deadening,

dulling, numbing; hypnotizing, mesmerizing, stupefying

near ant arousing, awakening, energizing, invigorating, rousing, stimulating, wakening, waking

ant stimulant

hypnotism *n* the art or act of inducing in a person a sleep-like state during which he or she readily follows suggestions — see HYPNOSIS

hypnotize *vb* to hold the attention of as if by a spell — see ENTHRALL 1

hypocrisy *n* the pretending of having virtues, principles, or beliefs that one in fact does not have ⟨the *hypocrisy* of people who claim to care about the environment but ride around in gas-guzzlers⟩

syn cant, dissembling, dissimulation, insincerity, piousness, sanctimoniousness

rel deception, deceptiveness, dishonesty, falsity, pretense, pretension, pretentiousness, self-righteousness, self-satisfaction; duplicity, fakery, falseness, fraudulentness, shamming; artificiality, glibness, oiliness, smoothness, unctuousness

near ant candor, honesty, openness, probity, straightforwardness, truthfulness; artlessness, guilelessness, naturalness, unaffectedness

ant genuineness, sincerity

hypocritical *adj* not being or expressing what one appears to be or express — see INSINCERE

hypodermic *n* a slender hollow instrument by which material is put into or taken from the body through the skin — see NEEDLE 1

hypodermic needle *n* a slender hollow instrument by which material is put into or taken from the body through the skin — see NEEDLE 1

hypodermic syringe *n* a slender hollow instrument by which material is put into or taken from the body through the skin — see NEEDLE 1

hypothesis *n* an idea that is the starting point for making a case or conducting an investigation — see THEORY

hypothetical *adj* existing only as an assumption or speculation — see THEORETICAL 1

hysteria *n* a state of wildly excited activity or emotion — see FRENZY

hysterical *adj* **1** causing or intended to cause laughter — see FUNNY 1

2 feeling overwhelming fear or worry — see FRANTIC 1

I

ice–cold *adj* having a low or subnormal temperature — see COLD 1

icy *adj* **1** having a low or subnormal temperature — see COLD 1

2 lacking in friendliness or warmth of feeling — see COLD 2

idea *n* something imagined or pictured in the mind ⟨my *idea* of the perfect vacation spot is an unspoiled beach⟩

syn concept, conception, image, impression, notion, picture, thought

rel apprehension, premonition, presentiment; chimera, illusion, phantasm; caprice, conceit, fancy, freak, notion, vagary, whim; observation, perception, reflection; assumption, belief, conclusion, conviction; conjecture, guess, hunch, hypothesis, speculation, supposition, surmise, theory; brainstorm, inspiration

near ant actuality, fact, reality

ideal *adj* being entirely without fault or flaw — see PERFECT 1

ideal *n* **1** someone of such unequaled perfection as to deserve imitation ⟨she's our *ideal* of the concerned, caring physician⟩

syn beau ideal, classic, exemplar, model, nonpareil, paragon

rel role model; embodiment, epitome, incarnation, manifestation, personification; archetype, example, paradigm, pattern; guideline, principle, rule; gauge (*also* gage), standard, touchstone; essence, quintessence; acme, apex, culmination, peak, pinnacle, summit, zenith

2 the most perfect type or example — see QUINTESSENCE 1

idealist *n* one whose conduct is guided more by the image of perfection than by the real world ⟨an *idealist* sees the best in everyone, regardless of how they behave⟩

syn dreamer, romantic, romanticist, utopian, visionary

rel sentimentalist; daydreamer, optimist, theorist; perfectionist; thinker

near ant cynic, defeatist, pessimist

ant pragmatist, realist

idealize *vb* to represent or think of as better than reality ⟨he had a tendency to *idealize* his heroes and believe they could do no wrong⟩

syn glamorize (*also* glamourize), glorify, romanticize

rel daydream, imagine, romance, theorize, vision; better, perfect

near ant blame, condemn, criticize, denounce; worsen

ideally *adv* without any flaws or errors — see PERFECTLY 1

idée fixe *n* something about which one is constantly thinking or concerned — see FIXATION

identical *adj* **1** being one and not another — see SAME 2

2 resembling another in every respect — see SAME 1

identicalness *n* the state of being exactly alike — see IDENTITY 1

identify *vb* **1** to find out or establish the identity of ⟨with a quick look at everyone's tongue, Mom was able to *identify* the person who had sneaked a piece of blueberry pie⟩

syn distinguish, pinpoint, single (out)

rel diagnose; determine, find; locate, pick out, place, recognize, spot; check, examine, inspect, investigate, notice, observe, scrutinize; betray, disclose, discover, reveal

near ant camouflage, conceal, disguise, hide; counterfeit, feign, sham, simulate

2 to think of (something) in combination — see ASSOCIATE 2

identifying *adj* serving to identify as belonging to an individual or group — see CHARACTERISTIC 1

identity *n* **1** the state of being exactly alike ⟨although the covers of the two paperback editions of the novel are different, there's a complete *identity* in the texts⟩

syn identicalness, sameness

rel oneness, homogeneity, homology; equality, equivalence; accordance, agreement, conformity, congruity, correspondence, likeness, resemblance, similarity

near ant alteration, change, modification, variation; distinction, distinctiveness, distinctness, exoticness, individuality, separateness, separation, uniqueness, unusualness; deviance, divergence; variance; incompatibility, incongruity, incongruousness; contrast

ant difference, disagreement, discrepancy, disparateness, disparity, dissimilarity, unlikeness

2 the set of qualities that make a person different from other people — see INDIVIDUALITY

ideology *n* the basic beliefs or guiding principles of a person or group — see CREED 1

idiocy *n* a foolish act or idea — see FOLLY 1

idiom *n* a sequence of words having a specific meaning — see PHRASE

idiosyncrasy *n* an odd or peculiar habit ⟨his only *idiosyncrasy* was collecting pencil erasers and making little dolls out of them⟩

---

syn synonym(s) *rel* related words
ant antonym(s) *near ant* near antonym(s)

syn crotchet, eccentricity, mannerism, oddity, peculiarity, quirk, singularity, trick

rel affectation, airs; attribute, characteristic, mark, property, trait; custom, habit, pattern, practice (*also* practise), way, wont; addiction; abnormality, perversion; disposition, genius, leaning, partiality; bent, inclination, penchant, predilection, predisposition, proclivity, propensity, tendency, turn; attitude, character, humor, identity, individuality, nature, personality, temperament

near ant conformity, sameness

idiot *n* a stupid person ⟨only an *idiot* would jump off a bridge just because their friends told them to⟩

syn blockhead, cretin, dodo, dolt, donkey, dope, dork [*slang*], dumbbell, dummy, dunce, fathead, goon, half-wit, ignoramus, imbecile, jackass, knothead, moron, nincompoop, ninny, nitwit, numskull (*or* numbskull), pinhead, simpleton, stock, turkey

rel booby, fool, goose, loony (*also* looney), lunatic, madman, nut, zany; loser; gawk; featherbrain, scatterbrain; beast, boor, cad, churl, clown, creep, cur, heel, jerk, skunk, snake, stinker, villain

near ant egghead, intellectual, sage, thinker

ant brain, genius

idle *vb* to spend time doing nothing ⟨she likes to *idle* during the summer even though her parents always tell her to get out and do something⟩

syn dally, dawdle, dillydally, hang around, hang out, loaf, loll, lounge

rel fiddle, fool, mess, monkey, play; potter, putter, trifle; estivate, hibernate; lag, linger, loiter, poke, relax, rest, tarry; amble, mosey, saunter, stroll; bum, furlough, goldbrick, malinger

phrases kill time, lie around, mark time, waste time

near ant drudge, grind, grub, hump, hustle, labor, moil, peg, plod, plow, plug, slave, sweat, toil, travail, work; apply, buckle (down); exert, run out

idle *adj* **1** not being in a state of use, activity, or employment — see INACTIVE 2

2 not easily aroused to action or work — see LAZY

idleness *n* **1** an inclination not to do work or engage in activities — see LAZINESS

2 lack of action or activity — see INACTION

3 lack of use — see DISUSE

idler *n* a lazy person — see LAZYBONES

idolater *or* **idolator** *n* a person who does not worship the God of the Bible — see HEATHEN 1

idolatry *n* excessive admiration of or devotion to a person — see WORSHIP

idolization *n* excessive admiration of or devotion to a person — see WORSHIP

idolize *vb* to love or admire too much ⟨she *idolized* her big sister⟩

syn adore, adulate, canonize, deify, dote (on), worship

rel appreciate, cherish, esteem, prize, treasure, value; fancy, favor, like, prefer; regard; respect, revere, venerate; approve, endorse (*also* indorse), support

near ant abhor, abominate, despise, detest, disdain, dislike, hate, loathe; belittle, deprecate, disparage, put down

idolizing *adj* reflecting great admiration or devotion — see WORSHIPFUL

ignitable *adj* capable of catching or being set on fire — see COMBUSTIBLE

ignite *vb* to set (something) on fire — see BURN 2

ignited *adj* being on fire — see ABLAZE 1

ignoble *adj* **1** belonging to the class of people of low social or economic rank ⟨an *ignoble* child cannot grow up to be king⟩

syn baseborn, common, humble, inferior, low, lower-class, lowly, mean, plebeian, proletarian, vulgar

rel bourgeois, middle-class; peasant, plain, poor, simple, working-class

near ant eminent, illustrious, notable, prominent

ant aristocratic, high, highborn, lofty, noble, wellborn

2 not following or in accordance with standards of honor and decency ⟨cheating on a test is an *ignoble* act and can get you expelled⟩

syn base, contemptible, despicable, detestable, dirty, dishonorable, low, mean, snide, sordid, vile, wretched

rel bad, black, evil, foul, immoral, iniquitous, wicked, wrong; cruel, nasty, vicious; blamable, blameworthy, censurable, reprehensible; corrupt, debased, debauched, degenerate, depraved, dissolute, perverted; atrocious, villainous; unethical, unprincipled, unscrupulous; discreditable, disgraceful, disreputable, ignominious, shameful

near ant ethical, honest, just, principled, righteous, right-minded, scrupulous; commendable, excellent, exemplary, good, moral, right; decent, proper, reputable, respectable, seemly; blameless, guiltless; incorruptible, irreproachable; uncorrupted, unerring

ant high, high-minded, honorable, lofty, noble, straight, upright, venerable, virtuous

ignominious *adj* not respectable — see DISREPUTABLE

ignominy *n* the state of having lost the esteem of others — see DISGRACE 1

ignoramus *n* a stupid person — see IDIOT

ignorance *n* **1** the state of being unaware or uninformed ⟨*ignorance* of the law is no excuse⟩

syn obliviousness, unawareness, unfamiliarity

rel callowness, greenness, inexperience, innocence, naïveté (*also* naivete), rawness, simpleness, unsophistication

near ant experience, know-how; sophistication

ant acquaintance, awareness, familiarity

2 the state of being unlearned ⟨with such vast sums spent on education, the level of *ignorance* among graduating seniors is a national disgrace⟩

syn illiteracy

rel brainlessness, dumbness, idiocy, imbecility, stupidity; philistinism; foolishness, mindlessness, senselessness, witlessness

near ant education, instruction, training; enlightenment, knowledge; erudition, scholarship

ant learning, literacy

ignorant *adj* **1** lacking in education or the knowledge gained from books ⟨the teacher was committed to educating the children of those poor, *ignorant* farmers⟩

syn benighted, dark, illiterate, nonliterate, simple, uneducated, uninstructed, unlearned, unlettered, unread, unschooled, untaught, untutored

rel lowbrow, uncultivated, uncultured; callow, green, inexperienced, innocent, naive (*or* naïve); unsophisticated; raw, untrained; brainless, dumb, idiotic, imbecilic, moronic, stupid, witless; foolish, senseless, silly

near ant brilliant, intelligent, smart; experienced, expert, trained; erudite, learned, scholarly; cultivated, cultured, highbrow, intellectual; sophisticated; acquainted, aware, familiar

ant educated, knowledgeable, literate, schooled

2 not informed about or aware of something ⟨he was *ignorant* of their plans⟩

syn oblivious, unacquainted, unaware, unconscious, ungrounded, uninformed, unknowing, unmindful, unwitting

rel uneducated, unschooled, untaught; absent, absentminded, abstracted, heedless, inattentive

near ant conversant, educated, knowledgeable, schooled, taught; heedful, observant; sensitive, sentient

ant acquainted, aware, cognizant, conscious, conversant, grounded, informed, knowing, mindful, witting

ignore *vb* **1** to fail to give proper attention to — see NEGLECT 1

2 to overlook or dismiss as of little importance — see EXCUSE 1

ilk *n* a number of persons or things that are grouped together because they have something in common — see SORT 1

ill *adj* **1** affected with nausea — see NAUSEOUS

2 causing or capable of causing harm — see HARMFUL

3 temporarily suffering from a disorder of the body — see SICK 1

ill *adv* in a manner so as to cause loss or suffering — see HARDLY 1

ill *n* **1** an abnormal state that disrupts a plant's or animal's normal bodily functioning — see DISEASE

2 that which is morally unacceptable — see EVIL

---

syn synonym(s)   *rel* related words
ant antonym(s)   *near ant* near antonym(s)

ill–advised *adj* showing poor judgment especially in personal relationships or social situations — see INDISCREET

ill–bred *adj* **1** lacking in refinement or good taste — see COARSE 2

2 showing a lack of manners or consideration for others — see IMPOLITE

illegal *adj* **1** contrary to or forbidden by law ⟨it is *illegal* to steal⟩

syn criminal, illegitimate, illicit, unlawful, wrongful

rel bad, evil, immoral, shameful, sinful, unethical, wicked, wrong; blamable, blameworthy, censurable, reprehensible; banned, barred, disallowed, discouraged, forbidden, interdicted, outlawed, prohibited, proscribed; unauthorized, unlicensed, unsanctioned; corrupt, unprincipled, unscrupulous, villainous

near ant ethical, good, just, principled, right, righteous, virtuous; allowed, permitted; authorized, licensed (*also* licenced); approved, endorsed, sanctioned; abetted, encouraged, promoted, suggested, supported; correct, decent, decorous, proper, seemly

ant lawful, legal, legitimate

2 not being in accordance with the rules or standards of what is fair in sport — see FOUL 2

illegitimate *adj* **1** born to a father and mother who are not married ⟨despite being *illegitimate*, Alexander Hamilton rose to greatness⟩

syn baseborn, bastard, misbegotten

rel fatherless, motherless; adopted, orphaned

ant legitimate

2 contrary to or forbidden by law — see ILLEGAL 1

ill–fated *adj* having, prone to, or marked by bad luck — see UNLUCKY

ill–favored *adj* unpleasant to look at — see UGLY 1

ill–humored *adj* having or showing a habitually bad temper — see ILL-TEMPERED

illicit *adj* contrary to or forbidden by law — see ILLEGAL 1

illimitable *adj* being or seeming to be without limits — see INFINITE

illiteracy *n* the state of being unlearned — see IGNORANCE 2

illiterate *adj* lacking in education or the knowledge gained from books — see IGNORANT 1

ill–mannered *adj* showing a lack of manners or consideration for others — see IMPOLITE

ill–natured *adj* having or showing a habitually bad temper — see ILL-TEMPERED

illness *n* **1** an abnormal state that disrupts a plant's or animal's normal bodily functioning — see DISEASE

2 the condition of not being in good health — see SICKNESS 1

illogical *adj* not using or following good reasoning ⟨the *illogical* claim that playing basketball makes people taller because one sees so many tall players⟩ ⟨*illogical* people are likely to believe every sensational claim on TV⟩

syn fallacious, invalid, irrational, nonrational, unreasonable, unreasoning, unsound, weak

rel misleading, specious; ill-advised, unconsidered, unreasoned; inconsistent; absurd, asinine, foolish, meaningless, nonsensical, preposterous, senseless, silly; odd, peculiar, strange, unusual, weird; insane, mad, nutty, wacky; disordered, disorganized, rambling, random; unconvincing, unsatisfying; inexplicable, unaccountable, unexplainable

near ant commonsense, sane, sensible, sober, wise; enlightened, informed, just, justified, reasoned; ordered, organized; clear, cogent, compelling, convincing, credible, persuasive, plausible, satisfying, solid; certain, sure, true; confirmed, corroborated, demonstrated, established, substantiated, validated, well-founded

ant logical, rational, reasonable, sound, valid

ill-starred *adj* having, prone to, or marked by bad luck — see UNLUCKY

ill-tempered *adj* having or showing a habitually bad temper ⟨an *ill-tempered* cat will scratch⟩

syn bearish, bilious, cantankerous, disagreeable, dyspeptic, ill-humored, ill-natured, ornery, splenetic, surly

rel choleric, crabby, cranky, crotchety, fussy, grouchy, grumpy, querulous; irascible, irritable, peevish, petulant, quick-tempered, snappish, testy, touchy; argumentative, contentious, contrary; angry, exasperated, indignant, irate, mad, upset, uptight; depressed, dour, glum, morose, sullen

near ant agreeable, amicable, congenial, friendly, pleasant; benign, gentle, kind, nice, sweet; bubbly, cheerful, cheery, effervescent, exuberant, high-spirited, lighthearted, lively, joyful, vivacious; content, glad, happy; calm, placid, serene; long-suffering, patient, tolerant

ant amiable, good-natured, good-tempered

ill-treat *vb* to inflict physical or emotional harm upon — see ABUSE 1

illuminate *vb* **1** to supply with light ⟨a floor lamp *illuminates* a living room rather nicely⟩

syn illumine, irradiate, light, lighten

rel brighten; beam, beat (down), radiate, shine; floodlight; highlight, spotlight; blaze, burn, fire, flame, glare, glow, ignite, incinerate, kindle; bedazzle, blind, daze, dazzle; gleam, glisten, glitter

near ant dim, dull, obscure; cover, shroud, veil; douse, extinguish, put out, quench, snuff (out)

ant blacken, darken

2 to make plain or understandable — see EXPLAIN 1

illuminated *adj* filled with much light — see BRIGHT 2

illumination *n* **1** a statement that makes something clear — see EXPLANATION 1

2 the quality or state of having or giving off light — see BRILLIANCE 1

3 the steady giving off of the form of radiation that makes vision possible — see LIGHT 1

illuminative *adj* serving to explain — see EXPLANATORY

illumine *vb* to supply with light — see ILLUMINATE 1

illumined *adj* filled with much light — see BRIGHT 2

ill-use *vb* to inflict physical or emotional harm upon — see ABUSE 1

illusion *n* **1** a conception or image created by the imagination and having no objective reality — see FANTASY 1

2 a false idea or belief — see FALLACY 1

illustrate *vb* **1** to show or make clear by using examples ⟨she *illustrated* her point with a story about her last experiment and the results it provided⟩

syn demonstrate, exemplify, instance

rel cite, mention, quote; name, specify; analyze, break down; clarify, clear (up), explain, explicate, expound; edify, elucidate, enlighten; illuminate; construe, interpret; simplify, spell out; detail, enumerate, list

near ant becloud, blur, cloud, darken, fog, muddy, obscure; confuse, perplex, puzzle

2 to make plain or understandable — see EXPLAIN 1

illustration *n* **1** something that visually explains or decorates a text ⟨the book on birds had gorgeous *illustrations*⟩

syn diagram, figure, graphic, plate

rel drawing, illumination, image, pictogram, pictograph, picture; caption, key, legend; depiction, portrait, portrayal, representation; clarification, elucidation, explanation, explication, exposition

2 a statement that makes something clear — see EXPLANATION 1

3 a two-dimensional design intended to look like a person or thing — see PICTURE 1

4 one of a group or collection that shows what the whole is like — see EXAMPLE 1

illustrative *adj* serving to explain — see EXPLANATORY

illustrious *adj* standing above others in rank, importance, or achievement — see EMINENT

image *n* **1** something or someone that strongly resembles another ⟨the girl is growing up to be the perfect *image* of her mother⟩

syn carbon copy, counterpart, double, duplicate, duplication, facsimile, likeness, match, picture, replica, ringer, spit

rel effigy, portrait, portrayal; companion, counterpart, fellow, mate; equal, equivalent, identical twin; analogue (*or* analog), parallel

near ant antithesis, converse, opposite, reverse

2 a two-dimensional design intended to look like a person or thing — see PICTURE 1

3 something imagined or pictured in the mind — see IDEA

image vb **1** to present a picture of — see PICTURE 1

2 to give a representation or account of in words — see DESCRIBE 1

3 to reproduce or show (an exact likeness) as a mirror would — see REFLECT

imaginary adj not real and existing only in the imagination ⟨his *imaginary* friend had purple hair⟩

syn chimerical, fabulous, fanciful, fantastic, fictional, fictitious, imagined, invented, made-up, make-believe, mythical (*or* mythic), phantasmal, phantom, pretend, unreal

rel fabled, legendary, romantic; abstract, hypothetical, theoretical (*also* theoretic); unbelievable, unconvincing, unlikely; conceived, envisaged, pictured, visualized; deceptive, delusional, delusive, hallucinatory, illusory; concocted, fabricated

near ant authentic, genuine, true; factual, verifiable, verified; believable, convincing, realistic; corporeal, material, physical, solid, substantial; palpable, tangible

ant actual, existent, existing, real

imagination n the ability to form mental images of things that either are not physically present or have never been conceived or created by others ⟨a cartoonist needs a good *imagination* in order to think up and draw interesting cartoons⟩

syn creativity, fancy, fantasy (*also* phantasy), imaginativeness, invention, inventiveness

rel brainstorm, brainstorming, inspiration; fecundity, fertility; ingenuity, originality; versatility; chimera, daydream, delusion, dream, figment, hallucination, illusion, mirage, phantasm, pipe dream; envisaging, visualization

near ant literalness

imaginative adj **1** having the skill and imagination to create new things — see CREATIVE 1

2 showing a use of the imagination and creativity especially in inventing — see CLEVER 1

imaginativeness n **1** the ability to form mental images of things that either are not physically present or have never been conceived or created by others — see IMAGINATION

2 the skill and imagination to create new things — see CREATIVITY 1

imagine vb **1** to form a mental picture of ⟨she *imagined* meeting the members of her favorite rock band face-to-face⟩

syn conceive, dream, envisage, fancy, picture, vision, visualize

rel daydream, stargaze; hallucinate; reflect, relive, reminisce; contemplate, meditate, muse, ponder, ruminate; concoct, fabricate, invent, make up, manufacture, plan, project

2 to have as an opinion — see BELIEVE 2

imagined adj not real and existing only in the imagination — see IMAGINARY

imbecile n a stupid person — see IDIOT

imbecility n a foolish act or idea — see FOLLY 1

imbibe vb **1** to swallow in liquid form — see DRINK 1

2 to take in (something liquid) through small openings — see ABSORB 1

imbue vb to cause (as a person) to become filled or saturated with a certain quality or principle — see INFUSE

imitate vb **1** to use (someone or something) as the model for one's speech, mannerisms, or behavior ⟨teenage boys who *imitate* whichever rock stars are hot⟩

syn ape, copy, emulate, mime, mimic

rel burlesque, caricature, lampoon, mock, parody, travesty; impersonate, perform, play; pantomime

2 to copy or exaggerate (someone or something) in order to make fun of — see MIMIC 1

3 to make an exact likeness of — see COPY 1

imitation adj being such in appearance only and made with or manufactured from usually cheaper materials ⟨you have to be careful not to buy an *imitation* diamond passed off as the real thing⟩

syn artificial, factitious, bogus, fake, false, man-made, mimic, mock, sham, simulated, substitute, synthetic

rel dummy, phony (*also* phoney); cultured, manufactured; unauthentic; adulterated, doctored, fudged, juggled, manipulated, tampered (with); concocted, fabricated; counterfeit, deceptive, forged, fraudulent, misleading; affected, feigned, pseudo, spurious

near ant authentic, bona fide, legitimate, true; premium, quality, valuable; pure, unadulterated

ant genuine, natural, real

imitation n something that is made to look exactly like something else — see COPY

imitative adj using or marked by the use of something else as a basis or model ⟨your writing style tends to be *imitative* of whichever author you've recently read⟩

syn apish, emulative, formulaic, mimetic, mimic, slavish, unoriginal

rel copied, cribbed, plagiarized; artificial, bogus, factitious, fake, false, imitation, man-made, mock, sham, simulated, substitute, synthetic; duplicated, photocopied, reduplicated, reproduced, transcribed; backup; counterfeit, deceptive, forged, fraudulent, misleading; uninspired

near ant authentic, bona fide, legitimate, true; genuine, natural, real; classic, ideal, model

ant archetypal, original

imitator n a person who adopts the appearance or behavior of another especially in an obvious way — see COPYCAT

2 a person who imitates another's voice and mannerisms for comic effect — see MIMIC

immaculate *adj* **1** free from any trace of the coarse or indecent — see CHASTE

2 free from dirt or stain — see CLEAN 1

immaterial *adj* **1** not composed of matter ⟨it is only possible to study *immaterial* forces like gravity by observing their effects on the physical world⟩

syn bodiless, incorporeal, insubstantial, nonmaterial, nonphysical, spiritual, unsubstantial

rel metaphysical, supernatural; impalpable, insensible, intangible, invisible; airy, diaphanous, ethereal, tenuous, thin, vaporous

near ant animal, carnal, fleshly; detectable, discernable, noticeable, observable, palpable, sensible, tangible, visible; bulky, heavy, massive, solid

ant bodily, corporeal, material, physical, substantial

2 not having anything to do with the matter at hand — see IRRELEVANT

immature *adj* **1** being in the early stage of life, growth, or development — see YOUNG

2 having or showing the annoying qualities (as silliness) associated with children — see CHILDISH

3 lacking in adult experience or maturity — see CALLOW

immeasurable *adj* being or seeming to be without limits — see INFINITE

immediacy *n* the state or condition of being near — see PROXIMITY

immediate *adj* **1** done or occurring without any noticeable lapse in time — see INSTANTANEOUS

2 done or working without something else coming in between — see DIRECT 1

3 done, carried out, or given without delay — see PROMPT 1

4 not being distant in time, space, or significance — see CLOSE 2

immediately *adv* without delay ⟨if you don't leave *immediately*, you'll be late for school and probably get in trouble⟩

syn directly, forthwith, instantly, now, promptly, pronto, right away, right now, straightaway, straightway

rel away, freely; anon, momentarily, shortly, soon; apace, briskly, fast, fleetly, full-tilt, posthaste, quick, quickly, rapidly, readily, snappily, speedily, swift, swiftly; abruptly, presto, suddenly, unexpectedly; hastily, impetuously, impulsively, rashly, recklessly; exactly, opportunely, punctually, seasonably

phrases at once, on the line, on the spot

near ant slowly; late, tardily

immense *adj* unusually large — see HUGE

immenseness *n* the quality or state of being very large — see IMMENSITY

immensity *n* the quality or state of being very large ⟨the *immensity* of the mountain was awe-inspiring, especially up close⟩

syn enormity, enormousness, hugeness, immenseness, magnitude, massiveness, vastness

rel bigness, extensiveness, greatness, largeness, voluminousness, weightiness; awesomeness, grandness, stupendousness; excessiveness, extravagance, extremeness, immoderacy

near ant littleness, puniness, smallness; triviality, unimportance

ant diminutiveness, minuteness, tininess

immerse *vb* **1** to hold the attention of — see ENGAGE 1

2 to sink or push (something) briefly into or as if into a liquid — see DIP 1

immersed *adj* having the mind fixed on something — see ATTENTIVE

immersing *adj* holding the attention or provoking interest — see INTERESTING

immersion *n* a focusing of the mind on something — see ATTENTION 1

immigrant *n* one that leaves one place to settle in another — see EMIGRANT

imminent *adj* giving signs of immediate occurrence ⟨a storm is *imminent*, so you should seek shelter now⟩

syn impending, pending, threatening

rel approaching, coming, forthcoming, future, near, nearing, oncoming, upcoming; brewing, gathering; likely, possible, probable; inevitable, unavoidable; menacing, ominous, portentous; anticipated, awaited, expected, foreseen, predicted

near ant distant, far-off, remote; eventual, ultimate; bygone, former, past; late, recent

2 being soon to appear or take place — see FORTHCOMING

immobile *adj* **1** fixed in a place or position — see STATIONARY 1

2 incapable of moving or being moved — see IMMOVABLE 1

immobilize *vb* to render powerless, ineffective, or unable to move — see PARALYZE

immoderate *adj* going beyond a normal or acceptable limit in degree or amount — see EXCESSIVE

immodest *adj* showing a lack of proper social reserve or modesty — see PRESUMPTUOUS 1

immolate *vb* to give up as an offering to a god — see SACRIFICE

immolation *n* something offered to a god — see SACRIFICE

immoral *adj* **1** not conforming to a high moral standard; morally unacceptable — see BAD 2

2 not guided by or concerned for what is right — see UNPRINCIPLED

immorality *n* **1** immoral conduct or practices harmful or offensive to society — see VICE 1

2 that which is morally unacceptable — see EVIL

immortal *adj* lasting forever — see EVERLASTING

immortality *n* unending existence after death — see ETERNITY 2

immortalize *vb* to give eternal or lasting existence to — see PERPETUATE

immovable *adj* **1** incapable of moving or being moved ⟨that boulder is *immovable*, even with a bulldozer⟩

syn immobile, irremovable, nonmotile, nonmoving, unbudging, unmovable

rel motionless, moveless, static, stationary, still, unmoving; fast, fixed, rooted, steadfast, stuck, wedged

near ant portable, removable, transferable, transportable

ant mobile, motile, movable (*or* moveable), moving

2 sticking to an opinion, purpose, or course of action in spite of reason, arguments, or persuasion — see OBSTINATE

immunity *n* freedom from punishment, harm, or loss — see IMPUNITY

immure *vb* **1** to close or shut in by or as if by barriers — see ENCLOSE 1

2 to put in or as if in prison — see IMPRISON

immurement *n* the act of confining or the state of being confined — see INTERNMENT

immutability *n* the state of continuing without change — see CONSTANCY 1

immutable *adj* not capable of changing or being changed — see INFLEXIBLE 1

imp *n* **1** an appealingly mischievous person — see SCAMP 1

2 an evil spirit — see DEMON

impact *n* **1** a forceful coming together of two things ⟨the glass shattered on *impact* with the floor⟩

syn bump, collision, concussion, crash, jar, jolt, shock, smash, strike, wallop

rel blow, buffet, hit, knock, punch, rap, slap, thump; bashing, battering, bludgeoning, clobbering, hammering, lambasting, licking, pounding, pummelling, thrashing; contact, encounter, meeting, touch

2 the power to bring about a result on another — see EFFECT 2

3 the quality of an utterance that provokes interest and produces an effect — see ¹PUNCH 1

impact *vb* **1** to act upon (a person or a person's feelings) so as to cause a response — see ¹AFFECT 1

2 to come into usually forceful contact with something — see HIT 2

impair *vb* to reduce the soundness, effectiveness, or perfection of — see DAMAGE 1

impale *vb* to penetrate or hold (something) with a pointed object ⟨*impale* a marshmallow or two on that stick and let's start toasting⟩

syn gore, harpoon, lance, pierce, puncture, skewer, spear, spike, stab, stick, transfix

rel spindle; perforate; jab, poke, prick, punch, thrust; cut, knife, slice

impalpable *adj* **1** not capable of being perceived by the sense of touch — see INTANGIBLE

2 not perceptible by a sense or by the mind — see IMPERCEPTIBLE

impart *vb* to cause (something) to pass from one to another — see COMMUNICATE 1

impartial *adj* marked by justice, honesty, and freedom from bias — see FAIR 2

impartiality *n* lack of favoritism toward one side or another — see DETACHMENT 1

impassable *adj* impossible to get through or into — see IMPENETRABLE 1

impasse *n* a point in a struggle where neither side is capable of winning or willing to give in ⟨if we cannot ever agree on which movie to see tonight, we are at an *impasse*⟩

syn deadlock, halt, stalemate, standstill

rel dead end; bottleneck, corner, dilemma, fix, hole, jam, pickle, pinch, plight, predicament, quagmire, quandary, spot; difficulty; problem

impassioned *adj* having or expressing great depth of feeling — see FERVENT

impassive *adj* **1** not feeling or showing emotion ⟨she remained *impassive* as they told her the bad news⟩

syn apathetic, cold-blooded, phlegmatic, stoic (*or* stoical), stolid, undemonstrative, unemotional

rel cold, cool, dispassionate, unmoved; calm, collected, composed; imperturbable, unflappable; reserved, reticent, taciturn; blank, deadpan, dry, empty, expressionless, inexpressive, vacant, wooden; enigmatic (*also* enigmatical), impenetrable, inscrutable; aloof, detached, unconcerned, unsentimental; impersonal, objective, unresponsive; hardhearted, pitiless, unfeeling; inconsiderate, thoughtless

near ant blazing, burning, fiery, flaming, glowing, red-hot; ardent, enthusiastic, gung ho, zealous; gushing, maudlin, mawkish, mushy, sentimental; dramatic, histrionic, melodramatic; compassionate, responsive, sympathetic; reactive, sensitive

ant demonstrative, emotional, fervent, fervid, hot-blooded, impassioned, passionate

2 not expressing any emotion — see BLANK 1

impassivity *n* a lack of emotion or emotional expressiveness — see APATHY 1

impatience *n* urgent desire or interest — see EAGERNESS

impatient *adj* **1** showing urgent desire or interest — see EAGER

2 unable or unwilling to endure — see INTOLERANT 1

impeach *vb* to make a claim of wrongdoing against — see ACCUSE

impeccability *n* the quality or state of being free from guilt or blame — see INNOCENCE 1

impeccable *adj* **1** being entirely without fault or flaw — see PERFECT 1

---

syn synonym(s)   *rel* related words
ant antonym(s)   *near ant* near antonym(s)

2 free from guilt or blame — see INNOCENT 2

impeccably *adv* without any flaws or errors — see PERFECTLY 1

impecunious *adj* lacking money or material possessions — see POOR 1

impecuniousness *n* the state of lacking sufficient money or material possessions — see POVERTY 1

impede *vb* to create difficulty for the work or activity of — see HAMPER

impediment *n* something that makes movement or progress more difficult — see ENCUMBRANCE

impel *vb* to set or keep in motion — see MOVE 2

impend *vb* to be about to happen — see LOOM

impend (over) *vb* to remain poised to inflict harm, danger, or distress on — see THREATEN

impending *adj* **1** being soon to appear or take place — see FORTHCOMING

2 giving signs of immediate occurrence — see IMMINENT 1

impenetrable *adj* **1** impossible to get through or into ⟨the ancient temple was surrounded by vast stretches of *impenetrable* jungle⟩

syn impassable, impermeable, impervious

rel close, compact, dense, thick; compressed, condensed; sturdy, substantial, tough; firm, frozen, hard, solid, stiff; inflexible, rigid, unbending, unyielding

near ant soft, squishy; bendable, elastic, flexible, giving, malleable, pliable, yielding; absorbent, porous

ant negotiable, passable, penetrable, permeable

2 being beyond one's powers to know, understand, or explain — see MYSTERIOUS 1

3 impossible to understand — see INCOMPREHENSIBLE

4 not allowing penetration (as by gas, liquid, or light) — see TIGHT 1

impenitent *adj* not sorry for having done wrong — see REMORSELESS

imperative *adj* **1** forcing one's compliance or participation by or as if by law — see MANDATORY

2 impossible to do without — see ESSENTIAL 1

3 needing immediate attention — see ACUTE 2

imperceptible *adj* not perceptible by a sense or by the mind ⟨a slight difference in hue between the two glasses that's *imperceptible* unless they're placed side by side⟩

syn impalpable, inappreciable, indistinguishable, insensible

rel inaudible, intangible, invisible; inconspicuous, indistinct, unnoticeable, unseeable, unseen; faint, insignificant, slight, trivial; buried, concealed, covert, disguised, hidden, obscure, shrouded, unapparent, vague

near ant audible, observable, tangible, visible; clear, conspicuous, evident, eye-catching, manifest, noticeable, obvious, plain, prominent, striking; apparent, distinct, significant, straightforward

ant appreciable, discernible, palpable, perceptible, sensible

imperfect *adj* having a fault — see FAULTY

imperfection *n* something that spoils the appearance or completeness of a thing — see BLEMISH

imperil *vb* to place in danger — see ENDANGER

imperilment *n* the state of not being protected from injury, harm, or evil — see DANGER 1

imperious *adj* **1** fond of ordering people around — see BOSSY

2 having a feeling of superiority that shows itself in an overbearing attitude — see ARROGANT

3 having or showing a tendency to force one's will on others without any regard to fairness or necessity — see ARBITRARY

4 needing immediate attention — see ACUTE 2

imperiousness *n* an exaggerated sense of one's importance that shows itself in the making of excessive or unjustified claims — see ARROGANCE

imperishable *adj* impossible to destroy — see INDESTRUCTIBLE

impermanent *adj* **1** intended to last, continue, or serve for a limited time — see TEMPORARY 1

2 lasting only for a short time — see MOMENTARY

impermeable *adj* **1** impossible to get through or into — see IMPENETRABLE 1

2 not allowing penetration (as by gas, liquid, or light) — see TIGHT 1

impermissible *adj* that may not be permitted ⟨chewing gum is an *impermissible* activity in school⟩

syn banned, barred, forbidden, interdicted, outlawed, prohibited, proscribed, taboo (*also* tabu)

rel intolerable, unacceptable, unbearable, unendurable; illegal, illegitimate, illicit, improper, inappropriate, unadvisable, unauthorized, unlawful, unlicensed, unmentionable; unseemly, unsuitable; objectionable; disallowed, disapproved, discouraged; refused, rejected, revoked, unsanctioned, vetoed; repressed, suppressed; precluded, prevented, stopped; excluded, ruled out, shut out; blocked, hindered, impeded, obstructed

near ant acceptable, bearable, endurable, tolerable; accepted, accredited, allowed, appropriate, approved, authorized, certified, endorsed, lawful, legal, legitimate, licensed (*also* licenced), OK (*or* okay), permitted, warranted; accorded, granted, sanctioned, vouchsafed; brooked, condoned, countenanced; encouraged, promoted, supported; commanded, mandatory, ordered, required; proper, seemly, suitable, tolerated, unobjectionable *ant* allowable, licensable, permissible, permissive, sufferable

impersonate *vb* **1** to pretend to be (what one is not) in appearance or behavior ⟨a school intruder was caught trying to *impersonate* a teacher⟩

syn masquerade (as), play, pose (as)

rel ape, copy, imitate, mime, mimic, mock, parody, travesty; act, perform, portray

2 to present a portrayal or performance of — see ACT 1

impersonator *n* **1** a person who imitates another's voice and mannerisms for comic effect — see MIMIC

2 one who acts professionally (as in a play, movie, or television show) — see ACTOR

impertinence *n* **1** disrespectful or argumentative talk given in response to a command or request — see BACK TALK

2 rude behavior — see DISCOURTESY

impertinent *adj* **1** displaying or marked by rude boldness — see NERVY 1

2 showing a lack of manners or consideration for others — see IMPOLITE

imperturbability *n* evenness of emotions or temper — see EQUANIMITY

imperturbable *adj* not easily panicked or upset — see UNFLAPPABLE

impervious *adj* **1** not allowing penetration (as by gas, liquid, or light) — see TIGHT 1

2 impossible to get through or into — see IMPENETRABLE 1

impetus *n* something that arouses action or activity — see IMPULSE

impiety *n* an act of great disrespect shown to God or to sacred ideas, people, or things — see BLASPHEMY

impinge *vb* to come into usually forceful contact with something — see HIT 2

impious *adj* not showing proper reverence for the holy or sacred — see IRREVERENT

impish *adj* tending to or exhibiting reckless playfulness — see MISCHIEVOUS 1

impishness *n* **1** a natural disposition for playful behavior — see PLAYFULNESS

2 playful, reckless behavior that is not intended to cause serious harm — see MISCHIEF 1

implacable *adj* **1** sticking to an opinion, purpose, or course of action in spite of reason, arguments, or persuasion — see OBSTINATE

2 showing no signs of slackening or yielding in one's purpose — see UNYIELDING 1

implant *vb* to set solidly in or as if in surrounding matter — see ENTRENCH

implausible *adj* too extraordinary or improbable to believe — see INCREDIBLE

implement *n* an article intended for use in work ⟨gardening *implements* such as hoes, spades, and pruners⟩

syn device, instrument, tool, utensil

rel apparatus, appliance, mechanism; contraption, contrivance, gadget, gizmo (or gismo), jigger

implement *vb* to carry out effectively — see ENFORCE

implementation *n* the doing of an action — see COMMISSION 2

implicit *adj* understood although not put into words ⟨the *implicit* agreement in the outing club is that every member pays his or her own way on all trips⟩

syn implied, tacit, unexpressed, unspoken, unvoiced, wordless

rel inferred; unannounced, undeclared, unsaid, untold; hinted, intimated, suggested

near ant apparent, blatant, evident, obvious, plain, straightforward; unambiguous, unequivocal, unmistakable

ant explicit, express, expressed, spoken, stated

implied *adj* understood although not put into words — see IMPLICIT

implore *vb* to make a request to (someone) in an earnest or urgent manner — see BEG

imploring *adj* asking humbly — see SUPPLIANT

imply *vb* to convey an idea indirectly — see HINT

impolite *adj* showing a lack of manners or consideration for others ⟨the librarian was shocked that anyone could be so *impolite* as to continue talking despite repeated warnings to be quiet⟩

syn discourteous, ill-bred, ill-mannered, impertinent, inconsiderate, rude, thoughtless, uncalled-for, uncivil, ungracious, unmannerly

rel audacious, bold, bold-faced, brash, brassy, disrespectful, impudent, insolent, saucy, shameless; boorish, churlish, clownish, loutish, uncouth, vulgar; undiplomatic, unsportsmanlike; abrupt, blunt, brusque, crusty, curt, gruff, sharp, snippy; antisocial, crabbed, cross, disagreeable, grumpy, sullen, surly; improper, inappropriate, incorrect, indecent, indecorous, unseemly; arrogant, conceited, presumptuous, pretentious

near ant humble, meek, modest, unassertive; deferential, dutiful, respectful, submissive, yielding; acceptable, appropriate, becoming, befitting, correct, decent, decorous, fit, fitting, good, meet, proper, respectable, right, seemly, suitable; affable, cordial, friendly, genial, hospitable, sociable; felicitous, graceful

ant civil, considerate, courteous, genteel, gracious, mannerly, polite, thoughtful, well-bred

impoliteness *n* rude behavior — see DISCOURTESY

import *n* **1** the quality or state of being important — see IMPORTANCE

2 the idea that is conveyed or intended to be conveyed to the mind by language, symbol, or action — see MEANING 1

import *vb* **1** to be of importance — see MATTER

---

2 to communicate or convey (as an idea) to the mind — see MEAN 1

importance *n* the quality or state of being important ⟨a final exam has great *importance*⟩

syn consequence, import, magnitude, moment, significance, weight, weightiness

rel celebrity, distinction, eminence, fame, note, noteworthiness, notoriety, preeminence, prominence, renown; store, substance, value, worth, worthiness; gravity, seriousness; authority, potency, power; mark, name, report, reputation, repute; cachet, position, prestige, rank, standing, stature; glory, greatness, honor, illustriousness

near ant paltriness, pettiness, worthlessness; disgrace, dishonor, disrepute, ignominy, odium, opprobrium, shame; anonymity; obscurity

ant insignificance, littleness, slightness, smallness, triviality, unimportance

important *adj* **1** having great meaning or lasting effect ⟨the discovery of penicillin was a very *important* event in the history of medicine⟩

syn big, consequential, eventful, major, material, meaningful, momentous, significant, substantial, weighty

rel decisive, fatal, fateful, strategic; earnest, grave, serious, sincere; distinctive, exceptional, impressive, outstanding, prominent, remarkable; valuable, worthwhile, worthy; distinguished, eminent, great, illustrious, preeminent, prestigious; famous, notorious, renowned; all-important, critical, crucial

near ant inconsiderable, minor, paltry, petty, worthless; anonymous, nameless, obscure, uncelebrated, unknown

ant insignificant, little, minor, slight, small, trivial, unimportant

2 having great power or influence ⟨Rachel Carson was an *important* figure in the environmental movement⟩

syn influential, mighty, potent, powerful, puissant, significant, strong

rel high-level, senior, top; able, capable, competent, effective, efficient; authoritarian, autocratic, despotic, dictatorial, magisterial, tyrannical (*also* tyrannic); distinguished, dominant, eminent, famous, great, illustrious, notorious, preeminent, prestigious, renowned; dynamic, energetic, forceful, robust, sturdy, tough, vigorous

near ant feeble, flimsy, frail, infirm; anonymous, obscure; incapable, incompetent, ineffective, inept, unfit, useless

ant impotent, insignificant, little, powerless, unimportant, weak

3 having a feeling of superiority that shows itself in an overbearing attitude — see ARROGANT

4 having too high an opinion of oneself — see CONCEITED

importune *vb* to make a request to (someone) in an earnest or urgent manner — see BEG

impose *vb* to establish or apply as a charge or penalty ⟨every town *imposes* a fine for speeding⟩

syn assess, charge, exact, fine, lay, levy, put

rel dock, mulct, penalize, tax; extort, shake down, wrest, wring; bleed, fleece, gouge, milk, skin, squeeze; coerce, compel, force; inflict, wreak; set; reapply, re-impose, relay

near ant abate, diminish, lessen; forgive, release

ant remit

impose (on *or* upon) *vb* to take unfair advantage of — see EXPLOIT 1

imposing *adj* **1** having or showing a serious and reserved manner — see DIGNIFIED

2 large and impressive in size, grandeur, extent, or conception — see GRAND 1

imposition *n* a charge usually of money collected by the government from people or businesses for public use — see TAX

impossible *adj* incapable of being solved or accomplished ⟨the (seemingly *impossible* problem of world hunger⟩ ⟨fitting everything in my backpack seemed an *impossible* task⟩

syn hopeless, unachievable, unattainable, unsolvable

rel impracticable, impractical; doubtful, dubious, far-fetched, improbable, unlikely; implausible, inconceivable, incredible, unbelievable, unthinkable; futile, useless; absurd, fantastic, outlandish, preposterous, ridiculous

near ant practicable, practical, reasonable; likely, probable; acceptable, believable, conceivable, credible, plausible

ant achievable, attainable, doable, feasible, possible, realizable, workable

impost *n* a charge usually of money collected by the government from people or businesses for public use — see TAX

impostor *or* **imposter** *n* one who makes false claims of identity or expertise ⟨the man who claimed to be a prince turned out to be an *impostor*⟩

syn charlatan, fake, faker, fraud, hoaxer, humbug, mountebank, phony (*also* phoney), pretender, quack

rel imitator, impersonator, mimic; actor, bluffer, counterfeiter, deceiver, dissembler, duper, feigner, misleader, trickster; poseur

near ant adept, expert, master, professional, virtuoso, whiz, wizard

impotence *n* the lack of sufficient ability, power, or means — see INABILITY

impotent *adj* **1** not able to produce fruit or offspring — see STERILE 1

2 unable to act or achieve one's purpose — see POWERLESS

impoverished *adj* **1** lacking money or material possessions — see POOR 1

2 producing inferior or only a small amount of vegetation — see BARREN 1

impoverishment *n* the state of lacking sufficient money or material possessions — see POVERTY 1

impracticable *adj* not capable of being put to use or account — see IMPRACTICAL

impractical *adj* not capable of being put to use or account ⟨the flimsy little toy shovel was cute, but completely *impractical* for digging up tree stumps⟩

syn impracticable, inoperable, nonpractical, unusable, unworkable, useless

rel unsuitable; inaccessible, unattainable, unavailable, unobtainable, unreachable; dead, dormant, fallow, free, idle, inactive, inert, inoperative, latent; arrested, interrupted, suspended; unrealistic

near ant accessible, available, obtainable, reachable; all-around (*also* all-round), handy; active, alive, busy, employed, functioning, operating, operative, running, working

ant applicable, feasible, functional, operable, operational, practicable, practical, usable, useful, workable

imprecate *vb* to ask a divine power to send harm or evil upon — see CURSE 1

imprecation *n* a prayer that harm will come to someone — see CURSE 1

imprecise *adj* not precisely correct — see INEXACT 1

impregnable *adj* incapable of being defeated, overcome, or subdued — see INVINCIBLE

impregnate *vb* to wet thoroughly with liquid — see SOAK 1

impress *n* a perceptible trace left by pressure — see PRINT 1

impress *vb* 1 to act upon (a person or a person's feelings) so as to cause a response — see ¹AFFECT 1

2 to produce a vivid impression of — see ENGRAVE 2

impression *n* 1 a perceptible trace left by pressure — see PRINT 1

2 something imagined or pictured in the mind — see IDEA

impressionist *n* a person who imitates another's voice and mannerisms for comic effect — see MIMIC

impressive *adj* having the power to affect the feelings or sympathies — see MOVING

imprimatur *n* an acceptance of something as satisfactory — see APPROVAL 1

imprint *n* 1 a mark or series of marks left on a surface by something that has passed along it — see TRACK 1

2 a perceptible trace left by pressure — see PRINT 1

imprint *vb* to produce a vivid impression of — see ENGRAVE 2

imprison *vb* to put in or as if in prison ⟨in this society, we try to *imprison* criminals so that they can't do any more harm⟩

syn commit, confine, immure, incarcerate, intern, jail, jug, lock (up)

rel constrain, limit, restrain, restrict, shut; apprehend, arrest, capture, catch, detain; impress, shanghai; hold, keep; enslave, subjugate

near ant emancipate, manumit

ant discharge, free, liberate, release

imprisoned *adj* taken and held prisoner — see CAPTIVE

imprisonment *n* the act of confining or the state of being confined — see INTERNMENT

improbable *adj* not likely to be true or to occur ⟨it is *improbable* that we will be allowed to stay out all night⟩

syn doubtful, dubious, far-fetched, flimsy, questionable, unapt, unlikely

rel implausible, impossible, inconceivable, incredible, last, unbelievable, unthinkable; absurd, outlandish, preposterous, ridiculous; outside, remote, slight

near ant believable, conceivable, credible, plausible; possible; liable

ant likely, probable

impromptu *adj* made or done without previous thought or preparation — see EXTEMPORANEOUS

improper *adj* not appropriate for a particular occasion or situation — see INAPPROPRIATE

improperly *adv* in a mistaken or inappropriate way — see WRONGLY

impropriety *n* 1 the quality or state of not being socially proper ⟨the *impropriety* of the song that the campers sang for the visitors was embarrassing⟩

syn inappropriateness, incorrectness, indecency, unfitness

rel coarseness, crudeness; imprudence, indiscretion

near ant discretion, prudence; etiquette

ant appropriateness, correctness, decency, decorousness, fitness, propriety, rightness, seemliness, suitability

2 a socially improper or unsuitable act or remark ⟨such *improprieties* as asking people how much money they make⟩

syn familiarity, gaffe, indiscretion, solecism

rel blunder, error, flub, fumble, goof, lapse, miscue, misstep, mistake, slip, slipup, stumble; discourtesy, incivility, offense (*or* offence); boner, howler, screamer; foul-up, muff; misapprehension, miscalculation, misconception, misjudgment, misstatement, misunderstanding

near ant manners, proprieties

ant amenity, civility, courtesy, formality, gesture

improve *vb* to make better ⟨a little salt would *improve* this bland food⟩

syn ameliorate, amend, better, enhance, enrich, meliorate, perfect, refine

rel correct, emend, rectify, reform, remedy; help; edit, revise; upgrade; fortify, intensify, strengthen; retouch, touch up

near ant damage, harm, hurt, impair, injure, spoil, tarnish; blemish, blight, deface, disfigure, flaw, mar; diminish, lessen, lower, reduce

ant worsen

---

improved *adj* being far along in development — see ADVANCED 1

improvement *n* an instance of notable progress in the development of knowledge, technology, or skill — see ADVANCE 2

improvident *adj* not thinking about and providing for the future ⟨the *improvident* view that the wearing away of the ozone layer need not concern us⟩

syn myopic, shortsighted

rel careless, heedless, imprudent, incautious, injudicious, unwise; extravagant, prodigal, profligate, spendthrift, thriftless, unthrifty; indulgent, lavish, reckless, wasteful

near ant careful, judicious, prudent, sensible, wise; economical, economizing, frugal, scrimping, sparing, thrifty; conserving, preserving, saving

ant farsighted, forehanded, foreseeing, foresighted, forethoughtful, provident

improvise *vb* to perform, make, or do without preparation ⟨since the award was a complete surprise, I *improvised* an acceptance speech⟩

syn ad-lib, extemporize

rel concoct, contrive, cook (up), devise, hatch, invent, make up, think up; cobble (together *or* up), dash (off)

near ant arrange, prepare, ready; consider, contemplate, ponder, study, think; practice (*or* practise), rehearse

improvised *adj* made or done without previous thought or preparation — see EXTEMPORANEOUS

imprudent *adj* showing poor judgment especially in personal relationships or social situations — see INDISCREET

impudence *n* 1 disrespectful or argumentative talk given in response to a command or request — see BACK TALK

2 rude behavior — see DISCOURTESY

impudent *adj* displaying or marked by rude behavior — see NERVY 1

impulse *n* something that arouses action or activity ⟨the new auto factory was just the *impulse* that the local economy needed⟩

syn boost, encouragement, goad, impetus, incentive, incitement, instigation, momentum, motivation, provocation, spur, stimulant, stimulus, yeast

rel inducement, invitation; cause, consideration, motive, reason

impulsive *adj* 1 caused by or suggestive of an irresistible urge — see COMPULSIVE

2 prone to sudden illogical changes of mind, ideas, or actions — see WHIMSICAL

impulsiveness *n* an inclination to sudden illogical changes of mind, ideas, or actions — see WHIMSICALITY

impunity *n* freedom from punishment, harm, or loss ⟨she mistakenly believed that she could insult people with *impunity*⟩

syn exemption, immunity

rel armor, defense, guard, protection, safeguard, safety; security, shield; buffer, bumper, screen; absolution, absolving, dispensation, forgiveness

near ant exposure, liability, susceptibility, vulnerability

impure *adj* containing foreign or lower-grade substances ⟨be careful, because *impure* motor oil can damage your car's engine⟩

syn adulterated, alloyed, contaminated, dilute, diluted, polluted, tainted, thinned, weakened

rel befouled, besmirched, corrupted, debased, defiled, dirtied, fouled, soiled, spoiled, sullied; blended, commingled, incorporated, intermingled, intermixed, merged, mingled, mixed; coalesced, combined, compounded; cheapened, doctored

near ant clarified, filtered, purified, refined; neat, plain, straight; concentrated, strong; uncombined; pasteurized

ant pure, unadulterated, unalloyed, uncontaminated, undiluted, unpolluted, untainted

impurity *n* something that is or that makes impure ⟨*impurities* in the water made it cloudy⟩

syn adulterant, contaminant, defilement, pollutant

rel blot, blotch, spot, stain, taint; dirt, filth, grime; blemish, defect, disfigurement, fault, flaw; abnormality, imperfection, irregularity

near ant clarifier, filter, purifier, refiner; cleanliness, immaculateness, purity

impute *vb* to explain (something) as being the result of something else — see CREDIT 1

in *adj* 1 being in the latest or current fashion — see STYLISH

2 enjoying widespread favor or approval — see POPULAR 1

in *adv* at, within, or to a short distance or time — see NEAR 1

inability *n* the lack of sufficient ability, power, or means ⟨the apparent *inability* of young children to sit still⟩

syn impotence, inadequacy, incapability, incapacity, incompetence, ineptitude, powerlessness

rel inaptitude; ineffectiveness, ineffectualness, inefficiency

near ant aptitude, bent, flair, talent; effectiveness, effectualness, efficaciousness, efficiency; fitness, suitability; power, strength

ant ability, adequacy, capability, capacity, competence, potency

inaccessible *adj* hard or impossible to get to or get at ⟨my pen is *inaccessible* now that it's fallen down the crack behind my desk⟩

syn inconvenient, unapproachable, unattainable, unavailable, unobtainable, unreachable, untouchable

rel distant, far, faraway, far-off, remote, removed; apart, hidden, isolated, out-of-the-way, secluded

near ant close, near, nearby

ant accessible, approachable, attainable, convenient, obtainable, reachable

inaccuracy *n* an unintentional departure from truth or accuracy — see ERROR 1

inaccurate *adj* **1** not being in agreement with what is true — see FALSE 1

2 not precisely correct — see INEXACT 1

inaccurately *adv* in a mistaken or inappropriate way — see WRONGLY

inaction *n* lack of action or activity ⟨as a result of the park department's *inaction*, the city's pools are not ready to open for the summer⟩

syn dormancy, idleness, inactivity, inertness, nonaction, quiescence

rel indolence, languor, lassitude, laziness, lethargy, listlessness, sleepiness, sloth, sluggishness

near ant animateness, briskness, liveliness, sprightliness; business, diligence, employment, industriousness, occupation

ant action, activeness, activity

inactive *adj* **1** slow to move or act ⟨it's easiest to catch snakes early in the morning, while they're still cold and *inactive*⟩

syn dull, inert, lethargic, quiescent, sleepy, sluggish, torpid

rel apathetic, indolent, languorous, lazy, lazyish, listless, slothful; dormant, inanimate, motionless, sedentary, static, still; dead; dopey, drugged

near ant busy, engaged, occupied, working; animated, dynamic, energetic, lively, sprightly, vigorous; assiduous, diligent, hardworking, industrious

ant active

2 not being in a state of use, activity, or employment ⟨an *inactive* oil well⟩

syn dead, dormant, fallow, free, idle, inert, inoperative, latent, off, vacant

rel arrested, interrupted, suspended; asleep, lifeless, quiescent, sleepy; inoperable, unusable, unworkable, useless; dead, dull, slow

phrases out of commission

near ant functional, operable, operational, workable; assiduous, industrious; energetic, vigorous; feasible, practical, usable, useful, viable

ant active, alive, busy, employed, functioning, on, operating, operative, running, working

inactivity *n* **1** lack of action or activity — see INACTION

2 lack of use — see DISUSE

inadequacy *n* **1** a falling short of an essential or desirable amount or number — see DEFICIENCY

2 the lack of sufficient ability, power, or means — see INABILITY

inadequate *adj* not coming up to a usual standard or meeting a particular need — see SHORT 3

inadequately *adv* in an unsatisfactory way — see BADLY

inadvertent *adj* happening by chance — see ACCIDENTAL

inadvisable *adj* showing poor judgment especially in personal relationships or social situations — see INDISCREET

inane *adj* having no meaning — see MEANINGLESS

inanity *n* **1** a foolish act or idea — see FOLLY 1

2 lack of good sense or judgment — see FOOLISHNESS

inapplicability *n* the quality or state of not having anything to do with the matter at hand — see IRRELEVANCE

inapplicable *adj* not having anything to do with the matter at hand — see IRRELEVANT

inappreciable *adj* not perceptible by a sense or by the mind — see IMPERCEPTIBLE

inappropriate *adj* not appropriate for a particular occasion or situation ⟨a bathing suit is *inappropriate* dress for strolling the streets of this seaside village⟩

syn graceless, improper, inapt, incongruous, incorrect, indecorous, inept, infelicitous, unapt, unbecoming, unfit, unhappy, unseemly, unsuitable, wrong

rel inopportune, unfortunate, unseasonable, untimely; immaterial, irrelevant; incompatible, uncongenial, unharmonious; bad, naughty, sinful; blamable, blameworthy, censurable; banned, barred, disallowed; forbidden, interdicted, outlawed, prohibited, proscribed; awkward, gauche, ungraceful; unacceptable, unsatisfactory

near ant fortunate, opportune, seasonable, timely; apt, material, relevant; compatible, congenial, harmonious; allowed, authorized, permitted; approved, endorsed, licensed (*also* licenced), sanctioned; abetted, encouraged, promoted, supported; acceptable, adequate, satisfactory; commendable, creditable, exemplary; blameless, irreproachable

ant appropriate, becoming, befitting, correct, decorous, felicitous, fit, fitting, genteel, happy, meet, proper, right, seemly, suitable

inappropriately *adv* in a mistaken or inappropriate way — see WRONGLY

inappropriateness *n* **1** the quality or state of being unsuitable or unfitting ⟨I cannot even begin to describe the *inappropriateness* of such language for the dinner table⟩

syn inaptness, incorrectness, infelicity, unfitness, wrongness

rel inadmissibility, inapplicability, extraneousness, inadequacy, irrelevance, meaninglessness, pointlessness, senselessness; inauspiciousness, intolerability, undesirability, undesirableness, unsatisfactorability, uselessness

near ant admissibility, applicability, bearing, connection, materiality, pertinence, pointedness, relevance

ant appropriateness, aptness, correctness, felicitousness, felicity, fitness, fittingness, rightness, seemliness, suitability, suitableness

2 the quality or state of not being socially proper — see IMPROPRIETY 1

inapt *adj* not appropriate for a particular occasion or situation — see INAPPROPRIATE

inaptly *adv* in a mistaken or inappropriate way — see WRONGLY

inaptness *n* the quality or state of being unsuitable or unfitting — see INAPPROPRIATENESS 1

inarticulate *adj* unable to speak — see MUTE 1

inasmuch as *conj* for the reason that — see SINCE

inaugural *adj* coming before all others in time or order — see FIRST 1

inaugural *n* the process or an instance of being formally placed in an office or organization — see INSTALLATION 1

inaugurate *vb* **1** to be responsible for the creation and early operation or use of — see FOUND

2 to put into an office or welcome into an organization with special ceremonies — see INSTALL 1

inauguration *n* the process or an instance of being formally placed in an office or organization — see INSTALLATION 1

inaugurator *n* a person who establishes a whole new field of endeavor — see FATHER 2

inauspicious *adj* being or showing a sign of evil or calamity to come — see OMINOUS

inauthentic *adj* being such in appearance only and made or manufactured with the intention of committing fraud — see COUNTERFEIT

inborn *adj* **1** being a part of the innermost nature of a person or thing — see INHERENT

2 genetically passed or capable of being passed from parent to offspring — see HEREDITARY

inbred *adj* being a part of the innermost nature of a person or thing — see INHERENT

incandescence *n* the steady giving off of the form of radiation that makes vision possible — see LIGHT 1

incandescent *adj* giving off or reflecting much light — see BRIGHT 1

incantation *n* a spoken word or set of words believed to have magic power — see SPELL 1

incapability *n* the lack of sufficient ability, power, or means — see INABILITY

incapable *adj* lacking qualities (as knowledge, skill, or ability) required to do a job — see INCOMPETENT

incapacitate *vb* to render powerless, ineffective, or unable to move — see PARALYZE

incapacitated *adj* deprived of the power to perform one or more natural bodily activities — see DISABLED

incapacity *n* the lack of sufficient ability, power, or means — see INABILITY

incarcerate *vb* to put in or as if in prison — see IMPRISON

incarcerated *adj* taken and held prisoner — see CAPTIVE

incarceration *n* the act of confining or the state of being confined — see INTERNMENT

incarnate *vb* to represent in visible form — see EMBODY 2

incarnation *n* a visible representation of something abstract (as a quality) — see EMBODIMENT

incautious *adj* not paying or showing close attention especially for the purpose of avoiding trouble — see CARELESS 1

incautiousness *n* failure to take the care that a cautious person usually takes — see NEGLIGENCE 1

incendiary *n* **1** a person who deliberately and unlawfully sets fire to a building or other property — see ARSONIST

2 a person who stirs up public feelings especially of discontent — see AGITATOR

incense *n* a sweet or pleasant smell — see FRAGRANCE

incense *vb* to make angry — see ANGER

incensed *adj* feeling or showing anger — see ANGRY

incentive *n* something that arouses action or activity — see IMPULSE

inception *n* the point at which something begins — see BEGINNING

incertitude *n* a feeling or attitude that one does not know the truth, truthfulness, or trustworthiness of someone or something — see DOUBT

incessant *adj* going on and on without any interruptions — see CONTINUOUS

incessantly *adv* on every relevant occasion — see ALWAYS 1

inch *n* **1** a very small distance or degree — see HAIR 1

2 an individual part of a process, series, or ranking — see DEGREE 1

inch *vb* **1** to advance gradually beyond the usual or desirable limits — see ENCROACH

2 to move slowly — see CRAWL 2

incident *n* something that happens — see EVENT 1

incidental *adj* happening by chance — see ACCIDENTAL

incipiency *n* the point at which something begins — see BEGINNING

incise *vb* **1** to cut (as letters or designs) on a hard surface — see ENGRAVE 1

2 to penetrate with a sharp edge (as a knife) — see CUT 1

incision *n* a long deep cut — see GASH

incite *vb* **1** to cause or encourage the development of ⟨the rock band's failure to show up *incited* a riot, as the crowd had waited for hours⟩

syn abet, ferment, foment, instigate, provoke, raise, stir (up), whip (up)

rel forward, foster, further, promote, sow, stimulate; set off, trigger; excite, galvanize, inflame, inspire, rouse; activate, energize, quicken, vitalize

near ant check, curb, discourage, inhibit, restrain; calm, soothe, subdue, tranquilize (*also* tranquillize)

2 to rouse to strong feeling or action — see PROVOKE 1

incitement *n* **1** something that arouses a strong response from another — see PROVOCATION 1

2 something that arouses action or activity — see IMPULSE

inciter *n* a person who stirs up public feelings especially of discontent — see AGITATOR

inciting *adj* serving or likely to arouse a strong reaction — see PROVOCATIVE

incivility *n* rude behavior — see DISCOURTESY

inclement *adj* marked by wet and windy conditions — see FOUL 1

inclination *n* **1** a habitual attraction to some activity or thing ⟨her natural *inclination* to help people in need⟩

syn bent, devices, disposition, genius, leaning, partiality, penchant, predilection, predisposition, proclivity, propensity, tendency, turn

rel bias, prejudice; aptitude, faculty, flair, gift, knack, talent; addiction, fondness, liking; forte, speciality, specialty; convention, custom, habit, pattern, practice (*also* practise), routine, trick, way, wont; oddity, peculiarity, quirk, singularity

near ant aversion, dislike, distaste; impartiality, neutrality, objectivity; apathy, disinterestedness, indifference

2 the act of positioning or an instance of being positioned at an angle — see TILT

3 the degree to which something rises up from a position level with the horizon — see SLANT

incline *n* the degree to which something rises up from a position level with the horizon — see SLANT

incline *vb* **1** to set or cause to be at an angle — see LEAN 1

2 to show a liking or proneness (for something) — see LEAN 2

inclined *adj* **1** having a desire or inclination (as for a specified course of action) — see WILLING 1

2 having a liking or affection — see FOND 1

3 having a tendency to be or act in a certain way — see PRONE 1

4 running in a slanting direction — see DIAGONAL

inclining *adj* bending downward or forward — see NODDING

include *vb* to have as part of a whole ⟨the test *included* some hard essay questions⟩

syn carry, comprehend, contain, embrace, encompass, entail, involve, number, take in

rel comprise, consist (of); have, hold, own, possess; admit, receive; compose, constitute, form, make; assimilate, embody, incorporate, integrate

near ant bar, debar, preclude, prevent, prohibit; deny, refuse, reject; eliminate, except, rule out; lose, mislay, misplace

ant exclude, omit

inclusive *adj* covering everything or all important points — see ENCYCLOPEDIC

incognito *adj* not named or identified by a name — see NAMELESS 1

incoherent *adj* **1** not clearly or logically connected ⟨the thriller's *incoherent* plot left movie audiences wondering who did what⟩

syn disconnected, disjointed, unconnected

rel baffling, bewildering, confounding, confused, confusing, disordered, disorderly, disorganized, muddled, perplexing, puzzling; disconcerting, frustrating; fallacious, illogical, inconsistent, invalid, irrational, unsound; absurd, asinine, eccentric, foolish, odd, peculiar, strange, unreasonable, unusual, weird; meaningless, nonsensical, nutty, preposterous, ridiculous, senseless, silly; unconvincing, unsatisfying; inexplicable, unaccountable, unexplainable

near ant ordered, orderly, organized; logical, rational, reasonable, sensible, solid, sound, valid; cogent, compelling, convincing, persuasive, plausible, satisfying; clear, lucid, perspicuous

ant coherent, connected

2 consisting of particles that do not stick together — see LOOSE 2

incombustible *adj* incapable of being burned ⟨we keep our important papers in an *incombustible* safe in the basement⟩

syn fireproof, noncombustible, nonflammable, noninflammable, uninflammable

rel nonexplosive

near ant ablaze, afire, blazing, burning, fiery; consumable; explosive, incendiary, volcanic

ant burnable, combustible, flammable, ignitable, inflammable

income *n* an increase usually measured in money that comes from labor, business, or property ⟨her summer job gave her some extra *income*⟩

syn earnings, gain(s), proceeds, profit, return, revenue, yield

rel killing, windfall; salary, tips, wages; capital, finances, funds, money

near ant cost, expenditures, expenses, outgo, outlay

incommode *vb* to cause discomfort to or trouble for — see INCONVENIENCE

incommoding *adj* causing difficulty, discomfort, or annoyance — see INCONVENIENT 1

incommunicable *adj* beyond the power to describe — see INDESCRIBABLE

incomparable *adj* having no equal or rival for excellence or desirability — see ONLY 1

incompatible *adj* not being in agreement or harmony — see INCONSISTENT

incompetence *n* the lack of sufficient ability, power, or means — see INABILITY

incompetent *adj* lacking qualities (as knowledge, skill, or ability) required to do a job ⟨an *incompetent* carpenter had built the deck, and the railings were loose already⟩
syn incapable, inept, inexpert, unfit, unqualified, unskilled, unskillful
rel ineffective, ineffectual, inefficient; callow, green, inexperienced, raw; unequipped, unprepared, untrained; useless, worthless; ineligible; wanting
near ant prepared, ready, trained; experienced, practiced (*or* practised), seasoned, veteran
ant able, capable, competent, expert, fit, qualified, skilled, skillful

incomplete *adj* lacking some necessary part ⟨an *incomplete* puzzle that has several pieces missing⟩
syn deficient, fragmental, fragmentary, halfway, partial
rel broken, damaged, flawed, impaired, imperfect, injured, marred, spoiled; sketchy, uncompleted, unfinished
near ant flawless, perfect, unbroken, undamaged, unimpaired, uninjured, unmarred; completed, finished
ant complete, entire, full, intact, whole

incompletely *adv* in some measure or degree — see PARTLY

incomprehensible *adj* impossible to understand ⟨rocket science is *incomprehensible* to most people⟩
syn impenetrable, unfathomable, unintelligible
rel abstruse, enigmatic (*also* enigmatical), esoteric, inscrutable, recondite; cryptic, mysterious, obscure; unanswerable, unknowable; baffling, bewildering, confounding, confusing, mystifying, perplexing, puzzling
near ant basic, elementary, rudimentary; easy, simple; coherent, connected, ordered, orderly, organized; clear, cogent, compelling, convincing, lucid, perspicuous, plain, straightforward
ant fathomable, intelligible, understandable

inconceivable *adj* too extraordinary or improbable to believe — see INCREDIBLE

incongruity *n* someone or something with qualities or features that seem to conflict with one another — see CONTRADICTION 1

incongruous *adj* **1** not appropriate for a particular occasion or situation — see INAPPROPRIATE
2 not being in agreement or harmony — see INCONSISTENT

inconsequential *adj* **1** lacking importance — see UNIMPORTANT
2 so small or unimportant as to warrant little or no attention — see NEGLIGIBLE

inconsiderable *adj* **1** lacking importance — see UNIMPORTANT
2 so small or unimportant as to warrant little or no attention — see NEGLIGIBLE 1

inconsiderate *adj* showing a lack of manners or consideration for others — see IMPOLITE

inconsideration *n* rude behavior — see DISCOURTESY

inconsistent *adj* not being in agreement or harmony ⟨*inconsistent* theories make it difficult to settle on one explanation⟩
syn clashing, conflicting, disagreeing, discordant, discrepant, incompatible, incongruous, inharmonious
rel irreconcilable; antagonistic, antithetical, contradictory, contrary, opposing, opposite
near ant akin, like, similar
ant agreeing, compatible, congruous, consistent, consonant, harmonious, nonconflicting

inconsolable *adj* feeling unhappiness — see SAD 1

inconspicuous *adj* not readily seen or noticed — see UNOBTRUSIVE

inconstancy *n* lack of faithfulness especially to one's husband or wife — see INFIDELITY 1

inconstant *adj* **1** likely to change frequently, suddenly, or unexpectedly — see FICKLE 1
2 not true in one's allegiance to someone or something — see FAITHLESS

incontestable *adj* not capable of being challenged or proved wrong — see IRREFUTABLE

incontestably *adv* without any question — see INDEED 1

incontrovertible *adj* not capable of being challenged or proved wrong — see IRREFUTABLE

incontrovertibly *adv* without any question — see INDEED 1

inconvenience *n* something that is a source of irritation — see ANNOYANCE 3

inconvenience *vb* to cause discomfort or trouble for ⟨he *inconvenienced* his sister by moving into her tiny apartment⟩
syn discommode, disoblige, disturb, incommode, trouble
rel burden, encumber, saddle, weigh; hamper, hamstring, hinder, hobble, impede; aggravate, anger, annoy, bother, bug, exasperate, gall, get, nettle, peeve, pique, put out, rile, vex; grate, inflame, provoke; agitate, perturb, upset
near ant aid, assist, help; ease, facilitate; appease, conciliate, mollify, pacify, placate; delight, gladden, gratify, please; comfort, console, content
ant accommodate, oblige

inconvenient *adj* **1** causing difficulty, discomfort, or annoyance ⟨the unexpected visitors showed up at an *inconvenient* time⟩
syn awkward, discommoding, disobliging, incommoding
rel bothersome, burdensome, onerous, troublesome; annoying, exasperating, irritating
near ant acceptable, bearable, tolerable; advantageous, desirable, good, helpful
ant convenient
2 hard or impossible to get to or get at — see INACCESSIBLE

incorporate *vb* **1** to make a part of a body or system — see EMBODY 1

2 to turn into a single mass that is more or less the same throughout — see BLEND 1

incorporeal *adj* not composed of matter — see IMMATERIAL 1

incorrect *adj* **1** having an opinion that does not agree with truth or the facts ⟨you're *incorrect* about the date of the final exam—it's next Tuesday, not Wednesday⟩

syn mistaken, wrong

rel confused, misguided, misled; erroneous, false; deceived, deluded, tricked

phrases all wet, full of it

near ant informed; accurate, exact, precise

ant correct, right

2 not appropriate for a particular occasion or situation — see INAPPROPRIATE

3 not being in agreement with what is true — see FALSE 1

incorrectly *adv* in a mistaken or inappropriate way — see WRONGLY

incorrectness *n* **1** the quality or state of being unsuitable or unfitting — see INAPPROPRIATENESS 1

2 the quality or state of not being socially proper — see IMPROPRIETY 1

incorrigible *adj* not capable of being cured or reformed — see HOPELESS 1

increase *n* **1** something added (as by growth) ⟨shortly after he turned 12, he had a sudden height *increase*⟩

syn accretion, accrual, addendum, addition, augmentation, boost, expansion, gain, increment, plus, proliferation, raise, rise, supplement

rel accumulation; complement; appendix, continuation, extension, uptrend, upturn; jump

near ant deduction

ant abatement, decrease, diminishment, lessening, lowering, reduction

2 the act or process of becoming greater in number — see MULTIPLICATION

increase *vb* **1** to make greater in size, amount, or number ⟨if you *increase* the number by two, how much do you have now?⟩

syn add (to), aggrandize, amplify, augment, boost, compound, enlarge, escalate, expand, extend, multiply, raise, swell, up

rel skyrocket; blow up, dilate, distend, inflate; elongate, lengthen, prolong; protract; enhance, heighten, intensify, magnify; complement, supplement; beef (up), reinforce, strengthen; maximize; accumulate, amass, collect; follow up, parlay

near ant abbreviate, abridge, curtail, shorten; compress, condense, constrict, cut back, retrench

ant abate, contract, decrease, diminish, lessen, lower, reduce, subtract (from)

2 to become greater in extent, volume, amount, or number ⟨the number of In-

ternet users *increased* rapidly during the 1990s⟩

syn accumulate, appreciate, balloon, build (up), burgeon, enlarge, escalate, expand, mount, multiply, mushroom, proliferate, rise, snowball, swell, wax

rel rocket, skyrocket; heighten, intensify; blow up, distend, inflate; crest, peak, surge

ant contract, decrease, diminish, lessen, wane

increased *adj* being at a higher level than average — see HIGH 2

incredible *adj* too extraordinary or improbable to believe ⟨she came in on Monday with an *incredible* story about monsters eating her homework⟩

syn fantastic, implausible, inconceivable, unbelievable, unconvincing, unimaginable, unthinkable

rel doubtful, dubious, far-fetched, fishy, flimsy, questionable, suspect, unlikely, unreasonable; hopeless, impossible; absurd, outlandish, preposterous, ridiculous; indefensible, insupportable, untenable

near ant likely, possible, probable; reasonable

ant believable, conceivable, convincing, credible, imaginable, plausible

incredulity *n* refusal to accept as true — see DISBELIEF

incredulous *adj* inclined to doubt or question claims — see SKEPTICAL 1

increment *n* something added (as by growth) — see INCREASE 1

incremental *adj* **1** proceeding or changing by steps or degrees — see GRADUAL

2 produced by a series of additions of identical or similar things — see CUMULATIVE

incriminate *vb* to make a claim of wrongdoing against — see ACCUSE

incubate *vb* to cover and warm eggs to hatch them — see SET 1

incubus *n* an evil spirit — see DEMON

inculcate *vb* to cause (as a person) to become filled or saturated with a certain quality or principle — see INFUSE

incumbent *adj* forcing one's compliance or participation by or as if by law — see MANDATORY

incurable *adj* not capable of being cured or reformed — see HOPELESS 1

incurious *adj* having or showing a lack of interest or concern — see INDIFFERENT 1

incursion *n* a sudden attack on and entrance into hostile territory — see RAID 1

indecency *n* **1** the quality or state of being obscene — see OBSCENITY 1

2 the quality or state of not being socially proper — see IMPROPRIETY 1

indecent *adj* depicting or referring to sexual matters in a way that is unacceptable in polite society — see OBSCENE 1

indecision *n* the act or an instance of pausing because of uncertainty about the right course of action — see HESITATION

---

syn synonym(s)   *rel* related words
ant antonym(s)   *near ant* near antonym(s)

indecorous *adj* not appropriate for a particular occasion or situation — see INAPPROPRIATE

indeed *interj* how surprising, doubtful, or unbelievable — see NO

indeed *adv* **1** without any question ⟨I know that you can *indeed* do better than that⟩

syn assuredly, certainly, definitely, doubtless, forsooth, incontestably, incontrovertibly, indisputably, really, surely, truly, undeniably, undoubtedly, unquestionably

rel conceivably, likely, perhaps, possibly, probably; clearly, obviously, unmistakably

phrases by all means, for sure

2 not merely this but also — see EVEN

indefatigable *adj* showing no signs of weariness even after long hard effort — see TIRELESS

indefatigably *adv* with great effort or determination — see HARD 1

indefensible *adj* too bad to be excused or justified — see INEXCUSABLE

indefinable *adj* beyond the power to describe — see INDESCRIBABLE

indefinite *adj* **1** being or seeming to be without limits — see INFINITE

2 not clearly expressed — see VAGUE 1

3 not seen or understood clearly — see FAINT 1

indelicacy *n* the quality or state of lacking refinement or good taste — see VULGARITY 1

indelicateness *n* the quality or state of lacking refinement or good taste — see VULGARITY 1

indemnification *n* payment to another for a loss or injury — see COMPENSATION 1

indemnify *vb* to provide (someone) with a just payment for loss or injury — see COMPENSATE 1

indemnity *n* payment to another for a loss or injury — see COMPENSATION 1

indentation *n* **1** a sunken area forming a separate space — see HOLE 1

2 a V-shaped cut usually on an edge or a surface — see NOTCH 1

indented *adj* curved inward — see HOLLOW

independence *n* **1** the ability to care for one's self — see SELF-SUFFICIENCY

2 the state of being free from the control or power of another — see FREEDOM 1

independent *adj* **1** able to take care of oneself without outside help — see SELF-SUFFICIENT

2 not being under the rule or control of another — see FREE 1

independently *adv* without aid or support — see ALONE 1

in-depth *adj* covering everything or all important points — see ENCYCLOPEDIC

indescribable *adj* beyond the power to describe ⟨the *indescribable* immensity of Mount Everest⟩

syn incommunicable, indefinable, ineffable, inexpressible, nameless, unspeakable, unutterable

rel inconceivable, incredible, unbelievable, unimaginable, unthinkable; characterless, featureless, nondescript

near ant conceivable, imaginable, thinkable

ant communicable, definable, expressible, speakable

indestructible *adj* impossible to destroy ⟨diamonds are widely considered to be *indestructible,* because they are one of the hardest known substances⟩

syn imperishable, inextinguishable

rel incorruptible; deathless, immortal, perpetual, undying; indelible; durable, enduring, lasting, permanent, unbreakable; strong, sturdy, tough

near ant mortal; impermanent, transient, transitory; breakable, delicate, flimsy, fragile, frail

ant destructible, extinguishable, perishable

index *n* an arrow-shaped piece on a dial or scale for registering information — see POINTER 1

index *vb* to put (someone or something) on a list — see ¹LIST 2

Indian *n* a member of any of the native peoples of the western hemisphere usually not including the Eskimos — see AMERICAN INDIAN

indicate *vb* to convey an idea indirectly — see HINT

indication *n* a slight or indirect pointing to something (as a solution or explanation) — see HINT 1

indicative *adj* indicating something ⟨a wide-eyed look that is *indicative* of his constant curiosity⟩

syn denotative, denoting, significant, signifying, telltale

rel alluding, allusive, referring; characteristic, symptomatic; demonstrative, exhibiting, expressive; symbolic (*also* symbolical); connoting, hinting, implying, insinuating, suggestive

indicator *n* an arrow-shaped piece on a dial or scale for registering information — see POINTER 1

indict *vb* to make a claim of wrongdoing against — see ACCUSE

indictment *n* a formal claim of criminal wrongdoing against a person — see CHARGE 1

indifference *n* lack of interest or concern ⟨he felt only *indifference* towards his schoolwork⟩

syn apathy, casualness, disinterestedness, disregard, insouciance, nonchalance, unconcern

rel halfheartedness, lukewarmness; carelessness, heedlessness, recklessness, unawareness; lethargy, listlessness; calmness, detachment, dispassion; callousness, hardheartedness, hardness, insensitivity; impassivity, phlegm; aloofness, coldness

near ant attentiveness, awareness, conscientiousness, heedfulness; sensitivity, warmheartedness; bias, partiality, prejudice; ardor, fervency, passion, warmth, zeal

ant concern, interest, regard

indifferent *adj* 1 having or showing a lack of interest or concern ⟨*indifferent* about the result of the football game⟩

syn apathetic, casual, disinterested, incurious, insouciant, nonchalant, perfunctory, unconcerned, uncaring, uninterested

rel halfhearted, lukewarm; aloof, cold, numb, remote, unemotional; calm, detached, dispassionate; careless, heedless, mindless; impassive, phlegmatic, stoic (*or* stoical), stolid; lethargic, listless; unawed, undazzled, unimpressed

near ant attentive, aware, conscientious, heedful, mindful; caring, sensitive, warmhearted; ardent, fervent, passionate, warm, zealous

ant concerned, interested

2 of average to below average quality — see MEDIOCRE 1

indigence *n* the state of lacking sufficient money or material possessions — see POVERTY 1

indigenous *adj* belonging to a particular place by birth or origin — see NATIVE 1

indigent *adj* lacking money or material possessions — see POOR 1

indignant *adj* feeling or showing anger — see ANGRY

indignation *n* an intense emotional state of displeasure with someone or something — see ANGER

indignity *n* an act or expression showing scorn and usually intended to hurt another's feelings — see INSULT

indirect *adj* not straightforward or direct ⟨the cab driver took a very *indirect* route to the hotel⟩ ⟨a long-winded, *indirect* answer to a very simple question⟩

syn circuitous, circular, roundabout

rel crooked, serpentine, sinuous, tortuous, twisting, winding; meandering, rambling, wandering; circumlocutory, long-winded, prolix, verbose; deceitful, deceptive, devious, dishonest, duplicitous, insidious, misleading, sneaky, underhand, underhanded; calculating, crafty, cunning, subtle, tricky

near ant candid, forthright, frank, honest, open, plain, unconcealed, undisguised

ant direct, straight, straightforward

indiscreet *adj* showing poor judgment especially in personal relationships or social situations ⟨telling a friend's secrets is *indiscreet*, and unkind as well⟩

syn ill-advised, imprudent, inadvisable, injudicious, tactless, unadvisable, unwise

rel dumb, idiotic, moronic, stupid; inconsiderate, thoughtless; ill-mannered, improper, inappropriate, indecorous, unbecoming, uncivil, unseemly; foolish, harebrained, nonsensical, preposterous, senseless, silly

near ant intelligent, logical, rational, sensible, smart, sound; appropriate, becoming, civil, decorous, proper, seemly; sage, sane, sapient

ant advisable, discreet, judicious, prudent, tactful, wise

indiscretion *n* a socially improper or unsuitable act or remark — see IMPROPRIETY 2

indispensable *adj* impossible to do without — see ESSENTIAL 1

indisposed *adj* 1 having doubts about the wisdom of doing something — see HESITANT

2 temporarily suffering from a disorder of the body — see SICK 1

indisposition *n* the condition of not being in good health — see SICKNESS 1

indisputable *adj* not capable of being challenged or proved wrong — see IRREFUTABLE

indisputably *adv* without any question — see INDEED 1

indistinct *adj* not seen or understood clearly — see FAINT 1

indistinguishable *adj* 1 not perceptible by a sense or by the mind — see IMPERCEPTIBLE

2 not seen or understood clearly — see FAINT 1

3 resembling another in every respect — see SAME 1

individual *adj* 1 of, relating to, or belonging to a single person ⟨everyone has his or her own *individual* opinion about the subject, but you will have to work together⟩

syn individualized, particular, peculiar, personal, personalized, private, privy, separate, singular, unique

rel characteristic, distinctive, intimate; identifying, idiosyncratic; special, specific; independent, nonconformist, self-directed, self-sufficient; custom, customized, specialized

near ant broad, prevailing, prevalent, widespread; common, normal, regular, typical

ant general, generic, popular, public, shared, universal

2 not the same or shared — see SEPARATE 1

3 serving to identify as belonging to an individual or group — see CHARACTERISTIC 1

individual *n* 1 a member of the human race — see HUMAN

2 one that has a real and independent existence — see ENTITY

individualist *n* a person who does not conform to generally accepted standards or customs — see NONCONFORMIST 1

individuality *n* the set of qualities that make a person different from other people ⟨her *individuality* showed through in everything she did⟩

syn character, identity, personality, selfhood, self-identity

rel distinctiveness, oneness, peculiarity, separateness, singleness, singularity,

uniqueness; disposition, humor, nature, temper, temperament; independence
near ant conformity, conventionality

individualized *adj* of, relating to, or belonging to a single person — see INDIVIDUAL 1

indoctrinate *vb* to cause to acquire knowledge or skill in some field — see TEACH

indolence *n* an inclination not to do work or engage in activities — see LAZINESS

indolent *adj* not easily aroused to action or work — see LAZY

indomitable *adj* incapable of being defeated, overcome, or subdued — see INVINCIBLE

indubitable *adj* not capable of being challenged or proved wrong — see IRREFUTABLE

induce *vb* **1** to be the cause of (a situation, action, or state of mind) — see EFFECT
2 to cause (someone) to agree with a belief or course of action by using arguments or earnest requests — see PERSUADE

inducement *n* the act of reasoning or pleading with someone to accept a belief or course of action — see PERSUASION 1

inducing *n* the act of reasoning or pleading with someone to accept a belief or course of action — see PERSUASION 1

induct *vb* to put into an office or welcome into an organization with special ceremonies — see INSTALL 1

inductee *n* a person forced or required to enroll in military service — see CONSCRIPT

induction *n* the process or an instance of being formally placed in an office or organization — see INSTALLATION 1

indulge *vb* to give in to (a desire) ⟨the grandparents generally *indulged* the child's wishes⟩
syn cater (to), gratify, humor
rel bask, luxuriate, revel, wallow; coddle, mollycoddle, pamper, spoil; delight, please, pleasure; sate, satiate, satisfy
near ant bridle, check, constrain, curb, inhibit, restrain, stifle

indulgence *n* **1** an act of kind assistance — see FAVOR 1
2 something adding to pleasure or comfort but not absolutely necessary — see LUXURY 1

industrious *adj* involved in often constant activity — see BUSY 1

industriously *adv* with great effort or determination — see HARD 1

industriousness *n* attentive and persistent effort — see DILIGENCE

industry *n* attentive and persistent effort — see DILIGENCE

inebriate *n* being under the influence of alcohol — see DRUNK 1

inebriate *n* a person who makes a habit of getting drunk — see DRUNK

inebriated *adj* being under the influence of alcohol — see DRUNK

ineffable *adj* beyond the power to describe — see INDESCRIBABLE

ineffective *adj* **1** not producing the desired result ⟨an *ineffective* effort to move the bookcase⟩
syn ineffectual, inefficient, inexpedient
rel abortive, bootless, fruitless, futile, nonproductive, pointless, unavailing, unproductive, unprofitable, unsuccessful, useless, worthless
near ant availing, beneficial, helpful, productive, profitable, successful, useful, worthwhile
ant effective, effectual, efficacious, efficient, expedient
2 producing no results — see FUTILE

ineffectual *adj* **1** not producing the desired result — see INEFFECTIVE 1
2 producing no results — see FUTILE

inefficient *adj* not producing the desired result — see INEFFECTIVE 1

inelegant *adj* **1** lacking social grace and assurance — see AWKWARD 1
2 marked by an obvious lack of style or good taste — see TACKY 1

inept *adj* **1** lacking qualities (as knowledge, skill, or ability) required to do a job — see INCOMPETENT
2 not appropriate for a particular occasion or situation — see INAPPROPRIATE
3 showing or marked by a lack of skill and tact (as in dealing with a situation) — see AWKWARD 2

ineptitude *n* the lack of sufficient ability, power, or means — see INABILITY

inequity *n* the state of being unfair or unjust — see INJUSTICE 1

inert *adj* **1** not being in a state of use, activity, or employment — see INACTIVE 2
2 slow to move or act — see INACTIVE 1

inertia *n* an inclination not to do work or engage in activities — see LAZINESS

inertness *n* lack of action or activity — see INACTION

inescapable *adj* impossible to avoid or evade — see INEVITABLE

inescapably *adv* because of necessity — see NEEDS

inevitable *adj* impossible to avoid or evade ⟨getting wet is *inevitable* if you are going to try to give your dog a bath⟩
syn certain, inescapable, necessary, sure, unavoidable
rel decided, definite, settled; likely, possible, probable; destined, fated, foreordained, predestined, predetermined, preordained; inexorable, relentless, unremitting
phrases in the bag
near ant preventable (*also* preventible); doubtful, dubious, questionable, shaky, unclear; undecided, unsettled; undependable, unreliable; improbable, unlikely
ant avoidable, escapable, uncertain, unsure

inevitably *adv* because of necessity — see NEEDS

inexact *adj* **1** not precisely correct ⟨a thousand is an *inexact* figure for the number of islands in the St. Lawrence River⟩
syn imprecise, inaccurate, loose

rel approximate; erroneous, false, incorrect, off, wrong; general, indefinable, indefinite, indeterminate, indistinct, undefined, undetermined, unsettled, vague; faulty, flawed, mistaken; specious; distorted, fallacious, misleading; doubtful, dubious, questionable, uncertain; inconclusive, indecisive; debatable, disputable; invalidated, unconfirmed, unsubstantiated, unsupported

near ant certain, incontestable, indubitable, positive, sure, undeniable, unquestionable; correct, errorless, factual, right, sound, true, valid; clear-cut, decisive, definable, defined, definite; incontrovertible, indisputable, irrefutable; absolute, unqualified; confirmed, corroborated, determined, established, substantiated, supported, validated

ant accurate, dead, exact, precise

2 not being in agreement with what is true — see FALSE 1

inexcusable *adj* too bad to be excused or justified ⟨spitting at a teacher is *inexcusable* behavior and will be severely punished⟩

syn indefensible, unforgivable, unjustifiable, unpardonable, unwarrantable

rel insufferable, insupportable, intolerable, unbearable, unendurable; abominable, atrocious, heinous, monstrous, outrageous, scandalous, shocking; egregious, flagrant, glaring, gross, rank; unacceptable, untenable; black, evil, iniquitous, vicious, wicked; base, contemptible, deplorable, despicable, dirty, execrable, ignoble, reprobate, vile, wretched; cruel, nasty; blamable, blameworthy, censurable, reprehensible; banned, barred, condemned, disallowed, forbidden, interdicted, outlawed, prohibited, proscribed

near ant acceptable, tolerable; authorized, legal, permissible; allowed, permitted, tolerated; approved, endorsed, sanctioned; abetted, encouraged, promoted, supported; ethical, good, moral, virtuous

ant defensible, excusable, forgivable, justifiable, pardonable

inexhaustible *adj* showing no signs of weariness even after long hard effort — see TIRELESS

inexpedient *adj* not producing the desired result — see INEFFECTIVE 1

inexpensive *adj* costing little — see CHEAP 1

inexperienced *adj* **1** lacking in adult experience or maturity — see CALLOW

2 lacking or showing a lack of expert skill — see AMATEURISH

inexpert *adj* **1** lacking or showing a lack of expert skill — see AMATEURISH

2 lacking qualities (as knowledge, skill, or ability) required to do a job — see INCOMPETENT

3 showing or marked by a lack of skill and tact (as in dealing with a situation) — see AWKWARD 2

inexplicable *adj* impossible to explain ⟨an *inexplicable* desire for ice cream at two in the morning⟩

syn unaccountable, unexplainable

rel indefinable, indescribable, inexpressible; enigmatic (*also* enigmatical), impenetrable, incomprehensible, inscrutable, mysterious, unfathomable, unknowable; irrational, unreasonable, unsound; foolish, mindless, senseless; absurd, odd, peculiar, strange, unusual, weird

near ant logical, rational, reasonable, understandable; sane, sensible, wise; compelling, convincing, persuasive, plausible, satisfying; confirmed, corroborated, determined, established, explained, substantiated, validated

ant accountable, explainable, explicable

inexpressible *adj* beyond the power to describe — see INDESCRIBABLE

inexpressive *adj* not expressing any emotion — see BLANK 1

inextinguishable *adj* impossible to destroy — see INDESTRUCTIBLE

infallible *adj* **1** not being or likely to be wrong ⟨a teacher with an *infallible* memory for names⟩

syn unerring, unfailing

rel errorless, faultless, flawless, impeccable; certain, foolproof, perfect, sure; dependable, reliable

near ant defective, faulty, flawed, imperfect; undependable, unreliable

ant fallible

2 not likely to fail ⟨an *infallible* cure for hiccups⟩

syn certain, sure, unfailing

rel dependable, reliable, surefire; deadly, unerring

near ant doubtful, questionable, uncertain

ant fallible

infamous *adj* not respectable — see DISREPUTABLE

infamy *n* the state of having lost the esteem of others — see DISGRACE 1

infant *n* a recently born person — see BABY

infantile *adj* having or showing the annoying qualities (as silliness) associated with children — see CHILDISH

infatuated (with) *adj* filled with an intense or excessive love for — see ENAMORED (OF)

infatuation *n* a strong but often short-lived liking for another person — see CRUSH 1

infectious *adj* exciting a similar feeling or reaction in others — see CONTAGIOUS 2

infelicitous *adj* not appropriate for a particular occasion or situation — see INAPPROPRIATE

infelicity *n* the quality or state of being unsuitable or unfitting — see INAPPROPRIATENESS 1

infer *vb* **1** to form an opinion through reasoning and information ⟨he *inferred* that she had left because her coat was gone⟩

syn conclude, deduce, extrapolate, gather, judge, reason, understand

---

syn synonym(s) **rel** related words
ant antonym(s) **near ant** near antonym(s)

rel conjecture, guess, speculate, surmise; construe, interpret; contemplate, rationalize, think; ascertain, dope (out), find out

phrases draw a conclusion

2 to convey an idea indirectly — see HINT

inferable *adj* being or provable by reasoning in which the conclusion follows necessarily from given information — see DEDUCTIVE

inference *n* an opinion arrived at through a process of reasoning — see CONCLUSION 1

inferior *adj* **1** situated lower down ⟨creatures that inhabit the dark, *inferior* depths of the ocean⟩

syn lower, nether

rel lowest, nethermost; underlying

near ant highest, uppermost; overhanging, overhead

ant higher, superior, upper

2 of little or less value or merit ⟨a girl who has always felt *inferior* to her older sister⟩

syn mean, minor, secondary, second-class, second-rate

rel junior, lesser, lower, petty, smaller, subordinate, under; average, common, fair, middling, ordinary; amiss, bad, defective, unsatisfactory, wrong; deficient, inadequate, insufficient, unacceptable, littler, slighter, smaller; jerkwater, one-horse, two-bit

near ant major, more, primary, senior; choice, exceptional, first-class, first-rate, high-grade, premium, prime; acceptable, adequate, sufficient

ant greater, higher, superior

3 belonging to the class of people of low social or economic rank — see IGNOBLE 1

4 falling short of a standard — see BAD 1

5 having not so great importance or rank as another — see LESSER

6 of low quality — see CHEAP 2

inferior *n* one who is of lower rank and typically under the authority of another — see UNDERLING

inferno *n* a destructive burning — see FIRE

infertile *adj* **1** not able to produce fruit or offspring — see STERILE 1

2 producing inferior or only a small amount of vegetation — see BARREN 1

infest *vb* to spread or swarm over in a troublesome manner ⟨called in an exterminator because the house was *infested* with ants⟩

syn overrun

rel beset, overspread, overwhelm; abound, crawl, teem; annoy, pester, plague; contaminate, infect

infidelity *n* **1** lack of faithfulness especially to one's husband or wife ⟨*infidelity* can lead to divorce⟩

syn disloyalty, faithlessness, falseness, falsity, inconstancy, perfidiousness, perfidy, unfaithfulness

rel adultery; betrayal, double-cross, double-dealing, duplicity, sellout, treachery, treason; deceit, deception, lying

near ant staunchness, steadfastness; dependability, reliability; honesty, trustworthiness

ant allegiance, constancy, devotedness, devotion, faith, faithfulness, fealty, fidelity, loyalty

2 the act or fact of violating the trust or confidence of another — see BETRAYAL

infiltrate *vb* to introduce in a gradual, secret, or clever way — see INSINUATE

infinite *adj* being or seeming to be without limits ⟨the *infinite* expanse of outer space⟩

syn boundless, endless, illimitable, immeasurable, indefinite, limitless, measureless, unbounded, unfathomable, unlimited

rel abysmal, bottomless; countless, incalculable, inestimable, innumerable, unmeasured; inexhaustible; far-flung, immense, vast

near ant fathomable, measurable; depthless, shallow, superficial

ant bounded, circumscribed, confined, definite, finite, limited, restricted

infinitesimal *adj* very small in size — see TINY

infinity *n* endless time — see ETERNITY 1

infirm *adj* lacking bodily strength — see WEAK 1

infirmity *n* **1** an abnormal state that disrupts a plant's or animal's normal bodily functioning — see DISEASE

2 the quality or state of lacking physical strength or vigor — see WEAKNESS 1

inflame *vb* **1** to make angry — see ANGER

2 to set (something) on fire — see BURN 2

inflamed *adj* **1** being on fire — see ABLAZE 1

2 feeling or showing anger — see ANGRY

inflammable *adj* capable of catching or being set on fire — see COMBUSTIBLE

inflexibility *n* the quality or state of being demanding or unyielding (as in discipline or criticism) — see SEVERITY

inflexible *adj* **1** not capable of changing or being changed ⟨the *inflexible* law of gravity⟩

syn fixed, hard-and-fast, immutable, invariable, unalterable, unchangeable

rel changeless, constant, determinate, established, set, settled, stable, steadfast, steady, unaltered, unchanging, unvarying; immovable, unmovable

near ant adaptable, adjustable; fickle, fluctuating, inconstant, uncertain, unstable, varying

ant alterable, changeable, flexible, mutable, variable

2 incapable of or highly resistant to bending — see STIFF 1

3 not allowing for any exceptions or loosening of standards — see RIGID 1

4 sticking to an opinion, purpose, or course of action in spite of reason, arguments, or persuasion — see OBSTINATE

inflow *n* a flowing or coming in — see INFLUX

influence *n* **1** the power to direct the thinking or behavior of others usually indirectly ⟨a mayor who doesn't hesitate to use her *influence* to get business leaders behind civic improvements⟩

syn authority, clout, pull, sway, weight

rel command, dominance, dominion, mastery, predominance, scepter, sovereignty, supremacy; consequence, eminence, importance, moment; impact, impression, mark

near ant helplessness, impotence, powerlessness, weakness

2 the power to bring about a result on another — see EFFECT 2

influence *vb* to act upon (a person or a person's feelings) so as to cause a response — see ¹AFFECT 1

influential *adj* **1** having power over the minds or behavior of others ⟨in light of the effect that they have had, religious leaders such as Jesus and Muḥammad must be regarded as among the most *influential* people ever⟩

syn authoritative, forceful, weighty

rel controlling, dominating, masterful; dominant, predominant, sovereign, supreme; eminent, important, momentous

near ant helpless, impotent, powerless, weak; incapable, unable

2 having great power or influence — see IMPORTANT 2

influx *n* a flowing or coming in ⟨a sudden *influx* of people⟩

syn flux, inflow, inrush

rel deluge, flood, flow, inundation, overflow, spate, torrent; rush, stampede; flow, river, stream, tide

near ant emigration, exodus, flight

ant outflow, outpouring

inform *vb* **1** to give information (as to the authorities) about another's improper or unlawful activities — see SQUEAL 1

2 to give information to — see ENLIGHTEN 1

informal *adj* **1** not rigidly following established form, custom, or rules ⟨an *informal* meeting allowed everyone to get acquainted⟩

syn irregular, unceremonious, unconventional, unorthodox

rel unauthorized, unofficial; casual, easygoing, lax, loose, relaxed

near ant correct, decorous, proper; constrained, inhibited, restrained, rigid, stiff, stuffy, uptight

ant ceremonial, ceremonious, conventional, formal, orthodox, regular, routine

2 not designed for special occasions — see CASUAL 1

3 used in or suitable for speech and not formal writing — see COLLOQUIAL 1

informant *n* a person who provides secret information about another's wrongdoing — see INFORMER

information *n* a report of recent events or facts not previously known — see NEWS

informational *adj* providing useful information or knowledge — see INFORMATIVE

informative *adj* providing useful information or knowledge ⟨some Web sites for family vacation resorts are very *informative* and some are practically useless⟩

syn educational, educative, informational, instructional, instructive

rel comprehensive, detailed, full; edifying, elucidative, enlightening, explanatory, illuminating; chatty, gossipy, newsy; availing, beneficial, constructive, helpful, profitable; practical, serviceable, usable, useful, worthwhile

near ant impractical, unhelpful, unusable, useless

ant uninstructive

informed *adj* **1** based on sound reasoning or information — see GOOD 1

2 having information especially as a result of study or experience — see FAMILIAR 2

informer *n* a person who provides secret information about another's wrongdoing ⟨the *informer* who told the police about that conspiracy angered a lot of dangerous people⟩

syn betrayer, informant, snitcher, squealer, stool pigeon, talebearer, tattler, tattletale, telltale

rel collaborator; blabbermouth, gossip, gossiper; snoop, snooper, spy; notifier

infraction *n* a failure to uphold the requirements of law, duty, or obligation — see BREACH 1

infrequent *adj* not often occurring or repeated ⟨a shut-in who made *infrequent* trips to the store⟩

syn occasional, rare, sporadic

rel scarce, scattered, uncommon, unique, unusual; choppy, discontinuous, erratic, fitful, intermittent, irregular, spasmodic, spotty, unsteady

near ant common, ordinary, routine

ant frequent

infrequently *adv* not often — see SELDOM

infringe *vb* to fail to keep — see VIOLATE 1

infringement *n* a failure to uphold the requirements of law, duty, or obligation — see BREACH 1

infuriate *vb* to make angry — see ANGER

infuriated *adj* feeling or showing anger — see ANGRY

infuse *vb* to cause (as a person) to become filled or saturated with a certain quality or principle ⟨parents who *infuse* their children with strong moral values⟩

syn imbue, inculcate, ingrain, inoculate, invest, steep, suffuse

rel animate, enliven, invigorate; implant, instill, plant; impregnate, permeate, pervade, saturate; deluge, drown, fill, flood, inundate, overwhelm, submerge

near ant deprive, divest, strip; clear, empty; eliminate, remove, take away

ingenious *adj* having the skill and imagination to create new things — see CREATIVE 1

---

syn synonym(s)   *rel* related words
ant antonym(s)   *near ant* near antonym(s)

2 showing a use of the imagination and creativity especially in inventing — see CLEVER 1

ingeniousness *n* the skill and imagination to create new things — see CREATIVITY 1

ingenuity *n* the skill and imagination to create new things — see CREATIVITY 1

ingenuous *adj* **1** free from any intent to deceive or impress others — see GUILELESS

2 lacking in worldly wisdom or informed judgment — see NAIVE 1

ingenuously *adv* without any attempt to impress by deception or exaggeration — see NATURALLY 3

ingenuousness *n* the quality or state of being simple and sincere — see NAÏVETÉ 1

ingest *vb* **1** to take in as food — see EAT 1

2 to take into the stomach through the mouth and throat — see SWALLOW 1

ingrain *vb* **1** to cause (as a person) to become filled or saturated with a certain quality or principle — see INFUSE

2 to produce a vivid impression of — see ENGRAVE 2

3 to set solidly in or as if in surrounding matter — see ENTRENCH

ingrained *adj* being a part of the innermost nature of a person or thing — see INHERENT

ingratiating *adj* likely to win one's affection ⟨one of the orphans had a most *ingratiating* smile⟩

syn disarming, endearing, winning, winsome

rel adorable, charming, likable, lovable; affecting, poignant, touching; adulatory, deferential, groveling (*or* grovelling), kowtowing, obsequious, servile, sycophantic; drooling, slavering, slobbering; soapy, sugary, unctuous

near ant alienating, disaffecting, displeasing; repugnant, repulsive; arrogant, disdainful, haughty, insolent, proud, scornful

ingredient *n* one of the parts that make up a whole — see ELEMENT 1

inhabitable *adj* suitable for living in — see LIVABLE

inhabitant *n* one who lives permanently in a place ⟨the *inhabitants* of the town don't like the tourists⟩

syn denizen, dweller, habitant, occupant, resident, resider

rel aborigine, native; citizen, national, subject; colonist, émigré (*also* emigré), migrant, newcomer, settler; burgher, townie, villager

near ant alien, foreigner; guest, tourist, visitor; defector, escaper, evacuee, exile, expatriate, refugee

ant transient

inharmonious *adj* **1** not being in agreement or harmony — see INCONSISTENT 1

2 marked by or producing a harsh combination of sounds — see DISSONANT

inherent *adj* being a part of the innermost nature of a person or thing ⟨an *inherent* concept of justice⟩

syn essential, inborn, inbred, ingrained, innate, integral, intrinsic, natural

rel basic, constitutional, elemental, fundamental; congenital, hereditary, inherited, inmost, inner, interior; internal; characteristic, distinctive, peculiar; normal, regular, typical

near ant alien, foreign; accidental, coincidental, incidental; acquired; superficial, surface; exterior, external

ant adventitious, extraneous, extrinsic

inherently *adv* by natural character or ability — see NATURALLY 1

inheritable *adj* genetically passed or capable of being passed from parent to offspring — see HEREDITARY

inheritance *n* something that is or may be inherited ⟨a sense of humor was her *inheritance* from her mother⟩

syn bequest, birthright, heritage, legacy; patrimony

rel heirloom; bestowal, gift, offering, present

inherited *adj* genetically passed or capable of being passed from parent to offspring — see HEREDITARY

inheritor *n* a person who has the right to inherit property — see HEIR

inhibit *vb* **1** to create difficulty for the work or activity of — see HAMPER

2 to keep from exceeding a desirable degree or level (as of expression) — see CONTROL 1

3 to steer (a person) from an activity or course of action — see DISCOURAGE 2

inhibition *n* **1** the checking of one's true feelings and impulses when dealing with others — see CONSTRAINT 1

2 something that makes movement or progress more difficult — see ENCUMBRANCE

inhospitable *adj* marked by opposition or ill will — see HOSTILE 1

inhuman *adj* **1** difficult to endure — see HARSH 1

2 having or showing a lack of sympathy or tender feelings — see HARD 1

inhumane *adj* **1** having or showing a lack of sympathy or tender feelings — see HARD 1

2 having or showing the desire to inflict severe pain and suffering on others — see CRUEL 1

inhumanity *n* the willful infliction of pain and suffering on others — see CRUELTY

inimical *adj* **1** marked by opposition or ill will — see HOSTILE 1

2 opposed to one's interests — see ADVERSE 1

inimitable *adj* having no equal or rival for excellence or desirability — see ONLY 1

iniquitous *adj* not conforming to a high moral standard; morally unacceptable — see BAD 2

iniquity *n* **1** immoral conduct or practices harmful or offensive to society — see VICE 1

2 that which is morally unacceptable — see EVIL

initial *adj* coming before all others in time or order — see FIRST 1

initially *adv* in the beginning — see ORIGINALLY

initiate *vb* **1** to be responsible for the creation and early operation or use of — see FOUND

2 to impart knowledge of a new thing or situation to — see ACQUAINT 1

3 to put into an office or welcome into an organization with special ceremonies — see INSTALL 1

initiation *n* the process or an instance of being formally placed in an office or organization — see INSTALLATION 1

initiative *n* readiness to engage in daring or difficult activity — see ENTERPRISE 2

initiator *n* a person who establishes a whole new field of endeavor — see FATHER 2

inject *vb* to put among or between others — see INSERT

injudicious *adj* showing poor judgment especially in personal relationships or social situations — see INDISCREET

injure *vb* **1** to cause bodily damage to ⟨*injured* himself while skiing⟩
syn damage, harm, hurt, wound
rel batter, bruise, contuse, gash, gore, lacerate, scald, scar, scathe, tear; cripple, lame, maim, mangle, mutilate; afflict, torment, torture; lay up; blemish, impair, mar, scrape, spoil
near ant cure, fix, heal, mend, remedy
2 to reduce the soundness, effectiveness, or perfection of — see DAMAGE 1

injurious *adj* causing or capable of causing harm — see HARMFUL

injury *n* **1** something that causes loss or pain ⟨the harsh words were the worst *injury*⟩
syn damage, detriment, harm, hurt
rel disservice, injustice, outrage, wrong; affront, dart, indignity, insult, offense (*or* offence); crippling, mayhem, mutilation; defacement, disablement, disability, disfigurement; abrasion, bruise, bump, contusion, scald, scar, scathe, scrape, scratch, sear
near ant healing, recovery; cure, fix, remedy
2 unfair or inadequate treatment of someone or something or an instance of this — see DISSERVICE

injustice *n* **1** the state of being unfair or unjust ⟨the *injustice* of the coach's accusation that I'd been lazy frustrated and angered me⟩
syn inequity, unfairness, unjustness
rel dirtiness, foulness
ant equity, fairness, justice
2 unfair or inadequate treatment of someone or something or an instance of this — see DISSERVICE

inkling *n* a slight or indirect pointing to something (as a solution or explanation) — see HINT 1

---

syn synonym(s)   *rel* related words
ant antonym(s)   *near ant* near antonym(s)

inlet *n* a part of a body of water that extends beyond the general shoreline — see GULF 1

inn *n* a place that provides rooms and usually a public dining room for overnight guests — see HOTEL

innards *n pl* the internal organs of the body — see GUT 1

innate *adj* being a part of the innermost nature of a person or thing — see INHERENT

innately *adv* by natural character or ability — see NATURALLY 1

inner *adj* **1** situated farther in ⟨an *inner* area of the national park that is some distance from the nearest road⟩
syn inside, interior, internal, inward
rel inmost, innermost; central, mid, middle
near ant outermost, outmost
ant exterior, external, outer, outside, outward
2 of or relating to the mind — see MENTAL 1

innocence *n* **1** the quality or state of being free from guilt or blame ⟨the accused criminal eventually proved her *innocence* and was released⟩
syn blamelessness, faultlessness, guiltlessness, impeccability
rel decency, goodness, honesty, incorruptibility, integrity, righteousness, uprightness, virtuousness; morality, virtue; chastity, purity; harmlessness, inoffensiveness
near ant blame, fault, responsibility; corruption, criminality, depravity, evil, immorality, reprehensibleness, sinfulness, wickedness; harmfulness, offensiveness
ant blameworthiness, culpability, guilt, guiltiness
2 the quality or state of being simple and sincere — see NAÏVETÉ 1

innocent *adj* **1** free from sin ⟨an *innocent* baby⟩
syn pure
rel chaste, moral, virtuous; immaculate, spotless, unblemished, unstained, unsullied; decent, ethical, good, honest, honorable, righteous, upright, virtuous; blameless, guiltless
near ant lascivious, lewd, lustful, unchaste; evil, immoral, iniquitous, reprobate, unrighteous, wicked; corrupt, debased, debauched, degenerate, depraved, dissolute, erring, fallen, lost, perverted; condemned, damned
ant impure, sinful
2 free from guilt or blame ⟨the robbery suspect was found to be *innocent*⟩
syn blameless, clear, faultless, guiltless, impeccable, irreproachable
rel absolved, acquitted, cleared, exonerated, vindicated; ethical, law-abiding, moral, righteous, upright, virtuous
phrases in the clear
near ant blamable, blameworthy, censurable, culpable, impeachable, indictable, punishable; accused, impeached, in-

dicted; condemned, convicted; hangdog, shamed, shamefaced

ant guilty

3 free from any intent to deceive or impress others — see GUILELESS

4 lacking in worldly wisdom or informed judgment — see NAIVE 1

5 not causing injury or hurt — see HARMLESS

innocent *n* an innocent or gentle person — see LAMB

innocently *adv* **1** without any attempt to impress by deception or exaggeration — see NATURALLY 3

2 with purity of thought and deed — see PURELY

innocuous *adj* not causing injury or hurt — see HARMLESS

innovate *vb* to be responsible for the creation and early operation or use of — see FOUND

innovation *n* something (as a device) created for the first time through the use of the imagination — see INVENTION 1

innovative *adj* having the skill and imagination to create new things — see CREATIVE 1

innovator *n* one who creates or introduces something new — see INVENTOR

innumerable *adj* too many to be counted — see COUNTLESS

inoculate *vb* to cause (as a person) to become filled or saturated with a certain quality or principle — see INFUSE

inoffensive *adj* not causing injury or hurt — see HARMLESS

inoperable *adj* **1** not being in working order ⟨we have several *inoperable* cars on the property⟩

syn inoperative, malfunctioning, nonfunctional, nonfunctioning, nonoperating

rel broken; off; deactivated, deadlocked, ineffective, ineffectual, nonproductive, unproductive, unusable, unworkable, useless

phrases on the blink, out of commission

near ant effective, effectual, employable, performing, producing, productive, serving, usable, useful, viable, workable

ant functional, functioning, operable, operating, operational, operative, running, working

2 not capable of being put to use or account — see IMPRACTICAL

inoperative *adj* **1** not being in a state of use, activity, or employment — see INACTIVE 2

2 not being in working order — see INOPERABLE 1

inopportune *adj* occurring before the usual or expected time — see EARLY 2

inopportunely *adv* before the usual or expected time — see EARLY

inordinate *adj* going beyond a normal or acceptable limit in degree or amount — see EXCESSIVE

inordinately *adv* beyond a normal or acceptable limit — see TOO 1

inquest *n* a systematic search for the truth or facts about something — see INQUIRY 1

inquire (into) *vb* to search through or into — see EXPLORE 1

inquire (of) *vb* to put a question or questions to — see ASK 1

inquiry *n* **1** a systematic search for the truth or facts about something ⟨an *inquiry* into the origins of the universe⟩

syn delving, examination, exploration, inquest, inquisition, investigation, probe, probing, research, study

rel quest; audit, check; checkup, diagnosis, inspection; hearing, interrogation, trial; feeler, query, question; poll, questionnaire; challenge, cross-examination, grilling, quiz

2 an act or instance of asking for information — see QUESTION 2

inquisition *n* a systematic search for the truth or facts about something — see INQUIRY 1

inquisitive *adj* interested in what is not one's own business — see CURIOUS 1

inquisitiveness *n* an eager desire to find out about things that are often none of one's business — see CURIOSITY 1

inroad *n* a sudden attack on and entrance into hostile territory — see RAID 1

inrush *n* a flowing or coming in — see INFLUX

insane *adj* **1** having or showing a very abnormal or sick state of mind ⟨only an *insane* person would jump off a skyscraper⟩

syn balmy, bananas, batty, crackbrained, cracked, crazed, crazy, cuckoo, daffy, daft, demented, deranged, loco, loony (*also* looney), lunatic, mad, maniacal (*also* maniac), mental, moonstruck, nuts, nutty, screwy, unbalanced, unsound, wacky

rel dotty, off; aberrant, delusional, disordered; eccentric, odd, queer, strange; foolish, senseless, witless; irrational, unreasonable; berserk, delirious; depressed; distraught, frantic, frenzied, hysterical

phrases around the bend, off one's rocker, out of one's head (*or* mind)

near ant clear, lucid, rational, reasonable; judicious, sensible, wise; healthy, normal

ant balanced, sane, sound

2 conceived or made without regard for reason or reality — see FANTASTIC 1

3 showing or marked by a lack of good sense or judgment — see FOOLISH 1

insanity *n* **1** a serious mental disorder that prevents one from living a safe and normal life ⟨his *insanity* requires that he spend the rest of his life in a mental hospital⟩

syn aberration, dementia, derangement, lunacy, madness, mania

rel irrationality, unreasonableness; delirium, frenzy, hysteria; neurosis, psychosis, schizophrenia; delusion, hallucination, obsession, phobia; abnormality, unsoundness *near ant* lucidity, rationality, reasonableness; normality, soundness

ant mind, saneness, sanity

2 a foolish act or idea — see FOLLY 1

3 lack of good sense or judgment — see FOOLISHNESS 1

inscribe *vb* 1 to cut (as letters or designs) on a hard surface — see ENGRAVE 1

2 to enter in a list or roll — see ENROLL 1

3 to put (someone or something) on a list — see ¹LIST 2

inscrutable *adj* 1 being beyond one's powers to know, understand, or explain — see MYSTERIOUS 1

2 having an often intentionally veiled or uncertain meaning — see OBSCURE 1

insecure *adj* not tightly fastened, tied, or stretched — see LOOSE 1

insecurity *n* the quality or state of not being firmly fixed in position — see INSTABILITY

insensate *adj* having or showing a lack of sympathy or tender feelings — see HARD 1

insensibility *n* 1 a lack of emotion or emotional expressiveness — see APATHY 1

2 a temporary or permanent state of unconsciousness — see FAINT

insensible *adj* 1 having lost consciousness — see UNCONSCIOUS 1

2 not perceptible by a sense or by the mind — see IMPERCEPTIBLE

insensitive *adj* 1 having or showing a lack of sympathy or tender feelings — see HARD 1

2 lacking in sensation or feeling — see NUMB

inseparability *n* the state of being in a very personal or private relationship — see FAMILIARITY 1

insert *vb* to put among or between others ⟨*inserted* a book in its proper place on the shelf⟩

syn fit (in *or* into), inject, insinuate, interject, interpolate, interpose, introduce

rel inlay, inset, install, weave, work (in); cram, sandwich, shove, thrust, wedge; add, append, attach

near ant eject, eliminate, exclude, expel, extract, withdraw; deduct, detach, subtract; reject

inside *adj* 1 not known or meant to be known by the general populace — see PRIVATE 1

2 situated farther in — see INNER 1

inside *n* 1 an interior or internal part ⟨the *inside* of the clock features an amazingly complex mechanism⟩

syn interior, within

rel bowels, guts, innards; stuffing; recesses; center, core, heart

near ant border, boundary, brim, brink, edge, end, extremity, fringe, limit, lip, margin, perimeter, periphery, rim

ant exterior, outside

2 *usually* **insides** *pl* the internal organs of the body — see GUT 1

insight *n* the ability to understand inner qualities or relationships — see WISDOM 1

insightful *adj* having or showing deep understanding and intelligent application of knowledge — see WISE 1

insignificant *adj* 1 lacking importance — see UNIMPORTANT

2 so small or unimportant as to warrant little or no attention — see NEGLIGIBLE 1

insincere *adj* not being or expressing what one appears to be or express ⟨the *insincere* compliments of a spiteful gossip⟩

syn artificial, backhanded, double-dealing, feigned, hypocritical, left-handed, mealy, mealymouthed, two-faced, unctuous

rel empty, hollow, meaningless; deceitful, devious, dishonest, untruthful; facile, glib, superficial; bogus, counterfeit, fake, false, phony (*also* phoney); sham; facetious, jocular

near ant candid, direct, forthright, frank, open, plain, straightforward

ant genuine, heartfelt, honest, sincere, unfeigned

insincerity *n* the pretending of having virtues, principles, or beliefs that one in fact does not have — see HYPOCRISY

insinuate *vb* 1 to introduce in a gradual, secret, or clever way ⟨the spy *insinuated* himself into the terrorist organization⟩

syn infiltrate, slip, sneak, work (in), worm

rel creep, edge, wiggle; insert, interpolate, interpose, introduce

2 to convey an idea indirectly — see HINT

3 to put among or between others — see INSERT

insipid *adj* 1 lacking in taste or flavor ⟨an apple pie with a mushy, *insipid* filling that strongly resembled soggy cardboard⟩

syn flat, flavorless, savorless, tasteless

rel bland, dilute, thin, watery, weak; plain, unflavored

near ant disgusting, distasteful, loathsome, sickening, unappetizing, unpalatable; appetizing, delectable, delicious, palatable, toothsome; piquant, seasoned, spicy; flavored; heavy, rich

ant flavorful, savory, tasty

2 lacking in qualities that make for spirit and character — see WISHY-WASHY 1

insist *vb* to state as a fact usually forcefully — see CLAIM 1

insist (on) *vb* to ask for (something) earnestly or with authority — see DEMAND 1

insistence *n* a solemn and often public declaration of the truth or existence of something — see PROTESTATION

insistent *adj* continuing despite difficulties, opposition, or discouragement — see PERSISTENT

insolence *n* 1 disrespectful or argumentative talk given in response to a command or request — see BACK TALK

2 rude behavior — see DISCOURTESY

insolent *adj* 1 displaying or marked by rude boldness — see NERVY 1

---

syn synonym(s)   *rel* related words

ant antonym(s)   *near ant* near antonym(s)

insouciance *n* lack of interest or concern — see INDIFFERENCE

insouciant *adj* **1** having or showing a lack of concern or seriousness — see CAREFREE

2 having or showing a lack of interest or concern — see INDIFFERENT 1

inspect *vb* to look over closely (as for judging quality or condition) ⟨*inspected* the animal before the show⟩
syn audit, check (out), examine, review, scan, scrutinize, survey
rel notice, observe, watch; peruse, pore (over); analyze, dissect; delve (into), explore, investigate, probe, research, study; categorize, classify
phrases go over
near ant skim; glance (at *or* over); miss, overlook

inspection *n* a close look at or over someone or something in order to judge condition ⟨a room *inspection* should include looking under the bed⟩
syn audit, check, checkup, examination, review, scan, scrutiny, survey
rel analysis, dissection; exploration, investigation, probe, research, study; inquisition, interrogation; perusal; observation, surveillance, watch

inspire *vb* to fill with courage or strength of purpose — see ENCOURAGE 1

inspiring *adj* causing great emotional or mental stimulation — see EXCITING 1

instability *n* the quality or state of not being firmly fixed in position ⟨the *instability* of the bridge became apparent when it suddenly collapsed⟩
syn insecurity, precariousness, shakiness, unsteadiness
rel insubstantiality, unsoundness; changeability, inconstancy, mutability
near ant firmness, soundness, substantiality
ant fixedness, security, stability, steadiness

install *vb* **1** to put into an office or welcome into an organization with special ceremonies ⟨*installed* her as the new principal⟩
syn baptize, inaugurate, induct, initiate, instate, invest
rel swear in; accept, admit, receive, take in; enlist, enroll (*also* enrol)
near ant can, discharge, fire, terminate; muster out

2 to establish or place comfortably or snugly — see ENSCONCE 1

installation *n* **1** the process or an instance of being formally placed in an office or organization ⟨the *installation* of a new president takes place once every four years⟩
syn baptism, inaugural, inauguration, induction, initiation, installment, investiture
rel enlistment, enrollment; promotion
near ant discharge, removal

2 a structure that is designed and built for a particular purpose — see FACILITY

installment *n* the process or an instance of being formally placed in an office or organization — see INSTALLATION 1

instance *n* one of a group or collection that shows what the whole is like — see EXAMPLE

instance *vb* **1** to give as an example — see QUOTE 1

2 to make reference to or speak about briefly but specifically — see MENTION 1

3 to show or make clear by using examples — see ILLUSTRATE 1

instant *adj* **1** done or occurring without any noticeable lapse in time — see INSTANTANEOUS

2 needing immediate attention — see ACUTE 2

instant *n* a very small space of time ⟨it all happened in an *instant*⟩
syn flash, jiffy, minute, moment, second, shake, split second, trice, twinkle, twinkling, wink
rel microsecond, nanosecond; snatch, spurt
near ant aeon (*or* eon), age, eternity; infinity, lifetime

instantaneous *adj* done or occurring without any noticeable lapse in time ⟨the thunder following the lightning was nearly *instantaneous*⟩
syn immediate, instant, straightaway
rel summary; fast, hit-and-run, prompt, quick, rapid, speedy, swift
near ant dilatory, tardy; slow, sluggish; prolonged, protracted; deferred, delayed

instantly *adv* without delay — see IMMEDIATELY

instate *vb* to put into an office or welcome into an organization with special ceremonies — see INSTALL 1

instead *adv* as a substitute ⟨I was offered a ride, but I chose to walk *instead*⟩
syn first, rather
rel alternatively, alternately

instigate *vb* **1** to cause or encourage the development of — see INCITE 1

2 to rouse to strong feeling or action — see PROVOKE 1

instigating *adj* serving or likely to arouse a strong reaction — see PROVOCATIVE

instigation *n* **1** something that arouses a strong response from another — see PROVOCATION 1

2 something that arouses action or activity — see IMPULSE

instigator *n* a person who stirs up public feelings especially of discontent — see AGITATOR

instinctive *adj* done instantly and without conscious thought or decision — see AUTOMATIC 1

instinctual *adj* done instantly and without conscious thought or decision — see AUTOMATIC 1

institute *n* **1** a group of persons formally joined together for some common interest — see ASSOCIATION 2

2 a public organization with a particular purpose or function — see INSTITUTION 1

institute *vb* to be responsible for the creation and early operation or use of — see FOUND

instituter *or* **institutor** *n* a person who establishes a whole new field of endeavor — see FATHER 2

institution *n* 1 a public organization with a particular purpose or function ⟨a charitable *institution* devoted to raising funds to feed the hungry⟩
  syn establishment, foundation, institute
  rel body, collective, group; corporation, enterprise; charity, philanthropy; think tank
  2 a group of persons formally joined together for some common interest — see ASSOCIATION 2

instruct *vb* 1 to cause to acquire knowledge or skill in some field — see TEACH
  2 to give information to — see ENLIGHTEN 1
  3 to issue orders to (someone) by right of authority — see COMMAND 1

instruction *n* 1 a statement of what to do that must be obeyed by those concerned — see COMMAND 1
  2 the act or process of imparting knowledge or skills to another — see EDUCATION 1

instructional *adj* providing useful information or knowledge — see INFORMATIVE

instructive *adj* providing useful information or knowledge — see INFORMATIVE

instructor *n* a person whose occupation is to give formal instruction in a school — see TEACHER

instrument *n* 1 a written or printed paper giving information about or proof of something — see CERTIFICATE
  2 an article intended for use in work — see IMPLEMENT
  3 something used to achieve an end — see AGENT 1

instrumentalist *n* a person who plays a musical instrument — see MUSICIAN 1

instrumentality *n* something used to achieve an end — see AGENT 1

insubordinate *adj* given to resisting authority or another's control — see DISOBEDIENT

insubordination *n* refusal to obey — see DISOBEDIENCE

insubstantial *adj* 1 being of a material lacking in sturdiness or substance — see FLIMSY 1
  2 not composed of matter — see IMMATERIAL 1

insufferable *adj* more than can be put up with — see UNBEARABLE

insufficiency *n* a falling short of an essential or desirable amount or number — see DEFICIENCY

insufficient *adj* not coming up to a usual standard or meeting a particular need — see SHORT 3

insular *adj* not broad or open in views or opinions — see NARROW 2

insulate *vb* to set or keep apart from others — see ISOLATE

insulation *n* the state of being alone or kept apart from others — see ISOLATION

insult *n* an act or expression showing scorn and usually intended to hurt another's feelings ⟨yelling an *insult* at the bully was not a very smart thing to do⟩
  syn affront, barb, dart, dig, epithet, indignity, name, offense (*or* offence), outrage, put-down, sarcasm, slight, slur
  rel gibe (*or* jibe), jeer, sneer, taunt; abuse, invective, vituperation; disapproval, opprobrium; disgrace, dishonor, shame; attack, criticism, slam; torment, torture
  near ant accolade, commendation, compliment; acclaim, applause, praise; adulation, flattery

insult *vb* to cause hurt feelings or deep resentment in ⟨*insulted* the people by saying their home was ugly⟩
  syn affront, dis [*slang*], offend, outrage, slight, wound
  rel cut, snub; displease, distress, disturb, hurt, pain, trouble, upset; jeer, mock, ridicule, sneer (at); taunt; defame, disparage, libel, malign, revile, slander, slur, smear; oppress, persecute, torment, torture
  near ant acclaim, applaud, approve, hail; commend, compliment, eulogize, praise; adulate, flatter; exalt, glorify, honor; delight, gratify, please, satisfy

insupportable *adj* more than can be put up with — see UNBEARABLE

insure *vb* to make sure, certain, or safe — see ENSURE

insurgency *n* open fighting against authority (as one's own government) — see REBELLION

insurgent *adj* taking part in a rebellion — see REBELLIOUS 1

insurgent *n* a person who rises up against authority — see REBEL

insurmountable *adj* incapable of being defeated, overcome, or subdued — see INVINCIBLE

insurrection *n* open fighting against authority (as one's own government) — see REBELLION

insurrectionary *adj* taking part in a rebellion — see REBELLIOUS 1

insurrectionary *n* a person who rises up against authority — see REBEL

insurrectionist *n* a person who rises up against authority — see REBEL

intact *adj* not lacking any part or member that properly belongs to it — see COMPLETE 1

intangible *adj* not capable of being perceived by the sense of touch ⟨electrical energy is completely *intangible*⟩
  syn impalpable
  rel bodiless, immaterial, incorporeal, insubstantial, unsubstantial; ethereal, spiritual, unreal

---

syn synonym(s)   **rel** related words
ant antonym(s)   **near ant** near antonym(s)

near ant tactile; corporeal, physical; embodied, material, real, solid, substantial
ant palpable, tangible, touchable

integer *n* a character used to represent a mathematical value — see NUMBER

integral *adj* 1 being a part of the innermost nature of a person or thing — see INHERENT

2 impossible to do without — see ESSENTIAL 1

3 not lacking any part or member that properly belongs to it — see COMPLETE 1

integrate *vb* 1 to make a part of a body or system — see EMBODY 1

2 to turn into a single mass that is more or less the same throughout — see BLEND 1

integrity *n* 1 conduct that conforms to an accepted standard of right and wrong — see MORALITY 1

2 devotion to telling the truth — see HONESTY 1

3 faithfulness to high moral standards — see HONOR 1

intellect *n* 1 a very smart person — see GENIUS 1

2 the ability to learn and understand or to deal with problems — see INTELLIGENCE 1

intellectual *adj* 1 much given to learning and thinking ⟨as the daughter of college professors, she's used to being around *intellectual* people⟩
syn cerebral, highbrow
rel cultivated, cultured; erudite, learned, literate, scholarly, well-read; academic, bookish, professorial; didactic, pedantic; high-hat, snobbish, snobby, snooty; educated, schooled; brainy, bright, brilliant, clever, intelligent, quick-witted, smart
near ant uncultivated, uncultured; ignorant, illiterate, uneducated, unlettered, unread; dumb, foolish, idiotic, moronic, slow, stupid, unintelligent
ant lowbrow, nonintellectual

2 of or relating to the mind — see MENTAL 1

intelligence *n* 1 the ability to learn and understand or to deal with problems ⟨high scores on this test supposedly demonstrate great *intelligence*⟩
syn brain(s), gray matter, intellect, reason, sense
rel acumen, alertness, astuteness, discernment, insight, judgment (*or* judgement), mentality, perception, perspicacity; sagacity, sapience, wisdom, wit; head, mind, skull
near ant denseness, density, doltishness, dopiness, dullness (*also* dulness), dumbness, fatuity, feeblemindedness, foolishness, idiocy, imbecility, senselessness, simpleness, slowness, stupidity

2 a report of recent events or facts not previously known — see NEWS

intelligent *adj* 1 having or showing quickness of mind ⟨the dolphin is considered one of the most *intelligent* animals⟩ ⟨running for help was an *intelligent* response to the emergency⟩
syn alert, brainy, bright, brilliant, clever, keen, nimble, quick, quick-witted, sharp, sharp-witted, smart
rel apt, ingenious, resourceful; acute, astute, discerning, insightful, knowing, perceptive, perspicacious, sagacious, sapient, savvy, wise; cerebral, erudite, highbrow, knowledgeable, learned, literate, scholarly, well-read; educated, informed, schooled, skilled, trained; creative, inventive, judicious, prudent, sage, sane, sapient, sensible, sound, wise; crafty, cunning, foxy, shrewd, wily; logical, rational, reasonable
near ant retarded; foolish, idiotic, imbecile, imbecilic, moronic, silly, witless; ignorant, illiterate, lowbrow, nonintellectual, unacademic, uneducated, uninformed
ant brainless, dense, doltish, dorky, dull, dumb, mindless, obtuse, simple, slow, stupid, thick, unintelligent

2 having the ability to reason — see RATIONAL 1

intemperate *adj* showing no signs of being under control — see RAMPANT 1

intend *vb* to have in mind as a purpose or goal ⟨he *intends* to be the president of a large corporation someday⟩
syn aim, aspire, contemplate, design, mean, meditate, plan, propose
rel dream, hope, wish; consider, debate, mull (over), ponder; attempt, endeavor, strive, struggle, try; plot, scheme; accomplish, achieve, effect, execute, perform
phrases figure on

intended *n* the person to whom one is engaged to be married — see BETROTHED

intense *adj* extreme in degree, power, or effect ⟨the *intense* cold of the polar regions⟩
syn deep, explosive, exquisite, fearful, ferocious, fierce, furious, hard, heavy, intensive, profound, terrible, vehement, vicious, violent
rel accentuated, aggravated, concentrated, deepened; emphasized, enhanced, heightened, intensified, magnified; stressed; exhaustive, thorough; harsh, rigorous, severe
near ant feeble, weak; shallow, superficial; moderated, qualified; alleviated, eased, lightened, toned (down); abated, decreased, diminished, lessened, reduced, subdued
ant light, moderate, soft

intensely *adv* with great effort or determination — see HARD 1

intensify *vb* to make markedly greater in measure or degree ⟨*intensified* her efforts to move that bookcase by herself⟩
syn amplify, beef (up), boost, consolidate, deepen, enhance, heighten, magnify, redouble, step up, strengthen
rel broaden, enlarge, expand, extend, lengthen; accelerate, hasten, quicken; accentuate, emphasize, stress; augment, reinforce, supplement; maximize; enliven, jazz (up); aggravate, exacerbate

near ant decrease, diminish, lessen, let up (on), reduce, subdue, tone (down), weaken; dwindle, recede, subside, taper (off), wane; alleviate, ease, lighten

ant abate, moderate

intensity *n* **1** depth of feeling — see ARDOR 1

2 the quality or state of being forceful (as in expression) — see VEHEMENCE 1

intensive *adj* extreme in degree, power, or effect — see INTENSE

intensively *adv* with great effort or determination — see HARD 1

intent *adj* **1** fully committed to achieving a goal — see DETERMINED 1

2 having the mind fixed on something — see ATTENTIVE

intent *n* **1** something that one hopes or intends to accomplish — see GOAL

2 the idea that is conveyed or intended to be conveyed to the mind by language, symbol, or action — see MEANING 1

intention *n* something that one hopes or intends to accomplish — see GOAL

intentional *adj* made, given, or done with full awareness of what one is doing ⟨I'm fairly sure that your "accidental" attack on your sister with a water balloon was really *intentional*⟩

syn deliberate, purposeful, willful (*or* wilful)

rel knowing, witting; designed, intended, planned; conscious; advised, calculated, considered, measured, reasoned, studied, thoughtful, weighed; premeditated; discretionary, elective, optional, volunteer

near ant inadvertent, unwitting; accidental, chance, haphazard, hit-or-miss, incidental, random; aimless, desultory, purposeless; abrupt, impetuous, sudden; coerced, forced, involuntary; compulsory, mandatory, necessary, nonelective, obligatory, ordered, required; casual; extemporaneous, impromptu, impulsive, instinctive, spontaneous, unforced, unpremeditated

ant unintentional

intentionally *adv* with full awareness of what one is doing ⟨the witness *intentionally* gave misleading answers to the questions⟩

syn consciously, deliberately, designedly, knowingly, purposefully, purposely, willfully, wittingly

rel calculatingly, studiedly; voluntarily, willingly

phrases on purpose

near ant accidentally, incidentally, randomly; involuntarily, unwillingly; impulsively, instinctively, spontaneously

ant inadvertently, unconsciously, unintentionally, unknowingly, unwittingly

intently *adv* with great effort or determination — see HARD 1

intentness *n* a mental state free of jesting or trifling — see EARNESTNESS

inter *vb* to place (a dead body) in the earth, a tomb, or the sea — see BURY 1

interaction *n* doings between individuals or groups — see RELATION 1

intercede *vb* to act as a go-between for opposing sides — see INTERVENE

intercessor *n* one who works with opposing sides in order to bring about an agreement — see MEDIATOR

intercommunicate *vb* to engage in an exchange of information or ideas — see COMMUNICATE 2

intercourse *n* **1** doings between individuals or groups — see RELATION 1

2 sexual union involving penetration of the vagina by the penis — see SEXUAL INTERCOURSE

interdict *n* an order that something not be done or used — see PROHIBITION 2

interdict *vb* to order not to do or use or to be done or used — see FORBID

interdicted *adj* that may not be permitted — see IMPERMISSIBLE

interdicting *n* the act of ordering that something not be done or used — see PROHIBITION 1

interdiction *n* **1** an order that something not be done or used — see PROHIBITION 2

2 the act of ordering that something not be done or used — see PROHIBITION 1

interest *n* **1** a legal right to participation in the advantages, profits, and responsibility of something ⟨all of the workers at the food cooperative have an *interest* in it⟩

syn claim, share, stake

rel ownership, part, partnership, possession, title

2 the state of doing well especially in relation to one's happiness or success — see WELFARE

interest *vb* to hold the attention of — see ENGAGE 1

interesting *adj* holding the attention or provoking interest ⟨the history lecture was so *interesting* that I didn't fall asleep after all⟩

syn absorbing, arresting, engaging, engrossing, enthralling, fascinating, gripping, immersing, intriguing, involving, riveting

rel breathtaking, electric, electrifying, exciting, exhilarating, galvanizing, inspiring, rousing, stimulating, stirring, thrilling; provocative, tantalizing; emphatic, showy, splashy, striking; alluring, attractive, bewitching, captivating, charming, enchanting, spellbinding; hypnotizing, mesmerizing; curious, odd, unusual, weird; amazing, astonishing, astounding, eye-opening, fabulous, marvelous (*or* marvellous), surprising, wonderful, wondrous; amusing, entertaining

near ant tiresome, tiring, wearisome, wearying; unexciting; dreary, humdrum, pedestrian; demoralizing, discouraging, disheartening, dispiriting

ant boring, drab, dry, dull, heavy, monotonous, tedious, uninteresting

interfere *vb* to interest oneself in what is not one's concern ⟨a strong resentment

---

interruption# interruption 393

of outsiders who *interfered* with their traditional ways of doing things⟩

syn butt in, intrude, meddle, mess, nose,
obtrude, poke, pry, snoop

rel intercede, interpose, intervene; encroach, infringe, invade, trespass; fiddle,
fool, monkey, play, tamper

near ant avoid, eschew, shun; disregard,
ignore, neglect, overlook

interfere (with) *vb* to create difficulty for
the work or activity of — see HAMPER

interference *n* something that makes
movement or progress more difficult —
see ENCUMBRANCE

interferer *n* a person who meddles in the
affairs of others — see BUSYBODY

interfering *adj* thrusting oneself where
one is not welcome or invited — see IN-
TRUSIVE

interim *adj* intended to last, continue, or
serve for a limited time — see TEMPO-
RARY 1

interim *n* a break in continuity — see
GAP 2

interior *adj* situated farther in — see
INNER 1

interior *n* an interior or internal part —
see INSIDE 1

interject *vb* to put among or between others — see INSERT

interlace *vb* **1** to cause to twine about one
another — see INTERTWINE 1

2 to scatter or set here and there among
other things — see THREAD 1

3 to twist together into a usually confused mass — see ENTANGLE 1

interloper *n* a person who meddles in the
affairs of others — see BUSYBODY

interlude *n* a break in continuity — see
GAP 2

intermediary *adj* occupying a position
equally distant from the ends or extremes
— see MIDDLE 1

intermediary *n* one who works with opposing sides in order to bring about an
agreement — see MEDIATOR

intermediate *adj* **1** being about midway
between extremes of amount or size —
see MIDDLE 2

2 occupying a position equally distant
from the ends or extremes — see MID-
DLE 1

interment *n* the act or ceremony of putting a dead body in its final resting place
— see BURIAL

intermingle *vb* to turn into a single mass
that is more or less the same throughout
— see BLEND 1

intermission *n* a break in continuity —
see GAP 2

intermittent *adj* **1** occurring or appearing
at intervals ⟨*intermittent* showers had me
opening and closing my umbrella all day
long⟩

syn continual, periodic, periodical, recurrent, recurring

rel alternate, alternating, cyclic (*or* cyclical), rhythmic (*or* rhythmical), seasonal,
serial; erratic, fitful, irregular, occasional,
spasmodic, sporadic, spotty, unsteady

near ant eternal, everlasting, interminable, perpetual

ant constant, continuous, incessant, unceasing

2 lacking in steadiness or regularity of occurrence — see FITFUL

intermix *vb* to turn into a single mass that
is more or less the same throughout —
see BLEND 1

intermixture *n* a distinct entity formed by
the combining of two or more different
things — see BLEND

intern *vb* to put in or as if in prison — see
IMPRISON

internal *adj* situated farther in — see
INNER 1

interned *adj* taken and held prisoner —
see CAPTIVE

internee *n* one that has been taken and
held in confinement — see CAPTIVE

internment *n* the act of confining or the
state of being confined ⟨the *internment* of
Americans of Japanese descent during
World War II is one of the more shameful
chapters in United States history⟩

syn captivity, confinement, immurement,
imprisonment, incarceration

rel bondage, enslavement, servitude; restraint, restriction; arrest, capture, entrapment; custody, detainment, detention

near ant emancipation, liberation, manumission, redemption, release; freedom,
independence, liberty

interpenetrate *vb* to spread throughout —
see PERMEATE

interpolate *vb* to put among or between
others — see INSERT

interpose *vb* **1** to act as a go-between for
opposing sides — see INTERVENE

2 to cause a disruption in a conversation
or discussion — see INTERRUPT

3 to put among or between others — see
INSERT

interposer *n* one who works with opposing sides in order to bring about an agreement — see MEDIATOR

interpret *vb* to make plain or understandable — see EXPLAIN 1

interpretation *n* a statement that makes
something clear — see EXPLANATION 1

interpretive *adj* serving to explain — see
EXPLANATORY

interring *n* the act or ceremony of putting
a dead body in its final resting place —
see BURIAL

interrogate *vb* **1** to put a question or questions to — see ASK 1

2 to put a series of questions to — see EX-
AMINE 1

interrupt *vb* to cause a disruption in a conversation or discussion ⟨it's rude to *interrupt* when someone is making an important point⟩

syn break (in), chime in, cut in, interpose, intrude

rel barge (in), bother; add, chip in, contribute, put in

interruption *n* **1** a break in continuity —
see GAP 2

2 a momentary halt in an activity — see PAUSE

intersect *vb* to divide by passing through or across ⟨the highway *intersects* that road⟩

syn bisect, cross

rel crisscross

intersection *n* a place where roads meet — see CROSSROAD 1

intersperse *vb* to scatter or set here and there among other things — see THREAD 1

intertwine *vb* **1** to cause to twine about one another ⟨*intertwined* two different colors of yarn⟩

syn interlace, interweave, lace

rel blend, fuse, join, link, mix

near ant disentangle, uncoil, untangle, untwine, unwind

2 to twist together into a usually confused mass — see ENTANGLE 1

interval *n* **1** a break in continuity — see GAP 2

2 an open space in a barrier (as a wall or hedge) — see GAP 1

intervene *vb* to act as a go-between for opposing sides ⟨*intervened* in the argument before any real harm was done⟩

syn intercede, interpose, mediate

rel butt in, interfere, intrude, meddle, obtrude, pry, snoop; arbitrate, moderate, negotiate; barge (in), bother; break (in), chime in, cut in; infringe, invade, trespass

near ant stand by; avoid, eschew; shun; disregard, ignore, overlook

interweave *vb* **1** to cause to twine about one another — see INTERTWINE 1

2 to scatter or set here and there among other things — see THREAD 1

3 to twist together into a usually confused mass — see ENTANGLE 1

intimacy *n* the state of being in a very personal or private relationship — see FAMILIARITY 1

intimate *adj* **1** closely acquainted — see FAMILIAR 1

2 not known or meant to be known by the general populace — see PRIVATE 1

intimate *n* a person who has a strong liking for and trust in another — see FRIEND 1

intimate *vb* to convey an idea indirectly — see HINT

intimation *n* a slight or indirect pointing to something (as a solution or explanation) — see HINT 1

intimidate *vb* to make timid or fearful by or as if by threats ⟨refusing to be *intimidated* by the manager's harsh stare, I demanded my money back⟩

syn browbeat, bully, cow, hector

rel affright, alarm, frighten, horrify, scare, shock, spook, startle, terrify; menace, terrorize, threaten; badger, harass, hound; bulldoze, coerce, compel, constrain, dragoon, force, make, oblige, press, pressure; demoralize, unman, un-

nerve; discompose, disconcert, disquiet, distress, disturb, perturb, upset

near ant cheer, comfort, console, reassure, solace, soothe; embolden, encourage, hearten, steel; convince, persuade

intimidating *adj* **1** causing fear — see FEARFUL 1

2 harsh and threatening in manner or appearance — see GRIM 1

intimidator *n* a person who teases, threatens, or hurts smaller or weaker persons — see BULLY 1

intolerable *adj* more than can be put up with — see UNBEARABLE

intolerant *adj* **1** unable or unwilling to endure ⟨*intolerant* of pain⟩

syn impatient

rel uncompromising, unforgiving, unyielding; complaining, fussing, griping, grumbling, protesting, squawking, whining

near ant accepting, forgiving, long-suffering, resigned, uncomplaining, willing; indulgent

ant abiding, enduring, forbearing, patient, tolerant

2 unwilling to grant other people social rights or to accept other viewpoints ⟨*intolerant* people supported racism⟩

syn bigoted, narrow, narrow-minded, prejudiced, small-minded

rel conservative, hidebound, old-fashioned, reactionary; insular, parochial, provincial; biased, one-sided, partial, partisan

near ant extreme, progressive, radical; impartial, objective, unbiased

ant broad-minded, liberal, open-minded, tolerant, unprejudiced

intone *vb* to utter in musical or drawn out tones — see CHANT 1

intoxicant *n* a fermented or distilled beverage that can make a person drunk — see ALCOHOL

intoxicate *vb* to cause a pleasurable stimulation of the feelings — see THRILL

intoxicated *adj* **1** being under the influence of alcohol — see DRUNK

2 experiencing or marked by overwhelming usually pleasurable emotion — see ECSTATIC

intoxication *n* a state of overwhelming usually pleasurable emotion — see ECSTASY

intractability *n* refusal to obey — see DISOBEDIENCE

intractable *adj* **1** given to resisting authority or another's control — see DISOBEDIENT

2 given to resisting control or discipline by others — see UNCONTROLLABLE

intrepid *adj* feeling or displaying no fear by temperament — see BRAVE

intrepidity *n* strength of mind to carry on in spite of danger — see COURAGE

intrepidness *n* strength of mind to carry on in spite of danger — see COURAGE

intricacy *n* **1** something that makes a situation more complicated or difficult — see COMPLICATION 1

---

syn synonym(s)   *rel* related words

ant antonym(s)   *near ant* near antonym(s)

2 the state or quality of having many interrelated parts or aspects — see COMPLEXITY 1

intricate *adj* **1** having many parts or aspects that are usually interrelated — see COMPLEX 1

2 made or done with great care or with much detail — see ELABORATE 1

intrigue *n* a secret plan for accomplishing evil or unlawful ends — see PLOT 1

intrigue *vb* **1** to engage in a secret plan to accomplish evil or unlawful ends — see PLOT

2 to hold the attention of — see ENGAGE 1

intriguing *adj* holding the attention or provoking interest — see INTERESTING

intrinsic *adj* being a part of the innermost nature of a person or thing — see INHERENT

intrinsically *adv* by natural character or ability — see NATURALLY 1

introduce *vb* **1** to make (one person) known (to another) socially ⟨a friend *introduced* him to the woman who later became his wife⟩
syn acquaint, present
rel address, greet, hail, meet

2 to present or bring forward for discussion ⟨the moderator *introduced* a new topic for the debate⟩
syn bring up, broach, moot, raise
rel allude (to), cite, mention, name, refer (to); offer, propose, suggest; air, express, speak (of), talk (about), vent, ventilate; interject, interrupt; debate, discuss, thrash (out *or* over)
near ant censor, hush (up), quiet, silence, suppress

3 to be responsible for the creation and early operation or use of — see FOUND

4 to impart knowledge of a new thing or situation to — see ACQUAINT 1

5 to put among or between others — see INSERT

introducer *n* one who creates or introduces something new — see INVENTOR

introduction *n* a short section (as of a book) that leads to or explains the main part ⟨a famous person wrote the *introduction* to that new textbook⟩
syn foreword, preamble, preface, prelude, prologue
rel beginning, commencement, initiation, opening, origin, origination, outset, start
near ant postscript; aftermath; cessation, close, closing, conclusion, end, finale, finish, stop, termination
ant epilogue

introductory *adj* coming before the main part or item usually to introduce or prepare for what follows — see PRELIMINARY

introverted *adj* not comfortable around people — see SHY 2

intrude *vb* **1** to cause a disruption in a conversation or discussion — see INTERRUPT

2 to interest oneself in what is not one's concern — see INTERFERE

intrude (upon) *vb* to thrust oneself upon (another) without invitation — see BOTHER 1

intruder *n* a person who meddles in the affairs of others — see BUSYBODY

intruding *adj* thrusting oneself where one is not welcome or invited — see INTRUSIVE

intrusive *adj* thrusting oneself where one is not welcome or invited ⟨that *intrusive* neighbor never knocks before coming in⟩
syn interfering, intruding, meddlesome, meddling, nosy (*or* nosey), obtrusive, officious, presumptuous, prying, snoopy
rel bold, brazen, impertinent, impudent, insolent, rude; invading, trespassing; curious, inquisitive; annoying, harassing, pestiferous
near ant quiet, reserved, reticent, retiring, silent, taciturn, withdrawn; inhibited, restrained, subdued
ant unobtrusive

inundate *vb* to cover or become filled with a flood — see FLOOD

inundation *n* a great flow of water or of something that overwhelms — see FLOOD

inure *vb* to make able to withstand physical hardship, strain, or exposure — see HARDEN 2

inured *adj* able to withstand hardship, strain, or exposure — see HARDY 1

invade *vb* to enter for conquest or plunder ⟨a superpower that had a tendency to *invade* and take over smaller and weaker countries⟩
syn foray (into), overrun, raid
rel despoil, loot, maraud, pillage, plunder, ravage, sack; conquer, crush, overcome, overpower, overwhelm, subdue, subjugate; assail, assault, attack; battle, combat, fight, war (with); encroach, infringe, trespass; besiege, blockade; occupy
near ant defend, guard, protect, shield; oppose, resist, withstand; capitulate (to), cede (to), submit (to), succumb (to), surrender (to), yield (to)

invader *n* one that starts armed conflict against another especially without reasonable cause — see AGGRESSOR

¹**invalid** *adj* chronically or repeatedly suffering from poor health — see SICKLY 1

²**invalid** *adj* **1** having no legal or binding force — see NULL 1

2 not being in agreement with what is true — see FALSE 1

3 not using or following good reasoning — see ILLOGICAL

4 having no basis in reason or fact — see GROUNDLESS

invalidate *vb* to put an end to by formal action — see ABOLISH

invariability *n* the state of continuing without change — see CONSTANCY 1

invariable *adj* not capable of changing or being changed — see INFLEXIBLE 1

invariably *adv* on every relevant occasion — see ALWAYS 1

invariant *adj* not varying — see UNIFORM

invasion *n* a sudden attack on and entrance into hostile territory — see RAID 1

invective *n* harsh insulting language — see ABUSE 1

invent *vb* to create or think of by clever use of the imagination ⟨they *invented* an explanation for the broken vase that would satisfy their grandmother⟩

syn concoct, contrive, cook (up), devise, fabricate, make up, manufacture, think (up)

rel coin, contrive, create, design, hatch, produce; daydream, dream, fantasize; conceive, envisage, imagine, picture, visualize

near ant copy, duplicate, imitate, mimic, replicate

invented *adj* not real and existing only in the imagination — see IMAGINARY

invention *n* **1** something (as a device) created for the first time through the use of the imagination ⟨his clever *invention* made people's lives easier⟩

syn coinage, concoction, contrivance, creation, innovation, wrinkle

rel contraption, device, gadget, gizmo (*or* gismo), novelty; design, product, work; dream, fantasy (*also* phantasy), picture, vision; conception, imagining, origination

near ant copy, duplicate, imitation

2 something that is the product of the imagination — see FICTION

3 the ability to form mental images of things that either are not physically present or have never been conceived or created by others — see IMAGINATION

4 the skill and imagination to create new things — see CREATIVITY 1

inventive *adj* having the skill and imagination to create new things — see CREATIVE 1

inventiveness *n* **1** the ability to form mental images of things that either are not physically present or have never been conceived or created by others — see IMAGINATION

2 the skill and imagination to create new things — see CREATIVITY 1

inventor *n* one who creates or introduces something new ⟨the *inventor* of the electric light bulb⟩

syn contriver, designer, developer, deviser, formulator, innovator, introducer, originator

rel author, creator, establisher, father, founder, inaugurator, originator; pioneer, researcher; builder, maker, producer; dreamer

near ant copier, duplicator, imitator

inventory *vb* to make a list of — see ¹LIST 1

invert *vb* to change the position of (an object) so that the opposite side or end is showing — see REVERSE 2

invertebrate *adj* lacking strength of will or character — see WEAK 2

invest *vb* **1** to cause (a person) to become filled or saturated with a certain quality or principle — see INFUSE

2 to furnish with something freely or naturally — see ENDOW 1

3 to give official or legal power to — see AUTHORIZE 1

4 to outfit with clothes and especially fine or special clothes — see CLOTHE 1

5 to put into an office or welcome into an organization with special ceremonies — see INSTALL 1

6 to surround (as a fortified place) with armed forces for the purpose of capturing or preventing commerce and communication — see BESIEGE

7 to surround or cover closely — see ENFOLD 1

investigate *vb* to search through or into — see EXPLORE 1

investigation *n* a systematic search for the truth or facts about something — see INQUIRY 1

investigator *n* a person whose business is solving crimes and catching criminals or gathering information that is not easy to get — see DETECTIVE

investiture *n* the process or an instance of being formally placed in an office or organization — see INSTALLATION 1

investment *n* the cutting off of an area by military means to stop the flow of people or supplies — see BLOCKADE

inveterate *adj* **1** firmly established over time ⟨he has an *inveterate* tendency to tell tall tales that began when he was just a little boy⟩

syn confirmed, deep-rooted, deep-seated, entrenched (*also* intrenched), hard-core, rooted, settled

rel fixed, immutable, set; implanted, inculcated, instilled; inborn, inbred, inherent, innate, natural; accustomed, chronic, customary, habitual, regular, typical, usual; abiding, enduring, lifelong, persistent, persisting

near ant brief, ephemeral, fleeting, impermanent, momentary, short-lived, temporary, transient

2 being such by habit and not likely to change — see HABITUAL 1

invidious *adj* having or showing mean resentment of another's possessions or advantages — see ENVIOUS

invidiousness *n* a painful awareness of another's possessions or advantages and a desire to have them too — see ENVY

invigorate *vb* to give life, vigor, or spirit to — see ANIMATE

invigorated *adj* made or become fresh in spirits or vigor — see NEW 4

invigorating *adj* having a renewing effect on the state of the body or mind — see TONIC

invincible *adj* incapable of being defeated, overcome, or subdued ⟨an *invincible* wrestler who has never lost a match⟩

syn impregnable, indomitable, insurmountable, invulnerable, unbeatable, unconquerable

rel inviolable, unassailable, untouchable; armored, defended, guarded, protected, safe, safeguarded, secure, shielded; un-

---

beaten, unconquered, undefeated, unsubdued

near ant exposed, imperiled, insecure, liable, open, susceptible, unguarded, unprotected, unsafe, unshielded; defenseless, helpless, powerless, weak

ant surmountable, vulnerable

inviolable *adj* not to be violated, criticized, or tampered with — see SACRED 1

invite *vb* to act so as to make (something) more likely — see COURT 1

invoice *n* a record of goods sold or services performed together with the costs due — see ¹BILL 1

involuntary *adj* **1** not made or done willingly or by choice ⟨my long stays on the sidelines during our football games were strictly *involuntary*⟩

syn coerced, forced, unintended, unintentional, unwilling

rel accidental, unplanned, unpremeditated; automatic, impulsive, instinctive, spontaneous, unprompted; inadvertent, unconscious, unknowing, unwitting

near ant advised, conscious, considered, knowing, planned, premeditated, purposeful; volitional

ant deliberate, intentional, unforced, voluntary, willful (*or* wilful), willing

2 done instantly and without conscious thought or decision — see AUTOMATIC 1

3 forcing one's compliance or participation by or as if by law — see MANDATORY

involution *n* the state or quality of having many interrelated parts or aspects — see COMPLEXITY 1

involve *vb* **1** to be the business or affair of — see CONCERN 2

2 to have as part of a whole — see INCLUDE

3 to hold the attention of — see ENGAGE 1

involved *adj* **1** having many parts or aspects that are usually interrelated — see COMPLEX 1

2 made or done with great care or with much detail — see ELABORATE 1

involving *adj* holding the attention or provoking interest — see INTERESTING

invulnerable *adj* incapable of being defeated, overcome, or subdued — see INVINCIBLE

inward *adj* situated farther in — see INNER 1

in-your-face *adj* having or showing a bold forcefulness in the pursuit of a goal — see AGGRESSIVE 1

iota *n* the smallest amount or part imaginable — see JOT

irascibility *n* readiness to show annoyance or impatience — see PETULANCE

irascible *adj* easily irritated or annoyed — see IRRITABLE

irate *adj* feeling or showing anger — see ANGRY

irateness *n* an intense emotional state of displeasure with someone or something — see ANGER

ire *n* an intense emotional state of displeasure with someone or something — see ANGER

ireful *adj* feeling or showing anger — see ANGRY

irk *vb* to disturb the peace of mind of (someone) especially by repeated disagreeable acts — see IRRITATE 1

irksome *adj* causing annoyance — see ANNOYING

iron *adj* not showing weakness or uncertainty — see FIRM 1

irons *n pl* something that physically prevents free movement — see BOND 1

irradiate *vb* to supply with light — see ILLUMINATE 1

irrational *adj* not using or following good reasoning — see ILLOGICAL

irrecoverable *adj* **1** not capable of being cured or reformed — see HOPELESS 1

2 not capable of being repaired, regained, or undone — see IRREPARABLE

irredeemable *adj* **1** not capable of being cured or reformed — see HOPELESS 1

2 not capable of being repaired, regained, or undone — see IRREPARABLE

irrefutable *adj* not capable of being challenged or proved wrong ⟨the *irrefutable* reply of "Because I like it!"⟩

syn incontestable, incontrovertible, indisputable, indubitable, unanswerable, undeniable, unquestionable

rel certain, definite, positive, sure; unambiguous, unequivocal; absolute, clear, conclusive, decisive; uncontested, undisputed

near ant controversial, debated, disputed; doubtful, dubious, inconclusive, indecisive, uncertain; ambiguous, equivocal

ant answerable, debatable, disputable, questionable

irregular *adj* **1** departing from some accepted standard of what is normal — see DEVIANT

2 lacking in steadiness or regularity of occurrence — see FITFUL

3 not having a level or smooth surface — see UNEVEN 1

4 not rigidly following established form, custom, or rules — see INFORMAL 1

5 not staying constant — see UNEVEN 2

irregularly *adv* without definite aim, direction, rule, or method — see HIT OR MISS

irrelevance *n* the quality or state of not having anything to do with the matter at hand ⟨the *irrelevance* of the comment brought conversation to a standstill⟩

syn extraneousness, inapplicability

rel inappropriateness, inaptness, unfitness, unsuitability; insignificance, unimportance; pointlessness, uselessness

near ant bearing, connection; appropriateness, aptness, fitness, suitability; importance, significance; usefulness

ant applicability, materiality, pertinence, relevance

irrelevant *adj* not having anything to do with the matter at hand ⟨*irrelevant* questions that merely disrupted the classroom lesson〉

syn extraneous, immaterial, inapplicable
rel inconsequential, insignificant, unimportant; meaningless, pointless, senseless, useless; inappropriate, inapt, unsuitable
phrases beside the point
near ant important, meaningful, significant; sensible, useful; appropriate, apt, fit, suitable
ant applicable, apposite, apropos, germane, material, pertinent, relevant

irreligious *adj* lacking religious emotions, principles, or practices 〈raised in an *irreligious* family where the subject of God was never even discussed〉

syn godless, nonreligious
rel ungodly, unholy; blasphemous, impious, irreverent, sacrilegious; agnostic, atheistic; unconsecrated, unhallowed; profane, secular, worldly
near ant devout, godly, holy, pious, prayerful, reverent, worshipful, worshipping (*also* worshiping); sanctimonious
ant religious

irremediable *adj* **1** not capable of being cured or reformed — see HOPELESS 1

2 not capable of being repaired, regained, or undone — see IRREPARABLE

irremovable *adj* incapable of moving or being moved — see IMMOVABLE 1

irreparable *adj* not capable of being repaired, regained, or undone 〈*irreparable* damage to the car〉

syn irrecoverable, irredeemable, irremediable, irretrievable, irreversible, unrecoverable, unredeemable
rel irreplaceable, irrevocable; unredeemed, unrepaired
near ant corrected, fixed, recovered, remedied, repaired
ant fixable, redeemable, remediable, retrievable

irreproachable *adj* **1** free from guilt or blame — see INNOCENT 2

2 being entirely without fault — see PERFECT 1

irresolution *n* the act or an instance of pausing because of uncertainty about the right course of action — see HESITATION

irresponsible *adj* having or showing a lack of concern for the consequences of one's actions — see RECKLESS 1

irretrievable *adj* **1** not capable of being cured or reformed — see HOPELESS 1

2 not capable of being repaired, regained, or undone — see IRREPARABLE

irreverence *n* an act of great disrespect shown to God or to sacred ideas, people, or things — see BLASPHEMY

irreverent *adj* not showing proper reverence for the holy or sacred 〈*irreverent* behavior during church services〉

syn blasphemous, impious, profane, sacrilegious

rel agnostic, atheistic; godless, irreligious, nonreligious, secular; ungodly, unholy; unconsecrated, unhallowed, unsanctified
near ant devout, godly, holy, prayerful, religious, worshipful, worshipping (*also* worshiping); consecrated, hallowed, sanctified
ant pious, reverent

irreversible *adj* not capable of being repaired, regained, or undone — see IRREPARABLE

irrigate *vb* to pour liquid over or through in order to cleanse — see FLUSH 1

irritability *n* readiness to show annoyance or impatience — see PETULANCE

irritable *adj* easily irritated or annoyed 〈that *irritable* old man always yells at people to stay off of his lawn〉

syn choleric, crabby, cranky, cross, crotchety, grouchy, grumpy, irascible, peevish, perverse, pettish, petulant, quick-tempered, short-tempered, snappish, snappy, snippy, testy, waspish
rel bearish, bilious, cantankerous, disagreeable, dyspeptic, ill-humored, ill-natured, ill-tempered, ornery, surly; sensitive, sulky, thin-skinned, touchy; hot-blooded, passionate
phrases out of sorts
near ant affable, cordial, friendly, genial, sociable; amiable, good-natured, good-tempered, well-disposed; carefree, easygoing, relaxed; obliging, patient, tolerant, uncomplaining, understanding

irritableness *n* readiness to show annoyance or impatience — see PETULANCE

irritant *n* something that is a source of irritation — see ANNOYANCE 3

irritate *vb* **1** to disturb the peace of mind of (someone) especially by repeated disagreeable acts 〈constant chatter *irritated* the student, who was trying to concentrate on a hard assignment〉

syn aggravate, annoy, bother, bug, chafe, exasperate, gall, get, grate, irk, nettle, peeve, persecute, pique, put out, rasp, rile, vex
rel hassle, heckle; nag; inflame, provoke, rouse; bait, harass, harry, pester; anger, enrage, incense, infuriate, madden; agitate, disturb, fret, perturb, upset; affront, insult, offend, outrage
phrases rub the wrong way
near ant appease, conciliate, mollify, oblige, pacify, placate, propitiate; delight, gladden, gratify, please, satisfy; comfort, console, content, quiet, soothe

2 to make sore by continued rubbing — see CHAFE 1

irritating *adj* causing annoyance — see ANNOYING

irritation *n* the feeling of impatience or anger caused by another's repeated disagreeable acts — see ANNOYANCE 2

irruption *n* a sudden attack on and entrance into hostile territory — see RAID 1

island *n* a fairly small area of land completely surrounded by water 〈they're taking a trip to an *island* in Hawaii for vacation〉

syn isle, islet

rel barrier reef, cay, coral reef, key; archipelago, atoll; cape, headland, peninsula, promontory

near ant continent, main, mainland

isle *n* a fairly small area of land completely surrounded by water — see ISLAND

islet *n* a fairly small area of land completely surrounded by water — see ISLAND

isolate *vb* to set or keep apart from others 〈*isolated* her in a corner for a five-minute punishment after she threw a book at her friend〉

syn cut off, insulate, seclude, segregate, separate, sequester

rel quarantine; confine, immure, incarcerate, intern, jail, lock (up), restrain, restrict; detach, disengage, remove; detain, hold, keep

near ant associate, connect, join, link, unite; discharge, free, liberate, loose, release

ant desegregate, integrate

isolated *adj* hidden from view — see SECLUDED

isolation *n* the state of being alone or kept apart from others 〈*isolation* always made the sociable child lonely〉

syn insulation, secludedness, seclusion, segregation, separateness, sequestration, solitariness, solitude

rel loneliness, lonesomeness; confinement, incarceration, internment, quarantine; retirement, withdrawal

near ant companionship, company

issuance *n* the act or process of giving out something to each member of a group — see DISTRIBUTION 1

issue *n* 1 a condition or occurrence traceable to a cause — see EFFECT 1

2 a place or means of going out — see EXIT 1

3 the descendants of a person, animal, or plant — see OFFSPRING

issue *vb* 1 to produce and release for distribution in printed form — see PUBLISH 1

2 to throw or give off — see EMIT 1

Italian sandwich *n* a large sandwich on a long split roll — see SUBMARINE

itch *n* a strong wish for something — see DESIRE

itch (for) *vb* to have an earnest wish to own or enjoy — see DESIRE

item *n* 1 a separate part in a list, account, or series 〈she got all the *items* on her grocery list except cereal〉

syn detail, particular, point

rel article, belonging, object, stuff, thing; characteristic, constituent, element, feature; ingredient; division, particle, piece, portion, section, segment

near ant aggregate, composite, compound, conglomerate; entirety, sum, total, totality, whole

2 a report of recent events or facts not previously known — see NEWS

itemize *vb* 1 to make a list of — see ¹LIST 1

2 to specify one after another — see ENUMERATE 1

itinerant *adj* traveling from place to place 〈an *itinerant* musician can see a lot of the world〉

syn errant, gallivanting (*also* galavanting), nomad (*or* nomadic), peripatetic, ranging, roaming, roving, vagabond, vagrant, wandering, wayfaring

rel drifting, footloose, meandering, rambling; sauntering, strolling, traipsing, walking

near ant immobile, settled, stationary

J

---

jab *n* a quick thrust — see ¹POKE

jabber *n* unintelligible or meaningless talk — see GIBBERISH

jabber *vb* 1 to engage in casual or rambling conversation — see CHAT

2 to speak rapidly, inarticulately, and usually unintelligibly — see BABBLE 1

jabberer *n* a person who talks constantly — see CHATTERBOX

jabberwocky *n* unintelligible or meaningless talk — see GIBBERISH

jack *n* 1 *slang* something (as pieces of stamped metal or printed paper) customarily and legally used as a medium of exchange, a measure of value, or a means of payment — see MONEY

2 a piece of cloth with a special design that is used as an emblem or for signaling — see FLAG 1

3 an adult male human being — see MAN 1

4 one who operates or navigates a seagoing vessel — see SAILOR

jack (up) *vb* 1 to lift with effort — see HEAVE 1

2 to move from a lower to a higher place or position — see RAISE 1

jackass *n* 1 a person who lacks good sense or judgment — see FOOL 1

2 a stupid person — see IDIOT

3 a sturdy and patient domestic mammal that is used especially to carry things — see DONKEY 1

jacked (up) *adj* being at a higher level than average — see HIGH 2

jacket *n* something that encloses another thing especially to protect it — see ¹CASE 1

jackpot *n* the total of the bets at stake at one time — see POT 1

jack–tar *n* one who operates or navigates a seagoing vessel — see SAILOR

jade *vb* to make weary and restless by being dull or monotonous — see ²BORE

jaded *adj* **1** depleted in strength, energy, or freshness — see WEARY 1

2 having one's patience, interest, or pleasure exhausted — see WEARY 2

jading *adj* causing weariness, restlessness, or lack of interest — see BORING

jagged *adj* **1** having an uneven edge or outline — see RAGGED 1

2 not having a level or smooth surface — see UNEVEN 1

jail *n* a place of confinement for persons held in lawful custody ⟨sentenced to three years in *jail* for his crime⟩
syn brig, gaol [*chiefly British*], guardroom, hoosegow, jug, lockup, pen, penitentiary, prison, stockade
rel bull pen; concentration camp, prison camp; dungeon, keep; reformatory, reform school
near ant freedom

jail *vb* to put in or as if in prison — see IMPRISON

jailbird *n* a person convicted as a criminal and serving a prison sentence — see CONVICT

jailed *adj* taken and held prisoner — see CAPTIVE

jam *n* a difficult, puzzling, or embarrassing situation from which there is no easy escape — see PREDICAMENT

jam *vb* **1** to fit (something) into a tight space — see CROWD 1

2 to prevent passage through — see CLOG 1

3 to put into (something) as much as can be held or contained — see FILL 1

jammed *adj* **1** containing or seeming to contain the greatest quantity or number possible — see FULL 1

2 firmly positioned in place and difficult to dislodge — see TIGHT 2

jam–pack *vb* to put into (something) as much as can be held or contained — see FILL 1

jam–packed *adj* **1** containing or seeming to contain the greatest quantity or number possible — see FULL 1

2 having little space between items or parts — see CLOSE 1

janitor *n* **1** a person who takes care of a property sometimes for an absent owner — see CUSTODIAN 1

2 a person who tends a door — see DOOR KEEPER

jar *n* **1** a forceful coming together of two things — see IMPACT 1

2 something that makes a strong impression because it is so unexpected — see SURPRISE 1

jar *vb* to be out of harmony or agreement usually noticeably — see CLASH

---

syn synonym(s)   *rel* related words
ant antonym(s)   *near ant* near antonym(s)

jargon *n* the special terms or expressions of a particular group or field — see TERMINOLOGY

jarring *adj* disagreeable to one's aesthetic or artistic sense — see HARSH 2

jaundice *n* a deep-seated ill will — see ENMITY

jaundiced *adj* **1** having or showing mean resentment of another's possessions or advantages — see ENVIOUS

2 marked by opposition or ill will — see HOSTILE 1

jaunt *n* a short trip for pleasure — see EXCURSION 1

jauntily *adv* **1** in a bright and showy way — see GAILY 3

2 in a quick and spirited manner — see GAILY 2

jaunty *adj* having much high-spirited energy and movement — see LIVELY 1

javelin *n* a weapon with a long straight handle and sharp head or blade — see SPEAR

jaw *vb* **1** to criticize (someone) severely or angrily especially for personal failings — see SCOLD

2 to engage in casual or rambling conversation — see CHAT

jazz *n* unintelligible or meaningless talk — see GIBBERISH

jazz (up) *vb* to give life, vigor, or spirit to — see ANIMATE

jazziness *n* the quality or state of having abundant or intense activity — see VITALITY 1

jazzy *adj* **1** attractively eye-catching in style ⟨that's a *jazzy* bathing suit, with all those spangles⟩
syn flashy, snazzy, splashy
rel cool, hip, neat; à la mode (*also* a la mode), chic, dashing; faddish, fashionable, in, modish, posh, ritzy, sharp, smart, snappy, spruce, stylish; custom, designer; garish, gaudy, loud, rakish, wild
near ant classic, elegant, genteel, polished, refined, sophisticated, stately, swank; plain, quiet, restrained, simple, understated

2 having much high-spirited energy and movement — see LIVELY 1

jealous *adj* **1** intolerant of rivalry or unfaithfulness ⟨became *jealous* whenever she paid attention to anyone but him⟩
syn possessive
rel controlling, demanding, grasping; covetous, envious, invidious, jaundiced; distrustful, mistrustful, suspicious
phrases green with envy
near ant undemanding; tolerant, trustful, trusting, understanding

2 having or showing mean resentment of another's possessions or advantages — see ENVIOUS

jealousy *n* a painful awareness of another's possessions or advantages and a desire to have them too — see ENVY

jeer *n* a vocal sound made to express scorn or disapproval — see CATCALL

jeer *vb* to make (someone or something) the object of unkind laughter — see RIDICULE

Jehovah *n* the being worshipped as the creator and ruler of the universe — see DEITY 2

jell *vb* 1 to take on a definite form — see FORM 1

2 to turn from a liquid into a substance resembling jelly — see COAGULATE

jelly *vb* to turn from a liquid into a substance resembling jelly — see COAGULATE

jeopardize *vb* to place in danger — see ENDANGER

jeopardizing *adj* involving potential loss or injury — see DANGEROUS

jeopardy *n* the state of not being protected from injury, harm, or evil — see DANGER 1

jerk *n* 1 a person whose behavior is offensive to others ⟨his constant rudeness and insensitivity made everyone think he was a real *jerk*⟩

syn beast, boor, cad, churl, clown, creep, cretin, cur, heel, joker, louse, lout, skunk, slob, snake, stinker

rel brute, Neanderthal, savage; rascal, rogue, scamp, villain; fool, jackass, nincompoop, nitwit; blockhead, dolt, goon, idiot

near ant hero, idol, role model

2 the act or an instance of applying force on something so that it moves in the direction of the force — see PULL 1

jerk *vb* 1 to move or cause to move with a sharp quick motion ⟨I *jerked* to one side to avoid getting hit⟩ ⟨*jerked* the leash to get the dog's attention⟩

syn buck, hitch, jolt, twitch, yank

rel bump, jounce, lurch, stagger; jiggle, shake; lug, pull, tug; pluck, tweak; grab, snap, snatch, wrench, wrest, wring

2 to make jerky or restless movements — see FIDGET

jerky *adj* 1 marked by a series of sharp quick motions ⟨made *jerky* progress walking with the new crutches⟩

syn bumpy, rough

rel choppy, erratic, fitful, irregular, spasmodic, spastic, unsteady

near ant calm, placid, smooth, steady, still

2 showing or marked by a lack of good sense or judgment — see FOOLISH 1

jest *n* 1 an attitude or manner not to be taken seriously — see FUN 2

2 something said or done to cause laughter — see JOKE 1

jest *vb* to make jokes — see JOKE

jester *n* 1 a person (as a writer) noted for or specializing in humor — see HUMORIST

2 a person formerly kept in a royal or noble household to amuse with jests and pranks — see FOOL 2

jesting *adj* marked by or expressive of mild or good-natured teasing — see QUIZZICAL

jesting *n* good-natured teasing or exchanging of clever remarks — see BANTER

jet *vb* 1 to flow out in great quantities or with force — see GUSH 1

2 to throw out or off (something from within) often violently — see ERUPT 1

jettison *n* the getting rid of whatever is unwanted or useless — see DISPOSAL 1

jettison *vb* to get rid of as useless or unwanted — see DISCARD

jetty *n* a structure used by boats and ships for taking on or landing cargo and passengers — see DOCK

jewel *n* 1 a usually valuable stone cut and polished for ornament — see GEM 1

2 an asset that brings praise or renown — see GLORY 2

3 someone or something unusually desirable — see PRIZE 1

jibe *vb* to be in agreement on every point — see CHECK 1

jiffy *n* a very small space of time — see INSTANT

jig *n* a clever often underhanded means to achieve an end — see TRICK 1

jigger *n* an interesting and often novel device with a practical use — see GADGET

jiggling *n* a series of slight movements by a body back and forth or from side to side — see VIBRATION

jim–dandy *adj* of the very best kind — see EXCELLENT

jim–dandy *n* something very good of its kind ⟨the brand new car was a *jim-dandy*⟩

syn beauty, corker, crackerjack, dandy, knockout, nifty, pip

rel marvel, wonder; gem, jewel, treasure

near ant disappointment, failure, lemon, loser

jimmy *vb* to raise, move, or pull apart with or as if with a lever — see PRY 1

jingle *n* 1 a series of short high ringing sounds — see TINKLE

2 a short musical composition for the human voice often with instrumental accompaniment — see SONG 1

jingle *vb* to make a repeated sharp light ringing sound ⟨the bell on the kitten's collar *jingled* as she walked⟩

syn chink, clink, tinkle

rel clack, clang, clank; clatter, rattle; ding, jangle, ping, ring

jingo *n* 1 one who shows excessive favoritism towards his or her country — see NATIONALIST

2 one who urges or attempts to cause a war — see WARMONGER

jingoism *n* excessive favoritism towards one's own country — see CHAUVINISM

jinx *n* something that brings bad luck ⟨believed the broken mirror was a *jinx*⟩

syn hex, hoodoo

rel curse, evil eye, spell; augury, omen, portent

near ant amulet, charm, talisman

jitters *n pl* a sense of panic or extreme nervousness ⟨always got the *jitters* right before a test⟩

syn dither, nerves, shakes, shivers, willies
rel cold sweat, creeps; anxiety, fear, hysteria; frazzle, nervous breakdown

near ant aplomb, composure, coolheadedness, equanimity, imperturbability, self-possession

jittery *adj* **1** easily excited by nature — see EXCITABLE

2 feeling or showing uncomfortable feelings of uncertainty — see NERVOUS 1

jive *vb* **1** to make fun of in a good-natured way — see TEASE 1

2 to make jokes — see JOKE

job *n* **1** an assignment at which one regularly works for pay ⟨a high-paying *job* as a banker⟩

syn appointment, berth, billet, capacity, function, place, position, post, situation
rel business, employment, occupation, profession; work; office, spot; calling, pursuit, vocation; line, racket; engagement; livelihood, living; assignment, mission, task

near ant avocation; joblessness, unemployment

2 a piece of work that needs to be done regularly — see CHORE 1

3 a specific task with which a person or group is charged — see MISSION

4 the action for which a person or thing is specially fitted or used or for which a thing exists — see ROLE

jobholder *n* one who works for another for wages or a salary — see EMPLOYEE

jocose *adj* indicative of or marked by high spirits or good humor — see MERRY

jocosely *adv* in a cheerful or happy manner — see GAILY 1

jocular *adj* given to or marked by mature intelligent humor — see WITTY

jocund *adj* indicative of or marked by high spirits or good humor — see MERRY

jog *vb* **1** to go at a pace faster than a walk — see RUN 1

2 to make short up-and-down movements — see NOD

joggle *vb* to make a series of small irregular or violent movements — see SHAKE 1

join *vb* **1** to be adjacent to — see ADJOIN 1

2 to become a member of — see ENTER 2

3 to come together to form a single unit — see UNITE 1

4 to participate or assist in a joint effort to accomplish an end — see COOPERATE 1

5 to put or bring together so as to form a new and longer whole — see CONNECT 1

joining *adj* having a border in common — see ADJACENT

joint *adj* used or done by a number of people as a group — see COLLECTIVE

joint *n* **1** a place where two or more things are united ⟨the leak was found at a *joint* in the pipe⟩

syn connection, coupling, junction, juncture
rel crux, link, tie; interconnection, intersection; abutment, articulation; seam, su-

ture; concourse, confluence, meeting; union

near ant crack, separation

2 a building, room, or suite of rooms occupied by a service business — see PLACE 2

jointly *adv* in or by combined action or effort — see TOGETHER 2

joke *n* **1** something said or done to cause laughter ⟨he was known for his hilarious *jokes*⟩

syn crack, gag, jest, laugh, pleasantry, quip, sally, waggery, wisecrack, witticism
rel funning, joking, wisecracking; antic, buffoonery, caper, monkeyshine(s), prank; caricature, lampoon, parody, put-on; banter, persiflage, raillery, repartee; facetiousness, funniness, hilariousness, humorousness; barb, humor, wit, wordplay

2 a poor, insincere, or insulting imitation of something — see MOCKERY 1

joke *vb* to make jokes ⟨he was known for his ability to *joke*⟩

syn banter, fool, fun, jest, jive, josh, kid, quip, wisecrack
rel chaff, mock, rally, razz, rib, ridicule, tease; caricature, lampoon, parody, satirize; amuse, divert, entertain

joker *n* **1** a person (as a writer) noted for or specializing in humor — see HUMORIST

2 a person whose behavior is offensive to others — see JERK 1

3 an adult male human being — see MAN 1

jokester *n* a person (as a writer) noted for or specializing in humor — see HUMORIST

joking *adj* marked by or expressive of mild or good-natured teasing — see QUIZZICAL

jollification *n* joyful or festive activity — see MERRYMAKING

jollity *n* joyful or festive activity — see MERRYMAKING

jolly *adj* indicative of or marked by high spirits or good humor — see MERRY

jolly *adv* to a great degree — see VERY 1

jolt *n* **1** a forceful coming together of two things — see IMPACT 1

2 something that makes a strong impression because it is so unexpected — see SURPRISE 1

jolt *vb* **1** to make a series of small irregular or violent movements — see SHAKE 1

2 to move or cause to move with a sharp quick motion — see JERK 1

3 to cause an often unpleasant surprise for — see SHOCK 1

josh *vb* **1** to make fun of in a good-natured way — see TEASE 1

2 to make jokes — see JOKE

joshing *adj* marked by or expressive of mild or good-natured teasing — see QUIZZICAL

joshing *n* good-natured teasing or exchanging of clever remarks — see BANTER

---

syn synonym(s)   *rel* related words
ant antonym(s)   *near ant* near antonym(s)

jot *n* the smallest amount or part imaginable ⟨it's obvious that he doesn't have a *jot* of interest in history⟩

syn hoot, iota, lick, modicum, rap, tittle, whit

rel ace, bit, crumb, dab, driblet, glimmer, hint, little, mite, nip, ounce, peanuts, ray, scruple, shade, shadow, shred, smidgen, snap, speck, spot, sprinkling, strain, streak, suspicion, touch, trace

jot (down) *vb* to make a written note of — see RECORD 1

jounce *vb* 1 to make a series of small irregular or violent movements — see SHAKE 1

2 to make short up-and-down movements — see NOD

journal *n* a publication that appears at regular intervals ⟨a monthly scientific *journal*⟩

syn gazette, magazine, newspaper, organ, paper, periodical, review

rel annual, bimonthly, biweekly, daily, monthly, quarterly, semimonthly, semiweekly, weekly, yearbook; broadside, extra, sheet, tabloid

journalist *n* a person employed by a newspaper, magazine, or radio or television station to gather, write, or report news — see REPORTER

journey *n* a going from one place to another usually of some distance ⟨they were hungry and tired after their long *journey*⟩

syn expedition, passage, peregrination, travel(s), trek, trip

rel errand, excursion, flight, hop, jaunt, junket, outing, sally, tour; cruise, sail, voyage; drive, ride, spin; odyssey, pilgrimage, progress, quest, safari

journey *vb* to take a trip especially of some distance — see TRAVEL 1

jovial *adj* indicative of or marked by high spirits or good humor — see MERRY

joviality *n* a mood characterized by high spirits and amusement and often accompanied by laughter — see MIRTH

jovially *adv* in a cheerful or happy manner — see GAILY 1

joy *n* 1 a feeling or state of well-being and contentment — see HAPPINESS 1

2 a source of great satisfaction — see DELIGHT 1

joy *vb* to feel or express joy or triumph — see EXULT

joyful *adj* experiencing pleasure, satisfaction, or delight — see GLAD 1

joyless *adj* feeling unhappiness — see SAD 1

joylessness *n* a state or spell of low spirits — see SADNESS

joyous *adj* experiencing pleasure, satisfaction, or delight — see GLAD 1

jubilant *adj* having or expressing feelings of joy or triumph — see EXULTANT

jubilee *n* a time or program of special events and entertainment in honor of something — see FESTIVAL

judge *n* 1 a person who impartially decides or resolves a dispute or controversy ⟨their father always played the role of *judge* when there was a disagreement⟩

syn arbiter, arbitrator, referee, umpire

rel justice, magistrate; intermediary, mediator, negotiator; conciliator, go-between, peacemaker, reconciler; decider

2 a public official having authority to decide questions of law ⟨the *judge* gave the defendant a suspended sentence⟩

syn bench, court, justice, magistrate

rel justice of the peace

near ant claimant, plaintiff; defendant

judge *vb* 1 to give an opinion about (something at issue or in dispute) ⟨the committee will *judge* the case based on the evidence⟩

syn adjudge, adjudicate, arbitrate, decide, determine, referee, rule (on), settle, umpire

rel consider, hear, ponder, weigh; size (up); mediate, moderate, negotiate; prosecute, try; find (for *or* against)

near ant equivocate, skirt

2 to decide the size, amount, number, or distance of (something) without actual measurement — see ESTIMATE 2

3 to form an opinion through reasoning and information — see INFER 1

judgment *or* **judgement** *n* 1 a decision made by a court or tribunal regarding a case it has heard — see SENTENCE

2 a position arrived at after consideration — see DECISION 1

3 an idea that is believed to be true or valid without positive knowledge — see OPINION 1

4 an opinion on the nature, character, or quality of something — see ESTIMATION 1

judicious *adj* 1 having or showing good judgment and restraint especially in conduct or speech — see DISCREET

2 suitable for bringing about a desired result under the circumstances — see EXPEDIENT

jug *n* 1 a place of confinement for persons held in lawful custody — see JAIL

2 a handled container for holding and pouring liquids that usually has a lip or a spout — see PITCHER

jug *vb* to put in or as if in prison — see IMPRISON

jugglery *n* the use of clever underhanded actions to achieve an end — see TRICKERY

juiciness *n* the quality or state of being full of juice — see SUCCULENCE

juicy *adj* full of juice ⟨she bit into the *juicy* orange⟩

syn fleshy, pulpy, succulent

rel sappy, watery

near ant dehydrated, dry, withered

jumble *n* 1 a state in which everything is out of order — see CHAOS

2 an unorganized collection or mixture of various things — see MISCELLANY 1

jumble *vb* to undo the proper order or arrangement of — see DISORDER

jumbled *adj* lacking in order, neatness, and often cleanliness — see MESSY

jumbo *adj* unusually large — see HUGE

jumbo *n* something that is unusually large and powerful — see GIANT

jump *n* **1** an act of leaping into the air ⟨her first *jump* from an airplane at the age of 12⟩
syn bound, hop, leap, spring, vault
rel bounce, lope, skip; caper, gambol; attack, pounce; dive, pitch, plunge
2 the more favorable condition or position in a competition — see ADVANTAGE 1

jump *vb* **1** to propel oneself upward or forward into the air ⟨*jumped* across the ditch⟩
syn bound, hop, leap, spring, vault
rel bounce, hurdle, lope, skip; buck; caper, cavort, frolic, gambol, romp; attack, pounce; shoot, skyrocket
2 to move suddenly and sharply (as in surprise) — see START 1

jump (on) *vb* **1** to take sudden, violent action against — see ATTACK 1
2 to criticize harshly and usually publicly — see ATTACK 2

jumpiness *n* a state of nervousness marked by sudden jerky movements ⟨the police detective interpreted the suspect's *jumpiness* as a sign of guilt⟩
syn edginess, fidgets, flightiness, restiveness, skittishness
rel agitation, anxiety, anxiousness, apprehension, apprehensiveness, disquiet, feverishness, nervousness, perturbation, uneasiness, upset, worry; nerves, tenseness, tension; dither, jitters, shakes, shivers, willies
near ant confidence, self-assurance, self-confidence, sureness; control, self-control; aplomb, calm, calmness, collectedness, composure, coolheadedness, coolness, ease, easiness, equanimity, imperturbability, self-possession

jumpy *adj* **1** easily excited by nature — see EXCITABLE
2 feeling or showing uncomfortable feelings of uncertainty — see NERVOUS 1

junction *n* **1** a place where two or more things are united — see JOINT 1
2 the act or an instance of joining two or more things into one — see UNION 1

juncture *n* **1** a particular and often important moment in time — see POINT 1
2 a place where two or more things are united — see JOINT 1
3 a time or state of affairs requiring prompt or decisive action — see EMERGENCY

junior *adj* having not so great importance or rank as another — see LESSER

junior *n* one who is of lower rank and typically under the authority of another — see UNDERLING

junk *n* discarded or useless material — see GARBAGE

junk *vb* to get rid of as useless or unwanted — see DISCARD

junket *n* a short trip for pleasure — see EXCURSION 1

junket *vb* to entertain with a fancy meal — see FEAST

junkie *also* **junky** *n* a person who regularly uses drugs especially illegally — see DOPER

junking *n* the getting rid of whatever is unwanted or useless — see DISPOSAL 1

junky *adj* **1** having no usefulness — see WORTHLESS
2 of low quality — see CHEAP 2

junto *n* a group of persons formally joined together for some common interest — see ASSOCIATION 2

jurisdiction *n* lawful control over the affairs of a political unit (as a nation) — see RULE 2

just *adj* **1** being what is called for by accepted standards of right and wrong ⟨a *just* punishment should fit the crime⟩
syn deserved, due, merited, right, rightful, warranted
rel applicable, appropriate, apt, fit, fitting, meet, proper, requisite, suitable; lawful, legal; accurate, correct
near ant incoherent, irrelevant; improper, inapplicable, inappropriate, inapt, inequitable; arbitrary, despotic
ant undeserved, undue, unjust, unwarranted
2 based on sound reasoning or information — see GOOD 1
3 conforming to a high standard of morality or virtue — see GOOD 2
4 following the accepted rules of moral conduct — see HONORABLE 1
5 guided by or in accordance with one's sense of right and wrong — see CONSCIENTIOUS 1
6 marked by justice, honesty, and freedom from bias — see FAIR 2

just *adv* **1** in a like manner ⟨you can do it *just* the way they do⟩
syn exactly, precisely
rel as well, dead, even, expressly, perfectly
phrases to a T
near ant slightly, somewhat, vaguely
2 by a very small margin ⟨I was *just* over the minimum height requirement for admittance to the amusement park ride⟩
syn barely, hardly, marginally, scarcely, slightly
rel minimally, minutely; approximately, more or less, roughly, somewhat
near ant definitely, easily, plainly, positively, quite, unquestionably; abundantly, completely, copiously, generously, greatly
ant considerably, significantly, substantially, well
3 nothing more than ⟨I was *just* kidding⟩
syn but, merely, only, simply
4 as stated or indicated without the slightest difference — see EXACTLY 1
5 for nothing other than — see SOLELY 1
6 not long ago — see NEWLY

justice *n* **1** the act or practice of giving to others what is their due ⟨they felt that *justice* had been done in the case⟩

syn equity, right

rel fairness, impartiality; goodness, virtue; honor; decorum

near ant bias, partiality, prejudice; corruption, foul play; crime

ant inequity, injustice, wrong

2 a public official having authority to decide questions of law — see JUDGE 1

justifiable *adj* capable of being defended with good reasoning against verbal attack — see TENABLE 1

justification *n* an explanation that frees one from fault or blame — see EXCUSE

justified *adj* based on sound reasoning or information — see GOOD 1

justify *vb* **1** to be an acceptable reason for ⟨you seem to think that losing a basketball game *justifies* a temper tantrum⟩

syn excuse

rel account (for), explain, rationalize; brush (aside *or* off), condone, disregard, forgive, gloss (over), ignore, pardon, pass over, remit, shrug off, wink (at)

2 to continue to declare to be true or proper despite opposition or objections — see MAINTAIN 2

jut *n* a part that sticks out from the general mass of something — see BULGE

jut *vb* to extend outward beyond a usual point — see BULGE

juvenile *adj* **1** being in the early stage of life, growth, or development — see YOUNG

2 having or showing the annoying qualities (as silliness) associated with children — see CHILDISH

3 lacking in adult experience or maturity — see CALLOW

juvenile *n* a young person who is between infancy and adulthood — see CHILD 1

juxtaposed *adj* having a border in common — see ADJACENT

keelhaul *vb* to criticize (someone) severely or angrily especially for personal failings — see SCOLD

keen *adj* **1** able to sense slight impressions or differences — see ²ACUTE 1

2 causing intense discomfort to one's skin — see CUTTING 1

3 having an edge thin enough to cut or pierce something — see SHARP 1

4 having or showing quickness of mind — see INTELLIGENT 1

5 of the very best kind — see EXCELLENT

6 showing urgent desire or interest — see EAGER

keen *n* a crying out in grief — see LAMENT 1

keen *vb* to make a long loud mournful sound — see HOWL 1

keenness *n* **1** a harsh or sharp quality — see EDGE 1

2 urgent desire or interest — see EAGERNESS

keep *vb* **1** to act properly in relation to ⟨*keep* the Sabbath by not working⟩

syn celebrate, commemorate, observe

rel bless, consecrate, sanctify, solemnize; honor, laud, praise; obey, respect, revere, reverence, venerate; remember

phrases live up to

near ant disregard, forget, ignore, neglect, overlook

ant break, transgress, violate

2 to continue to have in one's possession or power ⟨the money is yours to *keep*⟩ ⟨*keep* my secret and don't tell it to anyone⟩

syn hang on (to), hold, reserve, retain, withhold

rel conserve, preserve, save; enjoy, have, own, possess; conduct, control, detain, direct; bear, harbor

near ant abandon, cede, yield; contribute, donate, give; discard, dump; decline, reject, repudiate, spurn

ant hand over, relinquish, surrender

3 to do what is required by the terms of — see FULFILL 1

4 to place somewhere for safekeeping or ready availability — see STORE 1

keep (from) *vb* to resist the temptation of — see FORBEAR

keep (to) *vb* to give steadfast support to — see ADHERE

keeper *n* **1** a person or group that watches over someone or something — see GUARD 1

2 a person who takes care of a property sometimes for an absent owner — see CUSTODIAN 1

keeping *n* **1** responsibility for the safety and well-being of someone or something — see CUSTODY

2 the fact or state of having (something) at one's disposal — see POSSESSION 1

keepsake *n* something that serves to keep alive the memory of a person or event — see MEMORIAL

keep up *vb* **1** to continue to operate or to meet one's needs — see HOLD OUT

2 to keep in good condition — see MAINTAIN 1

3 to remain indefinitely in existence or in the same state — see CONTINUE 1

keg *n* an enclosed wooden vessel for holding beverages — see CASK

kerchief *n* a scarf worn on the head — see BANDANNA

kerf *n* a V-shaped cut usually on an edge or a surface — see NOTCH 1

key *adj* **1** coming before all others in importance — see FOREMOST 1

2 of the greatest possible importance — see CRUCIAL

key *n* **1** an explanatory list of the symbols on a map or chart — see LEGEND 1

2 something that allows someone to achieve a desired goal — see PASSPORT

key *vb* to bring to a state free of conflicts, inconsistencies, or differences — see HARMONIZE 2

keystone *n* an immaterial thing upon which something else rests — see BASE 1

kibitzer *n* a person who meddles in the affairs of others — see BUSYBODY

kick *n* **1** a pleasurably intense stimulation of the feelings — see THRILL

2 a source of great satisfaction — see DELIGHT 1

3 a feeling or declaration of disapproval or dissent — see OBJECTION

kick *vb* **1** to express dissatisfaction, pain, or resentment usually tiresomely — see COMPLAIN

2 to present an opposing opinion or argument — see OBJECT

kick in *vb* to make a donation as part of a group effort — see CONTRIBUTE 1

kick off *vb* to take the first step in (a process or course of action) — see BEGIN 1

kid *n* a young person who is between infancy and adulthood — see CHILD 1

kid *vb* **1** to make fun of in a good-natured way — see TEASE 1

2 to make jokes — see JOKE

kidding *adj* marked by or expressive of mild or good-natured teasing — see QUIZZICAL

kiddish *adj* having or showing the annoying qualities (as silliness) associated with children — see CHILDISH

kidnap *vb* to carry a person away by unlawful force or against his or her will ⟨the child was *kidnapped* and held for ransom⟩
syn abduct
rel impress, shanghai, waylay; snatch, spirit
phrases make away with
near ant deliver, ransom, redeem, rescue; restore, return

kill *vb* **1** to deprive of life ⟨the soldier was *killed* in battle⟩
syn croak [*slang*], destroy, dispatch, do in, fell, slay
rel annihilate, blot out, butcher, decimate, massacre, slaughter, wipe out; cut down, finish, nip, snuff; assassinate, execute, murder, smite
phrases do away with
near ant restore, resurrect, resuscitate, revive; nurture
ant animate

2 to reject by or as if by a vote — see NEGATIVE 1

3 to show (something written) to be no longer valid by drawing a cross over or a line through it — see X (OUT)

killer *adj* **1** likely to cause or capable of causing death — see DEADLY

2 requiring considerable physical or mental effort — see HARD 2

killer *n* a person who kills another person — see ASSASSIN

killjoy *n* a person who spoils the pleasure of others ⟨his constant negative attitude made him a real *killjoy* when others were trying to have fun⟩
syn party pooper, spoilsport
rel fuddy-duddy, goody-goody, old maid, stick-in-the-mud; defeatist, pessimist; complainer, grouch, sorehead, whiner
near ant cutup, live wire; carouser, celebrant, celebrator, merrymaker, reveler (*or* reveller), roisterer; libertine, playboy, rake

kilter *n* a state of being or fitness — see CONDITION 1

kin *n* **1** a group of persons who come from the same ancestor — see FAMILY 1

2 a person connected with another by blood or marriage — see RELATIVE

kind *adj* **1** given to or made with heedful anticipation of the needs and happiness of others — see THOUGHTFUL 1

2 having or marked by sympathy and consideration for others — see HUMANE 1

kind *n* **1** a number of persons or things that are grouped together because they have something in common — see SORT 1

2 one of the units into which a whole is divided on the basis of a common characteristic — see CLASS 2

kindhearted *adj* having or marked by sympathy and consideration for others — see HUMANE 1

kindheartedness *n* the capacity for feeling for another's unhappiness or misfortune — see HEART 1

kindle *vb* to set (something) on fire — see BURN 2

kindled *adj* being on fire — see ABLAZE 1

kindliness *n* **1** kindly concern, interest, or support — see GOODWILL 1

2 the capacity for feeling for another's unhappiness or misfortune — see HEART 1

kindly *adj* having or marked by sympathy and consideration for others — see HUMANE 1

kindly *adv* with good reason or courtesy — see WELL 4

kindness *n* **1** an act of kind assistance — see FAVOR 1

2 the capacity for feeling for another's unhappiness or misfortune — see HEART 1

kind of *adv* to some degree or extent — see FAIRLY

kindred *adj* **1** having a close connection like that between family members — see RELATED

2 having or marked by agreement in feeling or action — see HARMONIOUS 3

kindred *n* a group of persons who come from the same ancestor — see FAMILY 1

---

syn synonym(s)   **rel** related words
ant antonym(s)   **near ant** near antonym(s)

kinfolk *n pl* a group of persons who come from the same ancestor — see FAMILY 1

king *n* a person of rank, power, or influence in a particular field — see MAGNATE

kingdom come *n* a dwelling place of perfect bliss for the soul after death — see HEAVEN 1

kingly *adj* fit for or worthy of a royal ruler — see MONARCHICAL

kingpin *n* the person (as an employer or supervisor) who tells people and especially workers what to do — see BOSS

king-size *or* **king-sized** *adj* 1 unusually large — see HUGE

2 of great extent from end to end — see LONG 1

king's ransom *n* a very large amount of money — see FORTUNE 2

kinky *adj* different from the ordinary in a way that causes curiosity or suspicion — see ODD 2

kinsfolk *n pl* a group of persons who come from the same ancestor — see FAMILY 1

kinship *n* the fact or state of having something in common — see CONNECTION 1

kinsman *n* a person connected with another by blood or marriage — see RELATIVE

kirk *n*, *chiefly Scottish* a building for public worship and especially Christian worship — see CHURCH 1

kiss *vb* 1 to touch one another with the lips as a sign of love ⟨it's traditional for couples to *kiss* under the mistletoe at Christmastime⟩

syn make out, pet, smooch

rel smack; caress, fondle, hug; bill, cuddle, nestle, snuggle

2 to pass lightly across or touch gently especially in passing — see BRUSH

kisser *n*, *slang* 1 the front part of the head — see FACE 1

2 the opening through which food passes into the body of an animal — see MOUTH 1

kittenish *adj* affecting shyness or modesty in order to attract masculine interest — see COY 1

¹**kitty** *n* a small domestic animal known for catching mice — see CAT 1

²**kitty** *n* a sum of money set aside for a particular purpose — see FUND 1

knack *n* a special and usually inborn ability — see TALENT

knapsack *n* a soft-sided case designed for carrying belongings especially on the back — see PACK 1

knave *n* a mean, evil, or unprincipled person — see VILLAIN

knavery *n* playful, reckless behavior that is not intended to cause serious harm — see MISCHIEF 1

knavish *adj* tending to or exhibiting reckless playfulness — see MISCHIEVOUS 1

knell *vb* to make the clear sound heard when metal vibrates — see RING 1

knickknack *n* a small object displayed for its attractiveness or interest ⟨a variety of pretty porcelain *knickknacks* adorned the mantel⟩

syn bauble, curio, curiosity, gaud, gewgaw, novelty, ornamental, trinket

rel bric-a-brac, trumpery; trifle; figurine, objet d'art, ornament; souvenir

knife *n* an instrument with a sharp edge for cutting ⟨be careful in using the *knife* to split open the cardboard box⟩

syn blade, cutter

rel bayonet, bolo, bowie knife, dagger, dirk, machete, pocketknife, poniard, stiletto, switchblade; saber, steel, sword; scalpel

knob *n* a small uneven mass — see LUMP 1

knock *n* 1 a hard strike with a part of the body or an instrument — see ¹BLOW

2 bad luck or an example of this — see MISFORTUNE

knock *vb* 1 to come into usually forceful contact with something — see HIT 2

2 to deliver a blow to (someone or something) usually in a strong vigorous manner — see HIT 1

3 to express one's unfavorable opinion of the worth or quality of — see CRITICIZE

knock (about) *vb* to move about from place to place aimlessly — see WANDER

knock (down *or* over) *vb* to strike (someone) so forcefully as to cause a fall — see FELL 1

knockabout *adj* being rough or noisy in a high-spirited way — see BOISTEROUS

knock down *vb* to take apart — see DISASSEMBLE

knock off *vb* 1 to bring (as an action or operation) to an immediate end — see STOP 1

2 to stop doing (something) permanently — see QUIT 2

knockout *adj* very pleasing to look at — see BEAUTIFUL

knockout *n* 1 a lovely woman — see BEAUTY 2

2 a temporary or permanent state of unconsciousness — see FAINT

3 something very good of its kind — see JIM-DANDY

knot *n* 1 a number of things considered as a unit — see GROUP 1

2 a small rounded mass of swollen tissue — see BUMP 1

3 a uniting or binding force or influence — see BOND 2

4 a usually small number of persons considered as a unit — see GROUP 2

5 something that requires thought and skill for resolution — see PROBLEM 1

knot *vb* to twist together into a usually confused mass — see ENTANGLE 1

knothead *n* a stupid person — see IDIOT

knotty *adj* 1 having many parts or aspects that are usually interrelated — see COMPLEX 1

2 requiring exceptional skill or caution in performance or handling — see TRICKY

know *vb* 1 to have a practical understanding of ⟨he *knows* several languages⟩

syn comprehend, grasp, understand

rel appreciate, apprehend, fathom, perceive; have, possess

near ant misapprehend, misconceive, misinterpret, misunderstand
2 to come to a knowledge of (something) by living through it — see EXPERIENCE
know–how *n* knowledge gained by actually doing or living through something — see EXPERIENCE 1
knowing *adj* **1** having inside information — see WISE 2
2 having or showing a practical cleverness or judgment — see SHREWD
knowingly *adv* with full awareness of what one is doing — see INTENTIONALLY
knowledge *n* **1** a body of facts learned by study or experience ⟨the forest ranger shared some of his vast *knowledge* of the woods with us⟩
syn lore, science, wisdom
rel information, intelligence, lowdown, news; data, evidence, facts; acquaintance, awareness, familiarity, literacy

near ant ignorance, inexperience, unfamiliarity
2 the understanding and information gained from being educated — see EDUCATION 2
knowledgeable *adj* **1** having information especially as a result of study or experience — see FAMILIAR 2
2 having or displaying advanced knowledge or education — see EDUCATED
knuckle under *vb* **1** to cease resistance (as to another's arguments, demands, or control) — see YIELD 3
2 to yield to the control or power of enemy forces — see FALL 2
kook *n* a person of odd or whimsical habits — see ECCENTRIC
kooky *adj* showing or marked by a lack of good sense or judgment — see FOOLISH 1
kowtow *vb* to use flattery or the doing of favors in order to win approval especially from a superior — see FAWN

L

label *n* a slip (as of paper or cloth) that is attached to something to identify or describe it ⟨on its frame the painting had a *label* with its title and the name of the artist⟩
syn marker, tag, ticket
rel caption, legend; brand, emblem, logo, mark, symbol; badge, decal, plaque, seal, stamp, sticker
label *vb* **1** to attach an identifying slip to ⟨he *labeled* all of the poisonous materials with the familiar skull and crossbones⟩
syn mark, tag, ticket
rel caption, earmark, stamp; call, designate, identify, name, tab; brand, stigmatize
2 to give a name to — see NAME 1
labor *n* **1** a dull, unpleasant, or difficult piece of work — see CHORE 2
2 the active use of energy in producing a result — see EFFORT
3 very hard or unpleasant work — see TOIL
4 the act or process of giving birth to children — see CHILDBIRTH
labor *vb* to devote serious and sustained effort ⟨he *labored* most of the evening over the difficult homework assignment⟩
syn drudge, endeavor, fag, grub, hump, hustle, moil, peg (away), plod, plow, plug, slave, slog, strain, strive, struggle, sweat, toil, travail, work
rel apply (oneself), attempt, buckle (down), hammer (away), pitch in; attack, drive; essay, try; exercise, exert, overexert, overwork; eke out, grind (out), put

out, scratch; trudge, wade; employ, ply, use, utilize, wield
near ant break, ease (up), let up, slacken; bum, goldbrick, idle, loaf, lounge, shirk, slack (off); dawdle, poke, tarry; relax, rest; disport, frolic, gambol, play, recreate, rollick, romp, sport
ant dabble, fiddle (around), fool (around), mess (around), putter (around)
laborer *n* a person who does very hard or dull work — see SLAVE 2
laborious *adj* **1** involved in often constant activity — see BUSY 1
2 requiring considerable physical or mental effort — see HARD 2
3 requiring much time, effort, or careful attention — see DEMANDING 1
laboriously *adv* with great effort or determination — see HARD 1
laborsaving *adj* designed to replace or decrease human labor and especially physical labor ⟨a new *laborsaving* device let us clean the house in half the time⟩
syn automated, automatic, robotic, self-acting
rel mechanical, motorized; computerized; aiding, helping; easing, relieving; timesaving
labyrinth *n* a confusing and complicated arrangement of passages — see MAZE
labyrinthine *adj* having many parts or aspects that are usually interrelated — see COMPLEX 1
lace *n* **1** a length of braided, flexible material that is used for tying or connecting things — see CORD
2 a length of something formed of three or more strands woven together — see BRAID

---

syn synonym(s)   *rel* related words
ant antonym(s)   *near ant* near antonym(s)

lace vb **1** to cause to twine about one another — see INTERTWINE 1

2 to scatter or set here and there among other things — see THREAD 1

3 to strike repeatedly — see BEAT 1

laceration n a long deep cut — see GASH

lachrymose adj given to expressing strong emotion (as sorrow) by readily shedding tears — see TEARFUL 1

lacing n **1** a length of braided, flexible material that is used especially for tying or connecting things — see CORD

2 a length of something formed of three or more strands woven together — see BRAID

lack n **1** the fact or state of being absent ⟨the *lack* of news about the fate of the soldiers was frustrating⟩

syn absence, dearth, want

rel deficiency, deficit, inadequacy, insufficiency, meagerness, paucity, poverty, scantiness, scarceness, scarcity, shortage, skimpiness; deprivation, loss, necessity, need, needfulness, omission; privation; vacuum, void

near ant abundance, amplitude, bounty, plenitude, plenty, wealth; adequacy, sufficiency; excess, overabundance, oversupply, surfeit, surplus; deluge, flood; heap, mountain, peck, pile, pot, quantity, raft, stack, volume, wad; fund, pool, stock, supply; hoard, stockpile

ant presence

2 a falling short of an essential or desirable amount or number — see DEFICIENCY

3 a state of being without something necessary, desirable, or useful — see NEED 1

lackadaisical adj lacking bodily energy or motivation — see LISTLESS

lackey n a person hired to perform household or personal services — see SERVANT

lacking adj **1** not coming up to a usual standard or meeting a particular need — see SHORT 3

2 not present or in evidence — see ABSENT 2

laconic adj **1** marked by the use of few words to convey much information or meaning — see CONCISE

2 tending not to speak frequently (as by habit or inclination) — see SILENT 2

laconically adv in a few words — see SHORTLY 1

lad n **1** a male person who has not yet reached adulthood — see BOY

2 an adult male human being — see MAN 1

ladder n a scheme of rank or order — see ³SCALE 1

laddie n a male person who has not yet reached adulthood — see BOY

lade vb **1** to lift out with something that holds liquid — see DIP 2

2 to place a weight or burden on — see LOAD 1

lading n a mass or quantity of something taken up and carried, conveyed, or transported — see LOAD 1

ladle n a utensil with a bowl and a handle that is used especially in cooking and serving food — see SPOON

ladle vb to lift out with something that holds liquid — see DIP 2

lady n **1** an adult female human being — see WOMAN

2 the female partner in a marriage — see WIFE

3 a woman of high birth or social position — see GENTLEWOMAN

ladylove n a woman with whom one is in love — see GIRLFRIEND

lag vb **1** to lose bodily strength or vigor — see WEAKEN 1

2 to move or act slowly — see DELAY 1

laggard adj moving or proceeding at less than the normal, desirable, or required speed — see SLOW 1

laggard n someone who moves slowly or more slowly than others — see SLOWPOKE

laggardly adv at a pace that is less than usual, desirable, or expected — see SLOW

lagger n someone who moves slowly or more slowly than others — see SLOWPOKE

lagging adj moving or proceeding at less than the normal, desirable, or required speed — see SLOW

lagniappe n **1** something given in addition to what is ordinarily expected or owed — see BONUS

2 something given to someone without expectation of a return — see GIFT 1

laid-back adj having a relaxed, casual manner — see EASYGOING 1

lair n **1** a place where a person goes to hide — see HIDEOUT

2 the shelter or resting place of a wild animal — see DEN 1

lam n the act or an instance of getting free from danger or confinement — see ESCAPE 1

lam vb to get free from a dangerous or confining situation — see ESCAPE 1

lamb n an innocent or gentle person ⟨the new guys at football camp were *lambs* who hardly knew what awaited them⟩

syn angel, dove, innocent, sheep

rel fledgling, greenhorn, ingenue (*or* ingénue); cherub, saint; mollycoddle, sissy, softy (*or* softie), weakling, wimp; dupe, pigeon, sap, sucker

near ant bully, roughneck, rowdy, tough; beast, boor, cad, churl, clown, creep, cretin, cur, heel, jerk; shark, skunk, snake, stinker; rascal, rogue, scamp, villain

ant wolf

lambaste *or* **lambast** vb **1** to criticize (someone) severely or angrily especially for personal failings — see SCOLD

2 to criticize harshly and usually publicly — see ATTACK 2

3 to strike repeatedly — see BEAT 1

lambent adj giving off or reflecting much light — see BRIGHT 1

lame vb to cause severe or permanent injury to — see MAIM

lamella n a small thin piece of material that resembles an animal scale — see ²SCALE

lament n 1 a crying out in grief ⟨the national *lament* that was heard when President Kennedy was assassinated⟩

syn groan, howl, keen, lamentation, moan, plaint, wail

rel grieving, mourning, weeping; regret; complaint, outcry, protest

near ant cheering, laughing, smiling

ant exultation, rejoicing

2 a composition expressing one's grief over a loss ⟨a poem that is her *lament* for her late grandmother⟩

syn dirge, elegy, requiem, threnody

rel taps

near ant encomium, eulogy, paean, panegyric

lament vb 1 to feel or express sorrow for ⟨she *lamented* the loss of her beloved pet⟩

syn bemoan, bewail, deplore, grieve (for), mourn, wail (for)

rel elegize; complain (about), cry (for), groan (about), keen, moan, weep; regret, rue; deprecate, disapprove (of)

near ant beam, cheer, laugh, smile; boast, brag, crow

ant exult (in), glory (in), rejoice (in)

2 to feel sorry or dissatisfied about — see REGRET

lamentable adj 1 expressing or suggesting mourning — see MOURNFUL 1

2 of a kind to cause great distress — see REGRETTABLE

lamentation n a crying out in grief — see LAMENT 1

lamina n a small thin piece of material that resembles an animal scale — see ²SCALE

lamp n something that provides illumination — see LIGHT 2

lampoon n a creative work that uses sharp humor to point up the foolishness of a person, institution, or human nature in general — see SATIRE

lance n a weapon with a long straight handle and sharp head or blade — see SPEAR

lance vb to penetrate or hold (something) with a pointed object — see IMPALE

land n 1 a body of people composed of one or more nationalities usually with its own territory and government — see NATION

2 a broad geographical area — see REGION 2

3 the solid part of our planet's surface as distinguished from the sea and air — see EARTH 2

land vb 1 to stop at or near a place along the shore ⟨the Pilgrims *landed* at Plymouth after exploring Cape Cod Bay⟩

syn anchor, dock

rel moor, tie up; beach, ground; harbor; arrive, reach; debark, disembark

phrases drop anchor, make port

near ant embark, launch, sail

2 to get to a destination — see COME 2

3 to go ashore from a ship — see DISEMBARK

4 to come to rest after descending from the air — see ALIGHT

5 to receive as return for effort — see EARN 1

6 to take physical control or possession of (something) suddenly or forcibly — see CATCH 1

landfill n a place where discarded materials (as trash) are dumped — see DUMP 1

landing n a structure used by boats and ships for taking on or landing cargo and passengers — see DOCK

landlord n the owner of land or housing that is rented to another ⟨agreed to pay the *landlord* the rent on the first Monday of each month⟩

syn lessor, renter

rel landlady; laird, landholder, landowner; host, proprietor; slumlord

ant lessee, lodger, tenant

landmark n a point in a chain of events at which an important change (as in one's fortunes) occurs — see TURNING POINT

language n 1 the stock of words, pronunciation, and grammar used by a people as their basic means of communication ⟨Great Britain, the United States, Australia, and other countries where English is the dominant *language*⟩

syn lingo, mother tongue, speech, tongue, vocabulary

rel argot, cant, dialect, idiom, jargon, parlance, patois, patter, pidgin, slang, vernacular; colloquialism, localism, regionalism; terminology

2 the special terms or expressions of a particular group or field — see TERMINOLOGY

3 the way in which something is put into words — see WORDING

languid adj 1 lacking bodily energy or motivation — see LISTLESS

2 lacking bodily strength — see WEAK 1

3 moving or proceeding at less than the normal, desirable, or required speed — see SLOW 1

languish vb to lose bodily strength or vigor — see WEAKEN 2

languishing adj lacking bodily energy or motivation — see LISTLESS

languor n the quality or state of lacking physical strength or vigor — see WEAKNESS 1

languorous adj lacking bodily energy or motivation — see LISTLESS

lank adj not stiff in structure — see LIMP 1

lanky adj being tall, thin and usually loosejointed ⟨the *lanky* basketball star was great at slam-dunking⟩

syn gangling, gangly, rangy, spindling, spindly

rel angular, bony, gaunt, lank, rawboned, scrawny, skinny; lean, slender, slim, spare, thin; racy, reedy, spidery, stringy, twiggy, wiry; spindle-shanked

near ant chubby, chunky, heavyset, pudgy, squat, stocky, stout, stubby,

---

syn synonym(s)   **rel** related words

ant antonym(s)   **near ant** near antonym(s)

stumpy, sturdy, thick-bodied, thickset; muscle-bound

lap *n* a portion of a trip — see LEG 2

¹**lap** *vb* **1** to flow along or against — see WASH 1

2 to flow in a broken irregular stream — see GURGLE

3 to move with a splashing motion — see SLOSH

²**lap** *vb* **1** to lie over parts of one another — see OVERLAP

2 to surround or cover closely — see ENFOLD 1

lapping *n* a partial covering of one thing by an adjoining thing — see OVERLAP

lapse *n* **1** a change in status for the worse usually temporarily — see REVERSE 1

2 an unintentional departure from truth or accuracy — see ERROR 1

3 the stopping of a process or activity — see END 1

lapse *vb* to come to an end — see CEASE 1

larceny *n* the unlawful taking and carrying away of property without the consent of its owner — see THEFT 1

large *adj* of a size greater than average of its kind ⟨he was hungry, so he ordered the *large* pizza⟩

   syn big, bulky, considerable, goodly, good-sized, grand, great, handsome, hefty, hulking, largish, outsize (*also* outsized), oversize (*or* oversized), sizable (*or* sizeable), substantial, tidy, voluminous

   rel astronomical (*also* astronomic), bumper, cavernous, colossal, enormous, gigantic, gross, heroic, huge, immense, jumbo, king-size (*or* king-sized), major, mammoth, massive, monolithic, monstrous, monumental, prodigious, staggering, stupendous, super, tremendous, vast, vasty, whacking, whopping; excessive, exorbitant, extravagant, extreme, immoderate, inordinate; abundant, ample, appreciable, copious, plentiful; fat, thick; capacious, commodious, roomy, spacious

   near ant diminutive, microscopic (*or* microscopical), midget, miniature, minute, pint-size (*or* pint-sized), pocket-size (*also* pocket-sized), pygmy, smallish, teeny, teeny-weeny, tiny, wee; petite, slender, slight, slim, thin

   ant little, puny, small, undersized

largely *adv* **1** for the most part — see CHIEFLY

2 to a large extent or degree — see GREATLY 2

largeness *n* the quality or state of being large in size ⟨I was impressed by the *largeness* of the portions at the new restaurant⟩

   syn bigness, bulkiness, grandness, greatness, heftiness, substantiality, voluminousness

   rel enormity, enormousness, extensiveness, grossness, healthiness, hugeness, immenseness, immensity, magnitude, massiveness, stupendousness, vastness; excessiveness, extravagance, extremeness, immoderacy; abundance, ample-

ness, bountifulness, copiousness, liberality; adequacy, sufficiency; weightiness

   near ant diminutiveness, minuteness, tininess; slightness; meagerness, poorness, scantiness, scarceness, scarcity, skimpiness, slenderness, slimness, spareness, sparseness, stinginess; deficiency, inadequacy

   ant fineness, littleness, puniness, smallness

largess *or* **largesse** *n* **1** something given to someone without expectation of a return — see GIFT 1

2 the quality or state of being generous — see LIBERALITY

largish *adj* **1** of a size greater than average of its kind — see LARGE

2 sufficiently large in size, amount, or number to merit attention — see CONSIDERABLE 1

lariat *n* a rope or long leather thong with a noose used especially for catching livestock — see LASSO

lark *n* a time or instance of carefree fun — see FLING 1

lark *vb* to play and run about happily — see FROLIC 1

larva *n* a young wingless often wormlike form (as a grub or caterpillar) that hatches from the egg of many insects ⟨the *larva* looked ugly, but it was destined to hatch into a beautiful butterfly⟩

   syn naiad, nymph

lascivious *adj* **1** depicting or referring to sexual matters in a way that is unacceptable in polite society — see OBSCENE 1

2 having a strong sexual desire — see LUSTFUL

lasciviousness *n* the quality or state of being obscene — see OBSCENITY 1

lash *n* a long thin or flexible tool for striking — see WHIP

lash *vb* to strike repeatedly with something long and thin or flexible — see WHIP 1

lass *n* a young usually unmarried woman — see GIRL 1

lassie *n* a young usually unmarried woman — see GIRL 1

lassitude *n* a complete depletion of energy or strength — see FATIGUE

lasso *n* a rope or long leather thong with a noose used especially for catching livestock ⟨the cowpuncher skillfully tossed the *lasso* around the calf's neck⟩

   syn lariat, reata, riata

last *adj* following all others of the same kind in order or time ⟨*last* one in the pool is a rotten egg⟩

   syn closing, concluding, final, hindmost, latest, latter, rearmost, terminal, terminating, ultimate

   rel consequent, ensuing, eventual, following, succeeding; conclusive, crowning, decisive, definitive; farthest, furthest, remotest; lowermost, lowest, nethermost; endmost, extreme, outermost, outmost; penultimate

   near ant eminent, premier, superior

ant beginning, earliest, first, inaugural, initial, maiden, opening, original, primary, starting

last *vb* **1** to continue to operate or to meet one's needs — see HOLD OUT

2 to remain indefinitely in existence or in the same state — see CONTINUE 1

last word *n* a practice or interest that is very popular for a short time — see FAD

late *adj* **1** not arriving, occurring, or settled at the due, usual, or proper time ⟨I ran as fast as I could, but was still *late* for class⟩

syn behind, behindhand, belated, delinquent, latish, overdue, tardy

rel delayed, detained, postponed; dilatory, laggard, slow, sluggish

near ant opportune, seasonable, timely; prompt, punctual

ant early, premature

2 having been such at some previous time — see FORMER

3 no longer living — see DEAD 1

late *adv* not long ago — see NEWLY

lately *adv* not long ago — see NEWLY

latency *n* a state of temporary inactivity — see ABEYANCE

lateness *n* the quality or state of being late ⟨we were unable to get into the movie due to our *lateness* in arriving⟩

syn belatedness, delinquency, tardiness

rel dilatoriness, sluggishness

near ant promptness, punctuality

ant earliness

latent *adj* not being in a state of use, activity, or employment — see INACTIVE 2

later *adj* being, occurring, or carried out at a time after something else — see SUBSEQUENT

later *adv* following in time or place — see AFTER

lateral *adj* of, relating to, or located on one side — see SIDE

latest *adj* following all others of the same kind in order or time — see LAST

lather *n* **1** a light mass of fine bubbles formed in or on a liquid — see FOAM

2 a state of nervous or irritated concern — see FRET

lathery *adj* covered with, consisting of, or resembling foam — see FOAMY

latish *adj* not arriving, occurring, or settled at the due, usual, or proper time — see LATE 1

latitude *n* the right to act or move freely — see FREEDOM 2

latrine *n* a room furnished with a fixture for flushing body waste — see TOILET

latter *adj* following all others of the same kind in order or time — see LAST

laud *vb* **1** to declare enthusiastic approval of — see ACCLAIM

2 to proclaim the glory of — see PRAISE 1

laudable *adj* deserving of high regard or great approval — see ADMIRABLE

laugh *n* **1** an explosive sound that is a sign of amusement ⟨the child's frown turned into a *laugh* when he saw the clown⟩

syn cackle, chortle, chuckle, giggle, guffaw, laughter, snicker, snigger, titter

rel crow, whoop; grin, simper, smile, smirk

near ant cry, groan, moan, sob, wail

2 someone or something that is very funny — see SCREAM

3 something said or done to cause laughter — see JOKE 1

laugh *vb* to express scornful amusement by means of facial contortions — see SNEER

laugh (at) *vb* to make (someone or something) the object of unkind laughter — see RIDICULE

laughable *adj* **1** causing or intended to cause laughter — see FUNNY 1

2 so foolish or pointless as to be worthy of scornful laughter — see RIDICULOUS 1

laughing *adj* indicative of or marked by high spirits or good humor — see MERRY

laughingstock *n* a person or thing that is made fun of ⟨his nerdy clothes made him the *laughingstock* of the schoolyard⟩

syn butt, mark, mock, mockery, target

rel chump, dupe, fall guy, fool, gull, monkey, pigeon, sap, sucker, victim

near ant favorite, darling, pet

laughter *n* an explosive sound that is a sign of amusement — see LAUGH 1

launch *n* **1** a rising from a surface at the start of a flight (as of a rocket) — see LIFT-OFF

2 the point at which something begins — see BEGINNING

launch *vb* **1** to be responsible for the creation and early operation or use of — see FOUND

2 to take the first step in (a process or course of action) — see BEGIN 1

3 to send through the air especially with a quick forward motion of the arm — see THROW

laurels *n pl* public acknowledgment or admiration for an achievement — see GLORY 1

lavaliere *also* **lavalliere** *n* an ornament worn on a chain around the neck or wrist — see PENDANT

lavatory *n* a room furnished with a fixture for flushing body waste — see TOILET

lave *vb* to flow along or against — see WASH 1

lavish *adj* **1** going beyond a normal or acceptable limit in degree or amount — see EXCESSIVE

2 pouring forth in great amounts — see PROFUSE

3 showing obvious signs of wealth and comfort — see LUXURIOUS

lavish *vb* **1** to give readily and in large quantities — see RAIN 2

2 to use up carelessly — see WASTE 1

lavishly *adv* in a luxurious manner — see HIGH

syn synonym(s)	*rel* related words
ant antonym(s)	*near ant* near antonym(s)

lavishness *n* the quality or fact of being free or wasteful in the expenditure of money — see EXTRAVAGANCE 1

law *n* **1** a rule of conduct or action laid down by a governing authority and especially a legislator ⟨a record number of *laws* were passed in that legislative session⟩
syn act, enactment, ordinance, statute
rel decree, directive, edict, fiat, ruling; bylaw, regulation, rule; amendment, bill, legislation; common law, martial law; prohibition, restriction; canon, encyclical
2 a collection or system of rules of conduct — see CODE
3 the department of government that keeps order, fights crime, and enforces statutes — see POLICE 1

law-abiding *adj* readily giving in to the command or authority of another — see OBEDIENT

lawbreaker *n* a person who has committed a crime — see CRIMINAL

lawbreaking *adj* not restrained by or under the control of legal authority — see LAWLESS

lawbreaking *n* **1** a breaking of a moral or legal code — see OFFENSE 1
2 activities that are in violation of the laws of the state — see CRIME 1

lawful *adj* permitted by law — see LEGAL 1

lawfulness *n* the quality or state of being legal — see LEGALITY

lawgiver *n* a member of an organized body of persons having the authority to make laws — see LEGISLATOR

lawless *adj* not restrained by or under the control of legal authority ⟨the *lawless* rioters were destroying everything in sight⟩
syn anarchic, disorderly, lawbreaking, unruly
rel defiant, insubordinate, mutinous, rebellious, refractory, riotous; undisciplined; criminal, illegal, illegitimate, illicit, unlawful, wrongful
near ant lawful, legal, legalized, legitimate
ant law-abiding, orderly

lawlessness *n* **1** a state in which there is widespread wrongdoing and disregard for rules and authority — see ANARCHY
2 activities that are in violation of the laws of the state — see CRIME 1

lawmaker *n* a member of an organized body of persons having the authority to make laws — see LEGISLATOR

lawsuit *n* a court case for enforcing a right or claim ⟨she filed a *lawsuit* against the moving company that was responsible for breaking her furniture⟩
syn action, proceeding, suit
rel litigation; case, cause, complaint

lawyer *n* a person whose profession is to conduct lawsuits for clients or to advise about legal rights and obligations ⟨their *lawyers* told them that they couldn't use the park for the concert without permission from the city⟩
syn advocate, attorney, counsel, counselor (*or* counsellor)

rel pettifogger, shyster; district attorney, prosecutor; solicitor; jurist; lawgiver, lawmaker, legislator, solon

lax *adj* **1** failing to give proper care and attention — see NEGLIGENT
2 not bound by rigid standards — see EASYGOING 2
3 not tightly fastened, tied, or stretched — see LOOSE 1

laxness *n* failure to take the care that a cautious person usually takes — see NEGLIGENCE 1

lay *n* **1** a rhythmic series of musical tones arranged to give a pleasing effect — see MELODY
2 a short musical composition for the human voice often with instrumental accompaniment — see SONG 1

lay *vb* **1** to arrange something in a certain spot or position — see PLACE 1
2 to cause to come to rest at the bottom (as of a liquid) — see SETTLE 1
3 to establish or apply as a charge or penalty — see IMPOSE
4 to make ready in advance — see PREPARE 1
5 to put a layer of on a surface — see SPREAD 2
6 to risk (something) on the outcome of an uncertain event — see BET

lay away *vb* to put (something of future use or value) in a safe or secret place — see HOARD

lay down *vb* **1** to put into effect through legislative or authoritative action — see ENACT
2 to state clearly and strongly — see ASSERT 1
3 to give the rules about (something) clearly and exactly — see PRESCRIBE

layoff *n* the termination of the employment of an employee or a work force often temporarily ⟨many people lost their jobs in the *layoff*⟩
syn discharge, dismissal, furlough
rel closing, shutdown; downsizing

lay off *vb* to bring (as an action or operation) to an immediate end — see STOP 1

lay off (of) *vb* to stop doing (something) permanently — see QUIT 1

layout *n* **1** the way in which something is sized, arranged, or organized — see FORMAT 1
2 the way in which the elements of something (as a work of art) are arranged — see COMPOSITION 3

lay out *vb* **1** to hand over or use up in payment — see SPEND 1
2 to work out the details of (something) in advance — see PLAN 1

layover *n* a brief halt in a journey — see STOP 1

lay up *vb* to put (something of future use or value) in a safe or secret place — see HOARD

laziness *n* an inclination not to do work or engage in activities ⟨although she often talks about ambitious household projects, nothing even gets started because of her *laziness*⟩

syn idleness, indolence, inertia, shiftlessness, sloth

rel apathy, languor, lassitude, lethargy, listlessness, sluggishness; goldbricking, loafing

near ant enterprise, initiative; assiduity, diligence, perseverance; energy, pep, vigor, vim, vitality

ant drive, industriousness, industry

lazy *adj* not easily aroused to action or work ⟨the *lazy* dog just wanted to lie on the couch all day and sleep⟩

syn idle, indolent, shiftless, slothful

rel apathetic, languorous, lazyish, lethargic, listless, sluggish, torpid

near ant ambitious, diligent, enterprising, zealous; dynamic, energetic, exuberant, lively, vigorous

ant industrious

lazybones *n pl* a lazy person ⟨he's a *lazybones* who is never willing to do any work⟩

syn drone, idler, loafer, slouch, slug, sluggard

rel bum, ne'er-do-well; sleepyhead; dawdler, laggard, putterer, slowpoke, stick-in-the-mud, trifler; goldbrick, malingerer, shirker, slacker; dallier, lingerer, loiterer, lounger, saunterer; delayer, procrastinator; dropout, quitter

near ant live wire, powerhouse

ant doer, go-getter, hummer, hustler, rustler, self-starter

lea *n* open land over which livestock may roam and feed — see RANGE 1

lead *adj* highest in rank or authority — see HEAD

lead *n* **1** the person who has the most important role in a play, movie, or TV show — see STAR 2

2 the space or amount of space between two points, lines, surfaces, or objects — see DISTANCE

3 a piece of advice or useful information especially from an expert — see ¹TIP 1

4 a slight or indirect pointing to something (as a solution or explanation) — see HINT 1

lead *vb* **1** to point out the way for (someone) especially from a position in front ⟨the tour guide *led* the group through the museum⟩

syn conduct, direct, guide, marshal, pilot, route, show, steer, usher

rel precede; accompany, attend, chaperone (*or* chaperon), convoy, escort, see; control, manage

near ant dog, hound, shadow, tail, tailgate

ant follow, trail

2 to serve as leader of ⟨the honor of *leading* the soccer squad⟩

syn boss, captain, command, dominate, head, spearhead

rel control, direct, govern, handle, manage, oversee, regulate, superintend, supervise

near ant bow (to), comply (with), defer (to), follow, obey, serve, submit (to), yield (to)

3 to be at the front of ⟨the marching band *led* the parade⟩

syn head

rel precede; announce, herald; accompany, attend, escort, usher

near ant conclude, end, finish, stop, terminate; tail, tailgate; dog, follow, trail

4 to be positioned along a certain course or in a certain direction — see RUN 3

5 to give advice and instruction to (someone) regarding the course or process to be followed — see GUIDE 1

leaden *adj* **1** causing weariness, restlessness, or lack of interest — see BORING

2 of the color gray — see GRAY 1

leader *n* **1** a long hollow cylinder for carrying a substance (as a liquid or gas) — see PIPE 1

2 the person (as an employer or supervisor) who tells people and especially workers what to do — see BOSS

leading *adj* **1** coming before all others in importance — see FOREMOST 1

2 highest in rank or authority — see HEAD

lead on *vb* to lead away from a usual or proper course by offering some pleasure or advantage — see LURE

leafage *n* green leaves or plants — see GREENERY 1

leaflet *n* a short printed publication with no cover or with a paper cover — see PAMPHLET

leafy *adj* covered with a thick, healthy natural growth — see LUSH 1

league *n* **1** a group of persons formally joined together for some common interest — see ASSOCIATION 2

2 an association of persons, parties, or states for mutual assistance and protection — see CONFEDERACY

league *vb* to form or enter into an association that furthers the interests of its members — see ALLY

leak (out) *vb* to become known — see GET OUT 1

lean *adj* having a noticeably small amount of body fat — see THIN 1

lean *n* the degree to which something rises up from a position level with the horizon — see SLANT

lean *vb* **1** to set or cause to be at an angle ⟨just *lean* the ladder against the tree and climb up it⟩

syn angle, cant, cock, heel, incline, list, slant, slope, tilt, tip

rel bank; bend, deviate, swerve, veer; decline, descend, recline, retreat

near ant even, flatten, level, straighten

2 to show a liking or proneness (for something) ⟨his diet *leans* toward greasy food⟩

syn incline, run, tend, trend

rel go, gravitate; indicate, point, suggest

near ant avoid, shun, shy (from *or* away from)

---

syn synonym(s)   *rel* related words
ant antonym(s)   *near ant* near antonym(s)

3 to place reliance or trust — see DE-PEND 2

lean (toward) *vb* to show partiality toward — see PREFER 1

leaning *adj* running in a slanting direction — see DIAGONAL

leaning *n* 1 a prevailing or general movement or inclination — see TREND 1

2 a habitual attraction to some activity or thing — see INCLINATION 1

leap *n* an act of leaping into the air — see JUMP 1

leap *vb* to propel oneself upward or forward into the air — see JUMP 1

leaping *adj* passing from one topic to another — see DISCURSIVE

learn *vb* 1 to acquire complete knowledge, understanding, or skill in ⟨after months of trying, he finally *learned* the dance steps⟩

syn get, master, pick up

rel apprehend, comprehend, grasp, know, understand; absorb, assimilate, digest, imbibe; ascertain, descry, detect, determine, dig up, discern, discover, examine, find out, hear, hit (on *or* upon), run down, scare up, search (for), see, track (down), tumble (to), unearth; major (in), study; memorize

phrases get the hang (*or* knack) of

near ant forget, misunderstand; miss, overlook; disregard, ignore, neglect

ant unlearn

2 to come to an awareness — see DISCOVER 1

3 to come upon after searching, study, or effort — see FIND 1

4 to commit to memory — see MEMORIZE

learned *adj* 1 having or displaying advanced knowledge or education — see EDUCATED

2 suggestive of the vocabulary used in books — see BOOKISH

learnedness *n* the understanding and information gained from being educated — see EDUCATION 2

learning *n* the understanding and information gained from being educated — see EDUCATION 2

lease *vb* 1 to give the possession and use of (something) in return for periodic payment — see RENT 1

2 to take or get the temporary use of (something) for a set sum — see HIRE 1

least *adj* being the least in amount, number, or size possible — see MINIMAL

leather *n* 1 the hairless natural covering of an animal prepared for use ⟨the company claims to use only the finest *leathers* for its shoes and handbags⟩

syn hide, skin

rel coat, fleece, fur, pelt; alligator, buckskin, calfskin, chamois, cordovan, cowhide, deerskin, doeskin, goatskin, horsehide, kid, kidskin, lambskin, morocco, pigskin, seal, sharkskin, sheepskin, snakeskin, suede

2 the outer covering of an animal removed for its commercial value — see HIDE 1

leathery *adj* not easily chewed — see TOUGH 1

leave *n* 1 a period during which the usual routine of school or work is suspended — see VACATION

2 the approval by someone in authority for the doing of something — see PERMISSION

leave *vb* 1 to cause to remain behind ⟨you can *leave* your lunch in the refrigerator while we're outside⟩ ⟨lovers who promise never to *leave* one another⟩

syn abandon, desert, forsake, maroon, quit

rel discard, ditch, dump, fling, jettison, junk, scrap, shed, shuck (off), throw away, throw out; deliver, give up, hand over, relinquish, surrender, yield; retreat (from), take off (from), vacate, withdraw (from); abjure, cut off, disown, reject, renounce, repudiate, separate (from); sacrifice; distance; disregard, forget, ignore, neglect

phrases walk out on

near ant harbor, have, hold, keep, own, possess, reserve, retain, withhold; redeem, rescue, save

ant reclaim

2 to give by means of a will ⟨I'm going to *leave* all of my possessions to my children⟩

syn bequeath, will

rel deed; hand down, pass (down); devise

3 to give up (a job or office) — see QUIT 1

4 to put (something) into the possession or safekeeping of another — see GIVE 2

leave off *vb* 1 to bring (as an action or operation) to an immediate end — see STOP 1

2 to come to an end — see CEASE 1

leave-taking *n* 1 the act of leaving a place — see DEPARTURE

2 the act or process of two or more persons going off in different directions — see PARTING 1

leavings *n pl* a remaining group or portion — see REMAINDER 1

lecture *vb* 1 to criticize (someone) severely or angrily especially for personal failings — see SCOLD

2 to give a formal often extended talk on a subject — see TALK 1

leech *n* a person who is supported or seeks support from another without making an adequate return ⟨whenever the gang went out for pizza, the *leech* in the group always had an excuse for not paying his fair share⟩

syn hanger-on, parasite, sponge, sponger

rel dependent; deadbeat, idler; flunky (*also* flunkey), henchman, lackey, satellite, stooge, sycophant, toady, yes-man; cheapskate, miser, niggard, piker, scrooge, skinflint, tightwad

near ant benefactor, philanthropist, supporter

leer (at) *vb* to look at in a flirtatious or desiring way — see OGLE

leery *adj* inclined to doubt or question claims — see SKEPTICAL 1

leeward *adj* being in the direction that the wind is blowing — see DOWNWIND

left *n* a political belief stressing progress, the essential goodness of humankind, and individual freedom — see LIBERALISM

left–handed *adj* not being or expressing what one appears to be or express — see INSINCERE

leftover *n* an unused or unwanted piece or item typically of small size or value — see ¹SCRAP 1

leftovers *n* a remaining group or portion — see REMAINDER 1

leg *n* **1** a lower limb of an animal ⟨he broke his *leg* when he accidentally stepped in that gopher hole⟩
syn pin
rel member; foreleg, forelimb; calf, drumstick, shank, shin, thigh
2 a portion of a trip ⟨on the first *leg* of the cruise they went south to the Caribbean⟩
syn lap, stage
rel layover, stopover

leg (it) *vb* to go on foot — see WALK

legacy *n* something that is or may be inherited — see INHERITANCE

legal *adj* **1** permitted by law ⟨drinking is only *legal* if you are 21 years old⟩
syn lawful, legitimate
rel allowable, authorized, noncriminal, permissible; justifiable, warrantable; regulation, statutory; good, innocent, proper, right
near ant bad, corrupt, evil, immoral, iniquitous, reprobate, sinful, wicked, wrong; banned, criminal, forbidden, guilty, outlawed, prohibited, unauthorized, unjust; nonconstitutional, unconstitutional
ant illegal, illegitimate, illicit, unlawful, wrongful
2 following or according to the rules — see FAIR 3

legality *n* the quality or state of being legal ⟨the senator questioned the *legality* of the proposed program⟩
syn lawfulness, legitimacy
rel rightfulness, rightness; permissibility, permissibleness
near ant badness, immorality, iniquity, sinfulness, unjustness, wickedness, wrongness; criminality, unconstitutionality
ant illegality, illegitimacy, unlawfulness, wrongfulness

legal tender *n* something (as pieces of stamped metal or printed paper) customarily and legally used as a medium of exchange, a measure of value, or a means of payment — see MONEY

legate *n* a person sent on a mission to represent another — see AMBASSADOR

legatee *n* a person who has the right to inherit property — see HEIR

legend *n* **1** an explanatory list of the symbols on a map or chart ⟨the *legend* indicated that a large circle represented each city, while a small circle stood for a small town⟩
syn key
rel scale; caption; guide, table
2 an explanation or description accompanying a pictorial illustration — see CAPTION 1
3 a traditional but unfounded story that gives the reason for a current custom, belief, or fact of nature — see MYTH 1
4 the body of customs, beliefs, stories, and sayings associated with a people, thing, or place — see FOLKLORE

legendary *adj* based on, described in, or being a myth — see MYTHICAL 1

legerdemain *n* **1** the art or skill of performing tricks or illusions for entertainment — see MAGIC 2
2 the use of clever underhanded actions to achieve an end — see TRICKERY

legion *n* **1** a large body of men and women organized for land warfare — see ARMY 1
2 a great number of persons or things gathered together — see CROWD 1

legionary *n* a person engaged in military service — see SOLDIER

legionnaire *n* a person engaged in military service — see SOLDIER

legislate *vb* to put into effect through legislative or authoritative action — see ENACT

legislator *n* a member of an organized body of persons having the authority to make laws ⟨the *legislators* met in an all-night session to hammer out the details of the bill⟩
syn lawgiver, lawmaker, solon
rel assemblyman, assemblywoman; congressman, congresswoman; senator

legitimacy *n* the quality or state of being legal — see LEGALITY

legitimate *adj* permitted by law — see LEGAL 1

lei *n* an ornamental chain or string (as of beads) worn around the neck — see NECKLACE

leisure *n* freedom from activity or labor — see ¹REST 1

leisurely *adj* moving or proceeding at less than the normal, desirable, or required speed — see SLOW 1

leisurely *adv* at a pace that is less than usual, desirable, or expected — see SLOW

lemon *n* something that has failed — see FAILURE 3

lend *vb* to give to another for temporary use with the understanding that it or a like thing will be returned ⟨I can *lend* you my copy of the textbook until the weekend⟩ ⟨can you *lend* me five dollars?⟩
syn advance, loan
rel furnish, give, grant; lease, let [*chiefly British*], rent
near ant receive, take
ant borrow

---

syn synonym(s)　　*rel* related words
ant antonym(s)　　*near ant* near antonym(s)

length *n* the space or amount of space between two points, lines, surfaces, or objects — see DISTANCE

lengthen *vb* to make longer — see EXTEND 1

lengthening *n* the act of making longer — see EXTENSION 1

lengthy *adj* **1** of great extent from end to end — see LONG 1

2 lasting for a considerable time — see LONG 2

lenience *n* kind, gentle, or compassionate treatment especially towards someone who is undeserving of it — see MERCY 1

leniency *n* kind, gentle, or compassionate treatment especially towards someone who is undeserving of it — see MERCY 1

lenity *n* kind, gentle, or compassionate treatment especially towards someone who is undeserving of it — see MERCY 1

leprechaun *n* an imaginary being usually having a small human form and magical powers — see FAIRY

less *adj* having not so great importance or rank as another — see LESSER

lessen *vb* **1** to make smaller in amount, volume, or extent — see DECREASE 1

2 to grow less in scope or intensity especially gradually — see DECREASE 2

lesser *adj* having not so great importance or rank as another ⟨it was the *lesser* evil of the two choices⟩

syn inferior, junior, less, lower, minor, smaller, subordinate, under

rel little, mean, small; minute, petty; jerkwater, one-horse, second-class, secondrate, two-bit; secondary, subsidiary

near ant exceptional, first-class, first-rate

ant greater, higher, major, more, primary, prime, senior, superior

lesson *n* something assigned to be read or studied ⟨your *lesson* for tonight will be the chapter on chemical reactions⟩

syn assignment, reading

rel homework, schoolwork; lecture; drill, exercise, practice (*also* practise); etude, study

lessor *n* the owner of land or housing that is rented to another — see LANDLORD

let *n* something that makes movement or progress more difficult — see ENCUMBRANCE

let *vb* **1** to give permission to — see ALLOW

2 *chiefly British* to give the possession and use of (something) in return for periodic payment — see RENT 1

3 to make able or possible — see ENABLE 1

letdown *n* **1** the emotion felt when one's expectations are not met — see DISAPPOINTMENT 1

2 something that disappoints — see DISAPPOINTMENT 2

let down *vb* to fall short in satisfying the expectation or hope of — see DISAPPOINT

lethal *adj* likely to cause or capable of causing death — see DEADLY

lethargic *adj* slow to move or act — see INACTIVE 1

let on *vb* to take on a false or deceptive appearance — see PRETEND 1

letter *n* a message on paper from one person or group to another ⟨he wrote her a *letter* every week she was away⟩

syn dispatch, epistle, memo, memorandum, missive, note

rel airmail, card, electronic mail, e-mail, junk mail, mail, postal card, postcard; communication, report; encyclical

letter carrier *n* a person who delivers mail — see POSTMAN

letter-perfect *adj* being entirely without fault or flaw — see PERFECT 1

letup *n* a usually gradual decrease in the pace or level of activity of something — see SLOWDOWN

let up *vb* **1** to come to an end — see CEASE 1

2 to grow less in scope or intensity especially gradually — see DECREASE 2

levee *n* **1** a bank of earth constructed to control water — see DAM

2 a structure used by boats and ships for taking on or landing cargo and passengers — see DOCK

level *adj* having a surface without bends, breaks, or irregularities ⟨looked for a *level* place to land the plane⟩

syn even, flat, flush, plane, smooth

rel exact, uniform; aligned, regular, true; horizontal, tabular; plumb, straight, vertical

near ant inexact, irregular, unaligned; undulating, wavy

ant bumpy, coarse, lumpy, rough, uneven

level *n* the placement of someone or something in relation to others in a vertical arrangement — see RANK 1

level *vb* **1** to make equal in amount, degree, or status — see EQUALIZE

2 to make free from breaks, curves, or bumps — see EVEN 1

3 to point or turn (something) toward a target or goal — see AIM 1

4 to strike (someone) so forcefully as to cause a fall — see FELL 1

levelheaded *adj* based on sound reasoning or information — see GOOD 1

levelheadedness *n* the ability to make intelligent decisions especially in everyday matters — see COMMON SENSE

lever *vb* to raise, move, or pull apart with or as if with a lever — see ¹PRY 1

leviathan *n* something that is unusually large and powerful — see GIANT

levity *n* a lack of seriousness often at an improper time — see FRIVOLITY 1

levy *n* a charge usually of money collected by the government from people or businesses for public use — see TAX

levy *vb* to establish or apply as a charge or penalty — see IMPOSE

lewd *adj* **1** depicting or referring to sexual matters in a way that is unacceptable in polite society — see OBSCENE 1

2 having a strong sexual desire — see LUSTFUL

3 hinting at or intended to call to mind matters regarded as indecent — see SUGGESTIVE 1

lewdness *n* the quality or state of being obscene — see OBSCENITY 1

lexical *adj* of or relating to words or language — see VERBAL 1

lexicon *n* a reference book giving information about the meanings, pronunciations, uses, and origins of words listed in alphabetical order — see DICTIONARY

liability *n* **1** a feature of someone or something that creates difficulty for achieving success — see DISADVANTAGE

2 the state of being held as the cause of something that needs to be set right — see RESPONSIBILITY 1

3 the state of being left without shelter or protection against something harmful — see EXPOSURE 1

liable *adj* **1** being in a situation where one is likely to meet with harm ⟨because of his frail constitution, he's *liable* to diseases⟩

syn endangered, exposed, open, sensitive, subject (to), susceptible, vulnerable

rel likely, prone; uncovered, undefended, unguarded, unprotected, unscreened, unsecured, unsheltered, unshielded

phrases in jeopardy

near ant covered, guarded, protected, safeguarded, screened, secured, sheltered, shielded, warded

ant invulnerable, unexposed

2 being the one who must meet an obligation or suffer the consequences for failing to do so — see RESPONSIBLE 1

liaison *n* **1** the fact or state of having something in common — see CONNECTION 1

2 the state of having shared interests or efforts (as in social or business matters) — see ASSOCIATION 1

liar *n* a person who tells lies ⟨she knew he was a *liar* when he started claiming that he was an astronaut⟩

syn fabricator, fibber, prevaricator, storyteller

rel defamer, libeler (*or* libeller), slanderer; perjurer; distorter, falsifier; equivocator, palterer; gossip, gossiper, talebearer; charlatan, cheat, cheater, confidence man, counterfeiter, cozener, deceiver, defrauder, dissembler, dissimulator, doubledealer, fraud, hustler, mountebank, pretender

near ant square shooter

libation *n* a liquid suitable for drinking — see DRINK 1

libel *n* the making of false statements that damage another's reputation — see SLANDER

libel *vb* to make untrue and harmful statements about — see SLANDER

libeling *n* the making of false statements that damage another's reputation — see SLANDER

libelous *or* **libellous** *adj* causing or intended to cause unjust injury to a person's good name ⟨*libelous* statements about a celebrity for which the tabloid was sued⟩

syn defamatory, scandalous, slanderous

rel erroneous, false, inaccurate, incorrect, inexact, invalid, off, unsound, untrue, wrong; depreciative, depreciatory, derogatory, detractive, disparaging, uncomplimentary, unfavorable; invidious, objectionable; maligning, traducing, vilifying; hateful, malevolent, malicious, spiteful

near ant appreciative, complimentary, favorable; adulatory, commendatory, eulogistic, laudatory; accurate, correct, errorless, factual, right, sound, true, valid

liberal *adj* **1** not bound by traditional ways or beliefs ⟨parents who take a very *liberal* attitude toward letting their children stay out late⟩

syn broad-minded, nonconventional, nonorthodox, nontraditional, open-minded, progressive, radical, unconventional, unorthodox

rel advanced, contemporary, modern; forbearing, indulgent, lenient, permissive, tolerant; extreme; impartial, objective, unbiased

near ant hard, rigid, strict; doctrinal, dogmatic; bigoted, intolerant, narrow-minded; reactionary

ant conservative, conventional, nonprogressive, old-fashioned, orthodox, traditional

2 being more than enough without being excessive — see PLENTIFUL

3 giving or sharing in abundance and without hesitation — see GENEROUS 1

liberalism *n* a political belief stressing progress, the essential goodness of humankind, and individual freedom ⟨*liberalism* had always claimed to stand for the greatest social good⟩

syn left

rel radicalism, socialism

ant conservatism, right

liberality *n* the quality or state of being generous ⟨already known for his *liberality*, the billionaire continued to give away record amounts of money⟩

syn bountifulness, bounty, generosity, largess (*or* largesse), openhandedness, openheartedness, philanthropy, unselfishness

rel beneficence, charity; kindness; gift, gratuity, lagniappe; tribute; extravagance, improvidence, lavishness, prodigality, wastefulness; spendthrift; dissipating, squandering

near ant conserving, economizing, economy, frugality, husbandry, providence, scrimping, skimping, thrift; conservation, saving; husbanding, managing; scraping; cutting back

ant cheapness, closeness, meanness, miserliness, parsimony, penuriousness, pinching, stinginess, tightness

---

syn synonym(s)   **rel** related words

ant antonym(s)   **near ant** near antonym(s)

liberally *adv* in a generous manner — see WELL 2

liberate *vb* 1 to set free (as from slavery or confinement) — see FREE 1

2 to set free from entanglement or difficulty — see EXTRICATE

liberation *n* the act of setting free from slavery ⟨the *liberation* of the slaves was one of the key results of the Civil War⟩

syn emancipation, enfranchisement, freeing, manumission

rel deliverance, redemption, salvation; autonomy, freedom, independence, liberty, self-government, sovereignty

near ant bondage, serfdom, servitude, thralldom (*or* thraldom), yoke; captivity, enchainment, imprisonment, incarceration; conquest, subjugation

ant enslavement

libertine *n* a person who has sunk below the normal moral standard — see DEGENERATE

liberty *n* the state of being free from the control or power of another — see FREEDOM 1

library *n* 1 a place where books, periodicals, and records are kept for use but not for sale ⟨I went to the *library* to do some research for my report⟩

syn archive

rel stacks

2 an organized group of objects acquired and maintained for study, exhibition, or personal pleasure — see COLLECTION 1

licensable *adj* that may be permitted — see PERMISSIBLE

license *also* **licence** *vb* to give official or legal power to — see AUTHORIZE 1

license *or* **licence** *n* 1 the approval by someone in authority for the doing of something — see PERMISSION

2 the granting of power to perform various acts or duties — see COMMISSION 1

3 the right to act or move freely — see FREEDOM 2

licentious *adj* having a strong sexual desire — see LUSTFUL

licentiousness *n* immoral conduct or practices harmful or offensive to society — see VICE 1

lick *n* 1 a hard strike with a part of the body or an instrument — see ¹BLOW

2 a very small amount — see PARTICLE 1

3 the smallest amount or part imaginable — see JOT

lick *vb* 1 to strike repeatedly — see BEAT 1

2 to achieve a victory over — see BEAT 2

licking *n* failure to win a contest — see DEFEAT 1

lid *n* 1 a piece placed over an open container to hold in, protect, or conceal its contents — see COVER 1

2 *slang* a covering for the head usually having a shaped crown — see HAT

lie *n* a statement known by its maker to be untrue and made in order to deceive ⟨he wanted to deny the accusation, but he couldn't tell a *lie*⟩

syn fabrication, fairy tale, falsehood, falsity, fib, mendacity, prevarication, story, tale, untruth, whopper

rel distortion, exaggeration, half-truth; ambiguity, equivocation; defamation, libel, slander; perjury; bluff, pose, pretense (*or* pretence); humbug, jive, nonsense; fallacy, misconception, myth; misinformation, misrepresentation, misstatement; deceit, deceitfulness, dishonesty, duplicity, fraudulence

near ant fact, truism, verity; honesty, truthfulness, veracity; authentication, confirmation, substantiation, validation, verification

ant truth

lie *vb* 1 to make a statement one knows to be untrue ⟨would I *lie* to you about that?⟩

syn fabricate, fib, prevaricate

rel forswear, perjure; equivocate, fudge, palter; beguile, cozen, deceive, delude, dupe, fool, gull, hoax, hoodwink, kid, snow, take in, trick; defame, libel, slander; falsify, misrepresent, misstate; distort, garble; dissemble, dissimulate; misguide, misinform, mislead

phrases tell stories (*or* tales)

near ant assert, swear, testify; authenticate, confirm, substantiate, validate, verify

2 to be positioned along a certain course or in a certain direction — see RUN 3

3 to occupy a place or location — see STAND 1

lie detector *n* an instrument for detecting physical signs of the tension that goes with lying ⟨hooked the suspect up to a *lie detector* before interrogating him about the robbery⟩

syn polygraph

life *n* 1 a history of a person's life — see BIOGRAPHY

2 a member of the human race — see HUMAN

3 active strength of body or mind — see VIGOR 1

4 the period during which something exists, lasts, or is in progress — see DURATION 1

5 the way people live at a particular time and place — see CIVILIZATION 1

lifeless *adj* no longer living — see DEAD 1

lifelessness *n* the state of being dead — see DEATH 2

lifelike *adj* closely resembling the object imitated — see NATURAL 2

life span *n* the period during which something exists, lasts, or is in progress — see DURATION 1

lifestyle *n* the way people live at a particular time and place — see CIVILIZATION 1

lifetime *n* the period during which something exists, lasts, or is in progress — see DURATION 1

lift *n* 1 an act or instance of helping — see HELP 1

2 a means of getting to a destination in a vehicle driven by another — see RIDE

lift vb 1 to move from a lower to a higher place or position — see RAISE 1
2 to move or extend upward — see AS-CEND

lifted adj being positioned above a surface — see ELEVATED 1

lift-off n a rising from a surface at the start of a flight (as of a rocket) ⟨everyone was quiet in the control room as they waited for *lift-off*⟩
syn launch, takeoff
near ant crash; splashdown
ant landing

ligature n 1 something that physically prevents free movement — see BOND 1
2 a uniting or binding force or influence — see BOND 2

¹**light** adj 1 having little weight ⟨the suitcase was as *light* as a feather after all the clothes fell out⟩
syn airy, feathery, lightweight, underweight, weightless
rel bantam, diminutive, little, minute, small, smallish, puny, tiny, undersized, wee; flimsy, fragile, insubstantial; petite, slender, slight, slim, thin
near ant big, considerable, extensive, goodly, good-sized, great, handsome, huge, hulking, jumbo, king-size (*or* king-sized), large, largish, massive, oversize (*or* oversized), sizable (*or* sizeable), substantial, super, voluminous, whacking; bulky, cumbersome, unwieldy
ant heavy, hefty, leaden, overweight, ponderous, weighty
2 involving minimal difficulty or effort — see EASY 1
3 less plentiful than what is normal, necessary, or desirable — see MEAGER 1
4 moving easily — see GRACEFUL 1
5 not harsh or stern especially in manner, nature, or effect — see GENTLE 1
6 resembling air in lightness — see AIRY 1

²**light** adj 1 filled with much light — see BRIGHT 2
2 lacking intensity of color — see PALE 1
3 of light complexion — see FAIR 4

light n 1 the steady giving off of the form of radiation that makes vision possible ⟨he read poetry by the *light* of the moon⟩
syn blaze, flare, fluorescence, glare, gleam, glow, illumination, incandescence, luminescence, radiance, shine
rel flash, glimmer, glint, glitter, scintillation, shimmer, sparkle, twinkle; daylight, moonlight, sunlight; afterglow, aureole, aurora, beam, ray, shaft, streak, stream; glisten, gloss, luster (*or* lustre), polish, reflection, sheen
near ant blackness, dark, darkness, dimness, dusk, duskiness, gloom, night, shadow
2 something that provides illumination ⟨turn off the *light* when you go to bed⟩
syn beacon, lamp
rel arc lamp (*also* arc light), candelabra, candelabrum, candle, chandelier, dark

lantern, electric, flare, flash, flashbulb, flashcube, flashlight, floodlight, fluorescent lamp, gaslight, headlight, incandescent lamp, klieg light (*or* kleig light), lantern, light bulb, lighthouse, lighting, sconce, spotlight, streetlight
3 a person who is widely known and usually much talked about — see CELEBRITY 1

¹**light** vb to come to rest after descending from the air — see ALIGHT

²**light** vb 1 to set (something) on fire — see BURN 2
2 to supply with light — see ILLUMINATE 1

lighted *or* **lit** adj 1 filled with much light — see BRIGHT 2
2 being on fire — see ABLAZE 1

lighten vb to supply with light — see ILLUMINATE 1

light-footed adj moving easily — see GRACEFUL 1

light-headed adj 1 having a feeling of being whirled about and in danger of falling down — see DIZZY 1
2 lacking in seriousness or maturity — see GIDDY 1

light-headedness n a lack of seriousness often at an improper time — see FRIVOLITY 1

lighthearted adj having or showing a lack of concern or seriousness — see CAREFREE

lightheartedness n carefree freedom from constraint — see ABANDON

lighting out n the act of leaving a place — see DEPARTURE

lightly adv without difficulty — see EASILY

¹**lightness** n 1 the state or quality of having little weight ⟨the first thing I noticed about the little bird was its *lightness*; I could hardly tell I was holding it in my hand⟩
syn slightness, weightlessness
rel airiness, delicacy, etherealness; flimsiness, fluffiness, insubstantiality
near ant solidity, solidness, substantiality
ant heaviness, heftiness, massiveness, ponderousness, weightiness
2 a lack of seriousness often at an improper time — see FRIVOLITY 1

²**lightness** n the quality or state of having or giving off light — see BRILLIANCE 1

lightning adj moving, proceeding, or acting with great speed — see FAST 1

lightsome adj having or showing a good mood or disposition — see CHEERFUL 1

lightweight adj having little weight — see ¹LIGHT 1

lightweight n a person of no importance or influence — see NOBODY

like adj having qualities in common — see ALIKE

like adv to some degree or extent — see FAIRLY

like conj the way it would be or one would do if — see AS IF

¹**like** n 1 a number of persons or things that are grouped together because they have something in common — see SORT 1

2 one that is equal to another in status, achievement, or value — see EQUAL

²like *n* positive regard for something — see LIKING

like *vb* **1** to wish to have ⟨I'd *like* another slice of pizza, but I've already eaten more than I should have⟩

syn care (for), want

rel adore, delight (in), dig, enjoy, fancy, groove (on), like, love, relish, revel (in); covet, crave, die (for), wish (for), yearn (for)

2 to show partiality toward — see PREFER 1

3 to take pleasure in — see ENJOY 1

4 to see fit — see CHOOSE 2

likelihood *n* the quality or state of being likely to occur — see PROBABILITY 1

likeliness *n* the quality or state of being likely to occur — see PROBABILITY 1

likely *adj* **1** having a high chance of occurring ⟨if you don't do well in school, your *likely* fate is a low-paying job⟩

syn probable

rel conceivable, earthly, imaginable, possible, potential; apt, bound, certain, doubtless, inescapable, inevitable, necessary, sure, unavoidable

near ant impossible, inconceivable, unimaginable

ant doubtful, dubious, improbable, questionable, unlikely

2 having qualities which inspire hope — see HOPEFUL 1

3 worthy of being accepted as true or reasonable — see BELIEVABLE

likely *adv* without much doubt — see PROBABLY

liken *vb* **1** to describe as similar — see COMPARE 1

2 to regard or represent as equal or comparable — see EQUATE 1

likeness *n* **1** a two-dimensional design intended to look like a person or thing — see PICTURE 1

2 something or someone that strongly resembles another — see IMAGE 1

3 the quality or state of having many qualities in common — see SIMILARITY 1

likewise *adv* **1** in addition to what has been said — see MORE 1

2 in like manner — see ALSO 1

liking *n* positive regard for something ⟨I have a *liking* for dark chocolate⟩

syn appetite, fancy, favor, fondness, like, love, partiality, preference, relish, shine, taste, use

rel craving, desire, longing, thirst, yen; enthusiasm, interest, passion; bias, prejudice; bent, inclination, leaning, propensity, tendency; weakness

near ant apathy, disinclination; indifference, unconcern

ant aversion, disfavor, dislike, distaste, hatred, loathing

lily–livered *adj* having or showing a shameful lack of courage — see COWARDLY

limb *n* a major outgrowth from the main stem of a woody plant — see BRANCH 1

limber *adj* able to bend easily without breaking — see WILLOWY

limit *n* a real or imaginary point beyond which a person or thing cannot go ⟨there was no *limit* to the number of challenges they faced⟩

syn bound, boundary, ceiling, confines, end, extent, limitation, line, termination

rel extremity, fag end; border, brim, edge, margin, rim, verge; outside; bar, barrier, fence, hedge, restraint, stop, wall

limit *vb* **1** to set bounds or an upper limit for ⟨*limit* the note to a few words⟩

syn circumscribe, confine, restrict

rel bar, block, hinder, impede, obstruct; constrict, contract, lessen, narrow, pinch, squeeze, tighten; quell, repress, suppress; number; modify, qualify

near ant broaden, expand, widen; overextend, overreach

ant exceed

2 to mark the limits of ⟨adjectives *limit* the meanings of nouns⟩

syn bound, circumscribe, define, delimit, demarcate, mark (out), terminate

rel control, determine, govern; delineate, describe

limitation *n* **1** a real or imaginary point beyond which a person or thing cannot go — see LIMIT

2 something that limits one's freedom of action or choice — see RESTRICTION 1

3 the act or practice of keeping something (as an activity) within certain boundaries — see RESTRICTION 2

limited *adj* **1** having distinct or certain limits ⟨to avoid overcrowding, the number of tickets to the outdoor concerts is *limited*⟩

syn bounded, circumscribed, defined, definite, determinate, finite, measured, narrow, restricted

rel modified, qualified; detailed, exact, precise, specific; confined, constricted, moderate, modest; minute, puny, small, tiny; determined, fixed, settled

near ant bottomless, countless, incalculable, inestimable, inexhaustible, innumerable, unfathomable; general, indeterminate, nebulous, vague; enlarged, escalated, expanded; considerable, copious, plentiful; big, bulky, bumper, extensive, goodly, good-sized, great, handsome, hefty, hulking, jumbo, king-size (*or* king-sized), large, largish, oversize (*or* oversized), respectable, sizable (*or* sizeable), substantial, super, vast, voluminous, whacking; epic, grandiose, major; ample, broad, comprehensive, cosmopolitan, expansive, global, inclusive, universal, whole

ant boundless, dimensionless, endless, illimitable, immeasurable, indefinite, infinite, limitless, measureless, unbounded, undefined, unlimited, unmeasured

2 having a limit — see FINITE 1

limitless *adj* being or seeming to be without limits — see INFINITE

limp *adj* **1** not stiff in structure ⟨his broken arm was *limp* as he held it against his side⟩
syn droopy, flaccid, floppy, lank, yielding
rel flabby, mushy, semisoft, soft, squashy, squishy; delicate, flimsy, insubstantial; elastic, flexible, lax, loose, pliant, relaxed, resilient, springy, stretchy, supple
near ant firm, hard, indurated, solid, sound, strong; brittle, crisp; compact, dense, substantial
ant inflexible, resilient, rigid, stiff, sturdy, tense; firm, hard, indurated, solid, sound, strong

2 depleted in strength, energy, or freshness — see WEARY 1

3 lacking bodily energy or motivation — see LISTLESS

limp *vb* **1** to walk while favoring one leg ⟨she *limped* all day after stubbing her toe on the lawn sprinkler⟩
syn halt, hobble
rel hitch; blunder, falter, lurch, shuffle, stagger, stumble, teeter, totter, waver, wobble; dodder
near ant breeze, glide, sail
ant stride

2 to make progress in a clumsy, struggling manner — see FLOUNDER 1

limpid *adj* easily seen through — see CLEAR 1

limpidity *n* the state or quality of being easily seen through — see CLARITY 1

limpidness *n* the state or quality of being easily seen through — see CLARITY 1

line *n* **1** a series of persons or things arranged one behind another ⟨we waited in the *line* for lunch for what seemed like hours⟩
syn column, cue, file, queue, range, string, train
rel echelon, rank, row, tier; progression, sequence, succession; array

2 a way of acting or proceeding — see COURSE 1

3 the activity by which one regularly makes a living — see OCCUPATION

4 a region of activity, knowledge, or influence — see FIELD 2

5 a real or imaginary point beyond which a person or thing cannot go — see LIMIT

6 a long hollow cylinder for carrying a substance (as a liquid or gas) — see PIPE 1

7 a length of braided, flexible material that is used for tying or connecting things — see CORD

8 a group of vehicles traveling together or under one management — see FLEET

9 the direction along which something or someone moves — see PATH 1

10 a group of persons who come from the same ancestor — see FAMILY 1

11 the line of ancestors from whom a person is descended — see ANCESTRY

lineage *n* **1** the line of ancestors from whom a person is descended — see ANCESTRY

2 a group of persons who come from the same ancestor — see FAMILY 1

linear *adj* free from irregularities (as curves, bends, or angles) in course — see STRAIGHT 1

linger *vb* to move or act slowly — see DELAY 1

lingerer *n* someone who moves slowly or more slowly than others — see SLOWPOKE

lingo *n* **1** the stock of words, pronunciation, and grammar used by a people as their basic means of communication — see LANGUAGE 1

2 the special terms or expressions of a particular group or field — see TERMINOLOGY

linguistic *adj* of or relating to words or language — see VERBAL 1

link *n* **1** a rod-shaped portion of seasoned ground meat in a casing — see SAUSAGE

2 a uniting or binding force or influence — see BOND 2

link *vb* **1** to put or bring together so as to form a new and longer whole — see CONNECT 1

2 to think of (something) in combination — see ASSOCIATE 2

link (up) *vb* to come together to form a single unit — see UNITE 1

linkage *n* the fact or state of having something in common — see CONNECTION 1

linking *n* the act or an instance of joining two or more things into one — see UNION 1

linkup *n* the state of having shared interests or efforts (as in social or business matters) — see ASSOCIATION 1

lint *n* a soft airy substance or covering — see FUZZ

lionhearted *adj* feeling or displaying no fear by temperament — see BRAVE

liquefy *vb* to go from a solid to a liquid state ⟨the steel *liquefied* in the intense heat of the forge⟩
syn deliquesce, flux, fuse, melt, run, thaw
rel found, gutter, smelt, try; dissolve, render; soften, thin
near ant clot, coagulate, congeal, gel, jell, jelly, thicken
ant harden, set, solidify

liquid *adj* **1** capable of moving like a liquid — see FLUID 1

2 easily seen through — see CLEAR 1

liquidate *vb* **1** to destroy all traces of — see ANNIHILATE 1

2 to put to death deliberately — see MURDER 1

3 to give what is owed for — see PAY 2

liquor *n* a fermented or distilled beverage that can make a person drunk — see ALCOHOL

lissome *also* **lissom** *adj* **1** moving easily — see GRACEFUL 1

2 able to bend easily without breaking — see WILLOWY

¹list *n* a record of a series of items (as names or titles) usually arranged according to some system ⟨we put eggs, sour

---

syn synonym(s)   *rel* related words
ant antonym(s)   *near ant* near antonym(s)

cream, tomatoes, roast beef, and cheddar cheese on the shopping *list*⟩

syn canon, catalog (*or* catalogue), checklist, listing, menu, register, registry, roll, roster, schedule, table

rel agenda, bibliography, compilation, directory, docket, glossary, index, inventory, manifest, payroll; calendar, chronology, timetable

²list *n* the act of positioning or an instance of being positioned at an angle — see TILT

³list *n* a long narrow piece of material — see STRIP

¹list *vb* **1** to make a list of ⟨he *listed* the people on the team⟩

syn enumerate, inventory, itemize, numerate

rel count, mark, number; check (off), tick (off)

2 to put (someone or something) on a list ⟨her number isn't *listed* in the phone book⟩

syn catalog (*or* catalogue), enroll (*also* enrol), enter, index, inscribe, put down, record, register, schedule, slate

rel book, file, note; classify, compile, tabulate; reschedule

near ant delete

3 to enter in a list or roll — see ENROLL 1

4 to specify one after another — see ENUMERATE 1

²list *vb* to set or cause to be at an angle — see LEAN 1

listen *vb* to pay attention especially through the act of hearing ⟨would you *listen* to what I have to say?⟩

syn attend, hark, hear, hearken, heed, mind

phrases prick up one's ears

near ant discount, disregard

ant ignore, tune out

listen (to) *vb* to take notice of and be guided by — see HEED 1

listen in (on) *vb* to listen to (another in private conversation) — see EAVESDROP (ON)

listing *adj* **1** inclined or twisted to one side — see AWRY

2 running in a slanting direction — see DIAGONAL

listing *n* a record of a series of items (as names or titles) usually arranged according to some system — see ¹LIST

listless *adj* lacking bodily energy or motivation ⟨when I had the flu, I felt *listless* and worn-out⟩

syn enervated, lackadaisical, languid, languishing, languorous, limp, spiritless

rel indolent, lazy, slothful; lethargic, logy, sleepy, sluggish, torpid; exhausted, tired, weary; feeble, frail, weak; apathetic, impassive, phlegmatic, stolid; careless, heedless, thoughtless, unwary; inactive, inert

near ant active, dynamic, industrious; avid, eager, enthusiastic, keen, lively, vivacious; cheerful, chipper, perky, up; agog, alert, awake, dapper, open-eyed, sleepless, vigilant, watchful, wide-awake

ant ambitious, animated, energetic, enterprising, motivated

listlessness *n* the state of being bored — see BOREDOM

literal *adj* restricted to or based on fact — see FACTUAL 1

literary *adj* suggestive of the vocabulary used in books — see BOOKISH

literate *adj* having or displaying advanced knowledge or education — see EDUCATED

lithe *adj* **1** able to bend easily without breaking — see WILLOWY

2 moving easily — see GRACEFUL 1

lithesome *adj* moving easily — see GRACEFUL 1

litter *n* **1** an unorganized collection or mixture of various things — see MISCELLANY 1

2 discarded or useless material — see GARBAGE

littered *adj* lacking in order, neatness, and often cleanliness — see MESSY

little *adj* **1** having relatively little height — see SHORT 1

2 lacking importance — see UNIMPORTANT

3 not broad or open in views or opinions — see NARROW 2

4 not lasting for a considerable time — see SHORT 2

5 of a size that is less than average — see SMALL 1

little *adv* **1** in a very small quantity or degree ⟨we had *little* more than we needed to survive in the wilderness⟩

syn negligibly, nominally, slightly

rel meagerly, scantily; barely, hardly, just, marginally, minimally, scarcely

phrases a bit

near ant completely, entirely, purely, thoroughly, totally, utterly; eminently, exceptionally; appreciably, discernibly, noticeably, palpably; abundantly, plentifully; generously, handsomely, liberally; astronomically, grandly, hugely, monstrously, monumentally

ant awful, awfully, beastly, considerably, deadly, especially, exceedingly (*also* exceeding), extensively, extra, extremely, far, frightfully, full, greatly, heavily, highly, jolly, mightily, mighty, mortally, most, much, particularly, rattling, real, right, significantly, so, something, substantially, super, terribly, too, very, whacking

2 not often — see SELDOM

little *n* a very small amount — see PARTICLE 1

little by little *adv* by small steps or amounts — see GRADUALLY

littleness *n* the quality or state of being little in size — see SMALLNESS

littlest *adj* being the least in amount, number, or size possible — see MINIMAL

livable *also* **liveable** *adj* suitable for living in ⟨after adding some furniture and painting the walls, the apartment was *livable*⟩

syn habitable, inhabitable

rel comfortable, cozy, homelike, homey, intimate, snug; deluxe, lavish, luxuriant, luxurious, plush, sumptuous; opulent, palatial, rich; acceptable, bearable, endurable, sufferable, supportable, sustainable, tolerable

near ant uncomfortable; humble, Spartan; economical, frugal, spare, thrifty; intolerable, unacceptable, unbearable, unendurable, insupportable

ant uninhabitable, unlivable

live *adj* having or showing life — see ALIVE 1

live *vb* 1 to have a home ⟨he *lived* next door to the hospital⟩
syn abide, dwell, reside
rel lodge, settle, stay; frequent, hang out (at); haunt; inhabit, occupy; people, populate; lease, rent, sublet, tenant
2 to have life — see BE 1

liveliness *n* the quality or state of having abundant or intense activity — see VITALITY 1

lively *adj* 1 having much high-spirited energy and movement ⟨the *lively* puppy was racing around the dining room floor chasing after people's shoelaces⟩
syn active, animate, animated, bouncing, brisk, energetic, frisky, gay, jaunty, jazzy, peppy, perky, pert, racy, snappy, spanking, sparky, spirited, sprightly, springy, vital, vivacious, zippy
rel dapper, dashing, spiffy; agog, alert, awake, open-eyed, up, wide-awake; agile, nimble, spry; bright, buoyant, cheerful, chipper, effervescent, upbeat; eager, enthusiastic, keen; frolicsome, impish, playful; bubbly, exuberant, high-spirited; high-strung, nervous, skittish
phrases on the go
near ant indolent, lazy, unambitious; inert, lethargic, sleepy, sluggish, tired, torpid, weary; apathetic, impassive, phlegmatic, stolid; boring, dull, irksome, tedious
ant dead, inactive, inanimate, lackadaisical, languid, languishing, languorous, lifeless, limp, listless, spiritless, unanimated
2 marked by much life, movement, or activity — see ALIVE 2

liven (up) *vb* to give life, vigor, or spirit to — see ANIMATE

livery *n* the distinctive clothing worn by members of a particular group — see UNIFORM

live wire *n* an ambitious person who eagerly goes after what is desired — see GO-GETTER

livid *adj* lacking a healthy skin color — see PALE 2

living *adj* 1 being in effective operation — see ACTIVE 1
2 having being at the present time — see EXTANT 1
3 having or showing life — see ALIVE 1

---

syn synonym(s)   *rel* related words
ant antonym(s)   *near ant* near antonym(s)

load *n* 1 a mass or quantity of something taken up and carried, conveyed, or transported ⟨they placed a *load* of grain on the truck going to Florida⟩
syn burden, cargo, draft, freight, haul, lading, loading, payload, weight
rel consignment, boatload, carload, shipload, truckload; ballast, deadweight; overload, surcharge; bale, bundle, pack, package, packet, parcel, shipment; manifest; body, bulk, mass
2 **loads** *pl* a considerable amount — see LOT 2

load *vb* 1 to place a weight or burden on ⟨students complaining that their teachers were *loading* them with work⟩
syn burden, encumber, lade, lumber, saddle, weight
rel clog, clutter, fill, heap; press, weigh; strain, tax; overburden, overload, overtax, surcharge; handicap; afflict, oppress
near ant alleviate, ease, lighten, relieve
ant disencumber, unburden, unload
2 to put into (something) as much as can be held or contained — see FILL 1

loaded *adj* 1 containing or seeming to contain the greatest quantity or number possible — see FULL 1
2 having goods, property, or money in abundance — see RICH 1
3 *slang* being under the influence of alcohol — see DRUNK

loading *n* a mass or quantity of something taken up and carried, conveyed, or transported — see LOAD 1

loaf *vb* to spend time doing nothing — see IDLE

loafer *n* a lazy person — see LAZYBONES

loamy *adj* consisting or suggestive of earth — see EARTHY 1

loan *vb* to give to another for temporary use with the understanding that it or a like thing will be returned — see LEND

loath or **loth** *adj* having doubts about the wisdom of doing something — see HESITANT

loathe *vb* to dislike strongly — see HATE

loathing *n* 1 a dislike so strong as to cause stomach upset or queasiness — see DISGUST
2 a very strong dislike — see HATE 1

loathsome *adj* causing intense displeasure, disgust, or resentment — see OFFENSIVE 1

lob *vb* to send through the air especially with a quick forward motion of the arm — see THROW

lobby *n* 1 a centrally located room in a building that serves as a gathering or waiting area or as a passageway into the interior — see FOYER 1
2 the entrance room of a building — see HALL 1

local *n* a local unit of an organization — see CHAPTER

locale *n* the area or space occupied by or intended for something — see PLACE 1

locality *n* the area or space occupied by or intended for something — see PLACE 1

locate *vb* to come upon after searching, study, or effort — see FIND 1

location *n* the area or space occupied by or intended for something — see PLACE 1

loch *n, Scottish* a part of a body of water that extends beyond the general shoreline — see GULF 1

lock (up) *vb* to put in or as if in prison — see IMPRISON

locker *n* 1 a covered rectangular container for storing or transporting things — see CHEST

2 a storage case typically having doors and shelves — see CABINET

lockup *n* a place of confinement for persons held in lawful custody — see JAIL

loco *adj* having or showing a very abnormal or sick state of mind — see INSANE 1

locus *n* the area or space occupied by or intended for something — see PLACE 1

locution *n* a distinctive way of putting ideas into words — see STYLE 1

lodestone *n* something that attracts interest — see MAGNET

lodge *n* 1 a place that provides rooms and usually a public dining room for overnight guests — see HOTEL

2 an often small house for recreational or seasonal use — see COTTAGE

3 the meeting place of an organization — see CLUB 2

4 the shelter or resting place of a wild animal — see DEN 1

lodge *vb* 1 to provide with living quarters or shelter — see HOUSE 1

2 to establish or place comfortably or snugly — see ENSCONCE 1

3 to set solidly in or as if in surrounding matter — see ENTRENCH

lodged *adj* firmly positioned in place and difficult to dislodge — see TIGHT 2

lodger *n* one who rents a room or apartment in another's house — see TENANT

lodging *n* 1 the place where one lives — see HOME 1

2 **lodgings** *pl* a room or set of rooms in a private house or a block used as a separate dwelling place — see APARTMENT 1

loft *vb* to send through the air especially with a quick forward motion of the arm — see THROW

loftiest *adj* being at a point or level higher than all others — see TOP 1

loftiness *n* an exaggerated sense of one's importance that shows itself in the making of excessive or unjustified claims — see ARROGANCE

lofty *adj* 1 extending to a great distance upward — see HIGH 1

2 having a feeling of superiority that shows itself in an overbearing attitude — see ARROGANT

3 having or displaying feelings of scorn for what is regarded as beneath oneself — see PROUD 1

4 having, characterized by, or arising from a dignified and generous nature — see NOBLE 2

5 very dignified in form, tone, or style — see ELEVATED 2

log *vb* to make a written note of — see RECORD 1

logger *n* a person whose job is to cut down trees — see LUMBERJACK

logic *n* the thought processes that have been established as leading to valid solutions to problems ⟨I tried to use *logic* to figure out the solution to the puzzle⟩

syn reason, reasoning, sense

rel cogency, coherence, rationality, thought; analysis; deduction, induction

near ant incoherence, insanity, irrationality

logical *adj* 1 according to the rules of logic ⟨the lawyer won the case with a *logical* argument about the motives of the suspect⟩

syn analytic (*or* analytical), coherent, good, rational, reasonable, sensible, sound, valid

rel sane; thoughtful; scientific

near ant specious; crazy, insane; senseless, thoughtless

ant illogical, incoherent, invalid, irrational, unreasonable, unsound

2 based on sound reasoning or information — see GOOD 1

logo *n* a device, design, or figure used as an identifying mark — see EMBLEM

logy *adj* depleted in strength, energy, or freshness — see WEARY 1

loiter *vb* to move or act slowly — see DELAY 1

loiterer *n* someone who moves slowly or more slowly than others — see SLOWPOKE

loll *vb* 1 to be limp from lack of water or vigor — see DROOP 1

2 to refrain from labor or exertion — see REST 1

3 to spend time doing nothing — see IDLE

lone *adj* 1 being the one or ones of a class with no other members — see ONLY 2

2 not being in the company of others — see ALONE 1

lonely *adj* 1 not being in the company of others — see ALONE 1

2 sad from lack of companionship or separation from others — see LONESOME 1

loner *n* a person who does not conform to generally accepted standards or customs — see NONCONFORMIST 1

lonesome *adj* 1 sad from lack of companionship or separation from others ⟨a *lonesome* kitten left at the pound by its owners⟩

syn desolate, forlorn, lonely, lorn

rel friendless; abandoned, deserted, forgotten, forsaken, neglected; alone, lone, solitary; only, sole

near ant accompanied, attended, escorted

2 not being in the company of others — see ALONE 1

lone wolf *n* a person who does not conform to generally accepted standards or customs — see NONCONFORMIST 1

long *adj* 1 of great extent from end to end ⟨giraffes have *long* necks to help them reach leaves on tall trees⟩

syn elongated, extended, king-size (*or* king-sized), lengthy

rel extensive, far-reaching, longish, out-stretched; oblong, rectangular; big, considerable, good-sized, hefty, hulking, jumbo, large, largish, oversize (*or* oversized), sizable (*or* sizeable), substantial, super

near ant abbreviated, abridged, curtailed, diminished, shortened; diminutive, little, minute, puny, small, smallish, tiny, under-sized, wee

ant brief, short

2 lasting for a considerable time ⟨summer vacation seemed *long*, but we had to go back to school soon enough⟩

syn extended, far, great, lengthy, long-lived, long-range, long-term, marathon

rel endless, everlasting, interminable, persistent; longish, overlong, prolonged, protracted; permanent

near ant abrupt, sudden; abbreviated, condensed, curtailed; ephemeral, fleeting, momentary, transient, transitory; imper-manent

ant brief, short, short-lived, short-range, short-term

long (for) *vb* to have an earnest wish to own or enjoy — see DESIRE

longhand *n* writing done by hand — see HANDWRITING 2

longing *n* a strong wish for something — see DESIRE

long-lived *adj* **1** being of advanced years and especially past middle age — see ELDERLY

2 lasting for a considerable time — see LONG 2

long-range *adj* lasting for a considerable time — see LONG 2

longshoreman *n* one who loads and un-loads ships at a port — see DOCKWORKER

long-suffering *adj* accepting pains or hardships calmly or without complaint — see PATIENT 1

long-suffering *n* the capacity to endure what is difficult or disagreeable without complaining — see PATIENCE

long-term *adj* lasting for a considerable time — see LONG 2

long-winded *adj* using or containing more words than necessary to express an idea — see WORDY

long-windedness *n* the use of too many words to express an idea — see VERBIAGE

look *n* **1** facial appearance regarded as an indication of mood or feeling ⟨you should have seen the *look* on your face when we yelled "Surprise!"⟩

syn cast, countenance, expression, face, visage

rel frown, grimace, mouth, scowl; air, appearance, aspect, bearing, demeanor, manner, mien

2 an instance of looking especially briefly ⟨she gave the junk mail a quick *look* before throwing it in the garbage pail⟩

syn cast, eye, gander, glance, glimpse, peek, peep, regard, sight, view

rel gape, gaze, glare, leer, ogle, stare; squint

3 the outward form of someone or something especially as indicative of a quality — see APPEARANCE 1

4 looks *pl* the qualities in a person or thing that as a whole give pleasure to the senses — see BEAUTY 1

look *vb* **1** to give the impression of being — see SEEM

2 to make known (as an idea, emotion, or opinion) — see EXPRESS 1

look (at) *vb* to make note of (something) through the use of one's eyes — see SEE 1

look (into) *vb* to search through or into — see EXPLORE 1

look (toward) *vb* to stand or sit with the face or front toward — see FACE 1

looking glass *n* a smooth or polished surface (as of glass) that forms images by reflection — see MIRROR

lookout *n* **1** a high place or structure from which a wide view is possible ⟨we went up to the *lookout* on the top of the hill to watch the fireworks⟩

syn observatory, outlook

rel aerie, crow's nest, tower, watchtower

2 all that can be seen from a certain point — see VIEW 1

3 the act or state of being constantly attentive and responsive to signs of opportunity, activity, or danger — see VIGILANCE

4 a person or group that watches over someone or something — see GUARD 1

look up *vb* to go in search of — see SEEK 1

loom *vb* to be about to happen ⟨he could tell that trouble was *looming* when the bullies swaggered into the park⟩

syn brew, impend

rel advance, approach, close in, draw on, gather, near; lower (*also* lour), menace, threaten

near ant die down, diminish, disappear, dwindle, fade, vanish, wane; fall back, pass, recede, retreat, withdraw

loony *n* a person judged to be legally or medically insane — see LUNATIC 1

loony *also* **looney** *adj* **1** showing or marked by a lack of good sense or judgment — see FOOLISH 1

2 having or showing a very abnormal or sick state of mind — see INSANE 1

loop *n* a circular strip — see RING 2

loop *vb* to pass completely around — see ENCIRCLE 1

loose *adj* **1** not tightly fastened, tied, or stretched ⟨secure your neckerchief with a *loose* knot⟩

syn insecure, lax, loosened, relaxed, slack, slackened, unsecured

rel detached, free, unattached, unbound, undone, unfastened, untied; baggy; nonrestrictive

near ant constrained, restrained; attached, bound, fastened, tied

ant taut, tense, tight

2 consisting of particles that do not stick together ⟨the car wheels slipped on the *loose* gravel in the driveway⟩

syn incoherent, unconsolidated

rel nonadhesive; disconnected, disjointed, separate, unconnected; coarse, granular, rough

near ant connected, solid; compacted, compressed; adhesive, gluey, sticky

ant coherent, compact, dense, packed

3 not bound by rigid standards — see EASYGOING 2

4 not bound, confined, or detained by force — see FREE 3

5 not precisely correct — see INEXACT 1

loose *vb* 1 to cause (a projectile) to be driven forward with force — see SHOOT 1

2 to find emotional release for — see TAKE OUT 1

3 to set free (as from slavery or confinement) — see FREE 1

4 to set free (from a state of being held in check) — see RELEASE 1

loosen *vb* 1 to make less taut — see SLACKEN

2 to set free (as from slavery or confinement) — see FREE 1

3 to set free (from a state of being held in check) — see RELEASE 1

loosen (up) *vb* to free from obstruction or difficulty — see EASE 1

loosened *adj* not tightly fastened, tied, or stretched — see LOOSE 1

loot *n* valuables stolen or taken by force ⟨the burglar was caught when he stopped to examine the *loot* from the robbery⟩

syn booty, plunder, spoil, swag

rel prize; catch, haul, take; pilferage; windfall

loot *vb* to search through with the intent of committing robbery — see RANSACK 1

lop (off) *vb* to make (as hair) shorter with or as if with the use of shears — see CLIP

lope *vb* to move with a light bouncing step — see SKIP 1

lopsided *adj* inclined or twisted to one side — see AWRY

loquacious *adj* fond of talking or conversation — see TALKATIVE

Lord *n* the being worshipped as the creator and ruler of the universe — see DEITY 2

lord (it over) *vb* to assume or treat with an air of superiority — see CONDESCEND 2

lordliness *n* an exaggerated sense of one's importance that shows itself in the making of excessive or unjustified claims — see ARROGANCE

lordly *adj* 1 having a feeling of superiority that shows itself in an overbearing attitude — see ARROGANT

2 having or displaying feelings of scorn for what is regarded as beneath oneself — see PROUD 1

3 having, characterized by, or arising from a dignified and generous nature — see NOBLE 2

lore *n* 1 a body of facts learned by study or experience — see KNOWLEDGE 1

2 the body of customs, beliefs, stories, and sayings associated with a people, thing, or place — see FOLKLORE

lorn *adj* sad from lack of companionship or separation from others — see LONESOME 1

lose *vb* 1 to be unable to find or have at hand ⟨I always *lose* my keys⟩

syn mislay, misplace

near ant have

ant find, locate

2 to get rid of as useless or unwanted — see DISCARD

loser *n* something that has failed — see FAILURE 3

loss *n* 1 the act or an instance of not having or being able to find ⟨he was upset over the *loss* of his bike⟩

syn mislaying, misplacement

rel deprivation, dispossession; forfeit, forfeiture, penalty; sacrifice; bereavement

ant acquisition, gain

2 a person or thing harmed, lost, or destroyed — see CASUALTY 1

3 failure to win a contest — see DEFEAT 1

4 the amount by which something is lessened — see DECREASE

5 the state of being robbed of something normally enjoyed — see PRIVATION

6 the state or fact of being rendered nonexistent, physically unsound, or useless — see DESTRUCTION

lost *adj* no longer possessed ⟨they searched all over the house for the *lost* keys⟩

syn gone, mislaid, misplaced, missing

rel absent, castaway; irrecoverable, irretrievable; forgotten, unknown

near ant cherished, protected, treasured

ant owned, possessed, retained

lot *n* 1 a small piece of land that is developed or available for development ⟨we often played in the vacant *lot* down at the end of the street⟩

syn parcel, plat, plot, property, tract

rel patch; frontage; lease; development; real estate

2 a considerable amount ⟨they needed to do a *lot* of studying for the test⟩

syn abundance, barrel, bucket, bushel, deal, gobs, heap, loads, mass, mountain, much, oodles, peck, pile, plenitude, plenty, pot, profusion, quantity, raft, reams, scads, stack, volume, wad, wealth

rel embarrassment, excess, overabundance, overage, overkill, overmuch, oversupply, superabundance, superfluity, surfeit, surplus; deluge, flood, overflow

near ant atom, crumb, fragment, grain, iota, jot, modicum, molecule, particle, scrap, shred, tittle, whit; scattering, smattering; drop, morsel, shot; piece, portion, section; absence, dearth, lack, paucity, poverty, scarceness, scarcity, shortage, want; deficiency, deficit, inadequacy, insufficiency, meagerness, scantiness, skimpiness

ant ace, bit, dab, driblet, glimmer, hint, lick, little, mite, mouthful, ounce, peanuts, pinch, scruple, smidgen, speck, spot, sprinkling, suspicion, taste, touch, trace

3 a small area of usually open land — see FIELD 1

4 a number of things considered as a unit — see GROUP 1

5 a state or end that seemingly has been decided beforehand — see FATE 1

6 a group of people sharing a common interest and relating together socially — see GANG 2

7 a usually small number of persons considered as a unit — see GROUP 2

loud *adj* **1** marked by a high volume of sound ⟨*loud* music that could be heard all over the neighborhood⟩

syn blaring, blasting, booming, clamorous, clangorous, deafening, earsplitting, piercing, resounding, ringing, roaring, sonorous, stentorian, thunderous

rel brazen, dinning, discordant, noisy, obstreperous, raucous, rip-roaring, vociferous; grating, harsh, shrill, strident

near ant dead, quiet, silent, still; dreamy, peaceful, restful, soothing, tranquil; softened, toned (down)

ant gentle, low, soft

2 excessively showy — see GAUDY

lounge *n* a long upholstered piece of furniture designed for several sitters — see COUCH

lounge *vb* **1** to refrain from labor or exertion — see REST 1

2 to spend time doing nothing — see IDLE

louse *n* a person whose behavior is offensive to others — see JERK 1

louse up *vb* to make or do (something) in a clumsy or unskillful way — see BOTCH

lousy *adj* **1** arousing or deserving of one's loathing and disgust — see CONTEMPTIBLE 1

2 falling short of a standard — see BAD 1

3 extremely unsatisfactory — see WRETCHED 1

4 of low quality — see CHEAP 2

lout *n* **1** a big clumsy often slow-witted person — see OAF

2 a person whose behavior is offensive to others — see JERK 1

loutish *adj* having or showing crudely insensitive or impolite manners — see CLOWNISH

lovable *adj* having qualities that tend to make one loved ⟨she was a *lovable* child, always helpful and kind⟩

syn adorable, darling, dear, disarming, endearing, precious, sweet, winning

rel embraceable, kissable; beloved, cherished, treasured; attractive, beautiful, desirable, lovely; captivating, charming, fascinating; admirable, likable (*or* likeable), reputable, respectable; affable, agreeable, cheerful, cordial, friendly, genial, gracious, kind, pleasant; delightful, pleasing

near ant unloved; contemptible, disagreeable, disgusting, distasteful, heinous, hor-

rible, offensive, unlikable, unpleasant; frightful, grotesque, hideous, ill-favored, monstrous, ogreish, repellent (*also* repellant); repugnant, repulsive; ugly, unattractive, unsightly, vile

ant abhorrent, abominable, detestable, hateful, odious, unlovable

love *n* **1** a feeling of strong or constant regard for and dedication to someone ⟨her *love* for her children was truly selfless⟩

syn affection, attachment, devotedness, devotion, fondness, passion

rel appetite, favor, like, liking, partiality, preference, taste; craving, crush, desire, infatuation, longing, lust, yearning; ardor, eagerness, enthusiasm, fervor, zeal; esteem, regard, respect; adoration, idolatry, worship; allegiance, fealty, fidelity, loyalty

near ant allergy, animosity, antipathy, aversion, disfavor, dislike; abhorrence, disgust, repugnance, repulsion, revulsion; misanthropy

ant abomination, hate, hatred, loathing, rancor

2 a person with whom one is in love — see SWEETHEART

3 positive regard for something — see LIKING

love *vb* **1** to hold dear ⟨patriots who *loved* their country well enough to die for it⟩

syn appreciate, cherish, prize, treasure, value

rel delight (in), dig, enjoy, fancy, groove (on), like, relish, revel (in); admire, esteem, regard, respect, revere, reverence, venerate; enshrine, memorialize; adore, dote (on), idolize, worship

phrases set store (by *or* on)

near ant undervalue; abhor, abominate, despise, detest, execrate, hate, loathe; disdain, scorn, scout; belittle, decry, deprecate, depreciate, disparage; abandon, forget, neglect

2 to feel passion, devotion, or tenderness for ⟨a husband who *loves* his wife more than anything⟩

syn adore, cherish, worship

rel idealize, idolize; revere, reverence, venerate; delight (in), dote (on)

phrases fall for, lose one's heart (to)

near ant antagonize, displease; disapprove (of), disfavor, dislike; disgust, repulse, turn off

ant abhor, abominate, despise, detest, execrate, hate, loathe

3 to take pleasure in — see ENJOY 1

4 to touch or handle in a tender or loving manner — see FONDLE

love affair *n* a brief romantic relationship — see AFFAIR 1

loved *adj* granted special treatment or attention — see DARLING 1

loveliness *n* the qualities in a person or thing that as a whole give pleasure to the senses — see BEAUTY 1

lovely *adj* very pleasing to look at — see BEAUTIFUL

lover *n* a person with a strong and habitual liking for something — see FAN

---

syn synonym(s)   **rel** related words
ant antonym(s)   **near ant** near antonym(s)

loving *adj* feeling or showing love ⟨they were a *loving* family, supporting each other when times were bad⟩

syn adoring, affectionate, devoted, fond, tender, tenderhearted

rel caring, compassionate, considerate, cordial, doting, forgiving, friendly, kind, warmhearted; ardent, fervent, impassioned, passionate, warm; amatory, amorous, erotic; enamored, infatuated, lovesick; mushy, romantic, sentimental; brotherly, fatherly, motherly, sisterly

near *ant* aloof, detached, hardhearted, indifferent, pitiless, reserved, uncaring, unfeeling; disaffected, unconcerned, uninvolved; cold, frigid, unfriendly; hardboiled, unromantic, unsentimental

ant unloving

low *adj* 1 being near the equator ⟨we took a cruise to the *low* northern latitudes⟩

syn equatorial, tropical

near *ant* temperate

ant polar

2 belonging to or characteristic of an early level of skill or development — see PRIMITIVE 1

3 belonging to the class of people of low social or economic rank — see IGNOBLE 1

4 feeling unhappiness — see SAD 1

5 having a low musical pitch or range — see DEEP 2

6 having relatively little height — see SHORT 1

7 lacking bodily strength — see WEAK 1

8 lacking in refinement or good taste — see COARSE 2

9 not following or in accordance with standards of honor and decency — see IGNOBLE 2

10 not loud in pitch or volume — see SOFT 1

11 costing little — see CHEAP 1

lowbred *adj* lacking in refinement or good taste — see COARSE 2

lowbrow *adj* lacking in refinement or good taste — see COARSE 2

lowbrow *n* a person who is chiefly interested in material comfort and is hostile or indifferent to art and culture — see PHILISTINE

lowdown *n* information not generally available to the public — see DOPE 1

lower *adj* 1 having not so great importance or rank as another — see LESSER

2 situated lower down — see INFERIOR 1

¹**lower** *vb* 1 to cause to fall intentionally or unintentionally — see DROP 1

2 to go to a lower level — see DROP 2

3 to make smaller in amount, volume, or extent — see DECREASE 1

4 to grow less in scope or intensity especially gradually — see DECREASE 2

5 to reduce to a lower standing in one's own eyes or in others' eyes — see HUMBLE

²**lower** *also* **lour** *vb* 1 to take on a gloomy or forbidding look — see DARKEN 1

2 to look with anger and disapproval — see FROWN

lower *also* **lour** *n* a twisting of the facial features in disgust or disapproval — see GRIMACE

lower–class *adj* belonging to the class of people of low social or economic rank — see IGNOBLE 1

lowered *adj* directed down — see DOWNCAST 1

lowering *also* **louring** *adj* 1 covered over by clouds — see OVERCAST

2 harsh and threatening in manner or appearance — see GRIM 1

lowest *adj* being the least in amount, number, or size possible — see MINIMAL

low–grade *adj* of low quality — see CHEAP 2

lowliness *n* the absence of any feelings of being better than others — see HUMILITY

lowly *adj* 1 belonging to the class of people of low social or economic rank — see IGNOBLE 1

2 not having or showing any feelings of superiority, self-assertiveness, or showiness — see HUMBLE 1

lowly *adv* in manner showing no signs of pride or self-assertion ⟨the courtier bowed *lowly* before his king during the ceremony⟩

syn deferentially, humbly, meekly, modestly, sheepishly, submissively

rel fearfully, timidly; bashfully, diffidently, shyly; civilly, courteously, politely, respectfully

near *ant* fearlessly; discourteously, disdainfully, disrespectfully, impertinently, rashly, recklessly, saucily; impolitely, impudently, rudely, ungraciously

ant arrogantly, audaciously, boldly, brashly, brazenly, contemptuously, haughtily, pridefully, proudly, scornfully, swaggeringly

low–lying *adj* having relatively little height — see SHORT 1

lowness *n* 1 the quality or state of lacking refinement or good taste — see VULGARITY 1

2 the quality or state of lacking physical strength or vigor — see WEAKNESS 1

low–pressure *adj* having a relaxed, casual manner — see EASYGOING 1

low–spirited *adj* feeling unhappiness — see SAD 1

loyal *adj* firm in one's allegiance to someone or something — see FAITHFUL 1

loyalist *n* a person who loves his or her country and supports its interests and policies — see PATRIOT

loyalty *n* adherence to something to which one is bound by a pledge or duty — see FIDELITY

lozenge *n* a small mass containing medicine to be taken orally — see PILL

lubber *n* a big clumsy often slow-witted person — see OAF

lubberly *adj* lacking in physical ease and grace in movement or in the use of the hands — see CLUMSY 1

lubricate *vb* to coat (something) with a slippery substance in order to reduce fric-

tion ⟨it's not a good idea to use olive oil to *lubricate* the gears in an appliance⟩
syn grease, oil, slick, wax
near ant coarsen, rough, roughen

lubricated *adj* having or being a surface so smooth as to make sliding or falling likely — see SLICK 1

lucent *adj* 1 easily seen through — see CLEAR 1
2 giving off or reflecting much light — see BRIGHT 1

lucid *adj* 1 giving off or reflecting much light — see BRIGHT 1
2 having full use of one's mind and control over one's actions — see SANE
3 not subject to misinterpretation or more than one interpretation — see CLEAR 2

lucidity *n* 1 clearness of expression — see SIMPLICITY 2
2 the quality or state of having or giving off light — see BRILLIANCE 1

lucidness *n* clearness of expression — see SIMPLICITY 2

Lucifer *n* the supreme personification of evil often represented as the ruler of Hell — see DEVIL 1

luck *n* success that is partly the result of chance ⟨some people have all the *luck*⟩
syn fortunateness, fortune, luckiness
rel break, fluke, godsend, hit, serendipity, strike, windfall; chance, opportunity; coup, stroke
near ant knock, misadventure, mishap; adversity, curse, sorrow, tragedy, trouble; calamity, cataclysm, catastrophe, disaster; defeat, failure, fizzle, nonsuccess; accident, casualty; disappointment, letdown, setback; circumstance, destiny, doom, fate, lot, portion
ant mischance, misfortune, unluckiness
2 the uncertain course of events — see CHANCE 1

luckiness *n* success that is partly the result of chance — see LUCK 1

luckless *adj* having, prone to, or marked by bad luck — see UNLUCKY

lucky *adj* 1 having good luck ⟨the *lucky* gambler walked out of the casino with $10,000⟩
syn fortunate, happy
rel blessed, favored, gifted, privileged; fair, golden, promising
near ant cursed, disadvantaged
ant hapless, ill-fated, ill-starred, luckless, star-crossed, unfortunate, unhappy, unlucky
2 coming or happening by good luck especially unexpectedly — see FORTUNATE 1

lucrative *adj* yielding a profit — see PROFITABLE 1

lucre *n* 1 something (as pieces of stamped metal or printed paper) customarily and legally used as a medium of exchange, a measure of value, or a means of payment — see MONEY

2 the amount of money left when expenses are subtracted from the total amount received — see PROFIT 1

ludicrous *adj* 1 causing or intended to cause laughter — see FUNNY 1
2 so foolish or pointless as to be worthy of scornful laughter — see RIDICULOUS 1

lug *n* a big clumsy often slow-witted person — see OAF

lug *vb* 1 to cause to follow by applying steady force on — see PULL 1
2 to support and take from one place to another — see CARRY 1

lugubrious *adj* expressing or suggesting mourning — see MOURNFUL 1

lukewarm *adj* 1 having or giving off heat to a moderate degree — see WARM 1
2 showing little or no interest or enthusiasm — see TEPID 1

lukewarmness *n* the quality or state of being moderate in temperature — see WARMTH 1

lull *n* a momentary halt in an activity — see PAUSE

lulling *adj* tending to calm the emotions and relieve stress — see SOOTHING 1

lumber *n* tree logs as prepared for human use — see WOOD

lumber *vb* 1 to move heavily or clumsily ⟨the elephant *lumbered* through the jungle⟩
syn barge, clump, flounder, lump, pound, scuff, scuffle, shamble, shuffle, stamp, stomp, stumble, stump, tramp, tromp
rel drag, flop, haul; labor, plod, trudge; careen, lurch, stagger, sway, teeter, totter, waddle, weave, wobble
near ant float, hover, waft
ant breeze, coast, glide, slide, waltz, whisk
2 to make progress in a clumsy, struggling manner — see FLOUNDER 1
3 to make a low heavy rolling sound — see RUMBLE
4 to place a weight or burden on — see LOAD 1

lumbering *adj* lacking in physical ease and grace in movement or in the use of the hands — see CLUMSY 1

lumberjack *n* a person whose job is to cut down trees ⟨the sawmill gets most of its business from the *lumberjacks* up north⟩
syn logger
rel sawyer; forester

luminary *n* 1 a ball-shaped gaseous celestial body that shines by its own light — see STAR 1
2 a person who is widely known and usually much talked about — see CELEBRITY 1

luminescence *n* the steady giving off of the form of radiation that makes vision possible — see LIGHT 1

luminosity *n* the quality or state of having or giving off light — see BRILLIANCE 1

luminous *adj* giving off or reflecting much light — see BRIGHT 1

lump *n* 1 a small uneven mass ⟨she dumped a *lump* of clay on the table and started to sculpt⟩

---

syn synonym(s)   *rel* related words
ant antonym(s)   *near ant* near antonym(s)

syn blob, chunk, clod, clump, glob, gob, gobbet, hunk, knob, nub, nubble, nugget, wad

rel bead, drop, globule; block, body, bulk; particle, piece, portion; bit, chip, crumb, morsel, scrap

2 a small rounded mass of swollen tissue — see BUMP 1

3 an abnormal mass of tissue — see GROWTH 1

lump *vb* **1** to bring together in one body or place — see GATHER 1

2 to move heavily or clumsily — see LUMBER 1

lumpish *adj* lacking in physical ease and grace in movement or in the use of the hands — see CLUMSY 1

lumpy *adj* **1** having small pieces or lumps spread throughout — see CHUNKY 1

2 not having a level or smooth surface — see UNEVEN 1

lunacy *n* **1** a foolish act or idea — see FOLLY 1

2 a serious mental disorder that prevents one from living a safe and normal life — see INSANITY 1

3 lack of good sense or judgment — see FOOLISHNESS 1

lunatic *adj* having or showing a very abnormal or sick state of mind — see INSANE 1

2 showing or marked by a lack of good sense or judgment — see FOOLISH 1

lunatic *n* **1** a person judged to be legally or medically insane ⟨the *lunatic* was committed to an institution after running naked through the department store⟩

syn crackbrain, loony (*also* looney), maniac, neurotic, nut, psychopath, psychotic

rel madman, madwoman; deviant; paranoid, schizophrenic; character, crackpot, crank, eccentric, kook, oddball, screwball; case, patient

2 a person who lacks good sense or judgment — see FOOL 1

lurch *vb* **1** to make a series of unsteady side-to-side motions — see ROCK 1

2 to move forward while swaying from side to side — see STAGGER 1

lure *n* **1** something that persuades one to perform an action for pleasure or gain ⟨the promise of easy money is always the *lure* for some people to take up a life of crime⟩

syn allurement, bait, enticement, temptation, turn-on

rel appeal, call; attraction, goad, incentive, inducement, persuasion, seduction, spur; decoy, snare, trap

near ant caution, warning

2 something used to attract animals to a hook or into a trap — see BAIT 1

3 the act or pressure of giving in to a desire especially when ill-advised — see TEMPTATION 1

lure *vb* to lead away from a usual or proper course by offering some pleasure or advantage ⟨the hunter *lured* the lion into the open with the antelope carcass⟩

syn allure, beguile, decoy, entice, lead on, seduce, tempt

rel inveigle, persuade, rope (in), snow; catch, ensnare, entrap, snare; captivate, charm, enchant

near ant caution, ward (off), warn; drive (away *or* off), repulse, turn away

lurid *adj* **1** extremely disturbing or repellent — see HORRIBLE 1

2 lacking a healthy skin color — see PALE 2

3 arousing a strong and usually superficial interest or emotional reaction — see SENSATIONAL 1

luring *adj* having an often mysterious or magical power to attract — see FASCINATING 1

lurk *vb* to move about in a sly or secret manner — see SNEAK 1

lurker *n* someone who acts in a sly or secret manner — see SNEAK

luscious *adj* **1** very pleasing to the sense of taste — see DELICIOUS 1

2 pleasing to the physical senses — see SENSUAL

3 giving pleasure or contentment to the mind or senses — see PLEASANT

lusciousness *n* the quality of being delicious — see DELICIOUSNESS

lush *adj* **1** covered with a thick healthy natural growth ⟨they loved to go for picnics in the *lush* woodlands⟩

syn green, leafy, luxuriant, overgrown, verdant

rel fat, fecund, fertile, fruitful, productive, rich; dense, tangled

near ant bleak, depleted, infertile, poor, unproductive; arid, dead, desert, dry, parched

ant barren, leafless

2 growing thickly and vigorously — see RANK 1

lust (for *or* after) *vb* to have an earnest wish to own or enjoy — see DESIRE

lust *n* a strong wish for something — see DESIRE

luster *or* **lustre** *n* brightness created by light reflected from a surface — see SHINE 1

lusterless *adj* lacking a surface luster or gloss — see MATTE

lustful *adj* having a strong sexual desire ⟨the *lustful* student was always chasing after girls⟩

syn lascivious, lewd, licentious, passionate, wanton

rel prurient; dissipated, dissolute, libertine; corrupt, debauched, depraved, immoral, indecent

near ant celibate, chaste, decent, modest, moral, pure, virtuous; monastic, monkish; maidenly, virginal; innocent, lily-white

lustiness *n* the quality or state of having abundant or intense activity — see VITALITY 1

lustrous *adj* **1** giving off or reflecting much light — see BRIGHT 1

2 having a shiny surface or finish — see GLOSSY

lusty *adj* **1** having active strength of body or mind — see VIGOROUS 1

2 not showing weakness or uncertainty — see FIRM 1

luxuriant *adj* **1** covered with a thick, healthy natural growth — see LUSH 1

2 growing thickly and vigorously — see RANK 1

3 producing abundantly — see FERTILE

4 showing obvious signs of wealth and comfort — see LUXURIOUS

luxurious *adj* showing obvious signs of wealth and comfort ⟨the *luxurious* apartment was filled with the latest electronic gadgets and fine works of art⟩

syn deluxe, lavish, luxuriant, opulent, palatial, plush, sumptuous

rel costly, expensive; rich; extravagant, grandiose, ostentatious, pretentious, showy; awesome, awful, beautiful, gorgeous, grand, imposing, impressive, magnificent, majestic, splendid, stately; comfortable, cozy, homelike, homey, snug

near ant economical, frugal, meager (*or* meagre), spare, thrifty

ant ascetic, austere, humble, Spartan

luxuriously *adv* in a luxurious manner — see HIGH

luxury *n* something adding to pleasure or comfort but not absolutely necessary ⟨a private yacht is a *luxury*⟩

syn amenity, comfort, extra, frill, indulgence, superfluity

rel extravagance; dainty, delicacy, treat; accessory, option

ant basic, essential, fundamental, necessity, requirement

2 something that adds to one's ease — see COMFORT 2

lying *adj* telling or containing lies — see DISHONEST 1

lynx–eyed *adj* having unusually keen vision — see SHARP-EYED

lyric *adj* **1** having a pleasantly flowing quality suggestive of music ⟨they performed a slow, *lyric* dance for the audience⟩

syn euphonious, lyrical, mellifluous, mellow, melodic, melodious, musical

rel dulcet, golden, sweet

near ant disconnected, staccato; discordant, grating, harsh, jarring, strident

2 having qualities suggestive of poetry — see POETIC

lyric *n* **1** a composition using rhythm and often rhyme to create a lyrical effect — see POEM

2 a short musical composition for the human voice often with instrumental accompaniment — see SONG 1

lyrical *adj* **1** having a pleasantly flowing quality suggestive of music — see LYRIC 1

2 having qualities suggestive of poetry — see POETIC

ma *n* a female human parent — see MOTHER

macabre *adj* extremely disturbing or repellent — see HORRIBLE 1

Machiavellian *adj* not guided by or showing a concern for what is right — see UNPRINCIPLED

machinate *vb* **1** to engage in a secret plan to accomplish evil or unlawful ends — see PLOT

2 to plan out usually with subtle skill or care — see ENGINEER

machination *n* a secret plan for accomplishing evil or unlawful ends — see PLOT 1

machine *n* **1** a device that changes energy into mechanical motion — see ENGINE

2 a self-propelled passenger vehicle on wheels — see CAR

machinery *n* something used to achieve an end — see AGENT 1

mackintosh *or* **macintosh** *n* chiefly British a coat made of water-resistant material — see RAINCOAT

macrocosm *n* the whole body of things observed or assumed — see UNIVERSE

mad *adj* **1** feeling or showing anger — see ANGRY

2 having or showing a very abnormal or sick state of mind — see INSANE 1

3 marked by great and often stressful excitement or activity — see FURIOUS 1

4 showing or marked by a lack of good sense or judgment — see FOOLISH 1

mad (about) *adj* filled with an intense or excessive love for — see ENAMORED (OF)

madcap *adj* foolishly adventurous or bold — see FOOLHARDY 1

madden *vb* **1** to cause to go insane or as if insane — see CRAZE

2 to make angry — see ANGER

maddening *adj* causing annoyance — see ANNOYING

mademoiselle *n* a young usually unmarried woman — see GIRL 1

made–up *adj* not real and existing only in the imagination — see IMAGINARY

madhouse *n* **1** a place where insane people are cared for ⟨it was hard to believe that this place with the bright cheery walls was really a *madhouse*⟩

syn asylum

rel institution; hospice, hospital, sanatorium, sanitarium; home

2 a place of uproar or confusion ⟨our house is always a *madhouse* on school mornings, with five kids and two dogs running around⟩

syn babel, bedlam, circus, hell

rel commotion, havoc, pandemonium, racket, ruckus, tumult, turmoil; clamor, clatter, din, hubbub, noise; chaos, confusion, disarrangement, disarray, disorder, maelstrom, mess, muss

near ant heaven, paradise, utopia; order, orderliness, organization; calm, peace; hush, quiet, silence, soundlessness, stillness

madly *adv* **1** in a confused and reckless manner — see HELTER-SKELTER 1

2 in an enthusiastic manner — see SKY-HIGH

madness *n* **1** a serious mental disorder that prevents one from living a safe and normal life — see INSANITY 1

2 lack of good sense or judgment — see FOOLISHNESS 1

maelstrom *n* water moving rapidly in a circle with a hollow in the center — see WHIRLPOOL

maestro *n* a person with a high level of knowledge or skill in a field — see EXPERT

Mafia *n* a group involved in secret or criminal activities — see RING 1

magazine *n* **1** a building for storing goods — see STOREHOUSE

2 a place where military arms are stored — see ARMORY

3 a publication that appears at regular intervals — see JOURNAL

magic *adj* **1** being or appearing to be under a magic spell — see ENCHANTED

2 having seemingly supernatural qualities or powers — see MYSTIC 1

magic *n* **1** the power to control natural forces through supernatural means ⟨he claimed that he could summon a storm through *magic*⟩

syn bewitchment, black art, black magic, conjuring, enchantment, mojo, necromancy, sorcery, voodooism, witchcraft, witchery, wizardry

rel abracadabra, amulet, charm, fetish (*also* fetich), mascot, phylactery, talisman; curse, hex, incantation, jinx, spell; augury, divining, forecasting, foreknowing, foreseeing, foretelling, fortune-telling, predicting, presaging, prognosticating, prophesying, soothsaying; hoodoo, occultism, spiritualism; augur, omen; exorcism; alchemy

near ant science

2 the art or skill of performing tricks or illusions for entertainment ⟨they hired someone to do *magic* for their child's tenth birthday party⟩

syn conjuring, legerdemain

rel deception, trickery

phrases sleight of hand

3 the power of irresistible attraction — see CHARM 2

magical *adj* **1** being or appearing to be under a magic spell — see ENCHANTED

2 being so extraordinary or abnormal as to suggest powers which violate the laws of nature — see SUPERNATURAL 2

3 having seemingly supernatural qualities or powers — see MYSTIC 1

magician *n* **1** a person skilled in using supernatural forces ⟨the *magician* was able to turn birds purple with a simple spell⟩

syn charmer, conjurer (*or* conjuror), enchanter, necromancer, sorcerer, voodoo, witch, wizard

rel enchantress, hag, hex, sorceress, warlock; medicine man; foreseer, fortune-teller, prognosticator, prophesier, prophet, soothsayer; medium; exorcist

2 one who practices tricks and illusions for entertainment ⟨the famous *magician's* best trick was always pulling a rabbit out of a hat⟩

syn conjurer (*or* conjuror), prestidigitator, trickster

rel charmer, enchanter, enchantress

magistrate *n* a public official having authority to decide questions of law — see JUDGE 1

magnanimous *adj* having, characterized by, or arising from a dignified and generous nature — see NOBLE 2

magnanimously *adv* in a manner befitting a person of the highest character and ideals — see GREATLY 1

magnate *n* a person of rank, power, or influence in a particular field ⟨the film studio *magnate* had movie stars at his beck and call⟩

syn baron, czar (*also* tsar *or* tzar), king, mogul, prince, tycoon

rel big shot, bigwig, figure, nabob, notable, personage, VIP; celebrity, personality, star; moneybags, plutocrat

magnet *n* something that attracts interest ⟨the giant theme park is a *magnet* for tourists to the area⟩

syn attraction, draw, lodestone

rel capital, cynosure, mecca; allure, allurement, bait, enticement, fascination, lure, temptation, turn-on; appeal, call; incentive, inducement, persuasion, spur

magnetic *adj* having an often mysterious or magical power to attract — see FASCINATING 1

magnetism *n* the power of irresistible attraction — see CHARM 2

magnetize *vb* to attract or delight as if by magic — see CHARM 1

magnification *n* the representation of something in terms that go beyond the facts — see EXAGGERATION

magnificence *n* impressiveness of beauty on a large scale ⟨the *magnificence* of the great castle hallway is beyond description⟩

syn augustness, brilliance, gloriousness, glory, grandeur, grandness, majesty, nobility, nobleness, resplendence, splendor, stateliness, stupendousness, sublimeness, superbness *rel* awesomeness, marvelousness, wondrousness; lavishness, luxuriance, luxury, opulence, sumptuousness; grandiosity, ostentation, pretentiousness; flashiness, gaudiness, ornateness, showiness; extraordinariness, remarkableness

magnificent *adj* large and impressive in size, grandeur, extent, or conception — see GRAND 1

magnify *vb* 1 to add to the interest of by including made-up details — see EMBROIDER

2 to enhance the status of — see EXALT

3 to make markedly greater in measure or degree — see INTENSIFY

4 to proclaim the glory of — see PRAISE 1

magnitude *n* 1 the quality or state of being important — see IMPORTANCE

2 the quality or state of being very large — see IMMENSITY

3 the total amount of measurable space or surface occupied by something — see ¹SIZE

magnum opus *n* something (as a work of art) that is a great achievement and often its creator's greatest achievement — see MASTERPIECE

magpie *n* a person who talks constantly — see CHATTERBOX

maid *n* 1 a female domestic servant ⟨they hired a *maid* to do the housework after the baby was born⟩

syn charwoman, domestic, housekeeper, housemaid, maidservant

rel attendant, chambermaid, handmaiden (*also* handmaid), lady-in-waiting; nursemaid

2 a young usually unmarried woman — see GIRL 1

maiden *adj* 1 coming before all others in time or order — see FIRST 1

2 never having had sexual relations — see VIRGIN 1

maiden *n* a young usually unmarried woman — see GIRL 1

maidservant *n* a female domestic servant — see MAID 1

mail *n* communications or parcels sent or carried through the postal system ⟨whenever they were separated, the lovers always sent each other lots of *mail*⟩

syn matter, parcel post, post [*chiefly British*]

rel electronic mail, e-mail; dispatch, epistle, message, missive, note, postcard); airmail, rural free delivery, special delivery; junk mail

mail *vb* to send through the postal system ⟨if you don't *mail* that letter soon, it's going to arrive late⟩

syn post

rel airmail; address, consign; direct, dispatch, forward, remit, route, ship, transmit, transport; register

near ant receive

mail carrier *n* a person who delivers mail — see POSTMAN

mailman *n* a person who delivers mail — see POSTMAN

maim *vb* to cause severe or permanent injury to ⟨on-the-job accidents *maim* far too many workers every year⟩

syn cripple, disable, lame, mutilate

rel dismember, hamstring, hobble; batter, bruise, bung (up), mangle, maul, rough (up); gore, lacerate, wound; disfigure, scar; break, damage, harm, hurt, impair, injure; bash, beat, belt, bludgeon, buffet, drub, hammer, lace, lambaste (*or* lambast), lick, paste, pelt, pound, pummel, thump; bang, box, hit, punch, slap, smack, smash, sock, spank, swat, swipe, thrash, thwack, whack; flog, lash, wallop, whip; kill, murder; torment, torture

near ant cure, heal, remedy; doctor, fix, mend, patch; rebuild, recondition, reconstruct, rejuvenate, renew, renovate, repair, restore

main *adj* coming before all others in importance — see FOREMOST 1

main *n* 1 muscular strength — see MUSCLE 1

2 one of the great divisions of land on the globe or the main part of such a division — see MAINLAND

3 the main or greater part of something as distinguished from its appendages — see BODY 1

mainland *n* one of the great divisions of land on the globe or the main part of such a division ⟨the boat back to the *mainland* leaves once every two days⟩

syn continent, main

rel subcontinent, supercontinent

near ant island, isle, islet; atoll, barrier reef, cay, coral reef, key; cape, headland, peninsula, promontory

mainly *adv* for the most part — see CHIEFLY

mainstay *n* something or someone to which one looks for support — see DEPENDENCE 2

maintain *vb* 1 to keep in good condition ⟨he repairs and *maintains* antique cars as a hobby⟩

syn conserve, keep up, preserve, save

rel support, sustain; care (for), husband, manage; defend, guard, protect, safeguard, screen, shield; cure, fix, heal, remedy; mend, patch, rebuild, reconstruct

near ant disregard, ignore, neglect; break, damage, destroy, harm, hurt, impair, injure, ruin, wreck

2 to continue to declare to be true or proper despite opposition or objections ⟨part of debating is learning to *maintain* your position in the face of harsh challenges⟩

syn defend, justify, support, uphold

rel advocate, champion, espouse; confirm, vindicate, warrant; affirm, assert, avow, claim, contend, declare, insist, proclaim, profess, state; argue, debate, discuss; emphasize, stress, underline, underscore

---

syn synonym(s)   *rel* related words
ant antonym(s)   *near ant* near antonym(s)

near ant abandon, forsake, recant, retract, take back, withdraw; controvert, disprove, rebut, refute

3 to pay the living expenses of — see SUPPORT 2

4 to state (something) as a reason in support of or against something under consideration — see ARGUE 1

5 to state as a fact usually forcefully — see CLAIM 1

maintainable *adj* capable of being defended with good reasoning against verbal attack — see TENABLE 1

maintenance *n* the act or activity of keeping something in an existing and usually satisfactory condition ⟨I was hired to perform basic *maintenance* until the property could be sold⟩

syn conservation, conserving, preservation, preserving, upkeep

rel support, sustaining; care, guardianship; defense, guarding, protection, safeguarding, safekeeping

near ant dereliction, ignoring, neglect; damage, destruction, harm, hurt, injury, ruin

majestic *adj* **1** having or showing elegance — see ELEGANT 1

2 large and impressive in size, grandeur, extent, or conception — see GRAND 1

3 very dignified in form, tone, or style — see ELEVATED 2

majesty *n* **1** a dignified bearing or appearance befitting royalty ⟨even as a child, the princess possessed a certain *majesty* that would later serve her well⟩

syn augustness, stateliness

rel high-mindedness, magnanimity, nobility; haughtiness, lordliness, pompousness; dignity, poise; grandeur, grandness, greatness, impressiveness, magnificence, resplendence, splendor

2 dignified or restrained beauty of form, appearance, or style — see ELEGANCE 1

3 impressiveness of beauty on a large scale — see MAGNIFICENCE

major *adj* having great meaning or lasting effect — see IMPORTANT 1

majority *n* the state of being fully grown or developed — see MATURITY

make *vb* **1** to bring into being by combining, shaping, or transforming materials ⟨will you help me *make* the dough for the cookies?⟩

syn fabricate, fashion, form, frame, manufacture, produce

rel assemble, build, construct, erect, make up, put up, raise, rear, structure, throw up; craft, handcraft; forge, mold, shape; prefabricate; create, invent, originate; establish, father, institute, organize; concoct, contrive, cook up, design, devise, imagine, think (up); conceive, envisage, picture, visualize; refashion, remake, remanufacture

phrases put together

near ant disassemble, dismantle, take apart; break up, dismember; abolish, annihilate, demolish, destroy, devastate, eradicate, exterminate, extinguish, flatten, pulverize, raze, ruin, shatter, smash, wreck; break, damage, harm, hurt, impair; blow up, explode

2 to obtain (as a goal) through effort — see ACHIEVE 1

3 to be the cause of (a situation, action, or state of mind) — see EFFECT

4 to carry through (as a process) to completion — see PERFORM 1

5 to cause (a person) to give in to pressure — see FORCE

6 to decide the size, amount, number, or distance of (something) without actual measurement — see ESTIMATE 2

7 to form by putting together parts or materials — see BUILD

8 to give the impression of being — see SEEM

9 to go on a specified course or in a certain direction — see HEAD 1

10 to put into effect through legislative or authoritative action — see ENACT

11 to receive as return for effort — see EARN 1

12 to recognize the meaning of — see COMPREHEND 1

make-believe *adj* not real and existing only in the imagination — see IMAGINARY

make out *vb* **1** to meet one's day-to-day needs — see GET ALONG 1

2 to recognize the meaning of — see COMPREHEND 1

3 to touch one another with the lips as a sign of love — see KISS 1

make over *vb* **1** to change in form, appearance, or use — see CONVERT 2

2 to give over the legal possession or ownership of — see TRANSFER 1

3 to make different in some way — see CHANGE 1

Maker *n* the being worshipped as the creator and ruler of the universe — see DEITY 2

makeshift *adj* taking the place of one that came before — see NEW 1

makeshift *n* a temporary replacement ⟨when his belt broke, he used string as a *makeshift* until he could get home to replace it⟩

syn expedient, stopgap

rel recourse, refuge, resort; alternate, backup, standby, stand-in, substitute, understudy

near ant archetype, original, prototype

makeup *n* **1** preparations intended to beautify the face or hair ⟨she never left the house without applying her *makeup* and arranging her jewelry⟩

syn cosmetics, paint

rel greasepaint; camouflage; cold cream, cream, eye shadow, kohl, lipstick, lotion, mascara, oil, powder, rouge, vanishing cream

2 the way in which the elements of something (as a work of art) are arranged — see COMPOSITION 3

make up *vb* **1** to be all the substance of — see CONSTITUTE 1

2 to create or think of by clever use of the imagination — see INVENT

3 to form by putting together parts or materials — see BUILD

make up (for) *vb* to balance with an equal force so as to make ineffective — see OFFSET

making *n* the basic elements from which something can be developed ⟨she had all the *makings* of an excellent leader, but she needed some experience first⟩

syn material, raw material, stuff, substance

rel possibility, potential, potentiality; matter

maladroit *adj* showing or marked by a lack of skill and tact (as in dealing with a situation) — see AWKWARD 2

malady *n* an abnormal state that disrupts a plant's or animal's normal bodily functioning — see DISEASE

malcontent *adj* having a feeling that one has been wronged or thwarted in one's ambitions — see DISCONTENTED

male *adj* considered characteristic of or appropriate for men — see MASCULINE

male *n* an adult male human being — see MAN 1

malediction *n* a prayer that harm will come to someone — see CURSE 1

malefaction *n* a breaking of a moral or legal code — see OFFENSE 1

malefactor *n* **1** a person who commits moral wrongs — see EVILDOER 1

2 a person who has committed a crime — see CRIMINAL

malevolence *n* the desire to cause pain for the satisfaction of doing harm — see MALICE

malevolent *adj* having or showing a desire to cause someone pain or suffering for the sheer enjoyment of it — see HATEFUL

malevolently *adv* in a mean or spiteful manner — see NASTILY

malfeasance *n* improper or illegal behavior — see MISCONDUCT

malformed *adj* badly or imperfectly formed ⟨a clay sculpture of an eagle that was so *malformed* that it looked more like a feathered football⟩

syn deformed, distorted, misshapen, monstrous, shapeless

rel defaced, disfigured; aberrant, abnormal, freakish, mutant; asymmetrical (*or* asymmetric), crooked, disproportionate, irregular, lopsided, nonsymmetrical, overbalanced, unbalanced, unequal; horrible, horrific, terrible; ugly, unattractive

near ant flawless, perfect

ant shapely

malfunctioning *adj* not being in working order — see INOPERABLE 1

malice *n* the desire to cause pain for the satisfaction of doing harm ⟨there was no reason other than pure *malice* to spread such disgusting lies all over school⟩

syn cattiness, despite, hatefulness, malevolence, maliciousness, malignancy, malignity, meanness, nastiness, spite, spitefulness, spleen, venom, viciousness

rel abusiveness, cruelty; abhorrence, abomination, execration, hate, hatred, loathing; animosity, antagonism, antipathy, bitterness, enmity, grudge, hostility, ill will, jaundice, rancor, resentment; despicableness, invidiousness; vengefulness, vindictiveness; aversion, disgust, distaste, horror, repugnance, repulsion, revulsion; contempt, disdain; jealousy, pique, resentment, scorn; bile, rancor, virulence, vitriol

near ant devotion, love, passion; amiability, amicability, amity, civility, cordiality, friendliness, hospitality; adoration, ardor, infatuation, veneration, worship; affection, charity, kindliness; comity, empathy, friendship, goodwill, sympathy, understanding

malicious *adj* having or showing a desire to cause someone pain or suffering for the sheer enjoyment of it — see HATEFUL

maliciously *adv* in a mean or spiteful manner — see NASTILY

maliciousness *n* the desire to cause pain for the satisfaction of doing harm — see MALICE

malign *adj* having or showing a desire to cause someone pain or suffering for the sheer enjoyment of it — see HATEFUL

malign *vb* to make untrue and harmful statements about — see SLANDER

malignancy *n* the desire to cause pain for the satisfaction of doing harm — see MALICE

malignant *adj* having or showing a desire to cause someone pain or suffering for the sheer enjoyment of it — see HATEFUL

malignantly *adv* in a mean or spiteful manner — see NASTILY

maligning *n* the making of false statements that damage another's reputation — see SLANDER

malignity *n* the desire to cause pain for the satisfaction of doing harm — see MALICE

malleability *n* the quality or state of being easily molded — see PLASTICITY

malleable *adj* **1** capable of being easily molded or modeled — see PLASTIC

2 capable of being readily changed — see FLEXIBLE 1

malodorous *adj* having an unpleasant smell ⟨the garbage became quite *malodorous* after it sat there for two weeks⟩

syn fetid, foul, fusty, musty, noisome, rank, reeking, reeky, smelly, stinking, stinky, strong

rel putrid, rancid, stale; bad, disgusting, offensive, repulsive, revolting, vile; decayed, decaying, decomposed, decomposing, rotted, rotten, rotting, spoiled, spoiling; dirty, filthy, nasty, noxious; odoriferous, odorous

near ant flowery, fruity, spicy, woodsy

ant ambrosial, aromatic, fragrant, perfumed, redolent, savory, scented, sweet

---

syn synonym(s)   *rel* related words
ant antonym(s)   *near ant* near antonym(s)

maltreat *vb* **1** to inflict physical or emotional harm upon — see ABUSE 1

2 to abuse physically — see MANHANDLE 1

mama *n* a female human parent — see MOTHER

mammoth *adj* unusually large — see HUGE

mammoth *n* something that is unusually large and powerful — see GIANT

mammy *n* a female human parent — see MOTHER

man *n* **1** an adult male human being ⟨the children always feel better when there's a *man* or a woman around⟩

syn bloke [*chiefly British*], buck, cat [*slang*], chap [*chiefly British*], dude, fellow, gent, gentleman, guy, hombre, jack, joker, lad, male

rel master, mister, sir

2 a male romantic companion — see BOYFRIEND

3 a member of the human race — see HUMAN

4 the human race — see MANKIND

5 the male partner in a marriage — see HUSBAND

manacle *n* **1** something that physically prevents free movement — see BOND 1

2 something that makes movement or progress more difficult — see ENCUMBRANCE

manacle *vb* **1** to confine or restrain with or as if with chains — see BIND 1

2 to create difficulty for the work or activity of — see HAMPER

manage *vb* **1** to deal with (something) usually skillfully or efficiently — see HANDLE 1

2 to look after and make decisions about — see CONDUCT 1

3 to meet one's day-to-day needs — see GET ALONG 1

management *n* the act or activity of looking after and making decisions about something — see CONDUCT 1

manager *n* a person who manages or directs — see EXECUTIVE

managerial *adj* suited for or relating to the directing of things — see EXECUTIVE

managing *adj* highest in rank or authority — see HEAD

man-at-arms *n* a person engaged in military service — see SOLDIER

mandate *n* the granting of power to perform various acts or duties — see COMMISSION 1

mandatory *adj* forcing one's compliance or participation by or as if by law ⟨the tests are *mandatory* for all students wishing to graduate⟩

syn compulsory, forced, imperative, incumbent, involuntary, necessary, nonelective, obligatory, peremptory, required

rel all-important, essential, indispensable, needed, requisite; insistent, persistent, pressing, urgent; demanded, enforced, coercive

near ant chosen, discretionary; dispensable, unnecessary, unneeded, unwanted;

inconsequential, insignificant, nonessential, unimportant

ant elective, optional, voluntary

maneuver *vb* **1** to deal with (something) usually skillfully or efficiently — see HANDLE 1

2 to plan out usually with subtle skill or care — see ENGINEER

manful *adj* feeling or displaying no fear by temperament — see BRAVE

mangle *vb* to make or do (something) in a clumsy or unskillful way — see BOTCH

mangy *adj* showing signs of advanced wear and tear and neglect — see SHABBY 1

manhandle *vb* **1** to abuse physically ⟨charges that the police *manhandled* peaceful protesters⟩

syn maltreat, maul, mishandle, rough (up)

rel abuse, ill-treat, ill-use, mistreat, misuse; roughhouse, wrestle; bash, batter, beat, buffet, drub, lambaste (*or* lambast), lick, pound, pummel, slap, thrash; harm, hurt, injure, wound; oppress, persecute, wrong; ambush, assail, attack; clobber, fight, gang up (on), hit, jump, knock; torment, torture

near ant caress, fondle, pet; coddle, mollycoddle, pamper; care (for), foster, nurture

2 to inflict physical or emotional harm upon — see ABUSE 1

manhood *n* the set of qualities considered appropriate for or characteristic of men — see VIRILITY

mania *n* **1** a serious mental disorder that prevents one from living a safe and normal life — see INSANITY 1

2 something about which one is constantly thinking or concerned — see FIXATION

maniac *n* **1** a person judged to be legally or medically insane — see LUNATIC 1

2 a person with a strong and habitual liking for something — see FAN

maniacal *also* **maniac** *adj* having or showing a very abnormal or sick state of mind — see INSANE 1

manifest *adj* not subject to misinterpretation or more than one interpretation — see CLEAR 2

manifest *vb* **1** to make known (something abstract) through outward signs — see SHOW 2

2 to represent in visible form — see EMBODY 2

manifestation *n* a visible representation of something abstract (as a quality) — see EMBODIMENT

manifold *adj* being of many and various kinds ⟨the *manifold* attractions of that state make it an ideal destination for a family vacation⟩

syn divers, multifarious, myriad

rel multiform, multiple, multiplex, multitudinous; heterogeneous, miscellaneous, mixed, sundry, various; different, diverse, unlike, varied

near ant homogeneous, monolithic, unmixed, unvaried; alike, identical, same;

distinct, distinctive, individual, separate; alone, lone, only, sole, solitary; singular, unique

manikin *or* **mannikin** *n* 1 a three-dimensional representation of the human body used especially for displaying clothes — see MANNEQUIN 1

2 a person who poses with or wears merchandise (as clothes) often for pictorial advertising — see MODEL 2

manipulate *vb* 1 to control or take advantage of by artful, unfair, or insidious means ⟨*manipulated* their parents into agreeing to let them stay out later by telling their mother that their father agreed, and vice versa⟩

syn exploit, play (upon)

rel engineer, finagle, jockey, maneuver; beguile, bluff, cozen, deceive, delude, dupe, fool, gull, hoax, hoodwink, kid, snow, take in, trick; intrigue, machinate, plot, scheme; arrange, contrive, devise, finesse, mastermind; cheat, chisel, defraud, fleece, gyp, hustle, swindle

2 to deal with (something) usually skillfully or efficiently — see HANDLE 1

3 to plan out usually with subtle skill or care — see ENGINEER

mankind *n* the human race ⟨all of *mankind* stands to gain if world peace is finally achieved⟩

syn Homo sapiens, humanity, humankind, man

rel being, body, creature, fellowman, human, individual, mortal, party, person

manlike *adj* 1 considered characteristic of or appropriate for men — see MASCULINE

2 having qualities or traits that are traditionally considered inappropriate for a girl or woman — see UNFEMININE

manliness *n* the set of qualities considered appropriate for or characteristic of men — see VIRILITY

manly *adj* considered characteristic of or appropriate for men — see MASCULINE

man–made *adj* being such in appearance only and made with or manufactured from usually cheaper materials — see IMITATION

manna *n* 1 a source of great satisfaction — see DELIGHT 1

2 something that provides happiness or does good for a person or thing — see BLESSING 2

mannequin *n* 1 a three-dimensional representation of the human body used especially for displaying clothes ⟨the *mannequin* over there looks so real⟩

syn dummy, figure, form, manikin (*or* mannikin)

rel doll

2 a person who poses with or wears merchandise (as clothes) often for pictorial advertising — see MODEL 2

manner *n* 1 manners *pl* personal conduct or behavior as evaluated by an accepted standard of appropriateness for a social or professional setting ⟨her table *manners* were so impeccable that she even knew how to use all five forks⟩

syn etiquette, form, mores, proprieties

rel amenities, civilities, pleasantries; bearing, demeanor, deportment; courtesy, decorum, mannerliness, politeness; formalities, protocol, rules; air, attitude, carriage, poise, polish, pose, posture, presence; custom, habit, pattern, practice (*also* practise), trick, way, wont; convention, fashion, mode, style

2 a distinctive way of putting ideas into words — see STYLE 1

3 a number of persons or things that are grouped together because they have something in common — see SORT 1

4 the means or procedure for doing something — see METHOD

mannerism *n* an odd or peculiar habit — see IDIOSYNCRASY

mannerliness *n* speech or behavior that is a sign of good breeding — see POLITENESS

mannerly *adj* showing consideration, courtesy, and good manners — see POLITE 1

mannish *adj* 1 considered characteristic of or appropriate for men — see MASCULINE

2 having qualities or traits that are traditionally considered inappropriate for a girl or woman — see UNFEMININE

manor *n* a large impressive residence — see MANSION

manor house *n* a large impressive residence — see MANSION

manpower *n* a body of persons at work or available for work — see FORCE 1

mansion *n* a large impressive residence ⟨if I ever win the lottery, I'm going to buy a *mansion* in the mountains⟩

syn castle, château, countryseat, estate, hacienda, hall, manor, manor house, palace, villa

rel showplace; abode, domicile, dwelling, habitation, hearth, home, house, lodging(s), pad, place; housing, nest, quarter(s), residency, roof; aerie, penthouse; salon, suite, townhouse

man–size *or* **man–sized** *adj* considered characteristic of or appropriate for men — see MASCULINE

manta *n* any of several extremely large rays — see DEVILFISH

manta ray *n* any of several extremely large rays — see DEVILFISH

mantilla *n* a scarf worn on the head — see BANDANNA

mantle *n* 1 a sleeveless garment worn so as to hang over the shoulders, arms, and back — see ¹CAPE

2 something that covers or conceals like a piece of cloth — see CLOAK 1

mantle *vb* to surround or cover closely — see ENFOLD 1

manual *n* a book used for instruction in a subject — see TEXTBOOK

---

syn synonym(s)   *rel* related words
ant antonym(s)   *near ant* near antonym(s)

manufactory *n* a building or set of buildings for the manufacturing of goods — see FACTORY

manufacture *vb* **1** to bring into being by combining, shaping, or transforming materials — see MAKE 1

2 to create or think of by clever use of the imagination — see INVENT

manumission *n* the act of setting free from slavery — see LIBERATION

manumit *vb* to set free (as from slavery or confinement) — see FREE 1

manuscript *n* writing done by hand — see HANDWRITING 2

many *adj* being of a large but indefinite number ⟨a journey of *many* miles begins with a single step⟩
syn multiple, multiplex, multitudinous, numerous
rel countless, innumerable, numberless, uncountable, unnumbered, untold; several, some; miscellaneous, mixed, sundry, various; divers, manifold, multifarious, myriad
near ant countable, limited
ant few

map *n* an illustration of certain features of a geographical area ⟨there is a *map* of the United States on the wall over there⟩
syn chart
rel graph, graphic; relief map

map (out) *vb* to work out the details of (something) in advance — see PLAN 1

mar *vb* **1** to affect slightly with something morally bad or undesirable — see TAINT 1

2 to reduce the soundness, effectiveness, or perfection of — see DAMAGE 1

marathon *adj* lasting for a considerable time — see LONG 2

maraud *vb* to search through with the intent of committing robbery — see RANSACK 1

marble *vb* to mark with small spots especially unevenly — see SPOT 1

marbled *adj* having blotches of two or more colors — see PIED

march *n* **1** a region along the dividing line between two countries — see FRONTIER 1

2 forward movement in time or place — see ADVANCE 1

march *vb* **1** to move along with a steady regular step especially in a group ⟨the band had to practice for hours to be able to *march* in perfect step⟩
syn file, pace, parade, stride
rel goose-step; perambulate, step, traipse, tread; hike, tramp; lumber, plod, stamp, stomp, stride, trudge
near ant amble, meander, ramble, stroll, wander

2 to move forward along a course — see GO 1

margin *n* the line or relatively narrow space that marks the outer limit of something — see BORDER 1

margin *vb* to serve as a border for — see BORDER

marginally *adv* by a very small margin — see JUST 2

marine *adj* **1** of or relating to the sea ⟨he loves collecting little *marine* creatures while at the beach⟩
syn maritime, oceanic, pelagic
rel abyssal, deep-sea, deepwater, saltwater; admiralty, nautical, naval; undersea, underwater; hydrographic, oceanographic

2 of or relating to navigation of the sea ⟨a collection of *marine* instruments, including a sextant⟩
syn maritime, nautical, navigational
rel admiralty, naval; oceangoing, seafaring, seagoing; hydrographic, oceanographic

mariner *n* one who operates or navigates a seagoing vessel — see SAILOR

marital *adj* of or relating to marriage ⟨neither of them ever forgot their *marital* vows, no matter how hard things sometimes were⟩
syn conjugal, connubial, married, matrimonial, nuptial, wedded
rel espoused, matched, mated; bridal; wifely; affianced, betrothed, committed, engaged, pledged, promised

maritime *adj* **1** of or relating to navigation of the sea — see MARINE 2

2 of or relating to the sea — see MARINE 1

mark *n* **1** a person or thing that is made fun of — see LAUGHINGSTOCK

2 a person or thing that is the object of abuse, criticism, or ridicule — see TARGET 1

3 overall quality as seen or judged by people in general — see REPUTATION

4 something set up as an example against which others of the same type are compared — see STANDARD 1

5 something that one hopes or intends to accomplish — see GOAL

6 something that sets apart an individual from others of the same kind — see CHARACTERISTIC

7 something that spoils the appearance or completeness of a thing — see BLEMISH

8 the power to bring about a result on another — see EFFECT 2

mark *vb* **1** to attach an identifying slip to — see LABEL 1

2 to be an important feature of — see CHARACTERIZE 2

3 to make a written note of — see RECORD 1

mark (out) *vb* to mark the limits of — see LIMIT 2

mark down *vb* to lower the price or value of — see DEPRECIATE 1

marked *adj* likely to attract attention — see NOTICEABLE

marker *n* a slip (as of paper or cloth) that is attached to something to identify or describe it — see LABEL

market *vb* to offer for sale to the public ⟨local farmers *market* their garden-fresh produce in roadside stands all over the valley⟩
syn deal (in), merchandise, put up, retail, sell, vend

rel wholesale; hawk, peddle; barter, distribute, exchange, export, handle, trade, traffic (in); advertise, ballyhoo, boost, plug, promote, tout; bargain, chaffer, dicker, haggle, horse-trade, palter; auction; provide, supply; keep, stock

ant buy, purchase

marketable *adj* **1** fit to be offered for sale ⟨you'll need to clean that car up a bit before it's *marketable*⟩

syn salable (*or* saleable)

rel commercial, profitable; costly, fancy, fine, high-grade, precious, premium, prime, valuable; dear, expensive, extravagant

near ant damaged, shopworn; cheap, useless, worthless; bad, inferior, low-grade, substandard, unsatisfactory

ant nonsalable, unmarketable, unsalable **2** fit or likely to be sold especially on a large scale — see COMMERCIAL

marketplace *n* the buying and selling of goods especially on a large scale and between different places — see COMMERCE

market value *n* the amount of money for which something will find a buyer — see VALUE 1

marksman *n* a person skilled in shooting at a target ⟨only the best *marksmen* can hit the bull's-eye at 500 feet⟩

syn sharpshooter, shooter, shot

rel rifleman, trapshooter; gunman, gunner, sniper

maroon *vb* to cause to remain behind — see LEAVE 1

marriage *n* **1** a union representing a special kind of social and legal partnership between two people ⟨some religions consider *marriage* a sacrament⟩

syn match, matrimony, wedlock

rel bigamy, monogamy, polygamy; intermarriage, miscegenation, remarriage; attachment, commitment, relationship; betrothal, engagement, espousal, hand, pledge, promise, proposal, troth

near ant annulment, divorce, separation **2** a ceremony in which two people are united in matrimony — see WEDDING

married *adj* of or relating to marriage — see MARITAL

marry *vb* **1** to perform the ceremony of marriage for ⟨they chose a very nice priest to *marry* them⟩

syn wed

rel match, mate; conjoin, connect, unite; affiance

2 to give in marriage ⟨they worried about the cost of *marrying* off five daughters⟩

syn espouse, match, wed

rel commit, engage; affiance, betroth, pledge, promise

3 to take as a spouse ⟨he *married* his girlfriend three years ago, and they've been happy ever since⟩

syn espouse, wed

rel affiance, betroth, commit, engage, pledge, promise, propose; remarry

near ant separate (from)

ant divorce

4 to take a spouse ⟨she had always believed she would never *marry*, but fate proved her wrong⟩

syn wed

rel couple, mate; pair off, remarry

phrases tie the knot

near ant divorce, separate

5 to come together to form a single unit — see UNITE 1

marsh *n* spongy land saturated or partially covered with water — see SWAMP

marshal *vb* **1** to assemble and make ready for action — see MOBILIZE

2 to point out the way for (someone) especially from a position in front — see LEAD 1

3 to put into a particular arrangement — see ORDER 1

marshaling *or* **marshalling** *n* an act of gathering forces together to renew or attempt an effort — see RALLY 1

marshland *n* spongy land saturated or partially covered with water — see SWAMP

martial *adj* **1** of, relating to, or suitable for war or a warrior ⟨the young recruit looked all grown up in his new *martial* uniform⟩

syn military, soldierly

rel aggressive, bellicose, combative, contentious, guerrilla, pugnacious, quarrelsome, scrappy, truculent, warlike; belligerent, militant, warring; antagonistic, argumentative, fierce, gladiatorial, hot-tempered; mercenary

near ant civil, civilian, nonmilitary; conciliatory, nonviolent, pacific, peaceable, peaceful; affable, amiable, amicable, benevolent, complaisant, cordial, easygoing, friendly, genial, good-natured, gracious, ingratiating, obliging

ant unsoldierly

2 of or relating to the armed services — see MILITARY 1

martyr *vb* to cause persistent suffering to — see AFFLICT

marvel *n* something extraordinary or surprising — see WONDER 1

marveling *or* **marvelling** *adj* filled with amazement or wonder — see OPEN-MOUTHED

marvelous *or* **marvellous** *adj* **1** causing wonder or astonishment ⟨the sheer immensity of the ancient ruin known as Stonehenge is *marvelous* to behold⟩

syn amazing, astonishing, astounding, awesome, awful, eye-opening, fabulous, miraculous, portentous, prodigious, staggering, stunning, stupendous, sublime, surprising, wonderful, wondrous

rel incomprehensible, inconceivable, incredible, unbelievable, unimaginable, unthinkable; extraordinary, phenomenal, rare, sensational, spectacular; singular, uncommon, unique, unusual, unwonted; conspicuous, notable, noticeable, outstanding, remarkable; impressive, striking; animating, energizing, enlightening,

enlivening, exciting, galvanizing, invigorating, stimulating; alluring, attracting, attractive, beguiling, bewitching, captivating, charming, enchanting, entertaining, enthralling, fascinating, interesting
near ant unimpressive, uninspiring, unremarkable; boring, dull, jading, monotonous, tedious, tiring, uninspired, uninteresting, wearisome, weary, wearying; common, customary, mundane, normal, ordinary, typical, unexceptional, usual; draining, enervating, exhausting, fatiguing, wearing; debilitating, enfeebling; demoralizing, discouraging, disheartening, dispiriting

2 excitingly or mysteriously unusual — see EXOTIC

3 of the very best kind — see EXCELLENT

mascot *n* something worn or kept to bring good luck or keep away evil — see CHARM 1

masculine *adj* considered characteristic of or appropriate for men ⟨some people consider chest hair to be a particularly appealing *masculine* trait⟩
syn male, manlike, manly, mannish, mansize (*or* man-sized), virile
rel boyish, tomboyish
near ant girlish, sissy; feminine, womanish, womanlike, womanly; emasculated, impotent, weakened
ant effeminate, unmanly, unmasculine

masculinity *n* the set of qualities considered appropriate for or characteristic of men — see VIRILITY

mash *vb* **1** to apply external pressure on so as to force out the juice or contents of — see PRESS 2

2 to cause to become a pulpy mass — see CRUSH 1

mask *n* **1** a cover or partial cover for the face used to disguise oneself ⟨he loved his gorilla *mask* so much that he even tried to sleep with it on⟩
syn vizard
rel camouflage, disguise; bill, cloak, domino, hood, veil, visor (*also* vizor)
2 something that covers or conceals like a piece of cloth — see CLOAK 1

mask *vb* **1** to change the dress or looks of so as to conceal true identity — see DISGUISE

2 to keep secret or shut off from view — see ¹HIDE 1

masquerade *n* a display of emotion or behavior that is insincere or intended to deceive ⟨although she was deeply bored, she maintained a *masquerade* of polite interest as her guest droned on⟩
syn act, airs, charade, facade (*also* façade), front, guise, pose, pretense (*or* pretence), put-on, semblance, show
rel appearance, color, gloss; camouflage, cloak, disguise; affectation, deceit, deception, double-dealing, duplicity, fraud, guile; betrayal, double cross, faithlessness, falseness, falsity, infidelity, perfidy, treachery, treason, unfaithfulness; excuse, pretext

near ant candor, frankness, openheartedness, sincerity

masquerade (as) *vb* to pretend to be (what one is not) in appearance or behavior — see IMPERSONATE 1

mass *n* **1** masses *pl* the body of the community as contrasted with the elite ⟨the *masses* demanded the elimination of tax breaks for the rich⟩
syn commoners, herd, mob, people, plebeians, populace, rank and file
rel proletariat, rabble, riffraff, scum, trash; bourgeoisie, middle class; public
near ant aristocracy, gentry, nobility, upper class, upper crust
ant elite

2 a considerable amount — see LOT 2

3 a distinct and separate portion of matter — see BODY 2

4 the main or greater part of something as distinguished from its appendages — see BODY 1

massacre *n* the killing of a large number of people ⟨the infamous *massacre* of more than 200 Sioux at Wounded Knee, South Dakota⟩
syn butchery, carnage, slaughter
rel bloodshed, foul play, homicide, killing, manslaughter, murder, slaying; mortality; annihilation, decimation, demolishing, destruction, devastation, eradication, extermination; genocide; assassination, execution

massacre *vb* to kill on a large scale ⟨the country's rival ethnic groups began *massacring* one another⟩
syn butcher, mow (down), slaughter
rel assassinate, execute, murder, slay; annihilate, decimate, demolish, destroy, devastate, eradicate, exterminate, waste, wipe out

massive *adj* **1** having great weight — see HEAVY 1

2 unusually large — see HUGE

massively *adv* to a large extent or degree — see GREATLY 2

massiveness *n* **1** the quality or state of being very large — see IMMENSITY

2 the state or quality of being heavy — see WEIGHTINESS 1

mass-produced *adj* made beforehand in large numbers — see READY-MADE

master *adj* having or showing exceptional knowledge, experience, or skill in a field of endeavor — see PROFICIENT

master *n* **1** a person with a high level of knowledge or skill in a field — see EXPERT

2 one that defeats an enemy or opponent — see VICTOR 1

3 the person (as an employer or supervisor) who tells people and especially workers what to do — see BOSS

master *vb* **1** to achieve a victory over — see BEAT 2

2 to acquire complete knowledge, understanding, or skill in — see LEARN 1

masterful *adj* **1** accomplished with trained ability — see SKILLFUL 1

2 fond of ordering people around — see BOSSY

3 having a feeling of superiority that shows itself in an overbearing attitude — see ARROGANT

4 having or showing exceptional knowledge, experience, or skill in a field of endeavor — see PROFICIENT

masterfully *adv* in a skillful or expert manner — see WELL 3

masterfulness *n* **1** subtle or imaginative ability in inventing, devising, or executing something — see SKILL 1

2 an exaggerated sense of one's importance that shows itself in the making of excessive or unjustified claims — see ARROGANCE

masterly *adj* **1** accomplished with trained ability — see SKILLFUL 1

2 having or showing exceptional knowledge, experience, or skill in a field of endeavor — see PROFICIENT

mastermind *vb* to plan out usually with subtle skill or care — see ENGINEER

masterpiece *n* something (as a work of art) that is a great achievement and often its creator's greatest achievement ⟨Michelangelo's frescoes in the Sistine Chapel are often considered to be his *masterpieces*⟩

syn classic, magnum opus

rel pièce de résistance, showpiece; blockbuster, success; gem, jewel, prize, treasure

near ant debacle (*also* débâcle), disaster, failure, fiasco, fizzle, turkey

mastership *n* a highly developed skill in or knowledge of something — see COMMAND 2

mastery *n* **1** a highly developed skill in or knowledge of something — see COMMAND 2

2 the right or means to command or control others — see POWER 1

masticate *vb* to crush or grind with the teeth — see BITE (ON)

match *n* **1** a competitive encounter between individuals or groups carried on for amusement, exercise, or in pursuit of a prize — see GAME 1

2 a union representing a special kind of social and legal partnership between two people — see MARRIAGE 1

3 either of a pair matched in one or more qualities — see MATE 1

4 one that is equal to another in status, achievement, or value — see EQUAL

5 something or someone that strongly resembles another — see IMAGE 1

match *vb* **1** to be the exact counterpart of ⟨does this handbag's shade of blue *match* my navy blue pants?⟩ ⟨the rare blood type that exactly *matched* that of the transplant recipient⟩

syn correspond (to), equal, parallel

rel blend (with), coordinate (with), go (with), harmonize (with); complement,

supplement; counterbalance, counterpoise; echo, mirror, repeat; amount (to), approach, near; measure (up), partake (of), rival, suggest

2 to give in marriage — see MARRY 2

3 to produce something equal to (as in quality or value) — see EQUAL 1

matching *adj* having qualities in common — see ALIKE

matchless *adj* having no equal or rival for excellence or desirability — see ONLY 1

mate *n* **1** either of a pair matched in one or more qualities ⟨have you seen the *mate* to this glove anywhere?⟩

syn companion, fellow, half, match, twin

rel coordinate; counterpart, equal, equivalent, like, parallel, peer, rival; carbon copy, double, duplicate, identical twin, ringer; analogue (*or* analog), similarity

near ant antithesis, converse, opposite, reverse

2 a person frequently seen in the company of another — see ASSOCIATE 1

3 *chiefly British* a person who helps a more skilled person — see HELPER

4 the person to whom another is married — see SPOUSE

mate *vb* to engage in sexual intercourse — see COPULATE

material *adj* **1** relating to or composed of matter ⟨there's no *material* evidence, such as a dead body, that a murder has been committed⟩

syn concrete, physical, substantial

rel bodily, carnal, corporal, corporeal, fleshly; appreciable, detectable, discernible, noticeable, observable, palpable, perceptible, sensible, tangible; objective, phenomenal; bulky, heavy, massive, solid, weighty

near ant bodiless, disembodied, incorporeal; ethereal, insubstantial, unsubstantial; impalpable, imperceptible, insensible, intangible, invisible, unnoticeable; airy, diaphanous, tenuous, thin, vaporous; metaphysical, spiritual

ant immaterial, nonmaterial, nonphysical

2 having great meaning or lasting effect — see IMPORTANT 1

3 having to do with life on earth especially as opposed to that in heaven — see EARTHLY

4 having to do with the matter at hand — see PERTINENT

5 of or relating to the human body — see PHYSICAL 1

material *n* **1** the basic elements from which something can be developed — see MAKING

2 *usually* **materials** *pl* items needed for the performance of a task or activity — see EQUIPMENT

materialist *n* a person who is chiefly interested in material comfort and is hostile or indifferent to art and culture — see PHILISTINE

materiality *n* **1** something that actually exists — see FACT 2

---

syn synonym(s) *rel* related words
ant antonym(s) *near ant* near antonym(s)

2 the fact or state of being pertinent — see PERTINENCE

3 the quality of being actual — see FACT 1

materialize vb **1** to come into existence — see BEGIN 2

2 to come into view — see APPEAR 1

3 to come to one's attention especially gradually or unexpectedly — see ARISE 2

4 to represent in visible form — see EMBODY 2

matériel or **materiel** n items needed for the performance of a task or activity — see EQUIPMENT

maternal adj of, relating to, or characteristic of a mother — see MOTHERLY

maternity n motherly character or qualities ⟨she had such *maternity* at such a young age that all her classmates went to her for comfort⟩

syn motherliness

rel nurturance; fertility, fruitfulness, productivity, richness

mathematical adj meeting the highest standard of accuracy — see PRECISE 1

mating n sexual union involving penetration of the vagina by the penis — see SEXUAL INTERCOURSE

matriarch n a dignified usually elderly woman of some rank or authority ⟨even though she was 87, the *matriarch* of the family knew everything that was going on⟩

syn dame, dowager, matron

rel grandam (or grandame); headmistress, mistress; ma, mama, mammy, mom, momma

matriculate vb to enter in a list or roll — see ENROLL 1

matrimonial adj of or relating to marriage — see MARITAL

matrimony n a union representing a special kind of social and legal partnership between two people — see MARRIAGE 1

matron n a dignified usually elderly woman of some rank or authority — see MATRIARCH

matte also **mat** or **matt** adj lacking a surface luster or gloss ⟨I chose a paint with a *matte* finish so the walls wouldn't be too shiny⟩

syn dim, dull, dulled, flat, lusterless

rel tarnished, unpolished; cloudy, dingy, dirty, drab, mousy (or mousey), muddy; gray (also grey), leaden, pale; dark, darkened, dimmed, dusky, gloomy, murky, obscure, obscured, somber (or sombre)

near ant buffed, burnished, glazed, lacquered, polished, shellacked, varnished; satin, satiny; silken, silky; slick, slippery; gleaming, glimmering, glinting, glistening, glittering, scintillating, shimmering, shining, sparkling, twinkling; beaming, bedazzling, bright, brightened, brilliant, dazzling, effulgent, lucent, lucid, luminous, radiant, shining

ant glossy, lustrous, shiny, sleek

matter n **1** a major object of interest or concern (as in a discussion or artistic composition) ⟨that is not relevant to the *matter* under discussion⟩

syn content, motif, motive, question, subject, theme, topic

rel idea, point, purpose; issue, problem; body, bulk, burden, core, crux, fundamental, generality, gist, heart, kernel, keynote, main, marrow, mass, nub, nucleus, pith, purport, quick, staple, substance, sum; basis; bottom, essential, essentiality; affair, argument, debate

near ant aside, digression, interjection, parenthesis, tangent

2 something to be dealt with ⟨we must take care of this *matter* before it becomes a real problem⟩

syn affair, business, thing

rel problem; crisis, crossroad, emergency, exigency, juncture, strait, zero hour; concern, trouble, worry; care, lookout, responsibility; deadlock, impasse, stalemate; corner, fix, hole, hot water, pinch, predicament, scrape, spot

3 communications or parcels sent or carried through the postal system — see MAIL

4 something that requires thought and skill for resolution — see PROBLEM 1

matter vb to be of importance ⟨she believes that doing well in school really does *matter*⟩

syn count, import, mean, signify, weigh

rel affect, influence, sway; add up (to), amount (to)

phrases carry weight, cut ice

matter–of–fact adj **1** restricted to or based on fact — see FACTUAL 1

2 willing to see things as they really are and deal with them sensibly — see REALISTIC 1

maturation n the process of becoming mature ⟨a flower's *maturation* from bud to full bloom can take weeks⟩

syn development, growth, maturing, ripening

rel blossoming, flourishing, flowering; mellowing, softening

near ant decadence, decline, declining, deterioration; fading, shriveling, waning, wilting, withering; death, dying, expiring, perishing; regression, retrogression, reversion

mature adj **1** fully grown or developed ⟨I like pears when they're still hard, before they're *mature*⟩

syn adult, full-blown, full-fledged, full-grown, matured, ripe, ripened

rel aged, aging (or ageing), old; golden, mellow

near ant blooming, blossoming, burgeoning, flourishing, flowering; undeveloped, unfinished, unformed

ant green, immature, juvenile, unripened, young, youthful

2 having reached the date at which payment is required — see DUE 1

mature vb to become mature ⟨a young figure skater whose talent is still *maturing*⟩

syn age, develop, grow, grow up, progress, ripen

rel mellow, soften; bloom, blossom, burgeon, flourish, flower; open, unfold; advance, evolve

near ant decline, deteriorate; dry, fade, shrivel, wane, wilt, wither; regress, retrogress, revert; backslide, lapse, return

matured *adj* fully grown or developed — see MATURE 1

maturing *n* the process of becoming mature — see MATURATION

maturity *n* the state of being fully grown or developed ⟨people are legally considered to have reached *maturity* at eighteen years old in the United States⟩

syn adulthood, majority

rel manhood, womanhood; bloom, flush, heyday, prime; middle age, seniority

maudlin *adj* appealing to the emotions in an obvious and tiresome way — see CORNY

maul *vb* **1** to abuse physically — see MANHANDLE 1

2 to strike repeatedly — see BEAT 1

maunder *vb* **1** to move about from place to place aimlessly — see WANDER

2 to talk at length without sticking to a topic or getting to a point — see RAMBLE 1

maundering *adj* passing from one topic to another — see DISCURSIVE

maverick *n* a person who does not conform to generally accepted standards or customs — see NONCONFORMIST 1

mawkish *adj* appealing to the emotions in an obvious and tiresome way — see CORNY

mawkishness *n* the state or quality of having an excess of tender feelings (as of love, nostalgia, or compassion) — see SENTIMENTALITY

maxim *n* **1** an idea or statement about all of the members of a group or all the instances of a situation — see GENERALIZATION

2 an often stated observation regarding something from common experience — see SAYING

maximum *adj* **1** of the greatest or highest degree or quantity — see ULTIMATE 1

2 of the highest degree — see FULL 2

maximum *n* the greatest amount, number, or part — see MOST

maybe *adv* it is possible — see PERHAPS

mayhap *adv* it is possible — see PERHAPS

maze *n* a confusing and complicated arrangement of passages ⟨the mansion had a beautifully landscaped *maze* constructed of tall cypresses⟩

syn labyrinth

rel meander; jungle, quagmire; knot, snarl, tangle, web; entanglement, entrapment, snare, trap

meager *or* **meagre** *adj* less plentiful than what is normal, necessary, or desirable ⟨ever since he started the diet, his dinners have been more *meager* than he would like⟩

syn hand-to-mouth, light, niggardly, poor, scant, scanty, scarce, skimpy, slender, slim, spare, sparse, stingy

rel deficient, inadequate, insufficient, lacking, wanting; bare, mere, minimum; slight, small; barren, infertile, sterile, unfruitful, unproductive

near ant adequate, enough, sufficient; fat, fecund, fertile, fruitful, prolific, rich; lavish, luxuriant; blooming, bursting, flourishing, swarming, teeming, thriving

ant abundant, ample, bountiful, copious, generous, liberal, plenteous, plentiful

meal *n* food eaten or prepared for eating at one time ⟨all she wants to do is sit quietly after the large Thanksgiving *meal*⟩

syn chow, feed, mess, repast, table

rel board; breakfast, buffet, dinner, lunch, luncheon, refreshments, smorgasbord, snack, supper, tea; bite, gulp, morsel, serving, taste; banquet, feast, spread; bake, barbecue, clambake, cookout, fry, luau, picnic, potluck, roast

mealy *adj* not being or expressing what one appears to be or express — see INSINCERE

mealymouthed *adj* not being or expressing what one appears to be or express — see INSINCERE

mean *adj* **1** belonging to the class of people of low social or economic rank — see IGNOBLE 1

2 giving or sharing as little as possible — see STINGY 1

3 having or showing a desire to cause someone pain or suffering for the sheer enjoyment of it — see HATEFUL

4 not following or in accordance with standards of honor and decency — see IGNOBLE 2

5 of little or less value or merit — see INFERIOR 2

6 of the very best kind — see EXCELLENT

7 showing signs of advanced wear and tear and neglect — see SHABBY 1

mean *n* **1** a middle point between extremes ⟨that candidate's moderate views were seen as the *mean* that voters were looking for⟩

syn golden mean, medium, middle, midpoint

rel arithmetic mean, average; median, norm, par, standard

near ant maximum, minimum

2 means *pl* an action planned or taken to achieve a desired result — see MEASURE 1

3 means *pl* something used to achieve an end — see AGENT 1

4 means *pl* the total of one's money and property — see WEALTH 1

mean *vb* **1** to communicate or convey (as an idea) to the mind ⟨the national anthem *means* various things to various people⟩

syn denote, express, import, signify, spell

rel connote, imply, suggest; add up (to), amount (to); hint, insinuate, intimate; embody, epitomize, personify, represent, symbolize; advert, allude (to), mention,

---

syn synonym(s)   *rel* related words
ant antonym(s)   *near ant* near antonym(s)

refer (to); indicate, point (to), signal; announce, declare; elucidate, explain

2 to be of importance — see MATTER

3 to have in mind as a purpose or goal — see INTEND

meander *vb* to move about from place to place aimlessly — see WANDER

meaning *adj* clearly conveying a special meaning (as one's mood) — see EXPRESSIVE

meaning *n* **1** the idea that is conveyed or intended to be conveyed to the mind by language, symbol, or action ⟨the unmistakable *meaning* of the skier's upraised arms as he finished his spectacular run⟩
syn denotation, drift, import, intent, purport, sense, significance, signification
rel connotation; hint, implication, intimation, suggestion; message, tenor, theme; bottom, essence, essentiality, nature, soul, stuff; acceptance, definition; burden, crux, gist; core, heart, kernel, marrow, nub, nucleus, pith, point, quick; matter, motif, motive, subject, topic

2 something that one hopes or intends to accomplish — see GOAL

meaningful *adj* **1** clearly conveying a special meaning (as one's mood) — see EXPRESSIVE

2 having great meaning or lasting effect — see IMPORTANT 1

meaningless *adj* having no meaning ⟨this is an utterly *meaningless* bit of nonsense⟩
syn empty, inane, pointless, senseless
rel insignificant, trivial, unimportant; absurd, asinine, balmy, brainless, crazy, daffy, daft, dotty, fatuous, foolish, halfwitted, harebrained, insane, jerky, kooky, loony (*also* looney), lunatic, mad, mindless, nonsensical, nutty, preposterous, sappy, silly, unintelligent, unwise, wacky, weak-minded, witless, zany; irrational, unreasonable; aimless, haphazard, purposeless
near ant eloquent, expressive, pregnant, revealing, suggestive, telling; logical, rational, reasonable, valid
ant meaningful

meanly *adv* in a mean or spiteful manner — see NASTILY

meanness *n* the desire to cause pain for the satisfaction of doing harm — see MALICE

measly *adj* so small or unimportant as to warrant little or no attention — see NEGLIGIBLE 1

measure *n* **1** an action planned or taken to achieve a desired result ⟨such new security *measures* as metal detectors at all the entrances⟩
syn expedient, means, move, shift, step
rel act, deed, doing, feat, thing; procedure, proceeding, process; accomplishment, achievement, exploit; activity, affair, business, dealing, enterprise, event; attempt, endeavor, essay, initiative, operation, undertaking; effort, exertion, labor, pains, trouble, work; project, proposal, proposition; makeshift, resort, resource, stopgap

2 a given or particular mass or aggregate of matter — see AMOUNT

3 something set up as an example against which others of the same type are compared — see STANDARD 1

4 the recurrent pattern formed by a series of sounds having a regular rise and fall in intensity — see RHYTHM

5 the total amount of measurable space or surface occupied by something — see ¹SIZE

measure *vb* to find out the size, extent, or amount of ⟨for this experiment, you need to carefully *measure* all the chemicals before you mix them together⟩
syn gauge (*also* gage), scale, span
rel weigh; calibrate; lay off, mark (off); calculate, compute, figure, reckon, work out; conjecture, estimate, guess, judge, suppose; add up, sum, tally, total; ascertain, discover, dope (out), figure out, find out

measured *adj* **1** decided on as a result of careful thought — see DELIBERATE 1

2 having distinct or certain limits — see LIMITED 1

3 marked by or occurring with a noticeable regularity in the rise and fall of sound — see RHYTHMIC

measureless *adj* being or seeming to be without limits — see INFINITE

measurement *n* the total amount of measurable space or surface occupied by something — see ¹SIZE

measure up (to) *vb* to come near or nearer to in character or quality — see APPROXIMATE

meat *n* **1** animal and especially mammal tissue used as food ⟨we need to go shopping; there's only enough *meat* in the freezer for one more dinner⟩
syn flesh
rel game, poultry, variety meat

2 substances intended to be eaten — see FOOD

mecca *n* a thing or place that is of greatest importance to an activity or interest — see CENTER 1

mechanical *adj* **1** done instantly and without conscious thought or decision — see AUTOMATIC 1

2 lacking in natural or spontaneous quality — see ARTIFICIAL 1

medal *n* a piece of metal given in honor of a special event, a person, or an achievement ⟨the display case held an impressive array of military *medals* from World War II⟩
syn medallion, order
rel decoration, honor; crown, insignia, laurel, ribbon, title; badge, button, chevron, cockade, color, ensign, rosette; distinction; award, prize, trophy; citation, commendation

medallion *n* a piece of metal given in honor of a special event, a person, or an achievement — see MEDAL

meddle *vb* to interest oneself in what is not one's concern — see INTERFERE

meddler *n* a person who meddles in the affairs of others — see BUSYBODY

meddlesome *adj* thrusting oneself where one is not welcome or invited — see INTRUSIVE

meddling *adj* thrusting oneself where one is not welcome or invited — see INTRUSIVE

medial *adj* occupying a position equally distant from the ends or extremes — see MIDDLE 1

median *adj* 1 being about midway between extremes of amount or size — see MIDDLE 2

2 occupying a position equally distant from the ends or extremes — see MIDDLE 1

mediate *vb* to act as a go-between for opposing sides — see INTERVENE

mediator *n* one who works with opposing sides in order to bring about an agreement ⟨if you two cannot resolve this argument on your own, we'll have to bring in a *mediator*⟩

syn arbiter, arbitrator, conciliator, go-between, intercessor, intermediary, interposer, middleman, peacemaker

rel moderator; bargainer, negotiator; appeaser, pacifier, reconciler; broker; agent, attorney, deputy, factor, procurator, proxy; liaison; ambassador, emissary, envoy, messenger; delegate, representative; busybody, interferer, meddler; judge, referee, umpire; adviser (*or* advisor), counselor

medic *n* a person specially trained in healing human medical disorders — see DOCTOR

medication *n* a substance or preparation used to treat disease — see MEDICINE

medicine *n* a substance or preparation used to treat disease ⟨if you don't take all the doses of your *medicine*, you might get sick again⟩

syn cure, drug, medication, pharmaceutical, physic, remedy, specific

rel botanical, patent medicine, prescription; cordial, tonic; miracle drug, wonder drug; capsule, pill, tablet; injection, shot; liniment, lotion, ointment, potion, poultice, salve; syrup, tincture; antibiotic, antiseptic, serum

mediocre *adj* of average to below average quality ⟨your grades are *mediocre* and barely acceptable⟩

syn common, fair, indifferent, medium, middling, ordinary, passable, run-of-the-mill, second-rate, so-so

rel acceptable, adequate, all right, alright, decent, OK (*or* okay), reasonable, satisfactory, sufficient, sufficing, tolerable; moderate, modest; presentable, respectable; minimal, unexceptional; fine, good, nice

near ant distinguished, excellent, exceptional, exquisite, first-class, first-rate, matchless, maximum, optimal, optimum,

outstanding, peerless, preeminent, special, superior, supreme, top-notch; unmatched, unparalleled, unsurpassed; deficient, inadequate, insufficient, lacking, unacceptable, unsatisfactory, wanting

2 of low quality — see CHEAP 2

meditate *vb* 1 to give serious and careful thought to — see PONDER

2 to have in mind as a purpose or goal — see INTEND

meditation *n* long or deep thinking about spiritual matters — see CONTEMPLATION

meditative *adj* given to or marked by long, quiet thinking — see CONTEMPLATIVE

medium *adj* 1 being about midway between extremes of amount or size — see MIDDLE 2

2 occupying a position equally distant from the ends or extremes — see MIDDLE 1

3 of average to below average quality — see MEDIOCRE 1

medium *n* 1 a middle point between extremes — see MEAN 1

2 something used to achieve an end — see AGENT 1

3 the circumstances, conditions, or objects by which one is surrounded — see ENVIRONMENT

medley *n* an unorganized collection or mixture of various things — see MISCELLANY 1

meek *adj* not having or showing any feelings of superiority, self-assertiveness, or showiness — see HUMBLE 1

meekly *adv* in manner showing no signs of pride or self-assertion — see LOWLY

meekness *n* the absence of any feelings of being better than others — see HUMILITY

meet *adj* meeting the requirements of a purpose or situation — see FIT 1

meet *n* a competitive encounter between individuals or groups carried on for amusement, exercise, or in pursuit of a prize — see GAME 1

meet *vb* 1 to come upon face-to-face or as if face-to-face ⟨we never once *met* another car on that lonely country road⟩

syn chance (upon), encounter, happen (upon), stumble (upon)

rel accost, confront; face, greet, salute; collide (with), crash (into); crisscross, cross, pass; hit (upon), light (upon), tumble (to)

phrases bump into

near ant avoid, elude, escape, evade, shun

2 to come together into one body or place — see ASSEMBLE 1

3 to come upon unexpectedly or by chance — see HAPPEN (ON *OR* UPON)

4 to do what is required by the terms of — see FULFILL 1

5 to enter into contest or conflict with — see ENGAGE 2

6 to produce something equal to (as in quality or value) — see EQUAL 1

7 to put up with (something painful or difficult) — see BEAR 2

---

syn synonym(s)   *rel* related words
ant antonym(s)   *near ant* near antonym(s)

meeting *n* 1 a coming together of a number of persons for a specified purpose ⟨there will be another committee *meeting* next week to discuss the parish fair⟩
syn assembly, conference, congress, convention, convocation, council, gathering, get-together, huddle, powwow, roundtable, seminar
rel caucus, conclave, synod; demonstration, rally; conversation, dialogue (*also* dialog), discourse, discussion, palaver, talk; negotiation, parley; audience, interview, session
2 a body of people come together in one place — see GATHERING 1
3 the coming together of two or more things to the same point — see CONVERGENCE
meetly *adv* in a manner suitable for the occasion or purpose — see PROPERLY
megahit *n* a person or thing that is successful — see HIT 1
megalopolis *n* a thickly settled, highly populated area — see CITY
melancholy *adj* 1 causing unhappiness — see SAD 1
2 feeling unhappiness — see SAD 1
3 given to or marked by long, quiet thinking — see CONTEMPLATIVE
melancholy *n* a state or spell of low spirits — see SADNESS
mélange *n* an unorganized collection or mixture of various things — see MISCELLANY 1
melee *n* a rough and often noisy fight usually involving several people — see BRAWL 1
meliorate *vb* to make better — see IMPROVE
mellifluous *adj* having a pleasantly flowing quality suggestive of music — see LYRIC 1
mellow *adj* 1 having a pleasantly flowing quality suggestive of music — see LYRIC 1
2 not harsh or stern especially in manner, nature, or effect — see GENTLE 1
melodic *adj* having a pleasantly flowing quality suggestive of music — see LYRIC 1
melodious *adj* 1 having a pleasantly flowing quality suggestive of music — see LYRIC 1
2 having a pleasing mixture of notes — see HARMONIOUS 1
melodramatic *adj* 1 given to or marked by attention-getting behavior suggestive of stage acting — see THEATRICAL 1
2 having the general quality or effect of a stage performance — see DRAMATIC 1
melody *n* a rhythmic series of musical tones arranged to give a pleasing effect ⟨this week, we'll learn to play a more complicated *melody* on the saxophone⟩
syn air, lay, song, strain, tune, warble
rel descant; cadence, measure, meter, rhythm; ballad, ditty, hymn, lyric, madrigal
melt *vb* 1 to cease to be visible — see DISAPPEAR
2 to go from a solid to a liquid state — see LIQUEFY

member *n* 1 one of the parts that make up a whole — see ELEMENT 1
2 one of the pieces from which something is designed to be assembled — see PART 1
memento *n* something that serves to keep alive the memory of a person or event — see MEMORIAL
memo *n* 1 a message on paper from one person or group to another — see LETTER
2 a usually brief written reminder — see NOTE 1
3 a written communication giving information or directions — see MEMORANDUM 1
memoir *n* a history of a person's life — see BIOGRAPHY
memorandum *n* 1 a written communication giving information or directions ⟨I'm waiting for the *memorandum* that will explain the new vacation policy⟩
syn directive, memo, notice
rel announcement, declaration, proclamation, pronouncement; charge, command, dictate; directions, instructions, orders, word; encyclical, epistle, letter, mail, message, missive, note
2 a message on paper from one person or group to another — see LETTER
3 a usually brief written reminder — see NOTE 1
memorial *adj* serving to preserve the memory of a person, thing, or an event — see COMMEMORATIVE
memorial *n* something that serves to keep alive the memory of a person or event ⟨the Vietnam War *Memorial* is a starkly beautiful testimonial to the bravery of the soldiers who served in Vietnam⟩
syn commemorative, keepsake, memento, monument, remembrance, reminder, souvenir, token
rel memorabilia; relic, vestige; cairn, landmark, marker; testimonial, tribute
memorialize *vb* to be a memorial of — see COMMEMORATE 1
memorializing *adj* serving to preserve the memory of a person, thing, or an event — see COMMEMORATIVE
memorize *vb* to commit to memory ⟨everyone has to *memorize* a poem for next week⟩
syn con, learn, study
rel recall, recollect, relive, remember, reminisce, retain; accept, apprehend, comprehend, get, grasp, understand; absorb, digest
near ant forget; ignore, neglect, overlook
ant unlearn
memory *n* 1 the power or process of recalling what has been previously learned or experienced ⟨a photographic *memory* makes taking tests entirely too easy⟩
syn mind, recollection, remembrance, reminiscence
rel contemplation, musing, reflection, retrospection, thinking; awareness, cognizance, consciousness; apprehension, comprehension, understanding
near ant forgetfulness

2 a particular act or instance of recalling or the thing remembered ⟨I have only the vaguest *memory* of the family vacation we took the year I turned three⟩

syn recall, recollection, remembrance, reminiscence

rel flashback; memento, memorial, reminder, souvenir, token; association

3 the body of knowledge that has been retained in one's mind or the use of it — see HEART 2

menace *n* something that may cause injury or harm — see DANGER 2

menace *vb* **1** to place in danger — see ENDANGER

2 to remain poised to inflict harm, danger, or distress on — see THREATEN

menacing *adj* **1** being or showing a sign of evil or calamity to come — see OMINOUS

2 involving potential loss or injury — see DANGEROUS

ménage *n* those who live as a family in one house — see HOUSEHOLD

mend *vb* **1** to put into good shape or working order again ⟨that shirt will be as good as new when I'm finished *mending* it⟩

syn doctor, fix, patch, recondition, renovate, repair, revamp

rel overhaul, rebuild, reconstruct, refurbish; aid, cure, heal, help; condition, prepare, ready; care (for), maintain, service; rejuvenate, renew, restore; adjust, correct, modify, rectify, redress, reform, right; ameliorate, better, improve, meliorate

near ant break, damage, harm, hurt, impair, injure, mar, ruin, spoil, wreck; cripple, disable

2 to become healthy and strong again after illness or weakness — see CONVALESCE

3 to restore to a healthy condition — see HEAL 1

mendacious *adj* telling or containing lies — see DISHONEST 1

mendacity *n* **1** a statement known by its maker to be untrue and made in order to deceive — see LIE

2 the tendency to tell lies — see DISHONESTY 1

mendicant *n* a person who lives by public begging — see BEGGAR

mending *n* the process or period of gradually regaining one's health and strength — see CONVALESCENCE

menial *n* a person hired to perform household or personal services — see SERVANT *n*

menstruation *n* an occurrence of menstruating — see PERIOD 1

mental *adj* **1** of or relating to the mind ⟨a funny *mental* image made him laugh out loud⟩

syn cerebral, inner, intellectual, psychological (*also* psychologic)

rel cognitive, conscious; psychic (*also* psychical), telepathic; spiritual; alert, brainy, bright, clever, intelligent, quick-witted, rational, reasoning, smart, thinking

near ant bodily, carnal, corporal, corporeal, fleshly, physical, somatic

2 having or showing a very abnormal or sick state of mind — see INSANE 1

mention *vb* **1** to make reference to or speak about briefly but specifically ⟨you only *mentioned* in passing some of your accomplishments⟩

syn advert (to), cite, instance, name, note, notice, quote, refer (to), specify, touch (on *or* upon)

rel allude (to), hint (at), imply, infer, intimate, suggest; point (out), signal, signify; denominate, designate; indicate; bring up, broach, interject, interpolate, interpose, introduce; infiltrate, insinuate, worm; announce, declare, pronounce; elucidate, explain

near ant disregard, ignore, neglect, overlook, pass over, slight

2 to give as an example — see QUOTE 1

mentor *vb* to give advice and instruction to (someone) regarding the course or process to be followed — see GUIDE 1

menu *n* **1** a list of foods served at or available for a meal ⟨the *menu* at the fancy restaurant listed many dishes that I had never heard of⟩

syn bill of fare

rel chow, cuisine, fare, grub

2 a record of a series of items (as names or titles) usually arranged according to some system — see ¹LIST

mercenary *adj* having or marked by an eager and often selfish desire especially for material possessions — see GREEDY 1

merchandise *n* products that are bought and sold in business ⟨we stock only the finest-quality *merchandise* in this store⟩

syn commodities, goods, wares

rel line; export, import; inventory, staples, stock, stuff

merchandise *vb* to offer for sale to the public — see MARKET

merchandiser *n* **1** a buyer and seller of goods for profit — see MERCHANT

2 the person in a business deal who hands over an item in exchange for money — see VENDOR

merchant *n* a buyer and seller of goods for profit ⟨free trade agreements that are favored by *merchants* on both sides of the border⟩

syn dealer, merchandiser, trader, tradesman, trafficker

rel businessman; buyer, purchaser; hawker, peddler (*also* pedlar); retailer, seller, shopkeeper, storekeeper, vendor (*also* vender); jobber, middleman, wholesaler; distributor, provider, supplier

mercifulness *n* kind, gentle, or compassionate treatment especially towards someone who is undeserving of it — see MERCY 1

merciless *adj* having or showing a lack of sympathy or tender feelings — see HARD 1

---

syn synonym(s)   *rel* related words
ant antonym(s)   *near ant* near antonym(s)

mercurial *adj* likely to change frequently, suddenly, or unexpectedly — see FICKLE 1

mercy *n* **1** kind, gentle, or compassionate treatment especially towards someone who is undeserving of it ⟨always show your enemies *mercy*, because it makes you a better person⟩

syn charity, clemency, lenience, leniency, lenity, mercifulness, quarter

rel humanitarianism, philanthropy; empathy, pity, sympathy, understanding; commiseration, favor, grace; benevolence, care, compassion, gentleness, goodness, goodwill, kindliness, kindness, meekness, mildness, niceness, softness, tenderness; altruism, generosity, magnanimity, nobility; affection, devotion, love, worship

near ant reprisal, retaliation, retribution, revenge, vengeance; venom, vindictiveness, virulence, vitriol; brutality, cruelty, savagery, violence; castigation, chastisement, punishment, scolding; abhorrence, abomination, execration, hate, hatred, loathing; cattiness, malevolence, malice, malignity, meanness, spite, spitefulness, spleen; animosity, antagonism, antipathy, bitterness, enmity, grudge, hostility, jealousy, pique, resentment; bile, jaundice, rancor; hatefulness, invidiousness; coarseness, grimness, hardness, harshness, roughness

2 an act of kind assistance — see FAVOR 1

3 the capacity for feeling for another's unhappiness or misfortune — see HEART 1

mere *n, chiefly British* a small often deep body of water — see ¹POOL

mere *adj* being this and no more ⟨the *mere* idea of your traveling alone to Europe is ridiculous⟩

syn bare, very

rel absolute, sheer, simple, stark, utter; alone, only, singular, sole, solitary, solo, unique

merely *adv* nothing more than — see JUST 3

merge *vb* to turn into a single mass that is more or less the same throughout — see BLEND 1

merging *n* the act or an instance of joining two or more things into one — see UNION 1

meridian *n* the highest part or point — see HEIGHT 1

merit *n* **1** a quality that gives something special worth — see EXCELLENCE 2

2 the relative usefulness or importance of something as judged by specific qualities — see WORTH 1

merit *vb* to be or make worthy of (as a reward or punishment) — see EARN 2

merited *adj* being what is called for by accepted standards of right and wrong — see JUST 1

meritorious *adj* **1** deserving of high regard or great approval — see ADMIRABLE 1

2 having sufficient worth or merit to receive one's honor, esteem, or reward — see WORTHY

merrily *adv* in a cheerful or happy manner — see GAILY 1

merriment *n* **1** a mood characterized by high spirits and amusement and often accompanied by laughter — see MIRTH

2 joyful or festive activity — see MERRYMAKING

merriness *n* a mood characterized by high spirits and amusement and often accompanied by laughter — see MIRTH

merry *adj* indicative of or marked by high spirits or good humor ⟨Santa Claus has *merry*, twinkling blue eyes⟩

syn blithesome, festive, gay, gleeful, jocose, jocund, jolly, jovial, laughing, mirthful, sunny

rel amused, beaming, chuckling, giggling, smiling; bright, buoyant, carefree, cheerful, cheery, chipper, lighthearted, lightsome, upbeat; animated, jaunty, lively, perky, sprightly, vivacious; blessed, blissful, delighted, ecstatic, elated, enraptured, entranced, euphoric, exhilarated, exuberant, exultant, gladsome, happy, high, joyful, joyous, jubilant, overjoyed, radiant, rapturous, ravished, thrilled; amusing, facetious, flippant, funny, hilarious, jesting, joking, joshing, playful, witty; careless, cavalier, devil-may-care, easygoing, happy-go-lucky, insouciant, unconcerned; hopeful, optimistic, rosy, sanguine

near ant abject, aggrieved, anguished, blue, brokenhearted, dejected, depressed, despondent, disconsolate, disheartened, dispirited, downcast, downhearted, forlorn, heartbroken, heartsick, melancholy, sad, sorrowful, unhappy; crying, groaning, moaning, sobbing, wailing; discontented, disgruntled, moody; doleful, dolorous, joyless, lachrymose, mournful, plaintive, sorry, woeful; black, dark, desolate, gloomy, glum, gray (*also* grey); miserable, woebegone, wretched; dull, lethargic, listless, sluggish, torpid

merrymaker *n* one who engages in merrymaking especially in honor of a special occasion — see CELEBRANT

merrymaking *n* joyful or festive activity ⟨Christmas Eve is always an occasion of much *merrymaking* at our home⟩

syn conviviality, festivity, gaiety (*also* gayety), jollification, jollity, merriment, reveling, revelry

rel carousal, carouse; delight, diversion, entertainment, fun, pleasure, recreation, riot; glee, gleefulness, joviality, merriness, mirth, mirthfulness; carnival, celebration, party, revel; frolicking, gamboling, rollicking, romping; enjoyment, happiness, joy; binge, fling, frolic, gambol, lark, rollick, romp, spree; buffoonery, clownishness, flippancy, frivolity, funning, jesting, jocularity, joking, joshing, levity, lightheartedness, playfulness; zaniness

near ant blackness, darkness, gloominess, glumness, grief, grieving, heartbreak, miserableness, misery, mournfulness, mourning, wretchedness; anguish, dejection, depression, despondence, forlornness, melancholy, sorrow, unhappiness

mesa *n* a broad flat area of elevated land — see PLATEAU

mesh *n* a fabric made of strands loosely twisted, knotted, or woven together at regular intervals — see ¹NET 1

mesh *vb* to catch or hold as if in a net — see ENTANGLE 2

mesmerism *n* the art or act of inducing in a person a sleep-like state during which he or she readily follows suggestions — see HYPNOSIS

mesmerize *vb* to hold the attention of as if by a spell — see ENTHRALL 1

mess *n* **1** a state in which everything is out of order — see CHAOS

2 food eaten or prepared for eating at one time — see MEAL

3 something unpleasant to look at — see EYESORE

mess *vb* to interest oneself in what is not one's concern — see INTERFERE

mess (around) *vb* to spend time in aimless activity — see FIDDLE (AROUND)

mess (up) *vb* **1** to make or do (something) in a clumsy or unskillful way — see BOTCH

2 to undo the proper order or arrangement of — see DISORDER

mess (with) *vb* to handle thoughtlessly, ignorantly, or mischievously — see TAMPER

message *n* a piece of conveyed information — see COMMUNICATION

messed *adj* lacking in order, neatness, and often cleanliness — see MESSY

messenger *n* one that carries a message or does an errand ⟨the *messenger* comes by twice a day to pick up packages⟩

syn courier, go-between, page, runner

rel forerunner, harbinger, herald; agent, ambassador, delegate, deputy, emissary, envoy, representative; bearer, carrier, deliveryman, letter carrier, mail carrier, mailman

messy *adj* lacking in order, neatness, and often cleanliness ⟨you cannot go out to play until you clean up this *messy* room and put away all your toys⟩

syn chaotic, cluttered, confused, disarranged, disarrayed, disheveled (*or* dishevelled), disordered, disorderly, higgledy-piggledy, hugger-mugger, jumbled, littered, messed, muddled, mussed, mussy, pell-mell, rumpled, sloppy, topsy-turvy, tousled, tumbled, unkempt, untidy, upside-down

rel besmirched, blackened, dingy, dirty, filthy, foul, grimy, grubby, grungy, mucky, nasty, soiled, spotted, squalid, stained, sullied, unclean, uncleanly; dowdy, frowsy (*or* frowzy), slatternly, slovenly, uncombed; wrinkled; contaminated, defiled, polluted, tainted; knotted, snarled, tangled; seedy, shabby, sleazy, sordid; neglected, neglectful, negligent

phrases at sixes and sevens

near ant clean, cleaned, cleanly, hygienic, immaculate, sparkling, spick-and-span (*or* spic-and-span), spotless, stainless, unsoiled, unsullied; methodical, systematic; careful, fastidious, fussy, meticulous; combed, groomed, manicured; taintless, undefiled, unpolluted, untainted, wholesome

ant neat, ordered, orderly, organized, shipshape, snug, tidied, tidy, trim

metamorphose *vb* to change in form, appearance, or use — see CONVERT 2

metamorphosis *n* a change in form, appearance, or use — see CONVERSION

metaphor *n* an elaborate or fanciful way of expressing something — see CONCEIT 1

metaphorical *adj* expressing one thing in terms normally used for another — see FIGURATIVE

metaphysical *adj* of, relating to, or being part of a reality beyond the observable physical universe — see SUPERNATURAL 1

mete (out) *vb* to give out (something) in appropriate amounts or to appropriate individuals — see ADMINISTER 1

meter *n* the recurrent pattern formed by a series of sounds having a regular rise and fall in intensity — see RHYTHM

method *n* the means or procedure for doing something ⟨all experiments must be conducted using the proper scientific *method*⟩

syn approach, fashion, form, manner, strategy, style, system, tack, tactics, technique, way

rel mode; blueprint, design, game, ground plan, intrigue, layout, line, plan, plot, program, route, scheme; expedient, move, shift, step; practice (*also* practise), process, routine; project, proposal, proposition; policy

methodical *adj* following a set method, arrangement, or pattern ⟨a *methodical* study plan that included lists of points to memorize⟩

syn orderly, organized, regular, systematic, systematized

rel regularized, standardized; accurate, correct, exact, precise; detailed, specific; businesslike

near ant chaotic, disordered, disorderly, unordered

ant disorganized, haphazard, irregular, unsystematic

meticulous *adj* taking great care and effort — see PAINSTAKING

metric *adj* marked by or occurring with a noticeable regularity in the rise and fall of sound — see RHYTHMIC

metrical *adj* marked by or occurring with a noticeable regularity in the rise and fall of sound — see RHYTHMIC

metropolis *n* a thickly settled, highly populated area — see CITY

metropolitan *n* a person with the outlook, experience, and manners thought to be typical of big city dwellers — see COSMOPOLITAN

---

syn synonym(s)   *rel* related words
ant antonym(s)   *near ant* near antonym(s)

mettlesome *adj* marked by a lively display of strong feeling — see SPIRITED 1

mewl *vb* to utter feeble plaintive cries — see WHIMPER

microminiature *adj* very small in size — see TINY

microscopic *also* **microscopical** *adj* very small in size — see TINY

mid *adj* occupying a position equally distant from the ends or extremes — see MIDDLE 1

mid *prep* in or into the middle of — see AMONG

midday *n* the middle of the day — see NOON

middle *adj* **1** occupying a position equally distant from the ends or extremes ⟨you must mark the exact *middle* point of each of these lines in order to solve the problem⟩

syn halfway, intermediary, intermediate, medial, median, medium, mid, middlemost, midmost, midway

rel equidistant; central, inmost, inner, innermost, nearest

near ant outer, peripheral

ant extreme, farthest, farthermost, furthermost, furthest, outermost, outmost, remotest, utmost

2 being about midway between extremes of amount or size ⟨a house that is *middle* -sized for that neighborhood⟩ ⟨a man of *middle* height⟩

syn average, intermediate, median, medium, moderate, modest

rel reasonable; common, commonplace, conventional, normal, popular, regular, routine, standard, typical, usual; passable, tolerable

near ant excessive, extreme; rare, strange, uncommon, unusual; distinctive, idiosyncratic, special, unique; individual, peculiar, private

middle *n* **1** a middle point between extremes — see MEAN 1

2 an area or point that is an equal distance from all points along an edge or outer surface — see CENTER 2

3 the middle region of the human body — see MIDRIFF

4 the most intense or characteristic phase of something — see THICK

middleman *n* one who works with opposing sides in order to bring about an agreement — see MEDIATOR

middlemost *adj* occupying a position equally distant from the ends or extremes — see MIDDLE 1

middle-of-the-road *adj* avoiding major social change or extreme political ideas — see MODERATE 2

middling *adj* of average to below average quality — see MEDIOCRE 1

midget *n* a living thing much smaller than others of its kind — see DWARF 1

midmost *adj* occupying a position equally distant from the ends or extremes — see MIDDLE 1

midpoint *n* **1** a middle point between extremes — see MEAN 1

2 an area or point that is an equal distance from all points along an edge or outer surface — see CENTER 2

midriff *n* the middle region of the human body ⟨*midriff* -baring tops are popular this summer⟩

syn middle, waist, waistline

rel abdomen, torso, trunk

midst *n* **1** an area or point that is an equal distance from all points along an edge or outer surface — see CENTER 2

2 the most intense or characteristic phase of something — see THICK

midst *prep* in or into the middle of — see AMONG

midway *adj* occupying a position equally distant from the ends or extremes — see MIDDLE 1

mien *n* the outward form of someone or something especially as indicative of a quality — see APPEARANCE 1

might *n* the ability to exert effort for the accomplishment of a task — see POWER 2

mightily *adv* **1** to a great degree — see VERY 1

2 with great effort or determination — see HARD 1

3 in a vigorous and forceful manner — see HARD 3

mighty *adj* having great power or influence — see IMPORTANT 2

mighty *adv* to a great degree — see VERY 1

migrant *adj* having a way of life that involves moving from one region to another typically on a seasonal basis — see MIGRATORY

migrant *n* one that leaves one place to settle in another — see EMIGRANT

migratory *adj* having a way of life that involves moving from one region to another typically on a seasonal basis ⟨most of the apple crop is picked by *migratory* workers⟩ ⟨*migratory* birds heading south for the winter⟩

syn migrant, mobile

rel errant, itinerant, nomadic, peripatetic, ranging, roaming, roving, traveling (*or* travelling), vagabond, vagrant, wandering, wayfaring; ambulatory, drifting, footloose, gallivanting (*also* galavanting), lingering, meandering, rambling, sauntering, strolling, traipsing, walking

near ant immobile, stationary; established, fast, fixed, rooted, set, settled

ant nonmigratory, resident

mild *adj* **1** marked by temperatures that are neither too high nor too low — see CLEMENT

2 not harsh or stern especially in manner, nature, or effect — see GENTLE 1

milestone *n* a point in a chain of events at which an important change (as in one's fortunes) occurs — see TURNING POINT

milieu *n* the circumstances, conditions, or objects by which one is surrounded — see ENVIRONMENT

militancy *n* an inclination to fight or quarrel — see BELLIGERENCE

militant *adj* **1** feeling or displaying eagerness to fight — see BELLIGERENT
2 having or showing a bold forcefulness in the pursuit of a goal — see AGGRESSIVE 1

militant *n* one who is intensely or excessively devoted to a cause — see ZEALOT

militarist *n* one who urges or attempts to cause a war — see WARMONGER

military *adj* **1** of or relating to the armed services ⟨the colonel testified that revealing any more information would have required giving away *military* secrets⟩
syn martial, service
rel naval; GI, gladiatorial, mercenary, soldierly; aggressive, bellicose, combative, contentious, militant, militaristic, pugnacious, quarrelsome, scrappy, truculent, warlike
near ant civilian
ant nonmilitary
2 of, relating to, or suitable for war or a warrior — see MARTIAL 1

military *n* the combined army, air force, and navy of a nation — see ARMED FORCES

mill *n* a building or set of buildings for the manufacturing of goods — see FACTORY

mime *n* an actor in a story performed silently and entirely by body movements ⟨that annoying *mime* on the sidewalk is pretending to be in an invisible box again⟩
syn mimic, mummer, pantomime, pantomimist
rel entertainer, performer, player, trouper; imitator, impersonator, impressionist

mime *vb* to use (someone or something) as the model for one's speech, mannerisms, or behavior — see IMITATE 1

mimetic *adj* using or marked by the use of something else as a basis or model — see IMITATIVE

mimic *adj* **1** being such in appearance only and made with or manufactured from usually cheaper materials — see IMITATION
2 using or marked by the use of something else as a basis or model — see IMITATIVE

mimic *n* **1** a person who imitates another's voice and mannerisms for comic effect ⟨a gifted *mimic* who can do a terrific imitation of anyone's voice⟩
syn imitator, impersonator, impressionist
rel caricaturist, lampooner, mocker, parodist, satirist; mime, mummer, pantomimist; entertainer, performer, player, trouper; parrot
2 an actor in a story performed silently and entirely by body movements — see MIME

mimic *vb* **1** to copy or exaggerate (someone or something) in order to make fun of ⟨the comedian was famous for *mimicking* the President's distinctive lisp⟩

syn burlesque, caricature, imitate, mock, parody, take off (on), travesty
rel lampoon, satirize; deride, ridicule; ape, parrot; duplicate, emulate, replicate, reproduce; act, counterfeit, dissemble, fake, feign, pretend, sham, simulate; elaborate, embellish, embroider, exaggerate, magnify, pad, stretch; amplify, enhance, enlarge (upon), expand, flesh (out), overdraw, overstate; mime, pantomime; impersonate, perform, play
2 to use (someone or something) as the model for one's speech, mannerisms, or behavior — see IMITATE 1

mince *vb* to cut into small pieces — see CHOP

mind *vb* **1** to pay attention especially through the act of hearing — see LISTEN
2 *chiefly dialect* to bring back to mind — see REMEMBER
3 to act according to the commands of — see OBEY
4 to be cautious of or on guard against — see BEWARE (OF)
5 to have an interest or concern for — see CARE
6 to take charge of especially on behalf of another — see ²TEND 1
7 to take notice of and be guided by — see HEED 1

mind *n* **1** the part of a person that feels, thinks, perceives, wills, and especially reasons ⟨scientists still disagree about exactly where the *mind* is located⟩
syn cerebrum, head
rel brain, gray matter, intellect, intelligence, reason; acumen, alertness, astuteness, brilliance, insight, judgment (*or* judgement), mentality, perception, perspicacity, sagacity, sapience, wisdom, wit; awareness, cognizance, consciousness, self-awareness, self-consciousness
2 the normal or healthy condition of the mental abilities ⟨everyone used to tease him and tell him he was out of his *mind* when he swore he'd seen a flying saucer⟩
syn head, reason, saneness, sanity, wit
rel rationality, reasonableness, sense; health, healthfulness, healthiness, wholesomeness; lucidity, lucidness, normality, soundness; wisdom
near ant delusion, hallucination; delirium, frenzy, hysteria
ant derangement, insanity, lunacy, madness, mania
3 an idea that is believed to be true or valid without positive knowledge — see OPINION 1
4 the power or process of recalling what has been previously learned and experienced — see MEMORY 1

mindful *adj* having specified facts or feelings actively impressed on the mind — see CONSCIOUS

mindless *adj* **1** not having or showing an ability to absorb ideas readily — see STUPID 1
2 not paying or showing close attention especially for the purpose of avoiding trouble — see CARELESS 1

mindlessness *n* the quality or state of lacking intelligence or quickness of mind — see STUPIDITY 1

mine *n* a usually concealed explosive device designed to go off when disturbed — see BOOBY TRAP 1

mine *vb* to place hidden explosive devices in or under ⟨the troops *mined* the field before they gave it up to the enemy⟩
syn boobytrap
rel blow up, bomb; ambush, snare, trap; attack

mingle *vb* 1 to turn into a single mass that is more or less the same throughout — see BLEND 1
2 to take part in social activities — see SOCIALIZE

miniature *adj* very small in size — see TINY

miniature *n* an exact representation of something in greatly reduced size — see MODEL 1

minimal *adj* being the least in amount, number, or size possible ⟨the beached whales were returned to the sea with only *minimal* loss of life⟩
syn least, littlest, lowest, minimum, slightest
rel fewer, lesser, low, slight, small, smaller
near ant highest
ant full, greatest, largest, maximum, top, topmost, utmost

minimize *vb* to express scornfully one's low opinion of — see DECRY 1

minimum *adj* being the least in amount, number, or size possible — see MINIMAL

minion *n* a person or thing that is preferred over others — see FAVORITE

minister *n* 1 a person sent on a mission to represent another — see AMBASSADOR
2 a person specially trained and authorized to conduct religious services in a Christian church — see CLERGYMAN

minister (to) *vb* to attend to the needs and comforts of — see NURSE 1

ministerial *adj* of, relating to, or characteristic of the clergy — see CLERICAL

minor *adj* 1 having not so great importance or rank as another — see LESSER
2 of little or less value or merit — see INFERIOR 2
3 lacking importance — see UNIMPORTANT

minstrel *n* a person who writes poetry — see POET

minstrelsy *n* writing that uses rhythm, vivid language, and often rhyme to provoke an emotional response — see POETRY 1

mint *n* a very large amount of money — see FORTUNE 2

minus *n* a feature of someone or something that creates difficulty for achieving success — see DISADVANTAGE

minus *prep* not having — see WITHOUT 1

minute *adj* 1 including many small descriptive features — see DETAILED 1
2 lacking importance — see UNIMPORTANT

3 so small or unimportant as to warrant little or no attention — see NEGLIGIBLE 1
4 made or done with extreme care and accuracy — see FINE 2
5 very small in size — see TINY

minute *n* a very small space of time — see INSTANT

minutely *adv* with attention to all aspects or details — see THOROUGHLY 1

miracle *n* something extraordinary or surprising — see WONDER 1

miraculous *adj* 1 being so extraordinary or abnormal as to suggest powers which violate the laws of nature — see SUPERNATURAL 2
2 causing wonder or astonishment — see MARVELOUS 1

mire *n* 1 soft wet earth — see MUD
2 spongy land saturated or partially covered with water — see SWAMP

mire *vb* 1 to make dirty — see DIRTY
2 to place in conflict or difficulties — see EMBROIL

mirror *n* a smooth or polished surface (as of glass) that forms images by reflection ⟨breaking a *mirror* is supposed to bring seven years of bad luck⟩
syn looking glass
rel pier glass; reflector

mirror *vb* to reproduce or show (an exact likeness) as a mirror would — see REFLECT

mirth *n* a mood characterized by high spirits and amusement and often accompanied by laughter ⟨as charming as your mutual *mirth* is, could you refrain from nudging each other and giggling during class?⟩
syn cheer, cheerfulness, cheeriness, festivity, glee, gleefulness, hilarity, joviality, merriment, merriness, mirthfulness
rel frivolity, levity; carnival, gaiety (*also* gayety), jollification, jollity, reveling, revelry; brightness, buoyancy, good-humoredness, good-naturedness, humor, sunniness; insouciance, lightheartedness, playfulness; buffoonery, clownishness, flippancy, funning, jesting, jocularity, joking, joshing; animation, jauntiness, liveliness, perkiness, vivacity; joyfulness, joyousness, jubilation, rejoicing; frolicking, gamboling (*or* gambolling), rollicking, romping
near ant blues, dejection, depression, despondence, forlornness, sadness, sorrow, unhappiness; bile, gloom, melancholy, sourness, spleen; earnestness, graveness, gravity, grimness, seriousness, soberness, solemnity; discontent, disgruntlement, moodiness; dolefulness, dolorousness, joylessness, mournfulness, plaintiveness, woe, woefulness; blackness, darkness, gloominess, glumness; desolateness, desolation; heartbreak, miserableness, misery, mourning, wretchedness

mirthful *adj* indicative of or marked by high spirits or good humor — see MERRY

mirthfully *adv* in a cheerful or happy manner — see GAILY 1

mirthfulness *n* a mood characterized by high spirits and amusement and often accompanied by laughter — see MIRTH

miry *adj* full of or covered with soft wet earth — see MUDDY 1

misadventure *n* bad luck or an example of this — see MISFORTUNE

misanthrope *n* a person who distrusts other people and believes that everything is done for selfish reasons — see CYNIC

misanthropic *adj* having or showing a deep distrust of human beings and their motives — see CYNICAL

misapplication *n* incorrect or improper use — see MISUSE

misapply *vb* to put to a bad or improper use ⟨you've *misapplied* the theorem to certain problems that require a different formula⟩ ⟨kids who *misapply* their boundless energy and get into trouble⟩
  syn abuse, misuse, pervert, profane, prostitute
  rel degrade, twist; mismanage; corrupt, debase, desecrate
  near ant apply, employ, use, utilize; respect

misapprehend *vb* to fail to understand the true or actual meaning of — see MISUNDERSTAND

misapprehension *n* **1** a failure to understand correctly — see MISUNDERSTANDING 1
  2 a wrong judgment — see MISTAKE 1

misappropriate *vb* to take (something) without right and with an intent to keep — see STEAL 1

misbegotten *adj* born to a father and mother who are not married — see ILLEGITIMATE 1

misbehave *vb* to behave badly ⟨if the two of you *misbehave* in public like that again, you'll have to go to bed early for a week⟩
  syn act up, carry on
  rel misconduct; disobey; clown (around), cut up, fool (around), horse (around); show off; roughhouse
  phrases raise Cain, run riot
  near ant obey; acquit, act, bear, comport, demean, deport, quit; comply, conform; check, collect, compose, constrain, contain, control, curb, handle, inhibit, move, quiet, repress, restrain

misbehaving *adj* engaging in or marked by childish misbehavior — see NAUGHTY

misbehavior *n* improper or illegal behavior — see MISCONDUCT

miscalculate *vb* to make an incorrect judgment regarding ⟨they *miscalculated* how difficult the long trip would be⟩
  syn misconceive, misjudge, mistake
  rel misconstrue, misinterpret, misunderstand; overestimate, overrate, overvalue; underestimate, underrate, undervalue; miscount

---

syn synonym(s)   *rel* related words
ant antonym(s)   *near ant* near antonym(s)

miscarry *vb* to go wrong ⟨the scheme to save the dolphins *miscarried*, and all were lost⟩
  syn misfire
  rel miss; break down, conk (out), crash, die, fail, stall; fizzle, flop, flunk, fold, wash out; flounder, struggle; decline, slip, slump, wane
  phrases fall flat, fall short
  near ant prevail, succeed; flourish, prosper, thrive

miscellaneous *adj* consisting of many things of different sorts ⟨the bottom of the drawer was always a *miscellaneous* accumulation of odds and ends⟩
  syn assorted, heterogeneous, mixed, motley, patchwork, promiscuous, varied
  rel manifold, multifarious; multiple, multiplex, myriad; disparate, divergent, diverse, sundry, various; chaotic, cluttered, confused, disarranged, disarrayed, disheveled (*or* dishevelled), disordered, jumbled, littered, messed, messy, muddled; amalgamated, blended, combined, conglomerated, fused, incorporated, intermingled, intermixed, merged, mingled; unclassified, unsorted
  near ant monolithic, uniform; alike, identical, like, same; distinct, distinctive, individual, separate
  ant homogeneous

miscellaneousness *n* the quality or state of being composed of many different elements or types — see VARIETY 1

miscellany *n* **1** an unorganized collection or mixture of various things ⟨the box from the attic contained a *miscellany* of old records, family photo albums, and long-forgotten love letters⟩
  syn assortment, clutter, hash, hodgepodge, hotchpotch, jumble, litter, medley, mélange, mishmash, motley, muddle, potpourri, rummage, scramble, shuffle, tumble, variety, welter
  rel notions, odds and ends, sundries; accumulation, aggregation, conglomeration; catchall, patchwork; admixture, amalgam, blend, combination, composite, compound, fusion, intermixture, mix, mixture; chaos, confusion, disarrangement, disarray, disorder, mess, muddle, shambles; knot, snarl, tangle
  phrases odds and ends
  2 a collection of writings — see ANTHOLOGY

mischance *n* **1** a chance and usually sudden event bringing loss or injury — see ACCIDENT 1
  2 bad luck or an example of this — see MISFORTUNE

mischief *n* **1** playful, reckless behavior that is not intended to cause serious harm ⟨the children claimed that setting off a firecracker was harmless *mischief*, but they got a lecture anyway⟩
  syn devilishness, devilment, devilry (*or* deviltry), hob, impishness, knavery, mischievousness, rascality, roguishness, shenanigans, waggery, wickedness

rel diabolicalness, naughtiness; friskiness, playfulness, sportiveness; chicanery, hanky-panky, trickery; high jinks, monkeyshines, skylarking, tomfoolery; antic, caper, practical joke; aggravation, annoyance, exasperation, irritation

near ant gravity, seriousness, solemnity

2 a natural disposition for playful behavior — see PLAYFULNESS

3 an appealingly mischievous person — see SCAMP 1

mischievous *adj* **1** tending to or exhibiting reckless playfulness ⟨the children had been so *mischievous* that we had to pay the babysitter extra and then clean up the mess⟩

syn devilish, elvish, impish, knavish, pixieish, prankish, rascally, roguish, sly, waggish, wicked

rel antic, coltish, frisky, kittenish, playful, sportive; gay, happy, lighthearted, whimsical; energetic, lively, spirited, sprightly; artful, cunning, tricky; misbehaving, naughty; pestering, riling, teasing

near ant grave, grim, sober, solemn, stern

2 engaging in or marked by childish misbehavior — see NAUGHTY

3 causing or capable of causing harm — see HARMFUL

mischievousness *n* **1** a natural disposition for playful behavior — see PLAYFULNESS

2 playful, reckless behavior that is not intended to cause serious harm — see MISCHIEF 1

misconceive *vb* to make an incorrect judgment regarding — see MISCALCULATE

misconception *n* a false idea or belief — see FALLACY 1

misconduct *n* improper or illegal behavior ⟨some rough play got the hockey player fined for *misconduct* on the ice⟩

syn malfeasance, misbehavior, misdoing, wrongdoing

rel crime, malefaction, misdeed, sin, wrong; malpractice; familiarity, gaffe, impropriety, indiscretion; blunder, error, fault, flub, fumble, goof, lapse, miscue, misstep, mistake, slip, slipup, stumble

misconduct *vb* to manage badly — see MISMANAGE

misconstruction *n* a failure to understand correctly — see MISUNDERSTANDING 1

misconstrue *vb* to fail to understand the true or actual meaning of — see MISUNDERSTAND

misconstruing *n* a failure to understand correctly — see MISUNDERSTANDING 1

miscreant *n* a mean, evil, or unprincipled person — see VILLAIN

miscue *n* an unintentional departure from truth or accuracy — see ERROR 1

misdeed *n* a breaking of a moral or legal code — see OFFENSE 1

misdoing *n* **1** a breaking of a moral or legal code — see OFFENSE 1

2 improper or illegal behavior — see MISCONDUCT

miser *n* a mean grasping person who is usually stingy with money ⟨the *miser* liked to sit and play with his money⟩

syn cheapskate, niggard, piker, scrooge, skinflint, tightwad

rel hoarder, saver

near ant prodigal, profligate, spender, spendthrift, squanderer, waster, wastrel

miserable *adj* **1** causing or marked by an atmosphere lacking in cheer — see GLOOMY 1

2 feeling unhappiness — see SAD 1

3 of low quality — see CHEAP 2

4 showing signs of advanced wear and tear and neglect — see SHABBY 1

5 deserving of one's pity — see PATHETIC 1

miserliness *n* the quality of being overly sparing with money — see PARSIMONY

misery *n* **1** a situation or state that causes great suffering and unhappiness — see HELL 1

2 a state of great suffering of body or mind — see DISTRESS 1

misfire *vb* to go wrong — see MISCARRY

misfortune *n* bad luck or an example of this ⟨through sheer *misfortune* our car got a flat tire and we were late⟩ ⟨our *misfortunes* of the last year included the loss of a beloved pet⟩

syn adversity, knock, misadventure, mischance, mishap

rel calamity, cataclysm, catastrophe, disaster; tragedy; affliction, hardship, trial, tribulation; distress, misery, suffering, unhappiness; defeat, failure, fizzle, nonsuccess; curse, sorrow, trouble; accident, casualty; disappointment, letdown, setback; circumstance, destiny, doom, fate, lot, portion

near ant break, chance, fluke, godsend, hit, opportunity, stroke, windfall; accomplishment, achievement, success

ant fortune, luck

misgiving *n* **1** a feeling or attitude that one does not know the truth, truthfulness, or trustworthiness of someone or something — see DOUBT

2 an uneasy feeling about the rightness of what one is doing or going to do — see QUALM

3 suspicion or fear of future harm or misfortune — see APPREHENSION 1

misgovern *vb* to manage badly — see MISMANAGE

misguide *vb* to cause to believe what is untrue — see DECEIVE

mishandle *vb* **1** to inflict physical or emotional harm upon — see ABUSE 1

2 to abuse physically — see MANHANDLE 1

3 to manage badly — see MISMANAGE

mishap *n* **1** a chance and usually sudden event bringing loss or injury — see ACCIDENT 1

2 bad luck or an example of this — see MISFORTUNE

mishmash *n* an unorganized collection or mixture of various things — see MISCELLANY 1

misinform *vb* to cause to believe what is untrue — see DECEIVE

misinterpret *vb* **1** to change so much as to create a wrong impression or alter the meaning of — see GARBLE

2 to fail to understand the true or actual meaning of — see MISUNDERSTAND

misinterpretation *n* a failure to understand correctly — see MISUNDERSTANDING 1

misjudge *vb* to make an incorrect judgment regarding — see MISCALCULATE

misjudging *n* a wrong judgment — see MISTAKE 1

misjudgment *n* a wrong judgment — see MISTAKE 1

mislaid *adj* no longer possessed — see LOST

mislay *vb* to be unable to find or have at hand — see LOSE 1

mislaying *n* the act or an instance of not having or being able to find — see LOSS 1

mislead *vb* to cause to believe what is untrue — see DECEIVE

misleading *adj* tending or having power to deceive — see DECEPTIVE 1

mismanage *vb* to manage badly ⟨the business was *mismanaged* so seriously that it had to declare bankruptcy⟩

syn misconduct, misgovern, mishandle, misrule

rel abuse, ill-treat, ill-use, maltreat, mistreat, misuse; damage, harm, hurt, violate

near ant govern, handle, manage, rule; care (for), nurture; aid, help, protect, rescue

misplace *vb* to be unable to find or have at hand — see LOSE 1

misplaced *adj* no longer possessed — see LOST

misplacement *n* the act or an instance of not having or being able to find — see LOSS 1

misread *vb* to fail to understand the true or actual meaning of — see MISUNDERSTAND

misreading *n* a failure to understand correctly — see MISUNDERSTANDING 1

misrepresent *vb* **1** to change so much as to create a wrong impression or alter the meaning of — see GARBLE

2 to give a false idea of — see BELIE 1

misrule *n* a state in which there is widespread wrongdoing and disregard for rules and authority — see ANARCHY

misrule *vb* to manage badly — see MISMANAGE

miss *n* a young usually unmarried woman — see GIRL 1

miss *vb* **1** to fail to attend — see CUT 2

2 to fail to understand the true or actual meaning of — see MISUNDERSTAND

misshapen *adj* badly or imperfectly formed — see MALFORMED

missing *adj* **1** no longer possessed — see LOST

2 not present or in evidence — see ABSENT 2

3 not at a certain place — see ABSENT 1

mission *n* a specific task with which a person or group is charged ⟨your *mission* is to clean up the house before company arrives⟩

syn assignment, charge, job, operation, post

rel burden, chore, duty, need, obligation, requirement, responsibility; labor, work; commitment, pledge, promise; appointment, designation, nomination; compulsion, constraint, restraint

missive *n* a message on paper from one person or group to another — see LETTER

misspend *vb* to use up carelessly — see WASTE 1

misstate *vb* to change so much as to create a wrong impression or alter the meaning of — see GARBLE

misstep *n* an unintentional departure from truth or accuracy — see ERROR 1

mist *n* **1** a light or fine rain — see DRIZZLE

2 an atmospheric condition in which suspended particles in the air rob it of its transparency — see HAZE 1

mist *vb* to make dark, dim, or indistinct — see CLOUD 1

mistake *n* **1** a wrong judgment ⟨I made a *mistake* when I assumed that you were the one who broke the window⟩

syn misapprehension, misjudging, misjudgment

rel blunder, error, fault, flub, fumble, goof, inaccuracy, lapse, miscue, misstep, slipup, stumble; foul-up, muff; miscalculation, misstatement; misconception, misconstruction, misconstruing, misinterpretation

2 an unintentional departure from truth or accuracy — see ERROR 1

mistake *vb* **1** to fail to understand the true or actual meaning of — see MISUNDERSTAND

2 to make an incorrect judgment regarding — see MISCALCULATE

mistaken *adj* having an opinion that does not agree with truth or the facts — see INCORRECT 1

mistakenly *adv* in a mistaken or inappropriate way — see WRONGLY

mistreat *vb* to inflict physical or emotional harm upon — see ABUSE 1

mistrust *n* a feeling or attitude that one does not know the truth, truthfulness, or trustworthiness of someone or something — see DOUBT

mistrust *vb* to have no trust or confidence in — see DISTRUST

mistrustful *adj* **1** inclined to doubt or question claims — see SKEPTICAL 1

2 not feeling sure about the truth, wisdom, or trustworthiness of someone or something — see DOUBTFUL 1

mistrustfully *adv* with distrust — see ASKANCE

mistrustfulness *n* a feeling or attitude that one does not know the truth, truth-

syn synonym(s)   *rel* related words
ant antonym(s)   *near ant* near antonym(s)

fulness, or trustworthiness of someone or something — see DOUBT

misty *adj* filled with or dimmed by fine particles (as of dust or water) in suspension — see HAZY 1

misunderstand *vb* to fail to understand the true or actual meaning of ⟨you *misunderstood* that poem because you didn't look up the words you didn't know⟩

syn misapprehend, misconstrue, misinterpret, misread, miss, mistake

rel misconception

ant apprehend, catch, comprehend, conceive, fathom, grasp, know, make out, penetrate, perceive, savvy, see, seize, take in, understand

misunderstanding *n* 1 a failure to understand correctly ⟨people once thought that there were canals on Mars because of a common *misunderstanding* of a report by an Italian astronomer⟩

syn misapprehension, misconstruction, misconstruing, misinterpretation, misreading

rel misconception, mistake

near ant appreciation, apprehension, comprehension, conception, grasp, knowledge, perception, understanding; awareness, consciousness, realization

2 an often noisy or angry expression of differing opinions — see ARGUMENT 1

misusage *n* incorrect or improper use — see MISUSE

misuse *n* incorrect or improper use ⟨the warranty for this dryer is null and void if you subject the product to deliberate *misuse*⟩

syn abuse, misapplication, misusage, perversion

rel mishandling, mismanagement, mismanaging; maltreatment, mistreatment; damage, destruction, ruin, spoiling, wrecking; corruption, debasement, desecration, profanation, prostitution

near ant application, employment, use, utilization

misuse *vb* 1 to put to a bad or improper use — see MISAPPLY

2 to inflict physical or emotional harm upon — see ABUSE 1

mite *n* 1 a very small sum of money ⟨I have only a *mite* left to buy lunch for the rest of the week⟩

syn peanuts, pittance, shoestring, song

rel petty cash, pin money, pocket money, spending money

near ant capital, means, wherewithal; opulence, riches, treasure, wealth; heap, pile, pot; bonanza, mine, treasure trove, treasury

ant fortune, king's ransom, mint, wad

2 a living thing much smaller than others of its kind — see DWARF 1

3 a very small amount — see PARTICLE 1

mitigate *vb* to make more bearable or less severe — see HELP 2

mix *n* a distinct entity formed by the combining of two or more different things — see BLEND

mix *vb* 1 to turn into a single mass that is more or less the same throughout — see BLEND 1

2 to take part in social activities — see SOCIALIZE

mix (up) *vb* to undo the proper order or arrangement of — see DISORDER

mixed *adj* 1 being offspring produced by parents of different races, breeds, species, or genera ⟨our *mixed* dog has a greyhound's body but the features of a collie⟩

syn crossbred, hybrid, mongrel

rel dihybrid, trihybrid; crossbred, crossed, hybridized, interbred, outcrossed

near ant pedigreed; inbred

ant full-blooded, purebred, thoroughbred

2 consisting of many things of different sorts — see MISCELLANEOUS

mixture *n* a distinct entity formed by the combining of two or more different things — see BLEND

mix–up *n* an instance of confusion — see FOUL-UP

moan *n* 1 a long low sound indicating pain or grief ⟨she uttered an agonized *moan* and clutched her stomach⟩

syn groan, wail

rel blubbering, crying, sniveling, sobbing, weeping, whimpering, whining, yammering; keen, lament; bawl, cry, howl, shriek, squall, whimper, whine, yelp, yowl

near ant cackle, chuckle, chortle, giggle, guffaw, laugh, snicker, titter

2 a crying out in grief — see LAMENT 1

moan *vb* 1 to utter a moan ⟨he *moaned* and cried for days after his dog died⟩

syn groan, wail

rel cry, blubber, sob, weep; sniff, snivel, whimper, whine; bemoan, bewail, deplore, keen, lament, rue; bleed, grieve, mourn, sorrow, suffer; bawl, howl, shriek, squall, yammer, yelp, yowl

near ant cackle, chuckle, chortle, giggle, guffaw, laugh, snicker, titter

2 to express dissatisfaction, pain, or resentment usually tiresomely — see COMPLAIN

mob *n* 1 a great number of persons or things gathered together — see CROWD 1

2 a group involved in secret or criminal activities — see RING 1

3 the body of the community as contrasted with the elite — see MASS 1

mob *vb* to move upon or fill (something) in great numbers — see CROWD 2

mobile *adj* 1 capable of being moved especially with ease — see MOVABLE

2 having a way of life that involves moving from one region to another typically on a seasonal basis — see MIGRATORY

mobile home *n* a motor vehicle that is specially equipped for living while traveling — see CAMPER

mobilization *n* an act of gathering forces together to renew or attempt an effort — see RALLY 1

mobilize *vb* to assemble and make ready for action ⟨we are prepared to *mobilize* the troops on very short notice⟩

syn marshal, muster, rally

rel arrange, line up, order, organize; call (up), convene, summon; activate

near ant disarrange, disorder, disorganize; deactivate, dismiss

ant demobilize

mobster *n* a violent, brutal person who is often a member of an organized gang — see HOODLUM

mock *adj* **1** being such in appearance only and made with or manufactured from usually cheaper materials — see IMITATION

2 lacking in natural or spontaneous quality — see ARTIFICIAL 1

mock *n* a person or thing that is made fun of — see LAUGHINGSTOCK

mock *vb* **1** to copy or exaggerate (someone or something) in order to make fun of — see MIMIC 1

2 to make (someone or something) the object of unkind laughter — see RIDICULE

mocker *n* a person who causes repeated emotional pain, distress, or annoyance to another — see TORMENTOR

mockery *n* **1** a poor, insincere, or insulting imitation of something ⟨the resort's Old West show for tourists is a *mockery* of Native American culture⟩

syn caricature, farce, joke, parody, sham, travesty

rel burlesque, comedy; lampoon, takeoff; counterfeit, fake, feigning, pretense (*or* pretence), simulation

near ant homage, tribute

2 a person or thing that is made fun of — see LAUGHINGSTOCK

3 the making of unkind jokes as a way of showing one's scorn for someone or something — see RIDICULE

mod *adj* being or involving the latest methods, concepts, information, or styles — see MODERN

¹**mode** *n* **1** a distinctive way of putting ideas into words — see STYLE 1

2 a state of mind dominated by a particular emotion — see MOOD 1

²**mode** *n* a practice or interest that is very popular for a short time — see FAD

model *adj* constituting, serving as, or worthy of being a pattern to be imitated ⟨why can't you be like your sister, who is such a well-behaved *model* child?⟩

syn archetypal, classic, exemplary, paradigmatic, quintessential

rel ideal, nonpareil, special, unique; absolute, flawless, impeccable, perfect; bang-up, banner, capital, dandy, fine, first-class, first-rate, grand, great, groovy, jim-dandy, par excellence, prime, superb, superior, superlative, terrific, tip-top, top, top-notch, unsurpassed, wonderful; exceptional, fancy, high-grade

near ant bad, poor, substandard, unsatisfactory; atrocious, execrable, wretched; deficient, disappointing, failed, inadequate, inferior, poor; average, normal, ordinary, representative, typical; mediocre, second-class, second-rate

model *n* **1** an exact representation of something in greatly reduced size ⟨the dollhouse was a tiny, perfect *model* of the family's actual house⟩

syn miniature

rel copy, duplicate, duplication, imitation, replica, replication, reproduction; dwarf, midget, mini, pygmy

near ant archetype, original, prototype; blowup, enlargement

2 a person who poses with or wears merchandise (as clothes) often for pictorial advertising ⟨the most famous *models* can earn thousands of dollars an hour⟩

syn manikin, mannequin

rel figure, form; doll, dummy

3 someone of such unequaled perfection as to deserve imitation — see IDEAL 1

moderate *adj* **1** avoiding extremes in behavior or expression ⟨he was only a *moderate* drinker, stopping after a couple of glasses of wine⟩

syn temperate

rel controlled, curbed, disciplined, restrained, self-controlled; calculated, deliberate, measured; rational, reasonable; average, medio-cre, medium, modest, ordinary, run-of-the-mill, so-so; normal, ordinary, regular, routine, typical, usual

near ant excessive, extreme, inordinate, radical; irrational, unreasonable; extremist, fanatic (*or* fanatical), rabid, radical

ant immoderate, intemperate

2 avoiding major social change or extreme political ideas ⟨the principal's *moderate* position on cell phones is that students can use them at school but only for emergencies⟩

syn middle-of-the-road

rel conventional, orthodox, traditional, rational, reasonable; neutral

near ant excessive, conservative, reactionary, rightist; leftist, liberal, progressive; fanatic (*or* fanatical), revolutionary, revolutionist, subversive, violent; agitating, fomenting, incendiary, inciting, instigating, provocative, provoking; rabble-rousing; dissenting

ant extremist, radical

3 being about midway between extremes of amount or size — see MIDDLE 2

4 marked by temperatures that are neither too high nor too low — see CLEMENT

moderate *vb* to grow less in scope or intensity especially gradually — see DECREASE 2

moderately *adv* to some degree or extent — see FAIRLY

moderateness *n* an avoidance of extremes in one's actions, beliefs, or habits — see TEMPERANCE

moderation *n* an avoidance of extremes in one's actions, beliefs, or habits — see TEMPERANCE

moderator *n* a person in charge of a meeting — see CHAIR 1

---

syn synonym(s)   **rel** related words
ant antonym(s)   **near ant** near antonym(s)

modern *adj* being or involving the latest methods, concepts, information, or styles ⟨this hairstyle is absolutely the most *modern* fashion out there⟩

syn contemporary, current, hot, mod, modernistic, new, newfangled, new-fashioned, present-day, red-hot, space-age, ultramodern, up-to-date

rel fashionable, in, modish, stylish; last, latest; modernized, updated; futuristic, nontraditional

near ant anachronistic; aged, age-old, ancient, antediluvian, hoary, old, venerable; bygone, former, late, olden, past; antique, historic, historical; obsolete, outmoded, outworn; old-world; discarded, disused, moth-eaten; forgotten, remote; ageless, dateless, timeless

ant antiquated, archaic, dated, fusty, musty, noncontemporary, oldfangled, old-fashioned, old-time, out-of-date, passé

modern *n* a person with very modern ideas ⟨the leaders of the American suffragists were originally regarded by many people as uppity *moderns* who should have stayed in their place⟩

syn ultramodernist

rel leftist, liberal, progressive; extremist, radical; bohemian

near ant conservative, rightist, Tory; old hand, old-timer, veteran

ant antediluvian, dodo, fogy (*also* fogey), fossil, fuddy-duddy, reactionary, stick-in-the-mud

modernistic *adj* being or involving the latest methods, concepts, information, or styles — see MODERN

modest *adj* **1** being about midway between extremes of amount or size — see MIDDLE 2

2 free from any trace of the coarse or indecent — see CHASTE

3 not comfortable around people — see SHY 2

4 not having or showing any feelings of superiority, self-assertiveness, or showiness — see HUMBLE 1

modestly *adv* **1** in manner showing no signs of pride or self-assertion — see LOWLY

2 with purity of thought and deed — see PURELY

modesty *n* **1** the absence of any feelings of being better than others — see HUMILITY

2 the quality or state of being morally pure — see CHASTITY

modicum *n* the smallest amount or part imaginable — see JOT

modifiable *adj* capable of being readily changed — see FLEXIBLE 1

modification *n* the act, process, or result of making different — see CHANGE

modify *vb* **1** to limit the meaning of (as a noun) — see QUALIFY 1

2 to make different in some way — see CHANGE 1

modish *adj* **1** being in the latest or current fashion — see STYLISH

2 enjoying widespread favor or approval — see POPULAR 1

modishness *n* the state of enjoying widespread approval — see POPULARITY

mogul *n* a person of rank, power, or influence in a particular field — see MAGNATE

moiety *n* one of two equal or nearly equal parts — see HALF 1

moil *vb* to devote serious and sustained effort — see LABOR

moist *adj* slightly or moderately wet ⟨luckily, my new suede shoes are only a bit *moist* after I accidentally wore them in the rain⟩

syn damp, dank

rel dewy; clammy; humid, muggy, sticky; sultry, summery, sweltering, torrid, tropical; dripping, drenched, saturated, soaked, soaking, sodden, soggy, sopping, soppy, steeped, water-logged

near ant arid, dry, waterless; baked, burned, burnt, dehydrated, desert, droughty, dusty, parched, scorched, seared, sere

moisten *vb* to make or become slightly or moderately wet ⟨*moisten* the cloth before cleaning it with it⟩

syn dampen

rel drench, saturate, soak, steep; humidify; dip, immerge, immerse

near ant dehumidify, dehydrate, parch, scorch, sear

ant dry

moisture *n* the amount of water suspended in the air in tiny droplets ⟨dew is really just *moisture* from the air that condenses and collects when the temperature drops at night⟩

syn dampness, humidity

rel mugginess, stickiness, stuffiness; sultriness; clamminess, dankness, sogginess, wetness

near ant aridity, dehydration, dryness

mojo *n* **1** something worn or kept to bring good luck or keep away evil — see CHARM 1

2 the power to control natural forces through supernatural means — see MAGIC 1

molder *vb* to go through decomposition — see DECAY 1

molecule *n* a very small piece — see BIT 1

mollify *vb* **1** to lessen the anger or agitation of — see PACIFY

2 to make more bearable or less severe — see HELP 2

mollifying *adj* tending to lessen or avoid conflict or hostility — see PACIFIC 1

mollycoddle *n* a person without strength of character — see WEAKLING 2

mollycoddle *vb* to treat with great or excessive care — see BABY

molt *vb* to cast (a natural bodily covering or appendage) aside — see SHED 1

mom *n* a female human parent — see MOTHER

moment *n* **1** a particular point at which an event takes place — see OCCASION 1

2 the quality or state of being important — see IMPORTANCE

3 a very small space of time — see IN-STANT

4 the time currently existing or in progress — see PRESENT 1

momentarily *adv* at or within a short time — see SHORTLY 2

momentary *adj* lasting only for a short time ⟨the pain of the flu shot was only *momentary*⟩
syn ephemeral, evanescent, flash, fleeting, fugitive, impermanent, passing, short-lived, temporary, transient, transitory
rel brief, short; acting, interim
near ant lifelong
ant enduring, eternal, everlasting, lasting, long-lived, permanent, perpetual

momentous *adj* having great meaning or lasting effect — see IMPORTANT 1

momentum *n* something that arouses action or activity — see IMPULSE

momma *n* a female human parent — see MOTHER

monarch *n* one who rules over a people with a sole, supreme, and usually hereditary authority ⟨the ruling *monarch* of Britain at that time was Queen Elizabeth I⟩
syn autocrat, ruler, sovereign
rel czar (*also* tsar *or* tzar), emperor, empress, kaiser, king, lord, mogul, prince, queen, satrap, sultan; authoritarian, despot, dictator, overlord, potentate, tyrant; royalty

monarchal *or* **monarchial** *adj* fit for or worthy of a royal ruler — see MONARCHICAL

monarchical *also* **monarchic** *adj* fit for or worthy of a royal ruler ⟨guests who stay in the hotel's most expensive suite live in *monarchical* splendor⟩
syn kingly, monarchal (*or* monarchial), princely, queenly, regal, royal
rel aristocratic, baronial, imperial, lordly, noble, patrician

monastery *n* a residence for men under religious vows ⟨Gregory Mendel worked out his concepts of genetics by doing breeding experiments using pea plants in the *monastery's* garden⟩
syn abbey, cloister, friary, priory
rel house; convent, nunnery; lamasery

monetary *adj* of or relating to money, banking, or investments — see FINANCIAL

money *n* something (as pieces of stamped metal or printed paper) customarily and legally used as a medium of exchange, a measure of value, or a means of payment ⟨are you sure you have enough *money* to buy all that?⟩
syn bread [*slang*], cash, chips, currency, dough, gold, jack [*slang*], legal tender, lucre, pelf, tender, wampum [*slang*]
rel change, coinage, specie; paper money, scrip; banknote, cashier's check, check, draft, money order, note; bill, buck, dol-lar, greenback; bankroll, capital, finances, funds; mite, pittance; bundle, fortune, king's ransom, mint, wad; abundance, means, opulence, riches, treasure, wealth; resources, wherewithal; pin money, pocket money, spending money

moneyed *or* **monied** *adj* having goods, property, or money in abundance — see RICH 1

mongrel *adj* being offspring produced by parents of different races, breeds, species, or genera — see MIXED 1

mongrel *n* an offspring of parents with different genes especially when of different races, breeds, species, or genera — see HYBRID

monitor *vb* to pay continued close attention to (something) for a particular purpose ⟨police regularly *monitor* that road to record traffic density and catch speeders⟩
syn cover, watch
rel eye; behold, look, regard, see; gape, gawk, gaze, glare, goggle, peer, stare; glance, glimpse, peek, peep
phrases keep an eye on

monkey *n* an appealingly mischievous person — see SCAMP 1

monkey (around) *vb* **1** to engage in attention-getting playful or boisterous behavior — see CUT UP

2 to spend time in aimless activity — see FIDDLE (AROUND)

monkey (with) *vb* to handle thoughtlessly, ignorantly, or mischievously — see TAMPER

monkeying *n* wildly playful or mischievous behavior — see HORSEPLAY

monkeyshines *n pl* wildly playful or mischievous behavior — see HORSEPLAY

monochromatic *adj* having or consisting of a single color ⟨although marble and bronze sculptures are *monochromatic*, they can be amazingly lifelike⟩
syn solid
rel colored, colorful, pigmented; chromatic
near ant dappled (*also* dapple), marbled, shaded; mottled, piebald, pied, pinto; barred, brindled (*or* brindle); checkered, patterned, plaid, striped
ant motley, multicolored, polychromatic, varicolored, variegated

monopolize *vb* to have complete control over ⟨it is illegal in the United States to *monopolize* an entire industry or product⟩ ⟨you shouldn't *monopolize* that toy while your friends are waiting to play with it⟩
syn sew up
rel corner, hog; absorb, consume, engross; have, hold, own, possess; control, direct, govern, manage, reign (over), rule

monotonous *adj* causing weariness, restlessness, or lack of interest — see BORING

monotonousness *n* a tedious lack of variety — see MONOTONY

monotony *n* a tedious lack of variety ⟨the *monotony* of the cafeteria's selections was almost as bad as the quality⟩

---

syn synonym(s)   *rel* related words
ant antonym(s)   *near ant* near antonym(s)

syn monotonousness, sameness

rel uniformity; boredom, dullness (*also* dulness), ennui, restlessness, tediousness, tedium, tiresomeness, weariness, wearisomeness

near ant diversity, multiplicity, variety; variability, variation; absorption, engagement, engrossment, enthrallment, fascination, grip, interest, intrigue; animation, excitement, invigoration, stimulation

monster *adj* unusually large — see HUGE

monster *n* **1** a strange or horrible and often frightening creature ⟨both children insisted that their parents check under the bed for *monsters* every night⟩

syn monstrosity, ogre

rel ogre; bête noire, bogey (*also* bogy *or* bogie), bugaboo, bugbear; banshee, bogeyman, demon (*or* daemon), devil, fiend, fright, imp, incubus; horror; terror; abomination, anathema; abnormality, freak; mutant, mutation

2 a person, thing, or event that is not normal — see FREAK 1

3 a mean, evil, or unprincipled person — see VILLAIN 1

4 something that is unusually large and powerful — see GIANT

monstrosity *n* **1** a person, thing, or event that is not normal — see FREAK 1

2 a strange or horrible and often frightening creature — see MONSTER 1

3 something unpleasant to look at — see EYESORE

4 the quality of inspiring intense dread or dismay — see HORROR 1

5 the state or quality of being utterly evil — see ENORMITY 1

monstrous *adj* **1** badly or imperfectly formed — see MALFORMED

2 extremely disturbing or repellent — see HORRIBLE 1

3 unusually large — see HUGE

monstrously *adv* **1** beyond a normal or acceptable limit — see TOO 1

2 to a large extent or degree — see GREATLY 2

monthlies *n pl* an occurrence of menstruating — see PERIOD 1

monument *n* **1** a shaped stone laid over or erected near a grave and usually bearing an inscription to identify and preserve the memory of the deceased — see TOMBSTONE

2 something that serves to keep alive the memory of a person or event — see MEMORIAL

monumental *adj* **1** large and impressive in size, grandeur, extent, or conception — see GRAND 1

2 unusually large — see HUGE

mooch *vb* to move about from place to place aimlessly — see WANDER

mood *n* **1** a state of mind dominated by a particular emotion ⟨losing my favorite sweater left me in a bad *mood* for the rest of the day⟩

syn cheer, frame, humor, mode, spirit, temper

rel attitude, outlook, perspective, standpoint, viewpoint; emotion, feeling, heart, passion, sentiment; strain; belief, conviction, mind, opinion; expression, tone, vein; character, disposition, individuality, personality, temperament; responsiveness, sensibility, sensitiveness, sensitivity

2 a special quality or impression associated with something — see AURA

moody *adj* frequently influenced by moods and especially bad moods ⟨teenagers are often both *moody* and changeable⟩

syn temperamental

rel capricious, changeable, changeful, fickle, fluctuating, fluid, inconstant, mercurial, mutable, uncertain, unsettled, unstable, unsteady, variable, volatile, whimsical

near ant equable, even; changeless, constant, settled, stable, steady, unchanging

moonshine *n* **1** illegally produced liquor ⟨during Prohibition, *moonshine* and "bathtub gin" were made secretly⟩

syn bootleg

rel alcohol, booze, drink, grog, spirits

2 a fermented or distilled beverage that can make a person drunk — see ALCOHOL

3 unintelligible or meaningless talk — see GIBBERISH

moonstruck *adj* having or showing a very abnormal or sick state of mind — see INSANE 1

moor *vb* to put securely in place or in a desired position — see FASTEN 2

moot *adj* open to question or dispute — see DEBATABLE 1

moot *vb* **1** to present or bring forward for discussion — see INTRODUCE 2

2 to talk about (an issue) usually from various points of view and usually for the purpose of arriving at a decision or opinion — see DISCUSS

mope *vb* **1** to move about from place to place aimlessly — see WANDER

2 to silently go about in a bad mood — see SULK

mopes *n pl* a state or spell of low spirits — see SADNESS

moral *adj* **1** conforming to a high standard of morality or virtue — see GOOD 2

2 guided by or in accordance with one's sense of right and wrong — see CONSCIENTIOUS 1

moralist *n* a person who is greatly concerned with seemly behavior and morality especially regarding sexual matters — see PRUDE

morality *n* **1** conduct that conforms to an accepted standard of right and wrong ⟨the candidate claimed to be the best choice because of his unswerving *morality*⟩

syn character, decency, goodness, honesty, integrity, probity, rectitude, righteousness, uprightness, virtue, virtuousness

rel high-mindedness, honor, incorruptibility; appropriateness, correctness, decorousness, decorum, etiquette, fitness, propriety, seemliness; ethics, morals

near ant impropriety, indecency, indiscretion; debauchery, degeneracy, degradation, depravity, perversion; crookedness, dishonesty, underhandedness, unscrupulousness; lowness, meanness, viciousness, vileness; corruption, sin

ant badness, evil, immorality, wickedness

2 the code of good conduct for an individual or group — see ETHICS

morally *adv* with purity of thought and deed — see PURELY

morals *n pl* the code of good conduct for an individual or group — see ETHICS

morass *n* spongy land saturated or partially covered with water — see SWAMP

morbid *adj* causing or marked by an atmosphere lacking in cheer — see GLOOMY 1

mordant *adj* marked by the use of wit that is intended to cause hurt feelings — see SARCASTIC

more *adj* resulting in an increase in amount or number — see ADDITIONAL

more *adv* **1** in addition to what has been said ⟨the sci-fi movie was totally unbelievable and, what's *more*, it was boring⟩

syn additionally, again, also, besides, further, furthermore, likewise, moreover, then, too, withal, yet

phrases as well, in addition to, to boot

2 to a greater or higher extent ⟨the boxers for this bout are *more* evenly matched than the last two were⟩

syn better

more or less *adv* **1** very close to but not completely — see ALMOST

2 to some degree or extent — see FAIRLY

moreover *adv* in addition to what has been said — see MORE 1

mores *n pl* personal conduct or behavior as evaluated by an accepted standard of appropriateness for a social or professional setting — see MANNER 1

moribund *adj* nearly dead ⟨with its run-down look and empty aisles, the business appeared *moribund*⟩

syn dying

rel expiring, fading, passing away, sinking; decadent, declining, deteriorating; dead, deceased, defunct, departed, gone, passed away; terminal

near ant alive, animate, living; being, breathing, existing, subsisting, surviving; flourishing, prospering, thriving

morn *n* **1** the first appearance of light in the morning or the time of its appearance — see DAWN 1

2 the time from sunrise until noon — see MORNING 1

morning *n* **1** the time from sunrise until noon ⟨I hate getting up in the *morning* to go to school⟩

syn forenoon, morn

rel aurora, dawn, dawning, daybreak, daylight; cockcrow, sunrise, sunup; day, daytime, light

near ant dark, darkness, night, nighttime, twilight; dusk, evening, nightfall, sundown, sunset; afternoon

2 the first appearance of light in the morning or the time of its appearance — see DAWN 1

3 the point at which something begins — see BEGINNING

moron *n* a stupid person — see IDIOT

morose *adj* causing or marked by an atmosphere lacking in cheer — see GLOOMY 1

morsel *n* **1** a small piece or quantity of food ⟨I suppose you can have dessert, since you only left a couple *morsels* on your plate⟩

syn bite, mouthful, nibble, taste, tidbit (*also* titbit)

rel snack; appetizer, hors d'oeuvre; bit, chew, crumb, dab, driblet, hint, lick, nubbin, nugget, pinch, scrap, shred, smidgen (*also* smidgeon *or* smidgin), speck, spot, sprinkling, suspicion, touch, trace; dash, drop; gulp, swallow, swig

2 a very small piece — see BIT 1

mortal *adj* **1** likely to cause or capable of causing death — see DEADLY

2 of, relating to, or suggestive of death — see DEATHLY 1

3 relating to or characteristic of human beings — see HUMAN

mortal *n* a member of the human race — see HUMAN

mortally *adv* to a great degree — see VERY 1

mortician *n* a person who manages funerals and prepares the dead for burial or cremation — see FUNERAL DIRECTOR

mortification *n* the emotional state of being made self-consciously uncomfortable — see EMBARRASSMENT 1

mortify *vb* to throw into a state of self-conscious distress — see EMBARRASS 1

¹most *adv* to a great degree — see VERY 1

²most *adv* very close to but not completely — see ALMOST

most *adj* of the greatest or highest degree or quantity — see ULTIMATE 1

most *n* the greatest amount, number, or part ⟨this room will accommodate 50 people at the *most*⟩

syn maximum, outside

rel best, utmost

ant least, minimum

mostly *adv* for the most part — see CHIEFLY

mote *n* a very small piece — see BIT 1

moth–eaten *adj* **1** having passed its time of use or usefulness — see OBSOLETE

2 showing signs of advanced wear and tear and neglect — see SHABBY 1

3 used or heard so often as to be dull — see STALE

mother *n* a female human parent ⟨he dreaded telling his *mother* that her favorite figurine had gotten broken⟩

---

syn synonym(s)   **rel** related words
ant antonym(s)   **near ant** near antonym(s)

syn ma, mama, mammy, mom, momma, mum [*chiefly British*]

rel matriarch, matron

mother *vb* to attend to the needs and comforts of — see NURSE 1

motherland *n* the land of one's birth, residence, or citizenship — see COUNTRY 1

motherliness *n* motherly character or qualities — see MATERNITY

motherly *adj* of, relating to, or characteristic of a mother ⟨she showed a sweet *motherly* tenderness toward the tiny kitten she was taking care of⟩

syn maternal

rel parental; female, feminine, womanish, womanlike, womanly; matriarchal, matronly; caring, giving, nurturing

mother tongue *n* the stock of words, pronunciation, and grammar used by a people as their basic means of communication — see LANGUAGE 1

motif *n* 1 a major object of interest or concern (as in a discussion or artistic composition) — see MATTER 1

2 a unit of decoration that is repeated all over something (as a fabric) — see PATTERN 1

motion *n* the act or an instance of changing position — see MOVEMENT 1

motion *vb* to direct or notify by a movement or gesture ⟨the referee *motioned* the team captains to confer with him on the sideline⟩

syn beckon, flag, gesture, signal, wave

rel gesticulate, pantomime, sign; signalize; acquaint, advise, inform, relate, tell; flourish, shrug

motionlessly *adv* without motion — see STILL 1

motion picture *n* 1 a story told by means of a series of continuously projected pictures and a sound track — see MOVIE 1

2 motion pictures *pl* the art or business of making a movie — see MOVIE 2

motivation *n* something that arouses action or activity — see IMPULSE

motive *n* 1 a major object of interest or concern (as in a discussion or artistic composition) — see MATTER 1

2 a unit of decoration that is repeated all over something (as a fabric) — see PATTERN 1

3 something (as a belief) that serves as the basis for another thing — see REASON 2

motley *adj* 1 consisting of many things of different sorts — see MISCELLANEOUS

2 marked by a variety of usually vivid colors — see COLORFUL

motley *n* 1 a person formerly kept in a royal or noble household to amuse with jests and pranks — see FOOL 2

2 an unorganized collection or mixture of various things — see MISCELLANY 1

motor *n* 1 a device that changes energy into mechanical motion — see ENGINE

2 a self-propelled passenger vehicle on wheels — see CAR

motor *vb* to travel by a motorized vehicle — see DRIVE 2

motorboat *n* a boat equipped with a motor ⟨*motorboats* are banned on the lake because they are a hazard to swimmers⟩

syn powerboat, speedboat

rel cabin cruiser, cruiser, runabout

motorcade *n* a group of vehicles traveling together or under one management — see FLEET

motorcar *n* a self-propelled passenger vehicle on wheels — see CAR

motor home *n* a motor vehicle that is specially equipped for living while traveling — see CAMPER

motorist *n* a person who travels by automobile ⟨environmental organizations suggest that *motorists* get together and carpool to avoid using several cars and adding to pollution⟩

syn automobilist, driver

rel operator; chauffeur; carpooler

motor vehicle *n* a self-propelled passenger vehicle on wheels — see CAR

mottle *n* a small area that is different (as in color) from the main part — see SPOT 1

mottle *vb* to mark with small spots especially unevenly — see SPOT

mottled *adj* 1 having blotches of two or more colors — see PIED

2 marked with spots — see SPOTTED 1

mound *n* 1 a pile or ridge of granular matter (as sand or snow) — see ²BANK

2 a quantity of things thrown or stacked on one another — see ¹PILE 1

3 an area of high ground — see HEIGHT 4

mound *vb* 1 to form into a pile or ridge of earth ⟨he likes to sit on the beach and *mound* sand into sand castles⟩

syn bank, hill

rel heap, pile, pyramid, stack; embank; bunch, bundle, clump, lump, mass, wad; accumulate, amass, assemble, collect, gather, group

2 to lay or throw on top of one another — see PILE

¹**mount** *n* an elevation of land higher than a hill — see MOUNTAIN 1

²**mount** *n* something that holds up or serves as a foundation for something else — see SUPPORT 1

mount *vb* 1 to become greater in extent, volume, amount, or number — see INCREASE 2

2 to bring before the public in performance or exhibition — see PRESENT 1

3 to move or extend upward — see ASCEND

mountain *n* 1 an elevation of land higher than a hill ⟨my cousin likes to climb *mountains* just because she can⟩

syn alp, mount, peak

rel mountain range, seamount; mountaintop, pinnacle, precipice, summit

near ant basin, bowl, depression, hollow, vale, valley

2 a considerable amount — see LOT 2

3 a quantity of things thrown or stacked on one another — see ¹PILE 1

mountain lion *n* a large tawny cat of the wild — see COUGAR

mountainous *adj* unusually large — see HUGE

mountebank *n* one who makes false claims of identity or expertise — see IMPOSTOR

mounting *n* something that holds up or serves as a foundation for something else — see SUPPORT 1

mourn *vb* 1 to feel deep sadness or mental pain — see GRIEVE

2 to feel or express sorrow for — see LAMENT 1

mournful *adj* 1 expressing or suggesting mourning ⟨she had such a *mournful* expression that someone teasingly asked if her dog had died⟩

syn anguished, bemoaning, bewailing, deploring, doleful, dolorous, funeral, grieving, heartbroken, lamentable, lugubrious, plaintive, regretful, rueful, sorrowful, sorry, wailing, weeping, woeful

rel elegiac, melancholy; dejected, depressed, despondent, disconsolate, dispirited, downcast, downhearted, heartsick, inconsolable; careworn, sad, unhappy, woebegone; bawling, crying, groaning, howling, keening, moaning, yammering; bleeding, suffering; black, bleak, cheerless, comfortless, dark, darkening, desolate, dismal, dreary, funereal, gloomy, glum, gray (*also* grey), joyless, low, miserable, moody, morbid, morose, pathetic, pessimistic, piteous, saturnine, somber (*or* sombre), sullen, wretched

near ant delighted, exulting, glorying, happy, joyful, rejoicing, triumphant; bright, cheerful, cheering, cheery; laughing, smiling; blithe, blithesome, buoyant, gay, jocund, jolly, joyous, lighthearted, merry, mirthful; encouraging, hopeful, optimistic

2 feeling unhappiness — see SAD 1

mournfully *adv* with feelings of bitterness or grief — see HARD 2

mouse *vb* to move about in a sly or secret manner — see SNEAK 1

mousy *or* **mousey** *adj* easily frightened — see SHY 1

mouth *n* 1 the opening through which food passes into the body of an animal ⟨the baby chicks opened their *mouths* very wide and chirped piteously when their mother came back with worms⟩

syn kisser [*slang*], mug

rel countenance, face, puss [*slang*], visage; muzzle; jaws, mandible, maxilla; gullet, maw

2 a twisting of the facial features in disgust or disapproval — see GRIMACE

mouth *vb* to speak softly and unclearly — see MUMBLE

mouth (off) *vb* to talk as if giving an important and formal speech — see ORATE 1

mouthful *n* a small piece or quantity of food — see MORSEL 1

mouthpiece *n* a person who speaks for another or for a group — see SPOKESPERSON

movable *or* **moveable** *adj* capable of being moved especially with ease ⟨any furniture that is not *movable* will be covered with protective cloths by the painters⟩

syn mobile, portable

rel adjustable, flexible, modular; removable, transferable, transportable; motile, moving; unsteady, unstable; manageable

near ant motionless, moveless, static, stationary, still, stuck, unmoving, wedged; fast, fixed, rooted, steadfast

ant immobile, immovable, irremovable, unmovable

movables *or* **moveables** *n pl* 1 the movable articles in a room — see FURNITURE

2 transportable items that one owns — see POSSESSION 2

move *n* 1 an action planned or taken to achieve a desired result — see MEASURE 1

2 the act or an instance of changing position — see MOVEMENT 1

move *vb* 1 to change the place or position of ⟨I need you to *move* all your books off the chair before company gets here⟩

syn budge, dislocate, displace, disturb, remove, shift, transfer, transpose

rel bear, carry, convey, drive, haul, transmit, transport; transplant; replace, supersede, supplant; alter, make over, modify, redo, refashion, remake, remodel, revamp, revise, rework, vary

near ant fix, freeze, set, stabilize

2 to set or keep in motion ⟨the hands of the wall clock are *moved* by battery⟩

syn actuate, drive, impel, propel, work

rel activate, motivate, provoke; abet, ferment, foment, incite, raise, stir (up), whip (up); set off, trigger; excite, galvanize, inflame, inspire, motivate, rouse

near ant check, curb, inhibit, restrain

3 to change one's position ⟨don't *move* while I'm trying to draw your portrait⟩

syn budge, shift, stir

rel fidget, jiggle, squirm, twitch, wiggle, writhe; rouse

near ant remain, stay; stabilize

ant freeze

4 to act upon (a person or a person's feelings) so as to cause a response — see ¹AFFECT 1

5 to rouse to strong feeling or action — see PROVOKE 1

6 to cause (someone) to agree with a belief or course of action by using arguments or earnest requests — see PERSUADE

7 to cause to function — see ACTIVATE

8 to leave a place often for another — see GO 2

movement *n* 1 the act or an instance of changing position ⟨a sudden *movement* in the far corner of the room made her turn in that direction⟩

syn motion, move, shift, shifting, stir, stirring

rel dislocation, migration, relocation; locomotion, mobility, motility; fiddling, fidgeting, squirming, twitching, wriggling, writhing; flailing, flapping, waving

near ant immobility; inertia, inertness, stillness; ending, finish, halt, pause, stop, termination

ant motionlessness

2 a series of activities undertaken to achieve a goal — see CAMPAIGN

movie *n* **1** a story told by means of a series of continuously projected pictures and a sound track ⟨there was much excitement when it was announced that the popular children's book would be turned into a *movie*⟩

syn film, motion picture, moving picture, picture

rel animated cartoon, cartoon, docudrama, documentary, feature

2 movies *pl* the art or business of making a movie ⟨many a small-town girl has gone to Hollywood, dreaming of making it big in the *movies*⟩

syn cinema, film, motion pictures, pictures, screen

rel show business

moving *adj* having the power to affect the feelings or sympathies ⟨he gave a truly *moving* graduation speech that had some graduates in tears⟩

syn affecting, emotional, impressive, poignant, stirring, touching

rel eloquent, expressive, meaningful, significant; demonstrative, excitable, feeling, passionate, responsive, sensitive; exciting, provoking, rousing, stimulating; dramatic, histrionic, melodramatic, theatrical

near ant cold, cool, detached, dispassionate; deadpan

ant unemotional, unimpressive

moving picture *n* a story told by means of a series of continuously projected pictures and a sound track — see MOVIE 1

mow *vb* **1** to shorten the standing leafy plant cover of ⟨you really should *mow* the lawn before it gets much higher⟩

syn cut

rel clip, crop, dock, lop, manicure, pare, prune, trim; shave, shear

2 to bring down by cutting — see FELL 2

mow (down) *vb* to kill on a large scale — see MASSACRE

much *adv* **1** to a great degree — see VERY 1

2 to a large extent or degree — see GREATLY 2

3 very close to but not completely — see ALMOST

much *n* a considerable amount — see LOT 1

muck *n* **1** foul matter that mars the purity or cleanliness of something — see FILTH 1

2 soft wet earth — see MUD

mucky *adj* **1** full of or covered with soft wet earth — see MUDDY 1

2 not clean — see DIRTY 1

mud *n* soft wet earth ⟨we cannot play softball today because the field turned to *mud* after last night's heavy rain⟩

syn mire, muck, ooze, slime, slop, sludge, slush

rel gumbo, silt; clay, dirt, gravel, humus, loam, sand, soil

muddle *n* **1** a state in which everything is out of order — see CHAOS

2 a state of mental confusion — see HAZE 2

3 a state of mental uncertainty — see CONFUSION 1

4 an unorganized collection or mixture of various things — see MISCELLANY 1

muddle *vb* **1** to throw into a state of mental uncertainty — see CONFUSE 1

2 to undo the proper order or arrangement of — see DISORDER

muddled *adj* lacking in order, neatness, and often cleanliness — see MESSY

muddy *adj* **1** full of or covered with soft wet earth ⟨please do not walk in the house with *muddy* boots on, as you will get the carpet dirty⟩

syn miry, mucky, oozy, slimy, sludgy, slushy

rel clayey, loamy, silty; bedraggled; dirty, filthy, foul, grimy, grubby, grungy, impure, squalid, unclean, uncleanly

near ant clean, cleanly, immaculate, spotless, unsoiled, unsullied

2 having visible particles in liquid suspension — see CLOUDY 1

3 not clean — see DIRTY 1

muddy *vb* **1** to throw into a state of mental uncertainty — see CONFUSE 1

2 to make (something) unclear to the understanding — see CONFUSE 2

3 to make dirty — see DIRTY

muff *vb* to make or do (something) in a clumsy or unskillful way — see BOTCH

muffle *vb* to deaden the sound of ⟨the walls *muffled* their conversation so that only a low murmur was heard⟩

syn mute

rel insulate, soundproof; dampen, mellow, soften, subdue, tone (down); baffle; smother

near ant amplify, enhance, heighten, increase, magnify, strengthen

mug *n* **1** a round vessel equipped with a handle and designed for drinking — see CUP

2 a violent, brutal person who is often a member of an organized gang — see HOODLUM

3 the front part of the head — see FACE 1

4 the opening through which food passes into the body of an animal — see MOUTH 1

mug *vb* **1** to distort one's face ⟨every time their picture was snapped, both children *mugged* by sticking out their tongues or scrunching up their faces⟩

syn grimace

rel pout; contort, deform, twist, warp; frown, glare, gloom, glower, lower (*also* lour), scowl; gape, gaze, ogle, stare; growl, snarl, sneer; simper, smirk *phrases* make faces

near ant beam, grin, smile

2 to take a photograph of — see PHOTOGRAPH

muggy *adj* containing or characterized by an uncomfortable amount of moisture — see HUMID

mulct *n* a sum of money to be paid as a punishment — see FINE

mulct *vb* to rob by the use of trickery or threats — see FLEECE

mulish *adj* sticking to an opinion, purpose, or course of action in spite of reason, arguments, or persuasion — see OBSTINATE

mulishness *n* a steadfast adherence to an opinion, purpose, or course of action — see OBSTINACY

mull (over) *vb* to give serious and careful thought to — see PONDER

multicolored *adj* marked by a variety of usually vivid colors — see COLORFUL

multifarious *adj* being of many and various kinds — see MANIFOLD

multiple *adj* being of a large but indefinite number — see MANY

multiplex *adj* being of a large but indefinite number — see MANY

multiplication *n* the act or process of becoming greater in number ⟨there's been a steady *multiplication* in our attic of old video equipment since the revolution in consumer electronics⟩

syn accumulating, accumulation, addition, increase, proliferation

rel doubling, quadrupling, tripling; growth, rise, spread; enlargement, escalation, expansion; amplification, distention, inflation; accretion, accrual, augmentation; extension, lengthening

near ant compressing, compression, condensation, condensing, constricting, constriction, contracting, contraction, diminishing, diminishment, lessening, lowering, shrinking; retrenching, retrenchment, shortening

ant decrease

multiply *vb* **1** to bring forth offspring — see PROCREATE

2 to make greater in size, amount, or number — see INCREASE 1

3 to become greater in extent, volume, amount, or number — see INCREASE 2

multitude *n* a great number of persons or things gathered together — see CROWD 1

multitudinous *adj* being of a large but indefinite number — see MANY

mum *n, chiefly British* a female human parent — see MOTHER

mum *adj* deliberately refraining from speech — see SILENT 1

mumble *n* speech that is not clear enough to be understood ⟨please answer the question without your usual *mumble* and try to use complete sentences⟩

syn grunt, grunting, murmur, murmuring, mutter, muttering

rel undertone, whisper; babble, babbling, blab, blabbing, chatter, chattering, drivel, driveling (*or* drivelling), gabble, gabbling, jabber, jabbering, maundering, prattle, prattling, rambling

mumble *vb* to speak softly and unclearly ⟨I can't understand you if you *mumble*⟩

syn grunt, mouth, murmur, mutter

rel babble, blab, chatter, drivel, gabble, gibber, jabber, maunder, prattle, ramble; breathe, gasp, pant, whisper

near ant articulate, enunciate

ant speak out, speak up

mumbo jumbo *n* unintelligible or meaningless talk — see GIBBERISH

mummer *n* **1** an actor in a story performed silently and entirely by body movements — see MIME

2 one who acts professionally (as in a play, movie, or television show) — see ACTOR

mundane *adj* **1** having to do with the practical details of regular life ⟨they didn't want to be bothered with *mundane* concerns like doing the dishes while on vacation⟩

syn everyday, prosaic, workaday

rel earthly, temporal, worldly; average, common, commonplace, customary, familiar, garden, normal, ordinary, plain, popular, routine, run-of-the-mill, typical, unexceptional, unremarkable, usual; frequent, habitual, regular; expected, predictable

near ant high-minded, lofty, noble, sublime; aberrant, abnormal, atypical; exceptional, extraordinary, odd, peculiar, phenomenal, rare, singular, special, uncommon, uncustomary, unique, unusual, unwonted; bizarre, curious, funny, odd, outlandish, quaint, remarkable, strange, weird

2 having to do with life on earth especially as opposed to that in heaven — see EARTHLY

municipality *n* a thickly settled, highly populated area — see CITY

munificent *adj* giving or sharing in abundance and without hesitation — see GENEROUS 1

munificently *adv* in a generous manner — see WELL 2

murder *n* **1** a situation or state that causes great suffering and unhappiness — see HELL 2

2 the intentional and unlawful taking of another person's life — see HOMICIDE

murder *vb* **1** to put to death deliberately ⟨those people made me so mad I felt like I wanted to *murder* them⟩

syn dispatch, do in, execute, liquidate, slay

rel blot out, destroy, fell, kill, smite, zap; assassinate; butcher, massacre, mow (down), slaughter; annihilate, eliminate, eradicate, exterminate, wipe out

phrases do away with

2 to make or do (something) in a clumsy or unskillful way — see BOTCH

murderer *n* a person who kills another person — see ASSASSIN

murdering *adj* eager for or marked by the shedding of blood, extreme violence, or killing — see BLOODTHIRSTY

murderous *adj* **1** difficult to endure — see HARSH 1

2 requiring considerable physical or mental effort — see HARD 2

3 likely to cause or capable of causing death — see DEADLY

4 eager for or marked by the shedding of blood, extreme violence, or killing — see BLOODTHIRSTY

murk *n* **1** a time or place of little or no light — see DARK 1

2 an atmospheric condition in which suspended particles in the air rob it of its transparency — see HAZE 1

murkiness *n* the quality or state of having a veiled or uncertain meaning — see OBSCURITY 1

murky *adj* **1** being without light or without much light — see DARK 1

2 causing or marked by an atmosphere lacking in cheer — see GLOOMY 1

3 filled with or dimmed by fine particles (as of dust or water) in suspension — see HAZY 1

4 having an often intentionally veiled or uncertain meaning — see OBSCURE 1

5 not seen or understood clearly — see FAINT 1

murmur *n* **1** an expression of dissatisfaction, pain, or resentment — see COMPLAINT 1

2 speech that is not clear enough to be understood — see MUMBLE

murmur *vb* **1** to express dissatisfaction, pain, or resentment usually tiresomely — see COMPLAIN

2 to speak softly and unclearly — see MUMBLE

murmurer *n* an irritable and complaining person — see GROUCH

murmuring *n* speech that is not clear enough to be understood — see MUMBLE

muscle *n* **1** muscular strength ⟨I'm going to need someone with real *muscle* to help me move all this furniture⟩
syn brawn, main
rel force, might, potency, power, puissance, sinew
near ant impotence, weakness

2 the ability to exert effort for the accomplishment of a task — see POWER 2

muscle *vb* **1** to cause (a person) to give in to pressure — see FORCE

2 to force one's way — see PRESS 4

muscular *adj* **1** marked by a well-developed musculature ⟨Olympic runners tend to have very *muscular* legs⟩
syn brawny, sinewy
rel wiry; powerful, strong; beefy, burly, hefty, hulking, husky; able-bodied, athletic, herculean, mighty, robust, rugged, stalwart, strapping, sturdy
near ant nonathletic; delicate, feeble, fragile, frail, weak, weakly, wimpy; light, lightweight, slight; lean, slender, slim, svelte, sylphlike, thin, willowy; emaciated, gaunt, lank, rawboned, spare

ant scrawny, skinny

2 having muscles capable of exerting great physical force — see STRONG 1

museum *n* a building or part of a building in which objects of interest are displayed ⟨we're taking a trip to the *Museum* of Natural History as a special treat for science class⟩
syn gallery, salon
rel archives, collection, library; display, exhibition; studio

mush *n* **1** something (as a work of literature or music) that is too sentimental — see CORN

2 the state or quality of having an excess of tender feelings (as of love, nostalgia, or compassion) — see SENTIMENTALITY

mushroom *vb* to become greater in extent, volume, amount, or number — see INCREASE 2

mushy *adj* **1** appealing to the emotions in an obvious and tiresome way — see CORNY

2 giving easily to the touch — see SOFT 3

musical *adj* **1** having a pleasantly flowing quality suggestive of music — see LYRIC 1

2 having a pleasing mixture of notes — see HARMONIOUS 1

musicale *n* an entertainment featuring singing or the playing of musical instruments — see CONCERT

musician *n* **1** a person who plays a musical instrument ⟨the violinist was a famous and exquisitely talented *musician*⟩
syn instrumentalist, player
rel artist, performer; maestro, virtuoso; accompanist, recitalist, soloist; accordionist, bassoonist, clarinetist (*or* clarinettist), cornetist (*or* cornettist), drummer, fiddler, flautist, flutist, guitarist, harpist, oboist, organ-grinder, organist, percussionist, pianist, piper, saxophonist, trombonist, trumpeter, violinist

2 a person who writes musical compositions — see COMPOSER

muskeg *n* spongy land saturated or partially covered with water — see SWAMP

muss *vb* to undo the proper order or arrangement of — see DISORDER

mussed *adj* lacking in order, neatness, and often cleanliness — see MESSY

mussy *adj* lacking in order, neatness, and often cleanliness — see MESSY

must *n* something necessary, indispensable, or unavoidable — see ESSENTIAL 1

must *vb* to be under necessity or obligation to — see NEED 2

muster *n* a body of people come together in one place — see GATHERING 1

muster *vb* **1** to assemble and make ready for action — see MOBILIZE

2 to bring together in assembly by or as if by command — see CONVOKE

muster out *vb* to let go from office, service, or employment — see DISMISS 1

musty *adj* **1** having an unpleasant smell — see MALODOROUS

2 used or heard so often as to be dull — see STALE

mutable *adj* likely to change frequently, suddenly, or unexpectedly — see FICKLE 1

mutate *vb* to pass from one form, state, or level to another — see CHANGE 2

mute *adj* 1 unable to speak ⟨the child is both deaf and *mute* because her hearing was lost at birth⟩

  syn inarticulate, speechless, voiceless

  rel tongue-tied; incoherent, incomprehensible; closemouthed, laconic, taciturn, tight-lipped, uncommunicative; mum, nonspeaking, quiet, silent, wordless

  near ant communicative, gabby, garrulous, loquacious, talkative, talky, vocal; expatiating, speaking out, speaking up; articulating, speaking, talking; articulate, eloquent, fluent, voluble

  2 deliberately refraining from speech — see SILENT 1

mute *n* a device on a musical instrument that deadens or softens its tone ⟨I got in trouble for practicing my trumpet at three in the morning when the *mute* fell out, and I woke everyone up⟩ .

  syn damper

  rel muffler, quieter, softener

mute *vb* 1 to stop the noise or speech of — see SILENCE 1

  2 to deaden the sound of — see MUFFLE

muted *adj* 1 mostly or entirely without sound — see SILENT 3

  2 not excessively showy — see QUIET 2

muteness *n* incapacity for or restraint from speaking — see SILENCE 1

mutilate *vb* to cause severe or permanent injury to — see MAIM

mutineer *n* a person who rises up against authority — see REBEL

mutinous *adj* taking part in a rebellion — see REBELLIOUS 1

mutiny *n* open fighting against authority (as one's own government) — see REBELLION

mutiny *vb* to rise up against established authority — see REBEL

mutter *n* speech that is not clear enough to be understood — see MUMBLE

mutter *vb* 1 to express dissatisfaction, pain, or resentment usually tiresomely — see COMPLAIN

  2 to speak softly and unclearly — see MUMBLE

mutterer *n* an irritable and complaining person — see GROUCH

muttering *n* speech that is not clear enough to be understood — see MUMBLE

mutual *adj* used or done by a number of people as a group — see COLLECTIVE

myopic *adj* 1 able to see near things more clearly than distant ones — see NEARSIGHTED

  2 not thinking about and providing for the future — see IMPROVIDENT

myriad *adj* being of many and various kinds — see MANIFOLD

---

mysterious *adj* 1 being beyond one's powers to know, understand, or explain ⟨the huge stone statues on Easter Island are ancient, *mysterious*, and haunting⟩

  syn cryptic, darkling, deep, enigmatic (*also* enigmatical), impenetrable, inscrutable, mystic, occult, uncanny

  rel dark, murky, obscure, shadowy, vague; ambiguous, equivocal; incomprehensible, unfathomable, unintelligible; inexplicable, unaccountable, unexplainable; unanswerable, unknowable; metaphysical, mystical, supernatural; abstruse, esoteric, recondite; baffling, bewildering, confounding, confusing, mystifying, perplexing, puzzling

  near ant fathomable, intelligible, understandable; clear, obvious, open-and-shut, plain, straightforward, transparent

  2 having an often intentionally veiled or uncertain meaning — see OBSCURE 1

mystery *n* something hard to understand or explain ⟨why my sister dyed her hair bright blue is still a *mystery* to my parents⟩

  syn conundrum, enigma, mystification, puzzle, puzzlement, riddle, secret

  rel brainteaser, challenge, perplexity, poser, problem, stumper

mystic *adj* 1 having seemingly supernatural qualities or powers ⟨the notion that a cat has nine lives is based upon the belief that nine is a *mystic* number⟩

  syn magic, magical, occult, weird

  rel bewitched, enchanted, spellbound; bewitching, charming, conjuring, enchanting, wiling; awesome, extraordinary, marvelous (*or* marvellous), wondrous; divining, forecasting, foreknowing, fore-seeing, foretelling, fortune-telling, pre-dicting, presaging, prognosticating, prophesying, soothsaying

  near ant commonplace, ordinary, unremarkable

  2 being beyond one's powers to know, understand, or explain — see MYSTERIOUS 1

  3 having an often intentionally veiled or uncertain meaning — see OBSCURE 1

mystification *n* 1 a state of mental uncertainty — see CONFUSION 1

  2 something hard to understand and explain — see MYSTERY

mystify *vb* to throw into a state of mental uncertainty — see CONFUSE 1

myth *n* 1 a traditional but unfounded story that gives the reason for a current custom, belief, or fact of nature ⟨according to an ancient Greek *myth*, humans acquired fire from a giant who had stolen it from heaven⟩

  syn fable, legend

  rel allegory, parable; fabrication, fantasy (*also* phantasy), fiction, figment, invention; narrative, saga, story, tale, yarn

  2 the body of customs, beliefs, stories, and sayings associated with a people, thing, or place — see FOLKLORE

  3 a false idea or belief — see FALLACY 1

mythical *or* **mythic** *adj* 1 based on, described in, or being a myth ⟨for years the

Spanish conquistadors searched for the *mythical* El Dorado, a place of unimaginable riches⟩

syn fabled, fabulous, legendary

rel famed, romanticized, storied; fabricated, fantastic, fantastical, fictional, fictitious; fanciful; allegorical, mythological

near ant actual, real; historical; factual, true

2 not real and existing only in the imagination — see IMAGINARY

mythology *n* the body of customs, beliefs, stories, and sayings associated with a people, thing, or place — see FOLKLORE

nab *vb* **1** to take or keep under one's control by authority of law — see ARREST 1

2 to take physical control or possession of (something) suddenly or forcibly — see CATCH 1

nag *n* a large hoofed domestic animal that is used for carrying or drawing loads and for riding — see HORSE

nag *vb* to subject (someone) to constant scoldings and sharp reminders ⟨she kept *nagging* him to fix the furnace before the weather got any colder⟩

syn henpeck, hound, needle

rel carp (at), fuss (about *or* over), nitpick; annoy, badger, bait, bother, bug, chivy, harass, harry, hassle, irk, pester, plague, ride, vex, yap (at); egg, goad, incite, prod, prompt, spur, urge; exhort, insist, press, pressure, push; blandish, cajole, coax, wheedle; beg, importune, plead

near ant compliment; commend, laud, praise, recommend, tout; acclaim, applaud, eulogize, extol (*also* extoll)

naiad *n* **1** a mythical goddess represented as a young girl and said to live outdoors — see NYMPH 1

2 a young wingless often wormlike form (as a grub or caterpillar) that hatches from the egg of many insects — see LARVA

nail *vb* to take physical control or possession of (something) suddenly or forcibly — see CATCH 1

naive *or* **naïve** *adj* **1** lacking in worldly wisdom or informed judgment ⟨a first-time buyer who was so *naive* that he believed the salesman and paid good money for the rusty and broken-down car⟩

syn green, ingenuous, innocent, simple, simpleminded, uncritical, unknowing, unsophisticated, unsuspecting, unsuspicious, unwary, unworldly, wide-eyed

rel callow, dewy, inexperienced, raw; childlike, idealistic, impractical; believing, credulous, gullible, susceptible, trustful, trusting, unguarded; beguiled, duped, gulled, tricked; careless, heedless

near ant critical, doubting, incredulous, skeptical, suspecting, suspicious, unconvinced; careful, cautious, guarded, leery, wary, watchful; down-to-earth, hardheaded, pragmatic (*also* pragmatical), realistic, sober

ant cynical, experienced, knowing, sophisticated, worldly, worldly-wise

2 free from any intent to deceive or impress others — see GUILELESS

3 readily taken advantage of — see EASY 2

naively *adv* without any attempt to impress by deception or exaggeration — see NATURALLY 3

naïveté *also* **naivete** *n* **1** the quality or state of being simple and sincere ⟨her *naïveté* led her to leave her new bike outside the mall unchained while she shopped⟩

syn artlessness, greenness, guilelessness, ingenuousness, innocence, naturalness, simpleness, simplicity, unsophistication, unworldliness

rel candor, frankness, genuineness, honesty, openness, sincerity, straightforwardness; callowness, childishness, inexperience, rawness; carelessness, heedlessness; ignorance, obliviousness, unawareness; credulity, credulousness, gullibility; idealism, impracticality, optimism

near ant affectedness, artificiality, pretentiousness; deviousness, dishonesty, insincerity; disbelief, doubtfulness, incredulity, suspiciousness; carefulness, caution, wariness; pessimism, skepticism; maturity

ant artfulness, cynicism, sophistication, worldliness

2 readiness to believe the claims of others without sufficient evidence — see CREDULITY

naked *adj* **1** lacking or shed of clothing ⟨had recurrent nightmares about being *naked* in public⟩

syn bare, disrobed, nude, stripped, unclad, unclothed, undressed

rel denuded, peeled; raw, stark; unveiled

near ant covered, veiled; arrayed, caparisoned, decked (out), rigged (out), tricked (out); vested; decent

ant appareled (*or* apparelled), attired, clad, clothed, dressed, garbed, invested, robed; suited

2 lacking a usual or natural covering ⟨the winter trees were *naked* without their colorful fall leaves⟩

syn bald, bare, denuded, exposed, open, peeled, stripped, uncovered *rel* displayed, revealed; hairless, shaven; disrobed, unclad, unclothed, undressed; skinned; divested; unprotected, unsheltered

near ant mantled; overgrown, overrun, overspread; bearded, hairy

ant covered

3 free from all additions or embellishment — see PLAIN 1

name *adj* having a good reputation especially in a field of knowledge — see RESPECTABLE 1

name *n* **1** a word or combination of words by which a person or thing is regularly known ⟨introduced himself and then asked what my *name* was⟩

syn appellation, cognomen, denomination, denotation, designation, handle, title

rel christian name, forename, given name; family name, maiden name, surname; epithet, nickname, sobriquet (*also* soubriquet); alias, nom de plume, pen name, pseudonym; binomial, vernacular; misnomer; label, trademark

2 an act or expression showing scorn and usually intended to hurt another's feelings — see INSULT

3 outward and often deceptive indication — see APPEARANCE 2

4 overall quality as seen or judged by people in general — see REPUTATION

name *vb* **1** to give a name to ⟨decided to *name* her new puppy "Bubbles"⟩

syn baptize, call, christen, denominate, designate, dub, entitle, label, style, term, title

rel denote, specify; miscall, misname; nickname; rename

2 to make reference to or speak about briefly but specifically — see MENTION 1

3 to pick (someone) by one's authority for a specific position or duty — see APPOINT 2

4 to decide to accept (someone or something) from a group of possibilities — see CHOOSE 1

5 to decide upon (the time or date for an event) usually from a position of authority — see APPOINT 1

nameless *adj* **1** not named or identified by a name ⟨the victim of the crime will remain *nameless* to protect his privacy⟩ ⟨*nameless* editors who write TV listings in the newspaper⟩

syn anonymous, incognito, unbaptized, unchristened, unidentified, unnamed, untitled

rel unspecified; obscure, uncelebrated, unheard-of, unknown, unnoted, unremarkable

near ant denominated, designated, specified; labeled (*or* labelled), tabbed, titled; celebrated, famed, famous, known, notable, noted, noteworthy, remarkable, renowned, well-known

ant baptized, christened, dubbed, named, termed

2 beyond the power to describe — see INDESCRIBABLE

3 not widely known — see OBSCURE 2

namer *n* someone with the right or responsibility for making a selection — see SELECTOR

¹nap *n* a short sleep ⟨so tired that she needed to take a refreshing *nap* before soccer practice⟩

syn catnap, doze, drowse, forty winks, siesta, snooze, wink

rel repose, rest; slumber; bed

²nap *n* a soft airy substance or covering — see FUZZ

nap *vb* **1** to sleep lightly or briefly ⟨decided to let the kids *nap* for a few more minutes before waking them⟩

syn catnap, doze, drowse, slumber, snooze

rel relax, repose, rest; couch, lay, lie, roost; lull

near ant arise, arouse, awake, awaken, get up, rise, rouse, uprise, wake (up), waken

2 be in a state of sleep — see SLEEP 1

napping *adj* being in a state of suspended consciousness — see ASLEEP 1

napping *n* a natural periodic loss of consciousness during which the body restores itself — see SLEEP 1

narcotic *adj* **1** tending to calm the emotions and relieve stress — see SOOTHING 1

2 tending to cause sleep — see HYPNOTIC

narrate *vb* to give an oral or written account of in some detail — see TELL 1

narrative *n* **1** a relating of events usually in the order in which they happened — see ACCOUNT 1

2 a work with imaginary characters and events that is shorter and usually less complex than a novel — see STORY 1

narrow *adj* **1** being of less than usual width ⟨found a *narrow* opening in the fence that he was able to squeeze through⟩

syn fine, hairline, needlelike, skinny, slender, slim, thin

rel attenuated, elongated, linear; close, compressed, condensed, constricted, contracted, squeezed, tight, tightened; reedy, stalky, stringy, twiggy, wispy; spare

near ant chunky, squat, stocky, stumpy, thick, thickset; bulky, massive

ant broad, fat, wide

2 not broad or open in views or opinions ⟨a *narrow* person who thought that anyone who owned a television was morally corrupt⟩

syn insular, little, parochial, petty, provincial, sectarian, small, small-minded

rel inflexible, obdurate, obstinate, rigid, set, stubborn, unyielding, wrongheaded; bigoted, intolerant, narrow-minded; biased, discriminating, discriminatory, jaundiced, one-sided, partial, partisan, prejudiced; old-fashioned, reactionary, stodgy, straitlaced (*or* straightlaced); dogmatic, opinionated; limited

near ant impartial, nonpartisan, objective, unbiased, unprejudiced

---

syn synonym(s)   **rel** related words
ant antonym(s)   **near ant** near antonym(s)

ant broad-minded, catholic, cosmopolitan, liberal, open, open-minded, receptive, tolerant

3 having distinct or certain limits — see LIMITED 1

4 showing little difference in the standing of the competitors — see CLOSE 3

5 unwilling to grant other people social rights or to accept other viewpoints — see INTOLERANT 2

narrow-minded *adj* unwilling to grant other people social rights or to accept other viewpoints — see INTOLERANT 2

narrows *n pl* a narrow body of water between two land masses — see CHANNEL 2

nastily *adv* in a mean or spiteful manner ⟨he *nastily* stuck his foot out and tripped the front runner because he couldn't stand to see her win⟩

syn cattily, despitefully, hatefully, malevolently, maliciously, malignantly, meanly, spitefully, viciously, villainously, virulently, wickedly

rel contemptuously, deprecatingly, disdainfully, scornfully; acrimoniously, antagonistically, caustically, hostilely, invidiously, obnoxiously, rancorously, venomously; bitterly, enviously, jealously, resentfully; balefully, callously, cruelly, hardheartedly, heartlessly, inhumanely, mercilessly, pitilessly, ruthlessly, soullessly, unfeelingly; disagreeably, ill, ungraciously, unkindly; ill-naturedly, inconsiderately, insensitively, thoughtlessly; diabolically, fiendishly; misanthropically

near ant affably, agreeably, amiably, cordially, genially, good-humoredly, good-naturedly, graciously, nicely, pleasantly; altruistically, humanely; considerately, feelingly, lovingly, mercifully, sensitively, softheartedly, solicitously, soulfully, thoughtfully; compassionately, sympathetically; angelically, divinely, sweetly, tenderly

ant benevolently, benignantly, goodheartedly, kindheartedly, kindly

nastiness *n* **1** the desire to cause pain for the satisfaction of doing harm — see MALICE

2 the quality or state of being obscene — see OBSCENITY 1

3 the state or quality of being dirty — see DIRTINESS 1

nasty *adj* **1** arousing or deserving of one's loathing and disgust — see CONTEMPTIBLE 1

2 causing intense displeasure, disgust, or resentment — see OFFENSIVE 1

3 causing or feeling bodily pain — see PAINFUL 1

4 depicting or referring to sexual matters in a way that is unacceptable in polite society — see OBSCENE 1

5 having or showing a desire to cause someone pain or suffering for the sheer enjoyment of it — see HATEFUL

6 marked by wet and windy conditions — see FOUL 1

7 not clean — see DIRTY 1

8 not giving pleasure to the mind or senses — see UNPLEASANT

nation *n* a body of people composed of one or more nationalities usually with its own territory and government ⟨the American people became one *nation* when they adopted the Constitution in 1789⟩

syn commonwealth, country, land, sovereignty, state

rel city-state; domain, dominion, empire, kingdom, realm, republic; duchy, dukedom, principality, seigniory (*or* seignory), sultanate; democracy, dictatorship, monarchy, oligarchy, sovereign, theocracy; colony, dependency, province, settlement, soil; fatherland, homeland, motherland; power, superpower

national *adj* of or relating to a nation ⟨played the home team's *national* anthem before the start of the soccer game⟩

syn civil, public, state

rel civic, federal, municipal; government, governmental; domestic, internal; democratic, republican; nationwide

near ant global, international; alien, external, foreign

ant nonnational

national *n* a person who owes allegiance to a government and is protected by it — see CITIZEN 1

nationalism *n* **1** excessive favoritism towards one's own country — see CHAUVINISM

2 love and support for one's country — see PATRIOTISM

nationalist *adj* having or showing love and support for one's country — see PATRIOTIC

nationalist *n* one who shows excessive favoritism towards his or her country ⟨a staunch *nationalist* who favored any policy that would give the country more power in the international arena⟩

syn chauvinist, jingo

rel loyalist, patriot; hawk, warmonger

near ant internationalist; neutralist

nationalistic *adj* having or showing love and support for one's country — see PATRIOTIC

native *adj* **1** belonging to a particular place by birth or origin ⟨though she now lived in the Northeast, she was a *native* Midwesterner⟩

syn aboriginal, born, endemic, indigenous

rel domestic, local; original

near ant imported, introduced, transplanted; alien, exotic, foreign, strange; expatriate, immigrant

ant nonnative

2 being such as found in nature and not altered by processing or refining — see CRUDE 1

Native American *n* a member of any of the native peoples of the western hemisphere usually not including the Eskimos — see AMERICAN INDIAN

nativity *n* the act or instance of being born — see BIRTH 1

nattily *adv* in a strikingly neat and trim manner — see SMARTLY

natty *adj* being strikingly neat and trim in style or appearance — see SMART 1

natural *adj* **1** being such from birth or by nature ⟨from his first visits to the wading pool, we could tell he loved water and was a *natural* swimmer⟩
syn born, congenital
rel chronic, confirmed, habitual, ingrained, inveterate, proper, regular; constitutional, consummate; elemental, elementary, essential, hereditary, inborn, inherent, innate, intimate, intrinsic, native; instinctual, intuitive
near ant cultivated, developed, trained; alien, foreign, unnatural
ant nonnatural
2 closely resembling the object imitated ⟨the display of stuffed birds and plastic plants actually looked very *natural*⟩
syn lifelike, near, realistic
rel alike, like, living, matching; akin, analogous, approximate, comparable, resembling; accurate, close, faithful, true; convincing
near ant dissimilar, off, unalike, unlike; incomparable, unmatched; contrasted, contrasting, different, disparate; fake, mock, phony (*also* phoney), sham
ant nonnatural, nonrealistic, unrealistic
3 being a part of the innermost nature of a person or thing — see INHERENT
4 being such as found in nature and not altered by processing or refining — see CRUDE 1
5 existing without human habitation or cultivation — see WILD 2
6 free from any intent to deceive or impress others — see GUILELESS
7 relating to or characteristic of human beings — see HUMAN

naturally *adv* **1** by natural character or ability ⟨tour guides who are *naturally* outgoing and can easily approach and converse with strangers⟩
syn constitutionally, inherently, innately, intrinsically
rel elementally, essentially, fundamentally; instinctively, intuitively; intimately
near ant artificially, unnaturally
2 according to the usual course of things ⟨we *naturally* like to be as comfortable as possible⟩
syn commonly, generally, normally, ordinarily, typically, usually
rel customarily, habitually, regularly, routinely; familiarly; conventionally, traditionally
phrases of course
near ant oddly, peculiarly, queerly, strangely; anomalously, irregularly; radically
ant abnormally, atypically, extraordinarily, uncommonly, unusually
3 without any attempt to impress by deception or exaggeration ⟨he tried to act

naturally around the girl he had a crush on⟩
syn artlessly, guilelessly, ingenuously, innocently, naively, sincerely, unaffectedly, unfeignedly, unpretentiously
rel genuinely, honestly, simply, truly; freely, openheartedly, openly; candidly, frankly, matter-of-factly; informally, relaxedly, unceremoniously
near ant artfully, cannily, deceitfully, deceptively, deviously, dishonestly, falsely; archly, calculatingly, craftily, cunningly, furtively, insidiously, sharply, shiftily, slickly, slyly, underhand, underhanded, underhandedly; flatteringly, sycophantically, unctuously
ant affectedly, artificially, hypocritically, insincerely, pretentiously, unnaturally

naturalness *n* **1** carefree freedom from constraint — see ABANDON
2 the quality or state of being simple and sincere — see NAÏVETÉ 1

nature *n* **1** the set of qualities that makes a person, a group of people, or a thing different from others ⟨it was the violent *nature* of his stories that got them banned from school libraries⟩ ⟨her *nature* was such that lying was never an option for her⟩ ⟨the stoic *nature* of these people enables them to endure one calamity after another⟩
syn character, complexion, constitution, genius, personality, tone
rel distinctiveness, distinctness, individuality, singularity, uniqueness; attribute, characteristic, earmark, feature, flavor, hallmark, mark, point, property, savor, stamp, trait; disposition, grain, sort, temper, temperament; composition, makeup; essence, essentiality, soul, spirit, stuff, substance; habit, way
2 that part of the physical world that is removed from human habitation ⟨needed to get out of the office and be out in *nature* to clear his head⟩
syn open, open air, outdoors, out-of-doors, wild, wilderness
rel backwoods, bush, country, frontier, hinterland, sticks, up-country; outside, without; badland, barren, desert, waste, wasteland
3 a number of persons or things that are grouped together because they have something in common — see SORT 1
4 one's characteristic attitude or mood — see DISPOSITION 1
5 the quality or qualities that make a thing what it is — see ESSENCE
6 the whole body of things observed or assumed — see UNIVERSE

naught *also* **nought** *n* the numerical symbol 0 or the absence of number or quantity represented by it — see ZERO 1

naughty *adj* engaging in or marked by childish misbehavior ⟨told her to act her age and stop throwing temper tantrums like a *naughty* little girl⟩
syn bad, contrary, errant, froward, misbehaving, mischievous

rel defiant, disrespectful, ill-mannered, ill-natured, impolite, improper, impudent, indecorous, insolent, rude, uncouth, unmannerly; disobedient, headstrong, intractable, obstreperous, recalcitrant, refractory, transgressing, unruly, untoward, willful (*or* wilful); balky, restive, uncontrollable, ungovernable, wayward, wild; arch, elfish, impish, monkeying, monkeyish, ornery, pixieish, prankish, rascally, roguish, waggish; dissolute, perverse, wrongheaded; disorderly, rowdy, ruffianly; corrupt, evil, wicked; insurgent, mutinous, rebellious; disobliging, inconsiderate, selfish, thoughtless, unkind, unkindly; babyish, childish, immature, infantile, puerile

near ant acquiescent, compliant, complying, dutiful, obedient, submissive; clean, correct, decent, decorous, moral, proper, respectable; considerate, courteous, kindly, mannerly, polite, thoughtful; angelic, divine, heavenly; amenable, docile, governable, tractable; amiable, complaisant, good-natured, obliging, pleasant; discreet, modest; grown-up, mature

ant behaved, behaving, nice, orderly

nausea *n* **1** a disturbed condition of the stomach in which one feels like vomiting ⟨symptoms include fever accompanied by a loss of appetite and *nausea*⟩

syn qualmishness, queasiness, queerness, sickness, squeamishness

rel qualm; airsickness, morning sickness, motion sickness, seasickness

2 a dislike so strong as to cause stomach upset or queasiness — see DISGUST

nauseate *vb* to cause to feel disgust — see DISGUST

nauseated *adj* **1** affected with nausea — see NAUSEOUS

2 filled with disgust — see SICK 2

nauseating *adj* causing intense displeasure, disgust, or resentment — see OFFENSIVE 1

nauseous *adj* affected with nausea ⟨after eating the last four pieces of the two-week-old pizza, he was feeling a little *nauseous*⟩

syn ill, nauseated, qualmish, queasy (*also* queazy), queer, queerish, sick, sickish, squeamish

rel green, peaked, sickly; unsettled, upset, woozy

near ant settled; healthy, well

nautical *adj* of or relating to navigation of the sea — see MARINE 2

navigable *adj* capable of being traveled on — see PASSABLE 1

navigate *vb* to travel on water in a vessel — see SAIL 1

navigational *adj* of or relating to navigation of the sea — see MARINE 2

navigator *n* one who operates or navigates a seagoing vessel — see SAILOR

nay *adv* not merely this but also — see EVEN

nay *n* **1** a vote or decision against something — see NO 1

2 an unwillingness to grant something asked for — see DENIAL 1

Neanderthal *adj* not civilized — see SAVAGE 1

near *adj* **1** being the less far of two ⟨grab the comforter from the *near* side of the bed⟩

syn closer, hither, nigher, this

rel fore, forward, front, inside

near ant distant, remote, remoter; back, outside

ant far, farther, further, opposite, other, that

2 being such only when compared to something else — see COMPARATIVE

3 closely resembling the object imitated — see NATURAL 2

4 not being distant in time, space, or significance — see CLOSE 2

near *adv* **1** at, within, or to a short distance or time ⟨the campers were cold, so they moved *nearer* to the campfire⟩ ⟨as summer draws *near*, we usually start planning our annual vacation⟩

syn around, by, close, hard, in, nearby, nigh

rel hereabouts (*or* hereabout), thereabouts (*or* thereabout); along, alongside

phrases at close quarters, at hand

2 to a close degree ⟨copy the artist's drawing into your own sketchbook as *near* as you can⟩

syn closely, nearly

near ant distantly, remotely

3 very close to but not completely — see ALMOST

near *prep* close to — see AROUND 1

near *vb* **1** to come near or nearer — see APPROACH 1

2 to move closer to — see COME 1

nearby *adj* not being distant in time, space, or significance — see CLOSE 2

nearby *adv* at, within, or to a short distance or time — see NEAR 1

nearing *adj* being soon to appear or take place — see FORTHCOMING

nearly *adv* **1** to a close degree — see NEAR 2

2 very close to but not completely — see ALMOST

nearness *n* **1** the state of being in a very personal or private relationship — see FAMILIARITY 1

2 the state or condition of being near — see PROXIMITY

nearsighted *adj* able to see near things more clearly than distant ones ⟨I am a little *nearsighted* and need to wear glasses to drive⟩

syn myopic, shortsighted

rel astigmatic

ant farsighted

neat *adj* **1** being clean and in good order ⟨keep the kitchen *neat* so the cook doesn't have to work around piles of dirty dishes⟩

syn crisp, groomed, orderly, picked up, shipshape, snug, tidied, tidy, trim, uncluttered *rel* dapper, natty, prim, saucy, smart, spiffy, spruce; immaculate, spick-and-span (*or* spic-and-span), spotless; rakish, sleek, streamlined, taut; organized, straight, systematic

near ant seedy, shabby, slipshod, sloppy; dirty, filthy, foul, nasty, sordid, squalid; frowzy, rumpled, tousled, tumbled; disorganized, unsystematic

ant disheveled (*or* dishevelled), disordered, disorderly, messy, mussed, mussy, slovenly, unkempt, untidy

2 free from added matter — see PURE 1

3 of the very best kind — see EXCELLENT

nebulous *adj* **1** having an often intentionally veiled or uncertain meaning — see OBSCURE 1

2 not seen or understood clearly — see FAINT 1

nebulousness *n* the quality or state of having a veiled or uncertain meaning — see OBSCURITY 1

necessarily *adv* because of necessity — see NEEDS

necessary *adj* **1** forcing one's compliance or participation by or as if by law — see MANDATORY

2 impossible to avoid or evade — see INEVITABLE

3 impossible to do without — see ESSENTIAL 1

necessitate *vb* to have as a requirement — see NEED 1

necessity *n* something necessary, indispensable, or unavoidable — see ESSENTIAL 1

necklace *n* an ornamental chain or string (as of beads) worn around the neck ⟨found a lovely *necklace* to match the bracelet and ring her mother had given her⟩

syn choker, lei

rel rope, strand; bangle, lavaliere (*also* lavalliere), locket, pendant (*also* pendent)

necromancer *n* a person skilled in using supernatural forces — see MAGICIAN 1

necromancy *n* the power to control natural forces through supernatural means — see MAGIC 1

need *n* **1** a state of being without something necessary, desirable, or useful ⟨when it came time to wrap the presents, he found he was in *need* of adhesive tape⟩

syn absence, lack, needfulness, want

rel deficiency, deficit, inadequacy, insufficiency; dearth, meagerness, paucity, poverty, scantiness, scarceness, scarcity, shortage, skimpiness; defect, minus; deprivation, famishment, privation; demand, essential, necessity, requirement, requisite

near ant adequacy, enough, sufficiency; fund, pool, stock, supply; excess, fill, overabundance, oversupply, plenty, surfeit, surplus; hoard, stockpile

2 something necessary, indispensable, or unavoidable — see ESSENTIAL 1

3 something one must do because of prior agreement — see OBLIGATION

4 the state of lacking sufficient money or material possessions — see POVERTY 1

need *vb* **1** to have as a requirement ⟨a national crisis that *needs* a strong leader to solve it⟩

syn demand, necessitate, require, take, want, warrant

rel entail, involve; ask, beg, claim, clamor (for), cry (for); lack; command, enjoin, exact, insist, press, quest, stipulate

phrases call for

near ant own, possess

ant have, hold

2 to be under necessity or obligation to ⟨you *need* not stand when she enters the room⟩

syn have (to), must, ought (to), shall, should

rel will

needed *adj* impossible to do without — see ESSENTIAL 1

needful *adj* impossible to do without — see ESSENTIAL 1

needfulness *n* a state of being without something necessary, desirable, or useful — see NEED 1

neediness *n* the state of lacking sufficient money or material possessions — see POVERTY 1

needle *n* **1** a slender hollow instrument by which material is put into or taken from the body through the skin ⟨the nurse inserted the *needle* into his vein and collected some blood for testing⟩

syn hypodermic, hypodermic needle, hypodermic syringe, syringe

2 an arrow-shaped piece on a dial or scale for registering information — see POINTER 1

needle *vb* **1** to attack repeatedly with mean put-downs or insults — see TEASE 2

2 to subject (someone) to constant scoldings and sharp reminders — see NAG

needlelike *adj* being of less than usual width — see NARROW 1

needler *n* a person who causes repeated emotional pain, distress, or annoyance to another — see TORMENTOR

needless *adj* not needed by the circumstances or to accomplish an end — see UNNECESSARY

needlework *n* decorative stitching done on cloth with the use of a needle ⟨a school outing to the museum to see an exhibition of 18th century *needlework*⟩

syn embroidery

rel crewel, cross-stitch, needlepoint; hemstitch, fagoting (*or* faggoting), smocking; fancywork

needs *adv* because of necessity ⟨the dangers of global warming must *needs* be recognized—and recognized soon—by the industrialized nations of the world⟩

syn inescapably, inevitably, necessarily, perforce, unavoidably

rel involuntarily

ant unnecessarily

---

needy *adj* lacking money or material possessions — see POOR 1

ne'er *adv* at no time — see NEVER 1

nefarious *adj* not conforming to a high moral standard; morally unacceptable — see BAD 2

nefariousness *n* the state or quality of being utterly evil — see ENORMITY 1

negate *vb* **1** to declare not to be true — see DENY 1

2 to put an end to by formal action — see ABOLISH

3 to think not to be true or real — see DISBELIEVE

negation *n* a refusal to confirm the truth of a statement — see DENIAL 2

negative *adj* **1** marked by opposition or ill will — see HOSTILE 1

2 opposed to one's interests — see ADVERSE 1

negative *n* **1** a vote or decision against something — see NO 1

2 something that is as different as possible from something else — see OPPOSITE

negative *vb* **1** to reject by or as if by a vote ⟨though the rebuttal was very eloquent, he *negatived* it in favor of the first argument⟩ ⟨she *negatived* pizza for dinner, noting that they had already had it for three nights that week⟩
syn blackball, kill, veto
rel decline, disallow, disapprove, dismiss, refuse; blacklist
near ant admit, allow, approve, assent (to), pass, sanction; elect, support
ant confirm, ratify

2 to declare not to be true — see DENY 1

3 to show unwillingness to accept, do, engage in, or agree to — see DECLINE 1

neglect *n* **1** the state of being unattended to or not cared for ⟨the barn sat in *neglect* until it finally fell down⟩
syn desolation, dilapidation, disrepair, seediness
rel inattention, negligence; abandonment, desertion; decay, decrepitude, dereliction, deterioration, disintegration, ruin, ruination
near ant conservation, preservation
ant repair

2 the nonperformance of an assigned or expected action — see FAILURE 1

neglect *vb* **1** to fail to give proper attention to ⟨the news media *neglected* the real issues of the campaign and focused on personalities⟩
syn disregard, forget, ignore, overlook, overpass, pass over, slight, slur (over)
rel fail; miss, omit; brush (aside or off), reject, shrug off, slough (off); disdain, pooh-pooh, scorn; scant, skimp
near ant appreciate, cherish, prize, treasure, value; cultivate, foster, nurse, nurture; pamper; remember; listen (to), watch; follow, mark, note, notice, observe, remark
ant attend (to), heed, mind, regard, tend (to)

2 to leave undone or unattended to especially through carelessness ⟨she plays too much and *neglects* her homework⟩ ⟨I've *neglected* my garden, and now it's overgrown with weeds⟩
syn forget, shirk
rel slack (off)
near ant carry out, do, execute, perform; accomplish, achieve
ant attend (to), remember

3 to miss the opportunity or obligation ⟨the job applicant *neglected* to mention his criminal record⟩
syn fail, forget, omit
rel disregard, ignore, overlook, overpass, pass over, slight; slide, slip; default; skip
near ant heed, mind, remember; keep, observe; carry out, do, execute, perform, practice (or practise); discharge, fulfill (or fulfil), meet, satisfy; comply (with)

neglected *adj* showing signs of advanced wear and tear and neglect — see SHABBY 1

neglectful *adj* failing to give proper care and attention — see NEGLIGENT

neglecting *adj* failing to give proper care and attention — see NEGLIGENT

negligence *n* **1** failure to take the care that a cautious person usually takes ⟨exhibiting his usual *negligence*, he failed to set the emergency brake, and the car rolled down the steep hill and crashed into the telephone pole⟩
syn carelessness, dereliction, heedlessness, incautiousness, laxness, remissness, slackness
rel foolhardiness, rashness, recklessness, wildness; neglect, omission; delinquency, irresponsibility, malfeasance, malpractice, misconduct; misdirection, mishandling, mismanagement; forgetfulness, inattention, inattentiveness, obliviousness, shortsightedness, unwariness
near ant alertness, attention, attentiveness, awareness; circumspection, observance, vigilance, watchfulness; responsibility, responsibleness
ant care, carefulness, caution, cautiousness, heedfulness

2 the nonperformance of an assigned or expected action — see FAILURE 1

negligent *adj* failing to give proper care and attention ⟨has been *negligent* in taking care of the neighbor's dog, repeatedly forgetting to feed the poor animal⟩
syn careless, derelict, lax, neglectful, neglecting, remiss, slack
rel heedless, incautious, irresponsible, reckless, wild; unguarded, unwary; forgetful; disregardful, disregarding, inattentive, oblivious, thoughtless, unheeding, unmindful, unthinking; apathetic, disinterested, indifferent, unconcerned, uninterested; delinquent; loose
near ant meticulous, painstaking, punctilious; cautious, chary, circumspect, gingerly, guarded; alert, heedful, heeding, mindful, observant, regardful, regarding, vigilant, wary, watchful; foresighted, forethoughtful, provident, responsible; thinking, thoughtful; concerned, interested
ant attentive, careful, conscientious

negligible *adj* 1 so small or unimportant as to warrant little or no attention ⟨the two cents in change was such a *negligible* sum that she left the store without collecting the pennies from the cashier⟩

syn inconsequential, inconsiderable, insignificant, measly, minute, nominal, paltry, petty, picayune, piddling, slight, trifling, trivial

rel inferior, mean; imperceptible, inappreciable; little, puny, tiny; hairsplitting, nitpicking, pettifogging; one-horse, small-fry, two-bit

near ant serious, substantial, weighty; eventful, momentous; conspicuous, noteworthy, prominent, outstanding, remarkable, striking; appreciable, discernible, measurable

ant big, consequential, considerable, important, material, significant

2 lacking importance — see UNIMPORTANT

3 small in degree — see REMOTE 1

negligibly *adv* in a very small quantity or degree — see LITTLE 1

negotiable *adj* capable of being traveled on — see PASSABLE 1

negotiate *vb* 1 to bring about through discussion and compromise ⟨wanted to *negotiate* a higher salary before she accepted the job offer⟩

syn arrange, concert, conclude

rel settle (on *or* upon); bargain, chaffer, deal, dicker, haggle, horse-trade, palter; agree; contract, covenant; argue, debate, discuss, hammer (out), hash (over), reason, talk, talk over, work out

2 to deal with (something) usually skillfully or efficiently — see HANDLE 1

3 to plan out usually with subtle skill or care — see ENGINEER

4 to talk over or dispute the terms of a purchase — see BARGAIN

negotiation *n* the act or practice of each side giving up something in order to reach an agreement — see CONCESSION 1

neigh *vb* to make the cry typical of a horse ⟨the horses *neighed* when the rider came into the barn⟩

syn nicker, whinny

neighborhood *n* 1 an area (as of a city) set apart for some purpose or having some special feature — see DISTRICT

2 the people living in a particular area — see COMMUNITY 1

neighboring *adj* not being distant in time, space, or significance — see CLOSE 2

neighborly *adj* having or showing kindly feeling and sincere interest — see FRIENDLY 1

nemesis *n* 1 one who inflicts punishment in return for an injury or offense ⟨Batman is the Joker's main *nemesis* and always foils his wicked plots⟩

syn avenger, castigator, chastiser, punisher, scourge, vigilante

rel revenger; redresser, righter; requiter

near ant ransomer, redeemer, vindicator

2 suffering, loss, or hardship imposed in response to a crime or offense — see PUNISHMENT

neophyte *n* a person who is just starting out in a field of activity — see BEGINNER

neoplasm *n* an abnormal mass of tissue — see GROWTH 1

nerd *n* a person slavishly devoted to intellectual or academic pursuits ⟨was such a *nerd* she stayed home from the party to study for the exam on Monday⟩

syn bookworm, grind

rel egghead, highbrow, intellectual; brain, genius; scholar

near ant slacker, underachiever; lowbrow

nerve *n* 1 shameless boldness — see EFFRONTERY

2 strength of mind to carry on in spite of danger — see COURAGE

3 **nerves** *pl* a sense of panic or extreme nervousness — see JITTERS

nerve *vb* to prepare (oneself) mentally or emotionally — see FORTIFY 1

nerved *adj* inclined or willing to take risks — see BOLD 1

nerveless *adj* 1 lacking strength of will or character — see WEAK 2

2 not easily panicked or upset — see UNFLAPPABLE

nerviness *n* shameless boldness — see EFFRONTERY

nervous *adj* 1 feeling or showing uncomfortable feelings of uncertainty ⟨he was *nervous* about how he would do at the varsity basketball tryouts⟩

syn aflutter, anxious, dithery, edgy, het up, hung up, jittery, jumpy, nervy, perturbed, tense, troubled, uneasy, unquiet, upset, uptight, worried

rel aggrieved, bothered, concerned, disquieted, distraught, distressed, disturbed; apprehensive, foreboding, hesitant, misgiving; fretful, fretting, stewing, vexed; qualmish, qualmy; flustered, twittered, undone, unnerved, unstrung; obsessed, preoccupied, restless; fidgety, flighty, fluttery, high-strung, skittish, spooky

phrases keyed up, on edge, on pins and needles

near ant confident, self-assured, self-confident, sure; controlled, self-controlled

ant calm, collected, cool, easy, nerveless, relaxed

2 marked by or causing agitation or uncomfortable feelings ⟨a *nervous* silence filled the room as the teacher handed out the graded exams⟩

syn agitating, anxious, disquieting, distressful, distressing, disturbing, restless, tense, unnerving, unsettling, worrisome

rel bothersome, troublesome; foreboding, misgiving; discouraging, disheartening, strained; restive, restless, unrestful; awkward, embarrassing

near ant restful; pacific

ant calming, comfortable, easy, peaceful, quiet, quieting, tranquil

3 easily excited by nature — see EXCITABLE

---

syn synonym(s) **rel** related words
ant antonym(s) **near ant** near antonym(s)

nervousness *n* an uneasy state of mind usually over the possibility of an anticipated misfortune or trouble — see ANXIETY 1

nervy *adj* **1** displaying or marked by rude boldness ⟨the *nervy* waiter held up the small tip and called out to the departing customers, "Hope it doesn't break the bank!"⟩
syn arch, bold, bold-faced, brash, brassy, brazen, cheeky, cocky, fresh, impertinent, impudent, insolent, sassy, saucy
rel assertive, forward, obtrusive; audacious, defiant, disrespectful; shameless, unabashed, unblushing; bluff, blunt, curt; facetious, flip, flippant, pert, smart, smart-alecky (*or* smart-aleck)
near ant demure, humble, modest; courteous, genteel, mannerly, polite, proper; deferential, respectful; abashed, ashamed, blushing, embarrassed; gentle, mild; inconspicuous, unobtrusive
ant meek, mousy (*or* mousey), retiring, shy, timid
2 feeling or showing uncomfortable feelings of uncertainty — see NERVOUS 1
3 inclined or willing to take risks — see BOLD 1

nest *n* a place where a person goes to hide — see HIDEOUT

nest egg *n* a sum of money set aside for a particular purpose — see FUND 1

nestle *vb* **1** to lie close — see NUZZLE
2 to sit or recline comfortably or cozily — see SNUGGLE 1

¹net *n* **1** a fabric of strands loosely twisted, knotted, or woven together at regular intervals ⟨the basketball didn't go into the basket, it just hit the *net*⟩
syn mesh, netting, network
rel web, webbing; grille (*also* grill), lattice, screen, screening; filigree, lace
2 a device or scheme for capturing another by surprise — see TRAP 1
3 something that catches and holds — see WEB 1

²net *n* the amount of money left when expenses are subtracted from the total amount received — see PROFIT 1

nether *adj* situated lower down — see INFERIOR 1

netting *n* a fabric made of strands loosely twisted, knotted, or woven together at regular intervals — see ¹NET 1

nettle *vb* to disturb the peace of mind of (someone) especially by repeated disagreeable acts — see IRRITATE 1

nettling *adj* causing annoyance — see ANNOYING

network *n* **1** a fabric made of strands loosely twisted, knotted, or woven together at regular intervals — see ¹NET 1
2 something made up of many interdependent or related parts — see SYSTEM 1

neurotic *n* a person judged to be legally or medically insane — see LUNATIC 1

neuter *vb* to remove the sex organs of ⟨Dad agreed to buy us the dog on the condition that we have her *neutered* so she couldn't have puppies⟩
syn alter, desex
rel castrate, emasculate, geld; spay; sterilize

neutral *adj* not favoring or joined to either side in a quarrel, contest, or war ⟨Sweden remained *neutral* during World War II, refusing to join either side of the conflict⟩
syn nonpartisan, unallied
rel autonomous, independent, sovereign, unaffiliated; nonbelligerent; individualistic; disinterested, evenhanded, fair, impartial, unbiased, uninfluenced, unprejudiced; bipartisan
near ant biased, partial, partisan, prejudiced, unfair; affiliated, associated, federated; belligerent
ant allied, confederate

neutrality *n* lack of favoritism toward one side or another — see DETACHMENT 1

neutralize *vb* to balance with an equal force so as to make ineffective — see OFFSET

neutralizer *n* a force or influence that makes an opposing force ineffective or less effective — see COUNTERBALANCE

never *adv* **1** at no time ⟨I have *never* been out of the country⟩
syn ne'er
rel nevermore; not; infrequently, little, rarely, seldom
near ant eternally, everlastingly, evermore, invariably; frequently, often, recurrently, repeatedly
ant always, constantly, continuously, endlessly, ever, forever, perpetually
2 not in any degree, way, or under any condition ⟨though she turned down his offer of marriage twice, he was *never* convinced that she did not love him⟩
syn no, none, nothing, noway (*or* noways), nowise
rel nowhere near
phrases by no means, in no wise, nothing doing, on no account
near ant completely, extremely, full, fully, par excellence, right, very; altogether, exactly; somehow, someway (*also* someways); out
ant anyhow, anyway, anywise, at all, ever, half, however

nevertheless *adv* in spite of that — see HOWEVER

new *adj* **1** taking the place of one that came before ⟨after my bike was stolen, my scooter became my *new* mode of transportation⟩
syn backup, makeshift, substitute
rel alternate, alternative; different, other, separate; extra, spare; another, second; utility; successive; equivalent
near ant first, former; equal, identical, same; lasting, permanent
ant original
2 not known or experienced before ⟨Spanish was a *new* course of study for her⟩ ⟨the Americas were *new* lands for the European explorers⟩
syn fresh, novel, original, strange, unaccustomed, unfamiliar, unheard-of, unknown, unprecedented

rel innovative, unique; nontraditional, unconventional, untried; derivative, imitative

near ant conventional, established, traditional, tried, tried-and-true; derivative, imitative

ant familiar, old, time-honored, tired

3 recently made and never used before ⟨that unique scent that is the telltale sign of a *new* car⟩

syn brand-new, spick-and-span (*or* spic-and-span), unused

rel clean, fresh, pristine, unspoiled; untouched; newfangled, new-fashioned; natural, raw, virgin, unprocessed, untreated, unworked

near ant dirty, soiled, spoiled, stale; aged, beat-up, old, worn

ant hand-me-down, second hand, used

4 made or become fresh in spirits or vigor ⟨a little rest made him a *new* man after the exhausting basketball game⟩

syn energized, freshened, invigorated, reanimated, recreated, reenergized, refreshed, regenerated, renewed, resuscitated, revived

rel animated, enlivened, exhilarated, jazzed (up); resurrected; rested, untired, unwearied

near ant tired, weary; dampened, deadened; emasculated, unmanned; demoralized, disheartened, dispirited

ant drained, enervated, exhausted, weakened

5 being or involving the latest methods, concepts, information, or styles — see MODERN

new *adv* not long ago — see NEWLY

newborn *n* a recently born person — see BABY

newcomer *n* a person who is just starting out in a field of activity — see BEGINNER

newfangled *adj* being or involving the latest methods, concepts, information, or styles — see MODERN

new-fashioned *adj* being or involving the latest methods, concepts, information, or styles — see MODERN

newly *adv* not long ago ⟨as soon as he left the room, his dog jumped on the *newly* made bed and rumpled it again⟩

syn freshly, just, late, lately, new, now, only, recently

rel latterly

phrases of late

near ant ago, before, earlier, early, erstwhile, formerly, previously; heretofore, hitherto

ant anciently

newness *n* the quality or appeal of being new — see NOVELTY 1

news *n pl* a report of recent events or facts not previously known ⟨dropped by to give me the latest *news* about her daughter⟩

syn information, intelligence, item, story, tidings, word

rel announcement, communication, message; dope, lowdown, scoop, tidbit (*also* titbit); tip; gossip, rumor, tale, tattle; feedback

newspaper *n* a publication that appears at regular intervals — see JOURNAL

newsy *adj* having the style and content of everyday conversation — see CHATTY 1

next *adj* being the one that comes immediately after another ⟨my house is the *next* one⟩ ⟨turn at the *next* street, not this one⟩ ⟨she was *next* in line for concert tickets⟩

syn coming, ensuing, following, succeeding

rel consecutive, sequential, successive; posterior, subsequent; immediate; second

phrases on deck

near ant anterior, former; past; last

ant antecedent, foregoing, precedent, preceding, previous, prior

next-door *adj* not being distant in time, space, or significance — see CLOSE 2

next to *adv* very close to but not completely — see ALMOST

next to *prep* close to — see AROUND 1

nib *n* the jaws of a bird together with their hornlike covering — see BEAK

nibble *n* a small piece or quantity of food — see MORSEL 1

nibble *vb* to crush or grind with the teeth — see BITE (ON)

nice *adj* **1** following the established traditions of refined society and good taste — see PROPER 1

2 giving pleasure or contentment to the mind or senses — see PLEASANT

3 hard to please — see FINICKY

4 having an easygoing and pleasing manner especially in social situations — see AMIABLE

5 made or done with extreme care and accuracy — see FINE 2

nicely *adv* **1** in a pleasing way — see WELL 5

2 in a satisfactory way — see WELL 1

3 with good reason or courtesy — see WELL 4

niceness *n* the state or quality of having a pleasant or agreeable manner in socializing with others — see AMIABILITY 1

nicety *n* a single piece of information — see FACT 3

niche *n* **1** a hollowed-out space in a wall ⟨statues of various saints occupy the *niches* lining the abbey's many corridors⟩

syn alcove, nook, recess

rel corner, cranny, cubbyhole; cubicle; dent, indentation

2 the place where a plant or animal is usually or naturally found — see HOME 2

nick *n* a V-shaped cut usually on an edge or a surface — see NOTCH 1

nicker *vb* to make the cry typical of a horse — see NEIGH

nickname *n* a descriptive or familiar name given instead of or in addition to the one belonging to an individual ⟨his wavy hair earned him the *nickname* "Curly" early in life⟩

---

syn synonym(s)	*rel* related words
ant antonym(s)	*near ant* near antonym(s)

syn alias, cognomen, epithet, sobriquet (*also* soubriquet)

rel appellation, denomination, denotation, designation, handle, label, title; nom de plume, pen name, pseudonym

nifty *adj* of the very best kind — see EXCELLENT

nifty *n* something very good of its kind — see JIM-DANDY

niggard *adj* giving or sharing as little as possible — see STINGY 1

niggard *n* a mean grasping person who is usually stingy with money — see MISER

niggardly *adj* **1** giving or sharing as little as possible — see STINGY 1

2 less plentiful than what is normal, necessary, or desirable — see MEAGER

nigh *adj* not being distant in time, space, or significance — see CLOSE 2

nigh *adv* **1** at, within, or to a short distance or time — see NEAR 1

2 very close to but not completely — see ALMOST

nigher *adj* being the less far of two — see NEAR 1

night *adj* of, relating to, or occurring in the night — see NOCTURNAL

night *n* **1** the time from sunset to sunrise when there is no visible sunlight ⟨loved to sit outside at *night* and watch the stars⟩
syn dark, darkness, nighttime
rel dusk, evening, gloaming, nightfall, twilight; midnight
near ant dawn, daybreak, forenoon, morning; high noon, midday, noon, noonday, noontide, noontime; afternoon
ant day, daytime

2 a time or place of little or no light — see DARK 1

nightclub *n* a bar or restaurant offering special nighttime entertainment (as music, dancing, or comedy acts) ⟨decided to go dancing at a local *nightclub* after the long dinner and movie⟩
syn cabaret, café (*also* cafe), disco, discotheque, roadhouse
rel barroom, pub [*chiefly British*], public house [*chiefly British*], saloon, tavern; dive, speakeasy; canteen

nightdress *n* a loose pullover garment worn in bed — see NIGHTGOWN

nightfall *n* the time from when the sun begins to set to the onset of total darkness — see DUSK 1

nightgown *n* a loose pullover garment worn in bed ⟨decided to buy a flannel *nightgown* instead of pajamas⟩
syn nightdress, nightshirt
rel nightclothes; pajamas, pj's, pyjamas [*chiefly British*]; nightcap; lingerie

nightly *adj* of, relating to, or occurring in the night — see NOCTURNAL

nightmare *n* **1** a series of often striking pictures created by the imagination during sleep — see DREAM 1

2 a situation or state that causes great suffering and unhappiness — see HELL 2

nightmarish *adj* extremely disturbing or repellent — see HORRIBLE 1

nightshirt *n* a loose pullover garment worn in bed — see NIGHTGOWN

nightstick *n* a heavy rigid stick used as a weapon or for punishment — see CLUB 1

nighttime *adj* of, relating to, or occurring in the night — see NOCTURNAL

nighttime *n* the time from sunset to sunrise when there is no visible sunlight — see NIGHT 1

nil *n* the numerical symbol 0 or the absence of number or quantity represented by it — see ZERO 1

nimble *adj* **1** having or showing quickness of mind — see INTELLIGENT 1

2 moving easily — see GRACEFUL 1

nimbleness *n* ease and grace in physical activity — see DEXTERITY 2

nincompoop *n* **1** a person who lacks good sense or judgment — see FOOL 1

2 a stupid person — see IDIOT

ninny *n* **1** a person who lacks good sense or judgment — see FOOL 1

2 a stupid person — see IDIOT

¹**nip** *n* **1** a very small amount — see PARTICLE 1

2 an uncomfortable degree of coolness — see CHILL

²**nip** *n* the portion of a serving of a beverage that is swallowed at one time — see DRINK 2

nip *vb* **1** to make (as hair) shorter with or as if with the use of shears — see CLIP

2 to squeeze tightly between two surfaces, edges, or points — see PINCH 1

3 to take (something) without right and with an intent to keep — see STEAL 1

nip and tuck *adj* showing little difference in the standing of the competitors — see CLOSE 3

nipper *n* a male person who has not yet reached adulthood — see BOY

nipping *adj* having a low or subnormal temperature — see COLD 1

nippy *adj* **1** having a low or subnormal temperature — see COLD 1

2 having a powerfully stimulating odor or flavor — see SHARP 3

3 moving, proceeding, or acting with great speed — see FAST 1

4 uncomfortably cool — see CHILLY 1

nitpick *vb* to make often peevish criticisms or objections about matters that are minor, unimportant, or irrelevant — see QUIBBLE

nitpicker *n* a person given to harsh judgments and to finding faults — see CRITIC 1

nitwit *n* **1** a person who lacks good sense or judgment — see FOOL 1

2 a stupid person — see IDIOT

no *interj* how surprising, doubtful, or unbelievable ⟨*no*—you can't possibly mean that I failed that test! I studied for days!⟩
syn ah, aha, fie, indeed, pshaw, well, what, why
rel gee, ha, hello, hey, lo, oh; fiddlesticks, phooey, pooh; there; oops, ugh; egad, gad, the deuce, the devil, the dickens, zounds

no *adv* **1** not in any degree, way, or under any condition — see NEVER 2

2 certainly not — see HARDLY 2

no *n* **1** a vote or decision against something ⟨though I wanted spaghetti for dinner, the consensus was a decisive *no*⟩

syn nay, negative

rel con; blackball, veto; denial, negation, refusal

near ant pro; acceptance, approval, grace

ant positive, yea, yes

2 an unwillingness to grant something asked for — see DENIAL 1

nobility *n* impressiveness of beauty on a large scale — see MAGNIFICENCE

noble *adj* **1** of high birth, rank, or station ⟨despite his *noble* background, the prince is known for his unpretentious way with common people⟩

syn aristocratic, genteel, gentle, grand, highborn, patrician, upper-class, well-born

rel high, lofty, superior; elevated, ennobled, exalted; gentlemanly, kingly, knightly, ladylike, lordly, princely, queenly, regal, royal; high-level, senior

near ant inferior, knavish; bastard, illegitimate; ordinary, plain; abased, degraded; junior, subordinate

ant baseborn, common, humble, ignoble, low, lower-class, lowly, mean, plebeian

2 having, characterized by, or arising from a dignified and generous nature ⟨the factory owner had a kind, *noble* disposition that showed in his unstinting generosity toward the poor⟩ ⟨our country was founded on the *noble* ideas that are put forth in the founding fathers' writings⟩

syn chivalrous, elevated, gallant, great, greathearted, high, high-minded, lofty, lordly, magnanimous, sublime

rel ennobled, exalted, glorified; heroic, honorable, venerable, worthy; knightly, princely, regal; moving, inspiring, uplifting; august, magnificent, majestic

near ant sordid, squalid, vile, wretched; abominable, contemptible, despicable, detestable, hateful, offensive, repulsive, ugly; dastardly, dirty, lousy, sorry; little, mean, narrow, small-minded; degrading, discreditable, humiliating, ignominious; coarse, crude, vulgar

ant base, debased, degenerate, degraded, ignoble, low

3 following the accepted rules of moral conduct — see HONORABLE 1

4 large and impressive in size, grandeur, extent, or conception — see GRAND 1

5 of the very best kind — see EXCELLENT

6 standing above others in rank, importance, or achievement — see EMINENT

noble *n* a man of high birth or social position — see GENTLEMAN 1

nobleman *n* a man of high birth or social position — see GENTLEMAN 1

nobleness *n* impressiveness of beauty on a large scale — see MAGNIFICENCE

noblewoman *n* a woman of high birth or social position — see GENTLEWOMAN

nobly *adv* in a manner befitting a person of the highest character and ideals — see GREATLY 1

nobody *n* a person of no importance or influence ⟨she felt like a *nobody* until she won the National Spelling Bee⟩

syn lightweight, nonentity, nothing, shrimp, twerp, whippersnapper, zero, zilch

rel least; inferior, mediocrity, obscurity; figurehead, puppet

near ant chief, head, lead, leader; celebrity, luminary, notable, personality, star, superstar; authority, superior; great power, party, power

ant big shot, bigwig, eminence, figure, magnate, nabob, personage, somebody, VIP

nobody *pron* no person ⟨there is *nobody* home⟩ ⟨*nobody* wants to clean up that mess⟩

syn none, no one

near ant anybody, anyone; somebody, someone

ant everybody, everyone

nocturnal *adj* of, relating to, or occurring in the night ⟨he bought a new telescope so he could pursue his favorite *nocturnal* hobby of astronomy⟩

syn night, nightly, nighttime

rel late; midnight, overnight

near ant noon

ant daily, diurnal

nod *vb* to make short up-and-down movements ⟨though she couldn't see the rain, she knew it had started because she could see the flowers *nod* as raindrops hit them⟩

syn bob, bobble, jog, jounce, pump, seesaw

rel jerk, jiggle, shake, wiggle, wobble; oscillate, rock, sway, swing, undulate; drop, duck

nodding *adj* bending downward or forward ⟨some students, with *nodding* heads, were falling asleep during the boring lecture⟩

syn bowed, bowing, declined, declining, descendant (*or* descendent), descending, drooping, droopy, hanging, hung (*also* hanged), inclining, pendulous, sagging, stooping

rel floppy, limp; dangling, falling, pendent (*or* pendant); suspended; dipping, sinking, slumping

near ant erect, inflexible, rigid, stiff; elevated, raised, upraised

ant unbending, upright

noddle *n* the upper or front part of the body that contains the brain, the major sense organs, and the mouth — see HEAD 1

node *n* a small rounded mass of swollen tissue — see BUMP 1

nodule *n* a small rounded mass of swollen tissue — see BUMP 1

---

syn synonym(s)   *rel* related words

ant antonym(s)   *near ant* near antonym(s)

Noel *n* the season celebrating Christmas — see YULETIDE

noggin *n* the upper or front part of the body that contains the brain, the major sense organs, and the mouth — see HEAD 1

no–good *adj* having no usefulness — see WORTHLESS

no–good *n* a mean, evil, or unprincipled person — see VILLAIN

noise *n* 1 loud, confused, and usually unharmonious sound ⟨the blaring *noise* of traffic on Fifth Avenue made casual conversation impossible⟩

  syn bluster, cacophony, clamor, clangor, din, discordance, racket, roar

  rel discord, dissonance; commotion, furor, hubbub, hullabaloo, hurly-burly, rumpus, tumult, uproar; babel; clatter, jangle; bang, blast, boom, clap, crack, crash

  near ant calm, hush, lull; quietude, serenity, tranquillity (*or* tranquility)

  ant quiet, silence, still, stillness

  2 a violent shouting — see CLAMOR 1

noise (about) *vb* to make (as a piece of information) the subject of common talk without any authority or confirmation of accuracy — see RUMOR

noiseless *adj* mostly or entirely without sound — see SILENT 3

noisome *adj* 1 bad for the well-being of the body — see UNHEALTHY 1

  2 causing intense displeasure, disgust, or resentment — see OFFENSIVE 1

  3 having an unpleasant smell — see MALODOROUS

noisy *adj* 1 making loud, confused, and usually unharmonious sounds ⟨the *noisy* crowd moved up the street, shouting louder as they went along⟩

  syn clangorous, dinning, discordant

  rel cacophonous, dissonant; resounding, sonorous; clamorous, uproarious; blatant, obstreperous, strident, vociferous; blaring, booming, brassy, brazen, clanging, earsplitting

  near ant calm, hushed

  ant noiseless, quiet, silent, soundless, still

  2 full of or characterized by the presence of noise ⟨the crowded auditorium was *noisy*, packed with excited theatergoers eager for the show to start⟩ ⟨the manufacturing company was a *noisy* place, so we wore ear protection while we toured⟩

  syn clamorous, clangorous, clattering, clattery, resounding

  rel resonant, sonorous; buzzing, humming, murmuring; blustery, boisterous, raucous, rip-roaring, roaring, roistering, romping, rowdy; tumultuous, uproarious, woolly (*also* wooly); obstreperous, vociferous

  near ant calm, peaceful, serene, tranquil

  ant hushed, noiseless, quiet, silent, soundless, stilled, stilly

nomad *or* **nomadic** *adj* traveling from place to place — see ITINERANT

nomad *n* a person who roams about without a fixed route or destination ⟨after college she became quite the *nomad*, backpacking through Europe with no particular destination⟩

  syn drifter, gadabout, rambler, roamer, rover, stroller, vagabond, wanderer, wayfarer

  rel laggard, straggler; lingerer, loiterer, sojourner; bum, hobo, tramp; sightseer, traveler (*or* traveller); transient, vagrant; ambler, saunterer

  near ant homebody; denizen, dweller, habitant, inhabitant, resident, settler

nominal *adj* 1 being something in name or form only ⟨he was the *nominal* head of state—everyone knew the country was actually run by one of his advisers⟩

  syn formal, paper, titular

  rel so-called; phantom, virtual

  near ant actual, real, true

  2 so small or unimportant as to warrant little or no attention — see NEGLIGIBLE 1

nominally *adv* in a very small quantity or degree — see LITTLE 1

nonaction *n* lack of action or activity — see INACTION

nonbinding *adj* having no legal or binding force — see NULL 1

nonchalance *n* lack of interest or concern — see INDIFFERENCE

nonchalant *adj* having or showing a lack of interest or concern — see INDIFFERENT 1

noncombustible *adj* incapable of being burned — see INCOMBUSTIBLE

nonconflicting *adj* not having or showing any apparent conflict — see CONSISTENT

nonconformist *adj* deviating from commonly accepted beliefs or practices — see HERETICAL

nonconformist *n* 1 a person who does not conform to generally accepted standards or customs ⟨always the *nonconformist*, she insisted on wearing red on St. Patrick's Day and not green like everyone else⟩

  syn bohemian, deviant, individualist, loner, lone wolf, maverick

  rel character, codger, crackbrain, crackpot, crank, eccentric, freak, kook, nut, oddball, screwball, weirdo; misfit, outsider; anomaly

  near ant adherent, follower, supporter; sheep

  ant conformer, conformist

  2 a person who believes or teaches something opposed to accepted beliefs — see HERETIC

nonconformity *n* departure from a generally accepted theory, opinion, or practice — see HERESY

nonconventional *adj* not bound by traditional ways or beliefs — see LIBERAL 1

none *adv* 1 certainly not — see HARDLY 2

  2 in no degree, way, or under any condition — see NEVER 2

none *pron* no person — see NOBODY

nonelective *adj* forcing one's compliance or participation by or as if by law — see MANDATORY

nonentity *n* a person of no importance or influence — see NOBODY

nonessential *adj* not needed by the circumstances or to accomplish an end — see UNNECESSARY

nonetheless *adv* in spite of that — see HOWEVER

nonexistent *adj* not present or in evidence — see ABSENT 2

nonfictional *adj* restricted to or based on fact — see FACTUAL 1

nonflammable *adj* incapable of being burned — see INCOMBUSTIBLE

nonfunctional *adj* not being in working order — see INOPERABLE 1

nonfunctioning *adj* not being in working order — see INOPERABLE 1

noninflammable *adj* incapable of being burned — see INCOMBUSTIBLE

nonliterary *adj* used in or suitable for speech and not formal writing — see COLLOQUIAL 1

nonliterate *adj* lacking in education or the knowledge gained from books — see IGNORANT 1

nonmaterial *adj* not composed of matter — see IMMATERIAL 1

nonmotile *adj* incapable of moving or being moved — see IMMOVABLE 1

nonmoving *adj* 1 fixed in a place or position — see STATIONARY 1
2 incapable of moving or being moved — see IMMOVABLE 1

nonnative *adj* being, relating to, or characteristic of a country other than one's own — see FOREIGN 1

nonnative *n* a person who is not native to or known to a community — see STRANGER

no—nonsense *adj* not joking or playful in mood or manner — see SERIOUS 1

nonoperating *adj* not being in working order — see INOPERABLE 1

nonorthodox *adj* 1 deviating from commonly accepted beliefs or practices — see HERETICAL
2 not bound by traditional ways or beliefs — see LIBERAL 1

nonpareil *adj* having no equal or rival for excellence or desirability — see ONLY 1

nonpareil *n* someone of such unequaled perfection as to deserve imitation — see IDEAL 1

nonpartisan *adj* 1 marked by justice, honesty, and freedom from bias — see FAIR 2
2 not favoring or joined to either side in a quarrel, contest, or war — see NEUTRAL 1

nonphysical *adj* not composed of matter — see IMMATERIAL 1

nonplus *vb* to throw into a state of self-conscious distress — see EMBARRASS 1

nonpractical *adj* not capable of being put to use or account — see IMPRACTICAL

nonprofessional *adj* lacking or showing a lack of expert skill — see AMATEURISH

syn synonym(s)   **rel** related-words
ant antonym(s)   **near ant** near antonym(s)

nonpublic *adj* not known or meant to be known by the general populace — see PRIVATE 1

nonrational *adj* not using or following good reasoning — see ILLOGICAL

nonrealistic *adj* using elements of form (as color, line, or texture) with little or no attempt at creating a realistic picture — see ABSTRACT 2

nonreligious *adj* 1 lacking religious emotions, principles, or practices — see IRRELIGIOUS
2 not involving religion or religious matters — see PROFANE 1

nonresistant *adj* receiving or enduring without offering resistance — see PASSIVE

nonsense *n* 1 language, behavior, or ideas that are absurd and contrary to good sense ⟨told him to stop his mischievous *nonsense* and start behaving properly⟩ ⟨the discussion about building a time machine was complete *nonsense*⟩ ⟨a hundred years ago, the idea that man could walk on the moon was regarded as impractical *nonsense*⟩
syn bunk, claptrap, drivel, fiddlesticks, folly, foolishness, fudge, hogwash, humbug, humbuggery, piffle, rot, senselessness, silliness, slush, stupidity, trash
rel absurdity, asininity, fatuity, foolery, idiocy, imbecility, inanity, insanity, lunacy; absurdness, craziness, foolishness, madness, senselessness, witlessness; monkeyshines, shenanigans, tomfoolery; gas, hot air, jazz, moonshine, rigmarole, twaddle; double-talk
near ant levelheadedness, rationality, reasonableness, sensibleness; common sense, horse sense, sense; discernment, judgment (*or* judgement), wisdom
2 unintelligible or meaningless talk — see GIBBERISH

nonsensical *adj* 1 conceived or made without regard for reason or reality — see FANTASTIC 1
2 showing or marked by a lack of good sense or judgment — see FOOLISH 1

nonsensicalness *n* lack of good sense or judgment — see FOOLISHNESS 1

nonspecific *adj* relating to the main elements and not to specific details — see GENERAL 2

nonsuccess *n* a falling short of one's goals — see FAILURE 2

nontraditional *adj* not bound by traditional ways or beliefs — see LIBERAL 1

nonvalid *adj* 1 having no legal or binding force — see NULL 1
2 having no basis in reason or fact — see GROUNDLESS

nonviolent *adj* not involving violence or force — see PEACEFUL 2

nook *n* a hollowed-out space in a wall — see NICHE 1

noon *n* the middle of the day ⟨we eat a big lunch around *noon* then have dinner in the evening⟩
syn high noon, midday, noonday, noontide, noontime

rel forenoon, morning; afternoon, evening

noonday *n* the middle of the day — see NOON

no one *pron* no person — see NOBODY

noontide *n* the middle of the day — see NOON

noontime *n* the middle of the day — see NOON

norm *n* what is typical of a group, class, or series — see AVERAGE

normal *adj* **1** being of the type that is encountered in the normal course of events — see ORDINARY 1

2 having full use of one's mind and control over one's actions — see SANE

3 having or showing the qualities associated with the members of a particular group or kind — see TYPICAL 1

normal *n* what is typical of a group, class, or series — see AVERAGE

normalcy *n* the state or fact of being the way things usually are — see NORMALITY

normality *n* the state or fact of being the way things usually are ⟨the county slowly has returned to *normality* after a week of flash flooding⟩

syn normalcy, status quo

rel groove, routine, rut; currency, prevalence; conventionality; orderliness, peace

near ant irregularity, uncommonness, unusualness; disorderliness, disruptiveness; disruption, disturbance; anomalousness, deviance; exceptionalness, extraordinariness, noteworthiness, remarkableness; unconventionality

ant abnormality

normalize *vb* to make agree with a single established standard or model — see STANDARDIZE

normally *adv* according to the usual course of things — see NATURALLY 2

nose *vb* **1** to become aware of by means of the sense organs in the nose — see SMELL 1

2 to interest oneself in what is not one's concern — see INTERFERE

nosedive *n* the act or process of going to a lower level or altitude — see DESCENT 1

nose–dive *vb* to go to a lower level — see DROP 2

nosegay *n* a bunch of flowers — see BOUQUET 1

nosiness *n* an eager desire to find out about things that are often none of one's business — see CURIOSITY 1

nosy *or* **nosey** *adj* **1** interested in what is not one's own business — see CURIOUS 1

2 thrusting oneself where one is not welcome or invited — see INTRUSIVE

notable *adj* standing above others in rank, importance, or achievement — see EMINENT

notable *n* a person who is widely known and usually much talked about — see CELEBRITY 1

notation *n* a usually brief written reminder — see NOTE 1

notch *n* **1** a V-shaped cut usually on an edge or a surface ⟨lifted up the fence rail and put it in the *notch* cut into the post⟩

syn chip, hack, indentation, kerf, nick

rel punch; groove, score; slit, slot

2 a narrow opening between hillsides or mountains that can be used for passage — see CANYON

3 an individual part of a process, series, or ranking — see DEGREE 1

note *n* **1** a usually brief written reminder ⟨I'll make a *note* to myself so I don't forget to pick up some milk on the way home⟩

syn memo, memorandum, notation

rel memoir, minutes, report; line; document, writing

2 a message on paper from one person or group to another — see LETTER

3 a natural vocal sound made by an animal — see CALL 1

4 a piece of printed paper used as money — see ¹BILL 2

5 a special quality or impression associated with something — see AURA

6 overall quality as seen or judged by people in general — see REPUTATION

7 a briefly expressed opinion — see REMARK

note *vb* **1** to make a statement of one's opinion — see REMARK 1

2 to make a written note of — see RECORD 1

3 to make note of (something) through the use of one's eyes — see SEE 1

4 to make reference to or speak about briefly but specifically — see MENTION 1

5 to take notice of and be guided by — see HEED 1

noted *adj* widely known — see FAMOUS

notepad *n* a number of sheets of writing paper glued together at one edge — see PAD 1

noteworthiness *n* the fact or state of being above others in rank or importance — see EMINENCE 1

noteworthy *adj* standing above others in rank, importance, or achievement — see EMINENT

nothing *adv* not in any degree, way, or under any condition — see NEVER 2

nothing *n* **1** a person of no importance or influence — see NOBODY

2 something of little importance — see TRIFLE

3 the numerical symbol 0 or the absence of number or quantity represented by it — see ZERO 1

notice *n* **1** a published statement informing the public of a matter of general interest — see ANNOUNCEMENT

2 a state of being aware — see ATTENTION 2

3 a written communication giving information or directions — see MEMORANDUM 1

4 an essay evaluating or analyzing something — see CRITICISM

5 the act or an instance of telling beforehand of danger or risk — see WARNING 1

notice *vb* **1** to make note of (something) through the use of one's eyes — see SEE 1

2 to make reference to or speak about briefly but specifically — see MENTION 1

noticeable *adj* likely to attract attention ⟨the stain on the new carpet was quite *noticeable*, and nothing we did made it any lighter⟩

syn arresting, bold, catchy, conspicuous, dramatic, emphatic, eye-catching, flamboyant, marked, prominent, pronounced, remarkable, showy, splashy, striking

rel detectable, discernible, observable, perceptible, visible; outstanding, salient; distinguished, eminent, impressive, notable, noteworthy; highlighted, spotlighted; flagrant, glaring, screaming; flashy, garish, gaudy, glitzy, jazzy, loud, meretricious, swank (*or* swanky), tawdry; high-falutin, ostentatious, pretentious; extravagant, fancy, florid, glittery, spectacular; opulent, ornate, overdone, overwrought; absorbing, engrossing, enthralling, fascinating, interesting, riveting

near ant subtle; concealed, hidden, shrouded; dim, faint, obscure; insignificant, undistinguished, unimportant; modest, unaffected, unassuming, unpretentious; conservative, plain, quiet, simple, unaffected, understated; muted, restrained, subdued, subtle, toned-down

ant inconspicuous, unemphatic, unnoticeable, unobtrusive, unremarkable

notification *n* a published statement informing the public of a matter of general interest — see ANNOUNCEMENT

notion *n* **1** notions *pl* small useful items ⟨the fabric store had a wide variety of thread, pins, buttons, and other *notions*⟩

syn novelties, odds and ends, sundries

rel bauble(s), bric-a-brac, gewgaw(s), knickknack(s), trinket(s); hodgepodge, miscellany, variety

2 a sudden impulsive and apparently unmotivated idea or action — see WHIM

3 an idea that is believed to be true or valid without positive knowledge — see OPINION 1

4 something imagined or pictured in the mind — see IDEA

notoriety *n* the fact or state of being known to the public — see FAME

notorious *adj* **1** not respectable — see DISREPUTABLE

2 widely known — see FAMOUS

notwithstanding *adv* in spite of that — see HOWEVER

notwithstanding *prep* without being prevented by — see DESPITE

nourish *vb* **1** to help the growth or development of — see FOSTER 1

2 to supply with nourishment — see SUSTAIN 1

nourishing *adj* providing the substances necessary for health and bodily growth — see NUTRITIOUS

novel *adj* not known or experienced before — see NEW 2

novelette *n* a work with imaginary characters and events that is shorter and usually less complex than a novel — see STORY 1

novella *n* a work with imaginary characters and events that is shorter and usually less complex than a novel — see STORY 1

novelty *n* **1** the quality or appeal of being new ⟨the *novelty* of having a cat quickly wore off⟩

syn freshness, newness, originality

rel strangeness, unfamiliarity, unusualness; progressiveness; up-to-dateness; departure, divergence, innovation, offshoot, shoot

near ant banality, commonness, familiarity, staleness

2 novelties *pl* small useful items — see NOTION 1

3 a small object displayed for its attractiveness or interest — see KNICKKNACK

novice *n* a person who is just starting out in a field of activity — see BEGINNER

now *adv* **1** at the present time ⟨that company doesn't make those toys *now* because they are unsafe⟩

syn anymore, currently, nowadays, presently, right now, today

rel here

near ant away, far, farthest, remotest; heretofore, hitherto, since; ago, previously

ant before, formerly, long, once, then

2 not long ago — see NEWLY

3 on some occasions — see SOMETIMES

4 without delay — see IMMEDIATELY

now *conj* for the reason that — see SINCE

now *n* the time currently existing or in progress — see PRESENT 1

nowadays *adv* at the present time — see NOW 1

noway *or* **noways** *adv* not in any degree, way, or under any condition — see NEVER 2

no way *adv* certainly not — see HARDLY 2

nowise *adv* not in any degree, way, or under any condition — see NEVER 2

noxious *adj* **1** bad for the well-being of the body — see UNHEALTHY 1

2 causing or capable of causing harm — see HARMFUL

nth *adj* of the greatest or highest degree or quantity — see ULTIMATE 1

nub *n* **1** a small uneven mass — see LUMP 1

2 the central part or aspect of something under consideration — see CRUX

nubbin *n* a very small piece — see BIT 1

nubble *n* a small uneven mass — see LUMP 1

nubbly *adj* having small pieces or lumps spread throughout — see CHUNKY 1

nubby *adj* having small pieces or lumps spread throughout — see CHUNKY 1

nucleus *n* a thing or place that is of greatest importance to an activity or interest — see CENTER 1

nude *adj* lacking or shed of clothing — see NAKED 1

---

syn synonym(s)   *rel* related words
ant antonym(s)   *near ant* near antonym(s)

nudge *vb* to pass lightly across or touch gently especially in passing — see BRUSH

nugget *n* a small uneven mass — see LUMP 1

nuisance *n* **1** one who is obnoxiously annoying ⟨my little brother was being a *nuisance* by poking and prodding me throughout the long car trip⟩
syn annoyance, annoyer, gadfly, gnawer, persecutor, pest, tease, teaser
rel headache; harrier, heckler; hassle, plague; molester, tormentor, torturer
near ant charmer, smoothy (*or* smoothie)
2 something that is a source of irritation — see ANNOYANCE 3

null *adj* **1** having no legal or binding force ⟨the contract was *null* because the other person forgot to sign it⟩
syn invalid, nonbinding, nonvalid, null and void, void
rel illegal; useless, worthless; ineffective, ineffectual
near ant legal; working
ant binding, good, valid
2 having no usefulness — see WORTHLESS

null and void *adj* having no legal or binding force — see NULL 1

nullify *vb* to put an end to by formal action — see ABOLISH

numb *adj* lacking in sensation or feeling ⟨I sat in one position too long and now my feet are *numb*⟩
syn asleep, benumbed, dead, insensitive, numbed, unfeeling
rel chilled, nipped; anesthetized, deadened, drugged, stupefied; insensible, senseless, unconscious; inanimate, insensate
near ant awake
ant feeling, sensitive

numb *vb* to reduce or weaken in strength or feeling — see DULL 1

numbed *adj* lacking in sensation or feeling — see NUMB

number *n* a character used to represent a mathematical value ⟨asked him to write out the equation in *numbers*, not letters⟩
syn digit, figure, integer, numeral, whole number
rel decimal, fraction; cipher; symbol

number *vb* **1** to find the sum of (a collection of things) by noting each one as it is being added — see COUNT 1
2 to have a total of — see AMOUNT (TO) 1
3 to have as part of a whole — see INCLUDE

numberless *adj* too many to be counted — see COUNTLESS

numbing *adj* having a low or subnormal temperature — see COLD 1

numbness *n* a lack of emotion or emotional expressiveness — see APATHY 1

numeral *n* a character used to represent a mathematical value — see NUMBER

numerate *vb* **1** to make a list of — see ¹LIST 1
2 to specify one after another — see ENUMERATE 1

numerous *adj* being of a large but indefinite number — see MANY

numskull *or* **numbskull** *n* a stupid person — see IDIOT

nuptial *adj* of or relating to marriage — see MARITAL

nuptial *n, usually* **nuptials** *pl* a ceremony in which two people are united in matrimony — see WEDDING

nurse *n* a girl or woman employed to care for a young child or children ⟨sent his little son back to his *nurse* so that he could return to his study to work⟩
syn babysitter, nursemaid, nurser, sitter
rel mammy; governess

nurse *vb* **1** to attend to the needs and comforts of ⟨took some time to *nurse* his grandmother, helping her get from one room to the other and making sure she was warm⟩
syn care (for), minister (to), mother
rel cure, heal, remedy; doctor, treat; aid, conserve, preserve, provide (for), support; baby, coddle, mollycoddle, pamper, spoil; cater (to), humor; indulge
phrases look after, look out for, look to, see to, take care of
near ant brush (aside *or* off), forget, ignore, neglect, overlook, slight
2 to keep in one's mind or heart — see HARBOR 1
3 to treat with great or excessive care — see BABY

nursemaid *n* a girl or woman employed to care for a young child or children — see NURSE

nurser *n* a girl or woman employed to care for a young child or children — see NURSE

nurture *vb* **1** to help the growth or development of — see FOSTER 1
2 to provide (someone) with moral or spiritual understanding — see ENLIGHTEN 2
3 to supply with nourishment — see SUSTAIN 1

nut *n* **1** a person of odd or whimsical habits — see ECCENTRIC
2 a person who lacks good sense or judgment — see FOOL 1
3 a person with a strong and habitual liking for something — see FAN
4 a person judged to be legally or medically insane — see LUNATIC 1

nutrient *adj* providing the substances necessary for health and bodily growth — see NUTRITIOUS

nutritional *adj* providing the substances necessary for health and bodily growth — see NUTRITIOUS

nutritious *adj* providing the substances necessary for health and bodily growth ⟨opted for a *nutritious* snack and bought an apple instead of a candy bar⟩
syn nourishing, nutrient, nutritional, nutritive
rel dietary, dietetic; beneficial, healthful, healthy, restorative, salubrious, salutary, wholesome
near ant insalubrious, unhealthful, unhealthy, unwholesome
ant nonnutritious

nutritive *adj* providing the substances necessary for health and bodily growth — see NUTRITIOUS

nuts *adj* **1** having or showing a very abnormal or sick state of mind — see INSANE 1

2 showing urgent desire or interest — see EAGER

nuts (about) *adj* filled with an intense or excessive love for — see ENAMORED (OF)

nuttiness *n* lack of good sense or judgment — see FOOLISHNESS 1

nutty *adj* **1** having or showing a very abnormal or sick state of mind — see INSANE 1

2 showing or marked by a lack of good sense or judgment — see FOOLISH 1

nuzzle *vb* to lie close ⟨newborn puppies *nuzzling* against their mother to stay warm⟩
syn cuddle, nestle, snuggle
rel curl up; crouch, huddle
near ant blench, flinch, quail, recoil, shrink, shy, start, wince

nymph *n* **1** a mythical goddess represented as a young girl and said to live outdoors ⟨she bought the book of fairy tales for the beautiful engravings of *nymphs* and fairies featured between the stories⟩
syn dryad, naiad, oread
rel mermaid, siren

2 a young wingless often wormlike form (as a grub or caterpillar) that hatches from the egg of many insects — see LARVA

O

oaf *n* a big clumsy often slow-witted person ⟨it is not polite to call your brother a stupid *oaf*⟩
syn clod, gawk, hulk, lout, lubber, lug
rel chump, loser, schlemiel, turkey; ass, blockhead, dolt, donkey, dope, dumbbell, dummy, goon, half-wit, idiot, ignoramus, imbecile, jackass, moron, nincompoop, ninny, nitwit, simpleton; beast, boor, brute, cad, churl, clown, creep, cretin, cur, heel, louse, skunk, snake, stinker, villain; booby, fool, goose, loony (*also* looney), lunatic, madman, nut; featherbrain, scatterbrain; rascal, rogue, scamp
near ant brain, genius; egghead, intellectual, sage, thinker

oafish *adj* not having or showing an ability to absorb ideas readily — see STUPID 1

oafishness *n* the quality or state of lacking intelligence or quickness of mind — see STUPIDITY 1

oar *vb* to move a boat by means of oars — see ¹ROW

oarsman *n* a person who drives a boat forward by means of oars ⟨the only *oarsman* in a rowboat designed for two⟩
syn rower, sculler
rel coxswain, crewman; puller, sailor

oath *n* a person's solemn declaration that he or she will do or not do something — see PROMISE

obduracy *n* a steadfast adherence to an opinion, purpose, or course of action — see OBSTINACY

obdurate *adj* **1** having or showing a lack of sympathy or tender feelings — see HARD 1

2 sticking to an opinion, purpose, or course of action in spite of reason, arguments, or persuasion — see OBSTINATE

obedience *n* **1** a bending to the authority or control of another ⟨the drill sergeant demanded complete and unquestioning *obedience* from the recruits⟩
syn compliance, conformity, observance, submission, subordination
rel acquiescence, agreeability, amenability; docility, submissiveness; capitulation, surrender, yielding; servility, slavishness, subservience; inhibition, repression, restraint, suppression; control, discipline, order
near ant contrariness, frowardness, intractability, rebelliousness, recalcitrance, refractoriness; disrespect, impudence, insolence, rudeness; insurgency, insurrection, mutiny, revolt; hardheadedness, mulishness, obstinacy, perversity, stubbornness, willfulness; misbehavior, mischievousness, naughtiness; dissent, dissidence
ant disobedience, insubordination, noncompliance, rebelling, rebellion

2 a readiness or willingness to yield to the wishes of others — see COMPLIANCE 1

obedient *adj* readily giving in to the command or authority of another ⟨that boy is so *obedient* that he does everything the first time he is asked⟩
syn amenable, compliant, conformable, docile, law-abiding, submissive, tractable
rel acquiescent, agreeable, amiable, obliging; surrendering, yielding; obsequious, servile, slavish, subservient; decorous, disciplined, mannerly, orderly; constrained, curbed, inhibited, repressed, restrained; controllable, governable, manageable; gentle, meek, mild
near ant insurgent, mutinous; dogged, hardheaded, headstrong, mulish, obdurate, obstinate, peevish, pigheaded, self-

---

syn synonym(s)   *rel* related words
ant antonym(s)   *near ant* near antonym(s)

willed, stubborn, unyielding, willful (*or* wilful); obstreperous, restive, uncontrollable, ungovernable, unmanageable, wild; balky, defiant, perverse, resistant, wayward; bad, disorderly, errant, misbehaving, mischievous, naughty; ill-bred, undisciplined; dissident, nonconformist; disrespectful, ill-mannered, impolite, impudent, insolent, rude

ant contrary, disobedient, froward, insubordinate, intractable, rebellious, recalcitrant, refractory, unruly

obese *adj* having an excess of body fat — see FAT 1

obesity *n* the condition of having an excess of body fat — see CORPULENCE

obey *vb* to act according to the commands of ⟨it is important to *obey* your teachers immediately in the case of an emergency⟩ ⟨most people *obey* the law and wear their seat belts⟩

syn comply (with), conform (to), follow, mind, observe

rel defer (to), submit (to), surrender (to), yield (to); accede (to), acquiesce (to), agree (to), assent (to); attend, hear, heed, listen (to), mark, note, notice, regard, watch

phrases abide by

near ant challenge, dare; rebel (against); defy; direct, lead; brush off, disregard, ignore, overlook, overpass, pass over, tune out, wink (at); dismiss, pooh-pooh, shrug off; break, transgress, violate; deride, flout, scorn

ant disobey

object *n* 1 something material that can be perceived by the senses ⟨I kept tripping over countless little *objects* scattered about the darkened room⟩

syn thing

rel article, item, piece; being, entity, substance; commodity, good, ware; accessory, accompaniment, bauble, curio; knickknack, spangle, token, trinket

2 one that has a real and independent existence — see ENTITY

3 something that one hopes or intends to accomplish — see GOAL

object *vb* to present an opposing opinion or argument ⟨they *objected* to the conductor's insistence that their train tickets were not valid⟩

syn demur, expostulate (with), kick, protest, remonstrate (with)

rel cavil, quibble; challenge, dare, defy; conflict (with), debate, dispute, hassle, quarrel, squabble, wrangle; complain, inveigh (against); balk (at), stick (at); censure, criticize, denounce; disobey, rebel (against); demonstrate (against)

phrases take exception

near ant approve, sanction; accept; accede (to), acquiesce (to), agree (with), assent (to); comply (with), obey; advocate, champion, defend, maintain, support, sustain, uphold

objection *n* a feeling or declaration of disapproval or dissent ⟨pardon me, but I

have an *objection* to any plan that requires staying out all night⟩

syn challenge, complaint, demur, expostulation, fuss, protest, question, remonstrance

rel compunction, doubt, misgiving, qualm, scruple; difficulty, misunderstanding; cavil, quibble; argument, conflict, debate, dispute, dissent, hassle, quarrel, squabble; censure, criticism; defiance, disobedience, rebellion

near ant willingness; approval, sanction; acceptance, acquiescence, agreement, assent; compliance, obedience

objectionable *adj* provoking or likely to provoke protest ⟨that T-shirt displays *objectionable* images which are not appropriate for school⟩

syn censurable, exceptionable, obnoxious, offensive, reprehensible

rel bawdy, coarse, crude, dirty, filthy, foul, gross, indecent, lewd, nasty, obscene, smutty, vulgar; blamable, blameworthy, lascivious, pornographic, ribald, scurrilous; debasing, perverted, profane; racy, salty, suggestive; unacceptable, undesirable, unwanted, unwelcome; abhorrent, disgusting, loathsome, repellent (*also* repellant), repugnant, repulsive, revolting; disagreeable, displeasing, distasteful, unpleasant; bad, execrable, lousy, miserable; atrocious, infamous; indecent, indecorous, unbecoming; earthy, unprintable; naughty, wicked

near ant acceptable, agreeable, pleasant, pleasing, welcome; good; approved, endorsed, sanctioned; abetted, encouraged, promoted, supported; becoming, correct, decent, decorous, exemplary, seemly; blameless, commendable, creditable; immaculate, perfect, pure, spotless

ant inoffensive, unobjectionable

objective *adj* 1 based on observation or experience — see EMPIRICAL

2 marked by justice, honesty, and freedom from bias — see FAIR 2

3 restricted to or based on fact — see FACTUAL 1

objective *n* something that one hopes or intends to accomplish — see GOAL

objectivity *n* lack of favoritism toward one side or another — see DETACHMENT 1

obligate *vb* to cause (a person) to give in to pressure — see FORCE

obligation *n* something one must do because of prior agreement ⟨their financial *obligations* keep them from giving to charities as much as they would like⟩

syn burden, charge, commitment, duty, need, responsibility

rel pledge, promise; arrangement, prearrangement, setup; compact, contract, covenant, pact; payment, tribute; compulsion, constraint, restraint; must, requirement; coercion, duress, force; appointment, engagement, reservation

near ant grace, postponement, stay; discharge, exemption, release, waiver; alternative, choice, option, pick, preference, selection

obligatory *adj* forcing one's compliance or participation by or as if by law — see MANDATORY

oblige *vb* **1** to do a service or favor for ⟨I would appreciate it greatly if you could *oblige* me by bringing a dessert to the party⟩

syn accommodate, favor

rel humor, indulge; coddle, mollycoddle, pamper; appease, conciliate, mollify, pacify, placate; delight, gladden, gratify, please, satisfy; abet, aid, assist, help, support; attend, care (for), minister (to), relieve, succor

near ant bother, discommode, disturb, incommode, inconvenience, trouble; burden, encumber, saddle, weigh; desert, disappoint, fail, let down; constrain, hamper, hamstring, hinder, hobble, hold back, impede, obstruct, restrain; frustrate, oppose, sabotage, thwart

ant disoblige

2 to cause (a person) to give in to pressure — see FORCE

obliged *adj* feeling or expressing gratitude — see GRATEFUL 1

oblique *adj* **1** inclined or twisted to one side — see AWRY

2 running in a slanting direction — see DIAGONAL

obliquely *adv* in a line or direction running from corner to corner — see CROSSWISE

obliterate *vb* to destroy all traces of — see ANNIHILATE 1

obliteration *n* the state or fact of being rendered nonexistent, physically unsound, or useless — see DESTRUCTION

oblivion *n* a state of being disregardful or unconscious of one's surroundings, concerns, or obligations ⟨for two weeks each year the stressed-out couple enjoy the blissful *oblivion* that comes with a vacation at the beach⟩

syn forgetfulness, obliviousness

rel ignorance, unawareness, unconsciousness, unfamiliarity

near ant memory, recall, recollection, remembrance; alertness, awareness, cognizance, consciousness

oblivious *adj* not informed about or aware of something — see IGNORANT 2

obliviousness *n* **1** a state of being disregardful or unconscious of one's surroundings, concerns, or obligations — see OBLIVION

2 the state of being unaware or uninformed — see IGNORANCE 1

obnoxious *adj* **1** causing intense displeasure, disgust, or resentment — see OFFENSIVE 1

2 provoking or likely to provoke protest — see OBJECTIONABLE

obscene *adj* **1** depicting or referring to sexual matters in a way that is unacceptable in polite society ⟨*obscene* language and artwork is forbidden in this school⟩

syn bawdy, coarse, crude, dirty, filthy, foul, gross, indecent, lascivious, lewd, nasty, pornographic, ribald, smutty, unprintable, vulgar, wanton

rel earthy, racy, salty, suggestive; indecorous, unbecoming; debasing, perverted, profane; naughty, wicked; exceptionable, objectionable, unacceptable, undesirable, unwanted, unwelcome; abhorrent, disgusting, loathsome, offensive, repellent (*also* repellant), repugnant, repulsive, revolting; distasteful, obnoxious, unpleasant; blamable, blameworthy, censurable, reprehensible; atrocious, infamous; abusive, scurrilous

near ant priggish, prim, prudish, puritanical, straitlaced (*or* straightlaced), Victorian; correct, decorous, genteel, polite, proper, seemly; innocuous, inoffensive; acceptable, agreeable, desirable, pleasant, pleasing, welcome; appropriate, becoming, fit, meet, suitable; immaculate, perfect, pure, spotless; approved, endorsed, sanctioned

ant clean, decent

2 causing intense displeasure, disgust, or resentment — see OFFENSIVE 1

obscenity *n* **1** the quality or state of being obscene ⟨the issue of whether *obscenity* is a fundamental part of rap music⟩

syn bawdiness, coarseness, crudeness, dirt, dirtiness, filth, filthiness, foulness, grossness, indecency, lasciviousness, lewdness, nastiness, ribaldry, smuttiness, vulgarity

rel raciness, saltiness, suggestiveness; perversion, profanity; naughtiness, wickedness; loathsomeness, offensiveness, repulsiveness; distastefulness, obnoxiousness, unpleasantness

near ant priggishness, primness, prudery, prudishness, puritanism; correctness, decency, decorousness, decorum, seemliness; appropriateness, fitness, suitability, suitableness; immaculateness, perfection, purity, spotlessness

2 a disrespectful or indecent word or expression — see SWEARWORD

obscure *adj* **1** having an often intentionally veiled or uncertain meaning ⟨a fantasy writer who likes to put lots of *obscure* references and images in her tales of wizards and warlocks⟩

syn ambiguous, cryptic, dark, darkling, deep, enigmatic (*also* enigmatical), equivocal, inscrutable, murky, mysterious, mystic, nebulous, occult

rel abstruse, esoteric, recondite; bleary, cloudy, dim, faint, foggy, fuzzy, hazy, indefinite, indistinct, indistinguishable, shadowy, unclear, uncertain, undefined, undetermined, vague; impenetrable, incomprehensible, inexplicable; eerie, uncanny, weird; impalpable, inappreciable, intangible, invisible; unanswerable, unknowable; baffling, bewildering, confounding, confusing, mystifying, perplexing, puzzling, unfathomable; difficult, complex, complicated, obtuse

near ant comprehensible, fathomable, intelligible, knowable, understandable; bright, distinct, evident; certain, firm, strong, sure; defined, determined; direct, straightforward; definite, exact, explicit; appreciable, palpable, tangible, visible; blatant, patent, unmistakable

ant clear, obvious, plain, unambiguous, unequivocal

2 not widely known ⟨he's an *obscure* artist now, but he's sure to be famous someday⟩

syn anonymous, nameless, uncelebrated, unknown, unnoted, unsung

rel insignificant, minor, unimportant; undistinguished, unexceptional; unpopular; faceless

near ant fabled, fabulous, legendary; infamous; distinguished, eminent, exceptional, great, illustrious, leading, notable, outstanding, prestigious, remarkable; important, significant; favorite, popular, preferred; estimable, honorable, reputable, respectable; influential, major

ant celebrated, famed, famous, noted, notorious, prominent, renowned, well-known

3 being without light or without much light — see DARK 1

4 not seen or understood clearly — see FAINT 1

obscure *vb* **1** to keep secret or shut off from view — see ¹HIDE 2

2 to make dark, dim, or indistinct — see CLOUD 1

obscured *adj* being without light or without much light — see DARK 1

obscurity *n* **1** the quality or state of having a veiled or uncertain meaning ⟨the 16th-century astrologer's predictions are so filled with *obscurity* that people can interpret them any way they want⟩

syn ambiguity, ambiguousness, darkness, equivocalness, equivocation, murkiness, nebulousness, opacity

rel cloudiness, dimness, faintness, fogginess, fuzziness, haziness, indefiniteness, indistinctness, uncertainty, vagueness; impenetrability, incomprehensibility; deepness, profoundness; intangibility, invisibility; abstruseness; complexity, complication, difficulty, obtuseness

near ant comprehensibility, intelligibility; brightness, distinctness; certainty, surety; definiteness, exactness, explicitness; directness, straightforwardness; palpability, tangibility, visibility

ant clarity, clearness, obviousness, plainness

2 the quality or state of being mostly or completely unknown ⟨the singer languished in relative *obscurity* for years before becoming famous⟩

syn anonymity

rel oblivion; inconspicuousness, invisibility; insignificance, unimportance; unpopularity

near ant name, report, reputation, repute; popularity; importance, significance; distinction, eminence, glory, greatness, honor, illustriousness, note, preeminence, prominence; cachet, position, prestige, rank, standing, stature; acclaim, acknowledgment (*also* acknowledgement), praise, recognition; adoration, idolization

ant celebrity, fame, notoriety, renown

observable *adj* capable of being seen — see VISIBLE

observance *n* **1** an act of following a custom, rule, or law ⟨the *observance* of this family tradition would make your grandmother very happy⟩

syn observation

rel attention, heed, notice; respecting, upholding

near ant infraction, offense (*or* offence), sin, trespass, wrong; disregard, forgetting, ignoring, neglect, overlooking; delinquency, dereliction

ant breach, infringement, nonobservance, transgression, violation

2 an oft-repeated action or series of actions performed in accordance with tradition or a set of rules — see RITE

3 a bending to the authority or control of another — see OBEDIENCE 1

4 a state of being aware — see ATTENTION 2

observation *n* **1** a state of being aware — see ATTENTION 2

2 an act of following a custom, rule, or law — see OBSERVANCE 1

observational *adj* based on observation or experience — see EMPIRICAL

observatory *n* a high place or structure from which a wide view is possible — see LOOKOUT 1

observe *vb* **1** to act according to the commands of — see OBEY

2 to act properly in relation to — see KEEP 1

3 to keep one's eyes on — see WATCH 1

4 to make a statement of one's opinion — see REMARK 1

5 to make note of (something) through the use of one's eyes — see SEE 1

6 to take notice of and be guided by — see HEED 1

obsessed *adj* having extreme or relentless concern — see HUNG UP 1

obsession *n* something about which one is constantly thinking or concerned — see FIXATION

obsessive *adj* caused by or suggestive of an irresistible urge — see COMPULSIVE

obsolete *adj* having passed its time of use or usefulness ⟨the abacus was considered *obsolete* once the electronic calculator was invented⟩

syn antiquated, archaic, dated, moth-eaten, outdated, outmoded, out-of-date, outworn, passé

rel aging, obsolescent; discarded, disused; superannuated, worn-out; inoperable, unusable, unworkable, useless; dead, defunct, extinct; dormant, fallow, free, idle, inactive, inert, inoperative, latent; ancient, antediluvian, antique, fusty, musty, old, oldfangled, old-fashioned, old-time, old-world; aged, age-old, hoary, venerable; bygone, erstwhile, former, late, past; historic, historical

near ant contemporary, current, mod, modern, new, newfangled, new-fashioned, present-day, recent, ultramodern, up-to-date; fresh; modernized, refurbished, remodeled, renewed; functional, operable, operational, workable; active, alive, busy, employed, functioning, operating, operative

obstacle *n* something that makes movement or progress more difficult — see ENCUMBRANCE

obstinacy *n* a steadfast adherence to an opinion, purpose, or course of action ⟨the mindless *obstinacy* of those people who continue to insist that the earth is flat⟩

syn doggedness, hardheadedness, mulishness, obduracy, peevishness, persistence, pertinaciousness, pertinacity, self-will, stubbornness, tenaciousness, tenacity, willfulness

rel perverseness, perversity, resistance, waywardness, wrongheadedness; hardness, inflexibility, relentlessness, sternness, strictness; certainty, determination, firmness; inexorability, resolve, rigidity, rigidness, steadfastness; contrariness, defiance, disobedience, insubordination, recalcitrance

near ant broad-mindedness, open-mindedness, reasonableness, receptivity; acceptance, acquiescence, flexibility, pliability; compliance, docility, obedience; submission, surrender, willingness, yielding; slavishness, subservience

obstinate *adj* sticking to an opinion, purpose, or course of action in spite of reason, arguments, or persuasion ⟨the child was *obstinate* about wanting that specific toy, despite being offered several others⟩

syn adamant, adamantine, dogged, hard, hardened, hardheaded, hardhearted, headstrong, immovable, implacable, inflexible, mulish, obdurate, opinionated, ossified, pat, peevish, pertinacious, perverse, pigheaded, rigid, self-willed, stubborn, unbending, uncompromising, unrelenting, unyielding, willful (*or* wilful)

rel hidebound, narrow-minded; resistant, wayward, wrongheaded; persistent, tenacious; iron, relentless; grim, severe, stern, strict; determined, firm, inexorable, resolved, single-minded, steadfast, sure, unflinching; contrary, disobedient, froward, insubordinate, intractable, recalcitrant, refractory, uncooperative, ungovernable, unmanageable, unruly; defiant, insurgent, mutinous; indomitable, invincible, unconquerable; confirmed, inveterate, unregenerate; demanding, exacting

near ant docile, law-abiding, obedient, submissive, tractable; accepting, recep-

tive, responsive, willing; governable, manageable, reasonable, temperate; slavish, subservient

ant acquiescent, agreeable, amenable, compliant, complying, flexible, pliable, pliant, relenting, yielding

obstreperous *adj* engaging in or marked by loud and insistent cries especially of protest — see VOCIFEROUS

obstruct *vb* 1 to create difficulty for the work or activity of — see HAMPER

2 to prevent passage through — see CLOG 1

obstruction *n* something that makes movement or progress more difficult — see ENCUMBRANCE

obtain *vb* to receive as return for effort — see EARN 1

obtainable *adj* possible to get — see AVAILABLE 1

obtrude *vb* to interest oneself in what is not one's concern — see INTERFERE

obtrusive *adj* thrusting oneself where one is not welcome or invited — see INTRUSIVE

obtuse *adj* 1 lacking sharpness of edge or point — see DULL 1

2 not having or showing an ability to absorb ideas readily — see STUPID 1

obtuseness *n* the quality or state of lacking intelligence or quickness of mind — see STUPIDITY 1

obviate *vb* to keep from happening by taking action in advance — see PREVENT

obviating *n* the act or practice of keeping something from happening — see PREVENTION

obvious *adj* 1 not subject to misinterpretation or more than one interpretation — see CLEAR 2

2 very noticeable especially for being incorrect or bad — see EGREGIOUS

occasion *n* 1 a particular point at which an event takes place ⟨the *occasion* of our last meeting with our old friend was several years ago, unfortunately⟩

syn moment, time

rel flash, instant, jiffy, minute, second, shake, split second, trice, twinkle, wink; while

2 a favorable combination of circumstances, time, and place — see OPPORTUNITY

3 someone or something responsible for a result — see CAUSE 1

4 something that happens — see EVENT 1

occasional *adj* 1 lacking in steadiness or regularity of occurrence — see FITFUL

2 not often occurring or repeated — see INFREQUENT

occasionally *adv* on some occasions — see SOMETIMES

occult *adj* 1 being beyond one's powers to know, understand, or explain — see MYSTERIOUS 1

2 having an often intentionally veiled or uncertain meaning — see OBSCURE 1

3 having seemingly supernatural qualities or powers — see MYSTIC 1

---

syn synonym(s)   **rel** related words
ant antonym(s)   **near ant** near antonym(s)

occult *vb* to keep secret or shut off from view — see ¹HIDE 2

occupant *n* one who lives permanently in a place — see INHABITANT

occupation *n* the activity by which one regularly makes a living ⟨my primary *occupation* is as a stockbroker, but I'm a drummer in a rock band on the weekends⟩
syn calling, employment, line, profession, trade, vocation, work
rel racket; art, craft, handicraft; appointment, assignment, berth, billet, duty, function, job, office, place, position, post, situation; business, engagement, livelihood, living
near ant avocation, hobby, pursuit

occupied *adj* involved in often constant activity — see BUSY 1

occupy *vb* 1 to hold the attention of — see ENGAGE 1
2 to keep, control, or experience as one's own — see HAVE 1

occur *vb* to take place — see HAPPEN

occur (to) *vb* to come into the mind of ⟨it didn't *occur to* me to ask until much later⟩
syn dawn (on), strike
rel appear, arrive, come, emerge, materialize; con, learn, memorize; recall, recollect, remember, reminisce
near ant forget, unlearn; disregard, neglect, overlook

occurrence *n* something that happens — see EVENT 1

ocean *n* the whole body of salt water that covers nearly three-fourths of the earth ⟨the Vikings explored the *ocean* in small open boats, beginning in the eighth century⟩
syn blue, brine, deep, sea, seven seas
rel high seas, main, waters; basin; Davy Jones's locker

oceanic *adj* of or relating to the sea — see MARINE 1

ocular *adj* of, relating to, or used in vision — see VISUAL 1

odd *adj* 1 being one of a pair or set without a corresponding mate ⟨somehow, there's always at least one *odd* sock that comes out of the dryer⟩
syn unmatched, unpaired
rel alone, lone, only, single, singular, sole, solitary
ant matched, paired
2 different from the ordinary in a way that causes curiosity or suspicion ⟨one girl dyed her hair purple with pink polka dots, which was a rather *odd* effect⟩
syn bizarre, curious, far-out, funny, kinky, outlandish, out-of-the-way, outré, peculiar, quaint, queer, queerish, quirky, remarkable, screwy, strange, wacky, way-out, weird, wild
rel aberrant, abnormal, atypical, extraordinary, fantastic, flaky, freak, freakish, idiosyncratic, phenomenal, singular, unique, unusual, unwonted; conspicuous, notable, noticeable, outstanding, prominent, salient, striking; atrocious, outra-

geous, shocking; nonconformist, unconventional, unorthodox; eccentric, idiosyncratic; rare, uncommon, uncustomary; baffling, bewildering, confounding, mystifying, perplexing, puzzling
near ant average, commonplace, everyday, garden, ordinary, prosaic, routine, run-of-the-mill, typical, unexceptional, unremarkable, usual, workaday; conformist, conservative, conventional; expected, familiar, predictable; common, customary, frequent, habitual, regular, wonted
3 being out of the ordinary — see EXCEPTIONAL
4 noticeably different from what is generally found or experienced — see UNUSUAL 1

oddball *n* a person of odd or whimsical habits — see ECCENTRIC

oddity *n* 1 an odd or peculiar habit — see IDIOSYNCRASY
2 something strange or unusual that is an object of interest — see CURIOSITY 2

oddment *n* an unused or unwanted piece or item typically of small size or value — see ¹SCRAP 1

odds *n pl* a measure of how often an event will occur instead of another — see PROBABILITY 2

odds and ends *n pl* 1 small useful items — see NOTION 1
2 a remaining group or portion — see REMAINDER 1

odious *adj* causing intense displeasure, disgust, or resentment — see OFFENSIVE 1

odium *n* the state of having lost the esteem of others — see DISGRACE 1

odor *n* the quality of a thing that makes it perceptible to the sense organs in the nose — see SMELL

of *prep* 1 earlier than — see BEFORE 1
2 having to do with — see ABOUT 1

off *adv* from this or that place — see AWAY

off *adj* 1 falling short of a standard — see BAD 1
2 not being in a state of use, activity, or employment — see INACTIVE 2
3 not being in agreement with what is true — see FALSE 1
4 small in degree — see REMOTE 1

offbeat *adj* noticeably different from what is generally found or experienced — see UNUSUAL 1

offend *vb* 1 to commit an offense ⟨since this is the first time you've *offended*, we'll let you off lightly⟩
syn err, sin, transgress, trespass
rel breach, break, infringe, violate; backslide, lapse
phrases break the law, fall from grace
near ant forgive, justify; repent
2 to cause hurt feelings or deep resentment in — see INSULT

offender *n* a person who has committed a crime — see CRIMINAL

offense *or* **offence** *n* 1 a breaking of a moral or legal code ⟨wartime *offenses* that are crimes against all of humanity⟩

syn breach, crime, debt, error, lawbreaking, malefaction, misdeed, misdoing, sin, transgression, trespass, violation, wrongdoing

rel felony, misdemeanor; fault, foible, peccadillo; break, infringement; immorality, iniquity, sinfulness, vice, wickedness; criminality, illegality, lawlessness, unlawfulness

near ant blamelessness, faultlessness, guiltlessness, innocence; goodness, morality, righteousness, virtue, virtuousness

2 the act or action of setting upon with force or violence — see ATTACK 1

3 an act or expression showing scorn and usually intended to hurt another's feelings — see INSULT

4 the feeling of being offended or resentful after a slight or indignity — see PIQUE

offensive *adj* **1** causing intense displeasure, disgust, or resentment ⟨I find your disrespectful attitude toward religion very *offensive*⟩ ⟨the smell of rotting food is quite *offensive*⟩

syn abhorrent, abominable, appalling, awful, distasteful, dreadful, foul, hideous, horrendous, horrible, horrid, loathsome, nasty, nauseating, noisome, obnoxious, obscene, odious, repellent (*also* repellant), repugnant, repulsive, revolting, scandalous, shocking, sickening, ugly

rel exceptionable, objectionable; disagreeable, unpleasant; contemptible, despicable, detestable, hateful; unhealthy, unwholesome; execrable, lousy, miserable; atrocious, heinous, unspeakable; barbarous, unchristian, uncivilized, ungodly, unholy

near ant acceptable, agreeable, attractive, delectable, delightful, desirable, likable (*or* likeable), pleasant, pleasing, welcome; unobjectionable; healthy, wholesome

ant inoffensive

2 provoking or likely to provoke protest — see OBJECTIONABLE

offensive *n* the act or action of setting upon with force or violence — see ATTACK 1

offer *n* something which is presented for consideration — see PROPOSAL

offer *vb* **1** to put before another for acceptance or consideration ⟨I *offered* my boss an alternative to the plan that required me to work overtime⟩

syn extend, give, proffer, tender

rel pose, propose

near ant accept, receive, take; decline, refuse, reject; retract, withdraw; consider, contemplate, mull (over), ponder, study, think (over)

2 to set before the mind for consideration — see PROPOSE 1

3 to bring before the public in performance or exhibition — see PRESENT 1

4 to give up as an offering to a god — see SACRIFICE

---

syn synonym(s)   *rel* related words
ant antonym(s)   *near ant* near antonym(s)

offering *n* something offered to a god — see SACRIFICE

offhand *adj* made or done without previous thought or preparation — see EXTEMPORANEOUS

offhanded *adj* made or done without previous thought or preparation — see EXTEMPORANEOUS

office *n* a large unit of a governmental, business, or educational organization — see DIVISION 2

officeholder *n* a person who holds a public office — see OFFICIAL

officer *n* **1** a member of a force charged with law enforcement at the local level ⟨if you are ever lost, find the nearest *officer* and ask for help⟩

syn bobby [*British*], bull [*slang*], constable, cop, policeman, police officer

rel patrolman, policewoman; detective, inspector, plainclothesman; marshal, sheriff, trooper; captain, lieutenant, sergeant

2 a person who holds a public office — see OFFICIAL

official *adj* ordered or allowed by those in authority ⟨the *official* languages for those Olympic Games were French and English⟩

syn authorized, sanctioned

rel legal, permissible; approved, endorsed; abetted, encouraged, promoted, suggested, supported; certified, licensed (*also* licenced); authoritative, canonical, ex officio; semiofficial

near ant illegal, illicit, unlawful; unapproved, unendorsed, unlicensed

ant unauthorized, unofficial, unsanctioned

official *n* a person who holds a public office ⟨some of our best public *officials* do their jobs quietly and are never in the news⟩

syn functionary, officeholder, officer, public servant

rel bureaucrat; administrator, commissioner, director, executive, manager, superintendent, supervisor; chair, chairman

officious *adj* thrusting oneself where one is not welcome or invited — see INTRUSIVE

offing *n* time that is to come — see FUTURE 1

offset *n* a force or influence that makes an opposing force ineffective or less effective — see COUNTERBALANCE

offset *vb* to balance with an equal force so as to make ineffective ⟨if you get a high grade on this quiz, it will *offset* the D from your last one⟩

syn annul, cancel (out), compensate (for), correct, counteract, counterbalance, counterpoise, make up (for), neutralize

rel invalidate, negate, nullify; atone (for); outweigh, redeem; redress, relieve, remedy; override, overrule

offshoot *n* **1** a branch of a main stem especially of a plant ⟨we knew the rose bush had survived the winter when it began producing *offshoots* and turning green again⟩

syn outgrowth, shoot

rel excrescence, growth; bough, limb, twig; bud, floret; spray, sprig

2 something that naturally develops or is developed from something else — see DE-RIVATIVE

offspring *n* the descendants of a person, animal, or plant ⟨the racehorse's *offspring* all proved to be very good racers as well⟩ ⟨the couple celebrated their 50th wedding anniversary surrounded by three generations of *offspring*⟩

syn issue, posterity, progeny, seed, spawn

rel brood, hatch, litter, young; child, scion (*also* cion)

near ant ancestor, antecedent, forebear (*also* forbear), forefather, parent

offstage *adj or adv* off or away from the part of the stage visible to the audience ⟨please wait until you are *offstage* to start changing costumes⟩

syn backstage

rel upstage

phrases behind the scenes

oft *adv* many times — see OFTEN

often *adv* many times ⟨I seem to stumble *often* when I try to walk in high heels⟩

syn constantly, continually, frequently, oft, oftentimes (*or* ofttimes), repeatedly

rel always, consistently, continuously, perpetually; afresh, again, anew; commonly, ordinarily, regularly, routinely; intermittently, periodically, recurrently; generally, usually

phrases again and again, over and over, time after time, time and again

near ant occasionally, sometimes, sporadically, never; once

ant infrequently, rarely, seldom

oftentimes *or* **ofttimes** *adv* many times — see OFTEN

ogle *vb* to look at in a flirtatious or desiring way ⟨I do wish you two would stop *ogling* each other during class⟩

syn leer (at)

rel eye, gape, gawk, gaze, glare, goggle, peer, rubberneck, stare

ogre *n* **1** a strange or horrible and often frightening creature — see MONSTER 1

2 something or someone that causes fear or dread especially without reason — see BOGEY 1

oh *n* the numerical symbol 0 or the absence of number or quantity represented by it — see ZERO 1

oil *n* a picture created with usually oil paint — see PAINTING

oil *vb* to coat (something) with a slippery substance in order to reduce friction — see LUBRICATE

oiled *adj* having or being a surface so smooth as to make sliding or falling likely — see SLICK 1

oil painting *n* a picture created with usually oil paint — see PAINTING

oilskin *n* a coat made of water-resistant material — see RAINCOAT

OK *or* **okay** *adj* **1** being to one's liking — see SATISFACTORY 1

2 of a level of quality that meets one's needs or standards — see ADEQUATE

OK *or* **okay** *adv* **1** in a satisfactory way — see WELL 1

2 used to express agreement — see YES

OK *or* **okay** *n* an acceptance of something as satisfactory — see APPROVAL 1

OK *or* **okay** *vb* **1** to give official acceptance of something as satisfactory — see APPROVE

2 to have a favorable opinion of — see APPROVE (OF)

old *adj* **1** being of advanced years and especially past middle age — see ELDERLY

2 dating or surviving from the distant past — see ANCIENT 1

3 having been such at some previous time — see FORMER

older *adj* being of advanced years and especially past middle age — see ELDERLY

oldfangled *adj* pleasantly reminiscent of an earlier time — see OLD-FASHIONED 1

old-fashioned *adj* **1** pleasantly reminiscent of an earlier time ⟨an elegant, *old-fashioned* bun that was held in place with pearl hairpins⟩

syn antique, oldfangled, old-time, old-world, quaint

rel antiquated, obsolete; historic, historical, olden, traditional; outdated, outmoded, out-of-date, outworn, passé; dated, fusty, moth-eaten, musty; aged, age-old, ancient, antediluvian, fossilized, hoary, venerable; bygone, erstwhile, former, late, past; forgotten, remote; ageless, dateless; timeless

near ant fresh, new, up-to-date; chic, fashionable, smart, stylish; modernized, refurbished, remodeled, renewed

ant contemporary, hot, mod, modern, newfangled, new-fashioned, ultramodern

2 tending to favor established ideas, conditions, or institutions — see CONSERVA-TIVE 1

old hand *n* a person with long experience in a specified area — see VETERAN

old-maidish *adj* hard to please — see FINICKY

old man *n* **1** a male human parent — see FATHER 1

2 the male partner in a marriage — see HUSBAND

oldster *n* a person of advanced years — see SENIOR CITIZEN

old-time *adj* pleasantly reminiscent of an earlier time — see OLD-FASHIONED 1

old-timer *n* **1** a person of advanced years — see SENIOR CITIZEN

2 a person with long experience in a specified area — see VETERAN

old wives' tale *n* a false idea or belief — see FALLACY 1

old-world *adj* pleasantly reminiscent of an earlier time — see OLD-FASHIONED 1

omen *n* something believed to be a sign or warning of a future event ⟨some people believe that a black cat crossing your path is an *omen* that something bad is about to happen to you⟩

syn augury, auspice, boding, foreboding, foreshadowing, portent, prefiguring, presage

rel forerunner, harbinger, herald, precursor; foretaste, hint, inkling, intimation, suggestion; forewarning; forecast, foretelling, prediction, prognostication, prophecy; badge, mark, note, token

ominous *adj* being or showing a sign of evil or calamity to come ⟨that comment about downsizing from the company president sounded *ominous*⟩

syn baleful, dire, foreboding, inauspicious, menacing, portentous, sinister, threatening

rel black, dark, gloomy; unfavorable, unpromising; ill-fated, ill-starred, star-crossed, unfortunate, unlucky; evil, malign, malignant

near ant auspicious, benign, favorable, promising, propitious

omission *n* something left out ⟨the disk contains a selection of deleted scenes, and a couple of the *omissions* greatly add to the intelligibility of the movie's plot⟩

syn deletion

rel elimination; blank, skip; lapse, slip; deduction, reduction, subtraction

near ant inclusion; accretion, accrual, addendum, addition, augmentation, boost, gain, increase, increment, raise, rise, supplement

omit *vb* to miss the opportunity or obligation — see NEGLECT 3

omnibus *adj* covering everything or all important points — see ENCYCLOPEDIC

omnipotent *adj* having unlimited power or authority ⟨the nearly universal religious belief that God is *omnipotent* and can do anything⟩

syn all-powerful, almighty

rel great, sovereign, supreme, towering, transcendent; authoritative, chief, majestic, masterful; mighty, potent, powerful, strong; divine, godlike

near ant helpless, impotent, powerless; limited, restricted

omnipresent *adj* present in all places and at all times ⟨seeking some much-needed relief from the *omnipresent* noise of the big city⟩

syn ubiquitous, universal

rel boundless, endless, illimitable, immeasurable, indefinite, infinite, limitless, measureless, unbounded, unfathomable, unlimited

near ant bounded, circumscribed, confined, finite, limited, restricted

on *adj* being in effective operation — see ACTIVE 1

on *adv* 1 toward a point ahead in space or time — see ONWARD 1

2 toward or at a point lying in advance in space or time — see ALONG

on *prep* 1 having to do with — see ABOUT 1

2 in or into contact with — see AGAINST

oncoming *adj* being soon to appear or take place — see FORTHCOMING

one *adj* known but not named — see CERTAIN 1

one–dimensional *adj* having or showing a lack of depth of understanding or character — see SUPERFICIAL 2

onerous *adj* 1 difficult to endure — see HARSH 1

2 requiring much time, effort, or careful attention — see DEMANDING 1

one–sided *adj* inclined to favor one side over another — see PARTIAL 1

one–sidedness *n* an attitude that always favors one way of feeling or acting especially without considering any other possibilities — see BIAS

onetime *adj* having been such at some previous time — see FORMER

ongoing *adj* 1 being in progress or development ⟨we do seem to be making some headway on that *ongoing* project⟩ ⟨the ever *ongoing* quest for knowledge by men and women of science⟩

syn afoot, proceeding, under way

rel functioning, happening, operating, working; afloat, alive, going; advancing, gaining

near ant receding, regressing, retrogressing

ant arrested, halted, stalled, stopped

2 existing or in progress right now — see PRESENT 1

only *adj* 1 having no equal or rival for excellence or desirability ⟨the *only* way to really appreciate the beauty of the forest is to walk through it⟩

syn incomparable, inimitable, matchless, nonpareil, peerless, unequaled (*or* unequalled), unexampled, unmatched, unparalleled, unrivaled (*or* unrivalled), unsurpassable, unsurpassed

rel singular, unique; exceptional, extraordinary, rare, uncommon, unusual; A1, bang-up, banner, boss [*slang*], capital, classic, dandy, excellent, fabulous, fine, first-class, first-rate, grand, great, groovy, jim-dandy, keen, marvelous (*or* marvellous), mean, neat, par excellence, prime, superb, superior, superlative, terrific, tip-top, top-notch; better, preferred; exceptional, fancy, high-grade, special

near ant common, everyday, normal, ordinary, usual; inferior, lesser, worse, worst; bad, low, lousy; low-grade, substandard, unsatisfactory; mediocre, second-class, second-rate; atrocious, execrable, wretched

2 being the one or ones of a class with no other members ⟨that is the *only* possible right answer⟩ ⟨we were the *only* passengers on the tour bus⟩

syn alone, lone, singular, sole, solitary, special, unique

rel solo, unaccompanied, unattended; incomparable, inimitable, matchless, peerless, unequaled (*or* unequalled), un-

---

syn synonym(s)   **rel** related words
ant antonym(s)   **near ant** near antonym(s)

matched, unparalleled, unrivaled (*or* unrivalled), unsurpassable, unsurpassed; distinct, distinctive, individual, separate
near ant manifold, multifarious, myriad; assorted, heterogenous, miscellaneous, mixed, motley

only *adv* **1** for nothing other than — see SOLELY 1
2 not long ago — see NEWLY
3 nothing more than — see JUST 3
only *conj* if it were not for the fact that — see EXCEPT
onrush *n* forward movement in time or place — see ADVANCE 1
onset *n* **1** the act or action of setting upon with force or violence — see ATTACK 1
2 the point at which something begins — see BEGINNING
onslaught *n* the act or action of setting upon with force or violence — see ATTACK 1
onward *also* **onwards** *adv* **1** toward a point ahead in space or time ⟨we must continue to move *onward,* or we will die in this desert⟩
syn ahead, forth, forward, on
near ant backward
2 toward or at a point lying in advance in space or time — see ALONG
oodles *n* a considerable amount — see LOT 2
ooze *n* soft wet earth — see MUD
ooze *vb* to flow forth slowly through small openings — see EXUDE 1
oozy *adj* full of or covered with soft wet earth — see MUDDY 1
opacity *n* the quality or state of having a veiled or uncertain meaning — see OBSCURITY 1
opaque *adj* not seen or understood clearly — see FAINT 1
open *adj* **1** allowing passage without obstruction ⟨thank you for clearing out the hallway so that it's *open* again⟩
syn clear, cleared, free, unclogged, unclosed, unobstructed, unstopped
rel emptied, unoccupied, vacant; exposed, revealed; gaping, wide, yawning; unbarred, unbolted, unclasped, unfastened, unlatched, unlocked, unsealed; unbuttoned, unclenched, unfolded, unfurled, unzipped
near ant constricted, cramped, encumbered, hampered, hindered, impeded, interfered (with), trammeled; barricaded, blockaded, dammed
ant blocked, clogged, closed, jammed, obstructed, plugged, shut, stopped, stuffed, uncleared
2 freely available for use or participation by all ⟨the beach's *open* sand castle-building contest that every year attracts competitors of all ages and abilities⟩
syn free-for-all, public, unrestricted
rel collective, common, communal, shared; accessible, available, free; unregulated
near ant limited; inaccessible, unavailable
ant closed, exclusive, off-limits, private, restricted

3 being in a situation where one is likely to meet with harm — see LIABLE 1
4 free in expressing one's true feelings and opinions — see FRANK
5 lacking a usual or natural covering — see NAKED 2
6 not known by only a select few — see PUBLIC 1
7 not yet settled or decided — see PENDING 1
8 willing to consider new or different ideas — see OPEN-MINDED 1
open *n* that part of the physical world that is removed from human habitation — see NATURE 2
open *vb* **1** to change from a closed to an open position ⟨please *open* the door to let the cat out⟩
syn unclose
rel unbar, unbolt, unclasp, unfasten, unlatch, unlock; unbutton, unclench, unfold, unfurl, unzip; disengage, release, slip
near ant bar, bolt, clasp, fasten, latch, lock; button (up), zip (up)
ant close, shut
2 to arrange clear passage of (something) by removing obstructions ⟨we need to *open* this drain that's clogged with hair⟩
syn clear, free, unclog, unstop
rel ease, facilitate, loosen (up), smooth
near ant constrict, encumber, hamper, hinder, impede, interfere (with), obstruct, trammel; barricade, blockade
ant block, clog (up), close, dam (up), plug (up), stop
3 to arrange the parts of (something) over a wider area ⟨when we got too close, the cardinal *opened* its wings and flew to a higher branch⟩
syn expand, extend, fan (out), flare (out), spread (out), stretch (out), outspread, outstretch, unfold
rel overspread
near ant compact, compress, condense, reduce
ant close, contract, fold
4 to rid the surface of (as an area) from things in the way — see CLEAR 1
5 to take the first step in (a process or course of action) — see BEGIN 1
open-air *adj* of, relating to, or held in the open air — see OUTDOORS
open air *n* that part of the physical world that is removed from human habitation — see NATURE 2
open-and-shut *adj* not subject to misinterpretation or more than one interpretation — see CLEAR 2
open-eyed *adj* paying close attention usually for the purpose of anticipating approaching danger or opportunity — see ALERT 1
openhanded *adj* giving or sharing in abundance and without hesitation — see GENEROUS 1
openhandedness *n* the quality or state of being generous — see LIBERALITY
openhearted *adj* free in expressing one's true feelings and opinions — see FRANK

openheartedness *n* **1** the free expression of one's true feelings and opinions — see CANDOR

2 the quality or state of being generous — see LIBERALITY

opening *n* **1** a favorable combination of circumstances, time, and place — see OPPORTUNITY

2 a place in a surface allowing passage into or through a thing — see HOLE 1

3 an open space in a barrier (as a wall or hedge) — see GAP 1

open–minded *adj* **1** willing to consider new or different ideas ⟨all I ask is that you try to be *open-minded* when we present our suggestions⟩

syn broad-minded, open, receptive

rel impartial, neutral, objective, unbiased, unprejudiced; easygoing, tolerant; calm, detached, dispassionate; amenable, compliant; impressionable, suggestible, susceptible; persuadable, persuasible

near ant biased, one-sided, partial, partisan, prejudiced; bigoted, intolerant

ant narrow-minded

2 not bound by traditional ways or beliefs — see LIBERAL 1

openmouthed *adj* filled with amazement or wonder ⟨I was *openmouthed* at the stunning view from the mountaintop⟩

syn amazed, astonished, astounded, awed, awestruck, dumbfounded (*or* dumfounded), flabbergasted, marveling (*or* marvelling), wondering

rel startled, surprised; bemused, bewildered, puzzled; overwhelmed, staggered, stunned, stupefied

near ant unimpressed; disinterested, incurious, indifferent, unconcerned, uninterested; dispassionate, emotionless, impassive, unemotional; bored, jaded

openness *n* **1** the free expression of one's true feelings and opinions — see CANDOR

2 the state of being left without shelter or protection against something harmful — see EXPOSURE 1

open sesame *n* something that allows someone to achieve a desired goal — see PASSPORT

operable *adj* capable of or suitable for being used for a particular purpose — see USABLE 1

operate *vb* **1** to control the mechanical operation of ⟨do not *operate* heavy machinery, including cars, after taking this medication⟩

syn handle, run, work

rel use; maneuver, manipulate, ply, wield; command, control, direct, drive, guide, pilot, steer

2 to look after and make decisions about — see CONDUCT 1

3 to produce a desired effect — see ACT 2

4 to put into action or service — see USE 1

operating *adj* being in effective operation — see ACTIVE 1

operation *n* **1** a specific task with which a person or group is charged — see MISSION

2 a usually fixed or ordered series of actions or events leading to a result — see PROCESS 1

3 the act or activity of looking after and making decisions about something — see CONDUCT 1

4 the act or practice of employing something for a particular purpose — see USE 1

operational *adj* being in effective operation — see ACTIVE 1

operative *adj* being in effective operation — see ACTIVE 1

operative *n* **1** a person who tries secretly to obtain information from one country in the territory of another usually unfriendly country — see SPY

2 a person whose business is solving crimes and catching criminals or gathering information that is not easy to get — see DETECTIVE

opiate *adj* tending to cause sleep — see HYPNOTIC

opine *vb* to make a statement of one's opinion — see REMARK 1

opinion *n* **1** an idea that is believed to be true or valid without positive knowledge ⟨my *opinion* is that such interference was unnecessary⟩

syn belief, conviction, eye, feeling, judgment (*or* judgement), mind, notion, persuasion, sentiment, verdict, view

rel say; impression, perception, take; attitude; assumption, presumption, presupposition; conclusion, decision, determination; deliverance, esteem, estimate, estimation; credence, credit, faith; concept, conception, idea, thought; position, stand; comment, observation, reflection, remark; conjecture, guess, hunch, hypothesis, surmise, theory; advice, recommendation, suggestion; angle, outlook, perspective, point of view, shoes, slant, standpoint, viewpoint

near ant fact, truth

2 a position arrived at after consideration — see DECISION 1

opinionated *adj* sticking to an opinion, purpose, or course of action in spite of reason, arguments, or persuasion — see OBSTINATE

opponent *n* **1** one that takes a position opposite another in a competition or conflict ⟨in martial arts, before the match begins, always bow to your *opponent*⟩

syn adversary, antagonist, rival

rel equal, match; enemy, foe; archenemy, nemesis; competitor, contestant; bane, bête noire, curse; assailant, attacker, combatant, invader

near ant accomplice, ally, confederate, partner; advocate, champion, exponent, proponent, supporter

2 one that is hostile toward another — see ENEMY

opportune *adj* especially suitable for a certain time — see TIMELY 1

---

syn synonym(s)   *rel* related words
ant antonym(s)   *near ant* near antonym(s)

opportunist *n* one who does things only for his own benefit and with little regard for right and wrong — see SELF-SEEKER

opportunity *n* a favorable combination of circumstances, time, and place ⟨this art school could be a wonderful *opportunity* for you to finally develop your talent for painting⟩
syn chance, occasion, opening, room
rel break; play, way; juncture, pass

oppose *vb* **1** to refuse to give in to — see RESIST
2 to strive to reduce or eliminate — see FIGHT 2

opposite *adj* being as different as possible ⟨your suggestion that we hold the meeting at night is precisely *opposite* to our original plan for a nice daytime breakfast⟩
syn antipodal, antipodean, antithetical, contradictory, contrary, diametric (*or* diametrical), polar
rel adverse, negative, unfavorable; antagonistic, antipathetic, counter, hostile; converse, inverse, reverse; disparate, dissimilar, divergent, unalike, unlike
near ant alike, analogous, like, similar; equivalent, identical, same; synonymous
ant noncontradictory

opposite *n* something that is as different as possible from something else ⟨no matter what I say, you insist on the *opposite*⟩
syn antipode, antithesis, contrary, negative, reverse
rel negation; antonym; converse, inverse
near ant synonym; analogue, counterpart; carbon copy, copy, duplicate, replica

opposition *n* the inclination to resist — see RESISTANCE 1

oppress *vb* **1** to make sad — see DEPRESS 1
2 to subject to incapacitating emotional or mental stress — see OVERWHELM 1

oppression *n* a state or spell of low spirits — see SADNESS

oppressive *adj* difficult to endure — see HARSH 1

oppressively *adv* in a manner so as to cause loss or suffering — see HARDLY 1

oppressor *n* **1** a person who causes repeated emotional pain, distress, or annoyance to another — see TORMENTOR
2 a person who uses power or authority in a cruel, unjust, or harmful way — see DESPOT

opprobrium *n* the state of having lost the esteem of others — see DISGRACE 1

opt *vb* to come to a judgment after discussion or consideration — see DECIDE 1

opt (for) *vb* to decide to accept (someone or something) from a group of possibilities — see CHOOSE 1

optic *adj* of, relating to, or used in vision — see VISUAL 1

optical *adj* of, relating to, or used in vision — see VISUAL 1

optimism *n* an inclination to believe in the most favorable outcome ⟨your perpetual *optimism* even when things look bleak⟩
syn sanguinity

rel brightness, cheerfulness, perkiness, sunniness; hope, hopefulness, rosiness; idealism
near ant pessimism, skepticism; cynicism; desperation, discouragement, disheartenment, hopelessness; bleakness, cheerlessness, dreariness, gloom, gloominess; pragmatism, realism

optimistic *adj* having qualities which inspire hope — see HOPEFUL 1

option *n* **1** the act or power of making one's own choices or decisions — see FREE WILL
2 the power, right, or opportunity to choose — see CHOICE 1

optional *adj* subject to one's freedom of choice ⟨certain activities are *optional*, and you may choose not to participate if you wish⟩
syn discretionary, elective, voluntary
rel alternative, chosen; dispensable, unnecessary, unneeded, unwanted
near ant essential, indispensable, necessary, requisite
ant compulsory, mandatory, nonelective, obligatory, required

opulence *n* the total of one's money and property — see WEALTH 1

opulent *adj* **1** having goods, property, or money in abundance — see RICH 1
2 showing obvious signs of wealth and comfort — see LUXURIOUS

opulently *adv* in a luxurious manner — see HIGH

opus *n* a literary, musical, or artistic production — see COMPOSITION 1

oral *adj* **1** created by the body's organs of sound — see VOCAL
2 made or carried on through speaking rather than in writing — see VERBAL 2

orate *vb* **1** to talk as if giving an important and formal speech ⟨politicians will *orate* lengthily at any opportunity⟩
syn declaim, discourse, harangue, mouth (off)
rel rant, rave; lecture, preach; advertise, announce, broadcast, declare, proclaim, pronounce; speak, talk
2 to give a formal often extended talk on a subject — see TALK 1

oration *n* a usually formal discourse delivered to an audience — see SPEECH 1

oratorical *adj* marked by the use of impressive-sounding but mostly meaningless words and phrases — see RHETORICAL

oratory *n* **1** the art of speaking in public eloquently and effectively ⟨this debate class will teach you all to be skilled at *oratory*⟩
syn elocution
rel bombast, grandiloquence; rhetoric; discourse, speech, talk
2 language that is impressive-sounding but not meaningful or sincere — see RHETORIC 1

orb *n* a more or less round body or mass — see ¹BALL 1

orbit *vb* to pass completely around — see ENCIRCLE 1

orchestra *n* a usually large group of musicians playing together — see ²BAND 1

ordain *vb* **1** to determine the fate of in advance — see DESTINE

2 to give an order — see COMMAND 2

ordeal *n* a test of faith, patience, or strength — see TRIAL 1

order *n* **1** the way objects in space or events in time are arranged or follow one another ⟨you always keep your books in perfect alphabetical *order*⟩ ⟨we haven't found out the *order* of the speeches yet⟩

syn arrangement, array, disposal, disposition, distribution, ordering, sequence, setup

rel continuity; precedence, priority; chain, progression, succession; series; aligning, alignment, lining up; design, layout, pattern, structure, system

near ant confusion, disorder, disorganization, disruption, upset; disconnection, disjointedness

2 a group of persons formally joined together for some common interest — see ASSOCIATION 2

3 a number of persons or things that are grouped together because they have something in common — see SORT 1

4 a piece of metal given in honor of a special event, a person, or an achievement — see MEDAL

5 a state of being or fitness — see CONDITION 1

6 a statement of what to do that must be obeyed by those concerned — see COMMAND 1

7 one of the segments of society into which people are grouped — see CLASS 1

8 one of the units into which a whole is divided on the basis of a common characteristic — see CLASS 2

order *vb* **1** to put into a particular arrangement ⟨I've *ordered* all of my CDs according to type of music⟩ ⟨he likes to *order* his life so that there are few surprises⟩

syn arrange, array, classify, codify, dispose, draw up, marshal, organize, range, systematize

rel groom, make up, spruce (up), straighten (up), tidy (up); unscramble; align, line, line up, queue; alphabetize, file; emplace, place, set; display, lay out, map (out)

ant derange, disarrange, disarray, disorder, mess (up), muss (up), rumple, upset

2 to give a request or demand for ⟨they *ordered* hamburgers for lunch⟩

syn ask (for), request, requisition

rel commission, solicit; charter, hire, license (*also* licence)

phrases call for

3 to give an order — see COMMAND 2

4 to issue orders to (someone) by right of authority — see COMMAND 1

ordering *n* **1** a scheme of rank or order — see ³SCALE 1

2 the way objects in space or events in time are arranged or follow one another — see ORDER 1

orderly *adj* **1** being clean and in good order — see NEAT 1

2 following a set method, arrangement, or pattern — see METHODICAL

ordinance *n* a rule of conduct or action laid down by a governing authority and especially a legislator — see LAW 1

ordinarily *adv* according to the usual course of things — see NATURALLY 2

ordinary *adj* **1** being of the type that is encountered in the normal course of events ⟨it was a perfectly *ordinary* and undistinguished shirt⟩

syn average, common, commonplace, everyday, garden, normal, prosaic, routine, run-of-the-mill, standard, unexceptional, unremarkable, usual, workaday

rel regular, typical; familiar, homely, plain, popular, vulgar; natural; customary, wonted; insignificant, trivial, unimportant; customary, frequent, habitual; expected, predictable

near ant curious, funny, peculiar, quaint, queer; aberrant, atypical, irregular; rare, scarce; fantastic, phenomenal; bizarre, far-out, outrageous, outré, weird, wild; eccentric, idiosyncratic, nonconformist, unconventional, unorthodox; freak, freakish; conspicuous, notable, outstanding, prominent, salient, signal, striking; singular, unique

ant abnormal, exceptional, extraordinary, odd, out-of-the-way, strange, unusual

2 of average to below average quality — see MEDIOCRE 1

3 often observed or encountered — see COMMON 1

ordnance *n* large firearms (as cannon or rockets) — see ARTILLERY

oread *n* a mythical goddess represented as a young girl and said to live outdoors — see NYMPH 1

organ *n* **1** a publication that appears at regular intervals — see JOURNAL

2 something used to achieve an end — see AGENT 1

organization *n* a group of persons formally joined together for some common interest — see ASSOCIATION 2

organize *vb* to put into a particular arrangement — see ORDER 1

organized *adj* following a set method, arrangement, or pattern — see METHODICAL

orient *vb* to impart knowledge of a new thing or situation to — see ACQUAINT 1

orientate *vb* to impart knowledge of a new thing or situation to — see ACQUAINT 1

orifice *n* a place in a surface allowing passage into or through a thing — see HOLE 1

origin *n* the line of ancestors from whom a person is descended — see ANCESTRY

original *adj* **1** coming before all others in time or order — see FIRST 1

2 having the skill and imagination to create new things — see CREATIVE 1

---

syn synonym(s)   *rel* related words
ant antonym(s)   *near ant* near antonym(s)

3 not known or experienced before — see NEW 2

original *n* something from which copies are made ⟨please make copies to hand out, but keep the *original*⟩

syn archetype, prototype

rel example, paradigm, pattern; beau ideal, exemplar, classic, ideal, model, nonpareil, paragon; blueprint, draft

near ant copy, imitation, replica, reproduction; counterfeit, fake, forgery, sham

originality *n* 1 the quality or appeal of being new — see NOVELTY 1

2 the skill and imagination to create new things — see CREATIVITY 1

originally *adv* in the beginning ⟨we *originally* planned to go out tonight, but we changed our minds⟩

syn firstly, initially, primarily

rel incipiently; primitively

phrases at first

near ant finally, lastly, ultimately

originate *vb* to come into existence — see BEGIN 2

originator *n* 1 one who creates or introduces something new — see INVENTOR

2 a person who establishes a whole new field of endeavor — see FATHER 2

orison *n* an address to God or a deity — see PRAYER 1

ornament *n* something that decorates or beautifies — see DECORATION 1

ornament *vb* to make more attractive by adding something that is beautiful or becoming — see DECORATE

ornamental *adj* serving to add beauty — see DECORATIVE

ornamental *n* a small object displayed for its attractiveness or interest — see KNICKKNACK

ornate *adj* elaborately and often excessively decorated ⟨an *ornate* gambling casino that is designed to look like an Italian palace⟩

syn bedizened, florid, gingerbread, overdecorated, overwrought

rel arabesque, baroque, rococo; extravagant, flamboyant, spectacular, splashy; flashy, garish, gaudy, glitzy, loud, ostentatious, pretentious, showy, swank, tawdry; elaborate, extreme; adorned, arrayed, beautified, bedecked, decked, decorated, dressed, embellished, enriched, garnished, ornamented, trimmed; flowery, frilly, lacy; enhanced, heightened, intensified; bossed, chased, emblazoned, embossed, embroidered, flounced, fringed, garlanded, gilded, laced, wreathed

near ant bare, denuded, exposed, naked, stripped, uncovered; modest, unassuming, unpretentious; conservative, muted, quiet, restrained, subdued, tasteful, toned-down, understated, unobtrusive

ant austere, plain, severe, stark, unadorned

ornery *adj* having or showing a habitually bad temper — see ILL-TEMPERED

orthodox *adj* 1 following or agreeing with established form, custom, or rules — see FORMAL 1

2 tending to favor established ideas, conditions, or institutions — see CONSERVATIVE 1

oscillation *n* a series of slight movements by a body back and forth or from side to side — see VIBRATION

ossified *adj* sticking to an opinion, purpose, or course of action in spite of reason, arguments, or persuasion — see OBSTINATE

ostensible *adj* appearing to be true on the basis of evidence that may or may not be confirmed — see APPARENT 1

ostensibly *adv* to all outward appearances — see APPARENTLY

ostentation *n* excessive or unnecessary display ⟨the sheer *ostentation* of the rock star's mansion was overwhelming⟩

syn flamboyance, flashiness, garishness, gaudiness, glitz, ostentatiousness, pretentiousness, showiness, swank

rel extravaganza, pageant, parade, show; dazzle, pageantry, spectacle; adornment, decoration, dressing, embellishment, garnishment, ornamentation, trimming; extravagance, fanciness, luxuriousness, opulence, richness, sumptuousness; loudness, luridness; meretriciousness, tawdriness, vulgarity

near ant conservativeness, moderation, modesty, restraint, simplicity, understatement; elegance, gracefulness, tastefulness

ant austerity, plainness, severity

ostentatious *adj* 1 excessively showy — see GAUDY

2 self-consciously trying to present an appearance of grandeur or importance — see PRETENTIOUS 1

ostentatiousness *n* excessive or unnecessary display — see OSTENTATION

other *adj* 1 being not of the same kind — see DIFFERENT 1

2 resulting in an increase in amount or number — see ADDITIONAL

other *adv* in a different way — see OTHERWISE

otherwise *adv* in a different way ⟨a serious student who always does his best, for his conscience will not let him do *otherwise*⟩

syn differently, else, other

rel diversely, variously

near ant similarly

ant likewise

ought (to) *vb* to be under necessity or obligation to — see NEED 2

ounce *n* a very small amount — see PARTICLE 1

oust *vb* 1 to drive or force out — see EJECT 1

2 to remove from a position of prominence or power (as a throne) — see DEPOSE 1

out *adv* 1 in or into the open air — see OUTDOORS

2 with one's normal voice speaking the words — see ALOUD

out *adj* not at a certain place — see AB-
SENT 1

out *n* the act or a means of getting or keeping away from something undesirable —
see ESCAPE 2

out *vb* to become known — see GET OUT 1

out–and–out *adj* **1** having no exceptions
or restrictions — see ABSOLUTE 2

2 trying all possibilities — see EXHAUS-
TIVE

outbrave *vb* to oppose (something hostile
or dangerous) with firmness or courage
— see FACE 2

outbreak *n* a sudden and usually temporary growth of activity ⟨there was an immediate *outbreak* of paper shuffling and a
pretense of work when the teacher re-en-
tered the room⟩
syn burst, flare, flare-up, flash, flicker,
flurry, flutter, outburst, spurt
rel binge, jag, spree; boost, increase, pick-
up, upswing, upturn; epidemic, eruption,
explosion, paroxysm; deluge, flood, rush,
spate, surge; commotion, furor, uproar
near ant calm, doldrums, slump

outburst *n* **1** a sudden intense expression
of strong feeling ⟨when the coach suddenly started crying hysterically, everyone was shocked by the unexpected *outburst*⟩
syn agony, burst, eruption, explosion, fit,
flare, flare-up, flash, flush, gale, gush,
gust, paroxysm, spasm, storm
rel blowup, grouch, rage, tantrum; ecstasy, rapture, transport; delirium, frenzy,
furor

2 a sudden and usually temporary growth
of activity — see OUTBREAK

outcast *n* one who is cast out or rejected
by society ⟨they were convinced that
they would become total *outcasts* if they
didn't buy the newest fashions⟩
syn castaway, castoff, pariah, reject
rel untouchable; outsider; deportee, exile
near ant insider

outcome *n* a condition or occurrence
traceable to a cause — see EFFECT 1

outcry *n* a violent shouting — see CLAM-
OR 1

outdated *adj* having passed its time of use
or usefulness — see OBSOLETE

outdistance *vb* to be greater, better, or
stronger than — see SURPASS 1

outdo *vb* to be greater, better, or stronger
than — see SURPASS 1

outdoor *also* **outdoors** *adj* of, relating to,
or held in the open air ⟨an *outdoor* picnic
is always at the mercy of the weather, of
course⟩
syn open-air, out-of-door (*or* out-of-
doors)
rel airy; exterior, external, outer, outside,
outward; outermost, outmost
near ant inner, inside, interior, internal,
inward; inmost, innermost
ant indoor

---

syn synonym(s)   **rel** related words
ant antonym(s)   **near ant** near antonym(s)

outdoors *adv* in or into the open air
⟨please wait until you're *outdoors* to run
around and scream⟩
syn out, outside
rel without
near ant in, inside, within
ant indoors

outdoors *n* that part of the physical world
that is removed from human habitation
— see NATURE 2

outer *adj* situated on the outside or farther
out ⟨the *outer* edge of the blade of your
figure skate always wears out faster than
the inner because you use it more⟩
syn exterior, external, outside, outward
rel outermost, outlying, outmost; superficial, surface
near ant inmost, innermost
ant inner, inside, interior, internal, inward

outermost *adj* most distant from a center
— see EXTREME 1

outfit *n* **1** clothing chosen as appropriate
for a specific situation ⟨you'll need a special *outfit* for the scout troop⟩ ⟨do you
want to buy a new *outfit* for the Halloween party?⟩
syn costume, dress, garb, getup, guise,
togs
rel apparel, attire, clothes, duds, raiment;
fashion, mode, style; array, caparison,
vestments

2 a commercial or industrial activity or
organization — see ENTERPRISE 1

3 a group of people working together on
a task — see GANG 1

4 items needed for the performance of a
task or activity — see EQUIPMENT

5 the distinctive clothing worn by members of a particular group — see UNI-
FORM

outfit *vb* to provide (someone) with what is
needed for a task or activity — see FUR-
NISH 1

outflow *n* a flowing or going out ⟨there
was an immediate *outflow* of students
from the door when the bell rang⟩
syn exodus, gush, outpouring
rel drain, flow; ebb, reflux; rush, stampede; emigration, flight; discharge, ema-
nation, emission
near ant deluge, flood, inundation, overflow, spate, torrent; flow, river, stream,
tide
ant flux, inflow, influx, inrush

outfox *vb* to get the better of through cleverness — see OUTWIT

outgo *n* a payment made in the course of
achieving a result — see EXPENSE

outgoing *adj* likely to seek or enjoy the
company of others — see CONVIVIAL

outgrowth *n* **1** a branch of a main stem especially of a plant — see OFFSHOOT 1

2 a condition or occurrence traceable to
a cause — see EFFECT 1

3 something that naturally develops or is
developed from something else — see DE-
RIVATIVE

outing *n* a short trip for pleasure — see
EXCURSION 1

outlander *n* a person who is not native to or known to a community — see STRANGER

outlandish *adj* **1** different from the ordinary in a way that causes curiosity or suspicion — see ODD 2

2 excitingly or mysteriously unusual — see EXOTIC

outlast *vb* to last longer than ⟨I truly hope this car will *outlast* our previous one⟩ ⟨your work will probably *outlast* you⟩

syn outlive, outwear

rel survive; outstay; abide (beyond), endure (past), hold (past), hold out (past), last (beyond), persist (beyond); draw out, perpetuate; succeed

outlaw *vb* to order not to do or use or to be done or used — see FORBID

outlawed *adj* that may not be permitted — see IMPERMISSIBLE

outlawing *n* the act of ordering that something not be done or used — see PROHIBITION 1

outlay *n* a payment made in the course of achieving a result — see EXPENSE

outlet *n* a place or means of going out — see EXIT 1

outline *n* **1** a line that traces the outer limits of an object or surface ⟨place your hand on the paper and draw an *outline* around it⟩

syn contour, figure, silhouette

rel delineation, sketch; profile, skyline; form, cast, configuration, conformation, geometry, shape; framework, skeleton

2 a short statement of the main points — see SUMMARY

outline *vb* **1** to draw or make apparent the outline of ⟨she carefully *outlined* the tree before she started drawing in the leaves⟩

syn define, delineate, silhouette, sketch, trace

rel line; bound, fringe, margin, skirt; edge, hem, rim, trim; frame; circle, compass, encircle, girdle, girth, loop, ring, round, surround; chart, diagram, draw, map (out)

2 to make into a short statement of the main points (as of a report) — see SUMMARIZE

outlive *vb* to last longer than — see OUTLAST

outlook *n* **1** a high place or structure from which a wide view is possible — see LOOKOUT 1

2 a way of looking at or thinking about something — see POINT OF VIEW

3 all that can be seen from a certain point — see VIEW 1

out loud *adv* with one's normal voice speaking the words — see ALOUD

outmaneuver *vb* to get the better of through cleverness — see OUTWIT

outmoded *adj* having passed its time of use or usefulness — see OBSOLETE

outmost *adj* most distant from a center — see EXTREME 1

out–of–date *adj* having passed its time of use or usefulness — see OBSOLETE

out–of–door *or* **out–of–doors** *adj* of, relating to, or held in the open air — see OUTDOORS

out–of–doors *n* that part of the physical world that is removed from human habitation — see NATURE 2

out–of–the–way *adj* different from the ordinary in a way that causes curiosity or suspicion — see ODD 2

outpouring *n* a flowing or going out — see OUTFLOW

output *n* something produced by physical or intellectual effort — see PRODUCT 1

outrage *n* **1** an act or expression showing scorn and usually intended to hurt another's feelings — see INSULT

2 an intense emotional state of displeasure with someone or something — see ANGER

outrage *vb* **1** to cause hurt feelings or deep resentment in — see INSULT

2 to make angry — see ANGER

outraged *adj* feeling or showing anger — see ANGRY

outrank *vb* to be greater in importance than — see OUTWEIGH

outré *adj* different from the ordinary in a way that causes curiosity or suspicion — see ODD 2

outright *adj* having no exceptions or restrictions — see ABSOLUTE 2

outset *n* the point at which something begins — see BEGINNING

outshine *vb* to be greater, better, or stronger than — see SURPASS 1

outside *adj* **1** situated on the outside or farther out — see OUTER

2 small in degree — see REMOTE 1

outside *adv* in or into the open air — see OUTDOORS

outside *n* **1** an outer part or layer — see EXTERIOR

2 the greatest amount, number, or part — see MOST

outside *prep* **1** not including — see EXCEPT

2 out of the reach or sphere of — see BEYOND 2

outside of *prep* **1** not including — see EXCEPT

2 out of the reach or sphere of — see BEYOND 2

outsider *n* a person who is not native to or known to a community — see STRANGER

outsize *also* **outsized** *adj* **1** unusually large — see HUGE

2 of a size greater than average of its kind — see LARGE

outskirts *n pl* the area around a city — see ENVIRONS 1

outsmart *vb* to get the better of through cleverness — see OUTWIT

outspoken *adj* free in expressing one's true feelings and opinions — see FRANK

outspread *vb* to arrange the parts of (something) over a wider area — see OPEN 3

outstanding *adj* **1** not yet paid ⟨there are several *outstanding* bills left, but at least we paid the rest⟩

syn overdue, owed, owing, payable, unpaid, unsettled

rel due, mature

near ant prepaid

ant cleared, liquidated, paid (off *or* up), repaid, settled

2 standing above others in rank, importance, or achievement — see EMINENT

outstretch *vb* to arrange the parts of (something) over a wider area — see OPEN 3

outstrip *vb* to be greater, better, or stronger than — see SURPASS 1

outward *adj* situated on the outside or farther out — see OUTER

outwear *vb* to last longer than — see OUTLAST

outweigh *vb* to be greater in importance than ⟨the need to finish your homework *outweighs* your desire to see your favorite TV show⟩

syn outrank, overbalance, overshadow, overweigh

rel count, import, matter, mean, signify, weigh; dwarf; exceed, outstrip, surpass, transcend

outwit *vb* to get the better of through cleverness ⟨a plan to *outwit* their opponents at their own game⟩

syn fox, outfox, outsmart, outmaneuver, overreach

rel outguess, second-guess; baffle, balk, circumvent, foil, frustrate, thwart; cozen, deceive, dupe, fool, gull, trick; conquer, defeat, lick, overcome; bar, block, hinder, impede, obstruct

outworn *adj* having passed its time of use or usefulness — see OBSOLETE

oval *adj* having the shape of an egg ⟨the *Oval* Office in the White House⟩

syn elliptic (*or* elliptical), ovate, ovoid

ovate *adj* having the shape of an egg — see OVAL

ovation *n* enthusiastic and usually public expression of approval — see APPLAUSE

over *adj* brought or having come to an end — see COMPLETE 2

over *adv* **1** from one side to the other of an intervening space ⟨let's swim *over* to that island⟩

syn across, through

rel clear

2 yet another time — see AGAIN 1

3 to or in a higher place — see ABOVE

4 from beginning to end — see THROUGH 1

5 toward or in a lower position — see DOWN

over *prep* **1** higher than — see ABOVE

2 in the course of — see DURING

3 on or to the farther side of — see BEYOND 1

4 to the opposite side of — see ACROSS

5 in random positions within the boundaries of — see AROUND 1

overabundance *n* the state or an instance of going beyond what is usual, proper, or needed — see EXCESS

overactive *adj* being in a state of increased activity or agitation — see FEVERISH 1

overage *n* the state or an instance of going beyond what is usual, proper, or needed — see EXCESS

overall *adj* **1** belonging or relating to the whole — see GENERAL 1

2 relating to the main elements and not to specific details — see GENERAL 2

overall *adv* for the most part — see CHIEFLY

over and above *prep* in addition to — see BESIDES 1

overbalance *vb* to be greater in importance than — see OUTWEIGH

overbear *vb* to achieve a victory over — see BEAT 2

overbearing *adj* fond of ordering people around — see BOSSY

overbold *adj* foolishly adventurous or bold — see FOOLHARDY 1

overburden *vb* to fill or load to excess — see OVERLOAD

overcast *adj* covered over by clouds ⟨the dark, *overcast* sky made the whole day seem depressing⟩

syn beclouded, clouded, cloudy, dull, hazed, hazy, heavy, lowering (*also* louring), overclouded

rel bedimmed, befogged, blackened, darkened, darksome, dim, dimmed, dulled, dusky, misty, murky, obscure, obscured, overshadowed; sunless; black, bleak, cheerless, dark, desolate, dismal, drear, dreary, funereal, gloomy, glum, gray (*also* grey), somber (*or* sombre), sullen

near ant sunny, sunshiny; brightened, brilliant, dazzling, illuminated, illumined, lighted (*or* lit), lightened, radiant, shiny

ant cloudless

overcast *vb* to make dark, dim, or indistinct — see CLOUD 1

overcharge *vb* **1** to charge (someone) too much for goods or services ⟨I think that store may have *overcharged* us for the shoes, which were supposed to be on sale⟩

syn gouge, soak, sting, surcharge

rel cheat, defraud, stick; clip, fleece, skin

ant undercharge

2 to fill or load to excess — see OVERLOAD

overcloud *vb* to make dark, dim, or indistinct — see CLOUD 1

overclouded *adj* covered over by clouds — see OVERCAST

overcoat *n* a warm outdoor coat ⟨put your *overcoat* on—it's freezing out there!⟩

syn greatcoat, surcoat, topcoat

rel chesterfield, frock coat, mackinaw, ulster; jacket, parka; oilskin, raincoat, sou'wester; wrap

near ant undercoat

overcome *vb* **1** to achieve a victory over — see BEAT 2

---

syn synonym(s)   *rel* related words

ant antonym(s)   *near ant* near antonym(s)

2 to subject to incapacitating emotional or mental stress — see OVERWHELM 1

overconfident *adj* foolishly adventurous or bold — see FOOLHARDY 1

overcritical *adj* given to making or expressing unfavorable judgments about things — see CRITICAL 1

overdecorated *adj* elaborately and often excessively decorated — see ORNATE

overdo *vb* to describe or express in too strong terms — see OVERSTATE

overdraw *vb* to describe or express in too strong terms — see OVERSTATE

overdue *adj* **1** not arriving, or occurring, or settled at the due, usual, or proper time — see LATE 1

2 not yet paid — see OUTSTANDING 1

overeat *vb* to eat greedily or to excess — see GORGE 2

overeater *n* one who eats greedily or too much — see GLUTTON

overestimate *vb* to place too high a value on ⟨they *overestimated* their ability to do the work on such short notice⟩
syn overrate, overvalue
rel appreciate, cherish, prize, treasure, value; admire, esteem, regard, respect; adore, idolize, revere, reverence, venerate, worship
near ant belittle, decry, depreciate, disparage; despise, disdain, scorn; abhor, abominate, detest, loathe
ant underestimate, underrate, undervalue

overfamiliar *adj* showing a lack of proper social reserve or modesty — see PRESUMPTUOUS 1

overfill *vb* **1** to fill or load to excess — see OVERLOAD

2 to flow over the brim or top of — see OVERFLOW 1

overflow *n* **1** a great flow of water or of something that overwhelms — see FLOOD

2 the state or an instance of going beyond what is usual, proper, or needed — see EXCESS

overflow *vb* **1** to flow over the brim or top of ⟨the tea in the cup *overflowed* onto the saucer⟩
syn overfill, run over
rel boil over, spill, well (up); flow, flush, gush, pour, sluice, spout, spurt, stream; deluge, drown, engulf, flood, inundate, overwhelm, submerge, submerse, swamp; wash (over); brim, cascade, slop, slosh
near ant recede

2 to cover or become filled with a flood — see FLOOD

overgrown *adj* covered with a thick, healthy natural growth — see LUSH 1

overhang *n* a part that sticks out from the general mass of something — see BULGE

overhang *vb* **1** to extend outward beyond a usual point — see BULGE

2 to remain poised to inflict harm, danger, or distress on — see THREATEN

overhaul *vb* to move fast enough to get even with — see OVERTAKE

overhead *adv* to or in a higher place — see ABOVE

overhear *vb* to listen to (another in private conversation) — see EAVESDROP (ON)

overjoy *vb* **1** to fill with overwhelming emotion (as wonder or delight) — see ENTRANCE

2 to fill with great joy — see ELATE

overkill *n* the state or an instance of going beyond what is usual, proper, or needed — see EXCESS

overlap *n* a partial covering of one thing by an adjoining thing ⟨the orthodontist will try to fix that *overlap* of two of your upper incisors⟩
syn lapping, overlaying, overlying, overspreading
rel shingling

overlap *vb* to lie over parts of one another ⟨there were so many papers on the desk that many of them *overlapped*⟩
syn lap, overlay, overlie, overspread
rel shingle

overlay *vb* **1** to form a layer over — see COVER 2

2 to lie over parts of one another — see OVERLAP

overlaying *n* a partial covering of one thing by an adjoining thing — see OVERLAP

overlie *vb* **1** to lie over parts of one another — see OVERLAP

2 to form a layer over — see COVER 2

overload *vb* to fill or load to excess ⟨try not to *overload* your backpack, or you could end up with back problems⟩
syn overburden, overcharge, overfill
rel stuff; burden, charge, encumber, lade, load, lumber, saddle, weight
near ant lighten, unburden, unload

overlook *vb* **1** to look down on ⟨the fortress *overlooks* the city⟩
syn command, dominate
rel face, front

2 to fail to give proper attention to — see NEGLECT 1

overly *adv* beyond a normal or acceptable limit — see TOO 1

overlying *n* a partial covering of one thing by an adjoining thing — see OVERLAP

overmaster *vb* to subject to incapacitating emotional or mental stress — see OVERWHELM 1

overmatch *vb* to achieve a victory over — see BEAT 2

overmuch *adj* going beyond a normal or acceptable limit in degree or amount — see EXCESSIVE

overmuch *adv* beyond a normal or acceptable limit — see TOO 1

overmuch *n* the state or an instance of going beyond what is usual, proper, or needed — see EXCESS

overpass *vb* to fail to give proper attention to — see NEGLECT 1

overpower *vb* **1** to bring under one's control by force of arms — see CONQUER 1

2 to subject to incapacitating emotional or mental stress — see OVERWHELM 1

overpowering *n* the act or process of bringing someone or something under one's control — see CONQUEST

overpraise *n* excessive praise — see FLATTERY

overpraise *vb* to praise too much — see FLATTER 1

overrate *vb* to place too high a value on — see OVERESTIMATE

overreach *vb* **1** to get the better of through cleverness — see OUTWIT
2 to go beyond the limit of — see EXCEED

overripe *adj* having lost forcefulness, courage, or spirit — see EFFETE 1

overrun *vb* **1** to enter for conquest or plunder — see INVADE
2 to go beyond the limit of — see EXCEED
3 to spread or swarm over in a troublesome manner — see INFEST

oversee *vb* **1** to look after and make decisions about — see CONDUCT 1
2 to be in charge of — see BOSS 1
3 to take charge of especially on behalf of another — see ²TEND 1

overshadow *vb* **1** to make dark, dim, or indistinct — see CLOUD 1
2 to be greater in importance than — see OUTWEIGH

overshoot *vb* to go beyond the limit of — see EXCEED

oversight *n* **1** the act or activity of looking after and making decisions about something — see CONDUCT 1
2 an unintentional departure from truth or accuracy — see ERROR 1
3 the duty or function of watching or guarding for the sake of proper direction or control — see SUPERVISION 1
4 the nonperformance of an assigned or expected action — see FAILURE 1

oversize *or* **oversized** *adj* **1** unusually large — see HUGE
2 of a size greater than average of its kind — see LARGE

overspread *vb* **1** to form a layer over — see COVER 2
2 to lie over parts of one another — see OVERLAP

overspreading *n* a partial covering of one thing by an adjoining thing — see OVERLAP

overstate *vb* to describe or express in too strong terms ⟨it appears you've somewhat *overstated* your computer skills, if you can't find the "on" button!⟩
syn exaggerate, overdo, overdraw, put on
rel color, elaborate, embellish, embroider, magnify, pad, stretch; fudge, hedge; overemphasize, overlay
near ant belittle, minimize, play down
ant understate

overstatement *n* the representation of something in terms that go beyond the facts — see EXAGGERATION

overstep *vb* to go beyond the limit of — see EXCEED

---

oversupply *n* the state or an instance of going beyond what is usual, proper, or needed — see EXCESS

overtake *vb* to move fast enough to get even with ⟨she had to hurry to *overtake* her friends, who had forgotten their umbrellas⟩ ⟨the thunderstorm *overtook* them suddenly⟩
syn catch up (with), overhaul
rel chase, pursue; gain, reach; pass, surpass
near ant fall short

overthrow *n* failure to win a contest — see DEFEAT 1

overtop *vb* to be greater, better, or stronger than — see SURPASS 1

overturn *vb* to turn on one's side or upside down — see CAPSIZE

overvalue *vb* to place too high a value on — see OVERESTIMATE

overweening *adj* **1** having too high an opinion of oneself — see CONCEITED
2 going beyond a normal or acceptable limit in degree or amount — see EXCESSIVE
3 having a feeling of superiority that shows itself in an overbearing attitude — see ARROGANT

overweigh *vb* to be greater in importance than — see OUTWEIGH

overweight *adj* having an excess of body fat — see FAT 1

overwhelm *vb* **1** to subject to incapacitating emotional or mental stress ⟨just the thought of how much work there is to do *overwhelms* me⟩
syn carry away, crush, devastate, floor, oppress, overcome, overmaster, overpower, prostrate, snow under, swamp, whelm
rel deluge, drown; confute, defeat, refute; demoralize, distress, disturb, rock, shatter, stagger, unman, unnerve, upset
2 to cover or become filled with a flood — see FLOOD

overwrought *adj* **1** being in a state of increased activity or agitation — see FEVERISH 1
2 elaborately and often excessively decorated — see ORNATE

ovoid *adj* having the shape of an egg — see OVAL

owed *adj* not yet paid — see OUTSTANDING 1

owing *adj* not yet paid — see OUTSTANDING 1

owing to *prep* as the result of — see BECAUSE OF

own *vb* to keep, control, or experience as one's own — see HAVE 1

own (up) *vb* to accept the truth or existence of (something) usually reluctantly — see ADMIT

owner *n* one who has a legal or rightful claim to ownership — see PROPRIETOR

---

syn synonym(s)   *rel* related words
ant antonym(s)   *near ant* near antonym(s)

P

pa *n* a male human parent — see FATHER 1

pace *vb* to move along with a steady regular step especially in a group — see MARCH 1

pacific *adj* **1** tending to lessen or avoid conflict or hostility ⟨as a *pacific* gesture, we invited our feuding neighbors to our backyard barbecue⟩
syn appeasing, conciliating, conciliatory, disarming, mollifying, pacifying, peacemaking, placating, propitiatory
rel endearing, ingratiating; peaceable, peaceful; nonbelligerent, unaggressive, unassertive; calming, comforting, quieting, soothing; obliging, satisfying; affable, amiable, amicable, benevolent, gentle, kind, kindly; submissive, surrendering, yielding
near ant aggravating, annoying, exasperating, inflammatory, irritating, nettling, offensive, provocative, provoking, vexing; engaging, incensing, infuriating, maddening; antagonistic, hostile; aggressive, assertive, bellicose, belligerent, combative, contentious, pugnacious, quarrelsome, scrappy, truculent; martial, militant, military, warlike
ant antagonizing
2 inclined to live in peace and to avoid war — see PEACEFUL 1

pacifist *n* a person who opposes war or warlike policies — see DOVE 1

pacify *vb* to lessen the anger or agitation of ⟨the only thing that would *pacify* the child and end the tantrum was a new toy⟩
syn appease, conciliate, disarm, mollify, placate, propitiate
rel calm, comfort, console, content, quiet, soothe; endear (to), ingratiate; delight, gladden, gratify, please; blarney, flatter, overpraise, soft-soap; assuage, quench, sate, satiate, satisfy; cater (to), humor, indulge; blandish, cajole, coax, wheedle; coddle, mollycoddle, pamper, spoil
near ant aggravate, annoy, bother, bug, chafe, cross, exasperate, gall, get, grate, irk, irritate, nettle, peeve, pique, put out, rankle, rile, roil, ruffle, vex; provoke, rouse; harass, harry, pester; agitate, distress, disturb, fret, perturb, upset; affront, insult, offend
ant anger, enrage, incense, infuriate, madden, outrage

pacifying *adj* **1** tending to calm the emotions and relieve stress — see SOOTHING 1
2 tending to lessen or avoid conflict or hostility — see PACIFIC 1

pack *n* **1** a soft-sided case designed for carrying belongings especially on the back ⟨part of basic training is becoming accustomed to taking very long hikes with an eighty-pound *pack*⟩
syn backpack, knapsack, rucksack
rel haversack; grip, luggage, suitcase, traveling bag
2 a wrapped or sealed case containing an item or set of items — see PACKAGE 1

pack *vb* **1** to close up so that no empty spaces remain — see FILL 2
2 to put into (something) as much as can be held or contained — see FILL 1
3 to support and take from one place to another — see CARRY 1
4 to wear or have on one's person — see CARRY 2

pack (off) *vb* to cause to go or be taken from one place to another — see SEND

package *n* **1** a wrapped or sealed case containing an item or set of items ⟨Mom needed our help carrying all the *packages* and bags home from the store⟩
syn bundle, pack, packet, parcel
rel bag, poke [*chiefly Southern and Midland*], pouch, sack; box, container, crate
2 a number of things considered as a unit — see GROUP 1

packed *adj* **1** containing or seeming to contain the greatest quantity or number possible — see FULL 1
2 having little space between items or parts — see CLOSE 1

packet *n* a wrapped or sealed case containing an item or set of items — see PACKAGE 1

pact *n* **1** a formal agreement between two or more nations or peoples — see TREATY
2 an arrangement about action to be taken — see AGREEMENT 2

pad *n* **1** a number of sheets of writing paper glued together at one edge ⟨we'll need to buy a new *pad* for telephone messages soon⟩
syn notepad, tablet
rel album, notebook, scrapbook; booklet, pamphlet
2 a place set aside for sleeping — see BED 1
3 something that serves as a protective barrier — see CUSHION
4 the place where one lives — see HOME 1

pad *vb* **1** to add to the interest of by including made-up details — see EMBROIDER
2 to go on foot — see WALK

padding *n* **1** soft material that is used to fill the hollow parts of something — see FILLING
2 the representation of something in terms that go beyond the facts — see EXAGGERATION

paddle *vb* to move a boat by means of oars — see ¹ROW

padre *n* a person specially trained and authorized to conduct religious services in a Christian church — see CLERGYMAN

paean *n* a formal expression of praise — see ENCOMIUM

pagan *n* a person who does not worship the God of the Bible — see HEATHEN 1

page *n* one that carries a message or does an errand — see MESSENGER

pageant *n* a staged presentation often with music that consists of a procession of narrated or enacted scenes ⟨we always put on a Christmas *pageant* every year⟩
syn cavalcade
rel tableau; kaleidoscope, montage, panorama; drama, play; demonstration, performance, presentation, production; exhibition, extravaganza, show, spectacle; parade

pail *n* a round container that is open at the top and outfitted with a handle ⟨fetch me a *pail* full of water, please⟩
syn bucket
rel cauldron, kettle, pot; canteen, flagon, jar, jug, pitcher; bail, hod; tank, tub, vat

pain *n* 1 a sharp unpleasant sensation usually felt in some specific part of the body ⟨the child was crying because of a *pain* in her knee⟩
syn ache, pang, prick, smart, sting, stitch, throe, tingle, twinge
rel discomfort, distress, soreness, tenderness; agony, anguish, misery, suffering, torment, torture; inflammation, swelling; damage, harm, hurt, injury; backache, bellyache, charley horse, colic, earache, gripe, headache, stomachache, toothache
near ant comfort, ease
2 a state of great suffering of body or mind — see DISTRESS 1
3 **pains** *pl* strict attentiveness to what one is doing — see CARE 1
4 **pains** *pl* the active use of energy in producing a result — see EFFORT

pain *vb* to feel or cause physical pain — see HURT 1

painful *adj* 1 causing or feeling bodily pain ⟨her broken arm was too *painful* for her to go on the trip⟩
syn aching, hurting, nasty, sore
rel damaging, harmful, hurtful, injurious; raw, tender; bleeding, burning, chafing, cramping, festering; itching, nagging, pinching, pricking, prickling, smarting, stinging; inflamed, swollen; threatening, wounding
near ant curative, healing, helping, remedial
ant painless
2 hard to accept or bear especially emotionally — see BITTER 2

painfully *adv* with feelings of bitterness or grief — see HARD 2

painkiller *n* something (as a drug) that relieves pain ⟨a lot of *painkillers* have turned out to be addictive substances for patients⟩
syn analgesic, anesthetic
rel sedative, tranquilizer (*also* tranquilizer); narcotic, opiate

painless *adj* involving minimal difficulty or effort — see EASY 1

painlessly *adv* without difficulty — see EASILY

painstaking *adj* taking great care and effort ⟨she was always *painstaking* about her homework⟩
syn careful, conscientious, fussy, meticulous
rel assiduous, diligent, indefatigable, persevering, sedulous; exhaustive, thorough, thoroughgoing; attentive, observant, vigilant, watchful; accurate, precise; critical, demanding, discriminating, exacting, finicky, particular; cautious, chary, circumspect, gingerly, guarded, heedful, wary; deliberate, plodding, slow; studied, thoughtful; all-out, determined, dogged, intensive, tenacious, tireless, zealous
near ant cursory; heedless, inattentive, incautious, mindless, unguarded, unsafe, unwary; lax, neglectful, negligent, slipshod, sloppy, slovenly; imprecise; inaccurate, uncritical, undemanding, undiscriminating; bold, impetuous, rash, reckless; apathetic, indifferent, lackadaisical, lazy
ant careless

paint *n* preparations intended to beautify the face or hair — see MAKEUP 1

paint *vb* 1 to give a representation or account of in words — see DESCRIBE 1
2 to give color or a different color to — see COLOR 1

painting *n* a picture created with usually oil paint ⟨the Mona Lisa is a beautiful *painting* of a woman with a most mysterious smile⟩
syn canvas, oil, oil painting
rel fresco, mural, panorama; cartoon, drawing, etching, pastel, sketch, watercolor, work; masterpiece; pièce de résistance, showpiece
phrases work of art

pair *n* two things of the same or similar kind that match or are considered together ⟨a *pair* of blue socks⟩ ⟨the cheerleader and the computer nerd make quite a *pair* together⟩
syn brace, couple, duo, twain, twosome
rel span, yoke; partnership, team; companion, complement, doublet, fellow, half, match, mate, twin; counterpart, equal, equivalent, like, parallel, peer

pal *n* a person who has a strong liking for and trust in another — see FRIEND 1

pal (around) *vb* to come or be together as friends — see ASSOCIATE 1

palace *n* 1 a large impressive residence — see MANSION
2 a large, magnificent, or massive building — see EDIFICE 1
3 the residence of a ruler — see COURT 1

palatable *adj* 1 being to one's liking — see SATISFACTORY 1
2 giving pleasure or contentment to the mind or senses — see PLEASANT

---

syn synonym(s)   **rel** related words
ant antonym(s)   **near ant** near antonym(s)

3 very pleasing to the sense of taste — see DELICIOUS 1

palatial *adj* showing obvious signs of wealth and comfort — see LUXURIOUS

palaver *n* friendly, informal conversation or an instance of this — see CHAT

palaver *vb* to engage in casual or rambling conversation — see CHAT

pale *adj* 1 lacking intensity of color ⟨we chose a very *pale* pink for the walls of the room⟩

syn dull, dulled, faded, light, pastel, washed-out

rel flat, lackluster, lusterless, matte (*also* mat *or* matt); dim, faint; dirty, muddy; achromatic, colorless, uncolored, un-dyed, unpainted, unstained; blanched, bleached, washed, white, whitened; gray (*also* grey), indistinct, neutral

near ant bright, brilliant, vibrant, vivid; chromatic, colored, dyed, painted, stained, tinged, tinted; colorful, multicolored, polychromatic, polychrome, vari-colored, variegated; flashy, garish, gaudy, loud, showy, splashy

ant dark, deep, gay, rich

2 lacking a healthy skin color ⟨after a week with the flu, she was deathly *pale* and noticeably thinner⟩

syn ashen, ashy, blanched, cadaverous, livid, lurid, paled, pallid, pasty, peaked, wan

rel sallow, sick, sickly, waxen, waxy; white, whitened; deathlike; anemic, bloodless; untanned

near ant blooming, blushing, flushed, glowing, pink

ant florid, flush, rubicund, ruddy, sanguine

pale *vb* to make white or whiter by removing color — see WHITEN

paled *adj* lacking a healthy skin color — see PALE 2

palisade *n* a steep wall of rock, earth, or ice — see CLIFF

palliate *vb* 1 to make (something) seem less bad by offering excuses ⟨don't try to *palliate* your constant lying by claiming that everybody lies⟩

syn excuse, extenuate, gloss (over), gloze (over), whitewash

rel sugarcoat, varnish; apologize, atone, confess; explain, justify, rationalize; alleviate, lessen, lighten, mitigate, moderate, soften, temper; absolve, acquit, clear, exculpate, exonerate, vindicate

2 to make more bearable or less severe — see HELP 2

pallid *adj* lacking a healthy skin color — see PALE 2

palm off *vb* to offer (something fake, useless, or inferior) as genuine, useful, or valuable — see FOIST

palmy *adj* 1 having attained a desired end or state of good fortune — see SUCCESSFUL 1

2 marked by vigorous growth and well-being especially economically — see PROSPEROUS 1

palpable *adj* 1 able to be perceived by a sense or by the mind — see PERCEPTIBLE

2 capable of being perceived by the sense of touch — see TANGIBLE

3 not subject to misinterpretation or more than one interpretation — see CLEAR 2

palpitate *vb* to expand and contract in a rhythmic manner — see PULSATE

palpitation *n* a rhythmic expanding and contracting — see PULSATION

palsy *n* complete or partial loss of physical function (as motion or sensation) in a part of the body — see PARALYSIS

palter *vb* to talk over or dispute the terms of a purchase — see BARGAIN

paltry *adj* so small or unimportant as to warrant little or no attention — see NEGLIGIBLE 1

pamper *vb* to treat with great or excessive care — see BABY

pamphlet *n* a short printed publication with no cover or with a paper cover ⟨*pamphlets* about common safety precautions that we all can put into use⟩

syn booklet, brochure, circular, flier (*or* flyer), folder, leaflet

rel advertisement, catalog (*or* catalogue); tract; paperback, pocket book; guidebook, handbook, instructions, manual

pan *vb* to express one's unfavorable opinion of the worth or quality of — see CRITICIZE

panacea *n* something that cures all ills or problems — see CURE-ALL

pancake *n* a flat cake made from thin batter and cooked on both sides (as on a griddle) ⟨every Sunday morning, we have *pancakes* and bacon for breakfast⟩

syn flapjack, griddle cake, hotcake, slapjack

rel crepe (*or* crêpe); waffle

pandemonium *n* a state of noisy, confused activity — see COMMOTION

panegyric *n* a formal expression of praise — see ENCOMIUM

panel *n* 1 a meeting featuring a group discussion — see FORUM

2 a select group of persons assigned to consider or take action on some matter — see COMMITTEE

pang *n* a sharp unpleasant sensation usually felt in some specific part of the body — see PAIN 1

panhandler *n* a person who lives by public begging — see BEGGAR

panic *n* the emotion experienced in the presence or threat of danger — see FEAR

panic *vb* to strike with fear — see FRIGHTEN

panorama *n* all that can be seen from a certain point — see VIEW 1

panoramic *adj* covering everything or all important points — see ENCYCLOPEDIC

pan out *vb* 1 to come to be — see COME OUT 1

2 to turn out as planned or desired — see SUCCEED 1

pant *vb* to breathe hard, quickly, or with difficulty — see GASP

pant (after) *vb* to have an earnest wish to own or enjoy — see DESIRE

pantaloons *n pl* an outer garment covering each leg separately from waist to ankle — see PANTS

panther *n* a large tawny cat of the wild — see COUGAR

pantomime *n* **1** a movement of the body or limbs that expresses or emphasizes an idea or feeling — see GESTURE 1

2 an actor in a story performed silently and entirely by body movements — see MIME

pantomimist *n* an actor in a story performed silently and entirely by body movements — see MIME

pants *n pl* an outer garment covering each leg separately from waist to ankle ⟨you'll need a nice pair of *pants* for the job interview⟩

syn breeches, pantaloons, slacks, trousers

rel corduroys, denims, jeans; hose, legging (*or* leggin), pantsuit

papa *n* a male human parent — see FATHER 1

paper *adj* being something in name or form only — see NOMINAL 1

paper *n* **1** a piece of paper with information written or to be written on it — see FORM 2

2 a publication that appears at regular intervals — see JOURNAL

3 a short piece of writing done as a school exercise — see COMPOSITION 2

4 a short piece of writing typically expressing a point of view — see ESSAY 1

par *n* **1** something set up as an example against which others of the same type are compared — see STANDARD 1

2 the state or fact of being exactly the same in number, amount, status, or quality — see EQUIVALENCE

3 what is typical of a group, class, or series — see AVERAGE

parable *n* a story intended to teach a basic truth or moral about life — see ALLEGORY

parade *n* a body of individuals moving along in an orderly and often ceremonial way — see CORTEGE 2

parade *vb* **1** to move along with a steady regular step especially in a group — see MARCH 1

2 to present so as to invite notice or attention — see SHOW 1

paradigmatic *adj* constituting, serving as, or worthy of being a pattern to be imitated — see MODEL

paradise *n* **1** a place or state of great happiness ⟨Susan's idea of *paradise* was a world where no one had to go to work⟩

syn Eden, Elysium, heaven, utopia

rel dreamland, fairyland, promised land, wonderland; bliss, euphoria, gladness, joy

ant hell

2 a dwelling place of perfect bliss for the soul after death — see HEAVEN 1

3 a state of overwhelming usually pleasurable emotion — see ECSTASY

paradox *n* someone or something with qualities or features that seem to conflict with one another — see CONTRADICTION 1

paragon *n* someone of such unequaled perfection as to deserve imitation — see IDEAL 1

parallel *adj* having qualities in common — see ALIKE

parallel *n* **1** a point which two or more things share in common — see SIMILARITY 2

2 one that is equal to another in status, achievement, or value — see EQUAL

parallel *vb* to be the exact counterpart of — see MATCH 1

parallelism *n* the quality or state of having many qualities in common — see SIMILARITY 1

paralysis *n* complete or partial loss of physical function (as motion or sensation) in a part of the body ⟨the car accident left one athlete with *paralysis* from the waist down⟩

syn palsy

rel cerebral palsy, multiple sclerosis, poliomyelitis; debilitation, debility, decrepitude, enfeeblement, feebleness, frailness, weakness; infirmity, lameness; disability, impairment

near ant mobility, motility, sensation

paralytic *adj* affected with paralysis ⟨at first, he would not accept that he was now *paralytic* and needed help⟩

syn paralyzed

rel challenged, crippled, disabled, handicapped, maimed, mutilated; hobbled, lame, lamed; impaired, incapacitated; hamstrung; debilitated, decrepit, enfeebled, feeble, infirm, weak, weakened

near ant able-bodied

paralyze *vb* to render powerless, ineffective, or unable to move ⟨a blizzard *paralyzed* the city for two days⟩

syn cripple, disable, hamstring, immobilize, incapacitate, prostrate

rel attenuate, debilitate, enfeeble, sap, undermine, weaken; hobble, lame; maim, mutilate

near ant energize, galvanize, vitalize; fortify, strengthen; empower; refresh, rejuvenate, restore

paralyzed *adj* affected with paralysis — see PARALYTIC

paramount *adj* **1** coming before all others in importance — see FOREMOST 1

2 of the greatest or highest degree or quantity — see ULTIMATE 1

paraphernalia *n* **1** items needed for the performance of a task or activity — see EQUIPMENT

2 transportable items that one owns — see POSSESSION 2

paraphrase *n* an instance of expressing something in different words ⟨your essays on human rights should have some original thought and not be simply a *paraphrase* of what's in the textbook⟩

---

syn synonym(s)   *rel* related words
ant antonym(s)   *near ant* near antonym(s)

syn rephrasing, restatement, restating, re-wording, translating, translation

rel rehash; summary

near ant copy, transcript, transcription

ant quotation, quote

paraphrase *vb* to express something (as a text or statement) in different words ⟨could you *paraphrase* your diagnosis of my medical condition, using simpler language?⟩

syn rephrase, restate, reword, translate

rel summarize

near ant repeat; copy, reproduce, transcribe

ant quote

parasite *n* a person who is supported or seeks support from another without making an adequate return — see LEECH

parboil *vb* to cook in a liquid heated to the point that it gives off steam — see BOIL 2

parcel *n* **1** a number of things considered as a unit — see GROUP 1

2 a small area of usually open land — see FIELD 1

3 a small piece of land that is developed or available for development — see LOT 1

4 a usually small number of persons considered as a unit — see GROUP 2

5 a wrapped or sealed case containing an item or set of items — see PACKAGE 1

parcel (out) *vb* to give out (something) in appropriate amounts or to appropriate individuals — see ADMINISTER 1

parcel post *n* communications or parcels sent or carried through the postal system — see MAIL

parch *vb* to make dry — see DRY 1

pardon *n* release from the guilt or penalty of an offense ⟨the criminal is hoping for a Presidential *pardon*⟩

syn absolution, amnesty, forgiveness, remission, remittal

rel parole; acquittal, exculpation, exoneration, vindication; exemption, immunity, impunity, indemnity; commutation, commuting; reprieve

near ant conviction, sentence; assessment, charge, fine, imposition, levying; castigation, chastening, chastisement, condemnation

ant penalty, punishment, retribution

pardon *vb* **1** to cease to have feelings of anger or bitterness toward — see FORGIVE 1

2 to overlook or dismiss as of little importance — see EXCUSE 1

pardonable *adj* worthy of forgiveness — see VENIAL

pare *vb* to make (as hair) shorter with or as if with the use of shears — see CLIP

parentage *n* the line of ancestors from whom a person is descended — see ANCESTRY

parenthood *n* the caring for a child by its parents — see PARENTING

parenting *n* the caring for a child by its parents ⟨as the big day approaches, the expectant couple are starting to get worried about their fitness for *parenting*⟩

syn parenthood

rel raising, rearing, upbringing; fatherhood, fathering, paternity; maternity, motherhood, mothering

par excellence *adj* of the very best kind — see EXCELLENT

pariah *n* one who is cast out or rejected by society — see OUTCAST

parity *n* the state or fact of being exactly the same in number, amount, status, or quality — see EQUIVALENCE

park *n* the area around and belonging to a building — see GROUND 1

parley *n* **1** a meeting featuring a group discussion — see FORUM

2 an exchange of views for the purpose of exploring a subject or deciding an issue — see DISCUSSION 1

parley *vb* to exchange viewpoints or seek advice for the purpose of finding a solution to a problem — see CONFER 2

parliament *n* the highest lawmaking body of a political unit — see CONGRESS 1

parlor *n* a building, room, or suite of rooms occupied by a service business — see PLACE 1

parlous *adj* involving potential loss or injury — see DANGEROUS

parochial *adj* not broad or open in views or opinions — see NARROW 2

parody *n* **1** a work that imitates and exaggerates another work for comic effect ⟨the musical was a *parody* of *Romeo and Juliet*, with silly songs during the sad scenes⟩

syn burlesque, caricature, spoof, takeoff

rel lampoon, mockery, satire, travesty; comedy, farce, sketch, slapstick, squib; distortion, exaggeration; imitation, impersonation, mimicking

near ant archetype, original, prototype

2 a poor, insincere, or insulting imitation of something — see MOCKERY 1

parody *vb* to copy or exaggerate (someone or something) in order to make fun of — see MIMIC 1

paroxysm *n* **1** a sudden intense expression of strong feeling — see OUTBURST 1

2 a violent disturbance (as of the political or social order) — see CONVULSION

parrot *vb* to say after another — see REPEAT 3

parsimonious *adj* giving or sharing as little as possible — see STINGY 1

parsimony *n* the quality of being overly sparing with money ⟨her *parsimony* was so extreme that she'd walk five miles to the store to save a few cents on gas⟩

syn cheapness, closeness, miserliness, penuriousness, pinching, stinginess, tightness

rel conserving, economizing, economy, frugality, husbandry, providence, scrimping, skimping, thrift; conservation, saving; husbanding, managing

near ant extravagance, lavishness; dissipation, improvidence, prodigality, squandering, wastefulness

ant generosity, liberality, openhandedness, openheartedness, philanthropy

parson *n* a person specially trained and authorized to conduct religious services in a Christian church — see CLERGYMAN

part *adv* in some measure or degree — see PARTLY

part *n* **1** one of the pieces from which something is designed to be assembled ⟨the model car came in several small *parts* that had to be assembled⟩

syn member, partition, portion, section, segment

rel component, constituent, element, factor, ingredient, moiety, parcel; cut, length; bit, fragment, particle, scrap

near ant whole; aggregate, composite, compound, sum, total, totality

2 something belonging to, due to, or contributed by an individual member of a group — see SHARE 1

3 the action for which a person or thing is specially fitted or used or for which a thing exists — see ROLE

4 *usually* **parts** *pl* a broad geographical area — see REGION 2

part *vb* to set or force apart — see SEPARATE 1

partake *vb* to take a share or part ⟨we should all *partake* of this fine meal together⟩

syn participate, share

rel endure, experience, feel, see, taste, undergo; encounter, meet; accept, receive

partaker *n* one who takes part in something — see PARTICIPANT

partial *adj* **1** inclined to favor one side over another ⟨that judge is always *partial* to the defense, so be careful⟩

syn biased, one-sided, partisan, prejudiced

rel jaundiced, unfriendly, unsympathetic; colored, distorted, misrepresented, warped; convinced, influenced, persuaded, predisposed, prepossessed, swayed; affected, concerned, interested

near ant open, open-minded, persuasible, receptive; fair, honest, just, reasonable; bipartisan; autonomous, independent, unallied; aloof, detached, dispassionate, hardheaded, impersonal, objective, unemotional; apathetic, indifferent, unenthusiastic, uninterested

ant evenhanded, impartial, neutral, nonpartisan, unbiased, unprejudiced

2 having a liking or affection — see FOND 1

3 lacking some necessary part — see INCOMPLETE

partiality *n* **1** an attitude that always favors one way of feeling or acting especially without considering any other possibilities — see BIAS

2 a habitual attraction to some activity or thing — see INCLINATION 1

3 positive regard for something — see LIKING

partially *adv* in some measure or degree — see PARTLY

---

syn synonym(s)   **rel** related words
ant antonym(s)   **near ant** near antonym(s)

participant *n* one who takes part in something ⟨he seemed to be a willing *participant* in the prank⟩

syn partaker, participator, party, sharer

rel actor; accessory, aide, assistant, helper; colleague, partner

near ant bystander, looker-on, observer, onlooker, spectator, watcher

ant nonparticipant

participate *vb* to take a share or part — see PARTAKE

participator *n* one who takes part in something — see PARTICIPANT

particle *n* **1** a very small amount ⟨I did all but a *particle* of my work⟩

syn ace, bit, crumb, dab, driblet, glimmer, hint, lick, little, mite, nip, ounce, peanuts, ray, scruple, shade, shadow, shred, smidgen (*also* smidgeon *or* smidgin), snap, spark, speck, spot, sprinkling, strain, streak, suspicion, touch, trace

rel iota, jot, modicum, tittle, whit; atom, dot, fleck, flyspeck, grain, granule, molecule, morsel, mote, nubbin, patch, scrap; dash, drop, pinch; part, portion, section; bite, nibble, taste; handful, scattering, smattering; dose, shot; chip, flake, fragment, shard, shiver, sliver, smithereens, splinter; shred, tatter; clipping, paring, shaving

near ant abundance, barrel, bucket, bushel, deal, gobs, heaps, loads, mass, mountain, much, peck, pile, plenty, profusion, quantity, raft, scads, stack, wad, wealth; volume; embarrassment, excess, overabundance, overage, overflow, overkill, overmuch, oversupply, superabundance, superfluity, surfeit, surplus; chunk, hunk, lump, slab

2 a very small piece — see BIT 1

particular *adj* **1** hard to please — see FINICKY

2 of, relating to, or belonging to a single person — see INDIVIDUAL 1

3 tending to select carefully — see SELECTIVE

particular *n* **1** a separate part in a list, account, or series — see ITEM 1

2 a single piece of information — see FACT 3

particularity *n* **1** careful thoroughness of detail ⟨with great *particularity* she described the qualities she's looking for in a boyfriend⟩

syn explicitness, specificity

rel attentiveness, care, carefulness, conscientiousness, finickiness, fussiness, meticulousness; alertness, cautiousness, circumspection, heedfulness, safeness; discrimination; accuracy, exactitude, exactness, precision

near ant imprecision, inaccuracy, inexactness; indistinctness, vagueness

ant generality

2 a single piece of information — see FACT 3

particularized *adj* including many small descriptive features — see DETAILED 1

particularly *adv* to a great degree — see VERY 1

parting *adj* given, taken, or performed at parting ⟨she gave him a *parting* gift to remember her by⟩
syn farewell, valedictory
rel final, last, ultimate; departing, leaving

parting *n* 1 the act or process of two or more persons going off in different directions ⟨although their *parting* was sad, they knew they would see each other again⟩
syn farewell, leave-taking, separation
rel departure, egress, exit, exiting, exodus, going, leaving, quitting, running away; decampment, flight, withdrawal; abandonment, desertion, forsaking
near ant reunion; arrival, greeting, welcome; gathering, joining, meeting
2 the act of leaving a place — see DEPARTURE

partisan *adj* inclined to favor one side over another — see PARTIAL 1

partisan *n* 1 one who follows the opinions or teachings of another — see FOLLOWER
2 one who is intensely or excessively devoted to a cause — see ZEALOT

partisanship *n* an attitude that always favors one way of feeling or acting especially without considering any other possibilities — see BIAS

partition *n* 1 one of the pieces from which something is designed to be assembled — see PART 1
2 something that divides, separates, or marks off — see DIVISION 1
3 the act or process of a whole separating into two or more parts or pieces — see SEPARATION 1

partly *adv* in some measure or degree ⟨you're only *partly* right⟩
syn incompletely, part, partially
rel in part
near ant absolutely, dead, downright, plain, plumb, utterly
ant completely, entirely, totally, wholly

partner *n* the person to whom another is married — see SPOUSE

partnership *n* the state of having shared interests or efforts (as in social or business matters) — see ASSOCIATION 1

parturition *n* the act or process of giving birth to children — see CHILDBIRTH

party *n* 1 a social gathering ⟨we're all invited to the big *party* to celebrate the end of the term⟩
syn affair, blowout, event, fete (*or* fête), function, get-together, reception, shindig
rel ball, formal, prom; celebration, gala, occasion; orgy, saturnalia; benefit, clambake, hen party, housewarming, masquerade, mixer, shower, salon, soiree (*or* soirée), stag, tea
2 a group of people acting together within a larger group — see FACTION
3 a group of people working together on a task — see GANG 1
4 a member of the human race — see HUMAN
5 a usually small number of persons considered as a unit — see GROUP 2

6 one who takes part in something — see PARTICIPANT

party pooper *n* a person who spoils the pleasure of others — see KILLJOY

pass *n* 1 a narrow opening between hillsides or mountains that can be used for passage — see CANYON
2 a passage cleared for public vehicular travel — see WAY 1
3 a small sheet of plastic, paper, or paperboard showing that the bearer has a claim to something (as admittance) — see TICKET 1
4 an effort to do or accomplish something — see ATTEMPT

pass *vb* 1 to shift possession of (something) from one person to another ⟨could you please *pass* me the phone?⟩
syn hand, hand over, reach, transfer
rel relay; bear, carry; finger, handle, paw; cede, give, give up, release, relinquish, surrender
2 to come to an end — see CEASE 1
3 to put (something) into the possession or safekeeping of another — see GIVE 1
4 to put into effect through legislative or authoritative action — see ENACT
5 to take place — see HAPPEN

pass (on) *vb* to stop living — see DIE 1

pass (over) *vb* to make one's way through, across, or over — see TRAVERSE

passable *adj* 1 capable of being traveled on ⟨after the snowstorm, the roads might not be *passable* for the morning ride to school⟩
syn navigable, negotiable
rel clear, cleared, open, unclogged, unobstructed
near ant blocked, choked, clogged, closed, congested, dammed, jammed, obstructed; barricaded, blockaded
ant impassable
2 capable of being passed into or through — see PENETRABLE
3 of a level of quality that meets one's needs or standards — see ADEQUATE
4 of average to below average quality — see MEDIOCRE 1

passably *adv* in a satisfactory way — see WELL 1

passage *n* 1 an established course for traveling from one place to another ⟨the long *passage* down the Atlantic seaboard, around Cape Horn, and up the Pacific Coast to California⟩
syn approach, avenue, path, route, way
rel bypath, byway, lane; bypass, drive, freeway, highway, road, street, thoroughfare; trace, track, trail; airway; channel, watercourse, waterway; door, doorway, gate, gateway, portal
2 a going from one place to another usually of some distance — see JOURNEY
3 a journey over water in a vessel — see SAIL
4 a part taken from a longer work — see EXCERPT
5 forward movement in time or place — see ADVANCE 1

passageway n 1 a passage cleared for public vehicular travel — see WAY 1

2 a typically long narrow way connecting parts of a building — see HALL 2

pass away vb to stop living — see DIE 1

passé adj having passed its time of use or usefulness — see OBSOLETE

passel n 1 a number of things considered as a unit — see GROUP 1

2 a usually small number of persons considered as a unit — see GROUP 2

passing adj lasting only for a short time — see MOMENTARY

passing n the permanent stopping of all the vital bodily activities — see DEATH 1

passion n 1 a feeling of strong or constant regard for and dedication to someone — see LOVE 1

2 a strong but often short-lived liking for another person — see CRUSH 1

3 a strong wish for something — see DESIRE

4 a subjective response to a person, thing, or situation — see FEELING 1

5 depth of feeling — see ARDOR 1

6 passions pl general emotional condition — see FEELING 2

passionate adj 1 having a strong sexual desire — see LUSTFUL

2 having or expressing great depth of feeling — see FERVENT

passive adj receiving or enduring without offering resistance ⟨the student body was surprisingly passive about having recess shortened⟩

syn acquiescent, nonresistant, resigned, tolerant, tolerating, unresistant, unresisting, yielding

rel forbearing, long-suffering, patient, uncomplaining; agreeable, amenable, compliant, complying, conformist, docile, guidable, law-abiding, obedient, subordinate, tractable, willing; submissive, surrendering; amiable, obliging; slavish, subservient; disciplined, governable, manageable; apathetic, uncaring, unresponsive

near ant defiant; contrary, disobedient, insubordinate, insurgent, intractable, mutinous, rebellious, recalcitrant, refractory, uncontrollable, ungovernable, unruly; balky, perverse, wayward, wrongheaded; headstrong, willful (or wilful); indomitable; undisciplined, unmanageable; dissident, nonconformist

ant protesting, resistant, resisting, unyielding

pass off vb to offer (something fake, useless, or inferior) as genuine, useful, or valuable — see FOIST

pass out vb to lose consciousness — see FAINT

pass over vb 1 to fail to give proper attention to — see NEGLECT 1

2 to overlook or dismiss as of little importance — see EXCUSE 1

passport n something that allows someone to achieve a desired goal ⟨meeting that movie director could be your passport to a big acting career⟩

syn gateway, key, open sesame

rel password; accomplishment, achievement, success; manner, means, method, system, technique, way; blueprint, design, plan, scheme, strategy

password n a word or phrase that must be spoken by a person in order to pass a guard ⟨the password for the dance party will be changed next week⟩

syn countersign, watchword

rel shibboleth, sign; signal; hint, indication

past adj having been such at some previous time — see FORMER

past n the events or experience of former times ⟨we spent a pleasant evening recalling the past together⟩

syn auld lang syne, history, yesterday, yesteryear, yore

rel bygone; flashback; annals, chronicle, record; memoir; antiquity

near ant future, tomorrow; present

past prep on or to the farther side of — see BEYOND 1

paste vb to deliver a blow to (someone or something) usually in a strong vigorous manner — see HIT 1

pastel adj lacking intensity of color — see PALE 1

past master n a person with a high level of knowledge or skill in a field — see EXPERT

pastoral adj 1 of, relating to, associated with, or typical of open areas with few buildings or people — see RURAL

2 of, relating to, or characteristic of the clergy — see CLERICAL

pasturage n open land over which livestock may roam and feed — see RANGE 1

pasture n open land over which livestock may roam and feed — see RANGE 1

pasture vb to feed on grass or herbs — see ¹GRAZE

pasty adj lacking a healthy skin color — see PALE 2

pat adj sticking to an opinion, purpose, or course of action in spite of reason, arguments, or persuasion — see OBSTINATE

pat vb to touch or handle in a tender or loving manner — see FONDLE

patch n 1 a small area that is different (as in color) from the main part — see SPOT 1

2 a very small piece — see BIT 1

patch vb to put into good shape or working order again — see MEND 1

patch (together) vb to make or assemble roughly or hastily — see COBBLE (TOGETHER)

patchwork adj consisting of many things of different sorts — see MISCELLANEOUS

pate n the upper or front part of the body that contains the brain, the major sense organs, and the mouth — see HEAD 1

patent adj 1 not subject to misinterpretation or more than one interpretation — see CLEAR 2

---

syn synonym(s)   rel related words
ant antonym(s)   near ant near antonym(s)

2 very noticeable especially for being incorrect or bad — see EGREGIOUS

path n **1** the direction along which something or someone moves ⟨try to stay out of the *path* of the golf balls while playing⟩ ⟨I tripped over a rock directly in my *path*⟩

syn course, line, pathway, route, steps, track, way

rel circle, circuit, loop, orbit; flight path, trajectory; ascent, descent

2 a rough course or way formed by or as if by repeated footsteps — see TRAIL 1

3 an established course for traveling from one place to another — see PASSAGE 1

pathetic adj **1** deserving of one's pity ⟨the plight of the homeless family was quite *pathetic*⟩

syn heartbreaking, heartrending, miserable, piteous, pitiable, pitiful, poor, rueful, sorry, wretched

rel deplorable, lamentable, regrettable; emotional, impressive, inspiring; affecting, moving, poignant, stirring, touching; awful, horrible, terrible; distressing, disturbing, upsetting; grievous, sad, sorrowful, woeful

near ant unimpressive, uninspiring

2 causing unhappiness — see SAD 2

pathway n **1** a rough course or way formed by or as if by repeated footsteps — see TRAIL 1

2 the direction along which something or someone moves — see PATH 1

patience n the capacity to endure what is difficult or disagreeable without complaining ⟨my mother is endowed with nearly endless *patience*⟩

syn forbearance, long-suffering, sufferance, tolerance

rel acquiescence, resignation; passiveness, passivity; amenability, compliance, conformism, docility, obedience, subordination, tractability, willingness; discipline, self-control; submission, submissiveness

near ant defiance; contrariness, disobedience, insubordination, intractability, recalcitrance, resistance, willfulness

ant impatience

patient adj **1** accepting pains or hardships calmly or without complaint ⟨you were very *patient* about having to wait for me for so long⟩

syn forbearing, long-suffering, stoic (*or* stoical), tolerant, uncomplaining

rel lenient; acquiescent, passive, resigned, unresistant, unresisting, yielding; agreeable, amenable, compliant, complying, conformist, docile, law-abiding, obedient, submissive, subordinate, tractable, willing; slavish, subservient; amiable, obliging; collected, composed; constrained, contained, curbed, inhibited, repressed, restrained; disciplined, self-contained, self-controlled; apathetic, uncaring, unresponsive

near ant bored, tired, weary; defiant, resistant; contrary, disobedient, insubordinate, intractable, rebellious, recalcitrant,

refractory, ungovernable, unmanageable, unruly

ant complaining, fed up, impatient, protesting

2 continuing despite difficulties, opposition, or discouragement — see PERSISTENT

patient n an individual awaiting or under medical care and treatment ⟨the nurse asked the *patient* to change into a paper gown⟩

syn case

rel inpatient, outpatient; sufferer, victim; convalescent, nursling

patio n an open space wholly or partly enclosed (as by buildings or walls) — see COURT 2

patois n the special terms or expressions of a particular group or field — see TERMINOLOGY

patrician adj of high birth, rank, or station — see NOBLE 1

patrician n a man of high birth or social position — see GENTLEMAN 1

patrimony n something that is or may be inherited — see INHERITANCE

patriot n a person who loves his or her country and supports its interests and policies ⟨the contention that true *patriots* would be willing to do anything for their country⟩

syn loyalist

rel chauvinist; jingoist, nationalist; compatriot, countryman

near ant collaborator, quisling, spy, traitor; betrayer, deserter, recreant; renegade

patriotic adj having or showing love and support for one's country ⟨hanging a flag outside is a *patriotic* gesture⟩

syn nationalist, nationalistic

rel chauvinist; jingoist; constant, devoted, faithful, loyal, staunch (*or* stanch), steadfast, steady, true; ardent, fervent, fervid, impassioned, passionate

near ant traitorous, treasonous; disaffected, disloyal, faithless, false, fickle, inconstant, perfidious, recreant, treacherous, unfaithful

ant unpatriotic

patriotism n love and support for one's country ⟨her *patriotism* was so great that she quit her job to work for the war effort⟩

syn nationalism

rel chauvinism; jingoism; allegiance, constancy, devotion, faithfulness, fealty, loyalty, staunchness, steadfastness; fervency, fervidness, passion

near ant desertion, treason; disaffection, disloyalty, faithlessness, falseness, fickleness, inconstancy, perfidiousness, treachery, unfaithfulness

patron n **1** a person who buys a product or uses a service from a business — see CUSTOMER 1

2 a person who takes the responsibility for some other person or thing — see SPONSOR

3 one that helps another with gifts or money — see BENEFACTOR

patronize *vb* **1** to assume or treat with an air of superiority — see CONDESCEND 2
2 to promote the interests or cause of — see SUPPORT 1

patter *vb* to engage in casual or rambling conversation — see CHAT

patter *n* the special terms or expressions of a particular group or field — see TERMINOLOGY

pattern *n* **1** a unit of decoration that is repeated all over something (as a fabric) ⟨a quilt with tiny pink roses as the *pattern*⟩
syn design, figure, motif, motive
rel device; adornment, caparison, decoration, embellishment, frill, garnish, ornament, trim
2 a usual manner of behaving or doing — see HABIT
3 an established and often automatic or monotonous series of actions followed when engaging in some activity — see ROUTINE 1
4 the way in which the elements of something (as a work of art) are arranged — see COMPOSITION 3

patty *also* **pattie** *n* a small usually rounded mass of minced food that has been fried — see CAKE

paucity *n* a falling short of an essential or desirable amount or number — see DEFICIENCY

paunch *n* an enlarged or bulging abdomen — see POTBELLY

pauperism *n* the state of lacking sufficient money or material possessions — see POVERTY 1

pause *n* a momentary halt in an activity ⟨there was a brief *pause* for applause in her speech⟩
syn break, breath, breather, interruption, lull, recess
rel time-out; interim, interlude, intermission, interval, respite, rest; cessation, discontinuance, ending, expiration, finishing, lapse, stopping, termination; abeyance, moratorium, surcease, suspension; discontinuity, gap, hiatus
near ant continuation, endurance, persistence, progress, progression; extension, prolongation

pause *vb* to come to a temporary halt in one's activity ⟨he *paused* for a moment to tie his shoe⟩
syn break
rel break in, interrupt; cease, discontinue, end, finish, stop, terminate; knock off, lay off, quit; lapse, let up
near ant continue, persist; advance, progress; extend, prolong, stretch

pawn *n* **1** one that is or can be used to further the purposes of another ⟨she disliked being a *pawn* in her friends' power games⟩
syn puppet, tool
rel chump, dupe, foil, gull, sucker, victim; minion, stooge; yes-man

2 something given or held to assure that the giver will keep a promise — see PLEDGE 1

pawn *vb* to leave as a guarantee of repayment of a loan ⟨he *pawned* his watch in order to pay off his gambling debt⟩
syn hock, pledge
rel deposit, mortgage; bond
near ant buy (back), redeem, win (back)

pay *n* **1** the money paid regularly to a person for labor or services — see WAGE
2 something (as money) that is given or received in return for goods or services — see PAYMENT 2

pay *vb* **1** to give (someone) the sum of money owed for goods or services received ⟨we need to *pay* the cashier and then we can leave⟩
syn compensate, recompense, remunerate
rel reimburse, repay, requite; pay off, pay up, prepay
2 to give what is owed for ⟨you ought to *pay* that bill before it's overdue⟩
syn clear, discharge, foot, liquidate, pay off, pay up, quit, recompense, settle, spring (for), stand
ant repudiate
3 to hand over or use up in payment — see SPEND 1
4 to produce as revenue — see YIELD 2

payable *adj* not yet paid — see OUTSTANDING 1

paying *adj* yielding a profit — see PROFITABLE 1

paying *n* the act of offering money in exchange for goods or services — see PAYMENT 1

payload *n* a mass or quantity of something taken up and carried, conveyed, or transported — see LOAD 1

payment *n* **1** the act of offering money in exchange for goods or services ⟨they are very prompt in the *payment* of their credit card bills⟩
syn compensation, disbursement, giving, paying, remittal, remittance, remuneration
rel rendering, tendering; reimbursement, repayment; paying off, paying up, prepayment; overpayment
near ant underpayment
ant nonpayment, repudiation
2 something (as money) that is given or received in return for goods or services ⟨their *payment* for mowing the lawn was $20⟩ ⟨we finally mailed our last car *payment* last week⟩
syn compensation, consideration, pay, recompense, remittance, remuneration, requital
rel salary, stipend, wage(s); disbursement, expenditure, outlay; rebate, refund; indemnity, recoupment, redress, reparation, restitution; adjustment, settlement; deposit; reimbursement, repayment; prepayment; overpayment; rent, rental
3 the money paid regularly to a person for labor or services — see WAGE

---

syn synonym(s)   *rel* related words
ant antonym(s)   *near ant* near antonym(s)

payoff *n* the amount of money left when expenses are subtracted from the total amount received — see PROFIT 1

pay off *vb* to give what is owed for — see PAY 2

pay up *vb* to give what is owed for — see PAY 2

peace *n* 1 a state without war ⟨after a long and bitter war, the troubled region finally achieved *peace*⟩
syn peacefulness
rel accord, amity, concord, harmony; calm, quiet, serenity, tranquillity (*or* tranquility); order, stability; pacification
near ant conflict, contention, discord, dissidence, strife, trouble; tumult, turmoil, unrest, upheaval; fighting, warfare; action, battle, combat
ant war

2 a state of freedom from storm or disturbance — see CALM

3 peaceful coexistence — see HARMONY 2

peaceable *adj* 1 inclined to live in peace and to avoid war — see PEACEFUL 1

2 not involving violence or force — see PEACEFUL 2

peaceful *adj* 1 inclined to live in peace and to avoid war ⟨a *peaceful* tribe that had quietly inhabited these shores for centuries before the arrival of the Europeans⟩
syn pacific, peaceable
rel calm, mild, neutral, quiet, relaxed, serene, tranquil; affable, amiable, amicable, benevolent, gentle, kind, kindly; nonbelligerent, unaggressive; submissive, yielding
near ant militaristic; aggressive, bellicose, belligerent, combative, contentious, discordant, pugnacious, quarrelsome, scrappy, truculent; antagonistic, argumentative, fierce, gladiatorial, hostile, hot-tempered
ant warlike

2 not involving violence or force ⟨UN officials struggled to find a *peaceful* solution to the troublesome conflict⟩
syn nonviolent, peaceable
rel conciliatory, pacific, peacemaking; nonbelligerent, unaggressive, unassertive; appeasing, conciliating, mollifying, pacifying, placating; calming, quieting, soothing
near ant armed, martial, militant, military, warlike; aggressive, assertive, bellicose, belligerent, combative, contentious, quarrelsome; antagonistic, argumentative, fierce, gladiatorial, hostile; tempestuous, volcanic
ant forced, violent

3 free from disturbing noise or uproar — see QUIET 1

4 free from storms or physical disturbance — see CALM 1

peacefulness *n* 1 a state of freedom from storm or disturbance — see CALM

2 a state without war — see PEACE 1

peacemaker *n* one who works with opposing sides in order to bring about an agreement — see MEDIATOR

peacemaking *adj* tending to lessen or avoid conflict or hostility — see PACIFIC 1

peak *n* 1 an elevation of land higher than a hill — see MOUNTAIN 1

2 the highest part or point — see HEIGHT 1

3 the projecting front part of a hat or cap — see VISOR

peaked *adj* 1 lacking a healthy skin color — see PALE 2

2 tapering to a thin tip — see POINTED 1

3 temporarily suffering from a disorder of the body — see SICK 1

peal *vb* to make the clear sound heard when metal vibrates — see RING 1

peanuts *n pl* 1 a very small amount — see PARTICLE 1

2 a very small sum of money — see MITE 1

pearl *n* someone or something unusually desirable — see PRIZE 1

pebbly *adj* not having a level or smooth surface — see UNEVEN 1

peck *n* a considerable amount — see LOT 2

peculiar *adj* 1 being out of the ordinary — see EXCEPTIONAL

2 different from the ordinary in a way that causes curiosity or suspicion — see ODD 2

3 noticeably different from what is generally found or experienced — see UNUSUAL 1

4 of, relating to, or belonging to a single person — see INDIVIDUAL 1

5 serving to identify as belonging to an individual or group — see CHARACTERISTIC 1

peculiarity *n* 1 an odd or peculiar habit — see IDIOSYNCRASY

2 something that sets apart an individual from others of the same kind — see CHARACTERISTIC

pecuniary *adj* of or relating to money, banking, or investments — see FINANCIAL

pedagogue *n* a person whose occupation is to give formal instruction in a school — see TEACHER

peddle *vb* to sell from place to place usually in small quantities ⟨he traveled around the country *peddling* Bibles⟩
syn hawk
rel retail, wholesale; deal (in), distribute, high-pressure, hustle, market, merchandise, trade (in), vend

peddler *also* **pedlar** *n* one who sells things outdoors ⟨the *peddler* on the street corner selling baseball caps⟩
syn hawker, huckster
rel dealer, merchandiser, seller, vendor (*also* vender); concessionaire; black marketer, bootlegger, fence, fencer, hustler, smuggler, trader
near ant buyer, purchaser; consumer, end user, user

pedestrian *adj* causing weariness, restlessness, or lack of interest — see BORING

pedigree *n* the line of ancestors from whom a person is descended — see ANCESTRY

pedigreed *adj* of unmixed ancestry — see PUREBRED

peek *n* an instance of looking especially briefly — see LOOK 2

peek *vb* to take a quick or hasty look — see GLANCE 2

peel *vb* to remove the natural covering of ⟨she *peeled* an apple with great care⟩
syn bark, flay, hull, husk, shell, shuck, skin
rel bare, denude, expose, scale, strip; pare

peel (off) *vb* to rid oneself of (a garment) — see REMOVE 1

peeled *adj* lacking a usual or natural covering — see NAKED 2

peep *n* an instance of looking especially briefly — see LOOK 2

peep *vb* to make a short sharp sound like a small bird — see CHIRP

peer *n* one that is equal to another in status, achievement, or value — see EQUAL

peer *vb* to look long and hard in wonder or surprise — see GAPE

peerless *adj* having no equal or rival for excellence or desirability — see ONLY 1

peeve *n* **1** something that is a source of irritation — see ANNOYANCE 3
2 the feeling of being offended or resentful after a slight or indignity — see PIQUE

peeve *vb* to disturb the peace of mind of (someone) especially by repeated disagreeable acts — see IRRITATE 1

peeving *adj* causing annoyance — see ANNOYING

peevish *adj* **1** easily irritated or annoyed — see IRRITABLE 1
2 sticking to an opinion, purpose, or course of action in spite of reason, arguments, or persuasion — see OBSTINATE

peevishness *n* **1** a steadfast adherence to an opinion, purpose, or course of action — see OBSTINACY
2 readiness to show annoyance or impatience — see PETULANCE

peewee *n* a living thing much smaller than others of its kind — see DWARF 1

peg *n* an individual part of a process, series, or ranking — see DEGREE 1

peg *vb* **1** to arrange or assign according to type — see CLASSIFY 1
2 to send through the air especially with a quick forward motion of the arm — see THROW

peg (away) *vb* to devote serious and sustained effort — see LABOR

pelage *n* the hairy covering of a mammal especially when fine, soft, and thick — see FUR 1

pelagic *adj* of or relating to the sea — see MARINE 1

pelf *n* something (as pieces of stamped metal or printed paper) customarily and legally used as a medium of exchange, a measure of value, or a means of payment — see MONEY

pellet *n* a usually round or cone-shaped little piece of lead made to be fired from a firearm — see BULLET

pell-mell *adj* **1** acting or done with excessive or careless speed — see HASTY 1
2 lacking in order, neatness, and often cleanliness — see MESSY

pell-mell *adv* **1** in a confused and reckless manner — see HELTER-SKELTER 1
2 with excessive or careless speed — see HASTILY 1

pellucid *adj* easily seen through — see CLEAR 1

pelt *n* the outer covering of an animal removed for its commercial value — see HIDE 1

pelt *vb* **1** to proceed or move quickly — see HURRY 2
2 to send through the air especially with a quick forward motion of the arm — see THROW
3 to strike repeatedly — see BEAT 1

pen *n* **1** a place of confinement for persons held in lawful custody — see JAIL
2 an enclosure with an open framework for keeping animals — see CAGE

pen *vb* **1** to close or shut in by or as if by barriers — see ENCLOSE 1
2 to compose and set down on paper the words of — see WRITE 1

penal *adj* inflicting, involving, or serving as punishment — see PUNITIVE

penalize *vb* to inflict a penalty on for a fault or crime — see PUNISH

penalizing *adj* inflicting, involving, or serving as punishment — see PUNITIVE

penalty *n* **1** a feature of someone or something that creates difficulty for achieving success — see DISADVANTAGE
2 a sum of money to be paid as a punishment — see FINE
3 suffering, loss, or hardship imposed in response to a crime or offense — see PUNISHMENT

penchant *n* a habitual attraction to some activity or thing — see INCLINATION 1

pencil (in) *vb* to compose and set down on paper the words of — see WRITE 1

pendant *also* **pendent** *n* an ornament worn on a chain around the neck or wrist ⟨Navajo necklaces with *pendants* finely crafted in genuine sky-blue turquoise⟩
syn bangle, charm, lavalier (*also* lavaliere)
rel locket, teardrop

pendent *or* **pendant** *adj* extending freely from a support from above — see DEPENDENT 1

pending *adj* not yet settled or decided ⟨a decision is *pending* about whether to buy computers or sports equipment with this money⟩
syn open, undecided, undetermined, unresolved, unsettled
rel hanging; arguable, debatable, disputable, moot, uncertain, unsure
near ant confirmed, established; certain, sure
ant decided, determined, resolved, settled

---

syn synonym(s)   *rel* related words
ant antonym(s)   *near ant* near antonym(s)

2 being soon to appear or take place — see FORTHCOMING

3 giving signs of immediate occurrence — see IMMINENT 1

pendulous *adj* **1** bending downward or forward — see NODDING

2 extending freely from a support from above — see DEPENDENT 1

penetrable *adj* capable of being passed into or through ⟨unfortunately, our netting proved to be a rather *penetrable* barrier that allowed in our cabin a steady stream of mosquitoes⟩
syn passable, permeable, porous
rel absorbent
near ant airtight, watertight; close, compact, dense, thick
ant impassable, impenetrable, impermeable, impervious, nonporous

penetrate *vb* to go or come in or into — see ENTER 1

penetrating *adj* causing intense discomfort to one's skin — see CUTTING 1

peninsula *n* an area of land that juts out into a body of water — see ²CAPE

penitence *n* a feeling of responsibility for wrongdoing — see GUILT 1

penitent *adj* **1** feeling sorrow for a wrong that one has done — see CONTRITE 1

2 suffering from or expressive of a feeling of responsibility for wrongdoing — see GUILTY 2

penitentiary *n* a place of confinement for persons held in lawful custody — see JAIL

penman *n* a person who creates a written work — see AUTHOR 1

penmanship *n* **1** the form or style of a particular person's writing — see HANDWRITING 1

2 writing done by hand — see HANDWRITING 2

pennant *n* a piece of cloth with a special design that is used as an emblem or for signaling — see FLAG 1

penniless *adj* lacking money or material possessions — see POOR 1

pennon *n* a piece of cloth with a special design that is used as an emblem or for signaling — see FLAG 1

pensive *adj* given to or marked by long, quiet thinking — see CONTEMPLATIVE

penstock *n* a long hollow cylinder for carrying a substance (as a liquid or gas) — see PIPE 1

penthouse *n* a smaller structure added to a main building — see ANNEX

penumbra *n* partial darkness due to the obstruction of light rays — see SHADE 1

penurious *adj* **1** giving or sharing as little as possible — see STINGY 1

2 lacking money or material possessions — see POOR 1

penuriousness *n* **1** the quality of being overly sparing with money — see PARSIMONY

2 the state of lacking sufficient money or material possessions — see POVERTY 1

penury *n* the state of lacking sufficient money or material possessions — see POVERTY 1

peon *n* a person who does very hard or dull work — see SLAVE 2

people *n pl* **1** human beings in general ⟨despite the horrors she witnessed, Anne Frank never lost her faith in *people*⟩
syn folks, humanity, humankind, public, society, world
rel crowd, masses, mob, populace, proletariat, rabble, riffraff

2 the body of the community as contrasted with the elite — see MASS 1

3 a group of persons who come from the same ancestor — see FAMILY 1

pep *n* active strength of body or mind — see VIGOR 1

pep (up) *vb* to give life, vigor, or spirit to — see ANIMATE

pepper *vb* **1** to cover by or as if by scattering something over or on — see SCATTER 2

2 to mark with small spots especially unevenly — see SPOT

peppery *adj* marked by a lively display of strong feeling — see SPIRITED 1

peppiness *n* the quality or state of having abundant or intense activity — see VITALITY 1

peppy *adj* **1** having active strength of body or mind — see VIGOROUS 1

2 having much high-spirited energy and movement — see LIVELY 1

per *prep* using the means or agency of — see BY 2

perambulation *n* a relaxed journey on foot for exercise or pleasure — see WALK 1

per capita *adv* for each one — see APIECE

perceive *vb* **1** to have a vague awareness of — see FEEL 1

2 to make note of (something) through the use of one's eyes — see SEE 1

3 to recognize the meaning of — see COMPREHEND

percentage *n* a measure of how often an event will occur instead of another — see PROBABILITY 2

perceptible *adj* able to be perceived by a sense or by the mind ⟨you should note a *perceptible* temperature change when you add the second element⟩
syn appreciable, detectable, discernible, distinguishable, palpable, sensible
rel audible, observable, tangible, visible; clear, conspicuous, evident, eye-catching, manifest, noticeable, obvious, plain, prominent, striking; apparent, distinct, significant, straightforward
near ant inaudible, intangible, invisible; inconspicuous, indistinct, unnoticeable; faint, insignificant, slight, trivial; buried, concealed, covert, disguised, hidden, obscure, shrouded, vague
ant impalpable, imperceptible, inappreciable, indistinguishable, insensible

perception *n* **1** the ability to understand inner qualities or relationships — see WISDOM 1

2 the knowledge gained from the process of coming to know or understand something — see COMPREHENSION

perceptive *adj* **1** able to sense slight impressions or differences — see ACUTE 1

2 having or showing deep understanding and intelligent application of knowledge — see WISE 1

perceptiveness *n* the ability to understand inner qualities or relationships — see WISDOM 1

perch *vb* **1** to come to rest after descending from the air — see ALIGHT

2 to establish or place comfortably or snugly — see ENSCONCE 1

perchance *adv* it is possible — see PERHAPS

percolate *vb* to flow forth slowly through small openings — see EXUDE

percolate (into) *vb* to spread throughout — see PERMEATE

perdition *n* the place of punishment for the wicked after death — see HELL 1

peregrine *vb* to take a trip especially of some distance — see TRAVEL 1

peregrination *n* a going from one place to another usually of some distance — see JOURNEY

peremptoriness *n* an exaggerated sense of one's importance that shows itself in the making of excessive or unjustified claims — see ARROGANCE

peremptory *adj* **1** fond of ordering people around — see BOSSY

2 forcing one's compliance or participation by or as if by law — see MANDATORY

3 having a feeling of superiority that shows itself in an overbearing attitude — see ARROGANT

4 having or showing a tendency to force one's will on others without any regard to fairness or necessity — see ARBITRARY 1

perfect *adj* **1** being entirely without fault or flaw ⟨a stunningly *perfect* performance—not the slightest mistake—won her the gold medal in women's figure skating⟩

syn absolute, faultless, flawless, ideal, impeccable, irreproachable, letter-perfect, unblemished

rel consummate, expert, masterly; classic, dandy, excellent, fabulous, fine, first-class, first-rate, grand, great, marvelous (*or* marvellous), prime, superb, superior, superlative, terrific, top, top-notch, unsurpassed; completed, finished, perfected, polished; complete, entire, intact, whole; immaculate, unbruised, unmarred, unspoiled; exceptional, fancy, high-grade, special; accurate, correct, exact, precise; infallible, unerring, unfailing

near ant deficient, inadequate, incomplete, insufficient, wanting, unfinished, unpolished; fallible; blemished, blighted, broken, damaged, defaced, disfigured, impaired, injured, marred, spoiled, vitiated; atrocious, execrable, wretched; im-

precise, inaccurate, incorrect, inexact, wrong

ant bad, censurable, defective, faulty, flawed, imperfect, reproachable

2 having no exceptions or restrictions — see ABSOLUTE 2

3 not lacking any part or member that properly belongs to it — see COMPLETE 1

perfect *vb* **1** to bring (something) to a state where nothing remains to be done — see FINISH 1

2 to make better — see IMPROVE

perfection *n* the most perfect type or example — see QUINTESSENCE 1

perfectly *adv* **1** without any flaws or errors ⟨you did that handspring *perfectly* on your first try⟩

syn faultlessly, flawlessly, ideally, impeccably

rel excellently, fabulously, finely, grandly, greatly, marvelously, superbly, superiorly, superlatively, terrifically; exceptionally, fancily, specially

phrases to a nicety, to a T, to a turn

near ant deficiently, inadequately, incompletely, insufficiently; fallibly; atrociously, execrably, wretchedly

ant badly, defectively, faultily, imperfectly

2 to a full extent or degree — see FULLY 1

perfidious *adj* not true in one's allegiance to someone or something — see FAITHLESS

perfidiousness *n* lack of faithfulness especially to one's husband or wife — see INFIDELITY 1

perfidy *n* **1** lack of faithfulness especially to one's husband or wife — see INFIDELITY 1

2 the act or fact of violating the trust or confidence of another — see BETRAYAL

perforate *vb* to make a hole or series of holes in ⟨he *perforated* the sheet with his pencil and put it in his binder⟩

syn bore, drill, hole, pierce, punch, puncture

rel broach, tap; poke, prick; penetrate; burrow (into), excavate, gouge, groove, hollow; break, cut, gash, notch, rend, rupture, slash, split

near ant fill, patch, plug, seal

perforation *n* **1** a mark or small hole made by a pointed instrument — see PRICK 1

2 a place in a surface allowing passage into or through a thing — see HOLE 1

perforce *adv* because of necessity — see NEEDS

perform *vb* **1** to carry through (as a process) to completion ⟨she *performed* the task quickly and expertly⟩

syn accomplish, achieve, carry out, commit, compass, do, execute, follow through, fulfill (*or* fulfil), make

rel bring about, effect, effectuate, implement; engage (in), practice (*or* practise); work (at); reduplicate, reenact, repeat; actualize, attain, realize; complete, end, finish, wind up

phrases go through

near ant fail; skimp, slight, slur

---

2 to have a certain purpose — see FUNCTION

3 to present a portrayal or performance of — see ACT 1

4 to produce a desired effect — see ACT 2

performance *n* the doing of an action — see COMMISSION 2

perfume *n* a sweet or pleasant smell — see FRAGRANCE

perfume *vb* to fill or infuse with a pleasant odor or odor-releasing substance — see SCENT 1

perfumed *adj* having a pleasant smell — see FRAGRANT

perfunctory *adj* having or showing a lack of interest or concern — see INDIFFERENT 1

perhaps *adv* it is possible ⟨*perhaps* we will not have to take this exam, but I doubt it⟩
  syn conceivably, maybe, mayhap, perchance, possibly
  rel likely, probably; certainly, doubtless, surely, undoubtedly; presumably

peril *n* **1** something that may cause injury or harm — see DANGER 2
  2 the state of not being protected from injury, harm, or evil — see DANGER 1

perilous *adj* involving potential loss or injury — see DANGEROUS

perimeter *n* the line or relatively narrow space that marks the outer limit of something — see BORDER 1

period *n* **1** an occurrence of menstruating ⟨girls having their *period* will be excused from gym class⟩
  syn menstruation, monthlies
  rel menses
  2 an extent of time associated with a particular person or thing — see AGE 1

periodic *adj* **1** appearing in parts or numbers that follow regularly — see SERIAL
  2 appearing or occurring repeatedly from time to time — see REGULAR 1
  3 occurring or appearing at intervals — see INTERMITTENT 1

periodical *adj* **1** appearing in parts or numbers that follow regularly — see SERIAL
  2 occurring or appearing at intervals — see INTERMITTENT 1

periodical *n* a publication that appears at regular intervals — see JOURNAL

peripatetic *adj* traveling from place to place — see ITINERANT

peripheral *adj* available to supply something extra when needed — see AUXILIARY

periphery *n* the line or relatively narrow space that marks the outer limit of something — see BORDER 1

perish *vb* to stop living — see DIE 1

perk (up) *vb* **1** to become glad or hopeful — see CHEER (UP) 1
  2 to move from a lower to a higher place or position — see RAISE 1

perky *adj* having much high-spirited energy and movement — see LIVELY 1

permanent *adj* lasting forever — see EVERLASTING

permanently *adv* for all time — see EVER 1

permeable *adj* capable of being passed into or through — see PENETRABLE

permeate *vb* to spread throughout ⟨the smell of freshly baked bread *permeated* the house⟩
  syn interpenetrate, percolate (into), pervade, suffuse, transfuse
  rel diffuse (through), impregnate, pass (into), penetrate; fill (up); drench, infuse, saturate, soak, steep; flood, glut

permissible *adj* that may be permitted ⟨fortunately, that is a *permissible* shortcut to the answer⟩
  syn admissible, allowable, licensable
  rel acceptable, bearable, endurable, tolerable; accredited, allowed, authorized, certified, endorsed, licensed (*also* licenced), OK (*or* okay), permitted, sanctioned, warranted; mandatory, ordered, required
  near ant intolerable, unacceptable, unbearable, unendurable; objectionable; denied, disallowed, refused, rejected, vetoed; repressed, suppressed; outlawed
  ant banned, barred, forbidden, impermissible, inadmissible, interdicted, prohibited, proscribed

permission *n* the approval by someone in authority for the doing of something ⟨she asked for *permission* to have a piece of candy⟩ ⟨the President granted *permission* for the foreign diplomats to have special quarters⟩
  syn allowance, authorization, clearance, concurrence, consent, granting, leave, license (*or* licence), sanction, sufferance
  rel imprimatur, seal, signature, stamp; accreditation, certification; liberty, pass; concession, patent, permit; acceptance, acquiescence, agreement, assent, OK (*or* okay); accord, grant
  near ant denial, refusal, rejection, revocation; taboo; injunction, veto; deterrence, discouragement, repression, suppression; ban, embargo, exclusion
  ant interdiction, prohibition, proscription

permit *vb* **1** to give permission for or to approve of — see ALLOW 1
  2 to give permission to — see ALLOW 2
  3 to make able or possible — see ENABLE 1

pernicious *adj* causing or capable of causing harm — see HARMFUL

perpendicular *adj* rising straight up — see ERECT

perpetration *n* the doing of an action — see COMMISSION 2

perpetual *adj* lasting forever — see EVERLASTING

perpetually *adv* **1** for all time — see EVER 1
  2 on every relevant occasion — see ALWAYS 1

perpetuate *vb* to give eternal or lasting existence to ⟨we hope to *perpetuate* this holiday tradition⟩
  syn immortalize

rel commemorate, memorialize; celebrate, enshrine, honor; conserve, keep up, maintain, preserve, support, sustain; defend, guard, protect, safeguard

near ant extinguish, put out, snuff (out); annihilate, crush, decimate, demolish, destroy, devastate; eradicate, erase, expunge, extirpate, obliterate, wipe out

perpetuity *n* endless time — see ETERNITY 1

perplex *vb* **1** to make complex or difficult — see COMPLICATE

2 to throw into a state of mental uncertainty — see CONFUSE 1

perplexity *n* a state of mental uncertainty — see CONFUSION 1

perquisite *n* **1** a small sum of money given for a service over and above what is due — see ²TIP 1

2 something given in addition to what is ordinarily expected or owed — see BONUS

persecute *vb* **1** to cause persistent suffering to — see AFFLICT

2 to disturb the peace of mind of (someone) especially by repeated disagreeable acts — see IRRITATE 1

persecutor *n* **1** a person who causes repeated emotional pain, distress, or annoyance to another — see TORMENTOR

2 one who is obnoxiously annoying — see NUISANCE 1

persevere *vb* to continue despite difficulties, opposition, or discouragement ⟨although he was frustrated by the lack of financial resources and support, he *persevered* in his scientific research⟩

syn carry on, persist

rel hang on; follow through; knuckle down

phrases hang in there

near ant give up, quit, surrender, yield; falter, hesitate, vacillate, waver

persevering *adj* continuing despite difficulties, opposition, or discouragement — see PERSISTENT

persiflage *n* good-natured teasing or exchanging of clever remarks — see BANTER

persist *vb* **1** to continue despite difficulties, opposition, or discouragement — see PERSEVERE

2 to remain indefinitely in existence or in the same state — see CONTINUE 1

persistence *n* **1** continuing existence ⟨the *persistence* of the child's fever made us start to worry⟩

syn continuance, durability, endurance

rel longevity, staying power, tenacity; permanence; survival; continuation

near ant discontinuance; cessation, desisting, ending, finish, quitting, stop

2 uninterrupted or lasting existence — see CONTINUATION

3 a steadfast adherence to an opinion, purpose, or course of action — see OBSTINACY

persistent *adj* continuing despite difficulties, opposition, or discouragement ⟨although his first attempts were unsuccessful, he was *persistent* in his pursuit of a career in rock music⟩

syn dogged, insistent, patient, persevering, pertinacious, tenacious

rel assured, certain, dedicated, determined, firm, intent, positive, resolute, resolved, single-minded, sure; hardheaded, headstrong, mulish, obdurate, obstinate, opinionated, peevish, perverse, pigheaded, self-willed, stubborn, unyielding; unfaltering, unhesitating, unwavering; resistant, wayward, wrongheaded; constant, devoted, faithful, good, loyal, staunch (*or* stanch), steadfast, steady, true; indomitable, unconquerable; hard, inflexible, relentless, stern, unbending, unrelenting, unyielding

near ant quitting, surrendering, yielding; faltering, hesitant, hesitating, irresolute, vacillating, wavering; disloyal, faithless, false, fickle, inconstant, perfidious, traitorous, treacherous

person *n* a member of the human race — see HUMAN

personage *n* a person who is widely known and usually much talked about — see CELEBRITY 1

personal *adj* of, relating to, or belonging to a single person — see INDIVIDUAL 1

personality *n* **1** a person who is widely known and usually much talked about — see CELEBRITY 1

2 the set of qualities that make a person different from other people — see INDIVIDUALITY

3 the set of qualities that makes a person, a group of people, or a thing different from others — see NATURE 1

personalize *vb* to represent in visible form — see EMBODY 2

personalized *adj* of, relating to, or belonging to a single person — see INDIVIDUAL 1

personally *adv* in person and usually privately — see TÊTE-À-TÊTE

personalty *n* transportable items that one owns — see POSSESSION 2

personification *n* a visible representation of something abstract (as a quality) — see EMBODIMENT

personify *vb* to represent in visible form — see EMBODY 2

personnel *n* a body of persons at work or available for work — see FORCE 1

perspective *n* a way of looking at or thinking about something — see POINT OF VIEW

perspicuity *n* clearness of expression — see SIMPLICITY 2

perspicuous *adj* not subject to misinterpretation or more than one interpretation — see CLEAR 2

perspicuousness *n* clearness of expression — see SIMPLICITY 2

persuade *vb* to cause (someone) to agree with a belief or course of action by using arguments or earnest request ⟨she *per-*

---

syn synonym(s)   **rel** related words
ant antonym(s)   **near ant** near antonym(s)

suaded us that she can indeed communicate with the dead⟩ ⟨he *persuaded* his teachers to grant an extension⟩

syn argue, convince, get, induce, move, prevail (on *or* upon), satisfy, talk (into), win (over)

rel cajole, coax, exhort, urge; lead on, seduce, snow, tempt; incline, influence, move, prompt, sell, sway; attract, bring, draw, entice, interest; chew over, converse, debate, discuss, dispute, hash (over), moot; reason (with)

near ant dissuade

persuading *n* the act of reasoning or pleading with someone to accept a belief or course of action — see PERSUASION 1

persuasion *n* 1 the act of reasoning or pleading with someone to accept a belief or course of action ⟨the suffragists' gradual *persuasion* of the American people that voting rights had to be extended to women⟩

syn convincing, inducement, inducing, persuading, suasion

rel cajolery, coaxing, exhortation, urging; seduction, tempting; influencing, prompting, swaying; lobbying, pressuring

2 a body of beliefs and practices regarding the supernatural and the worship of one or more deities — see RELIGION 1

3 an idea that is believed to be true or valid without positive knowledge — see OPINION 1

persuasive *adj* having the power to persuade — see COGENT

persuasiveness *n* the capacity to persuade — see COGENCY 1

pert *adj* 1 having much high-spirited energy and movement — see LIVELY 1

2 making light of something usually regarded as serious or sacred — see FLIPPANT

pertain *vb* 1 to be the property of a person or group of persons — see BELONG 1

2 to have a relation or connection — see APPLY 1

pertain (to) *vb* to have (something) as a subject matter — see CONCERN 1

pertinacious *adj* 1 continuing despite difficulties, opposition, or discouragement — see PERSISTENT

2 sticking to an opinion, purpose, or course of action in spite of reason, arguments, or persuasion — see OBSTINATE

pertinaciousness *n* a steadfast adherence to an opinion, purpose, or course of action — see OBSTINACY

pertinacity *n* a steadfast adherence to an opinion, purpose, or course of action — see OBSTINACY

pertinence *n* the fact or state of being pertinent ⟨job applicants should question the *pertinence* of any questions about their personal lives⟩

syn applicability, bearing, connection, materiality, relevance, relevancy

rel appropriateness, aptness, fitness, suitability; importance, significance; usefulness

near ant inappropriateness, inaptness, unfitness, unsuitability; insignificance, unimportance; pointlessness, uselessness

ant extraneousness, inapplicability, irrelevance

pertinent *adj* having to do with the matter at hand ⟨he impressed the jury with his concise, *pertinent* answers to the attorney's questions⟩

syn applicable, apposite, apropos, germane, material, pointed, relative, relevant

rel appropriate, apt, fit, fitting, suitable; important, meaningful, significant; sensible, useful; admissible, allowable

phrases in point, to the point

near ant inconsequential, insignificant, unimportant; meaningless, purposeless, senseless, useless; inappropriate, inapt, unsuitable; inadmissible

ant extraneous, immaterial, inapplicable, irrelevant, pointless

pertly *adv* in a quick and spirited manner — see GAILY 2

pertness *n* shameless boldness — see EFFRONTERY

perturb *vb* to trouble the mind of; to make uneasy — see DISTURB 1

perturbation *n* an uneasy state of mind usually over the possibility of an anticipated misfortune or trouble — see ANXIETY 1

perturbed *adj* feeling or showing uncomfortable feelings of uncertainty — see NERVOUS 1

perturbing *adj* causing worry or anxiety — see TROUBLESOME

peruse *vb* to go over and mentally take in the content of — see READ

pervade *vb* to spread throughout — see PERMEATE

perverse *adj* 1 easily irritated or annoyed — see IRRITABLE

2 having or showing lowered moral character or standards — see CORRUPT

3 sticking to an opinion, purpose, or course of action in spite of reason, arguments, or persuasion — see OBSTINATE

perverseness *n* readiness to show annoyance or impatience — see PETULANCE

perversion *n* 1 a sinking to a state of low moral standards and behavior — see CORRUPTION 2

2 incorrect or improper use — see MISUSE

perversity *n* readiness to show annoyance or impatience — see PETULANCE

pervert *n* a person who has sunk below the normal moral standard — see DEGENERATE

pervert *vb* 1 to change so much as to create a wrong impression or alter the meaning of — see GARBLE

2 to lower in character or dignity — see DEBASE 1

3 to put to a bad or improper use — see MISAPPLY

perverted *adj* having or showing lowered moral character or standards — see CORRUPT

pessimist *n* **1** one who emphasizes bad aspects or conditions and expects the worst ⟨she's such a *pessimist* that she's convinced she'll fail every test⟩

syn defeatist

rel cynic, fatalist; pragmatist, realist

near ant dreamer, idealist, romantic, utopian, visionary; sentimentalist

ant optimist

2 a person who distrusts other people and believes that everything is done for selfish reasons — see CYNIC

pessimistic *adj* **1** emphasizing or expecting the worst ⟨with that *pessimistic* attitude, it's no wonder you're depressed⟩

syn defeatist, despairing, hopeless

rel cynical, fatalistic; desperate, discouraging, disheartening, inauspicious, unlikely, unpromising; bleak, cheerless, comfortless, dismal, dreary, gloomy, grim; contrary, hostile, negative

near ant auspicious, encouraging, fair, heartening, likely, promising, propitious; cheering, comforting, reassuring; favorable, good, positive; idealist, romantic, utopian, visionary

ant hopeful, optimistic, rose-colored, rosy, upbeat

2 having or showing a deep distrust of human beings and their motives — see CYNICAL

pest *n* **1** a widespread disease resulting in a high rate of death — see PLAGUE

2 one who is obnoxiously annoying — see NUISANCE 1

3 something that is a source of irritation — see ANNOYANCE 3

pester *vb* to thrust oneself upon (another) without invitation — see BOTHER 1

pestering *n* the act of making unwelcome intrusions upon another — see ANNOYANCE 1

pestilence *n* a widespread disease resulting in a high rate of death — see PLAGUE

pestilent *adj* likely to cause or capable of causing death — see DEADLY

pesty *adj* causing annoyance — see ANNOYING

pet *adj* granted special treatment or attention — see DARLING 1

pet *n* **1** a person or thing that is preferred over others — see FAVORITE

2 a state of resentful silence or irritability — see SULK

pet *vb* **1** to touch or handle in a tender or loving manner — see FONDLE

2 to touch one another with the lips as a sign of love — see KISS 1

petition *n* an earnest request — see PLEA 1

petition *vb* to make a request to (someone) in an earnest or urgent manner — see BEG

petitioner *n* one who asks earnestly for a favor or gift — see SUPPLICANT

pettish *adj* easily irritated or annoyed — see IRRITABLE

pettishness *n* readiness to show annoyance or impatience — see PETULANCE

petty *adj* **1** not broad or open in views or opinions — see NARROW 2

2 so small or unimportant as to warrant little or no attention — see NEGLIGIBLE 1

petulance *n* readiness to show annoyance or impatience ⟨I do not appreciate your *petulance* and eagerness to argue⟩

syn biliousness, crankiness, crossness, crotchetiness, grouchiness, grumpiness, huffiness, irascibility, irritability, irritableness, peevishness, perverseness, perversity, pettishness, testiness, waspishness

rel cantankerousness, disagreeableness, dyspepsia, fretfulness, orneriness, sulkiness, surliness; aggression, aggressiveness, bellicosity, belligerence, combativeness, contentiousness, contrariness, disputatiousness, fight, pugnacity, scrappiness, truculence; fussiness, querulousness, rudeness; oversensitiveness, sensitivity; antagonism, fierceness, hostility, unfriendliness; anger, exasperation, rage, wrath; hot-bloodedness, passion

near ant forbearance, patience, tolerance, understanding; affability, amicability, cordiality, friendliness, sociability; amiability, good-humoredness, good-naturedness, good-temperedness; coolness, serenity, tranquility; easygoingness, gentleness, kindliness, mildness

petulant *adj* easily irritated or annoyed — see IRRITABLE

pewter *adj* of the color gray — see GRAY 1

phantasm *n* **1** a conception or image created by the imagination and having no objective reality — see FANTASY 1

2 the soul of a dead person thought of especially as appearing to living people — see GHOST

phantasmal *adj* not real and existing only in the imagination — see IMAGINARY

phantom *adj* not real and existing only in the imagination — see IMAGINARY

phantom *n* the soul of a dead person thought of especially as appearing to living people — see GHOST

pharmaceutical *n* a substance or preparation used to treat disease — see MEDICINE

pharmacist *n* a person who prepares drugs according to a doctor's prescription — see DRUGGIST

pharmacy *n* a retail store where medicines and miscellaneous articles are sold — see DRUGSTORE

phase *n* **1** a certain way in which something appears or may be regarded — see ASPECT 1

2 an individual part of a process, series, or ranking — see DEGREE 1

phased *adj* proceeding or changing by steps or degrees — see GRADUAL

phenomenal *adj* **1** being out of the ordinary — see EXCEPTIONAL

2 being so extraordinary or abnormal as to suggest powers which violate the laws of nature — see SUPERNATURAL 2

---

syn synonym(s)   *rel* related words
ant antonym(s)   *near ant* near antonym(s)

phenomenon n something extraordinary or surprising — see WONDER 1

philanthropic adj having or showing a concern for the welfare of others — see CHARITABLE 1

philanthropy n 1 a gift of money or its equivalent to a charity, humanitarian cause, or public institution — see CONTRIBUTION

2 the giving of necessities and especially money to the needy — see CHARITY 1

3 the quality or state of being generous — see LIBERALITY

philharmonic n a usually large group of musicians playing together — see ²BAND 1

philistine n a person who is chiefly interested in material comfort and is hostile or indifferent to art and culture ⟨the town's *philistines* who think that spending on the arts is a waste of taxpayers' money⟩

syn lowbrow, materialist

rel capitalist, plutocrat; boor, cad, churl, clown, creep, cur, jerk, lout

near ant highbrow; egghead, intellectual, sage, thinker; brain, genius

philosophy n the basic beliefs or guiding principles of a person or group — see CREED 1

phlegm n a lack of emotion or emotional expressiveness — see APATHY 1

phlegmatic adj not feeling or showing emotion — see IMPASSIVE 1

phone vb to make a telephone call to — see CALL 2

phony also **phoney** adj 1 being such in appearance only and made or manufactured with the intention of committing fraud — see COUNTERFEIT

2 lacking in natural or spontaneous quality — see ARTIFICIAL 1

phony also **phoney** n 1 an imitation that is passed off as genuine — see FAKE 1

2 one who makes false claims of identity or expertise — see IMPOSTOR

photo n a picture created from an image recorded on a light-sensitive surface by a camera — see PHOTOGRAPH

photo vb to take a photograph of — see PHOTOGRAPH

photograph n a picture created from an image recorded on a light-sensitive surface by a camera ⟨the old *photograph* was faded but still clear enough to make out⟩

syn photo, print, shot, snap, snapshot

rel blowup, close-up, enlargement, still; daguerreotype, monochrome, tintype

photograph vb to take a photograph of ⟨we *photographed* the baby birds frequently⟩

syn mug, photo, shoot, snap

rel image, picture, retake; film, videotape

phrases capture on film

photographer n one who takes photographs ⟨we'll need to choose a *photographer* for the wedding⟩

syn shooter, shutterbug

rel cinematographer

phrase n a sequence of words having a specific meaning ⟨draw a literal representation of the *phrase* "to rain cats and dogs"⟩

syn expression, idiom

rel cliché; locution, term; epithet, expletive, name; byword, cry, motto, shibboleth, slogan, watchword; archaism, colloquialism, euphemism, modernism, neologism, provincialism, vulgarism

phrases figure of speech

phrase vb to convey in appropriate or telling terms ⟨he had trouble thinking of how to *phrase* his question for the visiting dignitary⟩

syn articulate, clothe, couch, express, formulate, put, say, state, word

rel craft, frame; hint, imply, insinuate, intimate, suggest; paraphrase, rephrase, restate, reword, summarize, translate; communicate, disclose, speak, tell; describe, render, write up

phraseology n 1 a distinctive way of putting ideas into words — see STYLE 1

2 the way in which something is put into words — see WORDING

phrasing n the way in which something is put into words — see WORDING

phylactery n something worn or kept to bring good luck or keep away evil — see CHARM 1

physic n a substance or preparation used to treat disease — see MEDICINE

physical adj 1 of or relating to the human body ⟨*physical* sensations such as heat and pain⟩

syn animal, bodily, carnal, corporal, corporeal, fleshly, material, somatic

rel anatomic (or anatomical), physiological; sensual, sensuous; hand-to-hand

near ant intellectual, mental, psychological (also psychologic); bodiless, immaterial, incorporeal, spiritual; ethereal, metaphysical, psychic (also psychical)

ant nonmaterial, nonphysical

2 relating to or composed of matter — see MATERIAL 1

physician n a person specially trained in healing human medical disorders — see DOCTOR

physique n the type of body that a person has ⟨she had a well-toned *physique*⟩

syn build, constitution, figure, form, frame, shape

rel anatomy, structure

picayune adj so small or unimportant as to warrant little or no attention — see NEGLIGIBLE 1

pick n 1 a person or thing that is chosen — see CHOICE 2

2 individuals carefully selected as being the best of a class — see ELITE

3 the power, right, or opportunity to choose — see CHOICE 1

pick vb 1 to catch or collect (a crop or natural resource) for human use — see HARVEST

2 to decide to accept (someone or something) from a group of possibilities — see CHOOSE 1

picked *adj* singled out from a number or group as more to one's liking — see SELECT 1

picked up *adj* being clean and in good order — see NEAT 1

picker *n* someone with the right or responsibility for making a selection — see SELECTOR

picket *n* a person or group that watches over someone or something — see GUARD 1

picking *n* the act or process of selecting — see SELECTION 1

pickle *n* a difficult, puzzling, or embarrassing situation from which there is no easy escape — see PREDICAMENT

pick up *vb* 1 to acquire complete knowledge, understanding, or skill in — see LEARN 1

2 to bring together in one body or place — see GATHER 1

3 to get possession of (something) by giving money in exchange for — see BUY

4 to increase in — see GAIN 1

5 to move from a lower to a higher place or position — see RAISE 1

6 to take or keep under one's control by authority of law — see ARREST 1

picky *adj* 1 hard to please — see FINICKY

2 tending to select carefully — see SELECTIVE

picnic *n* something that is easy to do — see CINCH

pictorial *adj* 1 consisting of or relating to pictures ⟨he's planning to do a primarily *pictorial* report on Africa⟩

syn graphic (*also* graphical), visual

rel photographic, video; drawn, painted, represented; illustrative; pictographic

2 producing a mental picture through clear and impressive description — see GRAPHIC 1

picture *n* 1 a two-dimensional design intended to look like a person or thing ⟨she produced a beautiful *picture* of her mother using watercolors⟩

syn illustration, image, likeness

rel delineation, depiction, representation; portrait; drawing, finger painting; etching, silhouette, sketch, watercolor; caricature, cartoon, doodle; collage, montage, photograph; hieroglyphic, ideogram; pictograph

2 a story told by means of a series of continuously projected pictures and a sound track — see MOVIE 1

3 a vivid representation in words of someone or something — see DESCRIPTION 1

4 position with regard to conditions and circumstances — see SITUATION 1

5 something or someone that strongly resembles another — see IMAGE 1

6 something imagined or pictured in the mind — see IDEA

7 **pictures** *pl* the art or business of making a movie — see MOVIE 2

picture *vb* 1 to present a picture of ⟨the famous painting that *pictures* the Founding Fathers signing the Declaration of Independence⟩

syn depict, image, portray, represent

rel delineate, describe, render; outline, sketch; illustrate, show; caricature

2 to form a mental picture of — see IMAGINE 1

3 to give a representation or account of in words — see DESCRIBE 1

picturesque *adj* producing a mental picture through clear and impressive description — see GRAPHIC 1

piddling *adj* so small or unimportant as to warrant little or no attention — see NEGLIGIBLE 1

piebald *adj* having blotches of two or more colors — see PIED

piece *n* 1 a broken or irregular part of something that often remains incomplete — see FRAGMENT

2 a literary, musical, or artistic production — see COMPOSITION 1

3 a portable weapon from which a shot is discharged by gunpowder — see GUN 1

piece *vb* to form by putting together parts or materials — see BUILD

piece by piece *adv* by small steps or amounts — see GRADUALLY

piecemeal *adj* proceeding or changing by steps or degrees — see GRADUAL

piecemeal *adv* 1 by small steps or amounts — see GRADUALLY

2 into parts or to pieces — see APART

pied *adj* having blotches of two or more colors ⟨although the mother's was pure black, the foal's coat was *pied*⟩

syn blotched, dappled (*also* dapple), marbled, mottled, piebald, pinto, splotched, spotted

rel shaded; checkered, motley, multicolored, polychromatic, polychrome, variegated; blotted, brindled (*or* brindle), specked, speckled, streaked; colored, colorful, pigmented; dotted, peppered, sprinkled; stippled; discolored, dyed, marked, stained; flecked, streaked; bespattered, spattered

near ant monochromatic, solid

pier *n* 1 a structure used by boats and ships for taking on or landing cargo and passengers — see DOCK

2 an upright shaft that supports an overhead structure — see PILLAR 1

pierce *vb* 1 to go or come in or into — see ENTER 1

2 to make a hole or series of holes in — see PERFORATE

3 to penetrate or hold (something) with a pointed object — see IMPALE

piercing *adj* 1 causing intense discomfort to one's skin — see CUTTING 1

2 marked by a high volume of sound — see LOUD 1

piety *n* 1 belief and trust in and loyalty to God — see FAITH 1

2 the quality or state of being spiritually pure or virtuous — see HOLINESS

---

syn synonym(s)   *rel* related words
ant antonym(s)   *near ant* near antonym(s)

piffle *n* **1** language, behavior, or ideas that are absurd and contrary to good reason — see NONSENSE 1

2 unintelligible or meaningless talk — see GIBBERISH

pigeon *n* one who is easily deceived or cheated — see DUPE

piggish *adj* having a huge appetite — see VORACIOUS 1

pigheaded *adj* sticking to an opinion, purpose, or course of action in spite of reason, arguments, or persuasion — see OBSTINATE

pigment *n* a substance used to color other materials ⟨I'm running out of the black *pigment*⟩
syn color, coloring, dye, dyestuff, stain, tincture
rel cast, hue, shade, tinge, tint, tone

pig out *vb* to eat greedily or to excess — see GORGE 2

pigpen *n* a dirty or messy place ⟨your room is a *pigpen* —so clean it up!⟩
syn hole, pigsty, shambles
rel chaos, confusion, disarrangement, disarray, disorder, jumble, mess, muddle; dump; clutter, litter, mishmash

pigsty *n* a dirty or messy place — see PIGPEN

¹pike *n* a passage cleared for public vehicular travel — see WAY 1

²pike *n* a weapon with a long straight handle and sharp head or blade — see SPEAR

³pike *n* the last and usually sharp or tapering part of something long and narrow — see POINT 2

piker *n* a mean grasping person who is usually stingy with money — see MISER

pikestaff *n* a weapon with a long straight handle and sharp head or blade — see SPEAR

pilaster *n* an upright shaft that supports an overhead structure — see PILLAR 1

¹pile *n* **1** a quantity of things thrown or stacked on one another ⟨a large *pile* of newspapers that needed to be disposed of⟩
syn cock, heap, hill, mound, mountain, rick, stack
rel bank, bar, drift, embankment; pyramid; barrow, cairn, pyre; accumulation, aggregate, assemblage, collection, conglomeration, gathering, grouping, hoard, jumble

2 a considerable amount — see LOT 2

²pile *n* **1** a soft airy substance or covering — see FUZZ

2 the hairy covering of a mammal especially when fine, soft, and thick — see FUR 1

pile *vb* to lay or throw on top of one another ⟨*piled* all the clothes on the chair before putting them away⟩
syn heap, mound, stack
rel bank; layer, pyramid; accumulate, amass, assemble, collect, gather, group, mass; bunch, clump, lump
ant unpile

pile (up) *vb* to gradually form into a layer, pile, or mass — see COLLECT 2

pilfer *vb* to take (something) without right and with an intent to keep — see STEAL 1

pilgrimage *vb* to take a trip especially of some distance — see TRAVEL 1

pill *n* a small mass containing medicine to be taken orally ⟨you'll have to take one of these *pills* every six hours for your flu⟩
syn capsule, lozenge, tablet
rel drug, medication, pharmaceutical, specific; miracle drug, wonder drug; potion, preparation; dosage, dose, drop, sleeping pill, tranquilizer (*also* tranquilizer)

pillage *vb* to search through with the intent of committing robbery — see RANSACK 1

pillar *n* **1** an upright shaft that supports an overhead structure ⟨the ancient Greek temple boasted graceful marble *pillars* with richly ornamented tops⟩
syn column, pier, pilaster, post, stanchion
rel caryatid, pedestal; buttress, flying buttress; needle, obelisk

2 something or someone to which one looks for support — see DEPENDENCE 2

pilot *adj* made or done as an experiment — see EXPERIMENTAL 1

pilot *n* one who flies or is qualified to fly an aircraft or spacecraft ⟨the airline is seeking experienced *pilots* to fly the new airplane⟩
syn airman, aviator, birdman, flier (*or* flyer)
rel ace, bush pilot, copilot, test pilot

pilot *vb* **1** to give advice and instruction to (someone) regarding the course or process to be followed — see GUIDE 1

2 to point out the way for (someone) especially from a position in front — see LEAD 1

pin *n* a lower limb of an animal — see LEG 1

pinch *n* **1** an instance of theft — see THEFT 2

2 the act of taking or holding under one's control by authority of law — see ARREST

pinch *vb* **1** to squeeze tightly between two surfaces, edges, or points ⟨the zipper on those jeans always *pinches* me⟩
syn nip
rel clasp, clutch, grasp, grip
near ant drop, free, loose, loosen, release

2 to take (something) without right and with an intent to keep — see STEAL 1

3 to take or keep under one's control by authority of law — see ARREST 1

pincher *n* one who steals — see THIEF

pinch–hit *vb* to serve as a replacement usually for a time only — see COVER 1

pinch hitter *n* a person or thing that takes the place of another — see SUBSTITUTE

pinching *adj* giving or sharing as little as possible — see STINGY 1

pinching *n* the quality of being overly sparing with money — see PARSIMONY

pine (for) *vb* to have an earnest wish to own or enjoy — see DESIRE

pinhead *n* a stupid person — see IDIOT

pinhole *n* a mark or small hole made by a pointed instrument — see PRICK 1

pining n a strong wish for something — see DESIRE

pinnacle n the highest part or point — see HEIGHT 1

pinpoint adj meeting the highest standard of accuracy — see PRECISE 1

pinpoint vb to find out or establish the identity of — see IDENTIFY 1

pinprick n a mark or small hole made by a pointed instrument — see PRICK 1

pinto adj having blotches of two or more colors — see PIED

pint–size or **pint–sized** adj of a size that is less than average — see SMALL 1

pioneer adj coming before all others in time or order — see FIRST 1

pioneer n a person who settles in a new region — see FRONTIERSMAN

pioneer vb to be responsible for the creation and early operation or use of — see FOUND

pious adj 1 firm in one's allegiance to someone or something — see FAITHFUL 1
2 showing a devotion to God and to a life of virtue — see HOLY 1

piousness n 1 the pretending of having virtues, principles, or beliefs that one in fact does not have — see HYPOCRISY
2 the quality or state of being spiritually pure or virtuous — see HOLINESS

pip n something very good of its kind — see JIM-DANDY

pipe n 1 a long hollow cylinder for carrying a substance (as a liquid or gas) ⟨the plumber came and fixed the water *pipe* that was leaking⟩
syn channel, conduit, duct, leader, line, penstock, trough, tube
rel drain, drainpipe, funnel, hydrant, main, smokestack, spout, stovepipe, tile, waterspout; pipeline, piping
2 an enclosed wooden vessel for holding beverages — see CASK

pipe vb 1 to cause to move to a central point or along a restricted pathway — see CHANNEL
2 to make a short sharp sound like a small bird — see CHIRP

pipe dream n a conception or image created by the imagination and having no objective reality — see FANTASY 1

pipeline n a direct way of passing along information or supplies ⟨an equipment hauler serves as the columnist's *pipeline* for gossip about the rock band⟩ ⟨the battle was ultimately lost because the enemy had destroyed our *pipeline* for resupply⟩
syn channel
rel conduit; grapevine, outlet; fountainhead, origin, source, wellspring; supplier; connection, contact

piping adj having a high musical pitch or range — see SHRILL

piping hot adj having a notably high temperature — see HOT 1

piquancy n the quality or state of being stimulating to the mind or senses ⟨a talk show host known for the quickness and *piquancy* of his wit⟩ ⟨I appreciated the *piquancy* of the peppers in the sauce⟩
syn pungency, zest
rel raciness, spiciness; fieriness, hotness; acuteness, keenness, sharpness; provocativeness; excitement, invigoration, stimulation, thrill; flavor, savor, tastiness
near ant flatness, tastelessness; dullness (*also* dulness), monotonousness, predictability, tediousness; blandness, thinness, weakness
ant insipidity

piquant adj sharp and pleasantly stimulating to the mind or senses ⟨a *piquant* tidbit of information about the new neighbors⟩ ⟨the *piquant* cuisine of India boasts some highly spiced dishes⟩
syn pungent, zesty
rel racy, spicy; fiery, hot; acute, keen; biting, bitter, cutting, mordant, trenchant; animating, energizing, enlightening, exciting, galvanizing, invigorating, provocative; appetizing, delectable, delicious, palatable, toothsome; flavorful, savory, tasty; absorbing, engaging, engrossing, enthralling, fascinating, gripping, interesting, intriguing
near ant flat, flavorless, savorless, tasteless; banal, boring, dull, monotonous, pedestrian, predictable, tedious, tiring, uninteresting, wearisome, wearying; bland, dilute, thin, watery, weak
ant insipid

pique n the feeling of being offended or resentful after a slight or indignity ⟨she's still in a *pique* over being snubbed by a so-called friend at the party⟩
syn dudgeon, huff, offense (*or* offence), peeve, resentment, umbrage
rel aggravation, anger, annoyance, bother, discomfort, exasperation, frustration, irritation, vexation; agitation, angriness, displeasure, distress, disturbance, indignation, irateness, ire, outrage, perturbation, upset; dander, temper; fit, pet, sulk(s), tantrum, tizzy; affront, insult
near ant satisfaction; appeasement, mollification, pacification; delight, pleasure

pique vb 1 to disturb the peace of mind of (someone) especially by repeated disagreeable acts — see IRRITATE 1
2 to rouse to strong feeling or action — see PROVOKE 1

piquing adj serving or likely to arouse a strong reaction — see PROVOCATIVE

piracy n the act or pursuit of robbing ships at sea ⟨many countries have harsh penalties for *piracy* now⟩
syn pirating
rel depredation, despoilment, despoliation, looting, marauding, pillaging, plunder, plundering, raiding, robbery; privateering; burglary, housebreaking, stealing, thieving; hijacking (*also* highjacking), rustling

pirate n someone who engages in robbery of ships at sea ⟨Sir Francis Drake was a British *pirate* who preyed on Spanish ships with the permission of the British queen⟩

syn buccaneer, corsair, freebooter, rover

rel looter, marauder, pillager, plunderer, raider, robber; privateer; burglar, housebreaker, stealer, thief; hijacker, rustler

pirating *n* the act or pursuit of robbing ships at sea — see PIRACY

pirouette *n* a rapid turning about on an axis or central point — see SPIN 1

pirouette *vb* to move in circles around an axis or center — see SPIN 1

pit *n* a sunken area forming a separate space — see HOLE 2

pit-a-pat *vb* to expand and contract in a rhythmic manner — see PULSATE

pitch *n* 1 an act or instance of diving — see DIVE 1

2 the degree to which something rises up from a position level with the horizon — see SLANT

pitch *vb* 1 to fix in an upright position — see ERECT 1

2 to cast oneself head first into deep water — see DIVE

3 to make a series of unsteady side-to-side motions — see ROCK 1

4 to send through the air especially with a quick forward motion of the arm — see THROW

pitch-black *adj* 1 being without light or without much light — see DARK 1

2 having the color of soot or coal — see BLACK 1

pitch-dark *adj* 1 being without light or without much light — see DARK 1

2 having the color of soot or coal — see BLACK 1

pitched *adj* running in a slanting direction — see DIAGONAL

pitcher *n* a handled container for holding and pouring liquids that usually has a lip or a spout ⟨please bring me the *pitcher* full of lemonade from the table⟩

syn flagon, jug

rel carafe, decanter; bucket, pail, pot; canteen, cup, flask, mug, stein; barrel, cask, hogshead, pipe, puncheon

pitch in *vb* to make a donation as part of a group effort — see CONTRIBUTE 1

pitchy *adj* having the color of soot or coal — see BLACK 1

piteous *adj* deserving of one's pity — see PATHETIC 1

pitfall *n* 1 a danger or difficulty that is hidden or not easily recognized ⟨buying a house can be full of *pitfalls* for the unwary⟩

syn booby trap, catch, snag

rel snare, trap, web; hazard, peril, risk; bombshell, surprise; bait, lure

2 something that may cause injury or harm — see DANGER 2

pith *n* the central part or aspect of something under consideration — see CRUX

pithily *adv* in a few words — see SHORTLY 1

pithiness *n* the quality or state of being marked by or using only few words to

convey much meaning — see SUCCINCTNESS

pithy *adj* marked by the use of few words to convey much information or meaning — see CONCISE

pitiable *adj* 1 arousing or deserving of one's loathing and disgust — see CONTEMPTIBLE 1

2 deserving pitying scorn (as for inadequacy) — see PITIFUL 1

3 deserving of one's pity — see PATHETIC 1

pitiful *adj* 1 deserving pitying scorn (as for inadequacy) ⟨that is a *pitiful* attempt at an essay on patriotism; you'll have to do it over⟩

syn contemptible, despicable, pitiable, sorry

rel deplorable, discreditable, disgraceful, disreputable, infamous, notorious; abhorrent, abominable, detestable, hateful, odious; bad, inferior, poor; disgusting, dishonorable, shameful; unworthy, worthless; scandalous, shocking, sordid, unsavory

near ant admirable, creditable, laudable, meritorious, praiseworthy; notable, noteworthy, noticeable, outstanding, reputable, worthy; excellent; flawless, perfect; honorable, noble; honest, straight

ant decent, presentable, respectable

2 arousing or deserving of one's loathing and disgust — see CONTEMPTIBLE 1

3 deserving of one's pity — see PATHETIC 1

pitiless *adj* having or showing a lack of sympathy or tender feelings — see HARD 1

pittance *n* a very small sum of money — see MITE 1

pitter-patter *vb* to expand and contract in a rhythmic manner — see PULSATE

pity *n* 1 a regrettable or blameworthy act — see CRIME 2

2 the capacity for feeling for another's unhappiness or misfortune — see HEART 1

pity *vb* to have sympathy for ⟨I always *pity* the people who have to work in this freezing weather⟩

syn bleed (for), commiserate (with), condole (with), feel (for), sympathize (with)

rel care (for); grieve (for), sorrow (for); love; tolerate, understand

near ant disregard, ignore, neglect, overlook; dislike, hate, scorn

pivot *n* the central part or aspect of something under consideration — see CRUX

pivot *vb* to move (something) in a curved or circular path on or as if on an axis — see TURN 1

pivotal *adj* of the greatest possible importance — see CRUCIAL

pixie *also* **pixy** *n* an imaginary being usually having a small human form and magical powers — see FAIRY

pixieish *adj* tending to or exhibiting reckless playfulness — see MISCHIEVOUS 1

placard *n* a sheet bearing an announcement for posting in a public place — see POSTER

placard *vb* 1 to affix (as a notice) to or on a suitable place — see ¹POST 1

2 to make known openly or publicly — see ANNOUNCE

placate *vb* to lessen the anger or agitation of — see PACIFY

placating *adj* tending to lessen or avoid conflict or hostility — see PACIFIC 1

place *n* 1 the area or space occupied by or intended for something ⟨the *place* chosen for the picnic⟩ ⟨there's the *place* where I left my umbrella⟩

syn locale, locality, location, locus, point, position, site, spot

rel scene; region, section, sector

2 a building, room, or suite of rooms occupied by a service business ⟨we're going to our favorite *place* to eat⟩

syn establishment, joint, parlor, salon

rel spot, station; facility, installation; studio; den, dive, hole

3 an assignment at which one regularly works for pay — see JOB 1

4 an extent or area available for or used up by some activity or thing — see ROOM 1

5 the action for which a person or thing is specially fitted or used or for which a thing exists — see ROLE

6 the place where one lives — see HOME 1

7 the placement of someone or something in relation to others in a vertical arrangement — see RANK 1

place *vb* 1 to arrange something in a certain spot or position ⟨he carefully *placed* the flowers in a vase⟩

syn deposit, dispose, fix, lay, position, put, set, set up, situate, stick

rel rearrange, reorder; orient; establish, locate, settle; assemble, collect; carry; berth, park; affix, anchor, wedge; lay out, line up, queue, rank; set down

near ant relocate, remove, take; banish; displace, replace, supplant

2 to arrange or assign according to type — see CLASSIFY 1

3 to decide the size, amount, number, or distance of (something) without actual measurement — see ESTIMATE 2

4 to take or have a certain position within a group arranged in vertical classes — see RANK 1

placid *adj* 1 free from emotional or mental agitation — see CALM 2

2 free from storms or physical disturbance — see CALM 1

placidity *n* 1 a state of freedom from storm or disturbance — see CALM

2 evenness of emotions or temper — see EQUANIMITY

plague *n* a widespread disease resulting in a high rate of death ⟨the Black Death was a *plague* that killed about one third of Europe's population in the Middle Ages⟩

syn pest, pestilence

rel epidemic, pandemic; affection, affliction, contagion, contagious disease, infection, infectious disease, infirmity, malady; curse, scourge

plague *vb* to cause persistent suffering to — see AFFLICT

plain *adj* 1 free from all additions or embellishment ⟨I like my hamburgers *plain*, with no ketchup or relish⟩ ⟨just give us the *plain* facts and none of your snide comments⟩

syn bald, bare, naked, simple, unadorned, undecorated, unvarnished

rel chaste, modest; unexaggerated, unsophisticated; denuded, divested, stripped; dry, laconic, terse; unpretentious; austere, bleak, severe, spartan, stark; inconspicuous, muted, restrained, subdued, toned (down), unobtrusive; conservative, quiet, understated

near ant flamboyant, flashy, garish, gaudy, glittery, glitzy, loud, ostentatious, showy, splashy, swank (or swanky), tawdry; bedizened, florid, lurid, ornate; exaggerated, overdecorated, overdone, overwrought; baroque, extravagant, rococo; arrayed, bedecked, decked-out, dressed, garnished, trimmed

ant adorned, decorated, embellished, fancy, ornamented

2 free from added matter — see PURE 1

3 free in expressing one's true feelings and opinions — see FRANK

4 going straight to the point clearly and firmly — see STRAIGHTFORWARD

5 not subject to misinterpretation or more than one interpretation — see CLEAR 2

plain *adv* in an honest and direct manner — see STRAIGHTFORWARD

plain *n* a broad area of level or rolling treeless country ⟨the first settlers in that area lived on the vast *plains* in lonely log cabins⟩

syn down, grassland, prairie, savanna (also savannah), steppe, tundra, veld (or veldt)

rel pampas; floodplain; bottom, bottomland, flat, lowland; plateau, table, tableland, upland

plainclothesman *n* a person whose business is solving crimes and catching criminals or gathering information that is not easy to get — see DETECTIVE

plainly *adv* in an honest and direct manner — see STRAIGHTFORWARD

plainness *n* 1 the free expression of one's true feelings and opinions — see CANDOR

2 the quality or state of having a form or structure of few parts or elements — see SIMPLICITY 1

plainspoken *adj* free in expressing one's true feelings and opinions — see FRANK

plaint *n* 1 a crying out in grief — see LAMENT 1

2 an expression of dissatisfaction, pain, or resentment — see COMPLAINT 1

plaintiff *n* the person in a legal proceeding who makes a charge of wrongdoing against another — see COMPLAINANT

plaintive *adj* expressing or suggesting mourning — see MOURNFUL 1

---

syn synonym(s)   *rel* related words
ant antonym(s)   *near ant* near antonym(s)

plait *n* a length of something formed of three or more strands woven together — see BRAID

plait *vb* to form into a braid — see BRAID

plan *n* **1** a method worked out in advance for achieving some objective ⟨there is a contingency *plan* in the office for handling almost any emergency⟩

syn arrangement, blueprint, design, game, ground plan, program, project, scheme, strategy, system

rel collusion, conspiracy, plot; maneuver, ruse, stratagem, subterfuge, trick; means, method, tactic, technique, way; conception, idea, proposal; aim, intention, purpose; diagram, formula, layout, map, policy, recipe, setup

2 something that one hopes or intends to accomplish — see GOAL

plan *vb* **1** to work out the details of (something) in advance ⟨we *planned* the school dance down to the smallest detail⟩

syn arrange, blueprint, calculate, chart, design, frame, lay out, map (out), project, schematize, scheme (out)

rel conspire, intrigue, machinate; draft, outline, sketch; aim, figure, intend, mean; contemplate, meditate, premeditate

2 to have in mind as a purpose or goal — see INTEND

plane *adj* having a surface without bends, breaks, or irregularities — see LEVEL

plane *vb* **1** to make free from breaks, curves, or bumps — see EVEN 1

2 to move through the air with or as if with outstretched wings — see FLY 1

planet *n* the celestial body on which we live — see EARTH 1

plant *n* a building or set of buildings for the manufacturing of goods — see FACTORY

plant *vb* to put or set into the ground to grow ⟨I'll *plant* the marigold seeds in the spring⟩

syn drill, put in, seed, sow

rel bed; replant, transplant; scatter; pot

near ant gather, harvest, reap

plantation *n* a settlement in a new country or region — see COLONY 1

planter *n* a person who cultivates the land and grows crops on it — see FARMER

plash *vb* **1** to flow in a broken irregular stream — see GURGLE

2 to move with a splashing motion — see SLOSH

3 to wet or soil by striking with something liquid or mushy — see SPLASH 2

plaster *n* a medicated covering used to heal an injury — see DRESSING 1

plastic *adj* capable of being easily molded or modeled ⟨Silly Putty is famous for being very *plastic*⟩

syn malleable

rel adaptable; ductile, pliable, pliant, supple, willowy; elastic, flexible, resilient, workable; bending, giving, tractable, yielding

near ant inflexible, rigid, stiff

plasticity *n* the quality or state of being easily molded ⟨we chose that type of clay for its greater *plasticity*⟩

syn malleability

rel adaptability; pliability, suppleness; elasticity, flexibility, resilience

near ant inflexibility, rigidity, stiffness

plat *n* a small area of usually open land — see FIELD 1

2 a small piece of land that is developed or available for development — see LOT 1

plate *n* a small thin piece of material that resembles an animal scale — see ²SCALE

2 something that visually explains or decorates a text — see ILLUSTRATION 1

plateau *n* a broad flat area of elevated land ⟨Native Americans have inhabited the *plateau* for centuries⟩

syn mesa, table, tableland

rel butte, dome, height, highland, upland

platform *n* a level usually raised surface ⟨you'll have to stand up there on the *platform* for your speech⟩

syn dais, podium, rostrum, stage, stand

rel altar, pulpit; balcony

platitude *n* an idea or expression that has been used by many people — see COMMONPLACE

plaudit *n usually* **plaudits** *pl* enthusiastic and usually public expression of approval — see APPLAUSE

plausible *adj* worthy of being accepted as true or reasonable — see BELIEVABLE

play *n* **1** activity engaged in to amuse oneself ⟨it's such a delight to watch the children in their *play*⟩

syn dalliance, frolic, frolicking, fun, recreation, relaxation, rollicking, sport

rel gamboling, romping; amusement, diversion, entertainment; delight, enjoyment, pleasure; friskiness, playfulness, sportiveness, wantonness; devilment, devilry (*or* deviltry), hob, impishness, mischief, mischievousness, rascality, roguishness, waggery; binge, fling, lark, revel, spree; hilarity, merrymaking, revelry; buffoonery, horseplay, tomfoolery

near ant drudgery, labor, work; duty, obligation, responsibility

2 a written work in which the story is told through speech and action that is intended to be acted out on stage ⟨we'll be putting on a school *play* using that stage⟩

syn drama, dramatization

rel comedy, melodrama, musical, musical comedy, tragedy, tragicomedy; magnum opus, opus, work; adaptation

3 an attitude or manner not to be taken seriously — see FUN 2

4 the act or practice of employing something for a particular purpose — see USE 1

play *vb* **1** to engage in activity for amusement ⟨you need some time to run and *play* in the yard after that hard work⟩

syn dally, disport, frolic, recreate, rollick, sport

rel gambol, romp; dabble, trifle; amuse, divert, entertain; delight, please; dabble, mess (around), putter; bum (around), dawdle, goldbrick, idle, loaf, lounge (around *or* about), relax, rest, slack (off), jest, joke, tease

near ant drudge, labor, plod, plug (away), slave, strain, strive, struggle, sweat, toil, work

2 to present a portrayal or performance of — see ACT 1

3 to pretend to be (what one is not) in appearance or behavior — see IMPERSONATE 1

4 to spend time in aimless activity — see FIDDLE (AROUND)

play (on *or* upon) *vb* to take unfair advantage of — see EXPLOIT 1

play (up) *vb* to indicate the importance of by giving prominent display — see EMPHASIZE

play (upon) *vb* to control or take advantage of by artful, unfair, or insidious means — see MANIPULATE 1

play (with) *vb* to handle thoughtlessly, ignorantly, or mischievously — see TAMPER

played out *adj* depleted in strength, energy, or freshness — see WEARY 1

player *n* **1** a person who plays a musical instrument — see MUSICIAN 1

2 one who acts professionally (as in a play, movie, or television show) — see ACTOR

playful *adj* given to good-natured joking or teasing ⟨the little girl was lighthearted and *playful*⟩

syn antic, coltish, elfish, fay, frisky, frolicsome, rollicking, sportive

rel kittenish; gay, happy, lighthearted, whimsical; energetic, lively, spirited, sprightly; devilish, knavish, rascally; amusing, diverting, enjoyable, entertaining, fun, pleasurable; dabbling, frivolous, trifling; delightful, pleasant, pleasing; jesting, joking, teasing

near ant dutiful, responsible; grave, grim, serious, solemn, somber (*or* sombre), stern, stolid; no-nonsense, priggish, starchy, stuffy; decorous, formal, proper, sedate, staid; guarded, inhibited, restrained

ant earnest, serious-minded, sober

playfulness *n* a natural disposition for playful behavior ⟨the *playfulness* of the kitten can be quite amusing⟩

syn friskiness, impishness, mischief, mischievousness, prankishness, sportiveness

rel devilment, devilry (*or* deviltry), hob, rascality, waggery; devilishness, diabolicalness, knavery; frivolousness; energy, liveliness, sprightliness; gaiety (*also* gayety), lightheartedness, whimsicality

near ant graveness, grimness, seriousness, solemnity, sternness; priggishness, starchiness, stuffiness; constraint, restraint, self-control

ant earnestness, soberness

playhouse *n* a building or part of a building where movies are shown — see THEATER 1

plea *n* **1** an earnest request ⟨the student made an impassioned *plea* for more time to finish the test⟩

syn appeal, cry, entreaty, petition, prayer, solicitation, suit, supplication

rel application; call, demand, insistence

2 an explanation that frees one from fault or blame — see EXCUSE

plead *vb* to state (something) as a reason in support of or against something under consideration — see ARGUE 1

plead (for) *vb* to make a request for — see ASK (FOR) 1

plead (to) *vb* to make a request to (someone) in an earnest or urgent manner — see BEG

pleader *n* one who asks earnestly for a favor or gift — see SUPPLICANT

pleading *adj* asking humbly — see SUPPLIANT

pleasant *adj* giving pleasure or contentment to the mind or senses ⟨the massage was extremely *pleasant* and relaxing⟩

syn agreeable, congenial, darling, delectable, delicious, delightful, dreamy, enjoyable, felicitous, good, grateful, gratifying, heavenly, luscious, nice, palatable, pleasing, pleasurable, satisfying, welcome

rel alluring, attractive, desirable, inviting, tempting; charming, enchanting, fascinating; calming, comforting, soothing; affable, amiable, amusing, cheerful, cheery, genial, goodly, good-natured, gracious, hospitable, kindly, personable; blissful, glad, happy, joyous; elating, exhilarating, intoxicating; ecstatic, euphoric, rapturous

near ant abominable, horrid, miserable, wretched; disgusting, distasteful, obnoxious, offensive, repellent (*also* repellant), repugnant, repulsive; abhorrent, detestable, hateful, odious; boring, commonplace, dull, flat, insipid, irksome, stale, tedious; displeasing, dissatisfying; depressing, disheartening, dismal, dreary, gloomy; black, blue, dejected, depressed, despondent, disconsolate, down, downcast, downhearted, forlorn, hangdog, heartbreaking, heartrending, heartsick, heartsore, inconsolable, joyless, lachrymose, low-spirited, sad, unhappy; bemoaning, bewailing, deploring, doleful, dolorous, grieving, lugubrious, mournful, plaintive, regretful, rueful, sorrowful, wailing, weeping; aggravating, annoying, exasperating, irritating, peeving, perturbing, vexing; forbidding; hostile, intimidating; angering, enraging, incensing, inflaming, infuriating, maddening, outraging, rankling, riling; distressing, disturbing, upsetting

ant disagreeable, unpalatable, unpleasant, unwelcome

pleasantly *adv* in a pleasing way — see WELL 5

---

syn synonym(s)   *rel* related words
ant antonym(s)   *near ant* near antonym(s)

pleasantness *n* the state or quality of having a pleasant or agreeable manner in socializing with others — see AMIABILITY 1

pleasantry *n* something said or done to cause laughter — see JOKE 1

please *vb* to give satisfaction to ⟨fresh flowers *please* me greatly⟩

syn content, delight, gladden, gratify, rejoice, satisfy, suit, warm

rel appease, mollify, pacify, placate, soothe; assuage, quench, sate, satiate; excite, tickle, titillate; overjoy, thrill; calm, comfort; humor, indulge; coddle, mollycoddle, pamper, spoil

near ant aggravate, annoy, bother, bug, chafe, cross, exasperate, gall, get, grate, irk, irritate, nettle, peeve, perturb, pique, put out, ruffle, vex; anger, enrage, incense, inflame, infuriate, madden, outrage, rankle, rile, roil; provoke, rouse; agitate, distress, disturb, fret, upset; harass, harry, pester; affront, insult, offend

ant displease

pleased *adj* **1** experiencing pleasure, satisfaction, or delight — see GLAD 1

2 feeling that one's needs or desires have been met — see CONTENT

pleasing *adj* giving pleasure or contentment to the mind or senses — see PLEASANT

pleasingly *adv* in a pleasing way — see WELL 5

pleasurable *adj* **1** giving pleasure or contentment to the mind or senses — see PLEASANT

2 providing amusement or enjoyment — see FUN

pleasure *n* **1** the feeling experienced when one's wishes are met ⟨nothing gives me more *pleasure* than a hot meal after a long day⟩

syn content, contentedness, contentment, delectation, delight, enjoyment, gladness, gratification, happiness, relish, satisfaction

rel bliss, felicity, glee, gleefulness, joy; amusement, diversion, entertainment; elatedness, elation, exhilaration, exultation, intoxication; ecstasy, euphoria, heaven, rapture; cheer, cheerfulness, exuberance, gaiety (*also* gayety), jollity, joyfulness, jubilation; comfort, ease, restfulness

near ant misery, sadness, unhappiness, wretchedness; anguish, desolation, joylessness, sorrow, woe; dejection, depression, despondency, dispiritedness, gloom, melancholy; aggravation, annoyance, exasperation, irritation, pique, vexation; anger, fury, rage; agitation, distress, disturbance, upset; discomfort, restlessness, uneasiness

ant discontent, discontentedness, discontentment, displeasure, dissatisfaction, unhappiness

2 a source of great satisfaction — see DELIGHT 1

3 someone or something that provides amusement or enjoyment — see FUN 1

pleat *vb* to form into a braid — see BRAID

plebeian *adj* belonging to the class of people of low social or economic rank — see IGNOBLE 1

plebeians *n pl* the body of the community as contrasted with the elite — see MASS 1

pledge *n* **1** something given or held to assure that the giver will keep a promise ⟨I was required to leave my keys as a *pledge* that I would bring the car back⟩

syn gage, guarantee, guaranty, pawn, security

rel bail, bond; deposit, down payment; surety, warranty; oath, promise, word; commitment, compact, contract, covenant; recognizance

2 a person's solemn declaration that he or she will do or not do something — see PROMISE

pledge *vb* **1** to obligate by prior agreement ⟨I would love to go to dinner with you, but I've *pledged* myself to a play with my parents that night⟩

syn commit, engage, troth

rel affiance, betroth, plight, promise, swear, vow; contract, enlist, enroll (*also* enrol), sign on, sign up

near ant renege

2 to leave as a guarantee of repayment of a loan — see PAWN

3 to make a solemn declaration of intent — see PROMISE 1

plenary *adj* not lacking any part or member that properly belongs to it — see COMPLETE 1

plenitude *n* **1** a considerable amount — see LOT 2

2 an amount or supply more than sufficient to meet one's needs — see PLENTY 1

plenteous *adj* being more than enough without being excessive — see PLENTIFUL

plentiful *adj* being more than enough without being excessive ⟨a *plentiful* amount of strawberries that will be more than enough for a couple of pies⟩

syn abundant, ample, bountiful, comfortable, generous, liberal, plenteous

rel abounding, overflowing, replete, rich, rife, teeming, wealthy; adequate, enough, sufficient; fat, fecund, fertile, fruitful, prolific; copious, galore, lavish, profuse; luxuriant

near ant deficient, inadequate, insufficient, lacking, wanting; meager (*or* meagre), niggardly, stingy; skimpy; least, minimum; light, slight, small; barren, infertile, sterile, unfruitful, unproductive

ant bare, minimal, scant

plentitude *n* an amount or supply more than sufficient to meet one's needs — see PLENTY 1

plenty *n* **1** an amount or supply more than sufficient to meet one's needs ⟨you'll have *plenty* of time to do your science project⟩

syn abundance, plenitude, plentitude, superabundance, wealth

rel adequacy, competence, competency, enough, sufficiency; amplitude, liberality; excess, overflow, overkill, oversupply, superfluity, surfeit, surplus; fecundity, fertility, fruitfulness, richness; lavishness, luxuriance

near ant paucity, poverty, scarcity; barrenness, infertility, sterility

ant deficiency, inadequacy, insufficiency

2 a considerable amount — see LOT 2

pliable *adj* able to bend easily without breaking — see WILLOWY

pliant *adj* able to bend easily without breaking — see WILLOWY

plod *vb* **1** to devote serious and sustained effort — see LABOR

2 to make progress in a clumsy, struggling manner — see FLOUNDER 1

3 to move slowly — see CRAWL 2

plop *vb* to throw or set down clumsily or casually — see FLOP 1

plot *n* **1** a secret plan for accomplishing evil or unlawful ends ⟨they uncovered a *plot* to assassinate the President just in time⟩

syn conspiracy, design, intrigue, machination, scheme

rel frame-up; manipulation, subterfuge, trickery; artifice, contrivance, maneuver, stratagem, trick; cabal, confederacy, ring; game, gimmick, racket; ground plan, program, strategy, system; collusion, complicity, connivance, conniving

2 a small area of usually open land — see FIELD 1

3 a small piece of land that is developed or available for development — see LOT 1

plot *vb* to engage in a secret plan to accomplish evil or unlawful ends ⟨mobsters were caught *plotting* to take over the company⟩

syn conspire, contrive, intrigue, machinate, scheme

rel brew, concoct, cook (up), hatch; connive, engineer, jockey, maneuver, manipulate; design, frame, lay out, map, plan, shape

plow *vb* **1** to cut into and turn over the sod of (a piece of land) using a bladed implement ⟨we'll have to get out there and *plow* and plant both fields before it rains⟩

syn break, furrow

rel cultivate, till; fallow; harrow, hoe, rake

2 to devote serious and sustained effort — see LABOR

ploy *n* a clever often underhanded means to achieve an end — see TRICK 1

pluck *n* **1** the act or an instance of applying force on something so that it moves in the direction of the force — see PULL 1

2 the strength of mind that enables a person to endure pain or hardship — see FORTITUDE

plug *vb* **1** to close up so that no empty spaces remain — see FILL 2

2 to devote serious and sustained effort — see LABOR

3 to provide publicity for — see PUBLICIZE 1

4 to strike with a missile from a gun — see SHOOT 3

plug (up) *vb* to prevent passage through — see CLOG 1

plugger *n* a person who does very hard or dull work — see SLAVE 2

plum *n* someone or something unusually desirable — see PRIZE 1

plumb *adj* rising straight up — see ERECT

plumb *adv* **1** in a direct line or course — see DIRECTLY 1

2 *chiefly dialect* to a full extent or degree — see FULLY 1

plumb *vb* to measure the depth of (as a body of water) typically with a weighted line — see ²SOUND 1

plume *n* something given in recognition of achievement — see AWARD

plume *vb* to think highly of (oneself) — see PRIDE

plummet *vb* to go to a lower level — see DROP 2

plump *adj* having an excess of body fat — see FAT 1

plump *adv* in a direct line or course — see DIRECTLY 1

plump *vb* to throw or set down clumsily or casually — see FLOP 1

plumpness *n* the condition of having an excess of body fat — see CORPULENCE

plunder *n* valuables stolen or taken by force — see LOOT

plunder *vb* to search through with the intent of committing robbery — see RANSACK 1

plunge *n* **1** an act or instance of diving — see DIVE 1

2 the act or process of going to a lower level or altitude — see DESCENT 1

plunge *vb* **1** to cast oneself head first into deep water — see DIVE

2 to go to a lower level — see DROP 2

3 to lead or extend downward — see DESCEND 1

plunk *vb* to throw or set down clumsily or casually — see FLOP 1

plus *n* something added (as by growth) — see INCREASE 1

plush *adj* showing obvious signs of wealth and comfort — see LUXURIOUS

ply *vb* to bring to bear especially forcefully or effectively — see EXERT

poach *vb* to cook in a liquid heated to the point that it gives off steam — see BOIL 2

po'boy *also* **poor boy** *n* a large sandwich on a long split roll — see SUBMARINE

pocket *adj* of a size that is less than average — see SMALL 1

pocket *n* available money — see FUND 2

pocket *vb* **1** to refrain from openly showing or uttering — see SUPPRESS 2

2 to take (something) without right and with an intent to keep — see STEAL 1

pocketbook *n* a container for carrying money and small personal items — see PURSE

pocket-size *also* **pocket-sized** *adj* of a size that is less than average — see SMALL 1

---

syn synonym(s) *rel* related words
ant antonym(s) *near ant* near antonym(s)

pockmark *n* something that spoils the appearance or completeness of a thing — see BLEMISH

pod *n* something that encloses another thing especially to protect it — see ¹CASE 1

podium *n* a level usually raised surface — see PLATFORM

poem *n* a composition using rhythm and often rhyme to create a lyrical effect ⟨your assignment is to write two *poems* about springtime⟩

syn lyric, song, verse

rel rhyme (*also* rime); ballad, lay; elegy, English sonnet, epic, epigram, haiku, jingle, lament, limerick, ode, psalm, sonnet; blank verse, free verse, minstrelsy, poesy, poetry

poesy *n* writing that uses rhythm, vivid language, and often rhyme to provoke an emotional response — see POETRY 1

poet *n* a person who writes poetry ⟨Emily Dickinson is famous as the *poet* who rarely left the house but often journeyed to the depths of the human heart⟩

syn bard, minstrel, versifier

rel poetess; poet laureate; troubadour; epigrammatist, rhymer, sonneteer

poetic *adj* having qualities suggestive of poetry ⟨your description of the sun setting over the Grand Canyon was a particularly *poetic* piece of writing⟩

syn lyric, lyrical, poetical

rel metric, metrical, rhyming, rhythmic (*or* rhythmical); rhapsodic (*also* rhapsodical); florid, flowery, grandiloquent, high-falutin, high-flown, ornate; figurative, metaphorical, symbolic (*also* symbolical)

near ant factual, literal, matter-of-fact

ant prosaic, prose, unpoetic

poetical *adj* having qualities suggestive of poetry — see POETIC

poetry *n* 1 writing that uses rhythm, vivid language, and often rhyme to provoke an emotional response ⟨not all *poetry* has to rhyme⟩

syn minstrelsy, poesy, song, verse

rel rhyme (*also* rime); blank verse, free verse

ant prose

2 the art or power of speaking or writing in a forceful and convincing way — see ELOQUENCE

poignancy *n* a harsh or sharp quality — see EDGE 1

poignant *adj* having the power to affect the feelings or sympathies — see MOVING

point *n* 1 a particular and often important moment in time ⟨it was at that *point* that I had to stop and check on the experiment⟩

syn juncture

rel flash, instant, jiffy, minute, moment, second, shake, split second, trice, twinkle, wink; bit, spell, stretch, while; brink, threshold, verge

2 the last and usually sharp or tapering part of something long and narrow ⟨be careful with the *point* on that umbrella, or you could hurt someone⟩

syn apex, cusp, end, pike, tip

rel prong, tine; barb, jag, prickle, snag, spike, sticker

3 a separate part in a list, account, or series — see ITEM 1

4 a single piece of information — see FACT 3

5 a small area that is different (as in color) from the main part — see SPOT 1

6 an area of high ground jutting into a body of water beyond the line of the coast — see HEADLAND 1

7 an area of land that juts out into a body of water — see ²CAPE

8 an individual part of a process, series, or ranking — see DEGREE 1

9 something that sets apart an individual from others of the same kind — see CHARACTERISTIC

10 the area or space occupied by or intended for something — see PLACE 1

11 the quality of an utterance that provokes interest and produces an effect — see ¹PUNCH 1

point (toward) *vb* to stand or sit with the face or front toward — see FACE 1

point (up) *vb* to indicate the importance of by giving prominent display — see EMPHASIZE

pointed *adj* 1 tapering to a thin tip ⟨the snake plant's long *pointed* leaves make it an easily recognized houseplant⟩

syn peaked, sharp, tipped

rel barbed, jagged, pronged, spiky

near ant dull, rounded

ant blunt

2 having to do with the matter at hand — see PERTINENT

pointer *n* 1 an arrow-shaped piece on a dial or scale for registering information ⟨the *pointer* on my bathroom scale must be stuck—I know I lost weight⟩

syn hand, index, indicator, needle

rel dial, face, gauge (*also* gage)

2 a piece of advice or useful information especially from an expert — see ¹TIP 1

pointless *adj* having no meaning — see MEANINGLESS

point of view *n* a way of looking at or thinking about something ⟨who actually has the right to possession of that wilderness area depends on your *point of view*⟩

syn angle, outlook, perspective, shoes, slant, standpoint, viewpoint

rel interpretation, spin; belief, conviction, eye, feeling, judgment (*or* judgement), mind, notion, opinion, perception, persuasion, sentiment, verdict, view; impression, take; wavelength; side; attitude, position, posture, stand

poise *n* a condition in which opposing forces are equal to one another — see BALANCE 1

poise *vb* to rest or move along the surface of a liquid or in the air — see FLOAT

poison *adj* containing or contaminated with a substance capable of injuring or killing a living thing — see POISONOUS

poison *n* a substance that by chemical action can kill or injure a living thing ⟨the

only way to get rid of rats is to leave out *poison*⟩
syn bane, toxin, venom
rel cancer, contagion, disease, virus; fungicide, germicide, herbicide, insecticide
near ant antidote, antivenin; cure; cure-all, elixir, panacea

poison *vb* 1 to affect slightly with something morally bad or undesirable — see TAINT 1

2 to make unfit for use by the addition of something harmful or undesirable — see CONTAMINATE

3 to lower in character or dignity — see DEBASE 1

poisoned *adj* containing or contaminated with a substance capable of injuring or killing a living thing — see POISONOUS

poisonous *adj* containing or contaminated with a substance capable of injuring or killing a living thing ⟨some evil person was leaving out *poisonous* meat for neighborhood dogs to eat⟩
syn envenomed, poison, poisoned, toxic, venomous
rel contagious, infectious; deleterious, harmful, hurtful, injurious, malignant, noxious, virulent; unhealthful, unhealthy, unwholesome; calamitous, deadly, fatal, lethal, murderous
near ant beneficial, curative, healthful, healthy, helpful, palliative, remedial, salubrious, salutary, wholesome; benign, harmless, innocuous, inoffensive; nonfatal, nonlethal
ant nonpoisonous, nontoxic, nonvenomous

¹**poke** *n* a quick thrust ⟨please stop giving the cat *pokes* while it's trying to sleep⟩
syn dab, dig, jab
rel punch; stab, stick; push, shove; jam, jerk, jog, nudge

²**poke** *n chiefly Southern & Midland* a container made of a flexible material (as paper or plastic) — see BAG 1

poke *vb* 1 to extend outward beyond a usual point — see BULGE

2 to interest oneself in what is not one's concern — see INTERFERE

3 to move or act slowly — see DELAY 1

4 to move slowly — see CRAWL 2

poking *adj* moving or proceeding at less than the normal, desirable, or required speed — see SLOW 1

poky *or* **pokey** *adj* moving or proceeding at less than the normal, desirable, or required speed — see SLOW 1

polar *adj* 1 being as different as possible — see OPPOSITE

2 having a low or subnormal temperature — see COLD 1

police *n* 1 the department of government that keeps order, fights crime, and enforces statutes ⟨the appearance of a ransom note meant that the teenager's disappearance was now a matter for the *police*⟩
syn law
rel judiciary, jurisprudence, justice

2 a body of officers of the law ⟨the National Guard will serve as backup for the metropolitan *police* in the event of violent protests⟩
syn constabulary, police force
rel constable, cop, gendarme, officer, policeman, police officer, policewoman, trooper

police force *n* a body of officers of the law — see POLICE 2

policeman *n* a member of a force charged with law enforcement at the local level — see OFFICER 1

police officer *n* a member of a force charged with law enforcement at the local level — see OFFICER 1

policy *n* a way of acting or proceeding — see COURSE 1

polish *n* 1 a high level of taste and enlightenment as a result of extensive intellectual training and exposure to the arts — see CULTURE 1

2 brightness created by light reflected from a surface — see SHINE 1

polish *vb* to make smooth or glossy usually by repeatedly applying surface pressure ⟨you'll need to *polish* your shoes with a clean rag before the performance⟩
syn buff, burnish, dress, gloss, grind, rub, shine, smooth
rel sleek, slick; coat, glaze; finish, veneer; brighten; rasp, sand, sandblast, sandpaper, scour, scrape, scrub
near ant rough (up), roughen, scuff (up)

polished *adj* 1 having a shiny surface or finish — see GLOSSY

2 having or showing a taste for the fine arts and gracious living — see CULTIVATED

polite *adj* 1 showing consideration, courtesy, and good manners ⟨it's only *polite* to hold the door for the person behind you⟩
syn civil, courteous, genteel, gracious, mannerly, well-bred
rel attentive, considerate, thoughtful; chivalrous, courtly, gallant; ceremonial, ceremonious; formal, suave, unctuous, urbane; elegant, refined; deferential, dutiful, respectful, submissive, yielding; acceptable, appropriate, becoming, befitting, correct, decent, decorous, fit, fitting, good, meet, proper, respectable, right, seemly, suitable; affable, cordial, friendly, genial, hospitable, sociable; felicitous, graceful; humble, meek, modest, unassertive
near ant heedless, inconsiderate, thoughtless; audacious, bold, bold-faced, brash, brassy, disrespectful, impertinent, impudent, insolent, saucy, shameless; boorish, churlish, clownish, loutish, uncouth, vulgar; casual, informal, unceremonious; improper, inappropriate, incorrect, indecent, indecorous, uncalled-for, unrespectable, unseemly; arrogant, conceited, presumptuous, pretentious

---

syn synonym(s) **rel** related words
ant antonym(s) **near ant** near antonym(s)

ant discourteous, ill-bred, ill-mannered, impolite, inconsiderate, rude, thoughtless, uncivil, ungracious, unmannerly

2 following the established traditions of refined society and good taste — see PROPER 1

politeness *n* speech or behavior that is a sign of good breeding ⟨the little girl's *politeness* greatly impressed her teacher⟩

syn civility, courteousness, courtesy, gentility, graciousness, mannerliness

rel attentiveness, consideration, thoughtfulness; ceremonialness, ceremoniousness, ceremony, formality; chivalrousness, chivalry, courtliness, gallantry; breeding, manners; suaveness, unctuousness, urbanity; elegance, refinement; deference, respect; decency, decorousness, decorum, propriety, respectability, seemliness; affability, cordiality, friendliness, geniality, hospitality, sociability; felicitousness, gracefulness; humility, meekness, modesty, shyness

near ant audaciousness, audacity, boldness, brashness, brassiness, disrespect, impertinence, impudence, insolence, sauciness, shamelessness; boorishness, churlishness, clownishness, loutishness, vulgarity; casualness, informality; impropriety, inappropriateness, incorrectness, indecency; inconsideration, thoughtlessness; arrogance, conceit, presumption, pretentiousness

ant discourteousness, discourtesy, impoliteness, incivility, rudeness, ungraciousness

politic *adj* suitable for bringing about a desired result under the circumstances — see EXPEDIENT

poll *n* the upper or front part of the body that contains the brain, the major sense organs, and the mouth — see HEAD 1

poll *vb* to go around and approach (people) with a request for opinions or information — see CANVASS

pollutant *n* something that is or that makes impure — see IMPURITY

pollute *vb* to make unfit for use by the addition of something harmful or undesirable — see CONTAMINATE

polluted *adj* containing foreign or lower-grade substances — see IMPURE

poltergeist *n* the soul of a dead person thought of especially as appearing to living people — see GHOST

poltroon *n* a person who shows a shameful lack of courage in the face of danger — see COWARD

polychromatic *adj* marked by a variety of usually vivid colors — see COLORFUL

polychrome *adj* marked by a variety of usually vivid colors — see COLORFUL

polygraph *n* an instrument for detecting physical signs of the tension that goes with lying — see LIE DETECTOR

pommel *vb* to strike repeatedly — see BEAT 1

pompous *adj* **1** having a feeling of superiority that shows itself in an overbearing attitude — see ARROGANT

2 having too high an opinion of oneself — see CONCEITED

3 self-consciously trying to present an appearance of grandeur or importance — see PRETENTIOUS 1

pompousness *n* **1** an exaggerated sense of one's importance that shows itself in the making of excessive or unjustified claims — see ARROGANCE

2 an often unjustified feeling of being pleased with oneself or with one's situation or achievements — see COMPLACENCE

ponder *vb* to give serious and careful thought to ⟨I'm *pondering* whether or not I should join another club⟩

syn chew over, cogitate, consider, contemplate, debate, deliberate, entertain, meditate, mull (over), question, ruminate, study, think (about *or* over), weigh

rel muse (upon), reflect (on *or* upon), reminisce; conclude, reason; second-guess, speculate; brood (about or over), fret (about *or* over), obsess (about *or* over); believe, conceive, opine; absorb, assimilate, digest, drink (in)

phrases cudgel one's brains

near ant disregard, ignore, overlook, slight; dismiss, pooh-pooh (*also* pooh), reject

ponderous *adj* **1** causing weariness, restlessness, or lack of interest — see BORING

2 having great weight — see HEAVY 1

ponderousness *n* the state or quality of being heavy — see WEIGHTINESS 1

pooch *n* a domestic mammal that is related to the wolves and foxes — see DOG

¹**pool** *n* a small often deep body of water ⟨when it rains, that small *pool* grows to almost the size of a lake⟩

syn mere [*chiefly British*], puddle

rel basin, hole, sinkhole; swimming pool; lake

²**pool** *n* **1** a body of persons at work or available for work — see FORCE 1

2 the number of individuals or amount of something available at any given time — see SUPPLY

3 a sum of money set aside for a particular purpose — see FUND 1

4 the total of the bets at stake at one time — see POT 1

poor *adj* **1** lacking money or material possessions ⟨every year, we make up a basket of food at Thanksgiving for a *poor* family in the neighborhood⟩

syn beggared, broke, destitute, impecunious, impoverished, indigent, needy, penniless, penurious, poverty-stricken, stone-broke

rel deprived, disadvantaged, underprivileged; bankrupt, bankrupted, insolvent; depressed, pinched, reduced, straitened; low, short

phrases hard up

near ant comfortable, prosperous

ant affluent, flush, moneyed (*or* monied), opulent, rich, wealthy, well-heeled, well-off, well-to-do

2 producing inferior or only a small amount of vegetation — see BARREN 1

3 less plentiful than what is normal, necessary, or desirable — see MEAGER

4 falling short of a standard — see BAD 1

5 of low quality — see CHEAP 2

6 deserving of one's pity — see PATHETIC 1

poorly *adj* temporarily suffering from a disorder of the body — see SICK 1

poorly *adv* in an unsatisfactory way — see BADLY

poorness *n* the state of lacking sufficient money or material possessions — see POVERTY 1

¹pop *n* a loud explosive sound — see CLAP 1

²pop *n* a male human parent — see FATHER 1

pop *vb* **1** to break open or into pieces usually because of internal pressure — see EXPLODE 1

2 to break suddenly with an explosive sound — see CRACK 1

3 to cause to break open or into pieces by or as if by an explosive — see BLAST 1

4 to strike with a missile from a gun — see SHOOT 1

pop (in) *vb* to make a brief visit — see CALL 3

populace *n* the body of the community as contrasted with the elite — see MASS 1

popular *adj* enjoying widespread favor or approval ⟨bell-bottom jeans were *popular* in the seventies⟩

syn fashionable, hot, in, modish, popularized, vogue

rel favorite, preferred; desirable, liked, wanted; celebrated, famed, famous, noted, notorious, prominent, renowned, well-known; fabled, fabulous, legendary; leading, notable, outstanding, remarkable; important, significant

near ant washed-up; despised, detested, disliked, hated, rejected; insignificant, unimportant; indistinguished, unexceptional; anonymous, nameless, obscure, unknown; inconspicuous

ant out, unpopular

2 accepted, used, or practiced by most people — see CURRENT 1

3 held by or applicable to a majority of the people — see GENERAL 3

4 of, relating to, or favoring political democracy — see DEMOCRATIC

popularity *n* the state of enjoying widespread approval ⟨the sudden *popularity* of low-cut blouses horrified my mother⟩

syn fashionableness, favor, hotness, modishness, vogue

rel craze, fad, mode, rage, style, trend; bandwagon; fame, notoriety, prominence, renown; enthusiasm, fervor, passion

near ant oblivion, obscurity

ant disfavor, unpopularity

popularized *adj* enjoying widespread favor or approval — see POPULAR 1

---

pore (over) *vb* to go over and mentally take in the content of — see READ

pornographic *adj* depicting or referring to sexual matters in a way that is unacceptable in polite society — see OBSCENE 1

porous *adj* capable of being passed into or through — see PENETRABLE

port *n* a part of a body of water protected and deep enough to be a place of safety for ships — see HARBOR 1

portable *adj* capable of being moved especially with ease — see MOVABLE

portal *n* a barrier by which an entry is closed and opened — see DOOR 1

portent *n* **1** something believed to be a sign or warning of a future event — see OMEN

2 something extraordinary or surprising — see WONDER 1

portentous *adj* **1** being or showing a sign of evil or calamity to come — see OMINOUS

2 causing wonder or astonishment — see MARVELOUS 1

porter *n chiefly British* a person who tends a door — see DOORKEEPER

portion *n* **1** a state or end that seemingly has been decided beforehand — see FATE 1

2 one of the pieces from which something is designed to be assembled — see PART 1

3 something belonging to, due to, or contributed by an individual member of a group — see SHARE 1

portion *vb* to give out (something) in appropriate amounts or to appropriate individuals — see ADMINISTER 1

portliness *n* the condition of having an excess of body fat — see CORPULENCE

portly *adj* having an excess of body fat — see FAT 1

portmanteau *n* a bag carried by hand and designed to hold a traveler's clothing and personal articles — see TRAVELING BAG

portrait *n* a vivid representation in words of someone or something — see DESCRIPTION 1

portray *vb* **1** to give a representation or account of in words — see DESCRIBE 1

2 to point out the chief quality or qualities of an individual or group — see CHARACTERIZE 1

3 to present a picture of — see PICTURE 1

4 to present a portrayal or performance of — see ACT 1

portrayal *n* a vivid representation in words of someone or something — see DESCRIPTION 1

pose *n* a display of emotion or behavior that is insincere or intended to deceive — see MASQUERADE

pose *vb* to set before the mind for consideration — see PROPOSE 1

pose (as) *vb* to pretend to be (what one is not) in appearance or behavior — see IMPERSONATE 1

position *n* **1** an assignment at which one regularly works for pay — see JOB 1

2 the action for which a person or thing is specially fitted or used or for which a thing exists — see ROLE

3 the area or space occupied by or intended for something — see PLACE 1

4 the place where someone is assigned to stand or remain — see STATION 1

5 the placement of someone or something in relation to others in a vertical arrangement — see RANK 1

position *vb* to arrange something in a certain spot or position — see PLACE 1

positive *adj* **1** expressing approval — see FAVORABLE 1

2 having or showing a mind free from doubt — see CERTAIN 2

positiveness *n* a state of mind in which one is free from doubt — see CONFIDENCE 2

possess *vb* to keep, control, or experience as one's own — see HAVE 1

possession *n* **1** the fact or state of having (something) at one's disposal ⟨a student who was found to have several overdue library books in his *possession*⟩

syn control, hands, keeping

rel ownership, proprietorship; authority, command, dominion, mastery, power; enjoyment, repossession; retention; claiming, collaring, commandeering, confiscation, procurement

near ant dispossession, relinquishment, surrendering, transferal

ant nonpossession

2 possessions *pl* transportable items that one owns ⟨we packed up all of our *possessions* and moved to a new house⟩

syn belongings, chattels, effects, holdings, movables (*or* moveables), paraphernalia, personalty, things

rel treasures, valuables; junk, stuff; appointments, fixtures, furnishings; property, tangibles; collateral

near ant real estate

possessive *adj* intolerant of rivalry or unfaithfulness — see JEALOUS 1

possessor *n* one who has a legal or rightful claim to ownership — see PROPRIETOR

possibility *n* **1** something that can develop or become actual — see POTENTIAL

2 something that might happen — see EVENT 2

possible *adj* **1** capable of being done or carried out ⟨I think that building the entire set in two days is *possible*, if difficult⟩

syn achievable, attainable, doable, feasible, practicable, realizable, viable, workable

rel practical, reasonable, sensible; likely, probable; acceptable, believable, conceivable, creditable, plausible; available, usable

near ant impractical, unrealistic; doubtful, dubious, far-fetched, improbable, unlikely; implausible, inconceivable, incredible, unbelievable; futile, useless, vain; absurd, fantastic, outlandish, preposterous, ridiculous; unthinkable

ant hopeless, impossible, impracticable, unachievable, unattainable, unworkable

2 existing only as a possibility and not in fact — see POTENTIAL

possibly *adv* it is possible — see PERHAPS

¹post *n chiefly British* communications or parcels sent or carried through the postal system — see MAIL

²post *n* **1** a specific task with which a person or group is charged — see MISSION

2 the place where someone is assigned to stand or remain — see STATION 1

3 an assignment at which one regularly works for pay — see JOB 1

³post *n* an upright shaft that supports an overhead structure — see PILLAR 1

¹post *vb* **1** to affix (as a notice) to or on a suitable place ⟨the student organizations always *post* their announcements on the cafeteria walls⟩

syn placard

rel nail, plaster, tack (up); advertise, announce, blaze, broadcast, call, declare, proclaim, promulgate, publicize, publish

near ant remove, take down

2 to make known openly or publicly — see ANNOUNCE

²post *vb* to assign to a place or position ⟨the police are planning to *post* an officer outside the hospital room of the witness⟩

syn detail, station

rel set; appoint; place, position

³post *vb* to send through the postal system — see MAIL

postdate *vb* to come after in time — see FOLLOW 1

poster *n* a sheet bearing an announcement for posting in a public place ⟨we put up a hundred *posters* announcing the concert⟩

syn bill, placard

rel billboard, sign, signboard; broadside, flier (*or* flyer), handbill, handout, playbill; ad, advertisement, announcement, bulletin, dispatch, release

posterior *adj* **1** being at or in the part of something opposite the front part — see BACK

2 being, occurring, or carried out at a time after something else — see SUBSEQUENT

posterior *n* the part of the body upon which someone sits — see BUTTOCKS

posterity *n* the descendants of a person, animal, or plant — see OFFSPRING

posthaste *adv* with great speed — see FAST 1

posthumous *adj* occurring after one's death ⟨the soldier was awarded a *posthumous* medal for valor⟩

syn postmortem

rel belated, delayed, late

posting *n* a published statement informing the public of a matter of general interest — see ANNOUNCEMENT

postman *n* a person who delivers mail ⟨the *postman* comes at around nine every morning⟩

syn letter carrier, mail carrier, mailman

rel messenger; postmaster

postmortem *adj* **1** occurring after one's death — see POSTHUMOUS

postmortem *n* examination of a dead body especially to find out the cause of death — see AUTOPSY

postmortem examination *n* examination of a dead body especially to find out the cause of death — see AUTOPSY

postpone *vb* to assign to a later time ⟨we'll have to *postpone* the decision until we have all the information⟩
syn defer, delay, hold off (on), hold up, put off, shelve
rel suspend; hesitate, pause, stay; detain, retard, slow; extend, lengthen, prolong, protract, stretch (out); wait
near ant act, deal (with), decide (upon), do, work (on)

postulate *n* something taken as being true or factual and used as a starting point for a course of action or reasoning — see ASSUMPTION

postulate *vb* to take as true or as a fact without actual proof — see ASSUME 2

posture *n* **1** a general way of holding the body ⟨a good upright *posture* will prevent backaches⟩
syn carriage, stance
rel attention; body language; pose, seat; bearing, behavior, conduct, demeanor, deportment; air, poise, presence; aspect, look, mien
2 position with regard to conditions and circumstances — see SITUATION 1

posy *n* a bunch of flowers — see BOUQUET 1

pot *n* **1** the total of the bets at stake at one time ⟨everyone got a bit nervous when the *pot* was more than a hundred dollars⟩
syn jackpot, pool
rel fund, kitty; bet, stake, wager
2 a considerable amount — see LOT 2

potable *adj* suitable for drinking ⟨around here, the only *potable* water comes from wells⟩
syn drinkable
rel clean, fresh, pure, uncontaminated, unpolluted; nonpoisonous
near ant contaminated, dirty, foul, polluted; poison, poisonous, toxic; unhealthful, unhealthy, unwholesome
ant undrinkable

potbelly *n* an enlarged or bulging abdomen ⟨he began exercising to get rid of his growing *potbelly* and tighten up his stomach⟩
syn paunch
rel belly, breadbasket [*slang*], gut, stomach, tummy; chubbiness, corpulence, fat, fatness, fleshiness, obesity, overweight, paunchiness, plumpness, portliness, pudginess; chunkiness, heaviness, stoutness

potency *n* the ability to exert effort for the accomplishment of a task — see POWER 2

potent *adj* **1** having an abundance of some characteristic quality (as flavor) — see FULL-BODIED
2 having great power or influence — see IMPORTANT 2
3 producing or capable of producing a desired result — see EFFECTIVE 1

potentate *n* a person who uses power or authority in a cruel, unjust, or harmful way — see DESPOT

potential *adj* existing only as a possibility and not in fact ⟨I can see a few *potential* problems with getting a puppy, but we'll wait and see if they come up⟩
syn possible
rel conceivable, imaginable, plausible, thinkable; likely, probable; conjectural, hypothetical, suppositional, theoretical (*also* theoretic); alleged, assumed, purported, reputed, supposed; achievable, attainable, doable, feasible, practicable, viable, workable
near ant authenticated, confirmed, demonstrated, established, proven, substantiated; authentic, bona fide, genuine, true
ant actual, existent, factual, real

potential *n* something that can develop or become actual ⟨a time when cloning was merely a *potential* and the stuff of science fiction⟩
syn eventuality, possibility, potentiality
rel likelihood, probability; latency
near ant actuality, reality; certainty

potentiality *n* something that can develop or become actual — see POTENTIAL

pother *n* **1** a state of nervous or irritated concern — see FRET
2 a state of noisy, confused activity — see COMMOTION

potpourri *n* an unorganized collection or mixture of various things — see MISCELLANY 1

potter (**around**) *vb* to spend time in aimless activity — see FIDDLE (AROUND)

potterer *n* a person who regularly or occasionally engages in an activity without being or becoming an expert at it — see AMATEUR

potter's field *n* a piece of land used for burying the dead — see CEMETERY

pottery *n* articles made of baked clay — see CROCKERY

pouch *n* a container made of a flexible material (as paper or plastic) — see BAG 1

poultice *n* a medicated covering used to heal an injury — see DRESSING 1

pounce (**on** *or* **upon**) *vb* to take sudden, violent action against — see ATTACK 1

pound *n* **1** a hard strike with a part of the body or an instrument — see ¹BLOW
2 an enclosure with an open framework for keeping animals — see CAGE

pound *vb* **1** to move heavily or clumsily — see LUMBER 1
2 to deliver a blow to (someone or something) usually in a strong vigorous manner — see HIT 1
3 to strike repeatedly — see BEAT 1
4 to shape with a hammer — see HAMMER 1

pour *vb* **1** to cause to flow in a stream ⟨she lifted the teakettle and *poured* some hot water through the spout⟩

syn stream

rel ladle, spoon; cascade, trickle; deluge, flood, inundate, overflow

2 to move in a stream — see FLOW 1

3 to flow out in great quantities or with force — see GUSH 1

4 to fall as water in a continuous stream of drops from the clouds — see RAIN 1

5 to give readily and in large quantities — see RAIN 2

pouring *adj* marked by or abounding with rain — see RAINY

pout *n* **1** a twisting of the facial features in disgust or disapproval — see GRIMACE

2 pouts *pl* a state of resentful silence or irritability — see SULK

pout *vb* to silently go about in a bad mood — see SULK

pouting *adj* given to or displaying a resentful silence and often irritability — see SULKY

poverty *n* **1** the state of lacking sufficient money or material possessions ⟨he dreamed of finding a good job and working his way out of *poverty* and debt⟩

syn beggary, destitution, impecuniousness, impoverishment, indigence, need, neediness, pauperism, penuriousness, penury, poorness, want

rel misery, woe, wretchedness; exigency, necessity; austerity, deprivation, privation; bankruptcy, insolvency; belt-tightening, pinching, straitening

near ant luxury, prosperity

ant affluence, opulence, richness, wealthiness

2 a falling short of an essential or desirable amount or number — see DEFICIENCY

poverty–stricken *adj* lacking money or material possessions — see POOR 1

powder *vb* to reduce to fine particles ⟨you have to *powder* the antibiotic tablet and mix it with food⟩

syn atomize, crush, grind, pulverize

rel grate; crumble, crunch; break, bust, dash, fracture, fragment; shatter, smash, splinter; mill

powdery *adj* consisting of very small particles — see FINE 1

power *n* **1** the right or means to command or control others ⟨the principal has nearly complete *power* over this school⟩

syn arm, authority, clutch, command, control, dominion, grip, hold, mastery, sway

rel clout, influence, pull, weight; jurisdiction; direction, management; dominance, predominance, sovereignty, supremacy; prerogative, privilege, right; eminence, importance, moment

near ant helplessness, weakness

ant impotence, powerlessness

2 the ability to exert effort for the accomplishment of a task ⟨the corporation has the *power* to accomplish almost anything⟩

⟨you'll need to build a bit more *power* in order to be a star pitcher⟩

syn energy, force, might, muscle, potency, puissance, sinew, strength, vigor

rel aptitude, capability, capacity, competence, competency; adequacy, effectiveness, effectualness, usefulness

near ant disability, inability, inaptitude, incapability, incapacity, incompetence, incompetency; ineffectiveness, ineffectualness, uselessness; helplessness, paralysis

ant impotence, powerlessness, weakness

3 a natural ability of the mind or body ⟨dogs have a very highly developed *power* of smell⟩

syn faculty

rel function; capability, capacity; aptitude, endowment, flair, genius, gift, instinct, knack, talent

near ant inability, incapability, incapacity; inaptitude, inaptness, ineptness

4 something with a usable capacity for doing work — see FUEL

powerboat *n* a boat equipped with a motor — see MOTORBOAT

powerful *adj* having great power or influence — see IMPORTANT 2

powerfully *adv* in a vigorous and forceful manner — see HARD 3

powerhouse *n* an ambitious person who eagerly goes after what is desired — see GO-GETTER

powerless *adj* unable to act or achieve one's purpose ⟨I wish I could help you, but I am *powerless* in this situation⟩

syn helpless, impotent, weak

rel incapable, incompetent, ineffective, ineffectual, inept, unfit, useless; feeble, frail, infirm, passive, spineless, supine, unaggressive

near ant able, capable, competent, effective, efficient; authoritarian, autocratic, despotic, dictatorial, magisterial, tyrannical (*also* tyrranic); dominant, dynamic, energetic, forceful, robust, sturdy, tough, vigorous; important, major, significant; high-level, senior, top

ant mighty, potent, powerful, puissant, strong

powerlessness *n* the lack of sufficient ability, power, or means — see INABILITY

powwow *n* **1** a coming together of a number of persons for a specified purpose — see MEETING 1

2 a meeting featuring a group discussion — see FORUM

powwow *vb* to exchange viewpoints or seek advice for the purpose of finding a solution to a problem — see CONFER 2

practicable *adj* **1** capable of being done or carried out — see POSSIBLE 1

2 capable of being put to use or account — see PRACTICAL 1

3 capable of or suitable for being used for a particular purpose — see USABLE 1

practical *adj* **1** capable of being put to use or account ⟨a *practical* and simple solution for the town's waste disposal⟩ ⟨she has some *practical* information on sightseeing in San Francisco⟩

syn applicable, functional, practicable, serviceable, usable, useful, workable, working

rel down-to-earth, pragmatic (*also* pragmatical), utilitarian; accessible, available, obtainable, reachable; all-around (*also* all-round), handy; active, alive, busy, employed, functioning, operating, operative

near ant abstract, academic, theoretical (*also* theoretic); inaccessible, unattainable, unavailable, unobtainable, unreachable; unsuitable

ant impracticable, impractical, unusable, unworkable, useless

2 willing to see things as they really are and deal with them sensibly — see REALISTIC 1

practical joke *n* a playful or mischievous act intended as a joke — see PRANK

practically *adv* very close to but not completely — see ALMOST

practice *also* **practise** *n* **1** a private performance or session in preparation for a public appearance — see REHEARSAL

2 a usual manner of behaving or doing — see HABIT

3 something done over and over in order to develop skill — see EXERCISE 2

practice *or* **practise** *vb* to do over and over so as to become skilled ⟨in order to play the guitar well, you need to *practice* fingering every single day⟩

syn exercise, rehearse

rel prepare (for), train (with); drill, repeat; work (at *or* on); review, study

practiced *or* **practised** *adj* **1** having or showing exceptional knowledge, experience, or skill in a field of endeavor — see PROFICIENT

2 accomplished with trained ability — see SKILLFUL

pragmatic *also* **pragmatical** *adj* willing to see things as they really are and deal with them sensibly — see REALISTIC 1

prairie *n* a broad area of level or rolling treeless country — see PLAIN

praise *vb* **1** to proclaim the glory of ⟨hymns that *praise* God⟩

syn bless, extol (*also* extoll), glorify, laud, magnify

rel adore, deify, idolize, worship; acclaim, applaud, commend, compliment, hail, salute; celebrate, cheer, eulogize, rhapsodize; cite; flatter; crack up, recommend, tout

near ant blame, censure, reprehend, reprobate; criticize, reprove; admonish, chide, rebuke, reprimand, reproach; castigate, lambaste (*or* lambast)

2 to declare enthusiastic approval of — see ACCLAIM

praiseworthy *adj* deserving of high regard or great approval — see ADMIRABLE

prance *vb* to walk with exaggerated arm and leg movements — see STRUT 1

prank *n* a playful or mischievous act intended as a joke ⟨as a *prank*, several stu-

dents managed to change all the classroom clocks to different times⟩

syn antic, caper, escapade, frolic, practical joke, trick

rel skylarking; adventure, experience, game, lark, time; high jinks, horseplay, play, roughhousing, rowdiness; shenanigans, tomfoolery; joking, kidding, teasing; gambit, hoax, maneuver, ploy; deed, feat, mission, performance, stunt; caprice, conceit, fancy, vagary, whim, whimsy; deceit, deception, delusion, fooling, fraud, hoodwinking, ruse, sham, stratagem, subterfuge, trickery, wile

prankish *adj* tending to or exhibiting reckless playfulness — see MISCHIEVOUS 1

prankishness *n* a natural disposition for playful behavior — see PLAYFULNESS

prate *vb* to engage in casual or rambling conversation — see CHAT

prattle *n* unintelligible or meaningless talk — see GIBBERISH

prattle *vb* **1** to engage in casual or rambling conversation — see CHAT

2 to speak rapidly, inarticulately, and usually unintelligibly — see BABBLE 1

prattler *n* a person who talks constantly — see CHATTERBOX

pray *vb* to make a request to (someone) in an earnest or urgent manner — see BEG

prayer *n* **1** an address to God or a deity ⟨he always directed a bedside *prayer* to God before going to sleep⟩

syn orison

rel collect, grace, invocation, litany, thanksgiving; evensong, matins, vespers; appeal, begging, beseeching, entreaty, imploring, petition, pleading, request, soliciting, suit, supplication

2 an earnest request — see PLEA 1

prayerful *adj* asking humbly — see SUPPLIANT

preacher *n* a person specially trained and authorized to conduct religious services in a Christian church — see CLERGYMAN

preamble *n* a short section (as of a book) that leads to or explains the main part — see INTRODUCTION

precariousness *n* the quality or state of not being firmly fixed in position — see INSTABILITY

precautionary *adj* concerned with or serving to keep something from happening — see PREVENTIVE

precede *vb* to go or come before in time ⟨there are two speeches which will *precede* yours⟩

syn antedate, forego, predate

ant follow, succeed

precedence *n* the right to one's attention before other things considered less important — see PRIORITY

precedent *adj* going before another in time or order — see PREVIOUS

preceding *adj* going before another in time or order — see PREVIOUS

preceptor *n* a person whose occupation is to give formal instruction in a school — see TEACHER

---

syn synonym(s)   *rel* related words
ant antonym(s)   *near ant* near antonym(s)

precious *adj* 1 commanding a large price — see COSTLY

2 granted special treatment or attention — see DARLING 1

3 having qualities that tend to make one loved — see LOVABLE

precipice *n* a steep wall of rock, earth, or ice — see CLIFF

precipitate *adj* acting or done with excessive or careless speed — see HASTY 1

precipitate *n* matter that settles to the bottom of a body of liquid — see DEPOSIT 1

precipitate *vb* to fall as water in a continuous stream of drops from the clouds — see RAIN 1

precipitately *adv* with excessive or careless speed — see HASTILY 1

precipitating *adj* marked by or abounding with rain — see RAINY

precipitation *n* excited and often showy or disorderly speed — see HURRY 1

precipitous *adj* 1 acting or done with excessive or careless speed — see HASTY 1

2 having an incline approaching the perpendicular — see STEEP 1

precipitously *adv* with excessive or careless speed — see HASTILY 1

precipitousness *n* excited and often showy or disorderly speed — see HURRY 1

précis *n* a short statement of the main points — see SUMMARY

precise *adj* 1 meeting the highest standard of accuracy ⟨a machine which takes very *precise* measurements⟩

syn accurate, close, delicate, exact, fine, hairline, mathematical, pinpoint, rigorous

rel correct, right, strict, true; definite, definitive; nice, subtle; careful, fastidious, finicky

near ant approximate, round; false, incorrect, untrue, wrong; careless, indefinite, unclear, vague; doubtful, dubious, questionable, unreliable, untrustworthy

ant coarse, imprecise, inaccurate, inexact, rough

2 being in agreement with the truth or a fact or a standard — see CORRECT 1

3 being neither more nor less than a certain amount, number, or extent — see EVEN 1

4 following an original exactly — see FAITHFUL 1

5 of a particular or exact sort — see EXPRESS 1

precisely *adv* 1 as stated or indicated without the slightest difference — see EXACTLY 1

2 in a like manner — see JUST 1

3 without any relaxation of standards or precision — see STRICTLY

preciseness *n* the quality or state of being very accurate — see PRECISION

precision *n* the quality or state of being very accurate ⟨the company that measures TV ratings prides itself on the *precision* of its calculations⟩

syn accuracy, closeness, delicacy, exactitude, exactness, fineness, preciseness, rigorousness, veracity

rel correctness, rightness, strictness, truth; definiteness, definitiveness; nicety, subtlety; care, carefulness, fastidiousness

near ant approximation, roundness; falseness, falsity, incorrectness, wrongness; carelessness, guesswork, looseness; indefiniteness, unclearness, vagueness

ant coarseness, impreciseness, imprecision, inaccuracy, inexactness, roughness

preclude *vb* to keep from happening by taking action in advance — see PREVENT

precluding *n* the act or practice of keeping something from happening — see PREVENTION

precocious *adj* occurring before the usual or expected time — see EARLY 2

precociously *adv* before the usual or expected time — see EARLY

preconception *n* an attitude, belief, or impression formed in advance of actual experience of something — see PREPOSSESSION 1

precursor *n* 1 one that announces or indicates the later arrival of another — see FORERUNNER 1

2 something belonging to an earlier time from which something else was later developed — see ANCESTOR 2

predaceous *or* **predacious** *adj* living by killing and eating other animals — see PREDATORY

predate *vb* to go or come before in time — see PRECEDE

predatory *adj* living by killing and eating other animals ⟨hawks are *predatory* and pose a danger to rabbits and other pets⟩

syn predaceous (*or* predacious), rapacious

rel carnivorous; aggressive, deadly, ferocious, fierce, savage, violent; untamed, wild

near ant herbivorous, vegetarian; gentle, submissive, tame

predecessor *n* something belonging to an earlier time from which something else was later developed — see ANCESTOR 2

predestine *vb* to determine the fate of in advance — see DESTINE

predetermine *vb* to determine the fate of in advance — see DESTINE

predicament *n* a difficult, puzzling, or embarrassing situation from which there is no easy escape ⟨if you had told the truth in the first place, we wouldn't be in this *predicament*⟩

syn corner, fix, hole, jam, pickle, spot

rel difficulty, dilemma, hot water, pinch, plight, quagmire, quandary, scrape, trouble; deadlock, halt, impasse, stalemate, standstill; clutch, crisis, crossroad, emergency, exigency, juncture, strait

predicate *vb* to find a basis — see BASE

predict *vb* to tell of or describe beforehand — see FORETELL

predicting *n* a declaration that something will happen in the future — see PREDICTION

prediction *n* a declaration that something will happen in the future ⟨we were all

amazed when the fortune-teller's *predictions* turned out to be true⟩
syn auguring, cast, forecast, forecasting, foretelling, predicting, presaging, prognosis, prognosticating, prognostication, prophecy, soothsaying
rel augury, omen, portent, sign; anticipation, foreknowledge; foresight; conjecture, guess, surmise
predictive *adj* being a sign of a later course of events — see PROPHETIC
predilection *n* a habitual attraction to some activity or thing — see INCLINATION 1
predisposition *n* a habitual attraction to some activity or thing — see INCLINATION 1
predominance *n* controlling power or influence over others — see SUPREMACY 1
predominant *adj* coming before all others in importance — see FOREMOST 1
predominantly *adv* for the most part — see CHIEFLY
preeminence *n* **1** exceptionally high quality — see EXCELLENCE 1
2 controlling power or influence over others — see SUPREMACY 1
3 the fact or state of being above others in rank or importance — see EMINENCE 1
preeminent *adj* **1** coming before all others in importance — see FOREMOST 1
2 highest in rank or authority — see HEAD
3 standing above others in rank, importance, or achievement — see EMINENT
preempt *vb* to take or make use of without authority or right — see APPROPRIATE 1
preface *n* a short section (as of a book) that leads to or explains the main part — see INTRODUCTION
prefer *vb* **1** to show partiality toward ⟨I generally *prefer* chocolate ice cream over vanilla⟩
syn favor, lean (toward), like
rel adore, cotton (to), delight (in), dig, enjoy, fancy, groove (on), relish, revel (in); choose, cull, handpick, name, pick, select, single (out), take; covet, crave, desire, want, wish (for); bias, prejudice; incline (towards), tend (to); admire, appreciate, cherish, prize, treasure, value
phrases be partial to
near ant disfavor, dislike; abhor, abominate, detest, hate, loathe; decline, refuse, reject, turn down; discard, jettison, throw away, throw out
2 to decide to accept (someone or something) from a group of possibilities — see CHOOSE 1
preferably *adv* by choice or preference — see RATHER 1
preference *n* **1** a person or thing that is preferred over others — see FAVORITE
2 positive regard for something — see LIKING
3 the power, right, or opportunity to choose — see CHOICE 1

preferment *n* a raising or a state of being raised to a higher rank or position — see ADVANCEMENT 1
preferred *adj* singled out from a number or group as more to one's liking — see SELECT 1
prefigure *vb* to give a slight indication of beforehand — see FORESHADOW
prefiguring *n* something believed to be a sign or warning of a future event — see OMEN
pregnancy *n* the state of containing unborn young within the body ⟨an elephant's *pregnancy* can last almost a year⟩
syn gestation
rel conception; begetting, breeding, generation, siring, spawning
near ant barrenness, infertility
pregnant *adj* **1** containing unborn young within the body ⟨we only realized that our cat had been *pregnant* when she unexpectedly delivered three kittens⟩
syn expectant, gravid
rel childbearing; brooding; conceiving, impregnated
phrases with child, with young
near ant barren, infertile; aborting, miscarrying; delivered
ant nonpregnant
2 clearly conveying a special meaning (as one's mood) — see EXPRESSIVE
prejudgment *n* an attitude, belief, or impression formed in advance of actual experience of something — see PREPOSSESSION 1
prejudice *n* **1** an attitude that always favors one way of feeling or acting especially without considering any other possibilities — see BIAS
2 hatred of or discrimination against a person or persons based on their race — see RACISM 2
prejudice *vb* to cause to have often negative opinions formed without sufficient knowledge ⟨all the bad stories I had heard about that teacher *prejudiced* me against him even before the first class⟩
syn bias
rel dispose, incline, predispose; influence, prepossess; convince, persuade, suggest
prejudiced *adj* **1** inclined to favor one side over another — see PARTIAL 1
2 unwilling to grant other people social rights or to accept other viewpoints — see INTOLERANT 2
prejudicial *adj* **1** causing or capable of causing harm — see HARMFUL
2 opposed to one's interests — see ADVERSE 1
preliminary *adj* coming before the main part or item usually to introduce or prepare for what follows ⟨we need to do some *preliminary* research in order to properly focus the experiment⟩
syn introductory, preparatory
rel introducing, prefacing, preparing, readying; premonitory, warning; basic, fundamental; ahead, early, former, preceding, previous, prior

---

syn synonym(s)   **rel** related words
ant antonym(s)   **near ant** near antonyms(s)

near ant after, behind, following, subsequent

prelude *n* a short section (as of a book) that leads to or explains the main part — see INTRODUCTION

premature *adj* occurring before the usual or expected time — see EARLY 2

prematurely *adv* before the usual or expected time — see EARLY

premier *adj* 1 coming before all others in time or order — see FIRST 1

2 highest in rank or authority — see HEAD

3 coming before all others in importance — see FOREMOST 1

premise *n* 1 something taken as being true or factual and used as a starting point for a course of action or reasoning — see ASSUMPTION

2 **premises** *pl* the area around and belonging to a building — see GROUND 1

premise *vb* to take as true or as a fact without actual proof — see ASSUME 2

premium *adj* commanding a large price — see COSTLY

premium *n* something given in recognition of achievement — see AWARD

premonition *n* a feeling that something bad will happen ⟨she had a *premonition* that her cat would somehow get hurt that day⟩
syn foreboding, presage, presentiment
rel anticipation, foreknowledge; insight, intuition; augury, omen, portent, sign; impression, suspicion; anxiety, apprehension, care, concern, disquiet, doubt, dread, fear, misgiving, unease, worry; foresight

preoccupation *n* something about which one is constantly thinking or concerned — see FIXATION

preoccupied *adj* lost in thought and unaware of one's surroundings or actions — see ABSENTMINDED 1

preparatory *adj* coming before the main part or item usually to introduce or prepare for what follows — see PRELIMINARY

prepare *vb* 1 to make ready in advance ⟨I think I *prepared* myself well for this test⟩ ⟨we *prepared* the classroom for the important visitors by getting rid of some unsightly clutter⟩
syn fit, fix, lay, ready
rel brace, fortify, steel; batten, gather, gear (up), mount, train; boot (up), prime; arrange, set, spread; arm, equip, furnish, outfit, provide, supply; incline, predispose; draft, draw (up), frame; warm (up)
2 to make competent (as by training, skill, or ability) for a particular office or function — see QUALIFY 2
3 to put (something) into proper and usually carefully worked out written form — see COMPOSE 1

prepared *adj* being in a state of fitness for some experience or action — see READY 1

prepossession *n* 1 an attitude, belief, or impression formed in advance of actual experience of something ⟨the foreign tourists' *prepossessions* about life in the U.S. had been formed by many hours of American TV shows⟩
syn preconception, prejudgment
rel bias, prejudice; conjecture, hypothesis, imagining, predetermination, presumption, presupposition, speculation, supposition, theorizing, theory; concept, thought
2 something about which one is constantly thinking or concerned — see FIXATION

preposterous *adj* 1 conceived or made without regard for reason or reality — see FANTASTIC 1
2 showing or marked by a lack of good sense or judgment — see FOOLISH 1
3 so foolish or pointless as to be worthy of scornful laughter — see RIDICULOUS 1

preposterousness *n* lack of good sense or judgment — see FOOLISHNESS 1

prerogative *n* something to which one has a just claim — see RIGHT 1

presage *n* 1 a feeling that something bad will happen — see PREMONITION
2 something believed to be a sign or warning of a future event — see OMEN

presage *vb* to tell of or describe beforehand — see FORETELL

presaging *n* a declaration that something will happen in the future — see PREDICTION

prescience *n* 1 the special ability to see or know about events before they actually occur — see FORESIGHT 1
2 concern or preparation for the future — see FORESIGHT 2

prescient *adj* having or showing awareness of and preparation for the future — see FORESIGHTED

prescribe *vb* to give the rules about (something) clearly and exactly ⟨in chess, you can move the various pieces only in certain *prescribed* ways⟩
syn define, lay down, specify
rel decree, dictate, ordain; assign, direct, fix, set, settle; arrange, order; choose, select; adjure, bid, charge, command, enjoin, instruct, tell; conduct, control, lead, manage; coerce, constrain, force; oblige, require

presence *n* 1 a position within view ⟨men should watch their language when in the *presence* of ladies⟩
syn sight
rel nearness, proximity
2 the outward form of someone or something especially as indicative of a quality — see APPEARANCE 1

present *adj* 1 existing or in progress right now ⟨I am very busy at the *present* moment⟩
syn current, extant, ongoing, present-day
rel contemporary, mod, modern, new, newfangled, new-fashioned, now, recent, red-hot, space-age, ultramodern, up-to-date; being, breathing, existing, living
near ant done, ended, finished, over; ancient, antediluvian, antiquated, antique, archaic, dated, fusty, musty, noncontem-

porary, obsolete, old, oldfangled, old-fashioned, old-time, out-of-date, outworn, passé; bygone, erstwhile, formerly

ant ago, past; future

2 being within the confines of a specified place ⟨all of you are required to be *present* for every class⟩

syn attending

rel accompanying, observing, participating; available; abounding; latent; breathing, existing, existent, extant, live

phrases in attendance, on hand

near ant departed, gone, retired; nonexistent; AWOL, truant; dead, departed, lost, vanished; delayed, late, overdue, tardy

ant absent, away, missing, out

present *n* **1** the time currently existing or in progress ⟨I cannot talk to you at *present*, but perhaps in a few minutes⟩

syn moment, now, today

rel phase, stage, state; tonight, tomorrow

near ant yesterday, yesteryear

ant past; future

2 something given to someone without expectation of a return — see GIFT 1

present *vb* **1** to bring before the public in performance or exhibition ⟨we will *present* a performance of *Our Town* this week⟩

syn carry, give, mount, offer, stage

rel display, exhibit, show; preview; act, impersonate, perform, play, portray; depict, dramatize, enact, render, represent; extend, proffer, tender

2 to make (one person) known (to another) socially — see INTRODUCE 1

3 to make a present of — see GIVE 1

presentation *n* something given to someone without expectation of a return — see GIFT 1

present–day *adj* **1** being or involving the latest methods, concepts, information, or styles — see MODERN

2 existing or in progress right now — see PRESENT 1

presentiment *n* a feeling that something bad will happen — see PREMONITION

presently *adv* **1** at or within a short time — see SHORTLY 2

2 at the present time — see NOW 1

preservation *n* **1** the act or activity of keeping something in an existing and usually satisfactory condition — see MAINTENANCE

2 the careful maintaining and protection of something valuable especially in its natural or original state — see CONSERVATION 1

preserve *vb* to keep in good condition — see MAINTAIN 1

preserving *n* the act or activity of keeping something in an existing and usually satisfactory condition — see MAINTENANCE

president *n* a person in charge of a meeting — see CHAIR 1

preside (over) *vb* to exercise authority or power over — see GOVERN 1

---

syn synonym(s)   *rel* related words
ant antonym(s)   *near ant* near antonym(s)

presiding *adj* highest in rank or authority — see HEAD

press *n* a great number of persons or things gathered together — see CROWD 1

press *vb* **1** to push steadily against with some force ⟨an old doorbell that requires you to *press* the button hard⟩

syn bear (down on), depress, shove, weigh (on *or* upon)

rel compress, squash, squeeze; compel, force, pressure; lean (on *or* against), muscle; drive, propel, thrust; compact, constrict, contract, crush, scrunch, wring; cram, jam, jam-pack, pack, stuff, wedge

2 to apply external pressure on so as to force out the juice or contents of ⟨my family will only drink juice from freshly *pressed* oranges⟩

syn crush, express, mash, squeeze

rel pulp, puree; extract, extrude

3 to gather into a closely packed group ⟨everyone *pressed* around me to see the pictures⟩

syn bunch, cluster, crowd, huddle

rel assemble, collect, congregate, flock, gather, herd, swarm, throng; encircle, mob, surround; embrace, hug

4 to force one's way ⟨we continued to *press* deeper and deeper into the tangled rain forest⟩

syn bulldoze, elbow, muscle, push

rel jostle; ram, shove, thrust

5 to cause (a person) to give in to pressure — see FORCE

6 to try to persuade (someone) through earnest appeals to follow a course of action — see URGE

press (for) *vb* to ask for (something) earnestly or with authority — see DEMAND 1

pressing *adj* needing immediate attention — see ACUTE 2

pressure *n* **1** the burden on one's emotional or mental well-being created by demands on one's time — see STRESS 1

2 the use of power to impose one's will on another — see FORCE 2

pressure *vb* to cause (a person) to give in to pressure — see FORCE

prestidigitator *n* one who practices tricks and illusions for entertainment — see MAGICIAN 2

prestigious *adj* **1** having a good reputation especially in a field of knowledge — see RESPECTABLE 1

2 standing above others in rank, importance, or achievement — see EMINENT

presto *adv* with great speed — see FAST 1

presumably *adv* **1** to all outward appearances — see APPARENTLY

2 without much doubt — see PROBABLY

presume *vb* **1** to form an opinion from little or no evidence — see GUESS 1

2 to take as true or as a fact without actual proof — see ASSUME 2

presumed *adj* appearing to be true on the basis of evidence that may or may not be confirmed — see APPARENT 1

presuming *adj* showing a lack of proper social reserve or modesty — see PRESUMPTUOUS 1

presumption n 1 shameless boldness — see EFFRONTERY

2 something taken as being true or factual and used as a starting point for a course of action or reasoning — see ASSUMPTION

presumptuous adj 1 showing a lack of proper social reserve or modesty ⟨it's a little *presumptuous* of you to assume that I'm your new best friend just because I invited you along⟩

syn bold, familiar, forward, free, immodest, overfamiliar, presuming

rel arrogant, complacent, conceited, egoistic, egotistic (or egotistical), important, overweening, pompous, prideful, proud, self-assertive, self-conceited, self-important, self-satisfied, smug, uppity, vain, vainglorious; cavalier, disdainful, haughty, lordly, pretentious, snobbish, stuck-up, supercilious, superior; audacious, brash, brassy, brazen, fresh, impertinent, impudent, pert, saucy; confident, self-assured, self-confident, sure; boastful, braggart, bragging; domineering, high-handed, imperious; self-centered, selfish

near ant humble, meek, unassertive; bashful, retiring, shy; diffident, self-doubting

ant modest, unassuming

2 having a feeling of superiority that shows itself in an overbearing attitude — see ARROGANT

3 thrusting oneself where one is not welcome or invited — see INTRUSIVE

presumptuousness n 1 an exaggerated sense of one's importance that shows itself in the making of excessive or unjustified claims — see ARROGANCE

2 shameless boldness — see EFFRONTERY

presuppose vb to take as true or as a fact without actual proof — see ASSUME 2

presupposition n something taken as being true or factual and used as a starting point for a course of action or reasoning — see ASSUMPTION

pretend adj not real and existing only in the imagination — see IMAGINARY

pretend vb 1 to take on a false or deceptive appearance ⟨I *pretended* that I was scared of the vacuum cleaner⟩

syn dissemble, let on

rel act, impersonate, masquerade, play, pose; affect, assume, counterfeit, fake, feign, profess, put on, simulate; camouflage, conceal, disguise, mask; bluff, feint *phrases* make a pretense, make a show, make believe, put on an act, put up a front

2 to present a false appearance of — see FEIGN

pretended adj lacking in natural or spontaneous quality — see ARTIFICIAL 1

pretender n one who makes false claims of identity or expertise — see IMPOSTOR

pretense or **pretence** n 1 the quality or state of appearing or trying to appear more important or more valuable than is the case ⟨she seemed to be a very down-to-earth woman who was completely free of *pretense*⟩

syn affectation, affectedness, grandiosity, pretension, pretentiousness

rel arrogance, complacency, conceit, egotism, pride, self-assertion, self-conceit, self-importance, self-satisfaction, smugness, vaingloriousness, vainglory, vainness, vanity; disdain, haughtiness, lordliness, snobbery, snobbishness, superciliousness, superiority; confidence, presumption, self-assurance, self-confidence, sureness; boastfulness, braggadocio; aggressiveness, assertiveness, audaciousness, boldness, brassiness, cheekiness, cockiness, forwardness, impudence, insolence, rudeness; grandiloquence; flashiness, gaudiness, ostentation, show, showiness

near ant demureness, humbleness, humility, meekness, modesty; bashfulness, diffidence, shyness, timidity; naturalness, sincerity

2 a display of emotion or behavior that is insincere or intended to deceive — see MASQUERADE

3 an entitlement to something — see CLAIM 1

4 an exaggerated sense of one's importance that shows itself in the making of excessive or unjustified claims — see ARROGANCE

pretension n 1 an entitlement to something — see CLAIM 1

2 an exaggerated sense of one's importance that shows itself in the making of excessive or unjustified claims — see ARROGANCE

3 the quality or state of appearing or trying to appear more important or more valuable than is the case — see PRETENSE 1

4 something that one hopes or intends to accomplish — see GOAL

pretentious adj 1 self-consciously trying to present an appearance of grandeur or importance ⟨the *pretentious* hosts served caviar at their party, even though they themselves dislike it⟩

syn affected, grandiose, highfalutin, ostentatious, pompous

rel grandiloquent, high-sounding, sententious; arrogant, complacent, conceited, egoistic, egotistic (or egotistical), important, overweening, prideful, proud, self-assertive, self-conceited, self-important, self-satisfied, smug, uppity, vain, vainglorious; cavalier, disdainful, haughty, lordly, snobbish, snobby, stuck-up, supercilious, superior; confident, self-assured, self-confident, sure; boastful, braggart, bragging; aggressive, assertive, audacious, bold, brassy, cheeky, cocky, forward, impudent, insolent, rude; flashy, flaunting, gaudy, showy

near ant demure, homely, humble, lowly, meek, retiring, unassertive, unassuming; bashful, diffident, mousy (or mousey), overmodest, passive, quiet, reserved, shy, timid *ant* modest, unpretentious

2 having a feeling of superiority that shows itself in an overbearing attitude — see ARROGANT

pretentiousness *n* **1** an exaggerated sense of one's importance that shows itself in the making of excessive or unjustified claims — see ARROGANCE

2 excessive or unnecessary display — see OSTENTATION

3 the quality or state of appearing or trying to appear more important or more valuable than is the case — see PRETENSE 1

preternatural *adj* of, relating to, or being part of a reality beyond the observable physical universe — see SUPERNATURAL 1

prettiness *n* the qualities in a person or thing that as a whole give pleasure to the senses — see BEAUTY 1

pretty *adj* very pleasing to look at — see BEAUTIFUL

pretty *adv* to some degree or extent — see FAIRLY

prevail *vb* **1** to achieve victory (as in a contest) — see WIN 1

2 to continue to operate or to meet one's needs — see HOLD OUT

prevail (on *or* upon) *vb* to cause (someone) to agree with a belief or course of action by using arguments or earnest requests — see PERSUADE

prevail (over) *vb* to achieve a victory over — see BEAT 2

prevailing *adj* **1** accepted, used, or practiced by most people — see CURRENT 1

2 held by or applicable to a majority of the people — see GENERAL 3

prevalence *n* the fact or state of happening often — see FREQUENCY

prevalent *adj* accepted, used, or practiced by most people — see CURRENT 1

prevaricate *vb* to make a statement one knows to be untrue — see LIE 1

prevarication *n* a statement known by its maker to be untrue and made in order to deceive — see LIE

prevaricator *n* a person who tells lies — see LIAR

prevent *vb* to keep from happening by taking action in advance ⟨a lot of problems would have been *prevented* if we'd just prepared better⟩

syn avert, forestall, help, obviate, preclude

rel anticipate, provide; negate, neutralize, nullify; avoid, save; baffle, balk, checkmate, deter, foil, frustrate, thwart; bar, block, hamper, hinder, impede, interfere (with), retard, stall; deflect, fend (off), head (off), stave off, stop, ward (off); avoid, circumvent, dodge, elude, escape, evade; forbid, inhibit, prohibit; arrest, check, halt, stop; counteract, offset

near ant abet, aid, assist; ease, facilitate, smooth; advance, cultivate, encourage, forward, foster, further, nurture, promote; allow, leave, let, permit

preventative *adj* concerned with or serving to keep something from happening — see PREVENTIVE

prevention *n* the act or practice of keeping something from happening ⟨good crowd control is crucial to the *prevention* of riots⟩

syn averting, forestallment, obviating, precluding

rel avoidance, circumvention; negation, neutralization, nullification; baffling, balking, checkmate, debarment, determent, deterrence, foiling, frustration, thwarting; bar, block, hindrance, interference; interdiction, prohibition

near ant aid, assistance; facilitation; advancement, cultivation, encouragement, nurture, promotion

preventive *adj* concerned with or serving to keep something from happening ⟨if you start taking this *preventive* medicine now, you may not get sick after all⟩

syn precautionary, preventative

rel deterrent, deterring; negating, neutralizing, nullifying; baffling, balking, foiling, frustrating, thwarting; blocking, hampering, hindering, impeding, retardant, stalling

near ant abetting, aiding, assisting; easing, facilitating, smoothing; encouraging, forwarding, fostering, furthering, nurturing, promoting

previous *adj* going before another in time or order ⟨the new instructor should consult with the *previous* teacher about the lesson plans⟩ ⟨the *previous* math problem also included a reference to store discounts⟩

syn antecedent, anterior, foregoing, precedent, preceding, prior

rel advance, early, premature; earliest, first, inaugural, initial, maiden, original, pioneer; preexisting, introductory, preliminary; erstwhile, former, whilom

near ant advanced, late; final, last, terminal, ultimate

ant after, ensuing, following, subsequent, succeeding

previously *adv* so as to precede something in order of time — see AHEAD 1

previous to *prep* earlier than — see BEFORE 1

prey *n* an animal that is hunted or killed ⟨rabbits are common *prey* for owls and hawks⟩

syn chase, quarry

rel game; kill, victim; creature, critter, beast, brute; target

near ant carnivore; chaser, hunter, pursuer; killer, murderer

ant predator

prey (on *or* upon) *vb* to seize and eat (something) as prey ⟨a fox has been *preying on* the chickens⟩

syn feed (on, upon, *or* off)

---

syn synonym(s)   *rel* related words
ant antonym(s)   *near ant* near antonym(s)

rel chase, hunt, pursue; destroy, dispatch, do in, fell, kill, slay

price *n* **1** the amount of money that is demanded as payment for something ⟨I really wanted to buy that shirt, but the *price* was more money than I had⟩

syn charge, cost, fee, figure

rel list price, market value, rate, tariff, unit price; carrying charge, overcharge, surcharge; deduction, discount, markdown, reduction, sale; deposit; down payment; account, bill, check, invoice, tab

2 the loss or penalty involved in achieving a goal ⟨I finished the essay, but the *price* was losing a night's sleep⟩

syn cost

rel expense, toll; forfeit, penalty, sacrifice

3 something offered or given in return for a service performed — see REWARD

prick *n* **1** a mark or small hole made by a pointed instrument ⟨the immunization shot left a *prick* on my arm that turned into a bruise⟩

syn perforation, pinhole, pinprick, punch, puncture, stab

rel gouge, groove, hollow; break, cut, gash, notch, rupture, slash, slit

2 a sharp unpleasant sensation usually felt in some specific part of the body — see PAIN 1

prickly *adj* likely to cause a scratch — see SCRATCHY 1

pride *n* **1** a reasonable or justifiable sense of one's worth or importance ⟨finishing that survival course gave me a real sense of *pride* and confidence in my abilities⟩

syn ego, pridefulness, self-esteem, self-regard, self-respect

rel confidence, self-assurance, self-confidence; dignity, face, honor, prestige

near ant disgrace, humiliation, shame; demureness, humbleness, humility, modesty; diffidence, meekness, shyness, timidity, timidness

2 an asset that brings praise or renown — see GLORY 2

3 an often unjustified feeling of being pleased with oneself or with one's situation or achievements — see COMPLACENCE

pride *vb* to think highly of (oneself) ⟨he *prides* himself on the quality of his writing⟩

syn flatter, plume

rel boast, brag, vaunt; congratulate, felicitate

prideful *adj* **1** having or displaying feelings of scorn for what is regarded as beneath oneself — see PROUD 1

2 having too high an opinion of oneself — see CONCEITED

pridefulness *n* **1** a reasonable or justifiable sense of one's worth or importance — see PRIDE 1

2 an often unjustified feeling of being pleased with oneself or with one's situation or achievements — see COMPLACENCE

priest *n* a person specially trained and authorized to conduct religious services in a Christian church — see CLERGYMAN

priestly *adj* of, relating to, or characteristic of the clergy — see CLERICAL

prim *adj* given to or marked by very conservative standards regarding personal behavior or morals — see STRAITLACED

primal *adj* relating to or occurring near the beginning of a process, series, or time period — see EARLY 1

primarily *adv* **1** in the beginning — see ORIGINALLY

2 for the most part — see CHIEFLY

primary *adj* **1** coming before all others in importance — see FOREMOST 1

2 done or working without something else coming in between — see DIRECT 1

3 highest in rank or authority — see HEAD

prime *adj* **1** highest in rank or authority — see HEAD

2 of the very best kind — see EXCELLENT

prime *n* **1** a state or time of great activity, thriving, or achievement — see BLOOM 1

2 individuals carefully selected as being the best of a class — see ELITE

primer *n* a book used for instruction in a subject — see TEXTBOOK

primeval *adj* relating to or occurring near the beginning of a process, series, or time period — see EARLY 1

primitive *adj* **1** belonging to or characteristic of an early level of skill or development ⟨*primitive* wooden tools were used before the Iron Age⟩

syn crude, low, rude, rudimentary

rel basic, simple, uncomplicated; homely, homespun, unsophisticated; early, primeval, primordial; backward, underdeveloped, undeveloped; aged, ancient, antediluvian, antiquated, antique, dated, fusty, hoary, musty, obsolete, old, oldfangled, old-fashioned, old-time, out-of-date, outworn, passé, past

near ant complex, complicated, intricate, involved, sophisticated; full-blown, full-grown, grown, mature, matured, perfected, ripe, ripened; civilized, cultivated, enlightened, refined; contemporary, current, latest, mod, modern, new, newfangled, new-fashioned, novel, now, present-day, space-age, ultramodern, up-to-date

ant advanced, developed, evolved, higher

2 relating to or occurring near the beginning of a process, series, or time period — see EARLY 1

primordial *adj* relating to or occurring near the beginning of a process, series, or time period — see EARLY 1

prince *n* a person of rank, power, or influence in a particular field — see MAGNATE

princely *adj* fit for or worthy of a royal ruler — see MONARCHICAL

principal *adj* **1** coming before all others in importance — see FOREMOST 1

2 highest in rank or authority — see HEAD

principal *n* the person who has the most important role in a play, movie, or TV show — see STAR 2

principally *adv* for the most part — see CHIEFLY

principled *adj* **1** following the accepted rules of moral conduct — see HONORABLE 1

2 guided by or in accordance with one's sense of right and wrong — see CONSCIENTIOUS 1

principles *n pl* **1** general or basic truths on which other truths or theories can be based ⟨if you don't learn the *principles* of algebra now, you won't understand much later on⟩

syn basics, elements, essentials, fundamentals, rudiments

rel basis, foundation, groundwork; nitty-gritty; belief, canon, doctrine, dogma, faith, philosophy; axiom, law, precept, tenet; rule, standard; theorem

near ant details, trivia

2 the code of good conduct for an individual or group — see ETHICS

print *n* **1** a perceptible trace left by pressure ⟨one telltale sign that I had been napping was the *print* left by the chenille bedspread on my cheek⟩

syn impress, impression, imprint, stamp

rel dent, hollow, indentation; mark, sign

2 a picture created from an image recorded on a light-sensitive surface by a camera — see PHOTOGRAPH

print *vb* to produce and release for distribution in printed form — see PUBLISH 1

prior *adj* going before another in time or order — see PREVIOUS

priority *n* the right to one's attention before other things considered less important ⟨the principal has decided to give your request *priority*, so you'll have a meeting early tomorrow morning⟩

syn precedence, right-of-way

rel preference; urgency; ascendancy, preeminence, primacy, supremacy; transcendence; order, progression, sequence, succession

prior to *prep* earlier than — see BEFORE 1

priory *n* a residence for men under religious vows — see MONASTERY

prison *n* a place of confinement for persons held in lawful custody — see JAIL

prisoner *n* one that has been taken and held in confinement — see CAPTIVE

pristine *adj* being in an original and unused or unspoiled state — see FRESH 1

private *adj* **1** not known or meant to be known by the general populace ⟨that he is planning to retire is *private* information until he makes a public announcement⟩

syn confidential, hushed, inside, intimate, nonpublic, privy, secret

rel classified, top secret; unadvertised, unannounced, undisclosed, unmentioned; clandestine, collusive, conspiratorial, covert; surreptitious, undercover, underhand, underhanded; personal; closeted, concealed, hidden; repressed, silenced, stifled, suppressed

near ant well-known; advertised, aired, announced, blazed, broadcast, declared, disclosed, divulged, enunciated, heralded, proclaimed, professed, promulgated, publicized, published, reported, spotlighted; general, popular, prevailing, vulgar; prevalent, rife, widespread; communal, shared

ant common, open, public

2 undertaken or done so as to escape being observed or known by others — see SECRET 1

3 of, relating to, or belonging to a single person — see INDIVIDUAL 1

privation *n* the state of being robbed of something normally enjoyed ⟨the constant *privation* of sleep was starting to affect my schoolwork⟩

syn deprivation, loss

rel lack, need, want; dispossession; denial, forfeit, forfeiture, penalty, sacrifice; bereavement

near ant ownership, possession; accumulation, acquiring, gain

privilege *n* something granted as a special favor ⟨you will have the *privilege* of leading the line today⟩

syn appanage, boon, concession, honor

rel courtesy; claim, entitlement, right; birthright; perquisite, prerogative; charter, grant, patent; exemption, immunity, waiver

near ant duty, obligation, responsibility

privy *adj* **1** not known or meant to be known by the general populace — see PRIVATE 1

2 undertaken or done so as to escape being observed or known by others — see SECRET 1

3 of, relating to, or belonging to a single person — see INDIVIDUAL 1

prize *n* **1** someone or something unusually desirable ⟨in her parents' view, her current boyfriend is certainly no *prize*⟩

syn catch, gem, jewel, pearl, plum, treasure

rel find, godsend, goody, valuable, windfall; booty, loot, spoil; glory, pride; jackpot, treasure trove

near ant lemon, loser

2 something given in recognition of achievement — see AWARD

¹prize *vb* **1** to draw out by force or with effort — see EXTRACT

2 to raise, move, or pull apart with or as if with a lever — see ¹PRY 1

²prize *vb* to hold dear — see LOVE 1

prizefighter *n* one that engages in the sport of fighting with the fists — see BOXER

probability *n* **1** the quality or state of being likely to occur ⟨the plot of the movie thriller was exciting and surprising but woefully lacking in *probability*⟩

syn likelihood, likeliness

---

rel credibility, plausibility; liability; feasibility, feasibleness, possibility, potentiality, reasonability, viability

near ant doubtfulness, dubiousness; impracticability, impracticality; implausibility, incredibility

ant improbability, unlikelihood, unlikeliness

2 a measure of how often an event will occur instead of another ⟨the *probability* of flipping a coin and getting heads fifty times in a row is not good⟩

syn chance, odds, percentage

rel outlook, prospect; possibility, potential, potentiality

probable *adj* **1** worthy of being accepted as true or reasonable — see BELIEVABLE

2 having a high chance of occurring — see LIKELY 1

probably *adv* without much doubt ⟨we would *probably* win with that bet⟩

syn doubtless, likely, presumably

rel mayhap, perchance, perhaps, possibly; conceivably, imaginably, plausibly, practically, reasonably; potentially; assuredly, certainly, clearly, conclusively, decisively, definitely, definitively, indubitably, positively, surely

near ant implausibly, inconceivably, incredibly, unbelievably

ant improbably

probe *n* a systematic search for the truth or facts about something — see INQUIRY 1

probe *vb* **1** to search through or into — see EXPLORE 1

2 to go into or range over for purposes of discovery — see EXPLORE 2

probing *n* a systematic search for the truth or facts about something — see INQUIRY 1

probity *n* **1** conduct that conforms to an accepted standard of right and wrong — see MORALITY 1

2 devotion to telling the truth — see HONESTY 1

3 faithfulness to high moral standards — see HONOR 1

problem *n* **1** something that requires thought and skill for resolution ⟨the *problem* of world hunger⟩

syn case, knot, matter, trouble

rel issue, question; challenge; corner, fix, hole, hot water, jam, pickle, predicament, situation; glitch, hitch, snag; conundrum, enigma, mystery, puzzle, puzzlement, riddle; brainteaser, perplexer, poser, stumper

ant answer, solution

2 an interrogative expression often used to test knowledge — see QUESTION 1

3 something that is a source of irritation — see ANNOYANCE 3

problematic *also* **problematical** *adj* **1** requiring exceptional skill or caution in performance or handling — see TRICKY

2 giving good reason for being doubted, questioned, or challenged — see DOUBTFUL 2

procedure *n* **1** a usually fixed or ordered series of actions or events leading to a result — see PROCESS 1

2 a way of acting or proceeding — see COURSE 1

proceed *vb* to move forward along a course — see GO 1

proceed (along) *vb* to make one's way through, across, or over — see TRAVERSE

proceeding *adj* being in progress or development — see ONGOING 1

proceeding *n* **1** a court case for enforcing a right or claim — see LAWSUIT

2 a usually fixed or ordered series of actions or events leading to a result — see PROCESS 1

proceeds *n pl* **1** an increase usually measured in money that comes from labor, business, or property — see INCOME

2 the amount of money left when expenses are subtracted from the total amount received — see PROFIT 1

process *n* **1** a usually fixed or ordered series of actions or events leading to a result ⟨the *process* by which the elastic fibers spun by silkworms is turned into soft, lustrous cloth⟩

syn course, operation, procedure, proceeding

rel fashion, manner, method, mode, style, system, technique, way; approach, blueprint, design, game plan, layout, plan, plot, program, scheme, strategy; accomplishment, achievement, attainment, enterprise, performance, undertaking, work; activity, functioning, movement

2 forward movement in time or place — see ADVANCE 1

procession *n* **1** a body of individuals moving along in an orderly and often ceremonial way — see CORTEGE 1

2 forward movement in time or place — see ADVANCE 1

proclaim *vb* to make known openly or publicly — see ANNOUNCE

proclivity *n* a habitual attraction to some activity or thing — see INCLINATION 1

procreate *vb* to bring forth offspring ⟨in life science class we learned how animals *procreate*⟩

syn breed, multiply, propagate, reproduce

rel bear, beget, engender, generate, get, mother, parent, produce, sire; hatch, spawn

procurable *adj* possible to get — see AVAILABLE 1

procurator *n* a person who acts or does business for another — see AGENT 2

procure *vb* to receive as return for effort — see EARN 1

prod *vb* **1** to urge or push forward with or as if with a pointed object ⟨my sister keeps *prodding* me with her pencil to move along faster⟩

syn goad, spur

rel chuck, jab, jog, nudge, poke; bore, drill, pierce, prick, punch, puncture, stab, stick; drive, propel

2 to try to persuade (someone) through earnest appeals to follow a course of action — see URGE

prodigal *adj* given to spending money freely or foolishly ⟨the *prodigal* child always spent her allowance the minute she got it⟩

syn extravagant, profligate, spendthrift, squandering, thriftless, unthrifty, wasteful

rel improvident, myopic, shortsighted; bountiful, generous, lavish, liberal, openhanded, openhearted, philanthropic; careless, heedless, imprudent, incautious, injudicious, unwise; indulgent, reckless, self-indulgent, splurging, wanton

near ant cheap, close, mean, miserly, niggardly, parsimonious, penurious, pinching, spare, sparing, stingy, tight, tightfisted; careful, judicious, prudent, sensible, wise; farsighted, forehanded, foresighted, forethoughtful, provident

ant conserving, economical, economizing, frugal, scrimping, skimping, thrifty

prodigal *n* someone who carelessly spends money ⟨the million-dollar lottery winner was such a *prodigal* that there was no money left after a few years⟩

syn profligate, spender, spendthrift, squanderer, waster, wastrel

near ant miser, skinflint, tightwad; conserver, saver

ant economizer

prodigality *n* **1** an instance of spending money or resources without care or restraint — see WASTE 1

2 the quality or fact of being free or wasteful in the expenditure of money — see EXTRAVAGANCE 1

prodigious *adj* **1** causing wonder or astonishment — see MARVELOUS 1

2 unusually large — see HUGE

prodigy *n* something extraordinary or surprising — see WONDER 1

produce *n* something produced by physical or intellectual effort — see PRODUCT 1

produce *vb* **1** to be the cause of (a situation, action, or state of mind) — see EFFECT

2 to bring forth from the womb — see BEAR 1

3 to bring into being by combining, shaping, or transforming materials — see MAKE 1

product *n* **1** something produced by physical or intellectual effort ⟨that book is the *product* of years of work⟩ ⟨a rebuilt car which is the *product* of several people's labor⟩

syn affair, fruit, handiwork, output, produce, production, thing, work, yield

rel article, commodity, object; goods, line, merchandise, wares; handcraft, handicraft; aftereffect, aftermath, conclusion, consequence, development, effect, issue, outcome, result, upshot; by-product, derivative, offshoot, outgrowth, residual, side effect, spin-off

2 a condition or occurrence traceable to a cause — see EFFECT 1

production *n* something produced by physical or intellectual effort — see PRODUCT 1

productive *adj* **1** having a role in deciding something's final form — see FORMATIVE

2 producing abundantly — see FERTILE

3 producing or capable of producing a desired result — see EFFECTIVE 1

productiveness *n* the power to produce a desired result — see EFFICACY

profane *adj* **1** not involving religion or religious matters ⟨it was hard to juggle the requirements of church and our more *profane* duties⟩

syn secular, temporal

rel atheistic, godless, irreligious, pagan; lay, nonclerical; nondenominational, nonsectarian; earthly, mundane, terrestrial, worldly; material, physical, substantial; bodily, carnal, corporal, fleshly; blasphemous, impious, irreverent, sacrilegious; unconsecrated, unhallowed, unsanctified

near ant divine, spiritual; consecrated, hallowed, holy, sanctified; churchly, devout, godly, pious, prayerful, reverent, worshipful; ethereal, insubstantial, metaphysical, unsubstantial; bodiless, immaterial, incorporeal, nonphysical

ant religious, sacred

2 not showing proper reverence for the holy or sacred — see IRREVERENT

profane *vb* **1** to lower in character or dignity — see DEBASE 1

2 to put to a bad or improper use — see MISAPPLY

3 to treat (a sacred place or object) shamefully or with great disrespect — see DESECRATE

profess *vb* **1** to present a false appearance of — see FEIGN

2 to state clearly and strongly — see ASSERT 1

3 to state as a fact usually forcefully — see CLAIM 1

profession *n* **1** a solemn and often public declaration of the truth or existence of something — see PROTESTATION

2 the activity by which one regularly makes a living — see OCCUPATION

proffer *n* something which is presented for consideration — see PROPOSAL

proffer *vb* **1** to put before another for acceptance or consideration — see OFFER 1

2 to set before the mind for consideration — see PROPOSE 1

proficiency *n* **1** a highly developed skill in or knowledge of something — see COMMAND 2

2 knowledge gained by actually doing or living through something — see EXPERIENCE 1

proficient *adj* having or showing exceptional knowledge, experience, or skill in a field of endeavor ⟨she is quite *proficient* at computer repair⟩ ⟨a *proficient* rendition of a difficult piano piece⟩

syn accomplished, ace, adept, consummate, crack, crackerjack, experienced,

---

syn synonym(s)   *rel* related words
ant antonym(s)   *near ant* near antonym(s)

expert, good, great, master, masterful, masterly, practiced (*or* practised), skilled, skillful, versed, veteran, virtuoso

rel adroit, clever, deft, dexterous (*also* dextrous), handy; gifted, talented; experienced, polished, refined; effective, effectual, efficient, workmanlike; able, capable, competent, fit, qualified; educated, knowledgeable, schooled, taught, trained, tutored; all-around (*also* all-round), well-rounded; long-term, old

near ant incapable, incompetent, inept, unable, unfit, unqualified; artless, crude, rude; ineffective, ineffectual, inefficient; ungifted, untalented; ignorant, unschooled, untaught, untrained, untutored; beginning, green, inexperienced, new, raw, untested, untried; rough, unpolished

ant amateur, amateurish, inexperienced, inexpert, unexperienced, unpracticed, unprofessional, unseasoned, unskilled, unskillful

proficiently *adv* in a skillful or expert manner — see WELL 3

profit *n* 1 the amount of money left when expenses are subtracted from the total amount received ⟨after we deducted the cost of sugar, lemons, and paper cups, the *profit* from a day of lemonade sales was about $20⟩

syn earnings, gain, lucre, net, payoff, proceeds, return

rel killing, windfall; gross; compensation, emolument, income, pay, payment, remittal, requital, salary, wages; interest, return, yield; (the) black; royalty

near ant cost, expenditure, expense, loss, outgo, outlay

2 an increase usually measured in money that comes from labor, business, or property — see INCOME

profit *vb* to provide with something useful or desirable — see BENEFIT

profitable *adj* 1 yielding a profit ⟨selling lemonade turned out to be a *profitable* venture⟩

syn fat, gainful, lucrative, paying, remunerative

rel advantageous, beneficial, rewarding, useful, worthwhile

ant unprofitable

2 conferring benefits; promoting or contributing to personal or social well-being — see BENEFICIAL

profligate *adj* given to spending money freely or foolishly — see PRODIGAL

profligate *n* 1 someone who carelessly spends money — see PRODIGAL

2 a person who has sunk below the normal moral standard — see DEGENERATE

profound *adj* 1 difficult for one of ordinary knowledge or intelligence to understand ⟨a *profound* observation about good and evil that few listeners fully grasped⟩

syn abstruse, deep, esoteric, recondite

rel erudite, learned, scholarly; academic, pedantic; complex, complicated, hard; darkling, enigmatic (*also* enigmatical), in-

scrutable, mysterious, mystic, uncanny; impenetrable, incomprehensible, unfathomable, unintelligible; ambiguous, cryptic; unanswerable, unknowable; baffling, bewildering, confounding, confusing, mystifying, perplexing, puzzling

near ant easy, facile, simple, straightforward; comprehensible, fathomable, intelligible, understandable; clear, obvious, plain

ant shallow

2 extreme in degree, power, or effect — see INTENSE

3 having no exceptions or restrictions — see ABSOLUTE 2

profoundness *n* the quality of being great in extent (as of insight) — see DEPTH 2

profundity *n* the quality of being great in extent (as of insight) — see DEPTH 2

profuse *adj* pouring forth in great amounts ⟨we received *profuse* thanks for our efforts⟩ ⟨a *profuse* rush of water from the collapsing dike⟩

syn copious, galore, gushing, lavish, riotous

rel abounding, abundant, ample, bounteous, bountiful, liberal, plenteous, plentiful; extravagant, luxuriant; fat, fecund, fertile; free, liberal, munificent, openhanded, unsparing, unstinting; excessive, immoderate; adequate, complete, enough, sufficient

near ant meager, niggardly, poor, scant, scanty, spare, sparse, stingy; deficient, inadequate, incomplete, insufficient, lacking, unsatisfactory, wanting; bare, mere, minimal; slight, small

ant dribbling, trickling

profusion *n* a considerable amount — see LOT 2

progeny *n* the descendants of a person, animal, or plant — see OFFSPRING

prognosis *n* a declaration that something will happen in the future — see PREDICTION

prognosticate *vb* to tell of or describe beforehand — see FORETELL

prognosticating *n* a declaration that something will happen in the future — see PREDICTION

prognostication *n* a declaration that something will happen in the future — see PREDICTION

prognosticator *n* one who predicts future events or developments — see PROPHET

program *n* 1 a listing of things to be presented or considered (as at a concert or play) ⟨the *program* will tell us the scheduled order of musical numbers⟩

syn agenda, calendar, docket, schedule, timetable

rel card, exercises; arrangement, order, organization

2 a method worked out in advance for achieving some objective — see PLAN 1

3 a way of acting or proceeding — see COURSE 1

progress *n* 1 forward movement in time or place — see ADVANCE 1

2 the act or process of going from the simple or basic to the complex or advanced — see DEVELOPMENT 1

progress *vb* **1** to become mature — see MATURE

2 to move forward along a course — see GO 1

progression *n* **1** a series of things linked together — see CHAIN 1

2 forward movement in time or place — see ADVANCE 1

3 the act or process of going from the simple or basic to the complex or advanced — see DEVELOPMENT 1

progressive *adj* **1** being far along in development — see ADVANCED 1

2 not bound by traditional ways or beliefs — see LIBERAL 1

prohibit *vb* to order not to do or use or to be done or used — see FORBID

prohibited *adj* that may not be permitted — see IMPERMISSIBLE

prohibiting *n* the act of ordering that something not be done or used — see PROHIBITION 1

prohibition *n* **1** the act of ordering that something not be done or used ⟨the principal's *prohibition* against the use of cell phones in the school building met with unanimous approval by the teachers⟩
syn banning, barring, enjoining, forbidding, interdicting, interdiction, outlawing, prohibiting, proscribing, proscription
rel bidding, charging, decreeing, dictation, direction, instruction; deterrence, discouragement, dissuading; repression, suppression; coercion, compulsion, constraint, force
near ant allowance, permission, sufferance, toleration; approval, endorsement; encouragement, promotion, support; compliance, obedience

2 an order that something not be done or used ⟨the school issued a *prohibition* against wearing clothing with obscene and provocative slogans⟩
syn ban, embargo, interdict, interdiction, proscription, veto
rel taboo (*also* tabu); injunction; constraint, inhibition, limitation, restraint, restriction; deterrent, discouragement; repression, suppression; prevention; denial, disallowance, negation, refusal, rejection; objection, protest
near ant sufferance, tolerance, toleration; allowance, allowing, authorization, consent, granting, leave, letting, license (*or* licence), licensing, permission, permitting, sanctioning; approval, endorsement; enabling, encouragement, facilitation, promotion, support; compliance, obedience; accession, acquiescence, agreement, assent
ant prescription

project *n* a method worked out in advance for achieving some objective — see PLAN 1

project *vb* **1** to extend outward beyond a usual point — see BULGE

2 to work out the details of (something) in advance — see PLAN 1

projection *n* a part that sticks out from the general mass of something — see BULGE

proletarian *adj* belonging to the class of people of low social or economic rank — see IGNOBLE 1

proletariat *n* people looked down upon as ignorant and of the lowest class — see RABBLE

proliferate *vb* to become greater in extent, volume, amount, or number — see INCREASE 2

proliferation *n* **1** something added (as by growth) — see INCREASE 1

2 the act or process of becoming greater in number — see MULTIPLICATION

prolific *adj* producing abundantly — see FERTILE

prolix *adj* using or containing more words than necessary to express an idea — see WORDY

prolixity *n* the use of too many words to express an idea — see VERBIAGE

prologue *n* a short section (as of a book) that leads to or explains the main part — see INTRODUCTION

prolong *vb* to make longer — see EXTEND 1

prolongation *n* the act of making longer — see EXTENSION 1

prolonging *n* the act of making longer — see EXTENSION 1

prom *n* a social gathering for dancing — see DANCE

prominence *n* an area of high ground — see HEIGHT 4

prominent *adj* **1** likely to attract attention — see NOTICEABLE

2 widely known — see FAMOUS

promiscuous *adj* consisting of many things of different sorts — see MISCELLANEOUS

promise *n* a person's solemn declaration that he or she will do or not do something ⟨he gave a *promise* that he would arrive on time⟩
syn oath, pledge, troth, vow, word
rel appointment, arrangement, commitment, engagement; compact, contract, covenant; assurance, guarantee, guaranty; bail, bond, deposit, gage, pawn, security, token, warranty

promise *vb* **1** to make a solemn declaration of intent ⟨I *promised* not to fight with my sister⟩
syn covenant, pledge, swear, vow
rel affiance, betroth, plight, troth; accede, agree, assent, consent; contract, engage, guarantee, undertake; affirm, assert, aver, avouch, avow, declare, insist, warrant
phrases give one's word

2 to show signs of a favorable or successful outcome — see BODE

promising *adj* **1** having qualities which inspire hope — see HOPEFUL 1

2 pointing toward a happy outcome — see FAVORABLE 2

promontory *n* **1** an area of high ground jutting out into a body of water beyond the line of the coast — see HEADLAND 1
2 an area of land that juts out into a body of water — see ²CAPE

promote *vb* **1** to move higher in rank or position ⟨the Navy *promoted* her to captain for her record of outstanding performance⟩
syn advance, elevate, raise, upgrade
rel forward, further; aggrandize, boost, heighten, improve, lift, uplift; commission, ennoble, knight; acclaim, applaud, celebrate, cite, commend, compliment, congratulate, decorate; eulogize, extol (*also* extoll), glorify, hail, honor, laud, praise, salute
near ant depose, dethrone, dismiss, expel, impeach, oust, overthrow, remove, unmake, unseat; demean, disgrace, dishonor, humble, humiliate, mortify, shame, take down; censure, condemn, damn, denounce, reprobate
ant abase, degrade, demote, downgrade, lower, reduce
2 to help the growth or development of — see FOSTER 1
3 to look after or assist the growth of by labor and care — see GROW 1
4 to provide publicity for — see PUBLICIZE 1

promoter *n* a person who actively supports or favors a cause — see EXPONENT 1

promotion *n* a raising or a state of being raised to a higher rank or position — see ADVANCEMENT 1

prompt *adj* **1** done, carried out, or given without delay ⟨*prompt* treatment of snakebites is always advisable⟩
syn immediate, punctual, timely
rel apt, quick, ready, willing; opportune, seasonable; early
near ant delinquent, latish, overdue; behind, behindhand, delayed, detained; dilatory, laggard, slow
ant belated, late, tardy
2 having or showing the ability to respond without delay or hesitation — see QUICK 1

prompt *vb* **1** to be the cause of (a situation, action, or state of mind) — see EFFECT 1
2 to try to persuade (someone) through earnest appeals to follow a course of action — see URGE

promptitude *n* the quality or habit of arriving on time ⟨the teacher's *promptitude* was such that you could set your watch by his morning arrival⟩
syn promptness, punctuality, timeliness
rel aptness, quickness, readiness, willingness; earliness
near ant belatedness, lateness; slowness
ant tardiness

promptly *adv* without delay — see IMMEDIATELY

promptness *n* the quality or habit of arriving on time — see PROMPTITUDE

promulgate *vb* to make known openly or publicly — see ANNOUNCE

prone *adj* **1** having a tendency to be or act in a certain way ⟨he was *prone* to emotional outbursts under stress⟩
syn apt, given, inclined, tending
rel choosing, preferring; disposed, likely, predisposed, willing
near ant averse, disinclined, indisposed, loath (*or* loth), unwilling
2 lying with the face downwards ⟨stretched out *prone* on the bed for a backrub⟩
syn prostrate
rel flat, recumbent; reclining, reposing; horizontal
near ant erect, raised, standing, upright, upstanding, vertical
ant supine

proneness *n* an established pattern of behavior — see TENDENCY 1

pronounced *adj* **1** likely to attract attention — see NOTICEABLE
2 very noticeable especially for being incorrect or bad — see EGREGIOUS

pronto *adv* **1** with great speed — see FAST 1
2 without delay — see IMMEDIATELY

proof *n* something presented in support of the truth or accuracy of a claim ⟨she presented *proof* that she had not cheated⟩
syn attestation, confirmation, corroboration, documentation, evidence, substantiation, testament, testimony, validation, witness
rel (the) goods; certificate, document, exhibit; demonstration, illustration; authentication, identification, manifestation, verification
near ant rebuttal, refutation; accusation, allegation, charge; assumption, conjecture, guess, presumption, surmise, suspicion
ant disproof

prop (up) *vb* **1** to hold up or serve as a foundation for — see SUPPORT 3
2 to provide (someone) with what is useful or necessary to achieve an end — see HELP 1

propagate *vb* **1** to bring forth offspring — see PROCREATE
2 to cause to become known over a considerable area or by many people — see SPREAD 1

propel *vb* **1** to apply force to (someone or something) so that it moves in front of one — see PUSH 1
2 to cause to function — see ACTIVATE
3 to set or keep in motion — see MOVE 2

propensity *n* **1** an established pattern of behavior — see TENDENCY 1
2 a habitual attraction to some activity or thing — see INCLINATION 1

proper *adj* **1** following the established traditions of refined society and good taste ⟨the formal ball called for *proper* attire—tuxedos and full-length gowns only⟩
syn correct, decent, decorous, genteel, nice, polite, respectable, seemly

rel acceptable, adequate, satisfactory, tolerable; dress, dressy, formal; dignified, elegant, gracious; priggish, prim, stuffy; apt, material, relevant; compatible, congenial, harmonious; allowed, authorized, kosher, permitted

near ant intolerable, unacceptable, unsatisfactory; casual, grungy, informal; seedy, shabby, tacky; banned, barred, disallowed; forbidden, interdicted, outlawed, prohibited, proscribed; awkward, gauche, ungraceful

ant improper, incorrect, indecent, indecorous, unbecoming, unseemly

2 being in agreement with the truth or a fact or a standard — see CORRECT 1

3 marked by or showing careful attention to set forms and details — see CEREMONIOUS 1

4 meeting the requirements of a purpose or situation — see FIT 1

5 serving to identify as belonging to an individual or group — see CHARACTERISTIC 1

properly *adv* in a manner suitable for the occasion or purpose ⟨the scouts were *properly* dressed for a week of camping⟩
syn appropriately, congruously, correctly, fittingly, happily, meetly, rightly, suitably

rel well; acceptably, adequately, passably, satisfactorily, tolerably; decently, decorously

near ant unacceptably, unsatisfactorily; inopportunely, unfortunately, unseasonably; inaptly, irrelevantly; awkwardly, ungracefully

ant improperly, inappropriately, incongruously, incorrectly, unsuitably, wrongly

property *n* **1** a small piece of land that is developed or available for development — see LOT 1

2 something that sets apart an individual from others of the same kind — see CHARACTERISTIC

prophecy *n* a declaration that something will happen in the future — see PREDICTION

prophesier *n* one who predicts future events or developments — see PROPHET

prophesy *vb* to tell of or describe beforehand — see FORETELL

prophet *n* one who predicts future events or developments ⟨a *prophet* who swore he could see wars before they happened⟩
syn augur, diviner, forecaster, foreseer, foreteller, fortune-teller, futurist, prognosticator, prophesier, seer, soothsayer

rel prophetess; mystic, oracle; astrologer

prophetic *or* **prophetical** *adj* being a sign of a later course of events ⟨the breaking of the cereal bowl was a *prophetic* start to a day filled with accidents and foul-ups⟩
syn predictive

rel baleful, dire, foreboding, menacing, portentous, sinister, threatening; inauspicious, unpromising; oracular; revelatory, telling

near ant auspicious, promising, propitious, rosy

propitiate *vb* to lessen the anger or agitation of — see PACIFY

propitiatory *adj* tending to lessen or avoid conflict or hostility — see PACIFIC 1

propitious *adj* **1** having qualities which inspire hope — see HOPEFUL 1

2 pointing toward a happy outcome — see FAVORABLE 2

proponent *n* a person who actively supports or favors a cause — see EXPONENT

proportion *n* **1** a balanced, pleasing, or suitable arrangement of parts — see HARMONY 1

2 something belonging to, due to, or contributed by an individual member of a group — see SHARE 1

3 the relationship in quantity, amount, or size between two or more things — see RATIO

4 the total amount of measurable space or surface occupied by something — see ¹SIZE

proportional *adj* corresponding in size, amount, extent, or degree ⟨each child receives an allowance *proportional* to his or her age and needs⟩
syn commensurate, proportionate

rel balanced, symmetrical; correlative, reciprocal; contingent, dependent, relative; akin, comparable, similar

phrases in proportion

near ant asymmetrical (*or* asymmetric), distorted, irregular, lopsided, nonsymmetrical, twisted, unsymmetrical; unbalanced

ant disproportionate

proportionate *adj* corresponding in size, amount, extent, or degree — see PROPORTIONAL

proposal *n* something which is presented for consideration ⟨the city council is accepting *proposals* for ways to use that land⟩
syn offer, proffer, proposition, suggestion

rel feeler, overture; motion; advancement, nomination, recommendation; presentation, submission, tender; arrangement, game, ground plan, layout, line, plan, plot, project, strategy, system; conception, idea, notion, thought

propose *vb* **1** to set before the mind for consideration ⟨he *proposed* that we go for a walk this afternoon⟩
syn advance, offer, pose, proffer, propound, suggest, vote

rel move; nominate, recommend; present, submit, tender; file, lay, lodge; arrange, calculate, chart, contrive, cover, frame, map, plan, plot, shape

phrases put forward

2 to have in mind as a purpose or goal — see INTEND

proposition *n* **1** an idea that is the starting point for making a case or conducting an investigation — see THEORY

---

syn synonym(s)   *rel* related words
ant antonym(s)   *near ant* near antonym(s)

2 something which is presented for consideration — see PROPOSAL

propound vb to set before the mind for consideration — see PROPOSE 1

proprieties n pl personal conduct or behavior as evaluated by an accepted standard of appropriateness for a social or professional setting — see MANNER 1

proprietor n one who has a legal or rightful claim to ownership ⟨I am the sole *proprietor* of my car⟩

  syn holder, owner, possessor

  rel homeowner, landowner

  near ant squatter; lessee, renter, tenant

propriety n socially acceptable behavior — see DECENCY 1

prorate vb to give out (something) in appropriate amounts or to appropriate individuals — see ADMINISTER 1

prosaic adj **1** being of the type that is encountered in the normal course of events — see ORDINARY 1

2 having to do with the practical details of regular life — see MUNDANE 1

proscribe vb to order not to do or use or to be done or used — see FORBID

proscribed adj that may not be permitted — see IMPERMISSIBLE

proscribing n the act of ordering that something not be done or used — see PROHIBITION 1

proscription n **1** the act of ordering that something not be done or used — see PROHIBITION 1

2 an order that something not be done or used — see PROHIBITION 1

proselyte n a person who has recently been persuaded to join a religious sect — see CONVERT 1

proselytize vb to persuade to change to one's religious faith — see CONVERT 1

prospect n **1** all that can be seen from a certain point — see VIEW 1

2 one who seeks an office, honor, position, or award — see CANDIDATE

prospect vb to go into or range over for purposes of discovery — see EXPLORE 2

prosper vb **1** to grow vigorously — see THRIVE 1

2 to reach a desired level of accomplishment — see SUCCEED 2

prospering adj marked by vigorous growth and well-being especially economically — see PROSPEROUS 1

prosperous adj **1** marked by vigorous growth and well-being especially economically ⟨a *prosperous* business that will soon be expanding⟩

  syn booming, flourishing, golden, palmy, prospering, roaring, successful, thriving

  rel affluent, moneyed (*or* monied), opulent, rich, substantial, wealthy, well-heeled, well-off, well-to-do; comfortable

  near ant declining, dying, failing, floundering, languishing, struggling; bankrupt, bankrupted, insolvent

  ant unsuccessful

2 having attained a desired end or state of good fortune — see SUCCESSFUL 1

3 growing thickly and vigorously — see RANK 1

prostitute n a woman who engages in sexual activities for money ⟨the town was horrified to discover that she had once been a *prostitute*⟩

  syn harlot, whore

  rel coquette, flirt, libertine, siren, tempter, temptress, wench

prostitute vb **1** to lower in character or dignity — see DEBASE 1

2 to put to a bad or improper use — see MISAPPLY

prostitution n the practice of engaging in sexual activities for money ⟨*prostitution* is illegal in most states⟩

  syn harlotry

prostrate adj **1** depleted in strength, energy, or freshness — see WEARY 1

2 lacking bodily strength — see WEAK 1

3 lying with the face downwards — see PRONE 2

prostrate vb **1** to diminish the physical strength of — see WEAKEN 1

2 to render powerless, ineffective, or unable to move — see PARALYZE

3 to subject to incapacitating emotional or mental stress — see OVERWHELM 1

prostrated adj lacking bodily strength — see WEAK 1

prostration n a complete depletion of energy or strength — see FATIGUE

protean adj able to do many different kinds of things — see VERSATILE

protect vb to drive danger or attack away from — see DEFEND 1

protection n **1** means or method of defending — see DEFENSE 1

2 someone that protects — see PROTECTOR

3 the state of not being exposed to danger — see SAFETY 1

protective adj intended to resist or prevent attack or aggression — see DEFENSIVE

protector n someone that protects ⟨a bigger girl served as her *protector* against bullies at school⟩

  syn custodian, defender, guard, protection

  rel bodyguard, champion; keeper, lookout, sentinel, sentry, warden, warder, watch, watchdog, watchman; conserver, keeper, preserver, saver

protest n a feeling or declaration of disapproval or dissent — see OBJECTION

protest vb **1** to state as a fact usually forcefully — see CLAIM 1

2 to present an opposing opinion or argument — see OBJECT

protestation n a solemn and often public declaration of the truth or existence of something ⟨the governor went on television to make a passionate *protestation* of his innocence in the bribery scandal⟩

  syn affirmation, assertion, avouchment, avowal, claim, declaration, insistence, profession

  rel announcement, declaration, proclamation, pronouncement; argument, justification, rationalization, reason; confirmation, vindication

near ant disclaimer; challenge, dispute, question; confutation, disproof, rebuttal, refutation; contradiction, denial, negation

ant disavowal

prototype *n* something from which copies are made — see ORIGINAL

protract *vb* to make longer — see EXTEND 1

protrude *vb* to extend outward beyond a usual point — see BULGE

protrusion *n* a part that sticks out from the general mass of something — see BULGE

protuberance *n* a part that sticks out from the general mass of something — see BULGE

proud *adj* **1** having or displaying feelings of scorn for what is regarded as beneath oneself ⟨the unemployed woman was too *proud* to take a job as a maid⟩

syn disdainful, haughty, highfalutin, lofty, lordly, prideful, superior

rel complacent, conceited, egoistic, egotistic (*or* egoistical), important, self-assertive, self-conceited, self-important, self-satisfied, smug, uppity, vain, vainglorious; arrogant, pretentious, snobbish, stuck-up, supercilious; cavalier, overbearing, overweening, peremptory, swaggering; high-sounding, pompous; condescending, patronizing; cocky, overconfident, presumptuous; bloated, boastful, bombastic; audacious, bold, brash, brassy, cheeky, cocksure, forward, impertinent, impudent, saucy; confident, presuming, self-assured, self-confident, sure; domineering, high-handed, imperious; self-centered, selfish; dominating, magisterial, masterful

near ant demure, homely, meek, unassuming, unpretentious; bashful, retiring, shy, timid; diffident, self-doubting; acquiescent, compliant, deferential, resigned, submissive, unassertive, yielding; apologetic, cowering, cringing, shrinking; passive, quiet, reserved, subdued, unobtrusive

ant humble, lowly, modest

2 having too high an opinion of oneself — see CONCEITED

3 large and impressive in size, grandeur, extent, or conception — see GRAND 1

provable *adj* capable of being proven as true or real — see VERIFIABLE

prove *vb* **1** to show the existence or truth of by evidence ⟨the prosecutor used DNA evidence to *prove* the defendant's guilt⟩

syn demonstrate, document, establish, substantiate, validate

rel back (up), buttress, corroborate; evidence, evince, record, support, witness; adduce, attest, authenticate, certify, iden-

tify; confirm, sustain, verify; clinch, nail, settle; depose, testify

near ant challenge, dispute, object; allege, assume, conjecture, guess, presume, surmise, suspect

ant disprove, rebut, refute

2 to come to be — see COME OUT 1

3 to gain full recognition or acceptance of — see ESTABLISH 1

provender *n* substances intended to be eaten — see FOOD

proverb *n* an often stated observation regarding something from common experience — see SAYING

provide *vb* to put (something) into the possession of someone for use or consumption — see FURNISH 1

provide (for) *vb* to pay the living expenses of — see SUPPORT 1

providence *n* **1** careful management of material resources — see ECONOMY

2 concern or preparation for the future — see FORESIGHT 2

3 *cap* the being worshipped as the creator and ruler of the universe — see DEITY 2

provident *adj* **1** careful in the management of money or resources — see FRUGAL

2 having or showing awareness of and preparation for the future — see FORESIGHTED

providential *adj* coming or happening by good luck especially unexpectedly — see FORTUNATE 1

province *n* a region of activity, knowledge, or influence — see FIELD 2

provincial *adj* not broad or open in views or opinions — see NARROW 1

provincial *n* an awkward or simple person especially from a small town or the country — see HICK

provision *n* **1** something upon which the carrying out of an agreement or offer depends — see CONDITION 2

2 provisions *pl* substances intended to be eaten — see FOOD

provision *vb* to provide food or meals for — see FEED 1

provisional *adj* intended to last, continue, or serve for a limited time — see TEMPORARY 1

proviso *n* something upon which the carrying out of an agreement or offer depends — see CONDITION 2

provocation *n* **1** something that arouses a strong response from another ⟨Dad only gets angry from the greatest of *provocations*⟩

syn excitement, incitement, instigation, stimulant, stimulation, stimulus

rel encouragement, goad, incentive, inducement, jog, prod, spur; induction, inspiration, motivation; aggravation, annoyance, bother, exasperation, frustration, hassle, headache, irritant, nuisance, peeve, pest

near ant subduing

2 something that arouses action or activity — see IMPULSE

provocative *adj* serving or likely to arouse a strong reaction ⟨a *provocative* editorial that sparked a heated discussion⟩

syn exciting, inciting, instigating, piquing, provoking, stimulating

rel explosive, fiery, incendiary, inflammatory, triggering; inducing, inspirational, inspiring, motivating, jeering, taunting, teasing; activating, energizing, galvanizing, quickening, vitalizing; angering, enraging, maddening, upsetting; aggravating, annoying, bothersome, exasperating, galling, irksome, irritating, pesky, vexatious, vexing

near ant subduing

provoke *vb* **1** to rouse to strong feeling or action ⟨his teasing finally *provoked* her to anger⟩ ⟨a strong chilling breeze *provoked* the picnickers to move inside⟩

syn arouse, encourage, excite, fire (up), incite, instigate, move, pique, stimulate, stir

rel fan, inflame, kindle, trigger; activate, energize, galvanize, induce, inspire, motivate, quicken, vitalize; abet, ferment, foment, raise, whip (up); anger, enrage, madden, upset; jeer, taunt, tease; aggravate, annoy, bother, exasperate, gall, get, irritate, vex

near ant calm, soothe, subdue, tranquilize (*also* tranquillize)

2 to cause or encourage the development of — see INCITE 1

provoking *adj* serving or likely to arouse a strong reaction — see PROVOCATIVE

proximity *n* the state or condition of being near ⟨the *proximity* of the curtains to the fireplace was a cause of concern to the safety inspector⟩

syn closeness, contiguity, immediacy, nearness

rel abutment, juxtaposition

ant distance, remoteness

proxy *n* a person who acts or does business for another — see AGENT 2

prude *n* a person who is greatly concerned with seemly behavior and morals especially regarding sexual matters ⟨it's not true that only a *prude* would object to being pressured for physical intimacy⟩

syn moralist, puritan

rel goody-goody; fuddy-duddy, old maid, prig, spoilsport

near ant libertarian, libertine

prudence *n* the ability to make intelligent decisions especially in everyday matters — see COMMON SENSE

prudent *adj* **1** having or showing good judgment and restraint especially in conduct or speech — see DISCREET

2 suitable for bringing about a desired result under the circumstances — see EXPEDIENT

prudery *n* a tendency to care a great deal about seemly behavior and morals especially in sexual matters ⟨such *prudery* regarding artistic depictions of the nude has no place on a college campus⟩

syn prudishness, puritanism

rel priggishness, primness; morality, virtue

near ant libertarianism

prudish *adj* given to or marked by very conservative standards regarding personal behavior or morals — see STRAITLACED

prudishness *n* a tendency to care a great deal about seemly behavior and morals especially in sexual matters — see PRUDERY

prune *vb* to make (as hair) shorter with or as if with the use of shears — see CLIP

¹pry *vb* **1** to raise, move, or pull apart with or as if with a lever ⟨it took some effort to *pry* up the trap door⟩

syn jimmy, lever, prize

rel elevate, hoist, lift, uplift; break, break up, detach, disengage, disjoin, divide, part, pull, separate; shift

near ant connect, join

2 to draw out by force or with effort — see EXTRACT

²pry *vb* to interest oneself in what is not one's concern — see INTERFERE

prying *adj* **1** interested in what is not one's own business — see CURIOUS 1

2 thrusting oneself where one is not welcome or invited — see INTRUSIVE

psalm *n* a religious song — see HYMN

psalmody *n* a book of hymns — see HYMNAL

pseudo *adj* lacking in natural or spontaneous quality — see ARTIFICIAL 1

pseudonym *n* a fictitious or assumed name ⟨the most notorious serial killer of the 19th century remains known only by the *pseudonym* of Jack the Ripper⟩

syn alias

rel nom de plume, pen name; appellation, designation; misnomer; epithet, nickname, sobriquet (*also* soubriquet)

pshaw *interj* how surprising, doubtful, or unbelievable — see NO

psyche *n* an immaterial force within a human being thought to give the body life, energy, and power — see SOUL 1

psychological *also* **psychologic** *adj* of or relating to the mind — see MENTAL 1

psychopath *n* a person judged to be legally or medically insane — see LUNATIC 1

psychotic *n* a person judged to be legally or medically insane — see LUNATIC 1

pub *n* a place of business where alcoholic beverages are sold to be consumed on the premises — see BARROOM

public *adj* **1** not known by only a select few ⟨it was *public* knowledge that they were expecting a baby⟩

syn open

rel general, popular; unclassified, well-known; advertised, aired, announced, broadcast, declared, disclosed, divulged, heralded, posted, proclaimed, promulgated, publicized, published, spotlighted; current, prevalent, rife, widespread; communal, shared; reported, reputed, rumored

near ant classified; unadvertised, unannounced, undisclosed; clandestine, collusive, conspiratorial, covert; surreptitious, undercover, underhand, underhanded; intimate, personal; concealed, repressed, reserved, silenced, stifled, suppressed, withheld; recanted, retracted, revoked
ant confidential, private, privy, secret

2 freely available for use or participation by all — see OPEN 2

3 of or relating to a nation — see NATIONAL

4 held by or applicable to a majority of the people — see GENERAL 3

5 used or done by a number of people as a group — see COLLECTIVE

public *n* human beings in general — see PEOPLE 1

public house *n* **1** a place that provides rooms and usually a public dining room for overnight guests — see HOTEL

2 *chiefly British* a place of business where alcoholic beverages are sold to be consumed on the premises — see BARROOM

publicity *n* newsworthy information released to the media that is designed to gain public attention or support for a person, business, or cause ⟨an endless flow of *publicity* for our charity event resulted in a great turnout⟩
syn ballyhoo
rel ad, advertisement, commercial, message, plug, promotion, spot, word; banner, bill, billboard, placard, poster, sign; advertising, marketing, propaganda; pronouncement, publication, release; broadcast, bulletin, dispatch, newscast, report, story; testimonial, write-up

publicize *vb* **1** to provide publicity for ⟨the movie studios widely *publicized* their summer blockbusters⟩
syn ballyhoo, plug, promote, tout
rel advertise; push; acclaim, hail, laud, praise; recommend, review; announce, broadcast, publish

2 to make known openly or publicly — see ANNOUNCE

public servant *n* **1** a person who holds a public office — see OFFICIAL

2 a worker in a government agency — see BUREAUCRAT

publish *vb* **1** to produce and release for distribution in printed form ⟨our local animal shelter *publishes* a newsletter⟩
syn get out, issue, print
rel serialize; contribute, edit, syndicate; manufacture, produce; distribute, market
near ant censor, suppress

2 to make known openly or publicly — see ANNOUNCE

puck *n* an imaginary being usually having a small human form and magical powers — see FAIRY

puddle *n* a small often deep body of water — see ¹POOL

pudginess *n* the condition of having an excess of body fat — see CORPULENCE

pudgy *adj* having an excess of body fat — see FAT 1

puerile *adj* **1** having or showing the annoying qualities (as silliness) associated with children — see CHILDISH

2 lacking in adult experience or maturity — see CALLOW

3 lacking in seriousness or maturity — see GIDDY 1

puff *n* a slight or gentle movement of air — see BREEZE 1

puff *vb* to breathe hard, quickly, or with difficulty — see GASP

pugilist *n* one that engages in the sport of fighting with the fists — see BOXER

pugnacious *adj* feeling or displaying eagerness to fight — see BELLIGERENT

pugnacity *n* an inclination to fight or quarrel — see BELLIGERENCE

puissance *n* the ability to exert effort for the accomplishment of a task — see POWER 2

puissant *adj* having great power or influence — see IMPORTANT 2

pule *vb* to utter feeble plaintive cries — see WHIMPER

pull *n* **1** the act or an instance of applying force on something so that it moves in the direction of the force ⟨I gave the door such a *pull* that when it suddenly opened, I nearly fell backwards⟩
syn draw, haul, jerk, pluck, tug, wrench, yank
rel drag, tow; hitch, jerk, twitch; grab, snatch
near ant heave, shove, thrust
ant push

2 the power to direct the thinking or behavior of others usually indirectly — see INFLUENCE 1

pull *vb* **1** to cause to follow by applying steady force on ⟨a team of horses *pulling* a heavy wagon⟩
syn drag, draw, hale, haul, lug, tow, tug
rel attract; jerk, yank; carry, convey, ferry, move, transport
near ant shove, thrust
ant drive, propel, push

2 to draw out by force or with effort — see EXTRACT

3 to injure by overuse, misuse, or pressure — see STRAIN 1

pull (out) *vb* to leave a place often for another — see GO 2

pulp *vb* to cause to become a pulpy mass — see CRUSH 1

pulpiness *n* the quality or state of being full of juice — see SUCCULENCE

pulpy *adj* **1** full of juice — see JUICY

2 giving easily to the touch — see SOFT 3

pulsate *vb* to expand and contract in a rhythmic manner ⟨the heart muscle *pulsates* regularly to pump blood⟩
syn beat, palpitate, pit-a-pat, pitter-patter, pulse, throb
rel fluctuate, oscillate, vibrate; quiver, tremble

pulsation *n* a rhythmic expanding and contracting ⟨you should press against the

---

syn synonym(s)   *rel* related words
ant antonym(s)   *near ant* near antonym(s)

artery in your wrist and count the *pulsations* to calculate your heart rate⟩

syn beat, palpitation, pulse, throb

rel fluctuation, oscillation, vibration; quiver, tremble, tremor

pulse *n* a rhythmic expanding and contracting — see PULSATION

pulse *vb* to expand and contract in a rhythmic manner — see PULSATE

pulverize *vb* 1 to bring to a complete end the physical soundness, existence, or usefulness of — see DESTROY 1

2 to reduce to fine particles — see POWDER

puma *n* a large tawny cat of the wild — see COUGAR

pummel *vb* to strike repeatedly — see BEAT 1

pump *vb* 1 to make short up-and-down movements — see NOD

2 to put a series of questions to — see EXAMINE 1

3 to remove (liquid) gradually or completely — see DRAIN 1

¹**punch** *n* 1 the quality of an utterance that provokes interest and produces an effect ⟨the real *punch* of the speech came in its closing lines⟩

syn cogency, effectiveness, force, forcefulness, impact, point

rel payoff; importance, significance; appeal, attraction, charm, fascination

2 active strength of body or mind — see VIGOR 1

3 a hard strike with a part of the body or an instrument — see ¹BLOW

²**punch** *n* a mark or small hole made by a pointed instrument — see PRICK 1

punch *vb* 1 to deliver a blow to (someone or something) usually in a strong vigorous manner — see HIT 1

2 to make a hole or series of holes in — see PERFORATE

3 to urge, push, or force onward — see DRIVE 1

puncheon *n* an enclosed wooden vessel for holding beverages — see CASK

punctual *adj* done, carried out, or given without delay — see PROMPT 1

punctuality *n* the quality or habit of arriving on time — see PROMPTITUDE

puncture *n* a mark or small hole made by a pointed instrument — see PRICK 1

puncture *vb* 1 to make a hole or series of holes in — see PERFORATE

2 to penetrate or hold (something) with a pointed object — see IMPALE

pungency *n* 1 a harsh or sharp quality — see EDGE 1

2 the quality or state of being stimulating to the mind or senses — see PIQUANCY

pungent *adj* 1 having a powerfully stimulating odor or flavor — see SHARP 3

2 marked by the use of wit that is intended to cause hurt feelings — see SARCASTIC

3 sharp and pleasantly stimulating to the mind or senses — see PIQUANT

puniness *n* the quality or state of being little in size — see SMALLNESS

punish *vb* to inflict a penalty on for a fault or crime ⟨the child was *punished* for breaking dishes on purpose⟩ ⟨if caught, the thief will be severely *punished*⟩

syn castigate, chasten, chastise, correct, discipline, penalize

rel assess, charge, dock, fine, impose, levy, mulct; convict, sentence; condemn, damn, denounce; criticize, reprove; wreak

near ant forfeit; get off, ransom; release; commute, reprieve; absolve, acquit, exculpate, exonerate, vindicate

ant excuse, pardon, spare

punisher *n* one who inflicts punishment in return for an injury or offense — see NEMESIS 1

punishment *n* suffering, loss, or hardship imposed in response to a crime or offense ⟨the child's *punishment* was confiscation of his toys for a day⟩

syn castigation, chastisement, correction, desert, discipline, nemesis, penalty, wrath

rel reprisal, retaliation, retribution, revenge, vengeance; assessment, charge, fine, mulct; example, sentence; confinement, imprisonment, incarceration; condemnation, damnation, denouncement; criticism, reproof

near ant amnesty, indemnity, pardon, parole; acquittal, exculpation, exoneration, vindication; exemption, immunity, impunity; release; commutation, reprieve; absolution, forgiveness, remission, remitment; condonation, disregard, overlooking

punitive *adj* inflicting, involving, or serving as punishment ⟨any misbehavior was immediately met with a *punitive* response⟩ ⟨the company had to pay a million dollars in *punitive* damages⟩

syn castigating, chastening, chastising, correcting, correctional, corrective, disciplinary, disciplining, penal, penalizing

rel retaliatory, retributive, retributory, revengeful; vengeful, wrathful

near ant compensatory; acquitting, exculpating, exculpatory, exonerating, vindicating; absolving, condoning, pardoning, remitting; commuting, reprieving

punk *adj* 1 falling short of a standard — see BAD 1

2 extremely unsatisfactory — see WRETCHED 1

3 temporarily suffering from a disorder of the body — see SICK 1

punk *n* a violent, brutal person who is often a member of an organized gang — see HOODLUM

puny *adj* of a size that is less than average — see SMALL 1

pupil *n* 1 one who attends a school — see STUDENT

2 one who follows the opinions or teachings of another — see FOLLOWER

puppet *n* 1 a small figure often of a human being used especially as a child's plaything — see DOLL 1

2 one that is or can be used to further the purposes of another — see PAWN 1

purchasable *adj* open to improper influence and especially bribery — see VENAL

purchase *vb* to get possession of (something) by giving money in exchange for — see BUY

pure *adj* **1** free from added matter ⟨I'm allergic to any jewelry that isn't *pure* silver⟩ ⟨the solution must be kept *pure* for the experiment to work⟩

syn absolute, fine, neat, plain, purified, refined, straight, unadulterated, unalloyed, undiluted, unmixed

rel clarified, filtered, refined; clean, uncontaminated, uncorrupted, undefiled, unpolluted, untainted; rendered, tried; concentrated, full-bodied, strong; uncombined

near ant befouled, besmirched, contaminated, corrupted, debased, defiled, fouled, polluted, soiled, spoiled, sullied, tainted; amalgamated, blended, coalesced, combined, commingled, compounded, incorporated, intermingled, intermixed, merged, mingled; conjoined, fused, joined, linked, united; cheapened, doctored, watered (down)

ant adulterated, alloyed, diluted, impure, mixed

2 free from any trace of the coarse or indecent — see CHASTE

3 free from sin — see INNOCENT 1

4 having no exceptions or restrictions — see ABSOLUTE 2

purebred *adj* of unmixed ancestry ⟨that horse is a *purebred* Arabian⟩

syn full-blooded, pedigreed, thoroughbred

rel inbred

near ant crossbred, crossed, hybridized, interbred, outcrossed

ant hybrid, mixed, mongrel

purely *adv* with purity of thought and deed ⟨the devout girl vowed to live her life *purely* and in the service of God⟩

syn chastely, innocently; morally, righteously; modestly, virtuously

rel decently, decorously, properly; priggishly, primly, prudishly

near ant indecently, obscenely, vulgarly; lasciviously, lewdly, lustfully

ant evilly, immorally, impurely, sinfully, wickedly

purge *vb* to free from moral guilt or blemish especially ceremonially — see PURIFY 1

purification *n* the act or fact of freeing from sin or moral guilt ⟨some people must undergo a ritual *purification* after certain activities⟩

syn cleansing, sanctification

rel rebirth, regeneration, restoration; grace, redemption, salvation; absolution, forgiveness, remission; acquittal, clearance, clearing, exoneration, vindication; atonement, expiation

near ant blasphemy, defilement, desecration, profanation, violation; corruption, debasement, perversion; contamination, pollution, sullying, tarnishing

purified *adj* free from added matter — see PURE 1

purify *vb* **1** to free from moral guilt or blemish especially ceremonially ⟨Catholics go to confession to be *purified*⟩

syn cleanse, purge, sanctify

rel amend, improve, refine; heal, regenerate, restore; elevate, ennoble, uplift; absolve, acquit, clear, exonerate, vindicate

near ant corrupt, debase, debauch, defile, degrade, demean, deprave, pervert, stain, warp; poison, profane, prostitute; sully, tarnish

2 to remove usually visible impurities from — see CLARIFY 1

puritan *n* a person who is greatly concerned with seemly behavior and morality especially regarding sexual matters — see PRUDE

puritanical *adj* given to or marked by very conservative standards regarding personal behavior or morals — see STRAITLACED

puritanism *n* a tendency to care a great deal about seemly behavior and morals especially in sexual matters — see PRUDERY

purity *n* the quality or state of being morally pure — see CHASTITY

purlieus *n pl* the area around a city — see ENVIRONS 1

purloin *vb* to take (something) without right and with an intent to keep — see STEAL 1

purloiner *n* one who steals — see THIEF

purport *n* the idea that is conveyed or intended to be conveyed to the mind by language, symbol, or action — see MEANING 1

purpose *n* **1** something that one hopes or intends to accomplish — see GOAL

2 the action for which a person or thing is specially fitted or used or for which a thing exists — see ROLE

purposeful *adj* **1** fully committed to achieving a goal — see DETERMINED 1

2 made, given, or done with full awareness of what one is doing — see INTENTIONAL

purposefully *adv* with full awareness of what one is doing — see INTENTIONALLY

purposefulness *n* firm or unwavering adherence to one's purpose — see DETERMINATION 1

purposely *adv* with full awareness of what one is doing — see INTENTIONALLY

purr *n* a monotonous sound like that of an insect in motion — see HUM

purse *n* a container for carrying money and small personal items ⟨I left my *purse* at home, so I can't buy anything after all⟩

syn bag, handbag, pocketbook

rel billfold, wallet; compact, vanity; poke, pouch, sack; backpack, haversack, knapsack, rucksack

pursue *vb* **1** to go after or on the track of — see FOLLOW 2

2 to go in search of — see SEEK 1

---

syn synonym(s)   *rel* related words
ant antonym(s)   *near ant* near antonym(s)

pursuing *n* the act of going after or in the tracks of another — see PURSUIT

pursuit *n* the act of going after or in the tracks of another ⟨the constant *pursuit* of the rock band by a horde of screaming fans as they roamed about the city⟩
syn chase, chasing, dogging, following, hounding, pursuing, shadowing, tagging, tailing, tracing, tracking, trailing
rel tagging along; path, track, trail; search, seeking

push *vb* 1 to apply force to (someone or something) so that it moves in front of one ⟨I had to *push* my damaged bike all the way home⟩
syn drive, propel, shove, thrust
rel impel, move; bear (down), compress, depress, jam, pressure, squash, squeeze, weigh (upon); bulldoze, compel, force, lean (on *or* against), muscle, ram
2 to force one's way — see PRESS 4

pushover *n* something that is easy to do — see CINCH

pusillanimous *adj* having or showing a shameful lack of courage — see COWARDLY

¹puss *n slang* the front part of the head — see FACE 1

²puss *n* a small domestic animal known for catching mice — see CAT 1

pussy *n* a small domestic animal known for catching mice — see CAT 1

pussyfoot *vb* 1 to avoid giving a definite answer or position — see EQUIVOCATE
2 to move about in a sly or secret manner — see SNEAK 1

put *vb* 1 to arrange something in a certain spot or position — see PLACE 1
2 to convey in appropriate or telling terms — see PHRASE
3 to decide the size, amount, number, or distance of (something) without actual measurement — see ESTIMATE 2
4 to establish or apply as a charge or penalty — see IMPOSE

put by *vb* to put (something of future use or value) in a safe or secret place — see HOARD

put–down *n* 1 an act or expression showing scorn and usually intended to hurt another's feelings — see INSULT
2 the act of making a person or a thing seem little or unimportant — see DEPRECIATION

put down *vb* 1 to express scornfully one's low opinion of — see DECRY 1
2 to make a written note of — see RECORD 1
3 to put (someone or something) on a list — see ¹LIST 2
4 to put a stop to (something) by the use of force — see QUELL 1

put in *vb* to put or set into the ground to grow — see PLANT

put off *vb* 1 to assign to a later time — see POSTPONE
2 to rid oneself of (a garment) — see REMOVE 1

put–on *adj* lacking in natural or spontaneous quality — see ARTIFICIAL 1

put–on *n* a display of emotion or behavior that is insincere or intended to deceive — see MASQUERADE

put on *vb* 1 to place on one's person ⟨I *put on* a coat and shoes to go outside⟩
syn don, slip (on *or* into), throw (on)
rel apparel, array, attire, bedeck, bedizen, bundle up, caparison, clothe, doll up, dress, garb, rig, robe, suit, trick, uniform; overdress
near ant disrobe, strip, undress
ant doff, remove, take off
2 to describe or express in too strong terms — see OVERSTATE
3 to present a false appearance of — see FEIGN

put out *vb* 1 to bring to bear especially forcefully or effectively — see EXERT
2 to cause to cease burning — see EXTINGUISH 1
3 to disturb the peace of mind of (someone) especially by repeated disagreeable acts — see IRRITATE 1

putrefaction *n* the process by which dead organic matter separates into simpler substances — see CORRUPTION 1

putrefied *adj* having undergone organic breakdown — see ROTTEN 1

putrefy *vb* to go through decomposition — see DECAY 1

putrid *adj* having undergone organic breakdown — see ROTTEN 1

putter (around) *vb* to spend time in aimless activity — see FIDDLE (AROUND)

putterer *n* a person who regularly or occasionally engages in an activity without being or becoming an expert at it — see AMATEUR

put up *vb* 1 to fix in an upright position — see ERECT 1
2 to form by putting together parts or materials — see BUILD
3 to offer for sale to the public — see MARKET
4 to provide with living quarters or shelter — see HOUSE 1

puzzle *n* something hard to understand or explain — see MYSTERY

puzzle *vb* to throw into a state of mental uncertainty — see CONFUSE 1

puzzle (out) *vb* to find an answer for through reasoning — see SOLVE

puzzlement *n* 1 a state of mental uncertainty — see CONFUSION 1
2 something hard to understand or explain — see MYSTERY

pygmy *adj* of a size that is less than average — see SMALL 1

pygmy *n* a living thing much smaller than others of its kind — see DWARF 1

quack *n* one who makes false claims of identity or expertise — see IMPOSTOR

quadrangle *n* an open space wholly or partly enclosed (as by buildings or walls) — see COURT 2

quaff *n* the portion of a serving of a beverage that is swallowed at one time — see DRINK 2

quaff *vb* to swallow in liquid form — see DRINK 1

quail *vb* 1 to draw back in fear, pain, or disgust — see FLINCH

2 to draw back or crouch down in fearful submission — see COWER

quaint *adj* 1 different from the ordinary in a way that causes curiosity or suspicion — see ODD 2

2 pleasantly reminiscent of an earlier time — see OLD-FASHIONED 1

quake *n* a shaking of the earth — see EARTHQUAKE

quake *vb* to make a series of small irregular or violent movements — see SHAKE 1

quaking *adj* marked by or given to small uncontrollable bodily movements — see SHAKY 1

qualification *n* 1 a skill, an ability, or knowledge that makes a person able to do a particular job ⟨the fashion firm was looking for an applicant who could list superior sewing skills among his or her *qualifications*⟩

syn capability, credentials, stuff

rel command, expertise, mastery, proficiency; ability, capacity, competence, competency, facility, faculty; flair, genius, gift, talent, forte, specialty; fitness, suitability, suitableness; makings, potentiality

2 something upon which the carrying out of an agreement or offer depends — see CONDITION 2

qualified *adj* having the required skills for an acceptable level of performance — see COMPETENT

qualify *vb* 1 to limit the meaning of (as a noun) ⟨*qualifying* the noun "adventure" in the title of your story with a descriptive adjective would make it more attention-grabbing⟩

syn modify, restrict

rel alter, distort, twist; narrow; compare, conjugate, decline, inflect

near ant broaden, expand, widen

2 to make competent (as by training, skill, or ability) for a particular office or function ⟨raising five children has *qualified* her to be an advice columnist on parenting⟩

syn equip, fit, prepare, ready, season

rel accustom, adapt, adjust, condition, groom, habituate, shape, tailor, train; authorize, entitle; empower, enable

3 to give a right to — see ENTITLE 1

4 to give official or legal power to — see AUTHORIZE 1

quality *n* 1 degree of excellence ⟨we expect a high *quality* of service in such a fancy restaurant⟩

syn caliber (*or* calibre), class, grade, rate

rel hallmark, standard; mark; footing, place, position, rank, standing, stature, status

2 high position within society — see RANK 2

3 something that sets apart an individual from others of the same kind — see CHARACTERISTIC

qualm *n* an uneasy feeling about the rightness of what one is doing or going to do ⟨she had no *qualms* about selling her old term papers to other students, even though it was against the academic honor code⟩

syn compunction, misgiving, scruple

rel conscience; distrust, doubt, mistrust, suspicion, uncertainty; qualmishness, unease, uneasiness; reluctance, unwillingness; demur, objection, protest; guilt, regret, remorse, self-reproach; shame; contrition, penitence, repentance

near ant aplomb, assurance, certainty, certitude, confidence, conviction, self-assurance, self-confidence, sureness

qualmish *adj* affected with nausea — see NAUSEOUS

qualmishness *n* 1 a disturbed condition of the stomach in which one feels like vomiting — see NAUSEA 1

2 the tendency to be or state of being squeamish — see DELICACY 3

quandary *n* a situation in which one has to choose between two or more equally unsatisfactory choices — see DILEMMA

quantity *n* 1 a considerable amount — see LOT 2

2 a given or particular mass or aggregate of matter — see AMOUNT

quarrel *n* an often noisy or angry expression of differing opinions — see ARGUMENT 1

quarrel *vb* to express different opinions about something often angrily — see ARGUE 2

quarreler *or* **quarreller** *n* a person who takes part in a dispute — see DISPUTANT

quarrelsome *adj* 1 feeling or displaying eagerness to fight — see BELLIGERENT

2 given to arguing — see ARGUMENTATIVE 1

---

syn synonym(s)   *rel* related words
ant antonym(s)   *near ant* near antonym(s)

quarry *n* an animal that is hunted or killed — see PREY

quarter *n* 1 an area (as of a city) set apart for some purpose or having some special feature — see DISTRICT

2 kind, gentle, or compassionate treatment especially towards someone who is undeserving of it — see MERCY 1

3 the place where someone is assigned to stand or remain — see STATION 1

4 **quarters** *pl* the place where one lives — see HOME 1

quarter *vb* to provide with living quarters or shelter — see HOUSE 1

¹**quash** *vb* to put a stop to (something) by the use of force — see QUELL 1

²**quash** *vb* to put an end to by formal action — see ABOLISH

quaver *vb* to sing with the alternation of two musical tones — see WARBLE

quavery *adj* marked by or given to small uncontrollable bodily movements — see SHAKY 1

quay *n* a structure used by boats and ships for taking on or landing cargo and passengers — see DOCK

queasiness *n* 1 a disturbed condition of the stomach in which one feels like vomiting — see NAUSEA 1

2 the tendency to be or state of being squeamish — see DELICACY 3

queasy *also* **queazy** *adj* affected with nausea — see NAUSEOUS

queenly *adj* fit for or worthy of a royal ruler — see MONARCHICAL

queer *adj* 1 affected with nausea — see NAUSEOUS

2 different from the ordinary in a way that causes curiosity or suspicion — see ODD 2

3 noticeably different from what is generally found or experienced — see UNUSUAL 1

queerish *adj* 1 affected with nausea — see NAUSEOUS

2 different from the ordinary in a way that causes curiosity or suspicion — see ODD 2

queerness *n* a disturbed condition of the stomach in which one feels like vomiting — see NAUSEA 1

quell *vb* 1 to put a stop to (something) by the use of force ⟨the National Guard was called in to help *quell* the late-night disturbances downtown⟩

syn clamp down (on), crack down (on), crush, put down, quash, repress, silence, snuff (out), squash, squelch, subdue, suppress

rel douse, extinguish, put out, quench; smother, stifle, strangle; annihilate, destroy, smash; exterminate, obliterate, wipe out; conquer, overcome, overwhelm, subjugate, vanquish

near ant abet, aid, assist, help, support; incite, instigate, provoke, stir; advance, encourage, foster, further, promote

2 to stop the noise or speech of — see SILENCE 1

quench *vb* 1 to cause to cease burning — see EXTINGUISH 1

2 to put a complete end to (a physical need or desire) — see SATISFY 1

quencher *n* a liquid suitable for drinking — see DRINK 1

querulous *adj* given to complaining a lot — see FUSSY 1

query *n* an act or instance of asking for information — see QUESTION 2

query *vb* 1 to demand proof of the truth or rightness of — see CHALLENGE 1

2 to put a question or questions to — see ASK 1

3 to put a series of questions to — see EXAMINE 1

quest *n* an act or process of looking carefully or thoroughly for someone or something — see SEARCH

quest *vb* 1 to ask for (something) earnestly or with authority — see DEMAND 1

2 to go in search of — see SEEK 1

3 to make a request for — see ASK (FOR) 1

question *n* 1 an interrogative expression often used to test knowledge ⟨because I have missed so many classes, I had a hard time answering every *question* on today's surprise quiz⟩

syn problem

rel brainteaser, conundrum, poser, puzzle, quiz, riddle, stickler, stumper

near ant answer, response, solution

2 an act or instance of asking for information ⟨after reading the brief statement to the reporters, the lawyer ended the press conference by saying, "No more *questions*, please"⟩ ⟨the dozens of *questions* researched by the reference librarians⟩

syn call, inquiry, request, query

rel questionnaire, survey; inquisition, interrogating, interrogation, questioning

3 a feeling or declaration of disapproval or dissent — see OBJECTION

4 a major object of interest or concern (as in a discussion or artistic composition) — see MATTER 1

question *vb* 1 to demand proof of the truth or rightness of — see CHALLENGE 1

2 to give serious and careful thought to — see PONDER

3 to have no trust or confidence in — see DISTRUST

4 to put a question or questions to — see ASK 1

5 to put a series of questions to — see EXAMINE 1

questionable *adj* 1 giving good reason for being doubted, questioned, or challenged — see DOUBTFUL 2

2 not likely to be true or to occur — see IMPROBABLE

3 open to question or dispute — see DEBATABLE 1

questioner *n* a person who is always ready to doubt or question the truth or existence of something — see SKEPTIC

questioning *adj* inclined to doubt or question claims — see SKEPTICAL 1

queue *n* a series of persons or things arranged one behind another — see LINE 1

quibble *vb* to make often peevish criticisms or objections about matters that are minor, unimportant, or irrelevant ⟨he spent the entire evening *quibbling* about the historical inaccuracies in the television series on World War II⟩

syn carp, cavil, fuss, nitpick

rel criticize, fault; beef, bellyache, complain, crab, croak, gripe, grouse, growl, grumble, moan, squawk, wail, whine, yammer; murmur, mutter

phrases split hairs

near ant applaud, commend, compliment, praise, recommend; approve, back, endorse (*also* indorse), support

quick *adj* **1** having or showing the ability to respond without delay or hesitation ⟨she was a *quick* wit, always ready with a pun or joke when the moment called for one⟩

syn alacritous, alert, expeditious, prompt, ready, willing

rel receptive, responsive; immediate, instant, instantaneous, summary; fast, hit-and-run, rapid, speedy, swift; eager, keen, sharp; apt, clever, smart

near ant unresponsive; dull, indolent, laggard, lazy, logy, slothful, slow, sluggish, tardy; dormant, idle, inactive, inert

2 having or showing quickness of mind — see INTELLIGENT 1

3 moving, proceeding, or acting with great speed — see FAST 1

quick *adv* with great speed — see FAST 1

quick *n* the seat of one's deepest thoughts and emotions — see CORE 1

quicken *vb* **1** to cause to move or proceed fast or faster — see HURRY 1

2 to give life, vigor, or spirit to — see ANIMATE

quickly *adv* with great speed — see FAST 1

quickness *n* a high rate of movement or performance — see SPEED

quick–tempered *adj* easily irritated or annoyed — see IRRITABLE

quick–witted *adj* having or showing quickness of mind — see INTELLIGENT 1

quiescence *n* **1** a state of temporary inactivity — see ABEYANCE

2 lack of action or activity — see INACTION

quiescent *adj* slow to move or act — see INACTIVE 1

quiet *adj* **1** free from disturbing noise or uproar ⟨left the din of the rock concert and went to a *quiet* restaurant where we could hear one another talk⟩

syn calm, hushed, peaceful, restful, serene, still, stilly, tranquil

rel noiseless, silent, soundless; speechless, wordless; dead, motionless, quiescent; muffled, muted, quieted

near ant crazy, tempestuous, wild

ant boisterous, clamorous, clattery, deafening, loud, noisy, raucous, rip-roaring, roistering, romping, rowdy, tumultuous, uproarious, woolly (*also* wooly)

2 not excessively showy ⟨she decided to wear a *quiet* business suit to the interview instead of her blue satin party dress⟩

syn conservative, muted, restrained, subdued, toned-down, understated, unpretentious

rel appropriate, fit, fitting, proper, suitable; modest, plain, simple, unadorned; inconspicuous, unobtrusive; tasteful; drab, mousy (*or* mousey); practical, sensible

near ant meretricious; graceless, inelegant, tacky, tasteless, vulgar; baroque, fancy, frilly, gilded, ornate, rococo; over-decorated, overdone, overwrought

ant flamboyant, flashy, garish, gaudy, glitzy, loud, ostentatious, splashy, swank (*or* swanky), tawdry

3 free from storms or physical disturbance — see CALM 1

4 hidden from view — see SECLUDED

5 mostly or entirely without sound — see SILENT 3

6 not loud in pitch or volume — see SOFT 1

quiet *n* **1** a state of freedom from storm or disturbance — see CALM

2 the near or complete absence of sound — see SILENCE 2

quiet *adv* without motion — see STILL 1

quiet *vb* **1** to become still and orderly ⟨told his rowdy class to *quiet* down during the lesson⟩

syn calm (down), cool, hush, settle (down)

rel relax, tranquilize (*also* tranquillize), unwind

near ant agitate, discompose, disrupt, disturb, provoke, rile, ruffle, stir; annoy, irritate

ant act up, carry on, cut up

2 to free from distress or disturbance — see CALM 1

quiet (down) *vb* to stop talking — see SHUT UP

quieted *adj* mostly or entirely without sound — see SILENT 3

quieting *adj* tending to calm the emotions and relieve stress — see SOOTHING 1

quietly *adv* without motion — see STILL 1

quietness *n* **1** a state of freedom from storm or disturbance — see CALM

2 the near or complete absence of sound — see SILENCE 2

quietude *n* **1** a state of freedom from storm or disturbance — see CALM

2 the near or complete absence of sound — see SILENCE 2

quietus *n* **1** a freeing from an obligation or responsibility — see RELEASE 1

2 the permanent stopping of all the vital bodily activities — see DEATH 1

quintessence *n* **1** the most perfect type or example ⟨the Parthenon in Greece was considered the *quintessence* of the perfectly proportioned building⟩

syn beau ideal, classic, epitome, exemplar, ideal, perfection

---

rel archetype, model, prototype; paradigm, standard; nonpareil, paragon; embodiment, incarnation, personification; acme, height, last word, ultimate, zenith
2 the quality or qualities that make a thing what it is — see ESSENCE

quintessential *adj* constituting, serving as, or worthy of being a pattern to be imitated — see MODEL

quip *n* something said or done to cause laughter — see JOKE 1

quip *vb* to make jokes — see JOKE

quirk *n* an odd or peculiar habit — see IDIOSYNCRASY

quirky *adj* different from the ordinary in a way that causes curiosity or suspicion — see ODD 2

quisling *n* one who betrays a trust or an allegiance — see TRAITOR

quit *adj* no longer burdened with something unpleasant or painful — see FREE 2

quit *vb* **1** to give up (a job or office) ⟨decided to *quit* his job at the fast-food restaurant⟩
syn leave, resign (from), retire (from), step down (from)
rel abandon, vacate; drop out (of), throw up
phrases give notice
near ant hire (out *or* on)
ant stay (at)
2 to stop doing (something) permanently ⟨told her it was high time she *quit* smoking⟩
syn discontinue, drop, give up, knock off, lay off (of)
rel break off, break up, close, conclude, end, expire, finish; pause, taper off; throw up; cease, desist, leave off
phrases have done (with)
near ant go, run on; hang on, hold on, persevere, persist; follow through, see out; resume; preserve, stay
ant carry on, continue, keep, keep up, maintain
3 to bring (as an action or operation) to an immediate end — see STOP 1
4 to cause to remain behind — see LEAVE 1
5 to cease resistance (as to another's arguments, demands, or control) — see YIELD 3
6 to come to an end — see CEASE 1
7 to give what is owed for — see PAY 2
8 to leave a place often for another — see GO 2
9 to manage the actions of (oneself) in a particular way — see BEHAVE

quite *adv* **1** to a full extent or degree — see FULLY 1
2 to some degree or extent — see FAIRLY

quittance *n* **1** a freeing from an obligation or responsibility — see RELEASE 1
2 payment to another for a loss or injury — see COMPENSATION 1

quitting *n* the act of leaving a place — see DEPARTURE

quiver *n* an instance of shaking involuntarily with fear or cold — see SHIVER 1

quiver *vb* to make a series of small irregular or violent movements — see SHAKE 1

quivering *n* a series of slight movements by a body back and forth or from side to side — see VIBRATION

quiz *vb* **1** to put a question or questions to — see ASK 1
2 to put a series of questions to — see EXAMINE 1

quiz *n* **1** a person who causes repeated emotional pain, distress, or annoyance to another — see TORMENTOR
2 a set of questions or problems designed to assess knowledge, skills, or intelligence — see EXAMINATION 1

quizzer *n* a person who causes repeated emotional pain, distress, or annoyance to another — see TORMENTOR

quizzical *adj* marked by or expressive of mild or good-natured teasing ⟨my puns are usually greeted with loud *quizzical* groans by my so-called friends⟩
syn bantering, chaffing, fooling, funning, jesting, joking, joshing, kidding, rallying, razzing, ribbing
rel bandying, quipping; deriding, derisive, derisory, jeering, mocking, ridiculing, taunting; contemptuous, sarcastic, scornful

quota *n* something belonging to, due to, or contributed by an individual member of a group — see SHARE 1

quotation *n* a passage referred to, repeated, or offered as an example ⟨the beautiful autumn day brought to mind this *quotation* from Thoreau: "So live in each season as it passes; breathe the air, drink the drink, taste the fruit, and resign yourself to the influences of each"⟩
syn citation, quote
rel allusion, reference; excerpt, extract; line, part, section

quote *n* a passage referred to, repeated, or offered as an example — see QUOTATION

quote *vb* **1** to give as an example ⟨I could *quote* to you a hundred instances in the past when you've lied to me⟩
syn adduce, cite, instance, mention
rel exemplify, represent; illustrate, refer (to); document, substantiate
2 to make reference to or speak about briefly but specifically — see MENTION 1
3 to say after another — see REPEAT 3

rabble *n* people looked down upon as ignorant and of the lowest class ⟨the crown prince was reminded that even the *rabble* of the realm deserved his attention and compassion⟩

syn proletariat, riffraff, scum, trash

rel dregs; herd, masses, mob, people, populace, public, rank and file; bourgeoisie, middle class, working class

near ant elect, establishment; gentlefolk, nobility

ant aristocracy, elite, gentry, society, upper class, upper crust

rabble–rouser *n* a person who stirs up public feelings especially of discontent — see AGITATOR

rabid *adj* **1** being very far from the center of public opinion — see EXTREME 2

2 feeling or showing anger — see ANGRY

3 marked by bursts of destructive force or intense activity — see VIOLENT 1

4 marked by great and often stressful excitement or activity — see FURIOUS 1

race *n* a group of persons who come from the same ancestor — see FAMILY 1

race *vb* **1** to engage in a contest — see COMPETE

2 to proceed or move quickly — see HURRY 2

raceway *n* an open man-made passageway for water — see CHANNEL 1

racial *adj* of, relating to, or reflecting the traits exhibited by a group of people with a common ancestry and culture ⟨humanitarian aid workers are often given special training to help them understand the *racial* differences between them and the people they will be serving⟩

syn ethnic, tribal

rel familial; folk; kin, kindred; cultural, multicultural, national

racialism *n* **1** the belief that certain races of people are by birth and nature superior to others — see RACISM 1

2 hatred of or discrimination against a person or persons based on their race — see RACISM 2

racialist *n* a person who believes that one race should control all others — see SUPREMACIST

racism *n* **1** the belief that certain races of people are by birth and nature superior to others ⟨Hitler's declaration of his belief in a "master race" was the first indication of the inherent *racism* of the Nazi movement⟩

syn racialism

rel apartheid, segregation; eugenics

near ant desegregation, integration

2 hatred of or discrimination against a person or persons based on their race ⟨the 1963 bombing of the Sixteenth Street Baptist Church in Birmingham, Alabama, was one of the most notorious incidents of *racism* that occurred during the civil rights movement of the 1960s⟩

syn prejudice, racialism

rel apartheid, jim crow, segregation; bigotry, intolerance, narrow-mindedness, narrowness

racist *n* a person who believes that one race should control all others — see SUPREMACIST

rack *vb* **1** to cause persistent suffering to — see AFFLICT

2 to injure by overuse, misuse, or pressure — see STRAIN 1

racket *n* **1** a scheme in which the victim is cheated out of his money after first gaining his trust — see CONFIDENCE GAME

2 loud, confused, and usually unharmonious sound — see NOISE 1

racketeer *n* a person who gets money from another by using force or threats ⟨the *racketeer* threatened to have his thugs vandalize the shop if the shopkeeper didn't pay him a monthly bribe⟩

syn blackmailer, extortioner, extortionist

rel crook, gangster, hoodlum, mafioso, mobster; bully, ruffian, thug; cheat, cheater, chiseler, gouger, gyp, hustler, profiteer, shark, sharper, swindler

racking *adj* intensely or unbearably painful — see EXCRUCIATING 1

rack up *vb* to gain (as points or runs in a game) as credit towards one's total number of points — see SCORE 2

racy *adj* **1** having much high-spirited energy and movement — see LIVELY 1

2 hinting at or intended to call to mind matters regarded as indecent — see SUGGESTIVE 1

radiance *n* **1** the quality or state of having or giving off light — see BRILLIANCE 1

2 the steady giving off of the form of radiation that makes vision possible — see LIGHT 1

radiant *adj* **1** having or being an outward sign of good feelings (as of love, confidence, or happiness) ⟨left the interview with a *radiant* smile on her face, confident she had gotten the job⟩ ⟨a *radiant* bride⟩

syn aglow, beaming, glowing, sunny

rel brilliant, dazzling, effulgent, gleaming, luminous, refulgent, shining, starry; blithe, blithesome, bright, cheerful, cheery, chipper, gay, gladsome, lightsome, merry, mirthful, optimistic, up-

---

beat; jocund, jovial, laughing; smiling; blooming, rosy

near ant flat, listless, stoic (*or* stoical), unemotional; dark, darkening, depressing, dismal, gloomy, glum, gray (*also* grey), melancholy, sullen; frowning, glaring, glowering, lowering (*also* louring), scowling

2 giving off or reflecting much light — see BRIGHT 1

radiate *vb* **1** to extend outwards from or as if from a central point ⟨the heat *radiating* from the fire⟩ ⟨the spokes of a bicycle wheel *radiate* from the hub towards the rim⟩

syn branch, diverge, fan (out)

rel diffuse, dispel, disperse, dissipate; fork, stem; divide, separate, split; scatter, splay, spread; arise, derive, emanate, flow, issue, proceed, spring

near ant approach, close in (on), near; center (on), centralize

ant concentrate, converge, focus, funnel, meet

2 to emit rays of light — see SHINE 1

radical *adj* **1** being very far from the center of public opinion — see EXTREME 2

2 not bound by traditional ways or beliefs — see LIBERAL 1

radical *n* a person who favors rapid and sweeping changes especially in laws and methods of government ⟨*radicals* staged large, violent protests in the hopes of toppling the government⟩

syn extremist, revolutionary, revolutionist

rel leftist, red; progressive, reformer; anarchist, subversive; agitator, insurgent, insurrectionist, rebel; secessionist, separatist

near ant conservative, reactionary, rightist, Tory

ant moderate

raffish *adj* lacking in refinement or good taste — see COARSE 2

raffishness *n* the quality or state of lacking refinement or good taste — see VULGARITY 1

raft *n* a considerable amount — see LOT 2

rage *n* **1** a state of wildly excited activity or emotion — see FRENZY

2 an intense emotional state of displeasure with someone or something — see ANGER

3 a practice or interest that is very popular for a short time — see FAD

rage *vb* **1** to express one's anger usually violently ⟨the bad call prompted the coach to *rage* about the refereeing, even throwing his clipboard at one referee⟩

syn bristle, fume, storm

rel blow up, flare (up), flip; bluster, carry on, fulminate, rampage, rant, rave, take on; burn, foam, seethe, smolder, steam; chafe, fret, stew

near ant allay, appease, pacify, soothe; check, collect, compose, contain, curb, hold in, rein, repress, restrain, smother, subdue, suppress; moderate, tone (down),

temper; ease, let up, relax; calm, cool, hush, quell, quiet, settle, still

2 to be excited or emotionally stirred up with anger — see BOIL 1

ragged *adj* **1** having an uneven edge or outline ⟨the Rocky Mountains cut an angular, *ragged* profile against the sky, in contrast to the rounded silhouette of the rolling, green Adirondack Mountains⟩

syn broken, craggy, jagged, scraggly, scraggy

rel saw-toothed, serrate, serrated; harsh, rough, rugged; irregular, nonuniform

near ant regular, uniform; flat, level, plane

ant clean, even, smooth, unbroken

2 worn or torn into or as if into rags ⟨finally convinced her to throw away her favorite pair of jeans, *ragged* from decades of yard work⟩

syn frayed, raggedy, ratty, seedy, shabby, tattered, threadbare, worn-out

rel dowdy, scruffy; dingy, faded; shredded; holey, patchy

3 not having a level or smooth surface — see UNEVEN 1

4 wearing torn or worn out clothes — see TATTERED 1

raggedy *adj* **1** wearing torn or worn out clothes — see TATTERED 1

2 worn or torn into or as if into rags — see RAGGED 2

rags *n pl* covering for the human body — see CLOTHING

ragtag *adj* wearing torn or worn out clothes — see TATTERED 1

raid *n* **1** a sudden attack on and entrance into hostile territory ⟨repeated Viking *raids* wore down the defenses of the seaside village⟩

syn descent, foray, incursion, inroad, invasion, irruption

rel pillage, plunder; aggression, assault, offense (*or* offence), offensive, onset, onslaught, siege, storm, strike; charge, sally, sortie; ambuscade, ambush, surprise; air raid, blitz, blitzkrieg, bombardment

2 the act or action of setting upon with force or violence — see ATTACK 2

raid *vb* **1** to enter for conquest or plunder — see INVADE

2 to take sudden, violent action against — see ATTACK 1

raider *n* one that starts armed conflict against another especially without reasonable cause — see AGGRESSOR

rail *n* **1** a protective barrier consisting of a horizontal bar and its supports — see RAILING

2 a roadway overlaid with parallel steel rails over which trains travel — see RAILROAD

rail (at *or* against) *vb* to criticize (someone) severely or angrily especially for personal failings — see SCOLD

railer *n* a person given to harsh judgments and to finding faults — see CRITIC 1

railing *n* a protective barrier consisting of a horizontal bar and its supports ⟨had to

put a *railing* on the balcony when the baby started walking⟩
syn balustrade, banister, guardrail, rail
rel handrail; taffrail; bar; fender

raillery *n* good-natured teasing or exchanging of clever remarks — see BANTER

railroad *n* a roadway overlaid with parallel steel rails over which trains travel ⟨Grandpa used to walk along the main *railroad* in town to get to school⟩
syn rail, railway, road
rel el, elevated, elevated railroad; monorail

railway *n* a roadway overlaid with parallel steel rails over which trains travel — see RAILROAD

raiment *n* covering for the human body — see CLOTHING

rain *n* **1** a steady falling of water from the sky in significant quantity ⟨Mom yelled at us to come in out of the *rain* before we caught cold⟩
syn cloudburst, deluge, downpour, rainfall, rainstorm, storm, wet
rel precipitation, shower; thunderstorm
near ant drizzle, mist, sprinkle

2 a heavy fall of objects ⟨the Norman invaders fled when the castle's defenders threw a *rain* of stones down upon them⟩
syn hail, shower, storm
rel barrage, broadside, cannonade, fusillade, salvo, volley; flood, gush, rush, spate, torrent; eruption, outbreak, outburst

rain *vb* **1** to fall as water in a continuous stream of drops from the clouds ⟨it started *raining* this morning and hasn't let up since⟩
syn pour, precipitate, storm
rel shower; hail, squall; deluge, flood
phrases rain cats and dogs
near ant drizzle, mist, spit, sprinkle

2 to give readily and in large quantities ⟨she *rained* praise upon her graduating students⟩ ⟨the squadron *rained* bombs on the enemy's fortifications⟩
syn heap, lavish, pour, shower
rel gush, stream; flood, inundate, overflow; bombard, hail
near ant hold back, keep, reserve, retain, withhold

raincoat *n* a coat made of water-resistant material ⟨grabbed my umbrella and *raincoat* before going out in the thunderstorm⟩
syn mackintosh (*or* macintosh) [*chiefly British*], oilskin, slicker, waterproof [*chiefly British*]
rel rainwear; poncho, sou'wester, trench coat

rainfall *n* a steady falling of water from the sky in significant quantity — see RAIN 1

rainstorm *n* a steady falling of water from the sky in significant quantity — see RAIN 1

rainy *adj* marked by or abounding with rain ⟨found that the cold, *rainy* weather made his joints swell and ache⟩
syn pouring, precipitating, stormy, wet
rel drizzling, drizzly, misty, spitting, sprinkling
near ant dry

raise *n* something added (as by growth) — see INCREASE 1

raise *vb* **1** to move from a lower to a higher place or position ⟨asked the students to *raise* their hands if they knew the answer⟩
syn boost, crane, elevate, heave, heft, heighten, hike, hoist, jack (up), lift, perk (up), pick up, up, uphold, uplift, upraise
rel ascend, mount, rise; rear, upend
near ant descend, fall, pitch, plunge, slip; bear, depress, press, push; sink, submerge
ant drop, lower

2 to bring to maturity through care and education — see BRING UP 1

3 to cause or encourage the development of — see INCITE 1

4 to draw out (something hidden, latent, or reserved) — see EDUCE

5 to fix in an upright position — see ERECT 1

6 to form by putting together parts or materials — see BUILD

7 to look after or assist the growth of by labor and care — see GROW 1

8 to make greater in size, amount, or number — see INCREASE 1

9 to move higher in rank or position — see PROMOTE 1

10 to present or bring forward for discussion — see INTRODUCE 2

raised *adj* **1** being at a higher level than average — see HIGH 2

2 being positioned above a surface — see ELEVATED 1

3 rising straight up — see ERECT

rake *vb* to look through (as a place) carefully or thoroughly in an effort to find or discover something — see SEARCH 1

rakishly *adv* in a bright and showy way — see GAILY 3

rally *n* **1** an act of gathering forces together to renew or attempt an effort ⟨in a last-minute *rally* the Confederates at Bull Run were able to turn a near defeat into an upset victory⟩
syn marshaling (*or* marshalling), mobilization, rallying
rel call-up, summons; convening, muster, mustering

2 a mass meeting for the purpose of displaying or arousing support for a cause or person ⟨a huge *rally* for the candidate on the eve of the election⟩
syn demonstration
rel assembly, convention, gathering; march; protest, sit-down, sit-down strike, sit-in, strike

3 the process or period of gradually regaining one's health and strength — see CONVALESCENCE

¹rally *vb* **1** to assemble and make ready for action — see MOBILIZE

---

syn synonym(s)   **rel** related words
ant antonym(s)   **near ant** near antonym(s)

2 to become healthy and strong again after illness or weakness — see CONVALESCE

3 to regain a former or normal state — see RECOVER 2

²**rally** vb to make fun of in a good-natured way — see TEASE 1

rallying n an act of gathering forces together to renew or attempt an effort — see RALLY 1

rallying adj marked by or expressive of mild or good-natured teasing — see QUIZZICAL

ram vb **1** to come into usually forceful contact with something — see HIT 2

2 to fit (something) into a tight space — see CROWD 1

ramble n a relaxed journey on foot for exercise or pleasure — see WALK

ramble vb **1** to talk at length without sticking to a topic or getting to a point ⟨the teenagers sat around the pizza parlor, *rambling* on about dating, homework, movies, and the local football team⟩

syn maunder, rattle, run on

rel deviate, digress, stray, wander; sidetrack; blab, chatter, gab, gabble, jabber, patter, prate, prattle

2 to move about from place to place aimlessly — see WANDER

rambler n a person who roams about without a fixed route or destination — see NOMAD

rambling adj **1** passing from one topic to another — see DISCURSIVE

2 using or containing more words than necessary to express an idea — see WORDY

rambunctious adj being rough or noisy in a high-spirited way — see BOISTEROUS

ramify vb to set or force apart — see SEPARATE 1

rampage n a state of wildly excited activity or emotion — see FRENZY

rampant adj **1** showing no signs of being under control ⟨the mayor promised to put a stop to the *rampant* crime that plagued the city⟩

syn intemperate, unbridled, unchecked, uncontrolled, uncurbed, ungoverned, unhampered, unhindered, unrestrained

rel uncontrollable, ungovernable; immoderate; riotous, uninhibited, wild

near ant moderate, tempered

ant checked, controlled, curbed, hampered, hindered, restrained, temperate

2 growing thickly and vigorously — see RANK 1

ramrod adj given to exacting standards of discipline and self-restraint — see SEVERE 1

ranch n a piece of land and its buildings used to grow crops or raise livestock — see FARM

rancor n a deep-seated ill will — see ENMITY

rancorous adj having or showing deep-seated resentment — see BITTER 1

random adj lacking a definite plan, purpose, or pattern ⟨since we were new in town, our choice of a vet for our dog was entirely *random*⟩

syn aimless, arbitrary, desultory, erratic, haphazard, hit-or-miss, scattered, slapdash, stray

rel accidental, casual, chance, fluky, fortuitous, inadvertent, incidental, lucky, unconsidered, unintended, unintentional, unplanned, unpremeditated; irregular, sporadic, spot; objectless, purposeless; indiscriminate, unsystematic; unaimed, undirected

near ant established, fixed, regular, set, stable, steady; constant, continuous, even; arranged, managed, orchestrated, ordered, planned; aware, conscious, deliberate, purposeful, thoughtful

ant methodical, nonrandom, orderly, systematic

randomly adv without definite aim, direction, rule, or method — see HIT OR MISS

range n **1** open land over which livestock may roam and feed ⟨knew exactly how many head of cattle were turned out on the *range* that morning to graze⟩

syn lea, pasturage, pasture

rel ranch, station; feedlot, stockyard, yard; grassland, pampas, prairie, savanna (also savannah), steppe

2 an area over which activity, capacity, or influence extends ⟨didn't know she had such a wide *range* of knowledge until I talked to her⟩

syn amplitude, breadth, compass, dimension(s), extent, reach, realm, scope, sweep, width

rel gamut, spectrum, spread; domain, field, sphere; horizon, panorama

3 the distance or extent between possible extremes ⟨an actor who can go through the full *range* of emotion, from joy to sorrow, in mere minutes⟩

syn gamut, scale, spectrum, spread, stretch

rel measure, pitch, scale; amplitude, compass, dimension(s), extent, reach, realm, scope, sweep, width

4 a relaxed journey on foot for exercise or pleasure — see WALK

5 a series of persons or things arranged one behind another — see LINE 1

6 an appliance that prepares food for consumption by heating it — see COOKER 1

7 the place where a plant or animal is usually or naturally found — see HOME 2

range vb **1** to arrange or assign according to type — see CLASSIFY 1

2 to move about from place to place aimlessly — see WANDER

3 to occur within a continuous range of variation — see RUN 4

4 to put into a particular arrangement — see ORDER 1

ranging adj traveling from place to place — see ITINERANT

rangy adj being tall, thin and usually loose-jointed — see LANKY

rank *adj* **1** growing thickly and vigorously ⟨covered with trumpet vines so *rank* you couldn't see the trellis beneath them⟩

syn lush, luxuriant, prosperous, rampant, weedy

rel lavish, profuse; overgrown, overrun; close, dense, thick

near ant dormant; blighted, stunted

ant sparse

2 having an unpleasant smell — see MALODOROUS

3 very noticeable especially for being incorrect or bad — see EGREGIOUS

rank *n* **1** the placement of someone or something in relation to others in a vertical arrangement ⟨attained the highest *rank* in Boy Scouting⟩

syn degree, footing, level, place, position, ranking, situation, standing, station, status

rel condition, echelon, estate, order, walk; capacity, function; rating

2 high position within society ⟨was born a woman of *rank* who socialized only with other members of the elite⟩

syn class, dignity, quality, standing

rel gentility, gentleness, nobility, nobleness; grandness, highness, loftiness; distinction, precedence, preeminence, primacy; caste, position, station, status; preferment

near ant debasement, degradation; subordinateness, subordination; baseness, commonness, inferiority, lowliness, lowness

3 a series of people or things arranged side by side — see ROW 1

4 *usually* **ranks** *pl* one of the units into which a whole is divided on the basis of a common characteristic — see CLASS 2

rank *vb* **1** to take or have a certain position within a group arranged in vertical classes ⟨my favorite pitcher *ranks* first in the league for number of consecutive outs⟩

syn be, grade, place, rate

rel seed; count; class, classify, set, sort; install, instate

2 to arrange or assign according to type — see CLASSIFY 1

rank and file *n* the body of the community as contrasted with the elite — see MASS 1

ranking *n* **1** a scheme of rank or order — see ³SCALE 1

2 the placement of someone or something in relation to others in a vertical arrangement — see RANK 1

rankle *vb* to make angry — see ANGER

rankling *adj* causing annoyance — see ANNOYING

ransack *vb* **1** to search through with the intent of committing robbery ⟨it was clear that the thieves who had *ransacked* the museum were professionals—they bypassed most of the exhibits and went straight for the vaults⟩

syn despoil, loot, maraud, pillage, plunder, sack, strip

rel burglarize; comb, hunt, rake, rifle, rummage; harry, raid; ravish

2 to look through (as a place) carefully or thoroughly in an effort to find or discover something — see SEARCH 1

ransom *vb* to free from captivity or punishment by paying a price ⟨the prince emptied the treasury to *ransom* his son from the kidnappers⟩

syn redeem

rel bail; deliver, rescue, save; emancipate, liberate; recover, regain, retrieve; release; buy; salvage

rant *n* **1** a long angry speech or scolding — see TIRADE

2 boastful speech or writing — see BOMBAST 1

rant *vb* to talk loudly and wildly ⟨when the salesclerk gave him incorrect change, he began *ranting* about the sorry state of math education today⟩

syn bluster, fulminate, rave, spout

rel sound off, speak out, speak up; blare, blurt out, bolt; declaim, harangue, mouth, orate, pontificate; carry on, rage, storm, take on

near ant grunt, murmur, mutter, slur; breathe, whisper

¹**rap** *n* **1** a formal claim of criminal wrongdoing against a person — see CHARGE 1

2 a hard strike with a part of the body or an instrument — see ¹BLOW

3 responsibility for wrongdoing or failure — see BLAME 1

²**rap** *n* friendly, informal conversation or an instance of this — see CHAT

³**rap** *n* the smallest amount or part imaginable — see JOT

¹**rap** *vb* **1** to deliver a blow to (someone or something) usually in a strong vigorous manner — see HIT 1

2 to strike or cause to strike lightly and usually rhythmically — see ¹TAP

²**rap** *vb* to engage in casual or rambling conversation — see CHAT

rapacious *adj* **1** having a huge appetite — see VORACIOUS 1

2 living by killing and eating other animals — see PREDATORY

3 having or marked by an eager and often selfish desire especially for material possessions — see GREEDY 1

rapaciousness *n* an intense selfish desire for wealth or possessions — see GREED

rapacity *n* an intense selfish desire for wealth or possessions — see GREED

rapid *adj* moving, proceeding, or acting with great speed — see FAST 1

rapid-fire *adj* moving, proceeding, or acting with great speed — see FAST 1

rapidity *n* a high rate of movement or performance — see SPEED

rapidly *adv* with great speed — see FAST 1

rapidness *n* a high rate of movement or performance — see SPEED

rapport *n* a friendly relationship marked by ready communication and mutual understanding ⟨his good *rapport* with his

---

syn synonym(s)   *rel* related words
ant antonym(s)   *near ant* near antonym(s)

students was one of the reasons why the school board named him Teacher of the Year⟩

syn communion, fellowship, rapprochement

rel accord, agreement, concord, harmony; oneness, solidarity, togetherness, unity; affinity, empathy, sympathy, understanding; amity, chumminess, companionship, friendship; reciprocity, symbiosis

near ant alienation, disaffection, estrangement; coldness, cold shoulder, distance, iciness; animosity, antagonism, enmity, hostility, rancor, spite

rapprochement *n* a friendly relationship marked by ready communication and mutual understanding — see RAPPORT

rapscallion *n* **1** a mean, evil, or unprincipled person — see VILLAIN

2 an appealingly mischievous person — see SCAMP 1

rapt *adj* having the mind fixed on something — see ATTENTIVE

rapture *n* a state of overwhelming usually pleasurable emotion — see ECSTASY

rapturous *adj* experiencing or marked by overwhelming usually pleasurable emotion — see ECSTATIC

rare *adj* **1** being out of the ordinary — see EXCEPTIONAL

2 having qualities that appeal to a refined taste — see CHOICE

3 not often occurring or repeated — see INFREQUENT

4 noticeably different from what is generally found or experienced — see UNUSUAL 1

rarely *adv* not often — see SELDOM

raring *adj* showing urgent desire or interest — see EAGER

rarity *n* something strange or unusual that is an object of interest — see CURIOSITY 2

rascal *n* **1** a mean, evil, or unprincipled person — see VILLAIN

2 an appealingly mischievous person — see SCAMP 1

rascality *n* playful, reckless behavior that is not intended to cause serious harm — see MISCHIEF 1

rascally *adj* tending to or exhibiting reckless playfulness — see MISCHIEVOUS 1

rash *adj* acting or done with excessive or careless speed — see HASTY 1

rashly *adv* with excessive or careless speed — see HASTILY 1

rasp *n* a harsh grating sound ⟨the rusted lock opened with a *rasp*⟩

syn creak, grind, scrape, scratch

rel clash, jangle, jar; croak; blast, bleat, bray, screech

rasp *vb* **1** to make smooth by friction — see GRIND 1

2 to pass roughly and noisily over or against a surface — see SCRAPE 1

3 to disturb the peace of mind of (someone) especially by repeated disagreeable acts — see IRRITATE 1

raspberry *n* a vocal sound made to express scorn or disapproval — see CATCALL

rasping *adj* harsh and dry in sound — see HOARSE

raspy *adj* harsh and dry in sound — see HOARSE

rat (on) *vb* to leave (a cause or party) often in order to take up another — see DEFECT

rate *n* **1** degree of excellence — see QUALITY 1

2 the relationship in quantity, amount, or size between two or more things — see RATIO

¹**rate** *vb* **1** to be or make worthy of (as a reward or punishment) — see EARN 2

2 to make an approximate or tentative judgment regarding — see ESTIMATE 1

3 to take or have a certain position within a group arranged in vertical classes — see RANK 1

4 to think of in a particular way — see CONSIDER 1

²**rate** *vb* to criticize (someone) severely or angrily especially for personal failings — see SCOLD

rather *adv* **1** by choice or preference ⟨I would *rather* go to the movies than stay at home⟩

syn first, preferably, readily, soon, willingly

rel alternately, alternatively, either, instead; electively, optionally; desirably, gladly, wishfully; voluntarily

near ant reluctantly; forcibly, willy-nilly

ant involuntarily, unwillingly

2 as a substitute — see INSTEAD

3 to some degree or extent — see FAIRLY

ratify *vb* to give official acceptance of something as satisfactory — see APPROVE

ratio *n* the relationship in quantity, amount, or size between two or more things ⟨the *ratio* of students to teachers in my school is nine to one⟩

syn proportion, rate

rel average; frequency; correspondence; percentage

near ant disproportion

ration *vb* to give as a share or portion — see ALLOT

rational *adj* **1** having the ability to reason ⟨human beings are *rational* creatures⟩

syn intelligent, reasonable, reasoning, thinking

rel analytic (*or* analytical), logical; brainy, cerebral, highbrow, intellectual; cognitive, mental; practical, sane, sensible

near ant brainless, mindless, stupid; illogical

ant irrational, nonrational, unintelligent, unreasonable, unreasoning, unthinking

2 according to the rules of logic — see LOGICAL 1

3 based on sound reasoning or information — see GOOD 1

rationale *n* a statement given to explain a belief or act — see REASON 1

rationalize *vb* to give the reason for or cause of — see EXPLAIN 2

rattle *vb* **1** to make a series of short sharp noises ⟨the children tromped through the

kitchen, making the plates on the shelf *rattle*⟩
syn clack, clatter
rel chink, chirp, clank, click, clink; clang, clash, crash; spatter, sputter
2 to engage in casual or rambling conversation — see CHAT
3 to talk at length without sticking to a topic or getting to a point — see RAMBLE 1
4 to throw into a state of self-conscious distress — see EMBARRASS 1

rattling *adj* moving, proceeding, or acting with great speed — see FAST 1

rattling *adv* to a great degree — see VERY 1

ratty *adj* showing signs of advanced wear and tear and neglect — see SHABBY 1
2 worn or torn into or as if into rags — see RAGGED 1

raucous *adj* being rough or noisy in a high-spirited way — see BOISTEROUS

ravage *vb* to bring destruction to (something) through violent action ⟨Hurricane Andrew *ravaged* Louisiana and Florida in 1992, causing $19 billion in damage⟩
syn destroy, devastate, ruin, scourge
rel despoil, foray, harry, loot, maraud, pillage, plunder, sack, strip; annihilate, desolate, extirpate, obliterate, smash, waste, wipe out, wreck; decimate, mow; demolish, raze; crush, overpower, overrun, overthrow, overwhelm
near ant recondition, recover, redeem, rehabilitate, restore

rave *vb* to make an exaggerated display of affection or enthusiasm — see GUSH 2
2 to talk loudly and wildly — see RANT

rave *n, often* **raves** *pl* enthusiastic and usually public expression of approval — see APPLAUSE

ravel (out) *vb* to separate the various strands of — see UNRAVEL 1

raven *adj* having the color of soot or coal — see BLACK 1

ravenous *adj* having a huge appetite — see VORACIOUS 1

ravine *n* a narrow opening between hillsides or mountains that can be used for passage — see CANYON

ravish *vb* to fill with overwhelming emotion (as wonder or delight) — see ENTRANCE

ravishing *adj* very pleasing to look at — see BEAUTIFUL

raw *adj* **1** not cooked ⟨you should wash your hands after handling *raw* chicken⟩
syn uncooked
rel unbaked, unheated; rare; underdone
near ant well-done; overdone; baked, boiled, braised, broiled, fried, grilled, heated, roasted, sautéed
ant cooked
2 being such as found in nature and not altered by processing or refining — see CRUDE 1
3 lacking in adult experience or maturity — see CALLOW

4 marked by wet and windy conditions — see FOUL 1
5 uncomfortably cool — see CHILLY 1
6 causing intense discomfort to one's skin — see CUTTING 1

raw deal *n* unfair or inadequate treatment of someone or something or an instance of this — see DISSERVICE

rawhide *vb* to strike repeatedly with something long and thin or flexible — see WHIP 1

raw material *n* the basic elements from which something can be developed — see MAKING

rawness *n* an uncomfortable degree of coolness — see CHILL

ray *n* **1** a narrow sharply defined line of light radiating from an object — see SHAFT 1
2 a very small amount — see PARTICLE 1

raze *vb* **1** to bring to a complete end the physical soundness, existence, or usefulness of — see DESTROY 1
2 to destroy (as a building) completely by knocking down or breaking to pieces — see DEMOLISH 1

razz *vb* to make fun of in a good-natured way — see TEASE 1

razzing *adj* marked by or expressive of mild or good-natured teasing — see QUIZZICAL

reach *n* **1** a wide space or area — see EXPANSE
2 an area over which activity, capacity, or influence extends — see RANGE 2

reach *vb* **1** to shift possession of (something) from one person to another — see PASS 1
2 to transmit information or requests to — see CONTACT

reachable *adj* situated within easy reach — see CONVENIENT

reacquire *vb* to get again in one's possession — see RECOVER 1

react *vb* to act or behave in response (as to a stimulus or influence) ⟨it was my first touchdown, and I didn't know how to *react* to the cheers of the crowd⟩
syn reply, respond
rel answer, return; retaliate; construe, interpret, read, take, understand
near ant act, behave; affect, cause, draw, effect

reaction *n* action or behavior that is done in return to other action or behavior ⟨we were startled by her extreme *reaction* to the bad grade⟩
syn reply, response, take
rel answer, return; backlash; rebound; revulsion, rise; jerk, start, twitch
near ant action, behavior; cause, effect

reactionary *adj* tending to favor established ideas, conditions, or institutions — see CONSERVATIVE

reactionary *n* **1** a person whose political beliefs are centered on tradition and keeping things the way they are — see CONSERVATIVE 1
2 a person with old-fashioned ideas — see FOGY

---

syn synonym(s)   **rel** related words
ant antonym(s)   **near ant** near antonym(s)

read *vb* to go over and mentally take in the content of ⟨he always *reads* the newspaper in the morning as he eats breakfast⟩
syn peruse, pore (over)
rel browse, dip (into), leaf (through); scan, skim, thumb (through); slog (through), wade (through); reread; proofread; decipher; review, study; apprehend, comprehend, get, grasp, make, make out, perceive, see, understand

readdress *vb* to consider again especially with the possibility of change or reversal — see RECONSIDER

readily *adv* 1 by choice or preference — see RATHER 1
2 without difficulty — see EASILY

reading *n* something assigned to be read or studied — see LESSON

ready *adj* 1 being in a state of fitness for some experience or action ⟨after studying for a whole month, she felt *ready* for the final exam⟩
syn fit, go, prepared, set
rel conditioned, primed; braced, fortified, steeled; qualified, trained
near ant unqualified, untrained
ant half-cocked, unprepared, unready
2 having a desire or inclination (as for a specified course of action) — see WILLING 1
3 having or showing the ability to respond without delay or hesitation — see QUICK 1
4 involving minimal difficulty or effort — see EASY 1

ready *vb* 1 to make competent (as by training, skill, or ability) for a particular office or function — see QUALIFY 2
2 to make ready in advance — see PREPARE 1
3 to prepare (oneself) mentally or emotionally — see FORTIFY 1

ready–made *adj* made beforehand in large numbers ⟨the store was full of inexpensive *ready-made* clothing⟩
syn mass-produced, store
rel ready-to-wear; commercial; prefabricated
near ant handcrafted, handmade, homemade; tailored, tailor-made
ant custom, custom-made

real *adj* 1 being exactly as appears or as claimed — see AUTHENTIC 1
2 existing in fact and not merely as a possibility — see ACTUAL
3 free from any intent to deceive or impress others — see GUILELESS

real *adv* to a great degree — see VERY 1

realistic *adj* 1 willing to see things as they really are and deal with them sensibly ⟨our guidance counselor encouraged us to be more *realistic* in our job choices, so we reluctantly gave up the idea of becoming professional snake charmers⟩
syn down-to-earth, earthy, hardheaded, matter-of-fact, practical, pragmatic (*also* pragmatical)
rel philistine, utilitarian; logical, no-nonsense, rational, reasonable, sane, sensible,

sound; hard-boiled, unromantic, unsentimental; cynical, disillusioned
near ant fanciful, fantastic, imaginative; romantic, sentimental; illogical, insane, irrational, unreasonable; theoretical (*also* theoretic)
ant idealistic, impractical, unrealistic, utopian, visionary
2 closely resembling the object imitated — see NATURAL 2

reality *n* 1 something that actually exists — see FACT 2
2 the fact of being or of being real — see EXISTENCE
3 the quality of being actual — see FACT 1

realizable *adj* capable of being done or carried out — see POSSIBLE 1

realization *n* the state of being actual or complete — see FRUITION

realize *vb* 1 to come to an awareness — see DISCOVER 1
2 to receive as return for effort — see EARN 1

really *adv* 1 in actual fact — see VERY 2
2 to tell the truth — see ACTUALLY 1
3 without any question — see INDEED 1

realm *n* 1 a region of activity, knowledge, or influence — see FIELD 2
2 an area over which activity, capacity, or influence extends — see RANGE 2

reams *n pl* a considerable amount — see LOT 2

reanalyze *vb* to consider again especially with the possibility of change or reversal — see RECONSIDER

reanimate *vb* to bring back to life, practice, or activity — see REVIVE 1

reanimated *adj* made or become fresh in spirits or vigor — see NEW 4

reanimation *n* the act or an instance of bringing something back to life, public attention, or vigorous activity — see REVIVAL

reap *vb* to catch or collect (a crop or natural resource) for human use — see HARVEST

reappraisal *n* a usually critical look at a past event — see REVIEW 1

rear *adj* being at or in the part of something opposite the front part — see BACK

rear *n* the part of the body upon which someone sits — see BUTTOCKS

rear *vb* 1 to bring to maturity through care and education — see BRING UP 1
2 to fix in an upright position — see ERECT 1
3 to form by putting together parts or materials — see BUILD
4 to look after or assist the growth of by labor and care — see GROW 1

rearmost *adj* following all others of the same kind in order or time — see LAST

rearward *adj* 1 being at or in the part of something opposite the front part — see BACK
2 directed, turned, or done toward the back — see BACKWARD

reason *n* 1 a statement given to explain a belief or act ⟨gave a good *reason* for her seemingly suspicious behavior⟩

syn argument, case, explanation, rationale

rel alibi, defense, excuse, justification; appeal, plea; guise, pretense (*or* pretence), pretext, rationalization

2 something (as a belief) that serves as the basis for another thing ⟨a firm belief that we are here on earth to help others is the *reason* for her tireless volunteer work⟩

syn grounds, motive, wherefore, why

rel antecedent, cause, occasion

3 an explanation that frees one from fault or blame — see EXCUSE

4 someone or something responsible for a result — see CAUSE 1

5 the ability to learn and understand or to deal with problems — see INTELLIGENCE 1

6 the normal or healthy condition of the mental abilities — see MIND 2

7 the thought processes that have been established as leading to valid solutions to problems — see LOGIC

reason *vb* **1** to form an opinion through reasoning and information — see INFER 1

2 to state (something) as a reason in support of or against something under consideration — see ARGUE 1

reasonable *adj* **1** according to the rules of logic — see LOGICAL 1

2 based on sound reasoning or information — see GOOD 1

3 costing little — see CHEAP 1

4 having the ability to reason — see RATIONAL 1

reasonably *adv* with good reason or courtesy — see WELL 4

reasoned *adj* **1** based on sound reasoning or information — see GOOD 1

2 being or provable by reasoning in which the conclusion follows necessarily from given information — see DEDUCTIVE

3 decided on as a result of careful thought — see DELIBERATE 1

reasoning *adj* having the ability to reason — see RATIONAL 1

reasoning *n* the thought processes that have been established as leading to valid solutions to problems — see LOGIC

reassure *vb* to ease the grief or distress of — see COMFORT 1

reata *n* a rope or long leather thong with a noose used especially for catching livestock — see LASSO

rebel *n* a person who rises up against authority ⟨the *rebel* would not submit peacefully, even after he was captured⟩

syn insurgent, insurrectionary, insurrectionist, mutineer, red, revolter, revolutionary, revolutionist, revolutionizer

rel challenger, defier, resister; anarchist; extremist, malcontent, radical

near ant loyalist, supporter; counterrevolutionary, counterrevolutionist

---

rebel *vb* to rise up against established authority ⟨the colonists *rebelled* when the unfair tax was imposed⟩

syn mutiny, revolt

rel defy, disobey; revolutionize

near ant obey, submit; attend, serve

rebel (against) *vb* to go against the commands, prohibitions, or rules of — see DISOBEY

rebellion *n* open fighting against authority (as one's own government) ⟨the *rebellion* would have failed if not for the aid sent by other countries⟩

syn insurgency, insurrection, mutiny, revolt, revolution, uprising

rel coup, coup d'état, overthrow; sedition, treachery, treason; sabotage, subversion

near ant counterrevolution

rebellious *adj* **1** taking part in a rebellion ⟨the *rebellious* troops fought a pitched battle with divisions still loyal to the government⟩

syn insurgent, insurrectionary, mutinous, revolutionary

rel seditious, traitorous, treacherous, treasonous

near ant loyal; obedient

2 given to resisting authority or another's control — see DISOBEDIENT

rebelliousness *n* refusal to obey — see DISOBEDIENCE

rebirth *n* the act or an instance of bringing something back to life, public attention, or vigorous activity — see REVIVAL

rebound *vb* **1** to regain a former or normal state — see RECOVER 2

2 to strike and fly off at an angle — see GLANCE 1

rebuff *n* treatment that is deliberately unfriendly — see COLD SHOULDER

rebuke *n* an often public or formal expression of disapproval — see CENSURE

rebuke *vb* **1** to criticize (someone) usually gently so as to correct a fault ⟨*rebuked* the toddler for his habit of telling fibs⟩

syn admonish, chide, reprimand, reproach, reprove

rel berate, castigate, chew out, dress down, flay, jaw, keelhaul, lambaste (*or* lambast), lecture, rail (at *or* against), scold, score, upbraid; abuse, assail, attack, bad-mouth, blame, blast, censure, condemn, criticize, crucify, denounce, dis [*slang*], excoriate, fault, knock, lash, pan, reprehend, slam; belittle, disparage, mock, put down; ridicule, scoff, scorn

near ant approve, endorse (*also* indorse), sanction; extol (*also* extoll), laud, praise

2 to criticize (someone) severely or angrily especially for personal failings — see SCOLD

3 to express public or formal disapproval of — see CENSURE 1

rebut *vb* to prove to be false — see DISPROVE

recalcitrance *n* refusal to obey — see DISOBEDIENCE

recalcitrant *adj* **1** given to resisting authority or another's control — see DISOBEDIENT

---

2 given to resisting control or discipline by others — see UNCONTROLLABLE

recall *n* **1** a particular act or instance of recalling or the thing remembered — see MEMORY 2

2 the act of putting an end to something planned or previously agreed to — see CANCELLATION

recall *vb* **1** to bring back to mind — see REMEMBER

2 to put an end to (something planned or previously agreed to) — see CANCEL 1

recant *vb* to solemnly or formally reject or go back on (as something formerly adhered to) — see ABJURE

recap *n* a short statement of the main points — see SUMMARY

recap *vb* to make into a short statement of the main points (as of a report) — see SUMMARIZE

recapitulate *vb* to make into a short statement of the main points (as of a report) — see SUMMARIZE

recapitulation *n* a short statement of the main points — see SUMMARY

recapture *vb* to get again in one's possession — see RECOVER 1

recast *vb* to make different in some way — see CHANGE 1

recede *vb* **1** to grow less in scope or intensity especially gradually — see DECREASE 2

2 to move back or away (as from something difficult, dangerous, or disagreeable) — see RETREAT 1

recently *adv* not long ago — see NEWLY

receptacle *n* something into which a liquid or smaller objects can be put for storage or transportation — see CONTAINER

reception *n* a social gathering — see PARTY 1

receptive *adj* willing to consider new or different ideas — see OPEN-MINDED 1

recess *n* **1** a hollowed-out space in a wall — see NICHE 1

2 a period during which the usual routine of school or work is suspended — see VACATION

3 a momentary halt in an activity — see PAUSE

4 a sunken area forming a separate space — see HOLE 2

recess *vb* to bring to a formal close for a period of time — see ADJOURN

recessed *adj* curved inward — see HOLLOW

recession *n* **1** a period of decreased economic activity — see DEPRESSION 1

2 an act of moving away especially from something difficult, dangerous, or disagreeable — see RETREAT 1

reciprocal *adj* related to each other in such a way that one completes the other — see COMPLEMENTARY

recite *vb* **1** to give an oral or written account of in some detail — see TELL 1

2 to give from memory — see REPEAT 2

reckless *adj* **1** having or showing a lack of concern for the consequences of one's actions ⟨the *reckless* skiers were making

everyone nervous by schussing down the mountainside at lightning speed⟩

syn daredevil, devil-may-care, foolhardy, irresponsible

rel adventurous, bold, daring, venturesome; hasty, headlong, hotheaded, impetuous, precipitate, rash, wild; nonchalant, unconcerned, unworried; careless, heedless, inattentive, incautious, unheeding; inconsiderate, thoughtless, unthinking

near ant careful, cautious, circumspect, heedful; overcareful, overcautious, timid

ant responsible

2 foolishly adventurous or bold — see FOOLHARDY 1

reckon *vb* **1** to decide the size, amount, number, or distance of (something) without actual measurement — see ESTIMATE 2

2 *chiefly dialect* to have as an opinion — see BELIEVE 2

3 to determine (a value) by doing the necessary mathematical operations — see CALCULATE 1

4 to place reliance or trust — see DEPEND 2

5 to think of in a particular way — see CONSIDER 1

reckoning *n* **1** the act of placing a value on the nature, character, or quality of something — see ESTIMATE 1

2 the act or process of performing mathematical operations to find a value — see CALCULATION

reclaim *vb* **1** to get again in one's possession — see RECOVER 1

2 to make better in behavior or character — see REFORM 1

3 to obtain (a raw material) by separating it from a by-product or waste product — see RECYCLE

reclamation *n* the act or process of getting something back — see RECOVERY 1

recluse *n* a person who lives away from others ⟨he was sick of cities and crowds, so he decided to go live by himself in the woods as a *recluse*⟩

syn anchorite, hermit, solitary

rel homebody, shut-in; monk

near ant socialite

recognize *vb* to show appreciation, respect, or affection for (someone) with a public celebration — see HONOR

recoil *vb* to draw back in fear, pain, or disgust — see FLINCH

recollect *vb* to bring back to mind — see REMEMBER

re-collect *vb* **1** to gain emotional or mental control of — see COLLECT 1

2 to get again in one's possession — see RECOVER 1

recollection *n* **1** a particular act or instance of recalling or the thing remembered — see MEMORY 2

2 the power or process of recalling what has been previously learned or experienced — see MEMORY 1

recommend *vb* to put forward as one's choice for or proper course of action — see ADVISE 2

recompense *n* **1** payment to another for a loss or injury — see COMPENSATION 1
2 something (as money) that is given or received in return for goods or services — see PAYMENT 2

recompense *vb* **1** to give (someone) the sum of money owed for goods or services received — see PAY 1
2 to give what is owed for — see PAY 2
3 to provide (someone) with a just payment for loss or injury — see COMPENSATE 1

reconceive *vb* to consider again especially with the possibility of change or reversal — see RECONSIDER

reconcile *vb* to bring to a state free of conflicts, inconsistencies, or differences — see HARMONIZE 1

recondite *adj* difficult for one of ordinary knowledge or intelligence to understand — see PROFOUND 1

recondition *vb* to put into good shape or working order again — see MEND 1

reconsider *vb* to consider again especially with the possibility of change or reversal ⟨the new information forced the general to *reconsider* his plan of attack⟩
syn readdress, reanalyze, reconceive, reevaluate, reexamine, rethink, review, reweigh
rel reappraise, reassess; amend, correct, emend, rectify, reform, remedy, revise
phrases change one's mind (about), go over, think better of, view in a new light
near ant assert, defend, maintain, uphold

reconsideration *n* a usually critical look at a past event — see REVIEW 1

record *n* **1** a relating of events usually in the order in which they happened — see ACCOUNT 1
2 an account of important events in the order in which they happened — see HISTORY 1

record *vb* **1** to make a written note of ⟨the reporter *recorded* the events of the evening in her notebook for later reference⟩
syn jot (down), log, mark, note, put down, register, set down
rel chronicle; chalk (up); score; rerecord
2 to put (someone or something) on a list — see ¹LIST 2

recount *vb* to give an oral or written account of in some detail — see TELL 1

recoup *vb* **1** to get again in one's possession — see RECOVER 1
2 to provide (someone) with a just payment for loss or injury — see COMPENSATE 1

recoupment *n* **1** payment to another for a loss or injury — see COMPENSATION 1
2 the act or process of getting something back — see RECOVERY 1

recourse *n* something that one uses to accomplish an end especially when the usual means is not available — see RESOURCE 1

recover *vb* **1** to get again in one's possession ⟨after fishing around in the garbage for ten minutes, I was able to *recover* my lost keys⟩
syn reacquire, recapture, reclaim, recollect, recoup, regain, repossess, retake, retrieve
rel recruit, replenish; redeem, repurchase; rescue
phrases get back
near ant lose, mislay, misplace
2 to regain a former or normal state ⟨after a disastrous first half, the team was able to *recover* toward the end of the game and manage a win⟩
syn rally, rebound, snap back
rel reanimate, revitalize, revive
phrases make a comeback
near ant decline, fail, worsen
3 to become healthy and strong again after illness or weakness — see CONVALESCE
4 to obtain (a raw material) by separating it from a by-product or waste product — see RECYCLE

recovery *n* **1** the act or process of getting something back ⟨the *recovery* of the sunken boat took over a week⟩
syn reclamation, recoupment, repossession, retrieval
rel recruitment, replenishment; redemption, rescue
near ant loss, misplacement
2 the process or period of gradually regaining one's health and strength — see CONVALESCENCE

recreant *adj* **1** having or showing a shameful lack of courage — see COWARDLY
2 not true in one's allegiance to someone or something — see FAITHLESS

recreant *n* **1** a person who abandons a cause or organization usually without right — see RENEGADE
2 a person who shows a shameful lack of courage in the face of danger — see COWARD
3 one who betrays a trust or an allegiance — see TRAITOR

recreate *vb* **1** to bring back to a former condition or vigor — see RENEW 1
2 to engage in activity for amusement — see PLAY 1

recreated *adj* made or become fresh in spirits or vigor — see NEW 4

recreation *n* **1** activity engaged in to amuse oneself — see PLAY 1
2 someone or something that provides amusement or enjoyment — see FUN 1
3 the act or activity of providing pleasure or amusement especially for the public — see ENTERTAINMENT 1

recruit *n* a person who is just starting out in a field of activity — see BEGINNER

rectifiable *adj* capable of being corrected — see REMEDIABLE

---

syn synonym(s)   *rel* related words
ant antonym(s)   *near ant* near antonym(s)

rectify *vb* to remove errors, defects, deficiencies, or deviations from — see CORRECT 1

rectifying *adj* serving to raise or adjust something to some standard or proper condition — see CORRECTIVE 1

rectitude *n* **1** conduct that conforms to an accepted standard of right and wrong — see MORALITY 1

2 faithfulness to high moral standards — see HONOR 1

recuperate *vb* to become healthy and strong again after illness or weakness — see CONVALESCE

recuperation *n* the process or period of gradually regaining one's health and strength — see CONVALESCENCE

recurrent *adj* occurring or appearing at intervals — see INTERMITTENT 1

recurring *adj* occurring or appearing at intervals — see INTERMITTENT 1

recycle *vb* to obtain (a raw material) by separating it from a by-product or waste product ⟨*recycling* the aluminum from pop cans is environmentally sound⟩
syn reclaim, recover
rel reuse; process

red *n* a person who rises up against authority — see REBEL

red–blooded *adj* having active strength of body or mind — see VIGOROUS 1

redden *vb* to develop a rosy facial color (as from excitement or embarrassment) — see BLUSH

redeem *vb* **1** to do what is required by the terms of — see FULFILL 1

2 to free from captivity or punishment by paying a price — see RANSOM

3 to free from the penalties or consequences of sin — see SAVE 1

4 to make better in behavior or character — see REFORM 1

redeemer *n* one that saves from danger or destruction — see SAVIOR

red–hot *adj* **1** being or involving the latest methods, concepts, information, or styles — see MODERN

2 having a notably high temperature — see HOT 1

3 having or expressing great depth of feeling — see FERVENT

redo *vb* **1** to make different in some way — see CHANGE 1

2 to make or do again — see REPEAT 4

redoing *n* the act, process, or result of making different — see CHANGE

redolence *n* **1** a sweet or pleasant smell — see FRAGRANCE

2 the quality of a thing that makes it perceptible to the sense organs in the nose — see SMELL

redolent *adj* having a pleasant smell — see FRAGRANT

redouble *vb* **1** to make markedly greater in measure or degree — see INTENSIFY

2 to make twice as great or as many — see DOUBLE 1

redoubtable *adj* causing fear — see FEARFUL 1

redraft *vb* to prepare for publication by correcting, rewriting, or updating — see EDIT

redress *n* payment to another for a loss or injury — see COMPENSATION 1

reduce *vb* **1** to bring to a lower grade or rank — see DEMOTE

2 to make smaller in amount, volume, or extent — see DECREASE 1

reduction *n* **1** something that is or may be subtracted — see DEDUCTION 1

2 the amount by which something is lessened — see DECREASE

redundancy *n* the use of too many words to express an idea — see VERBIAGE

reduplicate *vb* **1** to make an exact likeness of — see COPY 1

2 to make or do again — see REPEAT 4

reduplication *n* **1** something that is made to look exactly like something else — see COPY

2 the act of saying or doing over again — see REPEAT

reecho *vb* to continue or be repeated in a series of reflected sound waves — see REVERBERATE

reek *n* **1** a strong unpleasant smell — see STINK

2 an atmospheric condition in which suspended particles in the air rob it of its transparency — see HAZE 1

reek *vb* to give off an extremely unpleasant smell — see STINK

reeking *adj* having an unpleasant smell — see MALODOROUS

reeky *adj* having an unpleasant smell — see MALODOROUS

reel *n* a rapid turning about on an axis or central point — see SPIN 1

reel *vb* **1** to be in a confused state as if from being twirled around — see SPIN 2

2 to move forward while swaying from side to side — see STAGGER 1

reeling *adj* having a feeling of being whirled about and in danger of falling down — see DIZZY 1

reenergized *adj* made or become fresh in spirits or vigor — see NEW 4

reevaluate *vb* to consider again especially with the possibility of change or reversal — see RECONSIDER

reexamination *n* a usually critical look at a past event — see REVIEW 1

reexamine *vb* to consider again especially with the possibility of change or reversal — see RECONSIDER

refashion *vb* to make different in some way — see CHANGE 1

refashioning *n* the act, process, or result of making different — see CHANGE

refer *vb* to have a relation or connection — see APPLY 1

refer (to) *vb* **1** to make reference to or speak about briefly but specifically — see MENTION 1

2 to use or seek out as a source of aid, relief, or advantage — see RESORT (TO) 1

referee *vb* to give an opinion about (something at issue or in dispute) — see JUDGE 1

reference *n* relation to or concern with something specified — see RESPECT 1

refine *vb* to make better — see IMPROVE

refined *adj* **1** being far along in development — see ADVANCED 1

2 free from added matter — see PURE 1

3 having or showing a taste for the fine arts and gracious living — see CULTIVATED

4 having or showing elegance — see ELEGANT 1

5 made or done with extreme care and accuracy — see FINE 2

6 satisfying or pleasing because of fineness or mildness — see DELICATE 1

refinement *n* **1** an instance of notable progress in the development of knowledge, technology, or skill — see ADVANCE 2

2 a high level of taste and enlightenment as a result of extensive intellectual training and exposure to the arts — see CULTURE 1

3 dignified or restrained beauty of form, appearance, or style — see ELEGANCE

reflect *vb* to reproduce or show (an exact likeness) as a mirror would ⟨her face was *reflected* in the waters of the still pond⟩
syn image, mirror
rel copy, duplicate, imitate, reduplicate, repeat, replicate, reproduce

reflection *n* **1** a briefly expressed opinion — see REMARK

2 a cause of shame — see DISGRACE 2

reflective *adj* given to or marked by long, quiet thinking — see CONTEMPLATIVE

reform *vb* **1** to make better in behavior or character ⟨a *reformed* criminal who is now a productive member of society⟩
syn reclaim, redeem, rehabilitate
rel amend, improve; cleanse, purify, restore
near ant abase, corrupt, debauch, degrade, demean, demoralize, deprave, pervert, poison, profane, prostitute, subvert, warp

2 to remove errors, defects, deficiencies, or deviations from — see CORRECT 1

reformative *adj* serving to raise or adjust something to some standard or proper condition — see CORRECTIVE 1

reformatory *adj* serving to raise or adjust something to some standard or proper condition — see CORRECTIVE 1

refractoriness *n* refusal to obey — see DISOBEDIENCE

refractory *adj* **1** given to resisting authority or another's control — see DISOBEDIENT

2 given to resisting control or discipline by others — see UNCONTROLLABLE

refrain *n* a part of a song or hymn that is repeated every so often — see CHORUS 2

refrain (from) *vb* to resist the temptation of — see FORBEAR

refresh *vb* to bring back to a former condition or vigor — see RENEW 1

refreshed *adj* made or become fresh in spirits or vigor — see NEW 4

refreshen *vb* to bring back to a former condition or vigor — see RENEW 1

refreshing *adj* having a renewing effect on the state of the body or mind — see TONIC

refrigerate *vb* to cause to lose heat — see COOL 1

refuge *n* something (as a building) that offers cover from the weather or protection from danger — see SHELTER

refugee *n* a person forced to emigrate for political reasons — see ÉMIGRÉ 1

refulgence *n* the quality or state of having or giving off light — see BRILLIANCE 1

refulgent *adj* giving off or reflecting much light — see BRIGHT 1

refund *vb* to make a return payment to — see REPAY

refusal *n* an unwillingness to grant something asked for — see DENIAL 1

refuse *n* discarded or useless material — see GARBAGE

refuse *vb* **1** to be unwilling to grant — see DENY 2

2 to show unwillingness to accept, do, engage in, or agree to — see DECLINE 1

refute *vb* to prove to be false — see DISPROVE

regain *vb* to get again in one's possession — see RECOVER 1

regal *adj* **1** fit for or worthy of a royal ruler — see MONARCHICAL

2 large and impressive in size, grandeur, extent, or conception — see GRAND 1

regale *vb* **1** to cause (someone) to pass the time agreeably occupied — see AMUSE

2 to entertain with a fancy meal — see FEAST

regalia *n* dressy clothing — see FINERY

regard *n* **1** a feeling of great approval and liking — see ADMIRATION 1

2 an instance of looking especially briefly — see LOOK 2

3 relation to or concern with something specified — see RESPECT 1

4 regards *pl* best wishes — see COMPLIMENT

regard *vb* **1** to make note of (something) through the use of one's eyes — see SEE 1

2 to take notice of and be guided by — see HEED 1

3 to think of in a particular way — see CONSIDER 1

4 to think very highly or favorably of — see ADMIRE

regardful *adj* marked by or showing proper regard for another's higher status — see RESPECTFUL

regarding *prep* having to do with — see ABOUT 1

regardless *adv* in spite of everything ⟨the weather looked bad, but they were resolved to go on with their picnic *regardless*⟩
syn anyhow, anyway
rel nevertheless
phrases in any case, no matter

---

syn synonym(s)   **rel** related words
ant antonym(s)   **near ant** near antonym(s)

regenerate *vb* **1** to bring back to a former condition or vigor — see RENEW 1
2 to bring back to life, practice, or activity — see REVIVE 1

regenerated *adj* made or become fresh in spirits or vigor — see NEW 1

regeneration *n* the act or an instance of bringing something back to life, public attention, or vigorous activity — see REVIVAL

regime *also* **régime** *n* lawful control over the affairs of a political unit (as a nation) — see RULE 2

regimen *n* lawful control over the affairs of a political unit (as a nation) — see RULE 2

region *n* **1** a part or portion having no fixed boundaries ⟨if you look in the upper left *region* of the sky, you can see the constellation Orion⟩
syn area, demesne, field, zone
rel section; locale, locality, location, locus, place, point, position, site, spot
2 a broad geographical area ⟨corn is mostly grown in the central *regions* of the country⟩
syn belt, land, part(s), tract, zone
rel district, territory

¹**register** *n* a person whose job is to keep records — see CLERK 1

²**register** *n* a record of a series of items (as names or titles) usually arranged according to some system — see ¹LIST

register *vb* **1** to enter in a list or roll — see ENROLL 1
2 to make a written note of — see RECORD 1
3 to put (someone or something) on a list — see ¹LIST 2

registrar *n* a person whose job is to keep records — see CLERK 1

registration *n* the number of individuals registered ⟨there was a large *registration* for the popular swim classes at the community center⟩
syn enrollment, registry
rel class

registry *n* **1** a record of a series of items (as names or titles) usually arranged according to some system — see ¹LIST
2 the number of individuals registered — see REGISTRATION

regress *vb* to go back to a previous and usually lower state or level ⟨in extreme circumstances, people sometimes *regress* to the behavior they exhibited in childhood⟩
syn retrogress, revert
rel backslide, lapse, relapse; return
near ant grow, mature, ripen
ant advance, develop, evolve, progress

regression *n* the act or an instance of going back to an earlier and lower level especially of intelligence or behavior ⟨the *regression* to really childish behavior that boys often undergo when put in large groups⟩
syn retrogression, reversion
rel backslide, lapse, relapse; return; nondevelopment

near ant growth, maturation, ripening
ant advancement, development, evolution, progression

regret *n* a feeling of responsibility for wrongdoing — see GUILT 1

regret *vb* to feel sorry or dissatisfied about ⟨we *regret* any inconvenience that we may have caused you⟩
syn bemoan, deplore, lament, repent, rue
rel bewail, grieve (for), mourn, sorrow (for)

regretful *adj* **1** expressing or suggesting mourning — see MOURNFUL 1
2 feeling sorrow for a wrong that one has done — see CONTRITE 1

regretfully *adv* with feelings of bitterness or grief — see HARD 2

regrettable *adj* of a kind to cause great distress ⟨the explorers forged ahead despite the *regrettable* loss of some of their companions⟩
syn deplorable, distressful, distressing, grievous, heartbreaking, heartrending, lamentable, unfortunate, woeful
rel affecting, moving, poignant, touching; awful, dire, dreadful, fearful, terrible; horrible, horrifying, intolerable, unwhelming, shocking, sickening, unbearable; miserable, pitiful, wretched; calamitous, disastrous
near ant gratifying, pleasing, rewarding, satisfying; comforting, encouraging, heartening; cheering, heartwarming, inspiring; fortunate, happy, lucky

regular *adj* **1** appearing or occurring repeatedly from time to time ⟨what with one or another of our pets having problems, we've been *regular* visitors at the animal hospital⟩
syn constant, frequent, habitual, periodic, repeated, steady
rel chronic, confirmed, inveterate; expected, usual
near ant unexpected, unusual
ant inconstant, infrequent, irregular
2 following a set method, arrangement, or pattern — see METHODICAL
3 following or agreeing with established form, custom, or rules — see FORMAL 1
4 having no exceptions or restrictions — see ABSOLUTE 2
5 having or showing the qualities associated with the members of a particular group or kind — see TYPICAL 1

regular *n* a person engaged in military service — see SOLDIER

regularize *vb* to make agree with a single established standard or model — see STANDARDIZE

regulate *vb* **1** to keep from exceeding a desirable degree or level (as of expression) — see CONTROL 1
2 to look after and make decisions about — see CONDUCT 1

regulation *n* **1** a statement spelling out the proper procedure or conduct for an activity — see RULE 1
2 the act or activity of looking after and making decisions about something — see CONDUCT 1

3 the duty or function of watching or guarding for the sake of proper direction or control — see SUPERVISION 1

regulator *n* a mechanism for adjusting the operation of a device, machine, or system — see CONTROL 1

rehabilitate *vb* **1** to make better in behavior or character — see REFORM 1

2 to restore to a healthy condition — see HEAL 1

rehabilitation *n* the process or period of gradually regaining one's health and strength — see CONVALESCENCE

rehearsal *n* a private performance or session in preparation for a public appearance ⟨we made a few mistakes in *rehearsal*, but we were pretty sure that we'd be okay on opening night⟩

syn dry run, practice (*also* practise), trial

rel dress rehearsal; preview; drill, exercise

rehearse *vb* **1** to do over and over so as to become skilled — see PRACTICE

2 to give an oral or written account of in some detail — see TELL 1

3 to say or state again — see REPEAT 1

4 to specify one after another — see ENUMERATE 1

reimburse *vb* to make a return payment to — see REPAY

rein *n* the place of leadership or command — see HEAD 2

rein (in) *vb* to keep from exceeding a desirable degree or level (as of expression) — see CONTROL 1

reiterate *vb* **1** to make or do again — see REPEAT 4

2 to say or state again — see REPEAT 1

reiteration *n* the act of saying or doing over again — see REPEAT

reiterative *adj* marked by repetition — see REPETITIVE

reject *n* **1** one who is cast out or rejected by society — see OUTCAST

2 something separated from a group or lot for not being as good as the others — see CULL

reject *vb* **1** to be unwilling to grant — see DENY 2

2 to declare not to be true — see DENY 1

3 to get rid of as useless or unwanted — see DISCARD

4 to show unwillingness to accept, do, engage in, or agree to — see DECLINE 1

rejected *adj* left unoccupied or unused — see ABANDONED

rejection *n* **1** a refusal to confirm the truth of a statement — see DENIAL 2

2 an unwillingness to grant something asked for — see DENIAL 1

3 something separated from a group or lot for not being as good as the others — see CULL

rejoice *vb* **1** to feel or express joy or triumph — see EXULT

2 to give satisfaction to — see PLEASE

rejoicing *adj* having or expressing feelings of joy or triumph — see EXULTANT

rejoin *vb* to speak or write in reaction to a question or to another reaction — see ANSWER 1

rejoinder *n* something spoken or written in reaction especially to a question — see ANSWER 1

rejuvenate *vb* **1** to bring back to a former condition or vigor — see RENEW 1

2 to bring back to life, practice, or activity — see REVIVE 1

rejuvenation *n* the act or an instance of bringing something back to life, public attention, or vigorous activity — see REVIVAL

rekindle *vb* to bring back to life, practice, or activity — see REVIVE 1

relate *vb* **1** to form a close personal relationship — see COMMUNE

2 to give an oral or written account of in some detail — see TELL 1

3 to have a relation or connection — see APPLY 1

4 to think of (something) in combination — see ASSOCIATE 2

related *adj* having a close connection like that between family members ⟨the *related* fields of anthropology and archaeology⟩

syn affiliated, akin, allied, kindred

rel associated, connected; alike, analogous, comparable, correspondent, corresponding, like, matching, parallel, resembling, similar, such, suchlike; identical, same; germane, pertinent, relevant

near ant different, disparate, dissimilar, distinct, distinctive, distinguishable, diverse, other, unalike, unlike

ant unrelated

relation *n* **1 relations** *pl* doings between individuals or groups ⟨*relations* between the rival newspapers remained friendly despite their competition for the same stories⟩

syn dealings, interaction, intercourse

rel interrelationship

2 a person connected with another by blood or marriage — see RELATIVE

3 the fact or state of having something in common — see CONNECTION 1

4 the state of having shared interests or efforts (as in social or business matters) — see ASSOCIATION 1

relationship *n* **1** the fact or state of having something in common — see CONNECTION 1

2 the state of having shared interests or efforts (as in social or business matters) — see ASSOCIATION 1

relative *adj* **1** being such only when compared to something else — see COMPARATIVE

2 having to do with the matter at hand — see PERTINENT

relative *n* a person connected with another by blood or marriage ⟨it's always fun to see all your *relatives* at a big family gathering⟩

syn kin, kinsman, relation

---

syn synonym(s)   **rel** related words

ant antonym(s)   **near ant** near antonym(s)

rel in-law; kinswoman; blood, clan, family, folk, house, kindred, kinfolk, kinsfolk, line, lineage, people, race, stock, tribe

relatively *adv* to some degree or extent — see FAIRLY

relax *vb* 1 to get rid of nervous tension or anxiety ⟨she took deep breaths to *relax* before going on stage⟩

syn unwind

rel loosen (up), unbend; repose, rest; alleviate, comfort, ease, relieve; calm, compose, cool, quiet, settle

ant tense (up)

2 to make less taut — see SLACKEN

3 to refrain from labor or exertion — see REST 1

relaxation *n* 1 activity engaged in to amuse oneself — see PLAY 1

2 freedom from activity or labor — see ¹REST 1

relaxed *adj* 1 enjoying physical comfort — see COMFORTABLE 2

2 not bound by rigid standards — see EASYGOING 2

3 not tightly fastened, tied, or stretched — see LOOSE 1

relaxing *adj* tending to calm the emotions and relieve stress — see SOOTHING 1

release *n* 1 a freeing from an obligation or responsibility ⟨after they declared bankruptcy, the bank agreed to a *release* from their debt⟩

syn delivery, discharge, quietus, quittance

rel exemption, immunity, waiver

2 a document containing a declaration of an intentional giving up of a right, claim, or privilege — see WAIVER

3 a published statement informing the public of a matter of general interest — see ANNOUNCEMENT

release *vb* 1 to set free (from a state of being held in check) ⟨he *released* his anger with a great yell of frustration⟩

syn loose, loosen, uncork, unleash, unlock, unloose, unloosen

rel discharge, emancipate, enfranchise, free, liberate, manumit, spring, unbind, uncage, unchain, unfetter; air, express, vent

near ant manacle, shackle, trammel; bind, confine, enchain, fetter

ant bridle, check, constrain, contain, control, curb, govern, hold in, inhibit, regulate, rein (in), restrain, tame

2 to find emotional release for — see TAKE OUT 1

3 to set free (as from slavery or confinement) — see FREE 1

4 to set free from entanglement or difficulty — see EXTRICATE

5 to throw or give off — see EMIT 1

relent *vb* to grow less in scope or intensity especially gradually — see DECREASE 2

relentless *adj* showing no signs of slackening or yielding in one's purpose — see UNYIELDING 1

relevance *n* the fact or state of being pertinent — see PERTINENCE

relevancy *n* the fact or state of being pertinent — see PERTINENCE

relevant *adj* having to do with the matter at hand — see PERTINENT

reliability *n* worthiness as the recipient of another's trust or confidence ⟨we never had to question the *reliability* of the park rangers in an emergency⟩

syn dependability, reliableness, solidity, solidness, sureness, trustworthiness

rel infallibility

near ant doubtfulness, dubiousness

reliable *adj* worthy of one's trust — see DEPENDABLE

reliableness *n* worthiness as the recipient of another's trust or confidence — see RELIABILITY

reliance *n* 1 something or someone to which one looks for support — see DEPENDENCE 2

2 the quality or state of needing something or someone — see DEPENDENCE 1

relic *n* 1 a tiny often physical indication of something lost or vanished — see VESTIGE

2 something belonging to or surviving from an earlier period — see ANTIQUE

relief *n* 1 a feeling of ease from grief or trouble — see COMFORT 1

2 a person or thing that takes the place of another — see SUBSTITUTE

3 reduction of or freedom from pain — see EASE 1

relieve *vb* 1 to make more bearable or less severe — see HELP 2

2 to set (a person or thing) free of something that encumbers — see RID

religion *n* 1 a body of beliefs and practices regarding the supernatural and the worship of one or more deities ⟨the Jewish *religion* has followers in many parts of the globe⟩

syn credo, creed, cult, faith, persuasion

rel church, communion, denomination, sect; belief, doctrine, dogma, theology; monotheism, polytheism, theism

near ant agnosticism, atheism, secularism

2 belief and trust in and loyalty to God — see FAITH 1

religious *adj* 1 of, relating to, or used in the practice or worship services of a religion ⟨J.S. Bach wrote some of the most beautiful *religious* music in the world⟩

syn devotional, sacred, spiritual

rel blessed, consecrated, hallowed, holy, sacrosanct, sanctified; liturgical, ritual, sacramental

near ant earthly, mundane, worldly; irreligious, semireligious

ant nonreligious, profane, secular

2 showing a devotion to God and to a life of virtue — see HOLY 1

relinquish *vb* 1 to give (something) over to the control or possession of another usually under duress — see SURRENDER 1

2 to give up (as a position of authority) formally — see ABDICATE

relinquishment *n* the usually forced yielding of one's person or possessions to the control of another — see SURRENDER

relish *n* 1 positive regard for something — see LIKING

2 the feeling experienced when one's wishes are met — see PLEASURE 1

relish *vb* to take pleasure in — see ENJOY 1

reluctance *n* a lack of willingness or desire to do or accept something ⟨the mice showed an odd *reluctance* to eat the cheese we had put out for them⟩

syn disinclination, hesitance, hesitancy, unwillingness

rel faltering, hesitation, indecision, irresolution, shilly-shallying, staggering, vacillation, wavering, wobbling; distrust, distrustfulness, doubt, incertitude, misgiving, mistrust, mistrustfulness, skepticism, suspicion, uncertainty

near ant certainty, certitude, sureness, surety

ant inclination, willingness

reluctant *adj* having doubts about the wisdom of doing something — see HESITANT

rely *vb* to place reliance or trust — see DEPEND 2

remain *vb* to continue to be in a place for a significant amount of time — see STAY 1

remainder *n* 1 a remaining group or portion ⟨the *remainder* of the pills were saved in case they were needed later⟩

syn balance, leavings, leftovers, odds and ends, remains, remnant, residue, rest

rel fragment, scrap; oddment, scraping(s), stub, stump; excess, surplus

near ant bulk, most

2 an unused or unwanted piece or item typically of small size or value — see ¹SCRAP 1

remains *n pl* 1 the portion or bits of something left over or behind after it has been destroyed ⟨the *remains* of the house ripped apart by the tornado littered the block for weeks afterward⟩

syn ashes, debris, residue, rubble, ruins, wreck, wreckage

rel detritus, flotsam, jetsam; garbage, refuse, trash

2 a dead body — see CORPSE

3 a remaining group or portion — see REMAINDER 1

remake *vb* 1 to make different in some way — see CHANGE 1

2 to make or do again — see REPEAT 4

remaking *n* the act, process, or result of making different — see CHANGE

remark *n* a briefly expressed opinion ⟨the speaker made some short *remarks* about the new museum before officially opening the doors to visitors⟩

syn comment, note, observation, reflection

rel analysis, commentary, exposition; annotation; belief, conviction, eye, feeling, judgment (*or* judgement), mind, notion, opinion, persuasion, sentiment, verdict, view

remark *vb* 1 to make a statement of one's opinion ⟨he *remarked* on the attractiveness of the background music in the restaurant⟩

syn comment, note, observe, opine

rel articulate, express, say, speak, state, talk, tell, utter, verbalize, vocalize

2 to make note of (something) through the use of one's eyes — see SEE 1

remarkable *adj* 1 different from the ordinary in a way that causes curiosity or suspicion — see ODD 2

2 likely to attract attention — see NOTICEABLE

remediable *adj* capable of being corrected ⟨the problems with the local transportation system were severe but still *remediable*⟩

syn correctable, fixable, rectifiable, repairable, reparable

rel amendable, improvable, resolvable; redeemable

near ant irredeemable, irretrievable, unrecoverable

ant incorrigible, irremediable, irreparable

remedial *adj* serving to raise or adjust something to some standard or proper condition — see CORRECTIVE 1

remedy *n* 1 a substance or preparation used to treat disease — see MEDICINE

2 something that corrects or counteracts something undesirable — see CURE 1

remedy *vb* 1 to bring about recovery from — see CURE 1

2 to remove errors, defects, deficiencies, or deviations from — see CORRECT 1

remedying *adj* serving to raise or adjust something to some standard or proper condition — see CORRECTIVE 1

remember *vb* to bring back to mind ⟨I *remember* the fun we had last summer very clearly, but I can't *remember* anything I learned in school yesterday⟩

syn hark back (to), mind [*chiefly dialect*], recall, recollect, reminisce (about), think (of)

rel recapture, recur; educe, elicit, evoke, extract, remind; relive

phrases look back (on *or* upon)

near ant disregard, ignore, neglect, overlook; lose, miss; blank (out)

ant forget, unlearn

remembrance *n* 1 a particular act or instance of recalling or the thing remembered — see MEMORY 2

2 something that serves to keep alive the memory of a person or event — see MEMORIAL

3 the power or process of recalling what has been previously learned or experienced — see MEMORY 1

reminder *n* something that serves to keep alive the memory of a person or event — see MEMORIAL

reminisce (about) *vb* to bring back to mind — see REMEMBER

reminiscence *n* 1 a particular act or instance of recalling or the thing remembered — see MEMORY 2

---

syn synonym(s)   *rel* related words
ant antonym(s)   *near ant* near antonym(s)

2 the power or process of recalling what has been previously learned or experienced — see MEMORY 1

reminiscent *adj* provoking a memory or mental association — see SUGGESTIVE 2

remiss *adj* failing to give proper care and attention — see NEGLIGENT

remission *n* release from the guilt or penalty of an offense — see PARDON

remissness *n* failure to take the care that a cautious person usually takes — see NEGLIGENCE 1

remit *vb* **1** to grow less in scope or intensity especially gradually — see DECREASE 2
2 to overlook or dismiss as of little importance — see EXCUSE 1

remitment *n* the act of offering money in exchange for goods or services — see PAYMENT 1

remittable *adj* worthy of forgiveness — see VENIAL

remittal *n* release from the guilt or penalty of an offense — see PARDON

remittance *n* **1** something (as money) that is given or received in return for goods or services — see PAYMENT 1
2 the act of offering money in exchange for goods or services — see PAYMENT 1

remnant *n* **1** a remaining group or portion — see REMAINDER 1
2 an unused or unwanted piece or item typically of small size or value — see ¹SCRAP 1

remodel *vb* to make different in some way — see CHANGE 1

remodeling *n* the act, process, or result of making different — see CHANGE

remonstrance *n* a feeling or declaration of disapproval or dissent — see OBJECTION

remonstrate (with) *vb* to present an opposing opinion or argument — see OBJECT

remorse *n* a feeling of responsibility for wrongdoing — see GUILT 1

remorseful *adj* **1** feeling sorrow for a wrong that one has done — see CONTRITE 1
2 suffering from or expressive of a feeling of responsibility for wrongdoing — see GUILTY 2

remorsefulness *n* a feeling of responsibility for wrongdoing — see GUILT 1

remorseless *adj* not sorry for having done wrong ⟨the *remorseless* killer was sentenced to life in prison without chance of parole⟩
syn impenitent, unrepentant
rel compassionless, cruel, merciless, pitiless, ruthless, unmerciful; shameless, unashamed
near ant ashamed, hangdog, shamed, shamefaced
ant contrite, guilty, penitent, regretful, remorseful, repentant, sorry

remote *adj* **1** small in degree ⟨there's a *remote* chance that it'll rain today, so I brought an umbrella⟩
syn negligible, off, outside, slight, slim, small

near ant great, large; distinct, significant
ant good
2 having or showing a lack of friendliness or interest in others — see COOL 1
3 hidden from view — see SECLUDED
4 not close in time or space — see DISTANT 1

remotest *adj* most distant from a center — see EXTREME 1

removal *n* the getting rid of whatever is unwanted or useless — see DISPOSAL 1

remove *n* the space or amount of space between two points, lines, surfaces, or objects — see DISTANCE

remove *vb* **1** to rid oneself of (a garment) ⟨I *removed* my coat as soon as I got inside⟩
syn doff, peel (off), put off, take off
rel husk, shed
near ant wear
ant don, put on, slip (into)
2 to take away from a place or position ⟨he carefully *removed* the old manuscript from the shelf⟩
syn clear, draw, withdraw
rel demount, dislodge; abstract, cut, extract, pull; move, shift, transfer
near ant mount
ant place, put
3 to change the place or position of — see MOVE 1
4 to let go from office, service, or employment — see DISMISS 1

removed *adj* not close in time or space — see DISTANT 1

remunerate *vb* **1** to give (someone) the sum of money owed for goods or services received — see PAY 1
2 to provide (someone) with a just payment for loss or injury — see COMPENSATE 1

remuneration *n* **1** the act of offering money in exchange for goods or services — see PAYMENT 1
2 payment to another for a loss or injury — see COMPENSATION 1
3 something (as money) that is given or received in return for goods or services — see PAYMENT 2

remunerative *adj* yielding a profit — see PROFITABLE 1

rend *vb* to cause (something) to separate into jagged pieces by violently pulling at it — see TEAR 1

render *vb* to give (something) over to the control or possession of another usually under duress — see SURRENDER 1

rendezvous *vb* to come together into one body or place — see ASSEMBLE 1

rendezvous *n* **1** a place for spending time or for socializing — see HANGOUT
2 an agreement to be present at a specified time and place — see ENGAGEMENT 2

renegade *n* a person who abandons a cause or organization usually without right ⟨a band of *renegades* who had deserted their infantry units and were making their way to Mexico⟩
syn defector, deserter, recreant

rel betrayer, double-crosser, quisling, traitor, turncoat; chicken, coward, craven, dastard, poltroon; defier, insurgent, insurrectionary, insurrectionist, mutineer, rebel, red, revolter, revolutionary, revolutionist, revolutionizer

near ant adherent, disciple, follower, zealot

ant loyalist

renege *vb* to break a promise or agreement ⟨Dad promised to take me out for ice cream on the weekend, only to *renege* on Saturday morning⟩

syn back down, back off, cop out

rel chicken (out); disavow, recall, recant, retract, take back, withdraw

phrases go back on

near ant follow through; fulfill (*or* fulfil), honor

renew *vb* **1** to bring back to a former condition or vigor ⟨the trip to New York *renewed* our enthusiasm for travel⟩

syn freshen, recreate, refresh, refreshen, regenerate, rejuvenate, restore, revitalize, revive

rel make over, refurbish, rehabilitate, remake, remodel, renovate; refill, replenish, resupply

2 to begin again or return to after an interruption — see RESUME

3 to bring back to life, practice, or activity — see REVIVE 1

renewal *n* the act or an instance of bringing something back to life, public attention, or vigorous activity — see REVIVAL

renewed *adj* made or become fresh in spirits or vigor — see NEW 4

renounce *vb* **1** to give up (as a position of authority) formally — see ABDICATE

2 to solemnly or formally reject or go back on (as something formerly adhered to) — see ABJURE

renouncement *n* the act or practice of giving up or rejecting something once enjoyed or desired — see RENUNCIATION

renovate *vb* to put into good shape or working order again — see MEND 1

renown *n* the fact or state of being known to the public — see FAME

renowned *adj* widely known — see FAMOUS

rent *n* **1** a long deep cut — see GASH

2 an open space in a barrier (as a wall or hedge) — see GAP 1

rent *vb* **1** to give the possession and use of (something) in return for periodic payment ⟨we *rented* the apartment to a college student for $500 a month⟩

syn lease, let [*chiefly British*]

rel charter, hire; lodge; sublease, sublet

2 to take or get the temporary use of (something) for a set sum — see HIRE 1

renter *n* **1** one who rents a room or apartment in another's house — see TENANT

2 the owner of land or housing that is rented to another — see LANDLORD

renunciation *n* the act or practice of giving up or rejecting something once enjoyed or desired ⟨his *renunciation* of his smoking habit pleased his whole family⟩

syn abnegation, renouncement, repudiation, self-denial

rel denial, refusal; relinquishment, resignation, surrender

near ant acceptance; adoption, embrace, espousal

ant indulgence, self-indulgence

reopen *vb* to begin again or return to after an interruption — see RESUME

repair *n* a state of being or fitness — see CONDITION 1

repair *vb* to put into good shape or working order again — see MEND 1

repairable *adj* capable of being corrected — see REMEDIABLE

reparable *adj* capable of being corrected — see REMEDIABLE

reparation *n* payment to another for a loss or injury — see COMPENSATION 1

repartee *n* **1** a quick witty response — see RETORT 1

2 good-natured teasing or exchanging of clever remarks — see BANTER

repast *n* food eaten or prepared for eating at one time — see MEAL

repay *vb* to make a return payment to ⟨I *repaid* my friend the twenty dollars he had lent me⟩

syn refund, reimburse

rel quit, satisfy, settle

phrases pay back

repeal *n* the act of putting an end to something planned or previously agreed to — see CANCELLATION

repeal *vb* **1** to put an end to (something planned or previously agreed to) — see CANCEL 1

2 to put an end to by formal action — see ABOLISH

repeat *n* the act of saying or doing over again ⟨the news story will be broadcast on the six o'clock show, with a *repeat* on the 11 o'clock newscast⟩

syn duplication, reduplication, reiteration, repetition, replication

rel rerun

repeat *vb* **1** to say or state again ⟨I *repeated* the address over and over until I had it memorized⟩

syn din, rehearse, reiterate

rel echo, parrot; mouth

2 to give from memory ⟨*repeated* correctly all the verses she had memorized⟩

syn recite, say

rel declaim, mouth, orate, speak

near ant read

3 to say after another ⟨now *repeat* the oath after me⟩

syn echo, parrot, quote

rel mouth; copy, imitate, mimic

4 to make or do again ⟨try not to *repeat* your mistakes⟩

syn duplicate, redo, reduplicate, reiterate, remake, replicate

rel renew

---

syn synonym(s)   *rel* related words
ant antonym(s)   *near ant* near antonym(s)

repeated *adj* appearing or occurring repeatedly from time to time — see REGULAR 1

repeatedly *adv* many times — see OFTEN

repel *vb* 1 to drive back ⟨the defenders *repelled* the attacking army after several hours of fierce fighting⟩
syn fend (off), repulse, stave off
rel hold (off), resist, withstand; deflect, ward (off); rebuff, snub, spurn
near ant welcome
2 to cause to feel disgust — see DISGUST
3 to refuse to give in to — see RESIST

repelled *adj* filled with disgust — see SICK 2

repellent *also* **repellant** *adj* causing intense displeasure, disgust, or resentment — see OFFENSIVE 1

repent *vb* to feel sorry or dissatisfied about — see REGRET

repentance *n* a feeling of responsibility for wrongdoing — see GUILT 1

repentant *adj* 1 feeling sorrow for a wrong that one has done — see CONTRITE 1
2 suffering from or expressive of a feeling of responsibility for wrongdoing — see GUILTY 2

repercussion *n* the power to bring about a result on another — see EFFECT 2

repetition *n* the act of saying or doing over again — see REPEAT

repetitious *adj* marked by repetition — see REPETITIVE

repetitive *adj* marked by repetition ⟨the *repetitive* lyrics of so many rock songs⟩
syn reiterative, repetitious

rephrase *vb* to express something (as a text or statement) in different words — see PARAPHRASE

rephrasing *n* an instance of expressing something in different words — see PARAPHRASE

repine *vb* to express dissatisfaction, pain, or resentment usually tiresomely — see COMPLAIN

repine (for) *vb* to have an earnest wish to own or enjoy — see DESIRE

replace *vb* 1 to take the place of ⟨the old street lights were *replaced* with more energy-efficient models⟩
syn displace, substitute, supersede, supplant
rel preempt, usurp
2 to bring, send, or put back to a former or proper place — see RETURN 1

replacement *n* a person or thing that takes the place of another — see SUBSTITUTE

replete *adj* possessing or covered with great numbers or amounts of something specified — see RIFE

replica *n* 1 something or someone that closely resembles another — see IMAGE 1
2 something that is made to look exactly like something else — see COPY

replicate *vb* 1 to make an exact likeness of — see COPY 1
2 to make or do again — see REPEAT 4

replication *n* 1 something that is made to look exactly like something else — see COPY
2 the act of saying or doing over again — see REPEAT

reply *n* 1 action or behavior that is done in return to other action or behavior — see REACTION
2 something spoken or written in reaction especially to a question — see ANSWER 1

reply *vb* 1 to act or behave in response (as to a stimulus or influence) — see REACT
2 to speak or write in reaction to a question or to another reaction — see ANSWER 1

report *n* 1 a loud explosive sound — see CLAP 1
2 a relating of events usually in the order in which they happened — see ACCOUNT 1
3 overall quality as seen or judged by people in general — see REPUTATION

report *vb* to give an oral or written account of in some detail — see TELL 1

reporter *n* a person employed by a newspaper, magazine, or radio or television station to gather, write, or report news ⟨the *reporter* was careful to ask as many questions as possible without annoying anyone⟩
syn correspondent, journalist
rel announcer, broadcaster, newscaster; newsman, newspaperman; anchor, anchorman, anchorperson, anchorwoman, legman; columnist, commentator, copyreader, editor, sportswriter, staffer

repose *n* 1 a natural periodic loss of consciousness during which the body restores itself — see SLEEP 1
2 a state of freedom from storm or disturbance — see CALM
3 freedom from activity or labor — see ¹REST 1

repose *vb* to refrain from labor or exertion — see REST 1

repository *n* a building for storing goods — see STOREHOUSE

repossess *vb* to get again in one's possession — see RECOVER 1

repossession *n* the act or process of getting something back — see RECOVERY 1

reprehend *vb* 1 to declare to be morally wrong or evil — see CONDEMN 1
2 to express one's unfavorable opinion of the worth or quality of — see CRITICIZE

reprehensible *adj* 1 deserving reproach or blame — see BLAMEWORTHY
2 provoking or likely to provoke protest — see OBJECTIONABLE

represent *vb* 1 to point out the chief quality or qualities of an individual or group — see CHARACTERIZE 1
2 to present a picture of — see PICTURE 1
3 to serve as a material counterpart of — see SYMBOLIZE 1

representative *n* 1 a person who acts or does business for another — see AGENT 2
2 a person sent on a mission to represent another — see AMBASSADOR

3 one of a group or collection that shows what the whole is like — see EXAMPLE

representative *adj* **1** having or showing the qualities associated with the members of a particular group or kind — see TYPICAL 1

2 having the function or meaning of a symbol — see SYMBOLIC

repress *vb* **1** to put a stop to (something) by the use of force — see QUELL 1

2 to refrain from openly showing or uttering — see SUPPRESS 2

repression *n* the checking of one's true feelings and impulses when dealing with others — see CONSTRAINT 1

reprimand *n* an often public or formal expression of disapproval — see CENSURE

reprimand *vb* **1** to criticize (someone) severely or angrily especially for personal failings — see SCOLD

2 to criticize (someone) usually gently so as to correct a fault — see REBUKE 1

3 to express public or formal disapproval of — see CENSURE 1

reprisal *n* the act or an instance of paying back an injury with an injury — see REVENGE

reproach *n* **1** a cause of shame — see DISGRACE 2

2 an often public or formal expression of disapproval — see CENSURE

3 the state of having lost the esteem of others — see DISGRACE 1

reproach *vb* **1** to criticize (someone) severely or angrily especially for personal failings — see SCOLD

2 to criticize (someone) usually gently so as to correct a fault — see REBUKE 1

3 to express public or formal disapproval of — see CENSURE 1

reproachable *adj* deserving reproach or blame — see BLAMEWORTHY

reprobate *adj* having or showing lowered moral character or standards — see CORRUPT

reprobate *n* a mean, evil, or unprincipled person — see VILLAIN

reprobate *vb* to declare to be morally wrong or evil — see CONDEMN 1

reproduce *vb* **1** to bring forth offspring — see PROCREATE

2 to make an exact likeness of — see COPY 1

reproduction *n* something that is made to look exactly like something else — see COPY

reproof *n* an often public or formal expression of disapproval — see CENSURE

reprove *vb* **1** to criticize (someone) usually gently so as to correct a fault — see REBUKE 1

2 to express public or formal disapproval of — see CENSURE 1

3 to hold an unfavorable opinion of — see DISAPPROVE

republic *n* government in which the supreme power is held by the people and

used by them directly or indirectly through representation — see DEMOCRACY

republican *adj* of, relating to, or favoring political democracy — see DEMOCRATIC

repudiate *vb* **1** to declare not to be true — see DENY 1

2 to refuse to acknowledge as one's own or as one's responsibility — see DISCLAIM 1

3 to show unwillingness to accept, do, engage in, or agree to — see DECLINE 1

repudiation *n* **1** a refusal to confirm the truth of a statement — see DENIAL 2

2 the act or practice of giving up or rejecting something once enjoyed or desired — see RENUNCIATION

repugnance *n* a dislike so strong as to cause stomach upset or queasiness — see DISGUST

repugnant *adj* causing intense displeasure, disgust, or resentment — see OFFENSIVE 1

repulse *n* treatment that is deliberately unfriendly — see COLD SHOULDER

repulse *vb* **1** to cause to feel disgust — see DISGUST

2 to drive back — see REPEL 1

repulsed *adj* filled with disgust — see SICK 2

repulsion *n* a dislike so strong as to cause stomach upset or queasiness — see DISGUST

repulsive *adj* causing intense displeasure, disgust, or resentment — see OFFENSIVE 1

repulsiveness *n* the quality of inspiring intense dread or dismay — see HORROR 1

reputable *adj* having a good reputation especially in a field of knowledge — see RESPECTABLE 1

reputation *n* overall quality as seen or judged by people in general ⟨the college's athletic department has a good *reputation*, but the school's science facilities are a bit lacking⟩

syn character, mark, name, note, report, repute

rel credit, honor; celebrity, fame, notoriety, renown

near ant infamy

repute *n* overall quality as seen or judged by people in general — see REPUTATION

reputed *adj* **1** appearing to be true on the basis of evidence that may or may not be confirmed — see APPARENT 1

2 having a good reputation especially in a field of knowledge — see RESPECTABLE 1

request *n* an act or instance of asking for information — see QUESTION 1

request *vb* **1** to give a request or demand for — see ORDER 2

2 to make a request for — see ASK (FOR) 1

3 to make a request of — see ASK 2

requiem *n* a composition expressing one's grief over a loss — see LAMENT 2

require *vb* to have as a requirement — see NEED 1

syn synonym(s) *rel* related words
ant antonym(s) *near ant* near antonym(s)

required *adj* **1** forcing one's compliance or participation by or as if by law — see MANDATORY

2 impossible to do without — see ESSENTIAL 1

requirement *n* something necessary, indispensable, or unavoidable — see ESSENTIAL 1

requisite *adj* impossible to do without — see ESSENTIAL 1

requisite *n* something necessary, indispensable, or unavoidable — see ESSENTIAL 1

requisition *n* something that someone insists upon having — see DEMAND 1

requisition *vb* to give a request or demand for — see ORDER 2

requital *n* **1** payment to another for a loss or injury — see COMPENSATION 1

2 something (as money) that is given or received in return for goods or services — see PAYMENT 2

3 the act or an instance of paying back an injury with an injury — see REVENGE

requite *vb* **1** to provide (someone) with a just payment for loss or injury — see COMPENSATE 1

2 to punish in kind the wrongdoer responsible for — see AVENGE

rescind *vb* **1** to put an end to (something planned or previously agreed to) — see CANCEL 1

2 to put an end to by formal action — see ABOLISH

rescission *n* the act of putting an end to something planned or previously agreed to — see CANCELLATION

rescue *vb* to remove from danger or harm — see SAVE 2

rescuer *n* one that saves from danger or destruction — see SAVIOR

research *n* a systematic search for the truth or facts about something — see INQUIRY 1

research *vb* to search through or into — see EXPLORE 1

resemblance *n* **1** a point which two or more things share in common — see SIMILARITY 2

2 the quality or state of having many qualities in common — see SIMILARITY 1

resembling *adj* having qualities in common — see ALIKE

resentful *adj* **1** having or showing deep-seated resentment — see BITTER 1

2 having or showing mean resentment of another's possessions or advantages — see ENVIOUS

resentfully *adv* with feelings of bitterness or grief — see HARD 2

resentment *n* **1** a lingering ill will towards a person for a real or imagined wrong — see GRUDGE 1

2 a painful awareness of another's possessions or advantages and a desire to have them too — see ENVY

3 the feeling of being offended or resentful after a slight or indignity — see PIQUE

reservation *n* something upon which the carrying out of an agreement or offer depends — see CONDITION 2

reserve *n* **1** the checking of one's true feelings and impulses when dealing with others — see CONSTRAINT 1

2 a collection of things kept available for future use or need — see STORE

3 a person or thing that takes the place of another — see SUBSTITUTE

4 an interchangeable part or piece of equipment that is kept on hand for replacement of an original — see SPARE

reserve *vb* **1** to arrange to have something (as a hotel room) held for one's future use ⟨we made sure to *reserve* a kennel for our dog several months before the start of the family vacation⟩

syn bespeak, book

rel earmark; contract, engage, retain

2 to continue to have in one's possession or power — see KEEP 2

3 to keep or intend for a special purpose — see DEVOTE 1

reserved *adj* tending not to speak frequently (as by habit or inclination) — see SILENT 2

reside *vb* to have a home — see LIVE 1

residence *n* the place where one lives — see HOME 1

resident *n* one who lives permanently in a place — see INHABITANT

resider *n* one who lives permanently in a place — see INHABITANT

residue *n* **1** the portion or bits of something left over or behind after it has been destroyed — see REMAINS 1

2 a remaining group or portion — see REMAINDER 1

resign *vb* to give up (as a position of authority) formally — see ABDICATE

resign (from) *vb* to give up (a job or office) — see QUIT 1

resigned *adj* receiving or enduring without offering resistance — see PASSIVE

resilient *adj* able to revert to original size and shape after being stretched, squeezed, or twisted — see ELASTIC 1

resist *vb* to refuse to give in to ⟨it is important to *resist* the temptation to run away from your problems⟩

syn buck, defy, fight, oppose, repel, withstand

rel battle, combat, contend (with), counter; contest, dispute; baffle, balk, foil, frustrate, thwart; check, counter, hinder, obstruct, stem

ant bow (to), capitulate (to), give in (to), submit (to), succumb (to), surrender (to), yield (to)

resistance *n* **1** the inclination to resist ⟨there was much *resistance* to the idea of removing our baseball caps while eating⟩

syn defiance, opposition

rel demur, objection, protest, remonstrance; compunction, misgiving, reservation; disobedience, noncompliance

near ant compliance, obedience; acceptance, approval

ant acquiescence

2 a secret organization in a conquered country fighting against enemy forces ⟨soldiers from the *resistance* were cap-

tured after a short battle outside the foreign ministry⟩
syn underground
rel cabal, conspiracy
resolute *adj* fully committed to achieving a goal — see DETERMINED 1
resoluteness *n* firm or unwavering adherence to one's purpose — see DETERMINATION 1
resolution *n* **1** a position arrived at after consideration — see DECISION 1
2 firm or unwavering adherence to one's purpose — see DETERMINATION 1
resolvable *adj* capable of having the reason for or cause of determined — see SOLVABLE
resolve *n* firm or unwavering adherence to one's purpose — see DETERMINATION 1
resolve *vb* **1** to come to a judgment after discussion or consideration — see DECIDE 1
2 to find an answer for through reasoning — see SOLVE
3 to set or force apart — see SEPARATE 1
resolved *adj* fully committed to achieving a goal — see DETERMINED 1
resonant *adj* marked by conspicuously full and rich sounds or tones ⟨the orator's *resonant* voice filled the hall⟩
syn golden, resounding, reverberant, reverberating, ringing, round, sonorous, vibrant
rel deep, full, mellifluous, mellow, rich; loud, powerful, stentorian, thundering, thunderous
near ant cavernous, hollow; faint, low, murmurous, muted, smothered, soft, weak; thin, tinny
resonate *vb* to continue or be repeated in a series of reflected sound waves — see REVERBERATE
resort (to) *vb* **1** to use or seek out as a source of aid, relief, or advantage ⟨we were so desperate for better grades on our homework that we were forced to *resort to* spending all our evenings at the library⟩
syn go (to), refer (to), turn (to)
rel employ, use, utilize; depend (on), rely (on)
phrases fall back on
2 to go to or spend time in often — see FREQUENT
resort *n* **1** a place for spending time or for socializing — see HANGOUT
2 something that one uses to accomplish an end especially when the usual means is not available — see RESOURCE 1
resound *vb* to continue or be repeated in a series of reflected sound waves — see REVERBERATE
resounding *adj* **1** full of or characterized by the presence of noise — see NOISY 2
2 marked by a high volume of sound — see LOUD 1
3 marked by conspicuously full and rich sounds or tones — see RESONANT

4 marked by or uttered with forcefulness — see EMPHATIC 1
resource *n* **1** something that one uses to accomplish an end especially when the usual means is not available ⟨we used every possible *resource* to raise the funds needed to save our town's oldest house⟩
syn expedient, recourse, resort
rel hope, opportunity, possibility, relief; makeshift, replacement, stopgap, substitute
2 resources *pl* available money — see FUND 2
respect *n* **1** relation to or concern with something specified ⟨with *respect* to your application⟩
syn reference, regard
2 a feeling of great approval and liking — see ADMIRATION 1
3 respects *pl* best wishes — see COMPLIMENT
respect *vb* to think very highly or favorably of — see ADMIRE
respectable *adj* **1** having a good reputation especially in a field of knowledge ⟨no *respectable* dietician would advise people to eat just one kind of food⟩
syn esteemed, name, prestigious, reputable, reputed, respected
rel honorable, worthy; creditable, good, praiseworthy; celebrated, distinguished, famed, famous, honored, illustrious, notable, prominent, renowned, well-known
ant disreputable, loose
2 following accepted rules of moral conduct — see HONORABLE 1
3 following the established traditions of refined society and good taste — see PROPER 1
4 of a level of quality that meets one's needs or standards — see ADEQUATE
5 sufficiently large in size, amount, or number to merit attention — see CONSIDERABLE 1
respected *adj* having a good reputation especially in a field of knowledge — see RESPECTABLE 1
respectful *adj* marked by or showing proper regard for another's higher status ⟨the children were remarkably *respectful* while in the President's office⟩
syn deferential, dutiful, regardful
rel reverent, reverential, venerating, worshipful; fawning, groveling (*or* grovelling), obsequious, servile, subservient, sycophantic, toadying; civil, courteous, gracious, polite
near ant abusive, insulting, offensive; contemptuous, impudent, irreverent; discourteous, insolent, rude, uncivil
ant disrespectful
respecting *prep* having to do with — see ABOUT 1
respective *adj* not the same or shared — see SEPARATE 1
respire *vb* to inhale and exhale air — see BREATHE 1
resplendence *n* impressiveness of beauty on a large scale — see MAGNIFICENCE

---

syn synonym(s) **rel** related words
ant antonym(s) **near ant** near antonym(s)

respond *vb* **1** to act or behave in response (as to a stimulus or influence) — see REACT

2 to speak or write in reaction to a question or to another reaction — see ANSWER 1

response *n* **1** action or behavior that is done in return to other action or behavior — see REACTION

2 something spoken or written in reaction especially to a question — see ANSWER 1

responsibility *n* **1** the state of being held as the cause of something that needs to be set right ⟨*responsibility* for the accident lies with the driver who was speeding⟩

syn blame, fault, liability

rel accountability

2 something one must do because of prior agreement — see OBLIGATION

responsible *adj* **1** being the one who must meet an obligation or suffer the consequences for failing to do so ⟨each student is *responsible* for getting his or her own homework done on time⟩

syn accountable, answerable, liable

rel beholden, indebted, obligated, obliged

near ant exempt, immune

ant irresponsible, unaccountable

2 worthy of one's trust — see DEPENDABLE

¹**rest** *n* **1** freedom from activity or labor ⟨I'm looking forward to enjoying some *rest* at the end of the school term⟩

syn ease, leisure, relaxation, repose

rel catnapping, dozing, napping, resting, sleep, slumber, slumbering, snoozing; quiet, silence, stillness; calm, peace, peacefulness, placidity, restfulness, serenity, tranquillity (*or* tranquility)

near ant pressure, strain, stress, tension

ant exertion, labor, toil, work

2 a natural periodic loss of consciousness during which the body restores itself — see SLEEP 1

²**rest** *n* a remaining group or portion — see REMAINDER 1

rest *vb* **1** to refrain from labor or exertion ⟨a beach resort that caters to gung ho exercisers and athletes as well as vacationers who just want to *rest*⟩

syn bask, loll, lounge, relax, repose

rel bum, goldbrick, idle, loaf, slack (off)

near ant drudge, grub, hump, hustle, labor, moil, peg (away), plod, plow, plug, slave, slog, strain, strive, struggle, sweat, toil, travail, work; exercise, work out

2 be in a state of sleep — see SLEEP 1

3 to find a basis — see BASE

restart *vb* to begin again or return to after an interruption — see RESUME

restate *vb* to express something (as a text or statement) in different words — see PARAPHRASE

restatement *n* an instance of expressing something in different words — see PARAPHRASE

restating *n* an instance of expressing something in different words — see PARAPHRASE

restaurant *n* a public establishment where meals are served to paying customers for consumption on the premises ⟨when we get sick of cooking dinner at home, we like to go out to eat at a nice *restaurant*⟩

syn café (*also* cafe), diner, grill

rel cafeteria, coffeehouse, garden, luncheonette, lunchroom, snack bar, tearoom; bar, barroom, inn, tavern

restful *adj* free from disturbing noise or uproar — see QUIET 1

restfulness *n* a state of freedom from storm or disturbance — see CALM

resting *adj* being in a state of suspended consciousness — see ASLEEP 1

resting *n* a natural periodic loss of consciousness during which the body restores itself — see SLEEP 1

restitution *n* payment to another for a loss or injury — see COMPENSATION 1

restive *adj* **1** given to resisting authority or another's control — see DISOBEDIENT

2 lacking or denying rest — see RESTLESS 1

restiveness *n* **1** a disturbed or uneasy state — see UNREST

2 a state of nervousness marked by sudden jerky movements — see JUMPINESS

restless *adj* **1** lacking or denying rest ⟨the worried mother spent a *restless* night, tossing and turning in bed for hours⟩

syn restive, uneasy, unquiet, unrestful

rel agitated, distressed, disturbed, perturbed, troubled, unsettled; aflutter, anxious, dithery, edgy, fidgety, het up, hung up, jittery, jumpy, nervous, nervy, tense, upset, uptight, worried

near ant calm, easy, peaceful, quiet, relaxing, tranquil

ant restful

2 marked by or causing agitation or uncomfortable feelings — see NERVOUS 2

restlessness *n* **1** a disturbed or uneasy state — see UNREST

2 the state of being bored — see BOREDOM

restorative *adj* **1** good for the health — see HEALTHFUL

2 having a renewing effect on the state of the body or mind — see TONIC

restore *vb* **1** to bring back to a former condition or vigor — see RENEW 1

2 to bring, send, or put back to a former or proper place — see RETURN 1

restrain *vb* **1** to keep from exceeding a desirable degree or level (as of expression) — see CONTROL 1

2 to take or keep under one's control by authority of law — see ARREST 1

restrained *adj* not excessively showy — see QUIET 2

restraint *n* **1** the checking of one's true feelings and impulses when dealing with others — see CONSTRAINT 1

2 something that limits one's freedom of action or choice — see RESTRICTION 1

3 the power to control one's actions, impulses, or emotions — see WILL 1

restrict *vb* **1** to set bounds or an upper limit for — see LIMIT 1

2 to limit the meaning of (as a noun) — see QUALIFY 1

restricted *adj* having distinct or certain limits — see LIMITED 1

restriction *n* **1** something that limits one's freedom of action or choice ⟨my parents placed several *restrictions* on the party we were planning⟩

syn check, condition, constraint, curb, fetter, limitation, restraint

rel exception, proviso, qualification, reservation, stipulation, strings

near ant freedom, latitude

2 the act or practice of keeping something (as an activity) within certain boundaries ⟨the *restriction* of surfing to the southern end of the beach rankled some surfers⟩

syn confinement, limitation

rel constraint, restraint; isolation, segregation

rest room *n* a room furnished with a fixture for flushing body waste — see TOILET

result *n* **1** a condition or occurrence traceable to a cause — see EFFECT 1

2 something attained by mental effort and especially by computation — see ANSWER 2

result (in) *vb* to be the cause of (a situation, action, or state of mind) — see EFFECT

resultant *adj* coming as a result ⟨frequent trips to the ice cream parlor and the *resultant* gain in weight were starting to affect my tennis game⟩

syn attendant, consequent, consequential, due (to)

rel accompanying, coincident, concomitant

near ant causal

resultant *n* a condition or occurrence traceable to a cause — see EFFECT 1

resume *vb* to begin again or return to after an interruption ⟨we *resumed* the game as soon as the rain had passed⟩

syn continue, renew, reopen, restart

rel resuscitate, revive

near ant complete, conclude, consummate, end, finalize, finish; belay, break, can, cease, check, cut, desist, discontinue, drop, halt, knock off, leave off, quit, scuttle, shut off, stay, stop, terminate

résumé *or* **resume** *also* **resumé** *n* a short statement of the main points — see SUMMARY

resurgence *n* the act or an instance of bringing something back to life, public attention, or vigorous activity — see REVIVAL

resurrect *vb* to bring back to life, practice, or activity — see REVIVE 1

resurrection *n* the act or an instance of bringing something back to life, public attention, or vigorous activity — see REVIVAL

resuscitate *vb* to bring back to life, practice, or activity — see REVIVE 1

resuscitated *adj* made or become fresh in spirits or vigor — see NEW 4

resuscitation *n* the act or an instance of bringing something back to life, public attention, or vigorous activity — see REVIVAL

retail *vb* to offer for sale to the public — see MARKET

retain *vb* **1** to continue to have in one's possession or power — see KEEP 2

2 to keep, control, or experience as one's own — see HAVE 1

3 to provide with a paying job — see EMPLOY 1

retainer *n* a person hired to perform household or personal services — see SERVANT

retake *vb* to get again in one's possession — see RECOVER 1

retaliate *vb* to punish in kind the wrongdoer responsible for — see AVENGE

retaliation *n* the act or an instance of paying back an injury with an injury — see REVENGE

retard *vb* to cause to move or proceed at a less rapid pace — see SLOW 1

retardation *n* a usually gradual decrease in the pace or level of activity of something — see SLOWDOWN

retarding *n* a usually gradual decrease in the pace or level of activity of something — see SLOWDOWN

retch *vb* to discharge the contents of the stomach through the mouth — see VOMIT

rethink *vb* to consider again especially with the possibility of change or reversal — see RECONSIDER

reticent *adj* **1** given to keeping one's activities hidden from public observation or knowledge — see SECRETIVE

2 tending not to speak frequently (as by habit or inclination) — see SILENT 2

retinue *n* a body of employees or servants who accompany and wait on a person — see CORTEGE

retire *vb* **1** to go to one's bed in order to sleep — see BED

2 to let go from office, service, or employment — see DISMISS 1

3 to move back or away (as from something difficult, dangerous, or disagreeable) — see RETREAT 1

retire (from) *vb* to give up (a job or office) — see QUIT 1

retired *adj* hidden from view — see SECLUDED

retirement *n* an act of moving away especially from something difficult, dangerous, or disagreeable — see RETREAT 1

retiring *adj* **1** not comfortable around people — see SHY 2

2 not having or showing any feelings of superiority, self-assertiveness, or showiness — see HUMBLE 1

---

syn synonym(s)   *rel* related words
ant antonym(s)   *near ant* near antonym(s)

retiringness *n* the absence of any feelings of being better than others — see HUMILITY

retort *n* **1** a quick witty response ⟨the clever boy responded to the bully's threat with a rude *retort*⟩
syn comeback, repartee, riposte
rel back talk; crack, quip, sally, wisecrack, witticism; cut, insult, put-down
2 something spoken or written in reaction especially to a question — see ANSWER 1

retort *vb* to speak or write in reaction to a question or to another reaction — see ANSWER 1

retract *vb* to solemnly or formally reject or go back on (as something formerly adhered to) — see ABJURE

retreat *n* **1** an act of moving away especially from something difficult, dangerous, or disagreeable ⟨we made a strategic *retreat* when we realized that we were outnumbered⟩
syn recession, retirement, revulsion, withdrawal
rel flinch, recoil, shrinking
ant advancement
2 something (as a building) that offers cover from the weather or protection from danger — see SHELTER

retreat *vb* **1** to move back or away (as from something difficult, dangerous, or disagreeable) ⟨we *retreated* to the safety of the cellar at the first sign of the tornado⟩
syn back (away), fall back, recede, retire, withdraw
rel flinch, recoil, shrink; chicken (out); back down, backtrack; abandon, depart, evacuate, go, leave, quit, vacate
phrases give way, lose ground
near ant beard, brave, brazen, breast, confront, dare, defy, face, outbrave
ant advance
2 to hasten away from something dangerous or frightening — see RUN 2

retribution *n* the act or an instance of paying back an injury with an injury — see REVENGE

retrieval *n* the act or process of getting something back — see RECOVERY 1

retrieve *vb* to get again in one's possession — see RECOVER 1

retrograde *adj* directed, turned, or done toward the back — see BACKWARD

retrogress *vb* to go back to a previous and usually lower state or level — see REGRESS

retrogression *n* the act or an instance of going back to an earlier and lower level especially of intelligence or behavior — see REGRESSION

retrospect *n* a usually critical look at a past event — see REVIEW 1

retrospection *n* a usually critical look at a past event — see REVIEW 1

return *n* **1** something spoken or written in reaction especially to a question — see ANSWER 1

2 an increase usually measured in money that comes from labor, business, or property — see INCOME
3 the amount of money left when expenses are subtracted from the total amount received — see PROFIT 1

return *vb* **1** to bring, send, or put back to a former or proper place ⟨when I'm done reading a book, I always *return* it to the very shelf I got it from⟩
syn replace, restore
near ant remove, take
2 to produce as revenue — see YIELD 2
3 to speak or write in reaction to a question or to another reaction — see ANSWER 1

revamp *vb* **1** to make different in some way — see CHANGE 1
2 to prepare for publication by correcting, rewriting, or updating — see EDIT
3 to put into good shape or working order again — see MEND 1

revamping *n* the act, process, or result of making different — see CHANGE

reveal *vb* **1** to make known (as information previously kept secret) ⟨at the end of the book, the detective *reveals* the identity of the mysterious stranger⟩
syn bare, disclose, discover, divulge, expose, spill, tell, unbosom, uncloak, uncover, unmask, unveil
rel debunk, show up; unclothe, undrape; advertise, announce, blaze, broadcast, declare, placard, post, proclaim, promulgate, publicize, publish, sound; betray, blab, give away, leak, let on; inform, squeal, talk; communicate, impart, relate; acknowledge, admit, avow, concede, confess, own; disinter, unearth
phrases spill the beans (about)
near ant camouflage, disguise; gild, gloss (over), varnish, whitewash; becloud, bedim, befog, cloud, darken, eclipse, obscure, overcast, overshadow, shade
ant cloak, conceal, cover (up), enshroud, hide, mask, shroud, veil
2 to make known (something abstract) through outward signs — see SHOW 2

revealing *adj* clearly conveying a special meaning (as one's mood) — see EXPRESSIVE

revel *n* a time or instance of carefree fun — see FLING 1

revel (in) *vb* to take pleasure in — see ENJOY 1

revelation *n* the act or an instance of making known something previously unknown or concealed ⟨the *revelation* of the movie star's secret marriage by the tabloids⟩ ⟨a new biography of the former president that contains several shocking *revelations*⟩
syn disclosure, divulgence, exposure
rel bombshell, surprise; acknowledgment (*also* acknowledgement), admission, avowal, concession, confession
near ant concealment, cover-up

reveler *or* **reveller** *n* one who engages in merrymaking especially in honor of a special occasion — see CELEBRANT

reveling *n* joyful or festive activity — see MERRYMAKING

revelry *n* joyful or festive activity — see MERRYMAKING

revenge *n* the act or an instance of paying back an injury with an injury ⟨my *revenge* on the bully who stole my lunch money was the talk of the whole school⟩
syn reprisal, requital, retaliation, retribution, vengeance
rel counter, counterattack, counteroffensive; castigation, chastisement, correction; desert(s), discipline, nemesis, penalty, punishment, wrath; amends, compensation, indemnification, indemnity, quittance, recompense, recoupment, redress, remuneration, reparation(s), restitution
near ant clemency, grace, leniency, lenity, mercy; forgiveness, pardon, remission

revenge *vb* to punish in kind the wrongdoer responsible for — see AVENGE

revengeful *adj* likely to seek revenge — see VINDICTIVE

revenue *n* an increase usually measured in money that comes from labor, business, or property — see INCOME

reverberant *adj* marked by conspicuously full and rich sounds or tones — see RESONANT

reverberate *vb* to continue or be repeated in a series of reflected sound waves ⟨a room with nothing but hard surfaces will cause the music from your audio system to *reverberate*⟩
syn echo, reecho, resonate, resound, sound
near ant damp, dampen, deaden, dull, quiet

reverberating *adj* marked by conspicuously full and rich sounds or tones — see RESONANT

revere *vb* to offer honor or respect to (someone) as a divine power — see WORSHIP 1

revered *adj* deserving honor and respect especially by reason of age — see VENERABLE 1

reverence *vb* to offer honor or respect to (someone) as a divine power — see WORSHIP 1

reverend *adj* deserving honor and respect especially by reason of age — see VENERABLE 1

reverend *n* a person specially trained and authorized to conduct religious services in a Christian church — see CLERGYMAN

reverie *also* **revery** *n* the state of being lost in thought ⟨unfortunately, I was deep in *reverie* when the teacher called my name⟩
syn daydreaming, study, trance, woolgathering
rel contemplation, meditation, musing; absentmindedness, absorption, abstraction, preoccupation; chimera, conceit, daydream, delusion, dream, fancy, fantasy (*also* phantasy), figment, hallucination,

illusion, phantasm, pipe dream, unreality, vision

reversal *n* a change in status for the worse usually temporarily — see REVERSE 1

reverse *n* **1** a change in status for the worse usually temporarily ⟨the loss of my paper route was just the first of my financial *reverses* since the start of the new year⟩
syn lapse, reversal, setback
rel disappointment, frustration, letdown; comedown, decline, descent, down, downfall, fall; turnabout, turnaround; recession, regression, retrogression, reversion; relapse; breakdown, collapse, crash, meltdown, ruin, undoing
near ant status quo
2 something that is as different as possible from something else — see OPPOSITE

reverse *vb* **1** to change (as an opinion) to the contrary ⟨the principal refused to *reverse* his decision regarding the use of cellular phones⟩
syn switch
rel abrogate, overturn, repeal, rescind, revoke, strike (down); countermand, about-face, backtrack, revert
near ant maintain, support, uphold
2 to change the position of (an object) so that the opposite side or end is showing ⟨when one side of the cleaning cloth gets dirty, just *reverse* it⟩ ⟨you can *reverse* the jacket for a whole new look⟩
syn flip, invert, turn (over)
rel transpose; exchange, interchange, shift, switch; overturn, upset

reversion *n* the act or an instance of going back to an earlier and lower level especially of intelligence or behavior — see REGRESSION

revert *vb* to go back to a previous and usually lower state or level — see REGRESS

review *n* **1** a usually critical look at a past event ⟨a *review* of yesterday's football game gave us a lot of good ideas on how to improve for the next one⟩
syn reappraisal, reconsideration, reexamination, retrospect, retrospection
rel recap, recapitulation, rehash
near ant preview
2 a close look at or over someone or something in order to judge condition — see INSPECTION
3 a publication that appears at regular intervals — see JOURNAL
4 an essay evaluating or analyzing something — see CRITICISM

review *vb* **1** to consider again especially with the possibility of change or reversal — see RECONSIDER
2 to look over closely (as for judging quality or condition) — see INSPECT

reviewer *n* a person who makes or expresses a judgment on the quality of offerings in some field of endeavor — see CRITIC 2

revise *n* the act, process, or result of making different — see CHANGE

revise *vb* **1** to make different in some way — see CHANGE 1

syn synonym(s)   *rel* related words
ant antonym(s)   *near ant* near antonym(s)

2 to prepare for publication by correcting, rewriting, or updating — see EDIT

revision *n* the act, process, or result of making different — see CHANGE

revitalization *n* the act or an instance of bringing something back to life, public attention, or vigorous activity — see REVIVAL

revitalize *vb* **1** to bring back to a former condition or vigor — see RENEW 1

2 to bring back to life, practice, or activity — see REVIVE 1

revival *n* the act or an instance of bringing something back to life, public attention, or vigorous activity ⟨there was a *revival* of interest in the author's classic horror stories after a film version of his best-known story was released⟩

syn reanimation, rebirth, regeneration, rejuvenation, renewal, resurgence, resurrection, resuscitation, revitalization

rel renaissance, renascence; reactivation; rally, recovery, recuperation

near ant death, expiration, extinction

revive *vb* **1** to bring back to life, practice, or activity ⟨an effort to *revive* the once-common custom of celebrating May 1 as a springtime festival of games and dances⟩

syn reanimate, regenerate, rejuvenate, rekindle, renew, resurrect, resuscitate, revitalize

rel reactivate, restart

near ant extinguish, quench, suppress

2 to bring back to a former condition or vigor — see RENEW 1

3 to gain consciousness again — see COME TO

revived *adj* made or become fresh in spirits or vigor — see NEW 4

reviving *adj* having a renewing effect on the state of the body or mind — see TONIC

revocation *n* the act of putting an end to something planned or previously agreed to — see CANCELLATION

revoke *vb* to put an end to (something planned or previously agreed to) — see CANCEL 1

revolt *n* open fighting against authority (as one's own government) — see REBELLION

revolt *vb* **1** to cause to feel disgust — see DISGUST

2 to rise up against established authority — see REBEL

revolted *adj* filled with disgust — see SICK 2

revolter *n* a person who rises up against authority — see REBEL

revolting *adj* causing intense displeasure, disgust, or resentment — see OFFENSIVE 1

revolution *n* **1** a rapid turning about on an axis or central point — see SPIN 1

2 open fighting against authority (as one's own government) — see REBELLION

revolutionary *adj* being very far from the center of public opinion — see EXTREME 2

2 taking part in a rebellion — see REBELLIOUS 1

revolutionary *n* **1** a person who favors rapid and sweeping changes especially in laws and methods of government — see RADICAL

2 a person who rises up against authority — see REBEL

revolutionist *adj* being very far from the center of public opinion — see EXTREME 2

revolutionist *n* **1** a person who favors rapid and sweeping changes especially in laws and methods of government — see RADICAL

2 a person who rises up against authority — see REBEL

revolutionizer *n* a person who rises up against authority — see REBEL

revolve *vb* **1** to move (something) in a curved or circular path on or as if on an axis — see TURN 1

2 to move in circles around an axis or center — see SPIN 1

revulsion *n* **1** a dislike so strong as to cause stomach upset or queasiness — see DISGUST

2 an act of moving away especially from something difficult, dangerous, or disagreeable — see RETREAT 1

reward *n* something offered or given in return for a service performed ⟨there was a *reward* of twenty dollars for the return of her missing cat⟩

syn bounty, price

rel bonus, lagniappe, premium; bonanza, jackpot, treasure trove; award, decoration, distinction, honor, plume, premium, prize; gratuity, tip; desert(s), wages

reward *vb* to give something as a token of gratitude or admiration for a service or achievement ⟨the firefighters were *rewarded* by the city for their heroic actions with vacations⟩

syn award

rel cite, decorate, honor, remember; compensate, pay, recompense, requite; reimburse, repay; acclaim, applaud, commend, compliment, hail, praise, salute

rewarding *adj* making one feel good inside — see HEARTWARMING

reweigh *vb* to consider again especially with the possibility of change or reversal — see RECONSIDER

reword *vb* to express something (as a text or statement) in different words — see PARAPHRASE

rewording *n* an instance of expressing something in different words — see PARAPHRASE

rework *vb* **1** to make different in some way — see CHANGE 1

2 to prepare for publication by correcting, rewriting, or updating — see EDIT

reworking *n* the act, process, or result of making different — see CHANGE

rhapsodic *also* **rhapsodical** *adj* experiencing or marked by overwhelming usually pleasurable emotion — see ECSTATIC

rhapsodically *adv* in an enthusiastic manner — see SKY-HIGH

rhapsodize *vb* to make an exaggerated display of affection or enthusiasm — see GUSH 2

rhapsody *n* a state of overwhelming usually pleasurable emotion — see ECSTASY

rhetoric *n* **1** language that is impressive-sounding but not meaningful or sincere ⟨the mayor's promise to fight drugs was just *rhetoric*, since there was no money in the city budget for a drug program⟩
syn bombast, gas, grandiloquence, hot air, oratory, wind
rel claptrap, drivel, gibberish, hogwash, humbug, jabberwocky, jazz, moonshine, nonsense; affectedness, floweriness, grandiosity, loftiness, pomposity, pretension, pretentiousness; verboseness, verbosity, windiness, wordiness
2 the art or power of speaking or writing in a forceful and convincing way — see ELOQUENCE

rhetorical *adj* marked by the use of impressive-sounding but mostly meaningless words and phrases ⟨an essay on civic duty that was mostly *rhetorical*, full of flowery quotations but providing nothing helpful⟩
syn bombastic, gaseous, gassy, grandiloquent, oratorical, windy
rel elevated, florid, flowery, grandiose, highfalutin, high-flown, high-sounding, inflated, lofty, pompous, pretentious, stilted; overdone, verbose, wordy
near ant eloquent, well-spoken; bald, direct, matter-of-fact, plain, plainspoken, simple, stark, straightforward, unadorned, unaffected, unpretentious

rhythm *n* the recurrent pattern formed by a series of sounds having a regular rise and fall in intensity ⟨the steady *rhythm* of the rain falling on the roof⟩
syn beat, cadence, measure, meter
rel accent, accentuation, emphasis, stress; drum, throb; lilt, movement, sway; hexameter, pentameter, tetrameter, trimeter

rhythmic *or* **rhythmical** *adj* marked by or occurring with a noticeable regularity in the rise and fall of sound ⟨lulled to sleep by the *rhythmic* sound of her mother's voice reading the Bible⟩
syn cadenced, measured, metric, metrical
rel even, regular, steady, uniform; lilting, musical, swaying
ant unmeasured, unrhythmic

riata *n* a rope or long leather thong with a noose used especially for catching livestock — see LASSO

rib *vb* to make fun of in a good-natured way — see TEASE 1

ribald *adj* **1** depicting or referring to sexual matters in a way that is unacceptable in polite society — see OBSCENE 1
2 hinting at or intended to call to mind matters regarded as indecent — see SUGGESTIVE 1

ribaldry *n* the quality or state of being obscene — see OBSCENITY 1

ribbing *adj* marked by or expressive of mild or good-natured teasing — see QUIZZICAL

ribbon *n* a long narrow piece of material — see STRIP

rich *adj* **1** having goods, property, or money in abundance ⟨Tanya's dad works as chauffeur for the *richest* man in town, a big oil baron⟩
syn affluent, flush, loaded, moneyed (*or* monied), opulent, wealthy, well-heeled, well-off, well-to-do
rel comfortable, propertied, prosperous, successful; flourishing, prospering, thriving; advantaged, blessed, privileged
near ant deprived, disadvantaged, underprivileged; bankrupt, bankrupted, beggared, broke, indebted, insolvent, pauperized, ruined, stone-broke; depressed, pinched, reduced, straitened; low, short
ant destitute, impecunious, impoverished, indigent, needy, penniless, penurious, poor, poverty-stricken
2 containing much seasoning, fat, or sugar ⟨stay away from *rich* foods before you sing tonight⟩
syn heavy
rel buttery, fat, fatty, greasy, oily; caloric, calorific, fattening; cloying, filling, overfilling, satiating, sating; spicy, sugary; creamy, sauced
near ant natural, plain, simple; unseasoned; diet, nonfattening, slimming; nonfat
ant light
3 having an abundance of some characteristic quality (as flavor) — see FULL-BODIED
4 producing abundantly — see FERTILE

riches *n* the total of one's money and property — see WEALTH 1

richly *adv* in a luxurious manner — see HIGH

richness *n* the amusing quality or element in something — see HUMOR 1

rick *n* a quantity of things thrown or stacked on one another — see ¹PILE 1

ricochet *vb* to strike and fly off at an angle — see GLANCE 1

rid *vb* to set (a person or thing) free of something that encumbers ⟨worked two jobs to *rid* himself of debt⟩
syn clear, disburden, disencumber, free, relieve, unburden
rel discharge, emancipate, enfranchise, liberate, loose, loosen, manumit, release, spring, unbind, uncage, unchain, unfetter; bail (out), deliver, redeem, rescue; disengage, disentangle, extricate
near ant bog (down), fetter, restrain, shackle, subject, weigh (down), weight (down)
ant burden, encumber, saddle

riddance *n* the getting rid of whatever is unwanted or useless — see DISPOSAL 1

riddle *n* something hard to understand or explain — see MYSTERY

riddle vb to find an answer for through reasoning — see SOLVE

ride n a means of getting to a destination in a vehicle driven by another ⟨Laurie sometimes gets a *ride* to school from her neighbor⟩
syn lift, transportation
rel drive, spin, turn; joyride; conveyance, passage, transit, transport

ride vb 1 to attack repeatedly with mean put-downs or insults — see TEASE 2
2 to make fun of in a good-natured way — see TEASE 1
3 to rest or move along the surface of a liquid or in the air — see FLOAT

ride (out) vb to come safely through — see SURVIVE 1

ridge n the line formed when two sloping surfaces come together along their topmost edge ⟨pigeons roosting along the *ridge* of the roof⟩
syn crest
rel divide; backbone, chine, ridgepole, spine; eminence, peak, prominence, promontory, rise

ridicule n the making of unkind jokes as a way of showing one's scorn for someone or something ⟨the early efforts by the suffragists to obtain voting rights for women were met with *ridicule*⟩
syn derision, mockery
rel contempt, disdain, scorn; belittlement, deprecation, disparagement; insult, putdown; laughter, snickering; burlesque, caricature, mimicry, satire
near ant applause, approval, commendation, praise

ridicule vb to make (someone or something) the object of unkind laughter ⟨the term "big bang theory" was originally coined to *ridicule* the belief that the universe was created by a giant explosion⟩
syn deride, gibe (*or* jibe), jeer, laugh (at), mock, scout
rel scoff (at), scorn, sneer (at); badmouth, belittle, decry, disparage, poohpooh (*also* pooh), put down; chaff, jive, josh, kid, quiz, rally, razz, rib, ride, tease; bait, bug, harass, harry, hassle, heckle, needle, pester, target, taunt, torment; ape, burlesque, caricature, imitate, lampoon, mimic, parody, parrot, satirize, take off (on), travesty
phrases make fun of, poke fun at
near ant applaud, approve, commend, endorse (*also* indorse), sanction

ridiculer n a person who causes repeated emotional pain, distress, or annoyance to another — see TORMENTOR

ridiculous adj 1 so foolish or pointless as to be worthy of scornful laughter ⟨a movie thriller with such a *ridiculous* plot that it gets only guffaws from audiences⟩
syn absurd, comical, derisive, derisory, farcical, laughable, ludicrous, preposterous, risible, silly
rel asinine, brainless, dumb, fatuous, foolish, half-witted, harebrained, idiotic, imbecilic, inane, jerky, moronic, nonsensical, simpleminded, stupid, unwise,

weak-minded, witless; balmy, cockeyed, crazy, cuckoo, daffy, daft, dotty, insane, kooky, loony (*also* looney), lunatic, mad, nutty, screwball, senseless, wacky; fantastic, far-fetched, inconceivable, incredible, unbelievable, unreal, unreasonable
near ant earnest, serious, solemn; believable, conceivable, credible, logical, rational, realistic, reasonable, sensible
2 causing or intended to cause laughter — see FUNNY 1

rife adj possessing or covered with great numbers or amounts of something specified ⟨our school is *rife* with rumors about the incoming principal⟩
syn abounding, flush, fraught, replete, swarming, teeming, thick, thronging
rel brimming, bulging, bursting, chockfull (*or* chockful), crammed, crowded, fat, filled, full, jammed, jam-packed, loaded, packed, saturated, stuffed; clogged, congested, overcrowded, overfilled, overflowing, overfull, overloaded, overstuffed, surfeited; alive, animated, astir, bustling, busy, buzzing, humming, lively
near ant bare, barren, blank, devoid, empty, stark, vacant, void; depleted, drained, exhausted; deficient, incomplete, insufficient, short

riffraff n 1 discarded or useless material — see GARBAGE
2 people looked down upon as ignorant and of the lowest class — see RABBLE

rifle vb to look through (as a place) carefully or thoroughly in an effort to find or discover something — see SEARCH 1

rift n 1 an irregular usually narrow break in a surface created by pressure — see CRACK 1
2 an open space in a barrier (as a wall or hedge) — see GAP 1

rig n a horse-drawn wheeled vehicle for carrying passengers — see CARRIAGE 1

rig vb to provide (someone) with what is needed for a task or activity — see FURNISH 1

rig (out) vb to outfit with clothes and especially fine or special clothes — see CLOTHE 1

right adj 1 following an original exactly — see FAITHFUL 2
2 being exactly as appears or as claimed — see AUTHENTIC 1
3 being in agreement with the truth or a fact or a standard — see CORRECT 1
4 being what is called for by accepted standards of right and wrong — see JUST 1
5 conforming to a high standard of morality or virtue — see GOOD 2
6 free from irregularities (as curves, bends, or angles) in course — see STRAIGHT 1
7 having full use of one's mind and control over one's actions — see SANE
8 meeting the requirements of a purpose or situation — see FIT 1

right adv 1 as stated or indicated without the slightest difference — see EXACTLY 1

2 in a direct line or course — see DI-RECTLY 1

3 to a great degree — see VERY 1

right *n* **1** something to which one has a just claim ⟨everyone has the *right* to life, liberty, and the pursuit of happiness⟩

syn appanage, birthright, prerogative

rel due, entitlement, perquisite, privilege

2 an entitlement to something — see CLAIM 1

3 the act or practice of giving to others what is their due — see JUSTICE 1

right away *adv* without delay — see IMMEDIATELY

righteous *adj* **1** conforming to a high standard of morality or virtue — see GOOD 2

2 following the accepted rules of moral conduct — see HONORABLE 1

righteously *adv* with purity of thought and deed — see PURELY

righteousness *n* **1** conduct that conforms to an accepted standard of right and wrong — see MORALITY 1

2 faithfulness to high moral standards — see HONOR 1

rightful *adj* being what is called for by accepted standards of right and wrong — see JUST 1

rightist *n* a person whose political beliefs are centered on tradition and keeping things the way they are — see CONSERVATIVE

rightly *adv* in a manner suitable for the occasion or purpose — see PROPERLY

right-minded *adj* conforming to a high standard of morality or virtue — see GOOD 2

rightness *n* the quality or state of being especially suitable or fitting — see APPROPRIATENESS

right now *adv* **1** at the present time — see NOW 1

2 without delay — see IMMEDIATELY

right-of-way *n* the right to one's attention before other things considered less important — see PRIORITY

rigid *adj* **1** not allowing for any exceptions or loosening of standards ⟨*rigid* enforcement of drug laws⟩

syn exacting, inflexible, rigorous, strict, stringent, uncompromising

rel close, conscientious, scrupulous, undeviating; adamant, adamantine, determined, dogged, firm, relentless, resolved, single-minded, steadfast, stubborn, tenacious, unbending, unflinching; immovable, implacable, unrelenting, unyielding; austere, demanding, flinty, grim, hard, hardened, hardhearted, harsh, ironbound, severe, stern, tough

near ant acquiescent, compliant, compromising, pliable, pliant, relenting, yielding; easy, easygoing, gentle, indulgent, kindly, lenient, merciful, mild, pampering, soft, spoiling, tolerant

ant flexible, lax, loose, relaxed

2 given to exacting standards of discipline and self-restraint — see SEVERE 1

3 having a consistency that does not easily yield to pressure — see FIRM 2

4 incapable of or highly resistant to bending — see STIFF 1

5 sticking to an opinion, purpose, or course of action in spite of reason, arguments, or persuasion — see OBSTINATE

6 stretched with little or no give — see TAUT

rigidity *n* the quality or state of being demanding or unyielding (as in discipline or criticism) — see SEVERITY

rigidly *adv* without any relaxation of standards or precision — see STRICTLY

rigidness *n* the quality or state of being demanding or unyielding (as in discipline or criticism) — see SEVERITY

rigmarole *n* unintelligible or meaningless talk — see GIBBERISH

rigor *n* something that is a cause for suffering or special effort especially in the attainment of a goal — see DIFFICULTY 1

rigorous *adj* **1** given to exacting standards of discipline and self-restraint — see SEVERE 1

2 meeting the highest standard of accuracy — see PRECISE 1

3 not allowing for any exceptions or loosening of standards — see RIGID 1

rigorously *adv* without any relaxation of standards or precision — see STRICTLY

rigorousness *n* **1** the quality or state of being demanding or unyielding (as in discipline or criticism) — see SEVERITY

2 the quality or state of being very accurate — see PRECISION

rile *vb* to disturb the peace of mind of (someone) especially by repeated disagreeable acts — see IRRITATE 1

rile *vb* to make angry — see ANGER

riled *adj* feeling or showing anger — see ANGRY

riling *adj* causing annoyance — see ANNOYING

rill *n* a natural body of running water smaller than a river — see CREEK 1

rim *n* the line or relatively narrow space that marks the outer limit of something — see BORDER 1

rim *vb* to serve as a border for — see BORDER

rime *n* a covering of tiny ice crystals on a cold surface — see FROST

rime *vb* to cover with a hardened layer — see ENCRUST

ring *n* **1** a group involved in secret or criminal activities ⟨a *ring* of counterfeiters passing phony $20 bills⟩

syn cabal, conspiracy, gang, Mafia, mob, syndicate

rel circle, clan, clique, coterie, crowd; junta, oligarchy

2 a circular strip ⟨a metal *ring* encircled the barrel⟩

syn band, circle, eye, hoop, loop, round

rel belt, cincture, collar, girdle; wreath; coil, spiral

---

3 a communication by telephone — see CALL 3

4 a group of people sharing a common interest and relating together socially — see GANG 2

5 something with a perfectly round circumference — see CIRCLE 1

ring *vb* **1** to make the clear sound heard when metal vibrates ⟨I didn't hear the doorbell *ring*⟩

syn chime, knell, peal, toll

rel clang, clank, ding, jangle, jingle, ping, tinkle; resound, reverberate

2 to form a circle around — see SURROUND

3 to pass completely around — see ENCIRCLE 1

ring (up) *vb, chiefly British* to make a telephone call to — see CALL 2

ringer *n* something or someone that strongly resembles another — see IMAGE 1

ringing *adj* **1** marked by a high volume of sound — see LOUD 1

2 marked by conspicuously full and rich sounds or tones — see RESONANT

ringlet *n* a length of hair that forms a loop or series of loops — see CURL

rinse *vb* to pour liquid over or through in order to cleanse — see FLUSH 1

riot *n* someone or something that is very funny — see SCREAM

riotous *adj* **1** causing or intended to cause laughter — see FUNNY 1

2 pouring forth in great amounts — see PROFUSE

rip *n* a long deep cut — see GASH

rip *vb* **1** to cause (something) to separate into jagged pieces by violently pulling at it — see TEAR 1

2 to penetrate with a sharp edge (as a knife) — see CUT 1

3 to proceed or move quickly — see HURRY 2

4 to separate or remove by forceful pulling — see TEAR 2

ripe *adj* fully grown or developed — see MATURE 1

ripen *vb* to become mature — see MATURE

ripened *adj* fully grown or developed — see MATURE 1

ripening *n* the process of becoming mature — see MATURATION

rip–off *n* an instance of theft — see THEFT 2

rip off *vb* **1** to remove valuables from (a place) unlawfully — see ROB

2 to take (something) without right and with an intent to keep — see STEAL 1

riposte *n* a quick witty response — see RETORT 1

ripple *vb* to flow in a broken irregular stream — see GURGLE

rip–roaring *adj* causing great emotional or mental stimulation — see EXCITING 1

rise *n* **1** a raising or a state of being raised to a higher rank or position — see ADVANCEMENT 1

2 an area of high ground — see HEIGHT 4

3 an upward slope — see ASCENT 2

4 something added (as by growth) — see INCREASE 1

5 the act or an instance of rising or climbing up — see ASCENT 1

rise *vb* **1** to become greater in extent, volume, amount, or number — see INCREASE 2

2 to leave one's bed — see ARISE 1

3 to move or extend upward — see ASCEND

risible *adj* **1** causing or intended to cause laughter — see FUNNY 1

2 so foolish or pointless as to be worthy of scornful laughter — see RIDICULOUS 1

rising *n* the act or an instance of rising or climbing up — see ASCENT 1

risk *n* **1** something that may cause injury or harm — see DANGER 2

2 the state of not being protected from injury, harm, or evil — see DANGER 1

risk *vb* **1** to take a chance on ⟨Colette didn't want to *risk* running out of film on her trip, so she brought along a dozen rolls⟩

syn chance, gamble (on), hazard, venture

rel brave, challenge, dare, defy, face; compromise, endanger, imperil, jeopardize, menace; expose, subject; bet (on), wager

2 to place in danger — see ENDANGER

risky *adj* involving potential loss or injury — see DANGEROUS

rite *n* an oft-repeated action or series of actions performed in accordance with tradition or a set of rules ⟨the annual summer *rite* of loading up the car for the big family vacation⟩

syn ceremonial, ceremony, form, formality, observance, ritual, solemnity

rel amenities, civility, decorum, etiquette, graces, proprieties; convention, custom, habit, manners, mores, practice (*also* practise), standard, tradition, way; celebration, service

ritual *n* an oft-repeated action or series of actions performed in accordance with tradition or a set of rules — see RITE

rival *n* **1** one that is equal to another in status, achievement, or value — see EQUAL

2 one that takes a position opposite another in a competition or conflict — see OPPONENT 1

3 one who strives for the same thing as another — see COMPETITOR

rivalry *n* an earnest effort for superiority or victory over another — see CONTEST 1

rive *vb* to cause (something) to separate into jagged pieces by violently pulling at it — see TEAR 1

rivet *vb* to fix (as one's attention) steadily toward a central objective — see CONCENTRATE 2

riveting *adj* holding the attention or provoking interest — see INTERESTING

rivulet *n* a natural body of running water smaller than a river — see CREEK 1

road *n* **1** a passage cleared for public vehicular travel — see WAY 1

2 a roadway overlaid with parallel steel rails over which trains travel — see RAILROAD

roadhouse *n* a bar or restaurant offering special nighttime entertainment (as music, dancing, or comedy acts) — see NIGHTCLUB

roadway *n* a passage cleared for public vehicular travel — see WAY 1

roam *vb* to move about from place to place aimlessly — see WANDER

roamer *n* a person who roams about without a fixed route or destination — see NOMAD

roaming *adj* traveling from place to place — see ITINERANT

roar *n* 1 a violent shouting — see CLAMOR 1

2 loud, confused, and usually unharmonious sound — see NOISE 1

roar *vb* to make a long loud deep noise or cry ⟨its engine *roared* as the car sped away⟩

syn bellow, boom, growl, thunder

rel grumble, roll, rumble; blare, blast, peal, scream, screech, shriek, squall; cry, holler, hoot, shout, whoop, yell; caterwaul, howl, wail, yowl

near ant mumble, murmur, mutter, whisper; squeak, whimper

roaring *adj* 1 marked by a high volume of sound — see LOUD 1

2 marked by vigorous growth and well-being especially economically — see PROSPEROUS 1

roast *vb* to make fun of in a good-natured way — see TEASE 1

roasting *adj* having a notably high temperature — see HOT 1

rob *vb* to remove valuables from (a place) unlawfully ⟨in jail for *robbing* a bank⟩

syn burglarize, rip off, steal (from)

rel despoil, loot, pillage, plunder, sack, spoil, strip; bleed, break in, cheat, chisel, cozen, defraud, exploit, fleece, gyp, mulct, rook, squeeze, stick, swindle; hold up, mug, stick up

robber *n* one who steals — see THIEF

robbery *n* the unlawful taking and carrying away of property without the consent of its owner — see THEFT 1

robe *vb* to outfit with clothes and especially fine or special clothes — see CLOTHE 1

robotic *adj* designed to replace or decrease human labor and especially physical labor — see LABORSAVING

robust *adj* 1 enjoying health and vigor — see HEALTHY 1

2 having active strength of body or mind — see VIGOROUS 1

3 having an abundance of some characteristic quality (as flavor) — see FULL-BODIED

4 not showing weakness or uncertainty — see FIRM 1

robustness *n* 1 the condition of being sound in body — see HEALTH

2 the quality or state of having abundant or intense activity — see VITALITY 1

rock *vb* 1 to make a series of unsteady side-to-side motions ⟨the boat was *rocking* so much that Rosa felt seasick⟩

syn careen, lurch, pitch, roll, seesaw, sway, toss, wobble

rel blunder, dodder, falter, flounder, halt, hitch, hobble, jerk, reel, stagger, stumble, teeter, toddle, totter, tumble, waddle, weave; oscillate, undulate, wag, waggle

2 to swing unsteadily back and forth or from side to side — see TEETER 1

rock bottom *n* the lowest part, place, or point — see BOTTOM 3

rocket *vb* 1 to proceed or move quickly — see HURRY 2

2 to rise abruptly and rapidly — see SKYROCKET

rod *n* 1 a heavy rigid stick used as a weapon or for punishment — see CLUB 1

2 a straight piece (as of wood or metal) that is longer than it is wide — see BAR 1

rogue *n* 1 a mean, evil, or unprincipled person — see VILLAIN

2 an appealingly mischievous person — see SCAMP 1

roguish *adj* tending to or exhibiting reckless playfulness — see MISCHIEVOUS 1

roguishness *n* playful, reckless behavior that is not intended to cause serious harm — see MISCHIEF 1

roil *vb* 1 to be in a state of violent rolling motion — see SEETHE 1

2 to make angry — see ANGER

roiled *adj* 1 feeling or showing anger — see ANGRY

2 having visible particles in liquid suspension — see CLOUDY 1

roisterer *n* one who engages in merrymaking especially in honor of a special occasion — see CELEBRANT

role *also* **rôle** *n* the action for which a person or thing is specially fitted or used or for which a thing exists ⟨in science class we're studying the *role* of sunlight in the body's production of vitamin D⟩

syn capacity, function, job, part, place, position, purpose, task, work

rel affair, business, concern, involvement, participation; niche, office, post, situation; calling, occupation, pursuit, vocation; activity, assignment, charge, commission, duty, mission, responsibility, service, use

roll *n* 1 a rapid turning about on an axis or central point — see SPIN 1

2 a record of a series of items (as names or titles) usually arranged according to some system — see ¹LIST

roll *vb* 1 to form into a round compact mass — see WAD

2 to make a low heavy rolling sound — see RUMBLE

3 to make a series of unsteady side-to-side motions — see ROCK 1

4 to move (something) in a curved or circular path or as if on an axis — see TURN 1

5 to move in a stream — see FLOW 1

6 to move in circles around an axis or center — see SPIN 1

---

7 to move or proceed smoothly and readily — see FLOW 2

rollick *n* a time or instance of carefree fun — see FLING 1

rollick *vb* **1** to engage in activity for amusement — see PLAY 1

2 to play and run about happily — see FROLIC 1

rollicking *adj* given to good-natured joking or teasing — see PLAYFUL

rollicking *n* activity engaged in to amuse oneself — see PLAY 1

roly-poly *adj* having an excess of body fat — see FAT 1

romance *n* a brief romantic relationship — see AFFAIR 2

romantic *adj* excitingly or mysteriously unusual — see EXOTIC

romantic *n* one whose conduct is guided more by the image of perfection than by the real world — see IDEALIST

romanticist *n* one whose conduct is guided more by the image of perfection than by the real world — see IDEALIST

romanticize *vb* to represent or think of as better than reality — see IDEALIZE

romp *n* a time or instance of carefree fun — see FLING 1

romp *vb* to play and run about happily — see FROLIC 1

roof *n* **1** a raised covering over something for decoration or protection — see CANOPY

2 the place where one lives — see HOME 1

roof *vb* to provide with living quarters or shelter — see HOUSE 1

rook *vb* to rob by the use of trickery or threats — see FLEECE

rookie *n* a person who is just starting out in a field of activity — see BEGINNER

room *n* **1** an extent or area available for or used up by some activity or thing ⟨need more *room* to do a cartwheel⟩ ⟨made *room* for him on the bench⟩

syn elbowroom, place, space, way

rel capacity, range, scope; clearance, freedom, latitude, leeway, play

2 an area within a building that has been set apart from surrounding space by a wall ⟨finally had a *room* to himself when his brother went off to college⟩

syn apartment, cell, chamber, closet

rel accommodation, berth, booth, cabin, compartment, cubicle

3 a favorable combination of circumstances, time, and place — see OPPORTUNITY

roomer *n* one who rents a room or apartment in another's house — see TENANT

roomy *adj* more than adequate or average in capacity — see SPACIOUS

roost *vb* **1** to come to rest after descending from the air — see ALIGHT

2 to establish or place comfortably or snugly — see ENSCONCE 1

root *vb* to set solidly in or as if in surrounding matter — see ENTRENCH

root (out) *vb* **1** to destroy all traces of — see ANNIHILATE 1

2 to draw out by force or with effort — see EXTRACT

rooted *adj* firmly established over time — see INVETERATE 1

rope *n* a length of braided, flexible material that is used for tying or connecting things — see CORD

ropy *adj* being of a consistency that resists flow — see THICK 2

roquelaure *n* a sleeveless garment worn so as to hang over the shoulders, arms, and back — see ¹CAPE

rose-colored *adj* having qualities which inspire hope — see HOPEFUL 1

roster *n* a record of a series of items (as names or titles) usually arranged according to some system — see ¹LIST

rostrum *n* a level usually raised surface — see PLATFORM

rosy *adj* **1** having a healthy reddish skin tone — see RUDDY

2 having qualities which inspire hope — see HOPEFUL 1

rot *n* **1** language, behavior, or ideas that are absurd and contrary to good sense — see NONSENSE 1

2 the process by which dead organic matter separates into simpler substances — see CORRUPTION 1

3 unintelligible or meaningless talk — see GIBBERISH

rot *vb* **1** to become worse or of less value — see DETERIORATE

2 to go through decomposition — see DECAY 1

rotate *vb* **1** to move (something) in a curved or circular path on or as if on an axis — see TURN 1

2 to move in circles around an axis or center — see SPIN 1

rotation *n* a rapid turning about on an axis or central point — see SPIN 1

rote *n* **1** an established and often automatic or monotonous series of actions followed when engaging in some activity — see ROUTINE 1

2 the body of knowledge that has been retained in one's mind or the use of it — see HEART 2

rotten *adj* **1** having undergone organic breakdown ⟨*rotten*, smelly meat that should have been refrigerated⟩

syn addled, bad, corrupted, decayed, decomposed, putrefied, putrid, spoiled

rel curdled, fermented, rancid, sour, soured, turned; contaminated, defiled, fouled, polluted, tainted; corroded, crumbled, degenerated, deteriorated, disintegrated; decaying, decomposing, moldering, moldy, putrefying, rotting

near ant fresh, good, preserved; pristine, uncontaminated, undefiled, unpolluted, unspoiled, untainted, untouched

2 falling short of a standard — see BAD 1

3 not conforming to a high moral standard; morally unacceptable — see BAD 2

4 not giving pleasure to the mind or senses — see UNPLEASANT

5 extremely unsatisfactory — see WRETCHED 1

6 of low quality — see CHEAP 2

rotund *adj* having an excess of body fat — see FAT 1

rotundity *n* the condition of having an excess of body fat — see CORPULENCE

rough *adj* **1** covered with or as if with hair — see HAIRY 1

2 marked by bursts of destructive force or intense activity — see VIOLENT 1

3 marked by wet and windy conditions — see FOUL 1

4 not having a level or smooth surface — see UNEVEN 1

5 requiring considerable physical or mental effort — see HARD 1

6 difficult to endure — see HARSH 1

7 harsh and threatening in manner or appearance — see GRIM 1

8 hastily or roughly constructed — see RUDE 1

9 lacking in refinement or good taste — see COARSE 2

10 made of or resembling hair — see HAIRY 1

11 marked by a series of sharp quick motions — see JERKY 1

rough (up) *vb* to abuse physically — see MANHANDLE 1

roughened *adj* not having a level or smooth surface — see UNEVEN 1

roughhewn *adj* **1** hastily or roughly constructed — see RUDE 1

2 lacking in refinement or good taste — see COARSE 2

3 lacking social grace and assurance — see AWKWARD 1

roughhouse *n* wildly playful or mischievous behavior — see HORSEPLAY

roughhousing *n* wildly playful or mischievous behavior — see HORSEPLAY

roughly *adv* in a manner so as to cause loss or suffering — see HARDLY 1

roughneck *n* a violent, brutal person who is often a member of an organized gang — see HOODLUM

roughness *n* **1** a harsh or sharp quality — see EDGE 1

2 the quality or state of lacking refinement or good taste — see VULGARITY 1

round *adj* **1** having every part of the surface the same distance from the center ⟨*round* golf balls⟩ ⟨the earth is not perfectly *round*⟩
syn global, spherical
rel annular, circular, disklike (*or* dislike), ringlike; curved, looped, spiral; balled, rotund, rounded, roundish; elliptic (*or* elliptical), oval, ovate, ovoid

2 having an excess of body fat — see FAT 1

3 marked by conspicuously full and rich sounds or tones — see RESONANT 1

4 being neither more nor less than a certain amount, number, or extent — see EVEN 1

round *adv* **1** from beginning to end — see THROUGH 1

2 on all sides or in every direction — see AROUND 1

3 toward the opposite direction — see AROUND 2

round *n* **1** a circular strip — see RING 2

2 a series of events or actions that repeat themselves regularly and in the same order — see CYCLE 1

3 something with a perfectly round circumference — see CIRCLE 1

round *prep* in random positions within the boundaries of — see AROUND 1

round *vb* **1** to form into a round compact mass — see WAD

2 to pass completely around — see ENCIRCLE 1

3 to turn away from a straight line or course — see CURVE 1

round (off *or* out) *vb* **1** to bring (an event) to a natural or appropriate stopping point — see CLOSE 3

2 to serve as a completing element to — see COMPLEMENT

roundabout *adj* not straightforward or direct — see INDIRECT

roundly *adv* with attention to all aspects or details — see THOROUGHLY 1

roundtable *n* **1** a coming together of a number of persons for a specified purpose — see MEETING 1

2 a meeting featuring a group discussion — see FORUM

roundup *n* a short statement of the main points — see SUMMARY

round up *vb* to bring together in one body or place — see GATHER 1

rouse *vb* **1** to cause to stop sleeping — see WAKE 1

2 to cease to be asleep — see WAKE 2

rousing *adj* causing great emotional or mental stimulation — see EXCITING 1

rout *n* failure to win a contest — see DEFEAT 1

rout *vb* **1** to achieve a victory over — see BEAT 2

2 to defeat by a large margin — see WHIP 2

3 to drive or force out — see EJECT 1

route *n* **1** a passage cleared for public vehicular travel — see WAY 1

2 an established course for traveling from one place to another — see PASSAGE 1

3 the direction along which something or someone moves — see PATH 1

route *vb* to point out the way for (someone) especially from a position in front — see LEAD 1

routine *adj* **1** being of the type that is encountered in the normal course of events — see ORDINARY 1

2 following or agreeing with established form, custom, or rules — see FORMAL 1

3 often observed or encountered — see COMMON 1

routine *n* **1** an established and often automatic or monotonous series of actions followed when engaging in some activity ⟨part of my morning *routine* is drinking a

---

syn synonym(s)   **rel** related words
ant antonym(s)   **near ant** near antonym(s)

cup of hot chocolate while waiting for the bus⟩

syn groove, pattern, rote, rut, treadmill

rel custom, fashion, habit, practice (also practise), trick, wont; approach, manner, method, procedure, strategy, style, tack, way; design, plan, program, scheme; convention, policy, tradition

2 something done over and over in order to develop skill — see EXERCISE 2

rove *vb* to move about from place to place aimlessly — see WANDER

rover *n* **1** a person who roams about without a fixed route or destination — see NOMAD

2 someone who engages in robbery of ships at sea — see PIRATE

roving *adj* traveling from place to place — see ITINERANT

row *n* **1** a series of things or people arranged side by side ⟨stood in a *row* to have their picture taken⟩ ⟨three *rows* of eight jelly beans equals 24 jelly beans⟩

syn bank, rank

rel chain, column, cue, file, line, procession, queue, string, train; echelon, tier; array, sequence

2 a passage cleared for public vehicular travel — see WAY 1

3 a rough and often noisy fight usually involving several people — see BRAWL 1

4 a state of noisy, confused activity — see COMMOTION

5 an often noisy or angry expression of differing opinions — see ARGUMENT 1

¹row *vb* to move a boat by means of oars ⟨*rowed* around the lake⟩

syn oar, paddle, scull

rel canoe; pole, punt

²row *vb* to express different opinions about something often angrily — see ARGUE 2

rowdy *adj* being rough or noisy in a high-spirited way — see BOISTEROUS

rowdy *n* a violent, brutal person who is often a member of an organized gang — see HOODLUM

rower *n* a person who drives a boat forward by means of oars — see OARSMAN

royal *adj* **1** fit for or worthy of a royal ruler — see MONARCHICAL

2 large and impressive in size, grandeur, extent, or conception — see GRAND 1

rub *vb* **1** to damage or diminish by continued friction — see ABRADE 1

2 to make smooth by friction — see GRIND 1

3 to make smooth or glossy usually by repeatedly applying surface pressure — see POLISH

rubbed *adj* having a shiny surface or finish — see GLOSSY

rubberlike *adj* able to revert to original size and shape after being stretched, squeezed, or twisted — see ELASTIC 1

rubberneck *vb* to look long and hard in wonder or surprise — see GAPE

rubbery *adj* able to revert to original size and shape after being stretched, squeezed, or twisted — see ELASTIC 1

rubbish *n* discarded or useless material — see GARBAGE

rubbishy *adj* of low quality — see CHEAP 2

rubble *n* the portion or bits of something left over or behind after it has been destroyed — see REMAINS 1

rubicund *adj* having a healthy reddish skin tone — see RUDDY

rub out *vb* to destroy all traces of — see ANNIHILATE 1

rubric *n* a word or series of words often in larger letters placed at the beginning of a passage or at the top of a page in order to introduce or categorize — see HEADING

rucksack *n* a soft-sided case designed for carrying belongings especially on the back — see PACK 1

ruckus *n* **1** a rough and often noisy fight usually involving several people — see BRAWL 1

2 a state of noisy, confused activity — see COMMOTION

ruction *n* **1** a rough and often noisy fight usually involving several people — see BRAWL 1

2 a state of noisy, confused activity — see COMMOTION

ruddy *adj* having a healthy reddish skin tone ⟨his *ruddy* complexion runs in the family⟩

syn blooming, florid, flush, glowing, rosy, rubicund, sanguine

rel bronzed, brown, suntanned, tanned; flushed, pink, pinkish, warm; cherubic

near ant ashen, ashy, pale, pallid, pasty, sallow, wan, waxen, waxy; blanched, white, whitened; anemic, peaked, sick, sickly; bloodless, cadaverous, deathlike

rude *adj* **1** hastily or roughly constructed ⟨a *rude* shelter built from unfinished logs by some forgotten pioneer⟩

syn artless, clumsy, crude, rough, roughhewn, unrefined

rel defective, faulty, flawed, imperfect; imprecise, inexact; inartistic, undressed, unfinished, unpolished, unworked; amateur, amateurish, inexpert, unprofessional, unskilled, unskillful; primitive, rudimentary

near ant faultless, finished, meticulous, perfected, polished, well-done; adept, adroit, dexterous (also dextrous), expert, masterful, masterly, neat, practiced (or practised), skillful, workmanlike; artful, artistic, sophisticated; exact, precise

ant refined

2 belonging to or characteristic of an early level of skill or development — see PRIMITIVE 1

3 lacking in refinement or good taste — see COARSE 2

4 not civilized — see SAVAGE 1

5 showing a lack of manners or consideration for others — see IMPOLITE

rudeness *n* **1** rude behavior — see DISCOURTESY

2 the quality or state of lacking refinement or good taste — see VULGARITY 1

rudimentary *adj* **1** belonging to or characteristic of an early level of skill or development — see PRIMITIVE 1

2 of or relating to the simplest facts or theories of a subject — see ELEMENTARY

rudiments *n pl* general or basic truths on which other truths or theories can be based — see PRINCIPLES 1

rue *n* a feeling of responsibility for wrongdoing — see GUILT 1

rue *vb* to feel sorry or dissatisfied about — see REGRET

rueful *adj* **1** expressing or suggesting mourning — see MOURNFUL 1

2 feeling sorrow for a wrong that one has done — see CONTRITE 1

3 deserving of one's pity — see PATHETIC 1

ruefully *adv* with feelings of bitterness or grief — see HARD 2

ruffian *n* a violent, brutal person who is often a member of an organized gang — see HOODLUM

ruffle *n* a strip of fabric gathered or pleated on one edge and used as trimming ⟨likes lace curtains with *ruffles* and chintz curtains with *ruffles*⟩

syn flounce, frill, furbelow

rel border, edging, fringe, trim; pleat, ruff; bunting, skirting

rugged *adj* **1** able to withstand hardship, strain, or exposure — see HARDY 1

2 difficult to endure — see HARSH 1

3 harsh and threatening in manner or appearance — see GRIM 1

4 having muscles capable of exerting great physical force — see STRONG 1

5 not having a level or smooth surface — see UNEVEN 1

ruin *n* **1** the state or fact of being rendered nonexistent, physically unsound, or useless — see DESTRUCTION

2 ruins *pl* the portion or bits of something left over or behind after it has been destroyed — see REMAINS 1

ruin *vb* **1** to cause to lose one's fortune and become unable to pay one's debts ⟨*ruined* by the Great Chicago Fire of 1871, the industrialist was forced to sell his mansion and start all over again⟩

syn bankrupt, bust

rel beggar, impoverish, pauperize; break, reduce, straiten; clean (out), wipe out

near ant enrich, richen

2 to bring destruction to (something) through violent action — see RAVAGE

3 to bring to a complete end the physical soundness, existence, or usefulness of — see DESTROY 1

ruination *n* the state or fact of being rendered nonexistent, physically unsound, or useless — see DESTRUCTION

ruinous *adj* **1** bringing about ruin or misfortune — see FATAL 1

2 causing or tending to cause destruction — see DESTRUCTIVE 1

rule *n* **1** a statement spelling out the proper procedure or conduct for an activity ⟨read the *rules* that are posted before you use the pool⟩

syn bylaw, ground rule, regulation

rel code, constitution, decalogue; act, law, ordinance, statute; command, decree, dictate, directive, edict, fiat, order; axiom, fundamental, maxim, precept; moral, principle, value; prohibition, restriction; convention, custom, habit, manners, mores, practice (*also* practise), tradition, way; blueprint, canon, formula, guide, guideline, recipe, standard

2 lawful control over the affairs of a political unit (as a nation) ⟨the years during which Russia was under Communist *rule*⟩

syn administration, authority, governance, government, jurisdiction, regime (*also* régime), regimen

rel reign; dominion, power, sovereignty, supremacy, sway; command, leadership; direction, management, regulation, superintendence, supervision; dictatorship, domination, mastery, oppression, subjugation, tyranny

rule *vb* to exercise authority or power over — see GOVERN

rule (on) *vb* to give an opinion about (something at issue or in dispute) — see JUDGE 1

rule out *vb* to prevent the participation or inclusion of — see EXCLUDE

ruler *n* one who rules over a people with a sole, supreme, and usually hereditary authority — see MONARCH

ruling *n* **1** a decision made by a court or tribunal regarding a case it has heard — see SENTENCE

2 an order publicly issued by an authority — see EDICT 1

rumble *vb* to make a low heavy rolling sound ⟨when thunder *rumbled* in the distant sky, we wisely began packing up our stuff⟩

syn growl, grumble, lumber, roll

rel boom, drum, thunder

ruminant *adj* given to or marked by long, quiet thinking — see CONTEMPLATIVE

ruminate *vb* to give serious and careful thought to — see PONDER

rummage *n* an unorganized collection or mixture of various things — see MISCELLANY 1

rummage *vb* to look through (as a place) carefully or thoroughly in an effort to find or discover something — see SEARCH 1

rumor *vb* to make (as a piece of information) the subject of common talk without any authority or confirmation of accuracy ⟨for years people have been *rumoring* the principal's imminent retirement⟩

syn bruit (about), circulate, noise (about), whisper

rel bandy (about), blab, gossip; disclose, divulge, report, reveal, tell; hint, imply, insinuate, intimate, let on, suggest; broadcast, promulgate, propagate, spread

---

syn synonym(s)   **rel** related words
ant antonym(s)   **near ant** near antonym(s)

rump *n* the part of the body upon which someone sits — see BUTTOCKS

rumple *vb* 1 to create (as by crushing) an irregular mass of creases in — see CRUMPLE 1

2 to develop creases or folds — see WRINKLE 1

3 to undo the proper order or arrangement of — see DISORDER

rumpled *adj* lacking in order, neatness, and often cleanliness — see MESSY

rumpus *n* a state of noisy, confused activity — see COMMOTION

run *n* 1 a prevailing or general movement or inclination — see TREND 1

2 *chiefly Midland* a natural body of running water smaller than a river — see CREEK 1

3 the period during which something exists, lasts, or is in progress — see DURATION 1

4 the right to act or move freely — see FREEDOM 2

run *vb* 1 to go at a pace faster than a walk ⟨*ran* all the way to the bus stop, but still missed the bus⟩

syn dash, gallop, jog, scamper, sprint, trip, trot

rel bound, canter, leap, lope, skip, spring; foot (it), hoof (it), hotfoot (it), leg (it); nip, race, scuttle, step (along)

near ant amble, lumber, plod, saunter, shamble, shuffle, stroll; crawl, creep, poke; plod, trudge; hobble, limp

2 to hasten away from something dangerous or frightening ⟨rather than *run* from a black bear, it's better to hold your ground and make lots of noise⟩

syn bolt, break, flee, fly, retreat, run away, run off

rel abscond, clear out, decamp, elope, escape, light out, retreat, scat, scram, skip (out)

phrases beat it, turn tail

near ant beard, brave, confront, dare, defy, face

3 to be positioned along a certain course or in a certain direction ⟨the road *runs* along the river for a while⟩

syn extend, go, head, lead, lie

rel cross, cut, pass; follow, span, traverse

4 to occur within a continuous range of variation ⟨the electric bill *runs* between 30 and 50 dollars a month⟩

syn go, range, vary

rel alternate, move, shift; change, mutate; extend, reach, stretch, sweep

5 to move in a stream — see FLOW 1

6 to proceed or move quickly — see HURRY 2

7 to show a liking or proneness (for something) — see LEAN 2

8 to urge, push, or force onward — see DRIVE 1

9 to control the mechanical operation of — see OPERATE 1

10 to eventually have as a state or quality — see BECOME

11 to go from a solid to a liquid state — see LIQUEFY

12 to look after and make decisions about — see CONDUCT 1

13 to cause to function — see ACTIVATE

run away *vb* 1 to get free from a dangerous or confining situation — see ESCAPE 1

2 to hasten away from something dangerous or frightening — see RUN 2

run-down *adj* 1 showing signs of advanced wear and tear and neglect — see SHABBY 1

2 temporarily suffering from a disorder of the body — see SICK 1

run down *vb* to come upon after searching, study, or effort — see FIND 1

run-in *n* a brief clash between enemies or rivals — see ENCOUNTER

runner *n* one that carries a message or does an errand — see MESSENGER

running *adj* being in effective operation — see ACTIVE 1

running *n* the act or activity of looking after and making decisions about something — see CONDUCT 1

runny *adj* having an overly soft liquid consistency ⟨*runny* scrambled eggs⟩

syn soupy, watery

rel flowing, fluid, liquefied; dilute, diluted, thin, thinned, watered (down), weak; slushy, soggy, wet

near ant syrupy, viscid, viscous; creamy, heavy, thick, thickened, thickish; gelatinous, gluey, glutinous, gooey, gummy, sticky

run off *vb* 1 to drive or force out — see EJECT 1

2 to get free from a dangerous or confining situation — see ESCAPE 1

3 to hasten away from something dangerous or frightening — see RUN 2

run-of-the-mill *adj* 1 being of the type that is encountered in the normal course of events — see ORDINARY 1

2 of average to below average quality — see MEDIOCRE 1

run on *vb* 1 to engage in casual or rambling conversation — see CHAT

2 to remain indefinitely in existence or in the same state — see CONTINUE 1

3 to talk at length without sticking to a topic or getting to a point — see RAMBLE 1

run over *vb* to flow over the brim or top of — see OVERFLOW 1

runt *n* a living thing much smaller than others of its kind — see DWARF 1

run through *vb* to use up carelessly — see WASTE 1

rural *adj* of, relating to, associated with, or typical of open areas with few buildings or people ⟨grew up in a *rural* community where more than half the people were farmers⟩ ⟨a painter noted for his *rural* landscapes⟩

syn bucolic, country, pastoral, rustic

rel countrified (*also* countryfied), provincial; agrarian, agricultural *near ant* citified, urbanized; metropolitan, municipal; nonagricultural, nonfarm

ant urban

rush *n* 1 excited and often showy or disorderly speed — see HURRY 1

2 the act or action of setting upon with force or violence — see ATTACK 1

rush *vb* 1 to cause to move or proceed fast or faster — see HURRY 1

2 to flow out in great quantities or with force — see GUSH 1

3 to proceed or move quickly — see HURRY 2

4 to take sudden, violent action against — see ATTACK 1

rushed *adj* acting or done with excessive or careless speed — see HASTY 1

rustic *adj* of, relating to, associated with, or typical of open areas with few buildings or people — see RURAL

rustic *n* an awkward or simple person especially from a small town or the country — see HICK

rustle *vb* to proceed or move quickly — see HURRY 2

rustler *n* an ambitious person who eagerly goes after what is desired — see GO-GETTER

rut *n* an established and often automatic or monotonous series of actions followed when engaging in some activity — see ROUTINE 1

ruthless *adj* having or showing a lack of sympathy or tender feelings — see HARD 1

$$\text{S}$$

sable *adj* having the color of soot or coal — see BLACK 1

saccharine *adj* appealing to the emotions in an obvious and tiresome way — see CORNY

sacerdotal *adj* of, relating to, or characteristic of the clergy — see CLERICAL

sack *n* 1 a container made of a flexible material (as paper or plastic) — see BAG 1

2 a place set aside for sleeping — see BED 1

sack *vb* 1 to let go from office, service, or employment — see DISMISS 1

2 to search through with the intent of committing robbery — see RANSACK 1

sacred *adj* 1 not to be violated, criticized, or tampered with ⟨we took a *sacred* oath not to let anyone find our hideout⟩

syn holy, inviolable, sacrosanct, unassailable, untouchable

rel inviolate, pure; privileged, protected, shielded; exempt, immune

near ant blasphemous, irreverent, profane

2 of, relating to, or being God — see HOLY 3

3 of, relating to, or used in the practice or worship services of a religion — see RELIGIOUS 1

4 set apart or worthy of veneration by association with God — see HOLY 2

sacrifice *n* something offered to a god ⟨the herders selected their best lamb as a *sacrifice* in order to receive blessings from their god⟩

syn immolation, offering, victim

rel holocaust; contribution, donation

sacrifice *vb* to give up as an offering to a god ⟨in the Old Testament Abraham was willing to *sacrifice* even his son to God⟩

syn immolate, offer

rel consecrate, dedicate, devote; give, surrender, yield

sacrilege *n* an act of great disrespect shown to God or to sacred ideas, people, or things — see BLASPHEMY

sacrilegious *adj* not showing proper reverence for the holy or sacred — see IRREVERENT

sacristy *n* a room in a church building for sacred furnishings (as vestments) ⟨our choir robes were stored in the *sacristy*⟩

syn vestry

rel cloakroom

sacrosanct *adj* 1 not to be violated, criticized, or tampered with — see SACRED 1

2 set apart or worthy of veneration by association with God — see HOLY 2

sad *adj* 1 feeling unhappiness ⟨movies in which the hero dies always make us feel *sad*⟩

syn bad, blue, brokenhearted, crestfallen, dejected, depressed, despondent, disconsolate, doleful, down, downcast, downhearted, droopy, forlorn, gloomy, glum, heartbroken, heartsick, heartsore, inconsolable, joyless, low, low-spirited, melancholy, miserable, mournful, saddened, sorrowful, sorry, unhappy, woebegone, woeful, wretched

rel aggrieved, distressed, troubled; despairing, hopeless; disappointed, discouraged, disheartened, dispirited; suicidal; dolorous, lugubrious, plaintive, tearful; regretful, rueful; grieving, wailing, weeping; black, bleak, cheerless, comfortless, dark, darkening, depressing, desolate, dismal, drear, dreary, funereal, gray (*also*

syn synonym(s) *rel* related words
ant antonym(s) *near ant* near antonym(s)

grey), morbid, morose, murky, saturnine, somber (*or* sombre), sullen

near ant ecstatic, elated, enraptured, entranced, euphoric, exhilarated, exuberant, exultant; blithe, blithesome, gay, jocund, jolly, jovial, lightsome, merry, mirthful; excited, thrilled; hopeful, optimistic; encouraged, heartened; animated, jaunty, lively, perky, sprightly, vivacious; content, gratified, pleased, satisfied; beaming, grinning, laughing, smiling; boon, carefree, careless, cavalier, devil-may-care, easygoing, happy-go-lucky, insouciant, lighthearted, unconcerned

ant blissful, buoyant, buoyed, cheerful, cheery, chipper, delighted, glad, gladdened, gladsome, gleeful, happy, joyful, joyous, jubilant, sunny, upbeat

2 causing unhappiness ⟨the *sad* news about our uncle's death made my father cry⟩

syn depressing, dismal, drear, dreary, heartbreaking, heartrending, melancholy, pathetic, saddening, sorry, tearful, teary

rel discomforting, discomposing, disquieting, distressing, disturbing, perturbing; affecting, moving, poignant, touching; discouraging, disheartening, dispiriting

near ant heartening, heartwarming, inspiring, stimulating, stirring, uplifting; agreeable, pleasant, pleasurable; exhilarating, thrilling

ant cheering, cheery, glad, happy

sadden *vb* to make sad — see DEPRESS 1

saddened *adj* feeling unhappiness — see SAD 1

saddening *adj* causing unhappiness — see SAD 2

saddle *vb* to place a weight or burden on — see LOAD 1

sadism *n* the willful infliction of pain and suffering on others — see CRUELTY

sadistic *adj* having or showing the desire to in-flict severe pain and suffering on others — see CRUEL 1

sadly *adv* with feelings of bitterness or grief — see HARD 2

sadness *n* a state or spell of low spirits ⟨she was filled with *sadness* at the thought of having to leave her family⟩

syn blues, dejection, depression, desolation, despondency, disconsolateness, dispiritedness, doldrums, downheartedness, dreariness, dumps, forlornness, gloom, gloominess, heartsickness, joylessness, melancholy, mopes, oppression, unhappiness

rel melancholia, self-pity; anguish, dolor, grief, sorrow; dolefulness, mournfulness, somberness, sorrowfulness, woefulness; agony, distress, pain; misery, woe, wretchedness; discouragement, disheartenment; moodiness; despair, desperation, hopelessness; boredom, ennui, tedium

near ant gaiety (*also* gayety), gayness, glee, gleefulness, humor, jollity, joviality, lightheartedness, merriment, mirth, mirthfulness; cheer, cheerfulness, hopefulness, optimism, sunniness; content, contentedness, contentment, satisfaction; delight, gratification

ant bliss, blissfulness, ecstasy, elatedness, elation, euphoria, exhilaration, exuberance, exultation, felicity, gladness, gladsomeness, happiness, heaven, intoxication, joy, joyfulness, joyousness, jubilation, rapture, rapturousness

safe *adj* **1** not exposed to the threat of loss or injury ⟨the minute the rain started, we ran to a place where we were *safe* from getting wet⟩

syn all right, alright, secure

rel hale, healthy, intact, sound, well, whole; scatheless, unharmed, unhurt, uninjured, unscathed

near ant damaged, harmed, hurt, injured, scathed, wounded

ant endangered, imperiled, insecure, liable, threatened, unsafe, vulnerable

2 providing safety ⟨we tried to find a *safe* place to hide the candy⟩

syn secure, snug

rel guarding, protecting, safeguarding, sheltering, shielding; defended, guarded, protected, sheltered, shielded; impregnable, inviolable, invulnerable, unassailable, unconquerable

near ant undefended, unguarded, unprotected, vulnerable

ant dangerous, hazardous, insecure, risky, unsafe

3 having or showing a close attentiveness to avoiding danger or trouble — see CAREFUL 1

4 not causing injury or hurt — see HARMLESS

5 worthy of one's trust — see DEPENDABLE

safe *n* a specially reinforced container to keep valuables safe ⟨the hotel recommended that we keep all our valuables in its *safe* during our stay⟩

syn coffer, safe-deposit box, strongbox

rel vault; locker, storeroom, treasury; footlocker, trunk

safe–deposit box *n* a specially reinforced container to keep valuables safe — see SAFE

safeguard *n* means or method of defending — see DEFENSE 1

safeguard *vb* to drive danger or attack away from — see DEFEND 1

safekeeping *n* responsibility for the safety and well-being of someone or something — see CUSTODY

safeness *n* the state of not being exposed to danger — see SAFETY 1

safety *n* **1** the state of not being exposed to danger ⟨we were lucky to make it to *safety* just as the lions broke loose from their cage at the zoo⟩

syn protection, safeness, security

rel aegis, defense, guardianship, ward; guard, safeguard, screen, shield; asylum, harbor, haven, refuge, retreat, shelter; inviolability, invulnerability

near ant hazard, risk, threat; instability, precariousness *ant* danger, distress, endangerment, imperilment, jeopardy, peril, trouble

2 a protective device (as on a weapon) to prevent accidental operation ⟨the gun couldn't be fired as long as the *safety* was on⟩

syn guard

rel lock

sag *n* the extent to which something hangs or dips below a straight line ⟨if there's too much *sag* in the rod, the curtains will drag on the floor⟩

syn droop, slack, slackness

rel laxity, laxness, looseness

near ant tautness, tenseness, tension, tightness

sag *vb* **1** to be limp from lack of water or vigor — see DROOP 1

2 to decline gradually from a standard level — see SLIP 1

3 to lose bodily strength or vigor — see WEAKEN 2

sagacious *adj* having or showing deep understanding and intelligent application of knowledge — see WISE 1

sagaciousness *n* the ability to understand inner qualities or relationships — see WISDOM 1

sagacity *n* the ability to understand inner qualities or relationships — see WISDOM 1

sage *adj* having or showing deep understanding and intelligent application of knowledge — see WISE 1

sage *n* a person of deep wisdom or learning ⟨the young prince visited the *sage* to learn the meaning of life⟩

syn savant, scholar

rel brain, egghead, genius, highbrow, intellectual, thinker; guru, mahatma; rabbi; master, mentor, teacher

near ant blockhead, dodo, dolt, donkey, dope, dumbbell, dummy, dunce, fathead, fool, goon, half-wit, idiot, ignoramus, imbecile, jackass, knothead, know-nothing, moron, nincompoop, ninny, nitwit, numskull (*or* numbskull), pinhead, simpleton, stock, turkey

sageness *n* the ability to understand inner qualities or relationships — see WISDOM 1

sagging *adj* bending downward or forward — see NODDING

sail *n* a journey over water in a vessel ⟨we went for a brief *sail* on the bay to relax⟩

syn crossing, cruise, passage, voyage

sail *vb* **1** to travel on water in a vessel ⟨I can't *sail* when there's any breeze at all because I get seasick easily⟩

syn boat, cruise, navigate, voyage

rel yacht; coast; log

phrases make sail

2 to move or proceed smoothly and readily — see FLOW 2

3 to rest or move along the surface of a liquid or in the air — see FLOAT

sailboat *n* a boat equipped with one or more sails ⟨we were stuck in the *sailboat*

for an hour until the wind came up and we could move again⟩

syn bark, dinghy, windjammer

rel brigantine, caravel, catboat, clipper, corvette, cutter, frigate, galleon, galley, junk, ketch, lugger, outrigger, pinnace, schooner, shallop, ship, sloop, square-rigger, xebec, yacht, yawl; bottom, craft, vessel

sailor *n* one who operates or navigates a seagoing vessel ⟨the *sailors* were glad to be arriving in port after their long voyage⟩

syn gob, jack, jack-tar, mariner, navigator, salt, sea dog, seafarer, seaman, swab, tar

rel crewman, deckhand

saint *vb* to declare to be a saint and worthy of public respect ⟨Brigid of Sweden was *sainted* in October of 1391⟩

syn canonize

rel deify, worship; consecrate, hallow, sanctify; beatify, venerate

sainted *adj* showing a devotion to God and to a life of virtue — see HOLY 1

sainthood *n* the quality or state of being spiritually pure or virtuous — see HOLINESS

saintliness *n* the quality or state of being spiritually pure or virtuous — see HOLINESS

saintly *adj* showing a devotion to God and to a life of virtue — see HOLY 1

saintship *n* the quality or state of being spiritually pure or virtuous — see HOLINESS

salable *or* **saleable** *adj* **1** fit or likely to be sold especially on a large scale — see COMMERCIAL

2 fit to be offered for sale — see MARKETABLE 1

salary *n* the money paid regularly to a person for labor or services — see WAGE

sale *n* the transfer of ownership of something from one person to another for a price ⟨my neighbor tried to make a *sale*, but no one was interested in buying his old car⟩

syn deal, trade, transaction

rel auction; haggle, negotiation; bargain, buy; purchase; clearance; fair; garage sale, rummage sale, yard sale

salesclerk *n* a person employed to sell goods or services especially in a store — see SALESPERSON

salesman *n* a person employed to sell goods or services especially in a store — see SALESPERSON

salesperson *n* a person employed to sell goods or services especially in a store ⟨we asked a *salesperson* to see if they had any shoes in the stockroom in our size⟩

syn clerk, salesclerk, salesman

rel salespeople; saleswoman

saline *adj* of, relating to, or containing salt — see SALTY 1

salinity *n* the quality or state of being salty — see SALTINESS

saliva *n* the fluid that is secreted into the mouth by certain glands ⟨our mouths

---

filled with *saliva* when we smelled the delicious dinner⟩
syn slobber, spit, spittle
rel foam, froth; expectoration, sputum

salivate *vb* to let saliva or some other substance flow from the mouth — see DROOL

sallow *adj* lacking the warm skin color indicative of or associated with good health — see SICKLY 2

sally *n* 1 a short trip for pleasure — see EXCURSION 1
2 something said or done to cause laughter — see JOKE 1

sally (forth) *vb* to leave a place often for another — see GO 2

salon *n* 1 a building or part of a building in which objects of interest are displayed — see MUSEUM
2 a building, room, or suite of rooms occupied by a service business — see PLACE 2

saloon *n* a place of business where alcoholic beverages are sold to be consumed on the premises — see BARROOM

salt *adj* of, relating to, or containing salt — see SALTY 1

salt *n* one who operates or navigates a seagoing vessel — see SAILOR

salt away *vb* to put (something of future use or value) in a safe or secret place — see HOARD

saltiness *n* the quality or state of being salty ⟨the *saltiness* of the pretzels went well with the soda pop we were drinking⟩
syn brininess, salinity, saltness
near ant purity; sweetness

saltness *n* the quality or state of being salty — see SALTINESS

salty *adj* 1 of, relating to, or containing salt ⟨*salty* sea water is safe to swim in, but you really shouldn't swallow it⟩
syn briny, saline, salt
rel brackish
near ant sweet; clear, pure
2 hinting at or intended to call to mind matters regarded as indecent — see SUGGESTIVE 1

salubrious *adj* good for the health — see HEALTHFUL

salutary *adj* 1 conferring benefits; promoting or contributing to personal or social well-being — see BENEFICIAL
2 good for the health — see HEALTHFUL

salutation *n* 1 a formal expression of praise — see ENCOMIUM
2 an expression of goodwill upon meeting — see HELLO

salute *n* an expression of goodwill upon meeting — see HELLO

salute *vb* to declare enthusiastic approval of — see ACCLAIM

salvation *n* the saving from danger or evil ⟨we spent the night in the jungle praying for *salvation* from the dangerous animals⟩
syn deliverance
rel ransom, recovery, redemption, rescue; extrication; defense, protection, safeguarding; conservation, preservation

salvo *n* a rapid or overwhelming outpouring of many things at once — see BARRAGE

same *adj* 1 resembling another in every respect ⟨I bought the *same* shirt at the mall for five dollars less⟩
syn coequal, duplicate, equal, even, identical, indistinguishable
rel akin, alike, analogous, comparable, correspondent, corresponding, equivalent, like, matching, parallel, similar, such, suchlike, tantamount
near ant disparate, diverse, varied, various; distinct, distinctive
ant different, dissimilar, distinguishable, other, unalike, unlike
2 being one and not another ⟨that's the *same* guy I saw down at the beach yesterday⟩
syn identical, selfsame, very
near ant disparate, dissimilar, distinct, distinctive, distinguishable, diverse, unalike, unlike, varied, various
ant another, different, other

sameness *n* 1 a tedious lack of variety — see MONOTONY
2 the state of being exactly alike — see IDENTITY 1
3 the state or fact of being exactly the same in number, amount, status, or quality — see EQUIVALENCE

sample *n* 1 a number of things selected from a group to stand for the whole ⟨based on a *sample* of the menu items, we decided that this was the best restaurant in town⟩
syn cross section
rel case, example, exemplar, illustration, instance, representative, specimen; selection
2 one of a group or collection that shows what the whole is like — see EXAMPLE

sample *vb* to put (something) to a test — see TRY (OUT) 1

sanctification *n* 1 the act of making something holy through religious ritual — see CONSECRATION
2 the act or fact of freeing from sin or moral guilt — see PURIFICATION

sanctified *adj* set apart or worthy of veneration by association with God — see HOLY 2

sanctify *vb* 1 to free from moral guilt or blemish especially ceremonially — see PURIFY 1
2 to make holy through prayers or ritual — see BLESS 1

sanctimoniousness *n* the pretending of having virtues, principles, or beliefs that one in fact does not have — see HYPOCRISY

sanction *n* the approval by someone in authority for the doing of something — see PERMISSION

sanction *vb* to give official acceptance of something as satisfactory — see APPROVE

sanctioned *adj* ordered or allowed by those in authority — see OFFICIAL

sanctity *n* the quality or state of being spiritually pure or virtuous — see HOLINESS

sanctuary *n* **1** a place that is considered sacred (as within a religion) — see SHRINE

2 something (as a building) that offers cover from the weather or protection from danger — see SHELTER

sanctum *n* **1** a place that is considered sacred (as within a religion) — see SHRINE

2 something (as a building) that offers cover from the weather or protection from danger — see SHELTER

sand *vb* to make smooth by friction — see GRIND 1

sandwich *vb* to fit (something) into a tight space — see CROWD 1

sandy *adj* of a pale yellow or yellowish brown color — see BLOND

sane *adj* having full use of one's mind and control over one's actions ⟨the court ruled that the woman was indeed *sane* when she made out her will⟩

syn balanced, clearheaded, lucid, normal, right, stable

rel clear, logical, rational, reasonable; judicious, levelheaded, sensible; wise; healthy, sound

near ant balmy, bananas, batty, crackbrained, cracked, cuckoo, daffy, daft, dotty, loco [*slang*], loony (*also* looney), moonstruck, nuts, nutty, off, screwy, wacky; aberrant, disordered; delusional, neurotic, paranoid, psychotic, schizophrenic; eccentric, odd, queer, strange; foolish, senseless, witless; irrational, unreasonable; berserk, delirious, depressed, despondent; distraught, frantic, frenzied, hysterical

ant crazed, crazy, demented, deranged, insane, lunatic, mad, maniacal (*also* maniac), mental, unbalanced, unsound

saneness *n* the normal or healthy condition of the mental abilities — see MIND 2

sanguinary *adj* eager for or marked by the shedding of blood, extreme violence, or killing — see BLOODTHIRSTY

sanguine *adj* **1** eager for or marked by the shedding of blood, extreme violence, or killing — see BLOODTHIRSTY

2 having a healthy reddish skin tone — see RUDDY

3 having or showing a mind free from doubt — see CERTAIN 2

sanguinity *n* an inclination to believe in the most favorable outcome — see OPTIMISM

sanitary *adj* free from filth, infection, or dangers to health ⟨the nurse made sure that everything in the room was *sanitary* so that the baby wouldn't get sick⟩

syn aseptic, germfree, hygienic, sterile

rel antibacterial, antibiotic, antiseptic, germicidal; clean, immaculate, spick-and-span (*or* spic-and-span), spotless, stainless, unsoiled, unsullied; beneficial, healthful, healthy, restorative, salubrious, salutary, wholesome

near ant pathogenic; bedraggled, besmirched, dingy, dirty, draggled, dusty, filthy, foul, grimy, grubby, grungy, mucky, muddy, nasty, soiled, sordid, stained, sullied, unclean, uncleanly; insalubrious, noxious, unhealthful, unhealthy, unwholesome

ant insanitary, unhygienic, unsanitary

sanitary landfill *n* a place where discarded materials (as trash) are dumped — see DUMP 1

sanity *n* the normal or healthy condition of the mental abilities — see MIND 2

sans *prep* not having — see WITHOUT 1

sap *n* **1** active strength of body or mind — see VIGOR 1

2 one who is easily deceived or cheated — see DUPE

sap *vb* to diminish the physical strength of — see WEAKEN 1

sapience *n* the ability to understand inner qualities or relationships — see WISDOM 1

sapient *adj* having or showing deep understanding and intelligent application of knowledge — see WISE 1

sapped *adj* lacking bodily strength — see WEAK 1

sappiness *n* the state or quality of having an excess of tender feelings (as of love, nostalgia, or compassion) — see SENTIMENTALITY

sappy *adj* **1** appealing to the emotions in an obvious and tiresome way — see CORNY

2 showing or marked by a lack of good sense or judgment — see FOOLISH 1

sarcasm *n* an act or expression showing scorn and usually intended to hurt another's feelings — see INSULT

sarcastic *adj* marked by the use of wit that is intended to cause hurt feelings ⟨her *sarcastic* comments that my singing reminded her of the time her dog was sick⟩

syn acrid, biting, caustic, cutting, mordant, pungent, sardonic, satiric (*or* satirical), scalding, scathing, sharp, smart-alecky (*or* smart-aleck), tart

rel acid, acidic, cross, sour; incisive, trenchant; cynical, dry, ironic, wry; facetious, flippant, tongue-in-cheek; acrimonious, bitter, resentful; harsh, rough, severe, stringent; concise, crisp, curt, pithy, succinct, terse; backhanded, insincere

near ant amusing, droll, merry, playful, sportive, waggish; gentle, mild; bland; good-humored, good-natured; diplomatic, polite, smooth, suave, urbane; affable, cordial, genial, gracious

sardonic *adj* marked by the use of wit that is intended to cause hurt feelings — see SARCASTIC

sash *n* a strip of flexible material (as leather) worn around the waist — see ²BELT

---

syn synonym(s)   *rel* related words
ant antonym(s)   *near ant* near antonym(s)

sass *n* disrespectful or argumentative talk given in response to a command or request — see BACK TALK

sassy *adj* displaying or marked by rude boldness — see NERVY 1

Satan *n* the supreme personification of evil often represented as the ruler of Hell — see DEVIL 1

satanic *adj* of, relating to, or worthy of an evil spirit — see FIENDISH

sate *vb* **1** to fill with food to capacity — see GORGE 1
2 to put a complete end to (a physical need or desire) — see SATISFY 1

sated *adj* having one's appetite completely satisfied — see FULL 3

satiate *adj* having one's appetite completely satisfied — see FULL 3

satiate *vb* to put a complete end to (a physical need or desire) — see SATISFY 1

satiated *adj* having one's appetite completely satisfied — see FULL 3

satin *adj* **1** having a shiny surface or finish — see GLOSSY
2 smooth or delicate in appearance or feel — see SOFT 2

satiny *adj* **1** having a shiny surface or finish — see GLOSSY
2 smooth or delicate in appearance or feel — see SOFT 2

satire *n* a creative work that uses sharp humor to point up the foolishness of a person, institution, or human nature in general ⟨a *satire* about the music industry in which a handsome but untalented youth is turned into a rock star⟩
syn lampoon
rel burlesque, caricature, parody, spoof, takeoff; comedy, farce, sketch, slapstick, squib; derision, ridicule; mockery, travesty

satiric *or* **satirical** *adj* marked by the use of wit that is intended to cause hurt feelings — see SARCASTIC

satisfaction *n* **1** the feeling experienced when one's wishes are met — see PLEASURE 1
2 payment to another for a loss or injury — see COMPENSATION 1

satisfactorily *adv* **1** in a satisfactory way — see WELL 1
2 in or to a degree or quantity that meets one's requirements or satisfaction — see ENOUGH 1

satisfactoriness *n* the quality or state of meeting one's needs adequately — see SUFFICIENCY

satisfactory *adj* **1** being to one's liking ⟨we found the meal most *satisfactory*⟩
syn agreeable, all right, alright, copacetic (*also* copasetic *or* copesetic), fine, good, OK (*or* okay), palatable
rel delectable, delicious, delightful, dreamy, felicitous, gratifying, nice, pleasant, pleasing, scrumptious, welcome; acceptable, adequate, decent, passable, tolerable
ant disagreeable, unsatisfactory
2 of a level of quality that meets one's needs or standards — see ADEQUATE

satisfied *adj* **1** experiencing pleasure, satisfaction, or delight — see GLAD 1
2 feeling that one's needs or desires have been met — see CONTENT

satisfy *vb* **1** to put a complete end to (a physical need or desire) ⟨they *satisfied* their hunger after the game with a big pasta dinner⟩
syn assuage, quench, sate, satiate
rel cater (to), gratify, indulge; alleviate, lighten, relieve
near ant arouse, excite, pique, stimulate; tantalize, tease
2 to cause (someone) to agree with a belief or course of action by using arguments or earnest requests — see PERSUADE
3 to do what is required by the terms of — see FULFILL 1
4 to give satisfaction to — see PLEASE

satisfying *adj* **1** giving pleasure or contentment to the mind or senses — see PLEASANT
2 having the power to persuade — see COGENT
3 making one feel good inside — see HEARTWARMING

satisfyingly *adv* in a pleasing way — see WELL 5

saturate *vb* to wet thoroughly with liquid — see SOAK 1

saturated *adj* containing, covered with, or thoroughly penetrated by water — see WET

saturnine *adj* causing or marked by an atmosphere lacking in cheer — see GLOOMY 1

sauce *n* **1** a savory fluid food used as a topping or accompaniment to a main dish ⟨the chef poured *sauce* over the meat just before he served it⟩
syn dressing, gravy
rel condiment, relish, seasoning; fixing(s), garnish, topping; dip, marinade
2 disrespectful or argumentative talk given in response to a command or request — see BACK TALK
3 shameless boldness — see EFFRONTERY

sauciness *n* shameless boldness — see EFFRONTERY

saucy *adj* displaying or marked by rude boldness — see NERVY 1

saunter *n* a relaxed journey on foot for exercise or pleasure — see WALK

sausage *n* a rod-shaped portion of seasoned ground meat in a casing ⟨a couple of *sausages* and eggs make a good breakfast⟩
syn link
rel bologna, frankfurter, hot dog, knockwurst, liverwurst, pepperoni, salami, wiener

savage *adj* **1** not civilized ⟨Tarzan is usually portrayed as a noble but *savage* warrior of the jungle⟩
syn barbarous, heathen, heathenish, Neanderthal, rude, uncivil, uncivilized, uncultivated, wild
rel coarse, crude, primitive, rough; uncouth, uncultured

near *ant* cultured, enlightened, humane, sophisticated; genteel, polite, refined, urbane, well-bred
ant civilized

2 having or showing the desire to inflict severe pain and suffering on others — see CRUEL 1

3 living outdoors without taming or domestication by humans — see WILD 1

4 violently unfriendly or aggressive in disposition — see FIERCE 1

savage *n* **1** a mean, evil, or unprincipled person — see VILLAIN 1

2 an uncivilized person — see HEATHEN 2

savageness *n* the willful infliction of pain and suffering on others — see CRUELTY

savagery *n* the willful infliction of pain and suffering on others — see CRUELTY

savanna *also* **savannah** *n* a broad area of level or rolling treeless country — see PLAIN

savant *n* a person of deep wisdom or learning — see SAGE

save *prep* not including — see EXCEPT

save *vb* **1** to free from the penalties or consequences of sin ⟨the Christian belief that Jesus lived and died to *save* humanity⟩
syn deliver, redeem
rel reclaim, reform; forgive, pardon, remit; bless, hallow; consecrate, purify, sanctify

2 to remove from danger or harm ⟨the fire fighter *saved* my brother from the burning building⟩
syn bail out, deliver, rescue
rel salvage; emancipate, free, liberate, manumit; release; disentangle, extricate; recover
ant compromise, endanger, imperil, jeopardize

3 to avoid unnecessary waste or expense — see ECONOMIZE

4 to keep in good condition — see MAINTAIN 1

5 to keep or intend for a special purpose — see DEVOTE 1

saver *n* one that saves from danger or destruction — see SAVIOR

saving *conj* if it were not for the fact that — see EXCEPT

saving *prep* not including — see EXCEPT

savior *or* **saviour** *n* one that saves from danger or destruction ⟨the policeman proved to be our *savior*, arriving on the scene just as we were about to be mugged⟩
syn deliverer, redeemer, rescuer, saver
rel custodian, defender, guard, guardian, keeper, lookout, protector, sentinel, sentry, warden, warder, watch, watchman

savor *n* **1** the property of a substance that can be identified by the sense of taste — see TASTE 1

2 the quality of being delicious — see DELICIOUSNESS

savor *vb* to make more pleasant to the taste by adding something intensely flavored — see SEASON 1

savoriness *n* the quality of being delicious — see DELICIOUSNESS

savorless *adj* lacking in taste or flavor — see INSIPID 1

savory *adj* **1** having a pleasant smell — see FRAGRANT

2 very pleasing to the sense of taste — see DELICIOUS 1

savvy *n* knowledge gained by actually doing or living through something — see EXPERIENCE 1

saw *n* an often stated observation regarding something from common experience — see SAYING

saw-toothed *adj* notched or toothed along the edge — see SERRATED

say *vb* **1** to express (a thought or emotion) in words ⟨why don't you just *say* what's on your mind?⟩
syn articulate, speak, state, talk, tell, utter, verbalize, vocalize
rel air, discuss, express, give, look, sound, state, vent, ventilate, voice; advertise, announce, blaze, broadcast, declare, enunciate, proclaim, publicize, publish; affirm, allege, assert, aver, avouch, avow; breathe, drawl, gasp, mouth, murmur, shout, splutter, spout, whisper; couch, formulate, phrase, put, word; comment, remark
phrases put into words
near *ant* stifle, suppress

2 to convey in appropriate or telling terms — see PHRASE

3 to give from memory — see REPEAT 2

say *n* the right to express a wish, choice, or opinion — see VOICE 1

saying *n* an often stated observation regarding something from common experience ⟨there's an old *saying* that you should let sleeping dogs lie⟩
syn adage, aphorism, byword, epigram, maxim, proverb, saw
rel cliché, commonplace, platitude; expression, felicity; axiom, motto, precept, truism, truth; observation, reflection, remark

scabby *adj* arousing or deserving of one's loathing and disgust — see CONTEMPTIBLE 1

scads *n pl* a considerable amount — see LOT 2

scalawag *or* **scallywag** *n* a mean, evil, or unprincipled person — see VILLAIN

scalding *adj* **1** having a notably high temperature — see HOT 1

2 marked by the use of wit that is intended to cause hurt feelings — see SARCASTIC

¹**scale** *n* a device for measuring weight ⟨I hate getting on the bathroom *scale*⟩
syn balance
rel gravimeter

²**scale** *n* a small thin piece of material that resembles an animal scale ⟨*scales* of mica were embedded in the granite⟩
syn lamella, lamina, plate
rel chip, flake, sliver, splinter

---

syn synonym(s)   **rel** related words
ant antonym(s)   **near ant** near antonym(s)

³**scale** *n* **1** a scheme of rank or order ⟨a student who scored very highly on a standard intelligence *scale*⟩
syn graduation, ladder, ordering, ranking
rel arrangement, array, disposal, disposition, distribution, order, sequence, series
2 the distance or extent between possible extremes — see RANGE 3

scale *vb* to find out the size, extent, or amount of — see MEASURE

scaly *adj* composed of or covered with scales ⟨the snake's *scaly* skin was dry to the touch⟩
syn squamous
rel scalelike
near ant smooth
ant scaleless

scamp *n* **1** an appealingly mischievous person ⟨those little *scamps* are always getting into trouble, but no one has the heart to punish them⟩
syn devil, hellion, imp, mischief, monkey, rapscallion, rascal, rogue, urchin
rel cutup, madcap, skylarker; ragamuffin; brat, disrupter, nuisance; juvenile delinquent; gamin, gamine
near ant beast, boor, cad, churl, clown, creep, cretin, cur, heel, joker, louse, lout, skunk, snake, stinker; knave, scalawag (*or* scallywag); scoundrel, villain
2 a mean, evil, or unprincipled person — see VILLAIN

scamper *vb* to go at a pace faster than a walk — see RUN 1

scan *n* a close look at or over someone or something in order to judge condition — see INSPECTION

scan *vb* to look over closely (as for judging quality or condition) — see INSPECT

scandal *n* a cause of shame — see DISGRACE 2

scandalous *adj* **1** causing intense displeasure, disgust, or resentment — see OFFENSIVE 1
2 causing or intended to cause unjust injury to a person's good name — see LIBELOUS

scant *adj* less plentiful than what is normal, necessary, or desirable — see MEAGER

scant *vb* to use or give out in stingy amounts — see SPARE

scantiness *n* a falling short of an essential or desirable amount or number — see DEFICIENCY

scanty *adj* less plentiful than what is normal, necessary, or desirable — see MEAGER

scapegoat *n* a person or thing taking the blame for others ⟨companies often use the economy as a *scapegoat* to avoid taking responsibility for dropping sales⟩
syn fall guy, goat, whipping boy
rel victim; butt, dupe, fool, laughingstock, mockery, monkey; excuse

scar *n* something that spoils the appearance or completeness of a thing — see BLEMISH

scarce *adj* **1** less plentiful than what is normal, necessary, or desirable — see MEAGER
2 not coming up to a usual standard or meeting a particular need — see SHORT 3

scarcely *adv* **1** by a very small margin — see JUST 2
2 certainly not — see HARDLY 2

scarceness *n* a falling short of an essential or desirable amount or number — see DEFICIENCY

scarcity *n* a falling short of an essential or desirable amount or number — see DEFICIENCY

scare *vb* to strike with fear — see FRIGHTEN

scared *adj* filled with fear or dread — see AFRAID 1

scare up *vb* to come upon after searching, study, or effort — see FIND 1

scarp *n* a steep wall of rock, earth, or ice — see CLIFF

scary *adj* **1** causing fear — see FEARFUL 1
2 easily frightened — see SHY 1

scathe *vb* to criticize harshly and usually publicly — see ATTACK 2

scathing *adj* marked by the use of wit that is intended to cause hurt feelings — see SARCASTIC

scatter *vb* **1** to cause (members of a group) to move widely apart ⟨the noise of the backfiring car *scattered* the pigeons⟩
syn clear out, disband, dispel, disperse, dissipate
rel break up, isolate, part, segregate, separate, split up; diffuse, disseminate, diverge, spread
near ant agglutinate, conglomerate; unify, unite
ant assemble, cluster, collect, concentrate, congregate, gather
2 to cover by or as if by scattering something over or on ⟨the hillside was *scattered* with wildflowers⟩
syn bestrew, dot, pepper, sow, spray, sprinkle, strew
rel blanket, dust; stud; dapple, fleck, speckle, spot, stipple

scatterbrained *adj* lacking in seriousness or maturity — see GIDDY 1

scattered *adj* lacking a definite plan, purpose, or pattern — see RANDOM

scattering *n* **1** an act or process in which something scatters or is scattered ⟨the *scattering* of the protesters suddenly turned violent and chaotic⟩
syn disbandment, dispersal, dispersion, dissipation
near ant assembly, collection, concentration, gathering
2 a small number — see FEW

scenario *n* the written form of a story prepared for film production — see SCREENPLAY

scene *n* **1** the place and time in which the action for a portion of a dramatic work (as a movie) is set ⟨the first *scene* was the kitchen of a fancy restaurant during dinner⟩
syn background, setting

rel backdrop, scenery, set; tableau

2 an outburst or display of excited anger — see TANTRUM

3 position with regard to conditions and circumstances — see SITUATION 1

4 the array of painted backgrounds and furnishings used for a scene in a stage production — see SCENERY

scenery *n* the array of painted backgrounds and furnishings used for a scene in a stage production ⟨the *scenery* in the high school production was all hand-made⟩

syn scene, set

rel backdrop, drop; background, setting; prop, property

scent *n* **1** a sweet or pleasant smell — see FRAGRANCE

2 the quality of a thing that makes it perceptible to the sense organs in the nose — see SMELL 1

scent *vb* **1** to fill or infuse with a pleasant odor or odor-releasing substance ⟨fancy bars of soap *scented* with lavender⟩

syn perfume

near ant deodorize

2 to become aware of by means of the sense organs in the nose — see SMELL

3 to have a vague awareness of — see FEEL 1

scented *adj* having a pleasant smell — see FRAGRANT

schedule *n* **1** a listing of things to be presented or considered (as at a concert or play) — see PROGRAM 1

2 a record of a series of items (as names or titles) usually arranged according to some system — see ¹LIST

schedule *vb* to put (someone or something) on a list — see ¹LIST 2

scheduled *adj* being in accordance with the prescribed, normal, or logical course of events — see DUE 2

schematize *vb* to work out the details of (something) in advance — see PLAN 1

scheme *n* **1** a clever often underhanded means to achieve an end — see TRICK 1

2 a secret plan for accomplishing evil or unlawful ends — see PLOT 1

3 a method worked out in advance for achieving some objective — see PLAN 1

scheme *vb* to engage in a secret plan to accomplish evil or unlawful ends — see PLOT

scheme (out) *vb* to work out the details of (something) in advance — see PLAN 1

schism *n* **1** a lack of agreement or harmony — see DISCORD

2 the act or process of a whole separating into two or more parts or pieces — see SEPARATION 1

schmaltz *also* **schmalz** *n* something (as a work of literature or music) that is too sentimental — see CORN

schmaltzy *adj* appealing to the emotions in an obvious and tiresome way — see CORNY

scholar *n* **1** a person of deep wisdom or learning — see SAGE

2 a person with a high level of knowledge or skill in a field — see EXPERT

3 one who attends a school — see STUDENT

scholarly *adj* **1** having or displaying advanced knowledge or education — see EDUCATED

2 of or relating to schooling or learning especially at an advanced level — see ACADEMIC

scholarship *n* the understanding and information gained from being educated — see EDUCATION 2

scholastic *adj* of or relating to schooling or learning especially at an advanced level — see ACADEMIC

school *n* a place or establishment for teaching and learning ⟨one of the first *schools* in the country to admit girls as students⟩

syn academy, seminary

rel elementary school, grammar school, high school, junior high school, middle school, preparatory school, public school, secondary school, trade school; Sunday school, yeshiva (*also* yeshivah)

school *vb* to cause to acquire knowledge or skill in some field — see TEACH

schooling *n* the act or process of imparting knowledge or skills to another — see EDUCATION 2

schoolteacher *n* a person whose occupation is to give formal instruction in a school — see TEACHER

science *n* **1** a body of facts learned by study or experience — see KNOWLEDGE 1

2 the understanding and information gained from being educated — see EDUCATION 2

scintillate *vb* **1** to give off sparks — see SPARK 1

2 to shoot forth bursts of light — see FLASH 1

scoffer *n* a person who causes repeated emotional pain, distress, or annoyance to another — see TORMENTOR

scold *n* a person given to harsh judgments and to finding faults — see CRITIC 1

scold *vb* to criticize (someone) severely or angrily especially for personal failings ⟨he *scolded* the kids for not cleaning up the mess they had made in the kitchen⟩

syn berate, castigate, chew out, dress down, flay, jaw, keelhaul, lambaste (*or* lambast), lecture, rail (at *or* against), rate, rebuke, reprimand, reproach, score, upbraid

rel admonish, chide, remonstrate (with), reprove; abuse, assail, attack, bad-mouth, blame, blast, censure, condemn, criticize, crucify, denounce, dis [*slang*], excoriate, fault, knock, lash, pan, reprehend, slam; belittle, disparage, mock, put down; ridicule, scoff, scorn

phrases read the riot act (to), take to task

near ant approve, endorse (*also* indorse), sanction; extol (*also* extoll), laud, praise

---

syn synonym(s)   *rel* related words
ant antonym(s)   *near ant* near antonym(s)

scoop *n* 1 a utensil with a bowl and a handle that is used especially in cooking and serving food — see SPOON

2 information not generally available to the public — see DOPE 1

scoop *vb* to lift out with something that holds liquid — see DIP 2

scoot *vb* to proceed or move quickly — see HURRY 1

scope *n* an area over which activity, capacity, or influence extends — see RANGE 2

scorch *vb* to burn on the surface ⟨the picnickers kept *scorching* their marshmallows, deliberately sticking their skewers into the licking flames of the campfire⟩

syn char, sear, singe

rel fire, ignite, inflame, kindle, light; bake, cremate, incinerate; scald, scathe

scorching *adj* having a notably high temperature — see HOT 1

score *n* a lingering ill will towards a person for a real or imagined wrong — see GRUDGE 1

score *vb* 1 to mark with or as if with a line or groove ⟨the glassblower *scored* the glass rod first so that it would break cleanly⟩

syn groove, scribe, seam

rel abrade, file, graze, rasp, scarify, scratch

2 to gain (as points or runs in a game) as credit towards one's total number of points ⟨he *scored* the winning goal in the final minute of play⟩

syn rack up, tally

rel triumph, win; best, defeat

near ant lose

3 to obtain (as a goal) through effort — see ACHIEVE 1

4 to criticize (someone) severely or angrily especially for personal failings — see SCOLD

scorn *n* open dislike for someone or something considered unworthy of one's concern or respect — see CONTEMPT

scorn *vb* 1 to show contempt for ⟨*scorned* the religious traditions of their ancestors⟩

syn disdain, high-hat, slight, sniff (at), snub

rel scout; abhor, despise, detest, hate, loathe; disapprove (of), discountenance, disfavor, frown (on *or* upon)

phrases look down on, sneeze at

near ant cherish, prize, treasure, value; admire, esteem; revere, venerate, worship; accept, appreciate, approve (of), care (for), countenance, favor, OK (*or* okay), subscribe (to)

ant honor, respect

2 to ignore in a disrespectful manner ⟨she *scorned* the suggestions of her classmates for the parade float⟩

syn despise, disregard, flout

rel dismiss, forget, ignore, neglect, overlook, overpass, pass over, slight, slur (over)

near ant accept, approve; use

scorner *n* a person who causes repeated emotional pain, distress, or annoyance to another — see TORMENTOR

scornful *adj* 1 feeling or showing open dislike for someone or something regarded as undeserving of respect or concern — see CONTEMPTUOUS 1

2 intended to make a person or thing seem of little importance or value — see DEROGATORY

Scot *n* a person born or living in Scotland ⟨my grandfather was a *Scot*, but my grandmother was Welsh⟩

syn Scotchman, Scotsman, Scottie

Scotch *adj* of, relating to, or characteristic of the people of Scotland — see SCOTTISH

Scotchman *n* a person born or living in Scotland — see SCOT

Scots *adj* of, relating to, or characteristic of the people of Scotland — see SCOTTISH

Scotsman *n* a person born or living in Scotland — see SCOT

Scottie *n* a person born or living in Scotland — see SCOT

Scottish *adj* of, relating to, or characteristic of the people of Scotland ⟨golf was originally a *Scottish* game⟩

syn Scotch, Scots

scoundrel *n* a mean, evil, or unprincipled person — see VILLAIN

scour *vb* to look through (as a place) carefully or thoroughly in an effort to find or discover something — see SEARCH 1

scourge *n* 1 a long thin or flexible tool for striking — see WHIP

2 one who inflicts punishment in return for an injury or offense — see NEMESIS 1

scourge *vb* 1 to bring destruction to (something) through violent action — see RAVAGE

2 to strike repeatedly with something long and thin or flexible — see WHIP 1

scout *n* a member of the human race — see HUMAN

scout *vb* to make (someone or something) the object of unkind laughter — see RIDICULE

scout (up) *vb* to come upon after searching, study, or effort — see FIND 1

scowl *n* a twisting of the facial features in disgust or disapproval — see GRIMACE

scowl *vb* to look with anger or disapproval — see FROWN

scrabble *n* a forceful effort to reach a goal or objective — see STRUGGLE 1

scraggly *adj* having an uneven edge or outline — see RAGGED 1

scraggy *adj* 1 having an uneven edge or outline — see RAGGED 1

2 not having a level or smooth surface — see UNEVEN 1

scramble *n* an unorganized collection or mixture of various things — see MISCELLANY 1

scramble *vb* 1 to move (as up or over something) often with the help of the hands in holding or pulling — see CLIMB 1

2 to undo the proper order or arrangement of — see DISORDER

¹**scrap** *n* **1** an unused or unwanted piece or item typically of small size or value ⟨only a *scrap* of silk was left on the sewing table after they had finished the project⟩

syn end, fag end, leftover, oddment, remainder, remnant, stub

rel leavings, odds and ends, remains, residual, residue, scraping(s), stump; balance, rest; chip, flake, fragment, piece, sliver, splinter; ribbon(s), shred, tatter

near ant whole

2 a broken or irregular part of something that often remains incomplete — see FRAGMENT

3 a physical dispute between opposing individuals or groups — see FIGHT 1

4 a very small piece — see BIT 1

5 discarded or useless material — see GARBAGE

²**scrap** *n* an often noisy or angry expression of differing opinions — see ARGUMENT 1

¹**scrap** *vb* to express different opinions about something often angrily — see ARGUE 2

²**scrap** *vb* to get rid of as useless or unwanted — see DISCARD

scrape *n* **1** a brief clash between enemies or rivals — see ENCOUNTER

2 a harsh grating sound — see RASP

scrape *vb* **1** to pass roughly and noisily over or against a surface ⟨the rusty old gate *scraped* whenever anyone managed to open it⟩

syn grate, grind, rasp, scratch

rel rub; groan, whine

near ant glide, skate, slide

2 to damage by rubbing against a sharp or rough surface ⟨she *scraped* her knee when she fell down⟩

syn abrade, graze, scratch, scuff

rel bark, skin; chafe, fret, gall; claw, cut, lacerate; bruise, contuse

near ant polish, smooth, soften, wax

3 to get with great difficulty — see EKE OUT

4 to press or strike against or together so as to make a scraping sound — see GRIND 2

scrape (together) *vb* to bring together in one body or place — see GATHER 1

scrappiness *n* an inclination to fight or quarrel — see BELLIGERENCE

scrapping *n* the getting rid of whatever is unwanted or useless — see DISPOSAL 1

scrappy *adj* **1** feeling or displaying eagerness to fight — see BELLIGERENT

2 given to arguing — see ARGUMENTATIVE 1

scratch *n* a harsh grating sound — see RASP

scratch *vb* **1** to damage by rubbing against a sharp or rough surface — see SCRAPE 2

2 to pass roughly and noisily over or against a surface — see SCRAPE 1

3 to write or draw hastily or carelessly — see SCRIBBLE

scratch (out) *vb* **1** to compose and set down on paper the words of — see WRITE 1

2 to show (something written) to be no longer valid by drawing a cross over or a line through it — see X (OUT)

scratchy *adj* **1** likely to cause a scratch ⟨*scratchy* shrubbery that's intended to keep kids and pets off the old man's property⟩

syn brambly, prickly, thistly, thorny

rel burred; coarse, jagged, rough; irritating, itchy, stinging

near ant polished, smooth, soft, soothing; gentle

2 harsh and dry in sound — see HOARSE

scrawl *vb* to write or draw hastily or carelessly — see SCRIBBLE

scream *n* someone or something that is very funny ⟨that new comedy is a *scream*⟩

syn laugh, riot

rel howler; crack, gag, jest, joke, pleasantry, quip, sally, waggery, wisecrack, witticism; caution, sight

near ant bummer, downer

scream *vb* to cry out loudly and emotionally ⟨we *screamed* when the roller coaster began its thirty foot plunge⟩

syn howl, screech, shriek, shrill, squall, squeal, yelp, yell

rel bay, caterwaul, keen, squawk, wail, yawp (*or* yaup), yowl; bawl, call, cry, holler, shout, vociferate

near ant murmur, mutter, whisper

screaming *adj* **1** arousing a strong and usually superficial interest or emotional reaction — see SENSATIONAL 1

2 causing or intended to cause laughter — see FUNNY 1

screech *vb* to cry out loudly and emotionally — see SCREAM

screeching *adj* having a high musical pitch or range — see SHRILL

screen *n* **1** the art or business of making a movie — see MOVIE 2

2 means or method of defending — see DEFENSE 1

screen *vb* **1** to drive danger or attack away from — see DEFEND 1

2 to keep secret or shut off from view — see ¹HIDE 2

3 to pass through a filter — see STRAIN 2

4 to place a protective layer over — see COVER 3

screenplay *n* the written form of a story prepared for film production ⟨each actor was given a copy of the *screenplay* to study⟩

syn scenario, script

rel story, text

screw *vb* to twist (something) out of a natural or normal shape or condition — see CONTORT

screwball *adj* showing or marked by a lack of good sense or judgment — see FOOLISH 1

screwball *n* a person of odd or whimsical habits — see ECCENTRIC

syn synonym(s)   *rel* related words
ant antonym(s)   *near ant* near antonym(s)

screwing *n* the twisting of something out of its natural or normal shape or condition — see CONTORTION

screwlike *adj* turning around an axis like the thread of a screw — see SPIRAL

screwy *adj* **1** different from the ordinary in a way that causes curiosity or suspicion — see ODD 2

2 having or showing a very abnormal or sick state of mind — see INSANE 1

scribble *vb* to write or draw hastily or carelessly ⟨she *scribbled* a quick note on the pad by the door before leaving⟩
syn scratch, scrawl
rel doodle; jot (down); ink, inscribe, letter, pen, pencil, print, write

scribe *n* a person whose job is to keep records — see CLERK 1

scribe *vb* to mark with or as if with a line or groove — see SCORE 1

scrimmage *n* a physical dispute between opposing individuals or groups — see FIGHT 1

scrimmage (with) *vb* to oppose (someone) in physical conflict — see FIGHT 1

scrimp *vb* to avoid unnecessary waste or expense — see ECONOMIZE

scrimping *adj* careful in the management of money or resources — see FRUGAL

scrimping *n* careful management of material resources — see ECONOMY

script *n* **1** the form or style of a particular person's writing — see HANDWRITING 1

2 the written form of a story prepared for film production — see SCREENPLAY

3 writing done by hand — see HANDWRITING 2

Scripture *n* a book made up of the writings accepted by Christians as coming from God — see BIBLE

scrooge *n* a mean grasping person who is usually stingy with money — see MISER

scrounge *vb* to get with great difficulty — see EKE OUT

scrub *n* a living thing much smaller than others of its kind — see DWARF 1

scruffy *adj* showing signs of advanced wear and tear and neglect — see SHABBY 1

scrumptious *adj* very pleasing to the sense of taste — see DELICIOUS 1

scrunch *vb* **1** to create (as by crushing) an irregular mass of creases in — see CRUMPLE 1

2 to lie low with the limbs close to the body — see CROUCH

3 to press or strike against or together so as to make a scraping sound — see GRIND 2

scruple *n* **1** a very small amount — see PARTICLE 1

2 a very small piece — see BIT 1

3 an uneasy feeling about the rightness of what one is doing or going to do — see QUALM

scrupulous *adj* guided by or in accordance with one's sense of right and wrong — see CONSCIENTIOUS 1

scrupulousness *n* strict attentiveness to what one is doing — see CARE 1

scrutinize *vb* to look over closely (as for judging quality or condition) — see INSPECT

scrutiny *n* a close look at or over someone or something in order to judge condition — see INSPECTION

scuff *vb* **1** to damage by rubbing against a sharp or rough surface — see SCRAPE 2

2 to move heavily or clumsily — see LUMBER 1

scuffle *n* a physical dispute between opposing individuals or groups — see FIGHT 1

scuffle *vb* **1** to move heavily or clumsily — see LUMBER 1

2 to seize and attempt to unbalance one another for the purpose of achieving physical mastery — see WRESTLE

scull *vb* to move a boat by means of oars — see ¹ROW

sculler *n* a person who drives a boat forward by means of oars — see OARSMAN

sculpt *vb* to create a three-dimensional representation of (something) using solid material ⟨I *sculpted* a figure of a giraffe out of clay in art class today⟩
syn carve, sculpture
rel chisel, engrave, etch, grave, incise, inscribe; cast, form, model, mold, shape

sculpture *vb* to create a three-dimensional representation of (something) using solid material — see SCULPT

scum *n* people looked down upon as ignorant and of the lowest class — see RABBLE

scummy *adj* arousing or deserving of one's loathing and disgust — see CONTEMPTIBLE 1

scurry *vb* to proceed or move quickly — see HURRY 2

scurvy *adj* arousing or deserving of one's loathing and disgust — see CONTEMPTIBLE 1

scuttle *vb* to proceed or move quickly — see HURRY 2

sea *n* the whole body of salt water that covers nearly three-fourths of the earth — see OCEAN

sea devil *n* any of several extremely large rays — see DEVILFISH

sea dog *n* one who operates or navigates a seagoing vessel — see SAILOR

seafarer *n* one who operates or navigates a seagoing vessel — see SAILOR

seam *vb* to mark with or as if with a line or groove — see SCORE 1

seaman *n* one who operates or navigates a seagoing vessel — see SAILOR

sear *vb* **1** to burn on the surface — see SCORCH

2 to make dry — see DRY 1

search *n* an act or process of looking carefully or thoroughly for someone or something ⟨the *search* for the lost puppy took hours⟩
syn hunt, quest
rel chase, pursuit; reconnaissance, scout; canvas, survey; exploration, probe; forage

search vb **1** to look through (as a place) carefully or thoroughly in an effort to find or discover something ⟨we *searched* the closet for half an hour until we found the missing shoe⟩

syn comb, dig (through), dredge, hunt (through), rake, ransack, rifle, rummage, scour

rel audit, check (out), examine, inspect, investigate, review, scan, scrutinize, survey; ascertain, descry, detect, determine, discover, ferret (out), find, find out, get, hit (on *or* upon), learn, locate, run down, scare up, track (down); explore, probe, prospect, skirmish, snoop; browse, glance (over); look over; peruse, study

near ant hide; abandon, lose; ignore, neglect

2 to go into or range over for purposes of discovery — see EXPLORE 2

search (for *or* out) vb to go in search of — see SEEK 1

searing *adj* having a notably high temperature — see HOT 1

season vb **1** to make more pleasant to the taste by adding something intensely flavored ⟨the chef *seasoned* the vegetables as soon as they came out of the oven⟩

syn flavor, savor, spice

rel enhance, enrich, sauce; salt, pepper

2 to bring to a proper or desired state of fitness — see CONDITION 1

3 to make able to withstand physical hardship, strain, or exposure — see HARDEN 2

4 to make competent (as by training, skill, or ability) for a particular office or function — see QUALIFY 2

seasonable *adj* especially suitable for a certain time — see TIMELY 1

seasoning *n* **1** something (as a spice or herb) that adds an agreeable or interesting taste to food ⟨the stew was too bland before they added the *seasoning*⟩

syn flavor, flavoring, spice

rel sauce

2 something used to enhance the flavor of cooked or prepared food — see CONDIMENT

seat *n* **1** a place from which authority is exercised ⟨all applications had to be submitted at the county *seat* for proper processing⟩

syn command, headquarters

rel center, home; capital

2 the part of the body upon which someone sits — see BUTTOCKS

3 a thing or place that is of greatest importance to an activity or interest — see CENTER 1

seat vb to cause to sit down ⟨the usher *seated* them in the third row⟩

syn set down, sit

rel ensconce, settle; lay, lie, rest; place, put; recline, repose

seclude vb to set or keep apart from others — see ISOLATE

secluded *adj* hidden from view ⟨we stayed in a *secluded* resort, far away from the regular tourist crowds⟩

syn cloistered, covert, isolated, quiet, remote, retired, secret, sheltered

rel lonely, reclusive, solitary; private

near ant obvious, visible; exposed

secludedness *n* the state of being alone or kept apart from others — see ISOLATION

seclusion *n* the state of being alone or kept apart from others — see ISOLATION

second *n* a very small space of time — see INSTANT

secondary *adj* **1** taken or created from something original or basic ⟨history textbooks are *secondary* sources for historical information and do not represent original research⟩

syn derivative, secondhand

rel unoriginal; consequent, resultant

near ant fundamental, nonderivative; first, primary

ant basic, original

2 of little or less value or merit — see INFERIOR 2

second–class *adj* of little or less value or merit — see INFERIOR 2

secondhand *adj* taken or created from something original or basic — see SECONDARY 1

second–rate *adj* **1** of average to below average quality — see MEDIOCRE 1

2 of little or less value or merit — see INFERIOR 2

3 of low quality — see CHEAP 2

secrecy *n* the practice or habit of keeping secrets or keeping one's affairs secret ⟨in picking helpers for a surprise party, you'd very much want to choose people known for their *secrecy*⟩

syn closeness, secretiveness

rel discreetness, discretion, prudence; circumspection, wariness; reserve, reticence, silence, taciturnity; furtiveness, shiftiness, slyness, sneakiness, underhandedness; concealment, stealth, subterfuge

near ant candor, frankness, honesty, openness; imprudence, indiscretion

secret *adj* **1** undertaken or done so as to escape being observed or known by others ⟨a *secret* operation to rescue captive soldiers behind enemy lines⟩

syn clandestine, covert, furtive, huggermugger, private, privy, sneak, sneaking, sneaky, stealthy, surreptitious, undercover, underground, underhand, underhanded

rel classified, confidential, restricted, top secret, undisclosed; concealed, hidden, secreted, subterranean, unadvertised, unexposed

near ant acknowledged, avowed; aboveboard, straightforward, unconcealed, undisguised; unclassified, unrestricted; clear, evident, manifest, obvious, patent, plain

ant open, overt, public

---

syn synonym(s)   *rel* related words
ant antonym(s)   *near ant* near antonym(s)

2 working on missions in which one's objectives, activities, or true identity are not publicly revealed ⟨*secret* agents whose wartime exploits were known only by top government officials⟩

syn undercover

rel covert, private, secretive, subterranean

near ant overt

3 hidden from view — see SECLUDED

4 not known or meant to be known by the general populace — see PRIVATE 1

secret *n* **1** information shared only with another or with a select few ⟨they're best friends and are constantly sharing *secrets*⟩

syn confidence

rel dope, lowdown

near ant open secret

2 something hard to understand or explain — see MYSTERY

secrete *vb* to put into a hiding place — see ¹HIDE 1

secretion *n* the placing of something out of sight — see CONCEALMENT 1

secretive *adj* given to keeping one's activities hidden from public observation or knowledge ⟨the intelligence agency remained *secretive* despite the media's demands for more openness in government⟩

syn close, closemouthed, dark, reticent, uncommunicative

rel quiet, reserved, silent, taciturn, tight-lipped; discreet, prudent; clandestine, covert, furtive, hugger-mugger, secret, sneak, sneaky, stealthy, surreptitious, undercover, underhand, underhanded

near ant candid, frank, honest; blunt, outspoken, tactless

ant communicative, open

secretiveness *n* the practice or habit of keeping secrets or keeping one's affairs secret — see SECRECY

sect *n* a group of people acting together within a larger group — see FACTION

sectarian *adj* not broad or open in views or opinions — see NARROW 2

section *n* **1** an area (as of a city) set apart for some purpose or having some special feature — see DISTRICT

2 one of the pieces from which something is designed to be assembled — see PART 1

secular *adj* not involving religion or religious matters — see PROFANE 1

secure *adj* **1** firmly positioned in place and difficult to dislodge — see TIGHT 2

2 having or showing great faith in oneself or one's abilities — see CONFIDENT 1

3 not exposed to the threat of loss or injury — see SAFE 1

4 providing safety — see SAFE 2

secure *vb* **1** to drive danger or attack away from — see DEFEND 1

2 to make sure, certain, or safe — see ENSURE

3 to put securely in place or in a desired position — see FASTEN 2

4 to receive as return for effort — see EARN 1

security *n* **1** means or method of defending — see DEFENSE 1

2 something given or held to assure that the giver will keep a promise — see PLEDGE 1

3 the state of not being exposed to danger — see SAFETY 1

sedate *adj* not joking or playful in mood or manner — see SERIOUS 1

sedative *adj* tending to calm the emotions and relieve stress — see SOOTHING 1

sediment *n* matter that settles to the bottom of a body of liquid — see DEPOSIT 1

sediment *vb* to cause to come to rest at the bottom (as of a liquid) — see SETTLE 1

seduce *vb* to lead away from a usual or proper course by offering some pleasure or advantage — see LURE

seducer *n* one that tries to get a person to give in to a desire — see TEMPTER

seduction *n* the act or pressure of giving in to a desire especially when ill-advised — see TEMPTATION 1

seductive *adj* having an often mysterious or magical power to attract — see FASCINATING 1

seductiveness *n* the power of irresistible attraction — see CHARM 2

seductress *n* a woman whom men find irresistibly attractive — see SIREN

sedulous *adj* involved in often constant activity — see BUSY 1

sedulously *adv* with great effort or determination — see HARD 1

see *vb* **1** to make note of (something) through the use of one's eyes ⟨out of the corner of my eye I *saw* the deer run into the woods⟩

syn behold, descry, discern, distinguish, espy, eye, look (at), note, notice, observe, perceive, regard, remark, sight, spy, view, witness

rel identify, make out, pick out; attend (to), consider, heed, mark, mind; study, watch; examine, inspect, scan, scrutinize, survey; glance (at), glimpse, peer (at)

phrases get a load of [*slang*], lay eyes on, set eyes on

near ant disregard, ignore, neglect, overpass, pass over; miss, overlook

2 to come to a knowledge of (something) by living through it — see EXPERIENCE

3 to come to an awareness — see DISCOVER 1

4 to have a vague awareness of — see FEEL 1

5 to make a social call upon — see VISIT 1

6 to recognize the meaning of — see COMPREHEND 1

seeable *adj* capable of being seen — see VISIBLE

seed *n* the descendants of a person, animal, or plant — see OFFSPRING

seed *vb* to put or set into the ground to grow — see PLANT

seediness *n* the state of being unattended to or not cared for — see NEGLECT 1

seedy *adj* **1** showing signs of advanced wear and tear and neglect — see SHABBY 1

2 worn or torn into or as if into rags — see RAGGED 2

seeing *conj* for the reason that — see SINCE

seek *vb* **1** to go in search of ⟨the knights of the Round Table fervently *sought* the Holy Grail⟩
   syn cast about (for), cast around (for), forage (for), hunt, look up, pursue, quest, search (for *or* out)
   rel ferret (out), root (out)
   phrases look for
   near ant hide, lose; ignore, neglect
2 to make a request for — see ASK (FOR) 1
3 to make an effort to do — see ATTEMPT

seeker *n* one who seeks an office, honor, position, or award — see CANDIDATE

seem *vb* to give the impression of being ⟨I tried to cheer them up because they *seemed* depressed⟩
   syn act, appear, look, make, sound
   rel dissemble, pretend; resemble, suggest; hint, imply, insinuate

seeming *adj* appearing to be true on the basis of evidence that may or may not be confirmed — see APPARENT 1

seemingly *adv* to all outward appearances — see APPARENTLY

seemliness *n* the quality or state of being especially suitable or fitting — see APPROPRIATENESS

seemly *adj* following the established traditions of refined society and good taste — see PROPER 1

seep *vb* to flow forth slowly through small openings — see EXUDE

seer *n* one who predicts future events or developments — see PROPHET

seesaw *vb* **1** to make a series of unsteady side-to-side motions — see ROCK 1
2 to make short up-and-down movements — see NOD

seethe *vb* **1** to be in a state of violent rolling motion ⟨the water *seethed* with schools of feeding piranha⟩
   syn boil, churn, roil
   rel reel, spin, swirl, whirl; agitate, stir
   near ant abate, calm, subside
2 to be excited or emotionally stirred up with anger — see BOIL 1

segment *n* one of the pieces from which something is designed to be assembled — see PART 1

segregate *vb* to set or keep apart from others — see ISOLATE

segregation *n* the state of being alone or kept apart from others — see ISOLATION

seize *vb* **1** to recognize the meaning of — see COMPREHEND 1
2 to take or keep under one's control by authority of law — see ARREST 1
3 to take physical control or possession of (something) suddenly or forcibly — see CATCH 1

seizure *n* a sudden experiencing of a physical or mental disorder — see ATTACK 2

---

syn synonym(s)   *rel* related words
ant antonym(s)   *near ant* near antonym(s)

---

seldom *adv* not often ⟨we *seldom* go to the theater downtown because its prices are so high⟩
   syn infrequently, little, rarely
   rel ne'er, never
   phrases hardly ever
   near ant generally, usually; always, constantly, continuously, endlessly, eternally, ever, everlastingly, evermore, forever, invariably; recurrently, repeatedly
   ant frequently, often

select *adj* **1** singled out from a number or group as more to one's liking ⟨they use only *select* beans to make their coffee⟩
   syn chosen, elect, favored, picked, preferred, selected
   rel fashionable; exclusive; culled, screened, weeded (out), winnowed (out)
   near ant average, common, commonplace, ordinary, run-of-the-mill
2 having qualities that appeal to a refined taste — see CHOICE

select *vb* to decide to accept (someone or something) from a group of possibilities — see CHOOSE 1

selected *adj* singled out from a number or group as more to one's liking — see SELECT 1

selecting *n* the act or process of selecting — see SELECTION 1

selection *n* **1** the act or process of selecting ⟨his *selection* of a running mate was a long, tedious affair⟩
   syn choice, choosing, election, picking, selecting
   rel option; appointment, assignment, designation, naming, nomination
2 a person or thing that is chosen — see CHOICE 2

selective *adj* tending to select carefully ⟨we were highly *selective* about the music we listened to while trying out loudspeakers⟩
   syn choosy (*or* choosey), particular, picky
   rel fastidious, finicky, fussy; discerning, discriminating, judicious
   near ant indiscriminate
   ant nonselective

selector *n* someone with the right or responsibility for making a selection ⟨the librarians who are the *selectors* of the annual award for best children's book⟩
   syn chooser, namer, picker
   rel elector, voter

self-acting *adj* designed to replace or decrease human labor and especially physical labor — see LABORSAVING

self-admiration *n* an often unjustified feeling of being pleased with oneself or with one's situation or achievements — see COMPLACENCE

self-assertive *adj* having or showing a bold forcefulness in the pursuit of a goal — see AGGRESSIVE 1

self-assurance *n* great faith in oneself or one's abilities — see CONFIDENCE 1

self-assured *adj* having or showing great faith in oneself or one's abilities — see CONFIDENT 1

self–centered *adj* overly concerned with one's own desires, needs, or interests — see EGOCENTRIC

self–centeredness *n* excessive interest in oneself — see EGOISM

self–conceit *n* an often unjustified feeling of being pleased with oneself or with one's situation or achievements — see COMPLACENCE

self–conceited *adj* having too high an opinion of oneself — see CONCEITED

self–confidence *n* great faith in oneself or one's abilities — see CONFIDENCE 1

self–confident *adj* having or showing great faith in oneself or one's abilities — see CONFIDENT 1

self–containment *n* the power to control one's actions, impulses, or emotions — see WILL 1

self–control *n* 1 the power to control one's actions, impulses, or emotions — see WILL 1

2 the checking of one's true feelings and impulses when dealing with others — see CONSTRAINT 1

self–denial *n* the act or practice of giving up or rejecting something once enjoyed or desired — see RENUNCIATION

self–destruction *n* the act of deliberately killing oneself — see SUICIDE

self–determination *n* the act or power of making one's own choices or decisions — see FREE WILL

self–discipline *n* the power to control one's actions, impulses, or emotions — see WILL 1

self–esteem *n* 1 a reasonable or justifiable sense of one's worth or importance — see PRIDE 1

2 an often unjustified feeling of being pleased with oneself or with one's situation or achievements — see COMPLACENCE

3 great faith in oneself or one's abilities — see CONFIDENCE 1

self–governing *adj* 1 not being under the rule or control of another — see FREE 1

2 of, relating to, or favoring political democracy — see DEMOCRATIC

self–government *n* 1 government in which the supreme power is held by the people and used by them directly or indirectly through representation — see DEMOCRACY

2 the power to control one's actions, impulses, or emotions — see WILL 1

3 the state of being free from the control or power of another — see FREEDOM 1

selfhood *n* the set of qualities that make a person different from other people — see INDIVIDUALITY

self–identity *n* the set of qualities that make a person different from other people — see INDIVIDUALITY

self–importance *n* 1 an exaggerated sense of one's importance that shows itself in the making of excessive or unjustified claims — see ARROGANCE

2 an often unjustified feeling of being pleased with oneself or with one's situa-

tion or achievements — see COMPLACENCE

self–important *adj* having too high an opinion of oneself — see CONCEITED

self–interest *n* excessive interest in oneself — see EGOISM

selfish *adj* overly concerned with one's own desires, needs, or interests — see EGOCENTRIC

selfishness *n* excessive interest in oneself — see EGOISM

self–possessed *adj* free from emotional or mental agitation — see CALM 2

self–possession *n* 1 evenness of emotions or temper — see EQUANIMITY

2 the power to control one's actions, impulses, or emotions — see WILL 1

self–protective *adj* intended to resist or prevent attack or aggression — see DEFENSIVE

self–regard *n* 1 excessive interest in oneself — see EGOISM

2 a reasonable or justifiable sense of one's worth or importance — see PRIDE 1

self–reliance *n* the ability to care for one's self — see SELF-SUFFICIENCY

self–reliant *adj* able to take care of oneself without outside help — see SELF-SUFFICIENT

self–reproach *n* a feeling of responsibility for wrongdoing — see GUILT 1

self–respect *n* a reasonable or justifiable sense of one's worth or importance — see PRIDE 1

self–restraint *n* 1 the power to control one's actions, impulses, or emotions — see WILL 1

2 the checking of one's true feelings and impulses when dealing with others — see CONSTRAINT 1

self–rule *n* government in which the supreme power is held by the people and used by them directly or indirectly through representation — see DEMOCRACY

self–ruling *adj* of, relating to, or favoring political democracy — see DEMOCRATIC

selfsame *adj* being one and not another — see SAME 2

self–satisfaction *n* an often unjustified feeling of being pleased with oneself or with one's situation or achievements — see COMPLACENCE

self–satisfied *adj* having too high an opinion of oneself — see CONCEITED

self–seeker *n* one who does things only for his own benefit and with little regard for right and wrong ⟨he was accused of being a *self-seeker*, of being nice only to people who could do him favors⟩

syn opportunist, temporizer

rel egoist, egotist; conniver, machinator, plotter, schemer

self–seeking *adj* having a strong desire for personal advancement — see AMBITIOUS 1

2 overly concerned with one's own desires, needs, or interests — see EGOCENTRIC

self–starter *n* an ambitious person who eagerly goes after what is desired — see GO-GETTER

self–sufficiency *n* the ability to care for one's self ⟨*self-sufficiency* is a goal that all teenagers should work towards⟩

syn independence, self-reliance, self-support

rel autonomy, self-determination; potency, power, resilience, strength

near ant helplessness, impotence, inadequacy, weakness

ant dependence, reliance

self–sufficient *adj* able to take care of oneself without outside help ⟨the college student worked nights so that he would be *self-sufficient*⟩

syn independent, self-reliant, self-supporting

rel potent, powerful, resilient, strong

near ant helpless, inadequate, insufficient; impotent, weak

ant dependent, reliant

self–support *n* the ability to care for one's self — see SELF-SUFFICIENCY

self–supporting *adj* able to take care of oneself without outside help — see SELF-SUFFICIENT

self–will *n* a steadfast adherence to an opinion, purpose, or course of action — see OBSTINACY

self–willed *adj* sticking to an opinion, purpose, or course of action in spite of reason, arguments, or persuasion — see OBSTINATE

sell *vb* to offer for sale to the public — see MARKET

sell (for) *vb* to have a price of — see COST

sell (out) *vb* to be unfaithful or disloyal to — see BETRAY 1

seller *n* the person in a business deal who hands over an item in exchange for money — see VENDOR

sellout *n* the act or fact of violating the trust or confidence of another — see BETRAYAL

semblance *n* **1** a display of emotion or behavior that is insincere or intended to deceive — see MASQUERADE

2 outward and often deceptive indication — see APPEARANCE 2

semidarkness *n* a time or place of little or no light — see DARK 1

seminar *n* **1** a coming together of a number of persons for a specified purpose — see MEETING 1

2 a meeting featuring a group discussion — see FORUM

seminary *n* a place or establishment for teaching and learning — see SCHOOL

send *vb* to cause to go or be taken from one place to another ⟨they promised to *send* the package in the morning⟩

syn consign, pack (off), ship, transfer, transmit, transport

rel convey, deliver, hand over; advance, drop, launch, remit; address, forward; bestow, contribute, donate, give, present

near ant acquire, draw, earn, gain, garner, get, obtain, procure, secure

ant accept, receive

senior *adj* being of advanced years and especially past middle age — see ELDERLY

senior *n* **1** one who is older than another ⟨since the man next door is my *senior* by a number of years, I always address him as "Mr. Barton"⟩

syn elder

rel ancestor, forerunner, predecessor

near ant contemporary, peer; descendant (*or* descendent), successor

ant junior

2 one who is above another in rank, station, or office — see SUPERIOR

3 the senior member of a group — see DEAN

senior citizen *n* a person of advanced years ⟨more and more *senior citizens* are living active, rewarding lives⟩

syn ancient, elder, golden-ager, oldster, old-timer

rel senior; graybeard, patriarch; beldam (*or* beldame), grandam (*or* grandame); adult, grown-up

near ant adolescent, minor; child, cub, juvenile, kid

ant youngster, youth

sensation *n* **1** an indefinite physical response to a stimulus ⟨we felt just the barest *sensation* of warmth when we leaned against the radiator⟩

syn feel, feeling, sense

rel impression, perception; hint, suggestion

2 a practice or interest that is very popular for a short time — see FAD

3 something extraordinary or surprising — see WONDER 1

sensational *adj* **1** arousing a strong and usually superficial interest or emotional reaction ⟨the *sensational* news story caused a stir, but after a few days everyone forgot about it⟩

syn lurid, screaming

rel colorful, juicy, racy; dramatic, histrionic, melodramatic, theatrical; coarse, vulgar

near ant innocuous, inoffensive; dignified, formal, proper, restrained

2 of or relating to physical sensation or the senses — see SENSORY

3 of the very best kind — see EXCELLENT

sense *n* **1** an indefinite physical response to a stimulus — see SENSATION 1

2 the ability to learn and understand or to deal with problems — see INTELLIGENCE 1

3 the ability to make intelligent decisions especially in everyday matters — see COMMON SENSE

4 the idea that is conveyed or intended to be conveyed to the mind by language, symbol, or action — see MEANING 1

---

syn synonym(s)   **rel** related words
ant antonym(s)   **near ant** near antonym(s)

5 the thought processes that have been established as leading to valid solutions to problems — see LOGIC

sense *vb* to have a vague awareness of — see FEEL 1

senseless *adj* **1** having lost consciousness — see UNCONSCIOUS 1

2 having no meaning — see MEANINGLESS

3 not having or showing an ability to absorb ideas readily — see STUPID 1

4 showing or marked by a lack of good sense or judgment — see FOOLISH 1

senselessness *n* **1** lack of good sense or judgment — see FOOLISHNESS 1

2 language, behavior, or ideas that are absurd and contrary to good sense — see NONSENSE 1

3 the quality or state of lacking intelligence or quickness of mind — see STUPIDITY 1

sensibilities *n* general emotional condition — see FEELING 2

sensible *adj* **1** able to be perceived by a sense or by the mind — see PERCEPTIBLE

2 according to the rules of logic — see LOGICAL 1

3 based on sound reasoning or information — see GOOD 1

4 having specified facts or feelings actively impressed on the mind — see CONSCIOUS

sensibleness *n* the ability to make intelligent decisions especially in everyday matters — see COMMON SENSE

sensitive *adj* **1** able to sense slight impressions or differences — see ACUTE 1

2 being in a situation where one is likely to meet with harm — see LIABLE 1

3 easily injured without careful handling — see TENDER 1

4 of or relating to physical sensation or the senses — see SENSORY

sensor *n* a device that detects some physical quantity and responds usually with a transmitted signal ⟨the thief accidentally triggered the motion *sensor*, which alerted the police⟩

syn detector

rel eye; electric eye, photoelectric cell; alarm, trigger

sensory *adj* of or relating to physical sensation or the senses ⟨trying to listen to music while watching the TV and eating dinner caused a sort of *sensory* overload⟩

syn sensational, sensitive, sensuous

rel afferent, receptive; sensual

near ant extrasensory, intuitional

sensual *adj* pleasing to the physical senses ⟨the *sensual* feel of a velvet shirt against the skin⟩

syn carnal, fleshly, luscious, sensuous, voluptuous

rel bodily, corporeal; agreeable, delectable, delicious, delightful, dreamy, gratifying, palatable, pleasant, pleasing, pleasurable, scrumptious; epicurean, luxurious, self-indulgent

near ant harsh, painful, uncomfortable

sensuous *adj* **1** of or relating to physical sensation or the senses — see SENSORY

2 pleasing to the physical senses — see SENSUAL

sentence *n* a decision made by a court or tribunal regarding a case it has heard ⟨the court-martial pronounced a *sentence* of not guilty on all counts of cowardice⟩

syn doom, finding, holding, judgment (*or* judgement), ruling

rel verdict; injunction; decree, edict, order; declaration, deliverance, dictum, pronouncement; conclusion, decision, determination, opinion, resolution; discipline, penalty, punishment

sentence *vb* to impose a judicial punishment on ⟨the judge *sentenced* him to a fine of fifty dollars and time served⟩

syn condemn, damn, doom

rel adjudge, judge; castigate, chasten, chastise, correct, discipline, penalize, punish; conclude, decide, determine, find, opine, resolve

sentient *adj* having specified facts or feelings actively impressed on the mind — see CONSCIOUS

sentiment *n* **1** a subjective response to a person, thing, or situation — see FEELING 1

2 an idea that is believed to be true or valid without positive knowledge — see OPINION 1

sentimental *adj* appealing to the emotions in an obvious and tiresome way — see CORNY

sentimentalism *n* the state or quality of having an excess of tender feelings (as of love, nostalgia, or compassion) — see SENTIMENTALITY

sentimentality *n* the state or quality of having an excess of tender feelings (as of love, nostalgia, or compassion) ⟨the *sentimentality* of the story of star-crossed lovers only made it even more popular with moviegoers⟩

syn mawkishness, mush, sappiness, sentimentalism, sloppiness

rel emotion; sentiment; corn, schmaltz (*also* schmalz)

near ant cynicism, hardheadedness, hardheartedness

sentinel *n* a person or group that watches over someone or something — see GUARD 1

sentry *n* a person or group that watches over someone or something — see GUARD 1

separable *adj* capable of being split into two or more parts or pieces ⟨the outdated belief that the atom is the smallest particle of matter and is not *separable*⟩

syn divisible

rel detachable

near ant combinable, joinable

ant indivisible, inseparable

separate *adj* **1** not the same or shared ⟨we stayed in *separate* apartments on our vacation⟩

syn different, individual, respective

rel disparate, dissimilar, distinct, distinctive, distinguishable, diverse, unalike, varied

near ant identical, selfsame, very

ant same

2 not physically attached to another unit ⟨the housing development has 200 *separate* homes, each with its own enclosed yard⟩

syn detached, disconnected, discrete, freestanding, single, unattached, unconnected

rel independent, self-contained; individual, private

ant attached, connected, joined

3 not being under the rule or control of another — see FREE 1

4 of, relating to, or belonging to a single person — see INDIVIDUAL 1

separate *vb* **1** to set or force apart ⟨we tried to *separate* the gluey pages, but they were stuck tight⟩

syn break up, disconnect, disjoin, disjoint, dissever, dissociate, disunite, divide, divorce, part, ramify, resolve, sever, split, sunder, uncouple, unlink, unyoke

rel decompose, disassemble, dissolve; bisect, fractionate, halve, quarter, segment, subdivide; break, rend, rip, rupture, tear; cut off, insulate, isolate, seclude, segregate, sequester; detach, disengage, disentangle, untie

near ant assemble, associate, blend, combine, mingle, mix; connect, couple; unify; accumulate, agglutinate, attach, bind, cement, close, fasten, fuse, stick, weld

ant join, link, unify, unite

2 to go or move in different directions from a central point ⟨the searchers *separated* in order to cover more ground⟩

syn branch (out), diverge, divide, fork

rel bestrew, broadcast, clear out, disband, dispel, disperse, dissipate, distribute, scatter, sow; distance, recede, retreat

near ant assemble, gather, meet

ant converge, join

3 to arrange or assign according to type — see CLASSIFY 1

4 to set or keep apart from others — see ISOLATE

5 to understand or point out the difference — see DISTINGUISH 1

separateness *n* the state of being alone or kept apart from others — see ISOLATION

separation *n* **1** the act or process of a whole separating into two or more parts or pieces ⟨the *separation* of Czechoslovakia into the Czech Republic and Slovakia⟩

syn breakup, dissolution, disunion, division, fractionation, partition, schism, split

rel breach, rupture; decomposition, disassembly, segmentation, subdivision; dispersal, scattering; administration, apportionment, distribution; isolation, seclusion, segregation, sequestration

near ant assemblage, association; attachment, connection, link, linkage, linkup; combination, fusion

ant unification, union

2 the state of being kept distinct ⟨the *separation* of church and state is an important concept in the United States⟩

syn demarcation, discreteness, discrimination, distinction

rel differentiation

near ant blurring, confusion

3 a movement in different directions away from a common point — see DIVERGENCE

4 an open space in a barrier (as a wall or hedge) — see GAP 1

5 the act or process of two or more persons going off in different directions — see PARTING 1

sepulcher *or* **sepulchre** *n* a final resting place for a dead person — see GRAVE

sepulchral *adj* causing or marked by an atmosphere lacking in cheer — see GLOOMY 1

sepulture *n* **1** a final resting place for a dead person — see GRAVE

2 the act or ceremony of putting a dead body in its final resting place — see BURIAL

sequel *n* a condition or occurrence traceable to a cause — see EFFECT 1

sequence *n* **1** a condition or occurrence traceable to a cause — see EFFECT 1

2 a series of things linked together — see CHAIN 1

3 the way objects in space or events in time are arranged or follow one another — see ORDER 1

sequential *adj* following one after another without others coming in between — see CONSECUTIVE

sequester *vb* **1** to set or keep apart from others — see ISOLATE

2 to take ownership or control of (something) by right of one's authority — see CONFISCATE

sequestration *n* the state of being alone or kept apart from others — see ISOLATION

sere *adj* marked by little or no precipitation or humidity — see DRY 1

serene *adj* **1** free from disturbing noise or uproar — see QUIET 1

2 free from emotional or mental agitation — see CALM 2

3 free from storms or physical disturbance — see CALM 1

sereneness *n* a state of freedom from storm or disturbance — see CALM

serenity *n* **1** a state of freedom from storm or disturbance — see CALM

2 evenness of emotions or temper — see EQUANIMITY

serial *adj* appearing in parts or numbers that follow regularly ⟨"Uncle Tom's Cabin" first appeared as a *serial* novel from 1851 to 1852⟩

syn episodic, periodic, periodical

rel sequential; recurrent, regular

---

serious *adj* 1 not joking or playful in mood or manner ⟨our parents were quite *serious* when they told us not to stay out too late⟩

syn earnest, grave, humorless, no-nonsense, sedate, severe, sober, solemn, staid, uncomic, unfunny, unsmiling, weighty

rel harsh, stern, strict; dignified, distinguished, elevated, serious-minded

near ant antic, comic, comical, droll, farcical, funny, hilarious, hysterical, laughable, light, light-headed, ludicrous, ridiculous, risible, riotous, screaming, side-splitting, uproarious; featherbrained, flighty, frivolous, goofy, harebrained, lighthearted, puerile, scatterbrained; absurd, asinine, balmy, brainless, cockeyed, crazy, cuckoo, daffy, daft, dotty, fatuous, foolish, half-witted, insane, jerky, kooky, loony (*also* looney), lunatic, mad, nonsensical, nutty, preposterous, sappy, screwball, senseless, silly, unwise, wacky, weak-minded, witless, zany

ant facetious, flip, flippant, humorous, jesting, jocular, joking, playful

2 having a matter of importance as its topic ⟨a very *serious* film that dealt with the aftermath of the Gulf War⟩

syn grave, heavy, weighty

rel big, consequential, eventful, important, major, material, meaningful, momentous, significant, substantial

near ant insignificant, little, minor, slight, small, trivial, unimportant

ant light

3 involving potential loss or injury — see DANGEROUS

seriousness *n* a mental state free of jesting or trifling — see EARNESTNESS

sermon *n* a public speech usually by a member of the clergy for the purpose of giving moral guidance or uplift ⟨a *sermon* whose message was that we should love our neighbors as much as we love ourselves⟩

syn homily

rel lecture, speech; lesson

serpent *n* a limbless reptile with a long body — see SNAKE 1

serpentine *adj* marked by a long series of irregular curves — see CROOKED 1

serrate *adj* notched or toothed along the edge — see SERRATED

serrated *adj* notched or toothed along the edge ⟨you should use a *serrated* knife when cutting bread, so you don't squash the loaf⟩

syn saw-toothed, serrate

rel wavy

near ant flat, smooth

serried *adj* having little space between items or parts — see CLOSE 1

servant *n* a person hired to perform household or personal services ⟨the wealthy family had *servants* to clean and cook for them⟩

syn domestic, flunky (*also* flunkey), lackey, menial, retainer, steward

rel butler, footman, groom, houseboy, man, majordomo, manservant, servitor, valet; handmaiden (*also* handmaid), housekeeper, housemaid, lady-in-waiting, maid, maidservant, wench, woman; attendant, follower

near ant boss, captain, chief, foreman, head, headman, helmsman, kingpin, leader, taskmaster

ant master

serve *vb* 1 to be a servant for ⟨he *served* his master faithfully for twenty years⟩

syn slave (for), work (for)

phrases wait on, wait upon

2 to be enough ⟨they made the pasta *serve* for eight guests⟩

syn do, suffice

rel answer, suit; assuage, content, quench, sate, satiate, satisfy

3 to be fitting or proper — see DO 1

4 to behave toward in a stated way — see TREAT 1

5 to have a certain purpose — see FUNCTION

6 to provide with something useful or desirable — see BENEFIT

server *n* a person who serves food or drink ⟨we had barely finished ordering when the *server* brought our salads⟩

syn waiter

rel waitress; bartender; steward, stewardess

service *adj* of or relating to the armed services — see MILITARY 1

service *n* 1 an act of kind assistance — see FAVOR 1

2 the capacity for being useful for some purpose — see USE 2

3 the combined army, air force, and navy of a nation — see ARMED FORCES

serviceability *n* the capacity for being useful for some purpose — see USE 2

serviceable *adj* 1 capable of being put to use or account — see PRACTICAL 1

2 capable of or suitable for being used for a particular purpose — see USABLE 1

serviceableness *n* the capacity for being useful for some purpose — see USE 2

serviceman *n* a person engaged in military service — see SOLDIER

servility *n* the state of being a slave — see SLAVERY 1

servitude *n* the state of being a slave — see SLAVERY 1

set *adj* 1 being in a state of fitness for some experience or action — see READY 1

2 firmly positioned in place and difficult to dislodge — see TIGHT 2

3 fully committed to achieving a goal — see DETERMINED 1

4 having been established and usually not subject to change — see FIXED 1

5 of a particular or exact sort — see EXPRESS 1

set *n* 1 a group of people acting together within a larger group — see FACTION

2 a group of people sharing a common interest and relating together socially — see GANG 2

3 a number of things considered as a unit — see GROUP 1

4 one of the units into which a whole is divided on the basis of a common characteristic — see CLASS 2

5 the array of painted backgrounds and furnishings used for a scene in a stage production — see SCENERY

set *vb* **1** to cover and warm eggs to hatch them ⟨the hen *set* for days⟩
syn brood, hatch, incubate, sit
rel lay, spawn; pip

2 to decide upon (the time or date for an event) usually from a position of authority — see APPOINT 1

3 to make an approximate or tentative judgment regarding — see ESTIMATE 1

4 *chiefly dialect* to rest on the buttocks or haunches — see SIT 1

5 to point or turn (something) toward a target or goal — see AIM 1

6 to come to an agreement or decision concerning the details of — see ARRANGE 1

7 to put securely in place or in a desired position — see FASTEN 2

8 to turn from a liquid into a substance resembling jelly — see COAGULATE

9 to arrange something in a certain spot or position — see PLACE 1

10 to become physically firm or solid — see HARDEN 1

setback *n* a change in status for the worse usually temporarily — see REVERSE 1

set down *vb* **1** to cause to sit down — see SEAT

2 to make a written note of — see RECORD 1

set in *vb* to come into existence — see BEGIN 2

set off *vb* to cause to function — see ACTIVATE

settee *n* a long upholstered piece of furniture designed for several sitters — see COUCH

setting *n* **1** the circumstances, conditions, or objects by which one is surrounded — see ENVIRONMENT

2 the place and time in which the action for a portion of a dramatic work (as a movie) is set — see SCENE 1

settle *vb* **1** to cause to come to rest at the bottom (as of a liquid) ⟨the light rain will *settle* the dust in the air⟩ ⟨careful handling will *settle* the lees in the bottom of the wine bottle⟩
syn lay, sediment
rel filter, screen, sieve, sift, strain; resettle
near ant disturb, mix, stir
ant raise

2 to give an opinion about (something at issue or in dispute) — see JUDGE 1

3 to come to an agreement or decision concerning the details of — see ARRANGE 1

4 to come to rest after descending from the air — see ALIGHT

5 to establish or place comfortably or snugly — see ENSCONCE 1

6 to free from distress or disturbance — see CALM 1

7 to gain emotional or mental control of — see COLLECT 1

8 to give what is owed for — see PAY 2

9 to make final, definite, or beyond dispute — see CLINCH

10 to stop the noise or speech of — see SILENCE 1

settle (down) *vb* to become still and orderly — see QUIET 1

settled *adj* **1** firmly established over time — see INVETERATE 1

2 having been established and usually not subject to change — see FIXED 1

settlement *n* an arrangement about action to be taken — see AGREEMENT 2

settler *n* **1** a person who settles in a new region — see FRONTIERSMAN

2 one that leaves one place to settle in another — see EMIGRANT

setup *n* **1** the way in which something is sized, arranged, or organized — see FORMAT 1

2 the way objects in space or events in time are arranged or follow one another — see ORDER 1

set up *vb* **1** to arrange something in a certain spot or position — see PLACE 1

2 to be responsible for the creation and early operation or use of — see FOUND

3 to fix in an upright position — see ERECT 1

4 to form by putting together parts or materials — see BUILD

seven seas *n pl* the whole body of salt water that covers nearly three-fourths of the earth — see OCEAN

sever *vb* to set or force apart — see SEPARATE 1

severe *adj* **1** given to exacting standards of discipline and self-restraint ⟨a *severe*, uncompromising teacher who locked the classroom door precisely when the bell rang and let no one in afterward⟩
syn austere, authoritarian, flinty, hard, harsh, heavy-handed, ramrod, rigid, rigorous, stern, strict
rel demanding, exacting; uncharitable, unforgiving; adamant, adamantine, hardened, hardhearted, immovable, implacable, inflexible, ossified, unbending, uncompromising, unyielding; dour, gruff; ascetic, monastic; browbeating, bullying; determined, firm, resolved, single-minded, steadfast, unflinching; dogged, intractable, obstinate, relentless
near ant easy, easygoing, laid-back, undemanding; charitable, kind, merciful, patient, soft, softhearted; accepting, compromising, yielding; responsive, willing; acquiescent, agreeable, amenable, compliant, flexible, pliable, pliant
ant forbearing, indulgent, lax, lenient, tolerant

2 harsh and threatening in manner or appearance — see GRIM 1

3 not joking or playful in mood or manner — see SERIOUS 1

4 difficult to endure — see HARSH 1

---

syn synonym(s)   *rel* related words
ant antonym(s)   *near ant* near antonym(s)

5 requiring considerable physical or mental effort — see HARD 2

severely *adv* in a manner so as to cause loss or suffering — see HARDLY 1

severity *n* the quality or state of being demanding or unyielding (as in discipline or criticism) ⟨Jane's parents were legendary for the *severity* of their discipline—she never got away with so much as a white lie⟩
syn hardness, harshness, inflexibility, rigidity, rigidness, rigorousness, sternness, strictness
rel hardheartedness, implacability, obduracy; dourness, gruffness; asceticism, austerity, monasticism; determination, firmness, resolve, steadfastness; obstinacy, stubbornness
near ant forbearance, indulgence, kindness, lenience, patience, softness, tenderness, tolerance; responsiveness, willingness; compliance, pliability
ant flexibility, gentleness, laxness, mildness

sew *vb* to close up with a series of interlacing stitches ⟨luckily, Mom was able to *sew* the tear in my pants so skillfully that they looked as good as new⟩
syn darn, stitch
rel mend, patch, repair; baste, ease, fell, finish, overcast; crochet, knit, quilt

sew up *vb* to have complete control over — see MONOPOLIZE

sex *n* sexual union involving penetration of the vagina by the penis — see SEXUAL INTERCOURSE

sexual intercourse *n* sexual union involving penetration of the vagina by the penis ⟨many people believe that it's best to wait to experience *sexual intercourse* until you're mature enough to handle it⟩
syn coitus, copulating, copulation, intercourse, mating, sex, sexual relations
rel fornication; safe sex; sexuality
phrases making love

sexual relations *n pl* sexual union involving penetration of the vagina by the penis — see SEXUAL INTERCOURSE

sexy *adj* of, relating to, or expressing sexual attraction — see EROTIC

shabby *adj* **1** showing signs of advanced wear and tear and neglect ⟨*shabby* wallpaper that was peeling from the walls⟩
syn dilapidated, dog-eared, grungy, mangy, mean, miserable, moth-eaten, neglected, ratty, run-down, scruffy, seedy, tacky, threadbare
rel abandoned, desolate, forlorn; broken-down, decrepit, worn-out; bedraggled, dingy, ragged, tattered; decaying, deteriorated, deteriorating, ramshackle; broken, damaged, destroyed, harmed, hurt, impaired, injured, ruined, wrecked
phrases gone to seed
near ant brand-new, fresh, new; cared-for, kept-up, maintained; mended, patched, rebuilt, reconstructed; smart, spiffy, spruce
2 worn or torn into or as if into rags — see RAGGED 2

shack *n* a small, simply constructed, and often temporary dwelling ⟨a farmer's *shack* out in the fields that's used for lambing and as a shelter from storms⟩
syn cabin, camp, hovel, hut, hutch, shanty
rel lean-to, shed; cot, cottage, lodge; cabana; bungalow, chalet; hogan, wickiup, wigwam

shackle *n* **1** something that physically prevents free movement — see BOND 1
2 shackles *pl* something that makes movement or progress more difficult — see ENCUMBRANCE

shackle *vb* **1** to confine or restrain with or as if with chains — see BIND 1
2 to create difficulty for the work or activity of — see HAMPER

shade *n* **1** partial darkness due to the obstruction of light rays ⟨it was hard to see in the *shade* after being in the brilliant sunlight⟩ ⟨the trees cast *shade*⟩
syn penumbra, shadiness, shadow, umbra
rel blackness, dimness, duskiness, gloominess, murkiness, obscurity, somberness; cloudiness, dullness (*also* dulness)
near ant brightness, brilliance, effulgence, illumination, incandescence, light, lightness, lucidity, lucidness, luminosity, radiance
2 a time or place of little or no light — see DARK 1
3 a property that becomes apparent when light falls on an object and by which things that are identical in form can be distinguished — see COLOR 1
4 a very small amount — see PARTICLE 1
5 the soul of a dead person thought of especially as appearing to living people — see GHOST

shade *vb* to shelter (something) from light and heat ⟨the trees *shaded* us quite nicely from the noonday sun⟩
syn shadow
rel cloud, darken, dim, dull; canopy, cover, protect, screen
near ant illuminate, light, lighten; expose

shaded *adj* protected from the sun's rays — see SHADY 1

shadiness *n* partial darkness due to the obstruction of light rays — see SHADE 1

shadow *n* **1** a person whose business is solving crimes and catching criminals or gathering information that is not easy to get — see DETECTIVE
2 partial darkness due to the obstruction of light rays — see SHADE 1
3 shadows *pl* a time or place of little or no light — see DARK 1
4 a tiny often physical indication of something lost or vanished — see VESTIGE
5 a very small amount — see PARTICLE 1
6 the soul of a dead person thought of especially as appearing to living people — see GHOST

shadow *vb* **1** to go after or on the track of — see FOLLOW 2
2 to make dark, dim, or indistinct — see CLOUD 1

3 to shelter (something) from light and heat — see SHADE

shadowed *adj* protected from the sun's rays — see SHADY 1

shadowing *n* the act of going after or in the tracks of another — see PURSUIT

shadowy *adj* 1 not seen or understood clearly — see FAINT 1

2 protected from the sun's rays — see SHADY 1

shady *adj* 1 protected from the sun's rays ⟨a lovely *shady* spot in the park that was pleasantly cool⟩

syn shaded, shadowed, shadowy

rel canopied, covered, sheltered; cloudy; dark, darkened, darkish, darkling, darksome, dim, dimmed, dusky, gloomy, moonless, murky, obscure, obscured, pitch-black, pitch-dark, somber (*or* sombre), sunless

near ant bedazzling, bright, brightened, brilliant, dazzling, effulgent, illuminated, illumined, incandescent, light, lighted (*or* lit), lucent, lucid, luminous; beaming, lambent, radiant, shining; lustrous

ant sunny

2 given to or marked by cheating and deception — see DISHONEST 2

3 giving good reason for being doubted, questioned, or challenged — see DOUBTFUL 2

4 given to acting in secret and to concealing one's intentions — see SNEAKY 1

shaft *n* 1 a narrow sharply defined line of light radiating from an object ⟨*shafts* of late-afternoon sunlight pierced the blinds and streaked the floor⟩

syn beam, ray

rel moonbeam, sunbeam; laser, spotlight

2 a weapon with a long straight handle and sharp head or blade — see SPEAR

shaggy *adj* 1 covered with or as if with hair — see HAIRY 1

2 made of or resembling hair — see HAIRY 1

shake *vb* 1 to make a series of small irregular or violent movements ⟨the bus rattled and *shook* as it barreled down a rutted road⟩

syn agitate, convulse, joggle, jolt, jounce, quake, quiver, shudder, vibrate, wobble

rel rock, sway; quaver, shiver, tremble; dodder, waver; flicker, fluctuate, flutter, oscillate, wave; beat, palpitate, pit-a-pat, pitter-patter, pulsate, pulse, throb

2 to get or keep away from (as a responsibility) through cleverness or trickery — see ESCAPE 2

shake *n* 1 a very small space of time — see INSTANT

2 **shakes** *pl* a sense of panic or extreme nervousness — see JITTERS

shake up *vb* to cause an often unpleasant surprise for — see SHOCK 1

shakiness *n* the quality or state of not being firmly fixed in position — see INSTABILITY

shaking *adj* marked by or given to small uncontrollable bodily movements — see SHAKY 1

shaking *n* 1 a series of slight movements by a body back and forth or from side to side — see VIBRATION

2 the act or a means of getting or keeping away from something undesirable — see ESCAPE 2

shaky *adj* 1 marked by or given to small uncontrollable bodily movements ⟨the old man's hands were so *shaky* that I was afraid he'd drop the glass⟩

syn quaking, quavery, shaking, shuddering, shuddery, tottery, trembling, tremulous, wobbling, wobbly

rel shivering, shivery

near ant controlled, firm, settled, stable, steady

2 giving good reason for being doubted, questioned, or challenged — see DOUBTFUL 2

shall *vb* to be under necessity or obligation to — see NEED 2

shallow *adj* 1 lacking significant physical depth ⟨the dog quickly dug a *shallow* hole that was barely deep enough to accommodate his bone⟩

syn depthless, shoal

rel skin-deep, superficial, surface; fathomable, measurable; finite, limited, measured, restricted; even, flat, flush, horizontal, level, plane, smooth

near ant abysmal, abyssal, bottomless, boundless, endless, immeasurable, inestimable, infinite, limitless, measureless, unfathomable, unlimited, vast; navigable

ant deep

2 having or showing a lack of depth of understanding or character — see SUPERFICIAL 2

shallow *n*, *usually* **shallows** *pl* a place where a body of water (as a sea or river) is shallow — see SHOAL

sham *adj* 1 being such in appearance only and made with or manufactured from usually cheaper materials — see IMITATION

2 being such in appearance only and made or manufactured with the intention of committing fraud — see COUNTERFEIT

3 lacking in natural or spontaneous quality — see ARTIFICIAL 1

sham *n* 1 a poor, insincere, or insulting imitation of something — see MOCKERY 1

2 an imitation that is passed off as genuine — see FAKE 1

sham *vb* to present a false appearance of — see FEIGN

shamble *vb* to move heavily or clumsily — see LUMBER 1

shambles *n pl* 1 a dirty or messy place — see PIGPEN

2 a state in which everything is out of order — see CHAOS

shame *n* 1 a feeling of responsibility for wrongdoing — see GUILT 1

2 a regrettable or blameworthy act — see CRIME 2

---

syn synonym(s)   *rel* related words
ant antonym(s)   *near ant* near antonym(s)

3 the state of having lost the esteem of others — see DISGRACE 1

shame *vb* to reduce to a lower standing in one's own eyes or in others' eyes — see HUMBLE

shamed *adj* suffering from or expressive of a feeling of responsibility for wrongdoing — see GUILTY 2

shamefaced *adj* suffering from or expressive of a feeling of responsibility for wrongdoing — see GUILTY 2

shameful *adj* not respectable — see DISREPUTABLE

shanty *n* a small, simply constructed, and often temporary dwelling — see SHACK

shape *n* **1** a state of being or fitness — see CONDITION 1

2 the outward appearance of something as distinguished from its substance — see FORM 1

3 the type of body that a person has — see PHYSIQUE

shape *vb* to change (something) so as to make it suitable for a new use or situation — see ADAPT

shape (up) *vb* to take on a definite form — see FORM 1

shapeless *adj* **1** badly or imperfectly formed — see MALFORMED

2 having no definite or recognizable form — see FORMLESS

share *n* **1** something belonging to, due to, or contributed by an individual member of a group ⟨my *share* of the lottery winnings is over a million dollars⟩ ⟨Sue's *share* of the bill comes to $13.44⟩

syn allotment, allowance, cut, part, portion, proportion, quota

rel lot, ration; commission, percentage; member, partition, section, segment

near ant aggregate, composite, compound, sum, total, totality; whole

2 a legal right to participation in the advantages, profits, and responsibility of something — see INTEREST 1

share *vb* to take a share or part — see PARTAKE

shared *adj* used or done by a number of people as a group — see COLLECTIVE

sharer *n* one who takes part in something — see PARTICIPANT

shark *n* **1** a dishonest person who uses clever means to cheat others out of something of value — see TRICKSTER 1

2 a person with a high level of knowledge or skill in a field — see EXPERT

sharp *adj* **1** having an edge thin enough to cut or pierce something ⟨be careful, as that knife is *sharp* enough to slice off a finger⟩

syn cutting, edged, edgy, ground, honed, keen, sharpened, stropped, trenchant, whetted

rel clawlike; jabbing, jagged, lacerating, piercing, scratching, stabbing

near ant rounded, seamless, smooth; soft; even, flat, level, slick

ant blunt, blunted, dull, dulled, obtuse

2 causing intense mental or physical distress ⟨sudden *sharp* pains in your right lower belly can be a sign of appendicitis⟩

syn acute, agonizing, biting, excruciating, smart, smarting

rel bitter, cutting, keen, penetrating; piercing, raw, stinging; afflicting, distressing, disturbing, upsetting; cruel, grievous, harsh, heartrending, hurtful, lacerating, painful, paralyzing, severe, tormenting, torturous; insufferable, insupportable, intolerable, unacceptable, unbearable, unsupportable; appalling, awful, bad, dire, dreadful, ghastly, horrible, miserable, nasty, rotten, terrible, vile, wretched

near ant painless; acceptable, bearable, endurable, supportable, sustainable, tolerable; livable (*also* liveable), sufferable

ant dull

3 having a powerfully stimulating odor or flavor ⟨the cheese is so *sharp* that its rank aroma can practically clear a room⟩

syn nippy, pungent, strong

rel acid, acidic; acrid, bitter, harsh; piquant, spicy, tart, zesty; putrid, rancid, rank; acute, keen; animating, energizing, exciting, galvanizing, invigorating, provocative; appetizing, delectable, delicious, palatable, toothsome; flavorful, savory, tasty

near ant aged, mellow; gentle, soft; flat, flavorless, insipid; savorless, tasteless; dilute, thin, watery, weak

ant bland, mild, smooth

4 tapering to a thin tip — see POINTED 1

5 being in the latest or current fashion — see STYLISH

6 being strikingly neat and trim in style or appearance — see SMART 1

7 causing intense discomfort to one's skin — see CUTTING 1

8 given to or marked by cheating and deception — see DISHONEST 2

9 having or showing a practical cleverness or judgment — see SHREWD

10 having or showing quickness of mind — see INTELLIGENT 1

11 marked by the use of wit that is intended to cause hurt feelings — see SARCASTIC

12 able to sense slight impressions or differences — see ACUTE 1

13 uncomfortably cool — see CHILLY 1

sharp *adv* as stated or indicated without the slightest difference — see EXACTLY 1

sharpen *vb* to make sharp or sharper ⟨you need to *sharpen* your penknife's blade frequently in order to be able to whittle properly⟩

syn edge, grind, hone, strop, whet

rel file

near ant buff, burnish, gloss, polish, round, smooth

ant blunt, dull

sharpened *adj* having an edge thin enough to cut or pierce something — see SHARP 1

sharper *n* a dishonest person who uses clever means to cheat others out of something of value — see TRICKSTER 1

sharp–eyed *adj* having unusually keen vision ⟨a very *sharp-eyed* child found the last Easter egg, which was hidden in the flower arrangement⟩
syn clear-sighted, lynx-eyed
rel sighted; alert, attentive, aware, observant, observing, vigilant, watchful
near ant blind, eyeless, sightless, stone-blind, unseeing; astigmatic, myopic, near-sighted, shortsighted; unobservant, unobserving; purblind

sharply *adv* in a strikingly neat and trim manner — see SMARTLY

sharpness *n* 1 a harsh or sharp quality — see EDGE 1
2 an uncomfortable degree of coolness — see CHILL

sharpshooter *n* a person skilled in shooting at a target — see MARKSMAN

sharp–witted *adj* 1 having or showing a practical cleverness or judgment — see SHREWD
2 having or showing quickness of mind — see INTELLIGENT 1

shatter *vb* 1 to bring to a complete end the physical soundness, existence, or usefulness of — see DESTROY 1
2 to cause to break open or into pieces by or as if by an explosive — see BLAST 1
3 to cause to break with violence and much noise — see SMASH 1

shave *vb* 1 to make (as hair) shorter with or as if with the use of shears — see CLIP 2
2 to pass lightly across or touch gently especially in passing — see BRUSH

shaver *n* a male person who has not yet reached adulthood — see BOY

shear *vb* 1 to make (as hair) shorter with or as if with the use of shears — see CLIP

sheath *n* something that encloses another thing especially to protect it — see ¹CASE 1

sheathe *vb* to cover with something that protects ⟨sometimes shipbuilders *sheathe* a ship's bottom with copper for extra protection from barnacles and other threats⟩
syn face
rel apparel, array, clothe, dress, garb, robe; side, skin; embosom, embower, embrace, encase, enclose (*also* inclose), encompass, enshroud, envelop, enwrap, invest, lap, mantle, shroud, surround, swathe, veil, wrap; blanket, overlay, overspread
near ant bare, denude, expose, strip

shed *vb* 1 to cast (a natural bodily covering or appendage) aside ⟨a snake's skin doesn't grow as the snake does, so every so often the snake will *shed* its old skin⟩
syn exfoliate, molt, slough (*also* sluff)
rel flake, peel, scale; discard
2 to get rid of as useless or unwanted — see DISCARD

sheen *n* brightness created by light reflected from a surface — see SHINE 1

sheep *n* an innocent or gentle person — see LAMB

sheepish *adj* not comfortable around people — see SHY 2

sheepishly *adv* in manner showing no signs of pride or self-assertion — see LOWLY

sheer *adj* 1 very thin and easy to see through ⟨we had to get window shades because passersby could see right through our *sheer* curtains⟩
syn filmy, gauzy, gossamer, gossamery, transparent
rel clear, limpid, liquid, lucent, pellucid; lucid, translucent; dainty, delicate, flimsy, fragile, frail; colorless, uncolored
near ant opaque; cloudy, foggy, hazy, misty, murky, smoky (*also* smokey); drab, dull, lackluster, lusterless
2 having no exceptions or restrictions — see ABSOLUTE 2
3 having an incline approaching the perpendicular — see STEEP 1

sheer *vb* 1 to change one's course or direction — see TURN 3
2 to depart abruptly from a straight line or course — see SWERVE 1

sheet *vb* to form a layer over — see COVER 2

shell *n* 1 something that encloses another thing especially to protect it — see ¹CASE 1
2 the arrangement of parts that gives something its basic form — see FRAME 1

shell *vb* 1 to remove the natural covering of — see PEEL
2 to use bombs or artillery against — see BOMBARD

shellacking *n* failure to win a contest — see DEFEAT 1

shell–shocked *adj* suffering from high levels of physical and especially psychological stress — see STRESSED-OUT

shelter *n* something (as a building) that offers cover from the weather or protection from danger ⟨the sudden fierce storm forced us to run to the nearest *shelter*⟩
syn asylum, harbor, harborage, haven, refuge, retreat, sanctuary, sanctum
rel anchorage, mooring, port; cover, screen; abode, diggings, domicile, dwelling, habitation, house, housing, lodging, lodgment (*or* lodgement), pad, place, quarters, residence, rest, roof; den, lair, hermitage, hideaway, hideout; fastness, fort, fortress, palisade, stronghold; lean-to, shed, windbreak

shelter *vb* 1 to be or provide a shelter for ⟨the abandoned barn *shelters* a colony of stray cats⟩
syn harbor
rel cover, defend, protect, safeguard, screen, shield, ward; domicile, house, place; shade, shadow
near ant expose
2 to provide with living quarters or shelter — see HOUSE 1

sheltered *adj* hidden from view — see SECLUDED

shelve *vb* to assign to a later time — see POSTPONE

---

syn synonym(s)   *rel* related words
ant antonym(s)   *near ant* near antonym(s)

shenanigans *n pl* **1** playful, reckless behavior that is not intended to cause serious harm — see MISCHIEF 1

2 wildly playful or mischievous behavior — see HORSEPLAY

shepherd *vb* to give advice and instruction to (someone) regarding the course or process to be followed — see GUIDE 1

shibboleth *n* **1** an attention-getting word or phrase used to publicize something (as a campaign or product) — see SLOGAN

2 an idea or expression that has been used by many people — see COMMONPLACE

shield *n* means or method of defending — see DEFENSE 1

shield *vb* **1** to drive danger or attack away from — see DEFEND 1

2 to place a protective layer over — see COVER 3

shift *n* **1** an action planned or taken to achieve a desired result — see MEASURE 1

2 the act or an instance of changing position — see MOVEMENT 1

shift *vb* **1** to change the place or position of — see MOVE 1

2 to change one's position — see MOVE 3

3 to pass from one form, state, or level to another — see CHANGE 2

4 to give up (something) and take something else in return — see CHANGE 3

5 to meet one's day-to-day needs — see GET ALONG 1

shifting *n* the act or an instance of changing position — see MOVEMENT 1

shiftless *adj* not easily aroused to action or work — see LAZY

shiftlessness *n* an inclination not to do work or engage in activities — see LAZINESS

shifty *adj* **1** given to acting in secret and to concealing one's intentions — see SNEAKY 1

2 given to or marked by cheating and deception — see DISHONEST 2

shillelagh *n* a heavy rigid stick used as a weapon or for punishment — see CLUB 1

shilly-shally *vb* to show uncertainty about the right course of action — see HESITATE

shilly-shallying *n* the act or an instance of pausing because of uncertainty about the right course of action — see HESITATION

shimmer *vb* to shoot forth bursts of light — see FLASH 1

shindig *n* a social gathering — see PARTY 1

shindy *n* a state of noisy, confused activity — see COMMOTION

shine *n* **1** brightness created by light reflected from a surface ⟨the troop inspector insisted on nothing less than a dazzling *shine* from every pair of shoes in the line of review⟩

syn gloss, luster (*or* lustre), polish, sheen
rel glare, gleam, glimmer, glint, glisten, glow, shimmer; flicker, sparkle, twinkle; illumination, irradiation; iridescence, luminescence; brightness, brilliance, luminosity, radiance; finish, glaze

near ant dimness, dinginess, dirtiness, drabness, dullness (*also* dulness), flatness; grayness, paleness; cloudiness, gloom, murkiness, obscurity, somberness

2 the steady giving off of the form of radiation that makes vision possible — see LIGHT 1

3 positive regard for something — see LIKING

shine *vb* **1** to emit rays of light ⟨the sun appears to *shine* particularly brightly in summer because that is when it's closest to the Earth⟩

syn beam, radiate
rel blaze, burn, fire, flame, gleam, glimmer, glint, glisten, glitter, glow, shimmer; blink, flare, flash, flicker, scintillate, sparkle, twinkle, wink; beat (down); glare; brighten, illuminate, illumine, irradiate, light, lighten; bedazzle, blind, daze, dazzle

near ant blacken, darken; lower (*also* lour)

2 to make smooth or glossy usually by repeatedly applying surface pressure — see POLISH

shining *adj* giving off or reflecting much light — see BRIGHT 1

shiny *adj* giving off or reflecting much light — see BRIGHT 1

ship *n* a large craft for travel by water ⟨we chose to spend our vacation on a cruise *ship* traveling through the Caribbean⟩

syn boat, vessel
rel argosy, containership, corvette, cruiser, cutter, destroyer, ferryboat, flagship, freighter, icebreaker, ironclad, lightship, liner, man-of-war, merchantman, merchant ship, packet, steamer, supertanker, tanker, trader, tramp, transport, warship

ship *vb* to cause to go or be taken from one place to another — see SEND

shippable *adj* capable of being taken from one place to another by public carrier ⟨only boxes of five pounds and under are *shippable* by the postal service⟩

syn transferable, transmittable, transportable
rel addressable
ant nontransferable, receivable

shipshape *adj* being clean and in good order — see NEAT 1

shipwreck *n* the destruction or loss of a ship ⟨the *shipwreck* of much of the Spanish Armada ended Spain's plans for invading England⟩

syn shipwrecking, wreck, wreckage, wrecking
rel beaching, grounding, stranding; foundering, sinking
near ant salvage, salvaging

shipwreck *vb* to cause irreparable damage to (a ship) by running aground or sinking ⟨the helmsman fell asleep at the wheel and *shipwrecked* his yacht on the rocks⟩

syn strand, wreck
rel beach; founder, sink
near ant salvage

shipwrecking *n* the destruction or loss of a ship — see SHIPWRECK

shirk *vb* 1 to get or keep away from (as a responsibility) through cleverness or trickery — see ESCAPE 2

2 to leave undone or unattended to especially through carelessness — see NEGLECT 2

shirker *n* one who deliberately avoids work or duty — see SLACKER

shirty *adj, chiefly British* feeling or showing anger — see ANGRY

shiver *n* 1 an instance of shaking involuntarily with fear or cold ⟨Joe experienced a sudden *shiver* when confronted with the sight of the dark basement⟩

syn quiver, shudder, tremble

rel agitation, convulsing, jolt, quake, shake, tremor, vibration, wobble; fluctuation, flutter, oscillation, wave; beat, palpitation, pulsation, pulse, throb

2 **shivers** *pl* a sense of panic or extreme nervousness — see JITTERS

shivery *adj* having a low or subnormal temperature — see COLD 1

shoal *adj* lacking significant physical depth — see SHALLOW 1

shoal *n* a place where a body of water (as a sea or river) is shallow ⟨the *shoals* off Nantucket Island are famous as the final resting places of many ill-fated ships⟩

syn ford, shallows

rel bank, bar, sandbank, sandbar

near ant trench; abyss, deep, depth

shock *n* 1 a forceful coming together of two things — see IMPACT 1

2 the state of being strongly impressed by something unexpected or unusual — see SURPRISE 2

shock *vb* 1 to cause an often unpleasant surprise for ⟨Mom was *shocked* by the terrible news that her cousin had died in an accident⟩ ⟨Jack was *shocked* to find out that his grades were much lower than he realized⟩

syn appall, bowl (over), floor, jolt, shake up

rel affright, alarm, dismay, frighten, horrify, panic, scare, spook, startle, terrify, terrorize; disgust, nauseate, repel, revolt, sicken, turn off; displease, offend, outrage, scandalize; amaze, astound, awe; chill, daunt, demoralize, dispirit, unman, unnerve; discompose, disconcert, disquiet, disturb, perturb, unsettle, upset; crush, overpower, overwhelm

phrases knock for a loop

near ant cushion; delight, gratify, please, rejoice, tickle; charm, entice, tempt; cheer, comfort, console, solace, soothe; reassure

2 to make a strong impression on (someone) with something unexpected — see SURPRISE 1

3 to strike with fear — see FRIGHTEN

shocked *adj* 1 affected with sudden and great wonder or surprise — see THUNDERSTRUCK

2 filled with disgust — see SICK 2

shocking *adj* 1 causing a strong emotional reaction because unexpected — see SURPRISING 1

2 causing fear — see FEARFUL 1

3 causing intense displeasure, disgust, or resentment — see OFFENSIVE 1

4 extremely disturbing or repellent — see HORRIBLE 1

shoddy *adj* of low quality — see CHEAP 2

shoes *n pl* a way of looking at or thinking about something — see POINT OF VIEW

shoestring *n* a very small sum of money — see MITE 1

shoot *n* a branch of a main stem especially of a plant — see OFFSHOOT 1

shoot *vb* 1 to cause (a projectile) to be driven forward with force ⟨BB guns *shoot* small round metal pellets⟩

syn blast, discharge, fire, loose

rel launch, project; blaze (at), snipe (at); cast, catapult, fling, heave, hurl, pelt, pitch, sling, throw, toss

2 to cause a weapon to release a missile with great force ⟨soldiers train extensively to learn to *shoot* accurately and quickly⟩

syn blast, discharge, fire

rel blaze, pepper, snipe

3 to strike with a missile from a gun ⟨hunters can *shoot* deer only during the legally specified open season⟩

syn drill, gun, plug, pop

rel blaze, pepper; blast (at), fire (at); pick off; overshoot; snipe (at); croak [*slang*], destroy, dispatch, do in, fell, kill, slay; annihilate, blot out, butcher, decimate, massacre, slaughter, wipe out

4 to proceed or move quickly — see HURRY 2

5 to take a photograph of — see PHOTOGRAPH

6 to throw or give off — see EMIT 1

shoot (up) *vb* to rise abruptly and rapidly — see SKYROCKET

shooter *n* 1 a person skilled in shooting at a target — see MARKSMAN

2 one who takes photographs — see PHOTOGRAPHER

shop *n* 1 *also* **shoppe** an establishment where goods are sold to consumers ⟨the only *shop* which carries that game is halfway across the state⟩

syn bazaar, emporium, store

rel market, marketplace, outlet, showroom; boutique, department store, dime store, five-and-ten, thrift shop, variety store

2 a building or set of buildings for the manufacturing of goods — see FACTORY

¹**shore** *n* something that holds up or serves as a foundation for something else — see SUPPORT 1

²**shore** *n* the usually sandy or gravelly land bordering a body of water — see BEACH

shore (up) *vb* to hold up or serve as a foundation for — see SUPPORT 3

---

syn synonym(s)   *rel* related words
ant antonym(s)   *near ant* near antonym(s)

short *adj* **1** having relatively little height ⟨a lot of boys are *shorter* than the girls in middle school, but they quickly catch up by high school⟩

syn little, low, low-lying

rel dwarf, dwarfish; petite, slight; diminutive, little, pint-size (*or* pint-sized), small, smallish; bantam, bitty, dinky, miniature, minimized, minute, puny, teeny, teeny-weeny, tiny, undersized, wee; dumpy, flat, scrubby, squat, squatty, stubby, stumpy, stunted

near ant elevated, lifted, raised, uplifted, upswept; high-rise, statuesque; gangling, gangly, lanky, rangy

ant high, lofty, tall, towering

2 not lasting for a considerable time ⟨fortunately for those of us in the hot sun, the graduation speech was *short* and to the point⟩

syn brief, condensed, little

rel abbreviated, abridged, curtailed, cutback, shortened; compact, condensed; abrupt, sudden; ephemeral, fleeting, momentary, short-lived, transient, transitory; impermanent; compendious, concise, crisp, epigrammatic, laconic, pithy, succinct, summary, terse; short-range, short-term

near ant endless, everlasting, interminable, persistent, unending; longish, overlong, prolonged, protracted; permanent; enlarged, expanded, supplemented; long-range, long-term

ant extended, great, lengthy, long, long-lived, marathon

3 not coming up to a usual standard or meeting a particular need ⟨regrettably, the art supplies are *short* this year, so you'll have to share⟩

syn deficient, inadequate, insufficient, lacking, scarce, shy, wanting

rel hand-to-mouth, light, meager, niggardly, poor, scant, scanty, skimpy, slender, slim, spare, sparse, stingy; bare, mere, minimum; slight, small

near ant abundant, ample, bounteous, bountiful, copious, generous, liberal, plenteous, plentiful; enlarged, expanded, supplemented; abounding, overflowing, teeming; lavish, luxuriant, rich; big, considerable, hefty, jumbo, large, largish, oversize (*or* oversized), sizable (*or* sizeable), substantial, super

ant adequate, enough, sufficient

4 having a texture that readily breaks into little pieces under pressure — see CRISP 1

short *adv* with great suddenness ⟨the bicyclist ahead of me unexpectedly pulled up *short* and I plowed into him⟩

syn abruptly, suddenly

rel quickly; surprisingly, unexpectedly

near ant gradually, slowly; hesitantly

shortage *n* a falling short of an essential or desirable amount or number — see DEFICIENCY

shortchange *vb* to rob by the use of trickery or threats — see FLEECE

shortcoming *n* a defect in character — see FAULT 1

shorten *vb* to make less in extent or duration ⟨we decided to *shorten* the distance we had to walk home by cutting across the neighbor's lawn⟩ ⟨if Grandma has to go shopping today, you'll need to *shorten* your visit⟩

syn abbreviate, abridge, curtail, cut back

rel digest, summarize; abate, compress, constrict, contract, cut, cut down, pare, prune, trim; decrease, de-escalate, deflate, diminish, dock, dwindle, lessen, lower, moderate, modify, reduce, retrench, shrink, slash, taper

near ant enlarge, expand, supplement; add, aggrandize, amplify, augment, balloon, boost, dilate, escalate, heighten, increase, maximize, raise; blow up, distend, inflate, swell

ant elongate, extend, lengthen, prolong, protract

short–lived *adj* lasting only for a short time — see MOMENTARY

shortly *adv* **1** in a few words ⟨the sudden closing of the restaurant was announced only with a *shortly* worded sign: "Out of Business"⟩

syn briefly, compactly, concisely, crisply, laconically, pithily, succinctly, summarily, tersely

rel aphoristically; exactly, precisely; abruptly, bluntly, brusquely, curtly

phrases in a nutshell

near ant redundantly, repetitiously

ant diffusely, long-windedly, verbosely, wordily

2 at or within a short time ⟨the test will begin *shortly*, so don't go too far away to find a bathroom⟩

syn anon, momentarily, presently, soon

rel directly, forthwith, immediately, instantly, now, promptly, pronto, right away, right now, straightaway

phrases by and by

shortness *n* the condition of being short — see BREVITY 1

shortsighted *adj* **1** able to see near things more clearly than distant ones — see NEARSIGHTED

2 not thinking about and providing for the future — see IMPROVIDENT

short story *n* a work with imaginary characters and events that is shorter and usually less complex than a novel — see STORY 1

short–tempered *adj* easily irritated or annoyed — see IRRITABLE

short–term *adj* intended to last, continue, or serve for a limited time — see TEMPORARY 1

shot *n* **1** a directed propelling of a missile by a firearm or artillery piece ⟨cannon operators often had to use several *shots* to figure out the range of their targets⟩

syn blasting, discharge, firing

rel potshot; barrage, bombardment, broadside, burst, cannonade, fusillade, hail, salvo, storm, volley

2 an effort to do or accomplish something — see ATTEMPT

3 a picture created from an image recorded on a light-sensitive surface by a camera — see PHOTOGRAPH

4 a person skilled in shooting at a target — see MARKSMAN

5 the portion of a serving of a beverage that is swallowed at one time — see DRINK 2

should *vb* to be under necessity or obligation to — see NEED 1

shoulder *vb* to take to or upon oneself — see ASSUME 1

shout *n* a loud vocal expression of strong emotion ⟨Jason gave a sudden *shout* of surprise when the shower abruptly turned ice-cold⟩

syn cry, holler, hoot, howl, yell, yowl, whoop

rel scream, screech, shriek, squall, squeak, squeal, yelp; bellow, clamor, roar; caterwaul, wail

near ant mumble, murmur, mutter; gasp, whimper, whisper

shout *vb* to speak so as to be heard at a distance — see CALL 1

shove *vb* **1** to apply force to (someone or something) so that it moves in front of one — see PUSH 1

2 to push steadily against with some force — see PRESS 1

shove (off) *vb* to leave a place often for another — see GO 2

shovel *vb* to hollow out or form (something) by removing earth — see DIG 1

show *n* **1** an outward and often exaggerated indication of something abstract (as a feeling) for effect ⟨the children made a *show* of disgust when confronted with asparagus⟩

syn demonstration, display, exhibition, flaunting

rel act, pretense (*or* pretence), simulation; affectation, pose, sham; betrayal, disclosure

2 a display of emotion or behavior that is insincere or intended to deceive — see MASQUERADE

3 outward and often deceptive indication — see APPEARANCE 2

4 a public showing of objects of interest — see EXHIBITION 1

show *vb* **1** to present so as to invite notice or attention ⟨Julie made sure she *showed* the test paper with a big A on it to everyone in her family⟩

syn display, disport, exhibit, flaunt, flash, flaunt, parade, show off, sport, strut, unveil

rel brandish, flourish; advertise, air, broadcast, proclaim, publicize; divulge, talk (about), tell (of); bare, discover, reveal, uncloak, uncover

near ant camouflage, disguise, mask; conceal, cover, curtain, enshroud, hide, obscure, occult, shroud, veil

2 to make known (something abstract) through outward signs ⟨John's expressive face *shows* his every thought and emotion clearly⟩

syn bespeak, betray, demonstrate, display, expose, evince, give away, manifest, reveal

rel bare, disclose, unbosom, uncloak, uncover; advertise, air, broadcast, proclaim, publicize

near ant belie, misrepresent; distort, falsify, garble, twist; camouflage, disguise, gild, gloss (over), varnish, whitewash; conceal, counterfeit, cover, hide, mask, obscure, veil

3 to gain full recognition or acceptance of — see ESTABLISH 1

4 to give advice and instruction to (someone) regarding the course or process to be followed — see GUIDE 1

5 to point out the way for (someone) especially from a position in front — see LEAD 1

shower *n* **1** a heavy fall of objects — see RAIN 2

2 a rapid or overwhelming outpouring of many things at once — see BARRAGE

shower *vb* to give readily and in large quantities — see RAIN 2

showiness *n* excessive or unnecessary display — see OSTENTATION

show off *vb* **1** to engage in attention-getting playful or boisterous behavior — see CUT UP

2 to present so as to invite notice or attention — see SHOW 1

show up *vb* **1** to come into view — see APPEAR 1

2 to get to a destination — see COME 2

3 to reveal the true nature of — see EXPOSE 1

showy *adj* likely to attract attention — see NOTICEABLE

shred *n* a very small amount — see PARTICLE 1

shred *vb* to cause (something) to separate into jagged pieces by violently pulling at it — see TEAR 1

shrew *n* a bad-tempered scolding woman ⟨Rip Van Winkle went off into mountains to escape his wife, a *shrew* who made his life miserable⟩

syn fury, harpy, termagant, virago

rel carper, castigator, censurer, caviler (*or* caviller), critic, faultfinder, nitpicker, railer, scold; belittler, derider, detractor; pettifogger, quibbler

shrewd *adj* having or showing a practical cleverness or judgment ⟨a *shrewd* used car dealer who knew how to make the best possible deal⟩ ⟨*shrewd* investments that paid off big⟩

syn astute, canny, clear-sighted, hardheaded, knowing, sharp, sharp-witted, smart

rel artful, cagey (*also* cagy), crafty, cunning, devious, foxy, guileful, slick, sly, subtle, wily; discerning, insightful, perceptive, perspicacious, sagacious, sage, sapient, wise; experienced, veteran; discriminating, discriminative; agile, alert, brainy, bright, brilliant, clever, intelligent, keen, quick, quick-witted; apt, ingenious, resourceful; informed, knowledgeable, well-read

near ant artless, guileless, ingenuous, innocent, naive (*or* naïve); exploitable, gullible; undiscerning, unperceptive, unwise; dense, dull, obtuse; brainless, dumb, feebleminded, simple, slow, stupid, unintelligent, weak-minded; foolish, idiotic, imbecilic, moronic, silly, simple, thoughtless, witless; ignorant, uninformed

ant unknowing

shriek *vb* to cry out loudly and emotionally — see SCREAM

shrieking *adj* having a high musical pitch or range — see SHRILL

shrill *adj* having a high musical pitch or range ⟨the *shrill* sound of a policeman's whistle⟩

syn acute, high-pitched, piping, screeching, shrieking, squeaking, squeaky, treble, whistling

rel peeping, thin, tinny; piercing, earsplitting, piercing, penetrating, strident; squealing, whining, yelping

near ant gruff

ant bass, deep, low, throaty

shrill *vb* to cry out loudly and emotionally — see SCREAM

shrimp *n* 1 a living thing much smaller than others of its kind — see DWARF 1

2 a person of no importance or influence — see NOBODY

shrine *n* a place that is considered sacred (as within a religion) ⟨for centuries pilgrims have traveled to the *shrine* of Saint Thomas à Becket in Canterbury, England⟩

syn sanctuary, sanctum

rel reliquary

shrink *vb* 1 to become smaller in size or volume through the drawing together of particles of matter — see CONTRACT 2

2 to draw back in fear, pain, or disgust — see FLINCH

3 to grow less in scope or intensity especially gradually — see DECREASE 2

shrinkage *n* the amount by which something is lessened — see DECREASE

shroud *n* something that covers or conceals like a piece of cloth — see CLOAK 1

shroud *vb* 1 to keep secret or shut off from view — see ¹HIDE 2

2 to make dark, dim, or indistinct — see CLOUD 1

3 to surround or cover closely — see ENFOLD 1

shrug off *vb* to overlook or dismiss as of little importance — see EXCUSE 1

shuck *vb* to remove the natural covering of — see PEEL

shuck (off) *vb* to get rid of as useless or unwanted — see DISCARD

shudder *n* an instance of shaking involuntarily with fear or cold — see SHIVER 1

shudder *vb* to make a series of small irregular or violent movements — see SHAKE 1

shuddering *adj* marked by or given to small uncontrollable bodily movements — see SHAKY 1

shuddering *n* a series of slight movements by a body back and forth or from side to side — see VIBRATION

shuddery *adj* marked by or given to small uncontrollable bodily movements — see SHAKY 1

shuffle *n* an unorganized collection or mixture of various things — see MISCELLANY 1

shuffle *vb* 1 to move heavily or clumsily — see LUMBER 1

2 to undo the proper order or arrangement of — see DISORDER

shun *vb* to get or keep away from (as a responsibility) through cleverness or trickery — see ESCAPE 2

shunning *n* the act or a means of getting or keeping away from something undesirable — see ESCAPE 2

shush *vb* to stop the noise or speech of — see SILENCE 1

shut *vb* 1 to position (something) so as to prevent passage through an opening — see CLOSE 1

2 to stop the operations of — see CLOSE 2

shutdown *n* the stopping of a process or activity — see END 1

shutoff *n* the stopping of a process or activity — see END 1

shut off *vb* to bring (as an action or operation) to an immediate end — see STOP 1

shutterbug *n* one who takes photographs — see PHOTOGRAPHER

shut up *vb* to stop talking ⟨it's not polite to tell your classmates to *shut up*, even if you disagree with them⟩

syn clam up, hush, quiet (down)

rel calm (down), cool (down), settle (down); haw, hem

ant speak, talk

shy *adj* 1 easily frightened ⟨a *shy* cat who hid under the bed every time she heard any loud noise⟩

syn fainthearted, fearful, mousy (*or* mousey), scary, skittish, timid, timorous

rel chicken, chickenhearted, cowardly, craven, dastardly, lily-livered, jittery, jumpy, pusillanimous, spineless, unheroic, yellow; anxious, apprehensive, nervous; afraid, alarmed, horrified, panicked, panicky, scared, shocked, spooked, startled, terrified, terrorized

near ant brave, courageous, dauntless, doughty, fearless, gallant, greathearted, heroic, intrepid, lionhearted, stalwart, stout, stouthearted, valiant, valorous; assured, confident, self-assured, self-confident; determined, firm, game, plucky, resolute, unflinching, unswerving; mettlesome, spirited, spunky

ant adventuresome, adventurous, audacious, bold, daring, dashing, gutsy, hardy, venturous, venturesome

2 not comfortable around people ⟨a *shy* person who finds talking to anyone but a close friend to be an awkward and unpleasant experience⟩

syn bashful, coy, demure, diffident, introverted, modest, retiring, sheepish

rel antisocial, unsociable, unsocial; awkward, embarrassed, self-conscious, unadventurous, unassertive, unenterprising; inhibited, reserved, uneasy, uptight

near ant convivial, sociable, social; bold, dashing, forceful; brash, forward, uninhibited, unreserved

ant extroverted (*also* extraverted), immodest, outgoing

3 not coming up to a usual standard or meeting a particular need — see SHORT 3

sick *adj* **1** temporarily suffering from a disorder of the body ⟨Jessie was *sick* with a cold on Monday and had to stay home from school⟩

syn ailing, bad, down, ill, indisposed, peaked, poorly, punk, run-down, sickened, unhealthy, unsound, unwell

rel nauseated, nauseous, qualmish, queasy (*also* queazy), sickish, squeamish; airsick, carsick, seasick, dizzy, lighthearted, woozy; achy, feverish; diseased, disordered; feeble, frail, infirm, sickly, weak, weakly; afflicted, troubled; challenged, crippled, debilitated, disabled, incapacitated, lame

phrases out of sorts, under the weather

near ant cured; better, convalescing, improved, mending, recovering, recuperating, rehabilitated; hardy, hearty, lusty, robust, rugged, stalwart, strong, tough; blooming, bouncing, flourishing, flush, thriving

ant chipper, hale, healthful, healthy, sound, well, whole, wholesome

2 filled with disgust ⟨it makes me *sick* to think of someone hurting a helpless animal⟩

syn disgusted, nauseated, repelled, repulsed, revolted, shocked, sickened, squeamish

rel angry, displeased, mad, upset

near ant delighted, pleased, thrilled; beguiled, bewitched, captivated, charmed, enchanted, enthralled, fascinated, mesmerized

3 affected with nausea — see NAUSEOUS

4 having one's patience, interest, or pleasure exhausted — see WEARY 2

sicken *vb* to cause to feel disgust — see DISGUST

sicken (with) *vb* to become affected with (a disease or disorder) — see CONTRACT 1

sickened *adj* **1** temporarily suffering from a disorder of the body — see SICK 1

2 filled with disgust — see SICK 2

sickening *adj* causing intense displeasure, disgust, or resentment — see OFFENSIVE 1

sickish *adj* affected with nausea — see NAUSEOUS

sickly *adj* chronically or repeatedly suffering from poor health ⟨a *sickly* foal that seemed to catch everything that the other horses had⟩

syn ailing, invalid, weakly

rel bedridden; delicate, fragile, frail; dying, fading, incurable, moribund; challenged, crippled, debilitated, incapacitated, lame; decrepit, enfeebled, feeble, infirm, weak, weakened, worn-out

near ant able-bodied, nondisabled, nonhandicapped

ant healthy, well

sickness *n* **1** the condition of not being in good health ⟨Jamie pleaded *sickness* and tried to stay home from school every single time there was a spelling test scheduled⟩

syn illness, indisposition, unhealthiness, unsoundness

rel malaise; ailment, condition, disease, disorder, malady, trouble, upset; debility, decrepitude, feebleness, frailness, infirmity, lameness

near ant fettle, fitness, shape; hardiness, heartiness, lustiness, robustness, ruggedness, stamina, strength, toughness, vigor, vigorousness, vitality; bloom, flush, flushness; weal, welfare, well-being

ant health, healthiness, soundness, wellness, wholeness, wholesomeness

2 an abnormal state that disrupts a plant or animal's normal bodily functioning — see DISEASE 1

3 a disturbed condition of the stomach in which one feels like vomiting — see NAUSEA 1

side *adj* of, relating to, or located on one side ⟨please bring all deliveries to the *side* door⟩

syn lateral

rel left, right; one-sided

side *n* **1** a place, space, or direction away from or beyond a central point or line ⟨will everyone who wants to sign up for volleyball please stand off to this *side* of the gym?⟩

syn flank, hand

rel direction, face, outside, underpart, underside; lee, leeward, windward; left, right

2 a certain way in which something appears or may be regarded — see ASPECT 1

3 a group of people acting together within a larger group — see FACTION

sideboard *n* a storage case typically having doors and shelves — see CABINET

sidekick *n* a person who helps a more skilled person — see HELPER

side-splitting *adj* causing or intended to cause laughter — see FUNNY 1

sidestep *vb* **1** to avoid having to comply with (something) especially through cleverness — see CIRCUMVENT 1

2 to move suddenly aside or to and fro — see DODGE 1

sideways *adv* with one side faced forward ⟨I had to walk *sideways* to get between the two towering piles of boxes⟩

syn broadside, edgewise, sidewise

rel aslant, obliquely, indirectly; laterally, sideward (*or* sidewards)

near ant dead, direct, right, straight

---

syn synonym(s)   **rel** related words
ant antonym(s)   **near ant** near antonym(s)

sidewise *adv* with one side faced forward — see SIDEWAYS

siege *n* 1 a sudden experiencing of a physical or mental disorder — see ATTACK 2

2 the cutting off of an area by military means to stop the flow of people or supplies — see BLOCKADE

siesta *n* a short sleep — see ¹NAP

sigh *vb* to take in and let out a deep audible breath or to make a similar sound ⟨Mom always used to *sigh* loudly whenever she found a mess on the floor⟩ ⟨a breeze *sighed* through the leaves⟩

syn sough

rel gasp, huff, pant, puff, wheeze; breathe, respire; exhale, expire, inhale, inspire; yawn

sigh (for) *vb* to have an earnest wish to own or enjoy — see DESIRE

sight *n* 1 a position within view — see PRESENCE 1

2 an instance of looking especially briefly — see LOOK 2

3 something unpleasant to look at — see EYESORE

4 the ability to see — see EYESIGHT

sight *vb* to make note of (something) through the use of one's eyes — see SEE 1

sightless *adj* lacking the power of sight — see BLIND

sightly *adj* very pleasing to look at — see BEAUTIFUL

sightseer *n* a person who travels for pleasure — see TOURIST

sign *n* 1 a movement of the body or limbs that expresses or emphasizes an idea or feeling — see GESTURE 1

2 a written or printed mark that is meant to convey information to the reader — see CHARACTER 1

sign *vb* to write one's name on (as a document) ⟨you'll have to *sign* the contract for it to be legal⟩

syn autograph

rel countersign, endorse (*also* indorse), register, sign on; author, pen, pencil (in), scratch (out), scrawl, scribble, write

signal *adj* standing above others in rank, importance, or achievement — see EMINENT

signal *n* 1 an object intended to give public notice or warning ⟨stop signs are *signals* for vehicles to come to a full stop—not suggestions for slowing down, as some drivers seem to think⟩

syn flag, tocsin

2 a movement of the body or limbs that expresses or emphasizes an idea or feeling — see GESTURE 1

signal *vb* to direct or notify by a movement or gesture — see MOTION

significance *n* 1 the idea that is conveyed or intended to be conveyed to the mind by language, symbol, or action — see MEANING 1

2 the quality or state of being important — see IMPORTANCE

significant *adj* 1 clearly conveying a special meaning (as one's mood) — see EXPRESSIVE

2 indicating something — see INDICATIVE

3 having great meaning or lasting effect — see IMPORTANT 1

4 having great power or influence — see IMPORTANT 2

5 sufficiently large in size, amount, or number to merit attention — see CONSIDERABLE 1

signification *n* the idea that is conveyed or intended to be conveyed to the mind by language, symbol, or action — see MEANING 1

signify *vb* 1 to be of importance — see MATTER

2 to communicate or convey (as an idea) to the mind — see MEAN 1

signifying *adj* indicating something — see INDICATIVE

sign on (for) *vb* to become a member of — see ENTER 2

sign up (for) *vb* to become a member of — see ENTER 2

silence *n* 1 incapacity for or restraint from speaking ⟨the teacher expects complete *silence* from everyone during all tests⟩

syn dumbness, muteness, speechlessness, stillness

rel inarticulateness, voicelessness; reserve, reticence, reticency, taciturnity

near ant communication, speaking, talking; eloquence, fluency, volubility; chattiness, garrulousness, loquaciousness, loquacity, talkativeness; verboseness, verbosity, windiness, wordiness

2 the near or complete absence of sound ⟨the *silence* of the garden was refreshing after the din of the party inside⟩

syn hush, quiet, quietness, quietude, still, stillness

rel calm, lull, peacefulness, tranquillity (*or* tranquility)

near ant din, clamor, hubbub, racket, tumult, uproar

ant noise, sound

silence *vb* 1 to stop the noise or speech of ⟨the instructor quickly *silenced* anyone who tried to interrupt⟩ ⟨we need to have a repairman come and *silence* that door alarm⟩

syn hush, mute, quell, settle, shush, still

near ant agitate, stir

2 to put a stop to (something) by the use of force — see QUELL 1

silent *adj* 1 deliberately refraining from speech ⟨the *silent* child had to be prompted to say hello⟩

syn dumb, mum, mute, speechless, uncommunicative

rel inarticulate, tongue-tied; nonvocal, voiceless

near ant articulate, eloquent, fluent, voluble; gabby, garrulous, loquacious, talkative, talky; outspoken, unreserved, vocal

ant communicative, speaking, talking

2 tending not to speak frequently (as by habit or inclination) ⟨a naturally *silent* boy, he was often overshadowed by his louder siblings⟩

syn closemouthed, laconic, reserved, reticent, taciturn, tight-lipped, uncommunicative

rel inhibited, introverted, restrained; sedate, self-contained, sober, staid

near ant free-spoken, outspoken, vocal; blabby, gossipy, talebearing; long-winded, verbose, windy, wordy

ant chatty, communicative, conversational, gabby, garrulous, loquacious, talkative, talky, unreserved

3 mostly or entirely without sound ⟨the room was so *silent* that you could have heard a pin drop⟩

syn hushed, muted, noiseless, quiet, quieted, soundless, still

rel peaceful, tranquil

ant noisy, unquiet

silhouette *n* a line that traces the outer limits of an object or surface — see OUTLINE 1

silhouette *vb* to draw or make apparent the outline of — see OUTLINE 1

silken *adj* smooth or delicate in appearance or feel — see SOFT 2

silky *adj* smooth or delicate in appearance or feel — see SOFT 2

silliness *n* **1** lack of good sense or judgment — see FOOLISHNESS 1

2 language, behavior, or ideas that are absurd and contrary to good sense — see NONSENSE 1

silly *adj* **1** lacking in seriousness or maturity — see GIDDY 1

2 showing or marked by a lack of good sense or judgment — see FOOLISH 1

3 so foolish or pointless as to be worthy of scornful laughter — see RIDICULOUS 1

silver *adj* of the color gray — see GRAY 1

silver *n* eating and serving utensils — see TABLEWARE 1

silverware *n* eating and serving utensils — see TABLEWARE 1

silvery *adj* of the color gray — see GRAY 1

similar *adj* having qualities in common — see ALIKE

similarity *n* **1** the quality or state of having many qualities in common ⟨the *similarity* between the two essays is too great to be coincidental — one student virtually copied the other⟩

syn alikeness, community, correspondence, likeness, parallelism, resemblance, similitude

rel analogousness; equivalence, equivalency, parity; identicalness, identity, sameness; correlation, relationship; exchangeability, interchangeability; accordance, agreement, compatibility, conformity, congruity

near ant inequality; conflict, disagreement, discrepancy, disparity, variance; incompatibility, incongruity, incongruousness

ant dissimilarity, unlikeness

2 a point which two or more things share in common ⟨the only *similarity* between

this project and the last one is that both will involve some lab work⟩

syn correspondence, parallel, resemblance, similitude

rel counterpart, equal, equivalent

near ant difference, discrepancy; deviance, divergence; change, modification, variation

ant dissimilarity

similarly *adv* in like manner — see ALSO 1

similitude *n* **1** the quality or state of having many qualities in common — see SIMILARITY 1

2 a point which two or more things share in common — see SIMILARITY 2

simmer *vb* to cook in a liquid heated to the point that it gives off steam — see BOIL 2

simple *adj* **1** free from all additions or embellishment — see PLAIN 1

2 free from any intent to deceive or impress others — see GUILELESS

3 having no exceptions or restrictions — see ABSOLUTE 2

4 involving minimal difficulty or effort — see EASY 1

5 lacking in worldly wisdom or informed judgment — see NAIVE 1

6 lacking in education or the knowledge gained from books — see IGNORANT 1

7 not having or showing an ability to absorb ideas readily — see STUPID 1

simpleminded *adj* **1** lacking in worldly wisdom or informed judgment — see NAIVE 1

2 showing or marked by a lack of good sense or judgment — see FOOLISH 1

simpleness *n* **1** the quality or state of being simple and sincere — see NAÏVETÉ 1

2 the quality or state of lacking intelligence or quickness of mind — see STUPIDITY 1

simpleton *n* **1** a person who lacks good sense or judgment — see FOOL 1

2 a stupid person — see IDIOT

simplicity *n* **1** the quality or state of having a form or structure of few parts or elements ⟨the *simplicity* of this machine should enable everyone to learn how to use it⟩

syn plainness, unsophistication

rel homogeneity, unity

ant complexity, complication, elaborateness, intricacy, sophistication

2 clearness of expression ⟨the *simplicity* of this poem is beautiful⟩

syn clarity, explicitness, lucidity, lucidness, perspicuity, perspicuousness

rel incisiveness, directness, forthrightness, openness, straightforwardness

near ant ambiguity, equivocalness; incomprehensibility, unintelligibility; circuitousness, deviousness, indirectness, indistinctness; dimness, disjointedness, incoherence; faintness, fuzziness, muddiness, nebulousness, vagueness

ant obscurity

3 lack of good sense or judgment — see FOOLISHNESS 1

---

syn synonym(s)   *rel* related words
ant antonym(s)   *near ant* near antonym(s)

4 the quality or state of being simple and sincere — see NAÏVETÉ 1

simplify *vb* to make less complex ⟨you need to *simplify* this process somewhat or you'll never finish it today⟩

syn streamline

rel oversimplify; prune, strip (down), trim; purify, refine

near ant elaborate

ant complicate, perplex, sophisticate

simply *adv* **1** for nothing other than — see SOLELY 1

2 nothing more than — see JUST 3

simulate *vb* to present a false appearance of — see FEIGN

simulated *adj* **1** being such in appearance only and made with or manufactured from usually cheaper materials — see IMITATION

2 lacking in natural or spontaneous quality — see ARTIFICIAL 1

simultaneous *adj* existing or occurring at the same period of time — see CONTEMPORARY 1

simultaneously *adv* at one and the same time — see TOGETHER 1

sin *n* **1** a breaking of a moral or legal code — see OFFENSE 1

2 that which is morally unacceptable — see EVIL

3 immoral conduct or practices harmful or offensive to society — see VICE 1

4 a regrettable or blameworthy act — see CRIME 1

sin *vb* to commit an offense — see OFFEND 1

since *conj* for the reason that ⟨*since* I've done all my chores today, I should be allowed to go out and play⟩

syn as, because, for, inasmuch as, now, seeing, whereas

phrases as long as (*or* so long as), in view (*or* light) of the fact

sincere *adj* free from any intent to deceive or impress others — see GUILELESS

sincerely *adv* without any attempt to impress by deception or exaggeration — see NATURALLY 1

sinew *n* the ability to exert effort for the accomplishment of a task — see POWER 2

sinewy *adj* **1** having muscles capable of exerting great physical force — see STRONG 1

2 marked by a well-developed musculature — see MUSCULAR 1

sinful *adj* not conforming to a high moral standard; morally unacceptable — see BAD 2

sinfulness *n* the state or quality of being utterly evil — see ENORMITY 1

sing *vb* **1** to produce musical sounds with the voice ⟨it's relatively rare to find actors who can also *sing* well⟩

syn carol, chant, descant, vocalize

rel belt, croon, harmonize, hum, lilt, quaver, scat, sharp, slur, trill, troll, warble, yodel; serenade

2 to utter in musical or drawn out tones — see CHANT 1

3 to utter one's distinctive animal sound — see CRY 2

singe *vb* to burn on the surface — see SCORCH

singer *n* one who sings ⟨a famous opera *singer* will be performing tomorrow⟩

syn caroler (*or* caroller), songster, vocalist, vocalizer, voice

rel harmonizer, hummer, warbler, yodeler; serenader; cantor, chorist; songstress

single *adj* **1** not married ⟨there was such a shortage of *single* men in the neighborhood that he had his pick of girlfriends⟩

syn unattached, unmarried, unwed

rel fancy-free, footloose; marriageable, unmated, unpaired; divorced, separated

near ant mated, paired; affianced, betrothed, committed, engaged, pledged, promised; remarried

ant attached, espoused, married, wed

2 belonging only to the one person, unit, or group named — see SOLE 1

3 not physically attached to another unit — see SEPARATE 2

single (out) *vb* **1** to decide to accept (someone or something) from a group of possibilities — see CHOOSE 1

2 to find out or establish the identity of — see IDENTIFY 1

single–handedly *adv* without aid or support — see ALONE 1

singly *adv* without aid or support — see ALONE 1

singular *adj* **1** being out of the ordinary — see EXCEPTIONAL 1

2 noticeably different from what is generally found or experienced — see UNUSUAL 1

3 of, relating to, or belonging to a single person — see INDIVIDUAL 1

4 being the one or ones of a class with no other members — see ONLY 2

singularity *n* an odd or peculiar habit — see IDIOSYNCRASY

sinister *adj* being or showing a sign of evil or calamity to come — see OMINOUS

sink *vb* **1** to become worse or of less value — see DETERIORATE

2 to go to a lower level — see DROP 2

sinner *n* a person who commits moral wrongs — see EVILDOER 1

sinuous *adj* marked by a long series of irregular curves — see CROOKED 1

sip *n* the portion of a serving of a beverage that is swallowed at one time — see DRINK 2

sip *vb* to swallow in liquid form — see DRINK 1

siphon *vb* **1** to remove (liquid) gradually or completely — see DRAIN 1

2 to cause to move to a central point or along a restricted pathway — see CHANNEL

sire *vb* to become the father of — see FATHER

siren *n* a woman whom men find irresistibly attractive ⟨one of history's most famous *sirens*, Cleopatra charmed both Julius Caesar and Mark Antony⟩

syn enchantress, seductress, temptress

rel charmer, seducer

sissy *adj* having or displaying qualities more suitable for women than for men — see EFFEMINATE

sissy *n* a person who shows a shameful lack of courage in the face of danger — see COWARD

sit *vb* 1 to rest on the buttocks or haunches ⟨everybody needs to *sit* down, or no one will be able to see the movie⟩

syn set [*chiefly dialect*]

rel perch; lounge, slouch, sprawl, squat, straddle

near ant arise, get up, rise, stand

2 to cause to sit down — see SEAT

3 to cover and warm eggs to hatch them — see SET 1

4 to occupy a place or location — see STAND 1

site *n* the area or space occupied by or intended for something — see PLACE 1

sitter *n* a girl or woman employed to care for a young child or children — see NURSE

sitting duck *n* a person or thing that is the object of abuse, criticism, or ridicule — see TARGET 1

situate *vb* to arrange something in a certain spot or position — see PLACE 1

situation *n* 1 position with regard to conditions and circumstances ⟨the school's *situation* is improving with additional financial help⟩

syn footing, picture, posture, scene, status

rel rank, standing; place, spot, state; score, status quo

2 an assignment at which one regularly works for pay — see JOB 1

3 the placement of someone or something in relation to others in a vertical arrangement — see RANK 1

sixth sense *n* the power of seeing or knowing about things that are not present to the senses — see CLAIRVOYANCE

sizable *or* **sizeable** *adj* 1 of a size greater than average of its kind — see LARGE

2 sufficiently large in size, amount, or number to merit attention — see CONSIDERABLE 1

sizably *adv* to a large extent or degree — see GREATLY 2

size *n* the total amount of measurable space or surface occupied by something ⟨we worried that the immense *size* of the sofa would make getting it through the doorway impossible⟩

syn dimension, extent, magnitude, measure, measurement, proportion

rel area; capaciousness, commodiousness, roominess, spaciousness; ampleness, amplitude, bigness, bulk, bulkiness, enormousness, grandness, greatness, grossness, heftiness, hugeness, immenseness, immensity, largeness, mass, massiveness, monstrousness, stupendousness, tremen-

dousness, vastness, volume, voluminousness

size *n* a substance used to stick things together — see GLUE

sizzle *n* a sound similar to the speech sound \s\ stretched out — see HISS 1

sizzle *vb* to make a sound like that of stretching out the speech sound \s\ — see HISS

skeletal *adj* suffering extreme weight loss as a result of hunger or disease — see EMACIATED

skeleton *n* the arrangement of parts that gives something its basic form — see FRAME 1

skeptic *n* a person who is always ready to doubt or question the truth or existence of something ⟨the demand by *skeptics* that believers in Bigfoot produce some hard evidence of that hairy humanoid⟩

syn disbeliever, doubter, questioner, unbeliever

rel cynic, misanthrope, pessimist; derider, ridiculer, scoffer

near ant chump, dupe, gull, pigeon, sucker

skeptical *adj* 1 inclined to doubt or question claims ⟨it's good to be *skeptical* about what you see on TV⟩

syn disbelieving, distrustful, doubting, incredulous, leery, mistrustful, questioning, suspecting, suspicious, unbelieving

rel paranoid; critical, puzzled, quizzical; careful, cautious, guarded, leery, wary, watchful; cynical, experienced, knowing, sophisticated, worldly, worldly-wise; curious, inquiring, inquisitive, nosy (*or* nosey), snoopy; uncertain, unconvinced, undecided, undetermined, unsettled, unsure; hesitant

near ant green, ingenuous, innocent, naive (*or* naïve), simple, simpleminded, unknowing, unsophisticated, unworldly, wide-eyed; certain, confident, positive, sure; callow, inexperienced, raw; childlike, idealistic, impractical; beguiled, deceived, duped, gulled, tricked; careless, heedless, unsuspecting, unsuspicious, unwary

ant credulous, gullible, trustful, trusting, uncritical, unquestioning

2 not feeling sure about the truth, wisdom, or trustworthiness of someone or something — see DOUBTFUL 1

skeptically *adv* with distrust — see ASKANCE

skepticism *n* a feeling or attitude that one does not know the truth, truthfulness, or trustworthiness of someone or something — see DOUBT

sketch *n* 1 a picture using lines to represent the chief features of an object or scene — see DRAWING

2 a vivid representation in words of someone or something — see DESCRIPTION 1

sketch *vb* 1 to draw or make apparent the outline of — see OUTLINE 1

2 to give a representation or account of in words — see DESCRIBE 1

---

syn synonym(s)   *rel* related words

ant antonym(s)   *near ant* near antonym(s)

skewed *adj* inclined or twisted to one side — see AWRY

skewer *vb* to penetrate or hold (something) with a pointed object — see IMPALE

skill *n* **1** subtle or imaginative ability in inventing, devising, or executing something ⟨with unbelievable *skill*, the expert in origami transformed a few sheets of paper into a menagerie of exotic animals⟩
syn adeptness, adroitness, art, artfulness, artifice, artistry, cleverness, craft, cunning, deftness, masterfulness, skillfulness
rel dexterity, ease, finesse, handiness; experience, expertise, expertness, know-how, proficiency; creativity, ingenuity, inventiveness, knowledge, learning; aptitude, bent, flair, gift, knack, talent
near ant amateurishness, awkwardness, clumsiness, crudeness, rudeness; inability, inadequacy, incapability, incapacity, incompetence, ineffectiveness, ineffectualness, inefficiency
ant artlessness, ineptitude, ineptness, maladroitness
2 skills *pl* knowledge gained by actually doing or living through something — see EXPERIENCE 1

skilled *adj* having or showing exceptional knowledge, experience, or skill in a field of endeavor — see PROFICIENT

skillful *adj* **1** accomplished with trained ability ⟨the ice skater performed a *skillful* and graceful series of jumps⟩
syn adroit, artful, delicate, dexterous (*also* dextrous), expert, masterful, masterly, practiced (*or* practised), virtuoso, workmanlike
rel facile, smooth; artistic, creative, fancy, ingenious, neat; adept, clever, cunning; able, adequate, capable, competent
near ant awkward, clumsy, crude; ineffective, ineffectual; incompetent, inept
ant amateur, amateurish, artless, rude, unprofessional, unskillful
2 having or showing exceptional knowledge, experience, or skill in a field of endeavor — see PROFICIENT

skillfully *adv* in a skillful or expert manner — see WELL 3

skillfulness *n* subtle or imaginative ability in inventing, devising, or executing something — see SKILL 1

skim *vb* **1** to move or proceed smoothly and readily — see FLOW 2
2 to pass lightly across or touch gently especially in passing — see BRUSH
3 to strike and fly off at an angle — see GLANCE 1
4 to take a quick or hasty look — see GLANCE 2

skimp *vb* to avoid unnecessary waste or expense — see ECONOMIZE

skimp (on) *vb* to use or give out in stingy amounts — see SPARE

skimping *n* careful management of material resources — see ECONOMY

skimpy *adj* less plentiful than what is normal, necessary, or desirable — see MEAGER

skin *n* **1** an outer part or layer — see EXTERIOR
2 the outer covering of an animal removed for its commercial value — see HIDE 1
3 the hairless natural covering of an animal prepared for use — see LEATHER 1

skin *vb* **1** to remove the natural covering of — see PEEL
2 to rob by the use of trickery or threats — see FLEECE

skin–deep *adj* **1** lying on or affecting only the outer layer of something — see SUPERFICIAL 1
2 having or showing a lack of depth of understanding or character — see SUPERFICIAL 2

skinflint *n* a mean grasping person who is usually stingy with money — see MISER

skinny *adj* **1** being of less than usual width — see NARROW 1
2 having a noticeably small amount of body fat — see THIN 1

skip *vb* **1** to move with a light bouncing step ⟨children *skipping* across the playground⟩
syn bound, hop, lope, trip
rel caper, frisk, gambol, romp; skim, skitter; jump, leap, vault
near ant lumber, plod, trudge
2 to fail to attend — see CUT 2
3 to strike and fly off at an angle — see GLANCE 1

skipper *n* a person in overall command of a ship — see CAPTAIN 1

skirmish *n* **1** a brief clash between enemies or rivals — see ENCOUNTER
2 a physical dispute between opposing individuals or groups — see FIGHT

skirmish (with) *vb* to oppose (someone) in physical conflict — see FIGHT 1

skirt *n* the line or relatively narrow space that marks the outer limit of something — see BORDER 1

skirt *vb* **1** to avoid by going around — see DETOUR 1
2 to avoid having to comply with (something) especially through cleverness — see CIRCUMVENT 1
3 to be adjacent to — see ADJOIN 1
4 to serve as a border for — see BORDER

skirting *adj* having a border in common — see ADJACENT

skittish *adj* **1** easily excited by nature — see EXCITABLE
2 easily frightened — see SHY 1

skittishness *n* a state of nervousness marked by sudden jerky movements — see JUMPINESS

skulk *vb* to move about in a sly or secret manner — see SNEAK 1

skulker *n* someone who acts in a sly and secret manner — see SNEAK

skull *n* the case of bone that encloses the brain and supports the jaws of vertebrates ⟨anthropologists just found the *skull* of a prehistoric man in the desert⟩
syn cranium
rel braincase; death's-head; head, noddle, noggin, pate, poll; crown, scalp

skunk *n* a person whose behavior is offensive to others — see JERK 1

skunk *vb* **1** to defeat by a large margin — see WHIP 2

2 to achieve a victory over — see BEAT 2

sky *n* the expanse of air surrounding the earth ⟨the *sky* usually looks deep blue on a bright clear day⟩

syn blue, firmament, heaven(s), high

rel horizon, skyline

sky-high *adv* in an enthusiastic manner ⟨some reviewers had praised the movie *sky-high*, but we thought that it was just a so-so comedy⟩

syn enthusiastically, exuberantly, madly, rhapsodically

rel avidly, eagerly, excitedly, impatiently, keenly; fanatically, rabidly, zealously

near ant aloofly, disinterestedly, impassively, incuriously; hesitantly, reluctantly, unwillingly

ant apathetically, indifferently, lukewarmly, perfunctorily

skylark *vb* to engage in attention-getting playful or boisterous behavior — see CUT UP

skylarking *n* wildly playful or mischievous behavior — see HORSEPLAY

skyrocket *vb* to rise abruptly and rapidly ⟨the price of candy bars in the vending machine has *skyrocketed* over the past few months⟩

syn rocket, shoot (up), soar, zoom

rel accumulate, appreciate, balloon, build (up), burgeon, enlarge, escalate, expand, increase, mount, multiply, mushroom, proliferate, snowball, swell, wax; crest, peak, surge; heighten, intensify

near ant collapse, fall; contract, decrease, diminish, drop, lessen, wane

ant nose-dive, plummet, plunge, slump, tumble

skyward *adv* to or in a higher place — see ABOVE

slack *adj* **1** failing to give proper care and attention — see NEGLIGENT

2 not bound by rigid standards — see EASYGOING 2

3 not tightly fastened, tied, or stretched — see LOOSE 1

slack *n* **1** the extent to which something hangs or dips below a straight line — see SAG

2 slacks *pl* an outer garment covering each leg separately from waist to ankle — see PANTS

slack *vb* to make less taut — see SLACKEN

slacken *vb* to make less taut ⟨you'll need to *slacken* the rope a bit to get it free of that post⟩

syn ease, loosen, relax, slack

rel detach, free, unbind, undo, unfasten, untie

near ant attach, bind, fasten, tie; constrain, restrain

ant strain, stretch, tense, tighten

---

syn synonym(s)   *rel* related words

ant antonym(s)   *near ant* near antonym(s)

slackened *adj* not tightly fastened, tied, or stretched — see LOOSE 1

slacker *n* one who deliberately avoids work or duty ⟨there will be no *slackers* tolerated in this group—anyone who doesn't do their share will get booted out⟩

syn goldbrick, shirker

rel malingerer; dropout, quitter; drone, idler, lazybones, loafer, slouch, slug, sluggard; dallier, lingerer, loiterer, lounger, saunterer; dawdler, laggard, putterer, slowpoke

near ant live wire, powerhouse; doer, gogetter, hummer, hustler, rustler, selfstarter

slackness *n* **1** failure to take the care that a cautious person usually takes — see NEGLIGENCE 1

2 the extent to which something hangs or dips below a straight line — see SAG

slam *n* **1** a hard strike with a part of the body or an instrument — see BLOW 1

2 a loud explosive sound — see CLAP 1

slam *vb* **1** to shove into a closed position with force and noise ⟨the sulky child ran into her room and *slammed* the door loudly⟩

syn bang

rel close, shut, stop; bar, batten (down), bolt, chain, fasten, latch, lock, seal, secure

near ant open; unbar, unbolt, unfasten, unlatch, unlock, unseal

2 to deliver a blow to (someone or something) usually in a strong vigorous manner — see HIT 1

3 to come into usually forceful contact with something — see HIT 2

4 to criticize harshly and usually publicly — see ATTACK 2

slander *n* the making of false statements that damage another's reputation ⟨unhappy that she hadn't won, the girl resorted to *slander* and claimed that the winner's science project had actually been done by his father⟩

syn aspersing, blackening, defamation, defaming, libel, libeling, maligning, smearing, traducing, vilification, vilifying

rel aspersion, innuendo, smear; backbiting, detraction; abuse, invective, vituperation; attack, criticism, censure, denunciation; contempt, disdain, scorn; belittlement, disparagement; cattiness, despite, hatefulness, malevolence, malice, maliciousness, malignancy, malignity, meanness, nastiness, spite, spitefulness, spleen, venom, viciousness

near ant acclaim, accolade, applause, commendation, praise; esteem, honor, respect; adulation, flattery; adoration, reverence, veneration, worship

slander *vb* to make untrue and harmful statements about ⟨for some reason, that newspaper seems determined to *slander* one particular celebrity⟩

syn asperse, blacken, defame, libel, malign, smear, traduce, vilify *rel* belittle, detract, disparage; discredit, disgrace, dishonor, shame; abase, debase, degrade, humble, humiliate; disdain, scorn

near ant exalt, glorify, honor; acclaim, applaud, commend, praise; esteem, respect; admire, regard; adore, revere, venerate, worship

slanderous *adj* causing or intended to cause unjust injury to a person's good name — see LIBELOUS

slang *n* the special terms or expressions of a particular group or field — see TERMINOLOGY

slant *n* **1** the degree to which something rises up from a position level with the horizon ⟨the road has just enough of a *slant* to make bicycling up it a little strenuous⟩

syn cant, diagonal, grade, gradient, inclination, incline, lean, pitch, slope, tilt, upgrade

rel ascent, bank, climb, rise

near ant declension, declination, decline, declivity, descent, dip, downgrade, fall, receding

2 a way of looking at or thinking about something — see POINT OF VIEW

slant *vb* to set or cause to be at an angle — see LEAN 1

slanted *adj* **1** inclined or twisted to one side — see AWRY

2 running in a slanting direction — see DIAGONAL

slanting *adj* inclined or twisted to one side — see AWRY

slantways *adv* so as to slant — see SLANTWISE

slantwise *adj* **1** inclined or twisted to one side — see AWRY

2 running in a slanting direction — see DIAGONAL

slantwise *adv* so as to slant ⟨be careful not to lay the first boards *slantwise*, or the whole bookcase won't be straight⟩

syn slantways

rel down, downward (*or* downwards), up, upward (*or* upwards)

slap *n* a hard strike with a part of the body or an instrument — see ¹BLOW

slap *vb* to deliver a blow to (someone or something) usually in a strong vigorous manner — see HIT 1

slapdash *adj* lacking a definite plan, purpose, or pattern — see RANDOM

slapjack *n* a flat cake made from thin batter and cooked on both sides (as on a griddle) — see PANCAKE

slapstick *n* humorous entertainment — see COMEDY

slash *n* a long deep cut — see GASH

slash *vb* **1** to penetrate with a sharp edge (as a knife) — see CUT 1

2 to strike repeatedly with something long and thin or flexible — see WHIP 1

slate *adj* of the color gray — see GRAY 1

slate *vb* to put (someone or something) on a list — see ¹LIST 2

slated *adj* being in accordance with the prescribed, normal, or logical course of events — see DUE 2

slaty *adj* of the color gray — see GRAY 1

slaughter *n* the killing of a large number of people — see MASSACRE

slaughter *vb* to kill on a large scale — see MASSACRE

slave *n* **1** a person who is considered the property of another person ⟨many American *slaves* reached freedom in the North through the network known as the Underground Railroad⟩

syn bondman, bondsman, chattel, thrall

rel helot, serf; attendant, domestic, drudge, lackey, menial, servant

near ant freedman; enslaver, slave driver, slaveholder, slaver; master, taskmaster

ant freeman

2 a person who does very hard or dull work ⟨unappreciated office *slaves* who perform the necessary but tedious task of filing paperwork⟩

syn drudge, drudger, fag, grubber, laborer, peon, plugger, slogger, toiler, worker

rel workhorse; coolie, serf

near ant goldbrick, shirker; drone, idler, lazybones, loafer, slouch, slug, sluggard

slave *vb* to devote serious and sustained effort — see LABOR

slave (**for**) *vb* to be a servant for — see SERVE 1

slave driver *n* a boss who assigns much work — see TASKMASTER 1

slaver *vb* to let saliva or some other substance flow from the mouth — see DROOL

slavery *n* **1** the state of being a slave ⟨a child born into *slavery* was considered simply another addition to the master's wealth and property⟩

syn bondage, enslavement, servility, servitude, thrall, thralldom (*or* thraldom), yoke

rel peonage, serfdom; dependence, subjection, subjugation; captivity, enchainment, imprisonment, incarceration

near ant emancipation, enfranchisement, liberation, manumission; autonomy, independence, self-government, sovereignty

ant freedom, liberty

2 very hard or unpleasant work — see TOIL

slavish *adj* using or marked by the use of something else as a basis or model — see IMITATIVE

slavishly *adv* with great effort or determination — see HARD 1

slay *vb* **1** to deprive of life — see KILL 1

2 to put to death deliberately — see MURDER 1

slaying *n* the intentional and unlawful taking of another person's life — see HOMICIDE

sleazy *adj* of low quality — see CHEAP 2

sleek *adj* having a shiny surface or finish — see GLOSSY

sleep *n* **1** a natural periodic loss of consciousness during which the body restores itself ⟨eight hours of *sleep* or more are necessary for children and teenagers to function⟩

syn catnapping, dozing, napping, repose, rest, resting, slumber, slumbering, snoozing

rel catnap, doze, drowse, forty winks, nap, siesta, snooze, wink; oversleeping; dreaming, rapid eye movement

near ant insomnia, sleeplessness

ant consciousness, wakefulness

2 the state of being dead — see DEATH 2

sleep *vb* **1** be in a state of sleep ⟨the baby *slept* for the entire length of the car trip⟩

syn catnap, doze, nap, rest, slumber, snooze

rel drowse (off), nod (off); oversleep; dream, hibernate

near ant arise, arouse, awake, rise

2 to engage in sexual intercourse — see COPULATE

sleeper *n* one who sleeps ⟨Joe is a restless *sleeper* who always wakes up with the covers kicked off⟩

syn dozer, slumberer

rel nodder

near ant insomniac; riser, waker

sleepiness *n* the quality or state of desiring or needing sleep ⟨Sarah suffered such *sleepiness* in class that there were days when she could hardly keep her eyes open⟩

syn drowsiness, somnolence

rel lassitude, lethargy, sluggishness, torpor; dozing, resting, sleeping, slumbering; oversleeping

near ant awareness, consciousness

ant insomnia, sleeplessness, wakefulness

sleeping *adj* being in a state of suspended consciousness — see ASLEEP 1

sleepless *adj* not sleeping or able to sleep — see WAKEFUL

sleepy *adj* **1** desiring or needing sleep ⟨the *sleepy* children were carried up to bed⟩

syn drowsy, slumberous (*or* slumbrous), somnolent

rel asleep, dormant, dozing, resting, sleeping, slumbering; nodding, yawning

near ant restive, restless, sleepless

ant alert, awake, conscious, wakeful, wide-awake

2 slow to move or act — see INACTIVE 1

sleight *n* **1** a clever often underhanded means to achieve an end — see TRICK 1

2 mental skill or quickness — see DEXTERITY 1

3 ease and grace in physical activity — see DEXTERITY 2

slender *adj* **1** being of less than usual width — see NARROW 1

2 having a noticeably small amount of body fat — see THIN 1

3 less plentiful than what is normal, necessary, or desirable — see MEAGER

sleuth *n* a person whose business is solving crimes and catching criminals or gathering information that is not easy to get — see DETECTIVE

slice *n* a piece that has been separated from the whole by cutting — see CUT 1

slice *vb* **1** to cut into long slender pieces — see SLIVER

2 to penetrate with a sharp edge (as a knife) — see CUT 1

slick *adj* **1** having or being a surface so smooth as to make sliding or falling likely ⟨roads are often *slick* during the first hour of a rainstorm⟩

syn greased, greasy, lubricated, oiled, slicked, slippery, slithery

rel brushed, buffed, burnished, glossed, ground, polished, rubbed, shined; coated, glazed, waxed; soapy, waxy; rasped, sandblasted, sanded, sandpapered, scoured, scraped, scrubbed

near ant coarsened, rough, roughened, scuffed, uneven

2 clever at attaining one's ends by indirect and often deceptive means — see ARTFUL 1

slick *vb* to coat (something) with a slippery substance in order to reduce friction — see LUBRICATE

slicked *adj* having or being a surface so smooth as to make sliding or falling likely — see SLICK 1

slicker *n* a coat made of water-resistant material — see RAINCOAT

slickness *n* skill in achieving one's ends through indirect, subtle, or underhanded means — see CUNNING 1

slide *vb* **1** to move about in a sly or secret manner — see SNEAK 1

2 to move or proceed smoothly and readily — see FLOW 2

slight *adj* **1** lacking bodily strength — see WEAK 1

2 lacking importance — see UNIMPORTANT

3 of a size that is less than average — see SMALL 1

4 so small or unimportant as to warrant little or no attention — see NEGLIGIBLE 1

5 small in degree — see REMOTE 1

slight *n* an act or expression showing scorn and usually intended to hurt another's feelings — see INSULT

slight *vb* **1** to cause hurt feelings or deep resentment in — see INSULT

2 to deliberately ignore or treat rudely — see SNUB 1

3 to show contempt for — see SCORN 1

4 to fail to give proper attention to — see NEGLECT 1

slightest *adj* being the least in amount, number, or size possible — see MINIMAL

slighting *adj* intended to make a person or thing seem of little importance or value — see DEROGATORY

slightly *adv* **1** by a very small margin — see JUST 2

2 in a very small quantity or degree — see LITTLE 1

slightness *n* **1** the quality or state of being little in size — see SMALLNESS

---

2 the state or quality of having little weight — see ¹LIGHTNESS 1

slim *adj* **1** being of less than usual width — see NARROW 1

2 having a noticeably small amount of body fat — see THIN 1

3 less plentiful than what is normal, necessary, or desirable — see MEAGER

4 small in degree — see REMOTE 1

slime *n* soft wet earth — see MUD

slimy *adj* full of or covered with soft wet earth — see MUDDY 1

¹sling *vb* to place on an elevated point without support from below — see HANG 1

²sling *vb* to send through the air especially with a quick forward motion of the arm — see THROW

slink *vb* to move about in a sly or secret manner — see SNEAK 1

¹slip *n* a long narrow piece of material — see STRIP

²slip *n* **1** an unintentional departure from truth or accuracy — see ERROR 1

2 the act of going down from an upright position suddenly and involuntarily — see FALL 1

3 the act or an instance of getting free from danger or confinement — see ESCAPE 1

slip *vb* to decline gradually from a standard level 〈Susie's grades *slipped* somewhat after she joined five after-school activities〉

syn sag

rel drop, fall, slump; flag, sink, slacken, slow (down), weaken; abate, contract, decrease, de-escalate, die (down), diminish, dwindle, ebb, lessen, let up, lower, moderate, recede, relent, shrink, subside, taper, taper off, wane

near ant rocket, shoot (up), soar; balloon, burgeon, enlarge, escalate, expand, increase, mount, multiply, mushroom, proliferate, snowball, swell, wax; crest, peak, surge

2 to go down from an upright position suddenly and involuntarily — see FALL 1

3 to introduce in a gradual, secret, or clever way — see INSINUATE

4 to move about in a sly or secret manner — see SNEAK 1

5 to move or proceed smoothly and readily — see FLOW 2

slip (on or into) *vb* to place on one's person — see PUT ON 1

slippery *adj* **1** given to acting in secret and to concealing one's intentions — see SNEAKY 1

2 hard to find, capture, or isolate — see ELUSIVE

3 having or being a surface so smooth as to make sliding or falling likely — see SLICK 1

slipup *n* an unintentional departure from truth or accuracy — see ERROR 1

slit *n* a long deep cut — see GASH

slit *vb* to penetrate with a sharp edge (as a knife) — see CUT 1

slither *vb* to move slowly with the body close to the ground — see CRAWL 1

slithery *adj* having or being a surface so smooth as to make sliding or falling likely — see SLICK 1

sliver *n* a small flat piece separated from a whole — see CHIP 1

sliver *vb* to cut into long slender pieces 〈carefully *slivered* the rattan stems into strips for basketry〉

syn slice, splinter

rel chip, chop, dice, hash, mince; saw, scissor; cleave, rive, split; gash, incise, rip, slash, slit

slob *n* **1** a dirty or sloppy person 〈only a *slob* would let his bedroom get so messy that his own mother couldn't remember what the floor looked like〉

syn sloven

rel slattern, slut

near ant cleaner

ant old maid

2 a person whose behavior is offensive to others — see JERK 1

slobber *n* the fluid that is secreted into the mouth by certain glands — see SALIVA

slobber *vb* **1** to let saliva or some other substance flow from the mouth — see DROOL

2 to make an exaggerated display of affection or enthusiasm — see GUSH 2

slog *vb* **1** to deliver a blow to (someone or something) usually in a strong vigorous manner — see HIT 1

2 to devote serious and sustained effort — see LABOR

slogan *n* an attention-getting word or phrase used to publicize something (as a campaign or product) 〈within days, virtually everyone was familiar with the new-est advertising *slogan* for that brand of soda〉

syn cry, shibboleth, watchword

rel tag line; expression, idiom; cliché; maxim, motto

slogger *n* a person who does very hard or dull work — see SLAVE 2

slop *n* **1** soft wet earth — see MUD

2 slops *pl* solid matter discharged from an animal's alimentary canal — see DROPPING 1

slope *n* the degree to which something rises up from a position level with the horizon — see SLANT

slope *vb* to set or cause to be at an angle — see LEAN 1

sloped *adj* running in a slanting direction — see DIAGONAL

sloping *adj* running in a slanting direction — see DIAGONAL

sloppily *adv* in a careless or unfashionable manner 〈everyone dressed *sloppily* for the task of cleaning out the garage〉

syn dowdily, slovenly, unstylishly

rel slatternly; chaotically, messily, untidily; shabbily, sleazily; dingily, dirtily, filthily, foully, grubbily, nastily

near ant neatly, orderly, tidily; fashionably, modishly; carefully, fastidiously, fussily, meticulously; cleanly, immaculately, spotlessly

ant nattily, sharply, smartly, sprucely

sloppiness *n* the state or quality of having an excess of tender feelings (as of love, nostalgia, or compassion) — see SENTIMENTALITY

sloppy *adj* **1** lacking neatness in dress or person ⟨a *sloppy* child who always seems to have spilled something on his clothes⟩
syn dowdy, frowsy (*or* frowzy), slovenly, unkempt, untidy
rel slatternly, sluttish; chaotic, cluttered, confused, disarranged, disheveled (*or* dishevelled), disordered, messed, messy, muddled, mussed, mussy, rumpled, uncombed, wrinkled; shabby, sleazy; besmirched, blackened, dingy, dirty, filthy, foul, grimy, grubby, grungy, mucky, nasty, soiled, spotted, squalid, stained, sullied, unclean, uncleanly
near ant chic, fashionable, modish, stylish; combed, groomed; neat, ordered, orderly, tidy; careful, fastidious, fussy, meticulous; clean, cleaned, cleanly, immaculate, sparkling, spotless, stainless, unsoiled, unsullied
ant dapper, dashing, dolled up, sharp, smart, spruce
2 lacking in order, neatness, and often cleanliness — see MESSY
3 appealing to the emotions in an obvious and tiresome way — see CORNY

slosh *vb* to move with a splashing motion ⟨the baby gurgled contentedly as the water *sloshed* gently around him in the bathtub⟩
syn lap, plash, splash, swash
rel babble, bubble, gurgle, ripple

sloth *n* an inclination not to do work or engage in activities — see LAZINESS

slothful *adj* not easily aroused to action or work — see LAZY

slouch *n* a lazy person — see LAZYBONES

slough *also* **slue** *n* spongy land saturated or partially covered with water — see SWAMP

slough *also* **sluff** *vb* **1** to cast (a natural bodily covering or appendage) aside — see SHED 1
2 to get rid of as useless or unwanted — see DISCARD

sloven *n* a dirty or sloppy person — see SLOB 1

slovenly *adj* lacking neatness in dress or person — see SLOPPY 1

slovenly *adv* in a careless or unfashionable manner — see SLOPPILY

slow *adj* **1** moving or proceeding at less than the normal, desirable, or required speed ⟨because of the holiday, traffic to the beach was particularly *slow*⟩ ⟨*slow* readers⟩
syn crawling, creeping, dallying, dawdling, dilatory, dillydallying, dragging, laggard, lagging, languid, leisurely, poking, poky (*or* pokey), sluggish, tardy, unhurried
rel deliberate, measured; inactive, inert, lethargic, loafing, lounging; lingering, loitering, tarrying; ambling, inching, plodding, shuffling, strolling; decelerating, slowing; filibustering, procrastinating, stalling
near ant expeditious, prompt, ready; accelerated, hastened, quickened; hurried, rushed
ant barreling, bolting, breakneck, breathless, brisk, careering, dizzy, fast, fleet, flying, hasty, hurrying, lightning, quick, racing, rapid, rocketing, running, rushing, scooting, scudding, scurrying, snappy, speeding, speedy, swift, whirling, whirlwind, whisking, zipping
2 not having or showing an ability to absorb ideas readily — see STUPID 1

slow *adv* at a pace that is less than usual, desirable, or expected ⟨you need to go *slow* with this experiment, or you'll make mistakes⟩
syn laggardly, leisurely, slowly, sluggishly, tardily
rel carefully, cautiously, deliberately, purposefully; ploddingly
near ant immediately, posthaste, presto, promptly, pronto, readily, soon; impetuously, impulsively, rashly, recklessly; abruptly, suddenly
ant apace, briskly, fast, fleetly, full tilt, hastily, quick, quickly, rapidly, snappily, speedily, swift, swiftly

slow *vb* to cause to move or proceed at a less rapid pace ⟨if you don't *slow* your delivery down a bit, your speech will be over too soon⟩
syn brake, decelerate, retard
rel halt, stop; encumber, hamper, handicap, hinder, hobble, hold back, hold up, impede, inhibit, obstruct, tie up; arrest, check, constrain, curb, rein, restrain; baffle, foil, frustrate, sabotage, thwart
near ant drive, encourage, goad, propel, push, spur, stir, urge; advance, aid, dispatch, ease, expedite, facilitate, forward, further, help
ant accelerate, hasten, hurry, quicken, rush, speed (up), step up

slowdown *n* a usually gradual decrease in the pace or level of activity of something ⟨disease experts are encouraged by the recent *slowdown* in the spread of the virus⟩
syn braking, deceleration, letup, retardation, retarding
rel decline, drop, slump; ebb, remission, retreat, wane; flagging, weakening; arrest, check, halt, stoppage; collapse, crash, fall, plunge
ant acceleration, hastening, quickening

slowly *adv* at a pace that is less than usual, desirable, or expected — see SLOW

slowness *n* the quality or state of lacking intelligence or quickness of mind — see STUPIDITY 1

slowpoke *n* someone who moves slowly or more slowly than others ⟨quit being such a *slowpoke* this morning, or you'll be late⟩

---

syn crawler, creeper, dallier, dawdler, dragger, laggard, lagger, lingerer, loiterer, snail, stick-in-the-mud, straggler

rel latecomer; drone, idler, lazybones, loafer, lounger, slouch, slug, sluggard; delayer, procrastinator

near ant go-getter, hustler, scrambler; hurrier, rusher, speeder

ant speedster

sludge *n* soft wet earth — see MUD

sludgy *adj* full of or covered with soft wet earth — see MUDDY 1

¹**slug** *n* a hard strike with a part of the body or an instrument — see ¹BLOW

²**slug** *n* 1 a lazy person — see LAZYBONES

2 the portion of a serving of a beverage that is swallowed at one time — see DRINK 2

slug *vb* to deliver a blow to (someone or something) usually in a strong vigorous manner — see HIT 1

sluggard *n* a lazy person — see LAZY-BONES

sluggish *adj* 1 moving or proceeding at less than the normal, desirable, or required speed — see SLOW 1

2 slow to move or act — see INACTIVE 1

sluggishly *adv* at a pace that is less than usual, desirable, or expected — see SLOW

sluice *vb* to pour liquid over or through in order to cleanse — see FLUSH 1

slumber *n* a natural periodic loss of consciousness during which the body restores itself — see SLEEP 1

slumber *vb* 1 be in a state of sleep — see SLEEP 1

2 to sleep lightly or briefly — see NAP 1

slumberer *n* one who sleeps — see SLEEP-ER

slumbering *adj* being in a state of suspended consciousness — see ASLEEP 1

slumbering *n* a natural periodic loss of consciousness during which the body restores itself — see SLEEP 1

slumberous *or* **slumbrous** *adj* 1 desiring or needing sleep — see SLEEPY 1

2 tending to cause sleep — see HYPNOTIC

slump *n* a period of decreased economic activity — see DEPRESSION 1

slur *n* an act or expression showing scorn and usually intended to hurt another's feelings — see INSULT

slur (over) *vb* to fail to give proper attention to — see NEGLECT 1

slurp *vb* to swallow in liquid form — see DRINK 1

slush *n* 1 language, behavior, or ideas that are absurd and contrary to good sense — see NONSENSE 1

2 soft wet earth — see MUD

slushy *adj* full of or covered with soft wet earth — see MUDDY 1

sly *adj* 1 clever at attaining one's ends by indirect and often deceptive means — see ARTFUL 1

2 given to acting in secret and to concealing one's intentions — see SNEAKY 1

3 tending to or exhibiting reckless playfulness — see MISCHIEVOUS 1

slyness *n* skill in achieving one's ends through indirect, subtle, or underhanded means — see CUNNING 1

smack *n* a hard strike with a part of the body or an instrument — see ¹BLOW

smack *vb* to deliver a blow to (someone or something) usually in a strong vigorous manner — see HIT 1

smack–dab *adv* as stated or indicated without the slightest difference — see EX-ACTLY 1

small *adj* 1 of a size that is less than average ⟨a *small* cat who never weighed more than five pounds⟩

syn bantam, diminutive, dinky, dwarf, dwarfish, fine, little, pint-size (*or* pint-sized), pocket, pocket-size (*also* pocket-sized), puny, pygmy, slight, smallish, undersized

rel petite; scrubby, stunted; bitty, inappreciable, infinitesimal, micro, microscopic (*also* microscopical), midget, miniature, miniaturized, minute, teeny, teeny-weeny, tiny, wee; underweight; meager (*or* meagre), niggardly, poor, scant, scanty, scarce, skimpy, slender, slim, spare, sparse, stingy; deficient, inadequate, insufficient, lacking, wanting

near ant bulky, hefty, hulking, massive, voluminous; cavernous, colossal, elephantine, enormous, giant, gigantic, gross, Herculean, heroic, huge, immense, jumbo, mammoth, monolithic, monstrous, monumental, prodigious, staggering, stupendous, tremendous, vast; abundant, ample, appreciable, bountiful, copious, generous, healthy, liberal, plenteous, plentiful; fat, thick; broad, wide; boundless, cosmic, immeasurable, infinite; adequate, enough, sufficient

ant big, bumper, considerable, goodly, good-sized, grand, great, handsome, king-size (*or* king-sized), large, largish, outsize (*also* outsized), oversize (*or* oversized), sizable (*or* sizeable), substantial, super, whacking, whopping

2 small in degree — see REMOTE 1

3 lacking importance — see UNIMPOR-TANT

4 not broad or open in views or opinions — see NARROW 2

small arm *n* a portable weapon from which a shot is discharged by gunpowder — see GUN 1

smaller *adj* having not so great importance or rank as another — see LESSER

small–fry *adj* lacking importance — see UNIMPORTANT

smallish *adj* of a size that is less than average — see SMALL 1

small–minded *adj* 1 unwilling to grant other people social rights or to accept other viewpoints — see INTOLERANT 2

2 not broad or open in views or opinions — see NARROW 2

smallness *n* the quality or state of being little in size ⟨my grandmother was surprised by the *smallness* of the latest electronic devices⟩

syn diminutiveness, fineness, littleness, puniness, slightness

rel minuteness, tininess; meagerness, poorness, scantiness, scarceness, scarcity, skimpiness, slenderness, slimness, spareness, sparseness, stinginess; deficiency, inadequacy

near ant enormity, enormousness, grossness, hugeness, immenseness, immensity, stupendousness; extensiveness, vastness; excessiveness, extravagance, extremeness, immoderacy; abundance, ampleness, bountifulness, copiousness, healthiness, liberality; adequacy, sufficiency; heaviness, heftiness, weightiness; bulkiness, massiveness, voluminousness

ant bigness, grandness, greatness, largeness, magnitude

small talk *n* friendly, informal conversation or an instance of this — see CHAT

smart *adj* **1** being strikingly neat and trim in style or appearance ⟨dressed in their *smart* new uniforms, the cadets proudly paraded around the grounds of the military school⟩

syn dapper, natty, sharp, spruce

rel dressy, elegant, formal; neat, orderly, tidy; fashionable, modish, stylish; careful, fastidious, fussy, meticulous; clean, immaculate, spotless

near ant messy, untidy; shabby, sleazy; dingy, dirty, filthy, foul, grimy, grubby, nasty; dowdy, inelegant, unfashionable, unstylish

ant sloppy, slovenly

2 being in the latest or current fashion — see STYLISH

3 causing intense mental or physical distress — see SHARP 2

4 given to or marked by mature intelligent humor — see WITTY

5 making light of something usually regarded as serious or sacred — see FLIPPANT

6 having or showing a practical cleverness or judgment — see SHREWD

7 having or showing quickness of mind — see INTELLIGENT 1

8 having a wide and refined knowledge of the world especially from personal experience — see WORLDLY-WISE

smart *n* a sharp unpleasant sensation usually felt in some specific part of the body — see PAIN 1

smart *vb* to feel or cause physical pain — see HURT 1

smart aleck *n* a person who likes to show off in a clever but annoying way ⟨some *smart aleck* in the audience kept shouting clever insults at the speaker⟩

syn smarty (*or* smartie), wiseacre, wise guy

rel know-it-all; wisecracker; hotshot, show-off

smart-alecky *or* **smart-aleck** *adj* **1** making light of something usually regarded as serious or sacred — see FLIPPANT

2 marked by the use of wit that is intended to cause hurt feelings — see SARCASTIC

smarting *adj* **1** causing intense discomfort to one's skin — see CUTTING 1

2 causing intense mental or physical distress — see SHARP 2

smartly *adv* in a strikingly neat and trim manner ⟨the *smartly* dressed scouts marched at the head of the Memorial Day parade⟩

syn dashingly, nattily, sharply, sprucely

rel neatly, orderly, tidily, trimly; elegantly, fashionably, modishly, stylishly, swankily; carefully, fastidiously, fussily, meticulously; cleanly, immaculately, spotlessly

near ant dowdily, inelegantly, unstylishly; slatternly; messily, untidily; shabbily, sleazily; dingily, dirtily, filthily, foully, grubbily, nastily

ant sloppily, slovenly

smarty *or* **smartie** *n* a person who likes to show off in a clever but annoying way — see SMART ALECK

smash *n* **1** a forceful coming together of two things — see IMPACT 1

2 the violent coming together of two bodies into destructive contact — see CRASH 1

3 a hard strike with a part of the body or an instrument — see ¹BLOW

4 a loud explosive sound — see CLAP 1

5 a person or thing that is successful — see HIT 1

smash *vb* **1** to cause to break with violence and much noise ⟨deliberately *smashed* a glass against the brick fireplace⟩

syn crash, shatter

rel bust, fracture, fragment; bash, demolish, destroy, pulverize, ruin, wreck; shiver, splinter, split; crack, crunch, crush, snap

2 to cause to break open or into pieces by or as if by an explosive — see BLAST 1

3 to bring to a complete end the physical soundness, existence, or usefulness of — see DESTROY 1

4 to come into usually forceful contact with something — see HIT 2

smashup *n* the violent coming together of two bodies into destructive contact — see CRASH 1

smattering *n* a small number — see FEW

smear *vb* **1** to rub an oily or sticky substance over ⟨the toddler gleefully *smeared* her hair and face with maple syrup⟩

syn anoint, bedaub, besmear, daub

rel coat, paint, plaster; grease, oil; gum, lard, pitch, tar; begrime, besmirch, blacken, dirty, foul, grime, mire, muddy, smirch, smudge, soil, stain, sully

2 to make untrue and harmful statements about — see SLANDER

smearing *n* the making of false statements that damage another's reputation — see SLANDER

smell *n* the quality of a thing that makes it perceptible to the sense organs in the

---

syn synonym(s)　　*rel* related words
ant antonym(s)　　*near ant* near antonym(s)

nose ⟨the *smell* of vanilla is supposed to be very soothing⟩

syn odor, redolence, scent, sniff

rel whiff; aroma, bouquet, fragrance, perfume; ambrosia, lusciousness, savor, savoriness, spice, tang; acridness, fetidness, foulness, noisomeness, rancidity, rankness, stench, stink; incense, musk

smell vb **1** to become aware of by means of the sense organs in the nose ⟨we *smelled* the aroma of freshly baked cookies as soon as we walked in the house⟩

syn nose, scent, sniff, whiff

rel breathe, drink (in), inhale

2 to have a vague awareness of — see FEEL 1

smelly adj having an unpleasant smell — see MALODOROUS

smidgen also **smidgeon** or **smidgin** n a very small amount — see PARTICLE 1

smile vb **1** to express an emotion (as amusement) by curving the lips upward ⟨he *smiled* in pleasure when he saw the giant sign welcoming him home⟩

syn beam, grin

rel laugh, simper; smirk, sneer

near ant grimace; frown, glare, glower, scowl

2 to express scornful amusement by means of facial contortions — see SNEER

smirch n a mark of guilt or disgrace — see STAIN 1

smirch vb **1** to make dirty — see DIRTY

2 to reduce to a lower standing in one's own eyes or in others' eyes — see HUMBLE

smite vb to deliver a blow to (someone or something) usually in a strong vigorous manner — see HIT 1

smog n an atmospheric condition in which suspended particles in the air rob it of its transparency — see HAZE 1

smoggy adj filled with or dimmed by fine particles (as of dust or water) in suspension — see HAZY 1

smooch vb to touch one another with the lips as a sign of love — see KISS 1

smooth adj **1** having or showing very polished and worldly manners — see SUAVE

2 involving minimal difficulty or effort — see EASY 1

3 having a surface without bends, breaks, or irregularities — see LEVEL

smooth vb **1** to free from obstruction or difficulty — see EASE 1

2 to make free from breaks, curves, or bumps — see EVEN 1

3 to make smooth or glossy usually by repeatedly applying surface pressure — see POLISH

smoothly adv without difficulty — see EASILY

smother vb **1** to be or cause to be killed by lack of breathable air ⟨you should never play inside discarded appliances because you could become trapped and *smother*⟩

syn choke, stifle, strangle, suffocate

rel garrote (or garotte), throttle; asphyxiate; drown

near ant breathe, exhale, expire, inhale, inspire

2 to refrain from openly showing or uttering — see SUPPRESS 2

smudge vb to make dirty — see DIRTY

smug adj having too high an opinion of oneself — see CONCEITED

smugness n an often unjustified feeling of being pleased with oneself or with one's situation or achievements — see COMPLACENCE

smut n foul matter that mars the purity or cleanliness of something — see FILTH 1

smuttiness n the quality or state of being obscene — see OBSCENITY 1

smutty adj **1** depicting or referring to sexual matters in a way that is unacceptable in polite society — see OBSCENE 1

2 not clean — see DIRTY 1

snag n a danger or difficulty that is hidden or not easily recognized — see PITFALL 1

snail n someone who moves slowly or more slowly than others — see SLOWPOKE

snake n **1** a limbless reptile with a long body ⟨*snakes* are cold-blooded, so they regulate their body temperature by alternately basking in sunlight and seeking shade⟩

syn serpent, viper

rel adder, anaconda, asp, blacksnake, boa, bull snake, bushmaster, cobra, constrictor, copperhead, coral snake, cottonmouth moccasin, diamondback rattlesnake, fer-de-lance, garter snake, glass snake, gopher snake, green snake, hognose snake, indigo snake, king cobra, king snake, krait, mamba, milk snake, pit viper, puff adder, python, racer, rat snake, rattlesnake, sea serpent, sidewinder, water moccasin, water snake

2 a person whose behavior is offensive to others — see JERK 1

snake vb **1** to move about in a sly or secret manner — see SNEAK 1

2 to move slowly with the body close to the ground — see CRAWL 1

snap adj **1** involving minimal difficulty or effort — see EASY 1

2 made or done without previous thought or preparation — see EXTEMPORANEOUS

snap n **1** a loud explosive sound — see CLAP 1

2 a picture created from an image recorded on a light-sensitive surface by a camera — see PHOTOGRAPH

3 active strength of body or mind — see VIGOR 1

4 a weather condition marked by low temperatures — see COLD

5 a very small amount — see PARTICLE 1

6 something that is easy to do — see CINCH

snap vb **1** to speak sharply or irritably ⟨the shopkeeper finally *snapped* at one customer who couldn't seem to make up his mind⟩

syn bark, snarl

rel shout, yell; blow up, explode

2 to break suddenly with an explosive sound — see CRACK 1

3 to take a photograph of — see PHOTOGRAPH

snap (up) *vb* to take physical control or posses-sion of (something) suddenly or forcibly — see CATCH 1

snapback *n* the process or period of gradually regaining one's health and strength — see CONVALESCENCE

snap back *vb* **1** to become healthy and strong again after illness or weakness — see CONVALESCE

2 to regain a former or normal state — see RECOVER 2

snappily *adv* with great speed — see FAST 1

snappish *adj* easily irritated or annoyed — see IRRITABLE

snappy *adj* **1** being in the latest or current fashion — see STYLISH

2 easily irritated or annoyed — see IRRITABLE

3 having a low or subnormal temperature — see COLD 1

4 having much high-spirited energy and movement — see LIVELY 1

5 moving, proceeding, or acting with great speed — see FAST 1

snapshot *n* a picture created from an image recorded on a light-sensitive surface by a camera — see PHOTOGRAPH

snare *n* **1** a device or scheme for capturing another by surprise — see TRAP 1

2 something that catches and holds — see WEB 1

snare *vb* **1** to catch or hold as if in a net — see ENTANGLE 2

2 to take physical control or possession of (something) suddenly or forcibly — see CATCH 1

¹snarl *vb* to speak sharply or irritably — see SNAP 1

²snarl *vb* to twist together into a usually confused mass — see ENTANGLE 1

snatch *vb* to take physical control or possession of (something) suddenly or forcibly — see CATCH 1

snatching *n* an instance of theft — see THEFT 2

snazzy *adj* attractively eye-catching in style — see JAZZY 1

sneak *adj* undertaken or done so as to escape being observed or known by others — see SECRET 1

sneak *n* someone who acts in a sly and secret manner ⟨"Why, you little *sneak*," Mom exclaimed, "you made my birthday present right under my nose!"⟩
syn lurker, skulker
rel skunk, snake; sharper, slicker, swindler; stalker

sneak *vb* **1** to move about in a sly or secret manner ⟨the little kids *sneak* around upstairs when they're supposed to be in bed⟩

syn lurk, mouse, pussyfoot, skulk, slide, slink, slip, snake, steal
rel crawl, creep, edge, inch, worm; pad, tiptoe

2 to introduce in a gradual, secret, or clever way — see INSINUATE

sneakiness *n* skill in achieving one's ends through indirect, subtle, or underhanded means — see CUNNING 1

sneaking *adj* **1** given to acting in secret and to concealing one's intentions — see SNEAKY 1

2 undertaken or done so as to escape being observed or known by others — see SECRET 1

sneaky *adj* **1** given to acting in secret and to concealing one's intentions ⟨the *sneaky* little girl was clearly up to something⟩
syn furtive, shady, shifty, slippery, sly, sneaking, stealthy
rel devious, guileful; close, close-mouthed, reticent, secretive; clandestine, covert, dark; deceitful, deceiving, deceptive, tricky, underhand, underhanded; crooked, dishonest, double-dealing, two-faced; lying, mendacious, untrustworthy, untruthful; insidious, perfidious, treacherous
near ant aboveboard, forthright, straightforward; candid, frank, open, plain; honest, trustworthy, truthful

2 undertaken or done so as to escape being observed or known by others — see SECRET 1

sneer *vb* to express scornful amusement by means of facial contortions ⟨the most popular girl in school *sneered* every time she saw the "nerds"⟩
syn laugh, smile, snicker, snigger
rel sniff, snort; catcall, hoot, insult, jeer, mock, ridicule; decry, despise, disdain; scorn

snicker *n* an explosive sound that is a sign of amusement — see LAUGH 1

snicker *vb* to express scornful amusement by means of facial contortions — see SNEER

snide *adj* not following or in accordance with standards of honor and decency — see IGNOBLE 2

sniff *n* the quality of a thing that makes it perceptible to the sense organs in the nose — see SMELL

sniff *vb* to become aware of by means of the sense organs in the nose — see SMELL 1

sniff (at) *vb* to show contempt for — see SCORN 1

snigger *n* an explosive sound that is a sign of amusement — see LAUGH 1

snigger *vb* to express scornful amusement by means of facial contortions — see SNEER

snip *vb* to make (as hair) shorter with or as if with the use of shears — see CLIP

snippet *n* a very small piece — see BIT 1

snippy *adj* **1** being or characterized by direct, brief, and potentially rude speech or manner — see BLUNT 1

---

syn synonym(s) *rel* related words
ant antonym(s) *near ant* near antonym(s)

2 easily irritated or annoyed — see IRRITABLE

¹**snitch** vb to give information (as to the authorities) about another's improper or unlawful activities — see SQUEAL 1

²**snitch** vb to take (something) without right and with an intent to keep — see STEAL 1

snitcher n a person who provides secret information about another's wrongdoing — see INFORMER

snoop vb to interest oneself in what is not one's concern — see INTERFERE

snoopy adj **1** interested in what is not one's own business — see CURIOUS 1

2 thrusting oneself where one is not welcome or invited — see INTRUSIVE

snooze n a short sleep — see NAP

snooze vb **1** be in a state of sleep — see SLEEP 1

2 to sleep lightly or briefly — see ¹NAP 1

snoozing n a natural periodic loss of consciousness during which the body restores itself — see SLEEP 1

snort n **1** a vocal sound made to express scorn or disapproval — see CATCALL

2 the portion of a serving of a beverage that is swallowed at one time — see DRINK 2

snow vb to cause to believe what is untrue — see DECEIVE

snowball vb to become greater in extent, volume, amount, or number — see INCREASE 2

snow under vb **1** to defeat by a large margin — see WHIP 2

2 to subject to incapacitating emotional or mental stress — see OVERWHELM 1

snub n treatment that is deliberately unfriendly — see COLD SHOULDER

snub vb **1** to deliberately ignore or treat rudely ⟨the snob in town always *snubbed* anyone she thought was beneath her⟩

syn cold-shoulder, cut, slight

rel ostracize; brush (aside *or* off), disdain, rebuff, reject, repulse; disregard, forget, neglect, overlook, overpass, pass over, shrug off

2 to show contempt for — see SCORN 1

snuff (out) vb **1** to cause to cease burning — see EXTINGUISH 1

2 to destroy all traces of — see ANNIHILATE 1

3 to put a stop to (something) by the use of force — see QUELL 1

snug adj **1** being clean and in good order — see NEAT 1

2 providing physical comfort — see COMFORTABLE 1

3 enjoying physical comfort — see COMFORTABLE 2

4 firmly positioned in place and difficult to dislodge — see TIGHT 2

5 providing safety — see SAFE 2

snug vb to sit or recline comfortably or cozily — see SNUGGLE 1

snuggle vb **1** to sit or recline comfortably or cozily ⟨it's particularly nice to *snuggle* next to the fire on a snowy day⟩

syn cuddle, curl up, nestle, snug

rel huddle

2 to lie close — see NUZZLE

so adj being in agreement with the truth or a fact or a standard — see CORRECT 1

so adv **1** for this or that reason — see THEREFORE

2 in like manner — see ALSO 1

3 to a great degree — see VERY 1

soak n a person who makes a habit of getting drunk — see DRUNK 1

soak vb **1** to wet thoroughly with liquid ⟨we ran for home as soon as the rain started, but our clothes still ended up *soaked*⟩

syn drench, drown, impregnate, saturate, sop, souse, steep

rel marinate; presoak; dip, immerse, inundate, submerge; bathe, douse, wash, water, wet; infiltrate, penetrate, permeate

near ant dehydrate, dry; drain, empty, void

ant wring (out)

2 to charge (someone) too much for goods or services — see OVERCHARGE 1

3 to make wet — see WET

soak (up) vb to take in (something liquid) through small openings — see ABSORB 1

soaked adj containing, covered with, or thoroughly penetrated by water — see WET

soaking adj containing, covered with, or thoroughly penetrated by water — see WET

soap n a substance used for cleaning — see CLEANER

soar n the act or an instance of rising or climbing up — see ASCENT 1

soar vb **1** to move or extend upward — see ASCEND

2 to move through the air with or as if with outstretched wings — see FLY 1

3 to rise abruptly and rapidly — see SKYROCKET

sob vb to shed tears often while making meaningless sounds as a sign of pain or distress — see CRY 1

sober adj **1** not having one's mind affected by alcohol ⟨it's important to stay *sober* if you're going to be driving a car⟩

syn clearheaded, straight

rel abstemious, abstinent, dry, temperate

near ant alcoholic

ant befuddled, dissipated, drunk, drunken, high, inebriate, inebriated, intoxicated, loaded [*slang*], soused, tipsy

2 based on sound reasoning or information — see GOOD 1

3 not joking or playful in mood or manner — see SERIOUS 1

soberness n a mental state free of jesting or trifling — see EARNESTNESS

sobriety n a mental state free of jesting or trifling — see EARNESTNESS

sobriquet also **soubriquet** n a descriptive or familiar name given instead of or in addition to the one belonging to an individual — see NICKNAME

sociability n the quality or state of being social ⟨her *sociability* was called into question when she said she hated parties⟩

syn conviviality, gregariousness

rel amiability, friendliness, neighborliness; camaraderie, companionship, fellowship; boldness, brashness, extroversion (*or* extraversion), forwardness, immodesty

near ant bashfulness, coyness, diffidence, shyness, timidity, timidness; introversion; modesty

sociable *adj* **1** likely to seek or enjoy the company of others — see CONVIVIAL

2 showing a natural kindness and courtesy especially in social situations — see GRACIOUS 1

social *adj* likely to seek or enjoy the company of others — see CONVIVIAL

socialize *vb* to take part in social activities ⟨he likes to *socialize* with his coworkers after work ends⟩

syn associate, fraternize, hobnob, mingle, mix

phrases rub elbows, rub shoulders

near ant avoid, eschew, shun; slight, snub

society *n* **1** a group of persons formally joined together for some common interest — see ASSOCIATION 2

2 human beings in general — see PEOPLE 1

3 the feeling of closeness and friendship that exists between companions — see COMPANIONSHIP

4 the way people live at a particular time and place — see CIVILIZATION 1

sock *n* **1** a close-fitting covering for the foot and leg — see STOCKING

2 a hard strike with a part of the body or an instrument — see ¹BLOW

sock *vb* to deliver a blow to (someone or something) usually in a strong vigorous manner — see HIT 1

sod *n* the land of one's birth, residence, or citizenship — see COUNTRY 1

sodality *n* a group of persons formally joined together for some common interest — see ASSOCIATION 2

sodden *adj* containing, covered with, or thoroughly penetrated by water — see WET

sofa *n* a long upholstered piece of furniture designed for several sitters — see COUCH

soft *adj* **1** not loud in pitch or volume ⟨*soft* music played in the background while we ate⟩

syn dull, low, quiet

rel dead, silent, still; dreamy, peaceful, restful, soothing, tranquil; muffled, muted, softened, toned (down)

near ant brazen, dinning, discordant, noisy, obstreperous, raucous, rip-roaring, vociferous; grating, harsh, shrill, strident

ant blaring, blasting, booming, clamorous, clangorous, deafening, earsplitting, loud, piercing, resounding, ringing, roaring, sonorous, stentorian, thunderous

2 smooth or delicate in appearance or feel ⟨I like this sweater the best because it is so *soft* and comfortable⟩

syn cottony, downy, satin, satiny, silken, silky, velvety

rel creamy; delicate, fine, slick, smooth

near ant bumpy, lumpy, pebbly; broken, jagged, ragged, rugged; grainy, granular, gritty

ant coarse, harsh, rough, scratchy

3 giving easily to the touch ⟨*soft* mattresses make it very easy to fall asleep, but they have a tendency to get lumpy⟩

syn flabby, mushy, pulpy, spongy, squashy, squishy

rel unhardened; doughy, fleshy; droopy, flaccid, floppy, lank, limp, slack, yielding; compressible, malleable, pliable, pliant, workable

near ant inflexible, resilient, rigid, stiff, tense; resistant, sound, strong, sturdy, tough, unyielding; hardened, indurated, tempered

ant firm, hard, solid

4 involving minimal difficulty or effort — see EASY 1

5 lacking bodily strength — see WEAK 1

6 lacking strength of will or character — see WEAK 2

7 not harsh or stern especially in manner, nature, or effect — see GENTLE 1

8 providing physical comfort — see COMFORTABLE 1

soften *vb* **1** to diminish the physical strength of — see WEAKEN 1

2 to lessen the shock of — see CUSHION

softened *adj* lacking bodily strength — see WEAK 1

softhearted *adj* having or marked by sympathy and consideration for others — see HUMANE 1

softheartedness *n* the capacity for feeling for another's unhappiness or misfortune — see HEART 1

softness *n* the quality or state of lacking strength of will or character — see WEAKNESS 2

soft-soap *vb* **1** to get (someone) to do something by gentle urging, special attention, or flattery — see COAX

2 to praise too much — see FLATTER 1

soft soap *n* excessive praise — see FLATTERY

softy *or* **softie** *n* a person lacking in physical strength — see WEAKLING 1

soggy *adj* containing, covered with, or thoroughly penetrated by water — see WET

soil *n* **1** foul matter that mars the purity or cleanliness of something — see FILTH 1

2 the loose surface material in which plants naturally grow — see DIRT 1

3 the solid part of our planet's surface as distinguished from the sea and air — see EARTH 2

soil *vb* to make dirty — see DIRTY 1

soiled *adj* not clean — see DIRTY 1

sojourn *n* a temporary residing as another's guest — see VISIT 1

sojourn *vb* to reside as a temporary guest — see VISIT 2

solace *n* 1 a feeling of ease from grief or trouble — see COMFORT 1

2 the giving of hope and strength in times of grief, distress, or suffering — see CONSOLATION 1

solace *vb* to ease the grief or distress of — see COMFORT 1

solacing *n* the giving of hope and strength in times of grief, distress, or suffering — see CONSOLATION 1

solar plexus *n* the part of the body between the chest and the pelvis — see STOMACH

soldier *n* a person engaged in military service ⟨one of the goals of war is to keep as many *soldiers* as possible from being killed⟩

syn fighter, legionary, legionnaire, man-at-arms, regular, serviceman, warrior

rel servicewoman; cavalier, cuirassier, dragoon, trooper; dogface, doughboy, footman, foot soldier, infantryman; commando, marine, ranger; artilleryman, musketeer, rifleman; archer, lancer, spearman; Confederate, Continental, Federal, GI, guardsman, Rough Rider; guerilla, irregular, partisan; combatant, noncombatant; mercenary, soldier of fortune; veteran, war-horse; conscript, draftee, recruit; reservist

ant civilian

soldierly *adj* of, relating to, or suitable for war or a warrior — see MARTIAL 1

sole *adj* 1 belonging only to the one person, unit, or group named ⟨the landowner has *sole* rights to the property, so he can do whatever he wants to with it⟩

syn exclusive, single, unshared

rel proprietary

near ant joint, mutual, shared

ant nonexclusive

2 being the one or ones of a class with no other members — see ONLY 2

solecism *n* a socially improper or unsuitable act or remark — see IMPROPRIETY 2

solely *adv* 1 for nothing other than ⟨I fight *solely* for my country, not for money!⟩

syn alone, exclusively, just, only, simply

rel mainly, mostly, primarily

near ant additionally, also, likewise

2 without aid or support — see ALONE 1

solemn *adj* 1 having or showing a serious and reserved manner — see DIGNIFIED

2 not joking or playful in mood or manner — see SERIOUS 1

solemnity *n* 1 a mental state free of jesting or trifling — see EARNESTNESS

2 an oft-repeated action or series of actions performed in accordance with tradition or a set of rules — see RITE

solicit *vb* 1 to go around and approach (people) with a request for opinions or information — see CANVASS

2 to make a request for — see ASK (FOR) 1

3 to make a request of — see ASK 2

4 to make a request to (someone) in an earnest or urgent manner — see BEG

solicitation *n* an earnest request — see PLEA 1

soliciting *adj* asking humbly — see SUPPLIANT

solicitor *n* 1 one that tries to get a person to give in to a desire — see TEMPTER

2 one who asks earnestly for a favor or gift — see SUPPLICANT

solicitous *adj* 1 given to or made with heedful anticipation of the needs and happiness of others — see THOUGHTFUL 1

2 showing urgent desire or interest — see EAGER

solicitude *n* an uneasy state of mind usually over the possibility of an anticipated misfortune or trouble — see ANXIETY 1

solid *adj* 1 based on sound reasoning or information — see GOOD 1

2 having a consistency that does not easily yield to pressure — see FIRM 2

3 having or consisting of a single color — see MONOCHROMATIC

4 not showing weakness or uncertainty — see FIRM 1

5 worthy of one's trust — see DEPENDABLE

solidify *vb* 1 to become physically firm or solid — see HARDEN 1

2 to take on a definite form — see FORM 1

solidity *n* worthiness as the recipient of another's trust or confidence — see RELIABILITY

solidness *n* worthiness as the recipient of another's trust or confidence — see RELIABILITY

solitariness *n* the state of being alone or kept apart from others — see ISOLATION

solitary *adj* 1 being the one or ones of a class with no other members — see ONLY 2

2 not being in the company of others — see ALONE 1

solitary *n* a person who lives away from others — see RECLUSE

solitude *n* the state of being alone or kept apart from others — see ISOLATION

solo *adj* not being in the company of others — see ALONE 1

solon *n* a member of an organized body of persons having the authority to make laws — see LEGISLATOR

soluble *adj* capable of having the reason for or cause of determined — see SOLVABLE

solution *n* something attained by mental effort and especially by computation — see ANSWER 2

solvable *adj* capable of having the reason for or cause of determined ⟨I'm sure that the mystery of what happened to the missing pizza is *solvable*⟩

syn answerable, explainable, explicable, resolvable, soluble

rel analyzable, decipherable; feasible, workable

near ant impossible

ant inexplicable, insoluble, unexplainable, unsolvable

solve *vb* to find an answer for through reasoning ⟨it took me half an hour to *solve* the logic puzzle⟩
syn answer, break, crack, dope (out), figure out, puzzle (out), resolve, riddle, unravel, work, work out
rel clear (up), iron out, straighten (out), unscramble, untangle, untie; divine, guess; decipher, decode

somatic *adj* of or relating to the human body — see PHYSICAL 1

somber *or* **sombre** *adj* 1 being without light or without much light — see DARK 1
2 causing or marked by an atmosphere lacking in cheer — see GLOOMY 1

some *adj* known but not named — see CERTAIN 1

some *adv* very close to but not completely — see ALMOST

somebody *n* a person who is widely known and usually much talked about — see CELEBRITY 1

someday *adv* at a later time — see YET 1

something *adv* 1 to a great degree — see VERY 1
2 to some degree or extent — see FAIRLY

something *n* one that has a real and independent existence — see ENTITY

sometime *adj* having been such at some previous time — see FORMER

sometime *adv* at a later time — see YET 1

sometimes *adv* on some occasions ⟨*sometimes* I like to go skiing, and *sometimes* I prefer to stay inside where it's warm⟩
syn now, occasionally
rel intermittently, periodically; infrequently, rarely, seldom; irregularly, sporadically
phrases at times, from time to time, now and then, once in a while
near ant frequently, often, oftentimes (*or* ofttimes); commonly, ordinarily, regularly, usually; always, constantly, invariably; continually, continuously, incessantly, perpetually, unceasingly, uninterruptedly; endlessly, ever, interminably

somewhat *adv* to some degree or extent — see FAIRLY

somnolence *n* the quality or state of desiring or needing sleep — see SLEEPINESS

somnolent *adj* desiring or needing sleep — see SLEEPY 1

song *n* 1 a short musical composition for the human voice often with instrumental accompaniment ⟨she sang a short *song* for the talent show⟩
syn ballad, ditty, jingle, lay, lyric, vocal
rel anthem, canticle, carol, chorale, hymn, noel, psalm, spiritual; dirge, lament, requiem, threnody; hallelujah, paean; aria, barcarole (*or* barcarolle), blues, cantata, chantey (*or* chanty), chorus, croon, descant, glee, lullaby, madrigal, motet, part-song, pop, rocker, round, roundelay, serenade, troll

2 a composition using rhythm and often rhyme to create a lyrical effect — see POEM
3 a rhythmic series of musical tones arranged to give a pleasing effect — see MELODY
4 a very small sum of money — see MITE 1
5 writing that uses rhythm, vivid language, and often rhyme to provoke an emotional response — see POETRY 1

songster *n* one who sings — see SINGER

songwriter *n* a person who writes musical compositions — see COMPOSER

sonny *n* a male person who has not yet reached adulthood — see BOY

sonorous *adj* 1 marked by a high volume of sound — see LOUD 1
2 marked by conspicuously full and rich sounds or tones — see RESONANT

soon *adv* 1 at or within a short time — see SHORTLY 2
2 by choice or preference — see RATHER 1
3 with great speed — see FAST 1

soothe *vb* 1 to ease the grief or distress of — see COMFORT 1
2 to free from distress or disturbance — see CALM 1
3 to make more bearable or less severe — see HELP 2

soothing *adj* 1 tending to calm the emotions and relieve stress ⟨the *soothing* music eventually put the entire yoga class in the proper mood⟩
syn calming, comforting, dreamy, lulling, narcotic, pacifying, quieting, relaxing, sedative, tranquilizing (*also* tranquillizing)
rel hypnotic, opiate; anesthetic, deadening, depressant, numbing
near ant energizing, invigorating, stimulant, stimulating; aggravating, annoying, bothersome, exasperating, galling, grating, irksome, irritating, troublesome, vexing
2 not harsh or stern especially in manner, nature, or effect — see GENTLE 1

soothsayer *n* one who predicts future events or developments — see PROPHET

soothsaying *n* a declaration that something will happen in the future — see PREDICTION

sop *n* something given or promised in order to improperly influence a person's conduct or decision — see BRIBE

sop *vb* to wet thoroughly with liquid — see SOAK 1

sophisticate *n* a person with the outlook, experience, and manners thought to be typical of big city dwellers — see COSMOPOLITAN

sophisticate *vb* to make complex or difficult — see COMPLICATE

sophisticated *adj* 1 having a wide and refined knowledge of the world especially from personal experience — see WORLDLY-WISE
2 having many parts or aspects that are usually interrelated — see COMPLEX 1

---

syn synonym(s)   **rel** related words
ant antonym(s)   **near ant** near antonym(s)

3 having or showing very polished and worldly manners — see SUAVE

4 made or done with great care or with much detail — see ELABORATE 1

sophistication *n* the state or quality of having many interrelated parts or aspects — see COMPLEXITY 1

soppy *adj* containing, covered with, or thoroughly penetrated by water — see WET

sorcerer *n* a person skilled in using supernatural forces — see MAGICIAN 1

sorceress *n* a woman believed to have often harmful supernatural powers — see WITCH 1

sorcery *n* the power to control natural forces through supernatural means — see MAGIC 1

sordid *adj* **1** not clean — see DIRTY 1

2 not following or in accordance with standards of honor and decency — see IGNOBLE 2

sore *adj* **1** causing or feeling bodily pain — see PAINFUL 1

2 feeling or showing anger — see ANGRY

3 having or showing deep-seated resentment — see BITTER 1

sorely *adv* with feelings of bitterness or grief — see HARD 2

sorriness *n* deep sadness especially for the loss of someone or something loved — see SORROW

sorrow *n* deep sadness especially for the loss of someone or something loved ⟨he felt great *sorrow* at the loss of his beloved pet⟩

syn affliction, anguish, dolefulness, dolor, grief, heartache, heartbreak, sorriness, woe

rel agony, distress, pain, suffering, torment; blues, dejection, depression, desolateness, desolation, despondency, disconsolateness, dispiritedness, distress, doldrums, downheartedness, dreariness, dumps, forlornness, gloom, gloominess, heartsickness, joylessness, melancholy, miserableness, misery, mopes, oppression, sadness, unhappiness, wretchedness; regret, remorse, rue

near ant gaiety (*also* gayety), gayness, humor, jollity, joviality, lightheartedness, merriment, merrymaking, mirth, mirthfulness; hopefulness, optimism; enjoyment; content, contentedness

ant blessedness, bliss, blissfulness, cheer, cheerfulness, cheeriness, delight, ecstasy, elatedness, elation, euphoria, exhilaration, exuberance, exultation, gladness, gladsomeness, glee, gleefulness, happiness, joy, joyfulness, joyousness, jubilation, pleasure, rapture, rapturousness

sorrow *vb* to feel deep sadness or mental pain — see GRIEVE

sorrowful *adj* **1** expressing or suggesting mourning — see MOURNFUL 1

2 feeling unhappiness — see SAD 1

sorrowfully *adv* with feelings of bitterness or grief — see HARD 2

sorry *adj* **1** arousing or deserving of one's loathing and disgust — see CONTEMPTIBLE 1

2 causing unhappiness — see SAD 2

3 deserving pitying scorn (as for inadequacy) — see PITIFUL 1

4 feeling sorrow for a wrong that one has done — see CONTRITE 1

5 feeling unhappiness — see SAD 1

6 expressing or suggesting mourning — see MOURNING 1

7 deserving of one's pity — see PATHETIC 1

sort *n* **1** a number of persons or things that are grouped together because they have something in common ⟨I prefer jackets with zippers to the *sort* that close with buttons⟩

syn breed, class, description, feather, ilk, kind, like, manner, nature, order, type

rel model; sample, specimen; bracket, category, division, family, grade, group, lot, persuasion, rank(s), set

2 a member of the human race — see HUMAN

sort *vb* to arrange or assign according to type — see CLASSIFY 1

sort of *adv* to some degree or extent — see FAIRLY

so–so *adj* of average to below average quality — see MEDIOCRE 1

so–so *adv* in a satisfactory way — see WELL 1

sot *n* a person who makes a habit of getting drunk — see DRUNK 1

sough *vb* to take in and let out a deep audible breath or to make a similar sound — see SIGH

soul *n* **1** an immaterial force within a human being thought to give the body life, energy, and power ⟨many religions teach that the *soul* is immortal⟩

syn psyche, spirit

rel life, vitality

near ant body, flesh

2 a member of the human race — see HUMAN

3 the quality or qualities that make a thing what it is — see ESSENCE

4 the seat of one's deepest thoughts and emotions — see CORE 1

soulless *adj* having or showing a lack of sympathy or tender feelings — see HARD 1

sound *adj* **1** according to the rules of logic — see LOGICAL 1

2 enjoying health and vigor — see HEALTHY 1

3 marked by the ability to withstand stress without structural damage or distortion — see STABLE 1

sound *n* **1** a narrow body of water between two land masses — see CHANNEL 2

2 range of hearing — see EARSHOT

¹**sound** *vb* **1** to continue or be repeated in a series of reflected sound waves — see REVERBERATE

2 to give the impression of being — see SEEM

3 to make known (as an idea, emotion, or opinion) — see EXPRESS 1

4 to make known openly or publicly — see ANNOUNCE

²**sound** *vb* **1** to measure the depth of (as a body of water) typically with a weighted line ⟨the pilot *sounded* the river to make sure we weren't in any danger of running aground⟩

syn fathom, plumb

rel gauge (*also* gage), measure, scale

2 to cast oneself head first into deep water — see DIVE

soundless *adj* mostly or entirely without sound — see SILENT 3

soundness *n* **1** the ability to withstand force or stress without being distorted, dislodged, or damaged — see STABILITY 1

2 the condition of being sound in body — see HEALTH

sound off *vb* to voice one's opinions freely with force — see SPEAK UP

soup *n* an atmospheric condition in which suspended particles in the air rob it of its transparency — see HAZE 1

soupy *adj* **1** filled with or dimmed by fine particles (as of dust or water) in suspension — see HAZY 1

2 having an overly soft liquid consistency — see RUNNY

sour *adj* **1** causing or characterized by the one of the four basic taste sensations that is produced chiefly by acids ⟨the *sour* candy made our mouths all wrinkly inside⟩

syn acid, acidic, tart, vinegary

rel dry, soured, unsweetened; pungent, sharp, tangy; astringent, puckery; acetic; hyperacid

near ant sweet; bland, smooth

2 not giving pleasure to the mind or senses — see UNPLEASANT

sour *vb* to cause to change from friendly or loving to unfriendly or uncaring — see ESTRANGE

source *n* the beginning part of a stream — see HEADWATER

souring *n* the loss of friendship or affection — see ESTRANGEMENT

souse *n* a person who makes a habit of getting drunk — see DRUNK 1

souse *vb* **1** to make wet — see WET

2 to sink or push (something) briefly into or as if into a liquid — see DIP 1

3 to wet thoroughly with liquid — see SOAK 1

soused *adj* **1** being under the influence of alcohol — see DRUNK

2 containing, covered with, or thoroughly penetrated by water — see WET

souvenir *n* something that serves to keep alive the memory of a person or event — see MEMORIAL

sovereign *adj* **1** coming before all others in importance — see FOREMOST 1

2 not being under the rule or control of another — see FREE 1

sovereign *n* one who rules over a people with a sole, supreme, and usually hereditary authority — see MONARCH

sovereignty *n* **1** the state of being free from the control or power of another — see FREEDOM 1

2 a body of people composed of one or more nationalities usually with its own territory and government — see NATION

sow *vb* **1** to cover by or as if by scattering something over or on — see SCATTER 2

2 to put or set into the ground to grow — see PLANT

spa *n* a building or room used for sports activities and exercising — see GYM

space *n* **1** an extent or area available for or used up by some activity or thing — see ROOM 1

2 an indefinite but usually short period of time — see WHILE 1

space–age *adj* being or involving the latest methods, concepts, information, or styles — see MODERN

spacing *n* the space or amount of space between two points, lines, surfaces, or objects — see DISTANCE

spacious *adj* more than adequate or average in capacity ⟨almost all of the guests were able to fit into the *spacious* living room⟩

syn ample, capacious, commodious, roomy

rel broad, wide; big, bulky, considerable, generous, goodly, good-sized, grand, great, handsome, hefty, hulking, king-size (*or* king-sized), large, largish, outsize (*also* outsized), oversize (*or* oversized), sizable (*or* sizeable), substantial, super, voluminous; enormous, immense, vast; expansive, extended, extensive; boundless, limitless, unbounded

near ant confined, cramped, limited, narrow, restricted; small, snug, tight, tiny

span *vb* to find out the size, extent, or amount of — see MEASURE

spank *n* a hard strike with a part of the body or an instrument — see ¹BLOW

spanking *adj* having much high-spirited energy and movement — see LIVELY 1

spare *adj* **1** being over what is needed ⟨I had some *spare* time to kill, so I cleaned up my room a bit⟩

syn excess, extra, superfluous, supernumerary, surplus

rel accessory, additional, supplemental, supplementary; dispensable, extraneous, gratuitous, needless, nonessential, unessential, unnecessary, unneeded, unwanted

near ant inadequate, insufficient, meager, scant, scanty, scarce, short, sparse

2 giving or sharing as little as possible — see STINGY 1

3 having a noticeably small amount of body fat — see THIN 1

4 less plentiful than what is normal, necessary, or desirable — see MEAGER

spare *n* an interchangeable part or piece of equipment that is kept on hand for replacement of an original ⟨first we took

---

syn synonym(s)   *rel* related words
ant antonym(s)   *near ant* near antonym(s)

the burnt light bulb out, and then we replaced it with the *spare*⟩
syn extra, reserve
rel backup, substitute; stock; copy, double, duplicate, replacement
near ant archetype, original

spare *vb* to use or give out in stingy amounts ⟨I'll have a banana split and don't *spare* the whipped cream⟩
syn scant, skimp (on), stint (on)
rel dole (out), mete (out), portion (out), ration (out); pinch, shortchange
near ant lavish, rain

sparing *adj* 1 careful in the management of money or resources — see FRUGAL
2 giving or sharing as little as possible — see STINGY 1

spark *n* a very small amount — see PARTICLE 1

spark *vb* 1 to give off sparks ⟨the broken radio *sparked* and smoked the instant it was plugged in⟩
syn scintillate, sparkle
rel flash; burn
2 to cause to function — see ACTIVATE

sparkle *vb* 1 to give off sparks — see SPARK 1
2 to shoot forth bursts of light — see FLASH 1

sparky *adj* having much high-spirited energy and movement — see LIVELY 1

sparse *adj* less plentiful than what is normal, necessary, or desirable — see MEAGER

spasm *n* 1 a painful sudden tightening of a muscle — see CRAMP
2 a sudden intense expression of strong feeling — see OUTBURST 1

spasmodic *adj* lacking in steadiness or regularity of occurrence — see FITFUL

spat *n* an often noisy or angry expression of differing opinions — see ARGUMENT 1

spat *vb* to express different opinions about something often angrily — see ARGUE 2

spate *n* a great flow of water or of something that overwhelms — see FLOOD

spatter *vb* 1 to cause (something liquid or mushy) to move along in sheets — see SPLASH 1
2 to wet or soil by striking with something liquid or mushy — see SPLASH 2

spawn *n* the descendants of a person, animal, or plant — see OFFSPRING

spawn *vb* to be the cause of (a situation, action, or state of mind) — see EFFECT

speak *vb* 1 to express (a thought or emotion) in words — see SAY 1
2 to give a formal often extended talk on a subject — see TALK 1

speak (to *or* with) *vb* to communicate with by means of spoken words — see TALK 1

speaker *n* 1 a person in charge of a meeting — see CHAIR 1
2 a person who speaks for another or for a group — see SPOKESPERSON

speak out *vb* to voice one's opinions freely with force — see SPEAK UP

speak up *vb* to voice one's opinions freely with force ⟨she's never been afraid to *speak up* in class⟩

syn sound off, speak out, spout (off)
rel bawl, call, cry, holler, shout, sing (out), vociferate, yell; articulate, enunciate
phrases speak one's mind
near ant hush, suppress; quiet

spear *n* a weapon with a long straight handle and sharp head or blade ⟨the Roman gladiator thrust his *spear* triumphantly into the lion's side⟩
syn javelin, lance, pike, pikestaff, shaft
rel dart, spike; gaff, halberd, harpoon, trident

spear *vb* to penetrate or hold (something) with a pointed object — see IMPALE

spearhead *vb* to serve as leader of — see LEAD 2

special *adj* 1 being the one or ones of a class with no other members — see ONLY 2
2 granted special treatment or attention — see DARLING 1
3 of a particular or exact sort — see EXPRESS 1

speciality *n* something for which a person shows a special talent — see FORTE

specialized *adj* used by or intended for experts in a particular field of knowledge — see TECHNICAL

specialty *n* 1 a region of activity, knowledge, or influence — see FIELD 2
2 something for which a person shows a special talent — see FORTE

species *n* one of the units into which a whole is divided on the basis of a common characteristic — see CLASS 2

specific *adj* 1 of a particular or exact sort — see EXPRESS 1
2 so clearly expressed as to leave no doubt about the meaning — see EXPLICIT

specific *n* a substance or preparation used to treat disease — see MEDICINE

specificity *n* careful thoroughness of detail — see PARTICULARITY 1

specify *vb* 1 to give the rules about (something) clearly and exactly — see PRESCRIBE
2 to make reference to or speak about briefly but specifically — see MENTION 1

specimen *n* 1 a member of the human race — see HUMAN
2 one of a group or collection that shows what the whole is like — see EXAMPLE

specious *adj* tending or having power to deceive — see DECEPTIVE 1

speck *n* 1 a small area that is different (as in color) from the main part — see SPOT 1
2 a very small amount — see PARTICLE 1
3 a very small piece — see BIT 1

speck *vb* to mark with small spots especially unevenly — see SPOT

speckle *n* a small area that is different (as in color) from the main part — see SPOT 1

speckle *vb* to mark with small spots especially unevenly — see SPOT

speckled *adj* marked with spots — see SPOTTED 1

specs *n pl* a pair of lenses set in a frame that is held in place with ear supports and which are usually worn to correct vision — see GLASSES 1

spectacles *n pl* a pair of lenses set in a frame that is held in place with ear supports and which are usually worn to correct vision — see GLASSES 1

specter *or* **spectre** *n* the soul of a dead person thought of especially as appearing to living people — see GHOST

spectrum *n* the distance or extent between possible extremes — see RANGE 3

speculate *vb* to form an opinion from little or no evidence — see GUESS 1

speculation *n* a risky undertaking — see GAMBLE

speculative *adj* existing only as an assumption or speculation — see THEORETICAL 1

speech *n* **1** a usually formal discourse delivered to an audience ⟨the guest of honor gave a short *speech* in appreciation of the award⟩
syn address, declamation, harangue, oration, talk
rel diatribe, rant, tirade; eulogy, panegyric, tribute; keynote address, lecture; homily, sermon; monologue, soliloquy; pitch, presentation, spiel
2 the stock of words, pronunciation, and grammar used by a people as their basic means of communication — see LANGUAGE 1

speechless *adj* **1** deliberately refraining from speech — see SILENT 1
2 unable to speak — see MUTE 1

speechlessness *n* incapacity for or restraint from speaking — see SILENCE 1

speed *n* a high rate of movement or performance ⟨we did our homework with as much *speed* as possible so we could go to the movies⟩
syn celerity, fastness, fleetness, haste, hurry, quickness, rapidity, rapidness, speediness, swiftness, velocity
rel clip, pace, rate, tempo; drive, hustle; acceleration, rush; dispatch, expedition, expeditiousness, promptness
near ant languidness, languor, leisureliness, lethargy, torpor; reluctance; deliberateness, deliberation
ant slowness, sluggishness

speed *vb* to proceed or move quickly — see HURRY 1

speed (**up**) *vb* to cause to move or proceed fast or faster — see HURRY 1

speedboat *n* a boat equipped with a motor — see MOTORBOAT

speedily *adv* with great speed — see FAST 1

speediness *n* a high rate of movement or performance — see SPEED

speedy *adj* moving, proceeding, or acting with great speed — see FAST 1

spell *n* **1** a spoken word or set of words believed to have magic power ⟨the witch cast a *spell* that turned the prince into a toad⟩
syn bewitchment, charm, conjuration, enchantment, incantation
rel curse, hex, jinx; black magic, conjuring, magic, mojo, necromancy, sorcery, voodooism, witchcraft, witchery, wizardry
2 a sudden experiencing of a physical or mental disorder — see ATTACK 2
3 an indefinite but usually short period of time — see WHILE 1

spell *vb* **1** to cast a spell on — see BEWITCH 1
2 to communicate or convey (as an idea) to the mind — see MEAN 1

spellbind *vb* to hold the attention of as if by a spell — see ENTHRALL 1

spellbound *adj* being or appearing to be under a magic spell — see ENCHANTED

spell out *vb* to make plain or understandable — see EXPLAIN 1

spend *vb* **1** to hand over or use up in payment ⟨I always end up *spending* too much money at the mall⟩
syn disburse, expend, give, lay out, pay
rel lavish, rain; blow; squander, waste
near ant cache, hoard, save; acquire, earn, make
2 to make complete use of — see DEPLETE
3 to use up carelessly — see WASTE 1

spender *n* someone who carelessly spends money — see PRODIGAL

spendthrift *adj* given to spending money freely or foolishly — see PRODIGAL

spendthrift *n* someone who carelessly spends money — see PRODIGAL

spent *adj* depleted in strength, energy, or freshness — see WEARY 1

spew *vb* **1** to flow out in great quantities or with force — see GUSH 1
2 to throw out or off (something from within) often violently — see ERUPT 1

sphere *n* **1** a more or less round body or mass — see ¹BALL 1
2 a region of activity, knowledge, or influence — see FIELD 2

spherical *adj* having every part of the surface the same distance from the center — see ROUND 1

spice *n* **1** a sweet or pleasant smell — see FRAGRANCE
2 something (as a spice or herb) that adds an agreeable or interesting taste to food — see SEASONING 1

spice *vb* to make more pleasant to the taste by adding something intensely flavored — see SEASON 1

spick-and-span *or* **spic-and-span** *adj* **1** free from dirt or stain — see CLEAN 1
2 recently made and never used before — see NEW 3

spicy *adj* hinting at or intended to call to mind matters regarded as indecent — see SUGGESTIVE 1

spigot *n* a fixture for controlling the flow of a liquid — see FAUCET

spike *vb* to penetrate or hold (something) with a pointed object — see IMPALE

---

syn synonym(s)   *rel* related words
ant antonym(s)   *near ant* near antonym(s)

spill *n* the act of going down from an upright position suddenly and involuntarily — see FALL 1

spill *vb* to make known (as information previously kept secret) — see REVEAL 1

spin *n* **1** a rapid turning about on an axis or central point ⟨the ice skater moved into a tight *spin* at the end of her routine⟩
syn gyration, pirouette, reel, revolution, roll, rotation, twirl, wheel, whirl
rel circuit, circulation; coil, curl, curve, spiral, twist; circle, orbit; eddy, swirl
2 a state of mental confusion — see HAZE 2

spin *vb* **1** to move in circles around an axis or center ⟨after *spinning* around three times blindfolded, I tried to pin the tail on the donkey and almost fell over⟩
syn gyrate, pirouette, revolve, roll, rotate, turn, twirl, wheel, whirl
rel coil, curl, curve, round, spiral, twine, twist, wind; circle, orbit
2 to be in a confused state as if from being twirled around ⟨my head *spun* as I contemplated all the possible problems this could cause⟩
syn reel, swim, whirl
near ant calm, collect; settle, steady
3 to move (something) in a curved or circular path on or as if on an axis — see TURN 1

spinal column *n* a column of bones supporting the trunk of a vertebrate animal — see SPINE

spindling *adj* being tall, thin and usually loose-jointed — see LANKY

spindly *adj* being tall, thin and usually loose-jointed — see LANKY

spine *n* a column of bones supporting the trunk of a vertebrate animal ⟨he hurt his *spine* in the accident, but the doctor says he'll be walking again in no time⟩
syn backbone, chine, spinal column, vertebral column
rel back, spinal cord, vertebra

spineless *adj* **1** lacking strength of will or character — see WEAK 2
2 having or showing a shameful lack of courage — see COWARDLY

spinelessness *n* **1** the quality or state of lacking strength of will or character — see WEAKNESS 2
2 a shameful lack of courage in the face of danger — see COWARDICE

spin–off *n* something that naturally develops or is developed from something else — see DERIVATIVE

spiny *adj* requiring exceptional skill or caution in performance or handling — see TRICKY

spiral *adj* turning around an axis like the thread of a screw ⟨a *spiral* staircase takes visitors up into the Statue of Liberty⟩
syn coiling, corkscrew, helical, screwlike, winding
rel curving, curling, twisting
near ant lineal, linear, straight

spiral *vb* to follow a circular or spiral course — see WIND

spirit *n* **1** an immaterial force within a human being thought to give the body life, energy, and power — see SOUL 1
2 a state of mind dominated by a particular emotion — see MOOD 1
3 the soul of a dead person thought of especially as appearing to living people — see GHOST
4 spirits *pl* a fermented or distilled beverage that can make a person drunk — see ALCOHOL

spirited *adj* **1** marked by a lively display of strong feeling ⟨the town meeting featured a *spirited* debate about the proposed ban on skateboarding in the plaza downtown⟩
syn fiery, gingery, high-spirited, mettlesome, peppery, spunky
rel animate, animated, bouncing, bouncy, brisk, energetic, frisky, jaunty, jazzy, peppy, perky, pert, racy, snappy, spanking, sparky, sprightly, springy, vital, vivacious, zippy; ardent, fervent, impassioned, passionate
near ant boring, dull, lifeless
ant spiritless
2 having much high-spirited energy and movement — see LIVELY 1

spiritless *adj* lacking bodily energy or motivation — see LISTLESS

spiritual *adj* **1** not composed of matter — see IMMATERIAL 1
2 of, relating to, or used in the practice or worship services of a religion — see RELIGIOUS 1

spiritual *n* a religious song — see HYMN

¹**spit** *n* an area of land that juts out into a body of water — see CAPE

²**spit** *n* **1** something or someone that strongly resembles another — see IMAGE 1
2 the fluid that is secreted into the mouth by certain glands — see SALIVA

spite *n* the desire to cause pain for the satisfaction of doing harm — see MALICE

spiteful *adj* having or showing a desire to cause someone pain or suffering for the sheer enjoyment of it — see HATEFUL

spitefully *adv* in a mean or spiteful manner — see NASTILY

spitefulness *n* the desire to cause pain for the satisfaction of doing harm — see MALICE

spittle *n* the fluid that is secreted into the mouth by certain glands — see SALIVA

spit up *vb* to discharge the contents of the stomach through the mouth — see VOMIT

splash *vb* **1** to cause (something liquid or mushy) to move along in sheets ⟨I always *splash* water at my sister when we go to the pool⟩
syn spatter
rel dabble, lap, plash, wash
2 to wet or soil by striking with something liquid or mushy ⟨the bus *splashed* us as it passed⟩
syn bespatter, dash, plash, spatter, splatter
rel drench, drown, impregnate, saturate, soak, sop, souse, steep; bathe, douse, wash, water, wet; throw; spray; slop, sprinkle; squirt

3 to flow along or against — see WASH 1

4 to flow in a broken irregular stream — see GURGLE

5 to move with a splashing motion — see SLOSH

splashy *adj* **1** likely to attract attention — see NOTICEABLE

2 attractively eye-catching in style — see JAZZY 1

3 excessively showy — see GAUDY

splatter *vb* to wet or soil by striking with something liquid or mushy — see SPLASH 2

spleen *n* **1** an intense emotional state of displeasure with someone or something — see ANGER

2 the desire to cause pain for the satisfaction of doing harm — see MALICE

splendid *adj* **1** large and impressive in size, grandeur, extent, or conception — see GRAND 1

2 of the very best kind — see EXCELLENT

splendidly *adv* in a pleasing way — see WELL 5

splendor *n* **1** impressiveness of beauty on a large scale — see MAGNIFICENCE

2 the quality or state of having or giving off light — see BRILLIANCE 1

splenetic *adj* having or showing a habitually bad temper — see ILL-TEMPERED

splint *n* a small flat piece separated from a whole — see CHIP 1

splinter *n* a small flat piece separated from a whole — see CHIP 1

splinter *vb* to cut into long slender pieces — see SLIVER

split *adj* disagreeing with each other — see DIVIDED

split *n* **1** an irregular usually narrow break in a surface created by pressure — see CRACK 1

2 the act or process of a whole separating into two or more parts or pieces — see SEPARATION 1

split *vb* to set or force apart — see SEPARATE 1

split second *n* a very small space of time — see INSTANT

splotch *n* a small area that is different (as in color) from the main part — see SPOT 1

splotch *vb* to mark with small spots especially unevenly — see SPOT

splotched *adj* having blotches of two or more colors — see PIED

splotchy *adj* marked with spots — see SPOTTED 1

spoil *n* valuables stolen or taken by force — see LOOT

spoil *vb* **1** to affect slightly with something morally bad or undesirable — see TAINT 1

2 to go through decomposition — see DECAY 1

3 to reduce the soundness, effectiveness, or perfection of — see DAMAGE 1

4 to treat with great or excessive care — see BABY

spoilage *n* the process by which dead organic matter separates into simpler substances — see CORRUPTION 1

spoiled *adj* having undergone organic breakdown — see ROTTEN 1

spoilsport *n* a person who spoils the pleasure of others — see KILLJOY

spoken *adj* made or carried on through speaking rather than in writing — see VERBAL 2

spokesman *n* a person who speaks for another or for a group — see SPOKESPERSON

spokesperson *n* a person who speaks for another or for a group ⟨the *spokesperson* for the protesting students presented their demands to the principal⟩
syn mouthpiece, speaker, spokesman
rel spokeswoman; sayer, talker; agent, delegate, deputy, representative

sponge *n* a person who is supported by or seeks support from another without making an adequate return — see LEECH

sponge *vb* to take in (something liquid) through small openings — see ABSORB 1

sponger *n* a person who is supported by or seeks support from another without making an adequate return — see LEECH

spongy *adj* giving easily to the touch — see SOFT 3

sponsor *n* a person who takes the responsibility for some other person or thing ⟨you need a *sponsor* to recommend you in order to get into the exclusive country club⟩
syn backer, guarantor, patron, surety
rel chaperone (*or* chaperon); advocate, champion, supporter; benefactor, coach, mentor, teacher

spontaneity *n* carefree freedom from constraint — see ABANDON

spontaneous *adj* done instantly and without conscious thought or decision — see AUTOMATIC 1

spoof *n* a work that imitates and exaggerates another work for comic effect — see PARODY 1

spook *n* **1** a person who tries secretly to obtain information for one country in the territory of another usually unfriendly country — see SPY

2 the soul of a dead person thought of especially as appearing to living people — see GHOST

spook *vb* to strike with fear — see FRIGHTEN

spooked *adj* filled with fear or dread — see AFRAID 1

spooky *adj* **1** easily excited by nature — see EXCITABLE

2 fearfully and mysteriously strange or fantastic — see EERIE

spoon *n* a utensil with a bowl and a handle that is used especially in cooking and serving food ⟨it's easier to eat soup with a *spoon* than with a fork⟩
syn dipper, ladle, scoop
rel skimmer

spoon *vb* to lift out with something that holds liquid — see DIP 2

---

syn synonym(s)   *rel* related words
ant antonym(s)   *near ant* near antonym(s)

sporadic *adj* **1** lacking in steadiness or regularity of occurrence — see FITFUL

2 not often occurring or repeated — see INFREQUENT

sport *n* **1** activity engaged in to amuse oneself — see PLAY 1

2 an attitude or manner not to be taken seriously — see FUN 2

sport *vb* **1** to engage in activity for amusement — see PLAY 1

2 to play and run about happily — see FROLIC 1

3 to present so as to invite notice or attention — see SHOW 1

sportive *adj* given to good-natured joking or teasing — see PLAYFUL

sportiveness *n* a natural disposition for playful behavior — see PLAYFULNESS

sportsmanlike *adj* following or according to the rules — see FAIR 3

sportsmanly *adj* following or according to the rules — see FAIR 3

spot *n* **1** a small area that is different (as in color) from the main part ⟨in summer the white coat of the snow leopard is studded with brownish black *spots*⟩

syn blotch, dapple, dot, eyespot, fleck, mottle, patch, point, speck, speckle, splotch

rel birthmark, freckle, mole; blot, mark, smear, smudge, stain; spatter, splash

2 a difficult, puzzling, or embarrassing situation from which there is no easy escape — see PREDICAMENT

3 a mark of guilt or disgrace — see STAIN 1

4 a very small amount — see PARTICLE 1

5 the area or space occupied by or intended for something — see PLACE 1

spot *vb* to mark with small spots especially unevenly ⟨to give the effect of sunlight on water, the artist *spotted* the lake in his painting with flecks of gold paint⟩

syn blotch, dapple, dot, fleck, freckle, marble, mottle, pepper, speck, speckle, splotch, sprinkle, stipple

rel blot, dye, stain; streak, stripe; intersperse, stud; bespatter, spatter

spotless *adj* free from dirt or stain — see CLEAN 1

spotted *adj* **1** marked with spots ⟨the *spotted* tablecloth clashed with the stripes on the wallpaper⟩

syn dappled (*also* dapple), dotted, flecked, freckled, mottled, speckled, splotchy, spotty, stippled, variegated

rel spangled; marbled, moiré (*or* moire), veined; motley, multicolored; piebald, roan

near ant solid

2 having blotches of two or more colors — see PIED

spotting *n* the act or process of sighting or learning the existence of something for the first time — see DISCOVERY 1

spotty *adj* **1** lacking in steadiness or regularity of occurrence — see FITFUL

2 marked with spots — see SPOTTED 1

spouse *n* the person to whom another is married ⟨employees and their *spouses* are covered by the health plan⟩

syn consort, mate, partner

rel husband, man, old man; lady, wife

near ant single; bachelor; maid, maiden, spinster

spout *n* a pipe or channel for carrying off water from a roof — see GUTTER 1

spout *vb* **1** to flow out in great quantities or with force — see GUSH 1

2 to talk loudly and wildly — see RANT

3 to throw out or off (something from within) often violently — see ERUPT 1

spout (off) *vb* to voice one's opinions freely with force — see SPEAK UP

spray *vb* to cover by or as if by scattering something over or on — see SCATTER 2

spread *n* **1** a decorative cloth used as a top covering for a bed — see COUNTERPANE

2 a large fancy meal often accompanied by ceremony or entertainment — see FEAST

3 a wide space or area — see EXPANSE

4 the distance or extent between possible extremes — see RANGE 3

5 the space or amount of space between two points, lines, surfaces, or objects — see DISTANCE

spread *vb* **1** to cause to be known over a considerable area or by many people ⟨*spread* the news!⟩

syn broadcast, circulate, disseminate, propagate

rel radiate, sprawl; diffuse, dispense, disperse, dissipate, scatter, sow; communicate, pass (on); transmit

near ant conceal, hide, hold (in), secrete; contain, limit, restrict

2 to put a layer of on a surface ⟨we *spread* the fertilizer over the lawn evenly until it was fully covered⟩

syn apply, lay

rel dab, daub, plaster, smear; blanket, carpet, coat, cover, layer, overlay, overlie, overspread, sheet, surface

near ant peel, strip, uncover

3 to become known — see GET OUT 1

4 to cause (something) to pass from one to another — see COMMUNICATE 1

spread (out) *vb* to arrange the parts of (something) over a wider area — see OPEN 3

spreading *adj* exciting a similar feeling or reaction in others — see CONTAGIOUS 2

spree *n* a time or instance of carefree fun — see FLING 1

sprightliness *n* the quality or state of having abundant or intense activity — see VITALITY 1

sprightly *adv* in a quick and spirited manner — see GAILY 2

sprightly *adj* having much high-spirited energy and movement — see LIVELY 1

spring *n* an act of leaping into the air — see JUMP 1

spring *vb* **1** to come into existence — see BEGIN 2

2 to propel oneself upward or forward into the air — see JUMP 1

3 to set free (as from slavery or confinement) — see FREE 1

spring (for) *vb* to give what is owed for — see PAY 2

spring (up) *vb* to come to one's attention especially gradually or unexpectedly — see ARISE 2

springy *adj* **1** able to revert to original size and shape after being stretched, squeezed, or twisted — see ELASTIC 1

2 having much high-spirited energy and movement — see LIVELY 1

sprinkle *n* **1** a light or fine rain — see DRIZZLE

2 a small number — see FEW

sprinkle *vb* **1** to cover by or as if by scattering something over or on — see SCATTER 2

2 to mark with small spots especially unevenly — see SPOT

sprinkling *n* **1** a small number — see FEW

2 a very small amount — see PARTICLE 1

sprint *vb* to go at a pace faster than a walk — see RUN 1

sprite *n* an imaginary being usually having a small human form and magical powers — see FAIRY

spruce *adj* being strikingly neat and trim in style or appearance — see SMART 1

sprucely *adv* in a strikingly neat and trim manner — see SMARTLY

spry *adj* moving easily — see GRACEFUL 1

spryness *n* ease and grace in physical activity — see DEXTERITY 2

spume *n* a light mass of fine bubbles formed in or on a liquid — see FOAM

spunk *n* the strength of mind that enables a person to endure pain or hardship — see FORTITUDE

spunky *adj* marked by a lively display of strong feeling — see SPIRITED 1

spur *n* something that arouses action or activity — see IMPULSE

spur *vb* to urge or push forward with or as if with a pointed object — see PROD 1

spurious *adj* **1** being such in appearance only and made or manufactured with the intention of committing fraud — see COUNTERFEIT

2 lacking in natural or spontaneous quality — see ARTIFICIAL 1

spurn *vb* to show unwillingness to accept, do, engage in, or agree to — see DECLINE 1

spur-of-the-moment *adj* made or done without previous thought or preparation — see EXTEMPORANEOUS

spurt *n* a sudden and usually temporary growth of activity — see OUTBREAK

spurt *vb* **1** to flow out in great quantities or with force — see GUSH 1

2 to throw out or off (something from within) often violently — see ERUPT 1

sputter *vb* to speak rapidly, inarticulately, and usually unintelligibly — see BABBLE 1

spy *n* a person who tries secretly to obtain information for one country in the territory of another usually unfriendly country ⟨the government *spy* risked his life every day to get vital information back to his country⟩

syn operative, spook

rel counterspy, shadow

phrases secret agent, undercover agent

spy *vb* to make note of (something) through the use of one's eyes — see SEE 1

spying *n* the secret gathering of information on others — see ESPIONAGE

squabble *n* an often noisy or angry expression of differing opinions — see ARGUMENT 1

squabble *vb* to express different opinions about something often angrily — see ARGUE 2

squabbler *n* a person who takes part in a dispute — see DISPUTANT

squad *n* a group of people working together on a task — see GANG 1

squalidness *n* the state or quality of being dirty — see DIRTINESS 1

squall *n* **1** a disturbance of the atmosphere accompanied by wind and often by precipitation (as rain or snow) — see STORM 1

2 a state of noisy, confused activity — see COMMOTION

squall *vb* to cry out loudly and emotionally — see SCREAM

squally *adj* marked by wet and windy conditions — see FOUL 1

squamous *adj* composed of or covered with scales — see SCALY

squander *vb* to use up carelessly — see WASTE 1

squanderer *n* someone who carelessly spends money — see PRODIGAL

squandering *adj* given to spending money freely or foolishly — see PRODIGAL

square *adj* marked by justice, honesty, and freedom from bias — see FAIR 2

square *vb* **1** to be in agreement on every point — see CHECK 1

2 to influence someone with a bribe — see BRIBE

squarely *adv* as stated or indicated without the slightest difference — see EXACTLY 1

squash *vb* **1** to cause to become a pulpy mass — see CRUSH 1

2 to put a stop to (something) by the use of force — see QUELL 1

squashy *adj* giving easily to the touch — see SOFT 3

squat *adj* being compact and broad in build and often short in stature — see STOCKY

squat *vb* to lie low with the limbs close to the body — see CROUCH

squatty *adj* being compact and broad in build and often short in stature — see STOCKY

squawk *n* an expression of dissatisfaction, pain, or resentment — see COMPLAINT 1

squawk *vb* to express dissatisfaction, pain, or resentment usually tiresomely — see COMPLAIN

squeak *vb* to make a short shrill noise ⟨a loose board that *squeaked* every time we walked on the floor⟩
syn creak
rel cheep, peep; scream, screech, shriek, shrill, sing, squeal, yelp, yip

squeaking *adj* having a high musical pitch or range — see SHRILL

squeaky *adj* having a high musical pitch or range — see SHRILL

squeal *vb* **1** to give information (as to the authorities) about another's improper or unlawful activities ⟨as soon as the stool pigeon got to the police station, he *squealed* to the police about the whole smuggling operation⟩
syn inform, snitch, talk, tell
rel betray, give away, rat (on), turn in; blab, tattle; tip (off)
2 to cry out loudly and emotionally — see SCREAM

squealer *n* a person who provides secret information about another's wrongdoing — see INFORMER

squeamish *adj* **1** affected with nausea — see NAUSEOUS
2 filled with disgust — see SICK 2

squeamishness *n* **1** a disturbed condition of the stomach in which one feels like vomiting — see NAUSEA 1
2 the tendency to be or state of being squeamish — see DELICACY 3

squeeze *vb* **1** to apply external pressure on so as to force out the juice or contents of — see PRESS 2
2 to fit (something) into a tight space — see CROWD 1
3 to get with great difficulty — see EKE OUT
4 to reduce in size or volume by or as if by pressing parts or members together — see COMPRESS 1
5 to rob by the use of trickery or threats — see FLEECE

squeezing *n* the act or process of reducing the size or volume of something by or as if by pressing — see COMPRESSION

squelch *vb* to put a stop to (something) by the use of force — see QUELL 1

squinch *vb* **1** to lie low with the limbs close to the body — see CROUCH
2 to twist (something) out of a natural or normal shape or condition — see CONTORT

squinching *n* the twisting of something out of its natural or normal shape or condition — see CONTORTION

squire *vb* to go along with in order to provide assistance, protection, or companionship — see ACCOMPANY

squirm *vb* to make jerky or restless movements — see FIDGET

squirrel (away) *vb* to put (something of future use or value) in a safe or secret place — see HOARD

squirt *vb* to flow out in great quantities or with force — see GUSH 1

squishy *adj* giving easily to the touch — see SOFT 3

stab *n* **1** a mark or small hole made by a pointed instrument — see PRICK 1
2 an effort to do or accomplish something — see ATTEMPT

stab *vb* to penetrate or hold (something) with a pointed object — see IMPALE

stability *n* **1** the ability to withstand force or stress without being distorted, dislodged, or damaged ⟨the bridge was designed with such great *stability* that it supposedly will not collapse even under the harshest weather conditions⟩
syn firmness, soundness, steadiness, strength, sturdiness
rel dependability, durability, reliability; solidity, solidness; cohesion, toughness
near ant insecurity, weakness
ant instability, unsoundness, unsteadiness
2 the state of continuing without change — see CONSTANCY 1

stable *adj* **1** marked by the ability to withstand stress without structural damage or distortion ⟨the tower was *stable* enough to withstand the strongest winds without collapsing⟩
syn fast, firm, sound, stalwart, strong, sturdy
rel dependable, durable, reliable; solid; cohesive, tough
near ant insecure, weak
ant unsound, unstable, unsteady
2 having been established and usually not subject to change — see FIXED 1
3 having full use of one's mind and control over one's actions — see SANE
4 not undergoing a change in condition — see CONSTANT 1

stack *n* **1** a considerable amount — see LOT 2
2 a quantity of things thrown or stacked on one another — see ¹PILE 1

stack *vb* to lay or throw on top of one another — see PILE

stack up (against *or* with) *vb* to come near or nearer to in character or quality — see APPROXIMATE

stadium *n* a large usually roofless building for sporting events with tiers of seats for spectators ⟨the football game will be held at the new *stadium*, which seats 100,000 people⟩
syn bowl, circus, coliseum, colosseum
rel gym, gymnasium, spa; arena, hippodrome

staff *n* **1** a body of persons at work or available for work — see FORCE 1
2 a heavy rigid stick used as a weapon or for punishment — see CLUB 1

stage *n* **1** a level usually raised surface — see PLATFORM
2 a portion of a trip — see LEG 2
3 an individual part of a process, series, or ranking — see DEGREE 1
4 the public performance of plays — see DRAMA 1

stage *vb* to bring before the public in performance or exhibition — see PRESENT 1

stagger *vb* **1** to move forward while swaying from side to side ⟨I was so tired last night that I just *staggered* upstairs to bed without eating dinner⟩

syn careen, dodder, lurch, reel, teeter, totter, waddle

rel rock, sway, weave, wobble; clump, flounder, lumber, lump, pound, scuff, scuffle, shamble, shuffle, stamp, stomp, stumble, tramp, tromp

2 to show uncertainty about the right course of action — see HESITATE

staggering *adj* causing wonder or astonishment — see MARVELOUS 1

staid *adj* **1** not joking or playful in mood or manner — see SERIOUS 1

2 having or showing a serious and reserved manner — see DIGNIFIED

stain *n* **1** a mark of guilt or disgrace ⟨the *stain* of this cowardly act would haunt him for the rest of his career⟩

syn blot, brand, smirch, spot, stigma, taint

rel discredit, disgrace, dishonor, disrepute, guilt, ignominy, infamy, odium, opprobrium, reproach, shame

near ant award, credit, honor

2 a substance used to color other materials — see PIGMENT

stain *vb* **1** to affect slightly with something morally bad or undesirable — see TAINT 1

2 to give color or a different color to — see COLOR 1

3 to make dirty — see DIRTY

stained *adj* not clean — see DIRTY 1

stainless *adj* free from dirt or stain — see CLEAN 1

stake *n* **1** a legal right to participation in the advantages, profits, and responsibility of something — see INTEREST 1

2 the money or thing risked on the outcome of an uncertain event — see BET

stake *vb* **1** to provide money for — see FINANCE 1

2 to risk (something) on the outcome of an uncertain event — see BET

stale *adj* used or heard so often as to be dull ⟨viewers were bored by the *stale* story lines of the new crop of sitcoms⟩

syn banal, commonplace, hackney, hackneyed, moth-eaten, musty, stereotyped, threadbare, tired, trite

rel canned, unimaginative, uninspired, unoriginal; normal, ordinary, rote, routine, standard, stock; typical, usual; boring, drab, dreary, dry, dull, flat, heavy, humdrum, jading, leaden, monotonous, pedestrian, ponderous, prosaic, tame, tedious, tiresome, tiring, unanimated, undramatic, uninteresting, vapid, wearisome, weary, wearying; corny, maudlin, mawkish, mushy, saccharine, sappy, schmaltzy, sentimental, sloppy, sugarcoated, sugary

near ant animating, energizing, enlivening, exciting, galvanizing, invigorating, stimulating; absorbing, engaging, en-

grossing, gripping, interesting, intriguing, involving; atypical, extraordinary, uncommon, unusual

ant fresh, new, original

stalemate *n* **1** a point in a struggle where neither side is capable of winning or willing to give in — see IMPASSE

2 a situation in which neither participant in a contest, competition, or struggle comes out ahead of the other — see TIE 1

stalk *vb* **1** to seek out (game) for food or sport — see HUNT 1

2 to walk with exaggerated arm and leg movements — see STRUT 1

stall *vb* **1** to bring (something) to a standstill — see ¹HALT 1

2 to stop functioning — see FAIL 1

stalwart *adj* **1** feeling or displaying no fear by temperament — see BRAVE

2 having muscles capable of exerting great physical force — see STRONG 1

3 marked by the ability to withstand stress without structural damage or distortion — see STABLE 1

stamp *n* a perceptible trace left by pressure — see PRINT 1

stamp *vb* **1** to move heavily or clumsily — see LUMBER 1

2 to tread on heavily so as to crush or injure — see TRAMPLE

stamp (out) *vb* to destroy all traces of — see ANNIHILATE 1

stance *n* a general way of holding the body — see POSTURE 1

stanchion *n* an upright shaft that supports an overhead structure — see PILLAR 1

stand *n* a level usually raised surface — see PLATFORM

stand *vb* **1** to occupy a place or location ⟨the monument *stands* in the middle of the town plaza⟩

syn be, lie, sit

rel command, overlook; remain, rest, stay; await, wait; post, station

2 to put up with (something painful or difficult) — see BEAR 2

3 to give what is owed for — see PAY 2

standard *adj* **1** accepted, used, or practiced by most people — see CURRENT 1

2 being of the type that is encountered in the normal course of events — see ORDINARY 1

3 having or showing the qualities associated with the members of a particular group or kind — see TYPICAL 1

standard *n* **1** something set up as an example against which others of the same type are compared ⟨the animation in that movie set the *standard* against which all later animated cartoons were judged⟩

syn benchmark, criterion, grade, mark, measure, par, touchstone, yardstick

rel rule; case, example, instance; acme, apex, meridian, peak, pinnacle, summit, zenith

near ant aberration, abnormality, deviation

2 a piece of cloth with a special design that is used as an emblem or for signaling — see FLAG 1

---

syn synonym(s)   *rel* related words
ant antonym(s)   *near ant* near antonym(s)

3 what is typical of a group, class, or series — see AVERAGE

4 standards *pl* the code of good conduct for an individual or group — see ETHICS

standardize *vb* to make agree with a single established standard or model ⟨the plan is to *standardize* the test for reading comprehension so that we can see how students across the state compare⟩

syn formalize, homogenize, normalize, regularize

rel codify, organize, systematize; average, equalize, even; accredit, certify; control, govern, regulate; coordinate, harmonize, integrate, reconcile, synthesize

near ant customize, individualize, tailor

standby *n* something or someone to which one looks for support — see DEPENDENCE 2

stand-in *n* a person or thing that takes the place of another — see SUBSTITUTE

stand in *vb* to serve as a replacement usually for a time only — see COVER 1

standing *adj* **1** fixed in a place or position — see STATIONARY 1

2 rising straight up — see ERECT

standing *n* **1** high position within society — see RANK 2

2 the period during which something exists, lasts, or is in progress — see DURATION 1

3 the placement of someone or something in relation to others in a vertical arrangement — see RANK 1

standoff *n* a situation in which neither participant in a contest, competition, or struggle comes out ahead of the other — see TIE 1

standoffish *adj* having or showing a lack of friendliness or interest in others — see COOL 1

standout *n* a person who is widely known and usually much talked about — see CELEBRITY 1

stand out *vb* to extend outward beyond a usual point — see BULGE

standpoint *n* a way of looking at or thinking about something — see POINT OF VIEW

standstill *n* a point in a struggle where neither side is capable of winning or willing to give in — see IMPASSE

staple *n* the main or greater part of something as distinguished from its appendages — see BODY 1

star *adj* **1** of or relating to the stars — see STELLAR 1

2 standing above others in rank, importance, or achievement — see EMINENT

3 widely known — see FAMOUS

star *n* **1** a ball-shaped gaseous celestial body that shines by its own light ⟨it's difficult to see the *stars* at night in the middle of the city because of all the streetlights⟩

syn luminary, sun

rel constellation; dwarf, fixed star, giant star, lodestar (*also* loadstar), neutron star, nova, red giant, supernova, variable star, white dwarf

2 the person who has the most important role in a play, movie, or TV show ⟨when the *star* of the school play came down with the flu on opening night, her understudy got to go on⟩

syn lead, principal

rel leading lady, leading man; superstar; ingenue (*or* ingénue); starlet

near ant extra, supernumerary

3 a person who is widely known and usually much talked about — see CELEBRITY 1

starch *n* active strength of body or mind — see VIGOR 1

starchy *adj* marked by or showing careful attention to set forms and details — see CEREMONIOUS 1

star-crossed *adj* having, prone to, or marked by bad luck — see UNLUCKY

stare *vb* to look long and hard in wonder or surprise — see GAPE

stark *adj* **1** harsh and threatening in manner or appearance — see GRIM 1

2 having no exceptions or restrictions — see ABSOLUTE 2

3 lacking contents that could or should be present — see EMPTY 1

4 producing inferior or only a small amount of vegetation — see BARREN 1

starry *adj* of or relating to the stars — see STELLAR 1

start *n* the point at which something begins — see BEGINNING

start *vb* **1** to move suddenly and sharply (as in surprise) ⟨I *started* from my chair when I heard the sudden scream⟩

syn bolt, jump, startle

rel jerk, twitch; flinch, recoil; bound, leap, spring; react, respond

2 to be responsible for the creation and early operation or use of — see FOUND

3 to cause to function — see ACTIVATE

4 to come into existence — see BEGIN 2

5 to extend outward beyond a usual point — see BULGE

6 to take the first step in (a process or course of action) — see BEGIN 1

startle *vb* **1** to make a strong impression on (someone) with something unexpected — see SURPRISE 1

2 to move suddenly and sharply (as in surprise) — see START 1

3 to strike with fear — see FRIGHTEN

startling *adj* causing a strong emotional reaction because unexpected — see SURPRISING 1

starved *adj* feeling a desire or need for food — see HUNGRY 1

starving *adj* feeling a desire or need for food — see HUNGRY 1

stash *n* a supply stored up and often hidden away — see HOARD 1

stash *vb* to put (something of future use or value) in a safe or secret place — see HOARD

stashing *n* the placing of something out of sight — see CONCEALMENT 1

state *adj* of or relating to a nation — see NATIONAL

state *n* a body of people composed of one or more nationalities usually with its own territory and government — see NATION

state *vb* **1** to convey in appropriate or telling terms — see PHRASE

2 to express (a thought or emotion) in words — see SAY 1

3 to make known (as an idea, emotion, or opinion) — see EXPRESS 1

state house *n* the building in which a state legislature meets — see CAPITOL

stateliness *n* **1** a dignified bearing or appearance befitting royalty — see MAJESTY 1

2 dignified or restrained beauty of form, appearance, or style — see ELEGANCE

3 impressiveness of beauty on a large scale — see MAGNIFICENCE

stately *adj* **1** having or showing a serious and reserved manner — see DIGNIFIED

2 having or showing elegance — see ELEGANT 1

3 large and impressive in size, grandeur, extent, or conception — see ELEVATED 2

4 very dignified in form, tone, or style — see ELEVATED 2

statement *n* **1** a record of goods sold or services performed together with the costs due — see ¹BILL 1

2 an act, process, or means of putting something into words — see EXPRESSION 1

3 something that is said — see WORD 2

static *adj* fixed in a place or position — see STATIONARY 1

station *n* **1** the place where someone is assigned to stand or remain ⟨the soldiers remained at their *station* even though a huge enemy force was approaching⟩

syn position, post, quarter

rel assignment, detail

2 a regular stopping place ⟨the historic house was once a *station* on the Underground Railroad, the network that helped slaves reach freedom in the North⟩

syn stop, way station

rel depot, terminal; layover, stopover

3 the placement of someone or something in relation to others in a vertical arrangement — see RANK 1

station *vb* to assign to a place or position — see ²POST

stationary *adj* **1** fixed in a place or position ⟨a *stationary* bicycle is good for exercise, but you won't enjoy the scenery very much⟩

syn immobile, nonmoving, standing, static

rel immovable, irremovable, nonmotile, unmovable; frozen, motionless, stagnant, still, unbudging

near ant motile

ant mobile, movable (*or* moveable), moving, nonstationary

2 not undergoing a change in condition — see CONSTANT 1

statuette *n* a small statue — see FIGURINE

stature *n* the distance of something or someone from bottom to top — see HEIGHT 3

status *n* **1** position with regard to conditions and circumstances — see SITUATION 1

2 the placement of someone or something in relation to others in a vertical arrangement — see RANK 1

status quo *n* the state or fact of being the way things usually are — see NORMALITY

statute *n* a rule of conduct or action laid down by a governing authority and especially a legislator — see LAW 1

staunch *or* **stanch** *adj* firm in one's allegiance to someone or something — see FAITHFUL 1

stave off *vb* to drive back — see REPEL 1

¹stay *n* a temporary residing as another's guest — see VISIT 1

²stay *n* something that holds up or serves as a foundation for something else — see SUPPORT 1

stay *vb* **1** to continue to be in a place for a significant amount of time ⟨let's *stay* inside this pavilion until it stops raining⟩

syn abide, dwell, hang around, remain, stick around, tarry

rel await, hang on, hold on, wait; dally, linger, loiter; keep

ant go, leave, quit

2 to bring (something) to a standstill — see ¹HALT 1

3 to hold up or serve as a foundation for — see SUPPORT 3

4 to remain in place in readiness or expectation of something — see WAIT

5 to reside as a temporary guest — see VISIT 2

steadfast *adj* **1** firm in one's allegiance to someone or something — see FAITHFUL 1

steadfastness *n* adherence to something to which one is bound by a pledge or duty — see FIDELITY

steadiness *n* **1** the ability to withstand force or stress without being distorted, dislodged, or damaged — see STABILITY 1

2 the state of continuing without change — see CONSTANCY 1

steady *adj* **1** firm in one's allegiance to someone or something — see FAITHFUL 1

2 appearing or occurring repeatedly from time to time — see REGULAR 1

3 not undergoing a change in condition — see CONSTANT 1

4 not varying — see UNIFORM

5 worthy of one's trust — see DEPENDABLE

steal *n* something bought or offered for sale at a desirable price — see BARGAIN 1

steal *vb* **1** to take (something) without right and with an intent to keep ⟨the guy who tried to *steal* my car was sentenced to a year in jail⟩

syn appropriate, filch, hook, misappropriate, nip, pilfer, pinch, pocket, purloin, rip off, snitch, swipe, thieve

rel burglarize, fleece, rob; loot, pillage, plunder, sack; hijack (*or* highjack); pick, rifle; poach, rustle, shoplift; collar, grab,

---

grasp, nail, seize, snatch, take; mooch, sponge; abduct, kidnap, shanghai, spirit
phrases make away with, run off with, walk off with
near ant buy, purchase; bestow, contribute, donate, give, present
2 to move about in a sly or secret manner — see SNEAK 1

steal (from) *vb* to remove valuables from (a place) unlawfully — see ROB

stealer *n* one who steals — see THIEF

stealing *n* the unlawful taking and carrying away of property without the consent of its owner — see THEFT 1

stealthy *adj* **1** given to acting in secret and to concealing one's intentions — see SNEAKY 1
2 undertaken or done so as to escape being observed or known by others — see SECRET 1

steam *vb* to be excited or emotionally stirred up with anger — see BOIL 1

steaming *adj* feeling or showing anger — see ANGRY

steed *n* a large hoofed domestic animal that is used for carrying or drawing loads and for riding — see HORSE

steel *n* a hand weapon with a length of metal sharpened on one or both sides and usually tapered to a sharp point — see SWORD

steel *vb* **1** to fill with courage or strength of purpose — see ENCOURAGE 1
2 to make able to withstand physical hardship, strain, or exposure — see HARDEN 2
3 to prepare (oneself) mentally or emotionally — see FORTIFY 1

steely *adj* **1** harsh and threatening in manner or appearance — see GRIM 1
2 of the color gray — see GRAY 1

steep *adj* **1** having an incline approaching the perpendicular ⟨a very *steep* rock face that was nearly impossible to climb⟩
syn abrupt, bold, precipitous, sheer
rel perpendicular, plumb, straight, vertical; craggy, hilly, mountainous, scarped; angled, canted, cocked, heeled, inclined, listed, slanted, sloped, tilted, tipped
near ant gentle, gradual, moderate; even, flat, flush, horizontal, level, plane, smooth, unruffled, unwrinkled
ant easy
2 going beyond a normal or acceptable limit in degree or amount — see EXCESSIVE

steep *vb* **1** to cause (as a person) to become filled or saturated with a certain quality or principle — see INFUSE
2 to wet thoroughly with liquid — see SOAK 1

steer *vb* to point out the way for (someone) especially from a position in front — see LEAD 1

stellar *adj* **1** of or relating to the stars ⟨humankind's dream of *stellar* navigation is hampered by the vast distances between the stars, even in our own galaxy⟩
syn astral, star, starry
rel celestial, empyrean, heavenly; astronomical (*also* astronomic), astrophysical; astronautic (*or* astronautical); starlike, star-spangled
2 of the very best kind — see EXCELLENT

stench *n* a strong unpleasant smell — see STINK

stentorian *adj* marked by a high volume of sound — see LOUD 1

step *n* **1** an action planned or taken to achieve a desired result — see MEASURE 1
2 an individual part of a process, series, or ranking — see DEGREE 1
3 the mark or impression made by a foot — see FOOTPRINT
4 steps *pl* the direction along which something or someone moves — see PATH 1

step *vb* **1** to go on foot — see WALK
2 to perform a series of usually rhythmic bodily movements to music — see DANCE 1

step (along) *vb* to proceed or move quickly — see HURRY 2

step–by–step *adj* proceeding or changing by steps or degrees — see GRADUAL

step down (from) *vb* **1** to give up (a job or office) — see QUIT 1
2 to give up (as a position of authority) formally — see ABDICATE

steppe *n* a broad area of level or rolling treeless country — see PLAIN

step up *vb* to make markedly greater in measure or degree — see INTENSIFY

stereotype *n* an idea or statement about all of the members of a group or all the instances of a situation — see GENERALIZATION

stereotyped *adj* used or heard so often as to be dull — see STALE

sterile *adj* **1** not able to produce fruit or offspring ⟨*sterile* couples sometimes choose to adopt needy children⟩ ⟨the apple tree turned out to be *sterile*, never yielding a crop of apples⟩
syn barren, impotent, infertile, unfruitful
rel altered, desexed, neutered, sterilized; castrated, emasculated, gelded; spayed; fruitless, unproductive
near ant fecund, luxuriant, productive, prolific; enriched, fertilized, rich; impregnated, pregnant; potent; bearing, producing, yielding; blooming, bursting, flourishing, swarming, teeming
ant fat, fertile, fruitful
2 free from filth, infection, or dangers to health — see SANITARY

sterling *adj* of the very best kind — see EXCELLENT

stern *adj* **1** given to exacting standards of discipline and self-restraint — see SEVERE 1
2 harsh and threatening in manner or appearance — see GRIM 1

sternly *adv* in a manner so as to cause loss or suffering — see HARDLY 1

sternness *n* the quality or state of being demanding or unyielding (as in discipline or criticism) — see SEVERITY

stevedore *n* one who loads and unloads ships at a port — see DOCKWORKER

stew *n* 1 a state of nervous or irritated concern — see FRET

2 a state of noisy, confused activity — see COMMOTION

stew *vb* 1 to cook in a liquid heated to the point that it gives off steam — see BOIL 2

2 to experience concern or anxiety — see WORRY 1

steward *n* a person hired to perform household or personal services — see SERVANT

stick *vb* 1 to hold to something firmly as if by adhesion ⟨those magnets are strong enough to *stick* well to the refrigerator⟩

syn adhere, cleave, cling, hew

rel bind, cohere, fasten, fuse, glue, unite

near ant loosen; drop, fall

2 to arrange something in a certain spot or position — see PLACE 1

3 to penetrate or hold (something) with a pointed object — see IMPALE

4 to rob by the use of trickery or threats — see FLEECE

stick (to *or* with) *vb* to give steadfast support to — see ADHERE

stick around *vb* to continue to be in a place for a significant amount of time — see STAY 1

stick-in-the-mud *n* 1 a person with old-fashioned ideas — see FOGY

2 someone who moves slowly or more slowly than others — see SLOWPOKE

stick out *vb* 1 to extend outward beyond a usual point — see BULGE

2 to put up with (something painful or difficult) — see BEAR 2

sticks *n pl* the open rural area outside of big towns and cities — see COUNTRY 2

sticky *adj* 1 being of such a thick consistency as to readily cling to objects upon contact ⟨the *sticky* maple syrup was a mess to clean up⟩

syn adhesive, gelatinous, gluey, glutinous, gooey, gummy, viscid, viscous

rel ropy, tacky; adherent, tenacious

ant nonadhesive, nonviscous

2 containing or characterized by an uncomfortable amount of moisture — see HUMID

stiff *adj* 1 incapable of or highly resistant to bending ⟨use a *stiff* piece of paper for the project⟩

syn inflexible, rigid, stiffened, unyielding

rel inelastic; firm, hard, solid, sound, strong; brittle, crisp; compact, dense, substantial; arthritic, rheumatic, nonelastic, nonmalleable

near ant elastic, resilient, springy, stretchy, workable; malleable; droopy, flabby, flaccid, mushy, semisoft, soft, squashy, squishy; lank, limber, limp, lissome (*also* lissom), lithe, willowy

ant flexible, floppy, pliable, pliant, supple, yielding

2 difficult to endure — see HARSH 1

3 going beyond a normal or acceptable limit in degree or amount — see EXCESSIVE

4 having a consistency that does not easily yield to pressure — see FIRM 2

5 lacking social grace and assurance — see AWKWARD 1

6 requiring considerable physical or mental effort — see HARD 2

stiffened *adj* incapable of or highly resistant to bending — see STIFF 1

stiffly *adv* 1 in a manner so as to cause loss or suffering — see HARDLY 1

2 in a vigorous and forceful manner — see HARD 3

stifle *vb* 1 to be or cause to be killed by lack of breathable air — see SMOTHER 1

2 to refrain from openly showing or uttering — see SUPPRESS 2

stifling *adj* lacking fresh air — see STUFFY 1

stigma *n* a mark of guilt or disgrace — see STAIN 1

still *adj* 1 free from disturbing noise or uproar — see QUIET 1

2 free from storms or physical disturbance — see CALM 1

3 mostly or entirely without sound — see SILENT 3

still *adv* 1 without motion ⟨now, you have to sit very *still* while the hairdresser cuts your hair⟩

syn motionlessly, quiet, quietly

rel immovably; inactively

near ant movably

2 in spite of that — see HOWEVER

still *n* 1 a state of freedom from storm or disturbance — see CALM

2 the near or complete absence of sound — see SILENCE 2

still *vb* 1 to bring (something) to a standstill — see ¹HALT 1

2 to free from distress or disturbance — see CALM 1

3 to stop the noise or speech of — see SILENCE 1

stillness *n* 1 a state of freedom from storm or disturbance — see CALM

2 incapacity for or restraint from speaking — see SILENCE 1

3 the near or complete absence of sound — see SILENCE 2

stilly *adj* 1 free from disturbing noise or uproar — see QUIET 1

2 free from storms or physical disturbance — see CALM 1

stilted *adj* lacking social grace and assurance — see AWKWARD 1

stimulant *n* 1 something that arouses a strong response from another — see PROVOCATION 1

2 something that arouses action or activity — see IMPULSE

stimulate *vb* 1 to give life, vigor, or spirit to — see ANIMATE

2 to rouse to strong feeling or action — see PROVOKE 1

stimulating *adj* 1 causing great emotional or mental stimulation — see EXCITING 1

---

2 having a renewing effect on the state of the body or mind — see TONIC

3 serving or likely to arouse a strong reaction — see PROVOCATIVE

stimulation *n* something that arouses a strong response from another — see PROVOCATION 1

stimulative *adj* having a renewing effect on the state of the body or mind — see TONIC

stimulus *n* **1** something that arouses a strong response from another — see PROVOCATION 1

2 something that arouses action or activity — see IMPULSE

sting *n* a sharp unpleasant sensation usually felt in some specific part of the body — see PAIN 1

sting *vb* **1** to charge (someone) too much for goods or services — see OVERCHARGE 1

2 to rob by the use of trickery or threats — see FLEECE

stinginess *n* the quality of being overly sparing with money — see PARSIMONY

stinging *adj* causing intense discomfort to one's skin — see CUTTING 1

stingy *adj* **1** giving or sharing as little as possible ⟨until his redemption, Ebenezer Scrooge is the classic example of a very *stingy*, heartless miser⟩

syn cheap, close, closefisted, mean, niggard, niggardly, parsimonious, penurious, pinching, spare, sparing, stinting, tight, tightfisted, uncharitable

rel careful, chary, conserving, economical, economizing, frugal, saving, scrimping, skimping, thrifty; acquisitive, avaricious, avid, coveting, covetous, desirous, grasping, greedy, hoggish, itchy, mercenary, rapacious, selfish, shabby, small, sordid; begrudging, envious, grudging, resentful; inhospitable

near ant altruistic, selfless, unselfish; extravagant, free, handsome, lavish, profuse; be-neficent, benevolent, hospitable, humanitarian, philanthropic; compassionate, good-hearted, greathearted, kindly, magnanimous, openhearted; thriftless, unthrifty; dissipating, frittering, prodigal, profligate, spendthrift, splurging, squandering, wasteful, wasting

ant bounteous, bountiful, charitable, freehanded, generous, liberal, munificent, openhanded, unsparing, unstinting

2 less plentiful than what is normal, necessary, or desirable — see MEAGER

stink *n* a strong unpleasant smell ⟨the *stink* of burned plastic lingered in the kitchen for days after we accidentally melted a spatula on the stove⟩

syn reek, stench

rel acridness, fetidness, foulness, fustiness, malodorousness, mustiness, rancidity, rankness, staleness; badness, vileness; dirt, dirtiness, filth, filthiness, nastiness; odor, redolence, scent, sniff

near ant floweriness, lusciousness, savoriness, spiciness, sweetness; bouquet; ambrosia

ant aroma, fragrance, perfume

stink *vb* to give off an extremely unpleasant smell ⟨the dog *stinks* because she tangled with a skunk again⟩

syn reek

rel exhale, savor, smell; decay, decompose, rot, spoil; disgust, offend, repulse, revolt

stinker *n* a person whose behavior is offensive to others — see JERK 1

stinking *adj* having an unpleasant smell — see MALODOROUS

stinky *adj* having an unpleasant smell — see MALODOROUS

stint *n* **1** a fixed period of time during which a person holds a job or position — see TERM 1

2 a piece of work that needs to be done regularly — see CHORE 1

stint (on) *vb* to use or give out in stingy amounts — see SPARE

stinting *adj* giving or sharing as little as possible — see STINGY 1

stipend *n* the money paid regularly to a person for labor or services — see WAGE

stipple *vb* to mark with small spots especially unevenly — see SPOT

stippled *adj* marked with spots — see SPOTTED 1

stipulate (for) *vb* to ask for (something) earnestly or with authority — see DEMAND 1

stipulation *n* something upon which the carrying out of an agreement or offer depends — see CONDITION 2

stir *n* **1** a state of noisy, confused activity — see COMMOTION

2 the act or an instance of changing position — see MOVEMENT 1

stir *vb* **1** to cause (as a liquid) to move about in a circle especially repeatedly ⟨the recipe says to *stir* the mixture carefully until it's properly blended⟩

syn agitate, churn, swirl, whirl

rel beat, paddle, whip, whisk; reel, shake, wheel

2 to change one's position — see MOVE 3

3 to rouse to strong feeling or action — see PROVOKE 1

stir (up) *vb* to cause or encourage the development of — see INCITE 1

stirring *adj* **1** causing great emotional or mental stimulation — see EXCITING 1

2 having the power to affect the feelings or sympathies — see MOVING

stirring *n* the act or an instance of changing position — see MOVEMENT 1

stitch *n* a sharp unpleasant sensation usually felt in some specific part of the body — see PAIN 1

stitch *vb* to close up with a series of interlacing stitches — see SEW

stock *adj* accepted, used, or practiced by most people — see CURRENT 1

stock *n* **1** a group of persons who come from the same ancestor — see FAMILY 1

2 a stupid person — see IDIOT

3 firm belief in the integrity, ability, effectiveness, or genuineness of someone or something — see TRUST 1

4 the line of ancestors from whom a person is descended — see ANCESTRY

stockade *n* a place of confinement for persons held in lawful custody — see JAIL

stocking *n* a close-fitting covering for the foot and leg ⟨be sure to wear your thick wool *stockings* if it's cold today⟩

syn hose, sock

rel hosiery; anklet, bobby socks, bootee

stockpile *n* a supply stored up and often hidden away — see HOARD 1

stockpile *vb* to put (something of future use or value) in a safe or secret place — see HOARD

stocky *adj* being compact and broad in build and often short in stature ⟨he was a tough, *stocky* little boy, muscular and solid⟩

syn chunky, dumpy, heavyset, squat, squatty, stout, stubby, stumpy, thickset

rel beefy, brawny, bulky, burly, husky, sturdy, thick, thickish, weighty; chubby, corpulent, fat, fleshy, full, gross, heavy, obese, overweight, plump, portly, pudgy, roly-poly, rotund, round, tubby; paunchy, potbellied; flabby, soft

near ant delicate, fragile, frail, puny; lean, skinny, slender, slim, spare, thin; angular, bony, gaunt, lank, lanky, rawboned, sinewy; scraggy, scrawny, slight; anorexic, cadaverous, emaciated, haggard, skeletal, wasted; spindly, twiggy, waspish, weedy, willowy, wiry

stodgy *adj* causing weariness, restlessness, or lack of interest — see BORING

stoic *or* **stoical** *adj* **1** accepting pains or hardships calmly or without complaint — see PATIENT 1

2 not feeling or showing emotion — see IMPASSIVE 1

stolid *adj* **1** not expressing any emotion — see BLANK 1

2 not feeling or showing emotion — see IMPASSIVE 1

stomach *n* the part of the body between the chest and the pelvis ⟨please don't lean on my *stomach* — I just had a big meal⟩

syn abdomen, belly, breadbasket [*slang*], gut, solar plexus, tummy

rel middle, midriff, waist; paunch, potbelly; thorax

stomach *vb* to put up with (something painful or difficult) — see BEAR 2

stomachache *n* abdominal pain especially when focused in the digestive organs ⟨you can stay home from school tomorrow if you still have a *stomachache*⟩

syn bellyache

rel colic, cramps

stomp *vb* **1** to move heavily or clumsily — see LUMBER 1

2 to tread on heavily so as to crush or injure — see TRAMPLE

syn synonym(s)   *rel* related words
ant antonym(s)   *near ant* near antonym(s)

stone blind *adj* lacking the power of sight — see BLIND

stone-broke *adj* lacking money or material possessions — see POOR 1

stoneware *n* articles made of baked clay — see CROCKERY

stony *also* **stoney** *adj* having or showing a lack of sympathy or tender feelings — see HARD 1

stool pigeon *n* a person who provides secret information about another's wrongdoing — see INFORMER

stoop *vb* to descend to a level that is beneath one's dignity — see CONDESCEND 1

stooping *adj* bending downward or forward — see NODDING

stop *n* **1** a brief halt in a journey ⟨our guide called for a *stop* at the trail hut to eat and rest a bit⟩

syn layover, stopover

rel break, pause, rest

2 a regular stopping place — see STATION 2

3 something that makes movement or progress more difficult — see ENCUMBRANCE

4 the stopping of a process or activity — see END 1

stop *vb* **1** to bring (as an action or operation) to an immediate end ⟨please *stop* that running in the library⟩

syn break, break off, can, cease, cut (out), desist (from), discontinue, drop, end, halt, knock off, lay off, leave off, quit, shut off

rel complete, conclude, finish; close (down), deactivate; block, blockade, dam, delay, detain, hinder, hold, hold back, impede, obstruct, stem; call, suspend; arrest, brake, check, clamp down, rein (in), squash, squelch, stamp, stanch (*also* staunch), stunt, suppress, turn back; pause, stay, suspend; abolish, abort, annul, demolish, destroy, dissolve, kill, ruin, scuttle, snuff

phrases have done with, put the kibosh on

near ant carry on, continue, follow through, keep up, run on; advance, proceed, progress; actuate, drive, impel, propel, stir

2 to bring (something) to a standstill — see ¹HALT 1

3 to close up so that no empty spaces remain — see FILL 2

4 to come to an end — see CEASE 1

stop (**by** *or* **in**) *vb* to make a brief visit — see CALL 3

stop (**up**) *vb* to prevent passage through — see CLOG 1

stopcock *n* a fixture for controlling the flow of a liquid — see FAUCET

stopgap *n* a temporary replacement — see MAKESHIFT

stopover *n* a brief halt in a journey — see STOP 1

stoppage *n* the stopping of a process or activity — see END 1

storage *n* a building for storing goods — see STOREHOUSE

store *adj* made beforehand in large numbers — see READY-MADE

store *n* 1 a collection of things kept available for future use or need ⟨Dad has a *store* of funny stories for when conversation lags at company parties⟩
syn cache, deposit, hoard, reserve
rel budget, fund, nest egg, pool, reservoir, stock, stockpile, supply; accumulation, assemblage, collection, gathering
2 a supply stored up and often hidden away — see HOARD 1
3 an establishment where goods are sold to consumers — see SHOP 1

store *vb* 1 to place somewhere for safekeeping or ready availability ⟨we decided to *store* the lawn mower in the shed instead of the garage⟩
syn keep, stow
rel garage, house; file, pack, shelve
2 to put (something of future use or value) in a safe or secret place — see HOARD

storehouse *n* a building for storing goods ⟨the company has a large *storehouse* filled with lumber for manufacturing its line of furniture⟩
syn depository, depot, magazine, repository, storage, stowage, warehouse
rel cache, stockroom, storeroom; bank, bin, container, locker, safe-deposit box, strongbox; arsenal, dump

storm *n* 1 a disturbance of the atmosphere accompanied by wind and often by precipitation (as rain or snow) ⟨a winter *storm* bringing about six inches of snow⟩
syn squall, tempest
rel blizzard, hail storm, ice storm, northeaster, norther, rainstorm, sandstorm, snowstorm, southeaster, southwester, thunderstorm, windstorm; cyclone, hurricane, typhoon
2 a heavy fall of objects — see RAIN 2
3 a rapid or overwhelming outpouring of many things at once — see BARRAGE
4 a state of noisy, confused activity — see COMMOTION
5 a steady falling of water from the sky in significant quantity — see RAIN 1
6 a sudden intense expression of strong feeling — see OUTBURST 1
7 a violent disturbance (as of the political or social order) — see CONVULSION

storm *vb* 1 to express one's anger usually violently — see RAGE 1
2 to fall as water in a continuous stream of drops from the clouds — see RAIN 1
3 to take sudden, violent action against — see ATTACK 1

stormy *adj* 1 marked by bursts of destructive force or intense activity — see VIOLENT 1
2 marked by or abounding with rain — see RAINY
3 marked by sudden or violent disturbance — see CONVULSIVE
4 marked by turmoil or disturbance especially of natural elements — see WILD 3
5 marked by wet and windy conditions — see FOUL 1

story *n* 1 a work with imaginary characters and events that is shorter and usually less complex than a novel ⟨if you go right to bed, Daddy will read a *story* to you⟩
syn narrative, novelette, novella, short story, tale, yarn
rel exemplum, fable, parable; anecdote, joke; fairy tale, folktale, legend, myth, romance; account, annals, chronicle, history, record, report
2 a brief account of something interesting that happened especially to one personally ⟨Grandpa is always telling *stories* about what it was like growing up on a farm⟩
syn anecdote, tale, yarn
rel episode, event, happening, incident, occurrence; recital, recitation
3 a report of recent events or facts not previously known — see NEWS
4 a relating of events usually in the order in which they happened — see ACCOUNT 1
5 a rumor or report of a personal or sensational nature — see TALE 1
6 a statement known by its maker to be untrue and made in order to deceive — see LIE

storyteller *n* a person who tells lies — see LIAR

stout *adj* 1 able to withstand hardship, strain, or exposure — see HARDY 1
2 being compact and broad in build and often short in stature — see STOCKY
3 feeling or displaying no fear by temperament — see BRAVE
4 having muscles capable of exerting great physical force — see STRONG 1
5 not showing weakness or uncertainty — see FIRM 1

stouthearted *adj* feeling or displaying no fear by temperament — see BRAVE

stoutly *adv* in a vigorous and forceful manner — see HARD 3

stoutness *n* strength of mind to carry on in spite of danger — see COURAGE

stow *vb* 1 to place somewhere for safekeeping or ready availability — see STORE 1
2 to put (something of future use or value) in a safe or secret place — see HOARD

stowage *n* a building for storing goods — see STOREHOUSE

straggler *n* someone who moves slowly or more slowly than others — see SLOWPOKE

straight *adj* 1 free from irregularities (as curves, bends, or angles) in course ⟨in the wide, open spaces of the West some rural roads are incredibly *straight*⟩
syn linear, right, straightaway, straightforward
rel unbent, uncurled, untwisted; direct, undeviating, unswerving
near ant bowed, rounded; entwined, kinked, swirled, turned, turning, twined, twining, twisted, twisting, veering, warped; bending, coiled, coiling, corkscrew, curled, curling, curved, curving, looped, looping, spiral, spiraling (*or* spi-

ralling), winding; meandering, weaving; devious, serpentine, sinuous, zigzag, zig-zagging

ant crooked

2 conforming to a high standard of morality or virtue — see GOOD 2

3 free from added matter — see PURE 1

4 free in expressing one's true feelings and opinions — see FRANK

5 going straight to the point clearly and firmly — see STRAIGHTFORWARD 1

6 not having one's mind affected by alcohol — see SOBER 1

straight *adv* **1** in a direct line or course — see DIRECTLY 1

2 in an honest and direct manner — see STRAIGHTFORWARD

straightaway *adj* **1** done or occurring without any noticeable lapse in time — see INSTANTANEOUS

2 free from irregularities (as curves, bends, or angles) in course — see STRAIGHT 1

straightaway *adv* without delay — see IMMEDIATELY

straighten *vb* to cause to follow a line that is without bends or curls ⟨*straighten* that extension cord—it should be just long enough to reach the wall outlet⟩

syn unbend, uncurl

rel uncoil, unwind; disentangle, untangle, untwine, untwist

near ant arc, bend, bow, hook, round; entwine, kink, swirl, turn, twine, twist; coil, loop, spiral, wind

ant bend, crook, curl, curve

straightforward *also* **straightforwards** *adv* in an honest and direct manner ⟨she finally told him *straightforward* that she wasn't interested in a date⟩

syn directly, forthrightly, foursquare, plain, plainly, straight, straightforwardly

rel candidly, frankly, honestly, openheartedly, openly, unguardedly, unreservedly; artlessly, earnestly, sincerely; abruptly, bluntly, brusquely, curtly, gruffly, sharply; impolitely, inconsiderately, rudely, tactlessly; truthfully, veraciously

near ant long-windedly, verbosely, wordily; civilly, courteously, diplomatically, politely, tactfully; deceitfully, mendaciously, untruthfully; erroneously, fallaciously, falsely, hypocritically, insincerely; ambiguously, circuitously, equivocally, evasively, indirectly

straightforward *adj* **1** going straight to the point clearly and firmly ⟨a *straightforward* account of the football game with no digressions or personal comments⟩

syn direct, forthright, foursquare, plain, straight

rel aboveboard, candid, frank, free-spoken, honest, open, openhearted, outspoken, plainspoken, unguarded, unreserved; artless, earnest, sincere; uninhibited, unrestrained; abrupt, bluff, blunt, brusque, curt, gruff, sharp; impolite, in-

considerate, rude, tactless, undiplomatic; true, truthful, veracious

near ant circumlocutory, long-winded, prolix, verbose, wordy; inhibited, reserved, restrained; civil, courteous, polite, tactful; deceitful, lying, mendacious, untruthful; erroneous, fallacious, false; ambiguous, equivocal, evasive, misleading; double-dealing, hypocritical, two-faced

ant circuitous, indirect, roundabout

2 free from irregularities (as curves, bends, or angles) in course — see STRAIGHT 1

3 free in expressing one's true feelings and opinions — see FRANK

straightforwardly *adv* in an honest and direct manner — see STRAIGHTFORWARD

straightforwardness *n* the free expression of one's true feelings and opinions — see CANDOR

straightway *adv* without delay — see IMMEDIATELY

¹strain *n* **1** the line of ancestors from whom a person is descended — see ANCESTRY

2 a rhythmic series of musical tones arranged to give a pleasing effect — see MELODY

3 a very small amount — see PARTICLE 1

²strain *n* the burden on one's emotional or mental well-being created by demands on one's time — see STRESS 1

strain *vb* **1** to injure by overuse, misuse, or pressure ⟨in order to lift something heavy, squat down and lift with your legs, or you'll *strain* your back⟩

syn pull, rack, stretch, wrench

rel fray, tax, weaken; damage, harm, hurt, impair, wound; batter, bruise, tear; cripple, lame, mangle, mutilate

2 to pass through a filter ⟨better *strain* that coffee carefully to get all the grounds out⟩

syn filter, screen

rel percolate; refilter

3 to devote serious and sustained effort — see LABOR

4 to flow forth slowly through small openings — see EXUDE

5 to subject (a personal quality or faculty) to often excessive stress — see TRY (OUT) 2

strained *adj* lacking in natural or spontaneous quality — see ARTIFICIAL 1

strait *n* **1** a narrow body of water between two land masses — see CHANNEL 2

2 *often* **straits** *pl* a state of great suffering of body or mind — see DISTRESS 1

straitlaced *or* **straightlaced** *adj* given to or marked by very conservative standards regarding personal behavior or morals ⟨a very *straitlaced* old lady who believed women shouldn't even show a bare ankle in public⟩

syn prim, prudish, puritanical

rel priggish, staid, stuffy; genteel, proper, refined; decent, honest, moral, right, righteous, upright, virtuous

near ant liberated, permissive; bad, immoral, improper, indecent, lax, loose,

---

syn synonym(s)　　*rel* related words
ant antonym(s)　　*near ant* near antonym(s)

wicked; debauched, degenerate, degraded, depraved, perverted

strand *n* the usually sandy or gravelly land bordering a body of water — see BEACH

strand *vb* to cause irreparable damage to (a ship) by running aground or sinking — see SHIPWRECK

stranded *adj* resting on the shore or bottom of a body of water — see AGROUND

strange *adj* **1** different from the ordinary in a way that causes curiosity or suspicion — see ODD 1

2 excitingly or mysteriously unusual — see EXOTIC

3 not known or experienced before — see NEW 2

4 noticeably different from what is generally found or experienced — see UNUSUAL 1

stranger *n* a person who is not native to or known to a community ⟨the people of the island are quick to make *strangers* feel at home⟩

syn foreigner, nonnative, outlander, outsider

rel alien; outcast, pariah; drifter, transient, wanderer

near ant buddy, chum, comrade, confidant, crony, familiar, friend, intimate, pal; acquaintance, associate, cohort, colleague, companion, fellow, hearty, hobnobber, mate, partner, peer; adversary, antagonist, enemy, foe, opponent, rival; archenemy, nemesis; citizen, inhabitant, resident

ant native

strangle *vb* **1** to be or cause to be killed by lack of breathable air — see SMOTHER 1

2 to keep (someone) from breathing by exerting pressure on the windpipe — see CHOKE 1

3 to refrain from openly showing or uttering — see SUPPRESS 1

stratagem *n* a clever often underhanded means to achieve an end — see TRICK 1

strategy *n* **1** a method worked out in advance for achieving some objective — see PLAN 1

2 the means or procedure for doing something — see METHOD

stratum *n* one of the segments of society into which people are grouped — see CLASS 1

straw *adj* of a pale yellow or yellowish brown color — see BLOND

stray *adj* lacking a definite plan, purpose, or pattern — see RANDOM

streak *n* **1** a line or long narrow section differing in color from the background — see STRIPE

2 a very small amount — see PARTICLE 1

streak *vb* to make stripes on — see STRIPE

streaked *adj* having stripes — see STRIPED

stream *vb* **1** to cause to flow in a stream — see POUR 1

2 to move in a stream — see FLOW 1

3 to move or proceed smoothly and readily — see FLOW 2

streamer *n* a piece of cloth with a special design that is used as an emblem or for signaling — see FLAG 1

streamlet *n* a natural body of running water smaller than a river — see CREEK 1

streamline *vb* to make less complex — see SIMPLIFY

street *n* a passage cleared for public vehicular travel — see WAY 1

strength *n* **1** the ability to exert effort for the accomplishment of a task — see POWER 2

2 the ability to withstand force or stress without being distorted, dislodged, or damaged — see STABILITY 1

strengthen *vb* **1** to increase the ability of (as a muscle) to exert physical force ⟨lifting weights every day will eventually *strengthen* your muscles⟩ ⟨the Army makes new recruits run for miles in order to *strengthen* them⟩

syn beef (up), fortify, harden, toughen

rel anneal, temper; firm (up), tone (up); energize, invigorate, vitalize; restrengthen

near ant cripple, incapacitate, paralyze; damage, harm, hurt, impair, injure; break down, wear out; sap, undermine

ant debilitate, enervate, enfeeble, weaken

2 to make able to withstand physical hardship, strain, or exposure — see HARDEN 2

3 to make markedly greater in measure or degree — see INTENSIFY

4 to prepare (oneself) mentally or emotionally — see FORTIFY 1

strenuous *adj* **1** marked by or uttered with forcefulness — see EMPHATIC 1

2 requiring considerable physical or mental effort — see HARD 2

strenuously *adv* **1** in a vigorous and forceful manner — see HARD 3

2 with great effort or determination — see HARD 1

stress *n* **1** the burden on one's emotional or mental well-being created by demands on one's time ⟨with a full-time job and her college courses, the young woman is under a lot of *stress* right now⟩

syn pressure, strain, tension

rel load, weight; anxiety, concern, uneasiness, worry; aggravation, anger, annoyance, exasperation, irritation, persecution, trouble

near ant comfort, consolation

2 a special notice or importance given to something — see EMPHASIS 1

stress *vb* to indicate the importance of by giving prominent display — see EMPHASIZE

stressed–out *adj* suffering from high levels of physical and especially psychological stress ⟨I'm becoming *stressed-out* from trying to keep up with the demands of my school work and the grueling workouts for the football team⟩

syn shell-shocked

rel burned-out (*or* burnt-out), exhausted, tired, worn-out; undone, unmanned, unnerved, unstrung; edgy, nervous, tense, uneasy; agitated, disturbed, perturbed,

troubled, upset; aggravated, angry, annoyed, exasperated, irritated
near ant relaxed, rested

stretch *vb* **1** to revert to original size and shape after being stretched, squeezed, or twisted — see ELASTIC 1

stretch *n* **1** a wide space or area — see EXPANSE

2 an indefinite but usually short period of time — see WHILE 1

3 the distance or extent between possible extremes — see RANGE 3

4 the space or amount of space between two points, lines, surfaces, or objects — see DISTANCE

stretch *vb* **1** to add to the interest of by including made-up details — see EMBROIDER

2 to injure by overuse, misuse, or pressure — see STRAIN 1

3 to make longer — see EXTEND 1

4 to subject (a personal quality or faculty) to often excessive stress — see TRY (OUT) 2

stretch (out) *vb* **1** to arrange the parts of (something) over a wider area — see OPEN 3

stretchable *adj* able to revert to original size and shape after being stretched, squeezed, or twisted — see ELASTIC 1

stretching *n* **1** the act of making longer — see EXTENSION 1

2 the representation of something in terms that go beyond the facts — see EXAGGERATION

strew *vb* to cover by or as if by scattering something over or on — see SCATTER 2

strict *adj* **1** following an original exactly — see FAITHFUL 1

2 given to exacting standards of discipline and self-restraint — see SEVERE 1

3 not allowing for any exceptions or loosening of standards — see RIGID 1

strictly *adv* without any relaxation of standards or precision ⟨*strictly* speaking, Columbus did not discover America—the people living there had long known about it⟩ ⟨the rules must be *strictly* obeyed⟩
syn exactly, precisely, rigidly, rigorously
rel carefully, conscientiously, meticulously, scrupulously
ant imprecisely, inexactly, loosely

strictness *n* the quality or state of being demanding or unyielding (as in discipline or criticism) — see SEVERITY

stricture *n* an often public or formal expression of disapproval — see CENSURE

stride *vb* to move along with a steady regular step especially in a group — see MARCH 1

strife *n* a lack of agreement or harmony — see DISCORD

strike *n* **1** a work stoppage by a body of workers intended to force an employer to meet their demands ⟨the nurses will go on *strike* tomorrow unless they're finally given a pay raise⟩

---

syn walkout
rel shutdown, shutoff, sit-down, slowdown; lockout

2 the act or action of setting upon with force or violence — see ATTACK 1

3 a feature of someone or something that creates difficulty for achieving success — see DISADVANTAGE

4 a forceful coming together of two things — see IMPACT 1

strike *vb* **1** to refuse to work in order to force an employer to meet demands ⟨the union is calling for its members to *strike* until the mining company agrees to meet safety standards⟩
syn walk out
rel knock off, lay off; leave, quit, resign; decamp, depart, exit, go, leave, light out, part

2 to act upon (a person or a person's feelings) so as to cause a response — see ¹AFFECT 1

3 to come into the mind of — see OCCUR (TO)

4 to come into usually forceful contact with something — see HIT 2

5 to deliver a blow to (someone or something) usually in a strong vigorous manner — see HIT 1

6 to take apart — see DISASSEMBLE

7 to take sudden, violent action against — see ATTACK 1

strike (into) *vb* to take the first step in (a process or course of action) — see BEGIN 1

strike (out) *vb* to show (something written) to be no longer valid by drawing a cross over or a line through it — see X (OUT)

striking *adj* **1** likely to attract attention — see NOTICEABLE

2 very noticeable especially for being incorrect or bad — see EGREGIOUS

string *n* **1** a length of braided, flexible material that is used for tying or connecting things — see CORD

2 a series of persons or things arranged one behind another — see LINE 1

3 a series of things linked together — see CHAIN 1

string *vb* to put together into a series by means of or as if by means of a thread — see THREAD 2

string along *vb* to cause to believe what is untrue — see DECEIVE

stringent *adj* not allowing for any exceptions or loosening of standards — see RIGID 1

stringy *adj* resembling or having the texture of a mass of strings ⟨*stringy* hair that clearly needed a good washing⟩
syn fibrous
rel knotty, ropy, thready; sinewy, wiry

strip *n* a long narrow piece of material ⟨now tear the paper into *strips* and fold them up carefully⟩
syn list, ribbon, slip
rel band, bandage, belt, binding, strap, swath, tape

strip *vb* **1** to remove clothing from — see UNDRESS

---

2 to search through with the intent of committing robbery — see RANSACK 1

stripe *n* a line or long narrow section differing in color from the background ⟨the United States flag has seven red *stripes*⟩
syn band, bar, streak
rel blaze, crossbar, pinstripe

stripe *vb* to make stripes on ⟨the children carefully *striped* the paper with red and blue paint⟩
syn band, bar, streak
rel blaze

striped *adj* having stripes ⟨the zebra is a black-and-white *striped* animal⟩
syn barred, streaked
rel corded, tabby

stripling *n* a male person who has not yet reached adulthood — see BOY

stripped *adj* 1 lacking a usual or natural covering — see NAKED 2
2 lacking or shed of clothing — see NAKED 1

strive *vb* 1 to devote serious and sustained effort — see LABOR
2 to make an effort to do — see ATTEMPT

stroke *n* a hard strike with a part of the body or an instrument — see ¹BLOW

stroke *vb* to touch or handle in a tender or loving manner — see FONDLE

stroke (out) *vb* to show (something written) to be no longer valid by drawing a cross over or a line through it — see X (OUT)

stroll *n* a relaxed journey on foot for exercise or pleasure — see WALK

stroller *n* a person who roams about without a fixed route or destination — see NOMAD

strong *adj* 1 having muscles capable of exerting great physical force ⟨I need some *strong* people to help me move furniture⟩
syn brawny, muscular, rugged, sinewy, stalwart, stout
rel forceful, mighty, potent, powerful, puissant; able-bodied, athletic, fit, trim; beefy, burly, husky, strapping; masculine, virile; hard, inured, strengthened, sturdy, tough, toughened; energetic, energized, invigorated, lusty, red-blooded, robust, vigorous, vitalized; hale, healthy, hearty, sound
near ant challenged, disabled, incapacitated, paralyzed; impotent, powerless; puny, slight, small, unfit, unhealthy
ant delicate, feeble, frail, weak, wimpy
2 able to withstand hardship, strain, or exposure — see HARDY 1
3 having a powerfully stimulating odor or flavor — see SHARP 3
4 having an abundance of some characteristic quality (as flavor) — see FULL-BODIED
5 having an unpleasant smell — see MALODOROUS
6 having great power or influence — see IMPORTANT 2
7 having the power to persuade — see COGENT
8 marked by the ability to withstand stress without structural damage or distortion — see STABLE 1
9 not showing weakness or uncertainty — see FIRM 1

strongbox *n* a specially reinforced container to keep valuables safe — see SAFE

stronghold *n* a structure or place from which one can resist attack — see FORT

strongly *adv* in a vigorous and forceful manner — see HARD 3

strop *vb* to make sharp or sharper — see SHARPEN

stropped *adj* having an edge thin enough to cut or pierce something — see SHARP 1

structure *n* 1 something built as a dwelling, shelter, or place for human activity — see BUILDING
2 something put together by arranging or connecting an array of parts — see CONSTRUCTION 1
3 the arrangement of parts that gives something its basic form — see FRAME 1

struggle *n* 1 a forceful effort to reach a goal or objective ⟨a physically challenged child's determined *struggle* to make straight A's in school⟩
syn battle, fight, fray, scrabble
rel effort, exertion, labor, pains, trouble, work; drudgery, grind, sweat, toil, travail; combat, conflict, contest, strife, tussle, war, warfare; attempt, endeavor, essay, try
2 a physical dispute between opposing individuals or groups — see FIGHT 1
3 an earnest effort for superiority or victory over another — see CONTEST 1

struggle *vb* to devote serious and sustained effort — see LABOR

strut *vb* 1 to walk with exaggerated arm and leg movements ⟨the toy soldiers in the Christmas pageant *strutted* stiffly across the stage⟩
syn prance, stalk, swagger
rel flounce, mince, traipse; pussyfoot, tiptoe; parade, promenade; pad, step, tread; pace, stride; lumber, lurch, pound, shamble, shuffle, stagger
2 to present so as to invite notice or attention — see SHOW 1

stub *n* an unused or unwanted piece or item typically of small size or value — see ¹SCRAP 1

stubborn *adj* sticking to an opinion, purpose, or course of action in spite of reason, arguments, or persuasion — see OBSTINATE

stubbornness *n* a steadfast adherence to an opinion, purpose, or course of action — see OBSTINACY

stubby *adj* being compact and broad in build and often short in stature — see STOCKY

stuck *adj* firmly positioned in place and difficult to dislodge — see TIGHT 2

stuck-up *adj* having too high an opinion of oneself — see CONCEITED

student *n* one who attends a school ⟨a straight-A *student* at the local high school⟩

syn pupil, scholar

rel schoolboy, schoolchild, schoolgirl; schoolfellow, schoolmate; collegian, postgraduate, undergraduate; freshman, junior, senior, sophomore; underclassman, upperclassman

studied *adj* decided on as a result of careful thought — see DELIBERATE 1

study *n* **1** a systematic search for the truth or facts about something — see INQUIRY 1

2 the state of being lost in thought — see REVERIE

study *vb* **1** to use the mind to acquire knowledge ⟨you'll have to *study* hard and learn all about the Revolutionary War in order to pass the history test⟩

syn bone (up)

rel cram; analyze, deduce, find out; learn, read; research, restudy

phrases go over, go through

2 to commit to memory — see MEMORIZE

3 to give serious and careful thought to — see PONDER

stuff *n* **1** a skill, an ability, or knowledge that makes a person able to do a particular job — see QUALIFICATION 1

2 the basic elements from which something can be developed — see MAKING

3 the quality or qualities that make a thing what it is — see ESSENCE

stuff *vb* **1** to close up so that no empty spaces remain — see FILL 2

2 to fill with food to capacity — see GORGE 1

3 to fit (something) into a tight space — see CROWD 1

4 to prevent passage through — see CLOG 1

5 to put into (something) as much as can be held or contained — see FILL 1

stuffed *adj* **1** containing or seeming to contain the greatest quantity or number possible — see FULL 1

2 having one's appetite completely satisfied — see FULL 3

stuffer *n* one who eats greedily or too much — see GLUTTON

stuffing *n* soft material that is used to fill the hollow parts of something — see FILLING

stuffy *adj* **1** lacking fresh air ⟨the house was so *stuffy* after being closed up for a month⟩

syn breathless, close, stifling, suffocating

rel airless, unventilated; heavy, oppressive, thick

near ant bracing, brisk, invigorating, refreshed, sweet; ventilated

ant airy, breezy

2 causing weariness, restlessness, or lack of interest — see BORING

stumble *n* **1** an unintentional departure from truth or accuracy — see ERROR 1

2 the act of going down from an upright position suddenly and involuntarily — see FALL 1

stumble *vb* **1** to go down from an upright position suddenly and involuntarily — see FALL 1

2 to make progress in a clumsy, struggling manner — see FLOUNDER 1

3 to move heavily or clumsily — see LUMBER 1

stumble (on *or* onto) *vb* to come upon unexpectedly or by chance — see HAPPEN (ON *OR* UPON)

stumble (upon) *vb* to come upon face-to-face or as if face-to-face — see MEET 1

stumbling block *n* something that makes progress or movement more difficult — see ENCUMBRANCE

stump *vb* **1** to move heavily or clumsily — see LUMBER 1

2 to invite (someone) to take part in a contest or to perform a feat — see CHALLENGE 2

stumpy *adj* being compact and broad in build and often short in stature — see STOCKY

stun *vb* **1** to make senseless or dizzy by a blow ⟨a powerful uppercut to the jaw *stunned* the boxer and sent him crashing to the canvas⟩

syn daze

rel deaden, knock out, paralyze; benumb, numb, stupefy; bowl (over), knock (down)

phrases knock for a loop

2 to make a strong impression on (someone) with something unexpected — see SURPRISE 1

stunned *adj* **1** affected with sudden and great wonder or surprise — see THUNDERSTRUCK

2 suffering from mental confusion — see DIZZY 2

stunner *n* **1** a lovely woman — see BEAUTY 2

2 something that makes a strong impression because it is so unexpected — see SURPRISE 1

stunning *adj* **1** causing a strong emotional reaction because unexpected — see SURPRISING 1

2 causing wonder or astonishment — see MARVELOUS 1

3 very pleasing to look at — see BEAUTIFUL

stunt *n* an act of notable skill, strength, or cleverness — see FEAT 1

stunt *vb* to hold back the normal growth of ⟨unfortunately, an unusually dry summer seems to have permanently *stunted* the tree⟩

syn dwarf, suppress

rel arrest, catch, check, halt, hold up, stall, stay, still, stop; balk, block, hold back, impede, obstruct, stem

near ant advance, boost, encourage, forward, promote

stupefied *adj* **1** affected with sudden and great wonder or surprise — see THUNDERSTRUCK

2 suffering from mental confusion — see DIZZY 2

stupefy *vb* to make a strong impression on (someone) with something unexpected — see SURPRISE 1

stupefying *adj* causing a strong emotional reaction because unexpected — see SURPRISING 1

stupendous *adj* causing wonder or astonishment — see MARVELOUS 1

stupendously *adv* to a large extent or degree — see GREATLY 2

stupendousness *n* impressiveness of beauty on a large scale — see MAGNIFICENCE

stupid *adj* **1** not having or showing an ability to absorb ideas readily ⟨it's not nice to constantly call your brother *stupid* and ugly⟩ ⟨don't ask *stupid* questions⟩
syn brainless, dense, doltish, dopey, dorky [*slang*], dull, dumb, fatuous, half-witted, mindless, oafish, obtuse, senseless, simple, slow, thick, thickheaded, unintelligent, vacuous, weak-minded, witless
rel feebleminded, retarded, simpleminded; foolish, idiotic, imbecile, imbecilic, moronic; ignorant, illiterate, lowbrow, uneducated, uninformed, untaught, unthinking; absurd, asinine, balmy, cockeyed, crazy, cuckoo, daffy, daft, dotty, harebrained, insane, kooky, loony (*also* looney), lunatic, mad, nonsensical, nutty, preposterous, sappy, screwball, silly, unwise, wacky, zany; fallacious, illogical, invalid, irrational, unreasonable
near ant ingenious, resourceful; acute, astute, discerning, insightful, keen, knowing, perceptive, perspicacious, sagacious, sage, sapient, savvy, wise; cerebral, erudite, highbrow, intellectual, knowledgeable, learned, literate, scholarly, thinking, well-read; educated, informed, schooled, skilled, trained; crafty, cunning, foxy, shrewd, wily; judicious, prudent, sane, sensible, sound; logical, rational, reasonable, valid
ant apt, brainy, bright, brilliant; clever, intelligent, keen, nimble, quick, quick-witted, sharp, sharp-witted, smart
2 causing weariness, restlessness, or lack of interest — see BORING
3 showing or marked by a lack of good sense or judgment — see FOOLISH 1

stupidity *n* **1** the quality or state of lacking intelligence or quickness of mind ⟨the *stupidity* of the dialogue between the two romantic leads had movie audiences giggling uncontrollably⟩
syn brainlessness, denseness, density, doltishness, dopiness, dullness (*also* dulness), dumbness, fatuity, foolishness, mindlessness, oafishness, obtuseness, senselessness, simpleness, slowness, stupidness, vacuity, witlessness
rel absurdity, asininity, balminess, craziness, daftness, folly, idiocy, inanity, insanity, lunacy, madness, nonsensicalness, nuttiness, preposterousness, silliness, simplicity, wackiness, zaniness; fallacy, irrationality, unreasonableness

near ant acumen, alertness, astuteness, discernment, insight, judgment (*or* judgement), perception, perspicacity; sagacity, sageness, sapience, wisdom, wit; logicalness, rationality, reasonableness, soundness, validity
ant braininess, brightness, brilliance, cleverness, intelligence, keenness, quickness, quick-wittedness, sharpness, smartness
2 a foolish act or idea — see FOLLY 1
3 language, behavior, or ideas that are absurd and contrary to good sense — see NONSENSE 1

stupidness *n* the quality or state of lacking intelligence or quickness of mind — see STUPIDITY 1

sturdily *adv* in a vigorous and forceful manner — see HARD 3

sturdiness *n* the ability to withstand force or stress without being distorted, dislodged, or damaged — see STABILITY 1

sturdy *adj* **1** able to withstand hardship, strain, or exposure — see HARDY 1
2 marked by the ability to withstand stress without structural damage or distortion — see STABLE 1
3 not showing weakness or uncertainty — see FIRM 1

style *n* **1** a distinctive way of putting ideas into words ⟨I correctly identified the quotation because I recognized Mark Twain's inimitable *style*⟩
syn fashion, locution, manner, mode, phraseology, tone, vein
rel delivery, elocution; archaism, colloquialism, regionalism; acceptation, connotation, denotation, idiom
2 the means or procedure for doing something — see METHOD
3 a practice or interest that is very popular for a short time — see FAD

style *vb* to give a name to — see NAME 1

styleless *adj* marked by an obvious lack of style or good taste — see TACKY 1

stylish *adj* being in the latest or current fashion ⟨a pretty, *stylish* dress⟩
syn à la mode (*also* a la mode), chic, fashionable, in, modish, sharp, smart, snappy
rel dapper, dashing, natty, rakish, spiffy, spruce; posh, ritzy, swank (*or* swanky); elegant, graceful, handsome, majestic, refined, sophisticated, stately, tasteful, understated; dandyish, dudish, foppish; classic, exquisite, quiet, restrained, simple; affected, grandiose, pretentious
near ant tacky, unattractive, unbecoming; graceless, inelegant, tasteless, unhandsome; frowsy (*or* frowzy), sloppy, slovenly, unkempt, untidy; disheveled (*or* dishevelled); messy, mussy, rumpled, wrinkled; shabby, sleazy
ant dowdy, outmoded, styleless, unfashionable, unstylish

suasion *n* the act of reasoning or pleading with someone to accept a belief or course of action — see PERSUASION 1

suave *adj* having or showing very polished and worldly manners ⟨the *suave* gentleman was a great favorite of the elegant ladies who attended parties at the embassy〉

syn debonair, smooth, sophisticated, urbane

rel glib, slick, unctuous; civilized, cultivated, cultured, graceful, poised, polished, refined; cosmopolitan, smart, worldly-wise; experienced, knowing, practiced (*or* practised), schooled, seasoned; amiable, appealing, attractive; assured, calm, collected, composed, confident, cool, placid, secure, self-assured, self-confident, self-possessed, serene, tranquil, undisturbed, unperturbed

near ant awkward, clumsy, gauche, graceless, stiff, stilted, uncomfortable, uneasy, ungraceful, wooden; callow, green, inexperienced, raw; parochial, provincial, roughhewn, rustic; inelegant, philistine, uncivilized, uncultured, unrefined; unsophisticated, unworldly; gawky, lubberly, stodgy, ungainly; diffident, insecure

ant boorish, churlish, clownish, loutish, uncouth

¹sub *n* a large sandwich on a long split roll — see SUBMARINE

²sub *n* a person or thing that takes the place of another — see SUBSTITUTE

sub *vb* to serve as a replacement usually for a time only — see COVER 1

subdue *vb* **1** to achieve a victory over — see BEAT 2

2 to bring under one's control by force of arms — see CONQUER 1

3 to put a stop to (something) by the use of force — see QUELL 1

subdued *adj* not excessively showy — see QUIET 2

subduer *n* one that defeats an enemy or opponent — see VICTOR 1

subduing *n* the act or process of bringing someone or something under one's control — see CONQUEST

subject *n* **1** a major object of interest or concern (as in a discussion or artistic composition) — see MATTER 1

2 a person who owes allegiance to a government and is protected by it — see CITIZEN 1

subject *vb* to bring under one's control by force of arms — see CONQUER 1

subject (to) *adj* **1** determined by something else — see DEPENDENT 2

2 being in a situation where one is likely to meet with harm — see LIABLE 1

subjecting *n* the act or process of bringing someone or something under one's control — see CONQUEST

subjection *n* the act or process of bringing someone or something under one's control — see CONQUEST

subjugate *vb* to bring under one's control by force of arms — see CONQUER 1

subjugating *n* the act or process of bringing someone or something under one's control — see CONQUEST

subjugation *n* the act or process of bringing someone or something under one's control — see CONQUEST

sublime *adj* **1** causing wonder or astonishment — see MARVELOUS 1

2 having, characterized by, or arising from a dignified and generous nature — see NOBLE 2

sublimeness *n* impressiveness of beauty on a large scale — see MAGNIFICENCE

submarine *adj* living, lying, or occurring below the surface of the water — see UNDERWATER

submarine *n* a large sandwich on a long split roll 〈always orders a roast beef *submarine* with the works〉

syn grinder, hero, hoagie, Italian sandwich, po'boy (*also* poor boy), sub

submerge *vb* **1** to cover or become filled with a flood — see FLOOD

2 to sink or push (something) briefly into or as if into a liquid — see DIP 1

submerged *adj* living, lying, or occurring below the surface of the water — see UNDERWATER

submerse *vb* **1** to cover or become filled with a flood — see FLOOD

2 to sink or push (something) briefly into or as if into a liquid — see DIP 1

submission *n* **1** a bending to the authority or control of another — see OBEDIENCE 1

2 the usually forced yielding of one's person or possessions to the control of another — see SURRENDER

submissive *adj* readily giving in to the command or authority of another — see OBEDIENT

submissively *adv* in manner showing no signs of pride or self-assertion — see LOWLY

submissiveness *n* a readiness or willingness to yield to the wishes of others — see COMPLIANCE 1

submit *vb* **1** to cease resistance (as to another's arguments, demands, or control) — see YIELD 3

2 to give up and cease resistance (as to a liking, temptation, or habit) — see YIELD 1

3 to yield to the control or power of enemy forces — see FALL 2

submitting *n* the usually forced yielding of one's person or possessions to the control of another — see SURRENDER

subordinate *adj* having not so great importance or rank as another — see LESSER

subordinate *n* one who is of lower rank and typically under the authority of another — see UNDERLING

subordination *n* a bending to the authority or control of another — see OBEDIENCE 1

subpoena *n* a written notice ordering a person to appear in court — see SUMMONS

subscribe (to) *vb* to have a favorable opinion of — see APPROVE (OF)

---

syn synonym(s)   *rel* related words
ant antonym(s)   *near ant* near antonym(s)

subsequent *adj* being, occurring, or carried out at a time after something else ⟨I'll do the first problem as an example, but all *subsequent* efforts must be done on your own⟩
syn after, ensuing, later, posterior
rel behind, belated, delayed, late, slow; eventual, last, ultimate; following
near ant advance, early, premature
ant antecedent, anterior, fore, precedent, preceding, previous, prior

subsequently *adv* following in time or place — see AFTER

subside *vb* to grow less in scope or intensity especially gradually — see DECREASE 2

subsidize *vb* 1 to furnish (as an institution) with a regular source of income — see ENDOW 2
2 to provide money for — see FINANCE 1

subsidy *n* a sum of money allotted for a specific use by official or formal action — see APPROPRIATION

subsist *vb* to have life — see BE 1

subsistence *n* 1 the fact of being or of being real — see EXISTENCE
2 uninterrupted or lasting existence — see CONTINUATION

substance *n* 1 the basic elements from which something can be developed — see MAKING
2 the quality or qualities that make a thing what it is — see ESSENCE
3 the total of one's money and property — see WEALTH 1
4 one that has a real and independent existence — see ENTITY

substance abuser *n* a person who regularly uses drugs especially illegally — see DOPER

substandard *adj* falling short of a standard — see BAD 1

substantial *adj* 1 having great meaning or lasting effect — see IMPORTANT 1
2 of a size greater than average of its kind — see LARGE
3 relating to or composed of matter — see MATERIAL 1
4 sufficiently large in size, amount, or number to merit attention — see CONSIDERABLE 1

substantiality *n* the quality or state of being large in size — see LARGENESS

substantially *adv* for the most part — see CHIEFLY

substantiate *vb* 1 to gain full recognition or acceptance of — see ESTABLISH 1
2 to give evidence or testimony to the truth or factualness of — see CONFIRM
3 to represent in visible form — see EMBODY 2
4 to show the existence or truth of by evidence — see PROVE 1

substantiating *adj* serving to give support to the truth or factualness of something — see CORROBORATIVE

substantiation *n* something presented in support of the truth or accuracy of a claim — see PROOF

substitute *adj* 1 being such in appearance only and made with or manufactured from usually cheaper materials — see IMITATION
2 taking the place of one that came before — see NEW 1

substitute *n* a person or thing that takes the place of another ⟨you'll be getting a *substitute* until your regular teacher is feeling better⟩ ⟨if you like, you can use nuts as a *substitute* for coconut in that recipe⟩
syn backup, pinch hitter, relief, replacement, reserve, stand-in, sub
rel alternate, understudy; apology, makeshift, stopgap; agent, attorney, commissary, delegate, deputy, envoy, factor, procurator, proxy, representative, surrogate; assistant, second

substitute *vb* 1 to give up (something) and take something else in return — see CHANGE 3
2 to serve as a replacement usually for a time only — see COVER 1
3 to take the place of — see REPLACE 1

subterfuge *n* the use of clever underhanded actions to achieve an end — see TRICKERY

subtle *adj* 1 clever at attaining one's ends by indirect and often deceptive means — see ARTFUL 1
2 made or done with extreme care and accuracy — see FINE 2
3 satisfying or pleasing because of fineness or mildness — see DELICATE 1

subtleness *n* skill in achieving one's ends through indirect, subtle, or underhanded means — see CUNNING 1

subtlety *n* skill in achieving one's ends through indirect, subtle, or underhanded means — see CUNNING 1

subtract *vb* to take away (an amount or number) from a total ⟨if you *subtract* 10 from 23, you get 13⟩ ⟨you can *subtract* the time you spent daydreaming from your total homework time⟩
syn deduct, take off
rel decrease, diminish, discount, downsize, lessen, lower, reduce; abbreviate, abridge, clip, crop, curtail, cut, cut back, cut down, dock, pare, prune, retrench, shorten, slash, trim, truncate, whittle
near ant adjoin, annex, append, tack (on); add (to), complement, supplement; enhance, heighten, intensify; aggrandize, amplify, augment, boost, enlarge, escalate, expand, increase, raise
ant add

subtraction *n* the act or an instance of taking away from a total ⟨the dog was responsible for the unexplained *subtraction* in the number of potato chips on my sister's plate⟩
syn deduction
rel discount; abatement, decline, decrement, diminishment, diminution, drop, fall, loss, reduction, shrinkage; curtailment, cut, cutback
near ant boost, enlargement, gain, increase, increment, raise, rise; accretion,

accrual, accumulation, addendum, appendix, supplement
ant addition

suburbia *n* the area around a city — see ENVIRONS 1

subvert *vb* to lower in character or dignity — see DEBASE 1

succeed *vb* 1 to turn out as planned or desired ⟨the advertising campaign that finally *succeeded* used humor to sell the product⟩
syn click, deliver, go over, pan out, work out
rel catch on; flourish, prosper, thrive
phrases catch fire
near ant languish; flounder, struggle; decline, slip, slump, wane
ant collapse, fail, flop, flunk, fold, wash out

2 to reach a desired level of accomplishment ⟨if you want to *succeed* in show business, you have to feel comfortable in front of an audience⟩
syn flourish, prosper, thrive
rel prevail, triumph, win
phrases get ahead, make good, make it
near ant flounder, struggle
ant fail

3 to come after in time — see FOLLOW 1

succeeding *adj* 1 being the one that comes immediately after another — see NEXT

2 following one after another without others coming in between — see CONSECUTIVE

success *n* 1 a person or thing that is successful — see HIT 1

2 a successful result brought about by hard work — see ACCOMPLISHMENT 1

successful *adj* 1 having attained a desired end or state of good fortune ⟨the family runs several *successful* restaurants⟩
syn flourishing, going, palmy, prosperous, thriving, triumphant
rel coming, promising; booming, growing, roaring, robust
near ant futureless, hopeless, inauspicious, no-good; collapsing, failing, flopping, flunking, folding, washing-out; declining, slipping, slumping, waning; bankrupt, destroyed, ruined, wrecked
ant unsuccessful

2 marked by vigorous growth and well-being especially economically — see PROSPEROUS 1

successional *adj* following one after another without others coming in between — see CONSECUTIVE

successive *adj* following one after another without others coming in between — see CONSECUTIVE

succinct *adj* marked by the use of few words to convey much information or meaning — see CONCISE

succinctly *adv* in a few words — see SHORTLY 1

succinctness *n* the quality or state of being marked by or using only few words to convey much meaning ⟨Caesar's observation, "I came, I saw, I conquered," is famous for its *succinctness*⟩
syn brevity, briefness, compactness, conciseness, crispness, pithiness, terseness
rel abruptness, bluntness, brusqueness, curtness, shortness
near ant redundancy, repetitiousness
ant diffuseness, long-windedness, prolixity, verbosity, wordiness

succulence *n* the quality or state of being full of juice ⟨the *succulence* of the apple was such that the first bite sent juice running down my chin⟩
syn fleshiness, juiciness, pulpiness
rel sap, sappiness

succulent *adj* full of juice — see JUICY

succumb *vb* 1 to cease resistance (as to another's arguments, demands, or control) — see YIELD 3

2 to give up and cease resistance (as to a liking, temptation, or habit) — see YIELD 1

3 to stop living — see DIE 1

4 to yield to the control or power of enemy forces — see FALL 2

such *adj* having qualities in common — see ALIKE

suchlike *adj* having qualities in common — see ALIKE

suck (up) *vb* to take in (something liquid) through small openings — see ABSORB 1

sucker *n* one who is easily deceived or cheated — see DUPE

suddenly *adv* 1 with great suddenness — see SHORT

2 without warning — see UNAWARES

suds *n* a light mass of fine bubbles formed in or on a liquid — see FOAM

sudsy *adj* covered with, consisting of, or resembling foam — see FOAMY

sue (for) *vb* to make a request for — see ASK (FOR) 1

suer *n* the person in a legal proceeding who makes a charge of wrongdoing against another — see COMPLAINANT

suffer *vb* 1 to give permission to — see ALLOW 2

2 to come to a knowledge of (something) by living through it — see EXPERIENCE

3 to feel deep sadness or mental pain — see GRIEVE

4 to give permission for or to approve of — see ALLOW 1

sufferable *adj* capable of being endured — see BEARABLE

sufferance *n* 1 the approval by someone in authority for the doing of something — see PERMISSION

2 the capacity to endure what is difficult or disagreeable without complaining — see PATIENCE

suffice *vb* to be enough — see SERVE 2

sufficiency *n* the quality or state of meeting one's needs adequately ⟨the *sufficiency* of the portions is such that you will leave the restaurant with a full stomach but without doggie bags⟩

---

syn synonym(s)   *rel* related words
ant antonym(s)   *near ant* near antonym(s)

syn acceptability, adequacy, satisfactoriness

rel appropriateness, correctness, fitness, goodness, properness, rightness, seemliness, suitability, suitableness; bountifulness, copiousness; excess, overabundance, oversupply, surfeit, surplus; abundance, amplitude, plenitude, plenty

near ant lack, want; dearth, shortage; meagerness, paucity, poorness, poverty, rareness, rarity, scantiness, scarceness, scarcity, skimpiness; necessity, need, privation

ant inadequacy, insufficiency

sufficiently *adv* in or to a degree or quantity that meets one's requirements or satisfaction — see ENOUGH 1

suffocate *vb* to be or cause to be killed by lack of breathable air — see SMOTHER 1

suffocating *adj* lacking fresh air — see STUFFY 1

suffrage *n* the right to formally express one's position or will in an election — see VOTE 1

suffuse *vb* 1 to cause (as a person) to become filled or saturated with a certain quality or principle — see INFUSE

2 to spread throughout — see PERMEATE

sugarcoated *adj* appealing to the emotions in an obvious and tiresome way — see CORNY

sugary *adj* appealing to the emotions in an obvious and tiresome way — see CORNY

suggest *vb* 1 to convey an idea indirectly — see HINT

2 to put forward as one's choice for a wise or proper course of action — see ADVISE 2

3 to set before the mind for consideration — see PROPOSE 1

suggestion *n* 1 a slight or indirect pointing to something (as a solution or explanation) — see HINT 1

2 something which is presented for consideration — see PROPOSAL

suggestive *adj* 1 hinting at or intended to call to mind matters regarded as indecent ⟨making *suggestive* remarks to one's classmates will not be tolerated⟩

syn bawdy, lewd, racy, ribald, salty, spicy

rel leering; coarse, crude, earthy, foul, gross; dirty, filthy, lascivious, nasty, obscene, pornographic, smutty, unprintable, vulgar; indecorous, unbecoming; naughty, wicked; exceptionable, objectionable, unacceptable, undesirable, unwanted, unwelcome

near ant clean, decent; innocuous, inoffensive; priggish, prim, prudish, puritanical, straitlaced (*or* straightlaced), Victorian; correct, decorous, genteel, polite, proper, seemly; acceptable, agreeable, desirable, pleasant, pleasing, welcome; appropriate, becoming, fit, meet, suitable; immaculate, pure, spotless

2 provoking a memory or mental association ⟨a haunting and *suggestive* song about a long-lost love⟩

syn evocative, reminiscent

rel eloquent, expressive, meaningful, significant; affecting, emotional, moving, poignant, stirring, touching; exciting, provocative, provoking, rousing, stimulating

3 clearly conveying a special meaning (as one's mood) — see EXPRESSIVE

suicide *n* the act of deliberately killing oneself ⟨teenagers are more prone to *suicide* because they mistakenly believe their troubles are insurmountable⟩

syn self-destruction

rel martyrdom; foul play, homicide, murder, slaying; killing, manslaughter; assassination, execution; euthanasia, mercy killing

suit *n* 1 a court case for enforcing a right or claim — see LAWSUIT

2 an earnest request — see PLEA 1

suit *vb* 1 to be fitting or proper — see DO 1

2 to give satisfaction to — see PLEASE

3 to outfit with clothes and especially fine or special clothes — see CLOTHE 1

suitability *n* the quality or state of being especially suitable or fitting — see APPROPRIATENESS

suitable *adj* 1 having the required skills for an acceptable level of performance — see COMPETENT

2 meeting the requirements of a purpose or situation — see FIT 1

suitableness *n* the quality or state of being especially suitable or fitting — see APPROPRIATENESS

suitably *adv* in a manner suitable for the occasion or purpose — see PROPERLY

suitcase *n* a bag carried by hand and designed to hold a traveler's clothing and personal articles — see TRAVELING BAG

suite *n* 1 a body of employees or servants who accompany and wait on a person — see CORTEGE 1

2 a number of things considered as a unit — see GROUP 1

3 a room or set of rooms in a private house or a block used as a separate dwelling place — see APARTMENT 1

suitor *n* 1 a man who courts a woman usually with the goal of marrying her ⟨my sister finally married her *suitor* of six years on Sunday⟩

syn gallant, swain, wooer

rel beau, boyfriend, fellow, man; admirer, crush, steady; beloved, darling, dear, favorite, flame, honey, love, lover, sweet, sweetheart, valentine; date, escort; fiancé, intended

2 one who asks earnestly for a favor or gift — see SUPPLICANT

sulk *n* a state of resentful silence or irritability ⟨a child sitting in a *sulk* over a minor disagreement⟩

syn pet, pouts, sulkiness, sullenness

rel blues, dumps, mopes; surliness; biliousness, crankiness, crossness, crotchetiness, grouchiness, grumpiness, irascibility, irritability, peevishness, perverseness, perversity, pettishness, petulance, testiness, waspishness; cantankerousness, disagreeableness, orneriness *near ant* sociability; cheerfulness, gaiety (*also* gayety), gladsomeness, good-humoredness, high-spiritedness, lightheartedness, perkiness

sulk *vb* to silently go about in a bad mood ⟨the toddler *sulked* all day whenever he didn't get his way⟩

syn mope, pout

rel brood, dwell (on), mull (over), muse (over), ponder; frown, glower, lower (*also* lour), scowl; carry on, take on

sulkiness *n* a state of resentful silence or irritability — see SULK

sulky *adj* given to or displaying a resentful silence and often irritability ⟨our teenage daughter turns *sulky* if we refuse to let her borrow the car⟩

syn glum, pouting, sullen, surly

rel dour, gloomy, morose; choleric, crabby, cranky, cross, crotchety, grouchy, grumpy, irascible, irritable, peevish, perverse, pettish, petulant, quick-tempered, short-tempered, snappy, snippy, testy, waspish; brooding, moping; bearish, bilious, cantankerous, disagreeable, dyspeptic, ill-humored, ill-natured, ill-tempered, ornery; sensitive, temperamental, thinskinned, touchy

near ant sociable; cheerful, cheery, gladsome, good-humored, good-natured, perky

sullen *adj* **1** causing or marked by an atmosphere lacking in cheer — see GLOOMY 1

2 given to or displaying a resentful silence and often irritability — see SULKY

sullenness *n* a state of resentful silence or irritability — see SULK

sullied *adj* not clean — see DIRTY 1

sully *vb* to make dirty — see DIRTY

sultry *adj* **1** containing or characterized by an uncomfortable amount of moisture — see HUMID

2 having a notably high temperature — see HOT 1

sum *n* **1** a complete amount of something — see WHOLE

2 a short statement of the main points — see SUMMARY

sum *vb* to combine (numbers) into a single sum — see ADD 2

sum (to *or* into) *vb* to have a total of — see AMOUNT (TO) 1

summarily *adv* in a few words — see SHORTLY 1

summarization *n* a short statement of the main points — see SUMMARY

summarize *vb* to make into a short statement of the main points (as of a report) ⟨the closing minute of the newscast *summarizes* the main story of the day⟩

syn abstract, digest, encapsulate, epitomize, outline, recap, recapitulate, sum up, wrap up

rel abridge, condense, curtail, shorten; downsize, shrink; concentrate, consolidate; simplify, streamline

near ant amplify, elaborate (on *or* upon), enlarge (on *or* upon), expand

summary *adj* marked by the use of few words to convey much information or meaning — see CONCISE

summary *n* a short statement of the main points ⟨many book reports choose to begin with a *summary* of the book⟩

syn abstract, digest, encapsulation, epitome, outline, précis, recap, recapitulation, résumé (*or* resume *also* resumé), roundup, sum, summarization, synopsis

rel abbreviation, abridgment (*or* abridgement), condensation, curtailment, shortening; brief; rundown; simplification, streamlining

near ant amplification, enlargement, expansion

summation *n* a complete amount of something — see WHOLE

summit *n* the highest part or point — see HEIGHT 1

summon *vb* **1** to demand or request the presence or service of ⟨without explanation, the principal *summoned* me to his office⟩

syn call, hail

rel cite, subpoena; assemble, convene, convoke, muster; ask, bid, invite; command, order, request, requisition; beckon, demand, invoke

phrases send for

near ant dismiss, send (away), turn away

2 to call into being through the use of one's inner resources or powers ⟨managed to *summon* a bright smile despite the gloomy day⟩

syn conjure (up), gather (up)

rel educe, elicit, evoke, raise

3 to bring together in assembly by or as if by command — see CONVOKE

summons *n* a written notice ordering a person to appear in court ⟨if you ignore a court *summons*, you will be fined⟩

syn subpoena

rel warrant, writ

sumptuous *adj* showing obvious signs of wealth and comfort — see LUXURIOUS

sumptuously *adv* in a luxurious manner — see HIGH

sum up *vb* to make into a short statement of the main points (as of a report) — see SUMMARIZE

sun *n* **1** the light given off by the star around which the planet Earth revolves ⟨be sure to wear sunscreen if you plan to spend more than a few minutes in the *sun*⟩

syn sunlight, sunshine

rel sunburst; daylight

near ant cloudiness; penumbra, shade, shadiness, shadow, umbra

2 a ball-shaped gaseous celestial body that shines by its own light — see STAR 1

sunder *vb* to set or force apart — see SEPARATE 1

sundown *n* the time from when the sun begins to set to the onset of total darkness — see DUSK 1

---

syn synonym(s)   *rel* related words
ant antonym(s)   *near ant* near antonym(s)

sundowner *n, Australian* a homeless wanderer who may beg or steal for a living — see TRAMP

sundries *n pl* small useful items — see NOTION 1

sunken *adj* 1 curved inward — see HOLLOW

2 living, lying, or occurring below the surface of the water — see UNDERWATER

sunlight *n* the light given off by the star around which the planet Earth revolves — see SUN 1

sunny *adj* 1 having or being an outward sign of good feelings (as of love, confidence, or happiness) — see RADIANT 1

2 having or showing a good mood or disposition — see CHEERFUL 1

3 of or marked by high spirits or good humor — see MERRY

4 not stormy or cloudy — see FAIR 1

sunrise *n* the first appearance of light in the morning or the time of its appearance — see DAWN 1

sunset *n* the time from when the sun begins to set to the onset of total darkness — see DUSK 1

sunshine *n* the light given off by the star around which the planet Earth revolves — see SUN 1

sunshiny *adj* not stormy or cloudy — see FAIR 1

sunup *n* the first appearance of light in the morning or the time of its appearance — see DAWN 1

sup *n* the portion of a serving of a beverage that is swallowed at one time — see DRINK 2

sup *vb* to swallow in liquid form — see DRINK 1

super *adj* unusually large — see HUGE

super *adv* to a great degree — see VERY 1

superabundance *n* 1 an amount or supply more than sufficient to meet one's needs — see PLENTY 1

2 the state or an instance of going beyond what is usual, proper, or needed — see EXCESS

superb *adj* of the very best kind — see EXCELLENT

superbness *n* 1 exceptionally high quality — see EXCELLENCE 1

2 impressiveness of beauty on a large scale — see MAGNIFICENCE

supercilious *adj* having a feeling of superiority that shows itself in an overbearing attitude — see ARROGANT

superciliousness *n* an exaggerated sense of one's importance that shows itself in the making of excessive or unjustified claims — see ARROGANCE

superficial *adj* 1 lying on or affecting only the outer layer of something ⟨a *superficial* scratch that barely even broke the skin⟩

syn skin-deep, surface

rel depthless, shallow, shoal; two-dimensional

near ant deep, deep-rooted, deep-seated; subcutaneous, subterranean

2 having or showing a lack of depth of understanding or character ⟨a *superficial* analysis of how movie and video violence affects young people⟩

syn facile, one-dimensional, shallow, skin-deep

rel cursory, hasty, sketchy; aimless, desultory, haphazard, hit-or-miss, random; limited, narrow, restricted

near ant discerning, penetrating; definitive, hard; broad, complete, comprehensive, exhaustive, extensive, far-reaching, wide; general, global, inclusive; detailed, in-depth; critical

ant deep, profound

superfluity *n* 1 something adding to pleasure or comfort but not absolutely necessary — see LUXURY 1

2 the state or an instance of going beyond what is usual, proper, or needed — see EXCESS

superfluous *adj* being over what is needed — see SPARE 1

superheated *adj* having a notably high temperature — see HOT 1

superhuman *adj* 1 being so extraordinary or abnormal as to suggest powers which violate the laws of nature — see SUPERNATURAL 2

2 of, relating to, or being part of a reality beyond the observable physical universe — see SUPERNATURAL 1

superintend *vb* 1 to be in charge of — see BOSS 1

2 to look after and make decisions about — see CONDUCT 1

3 to take charge of especially on behalf of another — see ²TEND 1

superintendence *n* 1 the act or activity of looking after and making decisions about something — see CONDUCT 1

2 the duty or function of watching or guarding for the sake of proper direction or control — see SUPERVISION 1

superintendency *n* the duty or function of watching or guarding for the sake of proper direction or control — see SUPERVISION 1

superintendent *n* a person who manages or directs — see EXECUTIVE

superior *adj* 1 having a feeling of superiority that shows itself in an overbearing attitude — see ARROGANT

2 having or displaying feelings of scorn for what is regarded as beneath oneself — see PROUD 2

3 of the very best kind — see EXCELLENT

4 standing above others in rank, importance, or achievement — see EMINENT

superior *n* one who is above another in rank, station, or office ⟨if a customer is rude to you, report it to your *superior* and they'll handle it⟩

syn better, elder, senior

rel boss, chief, head, leader, master

near ant assistant, deputy

ant inferior, subordinate, underling

superiority *n* 1 an exaggerated sense of one's importance that shows itself in the making of excessive or unjustified claims — see ARROGANCE

2 exceptionally high quality — see EXCELLENCE 1

3 the fact or state of being above others in rank or importance — see EMINENCE 1

superlative *adj* of the very best kind — see EXCELLENT

supernal *adj* **1** of the very best kind — see EXCELLENT

2 of, relating to, or suggesting heaven — see CELESTIAL

supernatural *adj* **1** of, relating to, or being part of a reality beyond the observable physical universe ⟨Susie believes in ghosts, guardian angels, and other *supernatural* beings⟩

syn metaphysical, preternatural, superhuman, unearthly

rel occult; extrasensory; celestial, divine, heavenly

ant natural

2 being so extraordinary or abnormal as to suggest powers which violate the laws of nature ⟨he seems to read books with *supernatural* speed⟩

syn magical, miraculous, phenomenal, superhuman, uncanny, unearthly

rel bizarre, curious, far-out, funny, kinky, outlandish, out-of-the-way, outrageous, outré, peculiar, quaint, queer, queerish, quirky, remarkable, screwy, strange, wacky, way-out, weird, wild; baffling, bewildering, confounding, mystifying, perplexing, puzzling, shocking; aberrant, abnormal, atypical, extraordinary, fantastic, flaky, freak, freakish, idiosyncratic, rare, singular, uncommon, unique, unusual, unwonted; unconventional, uncustomary, unorthodox; conspicuous, notable, noticeable, outstanding, prominent, salient, striking

near ant average, commonplace, everyday, garden, ordinary, prosaic, routine, run-of-the-mill, typical, unexceptional, unremarkable, usual, workaday; expected, familiar, predictable; common, customary, frequent, habitual, regular, wonted

3 of, relating to, or being God — see HOLY 3

supernumerary *adj* being over what is needed — see SPARE 1

supersede *vb* to take the place of — see REPLACE 1

superstar *n* a person who is widely known and usually much talked about — see CELEBRITY 1

supervene *vb* to come after in time — see FOLLOW 1

supervise *vb* **1** to be in charge of — see BOSS 1

2 to look after and make decisions about — see CONDUCT 1

3 to take charge of especially on behalf of another — see ²TEND 1

supervision *n* **1** the duty or function of watching or guarding for the sake of proper direction or control ⟨our French teacher has *supervision* of all activities of the French Club⟩

syn care, charge, guidance, headship, oversight, regulation, superintendence, superintendency

rel monitoring, observing; administration, control, direction, management, running; leadership, piloting, shepherding, steering; government, reign, rule; aegis, guardianship, protection, tutelage

2 the act or activity of looking after and making decisions about something — see CONDUCT 1

supervisor *n* a person who manages or directs — see EXECUTIVE

supervisory *adj* suited for or relating to the directing of things — see EXECUTIVE

supplant *vb* to take the place of — see REPLACE 1

supple *adj* **1** able to bend easily without breaking — see WILLOWY

2 able to revert to original size and shape after being stretched, squeezed, or twisted — see ELASTIC 1

supplement *n* **1** something added (as by growth) — see INCREASE 1

2 something that serves to complete or make up for a deficiency in something else — see COMPLEMENT 1

supplemental *adj* available to supply something extra when needed — see AUXILIARY

supplementary *adj* **1** available to supply something extra when needed — see AUXILIARY

2 related to each other in such a way that one completes the other — see COMPLEMENTARY

suppliant *adj* asking humbly ⟨the *suppliant* student pleaded for a second chance⟩

syn beseeching, entreating, imploring, pleading, prayerful, soliciting, supplicant, supplicating

rel importunate, insistent, persistent

suppliant *n* one who asks earnestly for a favor or gift — see SUPPLICANT

supplicant *adj* asking humbly — see SUPPLIANT

supplicant *n* one who asks earnestly for a favor or gift ⟨the new governor soon had to deal with a long line of *supplicants* asking for jobs and other political favors⟩

syn petitioner, pleader, solicitor, suitor, suppliant

rel beggar, mendicant, panhandler; asker, requester, suer

supplicate *vb* to make a request to (someone) in an earnest or urgent manner — see BEG

supplicating *adj* asking humbly — see SUPPLIANT

supplication *n* an earnest request — see PLEA 1

supply *n* the number of individuals or amount of something available at any given time ⟨the *supply* of grown-ups willing to coach soccer seems to be shrink-ing⟩

syn budget, fund, pool

rel reserve, reservoir, resource; cache, hoard, stockpile; refill, renewal, replace-ment; kitty, nest egg, pot, purse; source, well, wellspring

supply *vb* 1 to provide (someone) with what is needed for a task or activity — see FURNISH 1

2 to put (something) into the possession of someone for use or consumption — see FURNISH 2

support *n* 1 something that holds up or serves as a foundation for something else ⟨if you don't add a couple more *supports* to that tower of blocks, it's going to fall down⟩

syn brace, bulwark, buttress, mount, mounting, shore, stay, underpinning

rel column, pedestal, pilaster, pillar; arch, bracket, cantilever; crutch, mainstay, peg, post, stake, stanchion, stand, stilt, truss; base, foundation, frame

2 an act or instance of helping — see HELP 1

3 something or someone to which one looks for support — see DEPENDENCE 2

support *vb* 1 to promote the interests or cause of ⟨my parents *support* the local schools both by volunteering and by fiercely opposing funding cuts at town meetings⟩

syn advocate, back, champion, endorse (*also* indorse), patronize

rel adopt, embrace, espouse; abet, aid, as-sist, prop (up), second; bolster, boost, buttress, reinforce; bail out, deliver, res-cue, save

phrases stand up for

near ant baffle, foil, frustrate, interfere, oppose, sabotage, thwart; desert, disap-point, fail, let down

2 to pay the living expenses of ⟨a young widow *supporting* a sick mother as well as two small children on a teacher's salary⟩

syn maintain, provide (for)

rel finance, fund, stake

phrases foot the bills for, take care of

3 to hold up or serve as a foundation for ⟨pillars *supporting* the bridge⟩

syn bear, bolster, brace, buttress, carry, prop (up), shore (up), stay, underpin, up-hold

rel steady, truss, underlie

4 to continue to declare to be true or proper despite opposition or objections — see MAINTAIN 2

5 to give evidence or testimony to the truth or factualness of — see CONFIRM

6 to provide (someone) with what is use-ful or necessary to achieve an end — see HELP 1

7 to put up with (something painful or difficult) — see BEAR 2

supportable *adj* 1 capable of being de-fended with good reasoning against ver-bal attack — see TENABLE 1

2 capable of being endured — see BEAR-ABLE

3 capable of being proven as true or real — see VERIFIABLE

supporter *n* 1 a person who actively sup-ports or favors a cause — see EXPONENT

2 someone associated with another to give assistance or moral support — see ALLY

supporting *adj* serving to give support to the truth or factualness of something — see CORROBORATIVE

supportive *adj* serving to give support to the truth or factualness of something — see CORROBORATIVE

suppose *vb* 1 to decide the size, amount, number, or distance of (something) without actual measurement — see ESTI-MATE 2

2 to form an opinion from little or no ev-idence — see GUESS 1

3 to have as an opinion — see BELIEVE 2

4 to take as true or as a fact without ac-tual proof — see ASSUME 2

supposed *adj* appearing to be true on the basis of evidence that may or may not be confirmed — see APPARENT 1

supposedly *adv* to all outward appear-ances — see APPARENTLY

supposition *n* 1 an idea that is the starting point for making a case or conducting an investigation — see THEORY

2 an opinion or judgment based on little or no evidence — see CONJECTURE

3 something taken as being true or factu-al and used as a starting point for a course of action or reasoning — see AS-SUMPTION

suppositional *adj* existing only as an as-sumption or speculation — see THEORET-ICAL 1

suppress *vb* 1 to keep from being publicly known ⟨the government tried to *suppress* the truth about that incident⟩

syn cover (up), hush (up)

rel censor, silence; repress, smother, squash, squelch, stifle

phrases keep a lid on

near ant debunk, expose, reveal, show up, uncloak, uncover, unmask; disclose, di-vulge, tell, unveil; broadcast, circulate, publish, spread; describe, narrate, recite, recount, rehearse, relate, report

2 to refrain from openly showing or ut-tering ⟨he managed to *suppress* a scream at the sight of the dead body⟩ ⟨*suppressed* her anger⟩

syn choke (back), pocket, repress, smother, stifle, strangle, swallow

rel control, govern, handle, manage; bri-dle, check, curb, hold back, quell; bottle up, contain, hold in; muffle, squelch

near ant loose, release, take out, unleash, vent

3 to hold back the normal growth of — see STUNT

4 to put a stop to (something) by the use of force — see QUELL 1

suppression *n* the checking of one's true feelings and impulses when dealing with others — see CONSTRAINT 1

supremacist *n* a person who believes that one race should control all others ⟨white *supremacists* were arrested for painting racial slurs on a church⟩
syn racialist, racist
rel segregationist; bigot

supremacy *n* 1 controlling power or influence over others ⟨the Roman empire had *supremacy* over the entire Mediterranean world⟩
syn ascendancy, dominance, dominion, predominance, preeminence
rel primacy, superiority; lordship, scepter, sovereignty; arm, authority, clutch, command, control, grip, hold, mastery, sway; take-over; direction, jurisdiction, management; clout, pull, weight; eminence, importance, moment; prerogative, privilege, right
near ant helplessness, weakness; impotence, powerlessness
2 exceptionally high quality — see EXCELLENCE 1

supreme *adj* 1 highest in rank or authority — see HEAD
2 coming before all others in importance — see FOREMOST 1
3 of the greatest or highest degree or quantity — see ULTIMATE 1

Supreme Being *n* the being worshipped as the creator and ruler of the universe — see DEITY 1

surcease *n* the stopping of a process or activity — see END 1

surcharge *vb* to charge (someone) too much for goods or services — see OVERCHARGE 1

surcoat *n* a warm outdoor coat — see OVERCOAT

sure *adj* 1 having or showing a mind free from doubt — see CERTAIN 2
2 impossible to avoid or evade — see INEVITABLE
3 not likely to fail — see INFALLIBLE 1
4 worthy of one's trust — see DEPENDABLE

surely *adv* without any question — see INDEED 1

sureness *n* 1 a state of mind in which one is free from doubt — see CONFIDENCE 2
2 worthiness as the recipient of another's trust or confidence — see RELIABILITY

surety *n* 1 a formal agreement to fulfill an obligation — see GUARANTEE 1
2 a person who takes the responsibility for some other person or thing — see SPONSOR

surf *n* a light mass of fine bubbles formed in or on a liquid — see FOAM

surface *adj* lying on or affecting only the outer layer of something — see SUPERFICIAL 1

surface *n* an outer part or layer — see EXTERIOR

surface *vb* 1 to come to one's attention especially gradually or unexpectedly — see ARISE 2

2 to penetrate the surface (as of water) from below — see BROACH 1

surfeit *n* the state or an instance of going beyond what is usual, proper, or needed — see EXCESS

surfeit *vb* to fill with food to capacity — see GORGE 1

surfeited *adj* having one's appetite completely satisfied — see FULL 3

surge *n* a moving ridge on the surface of water — see WAVE

surly *adj* 1 given to or displaying a resentful silence and often irritability — see SULKY
2 having or showing a habitually bad temper — see ILL-TEMPERED

surmise *n* an opinion or judgment based on little or no evidence — see CONJECTURE

surmise *vb* to form an opinion from little or no evidence — see GUESS 1

surmount *vb* to achieve a victory over — see BEAT 2

surpass *vb* 1 to be greater, better, or stronger than ⟨she always tried to *surpass* her older brother at anything he did⟩
syn beat, better, eclipse, excel, outdistance, outdo, outshine, outstrip, overtop, top, transcend
rel exceed, outpace, outrun, overpass; best, clobber, conquer, crush, defeat, drub, lick, master, overcome, overmatch, prevail (over), rout, skunk, subdue, surmount, thrash, trim, triumph (over), trounce, wallop, whip, win (against), worst; outweigh, overbear, overshadow
phrases go one better
near ant lose (to)
2 to go beyond the limit of — see EXCEED

surplus *adj* being over what is needed — see SPARE 1

surplus *n* the state or an instance of going beyond what is usual, proper, or needed — see EXCESS

surprise *also* **surprize** *vb* 1 to make a strong impression on (someone) with something unexpected ⟨I was very *surprised* when my parents offered to pay for guitar lessons⟩
syn amaze, astonish, astound, bowl (over), dumbfound (*also* dumfound), flabbergast, floor, shock, startle, stun, stupefy
rel befuddle, bewilder, confound, confuse, discomfit, disconcert, dismay, muddle, nonplus, perplex
phrases knock for a loop, take aback, take by surprise
2 to lie in wait for and attack by surprise — see AMBUSH

surprise *n* 1 something that makes a strong impression because it is so unexpected ⟨the birthday party was such a complete *surprise* that Jane was speechless for a moment⟩
syn bolt, bombshell, jar, jolt, stunner
rel shock, thunderclap; revelation, shocker

---

2 the state of being strongly impressed by something unexpected or unusual ⟨Danny stared in utter *surprise* at the deer in his living room⟩

syn amazement, astonishment, shock

rel awe, wonder, wonderment; startle; bewilderment, confusion, discomfiture, dismay

3 a scheme in which hidden persons wait to attack by surprise — see AMBUSH 1

surprising *adj* **1** causing a strong emotional reaction because unexpected ⟨the *surprising* news that they were going to have a baby had them rushing to buy nursery furniture⟩

syn amazing, astonishing, astounding, dumbfounding (*or* dumfounding), eye-opening, flabbergasting, shocking, startling, stunning, stupefying

rel unannounced, unanticipated, unexpected, unforeseen; awesome, awful, breathtaking, fabulous, marvelous (*or* marvellous), miraculous, portentous, prodigious, staggering, stupendous, sublime, wonderful, wondrous; extraordinary, phenomenal, rare, sensational, spectacular; befuddling, bewildering, confounding, confusing, discomfiting, disconcerting, dismaying, muddling, nonplussing, perplexing; incomprehensible, inconceivable, incredible, unbelievable, unimaginable, unthinkable; singular, uncommon, unique, unusual, unwonted; conspicuous, notable, noticeable, outstanding, remarkable; impressive, striking

near ant common, customary, mundane, normal, ordinary, typical, unexceptional, unremarkable, usual

2 causing wonder or astonishment — see MARVELOUS 1

surrender *n* the usually forced yielding of one's person or possessions to the control of another ⟨the police demanded the *surrender* of all hostages as a condition for allowing the hijackers safe passage out of the country⟩

syn capitulating, capitulation, relinquishment, submission, submitting

rel acceptance, acquiescence, concession; compromise; appeasement, conciliation; capture, fall

near ant resistance

surrender *vb* **1** to give (something) over to the control or possession of another usually under duress ⟨Annie *surrendered* the doll to her mother after a brief struggle⟩ ⟨the commander *surrendered* the garrison without having fired a single shot⟩

syn cede, deliver, give up, hand over, relinquish, render, turn over, yield

rel commit, consign, entrust; waive; renounce, resign; abandon, desert, discard, forsake, shed

near ant keep, retain, withhold

2 to cease resistance (as to another's arguments, demands, or control) — see YIELD 3

3 to give up (as a position of authority) formally — see ABDICATE

4 to give up and cease resistance (as to a liking, temptation, or habit) — see YIELD 1

5 to yield to the control or power of enemy forces — see FALL 2

surreptitious *adj* undertaken or done so as to escape being observed or known by others — see SECRET 1

surround *vb* to form a circle around ⟨she was *surrounded* by cheering fans within moments of scoring the winning goal⟩

syn circle, encircle, enclose (*also* inclose), encompass, ring

rel fence (in), hem (in), wall; besiege, entrench (*also* intrench), invest

surroundings *n pl* the circumstances, conditions, or objects by which one is surrounded — see ENVIRONMENT

surveillance *n* the act or state of being constantly attentive and responsive to signs of opportunity, activity, or danger — see VIGILANCE

survey *n* a close look at or over someone or something in order to judge condition — see INSPECTION

survey *vb* **1** to go around and approach (people) with a request for opinions or information — see CANVASS

2 to look over closely (as for judging quality or condition) — see INSPECT

survive *vb* **1** to come safely through ⟨the cat miraculously *survived* a two-story fall⟩

syn ride (out), weather

rel outlast, outlive; pull through; abide, continue, endure, hang on, last, lead, persist; be, breathe, exist, live, subsist; flourish, prosper, thrive

near ant croak [*slang*], decease, depart, die, expire, pass (on), pass away, perish, succumb; disappear, evaporate, fade, vanish; cease, end, stop

2 to continue to operate or to meet one's needs — see HOLD OUT

susceptibility *n* the quality or state of having little resistance to some outside agent ⟨Carol's unfortunate *susceptibility* to viruses meant she was nearly always sick⟩ ⟨Stephen had a well-known *susceptibility* to anyone with a pathetic story⟩

syn defenselessness, vulnerability, weakness

rel helplessness, powerlessness; passiveness, passivity; feebleness, frailness; exposure, liability, openness, sensitivity; receptiveness, receptivity; easiness, gullibility, naïveté (*also* naivete); credulity, credulousness

near ant immunity; impenetrability, indomitability, indomitableness, invincibility

ant invulnerability

susceptible *adj* **1** being in a situation where one is likely to meet with harm — see LIABLE 1

2 lacking protection from danger or resistance against attack — see HELPLESS 1

3 readily taken advantage of — see EASY 2

suspect *adj* giving good reason for being doubted, questioned, or challenged — see DOUBTFUL 2

suspect *vb* 1 to form an opinion from little or no evidence — see GUESS 1

2 to have no trust or confidence in — see DISTRUST

suspecting *adj* inclined to doubt or question claims — see SKEPTICAL 1

suspend *vb* 1 to bring to a formal close for a period of time — see ADJOURN

2 to place on an elevated point without support from below — see HANG 1

suspense *n* a state of temporary inactivity — see ABEYANCE

suspension *n* a state of temporary inactivity — see ABEYANCE

suspicion *vb, chiefly dialect* to form an opinion from little or no evidence — see GUESS 1

suspicion *n* 1 a feeling or attitude that one does not know the truth, truthfulness, or trustworthiness of someone or something — see DOUBT

2 a very small amount — see PARTICLE 1

suspicious *adj* 1 giving good reason for being doubted, questioned, or challenged — see DOUBTFUL 2

2 inclined to doubt or question claims — see SKEPTICAL 1

3 not feeling sure about the truth, wisdom, or trustworthiness of someone or something — see DOUBTFUL 1

suspiciously *adv* with distrust — see ASKANCE

sustain *vb* 1 to supply with nourishment ⟨a granola bar will *sustain* you long enough to last until lunch⟩

syn nourish, nurture

rel sate, satiate, satisfy; cloy, fill, surfeit; fortify, strengthen; feed; board, cater, provision

2 to come to a knowledge of (something) by living through it — see EXPERIENCE

3 to put up with (something painful or difficult) — see BEAR 2

sustainable *adj* 1 capable of being defended with good reasoning against verbal attack — see TENABLE 1

2 capable of being proven as true or real — see VERIFIABLE

3 capable of being endured — see BEARABLE

swab *n* one who operates or navigates a seagoing vessel — see SAILOR

swag *n* valuables stolen or taken by force — see LOOT

swagger *vb* 1 to praise or express pride in one's own possessions, qualities, or accomplishments often to excess — see BOAST

2 to walk with exaggerated arm and leg movements — see STRUT 1

swain *n* 1 a male romantic companion — see BOYFRIEND

2 a man who courts a woman usually with the goal of marrying her — see SUITOR 1

swallow *n* the portion of a serving of a beverage that is swallowed at one time — see DRINK 2

swallow *vb* 1 to take into the stomach through the mouth and throat ⟨try not to *swallow* the toothpaste, because it's not good for you⟩

syn down, ingest

rel drink, imbibe, sip; bolt, devour, gobble (up *or* down), gulp; consume, eat, mouth (down); gorge, scarf, scoff, wolf; chew, gnaw (at *or* on), lap, lick, nibble (on); dispatch, polish off

2 to refrain from openly showing or uttering — see SUPPRESS 2

3 to regard as right or true — see BELIEVE 1

swamp *n* spongy land saturated or partially covered with water ⟨be careful in the *swamp*, because alligators sometimes lurk there⟩

syn bog, fen, marsh, marshland, mire, morass, muskeg, slough (*also* slue), swampland

rel quagmire; muck, mud, ooze, slime, slop, sludge, slush

swamp *vb* 1 to cover or become filled with a flood — see FLOOD

2 to subject to incapacitating emotional or mental stress — see OVERWHELM 1

swampland *n* spongy land saturated or partially covered with water — see SWAMP

swank *or* **swanky** *adj* excessively showy — see GAUDY

swank *n* excessive or unnecessary display — see OSTENTATION

swankily *adv* in a bright and showy way — see GAILY 3

swap *n* a giving or taking of one thing of value in return for another — see EXCHANGE 1

swap *vb* to give up (something) and take something else in return — see CHANGE 3

swarm *n* a great number of persons or things gathered together — see CROWD 1

swarm *vb* to move upon or fill (something) in great numbers — see CROWD 2

swarming *adj* possessing or covered with great numbers or amounts of something specified — see RIFE

swash *vb* to move with a splashing motion — see SLOSH

swat *n* a hard strike with a part of the body or an instrument — see ¹BLOW

swat *vb* to deliver a blow to (someone or something) usually in a strong vigorous manner — see HIT 1

swathe *vb* to surround or cover closely — see ENFOLD 1

sway *n* 1 the power to bring about a result on another — see EFFECT 2

2 the power to direct the thinking or behavior of others usually indirectly — see INFLUENCE 1

3 the right or means to command or control others — see POWER 1

---

syn synonym(s)   *rel* related words
ant antonym(s)   *near ant* near antonym(s)

sway *vb* **1** to act upon (a person or a person's feelings) so as to cause a response — see ¹AFFECT 1

2 to make a series of unsteady side-to-side motions — see ROCK 1

swear *vb* **1** to use offensive or indecent language ⟨you're not allowed to *swear* in this house⟩

syn blaspheme, curse, cuss

rel confound, damn, execrate, imprecate; fulminate, rail, rant

2 to make a solemn declaration of intent — see PROMISE 1

3 to make a solemn declaration under oath for the purpose of establishing a fact — see TESTIFY

swearword *n* a disrespectful or indecent word or expression ⟨this is a list of *swearwords* that will not be permitted in my classroom⟩

syn curse, cuss, expletive, obscenity, vulgarism

rel profanity; execration, imprecation, malediction; epithet, name; oath

sweat *n* **1** the active use of energy in producing a result — see EFFORT

2 very hard or unpleasant work — see TOIL

sweat *vb* **1** to devote serious and sustained effort — see LABOR

2 to experience concern or anxiety — see WORRY 1

3 to work hard and long — see TOIL

4 to flow forth slowly through small openings — see EXUDE

sweep *n* an area over which activity, capacity, or influence extends — see RANGE 2

sweep *vb* **1** to move or proceed smoothly and readily — see FLOW 2

2 to turn away from a straight line or course — see CURVE 1

sweepstakes *n pl* a competitive encounter between individuals or groups carried on for amusement, exercise, or in pursuit of a prize — see GAME 1

sweet *adj* **1** granted special treatment or attention — see DARLING 1

2 having a pleasant smell — see FRAGRANT

3 having an easygoing and pleasing manner especially in social situations — see AMIABLE

4 having qualities that tend to make one loved — see LOVABLE

sweet *n* **1** a food having a high sugar content ⟨remember to brush your teeth after eating *sweets*⟩

syn confection, sweetmeat

rel confectionery; candy, dessert, pastry

2 a person with whom one is in love — see SWEETHEART

sweetheart *n* a person with whom one is in love ⟨I married my high-school *sweetheart* as soon as we both finished college⟩

syn beloved, darling, dear, flame, honey, love, sweet

rel beau, boyfriend, fellow, lover, man, swain; gal, girl, girlfriend, ladylove, mistress; date, escort; gallant, suitor, wooer; groom, husband; fiancé, intended; admirer, crush, steady

sweetmeat *n* a food having a high sugar content — see SWEET 1

sweetness *n* the state or quality of having a pleasant or agreeable manner in socializing with others — see AMIABILITY 1

swell *adj* of the very best kind — see EXCELLENT

swell *n* a moving ridge on the surface of water — see WAVE

swell *vb* **1** to become greater in extent, volume, amount, or number — see INCREASE 2

2 to make greater in size, amount, or number — see INCREASE 1

swelling *n* a small rounded mass of swollen tissue — see BUMP 1

sweltering *adj* having a notably high temperature — see HOT 1

swerve *vb* **1** to depart abruptly from a straight line or course ⟨the car *swerved* sharply to avoid the squirrel in the road⟩

syn sheer, veer, yaw

rel skew, slew (*also* slue); arc, arch, bend, bow, crook, curve, hook, round, sweep, wheel; circle, coil, curl, loop, spiral; turn, twist, wind; deviate, stray, wander, waver

ant straighten

2 to turn away from a straight line or course — see CURVE 1

3 to cause to turn away from a straight line — see BEND 1

swift *adj* moving, proceeding, or acting with great speed — see FAST 1

swift *adv* with great speed — see FAST 1

swiftly *adv* with great speed — see FAST 1

swiftness *n* a high rate of movement or performance — see SPEED

swig *n* the portion of a serving of a beverage that is swallowed at one time — see DRINK 2

swig *vb* to swallow in liquid form — see DRINK 1

swill *n* the portion of a serving of a beverage that is swallowed at one time — see DRINK 2

swill *vb* **1** to eat greedily or to excess — see GORGE 2

2 to swallow in liquid form — see DRINK 1

swiller *n* one who eats greedily or too much — see GLUTTON

swim *vb* to be in a confused state as if from being twirled around — see SPIN 2

swimmingly *adv* in a pleasing way — see WELL 5

swindle *n* a scheme in which the victim is cheated out of his money after first gaining his trust — see CONFIDENCE GAME

swindle *vb* to rob by the use of trickery or threats — see FLEECE

swindler *n* a dishonest person who uses clever means to cheat others out of something of value — see TRICKSTER 1

swing *vb* **1** to change one's course or direction — see TURN 3

2 to change the course or direction of (something) — see TURN 2

3 to deal with (something) usually skillfully or efficiently — see HANDLE 1

4 to move (something) in a curved or circular path on or as if on an axis — see TURN 1

5 to place on an elevated point without support from below — see HANG 1

swipe *n* a hard strike with a part of the body or an instrument — see ¹BLOW

swipe *vb* **1** to come into usually forceful contact with something — see HIT 2

2 to deliver a blow to (someone or something) usually in a strong vigorous manner — see HIT 1

3 to take (something) without right and with an intent to keep — see STEAL 1

swiping *n* an instance of theft — see THEFT 2

swirl *vb* **1** to cause (as a liquid) to move about in a circle especially repeatedly — see STIR 1

2 to move (something) in a curved or circular path on or as if on an axis — see TURN 1

swish *n* a sound similar to the speech sound \s\ stretched out — see HISS 1

swish *vb* to make a sound like that of stretching out the speech sound \s\ — see HISS

switch *n* **1** a long thin or flexible tool for striking — see WHIP

2 a quick jerky movement from side to side or up and down — see WAG 1

switch *vb* **1** to give up (something) and take something else in return — see CHANGE 3

2 to move from side to side or up and down with quick jerky motions — see WAG

3 to strike repeatedly with something long and thin or flexible — see WHIP 1

4 to change (as an opinion) to the contrary — see REVERSE 1

swoon *n* a temporary or permanent state of unconsciousness — see FAINT

swoon *vb* to lose consciousness — see FAINT

sword *n* a hand weapon with a length of metal sharpened on one or both sides and usually tapered to a sharp point ⟨once upon a time dueling with *swords* was the gentlemanly way to settle a point of honor⟩

syn blade, steel

rel broadsword, cutlass, rapier, saber (*or* sabre), scimitar

sycophant *n* a person who flatters another in order to get ahead ⟨my teacher isn't fooled by the class *sycophants*, who are always telling her what a wonderful teacher she is⟩

syn fawner, flunky (*also* flunkey), toady

rel yes-man; hanger-on, leech, parasite, sponge, sponger; henchman, lackey, minion, satellite, slave, stooge; admirer, cultist, devotee, enthusiast, fan, groveler (*or* groveller), idolater (*or* idolator), worship-

per (*or* worshiper), zealot; adherent, convert, disciple, follower, partisan, pupil, votary

symbol *n* **1** a device, design, or figure used as an identifying mark — see EMBLEM

2 a written or printed mark that is meant to convey information to the reader — see CHARACTER 1

symbolic *also* **symbolical** *adj* having the function or meaning of a symbol ⟨the teddy bear in the story was intended to be *symbolic* of a mother's love⟩

syn emblematic (*also* emblematical), representative

rel figurative, metaphorical; allegorical

ant nonsymbolic

symbolize *vb* to serve as a material counterpart of ⟨the flag *symbolizes* our country⟩

syn represent

rel embody, epitomize, incarnate, manifest, materialize, personalize, personify; exemplify, illustrate

phrases stand for

symmetry *n* a balanced, pleasing, or suitable arrangement of parts — see HARMONY 1

sympathetic *adj* **1** having or showing the capacity for sharing the feelings of another ⟨a *sympathetic* smile⟩ ⟨Jane was always a *sympathetic* listener⟩

syn compassionate, humane, understanding

rel gentle, sensitive, softhearted, tender, tenderhearted, warm, warmhearted; benevolent, benignant, charitable, kind; clement, lenient, merciful; cordial, friendly, good-natured, good-tempered, gracious; affectionate, loving

near ant inconsiderate, insensitive, thoughtless, unthinking; uncaring, unloving; merciless, pitiless, ruthless; grim, hard-bitten, hard-boiled, harsh, oppressive, rough, severe, stern, tough, ungentle; abusive, acrimonious, disagreeable, hateful, ill-natured, ill-tempered, malevolent, malicious, mean, rancorous, spiteful, surly, virulent

ant callous, cold-blooded, hardhearted, heartless, inhuman, inhumane, unfeeling, unsympathetic

2 having or marked by sympathy and consideration for others — see HUMANE 1

sympathize (with) *vb* to have sympathy for — see PITY

sympathizer *n* someone associated with another to give assistance or moral support — see ALLY

sympathy *n* **1** sorrow or the capacity to feel sorrow for another's suffering or misfortune ⟨although I'd never lost a relative, I felt great *sympathy* for the classmate whose grandfather died⟩

syn commiseration, compassion, feeling

rel condolence, regret; humanity, kindheartedness, kindliness, kindness, mercy, pity, softheartedness; affinity, empathy, rapport, sensitivity; altruism, benevolence, benignity, charity, generosity, goodwill, humanitarianism, philanthropy

near **ant** indifference, insensitivity, unconcern; cruelty, harshness; animosity, antipathy, dislike, hatred, hostility
ant callousness, hardheartedness, heartlessness
2 the capacity for feeling for another's unhappiness or misfortune — see HEART 1
symphonic *adj* having a pleasing mixture of notes — see HARMONIOUS 1
symphony *n* **1** a balanced, pleasing, or suitable arrangement of parts — see HARMONY 1
2 a usually large group of musicians playing together — see ²BAND 1
symphony orchestra *n* a usually large group of musicians playing together — see ²BAND 1
symposium *n* a meeting featuring a group discussion — see FORUM
symptomatic *adj* serving to identify as belonging to an individual or group — see CHARACTERISTIC 1
synchronous *adj* existing or occurring at the same period of time — see CONTEMPORARY 1
syndicate *n* **1** a group involved in secret or criminal activities — see RING 1
2 a number of businesses or enterprises united for commercial advantage — see CARTEL
synopsis *n* a short statement of the main points — see SUMMARY

synthetic *adj* being such in appearance only and made with or manufactured from usually cheaper materials — see IMITATION
syringe *n* a slender hollow instrument by which material is put into or taken from the body through the skin — see NEEDLE 1
syrupy *adj* being of a consistency that resists flow — see THICK 2
system *n* **1** something made up of many interdependent or related parts ⟨the national highway *system* allows travel from one end of the country to the other⟩ ⟨the democratic *system* of checks and balances in government⟩
syn complex, network
rel interlacement, Internet, net, web; aggregate, conglomerate, totality, whole
2 a method worked out in advance for achieving some objective — see PLAN 1
3 the means or procedure for doing something — see METHOD
systematic *adj* following a set method, arrangement, or pattern — see METHODICAL
systematize *vb* to put into a particular arrangement — see ORDER 1
systematized *adj* following a set method, arrangement, or pattern — see METHODICAL

T

tab *n* **1** a record of goods sold or services performed together with the costs due — see ¹BILL 1
2 the amount owed at a bar or restaurant or the slip of paper stating the amount — see CHECK 1
tabernacle *n* a building for public worship and especially Christian worship — see CHURCH 1
table *n* **1** a leg-mounted piece of furniture with a broad flat top designed for the serving of food ⟨we sat at the kitchen *table*, playing cards for hours on end⟩
syn board
rel coffee table, refectory table; bar, counter; buffet, sideboard
2 food eaten or prepared for eating at one time — see MEAL
3 a broad flat area of elevated land — see PLATEAU
4 a record of a series of items (as names or titles) usually arranged according to some system — see ¹LIST
5 substances intended to be eaten — see FOOD
tableland *n* a broad flat area of elevated land — see PLATEAU

tablet *n* **1** a number of sheets of writing paper glued together at one edge — see PAD 1
2 a small mass containing medicine to be taken orally — see PILL
table talk *n* friendly, informal conversation or an instance of this — see CHAT
tableware *n* **1** eating and serving utensils ⟨we ran short of *tableware*, so Emily went next door and borrowed some forks and knives⟩
syn flatware, silver, silverware
rel place setting, setting; silver plate; cutlery; chopstick, fork, knife, spoon, tablespoon, teaspoon
2 dishes used for eating or serving food or drink ⟨Betty would take out her good *tableware* only on special occasions, as when the mayor came to dinner⟩
syn dinnerware
rel setting; china, chinaware, crockery, earthenware, porcelain, pottery, stoneware, ware; crystal, glassware; plate, saucer; cup, glass, goblet, mug, teacup; bowl, casserole, charger, platter, tureen
taboo *also* **tabu** *adj* that may not be permitted — see IMPERMISSIBLE
tacit *adj* understood although not put into words — see IMPLICIT

taciturn *adj* tending not to speak frequently (as by habit or inclination) — see SILENT 2

tack *n* the means or procedure for doing something — see METHOD

tack (on) *vb* to join (something) to a mass, quantity, or number so as to bring about an overall increase — see ADD 1

tackle *n* items needed for the performance of a task or activity — see EQUIPMENT

tackle *vb* to start work on energetically — see ATTACK 3

tacky *adj* **1** marked by an obvious lack of style or good taste ⟨it was *tacky* to wear sneakers, but Tracey's dress shoes hurt her feet⟩ ⟨*tacky* plastic flowers⟩
syn cheesy, dowdy, inelegant, styleless, tasteless, trashy, unfashionable, unstylish
rel inappropriate, incorrect, unbecoming, unseemly, unsuitable, wrong; outmoded, out-of-date, passé; coarse, crude, unrefined, vulgar; cheap, common, inferior, junky, lousy, low-grade, second-rate, shoddy, sleazy, tawdry; gaudy, loud, ostentatious, overdone; showy, splashy
near ant appropriate, becoming, correct, fitting, proper, right, seemly, suitable; genteel, handsome, neat, quiet, refined, understated; contemporary, modern, up-to-date
ant elegant, fashionable, modish, ritzy, smart, stylish, tasteful
2 showing signs of advanced wear and tear and neglect — see SHABBY 1

tact *n* the ability to deal with others in touchy situations without offending them ⟨with supreme *tact*, Isabel suggested to her neighbor that her flower garden was probably not the best place for his dog to use as a bathroom⟩
syn diplomacy, tactfulness
rel considerateness, consideration, courtesy, delicacy, graciousness, thoughtfulness; civility, etiquette, mannerliness, manners, politeness; charm, gallantry, gentility, grace, gracefulness, suaveness, suavity; adroitness, deftness, dexterity, finesse; deference, regard, respect
near ant discourteousness, discourtesy, inconsiderateness, inconsideration, indelicacy, thoughtlessness, ungraciousness, unthoughtfulness; impoliteness, incivility; boorishness, brashness, brassiness, loutishness; awkwardness, gaucheness, gracelessness, maladroitness; disregard, disrespect, impertinence, impudence, insolence, rudeness
ant tactlessness

tactful *adj* having or showing tact ⟨Allie tried to be *tactful* when asked to comment on the short story that a classmate had written⟩
syn diplomatic
rel considerate, courteous, delicate, gracious, thoughtful; civil, mannerly, polite; charming, gallant, genteel, suave; deferential, regardful, respectful

near ant discourteous, inconsiderate, indelicate, thoughtless, ungracious, unthoughtful; ill-bred, ill-mannered, impolite, uncivil, unmannerly; boorish, brash, brassy, loutish; disregardful, disrespectful, impertinent, impudent, insolent, rude
ant tactless, undiplomatic

tactfulness *n* the ability to deal with others in touchy situations without offending them — see TACT

tactical *adj* suitable for bringing about a desired result under the circumstances — see EXPEDIENT

tactics *n pl* the means or procedure for doing something — see METHOD

tactless *adj* showing poor judgment especially in personal relationships or social situations — see INDISCREET

tad *n* a male person who has not yet reached adulthood — see BOY

tag *n* a slip (as of paper or cloth) that is attached to something to identify or describe it — see LABEL

tag *vb* **1** to attach an identifying slip to — see LABEL 1
2 to go after or on the track of — see FOLLOW 2

tagging *n* the act of going after or in the tracks of another — see PURSUIT

tail *n* a person whose business is solving crimes and catching criminals or gathering information that is not easy to get — see DETECTIVE

tail *vb* to go after or on the track of — see FOLLOW 2

tailing *n* the act of going after or in the tracks of another — see PURSUIT

tailored *adj* made or fitted to the needs or preferences of a specific customer — see CUSTOM-MADE

tailor-made *adj* made or fitted to the needs or preferences of a specific customer — see CUSTOM-MADE

taint *n* a mark of guilt or disgrace — see STAIN 1

taint *vb* **1** to affect slightly with something morally bad or undesirable ⟨criticism of her sister's singing that was *tainted* by envy⟩ ⟨a tendency toward conceitedness *taints* that athlete's status as a role model⟩
syn blemish, mar, poison, spoil, stain, tarnish, touch, vitiate
rel besmear, besmirch, blacken, cloud, dirty, discolor, smear, smirch, smudge, smut, soil, sully, tar; color, distort, twist; damage, deface, flaw, harm, hurt, impair; destroy, ruin, wreck
near ant cleanse, purify; elevate, ennoble, uplift
2 to make unfit for use by the addition of something harmful or undesirable — see CONTAMINATE

tainted *adj* containing foreign or lower-grade substances — see IMPURE

take *n* **1** action or behavior that is done in return to other action or behavior — see REACTION
2 the total amount collected or obtained especially at one time — see HAUL 1

take *vb* **1** to reach for and take hold of by embracing with the fingers or arms ⟨*take* my hand, or we'll get separated in this crowd⟩

syn clasp, grasp, grip, hold

rel clench, cling (to), clutch, hang on (to), hold on (to); catch, nab, seize, snatch

phrases lay hold of

near ant discharge, drop, free, liberate, release; give, hand, relinquish, unhand

2 to agree to receive whether willingly or reluctantly ⟨will you *take* that call?⟩ ⟨*took* a cut in pay⟩

syn accept, have

rel accede (to), assent (to), concede (to), consent (to), OK (*or* okay) (to), acquiesce (to), bow (to), capitulate (to), give in (to), submit (to), succumb (to), surrender (to), yield (to); bear, endure, shoulder, tolerate, swallow; adopt, embrace, welcome

near ant dissent (to), object (to), oppose, protest; hold off, resist, withstand

ant decline, refuse, reject, spurn, turn down

3 to become affected with (a disease or disorder) — see CONTRACT 1

4 to decide to accept (someone or something) from a group of possibilities — see CHOOSE 1

5 to get possession of (something) by giving money in exchange for — see BUY 1

6 to have as a requirement — see NEED 1

7 to make or have room for — see ACCOMMODATE 1

8 to produce a desired effect — see ACT 2

9 to put up with (something painful or difficult) — see BEAR 2

take (for) *vb* to think of in a particular way — see CONSIDER 1

take back *vb* to solemnly or formally reject or go back on (as something formerly adhered to) — see ABJURE

take down *vb* **1** to reduce to a lower standing in one's own eyes or in others' eyes — see HUMBLE

2 to take apart — see DISASSEMBLE

take in *vb* **1** to cause to believe what is untrue — see DECEIVE

2 to have as part of a whole — see INCLUDE

3 to provide with living quarters or shelter — see HOUSE 1

takeoff *n* **1** a rising from a surface at the start of a flight (as of a rocket) — see LIFT-OFF

2 a work that imitates and exaggerates another work for comic effect — see PARODY 1

take off *vb* **1** to leave a place often for another — see GO 2

2 to rid oneself of (a garment) — see REMOVE 1

3 to take away (an amount or number) from a total — see SUBTRACT

take off (on) *vb* to copy or exaggerate (someone or something) in order to make fun of — see MIMIC 1

take on *vb* **1** to enter into contest or conflict with — see ENGAGE 2

2 to provide with a paying job — see EMPLOY 1

take out *vb* **1** to find emotional release for ⟨*took out* his frustrations by splitting a cord of firewood⟩

syn loose, release, unleash, vent

phrases give way (to)

near ant control, govern, handle, manage; bridle, check, contain, curb, hold back, hold in, quell, restrain, smother; allay, lull, quiet, soothe, still; choke, inhibit, muffle, pocket, repress, stifle, strangle, swallow

ant bottle (up), repress, suppress

2 to go on a social engagement with — see DATE 1

take over *vb* **1** to serve as a replacement usually for a time only — see COVER 1

2 to take to or upon oneself — see ASSUME 1

take up *vb* to take for one's own use (something originated by another) — see ADOPT

taking *adj* very pleasing to look at — see BEAUTIFUL

tale *n* **1** a rumor or report of a personal or sensational nature ⟨don't believe the *tales* you hear about our neighbor's kid⟩

syn story, whisper

rel dirt, gossip, scuttlebutt, talebearing, talk, tattle; defamation, libel, slander; hearsay; fabrication, fairy tale, falsehood, falsity, fib, lie

2 a brief account of something interesting that happened especially to one personally — see STORY 2

3 a statement known by its maker to be untrue and made in order to deceive — see LIE

4 a work with imaginary characters and events that is shorter and usually less complex than a novel — see STORY 1

talebearer *n* a person who provides secret information about another's wrongdoing — see INFORMER

talent *n* a special and usually inborn ability ⟨Liza's musical *talent* was already apparent by the time she was five⟩ ⟨Jim's *talent* for coming up with really funny answers⟩

syn aptitude, endowment, faculty, flair, genius, gift, knack

rel bent, inclination, leaning, partiality, penchant, predilection, predisposition, proclivity, propensity, turn; ear, eye, head, mind, nose; feel, hang, instinct, touch, way; capability, competence, facility, proficiency, skill; capacity, power, potential

near ant disability, handicap, inability, incapacity; shortcoming, weakness

talisman *n* something worn or kept to bring good luck or keep away evil — see CHARM 1

talk *n* **1** a usually formal discourse delivered to an audience — see SPEECH 1

2 an exchange of views for the purpose of exploring a subject or deciding an issue — see DISCUSSION 1

3 friendly, informal conversation or an instance of this — see CHAT

talk *vb* **1** to give a formal often extended talk on a subject ⟨detective Connolly often *talks* at school assemblies about safety⟩

syn declaim, descant, discourse, expatiate, harangue, lecture, orate, speak

rel recite, soliloquize; mouth, spout; filibuster; stump; eulogize

phrases hold forth, take the floor

2 to engage in casual or rambling conversation — see CHAT

3 to express (a thought or emotion) in words — see SAY 1

4 to give information (as to the authorities) about another's improper or unlawful activities — see SQUEAL 1

5 to relate sometimes questionable or secret information of a personal nature — see GOSSIP

talk (into) *vb* to cause (someone) to agree with a belief or course of action by using arguments or earnest request — see PERSUADE 1

talk (to) *vb* to communicate with by means of spoken words ⟨Patty had never *talked* to a real live cowboy before⟩

syn chat (with), converse (with), speak (to *or* with)

rel accost, address, greet, hail, herald; inform, notify, tell

phrases engage in conversation

talkative *adj* fond of talking or conversation ⟨a *talkative* outgoing tour guide showed our school group around the city⟩

syn chatty, conversational, gabby, garrulous, loquacious, talky

rel communicative, expansive; demonstrative, effusive, gushing; outspoken, unreserved, vocal; articulate, fluent, glib, voluble; blabby, gossipy, talebearing; long-winded, prolix, verbose, windy, wordy; extroverted (*also* extraverted), gregarious, outgoing, sociable

near ant quiet, shy; mum, mute, silent, speechless, tongue-tied, wordless; evasive, nonvocal, secretive, self-contained, uncommunicative; aloof, introverted, unsociable, withdrawn

ant closemouthed, laconic, reserved, reticent, taciturn, tight-lipped

talker *n* a person who talks constantly — see CHATTERBOX

talk over *vb* to talk about (an issue) usually from various points of view and for the purpose of arriving at a decision or opinion — see DISCUSS

talky *adj* fond of talking or conversation — see TALKATIVE

tall *adj* **1** extending to a great distance upward — see HIGH 1

2 requiring considerable physical or mental effort — see HARD 2

tally *n* a total number obtained or recorded by noting each thing as it was being added — see COUNT 1

tally *vb* **1** to be in agreement on every point — see CHECK 1

2 to gain (as points or runs in a game) as credit towards one's total number of points — see SCORE 2

tame *adj* **1** changed from the wild state so as to become useful and obedient to humans ⟨every evening, a Canada goose is at the food trough with our *tame* geese⟩

syn domestic, domesticated, tamed

rel broken, housebroken, trained; docile, gentle

near ant unbroken, untrained

ant feral, nondomesticated, undomesticated, untamed, wild

2 causing weariness, restlessness, or lack of interest — see BORING

tame *vb* to keep from exceeding a desirable degree or level (as of expression) — see CONTROL 1

tamed *adj* changed from the wild state so as to become useful and obedient to humans — see TAME 1

tamper (with) *vb* to handle thoughtlessly, ignorantly, or mischievously ⟨someone has *tampered with* my computer files⟩

syn fiddle (with), fool (with), mess (with), monkey (with), play (with), tinker (with)

rel alter, doctor, manhandle, manipulate, misuse; butt in, interfere, intrude, meddle

tan *vb* to strike repeatedly with something long and thin or flexible — see WHIP 1

tangent *n* a departure from the subject under consideration ⟨in the middle of her description of her dog's symptoms, she went off on a *tangent* about its cute behavior⟩

syn digression, excursion

rel aside, parenthesis; rambling; circuitousness, circularity, circumlocution

tangible *adj* capable of being perceived by the sense of touch ⟨a firm belief in the existence of the soul, even though it is not at all *tangible*⟩

syn palpable, touchable

rel tactile; corporeal, physical; actual, concrete, embodied, existent, material, real, substantial; discernible, observable, perceptible, sensible

near ant bodiless, immaterial, incorporeal, insubstantial, nonmaterial, nonphysical, unsubstantial; abstract, ethereal, spiritual, unreal

ant impalpable, intangible

tangle *vb* **1** to catch or hold as if in a net — see ENTANGLE 2

2 to twist together into a usually confused mass — see ENTANGLE 1

tantrum *n* an outburst or display of excited anger ⟨had a *tantrum* when he found his little sister using his model paints⟩

syn blowup, explosion, fireworks, fit, huff, scene

rel eruption, flare-up, outburst, storm, uproar; agitation, delirium, distraction, frenzy, furor, furore, fury, hysteria, rage,

---

syn synonym(s) *rel* related words

ant antonym(s) *near ant* near antonym(s)

rampage, uproar; convulsion(s), paroxysm, seizure, spasm, upheaval; reaction, rise; dander, temper; pet, pouts, sulk(s)

tap *n* a fixture for controlling the flow of a liquid — see FAUCET

¹tap *vb* to strike or cause to strike lightly and usually rhythmically ⟨*tapped* her foot in time to the music⟩ ⟨kept *tapping* the desk with his pencil⟩

syn beat, drum, rap, thrum

rel bang, hammer, hit, knock, pound, thud, thump, thwack, whack; chink, clatter, clink, ping; pat; chuck, clap, flick, tip

²tap *vb* to remove (liquid) gradually or completely — see DRAIN 1

taper *vb* to grow less in scope or intensity especially gradually — see DECREASE 2

taper off *vb* to grow less in scope or intensity especially gradually — see DECREASE 2

tar *n* one who operates or navigates a seagoing vessel — see SAILOR

tardily *adv* at a pace that is less than usual, desirable, or expected — see SLOW

tardiness *n* the quality or state of being late — see LATENESS

tardy *adj* **1** moving or proceeding at less than the normal, desirable, or required speed — see SLOW 1

2 not arriving, occurring, or settled at the due, usual, or proper time — see LATE 1

target *n* **1** a person or thing that is the object of abuse, criticism, or ridicule ⟨Cinderella became the *target* of her stepsisters' envy⟩

syn butt, mark, sitting duck, victim

rel laughingstock, mockery; fall guy, goat, tattletale, whipping boy

near ant gossip, gossiper, talebearer, tattler, tattletale, troublemaker; defamer, libeler (*or* libeller), traducer; baiter, heckler, needler, ribber, taunter, teaser, tormentor, derider, insulter, mocker, ridiculer, scoffer, scorner; caricaturist, lampooner, parodist, satirist

2 a person or thing that is made fun of — see LAUGHINGSTOCK

3 something that one hopes or intends to accomplish — see GOAL

tarnish *vb* to affect slightly with something morally bad or undesirable — see TAINT 1

tarry *vb* **1** to continue to be in a place for a significant amount of time — see STAY 1

2 to move or act slowly — see DELAY 1

3 to reside as a temporary guest — see VISIT 2

tart *adj* **1** causing or characterized by the one of the four basic taste sensations that is produced chiefly by acids — see SOUR 1

2 marked by the use of wit that is intended to cause hurt feelings — see SARCASTIC

tartness *n* **1** a harsh or sharp quality — see EDGE 1

2 biting sharpness of feeling or expression — see ACRIMONY 1

task *n* **1** a piece of work that needs to be done regularly — see CHORE 1

2 the action for which a person or thing is specially fitted or used or for which a thing exists — see ROLE

taskmaster *n* **1** a boss who assigns much work ⟨pitiless *taskmaster* that he was, Ebenezer Scrooge only reluctantly let his ill-paid clerk have Christmas day off⟩

syn slave driver

rel enslaver; authoritarian, disciplinarian, discipliner, martinet, stickler; despot, dictator, oppressor, tyrant; dominator, overlord

2 the person (as an employer or supervisor) who tells people and especially workers what to do — see BOSS

taste *n* **1** the property of a substance that can be identified by the sense of taste ⟨Nora can't stand the *taste* of cherry-flavored cough syrup⟩

syn flavor, savor

rel relish, smack, tang; savoriness, tastiness; aftertaste

2 a small piece or quantity of food — see MORSEL

3 positive regard for something — see LIKING

taste *vb* **1** to come to a knowledge of (something) by living through it — see EXPERIENCE

2 to have a vague awareness of — see FEEL 1

tasteful *adj* having or showing elegance — see ELEGANT 1

tasteless *adj* **1** lacking in refinement or good taste — see COARSE 2

2 lacking in taste or flavor — see INSIPID 1

3 marked by an obvious lack of style or good taste — see TACKY 1

tastelessness *n* the quality or state of lacking refinement or good taste — see VULGARITY 1

tastiness *n* the quality of being delicious — see DELICIOUSNESS

tasty *adj* very pleasing to the sense of taste — see DELICIOUS 1

tatter *vb* to cause (something) to separate into jagged pieces by violently pulling at it — see TEAR 1

tattered *adj* **1** wearing torn or worn out clothes ⟨arrived at the refugee camp *tattered* and exhausted⟩

syn ragged, raggedy, ragtag

rel bedraggled, scruffy, shabby, threadbare

near ant decked (out), dolled up, dressed up; spiffy

2 worn or torn into or as if into rags — see RAGGED 2

tattle *vb* to relate sometimes questionable or secret information of a personal nature — see GOSSIP

tattler *n* a person who provides secret information about another's wrongdoing — see INFORMER

tattletale *n* a person who provides secret information about another's wrongdoing — see INFORMER

taunt *vb* to attack repeatedly with mean put-downs or insults — see TEASE 2

taunter *n* a person who causes repeated emotional pain, distress, or annoyance to another — see TORMENTOR

taut *adj* stretched with little or no give ⟨a *taut* clothesline⟩

syn drawn, rigid, tense, tight

rel firm, inflexible, stiff, tightened, unrelaxed, unyielding

near ant drooping, droopy, flaccid, floppy, hanging, lank, limp, loosened, relaxed, slackened, yielding

ant lax, loose, slack

tavern *n* **1** a place of business where alcoholic beverages are sold to be consumed on the premises — see BARROOM

2 a place that provides rooms and usually a public dining room for overnight guests — see HOTEL

tawdry *adj* excessively showy — see GAUDY

tawny *adj* of a pale yellow or yellowish brown color — see BLOND

tax *n* a charge usually of money collected by the government from people or businesses for public use ⟨the state sales *tax* boosted the final cost of my new computer⟩

syn assessment, duty, imposition, impost, levy

rel custom(s), excise, income tax, poll tax, sales tax, tariff, toll, tribute, withholding tax; surcharge, surtax; revenue

tax *vb* to subject (a personal quality or faculty) to often excessive stress — see TRY (OUT) 2

taxi *n* an automobile that carries passengers for a fare usually determined by the distance traveled — see TAXI

taxicab *n* an automobile that carries passengers for a fare usually determined by the distance traveled ⟨took a *taxicab* to the airport⟩

syn cab, hack, taxi

rel hackney; limousine; rickshaw (*also* ricksha)

taxing *adj* requiring much time, effort, or careful attention — see DEMANDING 1

teach *vb* to cause to acquire knowledge or skill in some field ⟨*taught* us about the basics of organic gardening⟩

syn educate, indoctrinate, instruct, school, train, tutor

rel coach, mentor, drill, fit, ground, prepare, prime, qualify; direct, guide, lead, rear; catechize, lecture, moralize, preach; implant, inculcate, instill (*also* instil); homeschool; edify, enlighten; brief, familiarize, impart (to), inform, verse; initiate, introduce, show; reeducate, retrain

teacher *n* a person whose occupation is to give formal instruction in a school ⟨a young man who ardently wants to become a *teacher* and teach first grade⟩

syn educator, instructor, pedagogue, preceptor, schoolteacher

rel headmaster, master, schoolmaster; headmistress, schoolmarm (*or* school-

ma'am), schoolmistress; coach, guide, guru, trainer; mentor, tutor; drillmaster; dean, don, professor; pedant; governess, homeschooler; catechist, lecturer, moralizer, preacher

teaching *n* the act or process of imparting knowledge or skills to another — see EDUCATION 1

team *n* a group of people working together on a task — see GANG 1

team (up) *vb* to participate or assist in a joint effort to accomplish an end — see COOPERATE 1

teamwork *n* the work and activity of a number of persons who individually contribute toward the efficiency of the whole ⟨it takes *teamwork* to pull off a successful fund-raiser⟩

syn collaboration, cooperation, coordination

rel fellowship, partnership; community, mutualism, symbiosis; synergism; communion, oneness, solidarity, togetherness, unity

tear *n* a long deep cut — see GASH

tear *vb* **1** to cause (something) to separate into jagged pieces by violently pulling at it ⟨angrily *tore* the letter to shreds⟩

syn rend, rip, rive, shred, tatter

rel break, cleave, rupture, split; cut, gash, incise, lacerate, slash; butcher, dismember, dissect, hack, mangle

2 to separate or remove by forceful pulling ⟨*tore* the book from his hand⟩

syn rip, wrench, wrest, yank

rel grab, nab, seize, snap (up), snatch; lop (off), nip, jerk; amputate, cut (off), dissever, sever; force, pry

near ant reattach

3 to proceed or move quickly — see HURRY 2

tear (out) *vb* to draw out by force or with effort — see EXTRACT

tear down *vb* **1** to bring to a complete end the physical soundness, existence, or usefulness of — see DESTROY 1

2 to destroy (as a building) completely by knocking down or breaking to pieces — see DEMOLISH 1

tearful *adj* **1** given to expressing strong emotion (as sorrow) by readily shedding tears ⟨a *tearful* woman who can be counted on to cry at every wedding, anniversary, and funeral⟩

syn lachrymose, teary

rel emotional; maudlin, mawkish, sentimental; bawling, blubbering, crying, keening, sniffling, sniveling, sobbing, wailing, weeping, whimpering; bemoaning, bewailing; doleful, dolorous, grieving, mournful, plaintive; funereal, gloomy, lugubrious; brokenhearted, sad, sorrowful, woeful

near ant grinning, laughing, smiling; blithe, blithesome, cheerful, cheery, gay, happy, lighthearted, lightsome, merry, mirthful, sunny

2 causing unhappiness — see SAD 2

teary *adj* **1** causing unhappiness — see SAD 2

2 given to expressing strong emotion (as sorrow) by readily shedding tears — see TEARFUL 1

tease *n* **1** a person who causes repeated emotional pain, distress, or annoyance to another — see TORMENTOR

2 one who is obnoxiously annoying — see NUISANCE 1

tease *vb* **1** to make fun of in a good-natured way ⟨Hilary liked to *tease* her twin brother about his girlfriend⟩

syn chaff, jive, josh, kid, rally, razz, rib, ride, roast

rel banter, joke; fool, fun, string along; jest, quip, wisecrack

2 to attack repeatedly with mean putdowns or insults ⟨some of the boys *teased* Michael because his parents were hog farmers⟩

syn bait, bug, hassle, heckle, needle, ride, taunt

rel haze; gibe (*or* jibe), mock, ridicule; annoy, bother, chafe, fret, nag, nettle, irritate, gall, get, gnaw (at), pester, trouble, vex; aggravate, exasperate, goad, test, try; aggrieve, agitate, bedevil, beleaguer, discomfort, disturb, perturb; badger, dog, hound; browbeat, bully, hector; harass, harry, persecute, plague, terrorize, torment, torture

phrases pick on

teaser *n* **1** a person who causes repeated emotional pain, distress, or annoyance to another — see TORMENTOR

2 one who is obnoxiously annoying — see NUISANCE 1

teasing *n* the act of making unwelcome intrusions upon another — see ANNOYANCE 1

technical *adj* used by or intended for experts in a particular field of knowledge ⟨although the owner's manual for the receiver was supposedly written for the average consumer, it's filled with *technical* language⟩

syn specialized

rel esoteric, especial, exclusive, limited, narrow, peculiar, restricted, special, specific, unique; authoritative, expert, professional, specialist (*or* specialistic)

near ant common, generalized, generic, nonexclusive, nonspecific, ordinary, universal; inexpert, lay, nonprofessional, unprofessional

ant general, nonspecialized, nontechnical

technique *n* the means or procedure for doing something — see METHOD

tedious *adj* causing weariness, restlessness, or lack of interest — see BORING

tedium *n* the state of being bored — see BOREDOM

teeming *adj* possessing or covered with great numbers or amounts of something specified — see RIFE

teeny *adj* very small in size — see TINY

teeny–weeny *adj* very small in size — see TINY

teeter *vb* **1** to swing unsteadily back and forth or from side to side ⟨*teetered* at the edge of the pool⟩

syn falter, rock, totter, waver, wobble

rel flounder, lurch, stumble, toddle; quaver, tremble; careen, reel, stagger, weave

2 to move forward while swaying from side to side — see STAGGER 1

3 to show uncertainty about the right course of action — see HESITATE

telephone *vb* to make a telephone call to — see CALL 2

tell *vb* **1** to give an oral or written account of in some detail ⟨*told* the story of how they had met⟩

syn describe, narrate, recite, recount, rehearse, relate, report

rel deliver, give, state, utter, voice; detail, enumerate, itemize, particularize; disclose, divulge, reveal; delineate, depict, express, render, sketch

2 to express (a thought or emotion) in words — see SAY 1

3 to find the sum of (a collection of things) by noting each one as it is being added — see COUNT 1

4 to give information (as to the authorities) about another's improper or unlawful activities — see SQUEAL 1

5 to give information to — see ENLIGHTEN 1

6 to issue orders to (someone) by right of authority — see COMMAND 1

7 to make known (as information previously kept secret) — see REVEAL 1

tell (on) *vb* to act upon (a person or a person's feelings) so as to cause a response — see ¹AFFECT 1

telling *adj* having the power to persuade — see COGENT

telltale *adj* indicating something — see INDICATIVE

telltale *n* a person who provides secret information about another's wrongdoing — see INFORMER

temerity *n* shameless boldness — see EFFRONTERY

temperance *n* an avoidance of extremes in one's actions, beliefs, or habits ⟨Mr. Grindell attributes his ripe old age to *temperance* in all things, especially eating and drinking⟩

syn moderateness, moderation, temperateness

rel constraint, control, discipline, restraint, self-control, self-discipline; asceticism, austerity, frugality, mortification, sacrifice, self-denial, self-deprivation; abnegation, abstention, avoidance, eschewal, forbearance; modesty, rationality, reasonableness; abstinence, soberness, sobriety

near ant excess, superfluity; extremeness, extremity; unconstraint, unrestraint; extremism, radicalness; irrationality, unreasonableness

ant excessiveness, immoderacy, intemperance, intemperateness

temper *n* **1** a special quality or impression associated with something — see AURA

2 a state of mind dominated by a particular emotion — see MOOD 1

3 one's characteristic attitude or mood — see DISPOSITION 1

temperament *n* one's characteristic attitude or mood — see DISPOSITION 1

temperamental *adj* **1** frequently influenced by moods and especially bad moods — see MOODY

2 likely to change frequently, suddenly, or unexpectedly — see FICKLE 1

temperate *adj* **1** avoiding extremes in behavior or expression — see MODERATE 1

2 marked by temperatures that are neither too high nor too low — see CLEMENT

temperateness *n* an avoidance of extremes in one's actions, beliefs, or habits — see TEMPERANCE

tempest *n* **1** a disturbance of the atmosphere accompanied by wind and often by precipitation (as rain or snow) — see STORM 1

2 a violent disturbance (as of the political or social order) — see CONVULSION

tempestuous *adj* **1** marked by bursts of destructive force or intense activity — see VIOLENT 1

2 marked by sudden or violent disturbance — see CONVULSIVE

3 marked by turmoil or disturbance especially of natural elements — see WILD 3

4 marked by wet and windy conditions — see FOUL 1

temple *n* a building for public worship and especially Christian worship — see CHURCH 1

temporal *adj* **1** having to do with life on earth especially as opposed to that in heaven — see EARTHLY

2 not involving religion or religious matters — see PROFANE 1

temporary *adj* **1** intended to last, continue, or serve for a limited time ⟨summer workers look for *temporary* accommodations in private homes⟩ ⟨a *temporary* cook until a permanent replacement can be found⟩

syn impermanent, interim, provisional, short-term

rel acting; alternate, proxy, substitute; expedient, improvised, makeshift; intermediary, intermediate, transitional; ephemeral, short-lived, transitory; conditional, contingent, limited, qualified, short-range, tentative; replaceable, terminable

near ant final, fixed, set, settled; unconditional, unlimited, unqualified; extended, lasting, long-range, standing; dateless, endless, enduring, eternal, everlasting, perpetual, timeless, unending

ant long-term, permanent

2 lasting only for a short time — see MOMENTARY

temporizer *n* one who does things only for his own benefit and with little regard for right and wrong — see SELF-SEEKER

tempt *vb* to lead away from a usual or proper course by offering some pleasure or advantage — see LURE

temptation *n* **1** the act or pressure of giving in to a desire especially when ill-advised ⟨resisted the *temptation* to go sailing and did his chores instead⟩

syn allurement, enticement, lure, seduction

rel appeal, attraction; beckoning, invitation; inducement, influence, persuasion, power, sway

2 something that persuades one to perform an action for gain — see LURE 1

tempter *n* one that tries to get a person to give in to a desire ⟨there is no greater *tempter* to put off studying than my dog when he wants to play⟩

syn baiter, seducer, solicitor

rel enchantress, siren, temptress; briber, inducer, persuader; corrupter (*or* corruptor), debaucher, undoer

temptress *n* a woman whom men find irresistibly attractive — see SIREN

tenable *adj* **1** capable of being defended against physical attack ⟨the soldiers' encampment on the open plain was not *tenable*, so they retreated to higher ground⟩

syn defensible

rel defended, guarded, protected, safeguarded, secure, secured, shielded; impregnable, indomitable, invincible, inviolable, invulnerable, unassailable, unbeatable, unconquerable, untouchable

near ant assailable, exposed, insecure, liable, open, susceptible, undefended, unguarded, unprotected, unsecured, unshielded; defenseless, helpless, powerless, vulnerable, weak

ant indefensible, untenable

2 capable of being defended with good reasoning against verbal attack ⟨the *tenable* theory that a giant meteor strike set off a chain of events resulting in the demise of the dinosaurs⟩

syn defendable, defensible, justifiable, maintainable, supportable, sustainable

rel rational, reasonable, sensible; acceptable, admissible, allowable, exceptionable, legitimate, passable, unobjectionable, viable, warrantable; confirmable, provable, verifiable; explainable, explicable

near ant absurd, irrational, ridiculous; extreme, outrageous, unreasonable; groundless, objectionable, unacceptable, unfounded; inexplicable, unexplainable

ant indefensible, insupportable, unjustifiable, untenable

tenacious *adj* continuing despite difficulties, opposition, or discouragement — see PERSISTENT

tenaciousness *n* a steadfast adherence to an opinion, purpose, or course of action — see OBSTINACY

tenacity *n* a steadfast adherence to an opinion, purpose, or course of action — see OBSTINACY

---

syn synonym(s)   *rel* related words
ant antonym(s)   *near ant* near antonym(s)

tenant *n* one who rents a room or apartment in another's house ⟨the laundry in the basement is for *tenants* only⟩

syn boarder, lodger, renter, roomer

rel roommate; guest, visitor; occupant, resident, resider

near ant landholder, landowner, proprietor; landlady; slumlord; host, innkeeper

ant landlord

¹**tend** *vb* to show a liking or proneness (for something) — see LEAN 2

²**tend** *vb* 1 to take charge of especially on behalf of another ⟨*tend* the store while I run an errand⟩

syn attend, care (for), mind, oversee, superintend, supervise

rel direct, manage; guard, patrol, protect, safeguard; baby, baby-sit, chaperone (*or* chaperon), mother, shepherd

phrases look after, see to

near ant abandon, disregard, forget, ignore, neglect

2 to look after or assist the growth of by labor and care — see GROW 1

3 to work by plowing, sowing, and raising crops on — see FARM

tendency *n* 1 an established pattern of behavior ⟨a *tendency* to drop things⟩ ⟨a *tendency* to make snap judgements⟩

syn aptness, proneness, propensity, way

rel bent, disposition, inclination, leaning, penchant, predilection, predisposition, proclivity; custom, habit, pattern, practice (*also* practise), routine, wont; oddity, peculiarity, quirk, singularity; trick

near ant averseness, disinclination, indisposition

2 a prevailing or general movement or inclination — see TREND 1

3 a habitual attraction to some activity or thing — see INCLINATION 1

tender *adj* 1 easily injured without careful handling ⟨a *tender* wound⟩ ⟨*tender* plants that cannot take the cold⟩ ⟨*tender* pride that got bruised when his girlfriend dumped him⟩

syn delicate, fragile, frail, sensitive

rel breakable, brittle; flimsy, puny, soft, weak; nonhardy, perishable, resistless, susceptible, unresistant, vulnerable, yielding

near ant durable, firm, flinty, hard, hardy, resistant, robust, rugged, solid, sound; stiff, stout, strong, sturdy, substantial; nonbreakable, unbreakable; hardened, inured, strengthened, tempered, toughened

ant tough

2 feeling or showing love — see LOVING

3 having or marked by sympathy and consideration for others — see HUMANE 1

4 lacking bodily strength — see WEAK 1

5 not harsh or stern especially in manner, nature, or effect — see GENTLE 1

tender *n* something (as pieces of stamped metal or printed paper) customarily and legally used as a medium of exchange, a measure of value, or a means of payment — see MONEY

tender *vb* to put before another for acceptance or consideration — see OFFER 1

tenderfoot *n* a person who is just starting out in a field of activity — see BEGINNER

tenderhearted *adj* 1 feeling or showing love — see LOVING

2 having or marked by sympathy and consideration for others — see HUMANE 1

tending *adj* having a tendency to be or act in a certain way — see PRONE 1

tenement *n* a room or set of rooms in a private house or a block used as a separate dwelling place — see APARTMENT 1

tense *adj* 1 feeling or showing uncomfortable feelings of uncertainty — see NERVOUS 1

2 marked by or causing agitation or uncomfortable feelings — see NERVOUS 2

3 stretched with little or no give — see TAUT

tension *n* the burden on one's emotional or mental well-being created by demands on one's time — see STRESS 1

tent *n* a raised covering over something for decoration or protection — see CANOPY

tentative *adj* determined by something else — see DEPENDENT 2

tenure *n* a fixed period of time during which a person holds a job or position — see TERM 1

tepid *adj* 1 showing little or no interest or enthusiasm ⟨the proposed table tennis club met with only a *tepid* response⟩

syn halfhearted, lukewarm, uneager, unenthusiastic

rel apathetic, disinterested, dispassionate, indifferent, neutral, uncaring, uninterested; lackadaisical, languid, listless, perfunctory, undemonstrative, unemotional, unresponsive; unfeeling, unsympathetic; chill, chilly, cold, cool, frigid, frosty, glacial, icy, unfriendly, wintry

near ant agog, ardent, avid, exuberant, gung ho, impassioned, raring; engaged, engrossed, interested; ready, willing; cordial, friendly, genial, warmhearted

ant eager, enthusiastic, hearty, keen, passionate, warm, wholehearted

2 having or giving off heat to a moderate degree — see WARM 1

term *n* 1 a fixed period of time during which a person holds a job or position ⟨elected for a two-year *term* as mayor⟩

syn hitch, stint, tenure, tour

rel shift, watch; go, turn; duration, standing, time; cycle, span, spell, stretch; life, life span, lifetime

2 a pronounceable series of letters having a distinct meaning especially in a particular field — see WORD 1

term *vb* to give a name to — see NAME 1

termagant *n* a bad-tempered scolding woman — see SHREW

terminal *adj* following all others of the same kind in order or time — see LAST

terminate *vb* 1 to bring (an event) to a natural or appropriate stopping point — see CLOSE 3

2 to come to an end — see CEASE 1

3 to mark the limits of — see LIMIT 2

terminated *adj* brought or having come to an end — see COMPLETE 2

terminating *adj* following all others of the same kind in order or time — see LAST

termination *n* **1** a real or imaginary point beyond which a person or thing cannot go — see LIMIT

2 the act of ceasing to exist — see DEATH 3

3 the stopping of a process or activity — see END 1

terminology *n* the special terms or expressions of a particular group or field ⟨the *terminology* favored by sportscasters⟩ ⟨medical *terminology* that can be hard for the patient to understand⟩

syn argot, cant, dialect, jargon, language, lingo, patois, patter, slang, vocabulary

rel colloquialism, idiom, localism, parlance, pidgin, provincialism, regionalism, speech, vernacular; journalese

terrestrial *adj* having to do with life on earth especially as opposed to that in heaven — see EARTHLY

terrible *adj* **1** causing fear — see FEARFUL 1

2 extreme in degree, power, or effect — see INTENSE

3 extremely disturbing or repellent — see HORRIBLE 1

4 extremely unsatisfactory — see WRETCHED 1

5 of low quality — see CHEAP 2

terribly *adv* to a great degree — see VERY 1

terrific *adj* of the very best kind — see EXCELLENT

terrified *adj* filled with fear or dread — see AFRAID 1

terrify *vb* to strike with fear — see FRIGHTEN

terrifying *adj* causing fear — see FEARFUL 1

territory *n* the place where a plant or animal is usually or naturally found — see HOME 2

terror *n* the emotion experienced in the presence or threat of danger — see FEAR

terrorize *vb* to strike with fear — see FRIGHTEN

terrorized *adj* filled with fear or dread — see AFRAID 1

terse *adj* marked by the use of few words to convey much information or meaning — see CONCISE

tersely *adv* in a few words — see SHORTLY 1

terseness *n* the quality or state of being marked by or using only few words to convey much meaning — see SUCCINCTNESS

test *n* **1** a procedure or operation carried out to resolve an uncertainty — see EXPERIMENT

2 a set of questions or problems designed to assess knowledge, skills, or intelligence — see EXAMINATION 1

test *vb* **1** to put (something) to a test — see TRY (OUT) 1

2 to subject (a personal quality or faculty) to often excessive stress — see TRY (OUT) 2

testament *n* something presented in support of the truth or accuracy of a claim — see PROOF

testify *vb* to make a solemn declaration under oath for the purpose of establishing a fact ⟨Mrs. Pattle was called to *testify* against the man whom she saw stealing her neighbor's car⟩

syn attest, depose, swear, witness

rel vouch; vow, promise

phrases bear witness

testify (to) *vb* to declare (something) to be true or genuine — see CERTIFY 1

testimony *n* something presented in support of the truth or accuracy of a claim — see PROOF

testiness *n* readiness to show annoyance or impatience — see PETULANCE

testy *adj* easily irritated or annoyed — see IRRITABLE

tête-à-tête *adv* in person and usually privately ⟨met *tête-à-tête* with the student's parents to discuss his disciplinary problems in class⟩

syn face-to-face, personally

rel familiarly, intimately; confidentially, secretly; directly, immediately

phrases in private

near ant distantly, indirectly; openly, publicly

tête-à-tête *n* friendly, informal conversation or an instance of this — see CHAT

text *n* a book used for instruction in a subject — see TEXTBOOK

textbook *n* a book used for instruction in a subject ⟨new, up-to-date middle school science *textbooks*⟩

syn handbook, manual, primer, text

rel schoolbook; grammar, reader, speller; tract, treatise; dictionary, lexicon, vocabulary, wordbook; encyclopedia, reference; bible, guide, guidebook

textile *n* a woven or knitted material (as of cotton or nylon) — see CLOTH

thankful *adj* feeling or expressing gratitude — see GRATEFUL 1

thankfulness *n* acknowledgment of having received something good from another — see THANKS

thankless *adj* **1** not showing gratitude ⟨a *thankless* guest who complained that my home cooking was not to her liking⟩

syn unappreciative, ungrateful

rel rude, thoughtless, ungracious

near ant beholden, indebted; gratified, pleased; courteous, gracious, thoughtful

ant appreciative, grateful, obliged, thankful

2 not likely to be appreciated by those who benefit ⟨the *thankless* job of cleaning up after a party⟩

syn unappreciated

rel uncredited, underrated, undervalued, unnoticed, unrecognized, unrewarded, unsung, unvalued

---

syn synonym(s)   *rel* related words
ant antonym(s)   *near ant* near antonym(s)

near ant credited, esteemed, honored, prized, recognized, regarded, rewarded, valued; creditable, meritorious, praiseworthy
ant appreciated, thanked

thanks *n pl* acknowledgment of having received something good from another ⟨to express our *thanks*, we'd like to present you with this plaque⟩
syn appreciation, appreciativeness, gratefulness, gratitude, thankfulness
rel thanksgiving; gratification, indebtedness, satisfaction; acknowledgment (*also* acknowledgement), recognition, tribute
ant ingratitude, thanklessness, ungratefulness

thaw *vb* to go from a solid to a liquid state — see LIQUEFY

thawed *adj* freed from a frozen state by exposure to warmth ⟨recommends cooking *thawed* fish within 24 hours⟩
syn defrosted, unfrozen
rel liquefied, melted, molten; deiced; heated, warmed
near ant chilled, iced, refrigerated; quick-frozen, refrozen, supercooled; congealed, glaciated, semisolid; frostbitten, frosty, icy
ant frozen, unthawed

theater *or* **theatre** *n* 1 a building or part of a building where movies are shown ⟨there's still one *theater* in town that shows movies for two dollars⟩
syn cinema, playhouse
rel nickelodeon; multiplex; drive-in
2 the public performance of plays — see DRAMA 1
3 a large room or building for enclosed public gatherings — see HALL 3

theatrical *adj* 1 given to or marked by attention-getting behavior suggestive of stage acting ⟨after stepping out of their hired limousine, the prom couple made a *theatrical* entrance in their evening clothes⟩
syn dramatic, histrionic, melodramatic
rel overacted, overdone, sensational, staged; conspicuous, elaborate, flamboyant, grandiose, ostentatious, showy; affected, artificial, exaggerated, formal, mannered, pretentious, self-conscious, studied, unnatural
near ant nondramatic, nontheatrical, unaffected, underplayed, unpretentious; muted, restrained, subdued, toned (down); conservative, discreet, inconspicuous; modest, quiet, plain, simple
ant undramatic, untheatrical
2 having the general quality or effect of a stage performance — see DRAMATIC 1

theatricals *n pl* the public performance of plays — see DRAMA 1

theft *n* 1 the unlawful taking and carrying away of property without the consent of its owner ⟨*theft* has never been a big problem at our school⟩
syn larceny, robbery, stealing, thievery
rel burglary, housebreaking; embezzlement, embezzling, graft, misappropriation; filching, pilfering, purloining, shop-

lifting; abduction, hijacking, kidnapping, shanghaiing; despoilment, despoliation, looting, pillage, plundering, rapine; poaching, rustling, smuggling; banditry, piracy
2 an instance of theft ⟨the police found the stolen car an hour after the *theft* was reported⟩
syn grab, pinch, rip-off, snatching, swiping
rel burglary, holdup, mugging, stickup; confidence game, con game

theme *n* 1 a major object of interest or concern (as in a discussion or artistic composition) — see MATTER 1
2 a short piece of writing done as a school exercise — see COMPOSITION 2
3 a short piece of writing typically expressing a point of view — see ESSAY 1

then *adv* in addition to what has been said — see MORE 1

theoretical *also* **theoretic** *adj* 1 existing only as an assumption or speculation ⟨the merits of the new testing procedures are purely *theoretical*, since no one has ever used them before⟩
syn conjectural, hypothetical, speculative, suppositional
rel alleged, assumed, presumed, presupposed, proposed, supposed, unproved, unproven, untested; academic, debatable, moot; abstract, conceptual, intellectual; nonclinical, nonpractical; nonempirical
near ant clinical, practical; concrete, defined, definite, distinct; attested, authenticated, confirmed, demonstrated, established, proven, substantiated, tested, time-tested, validated, verified; empirical (*also* empiric), observational
ant actual, factual, real
2 dealing with or expressing a quality or idea — see ABSTRACT 1

theory *n* an idea that is the starting point for making a case or conducting an investigation ⟨set out to prove her *theory* that people can't really taste any difference between colas, so they buy according to the product's image⟩
syn hypothesis, proposition, supposition
rel assumption, concession, premise, presumption, presupposition; generalization, guess, guesswork, inference, speculation, surmise; proffer, proposal, suggestion; feeling, hunch, impression, inkling, notion, suspicion; abstraction, concept, conception
near ant assurance, certainty, fact, knowledge

thereafter *adv* following in time or place — see AFTER

therefore *adv* for this or that reason ⟨it's snowing hard; *therefore* I think we should stay home⟩
syn accordingly, consequently, ergo, hence, so, thereupon, thus, wherefore

theretofore *adv* up to this or that time — see HITHERTO

thereupon *adv* for this or that reason — see THEREFORE

thesis *n* an idea or opinion that is put forth in a discussion or debate — see CONTENTION

thick *adj* **1** having or being of relatively great depth or extent from one surface to its opposite ⟨a *thick* board was laid across the pit⟩
syn chunky, fat
rel bulky, dense, hefty, thickish; broad, deep, wide
near ant narrow, shallow
ant skinny, slender, slim, thin
2 being of a consistency that resists flow ⟨*thick* maple syrup for pancakes⟩
syn ropy, syrupy, viscid, viscous
rel creamy, heavy, slushy, thickened, thickish, turbid, undiluted; gluey, glutinous, sticky; gelatinous, gooey, gummy, jellylike; concentrated, condensed
near ant flowing, fluid; dilute, diluted, liquid, watered (down), weak
ant runny, soupy, thin, watery
3 closely acquainted — see FAMILIAR 1
4 having a greater than usual measure across — see WIDE 1
5 having little space between items or parts — see CLOSE 1
6 not having or showing an ability to absorb ideas readily — see STUPID 1
7 possessing or covered with great numbers or amounts of something specified — see RIFE

thick *n* the most intense or characteristic phase of something ⟨in the *thick* of winter many Northerners are dreaming of tropical islands⟩
syn deep, depth, height, middle, midst
rel center, heart

thicket *n* a thick patch of shrubbery, small trees, or underbrush ⟨flushed a pheasant from a *thicket* of willows⟩
syn brake, brushwood, chaparral, coppice, copse, covert
rel canebrake; brush, bush, scrub, scrubland; bramble, jungle, tangle; grove, hedge, stand, woodlot; forest, greenwood, wildwood, wood, woodland

thickheaded *adj* not having or showing an ability to absorb ideas readily — see STUPID 1

thickness *n* the degree to which a fluid can resist flowing — see CONSISTENCY

thickset *adj* being compact and broad in build and often short in stature — see STOCKY

thief *n* one who steals ⟨sentenced the *thief* who stole Mrs. Stuckey's rosebushes to 30 hours of community service in the municipal rose garden⟩
syn pincher, purloiner, robber, stealer
rel burglar, housebreaker; embezzler, grafter; kleptomaniac; pickpocket, pilferer, rifler, shoplifter; abductor, hijacker, kidnapper, skyjacker; despoiler, looter, plunderer, ransacker, ravisher; poacher, rustler, smuggler; bandit, highwayman, pirate; grabber, mugger

thieve *vb* to take (something) without right and with an intent to keep — see STEAL 1

thievery *n* the unlawful taking and carrying away of property without the consent of its owner — see THEFT 1

thin *adj* **1** having a noticeably small amount of body fat ⟨after her bout with pneumonia, she looked *thinner*⟩
syn lean, skinny, slender, slim, spare
rel angular, bony, rawboned, scraggy, scrawny, sinewy; lank, lanky, rangy, reedy, spindling, spindly, twiggy, waspish, weedy, willowy, wiry; anorexic, cadaverous, emaciated, gaunt, haggard, pinched, skeletal, wasted, wizened; puny, meager (*or* meagre), slight
near ant beefy, bulky, chunky, fleshy, heavy, heavyset, stocky, stout, thick, thickset, weighty; brawny, burly, husky; dumpy, pudgy, roly-poly, squat, stubby; paunchy, potbellied; flabby, soft; buxom; fleshed-out, full, round
ant chubby, corpulent, fat, gross, obese, overweight, plump, portly, rotund, tubby
2 being of less than usual width — see NARROW 1
3 not containing very much of some important element — see WEAK 3

thin *vb* to alter (something) for the worse with the addition of foreign or lower-grade substances — see ADULTERATE

thing *n* **1** a member of the human race — see HUMAN
2 one that has a real and independent existence — see ENTITY
3 something done by someone — see ACTION 1
4 something material that can be perceived by the senses — see OBJECT 1
5 something produced by physical or intellectual effort — see PRODUCT 1
6 something that happens — see EVENT 1
7 something that one hopes or intends to accomplish — see GOAL
8 something to be dealt with — see MATTER 2
9 things *pl* transportable items that one owns — see POSSESSION 2

think *vb* to have as an opinion — see BELIEVE 2

think (about *or* over) *vb* to give serious and careful thought to — see PONDER

think (of) *vb* to bring back to mind — see REMEMBER

think (up) *vb* to create or think of by clever use of the imagination — see INVENT

thinker *n* a very smart person — see GENIUS 1

thinking *adj* having the ability to reason — see RATIONAL 1

thinned *adj* **1** containing foreign or lower-grade substances — see IMPURE
2 not containing very much of some important element — see WEAK 3

thirst *n* **1** a strong wish for something — see DESIRE
2 urgent desire or interest — see EAGERNESS

---

syn synonym(s)   *rel* related words
ant antonym(s)   *near ant* near antonym(s)

thirst (for) *vb* to have an earnest wish to own or enjoy — see DESIRE

thirsty *adj* **1** marked by little or no precipitation or humidity — see DRY 1

2 showing urgent desire or interest — see EAGER

this *adj* being the less far of two — see NEAR 1

thistly *adj* likely to cause a scratch — see SCRATCHY 1

thorn *n* something that is a source of irritation — see ANNOYANCE 3

thorny *adj* **1** likely to cause a scratch — see SCRATCHY 1

2 requiring exceptional skill or caution in performance or handling — see TRICKY

thorough *adj* **1** having no exceptions or restrictions — see ABSOLUTE 2

2 including many small descriptive features — see DETAILED 1

3 trying all possibilities — see EXHAUSTIVE

thoroughbred *adj* of unmixed ancestry — see PUREBRED

thoroughfare *n* a passage cleared for public vehicular travel — see WAY 1

thoroughgoing *adj* **1** having no exceptions or restrictions — see ABSOLUTE 2

2 trying all possibilities — see EXHAUSTIVE

thoroughly *adv* **1** with attention to all aspects or details ⟨they searched the grounds *thoroughly* for any sign of the intruder⟩

syn completely, comprehensively, detailedly, exhaustively, fully, minutely, roundly, totally

rel all-out, full blast, intensively; broadly, extensively, generally, globally, widely; conclusively, consummately, definitely, perfectly

phrases in detail

near ant aimlessly, desultorily, haphazardly, hit-or-miss, randomly; cursorily, imperfectly, inadequately, narrowly, shallowly, sketchily, summarily, superficially; indeterminately, nebulously, vaguely

2 to a full extent or degree — see FULLY 1

though *conj* in spite of the fact that — see ALTHOUGH

though *adv* in spite of that — see HOWEVER

thought *n* **1** a careful weighing of the reasons for or against something — see CONSIDERATION 1

2 something imagined or pictured in the mind — see IDEA

thoughtful *adj* **1** given to or made with heedful anticipation of the needs and happiness of others ⟨a *thoughtful* offer to watch the neighbors' children on moving day⟩ ⟨a *thoughtful* aunt who never forgets the birthday of a niece or nephew⟩

syn attentive, considerate, kind, solicitous

rel brotherly, good, good-hearted, helpful, hospitable, kindhearted, kindly, neighborly, nice; caring, compassionate, sympathetic, tender; chivalrous, courteous, courtly, gallant, gracious, polite; diplomatic, tactful; deferential, dutiful, obliging, regardful, respectful; altruistic, beneficent, benevolent, benignant, humane, selfless, unselfish; charitable, generous, magnanimous

near ant inattentive, uncaring, unheeding; inhospitable, unkind, unkindly, unneighborly; ill-bred, ill-mannered, impolite, rude, uncivil, uncourteous, unmannerly; unhelpful, unobliging; malevolent, malicious, mean, spiteful

ant heedless, inconsiderate, thoughtless, unthinking

2 decided on as a result of careful thought — see DELIBERATE 1

3 given to or marked by long, quiet thinking — see CONTEMPLATIVE

thoughtfully *adv* with good reason or courtesy — see WELL 4

thoughtless *adj* showing a lack of manners or consideration for others — see IMPOLITE

thrall *n* **1** a person who is considered the property of another person — see SLAVE 1

2 the state of being a slave — see SLAVERY 1

thralldom *or* **thraldom** *n* the state of being a slave — see SLAVERY 1

thrash *vb* **1** to achieve a victory over — see BEAT 2

2 to defeat by a large margin — see WHIP 2

3 to strike repeatedly with something long and thin or flexible — see WHIP 1

4 to strike repeatedly — see BEAT 1

thread *vb* **1** to scatter or set here and there among other things ⟨this history book *threads* excerpts from the diaries of pioneer women into its account of the settlement of the West⟩

syn interlace, intersperse, interweave, lace, weave, wreathe

rel insert, intermingle, mingle, mix; alternate, juxtapose; amalgamate, assimilate, blend, combine, commingle, embody, fuse, incorporate, integrate, merge

2 to put together into a series by means of or as if by means of a thread ⟨the reporter *threaded* his newspaper articles about the basketball team into a book that was essentially a chronicle of their championship season⟩

syn concatenate, string

rel chain, connect, join, link, unite; interlace, intersperse, intertwine, interweave, lace, weave, wreathe

threadbare *adj* **1** showing signs of advanced wear and tear and neglect — see SHABBY 1

2 used or heard so often as to be dull — see STALE

3 worn or torn into or as if into rags — see RAGGED 2

threat *n* something that may cause injury or harm — see DANGER 2

threaten *vb* to remain poised to inflict harm, danger, or distress on ⟨unless the home fans' unacceptable behavior and name-calling stops, the possibility of expulsion from the league *threatens* the school's basketball team⟩

syn hang (over), hover (over), impend (over), menace, overhang

rel endanger, hazard, imperil, jeopardize

threatening *adj* **1** giving signs of immediate occurrence — see IMMINENT 1

2 being or showing a sign of evil or calamity to come — see OMINOUS

3 involving potential loss or injury — see DANGEROUS

threefold *adj* having three units or parts — see TRIPLE

threesome *n* a group of three ⟨the *threesome* from Crystal Falls—Jocelyn, Katie, and Lynn—missed their plane and joined up with the rest of the group the next day⟩

syn triad, trinity, trio, triple, triplet, triumvirate

rel trilogy; triplicate; triplex

threnody *n* a composition expressing one's grief over a loss — see LAMENT 2

threshold *n* the point at which something begins — see BEGINNING

thrift *n* careful management of material resources — see ECONOMY

thriftless *adj* given to spending money freely or foolishly — see PRODIGAL

thrifty *adj* careful in the management of money or resources — see FRUGAL

thrill *n* a pleasurably intense stimulation of the feelings ⟨everyone gets a real *thrill* out of the Independence Day fireworks⟩

syn bang, exhilaration, kick, titillation

rel arousal, electrification, intoxication, stimulation; jolt, shock, surprise; delectation, delight, enjoyment, joy, lift, pleasure; amusement, diversion, entertainment, fun, treat

thrill *vb* to cause a pleasurable stimulation of the feelings ⟨was *thrilled* by the news of Betsy's promotion⟩

syn electrify, excite, exhilarate, galvanize, intoxicate, titillate, turn on

rel arouse, incite, inspire, provoke, stimulate; bewitch, captivate, charm, delight, enchant, enthrall (*or* enthral), hypnotize, mesmerize, rivet, spellbind; interest, intrigue, tantalize

near ant bore, jade, pall, tire, weary; deject, demoralize, discourage, dishearten, dispirit

thrilling *adj* causing great emotional or mental stimulation — see EXCITING 1

thrive *vb* **1** to grow vigorously ⟨these plants *thrive* with relatively little sunlight⟩

syn burgeon, flourish, prosper

rel luxuriate, overgrow, proliferate, shoot up; germinate, root, sprout; bloom, flower, fruit, produce, propagate, regenerate, seed

2 to reach a desired level of accomplishment — see SUCCEED 2

thriving *adj* **1** having attained a desired end or state of good fortune — see SUCCESSFUL 1

2 marked by much life, movement, or activity — see ALIVE 2

3 marked by vigorous growth and well-being especially economically — see PROSPEROUS 1

throaty *adj* **1** harsh and dry in sound — see HOARSE

2 having a low musical pitch or range — see DEEP 2

throb *n* a rhythmic expanding and contracting — see PULSATION

throb *vb* to expand and contract in a rhythmic manner — see PULSATE

throe *n* a sharp unpleasant sensation usually felt in some specific part of the body — see PAIN 1

throng *n* a great number of persons or things gathered together — see CROWD 1

throng *vb* to move upon or fill (something) in great numbers — see CROWD 2

thronging *adj* possessing or covered with great numbers or amounts of something specified — see RIFE

throttle *vb* to keep (someone) from breathing by exerting pressure on the windpipe — see CHOKE 1

through *adv* **1** from beginning to end ⟨read the letter *through* twice⟩ ⟨never once missed class the whole year *through*⟩

syn around, over, round, throughout

2 from one side to the other of an intervening space — see OVER 1

through *prep* **1** in or into the middle of — see AMONG

2 in random positions within the boundaries of — see AROUND 2

3 in the course of — see DURING

4 to the opposite side of — see ACROSS

5 along the way of — see BY 1

6 as the result of — see BECAUSE OF

7 using the means or agency of — see BY 2

through *adj* brought or having come to an end — see COMPLETE 2

throughout *prep* **1** in random positions within the boundaries of — see AROUND 2

2 in the course of — see DURING

throughout *adv* **1** from beginning to end — see THROUGH 1

2 in every place or in all places — see EVERYWHERE

throw *vb* to send through the air especially with a quick forward motion of the arm ⟨*threw* a life preserver to the drowning man⟩

syn cast, catapult, chuck, dash, fire, fling, heave, hurl, hurtle, launch, lob, loft, peg, pelt, pitch, sling, toss

rel bowl, flip, hook, pass, roll, shoot; buck, eject, impel, precipitate, project, propel, rifle, thrust

throw (on) *vb* to place on one's person — see PUT ON 1

throw away *vb* **1** to get rid of as useless or unwanted — see DISCARD

2 to use up carelessly — see WASTE 1

---

syn synonym(s)   **rel** related words
ant antonym(s)   **near ant** near antonym(s)

throwing away *n* the getting rid of whatever is unwanted or useless — see DISPOSAL 1

throw out *vb* **1** to drive or force out — see EJECT 1

2 to get rid of as useless or unwanted — see DISCARD

throw up *vb* **1** to discharge the contents of the stomach through the mouth — see VOMIT

2 to make or assemble roughly or hastily — see COBBLE (TOGETHER)

thrum *n* a monotonous sound like that of an insect in motion — see HUM

thrum *vb* to strike or cause to strike lightly and usually rhythmically — see ¹TAP

thrust *vb* to apply force to (someone or something) so that it moves in front of one — see PUSH 1

thud *n* a hard strike with a part of the body or an instrument — see ¹BLOW

thud *vb* to come into usually forceful contact with something — see HIT 2

thug *n* a violent, brutal person who is often a member of an organized gang — see HOODLUM

thumb *vb* to travel by securing free rides — see HITCHHIKE

thump *n* a hard strike with a part of the body or an instrument — see ¹BLOW

thump *vb* **1** to deliver a blow to (someone or something) usually in a strong vigorous manner — see HIT 1

2 to strike repeatedly — see BEAT 1

thunder *vb* to make a long loud deep noise or cry — see ROAR

thunderous *adj* marked by a high volume of sound — see LOUD 1

thunderstruck *adj* affected with sudden and great wonder or surprise ⟨Colin was *thunderstruck* when his parents told him he was adopted⟩

syn amazed, astonished, astounded, awestruck, bowled over, dumbfounded (*or* dumfounded), flabbergasted, shocked, stunned, stupefied

rel startled, surprised; aghast, appalled, dismayed, horrified; bewildered, confused, dazed, overwhelmed; agape, awed, awesome, openmouthed, wide-eyed, widemouthed

near ant casual, nonchalant, unruffled

ant unawed

thus *adv* for this or that reason — see THEREFORE

thus far *adv* up to this or that time — see HITHERTO

thwack *n* **1** a hard strike with a part of the body or an instrument — see ¹BLOW

2 a loud explosive sound — see CLAP 1

thwack *vb* to deliver a blow to (someone or something) usually in a strong vigorous manner — see HIT 1

thwart *vb* to prevent from achieving a goal — see FRUSTRATE

tick (off) *vb* to specify one after another — see ENUMERATE 1

ticket *n* **1** a small sheet of plastic, paper, or paperboard showing that the bearer has a claim to something (as admittance) ⟨only

people with *tickets* will be allowed past the front gates⟩

syn check, coupon, pass

rel certificate, note, token, voucher

2 a slip (as of paper or cloth) that is attached to something to identify or describe it — see LABEL

ticket *vb* to attach an identifying slip to — see LABEL 1

tickled *adj* experiencing pleasure, satisfaction, or delight — see GLAD 1

ticklish *adj* requiring exceptional skill or caution in performance or handling — see TRICKY

tidbit *also* **titbit** *n* **1** something that is pleasing to eat because it is rare or a luxury — see DELICACY 1

2 a small piece or quantity of food — see MORSEL 1

tide *n* a prevailing or general movement or inclination — see TREND 1

tidied *adj* being clean and in good order — see NEAT 1

tidings *n pl* a report of recent events or facts not previously known — see NEWS

tidy *adj* **1** being clean and in good order — see NEAT 1

2 of a size greater than average of its kind — see LARGE

3 sufficiently large in size, amount, or number to merit attention — see CONSIDERABLE 1

tie *n* **1** a situation in which neither participant in a contest, competition, or struggle comes out ahead of the other ⟨the competition for first place in the dessert division ended in a *tie* between the chocolate pecan pie and the walnut fudge tart⟩

syn dead heat, draw, stalemate, standoff

rel deadlock, impasse; photo finish; toss-up

2 a uniting or binding force or influence — see BOND 2

tie *vb* **1** to gather into a tight mass by means of a line or cord ⟨*tied* the newspapers into a bundle⟩

syn band, bind, gird, truss

rel cinch, cord, rope, strap, thread, wire; lash, leash, tether; interlace, intertwine, interweave, lace; entangle, knot, snarl, tangle, twist; coil, wind

near ant undo, unfasten, unlace, unlash, unloose, unloosen, unthread; unleash, untether; disentangle, uncoil, untangle, untwine, untwist, unwind

ant unbind, untie

2 to produce something equal to (as in quality or value) — see EQUAL 1

tie–up *n* the state of having shared interests or efforts in social or business matters) — see ASSOCIATION 1

tie up *vb* to create difficulty for the work or activity of — see HAMPER

tiff *n* an often noisy or angry expression of differing opinions — see ARGUMENT 1

tight *adj* **1** not allowing penetration (as by gas, liquid, or light) ⟨a *tight* hull that was no match for an iceberg⟩

syn impenetrable, impermeable, impervious

rel close, compact, dense, snug, thick; airtight, hermetic, watertight; lightproof, soundproof, waterproof

near ant absorbent, leaky, porous, unsealed

ant penetrable, permeable

2 firmly positioned in place and difficult to dislodge ⟨a *tight* screw that won't come loose⟩ ⟨a jar with a *tight* lid⟩

syn fast, firm, frozen, jammed, lodged, secure, set, snug, stuck, wedged

rel bonded, cemented, glued; anchored, clamped; embedded, entrenched (*also* intrenched); implanted; attached, bound, fastened, secured; immovable, unyielding

near ant detached, dislodged, freed, loosened, unattached, unbound, undone, unfastened, unsecured; movable (*or* moveable), yielding

ant insecure, loose

3 giving or sharing as little as possible — see STINGY 1

4 having little space between items or parts — see CLOSE 1

5 showing little difference in the standing of the competitors — see CLOSE 3

6 stretched with little or no give — see TAUT

tightfisted *adj* giving or sharing as little as possible — see STINGY 1

tight-lipped *adj* tending not to speak frequently (as by habit or inclination) — see SILENT 1

tightness *n* the quality of being overly sparing with money — see PARSIMONY

tightwad *n* a mean grasping person who is usually stingy with money — see MISER

till *vb* to work by plowing, sowing, and raising crops on — see FARM

tiller *n* a person who cultivates the land and grows crops on it — see FARMER

tilt *n* the act of positioning or an instance of being positioned at an angle ⟨indicated her approval with a slight forward *tilt* of her head⟩

syn angling, bend, cock, inclination, list, tip

rel turn, twist, veer; bow, dip, nod

tilt *vb* to set or cause to be at an angle — see LEAN 1

tilted *adj* **1** inclined or twisted to one side — see AWRY

2 running in a slanting direction — see DIAGONAL

tilting *adj* running in a slanting direction — see DIAGONAL

timber *n* **1** a dense growth of trees and shrubs covering a large area — see FOREST

2 tree logs as prepared for human use — see WOOD

timberland *n* a dense growth of trees and shrubs covering a large area — see FOREST

time *n* **1** a particular point at which an event takes place — see OCCASION 1

2 an exciting or noteworthy event that one experiences firsthand — see ADVENTURE

3 an extent of time associated with a particular person or thing — see AGE 1

4 the period during which something exists, lasts, or is in progress — see DURATION 1

timeliness *n* the quality or habit of arriving on time — see PROMPTITUDE

timely *adj* **1** especially suitable for a certain time ⟨a *timely* invitation to lunch that came just as I was starting to feel hungry⟩

syn opportune, seasonable

rel appropriate, apt, fit, fitting, meet, pat, proper, relevant, suitable; fortunate, lucky, propitious; anticipated, expected; prompt, punctual, undelayed

near ant improper, inappropriate, irrelevant, unfit, unsuitable; unfortunate, unlucky; behind, behindhand, belated, delayed, delinquent, late, latish, overdue, postponed, slow, tardy; anticipatory, early, precocious, premature; abrupt, sudden, unanticipated, unexpected

ant inopportune, unseasonable, untimely

2 done, carried out, or given without delay — see PROMPT 1

timepiece *n* a device to measure time ⟨the only *timepiece* she used at the cabin was a garden sundial⟩

syn chronometer, clock, timer

rel alarm clock, atomic clock, cuckoo clock, grandfather clock, time clock; hourglass, sandglass, sundial, water clock; chronograph, stopwatch, watch

timer *n* a device to measure time — see TIMEPIECE

timetable *n* a listing of things to be presented or considered (as at a concert or play) — see PROGRAM 1

timid *adj* easily frightened — see SHY 1

timidity *n* lack of willingness to assert oneself and take risks ⟨none of the scouts showed the least *timidity* about rappeling down the cliff⟩

syn faintheartedness, timidness, timorousness

rel bashfulness, constraint, embarrassment, inhibition, restraint, shyness, skittishness; hesitation, indecision, indecisiveness, irresoluteness, irresolution; alarm, anxiety, apprehension, concern, discomposure, dismay, fear, panic, upset, worry; cowardice, cowardliness, cravenness, spinelessness, yellowness

near ant assurance, confidence, self-assurance, self-confidence; composure, coolness, insouciance, nonchalance, unconcern; backbone, decisiveness, determination, fiber, firmness, fortitude, gameness, grit, gumption, mettle, resoluteness, resolution, spunk; bravery, courage, courageousness, daring, dauntlessness, doughtiness, fearlessness, intrepidity, intrepidness

ant audaciousness, audacity, boldness, guts, nerve

---

syn synonym(s)   *rel* related words
ant antonym(s)   *near ant* near antonym(s)

timidness *n* lack of willingness to assert oneself and take risks — see TIMIDITY

timorous *adj* easily frightened — see SHY 1

timorousness *n* lack of willingness to assert oneself and take risks — see TIMIDITY

tincture *n* a substance used to color other materials — see PIGMENT

tinge *n* a property that becomes apparent when light falls on an object and by which things that are identical in form can be distinguished — see COLOR 1

tinge *vb* to give color or a different color to — see COLOR 1

tingle *n* a sharp unpleasant sensation usually felt in some specific part of the body — see PAIN 1

tinker (with) *vb* to handle thoughtlessly, ignorantly, or mischievously — see TAMPER

tinkle *n* a series of short high ringing sounds ⟨Mrs. Mouse ignored the warning *tinkle* of the cat's bell, and now her children are orphans⟩

syn chime(s), jingle, tintinnabulation

rel clatter, jangle, rattle; chink, clang, clank, clink, dingdong, ping, ring, toll; chirr, ripple, trill, warble

tinkle *vb* to make a repeated sharp light ringing sound — see JINGLE

tint *vb* to give color or a different color to — see COLOR 1

tint *n* a property that becomes apparent when light falls on an object and by which things that are identical in form can be distinguished — see COLOR 1

tintinnabulation *n* a series of short high ringing sounds — see TINKLE

tiny *adj* very small in size ⟨the forest ranger showed us how every square foot of forest is alive with *tiny* creatures⟩

syn atomic, bitty, infinitesimal, microminiature, microscopic (*also* microscopical), miniature, minute, teeny, teeny-weeny, wee

rel diminutive, dwarf, little, midget, model, petite, pocket, pocket-size (*also* pocket-sized), pygmy, small, smallish; dinky, dwarfish, insignificant, pint-size (*or* pint-sized), puny, scrubby, undersized

near ant big, bulky, bumper, considerable, extensive, good, goodly, good-sized, grand, great, gross, handsome, hefty, hulking, jumbo, king-size (*or* king-sized), large, largish, major, outsize (*also* outsized), oversize (*or* oversized), sizable (*or* sizeable), substantial, super, whacking, whopping; formidable, grandiose, imposing, lofty, majestic, monolithic, staggering, stupendous, towering; boundless, cavernous, immeasurable, infinite, vast, vasty, voluminous

ant astronomical (*also* astronomic), colossal, cosmic, elephantine, enormous, giant, gigantic, herculean, heroic, huge, immense, mammoth, massive, monster, monstrous, monumental, mountainous, prodigious, titanic, tremendous

¹**tip** *n* **1** a piece of advice or useful information especially from an expert ⟨got some *tips* from a horticulturist on how to get my violets to bloom⟩

syn hint, lead, pointer

rel advice, advisement, assistance, counsel, guidance, recommendation, suggestion; caution, cautioning, sign, signal, telltale, tip-off, warning; brief, direction, feedback, instruction, observation; prompt, reminder, urging; answer, clue, solution

2 information not generally available to the public — see DOPE 1

²**tip** *n* **1** a small sum of money given for a service over and above what is due ⟨gave our waiter an extra large *tip* for such fantastic service⟩

syn gratuity, perquisite

rel donation, gift, lagniappe, largess (*or* largesse), present; bonus, favor, reward; contribution, offering

2 something given in addition to what is ordinarily expected or owed — see BONUS

³**tip** *n* the act of positioning or an instance of being positioned at an angle — see TILT

⁴**tip** *n* the last and usually sharp or tapering part of something long and narrow — see POINT 2

tip *vb* to set or cause to be at an angle — see LEAN 1

tipped *adj* tapering to a thin tip — see POINTED 1

tipping *adj* inclined or twisted to one side — see AWRY

tippler *n* a person who makes a habit of getting drunk — see DRUNK 1

tipsy *adj* being under the influence of alcohol — see DRUNK

tip–top *adj* of the very best kind — see EXCELLENT

tip–top *n* the highest part or point — see HEIGHT 1

tirade *n* a long angry speech or scolding ⟨after the inspection by the health department, Jay had to listen to his boss's *tirade* about keeping the restaurant's kitchen cleaner⟩

syn diatribe, harangue, rant

rel assault, attack, invective, lambasting, lashing, tongue-lashing, vituperation; berating, chewing out, rebuke, reprimand, reproach, reproof; abuse, castigation, censure, condemnation, criticism, denunciation; belittlement, deprecation, depreciation, disparagement, dissing; excoriation, execration, revilement; admonishment, admonition, lecture, sermon

near ant encomium, eulogy, panegyric, rhapsody, tribute; acclaim, acclamation, accolade, citation, homage, honor, praise; approval, blessing, commendation, endorsement, sanction; ovation, plaudit, rave

tire *vb* **1** to diminish the physical strength of — see WEAKEN 1

2 to make weary and restless by being dull or monotonous — see ²BORE

3 to use up all the physical energy of — see EXHAUST 1

tired *adj* **1** depleted in strength, energy, or freshness — see WEARY 1

2 having one's patience, interest, or pleasure exhausted — see WEARY 2

3 used or heard so often as to be dull — see STALE

tiredness *n* **1** a complete depletion of energy or strength — see FATIGUE

2 the state of being bored — see BOREDOM

tireless *adj* showing no signs of weariness even after long hard effort ⟨a *tireless* advocate for human rights⟩

syn indefatigable, inexhaustible, unflagging, untiring, unwearying, weariless

rel assiduous, conscientious, diligent, meticulous, painstaking, sedulous; determined, dogged, patient, persevering, persistent, pertinacious, plodding, relentless, steadfast, steady, stubborn, tenacious, unabating, unfailing, unfaltering, unflinching, unrelenting, unremitting, unwavering; active, busy, dynamic, energetic, feverish, spirited, vigorous; hard, industrious, intense, laborious, slavish, strenuous

near ant indolent, lackadaisical, laggard, lazy, listless, shiftless, slothful, sluggish; apathetic, casual, desultory, languid, spiritless; beat, broken, burned-out (*or* burnt-out), done in, drained, enervated, jaded, overtaxed, overworked, played out, sapped, spent, tuckered (out), wearied, worn-out

tirelessly *adv* with great effort or determination — see HARD 1

tiresome *adj* causing weariness, restlessness, or lack of interest — see BORING

tiring *adj* causing weariness, restlessness, or lack of interest — see BORING

titan *n* something that is unusually large and powerful — see GIANT

titanic *adj* unusually large — see HUGE

titillate *vb* to cause a pleasurable stimulation of the feelings — see THRILL

titillation *n* a pleasurably intense stimulation of the feelings — see THRILL

title *n* **1** a word or combination of words by which a person or thing is regularly known — see NAME 1

2 a word or series of words often in larger letters placed at the beginning of a passage or at the top of a page in order to introduce or categorize — see HEADING

3 the position occupied by the one who comes in first in a competition — see CROWN 2

title *vb* to give a name to — see NAME 1

titter *n* an explosive sound that is a sign of amusement — see LAUGH 1

tittle *n* **1** a very small piece — see BIT 1

2 the smallest amount or part imaginable — see JOT

titular *adj* being something in name or form only — see NOMINAL 1

tizzy *n* a state of nervous or irritated concern — see FRET

to *prep* earlier than — see BEFORE 1

toady *n* a person who flatters another in order to get ahead — see SYCOPHANT

toady *vb* to use flattery or the doing of favors in order to win approval especially from a superior — see FAWN

toast *vb* to cause to have or give off heat to a moderate degree — see WARM 1

toasty *adj* having or giving off heat to a moderate degree — see WARM 1

tocsin *n* **1** an object intended to give public notice or warning — see SIGNAL 1

2 something that tells of approaching danger or risk — see WARNING 2

today *adv* at the present time — see NOW 1

today *n* the time currently existing or in progress — see PRESENT 1

to-do *n* a state of noisy, confused activity — see COMMOTION

together *adv* **1** at one and the same time ⟨the two packages, although sent on different days, arrived *together*⟩

syn coincidentally, coincidently, concurrently, contemporaneously, simultaneously

rel close, immediately, narrowly, near

phrases at once

near ant apart, independently, individually, singly; consecutively, successively

ant separately

2 in or by combined action or effort ⟨working *together*, we can get this project done on time⟩

syn conjointly, jointly

rel collectively, mutually, reciprocally, unanimously, unitedly; cooperatively, symbiotically

phrases in concert

ant apart, independently, individually, separately, severally, singly, unilaterally

togs *n pl* **1** clothing chosen as appropriate for a specific situation — see OUTFIT 1

2 covering for the human body — see CLOTHING

toil *n* very hard or unpleasant work ⟨after years of *toil* in a sweatshop, Kim was finally able to start her own dressmaking business⟩

syn drudgery, grind, labor, slavery, sweat, travail

rel effort, exertion, pains, struggle, trouble; chore, duty, job, obligation, responsibility; routine, tedium, treadmill

near ant ease, leisure, relaxation, repose, rest; amusement, diversion, entertainment, recreation, sport; idleness, inactivity, inertia, inertness

ant fun, play

toil *vb* to devote serious and sustained effort — see LABOR

toiler *n* a person who does very hard or dull work — see SLAVE 2

toilet *n* a room furnished with a fixture for flushing body waste ⟨we were directed to the *toilets* in the church basement⟩

---

syn synonym(s)   *rel* related words
ant antonym(s)   *near ant* near antonym(s)

syn bath, bathroom, latrine, lavatory, rest room, washroom, water closet

rel commode; outhouse, privy

toilsome *adj* **1** requiring considerable physical or mental effort — see HARD 1

2 requiring much time, effort, or careful attention — see DEMANDING 1

token *n* something that serves to keep alive the memory of a person or event — see MEMORIAL

tolerable *adj* **1** capable of being endured — see BEARABLE

2 of a level of quality that meets one's needs or standards — see ADEQUATE

tolerably *adv* in a satisfactory way — see WELL 1

tolerance *n* the capacity to endure what is difficult or disagreeable without complaining — see PATIENCE

tolerant *adj* **1** accepting pains or hardships calmly or without complaint — see PATIENT 1

2 receiving or enduring without offering resistance — see PASSIVE

tolerate *vb* to put up with (something painful or difficult) — see BEAR 2

tolerating *adj* receiving or enduring without offering resistance — see PASSIVE

toll *vb* to make the clear sound heard when metal vibrates — see RING 1

tomb *n* a final resting place for a dead person — see GRAVE

tomboyish *adj* having qualities or traits that are traditionally considered inappropriate for a girl or woman — see UNFEMININE

tombstone *n* a shaped stone laid over or erected near a grave and usually bearing an inscription to identify and preserve the memory of the deceased ⟨the many *tombstones* marking the graves of children in the old cemetery reveal the harshness of pioneer life⟩

syn gravestone, headstone, monument

rel cross, marker, plaque, stone, table, tablet; monolith, obelisk, pillar; memorial, shrine

tome *n* a set of printed sheets of paper bound together between covers and forming a work of fiction or nonfiction — see BOOK 1

tomfoolery *n* wildly playful or mischievous behavior — see HORSEPLAY

tone *n* **1** a distinctive way of putting ideas into words — see STYLE 1

2 a property that becomes apparent when light falls on an object and by which things that are identical in form can be distinguished — see COLOR 1

3 the set of qualities that makes a person, a group of people, or a thing different from others — see NATURE 1

toned–down *adj* not excessively showy — see QUIET 2

tongue *n* the stock of words, pronunciation, and grammar used by a people as their basic means of communication — see LANGUAGE 1

tonic *adj* having a renewing effect on the state of the body or mind ⟨breathe in clear *tonic* mountain air⟩ ⟨never underestimate the *tonic* power of humor on a sick person⟩

syn bracing, invigorating, refreshing, restorative, reviving, stimulating, stimulative, vitalizing

rel conditioning, strengthening; animating, exhilarating, exhilarative, quickening, sharp; corrective, curative, curing, medicinal, rectifying, reformative, reformatory, remedial, remedying, reparative, therapeutic; beneficial, healthful, healthy, helpful, salubrious, salutary, wholesome

near ant deadening, debilitating, enervating, enfeebling, exhausting, numbing, sapping, weakening

too *adv* **1** beyond a normal or acceptable limit ⟨Ryan thought the test was *too* hard, but, on the other hand, he hadn't studied for it⟩

syn devilishly, excessively, exorbitantly, inordinately, monstrously, overly, overmuch, unacceptably, unduly

rel extravagantly, immoderately, intemperately; extortionately, inexcusably, intolerably, unbearably, unconsciously, unreasonably; improperly, inappropriately; abnormally, extraordinarily, freakishly, singularly, uncommonly, uncustomarily, unusually; astronomically, considerably, eminently, especially, exceedingly, exceptionally, extensively, extra, extremely, incredibly, remarkably, significantly, substantially, super, very, whacking

phrases to a fault

near ant acceptably, moderately, modestly, reasonably, temperately; barely, hardly, just, marginally, minimally, scarcely

ant deficiently, inadequately, insufficiently

2 in addition to what has been said — see MORE 1

3 to a great degree — see VERY 1

tool *n* **1** an article intended for use in work — see IMPLEMENT

2 one that is or can be used to further the purposes of another — see PAWN 1

3 one who is easily deceived or cheated — see DUPE

tooth and nail *adv* with all power or resources being used — see FULL BLAST

toothsome *adj* very pleasing to the sense of taste — see DELICIOUS 1

top *adj* **1** being at a point or level higher than all others ⟨an office in the *top* story of the building⟩ ⟨the *top* student in our graduating class⟩

syn highest, loftiest, topmost, upmost, uppermost

rel higher, loftier, upper; maximized, maximum, peaked, utmost; chief, first, foremost, head, leading, predominant, preeminent, premier, principal; dominant, dominating, eminent, prominent, towering; elevated, escalated, heightened, jacked (up), lifted, raised, uplifted, upraised *near ant* below, lower, under; low, lowered, low-lying, sunken

ant lowermost, lowest, nethermost, undermost

2 of the greatest or highest degree or quantity — see ULTIMATE 1

3 of the highest degree — see FULL 2

4 of the very best kind — see EXCELLENT

top *n* **1** a piece placed over an open container to hold in, protect, or conceal its contents — see COVER 1

2 the highest part or point — see HEIGHT 1

top *vb* to be greater, better, or stronger than — see SURPASS 1

topcoat *n* a warm outdoor coat — see OVERCOAT

topic *n* a major object of interest or concern (as in a discussion or artistic composition) — see MATTER 1

topmost *adj* **1** being at a point or level higher than all others — see TOP 1

2 of the highest degree — see FULL 2

top–notch *adj* of the very best kind — see EXCELLENT

topper *n* something (as a fact or argument) that is decisive or overwhelming — see CLINCHER

topple *vb* to go down from an upright position suddenly and involuntarily — see FALL 1

topsy–turvy *adj* lacking in order, neatness, and often cleanliness — see MESSY

torment *n* **1** a situation or state that causes great suffering and unhappiness — see HELL 2

2 a state of great suffering of body or mind — see DISTRESS 1

torment *vb* to cause persistent suffering to — see AFFLICT

tormenting *adj* **1** hard to accept or bear especially emotionally — see BITTER 2

2 intensely or unbearably painful — see EXCRUCIATING 1

tormentor *n* a person who causes repeated emotional pain, distress, or annoyance to another ⟨Phillip was relieved when his *tormentor* moved away, and he no longer had to take pains to avoid the bully⟩

syn baiter, heckler, mocker, needler, oppressor, persecutor, quiz, quizzer, ridiculer, scoffer, scorner, taunter, tease, teaser, torturer

rel belittler, derider, detractor, insulter; smart aleck, smarty (*or* smartie), wiseacre, wiseguy; lampooner, satirist; accuser, blamer, troublemaker; assailant, attacker, molester; bother, disturber, pest

near ant defender, deliverer, protector, rescuer, saviour; comforter, consoler, solace, soother, succorer

torpid *adj* **1** lacking bodily strength — see WEAK 1

2 slow to move or act — see INACTIVE 1

torrent *n* a great flow of water or of something that overwhelms — see FLOOD

torrid *adj* having a notably high temperature — see HOT 1

tortuous *adj* marked by a long series of irregular curves — see CROOKED 1

torture *n* **1** a situation or state that causes great suffering and unhappiness — see HELL 2

2 a state of great suffering of body or mind — see DISTRESS 1

torture *vb* to cause persistent suffering to — see AFFLICT

torturer *n* a person who causes repeated emotional pain, distress, or annoyance to another — see TORMENTOR

torturing *adj* intensely or unbearably painful — see EXCRUCIATING 1

torturous *adj* intensely or unbearably painful — see EXCRUCIATING 1

toss *vb* **1** to make a series of unsteady side-to-side motions — see ROCK 1

2 to make jerky or restless movements — see FIDGET

3 to send through the air especially with a quick forward motion of the arm — see THROW

toss (down *or* off) *vb* to swallow in liquid form — see DRINK 1

total *adj* **1** having no exceptions or restrictions — see ABSOLUTE 2

2 not lacking any part or member that properly belongs to it — see COMPLETE 1

3 trying all possibilities — see EXHAUSTIVE

total *n* a complete amount of something — see WHOLE

total *vb* **1** to have a total of — see AMOUNT (TO) 1

2 to combine (numbers) into a single sum — see ADD 2

totalitarianism *n* a system of government in which the ruler has unlimited power — see DESPOTISM

totality *n* a complete amount of something — see WHOLE

totally *adv* **1** to a full extent or degree — see FULLY 1

2 with attention to all aspects or details — see THOROUGHLY 1

tote *vb* to support and take from one place to another — see CARRY 1

totter *vb* **1** to move forward while swaying from side to side — see STAGGER 1

2 to swing unsteadily back and forth or from side to side — see TEETER 1

tottery *adj* marked by or given to small uncontrollable bodily movements — see SHAKY 1

touch *n* a very small amount — see PARTICLE 1

touch *vb* **1** to come into bodily contact with (something) so as to perceive a slight pressure on the skin ⟨be careful not to *touch* this pan—it's still hot⟩

syn feel

rel caress, embrace, finger, fondle, hug, paw, rub, stroke; brush, graze; clasp, clench, cling (to), clutch, grasp, grip, handle, palm; chuck, clap, dab, flick, pat, tag, tap, tip; hit, knock, pound, rap, whack

---

syn synonym(s) *rel* related words
ant antonym(s) *near ant* near antonym(s)

2 to act upon (a person or a person's feelings) so as to cause a response — see ¹AF-FECT 1

3 to affect slightly with something morally bad or undesirable — see TAINT 1

4 to be adjacent to — see ADJOIN 1

5 to be the business or affair of — see CONCERN 2

touch (on *or* upon) *vb* to make reference to or speak about briefly but specifically — see MENTION 1

touchable *adj* capable of being perceived by the sense of touch — see TANGIBLE

touch down *vb* to come to rest after descending from the air — see ALIGHT

touching *adj* **1** having a border in common — see ADJACENT

2 having the power to affect the feelings or sympathies — see MOVING

touch off *vb* to cause to function — see ACTIVATE

touchstone *n* something set up as an example against which others of the same type are compared — see STANDARD 1

touchy *adj* requiring exceptional skill or caution in performance or handling — see TRICKY

tough *adj* **1** not easily chewed ⟨her steak was so *tough* that she suggested the waiter use it as a hockey puck⟩
syn chewy, leathery
rel fibrous, gristly, sinewy, stringy; brittle, crunchy, hard
near ant mushy, soft
ant tender

2 able to withstand hardship, strain, or exposure — see HARDY 1

3 difficult to endure — see HARSH 1

4 requiring considerable physical or mental effort — see HARD 2

5 requiring exceptional skill or caution in performance or handling — see TRICKY

tough *n* a violent, brutal person who is often a member of an organized gang — see HOODLUM

toughen *vb* **1** to increase the ability of (as a muscle) to exert physical force — see STRENGTHEN 1

2 to make able to withstand physical hardship, strain, or exposure — see HARDEN 2

toughened *adj* able to withstand hardship, strain, or exposure — see HARDY 1

toughie *n* a violent, brutal person who is often a member of an organized gang — see HOODLUM

tour *n* a fixed period of time during which a person holds a job or position — see TERM 1

tour *vb* to take a trip especially of some distance — see TRAVEL 1

tourist *n* a person who travels for pleasure ⟨*tourists* from all over like to take pictures of the alligators in the bayou⟩
syn excursionist, sightseer, traveler (*or* traveller), tripper [*chiefly British*]
rel holidayer, vacationer, vacationist; guest, visitor; transient; journeyer, pilgrim, wayfarer

tournament *n* a competitive encounter between individuals or groups carried on for amusement, exercise, or in pursuit of a prize — see GAME 1

tourney *n* a competitive encounter between individuals or groups carried on for amusement, exercise, or in pursuit of a prize — see GAME 1

tousle *vb* to undo the proper order or arrangement of — see DISORDER

tousled *adj* lacking in order, neatness, and often cleanliness — see MESSY

tout *vb* **1** to praise or publicize lavishly and often excessively ⟨a new cleaning agent *touted* as the only product a homeowner needs for all his or her cleaning chores⟩
syn ballyhoo, crack up, glorify, trumpet
rel advance, advertise, announce, boost, herald, offer, plug, promote, publicize; assert, aver, claim, declare, lay down, make out, proclaim, pronounce

2 to declare enthusiastic approval of — see ACCLAIM

3 to provide publicity for — see PUBLICIZE 1

tow *vb* to cause to follow by applying steady force on — see PULL 1

toward *or* **towards** *prep* having to do with — see ABOUT 1

tower *n* a large, magnificent, or massive building — see EDIFICE 1

towering *adj* **1** extending to a great distance upward — see HIGH 1

2 going beyond a normal or acceptable limit in degree or amount — see EXCESSIVE

3 very dignified in form, tone, or style — see ELEVATED 2

town *n* a thickly settled, highly populated area — see CITY

townie *n* a person who lives in a town on a permanent basis — see BURGHER

toxic *adj* containing or contaminated with a substance capable of injuring or killing a living thing — see POISONOUS

toxin *n* a substance that by chemical action can kill or injure a living thing — see POISON

trace *n* **1** a mark or series of marks left on a surface by something that has passed along it — see TRACK 1

2 a passage cleared for public vehicular travel — see WAY 1

3 a rough course or way formed by or as if by repeated footsteps — see TRAIL 1

4 a tiny often physical indication of something lost or vanished — see VESTIGE

5 a very small amount — see PARTICLE 1

trace *vb* **1** to draw or make apparent the outline of — see OUTLINE 1

2 to go after or on the track of — see FOLLOW 2

tracing *n* the act of going after or in the tracks of another — see PURSUIT

track *n* **1** a mark or series of marks left on a surface by something that has passed along it ⟨a muddy *track* across the kitchen floor⟩
syn imprint, trace, trail

rel footprint, footstep, path, print, step, tread; artifact, evidence, leavings, mark, relic, remainder, remain(s), reminder, remnant, residual, residue, sign, spoor, telltale, token, vestige; clue, cue, hint, indication, inkling, intimation, suggestion; scent, shadow, whiff

2 a rough course or way formed by or as if by repeated footsteps — see TRAIL 1

3 the direction along which something or someone moves — see PATH 1

track *vb* to go after or on the track of — see FOLLOW 2

track (down) *vb* to come upon after searching, study, or effort — see FIND 1

tracking *n* the act of going after or in the tracks of another — see PURSUIT

tract *n* **1** a broad geographical area — see REGION 2

2 a small area of usually open land — see FIELD 1

3 a small piece of land that is developed or available for development — see LOT 1

tractable *adj* readily giving in to the command or authority of another — see OBEDIENT

trade *n* **1** a giving or taking of one thing of value in return for another — see EXCHANGE 1

2 an occupation requiring skillful use of the hands — see CRAFT 1

3 the activity by which one regularly makes a living — see OCCUPATION

4 the buying and selling of goods especially on a large scale and between different places — see COMMERCE

5 the transfer of ownership of something from one person to another for a price — see SALE

trade *vb* **1** to carry on the business of buying and selling goods or other property ⟨the U.S. agreed to *trade* with China⟩

syn deal, traffic

rel bargain, barter, horse-trade, negotiate, transact; auction, exchange, merchandise, rebuy, resell, swap; buy, purchase; distribute, market, peddle, retail, sell, supply, vend, wholesale; bootleg, fence, smuggle; corner, monopolize, undersell; invest, speculate

near ant boycott

2 to give up (something) and take something else in return — see CHANGE 3

trademark *n* **1** a device (as a word) identifying the maker of a piece of merchandise and legally reserved for the exclusive use of that person or company ⟨Kleenex is a *trademark* for a cleansing tissue⟩

syn brand

rel hallmark, imprint, label, logo, mark, name, service mark, stamp; copyright, patent

2 a device, design, or figure used as an identifying mark — see EMBLEM

trader *n* a buyer and seller of goods for profit — see MERCHANT

tradesman *n* **1** a buyer and seller of goods for profit — see MERCHANT

2 a person whose occupation requires skill with the hands — see ARTISAN

tradition *n* **1** an inherited or established way of thinking, feeling, or doing ⟨the town *tradition* of having the oldest resident ride at the head of the parade⟩

syn convention, custom

rel ethic, form, mode, mores, norm, values; birthright, inheritance, legacy; folklore, lore, superstition; culture, heritage, lifestyle

2 the body of customs, beliefs, stories, and sayings associated with a people, thing, or place — see FOLKLORE

traditional *adj* **1** based on customs usually handed down from a previous generation ⟨Ruben had a *traditional* Passover meal at his grandparents' house⟩

syn classical, conventional, customary

rel authentic, established, fixed, historical; common, habitual, orthodox, usual; ancestral, historic, old-time, old-world; aged, age-old, ancient, hoary, old, venerable; ageless, dateless, immemorial, timeless

near ant contemporary, current, modern, modernized, new, present-day, updated, up-to-date; futuristic, hot, latest, mod, modernistic, newfangled, new-fashioned, red-hot, space-age, ultramodern; nonconformist, nonorthodox, original, progressive, revolutionary, unorthodox, unusual

ant nontraditional, unconventional, uncustomary

2 tending to favor established ideas, conditions, or institutions — see CONSERVATIVE 1

traduce *vb* to make untrue and harmful statements about — see SLANDER

traducing *n* the making of false statements that damage another's reputation — see SLANDER

traffic *n* the buying and selling of goods especially on a large scale and between different places — see COMMERCE

traffic *vb* to carry on the business of buying and selling goods or other property — see TRADE 1

trafficker *n* a buyer and seller of goods for profit — see MERCHANT

tragedy *n* a sudden violent event that brings about great loss or destruction — see DISASTER

trail *n* **1** a rough course or way formed by or as if by repeated footsteps ⟨took a *trail* through the woods to get to the main road⟩

syn footpath, path, pathway, trace, track

rel bridle path; towpath; bypath, byroad, byway, passageway, walkway; detour, shortcut; course, passage, road, route, run, runway, way

2 a mark or series of marks left on a surface by something that has passed along it — see TRACK 1

trail *vb* to go after or on the track of — see FOLLOW 2

---

trailer *n* a motor vehicle that is specially equipped for living while traveling — see CAMPER

trailing *n* the act of going after or in the tracks of another — see PURSUIT

train *n* 1 a body of employees or servants who accompany and wait on a person — see CORTEGE 1

2 a group of vehicles traveling together or under one management — see FLEET

3 a series of persons or things arranged one behind another — see LINE 1

4 a series of things linked together — see CHAIN 1

train *vb* 1 to bring to a proper or desired state of fitness — see CONDITION 1

2 to cause to acquire knowledge or skill in some field — see TEACH

3 to fix (as one's attention) steadily toward a central objective — see CONCENTRATE 2

4 to point or turn (something) toward a target or goal — see AIM 1

trainer *n* a person who trains performers or athletes — see COACH

training *n* 1 something done over and over in order to develop skill — see EXERCISE 1

2 the act or process of imparting knowledge or skills to another — see EDUCATION 1

traipse *vb* 1 to go on foot — see WALK

2 to move about from place to place aimlessly — see WANDER

trait *n* something that sets apart an individual from others of the same kind — see CHARACTERISTIC

traitor *n* one who betrays a trust or an allegiance ⟨accused by her family of being a *traitor* when she sold their traditionally animal-friendly business to a competitor known to use animals for testing its products⟩

syn apostate, betrayer, double-crosser, quisling, recreant, turncoat

rel collaborationist, collaborator, subversive; conspirator, intriguer, plotter, schemer; defector, deserter, renegade; blabbermouth, gossip, gossiper, informant, informer, rat, snitcher, talebearer, talker, tattler, tattletale

traitorous *adj* not true in one's allegiance to someone or something — see FAITHLESS

trammel *n* something that makes movement or progress more difficult — see ENCUMBRANCE

trammel *vb* 1 to confine or restrain with or as if with chains — see BIND 1

2 to create difficulty for the work or activity of — see HAMPER

tramp *n* a homeless wanderer who may beg or steal for a living ⟨the police encouraged the *tramps* who were sleeping in the park to spend the bitterly cold night in the homeless shelter⟩

syn bum, hobo, sundowner [*Australian*], vagabond, vagrant

rel drifter, roamer, transient; beggar, derelict; dodger, malingerer, shirker, slacker; gamine, ragamuffin, urchin, waif

tramp *vb* 1 to move heavily or clumsily — see LUMBER 1

2 to tread on heavily so as to crush or injure — see TRAMPLE

trample *vb* to tread on heavily so as to crush or injure ⟨Isabel looked out her window and beheld the neighbor's Labrador retriever *trampling* her begonias⟩

syn stamp, stomp, tramp, tromp

rel override, run down, run over, step (on); mash, smash, squash; boot, kick

trance *n* the state of being lost in thought — see REVERIE

tranquil *adj* 1 free from disturbing noise or uproar — see QUIET 1

2 free from emotional or mental agitation — see CALM 2

3 free from storms or physical disturbance — see CALM 1

tranquilize *also* **tranquillize** *vb* to free from distress or disturbance — see CALM 1

tranquilizing *also* **tranquillizing** *adj* tending to calm the emotions and relieve stress — see SOOTHING 1

tranquillity *or* **tranquility** *n* 1 a state of freedom from storm or disturbance — see CALM

2 evenness of emotions or temper — see EQUANIMITY

transaction *n* the transfer of ownership of something from one person to another for a price — see SALE

transcend *vb* to be greater, better, or stronger than — see SURPASS 1

transfer *vb* 1 to give over the legal possession or ownership of ⟨Claire's grandfather agreed to *transfer* certain stocks to her when she turned 18⟩

syn alienate, assign, cede, deed, make over

rel bequeath, hand down, leave, pass down, will; bestow, confer, contribute, deliver, donate, grant, hand over, move, pass, present, release, relinquish, surrender, turn in, turn over, transmit, vest, yield; consign, entrust, trust; lease, lend, loan, rent

2 to cause (something) to pass from one to another — see COMMUNICATE 1

3 to cause to go or be taken from one place to another — see SEND

4 to change the place or position of — see MOVE 1

5 to put (something) into the possession or safekeeping of another — see GIVE 2

6 to shift possession of (something) from one person to another — see PASS 1

transferable *adj* capable of being taken from one place to another by public carrier — see SHIPPABLE

transfiguration *n* a change in form, appearance, or use — see CONVERSION

transfigure *vb* to change in form, appearance, or use — see CONVERT 2

transfix *vb* to penetrate or hold (something) with a pointed object — see IMPALE

transform *vb* to change in form, appearance, or use — see CONVERT 2

transformation *n* a change in form, appearance, or use — see CONVERSION

transfuse *vb* 1 to cause (something) to pass from one to another — see COMMUNICATE 1

2 to spread throughout — see PERMEATE

transgress *vb* 1 to commit an offense — see OFFEND 1

2 to fail to keep — see VIOLATE 1

transgression *n* 1 a breaking of a moral or legal code — see OFFENSE 1

2 a failure to uphold the requirements of law, duty, or obligation — see BREACH 1

transient *adj* lasting only for a short time — see MOMENTARY

transitory *adj* lasting only for a short time — see MOMENTARY

translate *vb* to express something (as a text or statement) in different words — see PARAPHRASE

translating *n* an instance of expressing something in different words — see PARAPHRASE

translation *n* an instance of expressing something in different words — see PARAPHRASE

transmit *vb* 1 to cause (something) to pass from one to another — see COMMUNICATE 1

2 to cause to go or be taken from one place to another — see SEND

3 to put (something) into the possession or safekeeping of another — see GIVE 2

transmittable *adj* 1 capable of being passed by physical contact from one person to another — see CONTAGIOUS 1

2 capable of being taken from one place to another by public carrier — see SHIPPABLE

transparency *n* the state or quality of being easily seen through — see CLARITY 1

transparent *adj* 1 easily seen through — see CLEAR 1

2 not subject to misinterpretation or more than one interpretation — see CLEAR 2

3 very thin and easy to see through — see SHEER 1

transpire *vb* to take place — see HAPPEN

transport *n* 1 a state of overwhelming usually pleasurable emotion — see ECSTASY

2 something used to carry goods or passengers — see CONVEYANCE

transport *vb* 1 to cause to go or be taken from one place to another — see SEND

2 to fill with great joy — see ELATE

3 to fill with overwhelming emotion (as wonder or delight) — see ENTRANCE

4 to force to leave a country — see BANISH 1

5 to support and take from one place to another — see CARRY 1

transportable *adj* capable of being taken from one place to another by public carrier — see SHIPPABLE

transportation *n* 1 a means of getting to a destination in a vehicle driven by another — see RIDE

2 something used to carry goods or passengers — see CONVEYANCE

transpose *vb* to change the place or position of — see MOVE 1

transversely *adv* in a line or direction running from corner to corner — see CROSSWISE

trap *n* 1 a device or scheme for capturing another by surprise ⟨undercover agents devised a *trap* to catch the counterfeiters⟩ ⟨a bear *trap*⟩

syn ambush, net, snare, web

rel entanglement, entrapment; booby trap, catch, hazard, pitfall, snag; deception, ploy, ruse, subterfuge, trick

2 a scheme in which hidden persons wait to attack by surprise — see AMBUSH 1

trap *vb* 1 to catch or hold as if in a net — see ENTANGLE 2

2 to take physical control or possession of (something) suddenly or forcibly — see CATCH 1

trash *n* 1 discarded or useless material — see GARBAGE

2 language, behavior, or ideas that are absurd and contrary to good sense — see NONSENSE 1

3 people looked down upon as ignorant and of the lowest class — see RABBLE

trashy *adj* 1 marked by an obvious lack of style or good taste — see TACKY 1

2 of low quality — see CHEAP 2

travail *n* very hard or unpleasant work — see TOIL

travail *vb* to devote serious and sustained effort — see LABOR

travel *vb* 1 to take a trip especially of some distance ⟨loves to *travel* and has been to 34 countries⟩

syn journey, peregrinate, pilgrimage, tour, trek, voyage

rel gallivant (*also* galavant), hop, jaunt, knock (about), ramble, roam, rove, traipse, wander; cruise, drive, fly, jet, motor, navigate, sail

2 to make one's way through, across, or over — see TRAVERSE

travel *n, often* travels *pl* a going from one place to another usually of some distance — see JOURNEY

traveler *or* **traveller** *n* a person who travels for pleasure — see TOURIST

traveling bag *n* a bag carried by hand and designed to hold a traveler's clothing and personal articles ⟨*traveling bags* made of lightweight but tough fabrics⟩

syn carryall, grip, handbag, portmanteau, suitcase

rel carpetbag, duffel bag, kit; backpack, haversack, knapsack, rucksack; attaché case, valise; baggage, bags, luggage

---

syn synonym(s)   *rel* related words
ant antonym(s)   *near ant* near antonym(s)

traverse *vb* to make one's way through, across, or over ⟨Julie watched the spider *traverse* the entire wall from floor to ceiling⟩
syn cover, crisscross, cross, cut (across), follow, go, pass (over), proceed (along), travel
rel hike, tread, walk; ride

travesty *n* a poor, insincere, or insulting imitation of something — see MOCKERY 1

travesty *vb* to copy or exaggerate (someone or something) in order to make fun of — see MIMIC 1

treacherous *adj* not true in one's allegiance to someone or something — see FAITHLESS

treachery *n* the act or fact of violating the trust or confidence of another — see BETRAYAL

tread *vb* to go on foot — see WALK

treadmill *n* an established and often automatic or monotonous series of actions followed when engaging in some activity — see ROUTINE 1

treason *n* the act or fact of violating the trust or confidence of another — see BETRAYAL

treasure *n* 1 an asset that brings praise or renown — see GLORY 2
2 someone or something unusually desirable — see PRIZE 1

treasure *vb* to hold dear — see LOVE 1

treat *n* 1 a source of great satisfaction — see DELIGHT 1
2 something that is pleasing to eat because it is rare or a luxury — see DELICACY 1

treat *vb* 1 to behave toward in a stated way ⟨she tries to *treat* all of her students fairly and equally, regardless of her personal feelings toward them⟩
syn act (toward), be (to), deal (with), handle, serve, use
rel consider, regard; react (to), respond (to)
2 to deal with (something) usually skillfully or efficiently — see HANDLE 1
3 to exchange viewpoints or seek advice for the purpose of finding a solution to a problem — see CONFER 2
4 to give medical treatment to — see DOCTOR 1

treat (of) *vb* to have (something) as a subject matter — see CONCERN 1

treaty *n* a formal agreement between two or more nations or peoples ⟨in accordance with a *treaty* between the United States and the tribes of the Pacific Northwest, commercial fishing of certain kinds of salmon is limited to Native Americans⟩
syn accord, alliance, compact, convention, covenant, pact
rel bargain, charter, contract, deal, settlement, understanding

treble *adj* 1 having a high musical pitch or range — see SHRILL
2 having three units or parts — see TRIPLE

trek *n* a going from one place to another usually of some distance — see JOURNEY

trek *vb* to take a trip especially of some distance — see TRAVEL 1

tremble *n* an instance of shaking involuntarily with fear or cold — see SHIVER 1

trembling *adj* marked by or given to small uncontrollable bodily movements — see SHAKY 1

trembling *n* a series of slight movements by a body back and forth or from side to side — see VIBRATION

tremendous *adj* unusually large — see HUGE

tremendously *adv* to a large extent or degree — see GREATLY 2

tremor *n* a shaking of the earth — see EARTHQUAKE

tremulous *adj* marked by or given to small uncontrollable bodily movements — see SHAKY 1

trench *n* a long narrow channel dug in the earth — see DITCH

trenchant *adj* having an edge thin enough to cut or pierce something — see SHARP 1

trend *n* 1 a prevailing or general movement or inclination ⟨according to the survey, there's a growing *trend* for companies to run their own day-care centers for the benefit of employees⟩
syn current, drift, leaning, run, tendency, tide, wind
rel curve, shift, swing, turn; custom, habit, propensity, tenor, way
2 a practice or interest that is very popular for a short time — see FAD

trend *vb* to show a liking or proneness (for something) — see LEAN 2

trepidation *n* the emotion experienced in the presence or threat of danger — see FEAR

trespass *n* 1 a breaking of a moral or legal code — see OFFENSE 1
2 a failure to uphold the requirements of law, duty, or obligation — see BREACH 1

trespass *vb* to commit an offense — see OFFEND 1

triad *n* a group of three — see THREESOME

triadic *adj* having three units or parts — see TRIPLE

trial *adj* made or done as an experiment — see EXPERIMENTAL 1

trial *n* 1 a test of faith, patience, or strength ⟨Nancy found living with her cousin a real *trial* and couldn't wait for the summer to end⟩
syn cross, crucible, gauntlet (*also* gantlet), ordeal
rel adversity, affliction, asperity, misfortune, mishap, privation, tragedy, tribulation, trouble, vicissitude, woe; challenge, complication, difficulty, grief, hardship, rigor; annoyance, discomfort, inconvenience, nuisance
2 a private performance or session in preparation for a public appearance — see REHEARSAL
3 a procedure or operation carried out to resolve an uncertainty — see EXPERIMENT
4 an effort to do or accomplish something — see ATTEMPT

tribal *adj* of, relating to, or reflecting the traits exhibited by a group of people with a common ancestry and culture — see RACIAL

tribe *n* a group of persons who come from the same ancestor — see FAMILY 1

tribulation *n* a state of great suffering of body or mind — see DISTRESS 1

tribunal *n* an assembly of persons for the administration of justice — see COURT 3

tribute *n* a formal expression of praise — see ENCOMIUM

trice *n* a very small space of time — see INSTANT

trick *n* 1 a clever often underhanded means to achieve an end ⟨used every *trick* in the book to get out of appearing in the fashion show featuring clothes for teens⟩
  syn artifice, device, dodge, gimmick, jig, ploy, scheme, sleight, stratagem, wile
  rel bluff, deception, feint; fraud, hoax, swindle

  2 a playful or mischievous act intended as a joke — see PRANK

  3 a usual manner of behaving or doing — see HABIT

  4 an act of notable skill, strength, or cleverness — see FEAT 1

  5 an odd or peculiar habit — see IDIOSYNCRASY

trick *vb* to cause to believe what is untrue — see DECEIVE

trickery *n* the use of clever underhanded actions to achieve an end ⟨Delia resorted to *trickery*—even loading up the fishing equipment—to induce her dog into the car for his vet appointment⟩
  syn artifice, chicanery, hanky-panky, jugglery, legerdemain, subterfuge, wile
  rel artfulness, caginess, craftiness, cunning, deviousness, foxiness, shadiness, sharpness, shiftiness, slickness, slipperiness, slyness, sneakiness, treachery, underhandedness, wiliness; deceit, deceitfulness, deception, deceptiveness, dishonesty, dissimulation, double-dealing, duplicity, guile, hypocrisy, insincerity; fakery, humbuggery, imposture, quackery; design, plotting, scheming, secrecy, stealth

trickle *vb* 1 to fall or let fall in or as if in drops — see DRIP

  2 to flow in a broken irregular stream — see GURGLE

trickster *n* 1 a dishonest person who uses clever means to cheat others out of something of value ⟨a heartless *trickster* swindled the elderly woman out of her life savings⟩
  syn cheat, cheater, confidence man, cozener, defrauder, dodger, hoaxer, shark, sharper, swindler
  rel double-crosser, double-dealer; bluffer, charlatan, fake, faker, humbug, imposter, mountebank, pretender, quack; adventurer, fox, knave, prankster, rascal,

rogue; slicker, smoothy (*or* smoothie); plotter, schemer, sneak

  2 one who practices tricks and illusions for entertainment — see MAGICIAN 2

tricky *adj* requiring exceptional skill or caution in performance or handling ⟨a *tricky* musical passage for the woodwind section⟩
  syn catchy, delicate, difficult, knotty, problematic (*also* problematical), spiny, thorny, ticklish, touchy, tough
  rel abstract, abstruse, complex, complicated, hard, intricate, involved, recondite; stubborn, troublesome, vexatious, vexing; burdensome, demanding, discommoding, exacting, importunate, inconvenient, onerous, oppressive, painful
  near ant easy, manageable, painless, straightforward, uncomplicated, undemanding, untroublesome

tried *adj* worthy of one's trust — see DEPENDABLE

tried–and–true *adj* worthy of one's trust — see DEPENDABLE

trifle *n* something of little importance ⟨let us not speak of *trifles* when our nation may be going to war⟩
  syn child's play, frippery, nothing, triviality
  rel naught, nothingness, smoke, zero; molehill, peanuts, pittance, song, straw, two bits; nonsense, trivia

trifle *vb* 1 to show a liking for someone of the opposite sex just for fun — see FLIRT

  2 to spend time in aimless activity — see FIDDLE (AROUND)

trifling *adj* 1 lacking importance — see UNIMPORTANT

  2 so small or unimportant as to warrant little or no attention — see NEGLIGIBLE 1

trigger *vb* to cause to function — see ACTIVATE

trill *vb* to sing with the alternation of two musical tones — see WARBLE

trim *adj* being clean and in good order — see NEAT 1

trim *n* 1 a state of being or fitness — see CONDITION 1

  2 something that decorates or beautifies — see DECORATION 1

trim *vb* 1 to achieve a victory over — see BEAT 2

  2 to defeat by a large margin — see WHIP 2

  3 to make (as hair) shorter with or as if with the use of shears — see CLIP

  4 to make more attractive by adding something that is beautiful or becoming — see DECORATE

trimmer *n* one that defeats an enemy or opponent — see VICTOR 1

trimming *n* failure to win a contest — see DEFEAT 1

trinity *n* a group of three — see THREESOME

trinket *n* a small object displayed for its attractiveness or interest — see KNICKKNACK

trio *n* a group of three — see THREESOME

trip *n* a going from one place to another usually of some distance — see JOURNEY

trip *vb* **1** to go at a pace faster than a walk — see RUN 1

2 to go down from an upright position suddenly and involuntarily — see FALL 1

3 to move with a light bouncing step — see SKIP 1

tripartite *adj* having three units or parts — see TRIPLE

triple *adj* having three units or parts ⟨a *triple* scoop of chocolate ice cream⟩

syn threefold, treble, triadic, tripartite, triplex

rel triplicate

triple *n* a group of three — see THREE-SOME

triplet *n* a group of three — see THREE-SOME

triplex *adj* having three units or parts — see TRIPLE

tripper *n, chiefly British* a person who travels for pleasure — see TOURIST

trippingly *adv* in a quick and spirited manner — see GAILY 2

trite *adj* used or heard so often as to be dull — see STALE

triumph *n* **1** a successful result brought about by hard work — see ACCOMPLISHMENT 1

2 an instance of defeating an enemy or opponent — see VICTORY

triumph *vb* **1** to achieve victory (as in a contest) — see WIN 1

2 to feel or express joy or triumph — see EXULT

triumph (over) *vb* to achieve a victory over — see BEAT 2

triumphant *adj* **1** having attained a desired end or state of good fortune — see SUCCESSFUL 1

2 having or expressing feelings of joy or triumph — see EXULTANT

triumvirate *n* a group of three — see THREESOME

trivial *adj* **1** lacking importance — see UNIMPORTANT

2 so small or unimportant as to warrant little or no attention — see NEGLIGIBLE 1

triviality *n* something of little importance — see TRIFLE

troll *n* an imaginary being usually having a small human form and magical powers — see FAIRY

tromp *vb* **1** to move heavily or clumsily — see LUMBER 1

2 to tread on heavily so as to crush or injure — see TRAMPLE

troop *n* **1** an organized group of stage performers — see COMPANY 1

2 *troops pl* the combined army, air force, and navy of a nation — see ARMED FORCES

tropical *adj* being near the equator — see LOW 1

trot *vb* **1** to go at a pace faster than a walk — see RUN 1

2 to proceed or move quickly — see HURRY 2

troth *n* **1** a person's solemn declaration that he or she will do or not do something — see PROMISE

2 the act or state of being engaged to be married — see ENGAGEMENT 1

troth *vb* to obligate by prior agreement — see PLEDGE 1

trouble *n* **1** an abnormal state that disrupts a plant's or animal's normal bodily functioning — see DISEASE

2 something that may cause injury or harm — see DANGER 2

3 something that requires thought and skill for resolution — see PROBLEM 1

4 the active use of energy in producing a result — see EFFORT

5 the state of not being protected from injury, harm, or evil — see DANGER 1

trouble *vb* **1** to experience concern or anxiety — see WORRY 1

2 to cause discomfort to or trouble for — see INCONVENIENCE

troubled *adj* feeling or showing uncomfortable feelings of uncertainty — see NERVOUS 1

troublesome *adj* causing worry or anxiety ⟨the *troublesome* news that there will be more cuts in the school budget⟩

syn discomforting, discomposing, disquieting, distressing, disturbing, perturbing, troubling, troublous, unsettling, upsetting, worrisome

rel daunting, demoralizing, discomfiting, disconcerting, discouraging, disheartening, dismaying, dispiriting

near ant calming, quieting, settling, soothing

ant reassuring, untroublesome

troubling *adj* causing worry or anxiety — see TROUBLESOME

troublous *adj* causing worry or anxiety — see TROUBLESOME

trough *n* **1** a long hollow cylinder for carrying a substance (as a liquid or gas) — see PIPE 1

2 a long narrow channel dug in the earth — see DITCH

3 a pipe or channel for carrying off water from a roof — see GUTTER 1

trounce *vb* **1** to achieve a victory over — see BEAT 2

2 to defeat by a large margin — see WHIP 2

trouncing *n* failure to win a contest — see DEFEAT 1

troupe *n* an organized group of stage performers — see COMPANY 1

trouper *n* one who acts professionally (as in a play, movie, or television show) — see ACTOR

trousers *n pl* an outer garment covering each leg separately from waist to ankle — see PANTS

truce *n* a temporary stopping of fighting ⟨both sides agreed to a 24-hour *truce* beginning at midnight on Christmas Eve⟩

syn armistice, cease-fire

rel accord, reconciliation; peace, peacetime

truck *n* a giving or taking of one thing of value in return for another — see EXCHANGE 1

truculence *n* an inclination to fight or quarrel — see BELLIGERENCE

truculent *adj* feeling or displaying eagerness to fight — see BELLIGERENT

trudge *vb* to make progress in a clumsy, struggling manner — see FLOUNDER 1

true *adj* 1 being exactly as appears or as claimed — see AUTHENTIC 1

2 being in agreement with the truth or a fact or a standard — see CORRECT 1

3 existing in fact and not merely as a possibility — see ACTUAL

4 firm in one's allegiance to someone or something — see FAITHFUL 1

5 following an original exactly — see FAITHFUL 2

6 free from any intent to deceive or impress others — see GUILELESS

7 restricted to or based on fact — see FACTUAL 1

8 worthy of one's trust — see DEPENDABLE

true–blue *adj* firm in one's allegiance to someone or something — see FAITHFUL 1

truism *n* an idea or expression that has been used by many people — see COMMONPLACE

truly *adv* 1 not merely this but also — see EVEN

2 to tell the truth — see ACTUALLY 1

3 without any question — see INDEED 1

trumpery *adj* of low quality — see CHEAP 2

trumpet *vb* to praise or publicize lavishly and often excessively — see TOUT 1

truncheon *n* a heavy rigid stick used as a weapon or for punishment — see CLUB 1

trunk *n* a covered rectangular container for storing or transporting things — see CHEST

truss *vb* to gather into a tight mass by means of a line or cord — see TIE 1

trust *n* 1 firm belief in the integrity, ability, effectiveness, or genuineness of someone or something ⟨a relationship of mutual *trust* between lawyer and client⟩

syn confidence, credence, faith, stock

rel acceptance, assurance, assuredness, certainty, certitude, conviction, positiveness, sureness; credit, dependence, hope, reliance

near ant disbelief, incredulity, unbelief; doubt, dubiousness, incertitude, nonconfidence, skepticism, suspicion, uncertainty

ant distrust, mistrust

2 a number of businesses or enterprises united for commercial advantage — see CARTEL

3 responsibility for the safety and well-being of someone or something — see CUSTODY

4 the right to take possession of goods before paying for them — see CREDIT 1

trust *vb* 1 to give a task, duty, or responsibility to — see ENTRUST 1

2 to put (something) into the possession or safekeeping of another — see GIVE 2

3 to regard as right or true — see BELIEVE 1

trustful *adj* having or showing trust in another — see TRUSTING 1

trusting *adj* 1 having or showing trust in another ⟨Delia couldn't look into her dog's *trusting* eyes as she drove him to the vet⟩

syn confiding, trustful

rel artless, childlike, credulous, guileless, gullible, innocent, naive (*also* naïve), simple, unsophisticated; dependent, hopeful, reliant; accepting, believing, certain, confident, convinced, overconfident, secure, sure, unquestioning, unsuspecting, unsuspicious, unwary

near ant disbelieving, incredulous, unbelieving, unconvinced, unpersuaded; hesitant, leery, oversuspicious, skeptical, suspicious, uncertain, unsure, wary

ant distrustful, doubtful, doubting, mistrustful

2 readily taken advantage of — see EASY 2

trustworthiness *n* worthiness as the recipient of another's trust or confidence — see RELIABILITY

trustworthy *adj* worthy of one's trust — see DEPENDABLE

trusty *adj* worthy of one's trust — see DEPENDABLE

truth *n* agreement with fact or reality ⟨there is no *truth* to her accusation that Emory cheated on the test⟩

syn factuality, verity

rel accuracy, actuality, authenticity, correctness; credibility, honesty, trustworthiness, truthfulness, veracity; dependability, reliability

near ant erroneousness, fallaciousness, fallacy; falsehood, fiction, inaccuracy, incorrectness; deceit, dishonesty, mendacity, untruthfulness

ant falseness, falsity, untruth

truthful *adj* being in the habit of telling the truth ⟨a *truthful* youngster who wouldn't just make up a story like that⟩

syn honest, veracious

rel candid, frank, open, plainspoken; believable, credible, veritable, true; conscientious, moral, principled, scrupulous; dependable, reliable, trustworthy, trusty

near ant fallacious, false, untrue; unbelievable, undependable, unreliable, untrustworthy; bluffing, dissembling, dissimulating, duplicitous, equivocating, hypocritical, insincere, posing, pretending; artful, deceitful, deceptive, devious, slick, slippery, sly, sneaky, treacherous, tricky, underhanded, wily

ant dishonest, fibbing, lying, mendacious, prevaricating, untruthful

truthfully *adv* to tell the truth — see ACTUALLY 1

truthfulness *n* devotion to telling the truth — see HONESTY 1

---

syn synonym(s) *rel* related words
ant antonym(s) *near ant* near antonym(s)

try *n* an effort to do or accomplish something — see ATTEMPT

try *vb* to make an effort to do — see ATTEMPT

try (out) *vb* **1** to put (something) to a test ⟨want to *try out* my new skateboard?⟩ ⟨*tried* his skill at archery⟩

syn sample, test

rel check out, examine, experiment (with), explore, feel (out), research

2 to subject (a personal quality or faculty) to often excessive stress ⟨you're *trying* my patience⟩

syn strain, stretch, tax, test

rel demand, exact, importune, press, pressure, push; aggravate, agitate, exasperate, get (to), gnaw (at), grate, harass, harry, hassle, irk, irritate, pain, pester

trying *adj* difficult to endure — see HARSH 1

tryst *n* an agreement to be present at a specified time and place — see ENGAGEMENT 2

tubby *adj* having an excess of body fat — see FAT 1

tube *n* a long hollow cylinder for carrying a substance (as a liquid or gas) — see PIPE 1

tucker (out) *vb* to use up all the physical energy of — see EXHAUST 1

tuckered (out) *adj* depleted in strength, energy, or freshness — see WEARY 1

tug *n* the act or an instance of applying force on something so that it moves in the direction of the force — see PULL 1

tug *vb* to cause to follow by applying steady force on — see PULL 1

tug–of–war *n* an earnest effort for superiority or victory over another — see CONTEST 1

tumble *n* **1** an unorganized collection or mixture of various things — see MISCELLANY 1

2 the act of going down from an upright position suddenly and involuntarily — see FALL 1

tumble *vb* **1** to go down from an upright position suddenly and involuntarily — see FALL 1

2 to go to a lower level — see DROP 2

3 to undo the proper order or arrangement of — see DISORDER

tumble (to) *vb* to recognize the meaning of — see COMPREHEND 1

tumbled *adj* lacking in order, neatness, and often cleanliness — see MESSY

tummy *n* the part of the body between the chest and the pelvis — see STOMACH

tumor *n* an abnormal mass of tissue — see GROWTH 1

tumult *n* **1** a state of noisy, confused activity — see COMMOTION

2 a violent disturbance (as of the political or social order) — see CONVULSION

3 a violent shouting — see CLAMOR 1

tumultuous *adj* **1** marked by sudden or violent disturbance — see CONVULSIVE

2 marked by turmoil or disturbance especially of natural elements — see WILD 3

tundra *n* a broad area of level or rolling treeless country — see PLAIN

tune *n* **1** a rhythmic series of musical tones arranged to give a pleasing effect — see MELODY

2 a state of consistency — see CONFORMITY 1

tuneful *adj* having a pleasing mixture of notes — see HARMONIOUS 1

turbid *adj* having visible particles in liquid suspension — see CLOUDY 1

turbulent *adj* **1** marked by bursts of destructive force or intense activity — see VIOLENT 1

2 marked by turmoil or disturbance especially of natural elements — see WILD 3

3 marked by wet and windy conditions — see FOUL 1

turkey *n* **1** a person who lacks good sense or judgment — see FOOL 1

2 a stupid person — see IDIOT

3 something that has failed — see FAILURE 3

turmoil *n* **1** a disturbed or uneasy state — see UNREST

2 a state of noisy, confused activity — see COMMOTION

turn *n* **1** a relaxed journey on foot for exercise or pleasure — see WALK

2 an act of kind assistance — see FAVOR 1

3 a habitual attraction to some activity or thing — see INCLINATION 1

4 something that curves or is curved — see BEND 1

turn *vb* **1** to move (something) in a curved or circular path on or as if on an axis ⟨*turned* the doorknob as quietly as possible⟩

syn pivot, revolve, roll, rotate, spin, swing, swirl, twirl, twist, twist, wheel, whirl

rel screw, unscrew; twiddle; crank, reel, wind; circulate

2 to change the course or direction of (something) ⟨the dog *turned* the stampeding flock of sheep around⟩ ⟨he *turned* his cart uphill⟩

syn deflect, divert, swing, veer, wheel, whip

rel avert, move, rechannel, shift, shunt, sidetrack, switch, transfer; swivel, twist, whirl, zigzag; bend, curve, sway; reverse, turn back

3 to change one's course or direction ⟨we *turned* left at the light⟩ ⟨the storm unexpectedly *turned* south and missed our area⟩

syn detour, deviate, sheer, swing, turn off, veer

rel tack, zigzag; double (back), turn back

4 to eventually have as a state or quality — see BECOME

5 to move in circles around an axis or center — see SPIN 1

turn (over) *vb* to change the position of (an object) so that the opposite side or end is showing — see REVERSE 2

turn (to) *vb* to use or seek out as a source of aid, relief, or advantage — see RESORT (TO) 1

turncoat *n* one who betrays a trust or an allegiance — see TRAITOR

turn down *vb* to show unwillingness to accept, do, engage in, or agree to — see DECLINE 1

turn in *vb* to go to one's bed in order to sleep — see BED

turning point *n* a point in a chain of events at which an important change (as in one's fortunes) occurs ⟨the *turning point* came when Victor finally admitted he was a werewolf⟩

syn climax, landmark, milestone

rel break, clincher, highlight; conversion, metamorphosis, transfiguration, transformation, turnabout, turnaround; clutch, crisis, crossroad(s), crunch, emergency, exigency, head, juncture, zero hour

turn off *vb* 1 to cause to feel disgust — see DISGUST

2 to change one's course or direction — see TURN 3

turn-on *n* something that persuades one to perform an action for pleasure or gain — see LURE 1

turn on *vb* 1 to cause a pleasurable stimulation of the feelings — see THRILL

2 to cause to function — see ACTIVATE

turn out *vb* to come to be — see COME OUT 1

turn over *vb* 1 to give (something) over to the control or possession of another usually under duress — see SURRENDER 1

2 to put (something) into the possession or safekeeping of another — see GIVE 2

turnpike *n* a passage cleared for public vehicular travel — see WAY 1

turn up *vb* 1 to come into view — see APPEAR 1

2 to get to a destination — see COME 2

tussle *n* a physical dispute between opposing individuals or groups — see FIGHT 1

tussle *vb* to seize and attempt to unbalance one another for the purpose of achieving physical mastery — see WRESTLE

tutelage *n* the act or process of imparting knowledge or skills to another — see EDUCATION 1

tutor *vb* 1 to cause to acquire knowledge or skill in some field — see TEACH

2 to give advice and instruction to (someone) regarding the course or process to be followed — see GUIDE 1

tutoring *n* the act or process of imparting knowledge or skills to another — see EDUCATION 1

twain *n* two things of the same or similar kind that match or are considered together — see PAIR

tweet *vb* to make a short sharp sound like a small bird — see CHIRP

twerp *n* a person of no importance or influence — see NOBODY

twice *adv* to two times the amount or degree — see DOUBLY

twilight *n* 1 a time or place of little or no light — see DARK 1

2 the time from when the sun begins to set to the onset of total darkness — see DUSK 1

twin *adj* consisting of two members or parts that are usually joined — see DOUBLE 1

twin *n* either of a pair matched in one or more qualities — see MATE 1

twine *vb* to follow a circular or spiral course — see WIND

twinge *n* a sharp unpleasant sensation usually felt in some specific part of the body — see PAIN 1

twinkle *n* a very small space of time — see INSTANT

twinkle *vb* 1 to shine with light at regular intervals — see BLINK 1

2 to shoot forth bursts of light — see FLASH 1

twinkling *n* a very small space of time — see INSTANT

twirl *n* a rapid turning about on an axis or central point — see SPIN 1

twirl *vb* 1 to move (something) in a curved or circular path on or as if on an axis — see TURN 1

2 to move in circles around an axis or center — see SPIN 1

twist *n* a forceful rotating or pulling motion for the purpose of dislodging something — see WRENCH 1

twist *vb* 1 to change so much as to create a wrong impression or alter the meaning of — see GARBLE

2 to follow a circular or spiral course — see WIND

3 to move (something) in a curved or circular path on or as if on an axis — see TURN 1

4 to move by or as if by a forceful rotation — see WRENCH 2

twisted *adj* marked by a long series of irregular curves — see CROOKED 1

twisting *adj* marked by a long series of irregular curves — see CROOKED 1

twisting *n* a forceful rotating or pulling motion for the purpose of dislodging something — see WRENCH 1

twitch *vb* 1 to make jerky or restless movements — see FIDGET

2 to move or cause to move with a sharp quick motion — see JERK 1

twitching *n* a series of slight movements by a body back and forth or from side to side — see VIBRATION

twitter *n* a state of nervous or irritated concern — see FRET

twitter *vb* 1 to engage in casual or rambling conversation — see CHAT

2 to make a short sharp sound like a small bird — see CHIRP

two-faced *adj* not being or expressing what one appears to be or express — see INSINCERE

twofold *adj* being twice as great or as many — see DOUBLE 2

---

syn synonym(s)   *rel* related words
ant antonym(s)   *near ant* near antonym(s)

twosome *n* two things of the same or similar kind that match or are considered together — see PAIR

tycoon *n* a person of rank, power, or influence in a particular field — see MAGNATE

type *n* **1** a number of persons or things that are grouped together because they have something in common — see SORT 1
2 one of the units into which a whole is divided on the basis of a common characteristic — see CLASS 2

typical *adj* **1** having or showing the qualities associated with the members of a particular group or kind ⟨*typical* behavior for a two-year-old⟩
syn archetypal, average, characteristic, normal, regular, representative, standard
rel common, conventional, customary, ordinary, usual, wonted; expected, familiar, habitual, predictable, routine, unexceptional, unremarkable; predominant, preponderant
near ant uncommon, unconventional, uncustomary, unusual, unwonted; distinctive, especial, exceptional, extraordinary, infrequent, noteworthy, rare, remarkable, singular, special, unexpected, unfamiliar, unique, unpredictable; eccentric, idiosyncratic, nonconformist, peculiar, unknown, unorthodox; curious, funny, odd, queer, strange; bizarre, fantastic, far-out, freak, freakish, out-of-the-way, outrageous, outré, unnatural, weird, wild
ant aberrant, abnormal, anomalous, atypical, deviant, irregular, nonrepresentative, nontypical
2 serving to identify as belonging to an individual or group — see CHARACTERISTIC 1

typically *adv* according to the usual course of things — see NATURALLY 2

tyrannical *also* **tyrannic** *adj* **1** exercising power or authority without interference by others — see ABSOLUTE 1
2 fond of ordering people around — see BOSSY

tyrannous *adj* **1** exercising power or authority without interference by others — see ABSOLUTE 1
2 fond of ordering people around — see BOSSY

tyranny *n* a system of government in which the ruler has unlimited power — see DESPOTISM

tyrant *n* a person who uses power or authority in a cruel, unjust, or harmful way — see DESPOT

tyro *n* a person who is just starting out in a field of activity — see BEGINNER

ubiquitous *adj* **1** often observed or encountered — see COMMON 1
2 present in all places and at all times — see OMNIPRESENT

ugly *adj* **1** unpleasant to look at ⟨her first attempt at painting was pretty *ugly* —a portrait of her sister that was not at all flattering⟩
syn grotesque, hideous, homely, ill-favored, unappealing, unattractive, unbeautiful, unhandsome, unlovely, unpleasing, unpretty, unsightly, vile
rel disgusting, repugnant, repulsive, revolting; unimposing, unprepossessing, unimpressive; plain, unaesthetic, unbecoming, unshapely
near ant becoming, bonny [*chiefly British*], cute, shapely; imposing, impressive, prepossessing
ant attractive, beauteous, beautiful, comely, cute, fair, gorgeous, handsome, lovely, pretty, stunning, taking
2 causing intense displeasure, disgust, or resentment — see OFFENSIVE 1

ultimate *adj* **1** of the greatest or highest degree or quantity ⟨the *ultimate* speed yet attained by a land-based vehicle⟩
syn consummate, maximum, most, nth, paramount, supreme, top, utmost, uttermost
rel unequaled (*or* unequalled), unmatched, unparalleled, unrivaled (*or* unrivalled); unsurpassed; topmost, upmost, uppermost
near ant littlest, smallest; lowest
ant least, minimal, minimum
2 following all others of the same kind in order or time — see LAST
3 most distant from a center — see EXTREME 1

ultimately *adv* at a later time — see YET 1

ultimatum *n* something that someone insists upon having — see DEMAND 1

ultra *adj* being very far from the center of public opinion — see EXTREME 2

ultramodern *adj* being or involving the latest methods, concepts, information, or styles — see MODERN

ultramodernist *n* a person with very modern ideas — see MODERN

umbra *n* **1** a time or place of little or no light — see DARK 1
2 partial darkness due to the obstruction of light rays — see SHADE 1

umbrage *n* the feeling of being offended or resentful after a slight or indignity — see PIQUE

umpire *vb* to give an opinion about (something at issue or in dispute) — see JUDGE 1

unabashed *adj* not embarrassed or ashamed ⟨*unabashed* by their booing and hissing, he continued with his performance⟩

syn unashamed, unblushing, unembarrassed

rel prideful, proud; bold, brassy, brazen, impudent, insolent, saucy, shameless; unapologetic, undaunted, undeterred, undismayed; unblinking, unflinching, unshrinking

near ant discomfited, disconcerted, nonplussed (*also* nonplused)

ant abashed, ashamed, embarrassed, shamefaced, sheepish

unacceptable *adj* falling short of a standard — see BAD 1

unacceptably *adv* 1 beyond a normal or acceptable limit — see TOO 1

2 in an unsatisfactory way — see BADLY

unacclimated *adj* not having acquired a habit or tolerance — see UNUSED 1

unaccompanied *adj* not being in the company of others — see ALONE 1

unaccountable *adj* impossible to explain — see INEXPLICABLE

unaccustomed *adj* 1 not having acquired a habit or tolerance — see UNUSED 1

2 not known or experienced before — see NEW 2

3 noticeably different from what is generally found or experienced — see UNUSUAL 1

unachievable *adj* incapable of being solved or accomplished — see IMPOSSIBLE

unacquainted *adj* not informed about or aware of something — see IGNORANT 2

unadapted *adj* not having acquired a habit or tolerance — see UNUSED 1

unadjusted *adj* not having acquired a habit or tolerance — see UNUSED 1

unadorned *adj* free from all additions or embellishment — see PLAIN 1

unadulterated *adj* 1 free from added matter — see PURE 1

2 having no exceptions or restrictions — see ABSOLUTE 2

unadvisable *adj* showing poor judgment especially in personal relationships or social situations — see INDISCREET

unaesthetic *adj* disagreeable to one's aesthetic or artistic sense — see HARSH 2

unaffected *adj* free from any intent to deceive or impress others — see GUILELESS

unaffectedly *adv* without any attempt to impress by deception or exaggeration — see NATURALLY 3

unaided *adv* without aid or support — see ALONE 1

unalike *adj* being not of the same kind — see DIFFERENT 1

unallied *adj* not favoring or joined to either side in a quarrel, contest, or war — see NEUTRAL

unalloyed *adj* 1 free from added matter — see PURE 1

2 having no exceptions or restrictions — see ABSOLUTE 2

unalterable *adj* not capable of changing or being changed — see INFLEXIBLE 1

unambiguous *adj* 1 not subject to misinterpretation or more than one interpretation — see CLEAR 2

2 so clearly expressed as to leave no doubt about the meaning — see EXPLICIT

unanimated *adj* causing weariness, restlessness, or lack of interest — see BORING

unanimity *n* the act or fact of being of one opinion about something — see AGREEMENT 1

unanimous *adj* having or marked by agreement in feeling or action — see HARMONIOUS 3

unanswerable *adj* not capable of being challenged or proved wrong — see IRREFUTABLE

unanticipated *adj* not expected — see UNEXPECTED

unappealing *adj* unpleasant to look at — see UGLY 1

unappeasable *adj* showing no signs of slackening or yielding in one's purpose — see UNYIELDING 1

unappetizing *adj* disagreeable or disgusting to the sense of taste — see DISTASTEFUL 1

unappreciated *adj* not likely to be appreciated by those who benefit — see THANKLESS 2

unappreciative *adj* not showing gratitude — see THANKLESS 1

unapproachable *adj* hard or impossible to get to or get at — see INACCESSIBLE

unapt *adj* 1 not appropriate for a particular occasion or situation — see INAPPROPRIATE

2 not likely to be true or to occur — see IMPROBABLE

unashamed *adj* not embarrassed or ashamed — see UNABASHED

unasked *adj* not searched or asked for — see UNSOUGHT

unassailable *adj* not to be violated, criticized, or tampered with — see SACRED 1

unassisted *adv* without aid or support — see ALONE 1

unassuming *adj* not having or showing any feelings of superiority, self-assertiveness, or showiness — see HUMBLE 1

unattached *adj* 1 not married — see SINGLE 1

2 not physically attached to another unit — see SEPARATE 2

unattainable *adj* 1 hard or impossible to get to or get at — see INACCESSIBLE

2 incapable of being solved or accomplished — see IMPOSSIBLE

unattractive *adj* unpleasant to look at — see UGLY 1

unauthentic *adj* being such in appearance only and made or manufactured with the intention of committing fraud — see COUNTERFEIT

unavailable *adj* hard or impossible to get to or get at — see INACCESSIBLE

---

syn synonym(s) *rel* related words
ant antonym(s) *near ant* near antonym(s)

unavailing *adj* producing no results — see FUTILE

unavoidable *adj* impossible to avoid or evade — see INEVITABLE

unavoidably *adv* because of necessity — see NEEDS

unaware *adj* not informed about or aware of something — see IGNORANT 2

unaware *adv* without warning — see UNAWARES

unawareness *n* the state of being unaware or uninformed — see IGNORANCE 1

unawares *adv* without warning ⟨the thunderstorm caught us *unawares*, and we scrambled to get off the ridge as lightning started to flash⟩

syn aback, suddenly, unaware, unexpectedly

rel abruptly, short

phrases all of a sudden

near ant slowly; obviously

unbalance *vb* to cause to go insane or as if insane — see CRAZE

unbalanced *adj* 1 having or showing a very abnormal or sick state of mind — see INSANE 1

2 not being in or able to maintain a state of balance — see UNSTABLE 1

unbaptized *adj* not named or identified by a name — see NAMELESS 1

unbearable *adj* more than can be put up with ⟨this heat is *unbearable* —when are we going to get air-conditioning?⟩

syn insufferable, insupportable, intolerable, unendurable, unsupportable

rel unacceptable; crushing, overwhelming; comfortless, harsh, painful, uncomfortable

near ant acceptable; adequate

ant endurable, sufferable, supportable, tolerable

unbeatable *adj* incapable of being defeated, overcome, or subdued — see INVINCIBLE

unbeautiful *adj* unpleasant to look at — see UGLY 1

unbecoming *adj* not appropriate for a particular occasion or situation — see INAPPROPRIATE

unbeknownst *also* **unbeknown** *adj* happening or existing without one's knowledge — see UNKNOWN 1

unbelief *n* refusal to accept as true — see DISBELIEF

unbelievable *adj* too extraordinary or improbable to believe — see INCREDIBLE

unbeliever *n* a person who is always ready to doubt or question the truth or existence of something — see SKEPTIC

unbelieving *adj* inclined to doubt or question claims — see SKEPTICAL

unbend *vb* to cause to follow a line that is without bends or curls — see STRAIGHTEN

unbending *adj* sticking to an opinion, purpose, or course of action in spite of reason, arguments, or persuasion — see OBSTINATE

unbiased *adj* marked by justice, honesty, and freedom from bias — see FAIR 2

unbidden *also* **unbid** *adj* not searched or asked for — see UNSOUGHT

unbind *vb* 1 to disengage the knotted parts of — see UNTIE

2 to set free (as from slavery or confinement) — see FREE 1

unblemished *adj* being entirely without fault or flaw — see PERFECT 1

unblock *vb* to rid the surface of (as an area) from things in the way — see CLEAR 1

unblushing *adj* not embarrassed or ashamed — see UNABASHED

unborn *adj* of a time after the present — see FUTURE

unbosom *vb* to make known (as information previously kept secret) — see REVEAL 1

unbound *adj* not bound, confined, or detained by force — see FREE 3

unbounded *adj* being or seeming to be without limits — see INFINITE

unbraid *vb* to separate the various strands of — see UNRAVEL 1

unbridled *adj* showing no signs of being under control — see RAMPANT 1

unbroken *adj* 1 going on and on without any interruptions — see CONTINUOUS

2 living outdoors without taming or domestication by humans — see WILD 1

unbudging *adj* incapable of moving or being moved — see IMMOVABLE 1

unburden *vb* 1 to empty or rid of cargo — see UNLOAD 1

2 to set (a person or thing) free of something that encumbers — see RID

unburdened *adj* no longer burdened with something unpleasant or painful — see FREE 2

uncage *vb* to set free (as from slavery or confinement) — see FREE 1

uncalled–for *adj* 1 not needed by the circumstances or to accomplish an end — see UNNECESSARY

2 showing a lack of manners or consideration for others — see IMPOLITE

uncanny *adj* 1 being beyond one's powers to know, understand, or explain — see MYSTERIOUS 1

2 being so extraordinary or abnormal as to suggest powers which violate the laws of nature — see SUPERNATURAL 2

3 fearfully and mysteriously strange or fantastic — see EERIE

uncataloged *adj* not appearing on a list — see UNLISTED

unceasing *adj* going on and on without any interruptions — see CONTINUOUS

uncelebrated *adj* not widely known — see OBSCURE 2

unceremonious *adj* not rigidly following established form, custom, or rules — see INFORMAL 1

uncertain *adj* 1 likely to change frequently, suddenly, or unexpectedly — see FICKLE 1

2 not feeling sure about the truth, wisdom, or trustworthiness of someone or something — see DOUBTFUL 1

uncertainty *n* a feeling or attitude that one does not know the truth, truthfulness, or trustworthiness of someone or something — see DOUBT

unchain *vb* to set free (as from slavery or confinement) — see FREE 1

unchangeable *adj* not capable of changing or being changed — see INFLEXIBLE 1

unchangeableness *n* the state of continuing without change — see CONSTANCY 1

unchanging *adj* 1 not undergoing a change in condition — see CONSTANT 1
2 not varying — see UNIFORM

uncharitable *adj* 1 giving or sharing as little as possible — see STINGY 1
2 having or showing a lack of sympathy or tender feelings — see HARD 1

unchecked *adj* showing no signs of being under control — see RAMPANT 1

unchristened *adj* not named or identified by a name — see NAMELESS 1

uncivil *adj* 1 not civilized — see SAVAGE 1
2 showing a lack of manners or consideration for others — see IMPOLITE

uncivilized *adj* not civilized — see SAVAGE

unclad *adj* lacking or shed of clothing — see NAKED 1

unclean *adj* not clean — see DIRTY 1

uncleanliness *n* the state or quality of being dirty — see DIRTINESS 1

uncleanly *adj* not clean — see DIRTY 1

uncleanness *n* the state or quality of being dirty — see DIRTINESS 1

unclear *adj* 1 not clearly expressed — see VAGUE 1
2 not seen or understood clearly — see FAINT 1

uncloak *vb* 1 to make known (as information previously kept secret) — see REVEAL 1
2 to reveal the true nature of — see EXPOSE 1

unclog *vb* 1 to arrange clear passage of (something) by removing obstructions — see OPEN 2
2 to free from obstruction or difficulty — see EASE 1

unclogged *adj* allowing passage without obstruction — see OPEN 1

unclose *vb* to change from a closed to an open position — see OPEN 1

unclosed *adj* allowing passage without obstruction — see OPEN 1

unclothe *vb* to remove clothing from — see UNDRESS

unclothed *adj* lacking or shed of clothing — see NAKED 1

unclouded *adj* not stormy or cloudy — see FAIR 1

uncluttered *adj* being clean and in good order — see NEAT 1

uncolored *adj* lacking an addition of color — see COLORLESS

uncomfortable *adj* 1 causing discomfort ⟨unfortunately, dressing up for the dance meant wearing an *uncomfortable* shirt⟩
syn comfortless, discomforting, harsh
rel aching, hurting, nasty, painful, sore; distressing, disturbing, upsetting; awkward, cumbersome, inconvenient, ungainly; uneasy
near ant easy, soothing; cozy, snug
ant comfortable
2 causing embarrassment — see AWKWARD 3
3 lacking social grace and assurance — see AWKWARD 1

uncomic *adj* not joking or playful in mood or manner — see SERIOUS 1

uncommon *adj* 1 being out of the ordinary — see EXCEPTIONAL
2 noticeably different from what is generally found or experienced — see UNUSUAL 1

uncommunicative *adj* 1 deliberately refraining from speech — see SILENT 1
2 given to keeping one's activities hidden from public observation or knowledge — see SECRETIVE
3 tending not to speak frequently (as by habit or inclination) — see SILENT 2

uncomplaining *adj* accepting pains or hardships calmly or without complaint — see PATIENT 1

uncomplimentary *adj* intended to make a person or thing seem of little importance or value — see DEROGATORY

uncompromising *adj* 1 not allowing for any exceptions or loosening of standards — see RIGID 1
2 sticking to an opinion, purpose, or course of action in spite of reason, arguments, or persuasion — see OBSTINATE

unconcern *n* lack of interest or concern — see INDIFFERENCE

unconcerned *adj* 1 having or showing a lack of concern or seriousness — see CAREFREE
2 having or showing a lack of interest or concern — see INDIFFERENT 1

unconditional *adj* having no exceptions or restrictions — see ABSOLUTE 2

unconfined *adj* not bound, confined, or detained by force — see FREE 3

uncongenial *adj* not giving pleasure to the mind or senses — see UNPLEASANT

unconnected *adj* 1 not clearly or logically connected — see INCOHERENT 1
2 not physically attached to another unit — see SEPARATE 2

unconquerable *adj* incapable of being defeated, overcome, or subdued — see INVINCIBLE

unconscionable *adj* 1 going beyond a normal or acceptable limit in degree or amount — see EXCESSIVE
2 not guided by or showing a concern for what is right — see UNPRINCIPLED

unconscious *adj* 1 having lost consciousness ⟨the guard was knocked *unconscious* by a blow to the head⟩
syn cold, insensible, senseless
rel semiconscious; anesthetized
near ant alert, awake, aware, up
ant conscious

---

syn synonym(s) *rel* related words
ant antonym(s) *near ant* near antonym(s)

2 not informed about or aware of something — see IGNORANT 2

unconsidered *adj* made or done without previous thought or preparation — see EXTEMPORANEOUS

unconsolidated *adj* consisting of particles that do not stick together — see LOOSE 2

uncontrollable *adj* given to resisting control or discipline by others ⟨the *uncontrollable* child kept throwing tantrums in public and creating scenes⟩

syn froward, headstrong, intractable, recalcitrant, refractory, ungovernable, unmanageable, unruly, untoward, wayward, willful (*or* wilful)

rel contrary, incorrigible, obstinate, perverse, self-willed, stubborn; undisciplined, unpunished; uncontrolled, ungoverned, wild; boisterous, rambunctious, rowdy; disobedient, insubordinate, rebellious; misbehaving, naughty

phrases out of hand

near ant docile, obedient, well-behaved; compliant, submissive, yielding

ant controllable, governable, tractable

uncontrolled *adj* showing no signs of being under control — see RAMPANT 1

unconventional *adj* **1** deviating from commonly accepted beliefs or practices — see HERETICAL

2 not bound by traditional ways or beliefs — see LIBERAL 1

3 not rigidly following established form, custom, or rules — see INFORMAL 1

unconvinced *adj* not feeling sure about the truth, wisdom, or trustworthiness of someone or something — see DOUBTFUL 1

unconvincing *adj* too extraordinary or improbable to believe — see INCREDIBLE

uncooked *adj* not cooked — see RAW 1

uncordial *adj* lacking in friendliness or warmth of feeling — see COLD 2

uncork *vb* to set free (from a state of being held in check) — see RELEASE 1

uncountable *adj* too many to be counted — see COUNTLESS

uncounted *adj* too many to be counted — see COUNTLESS

uncouple *vb* to set or force apart — see SEPARATE 1

uncouth *adj* **1** having or showing crudely insensitive or impolite manners — see CLOWNISH

2 lacking in refinement or good taste — see COARSE 2

uncover *vb* **1** to make known (as information previously kept secret) — see REVEAL 1

2 to reveal the true nature of — see EXPOSE 1

uncovered *adj* lacking a usual or natural covering — see NAKED 2

uncritical *adj* lacking in worldly wisdom or informed judgment — see NAIVE 1

uncrown *vb* to remove from a position of prominence or power (as a throne) — see DEPOSE 1

unctuous *adj* **1** not being or expressing what one appears to be or express — see INSINCERE

2 overly or insincerely flattering — see FULSOME

uncultivated *adj* **1** existing without human habitation or cultivation — see WILD 2

2 lacking in refinement or good taste — see COARSE 2

3 not civilized — see SAVAGE 1

uncultured *adj* lacking in refinement or good taste — see COARSE 2

uncurbed *adj* showing no signs of being under control — see RAMPANT 1

uncurious *adj* having or showing a lack of interest or concern — see INDIFFERENT 1

uncurl *vb* to cause to follow a line that is without bends or curls — see STRAIGHTEN

uncustomary *adj* **1** being out of the ordinary — see EXCEPTIONAL

2 noticeably different from what is generally found or experienced — see UNUSUAL 1

undaunted *adj* feeling or displaying no fear by temperament — see BRAVE

undeceive *vb* to free from mistaken beliefs or foolish hopes — see DISILLUSION

undecided *adj* **1** not yet settled or decided — see PENDING 1

2 not feeling sure about the truth, wisdom, or trustworthiness of someone or something — see DOUBTFUL 1

undecorated *adj* free from all additions or embellishment — see PLAIN 1

undefended *adj* lacking protection from danger or resistance against attack — see HELPLESS 1

undefined *adj* not seen or understood clearly — see FAINT 1

undemonstrative *adj* not feeling or showing emotion — see IMPASSIVE 1

undeniable *adj* not capable of being challenged or proved wrong — see IRREFUTABLE

undeniably *adv* without any question — see INDEED 1

under *adj* having not so great importance or rank as another — see LESSER

under *adv* in or to a lower place — see BELOW 1

under *prep* in a lower position than — see BELOW

underbelly *n* the side or part facing downward from something — see BOTTOM 1

underbody *n* the side or part facing downward from something — see BOTTOM 1

underclothes *n pl* clothing intended to be worn underneath other clothing — see UNDERWEAR

underclothing *n* clothing intended to be worn underneath other clothing — see UNDERWEAR

undercover *adj* **1** undertaken or done so as to escape being observed or known by others — see SECRET 1

2 working on missions in which one's objectives, activities, or true identity are not publicly revealed — see SECRET 2

undergarments *n pl* clothing intended to be worn underneath other clothing — see UNDERWEAR

undergo *vb* to come to a knowledge of (something) by living through it — see EXPERIENCE

underground *adj* undertaken or done so as to escape being observed or known by others — see SECRET 1

underground *n* a secret organization in a conquered country fighting against enemy forces — see RESISTANCE 2

underhand *adj* 1 given to or marked by cheating and deception — see DISHONEST 2

2 undertaken or done so as to escape being observed or known by others — see SECRET 1

underhanded *adj* 1 given to or marked by cheating and deception — see DISHONEST 2

2 undertaken or done so as to escape being observed or known by others — see SECRET 1

underline *vb* to indicate the importance of by giving prominent display — see EMPHASIZE

underling *n* one who is of lower rank and typically under the authority of another ⟨he instructed his *underlings* to carry out the order immediately⟩

syn inferior, subordinate

rel attendant, follower, retainer; domestic, menial, steward; flunky (*also* flunkey), henchman, lackey, minion; adjutant, aid, aide, assistant, coadjutor, deputy, second; helpmate, helpmeet, mate, sidekick

near ant boss, captain, chief, foreman, head, headman, helmsman, kingpin, leader, master, taskmaster

ant senior, superior

underlying *adj* of or relating to the simplest facts or theories of a subject — see ELEMENTARY

underneath *adv* in or to a lower place — see BELOW 1

underpin *vb* to hold up or serve as a foundation for — see SUPPORT 3

underpinning *n* 1 an immaterial thing upon which something else rests — see BASE 1

2 something that holds up or serves as a foundation for something else — see SUPPORT 1

underprivileged *adj* kept from having the necessities of life or a healthful environment — see DEPRIVED

underscore *vb* to indicate the importance of by giving prominent display — see EMPHASIZE

underside *n* the side or part facing downward from something — see BOTTOM 1

undersized *adj* of a size that is less than average — see SMALL 1

understand *vb* 1 to form an opinion through reasoning and information — see INFER 1

2 to have a practical understanding of — see KNOW 1

3 to recognize the meaning of — see COMPREHEND 1

understanding *adj* having or showing the capacity for sharing the feelings of another — see SYMPATHETIC 1

understanding *n* 1 an arrangement about action to be taken — see AGREEMENT 2

2 the knowledge gained from the process of coming to know or understand something — see COMPREHENSION

understated *adj* not excessively showy — see QUIET 2

undersurface *n* the side or part facing downward from something — see BOTTOM 1

undertake *vb* to take to or upon oneself — see ASSUME 1

undertaker *n* a person who manages funerals and prepares the dead for burial or cremation — see FUNERAL DIRECTOR

underwater *adj* living, lying, or occurring below the surface of the water ⟨*underwater* plants don't require as much light to grow as surface plants⟩ ⟨*underwater* exploring takes a long time because you can't move quickly⟩

syn aquatic, submarine, submerged, sunken

rel oceanic; abysmal, abyssal, deep, deepsea, deepwater

under way *adj* being in progress or development — see ONGOING 1

underwear *n* clothing intended to be worn underneath other clothing ⟨*underwear* has got to be the most boring thing that one could ever receive as a birthday present!⟩

syn underclothes, underclothing, undergarments, undies

rel lingerie; pantie (*or* panty), slip, underskirt; briefs, drawers, long johns, pants, shorts, underdrawers, underpants, undershirt, union suit; nightdress, nightgown, nightshirt, pajamas, pj's

near ant outerwear

underweight *adj* having little weight — see ¹LIGHT 1

underwrite *vb* to provide money for — see FINANCE 1

undesired *adj* not searched or asked for — see UNSOUGHT

undetermined *adj* 1 not seen or understood clearly — see FAINT 1

2 not yet settled or decided — see PENDING 1

undeviating *adj* not varying — see UNIFORM

undies *n pl* clothing intended to be worn underneath other clothing — see UNDERWEAR

undiluted *adj* free from added matter — see PURE 1

undisturbed *adj* free from emotional or mental agitation — see CALM 2

---

syn synonym(s)   *rel* related words
ant antonym(s)   *near ant* near antonym(s)

undivided *adj* not divided or scattered among several areas of interest or concern — see WHOLE 1

undo *vb* 1 to deprive of courage or confidence — see UNNERVE 1

2 to disengage the knotted parts of — see UNTIE

3 to trouble the mind of; to make uneasy — see DISTURB 1

undomesticated *adj* living outdoors without taming or domestication by humans — see WILD 1

undoubtedly *adv* without any question — see INDEED 1

undress *vb* to remove clothing from ⟨Mom *undressed* the mud-covered little toddler and plopped her in the bath⟩

syn disrobe, strip, unclothe

rel bare, denude, divest, expose, uncover, undrape, unveil; bark, flay, peel, skin

near ant apparel, array, attire, caparison, clothe, costume, cover, deck, dress, feather, garb, garment, invest, rig (out), vest; cloak, mantle; drape, swaddle, swathe; accoutre (*or* accouter), equip, furnish, outfit

ant dress, gown, robe

undressed *adj* 1 being such as found in nature and not altered by processing or refining — see CRUDE 1

2 lacking or shed of clothing — see NAKED 1

undue *adj* going beyond a normal or acceptable limit in degree or amount — see EXCESSIVE

unduly *adv* beyond a normal or acceptable limit — see TOO 1

undyed *adj* lacking an addition of color — see COLORLESS

undying *adj* lasting forever — see EVERLASTING

uneager *adj* showing little or no interest or enthusiasm — see TEPID 1

unearth *vb* to remove from place of burial — see EXHUME

unearthing *n* the act or process of sighting or learning the existence of something for the first time — see DISCOVERY 1

unearthly *adj* 1 being so extraordinary or abnormal as to suggest powers which violate the laws of nature — see SUPERNATURAL 2

2 fearfully and mysteriously strange or fantastic — see EERIE

3 of, relating to, or being part of a reality beyond the observable physical universe — see SUPERNATURAL 1

uneasiness *n* 1 a disturbed or uneasy state — see UNREST

2 an uneasy state of mind usually over the possibility of an anticipated misfortune or trouble — see ANXIETY 1

uneasy *adj* 1 feeling or showing uncomfortable feelings of uncertainty — see NERVOUS 1

2 lacking or denying rest — see RESTLESS 1

3 lacking social grace and assurance — see AWKWARD 1

uneducated *adj* lacking in education or the knowledge gained from books — see IGNORANT 1

unembarrassed *adj* not embarrassed or ashamed — see UNABASHED

unemotional *adj* not feeling or showing emotion — see IMPASSIVE 1

unending *adj* lasting forever — see EVERLASTING

unendurable *adj* more than can be put up with — see UNBEARABLE

unenjoyable *adj* not giving pleasure to the mind or senses — see UNPLEASANT

unenthusiastic *adj* showing little or no interest or enthusiasm — see TEPID 1

unequal *adj* not staying constant — see UNEVEN 2

unequaled *or* **unequalled** *adj* having no equal or rival for excellence or desirability — see ONLY 1

unequivocal *adj* 1 having no exceptions or restrictions — see ABSOLUTE 2

2 not subject to misinterpretation or more than one interpretation — see CLEAR 2

3 so clearly expressed as to leave no doubt about the meaning — see EXPLICIT

unerring *adj* not being or likely to be wrong — see INFALLIBLE 1

unessential *adj* not needed by the circumstances or to accomplish an end — see UNNECESSARY

unethical *adj* 1 not conforming to a high moral standard; morally unacceptable — see BAD 2

2 not guided by or showing a concern for what is right — see UNPRINCIPLED

uneven *adj* 1 not having a level or smooth surface ⟨we had to plane and sand down the *uneven* wooden board before we could paint it⟩

syn broken, bumpy, coarse, irregular, jagged, lumpy, pebbly, ragged, rough, roughened, rugged, scraggy

rel lopsided, unbalanced; inexact, irregular, unaligned; rutted, rutty, undulating, wavy; burred, harsh, nubbly, nubby, scraggly, scratchy; nonuniform

near ant exact, uniform; aligned, regular, true; horizontal, tabular; plumb, straight, vertical; flush

ant even, flat, level, plane, smooth

2 not staying constant ⟨the level of attendance at the ball park has been very *uneven* this season⟩

syn changing, erratic, fluctuating, irregular, unequal, unstable, unsteady, varying

rel capricious, changeable, changeful, choppy, fickle, fluid, inconsistent, inconstant, mercurial, mutable, uncertain, unsettled, variable, volatile

ant changeless, constant, stable, steady, unchanging, unvarying

3 inclined or twisted to one side — see AWRY

unexampled *adj* having no equal or rival for excellence or desirability — see ONLY 1

unexceptional *adj* being of the type that is encountered in the normal course of events — see ORDINARY 1

unexpected *adj* not expected ⟨the pop quiz was *unexpected*, but fortunately I was prepared⟩
  syn unanticipated, unforeseen, unlooked-for
  rel unintended, unplanned; improbable, unlikely; startling, surprising
  near ant predicted, prophesied
  ant anticipated, expected, foreseen

unexpectedly *adv* without warning — see UNAWARES

unexplainable *adj* impossible to explain — see INEXPLICABLE

unexpressed *adj* understood although not put into words — see IMPLICIT

unfailing *adj* 1 not being or likely to be wrong — see INFALLIBLE 1
  2 not likely to fail — see INFALLIBLE 2

unfailingly *adv* on every relevant occasion — see ALWAYS 1

unfair *adj* not being in accordance with the rules or standards of what is fair in sport — see FOUL 2

unfairness *n* the state of being unfair or unjust — see INJUSTICE 1

unfaithful *adj* not true in one's allegiance to someone or something — see FAITHLESS

unfaithfulness *n* 1 lack of faithfulness especially to one's husband or wife — see INFIDELITY 1
  2 the act or fact of violating the trust or confidence of another — see BETRAYAL

unfamiliar *adj* not known or experienced before — see NEW 2

unfamiliarity *n* the state of being unaware or uninformed — see IGNORANCE 1

unfashionable *adj* marked by an obvious lack of style or good taste — see TACKY 1

unfasten *vb* to disengage the knotted parts of — see UNTIE

unfathomable *adj* 1 being or seeming to be without limits — see INFINITE
  2 impossible to understand — see INCOMPREHENSIBLE

unfavorable *adj* opposed to one's interests — see ADVERSE 1

unfeeling *adj* 1 having or showing a lack of sympathy or tender feelings — see HARD 1
  2 lacking in sensation or feeling — see NUMB

unfeignedly *adv* without any attempt to impress by deception or exaggeration — see NATURALLY 3

unfeminine *adj* having qualities or traits that are traditionally considered inappropriate for a girl or woman ⟨in bygone days pants were considered *unfeminine*, and even women bicycling were expected to wear skirts⟩
  syn hoydenish, manlike, mannish, tomboyish, unladylike, unwomanly
  rel gentlemanly, male, manly, masculine

near ant effeminate, girlish, sissy, unmanly, unmasculine, womanish, womanlike; distaff, petticoat
  ant female, feminine, ladylike, womanly

unfetter *vb* to set free (as from slavery or confinement) — see FREE 1

unfit *adj* 1 lacking qualities (as knowledge, skill, or ability) required to do a job — see INCOMPETENT
  2 not appropriate for a particular occasion or situation — see INAPPROPRIATE

unfitness *n* 1 the quality or state of being unsuitable or unfitting — see INAPPROPRIATENESS 1
  2 the quality or state of not being socially proper — see IMPROPRIETY 1

unflagging *adj* showing no signs of weariness even after long hard effort — see TIRELESS

unflappable *adj* not easily panicked or upset ⟨the *unflappable* teacher never even blinked when the wall map came crashing down⟩
  syn imperturbable, nerveless, unshakable
  rel calm, collected, composed, cool, coolheaded, nonchalant, placid, self-possessed, serene, tranquil, undisturbed, unperturbed, unruffled, unshaken, untroubled, unworried
  near ant panicky; aflutter, anxious, dithery, edgy, het up, hung up, jittery, jumpy, nervous, nervy, perturbed, shaky, tense, troubled, uneasy, upset, uptight, worried
  ant perturbable, shakable

unfledged *adj* lacking in adult experience or maturity — see CALLOW

unflinching *adj* showing no signs of slackening or yielding in one's purpose — see UNYIELDING 1

unfold *vb* 1 to arrange the parts of (something) over a wider area — see OPEN 3
  2 to gradually become clearer or more detailed — see DEVELOP 1
  3 to produce flowers — see BLOOM

unforced *adj* done, made, or given with one's own free will — see VOLUNTARY 1

unforeseen *adj* not expected — see UNEXPECTED

unforgivable *adj* too bad to be excused or justified — see INEXCUSABLE

unformed *adj* having no definite or recognizable form — see FORMLESS

unfortunate *adj* 1 bringing about ruin or misfortune — see FATAL 1
  2 having, prone to, or marked by bad luck — see UNLUCKY
  3 of a kind to cause great distress — see REGRETTABLE

unfounded *adj* having no basis in reason or in fact — see GROUNDLESS

unfriendly *adj* 1 lacking in friendliness or warmth of feeling — see COLD 2
  2 marked by opposition or ill will — see HOSTILE 1
  3 opposed to one's interests — see ADVERSE 1

unfrozen *adj* freed from a frozen state by exposure to warmth — see THAWED

unfruitful *adj* not able to produce fruit or offspring — see STERILE 1

---

syn synonym(s)   **rel** related words
ant antonym(s)   **near ant** near antonym(s)

unfunny *adj* not joking or playful in mood or manner — see SERIOUS 1

ungainly *adj* **1** difficult to use or operate especially because of size, weight, or design — see CUMBERSOME

2 lacking in physical ease and grace in movement or in the use of the hands — see CLUMSY 1

ungentle *adj* harsh and threatening in manner or appearance — see GRIM 1

ungodly *adj* falling short of a standard — see BAD 1

ungovernable *adj* **1** given to resisting authority or another's control — see DISOBEDIENT

2 given to resisting control or discipline by others — see UNCONTROLLABLE

ungoverned *adj* showing no signs of being under control — see RAMPANT 1

ungraceful *adj* lacking social grace and assurance — see AWKWARD 1

ungracious *adj* showing a lack of manners or consideration for others — see IMPOLITE

ungraciousness *n* rude behavior — see DISCOURTESY

ungrateful *adj* not showing gratitude — see THANKLESS 1

ungrounded *adj* **1** having no basis in reason or fact — see GROUNDLESS

2 not informed about or aware of something — see IGNORANT 2

unguarded *adj* **1** free in expressing one's true feelings and opinions — see FRANK

2 lacking protection from danger or resistance against attack — see HELPLESS 1

3 not paying or showing close attention especially for the purpose of avoiding trouble — see CARELESS 1

unhampered *adj* showing no signs of being under control — see RAMPANT 1

unhandsome *adj* unpleasant to look at — see UGLY 1

unhandy *adj* **1** difficult to use or operate especially because of size, weight, or design — see CUMBERSOME

2 lacking in physical ease and grace in movement or in the use of the hands — see CLUMSY 1

unhappily *adv* with feelings of bitterness or grief — see HARD 2

unhappiness *n* a state or spell of low spirits — see SADNESS

unhappy *adj* **1** feeling unhappiness — see SAD 1

2 having, prone to, or marked by bad luck — see UNLUCKY

3 not appropriate for a particular occasion or situation — see INAPPROPRIATE

unhealthful *adj* bad for the well-being of the body — see UNHEALTHY 1

unhealthiness *n* the condition of not being in good health — see SICKNESS 1

unhealthy *adj* **1** bad for the well-being of the body ⟨we knew that the junk food at the carnival was *unhealthy*, but it tasted so good!⟩

syn noisome, noxious, unhealthful, unwholesome

rel insanitary, unhygienic, unsanitary; nonnutritious; poisonous, toxic; fatal, lethal, mortal

near ant hygienic, sanitary; nutritious

ant healthful, healthy

2 involving potential loss or injury — see DANGEROUS

3 temporarily suffering from a disorder of the body — see SICK 1

unheard–of *adj* not known or experienced before — see NEW 2

unheroic *adj* having or showing a shameful lack of courage — see COWARDLY

unhindered *adj* showing no signs of being under control — see RAMPANT 1

unhinge *vb* **1** to cause to go insane or as if insane — see CRAZE

2 to trouble the mind of; to make uneasy — see DISTURB 1

unhurried *adj* moving or proceeding at less than the normal, desirable, or required speed — see SLOW 1

unidentified *adj* **1** known but not named — see CERTAIN 1

2 not named or identified by a name — see NAMELESS 1

unification *n* the act or an instance of joining two or more things into one — see UNION 1

uniform *adj* not varying ⟨with flat-screen TVs, picture sharpness is *uniform* over the entire screen, even in the corners⟩

syn invariant, steady, unchanging, undeviating, unvarying, unwavering

rel immutable, invariable, unalterable, unchangeable

ant changing, deviating, varying

uniform *n* the distinctive clothing worn by members of a particular group ⟨the band *uniform* was brown with red and white stripes⟩

syn livery, outfit

rel fatigues, full dress, regimentals; costume, finery, regalia

unify *vb* **1** to bring (something) to a central point or under a single control — see CENTRALIZE

2 to come together to form a single unit — see UNITE 1

unimaginable *adj* too extraordinary or improbable to believe — see INCREDIBLE

unimportant *adj* lacking importance ⟨we figured that the details were *unimportant* as long as we got the basic design correct⟩

syn frivolous, inconsequential, inconsiderable, insignificant, little, minor, minute, negligible, slight, small, small-fry, trifling, trivial

rel jerkwater, one-horse; paltry, petty, worthless; anonymous, nameless, obscure, uncelebrated, unknown

near ant decisive, fatal, fateful; distinctive, exceptional, impressive, outstanding, prominent, remarkable; valuable, worthwhile, worthy; distinguished, eminent, great, illustrious, preeminent, prestigious; famous, notorious, renowned; all-important, basic, essential, fundamental *ant* big, consequential, eventful, important, major, material, meaningful, momentous, significant, substantial, weighty

uninflammable *adj* incapable of being burned — see INCOMBUSTIBLE

uninformed *adj* not informed about or aware of something — see IGNORANT 1

uninhibited *adj* showing feeling freely — see DEMONSTRATIVE

uninstructed *adj* lacking in education or the knowledge gained from books — see IGNORANT 1

unintelligent *adj* not having or showing an ability to absorb ideas readily — see STUPID 1

unintelligible *adj* impossible to understand — see INCOMPREHENSIBLE

unintended *adj* **1** happening by chance — see ACCIDENTAL

2 not made or done willingly or by choice — see INVOLUNTARY 1

unintentional *adj* **1** happening by chance — see ACCIDENTAL

2 not made or done willingly or by choice — see INVOLUNTARY 1

uninterested *adj* having or showing a lack of interest or concern — see INDIFFERENT 1

uninteresting *adj* causing weariness, restlessness, or lack of interest — see BORING

uninterrupted *adj* going on and on without any interruptions — see CONTINUOUS

uninvited *adj* not searched or asked for — see UNSOUGHT

union *n* **1** the act or an instance of joining two or more things into one ⟨the *union* of East Germany and West Germany that became possible after the fall of communism⟩

syn combination, combining, connecting, connection, consolidation, coupling, junction, linking, merging, unification

rel amalgamation, blend, commingling, compounding, fusion, intermingling, intermixture, mingling, mix, mixture; reunification, reunion

near ant detachment, divorcement, separation, severance

ant breakup, disconnection, dissolution, disunion, division, parting, partition, schism, split

2 an association of persons, parties, or states for mutual assistance and protection — see CONFEDERACY

3 the state of having shared interests or efforts (as in social or business matters) — see ASSOCIATION 1

unique *adj* **1** of, relating to, or belonging to a single person — see INDIVIDUAL 1

2 being out of the ordinary — see EXCEPTIONAL

3 being the one or ones of a class with no other members — see ONLY 2

4 noticeably different from what is generally found or experienced — see UNUSUAL 1

unison *n* the act or fact of being of one opinion about something — see AGREEMENT 1

unite *vb* **1** to come together to form a single unit ⟨using the microscope, we watched the water droplets *unite* into a single pool⟩

syn associate, coalesce, combine, conjoin, conjugate, connect, couple, fuse, join, link (up), marry, unify

rel mate, yoke; ally, confederate, league; chain, compound, hitch, hook; congregate, gather, meet; recombine, rejoin, reunify, reunite

near ant detach, disconnect, disjoin, disjoint, dissociate, disunite, divide, divorce, fractionate, isolate, resolve, uncouple, unyoke; disband, disperse, scatter

ant break up, dissever, part, section, separate, sever, split, sunder, unlink

2 to bring (something) to a central point or under a single control — see CENTRALIZE

3 to form or enter into an association that furthers the interests of its members — see ALLY

united *adj* **1** having or marked by agreement in feeling or action — see HARMONIOUS 3

2 used or done by a number of people as a group — see COLLECTIVE

unity *n* a balanced, pleasing, or suitable arrangement of parts — see HARMONY 1

universal *adj* **1** able to do many different kinds of things — see VERSATILE

2 belonging or relating to the whole — see GENERAL 1

3 covering everything or all important points — see ENCYCLOPEDIC

4 present in all places and at all times — see OMNIPRESENT

universe *n* the whole body of things observed or assumed ⟨the theory that the *universe* is constantly expanding⟩

syn cosmos, creation, macrocosm, nature, world

rel existence, reality

near ant nothingness, void

unjustifiable *adj* too bad to be excused or justified — see INEXCUSABLE

unjustness *n* the state of being unfair or unjust — see INJUSTICE 1

unkempt *adj* **1** lacking in order, neatness, and often cleanliness — see MESSY

2 lacking neatness in dress or person — see SLOPPY 1

unknowing *adj* **1** lacking in worldly wisdom or informed judgment — see NAIVE 1

2 not informed about or aware of something — see IGNORANT 2

unknown *adj* **1** happening or existing without one's knowledge ⟨*unknown* to me was the fact that while I was out, my family was hurriedly preparing a surprise birthday party⟩

syn unbeknownst (*also* unbeknown)

rel unperceived, unrecognized, unsuspected; unaware, unconscious, unmind-

---

syn synonym(s)   *rel* related words

ant antonym(s)   *near ant* near antonym(s)

ful; unknowing, unsuspecting, unwitting; ignorant, unacquainted, unfamiliar

2 not known or experienced before — see NEW 2

3 not widely known — see OBSCURE 2

unlade *vb* to empty or rid of cargo — see UNLOAD 1

unladylike *adj* having qualities or traits that are traditionally considered inappropriate for a girl or woman — see UNFEMININE

unlash *vb* to disengage the knotted parts of — see UNTIE

unlawful *adj* contrary to or forbidden by law — see ILLEGAL 1

unlearn *vb* to be unable to recall or think of — see FORGET 1

unlearned *adj* lacking in education or the knowledge gained from books — see IGNORANT 1

unleash *vb* **1** to set free (from a state of being held in check) — see RELEASE 1

2 to find emotional release for — see TAKE OUT 1

unlettered *adj* lacking in education or the knowledge gained from books — see IGNORANT 1

unlike *adj* being not of the same kind — see DIFFERENT 1

unlikely *adj* not likely to be true or to occur — see IMPROBABLE

unlikeness *n* the quality or state of being different — see DIFFERENCE 1

unlimited *adj* **1** being or seeming to be without limits — see INFINITE

2 not limited or specialized in application or purpose — see GENERAL 4

unlink *vb* to set or force apart — see SEPARATE 1

unlisted *adj* not appearing on a list ⟨she kept her phone number *unlisted* so as to reduce the number of unwanted calls⟩

syn uncataloged, unrecorded, unregistered

rel unwritten; unidentified, unspecified; undisclosed, unknown, unrevealed

ant cataloged (*or* catalogued), listed, recorded, registered

unliterary *adj* used in or suitable for speech and not formal writing — see COLLOQUIAL 1

unload *vb* **1** to empty or rid of cargo ⟨the dockworkers *unloaded* the ship⟩

syn disburden, discharge, disencumber, unburden, unlade, unpack

rel free, lighten, relieve; clear, empty, evacuate, vacate, void

near ant charge, cram, fill, heap, jam, jam-pack, stuff

ant load, pack

2 to get rid of as useless or unwanted — see DISCARD

unlock *vb* to set free (from a state of being held in check) — see RELEASE 1

unlooked–for *adj* not expected — see UNEXPECTED

unloose *vb* to set free (from a state of being held in check) — see RELEASE 1

unloosen *vb* to set free (from a state of being held in check) — see RELEASE 1

unlovely *adj* **1** not giving pleasure to the mind or senses — see UNPLEASANT

2 unpleasant to look at — see UGLY 1

unlucky *adj* having, prone to, or marked by bad luck ⟨the *unlucky* campers had rain all week⟩ ⟨I'm so *unlucky* I don't bother to play the lottery⟩ ⟨an *unlucky* throw of the dice⟩

syn hapless, ill-fated, ill-starred, luckless, star-crossed, unfortunate, unhappy

rel adverse, ill, inauspicious, unfavorable, unpromising, untoward; calamitous, catastrophic, disastrous; damned, doomed, tragic

near ant blessed, favored, gifted, privileged; auspicious, fair, favorable, golden, promising, propitious

ant fortunate, happy, lucky

unmake *vb* to remove from a position of prominence or power (as a throne) — see DEPOSE 1

unman *vb* **1** to deprive of courage or confidence — see UNNERVE 1

2 to lessen the courage or confidence of — see DISCOURAGE 1

unmanageable *adj* given to resisting control or discipline by others — see UNCONTROLLABLE

unmanly *adj* having or displaying qualities more suitable for women than for men — see EFFEMINATE

unmannerly *adj* showing a lack of manners or consideration for others — see IMPOLITE

unmarried *adj* not married — see SINGLE 1

unmask *vb* **1** to make known (as information previously kept secret) — see REVEAL 1

2 to reveal the true nature of — see EXPOSE 1

unmatched *adj* **1** being one of a pair or set without a corresponding mate — see ODD 1

2 having no equal or rival for excellence or desirability — see ONLY 1

unmelodious *adj* marked by or producing a harsh combination of sounds — see DISSONANT

unmerciful *adj* having or showing a lack of sympathy or tender feelings — see HARD 1

unmindful *adj* not informed about or aware of something — see IGNORANT 2

unmistakable *adj* not subject to misinterpretation or more than one interpretation — see CLEAR 2

unmitigated *adj* having no exceptions or restrictions — see ABSOLUTE 2

unmixed *adj* free from added matter — see PURE 1

unmoral *adj* not guided by or showing a concern for what is right — see UNPRINCIPLED

unmovable *adj* incapable of moving or being moved — see IMMOVABLE 1

unmusical *adj* marked by or producing a harsh combination of sounds — see DISSONANT

unnamed *adj* **1** known but not named —
see CERTAIN 1

2 not named or identified by a name —
see NAMELESS 1

unnatural *adj* **1** departing from some accepted standard of what is normal — see
DEVIANT

2 lacking in natural or spontaneous quality — see ARTIFICIAL 1

unnecessary *adj* not needed by the circumstances or to accomplish an end ⟨a
hair dryer was an *unnecessary* item on a
trip to the desert⟩

syn dispensable, gratuitous, needless,
nonessential, uncalled-for, unessential,
unwarranted

rel discretionary, elective, optional; extra,
extraneous, irrelevant, redundant, superfluous

near ant all-important, crucial, important, vital; imperative, pressing, urgent

ant essential, indispensable, necessary,
needed, needful, required

unnerve *vb* **1** to deprive of courage or confidence ⟨the riding accident so *unnerved*
me that for a while I was afraid to get
back on a horse⟩

syn demoralize, emasculate, undo,
unman, unstring

rel debilitate, enervate, enfeeble, weaken;
prostrate, sap, soften, tire, waste; fright-
en, scare, terrify, terrorize; daunt, discourage, dishearten, dismay, dispirit;
craze, derange, madden, unbalance, unhinge; discompose, disquiet, disturb, faze,
perturb, unsettle, upset

near ant fortify, strengthen; embolden,
encourage, hearten

ant nerve

2 to lessen the courage or confidence of
— see DISCOURAGE 1

unnerving *adj* marked by or causing agitation or uncomfortable feelings — see
NERVOUS 2

unnoted *adj* not widely known — see OB-
SCURE 2

unnoticeable *adj* not readily seen or noticed — see UNOBTRUSIVE

unnumbered *adj* too many to be counted
— see COUNTLESS

unobstructed *adj* allowing passage without obstruction — see OPEN 1

unobtainable *adj* hard or impossible to
get to or get at — see INACCESSIBLE

unobtrusive *adj* not readily seen or noticed ⟨the notice that an 18% tip would be
automatically added was so *unobtrusive*
we almost didn't see it at the bottom of
the menu⟩

syn inconspicuous, unnoticeable

rel unnoticed; impalpable, imperceptible,
inappreciable, indistinguishable, insensible; faint, indistinct, obscure; concealed,
hidden

near ant arresting, eye-catching, showy,
striking; apparent, blatant, clear, distinct,

evident, manifest, obvious, plain, unmistakable

ant conspicuous, noticeable

unoriginal *adj* using or marked by the use
of something else as a basis or model —
see IMITATIVE

unorthodox *adj* **1** deviating from commonly accepted beliefs or practices —
see HERETICAL

2 not bound by traditional ways or beliefs
— see LIBERAL 1

3 not rigidly following established form,
custom, or rules — see INFORMAL 1

unpack *vb* to empty or rid of cargo — see
UNLOAD 1

unpaid *adj* not yet paid — see OUTSTAND-
ING 1

unpainted *adj* lacking an addition of color
— see COLORLESS

unpaired *adj* being one of a pair or set
without a corresponding mate — see
ODD 1

unpalatable *adj* disagreeable or disgusting
to the sense of taste — see DISTASTEFUL 1

unparalleled *adj* having no equal or
rival for excellence or desirability — see
ONLY 1

unpardonable *adj* too bad to be excused
or justified — see INEXCUSABLE

unperturbed *adj* free from emotional or
mental agitation — see CALM 2

unplanned *adj* **1** happening by chance —
see ACCIDENTAL

2 made or done without previous thought
or preparation — see EXTEMPORANEOUS

unpleasant *adj* not giving pleasure to the
mind or senses ⟨the burnt pot roast had a
very *unpleasant* odor⟩

syn bad, disagreeable, displeasing, distasteful, nasty, rotten, sour, uncongenial,
unlovely, unpleasing, unsatisfying, unwelcome

rel abhorrent, abominable, appalling,
awful, beastly, disgusting, dreadful, foul,
hideous, horrendous, horrible, horrid, invidious, loathsome, nauseating, noisome,
obnoxious, obscene, odious, repellent
(*also* repellant), repugnant, repulsive, revolting, scandalous, shocking, sickening,
ugly, villainous; annoying, galling, irritating, vexing

near ant delectable, delicious, delightful,
dreamy, felicitous; affable, amiable,
friendly, genial, good-natured, good-tempered, gracious, sweet, well-disposed

ant agreeable, congenial, good, grateful,
gratifying, nice, palatable, pleasant, pleasing, pleasurable, satisfying, welcome

unpleasing *adj* **1** not giving pleasure to
the mind or senses — see UNPLEASANT

2 unpleasant to look at — see UGLY 1

unpolished *adj* lacking in refinement or
good taste — see COARSE 2

unprecedented *adj* not known or experienced before — see NEW 2

unpredictable *adj* likely to change frequently, suddenly, or unexpectedly — see
FICKLE 1

unprejudiced *adj* marked by justice, honesty, and freedom from bias — see FAIR 2

---

syn synonym(s)   *rel* related words
ant antonym(s)   *near ant* near antonym(s)

unpremeditated *adj* **1** happening by chance — see ACCIDENTAL

2 made or done without previous thought or preparation — see EXTEMPORANEOUS

unprepared *adj* made or done without previous thought or preparation — see EXTEMPORANEOUS

unpretending *adj* free from any intent to deceive or impress others — see GUILELESS

unpretentious *adj* **1** free from any intent to deceive or impress others — see GUILELESS

2 not excessively showy — see QUIET 2

3 not having or showing any feelings of superiority, self-assertiveness, or showiness — see HUMBLE 1

unpretentiously *adv* without any attempt to impress by deception or exaggeration — see NATURALLY 3

unpretty *adj* unpleasant to look at — see UGLY 1

unprincipled *adj* not guided by or showing a concern for what is right ⟨the *unprincipled* businessman made a lot of money—and didn't care how he made it⟩

syn cutthroat, immoral, Machiavellian, unconscionable, unethical, unmoral, unscrupulous

rel calculating, intriguing, opportunistic, scheming; merciless, pitiless, remorseless, ruthless; crooked, deceitful, dishonest; corrupt, debased, debauched, decadent, degenerate, degraded, demoralized, depraved, dissipated

near ant good, just, noble, righteous, virtuous

ant ethical, moral, principled, scrupulous

unprintable *adj* depicting or referring to sexual matters in a way that is unacceptable in polite society — see OBSCENE 1

unprocessed *adj* being such as found in nature and not altered by processing or refining — see CRUDE 1

unproductive *adj* **1** producing inferior or only a small amount of vegetation — see BARREN 1

2 producing no results — see FUTILE

unprofessional *adj* lacking or showing a lack of expert skill — see AMATEURISH

unprofitable *adj* producing no results — see FUTILE

unprogressive *adj* tending to favor established ideas, conditions, or institutions — see CONSERVATIVE 1

unprotected *adj* lacking protection from danger or resistance against attack — see HELPLESS 1

unqualified *adj* **1** having no exceptions or restrictions — see ABSOLUTE 2

2 lacking qualities (as knowledge, skill, or ability) required to do a job — see INCOMPETENT

3 not limited or specialized in application or purpose — see GENERAL 4

unquestionable *adj* not capable of being challenged or proved wrong — see IRREFUTABLE

unquestionably *adv* without any question — see INDEED 1

unquiet *adj* **1** feeling or showing uncomfortable feelings of uncertainty — see NERVOUS 1

2 lacking or denying rest — see RESTLESS 1

unravel *vb* **1** to separate the various strands of ⟨it took us forever to *unravel* the jumbled mass of Christmas tree lights⟩

syn disentangle, ravel (out), unbraid, unsnarl, untangle, untwine, untwist

rel smooth, straighten (out); undo, unlace, unstring, unthread, untie, unwind

near ant braid, knot, lace, tie, wind

ant entangle, snarl, tangle

2 to find an answer for through reasoning — see SOLVE

unreachable *adj* hard or impossible to get to or get at — see INACCESSIBLE

unread *adj* lacking in education or the knowledge gained from books — see IGNORANT 1

unreal *adj* **1** conceived or made without regard for reason or reality — see FANTASTIC 1

2 not real and existing only in the imagination — see IMAGINARY

unreality *n* a conception or image created by the imagination and having no objective reality — see FANTASY 1

unreasonable *adj* **1** having no basis in reason or fact — see GROUNDLESS

2 not using or following good reasoning — see ILLOGICAL

unreasoning *adj* not using or following good reasoning — see ILLOGICAL

unrecorded *adj* not appearing on a list — see UNLISTED

unrecoverable *adj* **1** not capable of being cured or reformed — see HOPELESS 1

2 not capable of being repaired, regained, or undone — see IRREPARABLE

unredeemable *adj* **1** not capable of being cured or reformed — see HOPELESS 1

2 not capable of being repaired, regained, or undone — see IRREPARABLE

unrefined *adj* **1** being such as found in nature and not altered by processing or refining — see CRUDE 1

2 hastily or roughly constructed — see RUDE 1

3 lacking in refinement or good taste — see COARSE 2

unregistered *adj* not appearing on a list — see UNLISTED

unrehearsed *adj* made or done without previous thought or preparation — see EXTEMPORANEOUS

unrelenting *adj* **1** sticking to an opinion, purpose, or course of action in spite of reason, arguments, or persuasion — see OBSTINATE

2 showing no signs of slackening or yielding in one's purpose — see UNYIELDING 1

unremarkable *adj* being of the type that is encountered in the normal course of events — see ORDINARY 1

unremitting *adj* going on and on without any interruptions — see CONTINUOUS

unrepentant *adj* not sorry for having done wrong — see REMORSELESS

unreserved *adj* 1 free in expressing one's true feelings and opinions — see FRANK

2 showing feeling freely — see DEMONSTRATIVE

unresistant *adj* 1 lacking protection from danger or resistance against attack — see HELPLESS 1

2 receiving or enduring without offering resistance — see PASSIVE

unresisting *adj* receiving or enduring without offering resistance — see PASSIVE

unresolved *adj* not yet settled or decided — see PENDING 1

unrest *n* a disturbed or uneasy state ⟨*unrest* gripped the city as the people nervously awaited the expected bombardment⟩ ⟨his stomach *unrest* was just a sign of stage fright⟩

syn disquiet, ferment, restiveness, restlessness, turmoil, uneasiness

rel fidgets; agitation, commotion, confusion, tumult, turbulence, upheaval; anarchy, chaos, disorder

near ant order, orderliness

ant calm, ease, peace, quiet

unrestful *adj* lacking or denying rest — see RESTLESS 1

unrestrained *adj* 1 not bound by rigid standards — see EASYGOING 2

2 not bound, confined, or detained by force — see FREE 3

3 showing feeling freely — see DEMONSTRATIVE

4 showing no signs of being under control — see RAMPANT 1

unrestraint *n* carefree freedom from constraint — see ABANDON

unrestricted *adj* 1 freely available for use or participation by all — see OPEN 2

2 not bound by rigid standards — see EASYGOING 2

3 not limited or specialized in application or purpose — see GENERAL 4

unrighteous *adj* not conforming to a high moral standard; morally unacceptable — see BAD 2

unripe *adj* lacking in adult experience or maturity — see CALLOW

unripened *adj* lacking in adult experience or maturity — see CALLOW

unrivaled *or* **unrivalled** *adj* having no equal or rival for excellence or desirability — see ONLY 1

unruliness *n* refusal to obey — see DISOBEDIENCE

unruly *adj* 1 given to resisting authority or another's control — see DISOBEDIENT

2 given to resisting control or discipline by others — see UNCONTROLLABLE

3 not restrained by or under the control of legal authority — see LAWLESS

unsafe *adj* 1 involving potential loss or injury — see DANGEROUS

2 not paying or showing close attention especially for the purpose of avoiding trouble — see CARELESS 1

unsatisfactorily *adv* in an unsatisfactory way — see BADLY

unsatisfactory *adj* falling short of a standard — see BAD 1

unsatisfying *adj* not giving pleasure to the mind or senses — see UNPLEASANT

unsavory *adj* 1 disagreeable or disgusting to the sense of taste — see DISTASTEFUL 1

2 not conforming to a high moral standard; morally unacceptable — see BAD 2

unsay *vb* to solemnly or formally reject or go back on (as something formerly adhered to) — see ABJURE

unschooled *adj* lacking in education or the knowledge gained from books — see IGNORANT 1

unscrupulous *adj* not guided by or showing a concern for what is right — see UNPRINCIPLED

unseasonable *adj* occurring before the usual or expected time — see EARLY 2

unseasonably *adv* before the usual or expected time — see EARLY

unseat *vb* to remove from a position of prominence or power (as a throne) — see DEPOSE 1

unsecured *adj* not tightly fastened, tied, or stretched — see LOOSE 1

unseemly *adj* not appropriate for a particular occasion or situation — see INAPPROPRIATE

unselfish *adj* giving or sharing in abundance and without hesitation — see GENEROUS 1

unselfishness *n* the quality or state of being generous — see LIBERALITY

unsettle *vb* to trouble the mind of; to make uneasy — see DISTURB 1

unsettled *adj* 1 likely to change frequently, suddenly, or unexpectedly — see FICKLE 1

2 not yet paid — see OUTSTANDING 1

3 not yet settled or decided — see PENDING 1

4 not feeling sure about the truth, wisdom, or trustworthiness of someone or something — see DOUBTFUL 1

unsettling *adj* 1 causing worry or anxiety — see TROUBLESOME

2 marked by or causing agitation or uncomfortable feelings — see NERVOUS 2

unshakable *adj* not easily panicked or upset — see UNFLAPPABLE

unshaken *adj* free from emotional or mental agitation — see CALM 2

unshaped *adj* having no definite or recognizable form — see FORMLESS

unshared *adj* belonging only to the one person, unit, or group named — see SOLE 1

unshielded *adj* lacking protection from danger or resistance against attack — see HELPLESS 1

unshorn *adj* covered with or as if with hair — see HAIRY 1

unsightly *adj* unpleasant to look at — see UGLY 1

unskilled *adj* 1 lacking or showing a lack of expert skill — see AMATEURISH

2 lacking qualities (as knowledge, skill, or ability) required to do a job — see INCOMPETENT

unskillful *adj* 1 lacking qualities (as knowledge, skill, or ability) required to do a job — see INCOMPETENT

2 lacking or showing a lack of expert skill — see AMATEURISH

unsmiling *adj* not joking or playful in mood or manner — see SERIOUS 1

unsnarl *vb* to separate the various strands of — see UNRAVEL 1

unsociable *adj* having or showing a lack of friendliness or interest in others — see COOL 1

unsoiled *adj* free from dirt or stain — see CLEAN 1

unsolicited *adj* not searched or asked for — see UNSOUGHT

unsolvable *adj* incapable of being solved or accomplished — see IMPOSSIBLE

unsophisticated *adj* lacking in worldly wisdom or informed judgment — see NAIVE 1

unsophistication *n* 1 the quality or state of being simple and sincere — see NAÏVETÉ 1

2 the quality or state of having a form or structure of few parts or elements — see SIMPLICITY 1

unsought *adj* not searched or asked for ⟨the meddling neighbor insisted on giving us *unsought* advice⟩

syn unasked, unbidden (*also* unbid), undesired, uninvited, unsolicited, unwanted, unwelcome

rel objectionable, offensive, unacceptable, undesirable; uncalled-for, unnecessary

near ant necessary, needed, required

ant desired, solicited, wanted, welcome

unsound *adj* 1 having or showing a very abnormal or sick state of mind — see INSANE 1

2 not being in agreement with what is true — see FALSE 1

3 not using or following good reasoning — see ILLOGICAL

4 temporarily suffering from a disorder of the body — see SICK 1

unsoundness *n* the condition of not being in good health — see SICKNESS 1

unsparing *adj* 1 giving or sharing in abundance and without hesitation — see GENEROUS 1

2 having or showing a lack of sympathy or tender feelings — see HARD 1

unspeakable *adj* beyond the power to describe — see INDESCRIBABLE

unspecialized *adj* not limited or specialized in application or purpose — see GENERAL 4

unspecified *adj* known but not named — see CERTAIN 1

unspoken *adj* understood although not put into words — see IMPLICIT

unsportsmanlike *adj* not being in accordance with the rules or standards of what is fair in sport — see FOUL 2

unstable *adj* 1 not being in or able to maintain a state of balance ⟨when we put the books down on the *unstable* desk, the whole stack went crashing to the floor⟩

syn unbalanced, unsteady

rel rickety, shaky, tottery, wobbly; cockeyed, lopsided, uneven

near ant even, level, straight; sound, sturdy, substantial

ant balanced, stable, steady

2 likely to change frequently, suddenly, or unexpectedly — see FICKLE 1

3 not staying constant — see UNEVEN 2

unstained *adj* lacking an addition of color — see COLORLESS

unsteadiness *n* the quality or state of not being firmly fixed in position — see INSTABILITY

unsteady *adj* 1 lacking in steadiness or regularity of occurrence — see FITFUL

2 likely to change frequently, suddenly, or unexpectedly — see FICKLE 1

3 not being in or able to maintain a state of balance — see UNSTABLE 1

4 not staying constant — see UNEVEN 2

unstop *vb* to arrange clear passage of (something) by removing obstructions — see OPEN 2

unstopped *adj* allowing passage without obstruction — see OPEN 1

unstring *vb* 1 to cause to go insane or as if insane — see CRAZE

2 to deprive of courage or confidence — see UNNERVE 1

unstructured *adj* having no definite or recognizable form — see FORMLESS

unstylish *adj* marked by an obvious lack of style or good taste — see TACKY 1

unstylishly *adv* in a careless or unfashionable manner — see SLOPPILY

unsubstantial *adj* 1 not composed of matter — see IMMATERIAL 1

2 being of a material lacking in sturdiness or substance — see FLIMSY 1

3 lacking bodily strength — see WEAK 1

unsubstantiated *adj* having no basis in reason or fact — see GROUNDLESS

unsuccessful *adj* producing no results — see FUTILE

unsuitable *adj* not appropriate for a particular occasion or situation — see INAPPROPRIATE

unsuitably *adv* in a mistaken or inappropriate way — see WRONGLY

unsullied *adj* free from dirt or stain — see CLEAN 1

unsung *adj* not widely known — see OBSCURE 2

unsupportable *adj* more than can be put up with — see UNBEARABLE

unsupported *adj* having no basis in reason or fact — see GROUNDLESS

unsure *adj* not feeling sure about the truth, wisdom, or trustworthiness of someone or something — see DOUBTFUL 1

unsurpassable *adj* having no equal or rival for excellence or desirability — see ONLY 1

unsurpassed *adj* **1** having no equal or rival for excellence or desirability — see ONLY 1

2 of the very best kind — see EXCELLENT

unsuspecting *adj* lacking in worldly wisdom or informed judgment — see NAIVE 1

unsuspicious *adj* lacking in worldly wisdom or informed judgment — see NAIVE 1

unsympathetic *adj* **1** having or showing a lack of sympathy or tender feelings — see HARD 1

2 lacking in friendliness or warmth of feeling — see COLD 2

3 marked by opposition or ill will — see HOSTILE 1

4 opposed to one's interests — see ADVERSE 1

untamed *adj* **1** existing without human habitation or cultivation — see WILD 2

2 living outdoors without taming or domestication by humans — see WILD 1

untangle *vb* **1** to separate the various strands of — see UNRAVEL 1

2 to set free from entanglement or difficulty — see EXTRICATE

untaught *adj* lacking in education or the knowledge gained from books — see IGNORANT 1

unthinkable *adj* too extraordinary or improbable to believe — see INCREDIBLE

unthrifty *adj* given to spending money freely or foolishly — see PRODIGAL

unthrone *vb* to remove from a position of prominence or power (as a throne) — see DEPOSE 1

untidy *adj* **1** lacking in order, neatness, and often cleanliness — see MESSY

2 lacking neatness in dress or person — see SLOPPY 1

untie *vb* to disengage the knotted parts of ⟨she always made sure to *untie* her shoelaces before removing her shoes⟩
    syn unbind, undo, unfasten, unlash
    rel unbraid, unlace; disentangle, ravel, unbraid, unravel, unsnarl, untangle, unwind; loose, loosen
    near ant braid, interlace, interweave, lace, wind; entangle, snarl, tangle
    ant bind, fasten, knot, lash, tie

untimely *adj* occurring before the usual or expected time — see EARLY 2

untiring *adj* showing no signs of weariness even after long hard effort — see TIRELESS

untitled *adj* not named or identified by a name — see NAMELESS 1

untold *adj* too many to be counted — see COUNTLESS

untouchable *adj* **1** hard or impossible to get to or get at — see INACCESSIBLE

2 not to be violated, criticized, or tampered with — see SACRED 1

untoward *adj* **1** given to resisting authority or another's control — see DISOBEDIENT

2 given to resisting control or discipline by others — see UNCONTROLLABLE

untreated *adj* being such as found in nature and not altered by processing or refining — see CRUDE 1

untroubled *adj* **1** free from emotional or mental agitation — see CALM 1

2 free from storms or physical disturbance — see CALM 1

untrue *adj* **1** not being in agreement with what is true — see FALSE 1

2 not true in one's allegiance to someone or something — see FAITHLESS

untruth *n* **1** a false idea or belief — see FALLACY 1

2 a statement known by its maker to be untrue and made in order to deceive — see LIE

3 the quality or state of being false — see FALLACY 2

untruthful *adj* **1** not being in agreement with what is true — see FALSE 1

2 telling or containing lies — see DISHONEST 1

untruthfulness *n* the tendency to tell lies — see DISHONESTY 1

untutored *adj* lacking in education or the knowledge gained from books — see IGNORANT 1

untwine *vb* to separate the various strands of — see UNRAVEL 1

untwist *vb* to separate the various strands of — see UNRAVEL 1

unusable *adj* not capable of being put to use or account — see IMPRACTICAL

unused *adj* **1** not having acquired a habit or tolerance ⟨while in Mexico we tried to stay out of the sun because we were simply *unused* to the tropical heat⟩
    syn unacclimated, unaccustomed, unadapted, unadjusted
    rel unhardened, unseasoned
    near ant unaffected, uninfluenced
    ant acclimated, accustomed, adapted, adjusted, habituated, used

2 recently made and never used before — see NEW 3

unusual *adj* **1** noticeably different from what is generally found or experienced ⟨finding some *unusual* shells by the hightide mark, we brought them home for our collection⟩
    syn curious, extraordinary, funny, odd, offbeat, peculiar, queer, rare, singular, strange, unaccustomed, uncommon, uncustomary, unique, weird
    rel bizarre, eccentric, far-out, outlandish, outré, way-out; aberrant, abnormal, atypical, exceptional, irregular; newsworthy, notable, noteworthy, noticeable, particular, remarkable, special
    near ant unexceptional; expected, predictable; familiar, normal, regular, typical
    ant common, ordinary, usual

2 being out of the ordinary — see EXCEPTIONAL

---

syn synonym(s)   *rel* related words
ant antonym(s)   *near ant* near antonym(s)

unutterable *adj* beyond the power to describe — see INDESCRIBABLE

unvarnished *adj* free from all additions or embellishment — see PLAIN 1

unvarying *adj* **1** not undergoing a change in condition — see CONSTANT 1

2 not varying — see UNIFORM

unveil *vb* **1** to make known (as information previously kept secret) — see REVEAL 1

2 to present so as to invite notice or attention — see SHOW 1

unvoiced *adj* understood although not put into words — see IMPLICIT

unwanted *adj* not searched or asked for — see UNSOUGHT

unwarrantable *adj* too bad to be excused or justified — see INEXCUSABLE

unwarranted *adj* **1** not needed by the circumstances or to accomplish an end — see UNNECESSARY

2 having no basis in reason or fact — see GROUNDLESS

unwary *adj* **1** lacking in worldly wisdom or informed judgment — see NAIVE 1

2 not paying or showing close attention especially for the purpose of avoiding trouble — see CARELESS 1

unwavering *adj* not varying — see UNIFORM

unwearying *adj* showing no signs of weariness even after long hard effort — see TIRELESS

unwed *adj* not married — see SINGLE 1

unwelcome *adj* **1** not giving pleasure to the mind or senses — see UNPLEASANT

2 not searched or asked for — see UNSOUGHT

unwell *adj* temporarily suffering from a disorder of the body — see SICK 1

unwholesome *adj* bad for the well-being of the body — see UNHEALTHY 1

unwieldy *adj* difficult to use or operate especially because of size, weight, or design — see CUMBERSOME

unwilling *adj* not made or done willingly or by choice — see INVOLUNTARY 1

unwillingness *n* a lack of willingness or desire to do or accept something — see RELUCTANCE

unwind *vb* to get rid of nervous tension or anxiety — see RELAX 1

unwise *adj* **1** showing or marked by a lack of good sense or judgment — see FOOLISH 1

2 showing poor judgment especially in personal relationships or social situations — see INDISCREET

unwitting *adj* **1** happening by chance — see ACCIDENTAL

2 not informed about or aware of something — see IGNORANT 2

unwomanly *adj* having qualities or traits that are traditionally considered inappropriate for a girl or woman — see UNFEMININE

unwonted *adj* being out of the ordinary — see EXCEPTIONAL

unworkable *adj* not capable of being put to use or account — see IMPRACTICAL

unworldliness *n* the quality or state of being simple and sincere — see NAÏVETÉ 1

unworldly *adj* lacking in worldly wisdom or informed judgment — see NAIVE 1

unworried *adj* free from emotional or mental agitation — see CALM 2

unwritten *adj* made or carried on through speaking rather than in writing — see VERBAL 2

unyielding *adj* **1** showing no signs of slackening or yielding in one's purpose ⟨the pioneers faced the challenge of settling the frontier with *unyielding* courage⟩

syn determined, dogged, grim, implacable, relentless, unappeasable, unflinching, unrelenting

rel hardheaded, headstrong, mulish, obdurate, opinionated, peevish, pertinacious, perverse, pigheaded, self-willed, stubborn, uncooperative, willful (*or* wilful); merciless, ruthless, unforgiving

near ant slackening, softening, yielding; impotent, invertebrate, slack, spineless, weak

2 having a consistency that does not easily yield to pressure — see FIRM 2

3 incapable of or highly resistant to bending — see STIFF 1

4 sticking to an opinion, purpose, or course of action in spite of reason, arguments, or persuasion — see OBSTINATE

unyoke *vb* to set or force apart — see SEPARATE 1

up *adj* **1** being at a higher level than average — see HIGH 2

2 brought or having come to an end — see COMPLETE 2

3 having information especially as a result of study or experience — see FAMILIAR 2

up *vb* **1** to make greater in size, amount, or number — see INCREASE 1

2 to move from a lower to a higher place or position — see RAISE 1

3 to move or extend upward — see ASCEND

upbeat *adj* **1** having or showing a good mood or disposition — see CHEERFUL 1

2 having qualities which inspire hope — see HOPEFUL 1

upbraid *vb* to criticize (someone) severely or angrily especially for personal failings — see SCOLD

upcoming *adj* being soon to appear or take place — see FORTHCOMING

up–country *n* a rural region that forms the edge of the settled or developed part of a country — see FRONTIER 2

upend *vb* to fix in an upright position — see ERECT 1

upgrade *n* **1** an upward slope — see ASCENT 2

2 a raising or a state of being raised to a higher rank or position — see ADVANCEMENT 1

3 the degree to which something rises up from a position level with the horizon — see SLANT

upgrade vb to move higher in rank or position — see PROMOTE 1

upheaval n a violent disturbance (as of the political or social order) — see CONVULSION

uphold vb 1 to continue to declare to be true or proper despite opposition or objections — see MAINTAIN 2

2 to hold up or serve as a foundation for — see SUPPORT 3

3 to move from a lower to a higher place or position — see RAISE 1

upkeep n the act or activity of keeping something in an existing and usually satisfactory condition — see MAINTENANCE

upland n an area of high ground — see HEIGHT 4

uplift vb to move from a lower to a higher place or position — see RAISE 1

uplifted adj being positioned above a surface — see ELEVATED 1

upmost adj being at a point or level higher than all others — see TOP 1

upon prep in or into contact with — see AGAINST

upper-class adj of high birth, rank, or station — see NOBLE 1

upper class n the highest class in a society — see ARISTROCRACY

upper crust n 1 individuals carefully selected as being the best of a class — see ELITE

2 the highest class in a society — see ARISTROCRACY

upper hand n the more favorable condition or position in a competition — see ADVANTAGE 1

uppermost adj being at a point or level higher than all others — see TOP 1

uppish adj having a feeling of superiority that shows itself in an overbearing attitude — see ARROGANT

uppity adj having a feeling of superiority that shows itself in an overbearing attitude — see ARROGANT

upraise vb 1 to move from a lower to a higher place or position — see RAISE 1

2 to fix in an upright position — see ERECT 1

upraised adj being positioned above a surface — see ELEVATED 1

upright adj 1 conforming to a high standard of morality or virtue — see GOOD 2

2 following the accepted rules of moral conduct — see HONORABLE 1

3 rising straight up — see ERECT

uprightness n 1 conduct that conforms to an accepted standard of right and wrong — see MORALITY 1

2 faithfulness to high moral standards — see HONOR 1

uprise vb 1 to leave one's bed — see ARISE 1

2 to move or extend upward — see ASCEND

uprising n open fighting against authority (as one's own government) — see REBELLION

uproar n 1 a state of noisy, confused activity — see COMMOTION

2 a state of wildly excited activity or emotion — see FRENZY

3 a violent disturbance (as of the political or social order) — see CONVULSION

4 a violent shouting — see CLAMOR 1

uproarious adj causing or intended to cause laughter — see FUNNY 1

uproot vb to draw out by force or with effort — see EXTRACT

upset adj feeling or showing uncomfortable feelings of uncertainty — see NERVOUS 1

upset n an act or instance of the order of things being disturbed ⟨the move to a new town is just the latest in a series of *upsets* for my family over the last year⟩

syn derangement, dislocation, disruption, disturbance

rel convulsion, revolution, upheaval

upset vb 1 to trouble the mind of; to make uneasy — see DISTURB 1

2 to turn on one's side or upside down — see CAPSIZE

3 to undo the proper order or arrangement of — see DISORDER

upsetting adj causing worry or anxiety — see TROUBLESOME

upshot n a condition or occurrence traceable to a cause — see EFFECT 1

upside-down adj lacking in order, neatness, and often cleanliness — see MESSY

upstanding adj 1 following the accepted rules of moral conduct — see HONORABLE 1

2 rising straight up — see ERECT

upsweep vb to move or extend upward — see ASCEND

uptight adj feeling or showing uncomfortable feelings of uncertainty — see NERVOUS 1

up-to-date adj 1 being or involving the latest methods, concepts, information, or styles — see MODERN

2 having information especially as a result of study or experience — see FAMILIAR 2

upturn vb to move or extend upward — see ASCEND

urbane adj having or showing very polished and worldly manners — see SUAVE

urbanize vb to accustom to the ways of the city — see CITIFY

urchin n an appealingly mischievous person — see SCAMP 1

urge n a strong wish for something — see DESIRE

urge vb to try to persuade (someone) through earnest appeals to follow a course of action ⟨our teacher *urged* us to do a good job on the assignment⟩

syn egg (on), encourage, exhort, goad, press, prod, prompt

rel drive, propel, spur, stimulate; hurry, hustle, push, rush; beseech, implore, importune; blandish, cajole, coax, soft-soap, wheedle; high-pressure, nag, needle, pressure; foment, incite, instigate, provoke, stir (up)

near ant deter, discourage, dissuade; brake, check, constrain, curb, hold back, inhibit, restrain

urgent *adj* needing immediate attention — see ACUTE 2

usable *adj* **1** capable of or suitable for being used for a particular purpose ⟨although the spade was *usable* as a snow shovel, it didn't do a very good job⟩

syn available, employable, exploitable, fit, functional, operable, practicable, serviceable, useful

rel applicable, relevant; doable, feasible; reusable

near ant outdated, outmoded

ant impracticable, inoperable, nonfunctional, unavailable, unemployable, unusable

2 capable of being put to use or account — see PRACTICAL 1

usage *n* the act or practice of employing something for a particular purpose — see USE 1

use *n* **1** the act or practice of employing something for a particular purpose ⟨the *use* of boom boxes was strictly prohibited in the park⟩

syn application, employment, exercise, operation, play, usage

rel exertion; reuse

near ant disuse

2 the capacity for being useful for some purpose ⟨the broken grill wasn't going to be of much *use* in cooking the hamburgers⟩

syn account, avail, service, serviceability, serviceableness, usefulness, utility

rel advantage, benefit, gain; aid, assistance, help; applicability, appropriateness, fitness, relevance; profit, value, worth

near ant inapplicability, inappropriateness

ant uselessness, worthlessness

3 positive regard for something — see LIKING

use *vb* **1** to put into action or service ⟨I think I'm going to need to *use* the large hammer for this project⟩

syn apply, employ, exercise, exploit, harness, operate, utilize

rel handle, manipulate, wield; direct, run, work; recycle, reuse

phrases draw on (or upon), make use of

near ant ignore, neglect; misapply, misuse

2 to behave toward in a stated way — see TREAT 1

3 to take unfair advantage of — see EXPLOIT 1

used *adj* being in the habit or custom — see ACCUSTOMED

useful *adj* **1** capable of being put to use or account — see PRACTICAL 1

2 capable of or suitable for being used for a particular purpose — see USABLE 1

usefulness *n* the capacity for being useful for some purpose — see USE 2

useless *adj* **1** not capable of being put to use or account — see IMPRACTICAL

2 producing no results — see FUTILE

user *n* a person who regularly uses drugs especially illegally — see DOPER

use up *vb* to make complete use of — see DEPLETE

usher *vb* to point out the way for (someone) especially from a position in front — see LEAD 1

usual *adj* **1** accepted, used, or practiced by most people — see CURRENT 1

2 being of the type that is encountered in the normal course of events — see ORDINARY 1

3 often observed or encountered — see COMMON 1

usually *adv* according to the usual course of things — see NATURALLY 2

usurp *vb* to take or make use of without authority or right — see APPROPRIATE 1

utensil *n* an article intended for use in work — see IMPLEMENT

utility *n* the capacity for being useful for some purpose — see USE 2

utilize *vb* to put into action or service — see USE 1

utmost *adj* **1** most distant from a center — see EXTREME 1

2 of the greatest or highest degree or quantity — see ULTIMATE 1

3 of the highest degree — see FULL 2

utopia *n* a place or state of great happiness — see PARADISE 1

utopian *n* one whose conduct is guided more by the image of perfection than by the real world — see IDEALIST

utter *adj* having no exceptions or restrictions — see ABSOLUTE 2

utter *vb* **1** to send forth using the vocal chords ⟨she tried not to *utter* a sound as the doctor gave her a flu shot⟩

syn emit

rel blurt (out), ejaculate, exclaim; gasp, groan, heave, hoot, moan, pant, quaver, snarl, sob, sputter, squawk, squeak, squeal, stammer, stutter, whimper, yowl; mouth, whisper

2 to express (a thought or emotion) in words — see SAY 1

utterance *n* **1** an act, process, or means of putting something into words — see EXPRESSION 1

2 something that is said — see WORD 2

uttered *adj* created by the body's organs of sound — see VOCAL

utterly *adv* **1** to a full extent or degree — see FULLY 1

2 to a large extent or degree — see GREATLY 1

uttermost *adj* of the greatest or highest degree or quantity — see ULTIMATE 1

vacancy *n* **1** empty space ⟨the vast *vacancy* that exists between our solar system and the nearest star having its own orbiting planets⟩

syn blank, blankness, emptiness, vacuity, void

rel nothingness; vacuum; bareness, barrenness, bleakness, desolateness, hollowness

near ant fullness, repleteness

ant fullness, repleteness

2 the quality or state of being empty ⟨the *vacancy* of the cavernous gymnasium was eerily apparent to me as I shot baskets alone⟩

syn bareness, emptiness, vacuity

rel hollowness; blankness, vacuum; void; barrenness, bleakness, desolateness; availability, clearness, openness; depletion, dryness, exhaustion

near ant completeness; abundance, fatness, repleteness

ant fullness

vacant *adj* **1** lacking contents that could or should be present — see EMPTY 1

2 not being in a state of use, activity, or employment — see INACTIVE 2

3 not expressing any emotion — see BLANK 1

vacate *vb* to remove the contents of — see EMPTY

vacated *adj* left unoccupied or unused — see ABANDONED

vacation *n* a period during which the usual routine of school or work is suspended ⟨we take a *vacation* at the beach for a week every year⟩

syn break, holiday [*chiefly British*], leave, recess

rel furlough, liberty; breather, relaxation, respite, rest; interim, intermission, interval; feast, holy day, legal holiday; honeymoon; idling, loafing, lounging, slacking off

near ant routine, work

vacation *vb* to take or spend a vacation ⟨Sue is hoping to *vacation* in Spain this summer⟩

syn holiday

rel escape, get away; break, ease up, let up, relax, rest; bum, goldbrick, idle, loaf, lounge, slack off

near ant drudge, endeavor, grub, hump, hustle, labor, moil, peg (away), plod, plow, plug, slave, slog, strain, strive, struggle, sweat, toil, travail, work

vacillate *vb* to show uncertainty about the right course of action — see HESITATE

---

syn synonym(s)   *rel* related words
ant antonym(s)   *near ant* near antonym(s)

vacillation *n* the act or an instance of pausing because of uncertainty about the right course of action — see HESITATION

vacuity *n* **1** empty space — see VACANCY 1

2 the quality or state of being empty — see VACANCY 2

3 the quality or state of lacking intelligence or quickness of mind — see STUPIDITY 1

vacuous *adj* not having or showing an ability to absorb ideas readily — see STUPID 1

vagabond *adj* traveling from place to place — see ITINERANT

vagabond *n* **1** a homeless wanderer who may beg or steal for a living — see TRAMP

2 a person who roams about without a fixed route or destination — see NOMAD

vagary *n* a sudden impulsive and apparently unmotivated idea or action — see WHIM

vagrant *adj* traveling from place to place — see ITINERANT

vagrant *n* a homeless wanderer who may beg or steal for a living — see TRAMP

vague *adj* **1** not clearly expressed ⟨Johnny gave as *vague* a reply to the test question as he could, hoping for partial credit⟩

syn fuzzy, indefinite, unclear

rel ambiguous, cryptic, dark, enigmatic (*also* enigmatical), equivocal, murky, nebulous, obscure, unintelligible; bleary, dim, faint, foggy, hazy, indeterminate, indistinguishable, uncertain, undefinable, undefined, undetermined; inexplicable, inscrutable, mysterious; baffling, bewildering, confounding, confusing, mystifying, perplexing, puzzling, unfathomable

near ant candid, direct, forthright, foursquare, frank, honest, open, openhearted, outspoken, plainspoken, straight, straightforward, unguarded; obvious, plain, unambiguous, understandable, unequivocal; comprehensible, fathomable, intelligible; defined, distinct; blatant, patent, unmistakable

ant clear, definite, explicit, specific

2 not seen or understood clearly — see FAINT 1

vain *adj* **1** having too high an opinion of oneself — see CONCEITED

2 producing no results — see FUTILE

vainglorious *adj* having too high an opinion of oneself — see CONCEITED

vaingloriousness *n* an often unjustified feeling of being pleased with oneself or with one's situation or achievements — see COMPLACENCE

vainglory *n* an often unjustified feeling of being pleased with oneself or with one's situation or achievements — see COMPLACENCE

vainness *n* an often unjustified feeling of being pleased with oneself or with one's situation or achievements — see COMPLACENCE

vale *n* an area of lowland between hills or mountains — see VALLEY

valedictory *adj* given, taken, or performed at parting — see PARTING

valiant *adj* feeling or displaying no fear by temperament — see BRAVE

valid *adj* 1 according to the rules of logic — see LOGICAL 1

2 based on sound reasoning or information — see GOOD 1

validate *vb* 1 to give evidence or testimony to the truth or factualness of — see CONFIRM

2 to show the existence or truth of by evidence — see PROVE 1

validation *n* something presented in support of the truth or accuracy of a claim — see PROOF

valley *n* an area of lowland between hills or mountains ⟨the *valley* will be the first to flood if the river rises⟩
syn dale, hollow, vale
rel canyon, dell, depression, dingle, glen, ravine, rift valley; basin, bowl
near ant alp, mount, peak; mountain range; mountaintop, pinnacle, precipice, summit

valor *n* strength of mind to carry on in spite of danger — see COURAGE

valorous *adj* feeling or displaying no fear by temperament — see BRAVE

valuable *adj* commanding a large price — see COSTLY

valuation *n* 1 the act of placing a value on the nature, character, or quality of something — see ESTIMATE 1

2 the amount of money for which something will find a buyer — see VALUE 1

3 the relative usefulness or importance of something as judged by specific qualities — see WORTH 1

value *n* 1 the amount of money for which something will find a buyer ⟨the real *value* of that house is close to a million dollars⟩
syn market value, valuation, worth
rel charge, cost, fee, figure, price; appraisal, assessment, estimate, estimation, evaluation; face value, list price, unit price

2 a quality that gives something special worth — see EXCELLENCE 2

3 the relative usefulness or importance of something as judged by specific qualities — see WORTH 1

value *vb* 1 to hold dear — see LOVE 1

2 to make an approximate or tentative judgment regarding — see ESTIMATE 1

valueless *adj* having no usefulness — see WORTHLESS

valve *n* a fixture for controlling the flow of a liquid — see FAUCET

vandal *n* a person who damages or destroys property on purpose ⟨a group of *vandals* broke into school and painted graffiti on the walls⟩

syn defacer
rel demolisher, desecrater (*or* desecrator), despoiler, destroyer, dynamiter, ravager, ruiner, saboteur, wrecker; looter, pillager, plunderer, spoiler
near ant conserver, preserver, protector, saver

vandalism *n* deliberate damaging or destroying of another's property ⟨anyone guilty of *vandalism* to school property will be expelled⟩
syn defacement
rel demolishing, demolition, desecrating, desecration, despoiling, despoilment, destruction, ravaging, ruin, ruination, wrecking; sabotage; looting, pillaging, plunder, plundering, sacking
near ant conservation, preservation, protection, saving

vandalize *vb* to deliberately cause the damage or destruction of another's property ⟨he decided to *vandalize* the store because the owner had kicked him out⟩
syn deface
rel desecrate, violate; break, damage, despoil, harm, hurt, impair, mar, shatter, spoil; demolish, destroy, devastate, ravage, raze, ruin, scourge, smash, tear down, waste, wipe out, wreck; sabotage; loot, pillage, plunder, sack
near ant conserve, preserve, protect, save; build, rebuild

vanguard *n* the leading or most important part of a movement — see FOREFRONT

vanish *vb* to cease to be visible — see DISAPPEAR

vanished *adj* no longer existing — see EXTINCT

vanity *n* an often unjustified feeling of being pleased with oneself or with one's situation or achievements — see COMPLACENCE

vanquish *vb* to bring under one's control by force of arms — see CONQUER 1

vanquisher *n* one that defeats an enemy or opponent — see VICTOR 1

vanquishing *n* the act or process of bringing someone or something under one's control — see CONQUEST

vantage *n* the more favorable condition or position in a competition — see ADVANTAGE 1

variable *adj* 1 capable of being readily changed — see FLEXIBLE 1

2 likely to change frequently, suddenly, or unexpectedly — see FICKLE 1

variance *n* a lack of agreement or harmony — see DISCORD

variation *n* the act, process, or result of making different — see CHANGE

varicolored *adj* marked by a variety of usually vivid colors — see COLORFUL

varied *adj* consisting of many things of different sorts — see MISCELLANEOUS

variegated *adj* 1 marked by a variety of usually vivid colors — see COLORFUL

2 marked with spots — see SPOTTED 1

variety *n* 1 the quality or state of being composed of many different elements or

types ⟨the sheer *variety* of the city's ethnic restaurants was dazzling⟩
syn assortment, diverseness, diversity, miscellaneousness, variousness
rel heterogeneousness; disparateness, disparity, dissimilarity, distinction, distinctiveness, distinctness, unlikeness
near ant homogeneity, likeness, sameness, similarity; fewness, paucity
2 an unorganized collection or mixture of various things — see MISCELLANY 1
variousness *n* the quality or state of being composed of many different elements or types — see VARIETY 1
varlet *n* a mean, evil, or unprincipled person — see VILLAIN
vary *vb* **1** to be unlike; to not be the same — see DIFFER 1
2 to make different in some way — see CHANGE 1
3 to occur within a continuous range of variation — see RUN 4
4 to pass from one form, state, or level to another — see CHANGE 2
varying *adj* not staying constant — see UNEVEN 2
vast *adj* unusually large — see HUGE
vastly *adv* to a large extent or degree — see GREATLY 2
vastness *n* the quality or state of being very large — see IMMENSITY
vasty *adj* unusually large — see HUGE
¹vault *n* an underground burial chamber — see CRYPT
²vault *n* an act of leaping into the air — see JUMP 1
vault *vb* to propel oneself upward or forward into the air — see JUMP 1
veer *vb* **1** to change one's course or direction — see TURN 3
2 to change the course or direction of (something) — see TURN 2
3 to depart abruptly from a straight line or course — see SWERVE 1
vegetation *n* green leaves or plants — see GREENERY 1
vehemence *n* **1** the quality or state of being forceful (as in expression) ⟨the *vehemence* in her voice when she said that she never gossiped surprised me⟩
syn aggressiveness, assertiveness, emphasis, fierceness, forcefulness, intensity, vigorousness
rel potency, power, strength; eloquence; fervency, insistence, passion, warmth; absoluteness, clearness, incisiveness, plainness
near ant ambiguity, equivocation
ant feebleness, mildness, weakness
2 depth of feeling — see ARDOR 1
vehement *adj* **1** marked by or uttered with forcefulness — see EMPHATIC 1
2 extreme in degree, power, or effect — see INTENSE
3 having or expressing great depth of feeling — see FERVENT

---

vehicle *n* **1** something used to achieve an end — see AGENT 1
2 something used to carry goods or passengers — see CONVEYANCE
veil *n* something that covers or conceals like a piece of cloth — see CLOAK 1
veil *vb* **1** to keep secret or shut off from view — see ¹HIDE 2
2 to surround and cover closely — see ENFOLD 1
vein *n* a distinctive way of putting ideas into words — see STYLE 1
veld *or* **veldt** *n* a broad area of level or rolling treeless country — see PLAIN
velocity *n* a high rate of movement or performance — see SPEED
velvety *adj* smooth or delicate in appearance or feel — see SOFT 2
venal *adj* open to improper influence and especially bribery ⟨that judge is known for being *venal* and easily bought⟩
syn bribable, corruptible, purchasable
rel hack, mercenary; crooked, cutthroat, dishonest, unethical, unprincipled, unscrupulous; corrupt, debased, debauched, degenerate, degraded, demoralized, depraved, dissipated, dissolute, perverse, perverted, warped; bad, evil, immoral, iniquitous, nefarious, sinful, vicious, wicked
near ant ethical, honest, principled; good, moral, righteous, virtuous
ant incorruptible, uncorruptible
vend *vb* to offer for sale to the public — see MARKET
vendor *also* **vender** *n* the person in a business deal who hands over an item in exchange for money ⟨we're thinking of making a deal with that other software *vendor*⟩
syn dealer, merchandiser, seller
rel auctioneer, concessionaire; blackmarketer, bootlegger, fence, fencer, hustler, smuggler, trader; distributor, retailer; sacrificer; wholesaler; hawker, huckster, peddler (*also* pedlar); salesclerk, salesman, salesperson, saleswoman; exporter, handler; bargainer, haggler, horse trader, palterer
near ant consumer, end user, user
ant buyer, purchaser
veneer *n* an outer part or layer — see EXTERIOR
venerable *adj* **1** deserving honor and respect especially by reason of age ⟨the *venerable* old man was a cherished source of advice and wisdom for the villagers⟩
syn hallowed, revered, reverend, venerated
rel honorable, reputable, respectable; honored, respected, reverenced; admirable, estimable, redoubtable; good, moral, righteous
near ant bad, discreditable, disgraceful, dishonorable, disreputable, ignominious, infamous, loose, notorious, shameful; immoral, seamy, shady, sordid, unsavory, vile, wicked; base, contemptible, despicable, detestable, dirty, low, mean, wretched

2 dating or surviving from the distant past — see ANCIENT 1

venerate *vb* to offer honor or respect to (someone) as a divine power — see WORSHIP 1

venerated *adj* deserving honor and respect especially by reason of age — see VENERABLE 1

vengeance *n* the act or an instance of paying back an injury with an injury — see REVENGE

vengeful *adj* likely to seek revenge — see VINDICTIVE

venial *adj* worthy of forgiveness ⟨stealing pencils is a *venial* offense⟩

syn excusable, forgivable, pardonable, remittable

rel justifiable, redeemable; allowable; insignificant, minor, trifling, trivial; harmless, tolerable

near ant abominable, criminal, damning, evil, heinous; sinful, vile, wicked

ant inexcusable, mortal, unforgivable, unpardonable

venom *n* **1** a substance that by chemical action can kill or injure a living thing — see POISON

2 the desire to cause pain for the satisfaction of doing harm — see MALICE

venomous *adj* containing or contaminated with a substance capable of injuring or killing a living thing — see POISONOUS

vent *vb* **1** to find emotional release for — see TAKE OUT 1

2 to make known (as an idea, emotion, or opinion) — see EXPRESS 1

3 to throw or give off — see EMIT 1

ventilate *vb* to make known (as an idea, emotion, or opinion) — see EXPRESS 1

venture *n* a risky undertaking — see GAMBLE

venture *vb* **1** to place in danger — see ENDANGER

2 to take a chance on — see RISK 1

venturesome *adj* **1** inclined or willing to take risks — see BOLD 1

2 involving potential loss or injury — see DANGEROUS

venturous *adj* inclined or willing to take risks — see BOLD 1

veracious *adj* **1** being in the habit of telling the truth — see TRUTHFUL

2 following an original exactly — see FAITHFUL 2

veracity *n* **1** devotion to telling the truth — see HONESTY 1

2 the quality or state of being very accurate — see PRECISION

verbal *adj* **1** of or relating to words or language ⟨the child didn't yet have the *verbal* skills needed to tell the doctor about the pain he was experiencing⟩

syn lexical, linguistic

rel communicative, conversational

2 made or carried on through speaking rather than in writing ⟨a *verbal* agreement carries less force than a written contract⟩

syn oral, spoken, unwritten

rel implicit, informal; articulated, verbalized; given, pronounced, said, sounded, stated, told, voiced

near ant explicit, formal

ant written

verbalize *vb* to express (a thought or emotion) in words — see SAY 1

verbatim *adv* in the same words ⟨you can't just copy the encyclopedia article *verbatim* for your report—that's plagiarism⟩

syn directly, exactly

rel accurately, precisely; identically; literally

phrases word for word

near ant basically, essentially; carelessly; freely, imprecisely, inaccurately, loosely

ant inexactly

verbiage *n* the use of too many words to express an idea ⟨teachers loathe the *verbiage* that students resort to in order to pad a paper⟩

syn circumlocution, diffuseness, long-windedness, prolixity, redundancy, verboseness, verbosity, windiness, wordiness

rel circuitousness, circularity; tautology; reiteration, repetition, repetitiousness; embellishment, embroidering, exaggeration, hyperbole

near ant brevity, briefness, compactness, conciseness, crispness, pithiness, succinctness, terseness

verbose *adj* using or containing more words than necessary to express an idea — see WORDY

verboseness *n* the use of too many words to express an idea — see VERBIAGE

verbosity *n* the use of too many words to express an idea — see VERBIAGE

verdant *adj* covered with a thick, healthy natural growth — see LUSH 1

verdict *n* **1** a position arrived at after consideration — see DECISION 1

2 an idea that is believed to be true or valid without positive knowledge — see OPINION 1

verdure *n* green leaves or plants — see GREENERY 1

verge (on)*vb* **1** to be adjacent to — see ADJOIN 1

2 to come very close to being — see BORDER (ON)

verge *n* the line or relatively narrow space that marks the outer limit of something — see BORDER 1

verging *adj* having a border in common — see ADJACENT

verifiable *adj* capable of being proven as true or real ⟨we're not sure whether that's a *verifiable* hypothesis⟩ ⟨you need a *verifiable* note from your doctor to be excused from gym class⟩

syn confirmable, demonstrable, provable, supportable, sustainable

rel certifiable, documentable, warrantable; excusable, justifiable; alleged, assumed, conjectured, guessed, presumed, surmised, suspected

near ant debatable, disputable, refutable

ant insupportable, unsupportable

verify *vb* to give evidence or testimony to the truth or factualness of — see CONFIRM

verifying *adj* serving to give support to the truth or factualness of something — see CORROBORATIVE

verily *adv* 1 to tell the truth — see ACTUALLY 1

2 not merely this but also — see EVEN

veritably *adv* in actual fact — see VERY 2

verity *n* 1 agreement with fact or reality — see TRUTH

2 devotion to telling the truth — see HONESTY 1

vernacular *adj* used in or suitable for speech and not formal writing — see COLLOQUIAL 1

versatile *adj* able to do many different kinds of things ⟨a *versatile* baseball player can play any position⟩ ⟨this tool is *versatile* enough to serve as a wrench or pliers⟩

syn adaptable, all-around (*also* all-round), protean, universal

rel multipurpose; well-rounded; able, ace, adept, experienced, expert, masterful, skilled, skillful; adjustable, alterable, changeable, elastic, flexible, fluid, malleable, modifiable, variable

near ant limited; amateur, inexperienced

verse *n* 1 a composition using rhythm and often rhyme to create a lyrical effect — see POEM

2 writing that uses rhythm, vivid language, and often rhyme to provoke an emotional response — see POETRY 1

versed *adj* 1 having information especially as a result of study or experience — see FAMILIAR 2

2 having or showing exceptional knowledge, experience, or skill in a field of endeavor — see PROFICIENT

versifier *n* a person who writes poetry — see POET

vertebral column *n* a column of bones supporting the trunk of a vertebrate animal — see SPINE

vertical *adj* rising straight up — see ERECT

verve *adj* active strength of body or mind — see VIGOR 1

very *adj* 1 being one and not another — see SAME 2

2 being this and no more — see MERE

3 existing in fact and not merely as a possibility — see ACTUAL

very *adv* 1 to a great degree ⟨that was a *very* brave thing to do⟩

syn awful, awfully, beastly, deadly, especially, exceedingly (*also* exceeding), extra, extremely, far, frightfully, full, greatly, heavily, highly, hugely, jolly, mightily, mighty, mortally, most, much, particularly, rattling, real, right, so, something, super, terribly, too, whacking

rel completely, entirely, purely, thoroughly, totally, utterly; eminently, exceptionally; considerably, extensively, significantly, substantially; appreciably, discernibly, noticeably, palpably; abundantly, plentifully; astronomically, grandly, monstrously, monumentally

phrases by far, far and away, good and, in particular

near ant meagerly, scantily; barely, hardly, just, marginally, minimally, scarcely

ant little, negligibly, nominally, slightly

2 in actual fact ⟨the *very* same thing happened to me⟩

syn actually, authentically, genuinely, really, veritably

rel accurately, exactly, just, precisely, right, sharp, smack-dab, squarely; almost, nearly, practically; literally, truly

phrases in truth

near ant apparently, ostensibly, outwardly, seemingly

ant professedly, supposedly

vessel *n* 1 a large craft for travel by water — see SHIP

2 a small buoyant structure for travel on water — see BOAT 1

3 a usually circular utensil for holding something (as food) — see DISH

4 something into which a liquid or smaller objects can be put for storage or transportation — see CONTAINER

vest *vb* to put (something) into the possession or safekeeping of another — see GIVE 2

vestibule *n* the entrance room of a building — see HALL 1

vestige *n* a tiny often physical indication of something lost or vanished ⟨a few strange words carved on a tree were the only *vestige* of the lost colony of Roanoke⟩

syn relic, shadow, trace

rel memento, remembrance, reminder; artifact; afterimage, aftertaste; balance, oddment, remainder, remnant, scrap, scraping(s); leavings, remains, residual, residue, rest

vestry *n* a room in a church building for sacred furnishings (as vestments) — see SACRISTY

vet *n* a person with long experience in a specified area — see VETERAN

veteran *adj* having or showing exceptional knowledge, experience, or skill in a field of endeavor — see PROFICIENT

veteran *n* a person with long experience in a specified area ⟨as a *veteran* of politics, she is often consulted by eager young hopefuls⟩

syn old hand, old-timer, vet

rel war-horse; expert, master, pro, professional

near ant apprentice, cub; boot, novitiate; amateur, dilettante; learner, student, trainee; candidate, entrant, probationer

ant beginner, colt, fledgling, freshman, greenhorn, neophyte, newcomer, novice, recruit, rookie, tenderfoot, tyro

veto *n* an order that something not be done or used — see PROHIBITION 2

veto *vb* to reject by or as if by a vote — see NEGATIVE 1

---

syn synonym(s)   *rel* related words
ant antonym(s)   *near ant* near antonym(s)

vex *vb* to disturb the peace of mind of (someone) especially by repeated disagreeable acts — see IRRITATE 1

vexation *n* 1 the act of making unwelcome intrusions upon another — see ANNOYANCE 1

2 the feeling of impatience or anger caused by another's repeated disagreeable acts — see ANNOYANCE 2

vexatious *adj* causing annoyance — see ANNOYING

vexing *adj* causing annoyance — see ANNOYING

via *prep* along the way of — see BY 1

viable *adj* capable of being done or carried out — see POSSIBLE 1

viands *n pl* substances intended to be eaten — see FOOD

vibrancy *n* the quality or state of having abundant or intense activity — see VITALITY 1

vibrant *adj* 1 marked by much life, movement, or activity — see ALIVE 2

2 marked by conspicuously full and rich sounds or tones — see RESONANT

vibrate *vb* to make a series of small irregular or violent movements — see SHAKE 1

vibration *n* a series of slight movements by a body back and forth or from side to side ⟨the *vibration* of the floor caused by thundering feet in the hallway⟩

syn jiggling, oscillation, quivering, shaking, shuddering, trembling, twitching

rel jiggle, palpitation, shake, shudder, tremor, twitch

vice *n* 1 immoral conduct or practices harmful or offensive to society ⟨that section of the city is legendary for crime and *vice*⟩

syn corruption, debauchery, depravity, immorality, iniquity, licentiousness, sin

rel bad, badness, blackness, evil, evildoing, ill, wickedness, wrong, villainy; atrociousness, evilness, heinousness, nefariousness, sinfulness, unscrupulousness, viciousness, vileness; devilry (*or* deviltry), fiendishness; corruptness, debasement, degeneracy, degeneration, depravedness, dissolution; indecency, lasciviousness, lewdness, looseness, perversion; abomination, anathema, taboo (*also* tabu); criminality, reprehensibleness; baseness, despicableness, dirtiness, lowness, meanness; lousiness, miserableness, wretchedness

near ant good, right; honesty, honor, integrity, legitimacy, probity, rectitude, scrupulousness, uprightness; goodness, righteousness, virtuousness; blamelessness; chastity, innocence, perfection, pureness, purity, spotlessness; cleanness, correctness, decency, decorousness, propriety, rightness, seemliness

ant morality, virtue

2 a defect in character — see FAULT 1

vicious *adj* 1 extreme in degree, power, or effect — see INTENSE

2 having or showing the desire to inflict severe pain and suffering on others — see CRUEL 1

3 not conforming to a high moral standard; morally unacceptable — see BAD 2

4 violently unfriendly or aggressive in disposition — see FIERCE 1

viciously *adv* in a mean or spiteful manner — see NASTILY

viciousness *n* 1 the desire to cause pain for the satisfaction of doing harm — see MALICE

2 the willful infliction of pain and suffering on others — see CRUELTY

victim *n* 1 a person or thing harmed, lost, or destroyed — see CASUALTY 1

2 a person or thing that is the object of abuse, criticism, or ridicule — see TARGET 1

3 something offered to a god — see SACRIFICE

victimize *vb* to rob by the use of trickery or threats — see FLEECE

victor *n* 1 one that defeats an enemy or opponent ⟨the computer is usually the *victor* in a chess match against a human opponent⟩

syn beater, conqueror, master, subduer, trimmer, vanquisher, whipper, winner

rel champion, finalist; ruler, subjugator

near ant pushover, quitter; failure, flop, washout

ant loser

2 the person who comes in first in a competition — see CHAMPION 1

victory *n* an instance of defeating an enemy or opponent ⟨with great effort, our team managed an upset *victory* in the final moments⟩

syn triumph, win

rel conquest, mastery, subjugation, vanquishing; landslide, shutout, sweep; success; takeover

near ant upset; collapse, debacle (*also* débâcle), failure, fizzle, flop, folding, nonsuccess, washout; decline, slip, slump, wane; lurch, setback

ant beating, defeat, licking, loss, overthrow, rout, shellacking, trimming, whipping

victuals *n pl* substances intended to be eaten — see FOOD

vie *vb* to engage in a contest — see COMPETE

view *n* 1 all that can be seen from a certain point ⟨the *view* of the mountains from the inn's porch is spectacular⟩

syn lookout, outlook, panorama, prospect, vista

rel landscape, scene, scenery; ken, sight

2 an idea that is believed to be true or valid without positive knowledge — see OPINION 1

3 an instance of looking especially briefly — see LOOK 2

view *vb* to make note of (something) through the use of one's eyes — see SEE 1

viewpoint *n* a way of looking at or thinking about something — see POINT OF VIEW

vigilance *n* the act or state of being constantly attentive and responsive to signs of opportunity, activity, or danger ⟨eternal *vigilance* is the price of freedom⟩

syn alertness, attentiveness, lookout, surveillance, watch, watchfulness

rel aliveness, awareness, consciousness, sensitivity; heedfulness, observance, observation; sleeplessness, wakefulness; care, carefulness, caution, chariness, wariness; preparation, readiness

near ant absentmindedness, absorption, abstraction, daydreaming, daze, distraction; engrossment, obliviousness, preoccupation; unawareness, unconsciousness; carelessness, heedlessness, inattention, inattentiveness; unwariness

vigilant *adj* paying close attention usually for the purpose of anticipating approaching danger or opportunity — see ALERT 1

vigilante *n* one who inflicts punishment in return for an injury or offense — see NEMESIS 1

vigor *n* **1** active strength of body or mind ⟨she was picked for the soccer team because of her *vigor* and enthusiasm⟩

syn bounce, dash, drive, energy, esprit, ginger, go, hardihood, life, pep, punch, sap, snap, starch, verve, vim, vitality, zing, zip

rel animation, briskness, jauntiness, liveliness, spiritedness, sprightliness, vivaciousness, vivacity; ardor, fervor, fire, passion, zeal; main, might, muscle, potency, power, puissance, strength; brawniness, fitness, hardiness, huskiness, virility; haleness, health, healthiness, soundness, wellness

near ant indolence, laziness; debilitation, debility, delicacy, delicateness, disablement, enfeeblement, faintness, feebleness, frailness, frailty, impotence, infirmity, powerlessness, puniness, slightness, softness, tenderness, weakness; enervation, exhaustion, prostration

ant lethargy, listlessness, sluggishness

2 the ability to exert effort for the accomplishment of a task — see POWER 2

vigorous *adj* **1** having active strength of body or mind ⟨he remains healthy and *vigorous* despite being over eighty years old⟩

syn dynamic, energetic, flush, gingery, lusty, peppy, red-blooded, robust, vital

rel animated, lively, spirited, sprightly, vivacious; energized, enlivened, invigorated, vitalized; firm, fortified, mettlesome, mighty, powerful, puissant, strong; refreshed, rejuvenated, revitalized; able-bodied, beefy, brawny, fit, fortified, hardy, husky, rugged, stalwart, stout, strapping, sturdy, tough; hale, healthy, sound; capable, competent

near ant delicate, effete, enervated, faint, feeble, frail, infirm, weak, weakened; impotent, powerless, prostrate, prostrated, sapped, tired; indolent, lackadaisical, languid, lazy; invertebrate, nerveless, soft, spineless, wimpy; ill, unhealthy, unsound,

unwell; broken-down, debilitated, decrepit, disabled, wasted, worn-out

ant lethargic, listless, sluggish, torpid

2 able to withstand hardship, strain, or exposure — see HARDY 1

3 marked by or uttered with forcefulness — see EMPHATIC 1

4 not showing weakness or uncertainty — see FIRM 1

vigorously *adv* in a vigorous and forceful manner — see HARD 3

vigorousness *n* the quality or state of being forceful (as in expression) — see VEHEMENCE 1

vile *adj* **1** not conforming to a high moral standard; morally unacceptable — see BAD 2

2 not following or in accordance with standards of honor and decency — see IGNOBLE 2

3 unpleasant to look at — see UGLY 1

vileness *n* the state or quality of being utterly evil — see ENORMITY 1

vilification *n* the making of false statements that damage another's reputation — see SLANDER

vilify *vb* to make untrue and harmful statements about — see SLANDER

vilifying *n* the making of false statements that damage another's reputation — see SLANDER

villa *n* a large impressive residence — see MANSION

villager *n* a person who lives in a town on a permanent basis — see BURGHER

villain *n* a mean, evil, or unprincipled person ⟨only a heartless *villain* would kidnap a baby for ransom⟩

syn beast, brute, devil, evildoer, fiend, heavy, knave, miscreant, monster, no-good, rapscallion, rascal, reprobate, rogue, savage, scalawag (*or* scallywag), scamp, scoundrel, varlet, wretch

rel blackguard; criminal, crook, culprit, felon, lawbreaker, malefactor, offender, transgressor; perpetrator, sinner, trespasser, wrongdoer; cad, heel; bravo, desperado, outlaw; convict, jailbird; assassin, cutthroat, gangster, gunman, hoodlum, racketeer, ruffian, thug; ne'er-do-well, trash

near ant angel, saint; hero

villainous *adj* not conforming to a high moral standard; morally unacceptable — see BAD 2

villainously *adv* in a mean or spiteful manner — see NASTILY

villainy *n* that which is morally unacceptable — see EVIL

vim *n* active strength of body or mind — see VIGOR 1

vindicate *vb* **1** to free from a charge of wrongdoing — see EXCULPATE

2 to give evidence or testimony to the truth or factualness of — see CONFIRM

vindicating *adj* serving to give support to the truth or factualness of something — see CORROBORATIVE

---

syn synonym(s)   *rel* related words
ant antonym(s)   *near ant* near antonym(s)

vindictive *adj* likely to seek revenge ⟨be careful not to annoy the *vindictive* old woman who lives down the street⟩
syn revengeful, vengeful
rel avenging; resentful, uncharitable, unforgiving; catty, cruel, despiteful, hateful, malevolent, malicious, malign, malignant, mean, nasty, sadistic, spiteful, vicious, virulent; grim, implacable, merciless, relentless, unrelenting; baleful, baneful, evil; harsh, hostile, inimical
near ant charitable, forgiving, merciful, relenting; benevolent, benign, benignant, loving; brotherly, compassionate, good, good-hearted, kind, kindhearted, kindly, sympathetic, warm, warmhearted; altruistic, humane, humanitarian, philanthropic; sweet, tender, tenderhearted; high-minded, magnanimous, noble

vinegary *adj* causing or characterized by the one of the four basic taste sensations that is produced chiefly by acids — see SOUR 1

violate *vb* 1 to fail to keep ⟨you *violated* the school rule against swearing at sporting events⟩
syn breach, break, infringe, transgress
rel disobey, rebel; brush off, disregard, ignore, overlook, overpass, pass over, tune out, wink (at); dismiss, pooh-pooh (*also* pooh), scorn, shrug off; defy, resist, withstand
near ant defer (to), serve, submit (to), surrender (to), yield (to); attend, hear, heed, listen (to); mark, note, notice, regard, watch
ant comply (with), conform (to), follow, mind, obey, observe
2 to treat (a sacred place or object) shamefully or with great disrespect — see DESECRATE

violation *n* 1 a breaking of a moral or legal code — see OFFENSE 1
2 a failure to uphold the requirements of law, duty, or obligation — see BREACH 1

violence *n* the use of brute strength to cause harm to a person or property ⟨the police believe that the woman died of natural causes rather than as a result of *violence*⟩
syn force, foul play
rel coercion, compulsion, constraint, duress, pressure; damage, detriment, harm, hurt, impairment, injury; crippling, maiming, mayhem, mutilation; assault, attack, bashing, battering, battery, batting, beating, belting, bludgeoning, buffeting, clubbing, drubbing, flogging, hammering, lacing, licking, mauling, pelting, pommeling, pounding, pummeling, thrashing, thumping, walloping, whaling, whipping; onslaught, outbreak, outrage, paroxysm, rampage, revolt, riot, shock, terror, threat, turbulence, upheaval, uproar; browbeating, bulldozing, bullying
near ant pacifism
ant nonviolence

violent *adj* 1 marked by bursts of destructive force or intense activity ⟨a *violent* fight that left several people badly hurt⟩
syn explosive, ferocious, fierce, furious, hot, rabid, rough, stormy, tempestuous, turbulent, volcanic
rel brutal, savage, vicious; antagonistic, hostile; aggressive, assertive, bellicose, belligerent, combative, contentious, gladiatorial, quarrelsome; frantic, frenzied, mad; destructive, ruinous
near ant calm, pacific, serene, tranquil; nonbelligerent, unaggressive, unassertive
ant nonviolent, peaceable, peaceful
2 extreme in degree, power, or effect — see INTENSE
3 marked by great and often stressful excitement or activity — see FURIOUS 1

VIP *n* a person who is widely known and usually much talked about — see CELEBRITY 1

viper *n* a limbless reptile with a long body — see SNAKE 1

virago *n* a bad-tempered scolding woman — see SHREW

virgin *adj* 1 never having had sexual relations ⟨*virgin* boys are sometimes unfairly teased⟩
syn maiden, virginal
rel chaste, modest, pure; innocent, untouched; abstinent, celibate; unmarried, unwed
2 being in an original and unused or unspoiled state — see FRESH 1

virginal *adj* never having had sexual relations — see VIRGIN 1

virile *adj* considered characteristic of or appropriate for men — see MASCULINE

virility *n* the set of qualities considered appropriate for or characteristic of men ⟨many cultures value *virility* as a sign of power⟩
syn manhood, manliness, masculinity
rel maleness; boyishness, mannishness, tomboyishness
near ant girlishness; femaleness; girlhood, maidenhood
ant femininity

virtually *adv* very close to but not completely — see ALMOST

virtue *n* 1 a quality that gives something special worth — see EXCELLENCE 2
2 conduct that conforms to an accepted standard of right and wrong — see MORALITY 1

virtuoso *adj* 1 accomplished with trained ability — see SKILLFUL
2 having or showing exceptional knowledge, experience, or skill in a field of endeavor — see PROFICIENT

virtuoso *n* a person with a high level of knowledge or skill in a field — see EXPERT

virtuous *adj* conforming to a high standard of morality or virtue — see GOOD 2

virtuously *adv* with purity of thought and deed — see PURELY

virtuousness *n* conduct that conforms to an accepted standard of right and wrong — see MORALITY 1

virulence *n* biting sharpness of feeling or expression — see ACRIMONY 1

virulent *adj* having or showing a desire to cause someone pain or suffering for the sheer enjoyment of it — see HATEFUL

virulently *adv* in a mean or spiteful manner — see NASTILY

visage *n* **1** facial appearance regarded as an indication of mood or feeling — see LOOK 1

2 the front part of the head — see FACE 1

viscera *n pl* the internal organs of the body — see GUT 1

viscid *adj* **1** being of a consistency that resists flow — see THICK 2

2 being of such a thick consistency as to readily cling to objects upon contact — see STICKY 1

viscosity *n* the degree to which a fluid can resist flowing — see CONSISTENCY

viscous *adj* **1** being of a consistency that resists flow — see THICK 2

2 being of such a thick consistency as to readily cling to objects upon contact — see STICKY 1

visible *adj* capable of being seen ⟨the *visible* light spectrum runs from red to violet⟩

syn apparent, observable, seeable, visual

rel external, outer, outward; detectable, discernible, noticeable, perceptible; clear, conspicuous, evident, eye-catching, manifest, obvious, plain, prominent, striking

near ant disappeared, dissolved, evanesced, evaporated, melted, vanished; imperceptible, inconspicuous, indistinct, unnoticeable; faint, insignificant, slight, vague; buried, concealed, covert, disguised, hidden, latent, obscure, shrouded

ant invisible, unseeable

vision *n* **1** a conception or image created by the imagination and having no objective reality — see FANTASY 1

2 a series of often striking pictures created by the imagination during sleep — see DREAM 1

3 the ability to see — see EYESIGHT

4 the soul of a dead person thought of especially as appearing to living people — see GHOST

vision *vb* to form a mental picture of — see IMAGINE 1

visionary *n* one whose conduct is guided more by the image of perfection than by the real world — see IDEALIST

visit *n* **1** a temporary residing as another's guest ⟨my aunt always looks forward to her week-long annual *visit* with her mother⟩

syn sojourn, stay

rel field trip; layover, stopover

2 a coming to see another briefly for social or business reasons — see CALL 2

visit *vb* **1** to make a social call upon ⟨the club ladies make a point of *visiting* everyone who moves into the neighborhood⟩

syn call (on *or* upon), see

rel look up, seek (out); frequent, hang out (at), haunt

phrases drop in on

near ant brush (off), cold-shoulder, ignore, snub

2 to reside as a temporary guest ⟨Johnny loves it when his friend Susie comes to *visit* for a month every summer⟩

syn sojourn, stay, tarry

rel frequent, hang out (at), haunt; inhabit, occupy

near ant abide, dwell, live, reside

3 to engage in casual or rambling conversation — see CHAT

4 to go to or spend time in often — see FREQUENT

5 to make a brief visit — see CALL 3

visitant *n* a person who visits another — see GUEST

visitation *n* a coming to see another briefly for social or business reasons — see CALL 2

visitor *n* a person who visits another — see GUEST 1

visor *also* **vizor** *n* the projecting front part of a hat or cap ⟨the *visor* of her baseball cap shades her eyes nicely⟩

syn bill, brim, peak

rel shade

vista *n* all that can be seen from a certain point — see VIEW 1

visual *adj* **1** of, relating to, or used in vision ⟨the eyes are the primary *visual* organs in humans⟩

syn ocular, optic, optical

rel seeing, sighted; focusing

ant nonvisual

2 capable of being seen — see VISIBLE

3 consisting of or relating to pictures — see PICTORIAL 1

visualize *vb* to form a mental picture of — see IMAGINE 1

vital *adj* **1** having active strength of body or mind — see VIGOROUS 1

2 having much high-spirited energy and movement — see LIVELY 1

3 impossible to do without — see ESSENTIAL 1

4 likely to cause or capable of causing death — see DEADLY

5 of the greatest possible importance — see CRUCIAL

vitality *n* **1** the quality or state of having abundant or intense activity ⟨a city known for the *vitality* of its entertainment and sports scenes⟩

syn animation, briskness, exuberance, jazziness, liveliness, lustiness, peppiness, robustness, sprightliness, vibrancy

rel buoyancy, jauntiness, springiness; brightness, cheer, cheerfulness, effervescence, vivacity, vivaciousness; eagerness, enthusiasm, keenness, spiritedness; friskiness, impishness, pertness, playfulness

near ant indolence, laziness; languor, lethargy, limpness, listlessness, sleepiness, sluggishness, torpor, weariness; apathy, impassivity; dullness (*or* dulness), tediousness, tedium

ant inactivity, lifelessness

2 active strength of body or mind — see VIGOR 1

---

syn synonym(s)   *rel* related words
ant antonym(s)   *near ant* near antonym(s)

vitalize *vb* to give life, vigor, or spirit to — see ANIMATE

vitalizing *adj* having a renewing effect on the state of the body or mind — see TONIC

vitals *n pl* the internal organs of the body — see GUT 1

vitiate *vb* 1 to affect slightly with something morally bad or undesirable — see TAINT 1

2 to reduce the soundness, effectiveness, or perfection of — see DAMAGE 1

vitriol *n* 1 biting sharpness of feeling or expression — see ACRIMONY 1

2 harsh insulting language — see ABUSE 1

vittles *n pl* substances intended to be eaten — see FOOD

vituperate *vb* to criticize harshly and usually publicly — see ATTACK 2

vituperation *n* harsh insulting language — see ABUSE 1

vivacious *adj* 1 having much high-spirited energy and movement — see LIVELY 1

2 joyously unrestrained — see EXUBERANT

vivid *adj* producing a mental picture through clear and impressive description — see GRAPHIC 1

vivify *vb* to give life, vigor, or spirit to — see ANIMATE

vizard *n* a cover or partial cover for the face used to disguise oneself — see MASK 1

vocabulary *n* 1 the special terms or expressions of a particular group or field — see TERMINOLOGY

2 the stock of words, pronunciation, and grammar used by a people as their basic means of communication — see LANGUAGE 1

vocal *adj* created by the body's organs of sound ⟨our cat is given to making strange *vocal* noises in the dead of night⟩

syn oral, uttered, voiced

rel articulate, articulated, spoken; breathed, drawled, gasped, mouthed, mumbled, murmured, muttered, shouted, spluttered, sputtered, whispered

near ant inarticulate; mute, quiet, silent; unexpressed, unspoken, unuttered, unvoiced

ant nonvocal

vocal *n* a short musical composition for the human voice often with instrumental accompaniment — see SONG 1

vocalist *n* one who sings — see SINGER

vocalize *vb* 1 to express (a thought or emotion) in words — see SAY 1

2 to produce musical sounds with the voice — see SING 1

vocalizer *n* one who sings — see SINGER

vocation *n* the activity by which one regularly makes a living — see OCCUPATION

vociferate *vb* to speak so as to be heard at a distance — see CALL 1

vociferous *adj* engaging in or marked by loud and insistent cries especially of protest ⟨*vociferous* opponents of the bill protested angrily outside the chambers of the legislature⟩

syn blatant, clamorous, obstreperous

rel clangorous, dinning, discordant, noisy; loudmouthed, outspoken, vocal; boisterous, rowdy, uproarious; cacophonous, dissonant, shrill, strident; blaring, booming, brassy, brazen

near ant noiseless, quiet, silent, soundless, still; calm, hushed, subdued

vogue *adj* enjoying widespread favor or approval — see POPULAR 1

vogue *n* 1 a practice or interest that is very popular for a short time — see FAD

2 the state of enjoying widespread approval — see POPULARITY

voice *n* 1 the right to express a wish, choice, or opinion ⟨everyone will have a *voice* in the decision of where to go for our field trip⟩

syn say, vote

rel part, role, share; enfranchisement, franchise, suffrage; judgment (*or* judgement), say-so; belief, conviction, opinion, sentiment, view

2 an act, process, or means of putting something into words — see EXPRESSION 1

3 one who sings — see SINGER

voice *vb* to make known (as an idea, emotion, or opinion) — see EXPRESS 1

voiced *adj* created by the body's organs of sound — see VOCAL

voiceless *adj* unable to speak — see MUTE 1

void *vb* to put an end to by formal action — see ABOLISH

void *adj* 1 having no legal or binding force — see NULL 1

2 lacking contents that could or should be present — see EMPTY 1

3 utterly lacking in something needed, wanted, or expected — see DEVOID 1

void *n* empty space — see VACANCY 1

void *vb* to remove the contents of — see EMPTY

volatile *adj* likely to change frequently, suddenly, or unexpectedly — see FICKLE 1

volcanic *adj* marked by bursts of destructive force or intense activity — see VIOLENT 1

volition *n* the act or power of making one's own choices or decisions — see FREE WILL

volley *n* a rapid or overwhelming outpouring of many things at once — see BARRAGE

volume *n* 1 a considerable amount — see LOT 2

2 a given or particular mass or aggregate of matter — see AMOUNT

3 a set of printed sheets of paper bound together between covers and forming a work of fiction or nonfiction — see BOOK 1

voluminous *adj* of a size greater than average of its kind — see LARGE

voluminousness *n* the quality or state of being large in size — see LARGENESS

voluntarily *adv* of one's own free will ⟨you took part in this *voluntarily*, so you have no cause to complain⟩
syn freely, willingly
rel consciously, knowingly, wittingly
phrases of one's own accord
near ant unconsciously, unknowingly, unwittingly
ant involuntarily, unwillingly

voluntary *adj* 1 done, made, or given with one's own free will ⟨a *voluntary* contribution to the school's fund-raising drive⟩
syn freewill, unforced, volunteer, willing
rel discretionary, elective, nonobligatory, optional; impulsive, instinctive, spontaneous, unforced, unpremeditated; conscious, deliberate, intentional, knowing, willful (*or* wilful)
near ant compulsory, mandatory, necessary, nonelective, obligatory, ordered, required
ant coerced, forced, involuntary
2 subject to one's freedom of choice — see OPTIONAL

volunteer *adj* done, made, or given with one's own free will — see VOLUNTARY 1

voluptuous *adj* pleasing to the physical senses — see SENSUAL

vomit *vb* to discharge the contents of the stomach through the mouth ⟨the children with the flu *vomited* every time they tried to eat something⟩
syn gag, heave, retch, spit up, throw up
rel disgorge, regurgitate; eject, expel, spew

voodoo *n* a person skilled in using supernatural forces — see MAGICIAN 1

voodooism *n* the power to control natural forces through supernatural means — see MAGIC 1

voracious *adj* 1 having a huge appetite ⟨it seemed like the *voracious* kitten was eating her weight in food every day⟩
syn gluttonous, greedy, hoggish, piggish, rapacious, ravenous
rel hearty, wolfish; devouring, gobbling, gorging, gormandizing, insatiable, unquenchable; empty, famished, hungry, starved, starving; malnourished, underfed, undernourished
near ant full, content, sated, satisfied
2 showing urgent desire or interest — see EAGER

vortex *n* water moving rapidly in a circle with a hollow in the center — see WHIRLPOOL

votary *n* one who follows the opinions or teachings of another — see FOLLOWER

vote *n* 1 the right to formally express one's position or will in an election ⟨in the United States, women were granted the *vote* by the Nineteenth Amendment in 1920⟩
syn enfranchisement, franchise, suffrage

rel say, voice
ant disenfranchisement
2 a piece of paper indicating a person's preferences in an election — see BALLOT
3 the right to express a wish, choice, or opinion — see VOICE 1

vote *vb* to set before the mind for consideration — see PROPOSE 1

vouch (for) *vb* to declare (something) to be true or genuine — see CERTIFY 1

vow *n* a person's solemn declaration that he or she will do or not do something — see PROMISE

vow *vb* to make a solemn declaration of intent — see PROMISE 1

voyage *n* a journey over water in a vessel — see SAIL

voyage *vb* 1 to take a trip especially of some distance — see TRAVEL 1
2 to travel on water in a vessel — see SAIL 1

vulgar *adj* 1 belonging to the class of people of low social or economic rank — see IGNOBLE 1
2 depicting or referring to sexual matters in a way that is unacceptable in polite society — see OBSCENE 1
3 held by or applicable to a majority of the people — see GENERAL 3
4 lacking in refinement or good taste — see COARSE 2
5 used in or suitable for speech and not formal writing — see COLLOQUIAL 1

vulgarism *n* a disrespectful or indecent word or expression — see SWEARWORD

vulgarity *n* 1 the quality or state of lacking refinement or good taste ⟨our cousins' general *vulgarity* and poor manners irritate my mother⟩
syn coarseness, commonness, crassness, crudeness, grossness, indelicacy, indelicateness, lowness, raffishness, roughness, rudeness, tastelessness
rel boorishness, churlishness, clownishness, loutishness, insensitivity, thoughtlessness; gracelessness, tackiness
near ant courtliness; elegance, grace, graciousness; consideration, sensitivity, thoughtfulness
ant cultivation, gentility, polish, refinement, tastefulness
2 the quality or state of being obscene — see OBSCENITY 1

vulnerability *n* 1 the quality or state of having little resistance to some outside agent — see SUSCEPTIBILITY
2 the state of being left without shelter or protection against something harmful — see EXPOSURE 1

vulnerable *adj* 1 being in a situation where one is likely to meet with harm — see LIABLE 1
2 lacking protection from danger or resistance against attack — see HELPLESS 1

---

syn synonym(s)   *rel* related words
ant antonym(s)   *near ant* near antonym(s)

wackiness *n* lack of good sense or judgment — see FOOLISHNESS 1

wacky *adj* **1** different from the ordinary in a way that causes curiosity or suspicion — see ODD 2

2 having or showing a very abnormal or sick state of mind — see INSANE 1

3 showing or marked by a lack of good sense or judgment — see FOOLISH 1

wad *n* **1** a considerable amount — see LOT 2

2 a small uneven mass — see LUMP 1

3 a very large amount of money — see FORTUNE 2

wad *vb* to form into a round compact mass ⟨she *wadded* up the paper and threw it in the wastebasket⟩
syn agglomerate, ball, roll, round
rel clump, lump; bead
near ant open, spread, unfold
ant unroll

waddle *vb* to move forward while swaying from side to side — see STAGGER 1

wade (into) *vb* to start work on energetically — see ATTACK 3

waft *n* a slight or gentle movement of air — see BREEZE 1

waft *vb* to rest or move along the surface of a liquid or in the air — see FLOAT

wag *n* **1** a quick jerky movement from side to side or up and down ⟨the dog gave its tail a single *wag* before it flopped back down⟩
syn switch, waggle
rel oscillation, swing; flap, flutter, wave; jerk, shake, twitch, wiggle

2 a person (as a writer) noted for or specializing in humor — see HUMORIST

wag *vb* to move from side to side or up and down with quick jerky motions ⟨the cat's tail *wagged* back and forth in annoyance⟩
syn switch, waggle
rel oscillate, swing; beat, flail, flap, flop, whip; flick, flicker, flutter, wave; jerk, shake, twitch, wiggle

wage *n, often* **wages** *pl* the money paid regularly to a person for labor or services ⟨the *wage* you earn is more than enough to support us comfortably⟩
syn emolument, hire, pay, payment, salary, stipend
rel minimum wage, take-home pay; compensation, recompense, remittance, remuneration, requital, return; check, commission, paycheck; recoupment, redress, reparation, restitution; reimbursement, repayment; profit, takings, yield

wager *n* the money or thing risked on the outcome of an uncertain event — see BET

wager *vb* to risk (something) on the outcome of an uncertain event — see BET

wagerer *n* one that bets (as on the outcome of a contest or sports event) — see BETTOR

waggery *n* **1** playful, reckless behavior that is not intended to cause serious harm — see MISCHIEF 1

2 something said or done to cause laughter — see JOKE 1

waggish *adj* tending to or exhibiting reckless playfulness — see MISCHIEVOUS 1

waggle *n* a quick jerky movement from side to side or up and down — see WAG 1

waggle *vb* to move from side to side or up and down with quick jerky motions — see WAG

wagon *n* a wheeled usually horse-drawn vehicle used for hauling — see CART

wail *n* **1** a crying out in grief — see LAMENT 1

2 a long low sound indicating pain or grief — see MOAN 1

wail *vb* **1** to express dissatisfaction, pain, or resentment usually tiresomely — see COMPLAIN

2 to make a long loud mournful sound — see HOWL 1

3 to utter a moan — see MOAN 1

wail (for) *vb* to feel or express sorrow for — see LAMENT 1

wailing *adj* expressing or suggesting mourning — see MOURNFUL 1

wain *n* a wheeled usually horse-drawn vehicle used for hauling — see CART

waist *n* the middle region of the human body — see MIDRIFF

waistline *n* the middle region of the human body — see MIDRIFF

wait *n* an instance or period of being prevented from going about one's business — see DELAY

wait *vb* to remain in place in readiness or expectation of something ⟨hurry up, as your sisters are already at the door *waiting* for you⟩
syn await, bide, hold on, stay
rel hang around, linger, stick around; anticipate, expect
phrases bide one's time

waiter *n* a person who serves food or drink — see SERVER

waiver *n* a document containing a declaration of an intentional giving up of a right, claim, or privilege ⟨before the hospital will treat you, you have to sign a *waiver* in which you give up your right to sue⟩
syn release
rel dispensation, exemption; abdication, relinquishment, renouncement; renunciation, surrender

wake *vb* **1** to cause to stop sleeping ⟨my banging around in the kitchen *woke* the cat⟩

syn arouse, awake, awaken, rouse, waken
rel raise, revive; reawake, reawaken; agitate, disturb, excite, provoke, stimulate, stir
near ant hypnotize, mesmerize; lay (down)
ant lull

2 to cease to be asleep ⟨I *woke* with a start when the door slammed⟩
syn arouse, awake, awaken, rouse, waken
rel arise, get up, rise, uprise; watch; revive; reawake, reawaken; shift, stir
near ant catnap, doze, drop (off), nap, nod, sleep, slumber, snooze; bed (down), couch, retire, turn in; oversleep

wakeful *adj* not sleeping or able to sleep ⟨the mother remained *wakeful* until her child returned home⟩
syn awake, sleepless, wide-awake
rel aroused, awakened, roused, wakened; aware, conscious; revived; reawakened
near ant drowsy, nodding, sleepy, slumberous, somnolent; dreaming; hypnotized, mesmerized
ant asleep, dormant, dozing, napping, resting, sleeping, slumbering

waken *vb* **1** to cause to stop sleeping — see WAKE 1

2 to cease to be asleep — see WAKE 2

walk *n* a relaxed journey on foot for exercise or pleasure ⟨we went for a long *walk* outside because it was such a nice night⟩
syn constitutional, perambulation, ramble, range, saunter, stroll, turn
rel parade, promenade; expedition, hike, march, peregrination, tramp, travel, trek, trip; excursion, jaunt, junket, outing, sally, spin, tour; pilgrimage, progress, safari

walk *vb* to go on foot ⟨I *walked* slowly to school⟩
syn foot (it), hoof (it), leg (it), pad, step, traipse, tread
rel parade, promenade; march, pace, stride; hike, peregrinate, trek; amble, perambulate, ramble, saunter, stroll, wander; clump, stomp, stump, tramp, tromp; plod, trudge; hobble, limp; mince, prance, pussyfoot, tiptoe; stalk, strut, swagger; lumber, lurch, pound, shamble, shuffle, stagger; nip, trip, trot

walking out *n* the act of leaving a place — see DEPARTURE

walkout *n* a work stoppage by a body of workers intended to force an employer to meet their demands — see STRIKE 1

walk out *vb* **1** to leave a place often for another — see GO 2

2 to refuse to work in order to force an employer to meet demands — see STRIKE 1

wall *n* **1** a physical object that blocks the way — see BARRIER

2 means or method of defending — see DEFENSE 1

wall (in) *vb* to close or shut in by or as if by barriers — see ENCLOSE 1

wallop *n* **1** a forceful coming together of two things — see IMPACT 1

2 a hard strike with a part of the body or an instrument — see ¹BLOW

wallop *vb* **1** to strike repeatedly — see BEAT 1

2 to achieve a victory over — see BEAT 2

3 to defeat by a large margin — see WHIP 2

4 to deliver a blow to (someone or something) usually in a strong vigorous manner — see HIT 1

wampum *n slang* something (as pieces of stamped metal or printed paper) customarily and legally used as a medium of exchange, a measure of value, or a means of payment — see MONEY

wan *adj* lacking a healthy skin color — see PALE 2

wander *vb* to move about from place to place aimlessly ⟨we just went outside and *wandered* around until it was time to go⟩
syn gad (about), gallivant (*also* galavant), knock (about), maunder, meander, mooch, mope, ramble, range, roam, rove, traipse
rel amble, saunter, stroll; bum, hobo; straggle, stray; prowl, tramp, travel

wanderer *n* a person who roams about without a fixed route or destination — see NOMAD

wandering *adj* traveling from place to place — see ITINERANT

wane *vb* to grow less in scope or intensity especially gradually — see DECREASE 2

wangle *vb* to plan out usually with subtle skill or care — see ENGINEER

want *n* **1** the fact or state of being absent — see LACK 1

2 a falling short of an essential or desirable amount or number — see DEFICIENCY

3 a state of being without something necessary, desirable, or useful — see NEED 1

4 the state of lacking sufficient money or material possessions — see POVERTY 1

want *vb* **1** to have an earnest wish to own or enjoy — see DESIRE

2 to have as a requirement — see NEED 1

3 to see fit — see CHOOSE 2

4 to wish to have — see LIKE 1

wanting *adj* **1** falling short of a standard — see BAD 1

2 not coming up to a usual standard or meeting a particular need — see SHORT 3

3 not present or in evidence — see ABSENT 2

wanting *prep* not having — see WITHOUT 1

wanton *adj* **1** depicting or referring to sexual matters in a way that is unacceptable in polite society — see OBSCENE 1

2 having a strong sexual desire — see LUSTFUL

3 having or showing the desire to inflict severe pain and suffering on others — see CRUEL 1

wantonness *n* the willful infliction of pain and suffering on others — see CRUELTY

---

syn synonym(s)   **rel** related words
ant antonym(s)   **near ant** near antonym(s)

war *n* **1** a state of armed violent struggle between states, nations, or groups ⟨the United States declared *war* on Japan after the bombing of Pearl Harbor⟩

syn conflict, hostilities, hot war

rel civil war, cold war, holy war, limited war, world war; action, battle, engagement; combat, fighting, warfare; belligerency; wartime

near ant demilitarization, demobilization, disarmament; pacification; cease-fire, truce; calm, peacefulness, tranquility

ant peace

2 a lack of agreement or harmony — see DISCORD

war (against) *vb* to oppose (someone) in physical conflict — see FIGHT 1

warble *n* a rhythmic series of musical tones arranged to give a pleasing effect — see MELODY

warble *vb* to sing with the alternation of two musical tones ⟨the skylark *warbled* prettily outside our window⟩

syn quaver, trill

rel slur; yodel; belt, carol, chant, chorus, croon, descant, harmonize, troll, vocalize; lilt, scat

ward *n* **1** means or method of defending — see DEFENSE 1

2 responsibility for the safety and well-being of someone or something — see CUSTODY

ward *vb* to drive danger or attack away from — see DEFEND 1

warden *n* **1** a person or group that watches over someone or something — see GUARD 1

2 a person who takes care of a property sometimes for an absent owner — see CUSTODIAN 1

warder *n* a person or group that watches over someone or something — see GUARD 1

warehouse *n* a building for storing goods — see STOREHOUSE

wares *n pl* products that are bought and sold in business — see MERCHANDISE

warfare *n* **1** a lack of agreement or harmony — see DISCORD

2 an earnest effort for superiority or victory over another — see CONTEST 1

wariness *n* a close attentiveness to avoiding danger — see CAUTION 1

warlike *adj* feeling or displaying eagerness to fight — see BELLIGERENT

warm *adj* **1** having or giving off heat to a moderate degree ⟨the pan was still *warm*, but no longer too hot to touch⟩

syn heated, lukewarm, tepid, toasty, warmed

rel thawed; broiling, burning, fiery, hot, piping hot, red-hot, roasting, scalding, scorching, searing, sultry, sweltering, torrid; overheated, roasted, superheated, sweltering; blazing, glowing, molten, sizzling; reheated

near ant arctic, bitter, bleak, chill, chilly, cold, freezing, frigid, frosty, glacial, ice-cold, iced, icy, nippy, polar, raw, sharp, snappy, snowy, subfreezing, subzero, wintry; unthawed; frosted; benumbed, nipped, numb

ant chilled, cool, cooled, refrigerated, unheated

2 having or expressing great depth of feeling — see FERVENT

3 having or showing kindly feeling and sincere interest — see FRIENDLY 1

4 showing or expressing acceptance or approval — see POSITIVE

warm *vb* **1** to cause to have or give off heat to a moderate degree ⟨you'll need to *warm* the food in the microwave⟩

syn heat, toast

rel overheat, superheat; reheat; burn, char, fire, scald, scorch, sear

near ant freeze, frost, ice

ant chill, cool, refrigerate

2 to give satisfaction to — see PLEASE

warm–blooded *adj* having or expressing great depth of feeling — see FERVENT

warmed *adj* having or giving off heat to a moderate degree — see WARM 1

warmhearted *adj* **1** having or marked by sympathy and consideration for others — see HUMANE 1

2 having or showing kindly feeling and sincere interest — see FRIENDLY 1

warmness *n* the quality or state of being moderate in temperature — see WARMTH 1

warmonger *n* one who urges or attempts to cause a war ⟨fortunately, the *warmongers* met with overwhelming opposition⟩

syn hawk, jingo, militarist

rel agitator, firebrand, fomenter, instigator, rabble-rouser; belligerent, combatant, militant; chauvinist

near ant peacemaker

ant dove, pacifist

warmth *n* **1** the quality or state of being moderate in temperature ⟨the cozy *warmth* of the inn's parlor was a welcome relief from the wintry weather outside⟩

syn lukewarmness, warmness

rel glow, radiance; heat, hotness, sultriness, stuffiness

near ant bitterness, bleakness, cold, coldness, frigidity, frostiness, iciness, rawness, sharpness; frost

ant chill, chilliness, coolness

2 depth of feeling — see ARDOR 1

warn *vb* to give notice to beforehand especially of danger or risk ⟨Dad *warned* us that if we continued playing so rough, someone was sure to get hurt⟩

syn alert, caution, forewarn

rel augur, forecast, foretell, predict, presage, prognosticate, prophesy; advise, apprise, inform, notify; admonish; bode, forebode, portend

near ant imperil, risk

warning *adj* serving as or offering a warning — see CAUTIONARY

warning *n* **1** the act or an instance of telling beforehand of danger or risk ⟨she delivered a strict *warning* that anyone who was caught cheating would get expelled⟩

syn admonition, alarm, alert, caution, forewarning, notice

rel auguring, augury, forecasting, foretelling, predicting, prediction, presaging, prognosticating, prophecy, prophesying; apprising, informing, notification, notifying; advice, counsel, guidance, recommendation, suggestion; announcement, declaration

2 something that tells of approaching danger or risk ⟨the ominously darkening sky was a *warning* that a tornado was approaching⟩

syn caution, tocsin

rel omen, portent; notification; buoy, knell, sign, signal; foretaste, foretoken; announcement, declaration

warp *vb* **1** to change so much as to create a wrong impression or alter the meaning of — see GARBLE

2 to lower in character or dignity — see DEBASE 1

3 to twist (something) out of a natural or normal shape or condition — see CONTORT

warped *adj* having or showing lowered moral character or standards — see CORRUPT

warping *n* the twisting of something out of its natural or normal shape or condition — see CONTORTION

warrant *vb* **1** to assume responsibility for the satisfactory quality or performance of ⟨the computer company unconditionally *warrants* all of its products for one full year⟩

syn guarantee

rel attest, authenticate, avouch, certify, testify (to), vouch (for), witness; assure, bond, contract, covenant; pledge, plight, swear, vow; adhere, assert, declare, insist; insure

2 to give official acceptance of something as satisfactory — see APPROVE

3 to have as a requirement — see NEED 1

4 to state as a fact usually forcefully — see CLAIM 1

warranted *adj* being what is called for by accepted standards of right and wrong — see JUST 1

warranty *n* a formal agreement to fulfill an obligation — see GUARANTEE 1

warrior *n* a person engaged in military service — see SOLDIER

wary *adj* having or showing a close attentiveness to avoiding danger or trouble — see CAREFUL 1

wash *vb* **1** to flow along or against ⟨crystal-clear waters gently *wash* the island's unspoiled beaches⟩

syn lap, lave, splash

rel gurgle, ripple, slosh

2 to flow in a broken irregular stream — see GURGLE

3 to make wet — see WET

4 to pour liquid over or through in order to cleanse — see FLUSH 1

washed *adj* containing, covered with, or thoroughly penetrated by water — see WET

washed–out *adj* lacking intensity of color — see PALE 1

washed–up *adj* having lost forcefulness, courage, or spirit — see EFFETE 1

washout *n* something that has failed — see FAILURE 3

wash out *vb* **1** to be unsuccessful — see FAIL 2

2 to make white or whiter by removing color — see WHITEN

3 to use up all the physical energy of — see EXHAUST 1

washroom *n* a room furnished with a fixture for flushing body waste — see TOILET

waspish *adj* easily irritated or annoyed — see IRRITABLE

waspishness *n* readiness to show annoyance or impatience — see PETULANCE

wassail *n* a bout of drinking — see CAROUSE

wastage *n* the state or fact of being rendered nonexistent, physically unsound, or useless — see DESTRUCTION

waste *adj* producing inferior or only a small amount of vegetation — see BARREN 1

waste *n* **1** an instance of spending money or resources without care or restraint ⟨it seems like a *waste* to spend my entire paycheck on a bigger TV⟩

syn extravagance, prodigality

rel indulgence, luxury, splurge; loss, wastage; generosity, liberality, openhandedness, profligacy; improvidence, shortsightedness; overindulgence, self-indulgence; excess, immoderacy, overkill; carelessness, heedlessness, imprudence, incautiousness; recklessness

near ant necessity; economizing, economy, frugality, saving, scrimping, skimping; austerity, moderation, restraint, temperance, temperateness

2 discarded or useless material — see GARBAGE

3 land that is uninhabited or not fit for crops — see WASTELAND

4 solid matter discharged from an animal's alimentary canal — see DROPPING 1

waste *vb* **1** to use up carelessly ⟨he *wasted* most of his allowance by buying comic books⟩

syn blow, dissipate, fritter (away), lavish, misspend, run through, spend, squander, throw away

rel splurge; consume, deplete, exhaust, impoverish; indulge, overindulge; disburse, expend, lay out

near ant economize, scrimp, skimp; preserve, protect, save; hoard, lay up

ant conserve

2 to bring to a complete end the physical soundness, existence, or usefulness of — see DESTROY 1

3 to diminish the physical strength of — see WEAKEN 1

---

waste (away) *vb* to lose bodily strength or vigor — see WEAKEN 2

wasted *adj* **1** lacking bodily strength — see WEAK 1

2 suffering extreme weight loss as a result of hunger or disease — see EMACIATED

wasteful *adj* given to spending money freely or foolishly — see PRODIGAL

wastefulness *n* the quality or fact of being free or wasteful in the expenditure of money — see EXTRAVAGANCE 1

wasteland *n* land that is uninhabited or not fit for crops ⟨with proper irrigation and fertilizer, they turned the desert *wasteland* into a fertile plain⟩
syn barren, desert, desolation, waste
rel badland; bush, brush; dust bowl; hinterland, upland; open, open air, outdoors, out-of-doors; nature, wild, wilderness

waster *n* someone who carelessly spends money — see PRODIGAL

wastrel *n* someone who carelessly spends money — see PRODIGAL

watch *n* **1** a person or group that watches over someone or something — see GUARD 1

2 the act or state of being constantly attentive and responsive to signs of activity, opportunity, or danger — see VIGILANCE

watch *vb* **1** to keep one's eyes on ⟨I turned my head to continue *watching* the bird as it flew away⟩
syn eye, observe
rel behold, look, regard, see, view; gape, gawk, gaze, glare, goggle, peer, rubberneck, stare; guard, wake, ward; monitor, read; spy; glance, glimpse, peek, peep
near ant blink, wink

2 to take notice of and be guided by — see HEED 1

3 to pay continued close attention to (something) for a particular purpose — see MONITOR

4 to have an interest or concern for — see CARE

watch (for) *vb* to believe in the future occurrence of (something) — see EXPECT

watchful *adj* paying close attention usually for the purpose of anticipating approaching danger or opportunity — see ALERT 1

watchfulness *n* the act or state of being constantly attentive and responsive to signs of opportunity, activity, or danger — see VIGILANCE

watchman *n* **1** a person or group that watches over someone or something — see GUARD 1

2 a person who takes care of a property sometimes for an absent owner — see CUSTODIAN 1

watch out (for) *vb* to be cautious of or on guard against — see BEWARE (OF)

watchword *n* **1** a word or phrase that must be spoken by a person in order to pass a guard — see PASSWORD

2 an attention-getting word or phrase used to publicize something (as a campaign or product) — see SLOGAN

water *vb* to make wet — see WET

water (down) *vb* to alter (something) for the worse with the addition of foreign or lower-grade substances — see ADULTERATE

water closet *n* a room furnished with a fixture for flushing body waste — see TOILET

watercourse *n* an open man-made passageway for water — see CHANNEL 1

watercraft *n* a small buoyant structure for travel on water — see BOAT 1

watered *adj* containing, covered with, or thoroughly penetrated by water — see WET

waterfall *n* a fall of water usually from a great height ⟨I used to like to throw sticks in the stream and watch them go over the *waterfall*⟩
syn cascade, cataract, fall(s)
rel rapid(s), white water; eddy, riffle; undertow, vortex, whirlpool

waterless *adj* marked by little or no precipitation or humidity — see DRY 1

waterlogged *adj* containing, covered with, or thoroughly penetrated by water — see WET

waterproof *n chiefly British* a coat made of water-resistant material — see RAINCOAT

waterproof *adj* made of or treated with material that does not allow water to penetrate ⟨luckily, my backpack is *waterproof*, so my notes didn't get wet⟩
syn waterproofed, watertight
rel rainproof; water-repellent, water-resistant; nonabsorbent, nonporous
near ant absorbent, porous

waterproofed *adj* made of or treated with material that does not allow water to penetrate — see WATERPROOF

waterspout *n* a pipe or channel for carrying off water from a roof — see GUTTER 1

watertight *adj* made of or treated with material that does not allow water to penetrate — see WATERPROOF

waterway *n* an open man-made passageway for water — see CHANNEL 1

watery *adj* **1** containing, covered with, or thoroughly penetrated by water — see WET

2 having an overly soft liquid consistency — see RUNNY

3 not containing very much of some important element — see WEAK 3

wave *n* a moving ridge on the surface of water ⟨the toddler was almost knocked down by the *waves* created by the speedboat⟩
syn billow, surge, swell
rel sea(s); breaker, whitecap; curl; comber, roller; eddy, riffle, ripple, wavelet; tidal wave, tsunami; undertow, vortex, whirlpool

wave *vb* to direct or notify by a movement or gesture — see MOTION

waver *vb* **1** to show uncertainty about the right course of action — see HESITATE

2 to swing unsteadily back and forth or from side to side — see TEETER 1

wavering *n* the act or an instance of pausing because of uncertainty about the right course of action — see HESITATION

wax *vb* **1** to become greater in extent, volume, amount, or number — see INCREASE

2 to coat (something) with a slippery substance in order to reduce friction — see LUBRICATE

3 to eventually have as a state or quality — see BECOME

way *n* **1** a passage cleared for public vehicular travel ⟨the town honored the local sports hero by naming after him a short *way* connecting two shopping centers⟩
syn artery, avenue, boulevard, drag, drive, expressway, freeway, highroad, highway, pass, passageway, pike, road, roadway, route, row, street, thoroughfare, trace, turnpike
rel causeway; alley, alleyway, bystreet, byway, catwalk, court, lane, place; approach, concourse, path, walkway; access; dead end; aisle, corridor, course, line; track, trail; channel; corduroy, tarmac; crossroad; bypass, overpass, underpass; cloverleaf, rotary

2 a usual manner of behaving or doing — see HABIT

3 an established course for traveling from one place to another — see PASSAGE 1

4 an established pattern of behavior — see TENDENCY 1

5 an extent or area available for or used up by some activity or thing — see ROOM 1

6 the direction along which something or someone moves — see PATH 1

7 the means or procedure for doing something — see METHOD

8 the opening through which one can enter or leave a structure — see DOOR 2

9 the power, right, or opportunity to choose — see CHOICE 1

10 the space or amount of space between two points, lines, surfaces, or objects — see DISTANCE

wayfarer *n* a person who roams about without a fixed route or destination — see NOMAD

wayfaring *adj* traveling from place to place — see ITINERANT

waylay *vb* to lie in wait for and attack by surprise — see AMBUSH

way–out *adj* different from the ordinary in a way that causes curiosity or suspicion — see ODD 2

way station *n* a regular stopping place — see STATION 2

wayward *adj* **1** given to resisting authority or another's control — see DISOBEDIENT

2 given to resisting control or discipline by others — see UNCONTROLLABLE

weak *adj* **1** lacking bodily strength ⟨the little boy was simply too *weak* to lift the box⟩

syn debilitated, delicate, effete, enervated, enfeebled, faint, feeble, frail, infirm, languid, low, prostrate, prostrated, sapped, slight, soft, softened, tender, torpid, unsubstantial, wasted, weakened, wimpy
rel challenged, disabled, incapacitated; paralyzed; broken-down, decrepit, worn out; impotent, powerless, puny; breakable, flimsy, fragile; dizzy, groggy, rocky, unsteady, woozy; exhausted, tired, weary; damaged, harmed, hurt, impaired, injured; resistless, susceptible, unresistant, vulnerable, yielding
near ant able-bodied, athletic, beefy, brawny, fit, husky, muscular, sinewy, strapping, virile; hard, hardy, lusty, robust, sturdy, tough; fortified, hardened, inured, strengthened, toughened; energetic, energized, invigorated, vigorous, vitalized; hale, healthy, sound; capable, competent; convalescing, recovering, recuperating
ant mighty, powerful, rugged, stalwart, stout, strong

2 lacking strength of will or character ⟨the opinion that overweight people are just *weak* individuals who easily give in to temptation⟩
syn characterless, effete, frail, invertebrate, nerveless, soft, spineless, weakened, wimpy, wishy-washy
rel forceless, ineffective, ineffectual; impotent, powerless; emasculated, unnerved; pliable, submissive; corrupt, unprincipled, unscrupulous, villainous; cowardly, craven, lily-livered
near ant ethical, good, moral, principled, right, righteous, upright, virtuous; determined, mettlesome, resolute; courageous, stalwart, stouthearted
ant backboned, firm, strong, tough

3 not containing very much of some important element ⟨the coffee came out too *weak* because I didn't put enough ground beans in⟩
syn dilute, diluted, thin, thinned, watery, weakened
rel adulterated, watered (down)
near ant enriched, fortified; concentrated, condensed, evaporated
ant full-bodied, rich, strong

4 not using or following good reasoning — see ILLOGICAL

5 unable to act or achieve one's purpose — see POWERLESS

weaken *vb* **1** to diminish the physical strength of ⟨several days of hardship in the desert had *weakened* them⟩
syn debilitate, enervate, enfeeble, prostrate, sap, soften, tire, waste
rel cripple, disable, incapacitate; deplete, depress, exhaust, impoverish, unman, wash out; damage, harm, hurt, impair, injure; break down, wear out; paralyze
near ant energize, invigorate, vitalize; harden, season, toughen
ant beef (up), fortify, recruit, strengthen

---

syn synonym(s)	*rel* related words
ant antonym(s)	*near ant* near antonym(s)

2 to lose bodily strength or vigor ⟨the bodybuilder *weakened* once she eased off on her workouts⟩

syn decay, droop, fail, flag, go, lag, languish, sag, waste (away), wilt

rel break down, wear out; yield

near ant convalesce, recover, recuperate; gain

2 to alter (something) for the worse with the addition of foreign or lower-grade substances — see ADULTERATE

weakened *adj* **1** containing foreign or lower-grade substances — see IMPURE

2 lacking bodily strength — see WEAK 1

3 lacking strength of will or character — see WEAK 2

4 not containing very much of some important element — see WEAK 3

weakening *n* a gradual sinking and wasting away of mind or body — see DECLINE 1

weakling *n* **1** a person lacking in physical strength ⟨he was a *weakling* until high school, when he started working out to put on muscle⟩

syn softy (*or* softie), wimp

rel pushover, sissy

ant powerhouse

2 a person without strength of character ⟨only a *weakling* would be willing to lie to save himself from punishment⟩

syn mollycoddle, wimp

rel coward, mouse

ant stalwart

weakly *adj* chronically or repeatedly suffering from poor health — see SICKLY 1

weak-minded *adj* **1** not having or showing an ability to absorb ideas readily — see STUPID 1

2 showing or marked by a lack of good sense or judgment — see FOOLISH 1

weakness *n* **1** the quality or state of lacking physical strength or vigor ⟨the flu left me with such *weakness* that I could hardly stand⟩

syn debilitation, debility, delicacy, delicateness, enfeeblement, faintness, feebleness, frailness, frailty, infirmity, languor, lowness

rel decay, decrepitude; breakdown, collapse, exhaustion, nervous breakdown, prostration; defenselessness, helplessness, softness, tenderness; disablement, incapacitation; damage, harm, hurt, impairment, injury

near ant energy, vitality; brawniness, fitness, huskiness, virility; hardness, ruggedness, stoutness, sturdiness, toughness; haleness, health, healthiness, soundness

ant hardihood, hardiness, robustness, strength, vigor

2 the quality or state of lacking strength of will or character ⟨in a moment of *weakness* he shoplifted the comic book⟩

syn frailness, frailty, softness, spinelessness

rel collapse; failing, flaw, foibles, peccadillo; evil, immorality, wickedness; corruption, corruptness

near ant discipline, self-discipline; goodness, morality, rightness, righteousness, uprightness, virtuousness

ant backbone, firmness, fortitude, mettle, resoluteness, strength

3 a defect in character — see FAULT 1

4 the quality or state of having little resistance to some outside agent — see SUSCEPTIBILITY

weal *n* the state of doing well especially in relation to one's happiness or success — see WELFARE

wealth *n* **1** the total of one's money and property ⟨her *wealth* increased to the point where she could afford several luxurious homes⟩

syn assets, capital, fortune, means, opulence, riches, substance, wherewithal

rel belongings, chattels, effects, holdings, paraphernalia, possessions, things; finances, money; king's ransom, mint, wad; abundance, affluence, prosperity, success; treasure, valuables; accession, acquisition, personalty, property; nest egg, reserve, resources, savings, treasury; collateral; heap, pile, pot; bonanza, mine, treasure trove

near ant debts, liabilities; indebtedness

2 a considerable amount — see LOT 2

3 an amount or supply more than sufficient to meet one's needs — see PLENTY 1

wealthy *adj* having goods, property, or money in abundance — see RICH 1

wear *n* **1** the result of long and hard use ⟨after several years, the carpet was finally showing *wear*⟩

syn wear and tear

rel abrasion, corrosion, erosion, erasure; decomposition, disintegration

near ant fixing, mending, patching, rebuilding, reconditioning, reconstruction, renovation, repair, revamping

2 covering for the human body — see CLOTHING

wear *vb* **1** to use up all the physical energy of — see EXHAUST 1

2 to damage or diminish by continued friction — see ABRADE 1

wear and tear *n* the result of long and hard use — see WEAR 1

wearied *adj* **1** depleted in strength, energy, or freshness — see WEARY 1

2 having one's patience, interest, or pleasure exhausted — see WEARY 2

weariless *adj* showing no signs of weariness even after long hard effort — see TIRELESS

weariness *n* **1** a complete depletion of energy or strength — see FATIGUE

2 the state of being bored — see BOREDOM

wearisome *adj* causing weariness, restlessness, or lack of interest — see BORING

wear out *vb* to use up all the physical energy of — see EXHAUST 1

weary *adj* **1** depleted in strength, energy, or freshness ⟨I am just too *weary* to do any more work tonight⟩

syn beat, burned-out (*or* burnt-out), bushed, dead, done in, drained, effete, exhausted, fatigued, jaded, limp, logy, played out, prostrate, spent, tired, tuckered (out), wearied, worn, worn-out

rel overtaxed, overworked; run-down; debilitated, enervated, enfeebled, sapped, weakened

phrases worn to a frazzle

near ant refreshed, rejuvenated, relaxed, rested, revitalized; active, energetic, invigorated, strengthened, strong, tireless, vitalized

ant untired

2 having one's patience, interest, or pleasure exhausted ⟨I am totally *weary* of this constant bickering⟩

syn bored, fed up, jaded, sick, tired, wearied

rel apathetic, disinterested, uninterested; glutted, sated, satiated, surfeited; dejected, demoralized, discouraged, disheartened, dispirited; beat, burned-out (*or* burnt-out), bushed, done in, drained, enervated, exhausted, fatigued, limp, played out, tuckered, worn-out; annoyed, frustrated, irritated; disgusted, nauseated, repulsed

near ant animated, energized, enlivened, excited, galvanized, invigorated, stimulated, vitalized; amused, entertained; beguiled, bewitched, captivated, charmed, enchanted, enthralled, fascinated, hypnotized, mesmerized; delighted, pleased, thrilled

ant absorbed, engaged, engrossed, gripped, interested, intrigued

3 causing weariness, restlessness, or lack of interest — see BORING

weary *vb* **1** to make weary and restless by being dull or monotonous — see ²BORE

2 to use up all the physical energy of — see EXHAUST 1

wearying *adj* causing weariness, restlessness, or lack of interest — see BORING

weather *vb* to come safely through — see SURVIVE 1

weave *vb* to scatter or set here and there among other things — see THREAD 1

web *n* **1** something that catches and holds ⟨he was caught in the *web* of branches⟩ ⟨she was trapped by her own *web* of lies⟩

syn entanglement, net, snare

rel mesh, trap; knot, snarl, tangle; labyrinth, maze; cobweb, spiderweb

2 a device or scheme for capturing another by surprise — see TRAP 1

wed *vb* **1** to give in marriage — see MARRY 2

2 to perform the ceremony of marriage for — see MARRY 1

3 to take a spouse — see MARRY 4

4 to take as a spouse — see MARRY 3

wedded *adj* of or relating to marriage — see MARITAL

wedding *n* a ceremony in which two people are united in matrimony ⟨they chose to have the *wedding* outdoors in the spring⟩

syn bridal, espousal, marriage, nuptial(s)

rel match, matrimony, wedlock; reception; engagement, hand, pledge, promise, proposal, troth

wedge *vb* to fit (something) into a tight space — see CROWD 1

wedged *adj* firmly positioned in place and difficult to dislodge — see TIGHT 2

wedlock *n* a union representing a special kind of social and legal partnership between two people — see MARRIAGE 1

wee *adj* very small in size — see TINY

weedy *adj* growing thickly and vigorously — see RANK 1

weep *vb* **1** to flow forth slowly through small openings — see EXUDE

2 to shed tears often while making meaningless sounds as a sign of pain or distress — see CRY 1

weeping *adj* expressing or suggesting mourning — see MOURNFUL 1

weigh *vb* **1** to be of importance — see MATTER

2 to give serious and careful thought to — see PONDER

weigh (on *or* upon) *vb* to push steadily against with some force — see PRESS 1

weighed *adj* decided on as a result of careful thought — see DELIBERATE 1

weight *n* **1** the amount that something weighs ⟨I'm not allowed to lift anything with a *weight* of over ten pounds⟩

syn heaviness, heft

rel mass; tonnage; deadweight; heftiness, massiveness, ponderousness, weightiness; solidity, solidness, substantiality; burdensomeness, cumbersomeness

2 the quality or state of being important — see IMPORTANCE

3 a mass or quantity of something taken up and carried, conveyed, or transported — see LOAD 1

4 a special notice or importance given to something — see EMPHASIS 1

5 the main or greater part of something as distinguished from its appendages — see BODY 1

6 the power to direct the thinking or behavior of others usually indirectly — see INFLUENCE 1

weight *vb* to place a weight or burden on — see LOAD 1

weightiness *n* **1** the state or quality of being heavy ⟨the *weightiness* of the bookcase made it difficult to move⟩

syn avoirdupois, heaviness, heftiness, massiveness, ponderousness

rel overweight; solidity, solidness, substantiality; bulk, bulkiness, hugeness; burdensomeness, cumbersomeness

near ant airiness, delicacy, etherealness; flimsiness, fluffiness, insubstantiality, slightness

ant lightness, weightlessness

2 the quality or state of being important — see IMPORTANCE

weightless *adj* having little weight — see ¹LIGHT 1

weightlessness *n* the state or quality of having little weight — see ¹LIGHTNESS 1

---

weighty *adj* **1** having a matter of importance as its topic — see SERIOUS 2

2 having great meaning or lasting effect — see IMPORTANT 1

3 having great weight — see HEAVY 1

4 not joking or playful in mood or manner — see SERIOUS 1

5 having power over the minds or behavior of others — see INFLUENTIAL 1

weird *adj* **1** different from the ordinary in a way that causes curiosity or suspicion — see ODD 2

2 fearfully and mysteriously strange or fantastic — see EERIE

3 having seemingly supernatural qualities or powers — see MYSTIC 1

4 noticeably different from what is generally found or experienced — see UNUSUAL 1

weirdo *n* a person of odd or whimsical habits — see ECCENTRIC

welcome *adj* giving pleasure or contentment to the mind or senses — see PLEASANT

welcome *n* an expression of goodwill upon meeting — see HELLO

welcome *vb* receive or accept gladly or readily ⟨the eager recruits *welcomed* every new project with which they were presented⟩

syn embrace

rel adopt, espouse, take up; greet, hail; enjoy, like, prefer; choose, cull, decide (on), elect, handpick, name, opt (for), pick, select, single (out), take

near ant decline, refuse, reject, turn down

welfare *n* the state of doing well especially in relation to one's happiness or success ⟨the social worker was pleased at the improvement in the child's *welfare*⟩

syn good, interest, weal, well-being

rel prosperity, success, successfulness; fitness, health, healthiness, robustness, soundness, wellness, wholeness, wholesomeness; bliss, felicity, happiness, joy; advantage, benefit, gain, sake; content, contentedness, gratification, satisfaction

near ant unhealthiness, unsoundness; misery, sadness, unhappiness, wretchedness

well *adv* **1** in a satisfactory way ⟨our current system for dividing household chores works *well*, so let's keep it⟩

syn acceptably, adequately, all right, fine, good, nicely, OK (*or* okay), passably, satisfactorily, so-so, tolerably

rel appropriately, congruously, correctly, decently, decorously, felicitously, fittingly, meetly, rightly, seemly, suitably

near ant unbearably; inappropriately, incorrectly, indecently, unsuitably

ant bad, badly, inadequately, intolerably, poorly, unacceptably, unsatisfactorily

2 in a generous manner ⟨the warm and gracious couple always treat overnight guests *well*⟩

syn bountifully, generously, handsomely, liberally, munificently

rel considerately, courteously, hospitably, kindly, nicely, reasonably, thoughtfully;

affably, amiably, cheerfully, cheerily, genially, good-naturedly, graciously

near ant contemptuously, disdainfully, rudely, scornfully; obnoxiously, provocatively; coldly, coolly, frigidly, hostilely; angrily, belligerently

ant stingily

3 in a skillful or expert manner ⟨she plays the piano very *well*⟩

syn ably, adeptly, capably, competently, expertly, masterfully, proficiently, skillfully

rel aptly; adroitly, deftly, dexterously

near ant inaptly

ant incapably, incompetently, inefficiently, ineptly, inexpertly, poorly, unskillfully

4 with good reason or courtesy ⟨we cannot *well* get out of going to your cousin's wedding⟩

syn considerately, courteously, kindly, nicely, reasonably, thoughtfully

rel pleasantly; excusably, justifiably

near ant contemptuously, disdainfully, rudely, scornfully

5 in a pleasing way ⟨the day went *well*, despite the rough beginning⟩

syn agreeably, delectably, deliciously, delightfully, dreamily, favorably, felicitously, gloriously, nicely, pleasantly, pleasingly, satisfyingly, splendidly, swimmingly

rel finely, grandly; advantageously, helpfully; fortunately, happily, luckily; prosperously, successfully

ant badly

6 to a full extent or degree — see FULLY 1

well *adj* enjoying health and vigor — see HEALTHY 1

well *interj* how surprising, doubtful, or unbelievable — see NO

well-being *n* the state of doing well especially in relation to one's happiness or success — see WELFARE

wellborn *adj* of high birth, rank, or station — see NOBLE 1

well-bred *adj* showing consideration, courtesy, and good manners — see POLITE 1

well-disposed *adj* having an easygoing and pleasing manner especially in social situations — see AMIABLE

well-founded *adj* based on sound reasoning or information — see GOOD 1

well-heeled *adj* having goods, property, or money in abundance — see RICH 1

well-known *adj* widely known — see FAMOUS

wellness *n* the condition of being sound in body — see HEALTH

well-nigh *adv* very close to but not completely — see ALMOST

well-off *adj* having goods, property, or money in abundance — see RICH 1

well-read *adj* having or displaying advanced knowledge or education — see EDUCATED

well-spoken *adj* able to express oneself clearly and well — see ARTICULATE

well-to-do *adj* having goods, property, or money in abundance — see RICH 1

welter *n* **1** a state of noisy, confused activity — see COMMOTION

2 an unorganized collection or mixture of various things — see MISCELLANY 1

wet *adj* containing, covered with, or thoroughly penetrated by water ⟨I left the car windows open while it rained, and the seats got all *wet*⟩

syn awash, bathed, doused, drenched, dripping, saturated, soaked, soaking, sodden, soggy, soppy, soused, washed, watered, waterlogged, watery

rel deluged, drowned, flooded, inundated, overflowed; submerged, swamped; hydrated; dipped, dunked, splashed; aqueous; steeped; flushed, irrigated, laved, rinsed, sluiced; clammy, damp, dank, humid, moist

near ant waterproof, water-resistant, water-repellent, watertight; baked, dehydrated, freeze-dried; droughty, parched, sere, sunbaked, thirsty; wrung

ant arid, dry, unwatered, waterless

2 marked by or abounding with rain — see RAINY

wet *n* a steady falling of water from the sky in significant quantity — see RAIN 1

wet *vb* to make wet ⟨you need to *wet* your hair thoroughly first⟩

syn bathe, douse, drench, soak, souse, wash, water

rel damp, dampen, humidify, hydrate, moisten; deluge, drown, flood, inundate, overflow; submerge, swamp; splash; impregnate, saturate, steep; flush, irrigate, lave, rinse, sluice; dip, dunk

near ant bake, dehydrate, evaporate, freeze-dry, parch; wring; dehumidify

ant dry

whack *n* **1** an effort to do or accomplish something — see ATTEMPT

2 a hard strike with a part of the body or an instrument — see ¹BLOW

3 a loud explosive sound — see CLAP 1

whack *vb* to deliver a blow to (someone or something) usually in a strong vigorous manner — see HIT 1

whacking *adj* unusually large — see HUGE

whacking *adv* to a great degree — see VERY 1

whale *n* something that is unusually large and powerful — see GIANT

whale *vb* **1** to deliver a blow to (someone or something) usually in a strong vigorous manner — see HIT 1

2 to strike repeatedly with something long and thin or flexible — see WHIP 1

3 to strike repeatedly — see BEAT 1

wharf *n* a structure used by boats and ships for taking on or landing cargo and passengers — see DOCK

what *interj* how surprising, doubtful, or unbelievable — see NO

wheedle *vb* to get (someone) to do something by gentle urging, special attention, or flattery — see COAX

wheel *n* a rapid turning about on an axis or central point — see SPIN 1

wheel *vb* **1** to change the course or direction of (something) — see TURN 2

2 to move (something) in a curved or circular path on or as if on an axis — see TURN 1

3 to move in circles around an axis or center — see SPIN 1

4 to turn away from a straight line or course — see CURVE 1

wheeze *vb* to breathe hard, quickly, or with difficulty — see GASP

whelm *vb* to subject to incapacitating emotional or mental stress — see OVERWHELM 1

when *conj* in spite of the fact that — see ALTHOUGH

where *adv* at, in, or to what place ⟨*where* will you be tonight?⟩

syn whereabouts (*also* whereabout), whither

rel wherever

whereabouts *also* **whereabout** *adv* at, in, or to what place — see WHERE

whereas *conj* for the reason that — see SINCE

wherefore *adv* for this or that reason — see THEREFORE

wherefore *n* something (as a belief) that serves as the basis for another thing — see REASON 2

wherewithal *n* **1** available money — see FUND 2

2 the total of one's money and property — see WEALTH 1

whet *vb* to make sharp or sharper — see SHARPEN

whetted *adj* having an edge thin enough to cut or pierce something — see SHARP 1

whiff *vb* to become aware of by means of the sense organs in the nose — see SMELL 1

while *conj* in spite of the fact that — see ALTHOUGH

while *n* **1** an indefinite but usually short period of time ⟨we stayed at school for a *while* longer⟩

syn bit, space, spell, stretch

rel lapse; season, span; day, epoch, era; flash, instant, jiffy, minute, moment, second, shake, spurt, trice, twinkle, twinkling, wink; aeon (*or* eon), age, eternity; interim, interlude, intermission, interval

2 the active use of energy in producing a result — see EFFORT

whilom *adj* having been such at some previous time — see FORMER

whilst *conj chiefly British* in spite of the fact that — see ALTHOUGH

whim *n* a sudden impulsive and apparently unmotivated idea or action ⟨on a *whim*, we stopped at the roadside stand to get ice cream⟩

syn caprice, fancy, freak, notion, vagary, whimsy (*also* whimsey)

rel capriciousness, freakishness, whimsicality; conceit; concept, conception, image, impression, picture, thought; brainstorm, inspiration

---

syn synonym(s)　　*rel* related words
ant antonym(s)　　*near ant* near antonym(s)

whimper vb to utter feeble plaintive cries ⟨the dog *whimpered* to be let in⟩

syn mewl, pule

rel fuss, snivel, snuffle, whine; bawl, cry, weep; peep, squeak; yelp; mumble, murmur, mutter

near ant scream, screech, shriek, squeal; howl, squall, wail, yowl; call, caterwaul, squawk; bellow, roar

whimsical *adj* prone to sudden illogical changes of mind, ideas, or actions ⟨it's hard to make plans with my *whimsical* best friend⟩

syn capricious, freakish, impulsive

rel mercurial, moody, temperamental, volatile; eccentric, flaky, quirky; arbitrary, erratic, fickle, inconstant, irregular, willful (*or* wilful); impractical, quixotic, romantic

near ant equable; levelheaded, logical, practical, reasonable, sensible; fast, fixed, hard-and-fast, immutable, inflexible, invariable, unalterable, unchangeable; changeless, constant, established, set, settled, stable, steadfast, steady, unchanging, unvarying

whimsicality *n* an inclination to sudden illogical changes of mind, ideas, or actions ⟨her *whimsicality* made her unpredictable⟩

syn capriciousness, freakishness, impulsiveness

rel moodiness, volatility; eccentricity, flakiness; changeability, unpredictability; arbitrariness, fickleness, inconstancy, irregularity, willfulness; changeability, flexibility, mutability, variability

near ant levelheadedness, practicality, reasonableness; fastness, fixedness, immutability, inflexibility, invariability; changelessness, constancy, stability, steadfastness, steadiness

whimsy *also* **whimsey** *n* a sudden impulsive and apparently unmotivated idea or action — see WHIM

whine vb to express dissatisfaction, pain, or resentment usually tiresomely — see COMPLAIN

whiner *n* 1 a person who makes frequent complaints usually about little things — see CRYBABY

2 an irritable and complaining person — see GROUCH

whinny vb to make the cry typical of a horse — see NEIGH

whip *n* a long thin or flexible tool for striking ⟨please do not use your belt as a *whip*⟩

syn flogger, lash, scourge, switch

rel blacksnake, cat-o'-nine-tails, cowhide, crop, knout, quirt, rawhide, strap; cane, club, cudgel, flail; stripe

whip vb 1 to strike repeatedly with something long and thin or flexible ⟨*whipped* the animal when it did not move fast enough to please him⟩

syn birch, cowhide, flagellate, flail, flog, hide, horsewhip, lash, rawhide, scourge, slash, switch, tan, thrash, whale

rel cane, club, cudgel; stripe; bang, bop, box, bust, clap, clip, clobber, clout, crack, cuff, hit, knock, lam, paste, punch, slap, slug, smack, smite, sock, spank, swat, swipe, thwack, wallop, whack; bash, batter, belt, bludgeon, buffet, bung, drub, hammer, lace, lambaste (*or* lambast), lick, mangle, maul, pelt, pound, pummel, rough, thump

2 to defeat by a large margin ⟨we *whipped* them 13-0 in the last game⟩

syn clobber, drub, rout, skunk, snow under, thrash, trim, trounce, wallop

rel beat, best, conquer, hurdle, lick, master, overbear, overcome, overmatch, prevail (over), subdue, surmount, throw, triumph (over), win (against), worst; crush, overpower, overthrow, subjugate, vanquish; exceed, outdo, surpass

3 to achieve a victory over — see BEAT 2

4 to change the course or direction of (something) — see TURN 2

5 to move or cause to move with a striking motion — see FLAP

6 to strike repeatedly — see BEAT 1

whip (up) vb to cause or encourage the development of — see INCITE 1

whipper *n* one that defeats an enemy or opponent — see VICTOR 1

whippersnapper *n* a person of no importance or influence — see NOBODY

whipping *n* failure to win a contest — see DEFEAT 1

whipping boy *n* a person or thing taking the blame for others — see SCAPEGOAT

whir *also* **whirr** vb to fly, turn, or move rapidly with a fluttering or vibratory sound ⟨the hummingbird *whirred* as it hovered over a flower⟩ ⟨our tires *whirred* as we traveled over the rough road⟩

syn buzz, drone, hum, whish, whiz (*or* whizz), zip, zoom

rel thrum; hiss, murmur, purr, rustle, sigh, whisper

whir *n* a monotonous sound like that of an insect in motion — see HUM

whirl *n* 1 a rapid turning about on an axis or central point — see SPIN 1

2 a state of mental uncertainty — see CONFUSION 1

3 a state of noisy, confused activity — see COMMOTION

whirl vb 1 to cause (as a liquid) to move about in a circle especially repeatedly — see STIR 1

2 to move (something) in a curved or circular path on or as if on an axis — see TURN 1

3 to move in circles around an axis or center — see SPIN 1

4 to proceed or move quickly — see HURRY 2

5 to be in a confused state as if from being twirled around — see SPIN 2

whirling *adj* having a feeling of being whirled about and in danger of falling down — see DIZZY 1

whirlpool *n* water moving rapidly in a circle with a hollow in the center ⟨in *The Odyssey*, Ulysses is trapped between the six-headed monster Scylla and Charybdis, a deadly *whirlpool* that threatens to suck his ship down⟩

syn maelstrom, vortex

rel eddy, swirl, whirl

whirlwind *adj* moving, proceeding, or acting with great speed — see FAST 1

whish *n* a sound similar to the speech sound \s\ stretched out — see HISS 1

whish *vb* 1 to fly, turn, or move rapidly with a fluttering or vibratory sound — see WHIRR

2 to make a sound like that of stretching out the speech sound \s\ — see HISS

whisk *vb* 1 to cause to move or proceed fast or faster — see HURRY 1

2 to move or proceed smoothly and readily — see FLOW 2

3 to proceed or move quickly — see HURRY 2

whisper *n* a rumor or report of a personal or sensational nature — see TALE 1

whisper *vb* to make (as a piece of information) the subject of common talk without any authority or confirmation of accuracy — see RUMOR

whistling *adj* having a high musical pitch or range — see SHRILL

whit *n* the smallest amount or part imaginable — see JOT

white *adj* 1 lacking an addition of color — see COLORLESS

2 not causing injury or hurt — see HARMLESS

whiten *vb* to make white or whiter by removing color ⟨years of sunlight had almost completely *whitened* the flag⟩

syn blanch, bleach, blench, decolorize, dull, fade, pale, wash out

rel brighten, lighten; dim, matte (*also* mat *or* matt); whitewash; frost, silver

near ant blacken; blotch, discolor, mottle, shade, splotch, spot, tarnish; color, dye, paint, stain, tinge, tint; burnish, polish, shine

ant darken, deepen

whitewash *vb* to make (something) seem less bad by offering excuses — see PALLIATE 1

whither *adv* at, in, or to what place — see WHERE

¹**whiz** *or* **whizz** *n* 1 a sound similar to the speech sound \s\ stretched out — see HISS 1

2 a monotonous sound like that of an insect in motion — see HUM

²**whiz** *n* 1 a person with a high level of knowledge or skill in a field — see EXPERT

2 a very smart person — see GENIUS 1

whiz *or* **whizz** *vb* 1 to make a sound like that of stretching out the speech sound \s\ — see HISS

2 to fly, turn, or move rapidly with a fluttering or vibratory sound — see WHIRR

whole *adj* 1 not divided or scattered among several areas of interest or concern ⟨you'll need to put your *whole* effort into this project⟩

syn all, concentrated, entire, exclusive, focused (*also* focussed), undivided

rel absolute, complete, full, thorough, total; comprehensive, intact, integral, perfect

near ant deficient, fragmental, fragmentary, incomplete, partial

ant diffuse, divided, scattered

2 enjoying health and vigor — see HEALTHY 1

3 not lacking any part or member that properly belongs to it — see COMPLETE 1

whole *n* a complete amount of something ⟨the landlord eventually refunded the *whole* of our deposit⟩

syn aggregate, full, sum, summation, total, totality

rel gross; completeness, comprehensiveness, entirety; bulk, lion's share, mass

phrases the whole kit and kaboodle, the whole shebang

near ant net

wholehearted *adj* characterized by unqualified enthusiasm — see HEARTY 1

wholeness *n* the condition of being sound in body — see HEALTH

whole number *n* a character used to represent a mathematical value — see NUMBER

wholesome *adj* 1 enjoying health and vigor — see HEALTHY 1

2 good for the health — see HEALTHFUL

wholesomeness *n* the condition of being sound in body — see HEALTH

wholly *adv* to a full extent or degree — see FULLY 1

whoop *n* a loud vocal expression of strong emotion — see SHOUT

whopper *n* 1 a statement known by its maker to be untrue and made in order to deceive — see LIE

2 something that is unusually large and powerful — see GIANT

whopping *adj* unusually large — see HUGE

whore *n* a woman who engages in sexual activities for money — see PROSTITUTE

why *interj* how surprising, doubtful, or unbelievable — see NO

why *n* something (as a belief) that serves as the basis for another thing — see REASON 2

wicked *adj* 1 not conforming to a high moral standard; morally unacceptable — see BAD 2

2 tending to or exhibiting reckless playfulness — see MISCHIEVOUS 1

wickedly *adv* in a mean or spiteful manner — see NASTILY

wickedness *n* 1 playful, reckless behavior that is not intended to cause serious harm — see MISCHIEF 1

2 the state or quality of being utterly evil — see ENORMITY 1

wide *adj* 1 having a greater than usual measure across ⟨the river was so *wide* that it was impossible to cross it in less than a day⟩

---

syn synonym(s)   **rel** related words

ant antonym(s)   **near ant** near antonym(s)

syn broad, fat, thick

rel expansive, extensive; commodious, roomy, spacious

near ant fine, hairlike; elongated; needlelike; close, compressed, condensed, constricted, contracted, squeezed, tight, tightened

ant narrow, skinny, slender, slim, thin

2 having considerable extent — see EXTENSIVE

wide–awake *adj* **1** not sleeping or able to sleep — see WAKEFUL

2 paying close attention usually for the purpose of anticipating approaching danger or opportunity — see ALERT 1

wide–eyed *adj* lacking in worldly wisdom or informed judgment — see NAIVE 1

widespread *adj* having considerable extent — see EXTENSIVE

width *n* an area over which activity, capacity, or influence extends — see RANGE 2

wield *vb* to bring to bear especially forcefully or effectively — see EXERT

wife *n* the female partner in a marriage ⟨a husband and *wife* who treat each other as equals in their marriage⟩

syn helpmate, helpmeet, lady

rel bride; consort, mate, partner, spouse; dowager, matron; homemaker, housewife

wiggle *vb* to make jerky or restless movements — see FIDGET

wight *n* a member of the human race — see HUMAN

wild *adj* **1** living outdoors without taming or domestication by humans ⟨*wild* animals can be shy or aggressive when confronted by humans⟩

syn feral, savage, unbroken, undomesticated, untamed

rel uncontrolled, unsubdued; bestial, brutal, brute; barbarous, uncivilized

near ant controlled, subdued; housebroken, trained; civilized, socialized

ant broken, busted, domestic, domesticated, tame, tamed

2 existing without human habitation or cultivation ⟨that land has been completely *wild* since the owners abandoned it⟩

syn natural, uncultivated, untamed

rel native; uninhabited; overgrown, untended; waste; undeveloped

near ant inhabited; developed

ant cultivated, tamed

3 marked by turmoil or disturbance especially of natural elements ⟨a *wild* night, full of wind and rain⟩

syn stormy, tempestuous, tumultuous, turbulent

rel blustery, rough, violent; brutal, harsh, severe; unsettled

near ant calm, halcyon, peaceful, placid, quiet, serene, tranquil

4 conceived or made without regard for reason or reality — see FANTASTIC 1

5 different from the ordinary in a way that causes curiosity or suspicion — see ODD 2

6 marked by great and often stressful excitement or activity — see FURIOUS 1

7 not civilized — see SAVAGE 1

wild *adv* in a confused and reckless manner — see HELTER-SKELTER 1

wild *n* that part of the physical world that is removed from human habitation — see NATURE 2

wilderness *n* that part of the physical world that is removed from human habitation — see NATURE 2

wildly *adv* in a confused and reckless manner — see HELTER-SKELTER 1

wile *n* **1** a clever often underhanded means to achieve an end — see TRICK 1

2 the use of clever underhanded actions to achieve an end — see TRICKERY

wile *vb* to attract or delight as if by magic — see CHARM 1

wiliness *n* **1** skill in achieving one's ends through indirect, subtle, or underhanded means — see CUNNING 1

2 the inclination or practice of misleading others through lies or trickery — see DECEIT

will *n* **1** the power to control one's actions, impulses, or emotions ⟨she kept her face still by sheer force of *will*⟩

syn restraint, self-containment, self-control, self-discipline, self-government, self-possession, self-restraint, willpower

rel self-denial; moderation, temperance; determination, nerve; command, control, discipline, mastery; aplomb, assurance, composure, confidence, coolness, equanimity, poise, self-confidence; discretion

near ant gratification, indulgence, self-indulgence; immoderacy, intemperance; overindulgence; demerit, failing, fault, feebleness, foible, frailty, shortcoming, vice, weakness

2 the act or power of making one's own choices or decisions — see FREE WILL

will *vb* **1** to give by means of a will — see LEAVE 2

2 to see fit — see CHOOSE 2

willful *or* **wilful** *adj* **1** given to resisting authority or another's control — see DISOBEDIENT

2 given to resisting control or discipline by others — see UNCONTROLLABLE

3 having or showing a tendency to force one's will on others without any regard to fairness or necessity — see ARBITRARY 1

4 made, given, or done with full awareness of what one is doing — see INTENTIONAL

5 sticking to an opinion, purpose, or course of action in spite of reason, arguments, or persuasion — see OBSTINATE

willfully *adv* with full awareness of what one is doing — see INTENTIONALLY

willfulness *n* **1** a steadfast adherence to an opinion, purpose, or course of action — see OBSTINACY

2 refusal to obey — see DISOBEDIENCE

willies *n pl* a sense of panic or extreme nervousness — see JITTERS

willing *adj* **1** having a desire or inclination (as for a specified course of action) ⟨I'm a little confused, but perfectly *willing* to do as you ask⟩

syn amenable, disposed, game, glad, inclined, ready

rel predisposed; agreeable, compliant, obedient, submissive; favorable, receptive; prepared, prompt, quick, responsive, swift

near ant averse, loath, reluctant

ant disinclined, unwilling

2 having or showing the ability to respond without delay or hesitation — see QUICK 1

3 done, made, or given with one's own free will — see VOLUNTARY 1

willingly *adv* **1** by choice or preference — see RATHER 1

2 of one's own free will — see VOLUNTARILY

willingness *n* cheerful readiness to do something — see ALACRITY

williwaw *n* a sudden brief rush of wind — see GUST 1

willowy *adj* able to bend easily without breaking ⟨the rattan's stems are split into *willowy* staves that are woven together to produce exquisite baskets⟩

syn flexible, limber, lissome (*also* lissom), lithe, pliable, pliant, supple

rel adaptable, ductile, elastic, fluid, malleable, modifiable, plastic, variable, yielding; flaccid, floppy

near ant inelastic, nonmalleable, unyielding; breakable, brittle, fragile

ant inflexible, rigid, stiff

willpower *n* the power to control one's actions, impulses, or emotions — see WILL 1

wilt *vb* **1** to be limp from lack of water or vigor — see DROOP 1

2 to lose bodily strength or vigor — see WEAKEN 2

3 to lose liveliness, force, or freshness — see WITHER

wily *adj* clever at attaining one's ends by indirect and often deceptive means — see ARTFUL 1

wimp *n* **1** a person lacking in physical strength — see WEAKLING 1

2 a person without strength of character — see WEAKLING 2

wimpy *adj* **1** lacking bodily strength — see WEAK 1

2 lacking strength of will or character — see WEAK 2

win *n* an instance of defeating an enemy or opponent — see VICTORY

win *vb* **1** to achieve victory (as in a contest) ⟨the kind of person who always has to *win*—even if the game is just for fun⟩

syn conquer, prevail, triumph

rel overcome, sweep; squeak, squeeze; contend, vie; succeed

phrases carry the day

near ant collapse, fail, flop, fold, wash out; flounder, struggle; decline, slip, slump, wane

ant lose

---

syn synonym(s)　　*rel* related words
ant antonym(s)　　*near ant* near antonym(s)

---

2 to receive as return for effort — see EARN 1

3 to obtain (as a goal) through effort — see ACHIEVE 1

win (against) *vb* to achieve a victory over — see BEAT 2

win (over) *vb* to cause (someone) to agree with a belief or course of action by using arguments or earnest requests — see PERSUADE

wince *vb* to draw back in fear, pain, or disgust — see FLINCH

¹wind *n* **1** noticeable movement of air in a particular direction ⟨there's a *wind* coming from underneath the front door⟩

syn current, draft

rel blast, blow, flurry, gale, gust, head wind, squall, tail wind, tempest, tornado, windstorm; breath, breeze, puff, waft, zephyr

2 a prevailing or general movement or inclination — see TREND 1

3 language that is impressive-sounding but not meaningful or sincere — see RHETORIC 1

²wind *n* something that curves or is curved — see BEND 1

wind *vb* to follow a circular or spiral course ⟨flowering vines *wind* around the porch's graceful columns⟩

syn coil, curl, entwine, spiral, twine, twist

rel arc, arch, bend, crook, curve, hook, sweep, swerve, turn, veer, wheel; swirl, whirl; circle, encircle, loop, interlace, intertwine, lace; bow, bulge; meander, weave, zigzag

near ant straighten

windfall *n* something that provides happiness or does good for a person or thing — see BLESSING 2

windiness *n* the use of too many words to express an idea — see VERBIAGE

winding *adj* **1** marked by a long series of irregular curves — see CROOKED 1

2 turning around an axis like the thread of a screw — see SPIRAL

windjammer *n* a boat equipped with one or more sails — see SAILBOAT

windup *n* the last part of a process or action — see FINALE

wind up *vb* **1** to bring (an event) to a natural or appropriate stopping point — see CLOSE 3

2 to come to an end — see CEASE 1

windy *adj* **1** marked by strong wind or more wind than usual ⟨one particularly *windy* day should shake the last of the autumn leaves from the trees⟩

syn blowy, blustery, breezy, gusty

rel drafty; stormy, tempestuous

near ant breathless, calm, motionless, still

2 marked by the use of impressive-sounding but mostly meaningless words and phrases — see RHETORICAL

3 using or containing more words than necessary to express an idea — see WORDY

wing *n* a group of people acting together within a larger group — see FACTION

wing *vb* to move through the air with or as if with outstretched wings — see FLY 1

wink *n* 1 a short sleep — see ¹NAP

2 a very small space of time — see INSTANT

wink *vb* 1 to rapidly open and close one's eyes ⟨she *winked* several times to get the dust and grit out of her eyes⟩

syn blink

rel bat, flutter; squint

2 to shine with light at regular intervals — see BLINK 1

3 to shoot forth bursts of light — see FLASH 1

4 to secretly sympathize with or pretend ignorance of something improper or unlawful — see CONNIVE

wink (at) *vb* to overlook or dismiss as of little importance — see EXCUSE 1

winner *n* 1 a person or thing that is successful — see HIT 1

2 one that defeats an enemy or opponent — see VICTOR 1

3 the person who comes in first in a competition — see CHAMPION 1

winning *adj* 1 having qualities that tend to make one loved — see LOVABLE

2 likely to win one's affection — see INGRATIATING

winsome *adj* likely to win one's affection — see INGRATIATING

wintry *adj* 1 having a low or subnormal temperature — see COLD 1

2 lacking in friendliness or warmth of feeling — see COLD 2

wipe out *vb* to destroy all traces of — see ANNIHILATE 1

wire *n* a length of braided, flexible material that is used for tying or connecting things — see CORD

wisdom *n* 1 the ability to understand inner qualities or relationships ⟨with age and experience comes *wisdom* —hopefully⟩ ⟨neither book learning nor simple intelligence should be confused with *wisdom*⟩

syn discernment, insight, perception, perceptiveness, sagaciousness, sagacity, sageness, sapience

rel acuity, acumen, astuteness, penetration, perspicacity, sensitivity, understanding; appreciation, apprehension, comprehension, grasp; braininess, brain(s), brightness, brilliance, canniness, cleverness, gray matter, intellect, intelligence, judgment (*or* judgement), mentality, power, reason, sense, smartness, wit; discrimination, judiciousness, prudence, sanity; logic, rationality

near ant density, dullness (*or* dulness), obtuseness; brainlessness, folly, foolishness, idiocy, imbecility, mindlessness, silliness, simpleness, stupidity, witlessness; illogic, irrationality, unreasonableness, unsoundness; craziness, insanity, lunacy, madness; preposterousness, senselessness, silliness, zaniness

2 a body of facts learned by study or experience — see KNOWLEDGE 1

3 the ability to make intelligent decisions especially in everyday matters — see COMMON SENSE

wise *adj* 1 having or showing deep understanding and intelligent application of knowledge ⟨a respected and *wise* old judge famous for her sensible rulings⟩

syn discerning, insightful, perceptive, sagacious, sage, sapient

rel acute, perspicacious; experienced; discriminating, discriminative; brainy, brilliant, bright, clever, intelligent, keen, nimble, quick, quick-witted, smart; cerebral, erudite, knowledgeable, learned, literate, scholarly; astute, sharp, shrewd; contemplative, reflective, thoughtful

near ant dense, dull, obtuse; brainless, dumb, feebleminded, foolish, idiotic, imbecilic, moronic, silly, simple, slow, stupid, thoughtless, unintelligent, witless; undiscriminating

ant undiscerning, unperceptive, unwise

2 having inside information ⟨they fooled everyone else, but I'd heard them talking and was *wise* to their true intentions⟩

syn hip, knowing

rel alerted, aware, clued, forewarned, informed, prepared, ready, warned; observant, observing, sharp, sharp-eyed; alert, attentive, open-eyed, vigilant, watchful

phrases in the know

near ant oblivious, unaware, unconscious, uninformed, unperceiving, unseeing, unwitting; heedless, unmindful, unobservant, unobserving; unprepared, unready, unwary

ant unknowing

3 suitable for bringing about a desired result under the circumstances — see EXPEDIENT

wise (up) *vb* to give information to — see ENLIGHTEN 1

wiseacre *n* a person who likes to show off in a clever but annoying way — see SMART ALECK

wisecrack *n* something said or done to cause laughter — see JOKE 1

wisecrack *vb* to make jokes — see JOKE

wise guy *n* a person who likes to show off in a clever but annoying way — see SMART ALECK

wish *vb* to see fit — see CHOOSE 2

wish (for) *vb* to have an earnest wish to own or enjoy — see DESIRE

wishy–washy *adj* 1 lacking in qualities that make for spirit and character ⟨this story is too *wishy-washy*; you need to add some verve to it⟩

syn banal, flat, insipid

rel unentertaining, unexciting, uninspiring, unrewarding, unsatisfying; bland, boring, drab, dreary, dry, dull, heavy, humdrum, jading, leaden, monotonous, pedestrian, ponderous, tedious, tiresome, tiring, uninteresting, wearisome, weary, wearying; inane; innocuous, inoffensive; mild, soft, subdued, tame, weak; common, commonplace, ordinary, stale, unexceptional

near ant piquant, poignant, pungent, racy, spicy; meaty, substantial; entertaining, exciting, galvanizing, inspiring, invigorating, thrilling

2 lacking strength of will or character — see WEAK 1

wit *n* **1** a person (as a writer) noted for or specializing in humor — see HUMORIST
2 the ability to make intelligent decisions especially in everyday matters — see COMMON SENSE
3 the normal or healthy condition of the mental abilities — see MIND 2

witch *n* **1** a woman believed to have often harmful supernatural powers ⟨in the old days women were sometimes accused of being *witches* and using evil magic to make the crops fail or an animal die suddenly⟩
syn enchantress, hag, hex, sorceress
rel charmer, conjuror (*or* conjurer), enchanter, necromancer, voodoo; magician, sorcerer, warlock, wizard
2 a mean or ugly old woman — see CRONE
3 a person skilled in using supernatural forces — see MAGICIAN 1

witchcraft *n* the power to control natural forces through supernatural means — see MAGIC 1

witchery *n* **1** the power of irresistible attraction — see CHARM 2
2 the power to control natural forces through supernatural means — see MAGIC 1

with *prep* **1** as the result of — see BECAUSE OF
2 using the means or agency of — see BY 2
3 without being prevented by — see DESPITE

withal *adv* **1** in addition to what has been said — see MORE 1
2 in spite of that — see HOWEVER

withdraw *vb* **1** to move back or away (as from something difficult, dangerous, or disagreeable) — see RETREAT 1
2 to solemnly or formally reject or go back on (as something formerly adhered to) — see ABJURE
3 to take away from a place or position — see REMOVE 2

withdrawal *n* an act of moving away especially from something difficult, dangerous, or disagreeable — see RETREAT 1

wither *vb* to lose liveliness, force, or freshness ⟨shortly after the moon landing, interest in the space program *withered*⟩ ⟨the old man seemed to *wither* suddenly when he turned eighty⟩
syn dry, wilt
rel mummify, shrivel, wizen; decline, fade, wane; decrease, diminish, lessen
near ant freshen, revive; flourish, prosper, thrive; develop, grow, increase, wax; crest, peak, surge

withhold *vb* **1** to be unwilling to grant — see DENY 2
2 to continue to have in one's possession or power — see KEEP 2

within *n* an interior or internal part — see INSIDE 1

without *prep* **1** not having ⟨spent two days *without* food⟩
syn minus, sans, wanting
2 out of the reach or sphere of — see BEYOND 2

withstand *vb* to refuse to give in to — see RESIST

witless *adj* **1** not having or showing an ability to absorb ideas readily — see STUPID 1
2 showing or marked by a lack of good sense or judgment — see FOOLISH 1

witlessness *n* **1** lack of good sense or judgment — see FOOLISHNESS 1
2 the quality or state of lacking intelligence or quickness of mind — see STUPIDITY 1

witness *n* something presented in support of the truth or accuracy of a claim — see PROOF

witness *vb* **1** to declare (something) to be true or genuine — see CERTIFY 1
2 to make note of (something) through the use of one's eyes — see SEE 1
3 to make a solemn declaration under oath for the purpose of establishing a fact — see TESTIFY

witticism *n* something said or done to cause laughter — see JOKE 1

wittingly *adv* with full awareness of what one is doing — see INTENTIONALLY

witty *adj* given to or marked by mature intelligent humor ⟨Susan is popular because she is so *witty* and fun-loving⟩ ⟨he's well-known for his *witty* retorts⟩
syn clever, facetious, humorous, jocular, smart
rel cerebral, highbrow, intellectual; bantering, frivolous, jesting, joking, joshing, teasing; antic, comic, comical, droll, farcical, funny, hysterical, laughable, ludicrous, ridiculous, riotous, risible, rollicking, screaming, side-splitting, uproarious; amusing, diverting, entertaining; mischievous, playful, prankish; jocose, jocund, jolly, jovial, laughing, merry, mirthful, sunny; scintillating, sparkling; flip, flippant, pert, smart-alecky (*or* smart-aleck); whimsical
near ant brainless, lowbrow, stupid, witless; corny, hackneyed, lame; humorless, uncomic, unfunny; earnest, grave, serious, sober, solemn, somber (*or* sombre); doleful, dolorous, lachrymose, plaintive, sorry, tearful, woeful

wizard *n* **1** a person skilled in using supernatural forces — see MAGICIAN 1
2 a person with a high level of knowledge or skill in a field — see EXPERT
3 a very smart person — see GENIUS 1

wizardry *n* the power to control natural forces through supernatural means — see MAGIC 1

---

syn synonym(s)   **rel** related words
ant antonym(s)   **near ant** near antonym(s)

wobble *vb* 1 to make a series of small irregular or violent movements — see SHAKE 1

2 to make a series of unsteady side-to-side motions — see ROCK 1

3 to show uncertainty about the right course of action — see HESITATE

4 to swing unsteadily back and forth or from side to side — see TEETER 1

wobbling *adj* marked by or given to small uncontrollable bodily movements — see SHAKY 1

wobbling *n* the act or an instance of pausing because of uncertainty about the right course of action — see HESITATION

wobbly *adj* marked by or given to small uncontrollable bodily movements — see SHAKY 1

woe *n* 1 a state of great suffering of body or mind — see DISTRESS 1

2 deep sadness especially for the loss of someone or something loved — see SORROW

woebegone *adj* feeling unhappiness — see SAD 1

woeful *adj* 1 expressing or suggesting mourning — see MOURNFUL 1

2 feeling unhappiness — see SAD 1

3 of a kind to cause great distress — see REGRETTABLE

woefully *adv* with feelings of bitterness or grief — see HARD 2

woman *n* an adult female human being ⟨for a while, the toddler called every *woman* "mama"⟩

syn female, lady

rel dame, gentlewoman; madam, madame, senora (*or* señora); beauty, belle, chick [*slang*], damsel, doll, gal, girl, ingenue (*or* ingénue), lass, lassie, mademoiselle, maid, maiden, miss, senorita (*or* señorita)

womanish *adj* 1 having or displaying qualities more suitable for women than for men — see EFFEMINATE

2 of, relating to, or marked by qualities traditionally associated with women — see FEMININE 1

womanlike *adj* 1 having or displaying qualities more suitable for women than for men — see EFFEMINATE

2 of, relating to, or marked by qualities traditionally associated with women — see FEMININE 1

womanly *adj* 1 having or displaying qualities more suitable for women than for men — see EFFEMINATE

2 of, relating to, or marked by qualities traditionally associated with women — see FEMININE 1

wonder *n* 1 something extraordinary or surprising ⟨the cunningly crafted miniature of our house is a *wonder*, perfect in every detail⟩

syn caution, flash, marvel, miracle, phenomenon, portent, prodigy, sensation

rel curiosity, sight, spectacle; apparition, appearance

2 the rapt attention and deep emotion caused by the sight of something extraordinary ⟨when we first saw the pyramids of Egypt, we gazed with openmouthed *wonder*⟩

syn admiration, amazement, astonishment, awe, wonderment

rel dread; fear; respect, reverence, veneration; curiosity, interest; shock, surprise; disbelief, incomprehension, incredulity; beguilement, bewitchment, captivation, enchantment, fascination; animation, enlightenment, enlivenment, excitement, invigoration, stimulation; absorption, engagement, engrossment, enthrallment, immersion, involvement

near ant apathy, disinterest, incuriosity, indifference, unconcern; boredom, doldrums, ennui, listlessness, restlessness, tedium, tiredness, weariness; cheerlessness, dispiritedness, joylessness, melancholy

wonderful *adj* 1 causing wonder or astonishment — see MARVELOUS 1

2 of the very best kind — see EXCELLENT

wondering *adj* filled with amazement or wonder — see OPENMOUTHED

wonderment *n* the rapt attention and deep emotion caused by the sight of something extraordinary — see WONDER 2

wondrous *adj* causing wonder or astonishment — see MARVELOUS 1

wont *adj* being in the habit or custom — see ACCUSTOMED

wont *n* a usual manner of behaving or doing — see HABIT

woo *vb* to act so as to make (something) more likely — see COURT 1

wood *n* tree logs as prepared for human use ⟨a huge load of *wood* outside the furniture maker's factory⟩

syn lumber, timber

rel beam, brace, pile, post, ridgepole, sill, splint, stake, stave, stick; bar, billet, block; cordwood, firewood

wood *n, often* **woods** *pl* a dense growth of trees and shrubs covering a large area — see FOREST

wooden *adj* lacking social grace and assurance — see AWKWARD 1

woodland *n* a dense growth of trees and shrubs covering a large area — see FOREST

wooer *n* a man who courts a woman usually with the goal of marrying her — see SUITOR 1

wool *n* the hairy covering of a mammal especially when fine, soft, and thick — see FUR 1

woolgathering *n* the state of being lost in thought — see REVERIE

woolly *also* **wooly** *adj* 1 made of or resembling hair — see HAIRY 2

2 covered with or as if with hair — see HAIRY 1

word *n* 1 a pronounceable series of letters having a distinct meaning especially in a particular field ⟨my doctor used all of these medical *words* that I didn't understand⟩

syn expression, term

rel linguistic form, monosyllable, morpheme; collocation, idiom, locution, phrase; archaism, coinage, colloquialism, euphemism, loan word, modernism, neologism

2 something that is said ⟨people who believe that the Bible is the literal *word* of God⟩
syn statement, utterance
rel communication, message; announcement, declamation, declaration, manifesto, proclamation, pronouncement

3 a report of recent events or facts not previously known — see NEWS

4 a person's solemn declaration that he or she will do or not do something — see PROMISE

5 a statement of what to do that must be obeyed by those concerned — see COMMAND 1

word *vb* to convey in appropriate or telling terms — see PHRASE

wordbook *n* a reference book giving information about the meanings, pronunciations, uses, and origins of words listed in alphabetical order — see DICTIONARY

wordiness *n* the use of too many words to express an idea — see VERBIAGE

wording *n* the way in which something is put into words ⟨it's important to get the *wording* of this law precisely correct⟩
syn diction, language, phraseology, phrasing
rel expression, formulation, locution; enunciation, phrase, speech, style, utterance, voice

wordless *adj* understood although not put into words — see IMPLICIT

wordy *adj* using or containing more words than necessary to express an idea ⟨your paper is two pages too long—it doesn't need to be so *wordy*⟩
syn circuitous, circumlocutory, diffuse, long-winded, prolix, rambling, verbose, windy
rel chatty, communicative, conversational, gabby, garrulous, loquacious, talkative, talky, voluble; redundant, repetitious, tautological; embellished, embroidered, exaggerated; bombastic, grandiloquent, highfalutin
near ant brief, short; aphoristic, epigrammatic, sententious; compendious, summary; abbreviated, abridged, condensed, shortened; abrupt, blunt, brusque, curt, laconic, snippy
ant compact, concise, crisp, pithy, succinct, terse

work *n* **1** a literary, musical, or artistic production — see COMPOSITION 1
2 something produced by physical or intellectual effort — see PRODUCT 1
3 the action for which a person or thing is specially fitted or used or for which a thing exists — see ROLE
4 the active use of energy in producing a result — see EFFORT
5 the activity by which one regularly makes a living — see OCCUPATION

6 works *pl* a building or set of buildings for the manufacturing of goods — see FACTORY

work *vb* **1** to be the cause of (a situation, action, or state of mind) — see EFFECT
2 to find an answer for through reasoning — see SOLVE
3 to have a certain purpose — see FUNCTION
4 to produce a desired effect — see ACT 2
5 to set or keep in motion — see MOVE 1
6 to control the mechanical operation of — see OPERATE 1
7 to devote serious and sustained effort — see LABOR

work (for) *vb* to be a servant for — see SERVE 1

work (in) *vb* to introduce in a gradual, secret, or clever way — see INSINUATE

workable *adj* **1** capable of being done or carried out — see POSSIBLE 1
2 capable of being put to use or account — see PRACTICAL 1

workaday *adj* **1** being of the type that is encountered in the normal course of events — see ORDINARY 1
2 having to do with the practical details of regular life — see MUNDANE 1
3 not designed for special occasions — see CASUAL 1

worker *n* **1** a person who does very hard or dull work — see SLAVE 2
2 one who works for another for wages or a salary — see EMPLOYEE

working *adj* **1** being in effective operation — see ACTIVE 1
2 capable of being put to use or account — see PRACTICAL 1
3 involved in often constant activity — see BUSY 1

workmanlike *adj* accomplished with trained ability — see SKILLFUL 1

workout *n* something done over and over in order to develop skill — see EXERCISE 2

work out *vb* **1** to find an answer for through reasoning — see SOLVE
2 to produce or bring about especially by long or repeated effort — see HAMMER (OUT)
3 to turn out as planned or desired — see SUCCEED 1
4 to determine (a value) by doing the necessary mathematical operations — see CALCULATE 1

workshop *n* a building or set of buildings for the manufacturing of goods — see FACTORY

world *n* **1** human beings in general — see PEOPLE 1
2 the celestial body on which we live — see EARTH 1
3 the whole body of things observed or assumed — see UNIVERSE

worldly *adj* **1** having a wide and refined knowledge of the world especially from personal experience — see WORLDLY-WISE

---

syn synonym(s)   **rel** related words
ant antonym(s)   **near ant** near antonym(s)

2 having to do with life on earth especially as opposed to that in heaven — see EARTHLY

worldly–wise *adj* having a wide and refined knowledge of the world especially from personal experience ⟨having followed their father on his military assignments all over the world, the Johnson kids have become very *worldly-wise*⟩

syn cosmopolitan, smart, sophisticated, worldly

rel suave, urbane; civilized, cultivated, cultured, polished, refined; experienced, knowing, practiced, schooled, seasoned; bored, cynical, jaded, skeptical; down-to-earth, pragmatic (*also* pragmatical), realistic, sober

near ant callow, green, inexperienced, raw; parochial, provincial, rustic; philistine, uncivilized, uncultured, unrefined; childlike, simple, simpleminded; idealistic, impractical; uncritical, unknowing

ant ingenuous, innocent, naïve (*or* naive), unsophisticated, unworldly, wide-eyed

worm *vb* **1** to advance gradually beyond the usual or desirable limits — see ENCROACH

2 to introduce in a gradual, secret, or clever way — see INSINUATE

3 to move slowly with the body close to the ground — see CRAWL 1

worn *adj* depleted in strength, energy, or freshness — see WEARY 1

worn–out *adj* **1** depleted in strength, energy, or freshness — see WEARY 1

2 worn or torn into or as if into rags — see RAGGED 2

worried *adj* feeling or showing uncomfortable feelings of uncertainty — see NERVOUS 1

worrisome *adj* **1** causing worry or anxiety — see TROUBLESOME

2 marked by or causing agitation or uncomfortable feelings — see NERVOUS 2

worry *n* an uneasy state of mind usually over the possibility of an anticipated misfortune or trouble — see ANXIETY 1

worry *vb* **1** to experience concern or anxiety ⟨they *worried* for days about the upcoming exam⟩

syn bother, fear, fret, stew, sweat, trouble

rel agonize; long, pine, yearn; chafe; despair

phrases care a hang, give a hang

near ant accept; abide, bear, endure, stick out, stomach, sustain, take, tolerate

2 to trouble the mind of; to make uneasy — see DISTURB 1

worsen *vb* to become worse or of less value — see DETERIORATE

worship *n* excessive admiration of or devotion to a person ⟨his *worship* of his big brother meant that he'd go to any extreme for his idol⟩

syn adulation, deification, idolization, worshiping (*also* worshipping)

rel adoration, deference, glorification, reverence, veneration; idealization, romanticization; affection, fancy, favor, fondness, like, liking, love; appreciation, esteem, regard, respect; approval

near ant condemnation, disapproval, disfavor, dislike, dismissal, disregard, hatred, loathing, scorn

worship *vb* **1** to offer honor or respect to (someone) as a divine power ⟨the ancient Greeks *worshiped* many different gods⟩

syn adore, deify, glorify, revere, reverence, venerate

rel admire, honor, love, regard, respect; dignify, exalt, magnify; extol (*also* extoll), laud, praise; delight, gratify, please, satisfy

near ant blaspheme, desecrate, profane, violate; affront, dishonor, disrespect, insult, offend, outrage, pique, ridicule, scorn, slight; displease; defame, disparage, libel, malign, slander, slur, smear

2 to feel passion, devotion, or tenderness for — see LOVE 2

3 to love or admire too much — see IDOLIZE

worshipful *adj* reflecting great admiration or devotion ⟨a movie fan's *worshipful* stare upon finally meeting her idol⟩ ⟨a teacher surrounded by *worshipful* little children⟩

syn adoring, adulatory, deifying, idolizing, worshipping (*also* worshiping)

rel glorifying, reverential, venerating; affectionate, fond, loving; appreciative, deferential, respectful; approving

near ant condemning, contemptuous, disapproving, hateful, loathing, scornful

worshipping *also* **worshiping** *n* excessive admiration of or devotion to a person — see WORSHIP

worshipping *also* **worshiping** *adj* reflecting great admiration or devotion — see WORSHIPFUL

worst *vb* to achieve a victory over — see BEAT 2

worth *n* **1** the relative usefulness or importance of something as judged by specific qualities ⟨money alone cannot determine the true *worth* of some things⟩

syn account, merit, valuation, value

rel assessment, estimation, evaluation; excellence, greatness, perfection; consequence, importance, significance, weight; desirability

near ant emptiness, worthlessness; baseness, cheapness, inferiority, meanness, paltriness, pettiness, poorness; deficiency, inadequacy, insufficiency, unacceptability

2 the amount of money for which something will find a buyer — see VALUE 1

worthless *adj* having no usefulness ⟨that expensive toy is *worthless* now that it's broken⟩

syn chaffy, empty, no-good, junky, null, valueless

rel base, cheap, inferior, lousy, low-grade, second-rate; bad, defective, flawed, imperfect, substandard, unsatisfactory; deficient, inadequate, insufficient, unacceptable

near ant invaluable, precious, priceless; cherished, esteemed, prized, treasured;

choice, exceptional, fancy, high-grade, special

ant useful, valuable, worthy

worthy *adj* having sufficient worth or merit to receive one's honor, esteem, or reward ⟨made charitable contributions to the American Red Cross and other *worthy* causes⟩ ⟨a *worthy* opponent in a tennis match⟩

syn deserving, good, meritorious

rel admirable, commendable, creditable, laudable, praiseworthy; invaluable, priceless; cherished, prized, treasured; choice, excellent, exceptional, fancy, high-grade, primary, prime, special

near ant base, cheap, inferior, second-rate, substandard; bad, defective, flawed, imperfect; deficient, inadequate, insufficient, unacceptable, unsatisfactory

ant no-good, undeserving, valueless, worthless

wound *vb* 1 to cause bodily damage to — see INJURE 1

2 to cause hurt feelings or deep resentment in — see INSULT

wraith *n* the soul of a dead person thought of especially as appearing to living people — see GHOST

wrangle *n* an often noisy or angry expression of differing opinions — see ARGUMENT 1

wrangle *vb* to express different opinions about something often angrily — see ARGUE 2

wrangler *n* a person who takes part in a dispute — see DISPUTANT

wrap *vb* 1 to encircle or bind with or as if with a belt — see GIRD 1

2 to surround or cover closely — see ENFOLD 1

wrap up *vb* 1 to bring (an event) to a natural or appropriate stopping point — see CLOSE 3

2 to make into a short statement of the main points (as of a report) — see SUMMARIZE 1

wrath *n* 1 an intense emotional state of displeasure with someone or something — see ANGER

2 suffering, loss, or hardship imposed in response to a crime or offense — see PUNISHMENT

wrathful *adj* feeling or showing anger — see ANGRY

wrathfulness *n* an intense emotional state of displeasure with someone or something — see ANGER

wreathe *vb* to scatter or set here and there among other things — see THREAD 1

wreck *n* 1 the portion or bits of something left over or behind after it has been destroyed — see REMAINS 1

2 the destruction or loss of a ship — see SHIPWRECK

3 the violent coming together of two bodies into destructive contact — see CRASH 1

wreck *vb* 1 to cause irreparable damage to (a ship) by running aground or sinking — see SHIPWRECK

2 to bring to a complete end the physical soundness, existence, or usefulness of — see DESTROY 1

wreckage *n* 1 the state or fact of being rendered nonexistent, physically unsound, or useless — see DESTRUCTION

2 the portion or bits of something left over or behind after it has been destroyed — see REMAINS 1

3 the destruction or loss of a ship — see SHIPWRECK

wrecking *n* the destruction or loss of a ship — see SHIPWRECK

wrench *n* 1 a forceful rotating or pulling motion for the purpose of dislodging something ⟨a sharp *wrench* only served to lodge the bent nail more securely into the wood⟩

syn twist, twisting, wrenching, wresting, wringing

rel draft, draw, extraction, pull, tug, yank; dislocation, displacement

2 the act or an instance of applying force on something so that it moves in the direction of the force — see PULL 1

wrench *vb* 1 to move by or as if by a forceful rotation ⟨with one last sharp yank, he *wrenched* the cap of the medicine bottle⟩

syn twist, wrest, wring

rel draw, dredge (up), extract, jerk, lug, pluck, pull, tug, tweak, yank; jimmy, lever, pry; budge, dislocate, displace, disturb, remove; shift, transfer, transpose

2 to injure by overuse, misuse, or pressure — see STRAIN 1

3 to separate or remove by forceful pulling — see TEAR 2

wrenching *n* a forceful rotating or pulling motion for the purpose of dislodging something — see WRENCH 1

wrest *vb* 1 to draw out by force or with effort — see EXTRACT 1

2 to get (as money) by the use of force or threats — see EXTORT

3 to get with great difficulty — see EKE OUT

4 to move by or as if by a forceful rotation — see WRENCH 1

5 to separate or remove by forceful pulling — see TEAR 2

wresting *n* a forceful rotating or pulling motion for the purpose of dislodging something — see WRENCH 1

wrestle *vb* to seize and attempt to unbalance one another for the purpose of achieving physical mastery ⟨the sisters *wrestled* on the floor over the last cookie⟩

syn grapple, scuffle, tussle

rel battle, clash (with), combat, contend, fight, war (against); duel, bash, batter, beat, buffet, hit, punch, slug, strike; box, spar; brawl, skirmish

wretch *n* a mean, evil, or unprincipled person — see VILLAIN

wretched *adj* 1 extremely unsatisfactory ⟨this paper is simply *wretched*—you'll have to rewrite it⟩

syn atrocious, awful, execrable, lousy, punk, rotten, terrible

rel bad, deficient, inferior, off, poor, substandard, unsatisfactory, wanting; contemptible, miserable, shameful; defective, faulty, flawed; low-grade, mediocre, reprehensible, second-rate; bum, useless, valueless, worthless; inadequate, insufficient, lacking; abominable, odious, vile

near ant choice, excellent, exceptional, first-class, first-rate, premium, prime, superior; adequate, sufficient; acceptable, satisfactory

ant great, marvelous (*or* marvellous), wonderful

2 arousing or deserving of one's loathing and disgust — see CONTEMPTIBLE 1

3 causing or marked by an atmosphere lacking in cheer — see GLOOMY 1

4 falling short of a standard — see BAD 1

5 feeling unhappiness — see SAD 1

6 not following or in accordance with standards of honor and decency — see IGNOBLE 2

7 of low quality — see CHEAP 2

8 deserving of one's pity — see PATHETIC 1

wretchedly *adv* with feelings of bitterness or grief — see SADLY 1

wriggle *vb* **1** to make jerky or restless movements — see FIDGET

2 to move slowly with the body close to the ground — see CRAWL 1

wring *vb* **1** to get (as money) by the use of force or threats — see EXTORT

2 to get with great difficulty — see EKE OUT

3 to move by or as if by a forceful rotation — see WRENCH 1

wringing *n* a forceful rotating or pulling motion for the purpose of dislodging something — see WRENCH 1

wrinkle *n* **1** a small fold in a soft and otherwise smooth surface ⟨the old woman's face creased into *wrinkles* as she smiled⟩ ⟨the curtains cascaded onto the floor in ripples and *wrinkles*⟩

syn crease, crimp, crinkle, furrow

rel corrugation, layer, loop, plait, pleat, ply, pucker, seam, tuck; crow's-foot

2 something (as a device) created for the first time through the use of the imagination — see INVENTION 1

wrinkle *vb* **1** to develop creases or folds ⟨if you don't keep clothes promptly after drying, they'll *wrinkle*⟩

syn crease, crinkle, furrow, rumple

rel collapse, crumple, double, fold

2 to create (as by crushing) an irregular mass of creases in — see CRUMPLE 1

write *vb* **1** to compose and set down on paper the words of ⟨*write* a theme in which you name your choice for the most important person in human history⟩

syn author, pen, pencil (in), scratch (out)

rel cast, compose, craft, draft, draw (up), formulate, frame, prepare; recast, redraft, revise, rewrite; letter, print, type, typewrite; record, take down, transcribe; au-

tograph, register, sign; couch, express, phrase, put, word

2 to engage in an exchange of written messages — see CORRESPOND 1

writer *n* a person who creates a written work — see AUTHOR 1

write off *vb* **1** to express scornfully one's low opinion of — see DECRY 1

2 to lower the price or value of — see DEPRECIATE 1

writhe *vb* to make jerky or restless movements — see FIDGET

wrong *adj* **1** falling short of a standard — see BAD 1

2 having an opinion that does not agree with truth or the facts — see INCORRECT 1

3 not appropriate for a particular occasion or situation — see INAPPROPRIATE

4 not being in agreement with what is true — see FALSE 1

5 not conforming to a high moral standard; morally unacceptable — see BAD 2

wrong *adv* off the desired or intended path or course ⟨all of our carefully laid plans went *wrong*⟩

syn afield, amiss, astray, awry

rel badly; faultily, improperly, inappropriately, incorrectly, mistakenly, wrongly; inadequately, insufficiently

near ant perfectly; auspiciously, favorably, promisingly; correctly, properly, rightly; appropriately, fittingly, suitably

ant aright, right, well

wrong *n* **1** that which is morally unacceptable — see EVIL

2 unfair or inadequate treatment of someone or something or an instance of this — see DISSERVICE

wrongdoer *n* a person who commits moral wrongs — see EVILDOER 1

wrongdoing *n* **1** a breaking of a moral or legal code — see OFFENSE 1

2 improper or illegal behavior — see MISCONDUCT

wrongful *adj* contrary to or forbidden by law — see ILLEGAL 1

wrongly *adv* in a mistaken or inappropriate way ⟨you have *wrongly* interpreted this passage in the Bible⟩

syn amiss, erroneously, faultily, improperly, inaccurately, inappropriately, inaptly, incorrectly, mistakenly, unsuitably

rel fallibly, imperfectly; extraneously, irrelevantly, meaninglessly, pointlessly, senselessly; inadequately, insufficiently; undesirably, unsatisfactorily; foolishly, unwisely

near ant infallibly, perfectly; meaningfully, pertinently, relevantly, sensibly; acceptably, adequately, satisfactorily, sufficiently; prudently, sagely, wisely

ant appropriately, aptly, correctly, fittingly, properly, right, rightly, suitably

wrongness *n* the quality or state of being unsuitable or unfitting — see INAPPROPRIATENESS 1

wroth *adj* feeling or showing anger — see ANGRY

X (out) *vb* to show (something written) to be no longer valid by drawing a cross over or a line through it ⟨*x out* the names of the people who have already left⟩

syn cancel, cross (out), delete, kill, scratch (out), strike (out), stroke (out)
rel blot out, efface, erase, expunge, obliterate, rub out, wipe out; cut, excise, remove

yammer *vb* to express dissatisfaction, pain, or resentment usually tiresomely — see COMPLAIN

yank *n* the act or an instance of applying force on something so that it moves in the direction of the force — see PULL 1

yank *vb* 1 to move or cause to move with a sharp quick motion — see JERK 1
2 to draw out by force or with effort — see EXTRACT
3 to separate or remove by forceful pulling — see EXTRACT 1

yard *n* 1 an open space wholly or partly enclosed (as by buildings or walls) — see COURT 2
2 the area around and belonging to a building — see GROUND 1

yardstick *n* something set up as an example against which others of the same type are compared — see STANDARD 1

yarn *n* 1 a brief account of something interesting that happened especially to one personally — see STORY 2
2 a work with imaginary characters and events that is shorter and usually less complex than a novel — see STORY 1

yaw *vb* to depart abruptly from a straight line or course — see SWERVE 1

yea *adv* 1 not merely this but also — see EVEN
2 used to express agreement — see YES

yeah *adv* used to express agreement — see YES

yearn (for) *vb* to have an earnest wish to own or enjoy — see DESIRE

yearning *n* a strong wish for something — see DESIRE

yeast *n* something that arouses action or activity — see IMPULSE

yell *n* a loud vocal expression of strong emotion — see SHOUT

yell *vb* 1 to cry out loudly and emotionally — see SCREAM
2 to speak so as to be heard at a distance — see CALL 1

yellow *adj* having or showing a shameful lack of courage — see COWARDLY

yellowness *n* a shameful lack of courage in the face of danger — see COWARDICE

yelp *vb* to cry out loudly and emotionally — see SCREAM

yen *n* a strong wish for something — see DESIRE

yes *adv* used to express agreement ⟨*yes*, I'll be ready for the test tomorrow⟩
syn all right, alright, aye (*also* ay), OK (*or* okay), yea, yeah
rel certainly, indeed, indisputably, undoubtedly, unquestionably
ant nay, no, no way

yesterday *n* the events or experience of former times — see PAST

yesteryear *n* the events or experience of former times — see PAST

yet *adv* 1 at a later time ⟨we may *yet* figure it out⟩
syn eventually, finally, someday, sometime, ultimately
phrases at last, at length, at long last
near ant ne'er, never, nevermore
2 in addition to what has been said — see MORE 1
3 in spite of that — see HOWEVER
4 up to this or that time — see HITHERTO

yet *conj* if it were not for the fact that — see EXCEPT

yield *n* 1 an increase usually measured in money that comes from labor, business, or property — see INCOME
2 something produced by physical or intellectual effort — see PRODUCT 1
3 the total amount collected or obtained especially at one time — see HAUL 1

yield *vb* 1 to give up and cease resistance (as to a liking, temptation, or habit) ⟨I finally *yielded* to temptation and had a bowl of ice cream⟩
syn bow, give in, submit, succumb, surrender
rel gratify, indulge, wallow; acquiesce (to), concede (to)

---

syn synonym(s)   *rel* related words
ant antonym(s)   *near ant* near antonym(s)

near ant battle, breast, combat, confront, counter, defy, face, meet, object, oppose, repel; thwart, withstand
ant hold off, resist

2 to produce as revenue ⟨I expect that stock to *yield* at least 14% profit this year⟩
syn give, pay, return
rel bring in, produce; afford, furnish, provide, supply

3 to cease resistance (as to another's arguments, demands, or control) ⟨after insisting that her answer was not incorrect, Mary *yielded* when her teacher threatened her with detention⟩
syn bow, budge, capitulate, concede, give in, knuckle under, quit, submit, succumb, surrender
rel acquiesce
near ant contend, fight
ant resist

4 to be the cause of (a situation, action, or state of mind) — see EFFECT

5 to fall down or in as a result of physical pressure — see COLLAPSE 1

6 to give (something) over to the control or possession of another usually under duress — see SURRENDER 1

yielding *adj* **1** receiving or enduring without offering resistance — see PASSIVE

2 not stiff in structure — see LIMP 1

yoke *n* the state of being a slave — see SLAVERY 1

yoke *vb* to put or bring together so as to form a new and longer whole — see CONNECT 1

yokel *n* an awkward or simple person especially from a small town or the country — see HICK

yon *adv* at or to a greater distance or more advanced point — see FARTHER

yonder *adv* at or to a greater distance or more advanced point — see FARTHER

yore *n* the events or experience of former times — see PAST

young *adj* being in the early stage of life, growth, or development ⟨a *young* cat requires more food than an older one⟩ ⟨a *young* tree that will eventually reach 50 feet tall⟩
syn adolescent, immature, juvenile, youngish, youthful
rel minor, underage; embryonic; callow, green, inexperienced, puerile, raw; babyish, childish, childlike, infantile; undeveloped, unfinished, unfledged, unformed, unripe, unripened; blooming, blossoming, burgeoning, flourishing, flowering
near ant aged, aging, elderly, old; full-blown, full-fledged; golden, mellow, ripe, ripened
ant adult, full-grown, mature, matured

youngish *adj* being in the early stage of life, growth, or development — see YOUNG

youngster *n* a young person who is between infancy and adulthood — see CHILD 1

youth *n* **1** a male person who has not yet reached adulthood — see BOY

2 a young person who is between infancy and adulthood — see CHILD 1

3 the state or time of being a child — see CHILDHOOD

youthful *adj* being in the early stage of life, growth, or development — see YOUNG

yowl *n* a loud vocal expression of strong emotion — see SHOUT

yowl *vb* to make a long loud mournful sound — see HOWL 1

yo-yo *n* a person who lacks good sense or judgment — see FOOL 1

yuletide *n* the season celebrating Christmas ⟨these days, as far as the stores are concerned, *yuletide* starts in September⟩
syn Christmastime, Noel
rel Advent; Christmas, nativity, Xmas, yule

yummy *adj* very pleasing to the sense of taste — see DELICIOUS 1

zaniness *n* lack of good sense or judgment — see FOOLISHNESS 1

zany *adj* showing or marked by a lack of good sense or judgment — see FOOLISH 1

zany *n* a comically dressed performer (as at a circus) who entertains with playful tricks and ridiculous behavior — see CLOWN 1

zap *vb* to deliver a blow to (someone or something) usually in a strong vigorous manner — see HIT 1

zealot *n* one who is intensely or excessively devoted to a cause ⟨some people called John a *zealot* because he was always crusading for human rights⟩

syn crusader, fanatic, militant, partisan
rel activist; dreamer, visionary; cultist, disciple, follower, idolizer, votary; addict, aficionado, buff, bug, devotee, enthusiast, fan, fancier, fiend, freak, lover, maniac, nut; backer, patron, promoter, supporter; booster, rooter, well-wisher; faddist
near ant dabbler, dilettante

zenith *n* the highest part or point — see HEIGHT 1

zephyr *n* a slight or gentle movement of air — see BREEZE 1

zero *n* **1** the numerical symbol 0 or the absence of number or quantity represented by it ⟨anything multiplied by *zero* comes out to zero⟩

syn aught, cipher, goose egg, naught (*also* nought), nil, nothing, oh, zilch, zip
rel blank, void

2 a person of no importance or influence — see NOBODY

zero hour *n* a time or state of affairs requiring prompt or decisive action — see EMERGENCY

zest *n* the quality or state of being stimulating to the mind or senses — see PIQUANCY

zesty *adj* sharp and pleasantly stimulating to the mind or senses — see PIQUANT

zigzag *vb* to move suddenly aside or to and fro — see DODGE 1

zilch *n* 1 a person of no importance or influence — see NOBODY

2 the numerical symbol 0 or the absence of number or quantity represented by it — see ZERO 1

zing *n* active strength of body or mind — see VIGOR 1

zip *n* 1 active strength of body or mind — see VIGOR 1

2 the numerical symbol 0 or the absence of number or quantity represented by it — see ZERO 1

zip *vb* 1 to fly, turn, or move rapidly with a fluttering or vibratory sound — see WHIRR

2 to make an irregular series of quick, sudden movements — see FLIT

3 to proceed or move quickly — see HURRY 2

zippy *adj* having much high-spirited energy and movement — see LIVELY 1

zone *n* 1 a broad geographical area — see REGION 2

2 a part or portion having no fixed boundaries — see REGION 1

zoom *n* a monotonous sound like that of an insect in motion — see HUM

zoom *vb* 1 to fly, turn, or move rapidly with a fluttering or vibratory sound — see WHIRR

2 to proceed or move quickly — see HURRY 2

3 to rise abruptly and rapidly — see SKYROCKET

---

syn synonym(s)   *rel* related words
ant antonym(s)   *near ant* near antonym(s)